NAVIGATOR SERIES

2000+ PROBLEMS

JEE Main & Advanced

Electrostatics & Current Electricity

PRADEEP BENIWAL
IIT Kharagpur

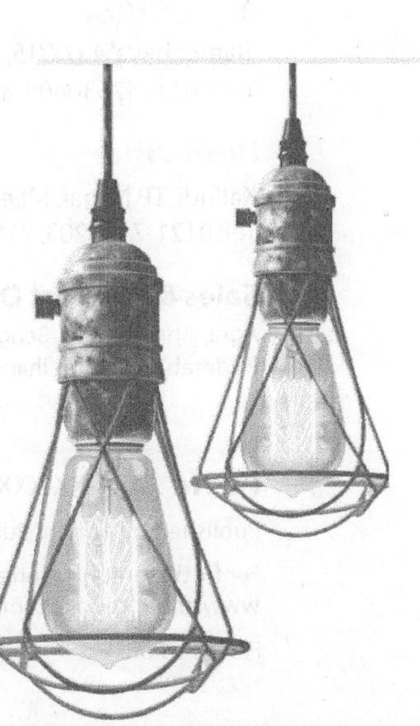

arihant
SUCCESS AND NOTHING LESS

ARIHANT PRAKASHAN (Series), MEERUT

卐 **Administrative & Production Offices**

Regd. Office

'Ramchhaya' 4577/15, Agarwal Road, Darya Ganj, New Delhi -110002
Tele: 011- 47630600, 43518550

Head Office

Kalindi, TP Nagar, Meerut (UP) - 250002
Tel: 0121-7156203, 7156204

卐 **Sales & Support Offices**

Agra, Ahmedabad, Bengaluru, Bareilly, Chennai, Delhi, Guwahati, Hyderabad, Jaipur, Jhansi, Kolkata, Lucknow, Nagpur & Pune.

卐 **PO No :** TXT-XX-XXXXXXX-X-XX

Published by Arihant Publications (India) Ltd.

For further information about the books published by Arihant, log on to www.arihantbooks.com or e-mail at info@arihantbooks.com

Follow us on

PREFACE

Physics is a subject that requires a lot of practice to master it and the best way to practice Physics is to solve more & more problems right from the beginner's level to the most complex ones. That's why, the search for a good Physics Problems book has always been the top notch task of each good student.

During the last 15 Years while teaching & mentoring thousands of students preparing for JEE Main, JEE Advanced, KVPY, Olympiads etc. I always felt the need of such a book that can offer quality problems of Physics for all the topics of different chapters. There are many problems books available in the market but unfortunately none of them serve the purpose perfectly.

To fulfil the need of a good Physics Problems book, I have prepared the book **JEE Navigator Electrostatics & Current Electricity**. All the problems given in this book are arranged conceptually and systematically in order to test the conceptual understanding & analytical ability of the students.

All the problems given in each chapter of this book have been developed with the utmost care and arranged in a way to enhance the problem-solving skills of the students & to boost their confidence to tackle complex JEE Problems.

The Points given below will help you to learn the basic structure of the book;

- Each chapter is divided into three major heads; **Level 1 'Starter Level', Level 2 'JEE Main Level' & Level 3 'JEE Advanced Level'.**
- **Level 1 'Starter Level'** consists of preliminary questions that test basic concepts. After completing this level student will have a solid understanding of fundamentals of the chapter necessary to solve the problems.
- **Level 2 'JEE Main Level'** has single choice correct questions and numerical value questions aimed especially for JEE Main.
- **Level 3 'JEE Advanced Level'** consists of various types of questions; MCQ with one or more than one correct answer, Comprehension Based Questions, Match the Columns and Numerical Value Questions as per the latest JEE Advanced Pattern.
- The problems given in JEE Advanced Level are made to be conceptually challenging resulting in practical and relevant practice for JEE Advanced.
- **Past Exams' Questions** of JEE Main & JEE Advanced are also covered in each chapter.
- Detailed solutions to all the problems have been provided at the end of every chapter just to help the students in case they stuck somewhere while solving some questions.

At the end, I can say confidently that if you rigorously practice the problems given in this book, then surely you will get an edge in Physics and will increase your chance of getting good JEE Score.

However, I have taken the utmost care while writing this book but if any error or whatsoever has skipped my attention, then please bring it to my notice so that it can be rectified. I would also like to appeal all my fellow Physics Teachers to have a look at the book and share their valuable suggestions for its further improvement.

Pradeep Beniwal
B.Tech, IIT Kharagpur
problemsinphysics@yahoo.com

CONTENTS

1. Electric Field 1-66

2. Electric Potential 67-122

3. Electric Dipole 123-144

4. Electric Flux 145-176

5. Conductors 177-216

6. Current Electricity 217-297

7. Electrical Instruments 298-351

8. Heating Effect of Current 352-386

9. Capacitance 387-453

10. Dielectrics 454-488

11. *R-C* Circuit 489-524

CHAPTER~01

ELECTRIC FIELD

LEVEL 01 Starter Level

1.1 Electric Charge

1 State True or False.

(i) Charge cannot exist without mass though mass can exist without charge.

(ii) Charge and mass both are conserved for an isolated system.

(iii) Electric charge of a body is always quantised.

(iv) Charge is relativistically invariant.

(v) An accelerated charged particle emits electromagnetic radiations in addition to producing electric and magnetic fields.

(vi) Relative permittivity of a medium lies between 0 and ∞.

(vii) A charged body and a neutral body cannot attract each other.

(viii) Repulsion is a sure test of electrification.

(ix) If two identical conductors having charges $+4e$ and $-2e$ are connected through a metallic wire, then charge on each conductor would be $+e$.

(x) When a positively charged rod is kept near a neutral conductor, they attract each other and when a negatively charged rod is kept near a neutral conductor, they repel each other.

2 A copper sphere contains about 2×10^{22} atoms. The charge on the nucleus of each atom is $+29e$. What fraction of the electrons must be removed from the sphere to give it a charge of $+2\mu C$?

3 A polythene piece rubbed with wool is found to have a negative charge of 3×10^{-7} C.

(i) Estimate the number of electrons transferred (from which to which?).

(ii) Is there a transfer of mass from wool to polythene?

4 Which of the following charges cannot exist?

(i) 1.6×10^{-18} C (ii) 1.6×10^{-20} C
(iii) 0.001 C (iv) $+2.5\,e$ (v) $-3.2\,e$

5 Two identical conducting spheres are charged by induction and then separated by a large distance; sphere-1 has charge $+Q$ and sphere-2 has charge $-Q$. A third sphere is initially uncharged. If sphere-3 is touched to sphere-1 and separated and then touched to sphere-2 and separated, what is the final charge on each of the three spheres?

1.2 Coulomb's Law

1 Two neutral objects are rubbed against each other and the electrostatic force of attraction between them is 3.6 N, when they are separated by a distance of 10 cm. How many electrons are transferred from one object to the other during rubbing?

2 Two equally charged identical metal sphere A and B repel each other with a force 20N . Another identical uncharged sphere C is touched to B and then placed at the mid-point between A and B. What is the net electric force on C?

3 Two point charges q_1 and q_2 repel each other with force F, when kept certain distance apart in air. If now both the charges are kept in water at the same separation,

(i) how much force q_1 and q_2 will exert on each other?

(ii) how much force each of them will experience?

(iii) how much force water will exert on each charge? (Relative permittivity of water = 80)

4 Two point charges $q_1 = 20\mu C$ and $q_2 = 25\mu C$ are placed at $(-1, 1, 1)$ m and $(3, 1, -2)$ m, with respect to a coordinate system. Find the electrostatic force on q_2.

5 A particle of mass m carrying charge q_1 is revolving around a fixed charge $-q_2$ in a circular path of radius r. Calculate the period of revolution and its speed also.

6 20 positively charged particles are kept fixed on the X-axis at points $x = 1\text{m}, 2\text{m}, 3\text{m}, \ldots, 20\text{m}$. The first particle has a charge $1.0\mu C$, the second $8.0\,\mu C$, the third $27\mu C$ and so on. Find the magnitude of the electric force acting on a $+10\mu C$ charge placed at the origin.

7 Four identical point charges each of magnitude q are placed at the corners of a square of side a. Find the net electrostatic force on any of the charges.

8 The distance between two fixed point charges $+4q$ and $+q$ is l. What charge Q is needed to achieve equilibrium for the entire system and where should it be placed?

9 A charge q_0 is placed at the centre of a regular pentagon having equal charges q at its corners. Assume that distance from centre to corner for pentagon $= a$

(i) Find the force on q_0.

(ii) If charge of one of the corners is removed, then find out magnitude of force acting on q_0.

(iii) If two adjacent charges are removed from corners, then find the magnitude of force acting on q_0.

10 Two spheres, each having mass m are suspended from a common point by two insulating strings each of length l. The spheres are identically charged and the separation between the spheres is d. Find the charge on each sphere.

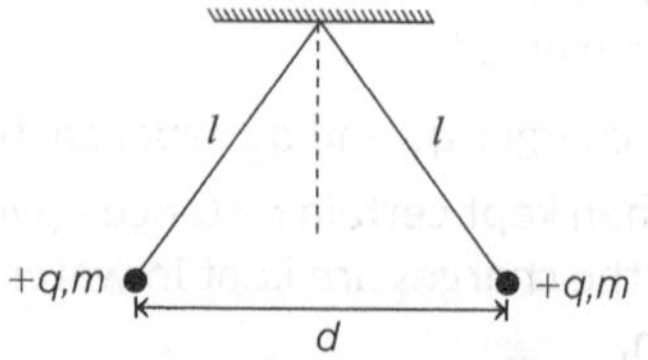

11 Find the force between a uniformly charged rod of length L and charge $+Q$ and a point charge $+q$ placed at a distance d from the centre of the rod at its axial position.

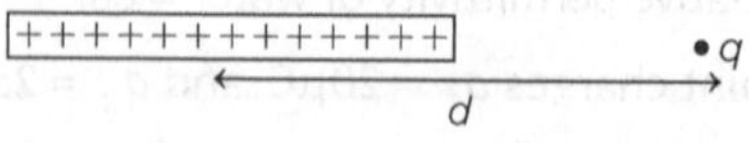

12 Two equal charges $+q$ are kept fixed at $x = -a$ and $x = +a$ along the X-axis. A particle of mass m and charge $+Q$ is brought to the origin and given a small displacement along the

(i) X-axis and (ii) Y-axis.

Describe the motion in the two cases.

13 (i) A particle A having a charge of $4\mu C$ and a mass of 600 g is fixed at the bottom of a smooth inclined plane of inclination 37°. Where should another particle B, having same charge and mass, be placed on the inclined plane, so that it may remain in equilibrium?

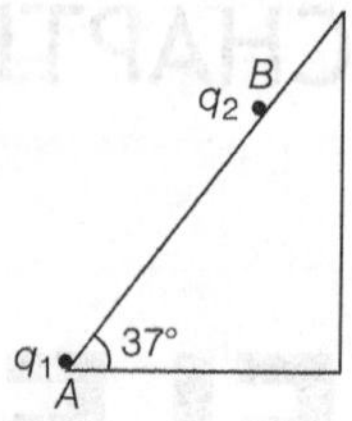

(ii) If B is replaced by a negative point charge of same mass and same amount of charge, then what will be its instantaneous acceleration? (Take, $g = 10\ \text{m/s}^2$)

14 A particle having a charge of $4\mu C$ is held fixed on a horizontal table. A second charged particle of same charge and mass 300 g stays in equilibrium on the table at a distance of d metre from the first charge. The coefficient of friction between the table and this second particle is $\mu = 0.3$. Find the range of d for which the second particle lies at rest. (Take, $g = 10\ \text{m/s}^2$)

1.3 Electric Field due to Point Charges

1 A point charge produces an electric field of magnitude 9.0 N/C at a distance of 20 cm from it. What is the magnitude of the charge?

2 An electric charge $Q = 10^{-10}$ C is placed at the point (1, 2, 3) m. Find the electric field intensity due to it at the point (2, 3, 4) m.

3 Find the magnitude of electric field intensity at point C in the following figures.

(i)

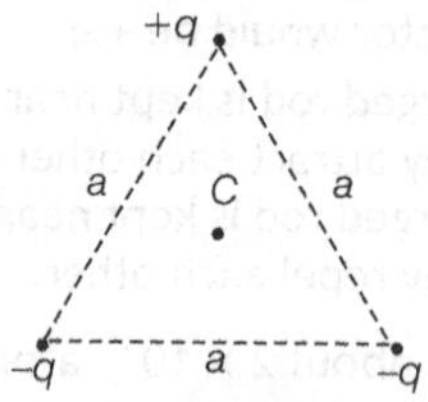

C is the centroid of equilateral triangle of side a

(ii)

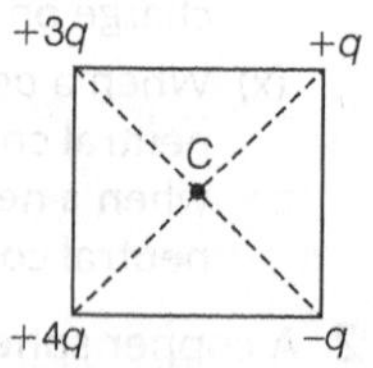

C is the centre of square of side a

(iii)

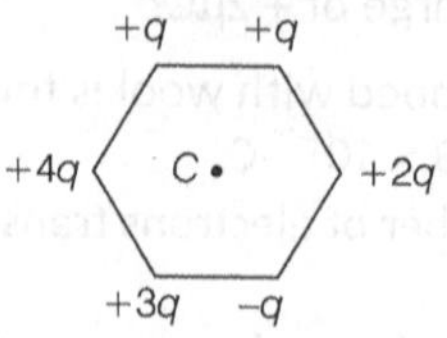

C is the centroid of regular hexagon of side a

4 Two point charges $+20\mu C$ and $-20\mu C$ are fixed at (5,0) and (– 5,0), respectively. Find electric field intensity at the following points.

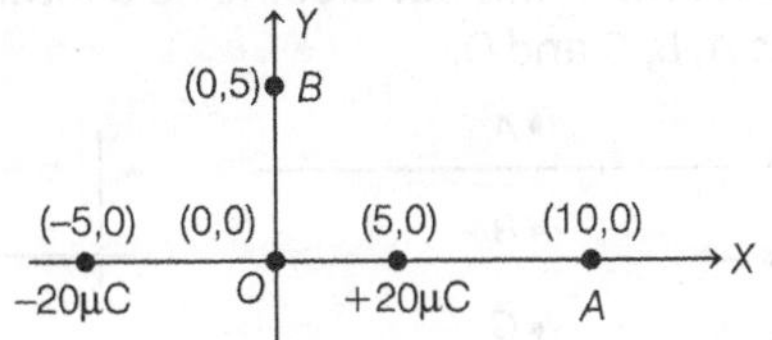

(i) (0, 0) (ii) (10, 0) (iii) (0, 5)

5 Two point charges A and B having charges of $+4\mu C$, and $-64\mu C$ respectively are held at a separation of 90 cm. Locate the point(s) on the line AB or on its extension, where the electric field is zero.

6 Three charges $q_1 = 4nC$, $q_2 = -2nC$ and $q_3 = 1nC$ are fixed along a straight line as shown in the figure.

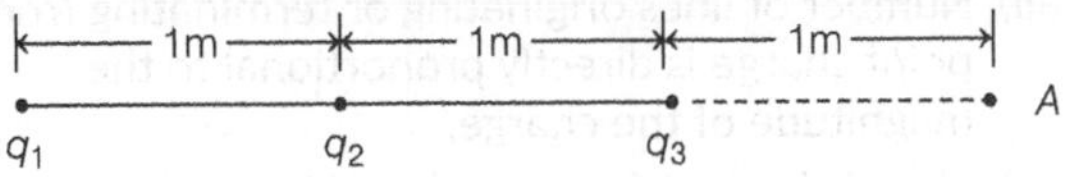

(i) Find electric field at a point A located at a distance of 1m to the right of q_3.

(ii) If a charge $Q = -2mC$ is placed at A, how much force will it experience?

7 12 equal charges q are located at the vertices of a regular 12 sided polygon.

(i) Find electric field at the centre of the polygon.

(ii) One of the charges is moved to the centre of the polygon. Its distance from all other charges is r. Find force acting on it.

8 A square of side L is placed in a horizontal plane and four equal charges +q are fixed at its vertices. A point P is located vertically above the centre of the square, at a height $\frac{L}{\sqrt{2}}$ from the plane of the square. Find the electric field at point P.

1.4 Electric Field due to Continuous Charge Distributions

1 Find electric field at the centre C for each charge configuration.

(i)
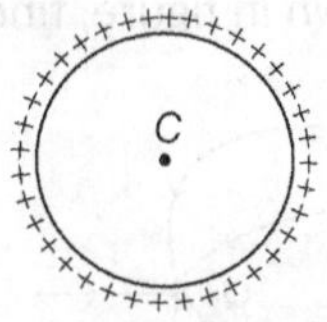

Uniformly charged ring of radius R and linear charge density λ.

(ii)
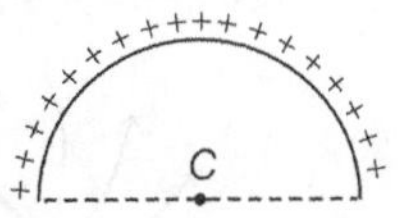

Uniformly charged half ring of radius R and linear charge density λ.

(iii)
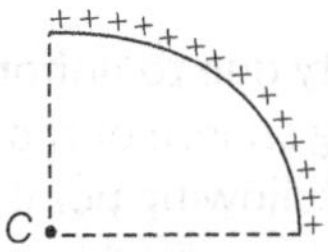

Uniformly charged quarter ring of radius R and linear charge density λ.

2 A circular wire of radius R carries a total charge Q distributed uniformly over its length. A small length dL of the wire is cut off. Find the electric field at the centre due to the remaining wire.

3 Two rings each of radius R carrying charges +Q and – Q are placed with their planes parallel and their centres $2\sqrt{3}R$ distance apart. Find electric field intensity at the mid-point P of line joining their centres.

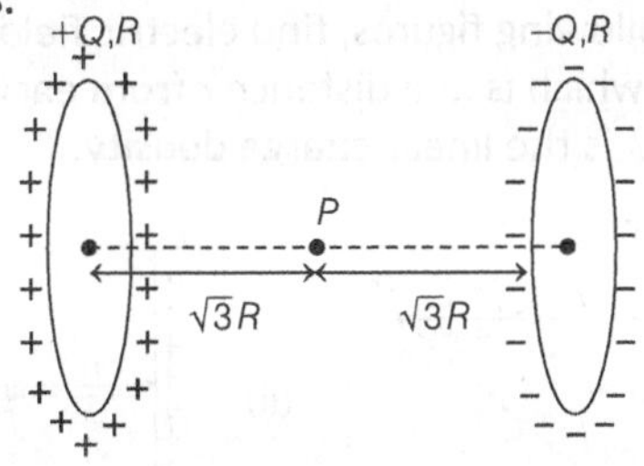

4 A ring of radius R has charge – Q distributed uniformly over it. Calculate the charge that should be placed at the centre of the ring such that the electric field becomes zero at a point on the axis of the ring at a distance R from the centre of the ring.

5 Derive the expression of electric field intensity at a point P which is situated at a distance x on the axis of uniformly charged disc of radius R and surface charge density σ.

6 Find out electric field intensity due to uniformly charged thin spherical shell of radius 10 cm having charge $+20\mu C$ at the following points

(i) At the centre (ii) 5 cm from centre

(iii) 20 cm from centre

7 Two concentric uniformly charged thin spherical shells of radius R and 2R have charges +Q and +2Q, respectively. Find electric field as a function of r for the following positions.

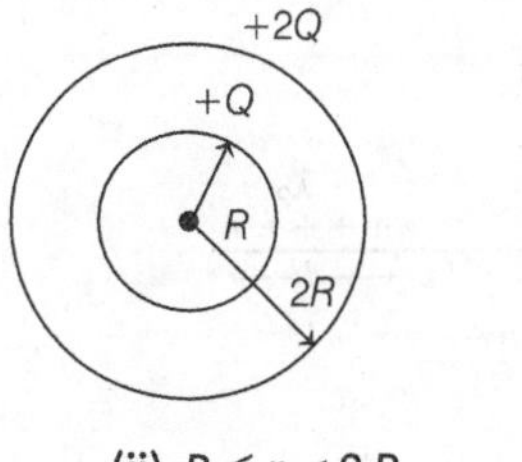

(i) $r < R$ (ii) $R \le r < 2R$ (iii) $r \ge 2R$

8 Find out electric field intensity due to uniformly charged solid non-conducting sphere of radius 10 cm having charge $+20\mu C$ at the following points.

(i) At the centre (ii) 5 cm from centre

(iii) 20 cm from centre

9 A non-conducting solid sphere of radius R has volume charge density that varies as $\rho = \rho_0 r$, where ρ_0 is a constant and r is distance from centre. Find out electric field intensity at the following positions.

(i) $r < R$ (ii) $r \geq R$

10 A 10 cm long rod carries a charge of $+50\mu C$ distributed uniformly along its length. Find the magnitude of the electric field at a point 10 cm from both the ends of the rod.

11 In the following figures, find electric field intensity at point P, which is at a distance r from each line charge. λ is the linear charge density.

(i)

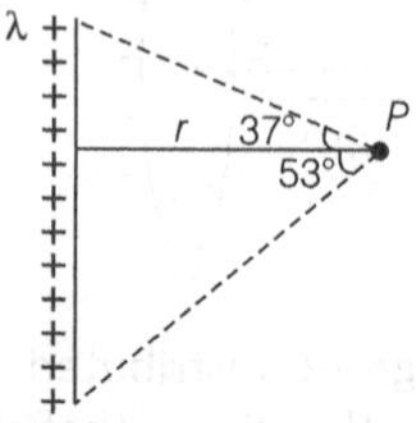

(ii)

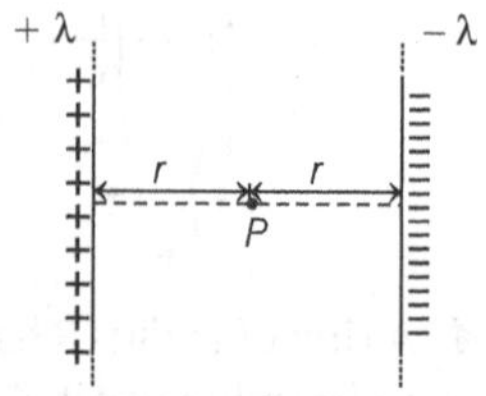

(iii)

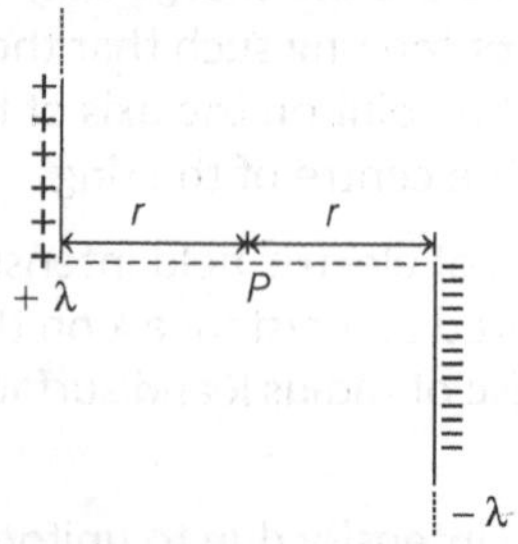

12 Find the force of interaction for the following charge configurations. λ is the linear charge density.

(i)

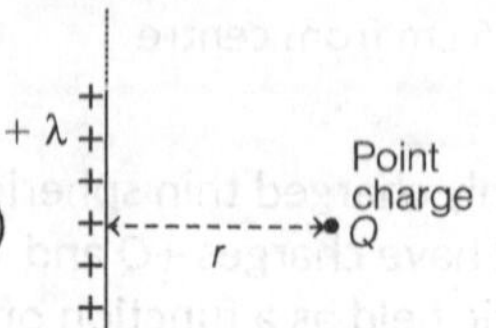

(ii)

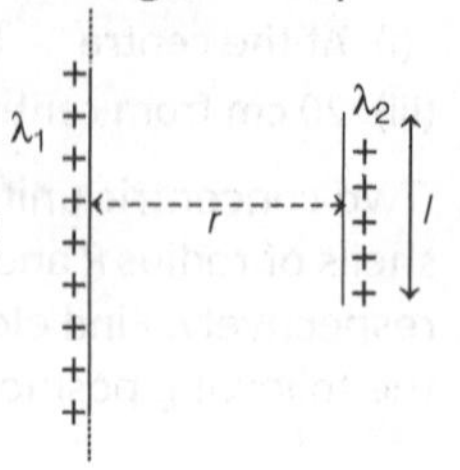

(iii)

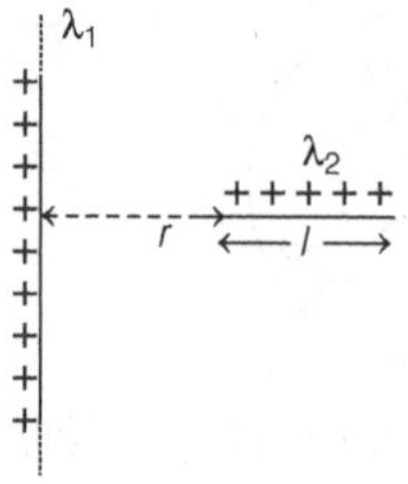

13 If three infinite charged sheets of uniform surface charge densities σ, 2σ and -4σ are placed as shown in figure, then find out electric field intensities at points A, B, C and D.

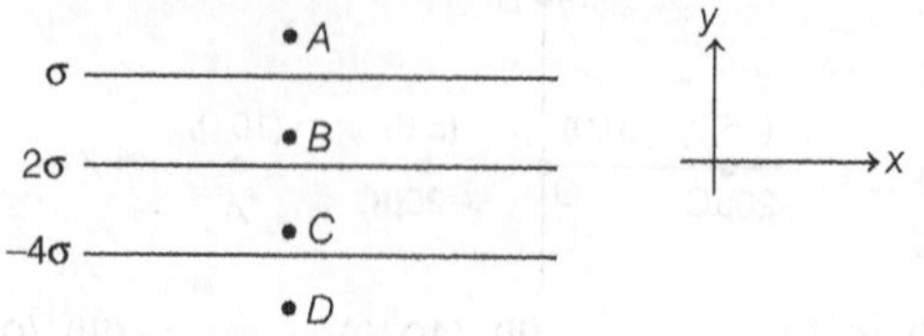

1.5 Electric Field Lines

1 State True or False.

(i) Electric line of force can pass through neutral point.

(ii) Electric field intensity is more, where electric field lines are closer.

(iii) Number of lines originating or terminating from a point charge is directly proportional to the magnitude of the charge.

(iv) Electric lines of force produced by static charges form closed loop.

(v) Two electric field lines can never intersect.

(vi) A charged particle need not always follow an electric line of force.

(vii) An electric line of force in the XY-plane is given by the equation, $x^2 + y^2 = 4$. A particle with unit positive charge, initially at rest at the point $x = 2$, $y = 0$ in the XY-plane will move along the circular line of force.

2 Draw electric field lines pattern for the following system of charges.

(i) Two point charges each $+q$ kept some distance apart.

(ii) Two point charges $+q$ and $-q$ kept some distance apart.

(iii) Three point charges each $+q$ lying on the vertices of an equilateral triangle.

(iv) Uniformly charged thin spherical shell.

(v) Uniformly charged solid non-conducting sphere.

(vi) A uniformly charged infinite thin non-conducting sheet.

3 From the field pattern shown in figure, find $\frac{Q_1}{Q_2}$.

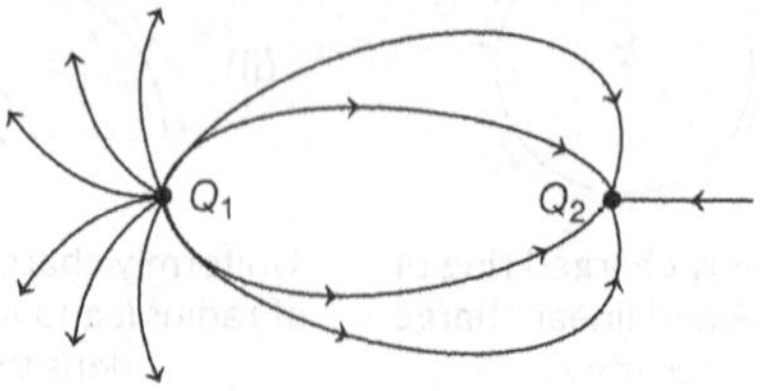

4 For the electric field shown in figure, electric field intensity at A is E_A and electric field intensity at B is E_B. Which is greater E_A or E_B?

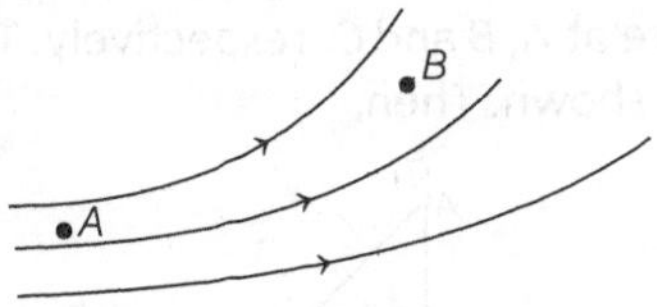

5 Which of the following electric field lines pattern are possible for static charges?

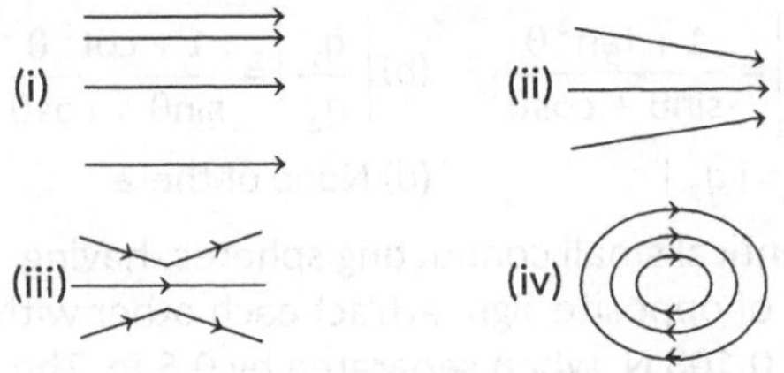

1.6 Motion of Charged Particles in External Electric Field

1 A ball of mass m and charge $-q$ is to be suspended in air in equilibrium. What electric field (magnitude and direction) is required to do so?

2 A small charged sphere of mass m is suspended by a string in a uniform field $E = \frac{mg}{q}$ at an angle of 37° with horizontal as shown in figure.

The sphere is in equilibrium. Find

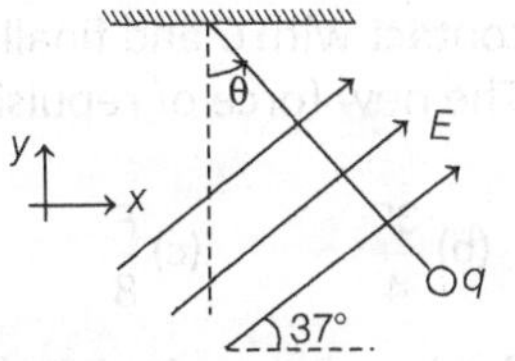

(i) the angle θ made by the string with vertical.
(ii) the tension in the string.

3 A simple pendulum has a bob of mass m and charge q connected to a string of length l, whose other end is fixed to the ceiling. Find time period of small oscillations of the simple pendulum, if

(i) a uniform vertical electric field of strength E pointing downward is switched ON.
(ii) a uniform vertical electric field of strength E pointing upward is switched ON.
(iii) a uniform horizontal electric field of strength E is switched ON.

4 A particle of mass m and charge q is thrown at a speed u against a uniform electric field E. How much distance will it travel before coming to momentarily rest? Also, find the time required till that moment. (Neglect gravity)

5 A uniform electric exists between two parallel charged plates as shown in figure. An electron-proton pair is released from rest from the middle of the gap between the plates. The electron hits the positive plate in time t_1 and the proton hits the negative plate in time t_2. Find $\frac{t_1}{t_2}$.

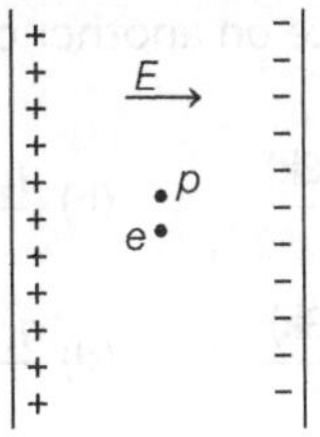

6 A uniform electric field $E = 91 \times 10^{-6}$ V/m is created between two parallel, charged plates as shown in figure. An electron enters the field symmetrically between the plates with a speed $v_0 = 4 \times 10^3$ m/s. The length of each plate is $l = 1$m. Find the angle of deviation of the path of the electron as it comes out of the field.

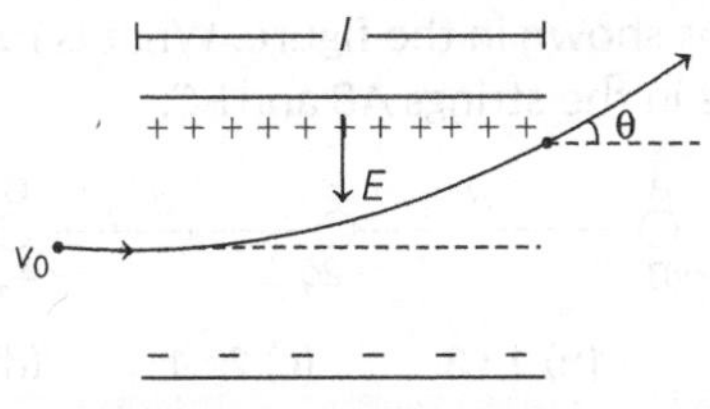

7 A particle of charge $-q$ and mass m moves in a circle of radius r around an infinitely long line charge of linear charge density $+\lambda$. Find its time period.

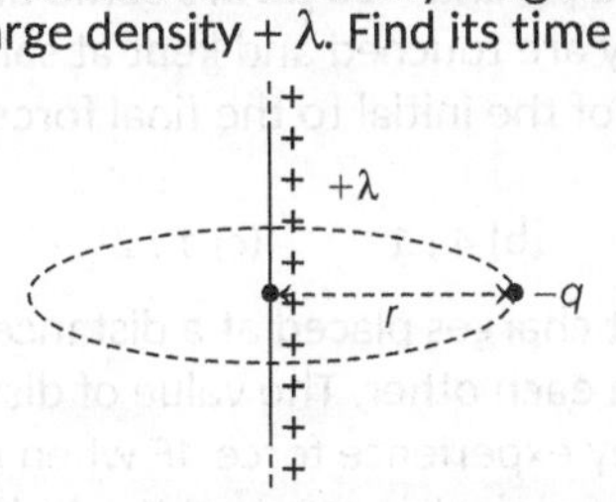

8 A proton is released from rest 10 cm from a large non-conducting thin sheet carrying a surface charge density of -2.21×10^{-9} C/m^2. Find the approximate time after which it shall strike the sheet. (Take, $\varepsilon_0 = 8.84 \times 10^{-12}$ C^2/N-m^2)

LEVEL 02 \ JEE Main Level

Single Choice Correct Questions

1 Two copper balls, each weighing 10 g are kept in air 10 cm apart. If one electron from every 10^6 atoms is transferred from one ball to the other, then find the Coulomb force between them. (Atomic weight of copper = 63.5 g)

(a) 2.0×10^{10} N (b) 2.0×10^8 N
(c) 2.0×10^6 N (d) 2.0×10^4 N

2 A charged particle q_1 is at position (2, – 1, 3). The electrostatic force on another charged particle q_2 at (0, 0, 0) is

(a) $\frac{q_1 q_2 (2\hat{i} - \hat{j} + 3\hat{k})}{56\ \pi\varepsilon_0}$ (b) $\frac{q_1 q_2 (2\hat{i} - \hat{j} + 3\hat{k})}{56\sqrt{14}\ \pi\varepsilon_0}$

(c) $\frac{q_1 q_2 (\hat{j} - 2\hat{i} - 3\hat{k})}{56\ \pi\varepsilon_0}$ (d) $\frac{q_1 q_2 (\hat{j} - 2\hat{i} - 3\hat{k})}{56\sqrt{14}\ \pi\varepsilon_0}$

3 Five balls, numbered 1 to 5, are suspended using separated threads. Pairs (1, 2), (2, 4), (4, 1) show electrostatic attraction, while pairs (2, 3) and (4, 5) show repulsion, therefore ball 1 must be

(a) positively charged (b) negatively charged
(c) neutral (d) Cannot say

4 Three charges $+q$, $+2q$ and $+4q$ are connected by strings as shown in the figure. What is ratio of tensions in the strings AB and BC.

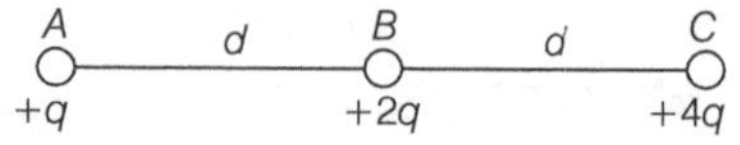

(a) 1 : 2 (b) 1 : 3 (c) 2 : 1 (d) 3 : 1

5 Two similar very small conducting spheres having charges 40 μC and – 20 μC are some distance apart. Now, they are touched and kept at same distance. The ratio of the initial to the final force between them is

(a) 8 : 1 (b) 4 : 1 (c) 1 : 2 (d) 1 : 1

6 Two point charges placed at a distance r in air exert a force F on each other. The value of distance R at which they experience force $4F$ when placed in a medium of dielectric constant $K = 16$ is

(a) r (b) $r/4$
(c) $r/8$ (d) $2r$

7 If a charge q is placed at the centre of the line joining two equal charges Q, such that the system is in equilibrium, then the value of q is

(a) $Q/2$ (b) $-Q/2$
(c) $Q/4$ (d) $-Q/4$

8 ABC is a right-angled triangle. Point charges q_1, q_2 and q_3 are at A, B and C, respectively. The force on q_3 is F as shown. Then,

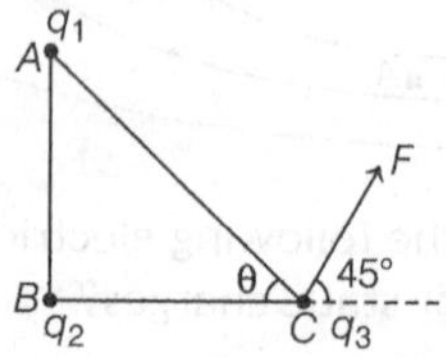

(a) $\left|\frac{q_1}{q_2}\right| = \frac{1 + \tan^2\theta}{\sin\theta + \cos\theta}$ (b) $\left|\frac{q_1}{q_2}\right| = \frac{1 + \cot^2\theta}{\sin\theta + \cos\theta}$

(c) $|q_1| = |q_2|$ (d) None of these

9 Two identical small conducting spheres, having charges of opposite sign, attract each other with a force of 0.108 N, when separated by 0.5 m. The spheres are connected by a conducting wire, which is then removed, and thereafter, they repel each other with a force of 0.036 N. The initial charges on the spheres are

(a) $\pm 5 \times 10^{-6}$ C and $\mp 15 \times 10^{-6}$ C
(b) $\pm 1.0 \times 10^{-6}$ C and $\mp 3.0 \times 10^{-6}$ C
(c) $\pm 2.0 \times 10^{-6}$ C and $\mp 6.0 \times 10^{-6}$ C
(d) $\pm 0.5 \times 10^{-6}$ C and $\mp 1.5 \times 10^{-6}$ C

10 Two spherical conductors B and C having equal radii and carrying equal charges repel each other with a force F, when kept apart at some distance. A third spherical conductor A having same radius as that of B but uncharged, is brought in contact with B, then brought in contact with C and finally removed away from both. The new force of repulsion between B and C is

(a) $\frac{F}{4}$ (b) $\frac{3F}{4}$ (c) $\frac{F}{8}$ (d) $\frac{3F}{8}$

11 A charge Q is placed at each of opposite corners of a square. A charge q is placed at each of the other two corners. If the net electrical force on Q is zero, then Q/q equals

(a) $-\frac{1}{\sqrt{2}}$ (b) $-2\sqrt{2}$ (c) – 1 (d) 1

12 Two charges, each equal to q, are kept at $x = -a$ and $x = +a$ on the X-axis. A particle of mass m and charge $q_0 = \frac{q}{2}$ is placed at the origin. If charge q_0 is given a small ($y << a$) displacement along the Y-axis, the net force acting on the particle is proportional to

(a) y (b) $-y$ (c) $\frac{1}{y^2}$ (d) $-\frac{1}{y^2}$

13 Four positive charges $(2\sqrt{2}-1)Q$ each are arranged at corners of a square. Another charge q is placed at the centre of the square. The system is in equilibrium, if q is

(a) $-7Q/4$ (b) $-4Q/7$
(c) $-Q$ (d) None of these

14 The electric force on $2\mu C$ charge placed at the centre O of two equilateral triangles each of side 10 cm, as shown in figure is P. If charge A, B, C, D, E and F are $2\,\mu C, 2\,\mu C, 2\,\mu C, -2\,\mu C, -2\,\mu C, -2\,\mu C$ respectively, then P is

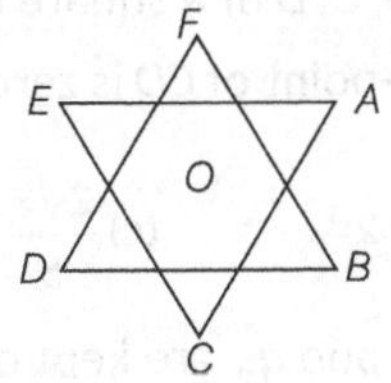

(a) 21.6 N (b) 64.8 N (c) 0 (d) 43.2 N

15 Two particles of equal mass m and charge q are placed at a distance of 16 cm. They do not experience any force. The value of $\frac{q}{m}$ is

(a) l (b) $\sqrt{\frac{\pi\varepsilon_0}{G}}$ (c) $\sqrt{\frac{G}{4\pi\varepsilon_0}}$ (d) $\sqrt{4\pi\varepsilon_0 G}$

16 Two small spheres each having the charge $+Q$ are suspended by insulating threads of length L from a hook. This arrangement is taken in space, where there is no gravitationect, then the angle between the two suspensial effons and the tension in each will be

(a) $180°, \frac{1}{4\pi\varepsilon_0}\frac{Q^2}{(2L)^2}$ (b) $90°, \frac{1}{4\pi\varepsilon_0}\frac{Q^2}{L^2}$
(c) $180°, \frac{1}{4\pi\varepsilon_0}\frac{Q^2}{2L^2}$ (d) $180°, \frac{1}{4\pi\varepsilon_0}\frac{Q^2}{L^2}$

17 Two small spherical balls each carrying a charge $Q = 10\,\mu C$ are suspended by two insulating threads of equal lengths 1 m each, from a point fixed in the ceiling. It is found that in equilibrium threads are separated by an angle 60° between them, as shown in the figure. What is the tension in the threads? (Given, $\frac{1}{4\pi\varepsilon_0} = 9\times10^9$ N-m/C^2)

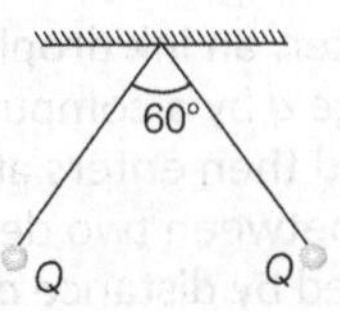

(a) 18 N (b) 1.8 N
(c) 0.18 N (d) None of these

18 Two identical charged spheres are suspended by strings of equal lengths. The strings make an angle of 30° with each other. When suspended in a liquid of density 2.7 g cm^{-3}, the angle remains the same. If density of the material of the sphere is 3.6 g cm^{-3}, the dielectric constant of the liquid is

(a) 1 (b) 4
(c) 3 (d) 2

19 Two pith balls with mass m are suspended from insulating threads. When the pith balls are given equal positive charge Q, they hang in equilibrium as shown. We now increase the charge on the left pith ball from Q to 2Q, while leaving its mass essentially unchanged. Which of the following diagrams best represents the new equilibrium configuration?

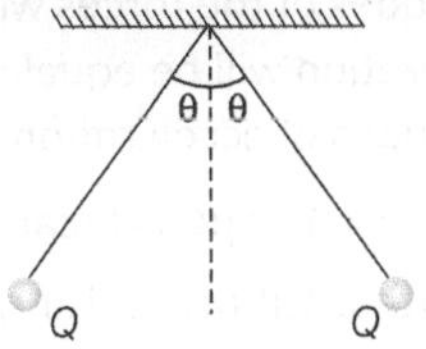

(a)
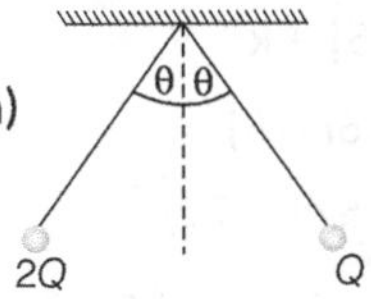

(b)
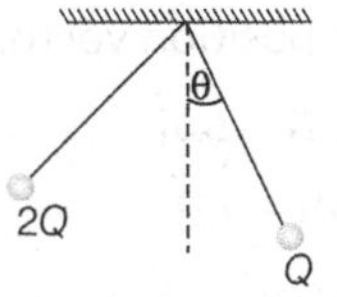

(c)
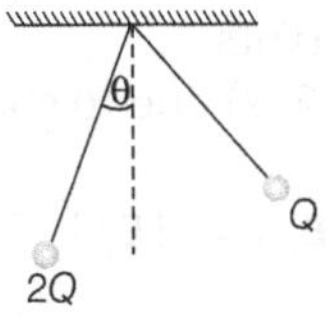

(d)
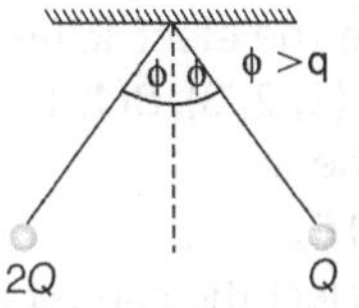

20 A point charge $+Q$ is placed at the centroid of an equilateral triangle. When a second charge $+Q$ is placed at a vertex of the triangle, the magnitude of the electrostatic force on the central charge is 8N. The magnitude of the net force on the central charge, when a third charge $+Q$ is placed at another vertex of the triangle is

(a) zero (b) 4 N
(c) $4\sqrt{2}$ N (d) 8 N

21 The number of electrons that should be removed from a coin of mass 1.6 g, so that it may float in electric field intensity 10^9 N/C directed upwards is

(a) 9.8×10^7
(b) 9.8×10^5
(c) 9.8×10^3
(d) 9.8×10^1

22 A particle of mass m and charge $+q$ is placed at rest in a uniform electric field as shown and released. The kinetic energy it attains after moving a distance y is (Neglect gravity)

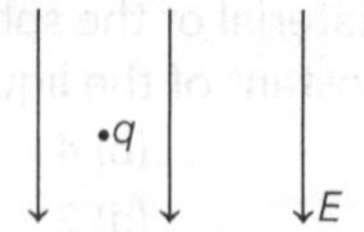

(a) $\frac{1}{2}qEy$ (b) qEy

(c) qE^2y (d) $\frac{1}{2}m(qEy)$

23 A proton and an electron are placed in a uniform electric field.

(a) The electric forces acting on them will be equal
(b) The magnitudes of the forces will be equal
(c) Their acceleration will be equal
(d) The magnitudes of acceleration will be equal

24 A point charge $q = 100\ \mu C$ is located in the XY-plane at the point with position vector $\mathbf{r}_0 = 2\hat{\mathbf{i}} + 3\hat{\mathbf{j}} + \hat{\mathbf{k}}$. What is the electric field vector (in kN/C) at the point with position vector $\mathbf{r} = 8\hat{\mathbf{i}} - 5\hat{\mathbf{j}} + \hat{\mathbf{k}}$?

(a) $4.2\hat{\mathbf{i}} - 5.6\hat{\mathbf{j}}$ (b) $6\hat{\mathbf{i}} - 8\hat{\mathbf{j}}$

(c) $54\hat{\mathbf{i}} - 72\hat{\mathbf{j}}$ (d) $5.4\hat{\mathbf{i}} - 7.2\hat{\mathbf{j}}$

25 A point charge q is placed at origin. Let $\mathbf{E}_A$, $\mathbf{E}_B$ and $\mathbf{E}_C$ be the electric field at three points A (1, 2, 3), B(1, 1, − 1) and C(2, 2, 2) due to charge q. Then,

(i) $\mathbf{E}_A \perp \mathbf{E}_B$ (ii) $|\mathbf{E}_B| = 4|\mathbf{E}_C|$

Select the correct alternative.

(a) Only (i) is correct
(b) Only (ii) is correct
(c) Both (i) and (ii) are correct
(d) Both (i) and (ii) are incorrect

26 Two charges $+5\ \mu C$ and $-10\ \mu C$ are placed 20 cm apart. The net electric field at the mid-point is

(a) 13.5×10^6 N/C directed towards $-10\ \mu C$
(b) 4.5×10^6 N/C directed towards $-10\ \mu C$
(c) 13.5×10^6 N/C directed towards $+5\ \mu C$
(d) 4.5×10^6 N/C directed towards $+5\ \mu C$

27 An infinite number of electric charges each equal to 5nC (magnitude) are placed along X-axis at $x = 1$ cm, $x = 2$ cm, $x = 4$ cm, $x = 8$ cm and so on. In the set up, if the successive charges have opposite sign, then electric field at $x = 0$ is

(a) 12×10^4 N/C (b) 24×10^4 N/C
(c) 36×10^4 N/C (d) 48×10^4 N/C

28 A hexagon of side L is placed in a horizontal plane and six equal charges q are fixed at its vertices. A point P is located vertically above the centre of the hexagon, at a height $L\sqrt{3}$ from the plane of the hexagon. Find the electric field at point P.

(a) $\frac{3\sqrt{3}q}{16\pi\varepsilon_0 L^2}$ (b) $\frac{3\sqrt{3}q}{4\pi\varepsilon_0 L^2}$

(c) $\frac{\sqrt{3}q}{16\pi\varepsilon_0 L^2}$ (d) $\frac{\sqrt{3}q}{4\pi\varepsilon_0 L^2}$

29 Point charges q, $-q$, $2Q$ and Q are placed in order at the corners A, B, C, D of a square of side $2b$. If the field at the mid-point of CD is zero, then $\frac{q}{Q}$ is

(a) 1 (b) 2 (c) $\frac{2\sqrt{2}}{5}$ (d) $\frac{5\sqrt{5}}{2}$

30 Two charges q_1 and q_2 are kept on X-axis and electric field at different points an X-axis is plotted against x. Choose correct statement about nature and magnitude of q_1 and q_2.

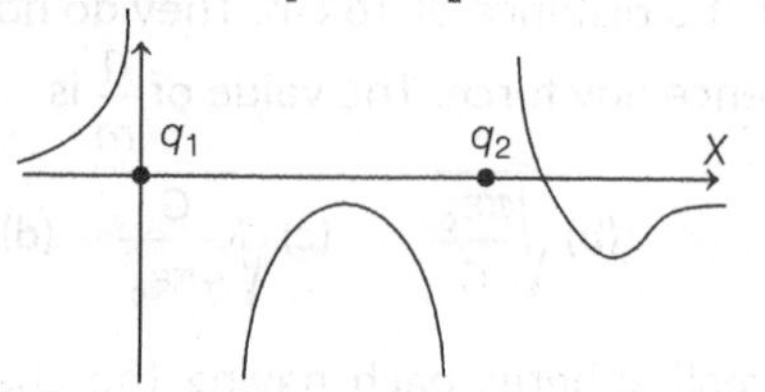

(a) q_1 + ve, q_2 − ve; $|q_1| > |q_2|$
(b) q_1 + ve, q_2 − ve; $|q_1| < |q_2|$
(c) q_1 − ve, q_2 + ve; $|q_1| > |q_2|$
(d) q_1 − ve, q_2 + ve; $|q_1| < |q_2|$

31 The figure shows some of the electric field lines corresponding to an electric field. The figure suggests

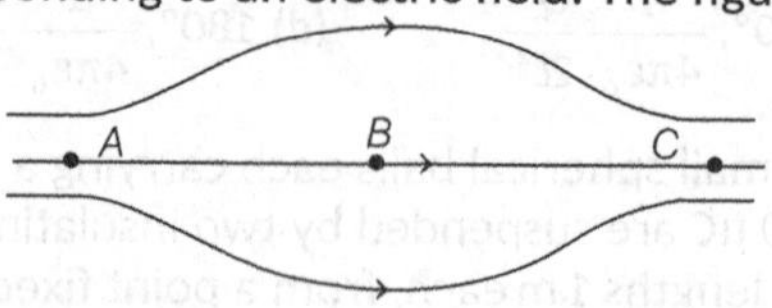

(a) $E_A > E_B > E_C$
(b) $E_A = E_B = E_C$
(c) $E_A = E_C > E_B$
(d) $E_A = E_C < E_B$

32 In an inkjet printer, an ink droplet of mass m is given a negative charge q by a computer controlled charging unit and then enters at speed v into the region midway between two deflecting plates of length L separated by distance d as shown in the figure. The electric field E is uniform in the regions between the plates.

Neglecting the gravitational force on the droplet, the maximum charge that it can have, so that it does not hit a plate is most closely approximated by

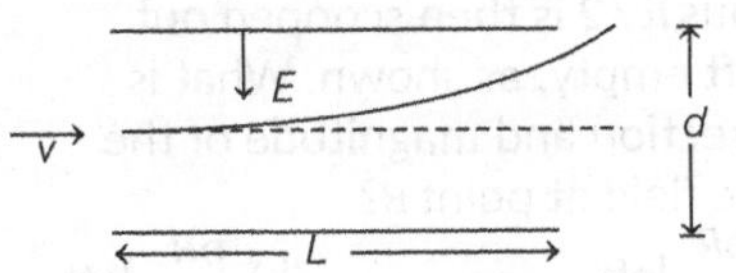

(a) $\frac{md}{E(vL)^2}$ (b) $\frac{mv^2}{dL^2}E$

(c) $\frac{m(vL)^2}{Ed}$ (d) $\frac{mv^2}{EL^2}d$

33 Two small sphere each of mass m are suspended by light string l metre in length as shown in the figure. Spheres have charges of q and $-q$ and are placed in the horizontal electric field. Electric field that enables the spheres to be in equilibrium at θ is

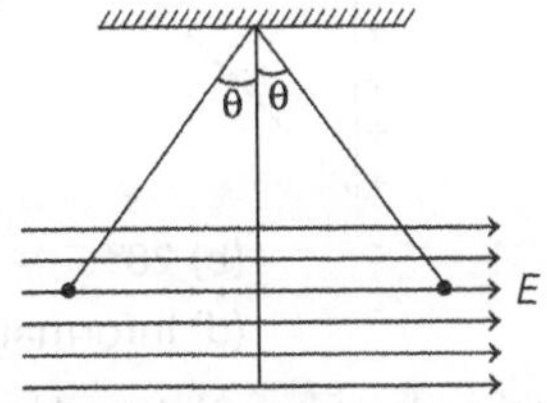

(a) $\frac{q}{4\pi\varepsilon_0}\frac{1}{(2l\sin\theta)^2}+\frac{mg\tan\theta}{q}$

(b) $\frac{mg\tan\theta}{q}-\frac{q}{4\pi\varepsilon_0}\frac{1}{(2l\sin\theta)^2}$

(c) $\frac{q}{4\pi\varepsilon_0}\frac{1}{(l\sin\theta)^2}+\frac{mg\tan\theta}{q}$

(d) $\frac{mg\tan\theta}{q}-\frac{q}{4\pi\varepsilon_0}\frac{1}{(l\sin\theta)^2}$

34 Two very long line charges of uniform charge density $+\lambda$ and $-\lambda$ are placed along same line with the separation between the nearest ends being $2a$, as shown in figure. The electric field intensity at point O is

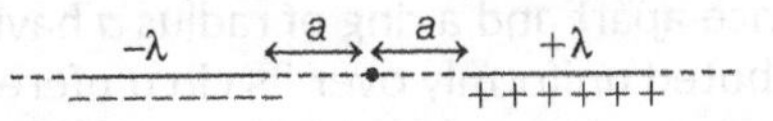

(a) $\frac{\lambda}{2\pi\varepsilon_0 a}$ (b) 0

(c) $\frac{\lambda}{\pi\varepsilon_0 a}$ (d) $\frac{\lambda}{4\pi\varepsilon_0 a}$

35 Which of the following graphs shows the correct variation of electric field as a function of x along the axis of a uniformly and positively charged ring of radius r and charge Q.

(a)

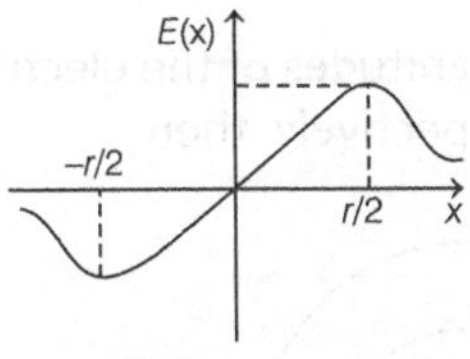

(b)

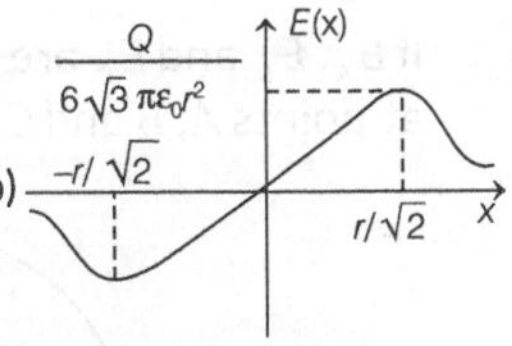

(c)

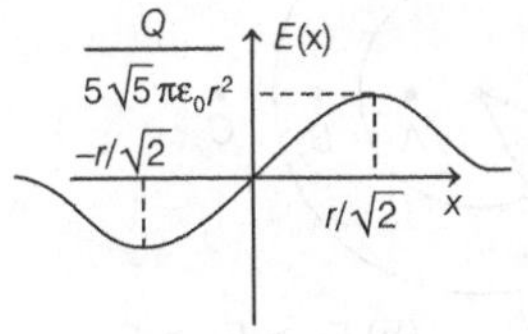

(d)

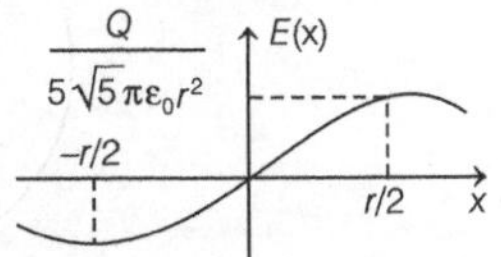

36 The charge per unit length of the four quadrant of the ring is 2λ, -2λ, λ, and $-\lambda$, respectively. The electric field at the centre is

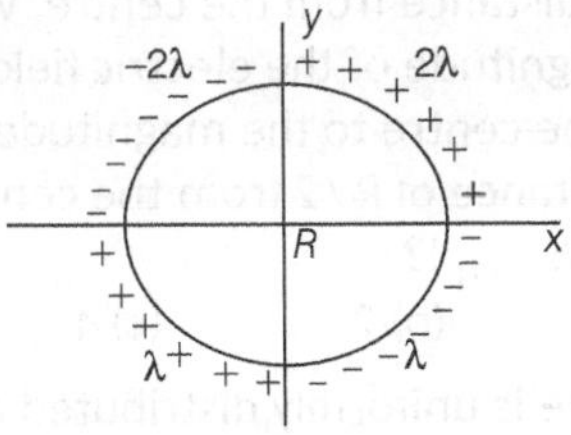

(a) $\frac{\lambda}{2\pi\varepsilon_0 R}\hat{i}$ (b) $\frac{\lambda}{2\pi\varepsilon_0 R}\hat{j}$

(c) $\frac{\sqrt{2}\lambda}{4\pi\varepsilon_0 R}\hat{i}$ (d) None of these

37 Two concentric rings, one of radius R and total charge $+Q$ and the second of radius $2R$ and total charge $-\sqrt{8}\,Q$, lie in XY-plane (i.e., $Z=0$ plane). The common centre of rings lies at origin and the common axis coincides with Z-axis. The charge is uniformly distributed on both rings. At what distance from origin is the net electric field on Z-axis zero?

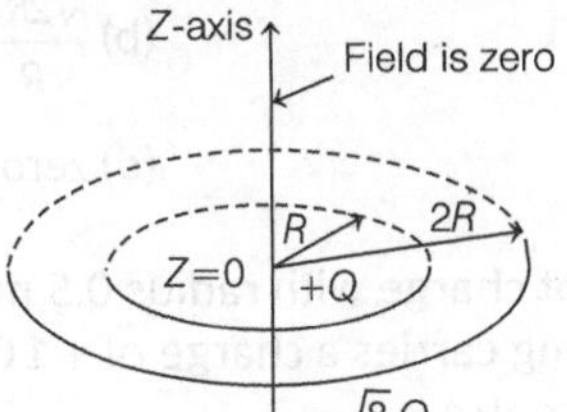

(a) $\sqrt{2}R$ (b) $2\sqrt{2}R$

(c) $2R$ (d) $\sqrt{3}R$

38 Consider two thin uniformly charged concentric shells of radii r and $2r$ having charges Q and $-Q$ respectively, as shown. Three points A, B and C are marked at distances $\frac{r}{2}$, $\frac{3r}{2}$ and $\frac{5r}{2}$ respectively from their common centre.

If E_A, E_B and E_C are magnitudes of the electric fields at points A, B and C respectively, then

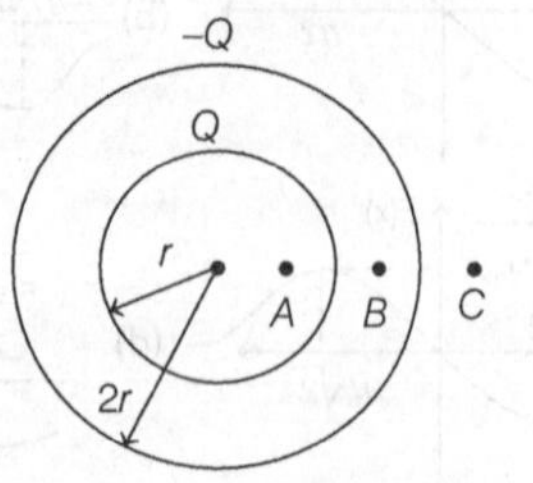

(a) $E_A > E_B > E_C$
(b) $E_C > E_B > E_A$
(c) $E_B > E_A = E_C$
(d) $E_B > E_A > E_C$

39 A sphere of radius R carries charge such that its volume charge density is proportional to the square of the distance from the centre. What is the ratio of the magnitude of the electric field at a distance $2R$ from the centre to the magnitude of the electric field at a distance of $R/2$ from the centre (i.e. $E_{r=2R}/E_{r=R/2}$)?

(a) 1 (b) 2 (c) 4 (d) 8

40 A charge is uniformly distributed on a wire, such that linear charge density is λ. Shape of the wire is shown in the figure, straight section is semi infinitely large. C is the centre of the semicircular portion of radius R. Considering all physical quantities in SI units, magnitude of electric field at C is $\left(K = \dfrac{1}{4\pi\varepsilon_0}\right)$

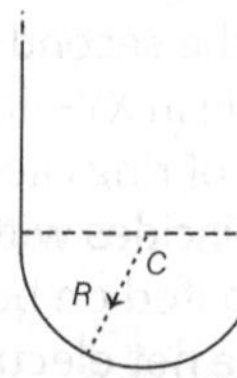

(a) $\dfrac{2K\lambda}{R}$
(b) $\dfrac{\sqrt{2}K\lambda}{R}$
(c) $\dfrac{K\lambda}{R}$
(d) zero

41 A ring of charge with radius 0.5 m has 0.002 π m gap. If the ring carries a charge of +1 C, the electric field at the centre is

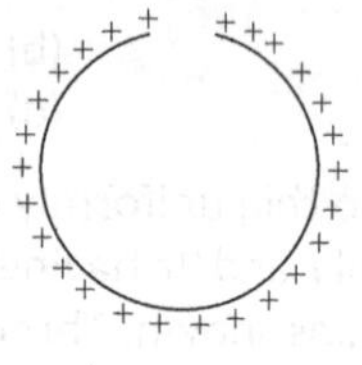

(a) 7.5×10^7 N/C
(b) 7.2×10^7 N/C
(c) 6.2×10^7 N/C
(d) 6.5×10^7 N/C

42 A positively charged sphere of radius R carries a volume charge density ρ (Figure). A spherical cavity of radius $R/2$ is then scooped out and left empty, as shown. What is the direction and magnitude of the electric field at point B?

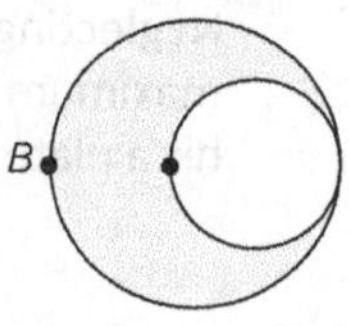

(a) $\dfrac{17\rho R}{54\varepsilon_0}$, left
(b) $\dfrac{\rho R}{6\varepsilon_0}$, left
(c) $\dfrac{17\rho R}{54\varepsilon_0}$, right
(d) $\dfrac{\rho R}{6\varepsilon_0}$, right

43 Consider a finite uniformly charged rod. Electric field at point P (shown) makes an angle θ with horizontal dotted line, then angle θ is

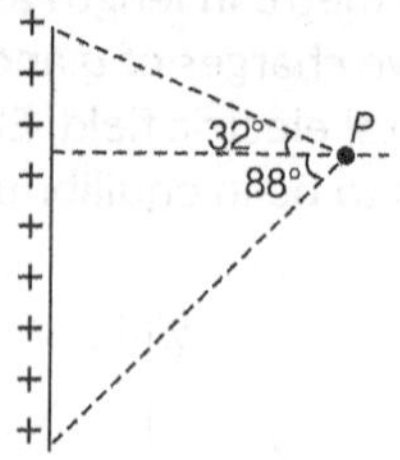

(a) 60°
(b) 28°
(c) 44°
(d) Information insufficient

44 Three charged rods of length L each are made of insulating material and form an equilateral triangle. They have linear charge densities of λ, λ and $-\lambda$ as shown in figure. Find the magnitude of electric field intensity at the centroid O of the triangle.

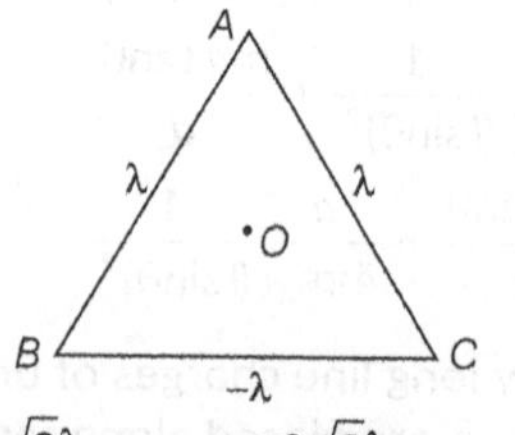

(a) $\dfrac{3\lambda}{2\pi\varepsilon_0 L}$
(b) $\dfrac{\sqrt{3}\lambda}{\pi\varepsilon_0 L}$
(c) $\dfrac{3\sqrt{3}\lambda}{2\pi\varepsilon_0 L}$
(d) $\dfrac{3\lambda}{\pi\varepsilon_0 L}$

45 Two point charges of charge $+q$ each are placed $2a$ distance apart and a ring of radius a having charge Cq distributed uniformly over its circumference is placed midways between them as shown in figure.If none of them accelerated when released, the value of C will be

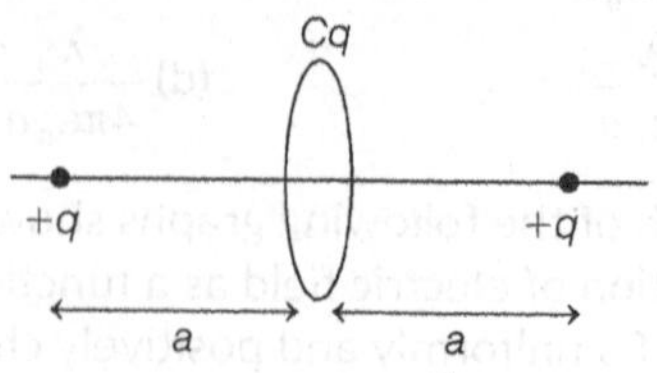

(a) $-\dfrac{1}{\sqrt{2}}$
(b) $-\sqrt{2}$
(c) $-\dfrac{1}{2\sqrt{2}}$
(d) $-2\sqrt{2}$

46 Consider a uniformly charged hemispherical shell shown alongside. Indicate the directions (not magnitude) of the electric field at the central point P_1 and an off-centre point P_2 on the drumhead of the shell.

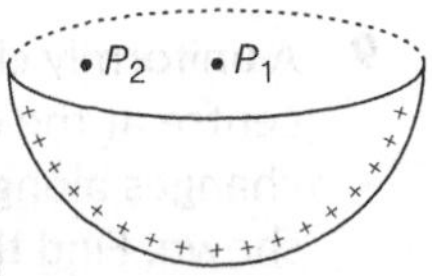

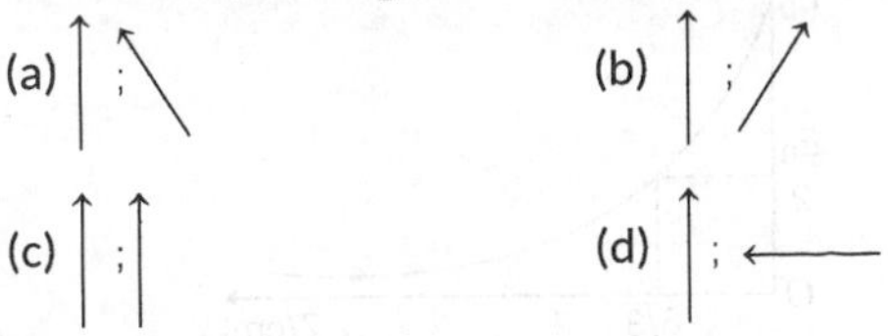

47 Using Thomson's model of the atom, consider an atom consisting of two electrons, each of charge $-e$, embedded in a sphere of charge $+2e$ and radius R. In equilibrium, each electron is at distance d from the centre of the atom. What is equilibrium separation between electrons?

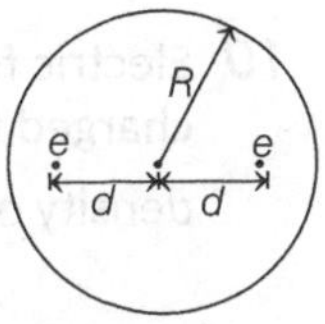

(a) R (b) $R/2$ (c) $R/3$ (d) $R/4$

48 A particle of mass m, charge $-Q$ is constrained to move along the axis of a ring of radius a. The ring carries a uniform charge density $+\lambda$ along its circumference. Initially, the particle lies in the plane of the ring at a point, where no net force acts on it. The period of oscillation of the particle when it is displaced slightly from its equilibrium position is

(a) $4\pi\sqrt{\dfrac{\varepsilon_0 ma^2}{\lambda Q}}$ (b) $2\pi\sqrt{\dfrac{2\varepsilon_0 ma^2}{\lambda Q}}$

(c) $2\pi\sqrt{\dfrac{4\varepsilon_0 ma^2}{\lambda Q}}$ (d) $2\pi\sqrt{\dfrac{\varepsilon_0 ma^2}{2\lambda Q}}$

49 A system consists of a uniformly charged ring of radius R carrying charge Q and a very long uniformly charged thread oriented along the axis of the ring, with one of its ends coinciding with the centre of the ring. The charge of the thread (per unit length) is equal to λ. The interaction force between the ring and the thread is

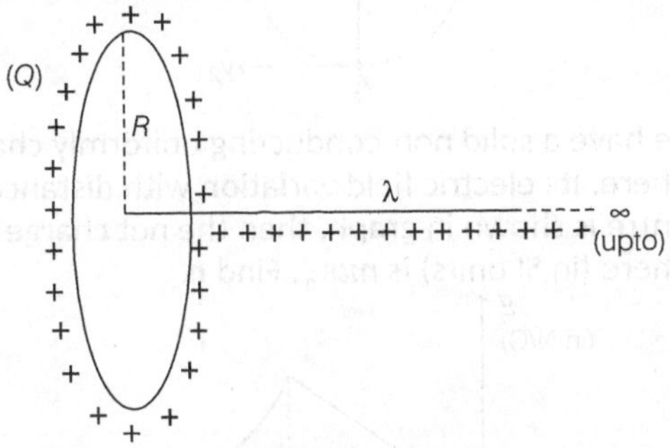

(a) $\dfrac{q\lambda}{4\pi\varepsilon_0 R}$ (b) $\dfrac{q\lambda}{2\pi\varepsilon_0 R}$ (c) $\dfrac{2q\lambda}{\pi\varepsilon_0 R}$ (d) zero

50 A disc is charged non-uniformly with charge per unit area depending on distance from the centre x as $\sigma = cx$. The radius of disc is 3 m and the electric field at a distance of 4 m from centre on it's axis is $\dfrac{1}{5\varepsilon_0}$ in SI units. Find c (in SI units).

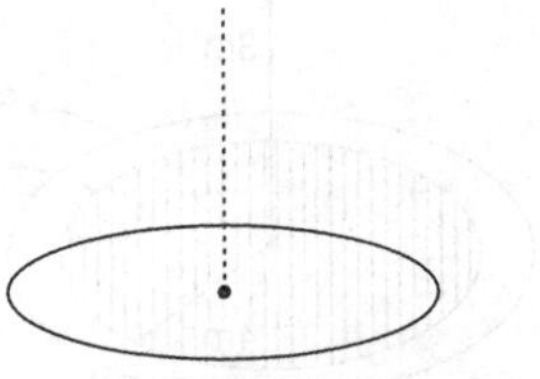

(a) 1 (b) 2

(c) 5 (d) 10

Numerical Value Questions

1 Two identical charge, 5μC each, are certain distance apart in the air. The largest charge to be transferred from one charge to another, so that their interaction force decreases 5 times when held at the same separation in a liquid of dielectric constant 2 is $\sqrt{n}$ μC. Find n.

2 A, B, C, D are the corners of a regular tetrahedron of side a. Three identical charges each Q are fixed at three corners B, C and D. The magnitude of electric field intensity at the corner A is $\dfrac{\sqrt{n}Q}{4\pi\varepsilon_0 a^2}$. Find n.

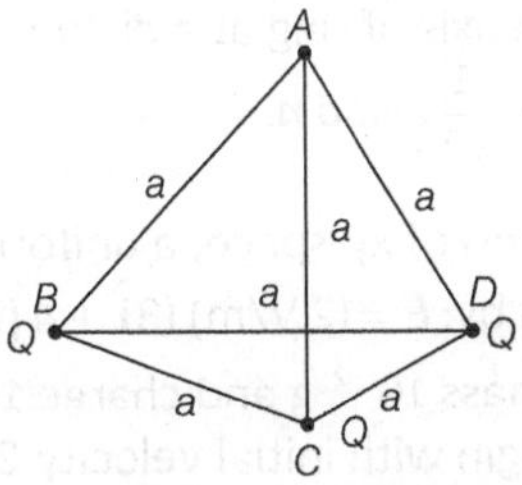

3 The curved wire, which is a part of a circle of radius R has a charge per unit length of $\lambda = \lambda_0 \sin 2\theta$, where θ is the angle shown in the figure. The electric field intensity at point O, the centre of the circle is $\dfrac{\sqrt{2}\lambda}{n\pi\varepsilon_0 R}$.

Find n.

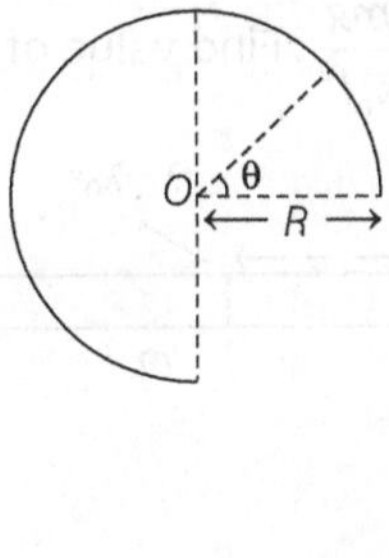

4 A disc of radius 4 m is uniformly charged with the charge of 1 μC. On the periphery of the disc, we stick a thin ring which has a uniform charge of – 1 μC. What is the electric field (in N/C) due to the combination at a point 3 m away from the centre of combination on the common axis?

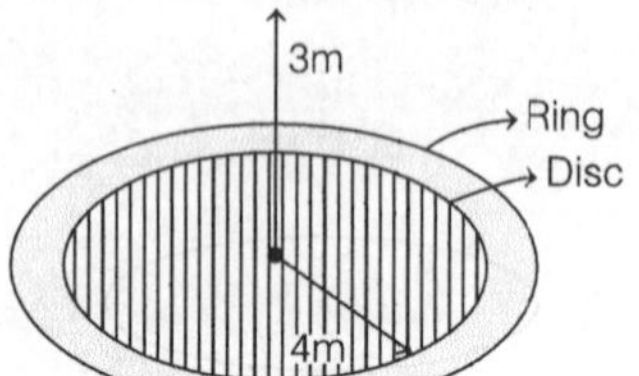

5 Three charged small spheres are suspended from point O with help of strings of length l as shown. All three charges are in equilibrium. Tension in middle string is $\frac{x}{10}$ N. Find x.

($m = 20$ g ; $q = 10$ μC; $l = 3$ m)

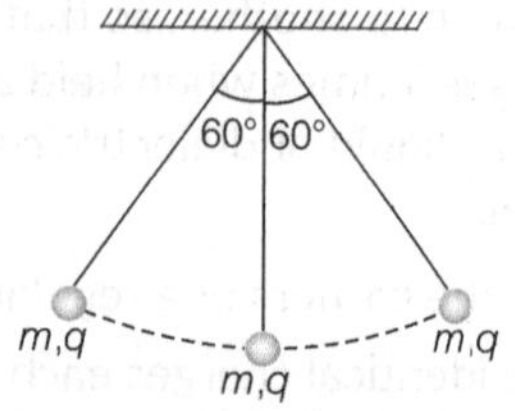

6 A point charge $-Q$ is placed at the centre of a uniformly charged ring of charge Q. Electric field at a point on the axis of ring at a distance x ($x >> R$) varies as $E \propto \frac{1}{x^n}$. Find n.

7 In a 2-D region of xy-space, a uniform electric field exists, given by: $E = (2\text{ V/m})(3\hat{\mathbf{i}} + 4\hat{\mathbf{j}})$. A charged particle of mass 10^{-2} g and charge 10^{-5} C is fired from the origin with initial velocity 20 m/s, directed along the negative y-direction. Find the minimum speed (in m/s) of the particle during its subsequent motion. Neglect gravity.

8 A rod of mass m (uniformly distributed) and length l is hinged about point O in a uniform vertical electric field as shown. Linear charge density of rod varies with x as $\lambda = \lambda_0 x$. Electric field for which rod remain horizontal is $\frac{nmg}{2\lambda_0 l^2}$. Find value of n.

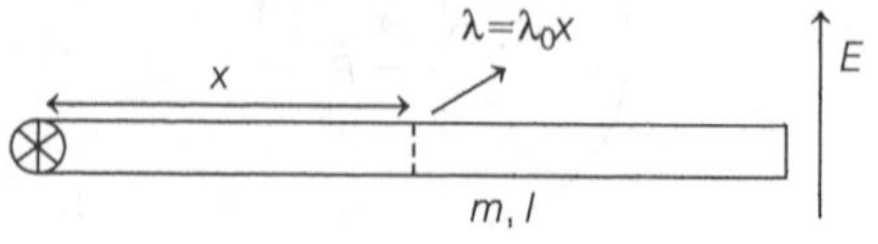

9 A uniformly charged disc lies in XY-plane with its centre at the origin. The strength of electric field (E) changes along the Z-axis according to the graph shown. Find the radius (in cm) of the disc.

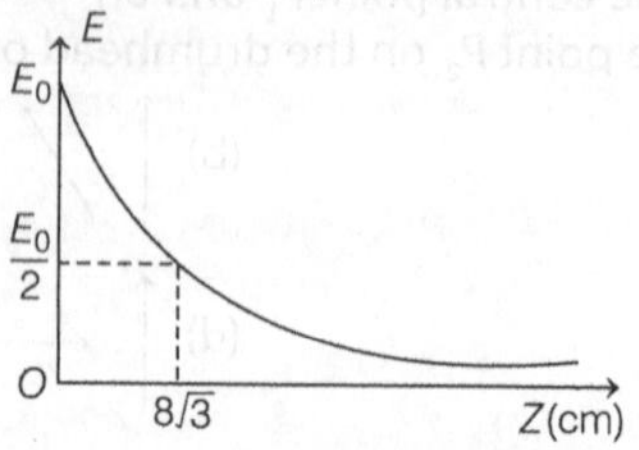

10 Electric field intensity at the centre of a uniformly charged thin hemispherical shell with surface charge density σ is $\frac{\sigma}{n\varepsilon_0}$. Find n.

11 In the YZ-plane, the entire region between $y = +a$ and $y = -a$ has a uniform surface charge density σ. The electric field at a point $(a, 0, 0)$ is $\frac{\sigma}{n\varepsilon_0}$. Find n.

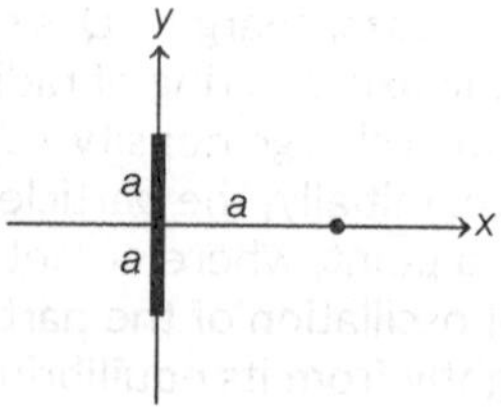

12 A ball of mass m with a charge q can rotate in a vertical plane at the end of a string of length $l = 10$ cm in a uniform electrostatic field whose lines of force are directed upwards. What horizontal velocity (in m/s) must be imparted to the ball in the upper position, so that the tension in the string in the lower position of the ball is 15 times the weight of the ball? (Given, $qE = 3\,mg$ and $g = 10\text{ m/s}^2$)

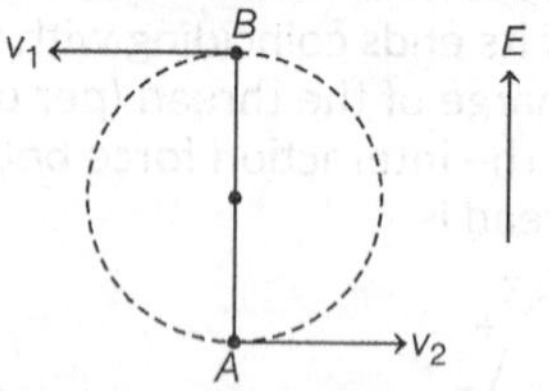

13 We have a solid non-conducting uniformly charged sphere. Its electric field variation with distance from centre is shown in graph, then the net charge on the sphere (in SI units) is $n\pi\varepsilon_0$. Find n.

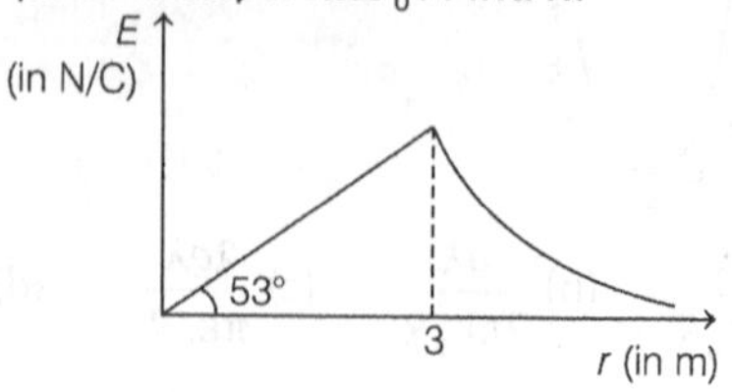

14 A 1kg ball is suspended in a uniform electric field with the help of a string fixed to a point. The ball is given a charge $\sqrt{5}$ C and the string make an angles 37° with the vertical in equilibrium position. In the equilibrium position, the tension is double the weight of the ball. Find the magnitude of the electric field in N/C.

15 An inclined plane making an angle of 37° with horizontal is placed in a uniform horizontal electric field E of 100 V/m. A block of mass 5 kg and charge 0.25 C is allowed to slide down from rest from a height of 6.75 m. If the coefficient of friction is 0.1, find the time(in seconds) taken by the block to reach the bottom. (Take, $g = 10\ m/s^2$)

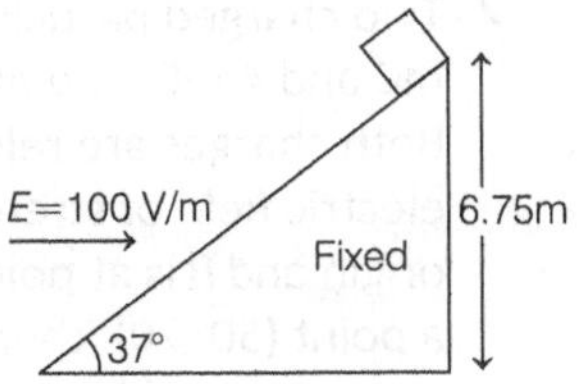

LEVEL 03 \ JEE Advanced Level

Single Choice Correct Questions

1 Identical charges of $-48\left(\frac{5}{4}-\frac{1}{\sqrt{3}}\right)$ μC are located at the vertices of a regular hexagon. What charge must be placed at the centre of the hexagon to set the whole system of charges in equilibrium?

(a) 29 μC
(b) 45 μC
(c) 59 μC
(d) 75 μC

2 Six point charges are placed at six corners of a cube as shown. Unit vector along direction of net electric field at centre of cube O is equal to

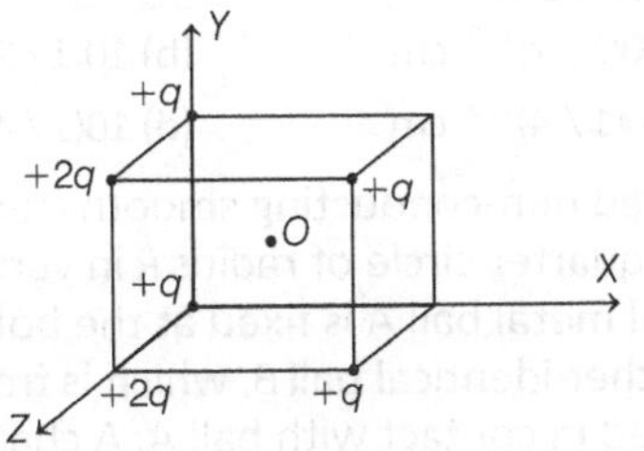

(a) $\frac{\hat{i}-\hat{k}}{\sqrt{2}}$ (b) $\frac{\hat{i}+\hat{k}}{\sqrt{2}}$

(c) $\frac{\hat{i}+\hat{j}}{\sqrt{2}}$ (d) $\frac{\hat{i}-\hat{j}}{\sqrt{2}}$

3 n identical point charges are kept symmetrically on the periphery of the circle $x^2+y^2=R^2$ in XY-plane. The resultant electric field at (0, 0, R) is E_1 and at (0, 0, $2R$) is E_2, the ratio of E_1/E_2 is

(a) $\frac{5\sqrt{5}}{4\sqrt{2}}$ (b) $\frac{5}{2}$

(c) 2 (d) $\frac{5\sqrt{5}}{2\sqrt{2}}$

4 A particle is uncharged and is thrown vertically upward from ground level with a speed of $5\sqrt{5}$ m/s in a region of space having uniform electric field. As a result, it attains a maximum height h. The particle is then given a positive charge $+q$ and reaches the same maximum height h when thrown vertically upward with a speed of 13 m/s. Finally, the particle is given a negative charge $-q$. Ignoring air resistance, determine the speed with which the negatively charged particle must be thrown vertically upward, so that it attains exactly the same maximum height h.

(a) 6 m/s (b) 8 m/s (c) 9 m/s (d) 10 m/s

5 Choose the incorrect statement.

(a) The electric field due to a discrete charge configuration is not defined at the locations of the discrete charges.
(b) For continuous volume charge distribution, it is defined at any point in the distribution.
(c) For a surface charge distribution, electric field is discontinuous across the surface.
(d) For a finite continuous volume charge distribution, electric field is discontinuous at the boundary.

6 In a horizontal uniform electric field, a small charged block of charge q is gently released on the top of a fixed sperical dome. The block slides down the dome without friction and breaks away from the surface of the dome at the angular position $\theta = \sin^{-1}\left(\frac{3}{5}\right)$ from vertical. The ratio of the force of gravity acting on the block to force of its interaction with the field is

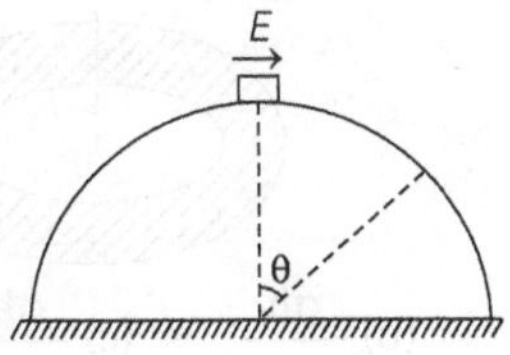

(a) 2.5 (b) 4 (c) 4.5 (d) 5

7 Two charged particles A and B are having charge -2 mC and 4 mC, and mass 2 kg and 1 kg, respectively. Both charges are released from rest in uniform electric field of strength 10 kN/C. Initially, A is at origin and B is at point (100, 100). At $t = 3$ sec, if B at a point (50, 70), then find the location of the point, where A would be at this time. (Assuming there is no gravity)

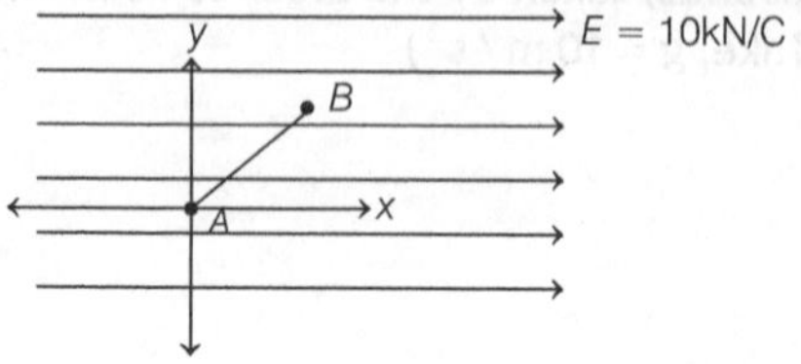

(a) (160, 30) (b) (90, 30) (c) (160, 15) (d) (70, 15)

8 A ring carries a uniform linear charge density on one half and the linear charge density of same magnitude but opposite sign on the other half.

(a) The component of electric field along the axis is zero at all points on the axis

(b) The component of electric field along the axis is zero only at the centre

(c) The resultant electric field at the centre is zero

(d) The resultant electric field at all points on the axis is zero except the centre

9 A non-conducting disc of mass = 2 kg, total charge = + 1C uniformly distributed, is placed on a rough horizontal non-conducting surface with its cross-section in vertical plane as shown. A uniform horizontal electric field E is now switched ON. The maximum magnitude of electric field E, so that the disc rolls purely is (Take, $g = 10\ \text{ms}^{-2}$)

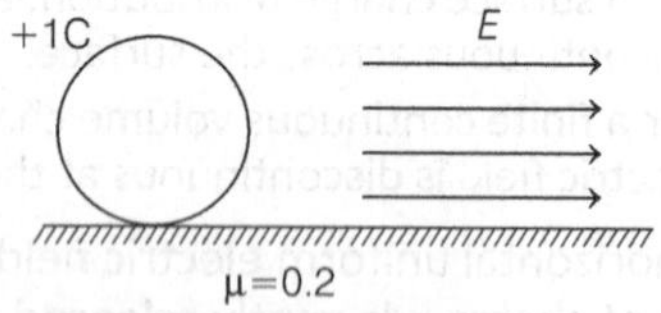

(a) 10 N/C (b) 12 N/C (c) 15 N/C (d) 20 N/C

10 A thin disc of radius $b = 2a$ has a concentric hole of radius a in it (see figure). It carries uniform surface charge σ on it. The electric field on its axis at height h ($h << a$) from its centre is given as

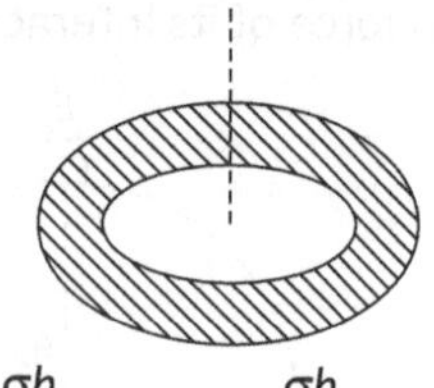

(a) $\dfrac{\sigma h}{4a\varepsilon_0}$ (b) $\dfrac{\sigma h}{2a\varepsilon_0}$ (c) $\dfrac{\sigma h}{8a\varepsilon_0}$ (d) $\dfrac{\sigma h}{a\varepsilon_0}$

11 A thin long strip whose cross-section is a semicircle carries a uniform surface charge of density σ on its inner surface. Find the electric field at a point O located midway on its axis.

(a) $\dfrac{\sigma}{2\pi\varepsilon_0}$ (b) $\dfrac{\sigma}{\pi\varepsilon_0}$

(c) $\dfrac{\sigma}{2\varepsilon_0}$ (d) $\dfrac{\sigma}{\varepsilon_0}$

12 Two small equally charged spheres, each of mass m, are suspended from the same point by silk threads of length l. The distance between the spheres $x << l$. Find the rate $\dfrac{dq}{dt}$ with which the charge leaks off each sphere, if they approach each other with velocity varying as $v = \dfrac{a}{\sqrt{x}}$, where a is a constant.

(a) $\dfrac{3a}{2}\sqrt{\dfrac{2\pi\varepsilon_0 mg}{l}}$ (b) $\dfrac{2a}{3}\sqrt{\dfrac{2\pi\varepsilon_0 mg}{l}}$

(c) $\dfrac{3a}{2}\sqrt{\dfrac{4\pi\varepsilon_0 mg}{l}}$ (d) $\dfrac{2a}{3}\sqrt{\dfrac{4\pi\varepsilon_0 mg}{l}}$

13 Two small equally charged identical conducting balls are suspended from long threads secured at one point. The charges and masses of the balls are such that they are in equilibrium when the distance between them is 10 cm (the length of the threads >> 10 cm.) One of the balls is then discharged. What will be the distance between the balls when equilibrium is restored?

(a) $10(1/2)^{1/3}$ cm (b) $10(1/2)^{3/2}$ cm

(c) $10(1/4)^{1/3}$ cm (d) $10(1/4)^{2/3}$ cm

14 A fixed non-conducting smooth track is in the shape of a quarter circle of radius R in vertical plane. A small metal ball A is fixed at the bottom of the track. Another identical ball B, which is free to move, is placed in contact with ball A. A charge Q is given to ball A which gets equally shared by the two balls. Ball B gets repelled and ultimately comes to rest in its equilibrium position, where its radius vector makes an angle $\theta = 60°$ with vertical. Mass of ball B is m. Find charge Q that was given to the balls.

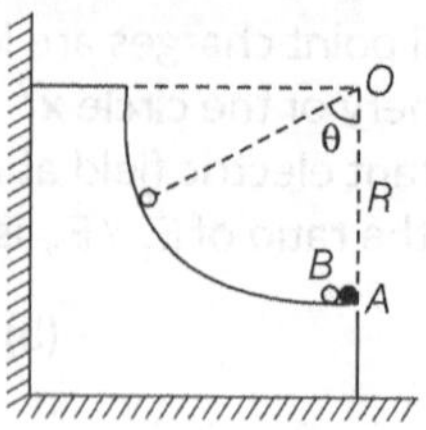

(a) $R\sqrt{\pi\varepsilon_0 mg}$ (b) $2R\sqrt{\pi\varepsilon_0 mg}$

(c) $3R\sqrt{\pi\varepsilon_0 mg}$ (d) $4R\sqrt{\pi\varepsilon_0 mg}$

15 A charged particle enters at point A and comes out from B. Its velocity makes angle α and β with electric field at these two points. Ratio of kinetic energy of charged particle at these two points will be

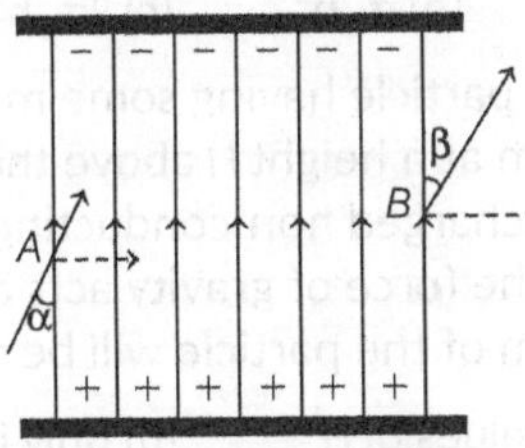

(a) $\frac{\sin^2\alpha}{\sin^2\beta}$ (b) $\frac{\sin^2\beta}{\sin^2\alpha}$

(c) $\frac{\cos^2\alpha}{\cos^2\beta}$ (d) $\frac{\cos^2\beta}{\cos^2\alpha}$

16 Two non-conducting infinite wires have shapes as shown in the figure. The linear charge densities of wire (1) and wire (2) are

$\begin{cases} x, & \text{if } x \le -a \text{ and } x \ge a \\ 0, & \text{if } -a < x < a \end{cases}$ $\begin{cases} y, & \text{if } y \le -a \text{ and } y \ge a \\ 0, & \text{if } -a < y < a \end{cases}$

respectively, where (x, y) are coordinates of point on the wire. An electron is released from origin, the unit vector along the direction of velocity of the electron just after its release will be

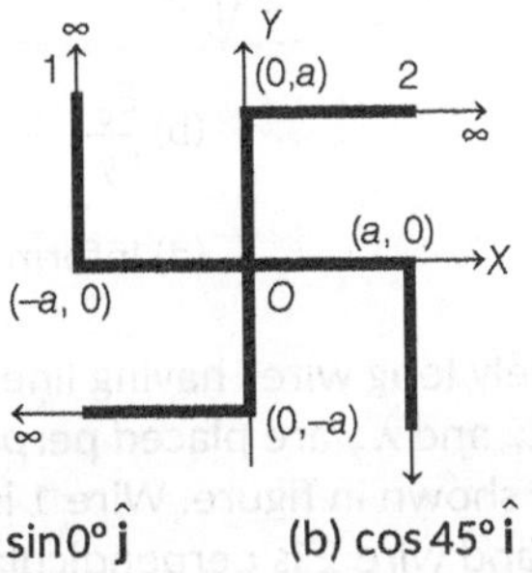

(a) $\cos 0°\hat{i} + \sin 0°\hat{j}$ (b) $\cos 45°\hat{i} + \sin 45°\hat{j}$

(c) $-\cos 0°\hat{i} + \sin 0°\hat{j}$ (d) $\cos 45°\hat{i} - \sin 45°\hat{j}$

17 Find the force experienced by the semicircular wire charged with a charge q, placed as shown in figure. Radius of the wire is R and the long line of charge with linear charge density λ is passing through its centre and perpendicular to the plane of wire.

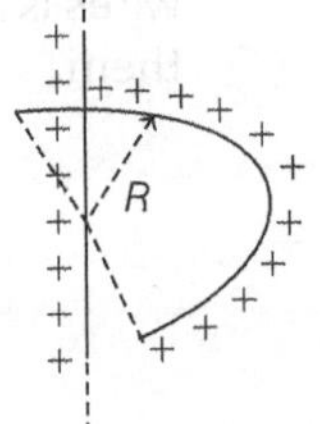

(a) $\frac{\lambda q}{2\pi^2\varepsilon_0 R}$ (b) $\frac{\lambda q}{\pi^2\varepsilon_0 R}$

(c) $\frac{\lambda q}{4\pi^2\varepsilon_0 R}$ (d) $\frac{\lambda q}{4\pi\varepsilon_0 R}$

18 A thin conducting ring of radius R has an electric charge $+Q$. If a point charge q is placed at the centre of the ring, the increment in tension in the ring will be

(a) $\frac{Qq}{8\pi\varepsilon_0 R^2}$ (b) $\frac{Qq}{4\pi\varepsilon_0 R^2}$

(c) $\frac{Qq}{8\pi^2\varepsilon_0 R^2}$ (d) $\frac{Qq}{4\pi^2\varepsilon_0 R^2}$

19 A spherical region of radius $3R$ have three different volume charge density $+\rho$, -2ρ and $+3\rho$ as shown. Electric field at point A is

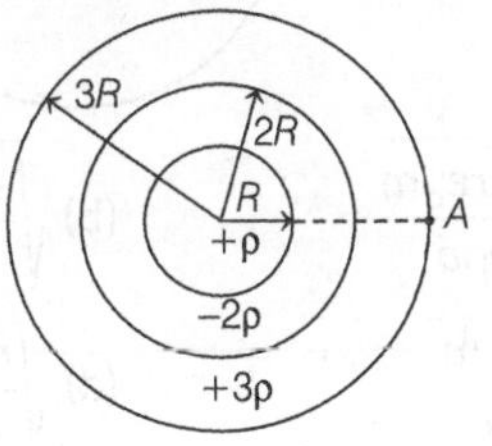

(a) $\frac{20\rho R}{27\varepsilon_0}$ (b) $\frac{25\rho R}{27\varepsilon_0}$ (c) $\frac{40\rho R}{27\varepsilon_0}$ (d) $\frac{44\rho R}{27\varepsilon_0}$

20 A square loop of side length a has a uniform linear charge density λ along its periphery. The loop lies in a horizontal plane. A particle having charge q is placed exactly above the centre of the square at a height a. The particle stays in equilibrium. Its mass is

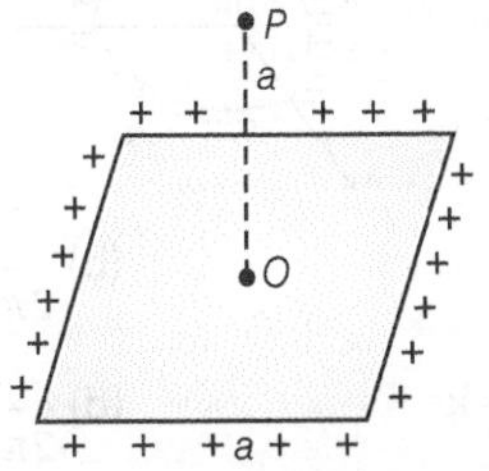

(a) $\frac{8q\lambda}{5\sqrt{6}\,\pi\varepsilon_0 ga}$ (b) $\frac{2q\lambda}{5\sqrt{3}\,\pi\varepsilon_0 ga}$

(c) $\frac{q\lambda}{5\sqrt{3}\,\pi\varepsilon_0 ga}$ (d) $\frac{2q\lambda}{5\sqrt{6}\,\pi\varepsilon_0 ga}$

21 The diagram shows a uniformly charged hemisphere of radius R. It has volume charge density ρ. If the magnitude of electric field at a point $2R$ distance above its centre is E, then what is the magnitude of electric field at the point which is $2R$ below its centre?

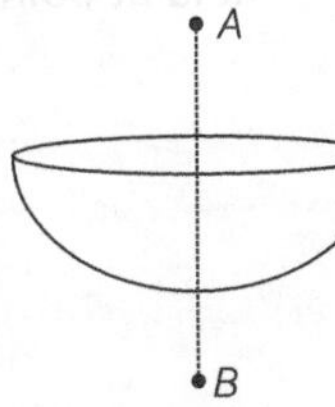

(a) $\frac{\rho R}{6\varepsilon_0} + E$ (b) $\frac{\rho R}{12\varepsilon_0} - E$ (c) $-\frac{\rho R}{6\varepsilon_0} + E$ (d) $\frac{\rho R}{24\varepsilon_0} + E$

22 A cavity of radius r is made inside a solid sphere. The volume charge density of the remaining sphere is ρ. An electron (charge e, mass m) is released inside the cavity from point P as shown in figure. The centre of sphere and centre of cavity are separated by a distance a. The time after which the electron again touches the sphere is

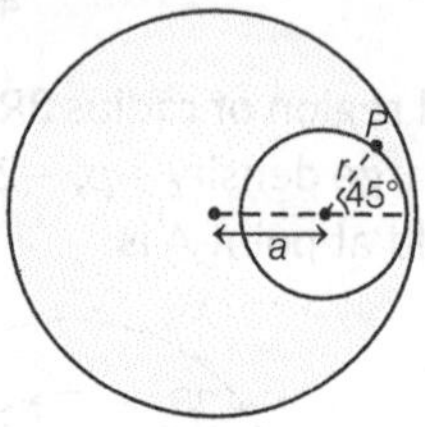

(a) $\sqrt{\dfrac{6\sqrt{2}r\varepsilon_0 m}{e\rho a}}$ (b) $\sqrt{\dfrac{\sqrt{2}r\varepsilon_0 m}{e\rho a}}$

(c) $\sqrt{\dfrac{6r\varepsilon_0 m}{e\rho a}}$ (d) $\sqrt{\dfrac{r\varepsilon_0 m}{e\rho a}}$

23 Three quarter circles (each of radius R) made of insulating material are uniformly charged with linear charge densities $-\lambda$, $+\lambda$ and $-\lambda$ and arranged in space as shown. Then, net electric field at centre is

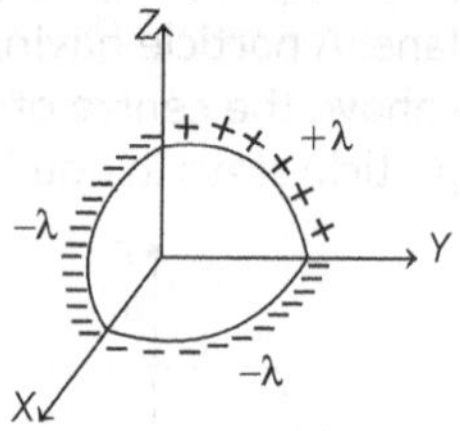

(a) $\dfrac{\lambda}{2\pi\varepsilon_0 R}\hat{i}$ (b) $\dfrac{\lambda}{2\pi\varepsilon_0 R}\hat{j}$

(c) $\dfrac{\lambda}{2\pi\varepsilon_0 R}\hat{k}$ (d) $\dfrac{\lambda}{2\pi\varepsilon_0 R}(\hat{j}+\hat{k})$

24 A hemispherical bowl of inner radii R and outer radii $2R$ is charged with volume charge density $\rho = \rho_0 \dfrac{r}{R}$, where r is the distance from the centre. The electric field at point O is

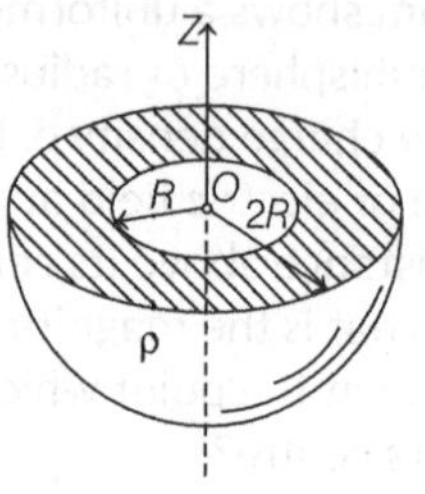

(a) $\dfrac{2\rho_0 R}{3\varepsilon_0}$ (b) $\dfrac{3\rho_0 R}{4\varepsilon_0}$ (c) $\dfrac{\rho_0 R}{2\varepsilon_0}$ (d) $\dfrac{3\rho_0 R}{8\varepsilon_0}$

25 A square of side b centred at the origin with sides parallel to axes of X and Y has surface charge density $\sigma(x, y) = \sigma_0 xy$ within its boundaries. Total charge on the square is

(a) zero (b) $\sigma_0 b^2$ (c) $2\sigma_0 b^2$ (d) $4\sigma_0 b^2$

26 A charged particle having some mass is resting in equilibrium at a height H above the centre of a uniformly charged non-conducting horizontal ring of radius R. The force of gravity acts downwards. The equilibrium of the particle will be stable

(a) for all values of H (b) only if $H > \dfrac{R}{\sqrt{2}}$

(c) only if $H < \dfrac{R}{\sqrt{2}}$ (d) only if $H = \dfrac{R}{\sqrt{2}}$

27 The electric field intensity at the centre of a uniformly charged hemispherical shell is E_0. Now, two portions of the hemisphere are cut from either side and remaining portion is shown in figure. If $\alpha = \beta = \dfrac{\pi}{3}$, then electric field intensity at centre due to remaining portion is

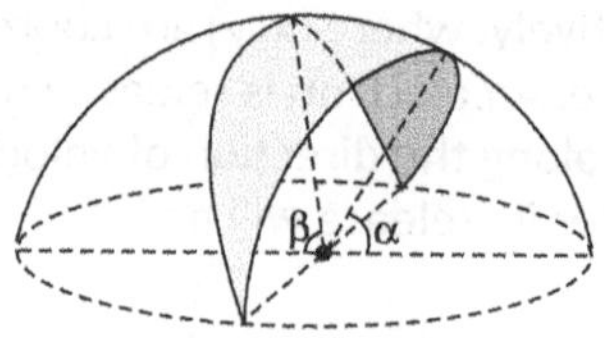

(a) $\dfrac{E_0}{3}$ (b) $\dfrac{E_0}{6}$

(c) $\dfrac{E_0}{2}$ (d) Information insufficient

28 Two infinitely long wires having linear charge densities λ_1 and λ_2 are placed perpendicular to one another as shown in figure. Wire 1 is in the plane of the paper and wire 2 is perpendicular to this plane. The symbol ⊙ indicates that the wire is going into the plane of the paper. Separation between the two wires is r. Find the force of interaction between them.

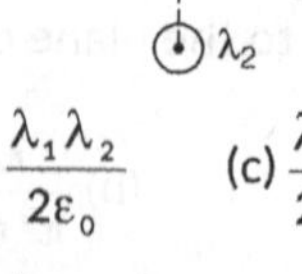

(a) $\dfrac{\lambda_1\lambda_2}{\varepsilon_0}$ (b) $\dfrac{\lambda_1\lambda_2}{2\varepsilon_0}$ (c) $\dfrac{\lambda_1\lambda_2}{2\pi\varepsilon_0}$ (d) $\dfrac{\lambda_1\lambda_2}{4\pi\varepsilon_0}$

29 A charged particle q of mass m is in equilibrium at a height h from a horizontal infinite line charge with uniform linear charge density λ. The charge lies in the vertical plane containing the line charge. The time period of small oscillations along vertical about its equilibrium position is

(a) $2\pi\sqrt{\dfrac{mh^2}{2K q\lambda}}$ (b) $2\pi\sqrt{\dfrac{mh^2}{K q\lambda}}$

(c) $2\pi\sqrt{\dfrac{2mh^2}{K q\lambda}}$ (d) $\pi\sqrt{\dfrac{mh^2}{K q\lambda}}$

30 A semicircular ring of radius R carries a uniform linear charge of λ. P is a point in the plane of the ring at a distance R from centre O. OP is perpendicular to AB. Find electric field intensity at point P.

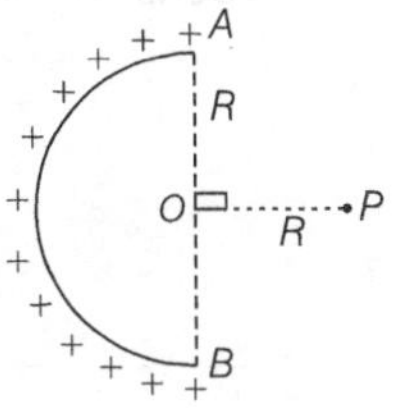

(a) $\dfrac{\lambda}{\pi\varepsilon_0 R}\ln(\sqrt{2}+1)$ (b) $\dfrac{\lambda}{2\pi\varepsilon_0 R}\ln(\sqrt{2}+1)$

(c) $\dfrac{2\lambda}{\pi\varepsilon_0 R}\ln(\sqrt{2}+1)$ (d) $\dfrac{\lambda}{4\pi\varepsilon_0 R}\ln(\sqrt{2}+1)$

31 In the figure shown, a very long wire and a semicircular ring of radius R are placed in the same plane. The centre of the ring is at a distance r from the wire. The wire has uniformly distributed line charge density λ and the ring has linear charge density $+\lambda$ on one half and $-\lambda$ on the other half as shown. Find the magnitude of net torque on the ring due to the wire.

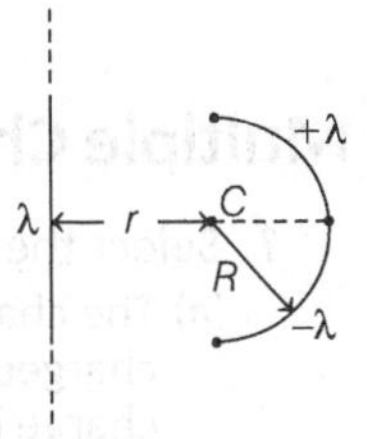

(a) $\dfrac{\lambda^2 R}{\pi\varepsilon_0}\ln\left(\dfrac{R+r}{r}\right)$ (b) $\dfrac{\lambda^2 R}{2\pi\varepsilon_0}\ln\left(\dfrac{R+r}{r}\right)$

(c) $\dfrac{\lambda^2 R}{\pi\varepsilon_0}\ln\left(\dfrac{R}{r}\right)$ (d) $\dfrac{\lambda^2 R}{2\pi\varepsilon_0}\ln\left(\dfrac{R}{r}\right)$

32 The charge and mass of two particles are $+Q$, M and $-q$, m, respectively. The particles separated by a distance L, are released from rest in a uniform electric field E. The electric field is parallel to line joining both the charges and is directed from negative to positive charge. For the separation between particles to remain constant, find the value of L. $\left(K = \dfrac{1}{4\pi\varepsilon_0}\right)$

(a) $\sqrt{\dfrac{(M+m)KQq}{E(qM+Qm)}}$ (b) $\sqrt{\dfrac{(M-m)KQq}{E(qM+Qm)}}$

(c) $\sqrt{\dfrac{(M+m)KQq^2}{E(qM-Qm)}}$ (d) $\sqrt{\dfrac{(M-m)KQ^2q}{E^2(qM-Qm)}}$

33 A light weight particle of charge Q is fixed at one end of an electrically insulated uniform elastic rod of natural length L, cross-sectional area A and Young's modulus Y. The rod is placed in space having uniform electric field of magnitude E and directed parallel to length of the rod as shown. Neglecting gravity, the magnitude of extension in this rod is

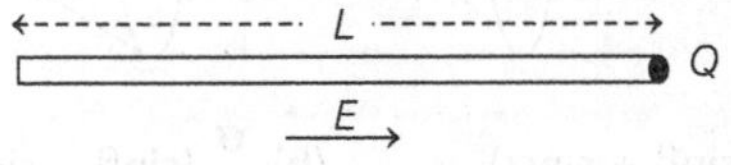

(a) 0 (b) $\dfrac{2QEL}{YA}$ (c) $\dfrac{QEL}{YA}$ (d) $\dfrac{QEL}{2YA}$

34 The electric field vector at point $P(a, a, a)$ due to three uniformly charged infinite wires 1, 2 and 3 with uniform charge density λ each kept along the X, Y and Z-axes respectively, as shown in figure is

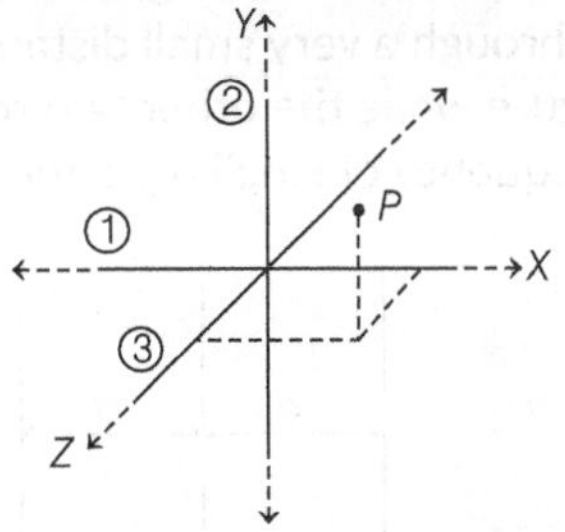

(a) $\dfrac{\lambda}{3\pi\varepsilon_0 a}(\hat{i}+\hat{j}+\hat{k})$ (b) $\dfrac{\lambda}{2\pi\varepsilon_0 a}(\hat{i}+\hat{j}+\hat{k})$

(c) $\dfrac{\lambda}{2\sqrt{2}\pi\varepsilon_0 a}(\hat{i}+\hat{j}+\hat{k})$ (d) $\dfrac{\sqrt{2}\lambda}{\pi\varepsilon_0 a}(\hat{i}+\hat{j}+\hat{k})$

35 A non-conducting infinite rod is placed along the Z-axis; the upper half of the rod (lying along $Z > 0$) is charged positively with a uniform linear charge density $+\lambda$, while the lower half ($Z < 0$) is charged negatively with a uniform linear charge density $-\lambda$. The origin is located at the junction of the positive and negative halves of the rod. A uniformly charged annular disc (surface charge density $= \sigma_0$) of inner radius R and outer radius $2R$ is placed in the XY-plane with its centre at the origin. The force on the rod due to the disc is

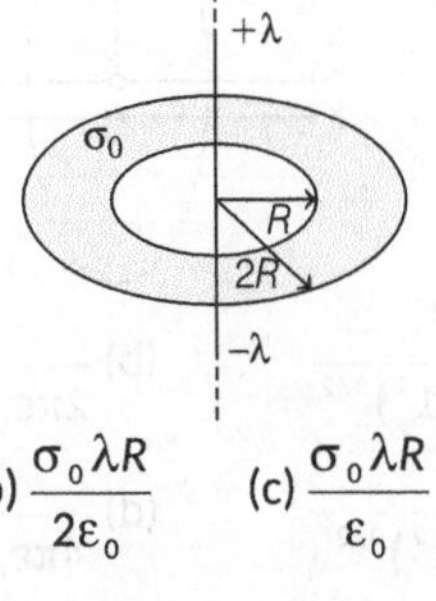

(a) $\dfrac{2\sigma_0\lambda R}{\varepsilon_0}$ (b) $\dfrac{\sigma_0\lambda R}{2\varepsilon_0}$ (c) $\dfrac{\sigma_0\lambda R}{\varepsilon_0}$ (d) $\dfrac{\sigma_0\lambda R}{3\varepsilon_0}$

36 A cylinder is uniformly charged on its curved surface with surface charge density σ. Radius of the cylinder is R. Calculate the electric field at point P on the axis of the cylinder, as shown in the figure.

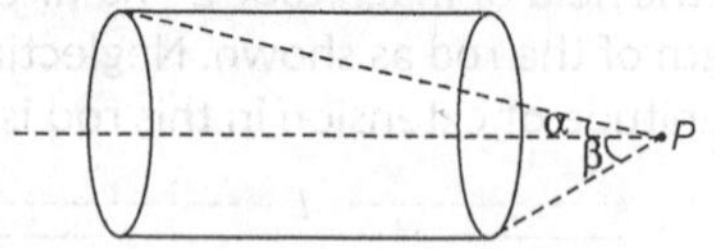

(a) $\frac{\sigma}{\varepsilon_0}(\sin\beta + \sin\alpha)$ (b) $\frac{\sigma}{\varepsilon_0}(\sin\beta - \sin\alpha)$

(c) $\frac{\sigma}{2\varepsilon_0}(\sin\beta + \sin\alpha)$ (d) $\frac{\sigma}{2\varepsilon_0}(\sin\beta - \sin\alpha)$

37 Three infinitely long, straight thin rods each carrying charge density $+\lambda$ and mass per unit length m are equally spaced as shown in figure. The middle rod is displaced through a very small distance x in the plane of figure while the other two rods held fixed. Find the frequency of small oscillations.

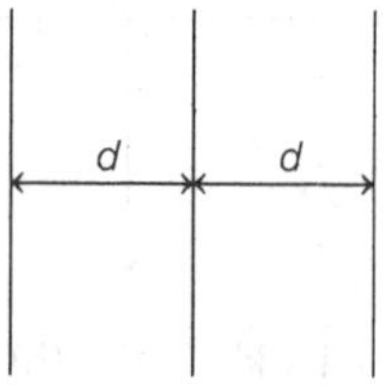

(a) $\frac{1}{2\pi}\sqrt{\frac{\lambda^2}{\pi\varepsilon_0 md^2}}$ (b) $\frac{1}{2\pi}\sqrt{\frac{\lambda^2}{2\pi\varepsilon_0 md^2}}$

(c) $\frac{1}{2\pi}\sqrt{\frac{2\lambda^2}{\pi\varepsilon_0 md^2}}$ (d) $\frac{1}{2\pi}\sqrt{\frac{\lambda^2}{4\pi\varepsilon_0 md^2}}$

38 Two identical charged particles of charge q are placed symmetrically on both the sides, on the axis of a uniformly charged ring of radius a with linear charge density λ as shown in the figure. The distance of the charge particle from centre of ring is l. Calculate tension in the ring due to presence to the charged particles.

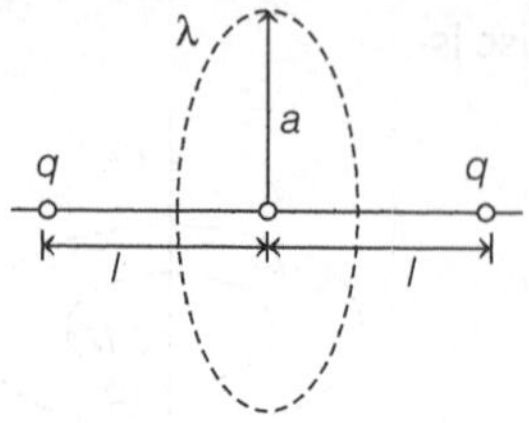

(a) $\frac{\lambda qa^2}{\pi\varepsilon_0(a^2+1^2)^{3/2}}$ (b) $\frac{\lambda qa^2}{2\pi\varepsilon_0(a^2+l^2)^{3/2}}$

(c) $\frac{2\lambda qa^2}{\pi\varepsilon_0(a^2+1^2)^{3/2}}$ (d) $\frac{\lambda qa^2}{4\pi\varepsilon_0(a^2+1^2)^{3/2}}$

39 In a free space, a thin rod carrying uniformly distributed negative charge $-q$ is placed symmetrically along the axis of a thin ring of radius R carrying uniformly distributed charge Q. The mass of the rod is m and length is $l = 2R$. The ring is fixed and the rod is free to move. The rod is displaced slightly along the axis of the ring and then released. Time period T of the small amplitude oscillations of the rod is

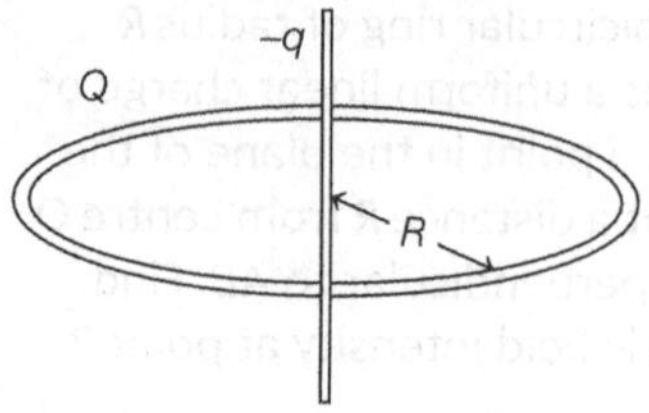

(a) $4\pi\left(\frac{\sqrt{2}\pi\varepsilon_0 R^3 m}{Qq}\right)^{1/2}$ (b) $4\pi\left(\frac{2\pi\varepsilon_0 R^3 m}{Qq}\right)^{1/2}$

(c) $4\pi\left(\frac{2\sqrt{2}\pi\varepsilon_0 R^3 m}{Qq}\right)^{1/2}$ (d) $4\pi\left(\frac{\pi\varepsilon_0 R^3 m}{Qq}\right)^{1/2}$

Multiple Choice(s) Correct Questions

1 Select the correct alternatives.
(a) The charge gained by the uncharged body from a charged body due to conduction is of same nature of charge initially present on charged body.
(b) The magnitude of charge increases with the increase in velocity of charge.
(c) Charge cannot exist without matter although matter can exist without charge.
(d) If three charges are in electrostatic equilibrium, then all three charges may be of same sign.

2 Two point charges (Q each) are placed at $(0, y)$ and $(0, -y)$. A point charge q of the same polarity can move along X-axis. Then,
(a) the force on q is maximum at $x = \pm y/\sqrt{2}$
(b) the charge q is in equilibrium at the origin
(c) the charge q performs an oscillatory motion about the origin
(d) for any position of q other than origin, the force is directed away from origin

3 The figure shows two point charges $q_1 = 2Q (> 0)$ and $q_2 = -Q$. The charges divide the line joining them in three parts I, II and III.

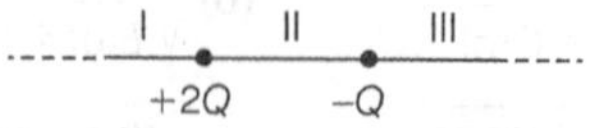

(a) Region III has a local maxima of electric field
(b) Region I has a local minima of electric field

(c) Equilibrium position for a test charge lies in region II

(d) The equilibrium (if there is any in region I,II or III) for constrained motion along the line joining the two charges is stable for a negative test charge

4 A particle of mass m and charge q is fastened to other end of a string fixed at point O. The whole system lies on a frictionless horizontal plane. Initially, the mass was at rest at A. A uniform electric field E in the direction shown is then switched ON.

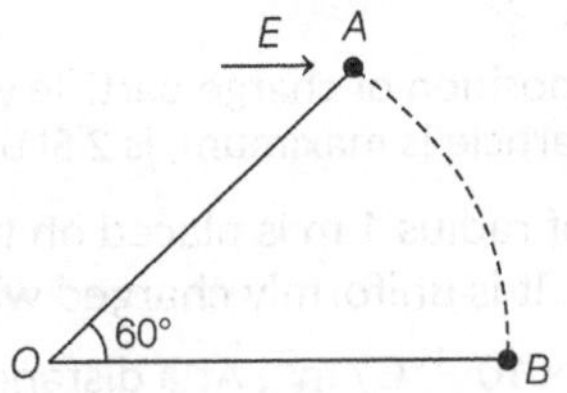

(a) The speed of the particle when it reaches point B is $\sqrt{\frac{qEl}{m}}$

(b) Tension in the string when the particle reaches point B is $2qE$

(c) Acceleration of the particle at point B is $\frac{qE}{m}$

(d) Angular momentum of particle about point O is conserved

5 In the given figure, initially an ideal sufficiently long spring is at its natural length when a constant electric field is switched ON. Choose correct option/options.

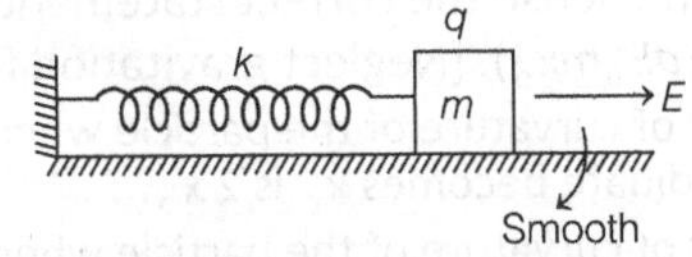

(a) Maximum elongation of spring is $\frac{2qE}{k}$

(b) Maximum compression of spring is $\frac{qE}{k}$

(c) Time period of SHM is $2\pi\sqrt{\frac{m}{k}}$

(d) It will perform SHM if and only if magnitude of field is small

6 A sphere of radius r carries a surface charge of density $\sigma = \mathbf{a}\cdot\mathbf{r}$, where $\mathbf{a}$ is a constant vector and $\mathbf{r}$ is the radius vector of a point on the sphere relative to its centre. Then,

(a) total charge on the sphere is zero

(b) if we cut the sphere in two part symmetrically by plane which is perpendicular to $\mathbf{a}$, then each sphere will have charge of magnitude $\pi r^3 a$

(c) field at centre of the sphere $= \frac{r}{3\varepsilon_0}(-\mathbf{a})$

(d) field at centre of the sphere $= \frac{r}{2\varepsilon_0}(-\mathbf{a})$

7 An electron is placed just in the middle between two long fixed line charges of charge density $+\lambda$ each. The wires are in the XY-plane (Do not consider gravity),

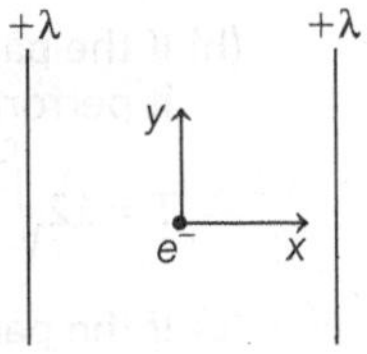

(a) the equilibrium of the electron will be unstable along x-direction

(b) the equilibrium of the electron will be neutral along y-direction

(c) the equilibrium of the electron will be stable along z-direction

(d) the equilibrium of the electron will be stable along y-direction

8 A particle of mass 2 kg and charge 1 mC is projected vertically with a velocity 10 ms^{-1}. There is a uniform horizontal electric field of 10^4 N/C,

(a) the horizontal range of the particle is 10 m

(b) the time of flight of the particle is 2 s

(c) the maximum height reached is 5 m

(d) the horizontal range of the particle is 0

9 An oil drop has a charge -9.6×10^{-19} C and has a mass 1.6×10^{-15} g. When allowed to fall, due to air resistance force, it attains a constant velocity. Then if a uniform electric field is to be applied vertically to make the oil drop ascend up with the same constant speed, which of the following are correct? ($g = 10\ ms^{-2}$) (Assume that the magnitude of resistance force is same in both the cases)

(a) The electric field is directed upward

(b) The electric field is directed downward

(c) The intensity of electric field is $\frac{1}{3} \times 10^2\ NC^{-1}$

(d) The intensity of electric field is $\frac{1}{6} \times 10^5\ NC^{-1}$

10 There is two concentric and coplanar ring of radius a and $3a$ with charge $-Q$ and $8Q$ uniformly distributed, fixed in YZ-plane with centre at origin. A particle of small positive charge q and mass m is at origin. [Neglect gravity]

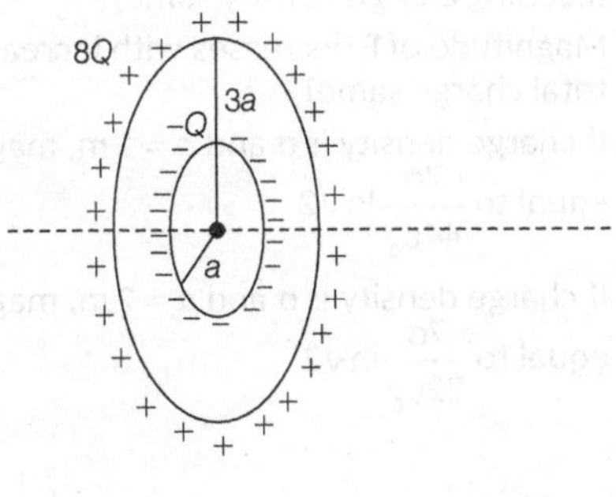

(a) If the particle is given a small push along X-axis, then it perform oscillatory motion of time period $T = 12\sqrt{\frac{3\pi^3 a^3 m\varepsilon_0}{19Qq}}$

(b) If the particle is given a small push along X-axis, then it perform oscillatory motion of time period $T = 12\sqrt{\frac{7\pi^3 a^3 m\varepsilon_0}{19Qq}}$

(c) If the particle is given a velocity along X-axis and it performs oscillatory motion, then amplitude of oscillation must be less than $\sqrt{\frac{7}{3}}\,a$

(d) If the particle is given a velocity along X-axis and it performs oscillatory motion, then amplitude of oscillation must be less than $\sqrt{\frac{5}{3}}\,a$

11 A simple pendulum of length l has a bob of mass m, with a charge q on it. A vertical sheet of charge, with charge σ per unit area, passes through the point of suspension of the pendulum. At equilibrium, the string makes an angle θ with the vertical. Its time period of oscillation is T in this position

(a) $\tan\theta = \frac{\sigma q}{2\varepsilon_0 mg}$ (b) $\tan\theta = \frac{\sigma q}{\varepsilon_0 mg}$

(c) $T < 2\pi\sqrt{\frac{l}{g}}$ (d) $T > 2\pi\sqrt{\frac{l}{g}}$

12 Consider a uniformly charged sheet $ABCD$, which is a part of an equilateral triangular sheet of a side a as shown in the figure. Choose the correct options regarding the electric field E at point O due to this sheet.

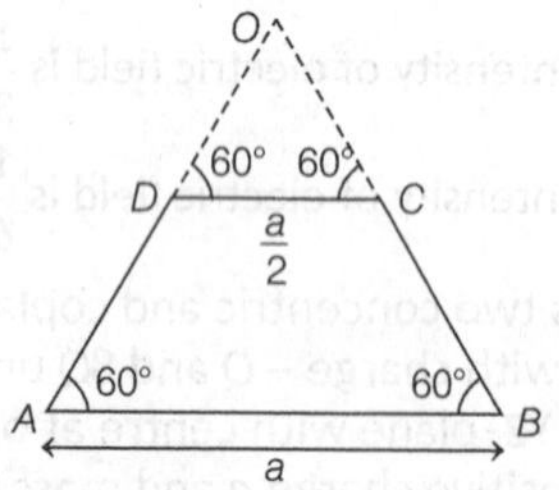

(a) Magnitude of **E** increases with the increase in a (keeping charge density same)

(b) Magnitude of **E** decreases with increase in a (keeping total charge same)

(c) If charge density is σ and $a = 1$ m, magnitude of E is equal to $\frac{7\sigma}{44\varepsilon_0}\ln\sqrt{2}$

(d) If charge density is σ and $a = 2$ m, magnitude of E is equal to $\frac{7\sigma}{22\varepsilon_0}\ln\sqrt{2}$

13 Electric field in a region is given as $\mathbf{E} = (10 - 5x)\hat{\mathbf{i}}$. A charge particle of mass 5 kg and charge $Q(= 1\,\text{C})$ is situated at origin and free to move in given electric field. Then, choose the correct options. (Neglect gravity)

(a) Motion of charge particle is oscillatory

(b) Maximum displacement of charge particle from origin is 4 SI units

(c) Maximum velocity gain by charge particle is 2 SI units

(d) The position of charge particle when velocity gained by particle is maximum, is 2 SI units

14 A disc of radius 1 m is placed on the horizontal ground. It is uniformly charged with charge density of $3.54 \times 10^{-11}\,\text{C/m}^2$. At a distance of $\frac{4}{3}$ m from the centre, we place a charge($Q = 10\,\mu\text{C}$, $m = 10^{-6}$ kg) vertically above the centre. When we release it,

(a) it's initial acceleration is $3\,\text{m/s}^2$ upwards

(b) it's initial acceleration is $6\,\text{m/s}^2$ downwards

(c) it's in equilibrium at a height of $\frac{5}{\sqrt{3}}$ m from the centre

(d) it's in equilibrium at a height of $\frac{1}{\sqrt{3}}$ m from the centre

15 A particle of mass m and charge q is projected in a region, where an electric field is existing and given by $\mathbf{E} = E_0\hat{\mathbf{i}}$, with a velocity $v_0\hat{\mathbf{j}}$ from the origin at time $t = 0$, then choose the correct statements (assuming $m^2 v_0^2 = 2qE_0 m x_0$). [Neglect gravitation force]

(a) Radius of curvature of the particle when its x-coordinate becomes x_0 is $2x_0$.

(b) Radius of curvature of the particle when its x-coordinate becomes x_0 is $4\sqrt{2}\,x_0$

(c) Speed of the particle when its x-coordinate becomes x_0 is $\sqrt{2}v_0$.

(d) Speed of the particle when its x-coordinate becomes x_0 is v_0.

16 A charged particle of mass $m = 1$ kg and charge $Q = 1$ C, is projected from (0, 10) with velocity **v**. Uniform electric field $(-10\hat{\mathbf{i}} + 5\hat{\mathbf{j}})$ N/C exists in the region. Gravity acts along negative y-direction. (Take, $g = 10\,\text{m/s}^2$). For $\mathbf{v} = 10\hat{\mathbf{i}}$,

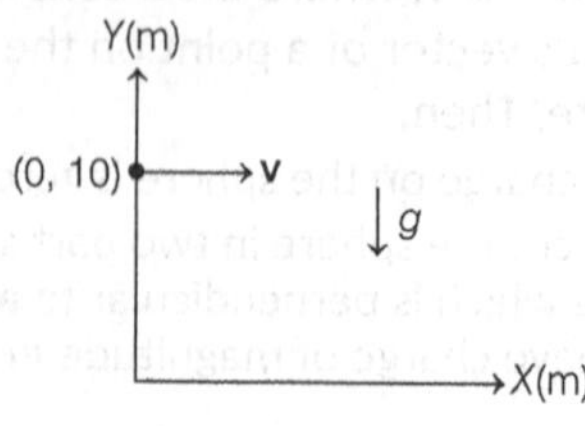

(a) particle passes through origin at some time
(b) time spent by charged particle in the first quadrant is 2 s
(c) while crossing origin, the trajectory makes equal angles with both X and Y-axes
(d) kinetic energy of particle at (0, 10) will be half the kinetic energy at origin

17 In a uniformly charged dielectric sphere, a very thin tunnel has been made along the diameter as shown in the figure below. A charge particle $-q$ having mass m is released from rest at one end of tunnel. For the situation described, mark out the correct statement (s). [Neglect gravity]

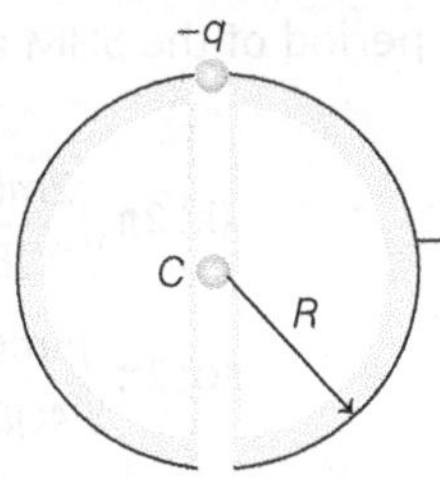

(a) Charged particle will perform SHM about centre of the sphere as mean position
(b) Time period of the particle is $2\pi\sqrt{\dfrac{4\pi\varepsilon_0 mR^3}{qQ}}$
(c) Particle will perform oscillation but not SHM
(d) Speed of the particle while crossing-mean position is $\sqrt{\dfrac{Qq}{4\pi\varepsilon_0 mR}}$

Comprehension Based Questions

Comprehension-1

Two point charges Q_a and Q_b are positioned at points A and B. The field strength to the right of charge Q_b on line that passes through two charges varies according to a law that is represented schematically in the figure. The field strength is assumed to be positive, if its direction coincides with the positive direction of X-axis.

The distance between the charges is $l = 21$ cm.

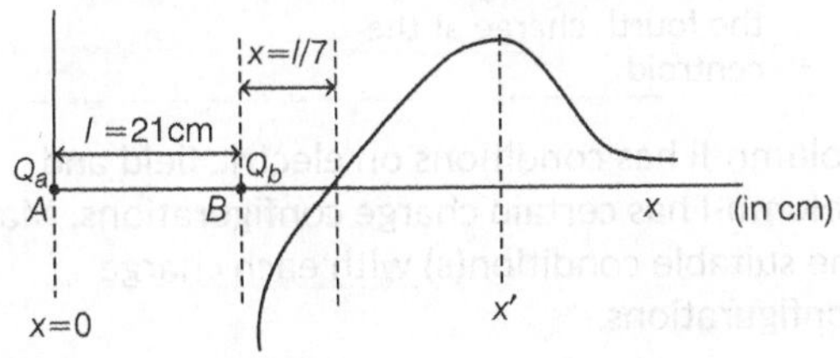

1 The signs of charges Q_a and Q_b are
(a) both positive (b) both negative
(c) positive and negative, respectively
(d) negative and positive, respectively

2 $\dfrac{|Q_a|}{|Q_b|}$ is
(a) 8 (b) 16 (c) 32 (d) 64

3 Find the coordinate x of the point, where the field strength is maximum.
(a) 25 (b) 28 (c) 30 (d) 36

Comprehension-2

Two charged small balls each of charge q and mass m when suspended from a common point by strings of length l in air, then these strings form an angle of 120° with each other. When the system is immersed in a liquid of dielectric constant K (relative density of liquid w.r.t. ball's material is 1/3), then the angle between the strings remains same.

4 Find the dielectric constant of the liquid.
(a) 3/2 (b) $\sqrt{3/2}$ (c) $\sqrt{3}$ (d) 3

5 Find the electrostatic force exerted by the liquid on one of the balls.
(a) $\dfrac{4Kq^2}{9l^2}$ (b) $\dfrac{Kq^2}{2l^2}$ (c) $\dfrac{Kq^2}{3l^2}$ (d) $\dfrac{Kq^2}{9l^2}$

6 If the total system is placed in a gravitational free space, then angle between the strings will be
(a) 0° (b) 90° (c) 180° (d) remain unchanged

Comprehension-3

A thin, homogeneous stick of mass m and length L may rotate in the vertical plane around a horizontal axle pivoted at one end of the stick. A small ball of mass m and charge Q is attached to the opposite end of this stick. The whole system is positioned in a constant horizontal electric field of magnitude $E = \dfrac{mg}{2Q}$. The stick is held horizontally at the beginning.

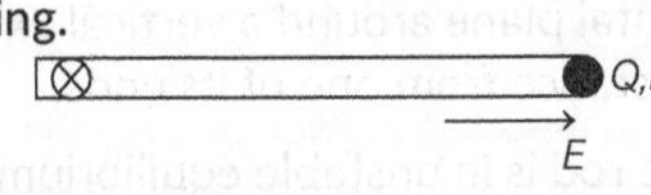

7 What is the acceleration of the small ball at the instance of releasing the stick?
(a) $\dfrac{3g}{2}$ (b) $\dfrac{3g}{4}$
(c) $\dfrac{9g}{8}$ (d) None of these

8 What is the speed of ball when rod becomes vertical?

(a) $\sqrt{\frac{3gl}{2}}$ (b) $\sqrt{2gl}$ (c) $\sqrt{\frac{3gl}{4}}$ (d) None of these

9 Magnitude of acceleration of the end of the stick, when it swings through the vertical position, is

(a) $\frac{3\sqrt{5}g}{2}$ (b) $\frac{3\sqrt{17}g}{8}$

(c) $\frac{3\sqrt{2}g}{4}$ (d) None of these

Comprehension-4

Consider a disc of radius 1 mm and uniform charge density 8.85 $\mu C/m^2$ kept at origin with its axis along x-direction. A rod of length 2 mm is kept along the X-axis at a distance 3m from origin. The linear charge density of the rod varies as $\lambda = (10^{-2} - 5l)$ C / m (l measured (in m) from one end of the rod in + ve x-direction)

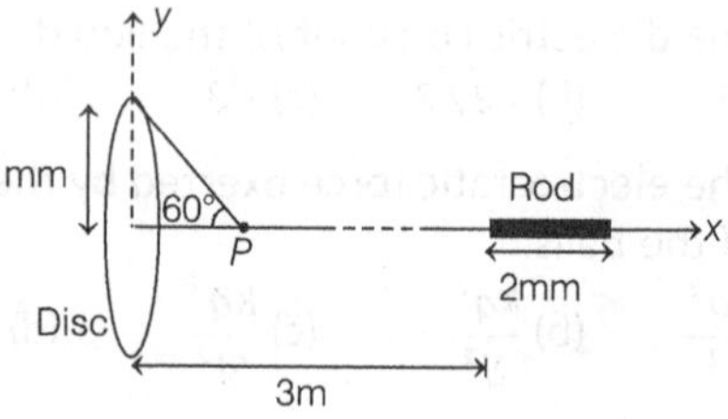

10 The magnitude of electric field at point P is

(a) 25×10^4 N/C (b) 10^4 N/C

(c) 24×10^4 N/C (d) 10^5 N/C

11 Find the force experienced by rod due to the disc.

(a) $\frac{25}{9} \times 10^{-7}$ N (b) $\frac{9}{25} \times 10^{-7}$ N

(c) $\frac{9}{16} \times 10^{-7}$ N (d) $\frac{16}{9} \times 10^{-7}$ N

Comprehension-5

There is an insulator rod of length L and of negligible mass with two small balls of mass m and electric charge Q attached to its ends. The rod can rotate in the horizontal plane around a vertical axis crossing it at a $L/4$ distance from one of its ends.

12 At first, the rod is in unstable equilibrium in a horizontal uniform electric field of field strength E. Then, we gently displace it from this position. Determine the maximum velocity attained by the ball which is closer to the axis in the subsequent motion.

(a) $\sqrt{\frac{2QEL}{m}}$ (b) $\sqrt{\frac{2QEL}{5m}}$ (c) $\sqrt{\frac{QEL}{5m}}$ (d) $\sqrt{\frac{4QEL}{5m}}$

13 In what position is the rod to be set so that, if displaced a little from that position it begins a harmonic oscillation about the axis A?

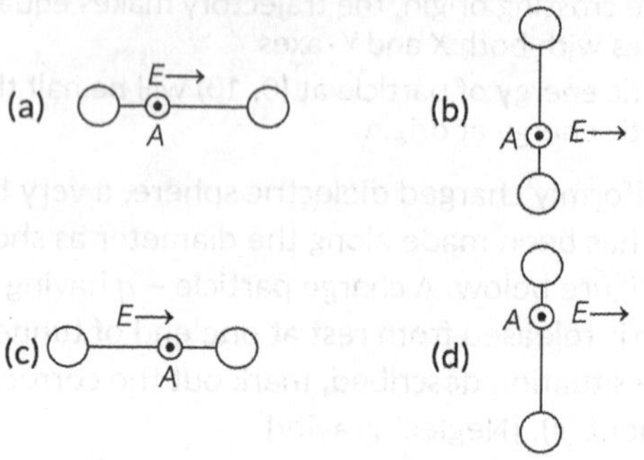

14 What is the time period of the SHM as mentioned in above question?

(a) $2\pi\sqrt{\frac{mL}{QE}}$ (b) $2\pi\sqrt{\frac{2mL}{3QE}}$

(c) $2\pi\sqrt{\frac{5mL}{QE}}$ (d) $2\pi\sqrt{\frac{5mL}{4QE}}$

Match the Columns Questions

1 **Match the following:** (Assume only electrostatic interaction forces) :

	Column-I		Column-II
(a)	Three charges are kept along a straight line	(p)	The system may be in equilibrium with proper choice of the value of charges.
(b)	Three charges are kept at the vertices of an equilateral triangle	(q)	The system will be in equilibrium for any value of the charges.
(c)	Three charges are kept at the three vertices of a square, and a fourth charge is kept at the point of intersection of the diagonals	(r)	The system will not be in equilibrium for any choice of the value of charges.
(d)	Three charges are kept at the vertices of an equilateral triangle with the fourth charge at the centroid	(s)	The equilibrium is unstable.

2 Column-II has conditions on electric field and Column-I has certain charge configurations. Match the suitable condition(s) with each charge configurations.

	Column-I		Column-II
(a)	Two point charges q and $-q$ are placed along X-axis and C is a point nearer to $+q$ 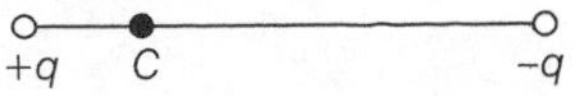	(p)	Electric field at the point C is towards right (positive x-direction)
(b)	A uniformly positively charged sphere with a spherical cavity inside such that centre C and O lie on X-axis 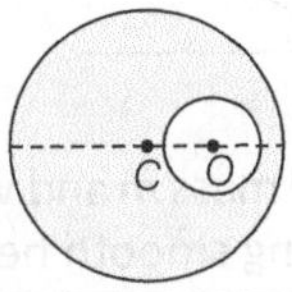	(q)	Electric field at the point C is zero
(c)	A regular hexagon with 5 charges as shown. Dotted line shows X-axis 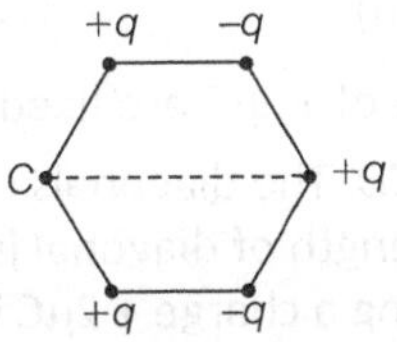	(r)	Electric field at the point C is towards left (negative x-direction)
(d)	A uniformly negatively charged sphere with a spherical cavity inside such that centre of cavity coincides with centre of sphere C 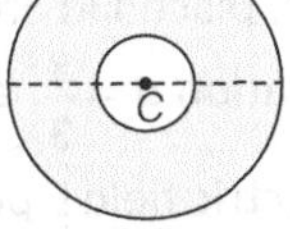	(s)	Electric field at the point C has two component one along negative x and other along positive y

3 Variation of electric field along the line joining two charges is given in Column-I. Relation between charges is given in Column-II, Match the proper variation. Take, electric field along right as positive

	Column-I		Column-II
(a)	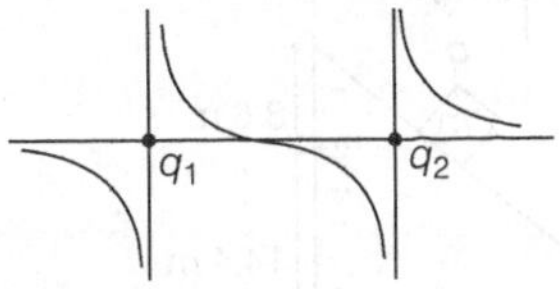	(p)	$\lvert q_1 \rvert > \lvert q_2 \rvert$ and $q_1 < 0;\ q_2 > 0$
(b)	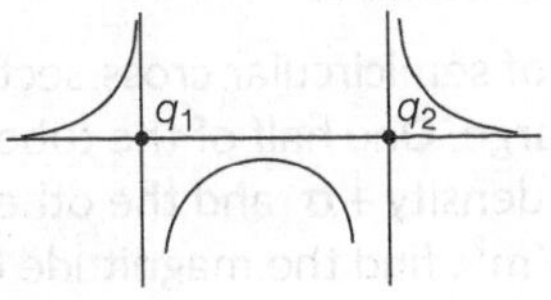	(q)	$\lvert q_1 \rvert = \lvert q_2 \rvert$ and $q_1 > 0;\ q_2 > 0$
(c)	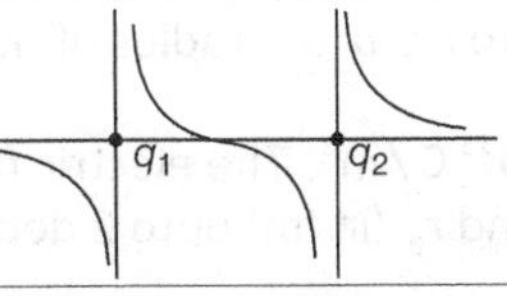	(r)	$\lvert q_1 \rvert = \lvert q_2 \rvert$ and $q_1 < 0;\ q_2 > 0$
(d)	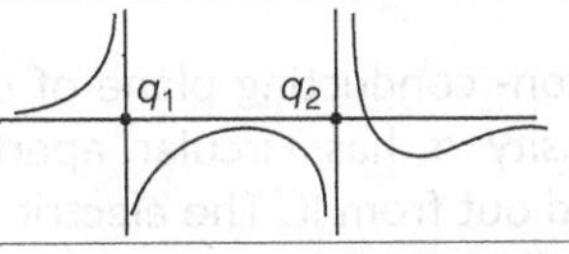	(s)	$\lvert q_2 \rvert > \lvert q_1 \rvert$ and $q_1 > 0;\ q_2 > 0$

4 An electron enters a uniform electric field between two parallel charged plates as shown in the diagram below. The electric field between the plates is assumed to be uniform. The fluorescent screen is placed very close to the end of the plates. The electric field across the plates is 11.5 N/C and the electron enter the field with a speed of 10^6 m/s, parallel to the plates. It is given that 1 eV $= 1.6 \times 10^{-19}$ J.

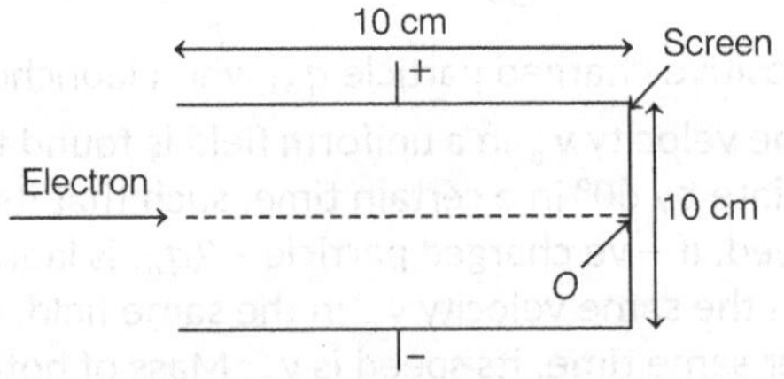

Match approximately Column-I with appropriate choices in Column-II.

	Column-I		Column-II
(a)	At what distance from O will the electron hit the screen (in cm)?	(p)	2
(b)	The speed of electron in vertical direction when it hits the plate (in 10^5 m/s)	(q)	0.2
(c)	The direction of electron's velocity with horizontal (in radians) at which it strikes the screen.	(r)	3
(d)	The kinetic energy possessed by electron (in eV) at the instant when it hits the screen.	(s)	1.0

Numerical Value Questions

1 The bob of a pendulum has mass $m = 1$ kg and charge $q = +40\ \mu$C. Length of pendulum is $l = 0.9$ m. The point of suspension also has the same charge $+40\ \mu$C. What the minimum speed u (in m/s) should be imparted to the bob, so that it can complete vertical circle?

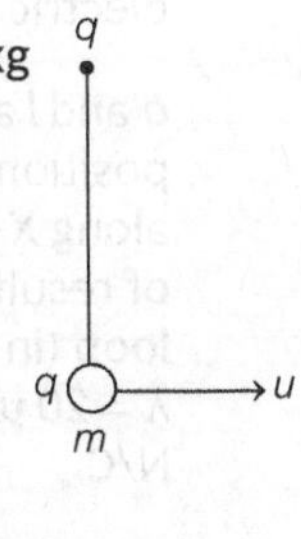

2 The charge density inside a nucleus is given by $\rho = \rho_0 \left(1 - \frac{r^2}{a^2}\right)$, where $r \le a$, a = radius of nucleus $= 3$ fm and $\rho_0 = 5 \times 10^{25}\ \text{C/m}^3$. The electric field is maximum at $r = r_0$. Find r_0 (in fm) upto 2 decimal places.

3 An infinitely large non- conducting plane of uniform surface charge density σ has circular aperture of certain radius curved out from it. The electric field at a point which is at a distance a from the centre of the aperture (perpendicular to the plane) is $\frac{\sigma}{2\sqrt{2}\,\varepsilon_0}$. If the radius of aperture is ka, then find the value of k.

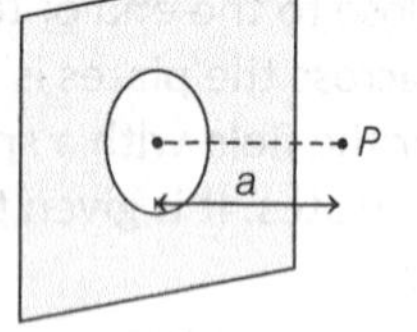

4 A positive charged particle q_0, when launched with some velocity $\mathbf{v}_0$ in a uniform field is found to deviate by 60° in a certain time, such that its speed is halved. If – ve charged particle $-2q_0$, is launched with the same velocity $\mathbf{v}_0$ in the same field, then after same time, its speed is v_2. Mass of both particles is same, then find value of $\frac{v_2^2}{v_0^2}$.

5 7 rods, AB, BC, CD, DE, EF, FG and GH are uniformly charged. Electric field due to each one is E at the centre of cube. Net electric field due to the entire combination is $\sqrt{n}E$. Find n.

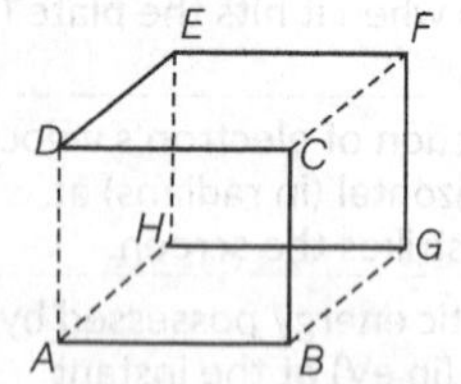

6 A square loop of side l each side having uniform linear charge density λ is placed in XY-plane as shown in the figure. There exists a non-uniform electric field $\mathbf{E} = \frac{a}{l}(x + l)\,\hat{\mathbf{i}}$, where a and l are constants and x is the position of the point from origin along X-axis. Find the magnitude of resultant electric force on the loop (in newtons), if $l = 10$ cm, $\lambda = 20\ \mu\text{C/m}$ and $a = 5 \times 10^5$ N/C.

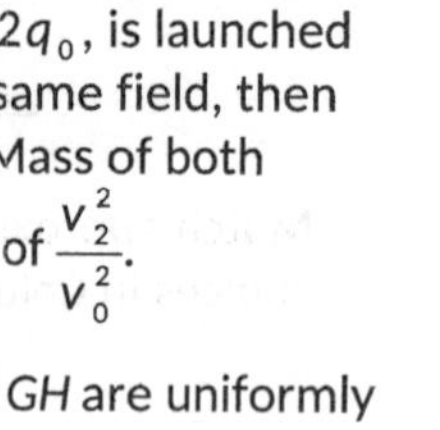

7 Find the magnitude of uniform electric field E in N/C (direction shown in figure), if an electron entering with velocity 100 m/s making 30° comes out making 60° (see figure), after a time numerically equal to $\frac{m}{e}$ of electron.

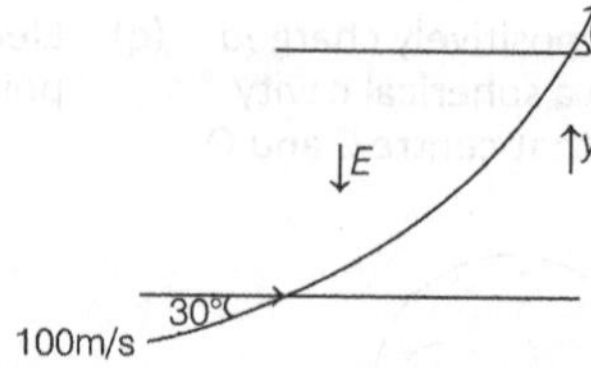

8 Two small spheres each of mass m and with a charge q lie inside a non-conducting smooth hemispherical bowl of radius R. The separation between the two charges in equilibrium is R. If $q = \frac{10^{-4}\ \text{C}}{n}$, then find n. (Take, $m = \sqrt{3}$ kg, $R = 1$ m)

9 Four point charges each of $+1\mu$C are fixed at the vertices of a square $ABCD$. The diagonals of the square intersect at O. Length of diagonal is 2m. A particle of mass 2g having a charge $+2\mu$C is released from a point 1 cm from O and 99cm from A. The motion of the particle is SHM with a period of $\frac{2\pi}{\sqrt{n}}$ s. Find the value of n neglecting gravity.

10 A small block of mass m is kept on the smooth inclined plane of angle 37°, placed in an elevator going upward with acceleration $a = \frac{g}{3}$, as shown in the figure. A horizontal electric field E perpendicular to the left and right vertical wall of the elevator exists. The charge on the block is $+q$. Find the time (in s), when the block collides with the vertical wall.

(Take, $g = 10\ \text{ms}^{-2}$ and $\frac{qE}{m} = 25\ \text{ms}^{-2}$)

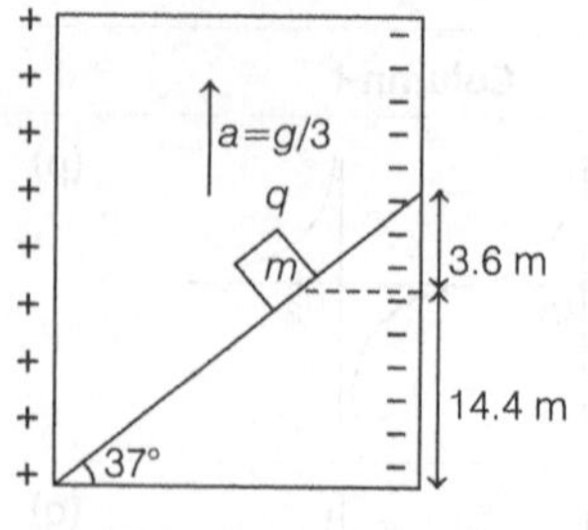

11 An infinitely long tube of semicircular cross-section is given some electric charge. One half of the tube is given a surface charge density $+\sigma$ and the other half of $-\sigma$. If $|\sigma| = 2\pi\varepsilon_0\ \text{C/m}^2$, find the magnitude of electric field(in N/C) at point O on the axis.

[The point O is some where near the centre on the axial line]

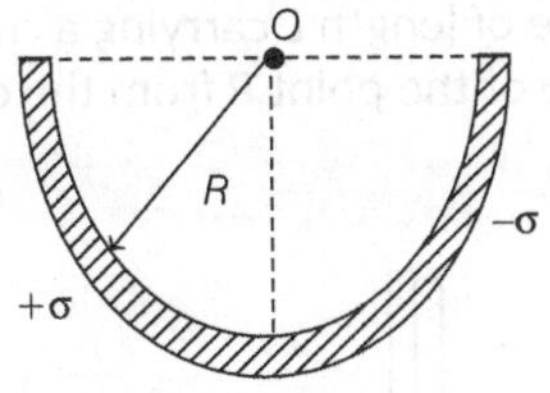

Previous Years' Questions

JEE Main

1 A thin metallic wire having cross-sectional area of $10^{-4}\ m^2$ is used to make a ring of radius 30 cm. A positive charge of 2π C is uniformly distributed over the ring, while another positive charge of 30 pC is kept at the centre of the ring. The tension in the ring is .... N, provided that the ring does not get deformed (neglect the influence of gravity).
$\left(\text{given, } \frac{1}{4\pi\varepsilon_0} = 9 \times 10^9 \text{ SI units}\right)$ **[2024, 27 Jan Shift-I]**

2 An electron is moving under the influence of the electric field of a uniformly charged infinite plane sheet S having surface charge density $+\sigma$. The electron at $t = 0$ is at a distance of 1 m from S and has a speed of 1 m/s. The maximum value of σ if the electron strikes S at $t = 1$ s is $\alpha\left[\frac{m\varepsilon_0}{e}\right]\frac{C}{m^2}$, the value of α is .... **[2024, 29 Jan Shift-I]**

3 A 10 μC charge is divided into two parts and placed at 1 cm distance so that the repulsive force between them is maximum. The charges of the two parts are **[2023, 13 April Shift-II]**

(a) 7 μC, 3 μC (b) 9 μC, 1 μC
(c) 5 μC, 5 μC (d) 8 μC, 2 μC

4 If two charges q_1 and q_2 are separated with distance d and placed in a medium of dielectric constant k. What will be the equivalent distance between charges in air for the same electrostatic force? **[2023, 24 Jan Shift-I]**

(a) $d\sqrt{k}$ (b) $2d\sqrt{k}$
(c) $1.5d\sqrt{k}$ (d) $k\sqrt{d}$

5 Three point charges q, $-2q$ and $2q$ are placed on X-axis at a distance $x = 0$, $x = 3/4R$ and $x = R$, respectively from origin as shown. If $q = 2 \times 10^{-6}$ C and $R = 2$ cm, the magnitude of net force experienced by the charge $-2q$ is .... N. **[2023, 13 April Shift-II]**

6 A point charge of 10 μC is placed at the origin. At what location on the X-axis should a point charge of 40 μC be placed so that the net electric field is zero at $x = 2$ cm on the X-axis ? **[2023, 25 Jan Shift-II]**

(a) $x = 8$ cm
(b) $x = -4$ cm
(c) $x = 4$ cm
(d) $x = 6$ cm

7 An electron revolves around an infinite cylindrical wire having uniform linear charge density 2×10^{-8} C-m^{-1} in circular path under the influence of attractive electrostatic field as shown in the figure. The velocity of electron with which it is revolving is ...... $\times 10^6$ ms^{-1}, Given, mass of electron $= 9 \times 10^{-31}$ kg **[2023, 10 April Shift-II]**

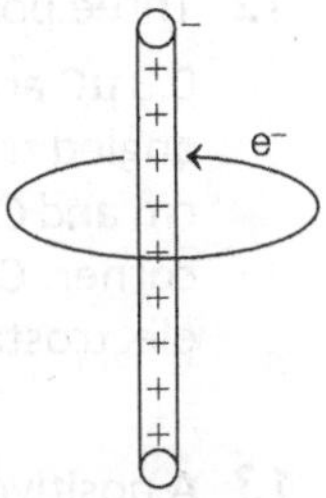

8 A uniform electric field of 10 N/C is created between two parallel charged plates (as shown in figure). An electron enters the field symmetrically between the plates with a kinetic energy 0.5 eV. The length of each plate is 10 cm. The angle (θ) of deviation of the path of electron as it comes out of the field is .... (in degree) **[2023, 25 Jan Shift-I]**

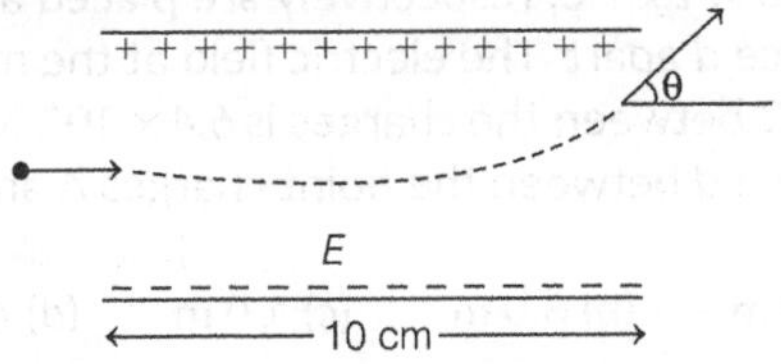

9 A stream of a positively charged particles having $\frac{q}{m} = 2 \times 10^{11}$ C/kg and velocity $\mathbf{v}_0 = 3 \times 10^7\ \hat{\mathbf{i}}$ m/s is deflected by an electric field $1.8\hat{\mathbf{j}}$ kV/m. The electric field exists in a region of 10 cm along x-direction. Due to the electric field, the deflection of the charge particles in the y-direction is .... mm **[2023, 24 Jan Shift-I]**

10 Two point charges Q each are placed at a distance d apart. A third point charge q is placed at a distance x from mid-point on the perpendicular bisector. The value of x at which charge q will experience the maximum coulomb's force is **[2022, 29 June Shift-II]**

(a) $x = d$ (b) $x = \frac{d}{2}$
(c) $x = \frac{d}{\sqrt{2}}$ (d) $x = \frac{d}{2\sqrt{2}}$

11 Two identical charged particles each having a mass 10 g and charge 2.0×10^{-7} C are placed on a horizontal table with a separation of L between them such that they stay in limited equilibrium. If the coefficient of friction between each particle and the table is 0.25, find the value of L. [Use, $g = 10\ ms^{-2}$] **[2022, 24 June Shift-II]**

(a) 12 cm (b) 10 cm (c) 8 cm (d) 5 cm

12 Three point charges of magnitude 5 μC, 0.16 μC and 0.3 μC are located at the vertices A, B and C of a right angled triangle whose sides are $AB = 3$ cm, $BC = 3\sqrt{2}$ cm and $CA = 3$ cm and point A is the right angle corner. Charge at point A, experiences .... N of electrostatic force due to the other two charges. **[2022, 26 July Shift-II]**

13 A positive charge particle of 100 mg is thrown in opposite direction to a uniform electric field of strength $1 \times 10^5\ NC^{-1}$. If the charge on the particle is 40 μC and the initial velocity is 200 ms^{-1}, how much distance it will travel before coming to the rest momentarily **[2022, 29 June Shift-I]**

(a) 1 m (b) 5 m
(c) 10 m (d) 0.5 m

14 Two point charges A and B of magnitude $+8 \times 10^{-6}$ C and -8×10^{-6} C, respectively are placed at a distance d apart. The electric field at the middle point O between the charges is $6.4 \times 10^4\ NC^{-1}$. The distance d between the point charges A and B is **[2022, 28 June Shift-II]**

(a) 2.0 m (b) 3.0 m (c) 1.0 m (d) 4.0 m

15 The three charges $q/2$, q and $q/2$ are placed at the corners A, B and C of a square of side a as shown in figure. The magnitude of electric field (E) at the corner D of the square, is **[2022, 28 June Shift-I]**

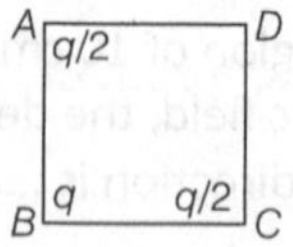

(a) $\frac{q}{4\pi\varepsilon_0 a^2}\left(\frac{1}{\sqrt{2}}+\frac{1}{2}\right)$

(b) $\frac{q}{4\pi\varepsilon_0 a^2}\left(1+\frac{1}{\sqrt{2}}\right)$

(c) $\frac{q}{4\pi\varepsilon_0 a^2}\left(1-\frac{1}{\sqrt{2}}\right)$

(d) $\frac{q}{4\pi\varepsilon_0 a^2}\left(\frac{1}{\sqrt{2}}-\frac{1}{2}\right)$

16 Find the electric field at point P (as shown in figure) on the perpendicular bisector of a uniformly charged thin wire of length L carrying a charge Q. The distance of the point P from the centre of the rod is $a = \frac{\sqrt{3}}{2}L$. **[2021, 26 Feb Shift I]**

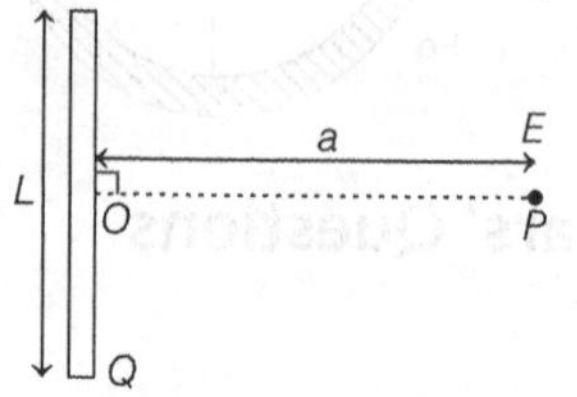

(a) $\frac{\sqrt{3}Q}{4\pi\varepsilon_0 L^2}$ (b) $\frac{Q}{3\pi\varepsilon_0 L^2}$ (c) $\frac{Q}{2\sqrt{3}\pi\ \varepsilon_0 L^2}$ (d) $\frac{Q}{4\pi\varepsilon_0 L^2}$

17 A cube of side a has point charges $+Q$ located at each of its vertices except at the origin, where the charge is $-Q$. The electric field at the centre of cube is **[2021, 24 Feb Shift-I]**

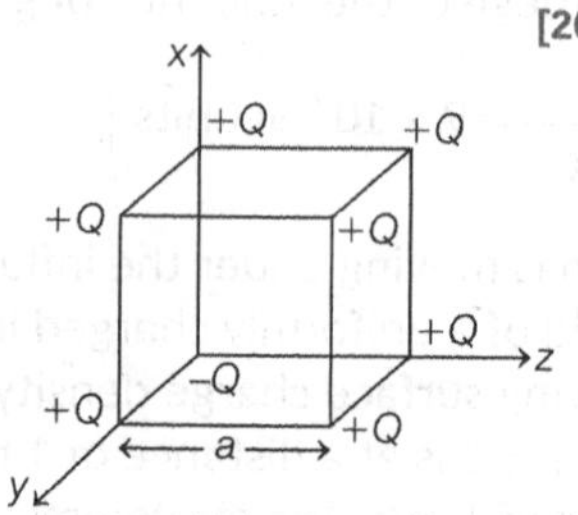

(a) $\frac{-Q}{3\sqrt{3}\pi\varepsilon_0 a^2}(\hat{x}+\hat{y}+\hat{z})$ (b) $\frac{Q}{3\sqrt{3}\pi\varepsilon_0 a^2}(\hat{x}+\hat{y}+\hat{z})$

(c) $\frac{-2Q}{3\sqrt{3}\pi\varepsilon_0 a^2}(\hat{x}+\hat{y}+\hat{z})$ (d) $\frac{2Q}{3\sqrt{3}\ \pi\varepsilon_0 a^2}(\hat{x}+\hat{y}+\hat{z})$

18 A thin infinite sheet charge and an infinite line charge of respective charge densities $+\sigma$ and $+\lambda$ placed parallel at 5 m distance from each other. Point P and Q are at $3/\pi$ m and $4/\pi$ m perpendicular distance from line charge towards sheet charge, respectively. E_p and E_Q are the magnitudes of resultant electric field intensities at point P and Q, respectively. If $\frac{E_P}{E_Q} = \frac{4}{a}$ for $2|\sigma| = |\lambda|$, then the value of a is .... **[2021, 13 April Shift-I]**

19 Two small spheres each of mass 10 mg are suspended from a point by threads 0.5 m long. They are equally charged and repel each other to a distance of 0.20 m. The charge on each of the sphere is $\frac{a}{21} \times 10^{-8}$ C. The value of a will be ....
[Given, $g = 10\ ms^{-2}$] **[2021, 25 Feb Shift-II]**

20 A certain charge Q is divided into two parts q and $(Q - q)$. How should the charges Q and q be divided, so that q and $(Q - q)$ placed at a certain distance apart experience maximum electrostatic repulsion ? **[2021, 20 July Shift-I]**

(a) $Q = \frac{q}{2}$
(b) $Q = 2q$
(c) $Q = 4q$
(d) $Q = 3q$

21 Find out the surface charge density at the intersection of point $X = 3$ m plane and X-axis, in the region of uniform line charge of 8 nC/m lying along the Z-axis in free space. **[2021, 16 March Shift-II]**

(a) 0.424 nC m^{-2}
(b) 47.88 nC m^{-2}
(c) 0.07 nC m^{-2}
(d) 4.0 nC m^{-2}

22 An infinite number of point charges, each carrying 1 μC charge, are placed along the Y-axis at $y = 1$ m, 2 m, 4 m, 8 m. The total force on a 1 C point charge, placed at the origin, is $x \times 10^3$ N. The value of x to the nearest integer, is ....

(Take, $\frac{1}{4\pi\varepsilon_0} = 9 \times 10^9$ N-m^2/C^2) **[2021, 18 March Shift-II]**

JEE Advanced

1 A uniform electric field, $\mathbf{E} = -400\sqrt{3}\hat{y}$ NC^{-1} is applied in a region. A charged particle of mass m carrying positive charge q is projected in this region with an initial speed of $2\sqrt{10} \times 10^6$ ms^{-1}. This particle is aimed to hit a target T, which is 5 m away from its entry point into the field as shown schematically in the figure. Take $\frac{q}{m} = 10^{10}$ Ckg^{-1}. Then, **(2020 Adv.)**

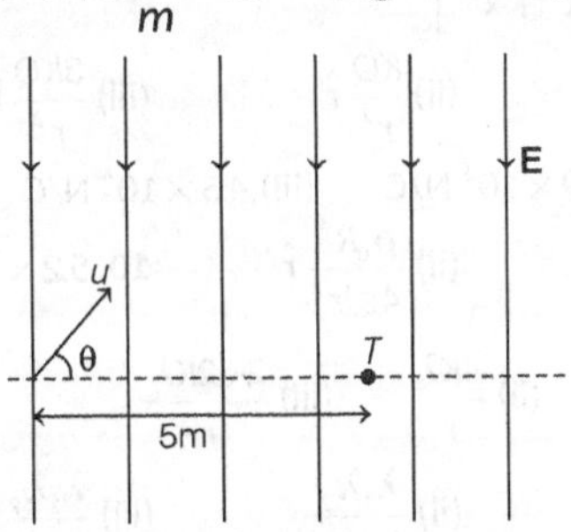

(a) the particle will hit T if projected at an angle 45° from the horizontal
(b) the particle will hit T if projected either at an angle 30° or 60° from the horizontal
(c) time taken by the particle to hit T could be $\sqrt{\frac{5}{6}}$ μs as well as $\sqrt{\frac{5}{2}}$ μs
(d) time taken by the particle to hit T is $\sqrt{\frac{5}{3}}$ μs

2 Two identical non-conducting solid spheres of same mass and charge are suspended in air from a common point by two non-conducting, massless strings of same length. At equilibrium, the angle between the strings is α. The spheres are now immersed in a dielectric liquid of density 800 kg m^{-3} and dielectric constant 21. If the angle between the strings remains the same after the immersion, then **(2020 Adv.)**

(a) electric force between the spheres remains unchanged
(b) electric force between the spheres reduces
(c) mass density of the spheres is 840 kg m^{-3}
(d) the tension in the strings holding the spheres remains unchanged

3 A particle of mass 10^{-3} kg and charge 1.0 C is initially at rest. At time $t = 0$, the particle comes under the influence of an electric field $\mathbf{E}(t) = E_0 \sin \omega t\,\hat{\mathbf{i}}$, where $E_0 = 1.0$ NC^{-1} and $\omega = 10^3$ rad s^{-1}. Consider the effect of only the electrical force on the particle. Then, the maximum speed (in ms^{-1}), attained by the particle at subsequent times is .... **[JEE Advanced 2019]**

4 The figures alongside depict two situations in which two infinitely long static line charges of constant positive line charge density λ are kept parallel to each other.

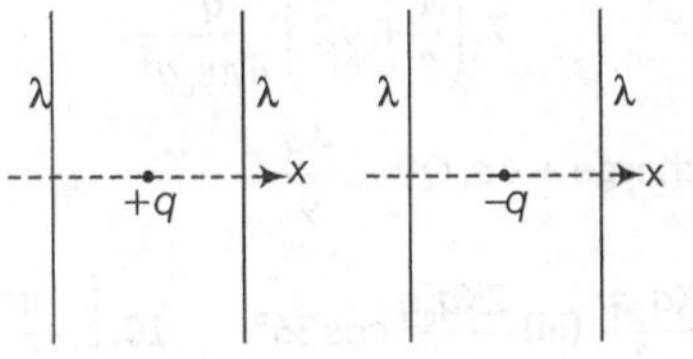

In their resulting electric field, point charges q and $-q$ are kept in equilibrium between them. The point charges are confined to move in the x direction only. If they are given a small displacement about their equilibrium positions, then the correct statements is/are **[JEE Advanced 2015]**

(a) both charges execute simple harmonic motion.
(b) both charges will continue moving in the direction of their displacement.

(c) charge $+q$ executes simple harmonic motion while charge $-q$ continues moving in the direction of its displacement.

(d) charge $-q$ executes simple harmonic motion while charge $+q$ continues moving in the direction of its displacement.

5 Four charges Q_1, Q_2, Q_3 and Q_4 of same magnitude are fixed along the X-axis at $X = -2a, -a, +a$ and $+2a$, respectively. A positive charge q is placed on the positive Y-axis at a distance $b > 0$. Four options of the signs of these charges are given in Column-I. The direction of the forces on the charge q is given in Column-II. Match Column I with Column II and select the correct answer using the code given below the lists. **[JEE Advanced 2014]**

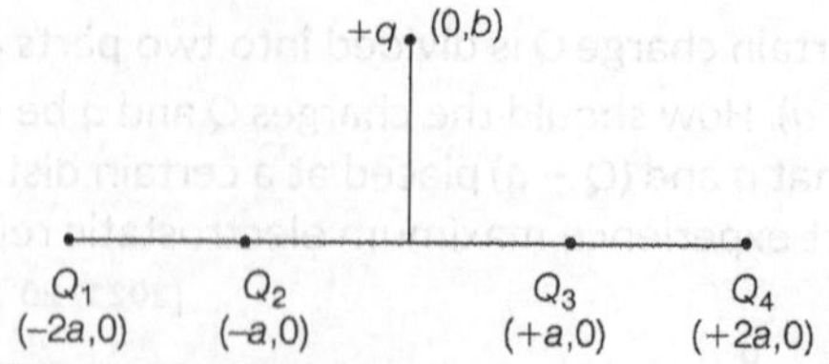

	Column-I		Column-II
A.	Q_1, Q_2, Q_3, Q_4 all positive	p.	$+X$
B.	Q_1, Q_2 positive; Q_3, Q_4 negative	q.	$-X$
C.	Q_1, Q_4 positive; Q_2, Q_3 negative	r.	$+Y$
D.	Q_1, Q_3 positive; Q_2, Q_4 negative	s.	$-Y$

Codes

(a) A-r, B-p, C-s, D-q (b) A-s, B-q, C-r, D-p

(c) A-r, B-p, C-q, D-s (d) A-s, B-q, C-p, D-r

Answer Key

Level 1

1.1 Electric Charge

1. (i) T (ii) F (iii) T (iv) T (v) T (vi) F (vii) F (viii) T (ix) F (x) F
2. 2.16×10^{-11}
3. (i) 1.875×10^{12} electrons from wool to polythene (ii) Yes
4. (ii), (iii), (iv) and (v)
5. $\frac{Q}{2}, -\frac{Q}{4}, -\frac{Q}{4}$

1.2 Coulomb's Law

1. 1.25×10^{13}
2. 20 N
3. (i) F (ii) $F/80$ (iii) $79\ F/80$
4. $0.036(4\hat{i} - 3\hat{k})$
5. $T = 4\pi r\sqrt{\frac{\pi\varepsilon_0 mr}{q_1 q_2}}, v = \sqrt{\frac{q_1 q_2}{4\pi\varepsilon_0 mr}}$
6. 18.9 N
7. $\left(\frac{1}{2} + \sqrt{2}\right)\frac{q^2}{4\pi\varepsilon_0 a^2}$
8. $\frac{2l}{3}$ from charge $+4q$, $Q = -\frac{4q}{9}$
9. (i) 0, (ii) $\frac{Kq_0 q}{a^2}$, (iii) $\frac{2Kq_0 q}{a^2}\cos 36°$
10. $\left(\frac{4\pi\varepsilon_0 mgd^3}{\sqrt{4l^2 - d^2}}\right)^{1/2}$
11. $\frac{4KqQ}{4d^2 - L^2}$
12. (i) SHM with $T = 2\pi\sqrt{\frac{\pi\varepsilon_0 ma^3}{Qq}}$ (ii) Accelerated translationally
13. (i) 20 cm from the bottom (ii) $12\ m/s^2$
14. $d \geq 0.4$ m

1.3 Electric Field Due to Point Charges

1. 4×10^{-11} C
2. $E = \frac{\sqrt{3}}{10}(\hat{i} + \hat{j} + \hat{k})$ N/C
3. (i) $\frac{6Kq}{a^2}$ (ii) $\frac{10Kq}{a^2}$ (iii) $\frac{4Kq}{a^2}$
4. (i) $14.4(-\hat{i})$ kN/C (ii) $6.4(\hat{i})$ kN/C (iii) $3.6\sqrt{2}(-\hat{i})$ kN/C
5. 30 cm from A along BA
6. (i) 8.5 N/C, right (ii) 0.017 N, left
7. (i) 0 (ii) $\frac{kq^2}{r^2}$
8. $\frac{q}{\sqrt{2}\pi\varepsilon_0 L^2}$

1.4 Electric Field Due to Continuous Charge Distributions

1. (i) 0 (ii) $\frac{2K\lambda}{R}$ (iii) $\frac{K\lambda}{R}$
2. $\frac{QdL}{8\pi^2\varepsilon_0 R^3}$
3. $\frac{\sqrt{3}KQ}{4R^2}$
4. $\frac{Q}{2\sqrt{2}}$
5. $\frac{\sigma}{2\varepsilon_0}\left[1 - \frac{x}{\sqrt{R^2 + x^2}}\right]$
6. (i) 0 (ii) 0 (iii) 4.5×10^6 N/C
7. (i) 0 (ii) $\frac{KQ}{r^2}\hat{r}$ (iii) $\frac{3KQ}{r^2}\hat{r}$
8. (i) 0 (ii) 9×10^6 N/C (iii) 4.5×10^6 N/C
9. (i) $\frac{\rho_0 r^2}{4\varepsilon_0}\hat{r}$ (ii) $\frac{\rho_0 R^4}{4\varepsilon_0 r^2}\hat{r}$
10. 5.2×10^7 N/C
11. (i) $\sqrt{2}\frac{K\lambda}{r}$ (ii) $\frac{4K\lambda}{r}$ (iii) $\frac{2\sqrt{2}K\lambda}{r}$
12. (i) $\frac{\lambda Q}{2\pi\varepsilon_0 r}$ (ii) $\frac{\lambda_1\lambda_2 l}{2\pi\varepsilon_0 r}$ (iii) $\frac{\lambda_1\lambda_2}{2\pi\varepsilon_0}\ln\left(1 + \frac{l}{r}\right)$
13. $E_A = \frac{-\sigma}{2\varepsilon_0}\hat{j}, E_B = \frac{-3\sigma}{2\varepsilon_0}\hat{j}, E_C = \frac{-7\sigma}{2\varepsilon_0}\hat{j}, E_D = \frac{\sigma}{2\varepsilon_0}\hat{j}$

1.5 Electric Field Lines

1. (i) F (ii) T (iii) T (iv) F (v) T (vi) T (vii) F

2.

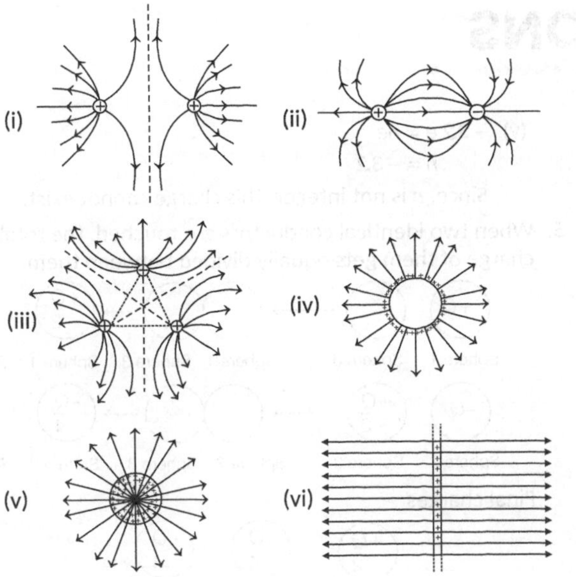

3. -2 4. $E_A > E_B$

5. (i) Not possible (ii) Possible (iii) Not possible (iv) Not possible

1.6 Motion of Charged Particles in External Electric Field

1. $\frac{mg}{q}$, vertically down 2. (i) $\theta = \tan^{-1}(2)$ (ii) $T = \frac{2mg}{\sqrt{5}}$

3. (i) $2\pi\sqrt{\frac{l}{g+\frac{qE}{m}}}$ (ii) $2\pi\sqrt{\frac{l}{g-\frac{qE}{m}}}$ (iii) $2\pi\sqrt{\frac{l}{\sqrt{g^2+\left(\frac{qE}{m}\right)^2}}}$

4. $\frac{mu^2}{2qE}, \frac{mu}{qE}$ 5. 0.0233 6. $\theta = \tan^{-1}\frac{eEl}{mv_0^2} = 45°$

7. $2\pi r\sqrt{\frac{2\pi\varepsilon_0 m}{\lambda q}}$ 8. 4 μs

Level 2

Single Choice Correct Questions

1. (b)	2. (d)	3. (c)	4. (b)	5. (a)
6. (c)	7. (d)	8. (a)	9. (b)	10. (d)
11. (b)	12. (a)	13. (a)	14. (d)	15. (d)
16. (a)	17. (b)	18. (b)	19. (d)	20. (d)
21. (a)	22. (b)	23. (b)	24. (d)	25. (c)
26. (a)	27. (c)	28. (a)	29. (d)	30. (c)
31. (c)	32. (d)	33. (a)	34. (a)	35. (b)
36. (a)	37. (a)	38. (c)	39. (b)	40. (d)
41. (b)	42. (a)	43. (b)	44. (d)	45. (a)
46. (c)	47. (a)	48. (b)	49. (a)	50. (a)

Numerical Questions

1. (15)	2. (6)	3. (6)	4. (234)	5. (3)
6. (4)	7. (12)	8. (3)	9. (24)	10. (4)
11. (4)	12. (5)	13. (144)	14. (6)	15. (5)

Level 3

Single Choice Correct Questions

1. (c)	2. (a)	3. (a)	4. (c)	5. (d)
6. (c)	7. (d)	8. (a)	9. (b)	10. (a)
11. (b)	12. (a)	13. (c)	14. (d)	15. (b)
16. (a)	17. (b)	18. (c)	19. (d)	20. (a)
21. (b)	22. (a)	23. (a)	24. (d)	25. (a)
26. (b)	27. (c)	28. (b)	29. (a)	30. (d)
31. (a)	32. (a)	33. (d)	34. (b)	35. (c)
36. (d)	37. (a)	38. (b)	39. (c)	

Multiple Choice(s) Correct Questions

1. (ac)	2. (abd)	3. (ad)	4. (abc)	5. (ac)
6. (abc)	7. (abc)	8. (abc)	9. (bc)	10. (ad)
11. (ac)	12. (bc)	13. (abcd)	14. (bd)	15. (bc)
16. (abcd)	17. (abd)			

Comprehension Based Questions

1. (c)	2. (d)	3. (b)	4. (a)	5. (d)
6. (c)	7. (c)	8. (a)	9. (b)	10. (c)
11. (a)	12. (c)	13. (a)	14. (d)	

Match the Column Questions

1. (a) → p, s; (b) → r; (c) → r; (d) → p, s
2. (a) → p; (b) → p; (c) → r; (d) → q
3. (a) → s; (b) → r; (c) → q; (d) → p
4. (a) → s; (b) → p; (c) → q; (d) → r

Numerical Value Questions

1. (6)	2. (2.24)	3. (1)	4. (7)	5. (1)
6. (6)	7. (100)	8. (3)	9. (18)	10. (1)
11. (2)				

Previous Year's Questions

JEE Main

1. (*)	2. (8)	3. (c)	4. (a)	5. (5440)
6. (d)	7. (8)	8. (68)	9. (2)	10. (d)
11. (a)	12. (17)	13. (d)	14. (b)	15. (a)
16. (c)	17. (c)	18. (6)	19. (630)	20. (b)
21. (a)	22. (12)			

JEE Advanced

1. (c)	2. (c)	3. (2)	4. (c)	5. (a)

SOLUTIONS

Level 1

1.1 Electric Charge

1. (i) Charge cannot exist without mass though mass can exist without charge.
   (ii) Charge of an isolated system is always conserved while mass of an isolated system is not always conserved. In nuclear reactions, mass gets converted into energy.
   (iii) Electric charge of a body is always quantised. It is integral multiple of $\pm e$.
   (iv) Charge is independent of frame of reference.
   (v) An accelerated charged particle emits electromagnetic radiations in addition to producing electric and magnetic fields.
   (vi) Relative permittivity of a medium lies between 1 and ∞, i.e. $\varepsilon_r \geq 1$.
   (vii) A charged body and a neutral conductor can attract through induction.
   (viii) Repulsion is a sure test of electrification as two bodies repel each other only when both of them are similarly charged.
   (ix) Since, number of electrons are very few, we cannot say that the total charge of the two identical conductors will be equally divided between them.
   (x) In induction, objects always attract.

2. Total number of electrons $= 2 \times 10^{22} \times 29$

   Number of electrons removed $= \dfrac{2 \times 10^{-6}}{1.6 \times 10^{-19}}$

   Fraction of electrons removed

   $$= \frac{\text{Number of electrons removed}}{\text{Total number of electrons}}$$

   $$= \frac{(2 \times 10^{-6})/(1.6 \times 10^{-19})}{2 \times 10^{22} \times 29} = 2.16 \times 10^{-11}$$

3. (i) Number of electrons transferred from wool to polythene $= \dfrac{3 \times 10^{-7}}{1.6 \times 10^{-19}} = 1.875 \times 10^{12}$

   (ii) Yes, wool loses mass and polythene gains mass.

4. $q = \pm ne$, where n is an integer.

   (i) $1.6 \times 10^{-18} = n(1.6 \times 10^{-19})$
   $n = 10$
   Since, n is integer, this charge can exist.

   (ii) $1.6 \times 10^{-20} = n(1.6 \times 10^{-19})$
   $n = 0.1$
   Since, n is not integer, this charge cannot exist.

   (iii) $0.001 = n(1.6 \times 10^{-19})$
   Since, n is integer, this charge cannot exist.

   (iv) $2.5e = ne$
   $\Rightarrow n = 2.5$
   Since, n is not integer, this charge cannot exist.

   (v) $-3.2\,e = ne$
   $n = -3.2$
   Since, n is not integer, this charge cannot exist.

5. When two identical conductors are touched, the total charge of them gets equally divided between them.

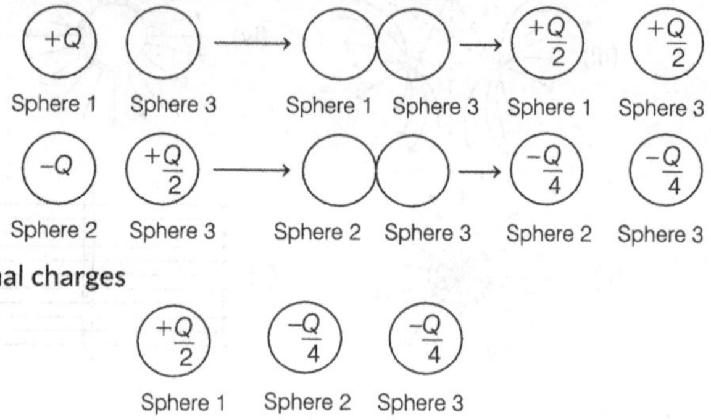

1.2 Coulomb's Law

1. After rubbing, lets say charges on them are $+q$ and $-q$.

   $$F = \frac{Kq_1q_2}{r^2}$$

   $$\Rightarrow \quad 3.6 = \frac{9 \times 10^9 \times q \times q}{(0.1)^2}$$

   $$\Rightarrow \quad q = 2 \times 10^{-6}\text{C}$$

   Number of electrons transferred $= \dfrac{2 \times 10^{-6}}{1.6 \times 10^{-19}} = 1.25 \times 10^{13}$

2. 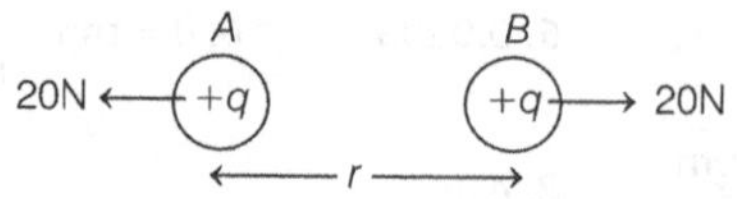

   $$\frac{Kq^2}{r^2} = 20$$

   When uncharged sphere C is touched with sphere B, final charges on them would be $+q/2$ and $+q/2$.

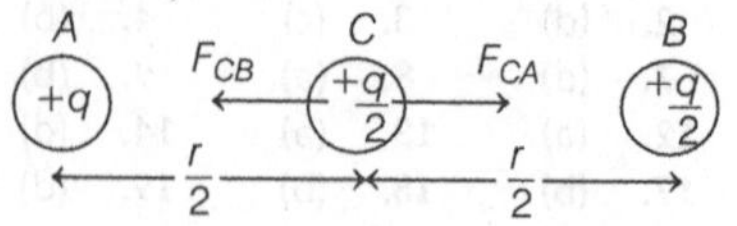

   $$F_{CA} = \frac{Kq\left(\frac{q}{2}\right)}{\left(\frac{r}{2}\right)^2} = 40\text{ N}, \quad F_{CB} = \frac{K\left(\frac{q}{2}\right)\left(\frac{q}{2}\right)}{\left(\frac{r}{2}\right)^2} = 20\text{ N}$$

   Net force experienced by $C = F_{CA} - F_{CB} = 40 - 20 = 20\text{ N}$

3. In air, $F = \dfrac{1}{4\pi\varepsilon_0}\dfrac{q_1q_2}{r^2}$

   In water, $F' = \dfrac{1}{4\pi\varepsilon_0\varepsilon_r}\dfrac{q_1q_2}{r^2} = \dfrac{F}{80}$

(i) Force between q_1 and q_2 remains unchanged.

(ii) Force on each of them $= F' = \dfrac{F}{80}$

(iii) Force exerted by water on each charge $= F - F'$

$$= F - \frac{F}{80} = \frac{79F}{80}$$

4. $$\mathbf{F}_{21} = \frac{Kq_1q_2}{|\mathbf{r}_2 - \mathbf{r}_1|^3}(\mathbf{r}_2 - \mathbf{r}_1)$$

$$= \frac{9\times10^9 \times 20\times10^{-6}\times25\times10^{-6}}{|4\hat{\mathbf{i}} + 0\hat{\mathbf{j}} - 3\hat{\mathbf{k}}|^3}(4\hat{\mathbf{i}} - 3\hat{\mathbf{k}})$$

$$= 0.036\,|4\hat{\mathbf{i}} - 3\hat{\mathbf{k}}|$$

5. $$\frac{Kq_1q_2}{r^2} = \frac{mv^2}{r}$$

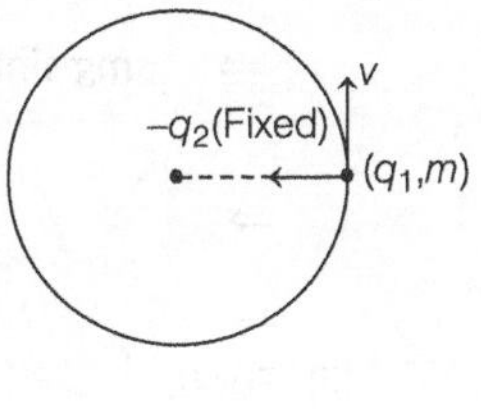

$$\Rightarrow \quad v = \sqrt{\frac{q_1q_2}{4\pi\varepsilon_0 mr}}$$

Time period, $T = \dfrac{2\pi r}{v} = 4\pi r\sqrt{\dfrac{\pi\varepsilon_0 mr}{q_1q_2}}$

6. $F = F_1 + F_2 + F_3 + \ldots + F_{20} = 9\times10^9 \times 10\times10^{-6}$

$$\left[\frac{10^{-6}}{1^2} + \frac{8\times10^{-6}}{2^2} + \frac{27\times10^{-6}}{3^2} + \ldots + \frac{20^3\times10^{-6}}{20^2}\right]$$

$$= 90\times10^{-3}(1+2+3+\ldots+20)$$

$$= 90\times10^{-3}\times\left(\frac{20(20+1)}{2}\right)$$

$$= 18.9\text{ N}$$

7. Net force on $A = \left(\dfrac{Kq^2}{a^2}\cos45°\right)\times2 + \dfrac{Kq^2}{(\sqrt{2}a)^2} = \left(\sqrt{2} + \dfrac{1}{2}\right)\dfrac{Kq^2}{a^2}$

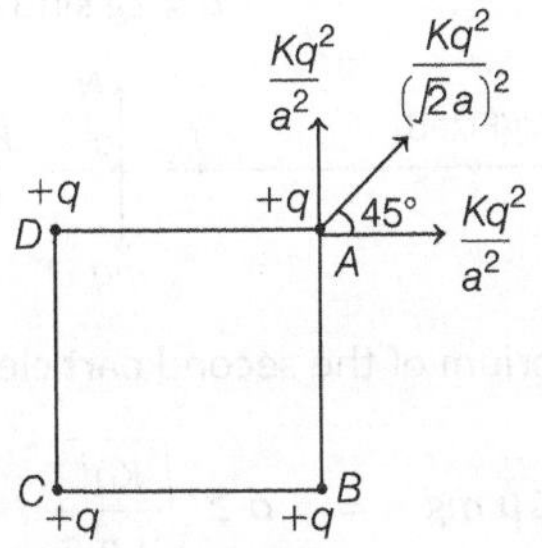

8.

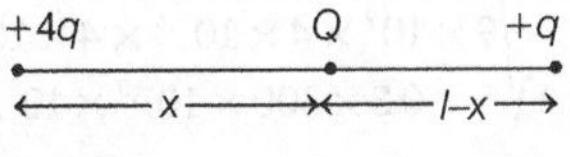

For equilibrium of Q,

$$\frac{K(4q)Q}{x^2} = \frac{KQq}{(l-x)^2}$$

$$\Rightarrow \quad \frac{l-x}{x} = \frac{1}{2} \quad \Rightarrow \quad x = \frac{2l}{3}$$

For equilibrium of $+q$,

$$\frac{K(4q)(q)}{l^2} + \frac{KQq}{(l-x)^2} = 0$$

$$\Rightarrow \quad Q = -\frac{4q}{9}$$

9. (i)

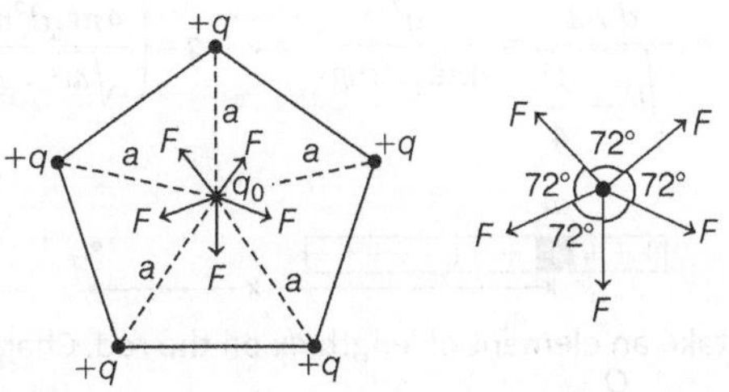

Net force on $q_0 = 0$

(ii)

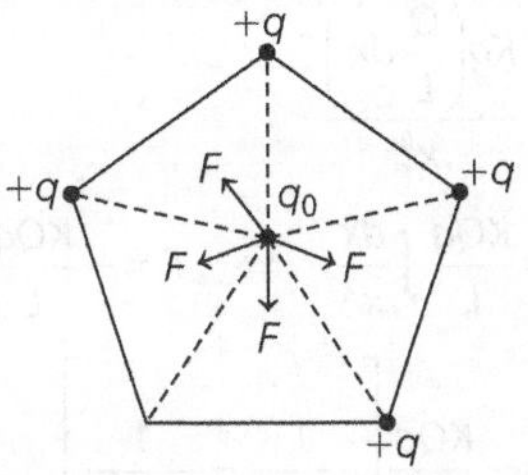

Resultant of the four forces acting on q_0 would be F directed towards the vacant corner.

$$F = \frac{kq_0q}{a^2}$$

(iii)

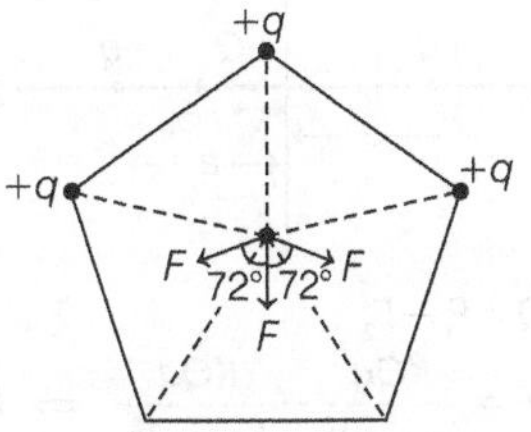

Resultant of the three forces acting on q_0

$$= (F\cos36°)\times2 = 2F\cos36°$$

$$= \frac{2kq_0q}{a^2}\cos36°$$

10.

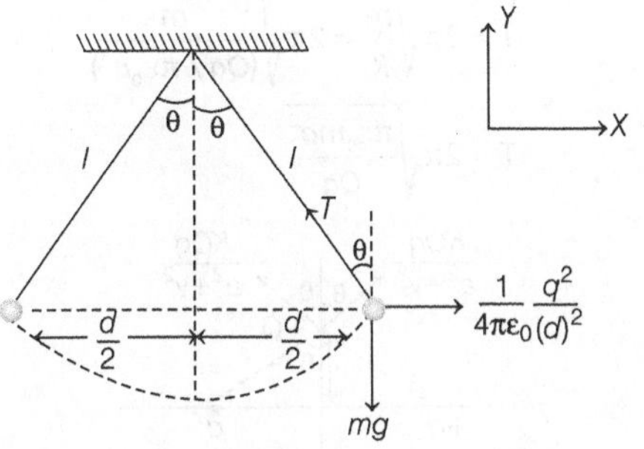

For equilibrium of sphere,

$$\Sigma F_x = 0$$

$$\Rightarrow \quad T\sin\theta = \frac{q^2}{4\pi\varepsilon_0 d^2} \quad \ldots\text{(i)}$$

$$\Sigma F_y = 0$$

$$\Rightarrow \quad T\cos\theta = mg \quad \ldots\text{(ii)}$$

Dividing Eq. (i) by Eq. (ii), we get

$$\tan\theta = \frac{q^2}{4\pi\varepsilon_0 d^2 mg}$$

$$\Rightarrow \frac{d/2}{\sqrt{l^2-\frac{d^2}{4}}}=\frac{q^2}{4\pi\varepsilon_0 d^2 mg} \Rightarrow q=\left(\frac{4\pi\varepsilon_0 d^3 mg}{\sqrt{4l^2-d^2}}\right)^{1/2}$$

11.

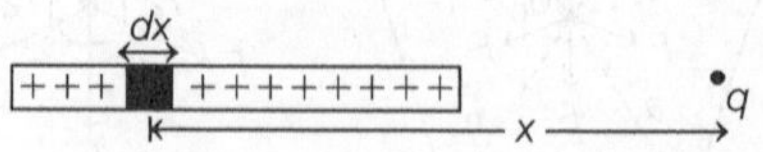

Lets take an element of length dx on the rod. Charge on the element $=\frac{Q}{L}dx$

$$dF=\frac{Kq\left(\frac{Q}{L}dx\right)}{x^2}$$

$$\Rightarrow \int dF=\frac{KQq}{L}\int\frac{dx}{x^2} \Rightarrow F=-\frac{KQq}{L}\left[\frac{1}{x}\right]_{d-\frac{L}{2}}^{d+\frac{L}{2}}$$

$$\Rightarrow F=-\frac{KQq}{L}\left[\frac{1}{d+\frac{L}{2}}-\frac{1}{d-\frac{L}{2}}\right] \Rightarrow F=\frac{4KQq}{4d^2-L^2}$$

12. (i)

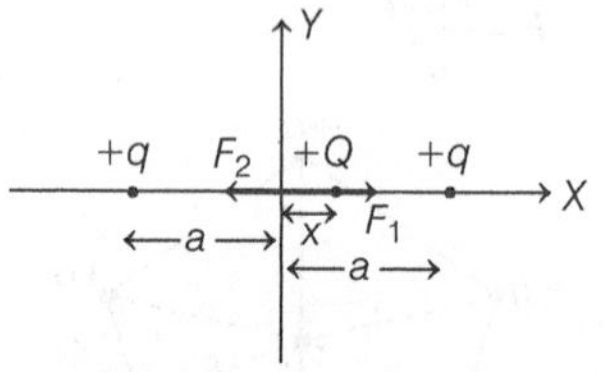

Net force on $Q=F_1-F_2$

$$F=\frac{KQq}{(a+x)^2}-\frac{KQq}{(a-x)^2} \Rightarrow F=\frac{(KQq)(-4ax)}{(a^2-x^2)^2}$$

$$\Rightarrow F=-\left(\frac{Qq}{\pi\varepsilon_0 a^3}\right)x \qquad \{\because x<<a\}$$

This is equation of SHM. So, particle will execute SHM.

$$T=2\pi\sqrt{\frac{m}{K}}=2\pi\sqrt{\frac{m}{(Qq/\pi\varepsilon_0 a^3)}}$$

$$T=2\pi\sqrt{\frac{\pi\varepsilon_0 ma^3}{Qq}}$$

(ii)

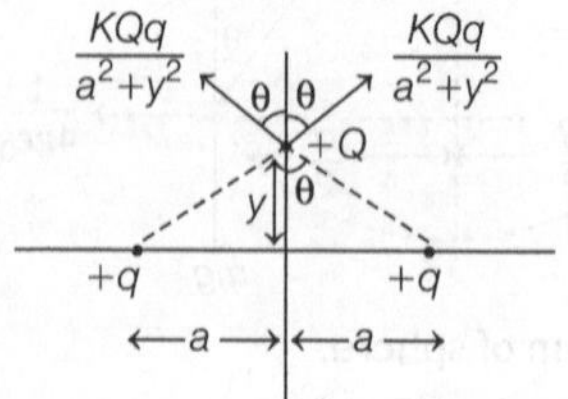

$$\text{Net force on Q along Y-axis}=\left(\frac{KQq}{a^2+y^2}\cos\theta\right)\times 2$$

$$\Rightarrow F=\frac{2KQq}{a^2+y^2}\frac{y}{\sqrt{a^2+y^2}}$$

$$\Rightarrow F=\frac{2KQqy}{(a^2+y^2)^{3/2}} \Rightarrow F=\frac{2KQqy}{a^3} \qquad (\because y<<a)$$

So, the particle will accelerate along the Y-axis.

13. (i)

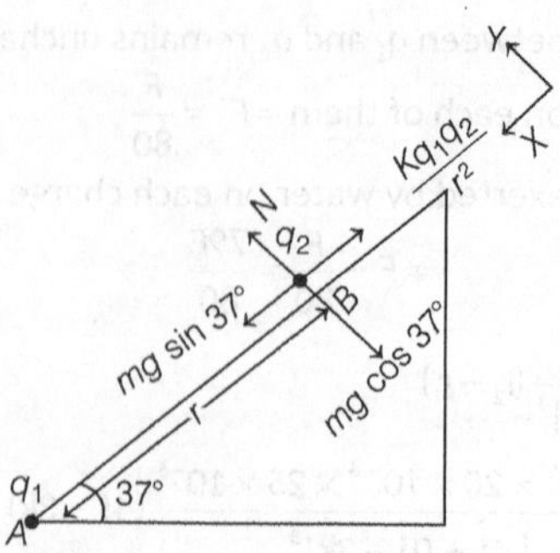

For equilibrium of B,

$$\Sigma F_x=0$$

$$\Rightarrow mg\sin 37^\circ=\frac{Kq_1q_2}{r^2} \Rightarrow r=\sqrt{\frac{Kq_1q_2}{mg\sin 37^\circ}}$$

$$\Rightarrow r=\sqrt{\frac{9\times10^9\times4\times10^{-6}\times4\times10^{-6}}{600\times10^{-3}\times10\times0.6}}$$

$$\Rightarrow r=0.2 \text{ m from the bottom}$$

(ii) For B, $\Sigma F_x=ma_x$

$$mg\sin 37^\circ+\frac{Kq^2}{r^2}=ma$$

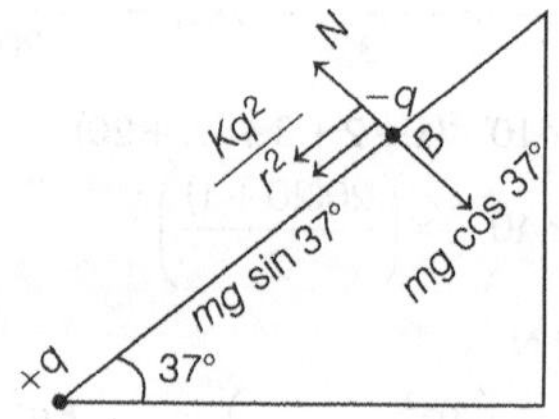

$$\Rightarrow mg\sin 37^\circ+mg\sin 37^\circ=ma$$

$$\Rightarrow a=2g\sin 37^\circ=12\text{ m/s}^2$$

14.

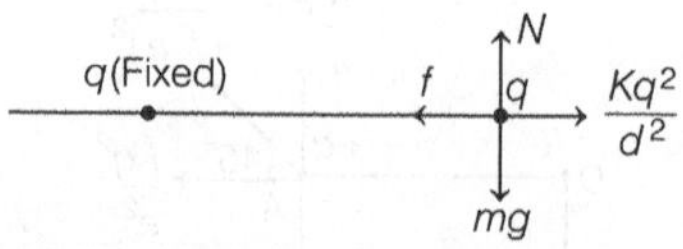

For the equilibrium of the second particle, $f=\frac{Kq^2}{d^2}$ and $f\le f_L$

$$\Rightarrow \frac{Kq^2}{d^2}\le\mu mg \Rightarrow d\ge\sqrt{\frac{Kq^2}{\mu mg}}$$

$$\Rightarrow d\ge\sqrt{\frac{9\times10^9\times4\times10^{-6}\times4\times10^{-6}}{0.3\times300\times10^{-3}\times10}}$$

$$\Rightarrow d\ge 0.4\text{ m}$$

1.3 Electric Field due to Point Charges

1. $E=\frac{Kq}{r^2} \Rightarrow 9=\frac{9\times10^9\times q}{(0.2)^2} \Rightarrow q=4\times10^{-11}\text{ C}$

2. $E=\frac{Kq}{|\mathbf{r}_2-\mathbf{r}_1|^3}(\mathbf{r}_2-\mathbf{r}_1)$

$$=\frac{9\times10^9\times10^{-10}}{|\hat{i}+\hat{j}+\hat{k}|^3}(\hat{i}+\hat{j}+\hat{k})=\frac{\sqrt{3}}{10}(\hat{i}+\hat{j}+\hat{k})\text{ N/C}$$

3. (i) $E = \dfrac{Kq}{(a/\sqrt{3})^2} = \dfrac{3Kq}{a^2}$

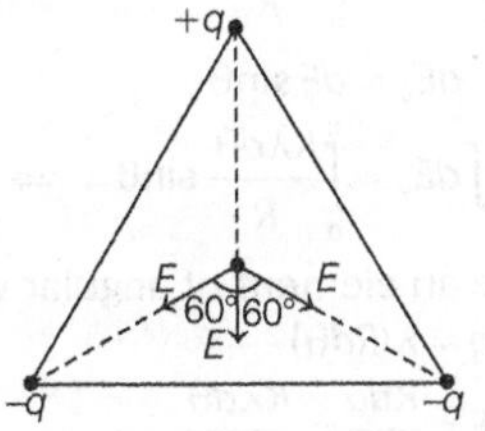

Net electric field at C

$$= E + E\cos 60^\circ + E\cos 60^\circ = 2E = 2\left(\frac{3Kq}{a^2}\right) = \frac{6Kq}{a^2}$$

(ii)

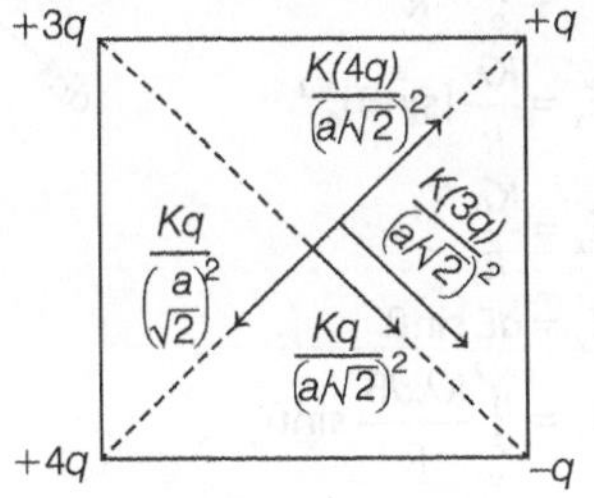

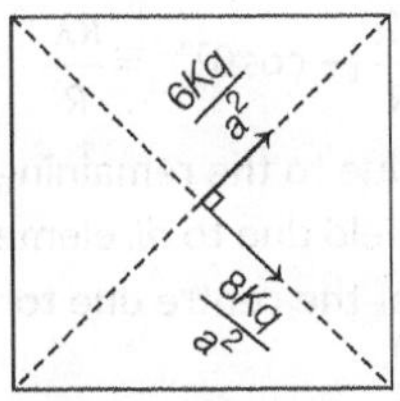

Net electric field at C

$$= \sqrt{\left(\frac{6Kq}{a^2}\right)^2 + \left(\frac{8Kq}{a^2}\right)^2} = \frac{10Kq}{a^2}$$

(iii)

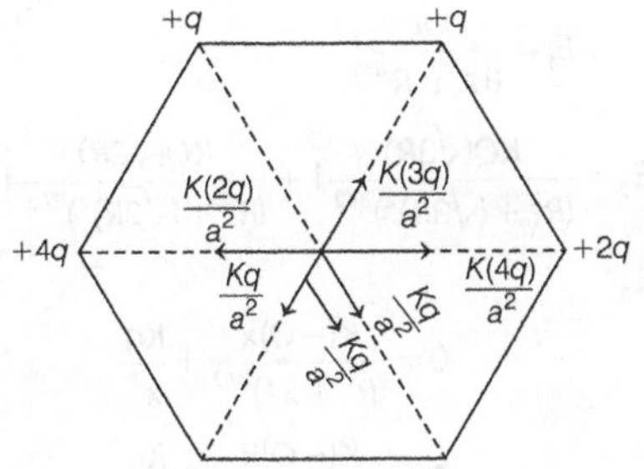

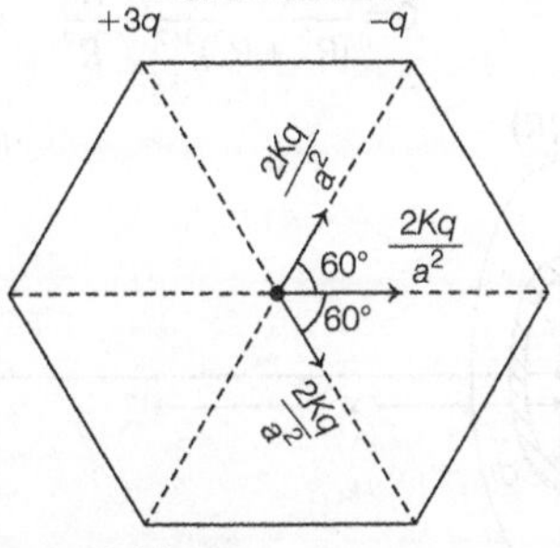

Net electric field at C

$$= \frac{2Kq}{a^2} + \left(\frac{2Kq}{a^2}\cos 60^\circ\right) \times 2 = \frac{4Kq}{a^2}$$

4. (i)

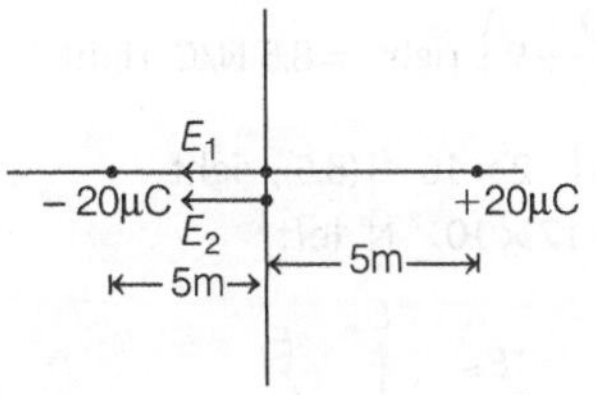

Electric field at origin $= (E_1 + E_2)(-\hat{\mathbf{i}})$

$$= \left(\frac{9\times10^9\times20\times10^{-6}}{5^2} + \frac{9\times10^9\times20\times10^{-6}}{5^2}\right)(-\hat{\mathbf{i}}) = 14.4\times10^3(-\hat{\mathbf{i}})\ \text{N/C}$$

(ii)

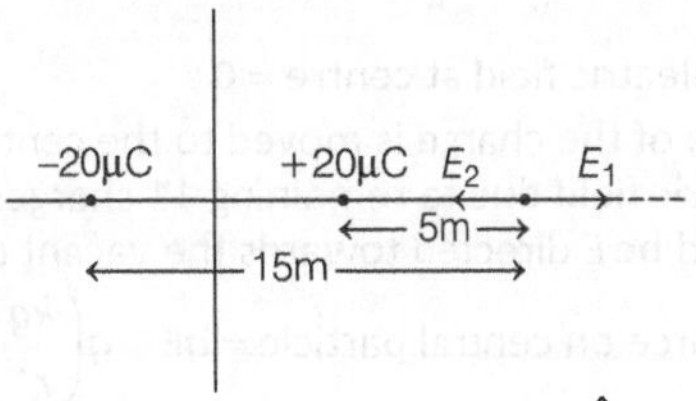

Net electric field at (10, 0) $= (E_1 - E_2)\hat{\mathbf{i}}$

$$= \left(\frac{9\times10^9\times20\times10^{-6}}{5^2} - \frac{9\times10^9\times20\times10^{-6}}{15^2}\right)\hat{\mathbf{i}}$$

$$= (6.4\times10^3\ \hat{\mathbf{i}})\ \text{N/C}$$

(iii)

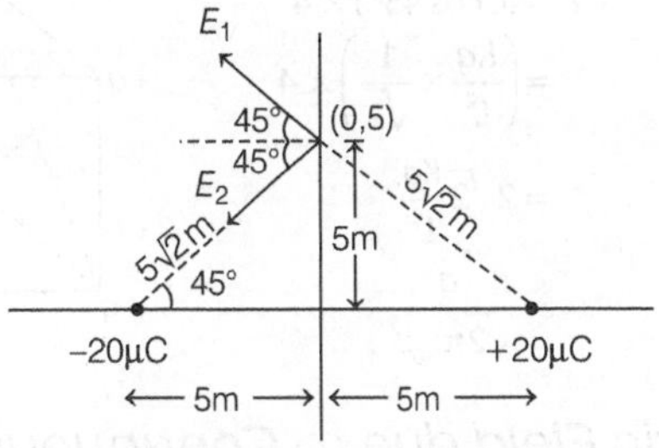

$$E_1 = E_2 = \frac{9\times10^9\times20\times10^{-6}}{(5\sqrt{2})^2} = 3.6\times10^3\ \text{N/C}$$

Net electric field at (0, 5)

$$= (E_1\cos 45^\circ + E_2\cos 45^\circ) - \hat{\mathbf{i}}$$

$$= (-3.6\sqrt{2}\times10^3\ \hat{\mathbf{i}})\ \text{N/C}$$

5.

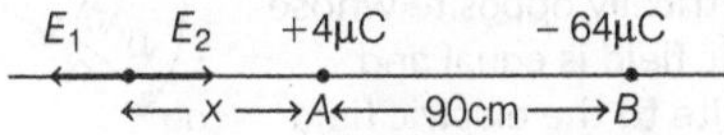

$$E_1 = E_2 \Rightarrow \frac{K(4\mu C)}{x^2} = \frac{K(64\mu C)}{(90+x)^2}$$

$$\Rightarrow \frac{90+x}{x} = 4 \Rightarrow x = 30\ \text{cm}$$

6. (i) Electric field at $A = \mathbf{E}_1 + \mathbf{E}_2 + \mathbf{E}_3$

$$\mathbf{E} = \left(\frac{Kq_1}{3^2} + \frac{Kq_2}{2^2} + \frac{Kq_3}{1^2}\right), \text{ right}$$

$$= \left(\frac{9\times10^9\times4\times10^{-9}}{9} + \frac{9\times10^9\times(-2\times10^{-9})}{4} + \frac{9\times10^9\times10^{-9}}{1}\right), \text{ right}$$

$$= \left(4 - \frac{9}{2} + 9\right), \text{ right } = 8.5 \text{ N/C, right}$$

(ii) $\mathbf{F} = q\mathbf{E} = (-2 \times 10^{-3})(8.5)$, right
$= 17 \times 10^{-3}$ N, left

7. (i)

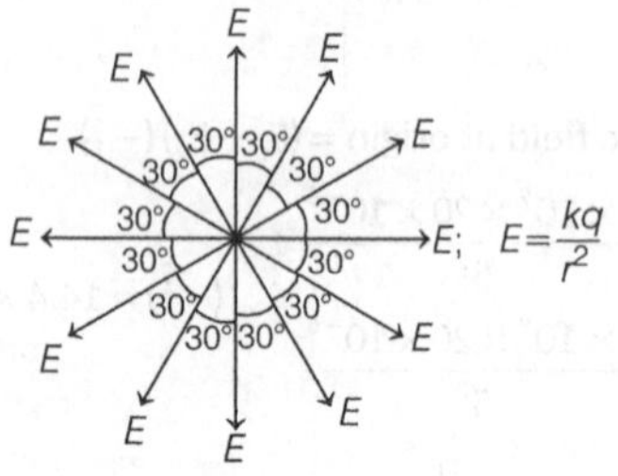

Net electric field at centre = 0

(ii) If one of the charge is moved to the centre, then electric field due to remaining 11 charges at the centre would be E directed towards the vacant corner.

So, force on central particle $= qE = q\left(\frac{kq}{r^2}\right) = \frac{kq^2}{r^2}$

8. $E = \frac{Kq}{L^2}$

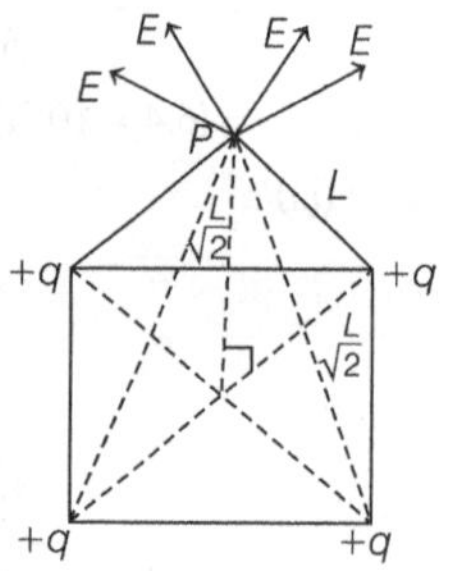

Net electric field at

$$P = (E\cos 45°) \times 4$$
$$= \left(\frac{Kq}{L^2} \times \frac{1}{\sqrt{2}}\right) \times 4$$
$$= 2\sqrt{2}\frac{Kq}{L^2}$$
$$= \frac{q}{\sqrt{2}\pi\varepsilon_0 L^2}$$

1.4 Electric Field due to Continuous Charge Distributions

1. (i) Electric field due to dq element at the centre is $\frac{Kdq}{R^2}$.

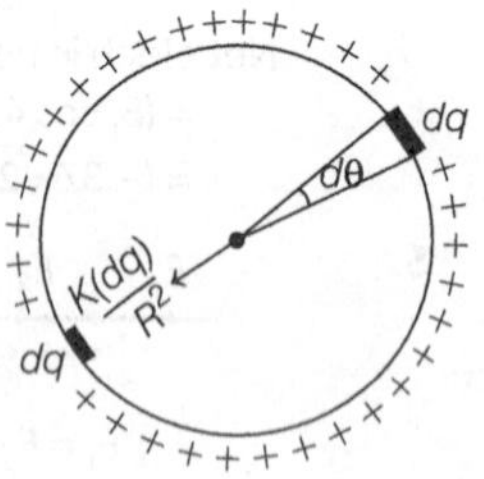

There is another dq element diametrically opposite whose electric field is equal and opposite to the electric field due to the first element.

So, net electric field at the centre would be zero.

(ii) Lets take an element of angular width $d\theta$ on the half ring.

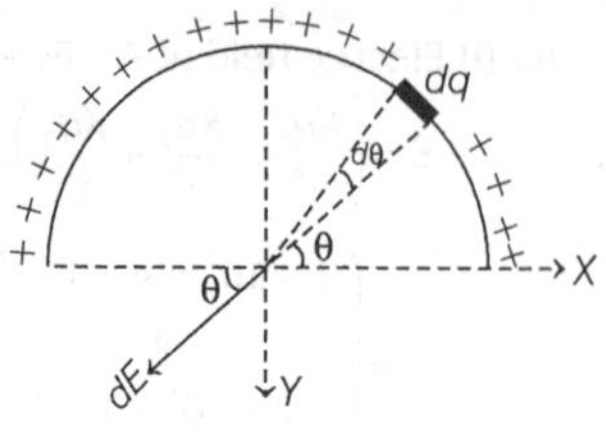

$$dq = \lambda(Rd\theta)$$
$$dE = \frac{Kdq}{R^2}$$
$$dE = \frac{K\lambda(Rd\theta)}{R^2}$$
$$dE_x = dE\cos\theta$$

$$\int dE_x = \int_0^{\pi} \frac{K\lambda d\theta}{R}\cos\theta \quad \Rightarrow \quad E_x = 0$$
$$dE_y = dE\sin\theta$$
$$\int dE_y = \int_0^{\pi} \frac{K\lambda d\theta}{R}\sin\theta \quad \Rightarrow \quad E_y = \frac{2K\lambda}{R}$$

(iii) Lets take an element of angular width $d\theta$ at an angle θ.

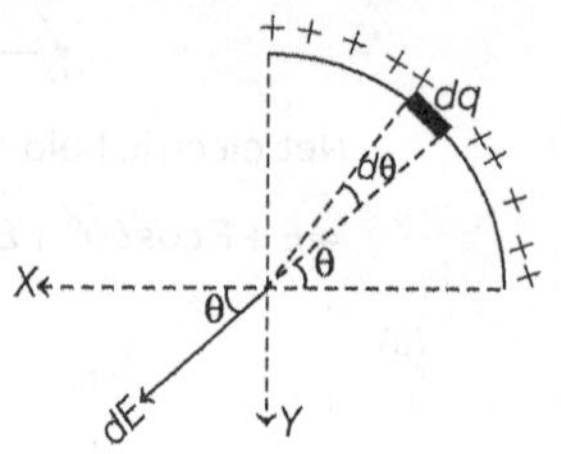

$$dq = \lambda(Rd\theta)$$
$$dE = \frac{Kdq}{R^2} = \frac{K\lambda d\theta}{R}$$
$$dE_x = dE\cos\theta$$
$$\Rightarrow \int dE_x = \int_0^{\pi/2} \frac{K\lambda d\theta}{R}\cos\theta$$
$$\Rightarrow E_x = \frac{K\lambda}{R}[\sin\theta]_0^{\pi/2}$$
$$\Rightarrow E_x = \frac{K\lambda}{R}$$
$$dE_y = dE\sin\theta$$
$$\Rightarrow \int dE_y = \int_0^{\pi/2} \frac{K\lambda d\theta}{R}\sin\theta$$
$$\Rightarrow E_y = \frac{K\lambda}{R}[-\cos\theta]_0^{\pi/2} = \frac{K\lambda}{R}$$

2. E_1 = Electric field due to the remaining ring and E_2 = electric field due to dL element.

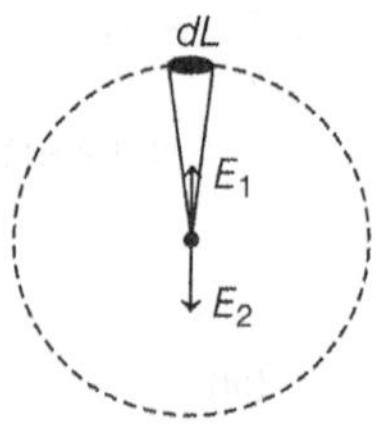

Net electric field at the centre due to the entire ring = 0

$$\Rightarrow E_1 = E_2$$
$$\Rightarrow E_1 = \frac{K\left(\frac{Q}{2\pi R}dL\right)}{R^2}$$
$$\Rightarrow E_1 = \frac{QdL}{8\pi^2\varepsilon_0 R^3}$$

3. $\mathbf{E} = \mathbf{E}_1 + \mathbf{E}_2 = \frac{KQ(\sqrt{3}R)}{(R^2 + (\sqrt{3}R)^2)^{3/2}}\hat{\mathbf{i}} + \frac{KQ(\sqrt{3}R)}{(R^2 + (\sqrt{3}R)^2)^{3/2}}\hat{\mathbf{i}} = \left(\frac{\sqrt{3}KQ}{4R^2}\right)\hat{\mathbf{i}}$

4. $\mathbf{E} = \mathbf{E}_1 + \mathbf{E}_2$

$$0 = \frac{K(-Q)x}{(R^2 + x^2)^{3/2}} + \frac{Kq}{x^2}$$
$$\Rightarrow \quad 0 = \frac{K(-Q)R}{(R^2 + R^2)^{3/2}} + \frac{Kq}{R^2} \quad \Rightarrow \quad q = \frac{Q}{2\sqrt{2}}$$

5. Disc (σ, R)

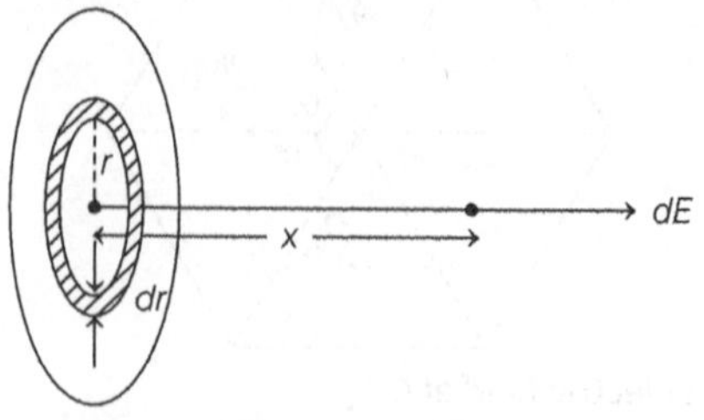

Lets take a ring of radius r and width dr.
Charge on the elemental ring, $dq = \sigma(2\pi r dr)$

$$dE = \frac{K(\sigma 2\pi r dr)\,x}{(r^2+x^2)^{3/2}}$$

$$\Rightarrow \quad \int dE = \int \frac{1}{4\pi\varepsilon_0}\frac{\sigma 2\pi r dr\, x}{(r^2+x^2)^{3/2}}$$

$$E = \frac{\sigma x}{2\varepsilon_0}\int_0^R \frac{rdr}{(r^2+x^2)^{3/2}}$$

Lets substitute $r^2 + x^2 = t^2$ and $rdr = tdt$

$$E = \frac{\sigma x}{2\varepsilon_0}\int_x^{\sqrt{R^2+x^2}} \frac{tdt}{t^3} = \frac{\sigma x}{2\varepsilon_0}\left[\frac{-1}{t}\right]_x^{\sqrt{R^2+x^2}}$$

$$\Rightarrow \quad E = \frac{\sigma}{2\varepsilon_0}\left(1 - \frac{x}{\sqrt{R^2+x^2}}\right)$$

6. (i) $E = 0$ as $r < R$

(ii) $E = 0$ as $r < R$

(iii) $E = \dfrac{Kq}{r^2}$ as $r > R = \dfrac{9\times10^9\times20\times10^{-6}}{(20\times10^{-2})^2} = 4.5\times10^6$ N/C

7. (i) $\mathbf{E} = \mathbf{E}_1 + \mathbf{E}_2 = 0 + 0 = 0$

(ii) $\mathbf{E} = \mathbf{E}_1 + \mathbf{E}_2 = \dfrac{KQ}{r^2}\hat{\mathbf{r}} + 0 = \dfrac{KQ}{r^2}\hat{\mathbf{r}}$

(iii) $\mathbf{E} = \mathbf{E}_1 + \mathbf{E}_2 = \dfrac{KQ}{r^2}\hat{\mathbf{r}} + \dfrac{K(2Q)}{r^2}\hat{\mathbf{r}} = \dfrac{3KQ}{r^2}\hat{\mathbf{r}}$

8. (i) $\mathbf{E} = 0$

(ii) $\mathbf{E} = \left(\dfrac{KQ}{R^3}r\right)\hat{\mathbf{r}} = \left(\dfrac{9\times10^9\times20\times10^{-6}}{(10\times10^{-2})^3}\times5\times10^{-2}\right)\hat{\mathbf{r}}$

$|\mathbf{E}| = 9\times10^6$ N/C

(iii) $\mathbf{E} = \dfrac{KQ}{r^2}\hat{\mathbf{r}} = \dfrac{9\times10^9\times20\times10^{-6}}{(20\times10^{-2})^2}\hat{\mathbf{r}}$

$|\mathbf{E}| = 4.5\times10^6$ N/C

9. (i) Lets take a spherical shell of radius x and thickness dx.

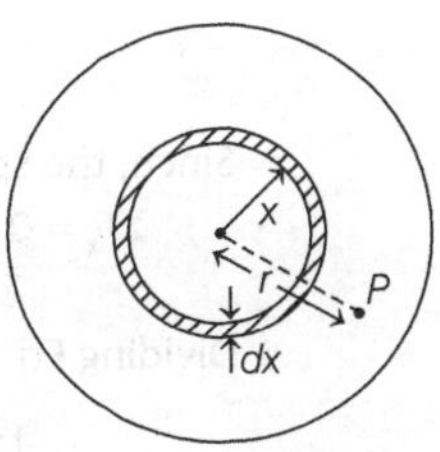

$$dE = \frac{Kdq}{r^2}$$

$$E = \int_0^r \frac{K(\rho_0 x\, 4\pi x^2\, dx)}{r^2}$$

$$= \frac{\rho_0 r^2}{4\varepsilon_0}\hat{\mathbf{r}}$$

(ii) $dE = \dfrac{Kdq}{r^2}$

$$\Rightarrow \quad \int dE = \int_0^R \frac{1}{4\pi\varepsilon_0}\frac{(\rho_0 x 4\pi x^2 dx)}{r^2} \quad \Rightarrow \quad E = \frac{\rho_0 R^4}{4\varepsilon_0 r^2}\hat{\mathbf{r}}$$

10.

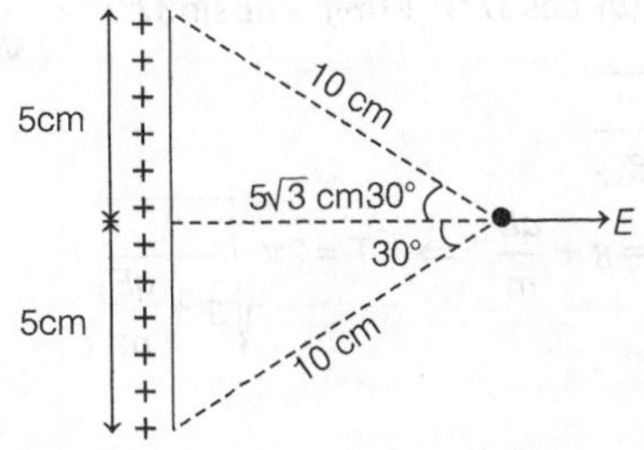

$$E = \frac{K\lambda}{r}(\sin\alpha + \sin\beta)$$

$$= \frac{9\times10^9\times(50\times10^{-6}/10\times10^{-2})}{5\sqrt{3}\times10^{-2}}(\sin30° + \sin30°)$$

$$= 3\sqrt{3}\times10^7 \text{ N/C} = 5.2\times10^7 \text{ N/C}$$

11. (i) $E_x = \dfrac{K\lambda}{r}(\sin\alpha + \sin\beta) = \dfrac{K\lambda}{r}(\sin37° + \sin53°)$

$$= \frac{K\lambda}{r}\left(\frac{3}{5} + \frac{4}{5}\right) = \frac{7K\lambda}{5r}$$

$$E_Y = \frac{K\lambda}{r}(\cos\alpha - \cos\beta) = \frac{K\lambda}{r}(\cos37° - \cos53°)$$

$$= \frac{K\lambda}{r}\left(\frac{4}{5} - \frac{3}{5}\right) = \frac{K\lambda}{5r}$$

$$E = \sqrt{E_x^2 + E_Y^2} = \sqrt{\left(\frac{7K\lambda}{5r}\right)^2 + \left(\frac{K\lambda}{5r}\right)^2} = \sqrt{2}\frac{K\lambda}{r}$$

(ii) $\mathbf{E} = \mathbf{E}_1 + \mathbf{E}_2 = \dfrac{2K\lambda}{r}\hat{\mathbf{i}} + \dfrac{2K\lambda}{r}\hat{\mathbf{i}}$

$$= \frac{4K\lambda}{r}\hat{\mathbf{i}}$$

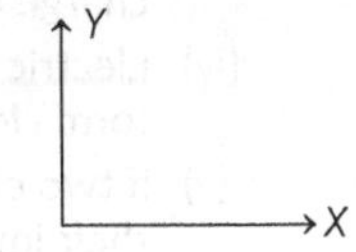

(iii) $\mathbf{E} = \mathbf{E}_1 + \mathbf{E}_2 = \left(\dfrac{K\lambda}{r}\hat{\mathbf{i}} - \dfrac{K\lambda}{r}\hat{\mathbf{j}}\right) + \left(\dfrac{K\lambda}{r}\hat{\mathbf{i}} - \dfrac{K\lambda}{r}\hat{\mathbf{j}}\right)$

$$= \frac{2K\lambda}{r}\hat{\mathbf{i}} - \frac{2K\lambda}{r}\hat{\mathbf{j}}$$

$$|\mathbf{E}| = \frac{2\sqrt{2}\,K\lambda}{r}$$

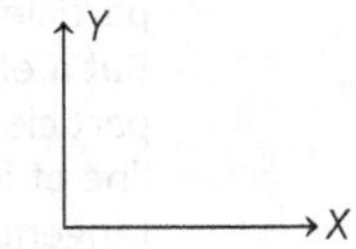

12. (i) $F = QE = Q\left(\dfrac{2K\lambda}{r}\right) = \dfrac{\lambda Q}{2\pi\varepsilon_0 r}$

(ii) $F = QE = (\lambda_2 l)\left(\dfrac{2K\lambda_1}{r}\right) = \dfrac{2K\lambda_1\lambda_2 l}{r} = \dfrac{\lambda_1\lambda_2 l}{2\pi\varepsilon_0 r}$

(iii)

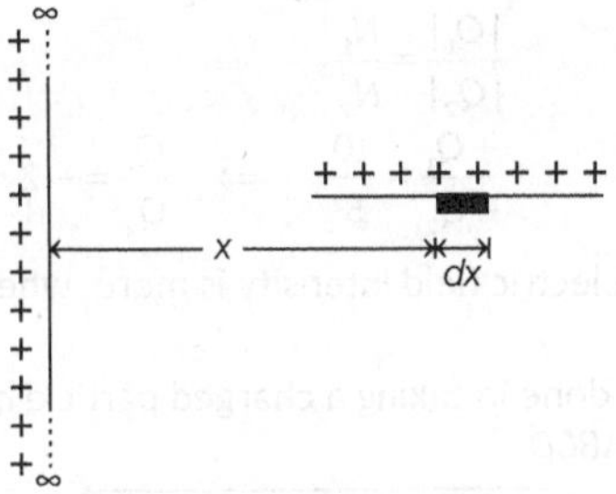

Lets take an element of width dx on the finite line charge.

$$dF = (\lambda_2 dx)\left(\frac{2K\lambda_1}{x}\right)$$

$$\int dF = \int_r^{l+r} \frac{2K\lambda_1\lambda_2\, dx}{x}$$

$$F = 2K\lambda_1\lambda_2 \ln\left(\frac{l+r}{r}\right) = \frac{\lambda_1\lambda_2}{2\pi\varepsilon_0}\ln\left(1 + \frac{l}{r}\right)$$

13. $\mathbf{E} = \mathbf{E}_1 + \mathbf{E}_2 + \mathbf{E}_3$

$$\mathbf{E}_A = \frac{\sigma}{2\varepsilon_0}\hat{j} + \frac{2\sigma}{2\varepsilon_0}\hat{j} - \frac{4\sigma}{2\varepsilon_0}\hat{j} = \frac{-\sigma}{2\varepsilon_0}\hat{j}$$

$$\mathbf{E}_B = \frac{-\sigma}{2\varepsilon_0}\hat{j} + \frac{2\sigma}{2\varepsilon_0}\hat{j} - \frac{4\sigma}{2\varepsilon_0}\hat{j} = \frac{-3\sigma}{2\varepsilon_0}\hat{j}$$

$$\mathbf{E}_C = \frac{-\sigma}{2\varepsilon_0}\hat{j} - \frac{2\sigma}{2\varepsilon_0}\hat{j} - \frac{4\sigma}{2\varepsilon_0}\hat{j} = \frac{-7\sigma}{2\varepsilon_0}\hat{j}$$

$$\mathbf{E}_D = \frac{-\sigma}{2\varepsilon_0}\hat{j} - \frac{2\sigma}{2\varepsilon_0}\hat{j} + \frac{4\sigma}{2\varepsilon_0}\hat{j} = \frac{\sigma}{2\varepsilon_0}\hat{j}$$

1.5 Electric Field Lines

1. (i) Electric field lines do not exist, where electric field is zero.

(ii) Electric field intensity is more, where electric field lines are closer.

(iii) Number of lines originating or terminating from a point charge is directly proportional to its magnitude.

(iv) Electric field lines produced by static charges do not form closed loop.

(v) If two electric field lines intersect, then the point of their intersection will have two directions of electric field which is not possible. Hence, electric field lines never intersect.

(vi) If electric field lines are straight, then a charged particle released from rest follow an electric field line. But if electric field lines are curved, then a charged particle released from rest will not follow the curved line of force as electric force on the charged particle is tangential and there is no force to provide centripetal acceleration on the curved path.

(vii) Electric force on the particle is tangential and there is no force to provide centripetal acceleration for the circular motion.

2. Number of lines originating from $Q_1 = 10$

Number of lines terminating on $Q_2 = 5$

$$\frac{|Q_1|}{|Q_2|} = \frac{N_1}{N_2}$$

$$\frac{+Q_1}{-Q_2} = \frac{10}{5} \Rightarrow \frac{Q_1}{Q_2} = -2$$

3. $E_A > E_B$ as electric field intensity is more, where lines are closer.

4. (i) Work done in taking a charged particle q around the loop $ABCD$

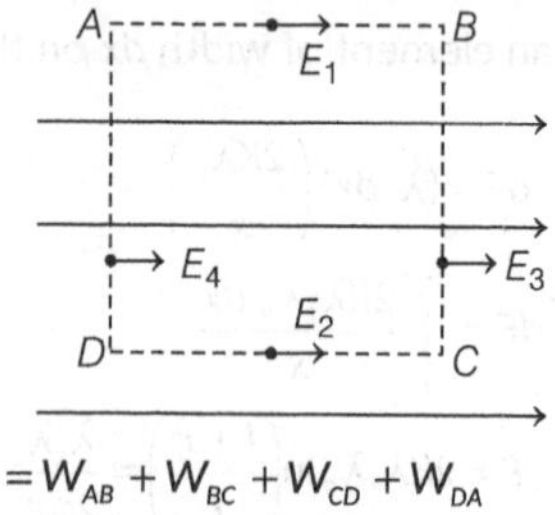

$$= W_{AB} + W_{BC} + W_{CD} + W_{DA}$$

$$= qE_1(AB) + 0 - qE_2(CD) + 0$$

$$= q(E_1 - E_2)AB \qquad (\because AB = CD)$$

Since, electric field lines are not uniformly spaced and they are closer on path AB than path CD.

So, $E_1 > E_2 \Rightarrow W > 0$

Electric field due to static charges is conservative and work done by electric force in a round trip is zero. So, this pattern is not possible.

(ii) It is possible.

(iii) Electric field lines cannot bend abruptly.

(iv) Electric field lines due to static charges cannot form closed loop.

1.6 Motion of Charged Particles in External Electric Field

1.

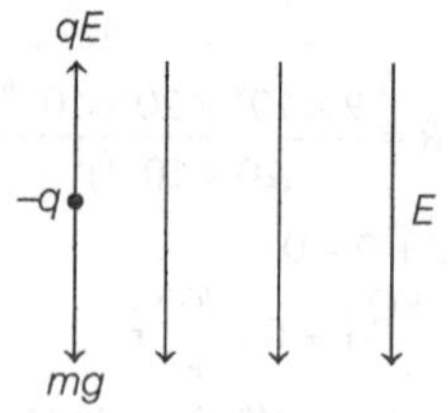

For equilibrium, $\Sigma F_y = 0$

$$\Rightarrow \qquad qE - mg = 0 \Rightarrow E = \frac{mg}{q}$$

$E = \dfrac{mg}{q}$, directed vertically down

2. (i)

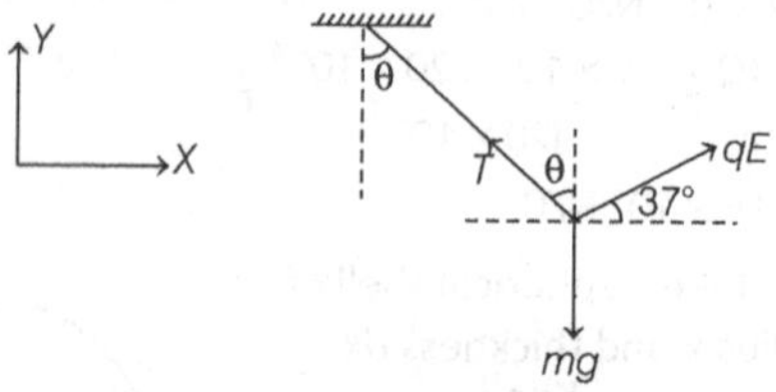

Since, the sphere is in equilibrium.

$$\Sigma F_x = 0 \Rightarrow T\sin\theta = qE\cos 37° \qquad \text{... (i)}$$

$$\Sigma F_y = 0 \Rightarrow T\cos\theta = mg - qE\sin 37° \qquad \text{... (ii)}$$

Dividing Eq. (i) by Eq. (ii), we get

$$\tan\theta = \frac{qE\cos 37°}{mg - qE\sin 37°}$$

$$\tan\theta = \frac{qE(4/5)}{qE - qE(3/5)} = 2$$

$$\Rightarrow \qquad \theta = \tan^{-1}(2)$$

(ii) From Eqs. (i) and (ii), we get

$$T = \sqrt{(qE\cos 37°)^2 + (mg - qE\sin 37°)^2} = \frac{2mg}{\sqrt{5}}$$

3. $T = 2\pi\sqrt{\dfrac{l}{g_{\text{eff}}}}$

(i) $g_{\text{eff}} = g + \dfrac{qE}{m} \Rightarrow T = 2\pi\sqrt{\dfrac{l}{g + \dfrac{qE}{m}}}$

(ii) $g_{eff} = g - \frac{qE}{m} \Rightarrow T = 2\pi\sqrt{\frac{l}{g - \frac{qE}{m}}}$

(iii) $g_{eff} = \sqrt{g^2 + \left(\frac{qE}{m}\right)^2} \Rightarrow T = 2\pi\sqrt{\frac{l}{\sqrt{g^2 + \left(\frac{qE}{m}\right)^2}}}$

4.

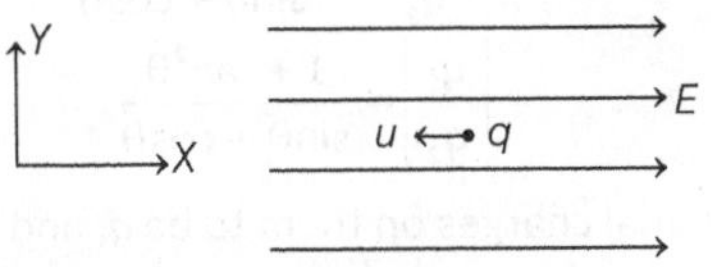

(i) $F = qE$

$\Rightarrow \quad ma = qE \Rightarrow a = \frac{qE}{m}$

$v^2 = u^2 + 2as \Rightarrow 0^2 = (-u)^2 + 2\left(\frac{qE}{m}\right)s$

$s = -\frac{mu^2}{2qE}$

Distance travelled $= \frac{mu^2}{2qE}$

(ii) $v = u + at$

$\Rightarrow \quad 0 = -u + \left(\frac{qE}{m}\right)t \Rightarrow t = \frac{mu}{qE}$

5. $a_p = \frac{eE}{m_p} \Rightarrow a_e = -\frac{eE}{m_e}$

$s = ut + \frac{1}{2}at^2$

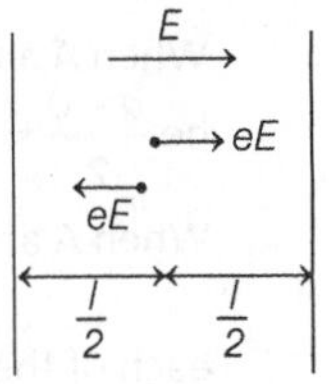

For electron; $-\frac{l}{2} = 0 + \frac{1}{2}\left(\frac{-eE}{m_e}\right)t_1^2$

$t_1 = \sqrt{\frac{m_e l}{eE}}$

For proton; $\frac{l}{2} = 0 + \frac{1}{2}\left(\frac{eE}{m_p}\right)t_2^2$

$t_2 = \sqrt{\frac{m_p l}{eE}}$

$\frac{t_1}{t_2} = \sqrt{\frac{m_e}{m_p}} = \sqrt{\frac{9.1 \times 10^{-31}}{1.673 \times 10^{-27}}}$

$= 2.33 \times 10^{-2} = 0.0233$

6.

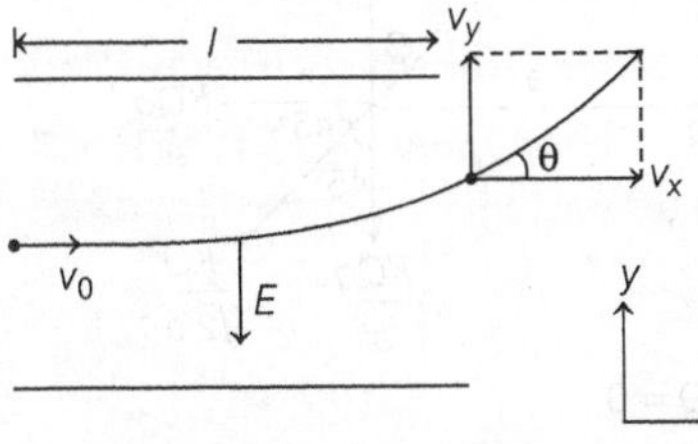

$\mathbf{F} = (-e)(-E\,\hat{\mathbf{j}}) \Rightarrow \mathbf{F} = eE\,\hat{\mathbf{j}}$

$a_x = 0$ and $a_y = \frac{eE}{m}$

$v_x = u_x + a_x t \Rightarrow v_x = v_0 + 0 = v_0$

$s_x = u_x t + \frac{1}{2}a_x t^2$

$l = v_0 t + 0 \Rightarrow t = \frac{l}{v_0}$

$v_y = u_y + a_y t = 0 + \left(\frac{eE}{m}\right)\frac{l}{v_0}$

$\tan\theta = \frac{v_y}{v_x} = \frac{(eE/m)\frac{l}{v_0}}{v_0} = \frac{eEl}{mv_0^2}$

$\theta = \tan^{-1}\left(\frac{eEl}{mv_0^2}\right) = 45°$

7. $q\left(\frac{2K\lambda}{r}\right) = \frac{mv^2}{r}$

$\Rightarrow \quad v = \sqrt{\frac{2K\lambda q}{m}}$

$T = \frac{2\pi r}{v} = \frac{2\pi r}{\sqrt{\frac{2K\lambda q}{m}}}$

$= 2\pi r\sqrt{\frac{m}{2K\lambda q}}$

$= 2\pi r\sqrt{\frac{2\pi\varepsilon_0 m}{\lambda q}}$

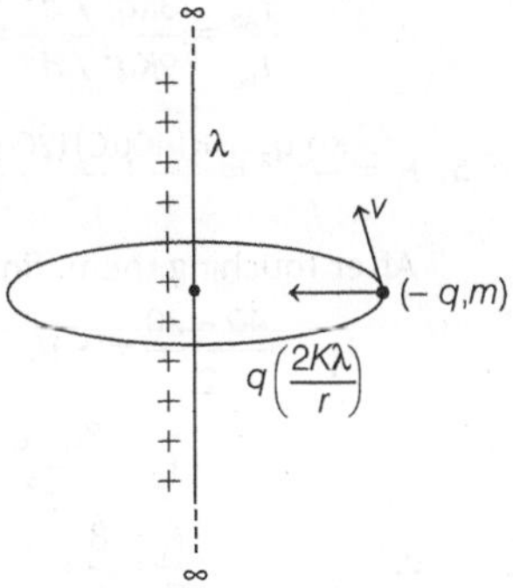

8. $F = qE$

$ma = q\left(\frac{\sigma}{2\varepsilon_0}\right) \Rightarrow a = \frac{q\sigma}{2\varepsilon_0 m}$

$s = ut + \frac{1}{2}at^2 \Rightarrow l = 0 + \frac{1}{2}\left(\frac{q\sigma}{2\varepsilon_0 m}\right)t^2$

$\Rightarrow \quad t = \sqrt{\frac{4\varepsilon_0 ml}{q\sigma}} = 4 \times 10^{-6}$ s

Level 2

Single Choice Correct Questions

1. Charge on each ball

$= \pm\frac{10}{63.5} \times 6 \times 10^{23} \times \frac{1}{10^6} \times 1.6 \times 10^{-19} = 1.512 \times 10^{-2}$ C

Force between the balls $= \frac{Kq_1q_2}{r^2}$

$= \frac{9 \times 10^9 \times (1.512 \times 10^{-2})^2}{(0.1)^2} = 2.0 \times 10^8$ N

2. $\mathbf{F}_{21} = \frac{Kq_1q_2}{|\mathbf{r}_2 - \mathbf{r}_1|^3}(\mathbf{r}_2 - \mathbf{r}_1) = \frac{1 \times q_1 \times q_2}{4\pi\varepsilon_0|-2\hat{\mathbf{i}} + \hat{\mathbf{j}} - 3\hat{\mathbf{k}}|^3}(-2\hat{\mathbf{i}} + \hat{\mathbf{j}} - 3\hat{\mathbf{k}})$

$= \frac{q_1q_2(-2\hat{\mathbf{i}} + \hat{\mathbf{j}} - 3\hat{\mathbf{k}})}{56\sqrt{14}\,\pi\,\varepsilon_0}$

3. Possible charges on the balls are

1	2	3	4	5
	+	+	–	–
	–	–	+	+

Since, ball 1 is attracting both balls 2 and 4, 1 must be neutral.

4.

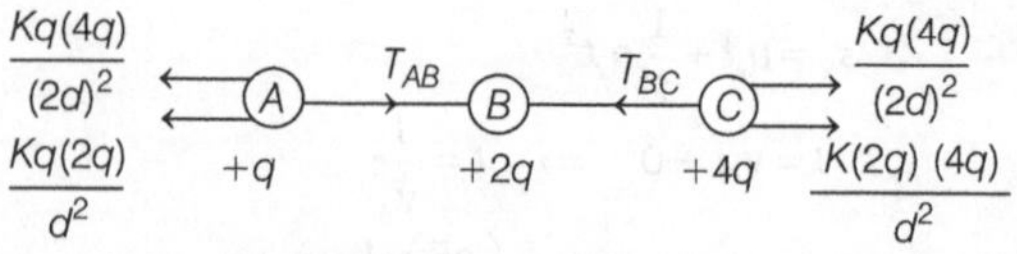

Since, A is in equilibrium, $\Sigma F = 0$

$$\Rightarrow \quad T_{AB} = \frac{Kq(4q)}{(2d)^2} + \frac{Kq(2q)}{d^2} = \frac{3Kq^2}{d^2}$$

Since, C is in equilibrium $\Sigma F = 0$

$$\Rightarrow \quad T_{BC} = \frac{Kq(4q)}{(2d)^2} + \frac{K(2q)(4q)}{d^2} = \frac{9Kq^2}{d^2}$$

$$\therefore \quad \frac{T_{AB}}{T_{BC}} = \frac{3Kq^2/d^2}{9Kq^2/d^2} = \frac{1}{3}$$

5. $F_1 = \frac{Kq_1q_2}{r^2} = \frac{K(40\mu C)(20\mu C)}{r^2}$

After touching them, final charge on each of them would be

$$\frac{40-20}{2} = +10\mu C$$

$$F_2 = \frac{Kq'_1q'_2}{r^2} = \frac{K(10\mu C)(10\mu C)}{r^2}$$

$$\therefore \quad \frac{F_1}{F_2} = \frac{8}{1}$$

6.

$$F = \frac{1}{4\pi\varepsilon_0}\frac{q_1q_2}{r^2} \quad \text{... (i)}$$

$$4F = \frac{1}{4\pi\varepsilon_0(16)}\frac{q_1q_2}{R^2} \quad \text{... (ii)}$$

From Eqs. (i) and (ii), we get

$$R = \frac{r}{8}$$

7.

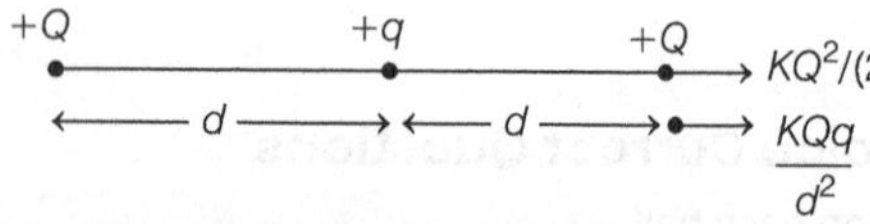

Central particle is already in equilibrium.

For equilibrium of $+Q$; $\Sigma F = 0$

$$\Rightarrow \quad \frac{KQ^2}{(2d)^2} + \frac{KQq}{d^2} = 0 \Rightarrow q = -\frac{Q}{4}$$

8.

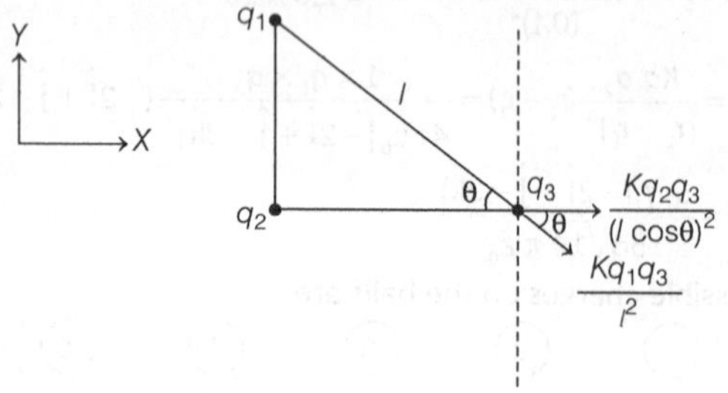

Force on $q_3 = \left(\frac{Kq_2q_3}{(l\cos\theta)^2} + \frac{Kq_1q_3}{l^2}\cos\theta\right)\hat{i} - \frac{Kq_1q_3}{l^2}\sin\theta\,\hat{j}$

$$\tan 45° = \frac{F_Y}{F_X} \quad \Rightarrow \quad 1 = \frac{-\frac{Kq_1q_3}{l^2}\sin\theta}{\frac{Kq_2q_3}{(l\cos\theta)^2} + \frac{Kq_1q_3}{l^2}\cos\theta}$$

$$\Rightarrow \quad \frac{Kq_1q_3}{l^2}(\sin\theta + \cos\theta) = -\frac{Kq_2q_3}{(l\cos\theta)^2}$$

$$\Rightarrow \quad \frac{q_1}{q_2} = -\frac{\sec^2\theta}{\sin\theta + \cos\theta}$$

$$\Rightarrow \quad \left|\frac{q_1}{q_2}\right| = \frac{1+\tan^2\theta}{\sin\theta + \cos\theta}$$

9. Lets take initial charges on them to be q_1 and $-q_2$.

$$0.108 = \frac{Kq_1q_2}{(0.5)^2} \quad \text{... (i)}$$

After connecting them, charge on each of them would be $\frac{q_1 - q_2}{2}$.

$$0.036 = \frac{K\left(\frac{q_1-q_2}{2}\right)\left(\frac{q_1-q_2}{2}\right)}{(0.5)^2} \quad \text{... (ii)}$$

Solving Eqs. (i) and (ii), we get

$$q_1 = \pm 1.0 \times 10^{-6}\text{ C} \quad \text{and} \quad q_2 = \mp 3.0 \times 10^{-6}\text{ C}$$

10.

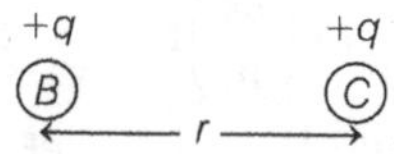

$$F = \frac{Kq^2}{r^2}$$

When A and B are touched, charges on each of them would be $\frac{q+0}{2} = \frac{q}{2}$.

When A and C are touched, charges on each of them would be $\frac{\frac{q}{2}+q}{2} = \frac{3q}{4}$

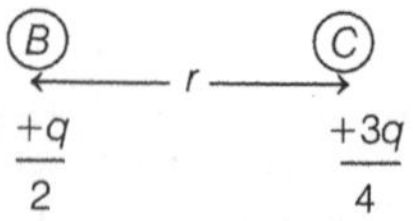

$$F' = \frac{K\left(\frac{q}{2}\right)\left(\frac{3q}{4}\right)}{r^2} = \frac{3F}{8}$$

11.

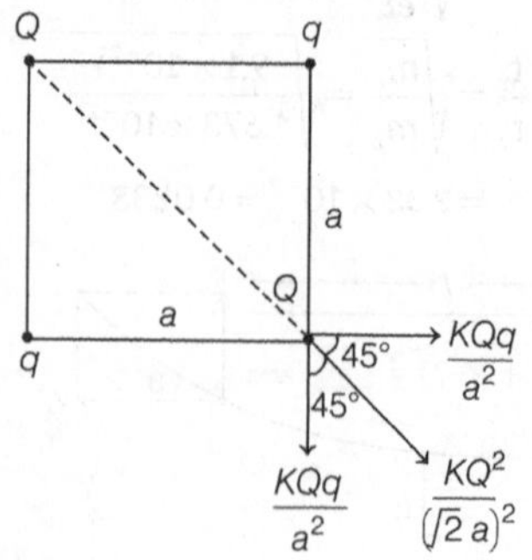

Net force on $Q = 0$

$$\Rightarrow \quad \frac{KQ^2}{2a^2} + \frac{KQq}{a^2}\cos 45° + \frac{KQq}{a^2}\cos 45° = 0$$

$$\Rightarrow \quad \frac{KQ^2}{2a^2} + \sqrt{2}\,\frac{KQq}{a^2} = 0 \quad \Rightarrow \quad \frac{Q}{q} = -2\sqrt{2}$$

12.

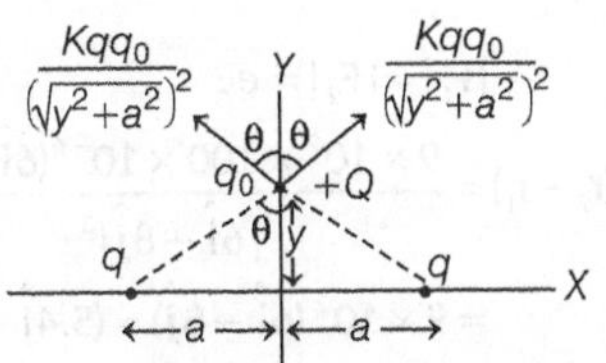

Net force on $q_0 = \dfrac{2Kqq_0}{y^2+a^2}\cos\theta$

$$F = \frac{2Kqq_0 y}{(a^2+y^2)^{3/2}}$$

$$F = \frac{2Kqq_0}{a^3}y \qquad (\because y << a)$$

$$F \propto y$$

13. $Q_0 = (2\sqrt{2}-1)Q$

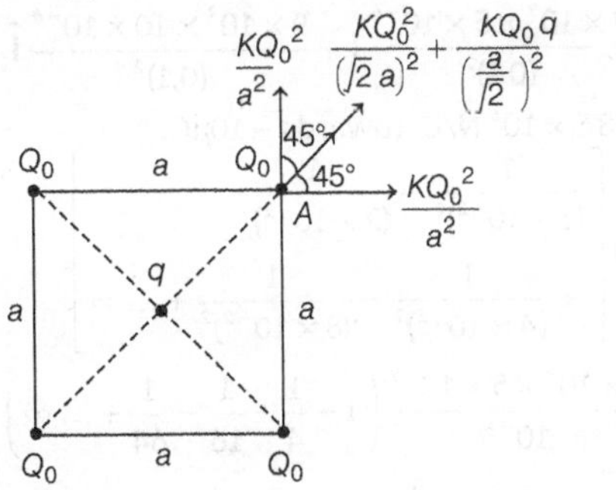

Net force on Q_0

$$= \frac{KQ_0^2}{(\sqrt{2}a)^2} + \frac{KQ_0 q}{\left(\dfrac{a}{\sqrt{2}}\right)^2} + \left(\frac{KQ_0^2}{a^2}\cos 45^\circ\right)\times 2 = 0$$

$$\Rightarrow \quad q = -\left(\frac{2\sqrt{2}+1}{4}\right)Q_0$$

$$\Rightarrow \quad q = -\left(\frac{2\sqrt{2}+1}{4}\right)(2\sqrt{2}-1)Q = -\frac{7Q}{4}$$

14. $F = \dfrac{Kq_1q_2}{r^2} = \dfrac{9\times10^9\times2\times10^{-6}\times2\times10^{-6}}{\left(\dfrac{0.1}{\sqrt{3}}\right)^2} = 10.8\text{ N}$

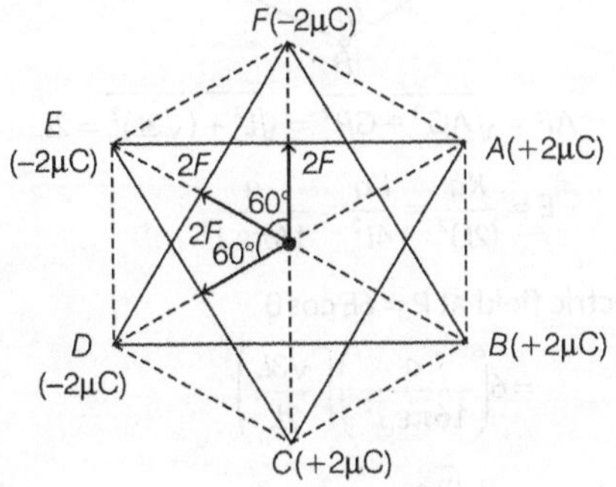

Net force on the central particle

$$= 2F + 2F\cos 60^\circ + 2F\cos 60^\circ = 4F$$
$$= 4(10.8) = 43.2\text{ N}$$

15.

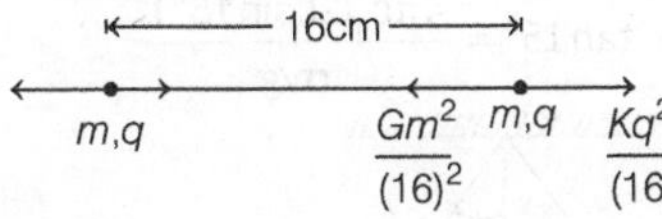

For equilibrium,

Gravitational force = Electrostatic force

$$\frac{Gm^2}{(16)^2} = \frac{Kq^2}{(16)^2} \Rightarrow \frac{q}{m} = \sqrt{\frac{G}{k}} = \sqrt{4\pi\varepsilon_0 G}$$

16. In gravity free space, angle between the two threads will be 180°.

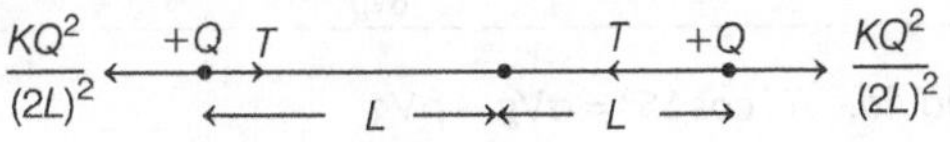

and $\quad T = \dfrac{KQ^2}{(2L)^2} = \dfrac{1}{4\pi\varepsilon_0}\dfrac{Q^2}{(2L)^2}$

17.

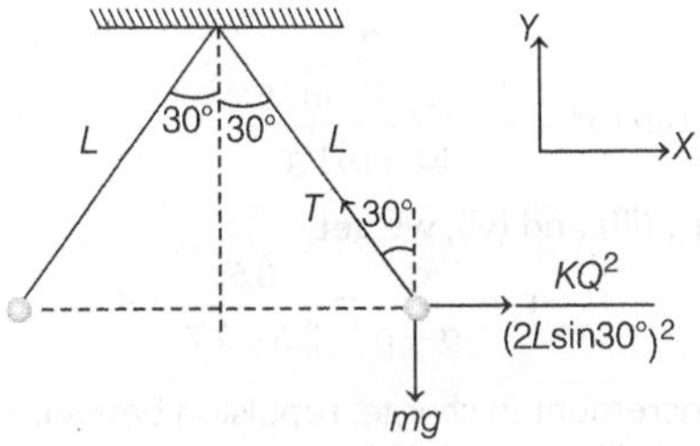

For equilibrium, $\Sigma F_x = 0$

$$\Rightarrow \quad T\sin 30^\circ = \frac{KQ^2}{(2L\sin 30^\circ)^2}$$

$$\Rightarrow \quad T\left(\frac{1}{2}\right) = \frac{9\times10^9\times10\times10^{-6}\times10\times10^{-6}}{\left(2(1)\left(\frac{1}{2}\right)\right)^2}$$

$$\Rightarrow \quad T = 1.8\text{ N}$$

18. In air,

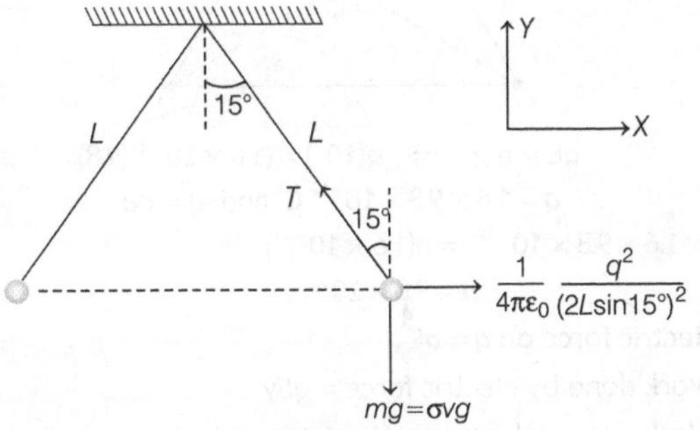

$$T\cos 15^\circ = \sigma vg \qquad \text{... (i)}$$

$$T\sin 15^\circ = \frac{1}{4\pi\varepsilon_0}\frac{q^2}{(2L\sin 15^\circ)^2} \qquad \text{... (ii)}$$

On dividing Eq. (ii) by Eq. (i), we get

$$\tan 15^\circ = \frac{\dfrac{q^2}{4\pi\varepsilon_0(2L\sin 15^\circ)^2}}{\sigma v g} \quad \text{... (iii)}$$

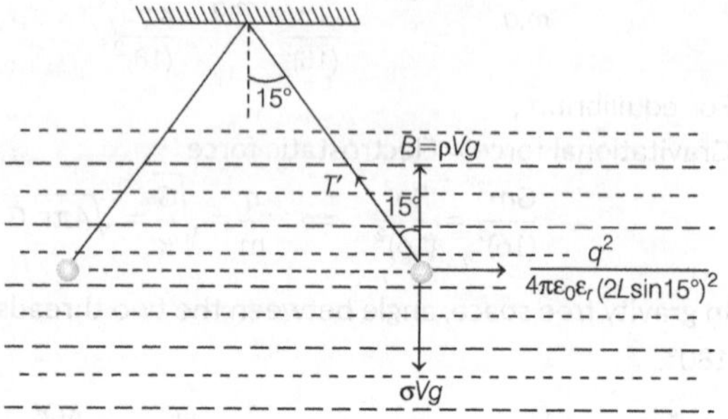

In liquid, $T'\cos 15^\circ = \sigma V g - \rho V g$ ... (iv)

$$T'\sin 15^\circ = \frac{q^2}{4\pi\varepsilon_0\varepsilon_r(2L\sin 15^\circ)^2} \quad \text{... (v)}$$

From Eqs. (iv) and (v), we get

$$\tan 15^\circ = \frac{\dfrac{q^2}{4\pi\varepsilon_0\varepsilon_r(2L\sin 15^\circ)^2}}{(\sigma-\rho)Vg} \quad \text{... (vi)}$$

From Eqs. (iii) and (vi), we get

$$\varepsilon_r = \frac{\sigma}{\sigma-\rho} = \frac{3.6}{3.6-2.7} = 4$$

19. Due to increment in charge, repulsion between the balls will increase and hence, angle between the strings will increase.

Symmetry would have been affected only if an external force would have changed.

20. Net force on the central particle

$$= 8\cos 60^\circ + 8\cos 60^\circ = 8\text{N}$$

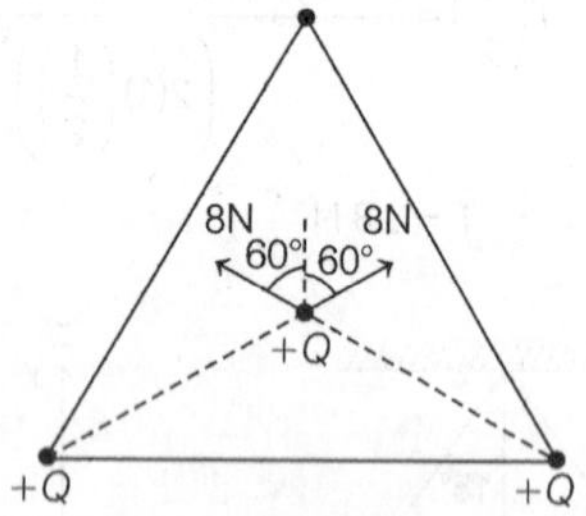

21. $qE = mg \Rightarrow q(10^9) = (1.6\times 10^{-3})(9.8)$

$q = 1.6\times 9.8\times 10^{-12}$ C and $q = ne$

$1.6\times 9.8\times 10^{-12} = n(1.6\times 10^{-19})$

$n = 9.8\times 10^7$

22. Electric force on $q = qE$

Work done by electric force $= qEy$

Work-energy theorem, $W = \Delta K$

$\Rightarrow \quad qEy = K_2 - 0 \Rightarrow K_2 = qEy$

23. $\mathbf{F} = q\mathbf{E}$

$\mathbf{F}_1$ = Force on proton $= (+e)\mathbf{E} = e\mathbf{E}$

$\mathbf{F}_2$ = Force on electron $= (-e)\mathbf{E} = -e\mathbf{E}$

$$|\mathbf{F}_1| = |\mathbf{F}_2| = eE$$

24. $\mathbf{E} = \dfrac{Kq}{|\mathbf{r}_2-\mathbf{r}_1|^3}(\mathbf{r}_2-\mathbf{r}_1) = \dfrac{9\times 10^9\times 100\times 10^{-6}(6\hat{\mathbf{i}}-8\hat{\mathbf{j}})}{|6\hat{\mathbf{i}}-8\hat{\mathbf{j}}|^3}$

$= 9\times 10^2(6\hat{\mathbf{i}}-8\hat{\mathbf{j}}) = (5.4\hat{\mathbf{i}}-7.2\hat{\mathbf{j}})$

25. $\mathbf{E}_A = \dfrac{Kq}{|\hat{\mathbf{i}}+2\hat{\mathbf{j}}+3\hat{\mathbf{k}}|^3}(\hat{\mathbf{i}}+2\hat{\mathbf{j}}+3\hat{\mathbf{k}})$

$\mathbf{E}_B = \dfrac{Kq}{|\hat{\mathbf{i}}+\hat{\mathbf{j}}-\hat{\mathbf{k}}|^3}(\hat{\mathbf{i}}+\hat{\mathbf{j}}-\hat{\mathbf{k}})$

$\mathbf{E}_C = \dfrac{Kq}{|2\hat{\mathbf{i}}+2\hat{\mathbf{j}}+2\hat{\mathbf{k}}|^3}(2\hat{\mathbf{i}}+2\hat{\mathbf{j}}+2\hat{\mathbf{k}})$

$\mathbf{E}_A\cdot\mathbf{E}_B = 0$

$\Rightarrow \quad \mathbf{E}_A \perp \mathbf{E}_B$ and $|\mathbf{E}_B| = 4|\mathbf{E}_C|$

26. $\mathbf{E} = \mathbf{E}_1 + \mathbf{E}_2$

$= \dfrac{9\times 10^9\times 5\times 10^{-6}}{(0.1)^2}\hat{\mathbf{i}} + \dfrac{9\times 10^9\times 10\times 10^{-6}}{(0.1)^2}\hat{\mathbf{i}}$

$= 13.5\times 10^6$ N/C, towards -10μC.

27. $E = Kq\left[\dfrac{1}{(1\times 10^{-2})^2} - \dfrac{1}{(2\times 10^{-2})^2} + \dfrac{1}{(4\times 10^{-2})^2} - \dfrac{1}{(8\times 10^{-2})^2} + \dots\infty\right]$

$E = \dfrac{9\times 10^9\times 5\times 10^{-9}}{10^{-4}}\left(1 - \dfrac{1}{4} + \dfrac{1}{16} - \dfrac{1}{64} + \dots\infty\right)$

$= 45\times 10^4 \times \dfrac{1}{1-\left(\dfrac{-1}{4}\right)} = 36\times 10^4$ N/C

28.

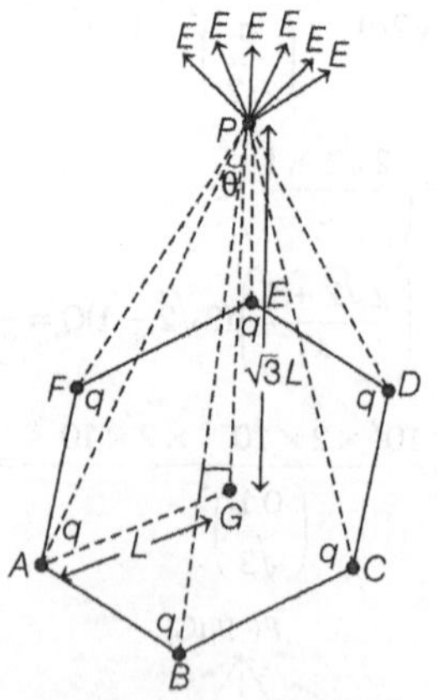

$$AP = \sqrt{AG^2 + GP^2} = \sqrt{L^2 + (\sqrt{3}L)^2} = 2L$$

$$E = \frac{Kq}{(2L)^2} = \frac{Kq}{4L^2} = \frac{q}{16\pi\varepsilon_0 L^2}$$

Net electric field at $P = 6E\cos\theta$

$$= 6\left(\frac{q}{16\pi\varepsilon_0 L^2}\right)\left(\frac{\sqrt{3}L}{2L}\right)$$

$$= \frac{3\sqrt{3}q}{16\pi\varepsilon_0 L^2}$$

29.

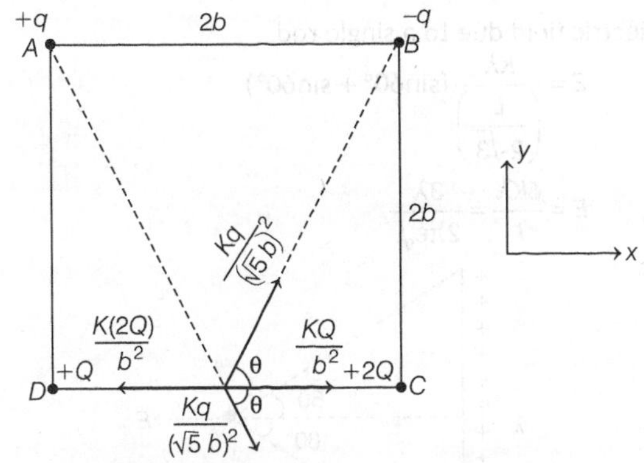

$$\Sigma E_x = 0$$

$$\Rightarrow \quad \frac{K(2Q)}{b^2} = \frac{KQ}{b^2} + \frac{Kq}{(\sqrt{5}\,b)^2}\cos\theta + \frac{Kq}{(\sqrt{5}\,b)^2}\cos\theta$$

$$\Rightarrow \quad \frac{KQ}{b^2} = \frac{2Kq}{5b^2}\left(\frac{b}{\sqrt{5}b}\right) \quad \Rightarrow \quad \frac{q}{Q} = \frac{5\sqrt{5}}{2}$$

30. Electric field between the two charges is negative. So, q_2 will be positive and q_1 will be negative.
Since, electric field is zero at a point closer to q_2, $|q_2| < |q_1|$.

31. Electric field intensity is more, where electric field lines are closer.
So, $E_A = E_C > E_B$

32. $\mathbf{F} = (-q)(-E\,\hat{\mathbf{j}})$

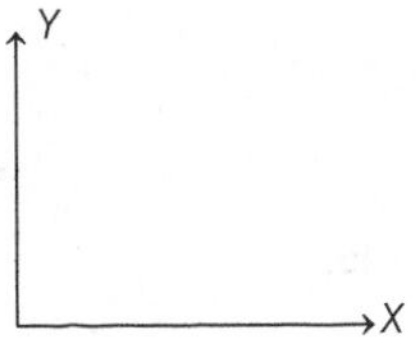

$$m\mathbf{a} = qE\hat{\mathbf{j}} \quad \Rightarrow \quad \mathbf{a} = \frac{qE}{m}\hat{\mathbf{j}}$$

$$s_x = u_x t + \frac{1}{2}a_x t^2$$

$$L = vt + 0 \quad \Rightarrow \quad t = \frac{L}{v}$$

For droplet to not hit the plate,

$$s_y < \frac{d}{2}$$

$$\Rightarrow \quad u_y t + \frac{1}{2}a_y t^2 < \frac{d}{2} \quad \Rightarrow \quad 0 + \frac{1}{2}\left(\frac{qE}{m}\right)\left(\frac{L}{v}\right)^2 < \frac{d}{2}$$

$$\Rightarrow \quad q < \frac{mv^2 d}{EL^2} \quad \Rightarrow \quad q_{max} = \frac{mv^2 d}{EL^2}$$

33.

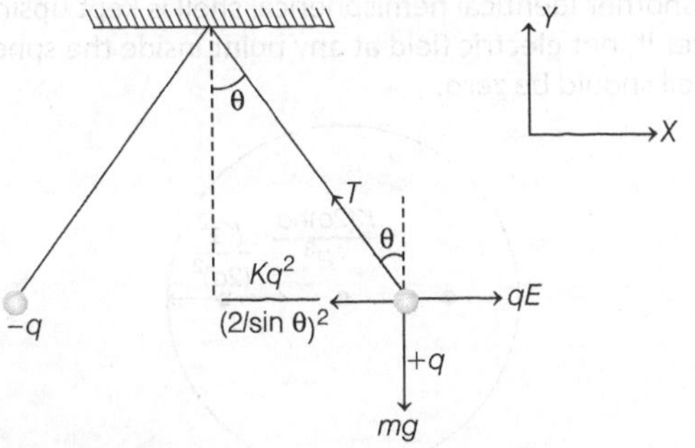

For equilibrium,

$$\Sigma F_x = 0$$

$$\Rightarrow \quad T\sin\theta = qE - \frac{Kq^2}{(2l\sin\theta)^2} \quad \text{... (i)}$$

$$\Sigma F_y = 0$$

$$\Rightarrow \quad T\cos\theta = mg \quad \text{... (ii)}$$

Dividing Eq. (i) by Eq. (ii), we get

$$\tan\theta = \frac{qE - \dfrac{Kq^2}{(2l\sin\theta)^2}}{mg}$$

$$\Rightarrow \quad E = \frac{Kq}{(2l\sin\theta)^2} + \frac{mg\tan\theta}{q}$$

34.

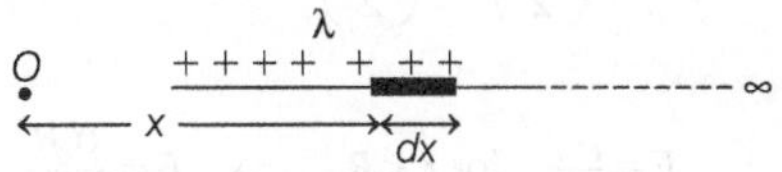

$$dE = \frac{K(\lambda\, dx)}{x^2}$$

$$\Rightarrow \quad \int dE = \frac{\lambda}{4\pi\varepsilon_0}\int_a^{\infty}\frac{dx}{x^2} \quad \Rightarrow \quad E = \frac{\lambda}{4\pi\varepsilon_0 a}$$

Electric field due to the other line charge will be same.

$$E_{net} = 2\left(\frac{\lambda}{4\pi\varepsilon_0 a}\right) = \frac{\lambda}{2\pi\varepsilon_0 a}$$

35. $E = \dfrac{KQx}{(r^2 + x^2)^{3/2}}$

Electric field is maximum at $x = \dfrac{r}{\sqrt{2}}$.

$$E_{max} = \frac{KQ(r/\sqrt{2})}{\left(r^2 + \left(\dfrac{r}{\sqrt{2}}\right)^2\right)^{3/2}} = \frac{KQ\left(\dfrac{1}{\sqrt{2}}\right)}{\left(\dfrac{3\sqrt{3}}{2\sqrt{2}}\right)r^2} = \frac{Q}{6\sqrt{3}\pi\varepsilon_0 r^2}$$

36.

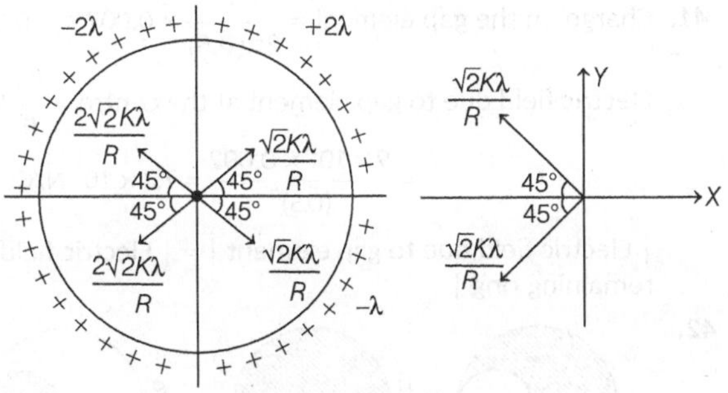

$$\text{Net electric field} = \left(\frac{\sqrt{2}K\lambda}{R}\cos 45° \times 2\right)(-\hat{\mathbf{i}})$$

$$= \frac{2K\lambda}{R}(-\hat{\mathbf{i}}) = \left(\frac{\lambda}{2\pi\varepsilon_0 R}\right)(-\hat{\mathbf{i}})$$

37. $\mathbf{E} = \mathbf{E}_1 + \mathbf{E}_2$

$$\Rightarrow \quad 0 = \frac{KQz}{(R^2 + z^2)^{3/2}}\hat{\mathbf{k}} - \frac{K(\sqrt{8}Q)z}{((2R)^2 + z^2)^{3/2}}\hat{\mathbf{k}}$$

$$\Rightarrow \quad \frac{KQz}{(R^2 + z^2)^{3/2}} = \frac{\sqrt{8}KQz}{((2R)^2 + z^2)^{3/2}}$$

$$\Rightarrow \quad 8(R^2 + z^2)^3 = (4R^2 + z^2)^3$$

$$\Rightarrow \quad 2(R^2 + z^2) = 4R^2 + z^2 \quad \Rightarrow \quad z = \sqrt{2}R$$

38. $\mathbf{E = E_1 + E_2}$

$$E_A = 0 + 0 = 0$$

$$E_B = \frac{KQ}{\left(\frac{3r}{2}\right)^2} + 0 = \frac{4KQ}{9r^2}$$

$$E_C = \frac{KQ}{\left(\frac{5r}{2}\right)^2} + \frac{K(-Q)}{\left(\frac{5r}{2}\right)^2} = 0 \;\Rightarrow\; E_B > E_A = E_C$$

39. $\rho = \rho_0 r^2$

$$E = \frac{\rho_0 r^3}{5\varepsilon_0} \text{ for } r < R \;\Rightarrow\; E = \frac{\rho_0 R^5}{5\varepsilon_0 r^2} \text{ for } r > R$$

$$E_{r=2R} = \frac{\rho_0 R^5}{5\varepsilon_0 (2R)^2} = \frac{\rho_0 R^3}{20\varepsilon_0}$$

$$E_{r=R/2} = \frac{\rho_0 (R/2)^3}{5\varepsilon_0} = \frac{\rho_0 R^3}{40\varepsilon_0} \;\Rightarrow\; \frac{E_{r=2R}}{E_{r=R/2}} = 2$$

40. Net electric field = 0

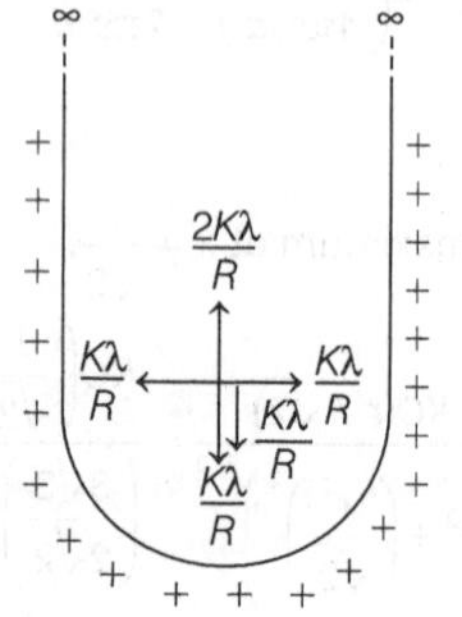

41. Charge on the gap element $= \dfrac{1}{2\pi(0.5)} \times 0.002\,\pi = 0.002$ C

Electric field due to gap element at the centre $= \dfrac{Kdq}{R^2}$

$$= \frac{9 \times 10^9 \times 0.002}{(0.5)^2} = 7.2 \times 10^7 \text{ N/C}$$

| Electric field due to gap element | = | Electric field due to remaining ring |

42.

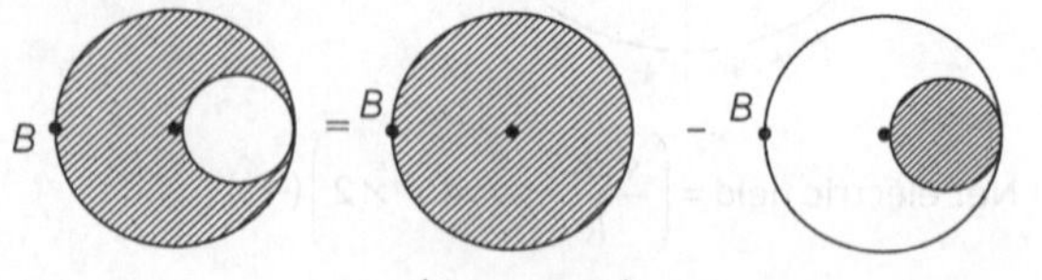

$$E_B = E_1 - E_2 = \frac{\rho R}{3\varepsilon_0} - \frac{K\left(\rho \frac{4}{3}\pi\left(\frac{R}{2}\right)^3\right)}{\left(\frac{3R}{2}\right)^2} = \frac{17\rho R}{54\varepsilon_0}, \text{ left}$$

43. $$\tan\theta = \frac{E_y}{E_x} = \frac{\frac{K\lambda}{r}(\cos\alpha - \cos\beta)}{\frac{K\lambda}{r}(\sin\alpha + \sin\beta)}$$

$$\Rightarrow\; \tan\theta = \tan\left(\frac{\beta - \alpha}{2}\right)$$

$$\Rightarrow\; \tan\theta = \tan 28^\circ \;\Rightarrow\; \theta = 28^\circ$$

44. Electric field due to a single rod,

$$E = \frac{K\lambda}{\left(\frac{L}{2\sqrt{3}}\right)}(\sin 60^\circ + \sin 60^\circ)$$

$$E = \frac{6K\lambda}{L} = \frac{3\lambda}{2\pi\varepsilon_0 L}$$

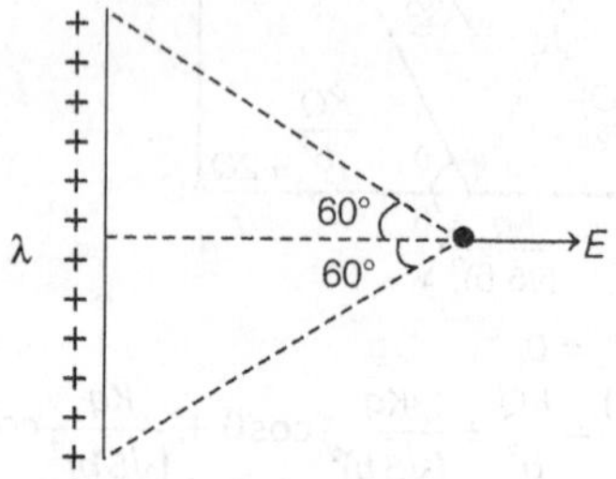

Net electric field at the centroid

$$= E + E\cos 60^\circ + E\cos 60^\circ$$

$$= 2E = 2\left(\frac{3\lambda}{2\pi\varepsilon_0 L}\right) = \frac{3\lambda}{\pi\varepsilon_0 L}$$

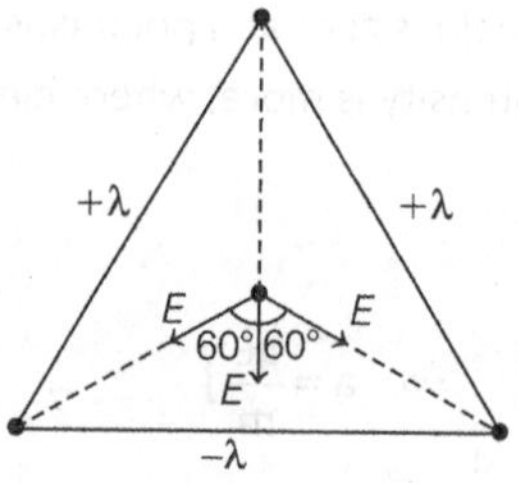

45.

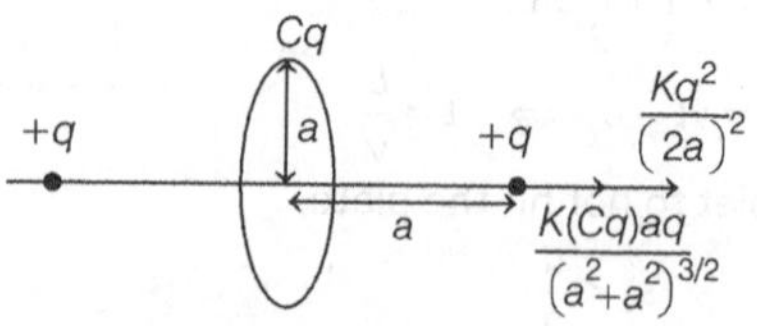

Net force on $+q = \dfrac{Kq^2}{4a^2} + \dfrac{KCq^2}{2\sqrt{2}a^2} = 0$

$$\Rightarrow \quad C = -\frac{2\sqrt{2}}{4} = -\frac{1}{\sqrt{2}}$$

46. If another identical hemispherical shell is kept upside down over it, net electric field at any point inside the spherical shell should be zero.

47.

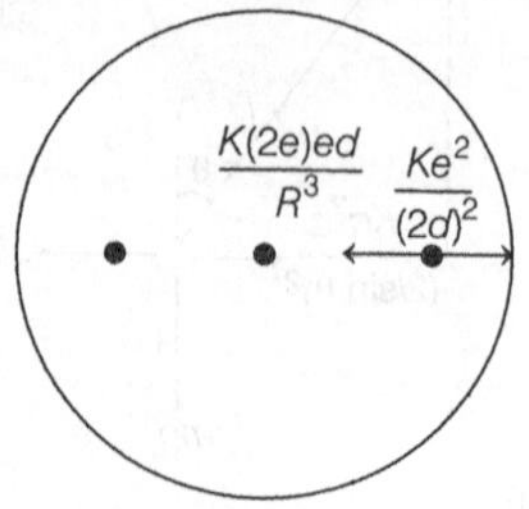

For equilibrium of electron,

$$\frac{K(2e)ed}{R^3} = \frac{Ke^2}{(2d)^2} \;\Rightarrow\; d = R/2$$

Separation between the electrons $= 2d = 2\left(\frac{R}{2}\right) = R$

48. $F = qE$

$$\Rightarrow \quad F = (-Q)\left(\frac{K(\lambda 2\pi a)\, x}{(a^2 + x^2)^{3/2}}\right)$$

$$\Rightarrow \quad F = -\frac{Qa\lambda}{2a^3\varepsilon_0} x \qquad (\because x << a)$$

$$\Rightarrow \quad F = -\left(\frac{Q\lambda}{2\varepsilon_0 a^2}\right) x$$

This is equation of SHM.

$$T = 2\pi\sqrt{\frac{m}{K}} = 2\pi\sqrt{\frac{m}{\frac{\lambda Q}{2\varepsilon_0 a^2}}} = 2\pi\sqrt{\frac{2m\varepsilon_0 a^2}{\lambda Q}}$$

49.

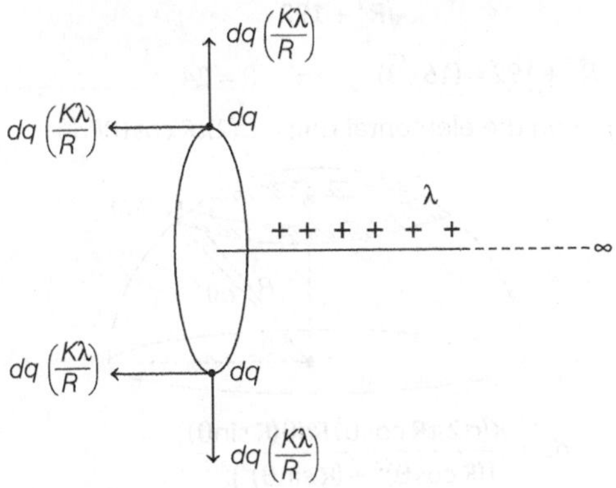

Net force in the plane of ring = 0

Net force perpendicular to the plane of the ring

$$= \int dq\left(\frac{K\lambda}{R}\right) = \frac{K\lambda}{R}\int dq = \frac{K\lambda q}{R} = \frac{\lambda q}{4\pi\varepsilon_0 R}$$

50. Lets divide the disc into rings. Take a ring of radius x and thickness dx.

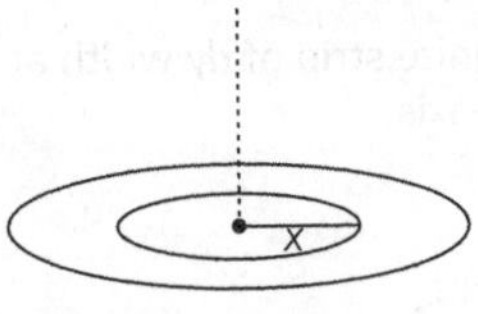

Charge on the ring $= dq = \sigma(2\pi x dx)$

$$= (cx)(2\pi x dx) = 2\pi c x^2 dx$$

Electric field due to this ring on the axis

$$= dE = \frac{1}{4\pi\varepsilon_0}\frac{dq(4)}{(4^2 + x^2)^{3/2}}$$

$$E = \int dE = \frac{1}{4\pi\varepsilon_0}\int_0^3 \frac{dq(4)}{(16 + x^2)^{3/2}}$$

$$= \frac{1}{4\pi\varepsilon_0}\int_0^3 \frac{(2\pi c x^2 dx)(4)}{(16 + x^2)^{3/2}} = \frac{c}{5\varepsilon_0}$$

So, $\quad \frac{c}{5\varepsilon_0} = \frac{1}{5\varepsilon_0}$

$\Rightarrow \quad c = 1$

Numerical Value Questions

1. Let the charge transferred to be x.

$$\frac{K(5\mu C)(5\mu C)}{r^2} = (5)\frac{K(5 - x)\mu C \times (5 + x)\mu C}{2r^2}$$

$$\Rightarrow \quad 25 - x^2 = 10$$

$$\Rightarrow \quad x = \sqrt{15}\ \mu C$$

2. $OA = \sqrt{AB^2 - OB^2}$

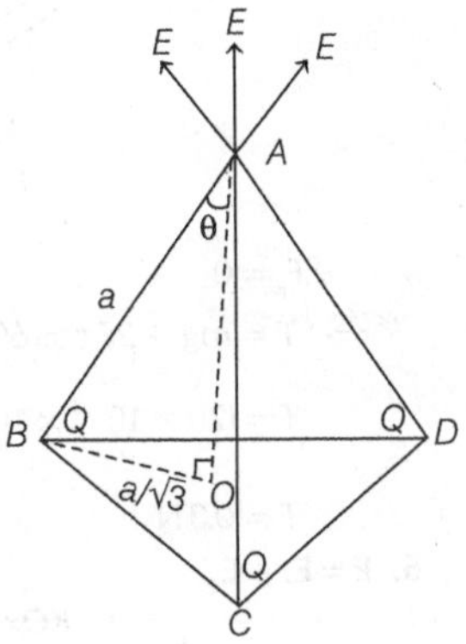

$$= \sqrt{a^2 - \frac{a^2}{3}} = \frac{\sqrt{2}a}{\sqrt{3}}$$

$$E = \frac{KQ}{a^2}$$

Net electric field at

$$A = (E\cos\theta) \times 3$$

$$= \frac{KQ}{a^2} \times \left(\frac{\sqrt{2}a/\sqrt{3}}{a}\right) \times 3$$

$$= \frac{\sqrt{6}Q}{4\pi\varepsilon_0 a^2}$$

So, $n = 6$

3. $dq = \lambda R d\theta = (\lambda_0 \sin 2\theta) R d\theta$

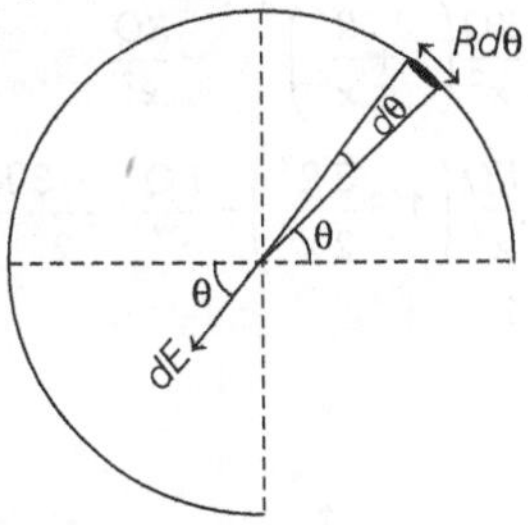

$$\mathbf{dE} = -dE\cos\theta\,\hat{i} - dE\sin\theta\,\hat{j}$$

$$\int d\mathbf{E} = -\int\frac{K(\lambda_0 \sin 2\theta)R d\theta \cos\theta}{R^2}\hat{i} - \int\frac{K\lambda_0 \sin 2\theta \sin\theta R d\theta}{R^2}\hat{j}$$

$$\Rightarrow \mathbf{E} = \frac{-K\lambda_0}{R}\left[2\int_0^{3\pi/2}\sin\theta\cos^2\theta\, d\theta\,\hat{i} + 2\int_0^{3\pi/2}\cos\theta\sin^2\theta\, d\theta\,\hat{j}\right]$$

$$\Rightarrow \mathbf{E} = \frac{-2K\lambda_0}{R}\left[\left[-\frac{\cos^3\theta}{3}\right]_0^{\frac{3\pi}{2}}\hat{i} + \left[\frac{\sin^3\theta}{3}\right]_0^{\frac{3\pi}{2}}\hat{j}\right]$$

$$\Rightarrow \quad \mathbf{E} = \frac{-2K\lambda_0}{R}\left[\frac{1}{3}\hat{i} + \frac{1}{3}\hat{j}\right]$$

$$\Rightarrow \quad |\mathbf{E}| = \frac{\sqrt{2}\,\lambda}{6\pi\,\varepsilon_0 R^2}$$

So, $\quad n = 6$

4. $\mathbf{E} = \mathbf{E}_1 + \mathbf{E}_2$

$$E = \frac{2KQ_1}{R^2}\left(1 - \frac{x}{\sqrt{R^2 + x^2}}\right) + \frac{KQ_2 x}{(R^2 + x^2)^{3/2}}$$

$$E = \frac{2 \times 9 \times 10^9 \times 1 \times 10^{-6}}{4^2}\left(1 - \frac{3}{5}\right) + \frac{9 \times 10^9 \times (-1 \times 10^{-6}) \times 3}{(5^2)^{3/2}}$$

$$E = 450 - 216 = 234$$

5.

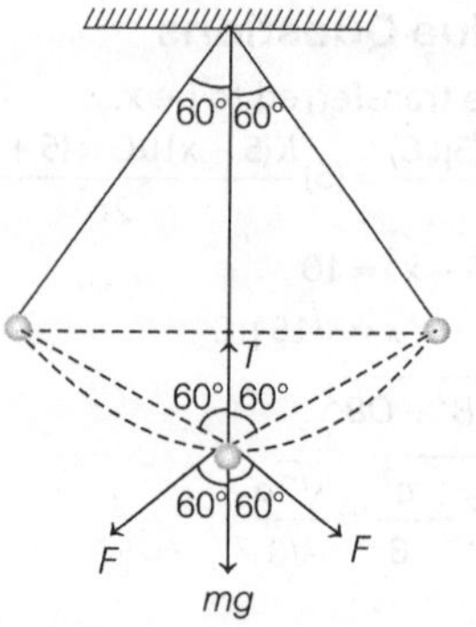

$\Sigma F_y = 0$

$\Rightarrow \quad T = mg + 2F\cos 60°$

$$T = (20\times10^{-3}\times10) + 2\left(\frac{9\times10^9\times(10\times10^{-6})^2}{(2\times3\times\sin 30°)^2}\right)\times\frac{1}{2}$$

$T = 0.3\,\text{N}$

6. $\mathbf{E} = \mathbf{E}_1 + \mathbf{E}_2$

$$E = \frac{KQx}{(R^2+x^2)^{3/2}} - \frac{KQ}{x^2} = \frac{KQx}{x^3\left(1+\frac{R^2}{x^2}\right)^{3/2}} - \frac{KQ}{x^2}$$

$$= \frac{KQ}{x^2}\left(1+\frac{R^2}{x^2}\right)^{-3/2} - \frac{KQ}{x^2}$$

$$= \frac{KQ}{x^2}\left(1-\frac{3}{2}\frac{R^2}{x^2}\right) - \frac{KQ}{x^2} = \frac{-3}{2}\frac{KQR^2}{x^4}$$

$$\Rightarrow \quad E \propto \frac{1}{x^4}$$

So, $n = 4$

7.

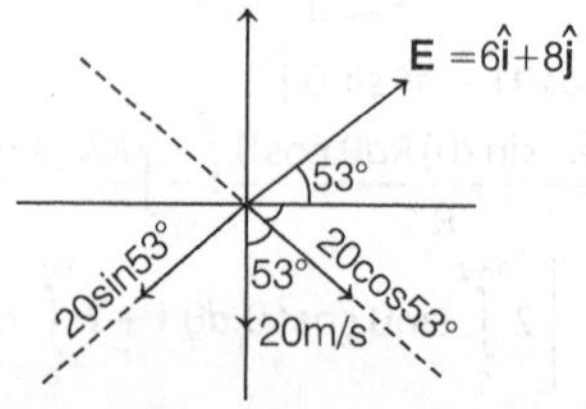

Component of velocity perpendicular to electric field remains constant. Velocity will be minimum when component of velocity along the electric field becomes zero. So, minimum speed = 20 cos 53° = 12 m/s

8.

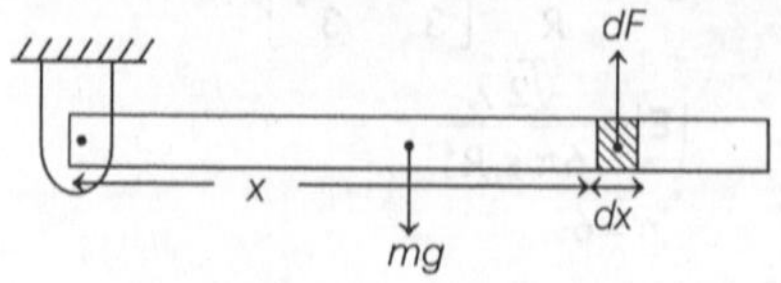

$dF = \lambda dx = \lambda_0 x dx$

$d\tau = dFx$

$$\int d\tau = \int_0^l (\lambda_0 x dx E)\,x$$

$$\tau = \frac{\lambda_0 l^3 E}{3}$$

For equilibrium of rod, $\Sigma\tau_{net} = 0$

$$\Rightarrow \quad mg\left(\frac{l}{2}\right) - \frac{\lambda_0 l^3 E}{3} = 0$$

$$\Rightarrow \quad E = \frac{3mg}{2\lambda_0 l^2}$$

So, $n = 3$

9. $E = \dfrac{\sigma}{2\varepsilon_0}\left(1 - \dfrac{x}{\sqrt{R^2+x^2}}\right)$

At $x = 0$; $E_0 = \dfrac{\sigma}{2\varepsilon_0}$

At $x = 8\sqrt{3}$; $\dfrac{E_0}{2} = E_0\left(1 - \dfrac{8\sqrt{3}}{\sqrt{(R^2+(8\sqrt{3})^2}}\right)$

$$\Rightarrow \quad \frac{1}{2} = 1 - \frac{8\sqrt{3}}{\sqrt{R^2+192}}$$

$\Rightarrow \quad R^2 + 192 = (16\sqrt{3})^2 \quad \Rightarrow \quad R = 24$

10. Charge on the elemental ring $= \sigma(2\pi R\cos\theta)Rd\theta$

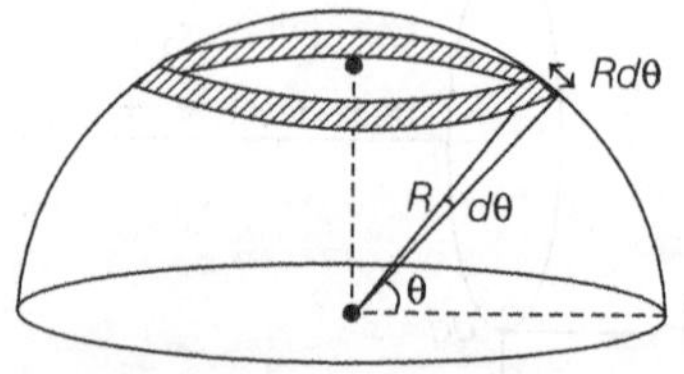

$$dE = \frac{K(\sigma 2\pi R\cos\theta)Rd\theta(R\sin\theta)}{((R\cos\theta)^2 + (R\sin\theta)^2)^{3/2}}$$

$$\int dE = \frac{\sigma}{2\varepsilon_0}\int_0^{\pi/2}\frac{\sin 2\theta}{2}d\theta = \frac{\sigma}{2\varepsilon_0}\left[\frac{-\cos 2\theta}{4}\right]_0^{\pi/2}$$

$$\Rightarrow \quad E = \frac{\sigma}{4\varepsilon_0}, \text{ so } n = 4$$

11. $\tan\theta = \dfrac{y}{a}$ and $dy = a\sec^2\theta d\theta$

Lets take an infinite strip of dy width at a distance y on either side of X-axis.

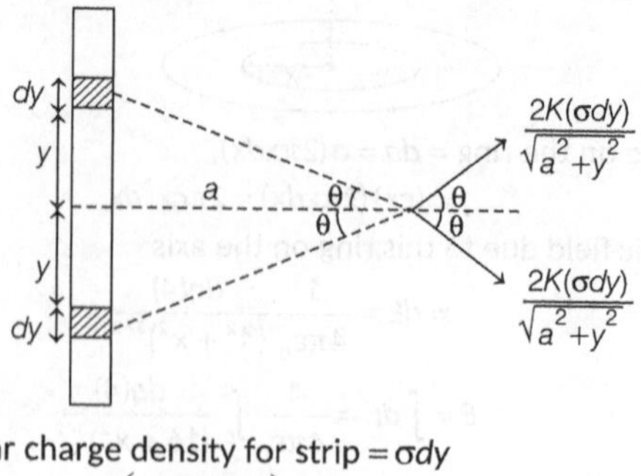

Linear charge density for strip $= \sigma dy$

$$E = \int 2\left(\frac{2K(\sigma dy)}{\sqrt{a^2+y^2}}\right)\cos\theta = \frac{\sigma}{\pi\varepsilon_0}\int_0^{\pi/4}\frac{a\sec^2\theta\, d\theta}{a\sec\theta}\cos\theta$$

$$= \frac{\sigma}{\pi\varepsilon_0}\int_0^{\pi/4}d\theta = \frac{\sigma}{\pi\varepsilon_0}\left(\frac{\pi}{4} - 0\right) = \frac{\sigma}{4\varepsilon_0}$$

12.

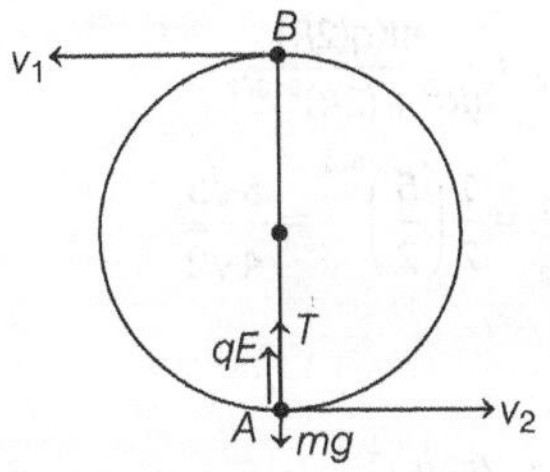

At the lowest position,

$$T + qE - mg = \frac{mv_2^2}{l}$$

$$15mg + 3mg - mg = \frac{mv_2^2}{l}$$

$$\Rightarrow \quad v_2 = \sqrt{17gl}$$

Applying work-energy theorem between A and B,

$$W_{mg} + W_T + W_{\text{electric}} = \Delta K - mg(2l) + 0 + qE(2l)$$

$$= \frac{1}{2}mv_1^2 - \frac{1}{2}m(\sqrt{17gl})^2$$

$$v_1 = \sqrt{25gl} = \sqrt{25 \times 10 \times 0.1} = 5$$

13. Electric field inside a solid sphere,

$$E = \frac{KQ}{R^3}r$$

$\Rightarrow$ Slope of E-r graph $= \tan 53° = \dfrac{KQ}{R^3}$

$$\Rightarrow \quad \frac{4}{3} = \frac{Q}{4\pi\varepsilon_0(3)^3}$$

$$\Rightarrow \quad Q = 144\,\pi\,\varepsilon_0$$

$$Q = 144\pi\varepsilon_0 = n\pi\varepsilon_0$$

$$\Rightarrow \quad n = 144$$

14. For equilibrium,

$$qE\cos\theta = T\sin 37° \quad \text{... (i)}$$

and $$qE\sin\theta = mg - T\cos 37° \quad \text{... (ii)}$$

Dividing Eq. (ii) by Eq. (i), we get

$$\tan\theta = \frac{mg - 2mg\cos 37°}{2mg\sin 37°} = \frac{-1}{2}$$

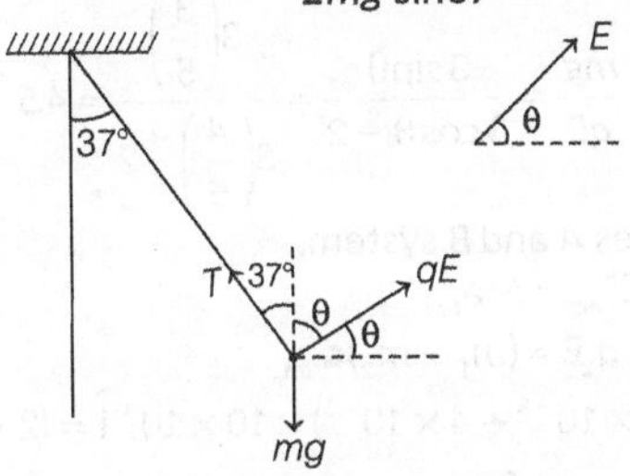

$$\Rightarrow \quad \cos\theta = \frac{2}{\sqrt{5}}$$

$$\Rightarrow \quad \sqrt{5}E\left(\frac{2}{\sqrt{5}}\right) = 2 \times 1 \times 10 \times \frac{3}{5}$$

$$\Rightarrow \quad E = 6\text{ N/C}$$

15.

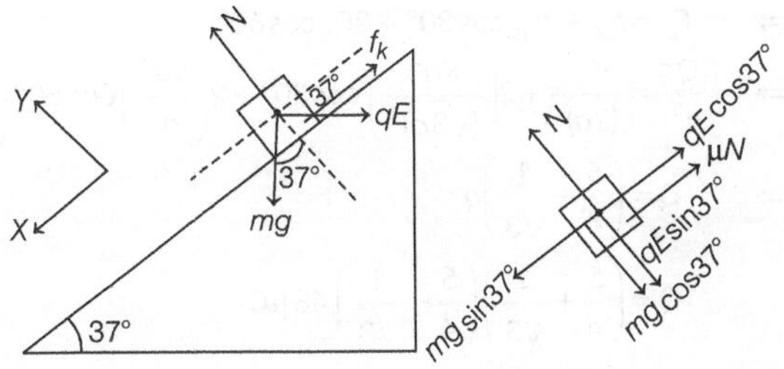

For block, $\Sigma F_y = 0$

$$\Rightarrow \quad N = mg\cos 37° + qE\sin 37°$$

$$\Sigma F_x = ma_x$$

$$mg\sin 37° - qE\cos 37° - \mu(mg\cos 37° + qE\sin 37°) = ma$$

$$\Rightarrow \quad 30 - 20 - 0.1(40 + 15) = 5a$$

$$\Rightarrow \quad a = 0.9\text{ m/s}^2$$

$$s_x = u_x t + \frac{1}{2}a_x t^2$$

$$\Rightarrow \quad \frac{6.75}{\sin 37°} = 0 + \frac{1}{2}(0.9)t^2$$

$$\Rightarrow \quad t = 5\text{ s}$$

Level 3

Single Option Correct Questions

1.

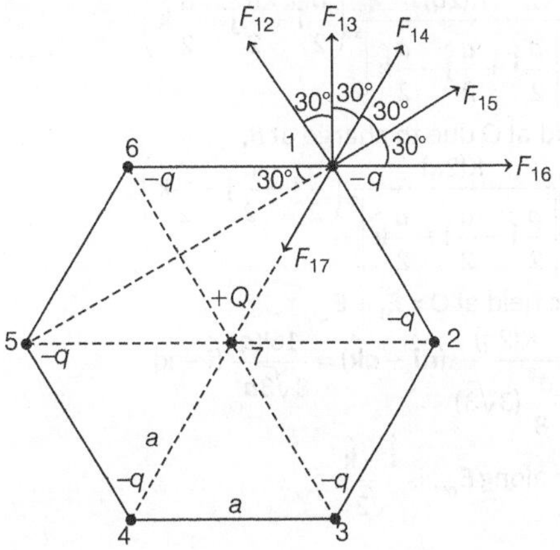

$$\text{Let } 48\left(\frac{5}{4} - \frac{1}{\sqrt{3}}\right) = q$$

$$F_{14} = \frac{Kq^2}{(2a)^2}$$

$$F_{15} = F_{13} = \frac{Kq^2}{(\sqrt{3}a)^2}$$

$$F_{16} = F_{12} = \frac{Kq^2}{a^2}$$

$$F_{17} = \frac{KQq}{a^2}$$

For equilibrium of particle 1,

$$F_{17} = F_{14} + F_{15}\cos 30° + F_{13}\cos 30° + F_{16}\cos 60° + F_{12}\cos 60°$$

$$\Rightarrow \quad F_{17} = F_{14} + 2F_{15}\cos 30° + 2F_{16}\cos 60°$$

$$\Rightarrow \quad \frac{KQq}{a^2} = \frac{Kq^2}{(2a)^2} + 2\left(\frac{Kq^2}{(\sqrt{3}a)^2}\right)\cos 30° + 2\left(\frac{Kq^2}{a^2}\right)\cos 60°$$

$$\Rightarrow \quad Q = \left(\frac{5}{4} + \frac{1}{\sqrt{3}}\right)q$$

$$Q = \left(\frac{5}{4} + \frac{1}{\sqrt{3}}\right)\left(\frac{5}{4} - \frac{1}{\sqrt{3}}\right) 48\,\mu C$$

$$Q = \left(\frac{25}{16} - \frac{1}{3}\right) 48\mu C = 59\mu C$$

2.

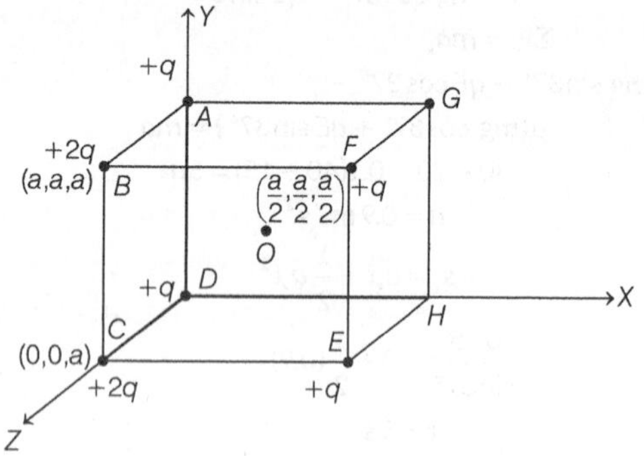

Electric field due to charges at D and F, A and E, will cancel out.

Electric field at O due to charge at C,

$$\mathbf{E}_1 = \frac{K(2q)}{\left|\frac{a}{2}\hat{\mathbf{i}} + \frac{a}{2}\hat{\mathbf{j}} - \frac{a}{2}\hat{\mathbf{k}}\right|^3}\left(\frac{a}{2}\hat{\mathbf{i}} + \frac{a}{2}\hat{\mathbf{j}} - \frac{a}{2}\hat{\mathbf{k}}\right)$$

Electric field at O due to charge at B,

$$\mathbf{E}_2 = \frac{K(2q)}{\left|\frac{a}{2}\hat{\mathbf{i}} - \frac{a}{2}\hat{\mathbf{j}} - \frac{a}{2}\hat{\mathbf{k}}\right|^3}\left(\frac{a}{2}\hat{\mathbf{i}} - \frac{a}{2}\hat{\mathbf{j}} - \frac{a}{2}\hat{\mathbf{k}}\right)$$

Net electric field at $O = \mathbf{E}_1 + \mathbf{E}_2$

$$\mathbf{E}_{net} = \frac{K(2q)}{\frac{a^3}{8}(3\sqrt{3})}(a\hat{\mathbf{i}} - a\hat{\mathbf{k}}) = \frac{16Kq}{3\sqrt{3}a^2}(\hat{\mathbf{i}} - \hat{\mathbf{k}})$$

Unit vector along $\mathbf{E}_{net}$ is $\dfrac{\hat{\mathbf{i}} - \hat{\mathbf{k}}}{\sqrt{2}}$.

3.

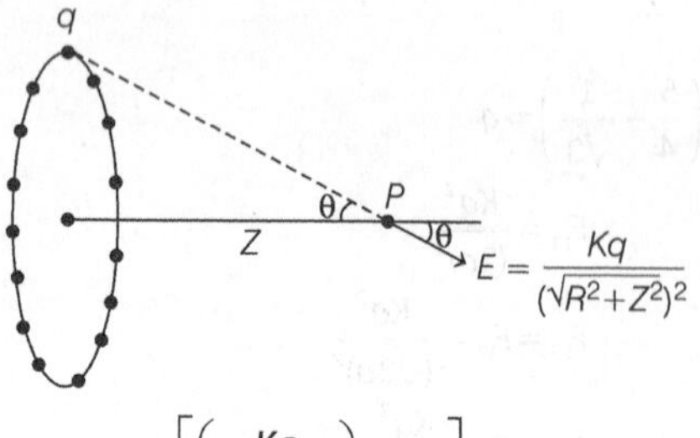

$$E_{net} = \left[\left(\frac{Kq}{R^2 + Z^2}\right)\cos\theta\right] n$$

$$E_{net} = \frac{nKq(Z)}{(R^2 + Z^2)^{3/2}}$$

$$E_1 = \frac{nKqR}{(R^2 + R^2)^{3/2}}$$

$$E_2 = \frac{nKq(2R)}{(R^2 + (2R)^2)^{3/2}}$$

$$\frac{E_1}{E_2} = \frac{1}{2}\left(\frac{5}{2}\right)^{3/2} = \frac{5\sqrt{5}}{4\sqrt{2}}$$

4. $h = \dfrac{u^2}{2g_{eff}}$

$$\Rightarrow \quad h = \frac{(5\sqrt{5})^2}{2g} \qquad \text{... (i)}$$

$$\Rightarrow \quad h = \frac{(13)^2}{2\left(g + \frac{qE}{m}\right)} \qquad \text{... (ii)}$$

$$\Rightarrow \quad h = \frac{u^2}{2\left(g - \frac{qE}{m}\right)} \qquad \text{... (iii)}$$

From Eqs. (i), (ii) and (iii), we get

$$u = 9 \text{ m/s}$$

5. (d)

6.

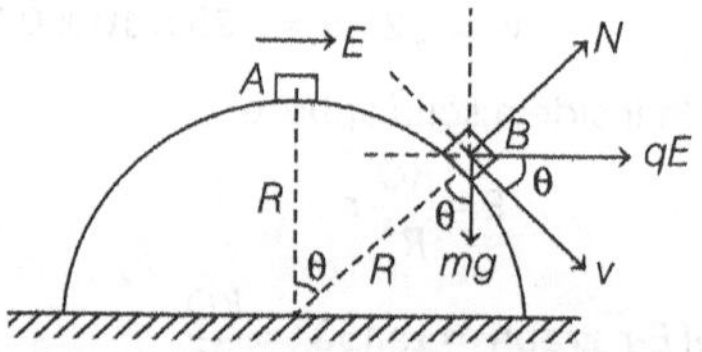

Applying work-energy theorem from A to B,

$$W_{mg} + W_N + W_{electric} = \Delta K$$

$$\Rightarrow \quad +mgR(1 - \cos\theta) + 0 + qE(R\sin\theta) = \frac{1}{2}mv^2 - 0 \qquad \text{... (i)}$$

At B, equation for circular motion is

$$mg\cos\theta - N - qE\sin\theta = \frac{mv^2}{R}$$

For losing contact, $N = 0$

$$\Rightarrow \quad mg\cos\theta - qE\sin\theta = \frac{mv^2}{R} \qquad \text{... (ii)}$$

From Eqs. (i) and (ii), we get

$$2mg(1 - \cos\theta) + 2qE\sin\theta = mg\cos\theta - qE\sin\theta$$

$$\Rightarrow \quad mg(3\cos\theta - 2) = 3qE\sin\theta$$

$$\Rightarrow \quad \frac{mg}{qE} = \frac{3\sin\theta}{3\cos\theta - 2} = \frac{3\left(\frac{3}{5}\right)}{3\left(\frac{4}{5}\right) - 2} = 4.5$$

7. For particles A and B system,

$$\Sigma\mathbf{F}_{ext} = M\mathbf{a}_{CM}$$

$$\Rightarrow \quad q_1\mathbf{E} + q_2\mathbf{E} = (m_1 + m_2)\mathbf{a}_{CM}$$

$$\Rightarrow \quad (-2\times 10^{-3} + 4\times 10^{-3})\times 10\times 10^3\,\hat{\mathbf{i}} = (2 + 1)\,\mathbf{a}_{CM}$$

$$\Rightarrow \quad \mathbf{a}_{CM} = \frac{20}{3}\hat{\mathbf{i}}$$

$$\mathbf{s}_{CM} = \mathbf{u}_{CM}t + \frac{1}{2}\mathbf{a}_{CM}t^2$$

$$\Rightarrow \quad \mathbf{s}_{CM} = 0 + \frac{1}{2}\left(\frac{20}{3}\right)\hat{\mathbf{i}}\,(3)^2$$

$$\Rightarrow \quad \mathbf{s}_{CM} = 30\hat{i}$$

$$\mathbf{s}_{CM} = \frac{m_1\mathbf{s}_1 + m_2\mathbf{s}_2}{m_1 + m_2}$$

$$\Rightarrow \quad 30\hat{i} = \frac{2(\mathbf{r}_1 - (0\hat{i} + 0\hat{j}) + 1((50-100)\,\hat{i} + (70-100)\hat{j})}{3}$$

$$\Rightarrow \quad \mathbf{r}_1 = 70\hat{i} + 15\hat{j}$$

So, *A* would be at (70, 15).

8.

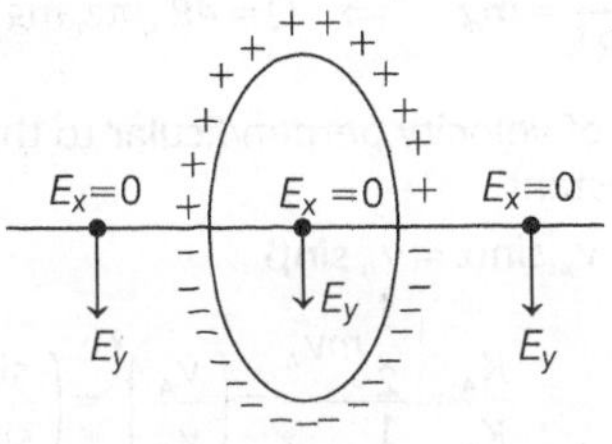

$$E_x = \frac{KQx}{(R^2 + x^2)^{3/2}} \Rightarrow E_x = 0 \qquad (\because Q = 0)$$

So, component of electric field along the axis is zero at all points on the axis.

9.

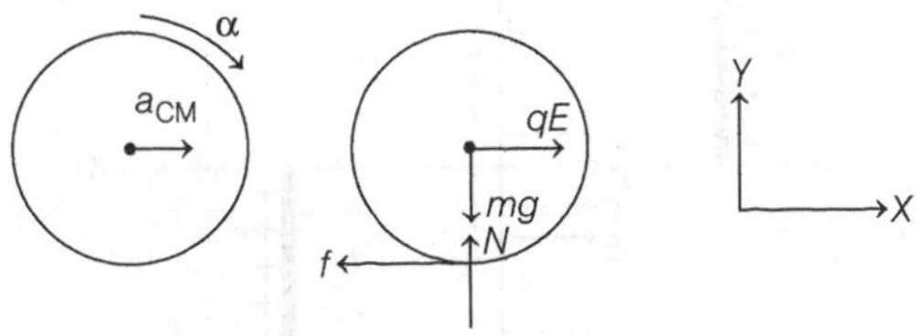

$$\Sigma F_x = ma_{CM}$$

$$\Rightarrow \quad qE - f = ma_{CM} \qquad \text{... (i)}$$

$$\Sigma\tau = I\alpha$$

$$\Rightarrow \quad fR = \left(\frac{mR^2}{2}\right)\alpha \qquad \text{... (ii)}$$

and for pure rolling, $a_{CM} = R\alpha$ ... (iii)

Solving Eqs. (i), (ii) and (iii), we get

$$a_{CM} = \frac{2qE}{3m} \text{ and } f = \frac{qE}{3}$$

$$f \le f_L$$

$$\frac{qE}{3} \le \mu N \quad \Rightarrow \quad E \le \frac{3\mu mg}{q}$$

$$\Rightarrow \quad E_{max} = \frac{3 \times 0.2 \times 2 \times 10}{1} = 12 \text{ N/C}$$

10.

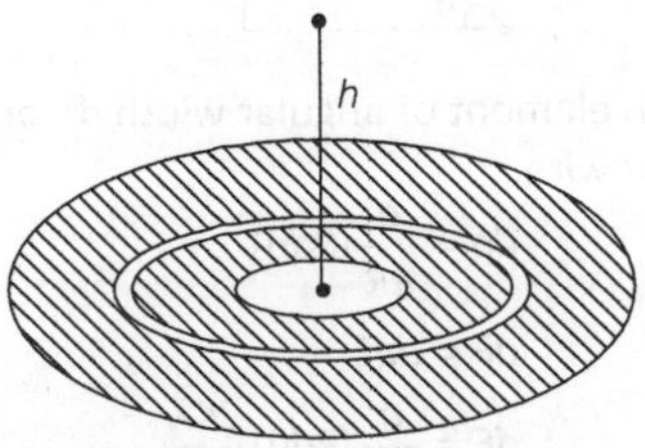

Lets take an elemental ring of radius *r* and width *dr*.

$$dq = \sigma(2\pi r dr)$$

$$\int dE = \int_a^{2a} \frac{K(\sigma 2\pi r\, dr)h}{(r^2 + h^2)^{3/2}}$$

$$E = \frac{\sigma h}{2\varepsilon_0} \int_a^{2a} \frac{r\,dr}{(r^2 + h^2)^{3/2}}$$

Substitute $r^2 + h^2 = t^2$ and $rdr = tdt$

$$E = \frac{\sigma h}{2\varepsilon_0} \int_{\sqrt{a^2+h^2}}^{\sqrt{4a^2+h^2}} \frac{tdt}{t^3}$$

$$\Rightarrow \quad E = \frac{\sigma h}{2\varepsilon_0}\left[\frac{1}{\sqrt{a^2 + h^2}} - \frac{1}{\sqrt{4a^2 + h}}\right]$$

$$= \frac{\sigma h}{2\varepsilon_0}\left(\frac{1}{a} - \frac{1}{2a}\right) \qquad (\because h << a)$$

$$= \frac{\sigma h}{4a\varepsilon_0}$$

11.

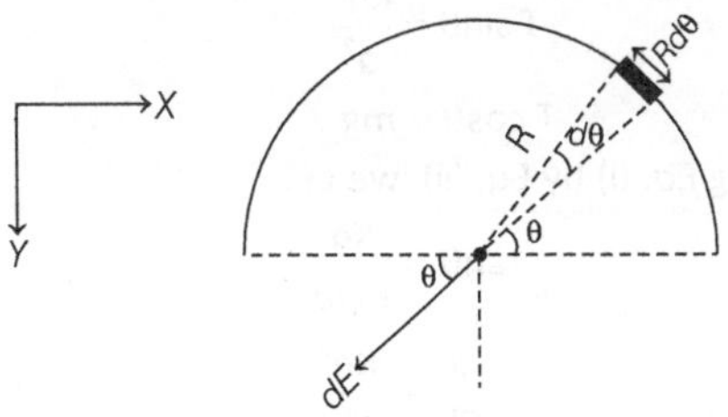

Lets take an infinite strip of width $Rd\theta$.

Linear charge density on the strip $= \sigma(Rd\theta)$

$$E_x = 0$$

$$dE_y = dE \sin\theta$$

$$\int dE_y = \int_0^{\pi} \frac{2K(\sigma R d\theta)}{R} \sin\theta \quad \Rightarrow \quad E_y = \frac{\sigma}{\pi\varepsilon_0}$$

12.

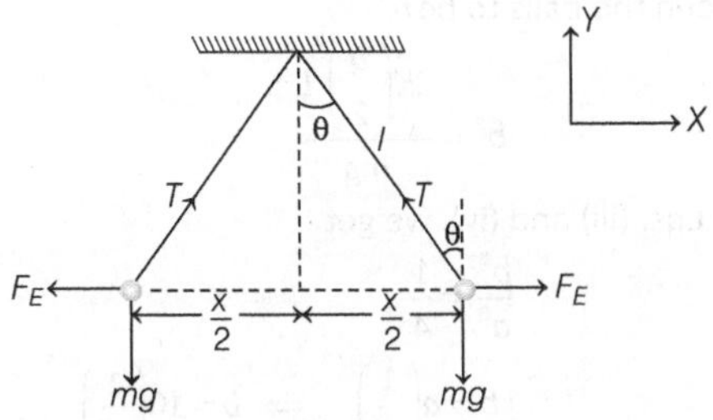

For equilibrium of the charges,

$$\Sigma F_y = 0$$

$$\Rightarrow \quad T\cos\theta = mg \qquad \text{... (i)}$$

$$\Sigma F_x = 0$$

$$\Rightarrow \quad T\sin\theta = F_E = \frac{Kq^2}{x^2} \qquad \text{... (ii)}$$

Dividing Eq. (ii) by Eq. (i), we get

$$\tan\theta = \frac{Kq^2/x^2}{mg}$$

$$\Rightarrow \quad \frac{x/2}{l} = \frac{Kq^2}{mgx^2} \Rightarrow q = \sqrt{\frac{2\pi\varepsilon_0 mg}{l}}\, x^{3/2}$$

Now, $\dfrac{dq}{dt} = \sqrt{\dfrac{2\pi\varepsilon_0 mg}{l}}\dfrac{3}{2}\sqrt{x}\dfrac{dx}{dt}$

$$= \sqrt{\frac{2\pi\varepsilon_0 mg}{l}}\frac{3}{2}\sqrt{x}\left(\frac{a}{\sqrt{x}}\right) = \frac{3a}{2}\sqrt{\frac{2\pi\varepsilon_0 mg}{l}}$$

13.

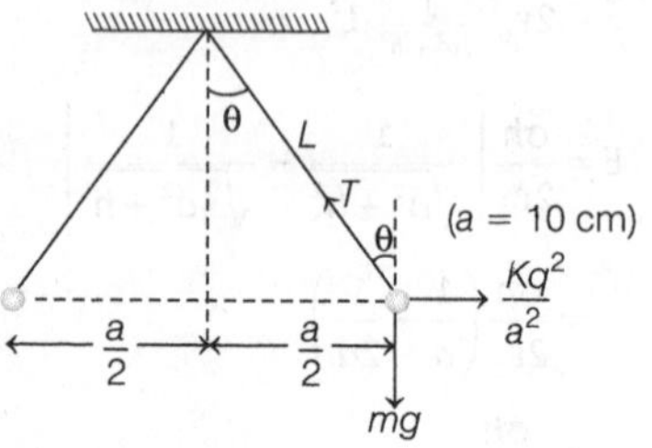

For equilibrium of balls,

$$T\sin\theta = \frac{Kq^2}{a^2} \quad \text{... (i)}$$

and $$T\cos\theta = mg \quad \text{... (ii)}$$

Dividing Eq. (i) by Eq. (ii), we get

$$\tan\theta = \frac{Kq^2}{mga^2}$$

$$\Rightarrow \quad \frac{a}{2L} = \frac{Kq^2}{mga^3}$$

$$\Rightarrow \quad a^3 = \frac{2Kq^2L}{mg} \quad \text{... (iii)}$$

When one of the balls is discharged, the balls come closer and touch each other. The charge on each ball after touching each other is $\frac{q}{2}$.

When equilibrium is restored, lets taken separation between the balls to be b.

$$b^3 = \frac{2K\left(\frac{q}{2}\right)^2 L}{mg} \quad \text{... (iv)}$$

From Eqs. (iii) and (iv), we get

$$\frac{b^3}{a^3} = \frac{1}{4}$$

$$\Rightarrow \quad b = a\left(\frac{1}{4}\right)^{1/3} \Rightarrow b = 10\left(\frac{1}{4}\right)^{1/3}$$

14.

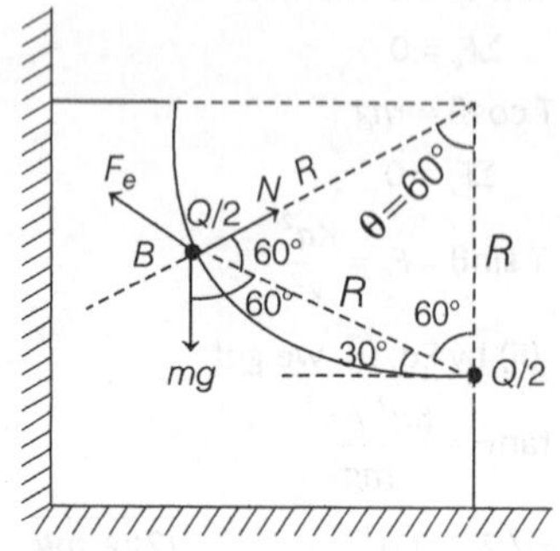

For equilibrium of ball B,

$$N\sin 60° = mg\sin 60° \quad \text{... (i)}$$

and $$F_e = N\cos 60° + mg\cos 60° \quad \text{... (ii)}$$

From Eqs. (i) and (ii), we get

$$F_e = mg$$

$$F_e = \frac{K\left(\frac{Q}{2}\right)\left(\frac{Q}{2}\right)}{R^2} = mg$$

$$\Rightarrow \quad \frac{Q^2}{16\pi\varepsilon_0 R^2} = mg \quad \Rightarrow \quad Q = 4R\sqrt{\pi\varepsilon_0 mg}$$

15. Component of velocity perpendicular to the electric field remains constant.

$$v_A\sin\alpha = v_B\sin\beta$$

$$\frac{K_A}{K_B} = \frac{\frac{1}{2}mv_A^2}{\frac{1}{2}mv_B^2} = \left(\frac{v_A}{v_B}\right)^2 = \left(\frac{\sin\beta}{\sin\alpha}\right)^2$$

16.

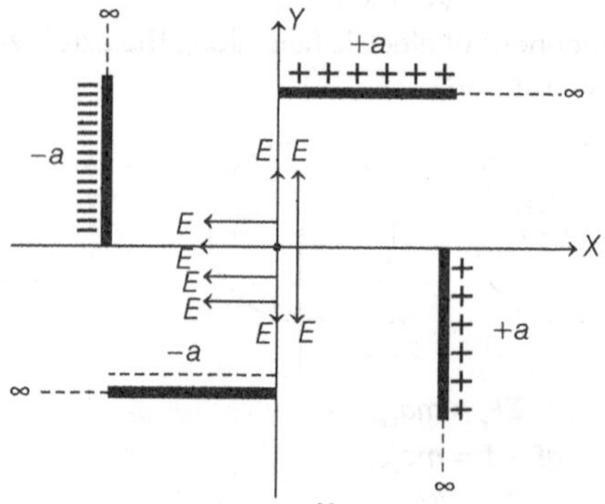

$$E = \frac{Ka}{a} = K$$

At origin, net electric field $= -4E\hat{\mathbf{i}} = -4K\hat{\mathbf{i}}$

$$\mathbf{F} = q\mathbf{E}$$

$$\mathbf{F} = (-e)(-4K\hat{\mathbf{i}}) = 4Ke\hat{\mathbf{i}}$$

So, unit vector along force on electron just after release is $\hat{\mathbf{i}}$.

17. The velocity of electron is $\cos 0° i + \sin 0° i$.

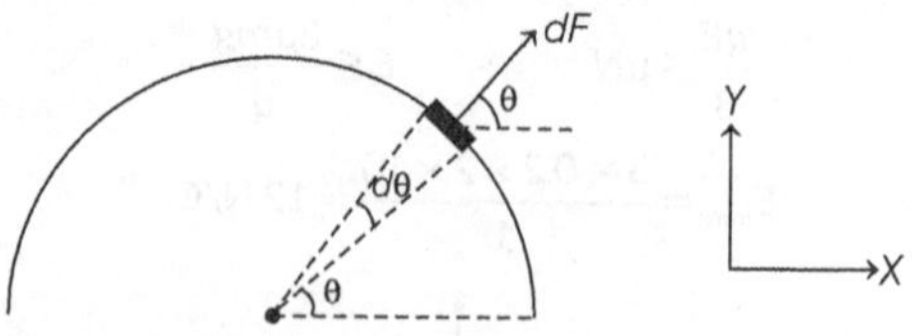

Lets take an element of angular width $d\theta$ on the semicircular wire.

$$dq = \frac{q}{\pi R}(Rd\theta)$$

$$dF = dqE$$

$$\Rightarrow \quad dF = \frac{q}{\pi R}(Rd\theta)\frac{2K\lambda}{R}$$

$$dF_x = dF\cos\theta$$

$$\Rightarrow \quad \int dF_x = 0 \quad \Rightarrow \quad F_x = 0$$

$$dF_y = dF\sin\theta$$

$$\Rightarrow \qquad \int dF_y = \int_0^{\pi} \frac{q}{\pi}\, d\theta\, \frac{2K\lambda}{R} \sin\theta$$

$$\Rightarrow \qquad F_y = \frac{\lambda q}{2\pi^2 \varepsilon_0 R} \int_0^{\pi} \sin d\theta = \frac{\lambda q}{\pi^2 \varepsilon_0 R}$$

18.

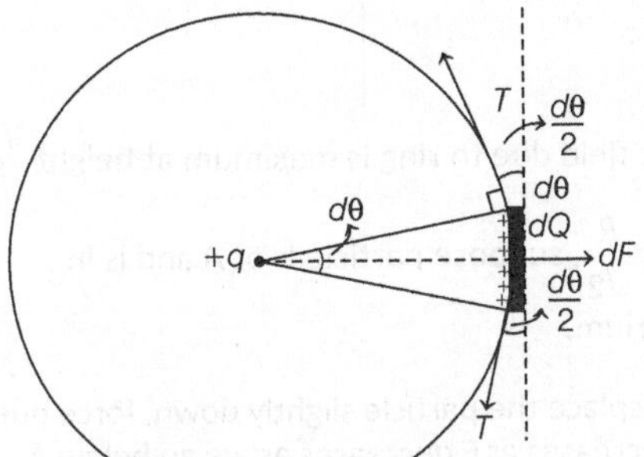

Increment in tension lets take T.

For equilibrium, $2T \sin\left(\frac{d\theta}{2}\right) = dF$

$$2T\frac{d\theta}{2} = \frac{K(dQ)q}{R^2}$$

$$\Rightarrow \qquad Td\theta = \frac{1}{4\pi\varepsilon_0}\frac{\left(\frac{Q}{2\pi R} R dQ\right)q}{R^2} \quad \Rightarrow T = \frac{Qq}{8\pi^2\varepsilon_0 R^2}$$

19. $E_A = \frac{KQ}{(3R)^2}$, where Q is the total charge.

$$Q = \rho\frac{4}{3}\pi R^3 + (-2\rho)\frac{4}{3}\pi((2R)^3 - R^3) + 3\rho \times \frac{4}{3}\pi\,((3R)^3 - (2R)^3)$$

$$Q = \rho\left(\frac{4}{3}\pi R^3\right)(1 - 14 + 57) = \frac{176}{3}\rho\pi R^3$$

$$E_A = \frac{1}{4\pi\varepsilon_0} \times \frac{1}{9R^2} \times \left(\frac{176}{3}\rho\pi R^3\right) = \frac{44\rho R}{27\varepsilon_0}$$

20.

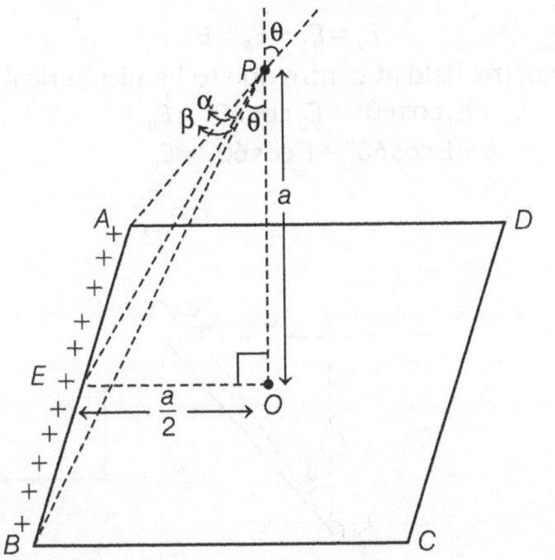

E = Electric field at P due to one side of square

$$PE^2 = OP^2 + OE^2 \qquad \Rightarrow \qquad PE = \frac{\sqrt{5}a}{2}$$

$$PB^2 = PE^2 + BE^2 \quad \Rightarrow PB = \sqrt{\left(\frac{\sqrt{5}a}{2}\right)^2 + \left(\frac{a}{2}\right)^2} = \sqrt{\frac{3}{2}}\,a$$

$$E = \frac{K\lambda}{r}(\sin\alpha + \sin\beta) = \frac{K\lambda}{\left(\frac{\sqrt{5}a}{2}\right)}\left(\frac{a/2}{\sqrt{\frac{3}{2}}a} + \frac{a/2}{\sqrt{\frac{3}{2}}a}\right) = \frac{K\lambda(2\sqrt{2})}{\sqrt{15}a}$$

$$\text{Net electric field at } P = 4E\cos\theta = 4\left(\frac{K\lambda 2\sqrt{2}}{\sqrt{15}a}\right)\left(\frac{a}{\sqrt{5}a/2}\right)$$

$$\Rightarrow \qquad E_{net} = \frac{16\sqrt{2}}{5\sqrt{3}}\frac{K\lambda}{a}$$

For equilibrium of particle,

$$mg = qE$$

$$\Rightarrow \qquad mg = q\left(\frac{16\sqrt{2}}{5\sqrt{3}}\frac{1}{4\pi\varepsilon_0}\frac{\lambda}{a}\right) \quad \Rightarrow m = \frac{8q\lambda}{5\sqrt{6}\,\pi\varepsilon_0 g a}$$

21. Lets put another identical hemisphere on hemisphere 1.

Due to complete sphere, electric field at A

$$= \frac{KQ}{(2R)^2} = \frac{K\left(\rho\frac{4}{3}\pi R^3\right)}{4R^2} = \frac{\rho R}{12\varepsilon_0}$$

$$E_A = E_1 + E_2$$

where, E_1 = electric field at A due to hemisphere 1,

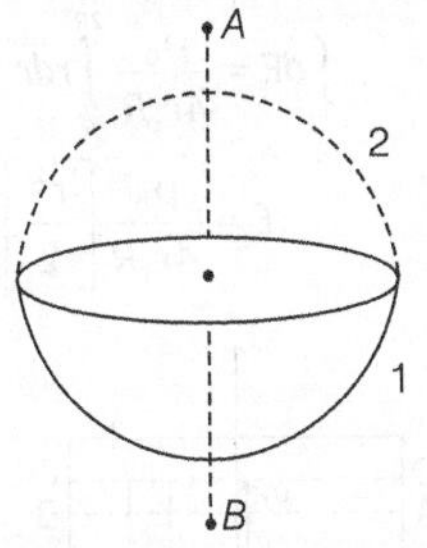

E_2 = electric field at A due to hemisphere 2

$$\frac{\rho R}{12\varepsilon_0} = E + E_2 \quad \Rightarrow \quad E_2 = \frac{\rho R}{12\varepsilon_0} - E$$

Electric field at B due to hemisphere 1 $= E_2$

$$= \frac{\rho R}{12\varepsilon_0} - E$$

22. Electric field inside cavity is uniform.

$$E = \frac{\rho a}{3\varepsilon_0}$$

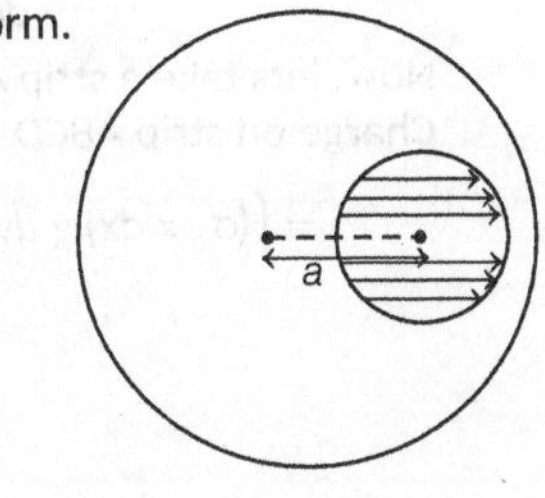

For electron, $s = ut + \frac{1}{2}at^2$

$$\Rightarrow \qquad 2r\cos 45° = 0 + \frac{1}{2}\left(\frac{eE}{m}\right)t^2$$

$$\Rightarrow \qquad t = \sqrt{\frac{6\sqrt{2}r\varepsilon_0 m}{e\rho a}}$$

23.

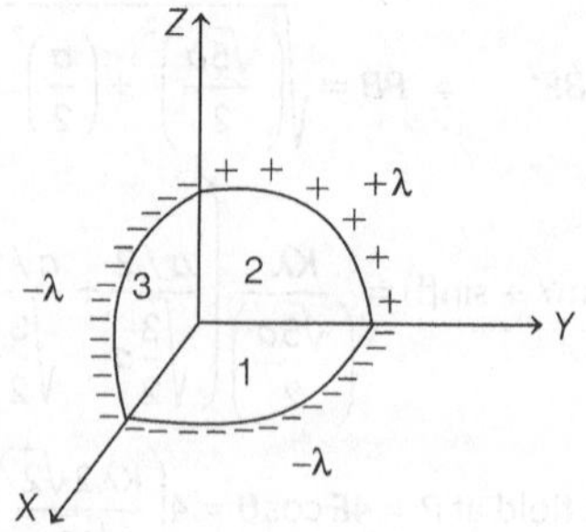

$$\mathbf{E} = \mathbf{E}_1 + \mathbf{E}_2 + \mathbf{E}_3$$

$$= \left(\frac{K\lambda}{R}\hat{\mathbf{i}} + \frac{K\lambda}{R}\hat{\mathbf{j}}\right) + \left(-\frac{K\lambda}{R}\hat{\mathbf{j}} - \frac{K\lambda}{R}\hat{\mathbf{k}}\right) + \left(\frac{K\lambda}{R}\hat{\mathbf{i}} + \frac{K\lambda}{R}\hat{\mathbf{k}}\right)$$

$$= \frac{2K\lambda}{R}\hat{\mathbf{i}} = \frac{\lambda}{2\pi\varepsilon_0 R}\hat{\mathbf{i}}$$

24. Electric field due to a uniformly charged hemispherical shell at its centre $= \frac{\sigma}{4\varepsilon_0}$.

Lets take an elemental hemispherical shell of radius r and thickness dr.

$$dq = \rho(2\pi r^2)\,dr$$

Surface charge density, $\sigma = \frac{dq}{2\pi r^2} = \rho dr$

$$dE = \frac{\rho dr}{4\varepsilon_0} = \frac{(\rho_0 r / R)dr}{4\varepsilon_0}$$

$$\Rightarrow \quad \int dE = \frac{\rho_0}{4\varepsilon_0 R}\int_R^{2R} r\,dr$$

$$\Rightarrow \quad E = \frac{\rho_0}{4\varepsilon_0 R}\left[\frac{r^2}{2}\right]_R^{2R} = \frac{3\rho_0 R}{8\varepsilon_0}$$

25.

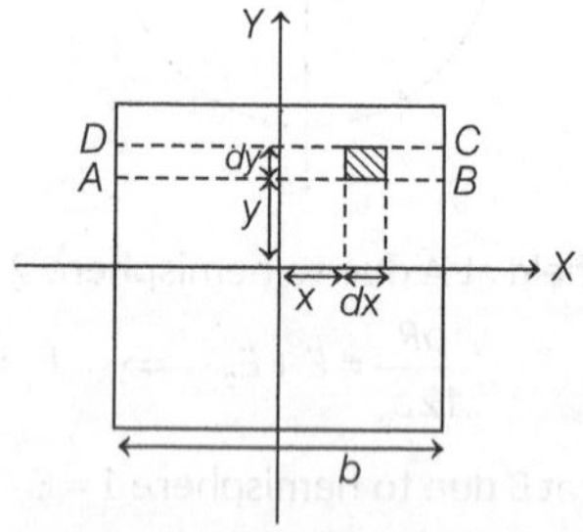

Lets take a rectangular element of length dx and breadth dy.

Charge on the element $= \sigma(dx\,dy)$

$$dq = \sigma_0 xy\,dx\,dy$$

Now, lets take a strip $ABCD$ at a height y and of width dy.

Charge on strip $ABCD$

$$= \int(\sigma_0 x\,dx)\,y\,dy = y\,dy\int_{-\frac{b}{2}}^{+b/2}\sigma_0 x\,dx \qquad (\because y \text{ is constant})$$

$$= y dy \sigma_0\left[\frac{x^2}{2}\right]_{-\frac{b}{2}}^{+b/2} = 0$$

This way, charge on all strips parallel to X-axis is zero. Hence, total charge on the plate is zero.

26.

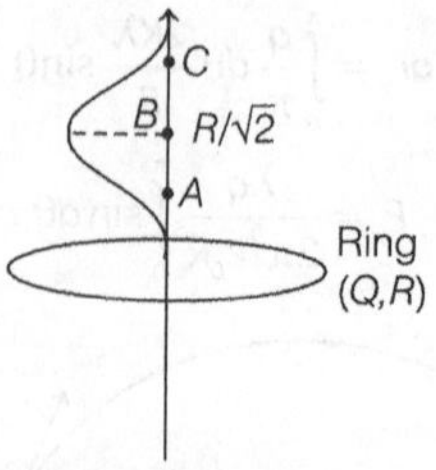

Electric field due to ring is maximum at height $\frac{R}{\sqrt{2}}$.

For $H < \frac{R}{\sqrt{2}}$, suppose particle is at A and is in equilibrium.

If we displace the particle slightly down, force due to electric field decreases as E decreases as we go below A.

So, net force on the particle is directed down and particle will not come back to its equilibrium position. So, equilibrium is unstable at A.

For $H > \frac{R}{\sqrt{2}}$, suppose the particle is at point C.

If we displace the particle down, electric field increases. So, particle will go back to its equilibrium position. Hence, equilibrium at C is stable.

For $H = \frac{R}{\sqrt{2}}$, equilibrium is unstable.

27. Lets take electric field due to the remaining portion as E.

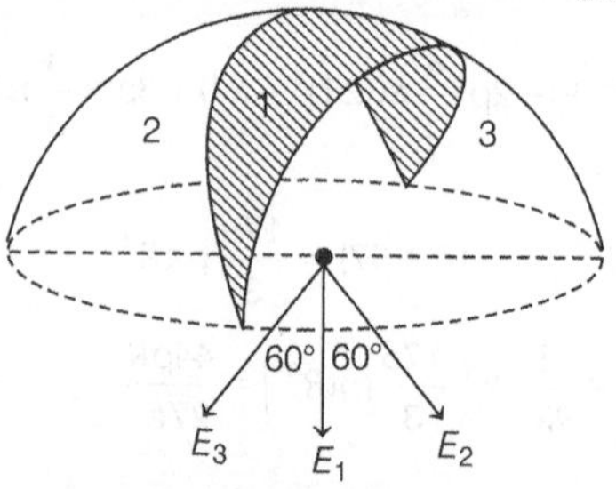

$$E_1 = E_2 = E_3 = E$$

Net electric field at centre due to hemispherical shell $= E_0$

$$\Rightarrow \quad E_1 + E_2\cos 60^\circ + E_3\cos 60^\circ = E_0$$

$$\Rightarrow \quad E + E\cos 60^\circ + E\cos 60^\circ = E_0$$

$$\Rightarrow \quad E = \frac{E_0}{2}$$

28.

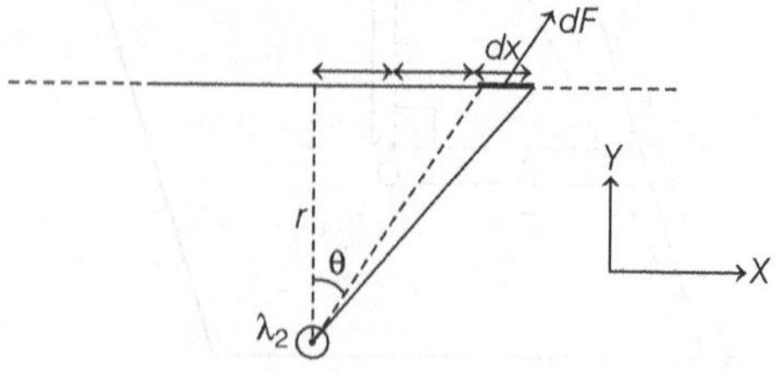

$$dF = \left(\frac{2K\lambda_2}{\sqrt{x^2 + r^2}}\right)(\lambda_1 dx)$$

$$dF_y = dF\cos\theta$$

$$\Rightarrow \qquad \int dF_y = \int \frac{2K\lambda_2\lambda_1}{\sqrt{x^2+r^2}}\,dx\cos\theta$$

Substitute $x = r\tan\theta$ and $dx = r\sec^2\theta\, d\theta$

$$F_y = \int_{-\pi/2}^{+\pi/2} \frac{2K\lambda_1\lambda_2 r\sec^2\theta\, d\theta\cos\theta}{r\sec\theta}$$

$$\Rightarrow \qquad F_y = 2K\lambda_1\lambda_2[\theta]_{-\pi/2}^{+\pi/2}$$

$$F_y = \frac{\lambda_1\lambda_2}{2\varepsilon_0} \text{ and } F_x = 0$$

29.

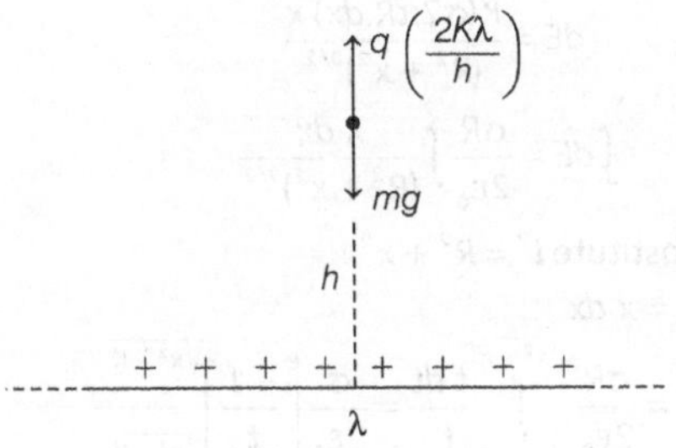

For equilibrium, $q\left(\frac{2K\lambda}{h}\right) = mg$

Lets displace the particle from its equilibrium position by distance y in downward direction.

$$F = mg - q\left(\frac{2K\lambda}{h-y}\right) \Rightarrow F = mg - \frac{2K\lambda q}{h\left(1-\frac{y}{h}\right)}$$

$$\Rightarrow \qquad F = mg - \frac{2K\lambda q}{h}\left(1-\frac{y}{h}\right)^{-1}$$

$$\Rightarrow \qquad F = mg - \frac{2K\lambda q}{h}\left(1+\frac{y}{h}\right) \qquad [\because y << h]$$

$$\Rightarrow \qquad F = -\left(\frac{2K\lambda q}{h^2}\right)y$$

This is equation of SHM.

Time period, $T = 2\pi\sqrt{\frac{m}{\left(\frac{2K\lambda q}{h^2}\right)}} = 2\pi\sqrt{\frac{mh^2}{2K\lambda q}}$

30.

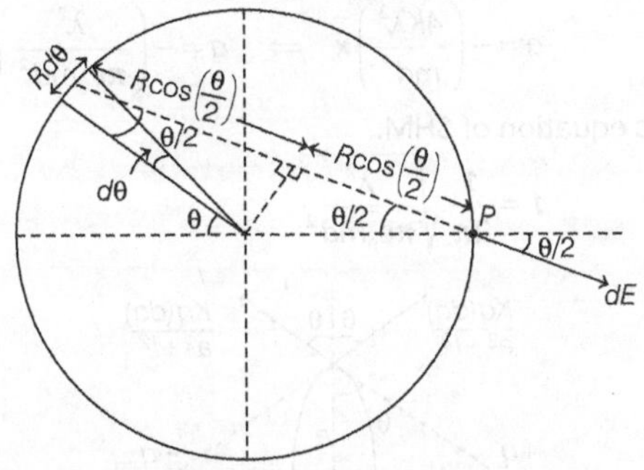

$$dE = \frac{K(\lambda R d\theta)}{\left(2R\cos\left(\frac{\theta}{2}\right)\right)^2}$$

$$dE_x = \int \frac{K\lambda R d\theta}{4R^2\cos^2\left(\frac{\theta}{2}\right)}\cos\left(\frac{\theta}{2}\right) = \frac{K\lambda}{4R}\int_{-\pi/2}^{+\pi/2}\sec\left(\frac{\theta}{2}\right)d\theta$$

$$= \frac{K\lambda}{4R}\times 2\left[\ln\left(\sec\left(\frac{\theta}{2}\right)+\tan\left(\frac{\theta}{2}\right)\right)\right]_{-\pi/2}^{+\pi/2}$$

$$= \frac{K\lambda}{2R}[\ln(\sqrt{2}+1) - \ln(\sqrt{2}-1)]$$

$$= \frac{K\lambda}{2R}\ln(\sqrt{2}+1)^2 = \frac{K\lambda}{R}\ln(\sqrt{2}+1)$$

31. $dq = \lambda R d\theta$

$$dF = \left(\frac{2K\lambda}{r+R\cos\theta}\right)(\lambda R\, d\theta)$$

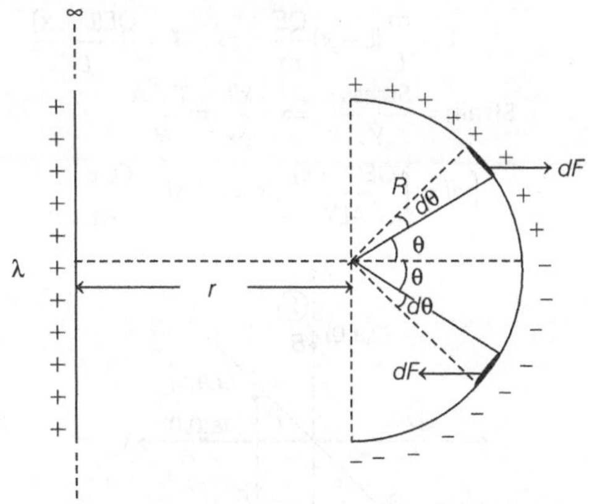

Torque due to couple, $d\tau = dF(2R\sin\theta)$

$$\int d\tau = \int \frac{2K\lambda^2 R d\theta}{r+R\cos\theta}(2R\sin\theta)$$

$$\Rightarrow \qquad \tau = 4K\lambda^2R^2\int_0^{\pi/2}\frac{\sin\theta d\theta}{r+R\cos\theta}$$

Lets substitute $t = r + R\cos\theta$,

$$dt = -R\sin\theta d\theta$$

$$= \frac{\lambda^2R^2}{\pi\varepsilon_0}\left(\frac{-1}{R}\right)\int_{r+R}^{r}\frac{dt}{t} = \frac{\lambda^2 R}{\pi\varepsilon_0}\ln\left(\frac{R+r}{r}\right)$$

32.

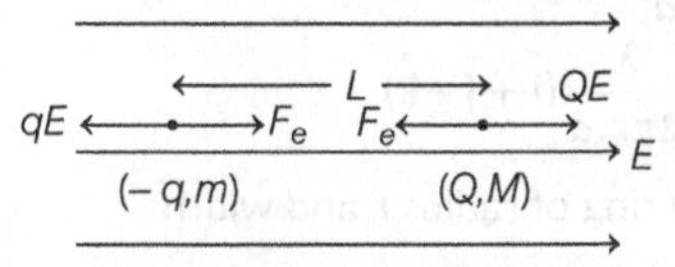

$$F_e = \frac{KQq}{L^2}$$

For separation to remain constant,

$$a_Q = a_{-q}$$

$$\Rightarrow \qquad \frac{QE - F_e}{M} = \frac{F_e - qE}{m}$$

$$\Rightarrow \qquad \frac{QE - \frac{KQq}{L^2}}{M} = \frac{\frac{KQq}{L^2} - qE}{m}$$

$$\Rightarrow \quad (M+m)\frac{KQq}{L^2} = (mQ+Mq)E$$

$$\Rightarrow \quad L = \sqrt{\frac{(M+m)KQq}{(qM+Qm)E}}$$

33.

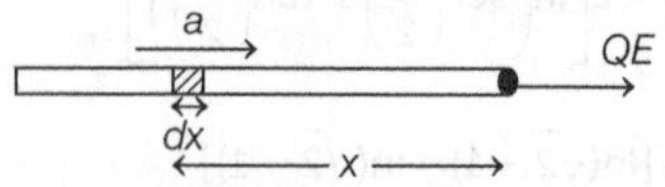

$$\Sigma F = ma$$

$$\Rightarrow \quad QE = ma \quad \Rightarrow \quad a = \frac{QE}{m}$$

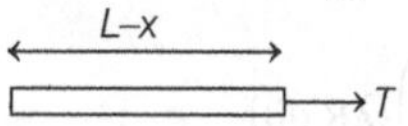

$$\Rightarrow \quad \Sigma F = ma$$

$$\Rightarrow \quad T = \frac{m}{L}(L-x)\frac{QE}{m} \quad \Rightarrow \quad T = \frac{QE(L-x)}{L}$$

$$\text{Strain} = \frac{\text{Stress}}{Y} \quad \Rightarrow \quad \frac{dl}{dx} = \frac{T/A}{Y}$$

$$\Rightarrow \quad \int dl = \int_0^L \frac{QE(L-x)}{ALY}dx \Rightarrow \Delta l = \frac{QEL}{2AY}$$

34.

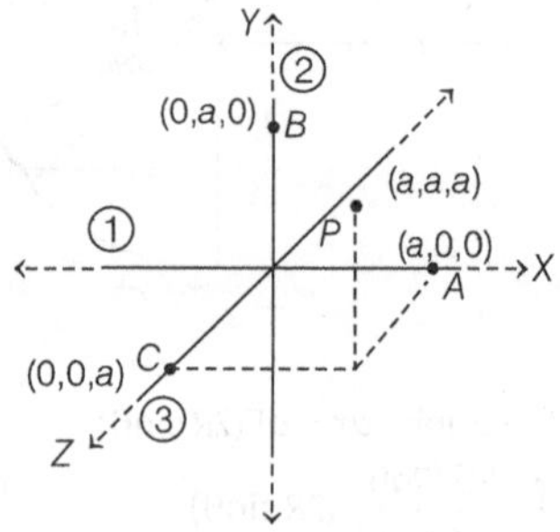

$$AP = BP = CP = \sqrt{2}a$$

$$\mathbf{E} = \mathbf{E}_1 + \mathbf{E}_2 + \mathbf{E}_3$$

$$\mathbf{E} = \frac{2K\lambda}{(AP)^2}\mathbf{AP} + \frac{2K\lambda}{(BP)^2}\mathbf{BP} + \frac{2K\lambda}{(CP)^2}\mathbf{CP}$$

$$= \frac{2K\lambda}{2a^2}(\mathbf{AP}+\mathbf{BP}+\mathbf{CP})$$

$$= \frac{K\lambda}{a^2}((a\hat{\mathbf{j}}+a\hat{\mathbf{k}})+(a\hat{\mathbf{i}}+a\hat{\mathbf{k}})+(a\hat{\mathbf{i}}+a\hat{\mathbf{j}}))$$

$$= \frac{\lambda}{2\pi\varepsilon_0 a}(\hat{\mathbf{i}}+\hat{\mathbf{j}}+\hat{\mathbf{k}})$$

35. Lets take a ring of radius r and width dr.

Force on the elemental ring,

$$dF = \left(\frac{2K\lambda}{r}\right)dq$$

$$\int dF = \int_R^{2R} \frac{2K\lambda}{r}\sigma_0 2\pi r\, dr$$

$$\Rightarrow \quad F = \frac{\lambda\sigma_0}{\varepsilon_0}[r]_R^{2R}$$

$$\Rightarrow \quad F = \frac{\sigma_0 \lambda R}{\varepsilon_0}$$

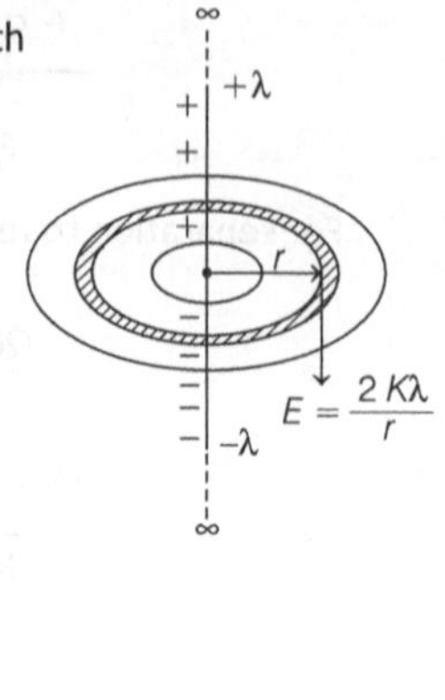

36.

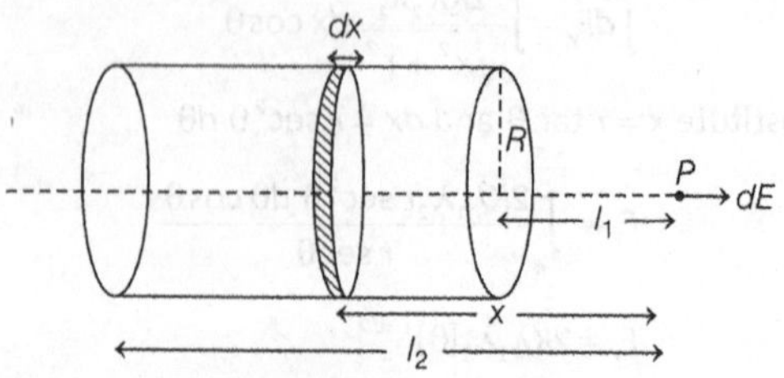

Lets take a ring of width dx.

$$dq = \sigma(2\pi R)\,dx$$

$$dE = \frac{K(\sigma 2\pi R\, dx)\,x}{(R^2+x^2)^{3/2}}$$

$$\Rightarrow \quad \int dE = \frac{\sigma R}{2\varepsilon_0}\int \frac{x\,dx}{(R^2+x^2)^{3/2}}$$

Lets substitute $t^2 = R^2 + x^2$

$\therefore \quad t\,dt = x\,dx$

$$E = \frac{\sigma R}{2\varepsilon_0}\int_{\sqrt{R^2+l_1^2}}^{\sqrt{R^2+l_2^2}} \frac{t\,dt}{t^3} = \frac{\sigma}{2\varepsilon_0}\left[\frac{-1}{t}\right]_{\sqrt{R^2+l_1^2}}^{\sqrt{R^2+l_2^2}}$$

$$E = \frac{\sigma}{2\varepsilon_0}\left(\frac{R}{\sqrt{R^2+l_1^2}} - \frac{R}{\sqrt{R^2+l_2^2}}\right) = \frac{\sigma}{2\varepsilon_0}(\sin\beta - \sin\alpha)$$

37.

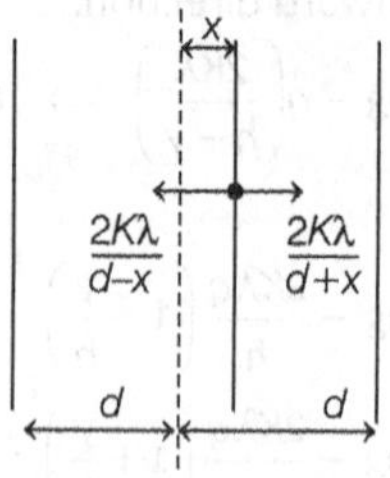

$$F = dqE_{\text{net}}$$

$$\Rightarrow \quad F = (\lambda dl)\left(\frac{2K\lambda}{d+x} - \frac{2K\lambda}{d-x}\right)$$

$$\Rightarrow \quad ma = -\frac{2K\lambda^2 dl}{d^2-x^2}(2x)$$

$$\Rightarrow \quad (mdl)\,a = -\frac{4K\lambda^2 dl}{d^2}x \qquad (\because x << d)$$

$$\Rightarrow \quad a = -\left(\frac{4K\lambda^2}{md^2}\right)x \quad \Rightarrow \quad a = -\left(\frac{\lambda^2}{\pi\varepsilon_0 md^2}\right)x$$

This is equation of SHM.

$$f = \frac{1}{2\pi}\sqrt{\frac{\lambda^2}{\pi\varepsilon_0 md^2}}$$

38.

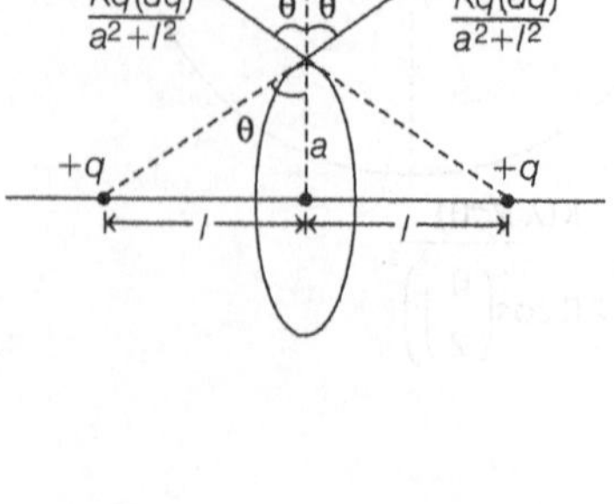

Lets take an element of angular width $d\phi$ on the ring.

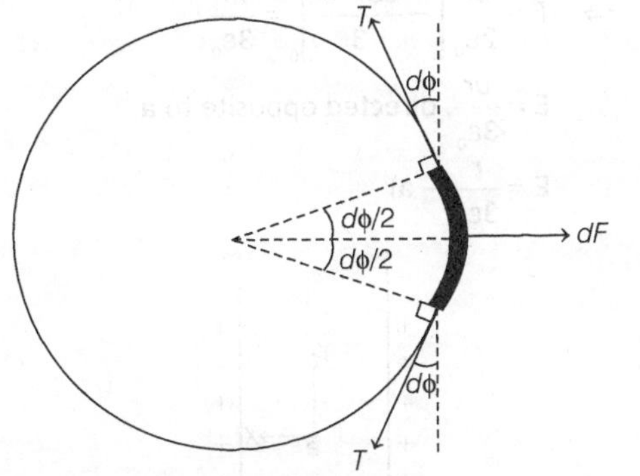

For equilibrium of $ad\phi$ element,

$$dF = 2T\sin\left(\frac{d\phi}{2}\right)$$

$$\Rightarrow \frac{2Kqdq}{a^2+l^2}\cos\theta = 2T\sin\left(\frac{d\phi}{2}\right)$$

$$\Rightarrow \frac{2Kq(\lambda a d\phi)\cos\theta}{a^2+l^2} = 2T\frac{d\phi}{2} \Rightarrow T = \frac{\lambda q a^2}{2\pi\varepsilon_0(a^2+l^2)^{3/2}}$$

39.

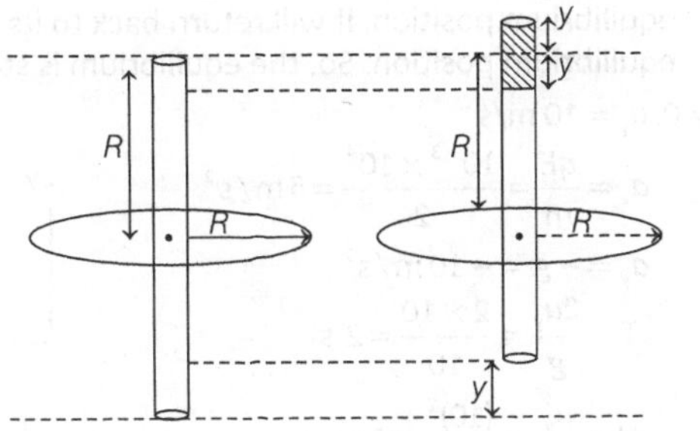

Lets displace the rod up by a distance y, where $y << l$.
The unbalanced force on the rod will be due to length $2y$.

$$F = qE$$

$$\Rightarrow F = \left(\frac{-q}{2R}2y\right)\frac{KQR}{(R^2+R^2)^{3/2}}$$

$$\Rightarrow ma = -\left(\frac{KQq}{R^3(2\sqrt{2})}\right)y \Rightarrow a = -\left(\frac{KQq}{2\sqrt{2}mR^3}\right)y$$

This is equation of SHM.

So, $$T = 2\pi\sqrt{\frac{2\sqrt{2}\times 4\pi\varepsilon_0 mR^3}{Qq}} = 4\pi\sqrt{\frac{2\sqrt{2}\,\pi\varepsilon_0 mR^3}{Qq}}$$

Multiple Choice(s) Correct Questions

1. (a) The charge gained by the uncharged body from a charged body due to conduction is of the same nature of charge initially present on the charged body.
   (b) Charge is relativistically invariant.
   (c) Charge cannot exist without matter although matter can exist without charge.
   (d) If three charges are in electrostatic equilibrium, then all three charges cannot be of same sign.

2. (a)

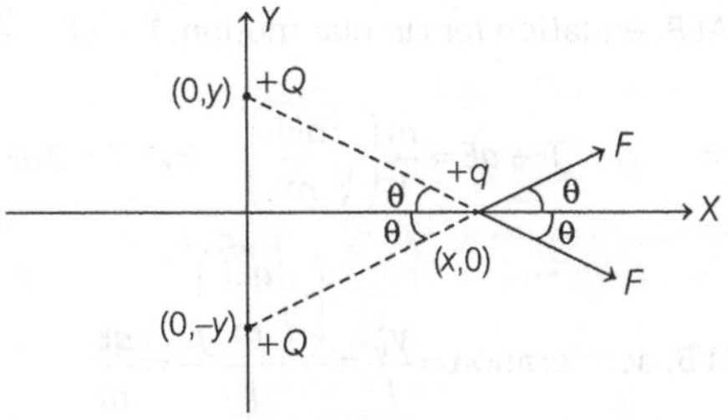

$$F = \frac{KQq}{(\sqrt{x^2+y^2})^2}$$

Net force on $q = 2F\cos\theta$

For F_{net} to be maximum, $\frac{dF_{net}}{dx} = 0$

$$\Rightarrow 2KQq\left[\frac{(x^2+y^2)^{3/2}(1) - \frac{3}{2}(x^2+y^2)^{1/2}(2x)\times x}{(x^2+y^2)^3}\right] = 0$$

$$\Rightarrow \frac{2KQq(x^2+y^2)^{1/2}}{(x^2+y^2)^3}(x^2+y^2-3x^2) = 0$$

$$\Rightarrow x^2 = \frac{y^2}{2} \Rightarrow x = \pm\frac{y}{\sqrt{2}}$$

(b) At origin, $F_{net} = 0$ $(\because x = 0)$
So, q is in equilibrium at origin.
(c) At origin, q is in unstable equilibrium.
So, it cannot perform oscillatory motion.
(d) For any position other than origin, the force is directed away from the origin.

3.

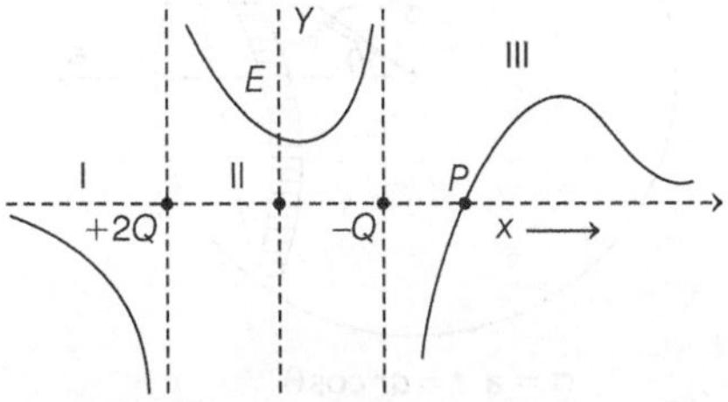

(a) Region III has a local maxima of electric field.
(b) Region I does not have any local maxima/minima.
(c) In region II, electric field is nowhere zero. So, test charge cannot be in equilibrium in region II.
(d) In region III, a negative test charge will be equilibrium at point P. If the negative test is displaced on either side of P, it has tendency to come back to P. So, equilibrium is stable.

4. (a) Applying work-energy theorem between position A and B,

$$W_T + W_{mg} + W_N + W_{electric} = \Delta K$$

$$\Rightarrow 0 + 0 + 0 + qE(l - l\cos 60°) = \frac{1}{2}mv_B^2 - 0$$

$$\Rightarrow v_B = \sqrt{\frac{qEl}{m}}$$

(b) At B, equation for circular motion, $T - qE = \dfrac{mv_B^2}{l}$

$$\Rightarrow \quad T - qE = \frac{m}{l}\left(\sqrt{\frac{qEl}{m}}\right)^2 \quad \Rightarrow \quad T = 2qE$$

(c) At B, acceleration $= \dfrac{v_B^2}{l} = \dfrac{\left(\sqrt{\dfrac{qEl}{m}}\right)^2}{l} = \dfrac{qE}{m}$

(d) About point O, angular momentum of particle is not conserved as torque due to electric force is non-zero.

5. (a) When the block comes to rest momentarily again, at that instant, the elongation will be maximum. Applying work-energy theorem,

$$W_{mg} + W_N + W_{SP} + W_{electric} = \Delta K$$

$$\Rightarrow \quad 0 + 0 + \frac{1}{2}K(0^2 - x_{max}^2) + qEx_{max} = 0 - 0$$

$$x_{max} = \frac{2qE}{K}$$

(b) The spring will not get compressed.

(c) $T = 2\pi\sqrt{\dfrac{m}{K}}$

Since, force due to electric field is constant.

(d) Since, the spring is ideal, it will perform SHM for any value of electric field.

6. (a)

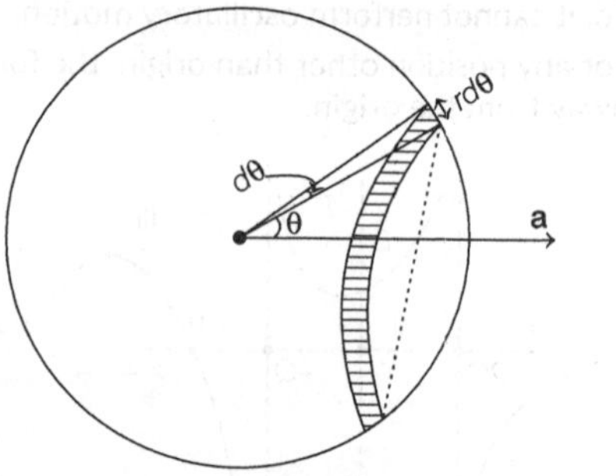

$$\sigma = \mathbf{a}\cdot\mathbf{r} = ar\cos\theta$$

Lets take an elemental ring of width $rd\theta$ as shown in figure.

$$dq = \sigma(2\pi r\sin\theta)\,rd\theta$$

$$\Rightarrow \quad dq = (ar\cos\theta)(2\pi r\sin\theta)\,rd\theta$$

$$\Rightarrow \quad \int dq = \pi r^3 a \int_0^{\pi} \sin 2\theta\, d\theta$$

$$\Rightarrow \quad q = 0$$

(b) $q = \pi r^3 a \displaystyle\int_0^{\pi/2} \sin 2\theta\, d\theta = \pi r^3 a\left[\frac{-\cos 2\theta}{2}\right]_0^{\pi/2} = \pi r^3 a$

(c) $dE = \dfrac{K\,dq\,r\cos\theta}{((r\sin\theta)^2 + (r\cos\theta)^2)^{3/2}}$

$$\Rightarrow \int dE = \int \frac{K(ar\cos\theta)(2\pi r\sin\theta)(rd\theta)(r\cos\theta)}{r^3}$$

$$\Rightarrow \quad E = \frac{ar}{2\varepsilon_0}\int_0^{\pi} \cos^2\theta\sin\theta d\theta$$

$$\Rightarrow \quad E = \frac{ar}{2\varepsilon_0}\left[-\frac{\cos^3\theta}{3}\right]_0^{\pi} = \frac{ar}{3\varepsilon_0}$$

$\mathbf{E} = \dfrac{ar}{3\varepsilon_0}$, **directed opposite to a**

$$\mathbf{E} = \frac{r}{3\varepsilon_0}(-\mathbf{a})$$

7.

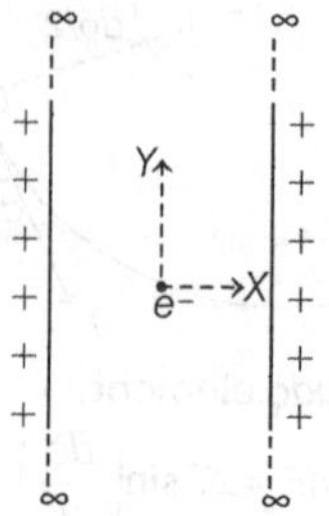

(a) If the particle is displaced along X-axis from the equilibrium position, it will not come back towards its equilibrium position. So, the equilibrium is unstable.

(b) The particle is in equilibrium at every point on the Y-axis. So, the equilibrium is neutral.

(c) If the particle is displaced along Z-axis from its equilibrium position, it will return back to its equilibrium position. So, the equilibrium is stable.

8. $u_x = 0; u_y = 10$ m/s

$$a_x = \frac{qE}{m} = \frac{10^{-3}\times 10^4}{2} = 5\,\text{m/s}^2$$

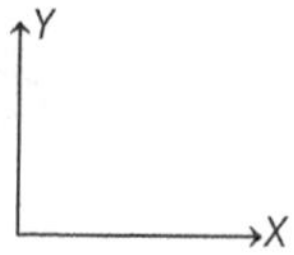

$$a_y = -g = -10\,\text{m/s}^2$$

$$T = \frac{2u_y}{g} = \frac{2\times 10}{10} = 2\text{ s}$$

$$H = \frac{u_y^2}{2g} = \frac{(10)^2}{2(10)} = 5\text{ m}$$

$$s_x = u_x t + \frac{1}{2}a_x t^2 \quad \Rightarrow \quad R = 0 + \frac{1}{2}(5)(2)^2 = 10\text{ m}$$

9. $\Sigma F = ma$

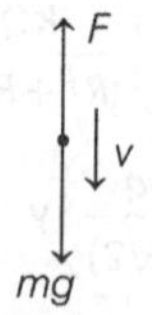

$$\Rightarrow \quad mg - F = 0 \quad \Rightarrow \quad F = mg$$

After applying electric field, the drop ascends up with the same constant speed.

$$\Rightarrow \quad qE - mg - F = 0$$

$$\Rightarrow \quad qE = mg + F$$

$$\Rightarrow \quad qE = 2mg$$

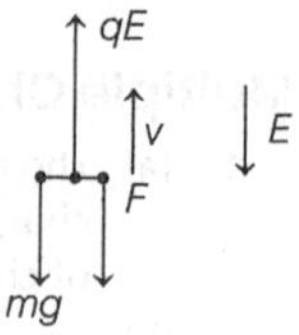

$$\Rightarrow \quad E = \frac{2mg}{q}$$

$$\Rightarrow \quad E = \frac{2(1.6\times 10^{-15}\times 10^{-3})(10)}{9.6\times 10^{-19}} = \frac{100}{3}\text{ N/C}$$

$\mathbf{E} = \dfrac{100}{3}$ **N/C, directed downward.**

10.

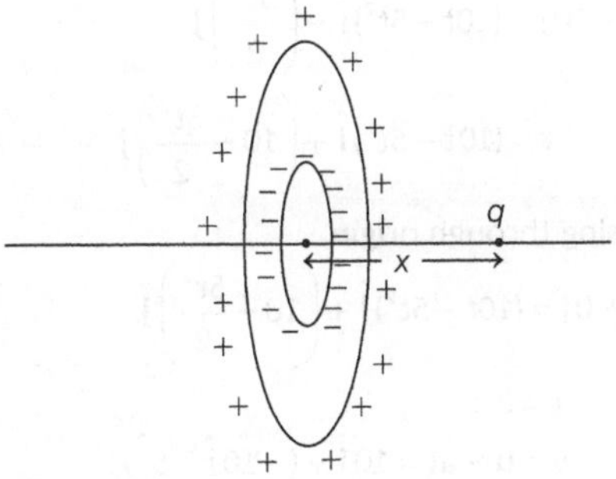

Lets displace the particle by a distance x from origin.

$$F = qE$$

$$\Rightarrow \quad F = q\left(\frac{K(8Q)x}{((3a)^2 + x^2)^{3/2}} + \frac{K(-Q)x}{(a^2 + x^2)^{3/2}}\right)$$

$$\Rightarrow \quad F = KQqx\left(\frac{8}{27a^3} - \frac{1}{a^3}\right) \qquad (\because x << a)$$

$$\Rightarrow \quad F = -\left(\frac{19KQq}{27a^3}\right)x$$

This is equation of SHM.

$$T = 2\pi\sqrt{\frac{27ma^3}{19KQq}} = 12\sqrt{\frac{3\pi^3 a^3 m\varepsilon_0}{19Qq}}$$

$$E = \frac{K(8Q)x}{((3a)^2 + x^2)^{3/2}} + \frac{K(-Q)x}{(a^2 + x^2)^{3/2}} = 0$$

$$\Rightarrow \quad 8x(a^2 + x^2)^{3/2} = x(9a^2 + x^2)^{3/2}$$

$$\Rightarrow \quad x = 0 \text{ and } x = \pm\sqrt{\frac{5}{3}}a$$

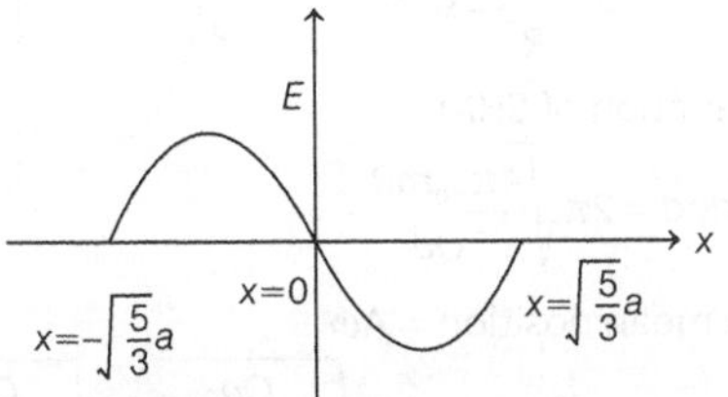

So, amplitude of oscillatory motion should be less than $\sqrt{\frac{5}{3}}a$.

11. For equilibrium,

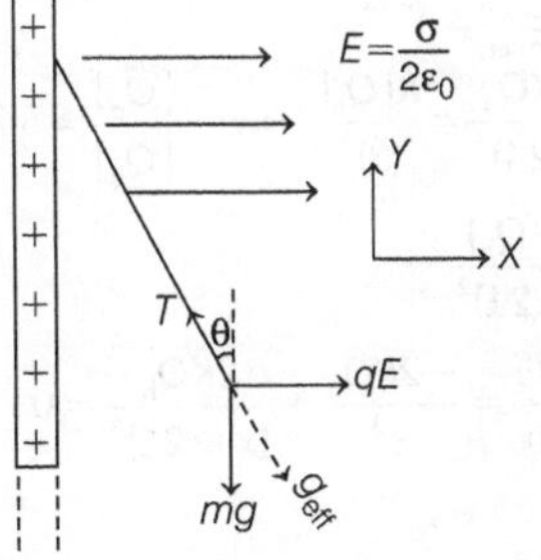

$$T\sin\theta = qE \qquad \text{...(i)}$$

and

$$T\cos\theta = mg \qquad \text{...(ii)}$$

Dividing Eq. (i) by Eq. (ii), we get

$$\tan\theta = \frac{qE}{mg} = \frac{q\sigma}{2\varepsilon_0 mg}$$

$$g_{eff} = \sqrt{g^2 + \left(\frac{qE}{m}\right)^2}$$

$$T = 2\pi\sqrt{\frac{l}{g_{eff}}}$$

Since, $g_{eff} > g$

$$\Rightarrow \quad T < 2\pi\sqrt{\frac{l}{g}}$$

12.

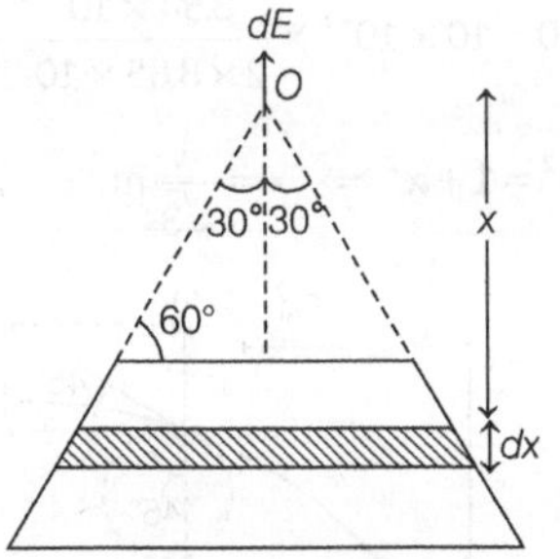

Lets take a strip of width dx at a distance x from the point O.

$$dE = \frac{K\lambda}{x}(\sin 30° + \sin 30°)$$

$$\int dE = \int_{\frac{a}{2}\sin 60°}^{a\sin 60°} \frac{1}{4\pi\varepsilon_0}\frac{(\sigma dx)}{x}$$

$$\Rightarrow \quad E = \frac{7\sigma}{88\varepsilon_0}[\ln x]_{\frac{a}{2}\sin 60°}^{a\sin 60°} = \frac{7\sigma}{88\varepsilon_0}\ln 2 = \frac{7\sigma}{44\varepsilon_0}\ln\sqrt{2}$$

If charge density (σ) is constant, then E is independent of a.

$$\sigma = \frac{Q}{\frac{\sqrt{3}}{4}\left(a^2 - \left(\frac{a}{2}\right)^2\right)} = \frac{16Q}{3\sqrt{3}\,a^2}$$

$$E = \frac{7}{44\varepsilon_0}\left(\frac{16Q}{3\sqrt{3}a^2}\right)\ln\sqrt{2}$$

If total charge is constant, then E decreases with increase in a.

13. $F = qE$

$$\Rightarrow \quad F = 1(10 - 5x)\hat{i} = 0 \Rightarrow x = 2$$

At $x = 2$, particle is in equilibrium.

So, the particle will execute SHM about mean position $x = 2$ with amplitude 2.

Maximum displacement from origin = 4m

Maximum velocity = $A\omega = 2\sqrt{\frac{5}{5}} = 2$ m/s

14. $E = \dfrac{\sigma}{2\varepsilon_0}\left(1 - \dfrac{x}{\sqrt{R^2 + x^2}}\right)$

At $x = \dfrac{4}{3}$, $E = \dfrac{3.54 \times 10^{-11}}{2 \times 8.85 \times 10^{-12}}\left(1 - \dfrac{4/3}{\sqrt{1^2 + \left(\frac{4}{3}\right)^2}}\right)$

$\Rightarrow \quad E = 0.4 \text{ N/C}$

$\Sigma F = ma \quad \Rightarrow \quad mg - qE = ma$

$\Rightarrow \quad 10^{-6} \times 10 - 0.4(10 \times 10^{-6}) = 10^{-6} a$

$\Rightarrow \quad a = 6 \text{ m/s}^2$, downwards

For equilibrium,

$mg = qE$

$\Rightarrow \quad 10^{-6} \times 10 = 10 \times 10^{-6} \times \dfrac{3.54 \times 10^{-11}}{2 \times 8.85 \times 10^{-12}}\left(1 - \dfrac{x}{\sqrt{1^2 + x^2}}\right)$

$\Rightarrow \quad (2x)^2 = 1 + x^2 \Rightarrow x = \dfrac{1}{\sqrt{3}} \text{ m}$

15.

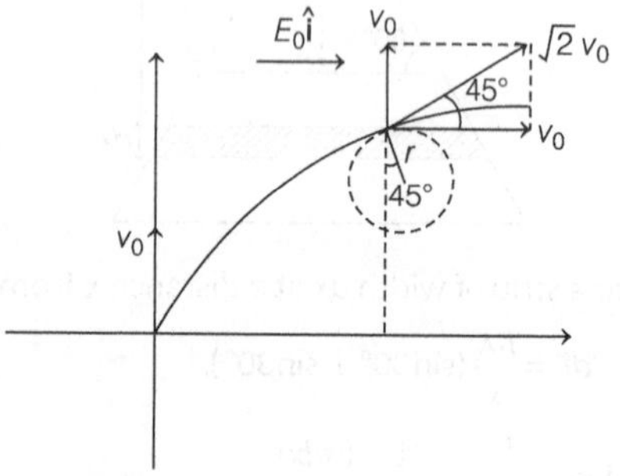

When x-coordinate is x_0.

$v_x^2 = u_x^2 + 2a_x s_x$

$v_x^2 = 0^2 + 2\left(\dfrac{qE_0}{m}\right)x_0$

$\Rightarrow \quad v_x = \sqrt{\dfrac{2qE_0x_0}{m}} = v_0$

$v_y = v_0$

Speed $= \sqrt{v_0^2 + v_0^2} = \sqrt{2}\, v_0$

Centripetal acceleration $= \dfrac{v_\perp^2}{r}$

$\dfrac{qE_0 \cos 45°}{m} = \dfrac{(\sqrt{2}v_0)^2}{r} \quad \Rightarrow \quad r = 4\sqrt{2}x_0$

16. $\mathbf{u} = 10\hat{\mathbf{i}}$

$\mathbf{F} = q\mathbf{E} + m\mathbf{g}$

$\Rightarrow \quad \mathbf{F} = 1(-10\hat{\mathbf{i}} + 5\hat{\mathbf{j}}) + 1(-10\hat{\mathbf{j}})$

$\Rightarrow \quad \mathbf{F} = -10\hat{\mathbf{i}} - 5\hat{\mathbf{j}}$

$\Rightarrow \quad \mathbf{a} = -10\hat{\mathbf{i}} - 5\hat{\mathbf{j}}$

$\mathbf{s} = \mathbf{u}t + \dfrac{1}{2}\mathbf{a}t^2$

$\Rightarrow \quad \mathbf{r} - (10\hat{\mathbf{j}}) = (10\hat{\mathbf{i}})t + \dfrac{1}{2}(-10\hat{\mathbf{i}} - 5\hat{\mathbf{j}})t^2$

$\Rightarrow \quad \mathbf{r} - 10\hat{\mathbf{j}} = (10t - 5t^2)\hat{\mathbf{i}} - \left(\dfrac{5t^2}{2}\right)\hat{\mathbf{j}}$

$\Rightarrow \quad \mathbf{r} = (10t - 5t^2)\hat{\mathbf{i}} + \left(10 - \dfrac{5t^2}{2}\right)\hat{\mathbf{j}}$

For passing through origin,

$0\hat{\mathbf{i}} + 0\hat{\mathbf{j}} = (10t - 5t^2)\hat{\mathbf{i}} + \left(10 - \dfrac{5t^2}{2}\right)\hat{\mathbf{j}}$

$\Rightarrow \quad t = 2 \text{ s}$

$\mathbf{v} = \mathbf{u} + \mathbf{a}t = 10\hat{\mathbf{i}} + (-10\hat{\mathbf{i}} - 5\hat{\mathbf{j}})t$

$= (10 - 10t)\,\hat{\mathbf{i}} - (5t)\,\hat{\mathbf{j}}$

$\tan\phi = \dfrac{v_y}{v_x} = \dfrac{-5t}{10 - 10t}$

At $t = 2\text{s}$, $\tan\phi = 1 \quad \Rightarrow \quad \phi = 45°$

So, while crossing origin, trajectory makes equal angles with both X and Y-axes.

At origin, $\mathbf{v} = (10 - 10t)\,\hat{\mathbf{i}} - 5t\,\hat{\mathbf{j}}$

$= (10 - 10 \times 2)\,\hat{\mathbf{i}} - (5 \times 2)\hat{\mathbf{j}} = -10\hat{\mathbf{i}} - 10\hat{\mathbf{j}}$

Kinetic energy at origin $= \dfrac{1}{2} \times 1 \times (10\sqrt{2})^2 = 100 \text{ J}$

Kinetic energy at $(0, 10) = \dfrac{1}{2} \times 1 \times 10^2 = 50 \text{ J}$

17. $\mathbf{F} = q\mathbf{E}$

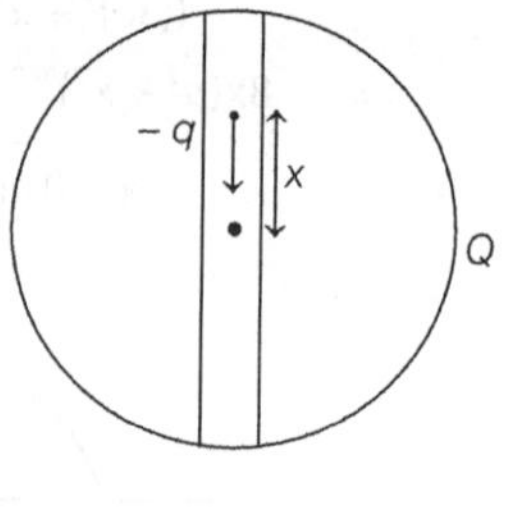

$F = (-q)\left(\dfrac{KQ}{R^3}x\right)$

$\Rightarrow \quad F = \dfrac{-KQq}{R^3}x$

This is equation of SHM.

Time period $= 2\pi\sqrt{\dfrac{4\pi\varepsilon_0 mR^3}{Qq}}$

Speed at mean position $= A\omega$

$= R\sqrt{\dfrac{Qq}{4\pi\varepsilon_0 mR^3}} = \sqrt{\dfrac{Qq}{4\pi\varepsilon_0 mR}}$

Comprehension Based Questions

1. Since, electric field is zero at a point right of charge B, Q_a and Q_b will be of opposite signs.

Electric field at points just right of B is negative. So, Q_b will be negative.

$\therefore$ Q_a is positive and Q_b is negative.

2. At $x = 24$ cm, $E_{net} = 0$

$\Rightarrow \quad \dfrac{KQ_a}{(24)^2} = \dfrac{K|Q_b|}{(3)^2} \quad \Rightarrow \quad \dfrac{|Q_a|}{|Q_b|} = 64$

3. $E = \dfrac{KQ_a}{x^2} + \dfrac{K(-Q_b)}{(x - 21)^2}$

$\dfrac{dE}{dx} = \dfrac{-2KQ_a}{x^3} + \dfrac{2KQ_b}{(x - 21)^3} = 0$

$$\Rightarrow \quad \frac{Q_a}{Q_b} = \frac{x^3}{(x-21)^3} = 64$$

$$\Rightarrow \quad x = 4x - 84$$

$$\Rightarrow \quad x = 28 \text{ cm}$$

4. In air for equilibrium,

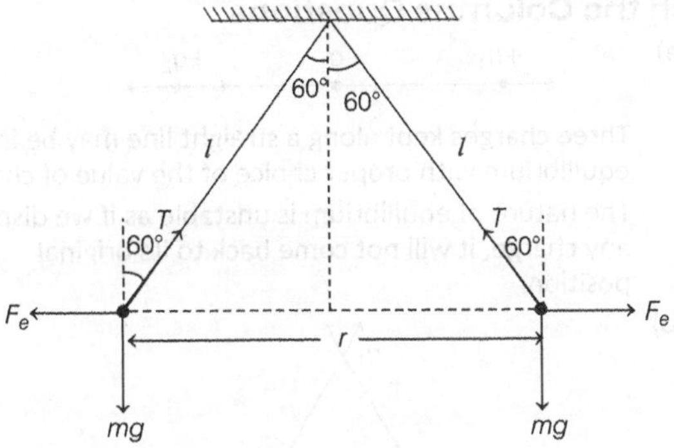

$$T\sin 60° = F_e = \frac{Kq^2}{r^2} \quad \text{... (i)}$$

$$T\cos 60° = mg \quad \text{... (ii)}$$

Dividing Eq. (i) by Eq. (ii), we get

$$\tan 60° = \frac{q^2}{4\pi\varepsilon_0 r^2 mg} \quad \text{... (iii)}$$

In liquid for equilibrium,

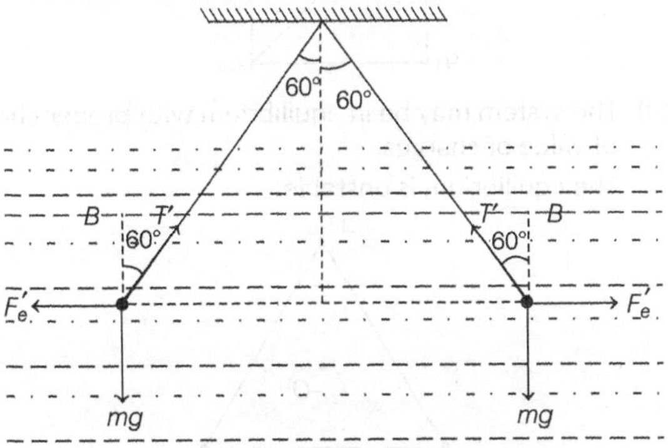

$$T'\sin 60° = \frac{q^2}{4\pi\varepsilon_0\varepsilon_r r^2} \quad \text{... (iv)}$$

$$T'\cos 60° = mg - B \quad \text{... (v)}$$

Dividing Eq. (iv) by Eq. (v), we get

$$\tan 60° = \frac{q^2}{4\pi\varepsilon_0\varepsilon_r(mg-B)} \quad \text{...(vi)}$$

Dividing Eq. (iii) by Eq. (vi), we get

$$\varepsilon_r = \frac{mg}{mg-B} = \frac{\sigma vg}{\sigma vg - \rho vg} = \frac{1}{1-\frac{\rho}{\sigma}} = \frac{1}{1-\frac{1}{3}} \Rightarrow \varepsilon_r = \frac{3}{2}$$

5. $F'_e = F_e - F_{\text{exerted by liquid on one of the balls}}$

$$\Rightarrow F_{\text{exerted by liquid on one of the balls}} = F_e - F'_e$$

$$= \frac{1}{4\pi\varepsilon_0}\frac{q^2}{r^2} - \frac{1}{4\pi\varepsilon_0\varepsilon_r}\frac{q^2}{r^2}$$

$$= \left(1-\frac{1}{\varepsilon_r}\right)\frac{1}{4\pi\varepsilon_0}\frac{q^2}{(2l\sin 60°)^2}$$

$$= \left(1-\frac{1}{3/2}\right)\frac{Kq^2}{\left(2l\left(\frac{\sqrt{3}}{2}\right)\right)^2} = \frac{Kq^2}{9l^2}$$

6. In gravity free space, due to repulsion between the balls, the strings will become horizontal. So, angle between them will be 180°.

7.

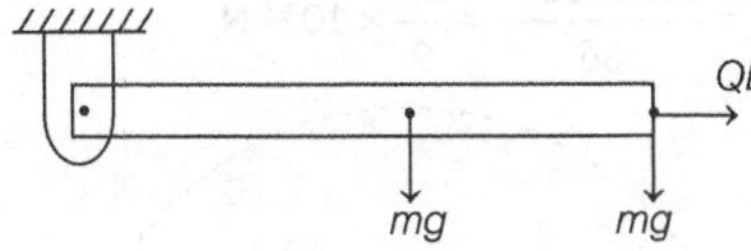

$$\tau = I\alpha$$

$$\Rightarrow \quad mg\left(\frac{l}{2}\right) + mgl + 0 = \left(\frac{ml^2}{3} + ml^2\right)\alpha$$

$$\Rightarrow \quad \alpha = \frac{9g}{8l}$$

For ball, tangential acceleration $= l\alpha = \frac{9g}{8}$

Centripetal acceleration $= \omega^2 l = 0$

So, net acceleration of ball $= \frac{9g}{8}$

8. Using work-energy theorem for (rod + ball) system,

$$W_{\text{gravity}} + W_{\text{electric}} + W_{\text{hinge}} = \Delta K_{\text{system}}$$

$$\Rightarrow \left(+mg\frac{l}{2} + mgl\right) - (QE)l + 0 = \frac{1}{2}\left(\frac{ml^2}{3} + ml^2\right)\omega^2 - 0$$

$$\Rightarrow \quad \omega = \sqrt{\frac{3g}{2l}}$$

Linear speed of ball $= \omega l = \sqrt{\frac{3gl}{2}}$

9. In vertical position, $\tau = I\alpha$

$$\Rightarrow \quad 0 + 0 - (QE)l = \left(\frac{ml^2}{3} + ml^2\right)\alpha$$

$$\alpha = -\frac{3QE}{4ml} = -\frac{3g}{8l}$$

Tangential acceleration $= l\alpha = \frac{3g}{8}$

Centripetal acceleration $= \omega^2 l = \frac{3g}{2}$

Net acceleration $= \sqrt{\left(\frac{3g}{8}\right)^2 + \left(\frac{3g}{2}\right)^2} = \frac{3\sqrt{17}}{8}g$

10. $\mathbf{E} = \mathbf{E}_1 + \mathbf{E}_2$

$$E = \frac{\sigma}{2\varepsilon_0}(1-\cos\theta) - \frac{Kq}{r^2}$$

$$= \frac{\sigma}{2\varepsilon_0}(1-\cos\theta) - \frac{K\left(\int_0^{2\,\text{mm}}(10^{-2} - 5l)\,dl\right)}{r^2}$$

$$= \frac{8.85\times10^{-6}}{2\times8.85\times10^{-12}}\left(1-\frac{1}{2}\right)-\frac{9\times10^{9}}{3^2}\left[10^{-2}l-\frac{5l^2}{2}\right]_0^{2\times10^{-3}}$$

$$= \frac{10^6}{4}-10^9\left[10^{-2}\times2\times10^{-3}-\frac{5}{2}\times4\times10^{-6}\right]$$

$$= 24\times10^4 \text{ N/C}$$

11. $F=\frac{Kq_1q_2}{r^2}=\frac{(8.85\times10^{-6}\times\pi(10^{-3})^2)(10^{-5})}{4\pi\times8.85\times10^{-12}\times3^2}$

$$=\frac{100\times10^{-7}}{36}=\frac{25}{9}\times10^{-7}\text{ N}$$

12.

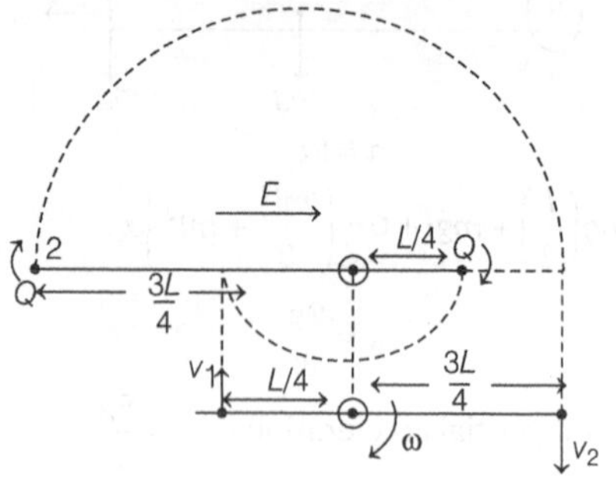

Using work-energy theorem,

$$W_{\text{electric}}=\Delta K$$

$$\Rightarrow \quad +QE\left(\frac{3L}{4}\times2\right)-QE\left(\frac{L}{4}\times2\right)$$

$$=\frac{1}{2}\left(m\left(\frac{L}{4}\right)^2+m\left(\frac{3L}{4}\right)^2\right)\omega^2-0$$

$$\Rightarrow \quad \omega=\sqrt{\frac{16QE}{5mL}}$$

Now, $v_1=\omega\left(\frac{L}{4}\right)=\left(\sqrt{\frac{16QE}{5mL}}\right)\left(\frac{L}{4}\right)=\sqrt{\frac{QEL}{5m}}$

13. The rod will oscillate about its stable equilibrium position. In stable equilibrium, potential energy is minimum.

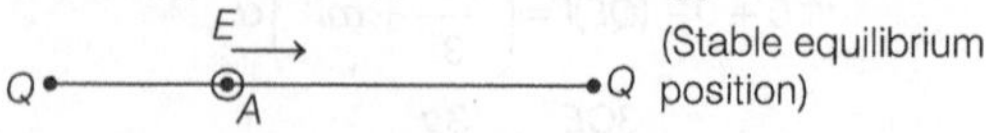

14.

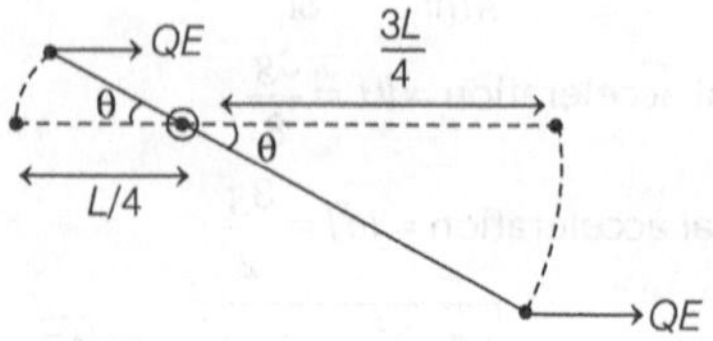

Lets rotate the rod by an angle θ from the stable equilibrium position.

Restoring torque $=QE\left(\frac{3L}{4}\right)\sin\theta-QE\left(\frac{L}{4}\right)\sin\theta$

$$\Rightarrow \quad \tau=-\left(\frac{QEL}{2}\right)\sin\theta$$

$$\Rightarrow \quad \left(\frac{5mL^2}{8}\right)\alpha=-\left(\frac{QEL}{2}\right)\theta \qquad (\because \theta \text{ is small})$$

$$\Rightarrow \quad \alpha=-\left(\frac{4QE}{5mL}\right)\theta$$

This is equation of SHM.

Hence, $T=2\pi\sqrt{\frac{5mL}{4QE}}$

Match the Columns Questions

1. (a)

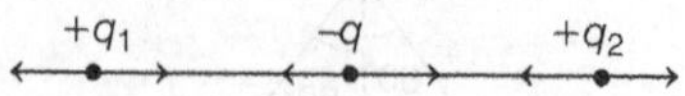

Three charges kept along a straight line may be in equilibrium with proper choice of the value of charges. The nature of equilibrium is unstable as if we displace any charge, it will not come back to its original position.

(b)

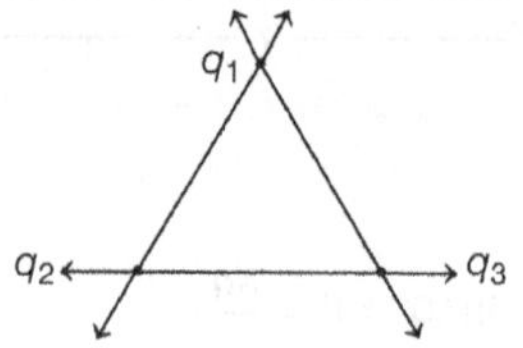

Net force on any of them can never be zero.

(c) Net force on q_2, q_3 and q_4 can never be zero.

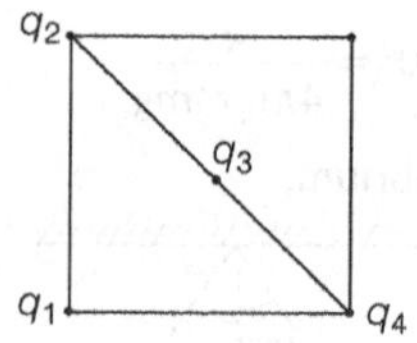

(d) The system may be in equilibrium with proper choice of value of charges.

The equilibrium is unstable.

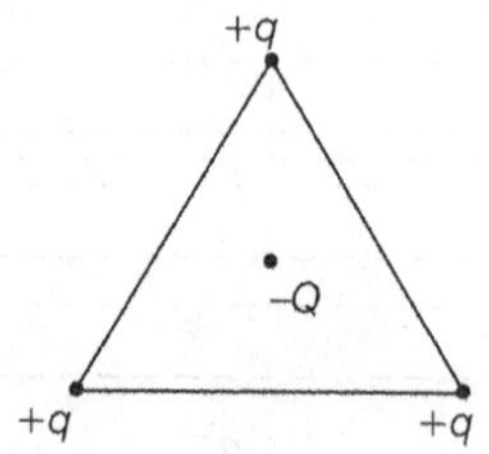

2. (a)

Electric field at C due to both the charges is directed right. So, net electric field is towards right.

(b)

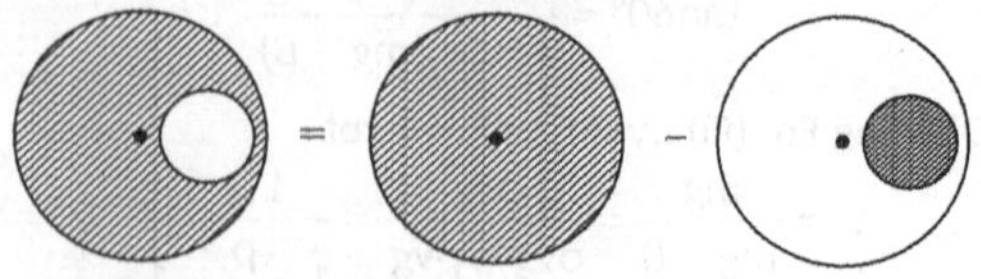

$\mathbf{E}_C=\mathbf{E}_1-\mathbf{E}_2$

$\mathbf{E}_1$ = Electric field due to complete sphere = 0

$\mathbf{E}_2$ = Electric field due to charge filled cavity.

$\mathbf{E}_C=0-\mathbf{E}_2=-\mathbf{E}_2$

$\mathbf{E}_2$ is towards left. So, $\mathbf{E}_C$ will be towards right.

(c)

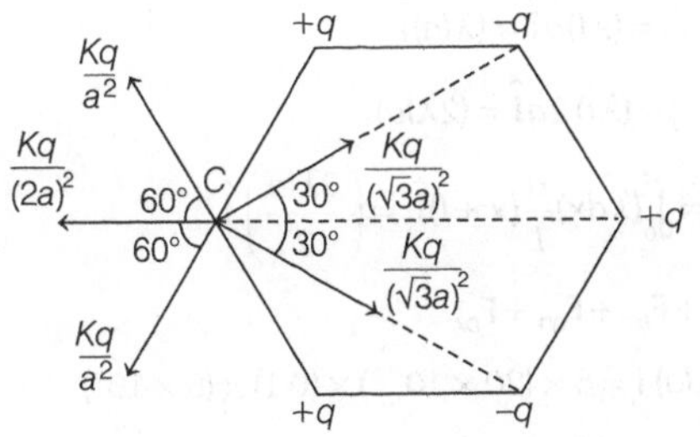

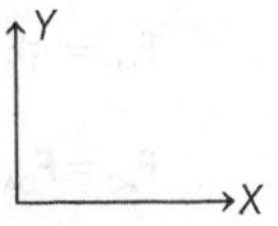

$$E_x = \left(\frac{Kq}{(\sqrt{3}a)^2}\cos 30^\circ\right)\times 2 - \left(\frac{Kq}{a^2}\cos 60^\circ\right)\times 2 - \frac{Kq}{(2a)^2}$$

$$E_x = \frac{Kq}{a^2}\left(\frac{1}{\sqrt{3}} - \frac{5}{4}\right)$$

$$E_y = \frac{Kq}{(\sqrt{3}a)^2}\sin 30^\circ - \frac{Kq}{(\sqrt{3}a)^2}\sin 30^\circ + \frac{Kq}{a^2}\sin 60^\circ - \frac{Kq}{a^2}\sin 60^\circ = 0$$

$E_x < 0$ and $E_y = 0$

So, electric field at C is directed left.

(d) Electric field at C is zero.

3. Apply the following tests

(a) Electric field will be zero in between the charges only if the charges are of same nature.

(b) Electric field will be zero in between the charges, closer to the smaller charge.

(c) Electric field may be zero on outer side of charges (on the line joining them), if they are unequal, closer to the smaller charge.

4. $\mathbf{E} = -11.5\,\hat{\mathbf{j}}$

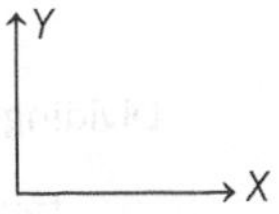

$$\mathbf{F} = q\mathbf{E} = (-e)(-11.5\hat{\mathbf{j}})$$

$$= 18.4\times 10^{-19}\hat{\mathbf{j}}$$

$$\mathbf{u} = 10^6\hat{\mathbf{i}}$$

(a) $s_x = u_x t + \frac{1}{2}a_x t^2$

$$10\times 10^{-2} = 10^6 t + 0$$

$$\Rightarrow \quad t = 10^{-7}\,\text{s}$$

$$s_y = u_y t + \frac{1}{2}a_y t^2 = 0 + \frac{1}{2}\left(\frac{18.4\times 10^{-19}}{9.2\times 10^{-31}}\right)(10^{-7})^2$$

$$= 0.01\text{ m} = 1\text{ cm}$$

(b) $v_y = u_y + a_y t = 0 + \left(\frac{18.4\times 10^{-19}}{9.2\times 10^{-31}}\right)(10^{-7}) = 2\times 10^5$ m/s

(c) $\tan\phi = \frac{v_y}{v_x} = \frac{2\times 10^5}{10^6} = 0.2$

(d) $K = \frac{1}{2}mv^2 = \frac{1}{2}m(\sqrt{v_x^2 + v_y^2})^2$

$$= \frac{1}{2}\times 9.2\times 10^{-31}(10^{12} + 4\times 10^{10})$$

$$= 4.784\times 10^{-19}\text{J} = 3\text{ eV}$$

Numerical Value Questions

1. $F = \frac{Kq^2}{l^2} = \frac{9\times 10^9\times(40\times 10^{-6})^2}{(0.9)^2}$

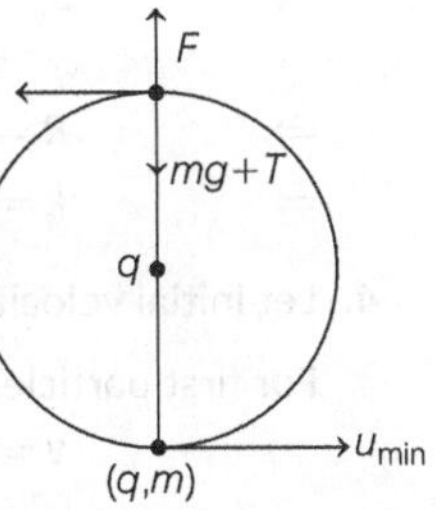

$$= \frac{160}{9}\text{ N}$$

Since $F > mg$, string will never get slack.

So, velocity of bob at the highest point can be zero.

Applying work-energy theorem between the lowest point and the highest point,

$$W_{mg} + W_T + W_{\text{electric}} = \Delta K$$

$$\Rightarrow \quad -mg(2l) + 0 + 0 = 0 - \frac{1}{2}mu_{\min}^2$$

$$u_{\min} = \sqrt{4gl} = 6$$

2. Take a spherical shell of radius x and thickness dx.

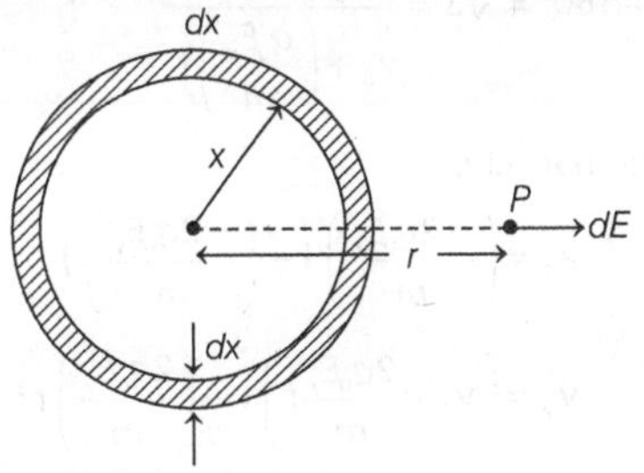

$$dE = \frac{Kdq}{r^2}$$

$$\Rightarrow \quad dE = \frac{1}{4\pi\varepsilon_0}\frac{\rho 4\pi x^2 dx}{r^2}$$

$$\Rightarrow \quad \int dE = \frac{1}{4\pi\varepsilon_0}\int_0^r \frac{\rho_0\left(1 - \frac{x^2}{a^2}\right)4\pi x^2 dx}{r^2}$$

$$\Rightarrow \quad E = \frac{\rho_0}{\varepsilon_0 r^2}\left[\frac{x^3}{3} - \frac{x^5}{5a^2}\right]_0^r \Rightarrow E = \frac{\rho_0}{\varepsilon_0}\left(\frac{r}{3} - \frac{r^3}{5a^2}\right)$$

For E to be maximum, $\frac{dE}{dr} = 0$

$$\Rightarrow \quad \frac{\rho_0}{\varepsilon_0}\left(\frac{1}{3} - \frac{3r^2}{5a^2}\right) = 0 \Rightarrow r = \frac{\sqrt{5}a}{3}$$

$$\Rightarrow \quad r_0 = \frac{\sqrt{5}(3\text{ fm})}{3} = \sqrt{5}\text{ fm} = 2.24\text{ fm}$$

3.

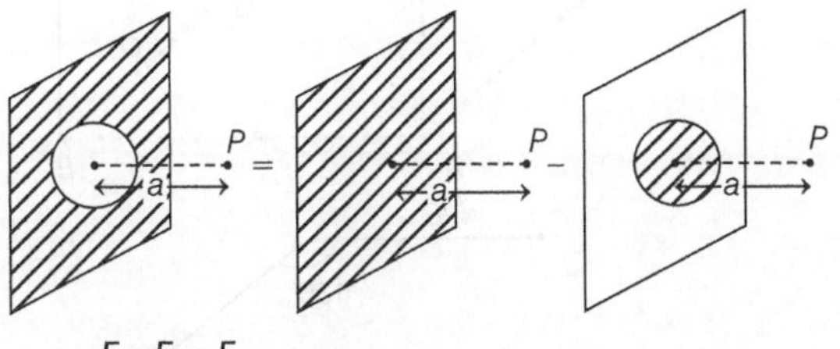

$$E = E_1 - E_2$$

$$\Rightarrow \quad E = \frac{\sigma}{2\varepsilon_0} - \frac{\sigma}{2\varepsilon_0}\left(1 - \frac{x}{\sqrt{R^2 + x^2}}\right)$$

$$\Rightarrow \quad E = \frac{\sigma}{2\varepsilon_0}\frac{x}{\sqrt{R^2+x^2}} \Rightarrow \frac{\sigma}{2\sqrt{2}\varepsilon_0} = \frac{\sigma}{2\varepsilon_0}\frac{a}{\sqrt{R^2+a^2}}$$

$$\Rightarrow \quad R = a = ka$$

$$\Rightarrow \quad k = 1$$

4. Let initial velocity be $\mathbf{v}_0 = v_0\hat{\mathbf{i}}$ and $\mathbf{E} = E_x\hat{\mathbf{i}} + E_y\hat{\mathbf{j}}$

For first particle,

$$\mathbf{v} = \mathbf{u} + \mathbf{a}t$$

$$\Rightarrow \quad \mathbf{v}_1 = \left(v_0 + \left(\frac{q_0E_x}{m}t\right)\right)\hat{\mathbf{i}} + \left(\frac{q_0E_y}{m}t\right)\hat{\mathbf{j}}$$

$$\left(v_0 + \left(\frac{q_0E_x}{m}t\right)\right)^2 + \left(\frac{q_0E_y}{m}t\right)^2 = \left(\frac{v_0}{2}\right)^2 \quad \text{... (i)}$$

$$\tan 60^\circ = \sqrt{3} = \frac{\left(\frac{q_0E_y}{m}\right)t}{v_0 + \left(\frac{q_0E_x}{m}\right)t} \quad \text{... (ii)}$$

For second particle,

$$\mathbf{a}_2 = \left(\frac{-2q_0E_x}{m}\right)\hat{\mathbf{i}} + \left(\frac{-2q_0E_y}{m}\right)\hat{\mathbf{j}}$$

$$\mathbf{v}_2 = \left(v_0 - \frac{2q_0E_x}{m}t\right)\hat{\mathbf{i}} - \left(\frac{2q_0E_y}{m}\right)t\hat{\mathbf{j}}$$

$$v_2^2 = \left[v_0 - \left(\frac{2q_0E_x}{m}\right)t\right]^2 + \left(\frac{2q_0E_y}{m}t\right)^2 \quad \text{... (iii)}$$

Solving Eqs. (i), (ii) and (iii), we get $\frac{v_2^2}{v_0^2} = 7$

5. Electric field due to rods AB and EF cancel out each other. Electric field due to rods CD and GH also cancel out each other.

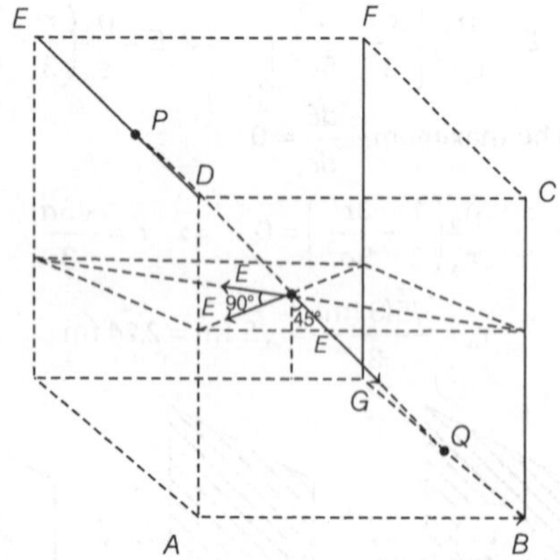

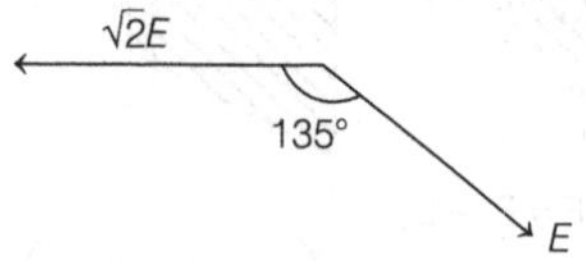

$$E_{\text{net}} = \sqrt{(\sqrt{2}E)^2 + E^2 + 2(\sqrt{2}E)E\cos 135^\circ} = E$$

$$\Rightarrow \quad \sqrt{n}E = 1 \Rightarrow n = 1$$

6. $\mathbf{F}_{AB} = q\mathbf{E}_{x=0} = (\lambda l)a\hat{\mathbf{i}} = (\lambda la)\hat{\mathbf{i}}$

$$\mathbf{F}_{CD} = q\mathbf{E}_{x=l} = (\lambda l)\,2a\hat{\mathbf{i}} = (2\lambda la)\hat{\mathbf{i}}$$

$$\mathbf{F}_{BC} = \mathbf{F}_{DA} = \int_0^l (\lambda dx)\frac{a}{l}(x+l)\hat{\mathbf{i}} = \left(\frac{3\lambda la}{2}\right)\hat{\mathbf{i}}$$

$$\mathbf{F}_{\text{net}} = \mathbf{F}_{AB} + \mathbf{F}_{BC} + \mathbf{F}_{CD} + \mathbf{F}_{DA}$$

$$= (6\lambda la)\hat{\mathbf{i}} = 6\times(20\times10^{-6})\times(0.1)\times(5\times10^5)$$

$$= 6\hat{\mathbf{i}} \Rightarrow |\mathbf{F}_{\text{net}}| = 6\text{ N}$$

7. Component of velocity perpendicular to velocity remains unchanged.

$$\Rightarrow \quad 100\cos 30^\circ = v\cos 60^\circ$$

$$\Rightarrow \quad v = 100\sqrt{3}\text{ m/s}$$

$$v_y = u_y + a_yt$$

$$\Rightarrow \quad 100\sqrt{3}\sin 60^\circ = 100\sin 30^\circ + (-e)\left(\frac{-E}{m}\right)\left(\frac{m}{e}\right)$$

$$\Rightarrow \quad E = 100\text{ N/C}$$

8.

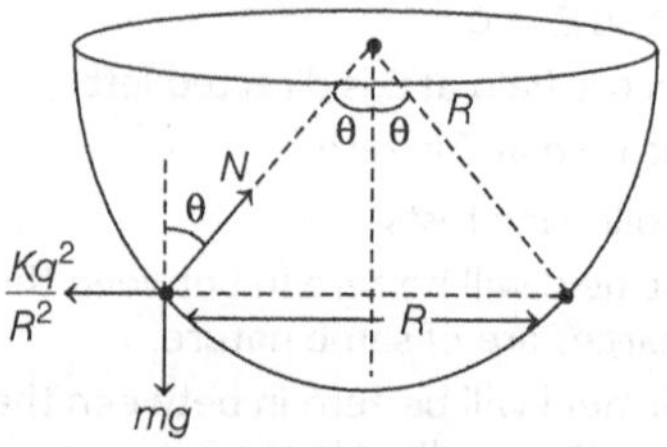

$$2R\sin\theta = R \Rightarrow \theta = 30^\circ$$

For equilibrium,

$$N\sin\theta = \frac{Kq^2}{R^2} \quad \text{... (i)}$$

$$N\cos\theta = mg \quad \text{... (ii)}$$

Dividing Eq. (i) by Eq. (ii), we get

$$\tan\theta = \frac{Kq^2}{mgR^2}$$

$$\Rightarrow \quad q = \sqrt{\frac{mg\tan\theta}{KR^2}} = \sqrt{\frac{\sqrt{3}\times10\times\left(\frac{1}{\sqrt{3}}\right)}{9\times10^9\times1^2}} = \frac{1}{3}\times10^{-4}\text{C}$$

9.

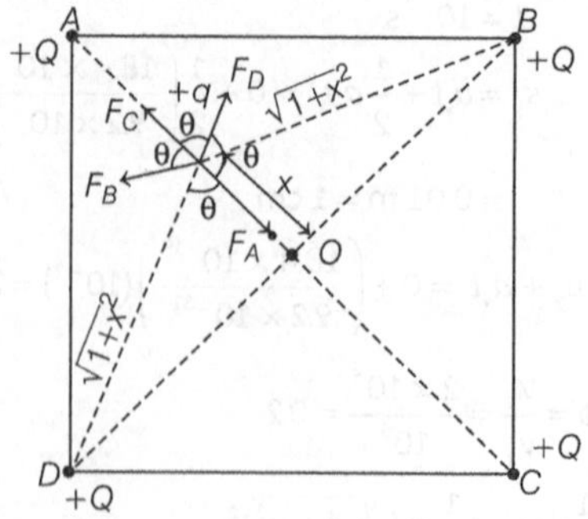

Restoring force

$$= -\left(\frac{KQq}{(1-x)^2} - \frac{KQq}{(1+x)^2} - \frac{2KQ}{(\sqrt{1+x^2})^2}\cos\theta\right)$$

$$\Rightarrow \quad F = -KQq\left(\frac{1}{(1-x)^2} - \frac{1}{(1+x)^2} - \frac{2x}{(1+x^2)^{3/2}}\right)$$

$$\Rightarrow \quad F = -KQq\left((1-x)^{-2} - (1+x)^{-2} - \frac{2x}{(1+x^2)^{3/2}}\right)$$

$$\Rightarrow \quad F = -KQq\,(1+2x-1+2x-2x) \qquad (\because x << 1)$$

$$F = -(2KQq)x$$

This is equation of SHM.

$$T = 2\pi\sqrt{\frac{m}{2KQq}} = 2\pi\sqrt{\frac{2\times10^{-3}}{2\times9\times10^9\times2\times10^{-6}\times10^{-6}}} = \frac{2\pi}{\sqrt{18}}$$

$$\Rightarrow \quad n = 18$$

10. Since, $qE\cos37° > \frac{4mg}{3}\sin37°$,

block will slide up the incline.

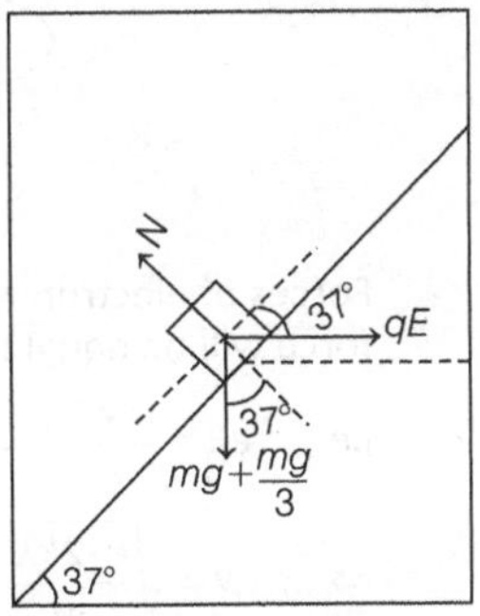

$$\Sigma F = ma$$

$$qE\cos37° - \frac{4mg}{3}\sin37° = ma$$

$$\Rightarrow \quad a = \frac{qE}{m}\left(\frac{4}{5}\right) - \frac{4g}{3}\left(\frac{3}{5}\right)$$

$$\Rightarrow \quad a = 20 - 8 = 12\,\text{m/s}^2$$

$$s = ut + \frac{1}{2}at^2$$

$$\Rightarrow \quad \frac{3.6}{\sin37°} = 0 + \frac{1}{2}(12)t^2 \Rightarrow t = 1\,\text{s}$$

11.

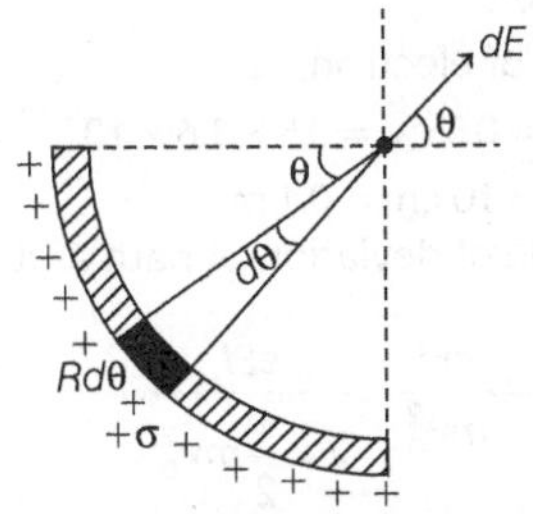

$$d\mathbf{E} = \frac{2K\lambda}{R}\cos\theta\,\hat{i} + \frac{2K\lambda}{R}\sin\theta\,\hat{j}$$

$$\int d\mathbf{E} = \int_0^{\frac{\pi}{2}}\frac{2K(\sigma R d\theta)}{R}\cos\theta\,\hat{i} + \int_0^{\pi/2}\frac{2K(\sigma R d\theta)}{R}\sin\theta\,\hat{j}$$

$$\mathbf{E} = \frac{\sigma}{2\pi\varepsilon_0}\hat{i} + \frac{\sigma}{2\pi\varepsilon_0}\hat{j}$$

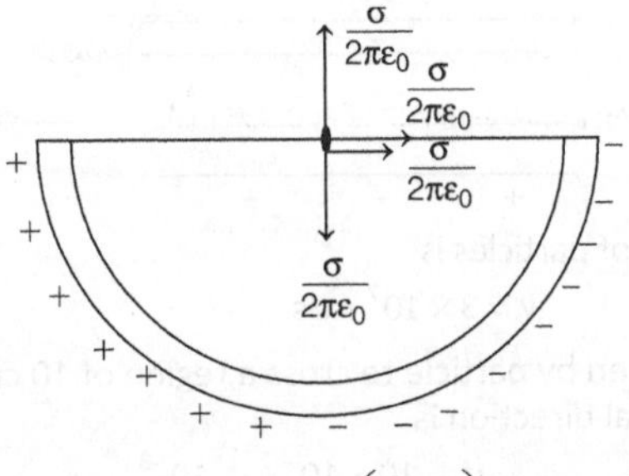

$$\text{Net electric field at centre} = 2\left(\frac{\sigma}{2\pi\varepsilon_0}\right) = \frac{\sigma}{\pi\varepsilon_0} = \frac{2\pi\varepsilon_0}{\pi\varepsilon_0} = 2$$

JEE Main

1. Consider an arc of $d\theta$, force on arc is balanced by component of tension.

$$F_e = \frac{kQ}{R^2}\times\frac{q}{2\pi}d\theta$$

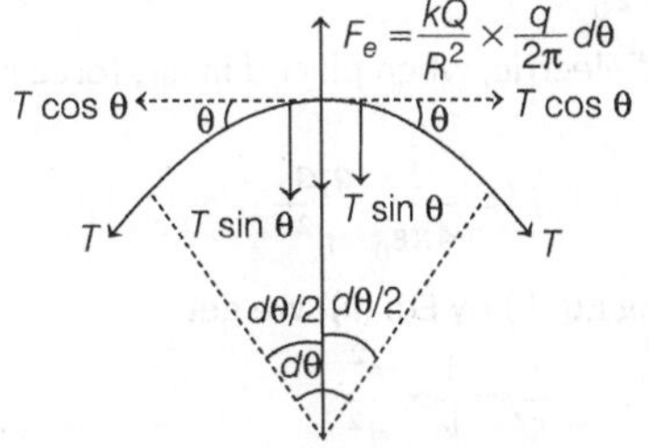

$$\text{So, } 2T\sin\frac{d\theta}{2} = F_e$$

$$F_e = \frac{kQq}{R^2}\left(\frac{d\theta}{2\pi}\right)$$

$$2T\sin\left(\frac{d\theta}{2}\right) = \frac{kQq}{R^2}\left(\frac{d\theta}{2\pi}\right)$$

$$\Rightarrow \quad T = \frac{\frac{kQq}{R^2}\left(\frac{d\theta}{2\pi}\right)}{2\sin\left(\frac{d\theta}{2}\right)} = \frac{\left(\frac{kQq}{\pi R^2}\right)}{2}$$

$$\text{As} \quad \frac{\sin\left(\frac{d\theta}{2}\right)}{\left(\frac{d\theta}{2}\right)} = 1 = \frac{9\times10^9\times2\pi\times30\times10^{-12}}{10^{-4}}$$

$$= 1696.4\times10 = 16964\,\text{N}$$

***Ans** not matching with NTA answer key.

2. Given, $u = 1$ m/s, $a = -\frac{\sigma e}{2\varepsilon_0 m}$

$$t = 1\,\text{s} \Rightarrow s = -1\,\text{m} \Rightarrow s = ut + \frac{1}{2}at^2$$

$$-1 = 1\times1 - \frac{1}{2}\frac{\sigma e}{2\varepsilon_0 m}(1)^2$$

$$-1 = 1 - \frac{1}{2}\frac{\sigma e}{2\varepsilon_0 m}$$

$$\frac{1}{2}\frac{\sigma e}{2\varepsilon_0 m} = 1 + 1 \Rightarrow \sigma = \frac{8\,\varepsilon_0 m}{e}$$

$$\alpha = 8$$

3. Divide charge, $q = 10\mu C$ into two parts,

$$q_1 = x, q_2 = q - x$$

$$F = \frac{K(x)(q-x)}{r^2} \quad \Rightarrow \quad F = \frac{K(x)(q-x)}{r^2}$$

For F to be maximum

$$\frac{dF}{dx} = 0 \quad \Rightarrow \quad q - 2x = 0 \quad \Rightarrow \quad x = \frac{q}{2}$$

$$q_1 = x = \frac{q}{2} = \frac{10\mu C}{2} = 5\mu C$$

$$q_2 = q - x = 10\mu C - 5\mu C = 5\mu C$$

Option (c) is correct.

4. Initially charges are placed in a medium of dielectric constant k.

$$F = \frac{q_1q_2}{4\pi\varepsilon d^2} = \frac{q_1q_2}{4\pi k\varepsilon_0 d^2} \quad \text{... (i)}$$

Here, $k = \frac{\varepsilon}{\varepsilon_0}$

Without dielectric, when placed in air, force between charges,

$$F' = \frac{1}{4\pi\varepsilon_0}\frac{q_1q_2}{r^2} \quad \text{... (ii)}$$

On dividing Eq. (i) by Eq. (ii), we get

$$\frac{F}{F'} = \frac{1}{k} \times \frac{r^2}{d^2}$$

When, $F = F'$, we get

$$1 = \frac{r^2}{kd^2}$$

$$r^2 = kd^2 \quad \Rightarrow \quad r = d\sqrt{k}$$

5. Given,

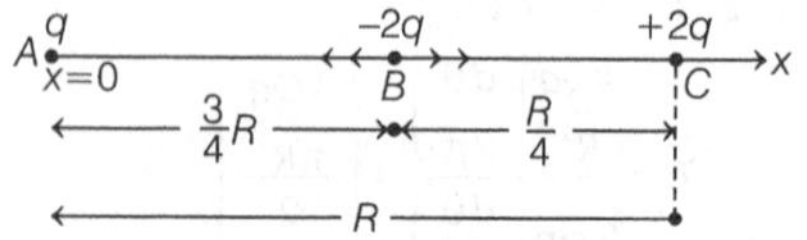

$$F_{BA} = \frac{kq \times 2q}{\left(\frac{3}{4}R\right)^2} \quad \Rightarrow \quad F_{BA} = \frac{16k \times 2q^2}{9R^2}$$

$$F_{BA} = \frac{32kq^2}{9R^2}$$

$$F_{BC} = \frac{k4q^2}{(R/4)^2} = \frac{64kq^2}{R^2}$$

$$F_B = F_{BC} - F_{BA} = \frac{64kq^2}{R^2} - \frac{32kq^2}{9R^2} = \frac{kq^2}{R^2}\left(64 - \frac{32}{9}\right)$$

$$= \frac{9 \times 10^9 \times (2 \times 10^{-6})^2}{(2 \times 10^{-2})^2} \times \frac{544}{9} = 5440 \text{ N}$$

6. Given,

$$q_0 = 10\,\mu\text{C} = 10^{-5}\text{C}$$

Let point charge of

$$q = 40\,\mu\text{ C} = 4 \times 10^{-5}\text{ C}$$

is placed at a distance x cm from origin O

According to given situation,

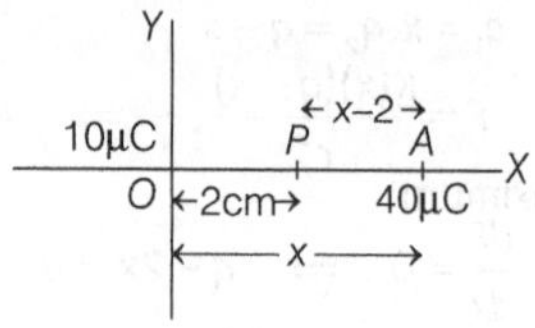

$$E_{OP} = E_{AP}$$

$$\Rightarrow \frac{1}{4\pi\varepsilon_0} \cdot \frac{10^{-5}}{(2 \times 10^{-2})^2} = \frac{1}{4\pi\varepsilon_0} \cdot \frac{4 \times 10^{-5}}{(x-2)^2 \times (10^{-2})^2}$$

$$\Rightarrow \frac{1}{(2 \times 10^{-2})^2} = \frac{4}{(x-2)^2 \times (10^{-2})^2}$$

$$\Rightarrow \frac{1}{2} = \frac{2}{x-2}$$

$$\Rightarrow x - 2 = 4$$

$$\Rightarrow x = 6 \text{ cm}$$

7. Given, charge density,

$$\lambda = \frac{q}{l} = 2 \times 10^{-8}\text{ Cm}^{-1}$$

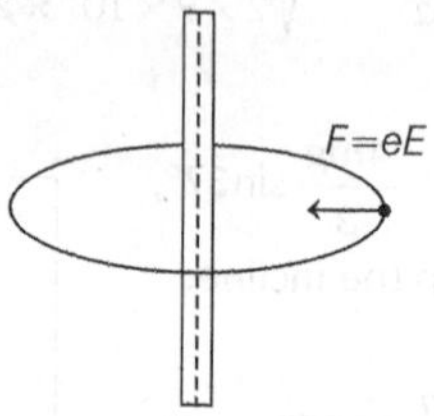

Forces of electron will be equilibrium when electrostatic force will be equal to centripetal force.

i.e., $eE = \frac{mv^2}{r} \quad \Rightarrow \quad e \cdot \frac{2k\lambda}{r} = \frac{mv^2}{r}$

$$\Rightarrow \quad v = \sqrt{\frac{e \cdot 2k\lambda}{m}} = \sqrt{\frac{1.6 \times 10^{-19} \times 2 \times 9 \times 10^9 \times 2 \times 10^{-8}}{9 \times 10^{-31}}}$$

$$= 8 \times 10^6 \text{ m/s}$$

8. Given, $E = 10$ N/C

Kinetic energy of electron,

$$K = 0.5 \text{ eV} = 0.5 \times 1.6 \times 10^{-19}\text{ J} = 3.2 \times 10^{-20}\text{ J}$$

$$l = 10 \text{ cm} = 0.1 \text{ m}$$

If θ be the angle of deviation of path as it comes out of the field, then

$$\tan\theta = \frac{eEl}{mv_0^2} = \frac{eEl}{2 \times \frac{1}{2}mv_0^2}$$

$$= \frac{eEl}{2K} = \frac{1.6 \times 10^{-19} \times 10 \times 0.1}{2 \times 3.2 \times 10^{-20}}$$

$$= \frac{1}{4} \times 10 = \frac{5}{2} = 2.5$$

$$\Rightarrow \quad \theta = \tan^{-1}(2.5) = 68°$$

9. Given situation is shown below,

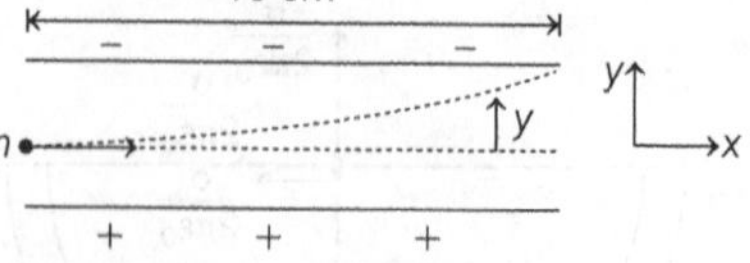

Velocity of particles is

$$v = 3 \times 10^7 \text{ m/s}$$

Time taken by particle to cross a region of 10 cm in horizontal direction is

$$t = \frac{d}{v} = \frac{10 \times 10^{-2}}{3 \times 10^7} = \frac{10^{-8}}{3}\text{ s}$$

Acceleration of particle in y-direction

$$a = \frac{F}{m} = \frac{qE}{m} = \frac{q}{m} \cdot E$$

$$= 2 \times 10^{11} \times 1.8 \times 10^3 \text{m/s}^2 = 3.6 \times 10^{14} \text{m/s}^2$$

Deflection y of charged particle using

$$s_y = u_y t + \frac{1}{2} a_y t^2 \; u_y = 0$$

displacement in y direction,

$$y = \frac{1}{2} \times 3.6 \times 10^{14} \times \left(\frac{10^{-8}}{3}\right)^2$$

$$= \frac{3.6}{2 \times 9} \times 10^{14-16} \text{ m}$$

$$= \frac{3.6}{18} \times 10^{-2+3} \text{ mm} = 2 \text{ mm}$$

10. The given situation is shown below

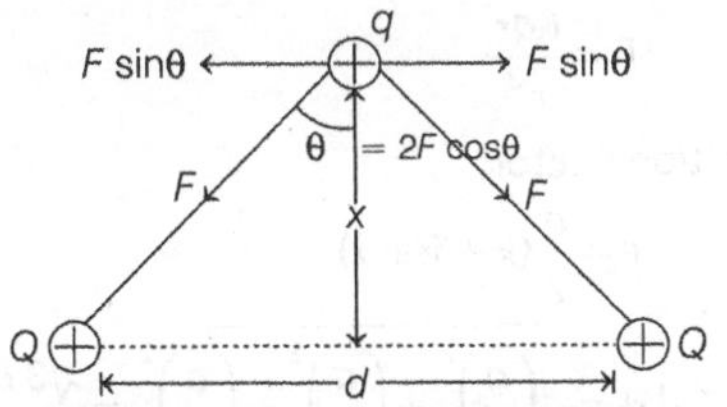

Net force on charge q = sum of components along perpendicular bisector

$$2F\cos\theta = \frac{2KQq}{\left(\frac{d^2}{4} + x^2\right)} \times \frac{x}{\left(\frac{d^2}{4} + x^2\right)^{1/2}}$$

$$\therefore \quad F_{\text{net}} = \frac{2KQq \cdot x}{\left(\frac{d^2}{4} + x^2\right)^{3/2}}$$

F_{net} is maximum, when $\frac{dF_{\text{net}}}{dx} = 0$

$$\Rightarrow \quad \frac{d}{dx}\left(2KQq \cdot \frac{x}{\left(\frac{d^2}{4} + x^2\right)^{3/2}}\right) = 0$$

$$\Rightarrow \quad \frac{\left(\frac{d^2}{4} + x^2\right)^{3/2} \cdot 1 - x \cdot \frac{3}{2}\left(\frac{d^2}{4} + x^2\right)^{1/2} \cdot 2x}{\left(\frac{d^2}{4} + x^2\right)^3} = 0$$

$$\Rightarrow \quad x = \frac{d}{2\sqrt{2}}$$

11. Masses of each charged particle,

$$m_1 = m_2 = 10\text{g} = 0.01 \text{ kg}$$

and charges on them,

$$q_1 = q_2 = 2 \times 10^{-7} \text{C}$$

$$\mu = 0.25$$

$$g = 10 \text{ m/s}^2$$

The given situation is shown in the figure below,

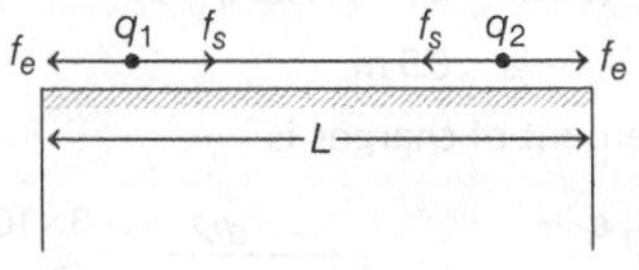

In the condition of limited equilibrium of either charge,

$$f_e = f_s$$

$$\frac{Kq_1 q_2}{L^2} = \mu \, mg$$

$$\Rightarrow \quad \frac{9 \times 10^9 \times 2 \times 10^{-7} \times 2 \times 10^{-7}}{L^2} = 0.25 \times 0.01 \times 10$$

$$\Rightarrow \quad L = 0.12 \text{ m} = 12 \text{ cm}$$

12. The given situation is shown below

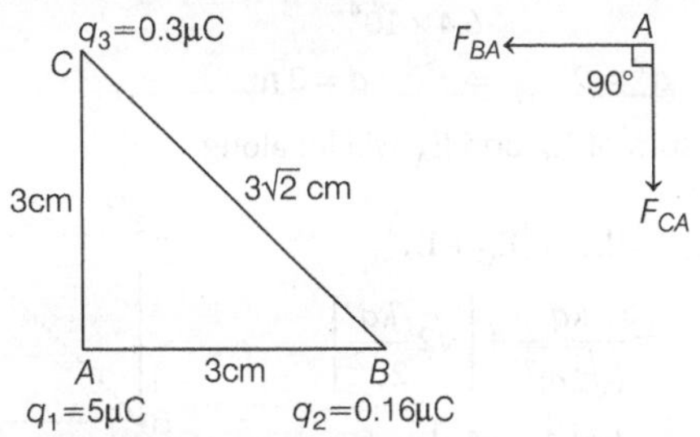

Here, $q_1 = 5\mu\text{C} = 5 \times 10^{-6}\text{C}$

$$q_2 = 0.16\mu\text{C} = 1.6 \times 10^{-7}\text{C}$$

$$q_3 = 0.3\mu\text{C} = 3 \times 10^{-7}\text{C}$$

Force on charge q_1 due to charge q_2,

$$F_{BA} = 9 \times 10^9 \frac{q_1 q_2}{(AB)^2} = 9 \times 10^9 \times \frac{5 \times 10^{-6} \times 1.6 \times 10^{-7}}{(3 \times 10^{-2})^2} = 8 \text{ N}$$

Force on charge q_1 due to charge q_3,

$$F_{CA} = 9 \times 10^9 \frac{q_1 q_2}{(AC)^2}$$

$$= 9 \times 10^9 \frac{5 \times 10^{-6} \times 3 \times 10^{-7}}{(3 \times 10^{-2})^2} = 15 \text{ N}$$

Net force experienced by charge on point A due to other two charges,

$$F = \sqrt{F_{CA}^2 + F_{BA}^2} = \sqrt{15^2 + 8^2} = \sqrt{289} = 17 \text{ N}$$

13. The given situation is shown below

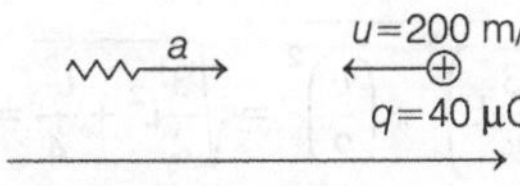

Acceleration of particle,

$$a = -\frac{F}{m} = -\frac{qE}{m} = -\left(\frac{40 \times 10^{-6} \times 1 \times 10^5}{100 \times 10^{-3} \times 10^{-3}}\right)$$

$$= -4 \times 10^4 \text{ m/s}^2$$

Now, using $v^2 - u^2 = 2as$, we have

$$0-(200)^2 = 2(-4\times10^4)\times s$$

or $\quad s = 0.5\text{ m}$

14. The arrangement of charges is

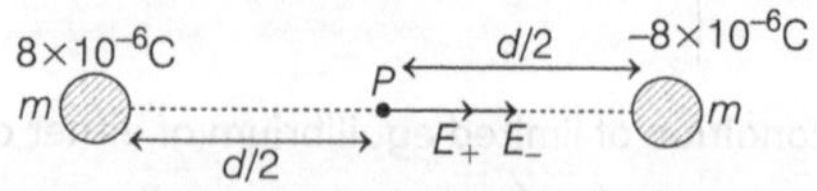

At mid-point net electric field is the sum of fields due to positive and negative charges.

$$\Rightarrow \quad E_{\text{net}}(\text{at } P) = 2\times\frac{Kq}{\left(\frac{d}{2}\right)^2} = \frac{8\times9\times10^9\times8\times10^{-6}}{d^2}$$

Given, $\quad E_{\text{net}} = 6.4\times10^4$ N/C

Hence, $d^2 = \dfrac{8\times9\times10^9\times8\times10^{-6}}{6.4\times10^4}$

$\Rightarrow \quad d^2 = 9 \quad \Rightarrow \quad d = 3\text{ m}$

15. Here, sum of $\mathbf{E}_C$ and $\mathbf{E}_A$ will lie along $\mathbf{E}_B$.

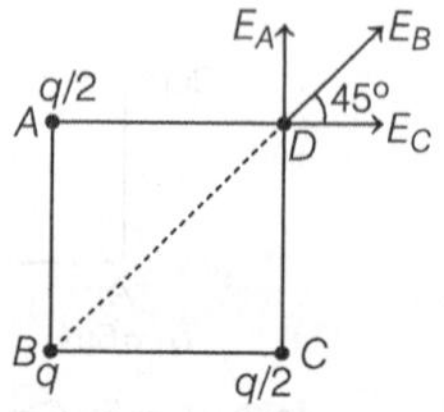

So, $|\mathbf{E}_{\text{net}}| = |\mathbf{E}_B| + |\mathbf{E}_C + \mathbf{E}_A|$

$$= \frac{kq}{(\sqrt{2}a)^2} + \left[\sqrt{2}\frac{kq}{2a^2}\right]$$

$$= \frac{kq}{a^2}\left[\frac{1}{2}+\frac{1}{\sqrt{2}}\right]$$

$$= \frac{q}{4\pi\varepsilon_0 a^2}\left[\frac{1}{\sqrt{2}}+\frac{1}{2}\right]$$

16. Given, length of conductor $= L$

Charge on conductor $= Q$

According to figure, $\; OP = a = \dfrac{\sqrt{3}}{2}L, \; OQ = \dfrac{L}{2}$

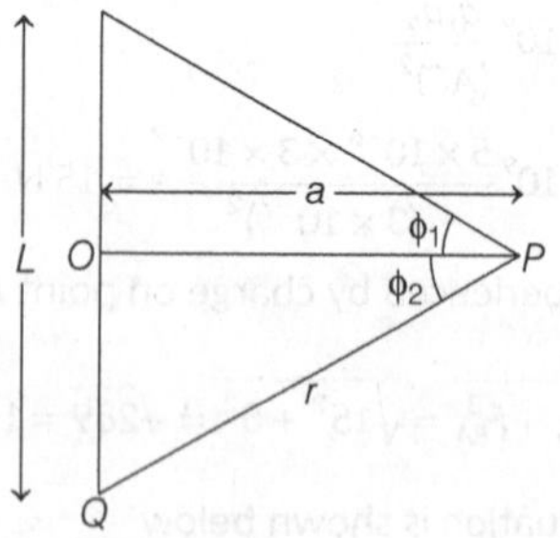

Let $\quad PQ = r = \sqrt{OP^2 + OQ^2}$

$$\Rightarrow \quad PQ = \sqrt{\left(\frac{\sqrt{3}}{2}L\right)^2 + \left(\frac{L}{2}\right)^2} = \sqrt{\frac{3}{4}L^2 + \frac{L^2}{4}} = L$$

and E be the electric field at point P.

Since, E (due to finite wire)

$$= \frac{k\lambda}{a}(\sin\phi_1 + \sin\phi_2) \qquad \text{...(i)}$$

Where, $k =$ Coulomb's constant $= \dfrac{1}{4\pi\varepsilon_0}$

$\lambda =$ linear charge density $= \dfrac{Q}{L}$

and $\sin\phi_1 = \sin\phi_2 = \dfrac{L/2}{L} = \dfrac{1}{2}$

On substituting the above value in Eq. (i), we get

$$E = \frac{k\lambda}{a} = \frac{1}{4\pi\varepsilon_0}\frac{Q}{L\cdot\frac{\sqrt{3}L}{2}} = \frac{1}{2\sqrt{3}\pi\varepsilon_0}\frac{Q}{L^2}$$

17. We can replace $-Q$ charge at origin by $+Q$ and $-2Q$. Now, due to $+Q$ charge at every corner of cube, electric field at centre of cube is zero. So, net electric field at centre is only due to $-2Q$ charge at origin. Vector form of electric field strength,

$$\mathbf{E} = \frac{Kq\mathbf{r}}{r^3}$$

Here, position vector,

$$r = \frac{a}{2}(\hat{\mathbf{x}}+\hat{\mathbf{y}}+\hat{\mathbf{z}})$$

$$\Rightarrow \quad |\mathbf{r}| = \sqrt{\left(\frac{a}{2}\right)^2+\left(\frac{a}{2}\right)^2+\left(\frac{a}{2}\right)^2} = \frac{\sqrt{3}\,a}{2}$$

$$\Rightarrow \quad \mathbf{E} = \frac{1}{4\pi\varepsilon_0}\times\frac{(-2Q)\,a/2}{\left(\frac{a}{2}\sqrt{3}\right)^3}\cdot(\hat{\mathbf{x}}+\hat{\mathbf{y}}+\hat{\mathbf{z}})$$

$$\mathbf{E} = \frac{-2Q(\hat{\mathbf{x}}+\hat{\mathbf{y}}+\hat{\mathbf{z}})}{3\sqrt{3}\,\pi a^2\varepsilon_0}$$

18. In the given question,

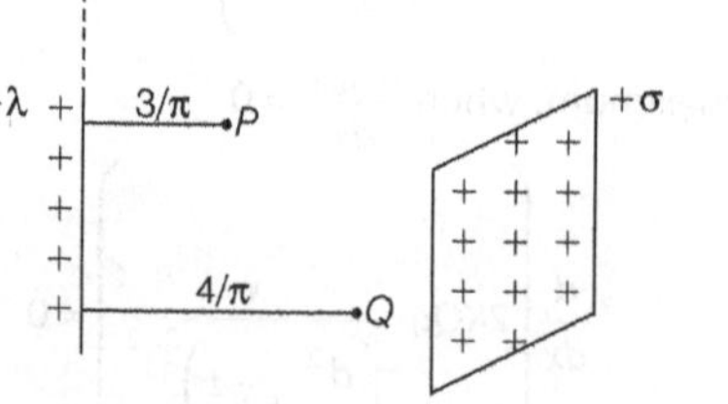

$$\frac{E_P}{E_Q} = \frac{\dfrac{\lambda}{2\pi\varepsilon_0\left(\frac{3}{\pi}\right)} - \dfrac{\sigma}{2\varepsilon_0}}{\dfrac{\lambda}{2\pi\varepsilon_0\left(\frac{4}{\pi}\right)} - \dfrac{\sigma}{2\varepsilon_0}} = \frac{4}{3}\left(\frac{\lambda-3\sigma}{\lambda-4\sigma}\right) = \frac{4}{3}\left(\frac{2\sigma-3\sigma}{2\sigma-4\sigma}\right)$$

$$= \frac{4}{3}\times\frac{1}{2} = \frac{2}{3} = \frac{4}{6} = \frac{4}{a} \quad \text{[Given]}$$

$\therefore \quad a = 6$

19. Given, mass of each spheres,

$$m = 10\text{ mg} = 10\times10^{-3}\text{ g}$$

Length of thread $(l) = 0.5$ m

Separation between charges, $d = 0.2$ m

Charge of each sphere, $q = \frac{a}{21} \times 10^{-8}$ C

Acceleration due to gravity (g) = 10 ms^{-2}

The situation can be shown as below,

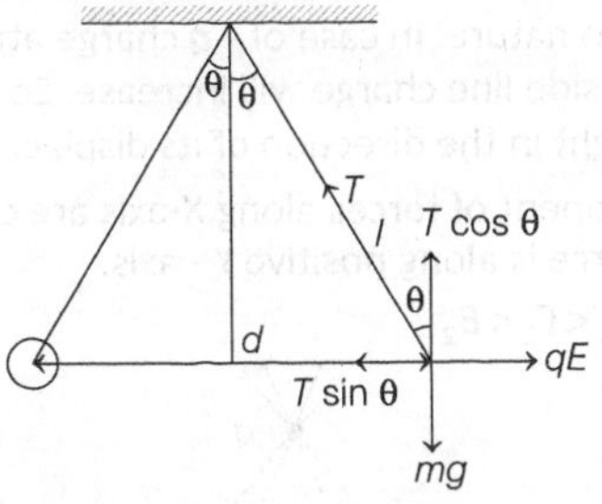

Taking component of tension (T)

$$T \cos\theta = mg \quad \text{...(i)}$$

$$T \sin\theta = qE = \frac{kq^2}{d^2} \quad \text{...(ii)}$$

$$\sin\theta = \frac{d/2}{l} = \frac{0.1}{0.5} = \frac{1}{5}$$

$$\cos\theta = \sqrt{1 - \sin^2\theta} = \sqrt{1 - 1/25} = \frac{\sqrt{24}}{5}$$

$$\therefore \quad \tan\theta = \frac{\sin\theta}{\cos\theta} = \frac{kq^2}{d^2 mg}$$

[Using Eqs. (i) and (ii)]

$$\Rightarrow \quad \frac{1/5}{\sqrt{24}/5} = \frac{kq^2}{d^2 mg}$$

$$\Rightarrow \quad \frac{1}{\sqrt{24}} = \frac{9 \times 10^9 \times q^2}{(0.2)^2 \times 10 \times 10^{-3} \times 10}$$

$$\Rightarrow \quad q = \sqrt{\frac{(0.2)^2 \times 10^{-1}}{\sqrt{24} \times 9 \times 10^9}}$$

$$\Rightarrow \quad q = 3 \times 10^{-7} \text{ C}$$

$$\Rightarrow \quad \frac{a}{21} \times 10^{-8} = 30 \times 10^{-8}$$

$$a = 630$$

20. Let's say the charge q and $(Q - q)$ are at r distance from each other. This can be shown as

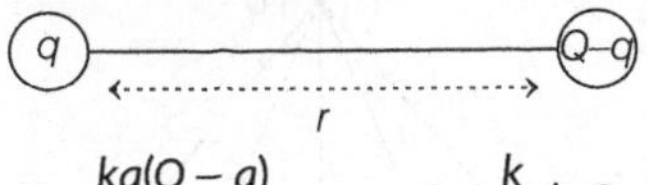

$$\therefore \quad F = \frac{kq(Q-q)}{r^2} \Rightarrow F = \frac{k}{r^2}(qQ - q^2)$$

As we know that $\frac{dF}{dq} = 0$, for maximum force.

$$\Rightarrow \quad \frac{dF}{dq} = \frac{d}{dq}\left[\frac{k}{r^2}(qQ - q^2)\right] = 0$$

$$\Rightarrow \quad \frac{k}{r^2}(Q - 2q) = 0 \Rightarrow Q = 2q$$

21. Given,

Linear charge density, $\lambda = 8$ nC/m $= 8 \times 10^{-9}$C/m

The relation between surface charge density and linear charge density can be given as

$$\frac{2k\lambda}{r} = \frac{\sigma}{\varepsilon_0} \quad \text{...(i)}$$

$$\Rightarrow \quad \sigma = \frac{2k\lambda\varepsilon_0}{r}$$

$$= \frac{2 \times 9 \times 10^9 \times 8 \times 10^{-9} \times 8.85 \times 10^{-12}}{3}$$

$$= 0.424 \times 10^{-9} \text{ C m}^{-2} = 0.424 \text{ nCm}^{-2}$$

22. The 1 C charge present in the origin and other 1μC charge are placed at 1 m, 2 m, 4 m, 8 m ...

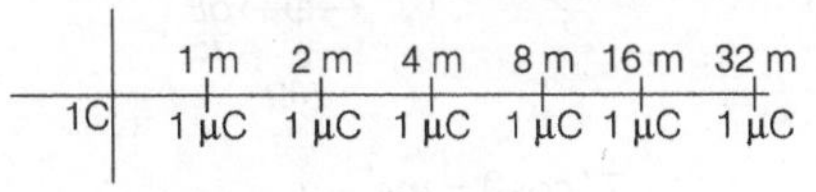

Using the Coulomb's law,

$$F = \frac{kq_1q_2}{r^2}$$

$$F = 9 \times 10^9 \times (1) \times 10^{-6}\left[1 + \frac{1}{2^2} + \frac{1}{4^2} + \frac{1}{8^2} + \dots\right]$$

$$= 9 \times 10^3 \times \left[\frac{1}{1 - \frac{1}{4}}\right] = 12 \times 10^3 \text{ N}$$

JEE Advanced

1. $a = \frac{qE}{m} = 10^{10} \times 400\sqrt{3}$ m/s^2

or $\quad a = 4\sqrt{3} \times 10^{12}$ m/s^2

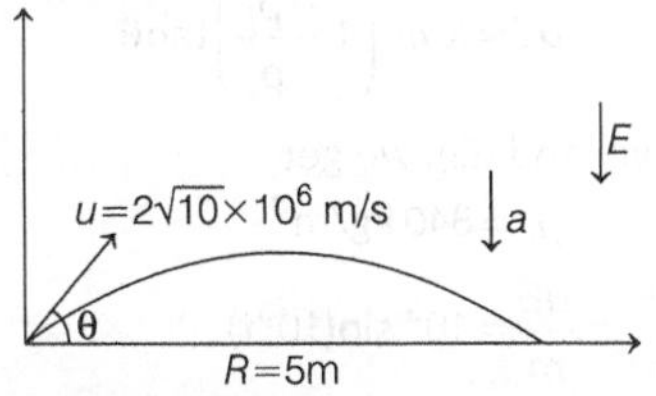

$$\therefore \quad R = \frac{u^2 \sin 2\theta}{a} \Rightarrow \sin 2\theta = \frac{Ra}{u^2}$$

$$\text{or} \quad \sin 2\theta = \frac{5 \times 4\sqrt{3} \times 10^{12}}{4 \times 10 \times 10^{12}}$$

$$\Rightarrow \quad \sin 2\theta = \frac{\sqrt{3}}{2}$$

$$\Rightarrow \quad 2\theta = 60°, 120°$$

$$\Rightarrow \quad \theta = 30° \text{ or } 60° \text{ for same range}$$

$$\therefore \quad T = \frac{2u\sin\theta}{a} = \frac{2 \times 2\sqrt{10} \times 10^6}{2 \times 4\sqrt{3} \times 10^{12}}$$

$$\Rightarrow \quad T = \sqrt{\frac{10}{12}} \times 10^{-6}$$

$$\Rightarrow \quad T = \sqrt{\frac{5}{6}} \times 10^{-6}$$

2. In air,

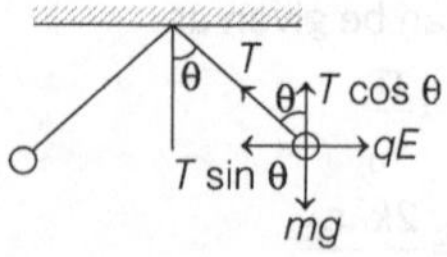

$$T\cos\theta = mg \quad \text{... (i)}$$
$$T\sin\theta = qE \quad \text{... (ii)}$$
$$qE = mg\tan\theta \quad \text{... (iii)}$$

In liquid,

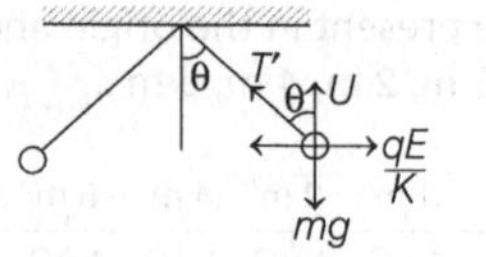

$$T'\cos\theta = mg - u$$
$$T'\cos\theta = mg\left(1+\frac{\rho_l}{\rho_s}\right) \quad \text{... (iv)}$$
$$T'\sin\theta = \frac{qE}{K} \quad \text{... (v)}$$

Dividing Eq. (v) by Eq.(ii), we get

$$\frac{T'}{T} = \frac{1}{K}$$
$$\Rightarrow \quad T' = \frac{T}{K} = \frac{T}{21} \quad \text{... (vi)}$$

Dividing Eq. (iv) by Eq. (v), we get

$$\frac{qE}{K} = mg\left(1-\frac{\rho_l}{\rho_s}\right)\tan\theta$$
$$qE = Kmg\left(1-\frac{\rho_l}{\rho_s}\right)\tan\theta \quad \text{... (vii)}$$

From Eqs. (vii) and (iii), we get

$$\rho_s = 840 \text{ kg/m}^3$$

3. $$a = \frac{F}{m} = \frac{qE}{m} = 10^3 \sin(10^3 t)$$

$$\frac{dv}{dt} = 10^3 \sin(10^3 t)$$

$$\Rightarrow \int_0^v dv = \int_0^t 10^3 \sin(10^3 t)\, dt$$

$$\therefore \quad v = \frac{10^3}{10^3}[1-\cos(10^3 t)]$$

Velocity will be maximum when $\cos(10^3 t) = -1$

$$v_{max} = 2$$

4. At centre both charges are in equilibrium, $+q$ charge is suppose displaced towards right, then repulsion on it will increase from right hand side line charge. Hence it starts oscillations. These small oscillations come out to be simple harmonic in nature. In case of $-q$ charge attraction from right hand side line charge will increase. So, net force is towards right in the direction of its displacement.

5. (A) Component of forces along X-axis are cancelled. So, net force is along positive Y - axis.

$$E_3 < E_1 < E_2$$

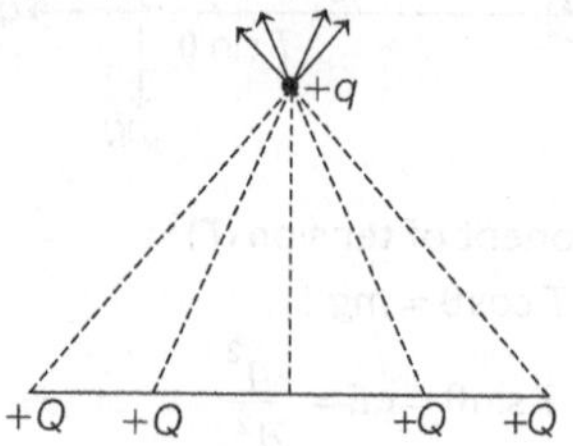

(B) Component of forces along Y-axis are cancelled and net force is along positive X-axis

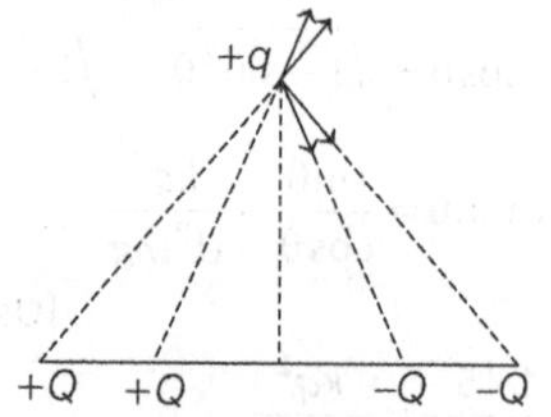

(C) Component of forces along X-axis are cancelled and net force is along negative Y-axis

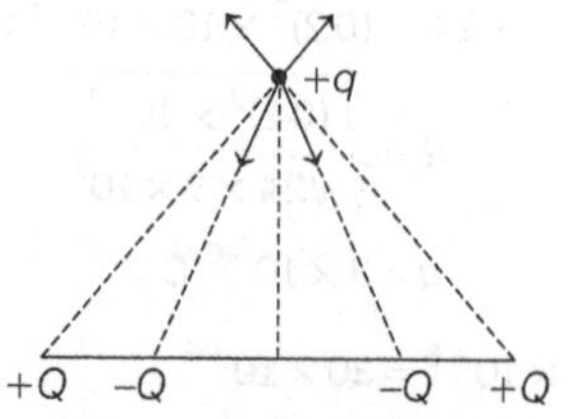

(D) Component of forces along Y-axis are cancelled and net force is along negative X-axis

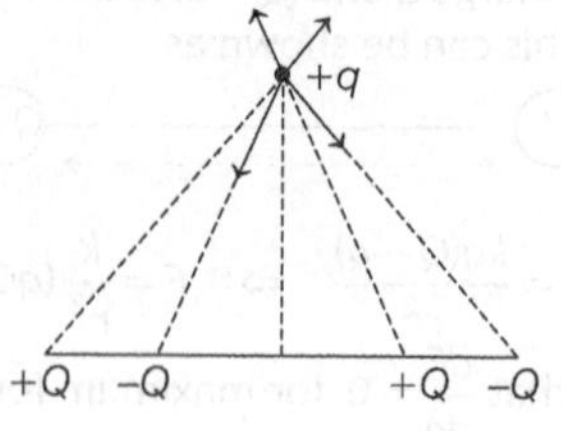

CHAPTER~02

ELECTRIC POTENTIAL

LEVEL 01 Starter Level

2.1 Electric Potential

1 A point charge + 2 C is taken from infinity to a point in an electric field, without changing its speed. If work done against electrostatic forces is – 40 J, then find the potential at that point.

2 A point charge + 20 μC is shifted slowly from infinity to a point *P* in an electric field. The potential of the point *P* is 1000 V.

(i) What is the work done by external agent against electric field?

(ii) What is the work done by electric field?

(iii) If a point charge + 30 μC is released from rest at point *P*, then find its kinetic energy at a large distance.

3 A point charge + 20 μC is shifted from infinity to a point *P* in an electric field. The potential of the point *P* is 1000 V. If the kinetic energy of the charged particle is found to increase by 10 mJ, when it is brought from infinity to point *P*, then

(i) what is the work done by electric field and

(ii) what is the total work done by external agent?

4 An electron is shifted slowly from infinity to a point *P* in an electric field. The potential of the point *P* is – 10 V.

(i) Find out work done by external agent against electric field.

(ii) What is the work done by electric field?

2.2 Electric Potential due to Point Charge(s)

1 Some point charges are kept at the vertices of the following shapes as shown. Find electric potential at point C for each case.

(i)

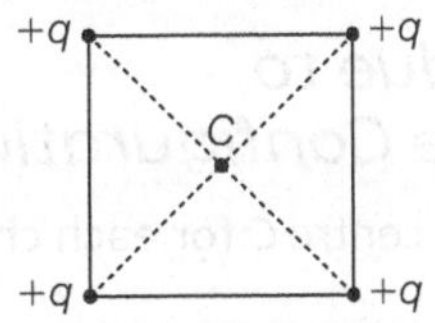

is the centre of the square of side *a*

(ii)

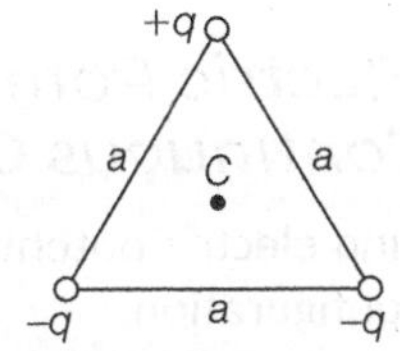

C is the centroid of the equilateral triangle of side *a*

(iii)

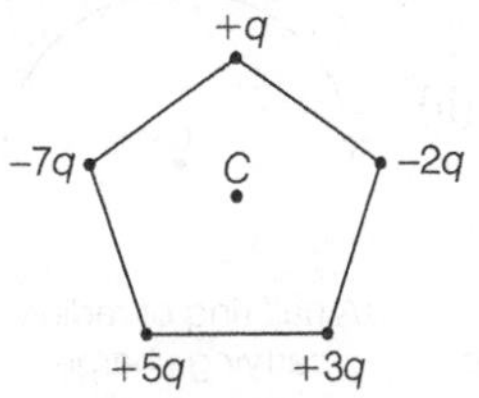

C is the centroid of regular pentagon of side *a*

2 Two point charges 2μC and – 4μC are situated at points (– 2,0) and (2, 0), respectively. Find out potential at points *A* (4, 0) and *B* (0, $\sqrt{5}$).

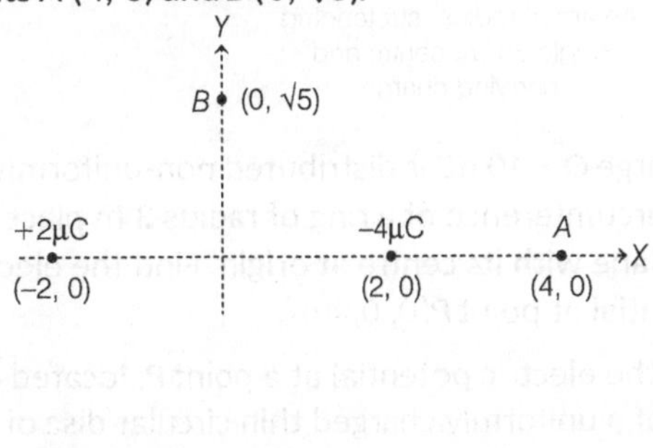

3 An infinite number of charges, each equal to q are placed along the X-axis at $x = 1, x = 2, x = 4, x = 8, \ldots$ and so on. Find the potential at the point $x = 0$ due to this set of charges. What will be the potential in the above set, if the consecutive charges have opposite signs?

4 Two particles A and B having charges of $+4\mu C$ and $-8\mu C$, respectively are held fixed at a separation of 60 cm. Locate the point(s) on the line AB, where the electric potential is zero.

5 Two point charges $+q$ and $-3q$ are placed at (0, 0) and (8,0), respectively. Find the locus of the zero potential points in the XY-plane.

6 A regular hexagon of side L is placed in a horizontal plane and six equal charges $+q$ are fixed at its vertices. A point P is located vertically above the centre of the hexagon, at a height $\sqrt{3}\,L$ from the plane of the hexagon. Find the electric potential at point P.

2.3 *Electric Potential due to Continuous Charge Configurations*

1 Find electric potential at the centre C for each charge configuration.

(i) 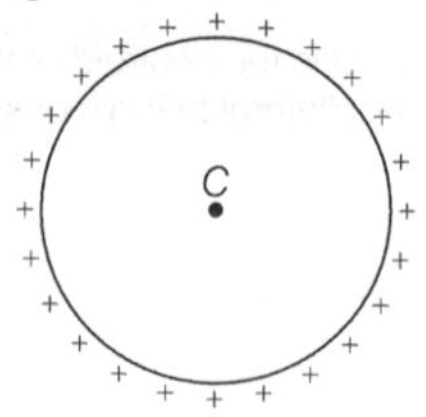

A non-uniformly charged ring of radius carrying charge

(ii) 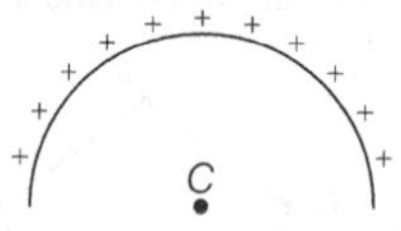

A half ring of radius carrying charge

(iii) 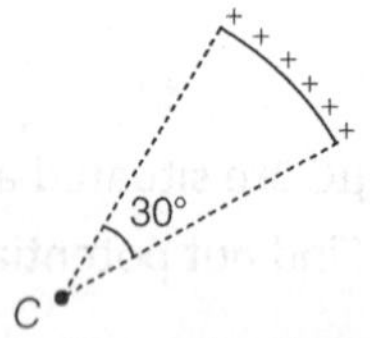

An arc of radius subtending angle 30° at centre and carrying charge

2 A charge $Q = 10$ nC is distributed non-uniformly over the circumference of a ring of radius 3 m placed on XY-plane with its centre at origin. Find the electric potential at point $P(0, 0, 4\text{m})$.

3 Find the electric potential at a point P, located on the axis of a uniformly charged thin circular disc of radius R and surface charge density σ at a distance x from the plane of the disc.

4 Find electric potential due to uniformly charged thin spherical shell of radius 10 cm carrying charge $+1.6\ \mu C$ at the following points.

(i) At the centre (ii) 4 cm from centre

(iii) 12 cm from centre

5 Two concentric spherical shells of radius R_1 and R_2 $(R_2 > R_1)$ are having uniformly distributed charges Q_1 and Q_2, respectively. Find out potential at points A, B and C. Distances of A, B and C from the common centre O can be taken as OA, OB and OC respectively, if required.

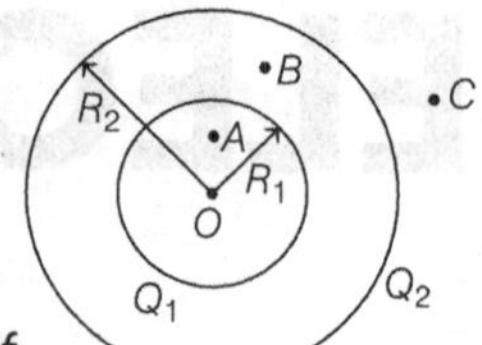

6 Find electric potential due to uniformly charged solid non-conducting sphere of radius 10 cm carrying charge $+1.6\ \mu C$ at the following points.

(i) At the centre

(ii) 5 cm from centre

(iii) 12 cm from centre

7 A solid sphere of radius R is uniformly charged with charge density ρ in its volume.

A spherical cavity of radius $\frac{R}{2}$ is made in the sphere as shown in the figure. Find the electric potential at the centre of the sphere.

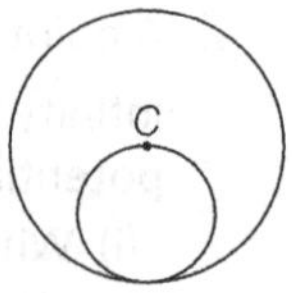

8 A charge Q is uniformly distributed over a thin rod AB of length L as shown in the figure. Find the electric potential at point P.

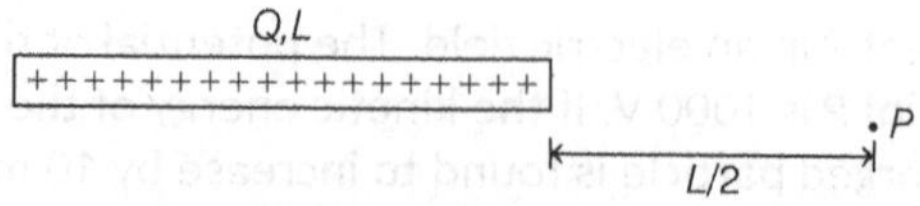

2.4 *Potential Difference*

1 20 J of work has to be done against an existing electric field to take a charge of 0.05 C from A to B. How much is the potential difference $V_B - V_A$?

2 An electron is accelerated through a potential difference of 45.5 V from rest. Find its final kinetic energy and speed.

3 The kinetic energy of a charged particle decreases by 20 J as it moves from a point at potential 50 V to a point at potential 100 V. Find the charge on the particle .

4 A particle of charge $+3 \times 10^{-9}$ C is in a uniform field directed to the left. It is released from rest and moves a distance of 5 cm, after which its kinetic energy is found to be 4.5×10^{-5} J.

(i) What work was done by the electrical force?

(ii) What is the magnitude of the electrical field?

(iii) What is the potential of the starting point with respect to the end point?

5 In the previous problem, suppose that another force in addition to the electrical force acts on the particle, so that when it is released from rest, it moves to the right. After, it has moved 5 cm, the additional force has done 9×10^{-5} J of work and the particle has 4.5×10^{-5} J of kinetic energy.

(i) What work was done by the electrical force?

(ii) What is the magnitude of the electric field?

(iii) What is the potential of the starting point with respect to the end point?

6 A charge of 8 mC is located at the origin. Find the work done by external agent in slowly taking a small charge of -2×10^{-9} C from a point A(0,0,0.03 m) to a point B(0,0.04m,0) *via* a point C(0,0.06m, 0.09m).

7 Four charges $+q, +q, -q, -q$ are fixed respectively at the corners A, B, C and D of a square of side a arranged in the given order. If E and F are the mid-points of sides BC, CD respectively, what will be the work done by external agent in carrying a charge Q slowly from E to F?

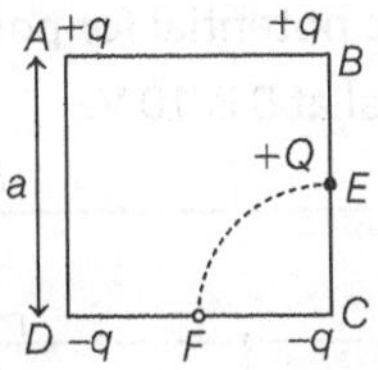

8 Two rings, each of radius R carry charges $+Q$ and $-Q$, respectively and they are held fixed with their planes parallel, such that their axes coincide and their centres are $\sqrt{3}R$ distance apart. Find the work done by external agent in slowly shifting a test charge $+q$ from the centre of the second ring to the centre of the first ring.

2.5 Potential Energy of a Point Charge

1 An α-particle is placed in an electric field at a point having electric potential 5 V. Find its potential energy.

2 Find the potential energy of a charge q_0 placed at the centre of regular hexagon of side a, if charge q is placed at each vertex of regular hexagon.

3 A particle of mass 2 g and charge 1 μC is held at rest on a frictionless horizontal surface at a distance of 1 m from a fixed charge 1 mC. If the particle is released, it will be repelled. Find the speed of the particle, when it is at distance of 10 m from the fixed charge.

4 Two identical charges $+5$ μC each are fixed at a distance 8 cm and a charged particle of mass 9×10^{-6} kg and charge -10 μC is placed at a distance 5 cm from each of them and is released from rest. Find the speed of the particle, when it is nearest to the two charges.

5 A particle of mass m, charge $q > 0$ and initial kinetic energy K is projected from infinity towards a heavy nucleus of charge Q assumed to have a fixed position. If the aim is perfect, find the distance of the closest approach.

6 A small point charge ($+q = 1$ μC, $m = 3$ kg) is thrown with speed $v_0 = 2$ m/s from a very long distance towards a fixed point charge ($+Q = 1$ mC). The initial line of motion of q is at a perpendicular distance of $d = 1$ m from the line passing from the centre of Q (as shown in figure). Find the distance of the closest approach between two point charges.

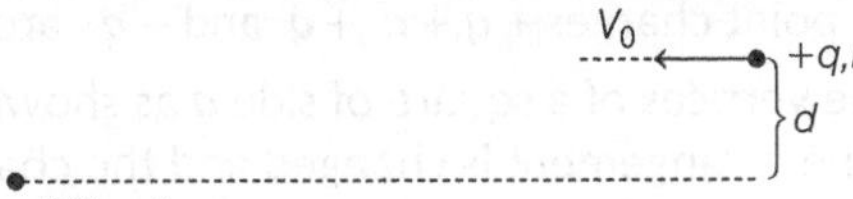

7 A particle having charge $-q$ and mass m is released from rest on the axis of a uniformly charged fixed ring of total charge Q and radius R from a distance $\sqrt{3}R$. Find out its speed, when it reaches the centre of ring.

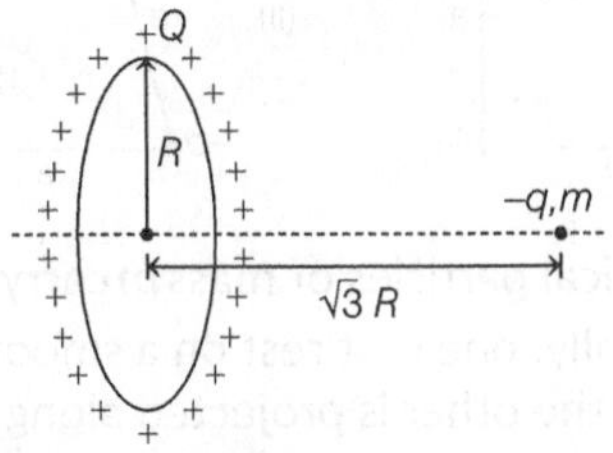

8 A solid uniformly charged fixed non-conducting sphere of total charge Q and radius R contains a tunnel of negligible diameter. If a point charge q of mass m is projected from point P as shown in figure, then find the minimum speed of projection u_{min}, so that the point charge comes out of the tunnel from the other end.

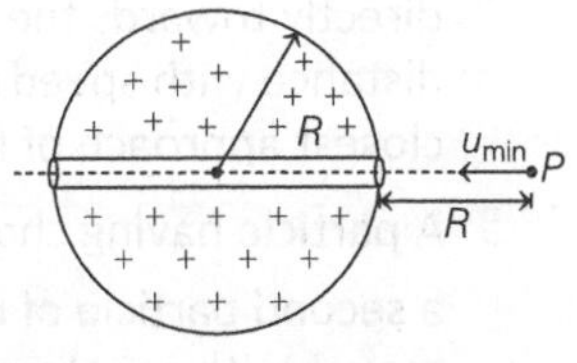

2.6 Potential Energy of a System of Point Charges

1 Calculate the electrostatic potential energy of the following systems of point charges.

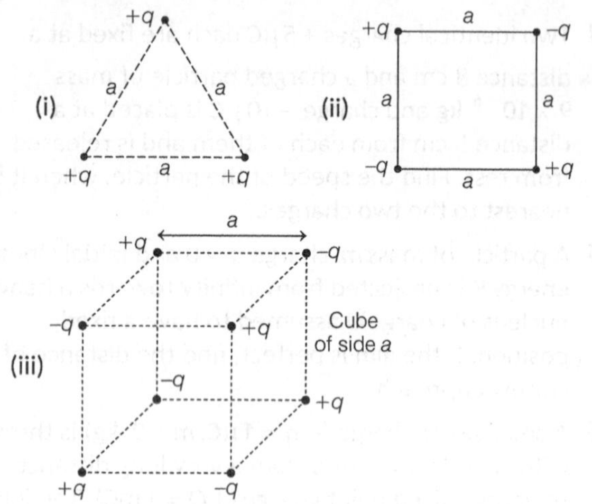

2 Two point charges $+15\ \mu C$ and $+10\ \mu C$ are 30 cm apart. Calculate the work done in bringing them closer to each other by 15 cm.

3 Four point charges $+q, +q, +q$ and $-q$ are placed at the vertices of a square of side a as shown in Fig. (i). The arrangement is changed and the charges are positioned at the vertices of a rhombus of side a as shown in Fig.(ii). Find the work done by external agent in changing the configuration.

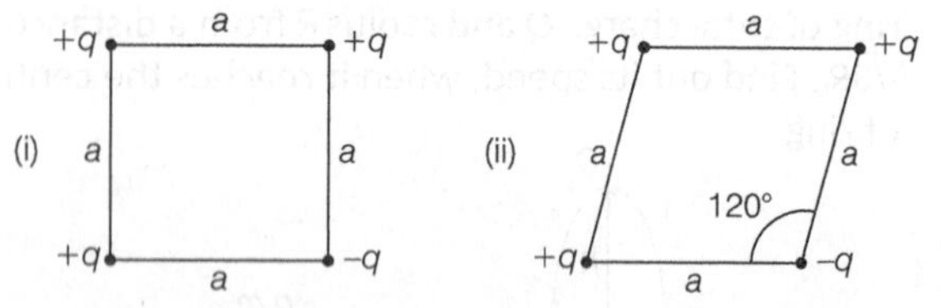

4 Two identical particles of mass m carry a charge Q each. Initially, one is at rest on a smooth horizontal plane and the other is projected along the plane directly towards the first particle from a large distance with speed u. Find the distance of the closest approach of them.

5 A particle having charge $+q$ is fixed at a point O and a second particle of mass m and having charge $-q_0$ moves with constant speed in a circle of radius r about the charge $+q$. Find energy required to be supplied to the moving charge to increase radius of the path to $2r$.

6 Three point charges each of charge $+20\ \mu C$ and mass 10 g are placed at the corners of an equilateral triangle of side 10 cm.

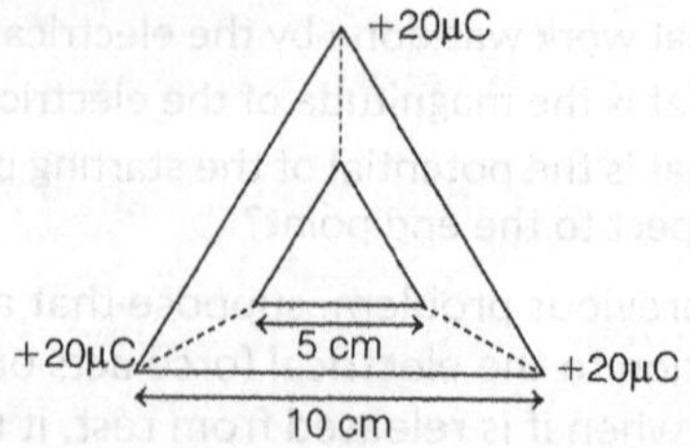

(i) Calculate the work required to move these charges to the corners of a smaller equilateral triangle of side 5 cm as shown in adjacent figure.

(ii) If all the charges are released from rest, when they are on equilateral triangle of side 10 cm, find their speeds when they lie on an equilateral triangle of side 20 cm.

(iii) If all the charges are released from rest, when they are on equilateral triangle of side 10 cm, find their speeds when they are at very large distance from each other.

(iv) If one of the charges is released from rest and the other two are held fixed when they are on equilateral triangle of side 10 cm, find its speed, when it reaches infinity.

2.7 Relation between Electric Field and Electric Potential

1 Find out electric potential for points A, C and D, if electric potential at B is 10 V.

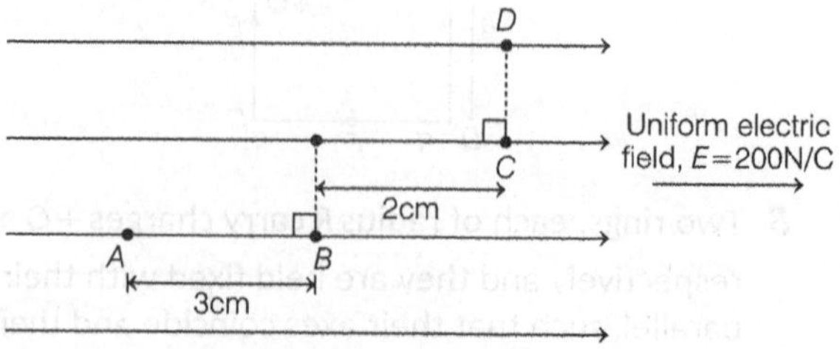

2 A uniform field of 8 N/C exists in space in positive x-direction.

(i) Taking the potential at the origin to be zero, write an expression for the potential at a general point (x, y, z).

(ii) If the potential at the origin is taken to be 80 V, what will be the expression for the potential at a general point?

(iii) What will be the potential at the origin, if the potential at infinity is taken to be zero?

3 An electric field $\mathbf{E} = (10\hat{\mathbf{i}} + 20\hat{\mathbf{j}})$ N/C exists in the space. If the potential at the origin is taken to be 100 V, find the potential at (3m, 4m).

4 If $\mathbf{E} = 6x^2\hat{\mathbf{i}} - 3y^2\hat{\mathbf{j}}$, then find $V(x, y)$.

5 If $\mathbf{E} = 2y\hat{\mathbf{i}} + 2x\hat{\mathbf{j}}$, then find $V(x, y)$, if the potential at (2,3) is 100 V.

6 If $V = x^2y + y^2z$, then find $\mathbf{E}(x, y, z)$.

7 The electric potential existing in space is $V(x, y, z) = 2(xy + yz + zx)$. Find the magnitude of the electric field at (5m, 7m, – 1 m).

8 A uniformly charged thin non-conducting infinite sheet of surface charge density σ is kept as shown in figure. Find the potential difference between points P and Q.

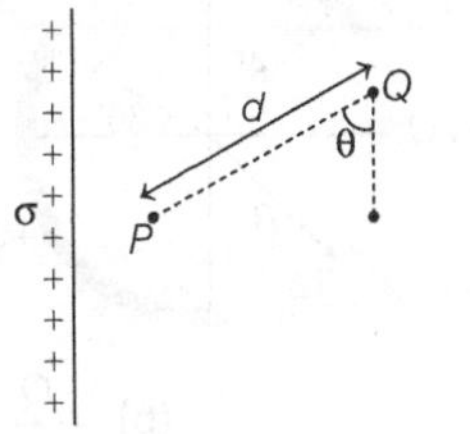

9 An infinite line of charge having charge density λ is lying along Y-axis. Find the work required in moving charge q from C to A along arc CA.

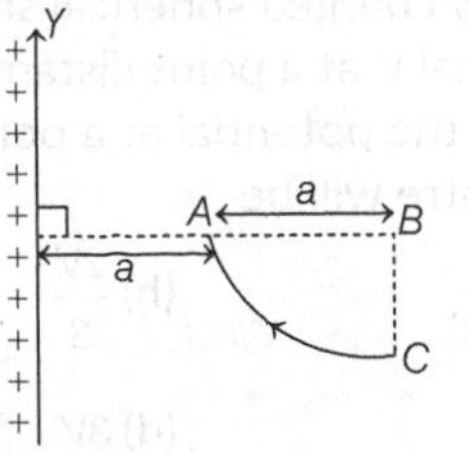

2.8 *Equipotential Surfaces*

1 Some equipotential surfaces are shown in the figure.
 (i) Compare electric field intensities at points A, B and C.
 (ii) Find the work done by external agent in shifting $+4\,\mu$C charge slowly from P to Q along the dotted path as shown in the figure.

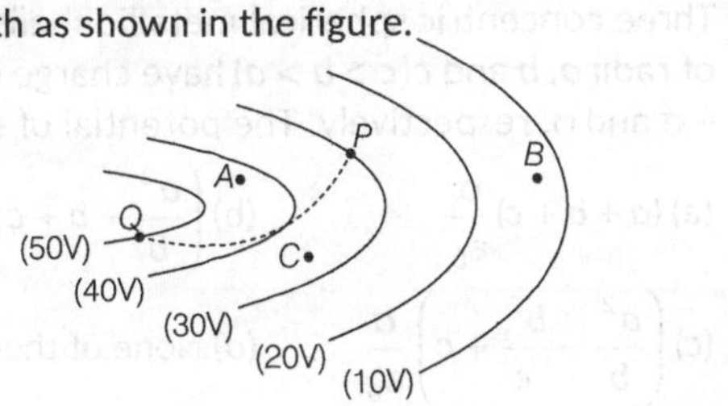

2 Some equipotential surfaces which are parallel planes are shown in figure.

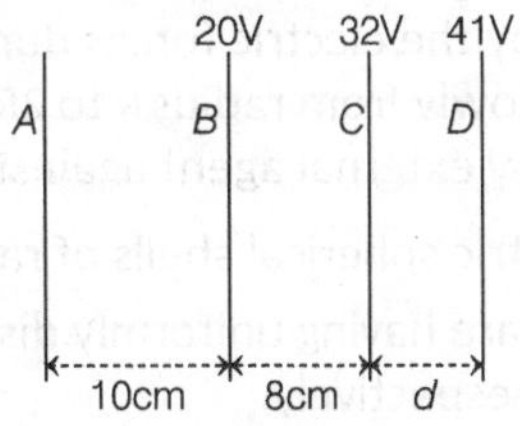

Find
 (i) magnitude and direction of electric field,
 (ii) separation d between equipotential surfaces C and D and
 (iii) potential of equipotential surface A.

3 Some equipotential surfaces are shown in figure. Find the magnitude and direction of the electric field.

(i)

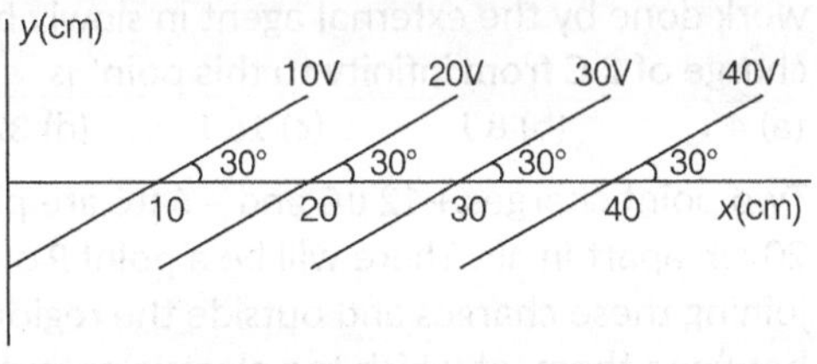

(ii)

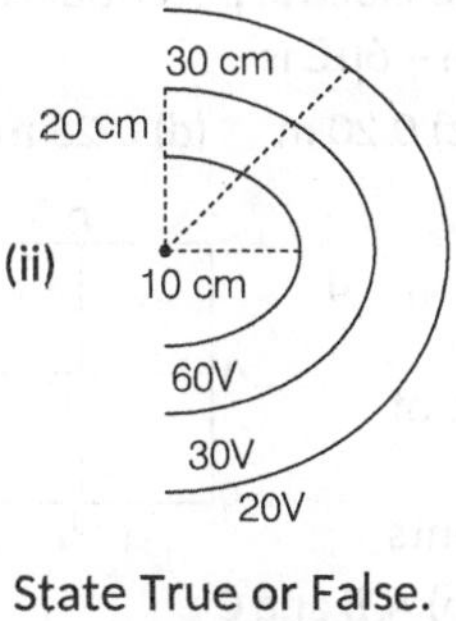

4 State True or False.
 (i) Equipotential surfaces and electric field lines cut at right angle.
 (ii) Two equipotential surfaces never intersect each other.
 (iii) Work done by external agent in shifting a test charge from one point to another on an equipotential surface is always zero.
 (iv) Electric field intensity is higher, where equipotential surfaces are closer.

2.9 *Self-Energy*

1 Find self-energy of the following.
 (i) Uniformly charged thin spherical shell of radius R carrying charge Q.
 (ii) Uniformly charged solid non-conducting sphere of radius R carrying charge Q.

2 A spherical shell of radius R with a uniform charge q has point charge q_0 at its centre. Find the work performed by the electric forces during the shell expansion slowly from radius R to $2R$. Also, find out work done by external agent against electric forces.

3 Two concentric spherical shells of radius R_1 and $R_2 (R_2 > R_1)$ are having uniformly distributed charges Q_1 and Q_2, respectively.

Find out total energy of the system.

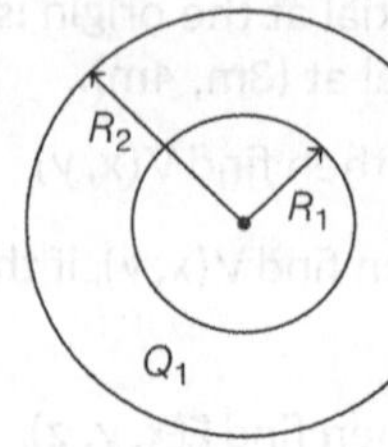

LEVEL 02 JEE Main Level

Single Choice Correct Questions

1 The electric field intensity at a point at a distance 2 m from a point charge q is 4 N/C. The amount of work done by the external agent in slowly bringing a charge of 2 C from infinity to this point is

(a) 4 J (b) 8 J (c) 16 J (d) 32 J

2 Two point charges + 12 μC and − 6 μC are placed 20 cm apart in air. There will be a point P on the line joining these charges and outside the region between them, at which the electric potential is zero. The distance of P from − 6μC is

(a) 0.10 m (b) 0.15 m (c) 0.20 m (d) 0.25 m

3 Figure represents a square carrying charges $+q, +q, -q, -q$ at its four corners as shown. A, C, P and Q are mid-points of respective sides. Then, the potential will be zero at points

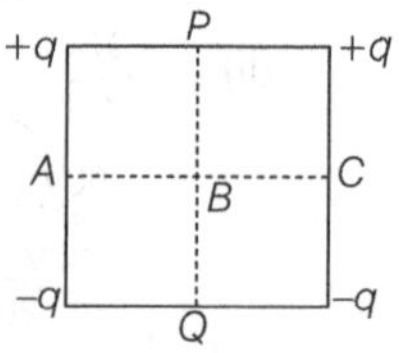

(a) A, B, C, P and Q (b) A, B and C
(c) A, P, C and Q (d) P, B and Q

4 In a regular polygon of n sides, each corner is at a distance r from the centre. Identical charges are placed at $(n-1)$ corners. At the centre, the intensity is E and the potential is V. The ratio V/E has magnitude

(a) rn (b) $r(n-1)$
(c) $(n-1)/r$ (d) $r(n-1)/n$

5 An infinite number of concentric rings carry a charge Q each alternately positive and negative. Their radii are 1m, 2m, 4m, 8m, ..., in geometric progression as shown in the figure. The potential at the centre of the rings will be

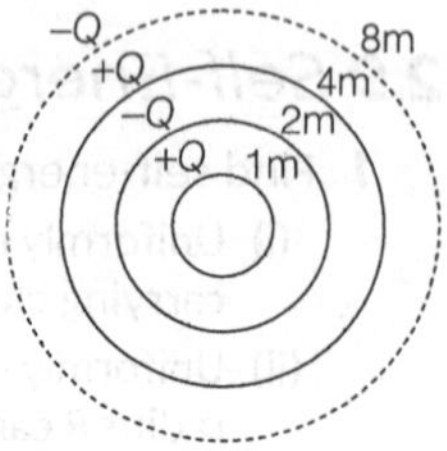

(a) zero (b) $\dfrac{Q}{12\pi\varepsilon_0}$ (c) $\dfrac{Q}{8\pi\varepsilon_0}$ (d) $\dfrac{Q}{6\pi\varepsilon_0}$

6 Figure shows three circular arcs, each of radius R and total charge as indicated. The net electric potential at the centre of curvature is

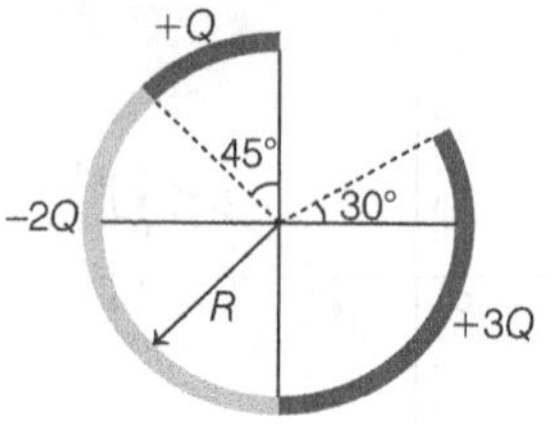

(a) $\dfrac{Q}{2\pi\varepsilon_0 R}$ (b) $\dfrac{Q}{4\pi\varepsilon_0 R}$

(c) $\dfrac{2Q}{\pi\varepsilon_0 R}$ (d) $\dfrac{Q}{\pi\varepsilon_0 R}$

7 If a uniformly charged spherical shell of radius 10 cm has a potential V at a point distant 5 cm from its centre, then the potential at a point distant 15 cm from the centre will be

(a) $\dfrac{V}{3}$ (b) $\dfrac{2V}{3}$

(c) $\dfrac{3}{2}V$ (d) $3V$

8 A solid sphere of radius R is charged uniformly. At what distance from its surface is the electrostatic potential half of the potential at the centre?

(a) R (b) $R/2$
(c) $R/3$ (d) $2R$

9 Three concentric spherical metallic shells A, B and C of radii a, b and $c (c > b > a)$ have charge densities σ, $-\sigma$ and σ, respectively. The potential of shell B is

(a) $(a+b+c)\dfrac{\sigma}{\varepsilon_0}$ (b) $\left(\dfrac{a^2}{b} - b + c\right)\dfrac{\sigma}{\varepsilon_0}$

(c) $\left(\dfrac{a^2}{b} - \dfrac{b^2}{c} + c\right)\dfrac{\sigma}{\varepsilon_0}$ (d) None of these

10 A total charge Q is distributed over two concentric hollow spheres of radii a and b $(b > a)$, such a way that their surface charge densities are equal. The potential at the common centre is given by

(a) $\frac{Q}{4\pi\varepsilon_0} \cdot \frac{(a+b)}{(a^2+b^2)}$ (b) $\frac{Q}{4\pi\varepsilon_0} \cdot \frac{(b-a)}{(a^2+b^2)}$

(c) $\frac{Q}{4\pi\varepsilon_0} \cdot \frac{(a+b)}{(a+b)^2}$ (d) $\frac{Q}{4\pi\varepsilon_0} \cdot \frac{(b-a)}{(a+b)^2}$

11 A wire having a uniform linear charge density λ is bent into the shape as shown in figure. Find the electric potential at point O.

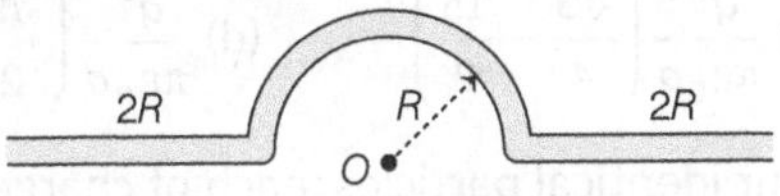

(a) $\frac{\lambda}{2\pi\varepsilon_0}(\pi + \ln 3)$ (b) $\frac{\lambda}{2\pi\varepsilon_0}(\pi + 2\ln 3)$

(c) $\frac{\lambda}{4\pi\varepsilon_0}(\pi + 2\ln 3)$ (d) $\frac{\lambda}{4\pi\varepsilon_0}(\pi + \ln 3)$

12 A charge is uniformly distributed inside a spherical body of radius $r_1 = 2r_0$ having a concentric cavity of radius $r_2 = r_0$ (ρ is charge density inside the sphere). Potential of a point P at a distance $\frac{3r_0}{2}$ from centre is

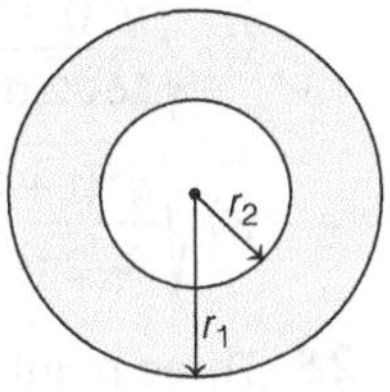

(a) $\frac{7\rho r_0^2}{6\varepsilon_0}$ (b) $\frac{101\rho r_0^2}{72\varepsilon_0}$

(c) $\frac{17\rho r_0^2}{72\varepsilon_0}$ (d) $\frac{84\rho r_0^2}{72\varepsilon_0}$

13 Consider a uniformly charged thin hemispherical shell. A, B and C are three points on the circular base of hemisphere, such that A is the centre. Let the potential at points A, B and C be V_A, V_B and V_C, respectively. Then,

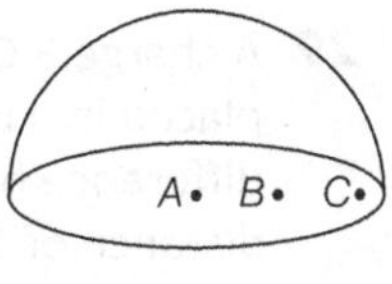

(a) $V_A > V_B > V_C$ (b) $V_C > V_B > V_A$

(c) $V_B > V_A$ and $V_B > V_C$ (d) $V_A = V_B = V_C$

14 Choose the correct statement.

(a) Wherever electric field is zero, potential has to be zero.

(b) Wherever potential is zero, electric field has to be zero.

(c) If electric field is constant in some part of space, electric potential will be zero in that space.

(d) If electric potential is constant in some part of space, electric field will be zero in that space.

15 If a charge is shifted from a low potential region to high potential region, the electrical potential energy

(a) increases (b) decreases

(c) remains constant (d) may increase or decrease

16 A ball of mass 1 g and charge 10^{-8} C moves from a point $A(V_A = 600 \text{ V})$ to the point B whose potential is zero. Velocity of the ball at the point B is 20 cm/s. The velocity of the ball at the point A is

(a) 16.7 m/s (b) 16.7 cm/s (c) 2.8 m/s (d) 2.8 cm/s

17 When a negative charge is released and moves in electric field, it moves toward a position of

(a) lower electric potential and lower potential energy

(b) lower electric potential and higher potential energy

(c) higher electric potential and lower potential energy

(d) higher electric potential and higher potential energy

18 A particle of charge Q and mass m travels through a potential difference V from rest. The final linear momentum of the particle is

(a) $\frac{mV}{Q}$ (b) $2Q\sqrt{mV}$ (c) $\sqrt{2mQV}$ (d) $\sqrt{\frac{2QV}{m}}$

19 A particle A has charge $+q$ and particle B has charge $+4q$ with each of them having the same mass m. When allowed to fall from rest through same electrical potential difference, the ratio of their speed $v_A : v_B$ will be

(a) 2 : 1 (b) 1 : 2 (c) 4 : 1 (d) 1 : 4

20 An α-particle moves towards a nucleus always at rest. The kinetic energy of the α-particle at a large distance is 10 MeV. If the atomic number of the nucleus is 50, then the minimum distance of approach is

(a) 1.44×10^{-14} m (b) 2.88×10^{-14} m

(c) 1.44×10^{-10} m (d) 2.88×10^{-10} m

21 Three particles of charge $+2Q$, $-Q$ and $-Q$ are placed at the corners of an equilateral triangle ABC as shown in the figure. Now, a fourth particle of charge $+Q$ is to be moved slowly from the centroid G to the mid-point D of side BC of the triangle. The work done by the external agent in order to move this fourth charge is given by

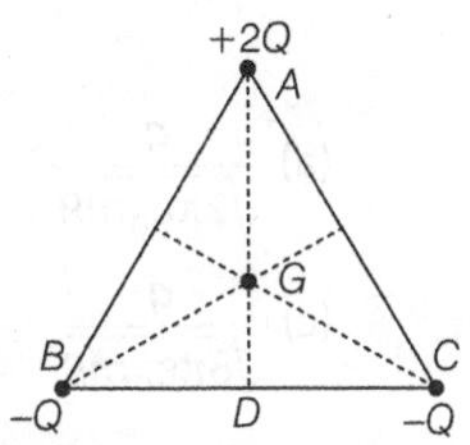

(a) $W = \frac{Q^2}{\pi\varepsilon_0 a}$ (b) $W = \frac{-Q^2}{\pi\varepsilon_0 a}\left(1 - \frac{1}{\sqrt{3}}\right)$

(c) $W = \frac{Q^2}{\pi\varepsilon_0 a}\left(1 - \frac{1}{\sqrt{3}}\right)$ (d) $W = \frac{Q^2}{\pi\varepsilon_0 a}$

22 A point charge Q is fixed. A small charge q and mass m is given a velocity v_0 from infinity and perpendicular distance r_0 as shown in figure. If distance of closest approach is $r_0/2$, the value of q is (Given, $mv_0^2 = \frac{Q^2}{4\pi\varepsilon_0 r_0}$)

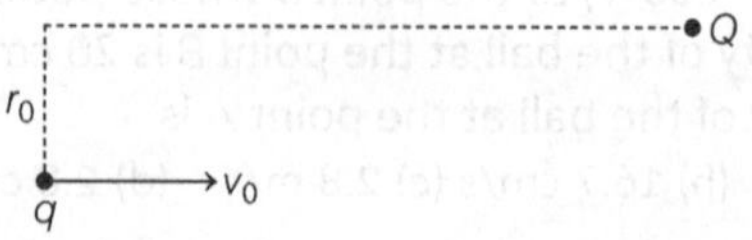

(a) $q = -\frac{Q}{4}$ (b) $q = -\frac{Q}{2}$

(c) $q = -\frac{3Q}{4}$ (d) $q = -Q$

23 A point charge q and mass m is just dropped from a height $a = 4R/3$ above a ring of charge Q and radius R. If q just reaches the centre of the ring, the value of q is (Given, $\frac{Q^2}{4\pi\varepsilon_0 R^2} = mg$)

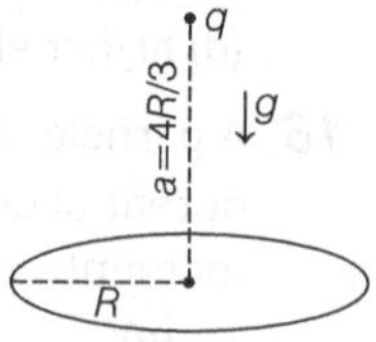

(a) $\frac{Q}{3}$ (b) $3Q$ (c) $\frac{10Q}{3}$ (d) $\frac{3Q}{10}$

24 A bullet of mass m and charge q is fired towards a solid uniformly charged sphere of radius R and total charge $+q$. If it strikes the surface of sphere with speed u, find the minimum speed u, so that it can penetrate through the sphere. (Neglect all resistance forces or friction acting on bullet except electrostatic forces.)

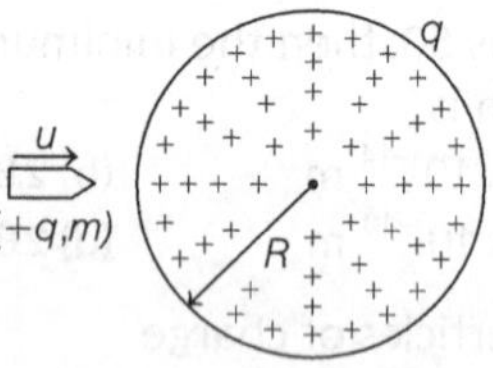

(a) $\frac{q}{\sqrt{2\pi\varepsilon_0 mR}}$ (b) $\frac{q}{\sqrt{4\pi\varepsilon_0 mR}}$

(c) $\frac{q}{\sqrt{8\pi\varepsilon_0 mR}}$ (d) $\frac{\sqrt{3}q}{\sqrt{4\pi\varepsilon_0 mR}}$

25 Three point charges Q, q and q are placed at the vertices of a right angle isosceles triangle as shown in figure. The net electrostatic energy of the configuration is zero, if q/Q is equal to

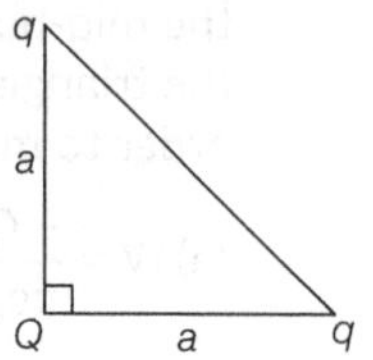

(a) -1 (b) $-\sqrt{2}$ (c) -2 (d) $-2\sqrt{2}$

26 Six charges of magnitude $+q$ and $-q$ are fixed at the corners of a regular hexagon of edge length a as shown in the figure. The electrostatic potential energy of the system of charged particles is

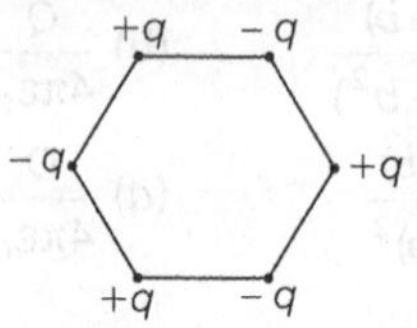

(a) $\frac{q^2}{\pi\varepsilon_0 a}\left(\frac{\sqrt{3}}{8} - \frac{15}{4}\right)$ (b) $\frac{q^2}{\pi\varepsilon_0 a}\left(\frac{\sqrt{3}}{2} - \frac{9}{4}\right)$

(c) $\frac{q^2}{\pi\varepsilon_0 a}\left(\frac{\sqrt{3}}{4} - \frac{15}{2}\right)$ (d) $\frac{q^2}{\pi\varepsilon_0 a}\left(\frac{\sqrt{3}}{2} - \frac{15}{8}\right)$

27 Four identical particles, each of charge q and mass m are released from rest simultaneously at the vertices of a square of side L. When their distance from the centre of the square doubles, the speed of each particle is

(a) $\sqrt{\frac{q^2(1+2\sqrt{2})}{16\sqrt{2}\pi\varepsilon_0 mL}}$ (b) $\sqrt{\frac{q^2(1+2\sqrt{2})}{16\pi\varepsilon_0 mL}}$

(c) $\sqrt{\frac{q^2(1+2\sqrt{2})}{8\sqrt{2}\pi\varepsilon_0 mL}}$ (d) $\sqrt{\frac{q^2(1+2\sqrt{2})}{4\sqrt{2}\pi\varepsilon_0 mL}}$

28 Three point charges q, $2q$ and $8q$ are to be placed on a straight line 9 cm long. The system possesses minimum potential energy, when

(a) $2q$ and q lie at ends with $8q$ at 3 cm from $2q$

(b) $2q$ and $8q$ lie at ends with q at 6 cm from $8q$

(c) q and $8q$ lie at ends with $2q$ at 6 cm from q

(d) $2q$ and $8q$ lie at ends with q at 3 cm from $8q$

29 A charge 3 C experiences a force 3000 N, when placed in a uniform electric field. The potential difference between two points separated by a distance of 1 cm along the field lines is

(a) 10 V (b) 90 V

(c) 1000 V (d) 9000 V

30 There is a uniform electric field in x-direction. If the work done by external agent in moving a charge of 0.2 C through a distance of 2 m slowly along the line making an angle of 60° with x-direction is 4 J, then the magnitude of E is

(a) $\sqrt{3}$N/C

(b) 4 N/C

(c) 5 N/C

(d) 20 N/C

31 The potential difference between points A and B in the given uniform electric field is

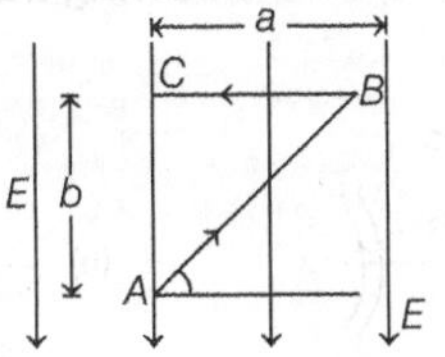

(a) Ea (b) Eb

(c) $E\sqrt{(a^2+b^2)}$ (d) $Eb/\sqrt{2}$

32 Let V_0 be the potential at the origin in an electric field $\mathbf{E} = E_x\hat{\mathbf{i}} + E_y\hat{\mathbf{j}}$. The potential at the point (x, y) is

(a) $V_0 - xE_x - yE_y$

(b) $V_0 + xE_x + yE_y$

(c) $xE_x + yE_y - V_0$

(d) $(\sqrt{x^2+y^2})\sqrt{E_x^2+E_y^2} - V_0$

33 Electric potential at (x, y, z) is given as $V = -xy^2\sqrt{z}$. The electric field at (2, 1, 1) is

(a) $\hat{\mathbf{i}} + 4\hat{\mathbf{j}} + \hat{\mathbf{k}}$ (b) $-\hat{\mathbf{i}} - 4\hat{\mathbf{j}} - 2\hat{\mathbf{k}}$

(c) $\hat{\mathbf{i}} + 2\hat{\mathbf{j}} + \hat{\mathbf{k}}$ (d) $-\hat{\mathbf{i}} - 2\hat{\mathbf{j}} - \hat{\mathbf{k}}$

34 Figure shows variation of potential V with distance y from origin along Y-axis. What is electric field at $y = 2.5$ m and $y = 5.5$ m?

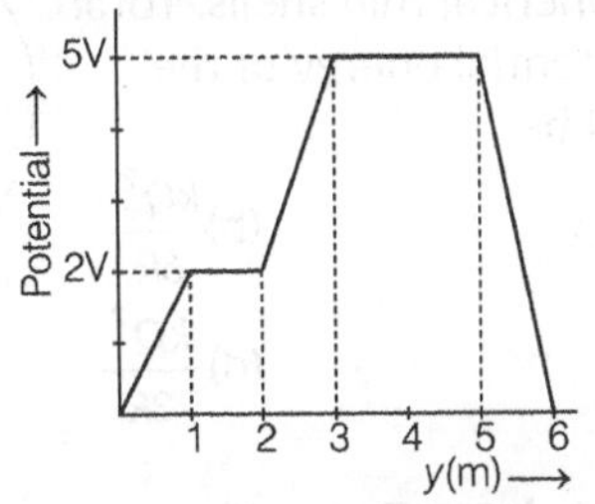

(a) $-3\hat{\mathbf{j}}, 5\hat{\mathbf{j}}$ (b) $2\hat{\mathbf{j}}, -5\hat{\mathbf{j}}$

(c) $3.5\hat{\mathbf{j}}, 2.5\hat{\mathbf{j}}$ (d) $3.5\hat{\mathbf{j}}, -2.5\hat{\mathbf{j}}$

35 There exists a uniform electric field in space. Electric field is parallel to XY-plane. The potential of points $A(2, 2)$, $B(-2, 2)$ and $C(2, 4)$ are 4 V, 16V and 12V, respectively. The electric field is

(a) $(4\hat{\mathbf{i}} + 5\hat{\mathbf{j}})$ V/m (b) $(3\hat{\mathbf{i}} + 4\hat{\mathbf{j}})$ V/m

(c) $-(3\hat{\mathbf{i}} + 4\hat{\mathbf{j}})$ V/m (d) $(3\hat{\mathbf{i}} - 4\hat{\mathbf{j}})$ V/m

36 Uniform electric field of magnitude 100 V/m in space is directed along the line $y = 3 + x$. Find the potential difference between points A (3, 1) and B (5, 3).

(a) 100 V (b) $200\sqrt{2}$ V

(c) 200 V (d) 0

37 A, B, C, D, P and Q are points in a uniform electric field. The potentials at these points are $V(A) = 2$ V, $V(P) = V(B) = V(D) = 5$ V and $V(C) = 8$ V. The electric field at P is

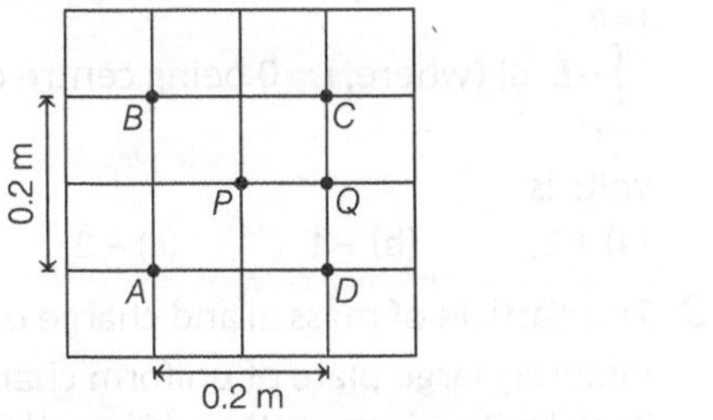

(a) 10 Vm^{-1} along PQ (b) $15\sqrt{2}$ Vm^{-1} along PA

(c) 5 Vm^{-1} along PC (d) 5 Vm^{-1} along PA

38 The equation of an equipotential line in an electric field is $y = 2x$, then the electric field strength vector at (1, 2) may be

(a) $4\hat{\mathbf{i}} + 8\hat{\mathbf{j}}$ (b) $4\hat{\mathbf{i}} - 8\hat{\mathbf{j}}$ (c) $8\hat{\mathbf{i}} + 4\hat{\mathbf{j}}$ (d) $-8\hat{\mathbf{i}} + 4\hat{\mathbf{j}}$

39 Figure shows equipotential surfaces for a two charges system. At which of the labelled points, will an electron have the highest potential energy?

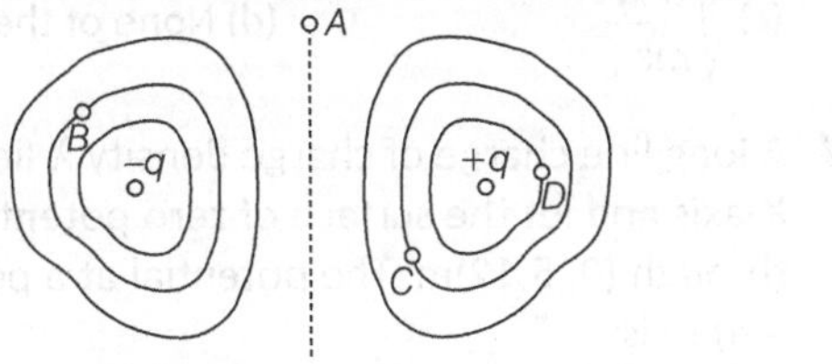

(a) Point A (b) Point B (c) Point C (d) Point D

40 An infinite non-conducting sheet of charge has a surface charge density of 10^{-7} C/m^2. The separation between two equipotential surfaces near the sheet whose potential differ by 5V is

(a) 0.88 cm (b) 0.88 mm (c) 0.88 m (d) 5×10^{-7} m

41 Figure below shows two equipotential lines in XY-plane for an electric field. The scales are marked. Electric field in the space between these equipotential lines are respectively

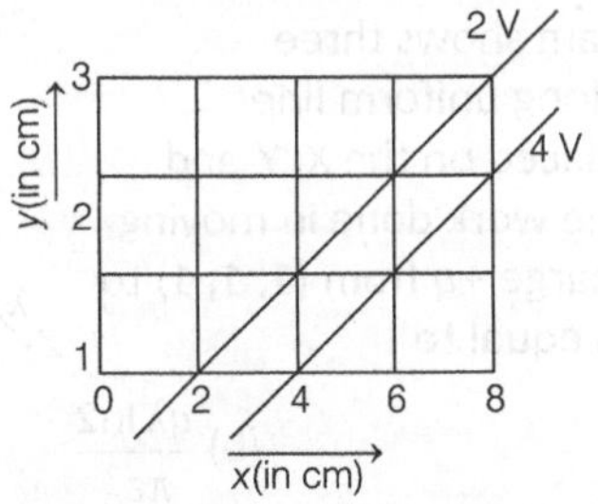

(a) $(100\hat{\mathbf{i}} - 200\hat{\mathbf{j}})$V/m (b) $(-100\hat{\mathbf{i}} + 200\hat{\mathbf{j}})$V/m

(c) $(200\hat{\mathbf{i}} + 100\hat{\mathbf{j}})$V/m (d) $(-200\hat{\mathbf{i}} - 100\hat{\mathbf{j}})$V/m

42 A non-conducting ring of radius 0.5 m carries a total charge of 1.11×10^{-10} C distributed non-uniformly on its circumference producing an electric field **E** everywhere in space. The value of the line integral $\int_{l=\infty}^{l=0} -\mathbf{E} \cdot d\mathbf{l}$ (where, $l = 0$ being centre of the ring) in volts is

(a) +2 (b) − 1 (c) − 2 (d) zero

43 The particle of mass m and charge q will touch the infinitely large plate of uniform charge density σ, if its velocity v is more than (Given that, $\sigma q > 0$)

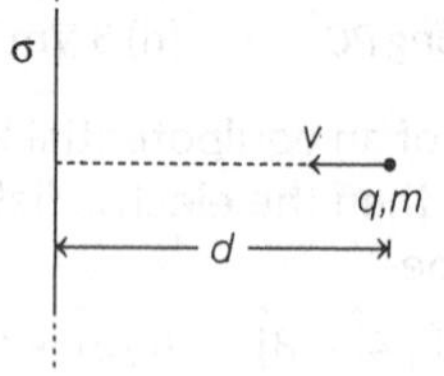

(a) zero (b) $\sqrt{\frac{2\sigma q d}{m\varepsilon_0}}$

(c) $\sqrt{\frac{\sigma q d}{m\varepsilon_0}}$ (d) None of these

44 A long line charge of charge density λ lies along the X-axis and let the surface of zero potential passes through (0, 5,12)m. The potential at a point (2, 3, – 4) m is

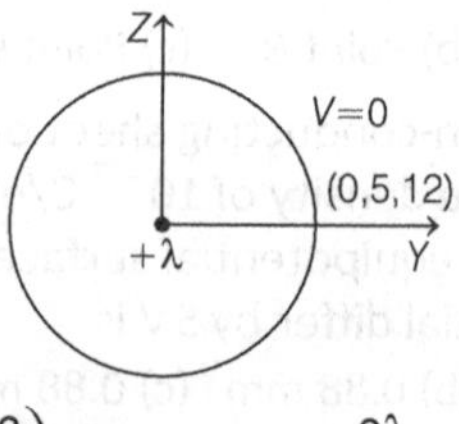

(a) $\frac{\lambda}{2\pi\varepsilon_0} \ln\left(\frac{13}{5}\right)$ (b) $\frac{2\lambda}{\pi\varepsilon_0} \ln\left(\frac{13}{5}\right)$

(c) $\frac{\lambda}{4\pi\varepsilon_0} \ln\left(\frac{13}{5}\right)$ (d) None of these

45 The diagram shows three infinitely long uniform line charges placed on the X, Y and Z-axes. The work done in moving a point charge $+q$ from (1, 1, 1) to (0, 1, 1) is equal to

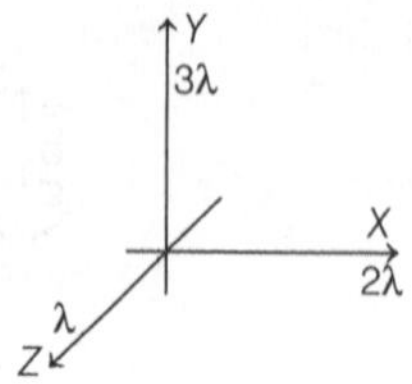

(a) $\frac{q\lambda \ln 2}{2\pi\varepsilon_0}$ (b) $\frac{q\lambda \ln 2}{\pi\varepsilon_0}$

(c) $\frac{3q\lambda \ln 2}{2\pi\varepsilon_0}$ (d) None of these

46 If the potential at any region varies in XY-plane as $V = axy$, which of the following field pattern is correct?

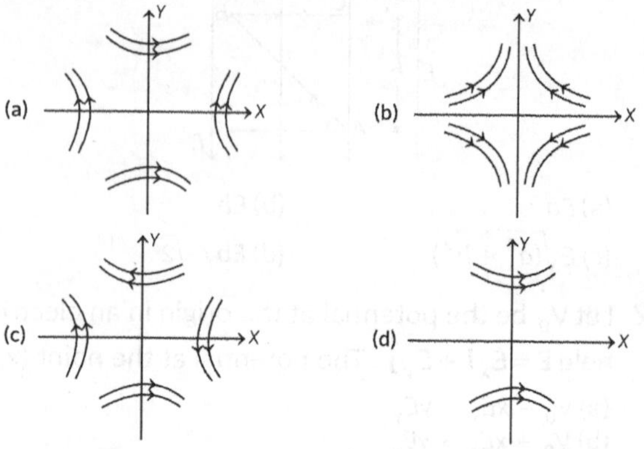

47 A soap bubble of spherical shape (radius R) is given charge Q as a result of which it expands to double its initial radius. The electrostatic potential energy stored in it will change by (as the radius expands from initial to final value)

(a) $\Delta U = \frac{-Q^2}{16\pi\varepsilon_0 R}$ (b) $\Delta U = \frac{Q^2}{8\pi\varepsilon_0 R}$

(c) $\Delta U = \frac{-Q^2}{4\pi\varepsilon_0 R}$ (d) $\Delta U = \frac{-Q^2}{32\pi\varepsilon_0 R}$

48 Shown in figure are two uniformly charged spherical thin shells. Total electric potential energy of the system will be

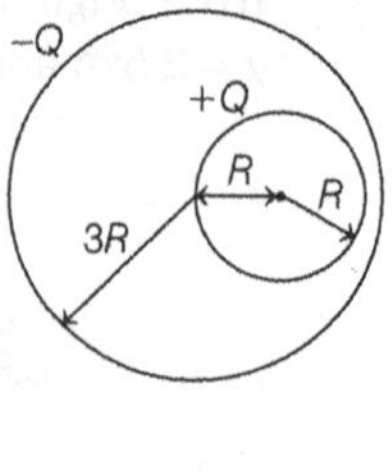

(a) $\frac{kQ^2}{12R}$ (b) $\frac{kQ^2}{6R}$

(c) $\frac{kQ^2}{2R}$ (d) $\frac{kQ^2}{3R}$

Numerical Value Questions

1 Two positive and two negative point charges $|Q| = 10$ nC are placed at the corners of a square insulator frame of side 5 m and the side of the frame are hinged together. The potential at the centre of the square frame is V_1. The frame is deformed into a rhombus as shown in figure. The potential at the centre of the rhombus frame is V_2. Find $V_2 - V_1$ (in volt).

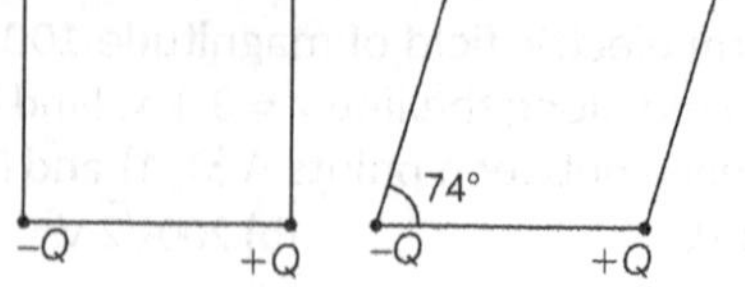

2 Two charges q and $-2q$ are placed at (–3, 0) and (3,0) in XY-plane. The locus of the point in the plane of the charges, where the field potential is zero is $(x+\alpha)^2 + y^2 = 4\beta^2$. Find the value of $(\alpha + \beta)$.

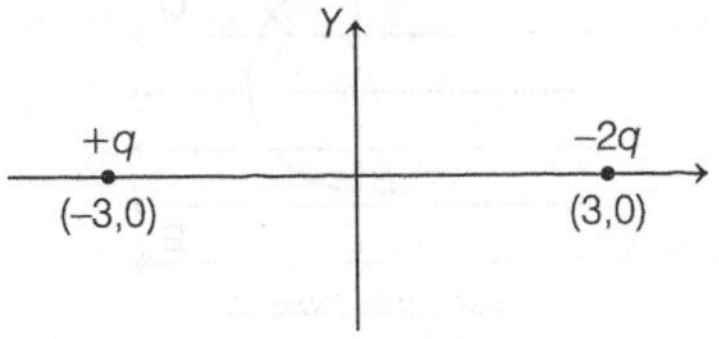

3 The charge on a ring of radius R varies according to the relation $\lambda = \lambda_0 \cos^2 \phi$, where λ_0 is a positive constant and ϕ is the azimuthal angle. The electric potential due to this ring at the centre is $\dfrac{\lambda_0}{n\varepsilon_0}$. Find the value of n.

4 A solid sphere of radius $\sqrt{60}$ cm is charged uniformly. Find the distance (in cm) of a point from its centre, where the electrostatic potential is 1.2 times the potential at the surface.

5 Figure shows the part of a hemisphere of radius $R = 2$ m and surface charge density $(\sigma) = 2\varepsilon_0 C/m^2$. Calculate the electric potential (in volt) at centre O.

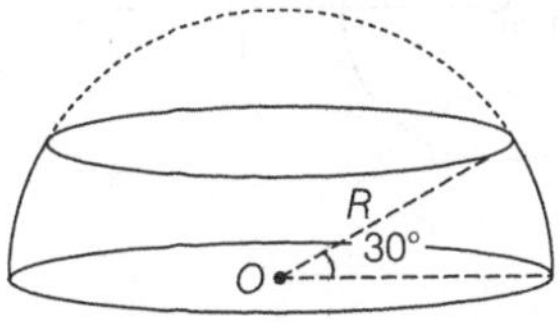

6 A positively charged particle starts at rest 25 cm from a second positively charged particle which is held stationary throughout the experiment. The first particle is released and accelerates directly away from the second particle. When the first particle has moved 25 cm, it has reached a velocity of $10\sqrt{2}$ m/s. What is the maximum velocity (in m/s) that the first particle will reach?

7 Two charge particles of opposite sign and magnitude Q each are projected directly away from each other with the same speed $\left(\dfrac{3Q^2}{32\pi\varepsilon_0 mr}\right)^{1/2}$, where r is the initial distance between the particles. Their masses are m and $2m$. The maximum distance between them is nr. Find the value of n.

8 Two small charged blocks of charges 5μC and 3μC are kept on a rough surface ($\mu = 0.5$) at a separation of 0.1 m. Find the separation (in cm) between the two blocks, when they come to rest.

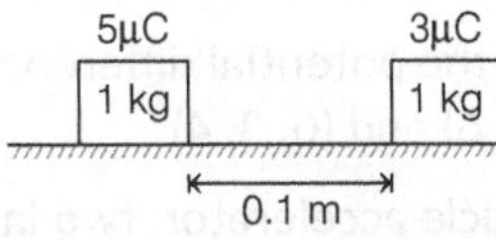

9 Two concentric rings of radii 2m and 4m are placed in YZ-plane with centre at origin and having charges $-\sqrt{2}$ μC and $+4$ μC, respectively. A particle with charge $+20\sqrt{6}$ μC and mass 10 g is thrown from a point far away from origin on X-axis towards origin. Find the minimum speed (in m/s) with which it is thrown, so that it will cross the origin.

10 Three charges 0.1 C each are placed on the corners of an equilateral triangle of side 1 m. If the energy is supplied to this system at the rate of 10 kW, how much time (in h) would be required to move one of the charges onto the mid-point of the line joining the other two?

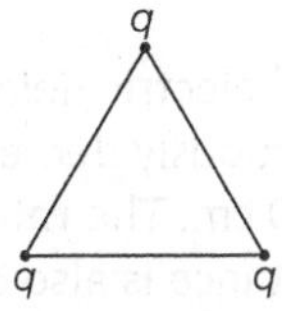

11 In a uniform electric field, the potential is 100 V at the origin of coordinates and 84 V at each of the points (1, 0, 0), (0, 2, 0) and (0, 0, 8). Find the potential (in V) at the point (3, 4, 5).

12 The electric potential (in volt) in a region is given by $V = 6x - 8xy^2 - 8y + 6yz - 4x^2$. Find electric force (in N) acting on a point charge of 2C placed at the origin.

13 A graph of the x-component of the electric field as a function of x in a region of space is shown. The y and z-components of the electric field are zero in this region. If the electric potential is 50 V at the origin, then find the potential (in V) at $x = 2.0$ m.

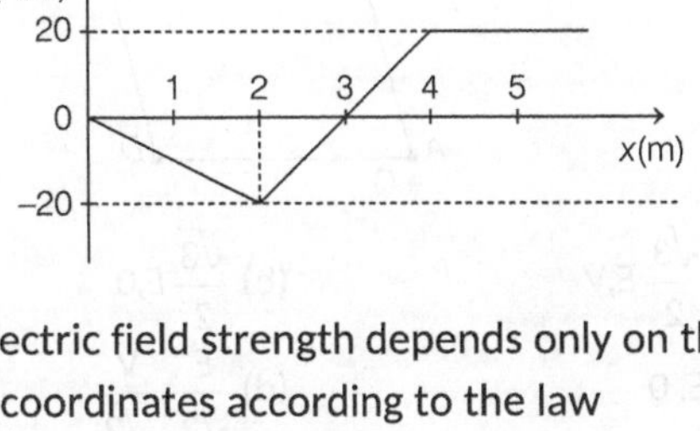

14 The electric field strength depends only on the x, y and z-coordinates according to the law

$E = \dfrac{a(x\hat{i} + y\hat{j} + z\hat{k})}{(x^2 + y^2 + z^2)^{3/2}}$, where $a = 280\ \text{Nm}^2/\text{C}$ is a constant. Find the potential difference (in V) between (3, 2, 6) and (0, 3, 4).

15 In a linear particle accelerator, two large plane uniformly charged are placed parallel to each other as shown in the figure. Figure also shows variation of potential between planes. A charged particle carrying a charge $q = 1.6 \times 10^{-19}$ C and having mass $m = 16 \times 10^{-31}$ kg is released from rest at $x = -10$ cm, determine time taken (in ns) by particle to strike the other plane. Neglect relativistic considerations.

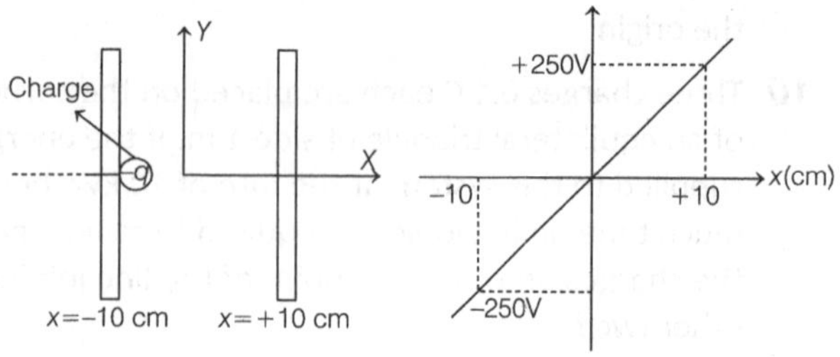

16 For a hypothetical electric field in x-direction, its potential is continuously decreasing and becoming half after every 20 cm. The rate of decreasing of potential with distance is also directly proportional to the potential itself. If the ratio of electric field and potential is $x \ln 2 (\text{m}^{-1})$. Find the value of x.

17 The charge $Q = \pi$ C is distributed on a thin semi-circular ring of radius $R = 2$m.

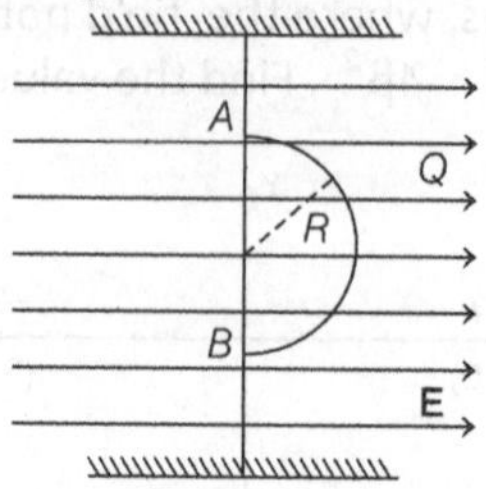

There is a uniform electrostatic field $|\mathbf{E}| = 2$N/C directed horizontally. The semi-circular ring can rotate freely about a fixed vertical axis AB. Initially, the ring is in static equilibrium as shown in figure. If we want to rotate it about the fixed axis by 90°, then minimum work required on the ring is x J. Find the value of x.

18 A particle of mass 2 g and charge $+1\,\mu$C is projected towards a non-conducting fixed spherical shell having the charge $+3\mu$C uniformly distributed on its surface. Find the minimum initial velocity (in m/s) of projection required, if the particle just grazes the shell.

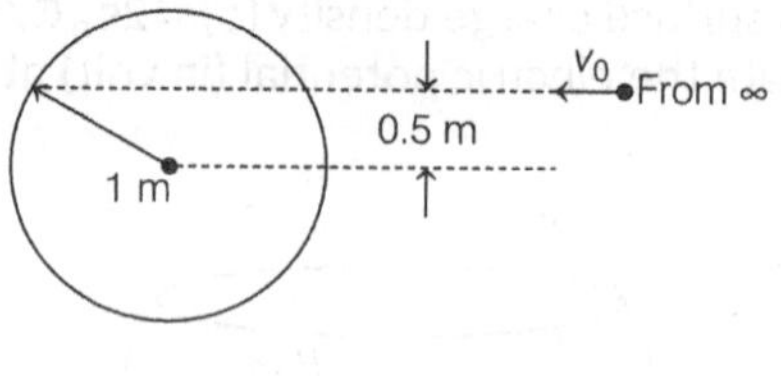

LEVEL 03 JEE Advanced Level

Single Choice Correct Questions

1 Consider a parallelogram $ABCD$, with angle $\angle B = 120°$. A charge $+Q$ placed at the corner A produces field E and potential V at corner D. If we now add charges $-2Q$ and $+Q$ at corners B and C respectively, then magnitude of field and potential at D will become respectively

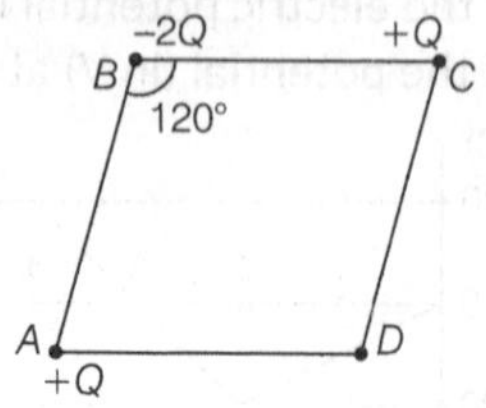

(a) $\dfrac{\sqrt{3}}{2}E, V$
(b) $\dfrac{\sqrt{3}}{2}E, 0$
(c) $E, 0$
(d) $\dfrac{E}{\sqrt{2}}, \dfrac{V}{\sqrt{2}}$

2 Two small equal point charges of magnitude q are suspended from a common point on the ceiling by insulating massless strings of equal lengths. They come to equilibrium with each string making angle θ from the vertical. If the mass of each charge is m, then the electrostatic potential at the centre of line joining them will be $\left(\dfrac{1}{4\pi\varepsilon_0} = k\right)$

(a) $2\sqrt{kmg \tan\theta}$
(b) $\sqrt{kmg \tan\theta}$
(c) $4\sqrt{kmg / \tan\theta}$
(d) $4\sqrt{kmg \tan\theta}$

3 In the diagram shown, there is a square, inside which there is another square and inside it there is another square and so on. On the vertex of each square, a charge is placed. On the vertex of the Nth square, a charge $+\frac{Q}{2^N}$ is placed. If the dimension of the outermost square is L and number of squares formed in this manner is infinite, then potential at the centre is

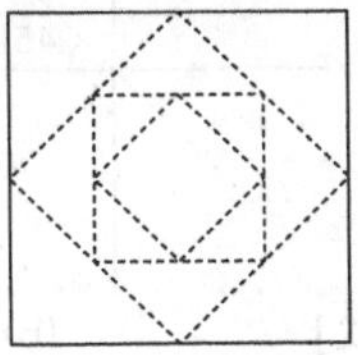

(a) $\frac{2Q(\sqrt{2}+1)}{\pi\varepsilon_0 L}$ (b) $\frac{Q(\sqrt{2}+1)}{\pi\varepsilon_0 L}$

(c) $\frac{4Q(\sqrt{2}+1)}{\pi\varepsilon_0 L}$ (d) None of these

4 A non-conducting semi-circular disc (as shown in figure) has a uniform surface charge density σ. The ratio of electric field to electric potential at the centre of the disc will be

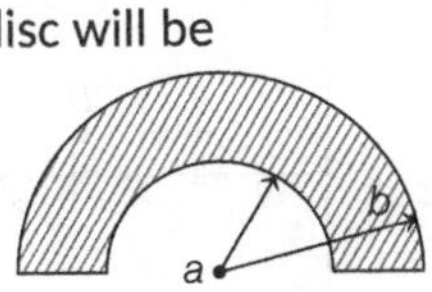

(a) $\frac{\ln b/a}{\pi(b-a)}$ (b) $\frac{2}{\pi}$

(c) $\frac{1}{\pi}\frac{\ln(b/a)^2}{(b-a)}$ (d) $\frac{\pi(b-a)}{2\ln(b/a)}$

5 A cone made of insulating material has a total charge Q spread uniformly over its sloping surface. The slant length is L. The energy required to take a test charge q from infinity to apex A of cone is

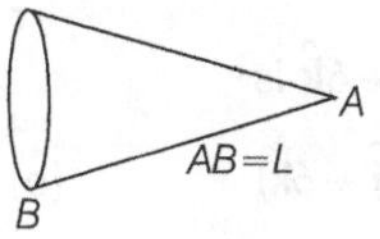

(a) $\frac{Qq}{2\pi\varepsilon_0 L}$ (b) $\frac{2Qq}{\pi\varepsilon_0 L}$

(c) $\frac{4Qq}{\pi\varepsilon_0 L}$ (d) $\frac{Qq}{\pi\varepsilon_0 L}$

6 The potential at the vertex A of a uniformly charged hemispherical surface of radius R and uniform surface charge density σ is

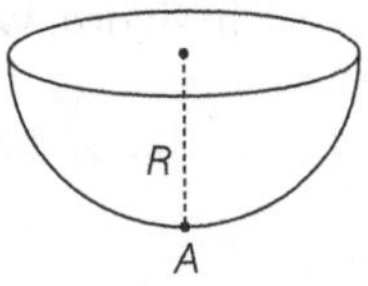

(a) $\frac{\sigma R}{2\varepsilon_0}$ (b) $\frac{2\sigma R}{\varepsilon_0}$

(c) $\frac{\sqrt{2}\sigma R}{\varepsilon_0}$ (d) $\frac{\sigma R}{\sqrt{2}\varepsilon_0}$

7 Q charge given to a uniform hemispherical charged distribution of radius R, then sum of potential at two diametrically opposite points $V_A + V_B$ is equal to

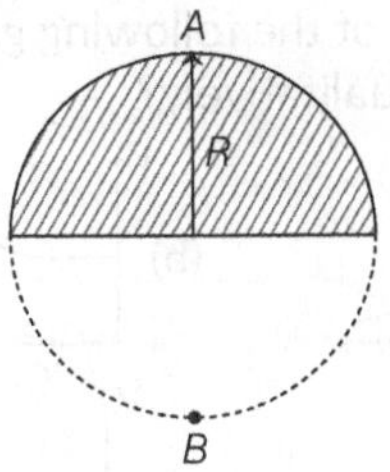

(a) $\frac{kQ}{R}$ (b) $\frac{2kQ}{R}$ (c) $\frac{kQ}{2R}$ (d) $\frac{kQ}{3R}$

8 Consider the potential at the corner of a uniformly charged cube of dimension L to be directly proportional to ρL^2, where ρ is the volume charge density. What is the value of the ratio of the potential at the centre to the potential at the corner of the cube?

(a) 4 : 1 (b) 3 : 2 (c) 8 : 1 (d) 2 : 1

9 A non-conducting sphere of radius $R = 5$ cm has its centre at origin O. It has a spherical cavity of radius $r = 1$ cm whose centre is at (0, 3 cm). Solid material of sphere has uniform positive charge density $\rho = \frac{10^{-6}}{\pi}$ C/m^3, then potential at point P (4 cm, 0) is

(a) 35.16 V (b) 34.92 V (c) 34.50 V (d) 34.20 V

10 Two charges lie on the X-axis. A rough sketch of the equipotential lines of these two charges is shown in figure. Which one of the following statement is true?

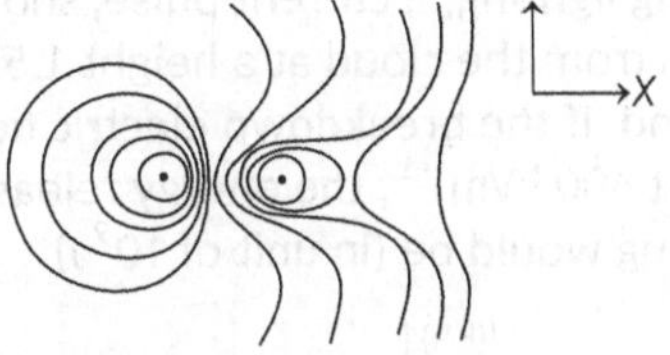

(a) The two charges have opposite signs and the charge on the left is smaller in magnitude than the charge on the right.

(b) The two charges have opposite signs and the charge on the left is larger in magnitude than the charge on the right.

(c) The two charges have the same sign and the charge on the left is smaller in magnitude than the charge on the right.

(d) The two charges have the same sign and the charge on the left is larger in magnitude than the charge on the right.

11 Two concentric spherical shells of radii r and $R (r < R)$ have surface charge densities $-\sigma$ and $+\sigma$, respectively. The variation of electric potential V with distance x from the centre O of the shells is plotted. Which of the following graphs best depict the variation qualitatively?

(a) 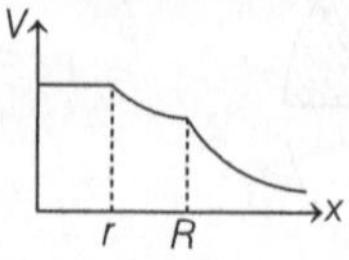
(b) 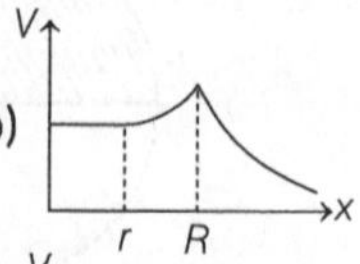
(c) 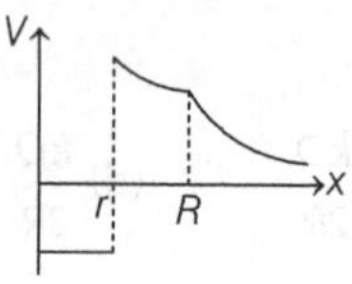
(d) 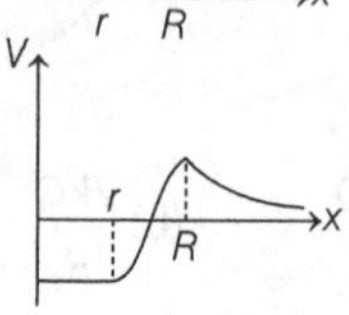

12 Two positive charges $+Q$ and $+4Q$ are placed at the ends of a straight line of length L. A negative charge $-Q$ is placed between the first two charges on the straight line at a distance $x (0 < x < L)$ from the charge $+Q$, then the graph of (electrostatic potential energy) of the system of three charges *versus* x is

(a) 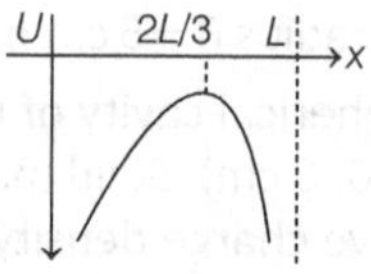
(b) 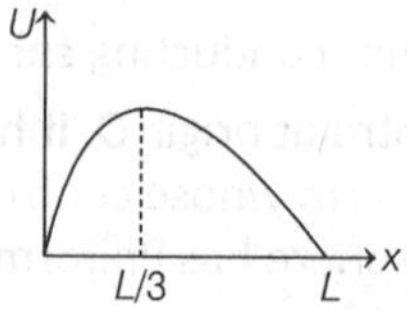
(c) 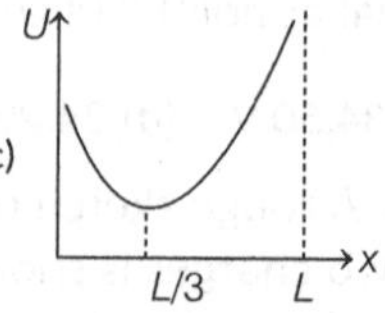
(d) 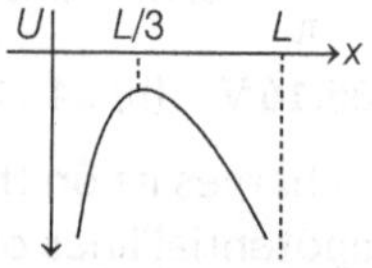

13 During lighting, a current pulse, shown in figure, flows from the cloud at a height 1.5 km to the ground. If the breakdown electric field of humid air is about 400 kVm^{-1}, the energy released during lighting would be (in unit of 10^9 J)

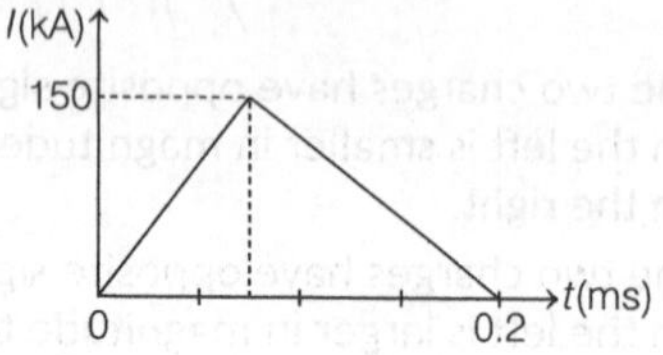

(a) 9
(b) 3.0
(c) 4.5
(d) 6.0

14 A uniform electric field exists only in XY-plane. When a student moves a distance 0.01 m along OP line, potential decreases by 0.02 V. The magnitude of electric field is $2\sqrt{5}$ V/m. When a student walks along OQ line (which is perpendicular to OP line), potential decreases. Then, electric field in vector form is

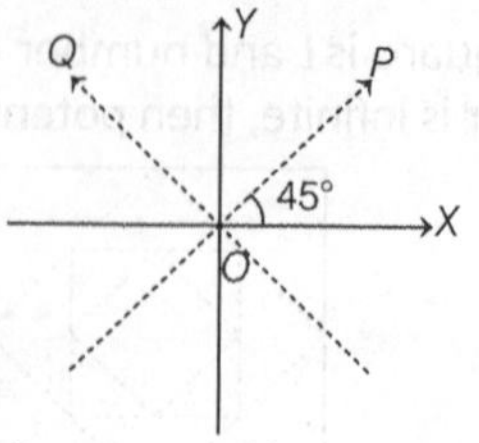

(a) $\sqrt{2}\hat{i} + 3\sqrt{2}\hat{j}$
(b) $3\sqrt{2}\hat{i} + \sqrt{2}\hat{j}$
(c) $-\sqrt{2}\hat{i} + 3\sqrt{2}\hat{j}$
(d) $-3\sqrt{2}\hat{i} + \sqrt{2}\hat{j}$

15 Between two infinitely long wires having linear charge densities $+\lambda$ and $-\lambda$, there are two points A and B as shown in the figure. The amount of work done by the electric field in moving a point charge q_0 from A to B is equal to

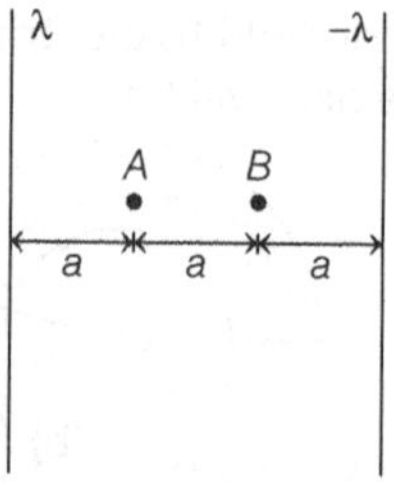

(a) $\frac{\lambda q_0}{2\pi\varepsilon_0}\ln 2$
(b) $-\frac{2\lambda q_0}{\pi\varepsilon_0}\ln 2$
(c) $\frac{2\lambda q_0}{\pi\varepsilon_0}\ln 2$
(d) $\frac{\lambda q_0}{\pi\varepsilon_0}\ln 2$

16 In an electric field, the potential at a point is given by the following relation, $V = \frac{343}{r^2}$. The electric field at $r = 3\hat{i} + 2\hat{j} + 6\hat{k}$ is

(a) $\frac{2}{7}(3\hat{i} + 2\hat{j} + 6\hat{k})$
(b) $\frac{1}{7}(3\hat{i} + 2\hat{j} + 6\hat{k})$
(c) $6\hat{i} + 4\hat{j} + 12\hat{k}$
(d) $-(3\hat{i} + 2\hat{j} + 6\hat{k})$

17 A non-conducting rod of length $2l$ with its left and right half given uniform linear charge densities $-\lambda$ and $+\lambda$ respectively is placed on the X-axis as shown in figure, which of the following is correct?

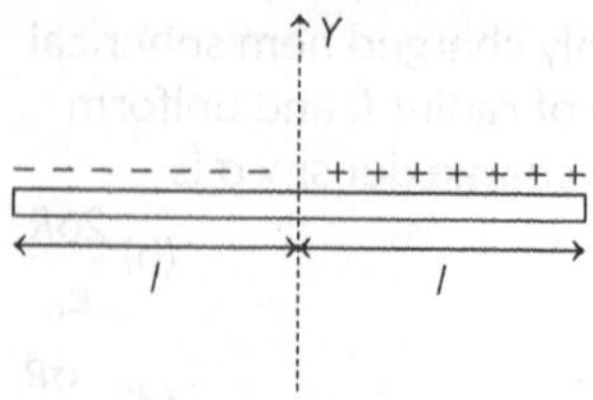

(a) The YZ-plane is an equipotential surface.

(b) The ZX-plane is an equipotential surface.

(c) The electric field at any point on the Y-axis is along the positive x-direction.

(d) The electric field at any point on the Z-axis is along the positive x-direction.

18 Two point charges of $+Q$ each have been placed at the positions $(-a/2, 0, 0)$ and $(a/2, 0, 0)$. The locus of the points in YZ-plane, where $-Q$ charge can be placed such that the total electrostatic potential energy of the system can become equal to zero, is represented by which of the following equations?

(a) $z^2+(y-a)^2=2a$ (b) $z^2+(y-a)^2=27a^2/4$

(c) $z^2+y^2=15a^2/4$ (d) None of these

19 On a semi-circular ring of radius $=4R$, charge $+3q$ is distributed in such a way that on one quarter $+q$ is uniformly distributed and on another quarter $+2q$ is uniformly distributed. Along its axis, a smooth non-conducting and uncharged pipe of length $6R$ is fixed axially as shown in figure. A small ball of mass m and charge $+q$ is thrown from one end of pipe with speed u. The minimum speed u_{min}, so that ball will come out from the other end of pipe is

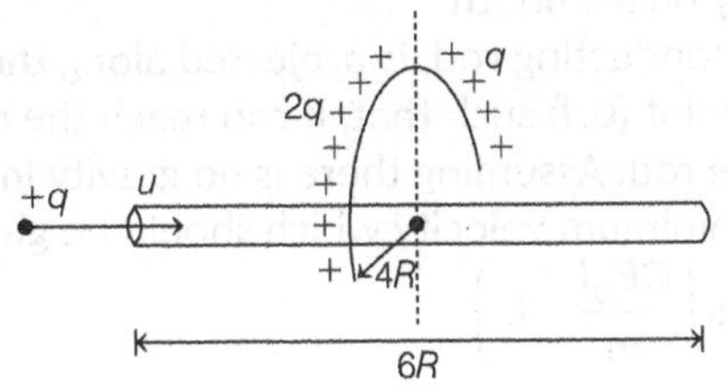

(a) $\sqrt{\dfrac{7q^2}{40\pi\varepsilon_0 mR}}$ (b) $\sqrt{\dfrac{3q^2}{40\pi\varepsilon_0 mR}}$

(c) $\sqrt{\dfrac{q^2}{40\pi\varepsilon_0 mR}}$ (d) $\sqrt{\dfrac{9q^2}{40\pi\varepsilon_0 mR}}$

20 An infinite dielectric sheet having charge density σ has a hole of radius R in it. An electron is released on the axis of the hole at a distance $\sqrt{3}R$ from the centre. The speed with which it crosses the plane of sheet is (e = charge on electron and m = mass of electron)

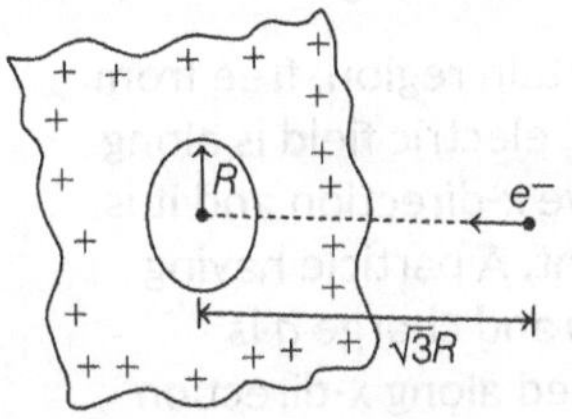

(a) $\sqrt{\dfrac{\sigma eR}{2m\varepsilon_0}}$ (b) $\sqrt{\dfrac{\sigma eR}{m\varepsilon_0}}$ (c) $\sqrt{\dfrac{2\sigma eR}{m\varepsilon_0}}$ (d) $\sqrt{\dfrac{3\sigma eR}{m\varepsilon_0}}$

21 A particle of mass m and charge $+q$ approaches from a very large distance towards a uniformly charged ring of radius R and charge $+q$, mass same as that of particle, with initial velocity v_0 along the axis of the ring as shown in the figure. The closest distance of approach between the ring and the particle is [Assume the space to be gravity free and frictionless]

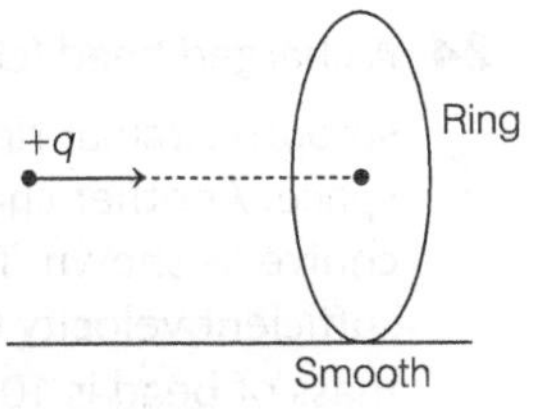

(a) $\sqrt{\dfrac{q^4}{\pi^2\varepsilon_0^2 m^2 v_0^4}-R^2}$ (b) $\sqrt{\dfrac{3q^4}{2\pi^2\varepsilon_0^2 m^2 v_0^4}+R^2}$

(c) $\sqrt{\dfrac{m^2 v_0^4}{2\pi^2 q^4 \varepsilon_0^2}-R^2}$ (d) $\sqrt{\dfrac{q^4}{4\pi^2\varepsilon_0^2 m^2 v_0^4}-R^2}$

22 A point charge Q of mass m is projected with some initial velocity v_0 from a very far off point as shown in figure. The sphere shown has a charge $-Q$, radius R and charge is uniformly distributed over its entire volume. Through out the process, this sphere stays stationary. Find, v_0, so that the point charge strikes the sphere at 45°. (Given that, $\alpha=\dfrac{Q^2}{4\pi\varepsilon_0 mR}$, $g=0$)

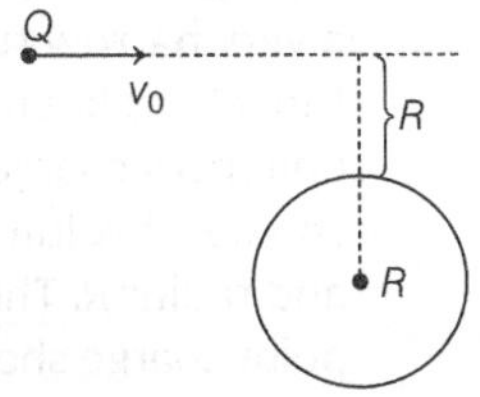

(a) $v_0=\sqrt{\dfrac{2}{7}\alpha}$ (b) $v_0=\sqrt{\dfrac{2}{3}\alpha}$

(c) $v_0=\sqrt{\dfrac{1}{7}\alpha}$ (d) $v_0=\sqrt{\dfrac{1}{3}\alpha}$

23 In space, a horizontal electric field $(E=(mg)/q)$ exists as shown in figure and a mass m is attached at the end of a light rod. If mass m is released from the position shown in figure, the angular velocity of the rod when it passes through the bottom most position is

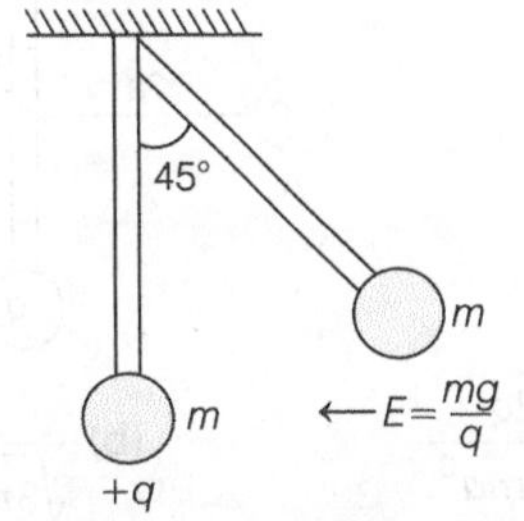

(a) $\sqrt{\dfrac{g}{l}}$ (b) $\sqrt{\dfrac{2g}{l}}$ (c) $\sqrt{\dfrac{3g}{l}}$ (d) $\sqrt{\dfrac{5g}{l}}$

24 A charged bead (charge $+4\mu C$) is threaded on a fixed smooth circular ring of radius 2 m in gravity free space. Another charge $+4\mu C$ is fixed at 1 m from centre as shown. The bead is projected with just sufficient velocity to complete the circular path. If mass of bead is 100 g, what is initial speed v_0?

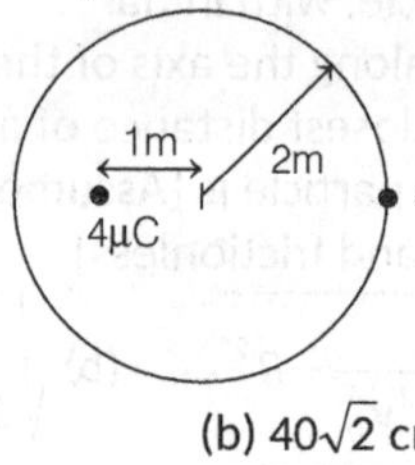

(a) $80\sqrt{3}$ cm/s (b) $40\sqrt{2}$ cm/s
(c) 10 m/s (d) $4\sqrt{5}$ m/s

25 A particle of charge $+q$ and mass m is projected with a velocity v inside a very narrow tunnel as shown. The tunnel has been made inside a uniformly charged non-conducting sphere of volume charge density ρ and radius R. The minimum velocity with which the point charge should be projected such that it can it reach the opposite end of the tunnel, is equal to

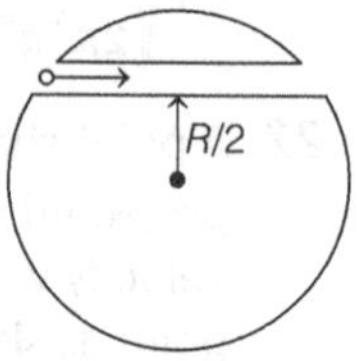

(a) $\left(\dfrac{q\rho R^2}{4m\varepsilon_0}\right)^{1/2}$ (b) $\left(\dfrac{q\rho R^2}{24m\varepsilon_0}\right)^{1/2}$

(c) $\left(\dfrac{q\rho R^2}{6m\varepsilon_0}\right)^{1/2}$

(d) zero because the initial and the final points are at same potential

26 Figure shows a ball having a charge q fixed at a point A. Two identical balls of mass m having charges $+q$ and $-q$ are attached to the end of a light rod of length $2a$. The system is released from the situation shown in figure. Find the angular velocity of the rod, when the rod turns through 90°.

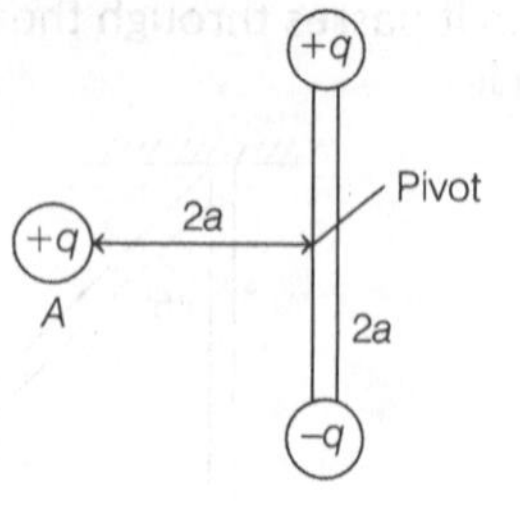

(a) $\dfrac{\sqrt{2}q}{3\pi\varepsilon_0 ma^3}$ (b) $\dfrac{q}{\sqrt{3\pi\varepsilon_0 ma^3}}$

(c) $\dfrac{q}{\sqrt{6\pi\varepsilon_0 ma^3}}$ (d) $\dfrac{\sqrt{2}q}{4\pi\varepsilon_0 ma^3}$

27 The mass m_1 and charge q_1 is released from rest from a very large distance along the axis of ring of radius R, charge q_2 and mass m_2.

Case-I Ring is kept fixed and speed of m_1, when it crosses the centre of ring is v_1.

Case-II Ring is free to move along the axis and speed of m_1, when it crosses the centre of the ring is v_2.

The value of $\left(\dfrac{v_1}{v_2}\right)$ is

(a) $\dfrac{m_1+m_2}{m_2}$ (b) $\dfrac{m_2}{m_1}$

(c) $\sqrt{\dfrac{m_1+m_2}{m_2}}$ (d) None of these

28 Electric field given by the vector $\mathbf{E} = \dfrac{E_0}{l}(x\hat{\mathbf{i}} + y\hat{\mathbf{j}})$ N/C is present in the XY-plane. A small ring of mass M carrying charge $+Q$, which can slide freely on a smooth non-conducting rod, is projected along the rod from the point $(0, l)$ such that, it can reach the other end of the rod. Assuming there is no gravity in the region, the minimum velocity which should be given to the ring is $\left(\dfrac{QE_0 l}{m} = 8\right)$

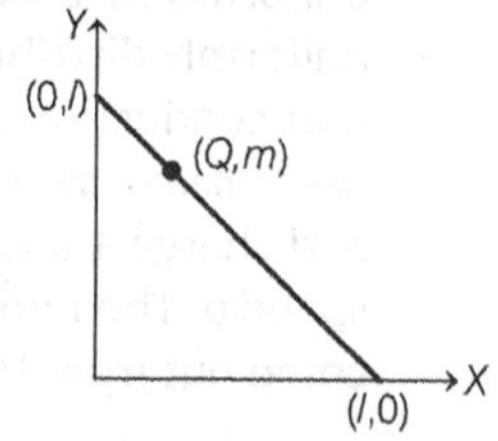

(a) 2 m/s (b) 3 m/s
(c) 2.5 m/s (d) 3.5 m/s

29 Two small balls of mass m, bearing a charge q each, are connected by a non-conducting thread of length $2l$. At a certain instant, the middle of the thread starts moving at a constant velocity v perpendicular to the direction of the thread at the initial instant. The minimum distance between the balls will be (Use, $q^2 = 4\pi\varepsilon_0 mv^2 l$)

(a) $\dfrac{l}{3}$ (b) $\dfrac{2l}{3}$ (c) l (d) $\dfrac{4l}{3}$

30 In a certain region, free from gravity, electric field is along negative x-direction and it is constant. A particle having mass m and charge q is projected along x-direction with speed v_0. An additional force $\mathbf{F} = \mathbf{C} \times \mathbf{v}$ is acting on the charge, where $\mathbf{v}$ is velocity vector and $\mathbf{C}$ is a constant vector. The charge

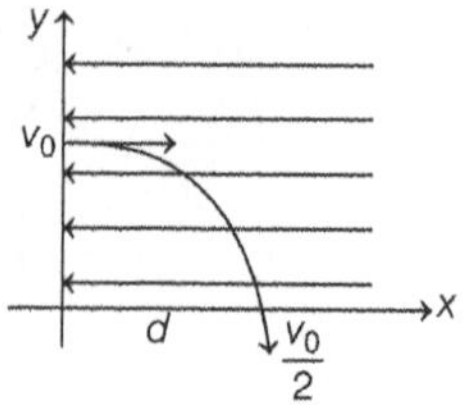

comes out of region with speed $\frac{v_0}{2}$, then the magnitude of electric field will be

(a) $\frac{3}{4}\frac{mv_0^2}{qd}$ (b) $\frac{4}{3}\frac{mv_0^2}{qd}$

(c) $\frac{3}{8}\frac{mv_0^2}{qd}$ (d) Cannot be determined

31 Four point charges are fixed along Y-axis as shown in the figure. A particle of mass m and charge $+Q$ is projected along the $+X$-axis towards centre O from large distance. Find the minimum velocity v_{min} of particle, so that it will reach at origin O. Take $Q^2 = 12\sqrt{5}\pi\varepsilon_0 m$. Neglect gravity.

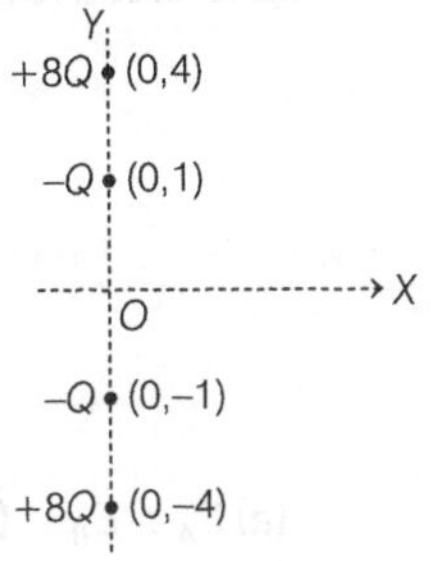

(a) 5 m/s (b) 6 m/s (c) 8 m/s (d) 10 m/s

Multiple Choice(s) Correct Questions

1 A small sphere is charged uniformly and placed at point $A(x, y)$ m, so that at point $B(8, 7)$ m, electric field strength is $\mathbf{E} = (54\hat{i} + 72\hat{j})$ N/C and potential is + 900 V. The dielectric strength of air is 3×10^6 V/m. Choose the correct option(s).

(a) Co-ordinate of point A are $(2, -1)$m

(b) Charge of the sphere is 2μC

(c) Minimum possible radius of sphere is $\sqrt{30}$ cm, so that air does not breakdown

(d) None of the above

2 At distance of 5 cm and 10 cm outwards from the surface of a uniformly charged solid sphere, the potentials are 100V and 75V, respectively. Then,

(a) potential at its surface is 150V

(b) the charge on the sphere is $(5/3) \times 10^{-9}$ C

(c) the electric field on the surface is 1500 V/m

(d) the electric potential at its centre is 225V

3 The electric potential decreases uniformly from 180 V to 20 V as one moves on the X-axis from $x = -2$ cm to $x = +2$ cm. The electric field at the origin

(a) must be equal to 40 V/cm

(b) may be equal to 40 V/cm

(c) may be greater than 40 V/cm

(d) may be less than 40 V/cm

4 Which of the following quantites depends on the choice of zero potential or zero potential energy?

(a) Potential at a particular point

(b) Change in potential energy of a two-charge system

(c) Potential energy of a two-charge system

(d) Potential difference between two points

5 Potential at a point x is 5 V and at a point y is -5V. A proton is moving towards x from y, then

(a) it must have kinetic energy more than 10 eV to reach x from y

(b) work done by **E** in motion from x to y is + 10 eV

(c) work done by **E** in motion from y to x is zero

(d) kinetic energy at y is more than kinetic energy at x, if particle is released at x

6 E and V are the electric field and electric potential at O. If the linear charge density of the system is λ, then

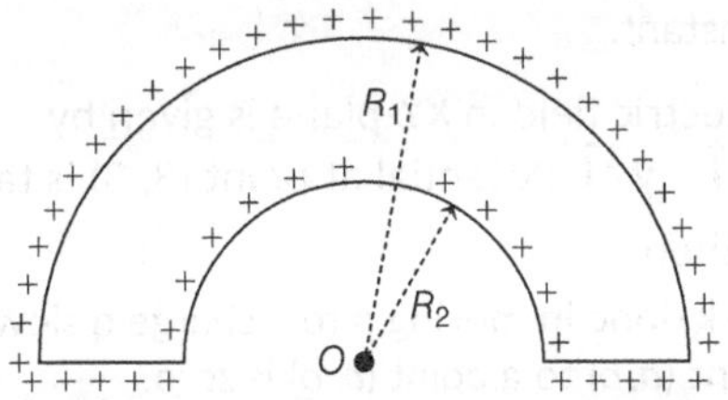

(a) $E = \frac{\lambda}{2\pi\varepsilon_0}\left(\frac{1}{R_1} + \frac{1}{R_2}\right)$ (b) $E = \frac{\lambda}{4\pi\varepsilon_0}\left(\frac{1}{R_1} + \frac{1}{R_2}\right)$

(c) $V = \frac{\lambda}{2\pi\varepsilon_0}\left[\pi + \ln\left(\frac{R_1}{R_2}\right)\right]$ (d) $V = \frac{\lambda}{4\pi\varepsilon_0}\left(\pi + \ln\frac{R_1}{R_2}\right)$

7 A wire having a uniform linear charge density λ, is bent in the form of a ring of radius R. Point A as shown in the figure, is in the plane of the ring but not at the centre. Two elements a_1 and a_2 of the ring subtend very small and equal angles at the point A. They are at distances r_1 and r_2 from the point A respectively

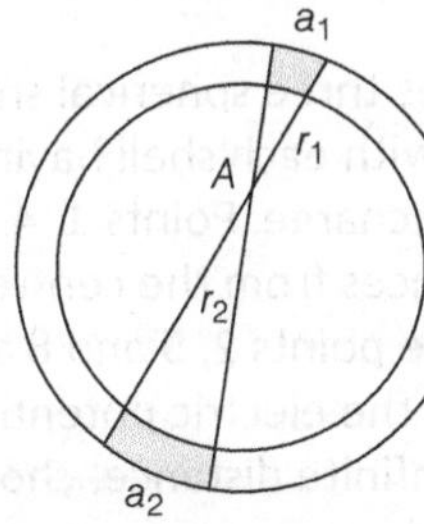

(a) The ratio of charge on elements a_1 and a_2 is r_1 / r_2.

(b) The element a_1 produces greater magnitude of electric field at A than element a_2.

(c) The elements a_1 and a_2 produce same potential at A.

(d) The element a_1 produces greater potential at A than element a_2.

8 A sphere of radius R_1 has charge density ρ uniform within its volume, except for a small spherical hollow region of radius R_2 located a distance a from centre (Take, zero potential at infinity).

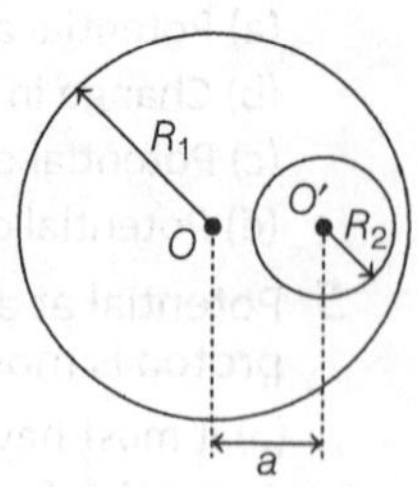

(a) Electric field at O' is $\dfrac{\rho a}{3\varepsilon_0}$

(b) Electric field at O' is $\dfrac{\rho a^3}{3\varepsilon_0}\hat{a}$

(c) Electric potential at O' is $\dfrac{\rho}{6\varepsilon_0}[3(R_1^2 - R_2^2) - a^2]$

(d) Electric potential at any point in hollow region is constant.

9 The electric field in XY-plane is given by $\mathbf{E} = x^2\hat{\mathbf{i}} + y^2\hat{\mathbf{j}}$. Potential at point (3, 3) is taken as zero, then

(a) work done in moving a test charge q slowly from a point (a, b) to a point (b, a) is zero.

(b) potential at any point on XY-plane can't exceed 18 unit for x and y in 1st quadrant.

(c) potential can't be defined as field is non-conservative in nature.

(d) equipotential curve are concentric circles with centre (3,3).

10 S_1 and S_2 are two equipotential surfaces on which the potentials are not equal.

(a) S_1 and S_2 cannot intersect

(b) S_1 and S_2 cannot both be plane surfaces

(c) In the region between S_1 and S_2, the field is maximum, where they are closest to each other

(d) A line of force from S_1 to S_2 must be perpendicular to both

11 Figure shows three spherical shells in separate situations, with each shell having the same uniform positive net charge. Points 1, 4 and 7 are at the same radial distances from the centre of their respective shells; so are points 2, 5 and 8 and so are points 3, 6 and 9. With the electric potential taken equals to zero at an infinite distance, choose correct statement(s).

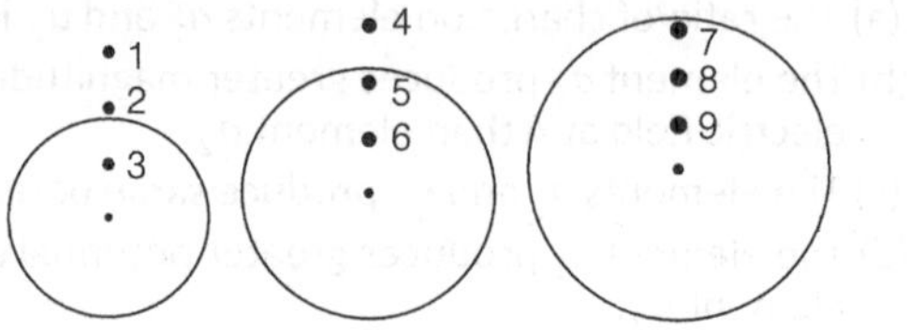

(a) Point 3 has highest potential.

(b) Points 1, 4 and 7 are at same potential.

(c) Point 1 has lowest potential.

(d) Points 5 and 8 are at different potential.

12 Which of the following is true for the figure showing electric lines of force?

(E is electric field, V is potential)

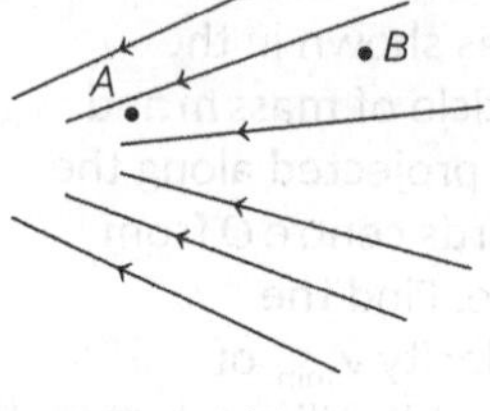

(a) $E_A > E_B$ (b) $E_B > E_A$ (c) $V_A > V_B$ (d) $V_B > V_A$

13 The potential as a function of x is plotted in figure. Which of the following is/are correct?

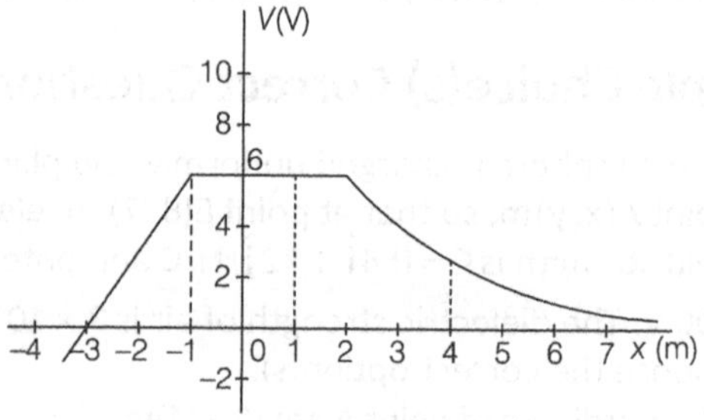

(a) The magnitude of electric field E_x at $x = -2$ m is 3 N/C

(b) The electric field E_x at $x = 1$ m is 6N/C

(c) The work done in moving a charge particle per unit charge from $x = -3$ m to $x = 1$ m is 6 J/C

(d) The work done in moving a charge particle per unit charge from $x = 2$ to $x = \infty$ is -6 J/C

14 In an electric field shown in figure, three equipotential surfaces are shown.

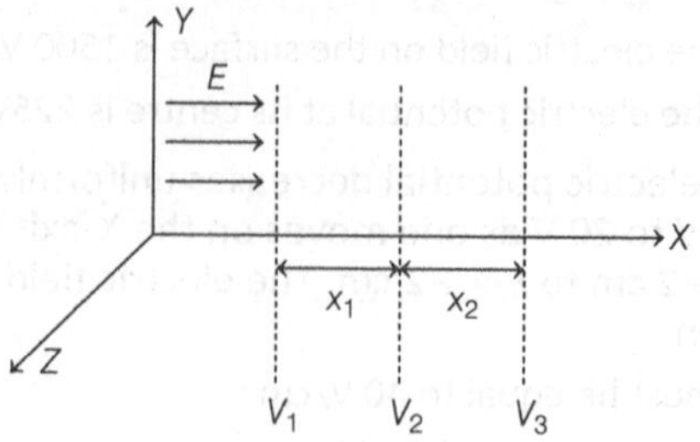

The function of electric field is $E = 2x^2$ V/m.

(a) If $V_1 - V_2 = V_2 - V_3$, then $x_1 > x_2$

(b) If $V_1 - V_2 = V_2 - V_3$, then $x_1 < x_2$

(c) $V_1 > V_2 > V_3$

(d) $V_1 < V_2 < V_3$

15 A fixed point charge Q is at origin. At $t = 0$, a charge q with mass m is at $x = a$ with leftward velocity v_0, which satisfies $\frac{kQq}{a} = 3mv_0^2$. The particle turns around and starts to move rightward at the position $b < a$.

(a) The ratio b/a is 6/7

(b) The ratio b/a is 3/7

(c) The velocity of the particle at a large distance from the origin is $\sqrt{7}\,v_0$

(d) The velocity of the particle at a large distance from the origin is zero

16 A uniform electric field of strength E exists in a region. An electron enters at point A perpendicularly with velocity v. It moves through the electric field and exits at point B, then

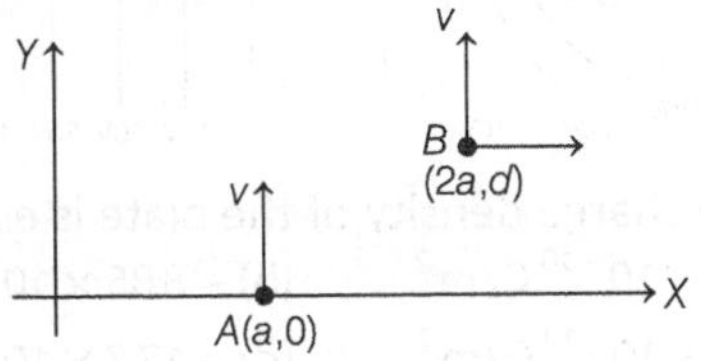

(a) $E = \frac{-2amv^2}{ed^2}\hat{i}$

(b) velocity at B is $\left(\frac{2av}{d}\right)\hat{i} + v\hat{j}$

(c) rate of work done by the electric field at B is $\frac{4ma^2v^3}{d^3}$

(d) rate of work done by the electric field at A is zero

17 Three charges are kept at the corners of a square as shown. A fourth charge q is brought slowly at the fourth corner from infinity, then choose the correct statement(s). (Take, reference potential energy at infinity to be zero and $k = \frac{1}{4\pi\varepsilon_0}$)

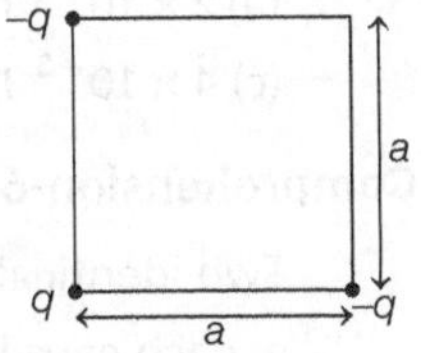

(a) Work done by electrostatic field is $\frac{kq^2}{a}\left(\frac{1-2\sqrt{2}}{\sqrt{2}}\right)$.

(b) Work done by external agent is $\frac{kq^2}{a}\left(\frac{1-2\sqrt{2}}{\sqrt{2}}\right)$.

(c) Total potential energy of the system after the charge is placed at the corner is $\frac{kq^2}{a}(\sqrt{2}-4)$.

(d) For the system thus achieved centre of square will be a point of equilibrium.

Comprehension Based Questions

Comprehension-1

Three charges $+3Q$, $+2Q$ and $-Q$ respectively, are located at a distance a from the origin as shown in the figure. The point P is located at a distance a from the origin. $\left(\text{Take, } k = \frac{1}{4\pi\varepsilon_0}\right)$

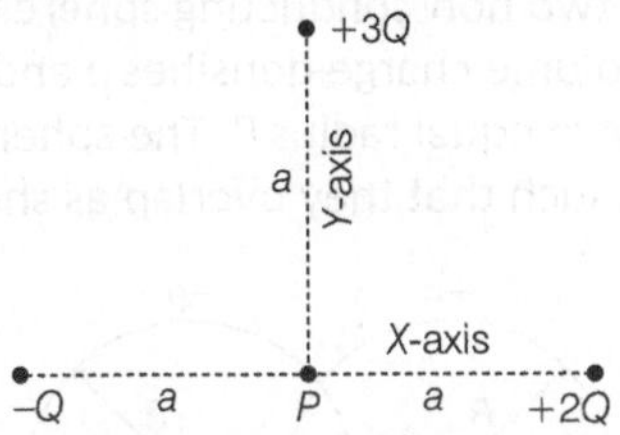

1 The magnitude of x and y-components of the electric field **E** at P are

(a) $E_x = 2E_y = \frac{k3Q}{a^2}$

(b) $E_x = E_y = -\frac{k3Q}{a^2}$

(c) $E_x = \frac{1}{2}, E_y = \frac{k3Q}{a^2}$

(d) $E_x = \frac{kQ}{a^2}, E_y = \frac{k3Q}{a^2}$

2 The electric potential energy U for the configuration of the three charges is

(a) $\frac{kQ^2}{a}\left(1-\frac{1}{\sqrt{2}}\right)$

(b) $\frac{kQ^2}{a}\left(\frac{1}{\sqrt{2}}+1\right)$

(c) $\frac{kQ^2}{a}\left(\frac{3}{\sqrt{2}}+1\right)$

(d) $\frac{kQ^2}{a}\left(\frac{3}{\sqrt{2}}-1\right)$

3 A fourth charge $+3Q$ is slowly moved in from infinity to point P. The work done by an external agent in this process must be

(a) $\frac{kQ^2}{a}\left(\frac{3}{\sqrt{2}}-1\right)$

(b) $\frac{kQ^2}{a}\left(\frac{3}{\sqrt{2}}+1\right)$

(c) $\frac{kQ^2}{a}\frac{4}{3}$

(d) $\frac{kQ^2}{a}(12)$

Comprehension-2

A point charge $q_1 = +6e$ fixed at the origin of a coordinate system and another point charge $q_2 = -10e$ is fixed at $x = 8$ nm, $y = 0$. The locus of all points in the XY-plane for which potential $V = 0$ (other than infinity) is a circle centred on the X-axis, as shown in figure.

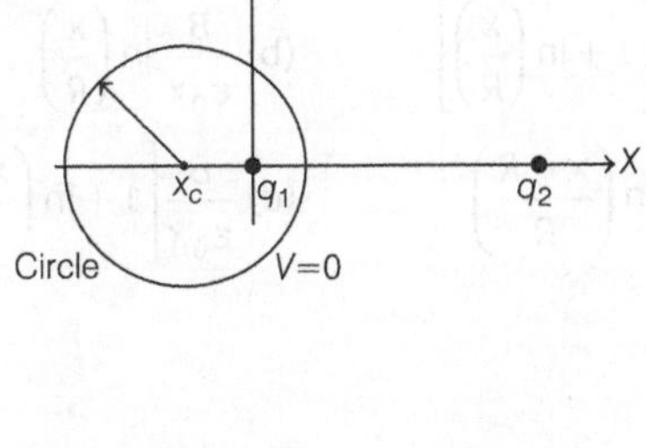

4 Radius R of the circle is
(a) 3 nm (b) 6 nm (c) 7.5 nm (d) 9 nm

5 X-coordinate of the centre of the circle is
(a) -2 nm (b) -3 nm (c) -4.5 nm (d) -7.5 nm

6 The potential at the centre of the circle is
(a) 0.32 V (b) 0.77 V (c) 1.2 V (d) -1.2 V

Comprehension-3

There are two non-conducting spheres having uniform volume charge densities ρ and $-\rho$. Both spheres have equal radius R. The spheres are now laid down such that they overlap as shown in the figure.

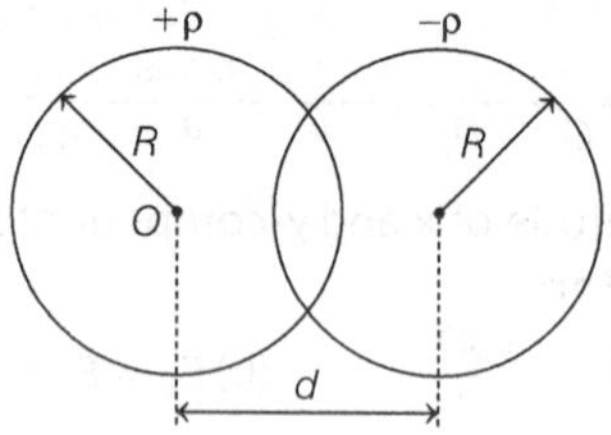

7 The electric field **E** in the overlap region is
(a) non-uniform (b) zero
(c) $\frac{\rho}{3\varepsilon_0}\mathbf{d}$ (d) $\frac{\rho}{3\varepsilon_0}\mathbf{r}$

8 The potential difference ΔV between the centres of the two spheres for $d = R$, is
(a) $\frac{\rho}{3\varepsilon_0}d^2$ (b) $\frac{\rho}{\varepsilon_0}d^2$ (c) zero (d) $\frac{2\rho}{\varepsilon_0}d^2$

Comprehension-4

An uncharged ball of radius R is placed at a point in space and the region outside (from R to ∞ measured from centre of the ball) the ball is non-uniformly charged with a charge density $\rho = \frac{B}{r^3}$ C/m^3, where B is a positive constant and r is the distance of a point measured from centre of the ball.

9 Electric potential at the centre of the ball is
(a) directly proportional to R
(b) directly proportional to R^2
(c) inversely proportional to R
(d) inversely proportional to R^2

10 Electric potential at a distance x from centre of the ball $(x > R)$ is
(a) $\frac{B}{\varepsilon_0 x}\left[1+\ln\left(\frac{x}{R}\right)\right]$ (b) $\frac{B}{\varepsilon_0 x}\ln\left(\frac{x}{R}\right)$
(c) $\frac{B}{\varepsilon_0 x}\ln\left(\frac{x-R}{R}\right)$ (d) $\frac{B}{\varepsilon_0 x}\left[1+\ln\left(\frac{x-R}{R}\right)\right]$

11 As we move away from ball's surface, electric potential
(a) decreases
(b) increases
(c) decreases then increases
(d) increases then decreases

Comprehension-5

The sketch below shows cross-sections of equipotential surfaces between a solid non-conducting sphere and large non-conducting sheet that are shown in black. Some points on the equipotential surfaces near them are marked as $A, B, C, \ldots$. The arrangement lies in air. (Take, $\varepsilon_0 = 8.85\times10^{-12}$ C^2/Nm^2)

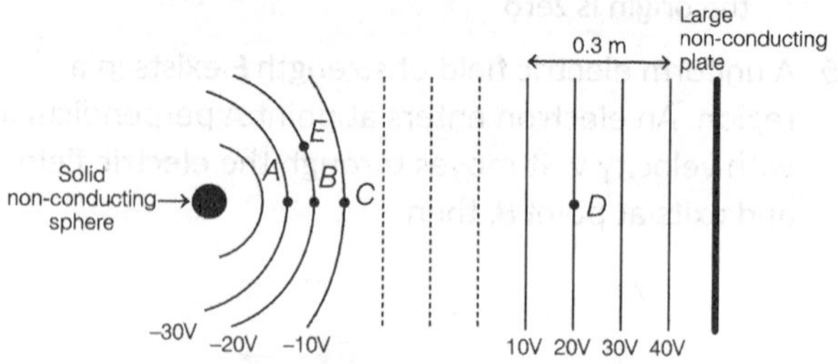

12 Surface charge density of the plate is equal to
(a) 8.85×10^{-10} C/m^2 (b) -8.85×10^{-10} C/m^2
(c) 17.7×10^{-10} C/m^2 (d) -17.7×10^{-10} C/m^2

13 A positive charge is placed at B. When it is released,
(a) no force will be exerted on it
(b) it will move towards A
(c) it will move towards C
(d) it will move towards E

14 How much work is required to slowly move a $-1\,\mu$C charge from E to D?
(a) 2×10^{-5} J (b) -2×10^{-5} J
(c) 4×10^{-5} J (d) -4×10^{-5} J

Comprehension-6

Two identical blocks A and B, each of mass $m = 600$ g, each carrying positive charge of $q = 40\mu$C are kept stationary on a smooth horizontal floor, When the blocks are released, due to electrostatic repulsion, A moves towards left while B towards right. After moving 40 cm, A comes in contact with a massless spring of force constant $k = 6400$ Nm^{-1}, while after moving 20 cm, B collides inelastically with a rigid wall as shown in figure.

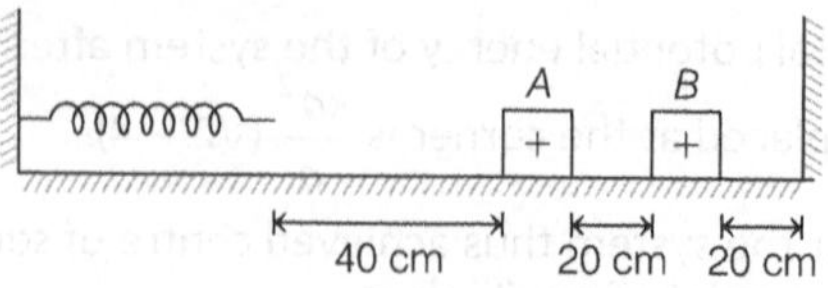

15 Velocity of A, when it comes in contact with the spring, is

(a) $10\ ms^{-1}$ (b) $15\ ms^{-1}$

(c) $20\ ms^{-1}$ (d) $30\ ms^{-1}$

16 Maximum compression of the spring is

(a) 20 cm (b) 10 cm

(c) 40 cm (d) 60 cm

Comprehension-7

A small charged sphere (mass M, charge Q) is connected by a light, inextensible, non-conducting string of length L to a fixed point $P(0, 2L)$. The sphere is at rest in equilibrium in the position A. The sphere is free to slide on a non-conducting, frictionless and horizontal surface (designated as OXY-plane).

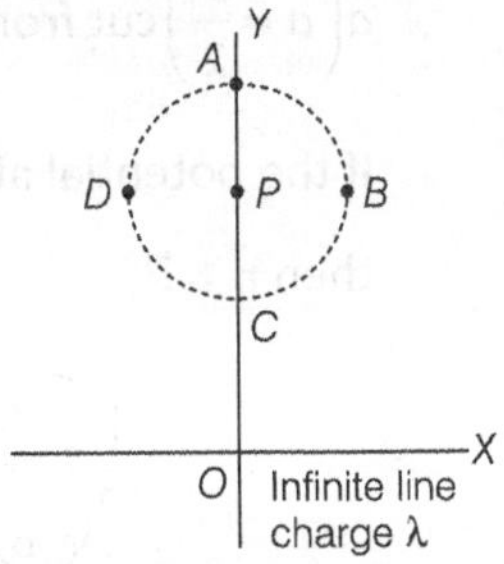

Along the X-axis lies an infinite line charge. The sphere is to be imparted a velocity $u\hat{i}$ at position A, so that it moves in a complete circle about the centre P. B, C, D are points on the circumference of the circle, BD parallel to line charge and AC normal to line charge.

17 The instantaneous tension in the string at the instant, the sphere is given the velocity $u\hat{i}$ is

(a) $\dfrac{Q\lambda}{6\pi\varepsilon_0 L}$ (b) $\dfrac{Mu^2}{L} - \dfrac{Q\lambda}{6\pi\varepsilon_0 L}$

(c) $\dfrac{Mu^2}{L} + \dfrac{Q\lambda}{6\pi\varepsilon_0 L}$ (d) $\dfrac{Q\lambda}{6\pi\varepsilon_0 L} - \dfrac{Mu^2}{L}$

18 The potential difference between points A and $B(V_A - V_B)$ is

(a) $\dfrac{\lambda}{4\pi\varepsilon_0}\ln\left(\dfrac{4}{3}\right)$ (b) $\dfrac{\lambda}{3\pi\varepsilon_0}\ln\left(\dfrac{3}{5}\right)$

(c) $\dfrac{\lambda}{2\pi\varepsilon_0}\ln\left(\dfrac{3}{2}\right)$ (d) $\dfrac{\lambda}{2\pi\varepsilon_0}\ln\left(\dfrac{2}{3}\right)$

19 The tension in the string, when the sphere reaches position B is

(a) $\dfrac{Q\lambda}{4\pi\varepsilon_0 L}$

(b) $\dfrac{Mu^2}{L} - \dfrac{Q\lambda}{\pi\varepsilon_0 L}\ln\left(\dfrac{3}{2}\right)$

(c) $\dfrac{Mu^2}{L} + \dfrac{Q\lambda}{\pi\varepsilon_0 L}\ln\left(\dfrac{3}{2}\right)$

(d) None of the above

Match the Columns Questions

1

Column I (Potential function)	Column II (Electric lines of force)
(a) $V = \dfrac{x}{y}$	(p) 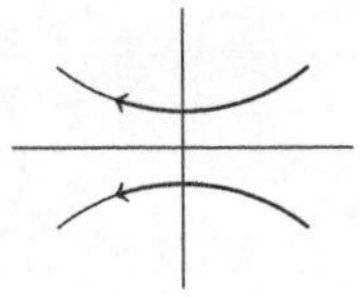
(b) $V = x^2 - y^2$	(q) 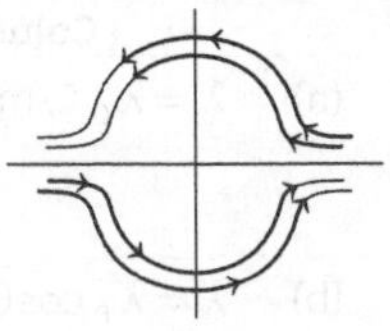
(c) $V = x^2 + y^2$	(r) 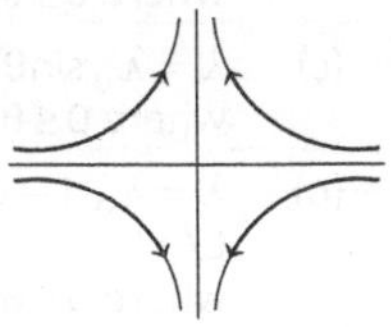
(d) $V = xy$	(s) 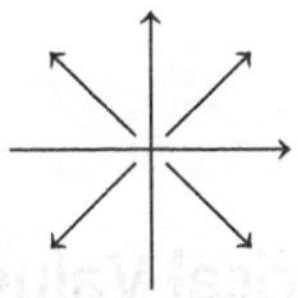

2 Two charged dielectric spheres A (solid) and B (hollow) of same radius R and masses $2\,m$ and m respectively, are kept on a horizontal rough surface. The two spheres A and B have charges $2Q$ and $-Q$, respectively and uniformly distributed. They are released from rest, when their centres are separated by very large distance. Assume that, there is no sliding.

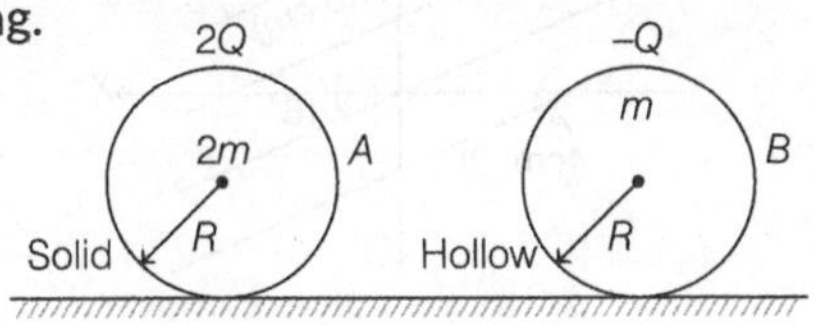

Column I	Column II
(a) Kinetic energy of system just before A and B meet	(p) $\dfrac{838kQ^2}{2345R}$
(b) Kinetic energy of A just before A and B meet	(q) $\dfrac{kQ^2}{R}$
(c) Kinetic energy of B just before A and B meet	(r) $\dfrac{25kQ^2}{67R}$
(d) Rotational kinetic energy of system just before A and B meet	(s) $\dfrac{42kQ^2}{67R}$

3 A non-conducting ring has linear charge density λ. Match the following column regarding this ring. θ is the angle measured from A.

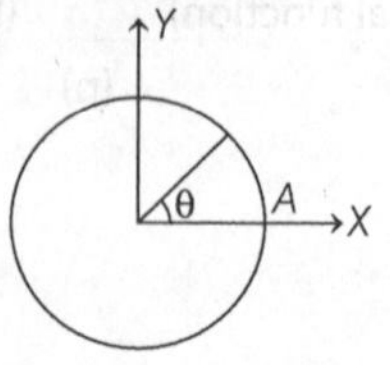

	Column I		Column II
(a)	$\lambda = \lambda_0$ C/m	(p)	Electric field at centre of the ring is in the direction to $(-\hat{j})$
(b)	$\lambda = \lambda_0 \cos\theta$ C/m, where $0 \le \theta \le 2\pi$	(q)	Electric field at centre of the ring is zero
(c)	$\lambda = \lambda_0 \sin\theta$ C/m, where $0 \le \theta \le 2\pi$	(r)	Electric potential at centre of ring is zero
(d)	$\lambda = \lambda_0(1-\cos 2\theta)$ C/m, where $0 \le \theta \le 2\pi$	(s)	Electric field intensity at centre of the ring is direction $(-\hat{i})$
		(t)	Electrostatics potential at centre of ring is positive

Numerical Value Questions

1 A uniform electric field of 400 V/m exists in space as shown in graph. Two points A and B are also shown with their co-ordinates. If the potential of A is 20 V, then find the potential of B (in V).

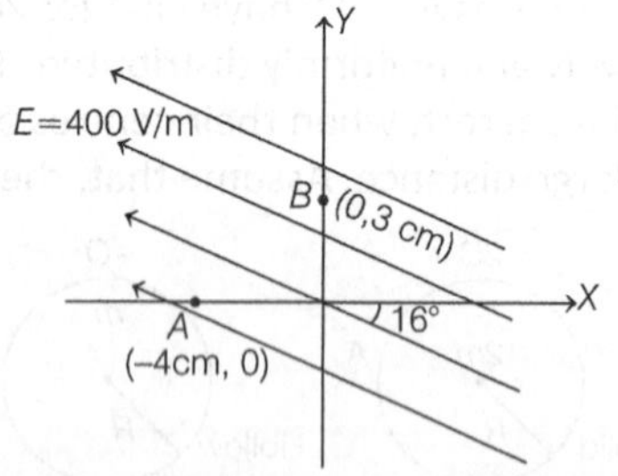

2 Consider the E versus x graph. What is the minimum velocity that should be given to a point charge $-Q$ of mass M, so that it can reach the origin?

Take, $Q = 1$ mC, mass of the charge as 1 mg, $E_0 = 20$ N/C, $L = 5$ m and $\sqrt{10} = 3.162$. (Assume particle is starting from $x = 3L$ and moving towards origin along X-axis)

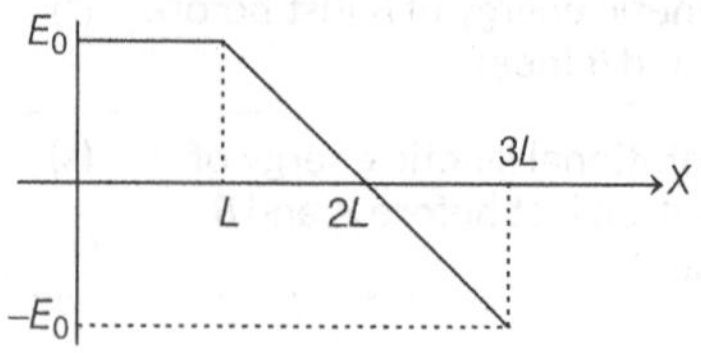

3 A total amount of positive charge Q is spread into a non-conducting flat circular annulus of inner radius a and outer radius $3a$. The charge is distributed, so that the charge density is given by $\sigma = \frac{k}{r^3}$, where r is the distance from the centre of the annulus to any point on it. The potential at the centre of annulus is $\frac{Q}{n\pi\varepsilon_0 a}$. Find n.

4 A uniformly charged hemisphere of radius b and charge density ρ has a hemispherical cavity of radius $a\left(a = \frac{b}{2}\right)$ cut from its centre.

If the potential at the centre of the cavity is $\frac{n\rho b^2}{16\varepsilon_0}$, then $n = ?$

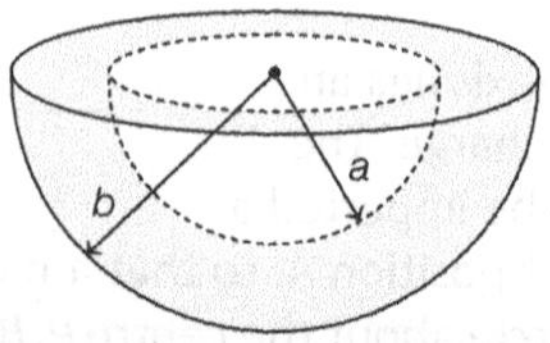

5 A non-conducting disc of radius $R = 6$ m and uniform positive surface charge density σ is placed on the ground, with its axis vertical. A particle of mass m and positive charge q is dropped, along the axis of the disc, from a height H with zero initial velocity. The particle has $\frac{q}{m} = \frac{4\varepsilon_0 g}{\sigma}$.

Find the value of H (in m), if the particle just reaches the disc.

6 Figure shows a thin rod of length L, which is uniformly charged with linear charge density λ kept on a smooth horizontal surface. Right end of rod is in contact with a vertical fixed wall. A block of mass m and charge q is projected with a velocity $v_0 = \sqrt{\frac{\lambda q}{m\pi\varepsilon_0}\ln 2}$ from a point very far from rod in the line of rod. If the distance of closest approach between the block and the left end A of the rod is $\frac{L}{n}$, then find n.

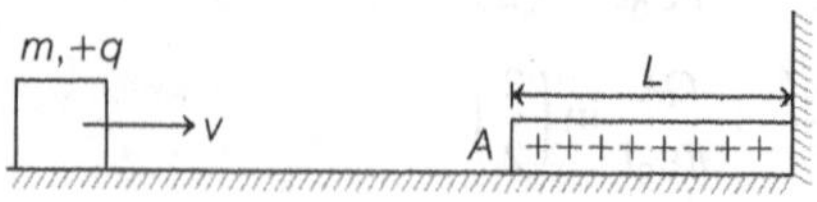

7 At the lower end of a vertically positioned insulator bar shown in the figure, there is a pearl of the mass $m = 10^{-4}$ kg and a charge of Q_1. Above it at a height $h_0 = 20$ cm, there is another pearl with the same mass m and electric charge Q_2 resting in equilibrium. At a given moment, we kick the lower pearl and it starts upwards at a velocity of $v_0 = 2$ m/s. How close (in cm) can the lower pearl get to the upper one at most? (The pearl can move along the bar without friction)

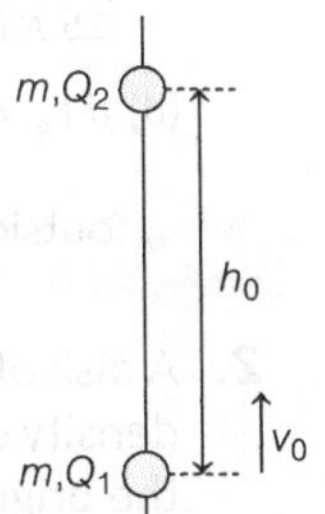

8 Four balls, each with mass m, are connected by four non-conducting strings to form a square with side a as shown in figure. The assembly is placed on a horizontal, non-conducting, frictionless surface. Balls 1 and 2 each have charge q and balls 3 and 4 are uncharged. Find the maximum speed of balls 3 and 4 after the string connected balls 1 and 2 is cut. If your answer is $\sqrt{\dfrac{Ykq^2}{Xam}}$ (where, $k = \dfrac{1}{4\pi\varepsilon_0}$), then fill value of $X + Y$, where X and Y are smallest positive integer.

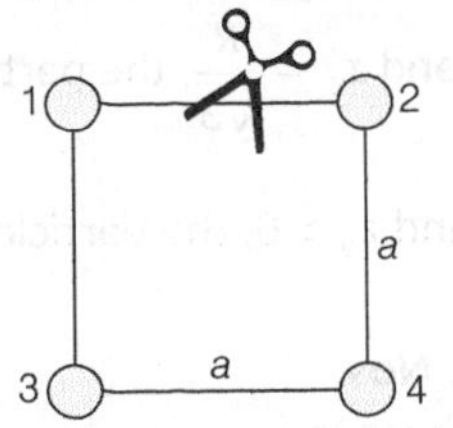

9 Two uniformly charged co-axial, identical rings (Radius R) are fixed as shown. A point charge q_0 is projected with speed v_0 along common axis of rings from large distance. Minimum value of v_0 for which the charge particle can just pass through both rings is given as $v_0 = \sqrt{\dfrac{kqq_0}{nmR}}$.

Find n. $\left(\text{Take, } k = \dfrac{1}{4\pi\varepsilon_0}\right)$

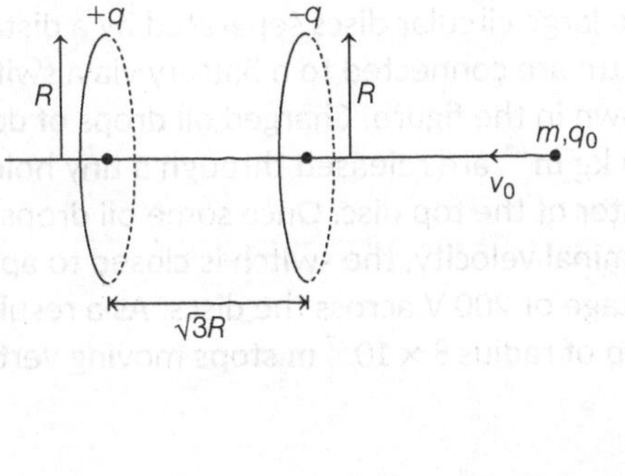

10 A bob of mass m and charge q is suspended from a point O of a vertical large thin non-conducting sheet of a surface charge density $+\sigma$. The bob is released from rest from horizontal. If $l = 1$ m, $\sigma q = 4\varepsilon_0 mg$, find velocity of the bob (in m/s), when $\theta = \sin^{-1}\left(\dfrac{3}{5}\right)$.

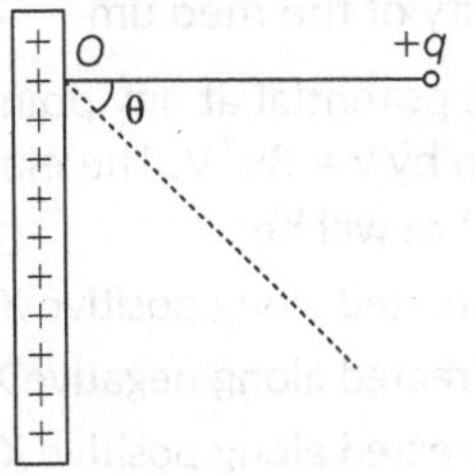

Previous Year's Questions

JEE Main

1 An electric charge 10^{-6} μC is placed at origin (0, 0) m of x-y coordinate system. Two points P and Q are situated at $(\sqrt{3}, \sqrt{3})$ m and $(\sqrt{6}, 0)$ m respectively. The potential difference between the points P and Q will be **[2024, 27 Jan Shift-I]**

(a) 3V (b) 0 V (c) $\sqrt{3}$ V (d) $\sqrt{6}$ V

2 Given below are two statements : one is labelled as **Assertion (A)** and other is labelled as **Reason (R)**.

Assertion (A) Work done by electric field on moving a positive charge on an equipotential surface is always zero.

Reason (R) Electric lines of forces are always perpendicular to equipotential surfaces.

In the light of the above statements, choose the **most appropriate** answer from the options given below **[2024, 27 Jan Shift-II]**

(a) (A) is not correct but (R) is correct.
(b) Both (A) and (R) but correct and (R) is not the correct explanation of (A).
(c) Both (A) and (R) are correct and (R) is the correct explanation of (A).
(d) (A) is correct but (R) is not correct.

3 Electric potential at a point 'P' due to a point charge of 5×10^{-9} C is 50 V. The distance of 'P' from the point charge is

(Assume, $\dfrac{1}{4\pi\varepsilon_0} = 9 \times 10^{+9}$ N-m^{2}C^{-2}) **[2023, 8 April Shift-II]**

(a) 90 cm (b) 3 cm (c) 0.9 cm (d) 9 cm

4 64 identical drops each charged upto potential of 10mV are combined to form a bigger drop. The potential of the bigger drop will be .... mV. **[2023, 12 April Shift-I]**

5 For a charged spherical ball, electrostatic potential inside the ball varies with r as $V = 2ar^2 + b$. Here, a and b are constant and r is the distance from the centre. The volume charge density inside the ball is $-\lambda a\varepsilon$. The value of λ is ....

ε = permittivity of the medium **[2023, 29 Jan Shift -II]**

6 If the electric potential at any point (x, y, z)m in space is given by $V = 3x^2$ V. The electric field at the point (1, 0, 3) m will be **[2022, 29 June Shift-II]**

(a) 3 Vm^{-1}, directed along positive X-axis.

(b) 3 Vm^{-1}, directed along negative X-axis.

(c) 6 Vm^{-1}, directed along positive X-axis.

(d) 6 Vm^{-1}, directed along negative X-axis.

7 27 identical drops are charged at 22 V each. They combine to form a bigger drop. The potential of the bigger drop will be .... V. **[2022, 25 June Shift-II]**

8 The average translational kinetic energy of N_2 gas molecules at ....°C becomes equal to the KE of an electron accelerated from rest through a potential difference of 0.1 V.

[Given, $K_B = 1.38\times 10^{-23}$ J/K] **[2021, 1 Sep Shift-II]**

9 27 similar drops of mercury are maintained at 10 V each. All these spherical drops combine into a single big drop. The potential energy of the bigger drop is .... times that of a smaller drop. **[2021, 26 Feb Shift-II]**

JEE Advanced

1. In the figure, the inner (shaded) region A represents a sphere of radius $r_A = 1$, within which of the electrostatic charge density varies with the radial distance r from the centre as $\rho_A = kr$, where k is positive. In the spherical shell B of outer radius r_B, the electrostatic charge density varies as $\rho_B = \frac{2k}{r}$. Assume that dimensions are taken care of. All physical quantities are in their SI units. **(2022 Adv.)**

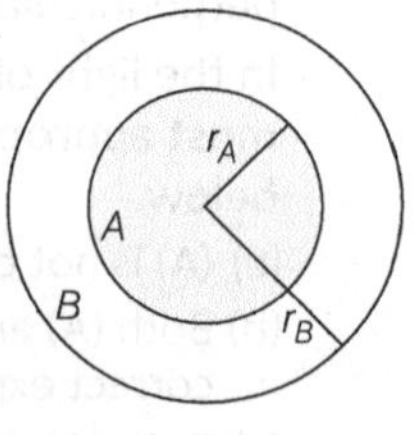

Which of the following statement(s) is(are) correct?

(a) If $r_B = \sqrt{\frac{3}{2}}$, then the electric field is zero everywhere outside B.

(b) If $r_B = \frac{3}{2}$, then the electric potential just outside B is $\frac{k}{\varepsilon_0}$.

(c) If $r_B = 2$, then the total charge of the configuration is $15\pi k$.

(d) If $r_B = \frac{5}{2}$, then the magnitude of the electric field just outside B is $\frac{13\pi k}{\varepsilon_0}$.

2. A disk of radius R with uniform positive charge density σ is placed on the XY-plane with its centre at the origin. The Coulomb potential along the Z-axis is

$V(z) = \frac{\sigma}{2\varepsilon_0}(\sqrt{R^2 + z^2} - z)$.

A particle of positive charge q is placed initially at rest at a point on the Z-axis with $z = z_0$ and $z_0 > 0$. In addition to the Coulomb force, the particle experiences a vertical force $\mathbf{F} = -c\mathbf{k}$ with $c > 0$. Let $\beta = \frac{2c\varepsilon_0}{q\sigma}$. Which of the following statement(s) is/are correct? **(2022 Adv.)**

(a) For $\beta = \frac{1}{4}$ and $z_0 = \frac{25}{7}R$, the particle reaches the origin.

(b) For $\beta = \frac{1}{4}$ and $z_0 = \frac{3}{7}R$, the particle reaches the origin.

(c) For $\beta = \frac{1}{4}$ and $z_0 = \frac{R}{\sqrt{3}}$, the particle returns back to $z = z_0$.

(d) For $\beta > 1$ and $z_0 > 0$, the particle always reaches the origin.

Question Stem (Q. Nos. 3 & 4) Two point charges $-Q$ and $+Q/\sqrt{3}$ are placed in the xy-plane at the origin (0, 0) and a point (2, 0) respectively, as shown in the figure.

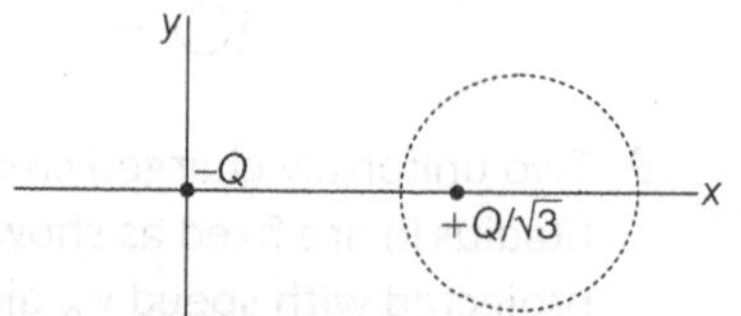

This results in an equipotential circle of radius R and potential $V = 0$ in the xy-plane with its centre at (b, 0). All lengths are measured in metre. **(2021 Adv.)**

3 The value of R is ____ metre.

4 The value of b is ____ metre.

5 Two large circular discs separated by a distance of 0.01m are connected to a battery via a switch as shown in the figure. Charged oil drops of density 900 kg m^{-3} are released through a tiny hole at the center of the top disc. Once some oil drops achieve terminal velocity, the switch is closed to apply a voltage of 200 V across the discs. As a result, an oil drop of radius 8×10^{-7} m stops moving vertically and floats between the discs. The number of electrons present in this oil drop is ________. (neglect the buoyancy force, take acceleration due to gravity $= 10\ \text{ms}^{-2}$ and charge on an electron (e) $= 1.6 \times 10^{-19}$ C) **(2020 Adv.)**

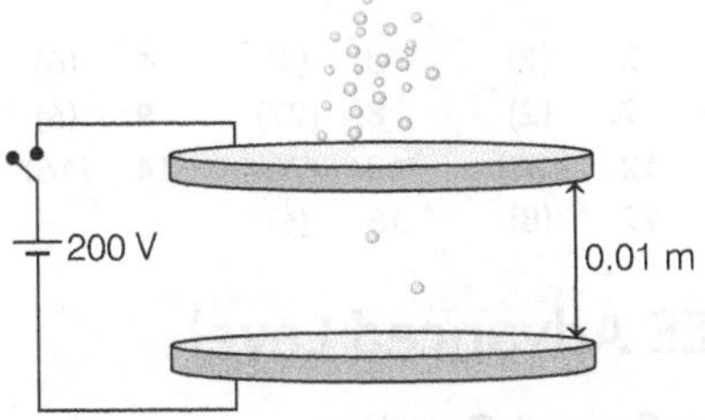

Passage (6-7) *There are two questions based on the following passage.*

Consider an evacuated cylindrical chamber of height h having rigid conducting plates at the ends and an insulating curved surface as shown in the figure. A number of spherical balls made of a light weight and soft material and coated with a conducting material are placed on the bottom plate. The balls have a radius $r << h$. Now, a high voltage source (HV) connected across the conducting plates, such that the bottom plate is at $+V_0$ and the top plate at $-V_0$. Due to their conducting surface, the balls will get charge, will become equipotential with the plate and are repelled by it. The balls will eventually collide with the top plate, where the coefficient of restitution can be taken to be zero due to te soft nature of the material of the balls. The electric field in the chamber can be considered to be that of a parallel plate capacitor. Assume that there are no collisions between the balls and the interaction between them is negligible. (Ignore gravity)

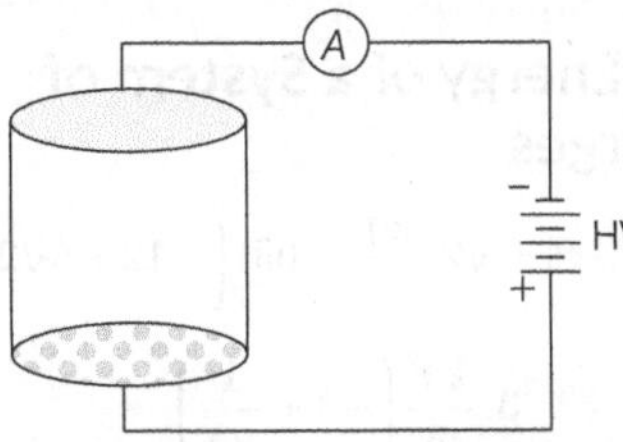

6 Which one of the following statement is correct? **[JEE Advanced 2016]**

(a) The balls will execute simple harmonic motion between the two plates.

(b) The balls will bounce back to the bottom plate carrying the same charge they went up with.

(c) The balls will stick to the top plate and remain there.

(d) The balls will bounce back to the bottom plate carrying the opposite charge they went up with.

7 The average current in the steady state registered by the ammeter in the circuit will be **[JEE Advanced 2016]**

(a) proportional to V_0^2.

(b) proportional to the potential V_0.

(c) zero

(d) proportions to $V_0^{1/2}$

Answer Key

Level 1 Starter Level

2.1 Electric Potential

1. -20 V 2. (i) 20 mJ (ii) -20 mJ (iii) 30 mJ
3. (i) -20 mJ (ii) 30 mJ 4. (i) 10 eV (ii) -10 eV

2.2 Electric Potential Due to Point Charge(s)

1. (i) $\frac{4\sqrt{2}kq}{a}$ (ii) $-\frac{\sqrt{3}kq}{a}$ (iii) 0
2. (i) $V_A = -15000$ V (ii) $V_B = -6000$ V
3. $V = \frac{q}{2\pi\varepsilon_0}, V = \frac{q}{6\pi\varepsilon_0}$ 4. 60 cm left of A and 20 cm right of A
5. $x^2 + y^2 + 2x - 8 = 0$ 6. $3kq/L$

2.3 Electric Potential Due to Continous Charge Configurations

1. (i) $\frac{kQ}{R}$ (ii) $\frac{kQ}{R}$ (iii) $\frac{kQ}{R}$ 2. 18 V
3. $\frac{\sigma}{2\varepsilon_0}(\sqrt{R^2+x^2} - x)$ 4. (i) 144 kV (ii) 144 kV (iii) 120 kV
5. (i) $\frac{kQ_1}{R_1} + \frac{kQ_2}{R_2}$ (ii) $\frac{kQ_1}{OB} + \frac{kQ_2}{R_2}$ (iii) $\frac{k(Q_1+Q_2)}{OC}$
6. (i) 216 kV, (ii) 198 kV (iii) 120 kV
7. $V = \frac{5\rho R^2}{12\varepsilon_0}$ 8. $\frac{Q\ln 3}{4\pi\varepsilon_0 L}$

2.4 Potential Difference

1. 400 V 2. 45.5 eV, 4×10^6 m/s 3. 0.4 C
4. (i) $+4.5 \times 10^{-5}$ J (ii) 3×10^5 N/C (iii) 1.5×10^4 V
5. (i) -4.5×10^{-5} J (ii) 3×10^5 N/C (iii) -1.5×10^4 V
6. 1.2 J 7. $\frac{Qq}{\pi\varepsilon_0 a}\left(\frac{1}{\sqrt{5}} - 1\right)$ 8. $\frac{kQq}{R}$

2.5 Potential Energy of a Point Charge

1. 10 eV 2. $\frac{6kqq_0}{a}$ 3. 90 m/s 4. 10^3 m/s

5. $\frac{Qq}{4\pi\varepsilon_0 K}$ 6. 2 m 7. $\sqrt{\frac{Qq}{4\pi\varepsilon_0 mR}}$ 8. $\sqrt{\frac{Qq}{2\pi\varepsilon_0 mR}}$

2.6 Potential Energy of a System of Point Charges

1. (i) $\frac{3kq^2}{a}$ (ii) $(-4+\sqrt{2})\frac{kq^2}{a}$ (iii) $\left(-12+6\sqrt{2}-\frac{4}{\sqrt{3}}\right)\frac{kq^2}{a}$

2. 4.5 J 3. $\frac{kq^2}{a}\left(-1+\frac{1}{\sqrt{3}}\right)$

4. $\frac{Q^2}{\pi\varepsilon_0 mu^2}$ 5. $\frac{qq_0}{16\pi\varepsilon_0 r}$ 6. (i) 108 J (ii) 60 m/s (iii) $60\sqrt{2}$ m/s (iv) 120 m/s

2.7 Relation between Electric Field and Electric Potential

1. $V_A = 16$ V, $V_C = 6$ V, $V_D = 6$V
2. (i) $V = -8x$ (ii) $V = 80 - 8x$ (iii) infinity
3. -10 V 4. $V = -4x^3 + y^3 + C$
5. $V = 112 - 2xy$ 6. $-2xy\hat{i} - (x^2 + 2yz)\hat{j} - y^2\hat{k}$
7. 28 V/m 8. $V_P - V_Q = \frac{\sigma d \sin\theta}{2\varepsilon_0}$ 9. $\frac{q\lambda \ln 2}{2\pi\varepsilon_0}$

2.8 Equipotential Surfaces

1. (i) $E_B > E_C > E_A$ (ii) 80 μJ
2. (i) 150 V/m towards left (ii) 6 cm (iii) 5 V
3. (i) 200 V/m at an angle of 120° with the X-axis
   (ii) $(6/r^2)$ V-m radially outward,
4. (i) True (ii) True (iii) False (iv) True

2.9 Self-Energy

1. (i) $\frac{kQ^2}{2R}$ (ii) $\frac{3kQ^2}{5R}$
2. $\frac{q(q_0+q/2)}{8\pi\varepsilon_0 R}, -\frac{q(q_0+q/2)}{8\pi\varepsilon_0 R}$
3. $\frac{Q_1^2}{8\pi\varepsilon_0 R_1} + \frac{Q_2^2}{8\pi\varepsilon_0 R_2} + \frac{Q_1Q_2}{4\pi\varepsilon_0 R_2}$

Level 2 JEE Main Level

Single Choice Correct Quesitons

1. (c)	2. (c)	3. (b)	4. (b)	5. (d)
6. (a)	7. (b)	8. (c)	9. (b)	10. (a)
11. (c)	12. (b)	13. (d)	14. (d)	15. (d)
16. (b)	17. (c)	18. (c)	19. (b)	20. (a)
21. (b)	22. (c)	23. (c)	24. (b)	25. (d)
26. (d)	27. (c)	28. (b)	29. (a)	30. (d)
31. (b)	32. (a)	33. (a)	34. (a)	35. (d)
36. (b)	37. (b)	38. (d)	39. (b)	40. (b)
41. (b)	42. (a)	43. (c)	44. (a)	45. (b)
46. (c)	47. (a)	48. (d)		

Numerical Value Questions

1. (15)	2. (7)	3. (4)	4. (6)	5. (1)
6. (20)	7. (2)	8. (27)	9. (6)	10. (5)
11. (10)	12. (20)	13. (70)	14. (16)	15. (40)
16. (5)	17. (8)	18. (6)		

Level 3 JEE Advanced Level

Single Choice Correct Questions

1. (c)	2. (d)	3. (b)	4. (c)	5. (a)
6. (d)	7. (b)	8. (d)	9. (a)	10. (b)
11. (b)	12. (d)	13. (a)	14. (c)	15. (d)
16. (a)	17. (a)	18. (c)	19. (b)	20. (b)
21. (a)	22. (a)	23. (b)	24. (a)	25. (a)
26. (c)	27. (c)	28. (a)	29. (b)	30. (c)
31. (b)				

Multiple Choice(s) Correct Questions

1. (ac)	2. (abcd)	3. (bc)	4. (ac)	5. (abd)
6. (ac)	7. (abc)	8. (ac)	9. (ab)	10. (acd)
11. (ad)	12. (ad)	13. (acd)	14. (ac)	15. (ac)
16. (abcd)	17. (bcd)			

Comprehension Based Questions

1. (b)	2. (d)	3. (d)	4. (c)	5. (c)
6. (b)	7. (c)	8. (a)	9. (c)	10. (a)
11. (a)	12. (c)	13. (b)	14. (d)	15. (a)
16. (b)	17. (c)	18. (d)	19. (b)	

Match the Columns Questions

1. a→ q; b→ r; c→ s; d→p
2. a→ q; b→ r, c→ s, d→ p
3. a→ q, t; b→ s, r; c→ p, r; d→q, t

Numerical Value Questions

1. 32	2. 316.20	3. 6	4. 3
5. 8	6. 3	7. 13.33	8. 4
9. 1	10. 2		

Previous Year's Questions

JEE Main

1. (b)	2. (c)	3. (a)	4. (160)	5. (12)
6. (d)	7. (198)	8. (500)	9. (243)	

JEE Advanced

1. (b)	2. (acd)	3. (1.73)	4. (3.00)	5. (6)
6. (d)	7. (a)			

SOLUTIONS

Level 1 Starter Level

2.1 Electric Potential

1. $V = \dfrac{W_{\text{ext } \infty \to P}}{q}\Bigg|_{\Delta K = 0} = \dfrac{-40}{2} = -20 \text{ V}$

2. (i) $W_{\text{ext } \infty \to P}\big|_{\Delta K = 0} = qV = (+20 \times 10^{-6})(1000) = 20 \text{ mJ}$

   (ii) $W_{\text{electric } \infty \to P} = -qV = -(20 \times 10^{-6})(1000) = -20 \text{ mJ}$

   (iii) Applying work-energy theorem,

   $$W_{\text{electric}} = \Delta K$$
   $$\Rightarrow \quad qV = K_\infty - 0$$
   $$\Rightarrow (+30 \times 10^{-6})(1000) = K_\infty$$
   $$\Rightarrow \quad K_\infty = 30 \text{ mJ}$$

3. (i) $W_{\text{electric } \infty \to P} = -qV = -(20 \times 10^{-6})(1000) = -20 \text{ mJ}$

   (ii) Using work-energy theorem,

   $$W_{\text{ext}} + W_{\text{electric}} = \Delta K$$
   $$\Rightarrow \quad W_{\text{ext}} - 20 \text{ mJ} = 10 \text{ mJ} - 0$$
   $$\Rightarrow \quad W_{\text{ext}} = 30 \text{ mJ}$$

4. (i) $W_{\text{ext } \infty \to P}\big|_{\Delta K = 0} = qV = (-e)(-10 \text{ V}) = 10 \text{eV}$

   (ii) $W_{\text{electric } \infty \to P} = -qV = -(-e)(-10 \text{ V}) = -10 \text{ eV}$

2.2 Electric Potential due to Point Charge(s)

1. (i) $V = V_1 + V_2 + V_3 + V_4 = \dfrac{kq}{a/\sqrt{2}} \times 4 = \dfrac{4\sqrt{2}kq}{a}$

   (ii) $V = V_1 + V_2 + V_3 = \dfrac{kq}{a/\sqrt{3}} + \dfrac{k(-q)}{a/\sqrt{3}} + \dfrac{k(-q)}{a/\sqrt{3}} = -\dfrac{\sqrt{3}kq}{a}$

   (iii) $V = V_1 + V_2 + V_3 + V_4 + V_5$

   $$= \frac{k}{r}(+5q + 3q - 2q + q - 7q) = 0$$

2. (i) $V_A = V_1 + V_2$

   $$= \frac{9 \times 10^9 \times (-4 \times 10^{-6})}{2} + \frac{9 \times 10^9 \times (+2 \times 10^{-6})}{6}$$
   $$= -15000 \text{ V}$$

   (ii) $V_B = V_1 + V_2$

   $$= \frac{9 \times 10^9 \times (-4 \times 10^{-6})}{\sqrt{2^2 + (\sqrt{5})^2}} + \frac{9 \times 10^9 \times 2 \times 10^{-6}}{\sqrt{2^2 + (\sqrt{5})^2}}$$
   $$= -6000 \text{ V}$$

3. 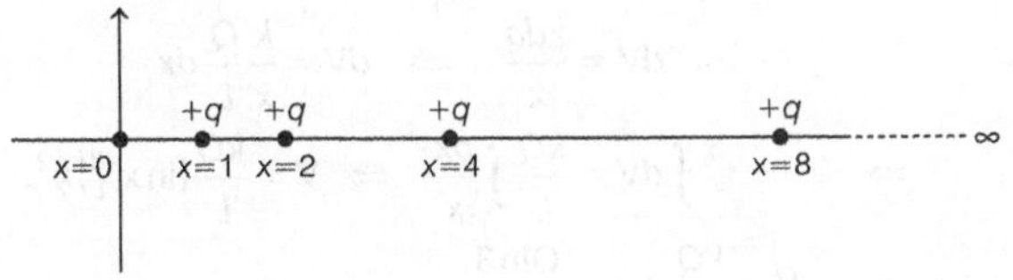

   $$V = V_1 + V_2 + V_3 + \ldots$$
   $$= \frac{kq}{1} + \frac{kq}{2} + \frac{kq}{4} + \frac{kq}{8} + \ldots \infty$$
   $$= kq\left(1 + \frac{1}{2} + \frac{1}{4} + \frac{1}{8} + \ldots \infty\right)$$
   $$= kq\left(\frac{1}{1 - \frac{1}{2}}\right) = \frac{q}{2\pi\varepsilon_0}$$

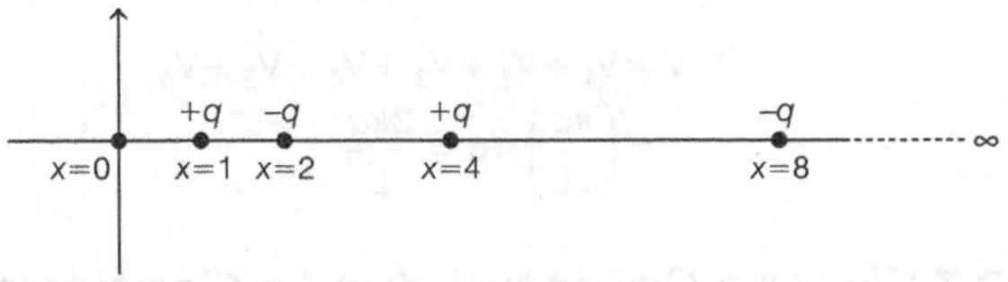

   $$V = V_1 + V_2 + V_3 + V_4 + \ldots$$
   $$= \frac{kq}{1} + \frac{k(-q)}{2} + \frac{k(+q)}{4} + \frac{k(-q)}{8} + \ldots \infty$$
   $$= kq\left(1 - \frac{1}{2} + \frac{1}{4} - \frac{1}{8} + \ldots \infty\right)$$
   $$= kq\left[\frac{1}{1 - \left(-\frac{1}{2}\right)}\right] = \frac{2kq}{3} = \frac{q}{6\pi\varepsilon_0}$$

4. 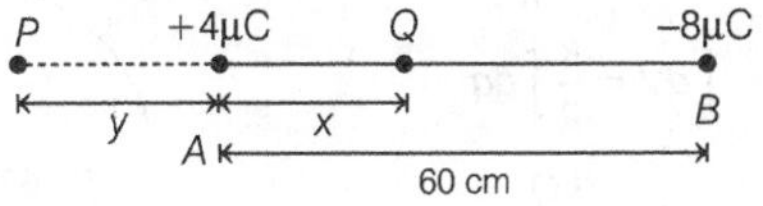

   $$V_Q = \frac{k(4\mu\text{C})}{x} + \frac{k(-8\mu\text{C})}{60 - x} = 0$$
   $$\Rightarrow \quad x = 20 \text{ cm}$$
   $$V_P = \frac{k(4\mu\text{C})}{y} + \frac{k(-8\mu\text{C})}{60 + y} = 0$$
   $$\Rightarrow \quad y = 60 \text{ cm}$$

5. 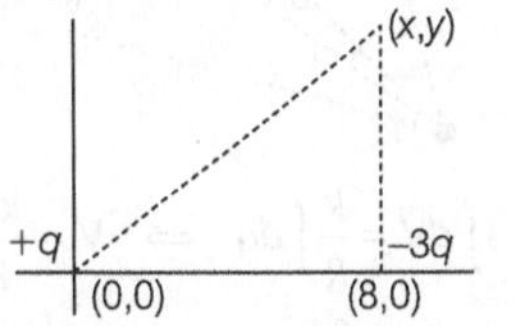

   $$V = V_1 + V_2$$
   $$\Rightarrow \quad 0 = \frac{kq}{\sqrt{x^2 + y^2}} + \frac{k(-3q)}{\sqrt{(x-8)^2 + y^2}}$$
   $$\Rightarrow \quad \sqrt{(x-8)^2 + y^2} = 3\sqrt{x^2 + y^2}$$
   $$\Rightarrow \quad (x-8)^2 + y^2 = 9x^2 + 9y^2$$
   $$\Rightarrow \quad 8x^2 + 8y^2 + 16x - 64 = 0$$
   $$\Rightarrow \quad x^2 + y^2 + 2x - 8 = 0$$

6.

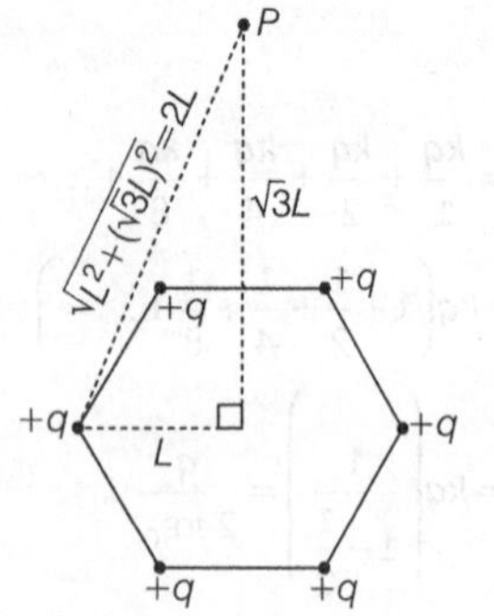

$$V = V_1 + V_2 + V_3 + V_4 + V_5 + V_6$$
$$= \left(\frac{kq}{2L}\right) \times 6 = \frac{3kq}{L}$$

2.3 Electric Potential due to Continuous Charge Configurations

1. (i) $dV = k\dfrac{dq}{R}$

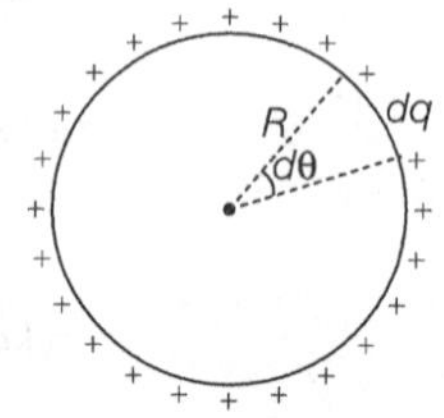

$$\Rightarrow \int dV = \frac{k}{R}\int dq$$
$$\Rightarrow V = \frac{kQ}{R}$$

(ii) $dV = k\dfrac{dq}{R}$

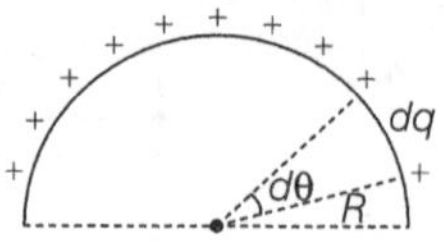

$$\Rightarrow \int dV = \frac{k}{R}\int dq$$
$$\Rightarrow V = \frac{kQ}{R}$$

(iii) $dV = k\dfrac{dq}{R}$

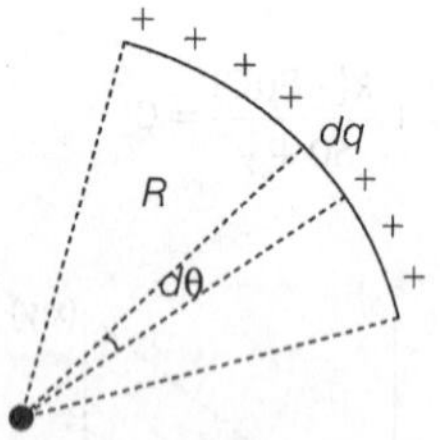

$$\Rightarrow \int dV = \frac{k}{R}\int dq \Rightarrow V = \frac{kQ}{R}$$

2. $V = \dfrac{kQ}{\sqrt{R^2+Z^2}} = \dfrac{9\times10^9 \times 10\times10^{-9}}{\sqrt{3^2+4^2}} = 18\text{ V}$

3.

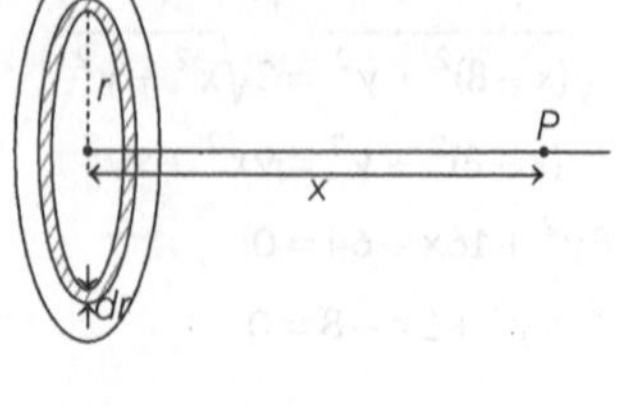

Lets take a ring of radius r and thickness dr on the disc,

$$dq = \sigma(2\pi r dr)$$
$$dV = \frac{kdq}{\sqrt{r^2+x^2}}$$
$$\Rightarrow V = \int_0^R \frac{1}{4\pi\varepsilon_0}\frac{2\pi r dr}{\sqrt{r^2+x^2}} \Rightarrow V = \frac{\sigma}{2\varepsilon_0}(\sqrt{R^2+x^2} - x)$$

4. (i) $V = \dfrac{kQ}{R} = \dfrac{9\times10^9 \times 1.6\times10^{-6}}{0.1} = 144\text{ kV}$

(ii) $V = \dfrac{kQ}{R} = 144\text{ kV}$

(iii) $V = \dfrac{kQ}{r} = \dfrac{9\times10^9 \times 1.6\times10^{-6}}{12\times10^{-2}} = 120\text{ kV}$

5. $V_A = V_1 + V_2 = \dfrac{kQ_1}{R_1} + \dfrac{kQ_2}{R_2}$

$$V_B = V_1 + V_2 = \frac{kQ_1}{OB} + \frac{kQ_2}{R_2}$$
$$V_C = V_1 + V_2 = \frac{kQ_1}{OC} + \frac{kQ_2}{OC} = \frac{k(Q_1+Q_2)}{OC}$$

6. (i) $V = \dfrac{3}{2}\dfrac{kQ}{R} = \dfrac{3}{2}\times\dfrac{9\times10^9\times1.6\times10^{-6}}{0.1} = 216\text{ kV}$

(ii) $V = \dfrac{kQ}{2R^3}(3R^2 - r^2)$

$$= \frac{9\times10^9\times1.6\times10^{-6}}{2\times(0.1)^3}[3(0.1)^2 - (0.05)^2] = 198\text{ kV}$$

(iii) $V = \dfrac{kQ}{r} = \dfrac{9\times10^9\times1.6\times10^{-6}}{12\times10^{-2}} = 120\text{ kV}$

7.

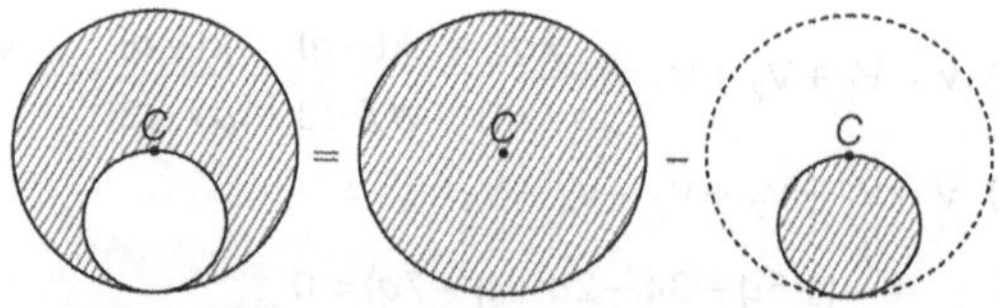

$$V = V_1 - V_2$$
$$= \frac{3}{2}\frac{k\left(\rho\frac{4}{3}\pi R^3\right)}{R} - \frac{k\left[\rho\frac{4}{3}\pi\left(\frac{R}{2}\right)^3\right]}{R/2} = \frac{5}{12}\frac{\rho R^2}{\varepsilon_0}$$

8.

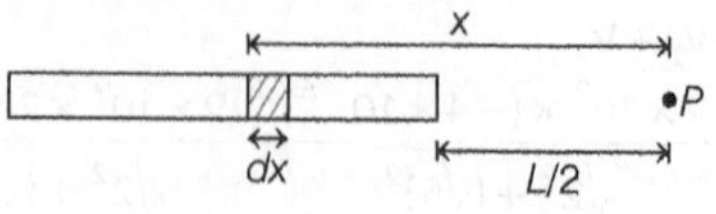

$$dq = \frac{Q}{L}dx$$
$$dV = \frac{kdq}{x} \Rightarrow dV = \frac{k}{x}\frac{Q}{L}dx$$
$$\Rightarrow \int dV = \frac{kQ}{L}\int\frac{dx}{x} \Rightarrow V = \frac{kQ}{L}(\ln x)_{L/2}^{3L/2}$$
$$\Rightarrow V = \frac{kQ}{L}\ln 3 = \frac{Q\ln 3}{4\pi\varepsilon_0 L}$$

2.4 Potential Difference

1. $V_B - V_A = \dfrac{W_{ext\ A\to B}|_{\Delta K=0}}{q} = \dfrac{20}{0.05} = 400\text{ V}$

2. $\Delta K = -q\Delta V$

$\Rightarrow \quad K - 0 = -(-e)(45.5\text{ V})$

$\Rightarrow \quad K = 45.5\text{ eV}$

$K = \dfrac{1}{2}mv^2 = 45.5\text{ eV}$

$\Rightarrow \quad \dfrac{1}{2}\times 9.1\times 10^{-31}\times v^2 = 45.5\times 1.6\times 10^{-19}$

$\Rightarrow \quad v = 4\times 10^6\text{ m/s}$

3. $\Delta K = -q(\Delta V)$

$\Rightarrow \quad -20 = -q(100-50)$

$\Rightarrow \quad q = 0.4\text{ C}$

4. (i) $W_{electric} = \Delta K$

$\Rightarrow \quad W_{electric} = 4.5\times 10^{-5} - 0$

$\Rightarrow \quad W_{electric} = 4.5\times 10^{-5}\text{ J}$

(ii) $W_{electric} = (qE)d$

$\Rightarrow \quad 4.5\times 10^{-5} = (3\times 10^{-9}E)\times 5\times 10^{-2}$

$\Rightarrow \quad E = 3\times 10^5\text{ N/C}$

(iii) $\Delta V = -\dfrac{W_{electric}}{q} = -\dfrac{4.5\times 10^{-5}}{3\times 10^{-9}} = -15\text{ kV}$

$\Rightarrow \quad V_2 - V_1 = -15\text{ kV}$

$\Rightarrow \quad V_1 - V_2 = 15\text{ kV} = 1.5\times 10^4\text{ V}$

5. (i) $W_{electric} + W_{ext} = \Delta K$

$\Rightarrow \quad W_{electric} + 9\times 10^{-5} = 4.5\times 10^{-5} - 0$

$\Rightarrow \quad W_{electric} = -4.5\times 10^{-5}\text{ J}$

(ii) $W_{electric} = (qE)d - 4.5\times 10^{-5}$

$= (3\times 10^{-9})E(-5\times 10^{-2})$

$\Rightarrow \quad E = 3\times 10^5\text{ N/C}$

(iii) $\Delta V = -\dfrac{W_{electric}}{q} = -\dfrac{(-4.5\times 10^{-5})}{3\times 10^{-9}}$

$\Rightarrow \quad V_2 - V_1 = 15\text{ kV}$

$\Rightarrow \quad V_1 - V_2 = -15\text{ kV} = -1.5\times 10^4\text{ V}$

6. $W_{ext} = q\Delta V = q(V_B - V_A)$

$= (-2\times 10^{-9})\left(\dfrac{9\times 10^9\times 8\times 10^{-3}}{0.04} - \dfrac{9\times 10^9\times 8\times 10^{-3}}{0.03}\right)$

$= 1.2\text{ J}$

7. $V_E = \dfrac{kq}{a/2} + \dfrac{k(-q)}{a/2} + \dfrac{kq}{\sqrt{5}a/2} + \dfrac{k(-q)}{\sqrt{5}a/2} = 0$

$V_F = \dfrac{k(-q)}{a/2}\times 2 + \dfrac{kq}{\sqrt{5}a/2}\times 2 = \dfrac{4kq}{a}\left(-1+\dfrac{1}{\sqrt{5}}\right)$

$W_{ext} = q\Delta V = Q(V_F - V_E)$

$= Q\left[\dfrac{4kq}{a}\left(\dfrac{1}{\sqrt{5}}-1\right) - 0\right]$

$= \dfrac{4kQq}{a}\left(\dfrac{1}{\sqrt{5}}-1\right) = \dfrac{Qq}{\pi\varepsilon_0 a}\left(\dfrac{1}{\sqrt{5}}-1\right)$

8.

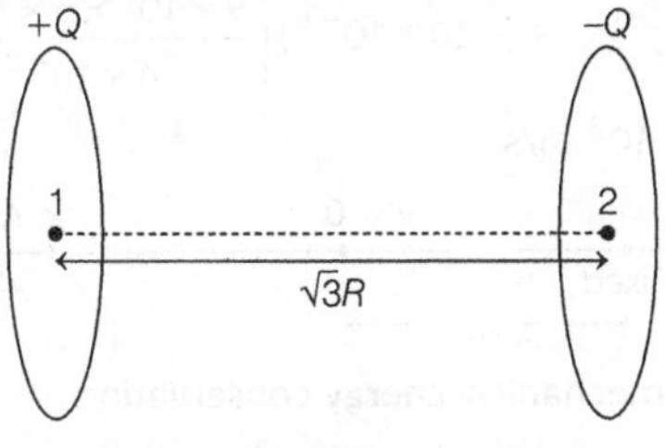

$V_1 = \dfrac{kQ}{R} + \dfrac{k(-Q)}{\sqrt{R^2+(\sqrt{3}R)^2}} = \dfrac{kQ}{2R}$

$V_2 = \dfrac{k(-Q)}{R} + \dfrac{k(Q)}{\sqrt{R^2+(\sqrt{3}R)^2}} = -\dfrac{kQ}{2R}$

$W_{ext} = q\Delta V = q(V_1 - V_2)$

$= q\left[\dfrac{kQ}{2R} - \left(\dfrac{-kQ}{2R}\right)\right] = \dfrac{kQq}{R}$

2.5 Potential Energy of a Point Charge

1. $U = qV = (+2e)(5\text{ V}) = 10\text{ eV}$

2. $U = qV = q_0\left(\dfrac{kq}{a}\times 6\right) = \dfrac{6kqq_0}{a}$

3.

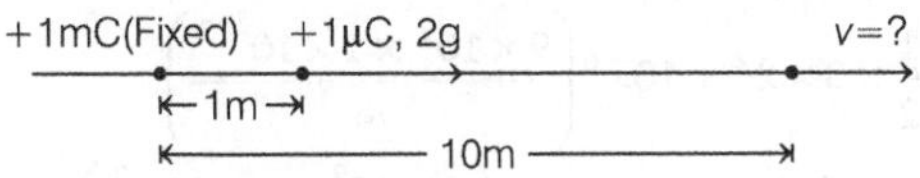

Applying mechanical energy conservation,

$K_1 + U_1 = K_2 + U_2$

$\Rightarrow 0 + 10^{-6}\left(\dfrac{9\times 10^9\times 1\times 10^{-3}}{1}\right)$

$= \dfrac{1}{2}\times 2\times 10^{-3}v^2 + 10^{-6}\left(\dfrac{9\times 10^9\times 1\times 10^{-3}}{10}\right)$

$\Rightarrow \quad v = \sqrt{8100} = 90\text{ m/s}$

4.

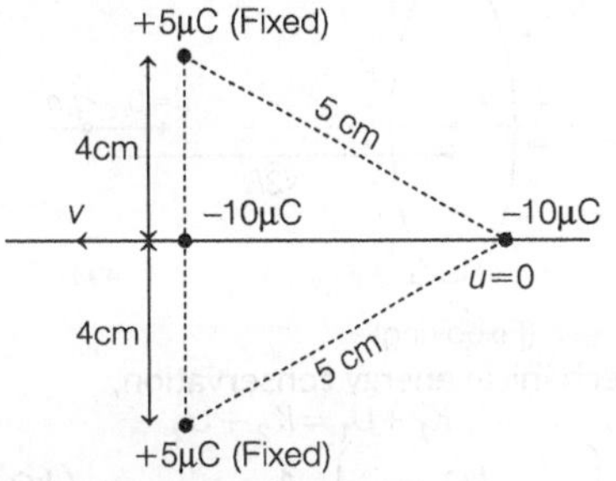

Applying mechanical energy conservation,

$K_1 + U_1 = K_2 + U_2$

$$\Rightarrow 0+(-10\times10^{-6})\left(\frac{9\times10^9\times5\times10^{-6}}{5\times10^{-2}}\times2\right)$$

$$=\frac{1}{2}\times9\times10^{-6}\times v^2$$

$$+(-10\times10^{-6})\left(\frac{9\times10^9\times5\times10^{-6}}{4\times10^{-2}}\times2\right)$$

$$\Rightarrow \quad v=10^3 \text{ m/s}$$

5.

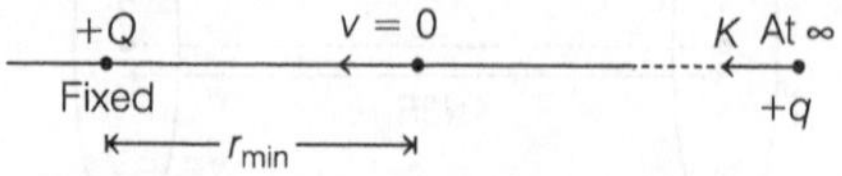

Applying mechanical energy conservation,

$$K_1+U_1=K_2+U_2$$

$$K+q\left(\frac{1}{4\pi\varepsilon_0}\frac{Q}{\infty}\right)=0+q\left(\frac{1}{4\pi\varepsilon_0}\frac{q}{r_{min}}\right)$$

$$\Rightarrow \quad r_{min}=\frac{Qq}{4\pi\varepsilon_0 K}$$

6.

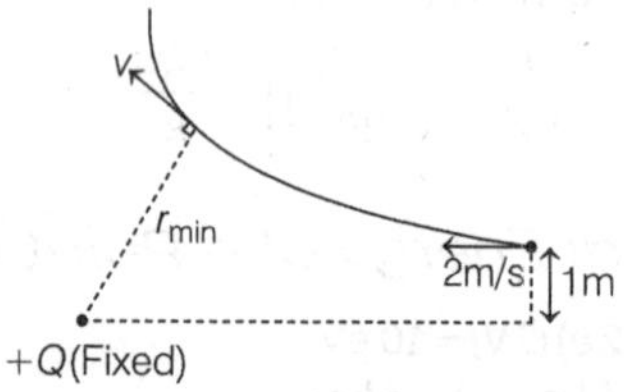

Applying mechanical energy conservation,

$K_1+U_1=K_2+U_2$

$$\Rightarrow \frac{1}{2}\times3\times2^2+10^{-6}\left(\frac{9\times10^9\times1\times10^{-3}}{\infty}\right)$$

$$=\frac{1}{2}\times3\times v^2+10^{-6}\left(\frac{9\times10^9\times1\times10^{-3}}{r_{min}}\right) \quad \text{... (i)}$$

Using conservation of angular momentum of q about Q,

$$3\times2\times1=3\times v\times r_{min}\times\sin90° \quad \text{... (ii)}$$

Solving Eqs. (i) and (ii), we get

$$r_{min}=2\text{m}$$

7.

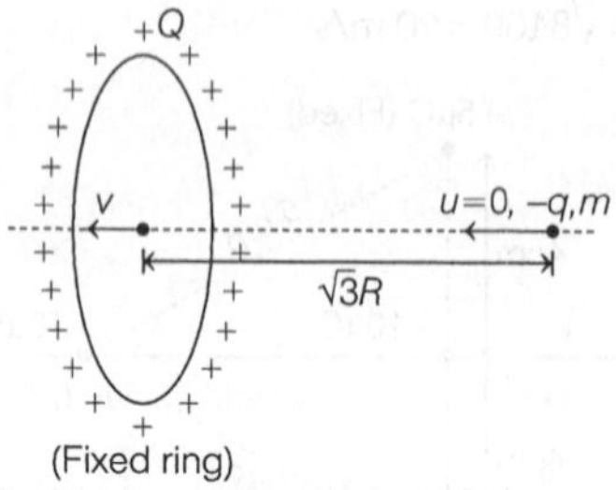

Using mechanical energy conservation,

$$K_1+U_1=K_2+U_2$$

$$0+(-q)\left(\frac{kQ}{\sqrt{R^2+(\sqrt{3}R)^2}}\right)=\frac{1}{2}mv^2+(-q)\left(\frac{kQ}{R}\right)$$

$$\Rightarrow \quad v=\sqrt{\frac{Qq}{4\pi\varepsilon_0 mR}}$$

8. We just need to make the point charge reach the centre of the sphere with negligible speed.

$$K_1+U_1=K_2+U_2$$

$$\Rightarrow \frac{1}{2}mu_{min}^2+q\left(\frac{kQ}{2R}\right)=0+q\left(\frac{3}{2}\frac{kQ}{R}\right) \Rightarrow u_{min}=\sqrt{\frac{Qq}{2\pi\varepsilon_0 mR}}$$

2.6 Potential Energy of a System of Point Charges

1. (i) $U=\frac{k(+q)(+q)}{a}\times3=\frac{3kq^2}{a}$

(ii) $U=\frac{k(+q)(-q)}{a}\times4+\frac{k(+q)(+q)}{\sqrt{2}a}+\frac{k(-q)(-q)}{\sqrt{2}a}$

$$=\frac{kq^2}{a}(-4+\sqrt{2})$$

(iii) $U=\left[\frac{k(+q)(-q)}{a}\right]\times12+\left[\frac{k(+q)(+q)}{\sqrt{2}a}\right]\times6$

$$+\left[\frac{k(-q)(-q)}{\sqrt{2}a}\right]\times6+\left[\frac{k(+q)(-q)}{\sqrt{3}a}\right]\times4$$

$$=\frac{kq^2}{a}\left(-12+\frac{12}{\sqrt{2}}-\frac{4}{\sqrt{3}}\right)$$

2. $W_{ext}=\Delta U=U_2-U_1$

$$=\frac{9\times10^9\times15\times10^{-6}\times10\times10^{-6}}{15\times10^{-2}}-\frac{9\times10^9\times15\times10^{-6}\times10\times10^{-6}}{30\times10^{-2}}$$

$$=9-4.5=4.5\text{ J}$$

3. $U_1=\left[\frac{k(+q)(+q)}{a}\right]\times2+\left[\frac{k(+q)(-q)}{a}\right]\times2$

$$+\frac{k(+q)(+q)}{\sqrt{2}a}+\frac{k(+q)(-q)}{\sqrt{2}a}$$

$\Rightarrow \quad U_1=0$

$$U_2=\left[\frac{k(+q)(+q)}{a}\right]\times2+\left[\frac{k(+q)(-q)}{a}\right]\times2$$

$$+\frac{k(+q)(+q)}{\sqrt{3}a}+\frac{k(+q)(-q)}{a}$$

$$\Rightarrow \quad U_2=\frac{kq^2}{a}\left(-1+\frac{1}{\sqrt{3}}\right)$$

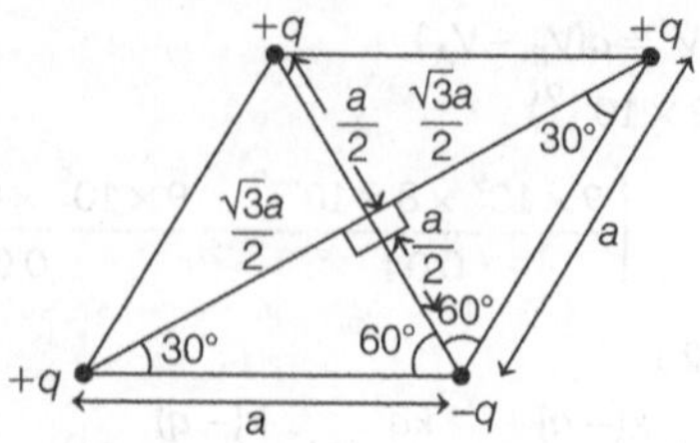

$$W_{ext}=\Delta U$$

$$=U_2-U_1=\frac{kq^2}{a}\left(-1+\frac{1}{\sqrt{3}}\right)-0$$

$$=\frac{kq^2}{a}\left(-1+\frac{1}{\sqrt{3}}\right)$$

4.

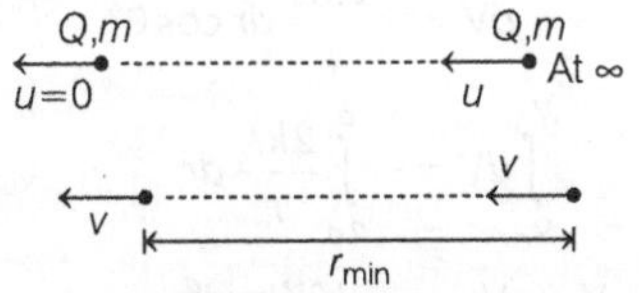

When the separation between the particles is minimum, their velocity of approach would be zero. So, both of them will have same velocity.

Using mechanical energy conservation,

$$K_1 + U_1 = K_2 + U_2$$

$$\left(0 + \frac{1}{2}mu^2\right) + Q\left(\frac{kQ}{\infty}\right) = \left(\frac{1}{2}mv^2 + \frac{1}{2}mv^2\right) + Q\left(\frac{kQ}{r_{min}}\right) \quad \text{... (i)}$$

Using linear momentum conservation,

$$0 + mu = mv + mv \quad \text{... (ii)}$$

Solving Eqs. (i) and (ii), we get

$$r_{min} = \frac{Q^2}{\pi\varepsilon_0 mu^2}$$

5. For circular motion,

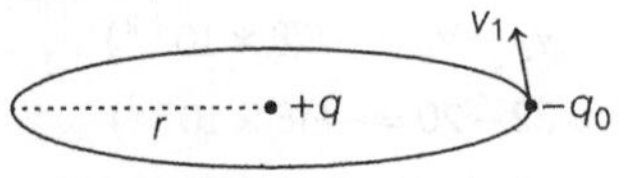

$$\frac{kqq_0}{r^2} = \frac{mv_1^2}{r}$$

$$\Rightarrow \quad v_1 = \sqrt{\frac{kqq_0}{mr}}$$

$$K_1 = \frac{1}{2}mv_1^2 = \frac{1}{2}m\left(\sqrt{\frac{kqq_0}{mr}}\right)^2 = \frac{kqq_0}{2r}$$

$$U_1 = \frac{k(+q)(-q_0)}{r} = -\frac{kqq_0}{r}$$

$$E_1 = K_1 + U_1 = \frac{kqq_0}{2r} - \frac{kqq_0}{r}$$

$$\Rightarrow \quad E_1 = -\frac{kqq_0}{2r}$$

$$E_2 = -\frac{kqq_0}{2(2r)} = -\frac{kqq_0}{4r}$$

$$W_{ext} = \Delta K + \Delta U = \Delta E$$

$$= E_2 - E_1$$

$$= -\frac{kqq_0}{4r} - \left(\frac{-kqq_0}{2r}\right) = \frac{qq_0}{16\pi\varepsilon_0 r}$$

6. (i) $$U_1 = \frac{9\times10^9 \times 20\times10^{-6} \times 20\times10^{-6}}{10\times10^{-2}} \times 3 = 108\text{ J}$$

$$U_2 = \frac{9\times10^9 \times 20\times10^{-6} \times 20\times10^{-6}}{5\times10^{-2}} \times 3 = 216\text{ J}$$

$$W_{ext} = \Delta U = U_2 - U_1 = 216 - 108 = 108\text{ J}$$

(ii) Applying mechanical energy conservation,

$$K_1 + U_1 = K_2 + U_2$$

$$(0+0+0) + \left(\frac{9\times10^9 \times 20\times10^{-6} \times 20\times10^{-6}}{10\times10^{-2}}\right)\times 3 = \left(\frac{1}{2}\times10\times10^{-3}v^2\right)\times 3 + \left(\frac{9\times10^9 \times 20\times10^{-6} \times 20\times10^{-6}}{20\times10^{-2}}\right)\times 3$$

$$\Rightarrow v = 60\text{ m/s}$$

(iii) Applying mechanical energy conservation,

$$K_1 + U_1 = K_2 + U_2$$

$$(0+0+0) + \left(\frac{9\times10^9 \times 20\times10^{-6} \times 20\times10^{-6}}{10\times10^{-2}}\right)\times 3 = \left(\frac{1}{2}\times10\times10^{-3}v^2\right)\times 3 + 0$$

$$\Rightarrow \quad v = 60\sqrt{2}\text{ m/s}$$

(iv) $K_1 + U_1 = K_2 + U_2$

$$0 + (20\times10^{-6})\left(\frac{9\times10^9 \times 20\times10^{-6} \times 2}{10\times10^{-2}}\right) = \frac{1}{2}\times10\times10^{-3}v^2 + 0$$

$$\Rightarrow \quad v = 120\text{ m/s}$$

2.7 Relation between Electric Field and Electric Potential

1. For uniform electric field, $\Delta V = -Ed$

$A \to B$;

$$\Delta V = -Ed \Rightarrow V_B - V_A = -Ed$$

$$\Rightarrow \quad 10 - V_A = -(200)(+3\times10^{-2})$$

$$\Rightarrow \quad V_A = 16\text{ V}$$

$B \to C$;

$$\Delta V = -Ed \Rightarrow V_C - V_B = -Ed$$

$$\Rightarrow \quad V_C - 10 = -(200)(+2\times10^{-2})$$

$$\Rightarrow \quad V_C = 6\text{V}$$

$C \to D$;

$$\Delta V = -Ed$$

$$V_D - V_C = -(200)(0) \Rightarrow V_D = V_C = 6\text{V}$$

2. (i) $\mathbf{E} = 8\hat{\mathbf{i}}$

$$dV = -\mathbf{E}\cdot d\mathbf{r}$$

$$\Rightarrow \quad dV = -(8\hat{\mathbf{i}})\cdot(dx\hat{\mathbf{i}} + dy\hat{\mathbf{j}} + dz\hat{\mathbf{k}})$$

$$\Rightarrow \quad \int_0^V dV = -8\int_{(0,0,0)}^{(x,y,z)} dx$$

$$\Rightarrow \quad [V]_0^V = -8[x]_0^x$$

$$\Rightarrow \quad V = -8x$$

(ii) $$\int_{80}^V dV = -8\int_{(0,0,0)}^{(x,y,z)} dx$$

$$\Rightarrow \quad V - 80 = -8x \Rightarrow V = 80 - 8x$$

(iii) $$\int_0^V dV = -8\int_{\infty}^0 dx \Rightarrow V = \infty$$

3. $\mathbf{E} = 10\hat{\mathbf{i}} + 20\hat{\mathbf{j}}$

$$dV = -\mathbf{E} \cdot d\mathbf{r}$$

$$\Rightarrow \quad dV = -(10\hat{\mathbf{i}} + 20\hat{\mathbf{j}}) \cdot (dx\hat{\mathbf{i}} + dy\hat{\mathbf{j}} + dz\hat{\mathbf{k}})$$

$$\Rightarrow \quad \int_{100}^{V} dV = -10\int_0^3 dx - 20\int_0^4 dy$$

$$\Rightarrow \quad [V]_{100}^{V} = -10[x]_0^3 - 20[y]_0^4$$

$$\Rightarrow V - 100 = -10(3-0) - 20(4-0)$$

$$\Rightarrow \quad V = -10\text{ V}$$

4. $dV = -\mathbf{E} \cdot d\mathbf{r}$

$$\Rightarrow \quad dV = -(6x^2\hat{\mathbf{i}} - 3y^2\hat{\mathbf{j}}) \cdot (dx\hat{\mathbf{i}} + dy\hat{\mathbf{j}})$$

$$\Rightarrow \quad \int dV = -6\int x^2 dx + 3\int y^2 dy$$

$$\Rightarrow \quad V = -4x^3 + y^3 + C$$

5. $dV = -\mathbf{E} \cdot d\mathbf{r}$

$$\Rightarrow \quad dV = -(2y\hat{\mathbf{i}} + 2x\hat{\mathbf{j}}) \cdot (dx\hat{\mathbf{i}} + dy\hat{\mathbf{j}} + dz\hat{\mathbf{k}})$$

$$\Rightarrow \quad \int dV = -\int (2y\,dx + 2x\,dy)$$

$$\Rightarrow \quad \int_{100}^{V} dV = -2\int_{(2,\,3)}^{(x,\,y)} (y\,dx + x\,dy)$$

$$\Rightarrow \quad \int_{100}^{V} dV = -2\int_{(2,\,3)}^{(x,\,y)} d(xy)$$

$$\Rightarrow \quad [V]_{100}^{V} = -2[xy]_{(2,\,3)}^{(x,\,y)}$$

$$\Rightarrow V - 100 = -2(xy - 6) \Rightarrow V = 112 - 2xy$$

6. $V = x^2y + y^2z$

$$E_x = \frac{-\partial V}{\partial x} = -2xy$$

$$E_y = \frac{-\partial V}{\partial y} = -x^2 - 2yz$$

$$E_z = \frac{-\partial V}{\partial z} = -y^2$$

$$\mathbf{E} = -2xy\hat{\mathbf{i}} - (x^2 + 2yz)\,\hat{\mathbf{j}} - y^2\hat{\mathbf{k}}$$

7. $V = 2(xy + yz + zx)$

$$\mathbf{E} = \frac{-\partial V}{\partial x}\hat{\mathbf{i}} - \frac{\partial V}{\partial y}\hat{\mathbf{j}} - \frac{\partial V}{\partial z}\hat{\mathbf{k}}$$

$$\Rightarrow \quad \mathbf{E} = -2(y+z)\,\hat{\mathbf{i}} - 2(x+z)\hat{\mathbf{j}} - 2(x+y)\hat{\mathbf{k}}$$

At $(5, 7, -1)$,

$$\mathbf{E} = -2(7-1)\hat{\mathbf{i}} - 2(5-1)\,\hat{\mathbf{j}} - 2(5+7)\hat{\mathbf{k}}$$

$$\Rightarrow \quad \mathbf{E} = -12\hat{\mathbf{i}} - 8\hat{\mathbf{j}} - 24\hat{\mathbf{k}}$$

$$|\mathbf{E}| = \sqrt{12^2 + 8^2 + 24^2} = 28\text{V/m}$$

8. $\Delta V = -Ed$

$P \to Q$:

$$V_Q - V_P = -\left(\frac{\sigma}{2\varepsilon_0}\right)(+d\sin\theta)$$

$$\Rightarrow \quad V_P - V_Q = \frac{\sigma d \sin\theta}{2\varepsilon_0}$$

9. $C \to A$;

$$dV = -\mathbf{E} \cdot d\mathbf{r}$$

$$\Rightarrow \quad dV = -\frac{2k\lambda}{r}dr\cos 0°$$

$$\Rightarrow \quad \int_{V_C}^{V_A} dV = -\int_{2a}^{a} \frac{2k\lambda}{r}dr$$

$$\Rightarrow \quad V_A - V_C = -2k\lambda[\ln r]_{2a}^{a}$$

$$\Rightarrow \quad V_A - V_C = \frac{\lambda}{2\pi\varepsilon_0}\ln 2$$

Now, $W_{\text{ext}} = q\Delta V = q(V_A - V_C) = \dfrac{q\lambda}{2\pi\varepsilon_0}\ln 2$

2.8 Equipotential Surfaces

1. (i) Electric field intensity is higher, where equipotential surfaces are closer.

So, $E_B > E_C > E_A$

(ii) $W_{(\text{ext})P \to Q} = \Delta U + \Delta K = q\Delta V + 0 = q(V_Q - V_P)$

$$= (4 \times 10^{-6})(50 - 30)$$

$$= 80 \times 10^{-6}\text{ J} = 80\,\mu\text{J}$$

2. (i) In going from B to C,

$$\Delta V = -Ed$$

$$\Rightarrow \quad V_C - V_B = -E(8 \times 10^{-2})$$

$$\Rightarrow \quad 32 - 20 = -E(8 \times 10^{-2})$$

$$\Rightarrow \quad E = -150\text{ V/m}$$

So, electric field is 150 V/m, towards left.

(ii) In going from C to D,

$$\Delta V = -Ed$$

$$\Rightarrow \quad 41 - 32 = -(-150) \times (d)$$

$$\Rightarrow \quad d = 0.06\text{ m} = 6\text{ cm}$$

(iii) $A \to B$;

$$\Delta V = -Ed$$

$$\Rightarrow \quad 20 - V_A = -(-150)(10 \times 10^{-2})$$

$$\Rightarrow \quad V_A = 5\text{V}$$

3. (i) Since, equipotential surfaces are uniformly spaced parallel planes, electric field will be uniform. Electric field direction will be perpendicular to the equipotential surfaces.

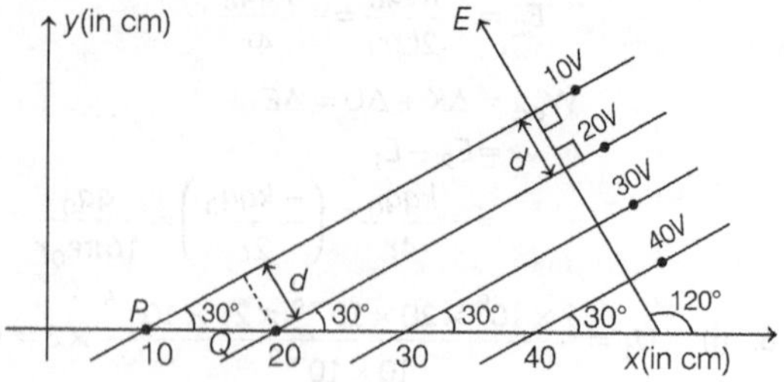

$P \to Q$,

$$\Delta V = -Ed$$

$$\Rightarrow \quad (20 - 10) = -E(10\sin 30° \times 10^{-2})$$

$$\Rightarrow \quad E = -200\text{ V/m}$$

$\mathbf{E} = 200$ V/m, at an angle of 120° with X-axis.

(ii) For each equipotential surface,

$$Vr = \text{constant}$$
$$Vr = 60\times 0.1 = 30\times 0.2 = 20\times 0.3$$
$$\Rightarrow \quad Vr = 6$$
$$\Rightarrow \quad V = \frac{6}{r}$$
$$E = -\frac{dV}{dr} = \frac{6}{r^2}$$
$$\mathbf{E} = \frac{6}{r^2}\text{V-m, radially outward}$$

4. (i) Equipotential surfaces and electric field lines are perpendicular.

(ii) Two equipotential surfaces never intersect each other. If they intersect, then the point of intersection will have two potentials which is not possible.

(iii) $W_{ext} = \Delta U + \Delta K = q\Delta V + \Delta K$

If a test charge is shifted slowly from one point to another on an equipotential surface, then work done by external agent is zero.

(iv) Electric field intensity is higher, where equipotential surfaces are closer.

2.9 *Self-Energy*

1. (i)

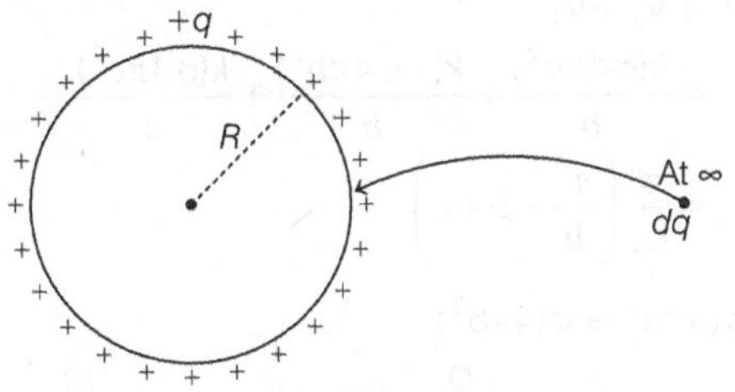

Lets take charge on shell at any instant as q.

We have to put dq charge on the shell now. Work done to put dq charge is dW_{ext}.

$$dW_{ext} = dqV$$
$$\Rightarrow \quad dW_{ext} = dq\left(\frac{kq}{R}\right) \quad \Rightarrow \quad \int dW_{ext} = \frac{k}{R}\int_0^Q q\,dq$$
$$\Rightarrow \quad W_{ext} = \frac{k}{R}\left[\frac{q^2}{2}\right]_0^Q \quad \Rightarrow \quad U = \frac{kQ^2}{2R}$$

Work done by the external agent in charging the shell to charge Q will be stored as electrical potential energy or self-energy of the shell.

(ii)

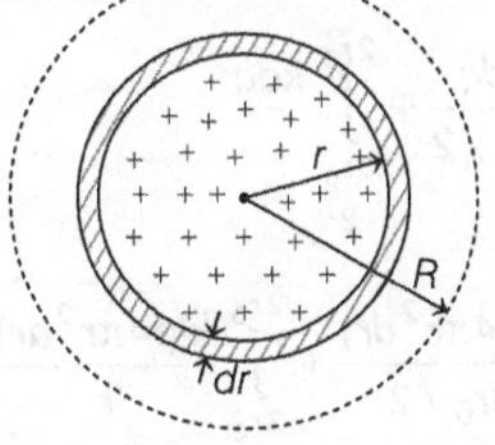

Lets say that the sphere is charged upto radius r and we have to add a layer of charge of dr thickness.

$$dW_{ext} = Vdq$$
$$\Rightarrow \quad dW_{ext} = \left(\frac{kq}{r}\right)(\rho 4\pi r^2 dr)$$
$$\Rightarrow \quad \int dW_{ext} = \int \frac{k}{r}\left(\rho \frac{4}{3}\pi r^3\right)(\rho 4\pi r^2 dr)$$
$$\Rightarrow \quad W_{ext} = \frac{16k\rho^2\pi^2}{3}\int_0^R r^4 dr$$
$$\Rightarrow \quad U = \frac{16\,k\rho^2\pi^2}{3}\left[\frac{r^5}{5}\right]_0^R$$
$$= \frac{16k}{3}\left(\frac{Q}{\frac{4}{3}\pi R^3}\right)^2 \pi^2\left(\frac{R^5}{5}\right) = \frac{3kQ^2}{5R}$$

2.

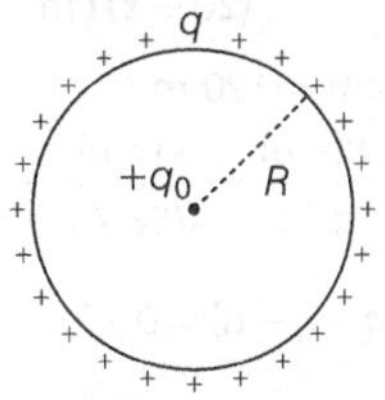

$$U_1 = \frac{kq^2}{2R} + q_0\left(\frac{kq}{R}\right)$$

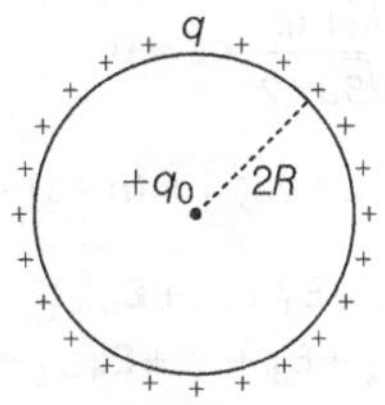

$$U_2 = \frac{kq^2}{2(2R)} + q_0\left(\frac{kq}{2R}\right)$$
$$W_{electric} = -\Delta U = U_1 - U_2$$
$$= \frac{kq^2}{4R} + \frac{kqq_0}{2R}$$
$$= \frac{q(q/2 + q_0)}{8\pi\varepsilon_0 R}$$
$$W_{ext} = \Delta U = U_2 - U_1 = -\frac{q(q/2+q_0)}{8\pi\varepsilon_0 R}$$

3. Total energy = Self-energy of shell 1 + Self-energy of shell 2 + Mutual electric potential energy

$$= \frac{kQ_1^2}{2R_1} + \frac{kQ_2^2}{2R_2} + Q_2\left(\frac{kQ_1}{R_2}\right)$$
$$= \frac{Q_1^2}{8\pi\varepsilon_0 R_1} + \frac{Q_2^2}{8\pi\varepsilon_0 R_2} + \frac{Q_1 Q_2}{4\pi\varepsilon_0 R_2}$$

Level 2

Single Choice Correct Questions

1. $E = \dfrac{kq}{r^2} = 4$

$$\Rightarrow \quad \frac{kq}{2^2} = 4 \Rightarrow kq = 16$$

$$W_{\text{ext})\,\infty \to P} = q'V$$

$$= 2\left(\frac{kq}{r}\right) = 2\left(\frac{16}{2}\right) = 16 \text{ J}$$

2.

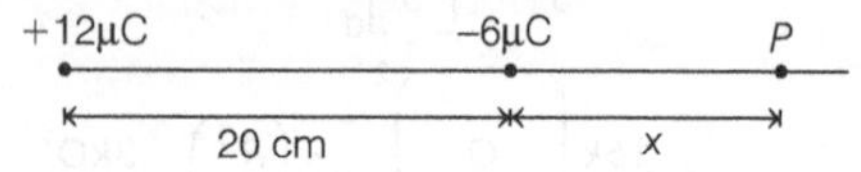

At point P,

$$V = V_1 + V_2 = \frac{k(+12\mu\text{C})}{(20+x)\text{ cm}} + \frac{k(-6\mu\text{C})}{x\text{ cm}} = 0$$

$$\Rightarrow \quad x = 20\text{ cm} = 0.20\text{ m}$$

3. $V_A = V_C = \dfrac{k(+q)}{a/2} + \dfrac{k(-q)}{a/2} + \dfrac{k(+q)}{\sqrt{5}a/2} + \dfrac{k(-q)}{\sqrt{5}a/2} = 0$

$$V_B = \frac{k}{a/\sqrt{2}}(+q - q + q - q) = 0$$

$$V_P = \frac{k(+q)}{a/2} \times 2 + \frac{k(-q)}{\sqrt{5}a/2} \times 2 \neq 0$$

$$V_Q = \frac{k(-q)}{a/2} \times 2 + \frac{k(+q)}{\sqrt{5}a/2} \times 2 \neq 0$$

4. $V = V_1 + V_2 + V_3 + \ldots + V_{n-1} = (n-1)\dfrac{kq}{r}$

$$\mathbf{E} = \mathbf{E}_1 + \mathbf{E}_2 + \mathbf{E}_3 + \ldots + \mathbf{E}_{n-1}$$

$$\Rightarrow \quad \mathbf{E} = (\mathbf{E}_1 + \mathbf{E}_2 + \mathbf{E}_3 + \ldots + \mathbf{E}_{n-1} + \mathbf{E}_n) - \mathbf{E}_n$$

$$\Rightarrow \quad \mathbf{E} = 0 - \mathbf{E}_n$$

$$\Rightarrow \quad |\mathbf{E}| = |-\mathbf{E}_n| = \frac{kq}{r^2}$$

$$\frac{V}{E} = \frac{(n-1)kq/r}{kq/r^2} = (n-1)r$$

5. $V = V_1 + V_2 + V_3 + V_4 + \ldots$

$$= \frac{kQ}{1} + \frac{k(-Q)}{2} + \frac{kQ}{4} + \frac{k(-Q)}{8} + \ldots$$

$$= \frac{Q}{4\pi\varepsilon_0}\left(1 - \frac{1}{2} + \frac{1}{4} - \frac{1}{8} + \ldots\infty\right)$$

$$= \frac{Q}{4\pi\varepsilon_0} \frac{1}{1 - \left(-\frac{1}{2}\right)} = \frac{Q}{6\pi\varepsilon_0}$$

6. All charges are equidistant from the centre.

$$V = \frac{k}{R}(+Q - 2Q + 3Q) = \frac{2kQ}{R} = \frac{Q}{2\pi\varepsilon_0 R}$$

7. For $r < R$; $V = \dfrac{kQ}{R}$

So, $V = \dfrac{kQ}{(10\text{ cm})}$

$$\Rightarrow \quad kQ = V(10\text{ cm})$$

For $r > R$; $V = \dfrac{kQ}{r}$

$$\Rightarrow \quad V' = \frac{kQ}{(15\text{ cm})} = \frac{V(10\text{ cm})}{(15\text{ cm})} = \frac{2V}{3}$$

8. $V_{\text{centre}} = \dfrac{3}{2}\dfrac{kQ}{R}$

For inside point,

$$V = \frac{kQ}{2R^3}(3R^2 - r^2) = \frac{1}{2}\left(\frac{3}{2}\frac{kQ}{R}\right)$$

$$\Rightarrow \quad 2(3R^2 - r^2) = 3R^2 \Rightarrow r = \sqrt{\frac{3}{2}}R$$

Distance from surface $= R - \sqrt{\dfrac{3}{2}}R$

For outside point,

$$V = \frac{kQ}{r} = \frac{1}{2}\left(\frac{3}{2}\frac{kQ}{R}\right) \Rightarrow r = \frac{4R}{3}$$

Distance from surface $= \dfrac{4R}{3} - R = \dfrac{R}{3}$

9. $V = V_1 + V_2 + V_3$

$$= \frac{k(\sigma 4\pi a^2)}{b} + \frac{k(-\sigma 4\pi b^2)}{b} + \frac{k(\sigma 4\pi c^2)}{c}$$

$$= \frac{\sigma}{\varepsilon_0}\left(\frac{a^2}{b} - b + c\right)$$

10. $Q = \sigma(4\pi a^2) + \sigma(4\pi b^2)$

$$\Rightarrow \quad \sigma = \frac{Q}{4\pi(a^2 + b^2)}$$

$$V = V_1 + V_2 = \frac{k(\sigma 4\pi a^2)}{a} + \frac{k(\sigma 4\pi b^2)}{b}$$

$$= \frac{\sigma}{\varepsilon_0}(a+b) = \frac{Q(a+b)}{4\pi\varepsilon_0(a^2 + b^2)}$$

11. $V = V_1 + V_2 + V_3$

$$= \frac{k(\lambda\pi R)}{R} + \int_R^{3R}\frac{k(\lambda dx)}{x} + \int_R^{3R}\frac{k\lambda dx}{x}$$

$$= k\lambda\pi + k\lambda\ln 3 + k\lambda\ln 3 = k\lambda(\pi + 2\ln 3)$$

$$= \frac{\lambda}{4\pi\varepsilon_0}(\pi + 2\ln 3)$$

12. Lets take a spherical shell of radius r and thickness dr.

$$\int dV = \int_{r_0}^{\frac{3r_0}{2}} \frac{kdq}{3r_0/2} + \int_{\frac{3r_0}{2}}^{2r_0} \frac{kdq}{r}$$

$$\Rightarrow V = \int_{r_0}^{\frac{3r_0}{2}} \frac{k(\rho 4\pi r^2 dr)}{3r_0/2} + \int_{\frac{3r_0}{2}}^{2r_0} \frac{k(\rho 4\pi r^2 dr)}{r}$$

$$= \frac{\rho}{\varepsilon_0}\frac{2}{3r_0}\left[\frac{r^3}{3}\right]_{r_0}^{\frac{3r_0}{2}} + \frac{\rho}{\varepsilon_0}\left[\frac{r^2}{2}\right]_{\frac{3r_0}{2}}^{2r_0}$$

$$= \frac{\rho}{\varepsilon_0}\left[\frac{2}{9r_0}\left(\frac{27}{8}r_0^3 - r_0^3\right)\right] + \frac{\rho}{2\varepsilon_0}\left(4r_0^2 - \frac{9r_0^2}{4}\right) = \frac{101\rho r_0^2}{72\varepsilon_0}$$

13.

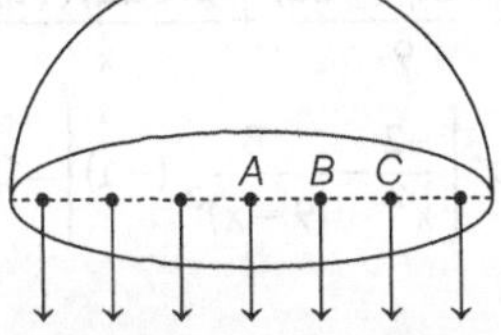

Electric field due to hemisphere at points lying on the diameter is perpendicular to the diameter. So, all points on the diameter are equipotential.

14. $E = -\frac{dV}{dr}$

If electric potential is constant in some part of space, then electric field will be zero in that space.

15. $U = qV$

If a positive charge is shifted from low potential region to high potential region, then its electrical potential energy increases.

If a negative charge is shifted from low potential region to high potential region, then its electrical potential energy decreases.

16. $K_1 + U_1 = K_2 + U_2$

$\Rightarrow \quad K_1 + qV_1 = K_2 + qV_2$

$$\Rightarrow \quad \frac{1}{2}\times 1\times 10^{-3}\times v_A^2 + 10^{-8}(600) = \frac{1}{2}\times 1\times 10^{-3}\times (0.2)^2 + 0$$

$\Rightarrow \quad v_A^2 = 0.04 - 0.012$

$\Rightarrow \quad v_A = \sqrt{0.028} = 0.167 \text{ m/s} = 16.7 \text{ cm/s}$

17. A negative charge released in an electric field will go against the direction of electric field. So, it will move toward a position of higher electric potential and lower potential energy.

18. $\Delta K = -q\Delta V$

$\Rightarrow \quad K_2 - K_1 = -(+Q)(-V)$

$\Rightarrow \quad K_2 - K_1 = QV$

Linear momentum, $p = \sqrt{2m(\text{KE})} = \sqrt{2mQV}$

19. $\Delta K = -q\Delta V$

$\Rightarrow \quad K_2 - K_1 = -q(-V) \quad \Rightarrow \quad K_2 = qV$

$\Rightarrow \quad \frac{1}{2}mv^2 = qV \quad \Rightarrow \quad v = \sqrt{\frac{2qV}{m}}$

Now, $$\frac{v_A}{v_B} = \frac{\sqrt{\frac{2qV}{m}}}{\sqrt{\frac{2(4q)V}{m}}} = \frac{1}{2}$$

20.

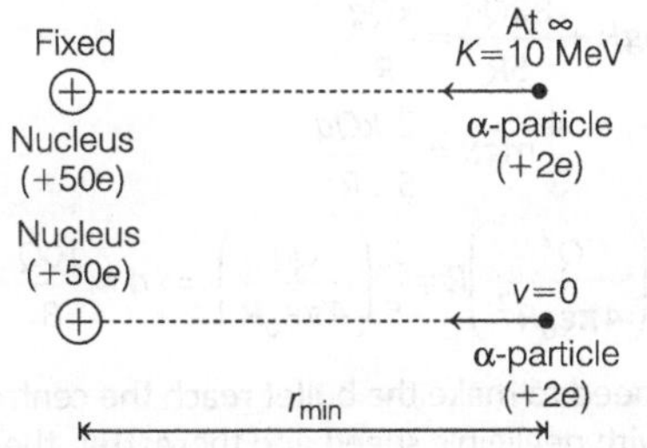

At the minimum distance of approach, speed of α-particle would be zero.

Applying mechanical conservation for α-particle,

$K_1 + U_1 = K_2 + U_2$

$$10 \text{ MeV} + 0 = 0 + \frac{k(+50e)(+2e)}{r_{min}}$$

$$\Rightarrow \quad r_{min} = \frac{9\times 10^9 \times 100 \times e \times e}{10\times 10^6 \times e}$$

$$= 14.4\times 10^{-15} \text{ or } 1.44\times 10^{-14} \text{ m}$$

21. $W_{ext} = \Delta U + \Delta K$

$$= q\Delta V + 0 = Q(V_D - V_G)$$

$$= Q\left[\left\{\frac{k(-Q)}{a/2}\times 2 + \frac{k(+2Q)}{\sqrt{3}a/2}\right\} - 0\right]$$

$$= \frac{-Q^2}{\pi\varepsilon_0 a}\left(1 - \frac{1}{\sqrt{3}}\right)$$

22.

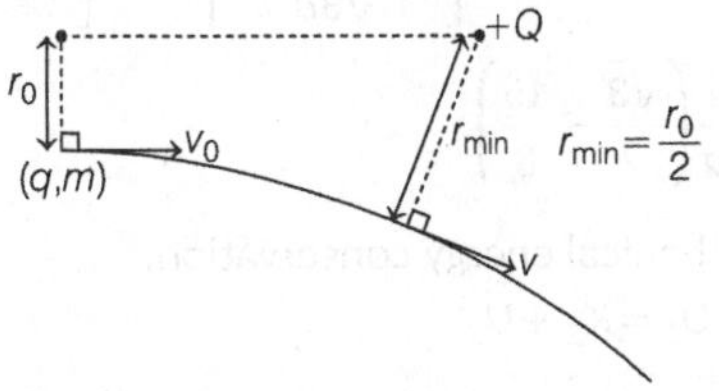

Using angular momentum conservation of q about Q,

$$mv_0 r_0 = mvr_{min} \quad \text{... (i)}$$

Using energy conservation,

$K_1 + U_1 = K_2 + U_2$

$$\frac{1}{2}mv_0^2 + 0 = \frac{1}{2}mv^2 + \frac{kQq}{r_{min}} \quad \text{... (ii)}$$

Solving Eqs. (i) and (ii), we get

$$q = -\frac{3Q}{4}$$

23. Using energy conservation, $K_1 + U_1 = K_2 + U_2$

$$\Rightarrow \quad 0 + \left[mg\frac{4R}{3} + q\left(\frac{kQ}{\sqrt{R^2 + \left(\frac{4R}{3}\right)^2}}\right)\right] = 0 + \left[0 + q\left(\frac{kQ}{R}\right)\right]$$

$$\Rightarrow \quad \frac{4}{3}mgR+\frac{3kQq}{5R}=\frac{kQq}{R}$$

$$\Rightarrow \quad \frac{4}{3}mgR=\frac{2}{5}\frac{kQq}{R}$$

$$\Rightarrow \quad \frac{4}{3}\left(\frac{Q^2}{4\pi\varepsilon_0 R^2}\right)R=\frac{2}{5}\left(\frac{Qq}{4\pi\varepsilon_0 R}\right)\Rightarrow q=\frac{10Q}{3}$$

24. We just need to make the bullet reach the centre of the sphere with negligible speed and thereafter, the bullet will come out of the sphere due to repulsion from sphere.

Applying mechanical energy conservation,

$$K_1+U_1=K_2+U_2 \Rightarrow \frac{1}{2}mu_{\min}^2+q\left(\frac{kq}{R}\right)=0+q\left(\frac{3}{2}\frac{kq}{R}\right)$$

$$\Rightarrow \quad U_{\min}=\frac{q}{\sqrt{4\pi\varepsilon_0 mR}}$$

25. $U=\frac{kQq}{a}+\frac{kQq}{a}+\frac{kq^2}{\sqrt{2}a}=0$

$$\Rightarrow \quad \frac{2kQq}{a}+\frac{kq^2}{\sqrt{2}a}=0 \Rightarrow \frac{q}{Q}=-2\sqrt{2}$$

26. Total number of pairs $= {}^6C_2=15$

$$U=\left[\frac{k(+q)(-q)}{a}\right]\times 6+\left[\frac{k(+q)(+q)}{\sqrt{3}a}\right]\times 3$$

$$+\left[\frac{k(-q)(-q)}{\sqrt{3}a}\right]\times 3+\left[\frac{k(+q)(-q)}{2a}\right]\times 3$$

$$\Rightarrow U=\frac{q^2}{\pi\varepsilon_0 a}\left(\frac{\sqrt{3}}{2}-\frac{15}{8}\right)$$

27. Applying mechanical energy conservation,

$$K_1+U_1=K_2+U_2$$

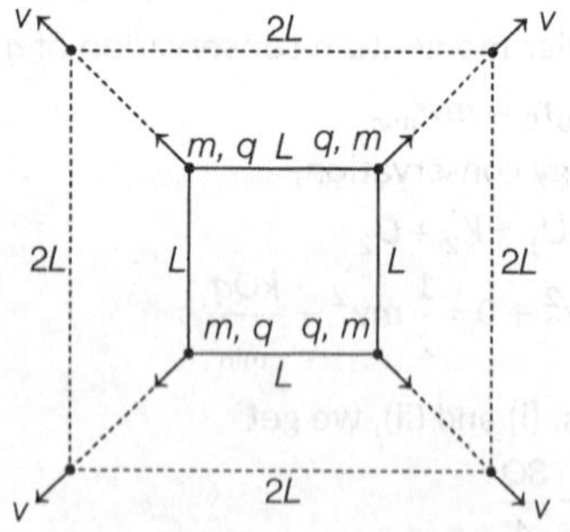

$$\Rightarrow (0+0+0+0)+\left(\frac{kq^2}{L}\times 4+\frac{kq^2}{\sqrt{2}L}\times 2\right)$$

$$=\left(\frac{1}{2}mv^2\right)\times 4+\left(\frac{kq^2}{2L}\times 4+\frac{kq^2}{2\sqrt{2}L}\times 2\right)$$

$$\Rightarrow \quad 4\left(\frac{1}{2}mv^2\right)=\frac{kq^2}{2L}\times 4+\frac{kq^2}{2\sqrt{2}L}\times 2$$

$$\Rightarrow \quad v=\sqrt{\frac{q^2(1+2\sqrt{2})}{8\sqrt{2}\pi\varepsilon_0 mL}}$$

28. For minimum potential energy of the system, the larger charges should be placed at the maximum separation possible, i.e. at the ends. Lets keep q charge at x distance from $+2q$.

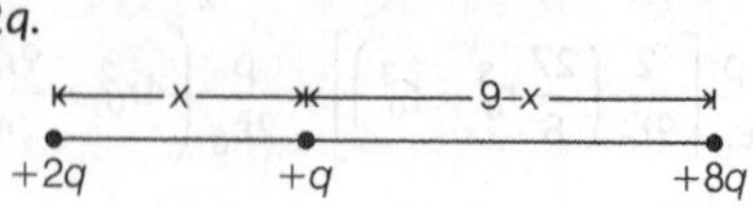

$$U=\frac{k(+8q)(+2q)}{9}+\frac{k(+2q)(+q)}{x}+\frac{k(+q)(+8q)}{9-x}$$

$$\frac{dU}{dx}=0+kq^2\left[\frac{-2}{x^2}-\frac{8}{(9-x)^2}(-1)\right]=0$$

$$\Rightarrow \quad x=3\text{ cm}$$

29. $F=qE$

$$\Rightarrow \quad 3000=3E \Rightarrow E=1000\text{ N/C}$$

$$\Delta V=Ed=(1000\text{N/C})(1\times 10^{-2}\text{m})=10\text{ V}$$

30. $W=(qE)s\cos\theta$

$$\Rightarrow \quad 4=(0.2E)(2)\cos 60^\circ$$

$$\Rightarrow \quad E=20\text{ N/C}$$

31. $\Delta V=Ed=Eb$

32. $dV=-\mathbf{E}\cdot d\mathbf{r}$

$$\Rightarrow \quad \int dV=-\int(E_x\hat{\mathbf{i}}+E_y\hat{\mathbf{j}})\cdot(dx\hat{\mathbf{i}}+dy\hat{\mathbf{j}})$$

$$\Rightarrow \quad \int_{V_0}^{V}dV=-\int_0^x E_x dx-\int_0^y E_y dy$$

$$\Rightarrow \quad V-V_0=-E_x[x]_0^x-E_y[y]_0^y$$

$$\Rightarrow \quad V=V_0-xE_x-yE_y$$

33. $V=-xy^2\sqrt{z}$

$$\mathbf{E}=-\frac{\partial V}{\partial x}\hat{\mathbf{i}}-\frac{\partial V}{\partial y}\hat{\mathbf{j}}-\frac{\partial V}{\partial z}\hat{\mathbf{k}}$$

$$=-(-y^2\sqrt{z})\hat{\mathbf{i}}-(-2xy\sqrt{z})\hat{\mathbf{j}}-\left(-\frac{xy^2}{2\sqrt{z}}\right)\hat{\mathbf{k}}$$

$$=y^2\sqrt{z}\hat{\mathbf{i}}+2xy\sqrt{z}\,\hat{\mathbf{j}}+\frac{xy^2}{2\sqrt{z}}\hat{\mathbf{k}}$$

At (2, 1, 1),

$$\mathbf{E}=(1^2\sqrt{1})\hat{\mathbf{i}}+[2(2)(1)\sqrt{1}]\,\hat{\mathbf{j}}+\left(\frac{2(1)^2}{2\sqrt{1}}\right)\hat{\mathbf{k}}=\hat{\mathbf{i}}+4\hat{\mathbf{j}}+\hat{\mathbf{k}}$$

34. $E_y=-\frac{dV}{dy}$

At $y=2.5$ m,

$$E_y=-\frac{dV}{dy}=-\text{ slope of V-y graph}=-\left(\frac{5-2}{1}\right)=-3$$

At $y=5.5$ m,

$$E_y=-\frac{dV}{dy}=-\text{ slope of V-y graph}=-\left[-\frac{(5-0)}{(1-0)}\right]=5$$

35. Lets take $\mathbf{E} = E_x\hat{\mathbf{i}} + E_y\hat{\mathbf{j}}$

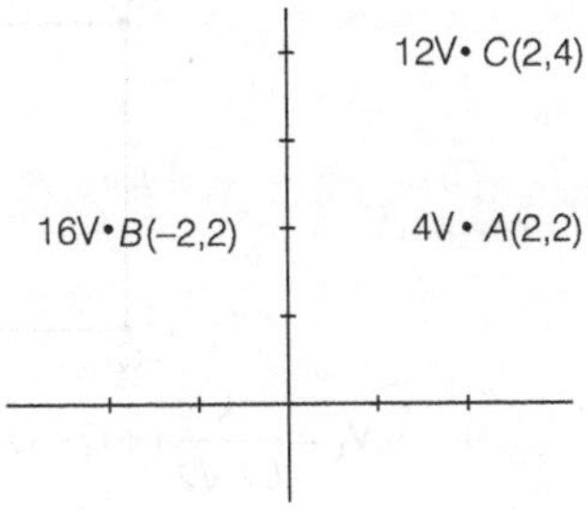

$B \rightarrow A$;

$$\Delta V = -Ed$$

$\Rightarrow \quad 4 - 16 = -E_x(4)$

$\Rightarrow \quad E_x = 3$

$A \rightarrow C$;

$$\Delta V = -Ed$$

$\Rightarrow \quad 12 - 4 = -E_y(2)$

$\Rightarrow \quad E_y = -4$

So, $\mathbf{E} = (3\hat{\mathbf{i}} - 4\hat{\mathbf{j}})$ V/m

36. $\mathbf{E} = \pm(100\cos 45°\,\hat{\mathbf{i}} + 100\sin 45°\,\hat{\mathbf{j}})$

$$= \pm(50\sqrt{2}\hat{\mathbf{i}} + 50\sqrt{2}\hat{\mathbf{j}})$$

$$\Delta\mathbf{r} = (5-3)\hat{\mathbf{i}} + (3-1)\hat{\mathbf{j}} = 2\hat{\mathbf{i}} + 2\hat{\mathbf{j}}$$

$$\Delta V = \mathbf{E}\cdot\Delta\mathbf{r} = \pm(50\sqrt{2}\hat{\mathbf{i}} + 50\sqrt{2}\hat{\mathbf{j}})\cdot(2\hat{\mathbf{i}} + 2\hat{\mathbf{j}})$$

$\Rightarrow \quad \Delta V = \pm 200\sqrt{2}$ V

$\Rightarrow \quad |\Delta V| = 200\sqrt{2}$ V

37.

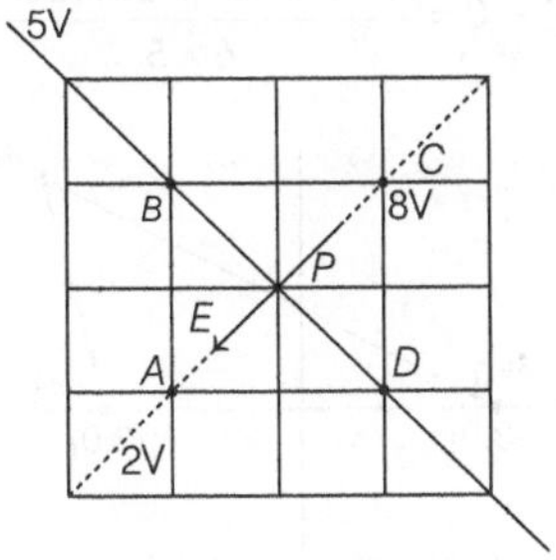

Line passing through points P, B and D is an equipotential surface.

So, electric field will be perpendicular to this line.

Direction of electric field will be from C to A as potential decreases in the direction of electric field.

In going from C to A,

$$\Delta V = -Ed$$

$\Rightarrow \quad 2 - 8 = -E(0.2\sqrt{2}) \Rightarrow E = 15\sqrt{2}$ V/m

$\mathbf{E} = 15\sqrt{2}$ V/m along PA

38.

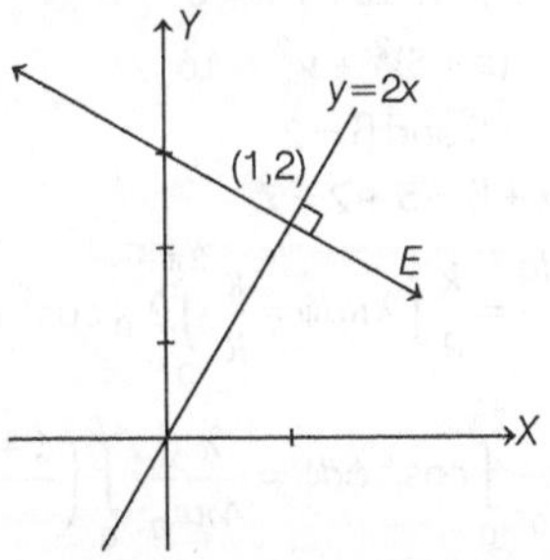

Electric field lines are perpendicular to equipotential surfaces.

m_1 = slope of equipotential surface = 2

m_2 = slope of electric field line

$$m_1 m_2 = -1$$

$\Rightarrow \quad 2m_2 = -1 \Rightarrow m_2 = \dfrac{-1}{2}$

In option (d), slope is $-\dfrac{1}{2}$.

39. $U = qV$

So, a negatively charged particle will have the highest potential energy, where electric potential is least.

Electric potential will be least closer to $-q$ charge, so potential energy of an electron will be highest at point B.

40. $|\Delta V| = Ed$

$\Rightarrow \quad 5 = \left(\dfrac{\sigma}{2\varepsilon_0}\right)d \Rightarrow 5 = \left(\dfrac{10^{-7}}{2\times 8.85\times 10^{-12}}\right)d$

$\Rightarrow \quad d = 8.85\times 10^{-4}$ m $= 0.885$ mm

41. $\mathbf{E} = E_x\hat{\mathbf{i}} + E_y\hat{\mathbf{j}}$

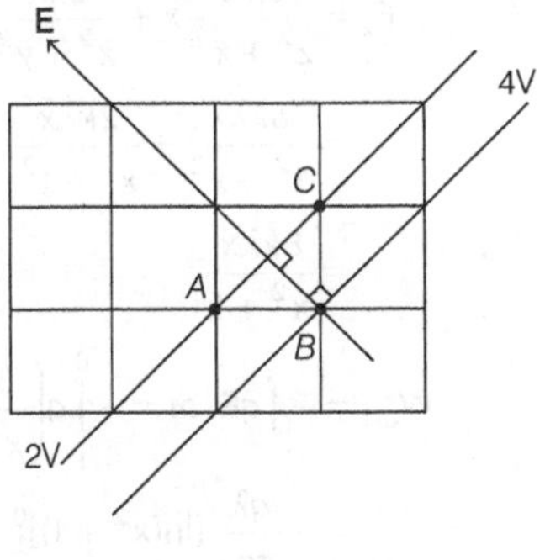

$A \rightarrow B$;

$$\Delta V = -Ed$$

$\Rightarrow$

$4 - 2 = -E_x(2\times 10^{-2})$

$\Rightarrow \quad E_x = -100$

$B \rightarrow C$;

$$\Delta V = -Ed$$

$2 - 4 = -E_y(1\times 10^{-2})$

$\Rightarrow \quad E_y = 200$

So, $\quad \mathbf{E} = -100\hat{\mathbf{i}} + 200\hat{\mathbf{j}}$ V/m

42. $\displaystyle\int_{l=\infty}^{l=0} -\mathbf{E}\cdot d\mathbf{l} = \Delta V = V_{\text{centre}} - V_{\text{infinity}}$

$$= \frac{kQ}{R} - \frac{kQ}{\sqrt{R^2 + (\infty)^2}}$$

$$= \frac{9\times 10^9 \times 1.11\times 10^{-10}}{0.5} - 0 = 1.998 \simeq 2$$

43. Loss in KE = Gain in PE

$\Rightarrow \quad -\Delta K = \Delta U$

$\Rightarrow \quad -\left(0 - \dfrac{1}{2}mv^2\right) = q\Delta V$

$\Rightarrow \quad \dfrac{1}{2}mv^2 = q\left(\dfrac{\sigma}{2\varepsilon_0}d\right) \Rightarrow v = \sqrt{\dfrac{q\sigma d}{m\varepsilon_0}}$

44. $\displaystyle\int dV = -\int \mathbf{E}\cdot d\mathbf{r}$

$\Rightarrow \quad \Delta V = -\displaystyle\int_{13}^{5} Edr\cos 0°$

$\Rightarrow \quad V - 0 = -\displaystyle\int_{13}^{5} \frac{2k\lambda}{r}\,dr$

$$\Rightarrow \quad V=\frac{-\lambda}{2\pi\varepsilon_0}\ln\left(\frac{5}{13}\right)=\frac{\lambda}{2\pi\varepsilon_0}\ln\left(\frac{13}{5}\right)$$

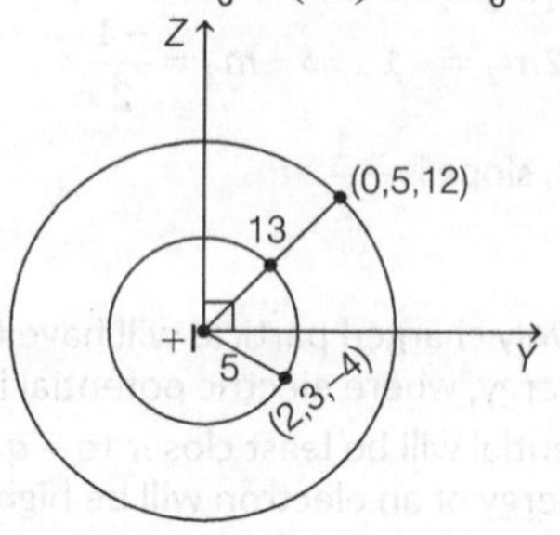

45. $\mathbf{E}=\mathbf{E}_1+\mathbf{E}_2+\mathbf{E}_3$

$$\mathbf{E}=\frac{2k(2\lambda)}{y^2+z^2}(y\hat{\mathbf{j}}+z\hat{\mathbf{k}})+\frac{2k(3\lambda)}{z^2+x^2}(z\hat{\mathbf{k}}+x\hat{\mathbf{i}})+\frac{2k\lambda}{x^2+y^2}(x\hat{\mathbf{i}}+y\hat{\mathbf{j}})$$

Work will be done only by x-component of electric field as displacement is parallel to X-axis.

$$E_x=\frac{6k\lambda}{z^2+x^2}x+\frac{2k\lambda}{x^2+y^2}x$$

$$=\frac{6k\lambda x}{1^2+x^2}+\frac{2k\lambda x}{x^2+1^2} \quad (\because y=1 \text{ and } z=1)$$

$$=\frac{8k\lambda x}{x^2+1}$$

$$W_{ext}=-\int q\mathbf{E}\cdot d\mathbf{r}=-\int_1^0 q\left(\frac{8k\lambda x}{x^2+1}\right)dx$$

$$=-\frac{q\lambda}{\pi\varepsilon_0}[\ln(x^2+1)]_1^0=\frac{q\lambda}{\pi\varepsilon_0}\ln 2$$

46. $V=axy$

$$\mathbf{E}=\frac{-\partial V}{\partial x}\hat{\mathbf{i}}-\frac{\partial V}{\partial y}\hat{\mathbf{j}}$$

$$\mathbf{E}=-ay\hat{\mathbf{i}}-ax\hat{\mathbf{j}}$$

$$\text{Slope}=\tan\theta=\frac{(-ax)}{(-ay)}$$

$$\Rightarrow \quad \frac{dy}{dx}=\frac{x}{y} \quad \Rightarrow \quad x\,dx=y\,dy$$

$$\Rightarrow \quad \int x\,dx=\int y\,dy \quad \Rightarrow \quad \frac{x^2}{2}=\frac{y^2}{2}+C'$$

$$\Rightarrow \quad x^2-y^2=C$$

which is equation of hyperbola.

47. $U_1=\dfrac{kQ^2}{2R}$

$$U_2=\frac{kQ^2}{2(2R)}$$

$$\Delta U=U_2-U_1=\frac{kQ^2}{4R}-\frac{kQ^2}{2R}=-\frac{kQ^2}{4R}=-\frac{Q^2}{16\pi\varepsilon_0 R}$$

48. $U=U_1+U_2+U_{12}=\dfrac{k(-Q)^2}{2(3R)}+\dfrac{kQ^2}{2R}+Q\left[\dfrac{k(-Q)}{3R}\right]=\dfrac{kQ^2}{3R}$

Numerical Value Questions

1.

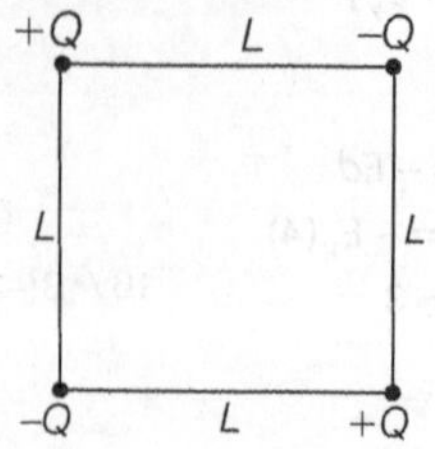

$$V_1=\frac{k}{L/\sqrt{2}}(+Q-Q+Q-Q)=0$$

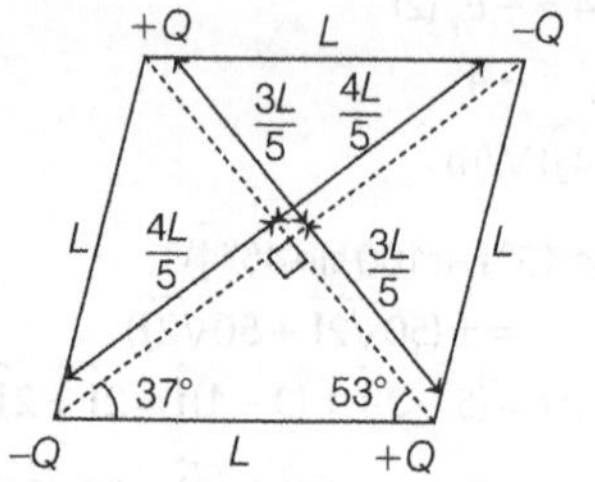

$$V_2=\frac{k(+Q)}{\frac{3L}{5}}\times 2+\frac{k(-Q)}{4L/5}\times 2=\frac{5kQ}{6L}$$

$$V_2-V_1=\frac{5kQ}{6L}-0=\frac{5\times 9\times 10^9\times 10\times 10^{-9}}{6\times 5}-0=15\text{ V}$$

2.

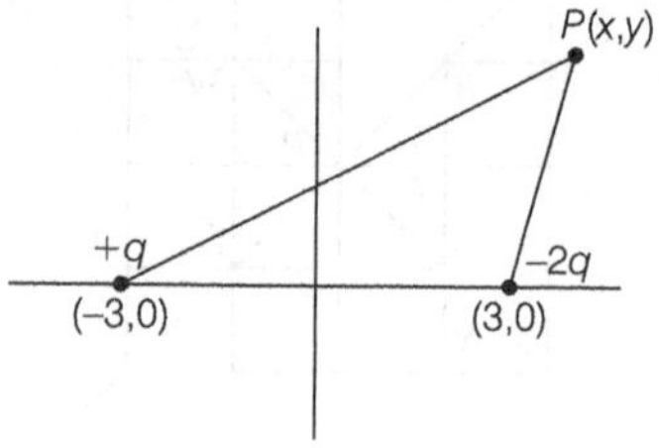

At point P,

$$V=V_1+V_2$$

$$V=\frac{k(-2q)}{\sqrt{(x-3)^2+y^2}}+\frac{k(+q)}{\sqrt{(x+3)^2+y^2}}=0$$

$$\Rightarrow \quad 2\sqrt{(x+3)^2+y^2}=\sqrt{(x-3)^2+y^2}$$

$$\Rightarrow \quad 4(x+3)^2+4y^2=(x-3)^2+y^2$$

$$\Rightarrow \quad 3x^2+3y^2+30x+27=0$$

$$\Rightarrow \quad x^2+y^2+10x+9=0$$

$$\Rightarrow \quad (x+5)^2+y^2=16$$

$$\Rightarrow \quad \alpha=5 \text{ and } \beta=2$$

$$\alpha+\beta=5+2=7$$

3. $V=\dfrac{kQ}{R}=\dfrac{k\int dq}{R}=\dfrac{k}{R}\int\lambda R\,d\phi=\dfrac{k}{R}\displaystyle\int_0^{2\pi}\lambda_0\cos^2\phi R\,d\phi$

$$=\frac{\lambda_0}{4\pi\varepsilon_0}\int_0^{2\pi}\cos^2\phi\,d\phi=\frac{\lambda_0}{4\pi\varepsilon_0}\int_0^{2\pi}\left(\frac{1+\cos 2\phi}{2}\right)d\phi$$

$$=\frac{\lambda_0}{8\pi\varepsilon_0}\left(\phi+\frac{\sin 2\phi}{2}\right)_0^{2\pi}=\frac{\lambda_0}{4\varepsilon_0}$$

So, $n=4$

4. $V=1.2\,V_{surface}$

$$\frac{kQ}{2R^3}(3R^2-r^2)=1.2\frac{kQ}{R}$$

$$\Rightarrow \quad 15R^2-5r^2=12R^2$$

$$\Rightarrow \quad r=\sqrt{\frac{3}{5}}R=\sqrt{\frac{3}{5}}\times\sqrt{60}=6\text{ cm}$$

5.

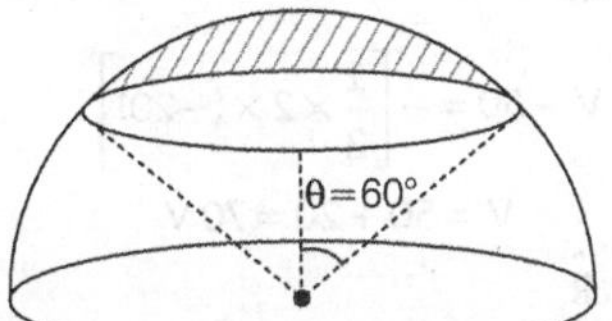

Solid angle subtended by the shaded part

$$=2\pi(1-\cos\theta)=2\pi(1-\cos 60°)=\pi$$

Solid angle subtended by the remaining hemisphere

$$=2\pi-\pi=\pi$$

$$V_{centre}=\frac{kQ}{R}=\frac{k}{R}\left[\sigma\left(\frac{4\pi R^2}{4\pi}\times\pi\right)\right]$$

$$=\frac{\sigma R}{4\varepsilon_0}=\frac{(2\varepsilon_0)(2)}{4\varepsilon_0}=1\text{ V}$$

6.

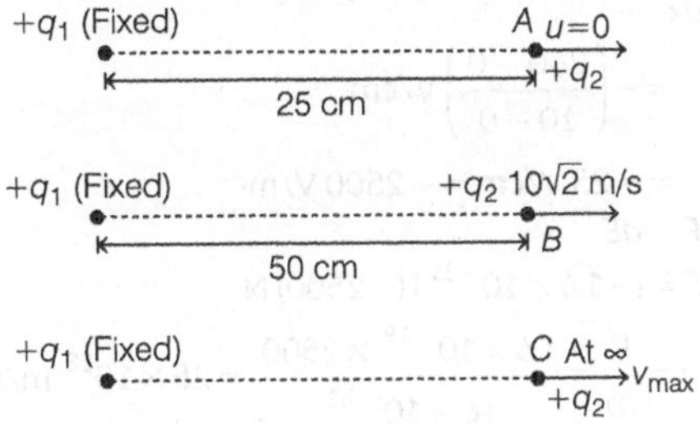

$A\rightarrow B$;

Using mechanical energy conservation,

$$K_1+U_1=K_2+U_2$$

$$\Rightarrow \quad 0+\frac{kq_1q_2}{(25\text{cm})}=\frac{1}{2}m(10\sqrt{2})^2+\frac{kq_1q_2}{(50\text{ cm})} \quad \text{... (i)}$$

$A\rightarrow C$;

Using mechanical energy conservation,

$$K_1+U_1=K_2+U_2$$

$$\Rightarrow \quad 0+\frac{kq_1q_2}{(25\text{cm})}=\frac{1}{2}mv_{max}^2+\frac{kq_1q_2}{\infty} \quad \text{... (ii)}$$

Solving Eqs. (i) and (ii), we get

$$v_{max}=20\text{ m/s}$$

7.

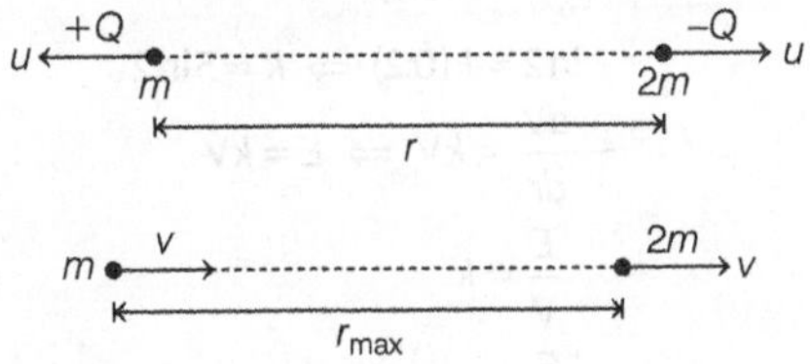

Using linear momentum conservation,

$$-mu+2mu=mv+2mv$$

$$\Rightarrow \quad v=\frac{u}{3} \quad \text{... (i)}$$

Using mechanical energy conservation,

$$K_1+U_1=K_2+U_2$$

$$\Rightarrow \quad \left[\frac{1}{2}mu^2+\frac{1}{2}(2m)u^2\right]+\frac{k(+Q)(-Q)}{r}$$

$$=\left(\frac{1}{2}mv^2+\frac{1}{2}2mv^2\right)+\frac{k(+Q)(-Q)}{r_{max}} \quad \text{... (ii)}$$

Solving Eqs. (i) and (ii), we get

$$r_{max}=2r$$

So, $n=2$

8.

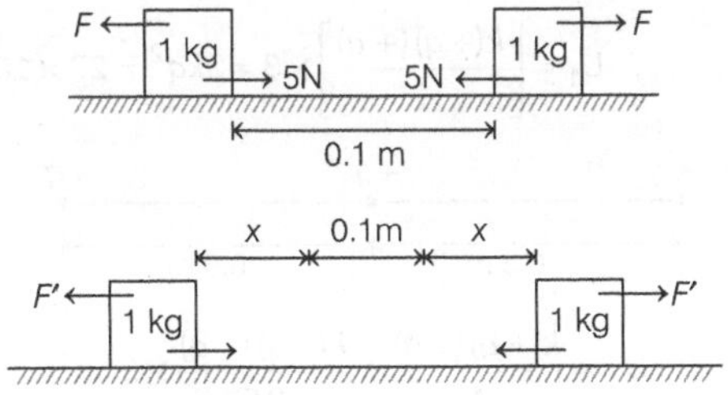

Using work-energy theorem,

$$W_{friction}+W_{electric}=\Delta K$$

$$\Rightarrow \quad (-5x)\times 2-\Delta U=(0+0)-(0+0)$$

$$\Rightarrow -10x-\left(\frac{9\times10^9\times5\times10^{-6}\times3\times10^{-6}}{0.1+2x}-\frac{9\times10^9\times5\times10^{-6}\times3\times10^{-6}}{0.1}\right)=0$$

$$\Rightarrow x=0.085\text{m}$$

Separation $=0.1+2x=0.1+2(0.085)=0.27\text{m}=27$ cm

9.

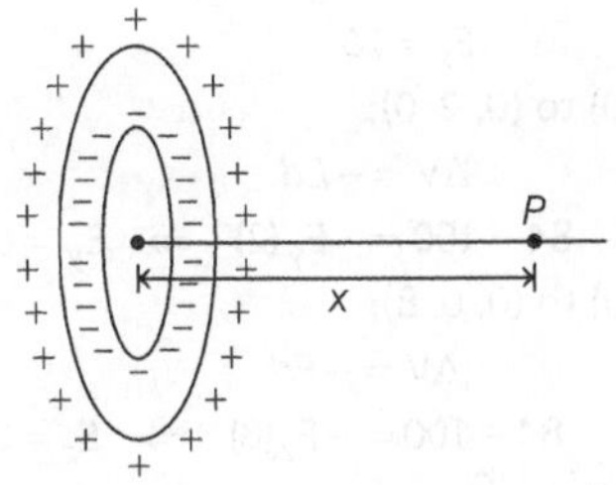

At point P,

$$E=\frac{k(-\sqrt{2}\mu C)x}{(2^2+x^2)^{3/2}}+\frac{k(4\mu C)x}{(4^2+x^2)^{3/2}}=0$$

$$\Rightarrow \quad x=2\sqrt{2}\text{ m}$$

We need to make the particle just reach P with negligible velocity as beyond P, the particle will be attracted by the two rings system.

Using mechanical energy conservation,

$$K_1+U_1=K_2+U_2$$

$$\Rightarrow \quad \frac{1}{2}mu^2 + 0 = 0 + q\left[\frac{k(-\sqrt{2}\times 10^{-6})}{\sqrt{2^2+(2\sqrt{2})^2}} + \frac{k(4\times 10^{-6})}{\sqrt{4^2+(2\sqrt{2})^2}}\right]$$

$$\Rightarrow \quad \frac{1}{2}\times 10\times 10^{-3}u^2 = (20\sqrt{6}\times 10^{-6})\left(\frac{9\times 10^9\times 10^{-6}}{\sqrt{6}}\right)$$

$$\Rightarrow \quad u^2 = 36 \quad \Rightarrow \quad u = 6 \text{ m/s}$$

10.

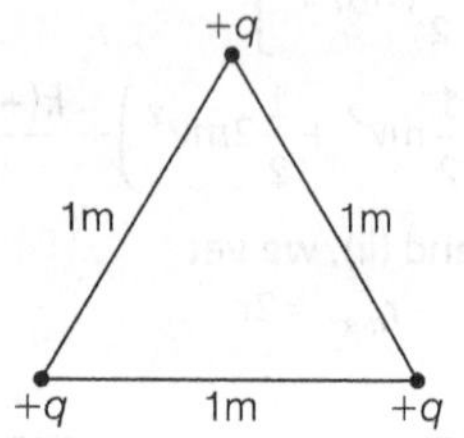

$$U_1 = \left[\frac{k(+q)(+q)}{1}\right]\times 3 = 3kq^2 = 27\times 10^7 \text{ J}$$

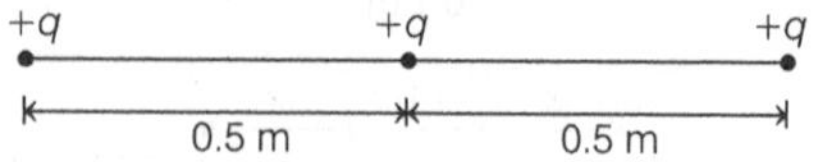

$$U_2 = \frac{k(+q)(+q)}{1} + \frac{k(+q)(+q)}{0.5}\times 2$$

$$= 5kq^2 = 45\times 10^7 \text{ J}$$

$$W_{ext} = \Delta U = U_2 - U_1 = 18\times 10^7 \text{ J}$$

Energy = Power × Time

$$\Rightarrow \quad 18\times 10^7 = 10\times 10^3 t$$

$$\Rightarrow \quad t = 18000 \text{ s} = 5 \text{ h}$$

11. $\mathbf{E} = E_x\hat{\mathbf{i}} + E_y\hat{\mathbf{j}} + E_z\hat{\mathbf{k}}$

From (0, 0, 0) to (1, 0, 0);

$$\Delta V = -Ed$$

$$\Rightarrow \quad 84 - 100 = -E_x \qquad \text{...(i)}$$

$$\Rightarrow \quad E_x = 16$$

From (0, 0, 0) to (0, 2, 0);

$$\Delta V = -Ed$$

$$\Rightarrow \quad 84 - 100 = -E_y(2) \quad \Rightarrow \quad E_y = 8$$

From (0, 0, 0) to (0, 0, 8);

$$\Delta V = -Ed$$

$$\Rightarrow \quad 84 - 100 = -E_z(8) \quad \Rightarrow \quad E_z = 2$$

So, $\mathbf{E} = 16\hat{\mathbf{i}} + 8\hat{\mathbf{j}} + 2\hat{\mathbf{k}}$

From (0, 0, 0) to (3, 4, 5);

$$\Delta V = -\mathbf{E}\cdot\Delta\mathbf{r}$$

$$\Rightarrow \quad V - 100 = -(16\hat{\mathbf{i}} + 8\hat{\mathbf{j}} + 2\hat{\mathbf{k}})\cdot(3\hat{\mathbf{i}} + 4\hat{\mathbf{j}} + 5\hat{\mathbf{k}})$$

$$\Rightarrow \quad V - 100 = -48 - 32 - 10$$

$$\Rightarrow \quad V = 100 - 90 = 10 \text{ V}$$

12. $V = 6x - 8xy^2 - 8y + 6yz - 4x^2$

$$E_x = -\frac{\partial V}{\partial x} = -6 + 8y^2 + 8x$$

$$E_y = -\frac{\partial V}{\partial y} = 16xy + 8 + 6z$$

$$E_z = -\frac{\partial V}{\partial z} = -6y$$

At origin, $E_x = -6, E_y = 8, E_z = 0$

$$\mathbf{E} = -6\hat{\mathbf{i}} + 8\hat{\mathbf{j}}$$

$$\mathbf{F} = q\mathbf{E} = 2(-6\hat{\mathbf{i}} + 8\hat{\mathbf{j}}) = -12\hat{\mathbf{i}} + 16\hat{\mathbf{j}}$$

$$|\mathbf{F}| = \sqrt{(12)^2 + (16)^2} = 20\text{N}$$

13. $\Delta V = -\int_0^2 E_x dx$

$$\Rightarrow \quad V - 50 = -\left[\frac{1}{2}\times 2\times(-20)\right]$$

$$\Rightarrow \quad V = 50 + 20 = 70 \text{ V}$$

14. $\mathbf{r} = x\hat{\mathbf{i}} + y\hat{\mathbf{j}} + z\hat{\mathbf{k}}$

$$\mathbf{E} = \frac{a\mathbf{r}}{r^3} = \left(\frac{ar}{r^3}\right)\hat{\mathbf{r}} \quad \Rightarrow \quad \mathbf{E} = \left(\frac{a}{r^2}\right)\hat{\mathbf{r}}$$

$$dV = -\mathbf{E}\cdot d\mathbf{r} \quad \Rightarrow \quad dV = -\left(\frac{a}{r^2}\right)\hat{\mathbf{r}}\cdot dr\hat{\mathbf{r}}$$

$$\Rightarrow \quad \int dV = -\int_7^5 \frac{a}{r^2}dr$$

$$\Rightarrow \quad \Delta V = -\left[-\frac{a}{r}\right]_7^5 = a\left(\frac{1}{5} - \frac{1}{7}\right) = 280\times\frac{2}{35} = 16 \text{ V}$$

15. $E = -\frac{dV}{dx} = -$ (Slope of V-x graph)

$$= -\left(\frac{250-0}{10-0}\right)\text{V/cm}$$

$$= -25 \text{ V/cm} = -2500 \text{ V/m}$$

$$F = qE$$

$$\Rightarrow \quad F = (-1.6\times 10^{-19})(-2500) \text{ N}$$

$$a = \frac{F}{m} = \frac{1.6\times 10^{-19}\times 2500}{16\times 10^{-31}} = 25\times 10^{13} \text{ m/s}$$

$$s = ut + \frac{1}{2}at^2$$

$$\Rightarrow \quad +20\times 10^{-2} = 0 + \frac{1}{2}(25\times 10^{13})t^2$$

$$\Rightarrow \quad t = 40\times 10^{-9}\text{ s} = 40 \text{ ns}$$

16. $-\frac{dV}{dr} \propto V$

$$\Rightarrow \quad -\frac{dV}{dr} = kV, \text{ where } k \text{ is a constant}$$

$$\Rightarrow \quad -\int_{V_0}^{V_0/2}\frac{dV}{V} = k\int_r^{r+0.2}dr$$

$$\Rightarrow \quad -[\ln V]_{V_0}^{V_0/2} = k[r]_r^{r+0.2}$$

$$\Rightarrow \quad \ln 2 = k(0.2) \Rightarrow k = 5\ln 2$$

Now, $-\frac{dV}{dr} = kV \Rightarrow E = kV$

$$\Rightarrow \quad \frac{E}{V} = k$$

$$\Rightarrow \quad \frac{E}{V} = 5\ln 2$$

17.
$$dU = dq(ER\cos\theta)$$
$$\Rightarrow \quad dU = \left(\frac{Q}{\pi R} R d\theta\right)(ER\cos\theta)$$
$$\Rightarrow \quad \int dU = \frac{QER}{\pi}\int_{-\pi/2}^{\pi/2} \cos\theta d\theta$$
$$\Rightarrow \quad \Delta U = \frac{2QER}{\pi}$$
$$= \frac{2(\pi)(2)(2)}{\pi} = 8\text{J}$$
$$W_{ext} = \Delta U = 8\text{J}$$

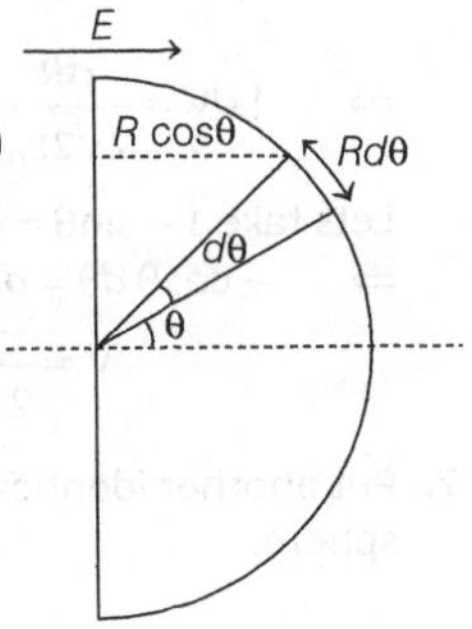

18.

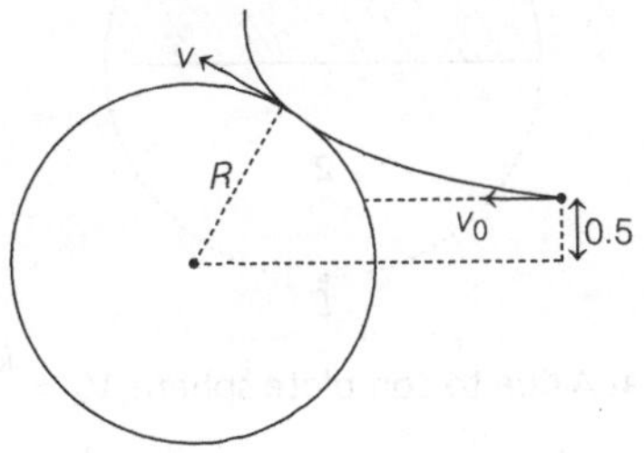

Using angular momentum conservation about the centre of the fixed shell,
$$mv_0(0.5) = mv(1) \quad \Rightarrow \quad v = \frac{v_0}{2}$$
Using energy conservation,
Loss in KE = Gain in PE
$$\frac{1}{2}mv_0^2 - \frac{1}{2}m\left(\frac{v_0}{2}\right)^2 = \frac{kq_1q_2}{R} - 0$$
$$v_0 = \sqrt{\frac{8kq_1q_2}{3mR}} = \sqrt{\frac{8\times 9\times 10^9 \times 3\times 10^{-6}\times 1\times 10^{-6}}{3\times 2\times 10^{-3}\times 1}}$$
$$= 6 \text{ m/s}$$

Level 3
Single Choice Correct Questions

1.

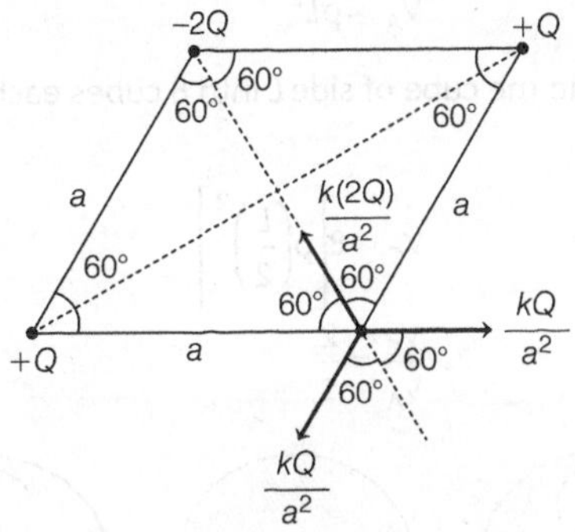

$$E = \frac{kQ}{a^2} \text{ and } V = \frac{kQ}{a}$$
$$\mathbf{E}_{net} = \mathbf{E}_1 + \mathbf{E}_2 + \mathbf{E}_3$$
$$\Rightarrow \quad E_{net} = \frac{2kQ}{a^2} - \frac{kQ}{a^2}\cos 60° - \frac{kQ}{a^2}\cos 60° = \frac{kQ}{a^2} = E$$
$$V_{net} = V_1 + V_2 + V_3 = \frac{kQ}{a} + \frac{kQ}{a} + \frac{k(-2Q)}{a} = 0$$

2.

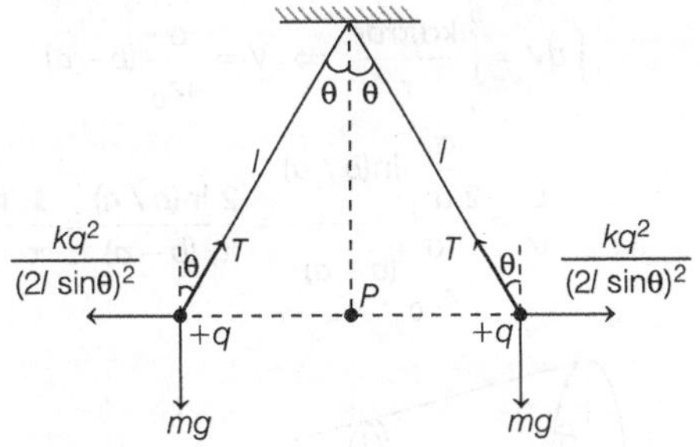

For equilibrium,
$$T\sin\theta = \frac{kq^2}{(2l\sin\theta)^2} \qquad \text{... (i)}$$
$$T\cos\theta = mg \qquad \text{... (ii)}$$
At point P,
$$V = V_1 + V_2 = \frac{kq}{l\sin\theta} + \frac{kq}{l\sin\theta} = \frac{2kq}{l\sin\theta}$$
From Eqs. (i) and (ii), we get
$$\frac{q}{l\sin\theta} = 2\sqrt{\frac{mg\tan\theta}{k}}$$
So, $$V = 2k\left(2\sqrt{\frac{mg\tan\theta}{k}}\right) = 4\sqrt{kmg\tan\theta}$$

3. $V = V_1 + V_2 + V_3 + \ldots$
$$= \left[\frac{k(Q/2)}{\frac{L}{\sqrt{2}}}\right]\times 4 + \left[\frac{k\left(\frac{Q}{2^2}\right)}{\frac{L}{2}}\right]\times 4 + \left[\frac{k\left(\frac{Q}{2^3}\right)}{\frac{L}{2\sqrt{2}}}\right]\times 4 + \ldots\ldots \infty$$
$$= \frac{4kQ}{L}\left(\frac{1}{\sqrt{2}} + \frac{1}{2} + \frac{1}{2\sqrt{2}} + \ldots\infty\right)$$
$$= \frac{Q}{\pi\varepsilon_0 L}\left(\frac{1/\sqrt{2}}{1-\frac{1}{\sqrt{2}}}\right) = \frac{Q}{\pi\varepsilon_0 L(\sqrt{2}-1)} = \frac{Q(\sqrt{2}+1)}{\pi\varepsilon_0 L}$$

4.

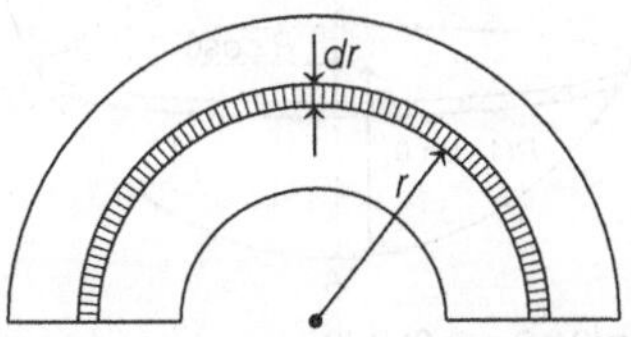

Lets take a semicircular strip of radius r and width dr.
$$dq = \sigma\pi r dr$$
$$dE = \frac{2k\lambda}{r} = \frac{2k\sigma dr}{r}$$

$$\int dE = \int_a^b \frac{2k\sigma dr}{r} \Rightarrow E = \frac{\sigma}{2\pi\varepsilon_0}\ln\left(\frac{b}{a}\right)$$

$$dV = \frac{kdq}{r}$$

$$\Rightarrow \int dV = \int_a^b \frac{k\sigma\pi r dr}{r} \Rightarrow V = \frac{\sigma}{4\varepsilon_0}(b-a)$$

$$\therefore \frac{E}{V} = \frac{\frac{\sigma}{2\pi\varepsilon_0}\ln(b/a)}{\frac{\sigma}{4\varepsilon_0}(b-a)} = \frac{2}{\pi}\frac{\ln(b/a)}{(b-a)} = \frac{1}{\pi}\frac{\ln(b/a)^2}{(b-a)}$$

5. 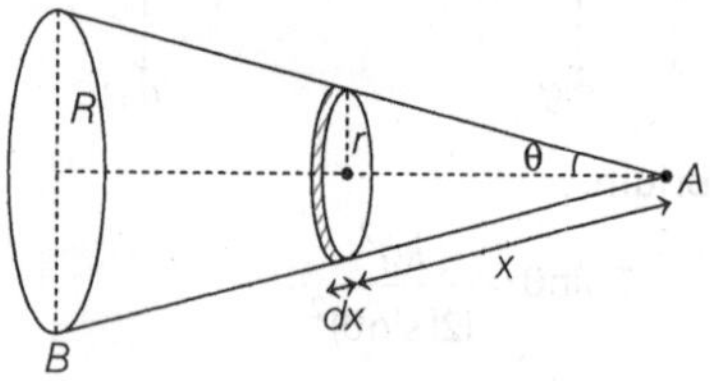

$$\sin\theta = \frac{r}{x} = \frac{R}{L}$$

Let divide the cone into rings as shown.

$$dq = \frac{Q}{\pi RL}(2\pi r dx)$$

$$dV = \frac{kdq}{x} = \frac{k}{x}\left(\frac{Q}{\pi RL}(2\pi r dx)\right)$$

$$dV = \frac{2kQ}{L}\frac{rdx}{Rx}$$

$$\Rightarrow dV = \frac{2kQ}{L}\frac{x}{L}\frac{dx}{x} \qquad \left(\because \frac{r}{R} = \frac{x}{L}\right)$$

$$\Rightarrow \int dV = \frac{2kQ}{L^2}\int_0^L dx$$

$$\Rightarrow V = \frac{2kQ}{L} = \frac{Q}{2\pi\varepsilon_0 L}$$

$$W_{ext} = qV = q\left(\frac{Q}{2\pi\varepsilon_0 L}\right) = \frac{Qq}{2\pi\varepsilon_0 L}$$

6. Lets divide the hemisphere into rings as shown.

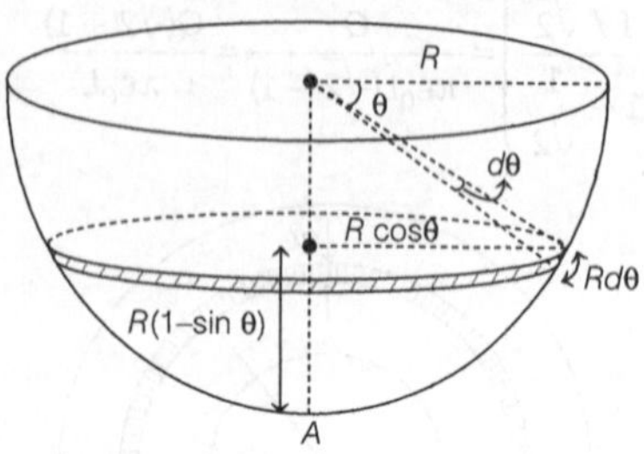

$$dq = \sigma(2\pi R\cos\theta)Rd\theta$$

At point A,

$$dV = \frac{kdq}{\sqrt{(R\cos\theta)^2 + [R(1-\sin\theta)]^2}}$$

$$\Rightarrow dV = \frac{\sigma R\cos\theta d\theta}{2\varepsilon_0\sqrt{2(1-\sin\theta)}}$$

$$\Rightarrow \int dV = \frac{\sigma R}{2\sqrt{2}\varepsilon_0}\int_0^{\pi/2}\frac{\cos\theta}{\sqrt{1-\sin\theta}}d\theta$$

Lets take $1-\sin\theta = t$

$\Rightarrow \quad -\cos\theta\, d\theta = dt$

$$V = \frac{\sigma R}{2\sqrt{2}\varepsilon_0}\int_1^0 \frac{-dt}{\sqrt{t}} = \frac{-\sigma R}{2\sqrt{2}\varepsilon_0}[2\sqrt{t}]_1^0 = \frac{\sigma R}{\sqrt{2}\varepsilon_0}$$

7. Put another identical hemisphere 2 to complete the sphere.

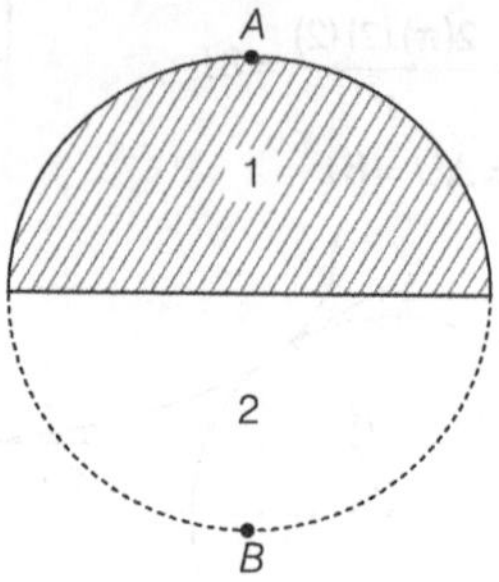

Potential at A due to complete sphere, $V_A = \frac{k(2Q)}{R}$

Potential at B due to complete sphere, $V_B = \frac{k(2Q)}{R}$

$$V_A + V_B = \frac{k(2Q)}{R} + \frac{k(2Q)}{R} \Rightarrow V_A + V_B = \frac{4kQ}{R}$$

Since, both the hemispheres are identical, $\frac{V_A + V_B}{2} = \frac{2kQ}{R}$

8. 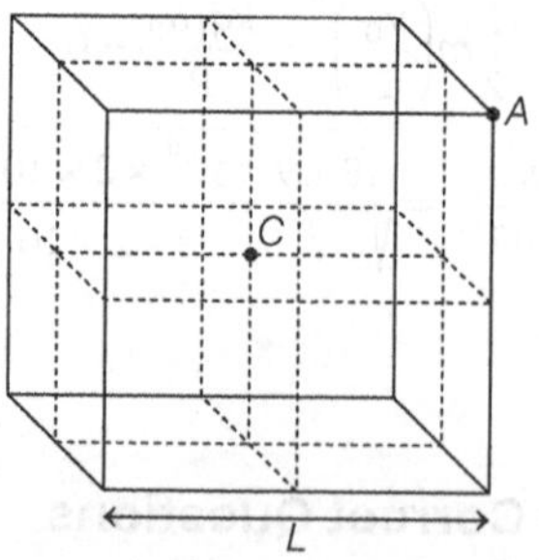

$$V_A \propto \rho L^2$$

Lets divide the cube of side L into 8 cubes each of side $\frac{L}{2}$ as shown,

So, $\quad V_C \propto 8\left[\rho\left(\frac{L}{2}\right)^2\right]$

$$\therefore \frac{V_C}{V_A} = \frac{2}{1}$$

9. 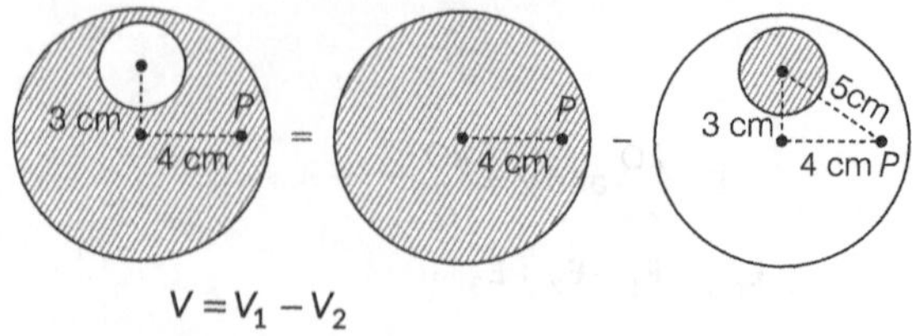

$$V = V_1 - V_2$$

$$V_1 = \frac{kQ}{2R}\left[3 - \left(\frac{r}{R}\right)^2\right]$$

$$= \frac{9\times 10^9 \times \left[\frac{10^{-6}}{\pi} \times \frac{4}{3}\pi(5\times 10^{-2})^3\right]}{2(5\times 10^{-2})}\left[3 - \left(\frac{4\times 10^{-2}}{5\times 10^{-2}}\right)^2\right] = 35.4 \text{ V}$$

$$V_2 = \frac{kq}{r'} = \frac{9\times 10^9 \times \left(\frac{10^{-6}}{\pi} \times \frac{4}{3}\pi(1\times 10^{-2})^3\right)}{5\times 10^{-2}}$$

$$= 0.24 \text{ V}$$

$$V = V_1 - V_2 = 35.4 - 0.24 = 35.16 \text{ V}$$

10. Null point is closer to the smaller charge. If the charges are of opposite signs, then null point is outside.
If the charges are of same signs, then null point is between the two charges.
In the given figure, there is a null point to the right of the right charge. So, the option (b) is correct.

11. For $x < r$;

$$V = V_1 + V_2$$

$$= \frac{k(-\sigma 4\pi r^2)}{r} + \frac{k(\sigma 4\pi R^2)}{R} = \frac{\sigma(R-r)}{\varepsilon_0}$$

For $r < x < R$;

$$V = V_1 + V_2 = \frac{k(-\sigma 4\pi r^2)}{x} + \frac{k(\sigma 4\pi R^2)}{R}$$

$$= \frac{\sigma}{\varepsilon_0}\left(\frac{-r^2}{x} + R\right)$$

For $x \geq R$;

$$V = V_1 + V_2$$

$$= \frac{k(-\sigma 4\pi r^2)}{x} + \frac{k(\sigma 4\pi R^2)}{x} = \frac{\sigma}{x\varepsilon_0}(R^2 - r^2)$$

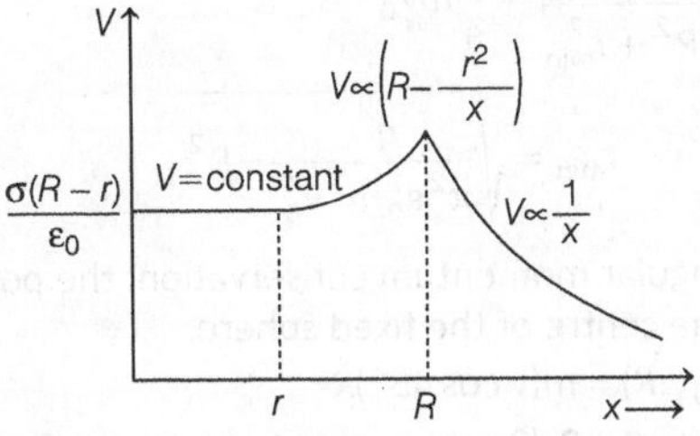

12.

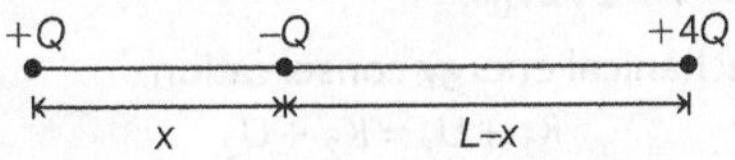

$$U = \frac{k(Q)(-Q)}{x} + \frac{k(-Q)(+4Q)}{L-x} + \frac{k(+Q)(+4Q)}{L}$$

$$U = kQ^2\left(\frac{-1}{x} - \frac{4}{L-x} + \frac{4}{L}\right)$$

$$\frac{dU}{dx} = kQ^2\left[\frac{1}{x^2} + \frac{4}{(L-x)^2}(-1)\right] = 0$$

$$\Rightarrow \quad x = \frac{L}{3}$$

$$x \to 0^+ \Rightarrow U \to -\infty$$

$$x \to L^- \Rightarrow U \to -\infty$$

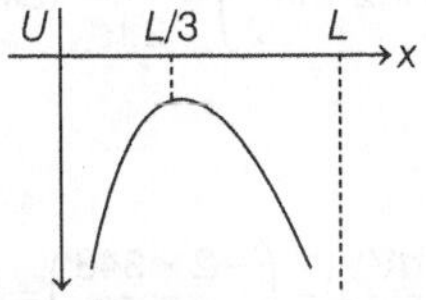

13. $q = \int i\,dt$ = Area under i - t curve

$$= \frac{1}{2}(0.2\times 10^{-3})(150\times 10^3) = 15 \text{ C}$$

$$V = Ed = (400\times 10^3)(1.5\times 10^3) = 6\times 10^8 \text{ V}$$

$$U = qV = 15\times(6\times 10^8) = 9\times 10^9 \text{ J}$$

14.

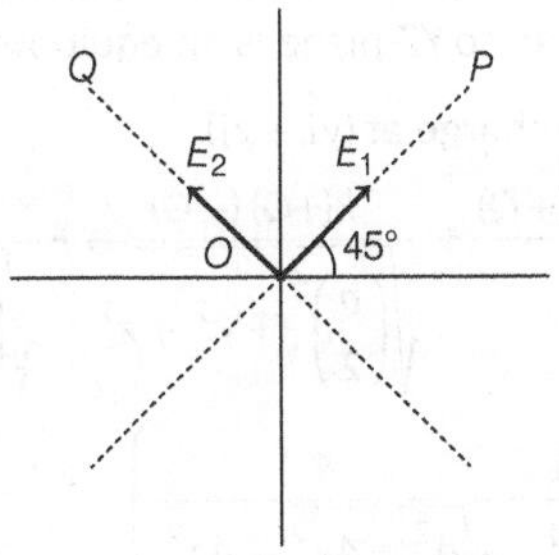

Lets take component of electric field along OP as E_1 and along OQ as E_2.
Along OP,

$$\Delta V = -Ed \quad \Rightarrow \quad -0.02 = -E_1(0.01)$$

$$\Rightarrow \quad E_1 = 2 \text{ V/m}$$

Net electric field $= \sqrt{E_1^2 + E_2^2}$

$$\Rightarrow \quad 2\sqrt{5} = \sqrt{2^2 + E_2^2} \Rightarrow E_2 = 4 \text{ V/m}$$

$$\mathbf{E} = (2\cos 45° - 4\cos 45°)\hat{\mathbf{i}} + (2\sin 45° + 4\sin 45°)\hat{\mathbf{j}}$$

$$= -\sqrt{2}\,\hat{\mathbf{i}} + 3\sqrt{2}\,\hat{\mathbf{j}}$$

15.

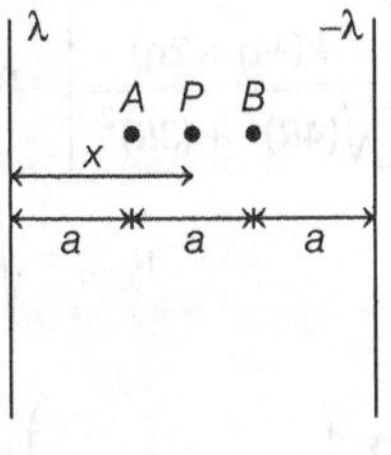

At point P,

$$\mathbf{E} = \mathbf{E}_1 + \mathbf{E}_2$$

$$E = \frac{2k\lambda}{x} + \frac{2k\lambda}{3a - x} = \frac{\lambda}{2\pi\varepsilon_0}\left(\frac{1}{x} + \frac{1}{3a - x}\right)$$

$$W=\int F dx=\int q_0 E dx$$

$$=\frac{q_0\lambda}{2\pi\varepsilon_0}\int_a^{2a}\left(\frac{1}{x}+\frac{1}{3a-x}\right)dx$$

$$=\frac{q_0\lambda}{2\pi\varepsilon_0}[\ln x]_a^{2a}-[\ln(3a-x)]_a^{2a}$$

$$=\frac{q_0\lambda}{2\pi\varepsilon_0}\left(\ln 2-\ln\frac{1}{2}\right)=\frac{q_0\lambda}{2\pi\varepsilon_0}(2\ln 2)=\frac{q_0\lambda\ln 2}{\pi\varepsilon_0}$$

16. $V=\dfrac{343}{r^2}$

$$E=-\frac{dV}{dr}=-\left(\frac{-2\times 343}{r^3}\right)=\frac{686}{r^3}$$

$$\mathbf{E}=E\hat{\mathbf{r}}=\frac{686}{r^3}\hat{\mathbf{r}}=\frac{686}{r^3}\left(\frac{\mathbf{r}}{r}\right)$$

$$=\frac{686}{r^4}\mathbf{r}=\frac{686}{7^4}(3\hat{\mathbf{i}}+2\hat{\mathbf{j}}+6\hat{\mathbf{k}})=\frac{2}{7}(3\hat{\mathbf{i}}+2\hat{\mathbf{j}}+6\hat{\mathbf{k}})$$

17. Electric field at any point on the YZ-plane is perpendicular to the YZ-plane, so YZ-plane is an equipotential surface.

18. Lets keep $-Q$ charge at $(y\hat{\mathbf{i}}+z\hat{\mathbf{j}})$.

$$U=\frac{k(+Q)(+Q)}{a}+\frac{k(+Q)(-Q)}{\sqrt{\left(\frac{a}{2}\right)^2+y^2+z^2}}+\frac{k(+Q)(-Q)}{\sqrt{\left(\frac{-a}{2}\right)^2+y^2+z^2}}$$

$$\Rightarrow 0=kQ^2\left(\frac{1}{a}-\frac{4}{\sqrt{a^2+4y^2+4z^2}}\right)$$

$$\Rightarrow \sqrt{a^2+4y^2+4z^2}=4a$$

$$\Rightarrow \quad 4y^2+4z^2=15a^2$$

$$\Rightarrow \quad y^2+z^2=\frac{15}{4}a^2$$

19. We just need to make the ball reach the centre of the semi-circular ring with negligible velocity and thereafter, the ball will come out of the pipe due to repulsion by the semi-circular ring.

Applying mechanical energy conservation,

$$K_1+U_1=K_2+U_2$$

$$\Rightarrow \frac{1}{2}mu_{\min}^2+(+q)\left[\frac{k(+q+2q)}{\sqrt{(4R)^2+(3R)^2}}\right]=0+(+q)\frac{k(+q+2q)}{4R}$$

$$\Rightarrow \quad u_{\min}=\sqrt{\frac{3q^2}{40\pi\varepsilon_0 mR}}$$

20. $E=E_1-E_2$

$$\Rightarrow \quad E=\frac{\sigma}{2\varepsilon_0}-\frac{\sigma}{2\varepsilon_0}\left(1-\frac{x}{\sqrt{R^2+x^2}}\right)$$

$$\Rightarrow \quad E=\frac{\sigma x}{2\varepsilon_0\sqrt{R^2+x^2}}$$

$$\Rightarrow \quad -\frac{dV}{dx}=\frac{\sigma x}{2\varepsilon_0\sqrt{R^2+x^2}}$$

$$\Rightarrow \quad \int -dV=\frac{\sigma}{2\varepsilon_0}\int_{\sqrt{3}R}^{0}\frac{x\,dx}{\sqrt{R^2+x^2}}$$

$$\Rightarrow \quad -\Delta V=\frac{\sigma}{2\varepsilon_0}[\sqrt{R^2+x^2}]_{\sqrt{3}R}^{0} \Rightarrow \Delta V=\frac{\sigma R}{2\varepsilon_0}$$

Now, loss in PE = gain in KE

$$\Rightarrow \quad -(-e)\left(\frac{\sigma R}{2\varepsilon_0}\right)=\frac{1}{2}mv^2 \Rightarrow v=\sqrt{\frac{\sigma e R}{m\varepsilon_0}}$$

21.

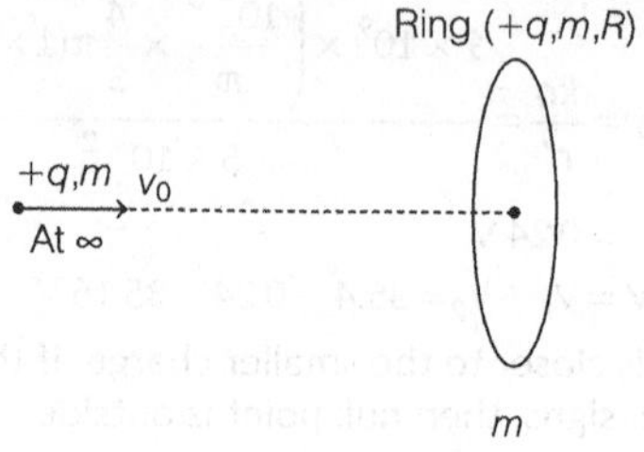

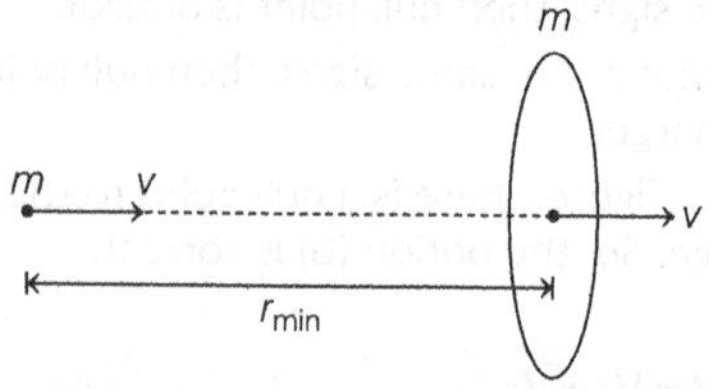

When the separation is minimum, their velocity of approach would be zero.

Using linear momentum conservation,

$$mv_0+0=mv+mv \Rightarrow v=\frac{v_0}{2}$$

Using mechanical energy conservation,

$$K_1+U_1=K_2+U_2$$

$$\Rightarrow \quad \left(\frac{1}{2}mv_0^2+0\right)+0=\left[\frac{1}{2}m\left(\frac{v_0}{2}\right)^2+\frac{1}{2}m\left(\frac{v_0}{2}\right)^2\right]+q\left(\frac{kq}{\sqrt{R^2+r_{\min}^2}}\right)$$

$$\Rightarrow \quad \frac{kq^2}{\sqrt{R^2+r_{\min}^2}}=\frac{1}{4}mv_0^2$$

$$\Rightarrow \quad r_{\min}=\sqrt{\frac{q^4}{\pi^2\varepsilon_0^2 m^2 v_0^4}-R^2}$$

22. Using angular momentum conservation, the point charge Q about the centre of the fixed sphere.

$$mv_0(2R)=m(v\cos 45^\circ)R$$

$$\Rightarrow \quad v=2\sqrt{2}v_0$$

Using mechanical energy conservation,

$$K_1+U_1=K_2+U_2$$

$$\Rightarrow \quad \frac{1}{2}mv_0^2+Q\left[\frac{k(-Q)}{\infty}\right]=\frac{1}{2}m(2\sqrt{2}v_0)^2+Q\left[\frac{k(-Q)}{R}\right]$$

$$v_0=\sqrt{\frac{2kQ^2}{7mR}}=\sqrt{\frac{2}{7}}\alpha$$

23. Using work-energy theorem,

$W_{mg} + W_{\text{electric}} + W_T = \Delta K$

$\Rightarrow + mg(l - l\cos 45°) + (qE)(l\sin 45°) + 0 = \frac{1}{2}(ml^2)\omega^2 - 0$

$\Rightarrow \quad mgl\left(1 - \frac{1}{\sqrt{2}}\right) + q\left(\frac{mg}{q}\right)\frac{l}{\sqrt{2}} = \frac{1}{2}(ml^2)\omega^2$

$\Rightarrow \quad \omega = \sqrt{\frac{2g}{l}}$

24.

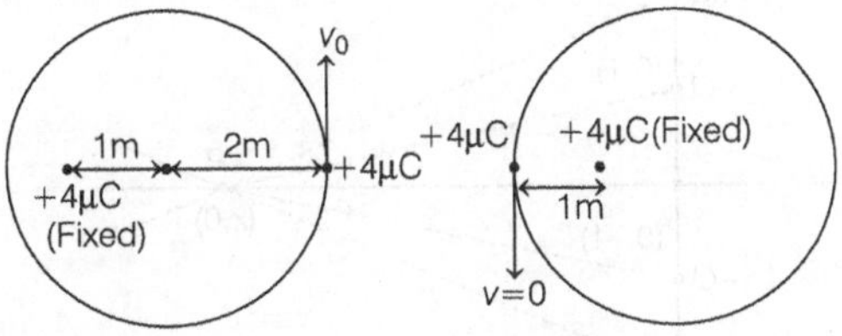

Using mechanical energy conservation,

$K_1 + U_1 = K_2 + U_2$

$\Rightarrow \frac{1}{2} \times 100 \times 10^{-3} v_0^2 + \frac{9 \times 10^9 \times 4 \times 10^{-6} \times 4 \times 10^{-6}}{3}$

$= 0 + \frac{9 \times 10^9 \times 4 \times 10^{-6} \times 4 \times 10^{-6}}{1}$

$\Rightarrow \quad v_0 = \frac{\sqrt{192}}{10}$ m/s

$= 0.8\sqrt{3}$ m/s

$= 80\sqrt{3}$ cm/s

25. We just need to make the particle reach the centre of the tunnel and thereafter, it will come out of the tunnel due to repulsion by the sphere.

Using mechanical energy conservation,

$K_1 + U_1 = K_2 + U_2$

$\frac{1}{2}mu_{\min}^2 + q\left(\frac{kQ}{R}\right) = 0 + q\frac{kQ}{2R}\left[3 - \left(\frac{R/2}{R}\right)^2\right]$

$\Rightarrow \quad u_{\min} = \sqrt{\frac{3kQq}{4mR}}$

$= \sqrt{\frac{3\left(\frac{1}{4\pi\varepsilon_0}\right)\left(\rho\frac{4}{3}\pi R^3\right)q}{4mR}}$

$= \sqrt{\frac{q\rho R^2}{4m\varepsilon_0}}$

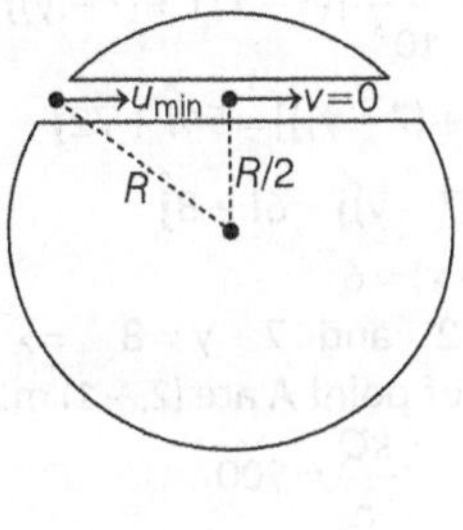

26. $U_1 = \frac{k(+q)(+q)}{\sqrt{5}a} + \frac{k(+q)(-q)}{\sqrt{5}a} + \frac{k(+q)(-q)}{2a} = -\frac{kq^2}{2a}$

$U_2 = \frac{k(+q)(-q)}{a} + \frac{k(+q)(-q)}{2a} + \frac{k(+q)(+q)}{3a} = \frac{-7}{6}\frac{kq^2}{a}$

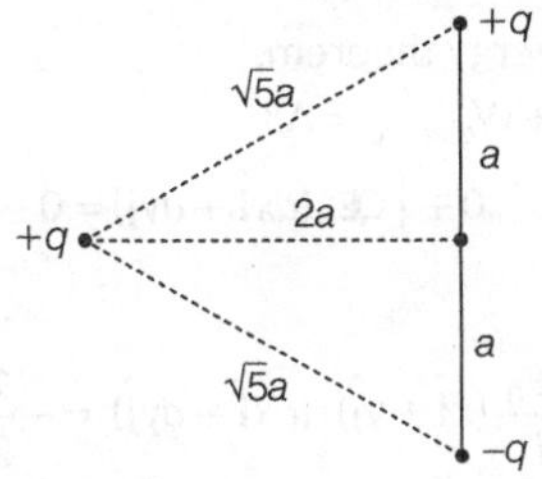

Loss in PE = Gain in KE

$\frac{-kq^2}{2a} - \left(\frac{-7}{6}\frac{kq^2}{a}\right) = \frac{1}{2}(ma^2 + ma^2)\omega^2 - 0$

$\Rightarrow \quad \omega = \sqrt{\frac{2kq^2}{3ma^3}} = \frac{q}{\sqrt{6\pi\varepsilon_0 ma^3}}$

27. Case -I

Loss in PE = Gain in KE of m_1

$\frac{kqq_1}{R} = \frac{1}{2}m_1v_1^2$ ... (i)

Case -II

Loss in PE = Gain in KE of m_1 and m_2

$\frac{kqq_1}{R} = \frac{1}{2}m_1v_2^2 + \frac{1}{2}m_2v_2'^2$ ... (ii)

Applying linear momentum conservation,

$0 + 0 = m_1v_2 - m_2v_2'$ ... (iii)

Solving Eqs. (i), (ii) and (iii), we get

$\frac{v_1}{v_2} = \sqrt{\frac{m_1 + m_2}{m_2}}$

28.

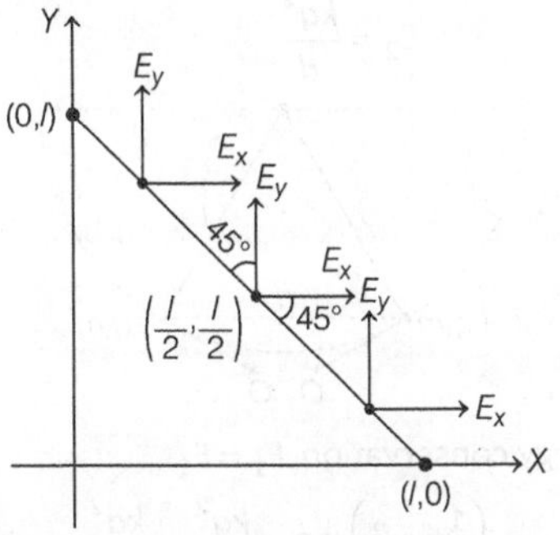

Component of electric field along the rod

$= E_x\cos 45° - E_y\cos 45° = 0$

$$\Rightarrow \quad \frac{E_0}{l}x\cos 45° - \frac{E_0 y}{l}\cos 45° = 0$$

$$\Rightarrow \quad x = y = \frac{l}{2}$$

We just need to make the particle reach the mid-point $\left(\frac{l}{2}, \frac{l}{2}\right)$ as thereafter component of electric field along the rod is directed towards $(l, 0)$.

Using work-energy theorem,

$$W_N + W_{\text{electric}} = \Delta K$$

$$\Rightarrow \quad 0 + \int Q\mathbf{E}\cdot(dx\hat{\mathbf{i}} + dy\hat{\mathbf{j}}) = 0 - \frac{1}{2}mu_{\min}^2$$

$$\Rightarrow \quad \int_{(0,\,l)}^{\left(\frac{l}{2},\frac{l}{2}\right)} \frac{QE_0}{l}(x\hat{\mathbf{i}} + y\hat{\mathbf{j}})\cdot(dx\hat{\mathbf{i}} + dy\hat{\mathbf{j}}) = -\frac{1}{2}mu_{\min}^2$$

$$\Rightarrow \quad \frac{QE_0}{l}\left[\frac{x^2}{2} + \frac{y^2}{2}\right]_{(0,\,l)}^{\left(\frac{l}{2},\frac{l}{2}\right)} = \frac{-1}{2}mu_{\min}^2$$

$$\Rightarrow \quad \frac{QE_0}{2l}\left(\frac{l^2}{2} - l^2\right) = -\frac{1}{2}mu_{\min}^2$$

$$\Rightarrow \quad u_{\min} = \sqrt{\frac{QE_0 l}{2m}} = 2\text{ m/s}$$

29. Let us go over to the inertial reference frame fixed to the moving centre of the thread.

Initially, with respect to the centre of the threads, the balls have velocity v each as shown.

$$E_1 = \left(\frac{1}{2}mv^2\right)\times 2 + \frac{kq^2}{2l}$$

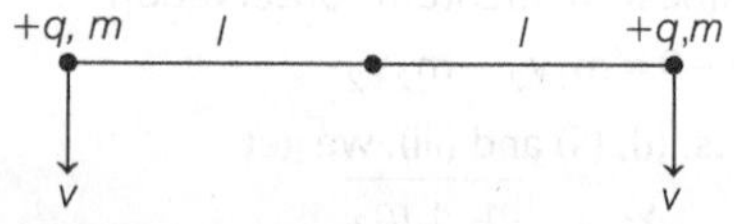

At the moment of the closest approach, the energy of the system,

$$E_2 = \frac{kq^2}{d}$$

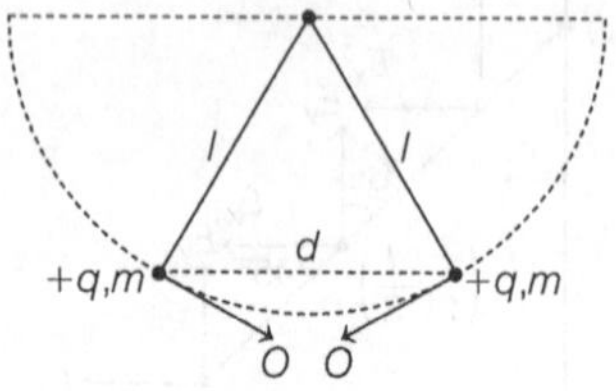

From energy conservation, $E_1 = E_2$

$$\Rightarrow \quad \left(\frac{1}{2}mv^2\right)\times 2 + \frac{kq^2}{2l} = \frac{kq^2}{d}$$

$$\Rightarrow \quad d = \frac{2q^2 l}{(q^2 + 8\pi\varepsilon_0 mv^2 l)} = \frac{2l}{3}$$

30. Using work-energy theorem for the particle,

$$W_{\text{electric}} + W_F = \Delta K$$

$$\Rightarrow qEd + 0 = \frac{1}{2}m\left(\frac{v_0}{2}\right)^2 - \frac{1}{2}mv_0^2 \qquad (\because W_F = 0 \text{ and } \mathbf{F}\perp\mathbf{v})$$

$$\Rightarrow \quad E = \frac{3mv_0^2}{8qd}$$

31.

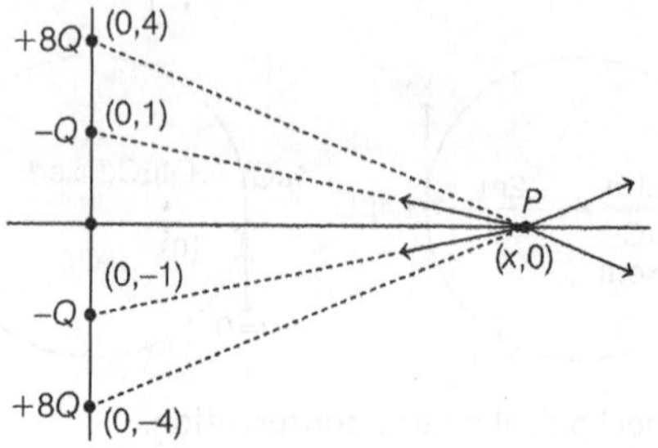

$$\text{At } P,\ E = \frac{k(8Q)}{(\sqrt{16 + x^2})^2}\frac{x}{\sqrt{16 + x^2}}\times 2 - \frac{kQ}{(\sqrt{1^2 + x^2})^2}\frac{x}{(\sqrt{1^2 + x^2})}\times 2 = 0$$

$$\Rightarrow 16 + x^2 = 4(1 + x^2) \Rightarrow x = 2$$

We just need to make the particle reach point (2, 0) with negligible velocity as after that electric field is directed towards the origin.

Using mechanical energy conservation,

$$K_1 + U_1 = K_2 + U_2$$

$$\frac{1}{2}mu_{\min}^2 + 0 = 0 + Q\left[\frac{k(8Q)}{\sqrt{2^2 + 4^2}}\times 2 + \frac{k(-Q)}{\sqrt{2^2 + 1^2}}\times 2\right]$$

$$u_{\min} = \sqrt{\frac{3Q^2}{\sqrt{5}\pi\varepsilon_0 m}} = 6\text{ m/s}$$

Multiple Choice(s) Correct Questions

1. $E = \frac{kQ}{r^2} = \sqrt{54^2 + 72^2} = 90$ V/m

$$V = \frac{kQ}{r} = 900\text{ V}$$

$$\frac{V}{E} = \frac{kQ/r}{kQ/r^2} = \frac{900}{90}$$

$$\Rightarrow \quad r = 10\text{ m and } kQ = 9000$$

$$\mathbf{E} = \frac{kQ}{r^3}\mathbf{r} = \frac{9000}{10^3}[(8 - x)\hat{\mathbf{i}} + (7 - y)\hat{\mathbf{j}}]$$

$$\Rightarrow \quad 9[(8 - x)\hat{\mathbf{i}} + (7 - y)\hat{\mathbf{j}}] = 54\hat{\mathbf{i}} + 72\hat{\mathbf{j}}$$

$$\Rightarrow \quad (8 - x)\hat{\mathbf{i}} + (7 - y)\hat{\mathbf{j}} = 6\hat{\mathbf{i}} + 8\hat{\mathbf{j}}$$

$$\Rightarrow \quad (8 - x) = 6$$

$$\Rightarrow \quad x = 2 \text{ and } 7 - y = 8 \quad \Rightarrow \quad y = -1$$

So, coordinates of point A are $(2, -1)$ m.

$$\frac{kQ}{r} = 900$$

$$\Rightarrow \quad \frac{9\times10^9 Q}{10} = 900 \Rightarrow Q = 10^{-6}\,\text{C} = 1\,\mu\text{C}$$

Electric field is maximum at surface of sphere,

$$E_{\text{surface}} = \frac{kQ}{R^2} < 3\times10^6$$

$$\Rightarrow \quad \frac{9000}{R^2} < 3\times10^6 \Rightarrow R^2 > 3\times10^{-3}$$

$$\Rightarrow \quad R > \sqrt{30}\times10^{-2}\text{ m} \Rightarrow R > \sqrt{30}\text{ cm}$$

$$\Rightarrow \quad R_{\min} = \sqrt{30}\text{ cm}$$

2. $$\frac{kQ}{(R+5)\text{cm}} = 100\text{ V} \quad \text{... (i)}$$

and $$\frac{kQ}{(R+10)\text{ cm}} = 75\text{ V} \quad \text{... (ii)}$$

Dividing Eq. (i) by Eq. (ii), we get

$$\frac{R+10}{R+5} = \frac{100}{75}$$

$$\Rightarrow \quad 3R + 30 = 4R + 20$$

$$\Rightarrow \quad R = 10\text{ cm}$$

(a) $V_{\text{surface}} = \dfrac{kQ}{R} = \dfrac{100\times15}{10} = 150\text{ V}$

(b) $\dfrac{kQ}{R} = 150$

$$\Rightarrow \quad \frac{9\times10^9 Q}{10\times10^{-2}} = 150$$

$$\Rightarrow \quad Q = \frac{5}{3}\times10^{-9}\text{C}$$

(c) $E_{\text{surface}} = \dfrac{kQ}{R^2} = \dfrac{100\times(15\text{ cm})}{(10\text{ cm})^2} = 1500\text{ V/m}$

(d) $V_{\text{centre}} = \dfrac{3kQ}{2R} = \dfrac{3}{2}(150) = 225\text{ V}$

3. Along X-axis,

$$\Delta V = -E_x d$$

$$\Rightarrow \quad 20 - 180 = -E_x(4\text{ cm})$$

$$\Rightarrow \quad E_x = 40\text{ V/cm}$$

$$\mathbf{E} = E_x\hat{\mathbf{i}} + E_y\hat{\mathbf{j}} + E_z\hat{\mathbf{k}}$$

If E_y and E_z are zero, then $E = 40$ V/cm.

If E_y and E_z are non-zero, then $E > 40$ V/cm.

4. Potential and potential energy depend on the choice of zero potential and zero potential energy, respectively.

5. (a) In going from y to x,

Gain in potential energy $= q\Delta V$

$$= (+e)[5 - (-5)]\text{ V} = 10\text{ eV}$$

So, KE > 10 eV

(b) $W_{\text{electric } x\to y} = -\Delta U = -q\Delta V$

$$= -(+e)(-5-5)\text{ V} \quad = +10\text{ eV}$$

(c) $W_{\text{electric } y\to x} = -q\Delta V = -(+e)[5-(-5)]\text{V}$

$$= -10\text{ eV}$$

(d) If the particle is released at x, then the particle will gain KE at the expense of loss of its potential energy.

6. $\mathbf{E} = \mathbf{E}_1 + \mathbf{E}_2$

$$E = \frac{2k\lambda}{R_1} + \frac{2k\lambda}{R_2} = \frac{\lambda}{2\pi\varepsilon_0}\left(\frac{1}{R_1} + \frac{1}{R_2}\right)$$

Electric field due to the two straight sections will cancel out each other.

$$V = V_1 + V_2 + V_3 + V_4$$

$$= \frac{k(\lambda_1\pi R_1)}{R_1} + \frac{k(\lambda_2\pi R_2)}{R_2} + \int_{R_2}^{R_1}\frac{k\lambda dx}{x} + \int_{R_2}^{R_1}\frac{k\lambda dx}{x}$$

$$= \frac{\lambda}{2\pi\varepsilon_0}\left[\pi + \ln\left(\frac{R_1}{R_2}\right)\right]$$

7. (a) $dq_1 = \lambda(r_1 d\theta)$

$$dq_2 = \lambda(r_2 d\theta)$$

$$\frac{dq_1}{dq_2} = \frac{r_1}{r_2}$$

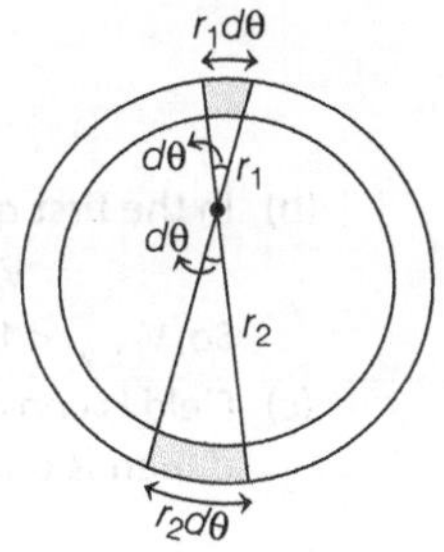

(b) $E_1 = \dfrac{kdq_1}{r_1^2} = \dfrac{k\lambda r_1 d\theta}{r_1^2}$

$$E_2 = \frac{kdq_2}{r_2^2} = \frac{k\lambda r_2 d\theta}{r_2^2}$$

$$\therefore \quad \frac{E_1}{E_2} = \frac{r_2}{r_1}$$

$$\Rightarrow \quad E_1 > E_2$$

$$\because \quad r_2 > r_1$$

(c) $V_1 = \dfrac{kdq_1}{r_1} = \dfrac{k\lambda r_1 d\theta}{r_1} = k\lambda d\theta$

$$V_2 = \frac{kdq_2}{r_2} = \frac{k\lambda r_2 d\theta}{r_2} = k\lambda d\theta$$

So, $V_1 = V_2$

8.

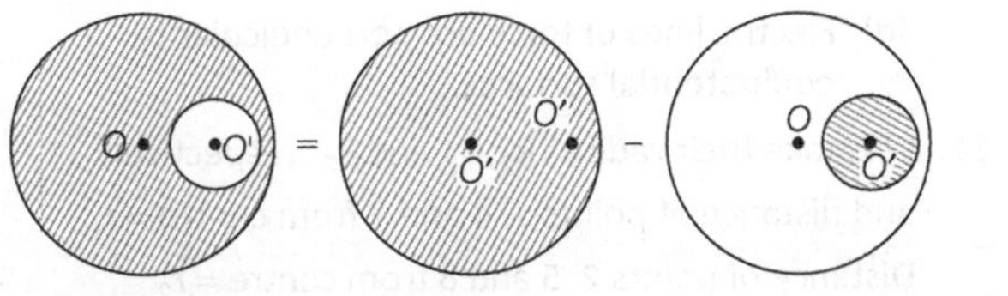

At point O',

$$\mathbf{E} = \mathbf{E}_1 - \mathbf{E}_2$$

$$\Rightarrow \quad \mathbf{E} = \frac{\rho a}{3\varepsilon_0} - 0 = \frac{\rho a}{3\varepsilon_0}$$

$$V = V_1 - V_2$$

$$\Rightarrow \quad V = \frac{k\left(\rho\frac{4}{3}\pi R_1^3\right)}{2R_1^3}(3R_1^2 - a^2) - \frac{3}{2}\times\frac{k\rho\frac{4}{3}\pi R_2^3}{R_2}$$

$$= \frac{\rho}{6\varepsilon_0}[3(R_1^2 - R_2^2) - a^2]$$

Electric potential in the hollow region is not constant as there exists a non-zero electric field in the hollow region.

9. $dV = -\mathbf{E}\cdot d\mathbf{r}$

$$\Rightarrow \quad dV = -(x^2\hat{\mathbf{i}} + y^2\hat{\mathbf{j}})\cdot(dx\hat{\mathbf{i}} + dy\hat{\mathbf{j}})$$

$$\Rightarrow \quad \int_0^V dV = -\int_3^x x^2\,dx - \int_3^y y^2 dy$$

$$\Rightarrow \quad [V]_0^V = -\left[\frac{x^3}{3}\right]_3^x - \left[\frac{y^3}{3}\right]_3^y$$

$$\Rightarrow \quad V - 0 = -\frac{x^3}{3} + 9 - \frac{y^3}{3} + 9$$

$$\Rightarrow \quad V = 18 - \frac{x^3}{3} - \frac{y^3}{3}$$

(a) $W_{ext} = q\Delta V$

$$= q(V_2 - V_1)$$

$$= q\left[\left(18 - \frac{b^3}{3} - \frac{a^3}{3}\right) - \left(18 - \frac{a^3}{3} - \frac{b^3}{3}\right)\right]$$

$$= 0$$

(b) In the first quadrant,

$V_{max} = 18$, when $x = 0$ and $y = 0$

So, $V_{(x,\,y)} < 18$ unit

(c) Field is conservative as work done by the electric field depends only on initial and final positions.

(d) $V = 18 - \frac{x^3}{3} - \frac{y^3}{3} = c$

$$\Rightarrow \quad x^3 + y^3 = 18 - 3c$$

So, equipotential surfaces are not concentric circles.

10. (a) Two equipotential surfaces never intersect each other.

(b) In a uniform electric field, equipotential surfaces are parallel planes.

(c) The electric field intensity is maximum, where equipotential surfaces are closest.

(d) Electric lines of force are perpendicular to equipotential surfaces.

11. Lets take their radii as R_1, R_2 and R_3, respectively and distance of points 1, 4 and 7 from centre $= r_1$

Distance of points 2, 5 and 8 from centre $= r_2$

Distance of points 3, 6 and 9 from centre $= r_3$

$$V_1 = \frac{kQ}{r_1}, V_2 = \frac{kQ}{r_2}, V_3 = \frac{kQ}{R_1}$$

$$V_4 = \frac{kQ}{r_1}, V_5 = \frac{kQ}{R_2}, V_6 = \frac{kQ}{R_2}$$

$$V_7 = V_8 = V_9 = \frac{kQ}{R_3}$$

(a) V_3 is maximum as $R_1 < R_2 < R_3$

(b) $V_1 = V_4 \neq V_7$

(c) Points 7, 8 and 9 have lowest potential as $R_3 > r_1$.

(d) $V_5 \neq V_8$

12. $E_A > E_B$ as electric field intensity is higher, where electric field lines are closer.

$V_A < V_B$ as potential decreases in the direction of electric field.

13. (a) $E_x = -\frac{dV}{dx} = -\frac{6-0}{[-1-(-3)]} = -3\text{N}/\text{C}$

(b) $E_x = -\frac{dV}{dx} = 0$

(c) $W_{ext} = q\Delta V = q(V_2 - V_1)$

$$\frac{W_{ext}}{q} = V_2 - V_1 = 6 - 0 = 6\ \text{J/C}$$

(d) $\frac{W_{ext}}{q} = \Delta V = V_2 - V_1$

$$= 0 - 6 = -6\ \text{J/C}$$

14. $dV = -\mathbf{E}\cdot d\mathbf{r}$

$$\Rightarrow \quad \int dV = -\int \mathbf{E}\cdot d\mathbf{r}$$

$$\Rightarrow \quad \Delta V = -\int \mathbf{E}\cdot d\mathbf{r}$$

As we move along X-axis, electric field increases.

So, $\quad V_1 - V_2 = V_2 - V_3 \quad \Rightarrow \quad x_2 < x_1$

In the direction of electric field, electric potential decreases.

So, $V_1 > V_2 > V_3$

15.

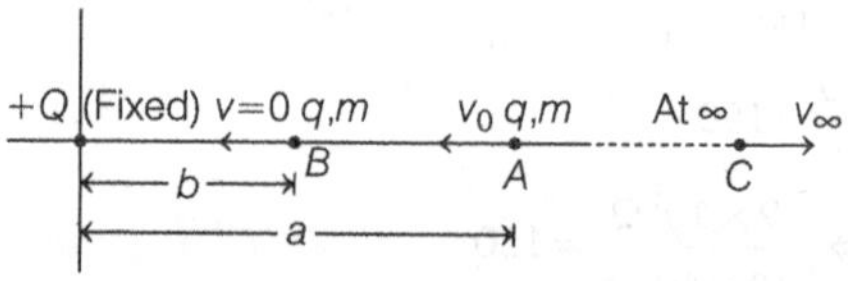

Using mechanical energy conservation between A and B,

$$K_1 + U_1 = K_2 + U_2$$

$$\frac{1}{2}mv_0^2 + \frac{kQq}{a} = 0 + \frac{kQq}{b}$$

$$\Rightarrow \quad \frac{kQq}{6a} + \frac{kQq}{a} = \frac{kQq}{b}$$

$$\Rightarrow \quad \frac{b}{a} = \frac{6}{7}$$

Using mechanical energy conservation between A and C,

$$K_1 + U_1 = K_2 + U_2$$

$$\frac{1}{2}mv_0^2 + \frac{kQq}{a} = \frac{1}{2}mv_\infty^2 + 0$$

$$\Rightarrow \quad v_\infty = \sqrt{7}v_0$$

16. (a) Lets take electric field as

$$\mathbf{E} = E_x\hat{\mathbf{i}} + E_y\hat{\mathbf{j}}$$

Since, y-component of velocity is constant,

$$\Rightarrow \quad E_y = 0$$

$$\mathbf{F} = q\mathbf{E}$$

$$\Rightarrow \quad m\mathbf{a} = (-e)(E_x\hat{\mathbf{i}}) \Rightarrow \mathbf{a} = -\left(\frac{eE_x}{m}\right)\hat{\mathbf{i}}$$

$$s_y = u_y t + \frac{1}{2}a_y t^2$$

$$\Rightarrow \quad d = vt + 0$$

$$\Rightarrow \quad t=\frac{d}{v}$$

$$s_x=u_xt+\frac{1}{2}a_xt^2$$

$$\Rightarrow \quad 2a-a=0+\frac{1}{2}\left(\frac{-eE_x}{m}\right)\left(\frac{d}{v}\right)^2$$

$$\Rightarrow \quad E_x=\frac{-2amv^2}{ed^2}$$

(b) $$v_x=u_x+a_xt=0+\left(\frac{-eE_x}{m}\right)\left(\frac{d}{v}\right)$$

$$=\frac{-e}{m}\left(-\frac{2amv^2}{ed^2}\right)\left(\frac{d}{v}\right)=\frac{2av}{d}$$

So, $\mathbf{v}=\left(\frac{2av}{d}\right)\hat{\mathbf{i}}+v\hat{\mathbf{j}}$

(c) Rate of work done at $B=\frac{dW}{dt}=P$

$$P=\mathbf{F}_B\cdot\mathbf{v}_B=(-e\mathbf{E})\cdot\mathbf{v}$$

$$=(-e)\left(\frac{-2amv^2}{ed^2}\hat{\mathbf{i}}\right)\cdot\left[\left(\frac{2av}{d}\right)\hat{\mathbf{i}}+v\hat{\mathbf{j}}\right]=\frac{4ma^2v^3}{d^3}$$

(d) Rate of work done at $A=\mathbf{F}_A\cdot\mathbf{v}_A$

$$=(-e)\left(\frac{-2amv^3}{ed^2}\hat{\mathbf{i}}\right)\cdot v\hat{\mathbf{j}}=0$$

17. (a) $W_{electric}=-q\Delta V=-q(V-0)$

$$=-q\left[\frac{k(-q)}{a}\times 2+\frac{k(+q)}{\sqrt{2}a}\right]=-\frac{kq^2}{a}\left(\frac{1-2\sqrt{2}}{\sqrt{2}}\right)$$

(b) $W_{ext}=q\Delta V=\frac{kq^2}{a}\left(\frac{1-2\sqrt{2}}{\sqrt{2}}\right)$

(c) $U=\frac{k(+q)(-q)}{a}\times 4+\frac{k(+q)(+q)}{\sqrt{2}a}+\frac{k(-q)(-q)}{\sqrt{2}a}$

$$=\frac{kq^2}{a}(\sqrt{2}-4)$$

(d) Electric field at the centre = 0

Comprehension Based Questions

1.

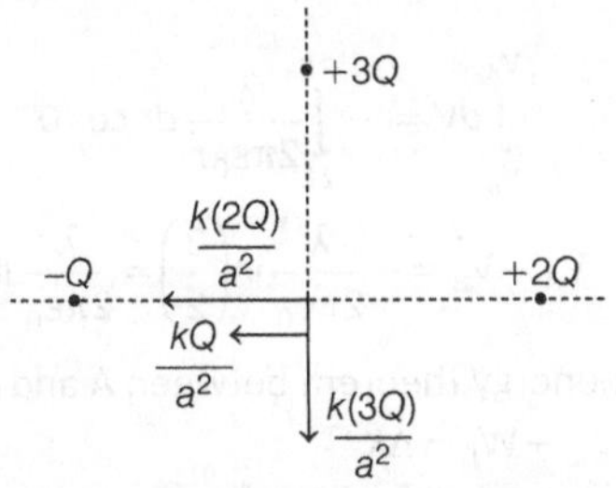

$$E_x=-\frac{k(2Q)}{a^2}-\frac{kQ}{a^2}=-\frac{k(3Q)}{a^2}$$

$$E_y=-\frac{k(3Q)}{a^2}$$

2. $U=U_{12}+U_{23}+U_{31}$

$$=\frac{k(+2Q)(+3Q)}{\sqrt{2}a}+\frac{k(+3Q)(-Q)}{\sqrt{2}a}+\frac{k(+2Q)(-Q)}{2a}$$

$$=\frac{kQ^2}{a}\left(\frac{3}{\sqrt{2}}-1\right)$$

3. $W_{ext}=\Delta U+\Delta K=q\Delta V+0$

$$=+3Q\left[\left\{\frac{k(+2Q)}{a}+\frac{k(+3Q)}{a}+\frac{k(-Q)}{a}\right\}-0\right]$$

$$=\frac{kQ^2}{a}(12)$$

4. Potential at point (x, y),

$$V=V_1+V_2$$

$$\Rightarrow \quad 0=\frac{k(+6e)}{\sqrt{x^2+y^2}}+\frac{k(-10e)}{\sqrt{(x-8)^2+y^2}}$$

$$\Rightarrow 9(x-8)^2+9y^2=25x^2+25y^2$$

$$\Rightarrow \quad x^2+y^2+9x-36=0$$

$$\Rightarrow \quad (x+4.5)^2+y^2=(7.5)^2$$

This is equation of circle.

Radius of circle = 7.5 nm

5. X-coordinate of the centre of circle = – 4.5 nm

6. At the centre (– 4.5, 0),

$$V=V_1+V_2=\frac{k(+6e)}{4.5\times 10^{-9}}+\frac{k(-10e)}{12.5\times 10^{-9}}$$

$$=1.92-1.152=0.768 \text{ V}$$

$$\simeq 0.77 \text{ V}$$

7. Electric field at any point inside a solid sphere $=\frac{\rho r}{3\varepsilon_0}$

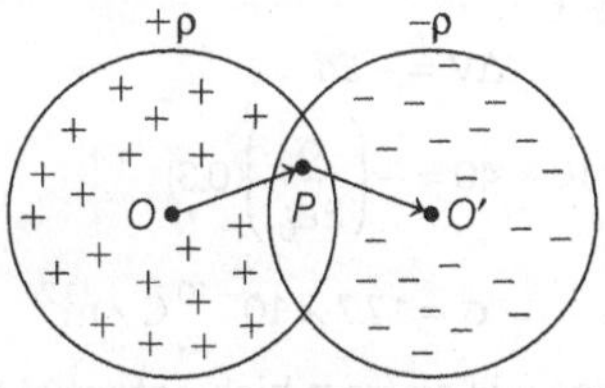

Lets take a point P in the overlap region.

$$\mathbf{E}=\mathbf{E}_1+\mathbf{E}_2$$

$$=\frac{\rho(\mathbf{OP})}{3\varepsilon_0}+\frac{\rho(\mathbf{PO'})}{3\varepsilon_0}$$

$$=\frac{\rho}{3\varepsilon_0}(\mathbf{OP}+\mathbf{PO'})$$

$$=\frac{\rho}{3\varepsilon_0}(\mathbf{OO'})=\left(\frac{\rho}{3\varepsilon_0}\right)\mathbf{d}$$

8. Electric field in the overlap region is uniform.

$$\Delta V=Ed=\left(\frac{\rho d}{3\varepsilon_0}\right)d=\frac{\rho d^2}{3\varepsilon_0}$$

9. Lets take a spherical shell of radius r and thickness dr.

Potential due to this shell at centre $= \frac{kdq}{r}$

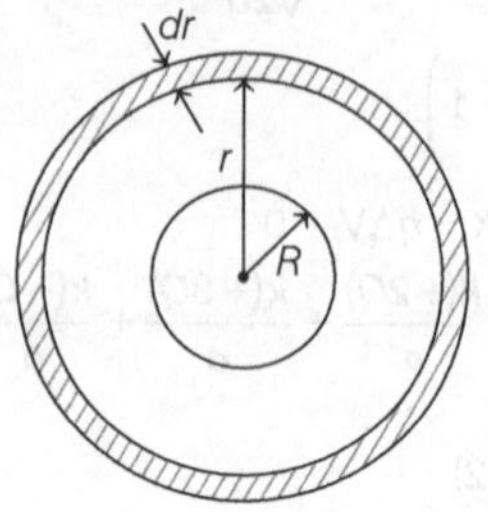

$$dV = \frac{k(\rho 4\pi r^2 dr)}{r}$$

$$\Rightarrow \quad \int dV = \int_R^{\infty} \frac{k(B/r^3)4\pi r^2 dr}{r}$$

$$\Rightarrow \quad V = \frac{B}{\varepsilon_0}\left[\frac{-1}{r}\right]_R^{\infty} \quad \Rightarrow \quad V = \frac{B}{\varepsilon_0 R}$$

10.

$$V = \int_R^x \frac{kdq}{x} + \int_x^{\infty} \frac{kdq}{r}$$

$$= \int_R^x \frac{k(B/r^3)4\pi r^2 dr}{x} + \int_x^{\infty} \frac{k(B/r^3)4\pi r^2 dr}{r}$$

$$= \frac{B}{\varepsilon_0 x}\ln\left(\frac{x}{R}\right) + \frac{B}{\varepsilon_0 x}$$

$$\Rightarrow \quad V = \frac{B}{\varepsilon_0 x}\left[1 + \ln\left(\frac{x}{R}\right)\right]$$

11. Electric field for $x > R$ is radially outward, so potential decreases, as we move away from ball's surface.

12. Near the sheet,

$$\Delta V = -Ed$$

$$\Rightarrow \quad 10 - 40 = -\left(\frac{\sigma}{2\varepsilon_0}\right)(0.3)$$

$$\Rightarrow \quad \sigma = 17.7 \times 10^{-10}\ \text{C/m}^2$$

13. Positive charge will go from high potential to low potential, so it will move towards A.

14. $W_{ext} = q\Delta V + \Delta K$

$$= (-1\times 10^{-6})[20 - (-20)] + 0 = -4 \times 10^{-5}\ \text{J}$$

15. Lets first find speed of each of them just before B hits the wall inelastically.

Using mechanical conservation,

$$K_1 + U_1 = K_2 + U_2$$

$$\Rightarrow (0+0) + \frac{9\times 10^9 \times 40\times 10^{-6} \times 40 \times 10^{-6}}{0.2}$$

$$= \left(\frac{1}{2}\times 0.6 v_0^2 + \frac{1}{2}\times 0.6 v_0^2\right) + \frac{9\times 10^9 \times 40\times 10^{-6}\times 40\times 10^{-6}}{0.6}$$

$$\Rightarrow v_0 = \sqrt{80}\ \text{m/s}$$

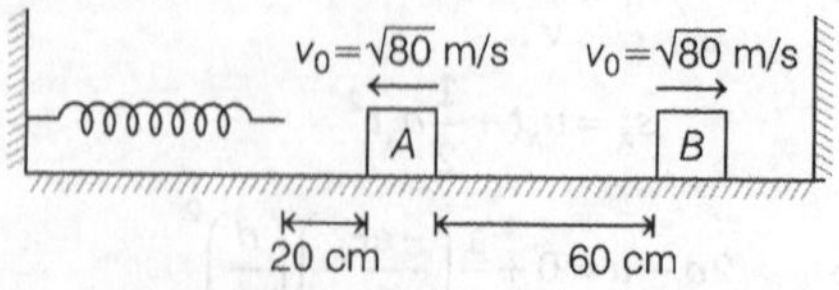

Now, after hitting wall, B will come to rest and A will travel further 20 cm to hit the spring.

For A, Further loss in PE= Further gain in KE

$$9\times 10^9 \times 40 \times 10^{-6} \times 40 \times 10^{-6}\left(\frac{1}{0.6} - \frac{1}{0.8}\right)$$

$$= \frac{1}{2}\times 0.6(v^2 - v_0^2)$$

$$\Rightarrow \quad v = 10\ \text{m/s}$$

16. After hitting the spring, lets take maximum compression to be x.

Further loss in PE + Further loss in KE = Gain in spring PE

$$\Rightarrow 9\times 10^9 \times 40\times 10^{-6} \times 40 \times 10^{-6}\left(\frac{1}{0.8} - \frac{1}{0.8 + x}\right)$$

$$+ \frac{1}{2}\times 0.6 \times 10^2 = \frac{1}{2}\times 6400 \times x^2$$

$$\Rightarrow \quad x = 10\ \text{cm}$$

17.

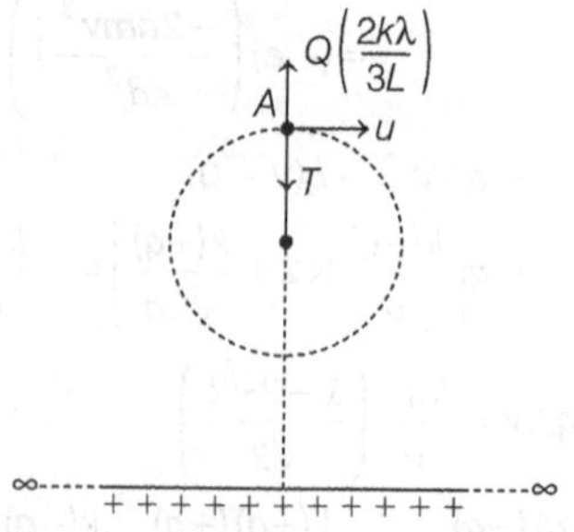

At point A, equation for circular motion is

$$T - Q\left(\frac{2k\lambda}{3L}\right) = \frac{Mu^2}{L}$$

$$\Rightarrow \quad T = \frac{Mu^2}{L} + \frac{Q\lambda}{6\pi\varepsilon_0 L}$$

18. $dV = -\mathbf{E}\cdot d\mathbf{r}$

$$\int_{V_B}^{V_A} dV = -\int_{2L}^{3L} \frac{\lambda}{2\pi\varepsilon_0 r} dr \cos 0^\circ$$

$$\Rightarrow \quad V_A - V_B = -\frac{\lambda}{2\pi\varepsilon_0}\ln\left(\frac{3}{2}\right) = \frac{\lambda}{2\pi\varepsilon_0}\ln\left(\frac{2}{3}\right)$$

19. Using work-energy theorem between A and B,

$$W_{electric} + W_T = \Delta K$$

$$\Rightarrow \quad -q\Delta V + 0 = \frac{1}{2}Mv^2 - \frac{1}{2}Mu^2$$

$$\Rightarrow \quad -Q(V_B - V_A) = \frac{1}{2}Mv^2 - \frac{1}{2}Mu^2$$

$$\Rightarrow \quad Q(V_A - V_B) = \frac{1}{2}Mv^2 - \frac{1}{2}Mu^2$$

$$\Rightarrow \quad v = \sqrt{u^2 + \frac{Q\lambda}{\pi\varepsilon_0 M}\ln\left(\frac{2}{3}\right)}$$

At position *B*, equation for circular motion,

$$T = \frac{Mv^2}{L}$$

$$\Rightarrow \quad T = \frac{Mu^2}{L} - \frac{Q\lambda}{\pi\varepsilon_0 L}\ln\left(\frac{3}{2}\right)$$

Match the Columns Questions

1. (a) $V = \frac{x}{y}$

$$\mathbf{E} = \frac{-\partial V}{\partial x}\hat{\mathbf{i}} - \frac{\partial V}{\partial y}\hat{\mathbf{j}}$$

$$\Rightarrow \quad \mathbf{E} = -\frac{1}{y}\hat{\mathbf{i}} + \frac{x}{y^2}\hat{\mathbf{j}}$$

Slope of electric field lines $= \frac{E_y}{E_x}$

$$\Rightarrow \quad \frac{dy}{dx} = \frac{x/y^2}{-1/y}$$

$$\Rightarrow \quad \frac{dy}{dx} = \frac{-x}{y}$$

$$\Rightarrow \quad \int x\,dx + \int y\,dy = 0$$

$$\Rightarrow \quad x^2 + y^2 = C$$

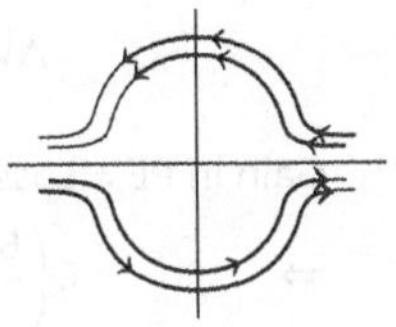

(b) $V = x^2 - y^2$

$$\mathbf{E} = \frac{-\partial V}{\partial x}\hat{\mathbf{i}} - \frac{\partial V}{\partial y}\hat{\mathbf{j}}$$

$$\Rightarrow \quad \mathbf{E} = -2x\hat{\mathbf{i}} + 2y\hat{\mathbf{j}}$$

Slope of electric field lines $= \frac{E_y}{E_x}$

$$\Rightarrow \quad \frac{dy}{dx} = \frac{+2y}{-2x}$$

$$\Rightarrow \quad \frac{dy}{y} + \frac{dx}{x} = C$$

$$\Rightarrow \quad \ln y + \ln x = C$$

$$\Rightarrow \quad \ln(xy) = C$$

$$\Rightarrow \quad xy = C'$$

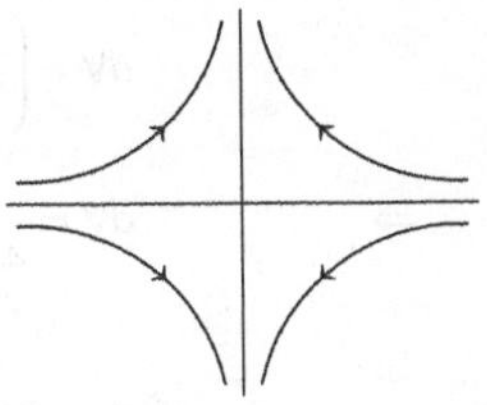

(c) $V = x^2 + y^2$

$$\mathbf{E} = \frac{-\partial V}{\partial x}\hat{\mathbf{i}} - \frac{\partial V}{\partial y}\hat{\mathbf{j}}$$

$$\Rightarrow \quad \mathbf{E} = -2x\hat{\mathbf{i}} - 2y\hat{\mathbf{j}}$$

Slope of electric field lines $= \frac{E_y}{E_x}$

$$\frac{dy}{dx} = \frac{-2y}{-2x}$$

$$\Rightarrow \quad \ln\left(\frac{y}{x}\right) = C \quad \Rightarrow \quad y = C'x$$

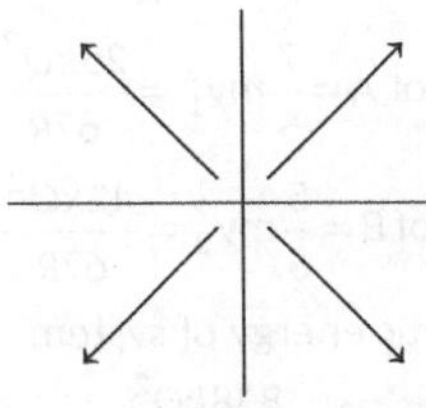

(d) $V = xy$

$$\Rightarrow \quad \mathbf{E} = \frac{-\partial V}{\partial x}\hat{\mathbf{i}} - \frac{\partial V}{\partial y}\hat{\mathbf{j}}$$

$$\Rightarrow \quad \mathbf{E} = -y\hat{\mathbf{i}} - x\hat{\mathbf{j}}$$

Slope of electric field lines $= \frac{E_y}{E_x} = \frac{-x}{-y}$

$$\frac{dy}{dx} = \frac{x}{y} \quad \Rightarrow \quad y^2 - x^2 = C$$

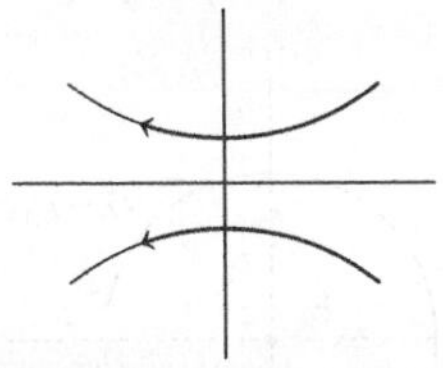

2. Let v_1 = velocity of COM of *A* and v_2 = velocity of COM of *B* just before they collide.

Loss in PE = Gain in KE

$$\Rightarrow \quad 0 - \frac{k(+2Q)(-Q)}{2R} = \frac{1}{2}(2m)v_1^2\left(1 + \frac{2}{5}\right) + \frac{1}{2}mv_2^2\left(1 + \frac{2}{3}\right)$$

$$\Rightarrow \quad \frac{7}{5}mv_1^2 + \frac{5}{6}mv_2^2 = \frac{kQ^2}{R} \qquad \text{... (i)}$$

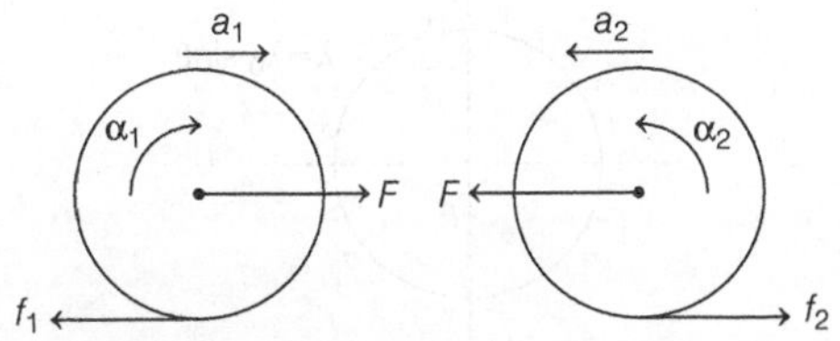

By taking torque about contact points,

$\tau = I\alpha$

$$\Rightarrow FR = \left[\frac{7}{5}(2m)R^2\right]\left(\frac{a_1}{R}\right) \text{ (For solid sphere)}$$

$$\text{and } FR = \left[\frac{5}{3}mR^2\right]\left[\frac{a_2}{R}\right] \text{ (For hollow sphere)}$$

$$\Rightarrow \quad 42a_1 = 25a_2$$

$$\Rightarrow \quad 42v_1 = 25v_2 \qquad \text{... (ii)}$$

Solving Eqs. (i) and (ii), we get

$$mv_1^2 = \frac{125kQ^2}{469R}$$

$$\text{and} \quad mv_2^2 = \frac{252kQ^2}{335R}$$

(a) Kinetic energy of system $= \dfrac{kQ^2}{R}$

(b) Kinetic energy of $A = \dfrac{7}{5}mv_1^2 = \dfrac{25kQ^2}{67R}$

(c) Kinetic energy of $B = \dfrac{5}{6}mv_2^2 = \dfrac{42kQ^2}{67R}$

(d) Rotational kinetic energy of system

$$= \frac{2}{5}mv_1^2 + \frac{1}{3}mv_2^2 = \frac{838kQ^2}{2345R}$$

3. (a)

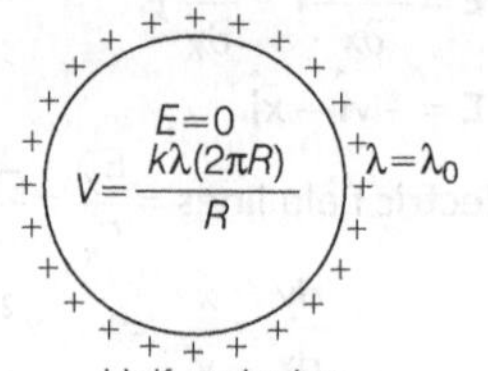

Uniformly ring

(b)

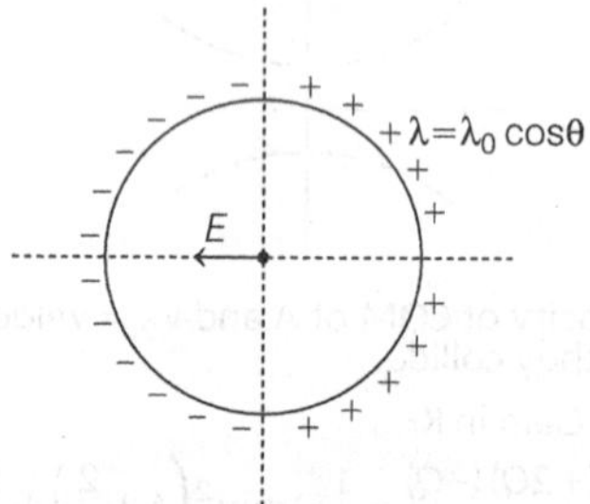

$$V = \int \frac{kdq}{R} = \int_0^{2\pi} \frac{k(\lambda_0 \cos\theta)Rd\theta}{R} = 0$$

(c)

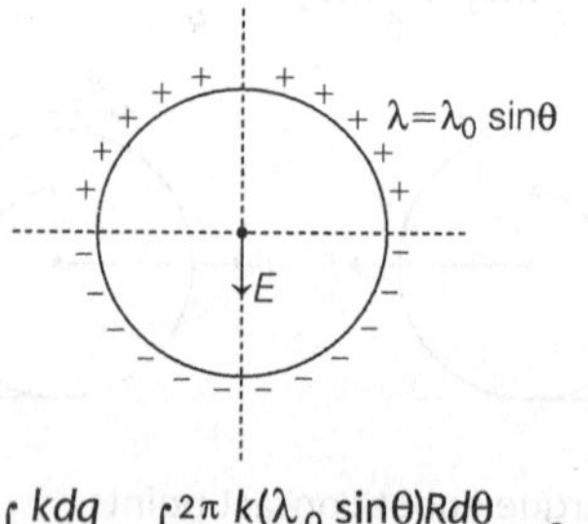

$$V = \int \frac{kdq}{R} = \int_0^{2\pi} \frac{k(\lambda_0 \sin\theta)Rd\theta}{R} = 0$$

(d) $\lambda = \lambda_0(1 - \cos 2\theta) = 2\lambda_0 \sin^2\theta$

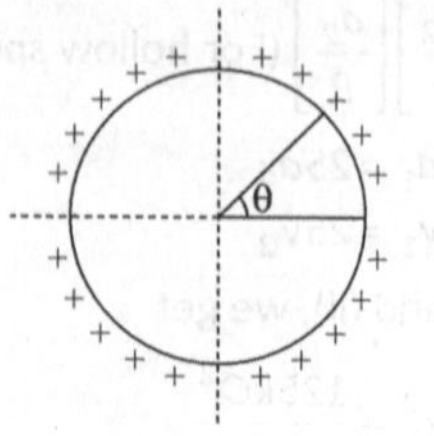

At centre, $E = 0$

$$V = \int \frac{kdq}{R} > 0$$

Numerical Value Questions

1.

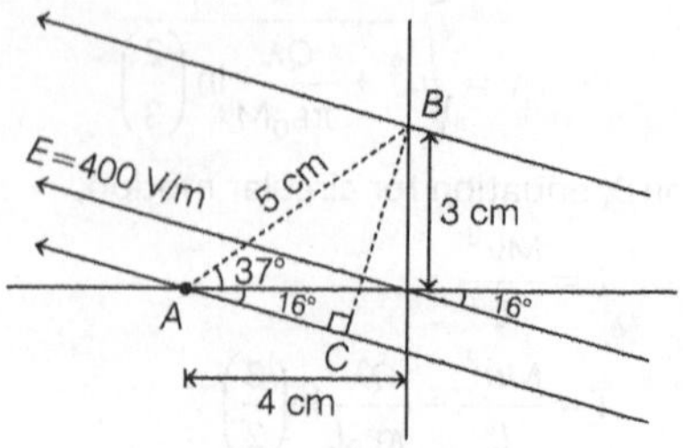

$$AB = \sqrt{4^2 + 3^2} = 5 \text{ cm}$$

$$AC = AB\cos 53^\circ = 5 \times \frac{3}{5} = 3 \text{ cm}$$

$$\Delta V = -Ed$$

$$\Rightarrow \quad V_B - V_A = -400(-3 \times 10^{-2}) = 12 \text{ V}$$

$$\Rightarrow \quad V_B - 20 = 12 \quad \Rightarrow \quad V_B = 32 \text{ V}$$

2. $-Q$ will experience repulsion from $x = 3L$ to $2L$ and attraction from $x = 2L$ to $x = 0$. So, we just need to make $-Q$ reach $x = 2L$ with negligible velocity.

From $x = 3L$ to $x = 2L$,

$$\Delta V = -\int E dx = -\left(\frac{-1}{2} \times E_0 \times L\right) = \frac{E_0 L}{2}$$

Gain in PE = Loss in KE

$$\Rightarrow \quad Q\left(\frac{E_0 L}{2}\right) = \frac{1}{2}mv_0^2 - 0$$

$$\Rightarrow \quad v_0 = \sqrt{\frac{QE_0 L}{m}} = \sqrt{\frac{10^{-3} \times 20 \times 5}{1 \times 10^{-3} \times 10^{-3}}}$$

$$= 100\sqrt{10} = 316.20 \text{ m/s}$$

3. $Q = \displaystyle\int_a^{3a} \frac{k}{r^3} 2\pi r dr = 2\pi k \left[\frac{-1}{r}\right]_a^{3a} = \frac{4\pi k}{3a} \quad \Rightarrow \quad k = \frac{3aQ}{4\pi}$

Potential at the centre,

$$dV = \left(\frac{1}{4\pi\varepsilon_0}\right)\frac{dq}{r}$$

$$\Rightarrow \quad dV = \frac{1}{4\pi\varepsilon_0} \frac{\sigma 2\pi r dr}{r}$$

$$\Rightarrow \quad \int dV = \frac{1}{4\pi\varepsilon_0} \int_a^{3a} \frac{\left(\frac{k}{r^3}\right) 2\pi r dr}{r}$$

$$\Rightarrow \quad \int dV = \frac{k}{2\varepsilon_0}\left[\frac{1}{(-2)r^2}\right]_a^{3a}$$

$$\Rightarrow \quad V = \frac{2k}{9\varepsilon_0 a^2} = \frac{2\left(\frac{3aQ}{4\pi}\right)}{9\varepsilon_0 a^2} = \frac{Q}{6\pi\varepsilon_0 a}$$

4. Potential at the centre of a hemispherical shell $= \frac{kQ}{R}$

Lets divide the hemisphere into thin hemispherical shells. Lets take a hemispherical shell of radius r and thickness dr.

Potential at its centre $= \frac{kdq}{r}$

$$dV = \frac{k(\rho^2 \pi r^2\, dr)}{r}$$

$$\int dV = \frac{\rho}{2\varepsilon_0}\int_a^b r dr$$

$$V = \frac{\rho}{2\varepsilon_0}\left[\frac{r^2}{2}\right]_a^b$$

$$= \frac{\rho}{4\varepsilon_0}\left(b^2 - \frac{b^2}{4}\right) = \frac{3\rho b^2}{16\varepsilon_0}$$

5. Loss in gravitational potential energy = Gain in electrostatic potential energy

$\Rightarrow mgH = q\Delta V$

$$\Rightarrow \quad mgH = q\left[\frac{\sigma R}{2\varepsilon_0} - \frac{\sigma}{2\varepsilon_0}(\sqrt{R^2+H^2} - H)\right]$$

$$\Rightarrow \quad gH = \frac{q}{m}\left(\frac{\sigma}{2\varepsilon_0}\right)[R + H - \sqrt{R^2+H^2}]$$

$$\Rightarrow \quad gH = \left(\frac{4\varepsilon_0 g}{\sigma}\right)\left(\frac{\sigma}{2\varepsilon_0}\right)(R + H - \sqrt{R^2+H^2})$$

$$\Rightarrow \quad H = \frac{4R}{3} = \frac{4\times 6}{3} = 8 \text{ m}$$

6.

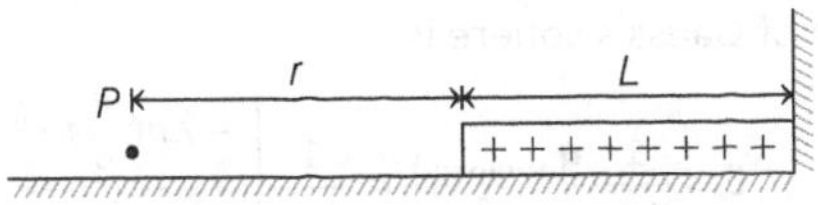

Potential at point P due to rod $= \int_r^{L+r} \frac{k\lambda dx}{x}$

$$\Rightarrow \quad V = \frac{\lambda}{4\pi\varepsilon_0}\ln\left(\frac{L+r}{r}\right)$$

For the block,

Loss in KE = Gain in PE

$$\Rightarrow \quad \frac{1}{2}mv_0^2 - 0 = q(V_2 - V_1)$$

$$\Rightarrow \quad \frac{1}{2}mv_0^2 = q\left[\left\{\frac{\lambda}{4\pi\varepsilon_0}\ln\left(\frac{L+r_{min}}{r_{min}}\right) - 0\right\}\right]$$

$$\Rightarrow \quad \frac{1}{2}m\left(\sqrt{\frac{\lambda q}{m\pi\varepsilon_0}\ln 2}\right)^2 = \frac{q\lambda}{4\pi\varepsilon_0}\ln\left(\frac{L+r_{min}}{r_{min}}\right)$$

$$\Rightarrow \quad \frac{L+r_{min}}{r_{min}} = 4$$

$$\Rightarrow \quad r_{min} = \frac{L}{3}$$

7. From equilibrium of Q_1, $\frac{1}{4\pi\varepsilon_0}\frac{Q_1Q_2}{h_0^2} = mg$

In centre of mass frame,

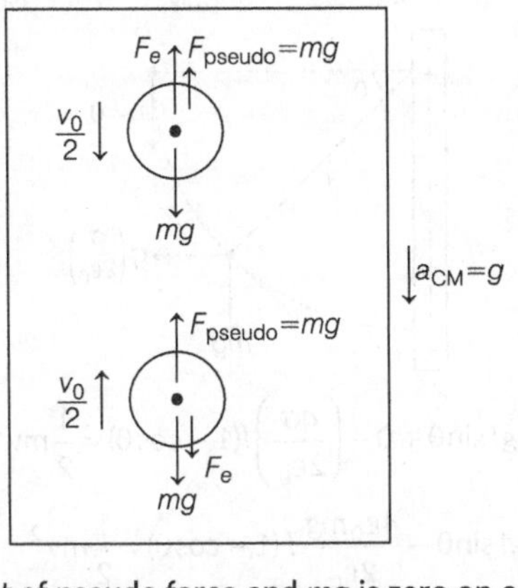

Resultant of pseudo force and mg is zero on each mass. At the closest distance, velocity of each mass is zero in COM frame. Lets take closest separation to be x.

Loss in KE = Gain in electrostatic PE

$$\Rightarrow \quad 2\left[\frac{1}{2}m\left(\frac{v_0}{2}\right)^2\right] = \frac{Q_1Q_2}{4\pi\varepsilon_0}\left(\frac{1}{x} - \frac{1}{h_0}\right)$$

$$\Rightarrow \quad x = 13.33 \text{ cm}$$

8.

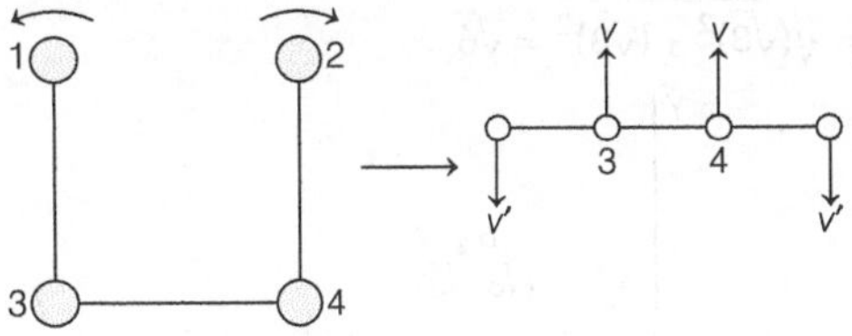

Speed of balls 3 and 4 will be maximum, when the string becomes horizontal.

Since, external force on the system of four balls is zero, linear momentum of system is conserved.

$$0 + 0 + 0 + 0 = mv + mv - mv' - mv'$$

$$\Rightarrow \quad v' = v$$

Using mechanical energy conservation,

Loss in PE = Gain in KE

$$\frac{kq^2}{a} - \frac{kq^2}{3a} = \frac{1}{2}mv^2 \times 4$$

$$v = \sqrt{\frac{kq^2}{3am}} = \sqrt{\frac{Ykq^2}{Xam}}$$

$$\Rightarrow \quad Y = 1 \text{ and } X = 3$$

$$\Rightarrow \quad X + Y = 4$$

9. Loss in KE = Gain in PE

$$\Rightarrow \quad \frac{1}{2}mv_0^2 - 0 = q_0\left[\frac{kq}{R} + \frac{k(-q)}{\sqrt{R^2+(\sqrt{3}R)^2}}\right] - 0$$

$$\Rightarrow \quad mv_0^2 = \frac{kqq_0}{R}$$

$$\Rightarrow \qquad v_0 = \sqrt{\frac{kqq_0}{mR}} = \sqrt{\frac{kqq_0}{nmR}} \Rightarrow n = 1$$

10. Using work-energy theorem, $W_{mg} + W_T + W_{\text{electric}} = \Delta K$

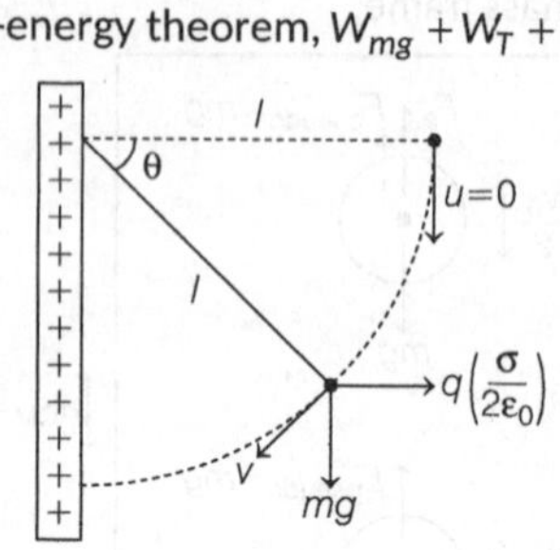

$$\Rightarrow \quad mgl\sin\theta + 0 - \left(\frac{q\sigma}{2\varepsilon_0}\right) l(1-\cos\theta) = \frac{1}{2}mv^2 - 0$$

$$\Rightarrow \quad mgl\sin\theta - \frac{4\varepsilon_0 mg}{2\varepsilon_0} l(1-\cos\theta) = \frac{1}{2}mv^2$$

$$\Rightarrow \quad v = \sqrt{2gl(\sin\theta + 2\cos\theta - 2)} = 2\text{ m/s}$$

Previous Year's Questions

JEE Main

1. Potential due to a point charge $V = \frac{kq}{r}$.

Here,

$OP = \sqrt{(\sqrt{3})^2 + (\sqrt{3})^2} = \sqrt{6}$

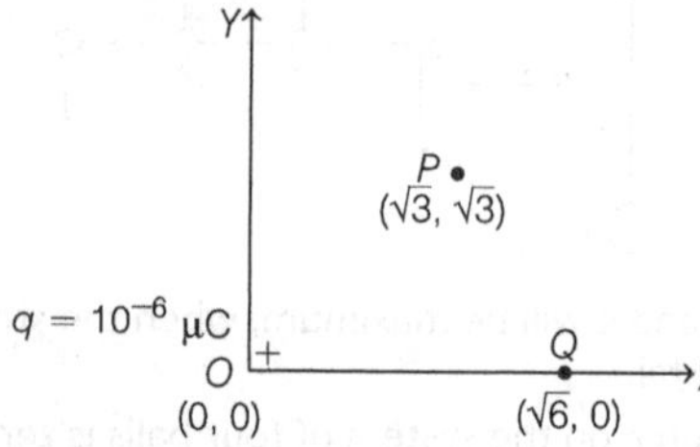

$\therefore \quad OP = OQ \Rightarrow V_P = V_Q$

Hence, $V_P - V_Q = 0$

2. Electric lines of force are always perpendicular to equipotential surface

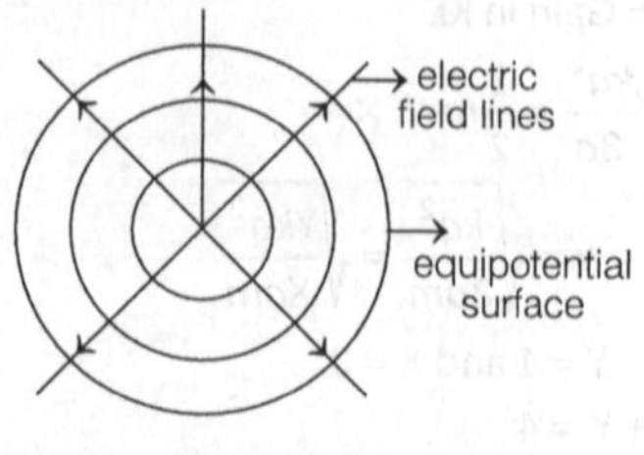

Work done by electric field on moving a positive charge on an equipotential surface is always zero.

3. Potential due to a point charge at a distance r is;

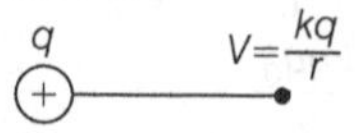

$$V = \frac{kq}{r}$$

Here, $q = 5 \times 10^{-9}$ C,

$V = 50$ V $k = 9 \times 10^9$ N - m^2/C^2

$$\text{So,} \quad r = \frac{kq}{V} = \frac{9\times 10^9 \times 5 \times 10^{-9}}{50} = \frac{45}{50} = 0.9\text{ m} = 90\text{ cm}$$

4. Given, potential of small drop = 10 mV

Let q be the charge of each drop.

$$V = \frac{kq}{r}$$

Now, for combination of 64 drop

$$64 \times \frac{4}{3}\pi r^3 = \frac{4}{3}\pi R^3$$

$$\Rightarrow \qquad R = 4r \text{ and } Q = 64q$$

Potential of bigger drop;

$$\frac{kQ}{R} = \frac{k64q}{4r} = \frac{16kq}{r} \Rightarrow 160\text{ mV}$$

5. Given, volume charge density inside a charged spherical ball is $\rho = -\lambda a \varepsilon$

As, charge density is constant, charge enclosed in a Gauss' sphere of radius r is;

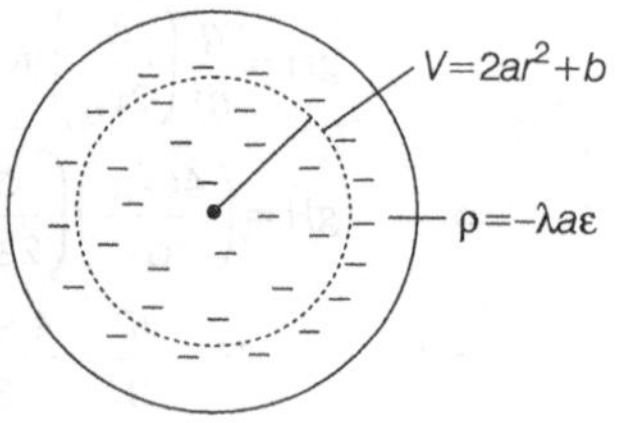

$$q = \rho \cdot V = -\lambda a\varepsilon\left(\frac{4}{3}\pi r^3\right)$$

by Gauss's law field on surface of Gauss's sphere is

$$E = \frac{1}{4\pi\varepsilon}\frac{q_{\text{enclosed}}}{r^2} = \frac{1}{4\pi\varepsilon}\left(\frac{-\lambda a\varepsilon \frac{4}{3}\pi r^3}{r^2}\right) = -\frac{\lambda}{3}ar$$

Now, using $E = \frac{-dV}{dr}$, we get

$$V = \int_0^r dV = -\int_0^r (Edr)$$

$$\text{or} \qquad V = \int_0^r \frac{\lambda}{3} ar\, dr = \frac{\lambda a}{3}\cdot\left(\frac{r^2}{2}\right)$$

$$\text{or} \qquad V = \frac{\lambda}{6}ar^2 \qquad \text{...(i)}$$

But potential is given,

$$V = 2ar^2 + b \qquad \text{...(ii)}$$

On comparing Eq. (i) and, Eq. (ii) we get

$$\frac{\lambda}{6} = 2 \text{ or } \lambda = 12$$

6. Electric field at some point (x, y, z),

$$E = -\frac{\partial V}{\partial x}\hat{i} - \frac{\partial V}{\partial y}\hat{j} - \frac{\partial V}{\partial z}\hat{k} = \frac{-\partial}{\partial x}(3x^2)\hat{i} = -6x\hat{i}$$

$$\text{As,} \qquad \frac{\partial V}{\partial y} = \frac{\partial}{\partial y}3x^2 = 0$$

Similarly, $\dfrac{\partial V}{\partial z} = 0$

Hence, E (at 1, 0, 3) $= -6\hat{i}$ V/m

So, direction of field will be along negative X-axis.

7. Potential at each charged drop

$$V = 22 \text{ V}$$

Let r and R be the radius of small and big drop respectively.

$\therefore$ Volume of big drop $= 27 \times$ Volume of small drop

$$\Rightarrow \quad \frac{4}{3}\pi R^3 = 27 \times \frac{4}{3}\pi r^3 \quad \Rightarrow \quad R = 3r$$

$\because$ Potential at small drop

$$V = 22 \text{ V}$$

or, $$\frac{1}{4\pi\varepsilon_0}\frac{q}{r} = 22 \quad \text{...(i)}$$

Potential of bigger drop,

$$V' = \frac{1}{4\pi\varepsilon_0}\frac{27q}{R} = \frac{1}{4\pi\varepsilon_0}\cdot\frac{27q}{3r} = 9\cdot\frac{1}{4\pi\varepsilon_0}\cdot\frac{q}{r}$$

$$= 9 \times 22 \quad \text{[From Eq. (i)]}$$

$$= 198 \text{ V}$$

8. Translational kinetic energy of dinitrogen (N_2)

$$KE = \frac{3}{2}K_B T$$

Kinetic energy of an electron $= eV$

$$\Rightarrow \quad \frac{3}{2}K_B T = eV$$

$$\Rightarrow \quad \frac{3}{2} \times 1.38 \times 10^{-23} \times T = 1.6 \times 10^{-19} \times (0.1)$$

$$T = 773 \text{ K} = 773 - 273°\text{C} = 500°\text{ C}$$

9. Given,

$$n = 27 \quad \Rightarrow \quad V_1 = 10 \text{ V}$$

Let q_1 be the charge of one drop, r_1 be its radius, r be the radius of bigger drop and q be its charge.

As, volume remains constant.

$$\therefore \quad 4/3\,\pi r^3 = 4/3\,\pi r_1^3 \times 27 \quad \Rightarrow \quad r = 3r_1$$

Electric potential $(V) = \dfrac{3kq_1^2}{5r}$

Where, k is Coulomb constant.

Therefore, potential energy of small drop,

$$U_s = \frac{3}{5}\frac{kq_1^2}{r_1} \quad \text{...(i)}$$

and potential energy of bigger drop,

$$U_B = \frac{3}{5}\frac{k(q_1 \times 27)^2}{r}$$

$$U_B = \frac{3}{5}\frac{k(27)^2 q_1^2}{3r_1} \quad \text{... (ii)}$$

On dividing Eq. (ii) by Eq. (i), we get

$$\frac{U_B}{U_s} = \frac{27 \times 27}{3} = 243$$

$$\Rightarrow \quad U_B = 243\,U_s$$

JEE Advanced

1. $$Q_{\text{total}} = \int_0^{r_A} kr(4\pi r^2)dr + \int_{r_A}^{r_B} \frac{2k}{r}(4\pi r^2)dr$$

$$= \frac{4\pi k}{4}r_A^4 + \frac{8\pi k}{2}(r_B^2 - r_A^2)$$

$$= \pi k + 4\pi k(r_B^2 - r_A^2)$$

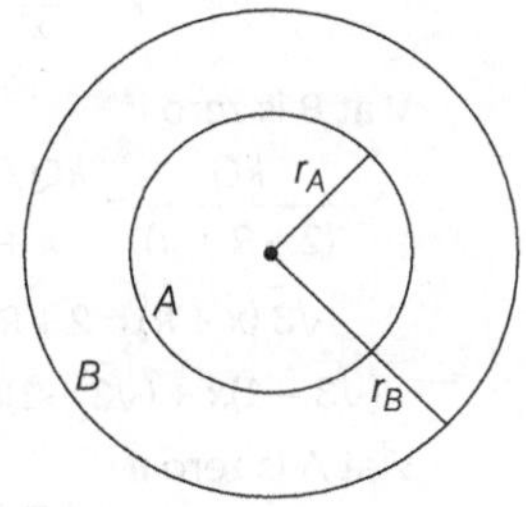

If $r_B = \sqrt{\dfrac{3}{2}}$,

$$Q_{\text{total}} = \pi k r_A^4 + 4\pi k\left(\frac{3}{2} - r_A^2\right)$$

$$= \pi k + 4\pi k\left(\frac{3}{2} - 1\right)$$

$$= \pi k + 2\pi k = 3\pi k$$

If $r_B = \dfrac{3}{2}$,

$$Q_{\text{total}} = \pi k + 4\pi k\left(\frac{9}{4} - 1\right) = \pi k + 4\pi k\left(\frac{5}{4}\right) = 6\pi k$$

$$V = \frac{1}{4\pi\varepsilon_0}\frac{6\pi k}{r_B} = \frac{3k}{2}\frac{2}{3\varepsilon_0} = \frac{k}{\varepsilon_0}$$

Option (b) is correct.

If $r_B = 2$,

$Q_{\text{total}} = \pi k + 4\pi k(4 - 1) = 13\pi k$

Option (c) is incorrect.

If $r_B = \dfrac{5}{2}$,

$$Q_{\text{total}} = \pi k + 4\pi k\left(\frac{25}{4} - 1\right)$$

$$= \pi k + \pi k(21) = 22\pi k$$

$$E = \frac{1}{4\pi\varepsilon_0}\frac{22\pi k}{25} \times 4 = \frac{22k}{25\varepsilon_0}$$

2. Applying work-energy theorem,

$$W_{EL} + W_{\text{ext}} = \Delta K = K_f - K_i$$

$$qV_f - qV_i + W_{\text{ext}} = K_f - 0$$

$$\frac{q\sigma}{2\varepsilon_0}[\sqrt{R^2 + Z^2} - Z] - \frac{q\sigma R}{2\varepsilon_0} + cZ = K_f$$

$$c = \frac{q\sigma B}{2\varepsilon_0}$$

Substitute values of β and Z, calculate kinetic energy K_f at $z = 0$.

If kinetic energy is positive, then particle will reach at origin.

If kinetic energy is negative, then particle will not reach at origin.

3. to 4.

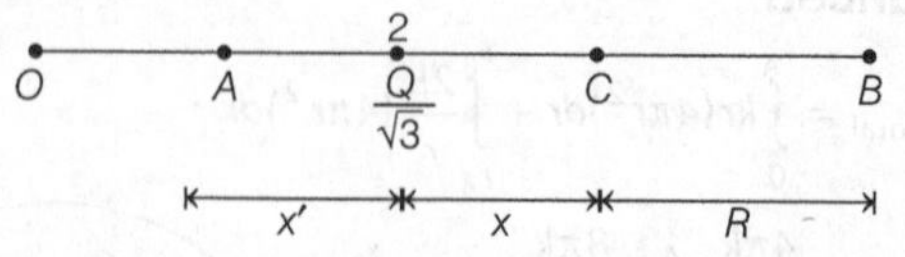

V at B is zero if

$$\frac{kQ}{(2+R+x)} = \frac{kQ/\sqrt{3}}{x+R} \qquad \left(\because k = \frac{1}{4\pi\varepsilon_0}\right)$$

$$\sqrt{3}\,(x+R) = 2+R+x$$

$$(\sqrt{3}-1)x + (\sqrt{3}-1)R = 2 \qquad \text{... (i)}$$

V at A is zero if

$$\frac{kQ}{2-x'} = \frac{\frac{kQ}{\sqrt{3}}}{x'} \Rightarrow \sqrt{3}x' = 2 - x'$$

$$x' = \frac{2}{\sqrt{3}+1} \Rightarrow x' + x = R$$

$$\frac{2}{\sqrt{3}+1} + x = R$$

$$2 + (\sqrt{3}+1)x = (\sqrt{3}+1)R$$

$$x = \frac{(\sqrt{3}+1)R - 2}{\sqrt{3}+1}$$

$$(\sqrt{3}+1)R - (\sqrt{3}+1)x = 2 \qquad \text{...(ii)}$$

Using Eqs. (i) and (ii), we get

$R = \sqrt{3}$ m = 1.73 m

$$x = \frac{(\sqrt{3}+1)\sqrt{3} - 2}{\sqrt{3}+1} = \frac{\sqrt{3}+1}{\sqrt{3}+1} = 1\text{ m}$$

Hence, the centre of circle is having x-coordinate $= b = 2 + x = 3.00$ m.

5. $qE = Mg$

$$\Rightarrow \qquad q = \frac{mg}{E} = \left(\frac{mg}{V/d}\right) = \frac{900 \times \frac{4}{5}\pi(8\times10^{-7})^3 \times 10}{\frac{200}{0.01}}$$

$$N = \frac{q}{e} = \frac{900 \times 4\pi \times 8^3 \times 10^{-21} \times 10 \times 0.01}{200 \times 1.6 \times 10^{-19}}$$

$$N = 6$$

6. Balls will gain positive charge and hence move towards negative plate.

On reaching negative plate, balls will attain negative charge and come back to positive plate.

So, balls will keep on oscillating.

But oscillation is not SHM,

as force on balls is not $\propto x$.

∴ (d) is correct.

7. As, the balls keep on carrying charge from one plate to another, current will keep on flowing. At bottom plate

$$\frac{kq}{r} = V_0 \qquad \left(\therefore k = \frac{1}{4\pi\varepsilon_0}\right)$$

$$\Rightarrow \qquad q = \frac{V_0 r}{k}$$

Inside the cylinder, electric field $E = [V_0 - (-V_0)]h$

$$= 2V_0 h.$$

⇒ Acceleration of each ball,

$$a = \frac{qE}{m} = \frac{2hr}{km}\cdot V_0^2$$

⇒ Time taken by the balls to reach the other plate,

$$t = \sqrt{\frac{2h}{a}} = \sqrt{\frac{2h.km}{2hrV_0^2}} = \frac{1}{V_0}\sqrt{\frac{km}{r}}$$

If there are n balls, then

$$\text{Average current, } i_{avg} = \frac{nq}{t} = n \times \frac{V_0 r}{k} \times V_0\sqrt{\frac{r}{km}}$$

$$\Rightarrow \qquad i_{avg} \propto V_0^2$$

CHAPTER~03

ELECTRIC DIPOLE

LEVEL 01 Starter Level

3.1 Electric Dipole Moment

1 An electron and a proton are at a distance of 1 Å. Find the electric dipole moment.

2 Find electric dipole moment of the following charge configurations.

(a) Three point charges are placed as shown.

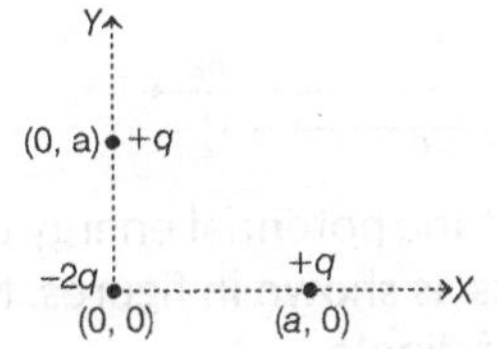

(b) Four point charges kept on a circle of radius R as shown.

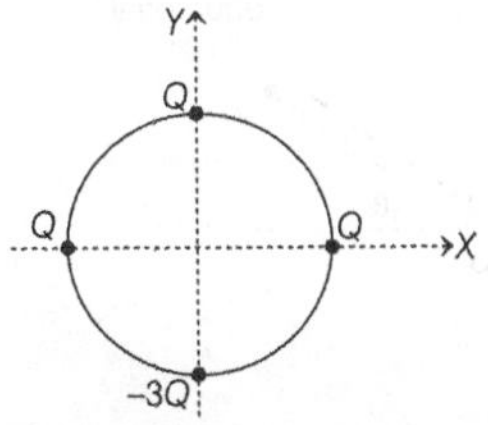

(c) Charge $+q$ is uniformly distributed on half-ring and a point charge $-q$ is kept at its centre.

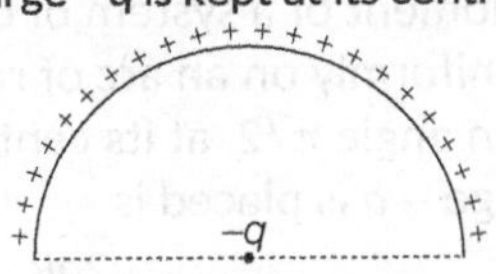

3.2 Electric Field due to Dipole

1 A dipole is placed at origin of coordinate system as shown in figure, find the electric field at point $P(0, y)$.

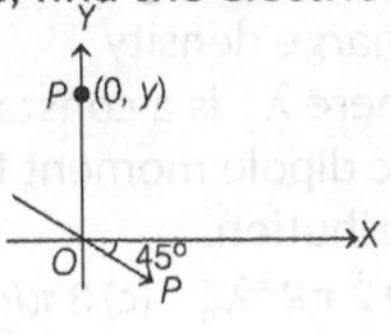

2 Find out the magnitude of electric field intensity at point (2 m, 0, 0) due to a dipole of dipole moment, $\mathbf{p} = (\hat{\mathbf{i}} + \sqrt{3}\hat{\mathbf{j}})$ C-m kept at origin.

3 Find the magnitude of the electric field at the point P in the configuration shown in figure for $d >> a$.

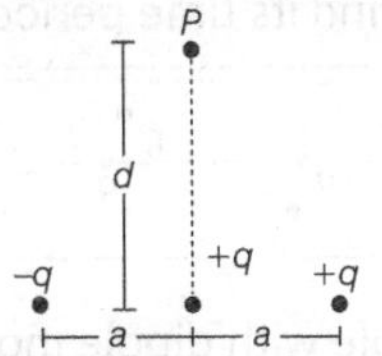

4 Two small electric dipoles of moment $p\hat{\mathbf{i}}$ and $-64\,p\,\hat{\mathbf{i}}$ are placed at (0,0) and (30,0) respectively, where will electric field intensity be zero?

3.3 Electric Potential due to Dipole

1 A dipole of dipole moment $\mathbf{p} = (2\hat{\mathbf{i}} - 3\hat{\mathbf{j}} + 4\hat{\mathbf{k}})$ μC-m is placed at point $A(2, -3, 1)$. Find the electric potential due to this dipole at the point $B(4, -1, 0)$.

2 Four short dipoles, each of dipole moment p are placed at the vertices of a square of side a. The direction of the dipole moments are shown in the figure. Find the electric potential at the centre O of the square.

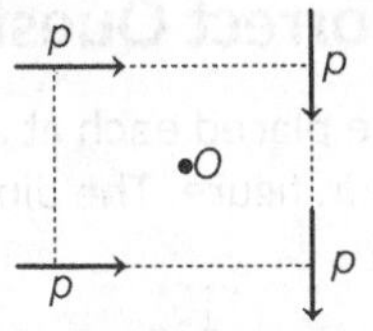

3 A charge q is carried slowly from a point $A(r, 135°)$ to point $B(r, 45°)$ following a path which is a quadrant of circle of radius r. If the dipole moment is p, then find out the work done by external agent.

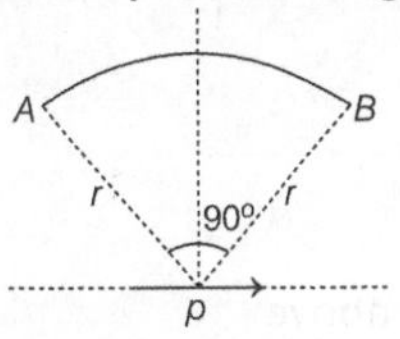

3.4 Dipole in External Uniform Electric Field

1 Two point charges of $-4\ \mu C$ and $+4\mu C$ are placed at points $A\ (1,0,4)$ and $B(2,-1,5)$ located in an electric field $\mathbf{E} = 0.2\ \hat{\mathbf{i}}$ V/cm. Find the force and torque acting on the dipole.

2 Figure shows an electric dipole formed by two particles fixed at the ends of a light rod of length l. The mass of each particle is m and the charges are $-q$ and $+q$. The system is placed in such a way that, the dipole axis is parallel to a uniform electric field E that exists in the region. The dipole is slightly rotated about its centre and released. Show that for small angular displacements, the motion is angular simple harmonic and find its time period.

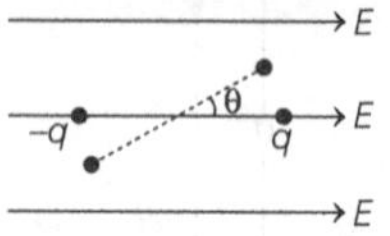

3 An electric dipole with dipole moment $\mathbf{p} = (2\hat{\mathbf{i}} + 3\hat{\mathbf{j}} - \hat{\mathbf{k}})\ \mu$C-m is placed in a uniform field $\mathbf{E} = (3\hat{\mathbf{i}} + 2\hat{\mathbf{k}}) \times 10^5$ N/C.

(i) What is the potential energy of the dipole?
(ii) If the dipole were to be rotated in the field $\mathbf{E}$, what is the maximum potential energy of the dipole?

4 What is the work done by the external agent in slowly rotating a dipole of dipole moment of p in a uniform electric field E from stable equilibrium orientation to unstable equilibrium orientation?

LEVEL 02 JEE Main Level

Single Choice Correct Questions

1 Four charges are placed each at a distance a from origin as shown in figure. The dipole moment of configuration is

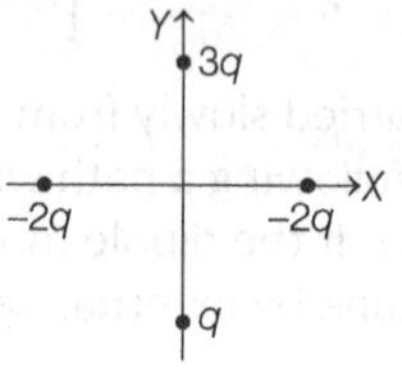

(a) $2qa\hat{\mathbf{j}}$
(b) $3qa\hat{\mathbf{j}}$
(c) $2aq(\hat{\mathbf{i}} + \hat{\mathbf{j}})$
(d) None of the above

3.5 Dipole External Non-Uniform Electric Field

1 Electric dipole of moment $\mathbf{p} = p\hat{\mathbf{i}}$ is kept at a point (x, y) in an electric field $\mathbf{E} = 4xy^2\ \hat{\mathbf{i}} + 4x^2y\ \hat{\mathbf{j}}$. Find the magnitude of force acting on the dipole.

2 Find out force experienced by short dipole of dipole moment p due to a point charge Q in following different arrangements as shown in figures.

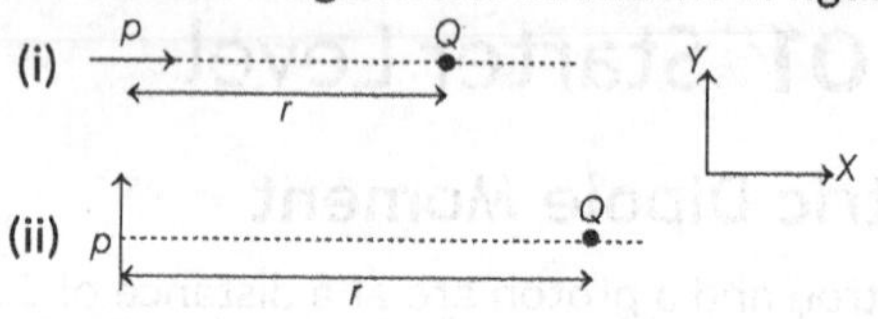

3 Find out force experienced by short dipole p_2 in the following arrangements as shown in figures.

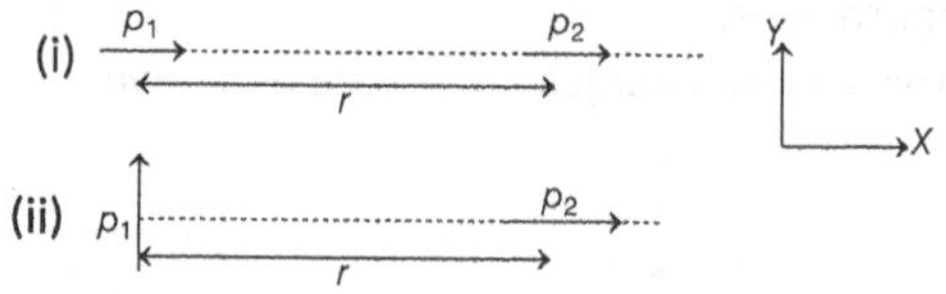

4 Find electrostatic potential energy of the following arrangements as shown in figures. Neglect self-energy of dipole.

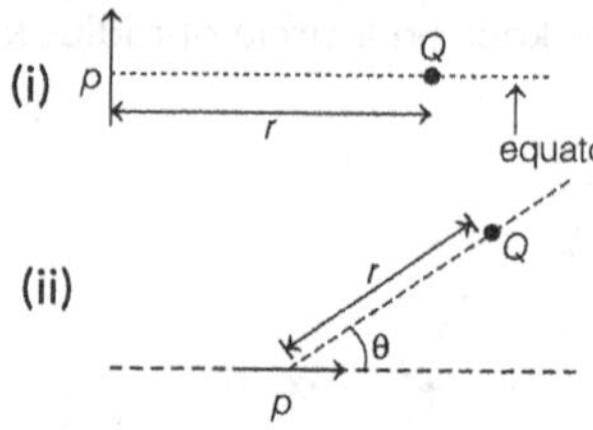

2 The dipole moment of a system of charge $+q$ distributed uniformly on an arc of radius R subtending an angle $\pi/2$, at its centre, where another charge $-q$ is placed is

(a) $\dfrac{2\sqrt{2}qR}{\pi}$ (b) $\dfrac{\sqrt{2}qR}{\pi}$
(c) $\dfrac{qR}{\pi}$ (d) $\dfrac{2qR}{\pi}$

3 A thin non-conducting ring of radius R has a linear charge density $\lambda = \lambda_0 \cos\theta$, where λ_0 is a constant. Find net electric dipole moment for this charge distribution.

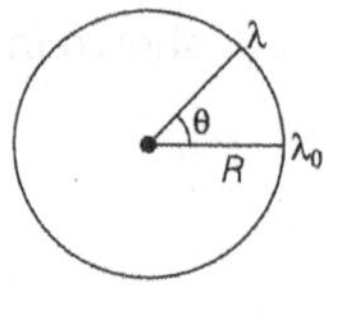

(a) $\pi R^2 \lambda_0$ (b) $2\pi R^2 \lambda_0$ (c) $3\pi R^2 \lambda_0$ (d) $4\pi R^2 \lambda_0$

4 A and B are two points on the axis and the perpendicular bisector, respectively of an electric dipole. A and B are far away from the dipole and at equal distance from it. The field at A and B are $\mathbf{E}_A$ and $\mathbf{E}_B$, then

(a) $\mathbf{E}_A = \mathbf{E}_B$ (b) $\mathbf{E}_A = 2\mathbf{E}_B$

(c) $\mathbf{E}_A = -2\mathbf{E}_B$

(d) $|\mathbf{E}_B| = \frac{1}{2}|\mathbf{E}_A|$ and $\mathbf{E}_B$ is perpendicular to $\mathbf{E}_A$

5 The electric field at point A due to dipole p is perpendicular to dipole. The angle θ is

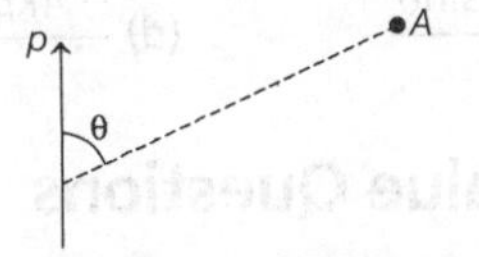

(a) 0° (b) 90° (c) $\tan^{-1}(2)$ (d) $\tan^{-1}\sqrt{2}$

6 Two equal charges Q are at opposite corners of a square of side a and an electric dipole of moment p is at a third corner, pointing towards one of the charges. If $p = 2\sqrt{2}\,aQ$, the field strength at the fourth corner of the square is

(a) $\frac{\sqrt{17/2}}{4\pi\varepsilon_0 a^2}Q$ (b) $\frac{\sqrt{17/4}}{4\pi\varepsilon_0 a^2}Q$

(c) $\frac{Q}{4\sqrt{2}\pi\varepsilon_0 a^2}$ (d) $\frac{\sqrt{3}Q}{4\pi\varepsilon_0 a^2}$

7 Two short dipoles $p(\hat{\mathbf{i}} + \hat{\mathbf{k}})$ and $4p\hat{\mathbf{k}}$ are located at (0, 0, 0) and (1m, 0, 2m), respectively. The resultant electric field due to the two dipoles at the point (1 m, 0, 0) is

(a) $\frac{p}{\pi\varepsilon_0}$ (b) $\frac{p}{2\pi\varepsilon_0}$ (c) $\frac{p}{\sqrt{2}\pi\varepsilon_0}$ (d) $\frac{\sqrt{2}p}{\pi\varepsilon_0}$

8 Figure shows an electric dipole of dipole moment $p = q(2a)$. For $r >> a$, what is potential of dipole at a point P with coordinates (x, y, z)?

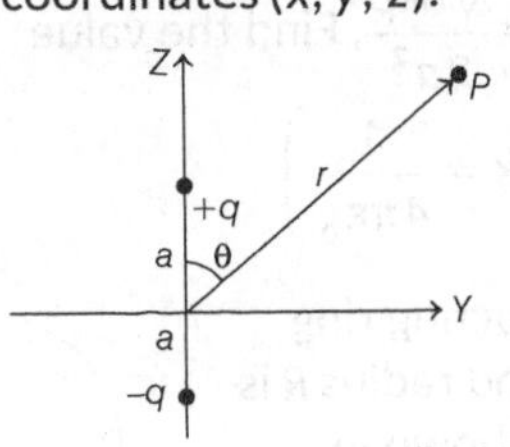

(a) $\frac{p}{4\pi\varepsilon_0}\frac{x}{(x^2 + y^2 + z^2)^{3/2}}$

(b) $\frac{p}{4\pi\varepsilon_0}\frac{y}{(x^2 + y^2 + z^2)^{3/2}}$

(c) $\frac{p}{4\pi\varepsilon_0}\frac{z}{(x^2 + y^2 + z^2)^{3/2}}$

(d) $\frac{p}{4\pi\varepsilon_0}\frac{xyz}{(x^2 + y^2 + z^2)^{3/2}}$

9 Find out work done by electric field in shifting a point charge $\frac{4\sqrt{2}}{27}$ μC from point P to S, which are shown in the figure. At point O, a dipole of dipole moment 2×10^{-6} C-m is kept

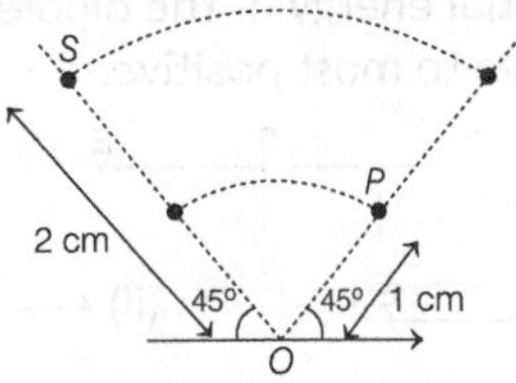

(a) (100/3) J (b) (200/3) J (c) 100 J (d) 200 J

10 Which of the following represents the equipotential lines of a dipole (two equal and opposite charges placed at small separation)?

(a) 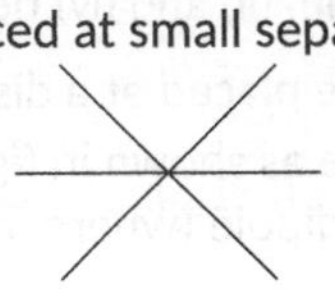 (b) 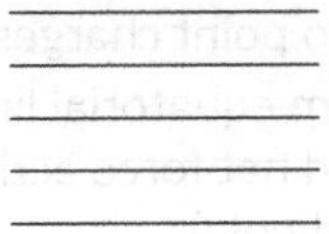

(c) 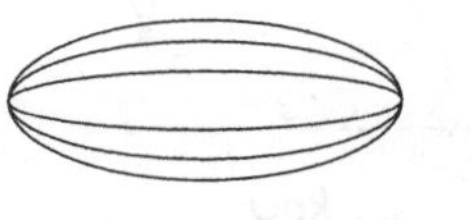 (d) 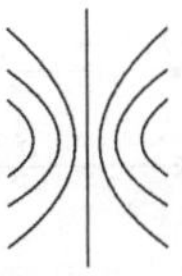

11 An electric dipole consists of two opposite charges each of magnitude 1.0 μC separated by a distance of 2.0 cm. The dipole is placed in an external field of 1.0×10^5 N/C. The maximum torque on the dipole is

(a) 0.2×10^{-3} N-m (b) 1.0×10^{-3} N-m

(c) 2.0×10^{-3} N-m (d) 4.0×10^{-3} N-m

12 An electric dipole with dipole moment $\mathbf{p} = (3\hat{\mathbf{i}} + 4\hat{\mathbf{j}}) \times 10^{-30}$ C-m is placed in an electric field $\mathbf{E} = 4000\,\hat{\mathbf{i}}$ (N/C). An external agent turns the dipole slowly until its electric dipole moment becomes $(-4\hat{\mathbf{i}} + 3\hat{\mathbf{j}}) \times 10^{-30}$ C-m. The work done by the external agent is equal to

(a) 4×10^{-28} J (b) -4×10^{-28} J

(c) 2.8×10^{-26} J (d) -2.8×10^{-26} J

13 An electric dipole is placed (not at infinity) in an electric field generated by a point charge,

(a) the net force on the dipole must be zero

(b) the net force on the dipole may be zero

(c) torque on the dipole due to the field must be zero

(d) torque on the dipole due to the field may be zero

14 An electric dipole of length 2 cm is placed with its axis making an angle of 30° to a uniform electric field of 10^5 N/C. If it experiences a torque of $10\sqrt{3}$ N-m, then potential energy of dipole is

(a) – 10 J (b) – 20 J (c) – 30 J (d) – 40 J

15 An electric dipole of dipole moment **p** is oriented parallel to a uniform electric field **E**, as shown. It is rotated to one of the four orientations shown below. Rank the final orientations according to the change in the potential energy of the dipole-field system, most negative to most positive.

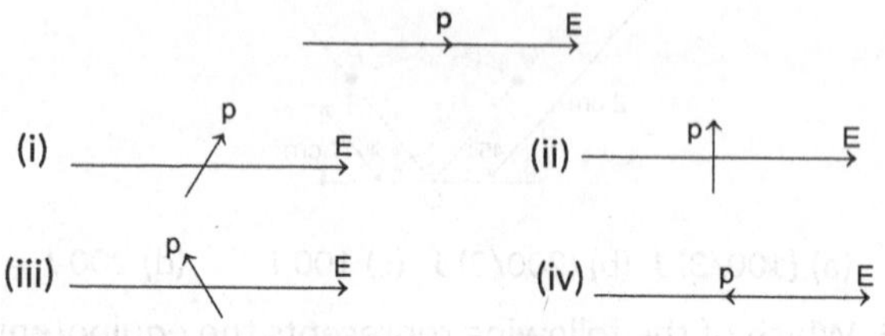

(a) (i), (ii), (iv), (iii) (b) (iv), (iii), (ii), (i)
(c) (i), (ii), (iii), (iv) (d) (iii), (ii) and (iv) tie, then (i)

16 Two point charges each Q are placed at a distance d from equatorial line of dipole as shown in figure. Find net force acting on the dipole (where, $d >>$ size of dipole).

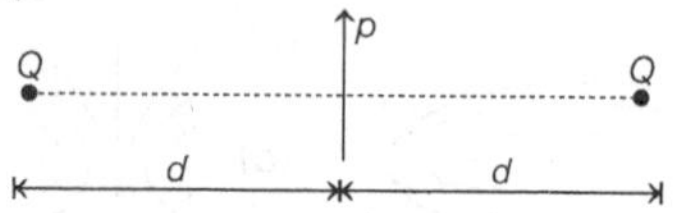

(a) 0 (b) $\frac{kpQ}{d^3}$
(c) $\frac{2kpQ}{d^3}$ (d) $\frac{4kpQ}{d^3}$

17 A small electric dipole **p** is placed on the X-axis at the point (1,0). The dipole vector forms an angle of 30° with the X-axis. Consider a non-uniform electric field to have been applied in the region given by the vector $\mathbf{E} = x^2\hat{\mathbf{i}} + y^2\hat{\mathbf{j}}$. What is the force acting on the dipole?

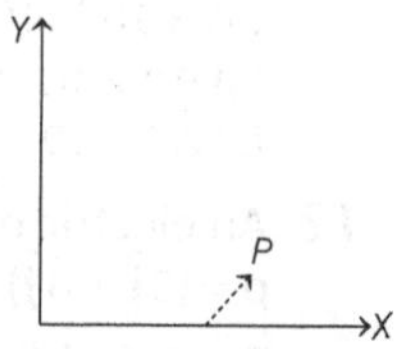

(a) $2\mathbf{p}\cos 30° (\hat{\mathbf{i}} + 2\hat{\mathbf{j}})$ (b) $2\mathbf{p}\cos 30° (\hat{\mathbf{i}})$
(c) $2\mathbf{p}\cos 30° (2\hat{\mathbf{j}})$ (d) None of these

18 A tiny electric dipole (H_2O molecule) of dipole moment **p** is placed at a distance r from an infinitely long wire, with its **p** normal to the wire in the same plane. If the linear charge density of the wire is λ, the electrostatic force acting on the dipole is equal to

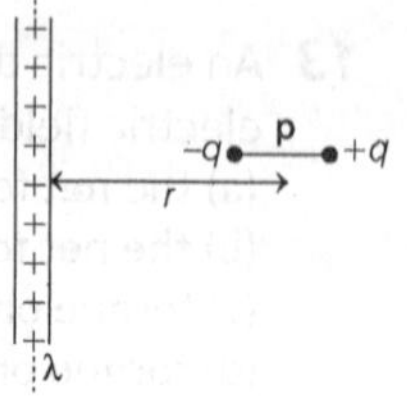

(a) $\frac{\lambda p}{4\pi\varepsilon_0 r}$ (b) $\frac{\lambda p}{\pi\varepsilon_0 r}$
(c) $\frac{2\lambda p}{\pi\varepsilon_0 r}$ (d) $\frac{\lambda p}{2\pi\varepsilon_0 r^2}$

19 Two short electric dipoles are placed as shown in figure. The energy of electric interaction between these dipoles will be

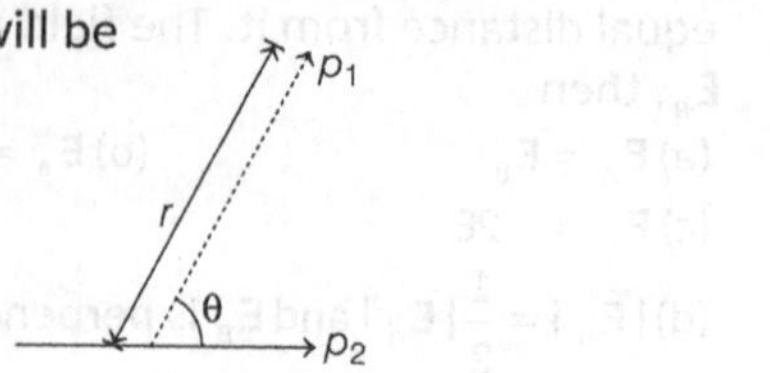

(a) $\frac{2kp_1p_2\cos\theta}{r^3}$ (b) $\frac{-2kp_1p_2\cos\theta}{r^3}$
(c) $\frac{-2kp_1p_2\sin\theta}{r^3}$ (d) $\frac{-4kp_1p_2\cos\theta}{r^3}$

Numerical Value Questions

1 An electric dipole is placed along X-axis at the origin as shown in the figure. Electric field at the point P is parallel to the Y-axis. If X-coordinate of P is $\sqrt{2}$ m, what is its Y-coordinate in metres?

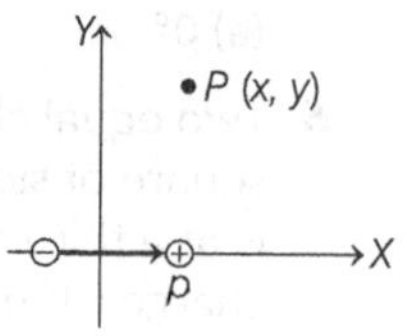

2 $ABCDEF$ is a regular hexagon of side a. At each vertex A, B and C, a point charge $+q$ is fixed and D, E, F, a point charge $-q$ is fixed. Intensity of electric field at a point lying on the line joining FC at a distance x away from the centre of hexagon ($x >> a$) is found to be $\frac{\sqrt{\alpha}aq}{2\pi\varepsilon_0 x^3}$, where α is an integer.

Find the value of α.

3 Three small dipoles of dipole moment p, each are placed at the three vertices of an equilateral triangle of side a as shown in figure. If total potential at the centroid G is given by $V = \frac{\sqrt{nkp}}{2a^2}$, Find the value of n. $\left(\text{Take, } k = \frac{1}{4\pi\varepsilon_0}\right)$

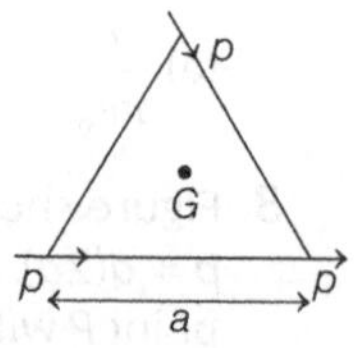

4 A non-conducting ring of mass m and radius R is charged as shown in figure. The charged density, i.e. charged per unit length is λ. It is then placed on a rough non-conducting horizontal surface plane. At time $t = 0$, a uniform electric field $\mathbf{E} = E_0\hat{\mathbf{i}}$ is switched on and the ring starts rolling without sliding. The friction force acting on the ring, when it starts moving is $n\lambda RE_0\hat{\mathbf{i}}$. Find the value of n.

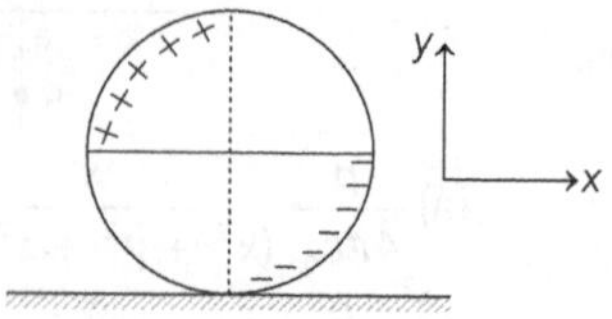

LEVEL 03 JEE Advanced Level

Single Choice Correct Questions

1 Three point charges $+2q$, $+q$ and $-q$ are located, respectively at $(0, a, a)$, $(0, -a, a)$ and $(0, 0, -a)$ as shown in figure. The dipole moment of this distribution is

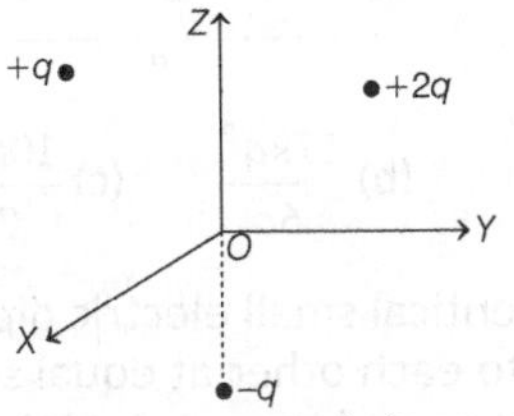

(a) $2qa$ in the YOZ plane at $\tan^{-1}\left(\frac{1}{4}\right)$ with Z-axis

(b) $\sqrt{17}qa$ in the YOZ plane at $\tan^{-1}\left(\frac{1}{4}\right)$ with Z-axis

(c) $\sqrt{5}\ qa$ in the XOY plane at $\tan^{-1}(4)$ with Y-axis

(d) $4qa$ in the XOY plane at $\tan^{-1}(4)$ with Y-axis

2 Two short dipoles of dipole moment p are placed at two corners of a square as shown in figure. What is the ratio of magnitudes of electric field intensity at two points O and A i.e. $E_{\text{at } O} : E_{\text{at } A}$?

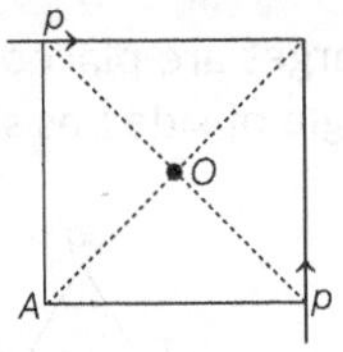

(a) 2 (b) $2\sqrt{2}$ (c) 4 (d) $\sqrt{2}$

3 A dipole of dipole moment p is placed at large distance a from a uniformly charged wire of mass m, length a and charge per unit length λ as shown in figure. The wire is free to rotate in the vertical plane about a horizontal axis passing through its lower end. Initial angular acceleration of the wire is

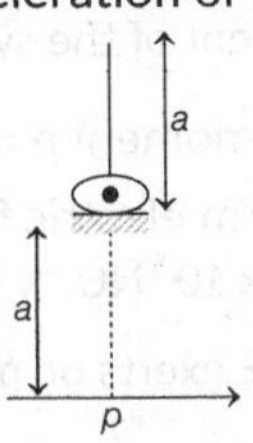

(a) $\frac{3p\lambda}{32\pi\varepsilon_0 ma^3}$ (b) $\frac{3p\lambda}{4\pi\varepsilon_0 ma^3}$

(c) $\frac{3p\lambda}{2\pi\varepsilon_0 ma^3}$ (d) $\frac{3p\lambda}{\pi\varepsilon_0 ma^3}$

4 A large sheet carries uniform surface charge density σ. A rod of length $2l$ has a linear charge density $+\lambda$ on one half and $-\lambda$ on the second half. The rod is hinged at mid-point O and makes an angle θ with the normal to the sheet. The torque experienced by the rod is

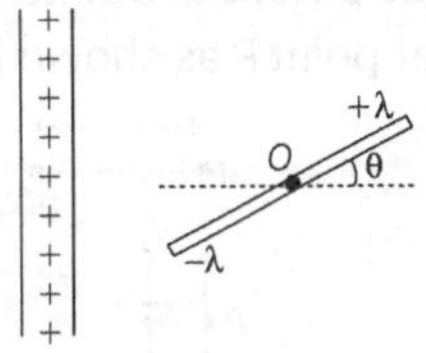

(a) 0 (b) $\frac{\sigma\lambda l^2}{2\varepsilon_0}\sin\theta$

(c) $\frac{\sigma\lambda l^2}{\varepsilon_0}\sin\theta$ (d) $\frac{\sigma\lambda l}{2\varepsilon_0}$

5 A particle A of mass $2m$ and carrying charge q is connected by a light rigid rod of length L to another particle B of mass m and carrying charge $-q$ as shown in figure. The system is placed in an electric field **E**. After the system settles into equilibrium, one particle is given a small push in the transverse direction, so that the rod makes a small angle θ_0 with the electric field. Find the maximum tension in the rod.

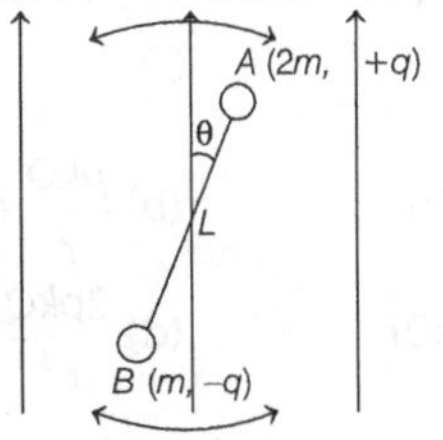

(a) $qE(1+\theta_0^2)$ (b) $qE\left(1+\frac{\theta_0^2}{2}\right)$

(c) $qE\left(1+\frac{\theta_0^2}{3}\right)$ (d) $qE\left(1-\frac{\theta_0^2}{2}\right)$

6 An electric dipole is kept on the axis of a uniformly charged ring at a distance $\frac{R}{\sqrt{2}}$ from the centre of the ring. The direction of the dipole moment is along the axis. If the dipole moment is p, charge of the ring is Q and radius of the ring is R, then the force on the dipole is

(a) $\frac{4kpQ}{3\sqrt{3}R^2}$ (b) $\frac{4kpQ}{3\sqrt{3}R^3}$ (c) $\frac{2kpQ}{3\sqrt{3}R^3}$ (d) zero

7 The equation of equipotential surfaces in XY-plane for a dipole kept at the origin and oriented along X-axis is

(a) $\dfrac{x}{(x^2+y^2)^{3/2}}=c$ (b) $\dfrac{y}{(y^2+x^2)^{3/2}}=c$

(c) $\dfrac{y^2}{(x^2+y^2)^{3/2}}=c$ (d) $\dfrac{x^2}{(x^2+y^2)^{3/2}}=c$

8 The electrostatic potential due to the charge configuration at point P as shown in figure for $b << a$.

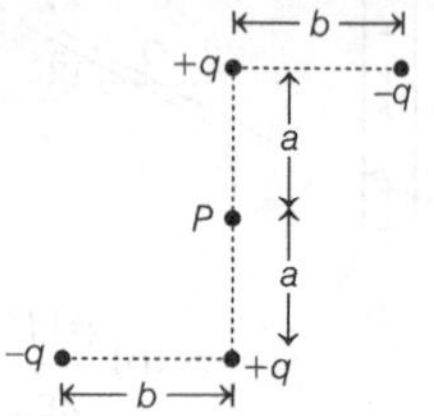

(a) $\dfrac{2q}{4\pi\varepsilon_0 a}$ (b) $\dfrac{2qb^2}{4\pi\varepsilon_0 a^3}$

(c) $\dfrac{qb^2}{4\pi\varepsilon_0 a^3}$ (d) zero

9 A point negative charge $-Q$ is placed at a distance r from a dipole with dipole moment p as shown in figure. The x-component of force acting on the charge $-Q$ is

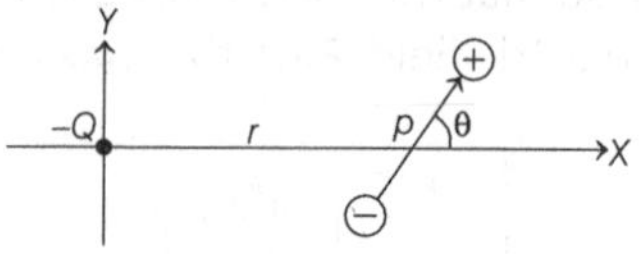

(a) $-\dfrac{pkQ}{r}\cos\theta\,\hat{i}$ (b) $\dfrac{pkQ}{r}\cos\theta\,\hat{i}$

(c) $-\dfrac{2pkQ}{r^3}\cos\theta\,\hat{i}$ (d) $\dfrac{2pkQ}{r^3}\cos\theta\,\hat{i}$

10 A wheel having mass m has charges $+q$ and $-q$ on diametrically opposite points. It remains in equilibrium on a rough inclined plane in the presence of uniform vertical electric field E. The value of E is

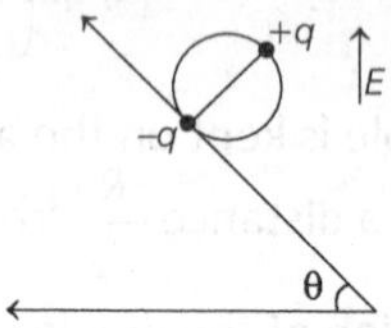

(a) $\dfrac{mg}{q}$ (b) $\dfrac{mg}{2q}$

(c) $\dfrac{mg\tan\theta}{2q}$ (d) None of these

11 The electrostatic potential energy due to interaction of a system of three point charges each $+q$ and a short dipole of dipole moment $p = qa/8$ as shown in figure is (neglect self-energy of dipole)

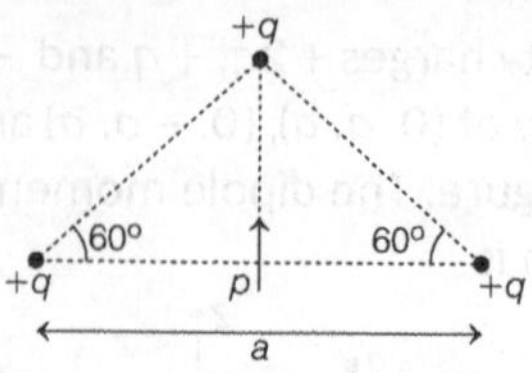

(a) $\dfrac{19kq^2}{6a}$ (b) $\dfrac{17kq^2}{6a}$ (c) $\dfrac{10kq^2}{3a}$ (d) $\dfrac{8kq^2}{3a}$

12 Three identical small electric dipoles are arranged parallel to each other at equal separation a as shown in the figure and there total interaction energy is U. Now, one of the end dipole is gradually reversed, how much work is done by the electric forces?

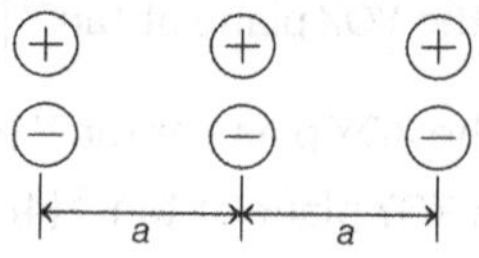

(a) $\dfrac{17U}{8}$ (b) $\dfrac{16\,U}{17}$ (c) $\dfrac{16\,U}{8}$ (d) $\dfrac{18\,U}{17}$

Multiple Choice(s) Correct Questions

1 Three points charges are placed at the corners of an equilateral triangle of side L as shown in the figure. Then,

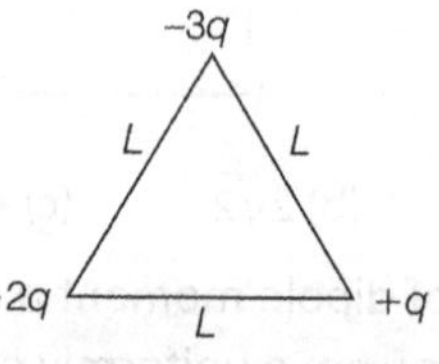

(a) the potential at the centroid of the triangle is zero

(b) the electric field at the centroid of the triangle is zero

(c) the dipole moment of the system is $\sqrt{7}\,qL$

(d) the dipole moment of the system is $\sqrt{3}\,qL$

2 An electric dipole moment $\mathbf{p} = (2.0\,\hat{i} + 3.0\hat{j})\,\mu$C-m is placed in an uniform electric field $\mathbf{E} = (3.0\,\hat{i} + 2.0\,\hat{k}) \times 10^5\,\text{NC}^{-1}$,

(a) the torque that $\mathbf{E}$ exerts on $\mathbf{p}$ is $(0.6\hat{i} - 0.4\hat{j} - 0.9\hat{k})$ N-m

(b) the potential energy of the dipole is -0.6 J

(c) the potential energy of the dipole is 0.6 J

(d) If the dipole is rotated in the electric field, the maximum potential energy of the dipole is 1.3 J

3 Imagine that, a dipole is at the centre of a spherical non-conducting surface. If the magnitude of electric field at a certain point on the surface of sphere is 10 N/C, then which of the following cannot be the magnitude of electric field anywhere on the surface of sphere?

(a) 4 N/C (b) 8 N/C
(c) 16 N/C (d) 32 N/C

4 For the situation shown in the figure below (assume $r >> $ length of dipole), mark out the correct statement(s).

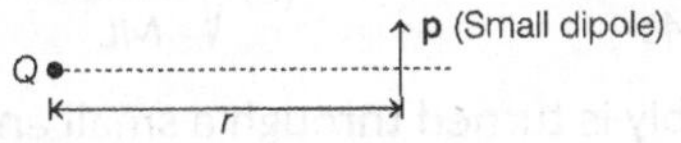

(a) Force acting on the dipole is zero.
(b) Force acting on the dipole is approximately $\frac{pQ}{4\pi\varepsilon_0 r^3}$ and is acting upward.
(c) Torque acting on the dipole is $\frac{pQ}{4\pi\varepsilon_0 r^2}$ in clockwise direction.
(d) Torque acting on the dipole is $\frac{pQ}{4\pi\varepsilon_0 r^2}$ in anti-clockwise direction.

5 Given a square frame of diagonal length $2r$ made of insulating wires. There is a short dipole, having dipole moment p, fixed in the plane of the figure lying at the centre of the square, making an angle θ as shown in figure. Four identical particles having charges of magnitude q each and alternatively positive and negative signs are placed at the four corners of the square. Select the correct alternative(s).

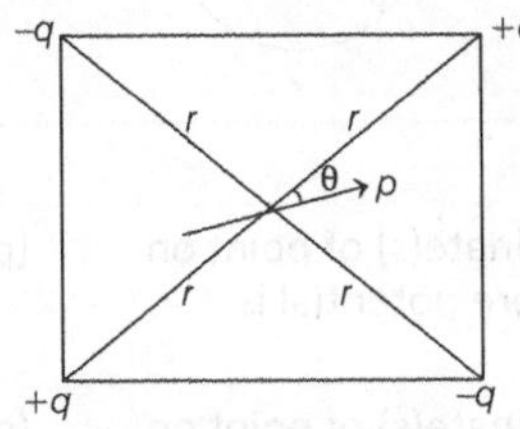

(a) Electrostatic force on the system of four charges due to dipole is $\frac{6kpq}{r^3}$
(b) Electrostatic force on the system of four charges due to dipole is $\frac{6kpq}{r^3}\cos\theta$
(c) Net torque on the system of four charges about the centre of the square due to dipole is zero
(d) Net torque on the system of four charges about the centre of the square due to dipole is $\frac{3kpq}{r^2}$

6 For a system of two dipoles $\mathbf{p}_1$ and $\mathbf{p}_2$ as shown in the figure, both dipoles are at origin and perpendicular to each other along X and Y-axes respectively, then

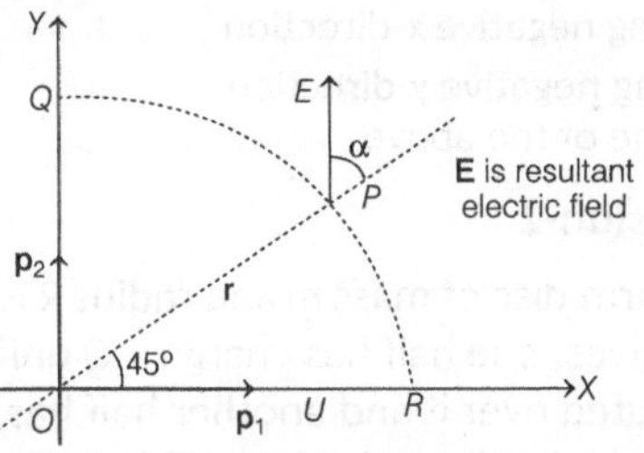

(a) work done in taking electron from P to R on QPR is zero
(b) $\tan\alpha = \frac{(p_1 + p_2)}{2(p_1 - p_2)}$
(c) $\tan\alpha = \frac{(p_1 - p_2)}{2(p_1 + p_2)}$
(d) $-\int_{\infty}^{r} \mathbf{E}\cdot d\mathbf{r} = \frac{p_1 + p_2}{4\sqrt{2}\pi\varepsilon_0 r^2}$

Comprehension Based Questions

Comprehension-1

A thin ring of radius R metres is placed in XY-plane, such that its centre lies on origin. The half ring in region $x < 0$ carries uniform linear charge density $+\lambda$ C/m and the remaining half-ring in region $x > 0$ carries uniform linear charge density $-\lambda$ C/m.

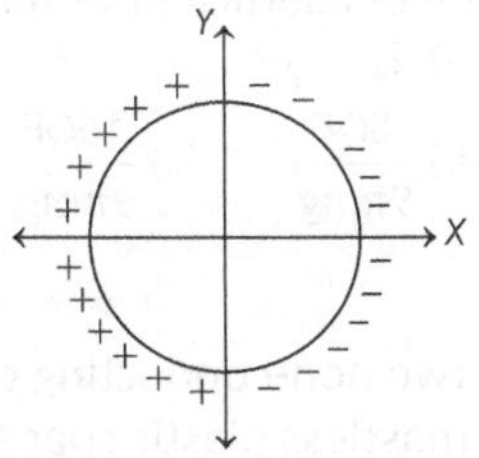

1 The dipole moment of the ring in C-m is

(a) $-(2\pi R^2\lambda)\,\hat{\mathbf{i}}$ (b) $(2\pi R^2\lambda)\,\hat{\mathbf{i}}$
(c) $-(4R^2\lambda)\,\hat{\mathbf{i}}$ (d) $(4R^2\lambda)\,\hat{\mathbf{i}}$

2 The electric potential (in V) at point P, whose coordinates are $\left(0\text{ m}, +\frac{R}{2}\text{m}\right)$ is

(a) $\frac{1}{4\pi\varepsilon_0}\frac{\lambda}{2}$ (b) 0
(c) $\frac{1}{4\pi\varepsilon_0}\frac{\lambda}{4}$ (d) Cannot be determined

3 The direction of electric field at point P, whose coordinates are $\left(0\text{ m}, +\frac{R}{2}\text{ m}\right)$ is

(a) along positive x-direction
(b) along negative x-direction
(c) along negative y-direction
(d) None of the above

Comprehension-2

A uniform disc of mass m and radius R is made up of two halves, one half has charge $+Q$ uniformly distributed over it and another half has charge $-Q$ uniformly distributed over it. This system is kept on rough surface in a uniform horizontal field E in a way, so that line of separation become parallel to field, system is released from rest, at $t = 0$ as shown in figure.

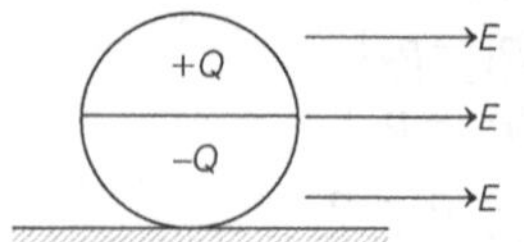

4 Torque of the electrostatic force about centre of mass at $t = 0$ is

(a) $\frac{8QER}{3\pi}$ (b) $\frac{QER}{9}$ (c) $\frac{16QER}{9\pi}$ (d) QER

5 Acceleration of centre of the disc at $t = 0$, if friction is sufficient to prevent slipping is

(a) $\frac{4QE}{9\pi m}$ (b) $\frac{8QE}{9\pi m}$ (c) $\frac{16QE}{9\pi m}$ (d) $\frac{2QE}{3m}$

6 Minimum value of coefficient of friction to prevent slipping at $t = 0$, is

(a) $\frac{4QE}{9\pi mg}$ (b) $\frac{8QE}{9\pi mg}$ (c) $\frac{16QE}{9\pi mg}$ (d) $\frac{2QE}{3mg}$

Comprehension-3

Figure shows two non-conducting charged rods separated by massless plastic spacers of length L. Entire assembly lies in an electric field $E = E_0\hat{\mathbf{k}}$. Assembly can rotate about Y-axis and initially is in YZ-plane. Mass of each rod is M. Now, assembly is turned through an angle $\theta = 60°$ in anti-clockwise sense as seen from left and released.

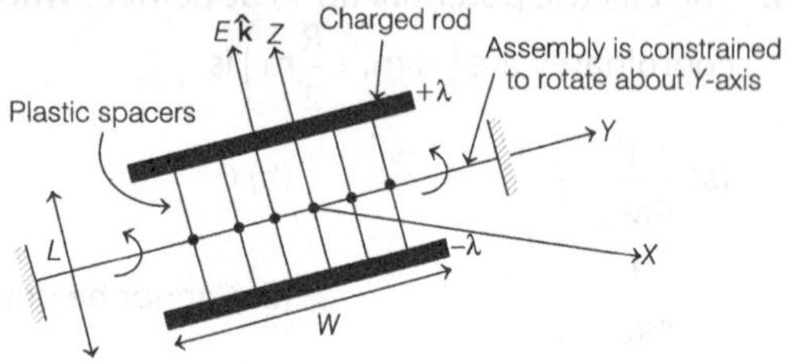

7 What is total mechanical energy of the assembly, taking reference position for potential energy, when it lies in XY-plane?

(a) $+\lambda WLE$ (b) $\frac{\lambda WLE}{2}$ (c) $-\frac{\lambda WLE}{2}$ (d) $-\lambda WLE$

8 What is angular velocity of assembly, when it comes back to YZ-plane?

(a) $\sqrt{\frac{4\lambda WE}{ML}}$ (b) $\sqrt{\frac{\lambda WE}{2ML}}$

(c) $\sqrt{\frac{\sqrt{3}\lambda WE}{2ML}}$ (d) $\sqrt{\frac{2\lambda WE}{ML}}$

9 If assembly is turned through a small angle from its stable equilibrium position, what is minimum time in which it will attain its equilibrium position?

(a) $2\pi\sqrt{\frac{ML}{\lambda WE}}$ (b) $\pi\sqrt{\frac{ML}{2\lambda WE}}$

(c) $3\pi\sqrt{\frac{ML}{\lambda WE}}$ (d) $\pi\sqrt{\frac{ML}{8\lambda WE}}$

Match the Columns Questions

1 Column I gives a situation in which two dipoles of dipole moment $p\hat{\mathbf{i}}$ and $\sqrt{3}\,p\hat{\mathbf{j}}$ are placed at origin. A circle of radius R with centre at origin is drawn as shown in figure. Column II gives co-ordinates of certain positions on the circle. Match the statements in Column I with the statements in Column II.

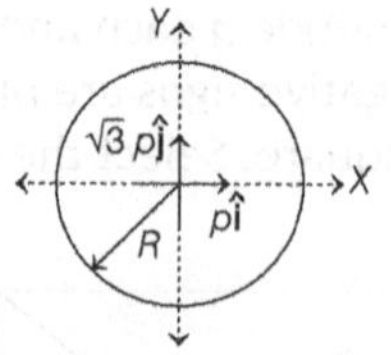

Column I	Column II
(a) The coordinate(s) of point on circle, where potential is maximum.	(p) $\left(\frac{R}{2}, \frac{\sqrt{3}R}{2}\right)$
(b) The coordinate(s) of point on circle, where potential is zero.	(q) $\left(-\frac{R}{2}, -\frac{\sqrt{3}R}{2}\right)$
(c) The coordinate(s) of point on circle, where magnitude of electric field intensity is $\frac{1}{4\pi\varepsilon_0}\frac{4p}{R^3}$.	(r) $\left(-\frac{\sqrt{3}R}{2}, \frac{R}{2}\right)$
(d) The coordinate(s) of point on circle, where magnitude of electric field intensity is $\frac{1}{4\pi\varepsilon_0}\frac{2p}{R^3}$.	(s) $\left(\frac{\sqrt{3}R}{2}, -\frac{R}{2}\right)$

2

Column I (Dipole **p** in an electric field **E**)	Column II (F = force, τ = torque and U = energy of dipole)
(a) 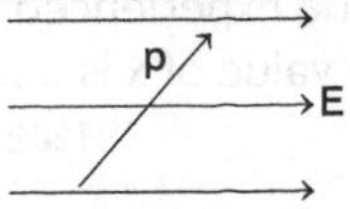 Uniform electric field	(p) $F \neq 0, \tau = 0$
(b) 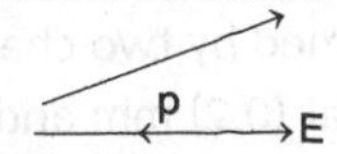 Non-uniform electric field	(q) $U = 0, F = 0$
(c) 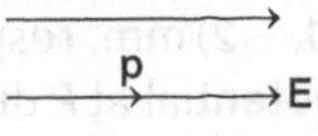 Uniform electric field	(r) $\tau \neq 0, F = 0$ and U = negative
(d) 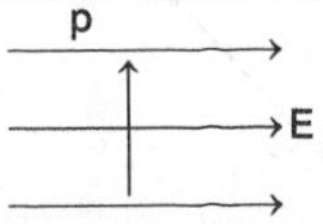 Uniform electric field	(s) U is minimum and $\tau = 0$

3 Two identical charged rings lie in XY-plane both having linear charge density λ varying as per $\lambda = \lambda_0 \cos\theta$ (λ_0 = constant), where θ is measured from $+X$-axis. Radius for both the rings is R.

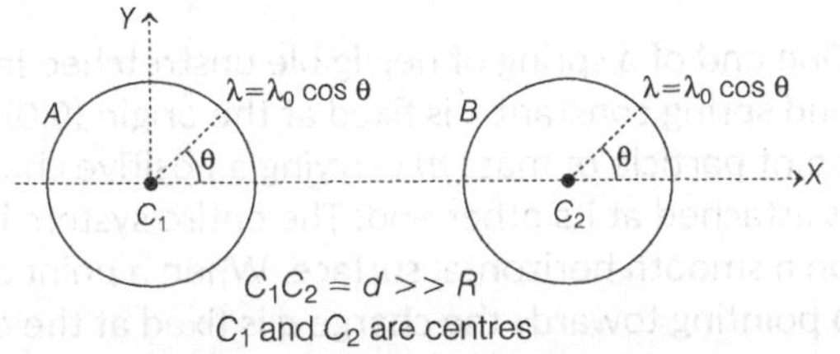

Column I	Column II
(a) Dipole moment of each ring is $x\lambda_0\pi R^2$, then x is	(p) 0
(b) Magnitude of work done by electric field in rotating ring B by 90° about X-axis is $\dfrac{xk\lambda_0^2\pi^2R^4}{2d^3}$, then x is	(q) 1
(c) Magnitude of work done by electric field in rotating ring B by 90° about Z-axis is $\dfrac{xk\lambda_0^2\pi^2R^4}{2d^3}$, then x is	(r) 6
(d) Electric force between the two rings is $\dfrac{xk\lambda_0^2\pi^2R^4}{d^4}$, then x is	(s) 4

Numerical Value Questions

1 Electric field intensity at point P due to below configuration for $r >> a$ is given by $n \times \dfrac{kpa}{r^m}$, where $p = qa$. Find the value of $m + n$.

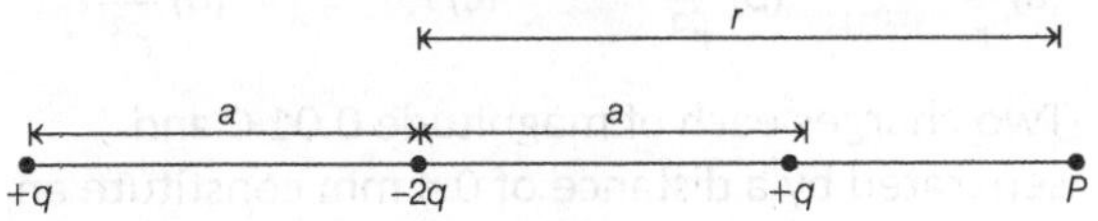

2 An infinite non-conducting plane with uniform charge density σ is kept parallel to YZ-plane and at a distance d from a dipole **p**, which itself is located at the origin. An equipotential surface for this system is spherical, centred at origin, having radius $R(< d)$. Given that, $R = \left(\dfrac{p}{n\pi\sigma}\right)^{1/3}$, find the integer n.

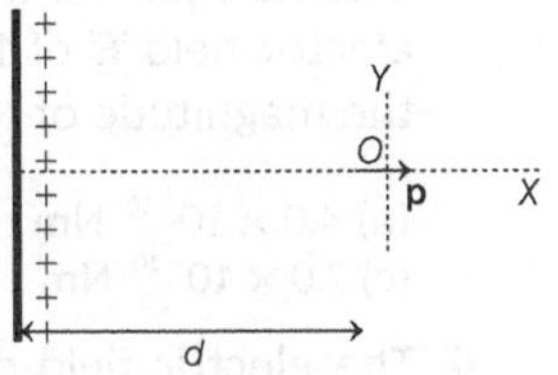

3 A uniform ring of mass m and radius R is placed freely in a gravity free region. Half of the ring positively charged with uniform linear charge density $+\lambda$ and other half is negatively charged with uniform charged density $-\lambda$. A uniform electric field E is switched on along the normal to the plane of the ring. If the angular speed of the ring, when it turns through an angle 90° is $n\left(\sqrt{\dfrac{\lambda E}{m}}\right)$, find the value of n.

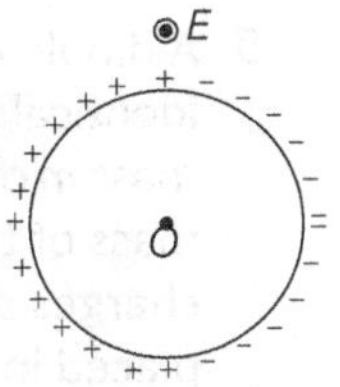

4 A non-conducting solid sphere of mass m and radius R having uniform charge densities $+\rho$ and $-\rho$ as shown in figure. It is then placed on a rough non-conducting horizontal plane. At $t = 0$, a uniform electric field $\mathbf{E} = E_0\hat{\mathbf{i}}$ N/C is switched on and the solid sphere starts rolling without sliding. The magnitude of frictional force at $t = 0$ is $\dfrac{2\rho\pi R^3 E_0}{K}$, find the value of K.

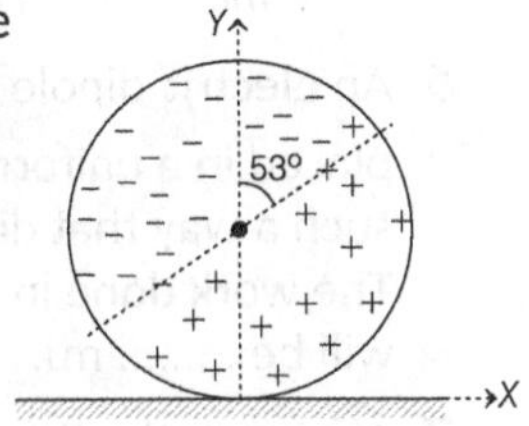

Previous Year's Questions

JEE Main

1 Two charges of $-4\,\mu C$ and $+4\,\mu C$ are placed at the points $A(1, 0, 4)$ m and $B(2, -1, 5)$ m located in an electric field $\mathbf{E} = 0.20\hat{\mathbf{i}}$ V/cm. The magnitude of the torque acting on the dipole is $8\sqrt{\alpha} \times 10^{-5}$ N-m, where $\alpha =$ .... **[2024, 27 Jan Shift-II]**

2 The electrostatic potential due to an electric dipole at a distance r varies as **[2024, 30 Jan Shift-I]**

(a) $\frac{1}{r}$ (b) $\frac{1}{r^3}$ (c) r (d) $\frac{1}{r^2}$

3 Two charges each of magnitude 0.01 C and separated by a distance of 0.4 mm constitute an electric dipole. If the dipole is placed in an uniform electric field 'E' of 10 dyne/C making 30° angle with E, the magnitude of torque acting on dipole is **[2023, 13 April Shift-I]**

(a) 4.0×10^{-10} Nm (b) 1.0×10^{-8} Nm
(c) 2.0×10^{-10} Nm (d) 1.5×10^{-9} Nm

4 The electric field due to a short electric dipole at a large distance (r) from centre of dipole on the equatorial plane varies with distance as **[2023, 15 April Shift-I]**

(a) $\frac{1}{r^2}$ (b) $\frac{1}{r^3}$ (c) $\frac{1}{r}$ (d) r

5 A dipole comprises of two charged particles of identical magnitude q and opposite in nature. The mass m of the positive charged particle is half of the mass of the negative charged particle. The two charges are separated by a distance l. If the dipole is placed in a uniform electric field E; in such a way that dipole axis makes a very small angle with the electric field, E. The angular frequency of the oscillations of the dipole when released is given by **[2023, 6 April Shift-II]**

(a) $\sqrt{\frac{8qE}{ml}}$ (b) $\sqrt{\frac{4qE}{3ml}}$ (c) $\sqrt{\frac{8qE}{3ml}}$ (d) $\sqrt{\frac{4qE}{ml}}$

6 An electric dipole of dipole moment is 6.0×10^{-6} Cm placed in a uniform electric field of 1.5×10^{3} NC^{-1} in such a way that dipole moment is along electric field. The work done in rotating dipole by 180° in this field will be .... mJ. **[2023, 8 April Shift-I]**

7 As shown the figure, a configuration of two equal point charges ($q_0 = +2\mu$C) is placed on an inclined plane. Mass of each point charge is 20 g. Assume that there is no friction between charge and plane. For the system of two point charges to be in equilibrium (at rest) the height $h = x \times 10^{-3}$ m.

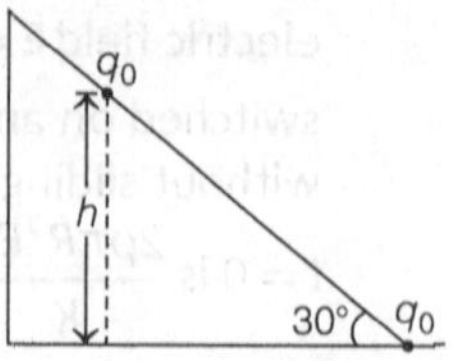

The value of x is .... **[2023, 11 April Shift-I]**

(Take, $\frac{1}{4\pi\varepsilon_0} = 9 \times 10^{9}$ Nm^{2}C^{-2}, g = 10 ms^{-2})

8 Two electric dipoles of dipole moments 1.2×10^{-30} C-m and 2.4×10^{-30} C-m are placed in two different uniform electric fields of strength 5×10^{4} NC^{-1} and 15×10^{4} NC^{-1}, respectively. The ratio of maximum torque experienced by the electric dipoles will be $1/x$ The value of x is .... **[2022, 28 July Shift-I]**

JEE Advanced

1. An electric dipole is formed by two charges $+q$ and $-q$ located in XY-plane at (0.2) mm and (0, – 2) mm, respectively, as shown in the figure. The electric potential at point P (100, 100) mm due to the dipole is V_0. The charges $+q$ and $-q$ are then moved to the points (– 1, 2) mm and (1, – 2) mm, respectively. What is the value of electric potential at P due to the new dipole? **(2023 Adv.)**

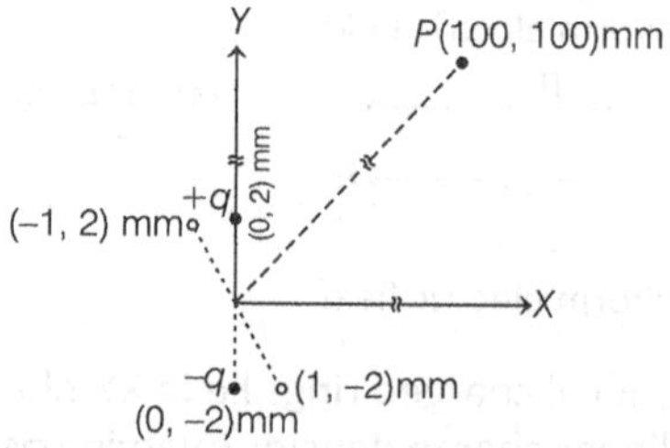

(a) $V_0/4$ (b) $V_0/2$
(c) $V_0/\sqrt{2}$ (d) $3V_0/4$

2. One end of a spring of negligible unstretched length and spring constant k is fixed at the origin (0,0). A point particle of mass m carrying a positive charge q is attached at its other end. The entire system is kept on a smooth horizontal surface. When a point dipole **p** pointing towards the charge q is fixed at the origin, the spring gets stretched to a length l and attains a new equilibrium position (see figure below). If the point mass is now displaced slightly by $\Delta l << l$ from its equilibrium position and released, it is found to oscillate at frequency $\frac{1}{\delta}\sqrt{\frac{k}{m}}$. The value of δ is ______. **(2020 Adv.)**

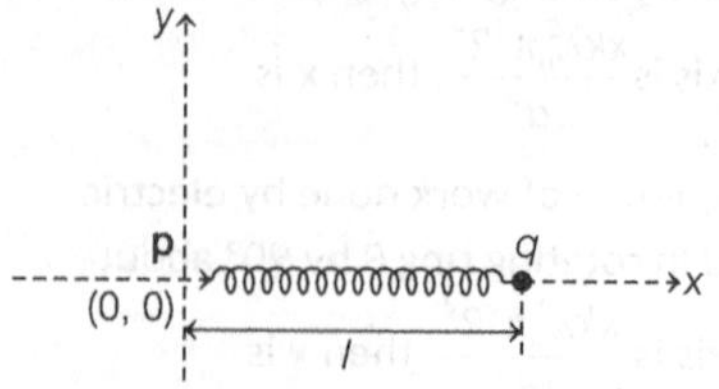

3 The electric field E is measured at a point P (0, 0, d) generated due to various charge distributions and the dependence of E on d is found to be different for different charge distributions. Column I contains different relations between E and d. Column II describes different electric charge distributions, along with their locations. Match the functions in Column I with the related charge distributions in Column II.

	Column I		Column II
A.	E is independent of d	p.	A point charge Q at the origin
B.	$E \propto \frac{1}{d}$	q.	A small dipole with point charges Q at $(0, 0, l)$ and $-Q$ at $(0, 0, -1)$. (Take, $2l << d$)
C.	$E \propto \frac{1}{d^2}$	r.	An infinite line charge coincident with the X-axis, with uniform linear charge density λ.
D.	$E \propto \frac{1}{d^3}$	s.	Two infinite wires carrying a uniform linear charge density parallel to the X- axis. The one along $(y = 0, z = l)$ has a charge density $+\lambda$ and the one along $(y = 0, z = -l)$ has a charge density $-\lambda$. (Take, $2l << d$).
		t.	Infinite plane charge coincident with the XY-plane with uniform surface charge density.

[JEE Advanced 2018]

(a) A $\rightarrow$ t; B $\rightarrow$ r,s; C $\rightarrow$ p; D $\rightarrow$ q

(b) A $\rightarrow$ t; B $\rightarrow$ r; C $\rightarrow$ p, s; D $\rightarrow$ q

(c) A $\rightarrow$ t; B $\rightarrow$ r; C $\rightarrow$ p, q; D $\rightarrow$ s

(d) A $\rightarrow$ s; B $\rightarrow$ q, r; C $\rightarrow$ p; D $\rightarrow$ t

Answer Key

Level 1 Starter Level

3.1 Electric Dipole Moment

1. 1.6×10^{-29} C-m, directed from electron to proton
2. (a) $qa(\hat{i} + \hat{j})$ (b) $4QR\hat{j}$ (c) $\frac{2qR}{\pi}\hat{j}$

3.2 Electric Field Due to Dipole

1. $\frac{kp}{\sqrt{2}y^3}(-\hat{i} - 2\hat{j})$ 2. $\frac{9\sqrt{7}}{8} \times 10^9$ V/m 3. $\frac{q\sqrt{d^2 + 4a^2}}{4\pi\varepsilon_0 d^3}$
4. $(-10, 0)$ and $(6, 0)$

3.3 Electric Potential Due to Dipole

1. -2000 V 2. $\frac{p}{\sqrt{2}\pi\varepsilon_0 a^2}$ 3. $\frac{\sqrt{2}\,qp}{4\pi\varepsilon_0 r^2}$

3.4 Dipole in External Uniform Electric Field

1. $F = 0, \tau = 8 \times 10^{-5}(\hat{j} + \hat{k})$ N-m 2. $T = 2\pi\sqrt{\frac{ml}{2qE}}$
3. (i) -0.4 J (ii) 1.35 J 4. $2pE$

3.5 Dipole External Non-Uniform Electric Field

1. $4py\sqrt{y^2 + 4x^2}$ 2. (i) $\frac{2kpQ}{r^3}(-\hat{i})$ (ii) $\frac{kpQ}{r^3}\hat{j}$
3. (i) $\frac{6kp_1p_2}{r^4}(-\hat{i})$ (ii) $\frac{3kp_1p_2}{r^4}(\hat{j})$ 4. (i) 0 (ii) $\frac{kpQ\cos\theta}{r^2}$

Level 2

1. (a)	2. (a)	3. (a)	4. (c)	5. (d)
6. (a)	7. (b)	8. (c)	9. (a)	10. (d)
11. (c)	12. (c)	13. (d)	14. (c)	15. (c)
16. (c)	17. (b)	18. (d)	19. (b)	

Numerical Value Questions

1. (2)	2. (7)	3. (27)	4. (1)

Level 3

1. (b)	2. (b)	3. (a)	4. (b)	5. (a)
6. (d)	7. (a)	8. (c)	9. (c)	10. (b)
11. (a)	12. (d)			

Multiple Choice(s) Correct Questions

1. (ac)	2. (abc)	3. (ad)	4. (bc)	5. (ac)
6. (cd)				

Comprehension Based Questions

1. (c)	2. (b)	3. (a)	4. (a)	5. (c)
6. (c)	7. (c)	8. (d)	9. (d)	

Match the Columns Questions

1. a $\rightarrow$ p; b $\rightarrow$ rs; c $\rightarrow$ pq; d $\rightarrow$ rs
2. a $\rightarrow$ r; b $\rightarrow$ p; c $\rightarrow$ s; d $\rightarrow$ q
3. a $\rightarrow$ q; b $\rightarrow$ p; c $\rightarrow$ s; d $\rightarrow$ r

Numerical Value Questions

1. 10 2. 2 3. 4 4. 7

Previous Year's Questions

JEE Main

1. (2)	2. (d)	3. (c)	4. (b)	5. (*)
6. (18)	7. (300)	8. (6)		

JEE Advanced

1. (b) 2. (3.14) 3. (b)

SOLUTIONS

Level 1

3.1 Electric Dipole Moment

1. $p = q(2a)$

$= 1.6 \times 10^{-19} \times 10^{-10}$

$= 1.6 \times 10^{-29}$ C-m

Direction is from electron to proton.

2. (a) Lets split $-2q$ into two point charges $-q$ each.

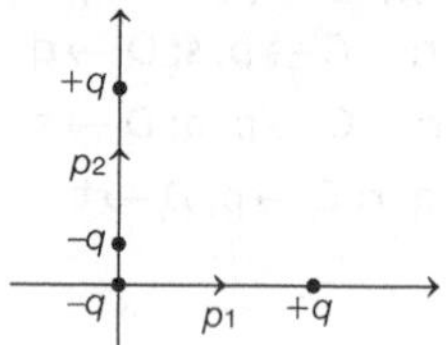

$p_1 = qa$ and $p_2 = qa$

$\mathbf{p} = p_1\hat{\mathbf{i}} + p_2\hat{\mathbf{j}}$

$= qa\hat{\mathbf{i}} + qa\hat{\mathbf{j}} = qa(\hat{\mathbf{i}} + \hat{\mathbf{j}})$

(b) Lets split $-3Q$ into three point charges $-Q$ each.

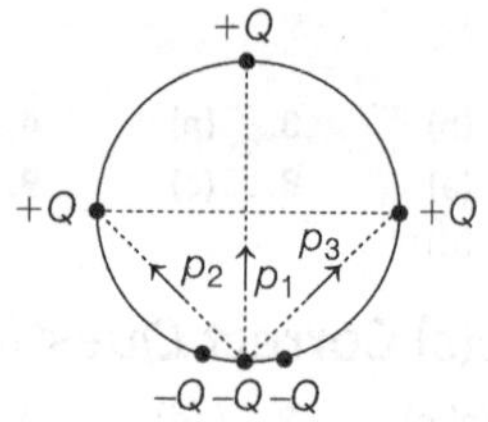

$p_1 = Q(2R),\ p_2 = Q(\sqrt{2}R)$

and $p_3 = Q(\sqrt{2}R)$

$\mathbf{p} = p_1\hat{\mathbf{j}} + (-p_2\cos 45°\,\hat{\mathbf{i}} + p_2\sin 45°\,\hat{\mathbf{j}})$

$+ (p_3\cos 45°\,\hat{\mathbf{i}} + p_3\sin 45°\,\hat{\mathbf{j}})$

$\Rightarrow \quad \mathbf{p} = \left(p_1 + \dfrac{p_2}{\sqrt{2}} + \dfrac{p_3}{\sqrt{2}}\right)\hat{\mathbf{j}} = 4QR\,\hat{\mathbf{j}}$

(c)

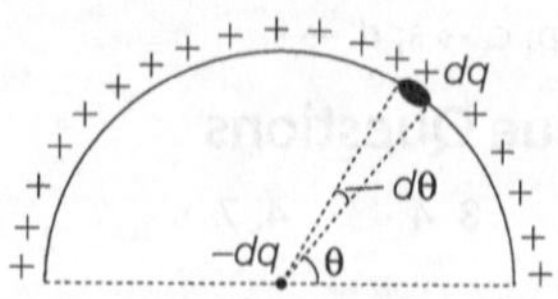

$dq = \dfrac{q}{\pi R}(R\,d\theta)$

$d\mathbf{p} = dp\cos\theta\,\hat{\mathbf{i}} + dp\sin\theta\,\hat{\mathbf{j}}$

$\Rightarrow \quad \int d\mathbf{p} = \int_0^{\pi}\left(\dfrac{q}{\pi R}R\,d\theta\right)R\cos\theta\,\hat{\mathbf{i}} + \int_0^{\pi}\left(\dfrac{q}{\pi R}R\,d\theta\right)R\sin\theta\,\hat{\mathbf{j}}$

$\Rightarrow \quad \mathbf{p} = \dfrac{2qR}{\pi}\,\hat{\mathbf{j}}$

3.2 Electric Field due to Dipole

1.

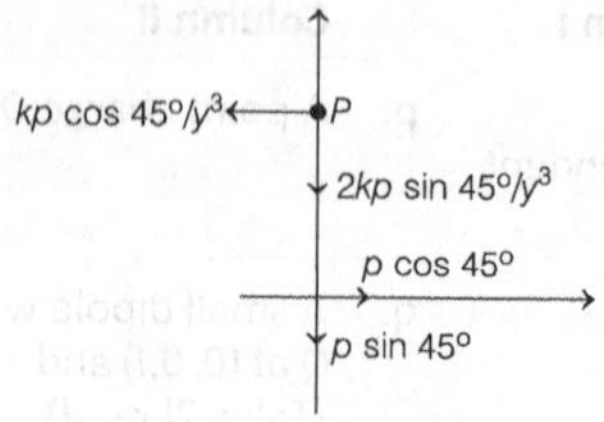

At point P,

$$\mathbf{E} = -\frac{kp\cos 45°}{y^3}\hat{\mathbf{i}} - \frac{2kp\sin 45°}{y^3}\hat{\mathbf{j}} = \frac{kp}{\sqrt{2}y^3}(-\hat{\mathbf{i}} - 2\hat{\mathbf{j}})$$

2.

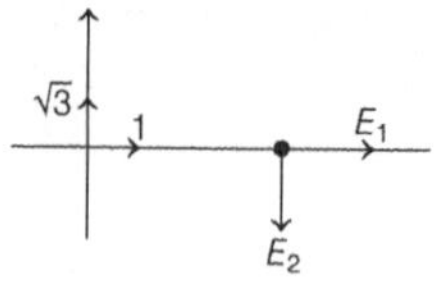

$$E_1 = \frac{2kp_x}{r^3} = \frac{2\times 9\times 10^9\times 1}{2^3} = \frac{9}{4}\times 10^9 \text{ N/C}$$

$$E_2 = \frac{kp_y}{r^3} = \frac{9\times 10^9\times\sqrt{3}}{2^3} = \frac{9\sqrt{3}}{8}\times 10^9 \text{ N/C}$$

$$\mathbf{E} = E_1\hat{\mathbf{i}} - E_2\hat{\mathbf{j}}$$

$$|\mathbf{E}| = \sqrt{E_1^2 + E_2^2} = \frac{9\sqrt{7}}{8}\times 10^9 \text{ V/m}$$

3. Leftmost and rightmost charges constitute an electric dipole of dipole moment $q(2a)$.

$\mathbf{E} = \mathbf{E}_1 + \mathbf{E}_2$

$\mathbf{E}_1$ = Electric field due to dipole $= \left[\dfrac{k(q(2a))}{d^3}\right](-\hat{\mathbf{i}})$

$\mathbf{E}_2$ = Electric field due to central $+q = \dfrac{kq}{d^2}\hat{\mathbf{j}}$

$\mathbf{E} = -\dfrac{2kqa}{d^3}\hat{\mathbf{i}} + \dfrac{kq}{d^2}\hat{\mathbf{j}}$

$|\mathbf{E}| = \dfrac{1}{4\pi\varepsilon_0}\dfrac{q}{d^3}(\sqrt{d^2 + 4a^2})$

4.

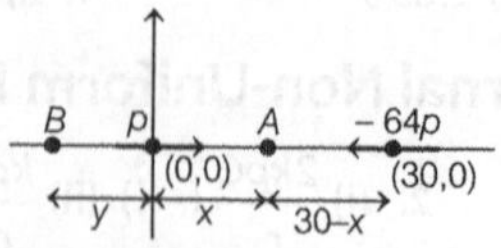

At point A, $E = \dfrac{kp}{x^3} + \dfrac{k(-64p)}{(30-x)^3} = 0$

$\Rightarrow \quad 4x = 30 - x \quad \Rightarrow \quad x = 6$ cm

At point B,

$E = \dfrac{kp}{y^3} + \dfrac{k(-64p)}{(30+y)^3} = 0$

$\Rightarrow \quad 4y = 30 + y$

$\Rightarrow \quad y = 10$ cm

3.3 Electric Potential due to Dipole

1. $\mathbf{p} = (2\hat{i} - 3\hat{j} + 4\hat{k})\,\mu\text{C-m}$

$$\mathbf{r} = \mathbf{r}_B - \mathbf{r}_A = 2\hat{i} + 2\hat{j} - \hat{k}$$

$$V = \frac{k(\mathbf{p}\cdot\mathbf{r})}{r^3} = \frac{9\times10^9(4-6-4)\times10^{-6}}{3^3} = -2000\text{ V}$$

2.

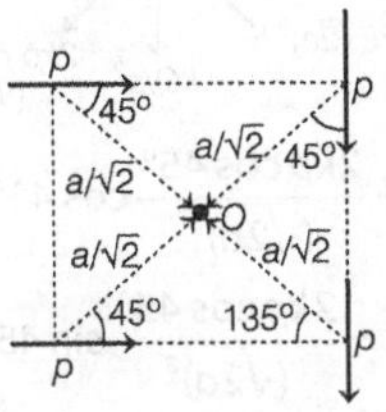

At point O,

$$V = V_1 + V_2 + V_3 + V_4$$

$$= \frac{kp\cos45^\circ}{(a/\sqrt{2})^2} + \frac{kp\cos45^\circ}{(a/\sqrt{2})^2} + \frac{kp\cos135^\circ}{(a/\sqrt{2})^2} + \frac{kp\cos45^\circ}{(a/\sqrt{2})^2}$$

$$= \frac{2\sqrt{2}kp}{a^2} = \frac{p}{\sqrt{2}\pi\varepsilon_0 a^2}$$

3. $W_{ext} = \Delta U + \Delta K$

$$= q\Delta V = q(V_B - V_A)$$

$$= q\left(\frac{kp\cos45^\circ}{r^2} - \frac{kp\cos135^\circ}{r^2}\right)$$

$$= \frac{\sqrt{2}kpq}{r^2} = \frac{1}{4\pi\varepsilon_0}\left(\frac{\sqrt{2}pq}{r^2}\right) = \frac{\sqrt{2}pq}{4\pi\varepsilon_0 r^2}$$

3.4 Dipole in External Uniform Electric Field

1. $\mathbf{p} = 4\times10^{-6}(\mathbf{r}_B - \mathbf{r}_A) = 4\times10^{-6}(\hat{i} - \hat{j} + \hat{k})$

$$\mathbf{F} = +q\mathbf{E} - q\mathbf{E} = 0$$

$$\tau = \mathbf{p}\times\mathbf{E} = 4\times10^{-6}(\hat{i} - \hat{j} + \hat{k})\times 20\hat{i}$$

$$= 8\times10^{-5}(\hat{j} + \hat{k})\text{ N-m}$$

2. $\tau = -pE\sin\theta$

$\Rightarrow$ $\tau = -(pE)\theta$ ($\because$ for small angles, $\sin\theta \simeq \theta$)

$\Rightarrow$ $I\alpha = -(pE)\theta$

$\Rightarrow$ $\alpha = -\left(\frac{pE}{I}\right)\theta$

which is equation of SHM.

$$T = 2\pi\sqrt{\frac{I}{pE}} = 2\pi\sqrt{\frac{m\left(\frac{l}{2}\right)^2 + m\left(\frac{l}{2}\right)^2}{qlE}} = 2\pi\sqrt{\frac{ml}{2qE}}$$

3. (i) $U = -\mathbf{p}\cdot\mathbf{E} = -(2\hat{i} + 3\hat{j} - \hat{k})\times10^{-6}\cdot(3\hat{i} + 2\hat{k})\times10^5$

$$= -(6-2)\times10^{-1} = -0.4\text{ J}$$

(ii) $U_{max} = pE$, when $\theta = 180^\circ$

$$= (\sqrt{14}\times10^{-6})(\sqrt{13}\times10^5)$$

$$= \frac{1}{10}(\sqrt{182}) = 1.35\text{ J}$$

4. $W_{ext} = \Delta U + \Delta K = (U_2 - U_1) + 0$

$$= pE - (-pE) = 2pE$$

3.5 Dipole in External Non-Uniform Electric Field

1. $F = p\left|\frac{\partial \mathbf{E}}{\partial x}\right| = p|\,4y^2\hat{i} + 8xy\hat{j}\,|$

$$= 4py\sqrt{y^2 + 4x^2}$$

2. (i) Force on Q due to dipole $= Q\mathbf{E}_{\text{due to dipole}} = Q\left(\frac{2kp}{r^3}\hat{i}\right)$

From Newton's third law,

Force on dipole due to $Q = \left(\frac{2kpQ}{r^3}\right)(-\hat{i})$

(ii) Force on Q due to dipole $= Q\mathbf{E}_{\text{due to dipole}} = Q\left(-\frac{kp}{r^3}\hat{j}\right)$

$$= \frac{kpQ}{r^3}(-\hat{j})$$

From Newton's third law,

Force on dipole due to $Q = \frac{kpQ}{r^3}\hat{j}$

3. (i) Force on p_2 dipole due to p_1 dipole $= p_2\frac{dE}{dr}$

$$= p_2\frac{d}{dr}\left(\frac{2kp_1}{r^3}\right)$$

$$= p_2\left(\frac{-6kp_1}{r^4}\right) = \frac{-6kp_1p_2}{r^4}$$

(ii) Force on p_2 dipole due to p_1 dipole

$$= p_2\frac{dE}{dr} = p_2\frac{d\left(-\frac{kp}{r^3}\right)}{dr} = \frac{3kp_1p_2}{r^4}$$

4. (i) $U = QV_{\text{due to dipole}} = Q(0) = 0$

(ii) $U = Q(V_{\text{due to }p\cos\theta\text{ dipole}} + V_{\text{due to }p\sin\theta\text{ dipole}})$

$$= Q\left[\frac{k(p\cos\theta)}{r^2} + 0\right] = \frac{kpQ\cos\theta}{r^2}$$

Level 2

Single Choice Correct Questions

1.

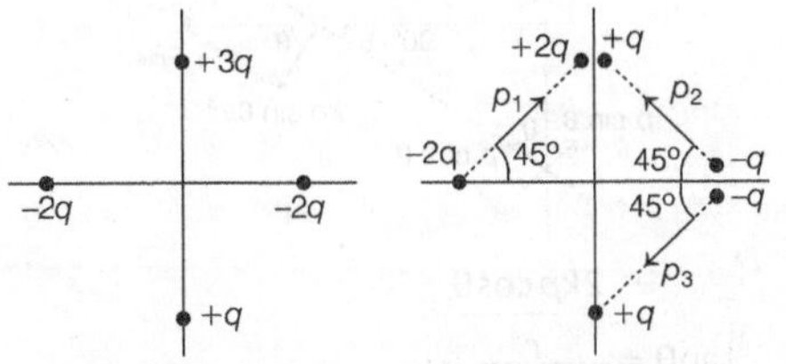

$$\mathbf{p}_1 = (2q)(\sqrt{2}a)(\cos45^\circ\hat{i} + \sin45^\circ\hat{j})$$

$$\mathbf{p}_2 = q(\sqrt{2}a)(-\cos45^\circ\hat{i} + \sin45^\circ\hat{j})$$

$$\mathbf{p}_3 = q(\sqrt{2}a)(-\cos45^\circ\hat{i} - \sin45^\circ\hat{j})$$

$$\mathbf{p} = \mathbf{p}_1 + \mathbf{p}_2 + \mathbf{p}_3 = (2qa)\hat{j}$$

2. $dq = \dfrac{q}{\pi R/2}(Rd\theta)$

$$\mathbf{dp} = dp\cos\theta\,\hat{\mathbf{i}} + dp\sin\theta\,\hat{\mathbf{j}}$$

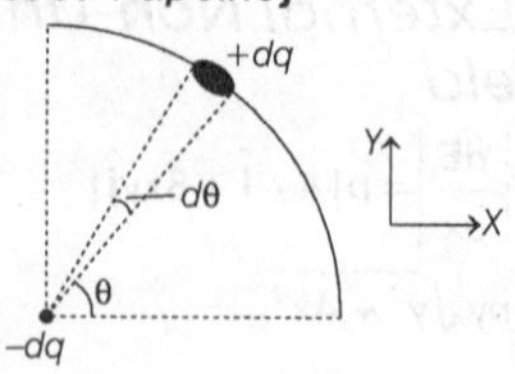

$$\Rightarrow \mathbf{dp} = \left(\frac{q}{\pi R/2}Rd\theta\right)R\cos\theta\,\hat{\mathbf{i}} + \left(\frac{q}{\pi R/2}Rd\theta\right)R\sin\theta\,\hat{\mathbf{j}}$$

$$\Rightarrow \int \mathbf{dp} = \frac{2qR}{\pi}\left(\int_0^{\pi/2}\cos\theta d\theta\,\hat{\mathbf{i}} + \int_0^{\pi/2}\sin\theta\, d\theta\,\hat{\mathbf{j}}\right)$$

$$\Rightarrow \quad \mathbf{p} = \frac{2qR}{\pi}(\hat{\mathbf{i}}+\hat{\mathbf{j}})$$

$$\Rightarrow \quad |\mathbf{p}| = \frac{2\sqrt{2}qR}{\pi}$$

3. $\mathbf{dp} = dq(2R\cos\theta)\hat{\mathbf{i}}$

$$\int \mathbf{dp} = \int(\lambda_0\cos\theta)Rd\theta(2R\cos\theta)\hat{\mathbf{i}}$$

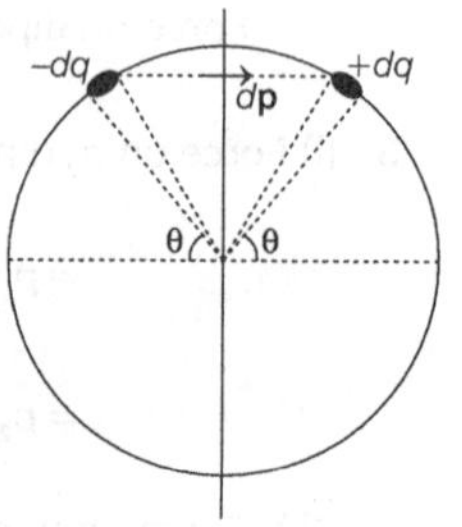

$$\Rightarrow \quad \mathbf{p} = 2\lambda_0 R^2\int_{-\pi/2}^{+\pi/2}\cos^2\theta d\theta$$

$$= \lambda_0 R^2\int_{\frac{-\pi}{2}}^{+\pi/2}(1+\cos 2\theta)\, d\theta$$

$$= \lambda_0 R^2\left[\theta + \frac{\sin 2\theta}{2}\right]_{-\pi/2}^{+\pi/2}$$

$$= \lambda_0 R^2\pi$$

4. $\mathbf{E}_A = \dfrac{2kp}{r^3}$ and $\mathbf{E}_B = \dfrac{-kp}{r^3}$

$$\Rightarrow \quad \mathbf{E}_A = -2\mathbf{E}_B$$

5.

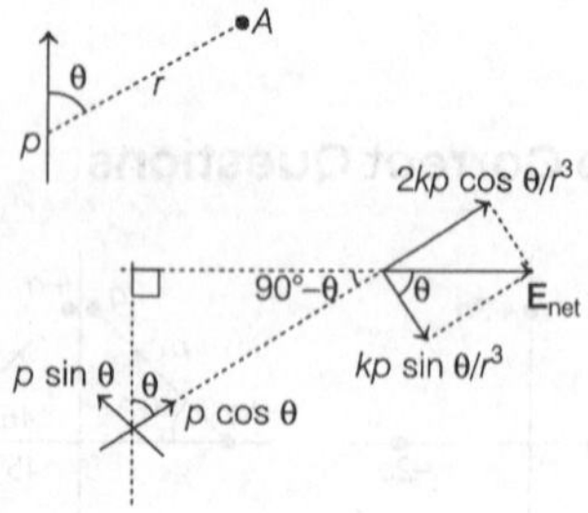

$$\tan\theta = \frac{\dfrac{2kp\cos\theta}{r^3}}{\dfrac{kp\sin\theta}{r^3}}$$

$$\Rightarrow \quad \tan\theta = 2\cot\theta$$

$$\Rightarrow \quad \tan^2\theta = 2$$

$$\Rightarrow \quad \theta = \tan^{-1}(\sqrt{2})$$

6.

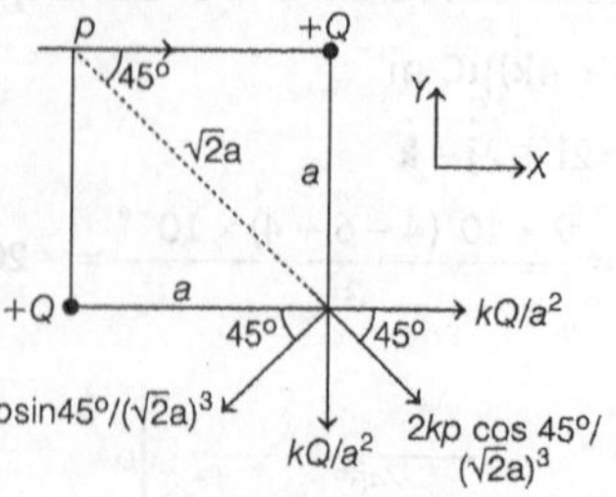

$$\mathbf{E} = \left(\frac{kQ}{a^2} + \frac{2kp\cos 45^\circ}{(\sqrt{2}a)^3}\cos 45^\circ - \frac{kp\sin 45^\circ}{(\sqrt{2}a)^3}\cos 45^\circ\right)\hat{\mathbf{i}} + \left(-\frac{kQ}{a^2} - \frac{2kp\cos 45^\circ}{(\sqrt{2}a)^3}\sin 45^\circ - \frac{kp\sin 45^\circ}{(\sqrt{2}a)^3}\sin 45^\circ\right)\hat{\mathbf{j}}$$

$$\Rightarrow \quad \mathbf{E} = \frac{3}{2}\frac{kQ}{a^2}\hat{\mathbf{i}} - \frac{5}{2}\frac{kQ}{a^2}\hat{\mathbf{j}}$$

$$\Rightarrow \quad |\mathbf{E}| = \frac{kQ}{2a^2}\sqrt{3^2+5^2} = \frac{\sqrt{17/2}}{4\pi\varepsilon_0 a^2}Q$$

7.

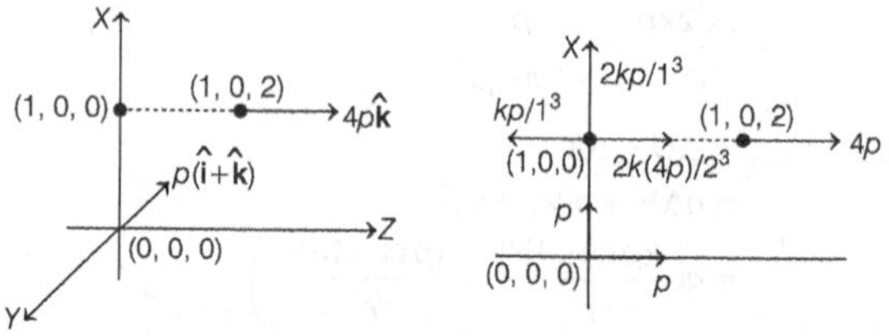

$$\mathbf{E} = \left(\frac{2k(4p)}{2^3} - \frac{kp}{1^3}\right)\hat{\mathbf{i}} + \left(\frac{2kp}{1^3}\right)\hat{\mathbf{j}}$$

$$\mathbf{E} = \frac{p}{2\pi\varepsilon_0}\hat{\mathbf{j}}$$

8. $V = \dfrac{k(\mathbf{p}\cdot\mathbf{r})}{r^3} = \dfrac{k(p\hat{\mathbf{k}})\cdot(x\hat{\mathbf{i}}+y\hat{\mathbf{j}}+z\hat{\mathbf{k}})}{(x^2+y^2+z^2)^{3/2}}$

$$= \frac{p}{4\pi\varepsilon_0}\frac{z}{(x^2+y^2+z^2)^{3/2}}$$

9. $W_{\text{electric}} = -\Delta U = U_1 - U_2 = q(V_1 - V_2)$

$$= q\left(\frac{kp\cos 45^\circ}{r_1^2} - \frac{kp\cos 135^\circ}{r_2^2}\right) = \frac{kpq}{\sqrt{2}}\left(\frac{1}{r_1^2}+\frac{1}{r_2^2}\right)$$

$$= \frac{9\times 10^9\times 2\times 10^{-6}}{\sqrt{2}}\times\left(\frac{4\sqrt{2}}{27}\right)\times 10^{-6}\left(\frac{1}{(10^{-2})^2}+\frac{1}{(2\times 10^{-2})^2}\right)$$

$$= \frac{100}{3}\text{ J}$$

10.

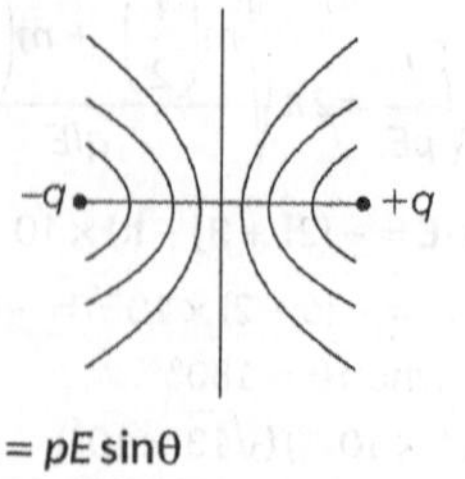

11. $\tau = pE\sin\theta$

$$\tau_{\max} = pE, \text{ when } \theta = 90^\circ$$

$$= (10^{-6}\times 2\times 10^{-2})(1.0\times 10^5)$$

$$= 2.0\times 10^{-3}\text{ N-m}$$

12. $$W_{ext} = \Delta U + \Delta K = (U_2 - U_1) + 0$$
$$= -\mathbf{p}_2 \cdot \mathbf{E} + \mathbf{p}_1 \cdot \mathbf{E} = (\mathbf{p}_1 - \mathbf{p}_2) \cdot \mathbf{E}$$
$$= [(7\hat{\mathbf{i}} + \hat{\mathbf{j}}) \times 10^{-30})] \cdot (4000\hat{\mathbf{i}}) = 2.8 \times 10^{-26} \text{ J}$$

13. Force on the dipole will be non-zero as electric field produced by a point charge is non-uniform.

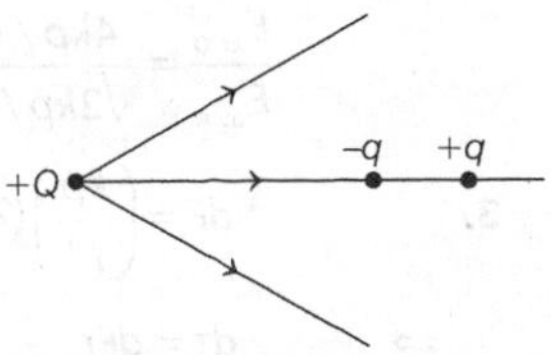

Torque will be zero, if the dipole is aligned along one of the electric field lines as shown in figure. For any other orientation of dipole, torque will be non-zero.

14. $\tau = pE\sin\theta$ and $U = -pE\cos\theta$

$$\Rightarrow \quad \frac{\tau}{U} = -\tan\theta$$

$$\Rightarrow \quad \frac{10\sqrt{3}}{U} = -\frac{1}{\sqrt{3}} \Rightarrow U = -30 \text{ J}$$

15.

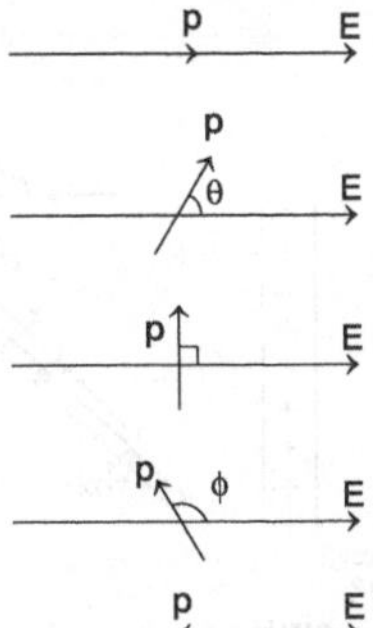

$U_0 = -pE$

$U_1 = -pE\cos\theta$

$U_2 = 0$

$U_3 = -pE\cos\phi$

$U_4 = pE$

$\Delta U_1 = U_1 - U_0 = pE(1 - \cos\theta)$, where $0° < \theta < 90°$.

$\Delta U_2 = U_2 - U_0 = pE$

$\Delta U_3 = U_3 - U_0 = pE(1 - \cos\phi)$, where $90° < \phi < 180°$.

$\Delta U_4 = U_4 - U_0 = 2pE$

$\Delta U_1 < \Delta U_2 < \Delta U_3 < \Delta U_4$

16. Force on each Q due to dipole $= QE$

$$= Q\left[\frac{kp}{d^3}(-\hat{\mathbf{j}})\right] = \frac{kpQ}{d^3}(-\hat{\mathbf{j}})$$

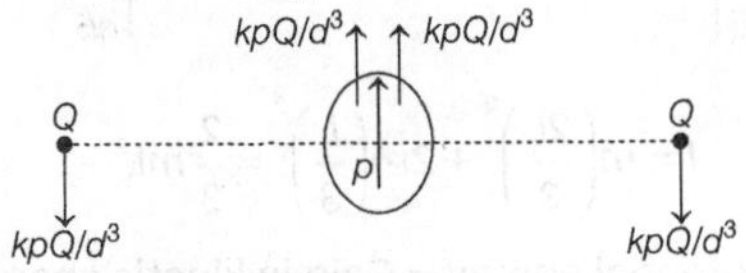

Net force on dipole $= \left(\frac{2kpQ}{d^3}\right)\hat{\mathbf{j}}$

17. $\mathbf{F} = (p\cos 30°)\frac{\partial E}{\partial x}\hat{\mathbf{i}} + (p\sin 30°)\frac{\partial E}{\partial y}\hat{\mathbf{j}}$

$\Rightarrow \mathbf{F} = (p\cos 30°)(2x\hat{\mathbf{i}}) + (p\sin 30°)(2y\hat{\mathbf{j}})$

$\Rightarrow \mathbf{F} = 2p(x\cos 30°\,\hat{\mathbf{i}} + y\sin 30°\,\hat{\mathbf{j}})$

At point (1, 0), $\mathbf{F} = (2p\cos 30°)(\hat{\mathbf{i}})$

18. $F = p\frac{dE}{dr} = p\frac{d\left(\frac{2k\lambda}{r}\right)}{dr} = \frac{-2kp\lambda}{r^2} = \frac{-\lambda p}{2\pi\varepsilon_0 r^2}$

19. $U = -\mathbf{p}_1 \cdot \mathbf{E}_{\text{due to } \mathbf{p}_2 \text{ dipole}}$

$$U = -(p_1\hat{\mathbf{r}}) \cdot \left(\frac{2kp_2\cos\theta}{r^3}\hat{\mathbf{r}} + \frac{kp\sin\theta}{r^3}\hat{\theta}\right)$$

$$U = -\frac{2kp_1p_2\cos\theta}{r^3}$$

Numerical Value Questions

1.

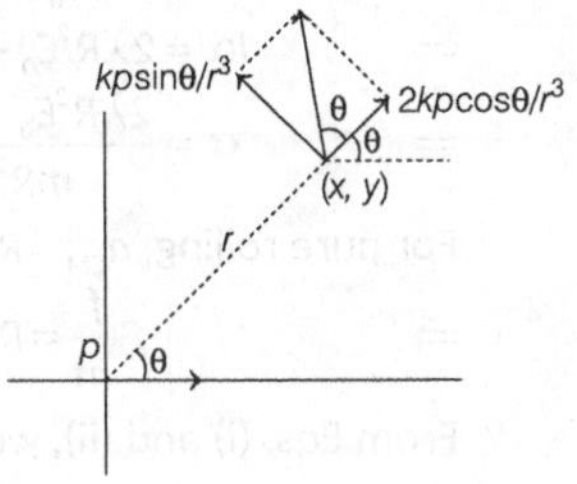

$$\tan\phi = \frac{\frac{kp\sin\theta}{r^3}}{\frac{2kp\cos\theta}{r^3}}$$

$$\tan\phi = \frac{\tan\theta}{2} \quad \text{... (i)}$$

$$\theta + \phi = 90° \quad \text{... (ii)}$$

∵ Net electric field is parallel to Y-axis.

$$\tan(90° - \theta) = \frac{\tan\theta}{2}$$

$$\Rightarrow \quad \tan\theta = \sqrt{2} \Rightarrow \frac{y}{x} = \sqrt{2}$$

$$\Rightarrow \quad y/\sqrt{2} = \sqrt{2} \Rightarrow y = 2$$

2.

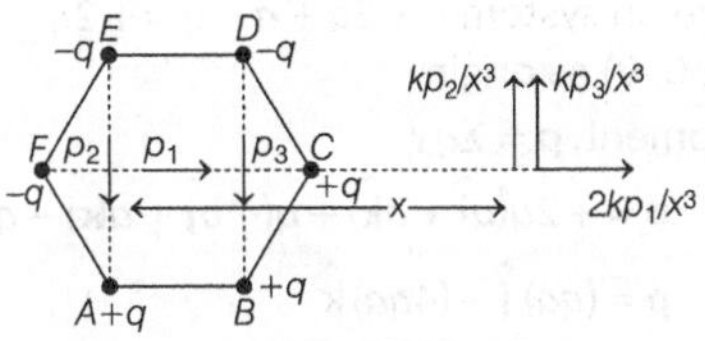

$$\mathbf{E} = \frac{2kp_1}{x^3}\hat{\mathbf{i}} + \left(\frac{Kp_2}{x^3} + \frac{Kp_3}{x^3}\right)\hat{\mathbf{j}}$$

$$\mathbf{E} = \frac{k}{x^3}(2p_1\hat{\mathbf{i}} + (p_2 + p_3)\hat{\mathbf{j}})$$

$$= \frac{k}{x^3}[2q(2a)\hat{\mathbf{i}} + (q\sqrt{3}a + q\sqrt{3}a)\hat{\mathbf{j}}]$$

$$= \frac{2kqa}{x^3}(2\hat{\mathbf{i}} + \sqrt{3}\hat{\mathbf{j}})$$

$$|\mathbf{E}| = \frac{\sqrt{7}aq}{2\pi\varepsilon_0 x^3}$$

3.

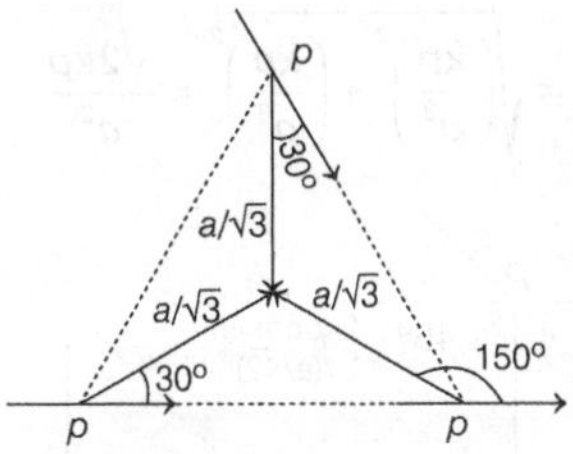

$$V = V_1 + V_2 + V_3$$

$$\Rightarrow \quad V = \frac{kp\cos 30°}{(a/\sqrt{3})^2} + \frac{kp\cos 150°}{(a/\sqrt{3})^2} + \frac{kp\cos 30°}{(a/\sqrt{3})^2}$$

$$\Rightarrow \quad V = \frac{3\sqrt{3}kp}{2a^2} = \frac{\sqrt{27}\,kp}{2a^2}$$

4. Net torque about the centre

$= (\int dF(2R\sin\theta)) - fR$

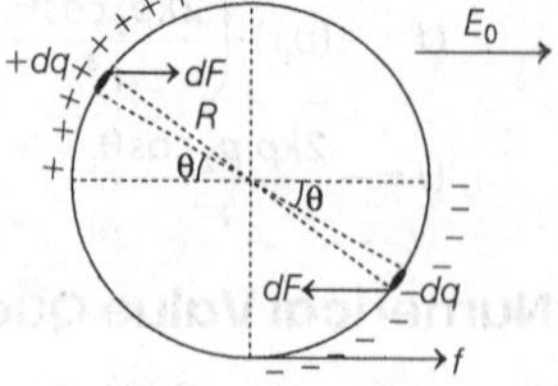

$\Rightarrow \tau = [\int dqE_0(2R\sin\theta)] - fR$

$\Rightarrow \tau = \int_0^{\pi/2} \lambda R d\theta\, E_0(2R\sin\theta) - fR$

$\Rightarrow \qquad \tau = 2\lambda E_0 R^2 - fR$

$\Rightarrow \qquad I\alpha = 2\lambda R^2 E_0 - fR$

$\Rightarrow \qquad \alpha = \dfrac{2\lambda R^2 E_0 - fR}{mR^2}$ ... (i)

For pure rolling, $a_{CM} = R\alpha$

$\Rightarrow \qquad \dfrac{f}{m} = R\alpha \Rightarrow \alpha = \dfrac{f}{mR}$ ... (ii)

From Eqs. (i) and (ii), we get

$$\frac{f}{mR} = \frac{2\lambda R^2 E_0 - fR}{mR^2} \Rightarrow f = \lambda R E_0$$

Level 3

Single Choice Correct Questions

1. Net charge on system $= +2q + q - q = +2q$

Taking (0, 0, 0) as origin,

Dipole moment, $\mathbf{p} = \Sigma q_i \mathbf{r}_i$

$\Rightarrow \qquad \mathbf{p} = +2q(a\hat{\mathbf{j}} + a\hat{\mathbf{k}}) + q(-a\hat{\mathbf{j}} + a\hat{\mathbf{k}}) - q(-a\hat{\mathbf{k}})$

$\Rightarrow \qquad \mathbf{p} = (qa)\,\hat{\mathbf{j}} + (4qa)\,\hat{\mathbf{k}}$

$|\mathbf{p}| = \sqrt{(qa)^2 + (4qa)^2} = \sqrt{17}qa$

$\mathbf{p} = \sqrt{17}qa$ in the YZ- plane at $\tan^{-1}\left(\dfrac{1}{4}\right)$ with the Z-axis.

2.

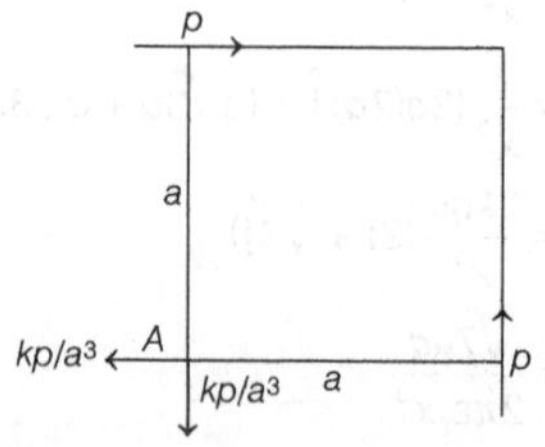

$$E_{\text{at }A} = \sqrt{\left(\frac{kp}{a^3}\right)^2 + \left(\frac{kp}{a^3}\right)^2} = \frac{\sqrt{2}kp}{a^3}$$

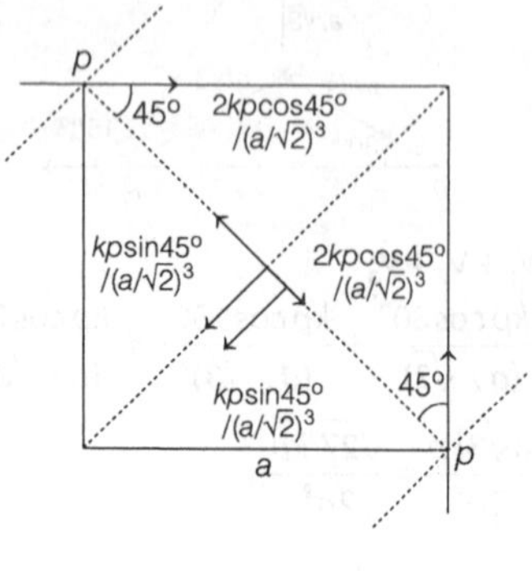

$$E_{\text{at O}} = \frac{kp\sin 45^\circ}{\left(\frac{a}{\sqrt{2}}\right)^3} + \frac{kp\sin 45^\circ}{\left(\frac{a}{\sqrt{2}}\right)^3} = \frac{4kp}{a^3}$$

$$\therefore \qquad \frac{E_{\text{at O}}}{E_{\text{at A}}} = \frac{4kp/a^3}{\sqrt{2}kp/a^3} = 2\sqrt{2}$$

3. $dF = \left(\dfrac{kp}{r^3}\right)(\lambda dr)$

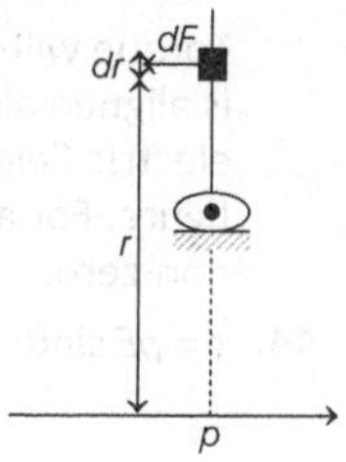

$\Rightarrow \qquad d\tau = dFr$

$\Rightarrow \qquad \int d\tau = \int_a^{2a}\left(\dfrac{kp}{r^3}\lambda dr\right)(r-a)$

$\Rightarrow \qquad \tau = kp\lambda\left[-\dfrac{1}{r} + \dfrac{a}{2r^2}\right]_a^{2a}$

$\Rightarrow \left(\dfrac{ma^2}{3}\right)\alpha = \dfrac{kp\lambda}{8a}$

$\Rightarrow \qquad \alpha = \dfrac{3kp\lambda}{8ma^3} = \dfrac{3p\lambda}{32\pi\varepsilon_0 ma^3}$

4. $dq = \lambda dx$

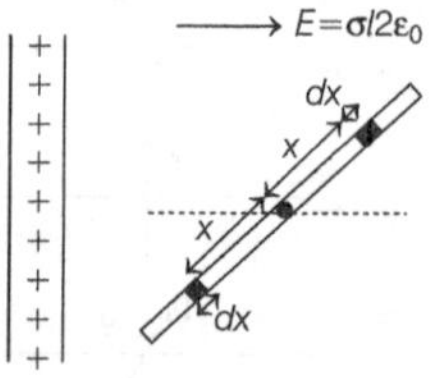

$\int dp = \int dq(2x)$

$\Rightarrow \qquad p = \int_0^l \lambda dx(2x)$

$\Rightarrow \qquad p = \lambda l^2$

Torque on the rod $= pE\sin\theta$

$= (\lambda l^2)\left(\dfrac{\sigma}{2\varepsilon_0}\right)\sin\theta = \dfrac{\sigma\lambda l^2}{2\varepsilon_0}\sin\theta$

5. Tension will be maximum in the equilibrium position. Lets first find angular speed ω in the equilibrium position.

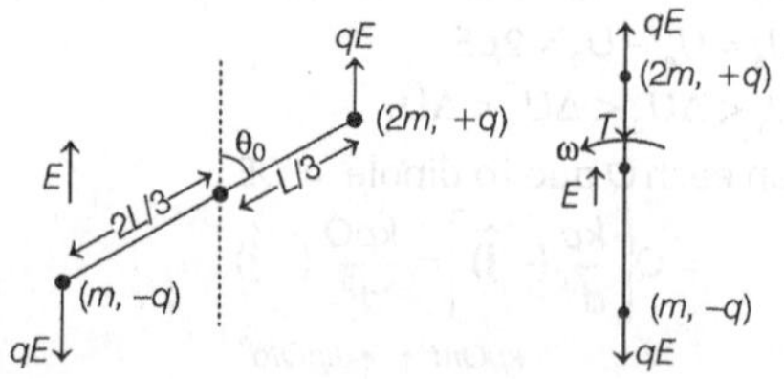

$$I = m\left(\frac{2L}{3}\right)^2 + 2m\left(\frac{L}{3}\right)^2 = \frac{2}{3}mL^2$$

Loss in potential energy = Gain in kinetic energy

$\Rightarrow -pE\cos\theta_0 - (-pE) = \dfrac{1}{2}\left(\dfrac{2}{3}mL^2\right)\omega^2 - 0$

$\Rightarrow \qquad \omega = \sqrt{\dfrac{3pE(1-\cos\theta_0)}{mL^2}}$

Circular motion equation for $2m$,

$T - qE = 2m\omega^2\left(\dfrac{L}{3}\right)$

$\Rightarrow \qquad T = qE + 2qE(1 - \cos\theta_0)$

$\Rightarrow \qquad T = qE + 2qE\left[2\sin^2\left(\dfrac{\theta_0}{2}\right)\right]$

$$\Rightarrow \quad T = qE + 2qE\left[2\left(\frac{\theta_0}{2}\right)^2\right] \quad \left[\because \sin\left(\frac{\theta_0}{2}\right) = \frac{\theta_0}{2} \text{ for small } \theta_0\right]$$

$$\Rightarrow \quad T = qE(1+\theta_0^2)$$

6. Electric field due to ring $= \dfrac{kQx}{(R^2+x^2)^{3/2}}$

$$F = \text{Force on dipole} = p\frac{dE}{dx}$$

At $x = \dfrac{R}{\sqrt{2}}, \dfrac{dE}{dx} = 0 \quad \Rightarrow F = 0$

7. At point P,

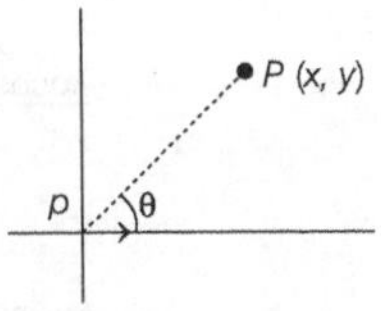

$$V = \frac{kp\cos\theta}{(\sqrt{x^2+y^2})^2}$$

$$V = \frac{kpx}{(x^2+y^2)^{3/2}} = \text{constant}$$

$$\Rightarrow \quad \frac{x}{(x^2+y^2)^{3/2}} = \text{constant}$$

8.

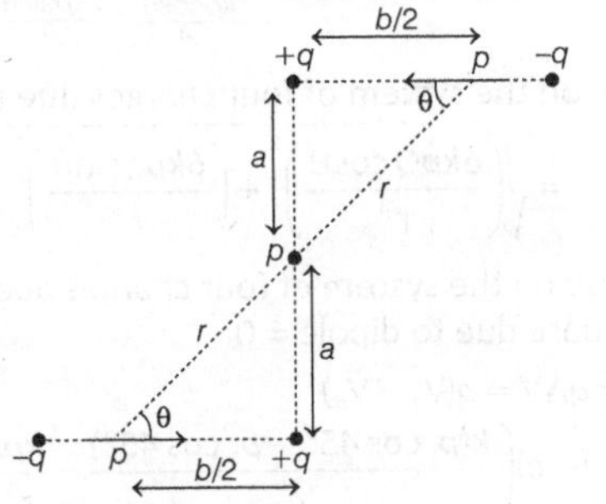

$$V = V_1 + V_2 = \frac{kp\cos\theta}{r^2} + \frac{kp\cos\theta}{r^2}$$

$$= \frac{2kp\cos\theta}{r^2} = 2\left(\frac{1}{4\pi\varepsilon_0}\right)\frac{qb(b/2)}{\left(a^2+\frac{b^2}{4}\right)\sqrt{a^2+\frac{b^2}{4}}}$$

$$= \frac{qb^2}{4\pi\varepsilon_0 a^3} \qquad (\because b << a)$$

9.

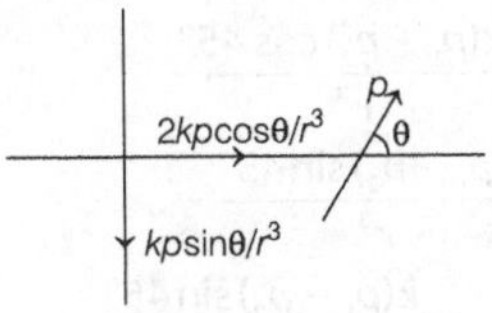

Electric field due to dipole $= \dfrac{2kp\cos\theta}{r^3}\hat{\mathbf{i}} - \dfrac{kp\sin\theta}{r^3}\hat{\mathbf{j}}$

$$\mathbf{F} = q\mathbf{E} = (-Q)\left(\frac{2kp\cos\theta}{r^3}\hat{\mathbf{i}} - \frac{kp\sin\theta}{r^3}\hat{\mathbf{j}}\right)$$

$$= \left(\frac{2kpQ\cos\theta}{r^3}\right)(-\hat{\mathbf{i}}) + \left(\frac{kpQ\sin\theta}{r^3}\right)(\hat{\mathbf{j}})$$

x-component of force $= \dfrac{-2kpQ\cos\theta}{r^3}\hat{\mathbf{i}}$

10.

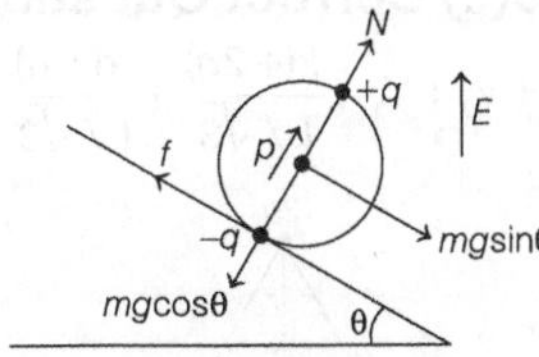

For equilibrium, $\Sigma\tau = 0$

About the point of contact.

$$\tau_{mg} + \tau_f + \tau_N + \tau_{\text{electric}} = 0$$

$$\Rightarrow (mg\sin\theta)R + 0 + 0 - pE\sin\theta = 0$$

$$\Rightarrow \quad E = \frac{mgR}{p} = \frac{mgR}{q(2R)} = \frac{mg}{2q}$$

11.

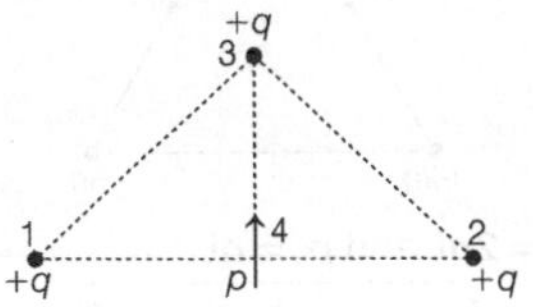

$^4C_2 = 6$ pairs

$$U = U_{12} + U_{23} + U_{31} + U_{41} + U_{42} + U_{43}$$

$$= \frac{kq^2}{a} + \frac{kq^2}{a} + \frac{kq^2}{a} + 0 + 0 + q\left(\frac{kp}{\left(\frac{\sqrt{3}a}{2}\right)^2}\right)$$

$$= \frac{3kq^2}{a} + \frac{4}{3}\frac{kpq}{a^2} = \frac{3kq^2}{a} + \frac{4}{3}\frac{k(qa/8)q}{a^2} = \frac{19}{6}\frac{kq^2}{a}$$

12.

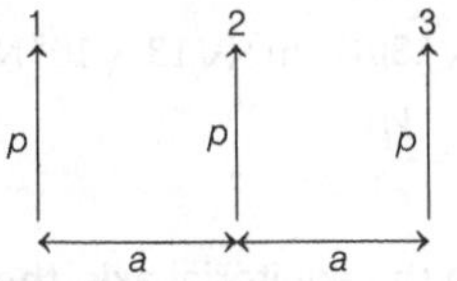

$$U = U_{12} + U_{23} + U_{31}$$

$$= -p\left(\frac{kp}{a^3}\right)\cos 180° - p\left(\frac{kp}{a^3}\right)\cos 180° - p\left[\frac{kp}{(2a)^3}\right]\cos 180°$$

$$= \frac{17}{8}\frac{kp}{a^3}$$

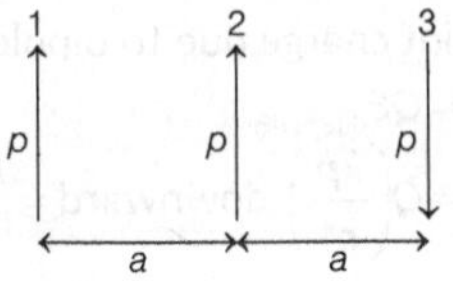

$$U' = U_{12} + U_{23} + U_{31}$$

$$= -p\left(\frac{kp}{a^3}\right)\cos 180° - p\left(\frac{kp}{a^3}\right)\cos 0° - p\left[\frac{kp}{(2a)^3}\right]\cos 0°$$

$$= -\frac{kp}{8a^3}$$

$$W_{\text{electric}} = -\Delta U = U - U'$$

$$= \frac{17}{8}\frac{kp}{a^3} - \left(-\frac{kp}{8a^3}\right) = \frac{18}{8}\left(\frac{kp}{a^3}\right) = \frac{18}{8}\left(\frac{8U}{17}\right) = \frac{18U}{17}$$

Multiple Choice(s) Correct Questions

1. (a) $V_{\text{centroid}} = V_1 + V_2 + V_3 = \dfrac{k(+2q)}{L/\sqrt{3}} + \dfrac{k(+q)}{L/\sqrt{3}} + \dfrac{k(-3q)}{L/\sqrt{3}} = 0$

(b)

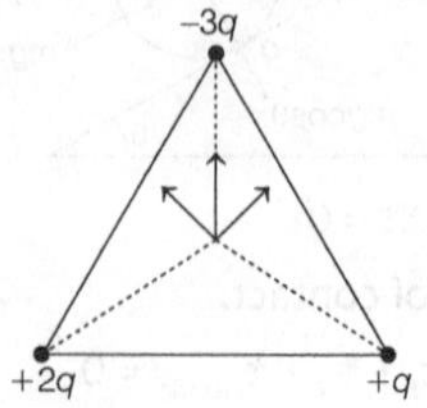

At the centroid, $\mathbf{E} \neq 0$

(c)

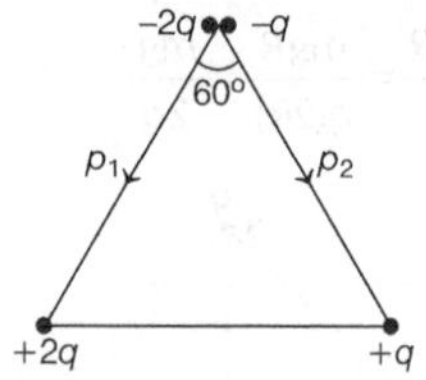

$p_1 = 2qL$ and $p_2 = qL$

$p_{\text{net}} = \sqrt{p_1^2 + p_2^2 + 2p_1p_2\cos\theta}$

$= \sqrt{(2qL)^2 + (qL)^2 + (2qL)(qL)\cos 60^\circ} = \sqrt{7}\, qL$

2. $\mathbf{p} = (2\hat{\mathbf{i}} + 3\hat{\mathbf{j}})\,\mu\text{C-m}$

$\mathbf{E} = (3\hat{\mathbf{i}} + 2\hat{\mathbf{k}}) \times 10^5$ N/C

(a) $\tau = \mathbf{p} \times \mathbf{E} = \begin{vmatrix} \hat{\mathbf{i}} & \hat{\mathbf{j}} & \hat{\mathbf{k}} \\ 2 & 3 & 0 \\ 3 & 0 & 2 \end{vmatrix} \times 10^{-1} = (0.6\hat{\mathbf{i}} - 0.4\hat{\mathbf{j}} - 0.9\hat{\mathbf{k}})$ N-m

(b) $U = -\mathbf{p}\cdot\mathbf{E} = -0.6$ J

(d) $V_{\max} = pE = (\sqrt{13}\mu\text{C - m})(\sqrt{13} \times 10^5\ \text{N/C}) = 1.3$ J

3. $E_{\max} = \dfrac{2kp}{r^3},\ E_{\min} = \dfrac{kp}{r^3}$

If the point is on the equitorial axis, then $E_{\min} = \dfrac{kp}{r^3} = 10.$

So, $10 \leq E \leq 20.$

If the point is on the axis, then $E_{\max} = \dfrac{2kp}{r^3} = 10.$

So, $5 \leq E \leq 10.$

4. Force on the point charge due to dipole

$= QE_{\text{due to dipole}}$

$= Q\left(\dfrac{kp}{r^3}\right)$, downward $= \dfrac{kpQ}{r^3}$, downward

From Newton's third law,

Force on dipole due to point charge $= \dfrac{kpQ}{r^3}$, upward

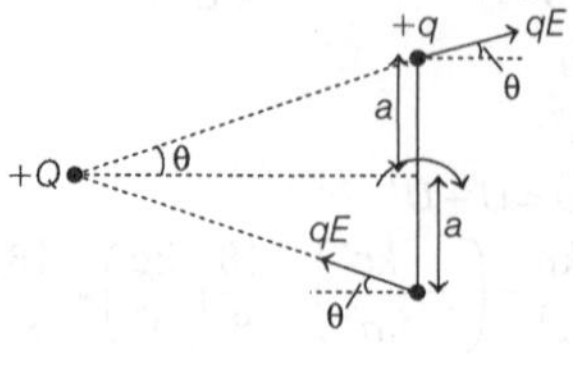

Torque on dipole $= (qE\cos\theta)\, a \times 2$, Clockwise

$= q(2a)\left(\dfrac{kQ}{(\sqrt{r^2+a^2})^2}\dfrac{r}{\sqrt{r^2+a^2}}\right)$, Clockwise

$= \dfrac{kpQ}{r^2}$, Clockwise $[\because a << r]$

$= \dfrac{1}{4\pi\varepsilon_0}\dfrac{pQ}{r^2}$, Clockwise

5.

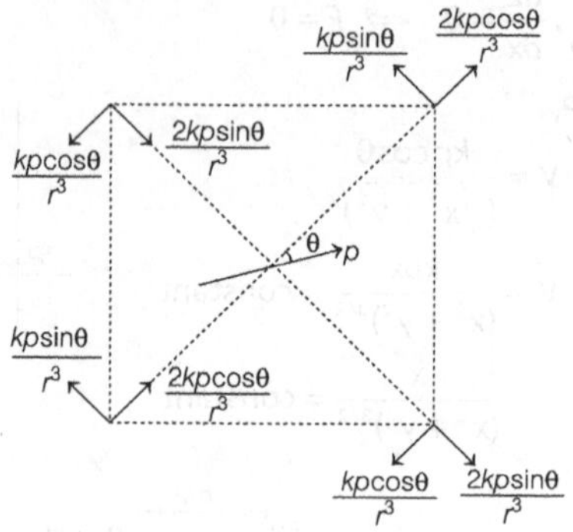

Net force on the system of four charges due to dipole

$= \sqrt{\left(\dfrac{6kpQ\cos\theta}{r^3}\right)^2 + \left(\dfrac{6kpq\sin\theta}{r^3}\right)^2} = \dfrac{6kpq}{r^3}$

Net torque on the system of four charges about the centre of the square due to dipole = 0

6. (a) $W_{\text{ext}} = q\Delta V = q(V_R - V_P)$

$= (-e)\left(\dfrac{k(p_1\cos 45^\circ + p_2\cos 45^\circ)}{r^2} - \dfrac{kp_1}{r^2}\right) \neq 0$

(c)

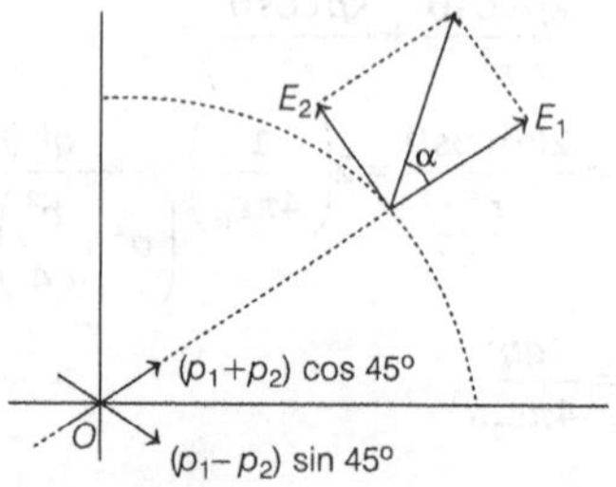

$E_1 = \dfrac{2k(p_1+p_2)\cos 45^\circ}{r^3}$

$E_2 = \dfrac{k(p_1-p_2)\sin 45^\circ}{r^3}$

$\tan\alpha = \dfrac{E_2}{E_1} = \dfrac{\dfrac{k(p_1-p_2)\sin 45^\circ}{r^3}}{\dfrac{2k(P_1+P_2)\cos 45^\circ}{r^3}}$

$\Rightarrow \quad \tan\alpha = \dfrac{p_1-p_2}{2(p_1+p_2)}$

(d) $-\displaystyle\int_\infty^r \mathbf{E}\cdot d\mathbf{r} =$ Potential at point P

$= \dfrac{kp_1\cos 45^\circ}{r^2} + \dfrac{kp_2\cos 45^\circ}{r^2} = \dfrac{(p_1+p_2)}{4\sqrt{2}\pi\varepsilon_0 r^2}$

Comprehension Based Questions

1.

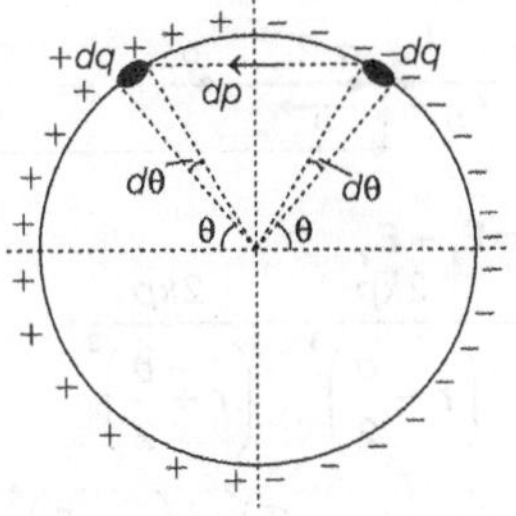

$$\mathbf{dp} = -\,dq(2R\cos\theta)\hat{\mathbf{i}}$$

$$\Rightarrow \quad \int \mathbf{dp} = -\int_{-\pi/2}^{\pi/2} (\lambda R d\theta)(2R\cos\theta)(\hat{\mathbf{i}})$$

$$\Rightarrow \quad \mathbf{p} = -(4R^2\lambda)\,\hat{\mathbf{i}}$$

2. Potential at the centre of ring $= \dfrac{k\int dq}{R} = 0$

Y-axis is the equatorial axis, so potential at all points on the equatorial axis would be same.

$$\Rightarrow \quad \text{Potential at}\left(0, \frac{R}{2}\right) = 0$$

3. Electric field on equatorial axis is opposite to direction of dipole moment, so electric field will be along positive x-direction.

4. $\mathbf{p} = Q\mathbf{r} = Q\left(\dfrac{8R}{3\pi}\right)\hat{\mathbf{j}}$

$$\tau = \mathbf{p} \times \mathbf{E} = \left[Q\left(\frac{8R}{3\pi}\right)\hat{\mathbf{j}}\right] \times (E)\,\hat{\mathbf{i}} = -\frac{8QRE}{3\pi}\hat{\mathbf{k}}$$

$$|\tau| = \frac{8QRE}{3\pi}$$

5. $f = ma_{CM}$ and $\tau_{net} = I\alpha$

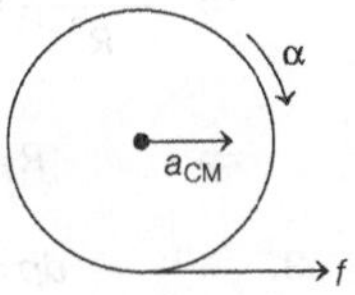

$$\Rightarrow \quad \frac{8QRE}{3\pi} - fR = \left(\frac{mR^2}{2}\right)\alpha$$

$$\Rightarrow \quad \frac{8QRE}{3\pi} - (ma_{CM})R = \left(\frac{mR^2}{2}\right)\left(\frac{a_{CM}}{R}\right)$$

(For pure rolling, $a_{CM} = R\alpha$)

$$\Rightarrow \quad a_{CM} = \frac{16QE}{9\pi m}$$

6. $f = ma_{CM} = m\left(\dfrac{16QE}{9\pi m}\right) = \dfrac{16QE}{9\pi}$

$$f \le f_L$$

$$\Rightarrow \quad \frac{16QE}{9\pi} \le \mu N \quad \Rightarrow \quad \frac{16QE}{9\pi} \le \mu(mg)$$

$$\Rightarrow \quad \mu \ge \frac{16QE}{9\pi mg} \quad \Rightarrow \quad \mu_{min} = \frac{16QE}{9\pi mg}$$

7. Dipole moment, $p = (\lambda W)L$

Potential energy, $U = -\mathbf{p}\cdot\mathbf{E} = -(\lambda WL)E\cos 60° = \dfrac{-\lambda WLE}{2}$

8. Loss in potential energy = Gain in kinetic energy

$$\Rightarrow \quad \frac{-\lambda WLE}{2} - (-\lambda WLE) = \frac{1}{2}I\omega^2 - 0$$

$$\Rightarrow \quad \frac{\lambda WLE}{2} = \frac{1}{2}\left[2M\left(\frac{L}{2}\right)^2\right]\omega^2 \quad \Rightarrow \quad \omega = \sqrt{\frac{2\lambda WE}{ML}}$$

9. $T = 2\pi\sqrt{\dfrac{I}{PE}} = 2\pi\sqrt{\dfrac{2M\left(\frac{L}{2}\right)^2}{(\lambda WL)E}}$

Required time $= \dfrac{T}{4} = \pi\sqrt{\dfrac{ML}{8\lambda WE}}$

Match the Columns Questions

1.

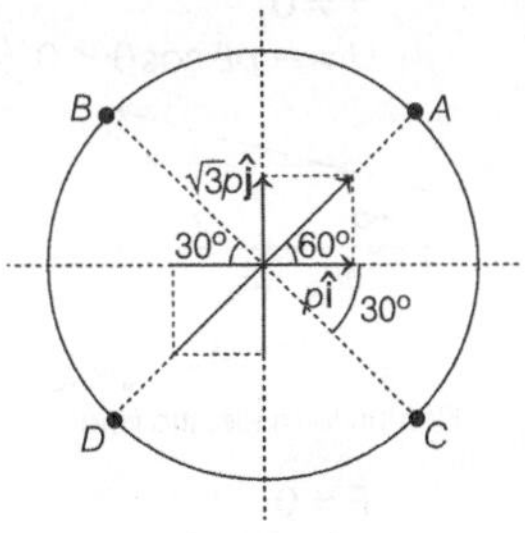

$$\mathbf{p} = p\hat{\mathbf{i}} + \sqrt{3}p\hat{\mathbf{j}}$$

$= 2p$ at 60° with X-axis

(a) Potential is maximum on the axis of the resultant dipole.

Co-ordinates of point $A = (R\cos 60°, R\sin 60°)$

$$= \left(\frac{R}{2}, \frac{\sqrt{3}R}{2}\right)$$

(b) Potential is zero on the equatorial axis of the resultant dipole.

Co-ordinate of $B = (-R\cos 30°, R\sin 30°)$

$$= \left(\frac{-\sqrt{3}R}{2}, \frac{R}{2}\right)$$

Co-ordinates of $C = (R\cos 30°, -R\sin 30°)$

$$= \left(\frac{\sqrt{3}R}{2}, -\frac{R}{2}\right)$$

(c) $$E_{max} = \frac{1}{4\pi\varepsilon_0}\left[\frac{2(2p)}{r^3}\right] = \frac{1}{4\pi\varepsilon_0}\left(\frac{4p}{r^3}\right)$$

Electric field is maximum at axis of the resultant dipole.

Co-ordinates of $A = (R\cos 60°, R\sin 60°)$

$$= \left(\frac{R}{2}, \frac{\sqrt{3}R}{2}\right)$$

Co-ordinates of $D = (-R\cos 60°, -R\sin 60°)$

$$= \left(\frac{-R}{2}, \frac{-\sqrt{3}R}{2}\right)$$

(d) $E_{min} = \frac{1}{4\pi\varepsilon_0}\left(\frac{2p}{r^3}\right)$

Electric field is minimum at equatorial axis of the resultant dipole.

Co-ordinates of $B = \left(\frac{-\sqrt{3}R}{2}, \frac{R}{2}\right)$

Co-ordinates of $D = \left(\frac{\sqrt{3}R}{2}, \frac{-R}{2}\right)$

2. (a)

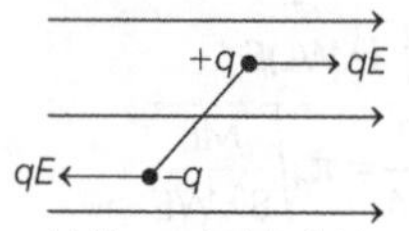

Uniform electric field

$F = 0$

$\tau \neq 0$

$U = -pE\cos\theta < 0$ ($\because \theta$ is acute)

(b)

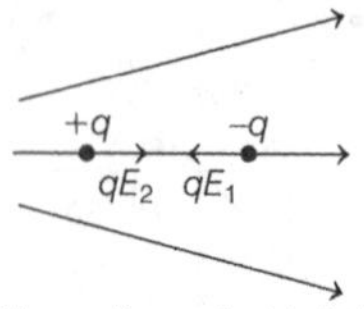

Non-uniform electric field

$F \neq 0$

$\tau = 0$

$U > 0$ ($\because$ **E** and **p** are anti-parallel)

(c)

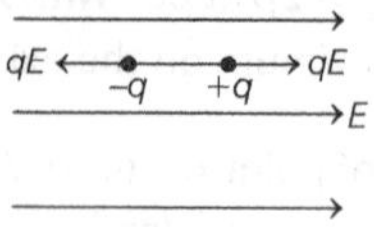

$F = 0$

$\tau = 0$

$U = -pE\cos 0° < 0$ and also minimum.

(d)

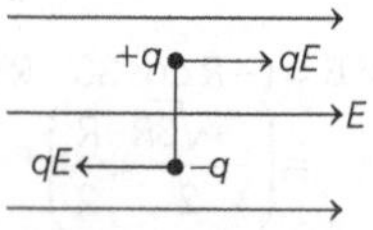

$F = 0$

$\tau = pE\sin 90° \neq 0$

$U = -pE\cos\theta = 0$

3. (a) (q) $dp = dq(2R\cos\theta)$

$\Rightarrow dp = (\lambda_0\cos\theta)Rd\theta(2R\cos\theta)$

$\Rightarrow \int dp = \lambda_0 R^2 \int_{-\pi/2}^{+\pi/2} 2\cos^2\theta\, d\theta \Rightarrow p = \lambda_0\pi R^2$

(b) (p) The orientation of dipole moment remains unchanged, so work done is zero.

(c) (p) $|W_{electric}| = |-\Delta U| = |pE\cos 0° - pE\cos 90°| = \frac{2kp^2}{d^3}$

(d) (r) $F = \frac{6kp_1p_2}{r^4} = \frac{6kp^2}{d^4}$

Numerical Type Questions

1.

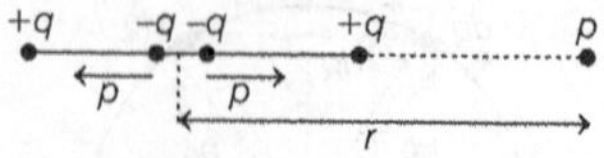

At point P, $\mathbf{E} = \mathbf{E}_1 + \mathbf{E}_2$

$$\Rightarrow E = \frac{2kp}{\left(r - \frac{a}{2}\right)^3} - \frac{2kp}{\left(r + \frac{a}{2}\right)^3}$$

$$\Rightarrow E = \frac{2kp(a)\left[\left(r + \frac{a}{2}\right)^2 + \left(r - \frac{a}{2}\right)^2 + r^2 - \frac{a^2}{4}\right]}{\left(r^2 - \frac{a^2}{4}\right)^3}$$

$$= \frac{2kpa\left(3r^2 + \frac{a^2}{4}\right)}{\left(r^2 - \frac{a^2}{4}\right)^3} = \frac{6kpa}{r^4} \quad [\because a << r]$$

So, $n = 6$ and $m = 4$ $\Rightarrow$ $m + n = 10$

2.

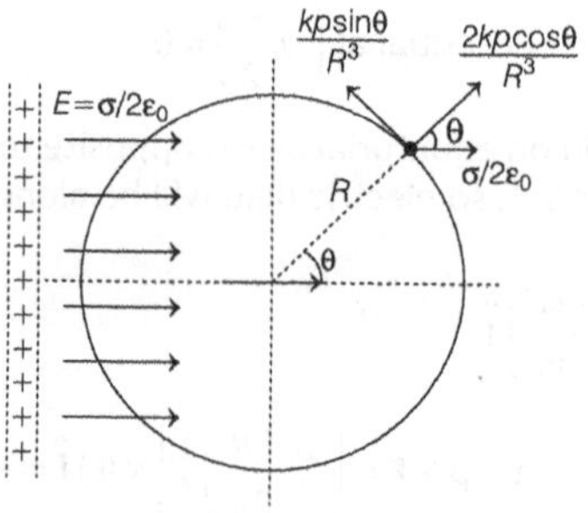

For potential to be constant on the circle, tangential component of resultant electric field should be zero.

$$\Rightarrow \frac{kp\sin\theta}{R^3} = \frac{\sigma}{2\varepsilon_0}\sin\theta \Rightarrow R^3 = \frac{2kp\varepsilon_0}{\sigma}$$

$$\Rightarrow R = \left(\frac{p}{2\pi\sigma}\right)^{1/3} \Rightarrow n = 2$$

3. $dp = dq(2R\cos\theta)$

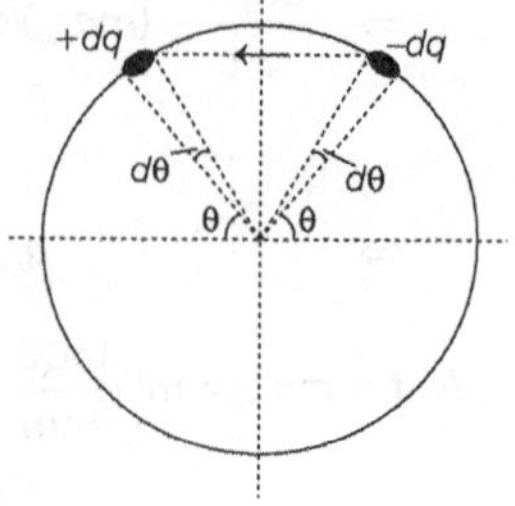

$$\Rightarrow \int dp = \int_{-\pi/2}^{+\pi/2} \lambda R\, d\theta\, (2R\cos\theta)$$

$$\Rightarrow p = 4\lambda R^2$$

Using mechanical energy conservation,

Loss in PE = Gain in KE

$$\Rightarrow 0 - (-\text{PE}) = \frac{1}{2}I\omega^2 - 0$$

$$\Rightarrow pE = \frac{1}{2}\left(\frac{mR^2}{2}\right)\omega^2$$

$$\Rightarrow 4\lambda R^2 E = \frac{1}{4}mR^2\omega^2 \Rightarrow \omega = 4\sqrt{\frac{\lambda E}{m}}$$

4.

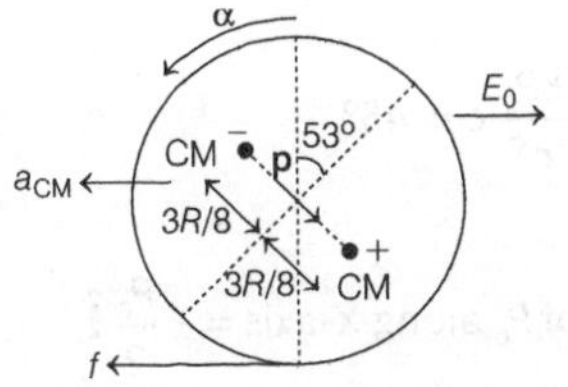

$$p = q\left(\frac{3R}{8}\times 2\right) = \rho\left(\frac{2}{3}\pi R^3\right)\left(\frac{3R}{4}\right) = \frac{\rho\pi R^4}{2}$$

$$\Sigma F_{ext} = ma_{CM} \Rightarrow f = ma_{CM}$$

$$\Sigma\tau = I\alpha$$

$$\Rightarrow \quad pE_0\sin 53° - fR = \frac{2}{5}mR^2\alpha$$

$$\Rightarrow \quad \left(\frac{\rho\pi R^4}{2}\right)E_0\left(\frac{4}{5}\right) - fR = \frac{2}{5}mR^2\left(\frac{a_{CM}}{R}\right)$$

$$\Rightarrow \quad \frac{2\rho\pi R^4 E}{5} - fR = \frac{2}{5}fR \Rightarrow f = \frac{2}{7}\rho\pi R^3 E_0$$

Hence, $K = 7$

Previous Year's Questions

JEE Main

1. Given,

$$q = 4\mu C$$
$$E = 0.20\hat{i}\,V/cm = 20\,\hat{i}\,V/m$$

position vector of point A, $r_A = \hat{i} + 4\hat{k}$

position vector of point B, $r_B = 2\hat{i} - \hat{j} + 5\hat{k}$

Dipole moment,

$$\mathbf{p} = q[\mathbf{r}_B - \mathbf{r}_A] = 4\times 10^{-6}[\hat{i} - \hat{j} + \hat{k}]$$

Torque, $\tau = \mathbf{p}\times\mathbf{E} = 4\times 10^{-6}[\hat{i} - \hat{j} + \hat{k}]\times 20\hat{i}$

$$= 80\times 10^{-6}[\hat{i}\times\hat{i} - \hat{j}\times\hat{i} + \hat{k}\times\hat{i}]$$
$$= 80\times 16^{-6}[0 + \hat{k} + \hat{j}]$$
$$|\tau| = 80\times 10^{-6}\sqrt{12+12}$$
$$= 8\sqrt{2}\times 10^{-5}\text{ N-m}$$
$$= 8\sqrt{\alpha}\times 10^{-5}\text{ N-m}$$
$$\therefore \quad \alpha = 2$$

2. Electric potential due to electric dipole is given by

$$V = \frac{1}{4\pi\varepsilon_0}\frac{p\cos\theta}{r^2}$$

where p is dipole moment.

$$\Rightarrow \quad V \propto \frac{1}{r^2}$$

3. Electric dipole moment

$$p = q\times 2l$$
$$p = 0.01\times 0.4\times 10^{-3} = 4\times 10^{-6}\text{ C-m}$$
$$E = 10\times 10^{-5}\text{ N/c}$$
$$|\tau| = |p\times E| = 4\times 10^{-6}\times 10\times 10^{-5}\sin 30°$$
$$= 2\times 10^{-10}\text{ N-m},$$

4. Electric field due to electric dipole on equilotrial plane at a distance r from its centre is given as

$$E = \frac{1}{4\pi\varepsilon_0}\cdot\frac{p}{r^3} \Rightarrow E \propto \frac{1}{r^3}$$

5. In this case since masses of both end are not same, therefore we need to find centre of mass about which dipole will oscillate and then we will find moment of Inertia about this axis, to find torque and hence ω, COM will be $\frac{1}{3}$ from $2m$ and $\frac{2L}{3}$ from m

MI about this axis.

$$I = 2m\times\left(\frac{L}{3}\right)^2 + m\left(\frac{2L}{3}\right)^2$$

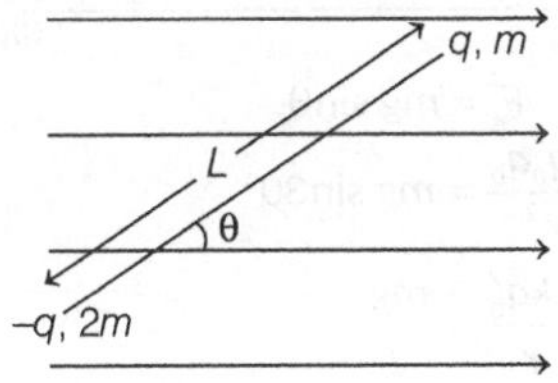

$$= \frac{2mL^2}{9} + \frac{4mL^2}{9} = \frac{6mL^2}{9} = \frac{2mL^2}{3},$$

Now, torque on the dipole, $\tau = I\alpha = \sin\theta$

Where, α is angular acceleration,

$$\therefore \quad \alpha = \frac{PE\sin\theta}{I}$$

$$\alpha = \left(\frac{PE}{I}\right)\theta \qquad \text{[For small angle } \sin\theta \approx \theta]$$

$$\alpha = \left(\frac{qEL}{I}\right)\theta \qquad [\because P = qL]$$

$$\alpha = \left(\frac{3qEL}{2mL^2}\right)\theta \qquad \left[\because I = \frac{2mL^2}{3}\right]$$

$$\alpha = \left(\frac{3qE}{2mL}\right)\theta \qquad \text{...(i)}$$

The above equation is similar to the equation for system excuting angular SHM.

Campare Eq. (i) with

$$\alpha = \omega^2\theta, \text{ then}$$

$$\omega^2 = \frac{3qE}{2mL} \Rightarrow \omega = \sqrt{\frac{3qE}{2mL}}$$

There is no correct option given.

6.

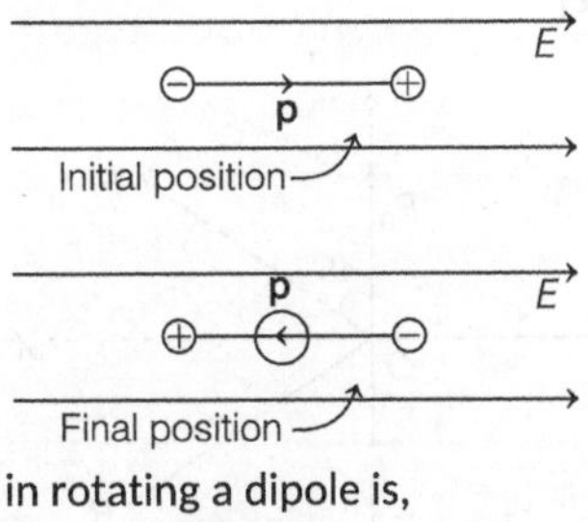

Work done in rotating a dipole is,

$$W_{\theta_1\to\theta_2} = -pE(\cos\theta_2 - \cos\theta_1)$$

Here, $\theta_1 = 0°, \theta_2 = 180°$

$$P = 6 \times 10^{-6} \text{ Cm},$$
$$E = 1.5 \times 10^3 \text{ NC}^{-1}$$

So, work done, W

$$= -6 \times 10^{-6} \times 1.5 \times 10^3 \times (\cos 180° - \cos 0°)$$
$$= 18 \times 10^{-3} \text{ J} = 18 \text{ mJ}$$

7. Point charge on equilibrium is at rest so,

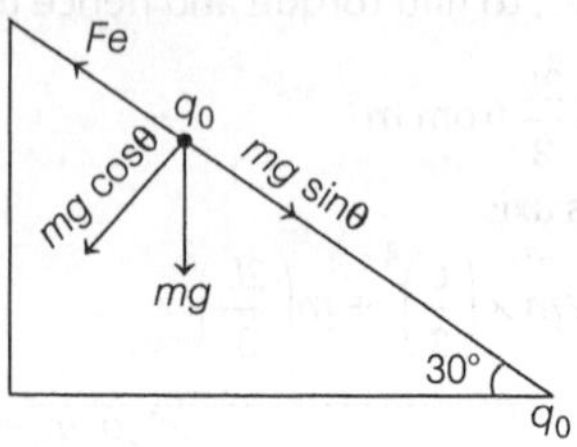

$$F_e = mg \sin\theta$$
$$\frac{kq_0q_0}{r^2} = mg \sin 30°$$
$$\frac{kq_0^2}{r^2} = \frac{mg}{2} \qquad \left[r = \frac{h}{\sin 30°}\right]$$
$$\frac{kq_0^2}{\left(\frac{h}{\sin 30}\right)^2} = \frac{mg}{2}$$
$$\frac{9 \times 10^9 \times (2 \times 10^{-6})^2}{4h^2} = \frac{20 \times 10^{-3} \times 10}{2}$$
$$\frac{9 \times 4 \times 10^9 \times 10^{-12}}{4h^2} = 10^{-1}$$
$$h^2 = 9 \times 10^{-2}$$
$$h = 0.3 \text{ m} = 300 \times 10^{-3} \text{ m}$$

Hence, $x = 300$

8. Given, for two electric dipole,

$$p_1 = 1.2 \times 10^{-30} \text{ C-m} \quad \text{and} \quad p_2 = 2.4 \times 10^{-30} \text{ C-m}$$
$$E_1 = 5 \times 10^4 \text{ NC}^{-1}$$
$$E_2 = 15 \times 10^4 \text{ NC}^{-1}$$

We know that maximum torque on electric dipole in electric field,

$$\tau_{max} = pE$$
$$\Rightarrow \frac{(\tau_{max})_1}{(\tau_{max})_2} = \frac{p_1E_1}{p_2E_2} = \frac{1.2 \times 10^{-30} \times 5 \times 10^4}{2.4 \times 10^{-30} \times 15 \times 10^4} = \frac{1}{6} = \frac{1}{x} \quad \text{(given)}$$
$$\therefore \quad x = 6$$

JEE Advanced

1.

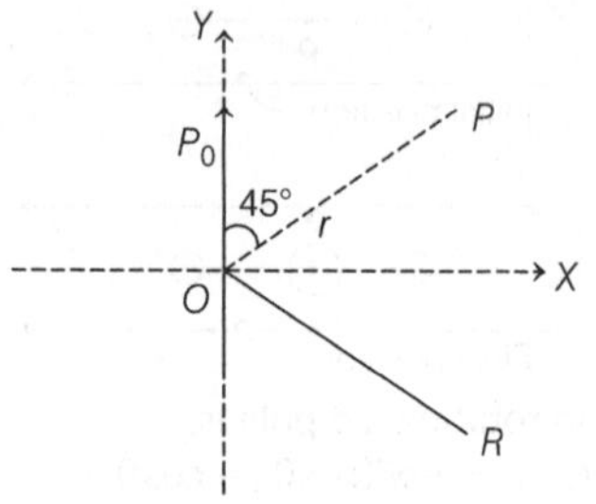

Case (i)

$$V_0 = \frac{kP_0}{r^2} \cos 45°$$

Case (ii)

Component of P_0' along X-axis $= -\frac{P_0}{2}\hat{\mathbf{i}}$

Component of P_0' along Y-axis $= P_0\hat{\mathbf{j}}$

Potential due to $P_0\hat{\mathbf{j}}$

$$\Rightarrow \frac{kP_0 \cos 45°}{r^2} = V_0$$

Potential due to $-\frac{P_0}{2}\hat{\mathbf{i}}$

2. Electrostatic force = Spring force

At l, $Fe = F_{sp}$ $\quad kl = \frac{2\alpha pq}{l^3} \qquad \left(\text{Here, } \alpha = \frac{1}{4\pi\varepsilon_0}\right)$

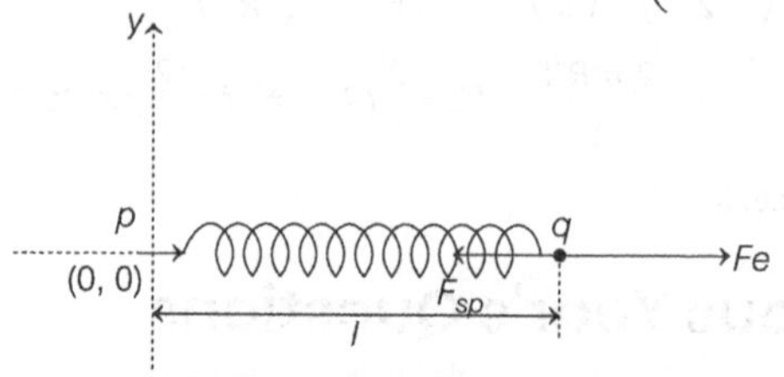

Now, the mass m is displaced by $\Delta l = x$ from the mean position

$$F_{net} = F_{sp} - Fe = k(l + x) - \frac{q(2\alpha p)}{(l + x)^3}$$
$$= k(x + l) - \frac{q(2\alpha p)}{l^3(1 + x/l)^3} = kx + kl - q\left(\frac{2\alpha p}{l^3}\right)\left(1 - \frac{3x}{l}\right)$$
$$= kx + kl - q\left(\frac{2\alpha p}{l^3}\right) + \frac{2\alpha pq}{l^3} \cdot \frac{3x}{l}$$

Substituting $\frac{2\alpha pq}{l^3} = kl$, we get

$$F_{net} = kx + kl\left(\frac{3x}{l}\right) = 4kx$$

This is restoring in nature.

Hence, $k_{eq} = 4k$ or $T = 2\pi\sqrt{\frac{m}{4k}} = \pi\sqrt{\frac{m}{k}}$

$$\therefore \quad f = \frac{1}{\pi}\sqrt{\frac{k}{m}}$$

So, $\delta = \pi = 3.14$

3. (p) $E = \frac{1}{4\pi\varepsilon_0}\frac{Q}{d^2} \Rightarrow E \propto \frac{1}{d^2}$

(q) $E_{axis} = \frac{1}{4\pi\varepsilon_0}\frac{2Q(2l)}{d^3} \Rightarrow E \propto \frac{1}{d^3}$

(r) $E = \frac{\lambda}{2\pi\varepsilon_0 d} \Rightarrow E \propto \frac{1}{d}$

(s) $E = \frac{\lambda}{2\pi\varepsilon_0(d - l)} - \frac{\lambda}{2\pi\varepsilon_0(d + l)} = \frac{\lambda(2l)}{2\pi\varepsilon_0 d^2} \Rightarrow E \propto \frac{1}{d^2}$

(t) $E = \frac{\sigma}{2\varepsilon_0} \Rightarrow$ E is independent of d

CHAPTER~04

ELECTRIC FLUX

LEVEL 01 Starter Level

4.1 Electric Flux

1 Find out the electric flux through an area $10\,m^2$ lying in XY-plane due to an electric field $\mathbf{E} = (3\hat{\mathbf{i}} - 4\hat{\mathbf{j}} + 10\hat{\mathbf{k}})\,Vm^{-1}$.

2 Find the electric flux through the ring of radius R in each of the following cases.

(i) 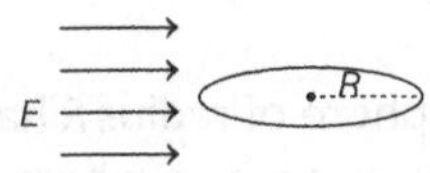

Uniform electric field E is parallel to the plane of the ring.

(ii) 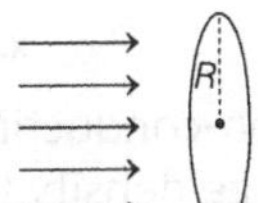

Uniform electric field E is normal to the plane of the ring.

(iii) 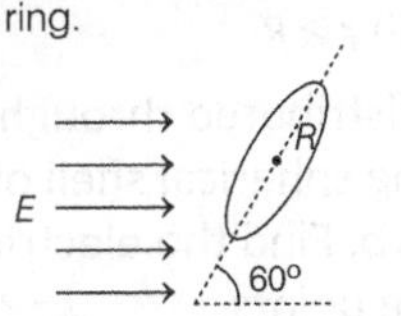

Uniform electric field E makes an angle of 60° with the plane of the ring.

3 Find the electric flux through the curved surface of the hemisphere in each of the following cases.

(i) 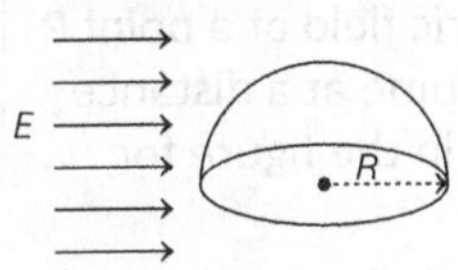

A uniform horizontal electric field E is parallel to the base of the hemisphere.

(ii) 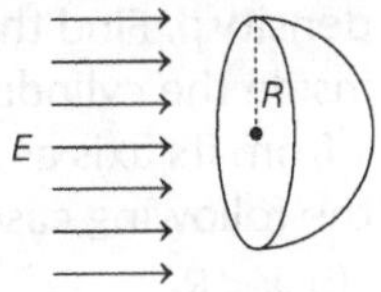

A uniform horizontal electric field E is perpendicular to the base of the hemisphere.

(iii) 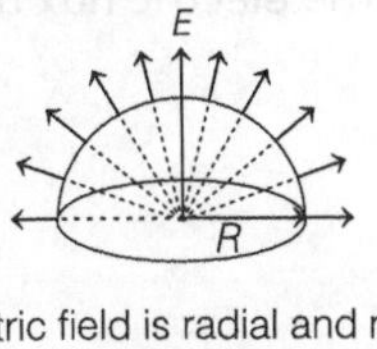

Electric field is radial and magnitude of electric field at any point on the curved surface of the hemisphere is E.

4 A cube of side 2 m has one corner at the origin of coordinates and extends along the positive X, Y and Z-axis. An electric field of magnitude 20 N/C exists in XY-plane and it makes an angle of 37° with the X-axis. Find the electric flux passing through each face of the cube.

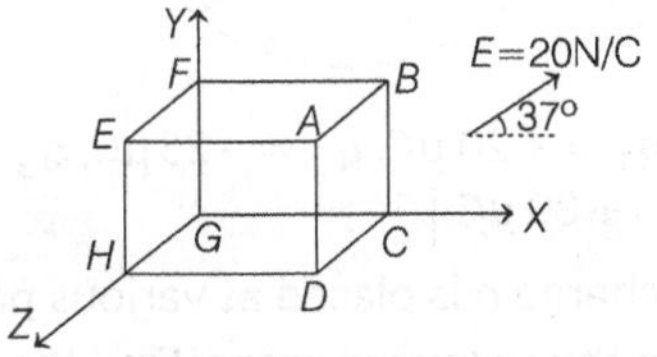

5 A uniform electric field $\mathbf{E} = E_0\,\hat{\mathbf{i}}$ exists in the region. Find the electric flux through each of the five faces of the triangular prism.

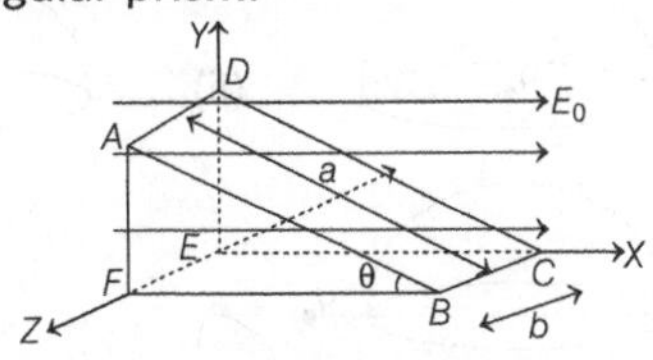

6 Find the electric flux entering the cone in each of the following cases.

(i) 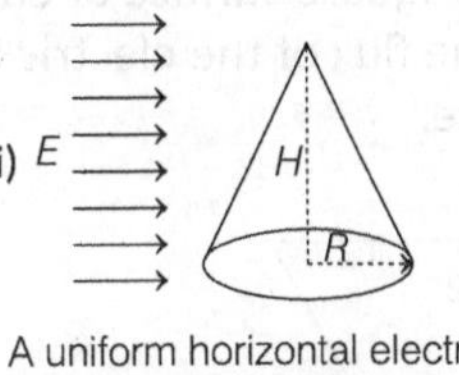

A uniform horizontal electric field E is present and axis of the cone is vertical.

(ii) 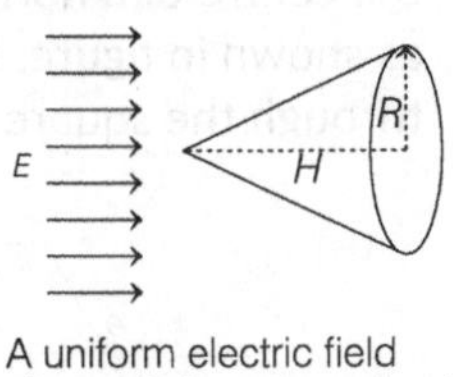

A uniform electric field directed along the axis of cone exists in the region.

(iii) 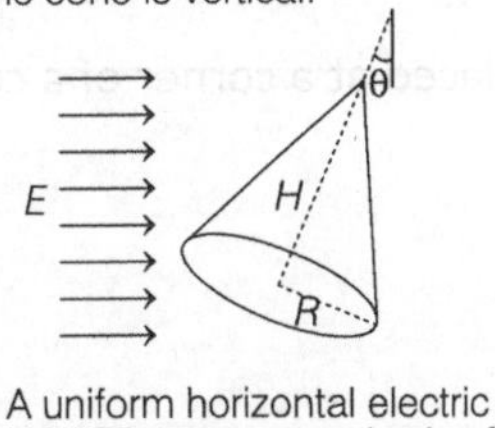

A uniform horizontal electric field E is present and axis of cone is tilted by an angle θ from vertical.

4.2 Gauss Law

1 A spherical surface encloses a point charge q. How the flux through the surface changes in each of the following cases?

(i) Radius of the spherical surface is doubled.
(ii) Charge q is shifted within the spherical surface.
(iii) Spherical surface is replaced with a cubical surface.
(iv) Another point charge q' is placed outside the surface.

2 The flux of the electric field, through the closed spherical surface S', is found to be four times that through the closed spherical surface S. Find the magnitude of the charge Q.

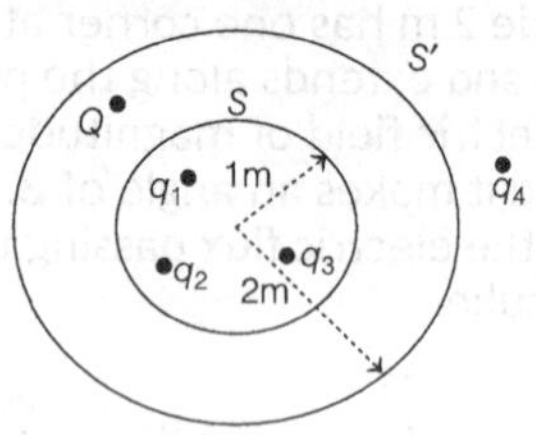

[Given, $q_1 = +20\,\mu\text{C}$, $q_2 = -25\,\mu\text{C}$, $q_3 = +9.75\,\mu\text{C}$ and $q_4 = +30\,\mu\text{C}$.]

3 A point charge q is placed at various positions as shown in the following cases. Find the electric flux due to this charge through the hemispherical surface for each case.

(i) 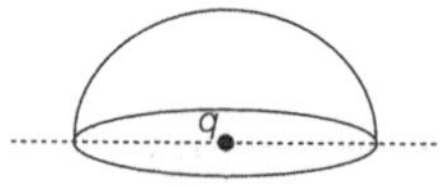

(ii) 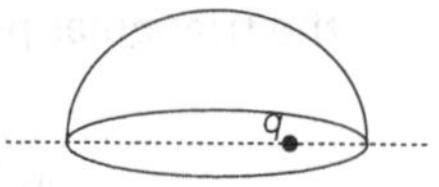

(iii) 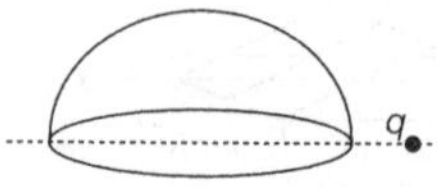

4 A point charge Q is placed at a distance $a/2$ above the centre of a horizontal, square surface of edge a as shown in figure. Find the flux of the electric field through the square surface.

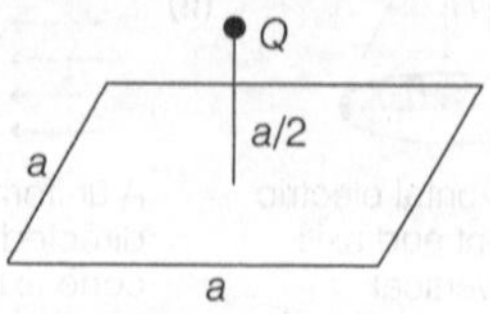

5 A point charge Q is placed at a corner of a cube as shown.

Find the flux of the electric field through the

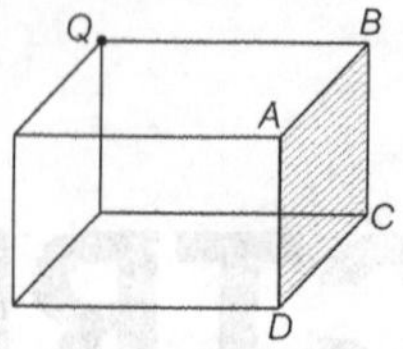

(i) cube (ii) face $ABCD$

6 The electric field in a region is radially outward with magnitude $E = Ba$, where B is a constant. Find the charge contained in a sphere of radius a centred at the origin.

7 Electric field in a region is given by $\mathbf{E} = -4x\hat{\mathbf{i}} + 6y\hat{\mathbf{j}}$.

Find the charge enclosed in the cube of side 1 m oriented as shown in the diagram.

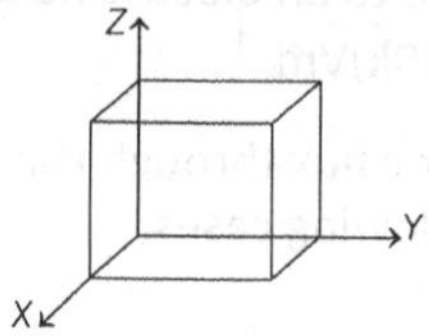

8 A non-conducting solid sphere of radius R has volume charge density that varies as $\rho = \rho_0 r$, where ρ_0 is a constant and r is distance from centre. Find out electric field intensities for the following positions.

(i) $r < R$ (ii) $r \geq R$

9 A charge Q is uniformly distributed throughout the volume of non-conducting spherical shell of inner radius a and outer radius b. Find the electric field intensity for the following points.

(i) $r < a$ (ii) $a \leq r < b$
(iii) $r \geq b$, where r is the distance of the point from the centre.

10 A long cylindrical volume (of radius R) contains a uniformly distributed charge of density ρ. Find the electric field at a point P inside the cylindrical volume at a distance x from its axis as shown in the figure for the following cases.

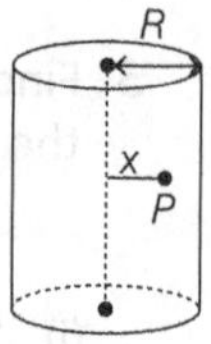

(i) $x < R$ (ii) $x \geq R$

11 A point charge q is placed at the apex of a cone of semi-vertex angle θ. Find the electric flux through the base of the cone.

LEVEL 02 JEE Main Level

Single Choice Correct Questions

1 A square of side a is lying in XY-plane, such that two of its sides are lying on the axes. If an electric field $\mathbf{E} = E_0 x\hat{\mathbf{k}}$ is applied on the square, the flux passing through the square is

(a) $E_0 a^3$ (b) $\frac{E_0 a^3}{2}$ (c) $\frac{E_0 a^3}{3}$ (d) $\frac{E_0 a^2}{2}$

2 A $+q_1$ charge is at centre of an imaginary spherical Gaussian surface S and $-q_1$ charge is placed nearby this $+q_1$ charge inside S. A charge $+q_2$ is located outside this Gaussian surface. Then, electric field on Gaussian surface will be

(a) due to $-q_1$ and q_2 (b) uniform
(c) due to all charges (d) zero

3 Electric charges are distributed in a small volume. The flux of the electric field through a spherical surface of radius 20 cm surrounding the total charge is 50 V-m. The flux over a concentric sphere of radius 40 cm will be

(a) 50 V-m (b) 75 V-m
(c) 100 V-m (d) 200 V-m

4 If the electric flux entering and leaving a closed surface are respectively, of magnitude ϕ_1 and ϕ_2, then the electric charge inside the surface will be

(a) $\frac{\phi_2 - \phi_1}{\varepsilon_0}$ (b) $(\phi_1 - \phi_2)\varepsilon_0$
(c) $\varepsilon_0(\phi_2 - \phi_1)$ (d) $\varepsilon_0(\phi_2 + \phi_1)$

5 An electric dipole is placed at the centre of a sphere. Mark the correct option.

(a) The electric field is zero at every point of the sphere.
(b) The flux of the electric field through the sphere is non-zero.
(c) The electric field is zero on a circle on the sphere.
(d) The electric field is not zero anywhere on the sphere.

6 Which of the following is false for a closed Gaussian surface?

(a) If the electric field is zero everywhere on the surface, then there can be no net charge enclosed by the surface.
(b) If the total electric flux through the surface is zero, then the total charge enclosed by the surface is zero.
(c) If the electric field is zero everywhere on the surface, then the total electric flux through the surface is zero.
(d) If the total electric flux through the surface is zero, then the electric field must be zero everywhere on the surface.

7 A point charge $+Q$ is positioned at the centre of the base of a square pyramid as shown. The flux through one of the four identical upper faces of the pyramid is

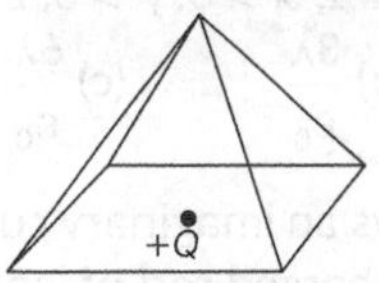

(a) $\frac{Q}{16\varepsilon_0}$ (b) $\frac{Q}{4\varepsilon_0}$
(c) $\frac{Q}{8\varepsilon_0}$ (d) None of these

8 A point charge q is placed at the corner of an equilateral prism. Then, the electric flux through the prism is

(a) $\frac{q}{8\varepsilon_0}$ (b) $\frac{q}{6\varepsilon_0}$ (c) $\frac{q}{12\varepsilon_0}$ (d) $\frac{q}{24\varepsilon_0}$

9 Four point charges q, $2q$, $3q$ and $4q$ are placed at the centre of the cube, at the mid-point of the edge, at the centre of the top face and at the corner of the cube, respectively as shown in figure. The total flux passing through the cube is

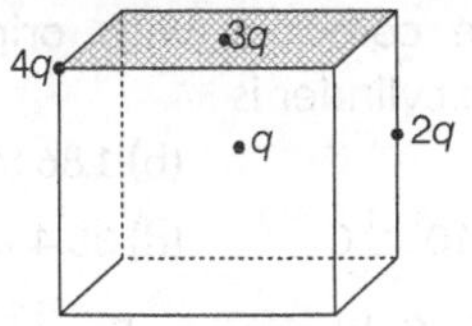

(a) $\frac{3q}{2\varepsilon_0}$ (b) $\frac{7q}{2\varepsilon_0}$ (c) $\frac{11q}{4\varepsilon_0}$ (d) $\frac{13q}{4\varepsilon_0}$

10 Eight point charges (can be assumed as uniformly charged small spheres and their centres at the corner of the cube) having value q each are fixed at vertices of a cube. The electric flux through square surface $ABCD$ of the cube is

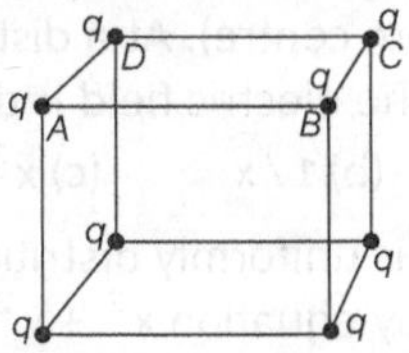

(a) $\frac{q}{24\varepsilon_0}$ (b) $\frac{q}{12\varepsilon_0}$ (c) $\frac{q}{6\varepsilon_0}$ (d) $\frac{q}{8\varepsilon_0}$

11 A long wire with a charge of λ per unit length passes through an imaginary cube of edge a. The maximum flux of the electric field through the cube will be

(a) $\frac{\lambda a}{\varepsilon_0}$ (b) $\frac{\sqrt{2}\lambda a}{\varepsilon_0}$ (c) $\frac{6\lambda a^2}{\varepsilon_0}$ (d) $\frac{\sqrt{3}\lambda a}{\varepsilon_0}$

12 Three uniformly charged wires with linear charge density λ are placed along X, Y and Z-axes, respectively. What is flux of electric field through Gaussian surface given by $x^2 + y^2 + z^2 = 1$; $x > 0; y > 0; z > 0$?

(a) $\frac{3\lambda}{2\varepsilon_0}$ (b) $\frac{3\lambda}{\varepsilon_0}$ (c) $\frac{6\lambda}{\varepsilon_0}$ (d) $\frac{3\lambda}{4\varepsilon_0}$

13 Figure (i) shows an imaginary cube of edge length L. An uniformly charged rod of length $2L$ moves towards left at a small but constant speed v. At $t = 0$, the left end of the rod just touches the centre of the face of the cube opposite to it. Which of the graphs shown in Fig. (ii) represents the flux of the electric field through the cube as the rod goes through it?

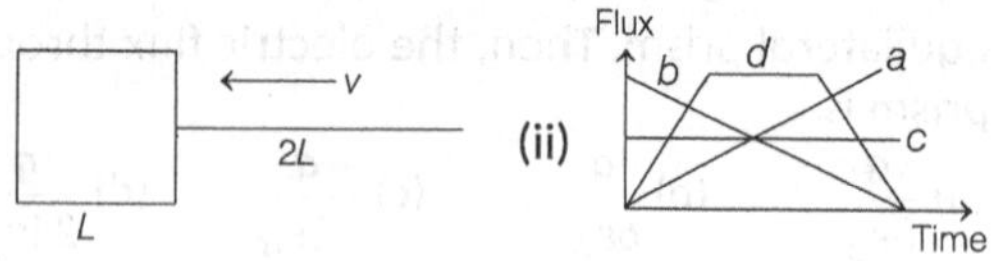

(a) a (b) b (c) c (d) d

14 The electric field in a region is given by $\mathbf{E} = 200\hat{\mathbf{i}}$ N/C for $x > 0$ and $-200\ \hat{\mathbf{i}}$ N/C for $x < 0$. A closed cylinder of length 2 m and cross-section area $10^2\ m^2$ is kept in such a way that the axis of cylinder is along X-axis and its centre coincides with origin. The total charge inside the cylinder is

(a) zero (b) 1.86×10^{-5} C
(c) 1.77×10^{-11} C (d) 35.4×10^{-8} C

15 An electric field given by $\mathbf{E} = 4\hat{\mathbf{i}} - 3(y^2 + 2)\hat{\mathbf{j}}$ passes through Gaussian cube of side 1 m placed at origin, such that its three sides represent X, Y and Z-axes. The magnitude of net charge enclosed within the cube is

(a) $4\varepsilon_0$ (b) $3\varepsilon_0$ (c) $5\varepsilon_0$ (d) zero

16 A solid sphere of radius R has a volume charge density $\rho = \rho_0 r^2$ (where, ρ_0 is a constant and r is the distance from centre). At a distance x from its centre (for $x < R$), the electric field is directly proportional to

(a) $1/x^2$ (b) $1/x$ (c) x^3 (d) x^2

17 1 μC charge is uniformly distributed on a spherical shell given by equation $x^2 + y^2 + z^2 = 25$. What will be intensity of electric field at a point (1, 1, 2)?

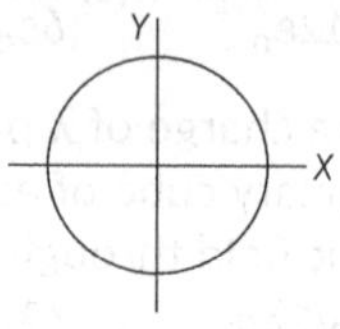

(a) 5 N/C (b) 45 N/C (c) $\frac{5\sqrt{3}}{2}$ N/C (d) Zero

18 If $\oint \mathbf{E} \cdot d\mathbf{S} = 0$ over a surface, then

(a) the electric field inside the surface and on it must be zero
(b) the electric field inside the surface is necessarily uniform
(c) all charges may be inside the surface
(d) the number of flux lines entering the surface must be equal to the number of flux lines leaving it

19 Figure shows four charges q_1, q_2, q_3 and q_4 fixed in space, then the total flux of electric field through a closed surface S, due to all charges q_1, q_2, q_3 and q_4 is

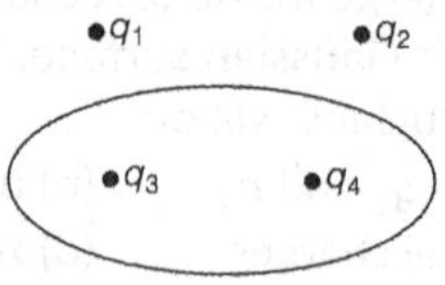

(a) not equal to the total flux through S due to charges q_3 and q_4
(b) equal to the total flux through S due to charges q_3 and q_4
(c) zero, if $q_1 + q_2 = q_3 + q_4$
(d) twice the total flux through S due to charges q_3 and q_4, if $q_1 + q_2 = q_3 + q_4$

20 In a certain region, **E** increases radially as $\mathbf{E} = 90r(-\hat{\mathbf{r}})$. The electric charge contained within a sphere of radius 2 m centred at the origin is

(a) 80 nC (b) – 80 nC
(c) 160 nC (d) – 160 nC

21 An infinite, uniformly charged sheet with surface charge density σ cuts through a spherical Gaussian surface of radius R at a distance x from its centre, as shown in the figure. The electric flux ϕ through the Gaussian surface is

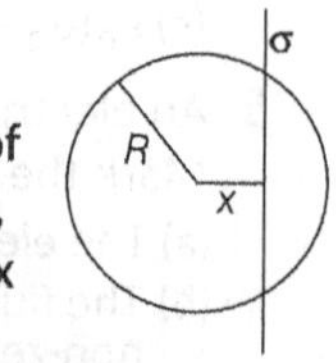

(a) $\frac{\pi R^2 \sigma}{\varepsilon_0}$ (b) $\frac{2\pi(R^2 - x^2)\sigma}{\varepsilon_0}$
(c) $\frac{\pi(R - x)^2 \sigma}{\varepsilon_0}$ (d) $\frac{\pi(R^2 - x^2)\sigma}{\varepsilon_0}$

22 A point charge q is placed at the centre of left circular end of a cylinder of length $l = 4$ cm and radius $R = 3$ cm as shown. Then, the electric flux through the curved surface of the cylinder is

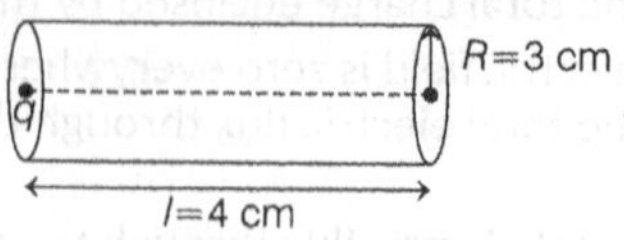

(a) $\frac{q}{5\varepsilon_0}$ (b) $\frac{2q}{5\varepsilon_0}$ (c) $\frac{3q}{5\varepsilon_0}$ (d) $\frac{4q}{5\varepsilon_0}$

23 Inside a uniformly charged infinitely long cylinder of radius R and volume charge density ρ there is a spherical cavity of radius $R/2$. A point P is located at a distance $2R$ from the axis of the cylinder as shown. Then, the electric field strength at the point P is

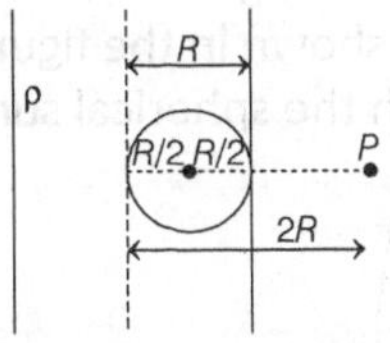

(a) $\frac{23\rho R}{54\varepsilon_0}$ (b) $\frac{23\rho R}{108\,\varepsilon_0}$ (c) $\frac{25\rho R}{54\varepsilon_0}$ (d) $\frac{25\rho R}{108\varepsilon_0}$

24 A point charge placed on the axis of an uniformly charged disc experiences a force F due to the disc. If the charge density on the disc is σ, the electric flux through the disc, due to the point charge will be

(a) $\frac{2\pi F}{\sigma}$ (b) $\frac{F}{2\pi\sigma}$ (c) $\frac{F^2}{\sigma}$ (d) $\frac{F}{\sigma}$

25 For a spherically symmetrical charge distribution, electric field at a distance r from the centre of sphere is $\mathbf{E} = kr^7\hat{\mathbf{r}}$, where k is a constant. What will be the volume charge density at a distance r from the centre of sphere?

(a) $\rho = 9k\varepsilon_0 r^6$ (b) $\rho = 5k\varepsilon_0 r^3$

(c) $\rho = 3k\varepsilon_0 r^4$ (d) $\rho = 9k\varepsilon_0 r^0$

Numerical Value Questions

1 A uniform electric field $E = 500$ N/C passes through a hemispherical surface of radius $R = 1.2$ m as shown in figure. If the net electric flux (in SI units) through the hemispherical surface only is $N\pi$, then find the value of N.

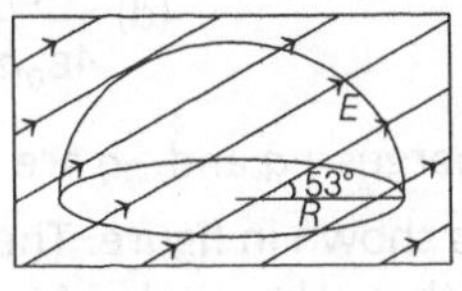

2 A point charge $+q$ is placed on the axis of a closed cylinder of radius R and height $25R/12$ as shown. If electric flux coming out from the curved surface of cylinder is $\frac{xq}{10\varepsilon_0}$, then calculate x.

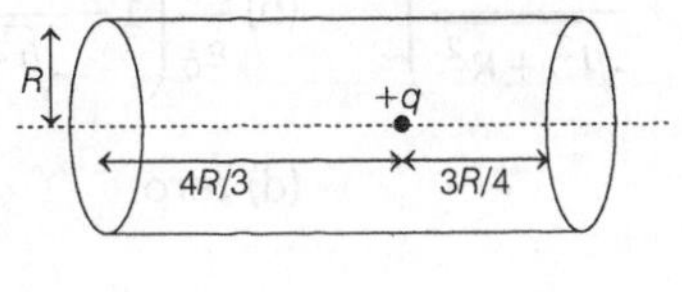

3 The length of each side of a cubical closed surface is l. A charge q is situated on one of the vertices of the cube as shown in figure. The flux passing through shaded faces of the cube is $\frac{q}{n\varepsilon_0}$. Find n.

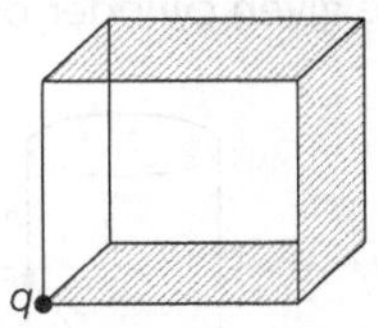

4 A very long uniformly charged thread oriented along the axis of a ring of radius $R = 2$ m rests on its centre with one of the ends. The charge on the thread per unit length is equal to $\lambda = 8.85 \times 10^{-10}$ Cm^{-1}. Find the flux (in SI unit) of the electric field through the ring.

5 Consider a triangular surface whose vertices are three points having coordinate $A(2a, 0, 0)$, $B(0, a, 0)$, $C(0, 0, a)$. If there is an uniform electric field $E_0\hat{\mathbf{i}} + 2E_0\hat{\mathbf{j}} + 3E_0\hat{\mathbf{k}}$, then flux linked to triangular surface ABC is $\frac{E_0 a^2}{2} \times N$. Find the value of N.

6 The volume charge density of a solid sphere of radius 24 m is proportional to the depth below the surface. Find the depth (in m) at which the electric intensity is maximum.

7 A non-uniform electric field in x-direction is increasing uniformly from 2 N/C at $x = 1$ m to 8 N/C at $x = 7$ m. The centre of cube is at $x = 2$ m. If the charge enclosed inside a small cube of side length 10 cm is $\beta \times 10^{-\alpha}$ C, then find the value of $(\alpha + \beta)$.

8 A sphere of radius R has charge density given by $\rho = \rho_0\left(1 - \frac{nr}{3R}\right)$, where ρ_0 is a constant, r is distance from centre of sphere. For a spherical Gaussian surface of radius R centred at the centre of sphere, the flux is zero. Find n.

9 A charge q is placed a distance above a square sheet of size $a \times a$ as shown in figure. If the flux through the square is $\frac{q}{n\varepsilon_0}$, then find n.

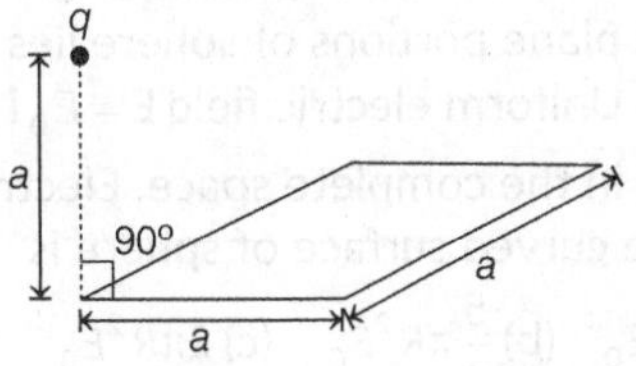

LEVEL 03 JEE Advanced Level

Single Choice Correct Questions

1 Electric field at point P is given by $\mathbf{E} = \mathbf{r}E_0$. The total flux through the given cylinder of radius R and height h is

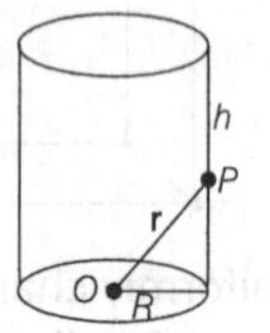

(a) $E_0\pi R^2h$ (b) $2E_0\pi R^2h$ (c) $3E_0\pi R^2h$ (d) $4E_0\pi R^2h$

2 An infinitely long metal cylinder of radius R and surface charge density σ is placed symmetrically with an imaginary surface of the shape of a prism. The length of prism is L and its 3 sides are all equal to $3R$. The flux through the prism is

(a) $\frac{\pi}{3}\frac{RL\sigma}{\varepsilon_0}$ (b) $\frac{\pi}{2}\frac{RL\sigma}{\varepsilon_0}$ (c) $\frac{\pi RL\sigma}{\varepsilon_0}$ (d) $\frac{2\pi RL\sigma}{\varepsilon_0}$

3 A ring of radius R having a linear charge density λ moves towards a solid imaginary sphere of radius $\frac{R}{2}$, so that the centre of ring passes through the centre of sphere. The axis of the ring is perpendicular to the line joining the centres of the ring and the sphere. The maximum flux through the sphere in this process is

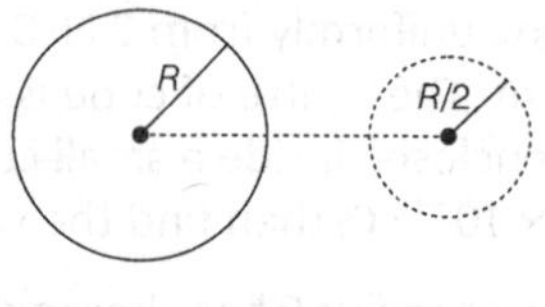

(a) $\frac{\lambda R}{\varepsilon_0}$ (b) $\frac{\lambda R}{2\varepsilon_0}$ (c) $\frac{\lambda\pi R}{4\varepsilon_0}$ (d) $\frac{\lambda\pi R}{3\varepsilon_0}$

4 Consider a hollow sphere of radius R, its quarter part is cut and kept, such that geometrical centre lies at origin as shown in figure. XY-axis lies in plane of paper and Z-axis is perpendicular to the plane of the paper. Sphere is kept in a manner, such that plane portions of sphere lies in ZX and YZ-plane. Uniform electric field $\mathbf{E} = E_0\hat{\mathbf{i}} + 2E_0\hat{\mathbf{j}} + 2E_0\hat{\mathbf{k}}$ (N/C) lies in the complete space. Electric flux coming out of the curved surface of sphere is

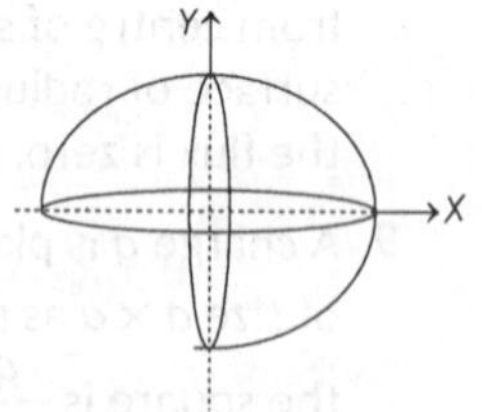

(a) $\frac{3}{2}\pi R^2E_0$ (b) $\frac{5}{2}\pi R^2E_0$ (c) $2\pi R^2E_0$ (d) zero

5 Consider an imaginary hemispherical surface. A semi-infinite wire of charge density λ is kept with one of its ends coinciding with centre of hemisphere and wire is kept along the symmetric axis of the hemisphere as shown in the figure. The electric flux passing through the spherical surface of the hemisphere is

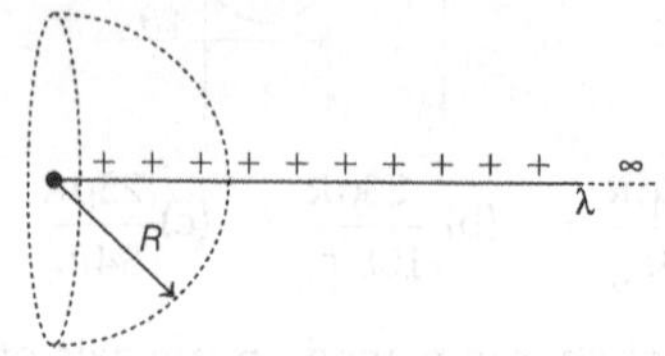

(a) $\frac{\lambda R}{3\varepsilon_0}$ (b) $\frac{\lambda R}{4\varepsilon_0}$

(c) $\frac{3}{4}\frac{\lambda R}{\varepsilon_0}$ (d) $\frac{\lambda R}{2\varepsilon_0}$

6 A charge Q is uniformly distributed over a square plate of side a. Another point charge q is placed at a height $\frac{a}{2}$ from the centre of square plate as shown in diagram. Force acting on the point charge q is

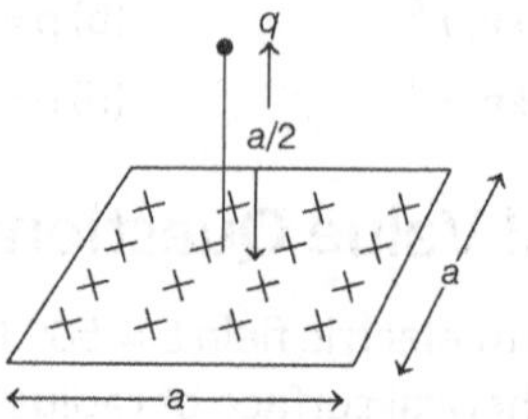

(a) $\frac{Qq}{4\pi\varepsilon_0 a^2}$ (b) $\frac{Qq}{6\pi\varepsilon_0 a^2}$

(c) $\frac{Qq}{6\varepsilon_0 a^2}$ (d) $\frac{Qq}{4\varepsilon_0 a^2}$

7 Two point charges $+q$ and $-q$ are separated by the distance $2l$ as shown in figure. The flux of electric field passing through a circle of radius R will be

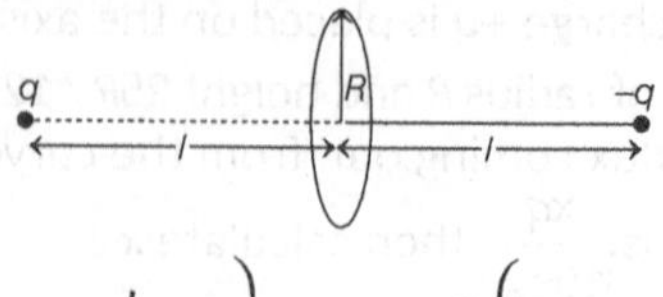

(a) $\frac{q}{\varepsilon_0}\left(1 + \frac{l}{\sqrt{l^2 + R^2}}\right)$ (b) $\frac{q}{\varepsilon_0}\left(1 - \frac{l}{\sqrt{l^2 + R^2}}\right)$

(c) $\frac{q}{\varepsilon_0}$ (d) zero

8 The electric field $\mathbf{E}_1$ at one face of a parallelopiped is uniform over the entire face and is directed out of the face. At the opposite face, the electric field $\mathbf{E}_2$ is also uniform over the entire face and is directed into that face (figure). The two faces in question are inclined at 30.0° from the horizontal, while $\mathbf{E}_1$ and $\mathbf{E}_2$ are both horizontal; $\mathbf{E}_1$ has a magnitude of 2.50×10^4 N/C, and $\mathbf{E}_2$ has a magnitude of 7.00×10^4 N/C. Assuming that, no other electric field lines cross the surfaces of the parallelopiped, the net charge contained within the parallelopiped is

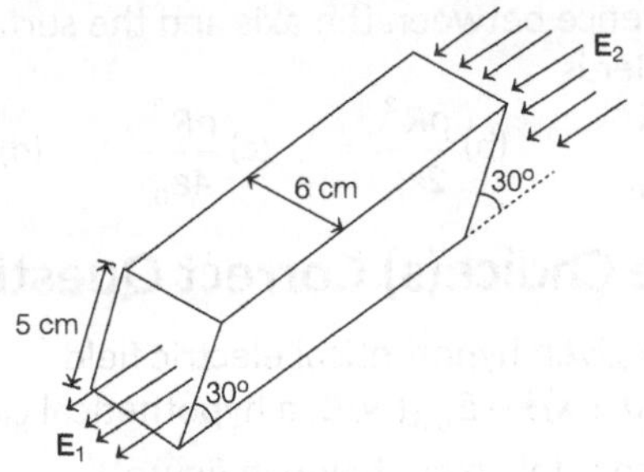

(a) $-67.5\,\varepsilon_0$ (b) $67.5\,\varepsilon_0$ (c) $105\,\varepsilon_0$ (d) $-105\,\varepsilon_0$

9 The volume charge density as a function of distance x from one face inside a unit cube is varying as shown in the figure. Then, the total flux (in SI units) through the cube is ($\rho_0 = 8.85\times10^{-12}$ C/m^3)

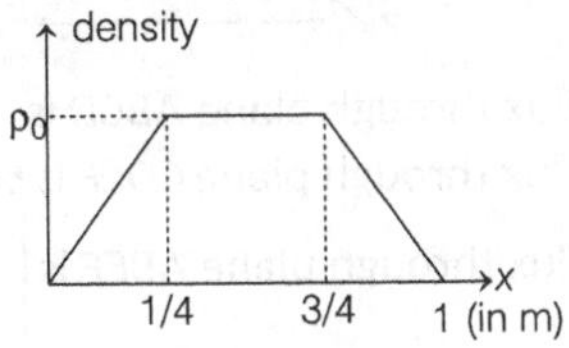

(a) 1/4 (b) 1/2
(c) 3/4 (d) 1

10 A charge $+Q$ is located somewhere inside a vertical cone, such that the depth of the charge from the free surface of the cone is H. It is found that the flux associated with the cone with the curved surface is $\frac{3Q}{5\varepsilon_0}$. If the charge is raised vertically through a height $2H$, then the flux through the curved surface is

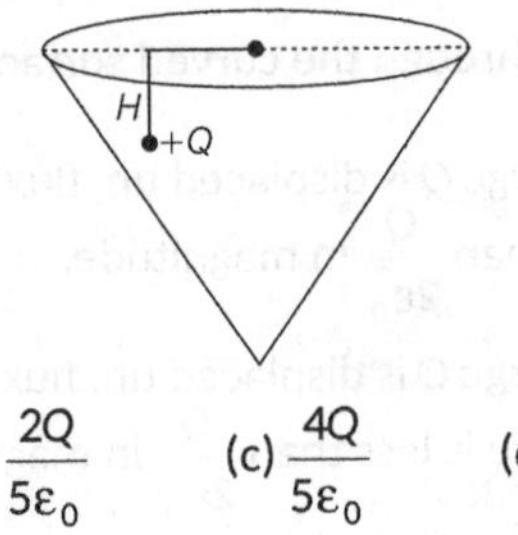

(a) $\frac{3Q}{5\varepsilon_0}$ (b) $\frac{2Q}{5\varepsilon_0}$ (c) $\frac{4Q}{5\varepsilon_0}$ (d) zero

11 Electric potential in a region varies as $V = (1500\text{ kV/m}^2)x^2$. Total electric charge lying inside the cube of side 10 cm shown in figure is (Take, $\varepsilon_0 = 8.9\times10^{-12}\text{ C}^2/\text{N-m}^2$)

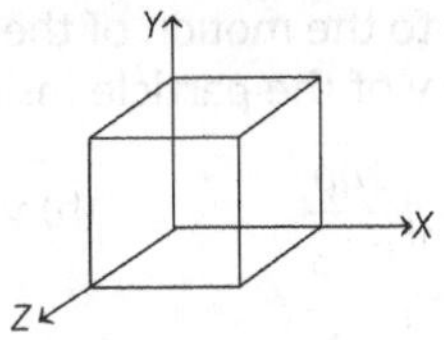

(a) -2.67×10^{-8} C (b) $+2.67\times10^{-8}$ C
(c) -5.24×10^{-8} C (d) $+5.24\times10^{-8}$ C

12 Figure shows two large cylindrical shells having uniform linear charge densities $+\lambda$ and $-\lambda$. Radius of inner cylinder is a and that of outer cylinder is b. A charged particle of mass m, charge q revolves in a circle of radius r. Then, its speed v is (Neglect gravity and assume the radii of both the cylinders to be very small in comparison to their lengths.)

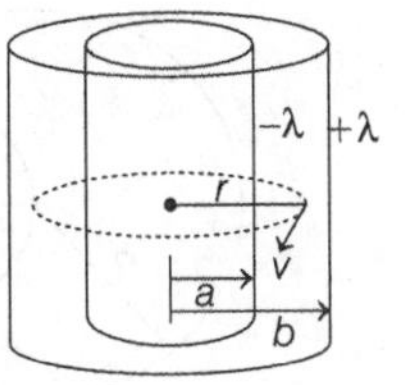

(a) $\sqrt{\frac{\lambda q}{2\pi\varepsilon_0 m}}$ (b) $\sqrt{\frac{2\lambda q}{\pi\varepsilon_0 m}}$ (c) $\sqrt{\frac{\lambda q}{\pi\varepsilon_0 m}}$ (d) $\sqrt{\frac{\lambda q}{4\pi\varepsilon_0 m}}$

13 Consider a solid insulating sphere of radius R with charge density varying as $\rho = \rho_0 r^2$ (ρ_0 is a constant and r is measured from centre). Consider two points A and B at distance x and y, respectively ($x < R$, $y > R$) from the centre. If magnitudes of electric fields at points A and B are equal, then

(a) $x^2 y = R^3$ (b) $x^3 y^2 = R^5$
(c) $x^2 y^3 = R^5$ (d) $\frac{x^4}{y} = R^5$

14 A system consists of a uniformly charged sphere of radius R and a surrounding medium filled by a charge with the volume density $\rho = \frac{\alpha}{r}$, where α is a positive constant and r is the distance from the centre of the sphere ($r > R$). The charge of the sphere for which the electric field intensity E outside the sphere is independent of R is

(a) $\frac{\alpha}{2\varepsilon_0}$ (b) $\frac{2}{\alpha\varepsilon_0}$
(c) $2\pi\alpha R^2$ (d) None of these

15 A large insulating thick sheet of thickness $2d$ carries a uniform charge per unit volume ρ. A particle of mass m, carrying a charge q having a sign opposite to that of the sheet, is released from the surface of the sheet. The sheet does not offer any mechanical resistance to the motion of the particle. The oscillation frequency ν of the particle inside the sheet is

(a) $\nu = \frac{1}{4\pi}\sqrt{\frac{2q\rho}{m\varepsilon_0}}$ (b) $\nu = \frac{1}{2\pi}\sqrt{\frac{2q\rho}{m\varepsilon_0}}$

(c) $\nu = \frac{1}{4\pi}\sqrt{\frac{q\rho}{m\varepsilon_0}}$ (d) $\nu = \frac{1}{2\pi}\sqrt{\frac{q\rho}{m\varepsilon_0}}$

16 An infinite long cylinder of radius R has a cylindrical cavity of radius $R/2$ just touching its surface. The region inside the cylinder is filled with uniform charge density ρ except in the cavity. A charge particle of charge q and mass m is thrown from point A in the cavity. AB is perpendicular to the diameter of the cavity passing through the axis of the cylinder. The minimum velocity u required at A for it to reach point B is

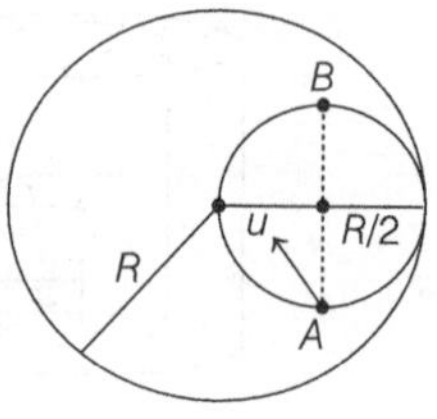

(a) $\sqrt{\frac{q\rho R^2}{4\varepsilon_0 m}}$ (b) $\sqrt{\frac{q\rho R^2}{2\varepsilon_0 m}}$

(c) $\sqrt{\frac{2q\rho R^2}{\varepsilon_0 m}}$ (d) $\sqrt{\frac{4q\rho R^2}{\varepsilon_0 m}}$

17 Two charges $+q_1$ and $-q_2$ are placed at A and B, respectively. A line of force emanates from q_1 at angle α with line AB and it terminates at an angle β as shown, then β is

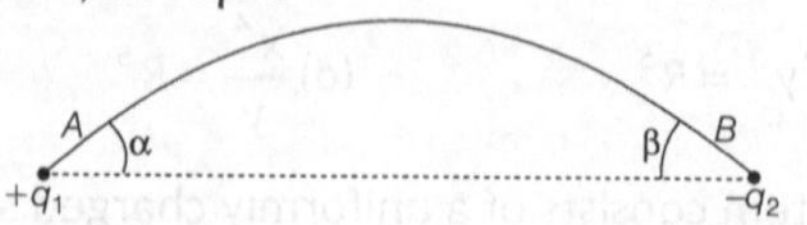

(a) $\sin^{-1}\left(\sqrt{\frac{q_1}{q_2}}\sin\frac{\alpha}{2}\right)$ (b) $2\sin^{-1}\left(\sqrt{\frac{q_1}{q_2}}\sin\alpha\right)$

(c) $\sin^{-1}\left(\sqrt{\frac{q_2}{q_1}}\sin\frac{\alpha}{2}\right)$ (d) $2\sin^{-1}\left(\sqrt{\frac{q_1}{q_2}}\sin\frac{\alpha}{2}\right)$

18 A cylindrical portion of radius r is removed from a solid sphere of radius R and uniform volume charge density ρ in such a way that the axis of the hollow cylinder coincides with one of the diameters of the sphere. (r is negligible compared to R). Then, the electric field intensity at point A is

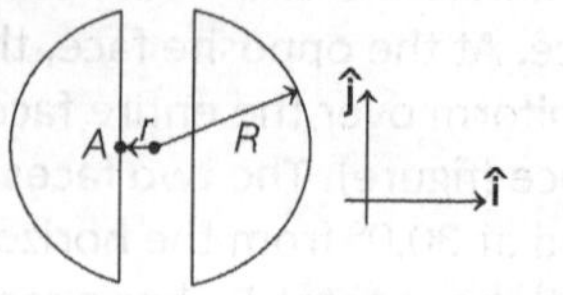

(a) $\frac{\rho r}{3\varepsilon_0}\hat{\mathbf{i}}$ (b) $-\frac{\rho r}{3\varepsilon_0}\hat{\mathbf{i}}$ (c) $\frac{\rho r}{6\varepsilon_0}\hat{\mathbf{i}}$ (d) $-\frac{\rho r}{6\varepsilon_0}\hat{\mathbf{i}}$

19 A long solid non-conducting cylinder of radius R has a uniform volume charge density ρ. The potential difference between the axis and the surface of the cylinder is

(a) $\frac{\rho R^2}{\varepsilon_0}$ (b) $\frac{\rho R^2}{2\varepsilon_0}$ (c) $\frac{\rho R^2}{4\varepsilon_0}$ (d) $\frac{2\rho R^2}{\varepsilon_0}$

Multiple Choice(s) Correct Questions

1 In the given hypothetical electric field $\mathbf{E} = [(d + x)\hat{\mathbf{i}} - E_0\hat{\mathbf{j}}]$ N/C, a hypothetical closed surface is taken as shown in figure.

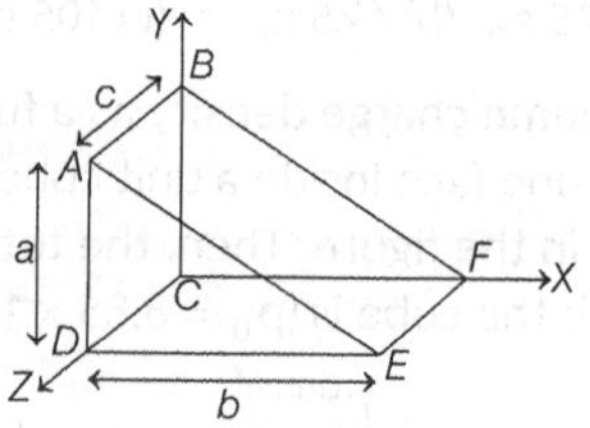

(a) Net flux through plane $ABCD$ is $-acd$ unit.

(b) Net flux through plane $CDEF$ is bcE_0 unit.

(c) Net flux through plane $ABEF$ is $\left[-bcE_0 + acd + \frac{acb}{2}\right]$ unit.

(d) Net charge enclosed by the closed surface is $abc\varepsilon_0$ unit.

2 A particle with charge Q is located immediately above the centre of the flat face of a hemisphere of radius R as shown in figure. Choose the correct statement(s).

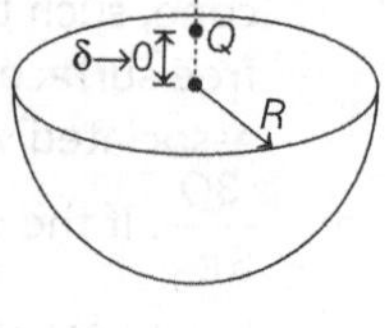

(a) Flux through the flat surface is $\frac{Q}{2\varepsilon_0}$

(b) Flux through the curved surface is $\frac{Q}{2\varepsilon_0}$.

(c) If charge Q is displaced up, flux through flat surface is less than $\frac{Q}{2\varepsilon_0}$ in magnitude.

(d) If charge Q is displaced up, flux through curved surface is less than $\frac{Q}{2\varepsilon_0}$ in magnitude.

3 A cuboid of dimension $[a \times a \times b]$ is shown in figure. Charge q is placed at the centre of edge having length b. If flux through face $ABCD$ is $\frac{q}{32\,\varepsilon_0}$, then select the correct statement(s).

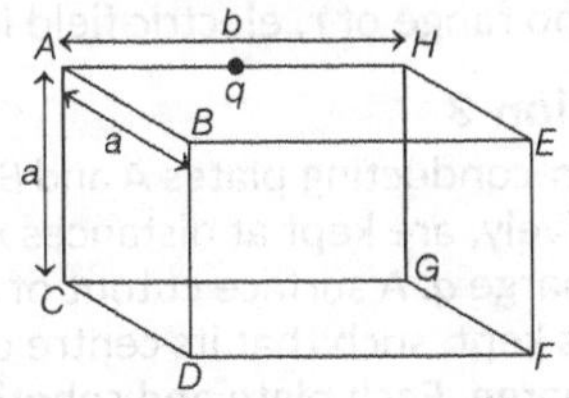

(a) Flux through the entire cuboid is $\frac{q}{4\varepsilon_0}$.

(b) Flux through the face $ABEH$ is zero.

(c) Flux through the face '$BEFD$' is $\frac{3q}{32\varepsilon_0}$.

(d) Flux through the face $BEFD$ is $\frac{q}{16\varepsilon_0}$.

4 Consider an infinite long wire with charge density as $\lambda = \lambda_0 + \alpha x^n$, kept along X-axis. A cube of side a is moved from 0 to $+\infty$ as shown in figure. Second figure shows the variation of flux through the cube. Choose the correct statement(s). (λ_0 and α are positive constants.)

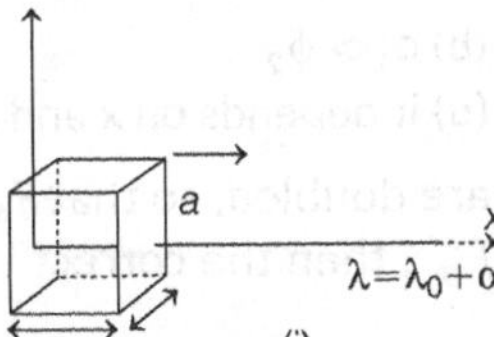

(i)

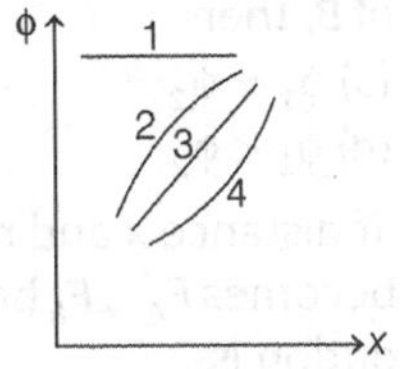

(ii)

(a) For $n = 0$ graph is (1) (b) For $n = 1$ graph is (3)

(c) For $n = 1$ graph is (4) (d) For $n = 0$ graph is (2)

5 A Gaussian surface

(a) must not pass through any discrete charge

(b) must pass through any material medium, whether conducting or non-conducting

(c) may pass through a continuous charge distribution

(d) may pass through a region, where no material medium is present

6 In the statement of Gauss's law, $\oint \mathbf{E}\cdot d\mathbf{s} = \frac{q_{\text{enclosed}}}{\varepsilon_0}$.

Select the correct alternative(s).

(a) The value of $\oint \mathbf{E}\cdot d\mathbf{s}$ does not depend on the shape of gaussian surface, if it encloses same charge.

(b) The electric field **E** also includes the contribution of charges outside the gaussian surface.

(c) If charge is moved inside the gaussian surface, $\mathbf{E}\cdot d\mathbf{s}$ at any point remains constant.

(d) If charge is moved inside the gaussian surface, electric field at every point on surface may change but $\oint \mathbf{E}\cdot d\mathbf{s}$ remains unchanged.

7 Consider a gaussian spherical surface, covering a dipole of charge q and $-q$, then

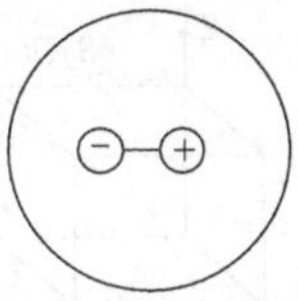

(a) $q_{\text{enclosed}} = 0$ (Net charge enclosed by the spherical surface)

(b) $\phi_{\text{net}} = 0$ (Net flux coming out the spherical surface)

(c) $E = 0$ at all points on the spherical surface

(d) $\oint \mathbf{E}\cdot d\mathbf{s} = 0$ (Surface integral of **E** over the spherical surface)

8 A spherical volume centred at the origin of coordinates with radius a, has a volume charge density $\rho(r) = +\frac{Q}{a}\left(\frac{1}{r^2}\right)$. The electric field

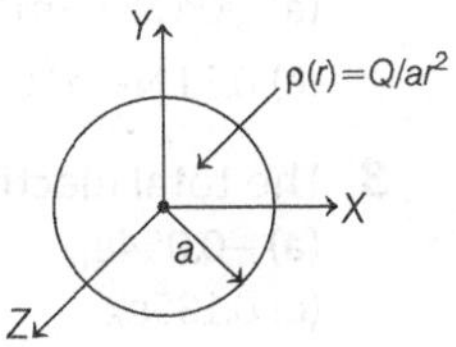

(a) at $r = \frac{a}{2}, E = \frac{2Q}{a^2\varepsilon_0}$ (b) at $r = a, E = \frac{Q}{a^2\varepsilon_0}$

(c) at $r = 2a, E = \frac{Q}{2a^2\varepsilon_0}$ (d) at $r = 4a, E = \frac{Q}{16a^2\varepsilon_0}$

9 A non-conducting rod AB of length $\sqrt{3}R$ has uniformly distributed charge of linear charge density λ. A non-conducting ring has uniformly distributed charge Q. Point A is the centre of ring and line AB is the axis of ring, perpendicular to plane of ring. Choose the correct statement(s).

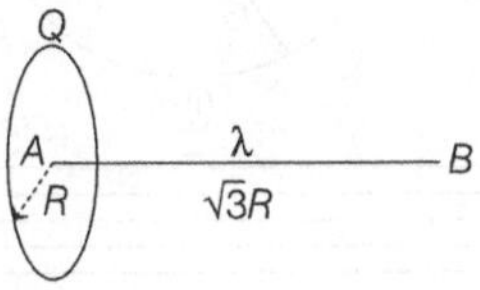

(a) The net electrostatic force on the ring due to charge on the rod is $\frac{Q\lambda}{8\pi\varepsilon_0 R}$.

(b) The net electrostatic force on the ring due to charge on the rod is $\frac{Q\lambda}{4\pi\varepsilon_0 R}$.

(c) The electrostatic flux through ring is $\frac{\lambda R}{\varepsilon_0}(\sqrt{3} - 1)$.

(d) The electrostatic flux through ring is $\frac{\lambda R}{2\varepsilon_0}(\sqrt{3} - 1)$.

Comprehension Based Questions

Comprehension-1

A cube has side of length, $L = 0.3$ m. It is placed with one corner at origin as shown in figure. The electric field is not uniform but is given by
$\mathbf{E} = (-5\text{NC}^{-1})x\hat{\mathbf{i}} + (3\text{NC}^{-1})z\hat{\mathbf{k}}$

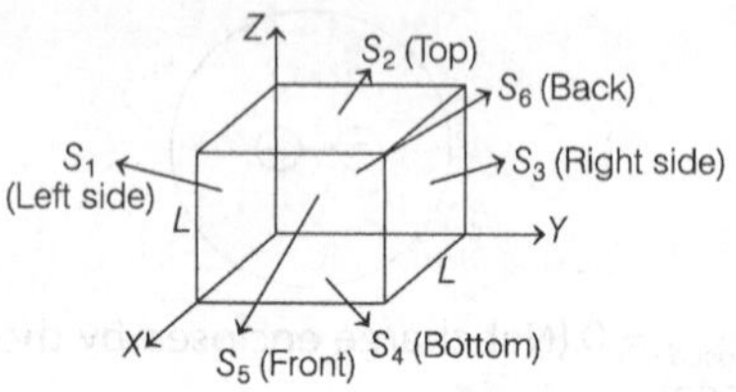

1 Which of the surfaces have zero flux?
(a) S_2, S_4 and S_5 (b) S_1, S_3, S_4 and S_6
(c) S_1, S_2 and S_3 (d) S_2, S_3 and S_4

2 The flux passing through the surface S_5 will be
(a) -0.135 N-m^{2}C^{-1} (b) -0.054 N-m^{2}C^{-1}
(c) 0.81 N-m^{2}C^{-1} (d) 0.054 N-m^{2}C^{-1}

3 The total electric charge inside the cube is
(a) $-0.054\varepsilon_0$ (b) $0.081\varepsilon_0$
(c) $0.135\varepsilon_0$ (d) $0.054\varepsilon_0$

Comprehension-2

A charged particle is suspended at the centre of two thin concentric spherical charged shells, made of non-conducting material. Figure (i) shows cross-section of the arrangement. Figure (ii) gives the net flux ϕ through a Gaussian sphere centred on the particle, as a function of the radius r of the sphere.

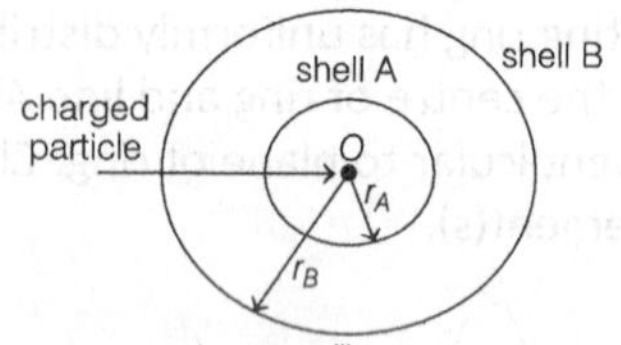

(i)

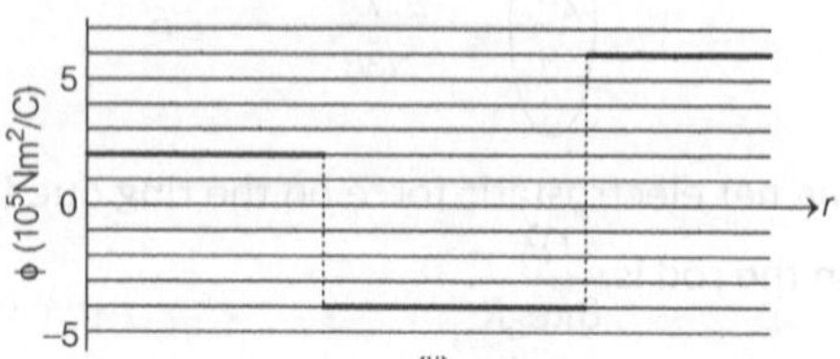

(ii)

4 What is the charge on the central particle?
(a) 0.2 μC (b) 2 μC (c) 1.77 μC (d) 3.4 μC

5 What is the charge on shell A?
(a) 5.31 μC (b) − 5.31 μC
(c) − 3.54 μC (d) − 1.77 μC

6 In which range of the values of r is the electric field zero?
(a) 0 to r_A
(b) r_A to r_B
(c) For $r > r_B$
(d) For no range of r, electric field is zero

Comprehension-3

Two non-conducting plates A and B of radii $2R$ and $4R$ respectively, are kept at distances x and $2x$ from the point charge q. A surface cutout of a non-conducting shell C is kept, such that its centre coincides with the point charge. Each plate and spherical surface carries surface charge density σ.

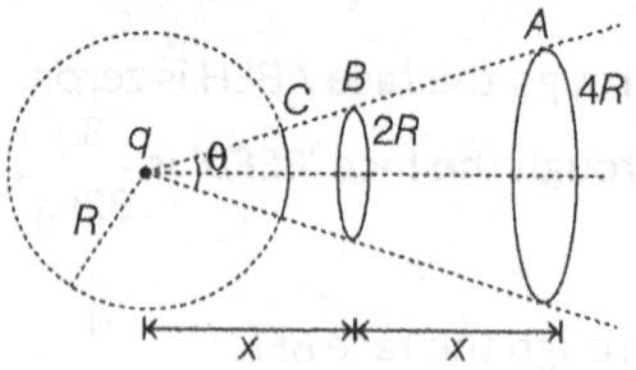

7 If F_A, F_B and F_C be the forces on plate A, plate B and spherical surface C due to charge q respectively, then
(a) $F_A = F_B = F_C$ (b) $F_C < F_B < F_A$
(c) $F_C > F_B > F_A$ (d) $F_A = F_B > F_C$

8 If ϕ_1 is flux through surface of B due to electric field of A and ϕ_2 be the flux through A due to electric field of B, then
(a) $\phi_1 = \phi_2$ (b) $\phi_1 > \phi_2$
(d) $\phi_1 < \phi_2$ (d) it depends on x and R

9 If distance x and radius R are doubled, so that F_A becomes F_A', F_B becomes F_B', then the correct option is
(a) $F_B > F_B'$ (b) $F_B' > F_B$
(c) $F_A' > F_B'$ (d) None of these

Comprehension-4

Electric field in a region is given by following equation $\mathbf{E} = \dfrac{K(\mathbf{r} - \mathbf{r_0})}{|\mathbf{r} - \mathbf{r_0}|^2}$, where $\mathbf{r} = x\hat{\mathbf{i}} + y\hat{\mathbf{j}}$ and $\mathbf{r_0} = \hat{\mathbf{i}} + \hat{\mathbf{j}}$ and an imaginary cube is made as shown in the diagram.

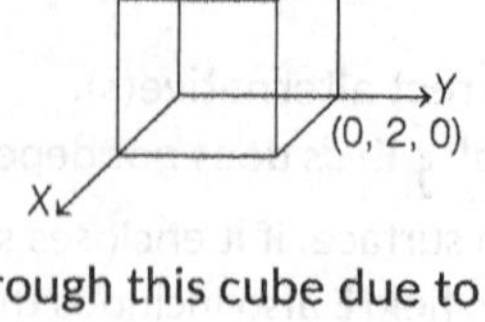

10 Total flux through this cube due to the given electric field is
(a) $4\pi K$ (b) $6\pi K$ (c) $16K$ (d) $8K$

11 Total charge encloses in this imaginary shown cube is

(a) $4K\pi\varepsilon_0$ (b) $8K\pi\varepsilon_0$

(c) $6K\pi\varepsilon_0$ (d) $2K\pi\varepsilon_0$

12 If $\mathbf{r}_0 = (2\hat{\mathbf{i}} + 2\hat{\mathbf{j}})$, then the value of total flux through the walls of the shown cube is

(a) $2K\pi$ (b) $K\pi$

(c) $4K\pi$ (d) $4K$

Match the Columns Questions

1 Match the Column I with Column II.

Column-I	Column-II
(a) 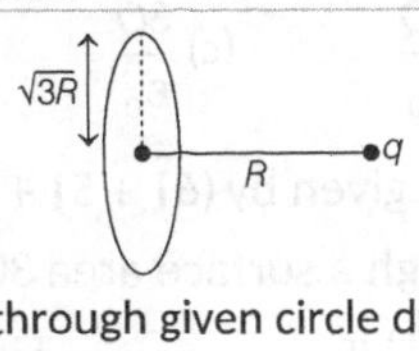 Flux through given circle due to point charge q	(p) 0
(b) 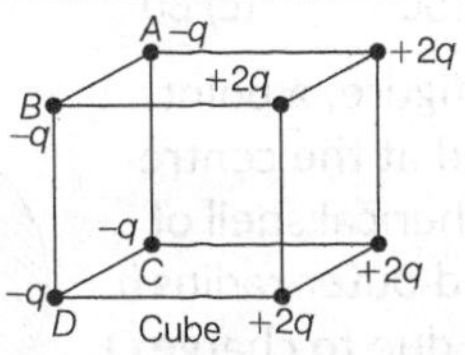 Net flux through surface $ABCD$	(q) $\dfrac{q}{2\varepsilon_0}$
(c) 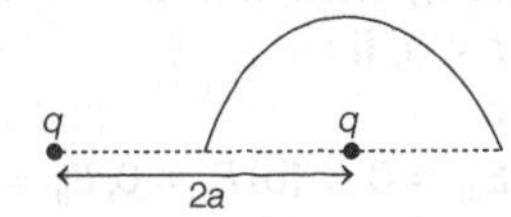 Net flux through given hemispherical surface	(r) $\dfrac{q}{3\varepsilon_0}$
(d) 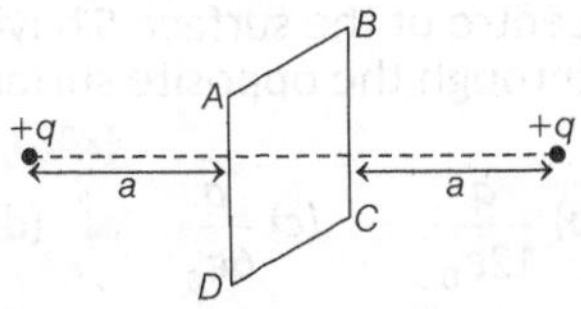 Net flux through surface $ABCD$	(s) $\dfrac{q}{4\varepsilon_0}$

2 Four particles having charges Q_1, Q_2, Q_3 and Q_4 are fixed at vertices of a square A, B, C and D as shown in figure. Let O be the centre of square and a dotted gaussian (closed) surface encloses charges Q_2 and Q_3 as shown. Match each statement in Column-I with the corresponding correct condition(s) given in Column-II.

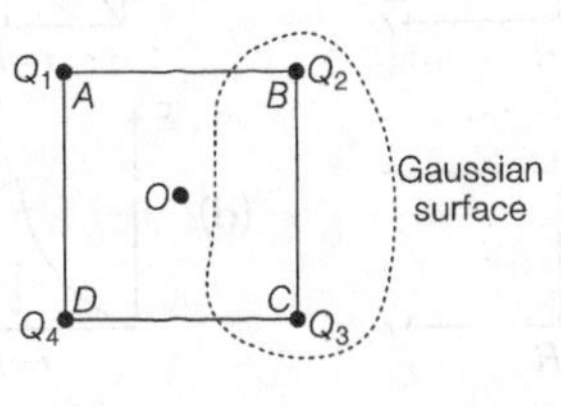

Column-I	Column-II
(a) The electric field at O is zero, if	(p) $Q_1 = Q_3 = +10\,\mu C$ and $Q_2 = Q_4 = -10\,\mu C$
(b) The potential at O is zero, if	(q) $Q_1 = Q_2 = +10\,\mu C$ and $Q_3 = Q_4 = -10\,\mu C$
(c) The flux through shown Gaussian surface is zero, if	(r) $Q_1 = Q_2 = +20\,\mu C$ and $Q_3 = Q_4 = -10\,\mu C$
(d) The electric field at O is parallel to **BC**, if	(s) $Q_1 = +10\,\mu C, Q_2 = +40\,\mu C$, $Q_3 = -40\,\mu C$ and $Q_4 = -10\,\mu C$
	(t) $Q_1 = Q_3 = +10\,\mu C$ and $Q_2 = Q_4 = -5\,\mu C$

3 Graph between electric potential and the X-coordinate is given and the electric field is along the X-axis. Then, find total charge in various cubes placed with one edge along positive X-axis.

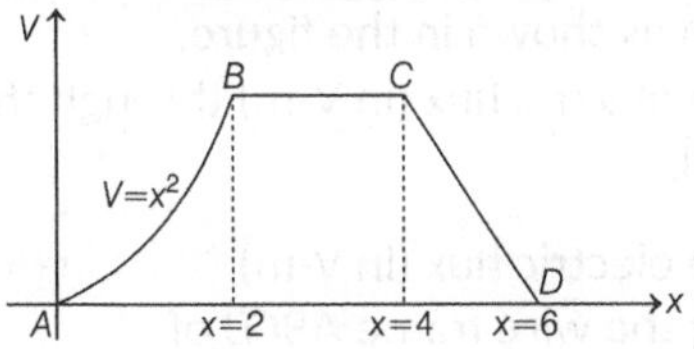

Column-I	Column-II
(a) Cube of 1 m edge with one corner at origin.	(p) Positive
(b) Cube of 1 m edge which lies between $X = 3$ to $X = 4$.	(q) Negative
(c) Cube of 2 m edge placed between the coordinate $X = 4$ to $X = 6$.	(r) Zero
(d) Cube of 6 m edge placed between the coordinate $X = 0$ to $X = 6$.	(s) Magnitude of charge is $2\varepsilon_0$ units.

Numerical Value Questions

1 Find the electrostatic flux (in V-m) through a rectangular area of $\dfrac{7}{47}\,\text{m}^2$ lying in a plane $2x + 3y + 6z = 10$ due to an electric field, $\mathbf{E} = (8\hat{\mathbf{i}} + 6\hat{\mathbf{j}} + 10\hat{\mathbf{k}})$ V/m.

2 A point charge is kept on the axis of circular non-conducting disc. The distance is, such that 1/10th of the total electric flux coming from the charge passes through the disc. By what distance (in cm) should the charge be moved along the axis, so that 1/5th of the total electric flux coming from the charge passes through the disc? The radius of the disc is 30 cm.

3 A point charge $q = 8.85 \times 10^{-9}$ C is placed at (0, d, 0), where $d = 1$ m. An insulating surface $ABCA$ is on the XZ-plane, which is bounded by a quarter circle AB and two equal length straight lines BC and CA as shown in the figure. Electric flux through the surface $ABCA$ in Nm^2/C is (nearest integer).

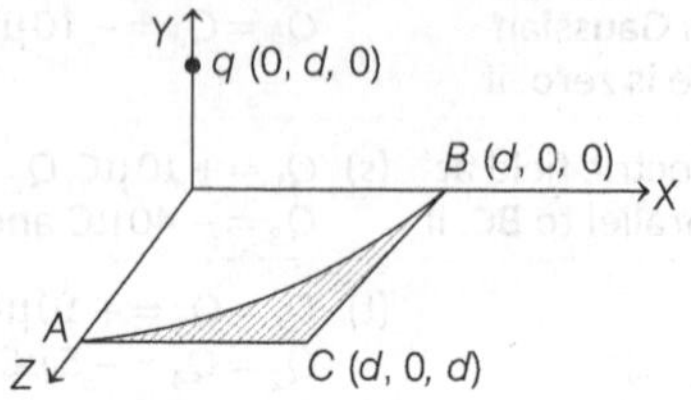

4 A dipole of dipole moment $p = 17.7\text{nC-m}$, is kept at the centre, along the axis of the hemispherical shell of radius $R = 50$ m as shown in the figure.
Find the electric flux (in V-m) through the surface of the shell.

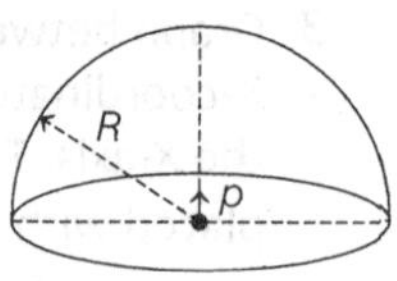

5 Find the electric flux (in V-m) crossing the wire frame $ABCD$ of length $l = 1$ m, width b and whose centre is at a distance, $OP = d\ (= b/2)$ from an infinite line of charge with linear charge density, $\lambda = 8.85 \times 10^{-10}$ C/m.
Consider that the plane of frame is perpendicular to line OP.

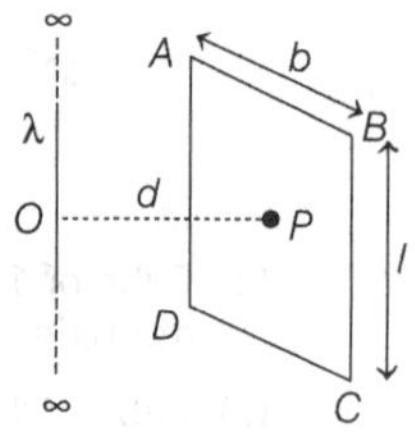

6 An infinitely long solid cylinder of radius R has a uniform charge density ρ. It has a spherical cavity of radius $R/2$ with its centre on the axis of the cylinder(as shown in figure). The magnitude of the electric field at point P, which is at a distance $2R$ from the axis of the cylinder, is given by $\dfrac{23\rho R}{6K\varepsilon_0}$.
The value of K is ....

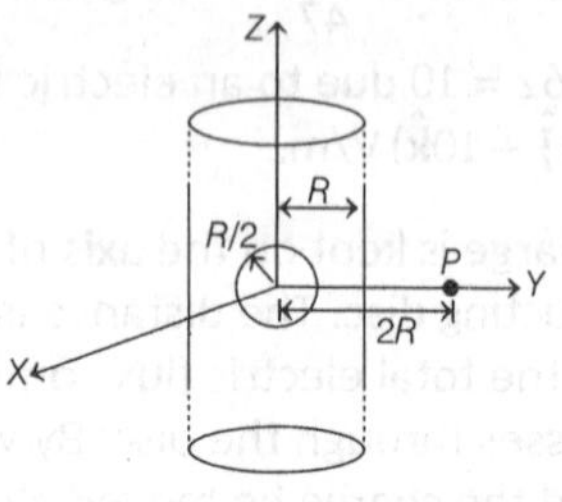

7 The visible portion of a lightning strike is preceded by an invisible stage in which a column of electrons extends downward from a cloud to the ground. Assume the, linear charge density along the column is 1.00×10^{-3} C/m. Treat the column of charge as, if it were straight and infinitely long. The dielectric strength for air is 3.00×10^{6} V/m? What will be the radius (in m) of a visible lightning bolt?

Previous Year's Questions

JEE Main

1 Two charges of $5Q$ and $-2Q$ are situated at the points $(3a, 0)$ and $(-5a, 0)$ respectively. The electric flux through a sphere of radius $4a$ having center at origin is **[2024, 29 Jan Shift-I]**

(a) $\dfrac{7Q}{\varepsilon_0}$ (b) $\dfrac{2Q}{\varepsilon_0}$ (c) $\dfrac{3Q}{\varepsilon_0}$ (d) $\dfrac{5Q}{\varepsilon_0}$

2 An electric field is given by $(6\hat{i} + 5\hat{j} + 3\hat{k})$ N\C. The electric flux through a surface area $30\hat{i}\ \text{m}^2$ lying in YZ-plane (in SI unit) is **[2024, 29 Jan Shift-II]**

(a) 90 (b) 150 (c) 60 (d) 180

3 As shown in the figure, a point charge Q is placed at the centre of conducting spherical shell of inner radius a and outer radius b. The electric field due to charge Q in three different regions I, II and III is given by (I : $r < a$, II : $a < r < b$, III : $r > b$) **[2023, 30 Jan Shift-II]**

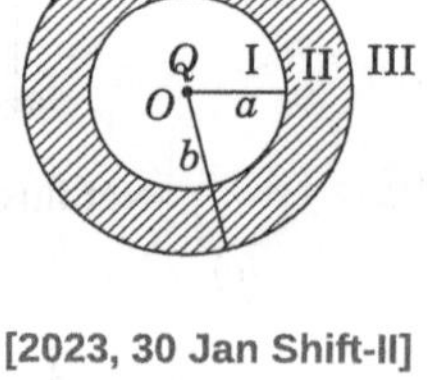

(a) $E_{\text{I}} \neq 0, E_{\text{II}} = 0, E_{\text{III}} = 0$ (b) $E_{\text{I}} = 0, E_{\text{II}} = 0, E_{\text{III}} \neq 0$
(c) $E_{\text{I}} \neq 0, E_{\text{II}} = 0, E_{\text{III}} \neq 0$ (d) $E_{\text{I}} = 0, E_{\text{II}} = 0, E_{\text{III}} = 0$

4 In a cuboid of dimension $2L \times 2L \times L$, a charge q is placed at the centre of the surface S having area of $4L^2$. The flux through the opposite surface to S is given by **[2023, 29 Jan Shift-I]**

(a) $\dfrac{q}{2\varepsilon_0}$ (b) $\dfrac{q}{12\varepsilon_0}$ (c) $\dfrac{q}{6\varepsilon_0}$ (d) $\dfrac{q}{3\varepsilon_0}$

5 Graphical variation of electric field due to a uniformly charged insulating solid sphere of radius R, with distance r from the centre O is represented by: **[2023, 8 April Shift-I]**

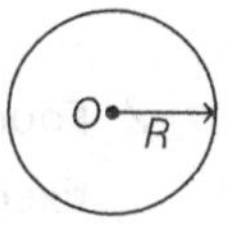

(a)
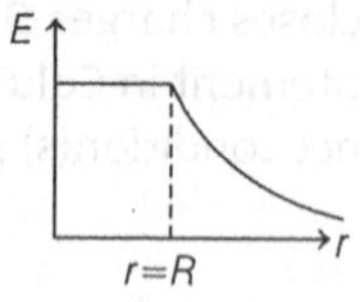

(b)
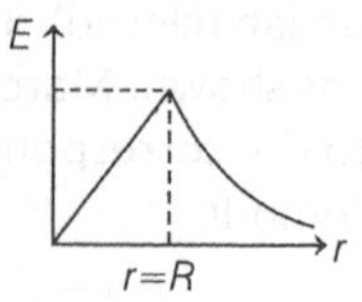

(c)
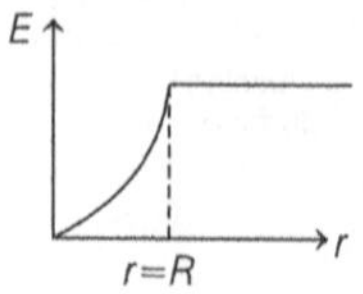

(d)
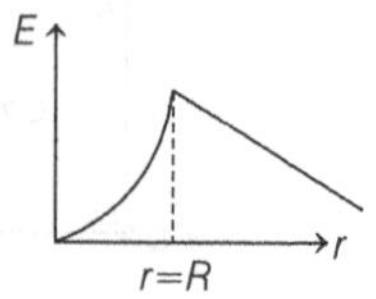

6 A cubical volume is bounded by the surfaces $x = 0$, $x = a, y = 0, y = a, z = 0, z = a$.
The electric field in the region is given by $\mathbf{E} = E_0 x\hat{\mathbf{i}}$. Where, $E_0 = 4 \times 10^4 \text{NC}^{-1}\text{m}^{-1}$. If $a = 2$ cm, the charge contained in the cubical volume is $Q \times 10^{-14}$ C. The value of Q is ....
(Take, $\varepsilon_0 = 9 \times 10^{-12} \text{C}^2/\text{N-m}^2$) **[2023, Feb Shift-II]**

7 As shown in figure, a cuboid lies in a region with electric field $\mathbf{E} = 2x^2\hat{\mathbf{i}} - 4y\hat{\mathbf{j}} + 6\hat{\mathbf{k}}$ N/C. The magnitude of charge within the cuboid is $n\varepsilon_0$C. The value of n is ....
(If dimension of cuboid is $1 \times 2 \times 3 \text{ m}^3$) **[2023, 30 Jan Shift-II]**

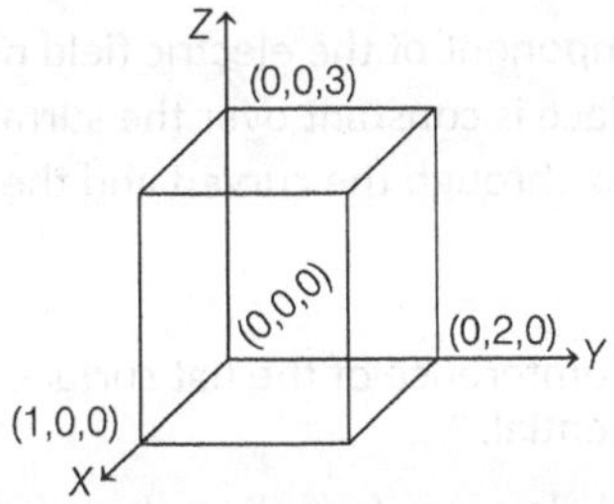

8 Expression for an electric field is given by $\text{E} = 4000x^2\hat{\mathbf{i}}$ V/m. The electric flux through the cube of side 20 cm when placed in electric field (as shown in the figure) is ....V-cm. **[2023, 31 Jan Shift-I]**

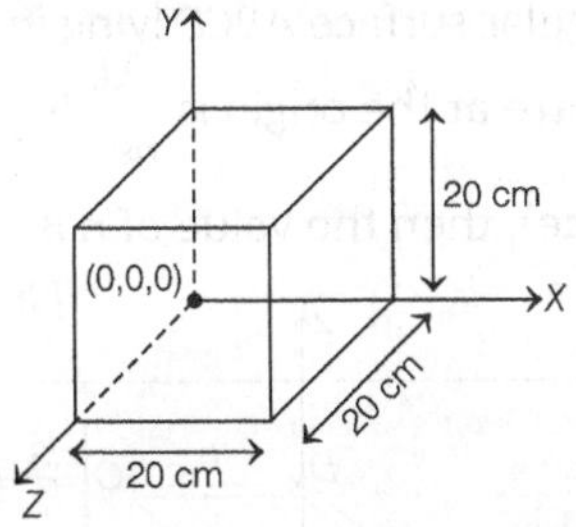

9 In the figure, a very large plane sheet of positive charge is shown. P_1 and P_2 are two points at distance l and $2l$ from the charge distribution. If σ is the surface charge density, then the magnitude of electric fields E_1 and E_2 at P_1 and P_2 respectively, are **[2022, 25 June Shift-I]**

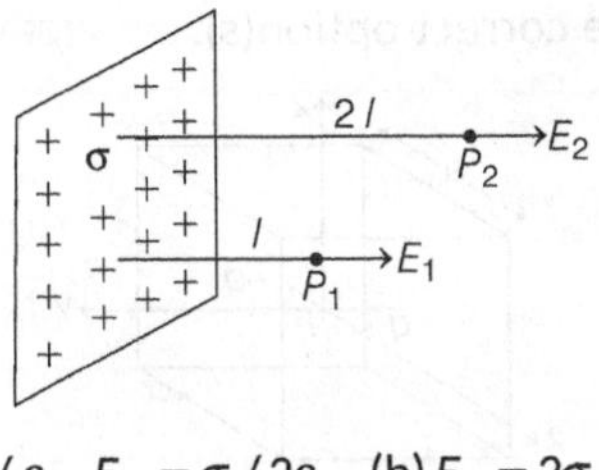

(a) $E_1 = \sigma/\varepsilon_0, E_2 = \sigma/2\varepsilon_0$ (b) $E_1 = 2\sigma/\varepsilon_0, E_2 = \sigma/\varepsilon_0$
(c) $E_1 = E_2 = \sigma/2\varepsilon_0$ (d) $E_1 = E_2 = \sigma/\varepsilon_0$

10 The volume charge density of a sphere of radius 6 m is $2\,\mu\text{C cm}^{-3}$. The number of lines of force per unit surface area coming out from the surface of the sphere is .... $\times 10^{10}$ NC^{-1}.
[Given, permittivity of vacuum, $\varepsilon_0 = 8.85 \times 10^{-12}$ C^2 N^{-1}-m^{-2}]. **[2022, 25 July shift-I]**

11 Given below are two statements, one is labelled as Assertion (A) and the other is labelled as Reason (R).
Assertion (A) If an electric dipole of dipole moment 30×10^{-5} C-m is enclosed by a closed surface, the net flux coming out of the surface will be zero.
Reason (R) Electric dipole consists of two equal and opposite charges.
In the light of the above statements, choose the most appropriate answer from the options given below. **[2021, 12 April Shift-I]**
(a) Both A and R are true and R is the correct explanation of A
(b) A is false but R is true
(c) Both A and R are true but R is not the correct explanation of A
(d) A is true but R is false

12 Given below are two statements:
Statement I An electric dipole is placed at the centre of a hollow sphere. The flux of electric field through the sphere is zero but the electric field is not zero anywhere in the sphere.
Statement II If R is the radius of a solid metallic sphere and Q be the total charge on it. The electric field at any point on the spherical surface of radius $r (< R)$ is zero but the electric flux passing through this closed spherical surface of radius r is not zero.
In the light of the above statements choose the correct answer from the options given below. **[2021, 26 Feb Shift-II]**
(a) Both Statement I and Statement II are true.
(b) Statement I is true but Statement II is false.
(c) Both Statement I and Statement II are false.
(d) Statement I is false but Statement II is true.

13 A charge q is placed at one corner of a cube as shown in figure. The flux of electrostatic field E through the shaded area is **[2021, 25 Feb Shift-II]**

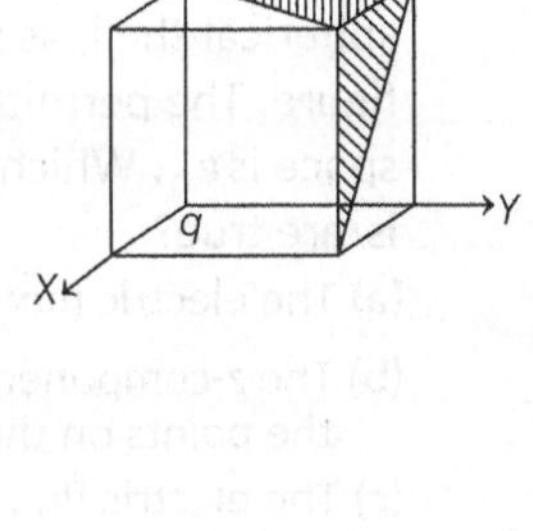

(a) $\frac{q}{48\varepsilon_0}$ (b) $\frac{q}{4\varepsilon_0}$
(c) $\frac{q}{8\varepsilon_0}$ (d) $\frac{q}{24\varepsilon_0}$

14 The total charge enclosed in an incremental volume of 2×10^{-9} m^3 located at the origin is ...... nC, if electric flux density of its field is found as $D = e^{-x} \sin y \hat{i} - e^{-x} \cos y \hat{j} + 2z\hat{k}$ C/m^2. **[2021, 22 July Shift-II]**

15 The electric field in a region is given by $E = \frac{2}{5}E_0 \hat{i} + \frac{3}{5}E_0 \hat{j}$ with $E_0 = 4.0 \times 10^3$ N/C. The flux of this field through a rectangular surface area 0.4 m^2 parallel to the yz-plane is .... N-m^2 C^{-1}. **[2021, 17 March Shift-II]**

JEE Advanced

1 A circular disc of radius R carries surface charge density $\sigma(r) = \sigma_0\left(1 - \frac{r}{R}\right)$, where σ_0 is a constant and r is the distance from the center of the disc. Electric flux through a large spherical surface that encloses the charged disc completely is ϕ_0. Electric flux through another spherical surface of radius $\frac{R}{4}$ and concentric with the disc is ϕ. Then, the ratio $\frac{\phi_0}{\phi}$ is__________. **(2022 Adv.)**

2 A charge q is surrounded by a closed surface consisting of an inverted cone of height h and base radius R, and a hemisphere of radius R as shown in the figure. The electric flux through the conical surface is $\frac{nq}{6\varepsilon_0}$ (in SI units). The value of n is .... **(2022 Adv.)**

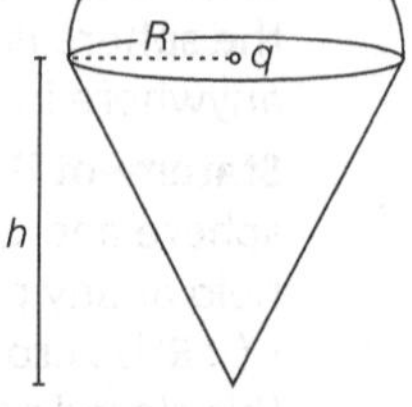

3 An infinitely long thin non-conducting wire is parallel to the Z-axis and carries a uniform line charge density λ. It pierces a thin non-conducting spherical shell of radius R in such a way that the arc PQ subtends an angle 120° at the centre O of the spherical shell, as shown in the figure. The permittivity of free space is ε_0. Which of the following statement(s) is/are true? **[JEE Advanced 2018]**

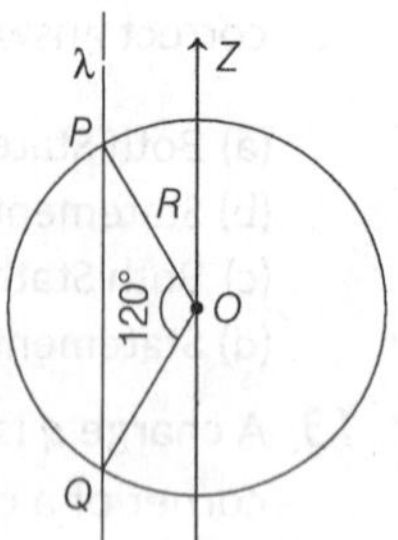

(a) The electric flux through the shell is $\sqrt{3}\, R\lambda / \varepsilon_0$.

(b) The z-component of the electric field is zero at all the points on the surface of the shell.

(c) The electric flux through the shell is $\sqrt{2}\, R\lambda / \varepsilon_0$.

(d) The electric field is normal to the surface of the shell at all points.

4 A point charge $+Q$ is placed just outside an imaginary hemispherical surface of radius R as shown in the figure. Which of the following statement(s) is/are correct? **[JEE Advanced 2017]**

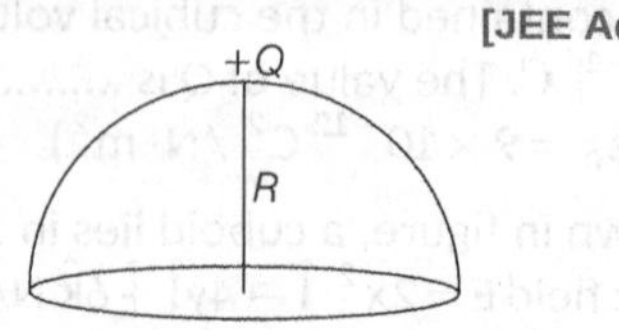

(a) The electric flux passing through the curved surface of the hemisphere is $-\frac{Q}{2\varepsilon_0}\left(1 - \frac{1}{\sqrt{2}}\right)$

(b) The component of the electric field normal to the flat surface is constant over the surface.

(c) Total flux through the curved and the flat surfaces, is $\frac{Q}{\varepsilon_0}$.

(d) The circumference of the flat surface is an equipotential.

5 An infinitely long uniform line charge distribution of charge per unit length λ lies parallel to the y-axis in the yz-plane at $z = \frac{\sqrt{3}}{2}a$ (see figure). If the magnitude of the flux of the electric field through the rectangular surface $ABCD$ lying in the xy-plane with its centre at the origin is $\frac{\lambda L}{n\varepsilon_0}$ (ε_0 = permittivity of free space), then the value of n is .... **[JEE Advanced 2015]**

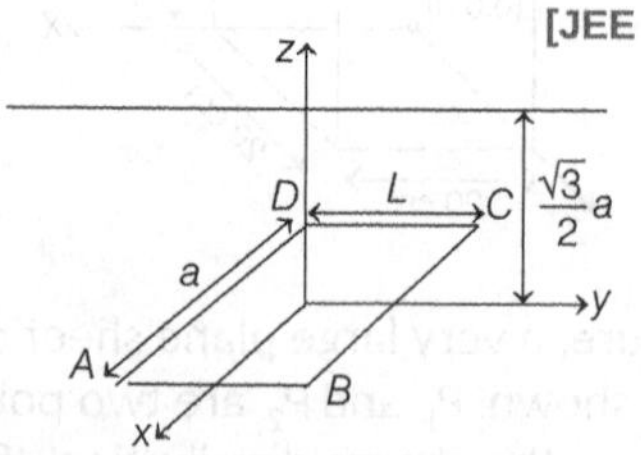

6 A cubical region of side a has its centre at the origin. It encloses three fixed point charges, $-q$ at $(0, -a/4, 0)$, $+3q$ at $(0, 0, 0)$ and $-q$ at $(0, +a/4, 0)$. Choose the correct option(s). **[JEE Advanced 2012]**

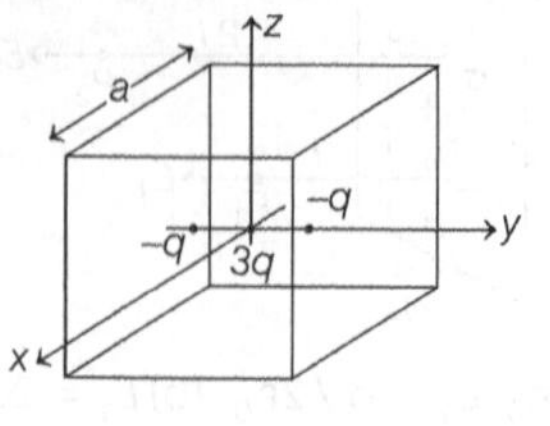

(a) The net electric flux crossing the plane $x = +a/2$ is equal to the net electric flux crossing the plane $x = -a/2$

(b) The net electric flux crossing the plane $y = +a/2$ is more than the net electric flux crossing the plane $y = -a/2$

(c) The net electric flux crossing the entire region is q/ε_0

(d) The net electric flux crossing the plane $z = +a/2$ is equal to the net electric flux crossing the plane $x = +a/2$

Answer Key

Level 1 Starter Level

4.1 Electric Flux

1. 100 V-m 2. (i) 0 (ii) $E\pi R^2$ (iii) $\frac{\sqrt{3}}{2}E\pi R^2$

3. (i) 0 (ii) $E\pi R^2$ (iii) $2E\pi R^2$

4. $\phi_{ABCD} = 64$ V - m, $\phi_{EFGH} = -64$ V - m, $\phi_{ABEF} = 48$ V - m, $\phi_{CDGH} = -48$ V - m, $\phi_{ADEH} = \phi_{BCFG} = 0$

5. $\phi_{ADEF} = -E_0\, ab\sin\theta$, $\phi_{ABCD} = E_0\, ab\sin\theta$, $\phi_{BCEF} = \phi_{ABF} = \phi_{CDE} = 0$

6. (i) ERH (ii) $E\pi R^2$ (iii) $E\cos\theta(HR) + E\sin\theta(\pi R^2)$

4.2 Gauss Law

1. No change in any case 2. 14.25 μC

3.(i) $\frac{q}{2\varepsilon_0}$ (ii) $\frac{q}{2\varepsilon_0}$ (iii) 0 4. $\phi = \frac{Q}{6\varepsilon_0}$ 5. (i) $\frac{q}{8\varepsilon_0}$ (ii) $\frac{q}{24\varepsilon_0}$

6. $4\pi\varepsilon_0 Ba^3$ 7. $q = 2\varepsilon_0$ 8. (i) $\frac{\rho_0 r^2}{4\varepsilon_0}\hat{r}$ (ii) $\frac{\rho_0 R^4}{4\varepsilon_0 r^2}\hat{r}$

9. (i) 0 (ii) $\frac{Q(r^3 - a^3)}{4\pi\varepsilon_0 r^2(b^3 - a^3)}$ (iii) $\frac{Q}{4\pi\varepsilon_0 r^2}$

10. (i) $\frac{\rho x}{2\varepsilon_0}$ (ii) $\frac{\rho R^2}{2\varepsilon_0 x}$ 11. $\frac{q(1-\cos\theta)}{2\varepsilon_0}$

Level 2 JEE Main Level

Single Choice Correct Questions

1. (b)	2. (c)	3. (a)	4. (c)	5. (d)
6. (d)	7. (c)	8. (c)	9. (b)	10. (c)
11. (d)	12. (d)	13. (d)	14. (d)	15. (b)
16. (c)	17. (d)	18. (d)	19. (b)	20. (b)
21. (d)	22. (b)	23. (d)	24. (d)	25. (a)

Numerical Value Questions

1. 576	2. 7	3. 12	4. 100	5. 11
6. 8	7. 23.85	8. 4	9. 24	

Level 3 JEE Advanced Level

Single Choice Correct Questions

1. (c)	2. (c)	3. (d)	4. (a)	5. (d)
6. (c)	7. (b)	8. (a)	9. (c)	10. (b)
11. (a)	12. (a)	13. (b)	14. (c)	15. (d)
16. (a)	17. (d)	18. (c)	19. (c)	

Multiple Choice(s) Correct Questions

1. (abc)	2. (abcd)	3. (abc)	4. (ab)	5. (acd)
6. (abd)	7. (abd)	8. (abd)	9. (ad)	

Comprehension Based Questions

1. (b)	2. (a)	3. (a)	4. (c)	5. (b)
6. (d)	7. (d)	8. (a)	9. (d)	10. (a)
11. (a)	12. (b)			

Match the Columns Questions

1. a → s; b → r; c → q; d → p
2. a → p,t; b → p,q,s; c → p,q,s; d → q,r,s
3. a → q,s; b → r; c → r; d → p

Numerical Value Questions

1. 2	2. 17.5	3. 5	4. 20
5. 25	6. 16	7. 6.00	

Previous Year's Questions

JEE Main

1. (d)	2. (d)	3. (c)	4. (c)	5. (b)
6. (288)	7. (12)	8. (640)	9. (c)	10. (45)
11. (a)	12. (b)	13. (d)	14. (4)	15. (640)

JEE Advanced

1. (6.40)	2. (3)	3. (ab)	4. (ad)	5. (6)
6. (a, c)				

SOLUTIONS

Level 1 Starter Level

4.1 Electric Flux

1. $\mathbf{E} = (3\hat{\mathbf{i}} - 4\hat{\mathbf{j}} + 10\hat{\mathbf{k}})$ V/m

$\mathbf{A} = (10\hat{\mathbf{k}})\text{m}^2$

$\phi = \mathbf{E}\cdot\mathbf{A} = (3\hat{\mathbf{i}} - 4\hat{\mathbf{j}} + 10\hat{\mathbf{k}})\cdot 10\hat{\mathbf{k}} = 100$ V-m

2. (i) $\phi = \mathbf{E}\cdot\mathbf{A} = EA\cos\theta = E(\pi R^2)\cos 90° = 0$

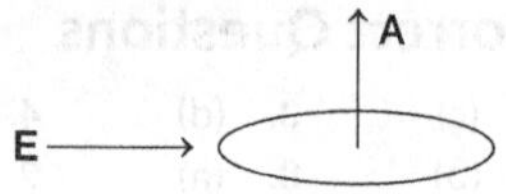

(ii) $\phi = \mathbf{E}\cdot\mathbf{A} = EA\cos\theta = E(\pi R^2)\cos 0° = E\pi R^2$

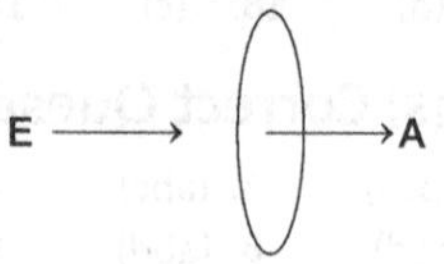

(iii) $\phi = \mathbf{E}\cdot\mathbf{A} = EA\cos\theta = E\pi R^2 \cos 30° = \dfrac{\sqrt{3}}{2}E\pi R^2$

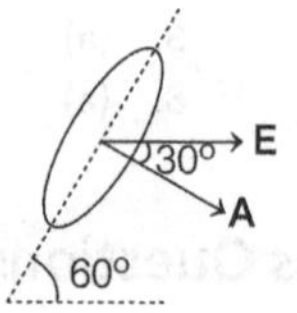

3. (i) Every electric field line entering the curved surface also leaves it. So, net flux through the curved surface of the hemisphere is zero.

(ii) $\phi = \mathbf{E}\cdot\mathbf{A} = E(A\cos\theta) = EA_{\text{projected}} = E\pi R^2$

(iii)

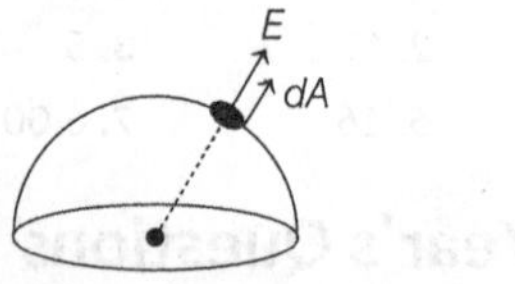

Lets take a small patch of area dA on the curved surface,

$d\phi = \mathbf{E}\cdot d\mathbf{A}$

$\Rightarrow \quad d\phi = E\,dA\cos 0°$

$\Rightarrow \quad \int d\phi = \int E\,dA$

$\Rightarrow \quad \phi = E\int dA$

$\Rightarrow \quad \phi = E(2\pi R^2)$

4. $\mathbf{E} = 20\cos 37°\,\hat{\mathbf{i}} + 20\sin 37°\,\hat{\mathbf{j}} = 16\,\hat{\mathbf{i}} + 12\,\hat{\mathbf{j}}$

$\phi_{ABCD} = \mathbf{E}\cdot\mathbf{A} = (16\hat{\mathbf{i}} + 12\hat{\mathbf{j}}).(4\hat{\mathbf{i}}) = 64$ V-m

$\phi_{EFGH} = \mathbf{E}\cdot\mathbf{A} = (16\hat{\mathbf{i}} + 12\hat{\mathbf{j}}).(-4\hat{\mathbf{i}}) = -64$ V-m

$\phi_{ABEF} = \mathbf{E}\cdot\mathbf{A} = (16\hat{\mathbf{i}} + 12\hat{\mathbf{j}}).(4\hat{\mathbf{j}}) = 48$ V-m

$\phi_{CDGH} = \mathbf{E}\cdot\mathbf{A} = (16\hat{\mathbf{i}} + 12\hat{\mathbf{j}}).(-4\hat{\mathbf{j}}) = -48$ V-m

$\phi_{ADEH} = \mathbf{E}\cdot\mathbf{A} = (16\hat{\mathbf{i}} + 12\hat{\mathbf{j}}).(4\hat{\mathbf{k}}) = 0$

$\phi_{BCFG} = \mathbf{E}\cdot\mathbf{A} = (16\hat{\mathbf{i}} + 12\hat{\mathbf{j}}).(-4\hat{\mathbf{k}}) = 0$

5. $\mathbf{E} = E_0\hat{\mathbf{i}}$

$\phi_{ADEF} = \mathbf{E}\cdot\mathbf{A} = (E_0\hat{\mathbf{i}})[ab\sin\theta(-\hat{\mathbf{i}})] = -E_0 ab\sin\theta$

$\phi_{ABF} = \mathbf{E}\cdot\mathbf{A} = (E_0\hat{\mathbf{i}})\left(\dfrac{1}{2}a^2\sin\theta\cos\theta\,\hat{\mathbf{k}}\right) = 0$

$\phi_{CDE} = \mathbf{E}\cdot\mathbf{A} = (E_0\hat{\mathbf{i}})\left[\dfrac{1}{2}a^2\sin\theta\cos\theta(-\hat{\mathbf{k}})\right] = 0$

$\phi_{BCEF} = \mathbf{E}\cdot\mathbf{A} = (E_0\hat{\mathbf{i}})[ab\cos\theta(-\hat{\mathbf{j}})] = 0$

$\phi_{ABCD} = \mathbf{E}\cdot\mathbf{A} = EA\cos\theta = EA_{\text{projected}}$

$= E_0(ab\sin\theta)$

6. (i)

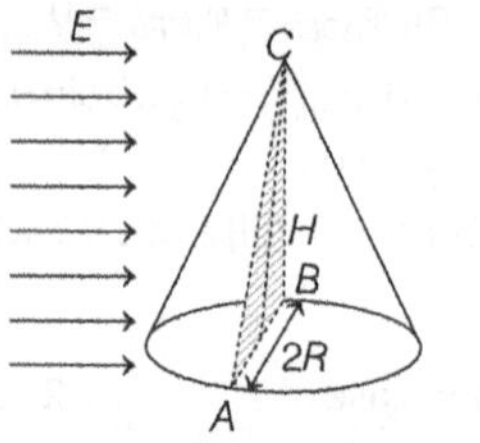

Area of $\Delta ABC = \dfrac{1}{2}\times \text{base} \times \text{height} = \dfrac{1}{2}(2R)H = RH$

Flux entering the cone $= \mathbf{E}\cdot\mathbf{A}$

$= E(A\cos\theta) = EA_{\text{projected}}$

$= E\left(\dfrac{1}{2}(2R)H\right) = ERH$

(ii)

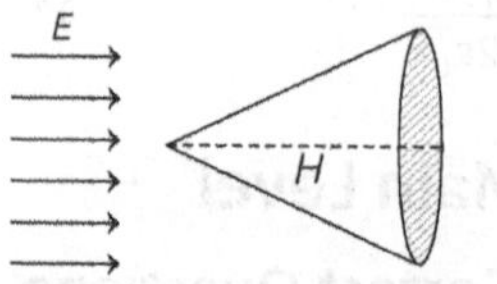

Flux entering the cone $= \mathbf{E}\cdot\mathbf{A} = E(A\cos\theta)$

$= EA_{\text{projected}} = E(\pi R^2)$

(iii)

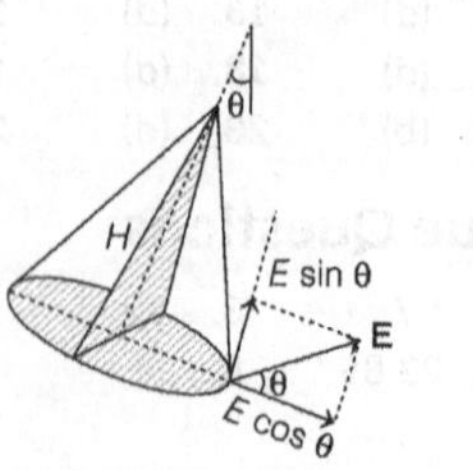

Lets make two components of electric field E as shown

$\phi = \phi_{\text{due to } E\cos\theta} + \phi_{\text{due to } E\sin\theta}$

$= (E\cos\theta)\left(\dfrac{1}{2}(2R)H\right) + (E\sin\theta)\,\pi R^2$

$= (E\cos\theta)HR + (E\sin\theta)\,\pi R^2$

4.2 Gauss Law

1. $\phi = \dfrac{q_{enclosed}}{\varepsilon_0}$

   Since, charge enclosed doesn't change in each case, flux will not change.

2. $\phi_{S'} = 4\phi_S$

   $\Rightarrow \quad \dfrac{q_1+q_2+q_3+Q}{\varepsilon_0} = 4\dfrac{(q_1+q_2+q_3)}{\varepsilon_0}$

   $\Rightarrow Q = 3(q_1+q_2+q_3) = 14.25\,\mu C$

3. (i) Lets put another hemisphere, so that the sphere is completed.

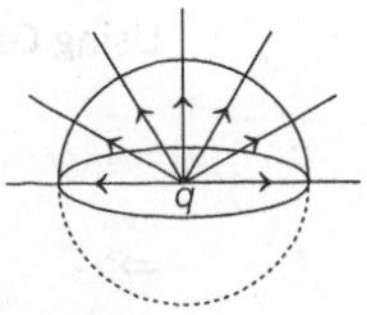

   Flux through sphere $= \dfrac{q}{\varepsilon_0}$

   Flux through the two hemispheres will be equal.

   So, flux through upper hemisphere $= \dfrac{1}{2}\left(\dfrac{q}{\varepsilon_0}\right) = \dfrac{q}{2\varepsilon_0}$

   (ii) The flux through the two hemispheres will be still equal.

   So, flux through upper hemisphere $= \dfrac{1}{2}\left(\dfrac{q}{\varepsilon_0}\right) = \dfrac{q}{2\varepsilon_0}$

   (iii)

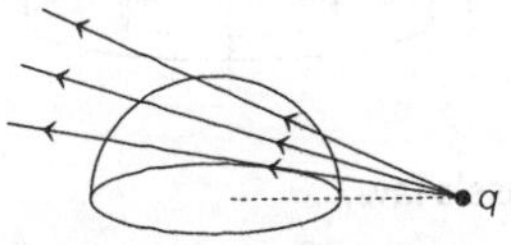

   Every electric field line emanating from q enters as well as leaves the curved surface of the hemisphere. So, flux is zero.

4. Put 5 more square surfaces to complete the cube as shown in figure.

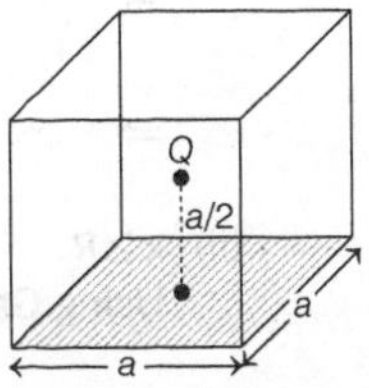

   Flux through the entire cube $= \dfrac{Q}{\varepsilon_0}$

   Flux through each square face $= \dfrac{q}{6\varepsilon_0}$

5. (i)

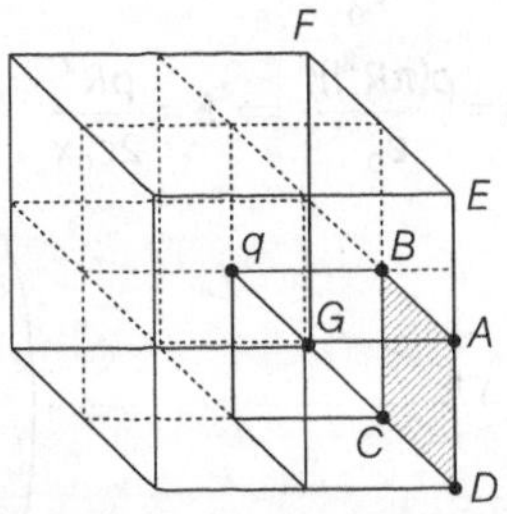

   Lets put 7 more cubes, so that charge q is centrally located.

   Total flux emanating from $\phi_E = \dfrac{q}{\varepsilon_0}$

   Flux passing through each of the 8 cubes

   $= \dfrac{1}{8}\left(\dfrac{q}{\varepsilon_0}\right) = \dfrac{q}{8\varepsilon_0}$

   (ii) Flux through face $DEFG = \dfrac{1}{6}\left(\dfrac{q}{\varepsilon_0}\right) = \dfrac{q}{6\varepsilon_0}$

   Flux through face $ABCD = \dfrac{1}{4}\left(\dfrac{q}{6\varepsilon_0}\right) = \dfrac{q}{24\varepsilon_0}$

6.

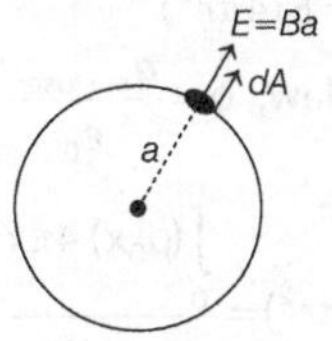

   Lets take a small patch of area dA.

   $$d\phi = \mathbf{E}\cdot d\mathbf{A}$$

   $$\Rightarrow \quad d\phi = E\,dA\cos 0^\circ \Rightarrow \int d\phi = \int E\,dA$$

   $$\Rightarrow \quad \phi = Ba\int dA = Ba(4\pi a^2)$$

   Using Gauss's law, $\phi = \dfrac{q_{enclosed}}{\varepsilon_0}$

   $$\Rightarrow \quad B(4\pi a^3) = \frac{q_{enclosed}}{\varepsilon_0}$$

   $$\Rightarrow \quad q_{enclosed} = 4\pi\varepsilon_0 Ba^3$$

7.

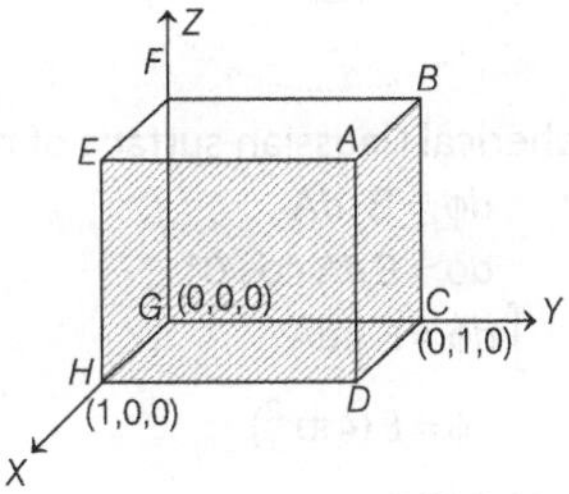

   $$\phi_{ABCD} = \mathbf{E}\cdot\mathbf{A} = (-4x\hat{\mathbf{i}}+6\hat{\mathbf{j}})\cdot\hat{\mathbf{j}} = 6$$

   $$\phi_{ADEH} = \mathbf{E}\cdot\mathbf{A} = (-4\hat{\mathbf{i}}+6y\hat{\mathbf{j}})\cdot\hat{\mathbf{i}} = -4$$

   $$\phi_{EFGH} = \mathbf{E}\cdot\mathbf{A} = (-4x\hat{\mathbf{i}})\cdot(-\hat{\mathbf{j}}) = 0$$

   $$\phi_{BCFG} = \mathbf{E}\cdot\mathbf{A} = (6y\hat{\mathbf{j}})\cdot(-\hat{\mathbf{i}}) = 0$$

   $$\phi_{ABEF} = \mathbf{E}\cdot\mathbf{A} = (-4x\hat{\mathbf{i}}+6y\hat{\mathbf{j}})\cdot\hat{\mathbf{k}} = 0$$

   $$\phi_{CDHG} = \mathbf{E}\cdot\mathbf{A} = (-4x\hat{\mathbf{i}}+6y\hat{\mathbf{j}})\cdot(-\hat{\mathbf{k}}) = 0$$

   Total flux through the cube $= 6 - 4 = 2$

   Using Gauss's law,

   $$\phi = \frac{q_{enclosed}}{\varepsilon_0} \Rightarrow 2 = \frac{q}{\varepsilon_0}$$

   $$\Rightarrow \quad q = 2\varepsilon_0$$

8. (i) $r < R$

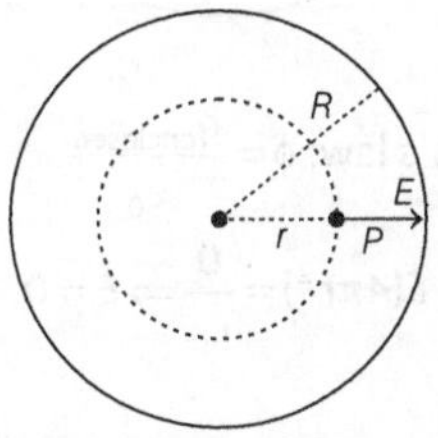

Take a spherical Gaussian surface of radius r.

$$d\phi = \mathbf{E} \cdot d\mathbf{A}$$

$$\Rightarrow \quad d\phi = E\, dA \cos 0°$$

$$\Rightarrow \quad \int d\phi = E \int dA$$

$$\phi = E(4\pi r^2)$$

Using Gauss's law, $\phi = \dfrac{q_{\text{enclosed}}}{\varepsilon_0}$

$$\Rightarrow \quad E(4\pi r^2) = \frac{\int_0^r (\rho_0 x)\, 4\pi x^2\, dx}{\varepsilon_0}$$

$$\Rightarrow \quad E = \frac{\rho_0 r^2}{4\varepsilon_0}$$

$$\Rightarrow \quad \mathbf{E} = \frac{\rho_0 r^2}{4\varepsilon_0}\hat{\mathbf{r}}$$

(ii) $r \geq R$

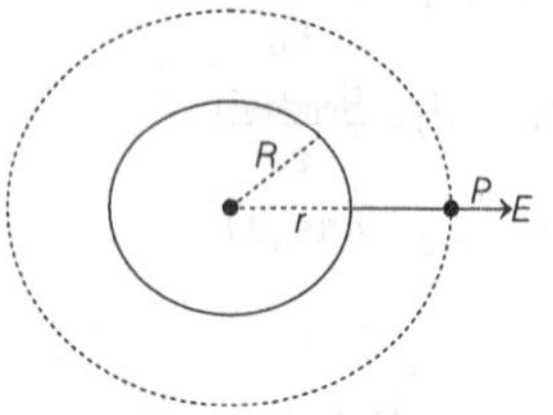

Take a spherical Gaussian surface of radius r as shown.

$$d\phi = \mathbf{E} \cdot d\mathbf{A}$$

$$\Rightarrow \quad d\phi = E\, dA \cos 0°$$

$$\Rightarrow \quad \int d\phi = E \int dA$$

$$\Rightarrow \quad \phi = E(4\pi r^2)$$

Using Gauss's law,

$$\phi = \frac{q_{\text{enclosed}}}{\varepsilon_0}$$

$$\Rightarrow \quad E(4\pi r^2) = \frac{\int_0^R (\rho_0 x)\, 4\pi x^2\, dx}{\varepsilon_0}$$

$$\Rightarrow \quad E = \frac{\rho_0 R^4}{4\varepsilon_0 r^2} \Rightarrow \mathbf{E} = \frac{\sigma_0 r^2}{4\varepsilon_0}\hat{\mathbf{r}}$$

9.

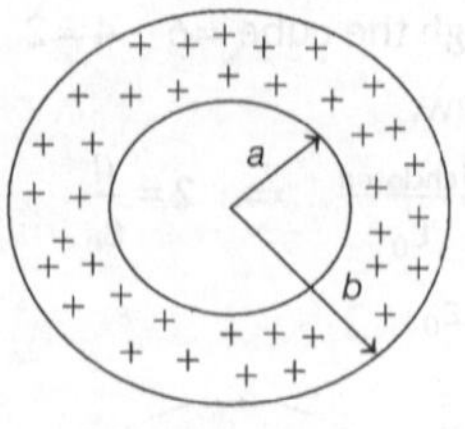

(i) $r < a$

Using Gauss's law, $\phi = \dfrac{q_{\text{enclosed}}}{\varepsilon_0}$

$$\Rightarrow \quad E(4\pi r^2) = \frac{0}{\varepsilon_0} \Rightarrow E = 0$$

(ii) $a \leq r < b$

Using Gauss's law,

$$\phi = \frac{q_{\text{enclosed}}}{\varepsilon_0}$$

$$\Rightarrow \quad E(4\pi r^2) = \frac{\dfrac{Q}{\frac{4}{3}\pi(b^3 - a^3)} \times \frac{4}{3}\pi(r^3 - a^3)}{\varepsilon_0}$$

$$\Rightarrow \quad E = \frac{Q(r^3 - a^3)}{4\pi\varepsilon_0 r^2(b^3 - a^3)}$$

(iii) $r \geq b$

Using Gauss's law,

$$\phi = \frac{q_{\text{enclosed}}}{\varepsilon_0}$$

$$\Rightarrow \quad E(4\pi r^2) = \frac{Q}{\varepsilon_0} \Rightarrow E = \frac{Q}{4\pi\varepsilon_0 r^2}$$

10. (i) $x < R$

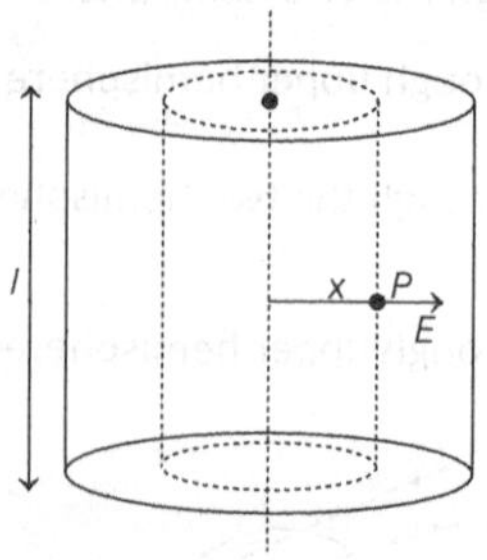

Using Gauss's law,

$$\phi = \frac{q_{\text{enclosed}}}{\varepsilon_0}$$

$$\Rightarrow \quad E(2\pi x l) = \frac{\rho(\pi x^2 l)}{\varepsilon_0}$$

$$\Rightarrow \quad E = \frac{\rho x}{2\varepsilon_0}$$

(ii) $x \geq R$

Using Gauss's law,

$$\phi = \frac{q_{\text{enclosed}}}{\varepsilon_0}$$

$$\Rightarrow E(2\pi x l) = \frac{\rho(\pi R^2 l)}{\varepsilon_0} \Rightarrow E = \frac{\rho R^2}{2\varepsilon_0 x}$$

11.

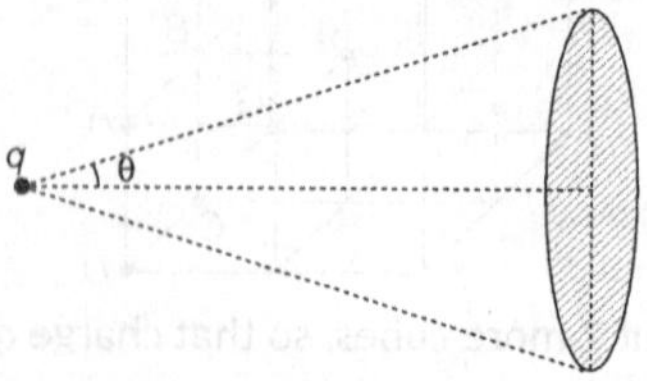

Ω = Solid angle subtended by the base of the cone at the apex $= 2\pi(1 - \cos\theta)$

Flux through the base $= \dfrac{(q/\varepsilon_0)}{4\pi} \times \Omega$

$$= \frac{(q/\varepsilon_0)}{4\pi} 2\pi(1 - \cos\theta) = \frac{q}{2\varepsilon_0}(1 - \cos\theta)$$

Level 2 JEE Main Level

Single Choice Correct Questions

1.

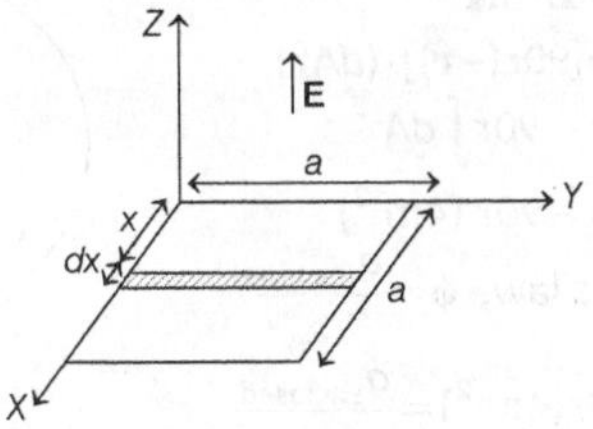

$d\phi$ = Flux through strip of width dx,

$d\phi = \mathbf{E} \cdot d\mathbf{A}$

$\Rightarrow \quad d\phi = (E_0 x\, dx\, \hat{\mathbf{k}}) \cdot (a\, dx\, \hat{\mathbf{k}})$

$\Rightarrow \quad \int d\phi = E_0 a \int_0^a x\, dx \quad \Rightarrow \quad \phi = \dfrac{E_0 a^3}{2}$

2. Electric field at any point on the Gaussian surface is due to all the charges inside as well as outside the Gaussian surface.

3. Since, charge enclosed is same, flux through the new Gaussian surface will be same.

4. Net electric flux $= \phi_2 - \phi_1$

Using Gauss's law,

$$\phi_{net} = \frac{q_{enclosed}}{\varepsilon_0}$$

$\Rightarrow \quad \phi_2 - \phi_1 = \dfrac{q_{enclosed}}{\varepsilon_0} \quad \Rightarrow \quad q_{enclosed} = (\phi_2 - \phi_1)\,\varepsilon_0$

5. Since, the charge enclosed is zero, flux through the Gaussian sphere is zero. Electric field is not zero anywhere on the sphere.

6. (a) $E = 0 \Rightarrow \phi = 0 \Rightarrow q_{enclosed} = 0$

(b) $\phi = 0 \Rightarrow q_{enclosed} = 0$

(c) $E = 0 \Rightarrow \phi = 0$

(d) $\phi = 0 \Rightarrow \oint \mathbf{E} \cdot d\mathbf{A} = 0 \Rightarrow E = 0$

7. Put another identical pyramid as shown in figure.

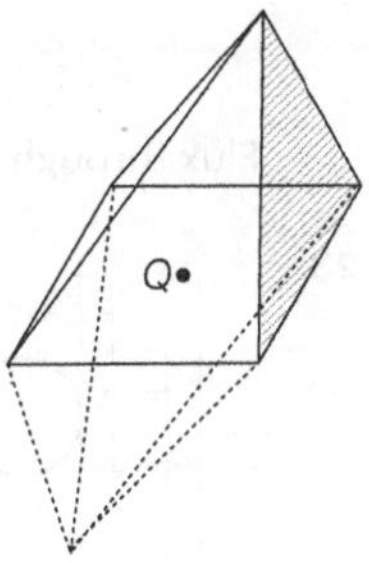

Total flux emanating from q will be equally divided between the two pyramids.

Flux through upper pyramid $= \dfrac{1}{2}\left(\dfrac{Q}{\varepsilon_0}\right)$

Flux through each face of upper pyramid $= \dfrac{1}{4}\left(\dfrac{Q}{2\varepsilon_0}\right) = \dfrac{Q}{8\,\varepsilon_0}$

8.

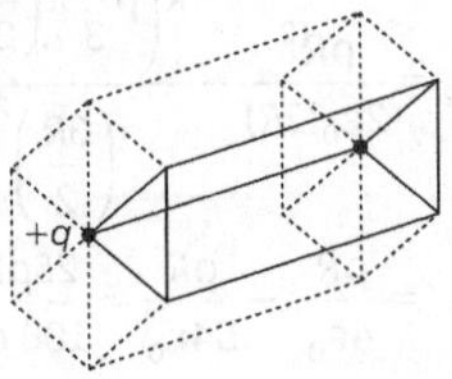

Lets put 5 more equilateral prisms as shown in figure.

Flux through hexagonal prism $= \dfrac{q}{2\varepsilon_0}$

Flux through each equilateral prism $= \dfrac{1}{6}\left(\dfrac{q}{2\varepsilon_0}\right) = \dfrac{q}{12\,\varepsilon_0}$

9. $\phi = \phi_q + \phi_{2q} + \phi_{3q} + \phi_{4q}$

$$= \frac{q}{\varepsilon_0} + \frac{1}{4}\left(\frac{2q}{\varepsilon_0}\right) + \frac{1}{2}\left(\frac{3q}{\varepsilon_0}\right) + \frac{1}{8}\left(\frac{4q}{\varepsilon_0}\right) = \frac{7q}{2\varepsilon_0}$$

10. Flux through face $ABCD$ due to charges at A, B, C and D is zero as no electric field emanated from these charges will pass through the face $ABCD$. Flux due to remaining four charges through the face $ABCD = 4\left(\dfrac{q}{24\,\varepsilon_0}\right) = \dfrac{q}{6\varepsilon_0}$

11. $$\phi = \frac{q}{\varepsilon_0}$$

$\Rightarrow \quad \phi_{max} = \dfrac{q_{max}}{\varepsilon_0} \quad \Rightarrow \quad \phi_{max} = \dfrac{\lambda l_{max}}{\varepsilon_0}$

The longest wire which is inside the cube is of length $\sqrt{3}a$.

$\Rightarrow \quad \phi_{max} = \dfrac{\sqrt{3}\lambda a}{\varepsilon_0}$

12. $x^2 + y^2 + z^2 = 1$ is equation of a sphere of radius 1 m centred at origin.

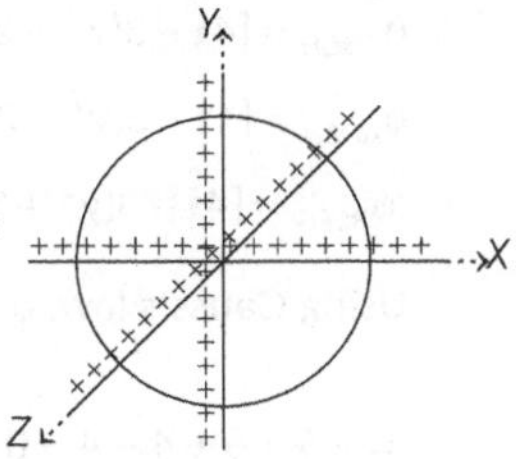

Flux through the complete sphere

$$= \frac{q_{enclosed}}{\varepsilon_0}$$

$\Rightarrow \quad \phi = \dfrac{\lambda(2) \times 3}{\varepsilon_0} \quad \Rightarrow \phi = \dfrac{6\lambda}{\varepsilon_0}$

$x^2 + y^2 + z^2 = 1;\ x > 0;\ y > 0;\ z > 0$ is the part of the sphere in the first octant.

Flux $= \dfrac{1}{8}\left(\dfrac{6\lambda}{\varepsilon_0}\right) = \dfrac{3\lambda}{4\varepsilon_0}$

13. First, the flux increases as the rod enters the cube. Then, flux becomes constant for time L/v as charged enclosed becomes constant and finally the flux decreases as the rod comes out of the cube. Hence graph (d) is the correct graph.

14.

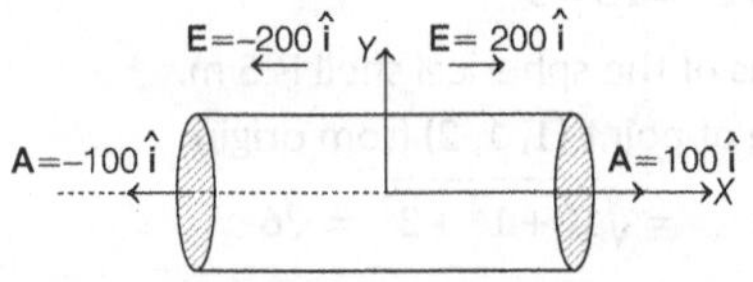

Flux through right flat face $= \mathbf{E} \cdot \mathbf{A}$

$$= (200\,\hat{\mathbf{i}}) \cdot (100\hat{\mathbf{i}}) = 2 \times 10^4$$

Flux through left flat face $= \mathbf{E} \cdot \mathbf{A}$

$$= (-200\,\hat{\mathbf{i}}) \cdot (-100\hat{\mathbf{i}}) = 2 \times 10^4$$

Flux through curved surface $= EA \cos 90° = 0$

Net flux through cylinder

$$= 2\times10^4 + 2\times10^4 + 0 = 4\times10^4$$

Using Gauss's law,

$$\phi = \frac{q_{\text{inside}}}{\varepsilon_0} \Rightarrow 4\times10^4 = \frac{q_{\text{inside}}}{8.85\times10^{-12}}$$

$$\Rightarrow \quad q_{\text{inside}} = 35.4\times10^{-8}\ \text{C}$$

15. Flux due to uniform electric field through a closed surface is zero. So, flux will be due to only the y-component which is non-uniform.

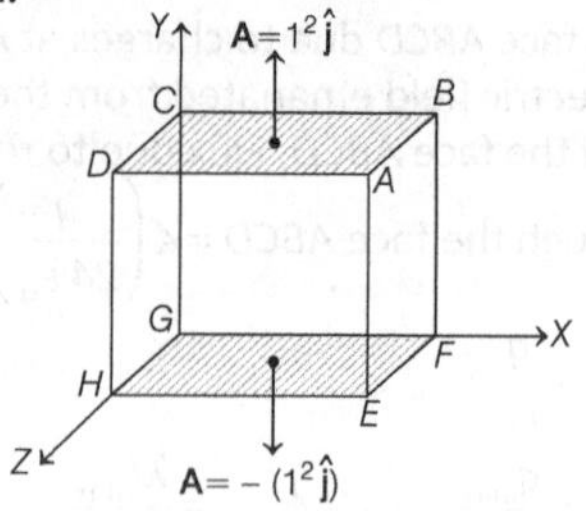

$$\phi_{ABCD} = \mathbf{E}\cdot\mathbf{A} = [4\hat{\mathbf{i}} - 3(1^2+2)\hat{\mathbf{j}}]\cdot(1^2\hat{\mathbf{j}}) = -9$$

$$\phi_{EFGH} = [4\hat{\mathbf{i}} - 3(0^2+2)\hat{\mathbf{j}}]\cdot(-1^2\hat{\mathbf{j}}) = 6$$

$$\phi_{ABEF} = [4\hat{\mathbf{i}} - 3(y^2+2)\hat{\mathbf{j}}]\cdot(1^2\hat{\mathbf{i}}) = 4$$

$$\phi_{CDGH} = [4\hat{\mathbf{i}} - 3(y^2+2)\hat{\mathbf{j}}]\cdot(-1^2\hat{\mathbf{i}}) = -4$$

$$\phi_{ADEH} = [4\hat{\mathbf{i}} - 3(y^2+2)\hat{\mathbf{j}}]\cdot(1^2\hat{\mathbf{k}}) = 0$$

$$\phi_{BCFG} = [4\hat{\mathbf{i}} - 3(y^2+2)\hat{\mathbf{j}}]\cdot(-1^2\hat{\mathbf{k}}) = 0$$

Using Gauss's law, $\phi = \dfrac{q_{\text{enclosed}}}{\varepsilon_0}$

$$\Rightarrow -9+6+4-4+0+0 = \frac{q_{\text{enclosed}}}{\varepsilon_0}$$

$$\Rightarrow \quad q_{\text{enclosed}} = -3\varepsilon_0 \quad \Rightarrow |q_{\text{enclosed}}| = 3\varepsilon_0$$

16. Using Gauss's law, $\phi = \dfrac{q_{\text{enclosed}}}{\varepsilon_0}$

$$\Rightarrow E(4\pi x^2) = \frac{\int_0^x (\rho_0 r^2)\,4\pi r^2 dr}{\varepsilon_0}$$

$$\Rightarrow \quad E = \frac{\rho_0 x^3}{5\varepsilon_0} \Rightarrow E \propto x^3$$

17. $x^2+y^2+z^2 = 25 = 5^2$

$\Rightarrow$ Radius of the spherical shell is 5 m.

Distance of point (1, 1, 2) from origin

$$= \sqrt{1^2+1^2+2^2} = \sqrt{6}$$

Since, $\sqrt{6} < 5$, the point lies inside the uniformly charged spherical shell. So, $E = 0$.

18. $\oint \mathbf{E}\cdot d\mathbf{S} = 0 \Rightarrow \phi = 0$

$\oint \mathbf{E}\cdot d\mathbf{S} = 0 \nRightarrow \mathbf{E} = 0$

So, number of flux lines entering the surface must be equal to number of flux lines leaving it.

19. According to Gauss's law, flux through a Gaussian surface is only due to charges inside. Flux due to charges outside is zero.

20.

$$d\phi = \mathbf{E}\cdot d\mathbf{A}$$

$$\Rightarrow \quad d\phi = [90r(-\hat{\mathbf{r}})]\cdot(dA\hat{\mathbf{r}})$$

$$\Rightarrow \quad \int d\phi = -90r\int dA$$

$$\Rightarrow \quad \phi = -90r\,(4\pi r^2)$$

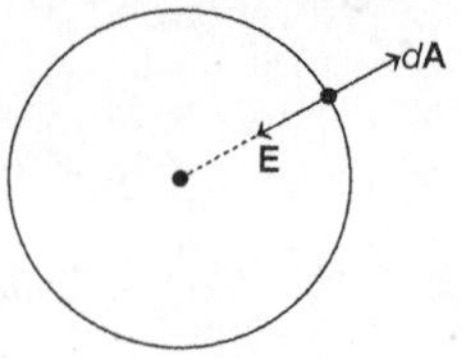

Using Gauss's law, $\phi = \dfrac{q_{\text{enclosed}}}{\varepsilon_0}$

$$\Rightarrow \quad -90r(4\pi r^2) = \frac{q_{\text{enclosed}}}{\varepsilon_0}$$

$$\Rightarrow \quad q_{\text{enclosed}} = -90\,(4\pi\varepsilon_0)\,r^3 = \frac{-90\times2^3}{9\times10^9} = -80\ \text{nC}$$

21.

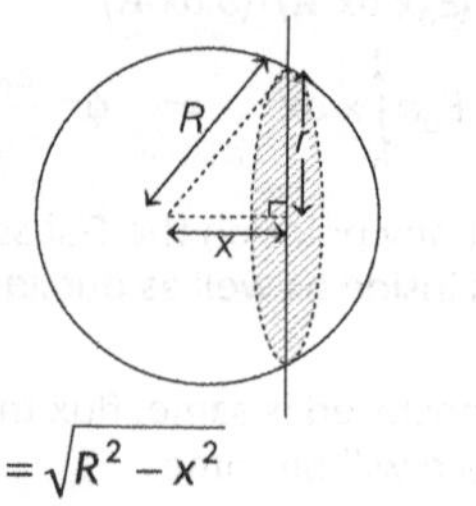

$$r = \sqrt{R^2 - x^2}$$

Area of sheet enclosed in the Gaussian sphere $= \pi r^2$

Charge enclosed $= \sigma\,\pi r^2$

$$\phi = \frac{\sigma\pi r^2}{\varepsilon_0} = \frac{\sigma\pi(R^2-x^2)}{\varepsilon_0}$$

22. Flux through cylinder $= \dfrac{q}{2\varepsilon_0}$

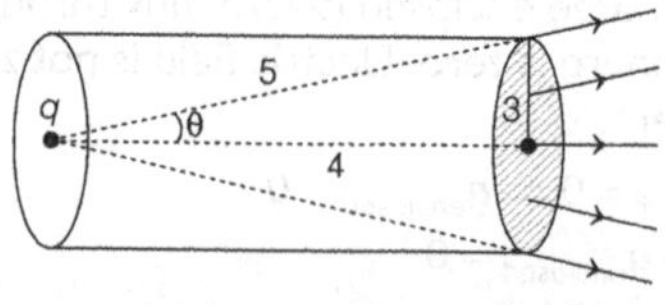

$$\text{Flux through the right flat face} = \frac{q/\varepsilon_0}{4\pi}[2\pi\,(1-\cos\theta)]$$

$$= \frac{q}{2\varepsilon_0}\left(1-\frac{4}{5}\right) = \frac{q}{10\,\varepsilon_0}$$

$$\text{Flux through curved surface} = \frac{q}{2\varepsilon_0} - \frac{q}{10\,\varepsilon_0} = \frac{2q}{5\varepsilon_0}$$

23.

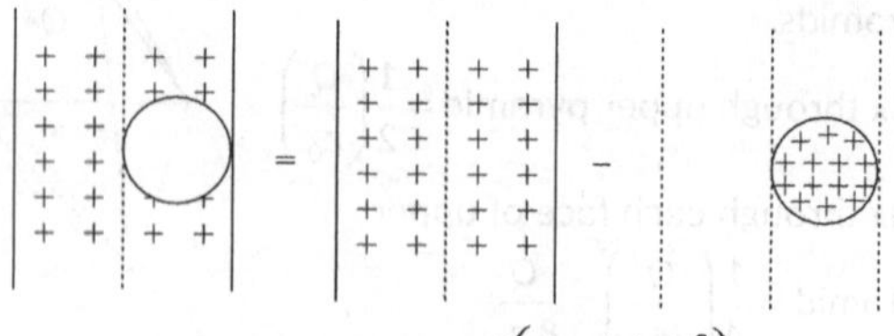

$$\mathbf{E} = \mathbf{E}_1 - \mathbf{E}_2 = \frac{\rho R^2}{2\varepsilon_0(2R)} - \frac{k\left(\rho\frac{4}{3}\pi\left(\frac{R}{2}\right)^3\right)}{\left(\frac{3R}{2}\right)^2}$$

$$= \frac{\rho R}{4\varepsilon_0} - \frac{\rho R}{54\varepsilon_0} = \frac{25\rho R}{108\,\varepsilon_0}$$

24.

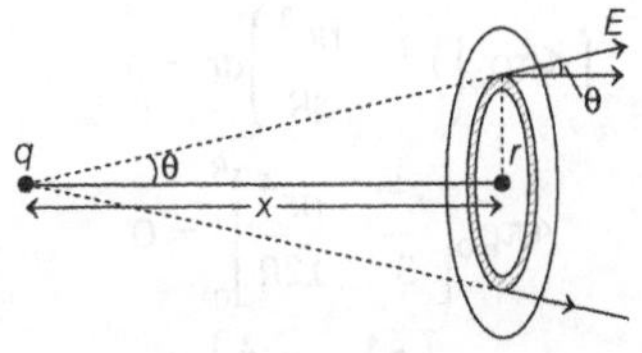

Lets take a ring of radius r and thickness dr on the disc.

Flux through the ring $= d\phi = E\,dA\cos\theta$

$\Rightarrow \quad d\phi = E(2\pi r dr)\cos\theta$

$\Rightarrow \quad d\phi = (2\pi r dr)(E\cos\theta)$

Multiplying by σ on both sides

$\Rightarrow \quad \sigma\, d\phi = (\sigma 2\pi\, r dr)(E\cos\theta)$

$\Rightarrow \quad \sigma\, d\phi = dq\,(E\cos\theta)$

$\Rightarrow \quad \sigma d\phi = dF \Rightarrow \sigma\int d\phi = \int dF$

$\Rightarrow \quad \phi = \dfrac{F}{\sigma}$

25.

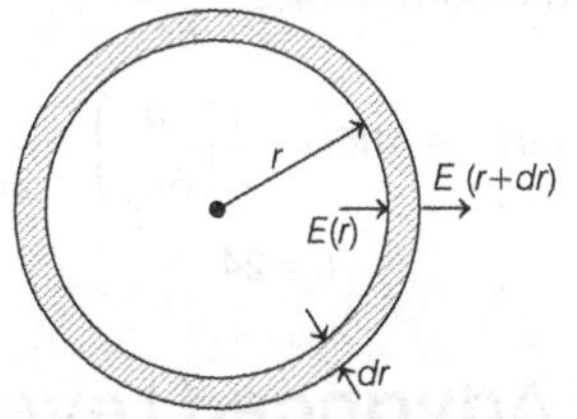

Lets take a spherical shell of radius r and thickness dr,

$$d\phi = E(r+dr)\,4\pi(r+dr)^2 - E(r)4\pi r^2$$

$$d\phi = 4\pi\,[E(r+dr)(r+dr)^2 - E(r)r^2] \quad \text{... (i)}$$

Using Gauss's law,

$$d\phi = \frac{dq}{\varepsilon_0} = \frac{\rho 4\pi r^2 dr}{\varepsilon_0} \quad \text{...(ii)}$$

From Eqs (i) and (ii), we get

$$\frac{\rho 4\pi r^2 dr}{\varepsilon_0} = 4\pi[E(r+dr)(r+dr)^2 - E(r)r^2]$$

$$\Rightarrow \quad \rho = \frac{\varepsilon_0}{r^2}\left(\frac{E(r+dr)(r+dr)^2 - E(r)r^2}{dr}\right)$$

$$\Rightarrow \quad \rho = \frac{\varepsilon_0}{r^2}\frac{d}{dr}(r^2E) = \frac{\varepsilon_0}{r^2}\frac{d}{dr}(r^2\,kr^7) = 9k\varepsilon_0 r^6$$

Numerical Value Questions

1. $\phi = \mathbf{E}\cdot\mathbf{A}_{\text{projected}}$

$\Rightarrow \quad \phi = (E\cos 53^\circ\,\hat{\mathbf{i}} + E\sin 53^\circ\,\hat{\mathbf{j}})\cdot(\pi R^2)\hat{\mathbf{j}}$

$\Rightarrow \quad \phi = (E\sin 53^\circ)\,\pi R^2$

$\Rightarrow \quad \phi = 500 \times \dfrac{4}{5} \times \pi\,(1.2)^2 = 576\pi$

2.

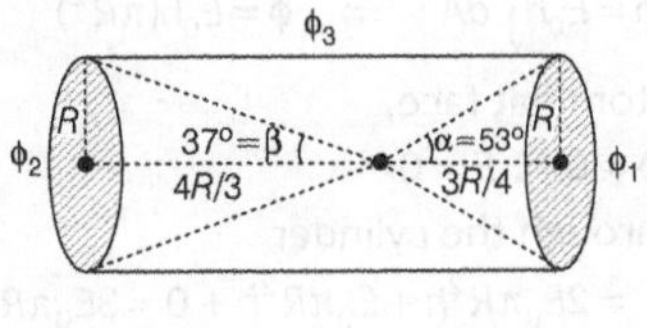

$$\phi_1 = \frac{q}{2\varepsilon_0}(1-\cos\alpha) = \frac{q}{2\varepsilon_0}\left(1-\frac{3}{5}\right) = \frac{q}{5\varepsilon_0}$$

$$\phi_2 = \frac{q}{2\varepsilon_0}(1-\cos\beta) = \frac{q}{2\varepsilon_0}\left(1-\frac{4}{5}\right) = \frac{q}{10\varepsilon_0}$$

$$\phi_1 + \phi_2 + \phi_3 = \frac{q}{\varepsilon_0}$$

$$\Rightarrow \quad \frac{q}{5\varepsilon_0} + \frac{q}{10\varepsilon_0} + \phi_3 = \frac{q}{\varepsilon_0} \quad \Rightarrow \quad \phi_3 = \frac{7q}{10\varepsilon_0}$$

3.

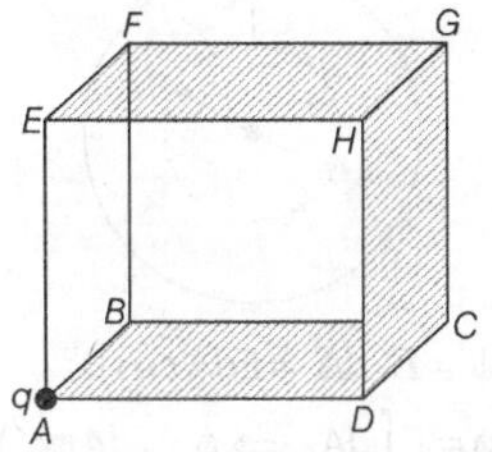

$$\phi_{ABCD} = 0,\ \phi_{CDGH} = \phi_{EFGH} = \frac{q}{24\varepsilon_0}$$

$$\phi = \phi_{ABCD} + \phi_{CDGH} + \phi_{EFGH}$$

$$= 0 + \frac{q}{24\varepsilon_0} + \frac{q}{24\varepsilon_0} = \frac{q}{12\varepsilon_0},\ \text{so } n = 12$$

4.

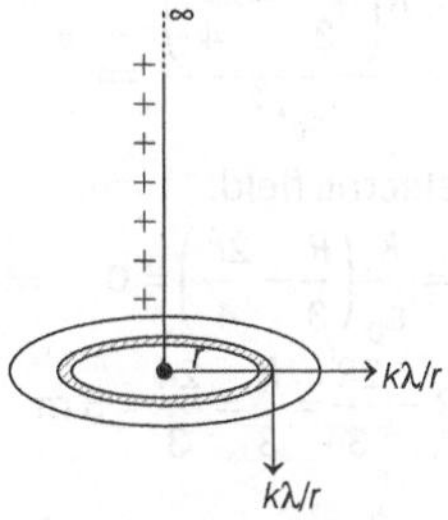

Lets take a ring of radius r and thickness dr flux through the ring $= d\phi$

$$\Rightarrow \quad d\phi = \left(\frac{k\lambda}{r}\right)(2\pi r dr) \Rightarrow \int d\phi = \frac{\lambda}{2\varepsilon_0}\int_0^R dr$$

$$\Rightarrow \quad \phi = \frac{\lambda R}{2\varepsilon_0} = \frac{8.85\times10^{-10}\times 2}{2\times 8.85\times10^{-12}} = 100\ \text{V-m}$$

5. $\mathbf{E} = E_0\hat{\mathbf{i}} + 2E_0\hat{\mathbf{j}} + 3E_0\hat{\mathbf{k}}$

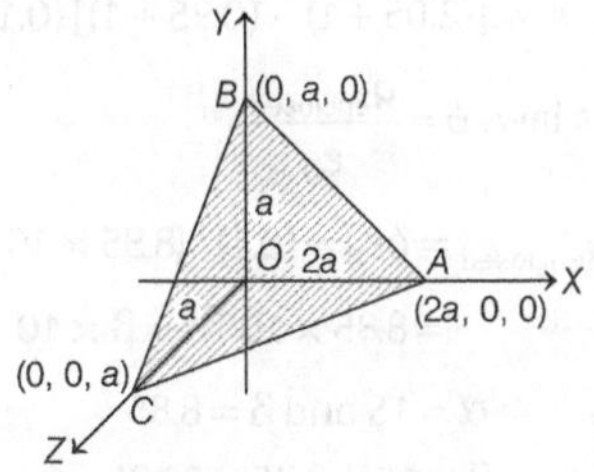

$$\mathbf{A} = \frac{1}{2}(2a)a\hat{\mathbf{k}} + \frac{1}{2}(2a)a\hat{\mathbf{j}} + \frac{1}{2}(a)a\hat{\mathbf{i}}$$

$$= \frac{a^2}{2}\hat{\mathbf{i}} + a^2\hat{\mathbf{j}} + a^2\hat{\mathbf{k}}$$

$$\phi = \mathbf{E}\cdot\mathbf{A} = (E_0\hat{\mathbf{i}} + 2E_0\hat{\mathbf{j}} + 3E_0\hat{\mathbf{k}})\cdot\left(\frac{a^2}{2}\hat{\mathbf{i}} + a^2\hat{\mathbf{j}} + a^2\hat{\mathbf{k}}\right)$$

$$= E_0\left(\frac{a^2}{2}\right) + 2E_0a^2 + 3E_0a^2 = \frac{11E_0a^2}{2}$$

So, $N = 11$

6. $\rho \propto h$

$\Rightarrow \quad \rho = Kh = k(R - r)$

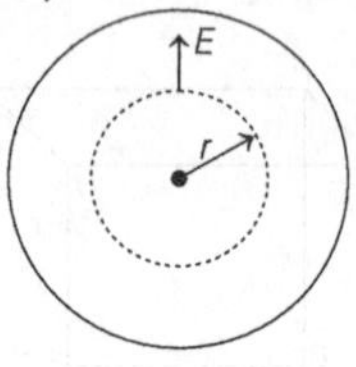

$$d\phi = \mathbf{E}\cdot d\mathbf{A} = EdA\cos 0^\circ$$

$\Rightarrow \quad \int d\phi = E\int dA \quad \Rightarrow \phi = E(4\pi r^2)$

Using Gauss's law,

$$\phi = E(4\pi r^2) = \frac{\int_0^r K(R-r)\,4\pi r^2 dr}{\varepsilon_0}$$

$\Rightarrow \quad E = \dfrac{K\left(\dfrac{Rr^3}{3} - \dfrac{r^4}{4}\right)}{\varepsilon_0 r^2} \Rightarrow E = \dfrac{K}{\varepsilon_0}\left(\dfrac{Rr}{3} - \dfrac{r^2}{4}\right)$

For maximizing electric field,

$$\frac{dE}{dr} = \frac{K}{\varepsilon_0}\left(\frac{R}{3} - \frac{2r}{4}\right) = 0 \quad \Rightarrow \quad r = \frac{2R}{3}$$

$$\text{Depth} = R - r = R - \frac{2R}{3} = \frac{R}{3} = \frac{24}{3} = 8\text{ m}$$

7.

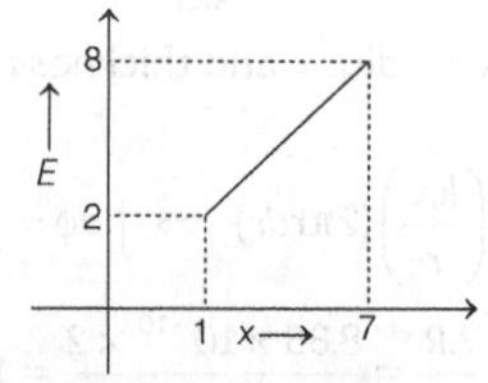

$$E = x + 1$$

$$\phi = E_{x=2.05}(0.1)^2 - E_{x=1.95}(0.1)^2$$

$$= [(2.05+1) - (0.95+1)](0.1)^2 = (0.1)^3$$

Using Gauss's law, $\phi = \dfrac{q_{\text{enclosed}}}{\varepsilon_0}$

$\Rightarrow \quad q_{\text{enclosed}} = \phi\varepsilon_0 = (0.1)^3(8.85\times 10^{-12})$

$$= 8.85\times 10^{-15} = \beta \times 10^{-\alpha}$$

$\Rightarrow \quad \alpha = 15 \text{ and } \beta = 8.85$

$\Rightarrow \quad \alpha + \beta = 15 + 8.85 = 23.85$

8. $\phi = 0 \Rightarrow q_{\text{enclosed}} = 0$

$\Rightarrow \quad \int \rho 4\pi r^2 dr = 0$

$\Rightarrow \quad \int \rho_0\left(1 - \dfrac{nr}{3R}\right)4\pi r^2 dr = 0$

$\Rightarrow \quad \int 4\pi\rho_0\left(r^2 - \dfrac{nr^3}{3R}\right)dr = 0$

$\Rightarrow \quad 4\pi\rho_0\left[\dfrac{r^3}{3} - \dfrac{nr^4}{12R}\right]_0^R = 0$

$\Rightarrow \quad 4\pi\rho_0\left[\dfrac{R^3}{3} - \dfrac{nr^4}{12R}\right] = 0 \Rightarrow n = 4$

9.

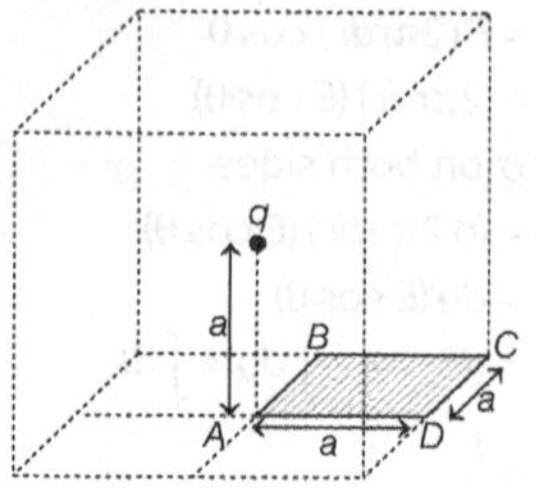

Flux through the bottom face $= \dfrac{q}{6\varepsilon_0}$

Flux through surface $ABCD = \dfrac{1}{4}\left(\dfrac{q}{6\varepsilon_0}\right) = \dfrac{q}{24\varepsilon_0}$

So, $\quad n = 24$

Level 3 JEE Advanced Level

Single Choice Correct Questions

1. For curved surface, $d\phi = \mathbf{E}\cdot d\mathbf{A}$

$\Rightarrow \quad d\phi = E_0 r\, dA\cos\theta$

$\Rightarrow \quad d\phi = E_0(r\cos\theta)dA \quad \Rightarrow \quad \int d\phi = E_0R\int dA$

$\Rightarrow \quad \phi = E_0R\,(2\pi Rh) = 2E_0\pi R^2 h$

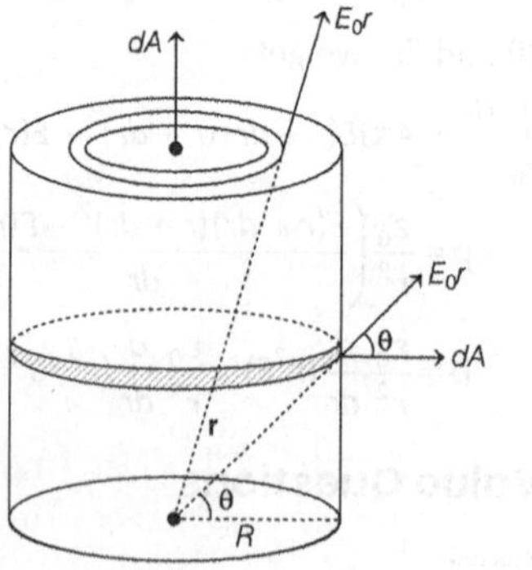

For the top flat face,

$$d\phi = \mathbf{E}\cdot d\mathbf{A} = (E_0 r)dA\cos(90^\circ - \theta)$$

$\Rightarrow \quad d\phi = E_0(r\sin\theta)\,dA$

$\Rightarrow \quad \int d\phi = E_0 h\int dA \quad \Rightarrow \quad \phi = E_0 h(\pi R^2)$

For the bottom flat face,

$$\phi = 0 \quad \because E = 0$$

Total flux through the cylinder

$$= 2E_0\pi R^2 h + E_0\pi R^2 h + 0 = 3E_0\pi R^2 h$$

2.

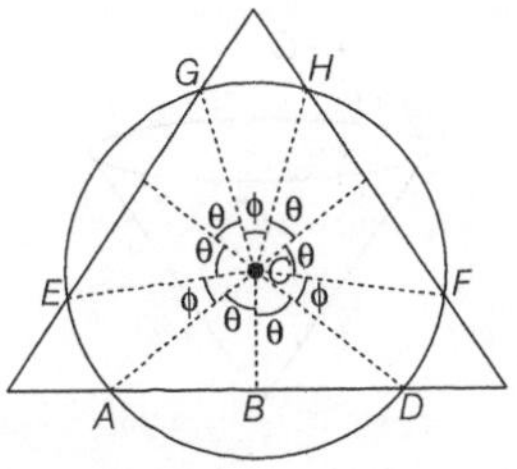

$$BC = \frac{1}{3}\left[\frac{\sqrt{3}}{2}(3R)\right] = \frac{\sqrt{3}R}{2}$$

$$\cos\theta = \frac{BC}{AC} = \frac{\sqrt{3}R/2}{R} \Rightarrow \theta = \frac{\pi}{6}$$

$$\Rightarrow \quad 6\theta + 3\phi = 2\pi \Rightarrow \phi = \frac{\pi}{3}$$

Area of cylinder enclosed in the prism $= 3\left(\frac{\pi}{3}R\right)L = \pi RL$

Using Gauss's law, $\phi = \frac{q_{\text{enclosed}}}{\varepsilon_0} = \frac{\sigma(\pi RL)}{\varepsilon_0}$

3.

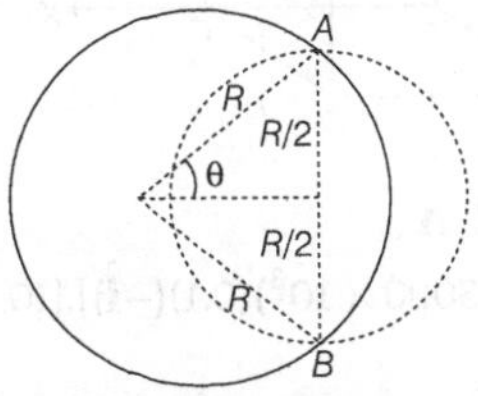

The flux through the sphere will be maximum, when maximum part of the ring is inside the sphere.

This will occur, when the chord *AB* is maximum. Now, the maximum length of chord *AB* is equal to diameter of sphere.

$$\sin\theta = \frac{R/2}{R} \Rightarrow \theta = \frac{\pi}{6}$$

So, the arc of ring inside the sphere subtends an angle of $\frac{\pi}{3}$ at the centre of ring.

Charge on the arc $= \lambda\left(\frac{\pi}{3}R\right)$

Using Gauss's law, $\phi = \frac{q_{\text{enclosed}}}{\varepsilon_0} = \frac{\lambda\pi R}{3\varepsilon_0}$

4.

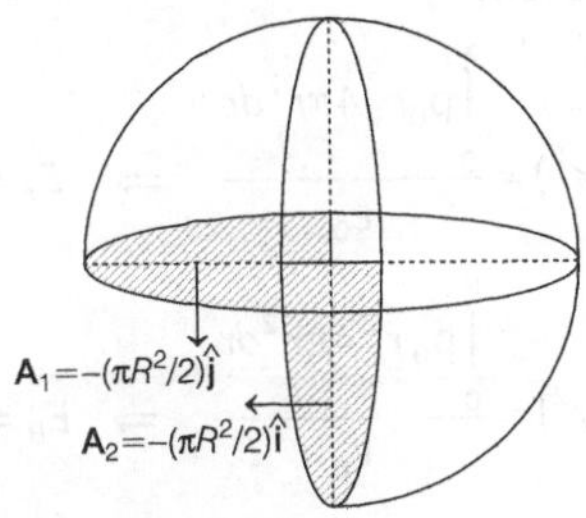

Flux through the flat faces

$$= \mathbf{E}\cdot\mathbf{A}_1 + \mathbf{E}\cdot\mathbf{A}_2$$

$$= (E_0\hat{\mathbf{i}} + 2E_0\hat{\mathbf{j}} + 2E_0\hat{\mathbf{k}})\cdot\left[\frac{\pi R^2}{2}(-\hat{\mathbf{i}}) + \left(\frac{\pi R^2}{2}\right)(-\hat{\mathbf{j}})\right]$$

$$= -E_0\frac{\pi R^2}{2} - E_0\pi R^2 \Rightarrow -\frac{3}{2}E_0\pi R^2$$

Total flux through a closed surface in a uniform electric field is zero. So, flux through the curved surface of sphere

$$= 0 - \left(-\frac{3}{2}E_0\pi R^2\right) = \frac{3}{2}E_0\pi R^2$$

5.

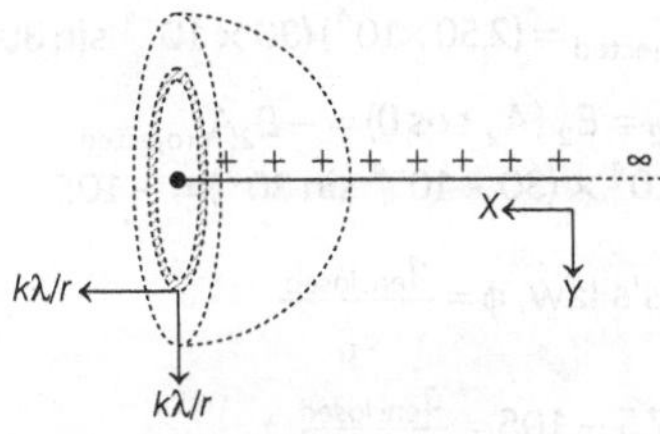

Lets first calculate flux through the flat base,

$$d\phi = \mathbf{E}\cdot d\mathbf{A}$$

$$\Rightarrow \quad d\phi = \left(\frac{K\lambda}{r}\right)2\pi r dr$$

$$\Rightarrow \quad \int d\phi = \frac{\lambda}{2\varepsilon_0}\int_0^R dr \quad \Rightarrow \quad \phi = \frac{\lambda R}{2\varepsilon_0}$$

Net flux through hemispherical surface,

$$\phi_{\text{net}} = \frac{q_{\text{enclosed}}}{\varepsilon_0}$$

$\Rightarrow$ Flux through flat base + Flux through the curved surface $= \frac{\lambda R}{\varepsilon_0}$

$\Rightarrow \frac{\lambda R}{2\varepsilon_0}$ + Flux through the curved surface $= \frac{\lambda R}{\varepsilon_0}$

$\Rightarrow$ Flux through the curved surface $= \frac{\lambda R}{2\varepsilon_0}$

6.

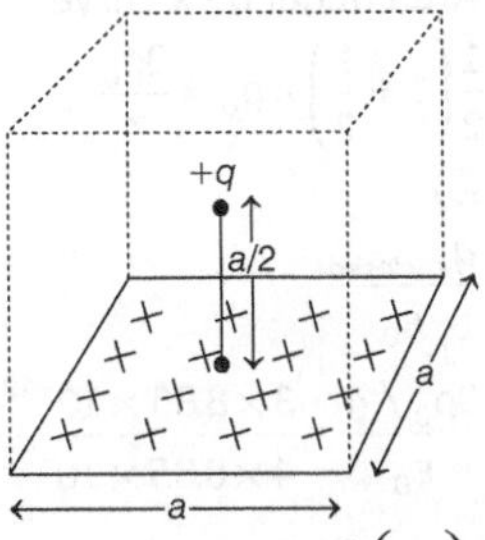

Flux through the square plate $= \frac{1}{6}\left(\frac{q}{\varepsilon_0}\right)$

$$\Rightarrow \quad \phi = \frac{q}{6\varepsilon_0}$$

$$F = \text{Force on the plate} = \sigma\,\phi = \left(\frac{Q}{a^2}\right)\frac{q}{6\varepsilon_0}$$

From Newton's third law,

Force on the point charge, $F = \frac{Qq}{6\varepsilon_0 a^2}$

7.

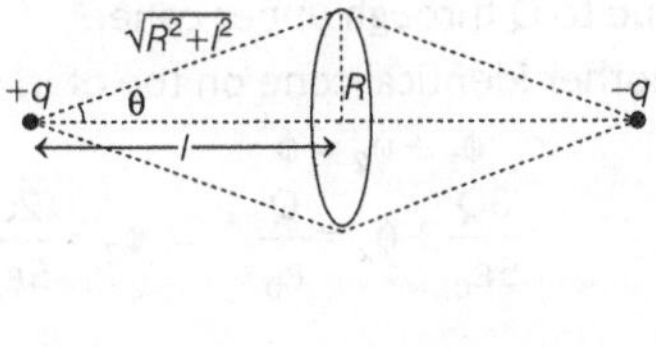

$$\phi = \phi_1 + \phi_2 = \frac{q}{2\varepsilon_0}(1-\cos\theta) + \frac{q}{2\varepsilon_0}(1-\cos\theta)$$

$$= \frac{q}{\varepsilon_0}\left(1 - \frac{l}{\sqrt{l^2+R^2}}\right)$$

8. $\phi_1 = \mathbf{E}_1 \cdot \mathbf{A}_1 = E_1 (A_1 \cos\theta)$

$$= E_1 A_{\text{projected}} = (2.50 \times 10^4)(30 \times 10^{-4} \sin 30°) = 37.5$$

$$\phi_2 = \mathbf{E}_2 \cdot \mathbf{A}_2 = E_2 (A_2 \cos\theta) = -E_2 A_{\text{projected}}$$

$$= -7 \times 10^4 \times (30 \times 10^{-4} \sin 30°) = -105$$

Using Gauss's law, $\phi = \dfrac{q_{\text{enclosed}}}{\varepsilon_0}$

$$\Rightarrow \quad 37.5 - 105 = \frac{q_{\text{enclosed}}}{\varepsilon_0}$$

$$-67.5 = \frac{q_{\text{enclosed}}}{\varepsilon_0} \quad \Rightarrow \quad q_{\text{enclosed}} = -67.5\varepsilon_0$$

9.

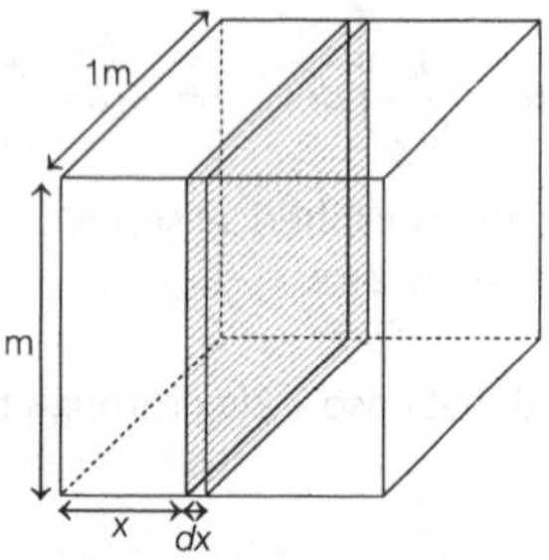

Charge in the shaded volume $= \rho(1^2\, dx)$

$$\Rightarrow \quad dq = \rho dx \quad \Rightarrow \quad \int dq = \int \rho dx$$

$\Rightarrow \quad q =$ Area under ρ - x curve

$$= \frac{1}{2}\left(1 + \frac{1}{2}\right) \times \rho_0 = \frac{3\rho_0}{4}$$

Using Gauss's law,

$$\phi = \frac{q_{\text{enclosed}}}{\varepsilon_0}$$

$$\phi = \frac{3\rho_0/4}{\varepsilon_0} = \frac{3 \times 8.85 \times 10^{-12}}{4 \times 8.85 \times 10^{-12}} = \frac{3}{4}$$

10.

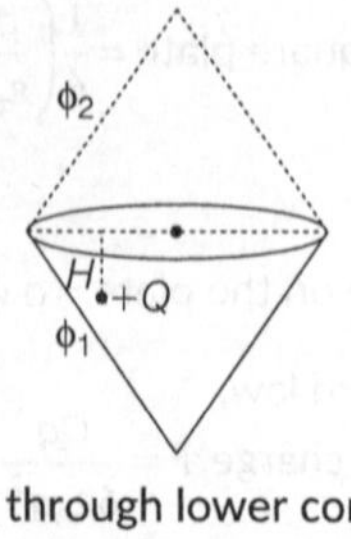

$\phi_1 =$ Flux due to Q through lower cone.

$\phi_2 =$ Flux due to Q through upper cone.

Lets put another identical cone on top of it.

$$\phi_1 + \phi_2 = \phi$$

$$\Rightarrow \quad \frac{3Q}{5\varepsilon_0} + \phi_2 = \frac{Q}{\varepsilon_0} \quad \Rightarrow \phi_2 = \frac{2Q}{5\varepsilon_0}$$

Now,

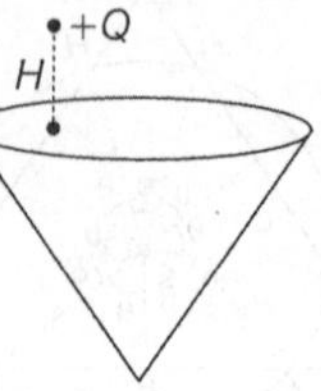

Flux due to Q through the lower cone $= \phi_2 = \dfrac{2Q}{5\varepsilon_0}$

11. $V = (1500 \times 10^3)x^2$

$$E = -\frac{dV}{dx} = -(3000 \times 10^3)x$$

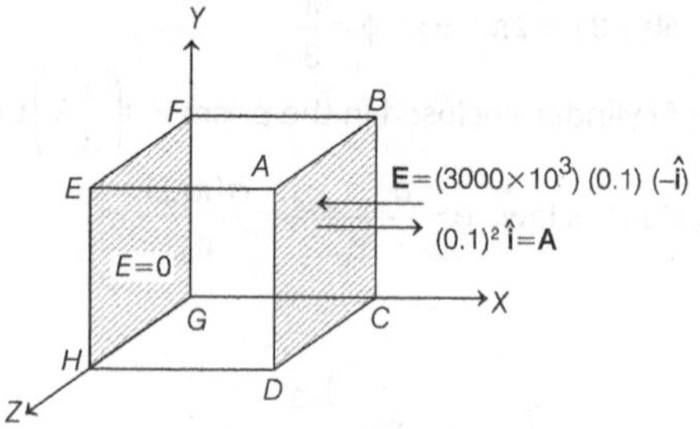

$$\phi_{ABCD} = \mathbf{E} \cdot \mathbf{A}$$

$$= [(3000 \times 10^3)(0.1)(-\hat{\mathbf{i}})].[(0.1)^2(\hat{\mathbf{i}})] = -3000$$

$$\phi_{EFGH} = 0$$

$\because \quad E = 0$

Using Gauss's law, $\phi = \dfrac{q_{\text{enclosed}}}{\varepsilon_0}$

$$\Rightarrow \quad (-3000 + 0 + 0 + 0 + 0 + 0) = \frac{q_{\text{enclosed}}}{\varepsilon_0}$$

$$\Rightarrow \quad q_{\text{enclosed}} = -3000 \times 8.9 \times 10^{-12} = -2.67 \times 10^{-8}\,\text{C}$$

12. $\mathbf{E} = \mathbf{E}_1 + \mathbf{E}_2$

$$\Rightarrow \quad \mathbf{E} = \frac{-2k\lambda}{r} + 0 = -\frac{2k\lambda}{r}$$

For circular motion,

$$q\left(\frac{2k\lambda}{r}\right) = \frac{mv^2}{r} \quad \Rightarrow \quad v = \sqrt{\frac{\lambda q}{2\pi\varepsilon_0 m}}$$

13. Using Gauss's law,

$$E_A(4\pi x^2) = \frac{\int_0^x \rho_0 r^2 4\pi r^2 dr}{\varepsilon_0} \quad \Rightarrow \quad E_A = \frac{\rho_0 x^3}{5\varepsilon_0}$$

and $$E_B(4\pi y^2) = \frac{\int_0^R \rho_0 r^2 4\pi r^2 dr}{\varepsilon_0} \quad \Rightarrow \quad E_B = \frac{\rho_0 R^5}{5\varepsilon_0 y^2}$$

$$E_A = E_B$$

$$\Rightarrow \quad \frac{\rho_0 x^3}{5\varepsilon_0} = \frac{\rho_0 R^5}{5\varepsilon_0 y^2} \quad \Rightarrow \quad x^3 y^2 = R^5$$

14. Using Gauss's law, $\phi = \dfrac{q_{\text{enclosed}}}{\varepsilon_0}$

$$\Rightarrow E(4\pi r^2) = \frac{Q + \int_R^r \frac{\alpha}{r} 4\pi r^2 dr}{\varepsilon_0}$$

$$\Rightarrow E(4\pi r^2) = \frac{1}{\varepsilon_0}[Q + 2\pi\alpha(r^2 - R^2)]$$

$$\Rightarrow \quad E = \frac{1}{4\pi\varepsilon_0}\left(\frac{Q}{r^2} + 2\pi\alpha - \frac{2\pi\alpha R^2}{r^2}\right)$$

$$\Rightarrow \quad E = \frac{1}{4\pi\varepsilon_0}\left[\frac{(Q - 2\pi\alpha R^2)}{r^2} + 2\pi\alpha\right]$$

For E to be independent of R,

$$\Rightarrow \quad Q - 2\pi\alpha R^2 = 0 \quad \Rightarrow \quad Q = 2\pi\alpha R^2$$

15.

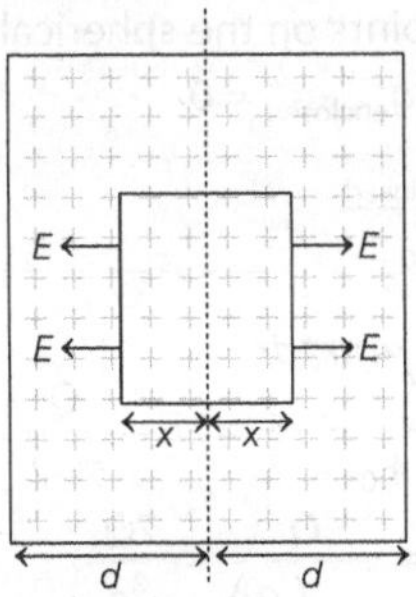

Lets first find electric field inside the sheet at a distance x from the centre of the sheet.

Take a cuboid shaped Gaussian surface as shown in figure.

$$\phi = \frac{q_{\text{enclosed}}}{\varepsilon_0}$$

$$\Rightarrow \quad EA + EA = \frac{\rho A(2x)}{\varepsilon_0} \quad \Rightarrow \quad E = \frac{\rho x}{\varepsilon_0}$$

Force on the particle $= (-q)E$

$$F = -\left(\frac{\rho q}{\varepsilon_0}\right)x \quad \Rightarrow \quad a = -\left(\frac{\rho q}{m\varepsilon_0}\right)x$$

This is equation of SHM,

$$\omega^2 = \frac{\rho q}{m\varepsilon_0} \quad \Rightarrow \quad \omega = \sqrt{\frac{\rho q}{m\varepsilon_0}}$$

$$\Rightarrow \quad \nu = \frac{1}{2\pi}\sqrt{\frac{\rho q}{m\varepsilon_0}}$$

16. Electric field inside a long solid cylinder $= \dfrac{\rho \mathbf{r}}{2\varepsilon_0}$

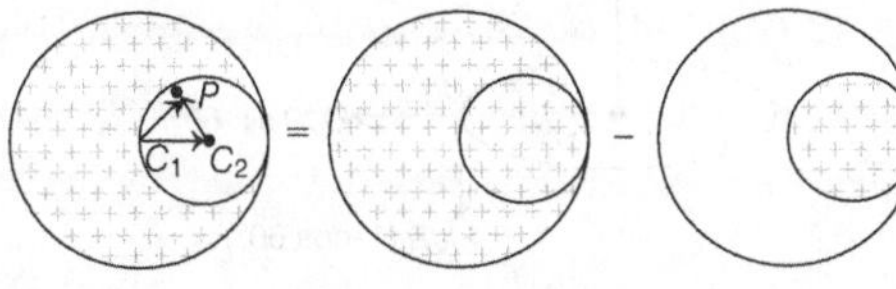

$$\mathbf{E} = \mathbf{E}_1 - \mathbf{E}_2$$

$$\Rightarrow \quad \mathbf{E} = \frac{\rho(\mathbf{C}_1\mathbf{P})}{2\varepsilon_0} - \frac{\rho(\mathbf{C}_2\mathbf{P})}{2\varepsilon_0} = \frac{\rho(\mathbf{C}_1\mathbf{C}_2)}{2\varepsilon_0}$$

So, electric field in the cylindrical cavity is uniform with magnitude $\rho(C_1C_2)$ and direction parallel to $\mathbf{C}_1\mathbf{C}_2$.

$$R_{\max} = \frac{u^2}{g_{\text{eff}}}, \text{ when } \theta = 45°$$

$$\Rightarrow \quad R = \frac{u^2}{\left[\frac{q}{m}\left(\frac{\rho R}{4\varepsilon_0}\right)\right]} \quad \Rightarrow \quad u = \sqrt{\frac{q\rho R^2}{4\varepsilon_0 m}}$$

17.

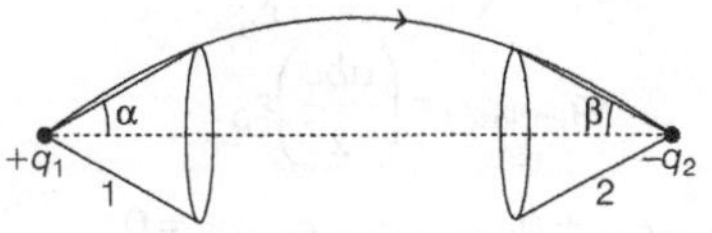

Flux through cone 1 = Flux through cone 2

$$\Rightarrow \quad \frac{q_1}{2\varepsilon_0}(1 - \cos\alpha) = \frac{q_2}{2\varepsilon_0}(1 - \cos\beta)$$

$$\Rightarrow \quad \frac{q_1}{2\varepsilon_0} 2\sin^2\left(\frac{\alpha}{2}\right) = \frac{q_2}{2\varepsilon_0} 2\sin^2\left(\frac{\beta}{2}\right)$$

$$\Rightarrow \quad \sqrt{\frac{q_2}{q_1}} = \frac{\sin\left(\frac{\alpha}{2}\right)}{\sin\left(\frac{\beta}{2}\right)} \quad \Rightarrow \quad \beta = 2\sin^{-1}\left[\sqrt{\frac{q_1}{q_2}}\sin\left(\frac{\alpha}{2}\right)\right]$$

18. $\mathbf{E} = \mathbf{E}_1 - \mathbf{E}_2$

where, $\mathbf{E}_1$ = Electric field due to complete sphere without cavity

and $\mathbf{E}_2$ = Electric field due to only cylindrical portion.

$$\Rightarrow \quad \mathbf{E} = \frac{\rho r}{3\varepsilon_0}(-\hat{\mathbf{i}}) - \frac{\rho r}{2\varepsilon_0}(-\hat{\mathbf{i}}) = \frac{\rho r}{6\varepsilon_0}\hat{\mathbf{i}}$$

19. $\Delta V = -\int \mathbf{E} \cdot d\mathbf{r}$

$$V_{\text{surface}} - V_{\text{axis}} = -\int_0^R \frac{\rho r}{2\varepsilon_0} dr = -\frac{\rho R^2}{4\varepsilon_0}$$

$$\Rightarrow V_{\text{axis}} - V_{\text{surface}} = \frac{\rho R^2}{4\varepsilon_0}$$

Multiple Choice(s) Correct Questions

1. (a) $\phi_{ABCD} = \int \mathbf{E} \cdot d\mathbf{A} = \int (d\hat{\mathbf{i}} - E_0\hat{\mathbf{j}}) \cdot d\mathbf{A}$

$$= (d\hat{\mathbf{i}} - E_0\hat{\mathbf{j}}) \cdot \int d\mathbf{A} = (d\hat{\mathbf{i}} - E_0\hat{\mathbf{j}}) \cdot (-ac\hat{\mathbf{i}}) = -acd$$

(b) $\phi_{CDEF} = \int \mathbf{E} \cdot d\mathbf{A} = \int [(d + x)\hat{\mathbf{i}} - E_0\hat{\mathbf{j}}] \cdot [cdx(-\hat{\mathbf{j}})]$

$$= \int_0^b E_0 c dx = bcE_0$$

(c) $\phi_{ABEF} = \int \mathbf{E} \cdot d\mathbf{A} = \int [(d + x)\hat{\mathbf{i}} - E_0\hat{\mathbf{j}}].(cdx\hat{\mathbf{j}} + cdy\hat{\mathbf{i}})$

$$= \int (d + x)\, c dy - \int_0^b E_0 c\, dx$$

$$= c^a\int \left[d + b\left(1 - \frac{y}{a}\right)\right] dy - cE_0\int_0^b dx$$

$$= c\left[d(y) + b\left(y - \frac{y^2}{2a}\right)\right]_0^a - CE_0[x]_0^b$$

$$= acd + \frac{acb}{2} - bcE_0$$

Total flux through the closed surface

$$= \phi_{ABCD} + \phi_{CDEF} + \phi_{ABEF} + \phi_{ADE} + \phi_{BCF}$$

$$= -acd + bcE_0 + \left(acd + \frac{acb}{2} - bcE_0\right) + 0 + 0$$

$$= \frac{abc}{2}\varepsilon_0$$

Using Gauss's law, $\phi = \frac{q_{enclosed}}{\varepsilon_0}$

$$\Rightarrow \quad q_{enclosed} = \left(\frac{abc}{2}\right)\varepsilon_0$$

2. $\phi_{\text{through flat surface}} + \phi_{\text{through curved surface}} = 0$

$$\Rightarrow \phi_{\text{through flat surface}} + \frac{Q}{2\varepsilon_0} = 0 \qquad (\because \delta < 0)$$

$$\Rightarrow \quad \phi_{\text{through flat surface}} = -\frac{Q}{2\varepsilon_0}$$

If charge Q is displaced up, then magnitude of flux through both flat surface and curved surface will decrease.

3. (a) Put three more cuboids, so that q is at the centre.

Flux through the 4 cuboids $= \frac{q}{\varepsilon_0}$

Flux through each cuboid $= \frac{1}{4}\left(\frac{q}{\varepsilon_0}\right) = \frac{q}{4\varepsilon_0}$

(b) $\phi_{ABEH} = \phi_{ACGH} = 0$

$\phi_{ABCD} = \phi_{EFGH} = \frac{q}{32\varepsilon_0}$

(c) $\phi_{BEFD} = \phi_{CDFG} = x$

$$\Rightarrow 0 + 0 + \frac{q}{32\varepsilon_0} + \frac{q}{32\varepsilon_0} + x + x = \frac{q}{4\varepsilon_0} \Rightarrow x = \frac{3q}{32\varepsilon_0}$$

4. For $n = 0 \Rightarrow \lambda = \lambda_0$

So, charge enclosed in the cube is $\lambda_0 a$, which is constant.

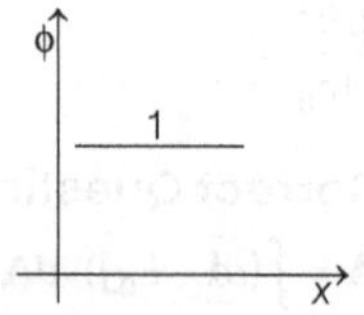

For $\quad \phi = \frac{q_{enclosed}}{\varepsilon_0} = \frac{\lambda_0 a}{\varepsilon_0} = \text{constant}$

$$n = 1 \Rightarrow \lambda = \lambda_0 + \alpha x$$

$$q_{enclosed} = \int_x^{x+a} (\lambda_0 + \alpha x)\, dx = \left[\lambda_0 x + \frac{\alpha x^2}{2}\right]_x^{x+a}$$

$$= \lambda_0 x + \frac{\alpha(2x+a)a}{2} = \frac{a^2}{2}\alpha + (\lambda_0 + a\alpha)x$$

$$\phi = \frac{q_{enclosed}}{\varepsilon_0} = \frac{1}{\varepsilon_0}\left(\frac{a^2}{2}\alpha + (\lambda_0 + a\alpha)x\right)$$

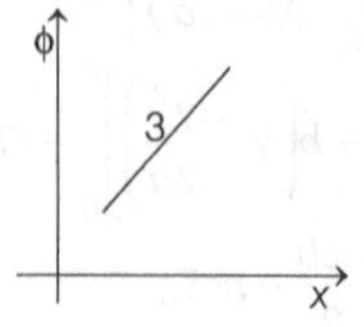

5. A Gaussian surface must not pass through any discrete charge as electric field is not defined at the location of a discrete charge.

A Gaussian surface can pass through any medium.

6. (a) Flux through a Gaussian surface doesn't depend on the shape of Gaussian surface, if it encloses same charge.

(b) $\mathbf{E}$ at any point is due to all the charges inside as well as outside.

(c) If charge is moved inside the Gaussian surface, $\mathbf{E}\cdot d\mathbf{S}$ will change as $\mathbf{E}$ will change.

(d) If charge is moved inside the Gaussian surface, flux through the Gaussian surface remains unchanged.

7. (a) $q_{enclosed} = +q - q = 0$

(b) $\phi_{net} = 0 \quad \because q_{enclosed} = 0$

(c) $E \neq 0$ at all points on the spherical surface

(d) $\oint \mathbf{E}\cdot d\mathbf{S} = 0 \because q_{enclosed} = 0$

8. For $r \le a$; $\phi = \frac{q_{enclosed}}{\varepsilon_0}$

$$E(4\pi r^2) = \frac{\int_0^r \frac{Q}{ar^2} 4\pi r^2 dr}{\varepsilon_0} \Rightarrow E = \frac{Q}{a\varepsilon_0 r}$$

At $\quad r = \frac{a}{2}; E = \frac{Q}{a\varepsilon_0\left(\frac{a}{2}\right)} = \frac{2Q}{a^2\varepsilon_0}$

$$r = a; E = \frac{Q}{a\varepsilon_0 a} = \frac{Q}{a^2\varepsilon_0}$$

For $\quad r > a$; $\phi = \frac{q_{enclosed}}{\varepsilon_0}$

$$\Rightarrow \quad E(4\pi r^2) = \frac{\int_0^a \frac{Q}{ar^2} 4\pi r^2 dr}{\varepsilon_0} \Rightarrow E = \frac{Q}{r^2\varepsilon_0}$$

At $r = 2a$; $E = \frac{Q}{(2a)^2\varepsilon_0} = \frac{Q}{4a^2\varepsilon_0}$

At $r = 4a$; $E = \frac{Q}{(4a)^2\varepsilon_0} = \frac{Q}{16a^2\varepsilon_0}$

9. (a)

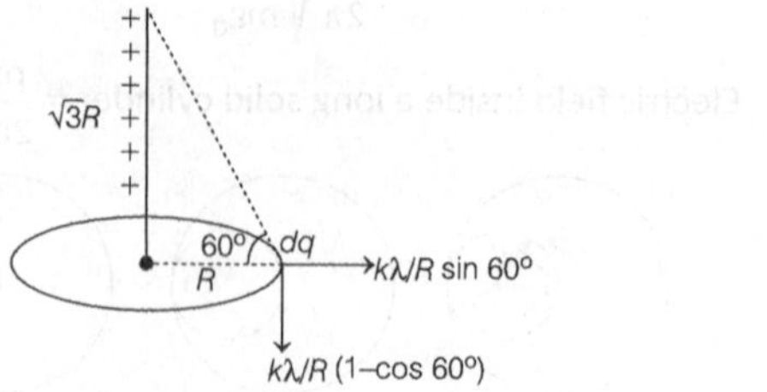

$$dF_y = dqE_y$$

$$\Rightarrow \quad \int dF_y = \int dq \frac{K\lambda}{2R}$$

$$\Rightarrow \quad F_y = \frac{K\lambda}{2R}\int dq = \frac{K\lambda}{2R}Q = \frac{Q\lambda}{8\pi\varepsilon_0 R}$$

(d)

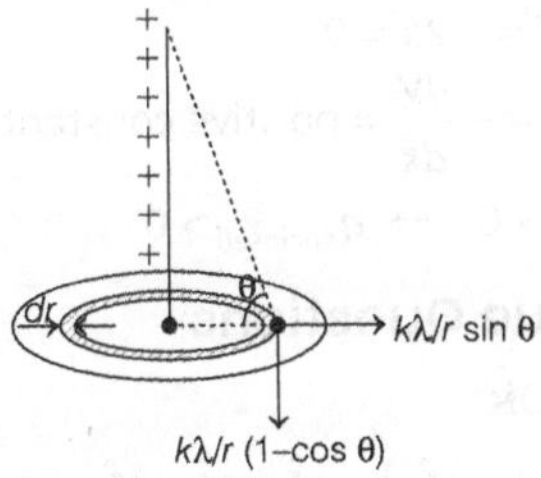

$$r=\sqrt{3}R\cot\theta$$

$$dr=-\sqrt{3}R\,\text{cosec}^2\theta\,d\theta$$

$$d\phi=\frac{K\lambda}{r}(1-\cos\theta)\,2\pi r\,dr$$

$$\int d\phi=\int\frac{\lambda}{2\varepsilon_0}(1-\cos\theta))(-\sqrt{3}R\,\text{cosec}^2\theta\,d\theta)$$

$$=-\frac{\lambda(\sqrt{3}R)}{2\varepsilon_0}\int_{90^\circ}^{60^\circ}\left(\text{cosec}^2\theta-\frac{\cos\theta}{\sin^2\theta}\right)d\theta$$

$$=-\frac{\sqrt{3}\lambda R}{2\varepsilon_0}\left[-\cot\theta+\frac{1}{\sin\theta}\right]_{90^\circ}^{60^\circ}$$

$$=-\frac{\sqrt{3}\lambda R}{2\varepsilon_0}\left[\left(-\frac{1}{\sqrt{3}}+0\right)+\left(\frac{1}{\sqrt{3}/2}-1\right)\right]$$

$$=\frac{\lambda R}{2\varepsilon_0}(\sqrt{3}-1)$$

Comprehension Based Questions

1. $\phi_{S_1}=0$

$\because$ **E** in ZX-plane and **A** along negative y-direction.

$\phi_{S_3}=0 \quad \because \mathbf{E}\perp\mathbf{A}$

$\phi_{S_4}=0 \quad \because E_Z=0$ in XY-plane

$\phi_{S_6}=0 \quad \because E_X=0$ in YZ-plane

2. $\phi_{S_5}=\int\mathbf{E}\cdot d\mathbf{A}=\int_0^{0.3}(-5\times0.3\hat{\mathbf{i}}+3z\hat{\mathbf{k}})\cdot(0.3dz\hat{\mathbf{i}})$

$$=-5\times0.3\times0.3\int_0^{0.3}dz=-0.135\text{ N-m}^2/\text{C}$$

3. $\phi_{S_2}=\int[-5x\,\hat{\mathbf{i}}+3(0.3)\hat{\mathbf{k}}]\cdot[(0.3)^2\hat{\mathbf{k}}]=0.081\text{ N-m}^2\text{C}^{-1}$

Using Gauss's law, $\phi=\dfrac{q_{\text{enclosed}}}{\varepsilon_0}$

$$\Rightarrow 0+0.081+0+0-0.135+0=\frac{q_{\text{enclosed}}}{\varepsilon_0}$$

$$\Rightarrow \quad q_{\text{enclosed}}=-0.054\,\varepsilon_0$$

4. For $r<r_A$, $\phi=\dfrac{q_{\text{enclosed}}}{\varepsilon_0}\Rightarrow 2\times10^5=\dfrac{q}{8.85\times10^{-12}}$

$$\Rightarrow \quad q=1.77\times10^{-6}\text{C}=1.77\mu\text{C}$$

5. For $r_A<r<r_B$

$$\phi=\frac{q_{\text{enclosed}}}{\varepsilon_0}$$

$$\Rightarrow \quad -4\times10^5=\frac{q+q_A}{8.85\times10^{-12}}$$

$$\Rightarrow \quad q_A=-5.31\times10^{-6}=-5.31\,\mu\text{C}$$

6. $\phi=E(4\pi r^2)$

Since, $\phi\neq0; E\neq0$

Therefore, the electric field will not be zero for range of r.

7. For A and B,

$$\phi=\int\mathbf{E}\cdot d\mathbf{S}$$

$$F=\int\sigma\mathbf{E}\cdot d\mathbf{S}$$

$$\Rightarrow \quad F=\sigma\int\mathbf{E}\cdot d\mathbf{S} \quad\Rightarrow\quad F=\sigma\,\phi$$

Since, flux due to q through plate A and plate B is same, force will be same. For C, for finding the force, we have to take the horizontal component of electric field but for flux, we don't have to take component of electric field.

So, $F_A=F_B>F_C$.

8. As force due to one plate on another plate is same. Hence, flux due to 1 in 2 and due to 2 in 1 will be same.

9. When x and R are increased, flux in the two plates due to charge q remains same. Hence, force due to charge q on plates doesn't change.

10. This field is due to a uniformly charged straight wire passing through (1, 1) in XY-plane and parallel to Z-axis.

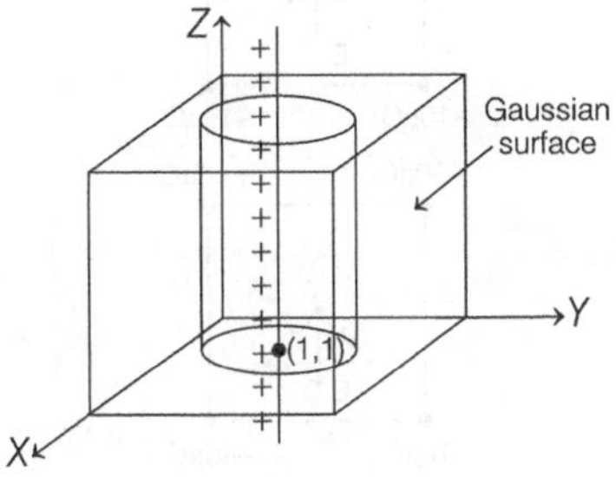

$$\phi=\int\mathbf{E}\cdot d\mathbf{S}=\frac{K}{r}(2\pi rl)\cos0^\circ=4\pi K$$

11. Using Gauss's law, $\phi=\dfrac{q_{\text{enclosed}}}{\varepsilon_0}$

$$\Rightarrow \quad q_{\text{enclosed}}=\phi\varepsilon_0=4\pi K\varepsilon_0$$

12. Now, total flux $=\dfrac{\phi}{4}=\dfrac{4\pi k}{4}=\pi K$

Match the Columns Questions

1. (a) $\phi=\dfrac{q}{2\varepsilon_0}(1-\cos\theta)=\dfrac{q}{2\varepsilon_0}(1-\cos60^\circ)=\dfrac{q}{4\varepsilon_0}$

(b) $\phi_{ABCD}=4\left(\dfrac{2q}{24\varepsilon_0}\right)=\dfrac{q}{3\varepsilon_0}$

(c) $\phi=\phi_1+\phi_2=\dfrac{q}{2\varepsilon_0}+0=\dfrac{q}{2\varepsilon_0}$

(d) Net flux through $ABCD=0$

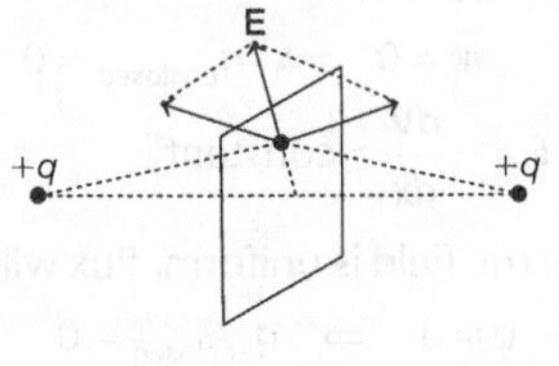

Net $\mathbf{E}$ at any point on surface $ABCD$ is parallel to surface. Hence, $\phi = 0$.

2. (a) Electric field at O is zero, if $Q_1 = Q_3$ & $Q_2 = Q_4$
So, $A \rightarrow p, t$

(b) Potential at $O = \dfrac{k(Q_1 + Q_2 + Q_3 + Q_4)}{a/\sqrt{2}} = 0$

$\Rightarrow Q_1 + Q_2 + Q_3 + Q_4 = 0$

So, $B \rightarrow p, q, s$

(c) $\phi = \dfrac{q_{enclosed}}{\varepsilon_0} = \dfrac{Q_2 + Q_3}{\varepsilon_0} = 0 \Rightarrow Q_2 + Q_3 = 0$

So, $C \rightarrow p, q, s$

(d) (q)

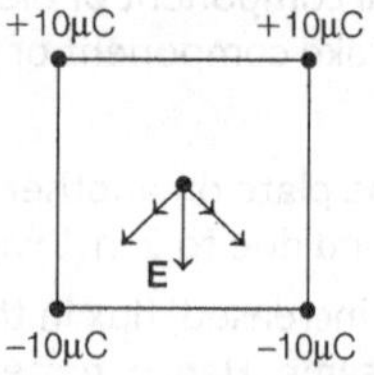

(r)

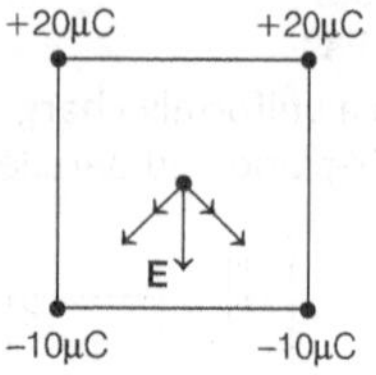

(s)

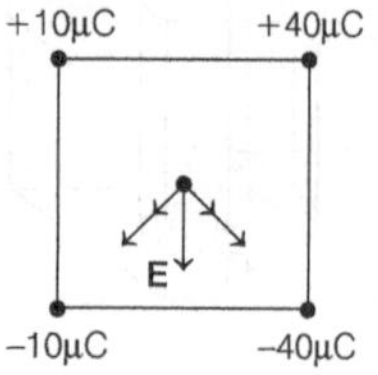

3. $E = -\dfrac{dV}{dx}$

(p)

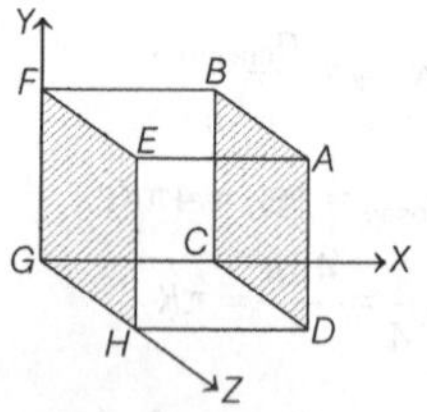

For $x < 2$, $E = -\dfrac{dV}{dx} = -2x$

At $x = 0, E = 0$

At $x = 1, E = -2$

$\phi_{EFGH} = 0 \quad (\because E = 0 \text{ at } x = 0)$

$\phi_{ABCD} = \mathbf{E} \cdot \mathbf{A} = (-2)(1) = -2$

$q_{enclosed} = \phi\varepsilon_0 = -2\,\varepsilon_0$

(q) For $3 \leq x < 4; E = 0$

$\Rightarrow \quad \phi = 0 \quad \Rightarrow q_{enclosed} = 0$

(r) $4 < x < 6; E = -\dfrac{dV}{dx} = \text{constant}$

Since electric field is uniform, flux will be zero.

$\phi = 0 \quad \Rightarrow \quad q_{enclosed} = 0$

(s) At $x = 0, E = -2x = 0$

At $x = 6; E = -\dfrac{dV}{dx} = \text{positive constant}$

So, $\quad \phi > 0 \quad \Rightarrow q_{enclosed} > 0$

Numerical Value Questions

1. $\mathbf{E} = 8\hat{\mathbf{i}} + 6\hat{\mathbf{j}} + 10\hat{\mathbf{k}}$

$$\mathbf{A} = \frac{7}{47}\left(\frac{2\hat{\mathbf{i}} + 3\hat{\mathbf{j}} + 6\hat{\mathbf{k}}}{\sqrt{49}}\right) = \frac{2\hat{\mathbf{i}} + 3\hat{\mathbf{j}} + 6\hat{\mathbf{k}}}{47}$$

$$\phi = \mathbf{E} \cdot \mathbf{A} = (8\hat{\mathbf{i}} + 6\hat{\mathbf{j}} + 10\hat{\mathbf{k}}) \cdot \left(\frac{2\hat{\mathbf{i}} + 3\hat{\mathbf{j}} + 6\hat{\mathbf{k}}}{47}\right) = \frac{94}{47} = 2$$

2.

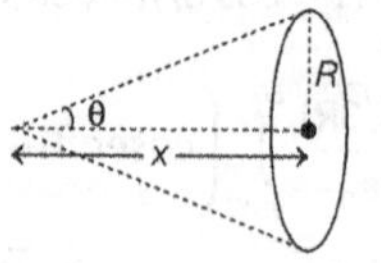

$$\phi = \frac{q}{2\varepsilon_0}(1 - \cos\theta) = \frac{q}{2\varepsilon_0}\left(1 - \frac{x}{\sqrt{R^2 + x^2}}\right)$$

$$\frac{1}{10}\left(\frac{q}{\varepsilon_0}\right) = \frac{q}{2\varepsilon_0}\left(1 - \frac{x}{\sqrt{R^2 + x^2}}\right)$$

$$\Rightarrow \quad \frac{1}{5} = 1 - \frac{x}{\sqrt{R^2 + x^2}}$$

$$\Rightarrow \quad \frac{x}{\sqrt{R^2 + x^2}} = \frac{4}{5}$$

$$\Rightarrow \quad 25x^2 = 16R^2 + 16x^2$$

$$\Rightarrow \quad x = \frac{4R}{3} = \frac{4(30)}{3} = 40 \text{ cm}$$

Now, $\quad \dfrac{1}{5}\left(\dfrac{q}{\varepsilon_0}\right) = \dfrac{q}{2\varepsilon_0}\left(1 - \dfrac{y}{\sqrt{R^2 + y^2}}\right)$

$$\Rightarrow \quad \frac{2}{5} = 1 - \frac{y}{\sqrt{R^2 + y^2}} \quad \Rightarrow \quad y = \frac{3R}{4} = 22.5 \text{ cm}$$

SHIFT $= x - y = 40 - 22.5 = 17.5$ cm

3.

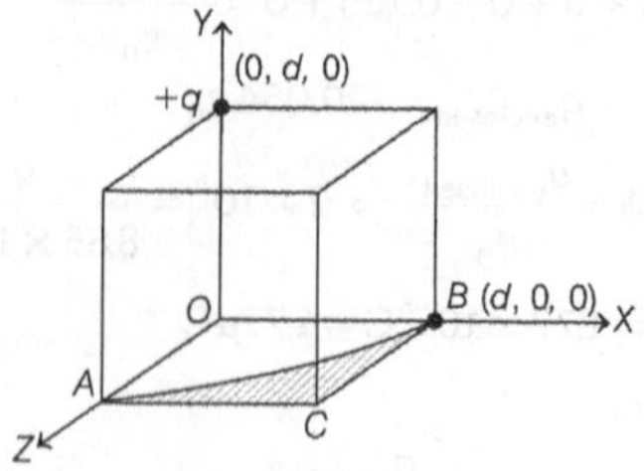

$$\phi_{OABC} = \frac{q}{24\varepsilon_0}$$

$$\phi_{OABO} = \frac{1}{4}\left[\frac{q}{2\varepsilon_0}(1 - \cos 45°)\right] = \frac{q}{8\varepsilon_0}\left(1 - \frac{1}{\sqrt{2}}\right)$$

$$\phi_{ABCA} = \phi_{OABC} - \phi_{OABO}$$

$$= \frac{q}{24\varepsilon_0} - \frac{q}{8\varepsilon_0}\left(1 - \frac{1}{\sqrt{2}}\right)$$

$$= \frac{q}{8\varepsilon_0}\left(\frac{1}{\sqrt{2}} - \frac{2}{3}\right)$$

$$= \frac{8.85 \times 10^{-9}}{8 \times 8.85 \times 10^{-12}}\left(\frac{1}{\sqrt{2}} - \frac{2}{3}\right)$$

$$= 125\left(\frac{1}{\sqrt{2}} - \frac{2}{5}\right) \approx 5$$

4.

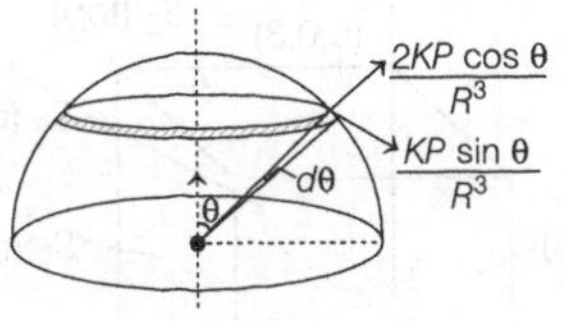

$$d\phi = \left(\frac{2KP\cos\theta}{R^3}\right)(2\pi R\sin\theta)\,(Rd\theta)$$

$$\int d\phi = \frac{P}{2R\varepsilon_0}\int_0^{+\pi/2} \sin 2\theta\, d\theta$$

$$\phi = \frac{P}{2\varepsilon_0 R}\left[\frac{-\cos 2\theta}{2}\right]_0^{\pi/2} = \frac{P}{2\varepsilon_0 R}$$

$$= \frac{17.7 \times 10^{-9}}{2 \times 8.85 \times 10^{-12} \times 50} = 20 \text{ V-m}$$

5.

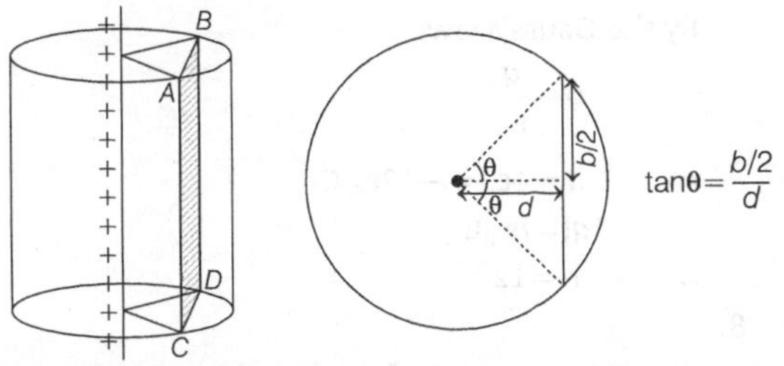

The number of lines passing through the plane surface *ABCD* is equal to number of lines passing through the curved surface.

$$\phi_{ABCD} = \phi_{\text{curved surface}} = \left(\frac{\lambda l}{\varepsilon_0}\right) \times \frac{2\theta}{2\pi}$$

$$= \frac{\lambda l}{\pi\varepsilon_0}\tan^{-1}\left(\frac{b}{2d}\right)$$

$$= \frac{\lambda l}{\pi\varepsilon_0}\tan^{-1}(1)$$

$$= \frac{\lambda l}{4\varepsilon_0} = \frac{8.85 \times 10^{-10} \times 1}{4 \times 8.85 \times 10^{-12}} = 25$$

6. $\mathbf{E} = \mathbf{E}_1 - \mathbf{E}_2$

where, $\mathbf{E}_1$ = electric field at point *P* due to long solid cylinder without cavity.

$\mathbf{E}_2$ = electric field at point *P* due to a uniformly charged solid sphere occupying the spherical cavity.

$$E = E_1 - E_2 = \frac{\rho R^2}{2\varepsilon_0(2R)} - \frac{1}{4\pi\varepsilon_0}\frac{\left[\rho \times \frac{4}{3}\pi\left(\frac{R}{2}\right)^3\right]}{(2R)^2}$$

$$= \frac{\rho R}{\varepsilon_0}\left(\frac{1}{4} - \frac{1}{96}\right) = \frac{23\rho R}{96\varepsilon_0}$$

Now, $$\frac{23\rho R}{96\varepsilon_0} = \frac{23\rho R}{6K\varepsilon_0}$$

$\Rightarrow$ $$K = 16$$

7.

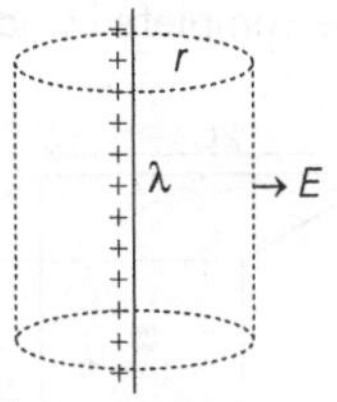

$$E = \frac{2k\lambda}{r}$$

$\Rightarrow$ $$3 \times 10^6 = \frac{2 \times 9 \times 10^9 \times 1 \times 10^{-3}}{r}$$

$\Rightarrow$ $$r = 6.00 \text{ m}$$

Previous Year's Questions

JEE Main

1. Given,

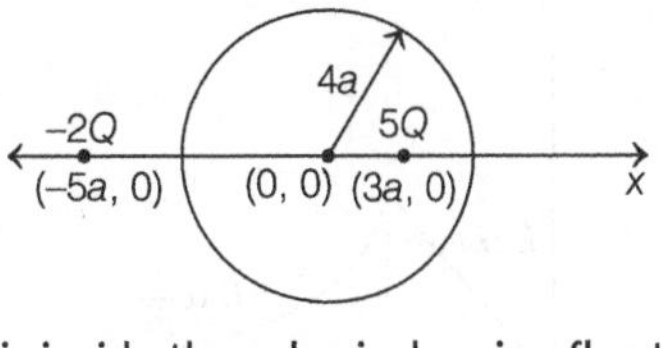

5*Q* charge is inside the spherical region flux through sphere $= \frac{5Q}{\varepsilon_0}$

2. Given,

$$\mathbf{E} = (6\hat{\mathbf{i}} + 5\hat{\mathbf{j}} + 3\hat{\mathbf{k}}) \text{ N/C}$$

$$\mathbf{A} = 30\hat{\mathbf{i}} \text{ m}^2$$

∴ Electric flux,

$$\phi = \mathbf{E} \cdot \mathbf{A}$$

$$= (6\hat{\mathbf{i}} + 5\hat{\mathbf{j}} + 3\hat{\mathbf{k}}) \cdot 30\hat{\mathbf{i}}$$

$$= 180 \text{ N-m}^2/\text{C}$$

3. Electric field in conducting materials is always zero. So, $E_{\text{II}} = 0$

If we make any Gaussian surface in region I and III, then it will enclose the charge Q.

Hence, by Gauss law,

$$\oint E \cdot ds = \frac{Q\text{enclosed}}{\varepsilon_0}$$

There will be electric field.

So, $E_I \neq 0$ and $E_{\text{III}} \neq 0$

4. Given, situation is as shown in figure.

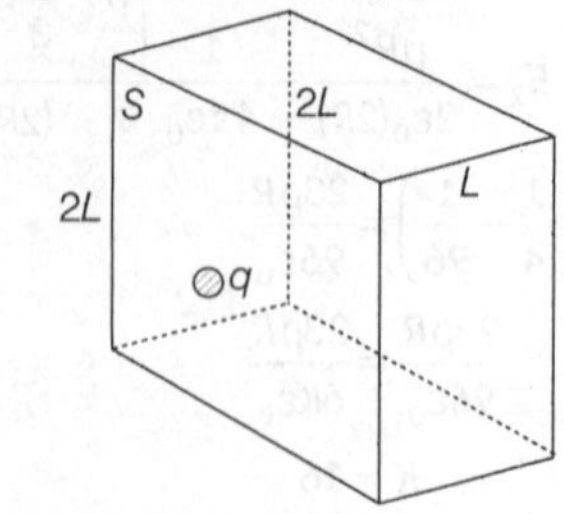

Now, we make cube complete by adding one more identical cuboid.

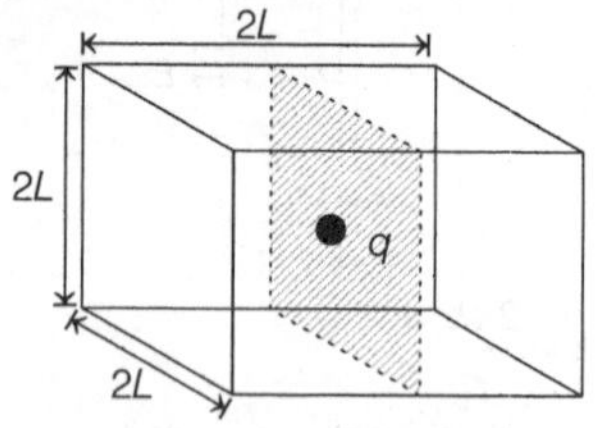

As, charge is placed symmetrically to above cube, flux through surface (one of face $= \frac{1}{6}\left(\frac{q}{\varepsilon_0}\right)$

5. For an insulator charged sphere,

$$E \propto r \,(r < R) \quad \text{and} \quad E \propto \frac{1}{r^2}(r > R)$$

So, graph between E and r will be same as given below

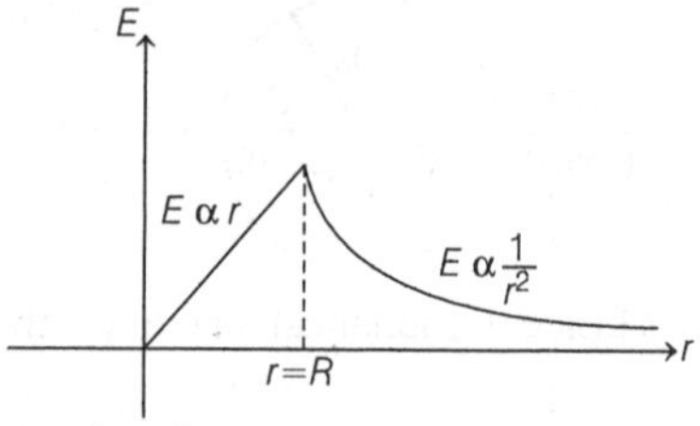

6. Drawing the cube given in question.

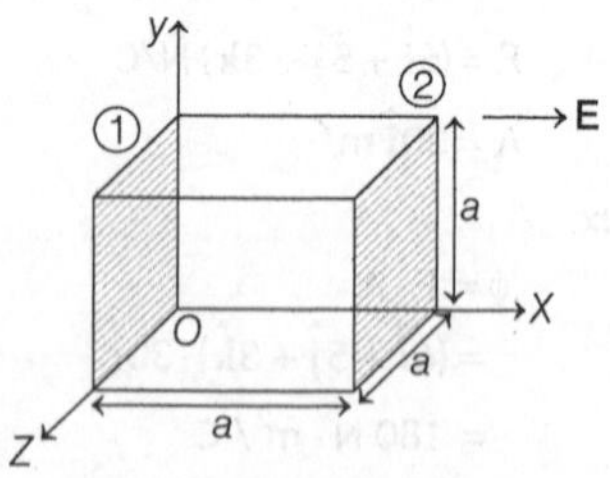

Since, electric field is along x-direction, so electric flux will be non zero only the shaded face.

Electric flux, $\phi = \mathbf{E} \cdot \mathbf{A} = EA\cos\theta$

At face 1, $\phi_1 = (0)a^2 = 0$ $\quad (\because E = 0)$

At face 2, $\phi_2 = \mathbf{E} \cdot \mathbf{A} = (E_0 a\hat{\mathbf{i}}) \cdot (a^2\hat{\mathbf{i}}) = E_0 a^3$

$$= 4 \times 10^4 \times (2 \times 10^{-2})^3$$

$$\phi_2 = 32 \times 10^{-2} \text{N/m}^2\text{-C}$$

Net flux, $\quad \phi = \phi_2 - \phi_1 = 32 \times 10^{-2}$ N/m^2 - C

From Gauss law,

$$\phi = \frac{q_{\text{enc}}}{\varepsilon_0}$$

$$\Rightarrow \quad q_{\text{enc}} = \phi\varepsilon_0 = 32 \times 10^{-2} \times 9 \times 10^{-12}$$

$$\Rightarrow \quad q_{\text{enc}} = 288 \times 10^{-14} \text{ C}$$

7. Given that

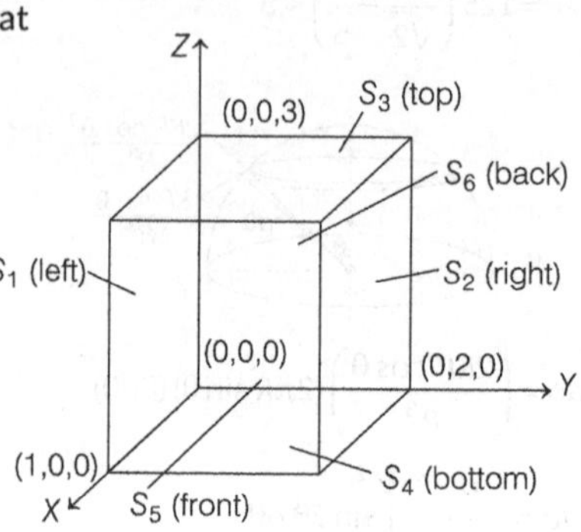

$$\mathbf{E} = (2x^2\hat{\mathbf{i}} - 4y\hat{\mathbf{j}} + 6\hat{\mathbf{k}}) \text{ N/C}$$

Total flux passing through the cuboid,

$$\phi = \sum_{i=1}^{6} \phi_i \quad [\text{where, } = \mathbf{E}.\mathbf{A}]$$

$$= -12 \text{ (N-m}^2\text{/C)}$$

By the Gauss's law,

$$\phi = \frac{q}{\varepsilon_0}$$

$\Rightarrow \quad q = \phi\varepsilon_0 = -12\varepsilon_0$ C

$|q| = n\varepsilon_0$C [Given]

$\therefore \quad n = 12$

8.

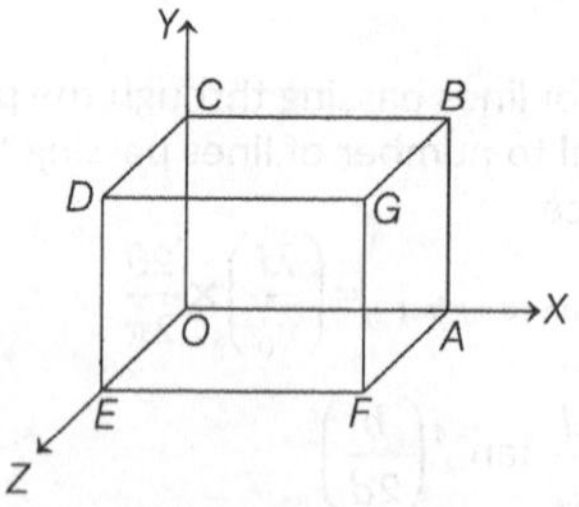

Since, the given electric field is along $\hat{\mathbf{i}}$ direction.

So, Electric flux through the faces which area vector is perpendicular to Electric field is zero.

$\therefore \quad \phi_{OAEF} = \phi_{BCDG} = \phi_{BCDG} = \phi_{OAFE} = 0$

At face $ABGF$,

$$\mathbf{E} = 4000\, x^2\, \hat{\mathbf{i}}$$

$$\mathbf{E} = 4000(0.2)^2\, \hat{\mathbf{i}} = 160 \text{ V/m}$$

At face $OCDE$,

$$\mathbf{E} = 4000(0)^2 = 0 \text{ V/m}$$

Net flux,

$$\phi_{cube} = \phi_{ABGE} - \phi_{OCDE}$$
$$= E_{ABGF} \times a^2 - E_{OCDE} \times a^2$$
$$= 160 \times (0.2)^2 - 0$$
$$= 6.4 \text{ V-m}$$
$$= 6.4 \times 100 \text{ V-cm}$$
$$\phi_{cube} = 640 \text{ V-cm}$$

9. Electric field due to plane charge distribution does not depend on distances of different points near it i.e., it is same at all points near it, which is equal to $\frac{\sigma}{2\varepsilon_0}$

i.e. $E_1 = E_2 = \frac{\sigma}{2\varepsilon_0}$

10. Number of field lines per unit area

$$= \frac{\text{Flux}}{\text{Area}} = \frac{Q}{\varepsilon_0 A} = \frac{\rho \times V}{\varepsilon_0 \times A} \qquad (\because Q = \rho \times V)$$

$$= \frac{\rho \times \frac{4}{3}\pi R^3}{\varepsilon_0 \times 4\pi R^2} = \frac{\rho \times R}{3\varepsilon_0} = \frac{2 \times 10^{-6} \times 10^6 \times 6}{8.85 \times 10^{-12} \times 3}$$

$$= \frac{4}{8.85} \times 10^{12} \approx 45 \times 10^{10} \text{ N/C}$$

11. Given, dipole moment, $p = 30 \times 10^{-5}$ C-m

Using Gauss' law, $\phi = \frac{Q_{in}}{\varepsilon_0} = 0 \qquad (\because Q_{in} = 0 \text{ for dipole})$

Thus, both A and R are true and R is the correct explanation of A.

12. Net charge on electric dipole $= +q - q = 0$

Hence, according to Gauss's law,

Electric flux, $\phi = \frac{q_{net}}{\varepsilon_0} = \frac{0}{\varepsilon_0} = 0$

Electric field due to electric dipole is non-zero and varies at point to point.

Hence, statement I is true.

Electric field due to charged solid sphere at a distance r from centre.

$$E = \frac{1}{4\pi\varepsilon_0} \cdot \frac{Qr}{R^3}$$

which is non-zero.

Hence, statement II is false.

Hence, option (b) is the correct.

13. Given, charge q is at one of the corner of the cube.

$\therefore$ Contribution of q in cube will be $q_{enclosed} = q/8$

As, only 3 faces of cube is allowing the flux lines to pass through it.

$$\therefore \quad \text{Flux } (\phi) = \frac{q_{enclosed}}{\varepsilon_0} = \frac{1}{3}\frac{q/8}{\varepsilon_0} = \frac{q}{24\varepsilon_0}$$

14. Given, incremental volume,

$$dV = 2 \times 10^{-9} \text{ m}^3$$

Electric flux denisty,

$$D = e^{-x} \sin y \hat{i} - e^{-x} \cos y \hat{j} + 2z\hat{k} \text{ C/m}^2$$

As we know that

$$\rho(x, y, z) = \nabla \cdot \Delta D = \frac{d}{dx}(e^{-x} \sin y) - \frac{d}{dy}(e^{-x} \cos y) + \frac{d}{dz}2z$$
$$= -e^{-x} \sin y + e^{-x} \sin y + 2$$
$$\rho(0, 0, 0) = 2 = \frac{Q}{dV}$$
$$\Rightarrow \quad Q = 2dV = 2 \times 2 \times 10^{-9} = 4 \times 10^{-9} = 4 \text{ nC}$$

15. Given,

The electric field in the region, $\mathbf{E} = \frac{2}{5}E_0\hat{i} + \frac{3}{5}E_0\hat{j}$

Here, $E_0 = 4 \times 10^3 \frac{\text{N}}{\text{C}}$

Area of the rectangular surface, $A = 0.4 \text{m}^2$

The direction of electric field vector and area vector is same, so the angle between the electric field vector and area vector is 0.

As we know the expression of electric flux,

$$\phi = E \cdot A \cos\theta \qquad \text{...(i)}$$

Here, E is the electric field vector and A is the surface area of the surfaces.

Consider the surface parallel to the Y-Z plane, so the area vector,

$$A = 0.4\hat{i} \text{ m}^2$$

Substituting the values in Eq. (i), we get

$$\phi = E \cdot A \cos 0°$$
$$\Rightarrow \quad \phi = \frac{2}{5}E_0(0.4)$$
$$\Rightarrow \quad \phi = \frac{2}{5}(4 \times 10^3)(0.4) = 640 \text{ Nm}^2\text{C}^{-1}$$

Hence, the electric flux of the surface parallel to the Y-Z plane is 640 Nm^2C^{-1}.

JEE Advanced

1.

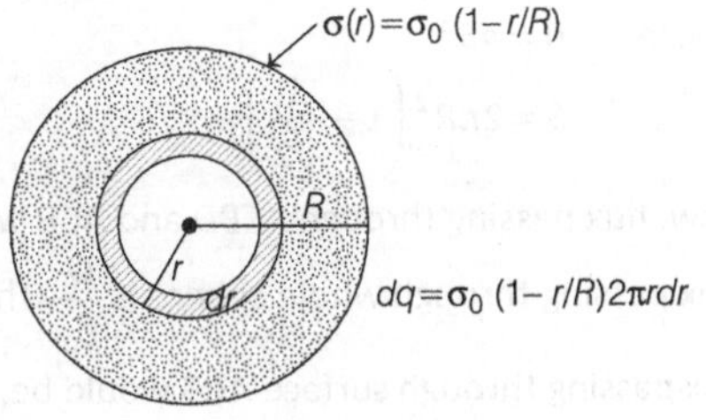

$$\phi_0 = \frac{\int dq}{\varepsilon_0} = \frac{\int_0^R \sigma_0\left(1 - \frac{r}{R}\right)2\pi r \, dr}{\varepsilon_0}$$

$$\phi_0 = \frac{\int dq}{\varepsilon_0} = \frac{\int_0^{R/4} \sigma_0\left(1 - \frac{r}{R}\right)2\pi r \, dr}{\varepsilon_0}$$

$$\therefore \quad \frac{\phi_0}{\phi} = \frac{\sigma_0 2\pi \int_0^R \left(r - \frac{r^2}{R}\right)dr}{\sigma_0 2\pi \int_0^{R/4}\left(r - \frac{r^2}{R}\right)dr} = \frac{\frac{R^2}{2} - \frac{R^2}{3}}{\frac{R^2}{32} - \frac{R^2}{3 \times 64}} = \frac{32}{5} = 6.40$$

2. Total flux from complete closed surface

$= \frac{q}{\varepsilon_0}$.

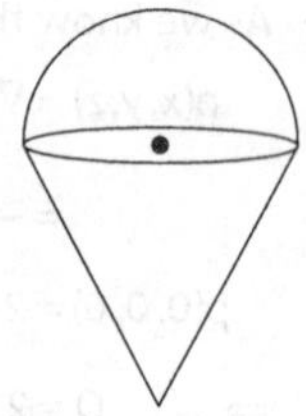

Half of the flux will pass through hemisphere.

$\therefore$ Flux through cone $= \frac{q}{2\varepsilon_0}$

or $\quad n = 3$

3. $PQ = (2)R \sin 60°$

$= (2R)\frac{\sqrt{3}}{2} = (\sqrt{3}R)$

$q_{\text{enclosed}} = \lambda(\sqrt{3}R)$

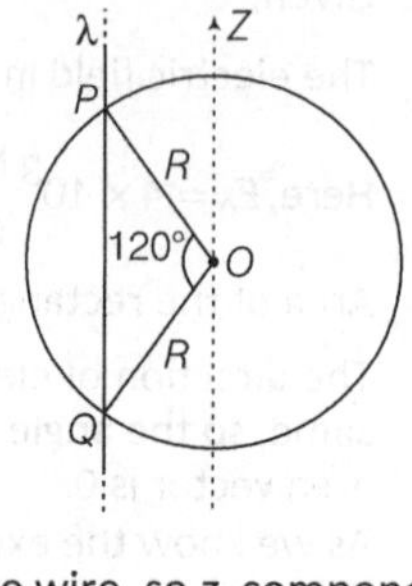

We have, $\phi = \frac{q_{\text{enclosed}}}{\varepsilon_0}$

$\Rightarrow \quad \phi = \left(\frac{\sqrt{3}\lambda R}{\varepsilon_0}\right)$

Also, electric field is perpendicular to wire, so z-component will be zero.

4. (a) Flux passing through curved surface and flat surface will be same and flux passing through flat surface can be obtained by the method discussed below.

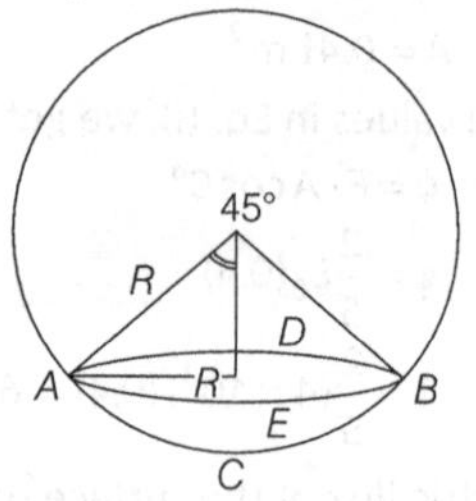

Area of spherical surface ACB,

$$S = 2\pi R^2 (1 - \cos\theta)$$

where, $\quad \theta = 45°$

$$\therefore \quad S = 2\pi R^2\left(1 - \frac{1}{\sqrt{2}}\right)$$

Now, flux passing through $AEBD$ and ACB will be same.

Flux passing through whole sphere is $\frac{Q}{\varepsilon_0}$. Therefore,

flux passing through surface ACB would be,

$$\phi = \left[\frac{(Q/\varepsilon_0)}{4\pi R^2}\right]\left[2\pi R^2\left(1 - \frac{1}{\sqrt{2}}\right)\right]$$

$$= \frac{Q}{2\varepsilon_0}\left(1 - \frac{1}{\sqrt{2}}\right)$$

(b) The component of the electric field perpendicular to the flat surface will decrease as we move away from the centre as the distance increases (magnitude of electric field decreases) as well as the angle between the normal and electric field will increase. Hence, the component of the electric field normal to the flat surface is not constant.

(c) Total flux ϕ due to charge Q is $\frac{Q}{\varepsilon_0}$.

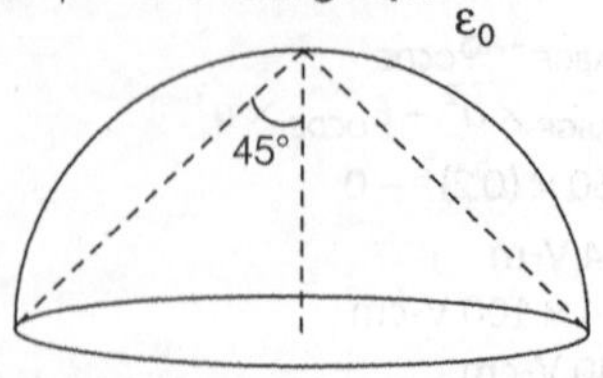

So, ϕ through the curved and flat surface will be less than $\frac{Q}{\varepsilon_0}$.

(d) Since, the circumference is equidistant from Q, it will be equipotential $V = \frac{KQ}{\sqrt{2}R}$.

where, $k = \frac{1}{4\pi\varepsilon_0}$

5. $ANBP$ is cross-section of a cylinder of length L. The line charge passes through the centre O and perpendicular to paper.

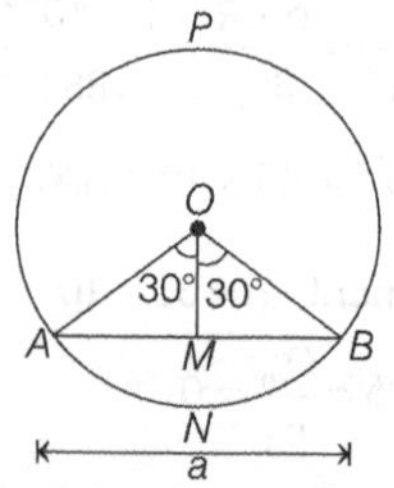

$AM = \frac{a}{2}, MO = \frac{\sqrt{3}a}{2}$

$$\therefore \quad \angle AOM = \tan^{-1}\left(\frac{AM}{OM}\right) = \tan^{-1}\left(\frac{1}{\sqrt{3}}\right) = 30°$$

Electric flux passing from the whole cylinder,

$$\phi_1 = \frac{q_{\text{in}}}{\varepsilon_0} = \frac{\lambda L}{\varepsilon_0}$$

$\therefore$ Electric flux passing through $ABCD$ plane surface (shown only AB) = Electric flux passing through cylindrical surface ANB

$$= \left(\frac{60°}{360°}\right)(\phi_1) = \frac{\lambda L}{6\varepsilon_0}$$

$\therefore \quad n = 6$

6. Option (a) is correct due to symmetry.

Option (b) is wrong again due to symmetry.

Option (c) is correct because as per Gauss's theorem, net electric flux passing through any closed surface $= \frac{q_{\text{in}}}{\varepsilon_0}$

Here, $\quad q_{\text{in}} = 3q - q - q = q$

$\therefore \quad$ Net electric flux $= \frac{q}{\varepsilon_0}$

Option (d) is wrong, because there is no symmetry in two given planes.

CHAPTER~05

CONDUCTORS

LEVEL 01 Starter Level

5.1 Conductors under Electrostatic Conditions

1 State true or false.

(i) Any excess charge given to a conductor resides on its surface.

(ii) Electric field inside a conductor is zero.

(iii) Electric lines of force can enter into conductors.

(iv) Electric field lines are always perpendicular to surface of a conductor.

(v) A conductor is an equipotential body.

(vi) If there is a cavity inside the conductor having no charge, then charge will always reside only on the outer surface of conductor.

(vii) Electric field due to the charges inside the cavity and due to the induced charges on the inner surface of the cavity is zero at any point outside the cavity.

(viii) Electric field due to the charges outside the conductor and due to the induced charges on the outer surface of the conductor is zero at any point inside the conductor.

(ix) When any conductor is grounded, then its charge becomes zero.

(x) When two conductors are connected, there will be charge flow till their charges become equal.

2 Find induced charges on inner and outer surfaces of conductor in the following cases.

(i)
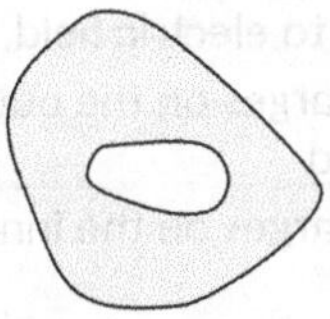

A neutral conductor with a cavity is given charge Q.

(ii)
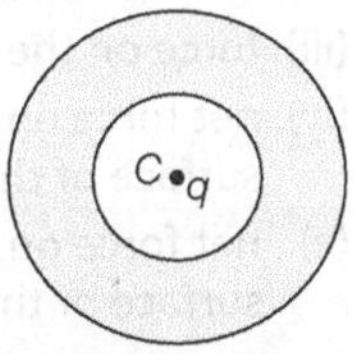

A neutral spherical conductor with a concentric spherical cavity has a point charge q at its centre C.

(iii)
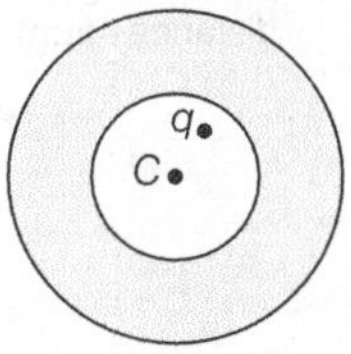

A spherical conductor with a concentric spherical cavity carries a charge Q. A point charge q is kept in the cavity OFF centre.

3 Find induced charges on all surfaces in the following cases. Surfaces are marked as 1, 2, 3, 4, 5, 6.

(i)
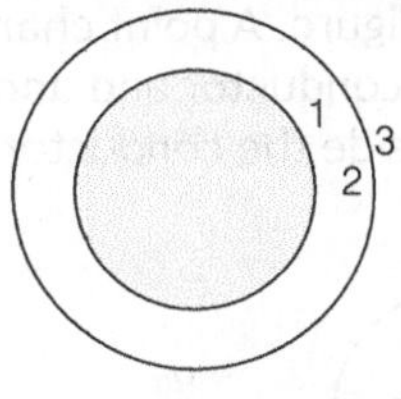

A solid metal sphere of charge $+20\,\mu C$ is surrounded by a thin metallic shell of charge $+10\,\mu C$.

(ii)
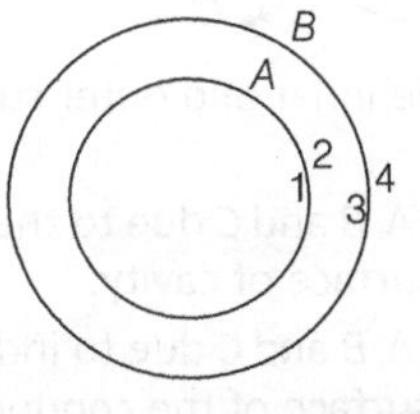

Two concentric thin metallic spherical shells A and B are given charges $+10\,\mu C$ and $-20\,\mu C$ respectively.

(iii)
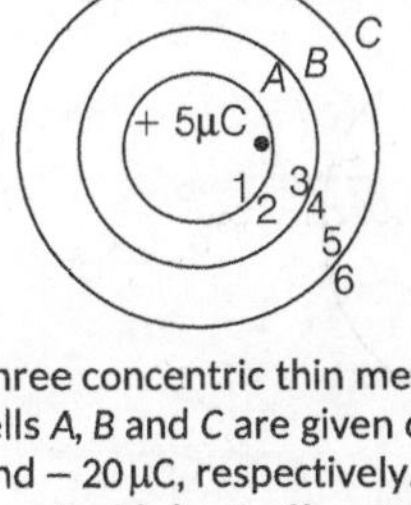

Three concentric thin metallic spherical shells A, B and C are given charges $+10\,\mu C$, 0 and $-20\,\mu C$, respectively. A point charge $+5\,\mu C$ is kept off centre as shown.

4 Find E and V at points A, B and C for each case.

(i)

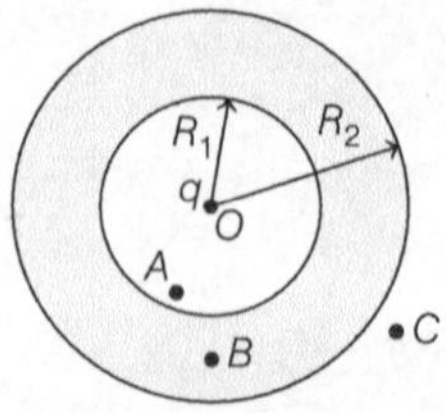

A neutral spherical conductor of inner radius R_1 and outer radius R_2 contains a point charge q placed at centre O.

(ii)

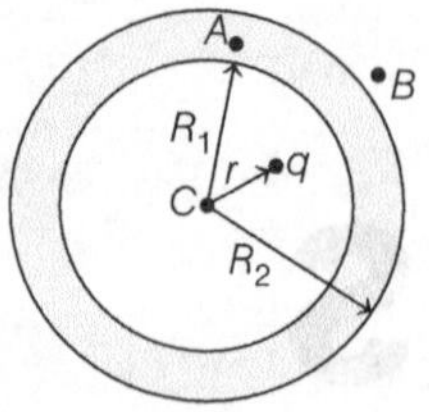

A neutral spherical conductor of radius R_2 with a concentric cavity of radius R_1 contains a point charge q placed at a distance r from its centre c.

(iii)

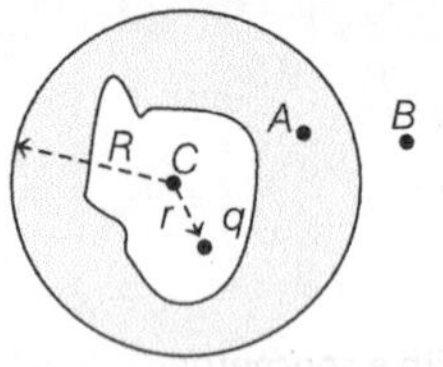

A neutral conductor of radius R with an irregular shaped cavity has a point charge q kept at a distance r from its centre c.

5 A spherical conductor of charge Q has an irregular shaped cavity as shown in figure. A point charge q is kept at the centre O of the conductor and another point charge q_0 is kept outside the conductor at point P. Find

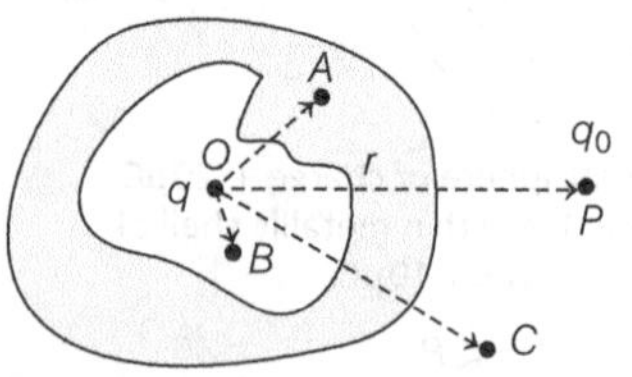

(i) induced charges on the inner and outer surfaces of the conductor.
(ii) electric field at points A, B and C due to the induced charges on the inner surface of cavity.
(iii) electric field at points A, B and C due to induced charges on the outer surface of the conductor.

6 An uncharged spherical conductor of radius R has a cubical shaped cavity as shown in figure. There is a point charge q outside the conductor at point P. Find

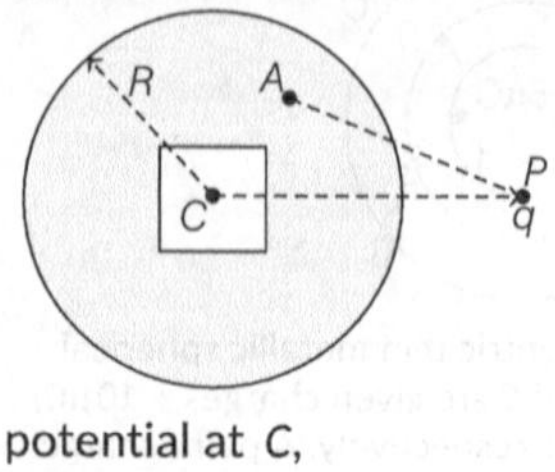

(i) electric potential at C,
(ii) electric potential at A and
(iii) electric potential at A due to induced charges on the conductor.

7 A neutral solid cubical metallic box has an irregular shaped cavity as shown in figure. A point charge q is kept at point A in the cavity. Find

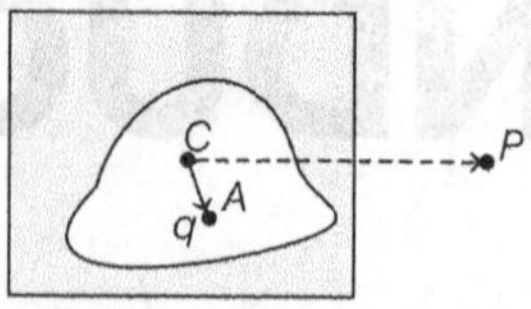

(i) potential at point P and
(ii) potential at point P due to induced charges on the cavity.

8 A point charge q is at the centre of a conducting spherical shell and another point charge q' is kept at distance r from centre outside the shell. Find

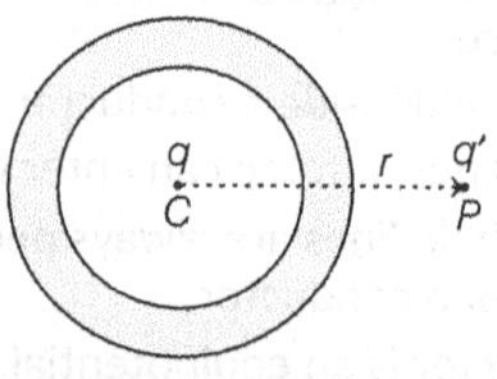

(i) net force acting on q,
(ii) force on q due to charges induced on the outer surface of the shell and
(iii) force on q' due to charges induced on the inner surface of the shell.

9 A neutral conductor has a cavity as shown in figure. A point charge q is kept inside cavity. A uniform electric field E exists in space. Find

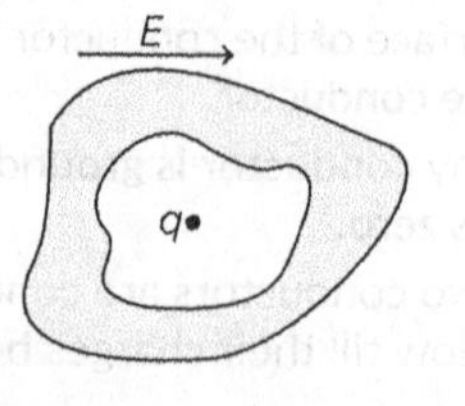

(i) net force acting on q,
(ii) net force acting on the conductor,
(iii) force on the conductor due to electric field,
(iv) net force on the induced charges on the outer surface of the conductor and
(v) net force on the induced charges on the inner surface of the cavity.

10 (i) What is the electric field near a conducting surface, if the local surface charge density is σ?
(ii) What is the electric pressure at the surface of a conductor, if the local surface charge density is σ?

5.2 Earthing of Conductors

1 An isolated metallic sphere of radius 10 cm carries charge + 50 μC. Find the charge flown through the switch to ground after it is closed.

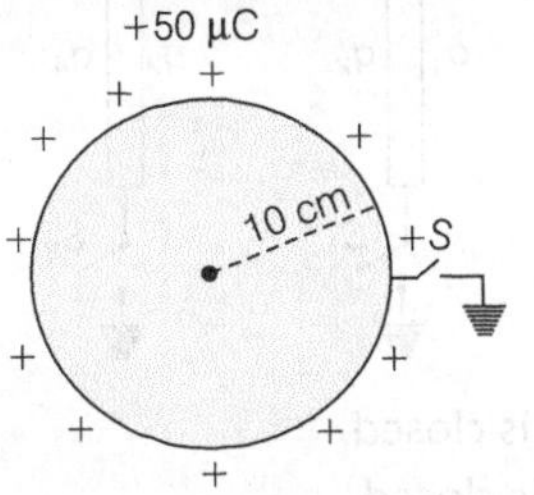

2 A spherical conductor of radius 10 cm carries charge + 50 μC. A point charge + 60 μC is placed 30 cm from the centre of the conductor. Find the charge on the conductor after closing the switch. Also, find the charge flown to the ground.

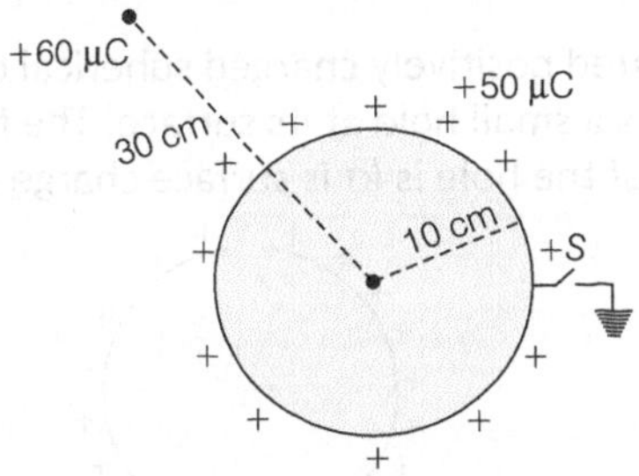

3 Two conducting thin spherical shells of radii R and $2R$ carry charges $-Q$ and $3Q$, respectively. How much charge will flow into the earth, if inner shell is grounded ?

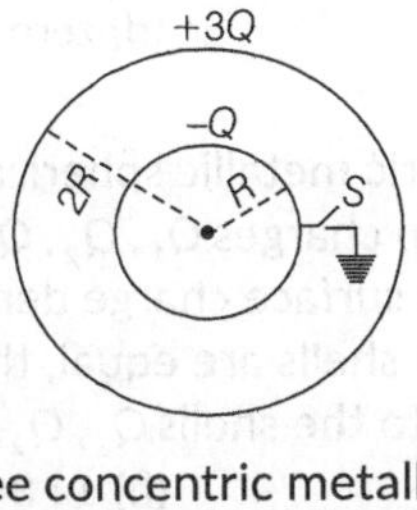

4 There are three concentric metallic spherical shells A, B and C of radius R, $2R$ and $3R$ with charges Q, $-3Q$, $4Q$, respectively as shown in figure. If switch is closed (i.e. its middle shell is earthed), then how much charge flows through switch to earth?

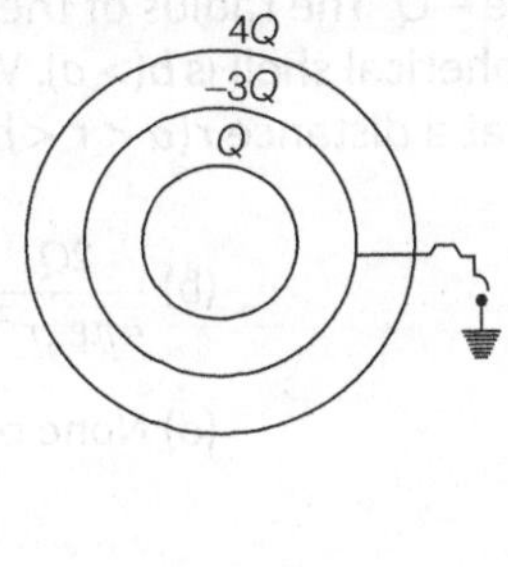

5 There are three concentric metallic thin spherical shells A, B and C with charges + 10 μC, – 20 μC, + 25 μC, respectively as shown in figure. Now, the outermost shell is earthed. How much charge flows through the switch to earth?

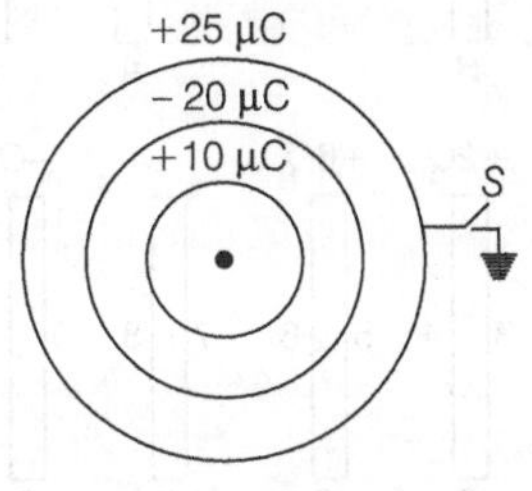

5.3 Connection of Conductors

1 The two conducting thin spherical shells are joined by a conducting wire and cut after sometime when charges stop flowing. Find out the charge on each sphere R after that. Also, find the heat produced in this process.

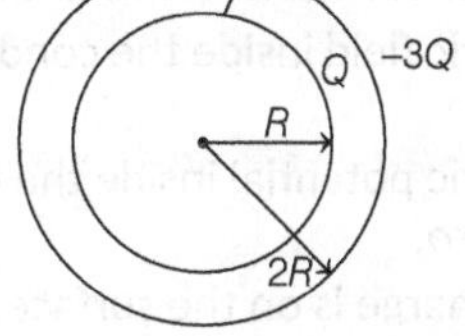

2 There are three concentric metallic thin spherical shells of radii R, $2R$ and $3R$ with charges Q, $-2Q$, $5Q$, respectively as shown in figure. Find charge on each spherical shell after joining the inner most shell and outer most shell by a conducting wire.

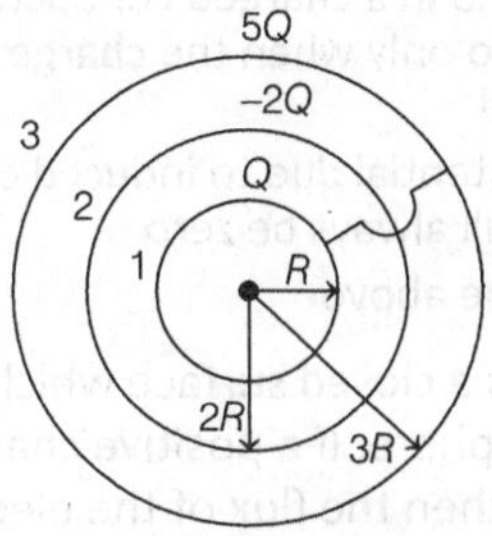

5.4 Parallel Conducting Plates

1 In each of the following cases, the parallel metallic plates kept at close separation are given charges as shown in figures. Find charges present on all surfaces marked as 1,2,3 for each case.

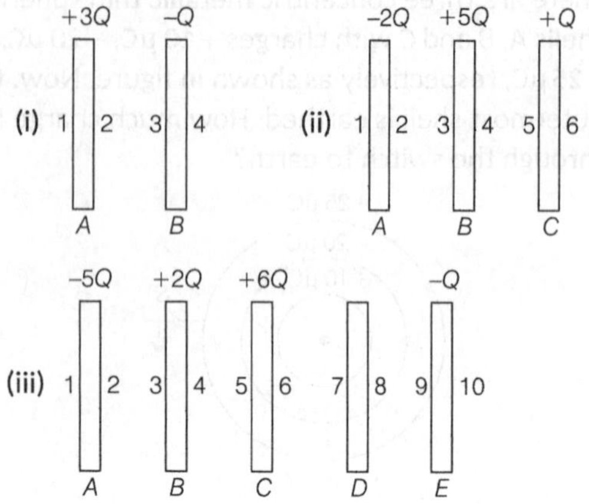

2 In figure, plate *A* has charge 100 μC and plate *B* has charge 60 μC. Find q_1, q_2, q_3 and q_4 when

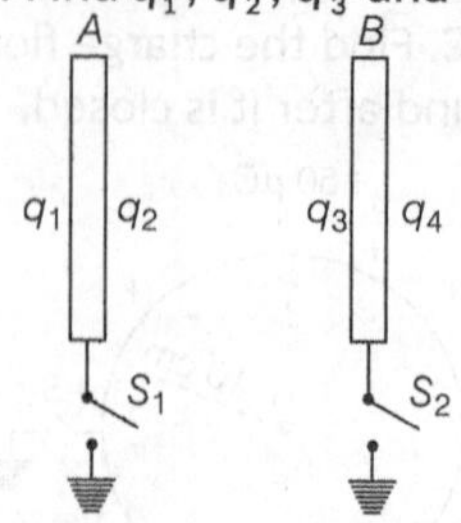

(i) only S_1 is closed,
(ii) only S_2 is closed,
(iii) both S_1 and S_2 are closed.

LEVEL 02 JEE Main Level

Single Choice Correct Questions

1 Which of the following statements about solid conductors in electrostatics is/are true?

I. The electric field inside the conductor is always zero.
II. The electric potential inside the conductor is always zero.
III. Any net charge is on the surface.

(a) Only I (b) Only III
(c) Both II and III (d) Both I and III

2 For a spherical shell,

(a) if potential inside it is zero, then it is necessarily electrically neutral
(b) electric field in a charged conducting spherical shell can be zero only when the charge is uniformly distributed
(c) electric potential due to induced charges at a point inside it will always be zero
(d) None of the above

3 Figure shows a closed surface which intersects a conducting sphere. If a positive charge is placed at the point *P*, then the flux of the electric field through the closed surface will

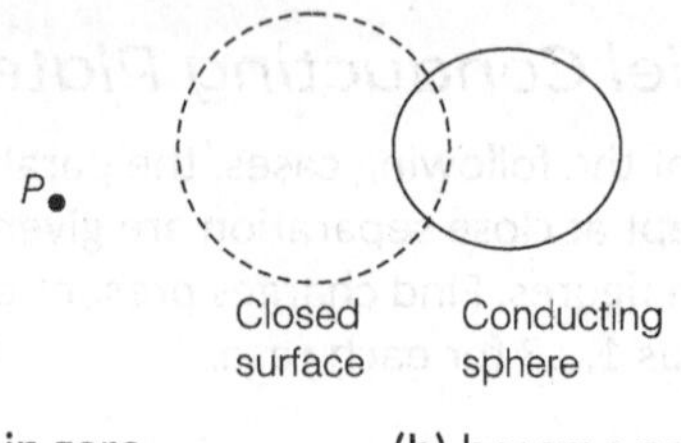

(a) remain zero (b) become positive
(c) become negative (d) become undefined

4 An isolated positively charged spherical conducting shell has a small hole at its surface. The field at the centre of the hole is (σ is surface charge density)

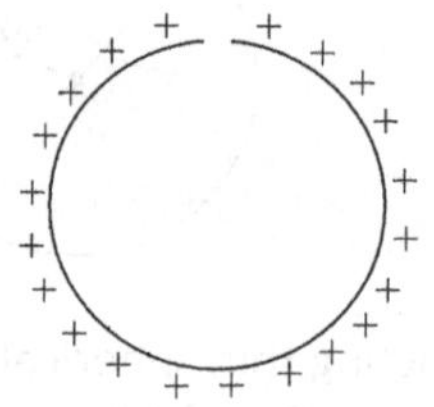

(a) $\frac{\sigma}{4\varepsilon_0}$ (b) $\frac{\sigma}{2\varepsilon_0}$
(c) $\frac{\sigma}{\varepsilon_0}$ (d) zero

5 Three concentric metallic spherical shells of radii *R*, 2*R*, 3*R* are given charges Q_1, Q_2, Q_3, respectively. It is found that the surface charge densities on the outer surfaces of the shells are equal, then the ratio of the charges given to the shells Q_1, Q_2, Q_3 is

(a) 1 : 2 : 3 (b) 1 : 3 : 5
(c) 1 : 4 : 9 (d) 1 : 8 : 18

6 A solid metallic sphere has a charge + 3Q. Concentric with this sphere is a conducting thin spherical shell having charge − Q. The radius of the sphere is *a* and that of the spherical shell is $b (> a)$. What is the electric field at a distance $r (a < r < b)$ from the centre?

(a) $\frac{Q}{2\pi\varepsilon_0 r^2}$ (b) $\frac{2Q}{4\pi\varepsilon_0 r^2}$
(c) $\frac{3Q}{4\pi\varepsilon_0 r^2}$ (d) None of these

7 A charge $+q$ is placed at a distance d from the centre of the uncharged metallic cube of side a. The electric field at the centre of the cube due to induced charges on the cube will be

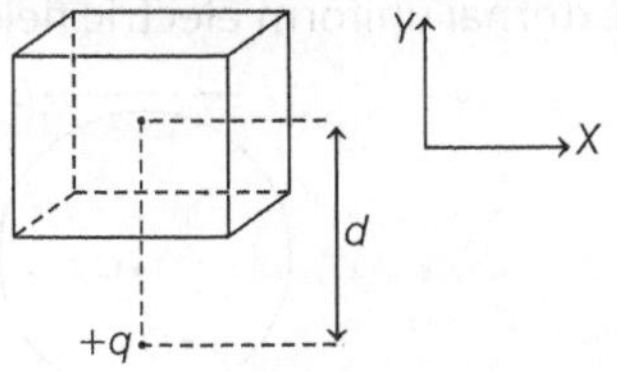

(a) zero (b) $\frac{q}{4\pi\varepsilon_0 d^2}(-\hat{\mathbf{j}})$

(c) $\frac{q}{4\pi\varepsilon_0 d^2}(\hat{\mathbf{j}})$ (d) $\frac{q}{4\pi\varepsilon_0\left(d-\frac{a}{2}\right)^2}(-\hat{\mathbf{j}})$

8 A spherical cavity of radius r is made in a conducting sphere of radius $2r$. A charge q is kept at the centre of cavity as shown in the figure. Find the magnitude of the total electric field at $(4r, 0, 0)$.

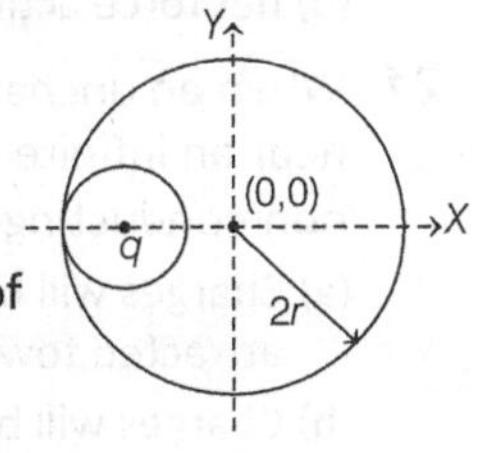

(a) $\frac{kq}{16r^2}$ (b) $\frac{4kq}{r^2}$ (c) $\frac{kq}{25r^2}$ (d) $\frac{4kq}{9r^2}$

9 A hollow spherical conductor has inner radius a and outer radius b. A positive point charge $+q$ is placed at the centre of the sphere. The conductor is uncharged. The potential at a distance r from centre $(a < r < b)$ is

(a) $V = kq\left[\frac{1}{r} + \frac{(b-a)}{ab}\right]$ (b) $V = \frac{kq}{r}$

(c) zero (d) $V = \frac{kq}{b}$

10 A point charge q is placed inside a neutral conducting spherical shell of inner radius $2R$ and outer radius $3R$ at a distance of R from the centre of the shell. The electric potential at the centre of shell will be $\frac{1}{4\pi\varepsilon_0}$ times, is

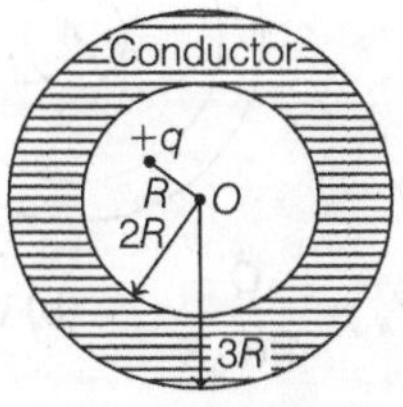

(a) $\frac{q}{2R}$ (b) $\frac{4q}{3R}$ (c) $\frac{5q}{6R}$ (d) $\frac{2q}{3R}$

11 Consider two concentric conducting spheres as shown in figure. The outer sphere is hollow and has a total charge of $+5\,\mu C$ charge on it; its inner radius is $R_1 = 9$ cm and its outer radius is $R_2 = 10$ cm. The inner sphere has a radius of 1 cm, is solid and has a charge $-3\mu C$ on it. What is the potential of the inner surface of the spherical shell?

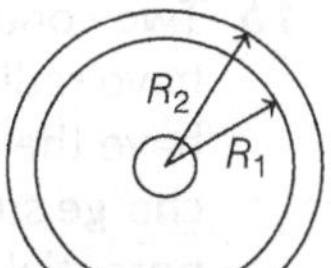

Assume that, the potential at infinite distance is zero.

(a) 180 kV (b) 300 kV

(c) 720 kV (d) None of these

12 A point charge q is placed at distance a from the centre of an uncharged thin spherical conducting shell of radius $R = 2a$. A point P is located at a distance $4a$ from the centre of the conducting shell as shown in figure. The electric potential due to induced charge on the inner surface of the conducting shell at point P is

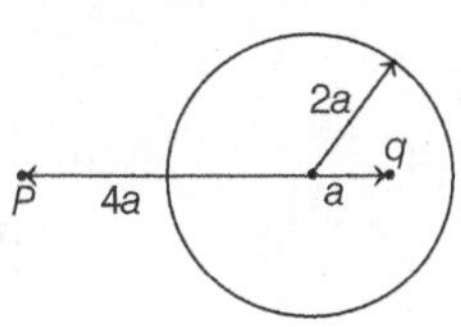

(a) $\frac{kq}{5a}$ (b) $-\frac{kq}{5a}$ (c) $\frac{kq}{4a}$ (d) $-\frac{kq}{4a}$

13 A small spherical conductor A of radius a is initially charged to a potential V and then placed inside an uncharged spherical conducting shell B of radius $6a$ as shown in figure. The potential of the spherical conductor A after closing the switch S is

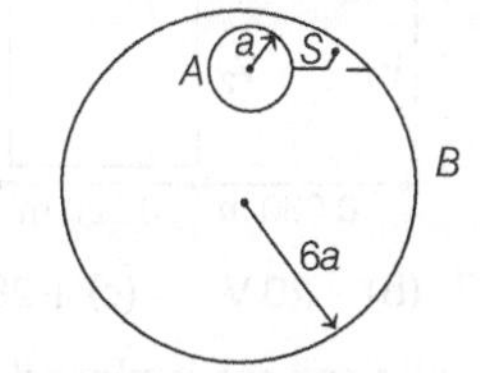

(a) V (b) $V/3$ (c) $V/2$ (d) $V/6$

14 S is a solid neutral conducting sphere. A point charge $q = 1 \times 10^{-6}$ C is placed at point A. C is the centre of sphere and AB is a tangent $BC = 3$ m and $AB = 4$ m. The electric potential at B due to induced charge on the sphere is

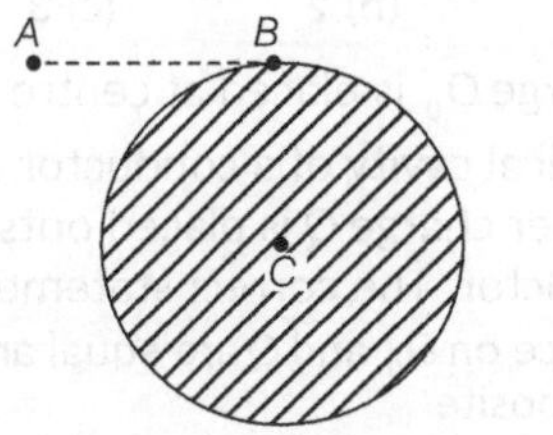

(a) 1.2 kV (b) $-$1.2 kV (c) $-$0.45 kV (d) 0.45 kV

15 Two conducting, concentric, hollow spheres A and B have radii a and b respectively, with A inside B. They have the same potential V. A is now given some charge such that its potential becomes zero. The potential of B will now be

(a) 0 (b) $V(1-a/b)$
(c) Va/b (d) $V(b-a)/(b+a)$

16 A point charge q is placed at a distance $3R$ from the centre of a hollow thin earthed conducting thin shell of radius R as shown in the figure. What is the electric potential due to the charge on spherical shell at a point A at a distance $\frac{R}{2}$ from centre of shell ?

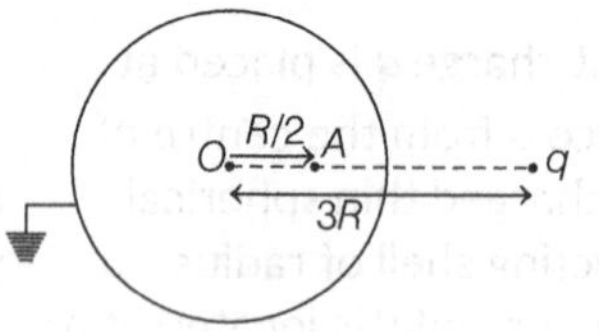

(a) $-\frac{1}{4\pi\varepsilon_0}\frac{q}{3R}$ (b) $-\frac{1}{4\pi\varepsilon_0}\frac{q}{2.5R}$
(c) Zero (d) None of these

17 An infinite conducting plate of thickness 0.020 m is surrounded by a uniform field $E = 400$ V/m directed left to right. Refer adjoining figure. Let the potential $V_0 = 0$ at a distance 0.020 m to the right of the plate. What is V_3, if the potential 0.030 m to the left of the plate?

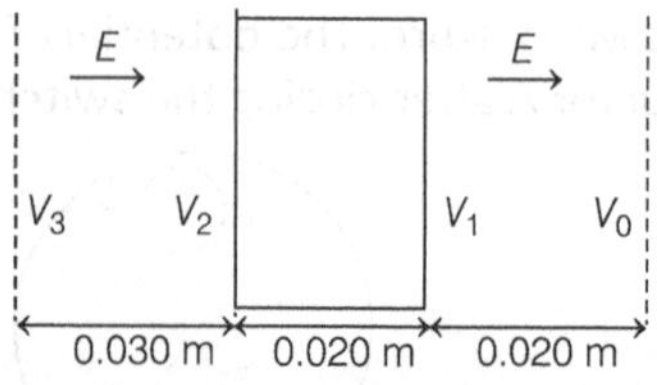

(a) – 28 V (b) – 20 V (c) + 28 V (d) + 20 V

18 A metallic solid sphere is placed in a uniform electric field. The lines of force follow the path(s) shown in figure as

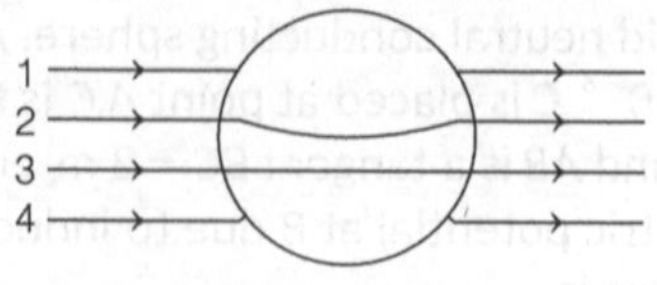

(a) 1 (b) 2 (c) 3 (d) 4

19 A charge Q_0 is placed at centre of spherical cavity of a conductor and another charge Q is placed outside the conductor. The correct statement is

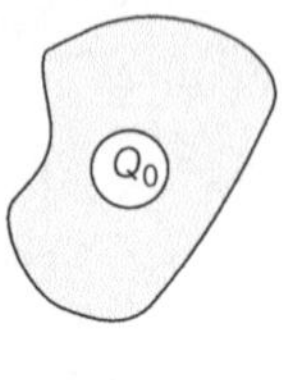

(a) force on Q_0 and Q are equal and opposite
(b) force on Q_0 is zero and force on Q is non-zero
(c) force on Q and Q_0 is zero
(d) force on Q_0 is non-zero and force on Q is zero

20 A positive point charge Q is kept (as shown in figure) inside a neutral conducting shell, whose centre is at C. An external uniform electric field E is applied, then

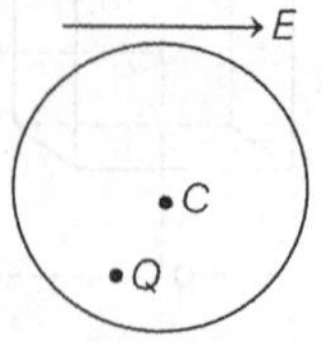

(a) force on Q due to E is zero
(b) net force on Q is zero
(c) net force acting on Q and conducting shell considered as a system is zero
(d) net force acting on the shell due to E is zero

21 When an uncharged cubical metal block is brought near an infinite uniformly charged non-conducting plane, choose the correct option.

(a) Charges will be induced on block and it will be attracted towards the plane
(b) Charges will be induced on block and it will be repelled from the plane
(c) Charges will be induced on block but it won't experience any force
(d) Either A or B depending on nature of metal

22 A metallic rod of length l rotates at angular velocity ω about an axis passing through one end and perpendicular to the rod . If mass of electron is m and its charge is $-e$, then the magnitude of potential difference between its two ends is

(a) $m\omega^2 l^2/2e$ (b) $m\omega^2 l^2/e$
(c) $m\omega^2 l/e$ (d) None of these

23 A and B are two concentric spheres of radii R and $2R$ respectively. A is given a charge $+Q$ and B is earthed. Which of the following is correct?

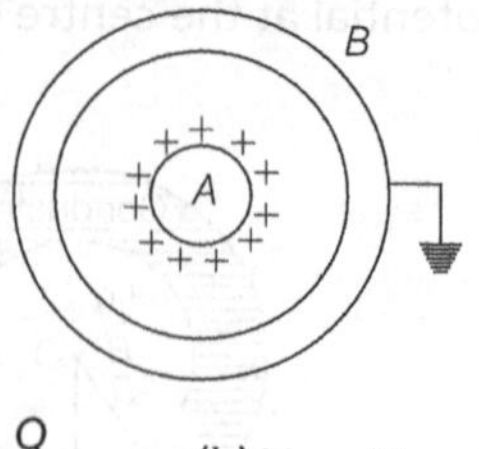

(a) $V_B = 0, V_A = \frac{Q}{4\pi\varepsilon_0 R}$ (b) $V_A = V_B = 0$

(c) $V_B = 0, V_A = \frac{Q}{8\pi\varepsilon_0 R}$ (d) $V_A = 0, V_B = \frac{Q}{2\pi\varepsilon_0 R}$

24 A conducting sphere of radius R and a concentric thick spherical shell of inner radius $2R$ and outer radius $3R$ is shown in figure. A charge $+10\,Q$ is given to the shell and inner sphere is earthed, then charge on inner sphere is

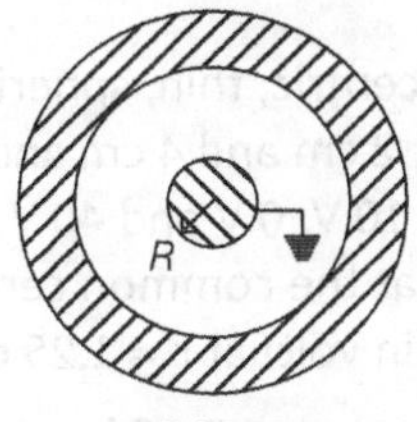

(a) $-4Q$ (b) $-10Q$
(c) zero (d) None of these

25 There are two uncharged identical metallic spheres 1 and 2 of radius r separated by a distance $d (d >> r)$. A charged metallic sphere of same radius having charge q is touched with one of the spheres. After sometime, it is moved away from the system. Now, the uncharged sphere is earthed, charge on the earthed sphere is

(a) q (b) $-q$
(c) $-qr/2d$ (d) zero

26 A system of three thin, concentric spherical metallic shells have radii a, b, c, where $a : b : c = 1 : 2 : 5$. Initially, charges $Q_1 = 24\,\mu C$ and $Q_2 = 30\,\mu C$ are given to the innermost and outermost.
How much charge passes through the switch S, when it is closed?

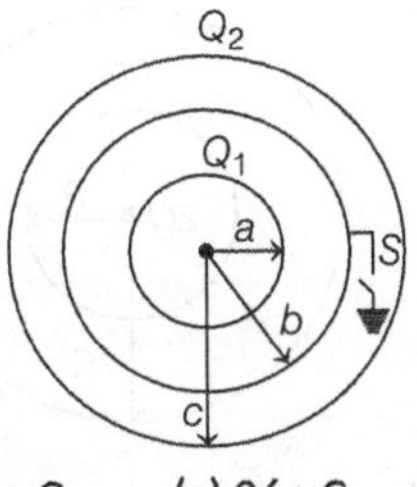

(a) 120 μC (b) 60 μC (c) 36 μC (d) zero

27 Consider a thin conducting shell of radius R carrying total charge Q. Two point charges Q and $2Q$ are placed on points A and B, which are at a distances of $R/2$ and $2R$ from the centre of the cell respectively as shown in the figure. If the cell is earthed, how much charge will flow to the earth?

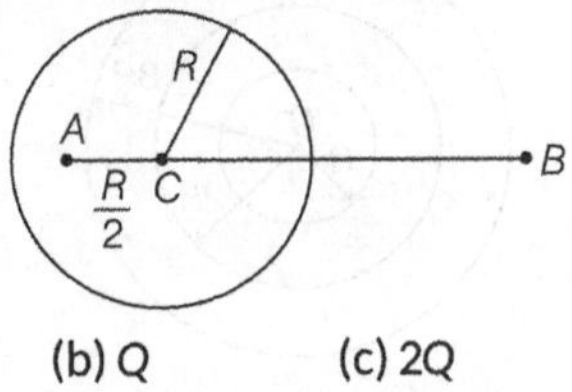

(a) $3Q$ (b) Q (c) $2Q$ (d) $Q/2$

28 Three concentric spherical conducting shells A, B and C of radii a, $2a$ and $4a$ are initially given charges $+Q$, $-2Q$ and $+Q$, respectively. The charge on the middle spherical shell B after switches S_1 and S_2 are simultaneously closed, will be

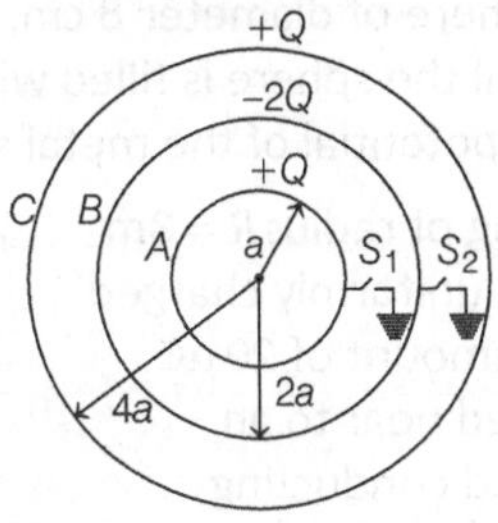

(a) $-Q$ (b) $-\frac{Q}{2}$ (c) $+Q$ (d) $+\frac{3Q}{2}$

29 In the figure shown below, the electric potential energy of the system is
(q is at the centre of the conducting neutral spherical shell of inner radius a and outer radius b and ignore self-energy of point charge)

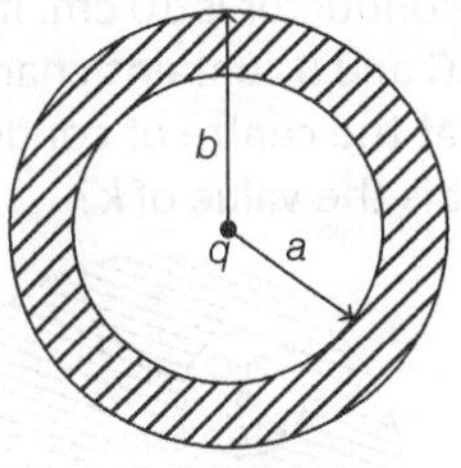

(a) zero (b) $\frac{kq^2}{2b}$
(c) $\frac{kq^2}{2b} - \frac{kq^2}{2a}$ (d) $\frac{kq^2}{2a} - \frac{kq^2}{2b}$

30 Two concentric spherical conducting shells of radii a and $2a$ are initially given charges $+2Q$ and $+Q$ respectively as shown in figure. The total heat dissipated after switch S has been closed is (Take, $k = \frac{1}{4\pi\varepsilon_0}$)

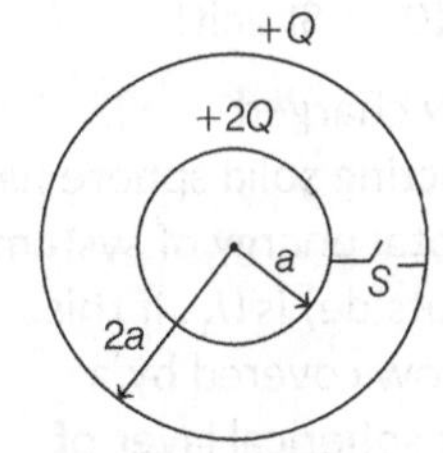

(a) $\frac{5kQ^2}{4a}$ (b) $\frac{kQ^2}{a}$
(c) $\frac{kQ^2}{2a}$ (d) $\frac{kQ^2}{4a}$

Numerical Value Questions

1 Mercury from a metal vessel maintained at a potential of 3V falls in spherical drops of 2 mm diameter through a small hole into a thin walled metal sphere of diameter 8 cm, isolated and placed in air until the sphere is filled with mercury. Calculate the final potential of the metal sphere (in volt).

2 A thin ring of radius $R = 3$m has been uniformly charged with an amount of 20 μC and placed near to an uncharged conducting sphere in such a way that the centre of the sphere O, lies on the rings axis at a distance of $l = 4$ m from the plane of the ring. The potential of the sphere is $n \times 10^4$ volt, find the value of n.

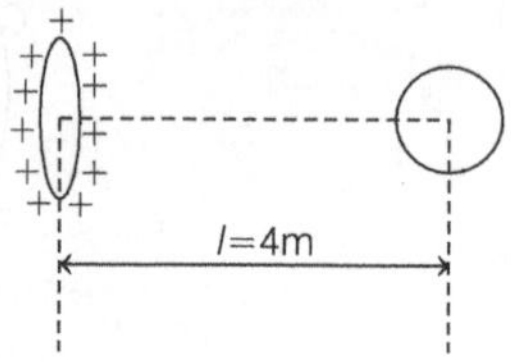

3 A neutral spherical conductor having cavity A and B of radius 1cm and 2cm, respectively. Radius of spherical conductor is 10 cm. If cavity A contains charge 2μC and B contains charge of $-1\,\mu$C, electric potential at the centre of conductor is $k \times 10^4$ volt, then what is the value of k?

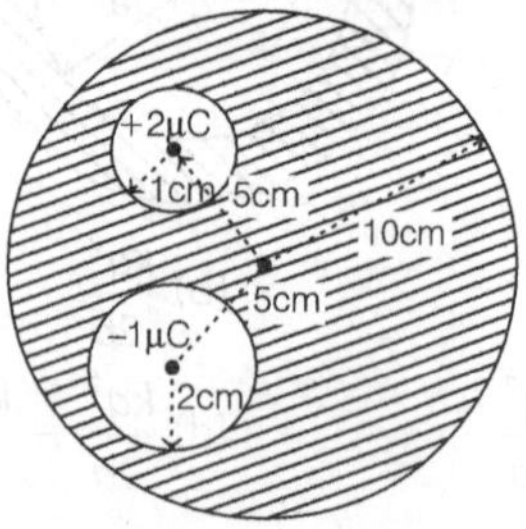

4 A metal sphere of radius a carries a charge Q. It is surrounded, out to radius b, by linear dielectric material of permittivity ε. Then, potential at the centre (relative to infinity) is given by α kV, find the value of α.
[Here, $Q = (4/3)\,\mu$C, $a = 1$m, $b = 2$m and $\varepsilon = 17.7 \times 10^{-12}$ SI unit]

5 A uniformly charged non-conducting solid sphere has a radius R. Total energy of system (inside + outside) is U_1. If this sphere is now covered by a conducting spherical layer of thickness $4R$, the total energy of system reduces to U_2. Find the ratio of $\frac{U_1}{U_2}$.

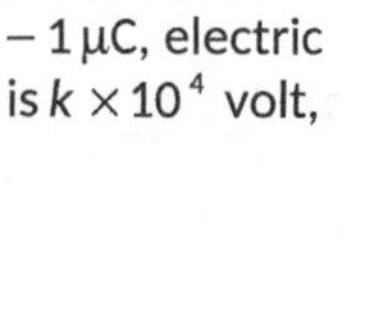

6 A thin spherical soap bubble has surface tension S. Its surface is charged with charge Q and its volume is V. It is found that when $Q^2 = n\pi\varepsilon_0 SV$, the excess pressure inside the bubble becomes zero. Find the value of n.

7 Three concentric, thin, spherical, metallic shells have radii 1 cm, 2 cm and 4 cm and they are held at potentials 10 V, 0 V and 40 V, respectively. Taking the origin at the common centre, calculate the potential (in volt) at $r = 1.25$ cm.

8 A point charge $q = 2$mC is moving towards the centre of an earthed conducting sphere of radius 2 m with a velocity 5 m/s. Find the current (in μA) flowing in the ammeter as shown in figure, when q is at a distance 5 m from the centre of sphere.

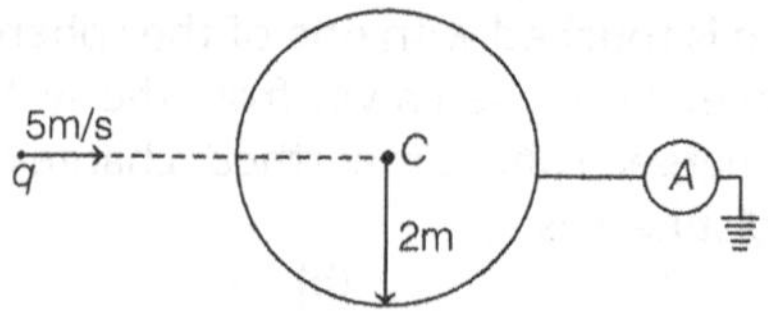

9 In the figure shown, a point charge $2Q$ is placed at the centre. The two concentric thin conducting spherical shells of radii R and $2R$ shown have charges $+Q$ and $-2Q$, respectively. Find the amount of heat generated (in joule) after the shell of radius R is earthed. (Take, $R = 1$ cm and $Q = 1\,\mu$C)

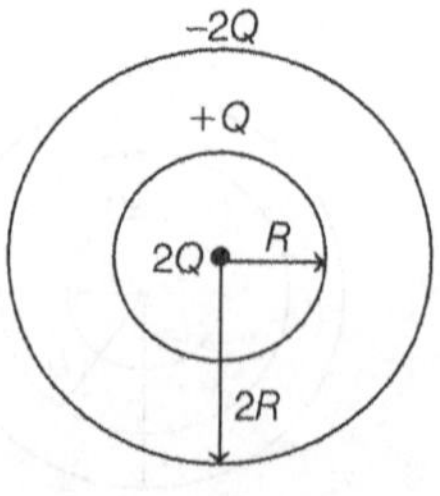

10 Three conducting concentric spherical shells of radii R, $2R$ and $3R$ carry equal charge densities. The innermost and the outermost spheres are now connected by a conducting wire. The ratio of potentials at the centre C before and after the connection is β. Find the value of 14β.

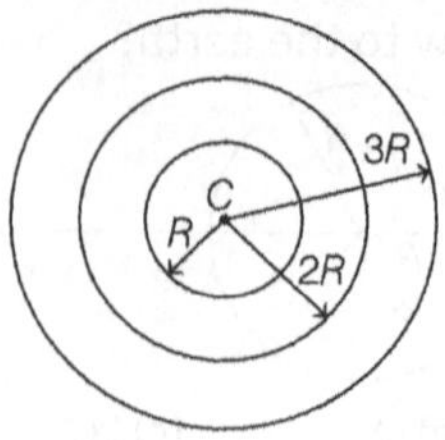

LEVEL 03 JEE Advanced Level

Single Choice Correct Questions

1 Two concentric conducting spherical shells of radii a_1 and $a_2\,(a_2 > a_1)$ are charged to potentials V_1 and V_2, respectively. The charge on the inner shell is

(a) $4\pi\varepsilon_0\left(\frac{V_1 - V_2}{a_2 - a_1}\right)a_1 a_2$ (b) $4\pi\varepsilon_0\left(\frac{V_1 - V_2}{a_2 + a_1}\right)a_1 a_2$

(c) $4\pi\varepsilon_0\left(\frac{V_1 + V_2}{a_2 - a_1}\right)a_1 a_2$ (d) $4\pi\varepsilon_0\left(\frac{V_1 + V_2}{a_2 + a_1}\right)a_1 a_2$

2 An ideal dipole of dipole moment **p** is placed infront of an uncharged conducting sphere of radius R as shown in figure. Potential at A due to the induced charges on the sphere is

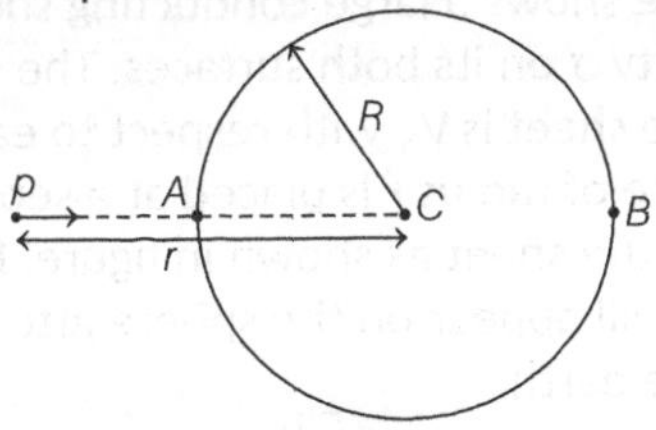

(a) $\frac{kp}{(r-R)^2}$ (b) $\frac{kp}{r^2} + \frac{kp}{(r-R)^2}$

(c) $\frac{kp}{r^2} - \frac{kp}{(r-R)^2}$ (d) $\frac{kp}{r^2}$

3 Two charges q_1 and q_2 are placed inside spherical cavities made inside uncharged conducting sphere of radius R as shown in figure. Electric field at P due to all the induced charges on the sphere is

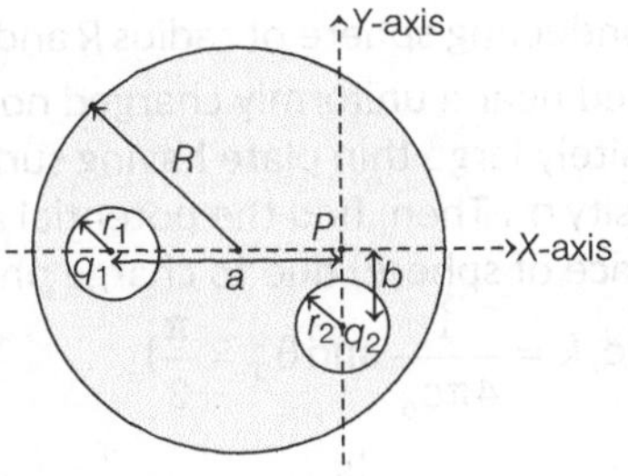

(a) $\frac{kq_1}{a^2}\hat{i} + \frac{kq_2}{b^2}\hat{j}$ (b) $-\frac{kq_1}{a^2}\hat{i} - \frac{kq_2}{b^2}\hat{j}$

(c) $\frac{kq_1}{r_1^2}\hat{i} + \frac{kq_2}{r_2^2}\hat{j}$ (d) $-\frac{kq_1}{r_1^2}\hat{i} - \frac{kq_2}{r_2^2}\hat{j}$

4 A charged particle $+q$ is placed inside a grounded metallic shell of inner and outer radii a and b respectively as shown in the figure. The particle is at a distance of $\left(\frac{a}{2}\right)$ from the centre of the shell, then the magnitude of potential at the centre of the sphere is equal to

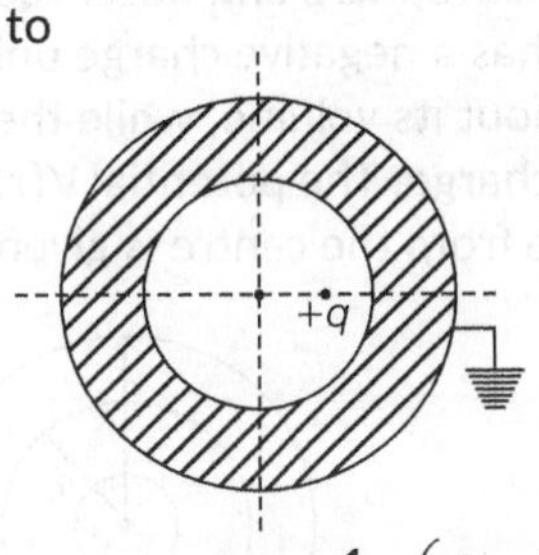

(a) zero (b) $\frac{1}{4\pi\varepsilon_0}\left(\frac{q}{b} + \frac{q}{a}\right)$

(c) $\frac{1}{4\pi\varepsilon_0}\left(\frac{q}{a}\right)$ (d) $\frac{1}{4\pi\varepsilon_0}\left(\frac{2q}{a} + \frac{q}{b}\right)$

5 A charged particle is brought near a neutral, isolated spherical conductor. Now, the switch S connecting the conductor to ground is closed. Which of the following statement(s) is/are incorrect?

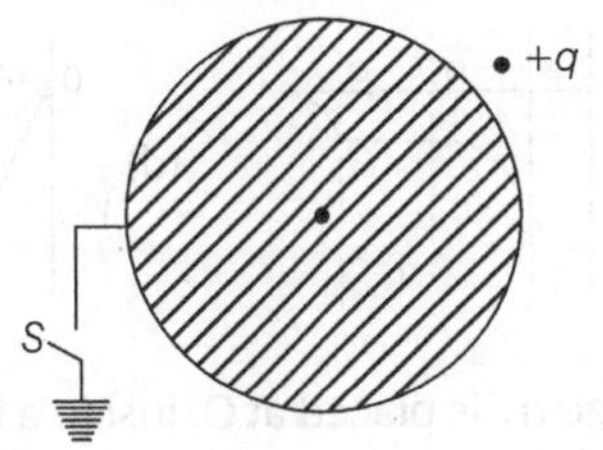

(a) The sphere draws negative charge, when grounded.
(b) The sphere's potential reduces to zero, when it is grounded.
(c) There will be zero induced charges on the surface of the sphere, when it is grounded.
(d) The sphere will attract the charged particle.

6 An ellipsoidal cavity is present inside a solid conducting sphere centred at the origin. The radius of the sphere is R and it is electrically neutral. On the XY-plane, the equation of the cavity can be given by the equation $(x^2/a^2) + (y^2/b^2) = 1$. If a point charge $+Q$ is placed at the centre of the cavity, then what is the potential at point A, having coordinates $(0, b)$?

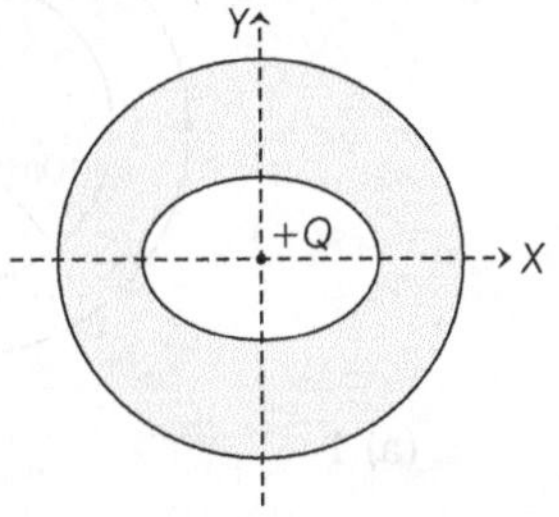

(a) $\frac{Q}{4\pi\varepsilon_0}\left(\frac{1}{b} - \frac{1}{R}\right)$ (b) $\frac{Q}{4\pi\varepsilon_0}\left(\frac{1}{b} + \frac{1}{R}\right)$

(c) $\frac{Q}{4\pi\varepsilon_0}\left(\frac{1}{a+b} - \frac{1}{R}\right)$ (d) $\frac{Q}{4\pi\varepsilon_0 R}$

7 A non-conducting sphere with radius a is concentric with and surrounded by a conducting spherical shell with inner radius b and outer radius c. The inner sphere has a negative charge uniformly distributed throughout its volume, while the spherical shell has no net charge. The potential $V(r)$ as a function of distance from the centre is given by

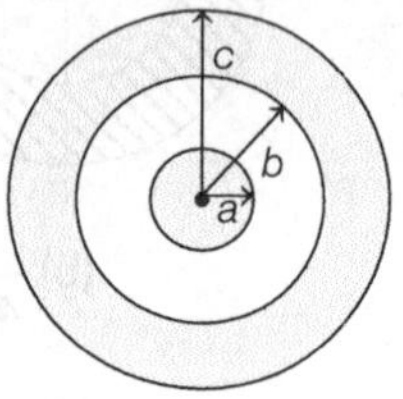

(a)
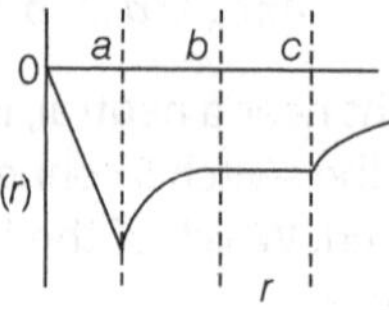

(b)
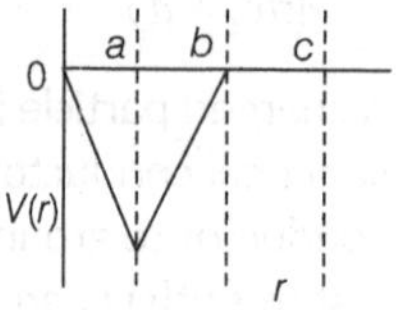

(c)
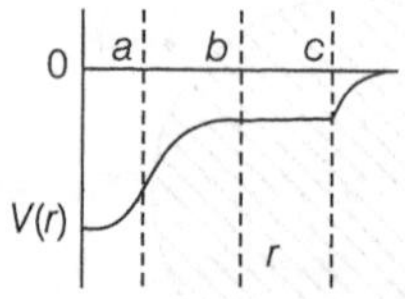

(d)
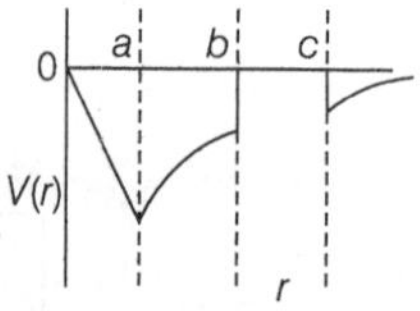

8 A charge q_1 is placed at O, inside a hollow conducting sphere having inner and outer radii as 10m and 11m as shown in figure. The force experienced by charge q_2 placed at point P is F_1. Instead of O, if q_1 is placed at O, force experience by q_2 is F_2 ($OO' = 5$ m, $OP = 12$ m). Then, F_1 / F_2 is

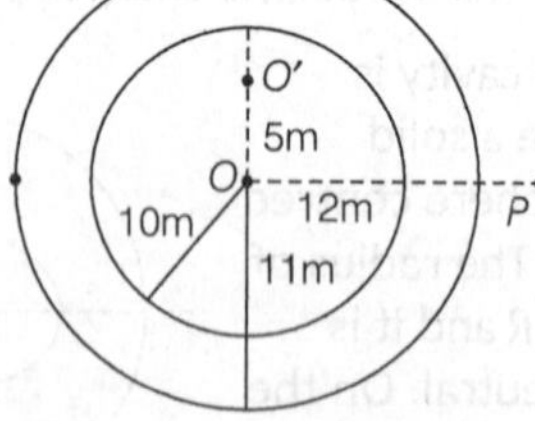

(a) 1 (b) $\left(\frac{12}{13}\right)^2$

(c) $\left(\frac{13}{12}\right)^2$ (d) $\left(\frac{4}{3}\right)^2$

9 There are two conducting concentric spherical thin shells of radius $\frac{3R}{4}$ and R. Thin shell of radius R is given a charge $4Q$. A point charge $-Q$ is also placed in the cavity at a distance $R/2$ from the centre as shown in figure. The electric potential at a distance $2R$ from the centre of concentric spherical shells along the line joining point charge is

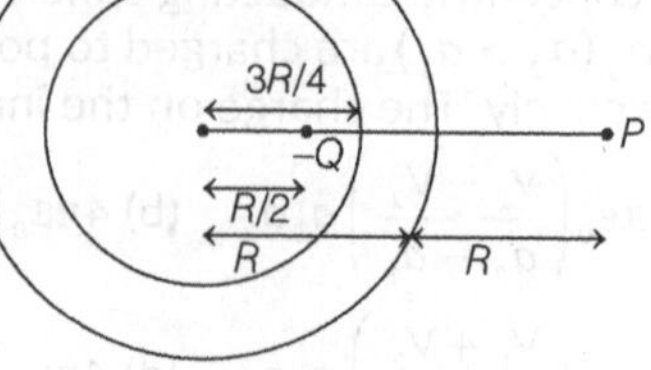

(a) $\frac{1}{8\pi\varepsilon_0}\frac{5Q}{R}$ (b) $-\frac{1}{8\pi\varepsilon_0}\frac{5Q}{R}$

(c) $\frac{1}{8\pi\varepsilon_0}\frac{3Q}{R}$ (d) $\frac{1}{2\pi\varepsilon_0}\frac{Q}{3R}$

10 Figure shows a large conducting sheet having charge density σ on its both surfaces. The surface potential of the sheet is V_0 with respect to earth. A conducting sphere of radius r is placed at a separation $l (l >> r)$ from the sheet as shown in figure. Find the charge that will appear on the sphere after it is connected to the earth.

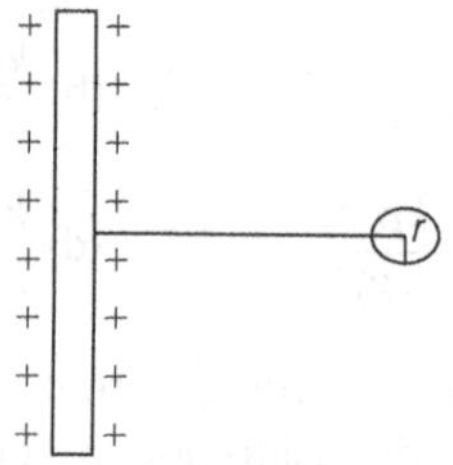

(a) $4\pi r(\sigma l - V_0 \varepsilon_0)$ (b) $4\pi r(\sigma l + V_0 \varepsilon_0)$

(c) $\pi r(\sigma l - V_0 \varepsilon_0)$ (d) Zero

11 A conducting sphere of radius R and charge Q is placed near a uniformly charged non-conducting infinitely large thin plate having surface charge density σ. Then, find the potential at point A (on the surface of sphere) due to charge on sphere.

(Take, $k = \frac{1}{4\pi\varepsilon_0}$ and $\theta_0 = \frac{\pi}{3}$)

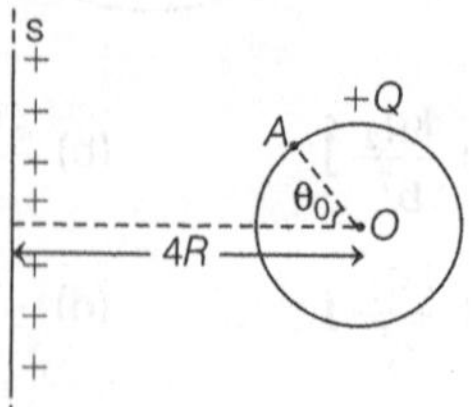

(a) $k\frac{Q}{R} - \frac{\sigma}{4\varepsilon_0}R$ (b) $k\frac{Q}{R} - \frac{\sigma R}{\varepsilon_0}$

(c) $k\frac{Q}{R}$ (d) None of these

12 A straight chain consisting of n identical metal balls is at rest in a region of free space as shown in figure. In the chain, each ball is connected with adjacent balls by identical conducting wires. Length l of a connecting wire is much larger than the radius r of a ball. A uniform electric field E pointing along the chain is switched ON in the region. Find magnitude of induced charges on one of the end ball.

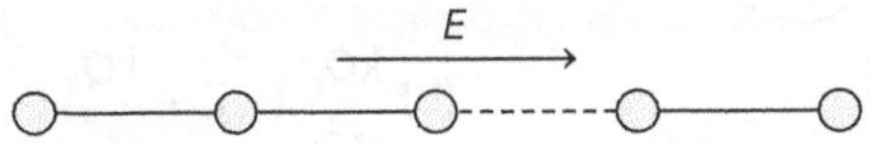

(a) $2\pi\varepsilon_0 rnlE$ (b) $2\pi\varepsilon_0 r(n-1)lE$
(c) $4\pi\varepsilon_0 r(n-1)lE$ (d) $4\pi\varepsilon_0 (n-1)^2 l^2 E$

13 In the figure, A, B, C and D are four concentric spheres of radii a, $2a$, $3a$ and $4a$ and contain charges $+3q$, $+6q$, $-9q$ and $+12q$, respectively. In the beginning, switches S_1 and S_2 are open. After earthing the sphere C, Δq_1 amount of charge flows from the sphere C to the earth. If the sphere B is also earthed, then Δq_2 amount of charge flows from the sphere B to the earth. Find the value of $\left|\dfrac{\Delta q_1}{\Delta q_2}\right|$.

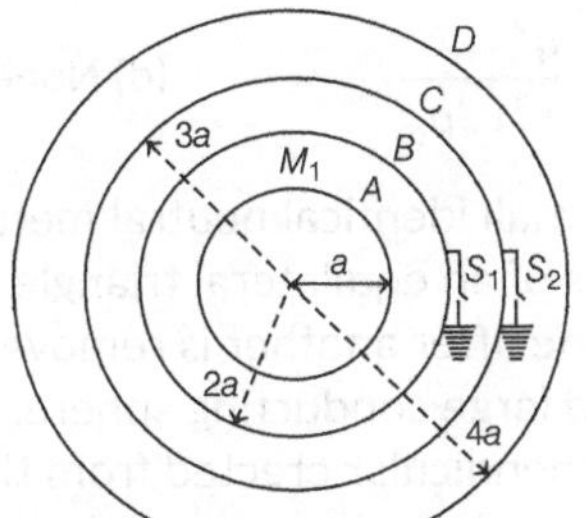

(a) 1 (b) 3/5 (c) 2/3 (d) 1/2

14 A thick hollow metallic sphere of inner and outer radii $2a$ and $4a$ respectively, encloses a solid concentric metallic sphere of radius a. These spheres are connected to the earth through switches S_1 and S_2 as shown in the figure. Initially, charge Q is given to the outer sphere with both S_1 and S_2 open. First, switch S_1 is closed and after sometime S_1 is opened. Then, S_2 is closed and after sometime S_2 is opened. This completes one cycle. The charge on the inner sphere after n cycles of earthing the inner and outer spheres is

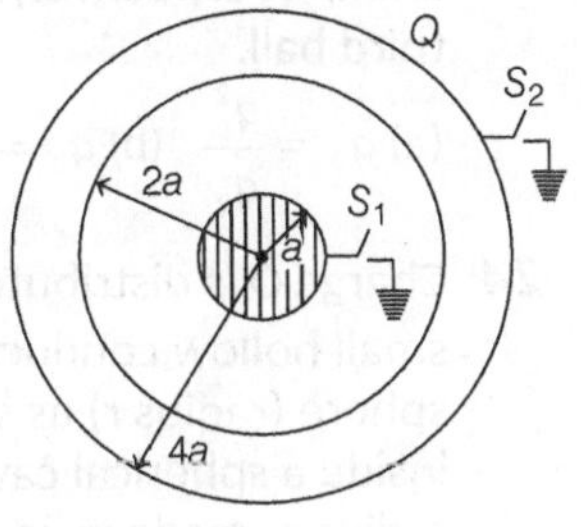

(a) $-Q/3$ (b) $-Q/3^n$
(c) $Q/3^n$ (d) None of these

15 Two non-conducting hemispherical surfaces, which are having uniform charge density σ are placed on smooth horizontal surface as shown in figure. Assuming springs are ideal, calculate compression in each spring, if both the hemispherical surfaces are just touching each other.

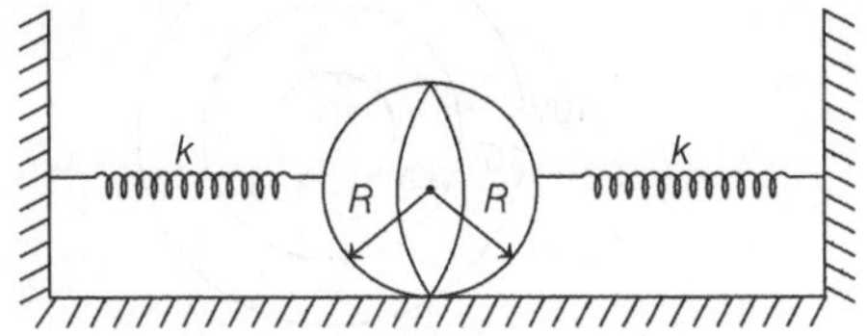

(a) $\dfrac{\sigma^2 R^2}{2\varepsilon_0 k}$ (b) R

(c) $\dfrac{\sigma^2 \pi R^2}{2\varepsilon_0 k}$ (d) None of these

16 Two concentric thin metal shells are shown in figure. Charge density on inner shell is σ_1, while that on outer shell is σ_2. Find the electrostatic pressure at any point of outer shell.

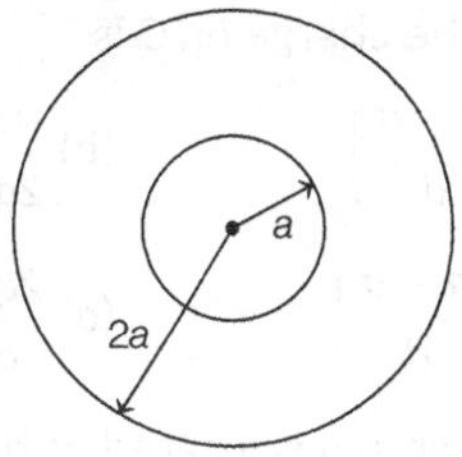

(a) $\dfrac{\sigma_2}{4\varepsilon_0}(\sigma_1+\sigma_2)$ (b) $\dfrac{\sigma_2}{4\varepsilon_0}(\sigma_1+2\sigma_2)$

(c) $\dfrac{\sigma_2}{4\varepsilon_0}(2\sigma_1+\sigma_2)$ (d) $\dfrac{\sigma_2}{2\varepsilon_0}(\sigma_1+\sigma_2)$

17 Electrically charged drops of mercury fall from altitude h into a spherical metal vessel of radius R in the upper part of which there is a small opening. The mass of each drop is m and charge is Q. What is the number n of last drop that can still enter the sphere?

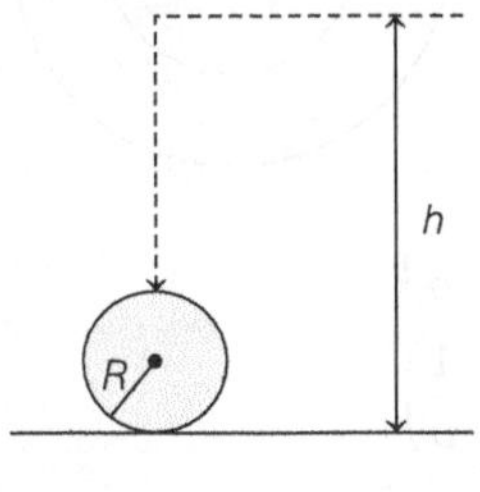

(a) $\dfrac{mg(h-R)R}{kQ^2}$ (b) $\dfrac{mg(h-2R)R}{kQ^2}$

(c) $\dfrac{mghR}{kQ^2}$ (d) $\dfrac{2mg(h-R)R}{kQ^2}$

18 The diagram shows three concentric conducting spherical shells having radii R, $2R$ and $3R$. The initial potential of each shell is as mentioned in the figure. If the inner most shell is earthed, then the charge present on its outer surface would be equal to

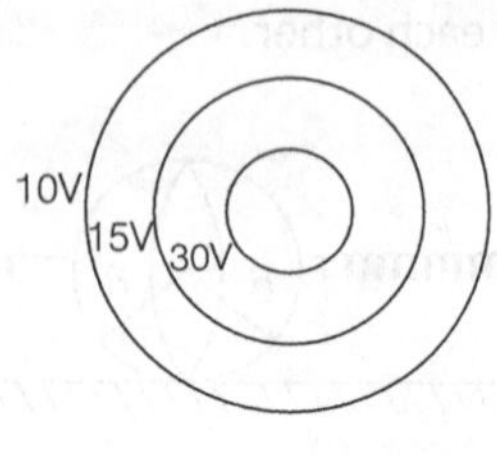

(a) zero (b) $40\pi\varepsilon_0 R$

(c) $4\pi\varepsilon_0 R$ (d) $-\pi\varepsilon_0 R$

19 Three identical metallic uncharged spheres A, B and C of radius a are kept on the corners of an equilateral triangle of side d. The fourth sphere of radius a ($d >> a$) which has a charge q touches A and is then removed to a position far away. B is earthed and then the earth connection is removed. C is then earthed, the charge on C is

(a) $\frac{qa}{2d}\left(\frac{2d-a}{2d}\right)$ (b) $\frac{qa}{2d}\left(\frac{2d-a}{d}\right)$

(c) $-\frac{qa}{2d}\left(\frac{d-a}{d}\right)$ (d) $\frac{2qa}{d}\left(\frac{d-a}{2d}\right)$

20 A point charge q is located at the centre O of a spherical uncharged conducting layer provided with small orifice. The inside and outside radii of the layer are equal to a and b, respectively. The amount of work that has to be performed to slowly transfer the charge q from the point O through the orifice and into infinity is

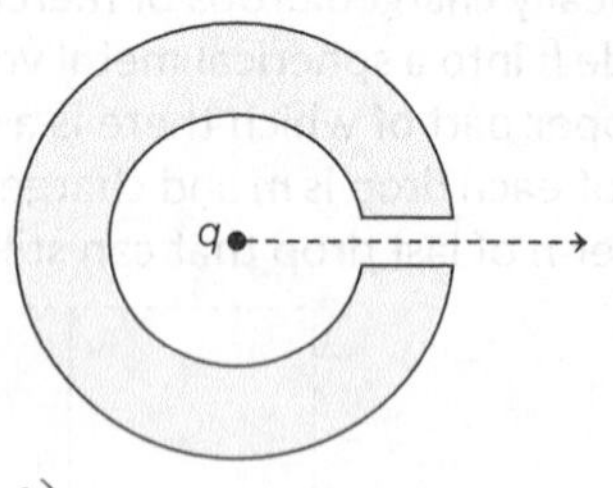

(a) $\frac{q^2}{4\pi\varepsilon_0}\left(\frac{1}{a}-\frac{1}{b}\right)$

(b) $\frac{q^2}{8\pi\varepsilon_0}\left(\frac{1}{a}-\frac{1}{b}\right)$

(c) $\frac{3q^2}{4\pi\varepsilon_0}\left(\frac{1}{a}-\frac{1}{b}\right)$

(d) $\frac{3q^2}{8\pi\varepsilon_0}\left(\frac{1}{a}-\frac{1}{b}\right)$

21 The density of charge at point P on the conductor is σ C/m^2. The resultant electric field near P (just outside) will be

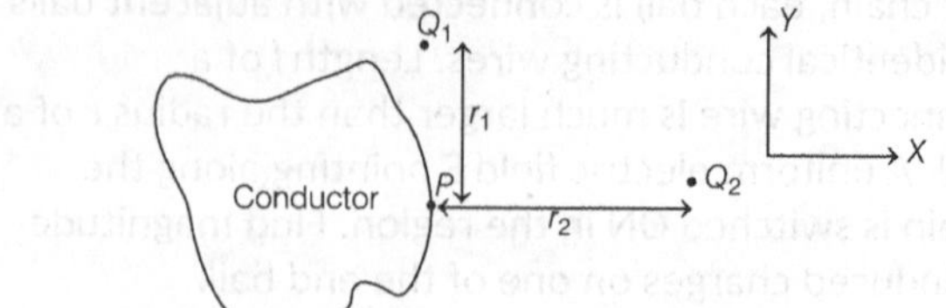

(a) $\frac{\sigma}{\varepsilon_0}\hat{i}$ (b) $\frac{kQ_1}{r_1^2}(-\hat{j})+\frac{kQ_2}{r_2^2}(-\hat{i})$

(c) $\frac{kQ_1}{r_1^2}(-\hat{j})+\frac{kQ_2}{r_2^2}(-\hat{i})+\frac{\sigma}{\varepsilon_0}(\hat{i})$

(d) $\frac{kQ_1}{r_1^2}(\hat{j})+\frac{kQ_2}{r_2^2}(\hat{i})+\frac{\sigma}{\varepsilon_0}(-\hat{i})$

22 An insulated soap bubble has radius r. It is then charged uniformly by total charge q. Neglecting surface tension, find the small increase in radius of bubble due to charging. Assume atmospheric pressure is p_0, temperature remains constant.

(a) $\frac{q^2}{32\pi^2 r^3\varepsilon_0 p_0}$ (b) $\frac{q^2}{48\pi^2 r^3\varepsilon_0 p_0}$

(c) $\frac{q^2}{96\pi^2 r^3\varepsilon_0 p_0}$ (d) None of these

23 Three small identical neutral metal balls are at the vertices of an equilateral triangle. The balls are in turn (one after another is removed) connected to an isolated large conducting sphere, whose centre is on the perpendicular erected from the plane of the triangle and passing through its centre. As a result, the first and second balls have acquired charges q_1 and q_2, respectively. Determine the charge q_3 of the third ball.

(a) $q_3=\frac{q_1^2}{q_2}$ (b) $q_3=\frac{q_2^2}{q_1}$ (c) $q_3=q_1$ (d) $q_3=q_2$

24 Charge Q is distributed on a small hollow conducting sphere (radius r) as shown inside a spherical cavity of radius r_1 made inside a solid conducting sphere of radius r_2 as shown in the figure. The total energy of the system is

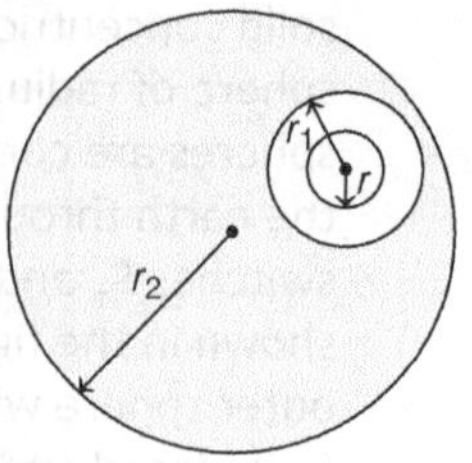

(a) $kQ^2\left(\frac{1}{2r_2}-\frac{1}{2r_1}+\frac{1}{2r}\right)$ (b) $kQ^2\left(\frac{1}{r_1}+\frac{1}{r_2}+\frac{1}{2r}\right)$

(c) $kQ^2\left(\frac{1}{2r_1}+\frac{1}{4r_2}+\frac{1}{2r}\right)$ (d) $kQ^2\left(\frac{1}{4r_1}+\frac{1}{2r_2}+\frac{1}{2r}\right)$

25 A charged large metal sheet is placed into uniform electric field, perpendicularly to the electric field lines. After placing the sheet into the field, the electric field on the left side of the sheet is $E_1 = 5 \times 10^5$ V/m and on the right, it is $E_2 = 3 \times 10^5$ V/m. The sheet experiences a net electric force of 0.08 N. Find the area of one face of the sheet. Assume, external field to remain constant after introducing the large sheet.

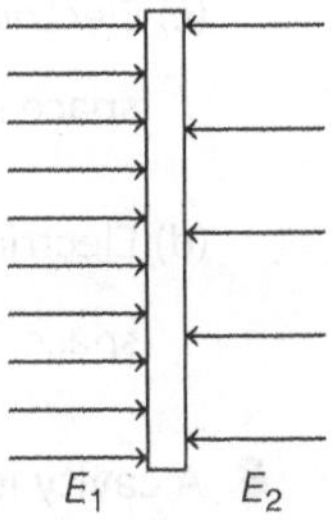

$\left(\text{Take, } \frac{1}{4\pi\varepsilon_0} = 9 \times 10^9 \text{ N-m}^2/\text{C}^2\right)$

(a) $3.6\,\pi \times 10^{-2}\,\text{m}^2$ (b) $0.9\,\pi \times 10^{-2}\,\text{m}^2$
(c) $1.8\,\pi \times 10^{-2}\,\text{m}^2$ (d) None of these

26 Three large plates are arranged as shown in figure. How much charge will flow through the key K, if it is closed?

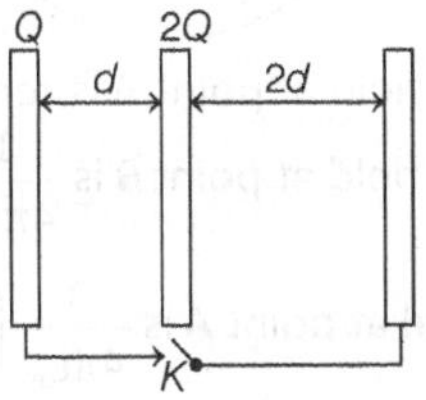

(a) $\frac{5Q}{6}$ (b) $\frac{4Q}{3}$
(c) $\frac{3Q}{2}$ (d) None of these

Multiple Choice(s) Correct Questions

1 A conducting ball is charged and another similar point charge is brought closer to the ball,
(a) the ball may attract the point charge
(b) the ball may repel the point charge
(c) the electric field inside the ball due to ball's charges is non- zero
(d) the net electric field inside the ball is zero

2 A conductor having total charge $+Q$ with a cavity, is placed inside a non-uniform electric field and there is no charge inside cavity. Then, in electrostatic conditions, the electric field
(a) inside the conductor is zero but non-zero in the cavity
(b) just outside the conductor is $\frac{\sigma}{\varepsilon_0}$, where σ is the local surface charge density
(c) inside the conductor is non-zero
(d) inside the conductor as well as cavity is zero

3 Figure shows a neutral metallic sphere with a point charge $+Q$ placed near its surface. Electrostatic equilibrium conditions exist on metallic sphere, mark the correct statements.

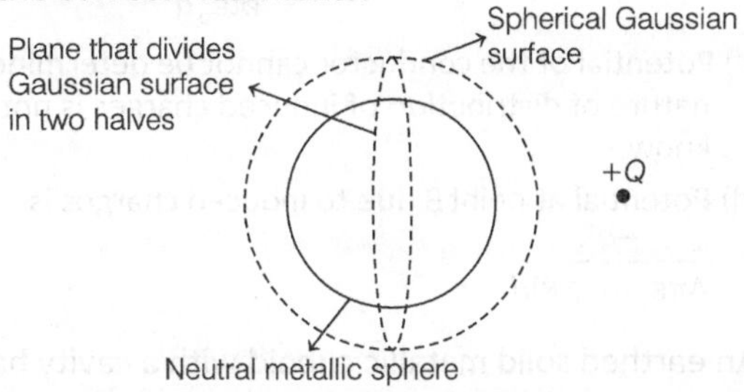

(a) Net flux through Gaussian surface due to charge Q is zero.
(b) Net flux through Gaussian surface due to charges appearing on the outer surface of metallic sphere must be zero.
(c) If point charge Q is displaced towards metallic sphere, magnitude of net flux through right hemispherical closed Gaussian surface increases.
(d) If point charge Q is displaced towards metallic sphere, charge distribution on outer surface of sphere will change.

4 There is a conductor with cavity of radius R as shown in figure. A point charge Q is placed at $R/2$ distance from centre of cavity. A point P is at r distance from centre of conductor, then

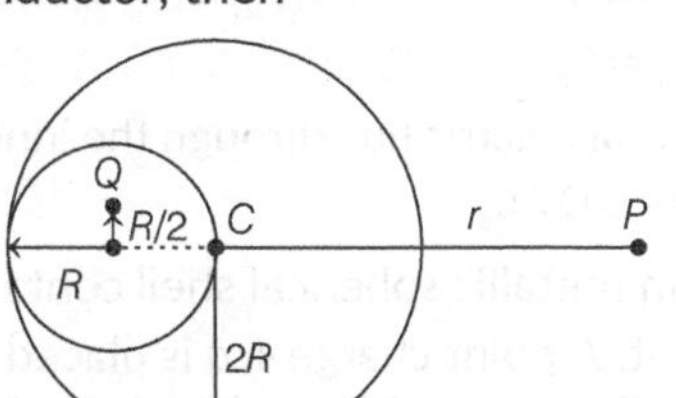

(a) charge density at inner surface of cavity will be non-uniform
(b) charge density at surface of conductor will be uniform
(c) electric field at point P is $\frac{Q}{4\pi\varepsilon_0 r^2}$
(d) force on charge Q is zero

5 For the situation shown in the figure below, mark out the correct statement(s).

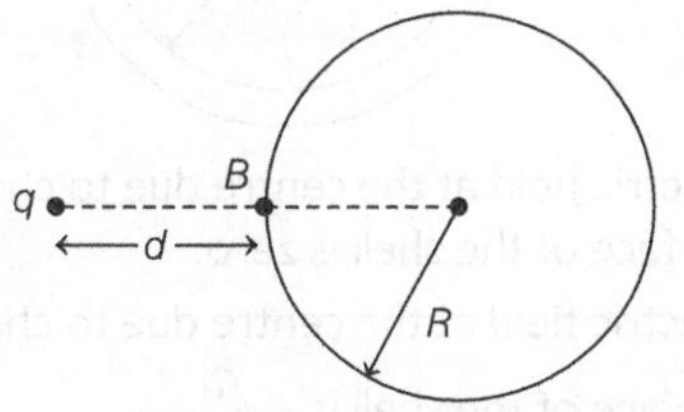

Hollow neutral conductor

(a) Potential of the conductor is $\dfrac{q}{4\pi\varepsilon_0(d+R)}$.

(b) Potential of the conductor is $\dfrac{q}{4\pi\varepsilon_0 d}$.

(c) Potential of the conductor cannot be determined as nature of distribution of induced charges is not known.

(d) Potential at point B due to induced charges is $\dfrac{-qR}{4\pi\varepsilon_0(d+R)d}$.

6 An earthed solid metallic cuboid with a cavity has a charged particle $+Q$ placed inside it and A and B are two points on the inner surface of the cavity as shown in figure. If σ, E and V represent the induced surface charge density, magnitude of electric field and electric potential, then which of the following statement(s) is/are correct?

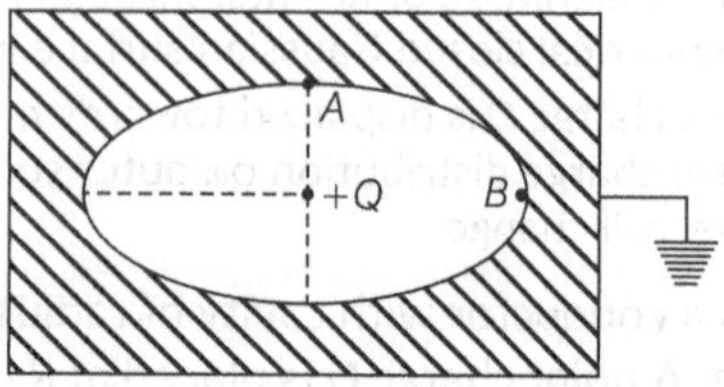

(a) $\sigma_A = \sigma_B$
(b) $V_A = V_B$
(c) $E_A = E_B$
(d) Total electric flux through the inner surface of the cavity is Q/ε_0.

7 A thin metallic spherical shell contains a charge Q over it. A point charge $+q$ is placed inside the shell at point T separated from the centre by distance a. Another point charge q_1 is placed outside the shell at a distance b from the centre as shown in the figure. Now, select the correct statement(s) from the following.

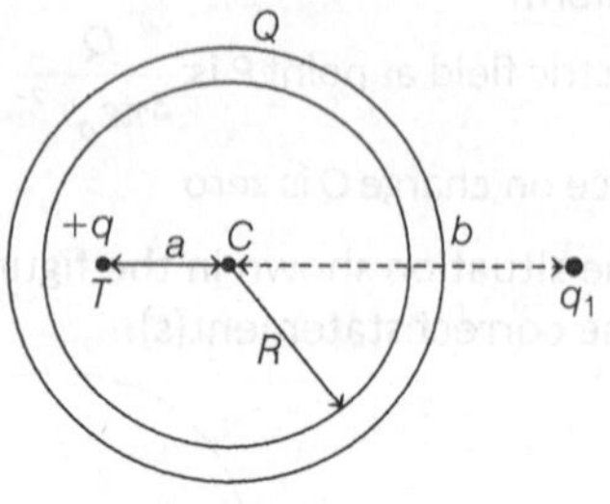

(a) Electric field at the centre due to charges over outer surface of the shell is zero.

(b) Electric field at the centre due to charges over outer surface of the shell is $\dfrac{q_1}{4\pi\varepsilon_0 b^2}$.

(c) Electric potential at the centre due to all charges in space is $\dfrac{1}{4\pi\varepsilon_0}\left(\dfrac{q}{a}-\dfrac{q}{R}+\dfrac{Q}{R}+\dfrac{q_1}{b}\right)$

(d) Electric potential at the centre due to all charges in space is $\dfrac{1}{4\pi\varepsilon_0}\left(\dfrac{q}{a}+\dfrac{Q}{R}+\dfrac{q_1}{b}\right)$.

8 A cavity is made inside a solid conducting sphere and a charge q is placed inside the cavity at the centre. A charge q_1 is placed outside the sphere as shown in the figure. Point A is inside the sphere and point B is inside the cavity, then

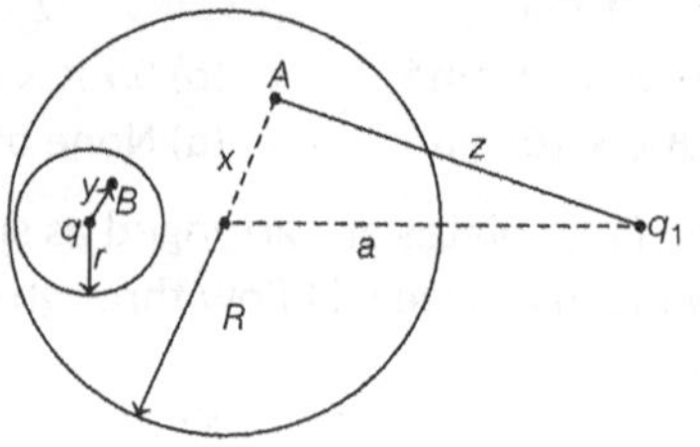

(a) electric field at point A is zero

(b) electric field at point B is $\dfrac{1}{4\pi\varepsilon_0}\dfrac{q}{y^2}$

(c) potential at point A is $\dfrac{1}{4\pi\varepsilon_0}\left(\dfrac{q_1}{a}+\dfrac{q}{R}\right)$

(d) potential at point B is $\dfrac{1}{4\pi\varepsilon_0}\left(\dfrac{q_1}{a}+\dfrac{q}{R}+\dfrac{q}{y}-\dfrac{q}{r}\right)$

9 As shown in figure, a point charge q_1 is placed inside a neutral conducting shell at a distance $\dfrac{R}{2}$ from the centre of shell. Another point charge q_2 is placed at a distance $\dfrac{\sqrt{7}}{2}R$ from the centre of shell. Choose the correct statement(s).

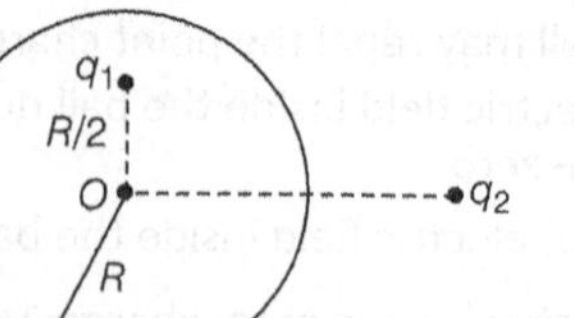

(a) The magnitude of force on q_1 due to induced charges at the inner surface of the shell is zero.

(b) The magnitude of force on q_1 due to induced charges at the outer surface of the shell is $\dfrac{q_1 q_2}{8\pi\varepsilon_0 R^2}$.

(c) The magnitude of force on q_2 due to induced charges at the inner surface of the shell is zero.

(d) The magnitude of force on q_2 due to induced charges at the inner surface of the shell is $\dfrac{q_1 q_2}{8\pi\varepsilon_0 R^2}$.

10 A thin conducting rod AB is introduced in between the two charges $+q_1$ and $-q_2$ as shown in figure. For this situation, mark the correct statement(s).

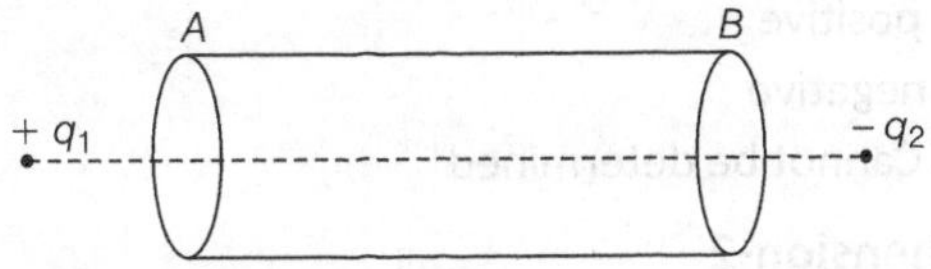

(a) The total force experienced by q_1 is vector sum of electric force experienced by $+q_1$ due to $-q_2$ and due to induced charges on rod.

(b) The end A will become negatively charged.

(c) The total magnitude of force acting on $+q_1$ will be greater than as compared to the case without rod.

(d) The total magnitude of force acting on $-q_2$ will be greater than as compared to the case without rod.

11 Two concentric shells have radii R and $2R$ charges q_A and q_B and potentials $2V$ and $(3/2)$ V respectively, if potential at infinity is zero. Now, shell B is earthed and let charges on them become q'_A and q'_B. Then,

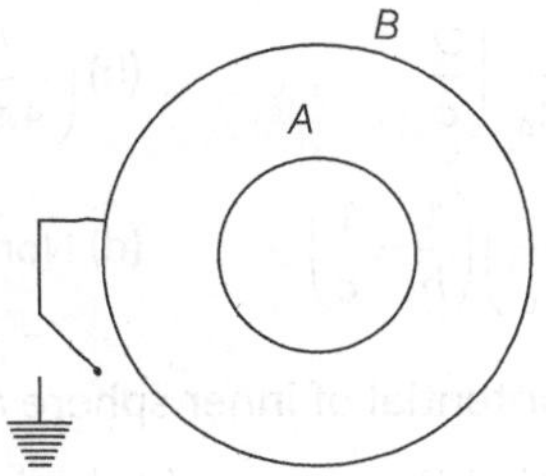

(a) $q_A / q_B = 1/2$

(b) $q'_A / q'_B = 1/2$

(c) potential of A after earthing becomes $(3/2)$ V

(d) potential difference between A and B after earthing becomes $V/2$

12 A solid conducting sphere of radius R is initially uncharged and Q charge is brought from infinity to point A, which is a distance $2R$ from centre of the sphere. B and D are points on sphere as shown in figure. Switch S is initially open, then

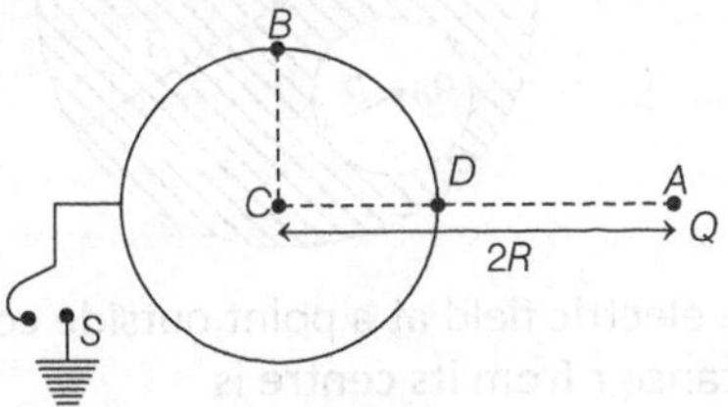

(a) $\dfrac{V_D}{V_B} = \dfrac{\sqrt{5}}{2-\sqrt{5}}$, where V_B and V_D are potential at B and D respectively due to induced charge on the sphere

(b) $V_B - V_D = \dfrac{Q}{4\pi\varepsilon_0 R}\left(\dfrac{1}{2} - \dfrac{1}{\sqrt{5}}\right)$, where V_B are V_D potential at B and D respectively due to induced charge on the sphere

(c) If switch is closed, then $Q/2$ flows from sphere to ground

(d) If switch is closed, then Q flows from sphere to ground

13 A spherical shell of radius R is given charge $3q$ on its surface and a point charge q is placed at distance $R/2$ from its centre C. Also, there is a charge $2q$ placed outside the shell at a distance of $2R$ as shown in figure. Then,

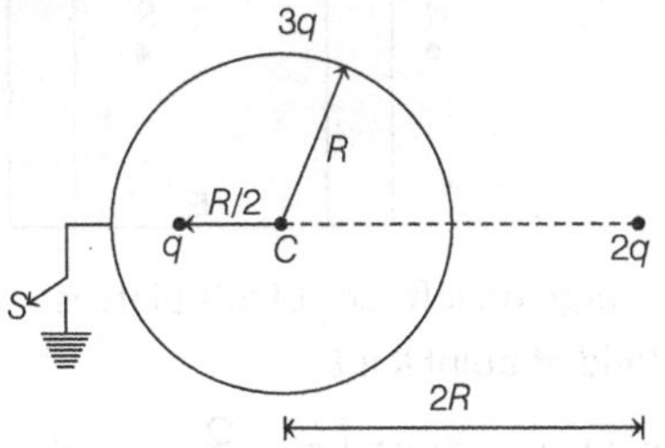

(a) the magnitude of electric field at the centre C due to charges on the outer surface of shell is $\dfrac{kq}{2R^2}$ before closing the switch S

(b) the electric potential at the centre C due to charges on the outer surface of shell is $\left(\dfrac{-kq}{R}\right)$ before closing the switch S

(c) the electric potential at the centre C due to charges on the outer surface of shell is $\left(\dfrac{-kq}{R}\right)$ after closing the switch S

(d) charge flown through the switch into earth after closing the switch S is $5q$

14 When isolated, the spherical shell A has a potential V. When connected by a conducting wire with initially uncharged spherical shell B and inside it, its potential is $(2/3)$ V. Find the correct options.

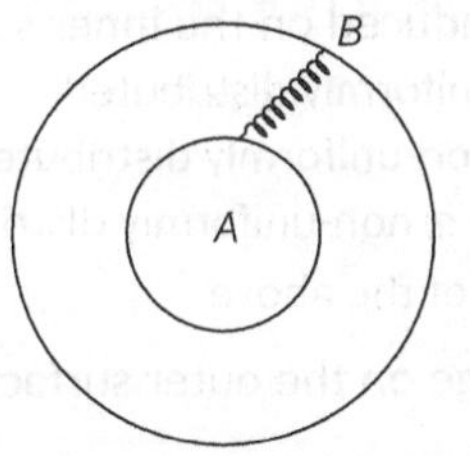

(a) If the radius of A is 2 cm, then radius of B will be 6 cm

(b) If the radius of A is 2 cm, then radius of B will be 3 cm

(c) The minimum charge on the shell B will be $8\pi\varepsilon_0 V$

(d) The minimum charge on the shell B will be $4\pi\varepsilon_0 aV$, where a is the radius of sphere A

15 Two large thin conducting plates with small gap in between are placed in a uniform electric field E (perpendicular to the plates). Area of each plate is A and charges $+Q$ and $-Q$ are given to these plates as shown in the figure. If points R, S and T as shown in the figure are three points in space, then the

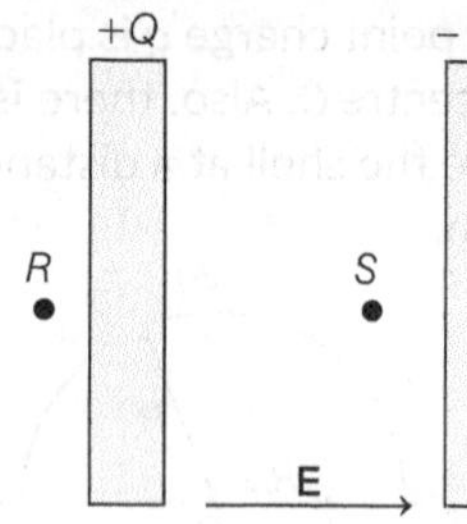

(a) charge on left face of left plate is $-\varepsilon_0 AE$

(b) field at point R is E

(c) field at point S is $\left(E + \dfrac{Q}{\varepsilon_0 A}\right)$

(d) field at point T is $\left(E + \dfrac{Q}{A\varepsilon_0}\right)$

Comprehension Based Questions

Comprehension-1

There is a cubical cavity inside a conducting sphere of radius R. A positive point charge Q is placed at the centre of the cube and another positive charge q is placed at a distance $l (> R)$ from the centre of the sphere. The sphere is earthed.

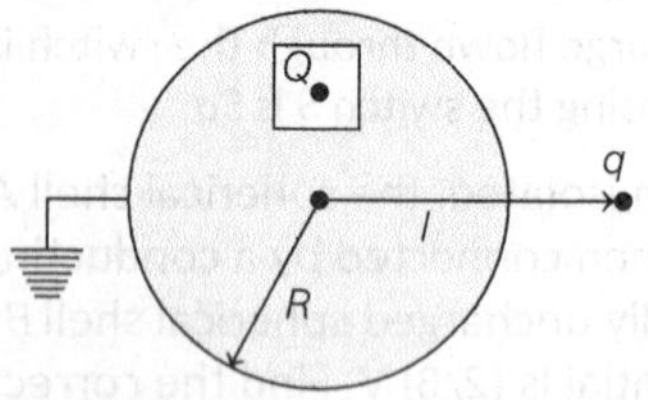

1 Charge induced on the inner surface of cavity is

(a) $-Q$, uniformly distributed

(b) $-Q$, non-uniformly distributed

(c) $-(Q + q)$ non-uniformly distributed

(d) None of the above

2 Net charge on the outer surface of conducting sphere is

(a) $+Q$ (b) $Q - qR/l$

(c) $-qR/l$ (d) None of these

3 Potential at a point inside the cavity is

(a) zero

(b) positive

(c) negative

(d) Cannot be determined

Comprehension-2

In the diagram shown, the outer conducting spherical shell (inner radius $= b$ and the outer radius $= c$) is electrically neutral and the inner conducting sphere (radius $= a$) carries charge $+Q$.

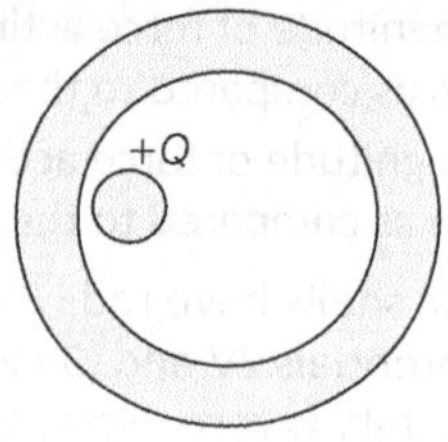

4 What is the potential of the outer spherical shell?

(a) $\left(\dfrac{1}{4\pi\varepsilon_0}\right)\dfrac{Q}{c}$ (b) $\left(\dfrac{Q}{4\pi\varepsilon_0}\right)\left(\dfrac{1}{c} - \dfrac{1}{a}\right)$

(c) $\left(\dfrac{Q}{4\pi\varepsilon_0}\right)\left(\dfrac{1}{b} - \dfrac{1}{c}\right)$ (d) None of these

5 If V_s is potential of inner sphere and V_c is the potential at the centre of spherical shell, then

(a) $V_c > V_s$ (b) $V_c < V_s$ (c) $V_c = V_s$

(d) None of the conclusions can be drawn from the given information

Comprehension-3

A conducting sphere of radius R has two spherical cavities of radius a and b. The cavities have charges q_a and q_b respectively at their centres, find

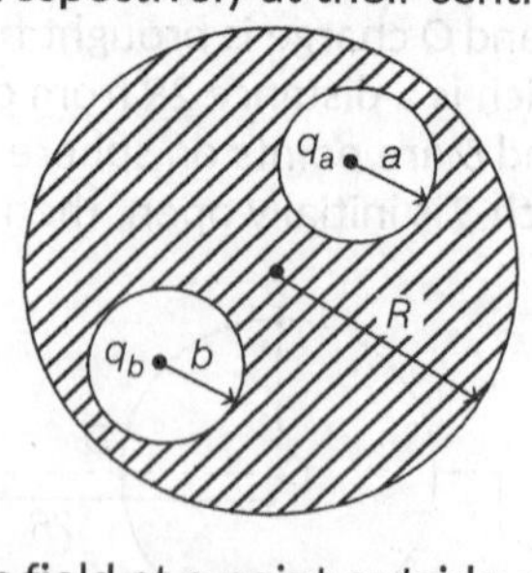

6 The electric field at a point outside conductor at a distance r from its centre is

(a) $\dfrac{q_a + q_b}{4\pi\varepsilon_0 r^2}$ (b) $\dfrac{q_a + q_b}{4\pi\varepsilon_0 R^2}$

(c) zero (d) Cannot find

7 The electric potential at a point inside cavity of radius b at a distance r from its centre is

(a) $\dfrac{q_b}{4\pi\varepsilon_0 r}$ (b) $-\dfrac{q_b}{4\pi\varepsilon_0 r}$ (c) $\dfrac{q_a + q_b}{4\pi\varepsilon_0 R}$ (d) $\dfrac{1}{4\pi\varepsilon_0}\left(\dfrac{q_a + q_b}{R} + \dfrac{q_b}{r} - \dfrac{q_b}{b}\right)$

8 Force on q_a is

(a) zero (b) $\dfrac{kq_a^2}{a^2}$

(c) $\dfrac{kq_a(q_a + q_b)}{R^2}$ (d) Cannot find

Comprehension-4

Four concentric hollow metallic spheres of radii R, $2R$, $3R$ and $4R$ have charges as shown in the figure, then the spheres 1 and 3, 2 and 4 are connected by conducting wires (both the connections are made at the same time).

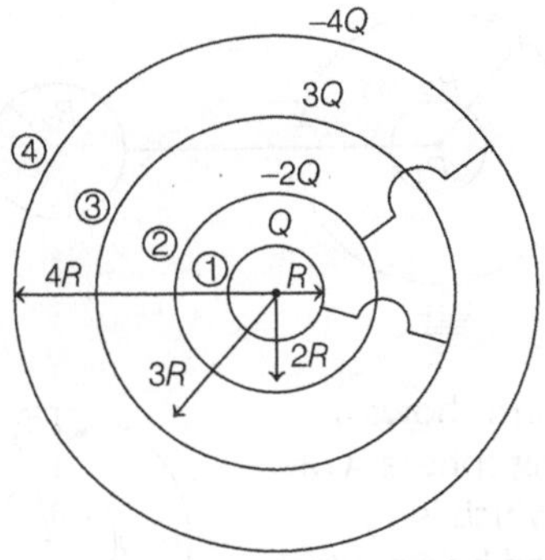

9 The charge on inner surface of third conductor is

(a) $-\dfrac{6Q}{5}$ (b) $+\dfrac{6Q}{5}$

(c) $-2Q$ (d) $+2Q$

10 The charge on fourth conductor is

(a) $+\dfrac{22Q}{5}$ (b) $+\dfrac{11Q}{3}$

(c) $-\dfrac{11Q}{3}$ (d) $-\dfrac{22Q}{5}$

11 The potential of conductor 1 is

(a) $\dfrac{3Q}{40\pi\varepsilon_0 R}$ (b) $-\dfrac{19Q}{40\pi\varepsilon_0 R}$

(c) $-\dfrac{3Q}{40\pi\varepsilon_0 R}$ (d) $\dfrac{19Q}{40\pi\varepsilon_0 R}$

12 The potential of conductor 2 is

(a) $-\dfrac{Q}{8\pi\varepsilon_0 R}$ (b) $\dfrac{Q}{8\pi\varepsilon_0 R}$

(c) $\dfrac{Q}{32\pi\varepsilon_0 R}$ (d) $-\dfrac{Q}{32\pi\varepsilon_0 R}$

Comprehension-5

Three identical parallel conducting plates A, B and C are placed as shown in figure. Switches S_1 and S_2 are open, and can connect A and C to earth when closed. $+Q$ charge is now given to B.

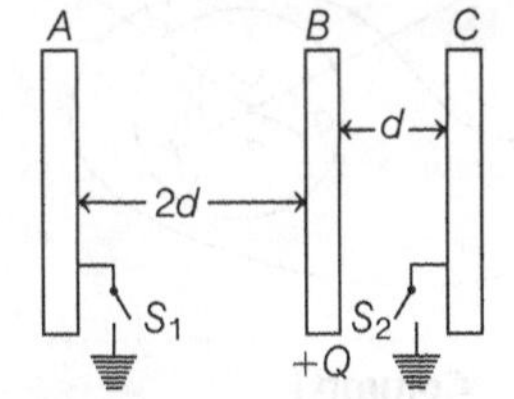

13 If S_1 is closed while S_2 is open, how much charge will pass through S_1?

(a) $Q/2$ (b) $2Q/3$ (c) $3Q/4$ (d) Q

14 If S_2 is closed while S_1 is open, how much charge will pass through S_2?

(a) $Q/2$ (b) $2Q/3$ (c) $3Q/4$ (d) Q

15 If S_1 and S_2 are closed simultaneously, how much charge will pass through S_2?

(a) $Q/2$ (b) $2Q/3$ (c) $3Q/4$ (d) Q

Match the Columns Questions

1 Figure shows three concentric thin spherical shells A, B and C of radii a, b and c, respectively. The shells A and C are given charges q and $-q$ respectively and the shell B is earthed. Find the charges appearing on the surfaces of B and C.

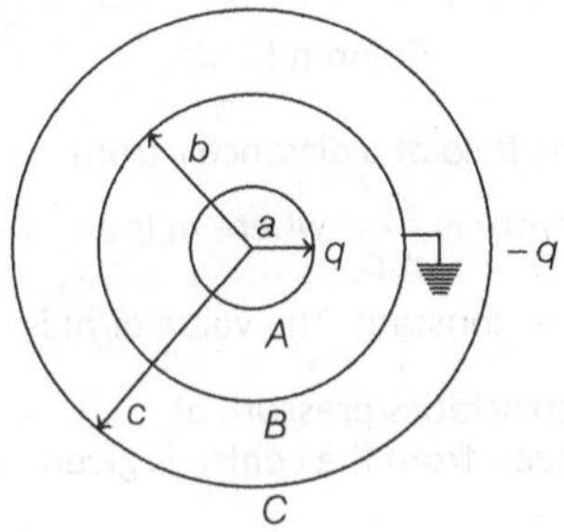

	Column I		Column II
(a)	Charge on outer surface of spherical shell C	(p)	$q/2$
(b)	Charge on inner surface of spherical shell C	(q)	$-q$
(c)	Charge on outer surface of spherical shell B	(r)	bq/c
(d)	Charge on inner surface of spherical shell B	(s)	$-bq/c$
		(t)	$q(b/c-1)$

2 In the shown figure, the conductor is uncharged and a charge q is placed inside a spherical cavity at a distance a from its centre C. Point P and charge $+Q$ are as shown in figure. a, b, c, d are known.

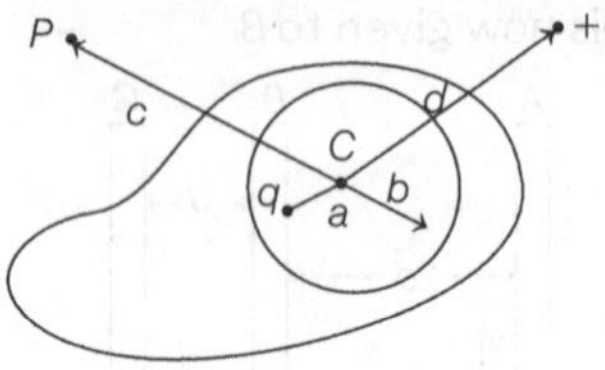

	Column I		Column II
(a)	Electric field due to induced charges on the inner surface of cavity at point P	(p)	zero
(b)	Electric potential due to charges on the inner surface of cavity and q at P	(q)	non-zero
(c)	Electric field due to induced charges on the outer surface of conductor and Q at C	(r)	value can be stated with the given data
(d)	Electric potential due to induced charges on the inner surface of cavity at C	(s)	value cannot be stated from the given data

3 A non-conducting sphere of radius R is given a volume charge density $\rho = kr$, where r is the distance of a point in the spherical volume from its centre and k is a positive constant. Match the physical quantities pertaining to the sphere in Column I with the values given in Column II.

	Column I		Column II
(a)	Electric field at a distance r from the centre is $\frac{kr^2}{m\varepsilon_0}$, where m is a positive constant. The value of m is	(p)	7
(b)	If electrostatics pressure at distance r from the centre is given by $p(r) = a(b - r^n)$, where a, b and n are constants, then $n =$	(q)	4
(c)	Electrostatic force of interaction between the left and right hemispheres is $\frac{k^2\pi R^6}{l\varepsilon_0}$, where l is a positive constant. The value of l is	(r)	5
(d)	Self-energy (Electrostatic) of the sphere is given by dR^e, where d and e are constants, then value of e is	(s)	6

Numerical Value Questions

1 The radius and surface tension of a spherical soap bubble be r and T, respectively. A charge is to be given to the bubble, so that its radius will become $2r$. Here, atmospheric pressure is p_0, temperature of air inside bubble remains constant and charge is assumed to uniformly distributed on the surface of bubble.

The final surface charge density is $\alpha \times 10^{-4}\ \text{C/m}^2$, find the value of α.

(Take, $p_0 = 10^4$ Pa, $T = 0.2$ N/m, $r = 0.12$ mm, $\varepsilon_0 = 9 \times 10^{-12}\ \text{C}^2/\text{N-m}^2$)

2 Two metal balls of radii R_1 and R_2, such that $R_2 = 2R_1$ are connected by a long thin conducting wire and has total charge $Q = 21\ \mu\text{C}$. Then, the ball of radius R_1 is placed inside a grounded metal sphere of radius $R = 3R_1$ as shown in figure. What charge (in μC) will flow through the wire in this process?

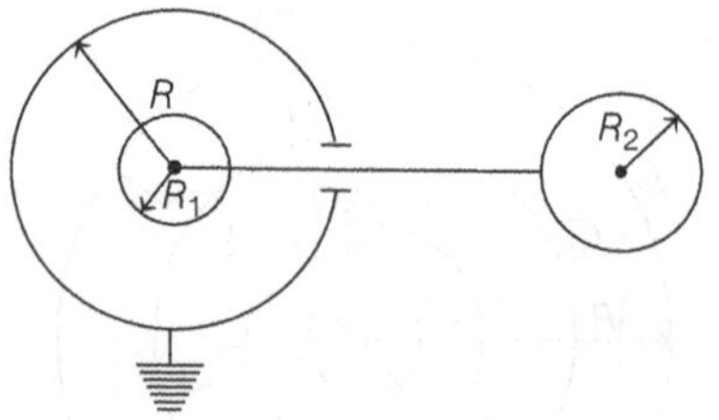

3 The diagram shows a conducting sphere A of radius a which is surrounded by a neutral conducting spherical shell B of radius $b (> a)$. Initially switches S_1, S_2 and S_3 are open and sphere A carries a charge Q. First, the switch S_1 is closed to connect the shell B with the ground and then opened. Now, the switch S_2 is closed, so that the sphere A is grounded and then S_2 is opened. Finally, the switch S_3 is closed to connect the spheres together. Find the heat (in joule) which is produced after closing the switch S_3.

(Take, $b = 4$ cm, $a = 2$ cm and $Q = 8\ \mu\text{C}$)

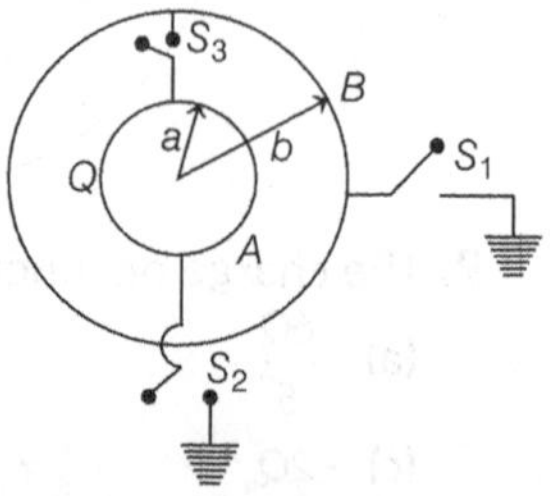

4 Two metal balls with radii of $r_1 = 3$ cm and $r_2 = 6$ cm at a distance of $R = 100$ cm from each other are connected to a battery with an electromotive force of $E = 100$ V. If the electric force between the balls is $\left(\frac{x}{9 \times 10^9}\right)$ N, then find the value of x.

5 A uniformly charged non-conducting shell of radius 1m and thickness $t = 1$ cm has a positive charge $Q = 10C$ and breaking stress $\frac{100}{\varepsilon_0} N/m^2$. Determine the minimum magnitude of a charge q (in C) located at the centre of shell for which the shell will tear apart. (Take, $\pi^2 = 10$)

Previous Year's Questions

JEE Main

1 Which of the following correctly represents the variation of electric potential (V) of a charged spherical conductor of radius (R) with radial distance (r) from the centre? **[2023, 31 Jan Shift-I]**

(a)

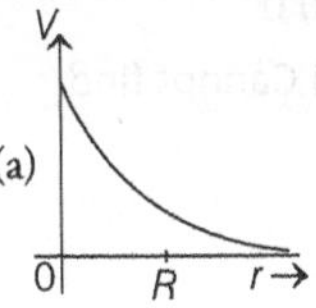

(b)

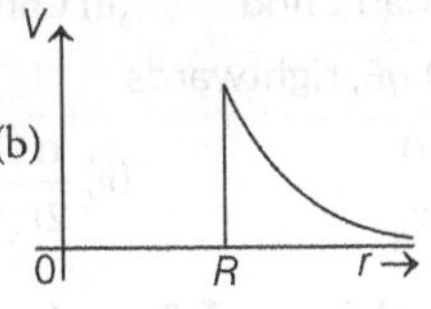

(c)

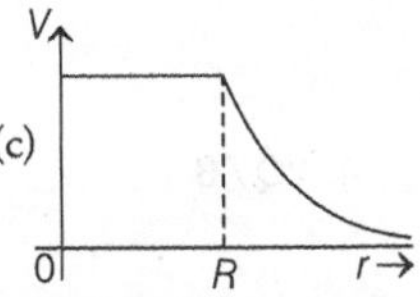

(d)

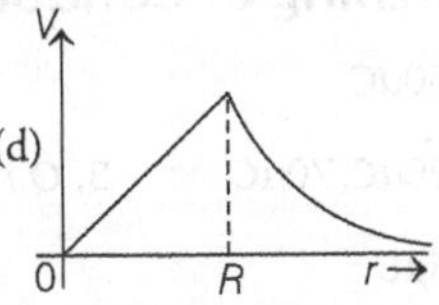

2 Two uniformly charged spherical conductors A and B of radii 5 mm and 10 mm are separated by a distance of 2 cm. If the spheres are connected by a conducting wire, then in equilibrium condition, the ratio of the magnitudes of the electric fields at the surface of the sphere A and B will be **[2022, 26 July Shift-II]**

(a) 1 : 2 (b) 2 : 1
(c) 1 : 1 (d) 1 : 4

3 Given below are two statements.

Statement I Electric potential is constant within and at the surface of each conductor.

Statement II Electric field just outside a charged conductor is perpendicular to the surface of the conductor at every point.

In the light of the above statements, choose the most appropriate answer from the options given below. **[2022, 29 July Shift-I]**

(a) Both Statement I and Statement II are correct.
(b) Both Statement I and Statement II are incorrect.
(c) Statement I is correct but Statement II is incorrect.
(d) Statement I is incorrect but Statement II is correct.

4 Sixty four conducting drops each of radius 0.02 m and each carrying a charge of $5\mu C$ are combined to form a bigger drop. The ratio of surface density of bigger drop to the smaller drop will be **[2022, 26 Jun Shift-II]**

(a) 1 : 4 (b) 4 : 1
(c) 1 : 8 (d) 8 : 1

JEE Advanced

1 A spherical metal shell A of radius R_A and a solid metal sphere B of radius $R_B (< R_A)$ are kept far apart and each is given charge $+Q$. Now they are connected by a thin metal wire. Then **[JEE Advanced 2011]**

(a) $(E)_{(A)\ inside} = 0$
(b) $Q_A > Q_B$
(c) $\frac{\sigma_A}{\sigma_B} = \frac{R_B}{R_A}$
(d) $(E)_{(A)\ on\ surface} < (E)_{(B)\ on\ surface}$

2 A uniformly charged thin spherical shell of radius R carries uniform surface charge density of σ per unit area. It is made of two hemispherical shells, held together by pressing them with force F (see figure). F is proportional to **[JEE Advanced 2010]**

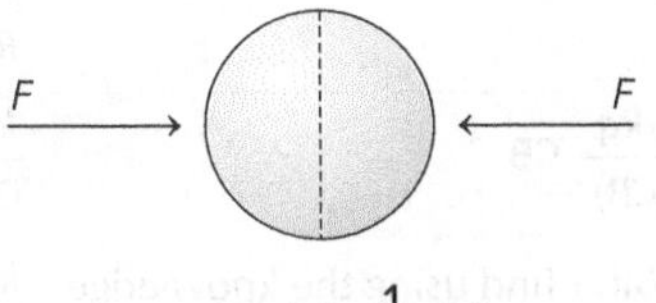

(a) $\frac{1}{\varepsilon_0}\sigma^2 R^2$ (b) $\frac{1}{\varepsilon_0}\sigma^2 R$

(c) $\frac{1}{\varepsilon_0}\frac{\sigma^2}{R}$ (d) $\frac{1}{\varepsilon_0}\frac{\sigma^2}{R^2}$

Answer Key

Level 1 Starter Level

5.1 Conductors under Electrostatic Conditions

1. (i) T (ii) T (iii) F (iv) T (v) T (vi) T (vii) T (viii) T (ix) F (x) F

2. (i) No charge on inner surface, Q on outer surface.
(ii) $-q$ charge uniformly distributed on inner surface, $+q$ uniformly distributed on outer surface.
(iii) $-q$ charge non-uniformly distributed on inner surface, $Q+q$ uniformly distributed on outer surface.

3. (i) $q_1 = +20\mu C$, $q_2 = -20\mu C$, $q_3 = +30\mu C$
(ii) $q_1 = 0$, $q_2 = +10\mu C$, $q_3 = -10\mu C$, $q_4 = -10\mu C$
(iii) $q_1 = -5\mu C$, $q_2 = +15\mu C$, $q_3 = -15\mu C$, $q_4 = +15\mu C$, $q_5 = -15\mu C$, $q_6 = -5\mu C$

4. (i)

	E	V
A	$\frac{kq}{(OA)^3}$ OA	$\frac{kq}{OA}+\frac{k(-q)}{R_1}+\frac{kq}{R_2}$
B	0	$\frac{kq}{R_2}$
C	$\frac{kq}{(OC)^3}$ OC	$\frac{kq}{OC}$

(ii)

	E	V
A	0	$\frac{kq}{R_2}$
B	$\frac{kq}{(CB)^3}$ CB	$\frac{kq}{CB}$
C	Can't find using the knowledge within JEE syllabus	$\frac{kq}{r}+\frac{k(-q)}{R_1}+\frac{kq}{R_2}$

(iii)

	E	V
A	0	$\frac{kq}{R}$
B	$\frac{kq}{(CB)^3}$ CB	$\frac{kq}{CB}$
C	Can't find	Can't find

5. (i) $-q$ on the inner surface, $Q+q$ on the outer surface.
(ii) $\mathbf{E}_A = \frac{kq}{(OA)^2}$ towards q, $\mathbf{E}_B$ cannot be found, $\mathbf{E}_C = \frac{kq}{(OC)^2}$ towards q
(iii) $E_A = \frac{kq_0}{(PA)^2}$ towards q_0, $E_B = \frac{kq_0}{(PB)^2}$ towards q_0, E_C cannot be found

6. (i) $\frac{kq}{CP}$ (ii) $\frac{kq}{CP}$ (iii) $\frac{kq}{CP}-\frac{kq}{AP}$

7. (i) Can't find (ii) $-\frac{kq}{AP}$

8. (i) 0 (ii) $\frac{kqq'}{r^2}$, rightwards (iii) $\frac{kqq'}{r^2}$, leftwards

9. (i) Can't find (ii) Can't find (iii) 0 (iv) qE, rightwards (v) Cannot find

10. (i) $\frac{\sigma}{\varepsilon_0}$ (ii) $\frac{\sigma^2}{2\varepsilon_0}$

5.2 Earthing of Conductors

1. $+50\mu C$
2. $-20\mu C, 70\mu C$
3. $Q/2$
4. $2Q/3$
5. $+15\mu C$

5.3 Connection of Conductors

1. Charge on the inner shell = 0 and outer shell = $-2Q$, heat produced = $\frac{kQ^2}{4R}$
2. Charge on innermost shell = $\frac{Q}{2}$, middle shell = $-2Q$, outermost shell = $\frac{5Q}{2}$

5.4 Parallel Conducting Plates

1. (i) $q_1 = Q, q_2 = 2Q, q_3 = -2Q, q_4 = Q$ (ii) $q_1 = 2Q, q_2 = -4Q, q_3 = 4Q, q_4 = Q, q_5 = -Q, q_6 = 2Q$
(iii) $q_1 = Q, q_2 = -6Q, q_3 = 6Q, q_4 = -4Q, q_5 = 4Q, q_6 = 2Q, q_7 = -2Q, q_8 = 2Q, q_9 = -2Q, q_{10} = Q$
2. (i) $q_1 = 0, q_2 = -60\,\mu C, q_3 = 60\,\mu C, q_4 = 0$
(ii) $q_1 = 0, q_2 = 100\,\mu C, q_3 = -100\,\mu C, q_4 = 0$
(iii) $q_1 = q_2 = q_3 = q_4 = 0$

Level 2 JEE Main Level

Single Choice Correct Questions

1. (d)	2. (d)	3. (c)	4. (b)	5. (b)
6. (c)	7. (b)	8. (a)	9. (d)	10. (c)
11. (a)	12. (b)	13. (d)	14. (c)	15. (b)

16. (b)	17. (d)	18. (d)	19. (b)	20. (d)
21. (c)	22. (a)	23. (c)	24. (a)	25. (c)
26. (c)	27. (a)	28. (b)	29. (c)	30. (b)

Numerical Value Questions

1. (4800)	2. (3.6)	3. (9)	4. (9)	5. (3)
6. (96)	7. (6)	8. (800)	9. (1.8)	10. (18)

Level 3 JEE Advanced Level

Single Choice Correct Questions

1. (a)	2. (c)	3. (b)	4. (c)	5. (c)
6. (d)	7. (c)	8. (a)	9. (c)	10. (a)
11. (a)	12. (b)	13. (a)	14. (b)	15. (c)
16. (b)	17. (b)	18. (a)	19. (c)	20. (b)
21. (a)	22. (c)	23. (b)	24. (a)	25. (a)
26. (a)				

Multiple Choice(s) Correct Questions

1. (abcd)	2. (bd)	3. (abcd)	4. (abc)	5. (ad)
6. (bd)	7. (bd)	8. (abcd)	9. (bd)	10. (abcd)
11. (ad)	12. (ac)	13. (acd)	14. (bd)	15. (abc)

Comprehension Based Questions

1. (b)	2. (c)	3. (b)	4. (a)	5. (d)
6. (a)	7. (d)	8. (a)	9. (b)	10. (d)
11. (c)	12. (a)	13. (d)	14. (d)	15. (b)

Match the Columns Questions

1. (a) $\rightarrow$ t, (b) $\rightarrow$ s, (c) $\rightarrow$ r, (d) $\rightarrow$ q
2. (a) $\rightarrow$ q, s; (b) $\rightarrow$ p, r; (c) $\rightarrow$ p,r; (d) $\rightarrow$ q, r
3. (a) $\rightarrow$ q, (b) $\rightarrow$ q, (c) $\rightarrow$ s, (d) $\rightarrow$ p

Numerical Value Questions

1. (4.5)	2. (2)	3. (1.8)	4. (4)	5. (27)

Previous Year's Questions

JEE Main

1. (c)	2. (b)	3. (a)	4. (b)

JEE Advanced

1. (a,b,c,d)	2. (a)

SOLUTIONS

Level 1 Starter Level

5.1 Conductors Under Electrostatic Conditions

1. (i) T (ii) T (iii) F (iv) T (v) T
   (vi) T (vii) T (viii) T (ix) F (x) F

2. (i)

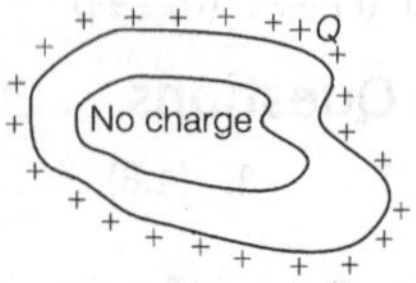

Due to repulsion, all charges will go to outer surface of the conductor. Charge on the inner surface will be zero.

(ii) Lets take a Gaussian surface in the conductor. Flux through the Gaussian surface is zero as electric field at every point on it is zero.

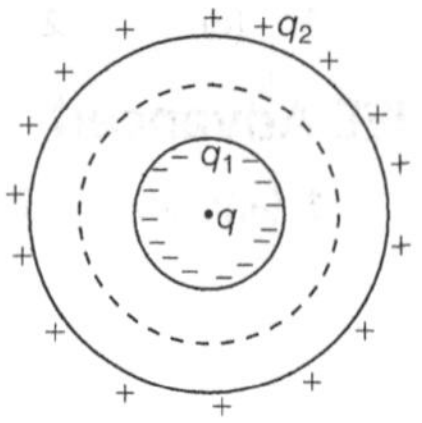

Using Gauss law,

$$\phi = 0$$

$$\Rightarrow \quad q_{\text{enclosed}} = 0$$

$$\Rightarrow \quad +q + q_1 = 0 \Rightarrow q_1 = -q$$

Since, conductor is neutral, $q_1 + q_2 = 0$

$$\Rightarrow \quad q_2 = -q_1 \Rightarrow q_2 = +q$$

So, charge on the inner surface is $-q$ distributed uniformly and charge on the outer surface $+q$ distributed uniformly.

(iii) Using Gauss law,

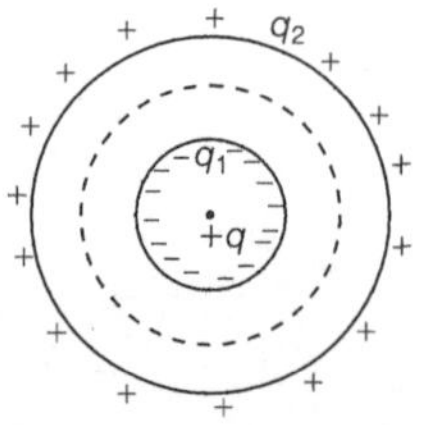

$$\phi = 0 \Rightarrow q_{\text{enclosed}} = 0$$

$$\Rightarrow \quad q + q_1 = 0 \Rightarrow q_1 = -q$$

Charge on the conductor $= Q$

$$q_1 + q_2 = Q$$

$$\Rightarrow \quad -q + q_2 = Q$$

$$\Rightarrow \quad q_2 = Q + q$$

Charge on the inner surface will be $-q$ non-uniformly distributed and charge on the outer surface will be $Q + q$ uniformly distributed.

3. (i) Entire charge $+20\,\mu C$ of solid sphere will be on its outer surface, so $q_1 = +20\,\mu C$.

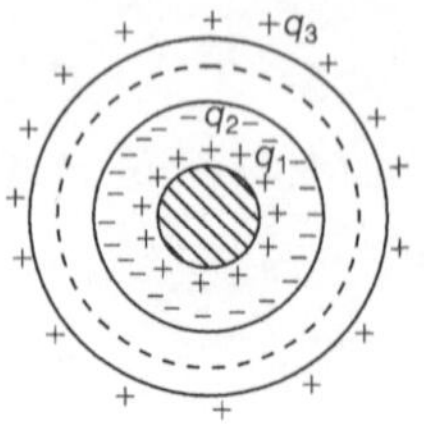

For the Gaussian surface inside the shell,

$$E = 0$$

$$\Rightarrow \quad \phi = 0$$

$$\Rightarrow \quad q_{\text{enclosed}} = 0$$

$$\Rightarrow \quad q_1 + q_2 = 0 \Rightarrow q_2 = -q_1 = -20\mu C$$

Total charge on the shell $= q_2 + q_3 = +10\mu C$

$$\Rightarrow \quad q_3 = +30\mu C$$

(ii) For the Gaussian surface within the inner shell,

$$E = 0 \Rightarrow \phi = 0$$

$$\Rightarrow \quad q_{\text{enclosed}} = 0 \Rightarrow q_1 = 0$$

Total charge on the inner shell $= +10\mu C$

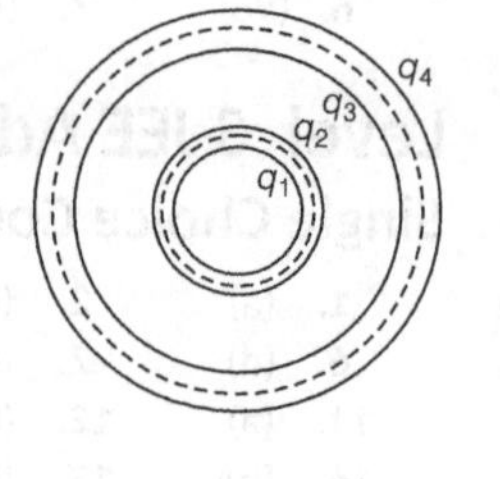

$$\Rightarrow \quad q_1 + q_2 = +10\mu C$$

$$\Rightarrow \quad q_2 = +10\mu C$$

For the Gaussian surface within the outer shell,

$$E = 0$$

$$\Rightarrow \quad \phi = 0 \Rightarrow q_{\text{enclosed}} = 0$$

$$\Rightarrow \quad q_1 + q_2 + q_3 = 0 \Rightarrow q_3 = -10\mu C$$

Total charge on the outer shell $= -20\mu C$

$$\Rightarrow \quad q_3 + q_4 = -20\mu C$$

$$\Rightarrow \quad q_4 = -10\mu C$$

(iii) For the Gaussian surface in shell A,

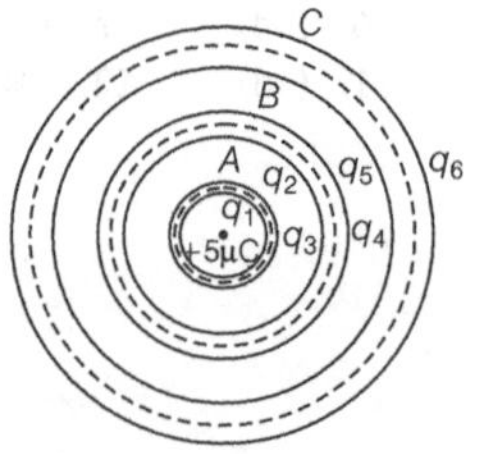

$$E = 0$$

$$\Rightarrow \quad \phi = 0$$

$$\Rightarrow \quad q_{\text{enclosed}} = 0$$

$$\Rightarrow \quad +5\,\mu C + q_1 = 0$$

$$\Rightarrow \quad q_1 = -5\mu C$$

Total charge on shell

$$A = +10\mu C$$

$$\Rightarrow \quad q_1 + q_2 = +10\mu C \Rightarrow q_2 = 15\mu C$$

For the Gaussian surface in shell B,

$$E = 0$$

$$\Rightarrow \quad \phi = 0 \Rightarrow q_{\text{enclosed}} = 0$$

$$\Rightarrow 5 + q_1 + q_2 + q_3 = 0 \Rightarrow q_3 = -15\mu C$$

Total charge on shell $B = 0$

$$\Rightarrow \quad q_3 + q_4 = 0 \Rightarrow q_4 = 15\mu C$$

For the Gaussian surface in shell C,

$$E = 0 \Rightarrow \phi = 0 \Rightarrow q_{\text{enclosed}} = 0$$

$$\Rightarrow 5 + q_1 + q_2 + q_3 + q_4 + q_5 = 0 \Rightarrow q_5 = -15\mu C$$

Total charge on shell $C = -20\mu C$

$$q_5 + q_6 = -20\mu C$$

$$\Rightarrow \quad q_6 = -5\mu C$$

4. (i)

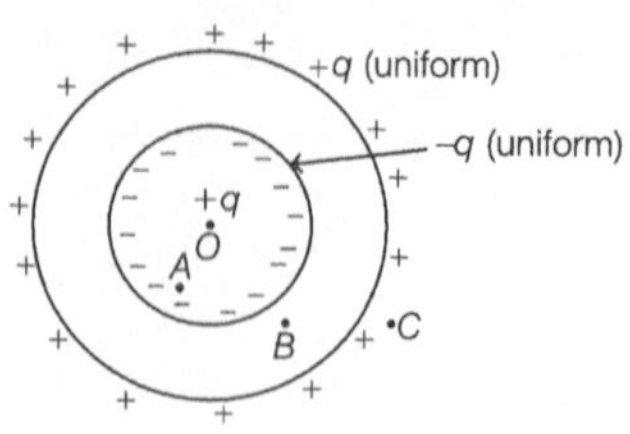

At point A,

$$\mathbf{E}_A = \left(\frac{kq}{(OA)^2}\right)(\hat{OA}) + 0 + 0 = \frac{kq}{(OA)^2}(\hat{OA})$$

$$V_A = \frac{kq}{(OA)} + \frac{k(-q)}{R_1} + \frac{kq}{R_2}$$

At point B,

$$\mathbf{E}_B = 0 \qquad (\because B \text{ is inside conductor})$$

$$V_B = \frac{kq}{R_2}$$

($\because$ potential at B due to the charges in the cavity is zero)

At point C,

$$\mathbf{E}_C = \frac{kq}{(OC)^2}(\hat{\mathbf{OC}})$$

($\because$ electric field at C due to charges in the cavity is zero)

$$V_C = \frac{kq}{(OC)}$$

($\because$ electric potential at C due to charges in the cavity is zero)

(ii) At point A,

$$\mathbf{E}_A = 0 \qquad (\because A \text{ is inside conductor})$$

$$V_A = \frac{kq}{R_2}$$

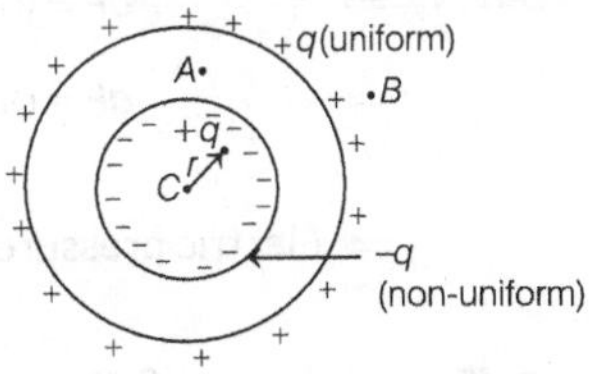

($\because$ potential at A due to the charges inside cavity is zero)

At point B,

$$\mathbf{E}_B = \frac{kq}{(CB)^2}(\hat{\mathbf{CB}})$$

($\because$ electric field at B due to charges inside cavity is zero)

$$V_B = \frac{kq}{(CB)}$$

($\because$ electric potential at B due to charges inside cavity is zero)

At centre C,

$\mathbf{E}_C$ = cannot find as we cannot write electric field at C due to $-q$ charge distributed non-uniformly using the knowledge within JEE Syllabus.

$$V_C = \frac{kq}{r} + \frac{k(-q)}{R_1} + \frac{k(+q)}{R_2}$$

(iii) At point A,

$$\mathbf{E}_A = 0 \qquad (\because A \text{ is inside conductor})$$

$$V_A = \frac{kq}{R}$$

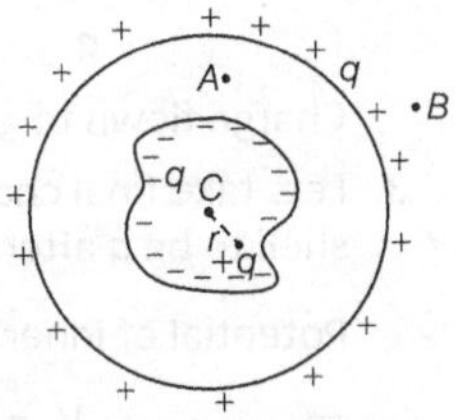

($\because$ potential at A due to charges in the cavity is zero)

At point B,

$$\mathbf{E}_B = \frac{kq}{(CB)^2}(\hat{\mathbf{CB}})$$

($\because$ electric field at B due to charges inside cavity is zero)

$$V_B = \frac{kq}{(CB)}$$

($\because$ electric potential at B due to charges inside cavity is zero)

At centre C,

$\mathbf{E}_C$ = cannot find as electric field due to $-q$ is unknown and V_C = cannot find as electric potential due to $-q$ is unknown.

5. (i) For the Gaussian surface,

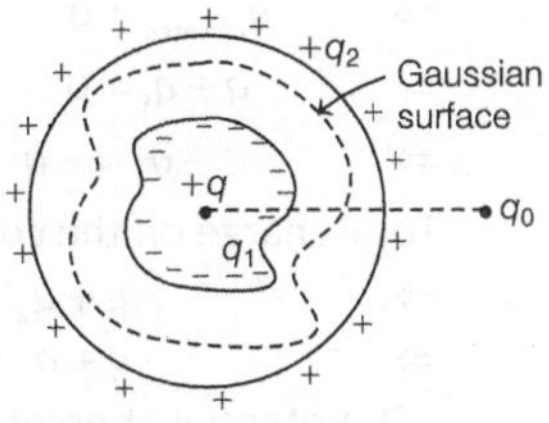

$$E = 0$$

$$\Rightarrow \quad \phi = 0$$

$$\Rightarrow \quad q_{\text{enclosed}} = 0$$

$$\Rightarrow \quad +q + q_1 = 0$$

$$\Rightarrow \quad q_1 = -q$$

Total charge on the conductor $= Q$

$$\Rightarrow \quad q_1 + q_2 = Q \Rightarrow -q + q_2 = Q$$

$$\Rightarrow \quad q_2 = Q + q$$

(ii) At point A, $\mathbf{E}_q + \mathbf{E}_{q_1} = 0$

$$\Rightarrow \quad \mathbf{E}_{q_1} = -\mathbf{E}_q = -\frac{kq}{(OA)^2}(\hat{\mathbf{OA}}) = \frac{kq}{(OA)^2}(\hat{\mathbf{AO}})$$

At point B, $\mathbf{E}_{q_1}$ cannot be found.

At point C, $\mathbf{E}_q + \mathbf{E}_{q_1} = 0$

$$\Rightarrow \quad \mathbf{E}_{q_1} = -\mathbf{E}_q = -\frac{kq}{(OC)^2}(\hat{\mathbf{OC}}) = \frac{kq}{(OC)^2}(\hat{\mathbf{CO}})$$

(iii) At point A, $\mathbf{E}_{q_2} + \mathbf{E}_{q_0} = 0$

$$\Rightarrow \quad \mathbf{E}_{q_2} = -\mathbf{E}_{q_0} = -\frac{kq_0}{(PA)^2}(\hat{\mathbf{PA}}) = \frac{kq_0}{(PA)^2}(\hat{\mathbf{AP}})$$

At point B, $\mathbf{E}_{q_2} + \mathbf{E}_{q_0} = 0$

$$\Rightarrow \quad \mathbf{E}_{q_2} = -\mathbf{E}_{q_0} = -\frac{kq_0}{(PB)^2}(\hat{\mathbf{PB}}) = \frac{kq_0}{(PB)^2}(\hat{\mathbf{BP}})$$

At point C, $\mathbf{E}_{q_2}$ cannot be found.

6.

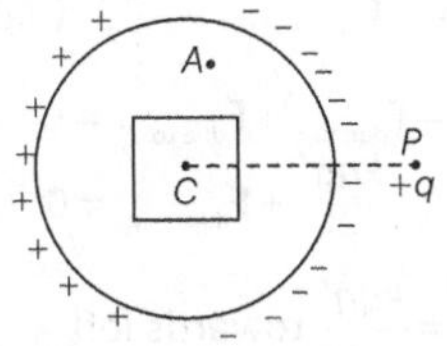

(i) At point C, $V = V_1 + V_2 = V_{\text{due to } q} + V_{\text{due to induced charges}}$

$$= \frac{kq}{PC} + \frac{k(0)}{R} = \frac{kq}{PC}$$

(ii) Potential at C and potential at A is same because there is no electric field in the cavity and the conductor.

So, $\quad V_A = V_C = \dfrac{kq}{PC}$

(iii) At point A, $V = V_{\text{due to } q} + V_{\text{due to induced charges}}$

$$\Rightarrow \quad \frac{kq}{PC} = \frac{kq}{AP} + V_{\text{due to induced charges}}$$

$$\Rightarrow \quad V_{\text{due to induced charges}} = \frac{kq}{PC} - \frac{kq}{AP}$$

7. For the Gaussian surface inside metal,

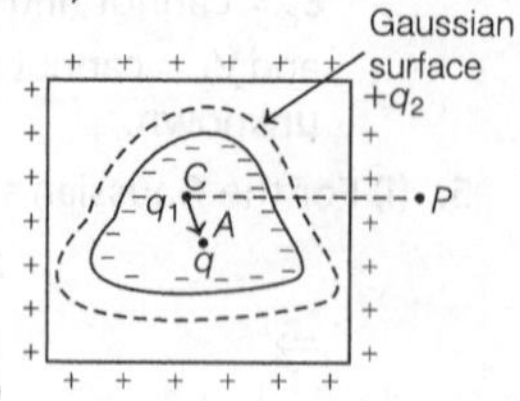

$$E = 0$$
$$\Rightarrow \quad \phi = 0$$
$$\Rightarrow \quad q_{enclosed} = 0$$
$$\Rightarrow \quad q + q_1 = 0$$
$$\Rightarrow \quad q_1 = -q$$

Total charge on the conductor = 0

$$\Rightarrow \quad q_1 + q_2 = 0$$
$$\Rightarrow \quad -q + q_2 = 0 \Rightarrow q_2 = q$$

(i) Potential at point P,

$$V_P = V_q + V_{q_1} + V_{q_2}$$
$$= \frac{kq}{PA} + \frac{k(-q)}{PA} + \text{(cannot find)}$$
$$= \text{Cannot find}$$

(ii) At point P, $V_{\text{due to } q} + V_{\text{due to } q_1} = 0$

$$\Rightarrow \quad \frac{kq}{AP} + V_{\text{due to } q_1} = 0$$
$$\Rightarrow \quad V_{\text{due to } q_1} = -\frac{kq}{AP}$$

8.

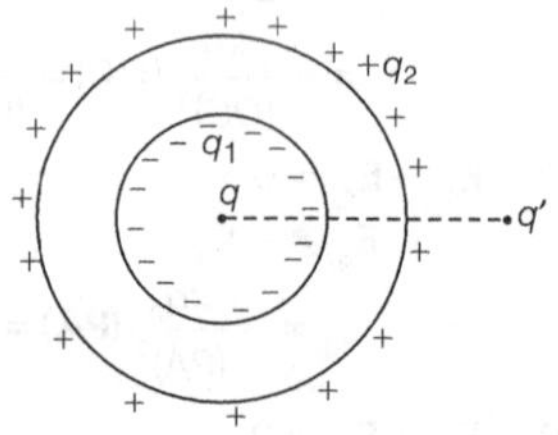

$q_1 = -q$ (uniform) and $q_2 = +q$ (non-uniform)

(i) Force on $q = \mathbf{F}_{\text{due to } q_1} + (\mathbf{F}_{\text{due to } q_2} + \mathbf{F}_{\text{due to } q'})$

$$= 0 + 0 = 0$$

(ii) Force on $q = \mathbf{F}_{\text{due to } q_2} + \mathbf{F}_{\text{due to } q'} = 0$

$$\Rightarrow \mathbf{F}_{\text{due to } q_2} = -\mathbf{F}_{\text{due to } q'} = -\frac{kqq'}{r^2} \text{ (rightwards)}$$

(iii) Force on $q' = \mathbf{F}_{\text{due to } q} + \mathbf{F}_{\text{due to } q_1} = 0$

$$\Rightarrow \quad \frac{kqq'}{r^2} + \mathbf{F}_{\text{due to } q_1} = 0$$
$$\Rightarrow \mathbf{F}_{\text{due to } q_1} = \frac{kqq'}{r^2} \text{ towards left}$$

9.

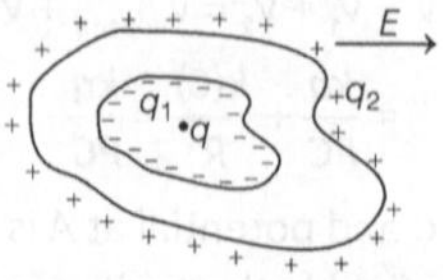

$q_1 = -q$ and $q_2 = +q$

(i) Force on $q = \mathbf{F}_{\text{due to } q_1} + (\mathbf{F}_{\text{due to } q_2} + \mathbf{F}_{\text{due to electric field}})$

= can't find + 0 = can't find

(ii) Force on conductor $= \mathbf{F}_{\text{due to } q_1} + \mathbf{F}_{\text{due to electric field}}$

= can't find + 0 = can't find

(iii) Force on the conductor due to electric field

$$= +qE + (-q)E = 0$$

(iv) Force on $q_2 = (\mathbf{F}_{\text{due to } q} + \mathbf{F}_{\text{due to } q_1}) + \mathbf{F}_{\text{due to electric field}}$

$= 0 + q\mathbf{E} = qE$, rightwards

(v) Force on $q_1 = \mathbf{F}_{\text{due to } q} + (\mathbf{F}_{\text{due to } q_2} + \mathbf{F}_{\text{due to electric field}})$

= can't find + 0 = can't find

10. (i) For the Gaussian cylinder,

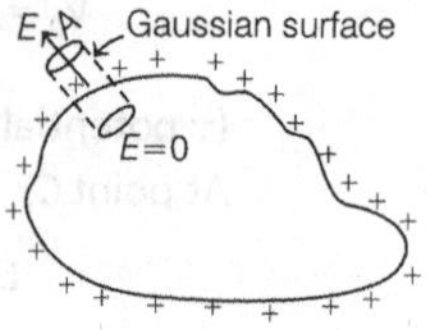

$$\phi = EA + 0 + 0 = EA$$

Using Gauss law,

$$\phi = \frac{q_{enclosed}}{\varepsilon_0}$$
$$\Rightarrow \quad EA = \frac{\sigma A}{\varepsilon_0} \Rightarrow E = \frac{\sigma}{\varepsilon_0}$$

(ii)

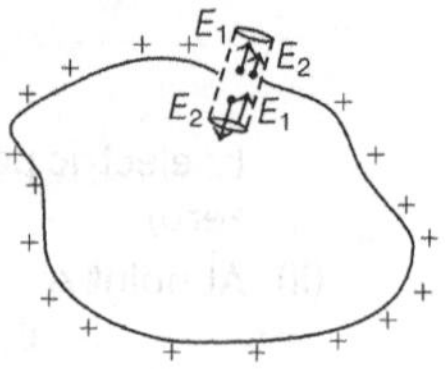

$$E_1 + E_2 = \frac{\sigma}{\varepsilon_0} \quad \text{...(i)}$$
$$E_1 - E_2 = 0 \quad \text{...(ii)}$$

From Eqs. (i) and (ii), we get

$$E_1 = \frac{\sigma}{2\varepsilon_0}$$
$$\Rightarrow \quad dF = (\sigma dA) E_1$$
$$\Rightarrow \quad dF = \sigma dA\left(\frac{\sigma}{2\varepsilon_0}\right) \Rightarrow \frac{dF}{dA} = \frac{\sigma^2}{2\varepsilon_0}$$
$$\Rightarrow \text{Electric pressure} = \frac{\sigma^2}{2\varepsilon_0}$$

5.2 Earthing of Conductors

1. Lets take charge on conductor q after earthing.

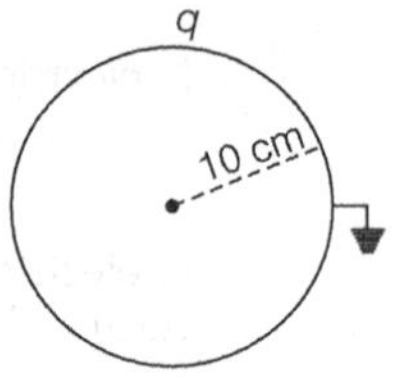

$$V_{conductor} = 0$$
$$\Rightarrow \quad \frac{kq}{(10 \text{ cm})} = 0$$
$$\Rightarrow \quad q = 0$$

Charge flown to ground $= 50 - 0 = 50\,\mu C$

2. Lets take charge on conductor after earthing to be q.

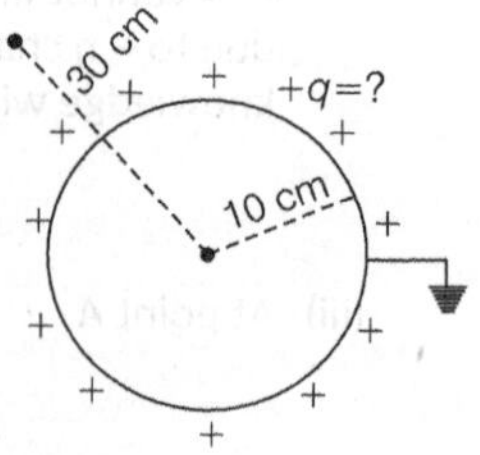

$$V_{conductor} = 0$$

At the centre of conductor,

$$\frac{k(q)}{(10 \text{ cm})} + \frac{k(+60\,\mu C)}{(30 \text{ cm})} = 0$$
$$q = -20\,\mu C$$

Charge flown to ground $= 50 - (-20) = 70\,\mu C$

3. Lets take final charge on the inner shell to be q after earthing.

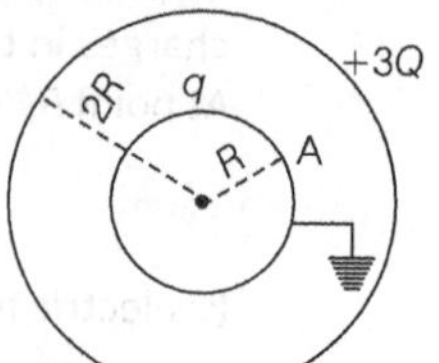

Potential of inner shell = 0

$$\Rightarrow \quad V_A = \frac{kq}{R} + \frac{k(3Q)}{2R} = 0$$
$$\Rightarrow \quad q = -\frac{3Q}{2}$$

$$\text{Charge flown to earth} = -Q - \left(-\frac{3Q}{2}\right) = +\frac{Q}{2}$$

4. Lets take final charge on the middle shell to be q after it has been earthed.

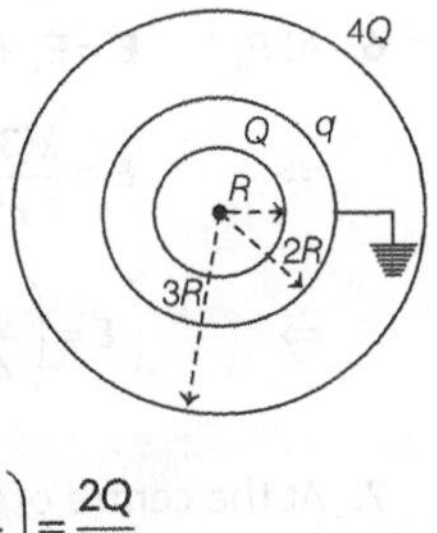

Potential of middle shell = 0

$$\Rightarrow \quad \frac{kQ}{2R} + \frac{kq}{2R} + \frac{k(4Q)}{3R} = 0$$

$$\Rightarrow \quad q = \frac{-11Q}{3}$$

$$\text{Charge flown to earth} = -3Q - \left(\frac{-11Q}{3}\right) = \frac{2Q}{3}$$

5. Lets take final charge on the outermost shell to be q after earthing.

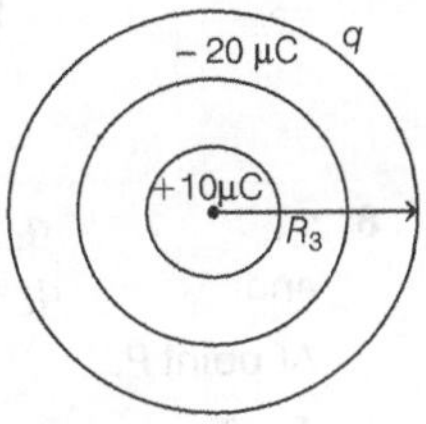

Potential of the outermost shell = 0

$$\Rightarrow \quad \frac{k(+10\mu C)}{R_3} + \frac{k(-20\mu C)}{R_3} + \frac{kq}{R_3} = 0$$

$$\Rightarrow \quad q = +10\,\mu C$$

Charge flown to earth = 25 – 10

$= 15\,\mu C$

5.3 Connection of Conductors

1.

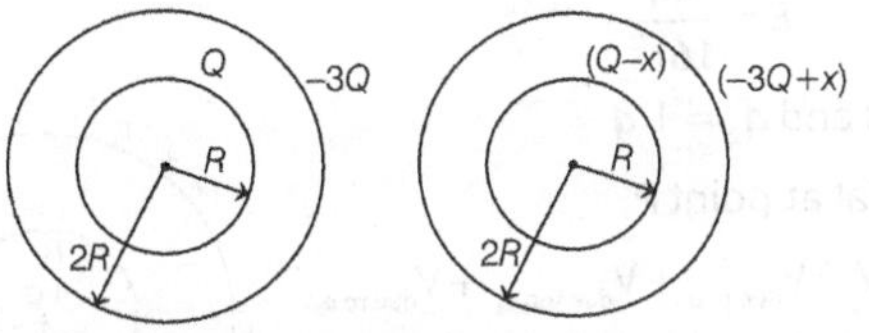

After connecting the shells,

$$V_{\text{inner shell}} = V_{\text{outer shell}}$$

$$\Rightarrow \quad \frac{k(Q-x)}{R} + \frac{k(-3Q+x)}{2R} = \frac{k(Q-x)}{2R} + \frac{k(-3Q+x)}{2R}$$

$$\Rightarrow \quad x = Q$$

Final charge on the inner shell = 0

Final charge on the outer shell = – 2Q

Heat produced = Loss in potential energy of system

$$= U_1 - U_2$$

$$= \left[\frac{kQ^2}{2R} + \frac{k(-3Q)^2}{2(2R)} + (-3Q)\frac{kQ}{2R}\right] - \left[0 + \frac{k(-2Q)^2}{2(2R)} + 0\right]$$

$$= \frac{kQ^2}{4R}$$

2. $V_{\text{innermost shell}} = V_{\text{outermost shell}}$

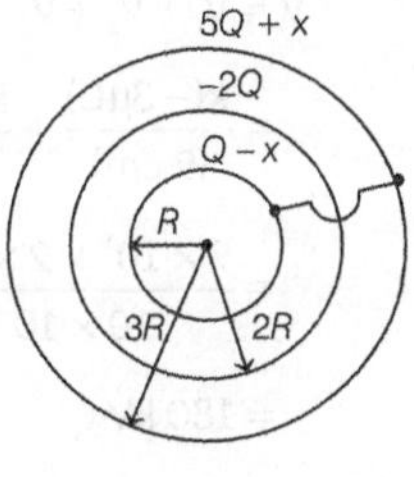

$$\Rightarrow \quad \frac{k(Q-x)}{R} + \frac{k(-2Q)}{2R} + \frac{k(5Q+x)}{3R}$$

$$= \frac{k(Q-x)}{3R} + \frac{k(-2Q)}{3R} + \frac{k(5Q+x)}{3R}$$

$$\Rightarrow \quad x = Q/2$$

Charge on the innermost shell

$$= Q - \frac{Q}{2} = \frac{Q}{2}$$

Charge on the middle shell = – 2Q

Charge on the outermost shell $= 2Q + Q/2 = 5Q/2$

5.4 Parallel Conducting Plates

1. (i)

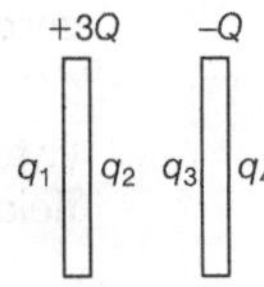

$$q_1 = q_4 = \frac{+3Q - Q}{2} = Q$$

$$q_1 + q_2 = 3Q$$

$$\Rightarrow \quad q_2 = 2Q$$

$$q_3 + q_4 = -Q$$

$$\Rightarrow \quad q_3 = -2Q$$

(ii)

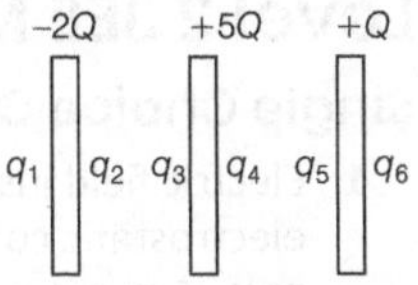

$$q_1 = q_6 = \frac{-2Q + 5Q + Q}{2} = 2Q$$

$$q_1 + q_2 = -2Q$$

$$\Rightarrow \quad q_2 = -4Q$$

$$q_3 = -q_2 = 4Q$$

$$q_3 + q_4 = 5Q$$

$$\Rightarrow \quad q_4 = Q$$

$$\Rightarrow \quad q_5 = -q_4 = -Q$$

(iii)

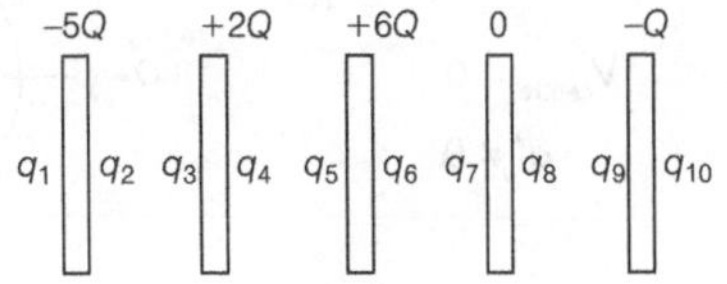

$$q_1 = q_{10} = \frac{-5Q + 2Q + 6Q + 0 - Q}{2} = Q$$

$$q_1 + q_2 = -5Q \;\Rightarrow\; q_2 = -6Q$$

$$q_3 = -q_2 \;\Rightarrow\; q_3 = 6Q$$

$$q_3 + q_4 = 2Q \;\Rightarrow\; q_4 = -4Q$$

$$q_5 = -q_4 \;\Rightarrow\; q_5 = 4Q$$

$$q_5 + q_6 = 6Q \;\Rightarrow\; q_6 = 2Q$$

$$q_7 = -q_6 \;\Rightarrow\; q_7 = -2Q$$

$$q_7 + q_8 = 0 \;\Rightarrow\; q_8 = 2Q$$

$$q_9 = -q_8 \;\Rightarrow\; q_9 = -2Q$$

2. (i) When S_1 is closed, potential of plate A becomes zero. So, charges on the outer faces of the two plates become zero.

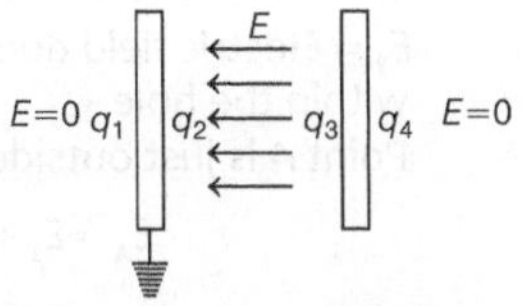

$$\Rightarrow \quad q_1 = q_4 = 0$$

$$q_3 + q_4 = 60\,\mu C$$

$$\Rightarrow \quad q_3 = 60\,\mu C$$

$$q_2 = -q_3$$

$$\Rightarrow \quad q_2 = -60\,\mu C$$

(ii) When S_2 is closed, plate B gets grounded and potential will be zero. So, charges on the outer faces of the two plates will be zero.

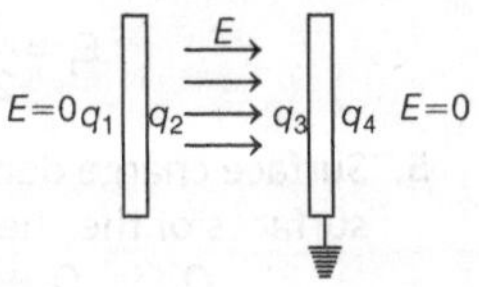

$$q_1 = q_4 = 0$$

$$q_1 + q_2 = +100\,\mu C$$

$$\Rightarrow \quad q_2 = +100\,\mu C$$

$$q_3 = -q_2$$

$$\Rightarrow \quad q_3 = -100\,\mu C$$

(iii) When both the switches are closed, both plates will get grounded.

So, potential of each of them will be zero.

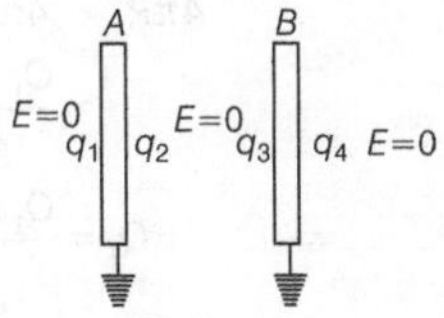

$$q_1 = q_4 = 0$$

($\because$ charges on outer faces of the two plates will be zero)

$$q_2 = q_3 = 0$$

($\because$ for the two plates to be at zero potential, electric field between them will be zero)

Level 2 JEE Main Level

Single Choice Correct Questions

1. Electric field inside a conductor is always zero under electrostatic conditions. Electric potential is not always zero. Any excess charge resides on the surface.

2. (a) $V_{\text{centre}} = \dfrac{kQ}{x} + \dfrac{kq'}{R}$

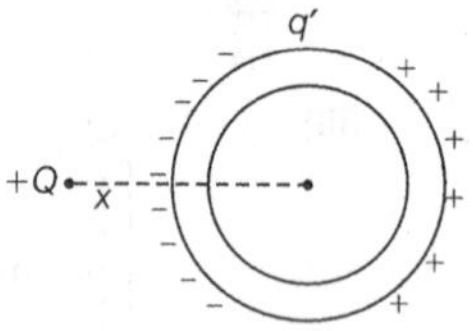

$\because$ $V_{\text{centre}} = 0$

$\Rightarrow$ $q' \neq 0$

(b) So, electric field in a charged conducting spherical shell can be zero even, if the charge is non-uniformly distributed.

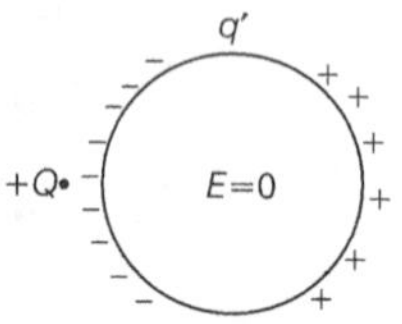

(c) Electric potential due to induced charges is zero only at the centre of the spherical shell.

3.

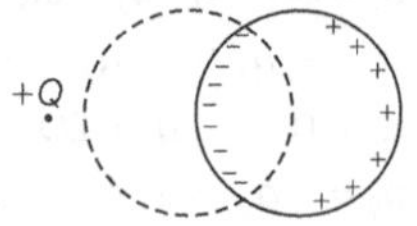

Due to negative induced charges inside the closed surface, flux will be negative.

4. E_1 = Electric field due to shell with hole

E_2 = Electric field due to part of shell within the hole.

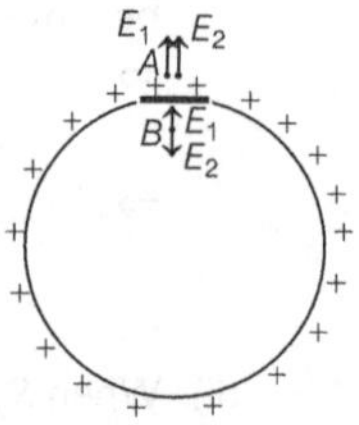

Point A is just outside the shell,

$$E_A = E_1 + E_2 = \frac{\sigma}{\varepsilon_0} \quad \text{... (i)}$$

Point B is just inside the shell,

$$E_B = E_1 - E_2 = 0 \quad \text{... (ii)}$$

From Eqs. (i) and (ii), we get

$$E_1 = \frac{\sigma}{2\varepsilon_0}$$

5. Surface charge densities on the outer surfaces of the shells are equal.

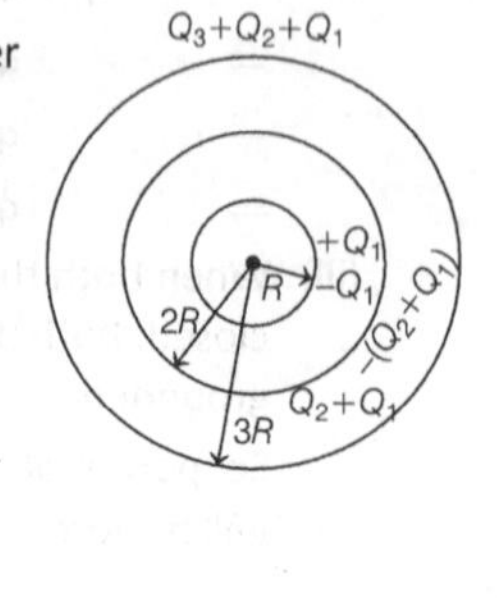

$$\Rightarrow \quad \frac{Q_1}{4\pi R^2} = \frac{Q_1 + Q_2}{4\pi(2R)^2} = \frac{Q_1 + Q_2 + Q_3}{4\pi(3R)^2}$$

$$\Rightarrow \quad Q_1 = \frac{Q_1 + Q_2}{4} = \frac{Q_1 + Q_2 + Q_3}{9}$$

$$\Rightarrow \quad Q_1 : Q_2 : Q_3 = 1 : 3 : 5$$

6. At P, $\mathbf{E} = \mathbf{E}_1 + \mathbf{E}_2 + \mathbf{E}_3$

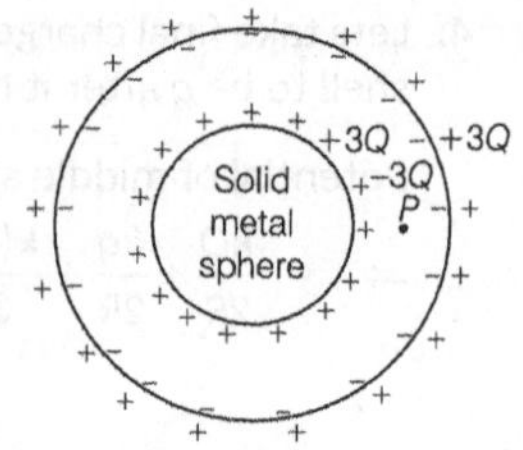

$$\Rightarrow \quad E = \frac{k(3Q)}{r^2} + 0 + 0$$

$$\Rightarrow \quad E = \left(\frac{1}{4\pi\varepsilon_0}\right)\frac{3Q}{r^2}$$

7. At the centre of the metallic cube,

$$\mathbf{E} = \mathbf{E}_{\text{due to induced charges}} + \mathbf{E}_{\text{due to } q} = 0$$

$$\Rightarrow \quad \mathbf{E}_{\text{due to induced charges}} = -\mathbf{E}_{\text{due to } q} = -\left(\frac{kq}{d^2}\hat{\mathbf{j}}\right) = -\frac{1}{4\pi\varepsilon_0}\frac{q}{d^2}\hat{\mathbf{j}}$$

8. $\because$ $q_1 = -q$

and $q_2 = +q$

At point P,

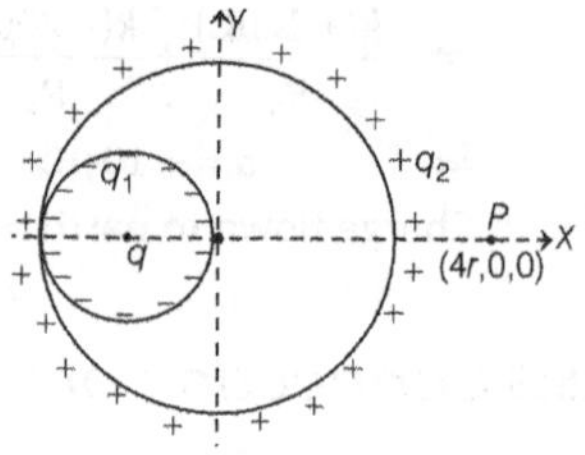

$$\mathbf{E} = (\mathbf{E}_{\text{due to } q} + \mathbf{E}_{\text{due to } q_1}) + \mathbf{E}_{\text{due to } q_2}$$

$$\Rightarrow \quad E = 0 + \frac{kq}{(4r)^2}$$

$$\Rightarrow \quad E = \frac{kq}{16r^2}$$

9. $q_1 = -q$ and $q_2 = +q$

Potential at point P,

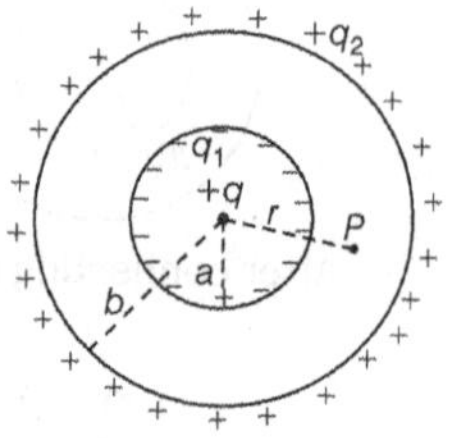

$$V = V_{\text{due to } q} + V_{\text{due top } q_1} + V_{\text{due to } q_2} = \frac{kq}{r} + \frac{kq_1}{r} + \frac{kq_2}{b}$$

$$\Rightarrow \quad V = \frac{kq}{r} + \frac{k(-q)}{r} + \frac{kq}{b} = \frac{kq}{b}$$

10. $q_1 = -q$ (non-uniform distribution)

$q_2 = +q$ (uniform distribution)

Potential at the centre,

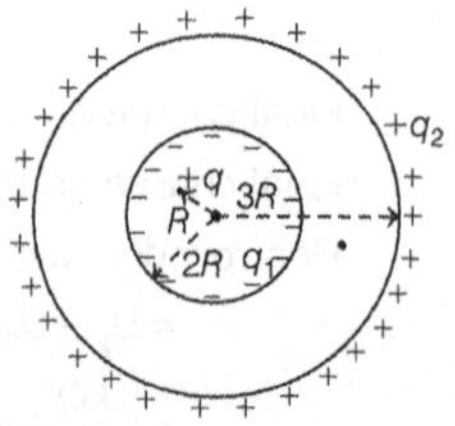

$$V = V_{\text{due to } q} + V_{\text{due to } q_1} + V_{\text{due to } q_2}$$

$$= \frac{kq}{R} + \frac{k(-q)}{2R} + \frac{kq}{3R} = \frac{5}{6}\frac{kq}{R}$$

11. Potential of the inner surface of the spherical shell,

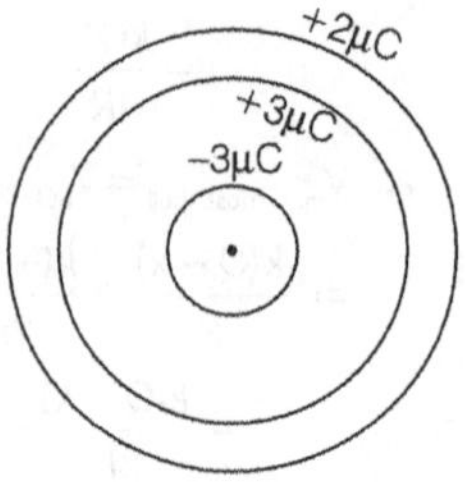

$$V = V_1 + V_2 + V_3$$

$$= \frac{k(-3\mu C)}{(9\text{ cm})} + \frac{k(+3\mu C)}{(9\text{ cm})} + \frac{k(+2\mu C)}{(10\text{ cm})}$$

$$= \frac{9 \times 10^9 \times 2 \times 10^{-6}}{10 \times 10^{-2}}$$

$$= 180 \text{ kV}$$

12. At point P,

$$V_{\text{due to } q} + V_{\text{due to induced charges on the inner surface}} = 0$$

$$\Rightarrow \quad V_{\text{due to induced charges on the inner surface}} = -V_{\text{due to } q} = \frac{-kq}{5a}$$

13. For conductor A, $V = \frac{kq}{a}$

When the switch is closed, all charges q of conductor A will be transferred to outer surface of the conducting shell B.

Potential at any point inside the shell $= \frac{kq}{(6a)} = \frac{V}{6}$

14. At point C,

$$V_C = V_{\text{due to } q} + V_{\text{due to induced charges}}$$

$$= \frac{kq}{AC} + 0 = \frac{kq}{AC}$$

Conductor is an equipotential body, so

$$V_B = V_C$$

Potential at B,

$$V_B = V_{\text{due to } q} + V_{\text{due to induced charges}}$$

$$\Rightarrow \quad \frac{kq}{AC} = \frac{kq}{AB} + V_{\text{due to induced charges}}$$

$$\Rightarrow V_{\text{due to induced charges}} = \frac{kq}{AC} - \frac{kq}{AB}$$

$$= \frac{9\times10^9\times10^{-6}}{5} - \frac{9\times10^9\times10^{-6}}{4}$$

$$= -0.45 \text{ kV}$$

15. Since, they have same potential, charge on the inner hollow sphere will be zero.

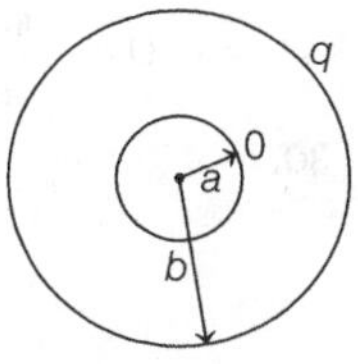

$$V = \frac{kq}{b}$$

Now, A is given charge, lets say x.

Potential of $A = 0$

$$\Rightarrow \quad \frac{kx}{a} + \frac{kq}{b} = 0 \Rightarrow x = -\frac{qa}{b}$$

Potential of $B = \frac{kx}{b} + \frac{kq}{b}$

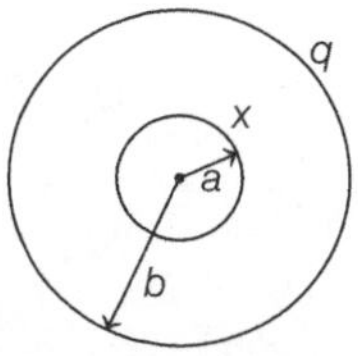

$$= \frac{k}{b}\left(\frac{-qa}{b}\right) + \frac{kq}{b}$$

$$= \frac{kq}{b}\left(1 - \frac{a}{b}\right) = V\left(1 - \frac{a}{b}\right)$$

16. Potential at A due to charges outside the conductor is zero, since the shell is grounded.

$$V_A = V_{\text{due to } q} + V_{\text{due to charges on the outer surface of shell}} = 0$$

$$\Rightarrow \quad V_{\text{due to charges on the outer surface of shell}} = -V_{\text{due to } q} = -\frac{kq}{(2.5R)}$$

17.

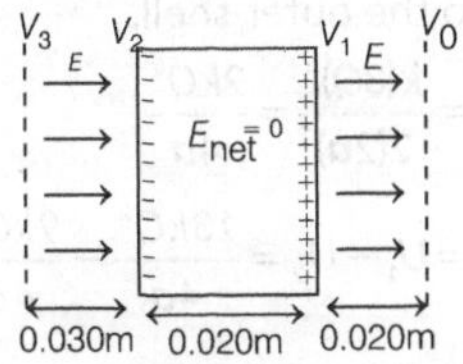

$$\Delta V = V_1 - V_0 = Ed = 400 \times 0.020$$

$$\Rightarrow \quad V_1 - 0 = 8 \quad \Rightarrow \quad V_1 = 8 \text{ V}$$

Inside the conducting plate, $E_{net} = 0$

$$\Rightarrow \quad V_2 = V_1 = 8 \text{ V}$$

$$\Delta V = V_3 - V_2 = Ed' = 400 \times 0.030$$

$$\Rightarrow \quad V_3 - 8 = 12 \Rightarrow V_3 = 20 \text{ V}$$

18. Electric field lines don't enter a conductor and at the surface, they are normal to the surface.

19. $q_1 = -Q_0$ (uniform)

and $q_2 = +Q$

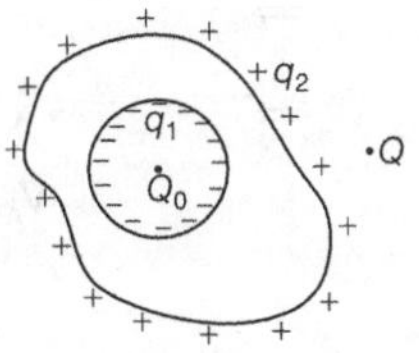

Force on Q_0,

$$\mathbf{F} = \mathbf{F}_{\text{due to } q_1} + (\mathbf{F}_{\text{due to } q_2} + \mathbf{F}_{\text{due to } Q})$$

$$= 0 + 0 = 0$$

Force on Q,

$$\mathbf{F} = (\mathbf{F}_{\text{due to } Q_0} + \mathbf{F}_{\text{due to } q_1}) + \mathbf{F}_{\text{due to } q_2}$$

$$= 0 + \mathbf{F}_{\text{due to } q_2} \neq 0$$

20.

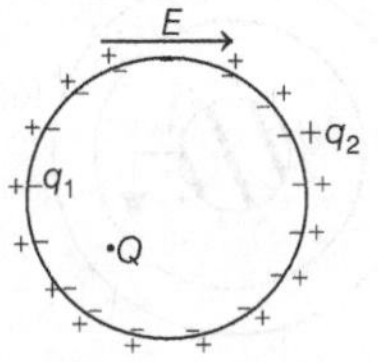

$q_1 = -Q$ (non-uniform); $q_2 = +Q$ (non-uniform)

(a) Force on Q due to $E = QE$

(b) Net force on $Q = \mathbf{F}_{\text{due to } q_1} + (\mathbf{F}_{\text{due to } q_2} + \mathbf{F}_{\text{due to } E})$

$$= \mathbf{F}_{\text{due to } q_1} + 0 = \mathbf{F}_{\text{due to } q_1} \neq 0$$

(c) Net force on Q and conducting shell considered as a system $= q_2E + q_1E + QE$

$$= QE - QE + QE = QE$$

(d) Net force on the shell due to $E = q_1E + q_2E$

$$= -QE + QE = 0$$

21.

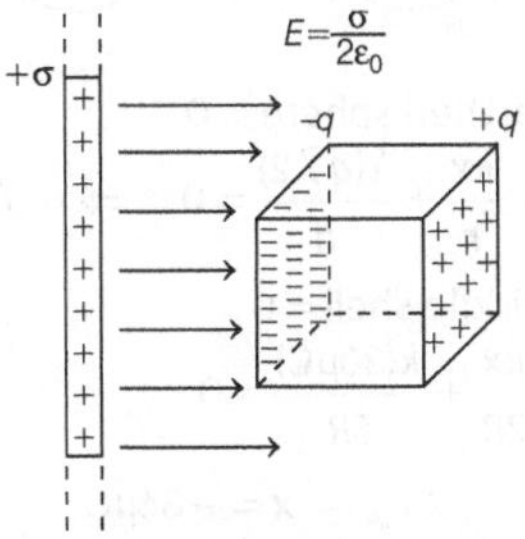

Charges will be induced on the block but force on the block due to a uniform electric field of the infinite non-conducting sheet will be zero, as total charge on the block is zero.

22.

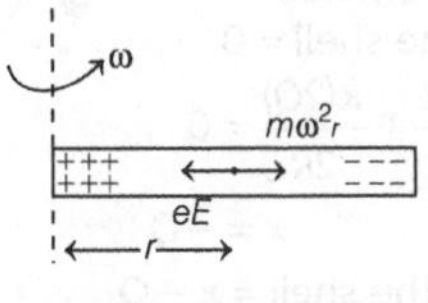

Due to centrifugal on free electrons, electrons will accumulate at the right end of the rod and there will be deficiency of electrons at the left end.

These induced charges will give rise to an electric field.

Electrons will stop accumulating at the right end when net force on free electron is zero.

$$\Delta V = \int E\,dr = \int_0^l \frac{m\omega^2 r}{e}\,dr = \frac{m\omega^2 l^2}{2e}$$

23. Since, B is earth, therefore $V_B = 0$

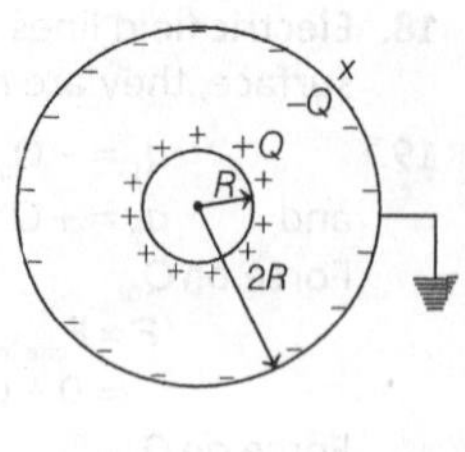

$$\Rightarrow \quad \frac{kQ}{2R} + \frac{k(x-Q)}{2R} = 0$$

$$\Rightarrow \quad x = 0$$

$$V_A = \frac{kQ}{R} + \frac{k(x-Q)}{2R}$$

$$= \frac{kQ}{2R} = \frac{Q}{8\pi\varepsilon_0 R}$$

24.

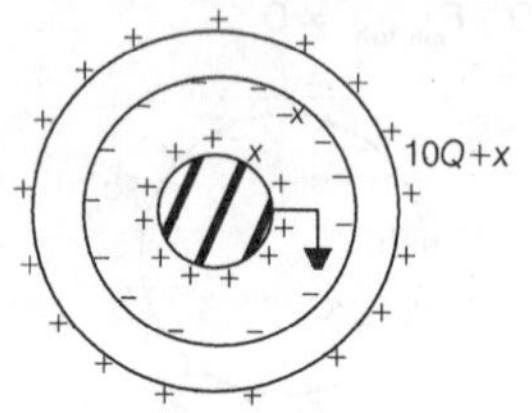

Potential of sphere = 0

$$\Rightarrow \quad \frac{kx}{R} + \frac{k(-x)}{2R} + \frac{k(10Q+x)}{3R} = 0 \Rightarrow x = -4Q$$

25. When uncharged sphere and the charged sphere are touched with each other, charge on each of them would be $\frac{q}{2}$.

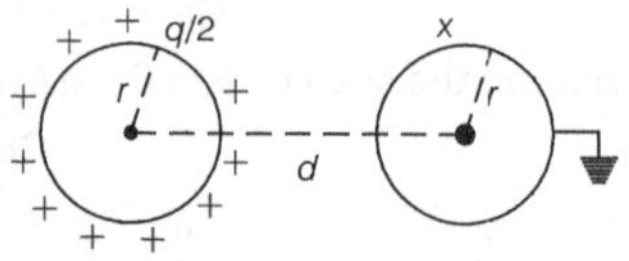

Potential of earthed sphere = 0

$$\Rightarrow \quad \frac{kx}{r} + \frac{k(q/2)}{d} = 0 \quad \Rightarrow \quad x = \frac{-qr}{2d}$$

26. Potential of middle shell = 0

$$\Rightarrow \quad \frac{k(24\mu C)}{2R} + \frac{kx}{2R} + \frac{k(30\mu C)}{5R} = 0$$

$$\Rightarrow \quad x = -36\mu C$$

Charge flown to earth $= 0 - (-36) = 36\mu C$

27. Lets take charge on outer surface of shell to be x after it has been earthed.

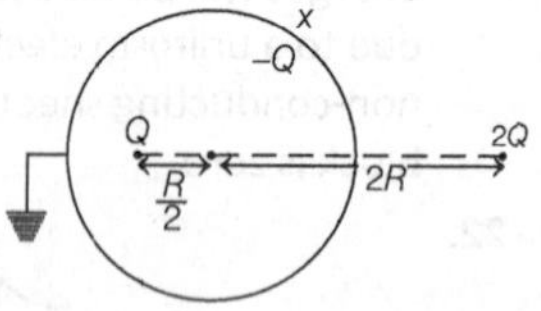

Potential due to outside charges inside the shell = 0

At the centre, $\frac{kx}{R} + \frac{k(2Q)}{2R} = 0$

$$x = -Q$$

Total charge on the shell $= x - Q$

$$= -Q - Q = -2Q$$

Charge flown to earth $= Q_1 - Q_2 = Q - (-2Q) = 3Q$

28. Potential of innermost shell = 0

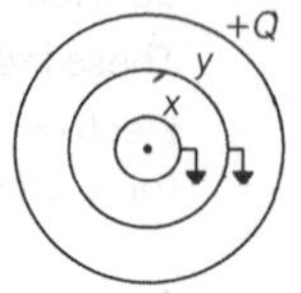

$$\Rightarrow \quad \frac{kx}{a} + \frac{ky}{2a} + \frac{kQ}{4a} = 0$$

$$\Rightarrow \quad 2x + y = \frac{-Q}{2} \quad \text{... (i)}$$

Potential of middle shell = 0

$$\frac{kx}{2a} + \frac{ky}{2a} + \frac{kQ}{4a} = 0$$

$$\Rightarrow \quad x + y = \frac{-Q}{2} \quad \text{... (ii)}$$

Solving Eqs. (i) and (ii), we get

$$x = 0 \text{ and } y = \frac{-Q}{2}$$

29.

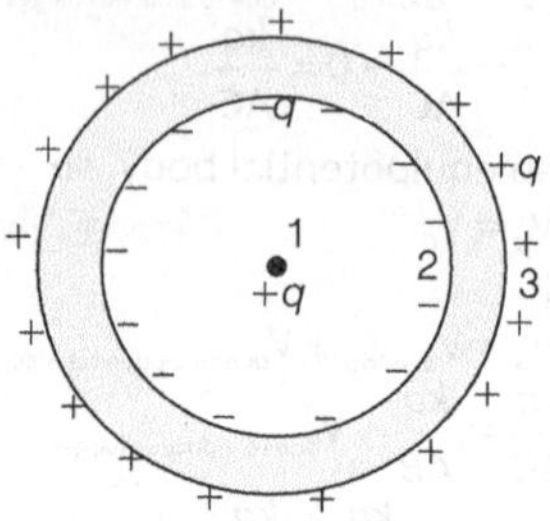

$$U = U_{12} + U_{23} + U_{31} + U_2 + U_3$$

$$\Rightarrow \quad U = (-q)\left(\frac{kq}{a}\right) + q\left[\frac{k(-q)}{b}\right] + q\left(\frac{kq}{b}\right) + \frac{k(-q)^2}{2a} + \frac{kq^2}{2b}$$

$$\Rightarrow \quad U = -\frac{kq^2}{a} - \frac{kq^2}{b} + \frac{kq^2}{b} + \frac{kq^2}{2a} + \frac{kq^2}{2b} = \frac{kq^2}{2b} - \frac{kq^2}{2a}$$

30.

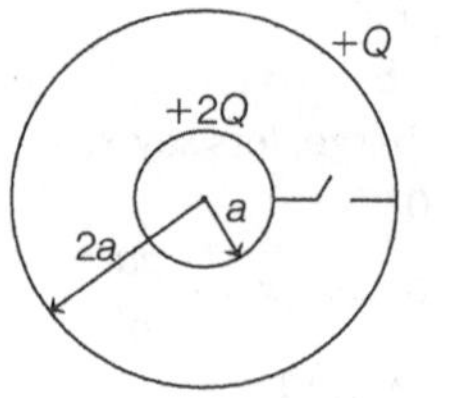

$$U_1 = \frac{k(2Q)^2}{2a} + \frac{kQ^2}{2(2a)} + Q\left[\frac{k(2Q)}{2a}\right] = \frac{13kQ^2}{4a}$$

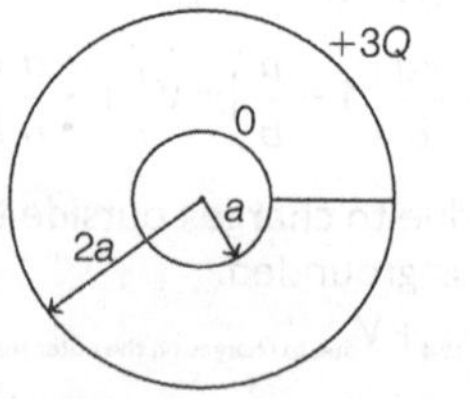

After closing the switch, the entire charge of inner shell will be transferred to the outer shell.

$$U_2 = \frac{k(3Q)^2}{2(2a)} = \frac{9kQ^2}{4a}$$

$$\text{Heat dissipated} = U_1 - U_2 = \frac{13kQ^2}{4a} - \frac{9kQ^2}{4a} = \frac{kQ^2}{a}$$

Numerical Value Questions

1. For each drop, $V = \frac{kq}{r} \Rightarrow 3 = \frac{kq}{1 \times 10^{-3}}$

$$n = \text{total number of drops inside the sphere} = \frac{\frac{4}{3}\pi R^3}{\frac{4}{3}\pi r^3}$$

$$= \left(\frac{4\times 10^{-2}}{1\times 10^{-3}}\right)^3 = 64\times 10^3$$

Final potential of sphere $= \dfrac{k(nq)}{R}$

$$= \frac{kq\times 64\times 10^3}{4\times 10^{-2}}$$

$$= \frac{3\times 10^{-3}\times 64\times 10^3}{4\times 10^{-2}} = 4800\text{ V}$$

2.

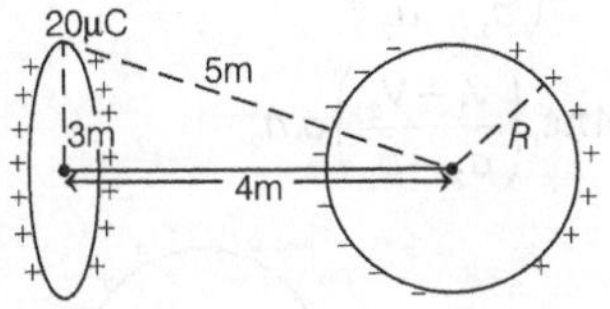

Potential of sphere,

Potential at the centre $= V_{\text{due to ring}} + V_{\text{due to induced charges}}$

$$= \frac{9\times 10^9\times 20\times 10^{-6}}{\sqrt{3^2+4^2}} + \frac{k(0)}{R} = 3.6\times 10^4\text{ V}$$

3.

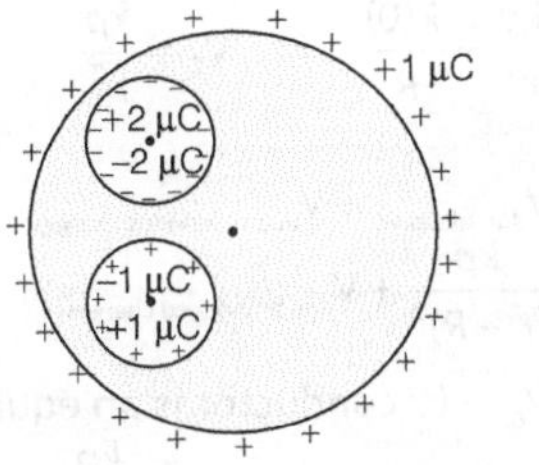

Electric potential at centre of conductor

$$= \frac{k(1\,\mu\text{C})}{(10\text{ cm})} = \frac{9\times 10^9\times 10^{-6}}{0.1} = 9\times 10^4\text{V}$$

4. $dV = -\mathbf{E}\cdot d\mathbf{r}$

$$\int_{V_C}^{0} dV = -\left[\int_0^a 0 + \int_a^b \frac{1Q}{4\pi\varepsilon r^2}dr + \int_b^\infty \frac{1}{4\pi\varepsilon_0}\frac{Q}{r^2}dr\right]$$

$$\Rightarrow \quad V_C = \frac{Q}{4\pi\varepsilon}\left(\frac{1}{a}-\frac{1}{b}\right) + \frac{Q}{4\pi\varepsilon_0}\left(\frac{1}{b}-\frac{1}{\infty}\right)$$

$$\Rightarrow \quad V_C = \frac{Q}{8\pi\varepsilon_0}\left(1-\frac{1}{2}\right) + \frac{Q}{4\pi\varepsilon_0}\left(\frac{1}{2}\right)$$

$$= \frac{3}{4}\left(\frac{1}{4\pi\varepsilon_0}\right)Q$$

$$= \frac{3}{4}\times 9\times 10^9\times \frac{4}{3}\times 10^{-6}$$

$$= 9\times 10^3\text{ V} = 9\text{ kV}$$

5.

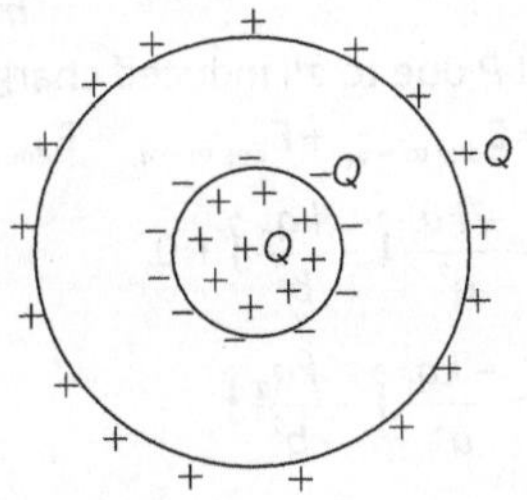

$$U_1 = \frac{3kQ^2}{5R}$$

$$U_2 = \frac{3kQ^2}{5R} + \frac{k(-Q)^2}{2R} + \frac{kQ^2}{2(5R)} + \left[\frac{k(-Q)}{5R}\right]Q + \frac{(kQ)Q}{5R} + \frac{(kQ)}{R}(-Q)$$

$$\Rightarrow \quad U_2 = \frac{kQ^2}{5R} \quad \Rightarrow \quad \frac{U_1}{U_2} = \frac{\dfrac{3kQ^2}{5R}}{\dfrac{kQ^2}{5R}} = 3$$

6. $\dfrac{\sigma^2}{2\varepsilon_0} = \dfrac{4S}{R}$

$$\Rightarrow \quad \frac{(Q/4\pi R^2)^2}{2\varepsilon_0} = \frac{4S}{R} \quad \Rightarrow \quad \frac{Q^2}{(16\pi^2R^4)2\varepsilon_0} = \frac{4S}{R}$$

$$\Rightarrow \quad Q^2 = 96\pi\varepsilon_0 S\left(\frac{4}{3}\pi R^3\right) \Rightarrow Q^2 = 96\pi\varepsilon_0 SV$$

So, $n = 96$

7. $\dfrac{kQ_1}{(1\text{cm})} + \dfrac{kQ_2}{(2\text{cm})} + \dfrac{kQ_3}{(4\text{cm})} = 10$ ... (i)

$\dfrac{kQ_1}{(2\text{cm})} + \dfrac{kQ_2}{(2\text{cm})} + \dfrac{kQ_3}{(4\text{cm})} = 0$ ... (ii)

$\dfrac{kQ_1}{(4\text{cm})} + \dfrac{kQ_2}{(4\text{cm})} + \dfrac{kQ_3}{(4\text{cm})} = 40$ ... (iii)

Solving Eqs. (i), (ii) and (iii), we get

$$kQ_1 = (10\text{V})(2\text{cm}) = 20\text{ V - cm}$$

$$kQ_2 = -180\text{V - cm}$$

$$kQ_3 = 320\text{ V - cm}$$

Potential at $r = 1.25$ cm,

$$V = \frac{kQ_1}{(1.25\text{cm})} + \frac{kQ_2}{(2\text{cm})} + \frac{kQ_3}{(4\text{cm})}$$

$$= \frac{20}{1.25} - \frac{180}{2} + \frac{320}{4} = 6\text{ V}$$

8.

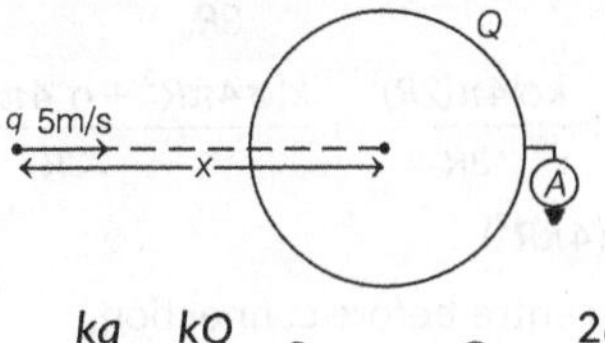

$$V_{\text{sphere}} = \frac{kq}{x} + \frac{kQ}{2} = 0 \quad \Rightarrow \quad Q = -\frac{2q}{x}$$

$$\Rightarrow \quad \frac{dQ}{dt} = -2q\left(\frac{-1}{x^2}\right)\frac{dx}{dt} = \frac{2\times 2\times 10^{-3}}{5^2}\times 5$$

$$= 0.8\times 10^{-3}\text{ A} = 800\times 10^{-6}\text{A} = 800\,\mu\text{A}$$

9.

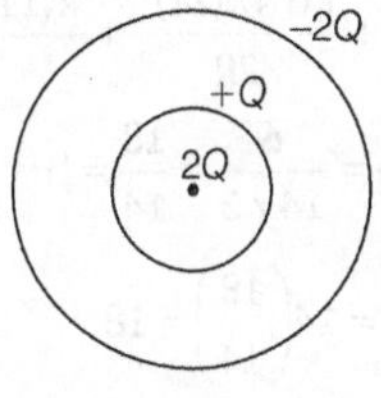

$$U_1 = \frac{kQ^2}{2R} + \frac{k(-2Q)^2}{2(2R)} + Q\left[\frac{k(2Q)}{R}\right] + (-2Q)\left[\frac{k(2Q)}{2R}\right] + (-2Q)\left(\frac{kQ}{2R}\right)$$

$$\Rightarrow \quad U_1 = \frac{kQ^2}{2R}$$

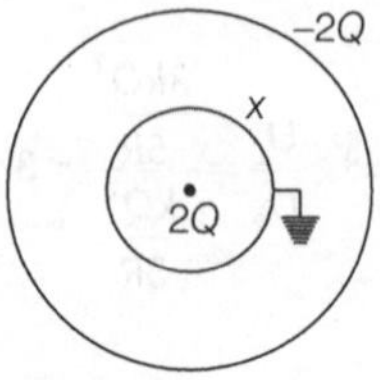

Potential of inner shell = 0

$$\Rightarrow \quad \frac{k(2Q)}{R} + \frac{kx}{R} + \frac{k(-2Q)}{2R} = 0$$

$$\Rightarrow \quad x = -Q$$

$$U_2 = \frac{k(-Q)^2}{2R} + \frac{k(-2Q)^2}{2(2R)} + (-Q)\left[\frac{k(2Q)}{2R}\right] + (-2Q)\left[\frac{k(2Q)}{2R}\right] + (-2Q)\left[\frac{k(-Q)}{2R}\right] = -\frac{3}{2}\frac{kQ^2}{R}$$

Heat generated $= U_1 - U_2$

$$= \frac{kQ^2}{2R} - \left(-\frac{3kQ^2}{2R}\right) = \frac{2kQ^2}{R}$$

$$= \frac{2 \times 9 \times 10^9 \times (10^{-6})^2}{1 \times 10^{-2}} = 1.8 \text{ J}$$

10.

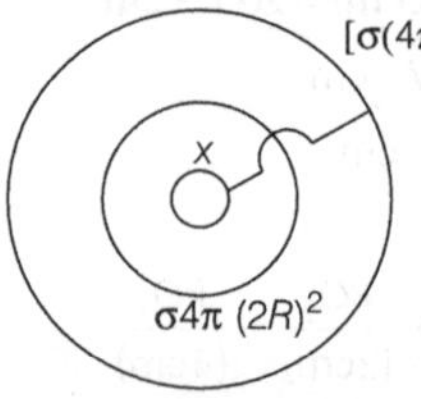

Potential of innermost shell = Potential of outermost shell

$$\frac{kx}{R} + \frac{k\sigma\, 4\pi(2R)^2}{2R} + \frac{k[\sigma 4\pi R^2 + \sigma\, 4\pi\,(3R)^2 - x]}{3R}$$

$$= \frac{kx}{3R} + \frac{k\sigma 4\pi(2R)^2}{3R} + \frac{k[\sigma 4\pi R^2 + \sigma\, 4\pi\,(3R)^2 - x]}{3R}$$

$$\Rightarrow \quad x = -\sigma(4\pi R^2)$$

Potential at centre before connection,

$$V_1 = \frac{k\sigma(4\pi R^2)}{R} + \frac{k\sigma\, 4\pi\,(2R)^2}{2R} + \frac{k\sigma 4\pi(3R)^2}{3R}$$

$$= 6k\sigma(4\pi R^2)$$

Potential at centre after connection,

$$V_2 = \frac{k(-\sigma 4\pi R^2)}{R} + \frac{k\sigma 4\pi(2R)^2}{2R} + \frac{k(11\sigma)4\pi R^2}{3R} = \frac{14k\sigma(4\pi R^2)}{3}$$

$$\frac{V_1}{V_2} = \frac{6}{14/3} = \frac{18}{14} = \beta$$

$$\Rightarrow \quad 14\beta = 14\left(\frac{18}{14}\right) = 18$$

Level 3 JEE Advanced Level

Single Choice Correct Questions

1.
$$V_1 = \frac{kQ_1}{a_1} + \frac{kQ_2}{a_2} \quad \text{... (i)}$$

$$V_2 = \frac{kQ_1}{a_2} + \frac{kQ_2}{a_2} \quad \text{... (ii)}$$

Subtracting Eq. (ii) from Eq. (i), we get

$$V_1 - V_2 = kQ_1\left(\frac{1}{a_1} - \frac{1}{a_2}\right)$$

$$\Rightarrow \quad Q_1 = 4\pi\varepsilon_0\left(\frac{V_1 - V_2}{a_2 - a_1}\right)a_1 a_2$$

2.

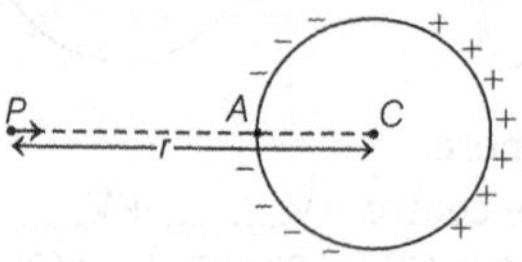

At centre C,

$$V_C = V_{\text{due to dipole}} + V_{\text{due to induced charges}}$$

$$V_C = \frac{kp}{r^2} + \frac{k(0)}{R} \Rightarrow V_C = \frac{kp}{r^2}$$

At point A,

$$V_A = V_{\text{due to dipole}} + V_{\text{due to induced charges}}$$

$$V_A = \frac{kp}{(r-R)^2} + V_{\text{due to induced charges}}$$

Now, $V_A = V_C$ ($\because$ conductor is an equipotential body)

$$\Rightarrow \quad \frac{kp}{(r-R)^2} + V_{\text{due to induced charges}} = \frac{kp}{r^2}$$

$$\Rightarrow \quad V_{\text{due to induced charges}} = \frac{kp}{r^2} - \frac{kp}{(r-R)^2}$$

3.

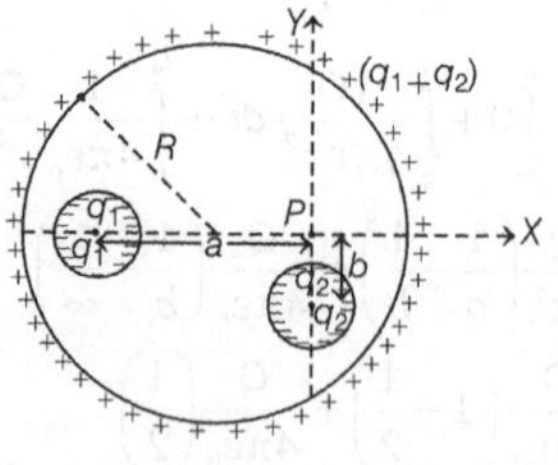

At P, $\mathbf{E}_{\text{due to } q_1} + \mathbf{E}_{\text{due to } -q_1} = 0$

$$\Rightarrow \quad \mathbf{E}_{\text{due to } -q_1} = -\mathbf{E}_{\text{due to } q_1} = -\frac{kq_1}{a^2}\hat{\mathbf{i}}$$

$$\mathbf{E}_{\text{due to } q_2} + \mathbf{E}_{\text{due to } -q_2} = 0$$

$$\Rightarrow \quad \mathbf{E}_{\text{due to } -q_2} = -\mathbf{E}_{\text{due to } q_2} = -\frac{kq_2}{b^2}\hat{\mathbf{j}}$$

Electric field at P due to all induced charges on the sphere,

$$\mathbf{E} = \mathbf{E}_{\text{due to } -q_1} + \mathbf{E}_{\text{due to } -q_2} + \mathbf{E}_{\text{due to } (q_1+q_2)}$$

$$= \frac{-kq_1}{a^2}\hat{\mathbf{i}} - \frac{kq_2}{b^2}\hat{\mathbf{j}} + 0$$

$$= \frac{-kq_1}{a^2}\hat{\mathbf{i}} - \frac{kq_2}{b^2}\hat{\mathbf{j}}$$

4.

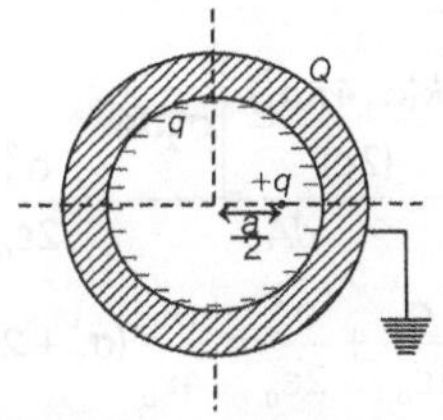

Potential of shell = 0 $\Rightarrow$ $Q = 0$

At the centre of shell,

$$V = V_{\text{due to }+q} + V_{\text{due to }-q}$$

$$= \frac{kq}{a/2} + \frac{k(-q)}{a} = \frac{1}{4\pi\varepsilon_0}\left(\frac{q}{a}\right)$$

5. To make potential of conductor zero, negative charge will flow from ground to conductor. There will be charges induced on the conductor due to q.

6.

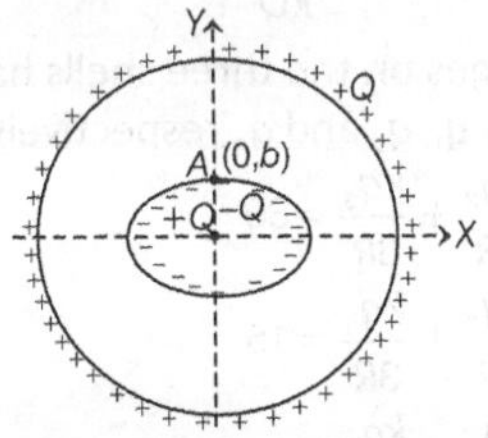

Potential at A will be only due to charge on the outer surface of the conducting sphere,

$$V_A = \frac{kQ}{R} = \frac{1}{4\pi\varepsilon_0}\left(\frac{Q}{R}\right)$$

7.

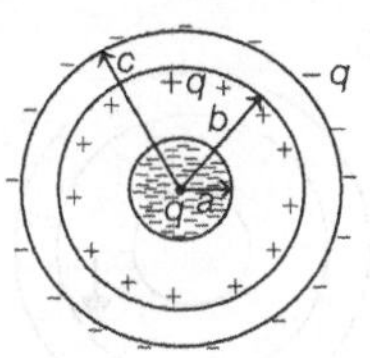

For $0 < r < a$,

$$V = \frac{k(-q)}{2a^3}(3a^2 - r^2) + \frac{kq}{b} + \frac{k(-q)}{c}$$

For $a \le r < b$,

$$V = \frac{k(-q)}{r} + \frac{kq}{b} + \frac{k(-q)}{c}$$

For $b \le r < c$,

$$V = \frac{k(-q)}{r} + \frac{kq}{r} + \frac{k(-q)}{c} = \text{constant}$$

For $r \ge c$,

$$V = \frac{k(-q)}{r} + \frac{kq}{r} + \frac{k(-q)}{r} = \frac{k(-q)}{r}$$

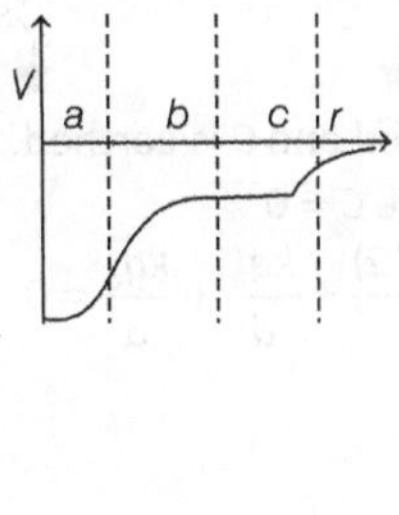

8. Force on q_2 is due to only charges on the outer surface of the sphere. When q_1 is shifted, charges on the outer surface don't change, so $F_1 = F_2$

9.

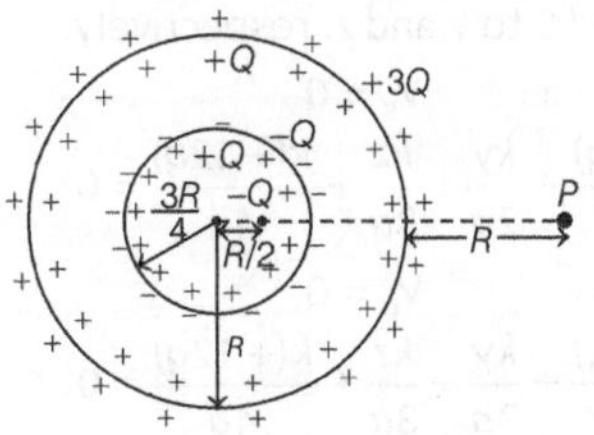

Potential at P will be only due to charges on the outer surface of the outermost shell,

$$V_P = \frac{k(3Q)}{(2R)} = \frac{1}{8\pi\varepsilon_0}\left(\frac{3Q}{R}\right)$$

10. Potential of sphere = 0

$$\Rightarrow \left(V_0 - \frac{\sigma}{\varepsilon_0}l\right) + \frac{kq}{r} = 0 \;\Rightarrow\; q = 4\pi r(\sigma l - V_0\varepsilon_0)$$

11. At the centre of sphere,

$$V_0 = V_{\text{due to sphere}} + V_{\text{due to sheet}} \;\Rightarrow\; V_0 = \frac{kQ}{R} + V_1$$

At point A on the surface of sphere,

$$V_A = V_{\text{due to sphere}} + V_{\text{due to sheet}}$$

$$V_A = V_{\text{due to sphere}} + \left[V_1 + \frac{\sigma}{2\varepsilon_0}\left(R\cos\frac{\pi}{3}\right)\right]$$

Since, conductor is an equipotential body.

$$V_0 = V_A$$

$$\Rightarrow \frac{kQ}{R} + V_1 = V_{\text{due to sphere}} + \left(V_1 + \frac{\sigma R}{4\varepsilon_0}\right)$$

$$\Rightarrow V_{\text{due to sphere}} = \frac{kQ}{R} - \frac{\sigma R}{4\varepsilon_0}$$

12.

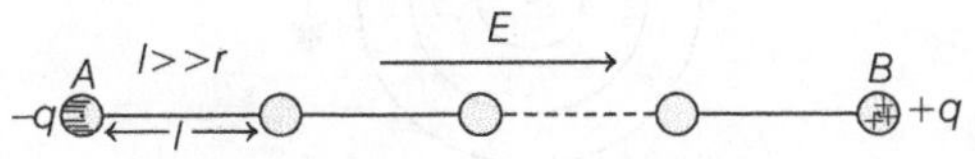

$$V_A = V_B \Rightarrow V_B - V_A = 0$$

$$\Rightarrow (V_B - V_A)_{\text{due to induced charges}} + (V_B - V_A)_{\text{due to electric field}} = 0$$

$$\Rightarrow \left[\left\{\frac{kq}{r} + \frac{k(-q)}{(n-1)l}\right\} - \left\{\frac{k(-q)}{r} + \frac{kq}{(n-1)l}\right\}\right] - (n-1)El = 0$$

$$\Rightarrow \frac{2kq}{r} - \frac{2kq}{(n-1)l} = (n-1)El$$

Since, $l >> r$

$$\frac{2kq}{r} = (n-1)El \Rightarrow q = 2\pi\varepsilon_0 r(n-1)El$$

13. After closing switch S_2, lets take charge on sphere C to be x.

$$V_C = 0$$

$$\Rightarrow \frac{k(+3q)}{3a} + \frac{k(+6q)}{3a} + \frac{kx}{3a} + \frac{k(+12q)}{4a} = 0$$

$$\Rightarrow x = -18q$$

Charge flown from sphere to earth $= -9q - (-18q)$

$$\Rightarrow \qquad \Delta q_1 = 9q$$

When both the switches are closed, lets take charges on sphere, B and C to y and z, respectively.

$$V_B = 0$$

$$\frac{k(+3q)}{2a} + \frac{ky}{2a} + \frac{kz}{3a} + \frac{k(+12q)}{4a} = 0 \qquad \text{... (i)}$$

$$V_C = 0$$

$$\frac{k(+3q)}{3a} + \frac{ky}{3a} + \frac{kz}{3a} + \frac{k(+12q)}{4a} = 0 \qquad \text{... (ii)}$$

Solving Eqs. (i) and (ii), we get

$$y = -3q$$

Charge flown from sphere B to earth $= 6q - (-3q)$

$$\Delta q_2 = 9q$$

$$\frac{\Delta q_1}{\Delta q_2} = 1$$

14. After closing S_1 for the first time, lets take charge on the inner sphere to be q.

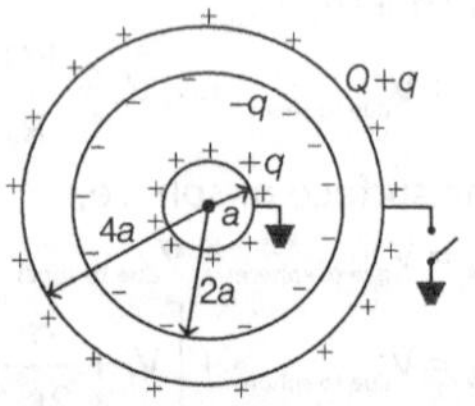

Potential of solid sphere = 0

$$\Rightarrow \quad \frac{kq}{a} + \frac{k(-q)}{2a} + \frac{k(Q+q)}{4a} = 0 \Rightarrow q = \frac{-Q}{3}$$

Now, after opening S_1 and closing S_2.

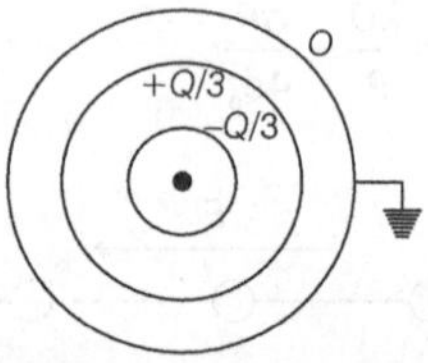

All charges on the outer surface will go to the earth.

After n cycles, charge on the inner sphere $= -\dfrac{Q}{3^n}$

15. Force on one hemisphere due to other,

$$F = \left(\frac{\sigma^2}{2\varepsilon_0}\right)(\pi R^2) \Rightarrow F = \frac{\sigma^2 \pi R^2}{2\varepsilon_0}$$

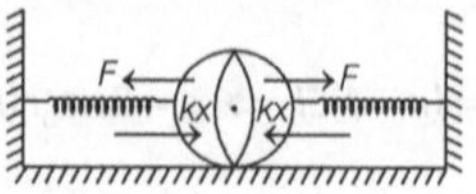

For equilibrium of each hemisphere,

$$F = kx$$

$$\Rightarrow \quad \frac{\sigma^2 \pi R^2}{2\varepsilon_0} = kx \Rightarrow x = \frac{\sigma^2 \pi R^2}{2\varepsilon_0 k}$$

16. $p = p_1 + p_2$

$$= \frac{\left[\dfrac{k(\sigma_1 4\pi a^2)}{(2a)^2}\right]\sigma_2 dA}{dA} + \frac{\sigma_2^2}{2\varepsilon_0}$$

$$= \frac{\sigma_1 \sigma_2}{4\varepsilon_0} + \frac{\sigma_2^2}{2\varepsilon_0} = \frac{\sigma_2}{4\varepsilon_0}(\sigma_1 + 2\sigma_2)$$

17. Let n drops have entered the vessel and $(n+1)$th drop fails to enter the vessel.

For $(n+1)$th drop,

Loss IN gravitational potential energy

= Gain in electrostatic potential energy

$$\Rightarrow \quad mg(h - 2R) = \frac{k(nQ)(Q)}{R}$$

$$\Rightarrow \quad n = \frac{mg(h-2R)R}{kQ^2}$$

18. Let initial charges on the three shells having radii $R, 2R$ and $3R$ be q_1, q_2 and q_3 respectively.

$$\frac{kq_1}{R} + \frac{kq_2}{2R} + \frac{kq_3}{3R} = 30 \qquad \text{...(i)}$$

$$\frac{kq_1}{2R} + \frac{kq_2}{2R} + \frac{kq_3}{3R} = 15 \qquad \text{...(ii)}$$

$$\frac{kq_1}{3R} + \frac{kq_2}{3R} + \frac{kq_3}{3R} = 10 \qquad \text{...(iii)}$$

Solving Eqs. (i), (ii) and (iii), we get

$$q_1 = 120\pi\varepsilon_0 R$$

$$q_2 = 0$$

$$q_3 = 0$$

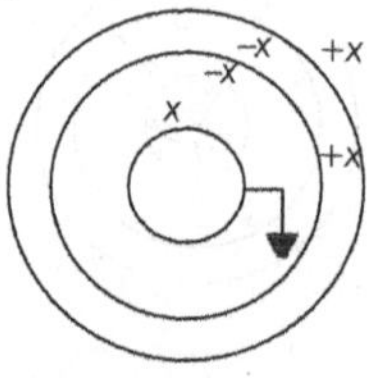

Potential of innermost shell = 0

$$\frac{kx}{R} + \frac{k(0)}{2R} + \frac{k(0)}{3R} = 0 \Rightarrow x = 0$$

19. When the fourth sphere touches sphere A, charge on each of them would be $q/2$.

When B is earthed, potential of sphere $B = 0$.

$$\Rightarrow \quad \frac{kq_B}{a} + \frac{k(q/2)}{d} + \frac{k(0)}{d} = 0 \Rightarrow q_B = \frac{-qa}{2d}$$

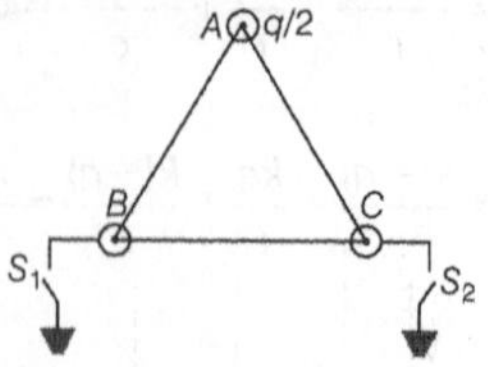

Now, B is unearthed and C is earthed.

Potential of sphere $C = 0$

$$\Rightarrow \quad \frac{k(q/2)}{d} + \frac{kq_B}{d} + \frac{kq_C}{a} = 0$$

$$\Rightarrow \quad \frac{kq}{2d} - \frac{kqa}{2d^2} + \frac{kq_c}{a} = 0$$

$$\Rightarrow \quad q_c = \frac{-qa}{2d}\left(\frac{d-a}{d}\right)$$

20.

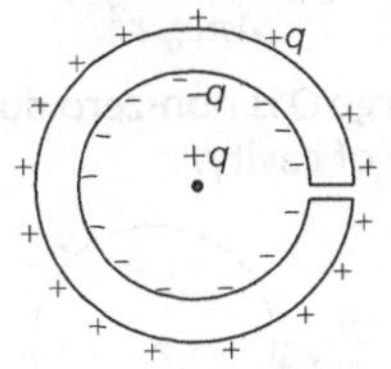

$$U_1 = \frac{k(-q)^2}{2(a)} + \frac{kq^2}{2b} + (-q)\left(\frac{kq}{a}\right) + (q)\left(\frac{kq}{b}\right) + q\left[\frac{k(-q)}{b}\right]$$

$$\Rightarrow \quad U_1 = \frac{kq^2}{2b} - \frac{kq^2}{2a} = \frac{q^2}{8\pi\varepsilon_0}\left(\frac{1}{b} - \frac{1}{a}\right)$$

$$U_2 = 0$$

$$W_{ext} = \Delta U + \Delta K = (U_2 - U_1) + 0 = \frac{q^2}{8\pi\varepsilon_0}\left(\frac{1}{a} - \frac{1}{b}\right)$$

21. Resultant electric field near $P = \left(\frac{\sigma}{\varepsilon_0}\right)\hat{i}$

22. For isothermal process, $pV = \text{constant}$

$$\Rightarrow \quad \frac{dV}{V} = -\frac{dp}{p}$$

$$\Rightarrow \quad 3\frac{dr}{r} = -\frac{dp}{p} \quad \Rightarrow \quad dr = -\frac{1}{3}\frac{dpr}{p}$$

$$\Rightarrow \quad dr = -\frac{1}{3}\frac{\left(-\frac{\sigma^2}{2\varepsilon_0}\right)r}{p_0} = \frac{q^2}{96\pi^2 r^3 \varepsilon_0 p_0}$$

23. Let L be the distance from the large conducting sphere to each of the three balls, d is the separation between the balls and r be the radius of each ball. If we connect the large sphere to the first ball, their potential become equal.

$$k\left(\frac{Q}{L} + \frac{q_1}{r}\right) = V \quad \text{... (i)}$$

where, Q is the charge of the large sphere and V is its potential.

If the large sphere is connected to the second ball,

$$k\left(\frac{Q}{L} + \frac{q_1}{d} + \frac{q_2}{r}\right) = V \quad \text{... (ii)}$$

(We assume that charge and potential of the large sphere change insignificantly in each charging of the balls)

When the larger sphere is connected to the third ball,

$$k\left(\frac{Q}{L} + \frac{q_1}{d} + \frac{q_2}{d} + \frac{q_3}{r}\right) = V \quad \text{... (iii)}$$

Solving Eqs. (i), (ii) and (iii), we get

$$q_3 = \frac{q_2^2}{q_1}$$

24.

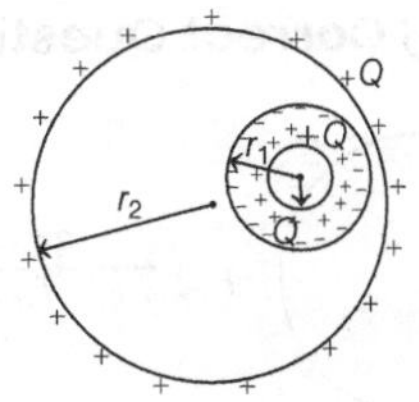

$$U = \frac{kQ^2}{2r} + \frac{k(-Q)^2}{2r_1} + \frac{kQ^2}{2r_2} + (-Q)\left(\frac{kQ}{r_1}\right)$$

$$= kQ^2\left(\frac{1}{2r_2} - \frac{1}{2r_1} + \frac{1}{2r}\right)$$

25.

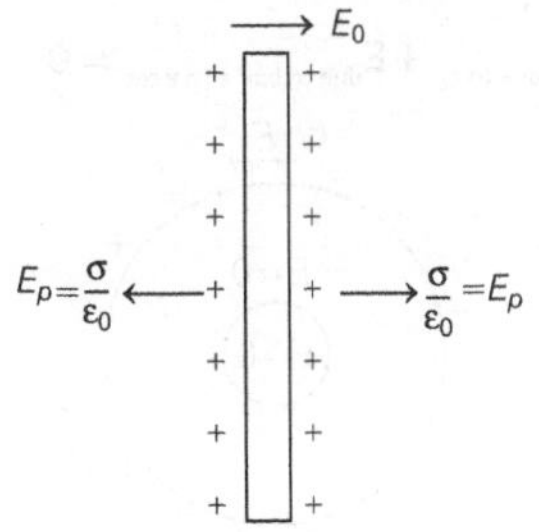

Lets take surface charge density on the plate to be σ and external uniform electric field lets take to be E_0.

$$E_0 - E_p = E_1 \quad \text{... (i)}$$

$$E_0 + E_p = -E_2 \quad \text{... (ii)}$$

Solving Eqs. (i) and (ii), we get

Electric field due to plate, $E_p = -4 \times 10^5$

$$\Rightarrow \quad \frac{\sigma}{\varepsilon_0} = -4 \times 10^5$$

$$\Rightarrow \quad \sigma = -4\varepsilon_0 \times 10^5$$

Force on the plate $= qE_0$

$$0.08 = (\sigma 2A)10^5$$

$$\Rightarrow \quad 0.08 = (4\varepsilon_0 \times 10^5) \times 2A \times 10^5$$

$$\Rightarrow \quad A = \frac{10^{-12}}{\varepsilon_0} = 10^{-12} \times 4\pi \times 10^9 \times 9$$

$$= 3.6\pi \times 10^{-2}\,\text{m}^2$$

26. Lets say x charge is transformed from the leftmost plate to the rightmost plate.

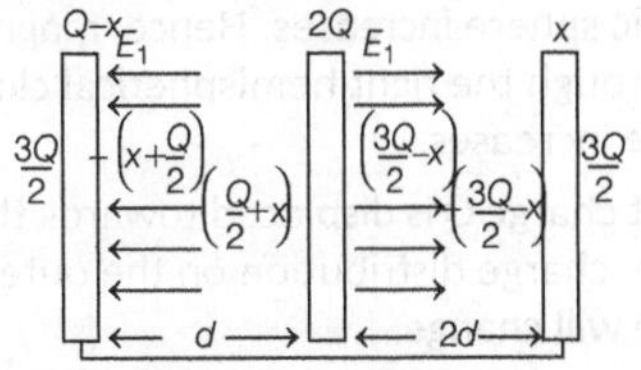

Leftmost and rightmost plates are at same potential.

$$\Rightarrow \quad E_1 d = E_2(2d)$$

$$\Rightarrow \quad \frac{\left(\frac{Q}{2} + x\right)}{A\varepsilon_0} d = \left(\frac{\frac{3Q}{2} - x}{A\varepsilon_0}\right) 2d \quad \Rightarrow \quad x = \frac{5Q}{6}$$

Multiple Choice(s) Correct Questions

1.

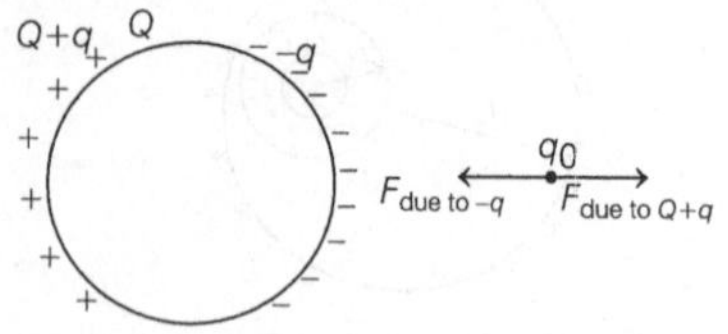

Due to induction, there will be shifting of charges on ball and net force can be attractive as well as repulsive depending upon the relative charge on them.

Net electric field inside the ball is zero but electric field inside the ball due to ball's charges is non-zero.

Inside the ball,

$$\mathbf{E}_{\text{net}} = \mathbf{E}_{\text{due to } q_0} + \mathbf{E}_{\text{due to ball's charges}} = 0$$

2.

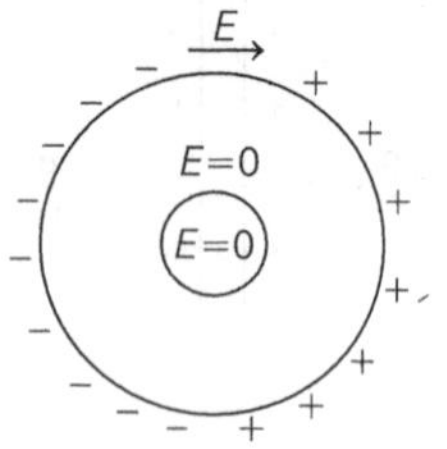

Electric field inside a chargeless cavity is zero.

Electric field just outside the conductor is $\frac{\sigma}{\varepsilon_0}$, where σ is the local surface charge density.

3.

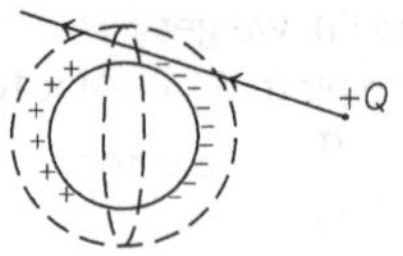

(a) Every electric field emanating from $+Q$ enters as well as leaves the spherical Gaussian surface. So, net flux through the Gaussian surface due to charge Q.

(b) Since, the metallic sphere is neutral, net induced charges on the outer surface are zero. So, net flux through the Gaussian sphere due to charges appearing on the outer surface of metallic sphere must be zero.

(c) If point charge Q is shifted towards the metallic sphere, magnitude of induced charges on the right half of the metallic sphere increases. Hence, magnitude of net flux through the right hemispherical closed Gaussian surface increases.

(d) If point charge Q is displaced towards the metallic sphere, charge distribution on the outer surface of sphere will change.

4.

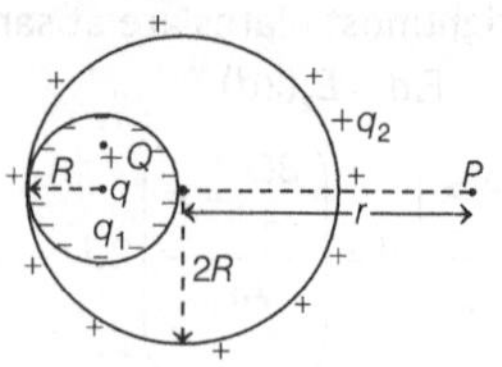

(a) $q_1 = -Q$ and charge distribution at the inner surface of cavity is non-uniform, since Q is kept off centre.

(b) $q_2 = +Q$ and charge distribution on the outer surface is uniform.

(c) Electric field at P will be only due to charges on the outer surface of conductor.

$$E = \frac{1}{4\pi\varepsilon_0}\frac{Q}{r^2}$$

(d) Force on charge Q is non-zero due to charges on the inner surface of cavity.

5.

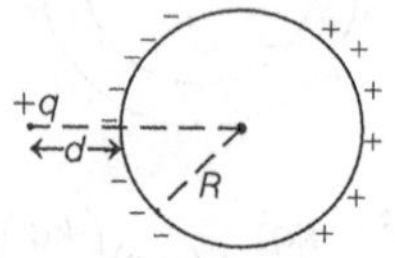

(a) Conductor is an equipotential body.

Potential at the centre,

$$V = V_{\text{due to } q} + V_{\text{due to induced charges}}$$

$$V = \frac{kq}{d+R} + \frac{k(0)}{R} = \frac{1}{4\pi\varepsilon_0}\left(\frac{q}{d+R}\right)$$

(d) Potential at $B = V_{\text{due to } q} + V_{\text{due to induced charges}}$

$$\Rightarrow \quad \frac{q}{4\pi\varepsilon_0(d+R)} = \frac{q}{4\pi\varepsilon_0 d} + V_{\text{due to induced charges}}$$

$$\Rightarrow V_{\text{due to induced charges}} = \frac{-qR}{4\pi\varepsilon_0 d(d+R)}$$

6. (a) $\sigma_A \neq \sigma_B$ as distances of A and B from charge Q are different.

(b) $V_A = V_B$, as A and B lie on the conductor.

(c) $E_A \neq E_B$, as $\sigma_A \neq \sigma_B$.

(d) $\phi = \frac{q_{\text{enclosed}}}{\varepsilon_0} = \frac{Q}{\varepsilon_0}$

7.

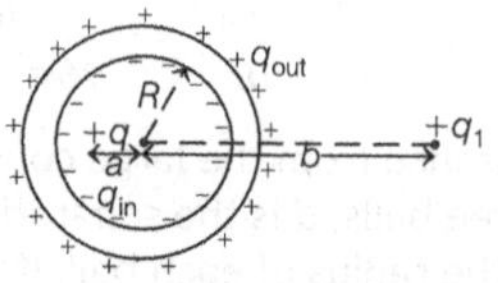

$q_{\text{in}} = -q$ (non-uniform distribution)

$q_{\text{out}} = Q + q$ (non-uniform distribution)

(a) At the centre, electric field due to charges outside the conductor and on the outer surface, the conductor is zero.

i.e. $\mathbf{E}_{\text{due to } q_{\text{out}}} + \mathbf{E}_{\text{due to } q_1} = 0$

$$\Rightarrow \quad \mathbf{E}_{\text{due to } q_{\text{out}}} \neq 0$$

(b) At the centre,

$$\mathbf{E}_{\text{due to } q_{\text{out}}} + \mathbf{E}_{\text{due to } q_1} = 0$$

$$\mathbf{E}_{\text{due to } q_{\text{out}}} = -\mathbf{E}_{\text{due to } q_1} = -\frac{kq_1}{b^2} = -\frac{1}{4\pi\varepsilon_0}\frac{q_1}{b^2}$$

$$|\mathbf{E}_{\text{due to } q_{\text{out}}}| = \frac{1}{4\pi\varepsilon_0}\frac{q_1}{b^2}$$

(d) At the centre,

$$V = V_{\text{due to } q} + V_{\text{due to } q_{\text{in}}} + V_{\text{due to } q_{\text{out}}} + V_{\text{due to } q_1}$$

$$= \frac{1}{4\pi\varepsilon_0}\frac{q}{a} + \frac{1}{4\pi\varepsilon_0}\frac{(-q)}{R} + \frac{1}{4\pi\varepsilon_0}\left(\frac{Q+q}{R}\right) + \frac{1}{4\pi\varepsilon_0}\left(\frac{q_1}{b}\right)$$

$$= \frac{1}{4\pi\varepsilon_0}\left(\frac{q}{a} + \frac{Q}{R} + \frac{q_1}{b}\right)$$

8.

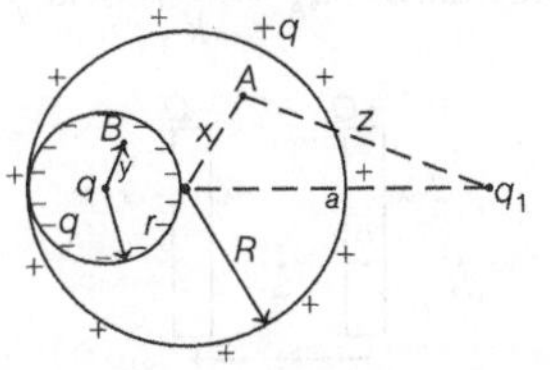

(a) Electric field at A is zero, as A is inside conductor.

(b) Electric field at B due to charges outside the conductor and on the outer surface of conductor is zero.

Electric field at B due to charges on the inner surface of cavity is also zero.

$$E_B = \frac{kq}{y^2} = \frac{1}{4\pi\varepsilon_0}\frac{q}{y^2}$$

(c) Potential at A and centre of sphere is same.

$$V_A = V_C = V_{\text{due to } q_1} + V_{\text{due to charges on the outer surface of sphere}} + V_{\text{due to charges in the cavity}}$$

$$= \frac{kq_1}{a} + \frac{kq}{R} + 0 = \frac{1}{4\pi\varepsilon_0}\left(\frac{q_1}{a} + \frac{q}{R}\right)$$

(d) Potential at B,

$$V_B = V_{\text{due to } q} + V_{\text{due to charges on the inner surface of cavity}} + V_{\text{due to charges outside the conductor}}$$

$$= \frac{kq}{y} + \frac{k(-q)}{r} + \left(\frac{kq_1}{a} + \frac{kq}{R}\right)$$

9.

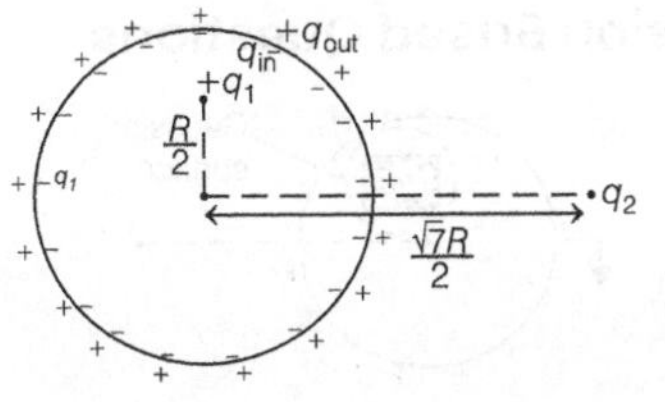

(a) Force on q_1 due to q_{in} is non-zero, as q_1 is kept off centre.

(b) Force on q_1 on due to q_2 and $q_{out} = 0$.

$\Rightarrow$ Force on q_1 due to q_{out} = – Force on q_1 due to q_2

$$= -\frac{kq_1q_2}{\left(\sqrt{\left(\frac{R}{2}\right)^2 + \left(\frac{\sqrt{7}R}{2}\right)^2}\right)^2} = -\frac{kq_1q_2}{2R^2}$$

(c) Force on q_2 due to q_1 and $q_{in} = 0$,

$\Rightarrow$ Force on q_2 due to q_{in} = – Force on q_2 and q_1

$$= -\frac{kq_1q_2}{2R^2}$$

10.

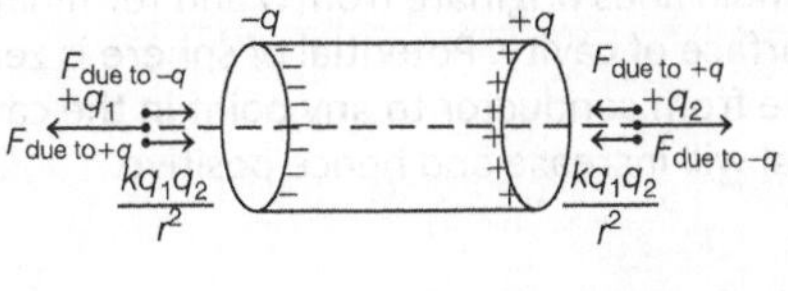

(a) Force on $q_1 = \mathbf{F}_{\text{due to} -q_2} + \mathbf{F}_{\text{due to induced charges}}$

(b) End A will become negatively charged.

(c) For q_1,

$$F_{\text{due to} -q} > F_{\text{due to} +q}$$

So, net force on $q_1 > \dfrac{kq_1q_2}{r^2}$

(d) For q_2,

$$F_{\text{due to} +q} > F_{\text{due to} -q}$$

So, net force on $q_2 > \dfrac{kq_1q_2}{r^2}$

11. $$V_A = \frac{kq_A}{R} + \frac{kq_B}{2R} = 2V \quad \text{... (i)}$$

$$V_B = \frac{kq_A}{2R} + \frac{kq_B}{2R} = \frac{3V}{2} \quad \text{... (ii)}$$

Solving Eqs. (i) and (ii), we get

$$\frac{q_A}{q_B} = \frac{1}{2}$$

After earthing B,

$$V_B = \frac{kq_A}{2R} + \frac{kq'_B}{2R} = 0$$

$$q'_B = -q_A \text{ and } q'_A = q_A$$

$$\Rightarrow \quad \frac{q'_A}{q'_B} = -1$$

$$V_A = \frac{kq'_A}{R} + \frac{kq'_B}{2R} = \frac{kq_A}{R} - \frac{kq_A}{2R} = \frac{kq_A}{2R} = \frac{1}{2}V$$

$$V_A - V_B = \frac{V}{2} - 0 = V/2$$

12.

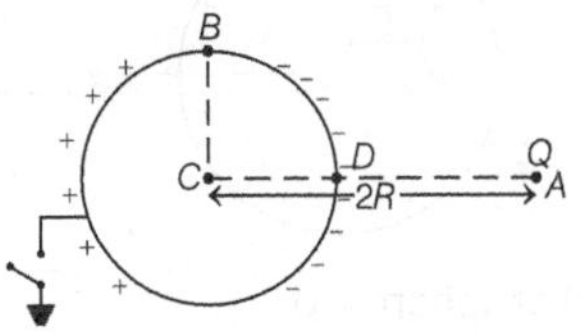

At C,

$$V_C = V_{\text{due to } Q} + V_{\text{due to induced charges}}$$

$$V_C = \frac{kQ}{2R} + \frac{k(0)}{R} \Rightarrow V_C = \frac{kQ}{2R}$$

At B,

Potential at $B = V_{\text{due to } Q} + V_{\text{due to induced charges}}$

$$\frac{kQ}{2R} = \frac{kQ}{\sqrt{5}R} + V_B \quad \left(\because \text{potential at } B = \frac{kQ}{2R}\right)$$

$$\Rightarrow \quad V_B = \frac{kQ}{R}\left(\frac{1}{2} - \frac{1}{\sqrt{5}}\right)$$

At D,

Potential at $D = V_{\text{due to } Q} + V_{\text{due to induced charges}}$

$$\Rightarrow \quad V_D = \frac{kQ}{2R} + \frac{kQ}{R} + V_D$$

$$\Rightarrow \quad V_D = -\frac{kQ}{2R}$$

$$\frac{V_D}{V_B} = \frac{-kQ/2R}{\frac{kQ}{R}\left(\frac{1}{2} - \frac{1}{\sqrt{5}}\right)} = \frac{\sqrt{5}}{2 - \sqrt{5}}$$

$$V_B - V_D = \frac{kQ}{R}\left(\frac{1}{2} - \frac{1}{\sqrt{5}}\right) - \left(-\frac{kQ}{2R}\right)$$
$$= \frac{kQ}{R}\left(1 - \frac{1}{\sqrt{5}}\right)$$

When switch is closed, potential of sphere = 0

At its centre,

$$\frac{kQ}{2R} + \frac{kx}{R} = 0$$

$$\Rightarrow \quad x = -\frac{Q}{2}$$

Charges flown from sphere to ground $= 0 - \left(\frac{-Q}{2}\right) = \frac{Q}{2}$

13.

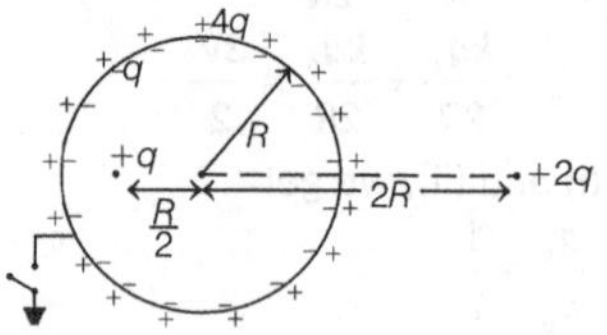

(a) At the centre, $\mathbf{E}_{\text{due to}+2q} + \mathbf{E}_{\text{due to}+4q} = 0$

$$\Rightarrow \quad \mathbf{E}_{\text{due to}+4q} = -\mathbf{E}_{\text{due to}+2q} = -\frac{k(2q)}{(2R)^2}$$

$$\Rightarrow \quad |\mathbf{E}_{\text{due to}+4q}| = \frac{kq}{2R^2}$$

(b) At the centre,

$$V_{\text{due to}+4q} = \frac{k(4q)}{R}$$

(c)

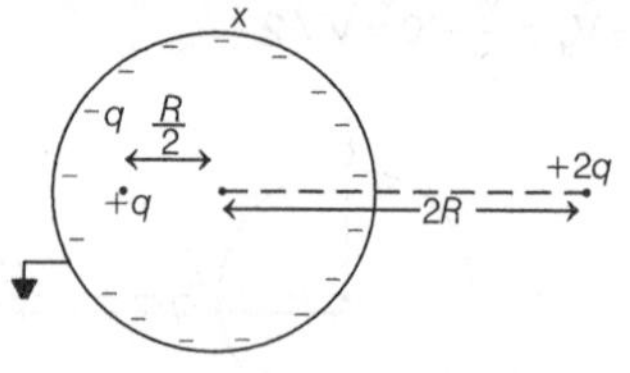

Potential of sphere = 0

$\Rightarrow$ Potential of sphere due to charges outside = 0.

$$\Rightarrow \quad \frac{kx}{R} + \frac{k(+2q)}{2R} = 0$$

$$x = -q$$

Potential at the centre C due to charges on the outer surface of shell is $\frac{k(-q)}{R}$.

(d) Charge flown into earth $= 4q - (-q) = 5q$

14. (b) $\frac{kq_A}{R_A} = V$ ... (i)

When shell A is connected to shell B by a conducting wire, all charges q_A of shell A will be transferred to shell B.

Now, potential of shell $A = \frac{2}{3}V$

$$\frac{kq_A}{R_B} = \frac{2}{3}V \quad \text{... (ii)}$$

Solving Eqs. (i) and (ii), we get

$$\frac{R_B}{R_A} = \frac{3}{2}$$

If $R_A = 2$ cm, then $R_B = \frac{3}{2} \times 2 = 3$ cm

(d) Charge on shell $B = q_A = \frac{R_A V}{k} = 4\pi\varepsilon_0 aV$

15.

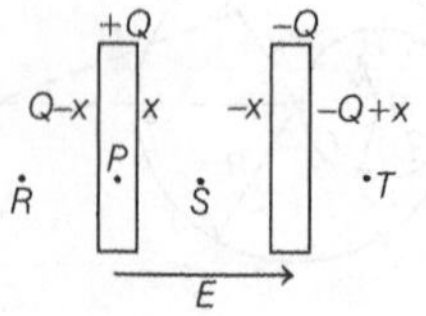

At P, $E_{\text{net}} = 0$

$$E + \frac{(Q-x)}{2A\varepsilon_0} - \frac{x}{2A\varepsilon_0} + \frac{x}{2A\varepsilon_0} - \frac{x-Q}{2A\varepsilon_0} = 0$$

$$\Rightarrow \quad E = \frac{x-Q}{A\varepsilon_0}$$

$$\Rightarrow \quad x = A\varepsilon_0 E + Q$$

$$Q - x = -A\varepsilon_0 E$$

At R, $E_{\text{net}} = E + \frac{Q-x}{2A\varepsilon_0} + \frac{x-Q}{2A\varepsilon_0} + \frac{x}{2A\varepsilon_0} - \frac{x}{2A\varepsilon_0} = E$

At S,

$$E_{\text{net}} = E + \frac{Q-x}{2A\varepsilon_0} - \frac{x-Q}{2A\varepsilon_0} + \frac{x}{2A\varepsilon_0} + \frac{x}{2A\varepsilon_0}$$
$$= E + \frac{Q-x}{A\varepsilon_0} + \frac{x}{A\varepsilon_0} = E + \frac{Q}{A\varepsilon_0}$$

At T,

$$E_{\text{net}} = E + \frac{Q-x}{2A\varepsilon_0} + \frac{x-Q}{2A\varepsilon_0} + \frac{x}{2A\varepsilon_0} - \frac{x}{2A\varepsilon_0} = E$$

Comprehension Based Questions

1.

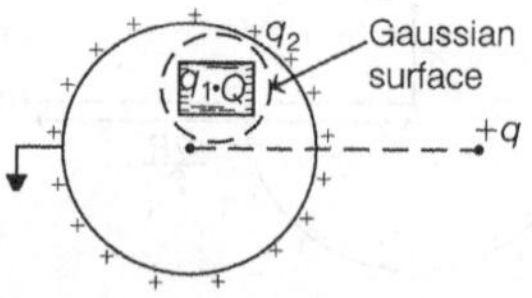

For the Gaussian surface,

$$E = 0$$

$$\Rightarrow \quad \phi = 0 \Rightarrow q_{\text{enclosed}} = 0$$

$$\Rightarrow Q + q_1 = 0 \Rightarrow q_1 = -Q$$

Distribution of $-Q$ on the inner surface of cavity will be non-uniform.

2. Since, the sphere is earthed, its potential will be zero. At the centre,

$$V = \frac{kq}{l} + \frac{kq_2}{R} = 0$$

$$\Rightarrow \quad q_2 = \frac{-qR}{l}$$

3. Electric field lines originate from Q and terminate on the inner surface of cavity. Potential of sphere is zero, so when we move from conductor to any point in the cavity, potential will increase and hence positive.

4.

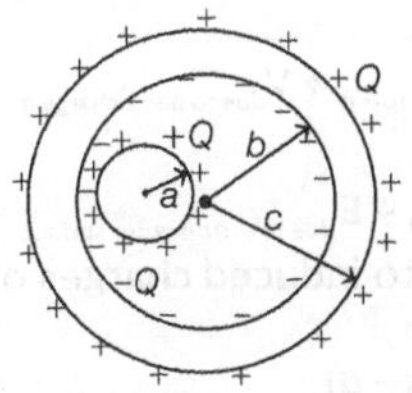

Potential outside the shell is only due to charges on the outer surface of the shell,

$$V = \frac{kQ}{c} = \left(\frac{1}{4\pi\varepsilon_0}\right)\frac{Q}{c}$$

5. If the entire conducting sphere is off centre, then $V_c < V_s$.
If centre lies on the conducting sphere, then $V_c = V_s$.

6.

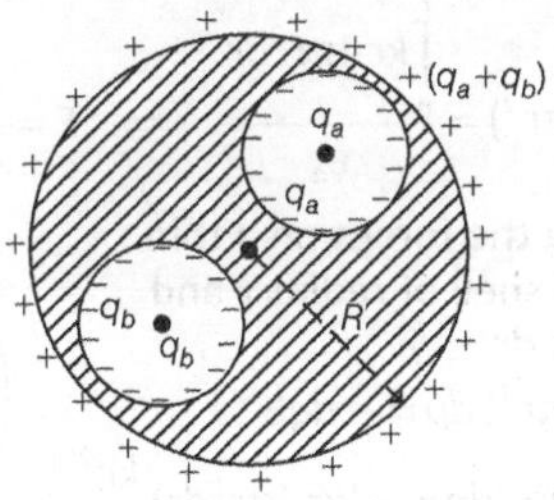

Electric field outside the conductor is only due to charges on the outer surface of conductor,

$$E = \frac{k(q_a+q_b)}{r^2}$$

7. $V = V_{\text{due to } q_a} + V_{\text{due to} - q_b} + V_{\text{due to}(q_a+q_b)} + V_{\text{due to } q_a \text{and} - q_a}$

$$\frac{kq_b}{r} + \frac{k(-q_b)}{b} + \frac{k(q_b+q_a)}{R} + 0$$

$$= \frac{1}{4\pi\varepsilon_0}\left(\frac{q_a+q_b}{R} + \frac{q_b}{r} - \frac{q_b}{b}\right)$$

8. Force on $q_a = \mathbf{F}_{\text{due to} - q_a} + \mathbf{F}_{\text{due to } q_b \text{and} - q_b} + \mathbf{F}_{\text{due to}(q_a+q_b)}$
$= 0 + 0 + 0 = 0$

9.

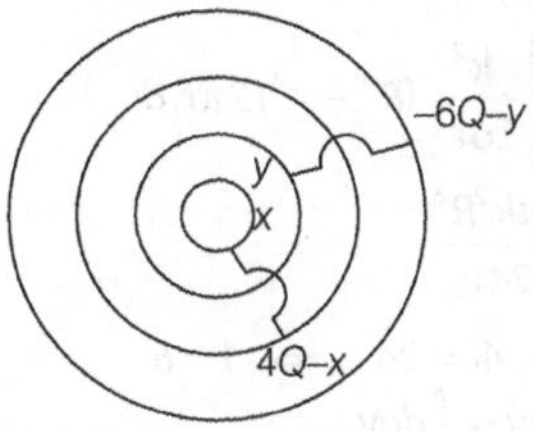

$$V_1 = V_3$$

$$\frac{kx}{R} + \frac{ky}{2R} + \frac{k(4Q-x)}{3R} + \frac{k(-6Q-y)}{4R}$$

$$= \frac{kx}{3R} + \frac{ky}{3R} + \frac{k(4Q-x)}{3R} + \frac{k(-6Q-y)}{4R}$$

$$\Rightarrow \quad x = -\frac{y}{4} \quad \text{... (i)}$$

$$V_2 = V_4$$

$$\frac{kx}{2R} + \frac{ky}{2R} + \frac{k(4Q-x)}{3R}$$

$$+ \frac{k(-6Q-y)}{4R} = \frac{kx}{4R} + \frac{ky}{4R} + \frac{k(4Q-x)}{4R} + \frac{k(-6Q-y)}{4R}$$

$$\Rightarrow \quad 2x + 3y = -4Q \quad \text{... (ii)}$$

Solving Eqs. (i) and (ii), we get

$$x = +\frac{2Q}{5} \text{ and } y = -\frac{8Q}{5}$$

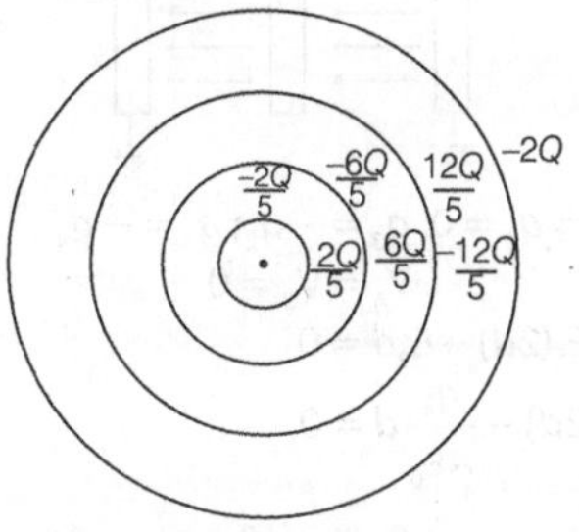

Charge on the inner surface of third conductor $= \frac{6Q}{5}$

10. Charge on the fourth conductor $= -6Q - y$

$$= -6Q + \frac{8Q}{5} = -\frac{22Q}{5}$$

11. $V_1 = \frac{kx}{R} + \frac{ky}{2R} + \frac{k(4Q-x)}{3R} + \frac{k(-6Q-y)}{4R}$

$$= \frac{-3kQ}{10R} = \frac{-3Q}{40\pi\varepsilon_0 R}$$

12. $V_2 = \frac{kx}{2R} + \frac{ky}{2R} + \frac{k(4Q-x)}{3R} + \frac{k(-6Q-y)}{4R}$

$$= \frac{-kQ}{2R} = \frac{-Q}{8\pi\varepsilon_0 R}$$

13. When S_1 is closed and S_2 is open,

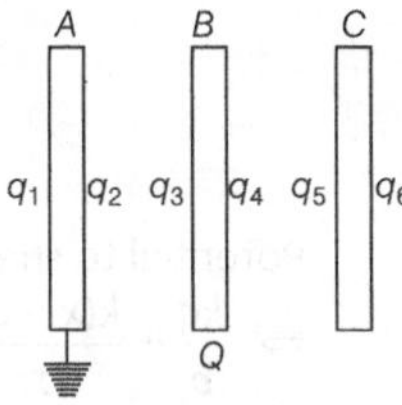

$q_1 = q_6 = 0$ (∵ potential of plate A is zero, so electric field outside the plates is zero. Hence, charges on outermost faces will be zero)

$$q_5 + q_6 = 0$$

(∵ plate C is neutral)

$$\Rightarrow \quad q_5 = 0$$

$$q_4 = -q_5 = 0$$

(∵ facing surfaces have equal and opposite charges)

$$q_3 + q_4 = Q \Rightarrow q_3 = Q \Rightarrow q_2 = -q_3$$

$$\Rightarrow \quad q_2 = -Q$$

(∵ facing surfaces have equal and opposite charges)

Charge flown through S_1 to earth $= 0 - (-Q) = Q$

14.

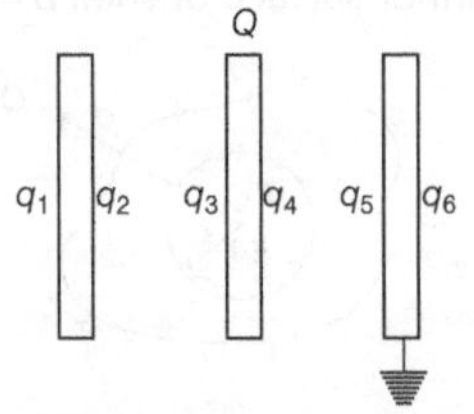

$$q_1 = q_6 = 0$$

$$q_1 + q_2 = 0 \Rightarrow q_2 = 0$$

$$q_3 = -q_2 \Rightarrow q_3 = 0$$

$$q_3 + q_4 = Q \Rightarrow q_4 = +Q$$

$$q_5 = -q_4 \Rightarrow q_5 = +Q$$

Charge flown through S_2 to earth $= 0 - (-Q) = Q$

15.

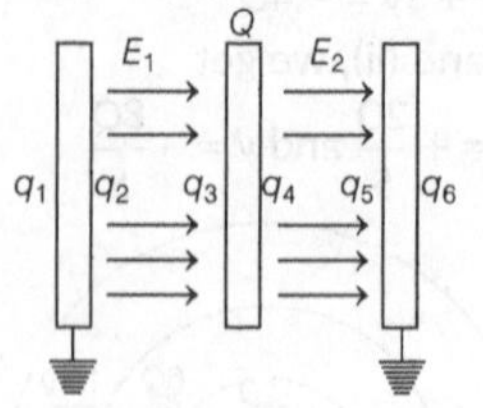

$$q_1 = q_6 = 0;\ q_3 = -q_2;\ q_5 = -q_4$$

$$V_A = V_C = 0$$

$$\Rightarrow \quad -E_1(2d) - E_2 d = 0$$

$$\Rightarrow \quad -\frac{q_2}{A\varepsilon_0}(2d) - \frac{q_4}{A\varepsilon_0}d = 0$$

$$\Rightarrow \quad q_4 = -2q_2$$

$$q_3 + q_4 = Q$$

$$\Rightarrow \quad -q_2 - 2q_2 = Q$$

$$\Rightarrow \quad q_2 = -\frac{Q}{3}$$

and $\quad q_5 = -q_4 = -(-2q_2) = -\dfrac{2Q}{3}$

Charge passing through $S_2 = 0 - \left(-\dfrac{2Q}{3}\right) = \dfrac{2Q}{3}$

Match the Columns Questions

1.

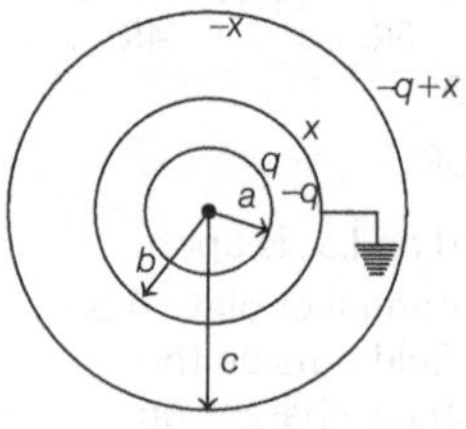

Potential to shell $B = 0$

$$\Rightarrow \quad \frac{kq}{b} + \frac{k(x-q)}{b} + \frac{k(-q)}{c} = 0 \Rightarrow x = \frac{bq}{c}$$

(a) Charge on outer surface of shell $C = x - q$

$$= \frac{bq}{c} - q = q\left(\frac{b}{c} - 1\right)$$

(b) Charge on inner surface of shell $C = -x = -\dfrac{bq}{c}$

(c) Charge on outer surface of shell $B = x = \dfrac{bq}{c}$

(d) Charge on inner surface of shell $B = -q$

2.

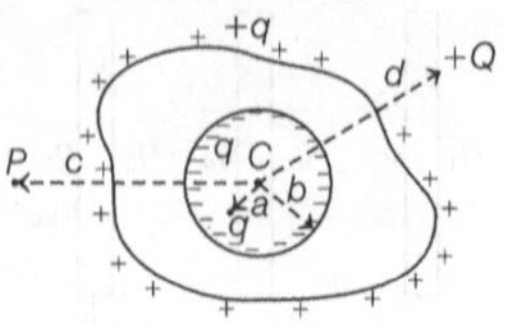

(a) At point P,

$$\mathbf{E}_{\text{due to}-q} + \mathbf{E}_{\text{due to point charge } q} = 0$$

$$\Rightarrow \quad \mathbf{E}_{\text{due to}-q} = -\mathbf{E}_{\text{due to point charge } q}$$

$\Rightarrow \mathbf{E}_{\text{due to}-q} \neq 0$ but value cannot be stated with the given data, as distance of point charge q from point P is unknown.

(b) At P,

$$V_{\text{due to}-q} + V_{\text{due to point charge } q} = 0$$

(c) At C,

$$\mathbf{E}_{\text{due to point charge } Q} + \mathbf{E}_{\text{due to}+q \text{ on outer surface}} = 0$$

(d) Potential due to induced charges on the inner surface of cavity at C

$$= \frac{k(-q)}{b}$$

3. (a) $\phi = \int \mathbf{E} \cdot d\mathbf{r} = \int EdA\cos 0° = E(4\pi r^2)$

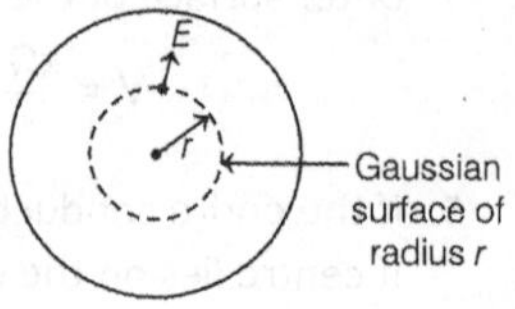

Using Gauss law,

$$\phi = \frac{q_{\text{enclosed}}}{\varepsilon_0}$$

$$E(4\pi r^2) = \frac{\int_0^r kr\, 4\pi r^2 dr}{\varepsilon_0} \Rightarrow E = \frac{kr^2}{4\varepsilon_0}$$

(b) Balancing the forces on a thin spherical shell of radius r and thickness dr

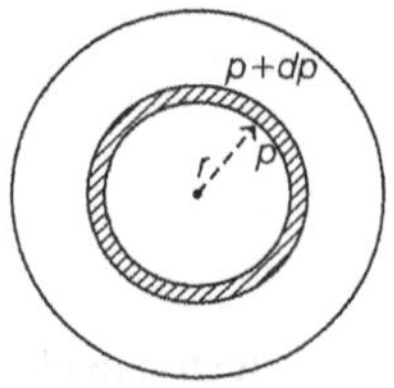

$$(4\pi r^2)\, dp = -dqE$$

$$\Rightarrow \quad 4\pi r^2 dp = -(kr\, 4\pi r^2 dr)\frac{kr^2}{4\varepsilon_0}$$

$$\Rightarrow \quad \int dp = -\frac{k^2}{4\varepsilon_0}\int r^3 dr$$

$$p = -\frac{k^2 r^4}{16\varepsilon_0} + C$$

At surface $p = 0$,

$$\Rightarrow \quad 0 = \frac{k^2R^4}{16\varepsilon_0} + C \Rightarrow C = +\frac{k^2R^4}{16\varepsilon_0}$$

$$p = \frac{k^2}{16\varepsilon_0}(R^4 - r^4)$$

(c) $\quad dF = \int p\, dA$

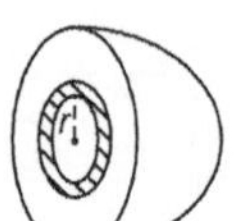

$$F = \int_0^R \frac{k^2}{16\varepsilon_0}(R^4 - r^4)\, 2\pi r\, dr$$

$$F = \frac{\pi k^2 R^6}{24\varepsilon_0}$$

So, $\quad 4l = 24 \Rightarrow l = 6$

(d) Self-energy $= \int dqV$

$$= \int_0^R (kr\, 4\pi r^2 dr)\left(\frac{\int_0^R kr\, 4\pi r^2 dr}{4\pi\varepsilon_0 r}\right)$$

$$= \int_0^R (kr\, 4\pi r^2 dr)\frac{4\pi k\left(\frac{r^4}{4}\right)}{4\pi\varepsilon_0 r}$$

$$= \frac{4\pi k^2}{\varepsilon_0}\int_0^R r^6 dr = \frac{4\pi k^2 R^7}{7\varepsilon_0} = dR^e$$

where, $e = 7$

Numerical Value Questions

1.

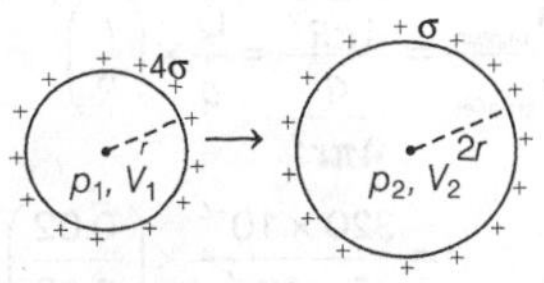

For isothermal process,

$$p_1V_1 = p_2V_2$$

$$\Rightarrow \left[p_0 + \frac{4T}{r} + \frac{(4\sigma)^2}{2\varepsilon_0}\right]\frac{4}{3}\pi r^3 = \left(p_0 + \frac{4T}{2r} + \frac{\sigma^2}{2\varepsilon_0}\right)\frac{4}{3}\pi(2r)^3$$

$$\Rightarrow p_0 + \frac{4T}{r} + \frac{8\sigma^2}{\varepsilon_0} = 8p_0 + \frac{16T}{r} + \frac{4\sigma^2}{\varepsilon_0}$$

$$\Rightarrow \frac{4\sigma^2}{\varepsilon_0} = \frac{12T}{r} + 7p_0$$

$$\Rightarrow \sigma = \sqrt{\left(\frac{7p_0}{4} + \frac{3T}{r}\right)\varepsilon_0}$$

$$= \sqrt{\left(\frac{7\times10^4}{4} + \frac{3\times0.2}{0.12\times10^{-3}}\right)9\times10^{-12}}$$

$$= 4.5\times10^{-4}\ \text{C/m}^2$$

2.

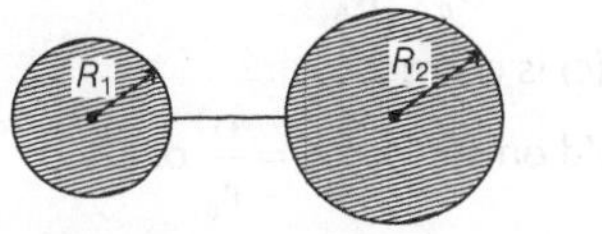

$$V_1 = V_2$$

$$\frac{kq_1}{R_1} = \frac{kq_2}{R_2} \Rightarrow q_2 = 2q_1$$

and $q_1 + q_2 = 21\mu C$

$\Rightarrow$ $q_1 = 7\mu C$ and $q_2 = 14\mu C$

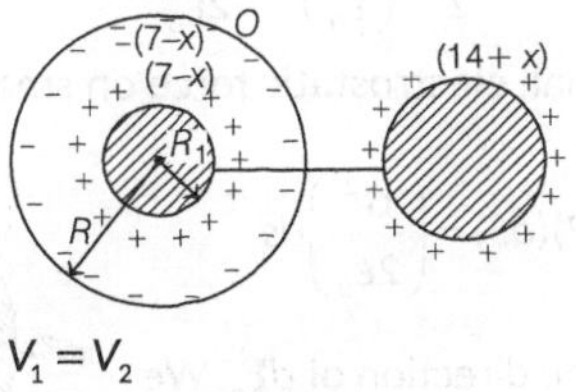

$$V_1 = V_2$$

$$\frac{k(7-x)}{R_1} + \frac{k[-(7-x)]}{R} = \frac{k(14+x)}{R_2}$$

$$\Rightarrow 7 - x + \frac{x-7}{3} = \frac{14+x}{2}$$

$$x = -2\mu C$$

So, charge flown through the wire $= 2\mu C$

3. When S_1 is closed, charge on the outer surface of shell will become zero.

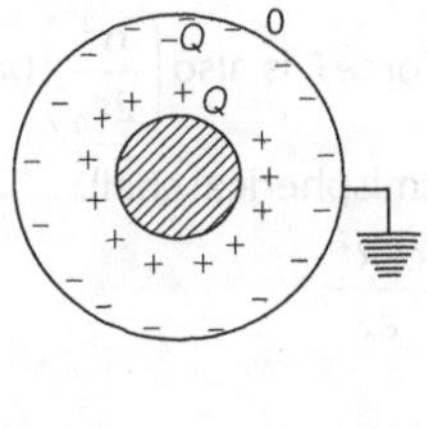

Now, S_1 is opened and S_2 is closed.

Lets take charge on sphere A to be x.

Potential of sphere $A = 0$

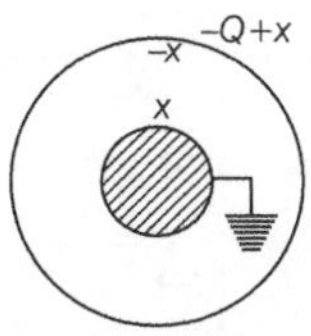

$$\Rightarrow \frac{kx}{a} + \frac{k(-Q)}{b} = 0$$

$$\Rightarrow x = \frac{Qa}{b} = \frac{Q(2\ \text{cm})}{(4\ \text{cm})} = Q/2$$

Now, S_2 is opened and S_3 is closed.

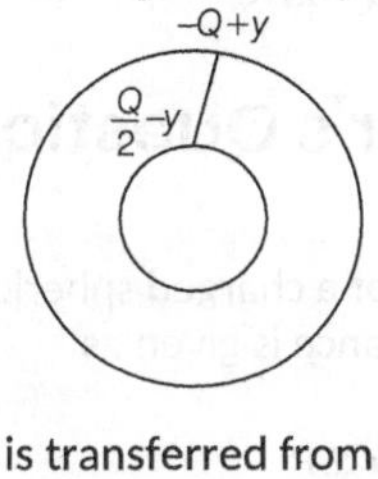

Lets say y charge is transferred from sphere A to shell B.

$$V_{\text{sphere}} = V_{\text{shell}}$$

$$\Rightarrow \frac{k\left(\frac{Q}{2} - y\right)}{a} + \frac{k(y-Q)}{b} = \frac{k(Q/2-y)}{b} + \frac{k(y-Q)}{b}$$

$$\Rightarrow y = Q/2$$

$$U_1 = \frac{k(Q/2)^2}{2a} + \frac{k(-Q)^2}{2b} + \left[\frac{k(Q/2)}{b}\right](-Q) = \frac{kQ^2}{8a}$$

$$U_2 = \frac{k(-Q/2)^2}{2b} = \frac{kQ^2}{8b}$$

$$\text{Heat produced} = U_1 - U_2 = \frac{kQ^2}{8a} - \frac{kQ^2}{8b} = 1.8\ \text{J}$$

4.

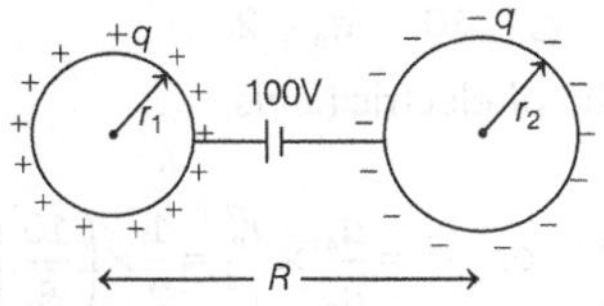

$$R >> r_1$$

and $R >> r_2$

$$V_1 - V_2 = 100$$

$$\Rightarrow \frac{kq}{r_1} - \frac{k(-q)}{r_2} = 100$$

$$\Rightarrow q = \frac{100r_1r_2}{k(r_1+r_2)} = \frac{100(3\times10^{-2})(6\times10^{-2})}{k(3\times10^{-2}+6\times10^{-2})} = \frac{2}{k}$$

$$\text{Force between the balls} = \frac{kq^2}{R^2} = \frac{k\left(\frac{2}{k}\right)^2}{1} = \frac{4}{k} = \frac{4}{9\times10^9}$$

$\therefore$ $x = 4$

5. $p = \left(\frac{kq}{R^2}\right)\sigma + \frac{\sigma^2}{2\varepsilon_0}$

$$\text{Stress} = \frac{F}{2\pi Rt}$$

$$S = \frac{p\pi R^2}{2\pi Rt} = \frac{\left[\frac{\sigma^2}{2\varepsilon_0} + \left(\frac{kq\sigma}{R^2}\right)\right]\pi R^2}{2\pi Rt}$$

$$\Rightarrow \quad S = \frac{\left[\dfrac{(Q/A)^2}{2\varepsilon_0} + \dfrac{kq\left(\dfrac{Q}{A}\right)}{R^2}\right]}{2\pi Rt}(\pi R^2)$$

$$\Rightarrow \quad q = \frac{2\varepsilon_0 A^2 tS}{QR} - \frac{Q}{2}$$

$$q = 27\text{ C}$$

Previous Year's Questions

JEE Main

1. Electric potential of a charged spherical conductor of radius (R) with radial distance is given as

$$V = \begin{cases} \dfrac{KQ}{R} & \text{If } r \le R \\ \dfrac{KQ}{r} & \text{If } r > R \end{cases}$$

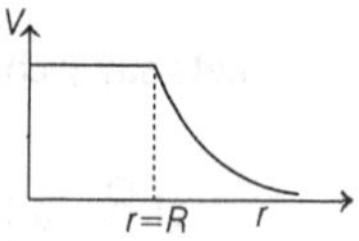

Now, plotting graph between V and r

2. When two conducting spheres are connected by a conducting wire, then charge will flow from the sphere of higher potential to the sphere of lower potential till both acquire the same potential.

$$\therefore \quad V_A = V_B$$

$$\text{or} \quad \frac{1}{4\pi\varepsilon_0}\frac{q_A}{r_A} = \frac{1}{4\pi\varepsilon_0}\frac{q_B}{r_B}$$

$$\text{or} \quad \frac{q_A}{q_B} = \frac{r_A}{r_B} = \frac{5}{10} \text{ or } \frac{q_A}{q_B} = \frac{1}{2}$$

Now, the ratio of electric fields,

$$\frac{E_1}{E_2} = \frac{K\dfrac{q_A}{r_A^2}}{K\dfrac{q_B}{r_B^2}} \quad \text{or} \quad \frac{E_1}{E_2} = \frac{q_A}{q_B} \times \frac{r_B^2}{r_A^2} = \frac{1}{2} \times \left(\frac{10}{5}\right)^2 \quad \text{or} \quad \frac{E_1}{E_2} = \frac{2}{1}$$

3. We know that $E = \dfrac{-\partial V}{\partial r}$

$\because$ From inside till surface, V = Constant

Since, electric field is zero along the surface of the conductor.

$\therefore E$ must be perpendicular to the surface of the conductors, so that its component along the surface of the conductors must be zero.

4. If R be the radius of combined big drop and r be the radius of small drop, then

Volume of big drop $= 64 \times$ Volume of small drop

$$\Rightarrow \quad \frac{4}{3}\pi R^3 = 64 \times \frac{4}{3}\pi r^3$$

$$\Rightarrow \quad R = 4r = 4 \times 0.02 = 0.08 \text{ m} \quad [\because r = 0.02 \text{ m}]$$

Charge on combined drop,

$$Q = 64 \times \text{Charge on one small drop}$$
$$= 64\,q = 64 \times 5 \quad [\because q = 5\,\mu\text{C}]$$
$$= 320\,\mu\text{C}$$

$$\therefore \quad \frac{\sigma_{\text{bigger}}}{\sigma_{\text{smaller}}} = \frac{\dfrac{Q}{4\pi R^2}}{\dfrac{q}{4\pi r^2}} = \frac{Q}{q} \times \left(\frac{r}{R}\right)^2$$

$$= \frac{320 \times 10^{-6}}{5 \times 10^{-6}} \times \left(\frac{0.02}{0.08}\right)^2 = \frac{4}{1} \quad \text{or} \quad 4:1$$

JEE Advanced

1. Inside a conducting shell electric field is always zero. Therefore, option (a) is correct. When the two are connected, their potentials become the same.

$$\therefore \quad V_A = V_B$$

$$\text{or} \quad \frac{Q_A}{R_A} = \frac{Q_B}{R_B} \quad \left(V = \frac{1}{4\pi\varepsilon_0}\frac{Q}{R}\right)$$

Since, $R_A > R_B \quad \therefore \quad Q_A > Q_B$

$\therefore$ Option (b) is correct.

Potential is also equal to, $V = \dfrac{\sigma R}{\varepsilon_0}$, $V_A = V_B$

$$\therefore \quad \sigma_A R_A = \sigma_B R_B$$

$$\text{or} \quad \frac{\sigma_A}{\sigma_B} = \frac{R_B}{R_A} \quad \text{or} \quad \sigma_A < \sigma_B$$

$\therefore$ Option (c) is correct.

Electric field on surface, $E = \dfrac{\sigma}{\varepsilon_0}$ or $E \propto \sigma$

Since, $\sigma_A < \sigma_B \quad \therefore \quad E_A < E_B$

$\therefore$ Option (d) is also correct.

$\therefore$ Correct options are (a), (b), (c) and (d).

2. Pressure or force per unit area is given by,

$$P = \frac{1}{2}\varepsilon_0 E^2 = \frac{1}{2}\varepsilon_0\left(\frac{\sigma}{\varepsilon_0}\right)^2 = \frac{\sigma^2}{2\varepsilon_0}$$

Therefore small electrostatic force on small area will be given by,

$$dF_e = (P)(dS) = \left(\frac{\sigma^2}{2\varepsilon_0}\right)ds$$

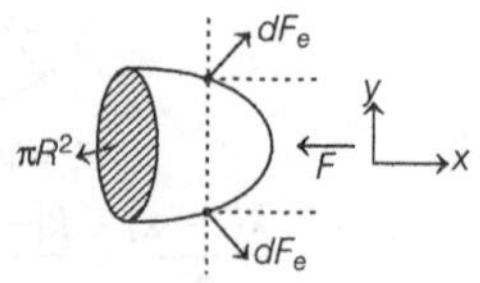

ds is also in the direction of $d\mathbf{F}_e$. We can see that y-components of dF_e are cancelled only x-components are left.

$$\therefore \quad F_e = \Sigma(dF_e)_x = \Sigma\left[\left(\frac{\sigma^2}{2\varepsilon_0}\right)ds\right]_x = \frac{\sigma^2}{2\varepsilon_0}\Sigma(ds)_x$$

Now, $\Sigma(ds)_x$ = projected area $= \pi R^2$

$$\therefore \quad F_e = \left(\frac{\sigma^2}{2\varepsilon_0}\right)(\pi R^2) \quad \text{towards right}$$

Hence, external force F is also $\left(\dfrac{\sigma^2}{2\varepsilon_0}\right)(\pi R^2)$ towards left for equilibrium of hemispherical shell.

$$\text{or} \quad F \propto \frac{\sigma^2 R^2}{\varepsilon_0}$$

CHAPTER~06

CURRENT ELECTRICITY

LEVEL 01 Starter Level

6.1 Electric Current, Current Density and Drift Velocity

1 The electric charge flowing through a cross-section of a wire is given by $q = (5t^2 - 2t + 3)$C. Find
(i) average current over time interval $t = 0$ to $t = 2$ s
(ii) current at $t = 2$ s.

2 The current through a wire depends on time as $i = i_0 + \alpha t$, where $i_0 = 10$ A and $\alpha = 4$ A/s. Find the charge crossed through a section of the wire in 10 s and average current for that interval.

3 The current passing through a wire decreases linearly from 10 A to 0 A in 8 s. Find total charge flown through the wire.

4 A conductor wire have 10^{23} free electrons/cm^3 carries a current of 20A. If the cross-section of the wire is 1 mm^2, then find the drift velocity of electrons.

5 An insulating pipe of cross-section area A contains an electrolyte which has two types of ions, their charges being $-e$ and $+2e$. A potential difference applied between the ends of the pipe result in the drifting of the two types of ions, having drift speed = v (– ve ion) and $v/4$ (+ve ion). Both ions have the same number per unit volume = n. Find the current flowing through the pipe.

6 The current density across a cylindrical wire of radius R varies according to the equation $J = J_0\left(1 - \frac{r}{R}\right)$, where J_0 is a constant and r is distance from the axis. Calculate the current flowing through the wire.

7 Calculate the electric field in a copper wire of cross-sectional area 2.0 mm^2 carrying a current of 10 A. The resistivity of copper $= 1.7 \times 10^{-8}$ Ω-m.

6.2 Resistance

1 What length of a copper wire of cross-sectional area 0.01 mm^2 will be needed to prepare a resistance of 340Ω? Resistivity of copper $= 1.7 \times 10^{-8}$ Ω-m.

2. If a wire of resistance R is stretched to double its length, find the new resistance.

3 A wire of resistance R is stretched, so that radius of its cross-section becomes one-third of its original radius. Find the new resistance.

4 Find the percentage change in resistance of a wire, if it is stretched to increase its length by
(i) 10% (ii) 0.3%

5 The dimensions of a conductor of specific resistance ρ are shown below. Find the resistance of the conductor across AB, CD and EF.

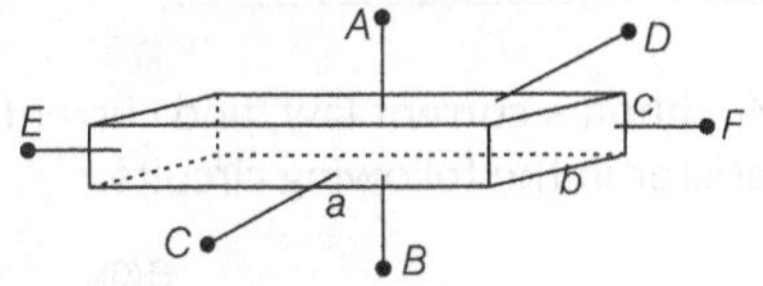

6 The temperature coefficient of resistivity of a wire is 1.25×10^{-3} per degree celsius. At 27°C, its resistance is 50 Ω. Find the temperature at which resistance of the wire will be 60Ω ?

7 Consider a conductor of length 40 cm, where a potential difference of 10V is maintained between the ends of the conductor. Find out the mobility of the electrons provided that the drift velocity of electrons is 5×10^{-6} m/s.

8 A resistor has colour code of brown, violet, yellow and gold as shown in the figure. What is its resistance?

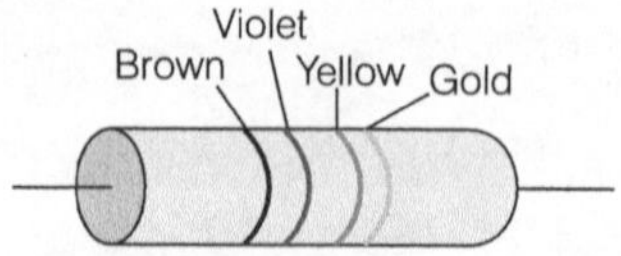

6.3 *Kirchhoff's Laws*

1 Find potential difference between points *A* and *B*.

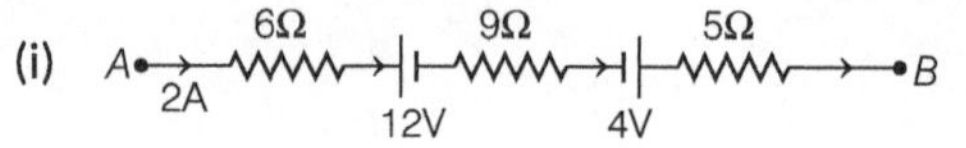

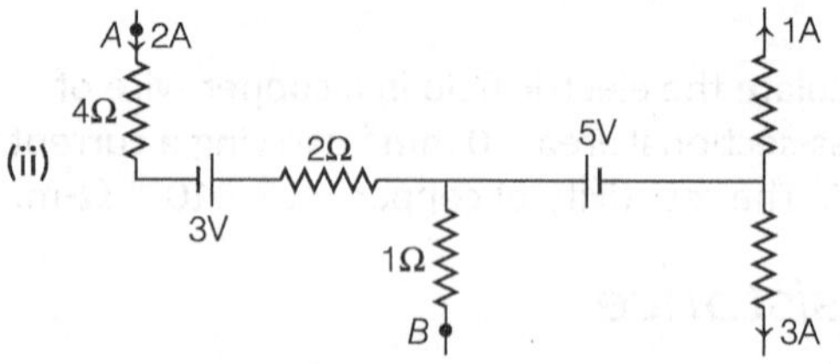

2 Using reference point, find current *i*.

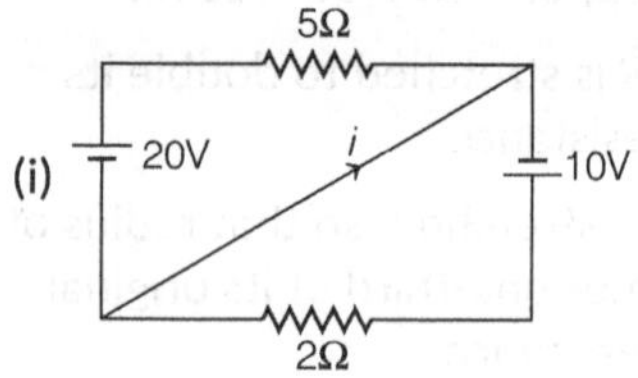

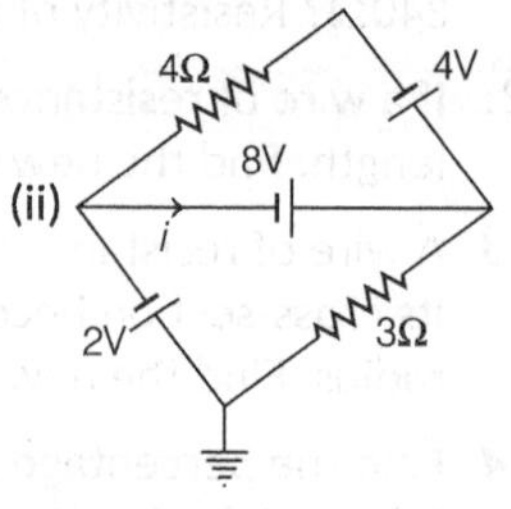

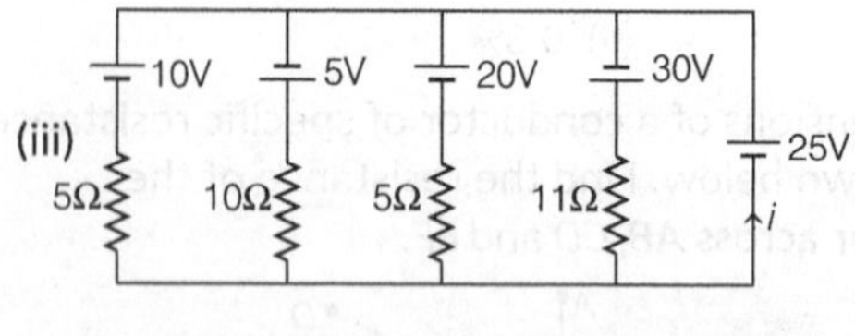

3 Using Kirchhoff's current law, find current through each resistor in the following circuits.

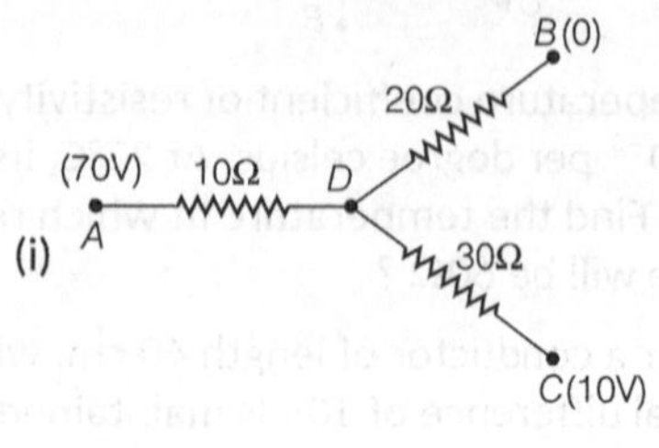

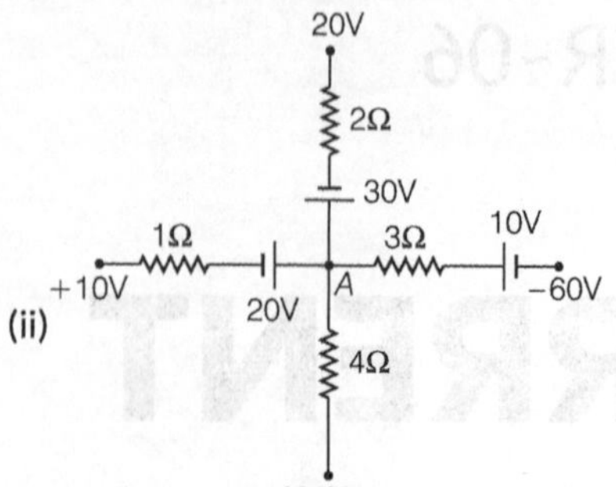

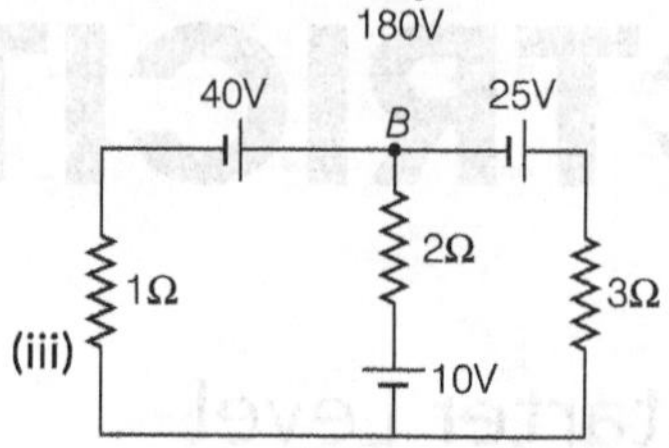

4 Using Kirchhoff's voltage law, find current in all the branches of the following circuits.

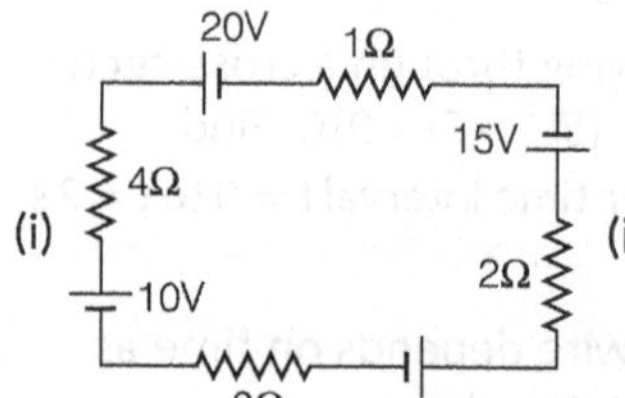

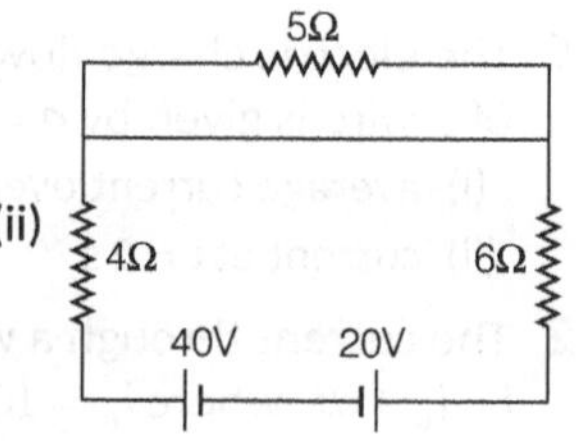

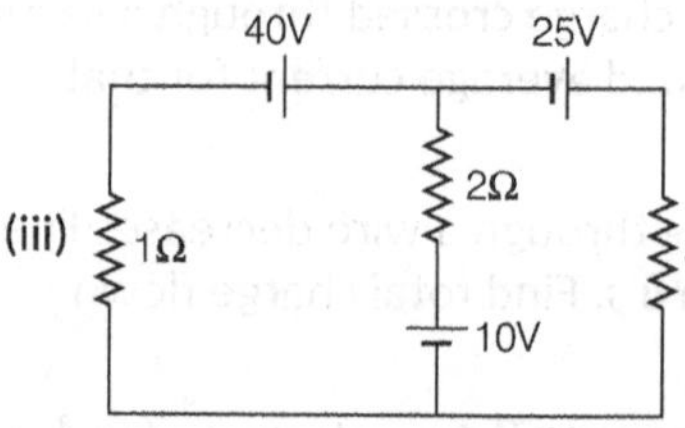

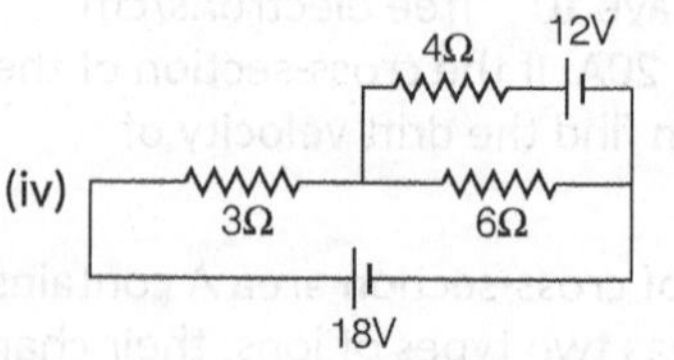

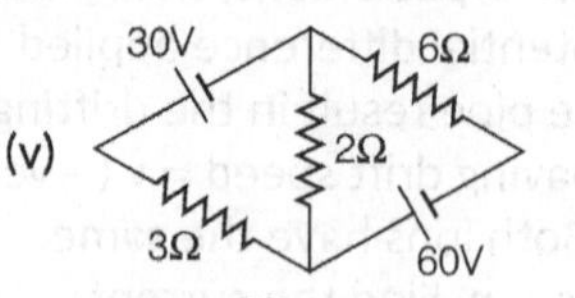

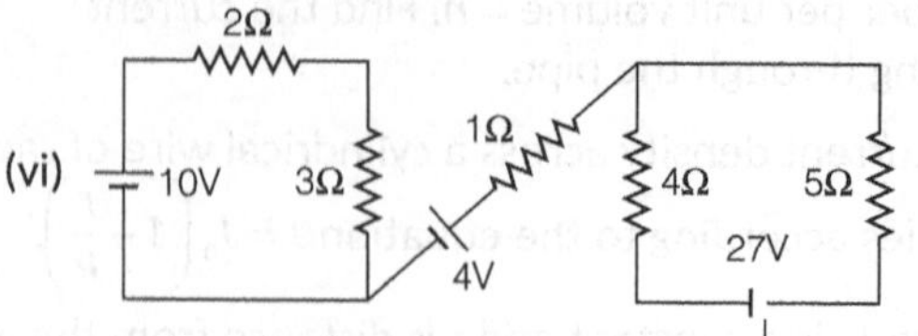

6.4 Battery as Source and Load

1 In the circuit shown in the figure, find

(i) the current in the circuit,

(ii) the potential difference across the terminals of the battery,

(iii) net power supplied by the battery.

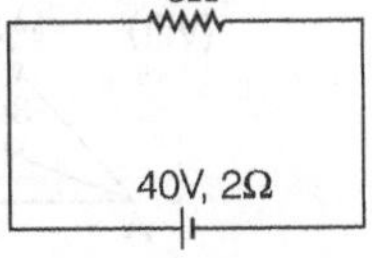

2 The potential difference between the terminals of a battery of emf 6.0 V and internal resistance 1Ω drops to 5.8 V when connected across an external resistor. Find the resistance of the external resistor.

3 The potential difference between the terminals of a 6.0 V battery is 7.2 V when it is being charged by a current of 2.0 A. What is the internal resistance of the battery?

4 Determine in each case,

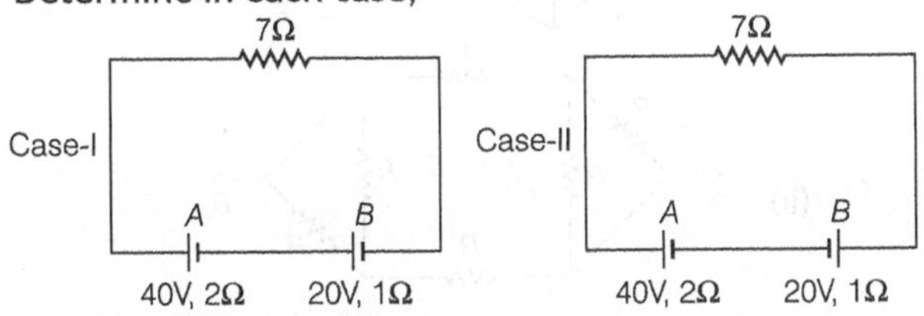

(i) current in the circuit,

(ii) potential difference between terminals of each battery,

(iii) power delivered or consumed by each battery.

6.5 Series and Parallel Combination Circuits

1 In the given circuit, determine

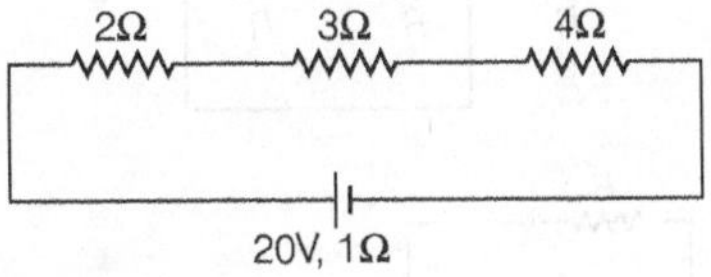

(i) current,

(ii) potential difference across 4 Ω resistance,

(iii) power dissipated in 3Ω resistance.

2 In the given circuit, determine

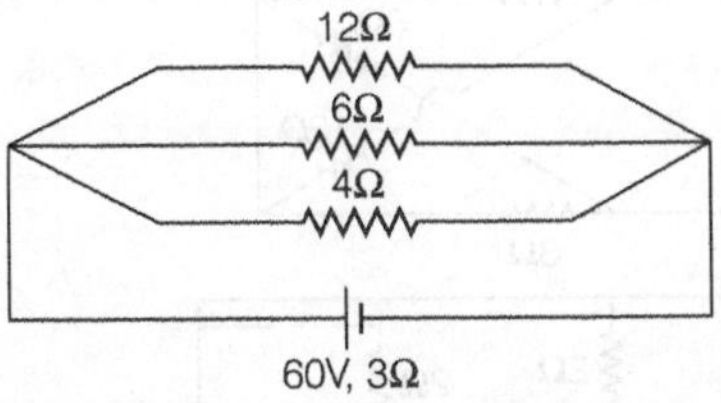

(i) current through the battery and 6Ω resistor,

(ii) potential difference across 12Ω resistor,

(iii) power dissipated in 4Ω resistor.

3 Find the current through the 3Ω resistor.

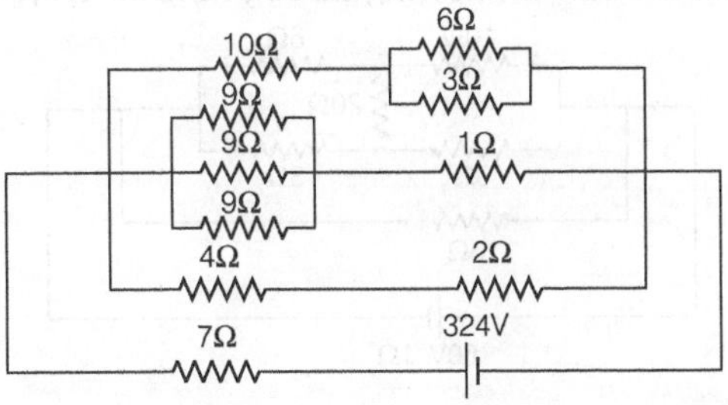

4 Find the current in 2Ω resistance.

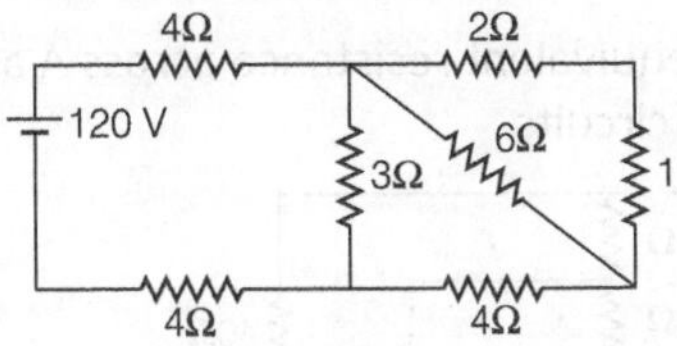

5 In the given circuit, current through 6Ω resistor is 4A. Find emf of the battery.

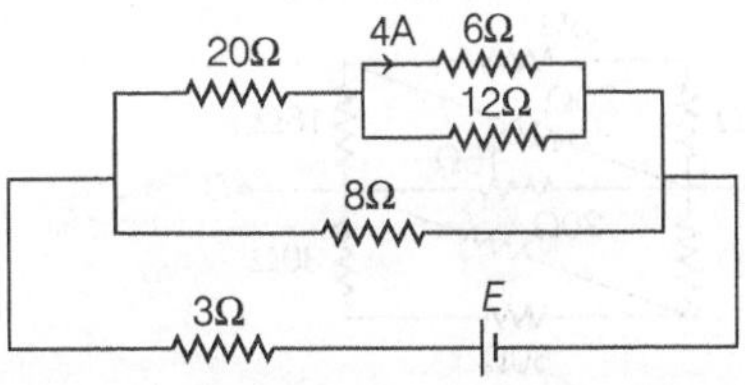

6 Find the current flowing through the segment *AB* of the circuit shown in figure.

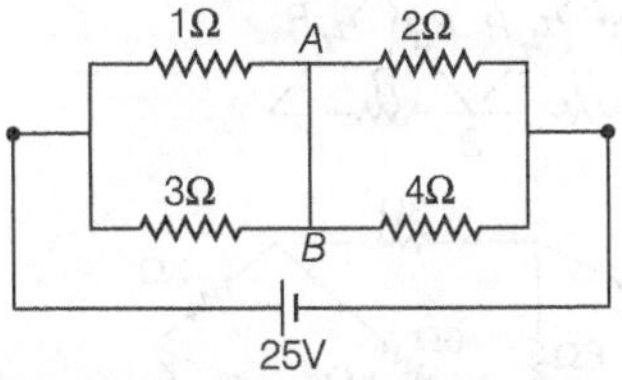

7 A current of 10A flows in a system of conductors as shown in the following figure. Find the potential difference $(V_A - V_B)$.

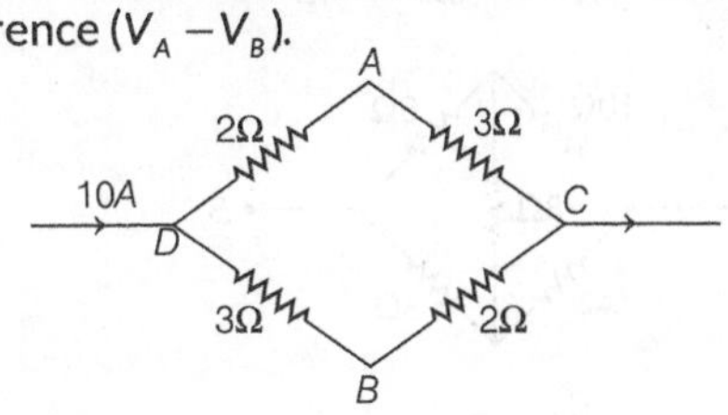

8 In the given circuit, if potential difference across *R* is 100 V, then find the value of *R*.

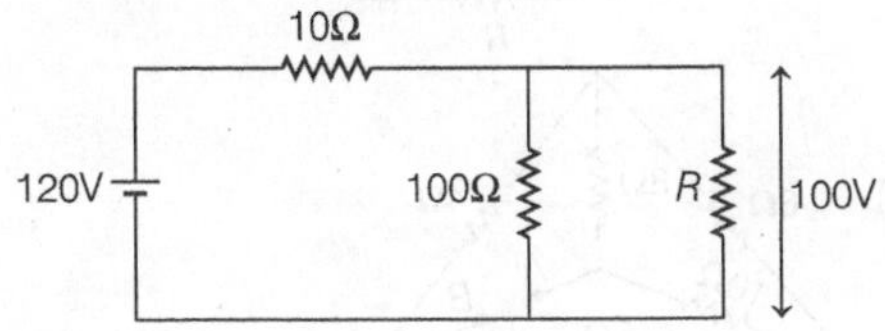

9 Find the current flowing through the battery.

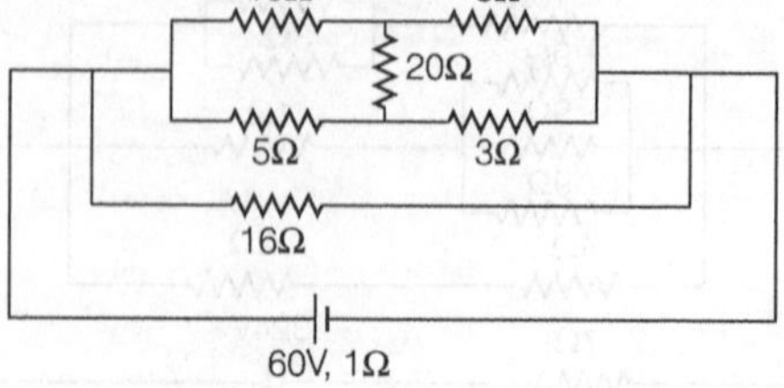

6.6 *Equivalent Resistance*

1 Find the equivalent resistance across *A* and *B* in the following circuits.

(i)
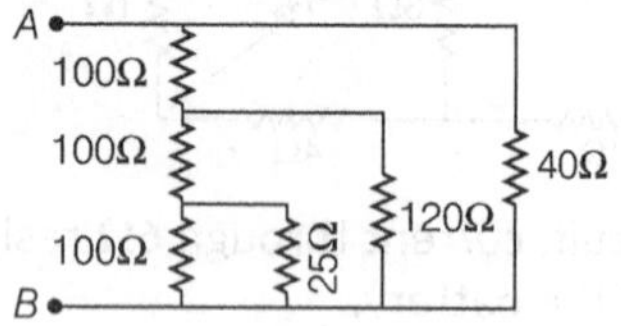

(ii)
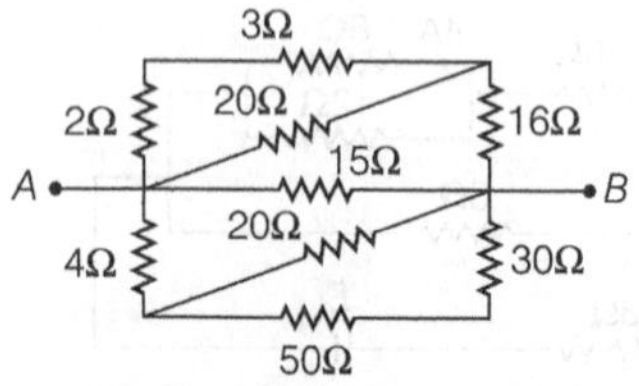

(iii)
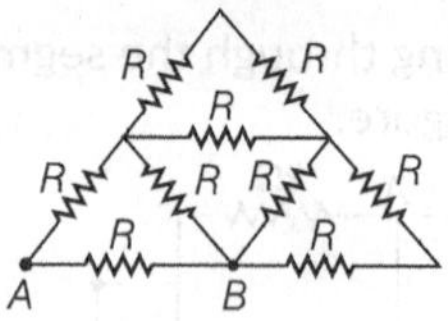

(iv)
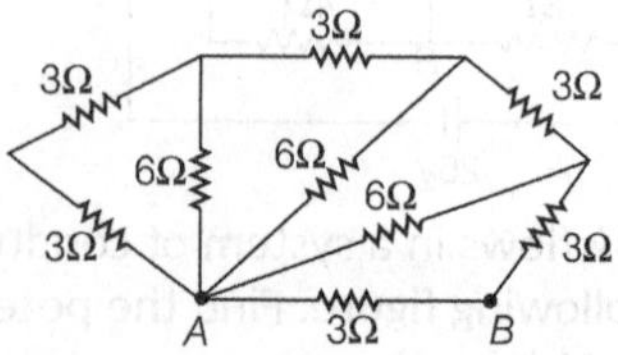

(v)
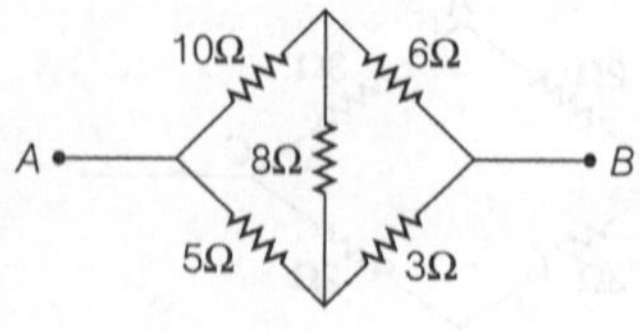

(vi)
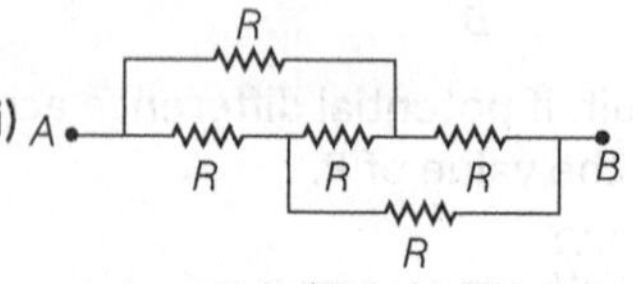

(vii)
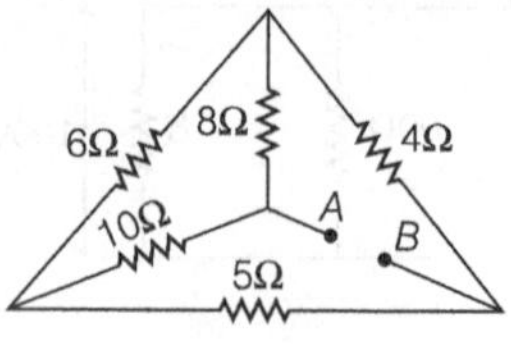

(viii)
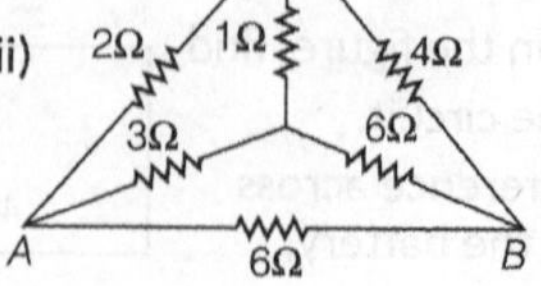

(ix)
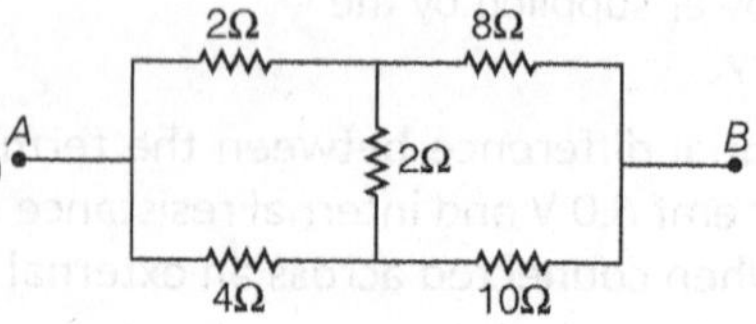

2 Find equivalent resistance across *A* and *B* in the following circuits.

(i)
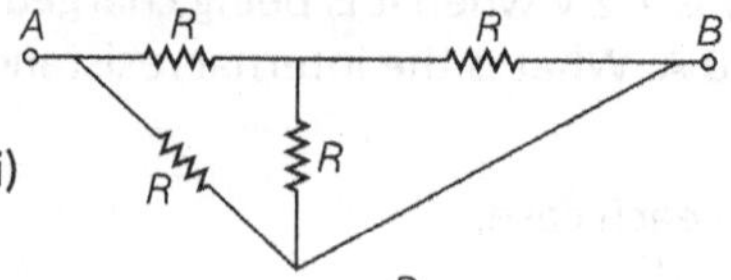

(ii)
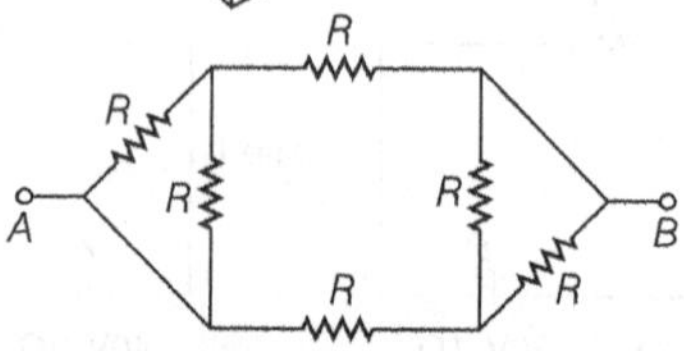

(iii)
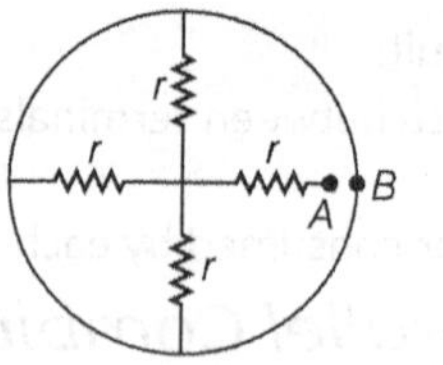

(iv)
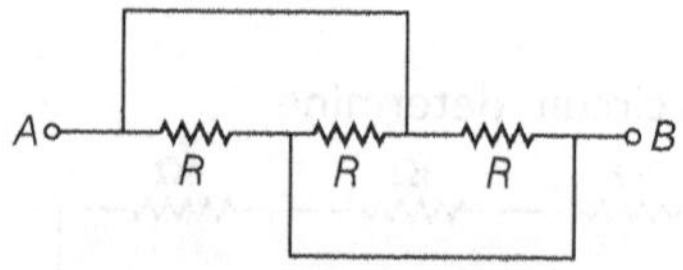

(v)
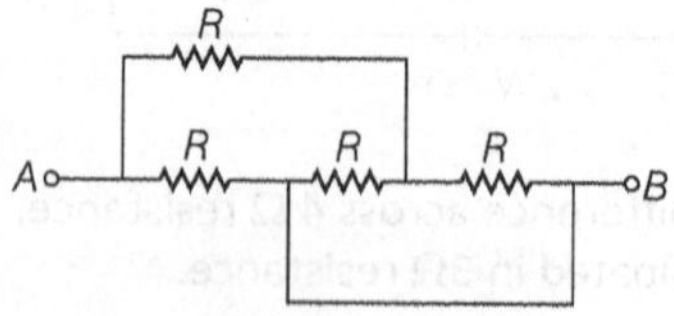

(vi)
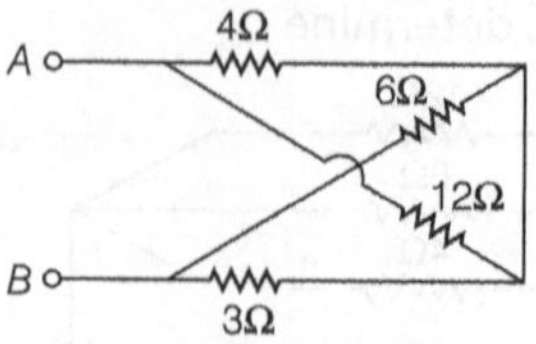

(vii)
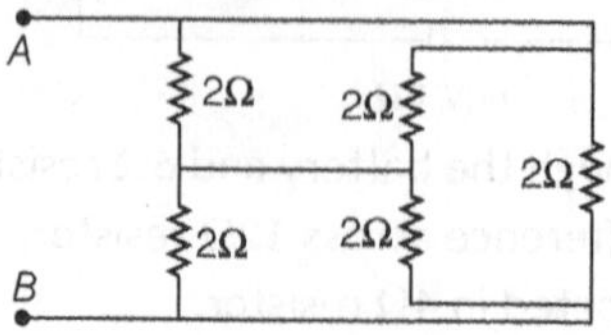

(viii)
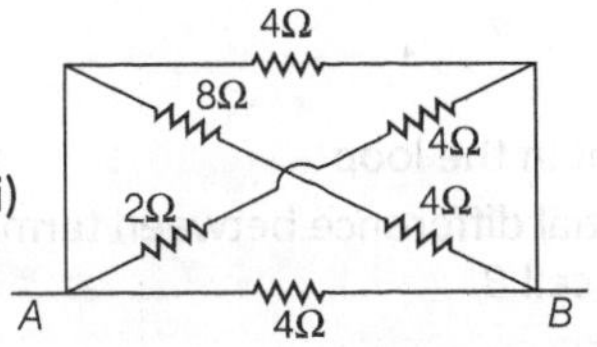

(ix)
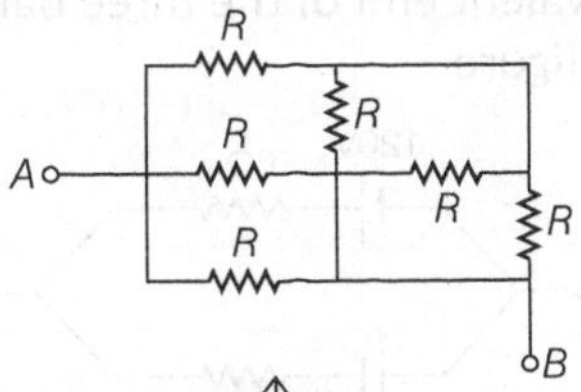

(x)
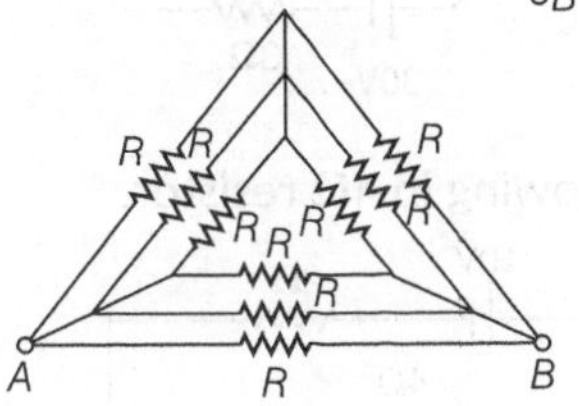

(xi)
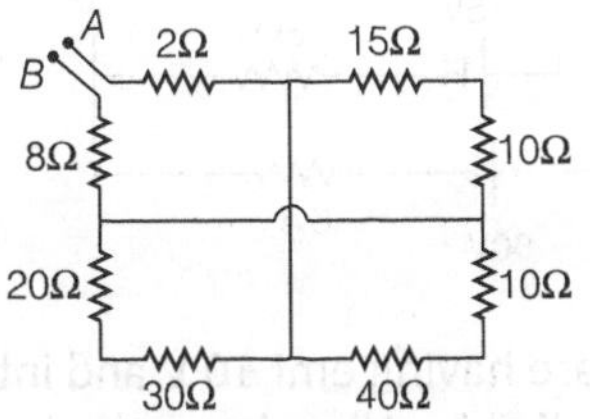

(xii)
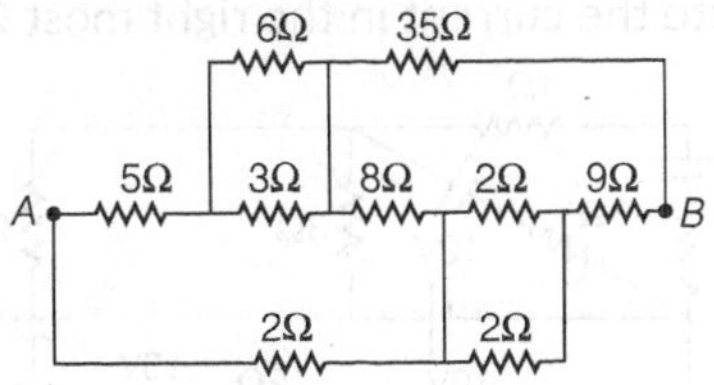

6.7 *Symmetric Circuits*

1 **Find equivalent resistance across *A* and *B* in the following circuits.**

(i)
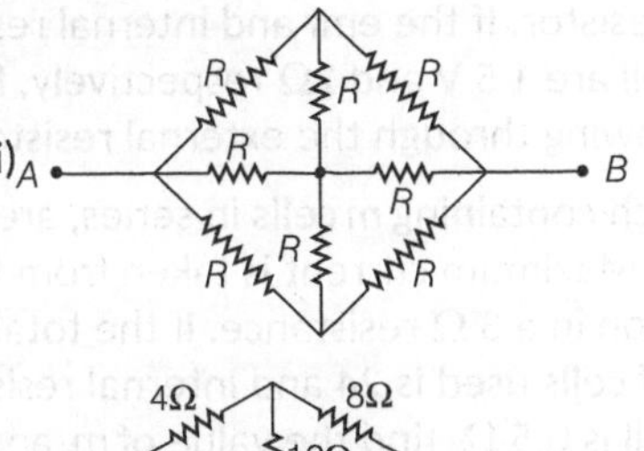

(ii)
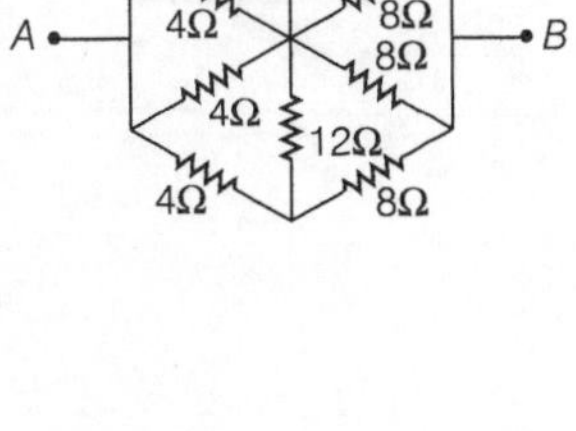

(iii)
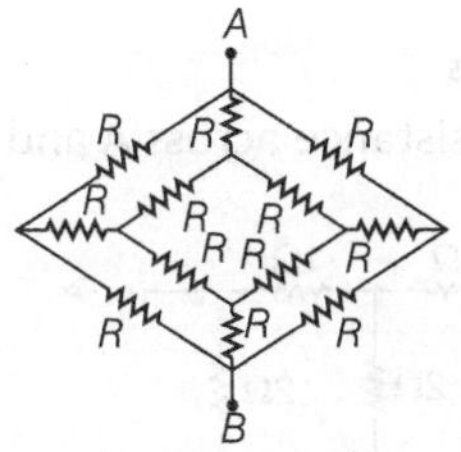

(iv)
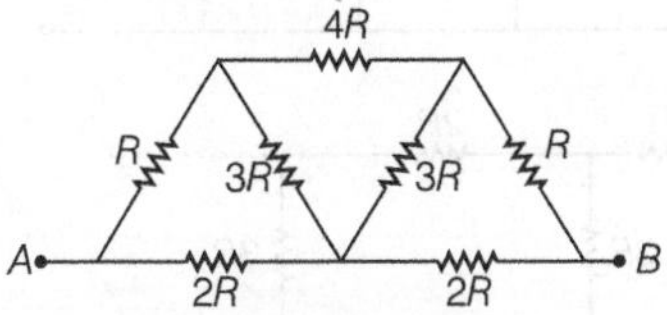

(v)
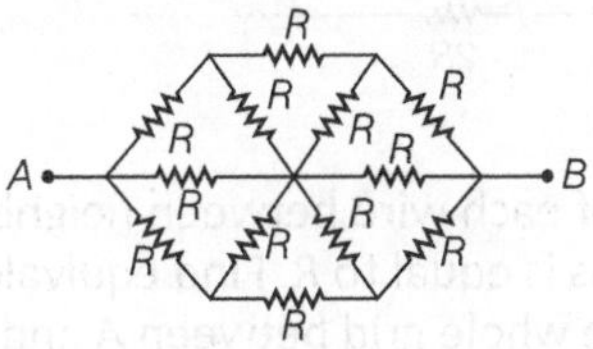

(vi)
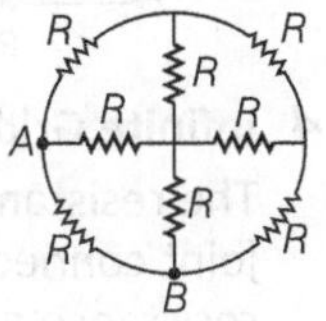

(vii)
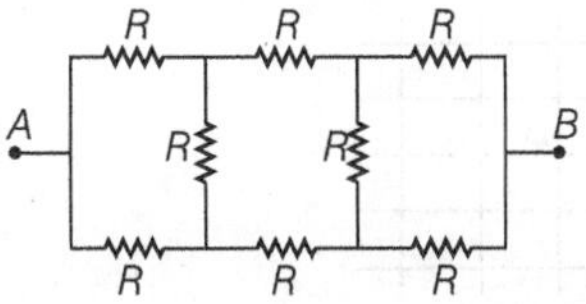

(viii)
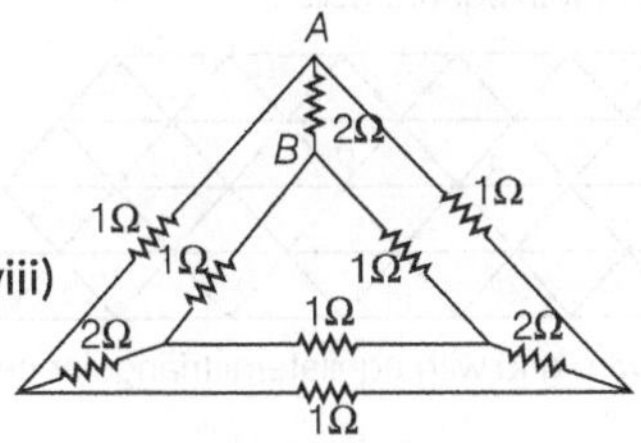

(ix)
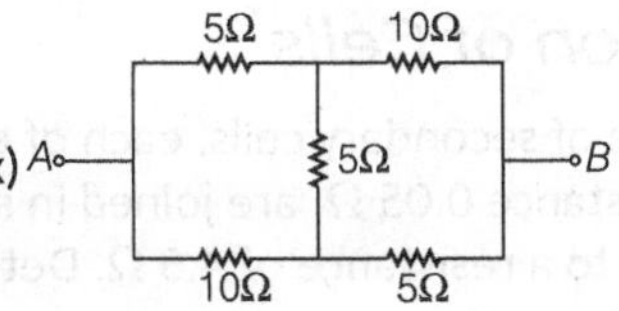

2 **Cube Problem**

Find the resistance of a wire frame shaped as a cube (figure) when measured between points

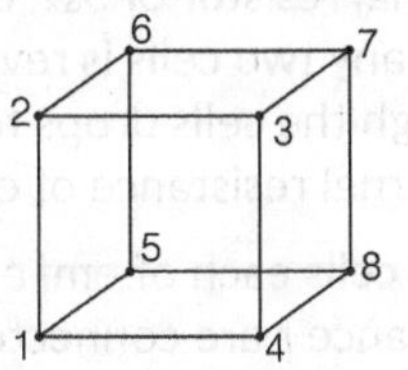

(i) 1-7
(ii) 1-3
(iii) 1-2

The resistance of each edge of the frame is *R*.

3 Infinite Ladder Circuits

Find the equivalent resistance across A and B in the following circuits.

(i)

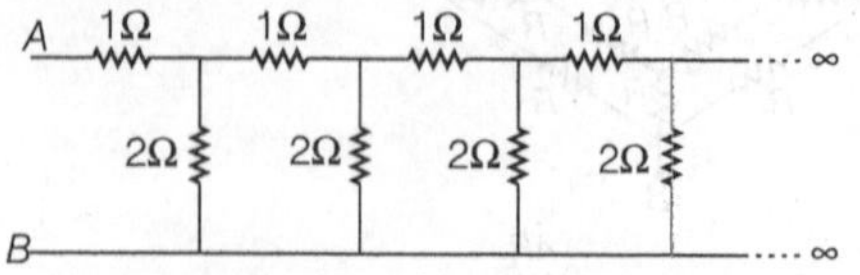

(ii)

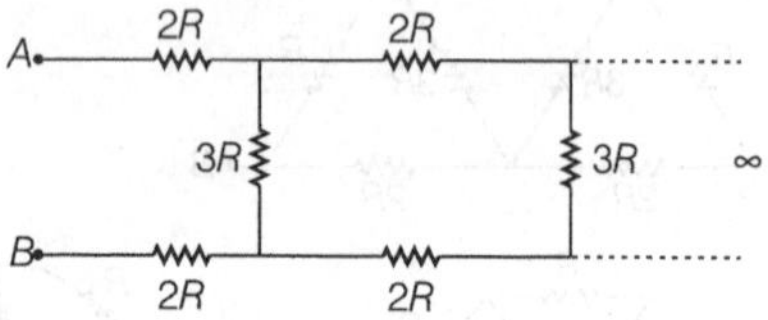

4 Infinite Grid

The resistance of each wire between neighbouring joint connections is equal to R. Find equivalent resistance of the whole grid between A and B.

(i)

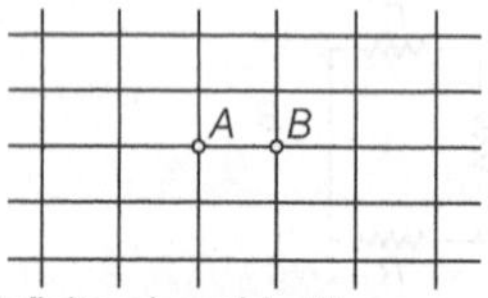

Infinite wire grid with square cells

(ii)

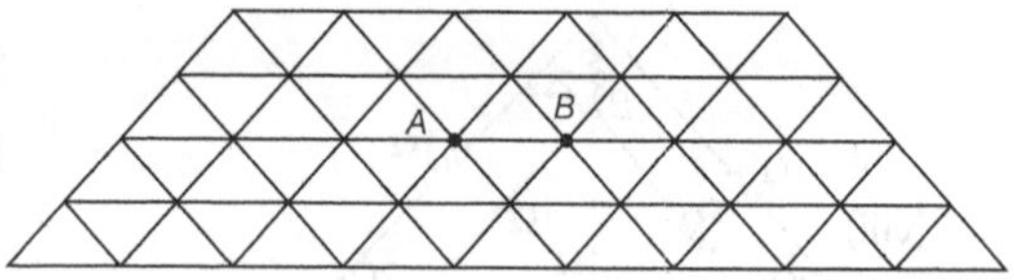

Infinite wire grid with equilateral triangular cells

6.8 *Combination of Cells*

1 10 lead-acid type of secondary cells, each of emf 3.0 V and internal resistance 0.05 Ω, are joined in series to provide a supply to a resistance of 4.5 Ω. Determine

(i) the current drawn from the supply and

(ii) its terminal voltage.

2 n indentical cells each of emf 6 V, connected in series with an external resistor of 5Ω, carry a current of 10 A. If polarties of any two cells is reversed, the current flowing through the cells drops to 6A. Find the value of n and the internal resistance of each cell.

3 Four identical cells each of emf ε and internal resistance r are connected in a conducting loop as shown in the figure.

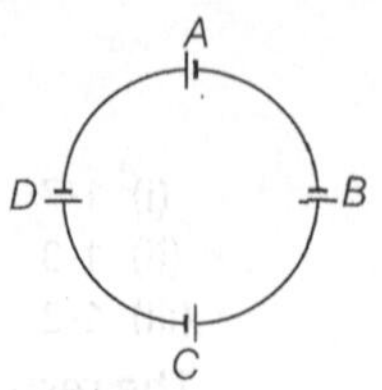

Find

(i) the current in the loop

(ii) the potential difference between terminals of cell A and cell B.

4 Find the equivalent emf of the three batteries as shown in the figure.

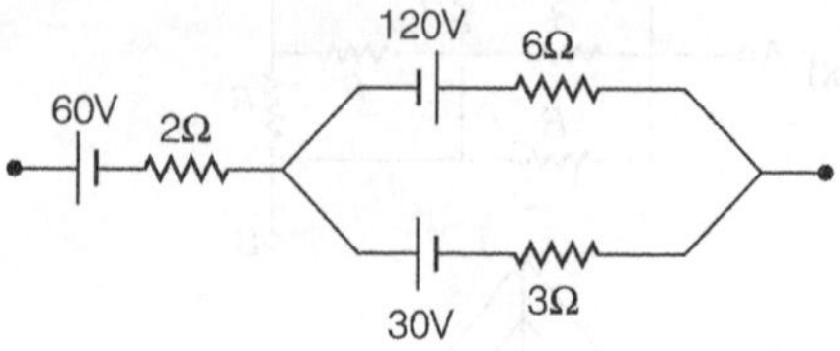

5 Find current flowing in 4Ω resistor.

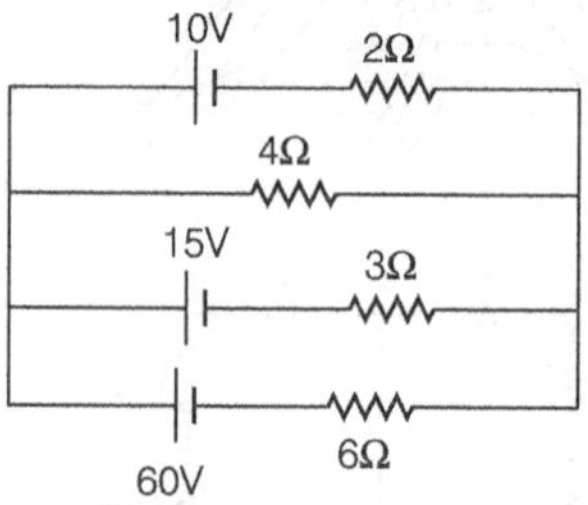

6 All batteries are having emf 10 V and internal resistance negligible. All resistors are in ohms. Calculate the current in the right most 2Ω resistor.

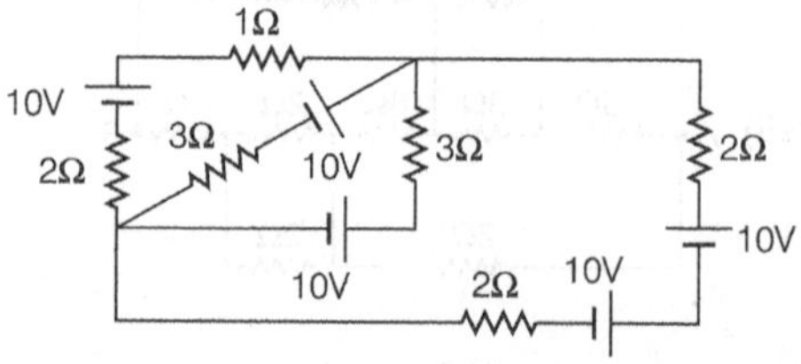

7 In a mixed grouping of identical cells, 8 rows are connected in parallel and each row contains 20 cells. This combination is connected across a 20 Ω external resistor. If the emf and internal resistance of each cell are 1.5 V and 2Ω respectively, find the current flowing through the external resistor.

8 n rows each containing m cells in series, are joined in parallel Maximum current is taken from this combination in a 3 Ω resistance. If the total number of cells used is 24 and internal resistance of each cell is 0.5 Ω, find the value of m and n.

LEVEL 02 JEE Main Level

Single Choice Correct Questions

1 The drift velocity of electrons in a conducting wire is of the order of 1 mm/s, yet the bulb glows very quickly after the switch is put on because

(a) the random speed of electrons is very high of the order of 10^6 m/s

(b) the electrons transfer their energy very quickly through collisions

(c) electric field is set up in the wire very quickly, producing a current through each cross-section, almost instantaneously

(d) All of the above

2 Two cylindrical rods of uniform cross-section radii r and $2r$, having free electrons per unit volume $2n$ and n respectively are joined in series. A current I flows through them in steady state. Then, the ratio of drift velocity of free electron in left rod to drift velocity of electron in the right rod is $\left(\frac{v_L}{v_R}\right)$ is

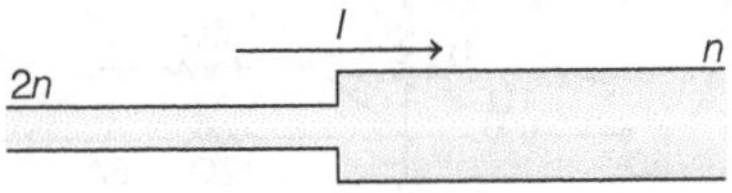

(a) 0.5 (b) 1

(c) 2 (d) 4

3 Find the average drift speed of conduction electrons in a copper wire of cross-sectional area 1.0×10^{-7} m^2 carrying a current of 1.5 A. Assume that each copper atom contributes roughly one conduction electron. The density of copper is 9.0×10^3 kg m^{-3} and its atomic mass is 63.5 u.

(a) 1.1 mm/s (b) 1.5 mm/s

(c) 2.2 mm/s (d) 2.5 mm/s

4 A current I flows through a cylindrical rod of uniform cross-section area A and resistivity ρ. The electric flux through the shaded cross-section of rod as shown in figure, is

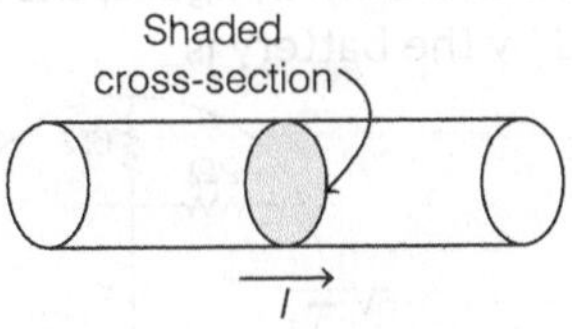

(a) $\frac{I}{\rho}$ (b) ρI

(c) $\frac{\rho I}{A}$ (d) $\frac{\rho A}{I}$

5 In a straight conductor of uniform cross-section charge q is flowing for time t. Let s be the specific charge of an electron. The momentum of all the free electrons per unit length of the conductor, due to their drift velocity only, is

(a) $\frac{q}{ts}$ (b) $\left(\frac{q}{ts}\right)^2$ (c) $\sqrt{\frac{q}{ts}}$ (d) qts

6 The current in a metallic conductor is plotted against voltage at two different temperatures T_1 and T_2. Which is correct?

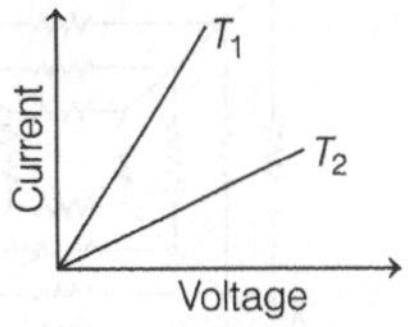

(a) $T_1 > T_2$ (b) $T_1 < T_2$

(c) $T_1 = T_2$ (d) None of these

7 A resistance wire has a resistance R. Half of this wire is stretched to double its length and half is twisted to double its thickness, then its new resistance becomes

(a) $\frac{17R}{8}$ (b) $\frac{17R}{16}$ (c) $\frac{65R}{32}$ (d) $\frac{65R}{16}$

8 The resistance of a wire at 20° C is 20Ω and at 500° C is 60Ω. At what temperature, resistance will be 25 Ω?

(a) 50°C (b) 60°C (c) 70°C (d) 80°C

9 Two resistors of resistances 400Ω and 800Ω at 0°C, having thermal coefficient of resistance α and 4α respectively, are connected in parallel. The equivalent thermal coefficient of resistance is

(a) 5α (b) $\frac{3\alpha}{2}$ (c) 2α (d) $\frac{4\alpha}{5}$

10 A non-conducting ring of radius R has a charge Q distributed unevenly over it. If it rotates with an angular velocity ω, the equivalent current will be

(a) 0 (b) $Q\omega$ (c) $\frac{Q\omega}{2\pi}$ (d) $\frac{Q\omega}{2R}$

11 Six resistors are connected between A and B as shown. The equivalent resistance between A and B of this network will be independent of the value of R, if x is equal to

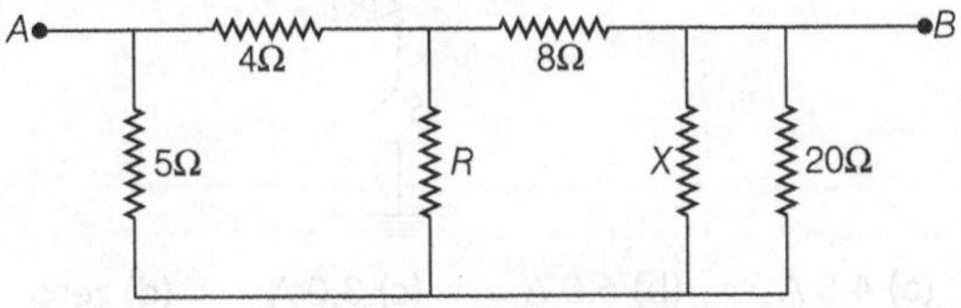

(a) 5 Ω (b) 10 Ω (c) 15 Ω (d) 20 Ω

12 The equivalent resistance between the points *A* and *B* is

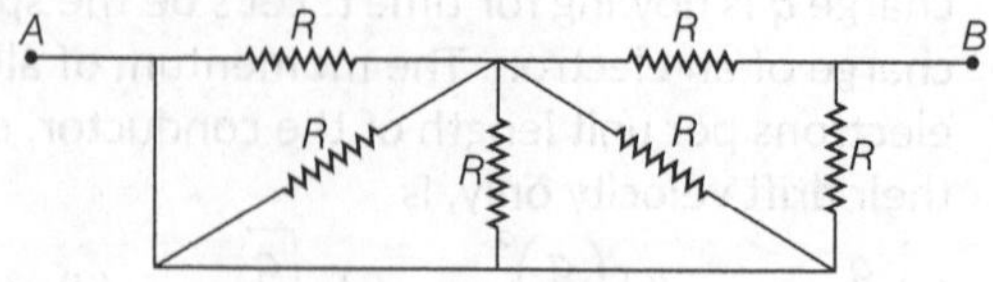

(a) $5R/9$ (b) $2R/3$ (c) $5R/6$ (d) $3R/5$

13 Sixteen resistors each of resistance *R* are connected in the circuit as shown in figure. The equivalent resistance across *A* and *B* is

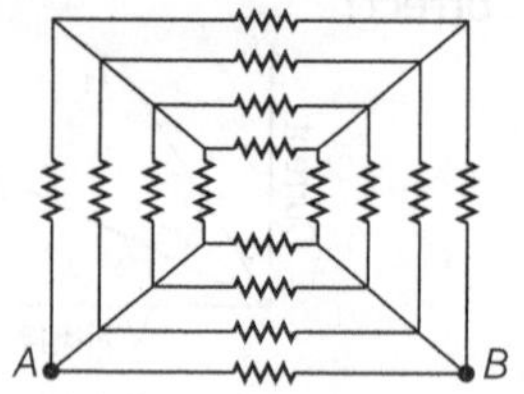

(a) $R/16$ (b) $R/8$ (c) $3R/16$ (d) $R/4$

14 The equivalent resistance between the points *A* and *B* is

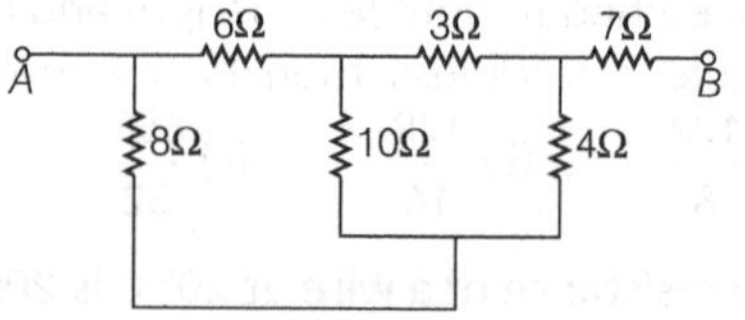

(a) $\frac{36}{7}\,\Omega$ (b) $10\,\Omega$

(c) $\frac{85}{7}\,\Omega$ (d) None of these

15 In the figure shown, find the equivalent resistance between *A* and *B*.

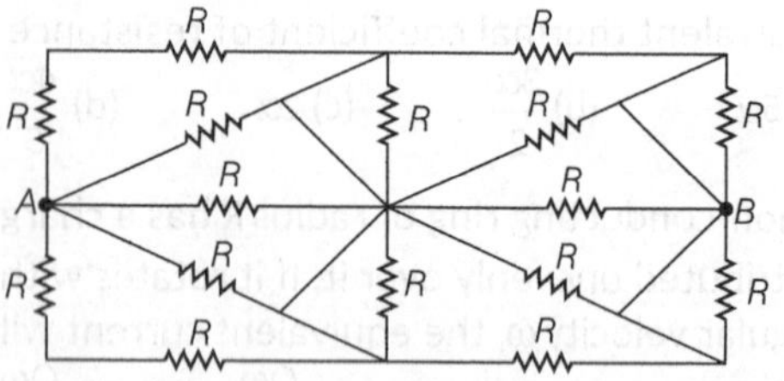

(a) $9R/10$ (b) $9R/20$ (c) $3R/10$ (d) $3R/20$

16 As the switch *S* is closed in the circuit shown in figure, current passing through it is

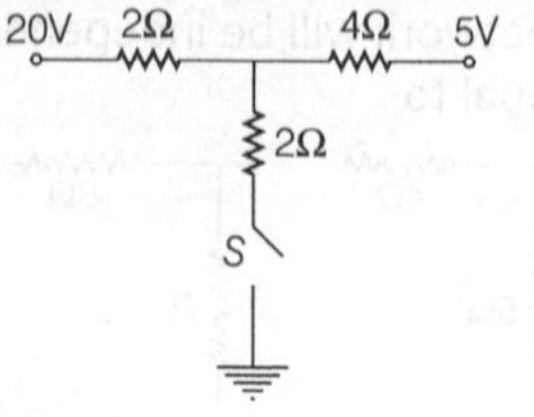

(a) 4.5 A (b) 6.0 A (c) 3.0 A (d) zero

17 The potential difference between points *A* and *B* in a section of a circuit as shown in figure is

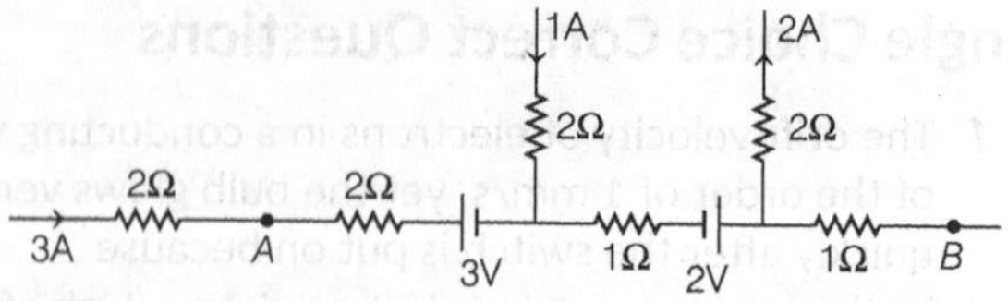

(a) 5 V (b) −13 V (c) 0 V (d) +13 V

18 In the circuit shown, each resistance is 2Ω. The potential V_1 as indicated in the circuit, is equal to

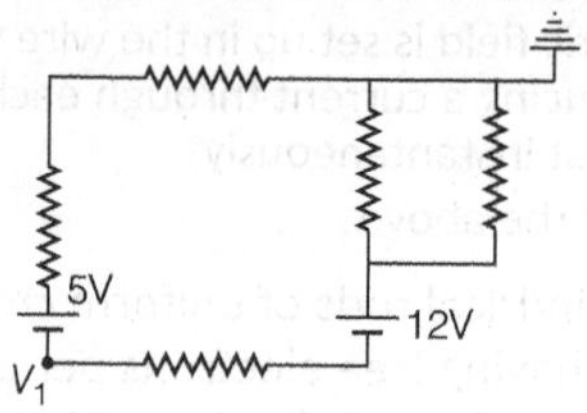

(a) 11 V (b) −11 V

(c) 9 V (d) −9 V

19 Figure shows a portion of circuit. The potential of point *D* is

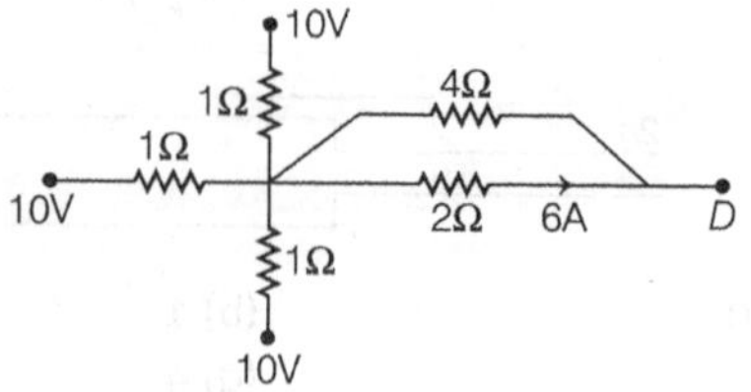

(a) −5 V (b) −10 V

(c) 5 V (d) 10 V

20 In the figure shown the current flowing through 2*R* is

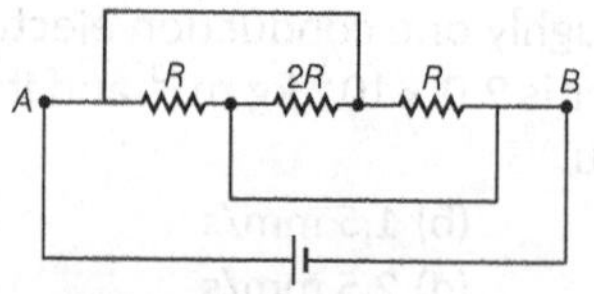

(a) from left to right

(b) from right to left

(c) no current

(d) None of the above

21 In the circuit shown in figure, the total current supplied by the battery is

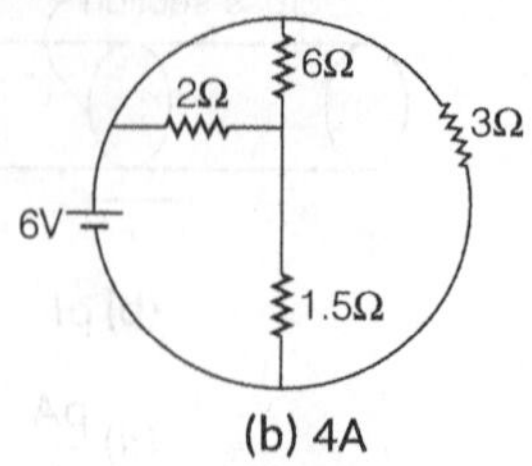

(a) 2A (b) 4A

(c) 1A (d) 6A

22 In the circuit shown, what is the potential difference V_{PQ}?

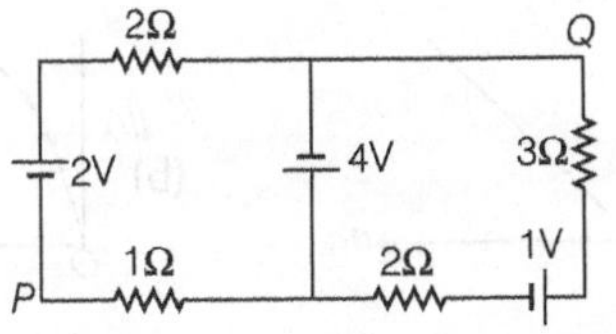

(a) +3V (b) +2V
(c) −2V (d) None of these

23 A 5V battery with internal resistance 2Ω and a 2 V battery with internal resistance 1Ω are connected to a 10 Ω resistor as shown in the figure. The current in the 10 Ω resistor is

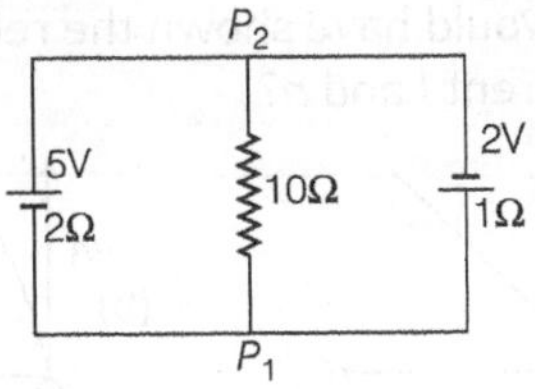

(a) 0.27 A, P_1 to P_2
(b) 0.03 A, P_2 to P_1
(c) 0.27 A, P_2 to P_1
(d) 0.03 A, P_1 to P_2

24 In the circuit as shown, a wire is connected between points *A* and *B*. How much current will flow through the wire *AB*?

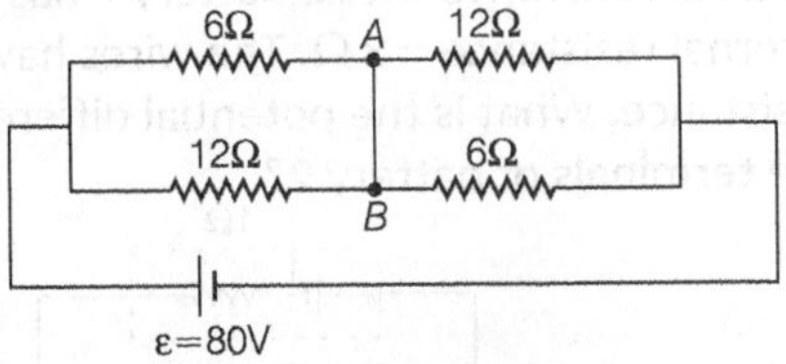

(a) Zero (b) (10/3) A
(c) (20/3) A (d) (5/3) A

25 In the given circuit, $R_B = 6\ \Omega$, $R_C = 3\ \Omega$, $R_D = 2\ \Omega$. The ratio of current through resistors *A*, *B*, *C* and *D* will be in the ratio

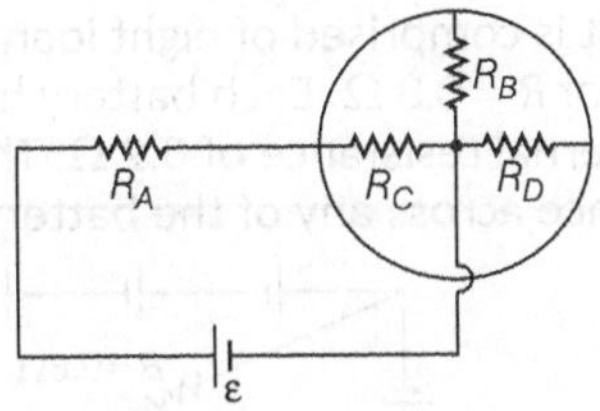

(a) 3 : 2 : 1 : 6
(b) 6 : 3 : 2 : 1
(c) 1 : 2 : 3 : 6
(d) 6 : 1 : 2 : 3

26 In the network shown in figure, the potential difference V_{ab} when the switch *S* is open, is

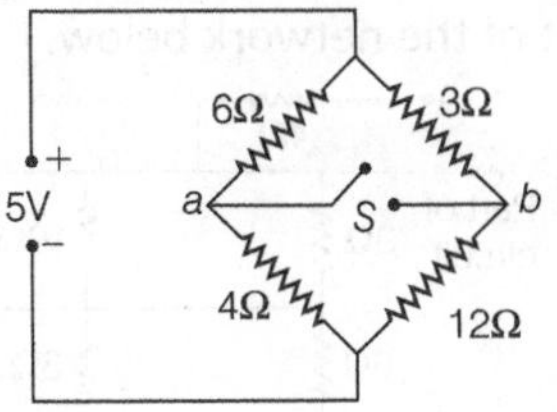

(a) 3 V (b) − 6 V (c) 9 V (d) 12 V

27 In the circuit shown, the value of *R* in ohm, that will result in no current through the 30 V battery, is

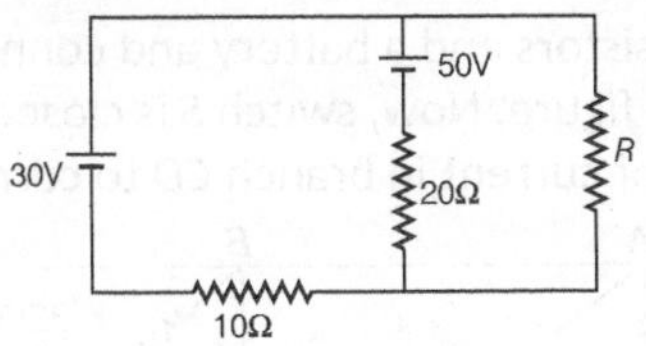

(a) 10 Ω (b) 25 Ω (c) 30 Ω (d) 40 Ω

28 Find the current through 10 V battery.

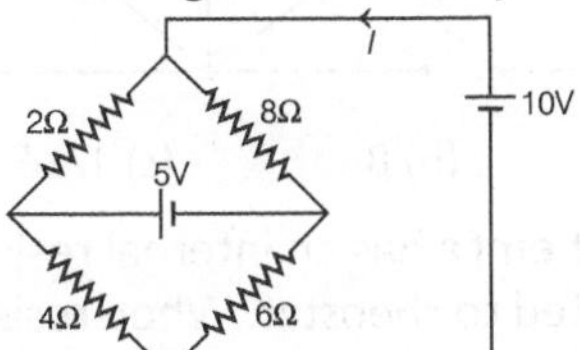

(a) 2.25 A (b) 2.5 A (c) 3 A (d) 5.5 A

29 Three carbon resistors R_1, R_2 and R_3 are joined as shown. Their colour code reads as

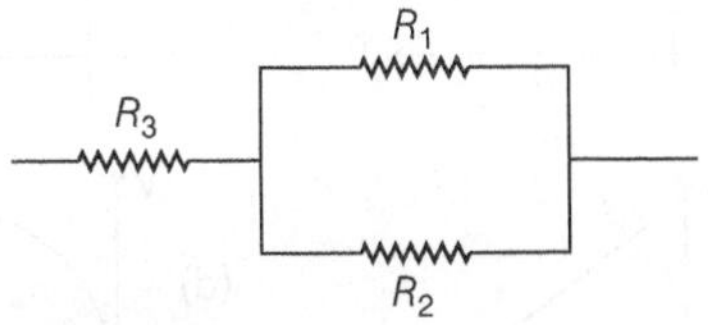

R_1 : Brown, Red, Brown
R_2 : Blue, Black, Black
R_3 : Orange, Black, Black
What is their equivalent resistance?
(a) 210 Ω (b) 180/7 Ω (c) 40 Ω (d) 70 Ω

30 The circuit is as given in figure. The current through the branch *BE* of the circuit is

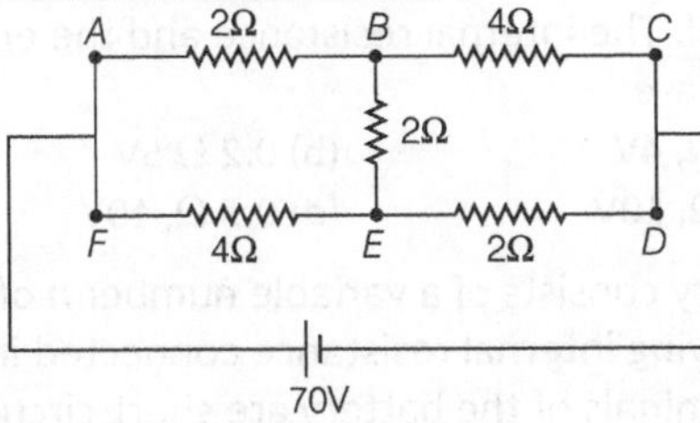

(a) 2A (b) 5 A (c) 7A (d) 10 A

31 Calculate the potential difference between points A and B and current flowing through the $6\ \Omega$ resistor in the part of the network below.

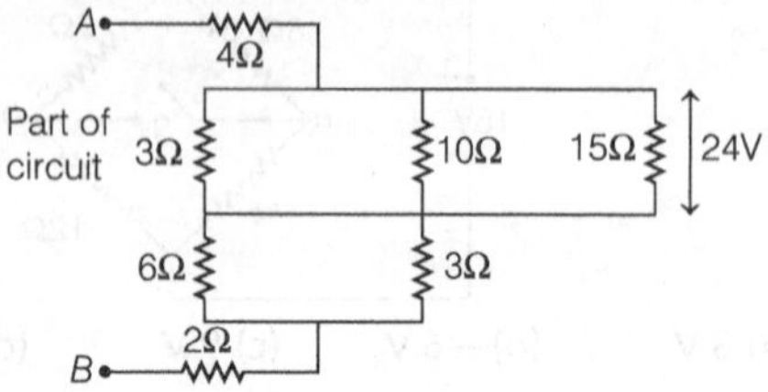

(a) 80 V, 6A (b) 80 V, 4 A
(c) 120 V, 6A (d) 120 V, 4A

32 Six resistors and a battery and connected as shown in the figure. Now, switch S is closed, then find the ratio of current in branch CD to current in branch AF.

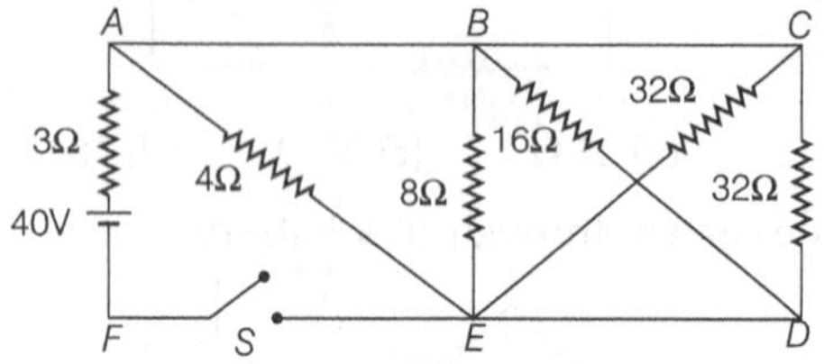

(a) 16 (b) 8 (c) 1/16 (d) 1/8

33 A cell of emf ε has an internal resistance r and is connected to rheostat. When resistance R of rheostat is changed, correct graph of potential difference across it is

(a)
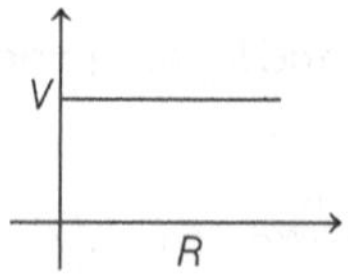

(b)
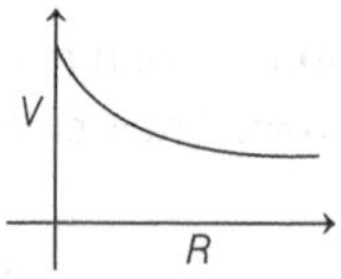

(c)
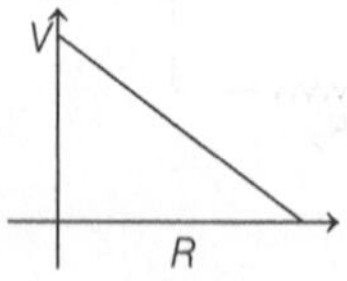

(d)
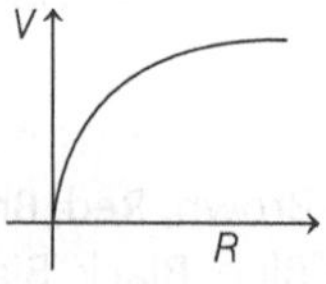

34 When a current of 4A flows within a battery from its positive to negative terminal, the potential difference across the battery is 12 V. The potential difference across the battery is 9 V when a current of 2A flows within it from its negative to its positive terminal. The internal resistance and the emf of the battery are

(a) $0.1\ \Omega$, 4V (b) $0.2\ \Omega$ 5V
(c) $0.5\ \Omega$, 10V (d) $0.7\ \Omega$, 10V

35 A battery consists of a variable number n of identical cells having internal resistance connected in series. The terminals of the battery are short-circuited and the current I measured. Which one of the graphs below shows the relationship between I and n?

(a)
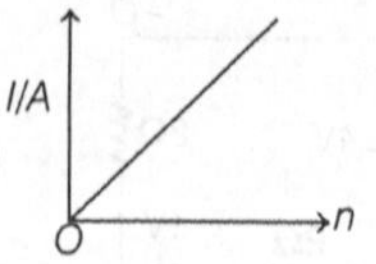

(b)
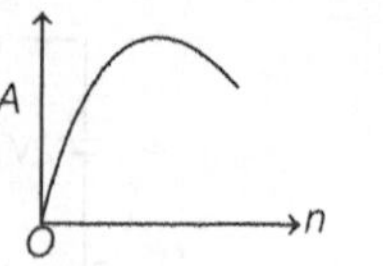

(c)
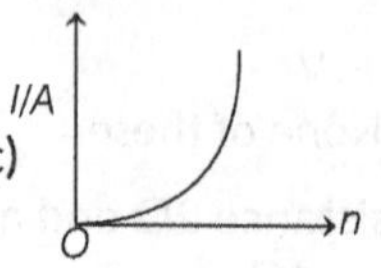

(d)
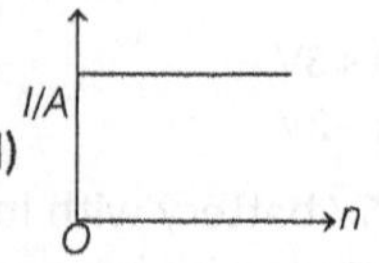

36 In previous problem, if the cells had been connected in parallel (instead of in series), which of the above graphs would have shown the relationship between total current I and n?

(a)
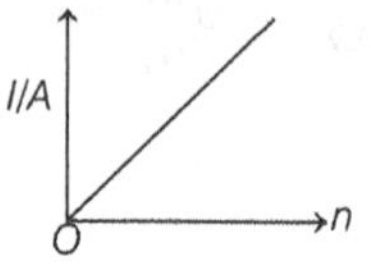

(b)
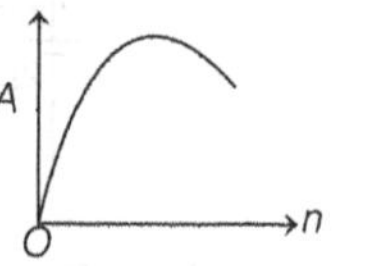

(c)
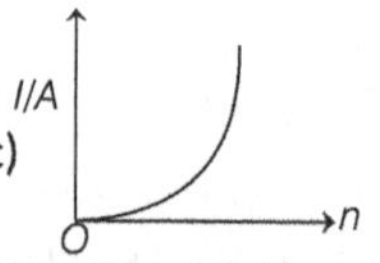

(d)
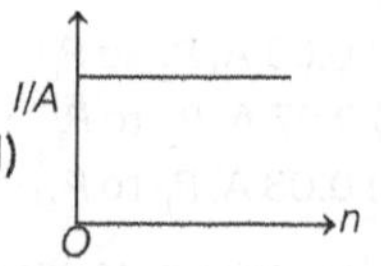

37 In the figure shown, battery 1 has emf = 6 V and internal resistance = $1\ \Omega$. Battery 2 has emf = 2V and internal resistance = $3\ \Omega$. The wires have negligible resistance. What is the potential difference across the terminals of battery 2?

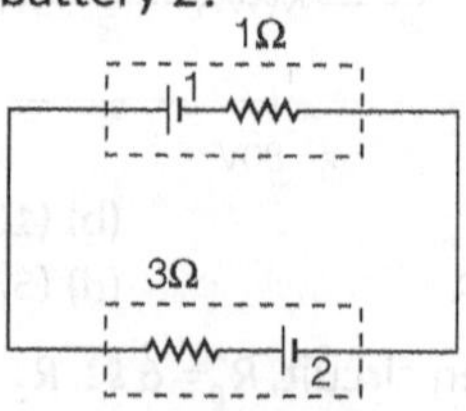

(a) 4 V (b) 1.5 V
(c) 5 V (d) 0.5 V

38 A circuit is comprised of eight identical batteries and a resistor $R = 0.8\ \Omega$. Each battery has an emf of 1.0 V and internal resistance of $0.2\ \Omega$. The voltage difference across any of the battery is

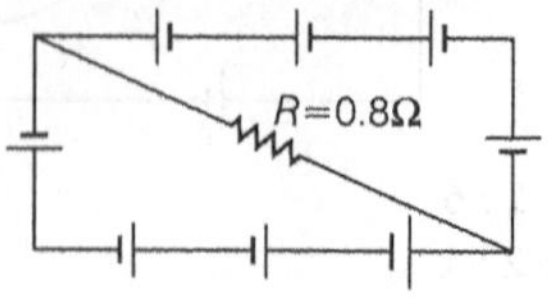

(a) 0.5 V (b) 1.0 V
(c) 0 (d) 2 V

39 Two batteries one of the emf 3 V, internal resistance 1 Ω and the other of emf 15 V, internal resistance 2 Ω are connected in series with a resistance R as shown. If the potential difference between a and b is zero, then resistance R in ohm is

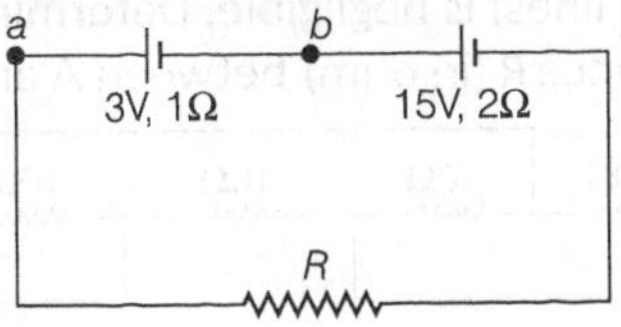

(a) 5 (b) 7 (c) 3 (d) 1

40 You are given 48 cells each of 2 V and internal resistance 1 Ω. How will you connect them so that the current through an external resistance of 3Ω is the maximum?

(a) 8 cells in series, 6 such groups in parallel
(b) 12 cells in series, 4 such groups in parallel
(c) 16 cells in series, 3 such groups in parallel
(d) 24 cells in series, 2 such groups in parallel

41 The value of current through 20 Ω resistor is

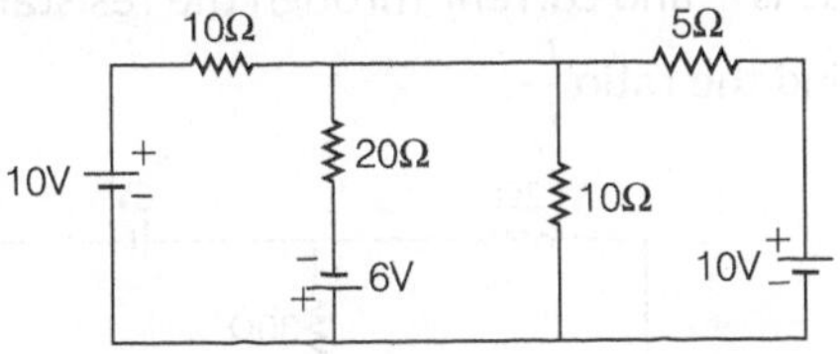

(a) 0.6 A (b) 0.8 A (c) 1.2 A (d) 1.8 A

42 In order to determine the emf of a storage battery, it was connected in series with a standard cell in a certain circuit and a current I_1 was obtained. When the battery is connected to the same circuit, opposite to the standard cell, a current I_2 flow in the external circuit from the positive pole of the storage battery was obtained. What is the emf ε_1 of the storage battery? The emf of the standard cell is ε_2.

(a) $\varepsilon_1 = \frac{I_1 + I_2}{I_1 - I_2}\varepsilon_2$ (b) $\varepsilon_1 = \frac{I_1 + I_2}{I_2 - I_1}\varepsilon_2$

(c) $\varepsilon_1 = \frac{I_1 - I_2}{I_1 + I_2}\varepsilon_2$ (d) $\varepsilon_1 = \frac{I_2 - I_1}{I_1 + I_2}\varepsilon_2$

43 The battery in the diagram is to be charged by the generator G. The generator has a terminal voltage of 120 V when the charging current is 10 A. The battery has an emf of 100 V and an internal resistance of 1 Ω. In order to charge the battery at 10 A charging current, the resistance R should be set at

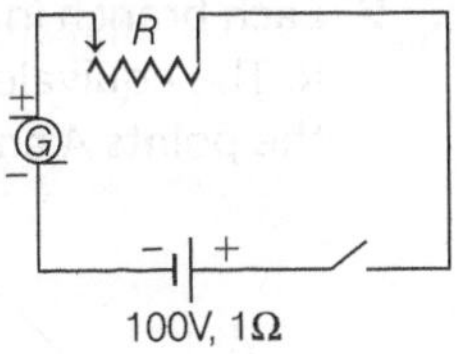

(a) 0.1 Ω (b) 0.5 Ω (c) 1.0 Ω (d) 5.0 Ω

44 In the circuit shown, the equivalent resistance between the points A and B is

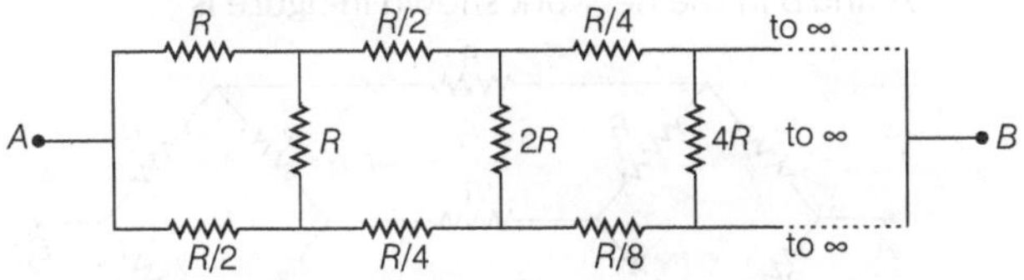

(a) R (b) $R/2$ (c) $4R/3$ (d) $2R/3$

45 Eight identical resistance r each are connected as shown. The equivalent resistance between AD is

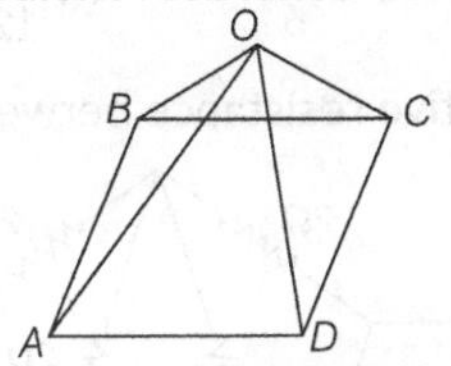

(a) $8R/15$ (b) $4R/15$
(c) $4R/5$ (d) $7R/10$

46 In the diagram shown, all the wires have resistance R. The equivalent resistance between the upper and lower dots shown in the diagram is

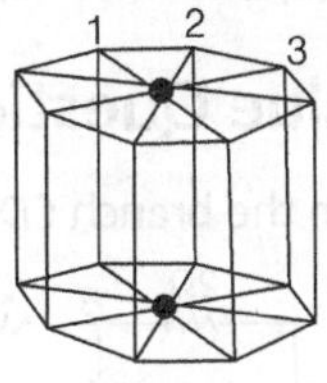

(a) $R/8$ (b) R
(c) $2R/5$ (d) $3R/8$

47 The equivalent resistance between the points A and B is (Each branch has resistance R)

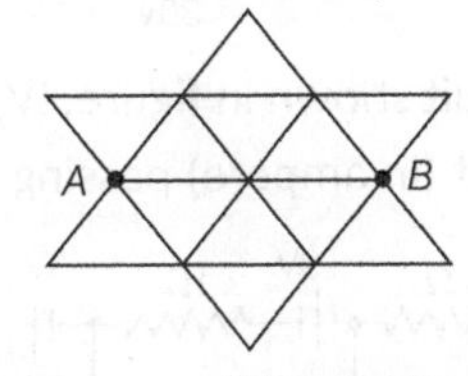

(a) $12R/25$ (b) $22R/25$
(c) $12R/35$ (d) $22R/35$

48 The resistance of all the wires between any two adjacent dots is R. Then, equivalent resistance between A and B as shown in figure is

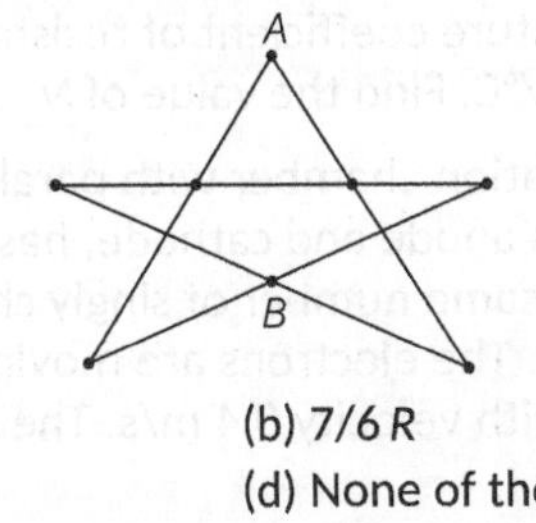

(a) 7/3 R (b) 7/6 R
(c) 14/8 R (d) None of these

49 The equivalent resistance between the terminal points A and B in the network shown in figure is

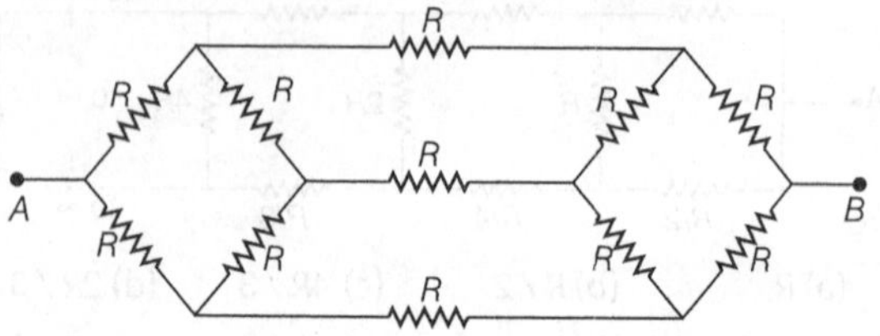

(a) $\frac{7R}{5}$ (b) $\frac{5R}{6}$ (c) $\frac{7R}{12}$ (d) $\frac{5R}{12}$

50 Find effective resistance between A and B.

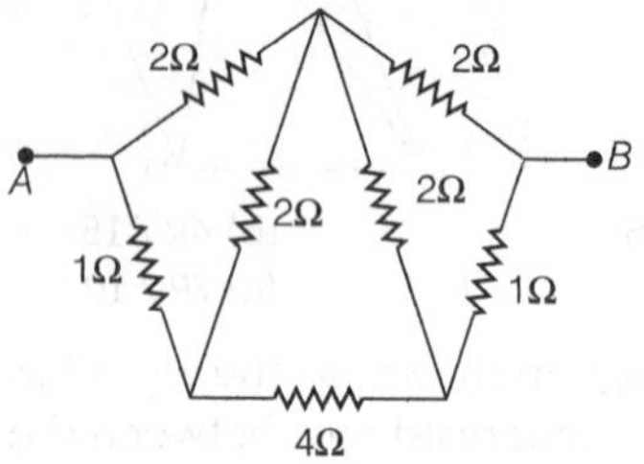

(a) 1 Ω (b) 2 Ω (c) 2/3 Ω (d) 3/4 Ω

Numerical Value Questions

1 Find current in the branch CD of the circuit (in ampere).

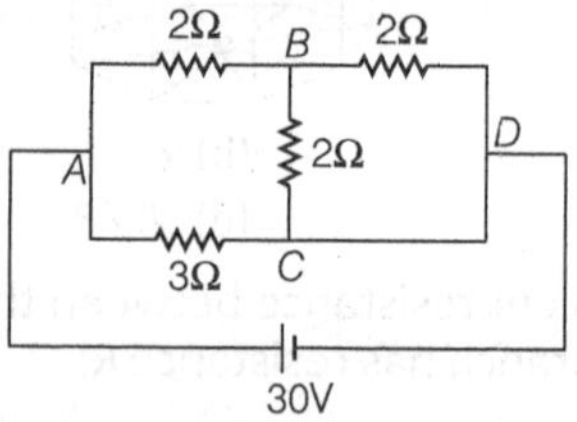

2 In the circuit shown in figure, $(V_A - V_B) = 16$ V. Find the current (in ampere) passing through 2 Ω resistor.

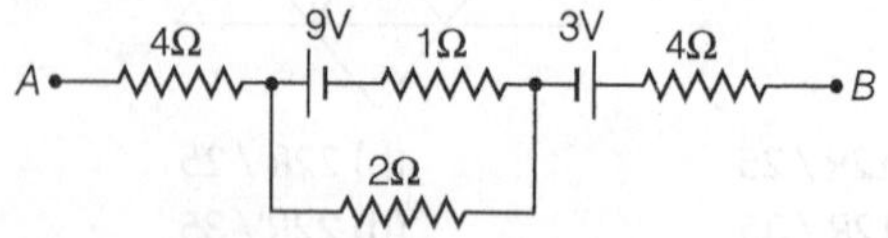

3 There is a cylindrical wire, whose temperature coefficient of resistivity is 6×10^{-3} /°C and coefficient of linear expansion is 1×10^{-3} /°C. The value of temperature coefficient of resistance is found be $N \times 10^{-3}$ /°C. Find the value of N.

4 An ionisation chamber with parallel conducting plates as anode and cathode, has 5×10^7 electrons and the same number of singly charged positive ions per cm^3. The electrons are moving towards the anode with velocity 0.4 m/s. The current density from anode to cathode is 4μ A/m^2. Find the velocity (in cm/s) of positive ions moving towards cathode.

5 Five 10Ω resistances are connected as shown in the figure. The resistance in the conducting wires (fully drawn lines) is negligible. Determine the resulting resistance R (in ohm) between A and B.

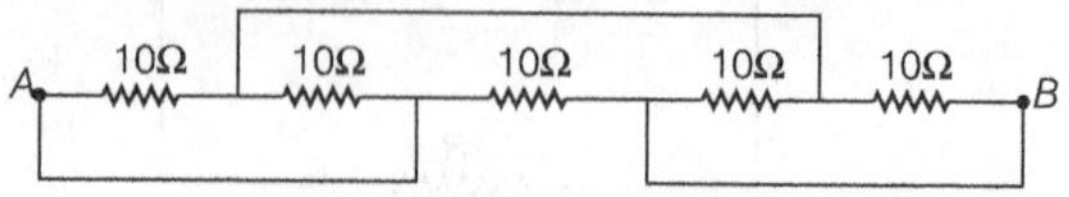

6 Find the effective resistance across terminals PQ in ohm.

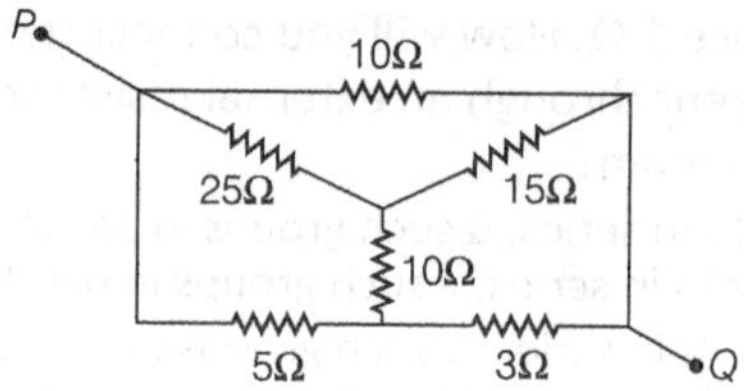

7 In the circuit shown, current through the resistance 2Ω is i_1 and current through the resistance 30Ω is i_2. Find the ratio $\frac{i_1}{i_2}$.

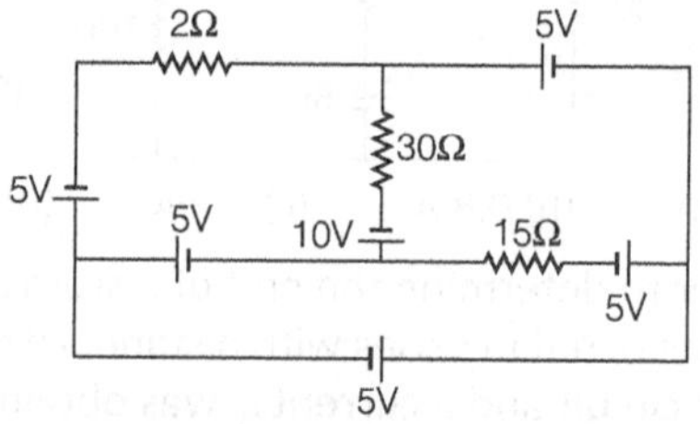

8 In the circuit, the electric current through the battery is .... ampere.

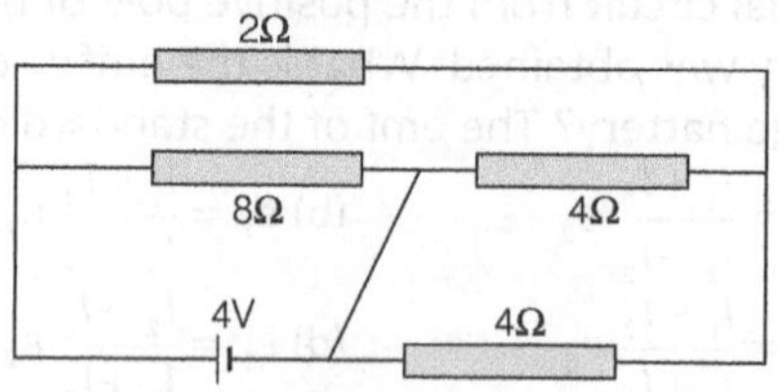

9 Each branch in the following circuit has a resistance R. The equivalent resistance of the circuit between the points A and B is x. Find the value of x / R.

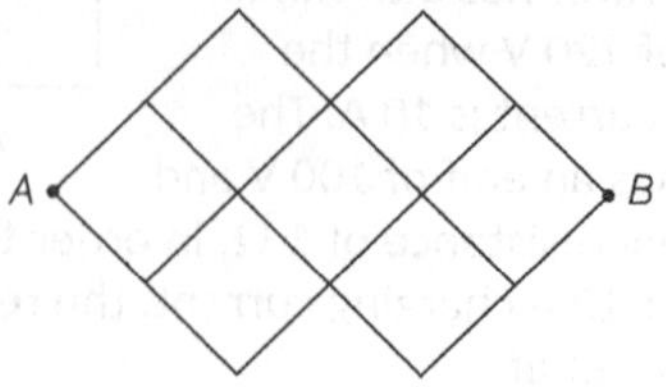

10 The equivalent resistance between the points *A* and *B* in the following circuit is $x\ \Omega$, then x is

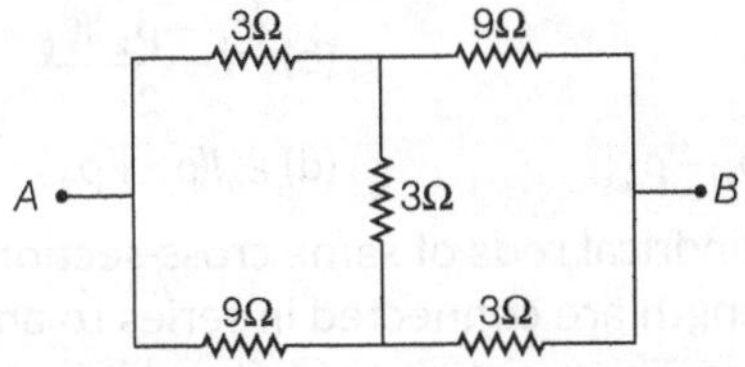

11 12 cells each of negligible internal resistance and having the same emf are connected in series and are kept in a closed box. Some of the cells are wrongly connected. This box is connected in series with an external resistor and two cells identical with the other cells. The current is 3A when the cells and box aid each other and is 2A when the cells and the box oppose each other. How many cells in the box are wrongly connected?

12 Eels are able to generate current with biological cells called electroplaques. The electroplaques in an Eel are arranged in 100 rows, each row stretching horizontally along the body of the fish containing 5000 electroplaques. The arrangement is suggestively shown below.

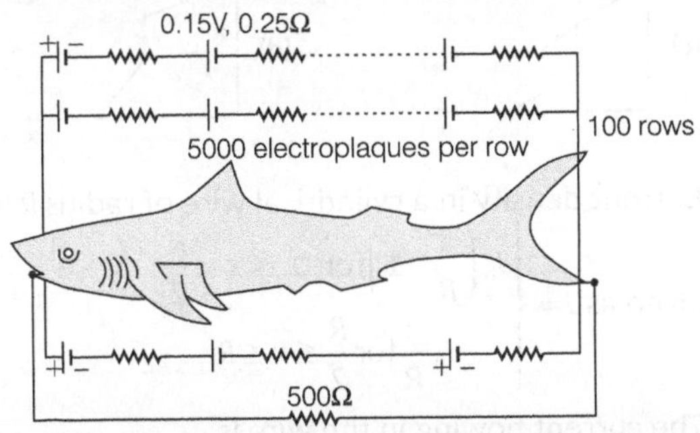

Each electroplaques has an emf of 0.15 V and internal resistance of 0.25 Ω. The water surrounding the Eel completes a circuit between the head and its tail. If the water surrounding it has a resistance of 500 Ω, find the current (in ampere upto 2 decimal places), which an Eel can produce in water.

13 Find equivalent resistance (in ohm) between *A* and *B* of the infinite network shown. Resistance of each $R = 100\sqrt{3}\ \Omega$.

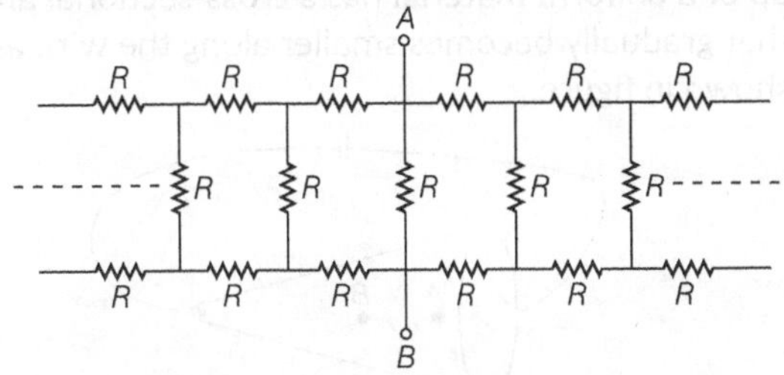

14 A network of twelve resistances each of resistance $R = 24\ \Omega$ form a square of squares as shown in the figure. The outer square is fitted in a metal ring of negligible resistance. Find the resistance between centre of the square and the ring.

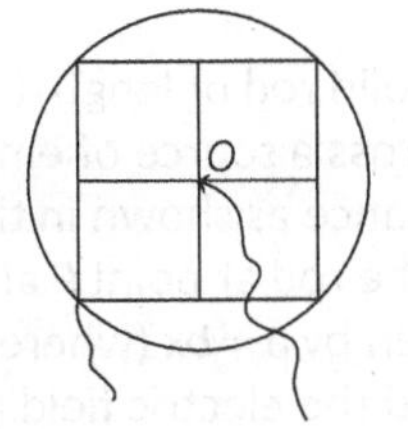

15 In the given network of resistors, each resistor has resistance $R = 12\ \Omega$. Find equivalent resistance (in ohm) across *A* and *B*.

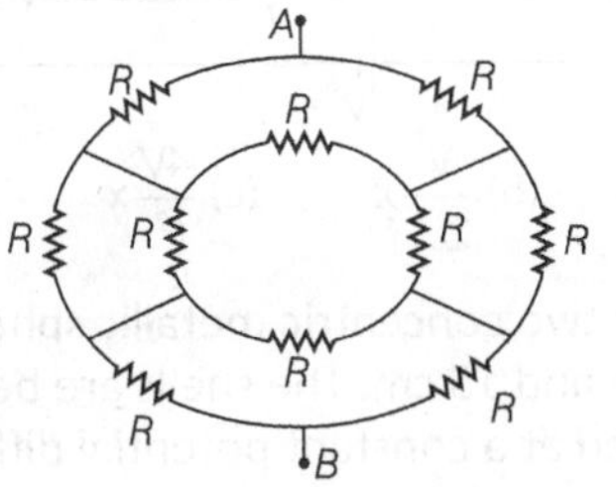

LEVEL 03 JEE Advanced Level

Single Choice Correct Questions

1 Suppose a current carrying cone shaped wire made up of a uniform material has a cross-sectional area that gradually becomes smaller along the wire as shown in figure.

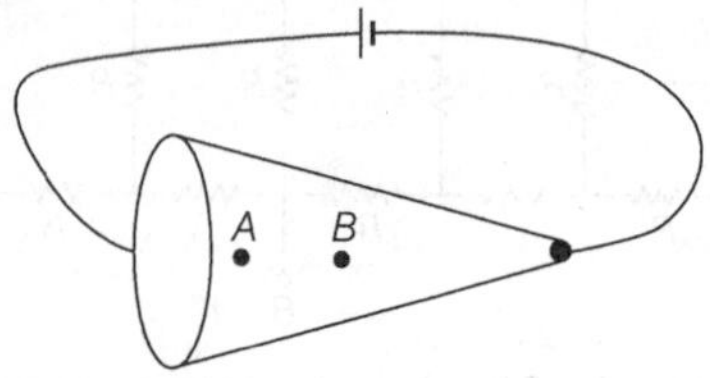

(a) Electric current is different in different portions of wire

(b) Current density at A is more than that of at point B

(c) Electric field at point A is lesser than that of point B

(d) Drift speed of electrons at point A is same as that of at point B

2 A cylindrical solid rod of length L and radius a is connected across a source of emf V and negligible internal resistance as shown in the figure. The resistivity of the rod at point P at a distance x from left end is given by $\rho = bx$ (where, b is a positive constant). Find the electric field at point P.

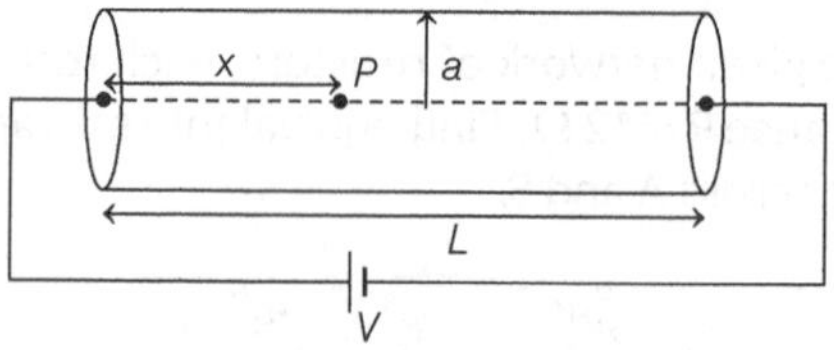

(a) $\frac{2V}{L^2}x$ (b) $\frac{V}{2L^2}x$ (c) $\frac{4V}{L^2}x$ (d) $\frac{8V}{L^2}x$

3 There are two concentric metallic spherical shells of radii 5 cm and 15 cm. The shells are being maintained at a constant potential difference of 10 V. The medium between the shells is filled with a material of resistivity 10^{-2} Ω-m. At a distance 10 cm from the centre, the electric field is

(a) 7.5 N/C (b) 75 N/C (c) 0.75 N/C (d) 750 N/C

4 Two long straight cylindrical conductors with resistivities ρ_1 and ρ_2 respectively are joined together as shown in figure. The radius of each of the conductor is a. If a uniform total current I flows through the conductors, the magnitude of the total free charge at the interface of the two conductor is

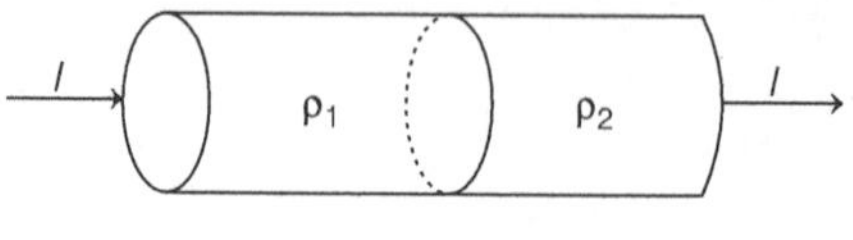

(a) zero (b) $\frac{(\rho_1 - \rho_2)I\varepsilon_0}{2}$

(c) $\varepsilon_0 I|\rho_1 - \rho_2|$ (d) $\varepsilon_0 I(\rho_1 + \rho_2)$

5 Two cylindrical rods of same cross-section area and same length are connected in series to an ideal cell as shown. The resistivity of left rod is ρ and that of right rod is 2ρ. Then, the variation of potential at any point P distant x from left end of combined rod system is given by

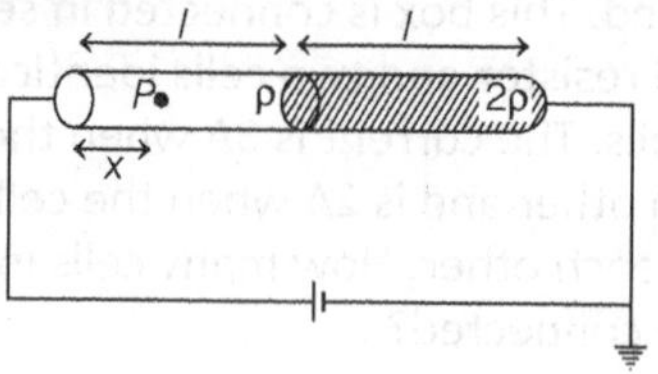

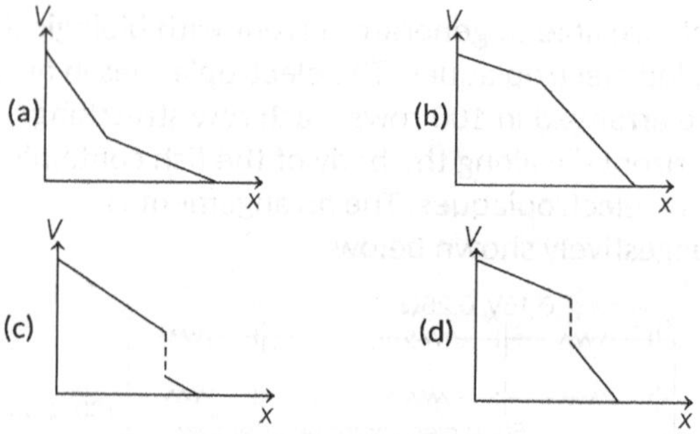

6 Current density in a cylindrical wire of radius R is given as $J = \begin{cases} J_0\left(\frac{x}{R} - 1\right) \text{for } 0 \le x < \frac{R}{2} \\ J_0 \frac{x}{R} \text{for } \frac{R}{2} \le x \le R \end{cases}$.

The current flowing in the wire is

(a) $\frac{7}{24}\pi J_0 R^2$ (b) $\frac{1}{6}\pi J_0 R^2$ (c) $\frac{7}{12}\pi J_0 R^2$ (d) $\frac{5}{12}\pi J_0 R^2$

7 A hemispherical metallic plate is buried in the earth with its plane surface parallel to the ground and touching the ground. A conducting pole is attached to the plate as shown in the figure. The pole carries a current I as shown. This current enters the plate and gets distributed uniformly on the surface of the plate. A man approaches the pole. If his steps are of length L and he is at a distance r_0 at some instant. Find the voltage, which will appear across his feet due to current I.

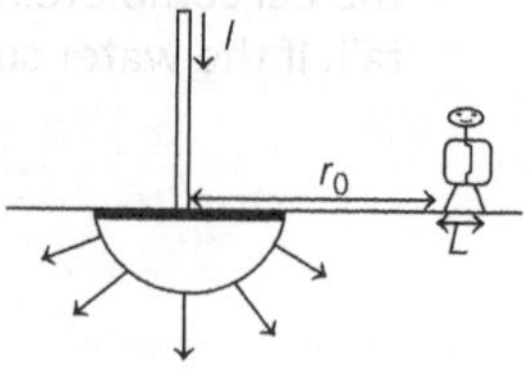

Assume that the conductivity of the earth is σ.

(a) $\dfrac{IL}{2\pi\sigma r_0(r_0+L)}$ (b) $\dfrac{IL}{4\pi\sigma r_0(r_0+L)}$

(c) $\dfrac{I}{2\pi\sigma L}\ln\left(\dfrac{r_0+L}{r_0}\right)$ (d) $\dfrac{I}{4\pi\sigma L}\ln\left(\dfrac{r_0+L}{r_0}\right)$

8 In order to increase the resistance of a given wire of uniform cross-section to four times its value, a fraction of its length is stretched uniformly till the full length of the wire becomes 1.5 times the original length, what is the value of this fraction?

(a) $\dfrac{1}{4}$ (b) $\dfrac{1}{8}$ (c) $\dfrac{1}{16}$ (d) $\dfrac{1}{6}$

9 A brass disc and a carbon disc of same radius are assembled alternatively to make a cylindrical conductor. The resistance of the cylinder is independent of the temperature. The ratio of thickness of the brass disc to that of the carbon disc is [α is temperature coefficient of resistance and neglect linear expansion]

(a) $\left|\dfrac{\alpha_C\rho_C}{\alpha_B\rho_B}\right|$ (b) $\left|\dfrac{\alpha_C\rho_B}{\alpha_B\rho_C}\right|$ (c) $\left|\dfrac{\alpha_B\rho_C}{\alpha_C\rho_B}\right|$ (d) $\left|\dfrac{\alpha_B\rho_B}{\alpha_C\rho_C}\right|$

10 A conducting rod of square cross-section is bent in a semi-circular shape of inner radius r as shown in figure. Length of side of cross-section is equal to a. Resistivity of material is ρ. The resistance of rod across its end will be (a is not small in comparison of r)

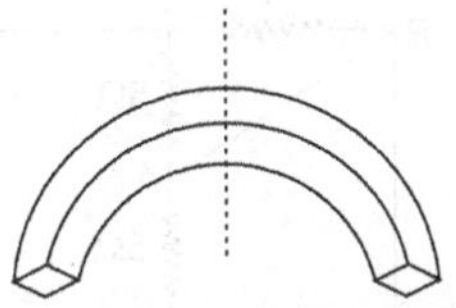

(a) $\dfrac{\pi\rho}{a\ln(1+a/r)}$ (b) $\dfrac{2\pi\rho}{a\ln(1+a/r)}$

(c) $\dfrac{\pi\rho(r+a)}{a^2}$ (d) $\dfrac{2\pi r\rho}{a^2}$

11 Maximum and minimum radii of given cylindrical conductor PQ are r_1 and r_2, then current through the battery will be (ρ = resistivity)

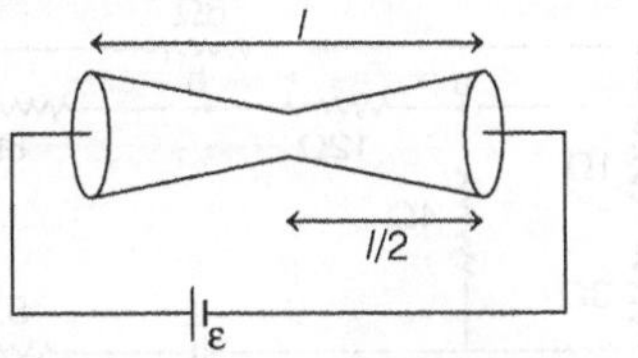

(a) $\dfrac{\pi\varepsilon r_1 r_2}{\rho l}$ (b) $\dfrac{2\pi\varepsilon r_1 r_2}{\rho l}$

(c) $\dfrac{\pi\varepsilon r_1 r_2}{2\rho l}$ (d) None of these

12 A metal rod of radius a is concentric with a metal cylindrical shell of radius b and length L. The space between rod and cylinder is tightly packed with a high resistance material of a resistivity ρ. A battery having a terminal voltage V is connected across the combination as shown. Neglect resistance of rod and cylinder. If I is the total current in the circuit, then I is

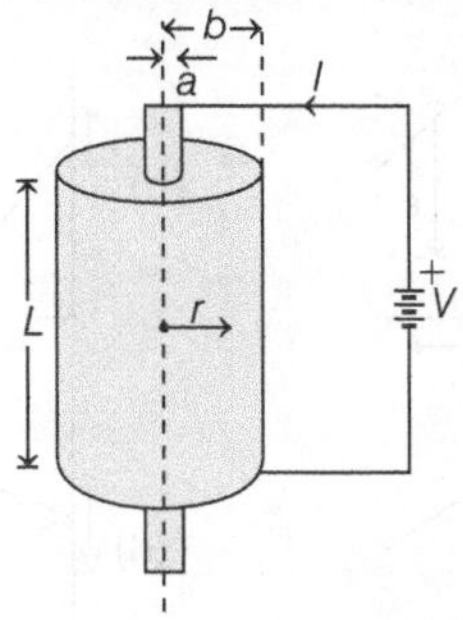

(a) $\dfrac{LV}{\rho}$ (b) $\dfrac{2\pi LV}{\rho(\ln b-\ln a)}$

(c) $\dfrac{4\pi LV}{\rho(\ln b-\ln a)}$ (d) $\dfrac{LV}{4\pi\rho(\ln b-\ln a)}$

13 Two current elements P and Q have current-voltage characteristics as shown below

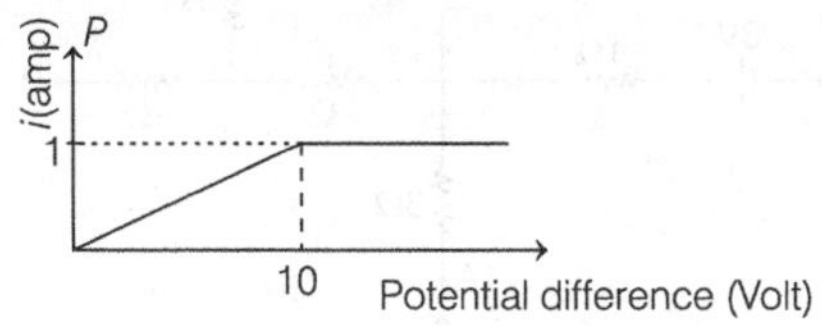

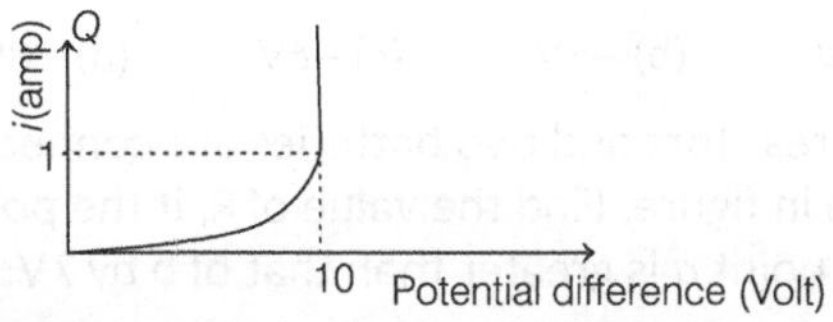

Which of the graphs given below represents current-voltage characteristics when P and Q are in series.

(a) 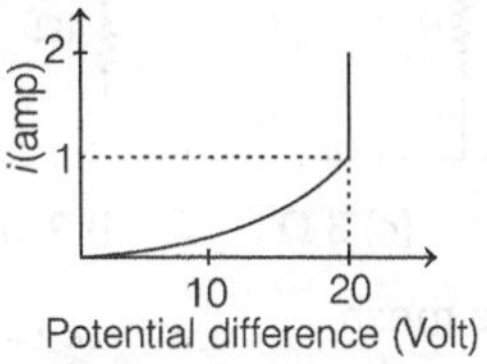

(b) 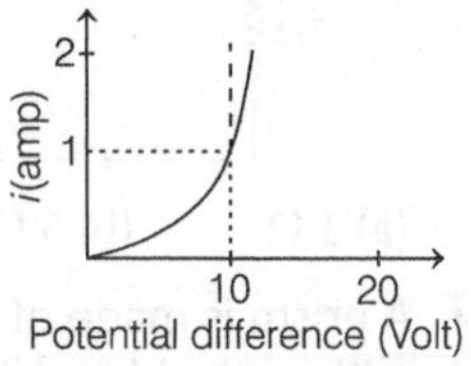

(c) 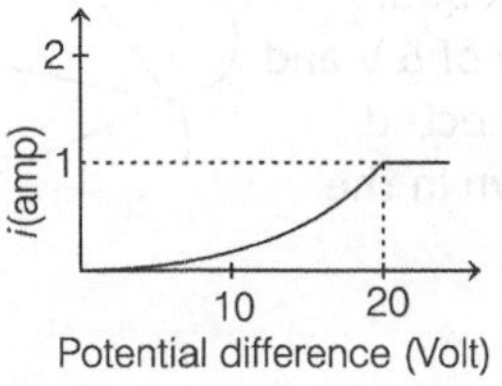

(d) 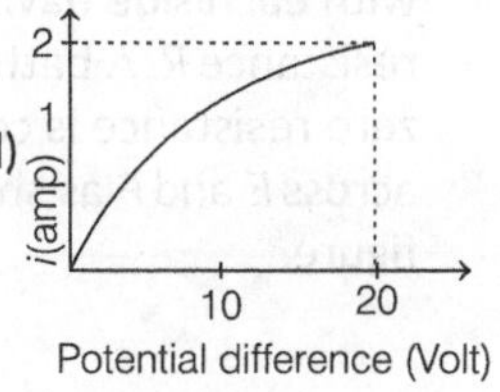

14 The two ends of a uniform conductor are joined to a cell of emf ε and some internal resistance. Starting from the mid-point *P* of the conductor, we move in the direction of the current and return to *P*. The potential *V* at every point on the path is plotted against the distance covered (*x*). Which of the following best represents the resulting curve?

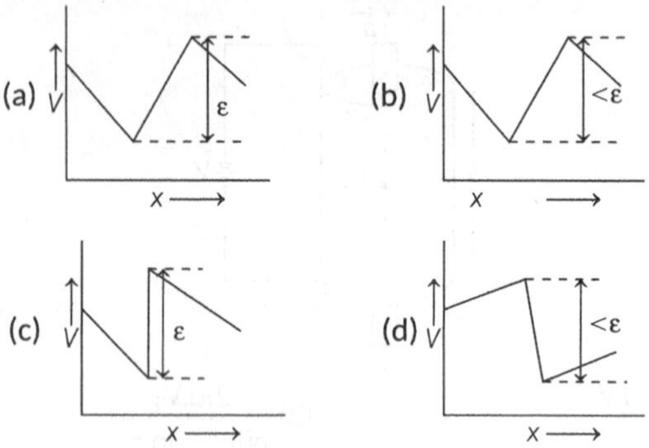

15 In the circuit given, find the potential of the point *P*.

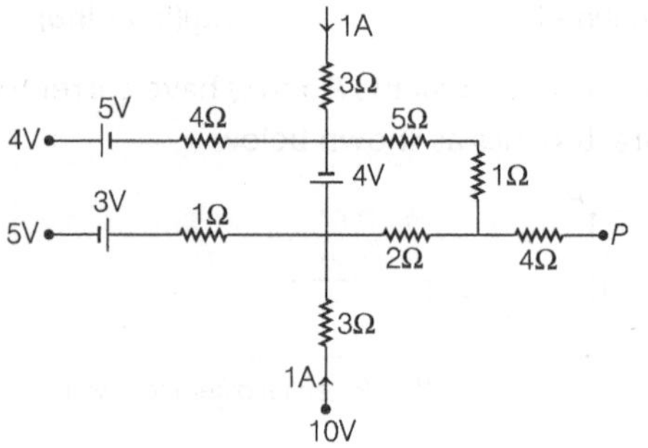

(a) –4V (b) –5V (c) –6V (d) –8V

16 Three resistors and two batteries are connected as shown in figure. Find the value of *R*, if the potential of the point *a* is greater than that of *b* by 7V.

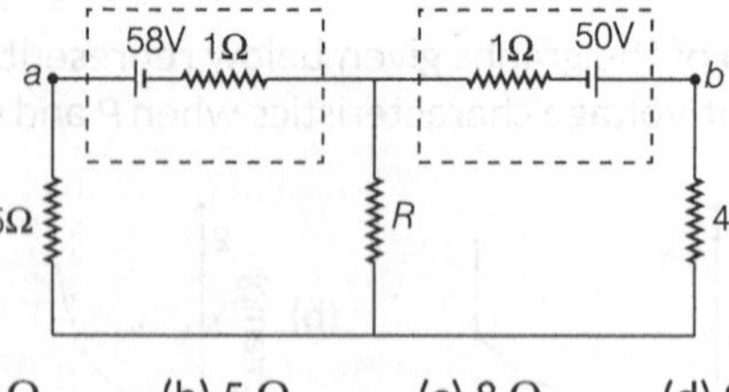

(a) 1 Ω (b) 5 Ω (c) 8 Ω (d) 9 Ω

17 A prism is made of wire mesh with each side having equal resistance *R*. A battery of 6 V and zero resistance is connected across *E* and *F* as shown in the figure.

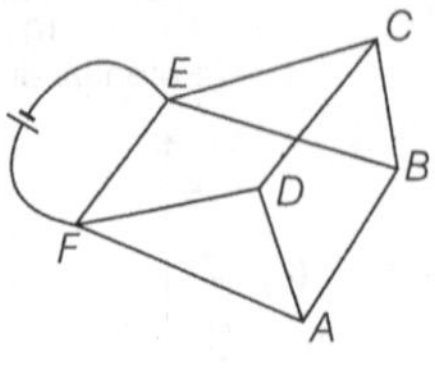

The current in the branch *AB*, if *R* is equal to 5Ω, is

(a) 0.6 A (b) 0.8 A
(c) 0.4 A (d) 0

18 What is potential difference between A and B?

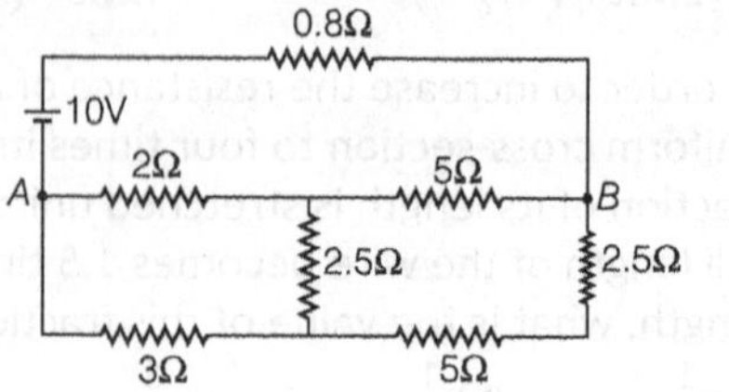

(a) 8.4 V (b) 2.4 V
(c) 4.2 V (d) 7.2 V

19 In the circuit shown, calculate the current through 6 V battery.

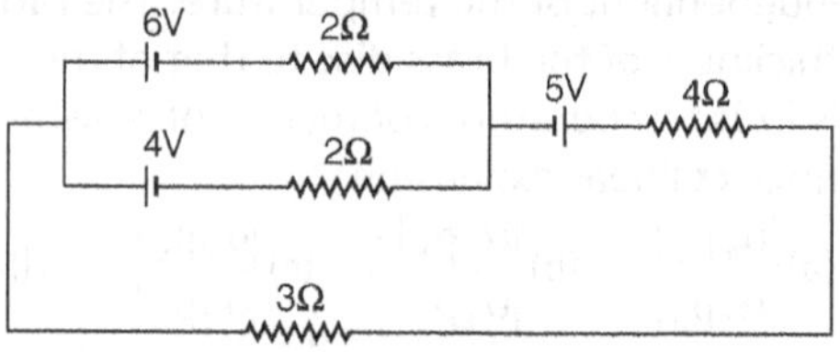

(a) 1/2 A (b) 1/4 A
(c) 1/8 A (d) None of these

20 In the circuit shown, find the current in branch *AB* of the circuit.

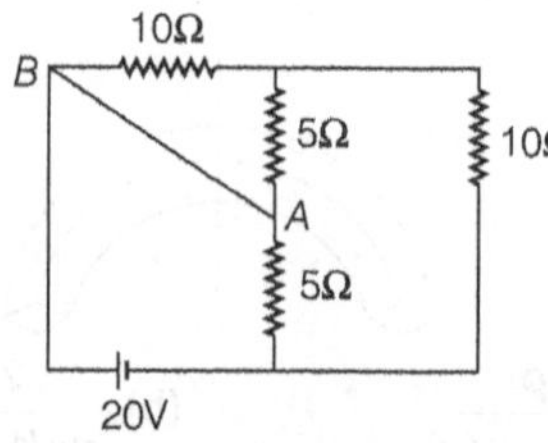

(a) 5A (b) 0.5 A
(c) $\frac{11}{3}$ A (d) Zero

21 In the circuit shown in the figure, the potential difference between points *a* and *b* is $V_a - V_b = 4$V. Find the emf *E* of the battery.

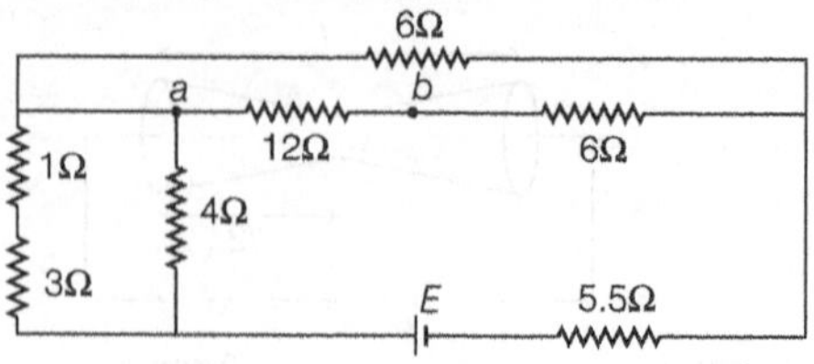

(a) 12 V (b) 16 V
(c) 20 V (d) 24 V

22 In the given circuit, three resistors of 3 Ω each, 3 cells ε_1 and ε_2 and ε_3 with internal resistance 3Ω each are connected. Currents in some branches are shown in the circuit. Find the emf of cell ε_3.

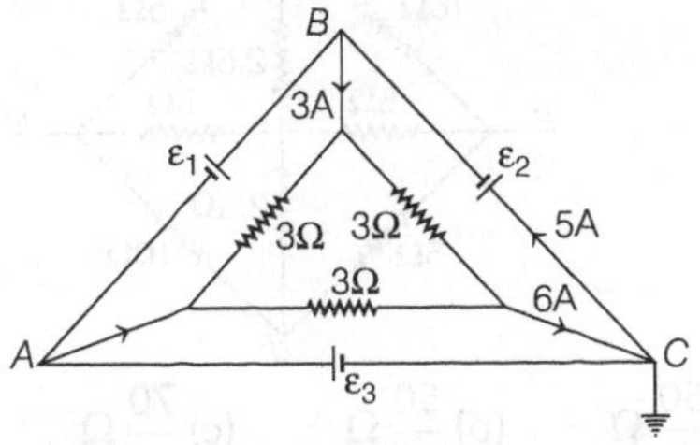

(a) 6 V (b) 9 V (c) 12 V (d) 15 V

23 Under what condition, current passing through the resistance R can be increased by short-circuiting the battery of emf ε_2. The internal resistances of the two batteries are r_1 and r_2, respectively.

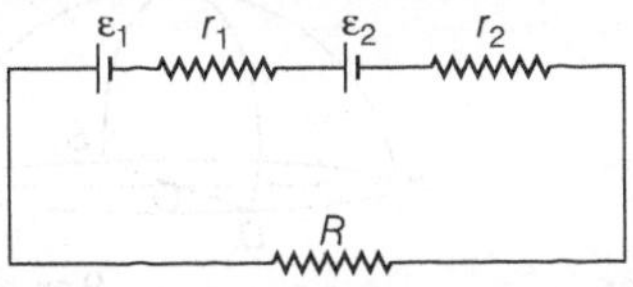

(a) $\varepsilon_2 r_1 > \varepsilon_1 (R + r_2)$ (b) $\varepsilon_1 r_2 > \varepsilon_2 (R + R_1)$
(c) $\varepsilon_2 r_2 > \varepsilon_1 (R + r_2)$ (d) $\varepsilon_1 r_1 > \varepsilon_2 (R + r_1)$

24 A long conductor of circular cross-section has radius r and length l as shown in the figure. The conductivity of the material near the axis is σ_1 and increases linearly with the distance from axis and becomes σ_2 near the surface. Find the current through the conductor, if a potential difference V is applied across the flat faces.

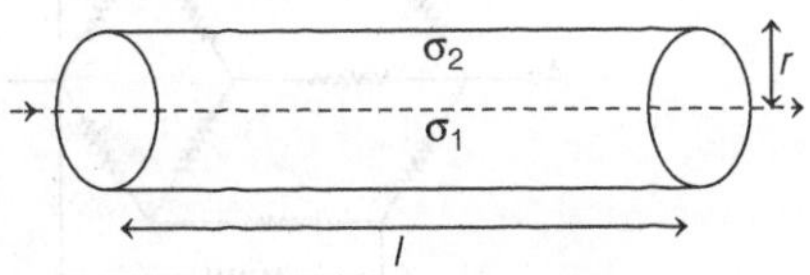

(a) $\dfrac{\pi r^2 V(\sigma_1 + \sigma_2)}{6l}$ (b) $\dfrac{2\pi r^2 V(\sigma_1 + \sigma_2)}{3l}$
(c) $\dfrac{\pi r^2 V(2\sigma_1 + \sigma_2)}{3l}$ (d) $\dfrac{\pi r^2 V(\sigma_1 + 2\sigma_2)}{3l}$

25 *ABCD* is a square, where each side is a uniform wire of resistance 1Ω. A point *E* lies on *CD* such that, if a uniform wire of resistance 1Ω is connected across *AE* and constant potential difference is applied across *A* and *C*, then *B* and *E* are equipotential. Then,

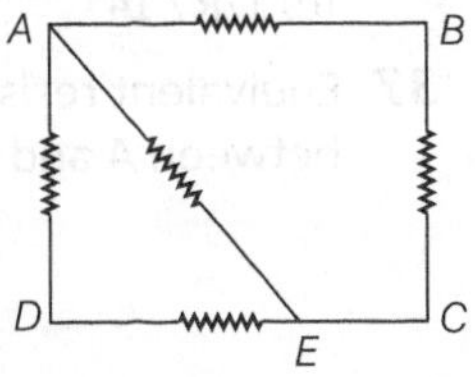

(a) $\dfrac{CE}{ED} = 1$ (b) $\dfrac{CE}{ED} = 2$ (c) $\dfrac{CE}{ED} = \dfrac{1}{\sqrt{2}}$ (d) $\dfrac{CE}{ED} = \sqrt{2}$

26 If the potential difference between *A* and *D* is *V*, what will be potential difference between *F* and *C*. Each of the resistance is *R*.

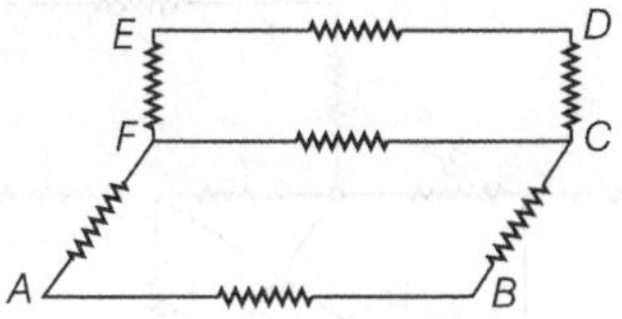

(a) V/3 (b) V/5
(c) V/7 (d) V/8

27 The current enters at *A* and comes out at *D*. Some of the resistance are shown. What should be resistance of wire *CB*, so that it draws double of the current that enters the wire *BF*?

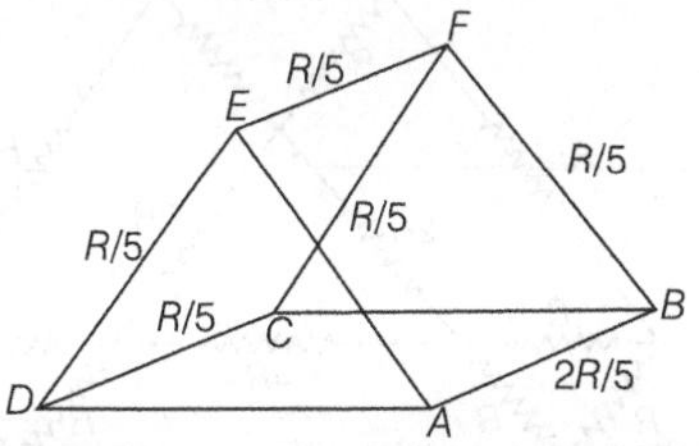

(a) $\dfrac{3R}{20}$ (b) $\dfrac{7R}{9}$ (c) $\dfrac{8R}{9}$ (d) $\dfrac{9R}{10}$

28 A source of emf ε = 10V and having negligible internal resistance is connected to a variable resistance. The resistance varies as shown in figure. The total charge that has passed through the resistor *R* during the time interval from t_1 to t_2 is

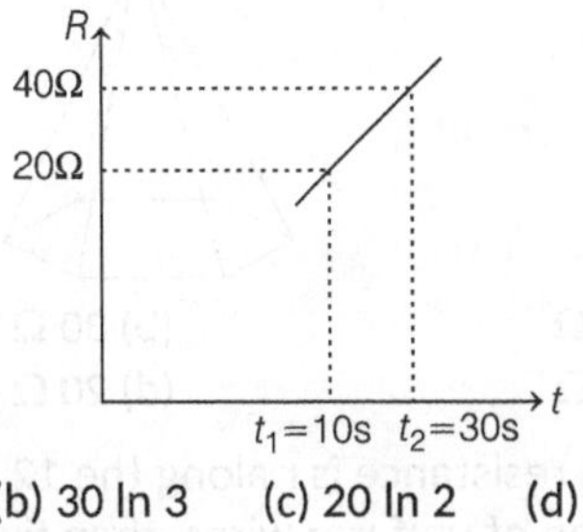

(a) 40 ln 4 (b) 30 ln 3 (c) 20 ln 2 (d) 10 ln 2

29 A wire has linear resistance ρ (in ohm/m). Find the equivalent resistance between points *A* and *B*, if the side of the big square is *d*.

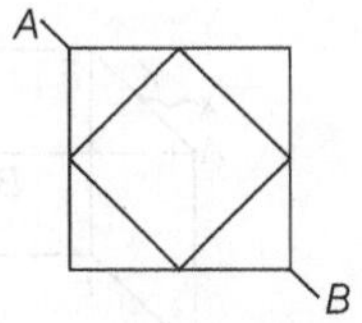

(a) $\dfrac{\rho d}{\sqrt{2}}$ (b) $\sqrt{2}\rho d$
(c) $2\rho d$ (d) None of these

30 The equivalent resistance between A and B in the arrangement of resistances as shown, is

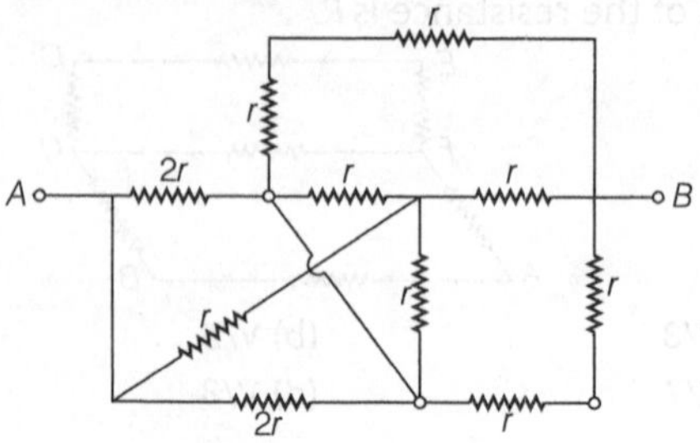

(a) $4r$ (b) $3r$ (c) $2.5\,r$ (d) r

31 For the shown circuit, find the effective resistance between the points A and B.

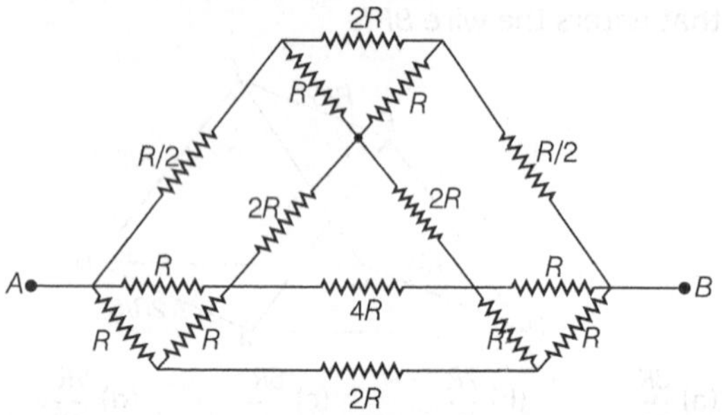

(a) R (b) $2R$
(c) $3R$ (d) $4R$

32 12 resistors (40 Ω each) are used to make a prism with hexagonal base as shown. Then, the resistance between two adjacent corners of the base is

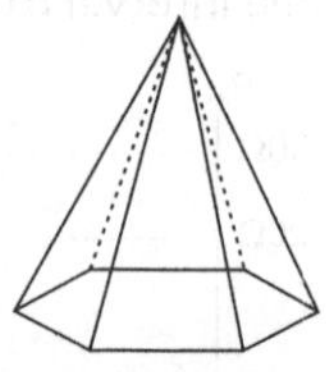

(a) 45 Ω (b) 30 Ω
(c) 22 Ω (d) 20 Ω

33 If each resistance is r along the 12 edges of a cubical skeleton of uniform wires, then find equivalent resistance between X and Y, where X and Y are the mid-points of two opposite edges of a face of the cube.

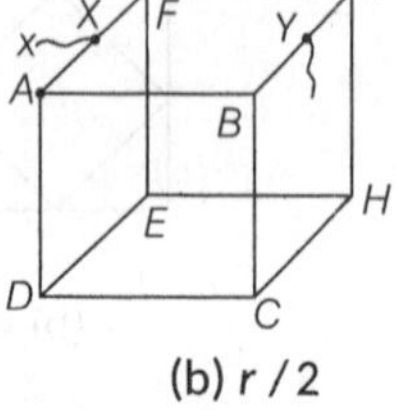

(a) $7r/8$ (b) $r/2$
(c) $4r/5$ (d) $7r/5$

34 Find the equivalent resistance of the network shown in figure between the points a and b.

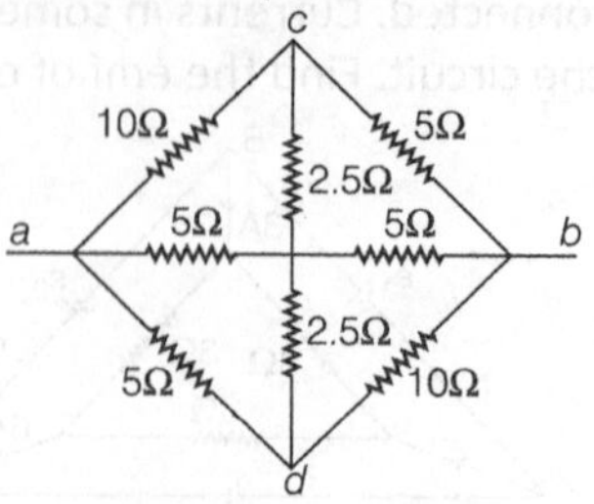

(a) $\frac{50}{13}\,\Omega$ (b) $\frac{50}{23}\,\Omega$ (c) $\frac{70}{29}\,\Omega$ (d) $\frac{70}{17}\,\Omega$

35 A hemispherical network of radius a is made by using a conducting wire of resistance per unit length r. The equivalent resistance across OP is

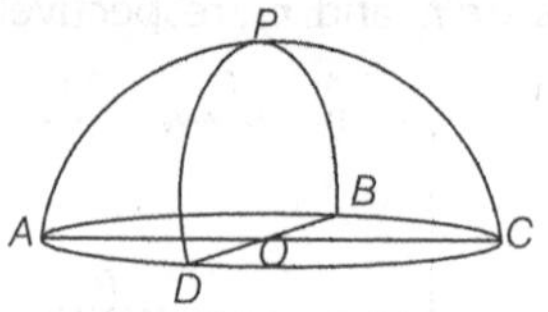

(a) $\frac{8ar}{(2+\pi)}$ (b) $\frac{8ar}{(2-\pi)}$
(c) $\frac{(2+\pi)ar}{8}$ (d) $\frac{(2-\pi)ar}{8}$

36 Find the equivalent resistance of the following group of resistance between A and B. Each resistance of the circuit is R.

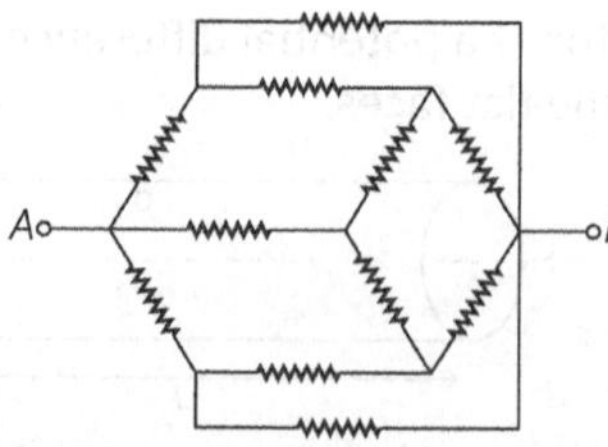

(a) $5R/14$
(b) $9R/14$
(c) $11R/14$
(d) $17R/14$

37 Equivalent resistance of the network given below between A and B will be (all resistances are R Ω)

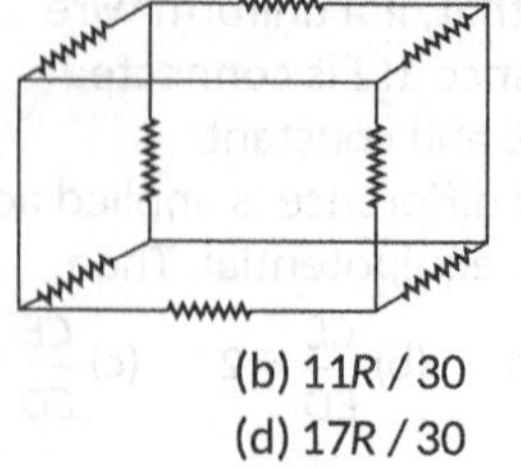

(a) $7R/30$ (b) $11R/30$
(c) $13R/30$ (d) $17R/30$

38 At what value of the resistance R_x in the circuit shown in figure will the total resistance between points A and B be independent of the number of loops? $[R = 2(\sqrt{3}+1)\,\Omega]$

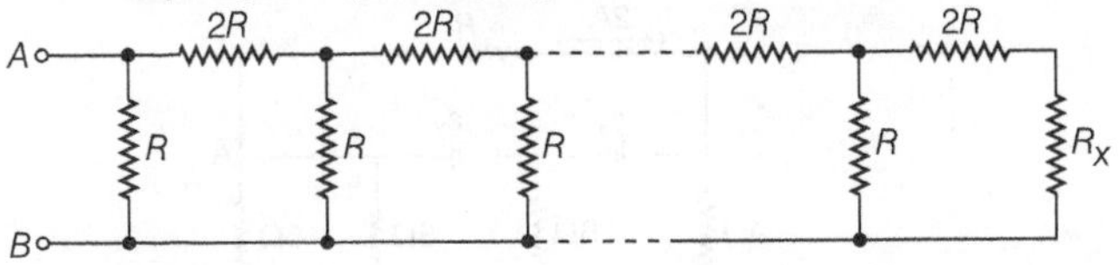

(a) $2\,\Omega$ (b) $4\,\Omega$ (c) $8\,\Omega$ (d) $16\,\Omega$

39 The circuit diagram shown consists of a large number of elements (each element has two resistors R_1 and R_2). The resistance of the resistors in each subsequent element differs by a factor of $K = 1/2$ from the resistance of the resistors in the previous elements. The equivalent resistance between A and B shown in figure is

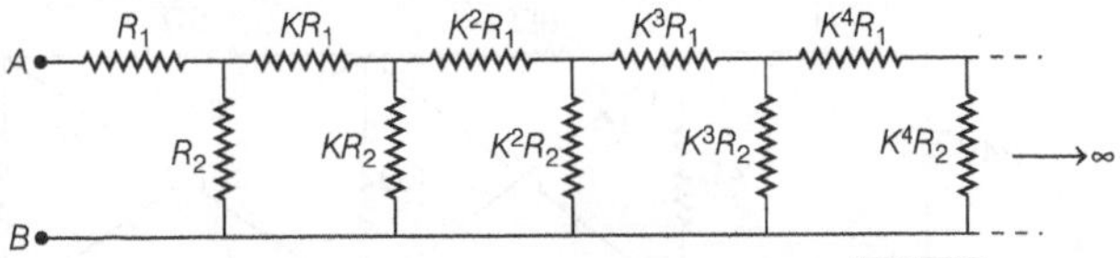

(a) $\dfrac{R_1 - R_2}{2}$ (b) $\dfrac{(R_1 - R_2) + \sqrt{6R_1R_2}}{2}$

(c) $\dfrac{(R_1 - R_2) + \sqrt{R_1^2 + R_2^2 + 6R_1R_2}}{2}$

(d) None of these

40 A frame made of thin homogeneous wire is shown in figure. Assume that the number of successively embedded equilateral triangle with sides decreasing by half tends to infinity. The side AB has a resistance $R = (\sqrt{7}+1)\,\Omega$. Find the equivalent resistance between A and B.

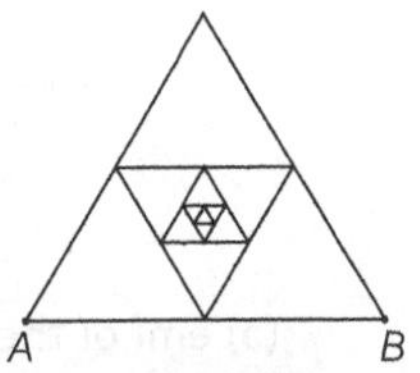

(a) $2\,\Omega$ (b) $3\,\Omega$ (c) $4\,\Omega$ (d) $6\,\Omega$

41 Determine the resultant resistance of the infinite circuit made of r resistance between A and B.

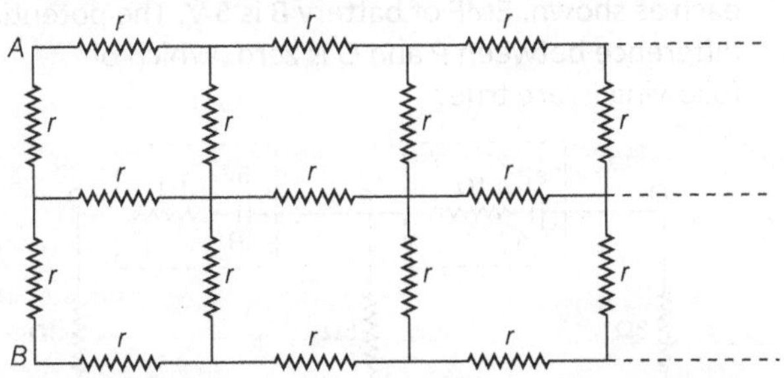

(a) $(\sqrt{5}+1)r$ (b) $(\sqrt{5}-1)r$

(c) $(\sqrt{3}-1)r$ (d) $(\sqrt{3}+1)r$

42 The circuit shown in the diagram extends to the right into infinity. Each battery has emf ε (unknown) and internal resistance r. Each resistor has the resistance $4r$. Value of emf of battery is

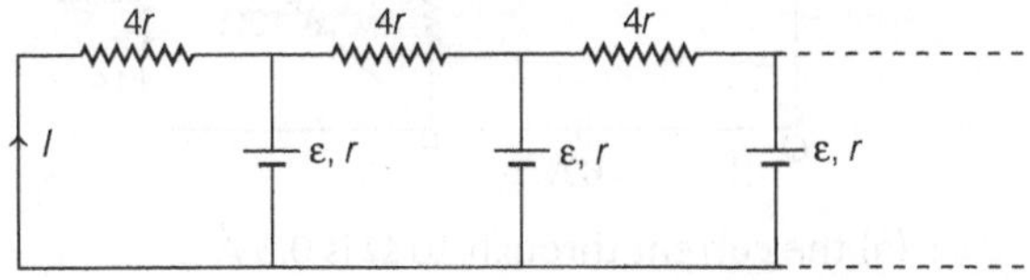

(a) $(\sqrt{2}-1)Ir$ (b) $(\sqrt{2}+1)Ir$

(c) $2(\sqrt{2}-1)Ir$ (d) $2(\sqrt{2}+1)Ir$

43 A window grill-like network of conductors is fitted in a ring of zero resistance. The interstices of the network are squares of side a and are made of uniform wire of resistance R per unit length. What is the effective resistance between the ring and the centre O.

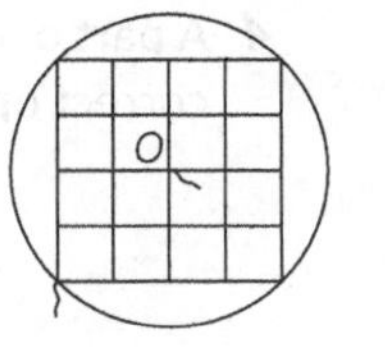

(a) $\dfrac{21}{40}ar$ (b) $\dfrac{31}{40}ar$

(c) $\dfrac{21}{50}ar$ (d) $\dfrac{31}{50}ar$

Multiple Choice(s) Correct Questions

1 Figure shows a solid resistance wire of uniform material but non-uniform cross-section area. A, B and C are the three sections. Current flowing is i, electric field at a section is E, potential is V and flux of electric field passing through a cross-section is ϕ, then

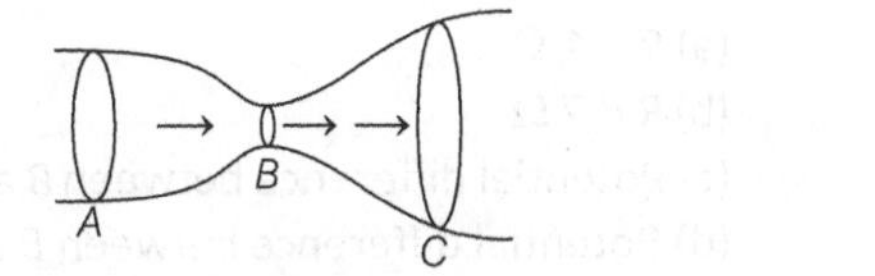

(a) $i_B > i_A > i_C$ (b) $E_B > E_A > E_C$

(c) $\phi_A = \phi_B = \phi_C$ (d) $V_B > V_A > V_C$

2 The resistivity of a cylindrical conductor carrying steady current along its length varies linearly with the distance from the current carrying end as given by $\rho = \rho_0\left(1 + \dfrac{x}{l}\right)$, where l is the length of the conductor and x is the distance from the current entry end. ρ_0 is a positive constant.

(a) Electric field varies linearly with x

(b) Electric potential difference across the length x varies linearly with x

(c) Volume charge density in the conductor is zero

(d) Volume charge density in the conductor is non-zero

3 In the circuit shown in diagram,

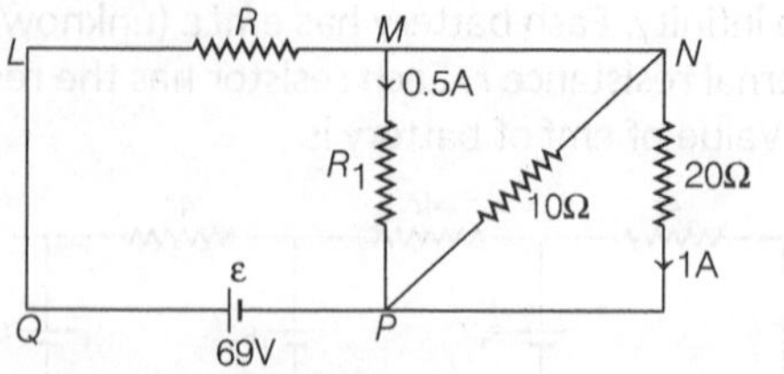

(a) the current through 10 Ω is 0.5 A
(b) the value of $R_1 = 40\ \Omega$
(c) the value of $R = 14\ \Omega$
(d) the potential difference across $R = 49$ V

4 A part of circuit is shown in figure. Choose the correct option(s).

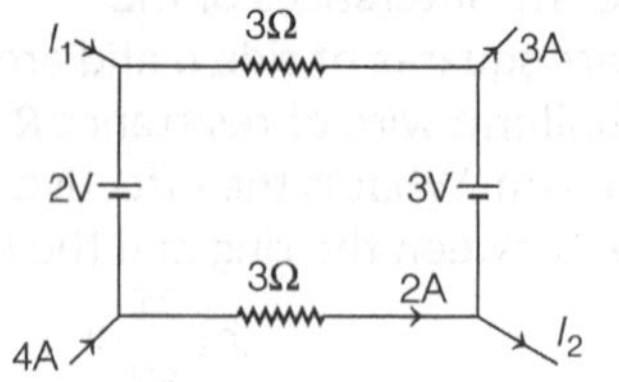

(a) $I_1 = 1/3$ A (b) $I_2 = 2/3$ A
(c) $I_1 = -1/3$ A (d) $I_2 = -2/3$ A

5 In the given circuit, the point *A* is 9V higher than point *B*.

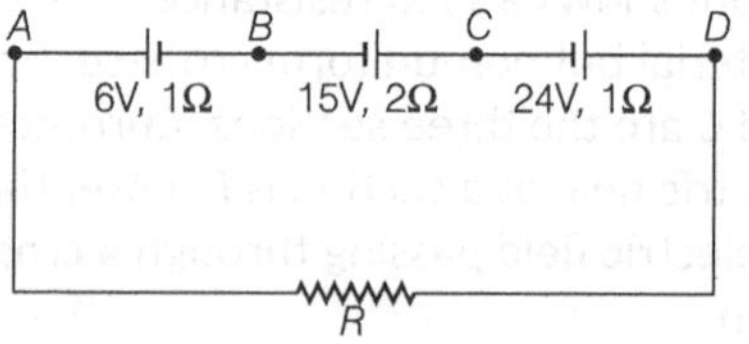

(a) $R = 1\ \Omega$
(b) $R = 7\ \Omega$
(c) Potential difference between *B* and *D* is 30 V
(d) Potential difference between *B* and *C* is 15 V

6 In the given diagram, choose correct options.

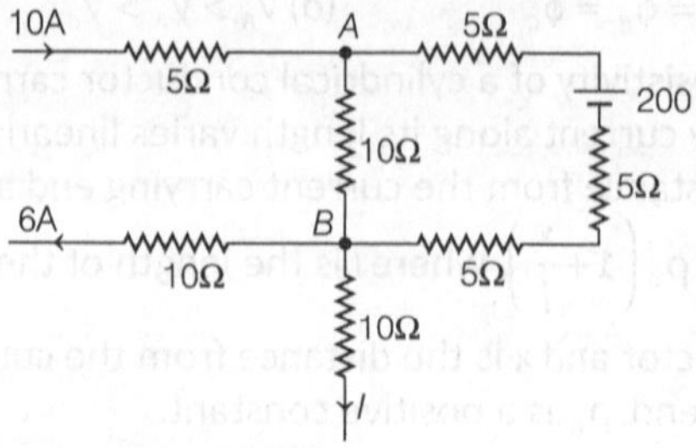

(a) The value of *I* is 4A
(b) The current from the cell is 4A
(c) Voltage drop across *AB* is 140 V
(d) The current from the cell is 10 A

7 In the circuit shown in figure, ε_1 and ε_2 are two ideal sources of unknown emfs. Some currents are shown. Potential difference appearing across 6 Ω resistance is $V_A - V_B = 10$ V,

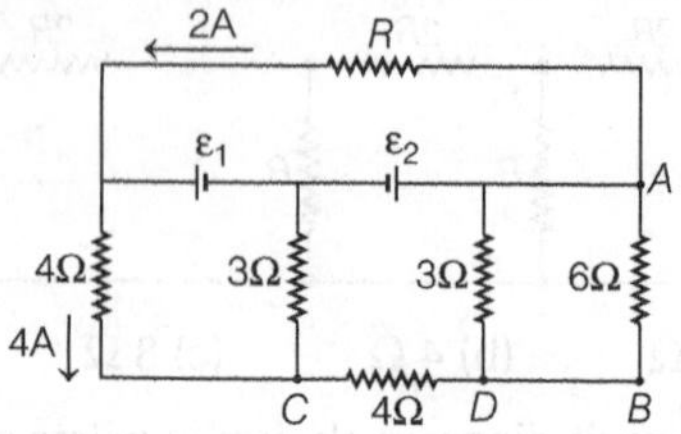

(a) the current in the 4 Ω resistor in between *C* and *D* is 5 A
(b) the unknown emf ε_1 is 43 V
(c) the unknown emf ε_2 is 57 V
(d) the resistance *R* is equal to 7 Ω

8 For the circuit shown in figure,

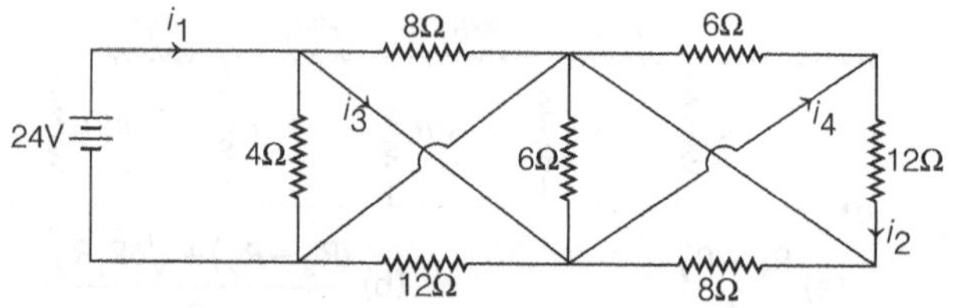

(a) $i_1 = 24$A (b) $i_2 = 2$A (c) $i_3 = 15$A (d) $i_4 = 6$A

9 An electric box contains three emf sources as shown in the figure. Then,

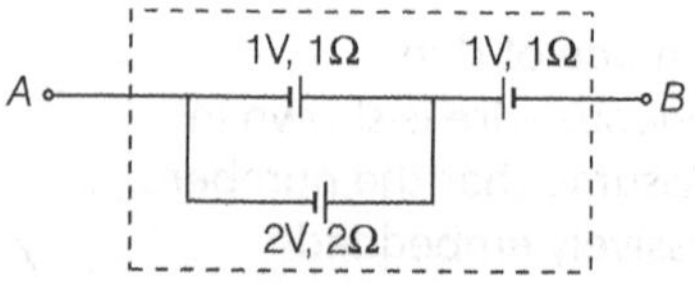

(a) emf of the electric box is 1/3 V
(b) point *B* is at higher potential than point *A*
(c) internal resistance of the box is 5/3Ω
(d) terminal voltage of 2V source is 4/3V

10 Two batteries *A* and *B* and three resistors are connected. Internal resistance of both batteries is 1 Ω each as shown. EMF of battery *B* is 5 V. The potential difference between *P* and *Q* is zero. Which of following is/are true?

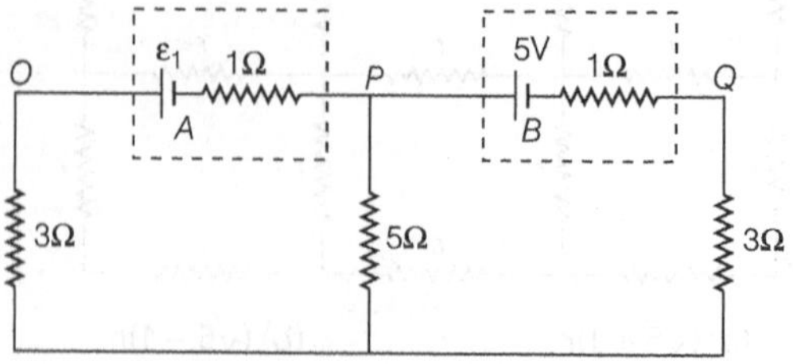

(a) The current through 5 Ω is 3 A
(b) The current through the battery A is 8 A
(c) The emf of the source A is 47 V
(d) The potential difference between O and P is 8V

11 Consider following circuit and select correct alternative(s).

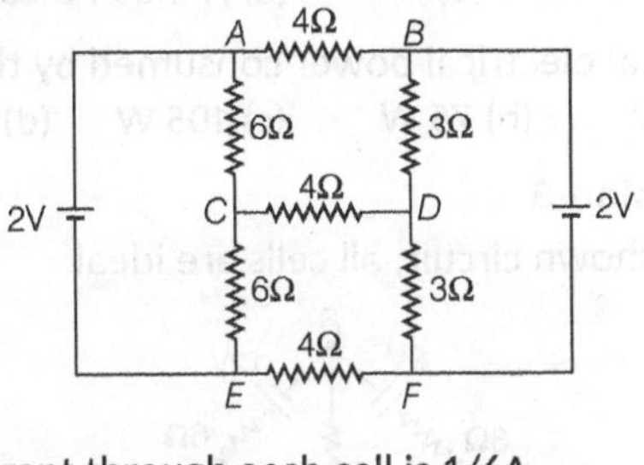

(a) Current through each cell is 1/6A
(b) Current through each 6Ω resistance is 1/6A
(c) Current through each 3Ω resistance is 1/3A
(d) Current through each 4Ω resistance is 1/2A

12 A battery of emf ε and internal resistance r is connected across a resistance R. Resistance R can be adjusted to any value greater than or equal to zero. A graph is plotted between the current (i) passing through the resistance and potential difference (V) across it. Select the correct alternative(s).

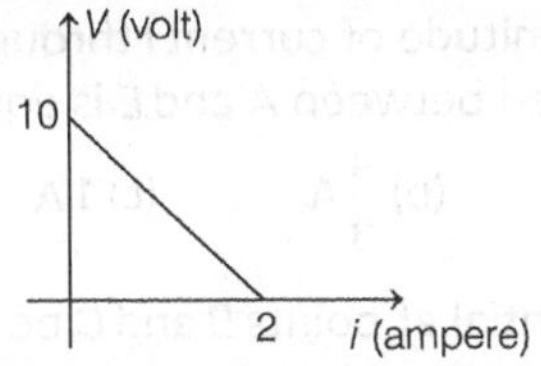

(a) internal resistance of the battery is 5Ω
(b) emf of the battery is 10 V
(c) Maximum current which can be taken from the battery is 2A
(d) V-i graph can never be a straight line as shown in figure

13 In the circuit shown in figure,

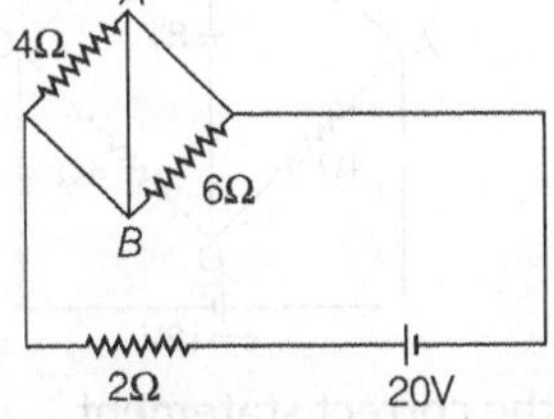

(a) power supplied by the battery is 200 W
(b) current flowing in the circuit is 5A
(c) potential difference across 4 Ω resistance is equal to the potential difference across 6Ω resistance
(d) current in wire AB is zero

14 In the circuit shown E, F, G and H are cells of emf 2V, 1V, 3V and 1V respectively and their internal resistances are 2Ω, 1Ω, 3Ω and 1Ω, respectively.

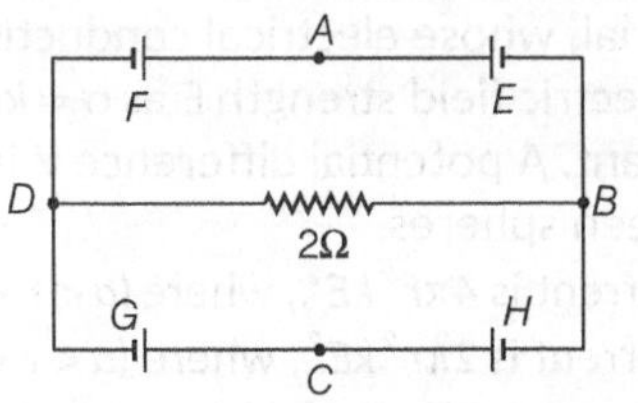

(a) $V_D - V_B = -2/13$V
(b) $V_D - V_B = 2/13$V
(c) $V_G = 21/13$V = potential difference across cell G
(d) $V_H = 19/13$V = potential difference across cell H

15 Which of the following options is/are correct regarding the below diagram?

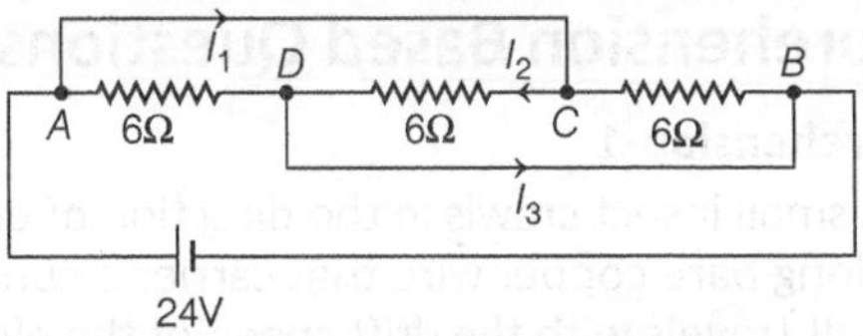

(a) $I_1 = 8$ A (b) $I_2 = 4$ A (c) $I_1 = 0$ (d) $I_3 = 8$ A

16 Consider 12 resistors arranged symmetrically in shape of bipyramid $ABCDEF$. The resistance of each resistor is R. The effective resistance between

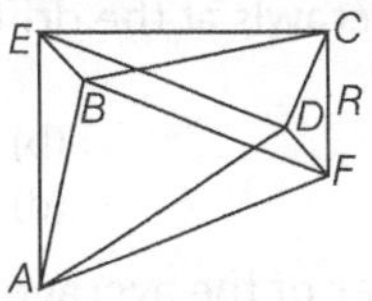

(a) E and F is $R/2$
(b) D and E is $5R/12$
(c) E and F is R
(d) A and C is $R/2$

17 Two circuits (shown below) are called 'circuit A' and circuit B, The equivalent resistance of circuit A is x and that of circuit B is y between 1 and 2.

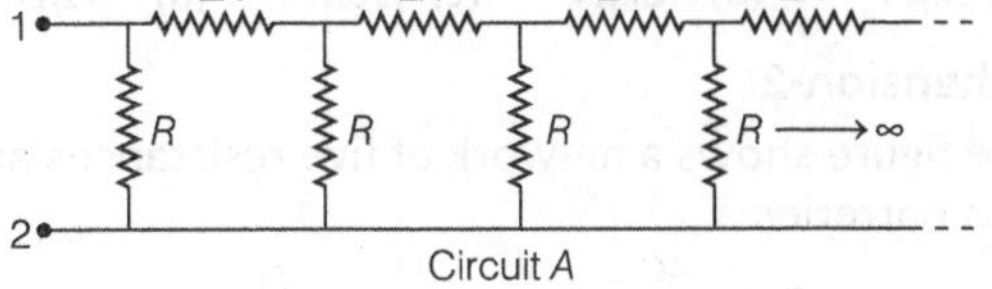

Circuit A

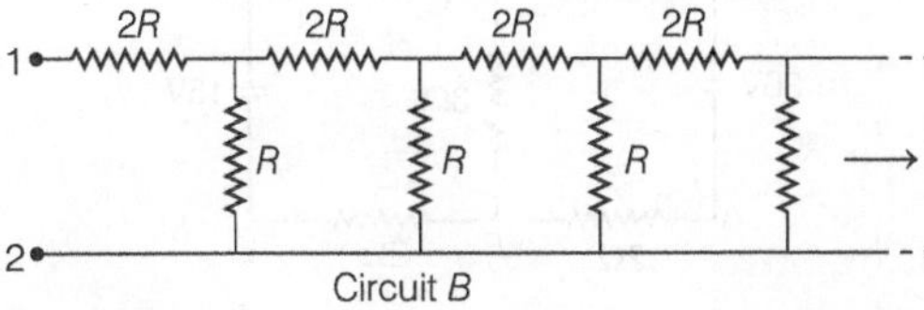

Circuit B

(a) $y > x$
(b) $y = (\sqrt{3}+1)R$
(c) $xy = 2R^2$
(d) $x - y = 2R$

18 A metal sphere of radius is surrounded by a concentric metal sphere of inner radius of b, where $b > a$. The space between the spheres is filled with a material, whose electrical conductivity σ varies with the electric field strength E as $\sigma = kE$, where k is a constant. A potential difference V is maintained between spheres.

(a) Current is $4\pi r^2 kE^2$, where $(a < r < b)$

(b) Current is $2\pi r^2 kE^2$, where $(a < r < b)$

(c) Potential difference between spheres is $V = \sqrt{\frac{1}{4\pi k}} \ln\left(\frac{b}{a}\right)$, where I is total current

(d) Potential difference between spheres is $V = \sqrt{\frac{1}{2\pi k}} \ln\left(\frac{b}{a}\right)$, where I is total current

Comprehension Based Questions

Comperehension-1

A small insect crawls in the direction of electron drift along bare copper wire that carries a current of 2.56 A. It travels with the drift speed of the electron in the wire of uniform cross-section area 1 mm^2. Number of free electrons for copper $= 8 \times 10^{22}$/cc and resistivity of copper $= 1.6 \times 10^{-8}$ Ω-m.

1 How much time would the caterpillar take to crawl 1.0 cm, if it crawls at the drift speed of the electrons in the wire?

(a) 50 s (b) 5 s
(c) 5000 s (d) None of these

2 What is order of the average time of collision for free electrons of copper?

(a) 10^{-14} s (b) 10^{-16} s (c) 10^{-11} s (d) 10^{-8} s

3 If the caterpillar starts from the point of zero potential at $t = 0$, it reaches a point of .... potential after 10 s.

(a) 82μV (b) −82μV (c) 41μV (d) −41μV

Comprehension-2

The figure shows a network of five resistances and two batteries

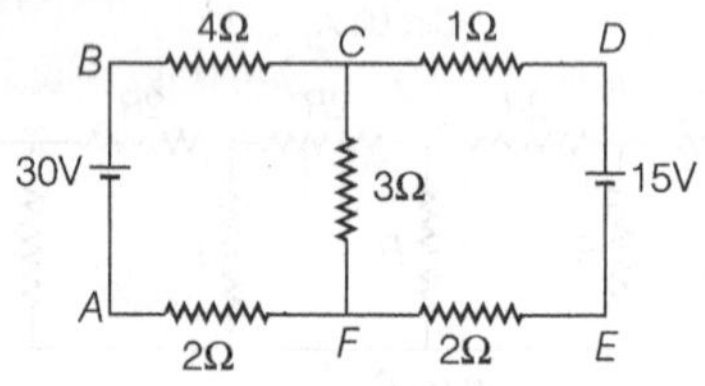

4 The current through the 30 V battery is

(a) 3A (b) 1A
(c) 2A (d) None of these

5 The current through the 15 V battery is

(a) zero (b) 1A
(c) 3A (d) None of these

6 Which of the batteries is getting charged?

(a) 30V (b) 15V
(c) Both (a) and (b) (d) None of these

7 The total electrical power consumed by the circuit is

(a) 15W (b) 75 W (c) 105 W (d) 90 W

Comprehension-3

In the shown circuit, all cells are ideal.

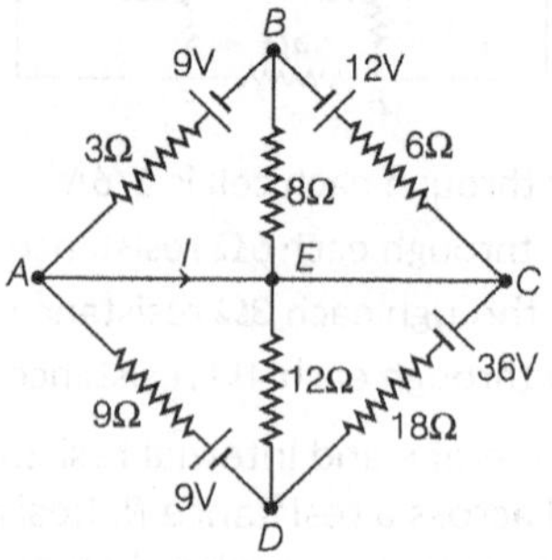

8 The magnitude of current through 8 Ω resistor connected between points B and E is equal to

(a) 0.25 A (b) 0.5 A (c) 1 A (d) 2 A

9 The magnitude of current I through conducting wire connected between A and E is equal to

(a) $\frac{1}{3}$A (b) $\frac{4}{3}$A (c) 1 A (d) zero

10 Let potential at points B and D be V_B and V_D, respectively. Then, $V_B - V_D$ is equal to

(a) 4V (b) −4 V (c) 20 V (d) −20 V

Comprehension-4

The given figure shows a network of resistances and a battery.

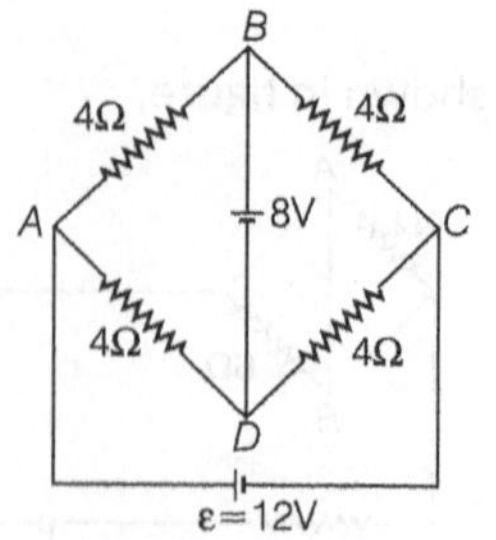

11 Identify the correct statement.

(a) The circuit satisfies the condition of a balanced Wheatstone bridge
(b) $V_B - V_D = 0$
(c) $V_B - V_D = 8$
(d) No current flows in the branch BD

12 Which of the two batteries is getting charged?

(a) 8 V battery (b) 12V battery
(c) None of these (d) Cannot be said

13 Choose the correct statement(s).

(a) The current coming out of the 8 V battery is 2A.
(b) The current coming out of the 12 V battery is 3A.
(c) The current flowing in all the 4Ω branches is same.
(d) The current flowing in the diagonally opposite branches is same.

Comprehension-5

In the circuit shown,

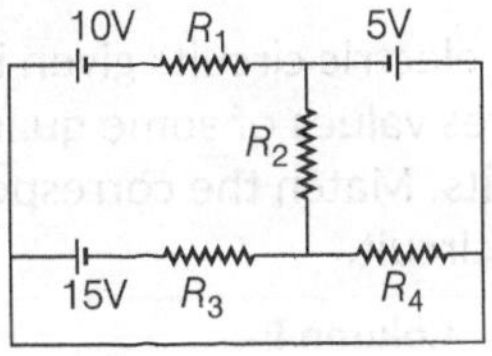

14 Current through R_2 is zero, if $R_4 = 2\ \Omega$ and $R_3 = 4\ \Omega$. In this case,

(a) current through R_3 is 2.5 A
(b) current through R_4 is 3A
(c) Both (a) and (b)
(d) None of the above

15 For what ratio $\frac{R_2}{R_4}$, current through R_3 will be zero?

(a) 1 : 1 (b) 1 : 2 (c) 1 : 3 (d) Not possible

Comprehension-6

In the circuit given below, both batteries are ideal. emf ε_1 of battery 1 has a fixed value, but emf ε_2 of battery 2 can be varied between 1.0 V and 10.0 V. The graph gives the currents through the two batteries as a function of ε_2, but are not marked as which plot corresponds to which battery. But for both plots, current is assumed to be negative when the direction of the current through the battery is opposite the direction of that battery's emf. (Direction of emf is from negative to positive)

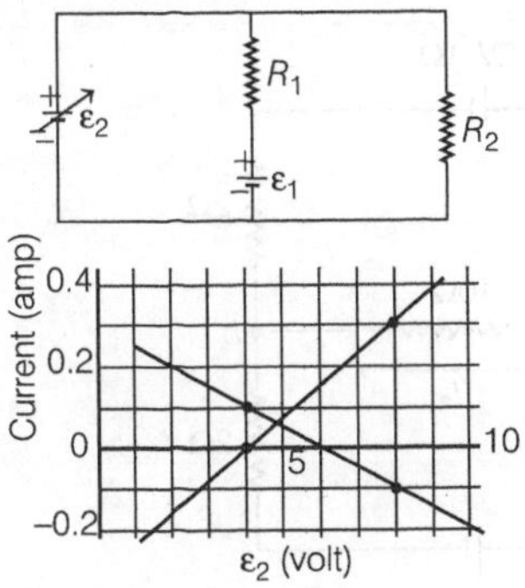

16 The value of emf ε_1 is

(a) 8 V (b) 6 V
(c) 4 V (d) 2 V

17 The resistance R_1 has value

(a) 10Ω (b) 20 Ω
(c) 30 Ω (d) 40 Ω

18 The resistance R_2 is equal to

(a) 10Ω (b) 20 Ω
(c) 30 Ω (d) 40 Ω

Match the Columns Questions

1 Column I gives physical quantities based on a situation in which an ideal cell of emf V is connected across a cylindrical rod of uniform cross-section area and conductivity (σ) as shown in figure. E, J, ϕ and i are electric field at, current density through, electric flux through and current through shaded cross-section respectively as shown in figure. Physical quantities in Column II are related to those in Column I. Match the expression in Column I with the statements in Column II.

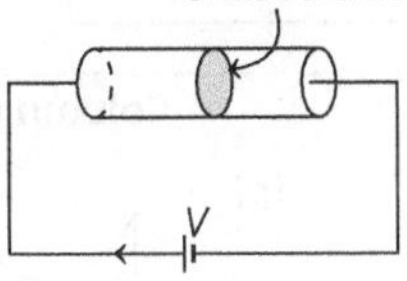

	Column I		Column II
(a)	$\frac{\phi}{i}$	(p)	Conductivity of rod
(b)	$\frac{E}{J}$	(q)	Resistance of rod
(c)	$\sigma\phi V$	(r)	Resistivity of rod
(d)	$\frac{V}{\sigma\phi}$	(s)	Power delivered to rod

2 Column I gives physical quantities of a situation in which a current i passes through two rods I and II of equal length that are joined in series. The ratio of free electron density (n), resistivity (ρ) and cross-section area (A) of both are in ratio $n_1 : n_2 = 2:1, \rho_1 : \rho_2 = 2:1$ and $A_1 : A_2 = 1:2$, respectively. Column II gives corresponding results. Match the ratios in Column I with the values in Column II.

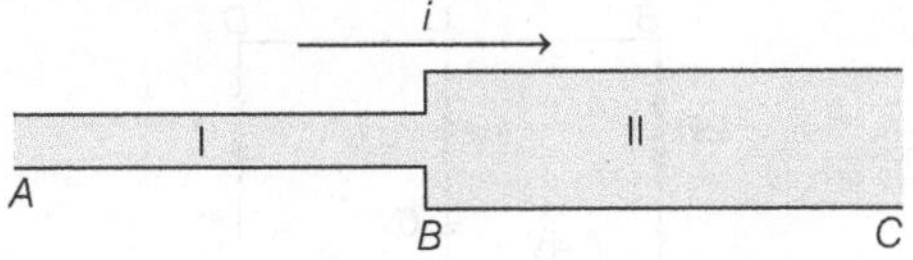

Column I	Column II
(a) $\dfrac{\text{Drift velocity of free electron in rod I}}{\text{Drift velocity of free electron in rod II}}$	(p) 0.5
(b) $\dfrac{\text{Electric field in rod I}}{\text{Electric field in rod II}}$	(q) 1
(c) $\dfrac{\text{Potential difference across rod I}}{\text{Potential difference across rod II}}$	(r) 2
(d) $\dfrac{\text{Average time taken by free electron to move from } A \text{ and } B}{\text{Average time taken by free electron to move from } B \text{ to } C}$	(s) 4

3 A resistor of varying cross-section is attached with a battery as shown. Variation of area from both ends are similar and areas are same at ends and maximum at centre. Match the approximate graphical representation of various physical properties in columns, where X-axis represents position from end A of resistor and Y-axis various physical properties.

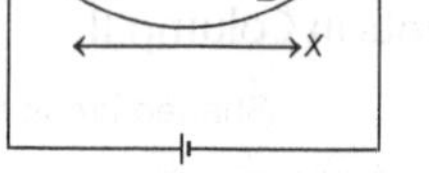

Column I	Column II
(a) *i* (current)	(p) 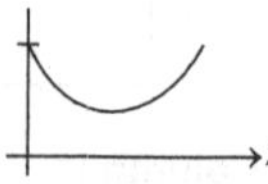
(b) *J* (current density)	(q) 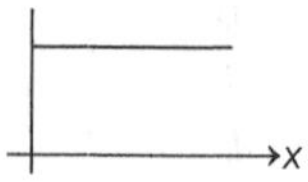
(c) *E* (electric field)	(r) 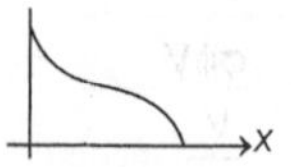
(d) V_d (potential)	(s) 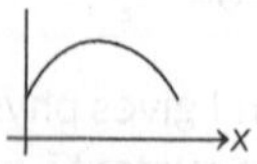
	(t) 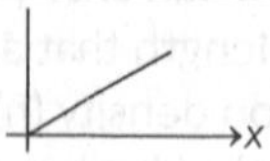

4 A circuit is shown in figure *R* is a non-zero variable with finite resistance. ε is some unknown emf with polarities are shown, then

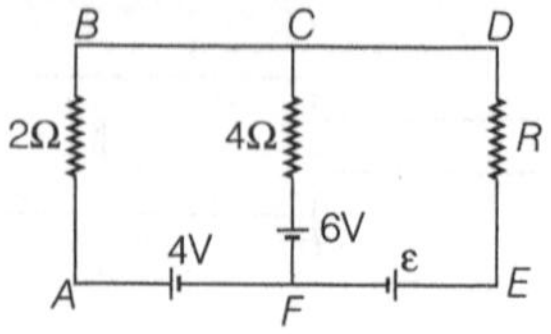

Column I	Column II
(a) Current passing through 4 Ω resistance can be zero	(p) possible, if ε = 6 V
(b) Current passing through 4 Ω resistance can be from *F* to *C* direction	(q) possible, if ε > 6 V
(c) Current passing through 4 Ω resistance can be from *C* to *F* direction	(r) possible, if ε < 6 V
(d) Current passing through 2 Ω resistance will be from *B* to *A* direction	(s) possible for any values of ε from zero to infinity

5 Consider the electric circuits given in Column I and Column II gives values of some quantities from electric circuits. Match the corresponding quantities with correct circuit.

Column I	Column II
(a) 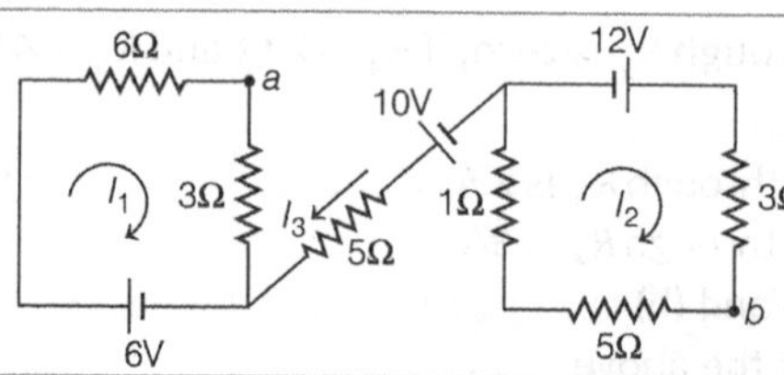	(p) $I_1 = \dfrac{1}{55}$ A
(b) 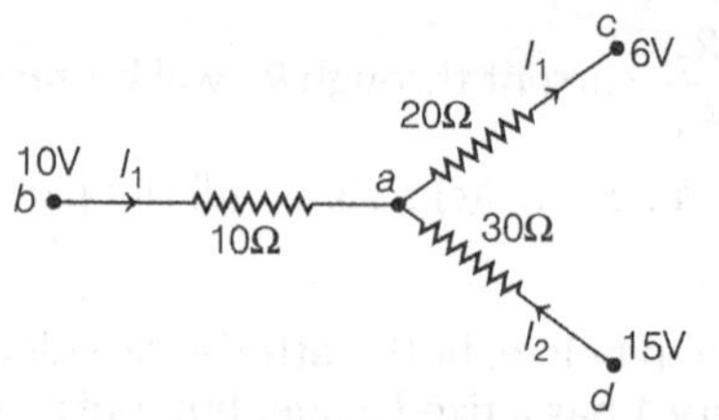	(q) $I_2 = \dfrac{-1}{121}$ A
(c) 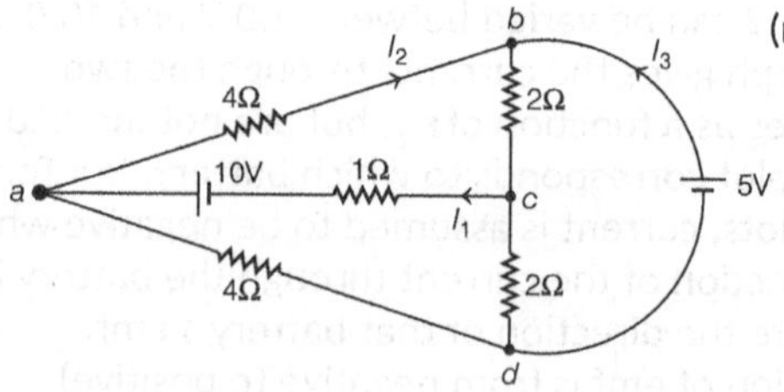	(r) $I_3 = \dfrac{15}{8}$ A
(d) 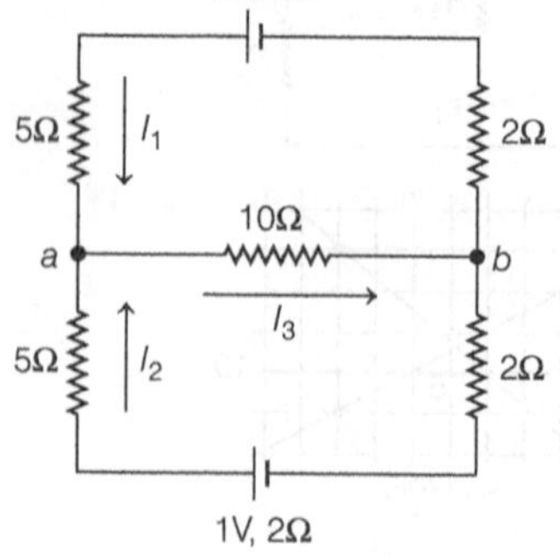	(s) $V_a - V_b = 4$V

6 In the network shown in figure, each resistance is R.

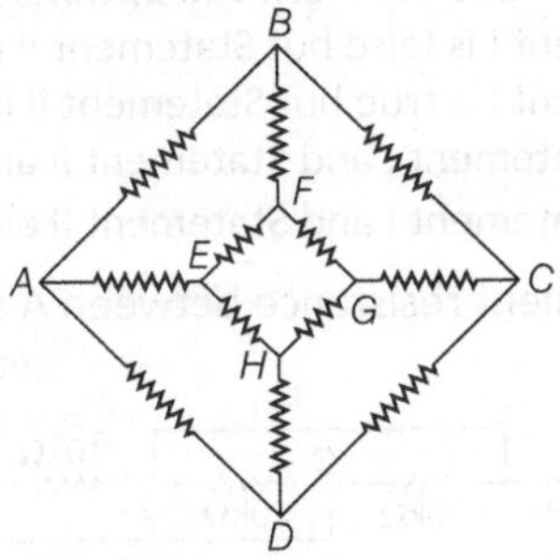

Column I		Column II	
(a)	Equivalent resistance between points A and E	(p)	$7R/12$
(b)	Equivalent resistance between points A and G	(q)	$5R/6$
(c)	Equivalent resistance between points A and C	(r)	$3R/4$
		(s)	$7R/8$

Numerical Value Questions

1 Each element in the finite chain of resistors shown in the figure is 1Ω. A current of 1 A flows through the final element. The potential difference V across the input terminals of the chain is N volt. Find N.

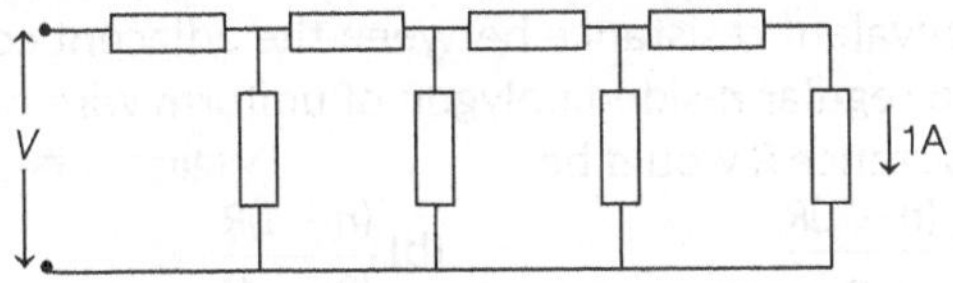

2 In the circuit diagram shown, find the current (in A) through the $1\ \Omega$ resistor.

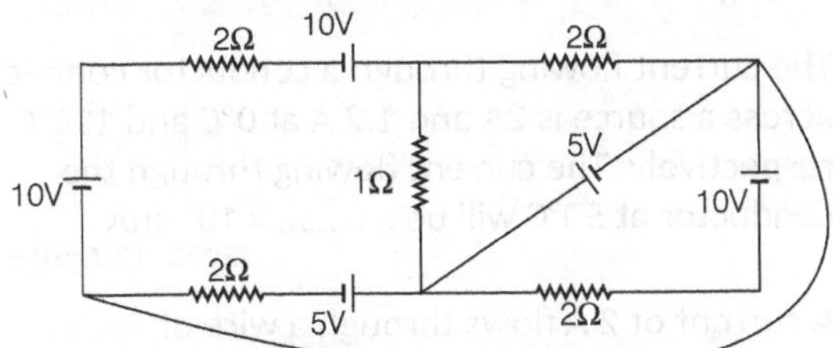

3 If the potential difference $V_A - V_B$ for the given circuit is $x/9$ V, then find x. All the cells are ideal and emf of each cell is 1 V.

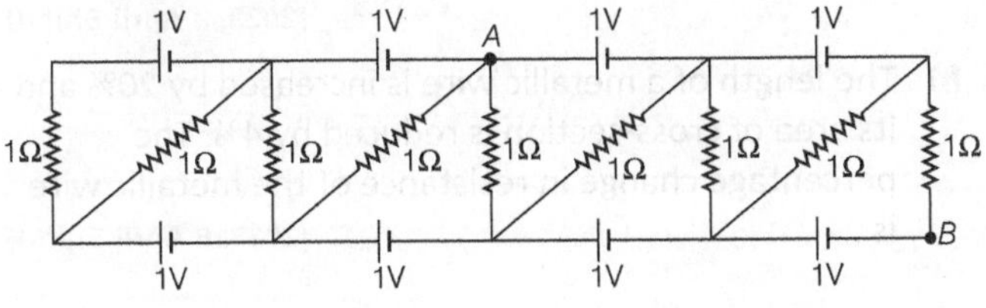

4 Figure shows a cell in which unit positive charge experience a constant non-electric force of 10N and a constant electric force of 8N in directions shown in the figure. Find the internal resistance (in ohm) of the cell.

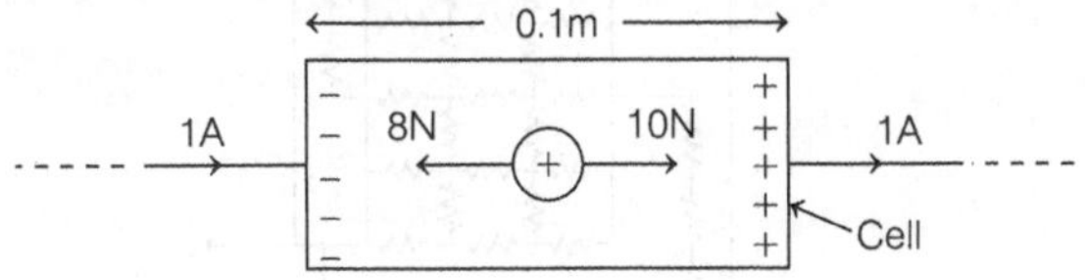

5 Find the current (in A) in the resistance R. Each resistance is of 2Ω.

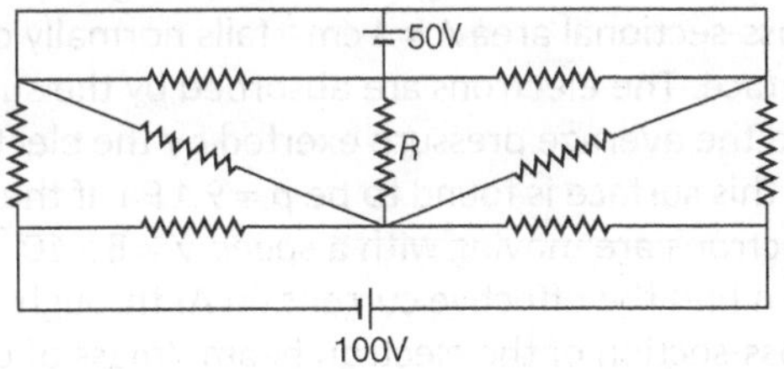

6 Consider an infinite mesh as shown in figure, where each side of the mesh has resistance $R = 24\Omega$. Consider hexagonal part $ABCDEF$ of infinite mesh and find equivalent resistance between A and B points of hexagon.

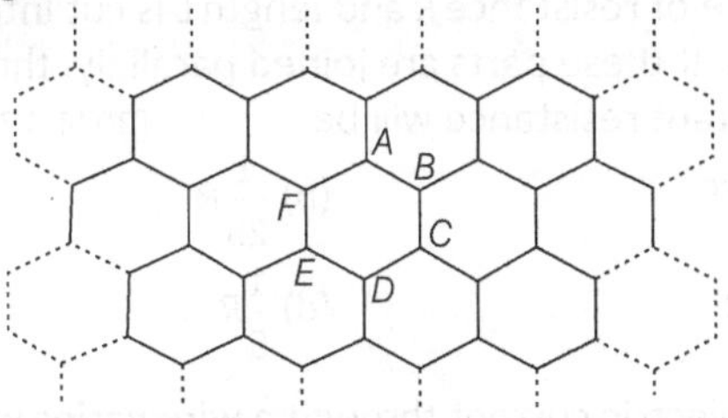

7 $ABCD$ is a square frame of conductor of electrical resistivity ρ. The frame lies in a vertical plane. PQ is an imaginary boundary separating space into two parts. Left of PQ, a uniform gravitational field g exists (figure), whereas no gravitational field is present right of PQ. Magnitude of charge on an electron is e and mass of electron is m. The electrical potential difference between A and B will be $\frac{kmgh}{4e}$. Find k.

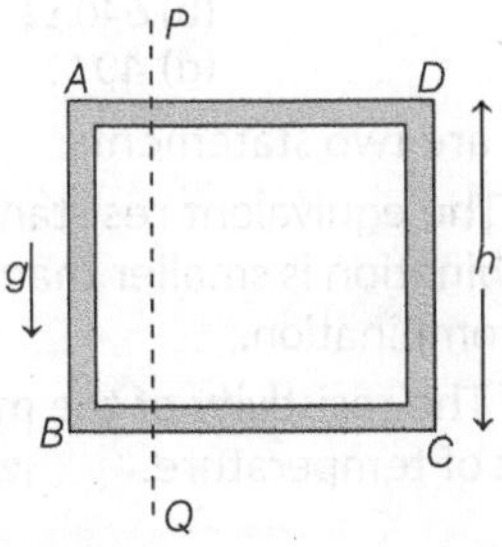

8 32 resistors are connected in a circuit as shown in the figure. The resistance of each resistor is 8Ω. Find equivalent resistance (in Ω) across AB.

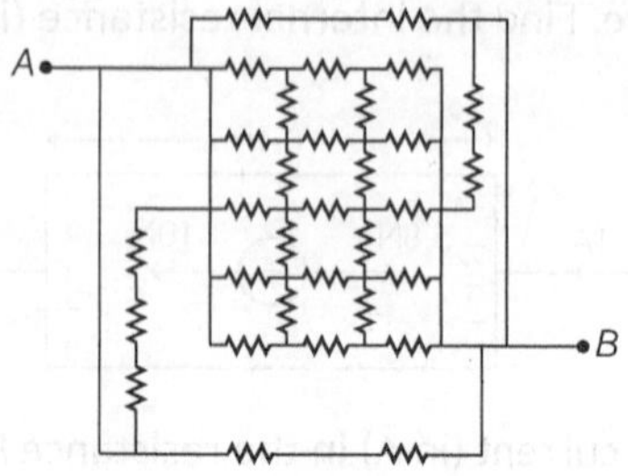

9 A beam of fast moving electrons having cross-sectional area $A = 1\text{ cm}^2$ falls normally on a flat surface. The electrons are absorbed by the surface and the average pressure exerted by the electrons on this surface is found to be $p = 9.1$ Pa. If the electrons are moving with a speed $v = 8\times10^7$ m/s, then find the effective current (in A) through any cross-section of the electron beam. (mass of electron $= 9.1\times10^{-31}$ kg)

Previous Year's Questions

JEE Main

1 A wire of resistance R and length L is cut into 5 equal parts. If these parts are joined parallely, then resultant resistance will be **[2024, 27 Jan Shift-I]**

(a) $25R$ (b) $\frac{1}{25}R$
(c) $5R$ (d) $\frac{1}{5}R$

2 The electric current through a wire varies with time as $I = I_0 + \beta t$, where $I_0 = 20$ A and $\beta = 3$ A/s. The amount of electric charge crossed through a section of the wire in 20 s is **[2024, 29 Jan Shift-I]**

(a) 1600 C (b) 800 C
(c) 80 C (d) 1000 C

3 A wire of resistance 160 Ω is melted and drawn into a wire one-fourth of its length. The new resistance of the wire will be **[2023, 12 April Shift-I]**

(a) 16 Ω (b) 640 Ω
(c) 10 Ω (d) 40 Ω

4 Given below are two statements.

Statement I The equivalent resistance of resistors in a series combination is smaller than least resistance used in the combination.

Statement II The resistivity of the material is independent of temperature. **[2023, 15 April Shift-I]**

In the light of above statements, choose the most appropriate answer from the options given below.

(a) Statement I is false but Statement II is true
(b) Statement I is true but Statement II is false
(c) Both Statement I and Statement II are true
(d) Both Statement I and Statement II are false

5 The equivalent resistance between A and B as shown in figure is **[2023, 8 April Shift-II]**

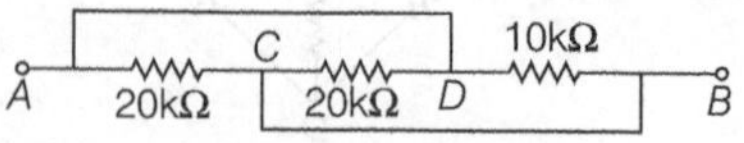

(a) 30 kΩ (b) 20 kΩ (c) 10 kΩ (d) 5 kΩ

6 The drift velocity of electrons for a conductor connected in an electrical circuit is v_d. The conductor is now replaced by another conductor with same material and same length but double the area of cross-section. The applied voltage remains same. The new drift velocity of electrons will be **[2023, 31 Jan Shift-I]**

(a) v_d (b) $v_d/2$
(c) $v_d/4$ (d) $2v_d$

7 The resistance of a wire is 5 Ω. Its new resistance in ohm if stretched to 5 times of its original length will be **[2023, 25 Jan Shift-II]**

(a) 5 (b) 25
(c) 125 (d) 625

8 Equivalent resistance between the adjacent corners of a regular n-sided polygon of uniform wire of resistance R would be **[2023, 1 Feb Shift-II]**

(a) $\frac{(n-1)R}{n}$ (b) $\frac{(n-1)R}{(2n-1)}$
(c) $\frac{(n-1)R}{n^2}$ (d) $\frac{n^2R}{n-1}$

9 The current flowing through a conductor connected across a source is 2A and 1.2 A at 0°C and 100°C respectively. The current flowing through the conductor at 50°C will be .... $\times 10^2$ mA. **[2023, 12 April Shift-I]**

10 A current of 2 A flows through a wire of cross-sectional area 25.0 mm^2. The number of free electrons in a cubic meter are 2.0×10^{28}. The drift velocity of the electrons is .... $\times 10^{-6}$ ms^{-1} (given, charge on electron $= 1.6\times10^{-19}$ C). **[2023, 8 April Shift-I]**

11 The length of a metallic wire is increased by 20% and its area of cross-section is reduced by 4%. The percentage change in resistance of the metallic wire is .... **[2023, 6 April Shift-I]**

12 A rectangular parallelopiped is measured as 1 cm $\times$ 1 cm $\times$ 100 cm. If its specific resistance is 3×10^{-7} Ω-m, then the resistance between its two opposite rectangular faces will be .... $\times 10^{-7}$ Ω. **[2023, 10 April Shift-II]**

13 If a copper wire is stretched to increase its length by 20%. The percentage increase in resistance of the wire is .... %. **[2023, 24 Jan Shift-II]**

14 A hollow cylindrical conductor has length of 3.14 m, while its inner and outer diameters are 4 mm and 8 mm, respectively. The resistance of the conductor is $n \times 10^{-3}$ Ω.
If the resistivity of the material is 2.4×10^{-8} Ω-m. The value of n is .... **[2023, 24 Jan Shift-I]**

15 Figure shows a part of an electric circuit. The potentials at points a, b and c are 30 V, 12 V and 2 V respectively. The current through the 20 Ω resistor will be **[2023, 6 April Shift-II]**

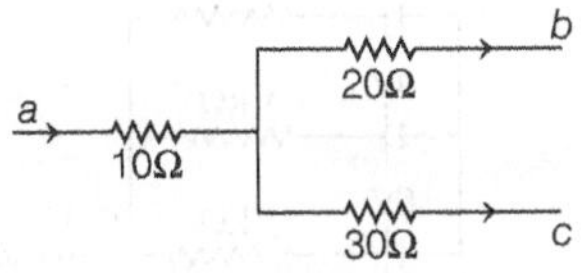

(a) 1.0 A (b) 0.4 A
(c) 0.2 A (d) 0.6 A

16 In the circuit diagram shown in figure given below, the current flowing through resistance 3Ω is $x/3$ A.
The value of x is .... **[2023, 11 April Shift-I]**

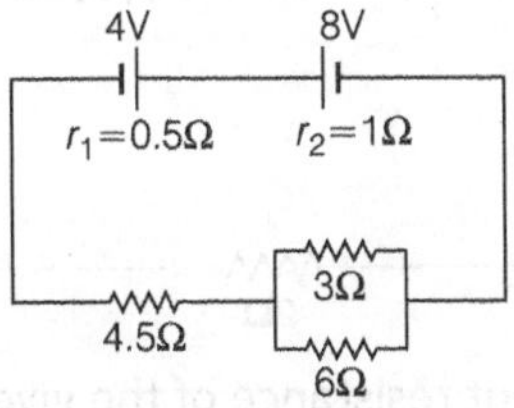

17 In the given circuit, the value of $\left|\dfrac{I_1 + I_3}{I_2}\right|$ is .... **[2023, 1 Feb Shift-II]**

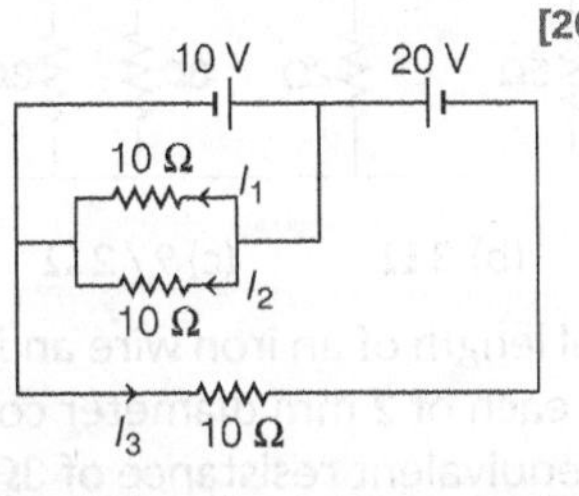

18 Two identical cells, when connected either in parallel or in series gives same current in an external resistance 5 Ω. The internal resistance of each cell will be .... Ω. **[2023, 31 Jan Shift-I]**

19 If the potential difference between B and D is zero, the value of x is $\dfrac{1}{n}$ Ω. The value of n is .... **[2023, 30 Jan Shift-II]**

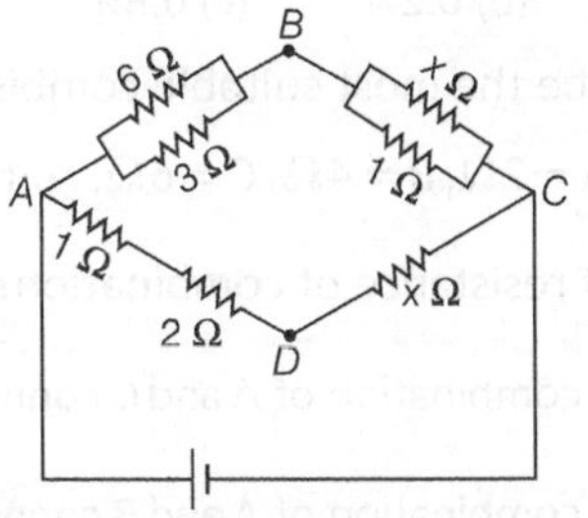

20 A 1 m long wire is broken into two unequal parts X and Y. The X part of the wire is stretched into another wire W. Length of W is twice the length of X and the resistance of W is twice that of Y. Find the ratio of length of X and Y. **2022, 29 July Shift-II]**

(a) 1 : 4 (b) 1 : 2 (c) 4 : 1 (d) 2 : 1

21 Resistance of the wire is measured as 2 Ω and 3 Ω at 10° C and 30° C respectively. Temperature coefficient of resistance of the material of the wire is **[2022, 28 June Shift-II]**

(a) 0.033 °C^{-1} (b) –0.033 °C^{-1}
(c) 0.011 °C^{-1} (d) 0.055 °C^{-1}

22 Two metallic wires of identical dimensions are connected in series. If σ_1 and σ_2 are the conductivities of these wires respectively, the effective conductivity of the combination is **[2022, 29 July Shift-I]**

(a) $\dfrac{\sigma_1 \sigma_2}{\sigma_1 + \sigma_2}$ (b) $\dfrac{2\sigma_1 \sigma_2}{\sigma_1 + \sigma_2}$ (c) $\dfrac{\sigma_1 + \sigma_2}{2\sigma_1 \sigma_2}$ (d) $\dfrac{\sigma_1 + \sigma_2}{\sigma_1 \sigma_2}$

23 A wire of resistance R_1 is drawn out so that its length is increased by twice of its original length. The ratio of new resistance to original resistance is **[2022, 28 July Shift-I]**

(a) 9 : 1 (b) 1 : 9 (c) 4 : 1 (d) 3 : 1

24 (A) The drift velocity of electrons decreases with the increase in the temperature of conductor.
(B) The drift velocity is inversely proportional to the area of cross-section of given conductor.
(C) The drift velocity does not depend on the applied potential difference to the conductor.
(D) The drift velocity of electron is inversely proportional to the length of the conductor.
(E) The drift velocity increases with the increase in the temperature of conductor.

Choose the correct answer from the options given below. **[2022, 27 July Shift-II]**

(a) (A) and (B) only (b) (A) and (D) only
(c) (B) and (E) only (d) (B) and (C) only

25 An aluminium wire is stretched to make its length, 0.4% larger. Then, percentage change in resistance is **[2022, 26 June Shift-I]**

(a) 0.4% (b) 0.2% (c) 0.8% (d) 0.6%

26 What will be the most suitable combination of three resistors $A = 2\Omega$, $B = 4\Omega$, $C = 6\Omega$, so that $\left(\frac{22}{3}\right)\Omega$ is equivalent resistance of combination? **[2022, June Shift-II]**

(a) Parallel combination of *A* and *C* connected in series with *B*.

(b) Parallel combination of *A* and *B* connected in series with *C*.

(c) Series combination of *A* and *C* connected in parallel with *B*.

(d) Series combination of *B* and *C* connected in series with *A*.

27 The current *I* flowing through the given circuit will be .... A. **[2022, 29 July Shift-I]**

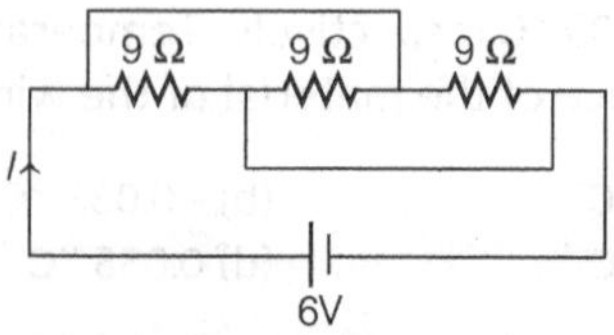

28 The length of a given cylindrical wire is increased to double of its original length. The percentage increase in the resistance of the wire will be ......% **[2022, 25 June Shift-II]**

29 All resistance in figure are 1 Ω each. The value of current *I* is $a/5$ A. The value of *a* is .... **[2022, 28 June Shift-II]**

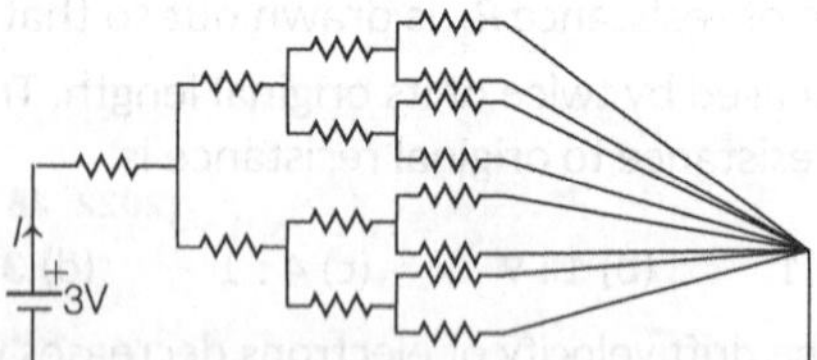

30 A 1 m long copper wire carries a current of 1 A. If the cross-section of the wire is 2.0 mm^2 and the resistivity of copper is 1.7×10^{-8} Ω-m, the force experienced by moving electron in the wire is ...... $\times 10^{-23}$ N. (Charge on electron $= 1.6 \times 10^{-19}$ C) **[2022, 27 July Shift-I]**

31 The combination of two identical cells, whether connected in series or parallel combination provides the same current through an external resistance of 2 Ω. The value of internal resistance of each cell is **[2022, 29 June Shift-II]**

(a) 2 Ω (b) 4 Ω (c) 6 Ω (d) 8 Ω

32 Two sources of equal emfs are connected in series. This combination is connected to an external resistance *R*. The internal resistances of the two sources are r_1 and r_2 ($r_1 > r_2$). If the potential difference across the source of internal resistance r_1 is zero, then the value of *R* will be **[2022, 27 July Shift-I]**

(a) $r_1 - r_2$ (b) $\frac{r_1 r_2}{r_1 + r_2}$ (c) $\frac{r_1 + r_2}{2}$ (d) $r_2 - r_1$

33 Two cells of same emf but different internal resistances r_1 and r_2 are connected in series with a resistance *R*. The value of resistance *R*, for which the potential difference across second cell is zero, is **[2022, 25 June Shift-II]**

(a) $r_2 - r_1$ (b) $r_1 - r_2$

(c) r_1 (d) r_2

34 In the given figure, the value of V_0 will be .... V. **[2022, 25 July Shift-I]**

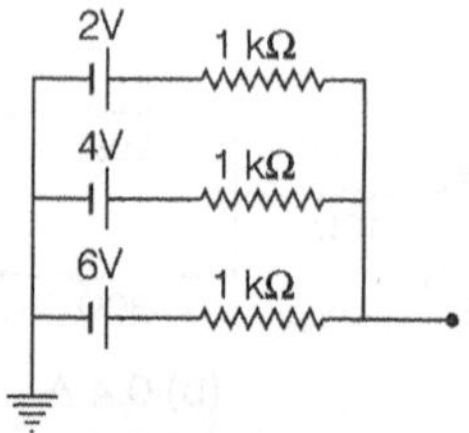

35 For the network shown below, the value of $V_B - V_A$ is _______ V. **[2022, 29 June Shift-I]**

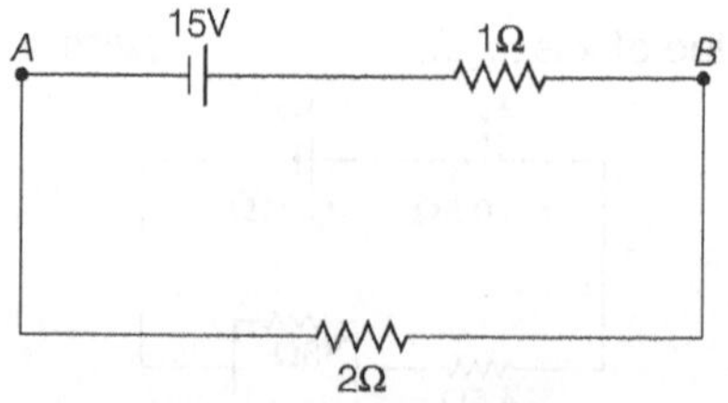

36 The equivalent resistance of the given circuit between the terminals *A* and *B* is **[2021, 31 Aug Shift-II]**

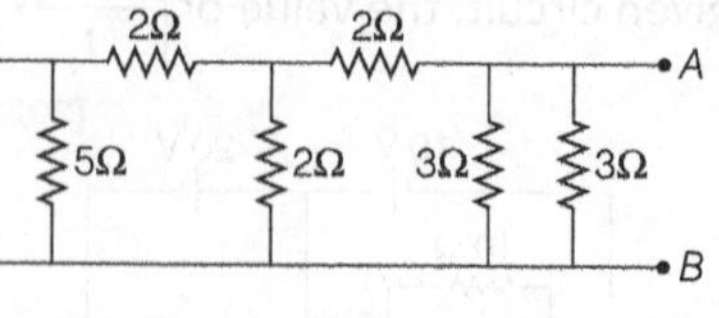

(a) 0 (b) 3 Ω (c) 9/2 Ω (d) 1 Ω

37 What equal length of an iron wire and a copper-nickel alloy wire, each of 2 mm diameter connected parallel to give an equivalent resistance of 3Ω?
(Given, resistivities of iron and copper-nickel alloy wire are 12 μΩ cm and 51 μΩ cm respectively) **[2021, 26 Aug Shift-I]**

(a) 82 m (b) 97 m (c) 110 m (d) 90 m

38 The resistance of a conductor at 15°C is 16 Ω and at 100°C is 20 Ω. What will be the temperature coefficient of resistance of the conductor? **[2021, 27 July Shift-II]**

(a) $0.010°C^{-1}$ (b) $0.033°C^{-1}$
(c) $0.003°C^{-1}$ (d) $0.042°C^{-1}$

39 A current of 5 A is passing through a non-linear magnesium wire of cross-section 0.04 m^2. At every point, the direction of current density is at an angle of 60° with the unit vector of area of cross-section. The magnitude of electric field at every point of the conductor is
(Take, resistivity of magnesium, $\rho = 44 \times 10^{-8}$ Ω-m) **[2021, 20 July Shift-I]**

(a) 11×10^{-2} V/m (b) 11×10^{-7} V/m
(c) 11×10^{-5} V/m (d) 11×10^{-3} V/m

40 A current of 10 A exists in a wire of cross sectional area of 5 mm^2 with a drift velocity of 2×10^{-3} ms^{-1}. The number of free electrons in each cubic metre of the wire is **[2021, 17 March Shift-I]**

(a) 2×10^6 (b) 625×10^{25}
(c) 2×10^{25} (d) 1×10^{23}

41 A conducting wire of length l, area of cross-section A and electric resistivity ρ is connected between the terminals of a battery. A potential difference V is developed between its ends, causing an electric current. If the length of the wire of the same material is doubled and the area of cross-section is halved, the resultant current would be **[2021, 16 March Shift-I]**

(a) $\frac{1}{4}\frac{VA}{\rho l}$ (b) $\frac{3}{4}\frac{VA}{\rho l}$ (c) $\frac{1}{4}\frac{\rho l}{VA}$ (d) $4\frac{VA}{\rho l}$

42 A current through a wire depends on time as $i = \alpha_0 t + \beta t^2$, where $\alpha_0 = 20$ A/s and $\beta = 8$ As^{-2}. Find the charge crossed through a section of the wire in 15 s. **[2021, 24 Feb Shift-I]**

(a) 260 C (b) 2100 C (c) 11250 C (d) 2250 C

43 Five equal resistances are connected in a network as shown in figure. The net resistance between the points A and B is **[2021, 26 Feb Shift-I]**

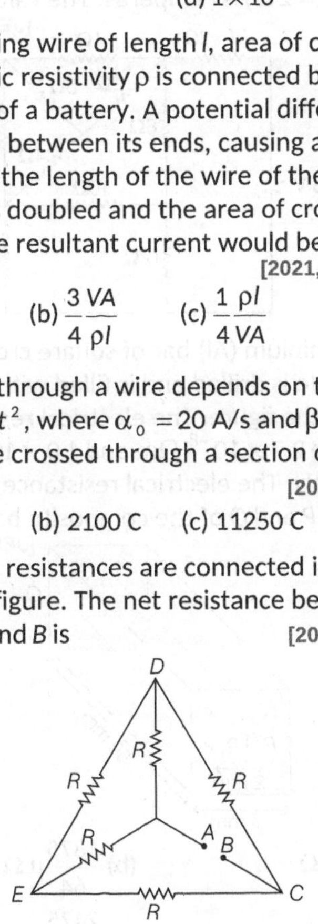

(a) R (b) $2R$ (c) $R/2$ (d) $3R/2$

44 A wire of 1 Ω has a length of 1 m. It is stretched till its length increases by 25 %. The percentage change in resistance to the nearest integer is **[2021, 26 Feb Shift-II]**

(a) 56% (b) 76% (c) 12.5% (d) 25%

45 In the given figure, switches S_1 and S_2 are in open condition. The resistance across ab when the switches S_1 and S_2 are closed is ...... Ω. **[2021, 20 July Shift-II]**

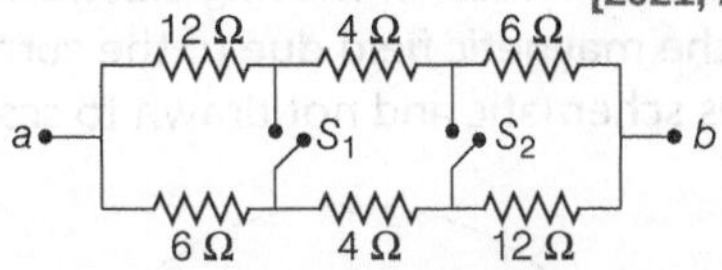

46 In the figure given, the electric current flowing through the 5 kΩ resistor is x mA. **[2021, 16 March Shift-I]**

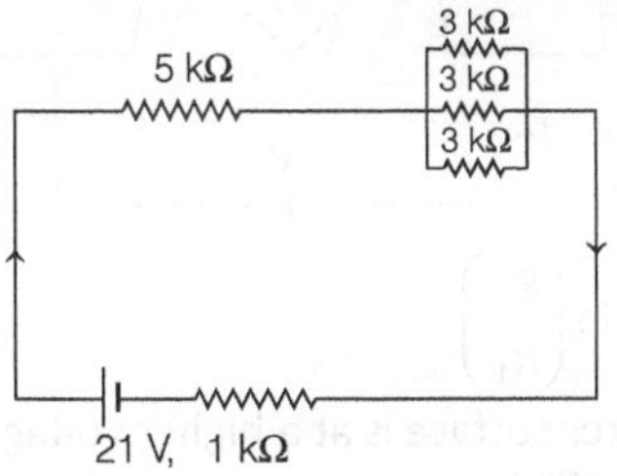

The value of x to the nearest Integer is ....

47 Two wires of same length and thickness having specific resistances 6 Ω- cm and 3 Ω-cm respectively are connected in parallel. The effective resistivity is ρ Ω-cm. The value of ρ to the nearest integer, is .... **[2021, 18 March Shift-II]**

48 A cylindrical wire of radius 0.5 mm and conductivity 5×10^7 S/m is subjected to an electric field of 10 mV/m. The expected value of current in the wire will be $x^3 \pi$ mA. The value of x is .... **[2021, 24 Feb Shift-II]**

49 A cell E_1 of emf 6 V and internal resistance 2 Ω is connected with another cell E_2 of emf 4 V and internal resistance 8 Ω (as shown in the figure). The potential difference across points X and Y is **[2021, 24 Feb Shift-I]**

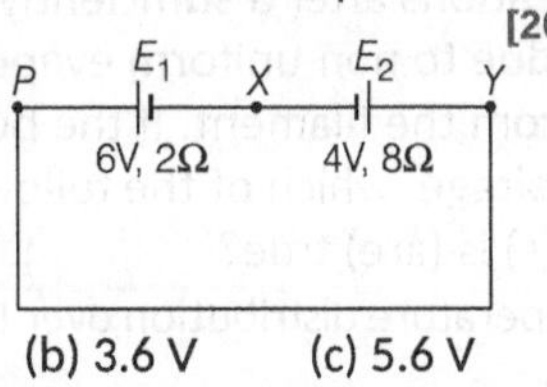

(a) 2.0 V (b) 3.6 V (c) 5.6 V (d) 10.0 V

50 In an electrical circuit, a battery is connected to pass 20 C of charge through it in a certain given time. The potential difference between two plates of the battery is maintained at 15 V. The work done by the battery is .... J. **[2021, 26 Feb Shift-I]**

JEE Advanced

1 Shown in the figure is a semicircular metallic strip that has thickness t and resistivity ρ. Its inner radius is R_1 and outer radius is R_2. If a voltage V_0 is applied between its two ends, a current I flows in it. In addition, it is observed that a transverse voltage ΔV develops between its inner and outer surfaces due to purely kinetic effects of moving electrons (ignore any role of the magnetic field due to the current). Then (figure is schematic and not drawn to scale) **(2020 Adv.)**

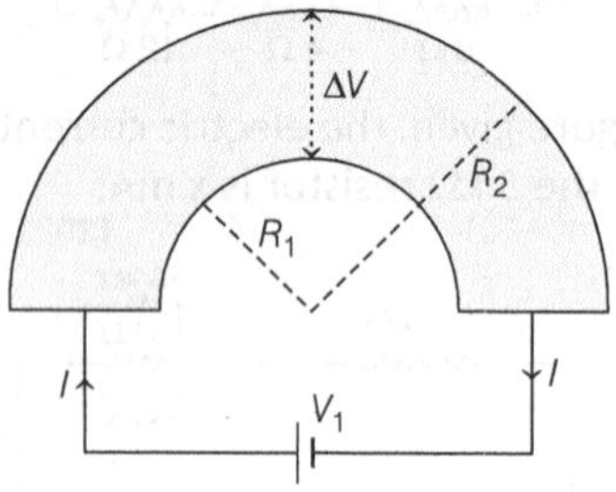

(a) $I = \dfrac{V_0 t}{\pi\rho} \ln\left(\dfrac{R_2}{R_1}\right)$

(b) the outer surface is at a higher voltage than the inner surface

(c) the outer surface is at a lower voltage than the inner surface

(d) $\Delta V \propto I^2$

2 Two batteries with emf 12 V and 13 V are connected in parallel across a load resistor of 10 Ω. The internal resistances of the two batteries are 1 Ω and 2 Ω, respectively. The voltage across the load lies between **[JEE Advanced 2016]**

(a) 11.7 V and 11.8 V (b) 11.6 V and 11.7 V

(c) 11.5 V and 11.6 V (d) 11.4 V and 11.5 V

3 An incandescent bulb has a thin filament of tungsten that is heated to high temperature by passing an electric current. The hot filament emits black-body radiation. The filament is observed to break up at random locations after a sufficiently long time of operation due to non-uniform evaporation of tungsten from the filament. If the bulb is powered at constant voltage, which of the following statement(s) is (are) true? **[JEE Advanced 2016]**

(a) The temperature distribution over the filament is uniform.

(b) The resistance over small sections of the filament decreases with time.

(c) The filament emits more light at higher band of frequencies before it breaks up.

(d) The filament consumes less electrical power towards the end of the life of the bulb.

4 An infinite line charge of uniform electric charge density λ lies along the axis of an electrically conducting infinite cylindrical shell of radius R. At time $t=0$, the space inside the cylinder is filled with a material of permittivity ε and electrical conductivity σ. The electrical conduction in the material follows Ohm's law. Which one of the following graphs best describes the subsequent variation of the magnitude of current density $j(t)$ at any point in the material? **[JEE Advanced 2016]**

(a)

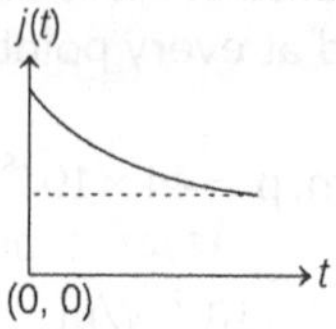

(b)

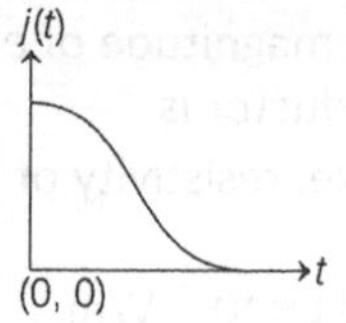

(c)

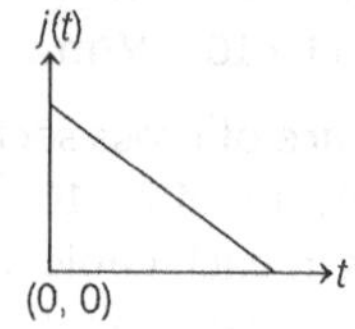

(d)

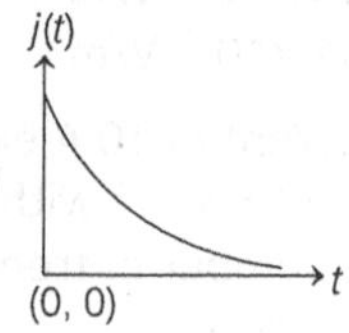

5 In the following circuit, the current through the resistor $R(=2\,\Omega)$ is I amperes. The value of I is **[JEE Advanced 2015]**

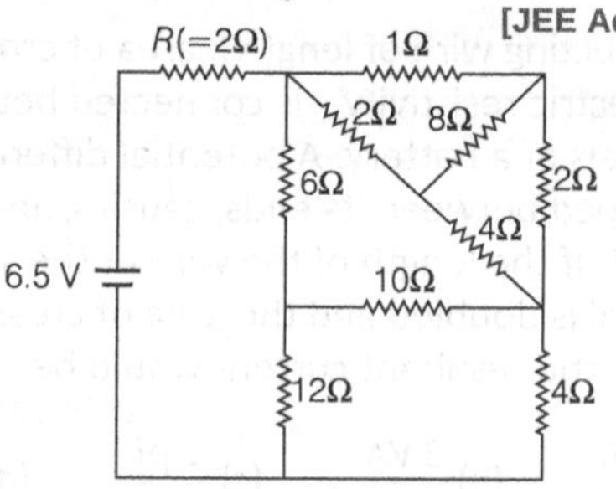

6 In an aluminium (Al) bar of square cross section, a square hole is drilled and is filled with iron (Fe) as shown in the figure. The electrical resistivities of Al and Fe are $2.7 \times 10^{-8}\,\Omega$m and $1.0 \times 10^{-7}\,\Omega$m, respectively. The electrical resistance between the two faces P and Q of the composite bar is **[JEE Advanced 2015]**

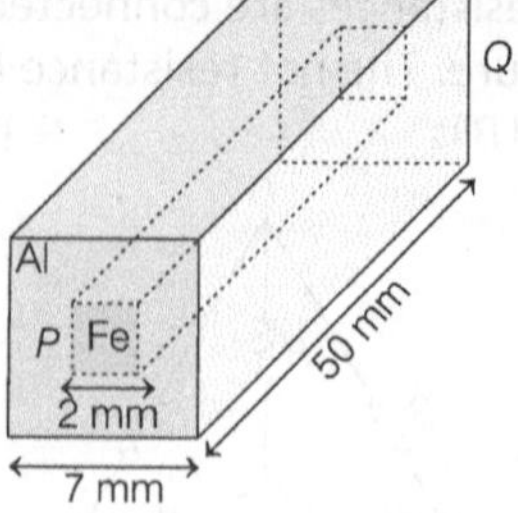

(a) $\dfrac{2475}{64}\,\mu\Omega$ (b) $\dfrac{1875}{64}\,\mu\Omega$

(c) $\dfrac{1875}{49}\,\mu\Omega$ (d) $\dfrac{2475}{132}\,\mu\Omega$

7 For the resistance network shown in the figure, choose the correct option(s). **[JEE Advanced 2012]**

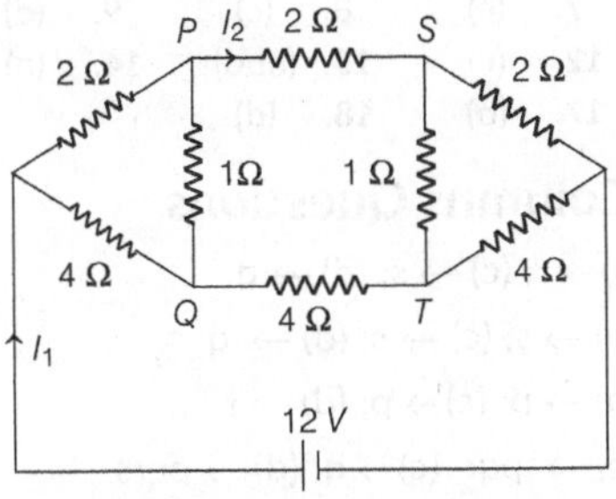

(a) The current through *PQ* is zero

(b) $I_1 = 3\,A$

(c) The potential at *S* is less than that at *Q*

(d) $I_2 = 2\,A$

8 Two batteries of different emfs and different internal resistances are connected as shown. The voltage across *AB* in volt is **[JEE Advanced 2011]**

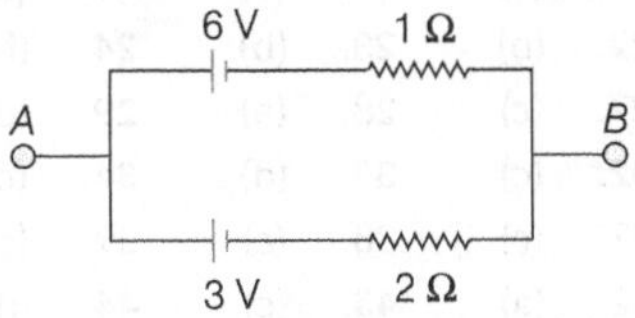

Answer Key

Level 1 Starter level

6.1 Electric Current, Current Density and Drift Velocity

1. (i) 8A (ii) 18 A 2. 300 C, 30 A 3. 40 C

4. $1.25 \times 10^{-3}\ ms^{-1}$ 5. 1.5 *nevA* 6. $\frac{J_0 \pi R^2}{3}$

7. 8.5×10^{-2} V/m

6.2 Resistance

1. 200 m 2. 4*R* 3. 81*R*

4. (i) 21% (ii) 0.6%

5. $R_{AB} = \frac{\rho c}{ab}, R_{CD} = \frac{\rho b}{ac}, R_{EF} = \frac{\rho a}{bc}$ 6. 187°C

7. $2 \times 10^{-7}\ m^2/V\text{-}s$ 8. $(17 \times 10^4 \pm 5\%)\ \Omega$

6.3 Kirchhoff's Laws

1. (i) 48 V (ii) 7V

2. (i) 1A (ii) 3A (iii) 12 A

3. (i) $i_{10\Omega} = 3A, i_{20\Omega} = 2A, i_{30\Omega} = 1A$

(ii) $i_{1\Omega} = 10A, i_{2\Omega} = 5A, i_{3\Omega} = 30A, i_{4\Omega} = 35A$

(iii) $i_{1\Omega} = 20A, i_{2\Omega} = 5A, i_{3\Omega} = 15A$

4. (i) 2.5 A (ii) $i_{4\Omega} = 2A, i_{5\Omega} = 0, i_{6\Omega} = 2A$

(iii) $i_{1\Omega} = 20A, i_{2\Omega} = 5A, i_{3\Omega} = 15A$

(iv) $i_{3\Omega} = 2A,\ i_{6\Omega} = 2A, i_{4\Omega} = 0$

(v) $i_{2\Omega} = 10A,\ i_{3\Omega} = 10/3A,\ i_{6\Omega} = 20/3A$

(vi) $i_{1\Omega} = 0,\ i_{2\Omega} = i_{3\Omega} = 2A,\ i_{4\Omega} = i_{5\Omega} = 3A$

6.4 Battery as Source and Load

1. (i) 4A (ii) 32 V (iii) 128 W 2. 29 Ω 3. 0.6 Ω

4. **Case I** (i) 6 A (ii) 28 V and 14 V

(iii) 168W (delivered) and 84W (delivered)

Case II (i) 2A (ii) 36 V and 22 V

(iii) 72 W (delivered) and 44 W (consumed)

6.5 Series and Parallel Combination Circuits

1. (i) 2A (ii) 8V (iii) 12 W

2. (i) 12 A and 4 A (ii) 24 V (iii) 144 W

3. 4 A 4. 8/3 A 5. 216 V 6. 1A

7. 5 V 8. 100 Ω 9. 12 A

6.6 Equivalent Resistance

1. (i) 32 Ω (ii) 6Ω (iii) 11*R*/18 (iv) 2 Ω (v) 16/3 Ω (vi) *R* (vii) 20/3 Ω (viii) 9/4Ω (ix) 226/39 Ω

2. (i) 3*R*/5 (ii) 3*R*/4 (iii) 4*r*/3 (iv) *R*/3 (v) 3*R*/5 (vi) 5Ω (vii) 1Ω (viii) 4/3 Ω (ix) 4*R*/11 (x) 2*R*/9 (xi) 22.5 Ω (xii) 28/3 Ω

6.7 Symmetric Circuits

1. (i) 2*R*/3 (ii) 3Ω (iii) 3*R*/4 (iv) 44*R*/21 (v) 4*R*/5 (vi) 8*R*/15 (vii) 3*R*/2 (viii) 1Ω (ix) 7Ω

2. (i) $\frac{5}{6}R$ (ii) $\frac{3}{4}R$ (iii) $\frac{7}{12}R$

3. (i) 2Ω (ii) 6*R* 4. (i) *R*/2 (ii) *R*/3

6.8 Combination of Cells

1. (i) 6A (ii) 27 V 2. $n = 10, r = 0.1\ \Omega$

3. (i) $\frac{\varepsilon}{2r}$ (ii) $\frac{\varepsilon}{2}$ and $\frac{3\varepsilon}{2}$ 4. 40 V 5. 4A

6. 2A 7. 1.2 A 8. $n = 2$ and $m = 12$

Level 2 JEE Main Level

Single Choice Correct Questions

1. (c)	2. (c)	3. (a)	4. (b)	5. (a)
6. (b)	7. (c)	8. (d)	9. (c)	10. (c)
11. (d)	12. (a)	13. (c)	14. (c)	15. (b)
16. (a)	17. (d)	18. (d)	19. (a)	20. (b)
21. (b)	22. (b)	23. (b)	24. (b)	25. (d)
26. (b)	27. (c)	28. (a)	29. (d)	30. (b)
31. (d)	32. (c)	33. (d)	34. (c)	35. (d)
36. (c)	37. (c)	38. (c)	39. (c)	40. (b)
41. (a)	42. (a)	43. (c)	44. (d)	45. (a)
46. (d)	47. (d)	48. (b)	49. (a)	50. (b)

Numercial Value Questions

1. (15)	2. (3.5)	3. (5)	4. (10)	5. (5)
6. (4)	7. (9)	8. (1.5)	9. (2.00)	10. (5)
11. (1)	12. (1.46)	13. (100)	14. (9)	15. (15)

Level 3 JEE Advanced Level

Single Choice Correct Questions

1. (c)	2. (a)	3. (b)	4. (c)	5. (b)
6. (d)	7. (a)	8. (b)	9. (a)	10. (a)
11. (a)	12. (b)	13. (c)	14. (b)	15. (b)
16. (c)	17. (c)	18. (a)	19. (a)	20. (a)
21. (b)	22. (c)	23. (b)	24. (d)	25. (d)
26. (c)	27. (a)	28. (d)	29. (a)	30. (d)
31. (a)	32. (c)	33. (a)	34. (d)	35. (c)
36. (b)	37. (b)	38. (b)	39. (c)	40. (a)
41. (b)	42. (d)	43. (a)		

Multiple Choice(s) Correct Questions

1. (bc)	2. (ad)	3. (bcd)	4. (bc)	5. (bc)
6. (abc)	7. (abcd)	8. (abcd)	9. (abcd)	10. (abc)
11. (bc)	12. (abc)	13. (ac)	14. (acd)	15. (abd)
16. (abd)	17. (abc)	18. (ac)		

Comprehension Based Questions

1. (a)	2. (a)	3. (a)	4. (a)	5. (b)
6. (d)	7. (c)	8. (c)	9. (d)	10. (a)
11. (c)	12. (c)	13. (abd)	14. (a)	15. (d)
16. (b)	17. (b)	18. (d)		

Match the Columns Questions

1. (a) → r; (b)→ r; (c) → s; (d) → q
2. (a) → q; (b) → s; (c) → s; (d) → q
3. (a) → q; (b) → p; (c)→ p; (d) → r
4. (a) → q; (b) → pqr; (c)→ q; (d) → pqrs
5. (a) → s; (b) → p; (c) → r ; (d) → q
6. (a) → p; (b) → q; (c) → r

Numerical Value Questions

1. (34)	2. (2.5)	3. (22)	4. (0.2)
5. (18.75)	6. (16)	7. (3)	8. (3)
9. (2)			

Previous Year's Questions

JEE Main

1 (b)	2 (d)	3 (c)	4 (d)	5 (d)
6 (a)	7 (c)	8 (c)	9 (15)	10 (25)
11 (25)	12 (3)	13 (44)	14 (2)	15 (b)
16 (1)	17 (2)	18 (5)	19 (2)	20 (b)
21 (a)	22 (b)	23 (c)	24 (a)	25 (c)
26 (b)	27 (2)	28 (300)	29 (8)	30 (136)
31 (a)	32 (a)	33 (a)	34 (4)	35 (10)
36 (d)	37 (b)	38 (c)	39 (c)	40 (b)
41 (a)	42 (c)	43 (a)	44 (a)	45 (10)
46 (3)	47 (2)	48 (5)	49 (c)	50 (300)

JEE Advanced

1 (acd)	2 (c)	3 (cd)	4 (a)	5 (1)
6 (b)	7 (abcd)	8 (5)		

SOLUTIONS

Level 1

6.1 Electric Current, Current Density and Drift Velocity

1. $q = 5t^2 - 2t + 3$

(i) $i_{avg} = \dfrac{\Delta q}{\Delta t} = \dfrac{q_2 - q_1}{t_2 - t_1} = \dfrac{19-3}{2-0} = 8A$

(ii) $i = \dfrac{dq}{dt} = 10t - 2$

At $t = 2$ s; $i = 10(2) - 2 = 18A$

2. $i = i_0 + \alpha t$

$$i = 10 + 4t$$

$$\Rightarrow \quad \int dq = \int_0^{10} (10 + 4t)\, dt$$

$$\Rightarrow \quad \Delta q = [10t + 2t^2]_0^{10}$$

$$\Rightarrow \quad \Delta q = 300 \text{ C}$$

Average current $= \dfrac{\Delta q}{\Delta t} = \dfrac{300}{10} = 30A$

3.

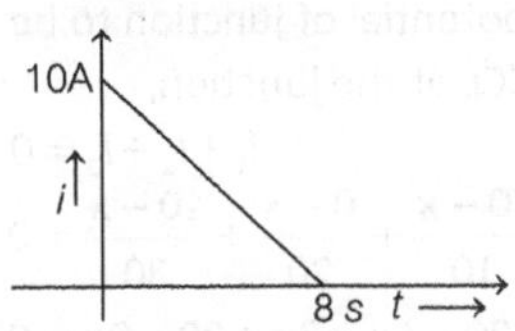

$q = \int i dt =$ Area under *i-t* curve

$= \dfrac{1}{2} \times 8 \times 10 = 40$ C

4. $i = nqAv_d$

$\Rightarrow \quad 20 = (10^{23} \times 10^6)(1.6 \times 10^{-19})(1 \times 10^{-6})v_d$

$\Rightarrow \quad v_d = 1.25 \times 10^{-3}$ m/s

5. $i = i_1 + i_2 = n_1 q_1 A_1 v_1 + n_2 q_2 A_2 v_2$

$$= n(-e)A(-v) + n(+2e)A\left(\frac{v}{4}\right) = \frac{3}{2} neAv = 1.5\, nevA$$

6. $i = \int JdA = \int_0^R J_0\left(1 - \dfrac{r}{R}\right) 2\pi r dr = 2\pi J_0\left[\dfrac{r^2}{2} - \dfrac{r^3}{3R}\right]_0^R = \dfrac{J_0 \pi R^2}{3}$

7. $J = \sigma E$

$$\Rightarrow \quad \frac{I}{A} = \left(\frac{1}{\rho}\right) E$$

$$\Rightarrow \quad E = \frac{\rho I}{A} = \frac{1.7 \times 10^{-8} \times 10}{2 \times 10^{-6}} = 8.5 \times 10^{-2} \text{ V/m}$$

6.2 Resistance

1.

$$R = \frac{\rho l}{A}$$

$$\Rightarrow \quad 340 = \frac{(1.7 \times 10^{-8}) l}{0.01 \times 10^{-6}} \quad \Rightarrow \quad l = 200 \text{ m}$$

2. Since, density is constant, $A_1 l_1 = A_2 l_2$

$$\Rightarrow \quad Al = A'(2l)$$

$$\Rightarrow \quad A' = \frac{A}{2}$$

$$R' = \frac{\rho(2l)}{(A/2)} = 4\frac{\rho l}{A} = 4R$$

3. Since, density is constant,

$$A_1 l_1 = A_2 l_2$$

$$\Rightarrow \quad \pi r_1^2 l_1 = \pi r_2^2 l_2$$

$$\Rightarrow \quad \pi r^2 l = \pi \left(\frac{r}{3}\right)^2 l'$$

$$\Rightarrow \quad l' = 9l$$

New resistance $= \dfrac{l\rho(9l)}{\pi\left(\dfrac{r}{3}\right)^2} = \dfrac{81\rho l}{\pi r^2} = 81R$

4. (i) Since, density is constant, $A_1 l_1 = A_2 l_2$

$$\Rightarrow \quad Al = A'(1.1l)$$

$$\Rightarrow \quad A' = \frac{A}{1.1}$$

R' = New resistance $= \dfrac{\rho(1.1l)}{(A/1.1)} = 1.21R$

% change is resistance $= \dfrac{R' - R}{R} \times 100$

$$= \left(\frac{1.21R - R}{R}\right) \times 100 = 21\%$$

(ii) $V = Al$

$$\Rightarrow \quad \frac{\Delta V}{V} = \frac{\Delta A}{A} + \frac{\Delta l}{l}$$

$$\Rightarrow \quad 0 = \frac{\Delta A}{A} + \frac{\Delta l}{l} \quad \Rightarrow \quad \frac{\Delta A}{A} = -\frac{\Delta l}{l}$$

$$R = \frac{\rho l}{A}$$

$$\frac{\Delta R}{R} = \frac{\Delta l}{l} - \frac{\Delta A}{A} = \frac{\Delta l}{l} - \left(-\frac{\Delta l}{l}\right) = 2\frac{\Delta l}{l}$$

% change in resistance

$$= \frac{\Delta R}{R} \times 100 = 2\left(\frac{\Delta l}{l} \times 100\right) = 2(0.3\%) = 0.6\%$$

5. $R = \dfrac{\rho l}{A}$

$$R_{AB} = \frac{\rho c}{ab} \Rightarrow R_{CD} = \frac{\rho b}{ac} \Rightarrow R_{EF} = \frac{\rho a}{bc}$$

6. $R' = R(1 + \alpha \Delta T)$

$$\Rightarrow \quad 60 = 50(1 + 1.25 \times 10^{-3}(T - 27))$$

$$\Rightarrow \quad T = 187° \text{ C}$$

7. Mobility $= \dfrac{\text{Drift velocity}}{\text{Electric field}}$

$$\mu = \frac{v_d}{V/l} = \frac{5\times10^{-6}}{\left(\frac{10}{0.4}\right)} = 2\times10^{-7}\ \text{m}^2/\text{V-s}$$

8. Brown = 1 (number)
Violet = 7 (number)
Yellow = 10^4 (multiplier)
Gold = 5% (tolerance)
$R = (17\times10^4 \pm 5\%)\,\Omega$

6.3 Kirchhoff's Laws

1. (i)

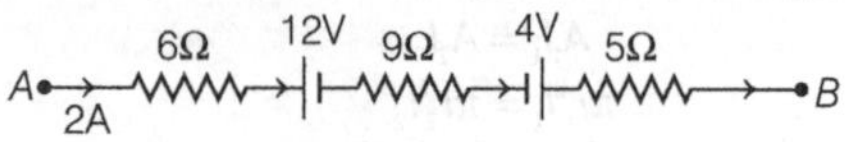

$$V_A - 2(6) - 12 - 2(9) + 4 - 2(5) = V_B$$

$\Rightarrow \quad V_A - V_B = 48$ V

(ii)

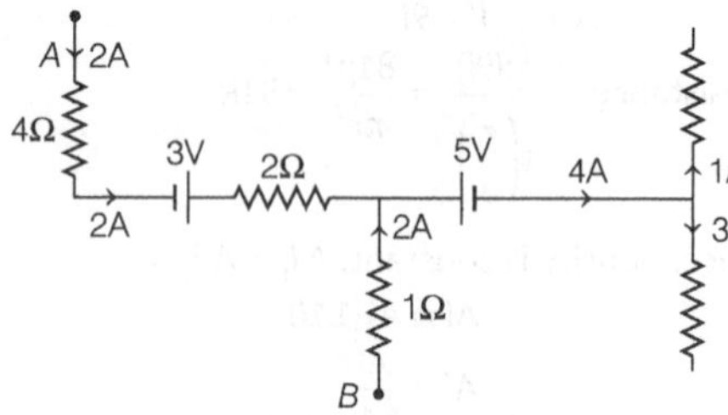

$$V_A - 2(4) + 3 - 2(2) + 2(1) = V_B$$

$\Rightarrow \quad V_A - V_B = 7$ V

2. (i)

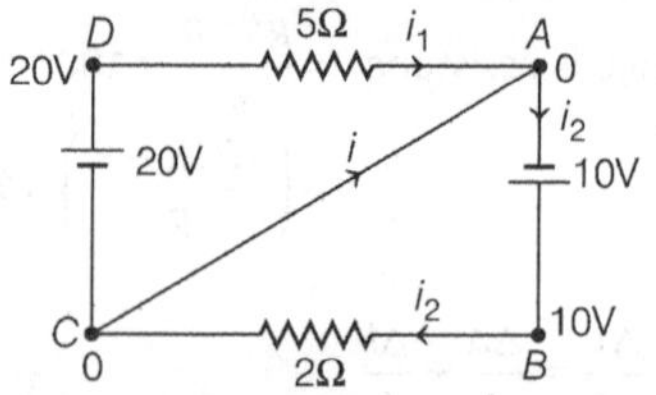

Lets take potential of point $A = 0$

$$i_1 = \frac{20-0}{5} = 4\text{A}$$

$$i_2 = \frac{10-0}{2} = 5\text{A}$$

Using KCL at junction A,

$$i_1 + i = i_2$$

$\Rightarrow \quad 4 + i = 5$

$\Rightarrow \quad i = 1$A

(ii) $V_A = 0$, $V_B = -2$V,

$V_D = 6$ V and $V_C = 2$V

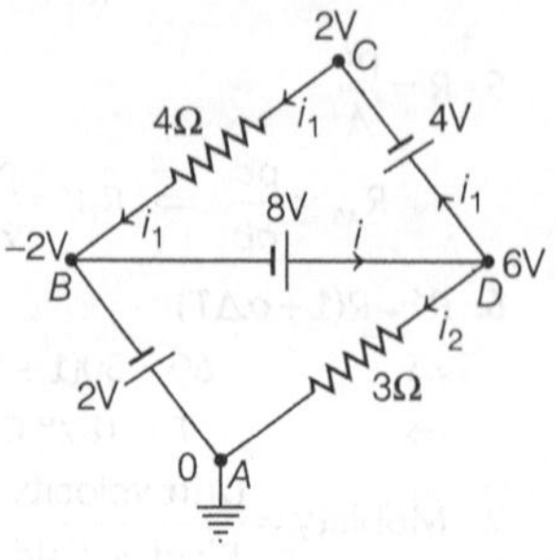

$$i_1 = \frac{2-(-2)}{4} = 1\text{A}$$

$$i_2 = \frac{6-0}{3} = 2\text{A}$$

Using KCL,

$$i = i_1 + i_2$$

$$= 1 + 2 = 3\text{A}$$

(iii)

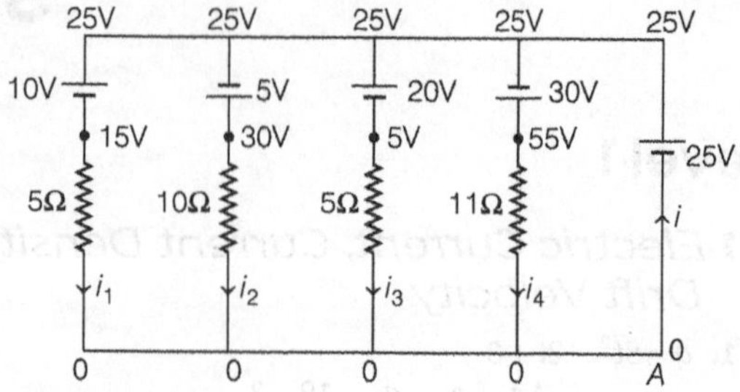

Lets take $V_A = 0$

$$i = i_1 + i_2 + i_3 + i_4$$

$$= \frac{15-0}{5} + \frac{30-0}{10} + \frac{5-0}{5} + \frac{55-0}{11}$$

$$= 3 + 3 + 1 + 5 = 12\text{A}$$

3. (i)

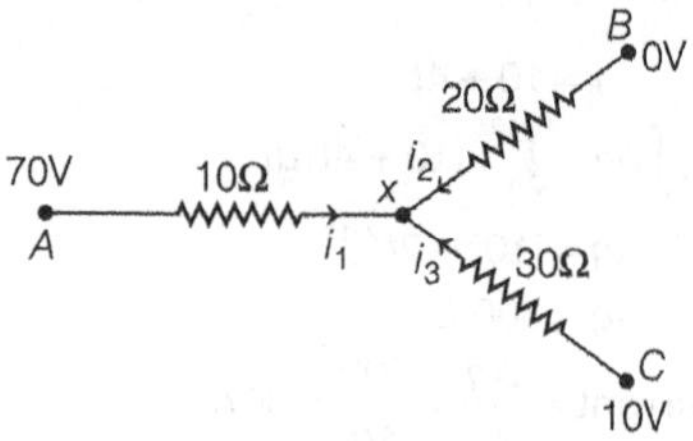

Lets take potential of junction to be x.
Applying KCL at the junction,

$$i_1 + i_2 + i_3 = 0$$

$$\frac{70-x}{10} + \frac{0-x}{20} + \frac{10-x}{30} = 0$$

$\Rightarrow \quad 420 - 6x - 3x + 20 - 2x = 0$

$\Rightarrow \quad 11x = 440 \Rightarrow x = 40$V

$$i_1 = \frac{70-40}{10} = 3\text{A}$$

$$i_2 = \frac{0-40}{20} = -2\text{A}$$

$$i_3 = \frac{10-40}{30} = -1\text{A}$$

(ii)

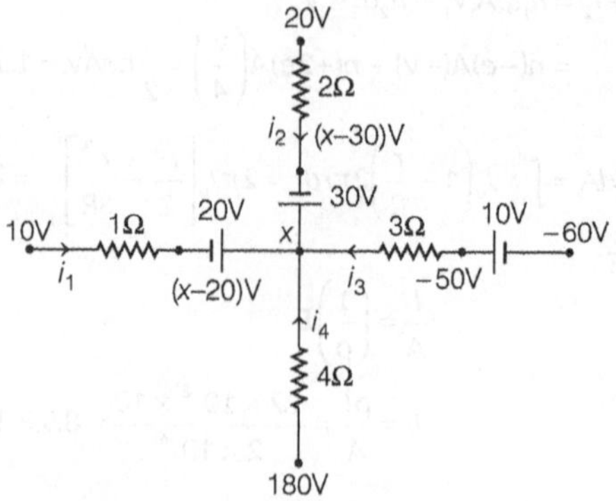

Lets take potential of the junction to be x.
Applying KCL at the junction,

$$i_1 + i_2 + i_3 + i_4 = 0$$

$$\Rightarrow \frac{10-(x-20)}{1} + \frac{20-(x-30)}{2} + \frac{-50-x}{3} + \frac{180-x}{4} = 0$$

$\Rightarrow 360 - 12x + 300 - 6x - 200 - 4x + 540 - 3x = 0$

$\Rightarrow \quad 25x = 1000$

$\Rightarrow \quad x = 40V$

$$i_1 = \frac{10-(40-20)}{1} = -10\text{ A}$$

$$i_2 = \frac{20-(40-30)}{2} = 5\text{A}$$

$$i_3 = \frac{-50-40}{3} = -30\text{A}$$

and $$i_4 = \frac{180-40}{4} = 35\text{A}$$

(iii)

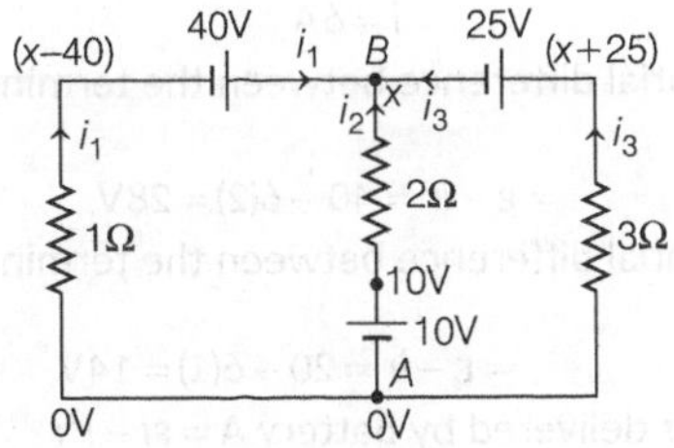

Lets take $V_A = 0$ and $V_B = x$

Applying KCL at junction B,

$$i_1 + i_2 + i_3 = 0$$

$$\Rightarrow \quad \frac{0-(x-40)}{1} + \frac{10-x}{2} + \frac{0-(x+25)}{3} = 0$$

$$\Rightarrow \quad 240 - 6x + 30 - 3x - 2x - 50 = 0$$

$$\Rightarrow \quad 11x = 220$$

$$\Rightarrow \quad x = 20V$$

$$i_1 = \frac{0-(20-40)}{1} = 20\text{A}$$

$$i_2 = \frac{10-20}{2} = -5\text{A}$$

$$i_3 = \frac{0-(20+25)}{3} = -15\text{A}$$

4. (i)

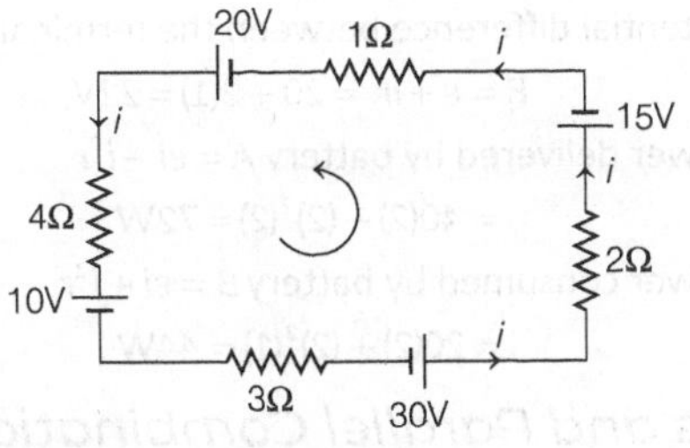

Lets take current in the loop to be i.

Applying KVL in the loop,

$$-i(1) + 20 - i(4) - 10 - i(3) + 30 - i(2) - 15 = 0$$

$$\Rightarrow \quad 10i = 25 \Rightarrow i = 2.5\text{A}$$

(ii)

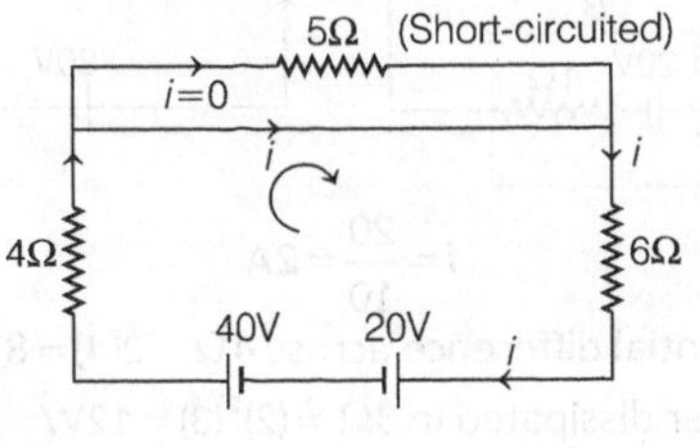

5Ω is short-circuited.

So, no current will flow through it.

Applying KVL in the loop,

$$+40 - i(4) - i(6) - 20 = 0$$

$$\Rightarrow \quad 10i = 20 \Rightarrow i = 2\text{A}$$

(iii)

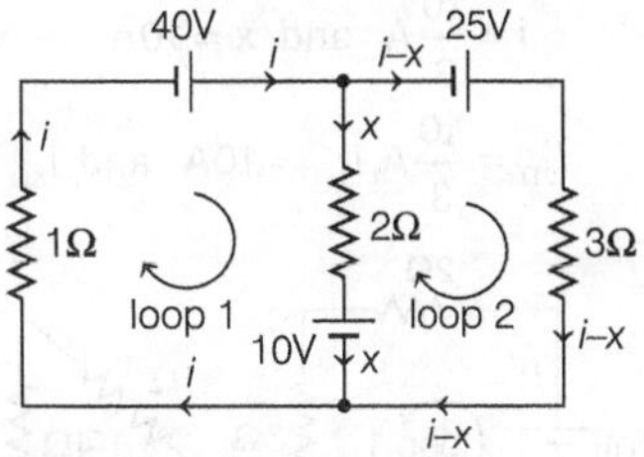

Applying KVL in loop 1,

$$+40 - 2x - 10 - i(1) = 0$$

$$\Rightarrow \quad i + 2x = 30 \quad \text{...(i)}$$

Applying KVL in loop 2,

$$+25 - 3(i - x) + 10 + 2x = 0$$

$$\Rightarrow \quad 3i - 5x = 35 \quad \text{...(ii)}$$

Solving Eqs. (i) and (ii), we get

$$i = 20\text{A}, \; x = 5\text{A}$$

So, $$i_{1\Omega} = 20\text{A}$$

$$i_{2\Omega} = 5\text{A} \quad \text{and} \quad i_{3\Omega} = 15\text{A}$$

(iv)

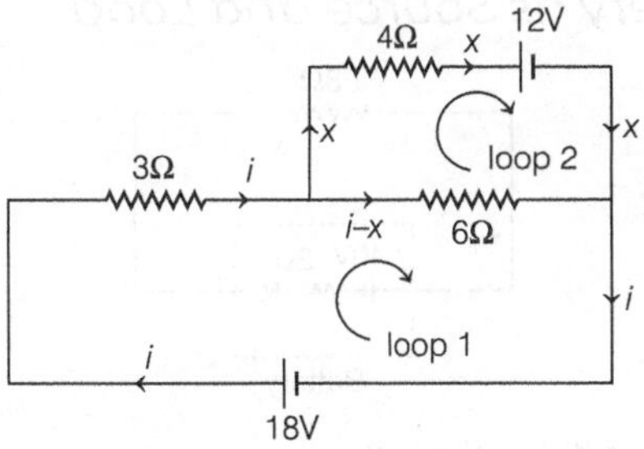

Applying KVL in loop 1,

$$+18 - 3i - 6(i - x) = 0$$

$$\Rightarrow \quad 3i - 2x = 6 \quad \text{...(i)}$$

Applying KVL in loop 2,

$$-4x - 12 + 6(i - x) = 0$$

$$3i - 5x = 6 \quad \text{...(ii)}$$

Solving Eqs. (i) and (ii), we get

$$i = 2\text{A and } x = 0$$

$$i_{3\Omega} = 2\text{A}, i_{6\Omega} = 2\text{A and } i_{4\Omega} = 0$$

(v)

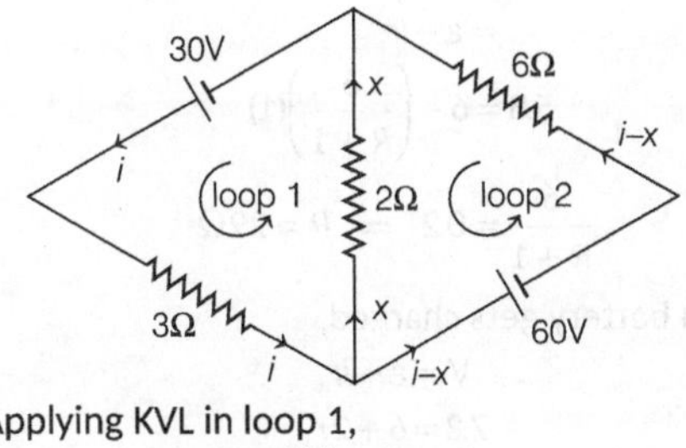

Applying KVL in loop 1,

$$+30 - i(3) - 2x = 0$$

$\Rightarrow \quad 3i + 2x = 30 \quad \text{...(i)}$

Applying KVL in loop 2,

$$-60 - 6(i - x) + 2x = 0$$

$\Rightarrow \quad -3i + 4x = 30 \quad \text{...(ii)}$

Solving Eqs. (i) and (ii), we get

$$i = \frac{10}{3}\text{A} \text{ and } x = 10\text{A}$$

So, $\quad i_{3\Omega} = \frac{10}{3}\text{A}, i_{2\Omega} = 10\text{A}$ and $i_{6\Omega} = \frac{20}{3}\text{A}$

(vi)

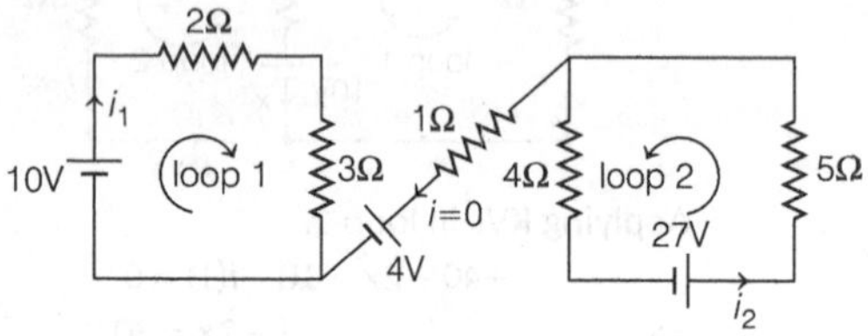

Current through 1Ω resistance will be zero.

In loop 1, using KVL,

$$+10 - 2i_1 - 3i_1 = 0$$

$\Rightarrow \quad i_1 = 2\text{A}$

In loop 2, using KVL,

$$+27 - 5i_2 - 4i_2 = 0$$

$\Rightarrow \quad i_2 = 3\text{A}$

6.4 *Battery as Source and Load*

1. (i)

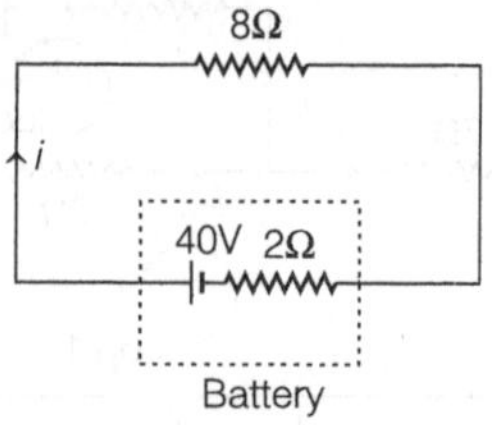

Using KVL in the loop,

$$+40 - i(8) - i(2) = 0$$

$\Rightarrow \quad i = 4\text{A}$

(ii) Potential difference across the terminals of battery

$$= \varepsilon - ir = 40 - 4(2) = 32\text{V}$$

(iii) Net power supplied by the battery

$$= \varepsilon i - i^2 r = 40 \times 4 - 4^2(2) = 128\text{W}$$

2. $i = \dfrac{\varepsilon}{R + r}$

Potential difference between the terminals of battery

$$= \varepsilon - ir$$

$\Rightarrow \quad 5.8 = 6 - \left(\dfrac{6}{R+1}\right)(1)$

$\Rightarrow \quad \dfrac{6}{R+1} = 0.2 \Rightarrow R = 29\Omega$

3. When a battery gets charged,

$$V = \varepsilon + ir$$

$\Rightarrow \quad 7.2 = 6 + 2r$

$\Rightarrow \quad r = 0.6\Omega$

4. **Case I**

(i)

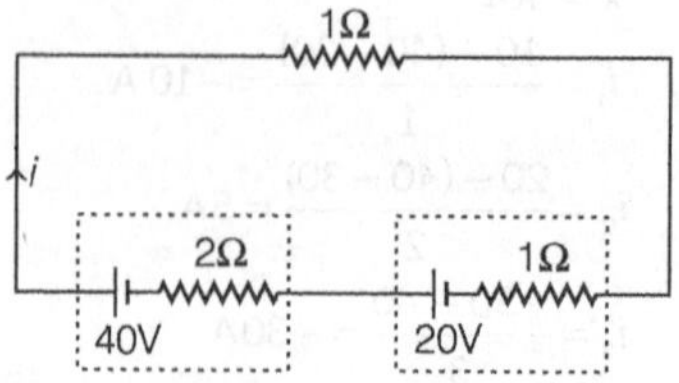

Using KVL,

$$+40 - i(7) - i(1) + 20 - i(2) = 0$$

$\Rightarrow \quad i = 6\text{A}$

(ii) Potential difference between the terminals of battery *A*

$$= \varepsilon - ir = 40 - 6(2) = 28\text{V}$$

Potential difference between the terminals of battery *B*

$$= \varepsilon - ir = 20 - 6(1) = 14\text{V}$$

(iii) Power delivered by battery $A = \varepsilon i - i^2 r$

$$= 40 \times 6 - 6^2(2) = 168\text{W}$$

Power delivered by battery $B = \varepsilon i - i^2 r$

$$= 20 \times 6 - 6^2(1) = 84\text{W}$$

Case II

(i)

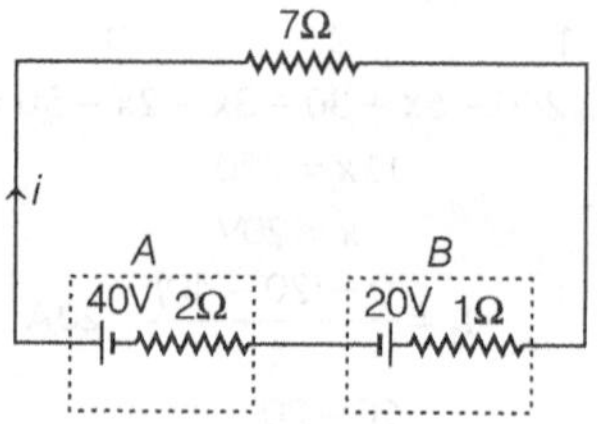

Using KVL, $\quad +40 - 2i - 7i - i - 20 = 0 \Rightarrow i = 2\text{A}$

(ii) Potential difference between the terminals of battery

$$A = \varepsilon - ir = 40 - 2(2) = 36\text{V}$$

Potential difference between the terminals of battery

$$B = \varepsilon + ir = 20 + 2(1) = 22\text{V}$$

(iii) Power delivered by battery $A = \varepsilon i - i^2 r$

$$= 40(2) - (2)^2(2) = 72\text{W}$$

Power consumed by battery $B = \varepsilon i + i^2 r$

$$= 20(2) + (2)^2(1) = 44\text{W}$$

6.5 *Series and Parallel Combination Circuits*

1. (i)

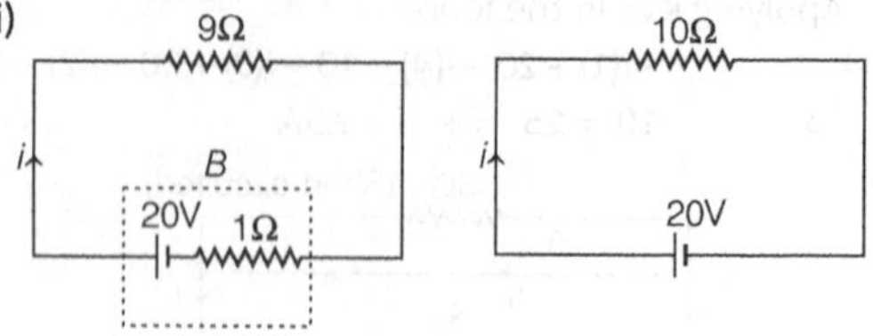

$$i = \frac{20}{10} = 2\text{A}$$

(ii) Potential difference across $4\Omega = 2(4) = 8\text{V}$

(iii) Power dissipated in $3\Omega = (2)^2(3) = 12\text{W}$

2. (i) $$\frac{1}{R_{eq}} = \frac{1}{12} + \frac{1}{6} + \frac{1}{4}$$

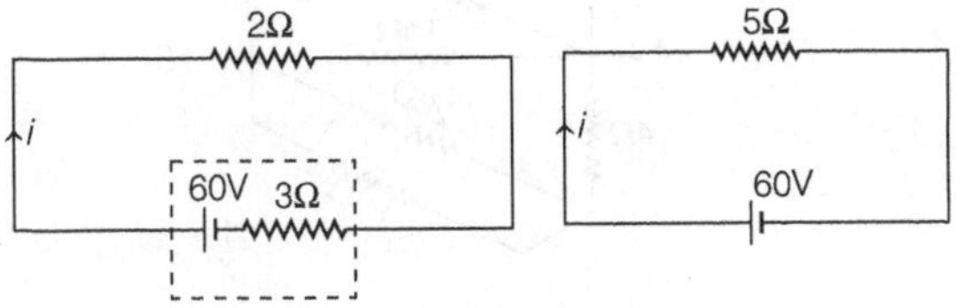

$\Rightarrow$ $$R_{eq} = 2\Omega$$

Current through battery, $i = \frac{60}{5} = 12A$

In parallel combination, current is split in the inverse ratio of resistances

i.e. $$\frac{1}{12} : \frac{1}{6} : \frac{1}{4} = 1:2:3$$

Current through $6\Omega = \frac{2}{(1+2+3)} \times 12 = 4A$

(ii) Potential difference across $12\Omega = iR_{eq} = 12 \times 2 = 24$ V

(iii) Power dissipated in $4\Omega = \frac{V^2}{R} = \frac{(24)^2}{4} = 144W$

3. $R_{eq} = 9\Omega$

Current through battery $= \frac{324}{9} = 36A$

In parallel combination, current is split in the inverse ratio of resistances

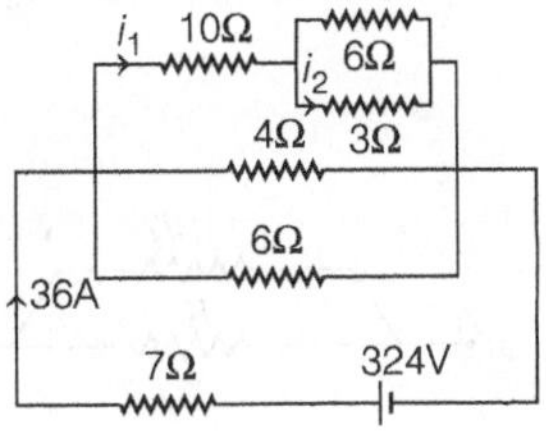

i.e. $$\frac{1}{12} : \frac{1}{4} : \frac{1}{6} = 1:3:2$$

$$i_1 = \frac{1}{6} \times 36 = 6A$$

$$i_2 = \frac{2}{3} \times 6 = 4A$$

4. $R_{eq} = 10\Omega$

Current through battery $= \frac{120}{10} = 12A$

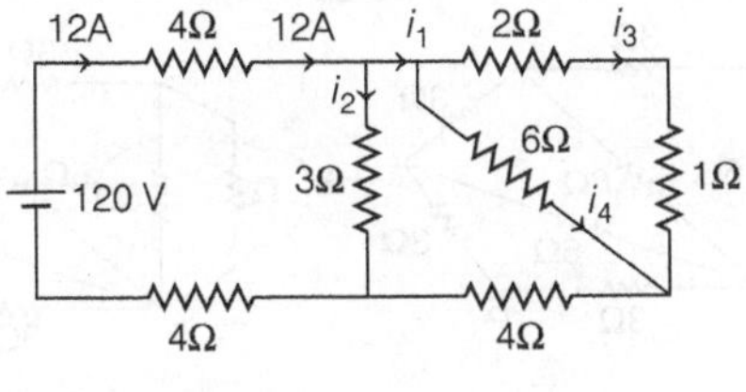

$$i_1 + i_2 = 12A \text{ and } \frac{i_1}{i_2} = \frac{1}{2}$$

$\Rightarrow$ $$i_1 = 4A$$

$$i_3 + i_4 = i_1 \text{ and } \frac{i_3}{i_4} = \frac{2}{1}$$

$$i_3 = \frac{2}{3}(i_1) = \frac{2}{3}(4) = \frac{8}{3}A$$

5. $R_{eq} = 9\Omega$

Current through battery $= \frac{E}{9}$

Current $\frac{E}{9}$ will split in the inverse ratio of resistances in the two parallel branches.

i.e. $$\frac{1}{24} : \frac{1}{8} = 1:3$$

Current through the top branch $= \frac{1}{4}\left(\frac{E}{9}\right) = \frac{E}{36}$

Current $\frac{E}{36}$ will split in the ratio $\frac{1}{6} : \frac{1}{12} = 2:1$

Current through $6\Omega = \frac{2}{3}\left(\frac{E}{36}\right) = 4$

$\Rightarrow$ $$E = 216V$$

6. $R_{eq} = \frac{1\times 3}{1+3} + \frac{2\times 4}{2+4} = \frac{25}{12}\Omega$

Current through battery $= \frac{25}{\left(\frac{25}{12}\right)} = 12A$

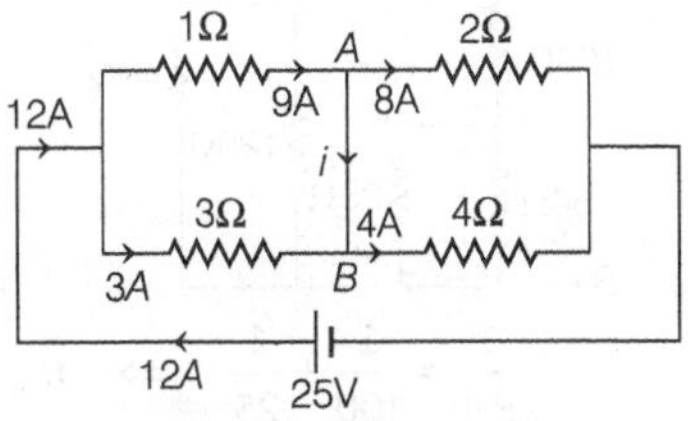

$$i = 9 - 8 = 1A$$

7.

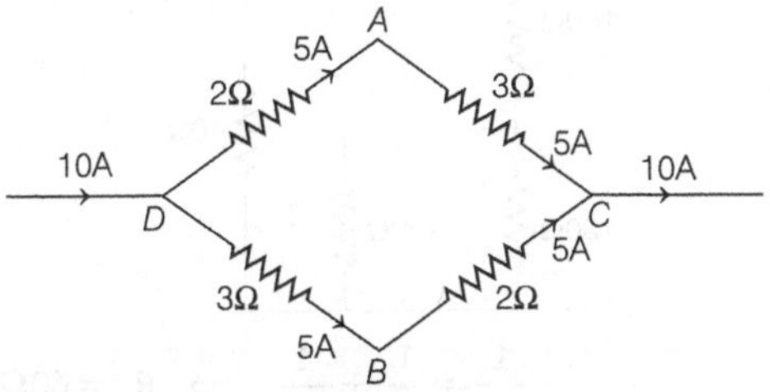

$$V_A - 5(3) + 5(2) = V_B$$

$\Rightarrow$ $$V_A - V_B = 5V$$

8. $R_{eq} = 10 + \frac{100R}{100+R} = \frac{1000 + 110R}{100+R}$

Current through battery $= \frac{120(100+R)}{(1000+110R)}$

Potential difference across $R = 100V$

$\Rightarrow$ $$i\left(\frac{100R}{100+R}\right) = 100$$

$\Rightarrow$ $$\left(\frac{120(100+R)}{1000+110R}\right)\left(\frac{100R}{100+R}\right) = 100$$

$\Rightarrow$ $$120R = 1000 + 110R$$

$\Rightarrow$ $$10R = 1000$$

$\Rightarrow$ $$R = 100\Omega$$

9. Wheatstone bridge is balanced. So, we can remove 20Ω resistance.

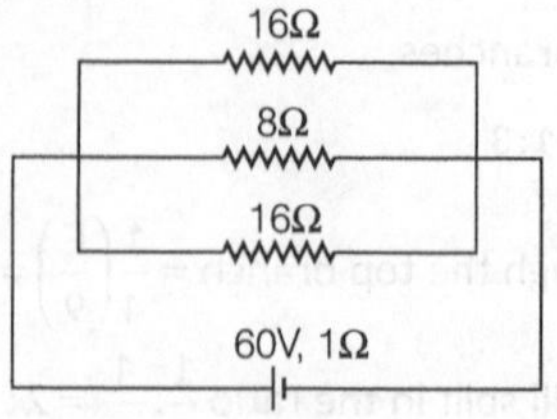

$$R_{eq} = \left(\frac{1}{16} + \frac{1}{8} + \frac{1}{16}\right)^{-1} + 1 = 5\Omega$$

$$\text{Current through battery} = \frac{60}{5} = 12\text{A}$$

6.6 *Equivalent Resistance*

1. (i)

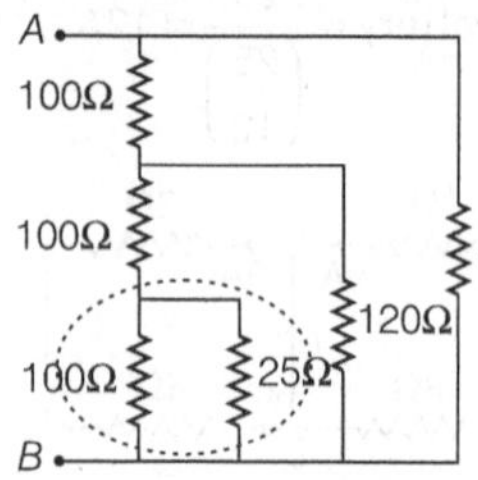

$$\frac{1}{R_{eq}} = \frac{1}{100} + \frac{1}{25} \Rightarrow R_{eq} = 20\Omega$$

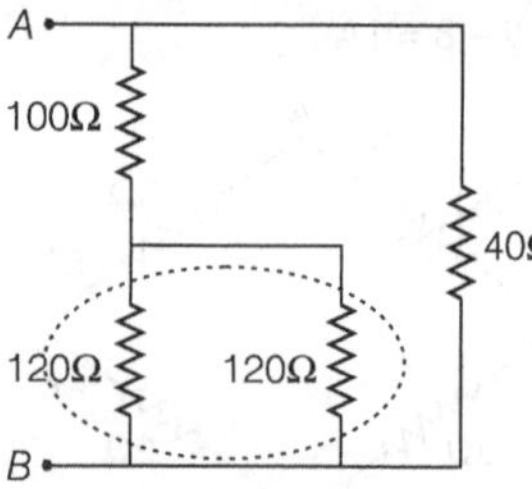

$$\frac{1}{R_{eq}} = \frac{1}{120} + \frac{1}{120} \Rightarrow R_{eq} = 60\Omega$$

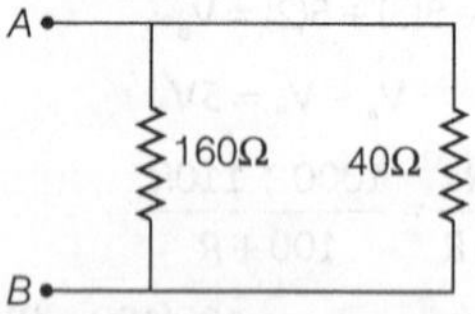

$$R_{eq} = \frac{160 \times 40}{160 + 40} = 32\Omega$$

(ii)

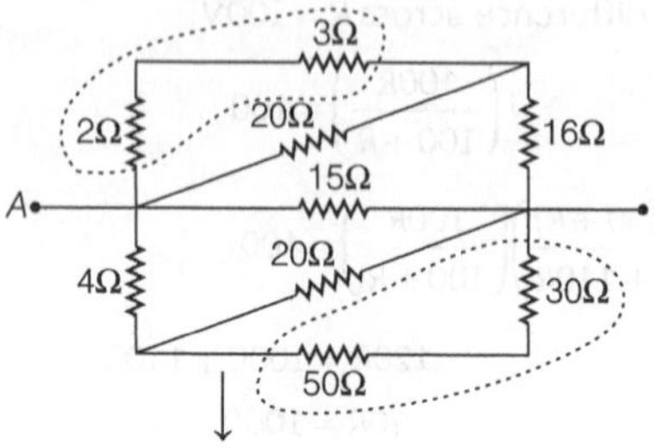

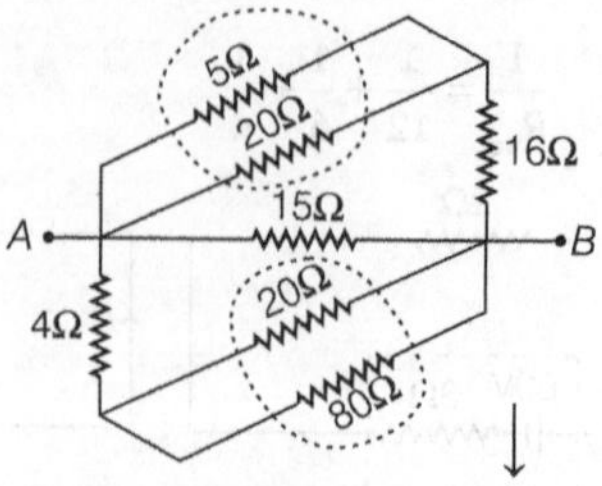

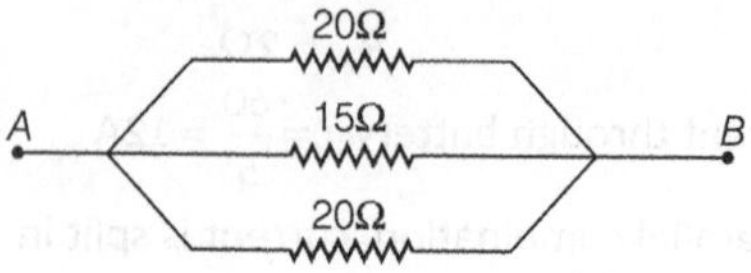

$$\frac{1}{R_{eq}} = \frac{1}{20} + \frac{1}{15} + \frac{1}{20}$$

$$\Rightarrow R_{eq} = 6\Omega$$

(iii)

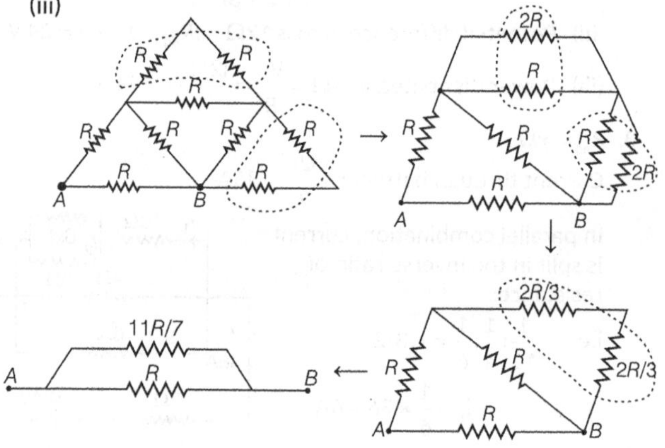

$$\frac{1}{R_{eq}} = \frac{1}{R} + \frac{1}{\frac{11R}{7}}$$

$$\Rightarrow R_{eq} = \frac{11R}{18}$$

(iv)

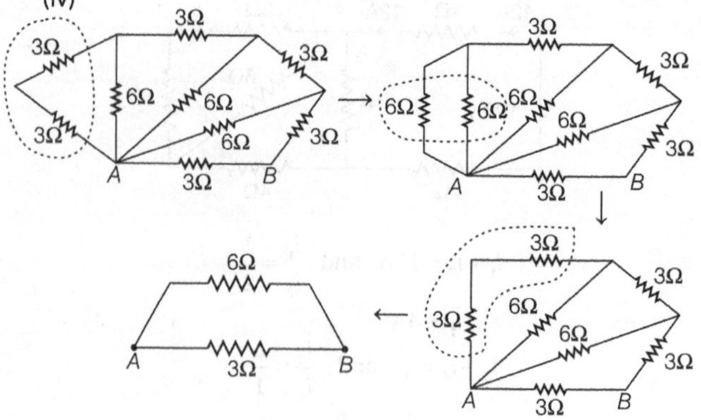

$$\frac{1}{R_{eq}} = \frac{1}{6} + \frac{1}{3} \Rightarrow R_{eq} = 2\Omega$$

(v)

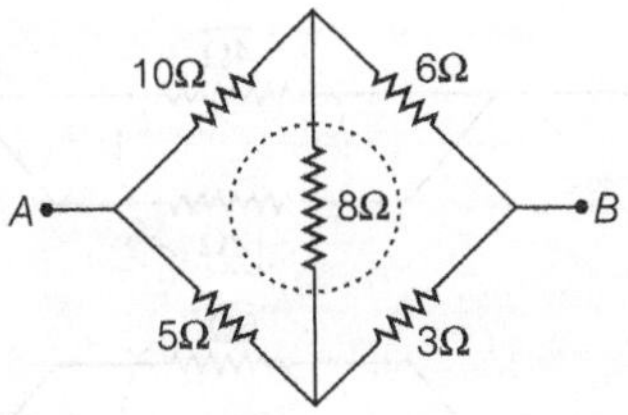

It is a balanced Wheatstone bridge. So, we can remove 8Ω resistor.

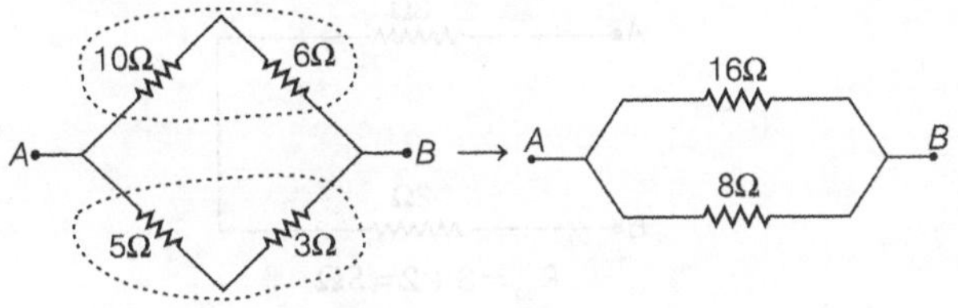

$$\frac{1}{R_{eq}} = \frac{1}{16} + \frac{1}{8} \Rightarrow R_{eq} = \frac{16}{3}\Omega$$

(vi)

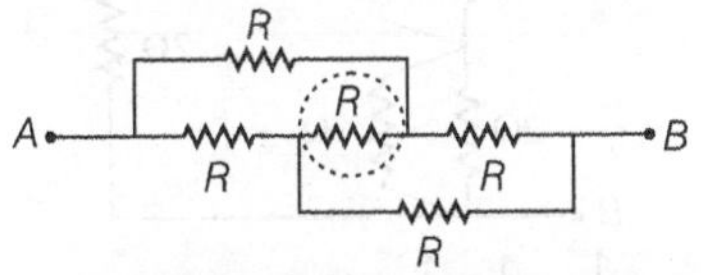

It is a balanced Wheatstone bridge.

So, we can remove middle R resistance.

$$\frac{1}{R_{eq}} = \frac{1}{2R} + \frac{1}{2R} \Rightarrow R_{eq} = R$$

(vii)

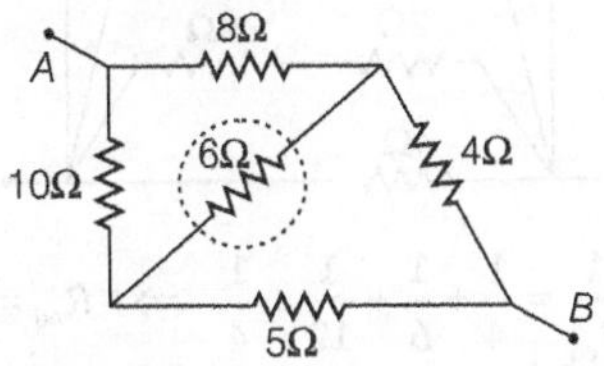

It is a balanced Wheatstone bridge. So, we can remove 6Ω resistance.

$$\frac{1}{R_{eq}} = \frac{1}{12} + \frac{1}{15}$$

$$\Rightarrow \quad R_{eq} = \frac{20}{3}\Omega$$

(viii)

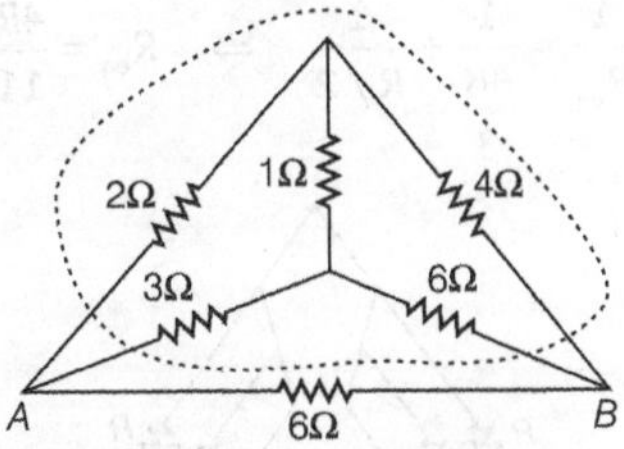

It is a balanced Wheatstone bridge.

So, we can remove 1Ω resistance.

$$\frac{1}{R_{eq}} = \frac{1}{6} + \frac{1}{9} + \frac{1}{6}$$

$$\Rightarrow \quad R_{eq} = \frac{9}{4}\Omega$$

(ix)

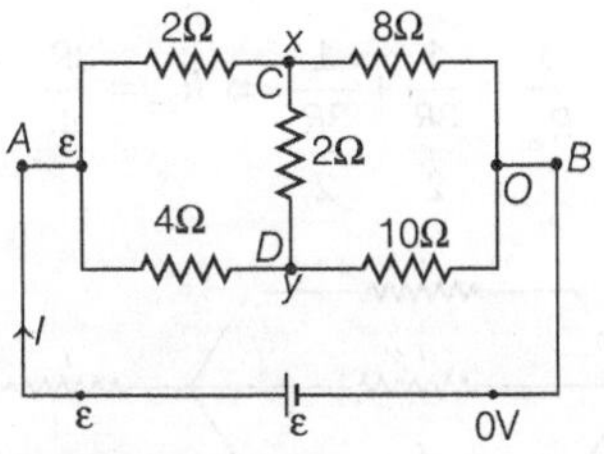

Lets take potential of junctions C and D to be x and y, respectively.

Applying KCL at junction C

$$\frac{\varepsilon - x}{2} + \frac{0 - x}{8} + \frac{y - x}{2} = 0$$

$$\Rightarrow \quad 4\varepsilon - 4x - x + 4y - 4x = 0$$

$$\Rightarrow \quad 9x - 4y = 4\varepsilon \qquad \text{...(i)}$$

Applying KCL at junction D,

$$\frac{\varepsilon - y}{4} + \frac{x - y}{2} + \frac{0 - y}{10} = 0$$

$$\Rightarrow \quad 5\varepsilon - 5y + 10x - 10y - 2y = 0$$

$$\Rightarrow \quad 17y - 10x = 5\varepsilon \qquad \text{...(ii)}$$

$$x = \frac{88\varepsilon}{113} \text{ and } y = \frac{85\varepsilon}{113}$$

$$I = \frac{\varepsilon - x}{2} + \frac{\varepsilon - y}{4} = \frac{39\varepsilon}{226}$$

$$R_{eq} = \frac{\varepsilon}{I} = \frac{226}{39}\Omega$$

2. (i)

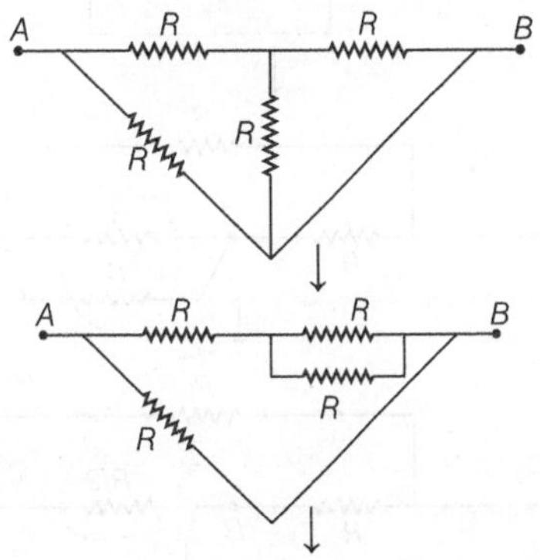

$$\frac{1}{R_{eq}} = \frac{1}{R} + \frac{1}{\frac{3R}{2}} \Rightarrow R_{eq} = \frac{3R}{5}$$

(ii)

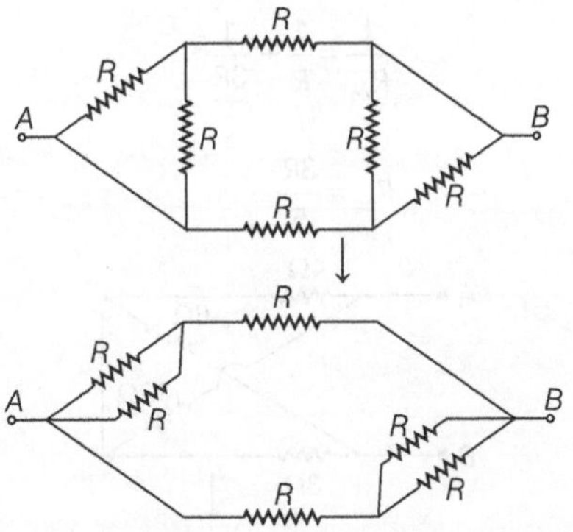

$$\frac{1}{R_{eq}} = \frac{1}{\frac{3R}{2}} + \frac{1}{\frac{3R}{2}} \Rightarrow R_{eq} = \frac{3R}{4}$$

(iii)

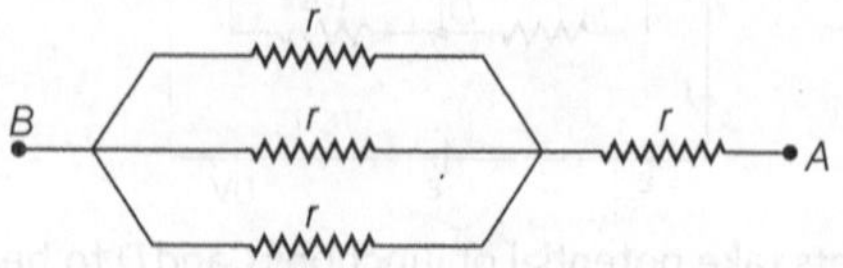

$$R_{eq} = r + \frac{r}{3} = \frac{4r}{3}$$

(iv)

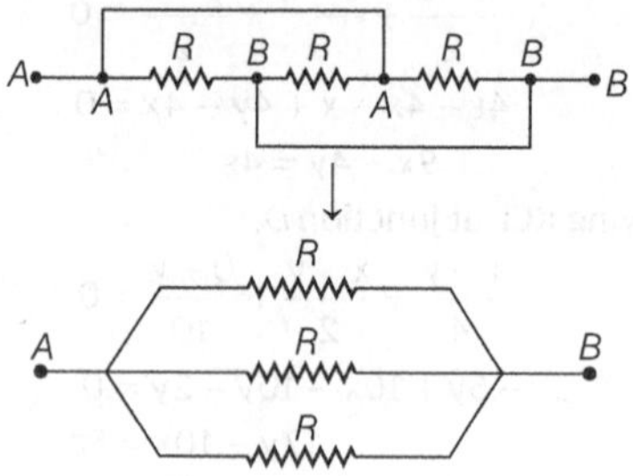

$$\frac{1}{R_{eq}} = \frac{1}{R} + \frac{1}{R} + \frac{1}{R} \Rightarrow R_{eq} = \frac{R}{3}$$

(v)

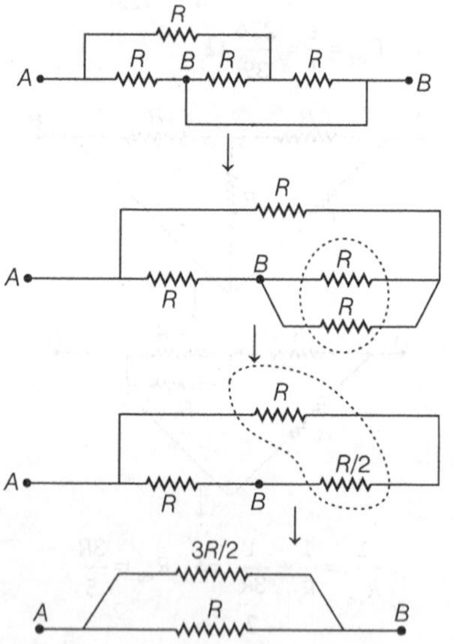

$$\frac{1}{R_{eq}} = \frac{1}{R} + \frac{1}{\frac{3R}{2}}$$

$$\Rightarrow \quad R_{eq} = \frac{3R}{5}$$

(vi)

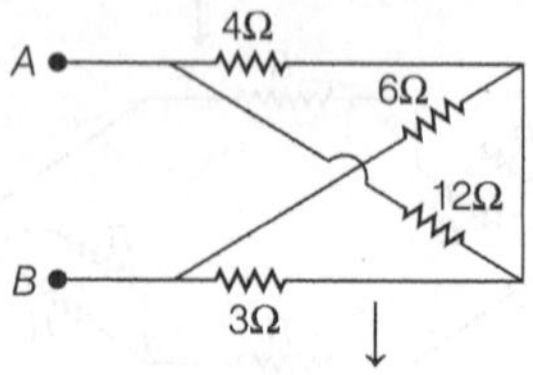

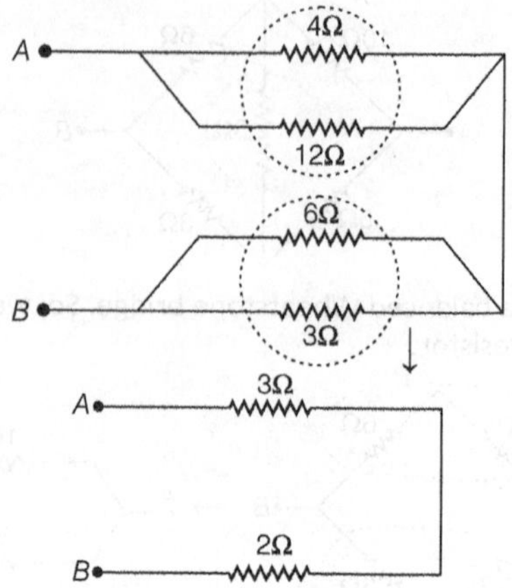

$$R_{eq} = 3 + 2 = 5\Omega$$

(vii)

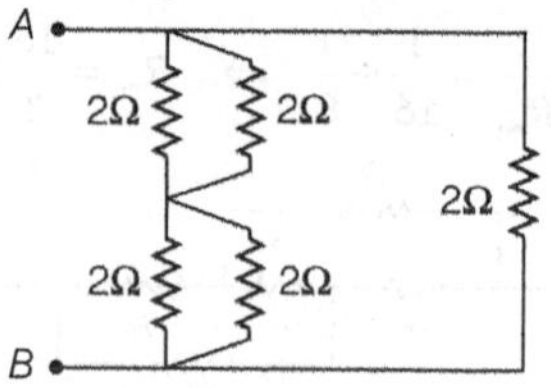

$$\frac{1}{R_{eq}} = \frac{1}{2} + \frac{1}{2} \quad \Rightarrow \quad R_{eq} = 1\Omega$$

(viii)

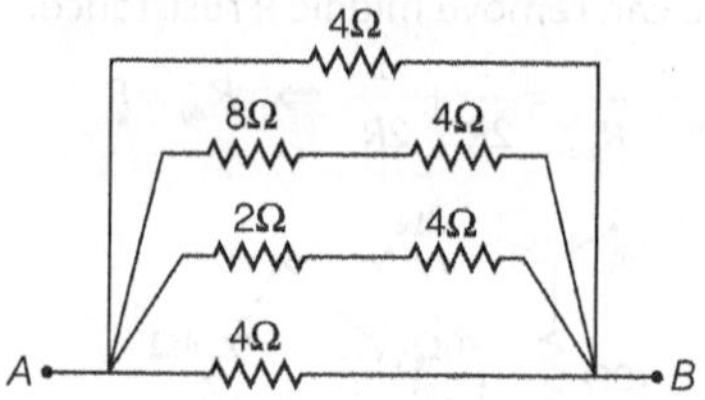

$$\frac{1}{R_{eq}} = \frac{1}{4} + \frac{1}{6} + \frac{1}{12} + \frac{1}{4} \quad \Rightarrow \quad R_{eq} = \frac{4}{3}\Omega$$

(ix)

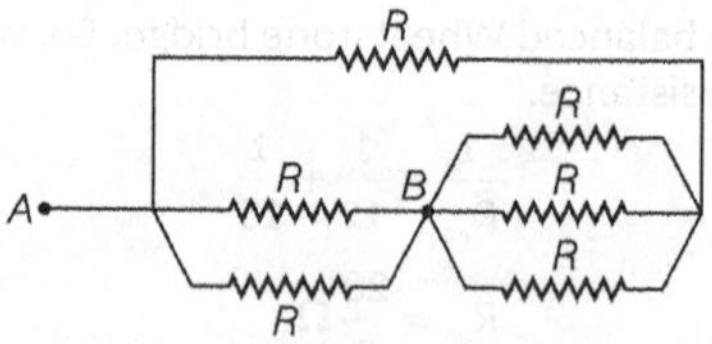

$$\frac{1}{R_{eq}} = \frac{1}{\frac{4R}{3}} + \frac{1}{R/2} \quad \Rightarrow \quad R_{eq} = \frac{4R}{11}$$

(x)

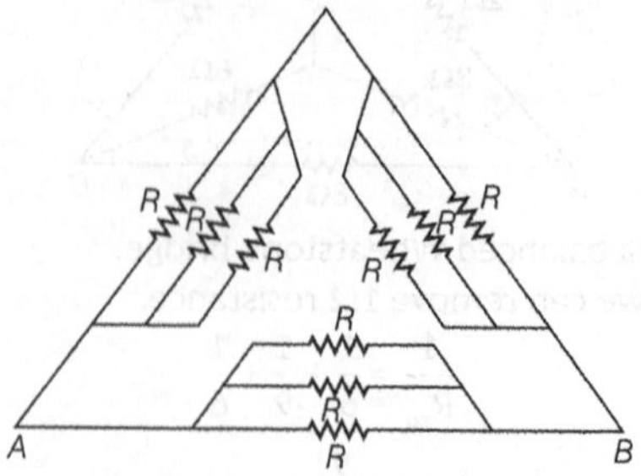

$$\frac{1}{R_{eq}}=\frac{1}{\frac{R}{3}}+\frac{1}{\frac{2R}{3}} \Rightarrow R_{eq}=\frac{2R}{9}$$

(xi)

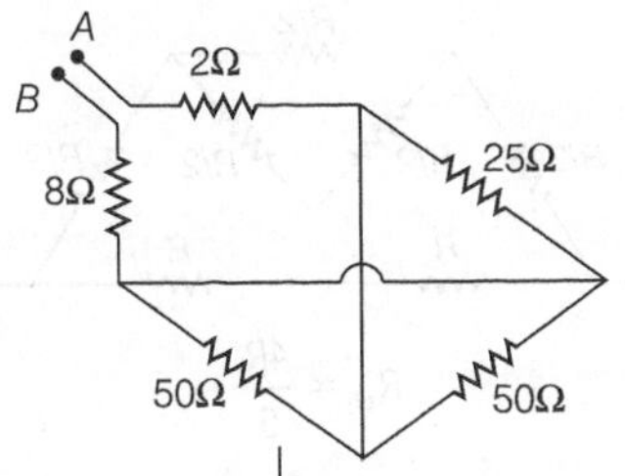

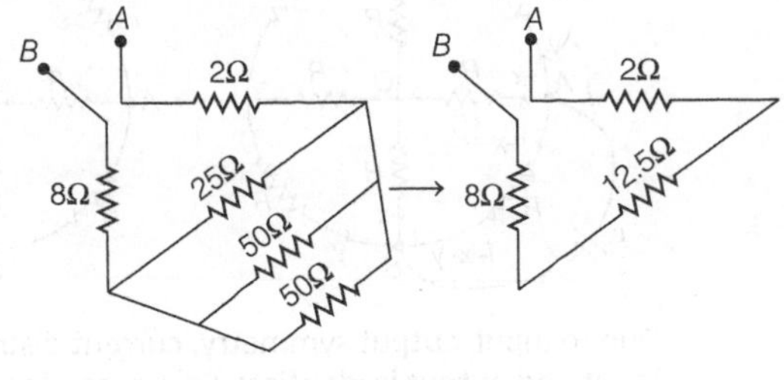

$$R_{eq}=8+2+12.5=22.5\,\Omega$$

(xii)

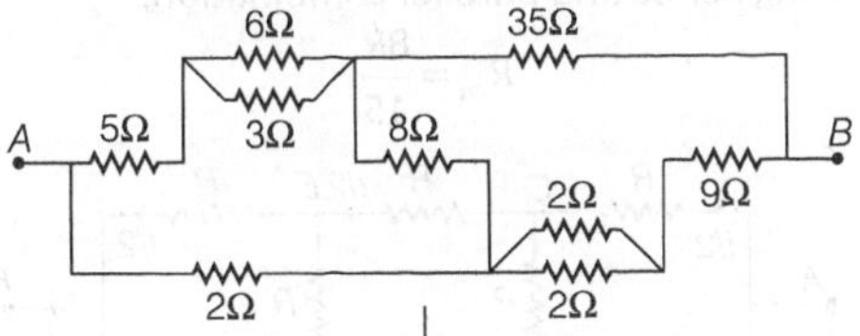

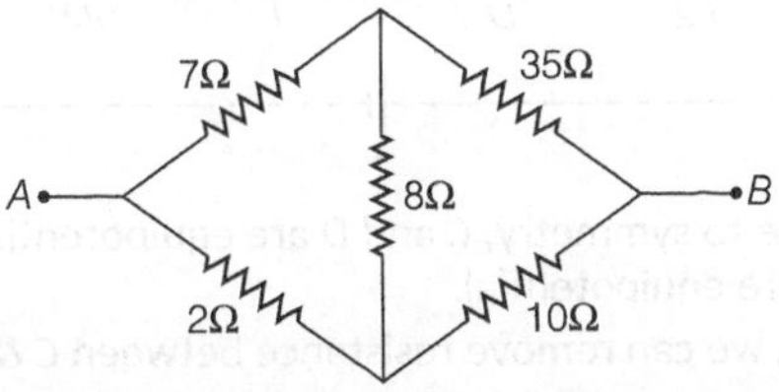

This is a balanced Wheatstone bridge. So, we can remove 8Ω resistance.

$$R_{eq}=\frac{42(12)}{42+12}=\frac{28}{3}\,\Omega$$

6.7 *Symmetric Circuits*

1. (i)

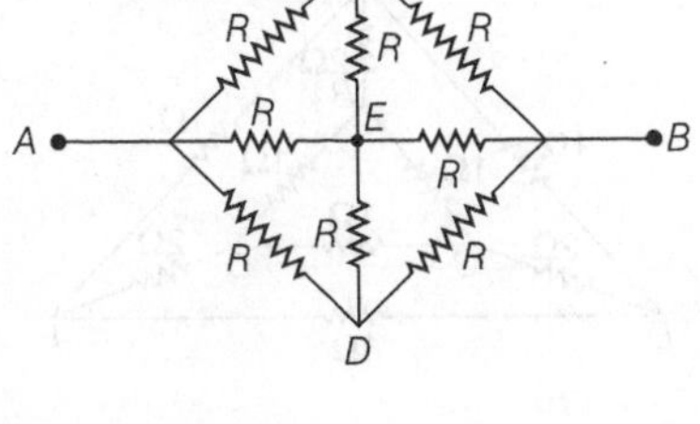

Due to symmetry, points *C* and *D* are equipotential. So, we can join *C* and *D*.

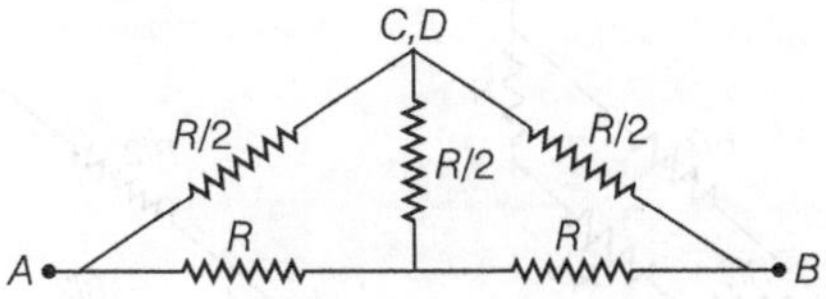

This is a balanced Wheatstone bridge.

So, we can remove the resistance between *C* and *E*.

$$\frac{1}{R_{eq}}=\frac{1}{2R}+\frac{1}{R} \Rightarrow R_{eq}=\frac{2R}{3}$$

(ii)

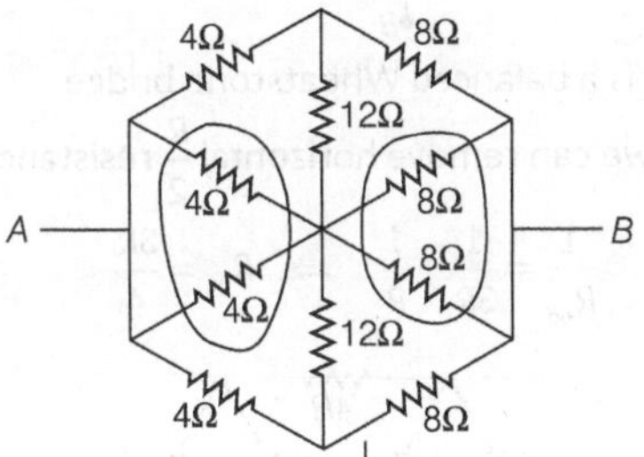

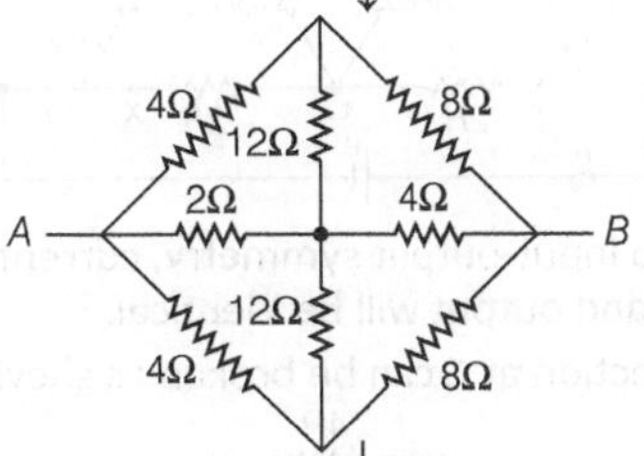

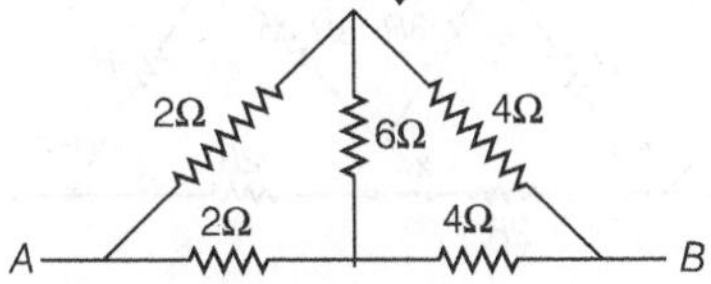

This is a balanced Wheatstone bridge.

So, we can remove 6Ω resistance.

$$\frac{1}{R_{eq}}=\frac{1}{6}+\frac{1}{6} \Rightarrow R_{eq}=3\,\Omega$$

(iii)

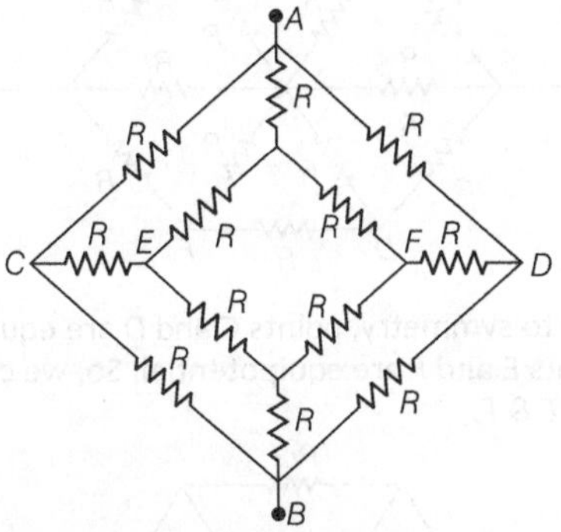

Due to symmetry, points *C* and *D* are equipotential and points *E* and *F* are equipotential.

So, we can join C and D and E and F.

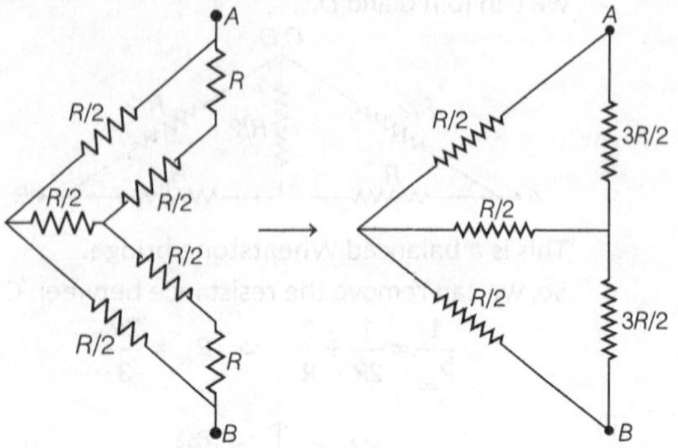

This is a balanced Wheatstone bridge.

So, we can remove horizontal $\frac{R}{2}$ resistance.

$$\frac{1}{R_{eq}}=\frac{1}{3R}+\frac{1}{R} \Rightarrow R_{eq}=\frac{3R}{4}$$

(iv)

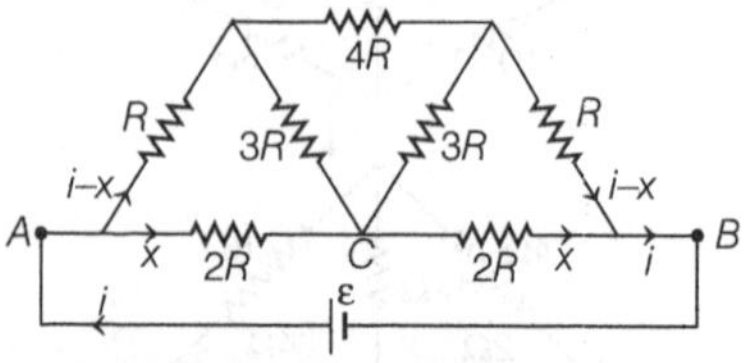

Due to input-output symmetry, current distribution at input and output will be identical.

So, junction at C can be broken as shown.

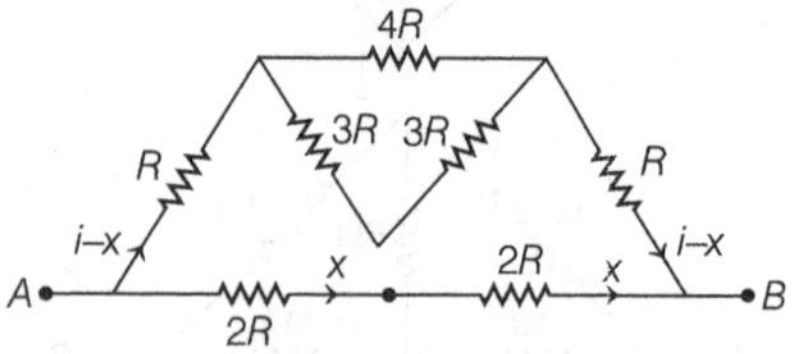

$$R_{eq}=\frac{44}{21}R$$

(v)

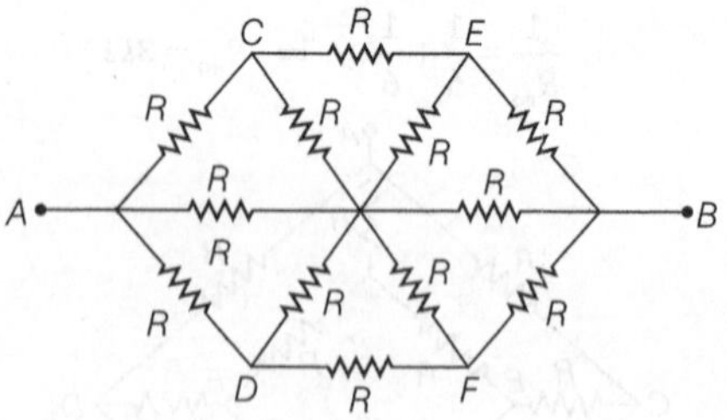

Due to symmetry, points C and D are equipotential and points E and F are equipotential. So, we can join C & D and E & F.

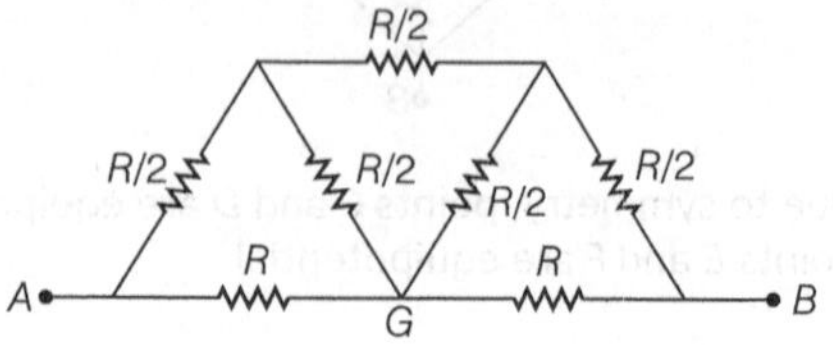

Due to input-output symmetry, current distribution at input and output will be identical. So, we can break junction at G.

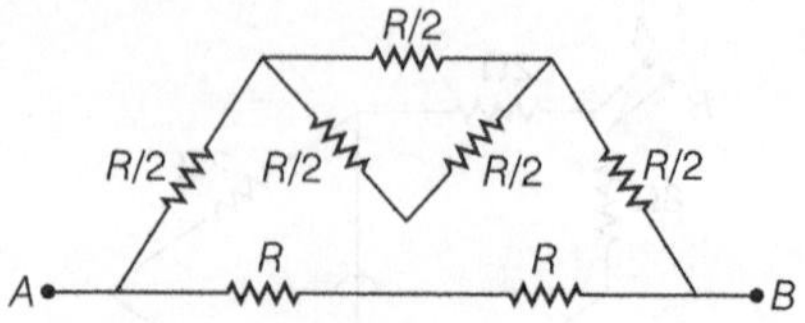

$$R_{eq}=\frac{4R}{5}$$

(vi)

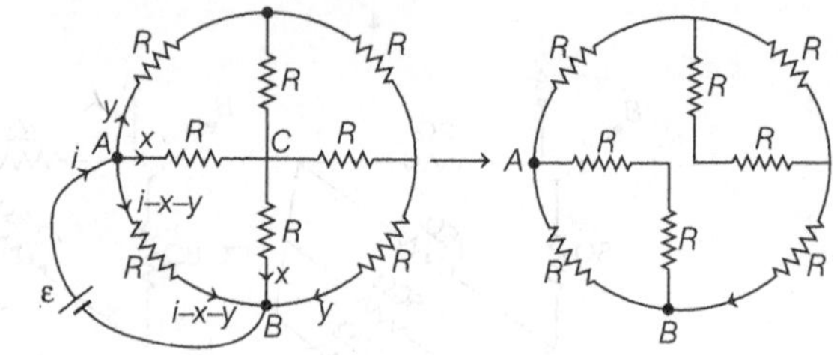

Due to input-output symmetry, current distribution at input and output is identical. So, we can break the junction at C.

Using series and parallel combination,

$$R_{eq}=\frac{8R}{15}$$

(vii)

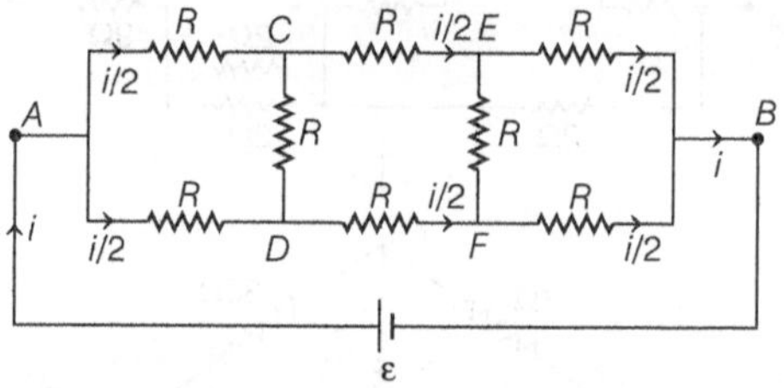

Due to symmetry, C and D are equipotential and E and F are equipotential.

So, we can remove resistance between C & D and E & F.

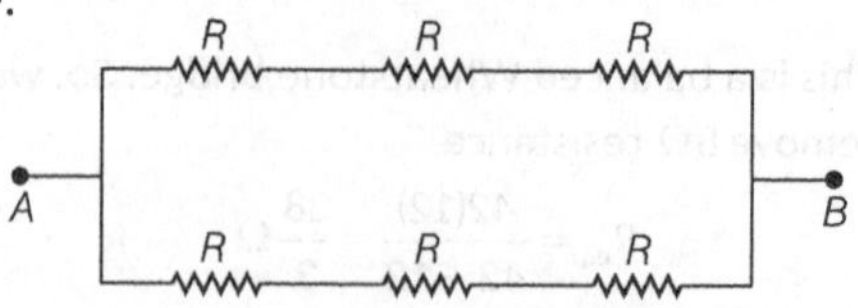

$$\frac{1}{R_{eq}}=\frac{1}{3R}+\frac{1}{3R} \Rightarrow R_{eq}=\frac{3R}{2}$$

(viii)

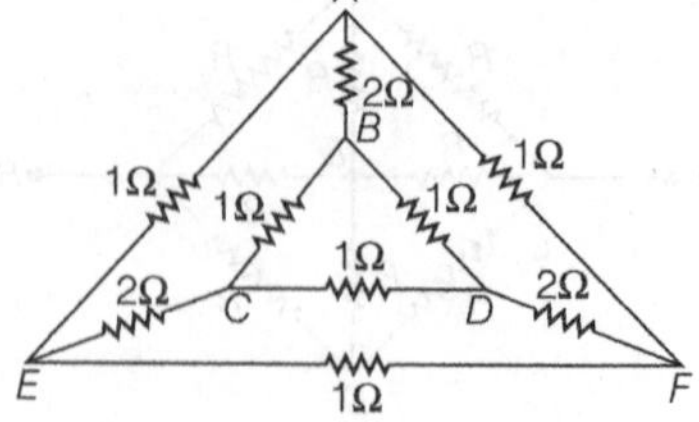

From symmetry, points C and D and E and F are equipotential. So, we can remove resistors between C & D and E & F.

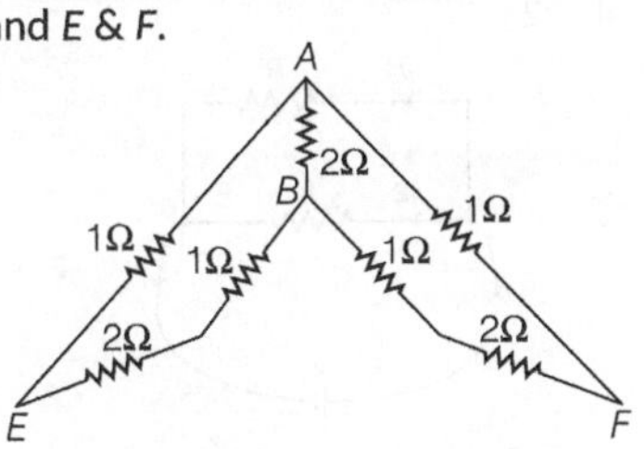

Using series and parallel combination

$$R_{eq} = 1\Omega$$

(ix)

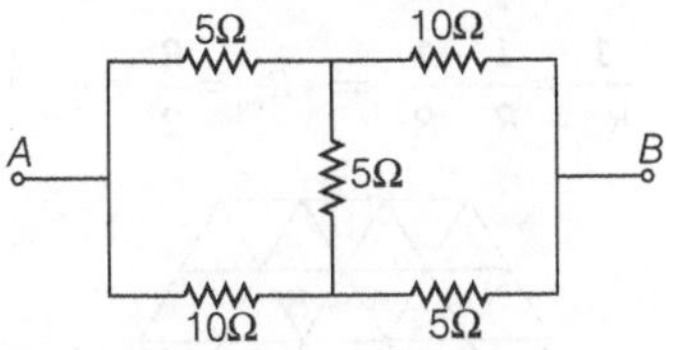

Due to cross-symmetry, potential drop across both 5Ω resistances will be same.

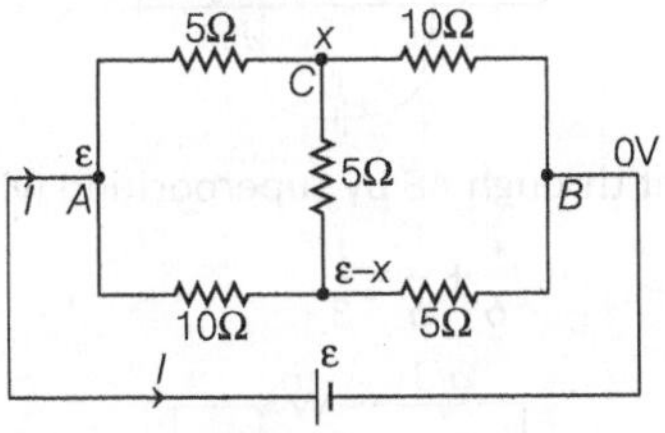

Applying KCL at junction C,

$$\frac{\varepsilon - x}{5} + \frac{(\varepsilon - x) - x}{5} + \frac{0 - x}{10} = 0$$

$$\Rightarrow \quad 2\varepsilon - 2x + 2\varepsilon - 4x - x = 0$$

$$\Rightarrow \quad x = \frac{4\varepsilon}{7}$$

$$I = \frac{\varepsilon - x}{5} + \frac{\varepsilon - (\varepsilon - x)}{10} = \frac{\varepsilon - \frac{4\varepsilon}{7}}{5} + \frac{\frac{4\varepsilon}{7}}{10} = \frac{\varepsilon}{7}$$

$$R_{eq} = \frac{\varepsilon}{I} = 7\Omega$$

2. (i)

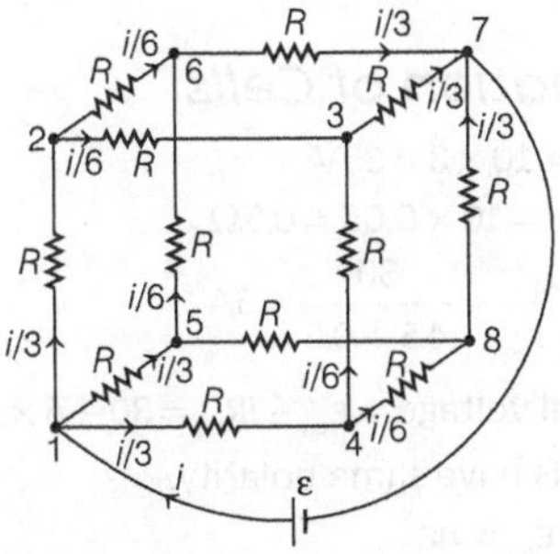

Applying KVL in the loop 12371,

$$+\varepsilon - \frac{i}{3}R - \frac{i}{6}R - \frac{i}{3}R = 0$$

$$\Rightarrow \quad \frac{\varepsilon}{i} = \frac{5R}{6} \Rightarrow R_{eq} = \frac{5R}{6}$$

(ii)

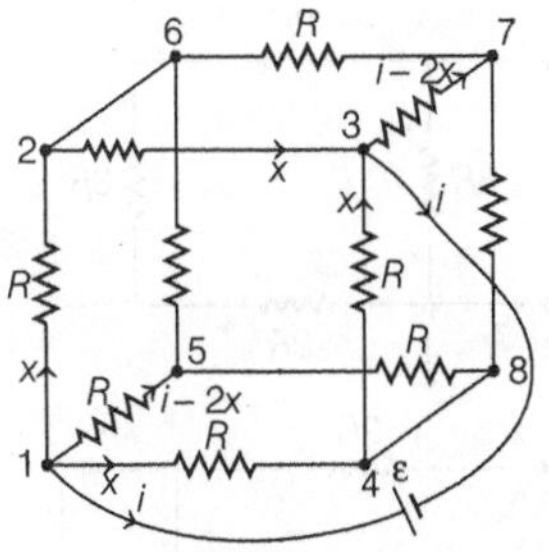

Due to input-output symmetry, current distribution at input and output is identical so, no current flows through resistors between 2 & 6 and 4 & 8.

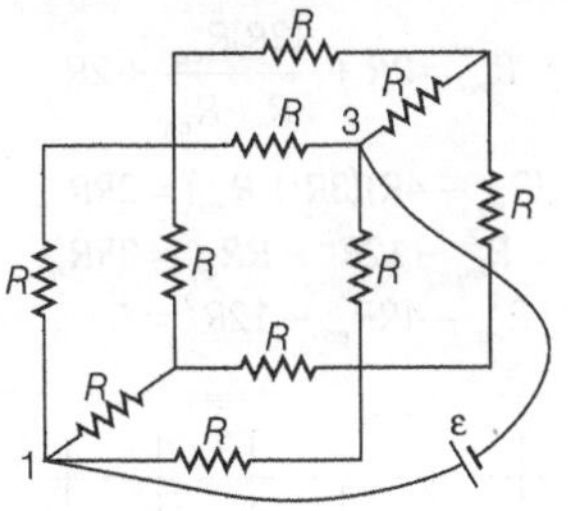

Using series and parallel combinations, $R_{eq} = \frac{3R}{4}$

(iii)

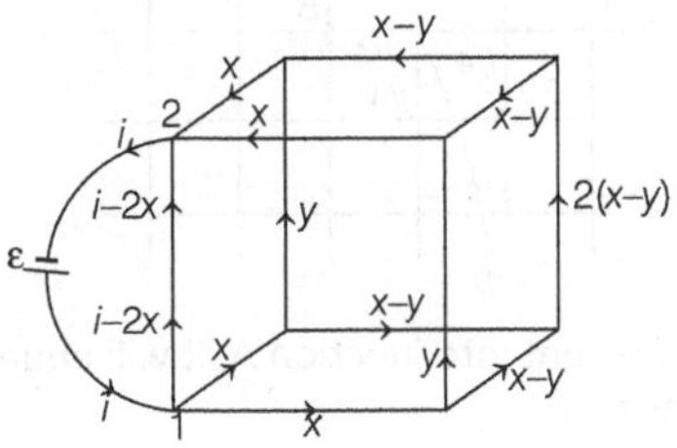

Using KVL,

$$+\varepsilon - (i - 2x)R = 0 \quad \text{...(i)}$$

$$+\varepsilon - xR - yR - xR = 0 \quad \text{...(ii)}$$

$$+\varepsilon - xR - (x - y)R - 2(x - y)R - (x - y)R - xR = 0 \quad \text{...(iii)}$$

Solving Eqs. (i), (ii) and (iii), we get

$$R_{eq} = \frac{\varepsilon}{i} = \frac{7R}{12}$$

3. (i)

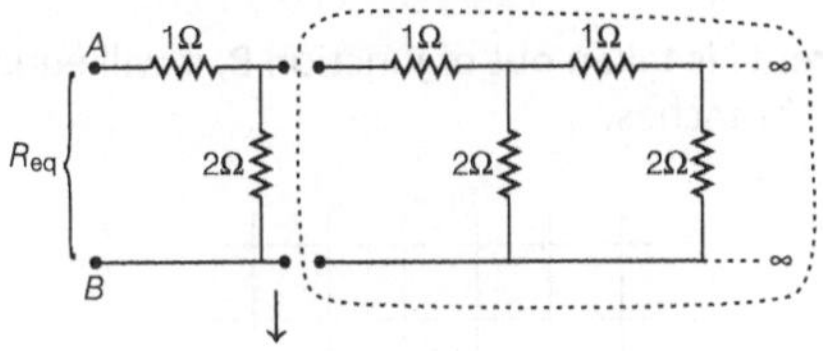

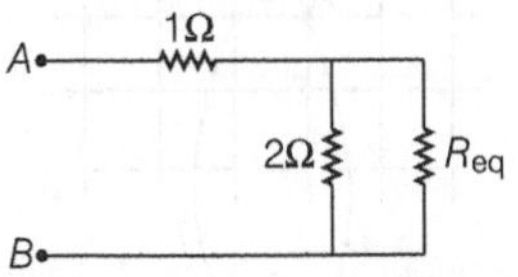

$$R_{eq} = 1 + \frac{2R_{eq}}{2 + R_{eq}}$$

$$\Rightarrow \quad 2R_{eq} + R_{eq}^2 = 2 + 3R_{eq}$$

$$\Rightarrow \quad R_{eq}^2 - R_{eq} - 2 = 0 \Rightarrow R_{eq} = 2\Omega$$

(ii)

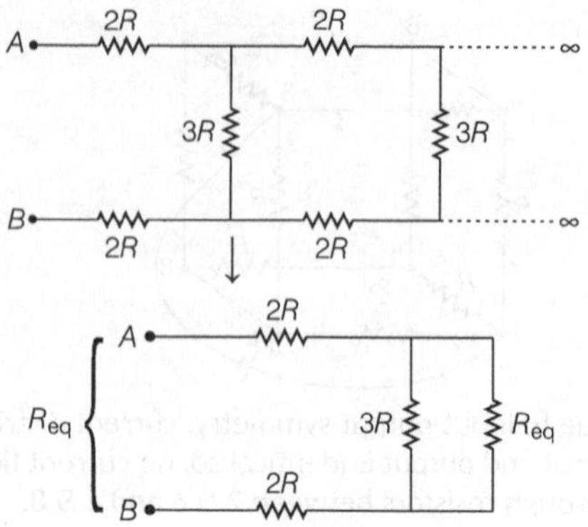

$$R_{eq}=2R+\frac{(3R)R_{eq}}{3R+R_{eq}}+2R$$

$$\Rightarrow \quad (R_{eq}-4R)(3R+R_{eq})=3RR_{eq}$$

$$\Rightarrow \quad R_{eq}^2-12R^2-RR_{eq}=3RR_{eq}$$

$$\Rightarrow \quad R_{eq}^2-4RR_{eq}-12R^2=0 \quad \Rightarrow \quad R_{eq}=6R$$

4. Case 1

(i)

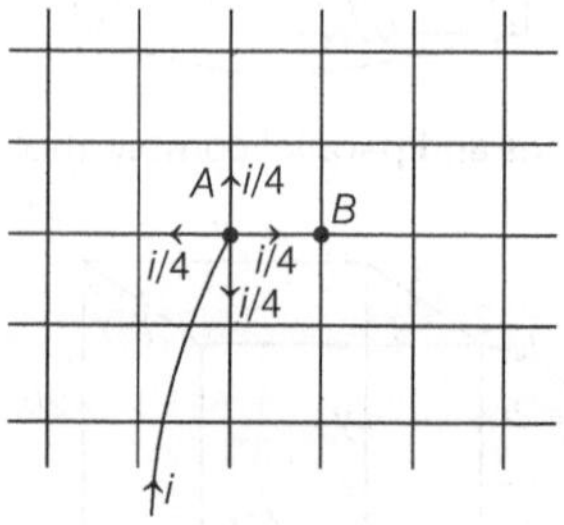

If a current *i* is sent into junction *A*, it will equally split in the four branches.

Case 2

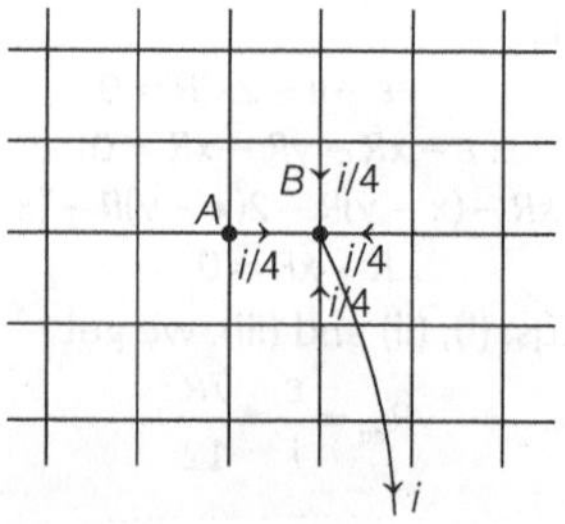

If a current *i* is taken out of junction *B*, it will equally split in the four branches.

Case 3

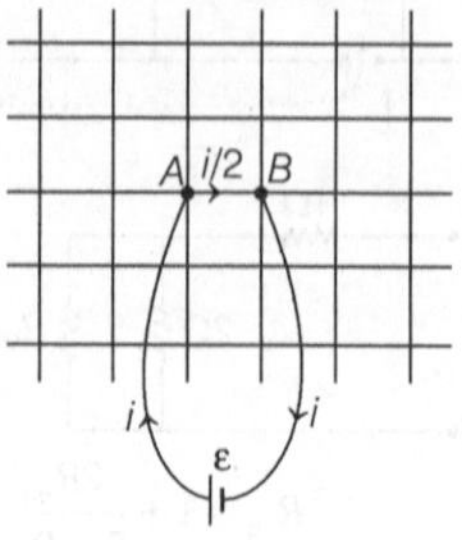

If a battery is connected across *AB*, current *i* enters at *A* and leaves at *B*.

By superposition of the first two cases, current through *AB* will be $\frac{i}{4}+\frac{i}{4}=\frac{i}{2}$.

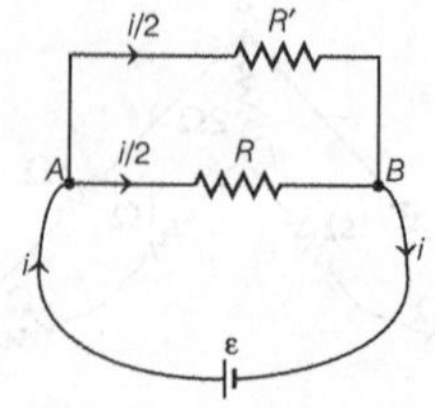

R' is resistance of remaining grid across *AB*.

$$\frac{i}{2}R'=\frac{i}{2}R \quad \Rightarrow \quad R'=R$$

$$\frac{1}{R_{eq}}=\frac{1}{R}+\frac{1}{R} \quad \Rightarrow \quad R_{eq}=\frac{R}{2}$$

(ii)

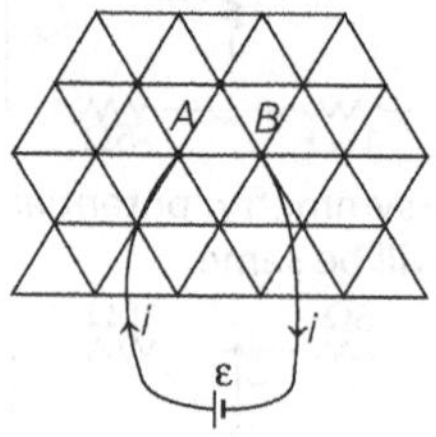

Current through *AB* by superposition will be

$$\frac{i}{6}+\frac{i}{6}=\frac{i}{3}$$

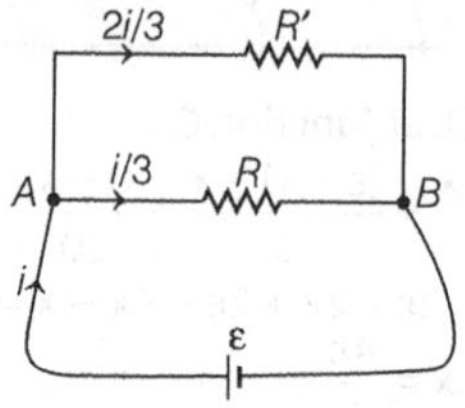

R' is the resistance of the remaining grid across *AB*.

$$\left(\frac{i}{3}\right)R=\left(\frac{2i}{3}\right)R' \quad \Rightarrow \quad R'=\frac{R}{2}$$

$$\frac{1}{R_{eq}}=\frac{1}{R}+\frac{1}{R/2} \quad \Rightarrow \quad R_{eq}=\frac{R}{3}$$

6.8 Combination of Cells

1. (i) $\varepsilon_{eq}=10\varepsilon=10\times 3=30\text{V}$

$$r_{eq}=10r=10\times 0.05=0.5\Omega$$

$$i=\frac{\varepsilon_{eq}}{R+r_{eq}}=\frac{30}{4.5+0.5}=6\text{A}$$

(ii) Terminal voltage $=\varepsilon_{eq}-iR_{eq}=30-6\times 0.5=27\text{ V}$

2. When all cells have same polarity,

$$\varepsilon_{eq}=n\varepsilon$$

$$r_{eq}=nr$$

and $$i=\frac{\varepsilon_{eq}}{R+r_{eq}} \Rightarrow 10=\frac{n(6)}{5+nr} \quad \text{...(i)}$$

When two cells are wrongly connected,

$$\varepsilon_{eq} = (n-2)\varepsilon - 2\varepsilon = (n-4)\varepsilon$$

$$r_{eq} = nr$$

and $\quad i = \dfrac{\varepsilon_{eq}}{R + r_{eq}} \Rightarrow 6 = \dfrac{(n-4)6}{5+nr}$ ....(ii)

Solving Eqs. (i) and (ii), we get

$$n = 10 \text{ and } r = 0.1\,\Omega$$

3. (i)

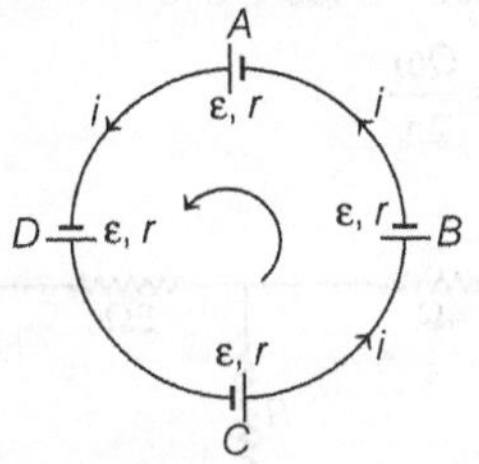

Applying KVL in the loop,

$$+\varepsilon + \varepsilon + \varepsilon - \varepsilon - ir - ir - ir - ir = 0$$

$$\Rightarrow \quad i = \frac{\varepsilon}{2r}$$

(ii) Potential difference across cell A

$$= \varepsilon - ir = \varepsilon - \left(\frac{\varepsilon}{2r}\right) r = \frac{\varepsilon}{2}$$

Potential difference across cell $B = \varepsilon + ir$

$$= \varepsilon + \left(\frac{\varepsilon}{2r}\right) r = \frac{3\varepsilon}{2}$$

4.

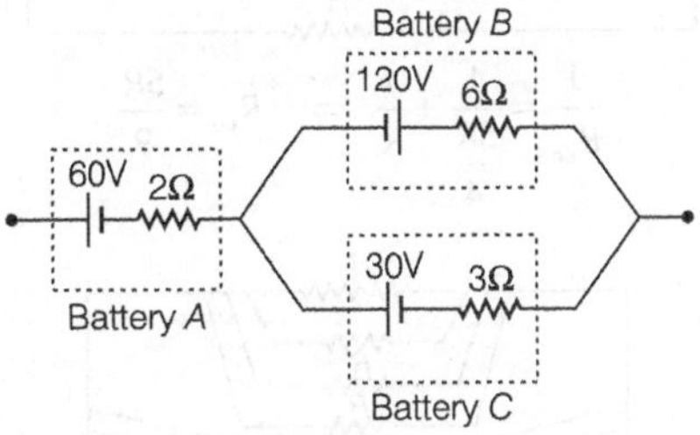

Battery B and C are in parallel.

$$\varepsilon_{eq} = \frac{\dfrac{\varepsilon_1}{r_1} + \dfrac{\varepsilon_2}{r_2}}{\dfrac{1}{r_1} + \dfrac{1}{r_2}} = \frac{\dfrac{120}{6} - \dfrac{30}{3}}{\dfrac{1}{6} + \dfrac{1}{3}} = 20\text{ V}$$

$$r_{eq} = \frac{r_1 r_2}{r_1 + r_2} = \frac{6 \times 3}{6+3} = 2\Omega$$

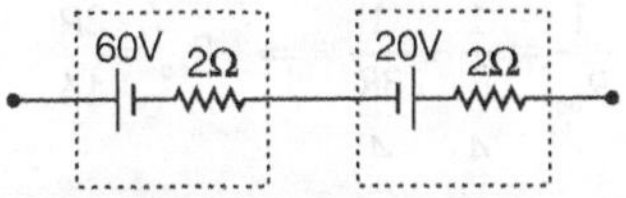

For series combination of cells,

$$\varepsilon_{eq} = \varepsilon_1 + \varepsilon_2 = 60 - 20 = 40\text{V}$$

$$r_{eq} = r_1 + r_2 = 2 + 2 = 4\Omega$$

5. $$\varepsilon_{eq} = \frac{\dfrac{\varepsilon_1}{r_1} + \dfrac{\varepsilon_2}{r_2} + \dfrac{\varepsilon_3}{r_3}}{\dfrac{1}{r_1} + \dfrac{1}{r_2} + \dfrac{1}{r_3}} = \frac{\dfrac{60}{6} + \dfrac{15}{3} + \dfrac{10}{2}}{\dfrac{1}{6} + \dfrac{1}{3} + \dfrac{1}{2}} = 20\text{V}$$

$$\frac{1}{r_{eq}} = \frac{1}{r_1} + \frac{1}{r_2} + \frac{1}{r_3}$$

$$\Rightarrow \quad \frac{1}{r_{eq}} = \frac{1}{6} + \frac{1}{3} + \frac{1}{2} \Rightarrow r_{eq} = 1\Omega$$

$$i = \frac{\varepsilon_{eq}}{R + r_{eq}} = \frac{20}{4+1} = 4\text{A}$$

6. $$\varepsilon_{eq} = \frac{\dfrac{\varepsilon_1}{r_1} + \dfrac{\varepsilon_2}{r_2} + \dfrac{\varepsilon_3}{r_3}}{\dfrac{1}{r_1} + \dfrac{1}{r_2} + \dfrac{1}{r_3}} = \frac{\dfrac{10}{3} + \dfrac{10}{3} + \dfrac{10}{3}}{\dfrac{1}{3} + \dfrac{1}{3} + \dfrac{1}{3}} = 10\text{V}$$

$$\frac{1}{r_{eq}} = \frac{1}{r_1} + \frac{1}{r_2} + \frac{1}{r_3}$$

$$\frac{1}{r_{eq}} = \frac{1}{3} + \frac{1}{3} + \frac{1}{3} \Rightarrow r_{eq} = 1\Omega$$

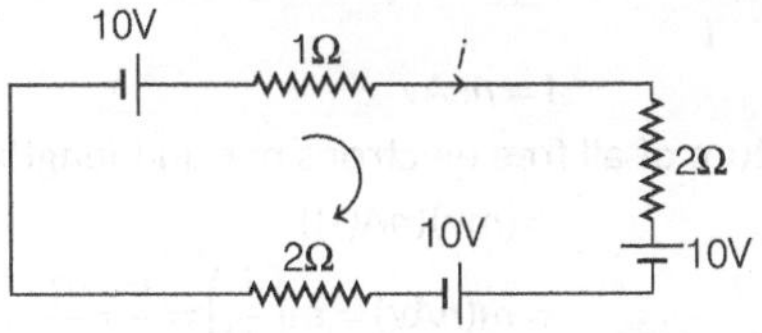

Using KVL in the loop,

$$+10 - i(1) - i(2) - 10 - 10 - i(2) = 0$$

$$i = -2\text{A} = 2\text{A, anti-clockwise}$$

7. $\varepsilon_{eq} = n\varepsilon = 20(1.5) = 30\text{ V}$

$$r_{eq} = \frac{nr}{m} = \frac{20(2)}{8} = 5\Omega$$

$$i = \frac{\varepsilon_{eq}}{R + r_{eq}} = \frac{30}{20+5} = 1.2\text{A}$$

8. For maximum current,

(Number of rows) $\times R$ = (Number of cells in each row) $\times r$

$$nR = mr$$

$\Rightarrow \quad n(3) = m(0.5) \Rightarrow m = 6n$ ...(i)

Total number of cells $= mn = 24$

$mn = 24$ ...(ii)

From Eqs. (i) and (ii), we get

$$m = 12 \text{ and } n = 2$$

Level 2 JEE Main Level

Single Choice Correct Questions

1. Electric field is set up in the wire very quickly, producing a current through each cross-section, almost instantaneously.

2. $I_1 = I_2 = I$

$$\Rightarrow \quad n_1 q_1 A_1 v_1 = n_2 q_2 A_2 v_2$$

$$\Rightarrow \quad (2n)eAv_L = (n)e(4A)v_R$$

$$\Rightarrow \quad \frac{v_L}{v_R} = \frac{2}{1}$$

3. Number of electrons per unit volume

$$= \frac{9\times10^3\times10^3}{63.5}\times6\times10^{23}\times1$$

$$i = nqAv_d$$

$$\Rightarrow v_d = \frac{i}{nqA}$$

$$= \frac{1.5}{\left(\frac{9\times10^3\times10^3}{63.5}\times6\times10^{23}\times1\right)(1.6\times10^{-19})(1\times10^{-7})}$$

$$= 1.1\times10^{-3}\text{ m/s} = 1.1\text{ mm/s}$$

4. $\phi = EA = \left(\frac{J}{\sigma}\right)A = \frac{\left(\frac{I}{A}\right)A}{\left(\frac{1}{\rho}\right)} = \rho I$

5. Current $= \frac{q}{t}$

$$i = neAv$$

Momentum of all free electrons per unit length

$$= (mv)(nA(1))$$

$$= m(nAv) = m\left(\frac{i}{e}\right) = \frac{i}{s} = \frac{q}{ts}$$

6. At higher temperature, resistance is more for a metallic conductor,

$$R = \frac{1}{\text{Slope of } i\text{ - }V \text{ graph}}$$

$$\Rightarrow \quad R_2 > R_1 \Rightarrow T_2 > T_1$$

7.

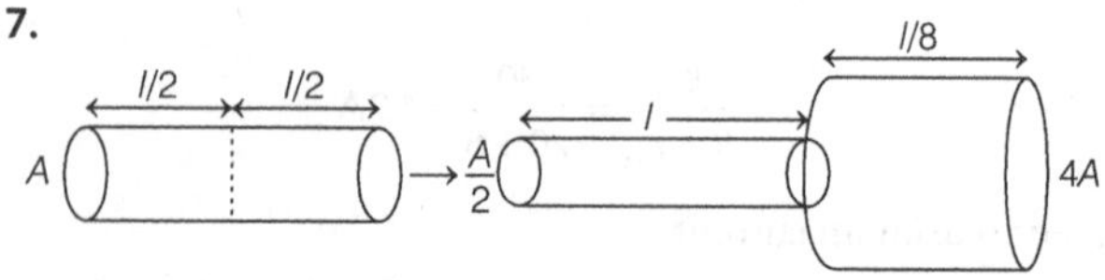

$$R = \frac{\rho l}{A}$$

$$R' = \frac{\rho l}{\left(\frac{A}{2}\right)} + \frac{\rho\left(\frac{l}{8}\right)}{4A} = \frac{65}{32}R$$

8. $R = R_0(1+\alpha\Delta T)$

$$60 = 20[1+\alpha(500-20)]$$

$$\alpha = \frac{1}{240}/°\text{C}$$

$$R = R_0(1+\alpha\Delta T)$$

$$\Rightarrow \quad 25 = 20\left(1+\frac{1}{240}(T-20)\right) \Rightarrow T = 80°\text{ C}$$

9. At 0°C, $R_1 = 400\Omega, R_2 = 800\Omega$

$$R_{eq} = \frac{400\times800}{400+800} = \frac{800}{3}\Omega$$

At t°C, $$\frac{1}{R'_{eq}} = \frac{1}{R'_1} + \frac{1}{R'_2}$$

$$\frac{1}{\frac{800}{3}(1+\alpha_{eq}t)} = \frac{1}{400(1+\alpha t)} + \frac{1}{800(1+4\alpha t)}$$

$$\Rightarrow \quad \frac{3}{800}(1-\alpha_{eq}t) = \frac{1}{400}(1-\alpha t) + \frac{1}{800}(1-4\alpha t)$$

$$\Rightarrow \quad \frac{3\alpha_{eq}t}{800} = \frac{\alpha t}{400} + \frac{4\alpha t}{800} \Rightarrow \alpha_{eq} = 2\alpha$$

10. $i = \frac{Q}{T} = \frac{Q}{\left(\frac{2\pi}{\omega}\right)} = \frac{Q\omega}{2\pi}$

11.

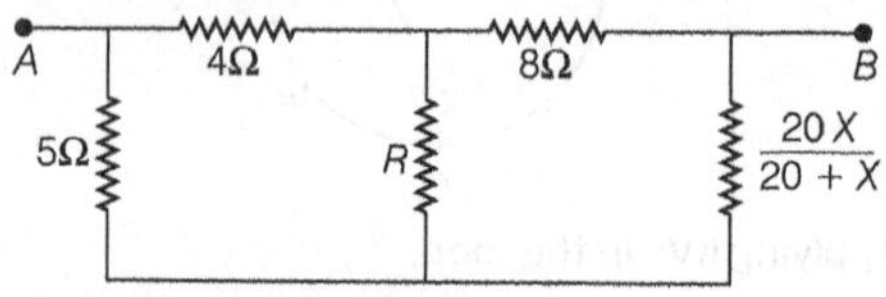

For equivalent resistance to be independent of R, it should be a balanced Wheatstone bridge.

$$\Rightarrow \quad 4\left(\frac{20X}{20+X}\right) = 8\times5 \Rightarrow x = 20\Omega$$

12.

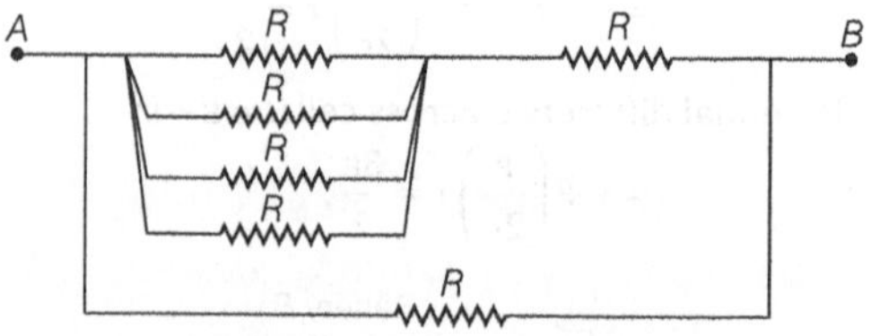

$$\frac{1}{R_{eq}} = \frac{1}{\frac{5R}{4}} + \frac{1}{R} \Rightarrow R_{eq} = \frac{5R}{9}$$

13.

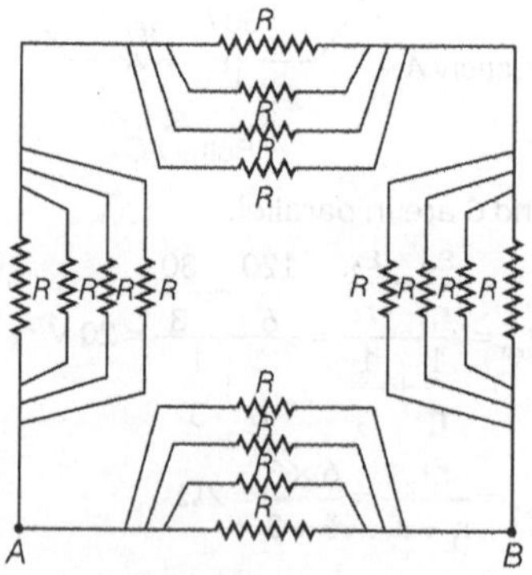

$$\frac{1}{R_{eq}} = \frac{1}{\frac{R}{4}} + \frac{1}{\frac{3R}{4}} \Rightarrow R_{eq} = \frac{3R}{16}$$

14.

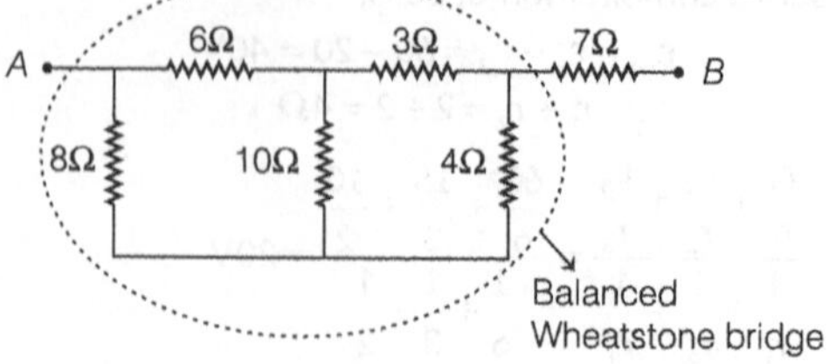

We can remove 10Ω resistance.

$$R_{eq} = \frac{36}{7} + 7 = \frac{85}{7}\,\Omega$$

15.

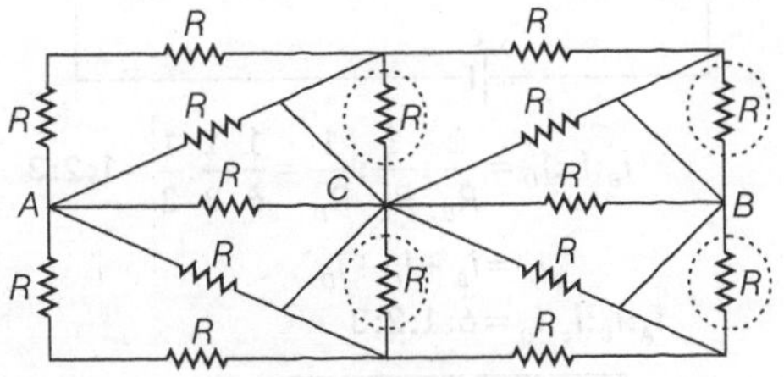

Circled resistors are short-circuited.

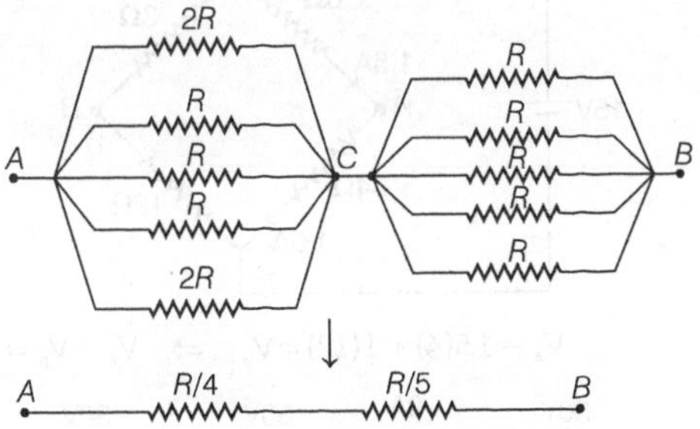

$$R_{eq} = \frac{R}{4} + \frac{R}{5} = \frac{9R}{20}$$

16.

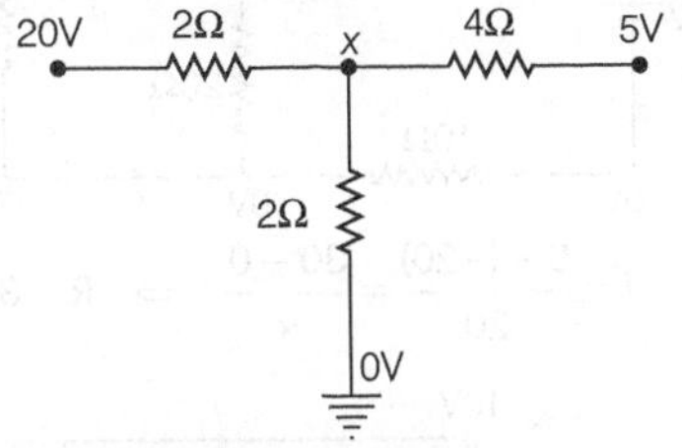

Lets take potential of juction to be x.

Applying KCL at the junction,

$$\frac{20-x}{2} + \frac{5-x}{4} + \frac{0-x}{2} = 0$$

$$\Rightarrow \quad 40 - 2x + 5 - x - 2x = 0$$

$$\Rightarrow \quad x = 9\text{V}$$

Current through the switch $= \frac{x-0}{2} = \frac{9-0}{2} = 4.5\text{A}$

17.

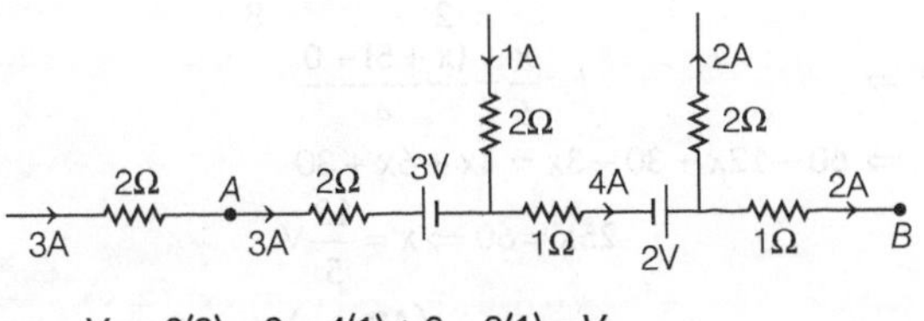

$$V_A - 3(2) - 3 - 4(1) + 2 - 2(1) = V_B$$

$$\Rightarrow \quad V_A - V_B = 13\text{V}$$

18.

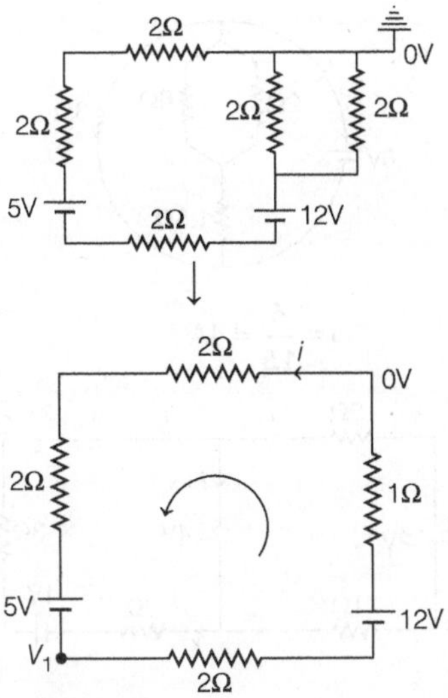

Using KVL in the loop,

$$+12 - i(1) - i(2) - i(2) - 5 - i(2) = 0$$

$$\Rightarrow \quad i = 1\text{A}$$

$$0 - i(2) - i(2) - 5 = V_1 \quad \Rightarrow \quad V_1 = -9\text{V}$$

19.

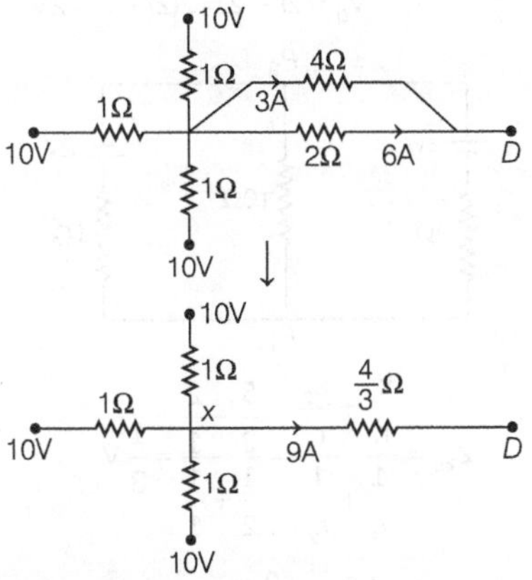

Lets take potential of the junction to be x.

Using KCL at the junction,

$$\frac{10-x}{1} + \frac{10-x}{1} + \frac{10-x}{1} = 9$$

$$\Rightarrow \quad x = 7\text{V} \quad \Rightarrow \quad \frac{x - V_D}{\frac{4}{3}} = 9$$

$$\Rightarrow \quad 7 - V_D = 12 \quad \Rightarrow \quad V_D = -5\text{V}$$

20.

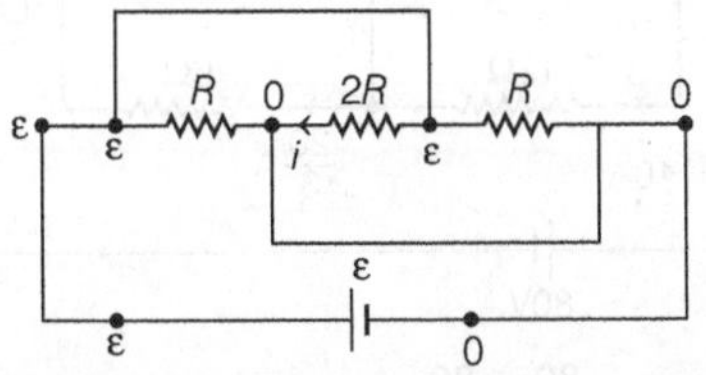

Current in a resistor flows from high potential to low potential. So, current in 2R resistance will be from right to left.

21.

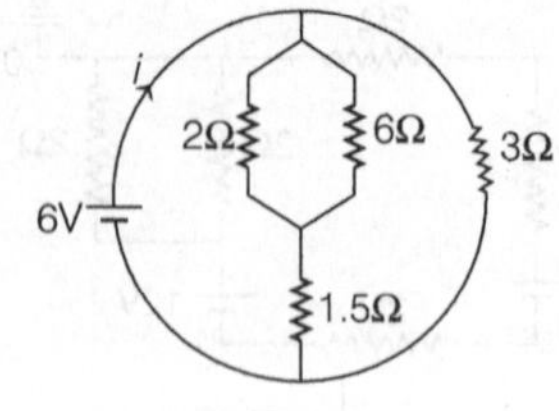

$$i = \frac{6}{1.5} = 4\text{A}$$

22.

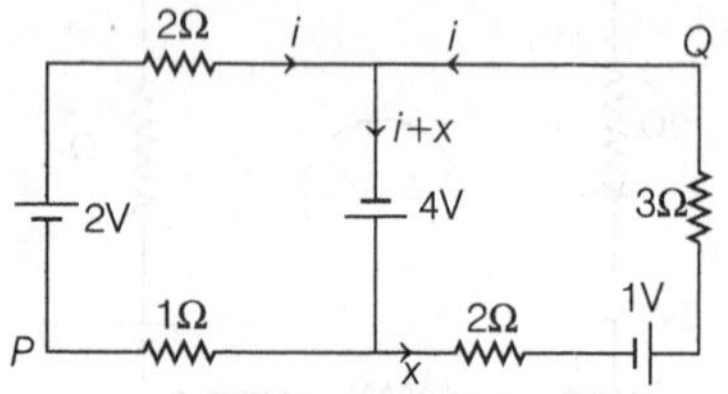

Using KVL,

$$+2 - 2i + 4 - i(1) = 0 \quad \Rightarrow \quad i = 2\text{A}$$

$$+4 - 2x + 1 - 3x = 0 \quad \Rightarrow \quad x = 1\text{A}$$

$$V_P + 2 - i(2) = V_Q$$

$$\Rightarrow \quad V_P - V_Q = 2i - 2 = 2(2) - 2 = 2\text{V}$$

23.

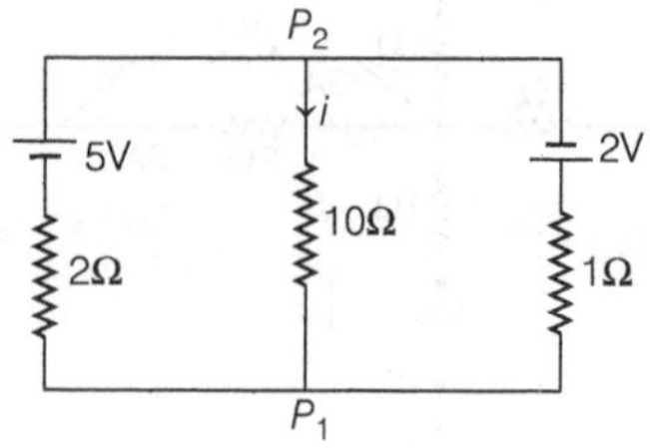

$$\varepsilon_{eq} = \frac{\frac{\varepsilon_1}{r_1} + \frac{\varepsilon_2}{r_2}}{\frac{1}{r_1} + \frac{1}{r_2}} = \frac{\frac{5}{2} - \frac{2}{1}}{\frac{1}{2} + \frac{1}{1}} = \frac{1}{3}\text{V}$$

$$r_{eq} = \frac{r_1 r_2}{r_1 + r_2} = \frac{2}{3}\Omega$$

$$i = \frac{\varepsilon_{eq}}{R + r_{eq}} = \frac{\frac{1}{3}}{10 + \frac{2}{3}} = \frac{1}{32}\text{A} = 0.03\text{A}$$

24.

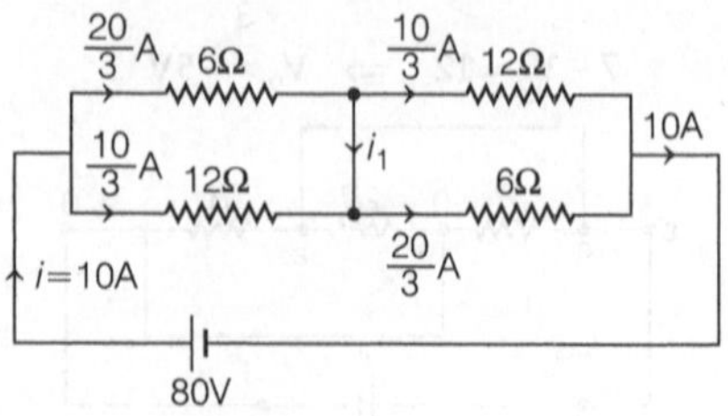

$$i = \frac{80}{R_{eq}} = \frac{80}{8} = 10\text{A}$$

$$i_1 = \frac{20}{3} - \frac{10}{3} = \frac{10}{3}\text{A}$$

25.

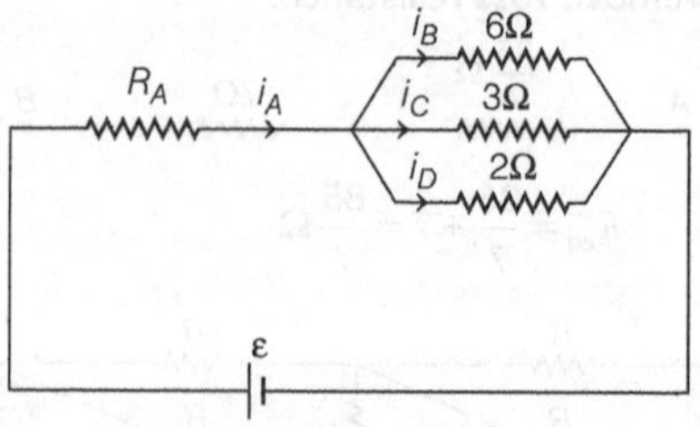

$$i_B : i_C : i_D = \frac{1}{R_B} : \frac{1}{R_C} : \frac{1}{R_D} = \frac{1}{6} : \frac{1}{3} : \frac{1}{2} = 1:2:3$$

$$i_A = i_B + i_C + i_D$$

$$\Rightarrow \quad i_A : i_B : i_C : i_D = 6:1:2:3$$

26.

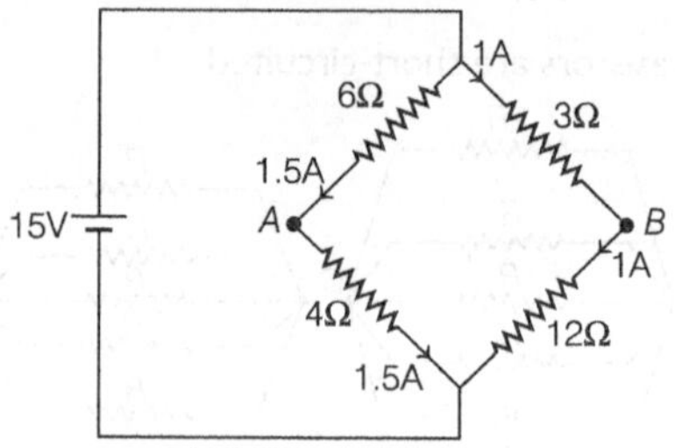

$$V_A - 1.5(4) + 1(12) = V_B \quad \Rightarrow \quad V_A - V_B = -6\text{V}$$

27.

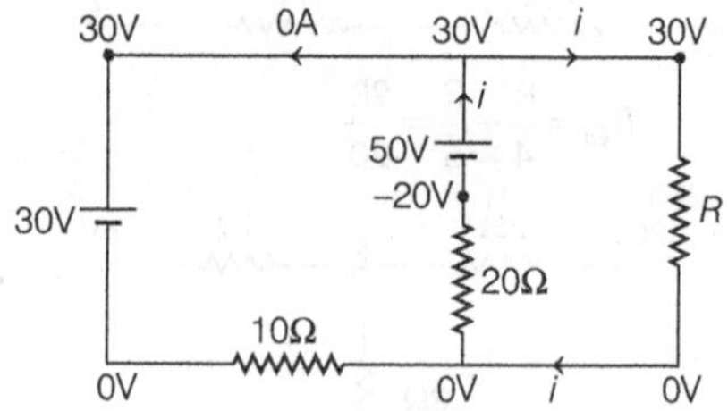

$$i = \frac{0 - (-20)}{20} = \frac{30 - 0}{R} \quad \Rightarrow \quad R = 30\Omega$$

28.

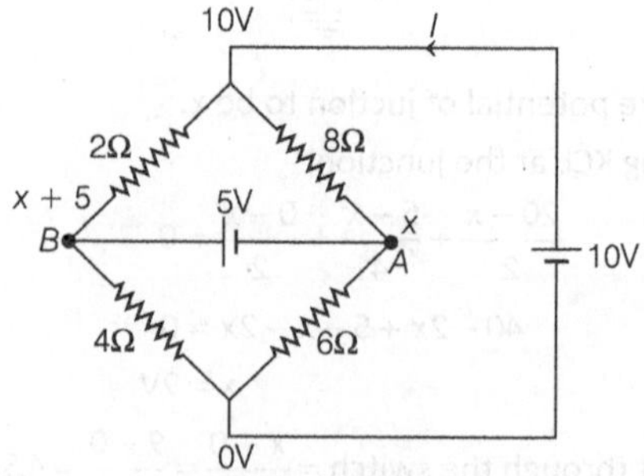

$$I = \frac{10 - (x+5)}{2} + \frac{10 - x}{8}$$

$$\Rightarrow \quad I = \frac{x}{6} + \frac{(x+5) - 0}{4}$$

$$\Rightarrow 60 - 12x + 30 - 3x = 4x + 6x + 30$$

$$25x = 60 \Rightarrow x = \frac{12}{5}\text{V}$$

$$I = \frac{12}{5} + \frac{\left(\frac{12}{5} + 5\right) - 0}{4} = 2.25\text{A}$$

29. R_1: Brown, Red, Brown $= 12 \times 10^1 = 120\ \Omega$

R_2: Blue, Black, Black $= 60 \times 10^0 = 60\ \Omega$

R_3: Orange, Black, Black $= 30 \times 10^0 = 30\ \Omega$

$$R_{eq} = \frac{R_1 R_2}{R_1 + R_2} + R_3 = \frac{120 \times 60}{120 + 60} + 30 = 70\ \Omega$$

30.

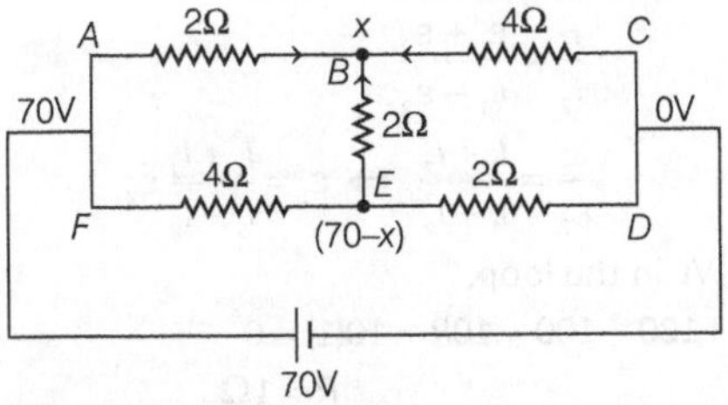

Applying KCL at junction B,

$$\frac{70 - x}{2} + \frac{0 - x}{4} + \frac{(70 - x) - x}{2} = 0$$

$$\Rightarrow \quad 140 - 2x - x + 140 - 4x = 0$$

$$\Rightarrow \quad 7x = 280 \quad \Rightarrow \quad x = 40\text{V}$$

Current through branch $BE = \dfrac{x - (70 - x)}{2}$

$$= \frac{2x - 70}{2} = \frac{2(40) - 70}{2} = 5\text{A}$$

31.

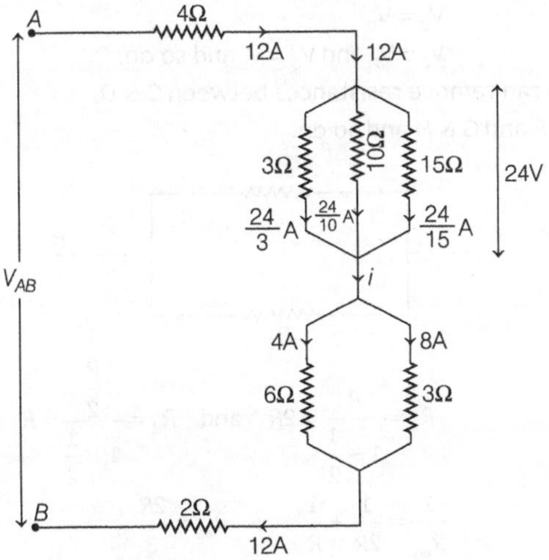

$$i = \frac{24}{15} + \frac{24}{10} + \frac{24}{3} = 12\text{A}$$

$$V_{AB} = 12(4) + 24 + 8(3) + 12(2) = 120\text{V}$$

Current through 6Ω resistor $= \dfrac{3}{3+6}(12) = 4\text{A}$

32.

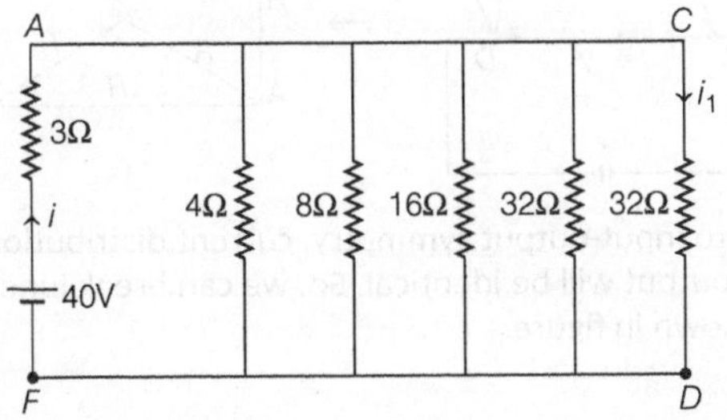

$$R_{eq} = 3 + \left(\frac{1}{4} + \frac{1}{8} + \frac{1}{16} + \frac{1}{32} + \frac{1}{32}\right)^{-1} = 3 + 2 = 5\Omega$$

i = Current through battery $= \dfrac{40}{5} = 8\text{A}$

$$i_1 = \left(\frac{\frac{1}{32}}{\frac{1}{4} + \frac{1}{8} + \frac{1}{16} + \frac{1}{32} + \frac{1}{32}}\right)(8)$$

$$i_1 = \frac{1}{2} \quad \Rightarrow \quad \frac{i_1}{i} = \frac{1/2}{8} = \frac{1}{16}$$

33.

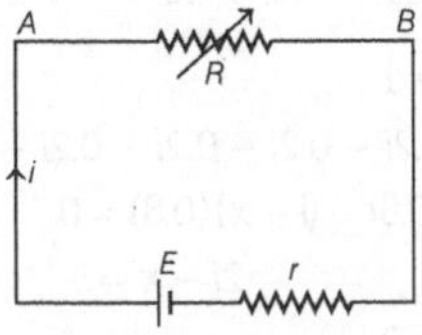

$$i = \frac{E}{R + r}$$

$$\Rightarrow \quad V = V_A - V_B = iR$$

$$V = \frac{ER}{R + r}$$

$$\Rightarrow \quad V = \frac{E}{1 + \frac{r}{R}}$$

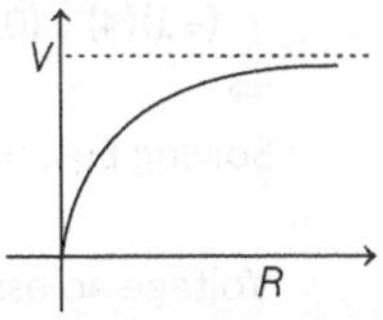

34. $12 = \varepsilon + ir$

$$\Rightarrow \quad 12 = \varepsilon + 4r \quad \text{...(i)}$$

$$9 = \varepsilon - ir$$

$$\Rightarrow \quad 9 = \varepsilon - 2r \quad \text{...(ii)}$$

Solving Eqs. (i) and (ii), we get

$$\varepsilon = 10\text{V}, \ r = 0.5\ \Omega$$

35. Applying KVL in the loop,

$$+n\varepsilon - i(nr) = 0$$

$$\Rightarrow \quad i = \frac{\varepsilon}{r}$$

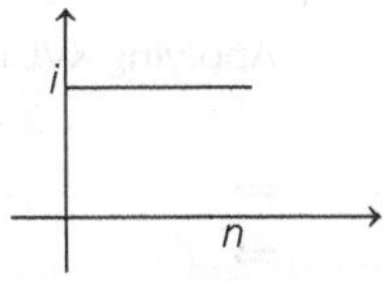

36.

$$\varepsilon_{eq} = \frac{\frac{\varepsilon}{r} + \frac{\varepsilon}{r} + \frac{\varepsilon}{r} + \dots}{\frac{1}{r} + \frac{1}{r} + \frac{1}{r} + \dots} = \varepsilon$$

$$r_{eq} = \left(\frac{1}{r} + \frac{1}{r} + \dots\right)^{-1} = \frac{r}{n}$$

$$i = \frac{\varepsilon_{eq}}{r_{eq}} = \frac{\varepsilon}{r/n} = \frac{n\varepsilon}{r}$$

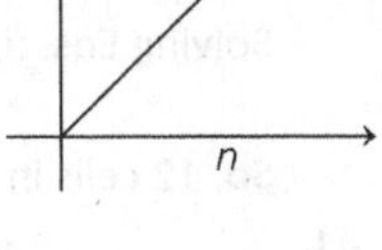

37.

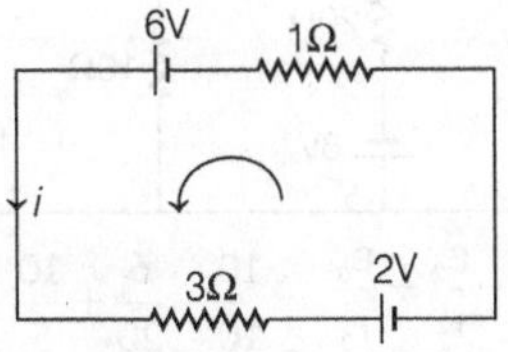

Using KVL in the loop,

$$+6 - i(3) - 2 - i(1) = 0 \quad \Rightarrow \quad i = 1\text{A}$$

Potential difference across terminals of battery 2

$$= \varepsilon + ir = 2 + 1(3) = 5\text{V}$$

38.

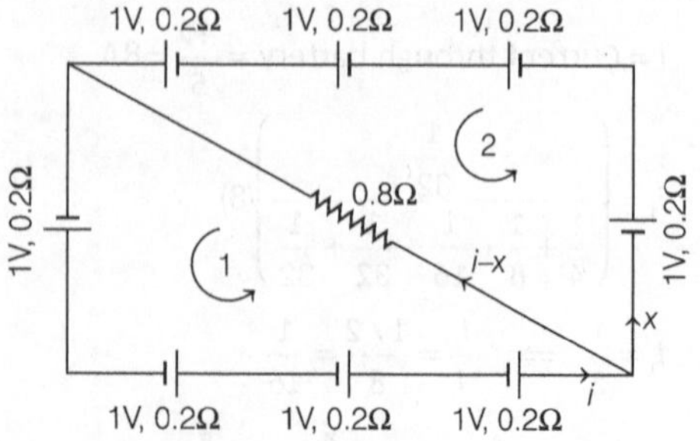

Using KVL in loop 1

$$+1+1+1+1-0.2i-0.2i-0.2i-0.2i-(i-x)(0.8)=0$$

$$\Rightarrow \quad 4-0.8i-(i-x)(0.8)=0$$

$$\Rightarrow \quad 2i-x=5 \quad \text{...(i)}$$

Using KVL in loop 2,

$$(+1)(4)-(0.2x)(4)+(i-x)(0.8)=0$$

$$\Rightarrow \quad 2x-i=5 \quad \text{...(ii)}$$

Solving Eqs. (i) and (ii), we get

$$i = 5\text{A and } x = 5\text{A}$$

Voltage across any of the battery $= \varepsilon - ir = 1 - 5(0.2) = 0$

39.

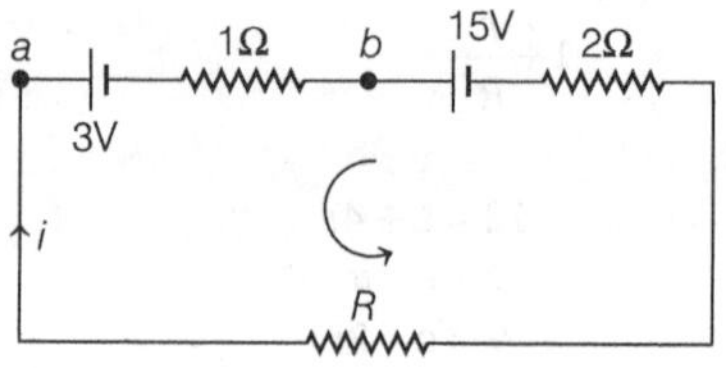

$$V_a - V_b = \varepsilon - ir$$

$$\Rightarrow \quad 0 = 3 - i(1) \Rightarrow i = 3\text{A}$$

Applying KVL in the loop,

$$+3 - iR - i(2) + 15 - i(1) = 0$$

$$\Rightarrow \quad (3+R)i = 18$$

$$\Rightarrow \quad (3+R)(3) = 18 \Rightarrow R = 3\Omega$$

40. Total number of cells $= mn = 48$ ...(i)

For maximum current,

$$nr = mR \Rightarrow n(1) = m(3) \quad \text{...(ii)}$$

Solving Eqs. (i) and (ii), we get

$$n = 12,\ m = 4$$

So, 12 cells in series, 4 such groups in parallel.

41.

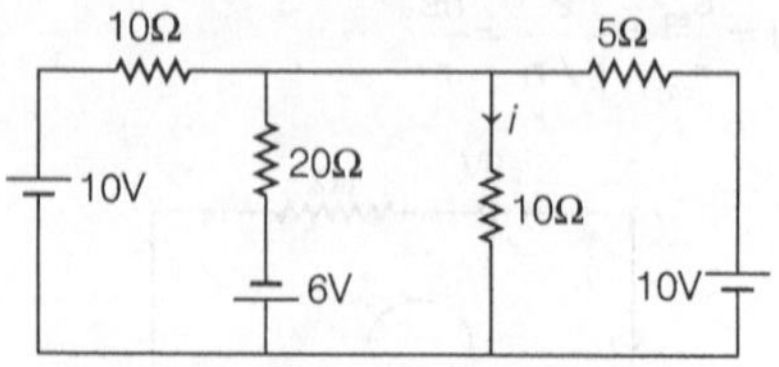

$$\varepsilon_{eq} = \frac{\dfrac{\varepsilon_1}{r_1}+\dfrac{\varepsilon_2}{r_2}+\dfrac{\varepsilon_3}{r_3}}{\dfrac{1}{r_1}+\dfrac{1}{r_2}+\dfrac{1}{r_3}} = \frac{\dfrac{10}{10}-\dfrac{6}{20}+\dfrac{10}{5}}{\dfrac{1}{10}+\dfrac{1}{20}+\dfrac{1}{5}} = \frac{54}{7}\text{V}$$

$$i = \frac{\varepsilon_{eq}}{R + r_{eq}} = \frac{\dfrac{54}{7}}{10+\dfrac{20}{7}} = \frac{54}{90} = \frac{3}{5} = 0.6\text{A}$$

42. $I_1 = \dfrac{\varepsilon_1+\varepsilon_2}{r_1+r_2}$ and $I_2 = \dfrac{\varepsilon_1-\varepsilon_2}{r_1+r_2}$

$$\Rightarrow \quad \frac{I_1}{I_2} = \frac{\varepsilon_1+\varepsilon_2}{\varepsilon_1-\varepsilon_2}$$

$$\Rightarrow \quad \frac{\varepsilon_1}{\varepsilon_2} = \frac{I_1+I_2}{I_1-I_2} \Rightarrow \varepsilon_1 = \frac{I_1+I_2}{I_1-I_2}\varepsilon_2$$

43. Using KVL in the loop,

$$+120-100-10R-10(1)=0$$

$$\Rightarrow \quad R = 1\Omega$$

44.

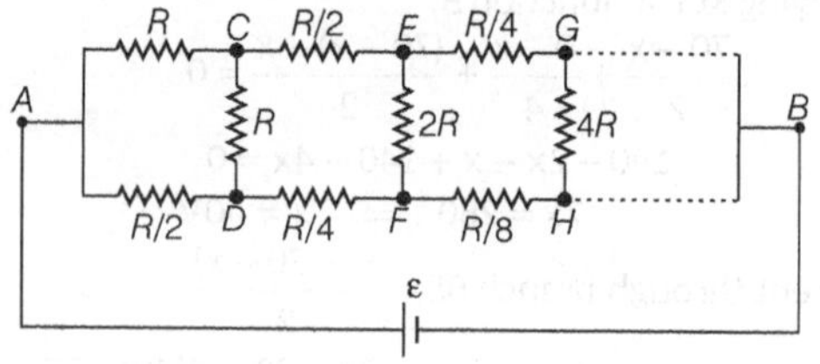

Resistance ratio in the top branch and the bottom branch is same.

So, $\quad V_C = V_D$

$V_E = V_F$ and $V_G = V_r$ and so on.

We can remove resistances between C & D, E & F and G & H and so on.

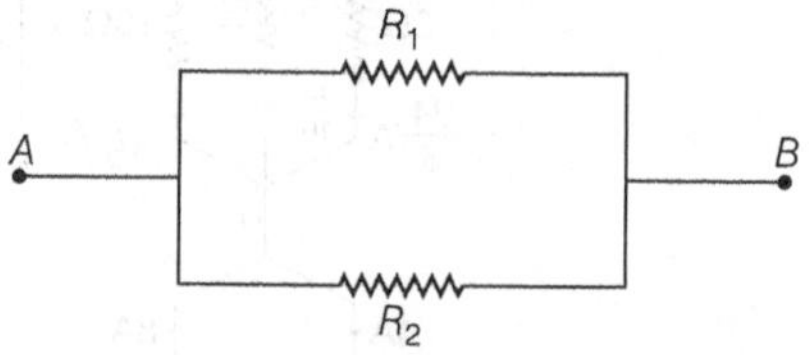

$$R_1 = \frac{R}{1-\dfrac{1}{2}} = 2R \quad \text{and} \quad R_2 = \frac{\dfrac{R}{2}}{1-\dfrac{1}{2}} = R$$

$$\frac{1}{R_{eq}} = \frac{1}{2R}+\frac{1}{R} \Rightarrow R_{eq} = \frac{2R}{3}$$

45.

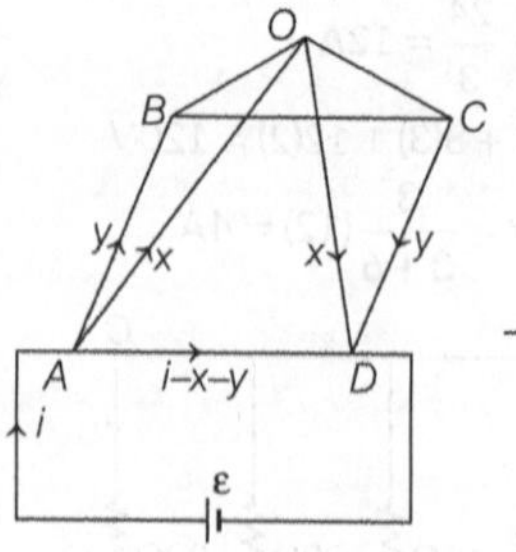

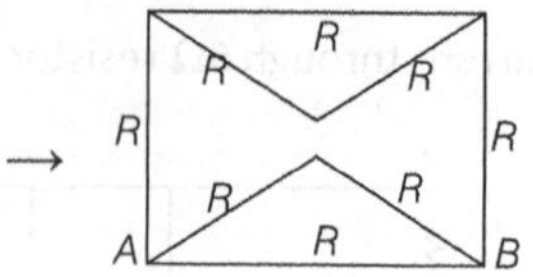

Due to input-output symmetry, current distribution at input and output will be identical. So, we can break junction at O as shown in figure.

Using series and parallel combination, $R_{eq} = \frac{8R}{15}$

46. Due to symmetry, points 1, 2, 3, ... are equipotential. So, we can remove resistors connected between these points.

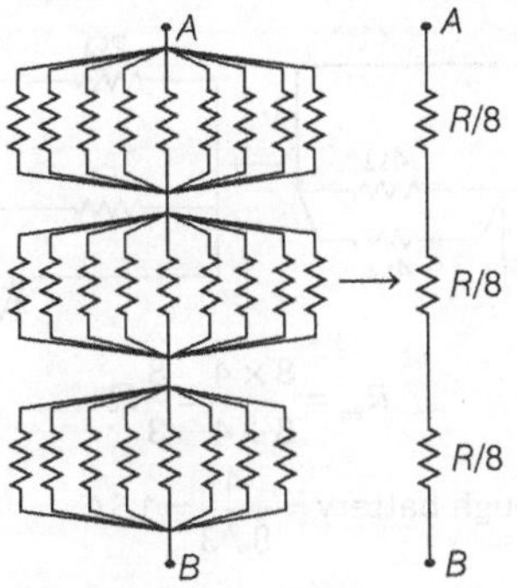

$$R_{eq} = \frac{R}{8} + \frac{R}{8} + \frac{R}{8} = \frac{3R}{8}$$

47.

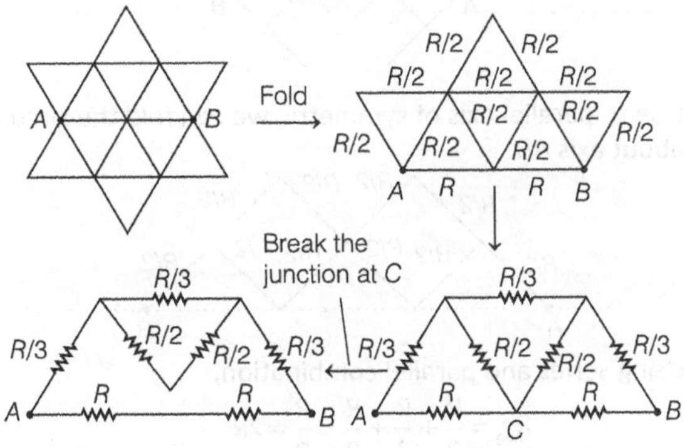

Using series and parallel combinations, $R_{eq} = \frac{22R}{35}$

48.

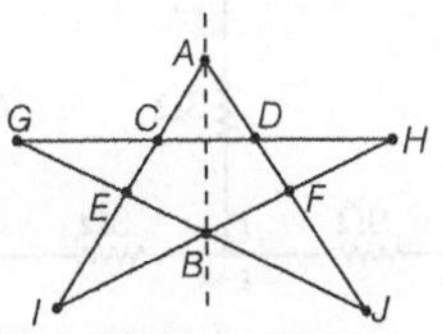

Due to symmetry, $V_C = V_D$ and $V_E = V_F$

$V_G = V_H$ and $V_I = V_J$

So, we can fold the circuit about axis passing through points A and B.

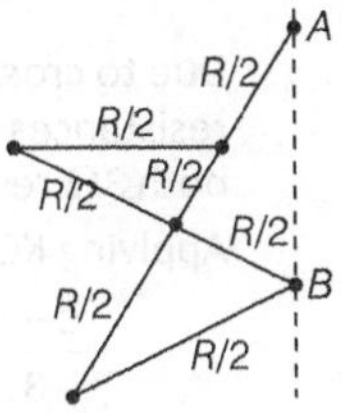

Using series and parallel combination,

$$R_{eq} = \frac{7R}{6}$$

49.

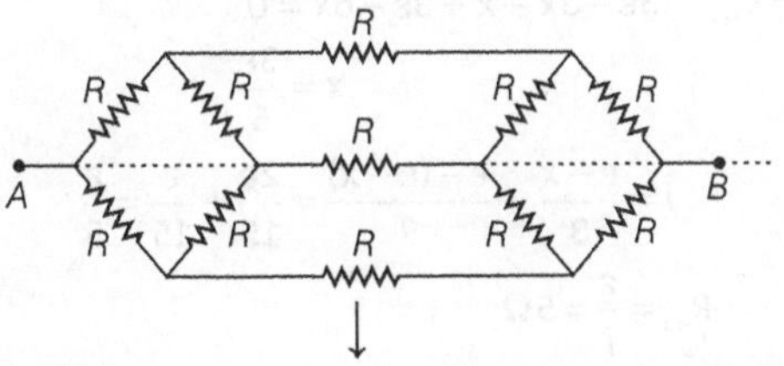

Folding about axis passing through points A and B

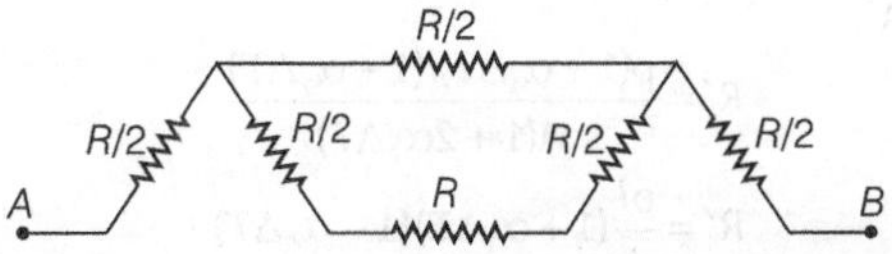

Using series and parallel combination now, $R_{eq} = \frac{7R}{5}$

50.

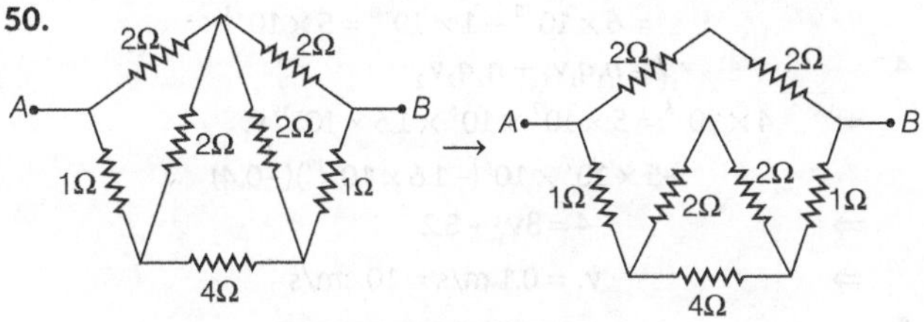

Using series and parallel combination, $R_{eq} = 2\Omega$

Numerical Value Questions

1.

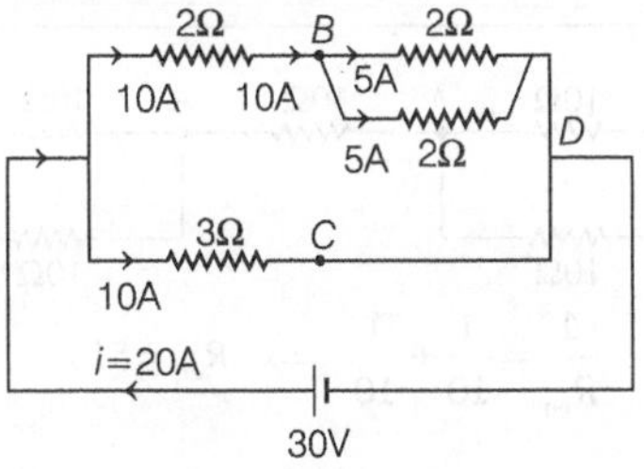

$$R_{eq} = 1.5\Omega$$

Current through battery $= \frac{30}{1.5} = 20A$

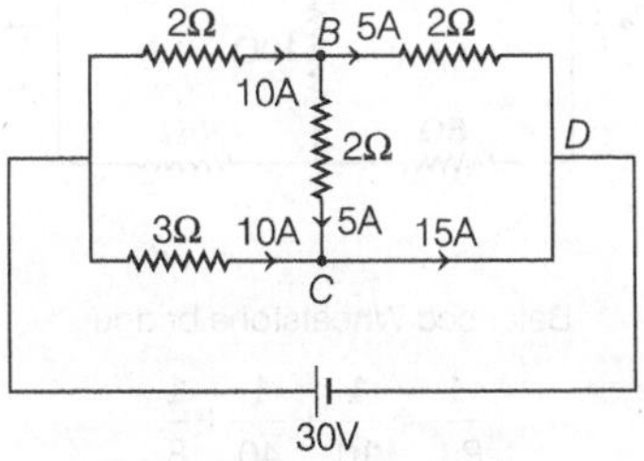

Current through branch $CD = 15A$.

2.

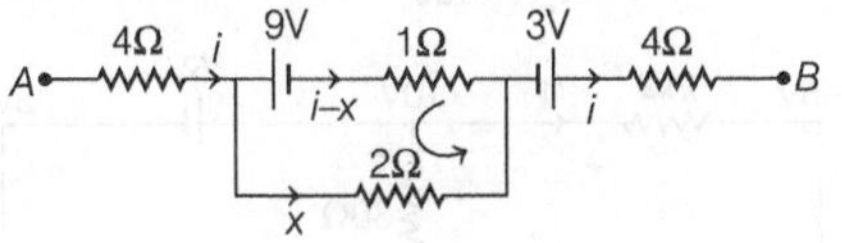

$$V_A - V_B = 16\text{ V}$$

$$V_A - 4i - 9 - 1(i - x) + 3 - 4i = 0$$

$$9i - x = 10 \quad \text{...(i)}$$

$$+9 - x(2) + (i - x)1 = 0$$

$$3x - i = 9 \quad \text{...(ii)}$$

Solving Eqs. (i) and (ii), we get

$$x = \frac{91}{26} = 3.5A$$

3. $R = \dfrac{\rho l}{A}$

$$R' = \frac{\rho(1+\alpha_1\Delta T)l(1+\alpha_2\Delta T)}{A(1+2\alpha_2\Delta T)}$$

$$R' = \frac{\rho l}{A}(1+\alpha_1\Delta T)(1-\alpha_2\Delta T)$$

$$R' = R(1+(\alpha_1-\alpha_2)\Delta T)$$

Temperature coefficient of resistance $= \alpha_1 - \alpha_2$

$$= 6\times10^{-3} - 1\times10^{-3} = 5\times10^{-3}$$

4. $J = n_1q_1v_1 + n_2q_2v_2$

$\Rightarrow \quad 4\times10^{-6} = 5\times10^{7}\times10^{6}\times1.6\times10^{-19}v_1$

$\quad +5\times10^{7}\times10^{6}(-1.6\times10^{-19})(-0.4)$

$\Rightarrow \quad 4 = 8v_1 + 3.2$

$\Rightarrow \quad v_1 = 0.1 \text{ m/s} = 10 \text{ cm/s}$

5.

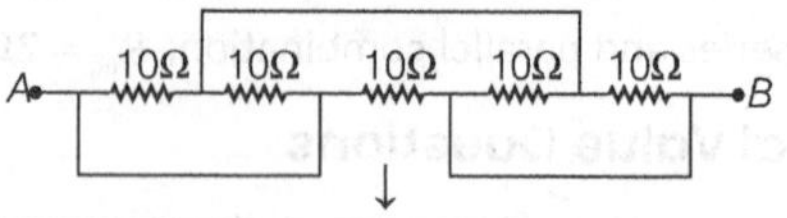

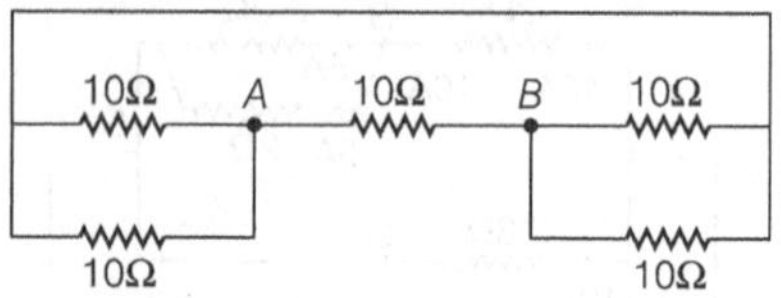

$$\frac{1}{R_{eq}} = \frac{1}{10} + \frac{1}{10} \Rightarrow R_{eq} = 5\Omega$$

6.

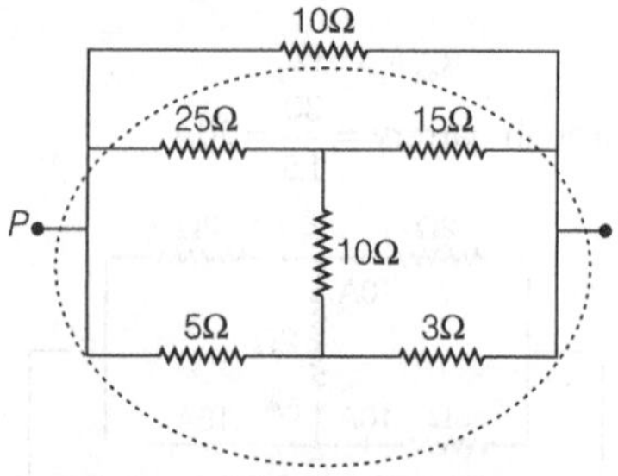

Balanced Wheatstone bridge

$$\frac{1}{R_{eq}} = \frac{1}{10} + \frac{1}{40} + \frac{1}{8}$$

$\Rightarrow \quad R_{eq} = 4\Omega$

7.

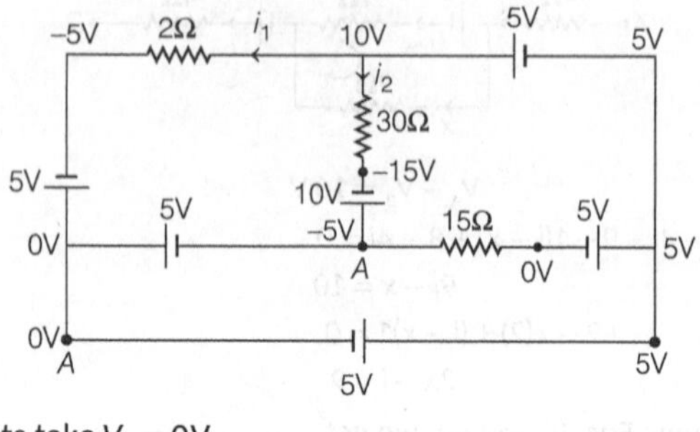

Lets take $V_A = 0V$

$$i_1 = \frac{10-(-5)}{2} = 7.5\text{A}$$

$$i_2 = \frac{10-(-15)}{30} = \frac{5}{6}\text{A} \Rightarrow \frac{i_1}{i_2} = \frac{\frac{15}{2}}{\frac{5}{6}} = 9$$

8.

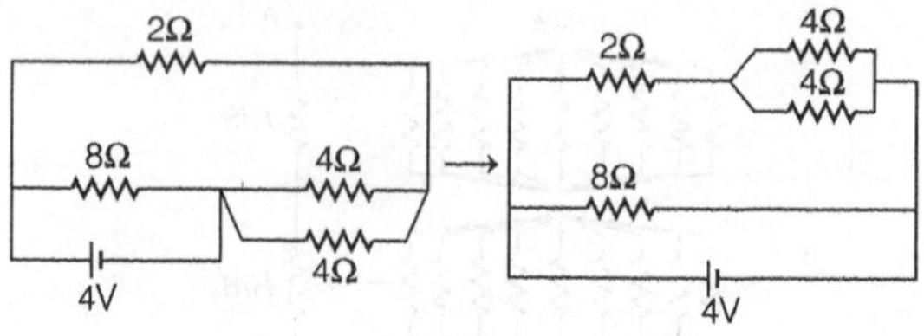

$$R_{eq} = \frac{8\times4}{8+4} = \frac{8}{3}\Omega$$

Current through battery $= \dfrac{4}{8/3} = 1.5\text{A}$

9.

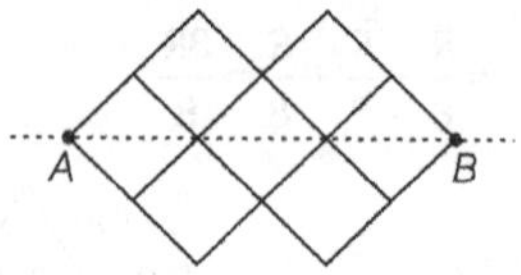

Due to parallel axis of symmetry, we can fold the circuit about axis *AB*.

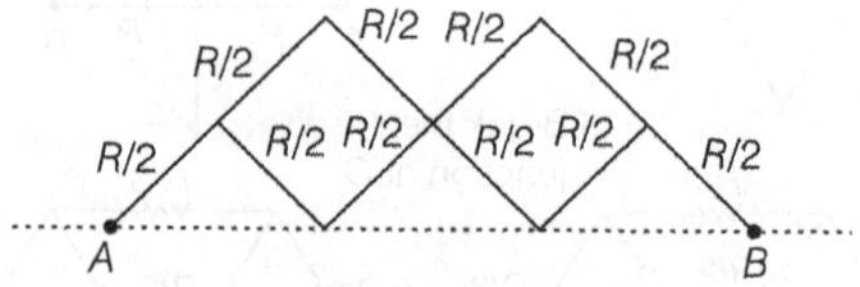

Using series and parallel combination,

$$R_{eq} = \frac{R}{2} + \frac{R}{2} + \frac{R}{2} + \frac{R}{2} = 2R$$

10.

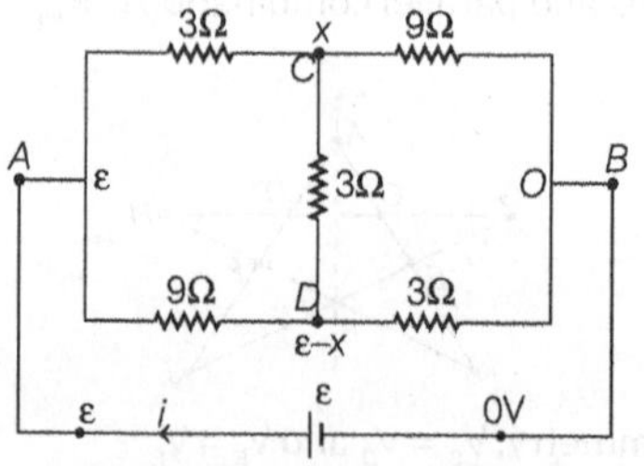

Due to cross-symmetry, current through both 3Ω resistances will be same. So, potential difference across both 3Ω resistances will be also same.

Applying KCL at junction *C*,

$$\frac{\varepsilon - x}{3} + \frac{0-x}{9} + \frac{(\varepsilon - x) - x}{3} = 0$$

$\Rightarrow \quad 3\varepsilon - 3x - x + 3\varepsilon - 6x = 0$

$\Rightarrow \quad x = \dfrac{3\varepsilon}{5}$

$$i = \frac{\varepsilon - x}{3} + \frac{\varepsilon - (\varepsilon - x)}{9} = \frac{2\varepsilon}{15} + \frac{\varepsilon}{15} = \frac{\varepsilon}{5}$$

$$R_{eq} = \frac{\varepsilon}{i} = 5\Omega$$

11. Lets take number of cells wrongly connected in the box to be n.

Equivalent emf of the box $= (12-n)\varepsilon - n\varepsilon = (12-2n)\varepsilon$

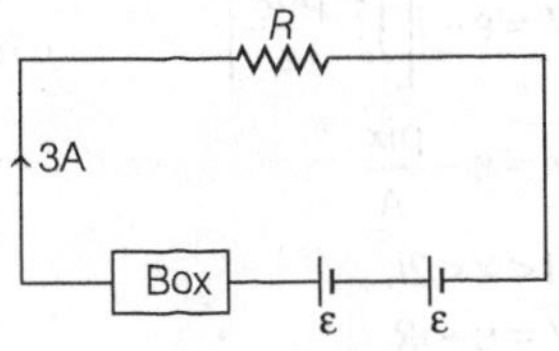

$$3 = \frac{(12-2n)\varepsilon + 2\varepsilon}{R} \quad \text{...(i)}$$

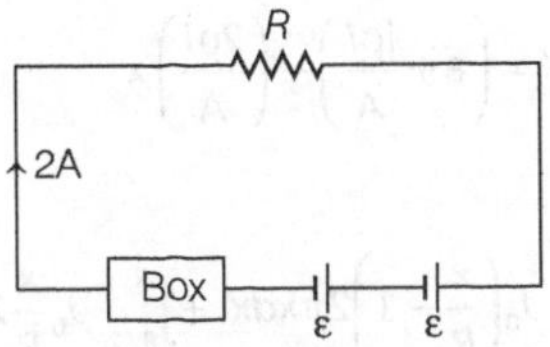

$$2 = \frac{(12-2n)\varepsilon - 2\varepsilon}{R} \quad \text{...(ii)}$$

Solving Eqs. (i) and (ii), we get

$$n = 1$$

12. $$\varepsilon_{eq} = n\varepsilon = 5000 \times 0.15 = 750\text{V}$$

$$r_{eq} = \frac{nr}{m} = \frac{5000 \times 0.25}{100} = 12.5\Omega$$

$$i = \frac{\varepsilon_{eq}}{R + r_{eq}} = \frac{750}{500 + 12.5} = 1.46 \text{ A}$$

13. Lets first find equivalent resistance of the following circuit.

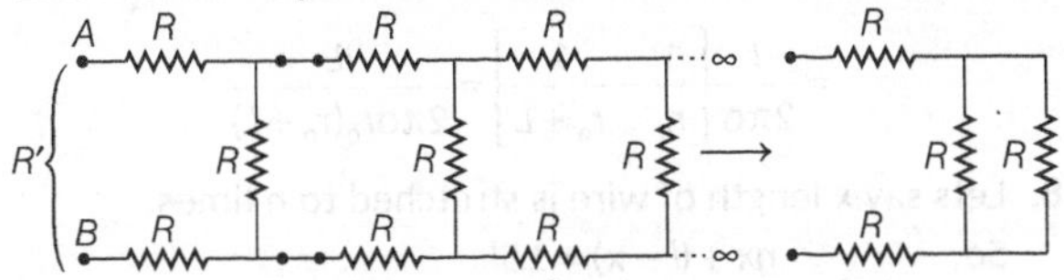

$$\Rightarrow \quad R' = R + \frac{RR'}{R+R'} + R$$

$$\Rightarrow \quad RR' + (R')^2 = 2R^2 + 3RR'$$

$$\Rightarrow \quad (R')^2 - 2RR' - 2R^2 = 0$$

$$\Rightarrow \quad R' = \frac{2 + \sqrt{4R^2 + 8R^2}}{2}$$

$$\Rightarrow \quad R' = (\sqrt{3}+1)R$$

Now, original circuit reduces to

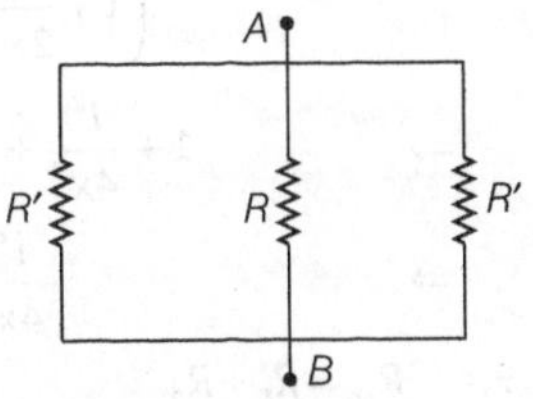

$$\frac{1}{R_{eq}} = \frac{1}{R'} + \frac{1}{R} + \frac{1}{R'}$$

$$R_{eq} = \frac{RR'}{2R + R'}$$

$$= \frac{R(\sqrt{3}+1)R}{2R + (\sqrt{3}+1)R}$$

$$= \frac{R}{\sqrt{3}} = \frac{100\sqrt{3}}{\sqrt{3}} = 100\Omega$$

14.

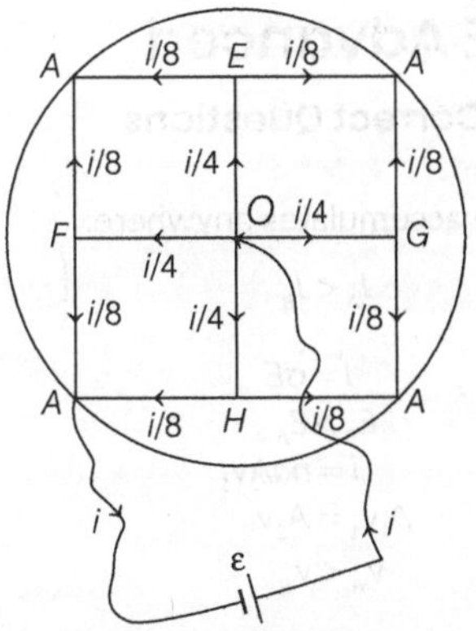

Due to symmetry, current entering at junction O will get equally divided in the four branches.

So, points E, F, G and H are equipotential.

$$R_{eq} = \frac{R}{4} + \frac{R}{8} = \frac{3R}{8} = \frac{3 \times 24}{8} = 9\Omega$$

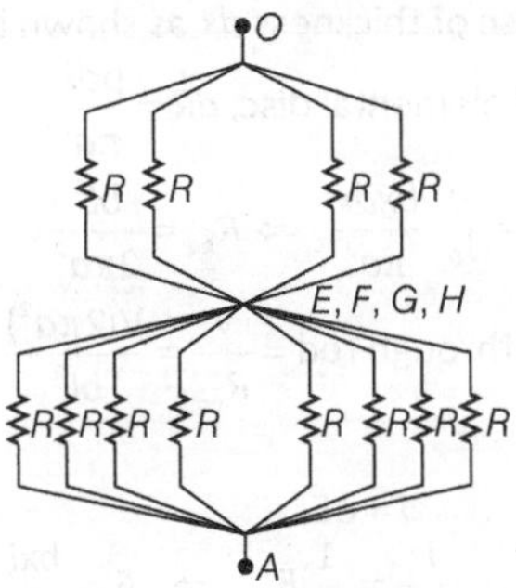

15.

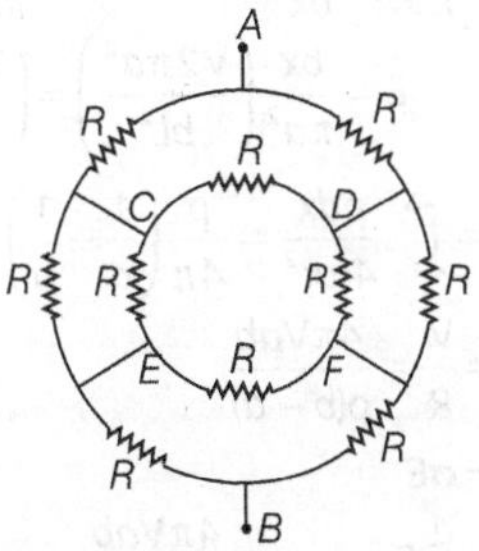

Due to symmetry, points C & D and E & F are equipotential. So, we can remove resistances between C & D and E & F.

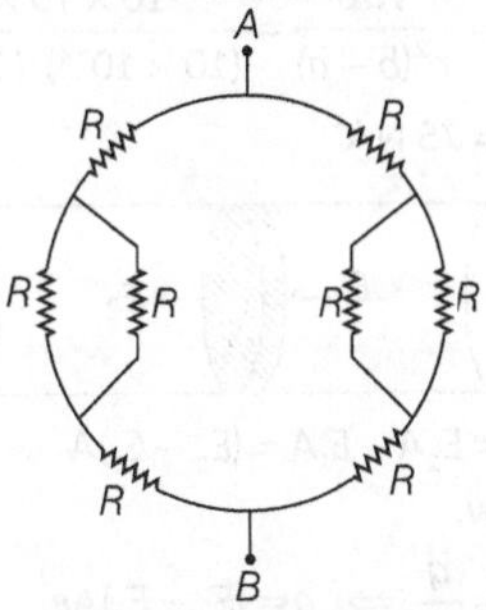

Using series and parallel combination,

$$R_{eq} = \frac{5R}{4} = \frac{5}{4}(12) = 15\Omega$$

Level 3 JEE Advanced

Single Choice Correct Questions

1. $i_A = i_B$

$\because$ No charge accumulates anywhere.

$$J_A < J_B \qquad \left(\because J = \frac{i}{\pi r^2} \text{ and } r_A > r_B\right)$$

$$J = \sigma E$$

$$\Rightarrow \quad E_B > E_A$$

$$i = nqAv_1$$

$$\Rightarrow \quad A_1 v_1 = A_2 v_2$$

$$\Rightarrow \quad v_A < v_B \qquad (\because r_A > r_B)$$

2.

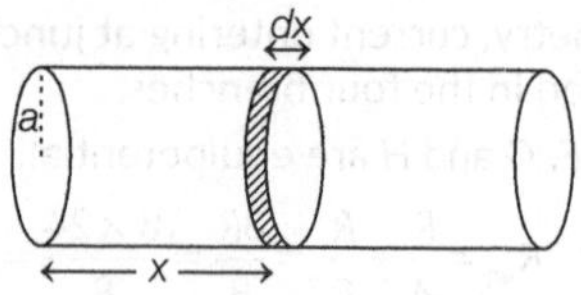

Lets take a disc of thickness dx as shown in figure.

Resistance of elemental disc, $dR = \dfrac{\rho dx}{\pi a^2}$

$$\Rightarrow \quad \int dR = \int_0^L \frac{bxdx}{\pi a^2} \Rightarrow R_{eq} = \frac{bL^2}{2\pi a^2}$$

$$i = \text{Current through rod} = \frac{V}{R_{eq}} = \frac{V(2\pi a^2)}{bL^2}$$

At point P,

$$J = \sigma E$$

$$\Rightarrow \quad \frac{i}{\pi a^2} = \frac{1}{bx} E \Rightarrow E = \frac{bxi}{\pi a^2}$$

$$E = \frac{bx}{\pi a^2}\left(\frac{V 2\pi a^2}{bL^2}\right) = \left(\frac{2V}{L^2}\right) x$$

3. $R = \text{Resistance} = \displaystyle\int_a^b \frac{\rho dx}{4\pi x^2} = \frac{\rho}{4\pi}\left(\frac{1}{a} - \frac{1}{b}\right)$

$$i = \frac{V}{R} = \frac{4\pi Vab}{\rho(b-a)}$$

$$J = \sigma E$$

$$\Rightarrow \quad \frac{i}{4\pi r^2} = \frac{1}{\rho} E \Rightarrow \frac{4\pi Vab}{4\pi r^2 \rho(b-a)} = \frac{1}{\rho} E$$

$$\Rightarrow \quad E = \frac{Vab}{r^2(b-a)} = \frac{10 \times 15 \times 10^{-2} \times 5 \times 10^{-2}}{(10 \times 10^{-2})^2 (15 \times 10^{-2} - 5 \times 10^{-2})}$$

$$= 75 \text{ N/C}$$

4.

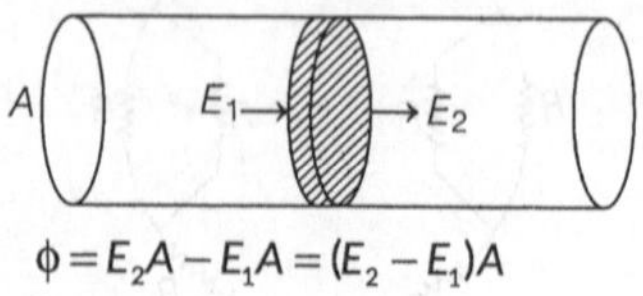

$$\phi = E_2 A - E_1 A = (E_2 - E_1) A$$

Using Gauss law,

$$\phi = \frac{q}{\varepsilon_0} \Rightarrow q = (E_2 - E_1) A \varepsilon_0$$

$$\Rightarrow \quad q = (\rho_2 J - \rho_1 J) A \varepsilon_0$$

$$\Rightarrow \quad q = (\rho_2 - \rho_1) I \varepsilon_0 \Rightarrow q = |\rho_1 - \rho_2| I \varepsilon_0$$

5. For $x < l$,

$$V = \varepsilon - iR$$

$$V = \varepsilon - i\left[\int_0^x \frac{\rho dx}{A}\right]$$

$$V = \varepsilon - \frac{\rho i x}{A}$$

For $l < x < 2l$,

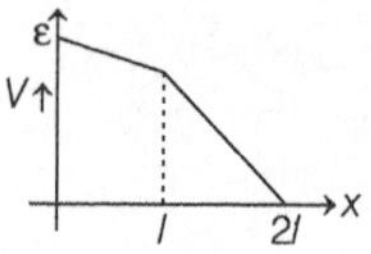

$$V = \varepsilon - iR$$

$$\Rightarrow \quad V = \varepsilon - i\left[\frac{\rho l}{A} + \frac{2\rho(x-l)}{A}\right]$$

$$\Rightarrow \quad V = \left(\varepsilon + \frac{i\rho l}{A}\right) - \left(\frac{2\rho i}{A}\right) x$$

6. $i = \int J dA$

$$i = \int_0^{R/2} J_0\left(\frac{x}{R} - 1\right) 2\pi x dx + \int_{R/2}^{R} J_0 \frac{x}{R} 2\pi x dx$$

$$= 2\pi J_0 \left[\frac{x^3}{3R} - \frac{x^2}{2}\right]_0^{R/2} + \frac{2\pi J_0}{R}\left[\frac{x^3}{3}\right]_{R/2}^{R} = \frac{5}{12}\pi J_0 R^2$$

7. $J = \dfrac{I}{2\pi r^2}$ and $J = \sigma E$

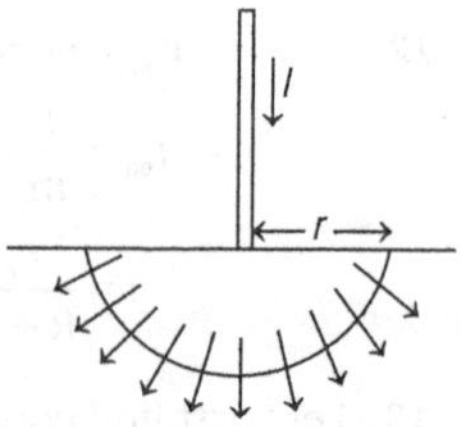

$$\Rightarrow \quad E = \frac{I}{2\pi\sigma r^2}$$

$$\int dV = \int \mathbf{E} \cdot dr$$

$$\Delta V = \frac{I}{2\pi\sigma}\int_{r_0}^{r_0+L} \frac{1}{r^2} dr$$

$$= \frac{I}{2\pi\sigma}\left[\frac{1}{r_0} - \frac{1}{r_0 + L}\right] = \frac{IL}{2\pi\sigma r_0 (r_0 + L)}$$

8. Lets say x length of wire is stretched to n times.

So, $\quad nx + (l - x) = 1.5l$

$$\Rightarrow \quad n = 1 + \frac{l}{2x} \qquad \text{...(i)}$$

$$R' = \frac{\rho n x}{A/n} + \frac{\rho(l-x)}{A} = 4\left(\frac{\rho l}{A}\right)$$

$$\Rightarrow \quad n^2 x + l - x = 4l$$

$$\Rightarrow \quad n^2 = \frac{3l}{x} + 1 \qquad \text{...(ii)}$$

From Eqs. (i) and (ii), we get

$$\left(1 + \frac{l}{2x}\right)^2 = \frac{3l}{x} + 1$$

$$\Rightarrow \quad 1 + \frac{l^2}{4x^2} + \frac{l}{x} = \frac{3l}{x} + 1$$

$$\Rightarrow \quad \frac{l^2}{4x^2} = \frac{2l}{x} \Rightarrow \frac{x}{l} = \frac{1}{8}$$

9. $R_{eq} = R_1 + R_2$

$$= \frac{\rho_C t_C}{A}(1 + \alpha_C \Delta T) + \frac{\rho_B t_B}{A}(1 + \alpha_B \Delta T)$$

$$= \frac{\rho_C t_C + \rho_B t_B}{A} + \frac{(\rho_C t_C \alpha_C + \rho_B t_B \alpha_B)\Delta T}{A}$$

For R_{eq} to be independent of temperature.

Coefficient of $\Delta T = 0$

$$\Rightarrow \quad \rho_C\alpha_C t_C + \rho_B\alpha_B t_B = 0$$

$$\Rightarrow \quad \frac{t_B}{t_C} = \left|\frac{\rho_C\alpha_C}{\rho_B\alpha_B}\right|$$

10. Lets take a strip of radius x and width dx.

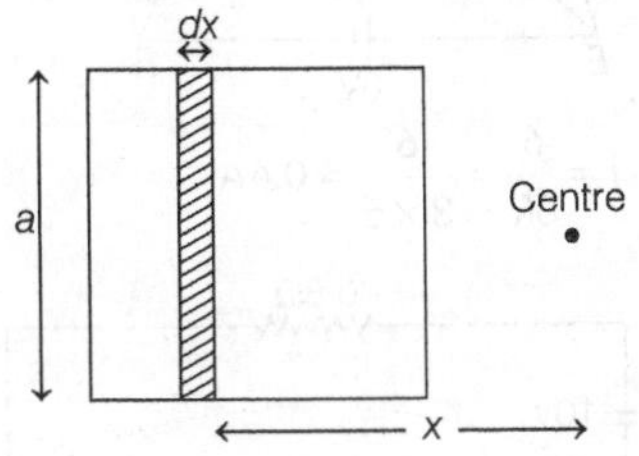

$$dR = \text{Resistance of strip} = \frac{\rho(\pi x)}{adx}$$

$$\frac{1}{R} = \int \frac{1}{dR} = \int_r^{r+a} \frac{1}{\frac{\rho\pi x}{adx}}$$

$$\frac{1}{R} = \frac{a}{\rho\pi}\ln\left(\frac{r+a}{r}\right) \Rightarrow R = \frac{\rho\pi}{a\ln\left(1+\frac{a}{r}\right)}$$

11. Lets first calculate resistance of a frustum.

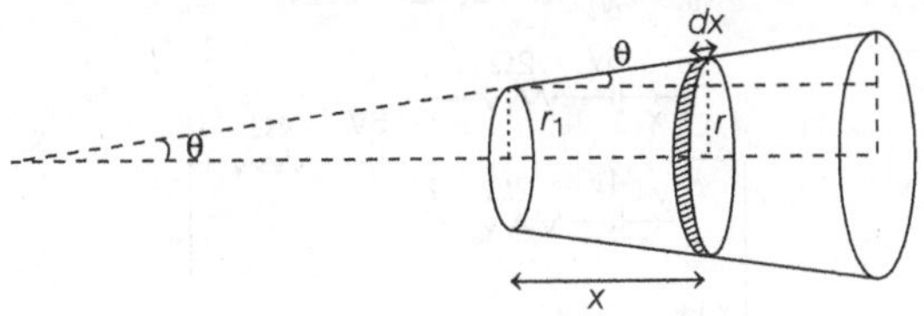

$$\tan\theta = \frac{r-r_1}{x} = \frac{r_2-r_1}{L}$$

$$r = \frac{(r_2-r_1)}{L}x + r_1 \Rightarrow dr = \left(\frac{r_2-r_1}{L}\right)dx$$

Resistance of elemental disc of radius r and thickness $dx = \frac{\rho dx}{\pi r^2}$

$$dR = \frac{\rho dx}{\pi r^2}$$

$$\int dR = \int_{r_1}^{r_2} \frac{\rho}{\pi r^2}\left(\frac{L}{r_2-r_1}\right)dr$$

$$R = \frac{\rho L}{\pi(r_2-r_1)}\left[-\frac{1}{r_1}\right]_{r_1}^{r_2} = \frac{\rho L}{\pi r_1 r_2}$$

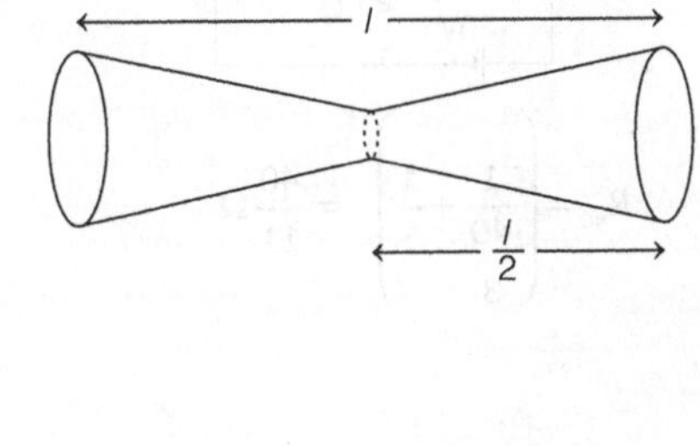

$$R_{eq} = R_1 + R_2 = \frac{\rho\frac{l}{2}}{\pi r_1 r_2} + \frac{\rho\frac{l}{2}}{\pi r_1 r_2} = \frac{\rho l}{\pi r_1 r_2}$$

$$i = \frac{\varepsilon}{R_{eq}} = \frac{\pi\varepsilon r_1 r_2}{\rho l}$$

12.

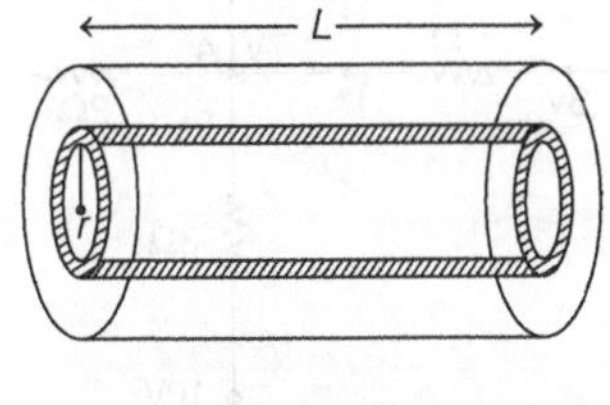

Lets take a cylindrical shell of radius r and thickness dr.

Resistance of elemental cylindrical shell $= \frac{\rho dr}{2\pi rL}$

$$\int dR = \int_a^b \frac{\rho dr}{2\pi rL}$$

$$R_{eq} = \frac{\rho}{2\pi L}\ln\left(\frac{b}{a}\right)$$

$$I = \frac{V}{R_{eq}} = \frac{V(2\pi L)}{\rho(\ln b - \ln a)}$$

13. For element P, upto 10V, resistance is constant and after 10V, current through it is constant and equal to 1A.

For element Q, upto 10V, resistance is gradually decreasing to zero.

When elements P and Q are connected in series,

$$R_{eq} = R_1 + R_2$$

Upto 20V, R_1 is constant and R_2 is gradually decreasing.

So, R_{eq} will gradually decrease and current will gradually increase. And after 20V, current will be constant 1A.

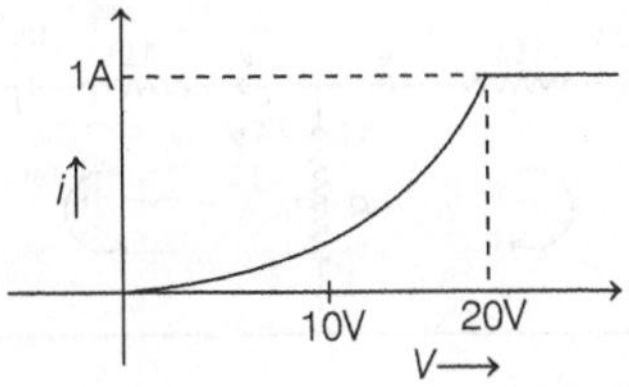

14.

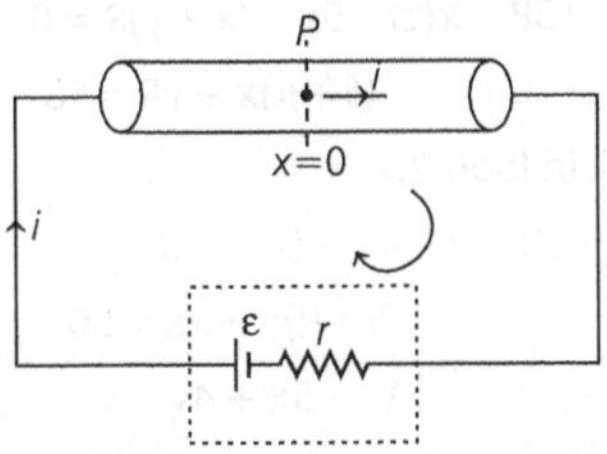

In a resistance, potential decreases in the direction of current.

Inside battery while going from cathode to anode, potential will increase but potential difference across the terminals of the battery will be $\varepsilon - ir$ which is less than ε.

15.

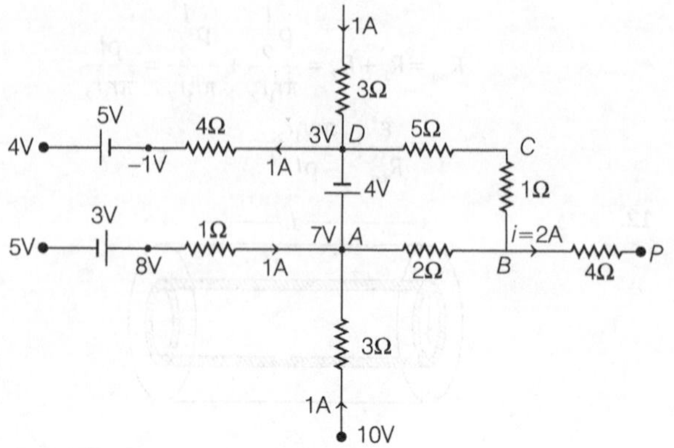

For 3Ω resistor, $1 = \dfrac{10 - V_A}{3}$

$\Rightarrow \quad V_A = 7\text{V}$

$V_D = 7 - 4 = 3\text{V}$

For 1 Ω resistor, $i = \dfrac{8-7}{1} = 1\text{V}$, right

For 4Ω resistor, $i = \dfrac{3-(-1)}{4} = 1\text{A}$, left

For loop *ABCD*,

Incoming current = Outgoing current

$$1 + 1 + 1 = 1 + i \Rightarrow i = 2\text{A}$$

Applying KCL at junction *B*,

$$\frac{3 - V_B}{6} + \frac{7 - V_B}{2} = 2 \Rightarrow V_B = 3\text{V}$$

For 4Ω resistor on the right side,

$$2 = \frac{3 - V_P}{4} \Rightarrow V_P = -5\text{V}$$

16.

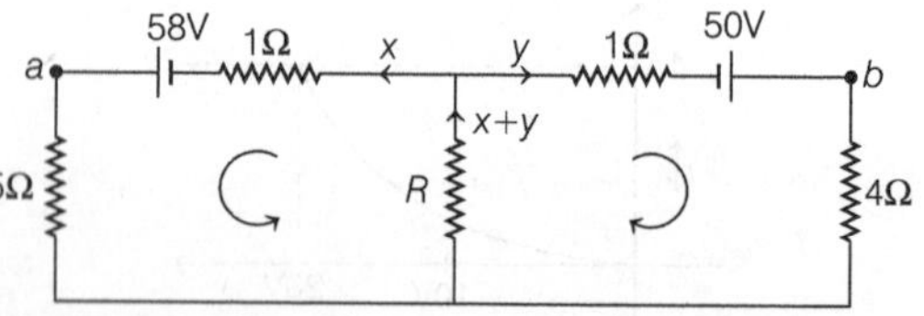

Applying KVL in loop 1,

$$+58 - x(1) - 5x - (x + y)R = 0$$

$$(6 + R)x + yR = 58 \quad \text{...(i)}$$

Applying KVL in loop 2,

$$+50 - y - 4y - (x + y)R = 0$$

$$(5 + R)y + xR = 50 \quad \text{...(ii)}$$

$$V_a - 5x + 4y = V_b$$

$$5x - 4y = V_a - V_b = 7$$

$$5x - 4y = 7 \quad \text{...(iii)}$$

Solving Eqs. (i), (ii) and (iii), we get

$R = 8\Omega, x = 3\text{A}$

and $\quad y = 2\text{A}$

17. Due to symmetry, *A* & *D* and *B* & *C* are equipotential. So, we can remove resistances between *A* & *D* and *B* & *C*.

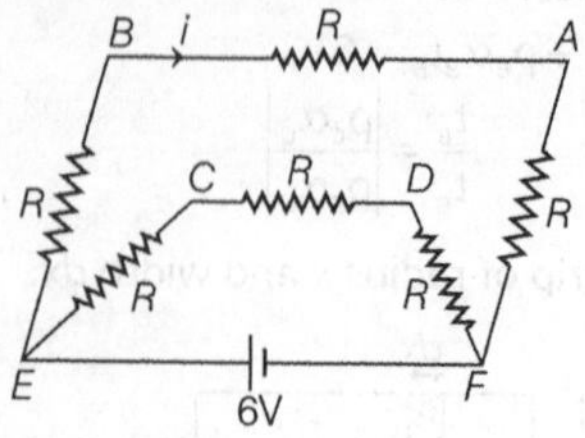

$$i = \frac{6}{3R} = \frac{6}{3 \times 5} = 0.4\text{A}$$

18.

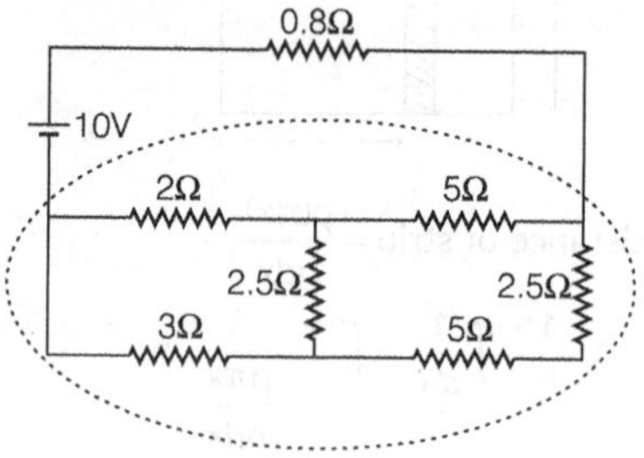

We can remove 2.5 Ω resistance.

$$i = \frac{10}{4.2 + 0.8} = 2\text{A}$$

$$V_B - V_A = iR = 2(4.2) = 8.4\text{V}$$

19.

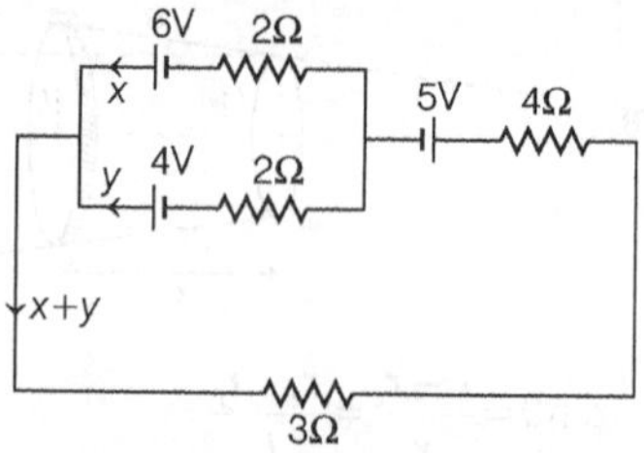

Using KVL,

$$+6 - 4 + 2y - 2x = 0$$

$$x - y = 1 \quad \text{...(i)}$$

$$+6 - 3(x + y) - 4(x + y) - 5 - x(2) = 0$$

$\Rightarrow$
$$9x + 7y = 1 \quad \text{...(ii)}$$

Solving Eqs. (i) and (ii), we get

$$x = \frac{1}{2}\text{A}$$

20.

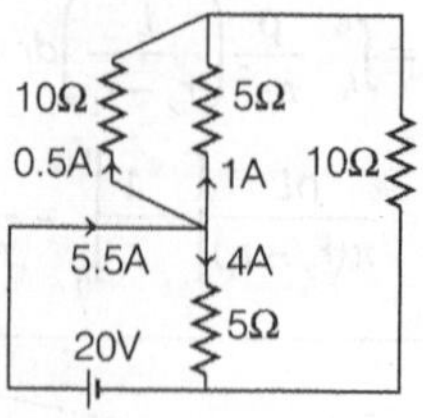

$$R_{eq} = \left(\frac{1}{\frac{40}{3}} + \frac{1}{5}\right)^{-1} = \frac{40}{11}\Omega$$

Current through battery $= \dfrac{20}{40/11} = 5.5\text{A}$

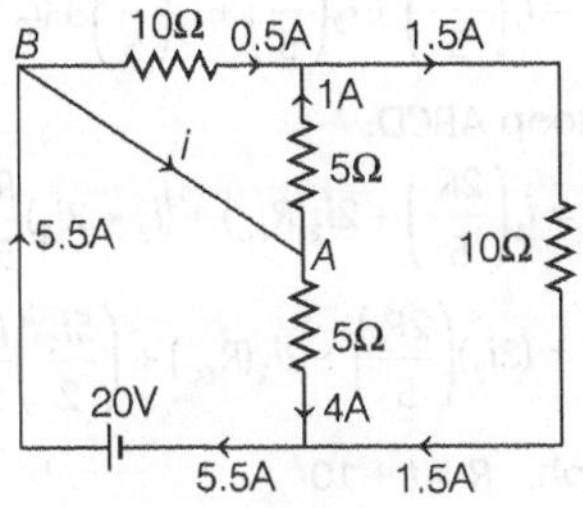

$i = 4 + 1 = 5\text{A}$

21.

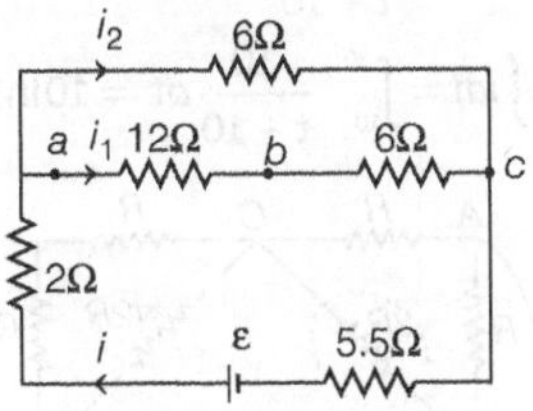

$$i_1 = \frac{V_a - V_b}{12} = \frac{4}{12} = \frac{1}{3}\text{A}$$

$$V_a - V_c = 18\left(\frac{1}{3}\right) = 6\text{V}$$

$$i_2 = \frac{V_a - V_c}{6} = \frac{6}{6} = 1\text{A}$$

$$i = i_1 + i_2 = 1 + \frac{1}{3} = \frac{4}{3}\text{A}$$

$$R_{eq} = 5.5 + 2 + \frac{18 \times 6}{18 + 6} = 12\Omega$$

$$\varepsilon = iR_{eq} = \frac{4}{3} \times 12 = 16\text{ V}$$

22.

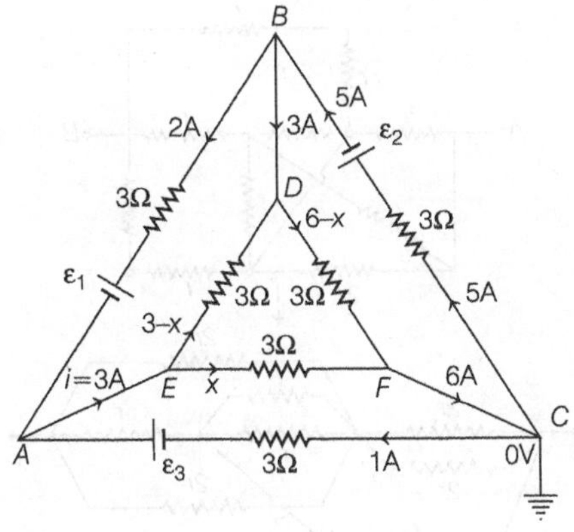

For ΔDEF,

Incoming current = Outgoing current

$$i + 3 = 6 \Rightarrow i = 3\text{A}$$

Using KVL in ΔDEF,

$$-3(3 - x) - 3(6 - x) + 3x = 0$$

$$-3 + x - 6 + x + x = 0 \Rightarrow x = 3\text{A}$$

Applying KVL in loop $AEFCA$,

$$-3x - 3 + \varepsilon_3 = 0$$

$$\varepsilon_3 = 3x + 3 = 12\text{V}$$

23.

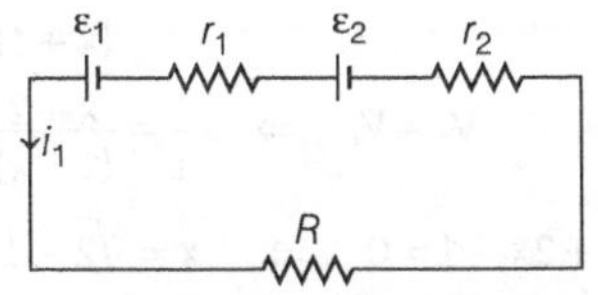

$$i_1 = \frac{\varepsilon_1 + \varepsilon_2}{R + r_1 + r_2}$$

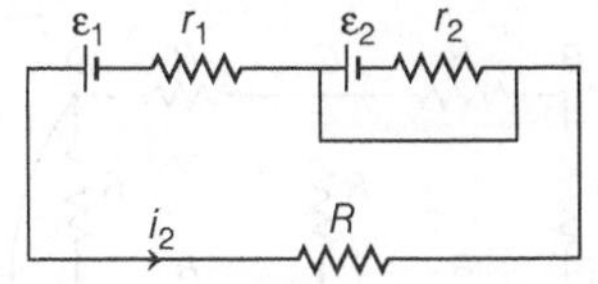

$$i_2 = \frac{\varepsilon_1}{R + r_1} \Rightarrow i_2 > i_1$$

$$\frac{\varepsilon_1}{R + r_1} > \frac{\varepsilon_1 + \varepsilon_2}{R + r_1 + r_2}$$

$$\Rightarrow \quad \varepsilon_1 R + \varepsilon_1 r_1 + \varepsilon_1 r_2 > \varepsilon_1 R + \varepsilon_1 r_1 + \varepsilon_2 R + \varepsilon_2 r_1$$

$$\Rightarrow \quad \varepsilon_1 r_2 > \varepsilon_2 (R + r_1)$$

24.

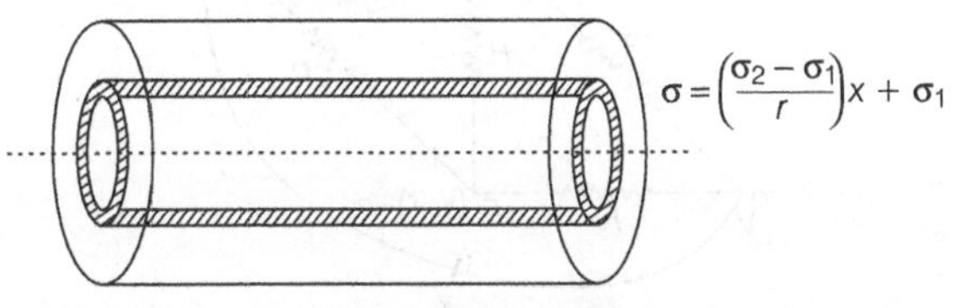

Lets take a cylindrical shell of radius x and thickness dx.

Resistance of elemental cylinder shell $= \dfrac{l}{\sigma 2\pi x dx}$

$$dR = \frac{l}{\sigma(2\pi x)dx}$$

All such cylindrical shells are in parallel combination.

$$\int \frac{1}{dR} = \int \frac{\sigma(2\pi x)dx}{l}$$

$$\frac{1}{R_{eq}} = \int_0^r \frac{[(\sigma_2 - \sigma_1)\frac{x}{r} + \sigma_1]2\pi x dx}{l}$$

$$\frac{1}{R_{eq}} = \left(\frac{(\sigma_2 - \sigma_1)}{3} + \frac{\sigma_1}{2}\right)\frac{2\pi r^2}{l}$$

$$\Rightarrow \quad R_{eq} = \frac{3l}{(\sigma_1 + 2\sigma_2)\pi r^2}$$

$$i = \frac{V}{R_{eq}} = \frac{\pi r^2 V(\sigma_1 + 2\sigma_2)}{3l}$$

25.

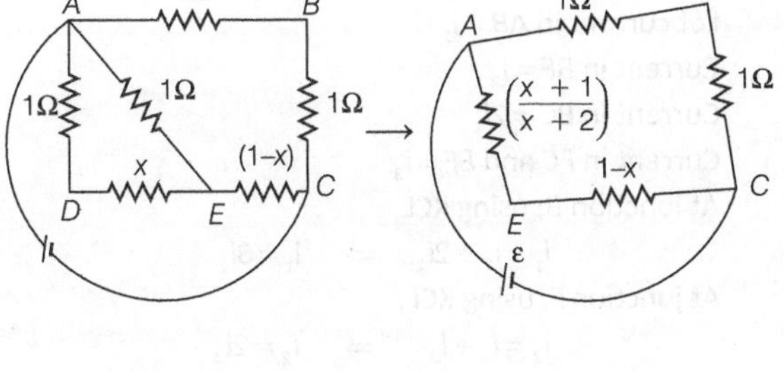

$$V_B = V_E \Rightarrow \frac{1}{1} = \frac{\frac{(x+1)}{x+2}}{(1-x)}$$

$$\Rightarrow \quad x^2 + 2x - 1 = 0 \Rightarrow x = \sqrt{2} - 1$$

Now, $\dfrac{CE}{ED} = \dfrac{1-x}{x} = \dfrac{1-(\sqrt{2}-1)}{\sqrt{2}-1} = \dfrac{2-\sqrt{2}}{\sqrt{2}-1} = \sqrt{2}$

26.

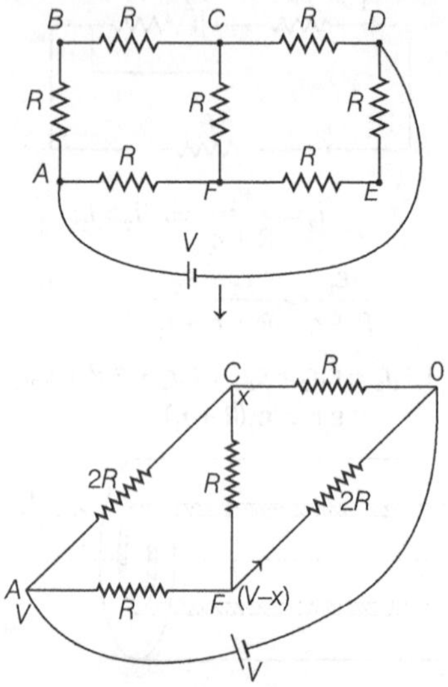

Applying KCL at junction C,

$$\frac{V-x}{2R} + \frac{(V-x)-x}{R} + \frac{0-x}{R} = 0$$

$$V - x + 2V - 4x - 2x = 0 \Rightarrow x = \frac{3V}{7}$$

$$V_F - V_C = (V-x) - x = V - 2x$$

$$= V - 2\left(\frac{3V}{7}\right) = \frac{V}{7}$$

27.

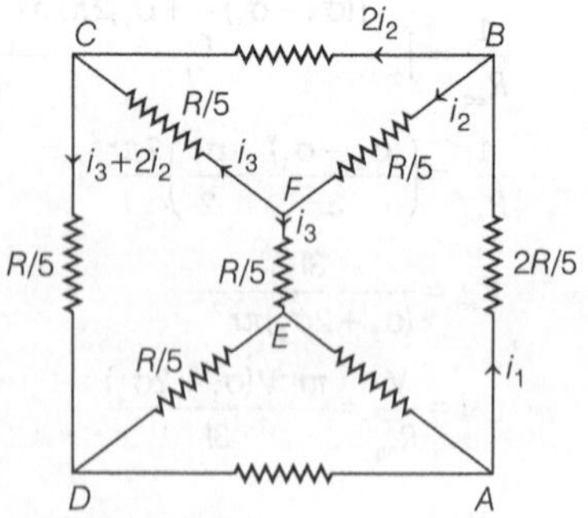

Let current in $AB = i_1$

Current in $BF = i_2$

Current in $BC = 2i_2$

Current in FC and $EF = i_3$

At junction B, using KCL,

$$i_1 = i_2 + 2i_2 \Rightarrow i_1 = 3i_2$$

At junction F, using KCL,

$$i_2 = i_3 + i_3 \Rightarrow i_2 = 2i_3$$

Using KVL in loop ABFCD,

$$V_A - V_D = i_1\left(\frac{2R}{5}\right) + i_2\left(\frac{R}{5}\right) + i_3\left(\frac{R}{5}\right) + (i_3 + 2i_2)\frac{R}{5} = 2i_2R$$

Using KVL in loop ABCD,

$$V_A - V_D = i_1\left(\frac{2R}{5}\right) + 2i_2(R_{BC}) + (i_3 + 2i_2)\frac{R}{5}$$

$$2i_2R = (3i_2)\left(\frac{2R}{5}\right) + 2i_2(R_{BC}) + \left(\frac{5i_2}{2}\right)\frac{R}{5} \Rightarrow R_{BC} = \frac{3R}{20}$$

28. From the graph, $R = t + 10$

Current, $i = \dfrac{10}{t+10}$

$$q = \int i\,dt = \int_{10}^{30} \frac{10}{t+10}\,dt = 10\ln 2$$

29.

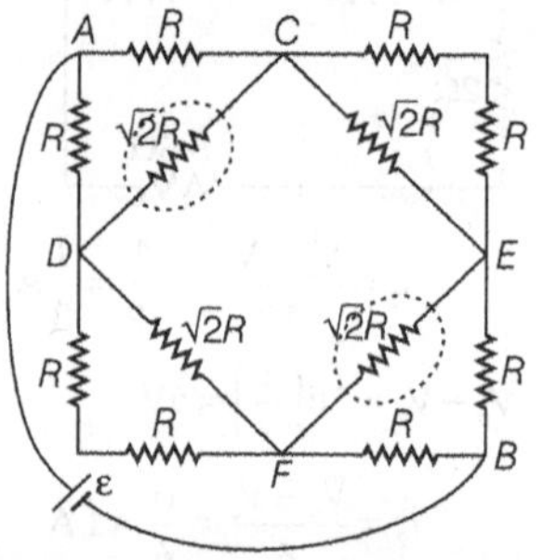

Due to parallel axis symmetry, points C & D and E & F are equipotential. So, we can remove resistances between C & D and E & F.

Now, using series and parallel combination,

$$R_{eq} = \sqrt{2}R = \sqrt{2}\left(\rho\frac{d}{2}\right) = \frac{\rho d}{\sqrt{2}}$$

30.

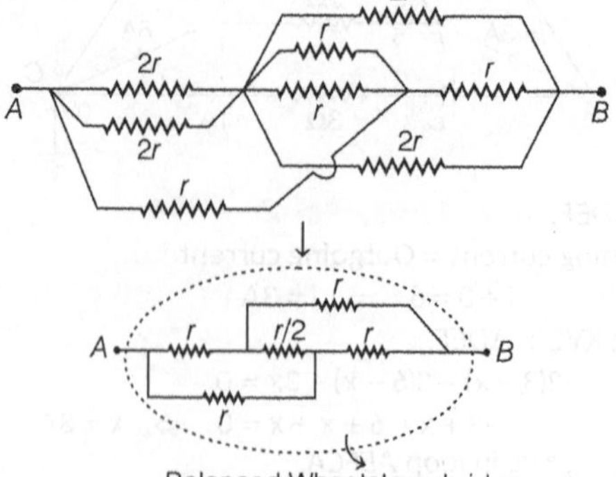

Balanced Wheatstone bridge

$R_{eq} = r$

31. Due to input-output symmetry in the upper circuit, current distribution will be identical at input and output.
So, we can break junction at C as shown.

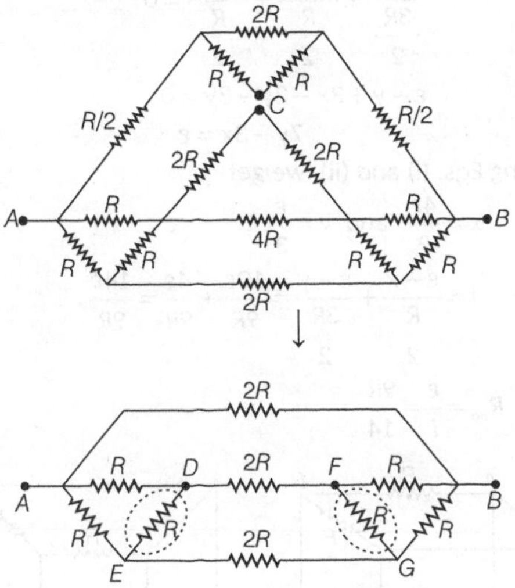

Due to symmetry, points D & E and F & G are equipotential. So, we can remove resistors between D & E and F & G.
Now, using series and parallel combinations,

$$R_{eq} = R$$

32.

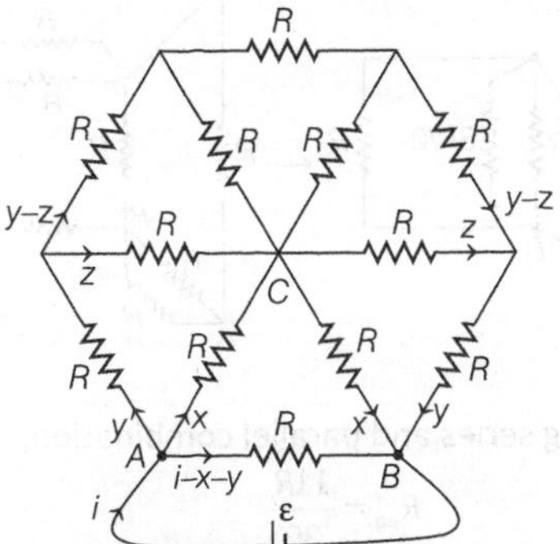

Due to input-output symmetry, current distribution at input and output is identical. So, we can break junction at C as shown.

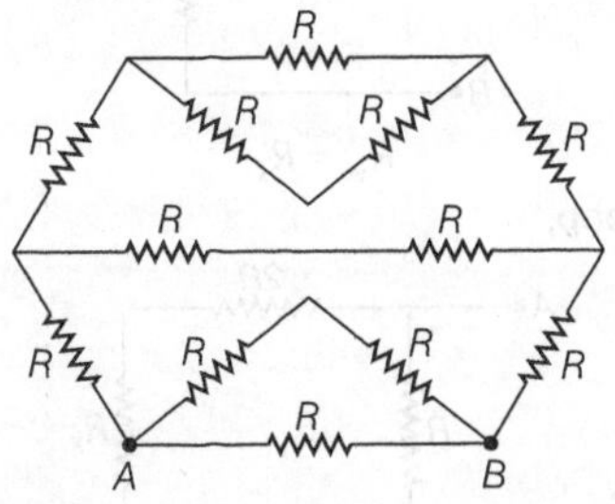

Now, using series and parallel combination,

$$R_{eq} = \frac{11R}{20} = \frac{11}{20}(40) = 22\,\Omega$$

33.

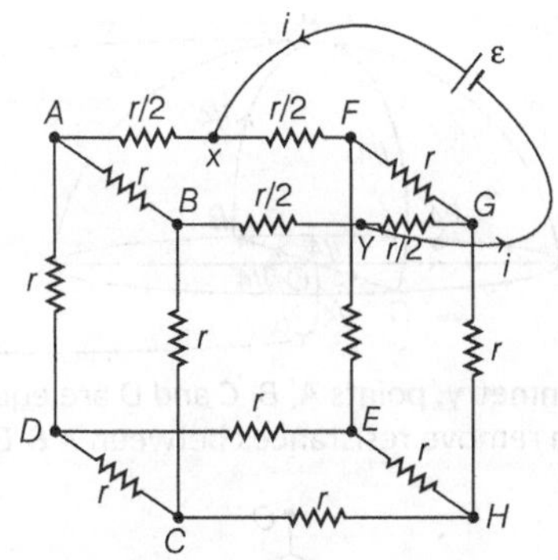

Due to symmetry, points D & E and C & H are equipotential. So, we can remove resistances between D & E and C & H.
Now, using series and parallel combination,

$$R_{eq} = \frac{7r}{8}$$

34.

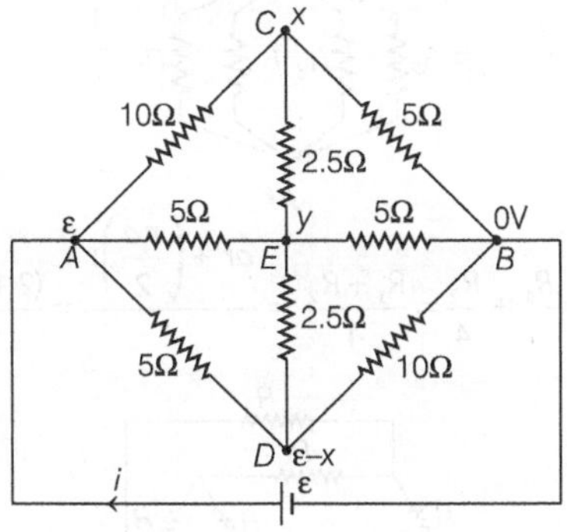

Applying KCL at junction C,

$$\frac{\varepsilon - x}{10} + \frac{y - x}{2.5} + \frac{0 - x}{5} = 0$$

$$\varepsilon - x + 4y - 4x - 2x = 0$$

$$7x - 4y = \varepsilon \quad \text{...(i)}$$

Applying KCL at junction E,

$$\frac{\varepsilon - y}{5} + \frac{x - y}{2.5} + \frac{\varepsilon - x - y}{2.5} + \frac{0 - y}{5} = 0$$

$$\varepsilon - y + 2x - 2y + 2\varepsilon - 2x - 2y - y = 0$$

$$\Rightarrow \quad y = \frac{\varepsilon}{2} \quad \text{...(ii)}$$

$$x = \frac{3\varepsilon}{7} \text{ and } y = \frac{\varepsilon}{2}$$

$$i = \frac{\varepsilon - x}{10} + \frac{\varepsilon - y}{5} + \frac{\varepsilon - (\varepsilon - x)}{5}$$

$$= \frac{4\varepsilon}{70} + \frac{\varepsilon}{10} + \frac{3\varepsilon}{35}$$

$$= \frac{17\varepsilon}{70}$$

$$R_{eq} = \frac{\varepsilon}{i} = \frac{70}{17}\,\Omega$$

35.

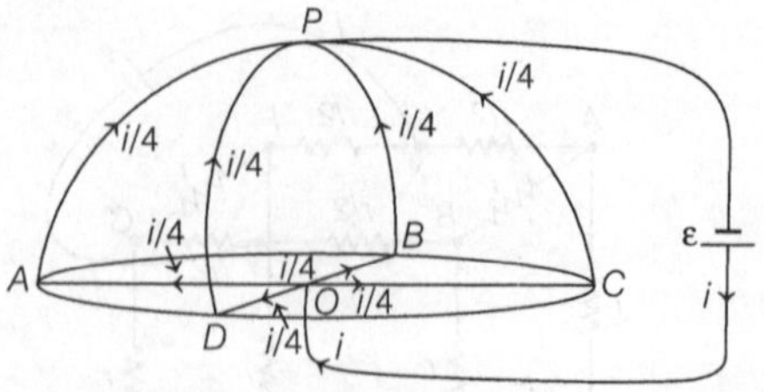

Due to symmetry, points A, B, C and D are equipotential. So, we can remove resistances between A & B, B & C, C & D and D & A.

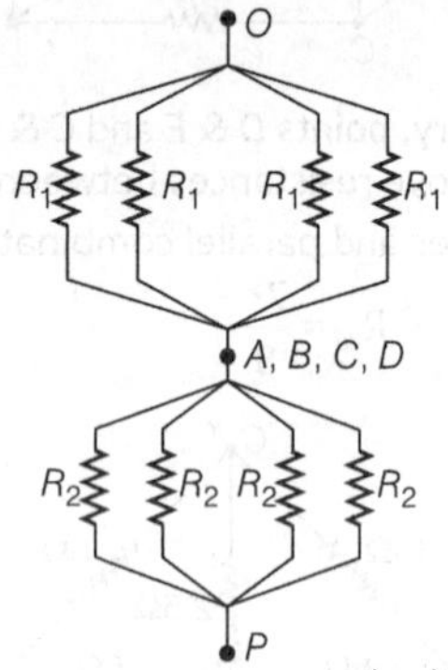

$$R_{eq} = \frac{R_1}{4} + \frac{R_2}{4} = \frac{R_1 + R_2}{4} = \frac{ar + \left(\frac{\pi a}{2}\right)r}{4} = \frac{(2+\pi)ar}{8}$$

36.

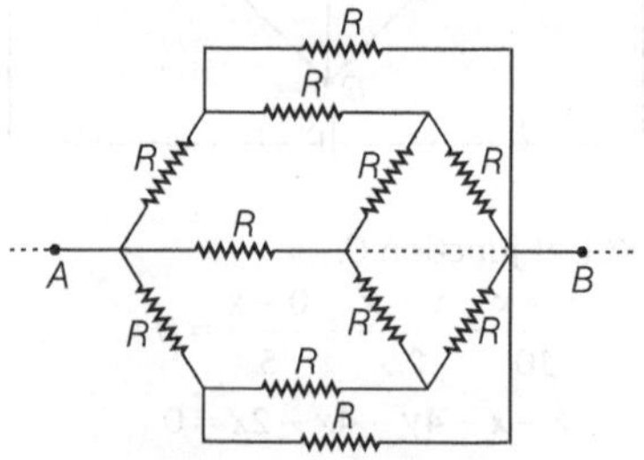

We can fold circuit about axis AB.

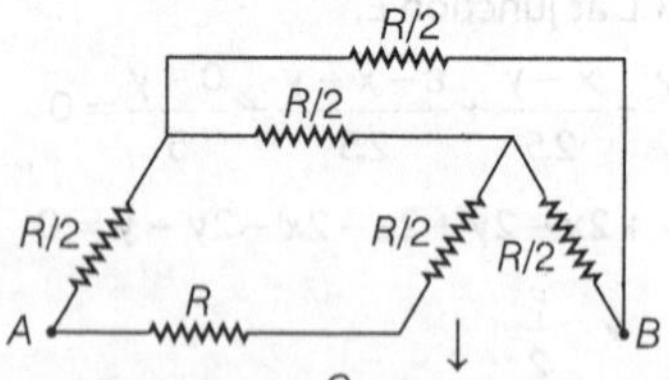

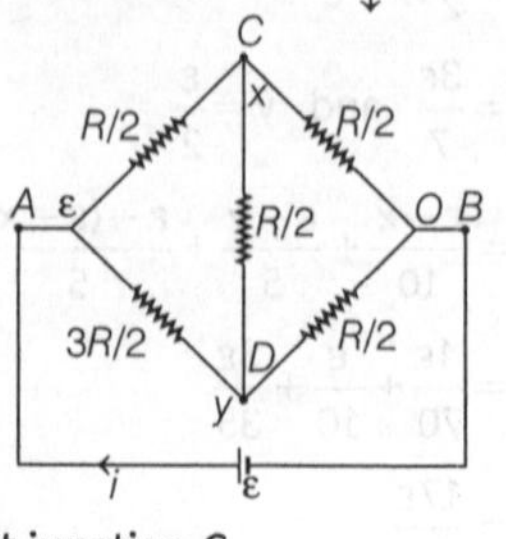

Applying KCL at junction C,

$$\frac{\varepsilon - x}{\frac{R}{2}} + \frac{y - x}{\frac{R}{2}} + \frac{0 - x}{\frac{R}{2}} = 0$$

$$\Rightarrow \quad 3x - y = \varepsilon \quad \text{...(i)}$$

Applying KCL at junction D,

$$\frac{\varepsilon - y}{\frac{3R}{2}} + \frac{x - y}{\frac{R}{2}} + \frac{0 - y}{\frac{R}{2}} = 0$$

$$\Rightarrow \quad \varepsilon - y + 3x - 3y - 3y = 0$$

$$7y - 3x = \varepsilon \quad \text{...(ii)}$$

Solving Eqs. (i) and (ii), we get

$$x = \frac{4\varepsilon}{9} \text{ and } y = \frac{\varepsilon}{3}$$

$$i = \frac{\varepsilon - x}{\frac{R}{2}} + \frac{\varepsilon - y}{\frac{3R}{2}} = \frac{10\varepsilon}{9R} + \frac{4\varepsilon}{9R} = \frac{14\varepsilon}{9R}$$

$$R_{eq} = \frac{\varepsilon}{i} = \frac{9R}{14}$$

37.

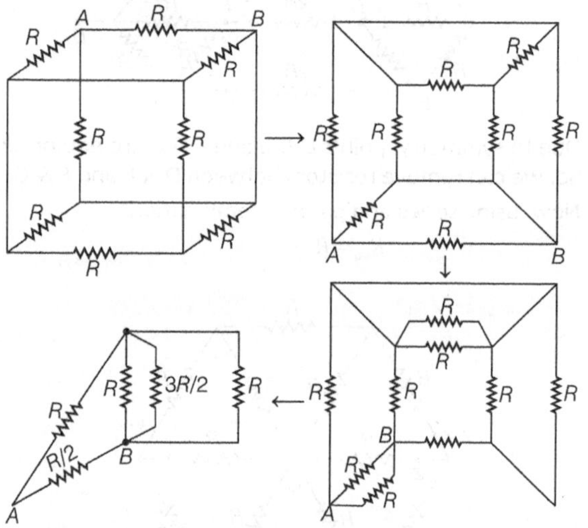

Now, using series and parallel combination,

$$R_{eq} = \frac{11R}{30}$$

38. With zero loop,

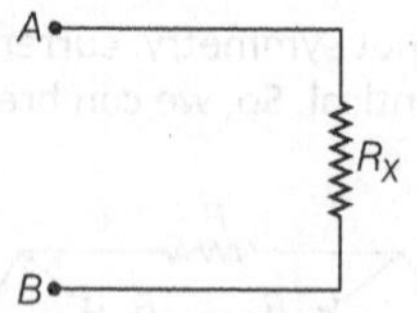

$$R_{eq} = R_x$$

With one loop,

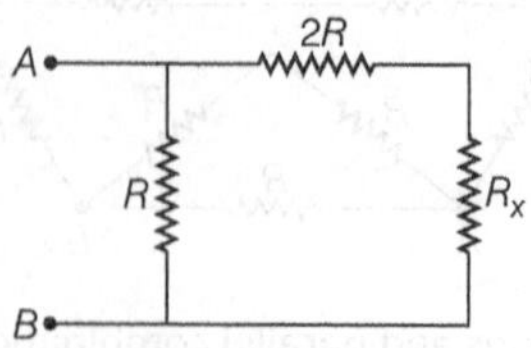

$$R_{eq} = \frac{(2R + R_x)R}{(2R + R_x) + R}$$

Since, equivalent resistance between A and B is independent of number of loops,

$$R_x = \frac{(2R + R_x)R}{3R + R_x}$$

$$\Rightarrow \quad 3RR_x + R_x^2 = 2R^2 + RR_x$$

$$\Rightarrow \quad R_x^2 + 2RR_x - 2R^2 = 0$$

$$R_x = \left(\frac{-2 + \sqrt{12}}{2}\right)R = (\sqrt{3} - 1)R$$

$$= (\sqrt{3} - 1)(2\sqrt{3} + 1) = 4\Omega$$

39.

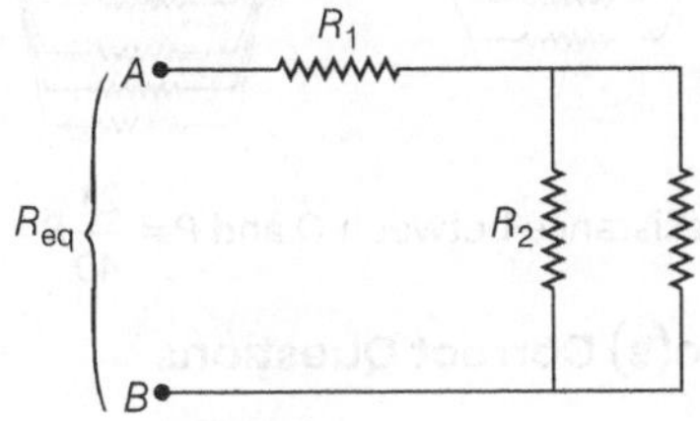

$$R_{eq} = R_1 + \frac{R_2(KR_{eq})}{R_2 + KR_{eq}}$$

$$R_{eq} = \frac{R_1R_2 + KR_1R_{eq} + KR_2R_{eq}}{R_2 + KR_{eq}}$$

$$\Rightarrow \quad R_{eq}R_2 + KR_{eq}^2 = R_1R_2 + KR_1R_{eq} + KR_2R_{eq}$$

$$\Rightarrow \quad KR_{eq}^2 + (R_2 - KR_1 - KR_2)R_{eq} - R_1R_2 = 0$$

$$\Rightarrow \quad R_{eq}^2 + (R_2 - R_1)R_{eq} - 2R_1R_2 = 0 \qquad \left[\because K = \frac{1}{2}\right]$$

$$R_{eq} = \frac{(R_1 - R_2) + \sqrt{(R_2 - R_1)^2 + 8R_1R_2}}{2}$$

$$= \frac{(R_1 - R_2) + \sqrt{R_1^2 + R_2^2 + 6R_1R_2}}{2}$$

40. Let equivalent resistance between A and $B = x$.

Since, the resistance is directly proportional to length of a conductor, the equivalent resistance between A_1 and B_1 will be $\frac{x}{2}$.

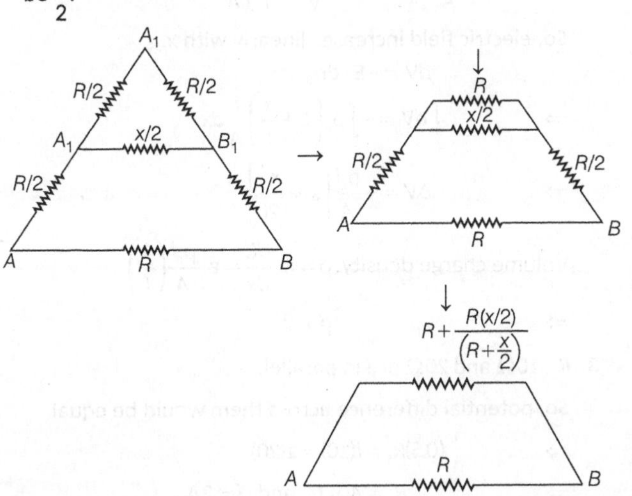

$$\frac{1}{x} = \frac{1}{R} + \frac{\left(R + \frac{x}{2}\right)}{R^2 + Rx}$$

$$\Rightarrow \quad \frac{R - x}{Rx} = \frac{2R + x}{2R(R + x)}$$

$$\Rightarrow \quad 2R^2 - 2x^2 = 2Rx + x^2$$

$$\Rightarrow \quad 3x^2 + 2Rx - 2R^2 = 0$$

$$\Rightarrow \quad x = \frac{-2R + \sqrt{28}\,R}{6}$$

$$x = \frac{(\sqrt{7} - 1)R}{3}$$

$$= \frac{(\sqrt{7} - 1)(\sqrt{7} + 1)}{3} = 2\Omega$$

41.

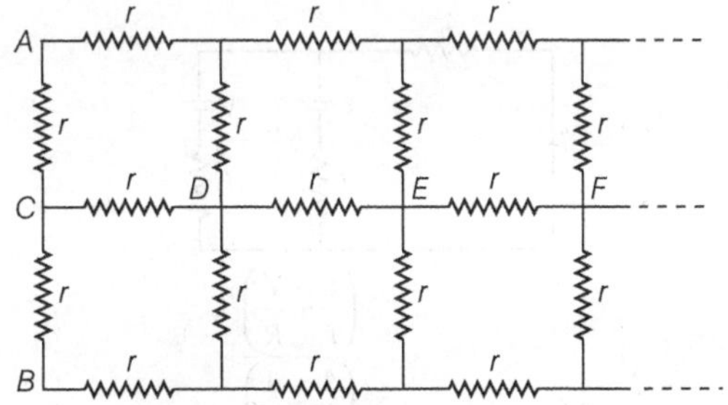

From symmetry, points C, D, E, F .... so on are equipotential. So, we can remove resistance connected between these points.

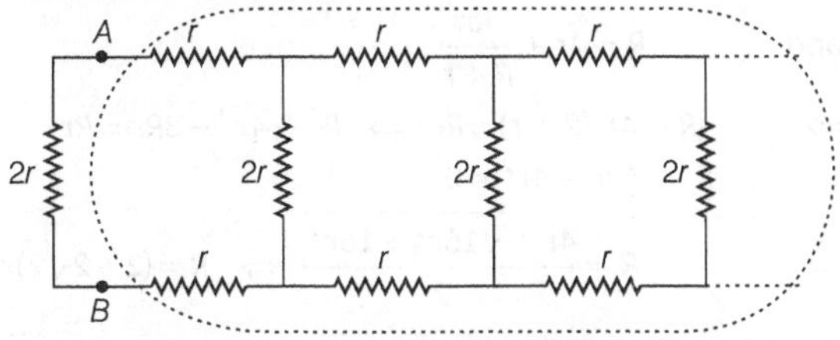

Lets first find resistance of circled part.

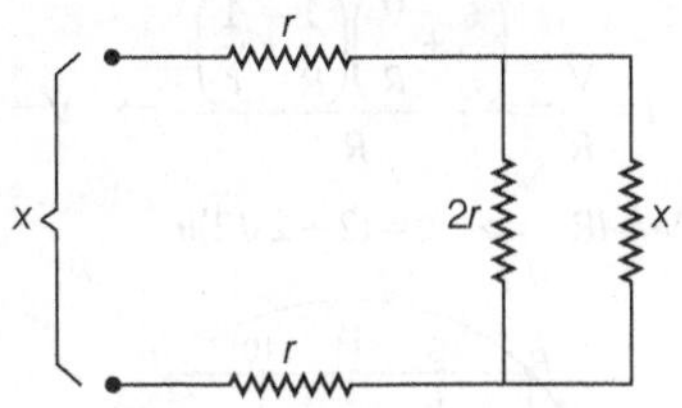

$$x = 2r + \frac{2rx}{2r + x}$$

$$\Rightarrow \quad x^2 - 2rx - 4r^2 = 0$$

$$\Rightarrow \quad x = \frac{2 + \sqrt{20}}{2} = (\sqrt{5} + 1)r$$

Now, $\frac{1}{R_{AB}} = \frac{1}{2r} + \frac{1}{(\sqrt{5} + 1)r}$

$$\Rightarrow \quad R_{AB} = \frac{2(\sqrt{5} + 1)}{(\sqrt{5} + 3)}r = (\sqrt{5} - 1)r$$

42.

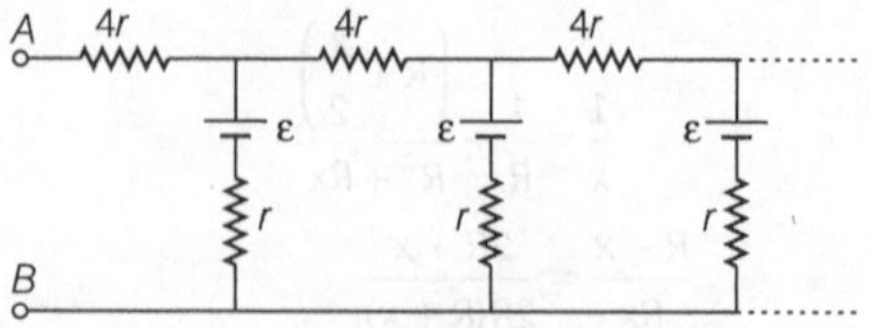

Let equivalent emf and equivalent internal resistance across A and B be V and R, respectively.

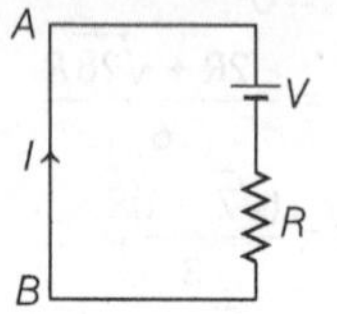

$$I = \frac{V}{R} \qquad \text{...(i)}$$

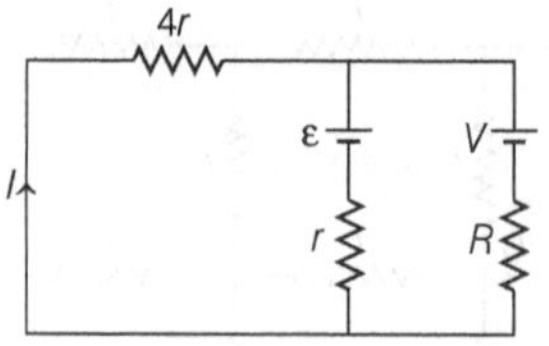

$$I = \frac{\varepsilon_{eq}}{r_{eq}} = \frac{\dfrac{\left(\dfrac{\varepsilon}{r}+\dfrac{V}{R}\right)}{\left(\dfrac{1}{R}+\dfrac{1}{r}\right)}}{\dfrac{Rr}{R+r}+4r} \qquad \text{...(ii)}$$

and $\qquad R = 4r + \dfrac{Rr}{R+r}$

$\Rightarrow \quad (R-4r)(R+r) = Rr \Rightarrow R^2 - 4r^2 - 3Rr = Rr$

$\Rightarrow \quad R^2 - 4Rr - 4r^2 = 0$

$\Rightarrow \quad R = \dfrac{4r + \sqrt{16r^2 + 16r^2}}{2} \Rightarrow R = (2+2\sqrt{2})r$

From Eqs. (i) and (ii), we get

$$I = \frac{V}{R} = \frac{\left(\dfrac{\varepsilon}{r}+\dfrac{V}{R}\right)\left(\dfrac{1}{R}+\dfrac{1}{r}\right)}{R} \Rightarrow V = \varepsilon$$

Now, $\quad V = IR \Rightarrow \varepsilon = (2+2\sqrt{2})Ir$

43.

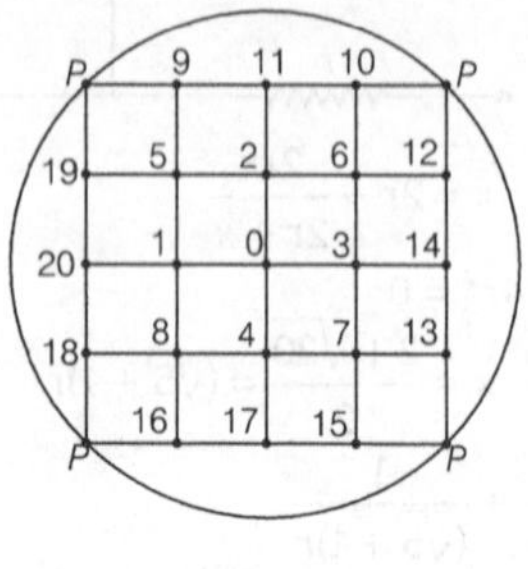

From symmetry, points 1, 2, 3, 4 are equipotential; 5, 6, 7, 8 are equipotential; 9, 10, 12, 13, 15, 16, 18, 19 are equipotential and 11, 14, 17, 20 are equipotential.

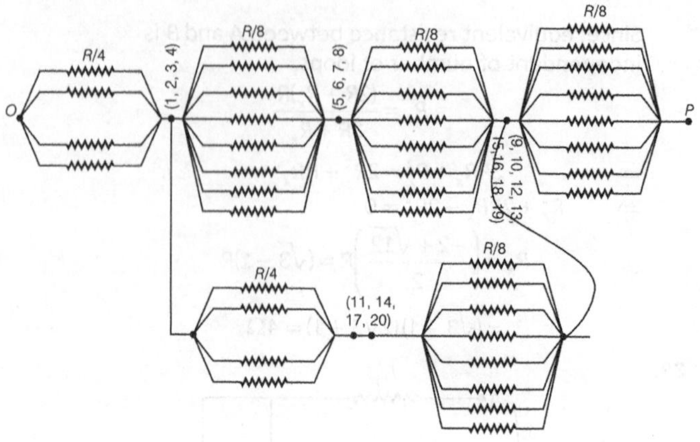

Equivalent resistance between O and $P = \dfrac{21}{40}R = \dfrac{21}{40}$ ar

Multiple Choice(s) Correct Questions

1. $i_A = i_B = i_C$

$\therefore$ No charge accumulates at any section.

$$J = \frac{i}{A}$$

$\Rightarrow \quad J_B > J_A > J_C \qquad (\because A_C > A_A > A_B)$

$\quad J = \sigma E$

$\Rightarrow \quad E_B > E_A > E_C$

$\quad \phi = EA$

$\Rightarrow \quad \phi = \left(\dfrac{J}{\sigma}\right)A \Rightarrow \phi = \left(\dfrac{i}{\sigma A}\right)A$

$\Rightarrow \quad \phi = \dfrac{i}{\sigma} \Rightarrow \phi_A = \phi_B = \phi_C$

$\quad V_C < V_B < V_A$

$\because$ Potential decreases in the direction of flow of current.

2. $J = \sigma E \Rightarrow \dfrac{i}{A} = \left(\dfrac{1}{\rho}\right)E$

$\Rightarrow \quad E = \dfrac{\rho i}{A} \Rightarrow E = \rho_0\left(1+\dfrac{x}{l}\right)\dfrac{i}{A}$

So, electric field increases linearly with x.

$\quad dV = -\mathbf{E}\cdot d\mathbf{r}$

$\Rightarrow \quad \int dV = -\int \rho_0\left(1+\dfrac{x}{l}\right)\dfrac{i}{A}dx$

$\Rightarrow \quad \Delta V = -\dfrac{\rho_0 i}{A}\left[x + \dfrac{x^2}{2l}\right]$

Volume charge density, $\rho = \varepsilon_0 \dfrac{dE}{dx} = \varepsilon_0 \dfrac{\rho_0 i}{A}\left(\dfrac{1}{l}\right)$

$\Rightarrow \quad \rho \neq 0$

3. R_1, 10Ω and 20Ω are in parallel.

So, potential difference across them would be equal.

$\Rightarrow \quad (0.5)R_1 = i(10) = 1(20)$

$\Rightarrow \quad R_1 = 40\Omega$ and $i = 2\text{A}$

Current through battery $= 0.5 + 2 + 1 = 3.5\text{A}$

$$3.5 = \frac{69}{R_{eq}}$$

$$\Rightarrow \quad 3.5 = \frac{69}{R + \left(\frac{1}{40} + \frac{1}{10} + \frac{1}{20}\right)^{-1}}$$

$$\Rightarrow \quad 3.5 = \frac{69}{R + \frac{40}{7}}$$

$$\Rightarrow \quad R = 14\Omega$$

Potential difference across $R = 3.5 \times 14 = 49\text{V}$

4. Applying KCL for the loop,

$$+I_1 + 4 - 3 - I_2 = 0$$

$$\Rightarrow \quad I_2 - I_1 = 1$$

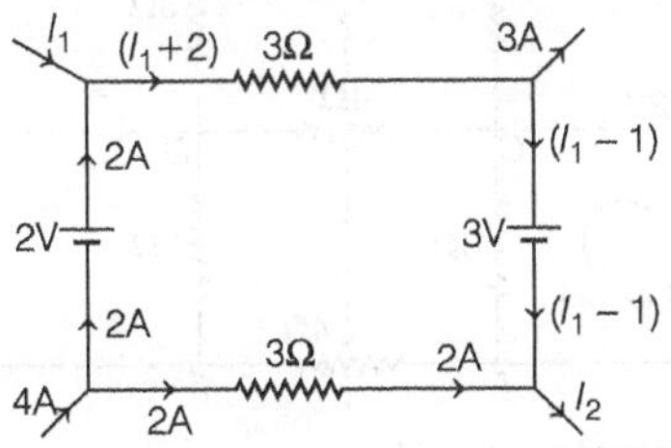

Applying KVL in the loop,

$$-2(3) + 3 + 3(I_1 + 2) - 2 = 0$$

$$\Rightarrow \quad -6 + 3 + 3I_1 + 6 - 2 = 0$$

$$\Rightarrow \quad 3I_1 = -1$$

$$\Rightarrow \quad I_1 = -\frac{1}{3}\text{A}$$

and $\quad I_2 = -\left(-\frac{1}{3}\right) = 1 \Rightarrow I_2 = \frac{2}{3}\text{A}$

5.

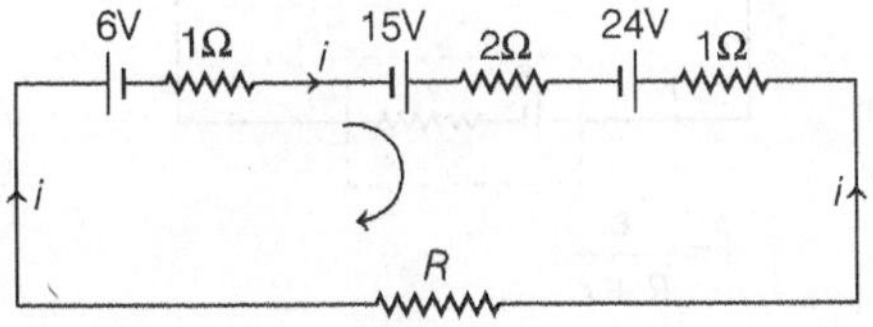

Applying KVL in the loop,

$$+15 + 24 - 6 - i(1) - i(2) - i(1) - iR = 0$$

$$\Rightarrow \quad i(R + 4) = 33 \quad \ldots\text{(i)}$$

$$V_A - V_B = 9\text{V}$$

$$\Rightarrow \quad 6 + i(1) = 9$$

$$\Rightarrow \quad i = 3\text{A}$$

Substituting in Eq. (i), we get

$$3(R + 4) = 33$$

$$\Rightarrow \quad R = 7\Omega$$

$$V_D - V_B = +15 + 24 - 2(3) - 1(3) = 30\text{V}$$

$$V_C - V_B = +15 - 3(2) = 9\text{V}$$

6.

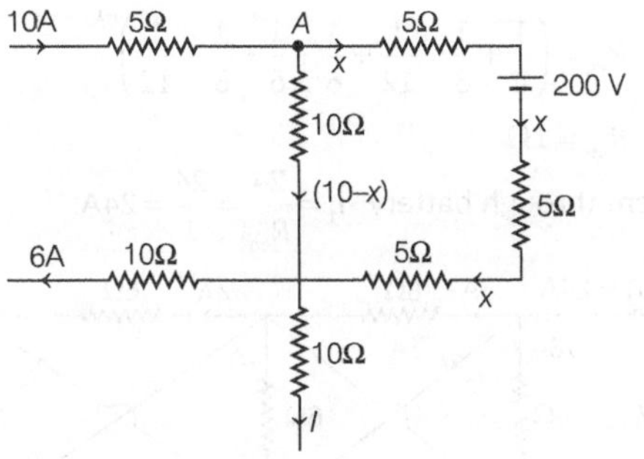

Applying KCL,

$$+10 - 6 - I = 0 \Rightarrow I = 4\text{A}$$

Applying KVL in the loop,

$$-5x - 200 - 5x - 5x + 10(10 - x) = 0$$

$$\Rightarrow \quad 25x = -100 \quad \Rightarrow \quad x = -4\text{A}$$

So, current from cell = 4A (up)

Current from 10Ω between A and $B = 10 - (-4) = 14A$

Voltage drop across $AB = 14 \times 10 = 140\text{V}$

7.

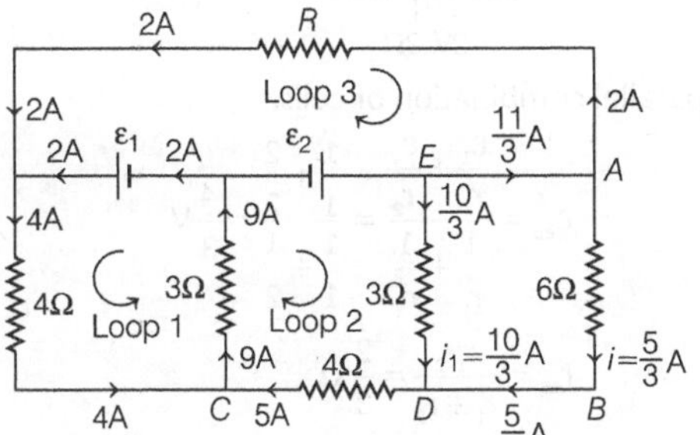

$$V_A - V_B = 10 \Rightarrow i(6) = 10 \quad \Rightarrow \quad i = \frac{5}{3}\text{A}$$

$$\Rightarrow \quad V_E - V_D = V_A - V_B = 10$$

$$\Rightarrow \quad 3i_1 = 10 \Rightarrow i_1 = \frac{10}{3}$$

Current through 4Ω resistor in between

$$C \text{ and } D = \frac{10}{3} + \frac{5}{3} = 5\text{A}$$

Applying KVL in loop 1,

$$+\varepsilon_1 - 4(4) - 9(3) = 0 \Rightarrow \varepsilon_1 = 43\text{V}$$

Applying KVL in loop 2,

$$+\varepsilon_2 - 3\left(\frac{10}{3}\right) - 4(5) - 9(3) = 0 \Rightarrow \varepsilon_2 = 57\text{V}$$

Applying KVL in loop 3,

$$+2(R) - \varepsilon_2 + \varepsilon_1 = 0$$

$$\Rightarrow \quad 2R - 57 + 43 = 0$$

$$\Rightarrow \quad R = 7\Omega$$

8.

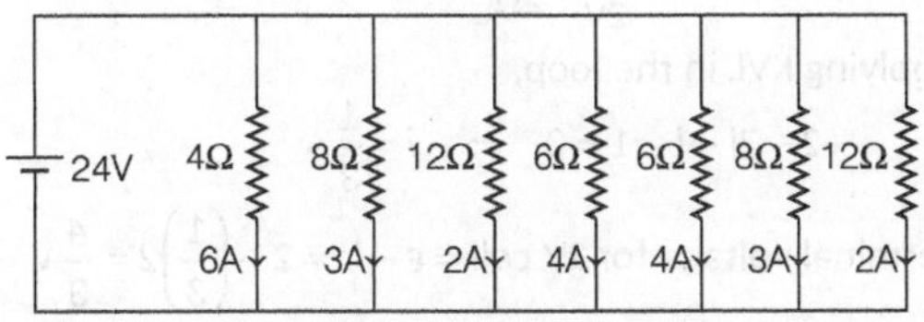

$$R_{eq} = \left(\frac{1}{4}+\frac{1}{8}+\frac{1}{12}+\frac{1}{6}+\frac{1}{6}+\frac{1}{8}+\frac{1}{12}\right)^{-1}$$

$$R_{eq} = 1\Omega$$

Current through battery, $i_1 = \frac{24}{R_{eq}} = \frac{24}{1} = 24\text{A}$

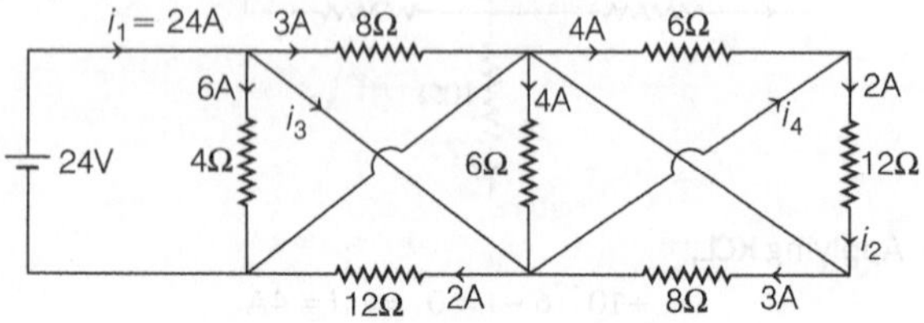

$$24 = 6 + i_3 + 3 \Rightarrow i_3 = 15\text{A}$$

$$i_2 = 2\text{A} \Rightarrow i_4 = 4 + 2 = 6\text{A}$$

9.

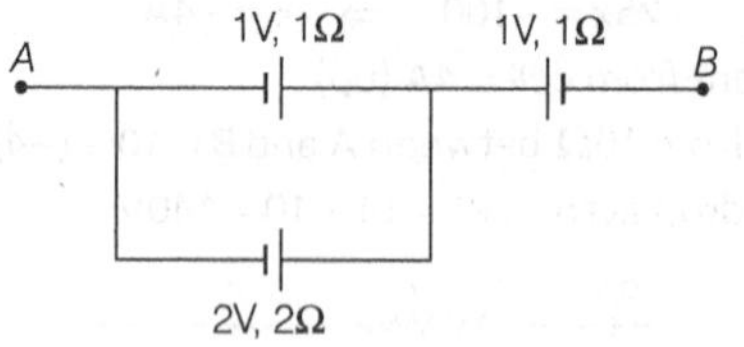

For parallel combination of cells,

$$\varepsilon_{eq} = \frac{\frac{\varepsilon_1}{r_1}+\frac{\varepsilon_2}{r_2}}{\frac{1}{r_1}+\frac{1}{r_2}} = \frac{\frac{1}{1}+\frac{2}{2}}{\frac{1}{1}+\frac{1}{2}} = \frac{4}{3}\text{V}$$

$$r_{eq} = \frac{r_1 r_2}{r_1 + r_2} = \frac{2}{3}\Omega$$

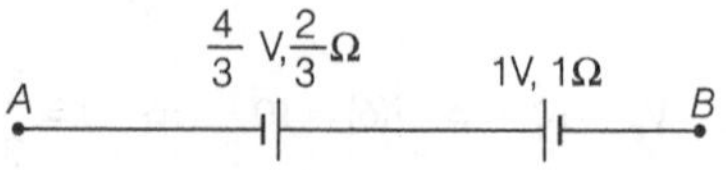

For series combination of cells,

$$\varepsilon_{eq} = \frac{4}{3} - 1 = \frac{1}{3}\text{V} \Rightarrow r_{eq} = \frac{2}{3} + 1 = \frac{5}{3}\Omega$$

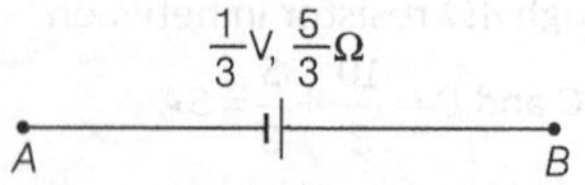

(a) emf of electric box is $\frac{1}{3}$V.

(b) Point B is higher potential than point A.

(c) Internal resistance of the box is $\frac{5}{3}\Omega$.

(d)

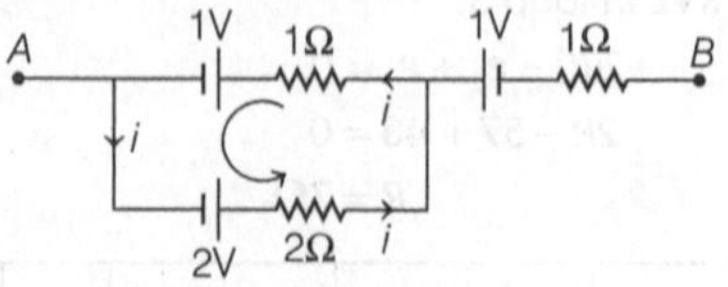

Applying KVL in the loop,

$$+2 - 2i - i - 1 = 0 \Rightarrow i = \frac{1}{3}\text{A}$$

Terminal voltage for 2V cell $= \varepsilon - ir = 2 - \left(\frac{1}{3}\right)2 = \frac{4}{3}$V

10. $V_P - V_Q = 0 \Rightarrow 5 - i(1) = 0 \Rightarrow i = 5\text{A}$

Applying KVL in loop 2,

$$+5 + 5x - 5 \times 3 - 1(5) = 0 \Rightarrow x = 3\text{A}$$

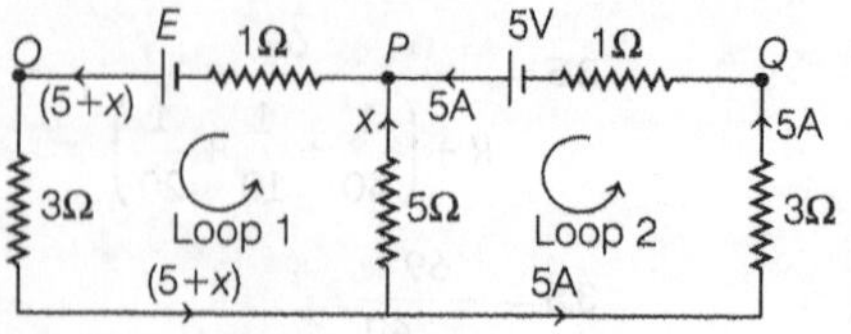

Applying KVL in loop 1,

$$+E - 3(5 + x) - 5x - 1(5 + x) = 0$$

$$\Rightarrow \quad E = 47\text{V}$$

$$V_O - V_P = E - Ir = 47 - 8(1) = 39\text{V}$$

11.

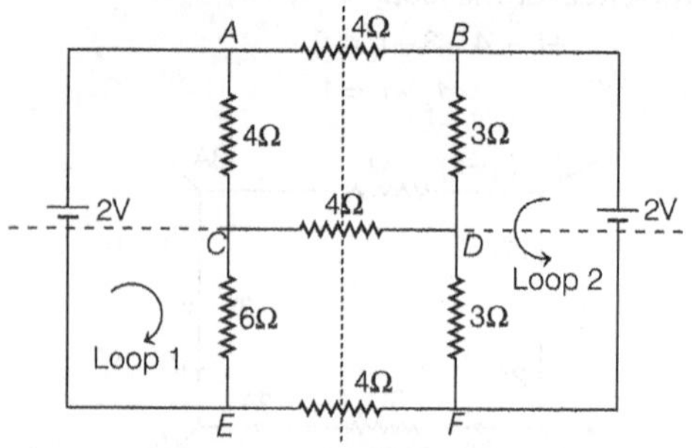

Due to symmetry, $V_A = V_B$;

$V_C = V_D$ and $V_E = V_F$

So, current through each 4Ω is zero.

Loop 1 and Loop 2 are independent from each other.

In loop 1, current $= \frac{2}{6+6} = \frac{1}{6}$A

In loop 2, current $= \frac{2}{3+3} = \frac{1}{3}$A

12.

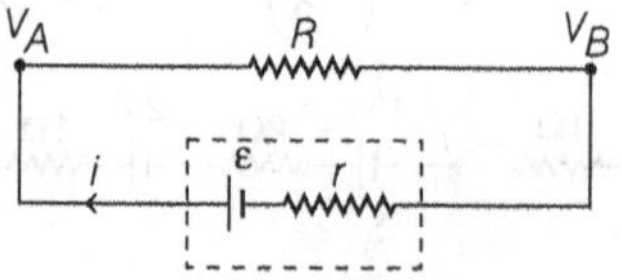

$$i = \frac{\varepsilon}{R + r}$$

$$V_A - V_B = \varepsilon - ir \Rightarrow V = \varepsilon - ir$$

$$i = 0 \Rightarrow V = \varepsilon = 10\text{V}$$

$$V = 0 \Rightarrow 0 = 10 - 2r$$

$$\Rightarrow \quad r = 5\Omega$$

Current is maximum when $V = 0$

$$\Rightarrow \quad i_{max} = 2\text{A}$$

13.

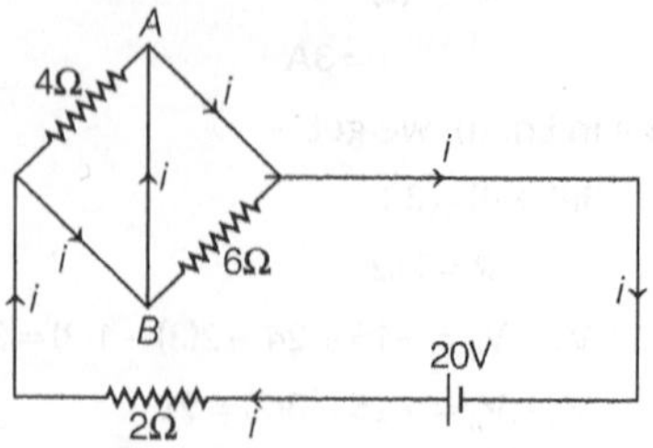

4Ω and 6Ω are short-circuited.

So, no current will flow through them.

Potential difference across 4Ω and 6Ω is zero.

$$i = \frac{20}{2} = 10\text{A}$$

Power supplied by battery $= 20 \times 10 = 200\text{W}$

Current in wire $AB = i = 10\text{A}$

14.

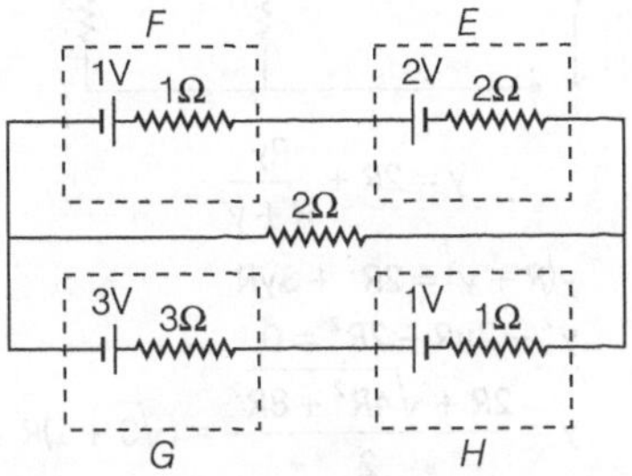

For cells E and F ; Equivalent emf $= 2 - 1 = 1\text{V}$

Equivalent internal resistance $= 3\Omega$

For cells G and H, equivalent emf $= 3 - 1 = 2\text{V}$

Equivalent internal resistance $= 4\Omega$

For parallel combination of cells

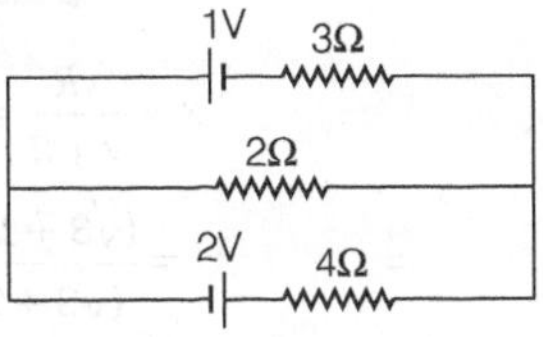

$$\text{Equivalent emf} = \frac{\frac{2}{4} - \frac{1}{3}}{\frac{1}{4} + \frac{1}{3}} = \frac{2}{7}\text{V}$$

Equivalent internal resistance

$$= \frac{3 \times 4}{3 + 4} = \frac{12}{7}\Omega$$

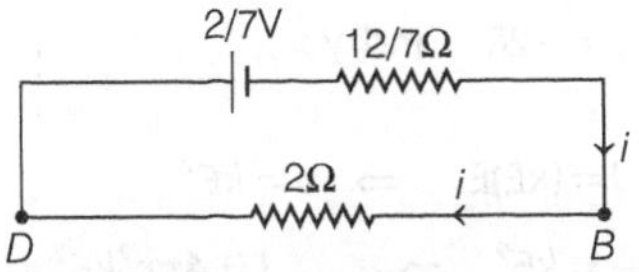

$$i = \frac{\frac{2}{7}}{\frac{12}{7} + 2} = \frac{1}{13}\text{A}$$

$$V_D - V_B = -iR = -\frac{1}{13}(2) = -\frac{2}{13}\text{V}$$

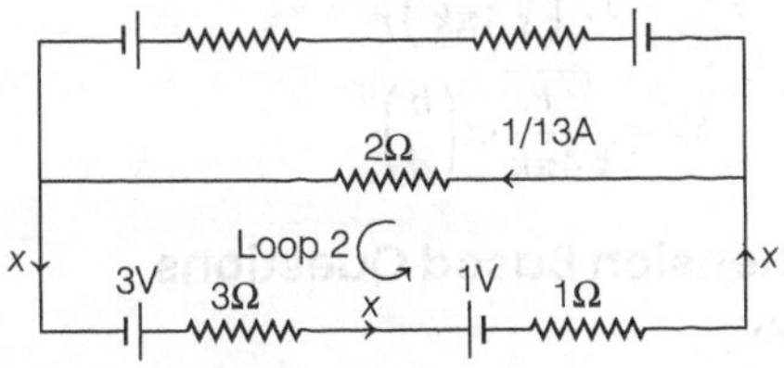

Applying KVL in loop 2,

$$-\frac{1}{13}(2) + 3 - 3x - 1 - x = 0 \quad \Rightarrow \quad x = \frac{6}{13}\text{A}$$

Potential difference across cell $G = E - ir$

$$= 3 - \left(\frac{6}{13}\right)(3) = \frac{21}{13}\text{V}$$

Potential difference across cell $H = E + ir$

$$= 1 + \left(\frac{6}{13}\right)1 = \frac{19}{13}\text{V}$$

15.

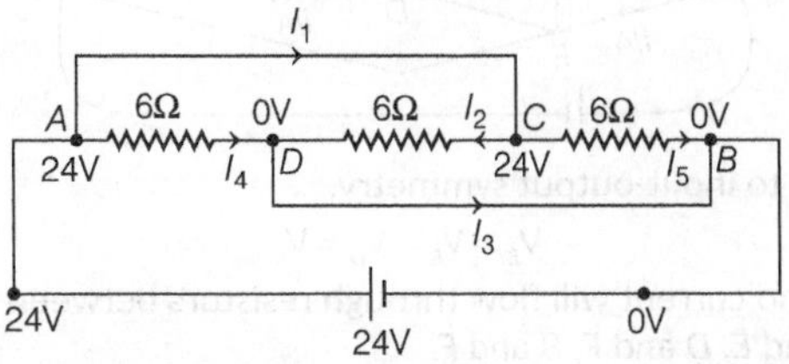

Lets take $V_B = 0 = V_D$

So, $\quad V_A = V_C = 24\text{V}$

$$I_2 = \frac{V_C - V_D}{R} = \frac{24 - 0}{6} = 4\text{A}$$

$$I_4 = \frac{V_A - V_D}{R} = \frac{24 - 0}{6} = 4\text{A}$$

$$I_5 = \frac{V_C - V_B}{R} = \frac{24 - 0}{6} = 4\text{A}$$

Using KCL at junction D,

$$I_3 = I_2 + I_4 = 4 + 4 = 8\text{A}$$

Using KCL at junction C,

$$I_1 = I_2 + I_5 = 4 + 4 = 8\text{A}$$

Between *E* and *F*

Dut to perpendicular axis of symmetry,

$$V_A = V_C$$

So, we can join points A and C.

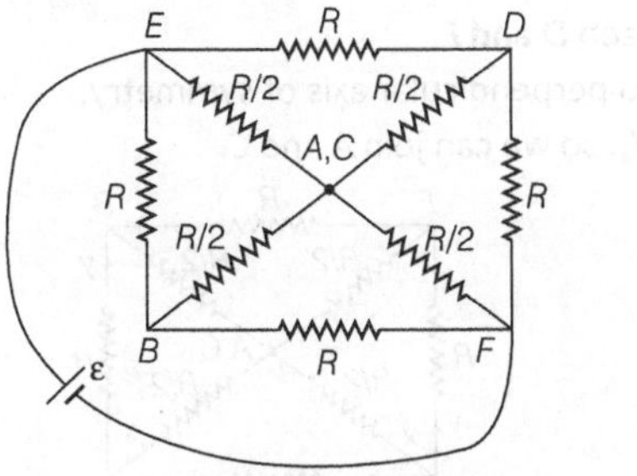

Due to perpendicular axis of symmetry,

$$V_B = V_D$$

So, we can join B and D.

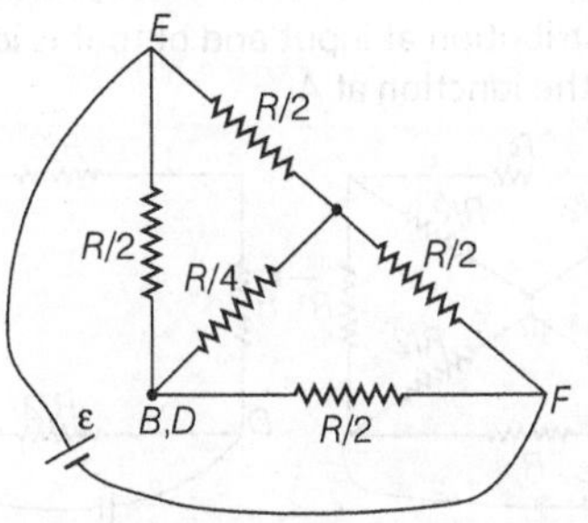

16. Between A and C

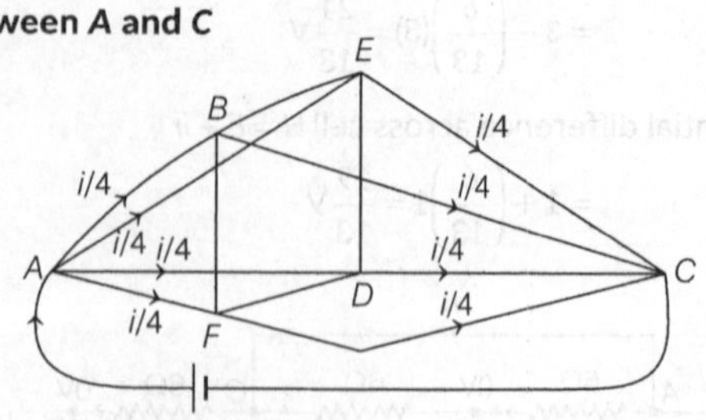

Due to input-output symmetry,

$$V_B = V_E = V_D = V_F$$

So, no current will flow through resistors between B and E, D and E, D and F, B and F.

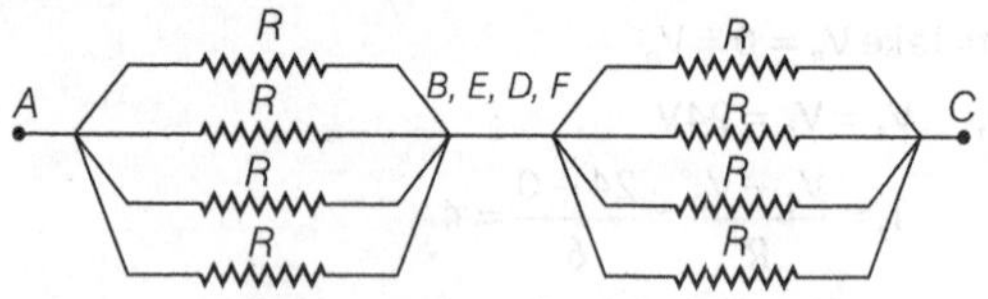

$$R_{eq} = \frac{R}{4} + \frac{R}{4} = \frac{R}{2}$$

This is a balanced Wheatstone bridge.

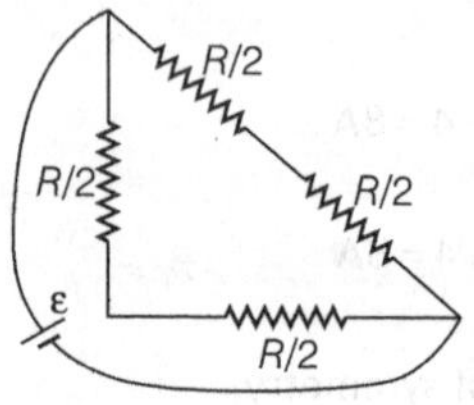

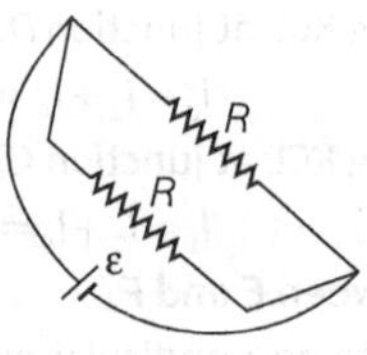

$$R_{eq} = \frac{R(R)}{R+R} = \frac{R}{2}$$

Between D and E,

Due to perpendicular axis of symmetry,

$V_C = V_A$, so we can join A and C.

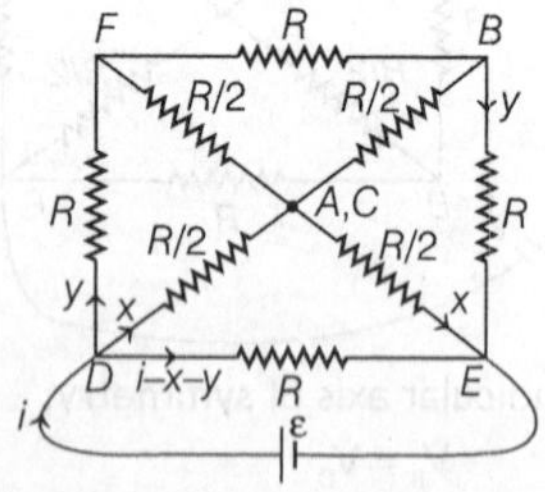

Due to perpendicular axis of symmetry,

current distribution at input and output is identical. So, we can break the junction at A.

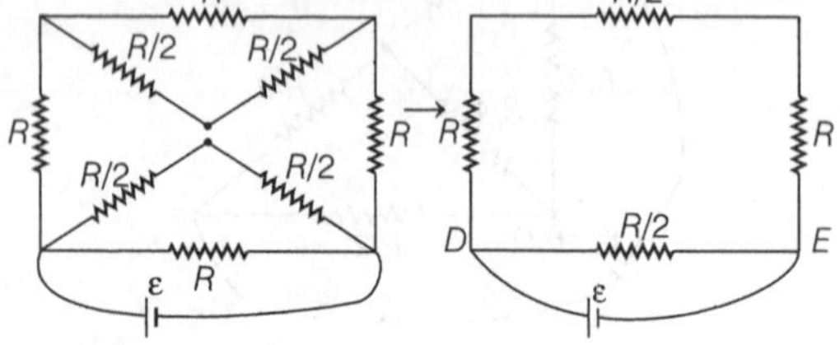

$$R_{eq} = \frac{\left(\frac{R}{2}\right)\left(\frac{5R}{2}\right)}{\frac{R}{2} + \frac{5R}{2}} = \frac{\frac{5R}{4}}{3R} = \frac{5R}{12}$$

17. For circuit B,

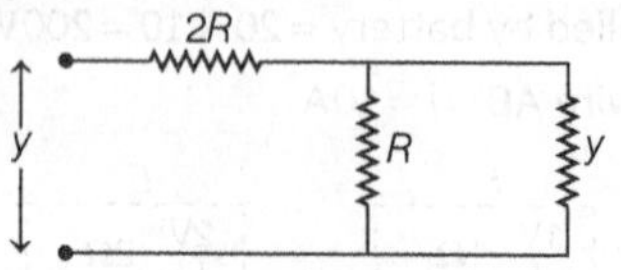

$$y = 2R + \frac{Ry}{R+y}$$

$$\Rightarrow \quad y(R+y) = 2R^2 + 3yR$$

$$\Rightarrow \quad y^2 - 2yR - 2R^2 = 0$$

$$\Rightarrow \quad y = \frac{2R + \sqrt{4R^2 + 8R^2}}{2} = (\sqrt{3}+1)R$$

For circuit A,

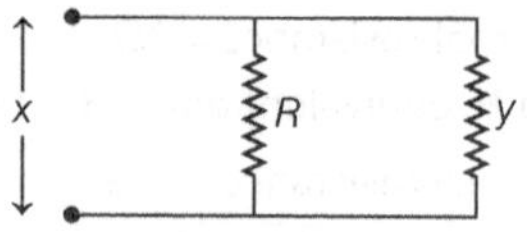

$$x = \frac{yR}{y+R} = \frac{(\sqrt{3}+1)R \times R}{(\sqrt{3}+1)R + R}$$

$$\Rightarrow \quad = \frac{(\sqrt{3}+1)R}{(\sqrt{3}+2)} \times \frac{(\sqrt{3}-2)}{(\sqrt{3}-2)}$$

$$= (\sqrt{3}-1)R$$

$$xy = (\sqrt{3}+1)R(\sqrt{3}-1)R = 2R^2$$

$$x - y = (\sqrt{3}-1)R - (\sqrt{3}+1)R$$

$$= -2R \quad \text{and } y > x$$

18. $J = \sigma E$

$$\Rightarrow \quad J = (kE)E \quad \Rightarrow \quad J = kE^2$$

$$\Rightarrow \quad \frac{I}{4\pi r^2} = kE^2 \quad \Rightarrow \quad I = 4\pi r^2 kE^2$$

$$E = \left(\sqrt{\frac{I}{4\pi k}}\right)\frac{1}{r}$$

$$dV = -\mathbf{E} \cdot d\mathbf{r}$$

$$\int dV = \int_a^b \left(\sqrt{\frac{I}{4\pi k}}\right)\frac{1}{r}\,dr$$

$$\Delta V = \sqrt{\frac{I}{4\pi k}} \ln\left(\frac{b}{a}\right)$$

Comprehension Based Questions

1. $i = nqAv_d$

$$\Rightarrow \quad 2.56 = (8 \times 10^{22} \times 10^6)(1.6 \times 10^{-19})(1 \times 10^{-6})v_d$$

$$\Rightarrow \quad v_d = 2 \times 10^{-4} \text{ m/s}$$

$$\text{Time taken} = \frac{\text{Distance}}{\text{Drift speed}} = \frac{1 \times 10^{-2}}{2 \times 10^{-4}} = 50 \text{ s}$$

2. $\rho = \dfrac{2m}{ne^2\tau}$

$\Rightarrow \tau = \dfrac{2m}{ne^2\rho} = \dfrac{2 \times 9.1 \times 10^{-31}}{8 \times 10^{28} \times (1.6 \times 10^{-19})^2 \times (1.6 \times 10^{-8})} \approx 10^{-14}$ s

3. Distance travelled = Drift speed × Time

$= 2 \times 10^{-4} \times 10 = 2 \times 10^{-3}$ m

$\Delta V = El = (J\rho)l$

$= \left(\dfrac{2.56}{1 \times 10^{-6}}\right)(1.6 \times 10^{-8})(2 \times 10^{-3})$

$= 8.192 \times 10^{-5}\ \text{V} = 81.92\mu\text{V} \approx 82\mu\text{V}$

4.

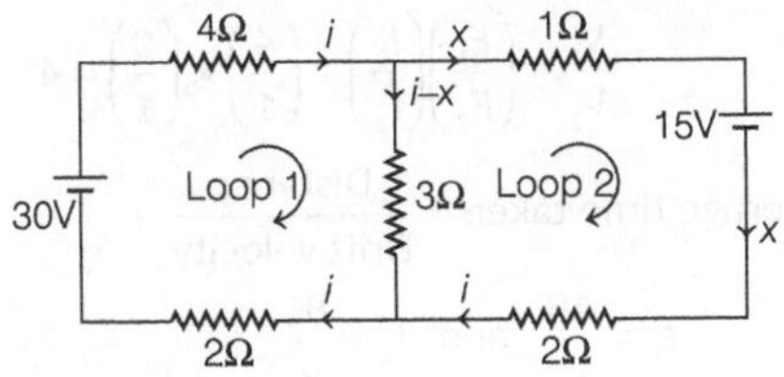

Applying KVL in loop 1,

$+30 - 4i - 3(i - x) - 2i = 0$

$\Rightarrow \quad 9i - 3x = 30$

$\Rightarrow \quad 3i - x = 10 \quad$ ...(i)

Applying KVL in loop 2,

$-x(1) - 15 - 2(x) + 3(i - x) = 0$

$\Rightarrow \quad i - 2x = 5 \quad$ ...(ii)

Solving Eqs. (i) and (ii), we get

$i = 3\text{A}$ and $x = -1\text{A}$

Current through 30V battery = 3A

5. Current through 15V battery = 1A

6. Both the batteries are discharging as current leaves their anode terminal.

7. Total power consummed = Total power supplied by both batteries

$= 30 \times 3 + 15 \times 1 = 105\text{W}$

8.

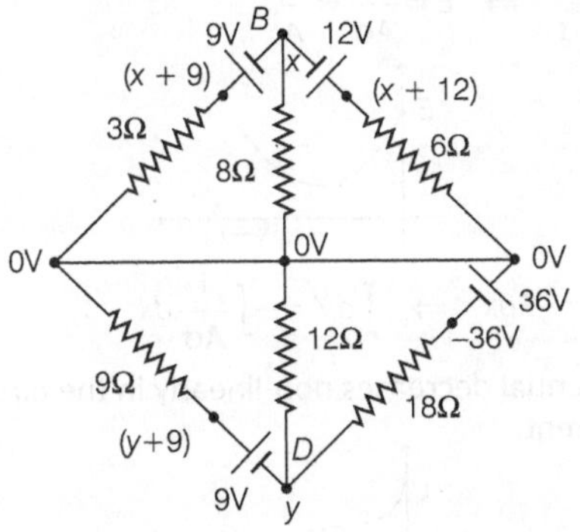

Using KCL at junction B,

$\dfrac{0-(x+9)}{3} + \dfrac{0-x}{8} + \dfrac{0-(x+12)}{6} = 0 \Rightarrow x = -8\text{V}$

Current through $BE = \dfrac{8-0}{8} = 1\text{A}$

9. Applying KCL at junction D,

$\dfrac{0-(y+9)}{9} + \dfrac{0-y}{12} + \dfrac{(-36-y)}{18} = 0$

$y = -12\text{V}$

$I = \dfrac{(x+9)-0}{3} + \dfrac{(y+9)-0}{9} = 0$

10. $V_B - V_D = x - y = -8 - (-12) = 4\text{V}$

11.

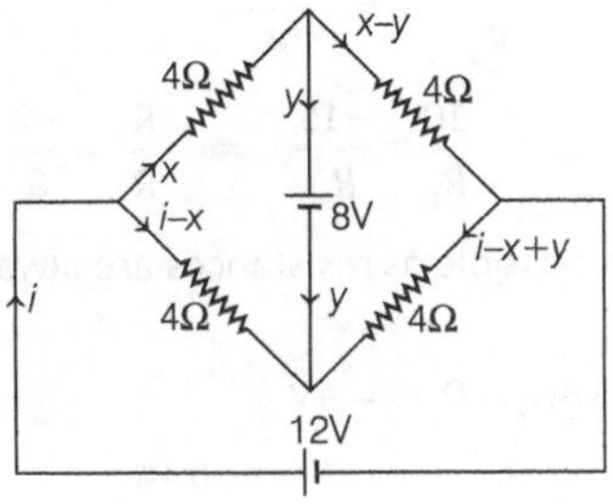

Using KVL,

$+12 - 4x - 4(x - y) = 0$

$\Rightarrow \quad 3 - x - x + y = 0$

$\Rightarrow \quad 2x = y + 3 \quad$ ...(i)

$-4x - 8 + 4(i - x) = 0$

$\Rightarrow \quad -x - 2 + i - x = 0$

$\Rightarrow \quad i - 2x = 2 \quad$ ...(ii)

$+8 - 4(x - y) + 4(i - x + y) = 0$

$\Rightarrow \quad 2 - x + y + i - x + y = 0$

$\Rightarrow \quad 2x - 2y = i + 2 \quad$ ...(iii)

Solving Eqs. (i), (ii) and (iii), we get

$i = 3\text{A},\ x = 0.5\text{A},\ y = -2\text{A}$

$V_B - V_D = 8\text{V}$

12. Both the batteries are discharging.

13. Current coming out of 12 V battery = 3A

Current coming out of 8V battery = $-y$ = 2A

The current flowing in the diagonally opposite branches is same.

14.

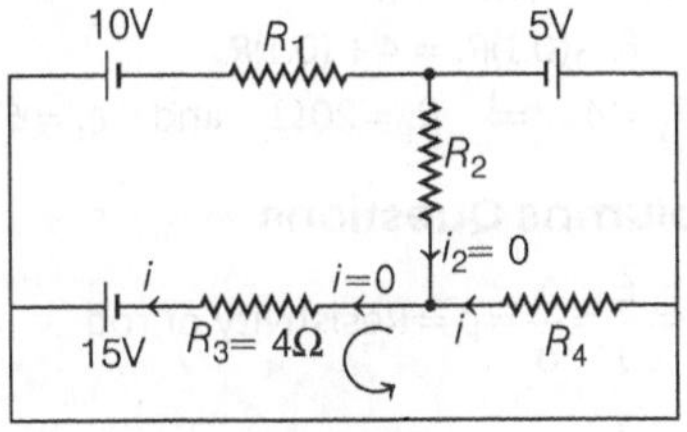

Using KVL,

$+15 - i(2) - i(4) = 0$

$\Rightarrow \quad i = 2.5\text{A}$

So, current through R_3 is 2.5 A.

15.

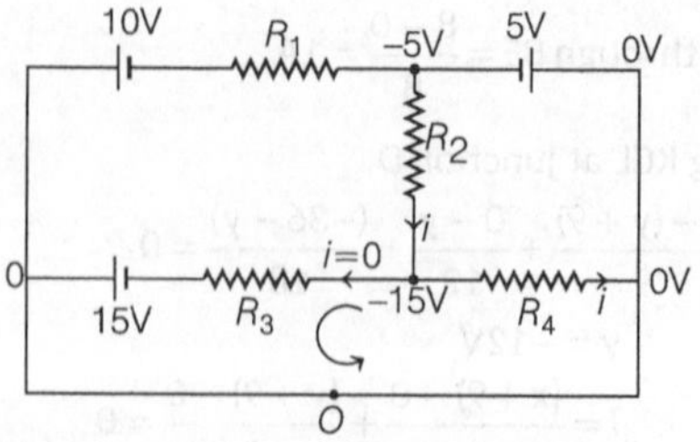

Current through R_2 = Current through R_4

$$\frac{-5-(-15)}{R_2}=\frac{-15-0}{R_4}$$

$$\Rightarrow \quad \frac{10}{R_2}=\frac{-15}{R_4} \Rightarrow \frac{R_2}{R_4}=\frac{-2}{3}$$

which is not possible as resistances are always positive.

16, 17. and 18.

$i_1 = 0.1\text{A}, i_2 = 0, \varepsilon_2 = 4\text{V}$

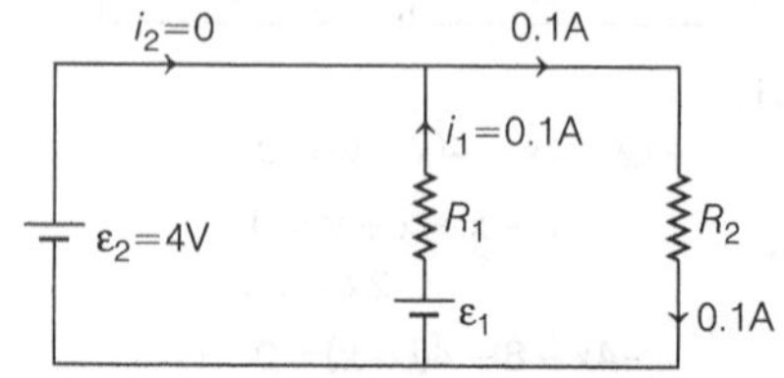

Using KVL,

$$+4-(0.1)R_2=0 \Rightarrow R_2=40\Omega$$

$$+\varepsilon_1-(0.1)R_1-(0.1)R_2=0$$

$$\Rightarrow \quad \varepsilon_1-(0.1)R_1=4 \quad \text{...(i)}$$

Now, $i_2 = 0.3\text{A}, i_1 = -0.1\text{A}$ and $\varepsilon_2 = 8\text{V}$

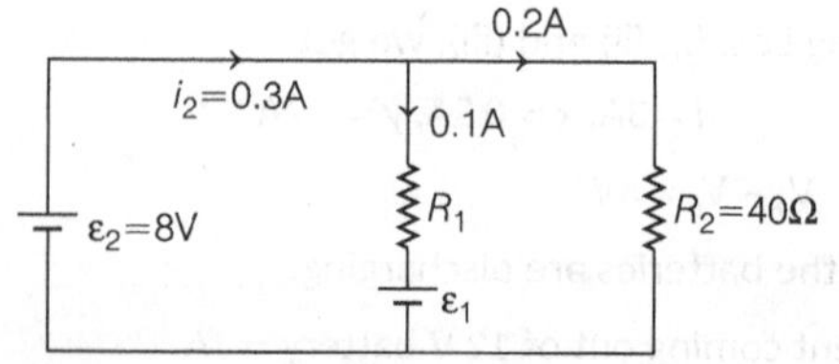

Using KVL,

$$+8-(0.1)R_1-\varepsilon_1=0$$

$$\Rightarrow \quad \varepsilon_1=8-(0.1)R_1 \quad \text{...(ii)}$$

From Eqs. (i) and (ii), we get

$$8-(0.1)R_1=4+(0.1)R_1$$

$$\Rightarrow \quad (0.2)R_1=4 \Rightarrow R_1=20\Omega \text{ and } \varepsilon_1=6\text{V}$$

Match the Columns Questions

1. (a) $\frac{\phi}{i}=\frac{EA}{i}=\frac{E}{J}=\frac{1}{\sigma}=\rho=$ Resistivity of rod

(b) $\frac{E}{J}=\frac{E}{\sigma E}=\frac{1}{\sigma}=\rho=$ Resistivity of rod

(c) $\sigma\phi V=\sigma(EA)V=\sigma\left(\frac{J}{\sigma}A\right)V=(JA)V$

$=iV=$ Power delivered to rod

(d) $\frac{V}{\sigma\phi}=\frac{V}{\sigma EA}=\frac{El}{\sigma EA}=\frac{\rho l}{A}=$ Resistance of rod

2. (a) $i_1=i_2$

$$\Rightarrow \quad n_1eA_1v_1=n_2eA_2v_2$$

$$\Rightarrow \quad \frac{v_1}{v_2}=\frac{n_2A_2}{n_1A_1}=\left(\frac{1}{2}\right)\left(\frac{2}{1}\right)=1$$

(b) $E=\rho J=\frac{\rho i}{A}$

$$\Rightarrow \quad \frac{E_1}{E_2}=\left(\frac{\rho_1}{\rho_2}\right)\left(\frac{A_2}{A_1}\right)=\left(\frac{2}{1}\right)\times\left(\frac{2}{1}\right)=4$$

(c) $V=El$

$$\frac{V_1}{V_2}=\left(\frac{E_1}{E_2}\right)\left(\frac{l_1}{l_2}\right)=\left(\frac{4}{1}\right)\times\left(\frac{1}{1}\right)=4$$

(d) Average time taken $=\frac{\text{Distance}}{\text{Drift velocity}}$

$$t_1=\frac{AB}{v_1} \text{ and } t_2=\frac{BC}{v_2}$$

$$\frac{t_1}{t_2}=\left(\frac{AB}{v_1}\right)\times\left(\frac{v_2}{BC}\right)=\left(\frac{v_2}{v_1}\right)\left(\frac{AB}{BC}\right)=1\times1=1$$

3. (a) Current is constant throughout the resistor.

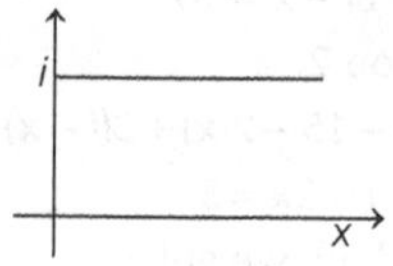

(b) Current density, $J=\frac{i}{A}\propto\frac{1}{A}$

Cross-section area first increases and then decreases. So, current density first decreases and then increases.

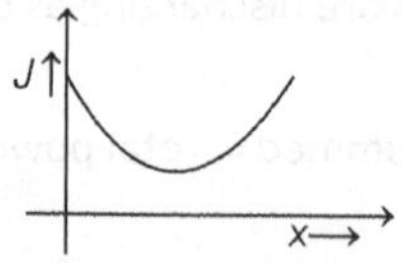

(c) $E=\frac{J}{\sigma} \Rightarrow E=\frac{i}{A\sigma}\propto\frac{1}{A}$

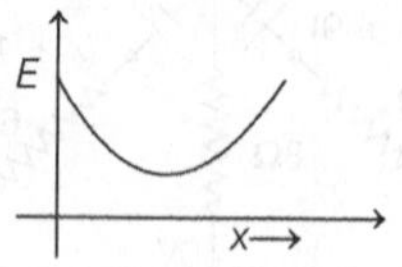

(d) $dV=-Edx \Rightarrow \int dV=-\int\frac{i}{A\sigma}dx$

Potential decreases non-linearly in the direction of current.

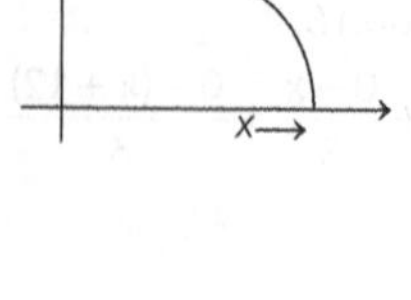

4.

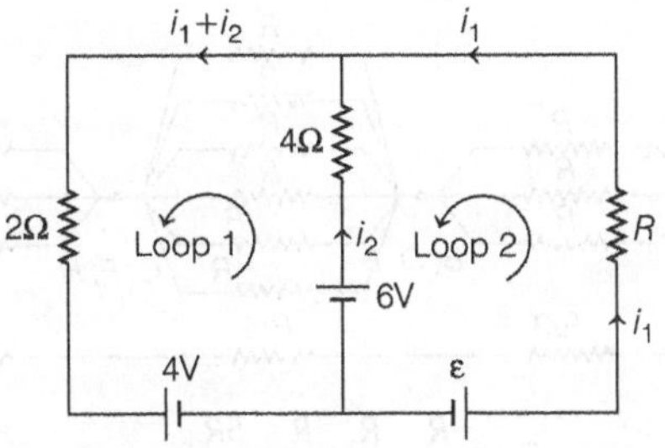

Using KVL in loop 1,

$$+6+i_1R-\varepsilon-i_2(4)=0$$

$$\Rightarrow \quad i_1R-i_2(4)=\varepsilon-6 \quad \text{...(i)}$$

Using KVL in loop 2,

$$+6-4i_2-2(i_1+i_2)-4=0$$

$$\Rightarrow \quad i_1+3i_2=1 \quad \text{...(ii)}$$

Solving Eqs. (i) and (ii), we get

$$i_1=\frac{3\varepsilon-14}{3R+4} \quad \text{and} \quad i_2=\frac{R+6-\varepsilon}{3R+4}$$

(a) $i_2=0 \Rightarrow R+6-e=0$

$$\Rightarrow \quad e=R+6$$

$$\Rightarrow \quad \varepsilon>6V \quad (\because R>0)$$

(b) $i_2>0$

$$\Rightarrow \quad R+6-\varepsilon>0 \Rightarrow e<R+6$$

which is possible for any finite value of ε, because R is finite.

(c) For current to be from C to F,

$$i_2<0 \Rightarrow \varepsilon>R+6$$

$$\Rightarrow \quad \varepsilon>6V \quad (\because R>0)$$

(d) For current in 2Ω from B to A,

$$i_1+i_2=\frac{R-8+2\varepsilon}{3R+4}>0$$

$$\Rightarrow \quad R-8+2\varepsilon>0 \Rightarrow \varepsilon>4-\frac{R}{2}$$

So, depending on value of R, ε can take any value from zero to infinity.

5. (a)

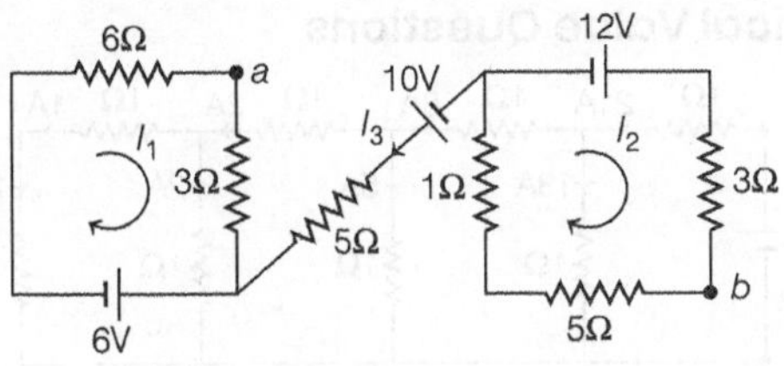

$$I_3=0$$

Applying KVL in loop 1,

$$+6-6I_1-3I_1=0 \Rightarrow I_1=\frac{2}{3}A$$

Applying KVL in loop 2,

$$+12-3I_2-5I_2-I_2=0$$

$$I_2=\frac{4}{3}A$$

$$V_a-3I_1-10+12-3I_2=V_b$$

$$\Rightarrow \quad V_a-V_b=3I_1+3I_2-2=3\left(\frac{2}{3}\right)+3\left(\frac{4}{3}\right)-2=4V$$

(b)

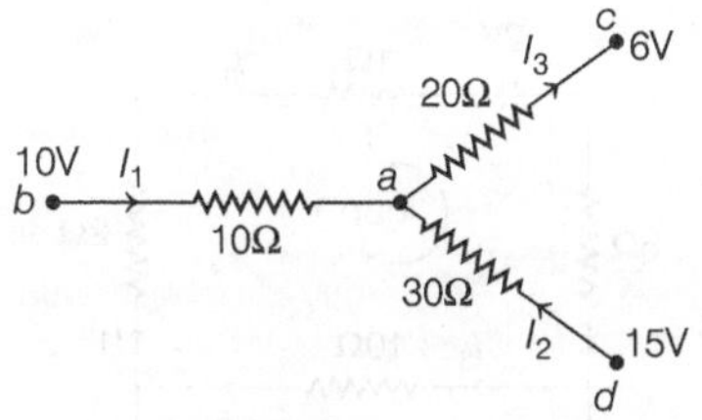

$$I_3=I_1+I_2$$

$$\Rightarrow \quad \frac{V_a-6}{20}=\frac{10-V_a}{10}+\frac{15-V_a}{30}$$

$$\Rightarrow \quad 3V_a-18=60-6V_a+30-2V_a$$

$$11V_a=108$$

$$\Rightarrow \quad V_a=\frac{108}{11}V$$

$$I_1=\frac{10-\frac{108}{11}}{10}=\frac{1}{55}A$$

$$I_2=\frac{15-\frac{108}{11}}{30}$$

$$=\frac{57}{30\times11}=\frac{19}{110}V$$

$$I_3=\frac{\frac{108}{11}-6}{20}=\frac{21}{110}V$$

(c)

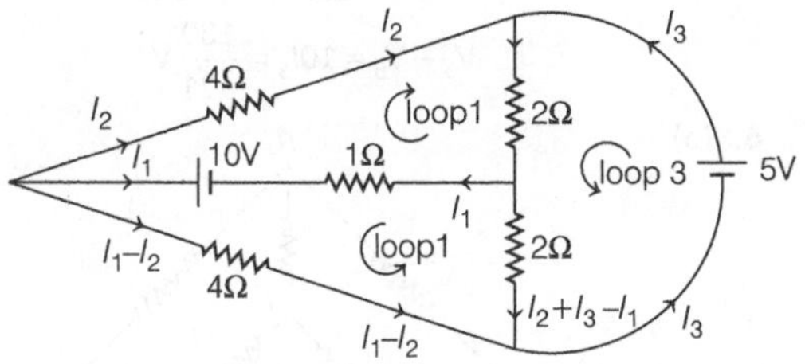

In loop 1,

$$+10-I_1-4I_2-2(I_2+I_3)=0$$

$$I_1+6I_2+2I_3=10 \quad \text{...(i)}$$

In loop 2,

$$-I_1+10-4(I_1-I_2)+2(I_2+I_3-I_1)=0$$

$$7I_1-6I_2-2I_3=10 \quad \text{...(ii)}$$

In loop 3,

$$+5-2(I_2+I_3)-2(I_2+I_3-I_1)=0$$

$$\Rightarrow \quad 4I_2+4I_3-2I_1=5 \quad \text{...(iii)}$$

Solving Eqs. (i), (ii) and (iii), we get

$$I_1=\frac{5}{2}A, I_2=\frac{5}{8}A$$

and $I_3=\frac{15}{8}A$

$$V_a-4I_2=V_b$$

$$V_a-V_b=4I_2=4\left(\frac{5}{8}\right)=\frac{5}{2}V$$

(d)

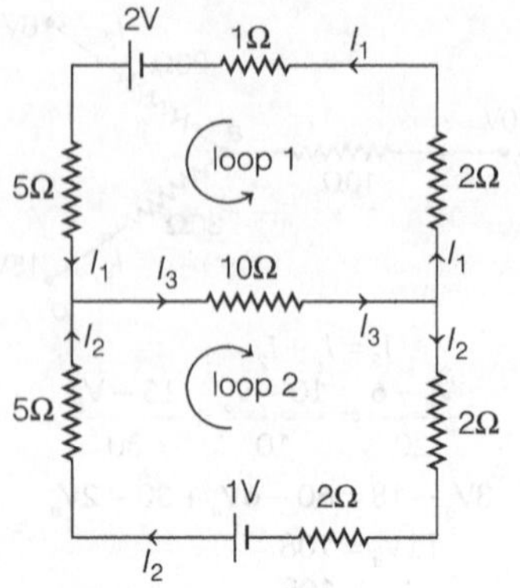

Applying KVL in loop 1,

$$+2-5I_1-10I_3-2I_1-I_1=0$$

$$\Rightarrow \quad 8I_1+10I_3=2$$

$$\Rightarrow \quad 4I_1+5I_3=1 \quad \text{...(i)}$$

Applying KVL in loop 2,

$$+1-5I_2-10I_3-2I_2-2I_2=0$$

$$9I_2+10I_3=1 \quad \text{...(ii)}$$

Applying KCL at junction *b*,

$$I_3=I_1+I_2 \quad \text{...(iii)}$$

Solving Eqs. (i), (ii) and (iii), we get

$$I_1=\frac{14}{121}\text{A}, I_2=\frac{-1}{121}\text{A} \text{ and } I_3=\frac{13}{121}\text{A}$$

$$V_a-V_b=10I_3=\frac{130}{121}\text{V}$$

6. (a)

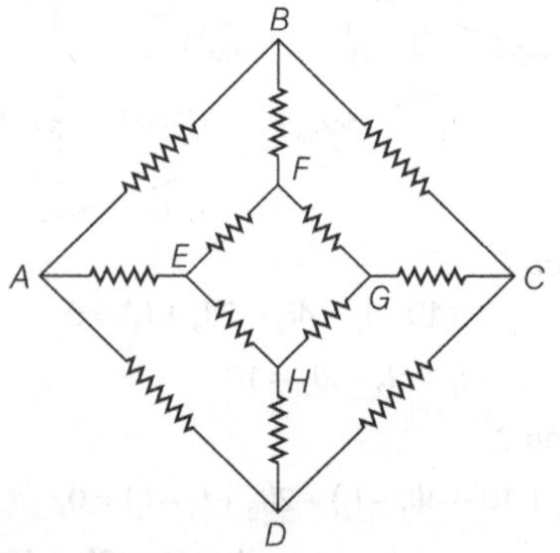

When battery is connected across *A* and *E*, $V_B=V_D$ and $V_F=V_H$ due to parallel axis of symmetry. So, we can join *B* & *D* and *F* & *H*.

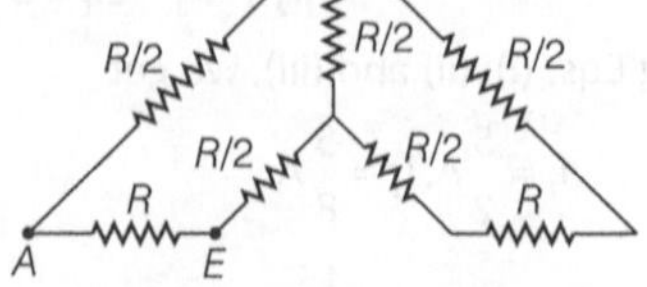

Using series and parallel combination,

$$R_{eq}=\frac{7R}{12}$$

(b) When battery is connected between *A* and *G*, points *B*, *E* and *D* will be at the same potential and points *C*, *F* and *H* are at the same potential.

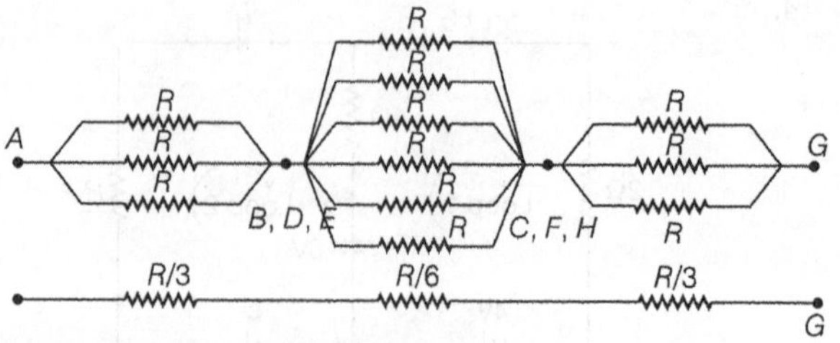

$$R_{eq}=\frac{R}{3}+\frac{R}{6}+\frac{R}{3}=\frac{5R}{6}$$

(c) When battery is connected across *A* and *C*, points *B* & *D* and *F* & *H* are equipotential.
So, we can join them.

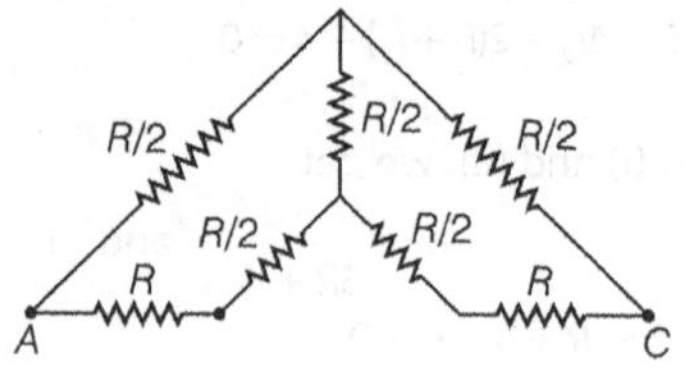

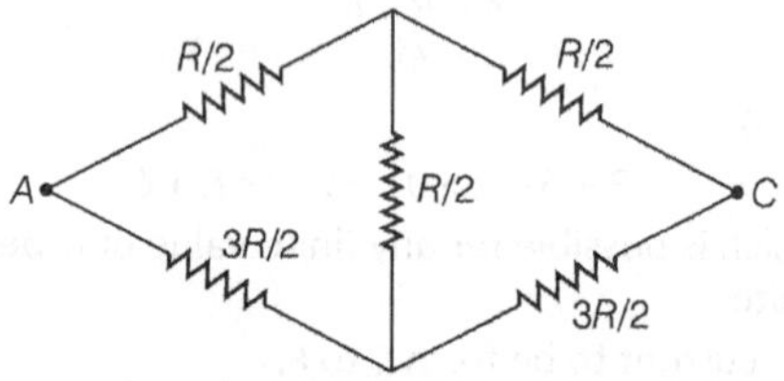

This is a balanced Wheatstone bridge.

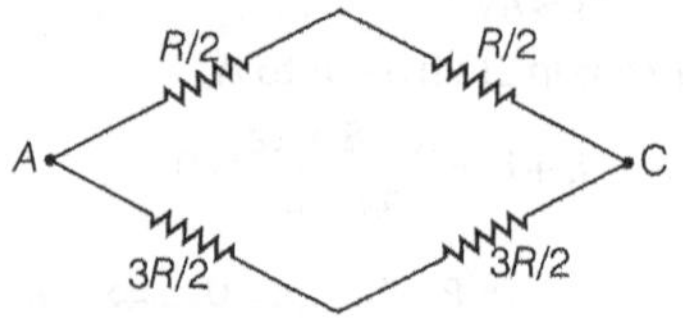

Using series and parallel combination, $R_{eq}=\frac{3R}{4}$

Numerical Value Questions

1.

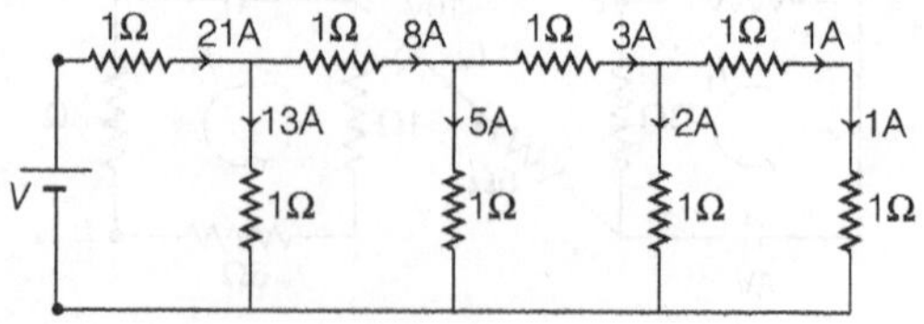

$$V=iR_{eq}=21\left(\frac{34}{21}\right)=34\text{ V}$$

2.

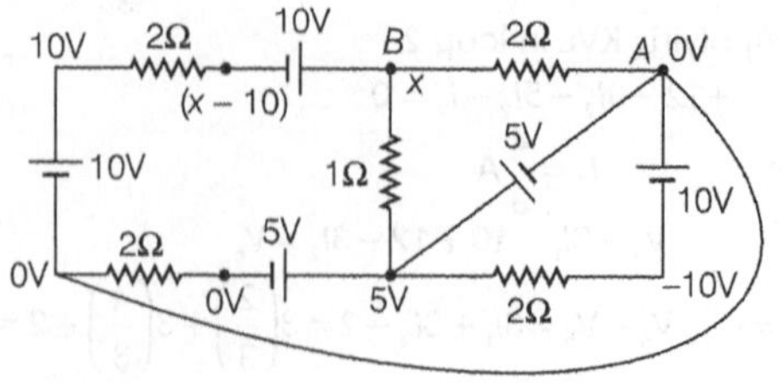

Let potential of A be 0 V and potential of B be x.

Applying KCL at junction B,

$$\frac{10-(x-10)}{2}+\frac{0-x}{2}+\frac{5-x}{1}=0$$

$$\Rightarrow \quad 20-x-x+10-2x=0 \Rightarrow x=7.5\,\text{V}$$

Current through 1Ω resistor $=\frac{x-5}{1}=2.5\,\text{A}$

3.

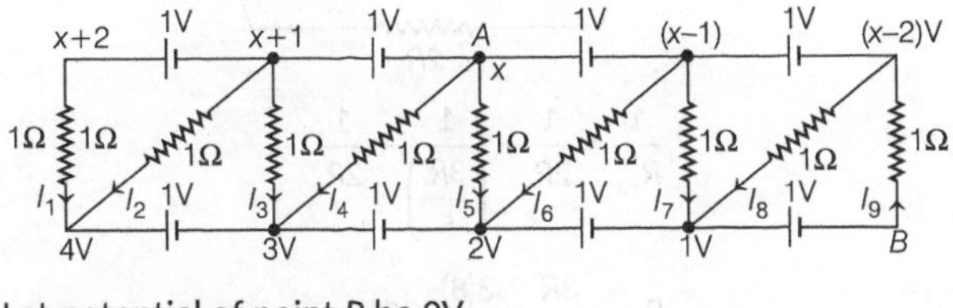

Let potential of point B be 0V and potential of point A be x.

$$I_9=I_1+I_2+I_3+I_4+I_5+I_6+I_7+I_8$$

$$\frac{0-(x-2)}{1}=\frac{(x+2)-4}{1}+\frac{(x+1)-4}{1}+\frac{(x+1)-3}{1}$$

$$+\frac{(x-3)}{1}+\frac{x-2}{1}+\frac{(x-1)-2}{1}+\frac{(x-1)-1}{1}+\frac{(x-2)-1}{1}$$

$$\Rightarrow \quad 2-x=8x-20$$

$$\Rightarrow \quad 9x=22 \quad \Rightarrow \quad x=\frac{22}{9}\,\text{V}$$

4. V = Potential difference across the cell

= Electric field × Width of cell

$=(8\,\text{N/C})\times(0.1\,\text{m}) = 0.8\,\text{V}$

ε = Emf of the cell $=10\times 1=10\,\text{V}$

$$V=\varepsilon-ir$$

$$0.8=1-1(r) \quad \Rightarrow \quad r=0.2\Omega$$

5.

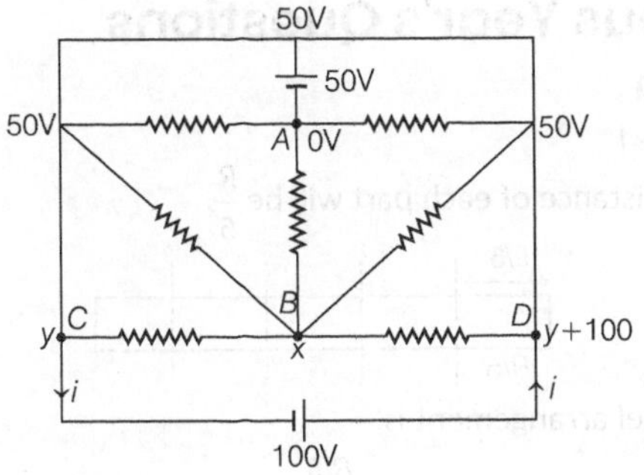

Applying KCL at junction B,

$$\frac{y-x}{2}+\frac{50-x}{2}+\frac{0-x}{2}+\frac{50-x}{2}+\frac{(y+100)-x}{2}=0$$

$$\Rightarrow \quad 2y-5x+200=0$$

$$\Rightarrow \quad 5x-2y=200 \qquad \text{...(i)}$$

At junction C,

$$i=\frac{50-y}{2}+\frac{x-y}{2} \qquad \text{...(ii)}$$

At junction D,

$$i=\frac{(y+100)-50}{2}+\frac{(y+100)-x}{2} \qquad \text{...(iii)}$$

From Eqs. (ii) and (iii), we get

$$i=\frac{50-y}{2}+\frac{x-y}{2}$$

$$=\frac{(y+100)-50}{2}+\frac{(y+100)-x}{2}$$

$$\Rightarrow \quad 50+x-2y=2y-x+150$$

$$\Rightarrow \quad x-2y=50 \qquad \text{...(iv)}$$

Solving Eqs. (i) and (iv), we get

$$x=37.5\,\text{V}$$

Current through $R=\frac{37.5-0}{2}=18.75\,\text{A}$

6.

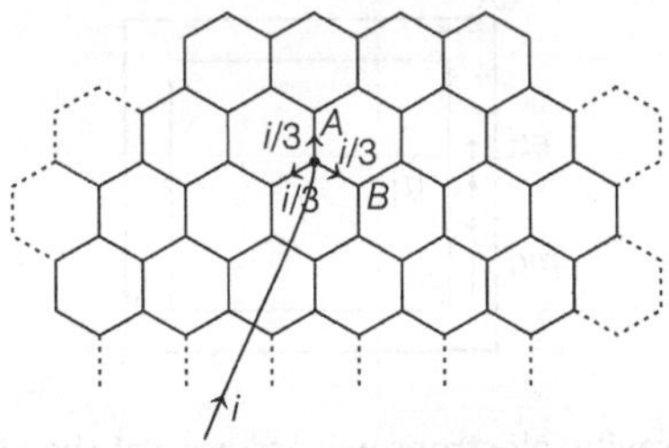

When a current i is sent at A, it is distributed equally in 3 branches.

Current through branch AB is $\frac{i}{3}$.

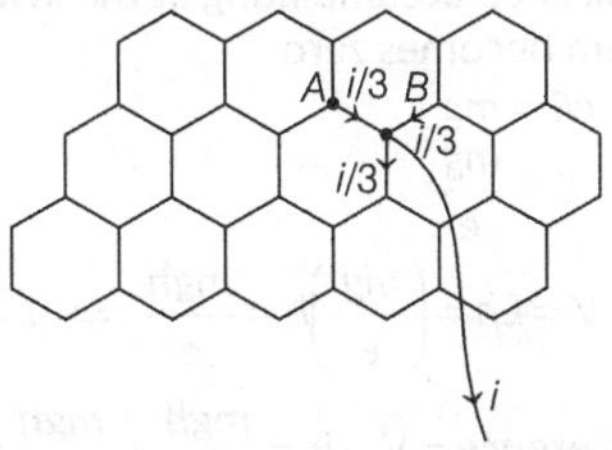

When a current i is taken out at B, it is distributed equally in 3 branches.

Current through branch AB is $\frac{i}{3}$.

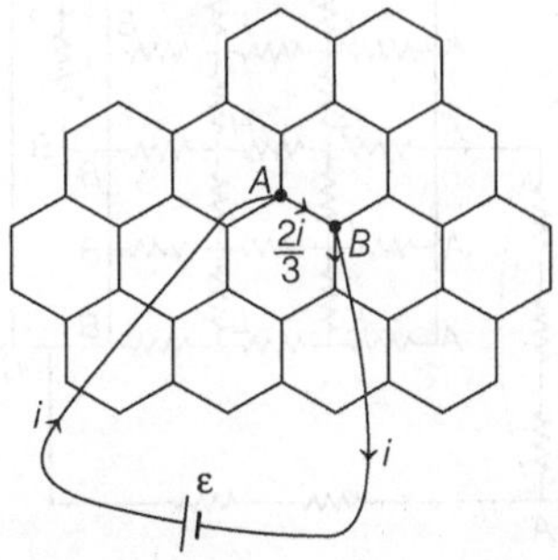

Now, if a battery is connected across A and B, current i enters at A and leaves at B.

By superposition of first two cases, current in branch AB will be now $\frac{i}{3}+\frac{i}{3}=\frac{2i}{3}$.

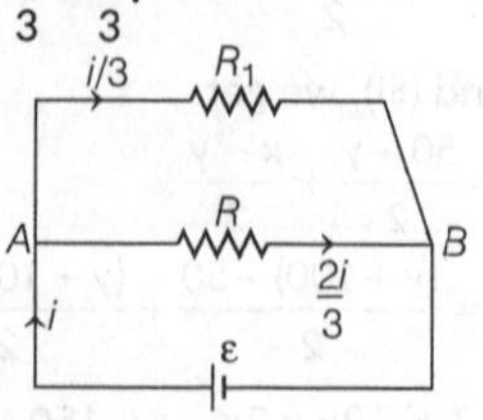

R_1 = Resistance of remaining grid across A and B,

$$(i/3)R_1=\left(\frac{2i}{3}\right)R \Rightarrow R_1=2R$$

$$R_{eq}=\frac{(2R)R}{2R+R}=\frac{2R}{3}=\frac{2(24)}{3}=16\Omega$$

7.

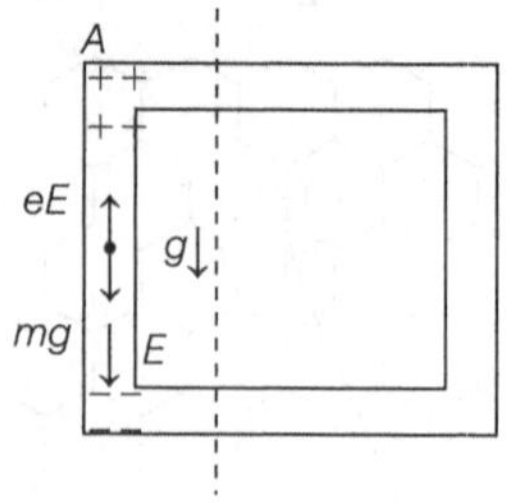

Due to gravity, electrons will accurate at the bottom and there will be deficiency of electrons at the top. Due to accumulation of positive and negative charges, an electric field will develop.

Electrons will keep accumulating at the lower end till net force on them becomes zero.

$$eE=mg$$

$$\Rightarrow \quad E=\frac{mg}{e}$$

$$V=Eh=\left(\frac{mg}{e}\right)h=\frac{mgh}{e} \Rightarrow i=\frac{V}{R}=\frac{mgh}{e(4r)}$$

$$\text{Potential difference}=V-ir=\frac{mgh}{e}-\frac{mgh}{e(4r)}r=\frac{3mgh}{4e}$$

8.

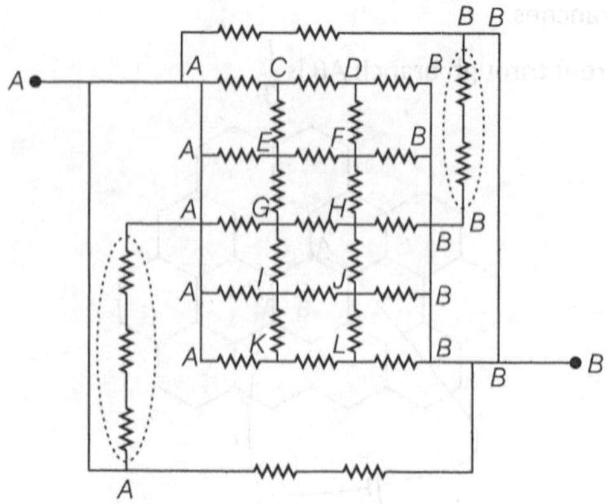

Circled resistors are short-circuited.

From symmetry, points C, E, G, I, K are equipotential.

Points D, F, H, J, L are also equipotential.

So, we can remove resistors connected between these points.

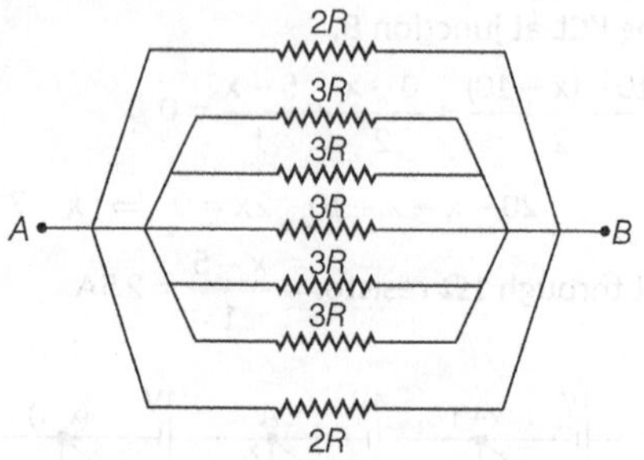

$$\frac{1}{R_{eq}}=\frac{1}{2R}+\frac{1}{\left(\frac{3R}{5}\right)}+\frac{1}{2R}$$

$$R_{eq}=\frac{3R}{8}=\frac{3(8)}{8}=3\Omega$$

9. $\text{Pressure}=\frac{\text{Force}}{\text{Area}}=\left(\frac{\Delta p}{\Delta t}\right)\frac{1}{A}$

$$\Rightarrow \quad 9.1=\left(\frac{\Delta p}{\Delta t}\right)\left(\frac{1}{1\times10^{-4}}\right)$$

$$\Rightarrow \quad \frac{\Delta p}{\Delta t}=9.1\times10^{-4}$$

Number of electrons incident per second $=\frac{i}{e}$

Change in momentum per second $=\left(\frac{i}{e}\right)mv$

$$\Rightarrow \quad \frac{imv}{e}=9.1\times10^{-4}$$

$$\Rightarrow \quad i=\frac{1.6\times10^{-19}\times9.1\times10^{-4}}{9.1\times10^{-31}\times8\times10^{7}}=2\text{A}$$

Previous Year's Questions

JEE Main

1. As $R \propto l$

$\therefore$ Resistance of each part will be $\frac{R}{5}$.

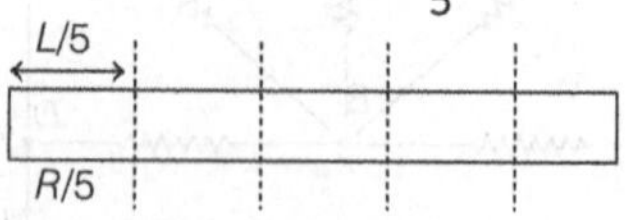

Parallel arrangement is,

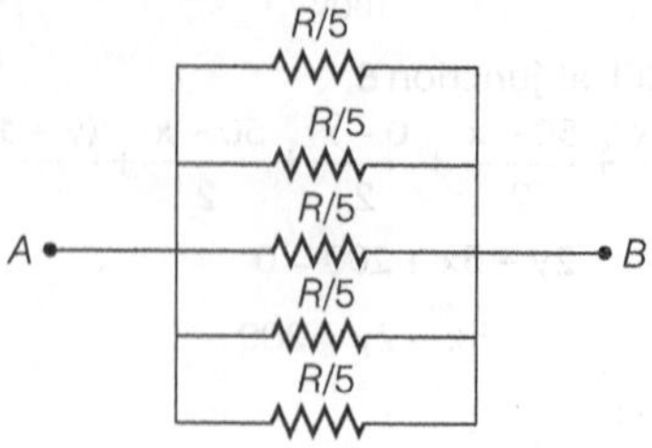

$$R_{eq}=\frac{R/5}{5}=\frac{R}{25}$$

2. $I = I_0 + \beta t$, where $I_0 = 20$ A

and $\beta = 3$ A/s

So, $I = 20 + 3t$

$$\Rightarrow \frac{dq}{dt} = 20 + 3t$$

$$\Rightarrow \int dq = \int (20 + 3t)dt$$

$$q = \int_0^{20} 20\, dt + \int_0^{20} 3t\, dt = \left[20t + \frac{3t^2}{2}\right]_0^{20}$$

$$q = 1000 \text{ C}$$

3. Given, resistance of the wire, $R = 160\,\Omega$

Let ρ be the resistivity of the wire. Since, volume remains constant, thus

$$A_1L_1 = A_2L_2$$

$$\Rightarrow A_1L = A_2\frac{L}{4} \qquad \left(\text{given}, L_2 = \frac{L_1}{4}\right)$$

$$\Rightarrow 4A_1 = A_2$$

Initially, $R_1 = \rho\frac{L_1}{A_1}$

Finally, $R_2 = \rho\frac{L_2}{A_2}$

$$\Rightarrow \frac{R_2}{R_1} = \frac{L_2A_1}{L_1A_2} = \frac{1}{4}\frac{A_1}{4A_1} = \frac{1}{16}$$

$$\Rightarrow R_2 = \frac{160}{16} = 10\,\Omega$$

4. In series combination, equivalent resistance,

$$R = R_1 + R_2 + R_3$$

Hence, equivalent resistance of resistors in series combination is more than largest resistance used in combination.

Therefore, statement I is incorrect. Resistivity of the material is dependent on temperature.

For metals, it increases with increase in temperature and for semi-conductor , it decreases with increase temperature. Thus, statement II is also incorrect.

5. Given circuit is;

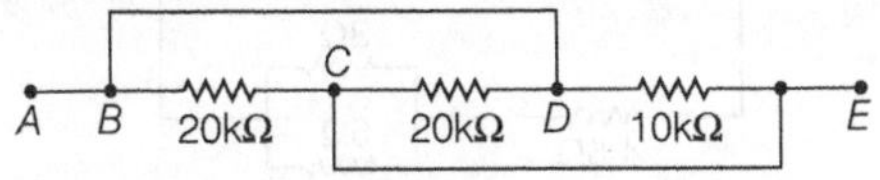

We radiance above circuit as;

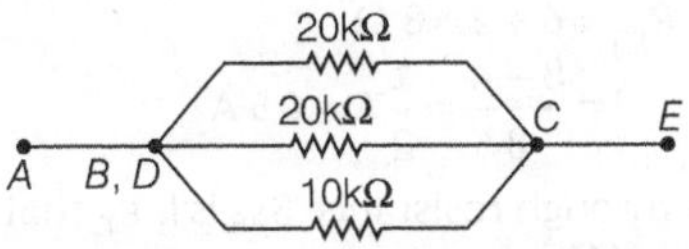

So, we have 3-resistances in parallel. Equivalent resistance of circuit is;

$$\frac{1}{R_{eq}} = \frac{1}{R_1} + \frac{1}{R_2} + \frac{1}{R_3}$$

$$= \frac{1}{20} + \frac{1}{20} + \frac{1}{10} = \frac{1+1+2}{20}$$

So, $R_{eq} = \frac{20}{4}\text{k}\,\Omega = 5\text{k}\,\Omega$

6. Drift velocity of electrons through conductor is given as,

$$v_d = \frac{I}{neA} \text{ or } v_d \propto \frac{I}{A}$$

$\because$ For same potential difference,

$$I \propto \frac{1}{R} \propto A$$

or $$v_d \propto \frac{A}{A} \text{ or } v_d \propto 1$$

So, drift velocity will not change.

7. Given, initial resistance of wire

$$R_1 = 5\,\Omega$$

If R_2 be the new resistance of the wire when wire is stretched to 5 times, then

$$R_2 = 5^2R_1 \qquad (\because R_2 = n^2R_1)$$

$$= 25 \times 5 = 125\,\Omega$$

8. When a uniform wire of resistance R is shaped into a regular n-sided polygon, the resistance of each side will be

$$R_1 = \frac{R}{n}$$

Let, R_1 and R_2 be the resistance between adjacent corners of a regular polygon.

$\therefore$ The resistance of $(n-1)$ side, $R_2 = \left(\frac{n-1}{n}\right)R$

Since, two parts are in parallel.

Therefore, $$R_{eq} = \frac{R_1R_2}{R_1 + R_2} = \frac{\left(\frac{R}{n}\right)\left(\frac{n-1}{n}\right)R}{\frac{R}{n} + \left(\frac{n-1}{n}\right)R}$$

$$\Rightarrow R_{eq} = \frac{(n-1)}{n^2}R$$

9. Given, current at 0°C = 2A

Current at 100°C = 1.2 A

For the same source we have

$$i_0R_0 = i_{100}R_{100}$$

$$\Rightarrow 2R_0 = 1.2R_0(1 + 100\alpha) \qquad \text{... (i)}$$

$$\Rightarrow 1 + 100\alpha = \frac{5}{3}$$

$$\Rightarrow 100\alpha = \frac{2}{3}$$

$$\Rightarrow 50\alpha = \frac{1}{3}$$

$$\therefore i_{50}R_{50} = i_0R_0 \qquad \text{[Same source]}$$

$$\Rightarrow i_{50} = \frac{i_0R_0}{R_{50}} = \frac{2 \times R_0}{R_0(1+50\alpha)} = \frac{2}{1+\frac{1}{3}}$$

$$= 1.5\text{A} = 15 \times 10^2\text{mA}$$

10. Drift velocity of electrons in a conductor is

$$I = nev_d A \quad \text{...(i)}$$

Here, number of electrons per meter cube $n = 2 \times 10^{28}\ \text{m}^{-3}$

Area of wire, $A = \pi r^2$

Charge of an electron, $e = 1.6 \times 10^{-19}$ C

Current in wire, $I = 2$A

So from Eq. (i) we have,

$$v_d = \frac{I}{neA}$$

$$= \frac{2}{2 \times 10^{28} \times 1.6 \times 10^{-19} \times 25 \times 10^{-6}}$$

$$= 0.25 \times 10^{-4}\ \text{ms}^{-1}$$

$$\Rightarrow \quad v_d = 25 \times 10^{-6}\ \text{ms}^{-1}$$

11. $R = \dfrac{\rho l}{A}$

Where $l' = 21.2l$, $A' = 0.96\ A$

$$R' = \frac{\rho \times 1.2l}{0.96A} = \frac{10}{8}R = 1.25R$$

It mean 25% increase in resistance.

12. Given, specific resistance, $\rho = 3 \times 10^{-7}\ \Omega\text{-m}$

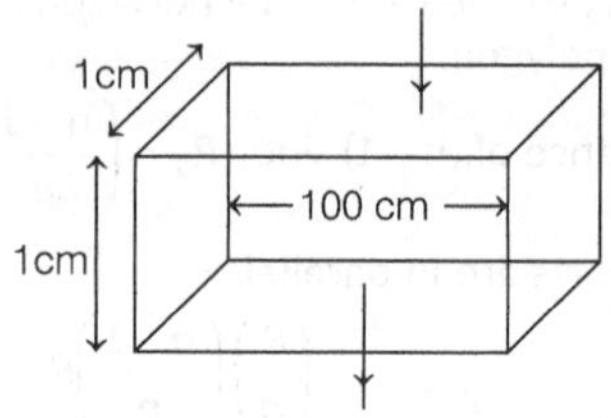

Resistance, $R = \rho \dfrac{l}{A}$.

Resistance through its two opposite faces will be

$$R = \frac{3 \times 10^{-7} \times (1 \times 10^{-2})}{100 \times 1 \times 10^{-4}} = 3 \times 10^{-7}\ \Omega$$

13. Resistance of stretched wire will be,

$$K = l \times A$$

$$l' = 20\% + l = \frac{120}{100}l = \frac{6}{5}l;$$

$$A = V/l$$

$$A' = V/l' = V/(6/5l) = \frac{5}{6}(V/l) = \frac{5}{6}A$$

$$R' = \rho\frac{l'}{A'} = \frac{\rho \cdot \frac{6}{5}l}{\frac{5}{6}A} = \frac{36}{25}\left(\rho\frac{l}{A}\right) = \frac{36}{25}R$$

So, % increase in resistance will be $\dfrac{\Delta R}{R} \times 100 = \dfrac{R'}{R} \times 100$

$$= \left(\frac{36}{25} - 1\right) \times 100$$

$$= 11 \times 4 = 44\%$$

14.

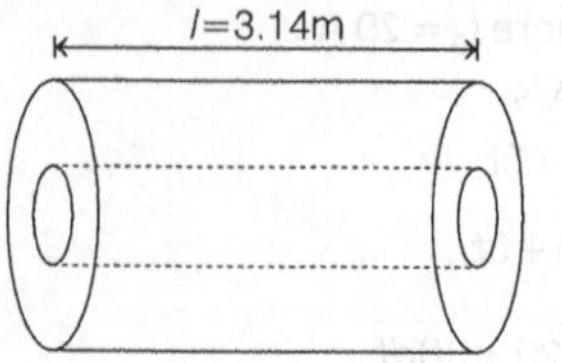

Inner diameter, $d_1 = 4\ \text{mm} = 4 \times 10^{-3}$ m

Outer diameter, $d_2 = 8\ \text{mm} = 8 \times 10^{-3}$ m

Resistance of conductor given is

$$R = \rho\frac{l}{A} = \frac{2.4 \times 10^{-8} \times 3.14}{\frac{\pi}{4}[(8 \times 10^{-3})^2 - (4 \times 10^{-3})^2]} = 2 \times 10^{-3}\ \Omega$$

Given, $R = n \times 10^{-3}\ \Omega$

So, $\quad n = 2$

15. Given,

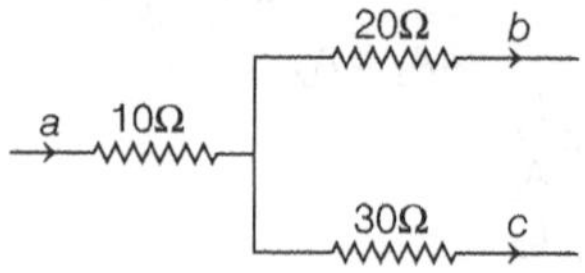

Let potential of the junction be x volts using junction law

$$i_1 + i_2 + i_3 = 0$$

or $\quad \dfrac{x - 30}{10} + \dfrac{x - 12}{20} + \dfrac{x - 2}{30} = 0$

$$\Rightarrow \frac{1}{60}[6x - 180 + 3x - 36 + 2x - 4] = 0$$

$$\frac{1}{60}[11x - 220] = 0 \quad \Rightarrow \quad x = \frac{220}{11} = 20\ \text{V}$$

Current through 20 Ω is $= \dfrac{x - 12}{20}$

$$i_2 = \frac{20 - 12}{20} = 0.4\ \text{A}$$

16

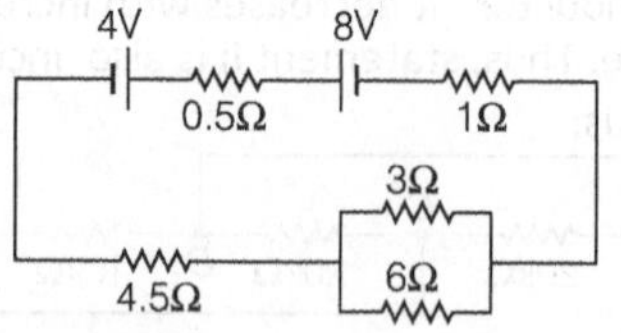

$$R_{eq} = 0{\cdot}5 + 1 + 4{\cdot}5 + 2$$

$$R_{eq} = 6 + 2 = 8\ \Omega$$

$$I = \frac{8 - 4}{8} = \frac{1}{2}\text{A} = 0.5\ \text{A}$$

Current through resistance 3Ω is I_1 ε_T that through resistance 6Ω is I_2

$$I_1 : I_2 = \frac{1}{3} : \frac{1}{6}$$

$$I_1 : I_2 = 2 : 1$$

and $\quad I_1 + I_2 = 0{\cdot}5\ \text{A}$

$$I_1 = \frac{2}{3} \times 0{\cdot}5 = \frac{1}{3}\ \text{A}$$

So, $\quad \dfrac{1}{3} = \dfrac{x}{3} \quad \Rightarrow \quad x = 1$

17. The given circuit may be reduced in following form

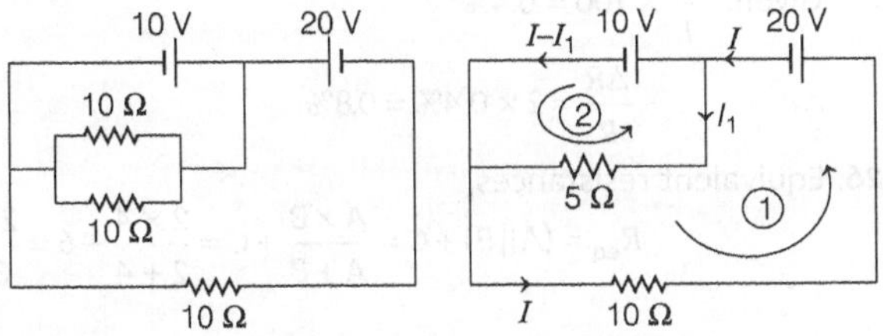

On applying KVL in loop-1 along the direction shown, we get

$$20-10-10I=0 \quad \Rightarrow \quad I=1\text{ A}$$

On applying KVL in loop-2 along the direction shown, we get

$$-10+5I'=0 \quad \Rightarrow \quad I'=2\text{A}$$

On comparing, we get $I_3=1\text{A}=I_1=\dfrac{I'}{2}=1\text{A}$

So, the value of $\left|\dfrac{I_1+I_3}{I_2}\right|=\left|\dfrac{1+1}{1}\right|=2$

18. The given condition is as follows

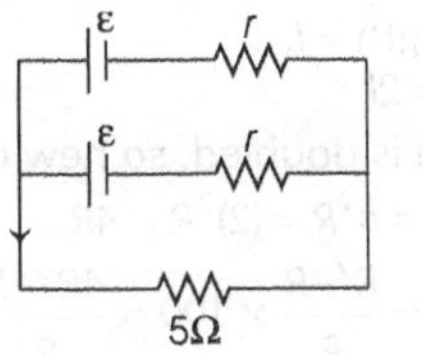

In parallel combination of cell,

$$r_{eq}=\frac{r_1r_2}{r_1+r_2}=\frac{r\times r}{r+r}=\frac{r}{2}$$

$$\varepsilon_{eq}=\frac{\varepsilon_1r_2+\varepsilon_2r_1}{r_1+r_2}=\frac{\varepsilon\times r+\varepsilon\times r}{r+r}=\varepsilon$$

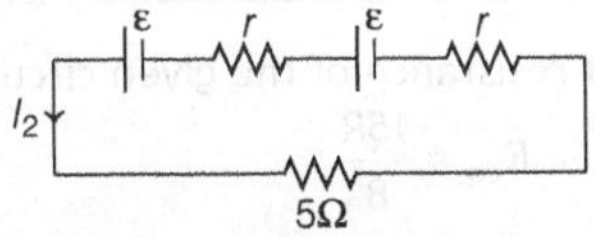

In series, $r_{eq}=r_1+r_2=r+r=2r$

$$\varepsilon_{eq}=\varepsilon_1+\varepsilon_2=\varepsilon+\varepsilon=2\varepsilon$$

$$I_2=\frac{\varepsilon_{eq}}{R+r_{eq}}=\frac{2\varepsilon}{5+2r}$$

Current through load, $I_1=\dfrac{\varepsilon_{eq}}{R+\dfrac{r}{2}}=\dfrac{\varepsilon}{5+\dfrac{r}{2}}$

According to question, $I_1=I_2$

$$\Rightarrow \quad \frac{\varepsilon}{5+\dfrac{r}{2}}=\frac{2\varepsilon}{5+2r}$$

or $\quad 5+\dfrac{r}{2}=\dfrac{5+2r}{2}$

$$\Rightarrow \quad 10+r=5+2r \Rightarrow r=5\,\Omega$$

19. The potential difference between point B and D is zero, hence it is the balanced Wheatstone bridge circuit.

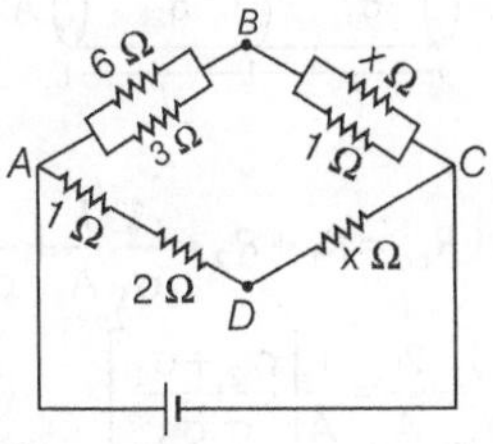

$$\therefore \quad \frac{R_{AB}}{R_{BC}}=\frac{R_{AD}}{R_{DC}}$$

$$\Rightarrow \quad \frac{\dfrac{6\times 3}{6+3}}{\dfrac{x\times 1}{x+1}}=\frac{1+2}{x} \quad \Rightarrow \quad \frac{2(x+1)}{x}=\frac{3}{x}$$

$$\Rightarrow \quad 2x^2+2x-3x=0 \quad \Rightarrow \quad 2x^2-x=0$$

$$\Rightarrow \quad x(2x-1)=0 \quad \Rightarrow \quad x=1/2=\frac{1}{n} \qquad \text{[Given]}$$

$$\therefore \quad n=2$$

20. According to the question,

$$I_w=2I_x \qquad \text{... (i)}$$

$$R_w=2R_y$$

$$\Rightarrow \quad \rho\frac{l_w}{A_w}=2\rho\frac{l_y}{A_y} \qquad \text{... (ii)}$$

$$\Rightarrow \quad \rho\frac{l_w}{A_w}=2\rho\frac{l_y}{A_y}$$

$$\Rightarrow \quad \frac{l_w}{A_w}=\frac{2l_y}{A_y},\ \frac{2l_x}{A_w}=\frac{2l_y}{A_y}$$

Also, $\quad l_x+l_y+l_y=1 \qquad$ ... (iii)

and $\quad A_xl_x=A_wl_w \qquad$ ...(iv)

From Eqs. (i) and (iv),

$$A_xl_x=A_w(2l_x);\ A_x=2A_w$$

From (ii), $\quad \dfrac{2l_x}{A_x/2}=\dfrac{2l_y}{A_y}$

$$\Rightarrow \quad \frac{2l_x}{l_y}=\frac{A_x}{A_y} \qquad \text{...(v)}$$

Since, $A_x=A_y \Rightarrow 2l_x=l_y,\ \dfrac{l_x}{l_y}=\dfrac{1}{2}$

21. Here, resistance of wire at 10 °C, $R_{10}=2\,\Omega$

Resistance of wire at 30° C, $R_{30}=3\,\Omega$

Resistance of any temperature T is given by

$$R_T=R_0(1+\alpha\Delta T)$$

$$\therefore \quad R_{10}=R_0(1+10\alpha)$$

or $\quad 2=R_0(1+10\alpha) \qquad$ ...(i)

Similarly, $\quad R_{30}=R_0(1+30\alpha)$

or $\quad 3=R_0(1+30\alpha) \qquad$ ...(ii)

On dividing Eq. (i) by Eq. (ii), we get

$$\frac{2}{3}=\frac{(1+10\alpha)}{(1+30\alpha)}$$

$$\Rightarrow \quad 2+60\alpha=3+30\alpha \Rightarrow \quad \alpha=\frac{1}{3}=0.033\,°\text{C}^{-1}$$

22. According to the question

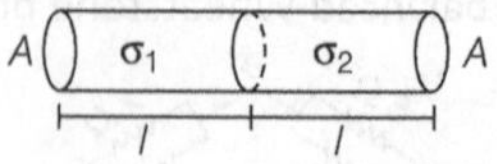

In series,

$$R_{eq} = R_1 + R_2 = \frac{1}{\sigma_1}\frac{l}{A} + \frac{1}{\sigma_2}\frac{l}{A}$$

$$\Rightarrow \quad \frac{1}{\sigma_{eq}}\frac{2l}{A} = \frac{l}{A}\left[\frac{\sigma_2+\sigma_1}{\sigma_1\sigma_2}\right] \qquad \left[\because R = \frac{1}{\sigma}\frac{\ell}{A}\right]$$

$$\Rightarrow \quad \sigma_{eq} = \frac{2\sigma_1\sigma_2}{(\sigma_1+\sigma_2)}$$

23. Given, initial resistance of wire $= R_1$

i.e. $R_2 = n^2 R_1$

Here, $n = 2$

$\therefore$ $R_2 = 2^2 R_1$

$\Rightarrow$ $R_2 = 4R_1 \Rightarrow R_2/R_1 = 4/1$

$R_2 : R_1 = 4:1$

24. We know, $v_d = \dfrac{eE\tau}{m}$

Where, τ = relaxation time

$\because$ $v_d \propto \tau$

On increasing temperature, τ decreases.

Thus, v_d decreases with increasing temperature.

$\therefore$ (A) is correct.

Now, $v_d = \dfrac{i}{neA}$

Clearly the drift velocity is inversely proportional to the area of cross-section.

We know, $E = \dfrac{V}{l}$ (Where, V = potential difference)

$\therefore$ $v_d = \dfrac{eV\tau}{ml}$

$v_d \propto V$

$\therefore$ (C) is wrong.

$\therefore$ v_d it is independent of length of conductor.

Hence, (D) is wrong.

(E) is also wrong.

25. Density,

$$d = \frac{\text{mass}}{\text{volume}} = \frac{\text{mass}}{\text{area} \times \text{length}}$$

$$d = \frac{m}{Al} \Rightarrow A = \frac{m}{ld}$$

$$\text{Resistance, } R = \frac{\rho l}{A} = \frac{\rho l}{m/ld} = \frac{\rho l^2 d}{m}$$

$$\therefore \quad R = \left[\frac{\rho d}{m}\right] l^2 = \text{constant} \times l^2$$

$$\frac{\Delta R}{R} = 2 \times \frac{\Delta l}{l}$$

% change in resistance is

$$\frac{\Delta R}{R} \times 100 = 2 \times \left[\frac{\Delta l}{l}\right] \times 100$$

Given, $\dfrac{\Delta l}{l} \times 100 = 0.4\%$

$$\therefore \quad \frac{\Delta R}{R} = 2 \times 0.4\% = 0.8\%$$

26. Equivalent resistances,

$$R_{eq} = (A \| B) + C = \frac{A \times B}{A+B} + C = \frac{2\times 4}{2+4} + 6 = \frac{22}{3}\,\Omega$$

27. Equivalent resistance of given circuit is given as

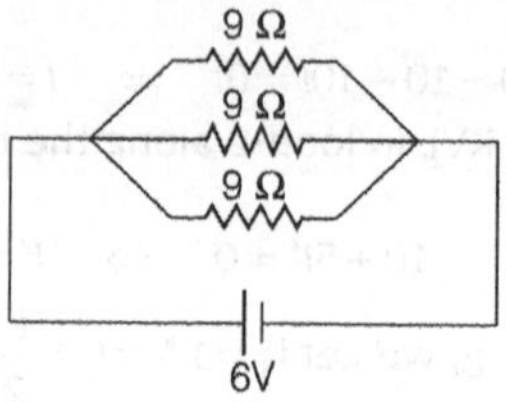

$$R_{eq} = \frac{9}{3}\Omega = 3\Omega;$$

$$\text{Now, } V = IR_{eq};\ I = \frac{V}{R_{eq}} = \frac{6}{3} = 2\text{A}$$

28. Let initial length $= l$,

final length $= 2l$

As the length is doubled, so new resistance

$$R' = n^2 R = (2)^2 R = 4R$$

$$\%\text{ resistance} = \frac{R'-R}{R} \times 100 = \frac{4R - R}{R} \times 100 = 300\ \%$$

29.

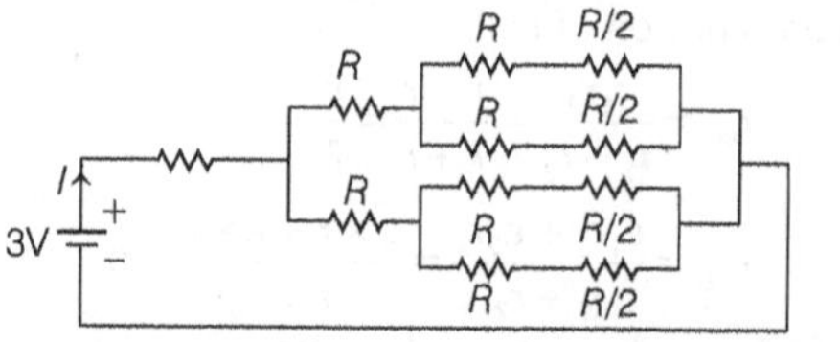

Equivalent resistance of the given circuit will be

$$R_{eq} = \frac{15R}{8}$$

Resistance of each resistor, $R = 1\,\Omega$

$$\therefore \quad R_{eq} = \frac{15}{8}\Omega$$

Now, current in the circuit,

$$I = \frac{V}{R_{eq}} = \frac{3\times 8}{15} = \frac{8}{5}\text{A}$$

So, $a = 8$

30. Given, $l = 1$ m, $I = 1$ A

$A = 2\text{mm}^2 = 2 \times 10^{-6}\text{m}^2$

$\rho = 1.7 \times 10^{-8}\,\Omega\text{-m}$

We know that

Current density,

$$\Rightarrow \quad J = \frac{E}{\rho} \qquad \left(\because \sigma = \frac{1}{\rho}\right)$$

$$\Rightarrow \quad \frac{I}{A} = \frac{E}{\rho} \qquad \left(\because J = \frac{I}{A}\right)$$

$$\Rightarrow \quad E = \frac{I\rho}{A} \quad \text{...(i)}$$

$\therefore$ Force on electron,

$$F = eE \quad \text{[From Eq. (i)]}$$

$$= \frac{eI\rho}{A} = \frac{1.6 \times 10^{-19} \times 1 \times 1.7 \times 10^{-8}}{2 \times 10^{-6}}$$

$$= 136 \times 10^{-23} \text{ N}$$

31. Let the internal resistance of cell is r and emf is ε. External resistance,

$$R = 2\,\Omega$$

When, they are in series

$$i = \frac{2\varepsilon}{R + 2r} \quad \text{...(i)}$$

When, they are in parallel

$$i' = \frac{\varepsilon}{R + r/2} \quad \text{...(ii)}$$

From (i) and (ii), $i = i'$

$$\Rightarrow \quad \frac{2\varepsilon}{R + 2r} = \frac{\varepsilon}{R + r/2}$$

$$\Rightarrow \quad 2R + r = R + 2r; R = r$$

$$\Rightarrow \quad r = 2\,\Omega$$

32. The circuit diagram for the given condition is shown below.

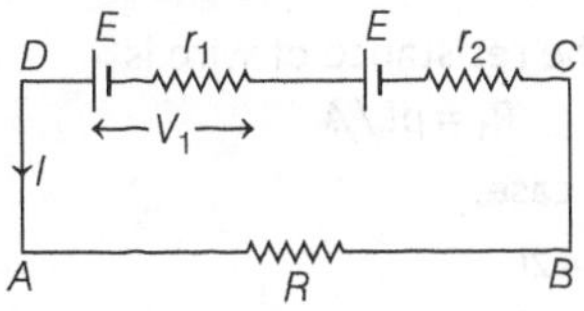

Given, $\quad V_1 = 0$

i.e $\quad E - Ir_1 = 0$

$$E = Ir_1 \quad \text{...(i)}$$

On applying KVL in loop $ABCDA$.

$$RI + Ir_2 - E + Ir_1 - E = 0$$

$$I(R + r_1 + r_2) = 2E$$

$$\Rightarrow \quad I(R + r_1 + r_2) = 2 \times Ir_1 \quad \text{[From Eq. (i)]}$$

$$\Rightarrow \quad R + r_1 + r_2 = 2r_1$$

$$\Rightarrow \quad R = 2r_1 - r_1 - r_2$$

$$\Rightarrow \quad R = r_1 - r_2$$

33. The circuit diagram for the given situation is shown below

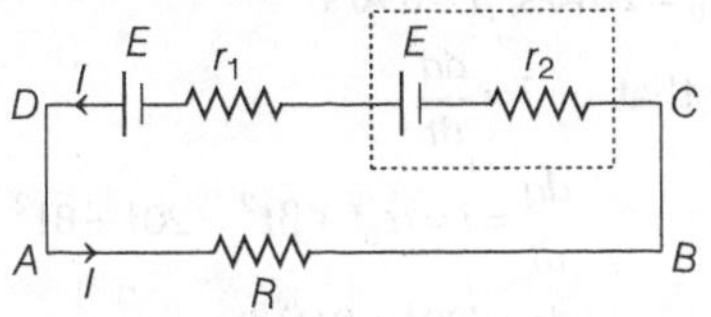

Since, potential difference across the second cell is zero.

i.e. $\quad V_2 = E - Ir_2 = 0$

$$\Rightarrow \quad I = \frac{E}{r_2} \quad \text{...(i)}$$

On applying KVL in loop $ABCDA$, we get

$$IR + Ir_2 - E + Ir_1 - E = 0$$

$$\Rightarrow \quad I(R + r_1 + r_2) = 2E$$

$$\Rightarrow \quad I = \frac{2E}{R + r_1 + r_2} \quad \text{...(ii)}$$

From Eqs. (i) and (ii), we get

$$\frac{E}{r_2} = \frac{2E}{R + r_1 + r_2}$$

$$\Rightarrow \quad R + r_1 + r_2 = 2r_2$$

$$\Rightarrow \quad R = r_2 - r_1$$

34. The given circuit diagram is shown below

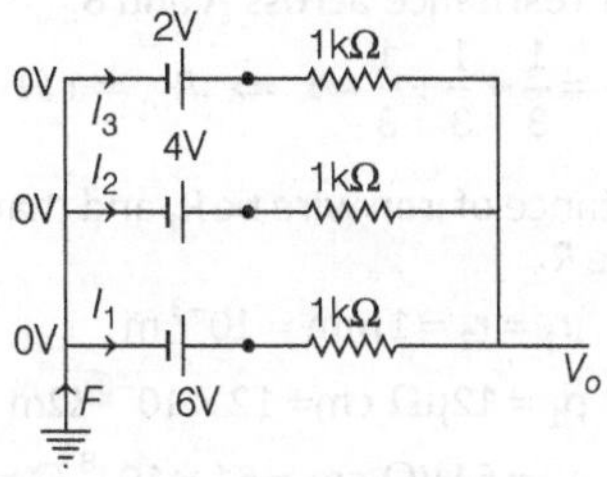

Using Kirchhoff's junction rule,

$$I_1 + I_2 + I_3 = 0$$

$$\frac{6 - V_0}{1 \times 10^3} + \frac{4 - V_0}{1 \times 10^3} + \frac{2 - V_0}{1 \times 10^3} = 0$$

$$\Rightarrow \quad 12 - 3V_0 = 0$$

$$\Rightarrow \quad V_0 = 4 \text{ V}$$

35. The circuit diagram is shown below

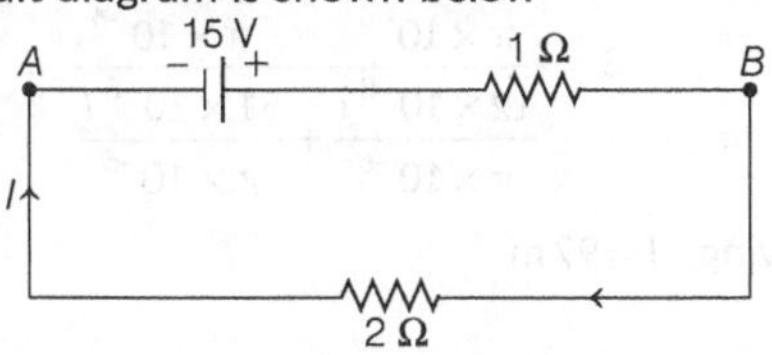

Current in circuit, $\quad I = \frac{V}{R_{total}} = \frac{15}{3} = 5$ A.

Now potential drop in 2 Ω resistance $= V_2 = IR$

$$= 5 \times 2 = 10 \text{ V}$$

Hence, $\quad V_{BA} = V_B - V_A = V_2 = 10$ V

36. In the given circuit, 5 Ω resistance is shorted. So, it .can be discarded.

Now, we get a resolved circuit as shown below

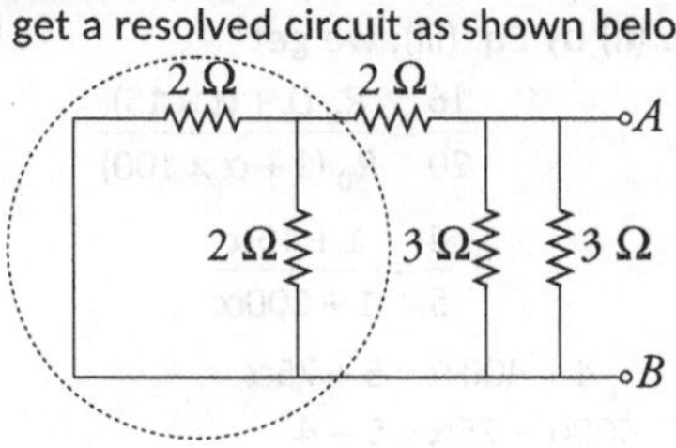

In parallel, $R_1 = \frac{2 \times 2}{2 + 2} = 1\,\Omega$

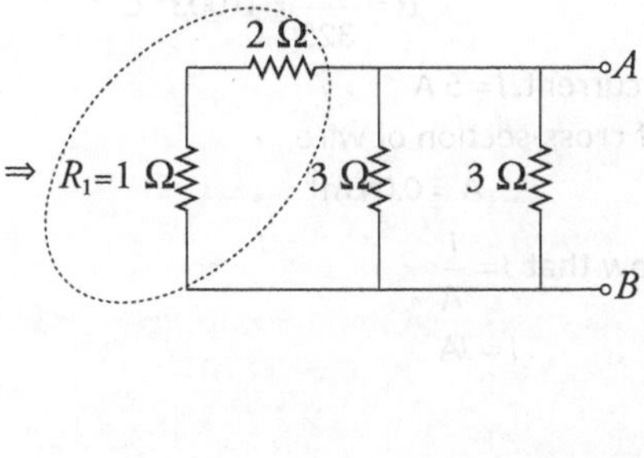

In series, $R_2 = R_1 + 2 = 1 + 2 = 3\Omega$

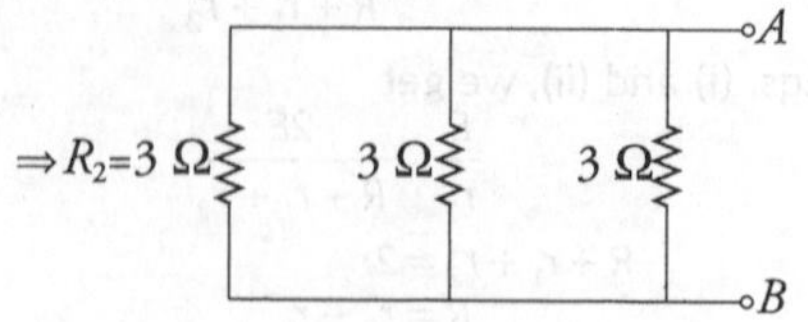

Here, all the three resistances (3 Ω) are parallel.

∴ Equivalent resistance across A and B,

$$\frac{1}{R_{eq}} = \frac{1}{3} + \frac{1}{3} + \frac{1}{3} = 1 \Rightarrow R_{eq} = 1\,\Omega$$

37. Let the resistance of iron wire be R_1 and that of copper nickel alloy wire be R_2

$$r_1 = r_2 = 1\,\text{mm} = 10^{-3}\,\text{m}$$

$$\rho_1 = 12\mu\Omega\ \text{cm} = 12 \times 10^{-8}\ \Omega\text{m}$$

$$\rho_2 = 51\mu\Omega\ \text{cm} = 51 \times 10^{-8}\ \Omega\text{m}$$

For parallel combination,

$$R_{eq} = \frac{R_1 R_2}{R_1 + R_2} \text{ and } 3 = \frac{\frac{\rho_1 l}{\pi r_1^2} \frac{\rho_2 l}{\pi r_2^2}}{\frac{\rho_1 l}{\pi r_1^2} + \frac{\rho_2 l}{\pi r_2^2}}$$

$$\Rightarrow \quad 3 = \frac{\frac{(12 \times 10^{-8}) l}{\pi \times 10^{-6}} \times \frac{51 \times 10^{-8} l}{\pi \times 10^{-6}}}{\frac{12 \times 10^{-8} l}{\pi \times 10^{-6}} + \frac{51 \times 10^{-8} l}{\pi \times 10^{-6}}}$$

On solving, $l = 97\,\text{m}$

38. Given,

Resistance of conductor at 15°C = 16 Ω

and resistance of conductor at 100°C = 20 Ω

∴ Using Eq. (i), we can write

$$16 = R_0[1 + \alpha(15 - T_0)] \quad \text{...(ii)}$$

and $$20 = R_0[1 + \alpha(100 - T_0)] \quad \text{...(iii)}$$

Assume that T_0 to be 0°C as per general convention and divide Eq. (ii) by Eq. (iii), we get

$$\frac{16}{20} = \frac{R_0(1 + \alpha \times 15)}{R_0(1 + \alpha \times 100)}$$

$$\Rightarrow \quad \frac{4}{5} = \frac{1 + 15\alpha}{1 + 100\alpha}$$

$$\Rightarrow \quad 4 + 400\alpha = 5 + 75\alpha$$

$$\Rightarrow \quad 400\alpha - 75\alpha = 5 - 4$$

$$\Rightarrow \quad 325\alpha = 1$$

$$\Rightarrow \quad \alpha = \frac{1}{325} = 0.003°\ \text{C}^{-1}$$

39. Given, current, $I = 5$ A

Area of cross-section of wire,

$$A = 0.04\,\text{m}^2$$

We know that $J = \frac{I}{A}$

$$\Rightarrow \quad I = JA$$

or $$\mathbf{I} = \mathbf{J} \cdot \mathbf{A} \text{ or } I = JA\cos\theta$$

Where, $J =$ Ocurrent density.

$$\Rightarrow \quad 5 = J\left(\frac{4}{100}\right) \times \cos(60°) \quad [\because \text{Given, } \theta = 60°]$$

$$J = 500 \times \frac{1}{2} \quad \left[\because \cos 60° = \frac{1}{2}\right]$$

$$\Rightarrow \quad J = 250\ \text{Am}^{-2}$$

The relation between electric field, current density and resistivity can be given as

$$\mathbf{E} = \rho \cdot \mathbf{J} = 44 \times 10^{-8} \times 250$$

$$[\because \text{Resistivity, } \rho = 44 \times 10^{-8}\ \Omega\text{-m}]$$

$$= 11 \times 10^{-5}\ \text{V/m}$$

40. Given, current, $I = 10$ A

Cross-sectional area,

$$A = 5\text{mm}^2 = 5 \times 10^{-6}\ \text{m}^2$$

Drift velocity, $v_d = 2 \times 10^{-3}\ \text{ms}^{-1}$

We know that, $I = neAv_d$

$$\Rightarrow \quad 10 = n \times 1.6 \times 10^{-19} \times 5 \times 10^{-6} \times 2 \times 10^{-3}$$

$$\Rightarrow \quad n = \frac{10}{1.6 \times 10^{-19} \times 5 \times 10^{-6} \times 2 \times 10^{-3}}$$

$$= 0.625 \times 10^{28} = 625 \times 10^{25}$$

41. Initially, the resistance of wire is

$$R_1 = \rho L / A$$

In second case,

Length, $l' = 2l$

Area, $A' = \frac{A}{2}$

$$\therefore \quad R_2 = \frac{\rho l'}{A'} = \frac{\rho(2l)}{(A/2)} = \frac{4\rho l}{A}$$

According to Ohm's law, $I = \frac{V}{R_2}$

$$\Rightarrow \quad I = \frac{V}{4\rho l / A} = \frac{1}{4}\frac{VA}{\rho l}$$

42. Given, $i = \alpha_0 t + \beta t^2$

Where, $\alpha_0 = 20\ \text{A/s}$, $\beta = 8\ \text{A/s}^2$

We know that $i = \frac{dq}{dt}$

$$\Rightarrow \quad \frac{dq}{dt} = i = \alpha_0 t + \beta t^2 = 20t + 8t^2$$

$$\Rightarrow \quad dq = (20t + 8t^2)dt$$

On integrating both sides, we get

$$\int_0^q dq = \int_0^{15} (20\,t + 8\,t^2)dt$$

$$q = \left[\frac{20t^2}{2} + \frac{8t^3}{3}\right]_0^{15} = 10 \times (15)^2 + \frac{8}{3} \times (15)^3$$

$$\therefore \quad q = 11250\ \text{C}$$

43. It is a balanced Wheatstone bridge, therefore resistance between E and D can be removed.

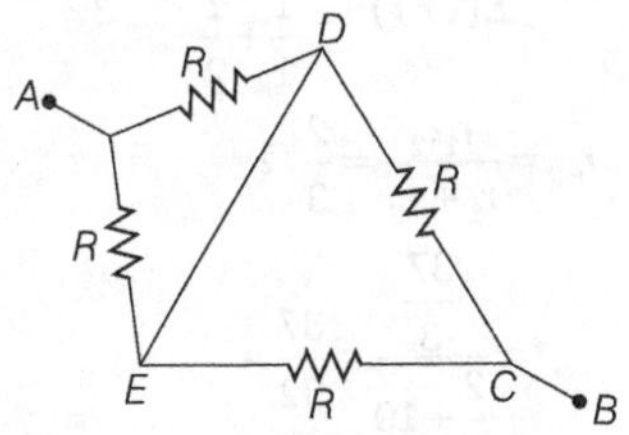

So, $$\frac{1}{R_{eq}}=\frac{1}{2R}+\frac{1}{2R}=\frac{1}{R} \Rightarrow R_{AB}=R_{eq}=R$$

44. As we know, $R=\frac{\rho l}{A}$

Original length, $l_0=1$ m

Change in length, $l_1=\frac{1\times 25}{100}=0.25$ m

New length $=1.25$ m

As volume of wire remains constant so

$$A_0 l_0 = A_1 l_1 \Rightarrow A_1=\frac{l_0 A_0}{l_1}$$

If length becomes 1.25 m area should decreases by 1.25.

$$R'=\frac{\rho(1.25)L}{A/1.25}=\frac{(1.25)^2\rho L}{A}$$

$\therefore$ $R'=1.5625\,R$ $\left[\therefore R=\frac{\rho L}{A}\right]$

Therefore, increase in resistance $=56.25$ %

45. When switches S_1 and S_2 are closed, then the given figure will be represented as follows

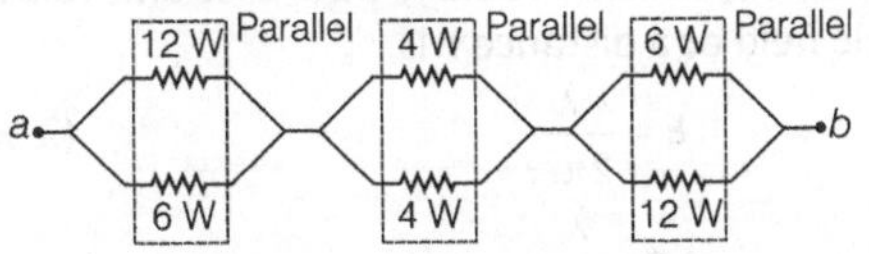

$\therefore$ The resistance across ab will be given as

$$R_{ab}=\frac{12\times 6}{12+6}+\frac{4\times 4}{4+4}+\frac{6\times 12}{6+12}$$

$$\Rightarrow \quad R_{ab}=\frac{72}{18}+2+\frac{72}{18}$$

$$\Rightarrow \quad R_{ab}=4+2+4=10\,\Omega$$

46. According to the figure given in question, all 3Ω resistances are in parallel combination. So, their equivalent resistance is

$$\frac{1}{R_{parallel}}=\frac{1}{3}+\frac{1}{3}+\frac{1}{3}$$

$$\frac{1}{R_{parallel}}=\frac{3}{3} \Rightarrow R_{parallel}=1\text{k}\Omega$$

Equivalent circuit

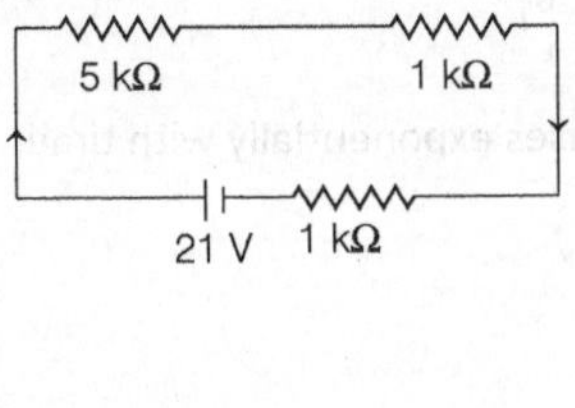

$5\text{ k}\Omega$ and $1\text{ k}\Omega$ are in series to the equivalent of all 3Ω resistances.

$$\therefore \quad R_{net}=5+1+R_{parallel} \quad \text{...(i)}$$

$$\Rightarrow \quad R_{net}=(5+1+1)\text{k}\Omega$$

$$=7\text{k}\Omega=7\times 10^3\,\Omega$$

$\therefore$ The value of electric current flowing through $5\text{k}\Omega$ resistor will be

$$I=\frac{V}{R_{net}}=\frac{21}{7\times 10^3}=3\times 10^{-3}\text{ A}=3\text{ mA}$$

47. Given, specific resistance for wire 1,

$$\rho_1=6\,\Omega\text{-cm}$$

Specific resistance for wire 2,

$$\rho_2=3\,\Omega\text{-cm}$$

Resistance, $R=\frac{\rho l}{A}$

For parallel connections,

$$R_{net}=\frac{R_1R_2}{R_1+R_2} \Rightarrow \frac{\rho l}{A}=\frac{\frac{\rho_1 l}{A}\times\frac{\rho_2 l}{A}}{\frac{\rho_1 l}{A}+\frac{\rho_2 l}{A}}$$

$$\Rightarrow \quad \rho=\frac{\rho_1\rho_2}{\rho_1+\rho_2}=\frac{6\times 3}{6+3}$$

$$\rho=2\,\Omega\text{-cm}$$

48. Given, radius of cylindrical wire, r

$$=0.5\text{ mm}=0.5\times 10^{-3}\text{ m}$$

Conductivity, $\sigma=5\times 10^7$ S/m

Electric field, $E=10$ mV/m $=10\times 10^{-3}$ V/m

We know that current density,

$$\therefore \quad J=\sigma E=5\times 10^7\times 10\times 10^{-3}$$

$$=5\times 10^5\text{ A/ m}^2$$

Also, $J=I/A \Rightarrow I=JA$

$$\Rightarrow \quad I=5\times 10^5\times\pi\times(0.5\times 10^{-3})^2$$

$$=5\times 10^5\times\pi\times 25\times 10^{-8}=125\,\pi\times 10^{-3}$$

$$\Rightarrow \quad x^3\,\pi\text{mA}=125\,\pi\text{ mA}$$

$$\Rightarrow \quad x=5$$

49. The circuit can be shown as below

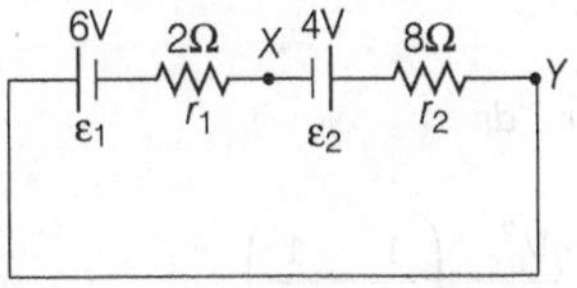

The current through the circuit,

$$I=\frac{\varepsilon_1-\varepsilon_2}{r_1+r_2}=\frac{6-4}{10}=\frac{1}{5}\text{ A}$$

$\therefore$ Potential difference across points X and Y is

$$V_{XY}=E_2+Ir_2=4+\frac{1}{5}\times 8=5.6=5.6\text{ V}$$

50. Given, charge passing through circuit,

$$q=20\text{ C}$$

Potential difference between two plates,

$$V=15\text{ V}$$

Let W be the amount of work done by battery.

$$\therefore \quad W=qV=20\times 15=300\text{ J}$$

JEE Advanced

1. All the elements are in parallel.

$$\therefore \quad \int \frac{1}{dr} = \int_{R_1}^{R_2} \frac{t\,dx}{\rho\pi x} \quad \Rightarrow \quad \frac{1}{r} = \frac{t}{\pi\rho} \ln\left(\frac{R_2}{R_1}\right)$$

$$\text{Resistance} = \frac{\pi\rho}{t\ln\left(\frac{R_2}{R_1}\right)}$$

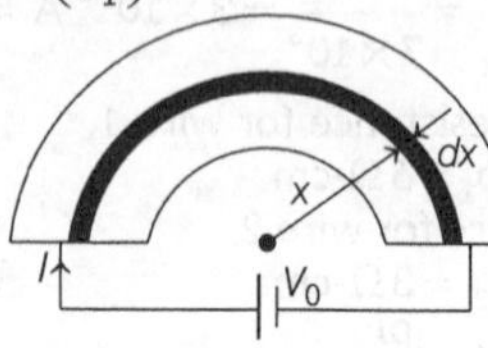

$$\therefore \quad I = \frac{V}{\text{Resistance}} = \frac{Vt}{\pi\rho}\ln\left(\frac{R_2}{R_1}\right)$$

$$eE = \frac{mv^2}{r}$$

$$I = neAV_d$$

$$\frac{V_0 t dr}{\rho\pi r} = ne(drt)V$$

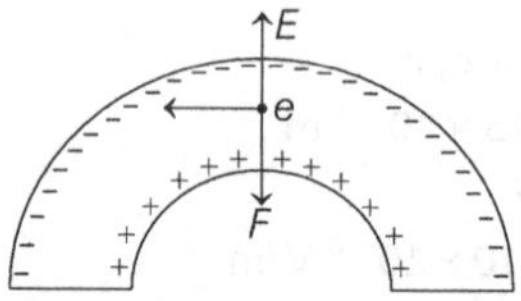

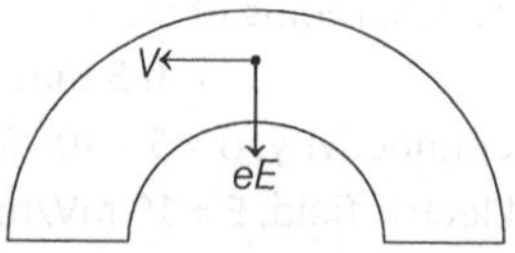

$$\Rightarrow \quad V = \sqrt{\frac{V_0}{\rho\pi n e r}}$$

$$\therefore \quad E = \frac{m}{er}\,\frac{V_0^2 t^2}{\rho^2\pi^2 n^2 e^2 r^2}$$

$$\Rightarrow \quad E = \frac{mV_0^2}{e^3 r^2 \rho^2 \pi^2 n^2}$$

$$dV = -Edr$$

$$dV = -\frac{K}{r^3}dr$$

$$V = K\int_{R_1}^{R_2} r^{-3}dr$$

$$\Delta V = \frac{mV_0^2}{e^3\rho^2\pi^2 n^2}\left(\frac{1}{r_1^2} - \frac{1}{r_2^2}\right)$$

$$\Delta V \propto V_0^2 \quad \Rightarrow \quad I \propto V_0$$

2.

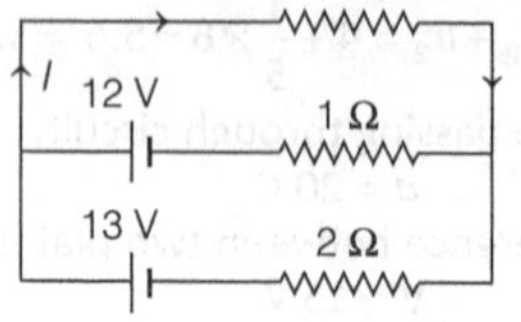

$$E_{eq} = \frac{\Sigma E/r}{\Sigma(1/r)} = \frac{\frac{12}{1}+\frac{13}{2}}{\frac{1}{1}+\frac{1}{2}} = \frac{37}{3}\text{V}$$

$$r_{eq} = \frac{r_1 r_2}{r_1 + r_2} = \frac{2}{3}\Omega$$

$$\Rightarrow \quad I = \frac{\frac{37}{3}}{\frac{2}{3}+10} = \frac{37}{32}\text{A}$$

$$\text{Voltage across load} = IR = \left(\frac{37}{32}\right)(10) = 11.56\text{ V}$$

3. Because of non-uniform evaporation at different section, area of cross-section would be different at different sections.

Region of highest evaporation rate would have rapidly reduced area and would become break up cross-section.

Resistance of the wire as whole increases with time.

Overall resistance increases hence power decreases.

$$\left(p = \frac{V^2}{R} \text{ or } p \propto \frac{1}{R} \text{ as } V \text{ is constant}\right).$$

At break up junction temperature would be highest, thus light of highest band frequency would be emitted at those cross-section.

4. Here charge per unit length λ is not constant and there is some conductivity of the material between line charge and shell. So free electrons will start flowing opposite to the electric field, which is radially outwards and value of this electric field at a distance r is,

$$E = \frac{\lambda}{2\pi\varepsilon r} \qquad (\lambda \neq \text{constant})$$

$$\neq \frac{\lambda}{2\pi\varepsilon_0 r}$$

Since free electrons are flowing radially inwards, so positive line charge will gradually decrease. Now,

$$I = -\frac{dq}{dt} = j(A) = (\sigma E)A \qquad [\text{as } j = \sigma E]$$

$$\therefore \quad -\frac{d}{dt}(\lambda l) = (\sigma)(2\pi r l)\frac{\lambda}{2\pi\varepsilon r} \qquad [q = \lambda l]$$

$$\therefore \quad \int_{\lambda_i}^{\lambda} \frac{d\lambda}{\lambda} = -\frac{\sigma}{\varepsilon}\int_0^t dt$$

Solving this equation, we get

$$\lambda = \lambda_i e^{-\frac{\sigma}{\varepsilon}t}$$

$$\text{Now,} \quad j = \sigma E = \sigma\left(\frac{\lambda}{2\pi\varepsilon r}\right) = \frac{\sigma\lambda_i}{2\pi\varepsilon r}e^{-\frac{\sigma}{\varepsilon}t}$$

$$j = j_i e^{-\frac{\sigma}{\varepsilon}t}$$

Thus j decreases exponentially with time.

5.

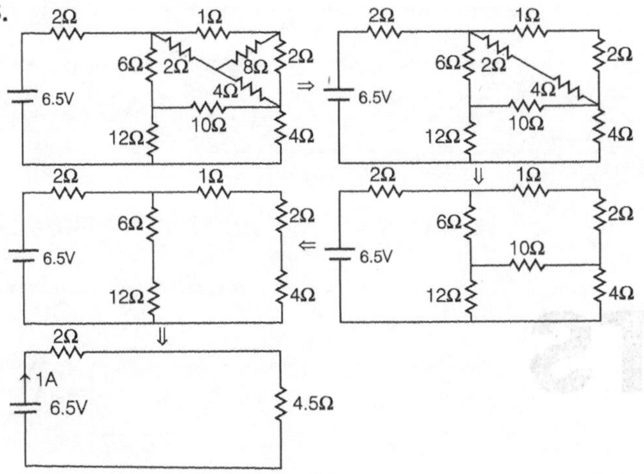

6. $\frac{1}{R} = \frac{1}{R_{Al}} + \frac{1}{R_{Fe}} = \left(\frac{A_{Al}}{\rho_{Al}} + \frac{A_{Fe}}{\rho_{Fe}}\right)\frac{1}{l}$

$$= \left[\frac{(7^2 - 2^2)}{2.7} + \frac{2^2}{1.0}\right]\frac{10^{-6}}{10^{-8}} \times \frac{1}{50 \times 10^{-3}}$$

Solving we get,

$$R = \frac{1875}{64} \times 10^{-6}\ \Omega$$

$$= \frac{1875}{64}\ \mu\Omega$$

7. Due to symmetry on upper side and lower side, points P and Q are at same potentials. Similarly, points S and T are at same potentials. Therefore, the simple circuit can be drawn as shown below

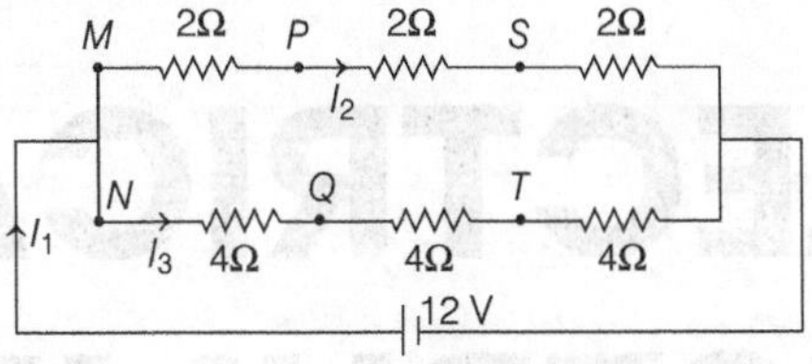

$$I_2 = \frac{12}{2+2+2} = 2\ \text{A}$$

$$I_3 = \frac{12}{4+4+4} = 1\ \text{A}$$

$\therefore$ $$I_1 = I_2 + I_3 = 3\ \text{A}$$

$$I_{PQ} = 0$$

because $$V_P = V_Q$$

$$V_{MS} = 2 \times 4 = 8\ \text{V}$$

$$V_{NQ} = 1 \times 4 = 4\ \text{V}$$

or $$V_S < V_Q$$

8. V_{AB} = Equivalent emf of two batteries in parallel (as current taken from the battery is zero).

$$= \frac{E_1/r_1 + E_2/r_2}{1/r_1 + 1/r_2} = \frac{(6/1)+(3/2)}{(1/1)+(1/2)} = 5\ \text{V}$$

$\therefore$ Answer is 5.

CHAPTER~07

ELECTRICAL INSTRUMENTS

LEVEL 01 Starter Level

7.1 *Galvanometer, Ammeter and Voltmeter*

1 What is the value of shunt which passes 10% of the main current through a galvanometer of 99 Ω?

2 The deflection of a moving coil galvanometer falls from 60 divisions to 12 divisions for the same value of current in the circuit, when a shunt of 12 Ω is connected. Find the resistance of the galvanometer.

3 A galvanometer has a resistance of 30 Ω and a full scale deflection current of 20 mA. What is the resistance needed and how is it to be connected to convert the galvanometer
(a) into an ammeter of 10 A range and
(b) into a voltmeter of 100 V range?

4 A moving coil galvanometer of resistance 20 Ω gives a full scale deflection when a current of 1 mA is passed through it. It is to be converted into an ammeter reading 20A on full scale, but the shunt of 0.005 Ω only is available. What resistance should be connected in series with the galvanometer coil?

5 A galvanometer with a scale divided into 100 equal divisions, has a current sensitivity of 10 division per mA and voltage sensitivity of 2 division per mV. What adoptions are required to use it (a) to read 5A full scale and (b) 1 division per volt ?

6 A galvanometer having 50 divisions provided with a variable shunt *S* is used to measure the current when connected in series with a resistance of 90 Ω and a battery of internal resistance 10 Ω. It is observed that when the shunt resistances are 10Ω, 50Ω respectively, the deflections are 9 and 30 divisions respectively. What is the resistance of the galvanometer?
Further if the full scale deflection of the galvanometer movement is 300 mA, find the emf of the cell.

7.2 *Measurement using Ammeter and Voltmeter*

1 (a) What is the reading of the ammeter in the circuits (a) and (b)?

(b) What is the percentage error in measuring the current through the ammeter in circuit (b)?

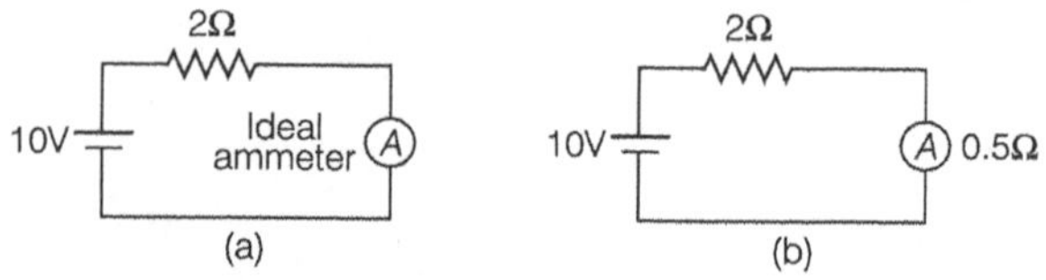

2 Find the reading of ammeter. Is this the current through 6 Ω?

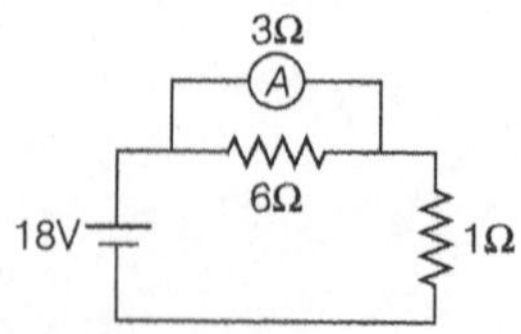

3 A voltmeter of resistance 400 Ω is used to measure the potential difference across the 100 Ω resistor in the circuit shown in the figure. (a) What will be the reading of the voltmeter? (b) What was the potential difference across 100 Ω before the voltmeter was connected ?

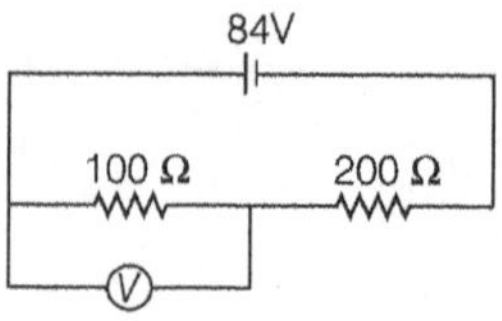

4 A cell of emf 3.4 V and internal resistance 3Ω connected to an ammeter having resistance 2Ω and to an external resistance of 100Ω. When a voltmeter is connected across the 100Ω resistance, the ammeter reading is 0.04 A. Find the voltage read by the voltmeter and its resistance. Had the voltmeter been an ideal one, what would have been its reading?

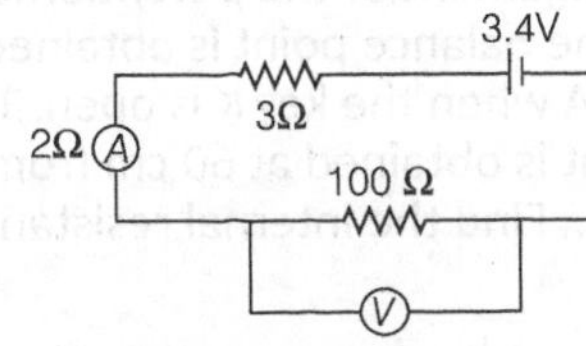

5 Find the reading of the ideal voltmeter as shown in figure.

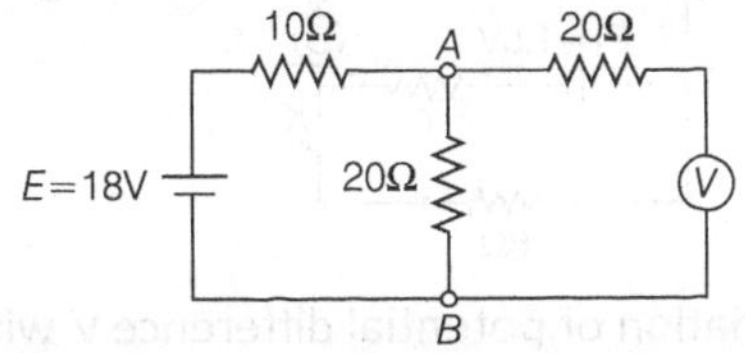

6 The emf E and the internal resistance r of the battery shown in figure are 50 V and 5.0 Ω, respectively. The external resistance R is 50 Ω. The resistances of the ammeter and voltmeter are 5.0Ω and 200Ω, respectively.

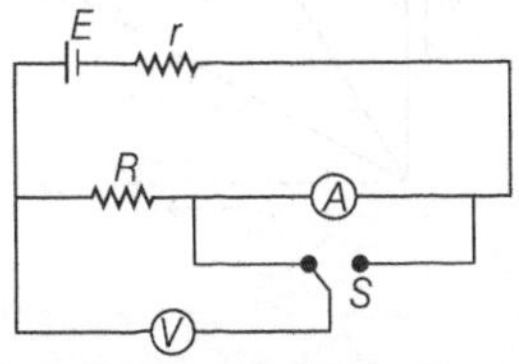

(a) Find the readings of the two meters.

(b) The switch is thrown to the other side. What will be the readings of the two meters now?

7.3 Meter Bridge

1 A meter bridge set-up with null deflection for the galvanometer is as shown in the figure. Find the value of the unknown resistor R.

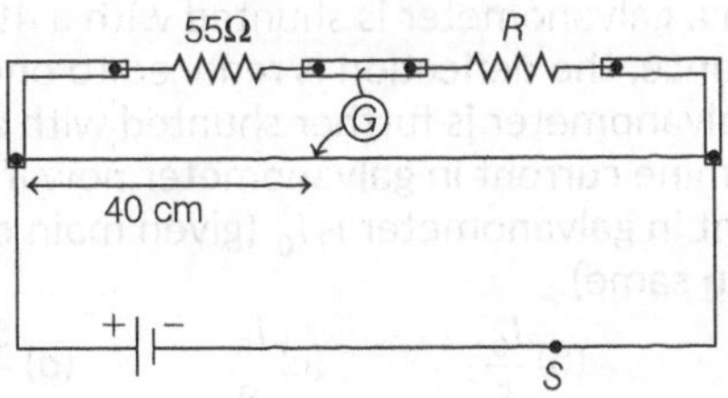

2 In the figure shown for which values of R_1 and R_2, the balance point for jockey is at 40 cm from A. When R_2 is shunted by a resistance of 10 Ω, balance shifts to 50 cm. Find R_1 and R_2. ($AB = 1$ m).

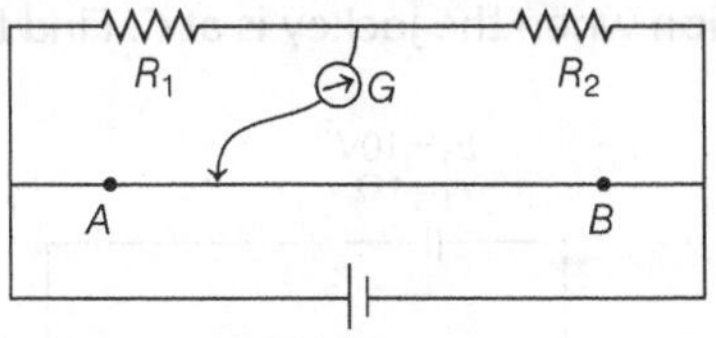

3 A meter bridge is set-up as shown, to determine an unknown resistance X using a standard 10Ω resistor. The galvanometer shows null point, when tapping key is at 52 cm mark. The end-corrections are 1 cm and 2 cm respectively for the ends A and B. Find value of X.

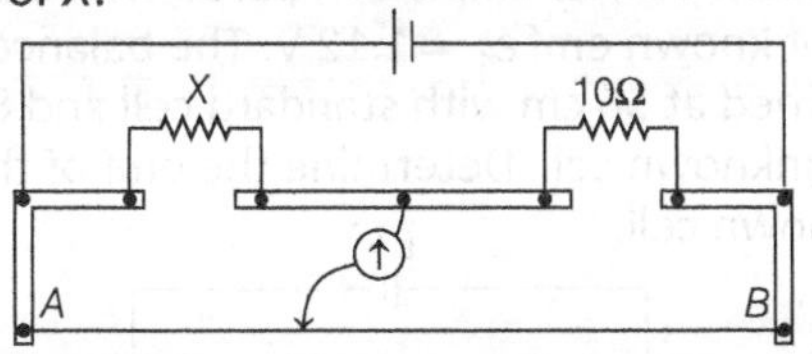

4 An unknown resistance is to be determined using resistances R_1, R_2 and R_3. If their corresponding null points are A, B and C, which of them will give most accurate reading?

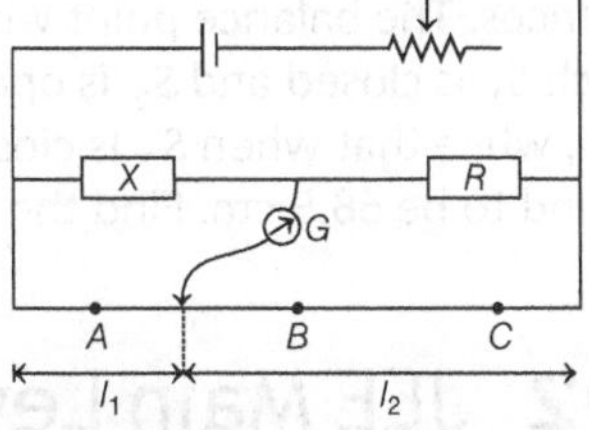

7.4 Potentiometer

1 In the primary circuit of a potentiometer as shown in figure, a potentiometer wire of length $L = 10$ m and resistance 10 Ω is joined in series with a resistance 20 Ω across a cell of emf $\varepsilon = 15$V. Find

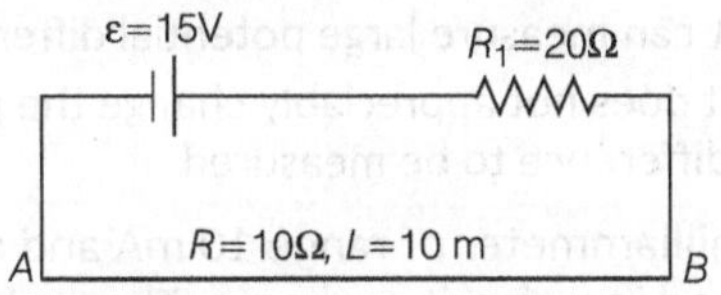

(a) current in primary circuit.

(b) potential drop across potentiometer wire AB.

(c) potential gradient.

(d) maximum potential difference which can be measured with the potentiometer.

2 In the figure, the potentiometer wire of length $l =$ 450 cm and resistance 9 Ω is joined to a cell of emf $E_1 = 10$ V and internal resistance $r_1 = 1\,\Omega$. Another cell of emf $E_2 = 5$ V and internal resistance $r_2 = 2\,\Omega$ is connected as shown. The galvanometer G shows no deflection when the jockey is at C. Find the length AC.

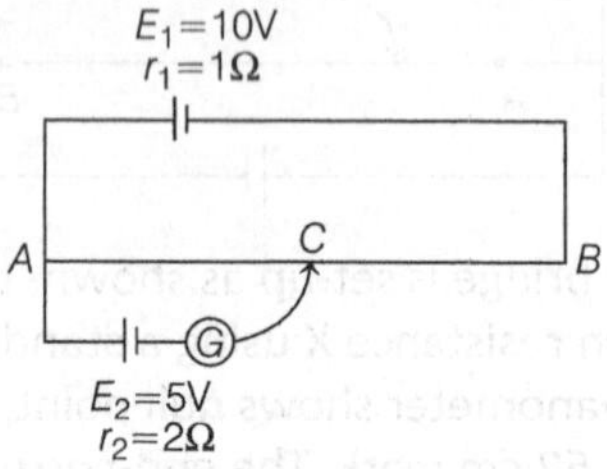

3 In an experiment to determine the emf of an unknown cell, its emf is compared with a standard cell of known emf $\varepsilon_1 = 1.12$ V. The balance point is obtained at 56 cm with standard cell and 80 cm with the unknown cell. Determine the emf of the unknown cell.

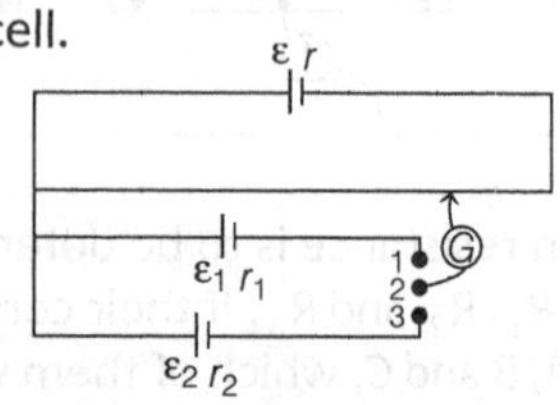

4 Figure shows a potentiometer circuit for comparing two resistances. The balance point with $R = 10\,\Omega$, when switch S_1 is closed and S_2 is open is found to be 58.3 cm, while that when S_2 is closed and S_1 is open is found to be 68.5 cm. Find the value of X.

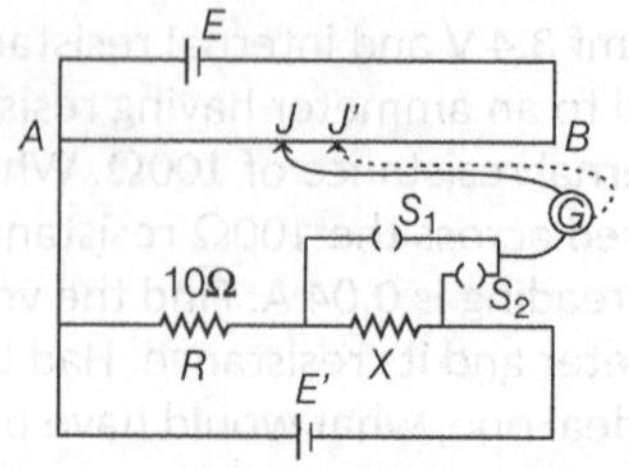

5 For the arrangement of the potentiometer shown in the figure, the balance point is obtained at a distance 75 cm from A when the key K is open. The second balance point is obtained at 60 cm from A when the key is closed. Find the internal resistance of the battery E_1.

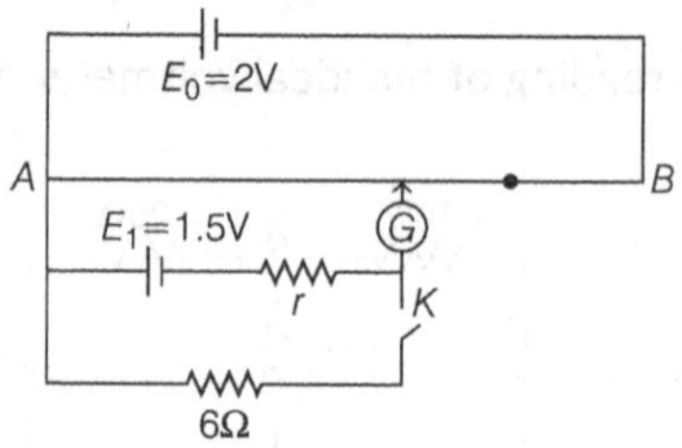

6 The variation of potential difference V with length l in case of two potentiometers X and Y is as shown in the given figure. Which one of these two will you prefer for comparing emf's of two cells and why?

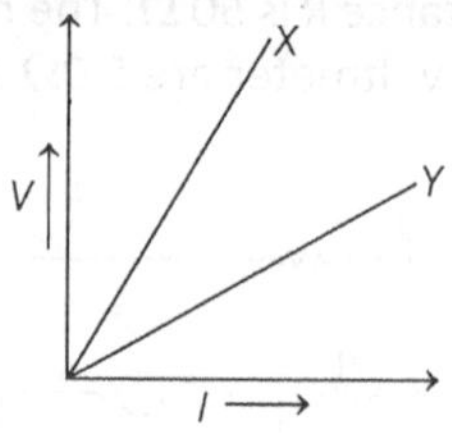

LEVEL 02 JEE Main Level

Single Choice Correct Questions

1 The net resistance of a voltmeter should be large to ensure that

(a) it does not get overheated
(b) it does not draw excessive current
(c) it can measure large potential differences
(d) it does not appreciably change the potential difference to be measured

2 A milliammeter of range 10 mA and resistance 9 Ω is joined in a circuit as shown. The metre gives full-scale deflection for current I when A and B are used as its terminals, i.e. current enters at A and leaves at B (C is left isolated). The value of I is

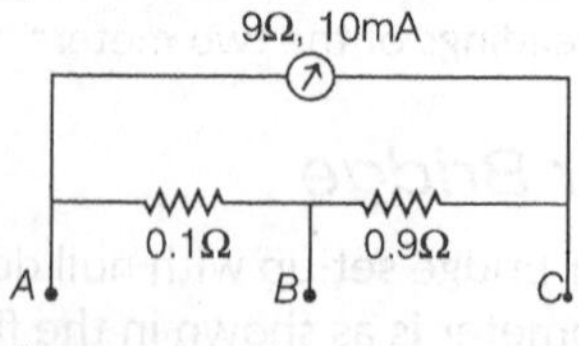

(a) 100 mA (b) 900 mA (c) 1 A (d) 1.1 A

3 When a galvanometer is shunted with a 4Ω resistance, the deflection is reduced to one-fifth. If the galvanometer is further shunted with a 2Ω wire, determine current in galvanometer now if initially current in galvanometer is I_0 (given main current remain same).

(a) $\frac{I_0}{13}$ (b) $\frac{I_0}{5}$ (c) $\frac{I_0}{8}$ (d) $\frac{5I_0}{13}$

4 A galvanometer has a resistance of 20 Ω and reads full-scale when 0.2 V is applied across it. To convert it into a 10 A ammeter, the galvanometer coil should have a

(a) 0.01 Ω resistor connected across it
(b) 0.02 Ω resistor connected across it
(c) 200 Ω resistor connected in series with it
(d) 2000 Ω resistor connected in series with it

5 A galvanometer coil has a resistance 90 Ω and full scale deflection current 10 mA. A 910 Ω resistance is connected in series with the galvanometer to make a voltmeter. If the least count of the voltmeter is 0.1 V, the number of divisions on its scale is

(a) 90 (b) 91
(c) 100 (d) None of these

6 An ammeter has resistance R_0 and range I. What resistance should be connected in parallel with it to increase its range to nI?

(a) $\frac{R_0}{n}$ (b) $R_0(n+1)$ (c) $\frac{R_0}{n+1}$ (d) $\frac{R_0}{n-1}$

7 The galvanometer deflection, when key K_1 is closed but K_2 is open, equals θ_0 (see figure). On closing K_2 also and adjusting R_2 to 5 Ω, the deflection in galvanometer becomes $\frac{\theta_0}{5}$. The resistance of the galvanometer is given by (Neglect the internal resistance of battery)

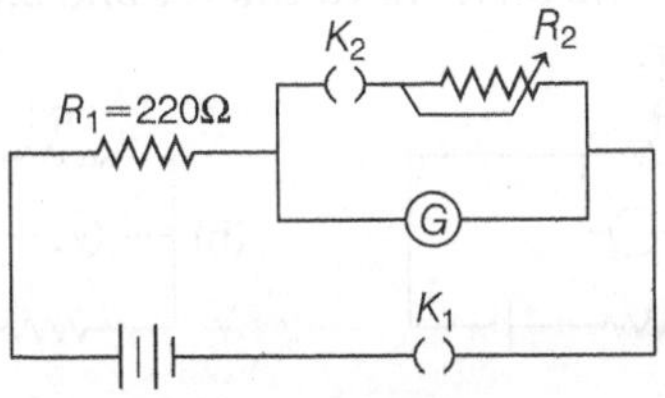

(a) 12 Ω (b) 25 Ω (c) 5 Ω (d) 22Ω

8 Two scales on a voltmeter measure voltage up to 20.0 V and 30.0 V. The resistance connected in series with the galvanometer is 1680 Ω for the 20.0 V scale and 2930 Ω for the 30.0V scale. The resistance of the galvanometer and the full scale current respectively are

(a) 320 Ω, 8 mA (b) 70 Ω, 10 mA
(c) 820 Ω, 10 mA (d) 820 Ω, 8 mA

9 A moving coil galvanometer has 150 equal divisions. Its current sensitivity is 10 divisions per milliampere and voltage sensitivity is 2 divisions per milli volt. In order that each division reads 1 V, the resistance in ohm needed to be connected in series, with the coil will be

(a) 99995 (b) 9995 (c) 1000 (d) 10000

10 The ammeter has range 1 A without shunt. The range can be varied by using different shunt resistances. The graph between shunt resistance and range will have the nature

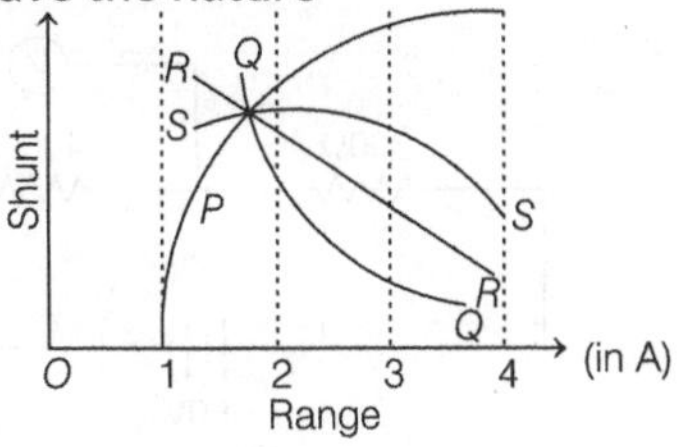

(a) P (b) Q (c) R (d) S

11 The reading of ammeter A_1 in figure is 2.4 A. Ammeter A_1 is ideal while the resistances of the ammeters A_2 and A_3 are 1 Ω and 3 Ω , respectively. The reading of ammeter A_3 will be

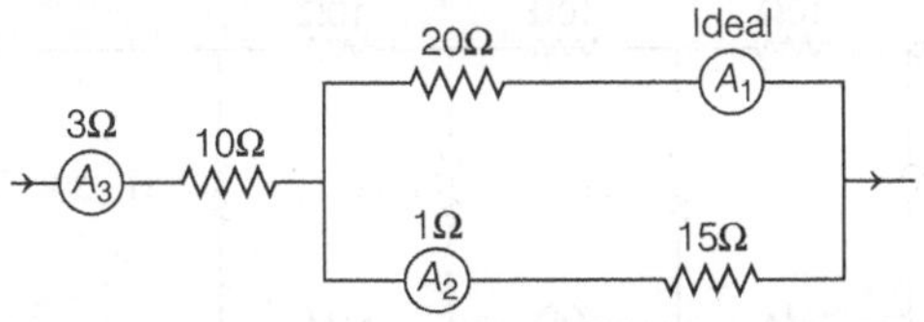

(a) 3.6 A (b) 4.8 A
(c) 5 A (d) 5.4 A

12 Voltmeter shown reads 18 V. The resistance of voltmeter, is

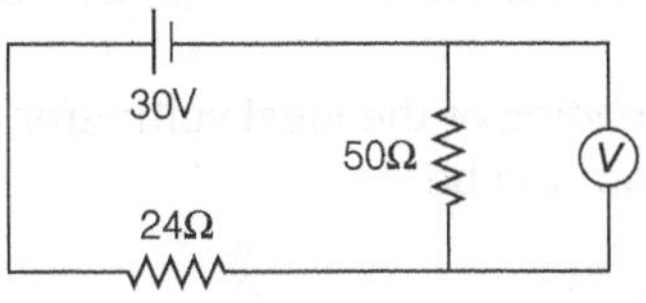

(a) 75 Ω (b) 120 Ω (c) $\frac{800}{7}$ Ω (d) $\frac{900}{7}$ Ω

13 By error, a student places moving coil voltmeter V (nearly ideal) in series with the resistance in a circuit in order to read the current, as shown in figure. The voltmeter reading will

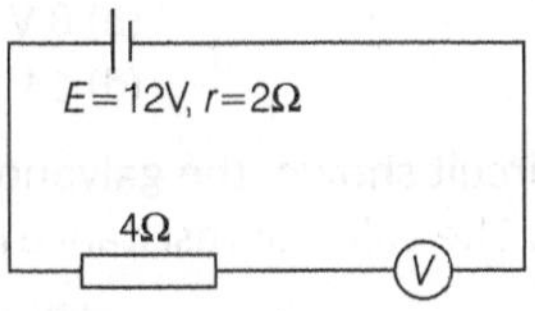

(a) 0 (b) 4V (c) 6V (d) 12V

14 Two resistances of 400 Ω and 800 Ω are connected in series with 6 V battery of negligible internal resistance. A voltmeter of resistance 10000 Ω is used to measure the potential difference across 400 Ω. The error in the measurement of potential difference in volts approximately is

(a) 0.01 (b) 0.02 (c) 0.03 (d) 0.05

15 In the circuit, a voltmeter reads 30 V when it is connected across 400 Ω resistance. What the same voltmeter will read when it is connected across the 300 Ω resistance?

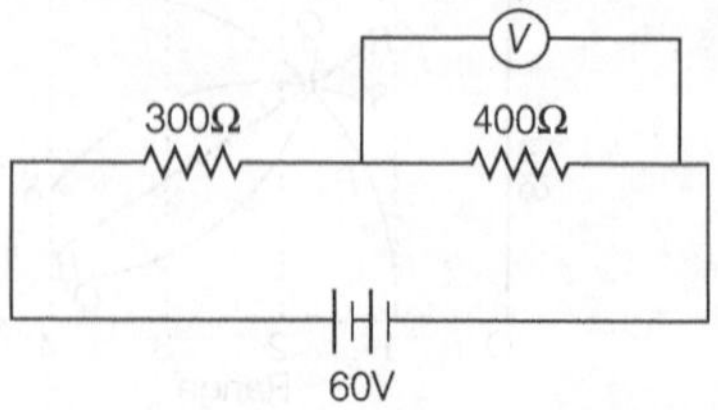

(a) 20 V (b) 22.5 V (c) 25 V (d) 32.5 V

16 An ammeter of resistance 10 Ω and a voltmeter of resistance 20 Ω are connected in a circuit as shown in figure. Reading of ammeter and voltmeter are respectively

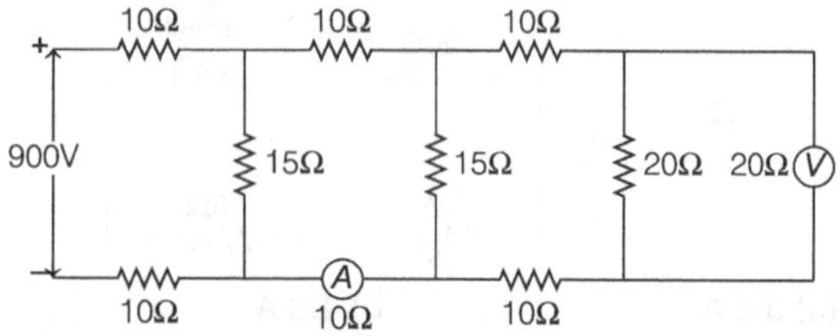

(a) $\frac{10}{3}$ A and $\frac{100}{3}$ V (b) 10 A and 100 V

(c) $\frac{10}{3}$ A and 100 V (d) 10 A and $\frac{100}{3}$ V

17 The reading of the ideal voltmeter in the adjoining diagram will be

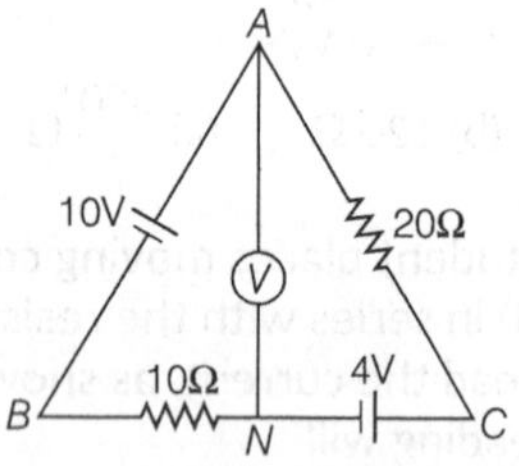

(a) 4 V (b) 8 V

(c) 12 V (d) 14 V

18 In the circuit shown, the galvanometer shows zero current. The value of resistance *R* is

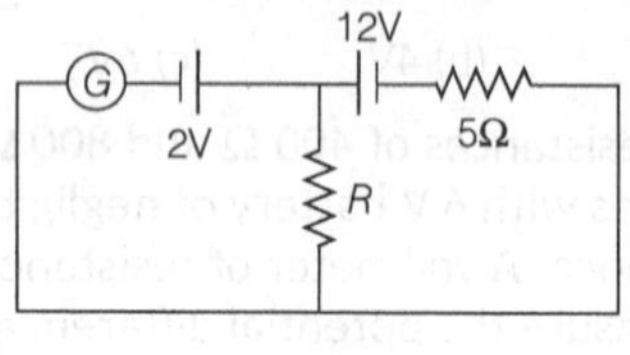

(a) 1 Ω (b) 2 Ω

(c) 4 Ω (d) 9 Ω

19 In the circuit shown, cells are of equal emf *E* but of different internal resistances $r_1 = 6\ \Omega$ and $r_2 = 4\ \Omega$. Reading of the ideal voltmeter connected across cell 1 is zero. Value of the external resistance *R* in ohm is equal to

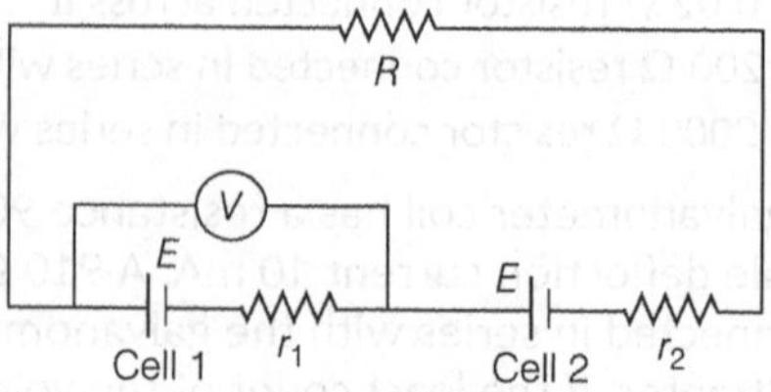

(a) 2 (b) 2.4

(c) 10 (d) 24

20 In the circuit shown the resistance of voltmeter is 10000 Ω and that of ammeter is 20 Ω. The ammeter reading is 0.10 A and voltmeter reading is 12 V, then *R* is equal to

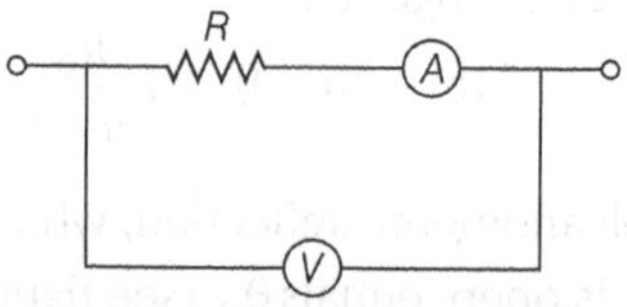

(a) 122 Ω (b) 140 Ω

(c) 116 Ω (d) 100 Ω

21 Which of the following wiring diagrams could be used to experimentally determine *R* using Ohm's law? Assume an ideal voltmeter and an ideal ammeter.

(a) 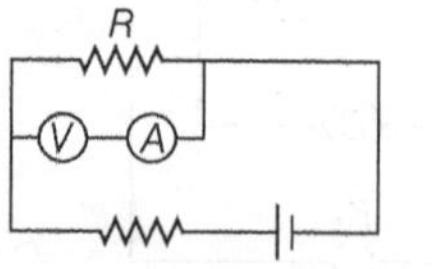

(b) 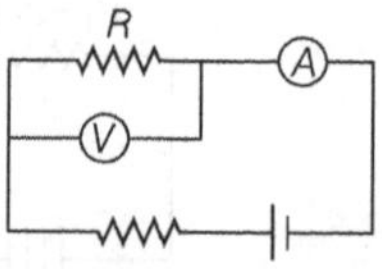

(c) 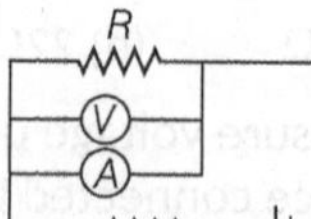

(d) 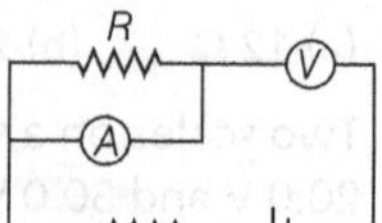

22 In the circuit shown, the reading of the ammeter is doubled after the switch is closed. Each resistor has a resistance = 1 Ω and the ideal cell has an emf = 10 V, then the ammeter has a coil resistance equal to

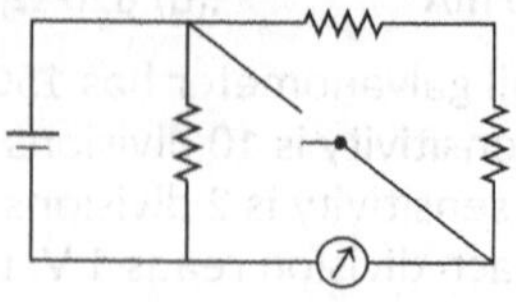

(a) 2 Ω (b) 1 Ω

(c) 2.5 Ω (d) None of these

23 In the circuit shown in the figure, reading of voltmeter is V_1 when only S_1 is closed, reading of voltmeter is V_2 when only S_2 is closed and reading of voltmeter is V_3 when both S_1 and S_2 are closed. Then,

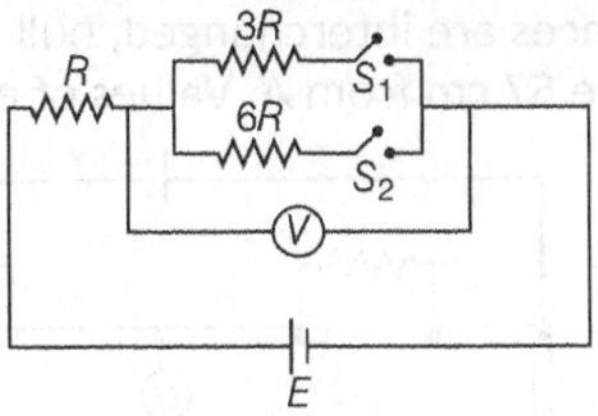

(a) $V_3 > V_2 > V_1$ (b) $V_2 > V_1 > V_3$
(c) $V_3 > V_1 > V_2$ (d) $V_1 > V_2 > V_3$

24 When an ammeter of negligible internal resistance is inserted in series with circuit, it reads 1 A. When a voltmeter of very large resistance is connected across X, it reads 1V. When the points A and B are short-circuited by a conducting wire, then the voltmeter measures 10 V across the battery. The internal resistance of the battery is

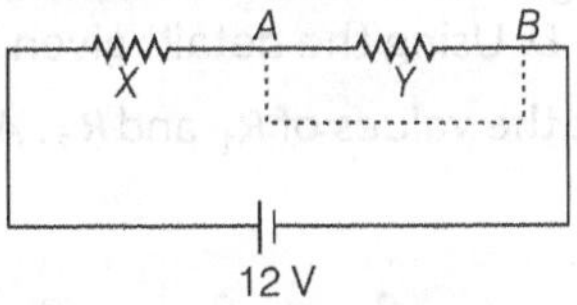

(a) 0 (b) 0.1 Ω (c) 0.2 Ω (d) 0.52 Ω

25 An ammeter and a voltmeter are joined in series to a cell and their readings are A and V ,respectively. If a resistance is now joined in parallel with the voltmeter

(a) both A and V will increase
(b) both A and V will decrease
(c) A will decrease, V will increase
(d) A will increase, V will decrease

26 The diagram besides shows a circuit used in an experiment to determine the emf and internal resistance of the cell C. A graph was plotted of the potential difference V between the terminals of the cell against the current I, which was varied by adjusting the rheostat. The graph is shown on the right; x and y are the intercepts of the graph with the axes as shown. What is the internal resistance of the cell?

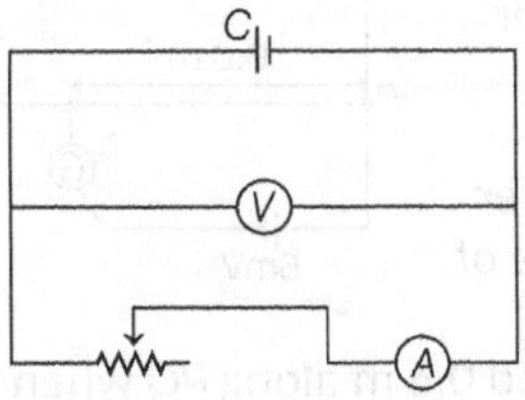

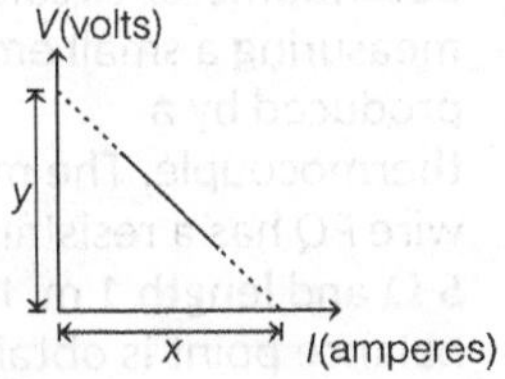

(a) x (b) y (c) $\frac{x}{y}$ (d) $\frac{y}{x}$

27 A potential difference of 220 V is maintained across a 12000 Ω rheostat, as shown in the figure. The voltmeter has a resistance of 6000 Ω and point C is at one-fourth of the distance from A to B. Therefore, the reading of the voltmeter will be

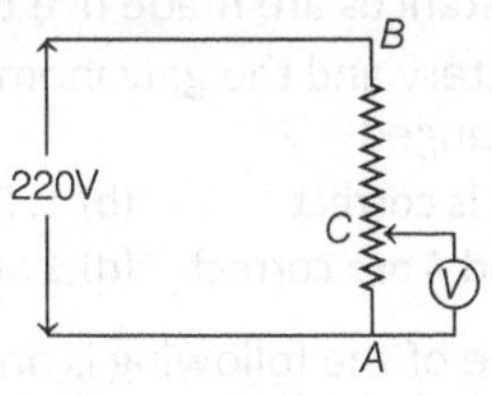

(a) 32 V (b) 36 V (c) 40 V (d) 42 V

28 A cell of internal resistance 1 Ω is connected across a resistor. A voltmeter having variable resistance G is used to measure potential difference across resistor. The plot of voltmeter reading V against G is shown. What is value of external resistor R?

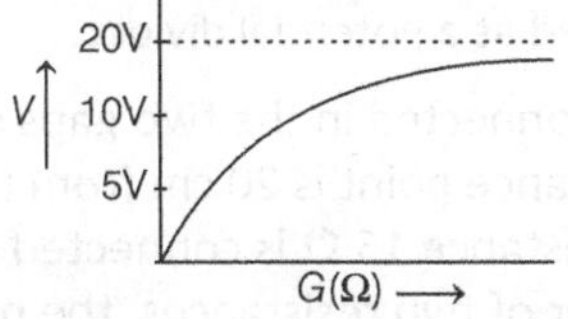

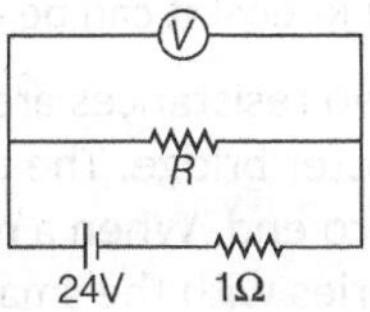

(a) 5 Ω (b) 4 Ω (c) 3 Ω (d) 1 Ω

29 An ammeter and a voltmeter are initially connected in series to a battery of zero internal resistance. When switch S_1 is closed, the reading of the voltmeter becomes half of the initial, whereas the reading of the ammeter becomes double.

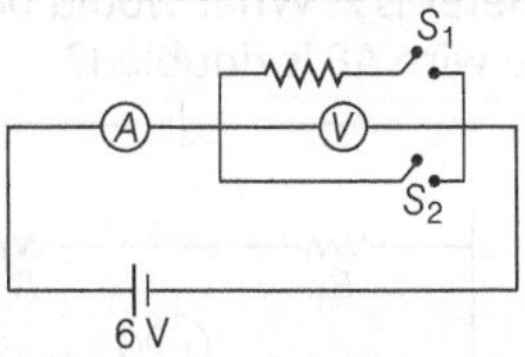

If now switch S_2 is also closed, then reading of ammeter becomes

(a) 3/2 times the initial value
(b) 3/2 times the value after closing S_1
(c) 3/4 times the value after closing S_1
(d) 3/4 times the initial value

30 A Wheatstone's bridge is balanced with a resistance of 625 Ω in the third arm, where P, Q and S are in the 1st, 2nd and 4th arm, respectively. If P and Q are interchanged, the resistance in the third arm has to be increased by 51 Ω to secure balance. The unknown resistance in the fourth arm is

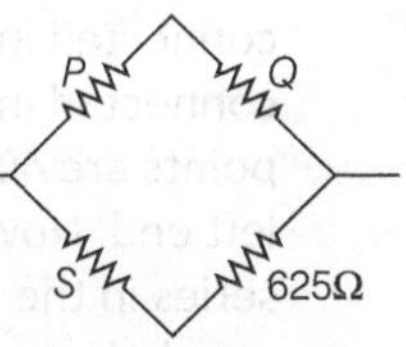

(a) 625 Ω (b) 650 Ω (c) 676 Ω (d) 600 Ω

31 In a balanced Wheatstone bridge, current in the galvanometer is zero. It remains zero, when
1. battery emf is increased
2. all resistances are increased by 10 Ω
3. all resistances are made five times
4. the battery and the galvanometer are interchanged

(a) Only 1 is correct (b) 1, 2 and 3 are correct
(c) 1, 3 and 4 are correct (d) 1 and 3 are correct

32 Which one of the following is an incorrect statement?
(a) The Wheatstone bridge is most sensitive, when all the four resistances are of the same order.
(b) Sensitivity of a potentiometer is directly proportional to its potential gradient.
(c) Potentiometer is a better device than voltmeter for measuring potential difference.
(d) Rheostat can be used as a potential divider.

33 Two resistances are connected in the two gaps of a meter bridge. The balance point is 20 cm from the zero end. When a resistance 15 Ω is connected in series with the smaller of two resistances, the null point shifts to 40 cm. The smaller of the two resistances has the value
(a) 3 Ω (b) 6 Ω (c) 9 Ω (d) 12 Ω

34 In the shown arrangement of the experiment of the meter bridge, if *AC* corresponding to null deflection of galvanometer is *x*. What would be its value, if the radius of the wire *AB* is doubled?

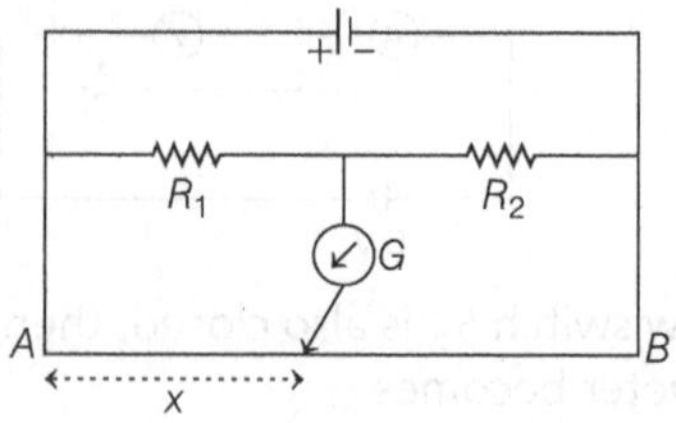

(a) *x* (b) $\frac{x}{4}$
(c) 4*x* (d) 2*x*

35 In a meter bridge experiment, resistance *X* is connected in the right gap. When R_1 and R_2 are connected in the left gap separately, the balance points are 40 cm and 50 cm respectively, from the left end. Now, if both R_1 and R_2 are connected in series in the left gap with *X* in the right gap, then the new balance point from the left end will be
(a) 50 cm
(b) 62.5 cm
(c) 75 cm
(d) Data insufficient for calculation

36 A meter bridge is set up as shown to determine end corrections at *A* and *B*. When a resistance of 15 Ω is used in left gap and of 20 Ω in right gap, then null point comes at a distance 42 cm from *A*. When these resistances are interchanged, null point comes at a distance 57 cm from *A*. Values of end corrections are

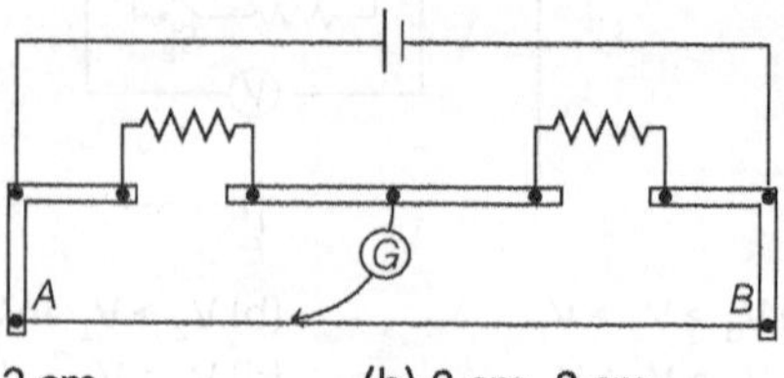

(a) 1 cm, 2 cm (b) 2 cm, 3 cm
(c) 3 cm, 4 cm (d) 3 cm, 2 cm

37 The diagram shows a modified meter bridge, which is used for measuring two unknown resistances at the same time. When the first galvanometer is used for obtaining the balance point, it is found at point *C*. Now the first galvanometer is removed and the second galvanometer is used, which gives balance point at *D*. Using the details given in the diagram, find out the values of R_1 and R_2. $AB = L$; $AC = \frac{L}{4}$ and $AD = \frac{2L}{3}$.

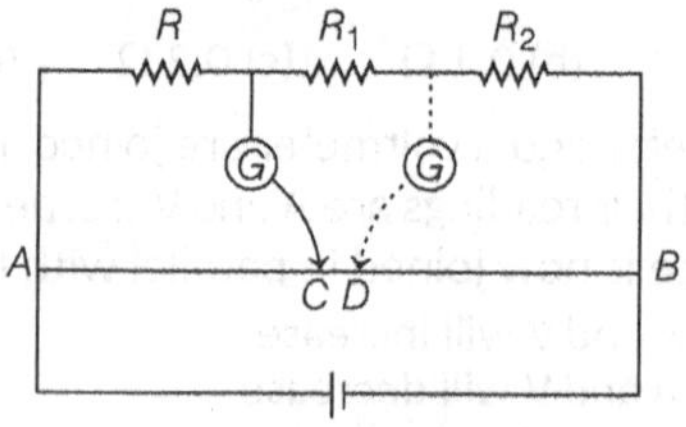

(a) $\frac{5R}{3}, \frac{4R}{3}$ (b) $\frac{3R}{5}, \frac{3R}{4}$ (c) $\frac{4R}{3}, \frac{5R}{3}$ (d) $\frac{3R}{4}, \frac{3R}{5}$

38 The resistance of a potentiometer wire 8 m long is 8 Ω. A high resistance box and a 2 V accumulator are connected in series with it. What should be the value of the resistance in the box, if it is desired to have a potential gradient of 1 μV/mm?
(a) 992 Ω (b) 1992 Ω
(c) 19992 Ω (d) None of these

39 Figure shows a simple potentiometer circuit for measuring a small emf produced by a thermocouple. The meter wire *PQ* has a resistance of 5 Ω and length 1 m. If a balance point is obtained 0.6 m along *PQ* when measuring an emf of 6 mV, what is the value of resistance *R*?

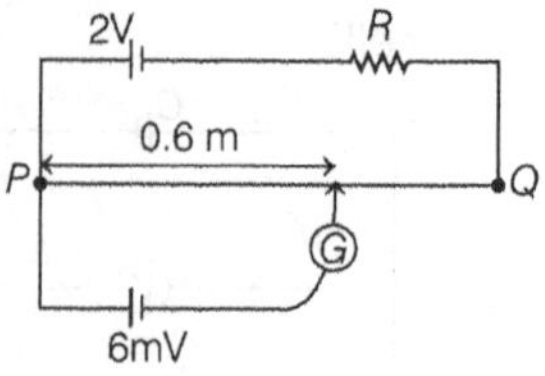

(a) 95 Ω (b) 995Ω (c) 195 Ω (d) 1995 Ω

40 In a potentiometer experiment, n identical cells each of emf E are used in series and the balancing length is found to be 58 cm of the wire. If the polarities of 2 cells out of n cells is reversed, then the balancing length becomes 29 cm. Value of n is

(a) 8 (b) 12 (c) 16 (d) 24

41 In the given potentiometer circuit, length of the wire AB is 3 m and resistance is $R = 4.5\ \Omega$. The length AC for no deflection in galvanometer is

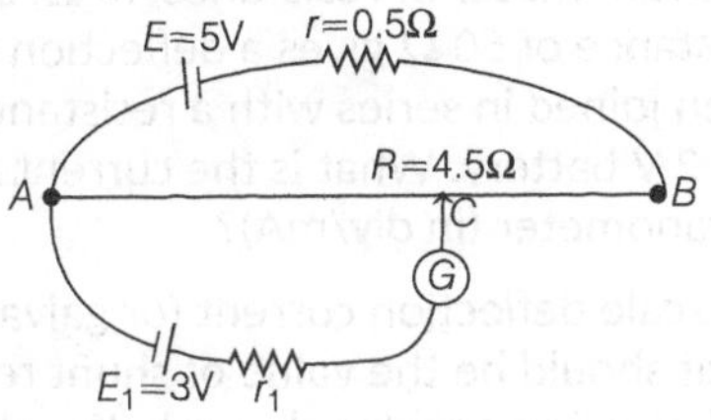

(a) 2 m
(b) 1.8 m
(c) dependent on r_1
(d) None of the above

42 Suppose a voltmeter of resistance 660 Ω reads the voltage of a very old cell to be 1.32 V while a potentiometer reads its voltage to be 1.44 V. The internal resistance of the cell is

(a) 30 Ω (b) 60 Ω
(c) 6 Ω (d) 0.6 Ω

43 The length of a potentiometer wire is l. A cell of emf E is balanced at a length $l/3$ from the positive end of the wire. If the length of the wire is increased by $l/2$, at what distance will the same cell give a balance point?

(a) $\frac{2l}{3}$ (b) $\frac{l}{2}$ (c) $\frac{l}{6}$ (d) $\frac{4l}{3}$

44 A standard cell of emf $E_1 = 6$ V and negligible internal resistance is connected to the terminals of a potentiometer of resistance 20 Ω. A storage battery of emf E_2 and negligible internal resistance is connected to a galvanometer as shown. On moving the jockey along AB, when AN is 16 Ω, the galvanometer shows null deflection. The emf of the storage battery E is

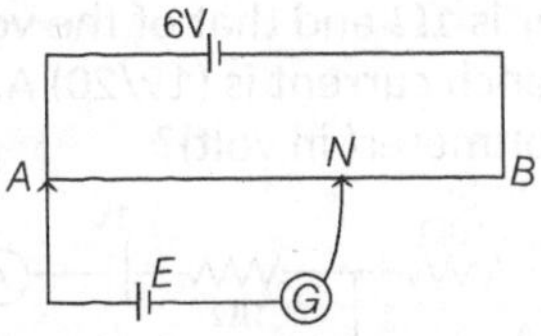

(a) 4.2 V (b) 4.5 V
(c) 4.8 V (d) 5.1 V

45 The sensitivity of a potentiometer can be increased by
(a) decreasing the length of potentiometer wire
(b) increasing the length of potentiometer wire
(c) increasing the emf of the cell in primary circuit
(d) decreasing the external resistance connected in primary circuit

46 A potentiometer wire AB is 100 cm long and has a total resistance of 10Ω. If the galvanometer shows zero deflection at the position C, then find the value of unknown resistance R.

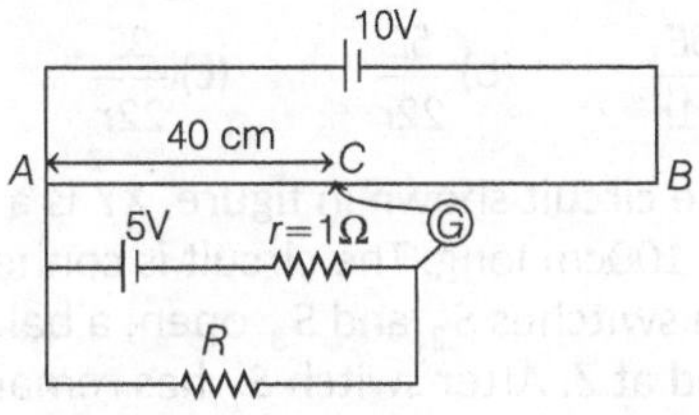

(a) 1 Ω (b) 2 Ω (c) 4 Ω (d) 8 Ω

47 Circuit for the measurement of resistance by potentiometer is shown. The galvanometer is first connected at point A and zero deflection is observed at length $PJ = 10$ cm. In second case, it is connected at point C and zero deflection is observed at a length 30 cm from P. Then, the unknown resistance X is

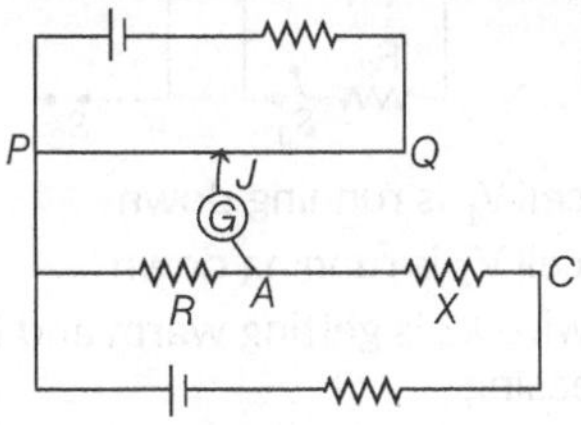

(a) $2R$ (b) $\frac{R}{2}$ (c) $\frac{R}{3}$ (d) $3R$

48 In the arrangement shown in figure when the switch S_2 is open, the galvanometer shows no deflection for $l = \frac{L}{2}$. When the switch S_2, is closed, the galvanometer shows no deflection for $l = \frac{5L}{12}$. The internal resistance r of 6 V cell and the emf E of the other battery are respectively

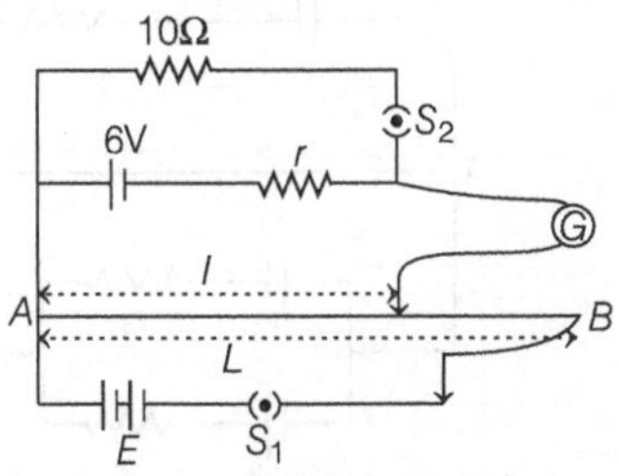

(a) 3 Ω, 8 V (b) 2 Ω, 12 V
(c) 2 Ω, 24 V (d) 3 Ω, 12 V

49 Consider the potentiometer circuit arranged as in figure. The potentiometer wire (resistance 15r) is 600 cm long. If the jockey touches the wire at a distance of 560 cm from A, what will be the current in the galvanometer?

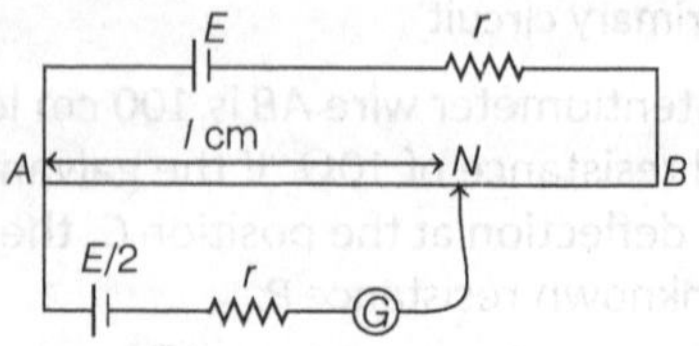

(a) $\frac{3E}{11r}$ (b) $\frac{5E}{22r}$ (c) $\frac{3E}{22r}$ (d) $\frac{5E}{11r}$

50 In the circuit shown in figure, XY is a potentiometer wire 100cm long. The circuit is connected as shown. With switches S_2 and S_3 open, a balance point is found at Z. After switch S_1 has remained closed for some time, it is found that contact at Z must be moved towards Y to maintain a balance. Which of the following is the most likely reason for this?

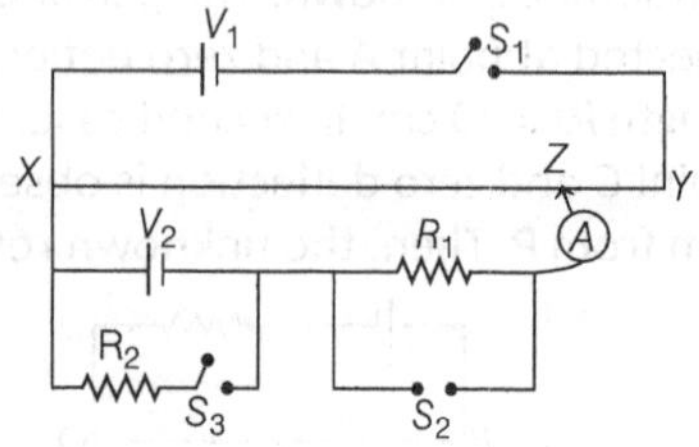

(a) The cell V_1 is running down
(b) The cell V_2 is running down
(c) The wire XZ is getting warm and its resistance is increasing
(d) The resistor R_1 is getting warm and increasing in value

51 A battery of emf $E_0 = 12$ V is connected across a 4m long uniform wire having resistance 4Ω/m. The cells of small emf $\varepsilon_1 = 2$ V and $\varepsilon_2 = 4$ V having internal resistances 2Ω and 6Ω respectively, are connected as shown in the figure. If galvanometer shows no deflection at the point N, the distance of point N from the point A is equal to

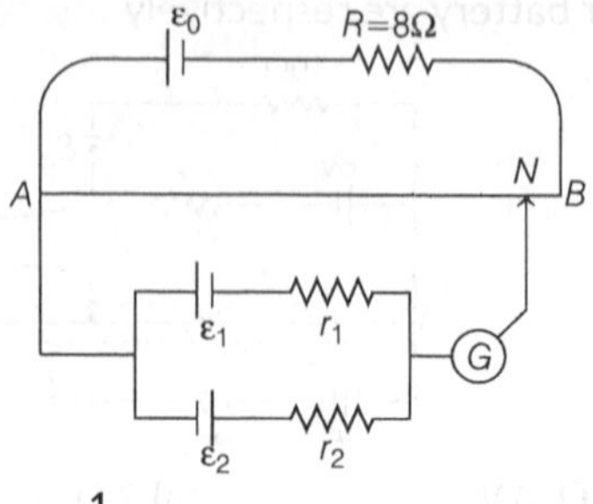

(a) $\frac{1}{6}$ m (b) $\frac{1}{3}$ m (c) 25 cm (d) 50 cm

Numerical Value Questions

1 A galvanometer, having a resistance of 50 Ω, gives a full scale deflection for a current of 0.05 A. Find the length in meter of a resistance wire of area of cross-section 2.97×10^{-2} cm that can be used to convert the galvanometer into an ammeter which can read a maximum of 5 A current. (Specific resistance of the wire $= 5 \times 10^{-7}$ Ω-m)

2 A galvanometer of resistance 40 Ω, shunted by a resistance of 50 Ω gives a deflection of 50 divisions when joined in series with a resistance of (1000/9) Ω and 2 V battery. What is the current senstivity of galvanometer (in div/mA)?

3 Full scale deflection current for galvanometer is 1 A. What should be the value of shunt resistance (in Ω), so that galvanometer shows half scale deflection.

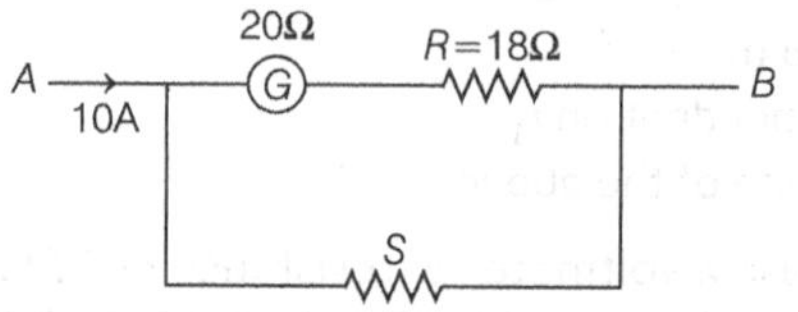

4 DC supply of 120V is connected to a large resistance X. A 100 V voltmeter of resistance 10 kΩ placed in series in the circuit reads 4V. This is an unusual use of voltmeter for measuring very high resistance. Find value of X (in kΩ).

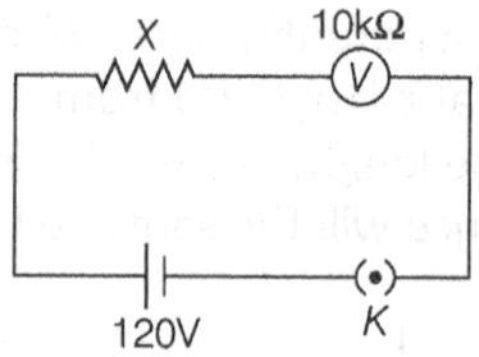

5 In the given circuit, the current flowing through the resistance 20Ω is 0.3 A while the ammeter reads 0.9 A. What is the value of R_1 (in Ω)?

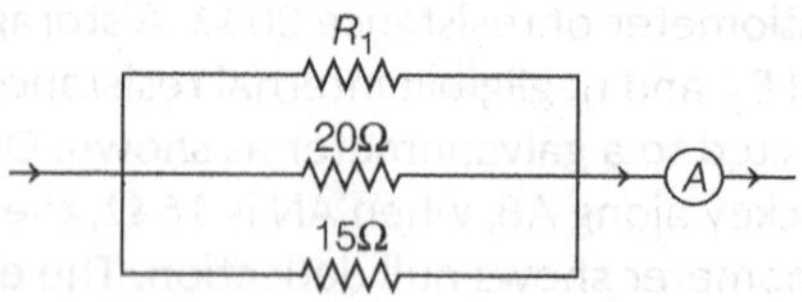

6 In the circuit shown, the coil resistance of the ammeter is 1Ω and that of the voltmeter is 20Ω. The main branch current is (19/20) A. What is the reading of the voltmeter(in volt)?

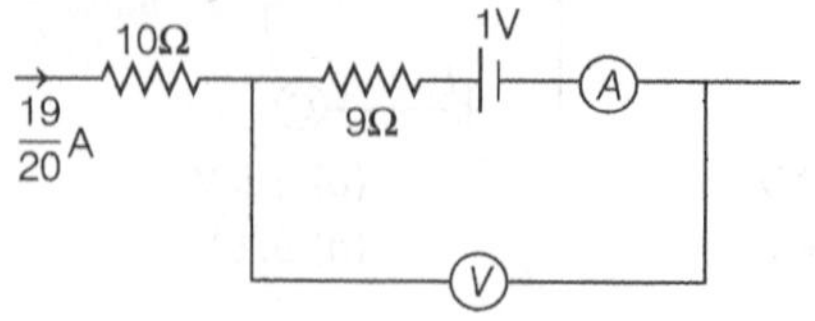

7 For the circuit shown in the figure. Find the emf (in mV) of the unknown battery E. The ammeter represented by the symbol A can be considered perfect (i.e. no resistance) and it reads the current in the wire to be 0.5 A in the direction shown.

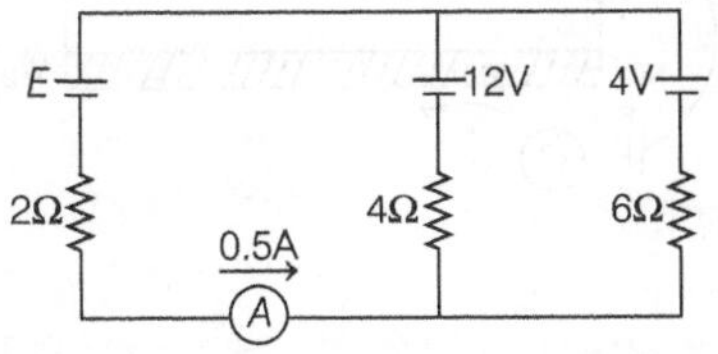

8 Two cells A and B of emf 1.3V and 1.5V respectively are arranged as shown in figure. The voltmeter reads 1.45 V. The voltmeter is assumed to be ideal. Find the ratio of internal resistances $\left(\frac{r_1}{r_2}\right)$ of the cells.

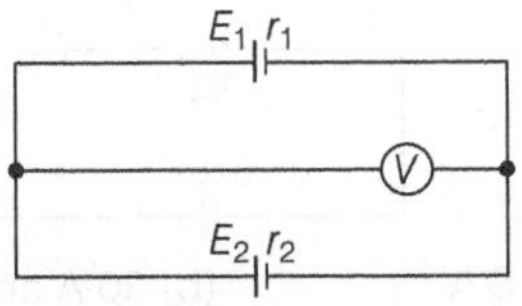

9 In the circuit shown, all voltmeters and ammeter are ideal. The internal resistance of battery is 20 Ω. The readings of voltmeter and ammeter are marked in the figure. What is resistance R_2 (in Ω)?

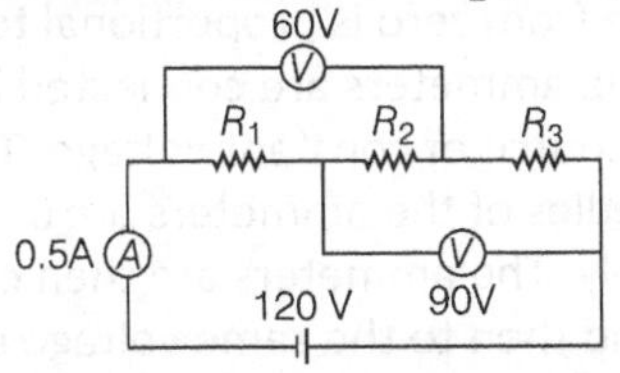

10 A resistance of 2Ω is connected across one gap of a meter bridge (the length of the wire is 100 cm) and an unknown resistance, greater than 2Ω, is connected across the other gap. When these resistances are interchanged, the balanced point shifts by 20 cm. Neglecting any end corrections, the unknown resistance is .... Ω.

11 The resistance of uniform wire AB is 9Ω. Find the resistance of part BC (in Ω) for which galvanometer G will show zero deflection.

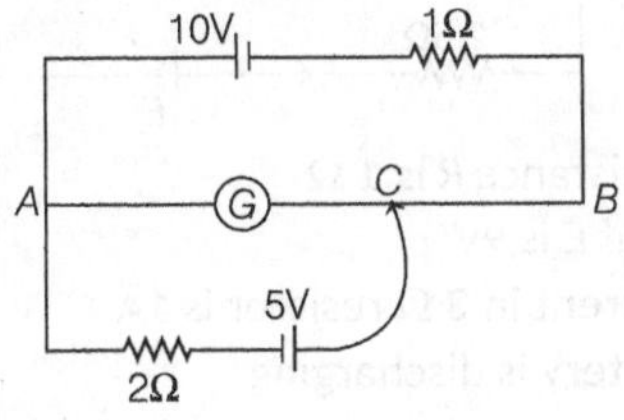

12 A 10 m long potentiometer wire has a resistance of 20Ω. It is connected in series with a battery of emf 3V and a resistance of 10 Ω. The internal resistance of cell is negligible. If the length can be read accurately up to 1 mm, the potentiometer can read voltage with an accuracy β mV. Then, what is the value of β?

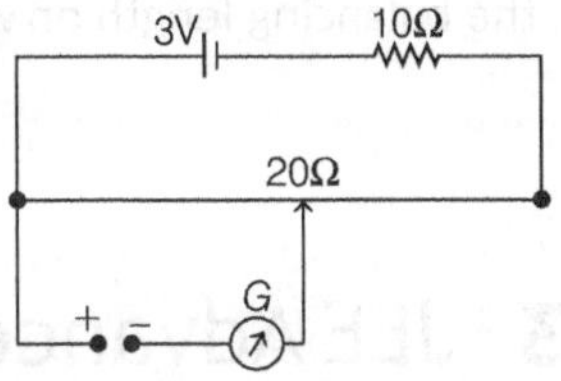

13 An ideal cell having a steady emf of 2 V is connected across the potentiometer wire of length 10 m. The potentiometer wire is of magnesium and having resistance of 11.5 Ω/m. An another cell gives a null point at 6.9 m. If a resistance of 5Ω is put in series with potentiometer wire, find the new position of the null point (in m).

14 A potentiometer circuit is arranged as shown in figure. AB is potentiometer wire of length 1m. Internal resistances of cells are shown in figure. Now, when only key K_1 is closed, balanced length AJ is 40 cm and when only K_2 closed, balanced length AJ becomes 55 cm. Find the balanced length AJ (in cm) when both the keys are closed.

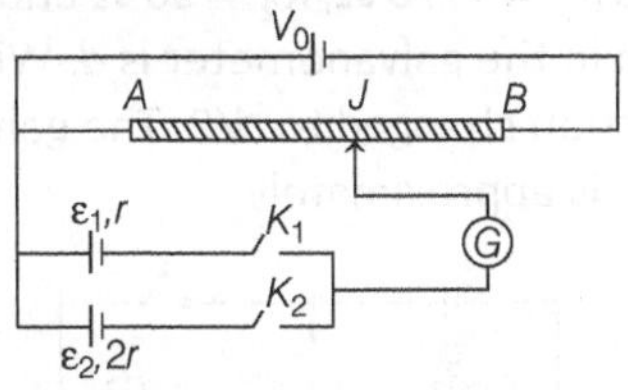

15 AB and CD are two uniform resistance wires of lengths 100 cm and 80 cm, respectively. The connections are shown in the figure. The cell of 5V is ideal while the other cell of emf E has internal resistance 2 Ω. A length of 20 cm of wire CD is balanced by 40 cm of wire AB. If the reading of the ideal ammeter is 2A, then find the emf E in volt. The other connecting wires have negligible resistance.

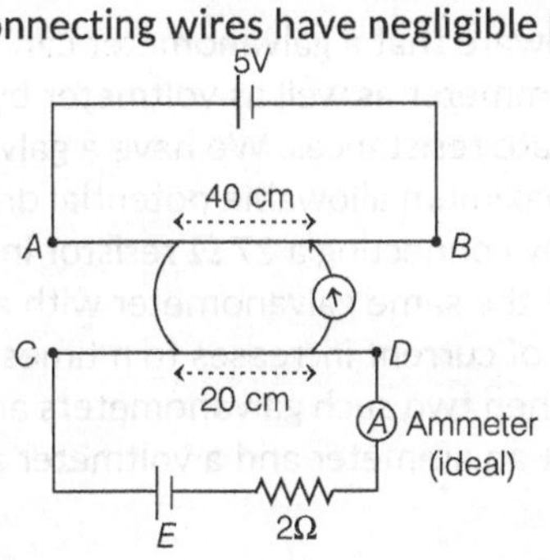

16 Two potentiometer wires w_1 and w_2 of equal length l, connected to a battery of emf ε_P and internal resistance 1Ω through two switches S_1 and S_2. A battery of emf ε is balanced on these potentiometer wires one by one. Potentiometer wire w_1 is of resistance $2\ \Omega$. When only S_1 is closed and S_2 is open, balancing length is $l/2$ on it. On closing S_2 and opening S_1, the balancing length on w_2 is found to be $\frac{2l}{3}$. Find the resistance (in Ω) of potentiometer wire w_2.

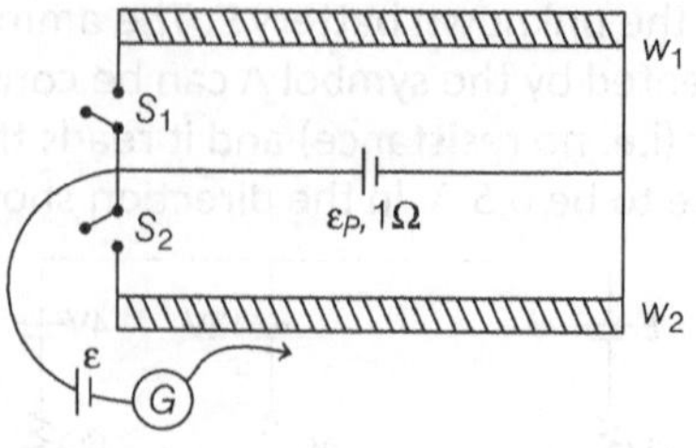

LEVEL 03 JEE Advanced Level

Single Choice Correct Questions

1 A galvanometer has a resistance of 3663 Ω. A shunt S is connected across it such that (1/34) of the total current passes through the galvanometer. The external resistance which must be connected in series with the main circuit, so that the total current in the main circuit remain unaltered even when the galvanometer is shunted is

(a) 3663 Ω (b) 111 Ω
(c) 107.7 Ω (d) 3555.3 Ω

2 To find the resistance of a galvanometer by the half deflection method, the following circuit is used with resistance $R_1 = 9970\ \Omega$, $R_2 = 30\ \Omega$ and $R_3 = 0$. The deflection in the galvanometer is d. With $R_3 = 107\ \Omega$, the deflection changed to $d/2$. The galvanometer resistance is approximately

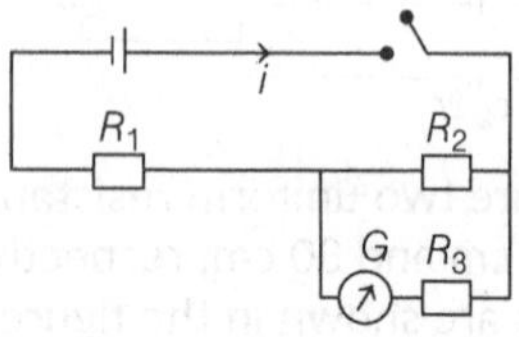

(a) 107 Ω (b) 137 Ω
(c) $\frac{107}{2}$ Ω (d) 77 Ω

3 We are aware that a galvanometer can be converted into an ammeter as well as voltmeter by using appropriate resistances. We have a galvanometer whose maximum allowable potential drop increases n times by connecting a 27 Ω resistor in series. When we shunt the same galvanometer with a 3Ω resistor, its range of current increases to n times the original value. When two such galvanometers are used to construct an ammeter and a voltmeter and are connected as shown, the current in galvanometer making up ammeter and voltmeter respectively are

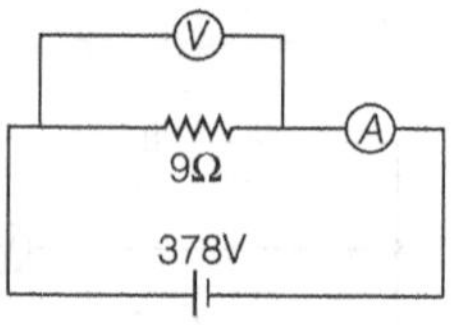

(a) 10 A and 8 A (b) 30 A and 10 A
(c) 32 A and 30 A (d) 8 A and 30 A

4 Two ammeters 1 and 2 have different internal resistances r_1 (known) and r_2 (unknown). Each ammeter has scale such that the angular deviation of the needle from zero is proportional to the current. Initially, the ammeters are connected in series and then to a source of constant voltage. The deviations of the needles of the ammeters are θ_1 and θ_2, respectively. The ammeters are then connected in parallel and then to the same voltage source. This time, the deviations of the needles are θ'_1 and θ'_2, respectively. r_2 in terms of $r_1, \theta_1, \theta_2, \theta'_1$ and θ'_2 is

(a) $r_1\frac{\theta_1\theta'_1}{\theta_2\theta'_2}$ (b) $r_1\frac{\theta_2\theta'_1}{\theta_1\theta'_2}$ (c) $r_1\frac{\theta_2\theta'_2}{\theta_1\theta'_1}$ (d) $r_1\frac{\theta_1\theta_2}{\theta'_1\theta'_2}$

5 In a circuit, voltmeter reads 3V and the ammeter reads 2A. Then, which of the following is incorrect?

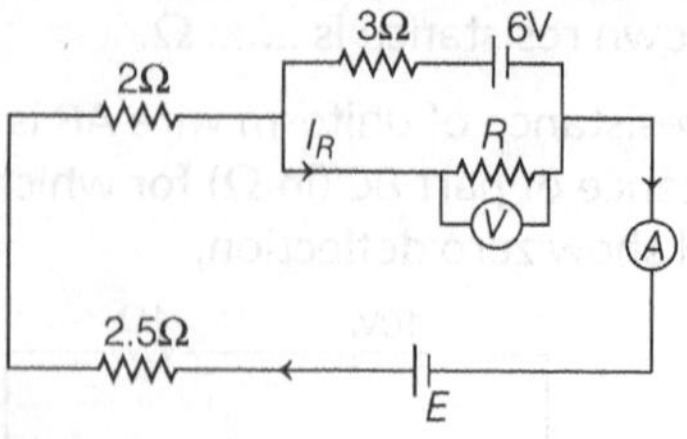

(a) The resistance R is 1 Ω
(b) The emf E is 9V
(c) The current in 3 Ω resistor is 1A
(d) 6 V battery is discharging

6 In the circuit shown, when switch S_1 is closed and S_2 is open, the ideal voltmeter shows a reading of 18V. When switch S_2 is closed and S_1 is open, the reading of voltmeter is 24V. When S_1 and S_2 both are closed, the voltmeter reading will be

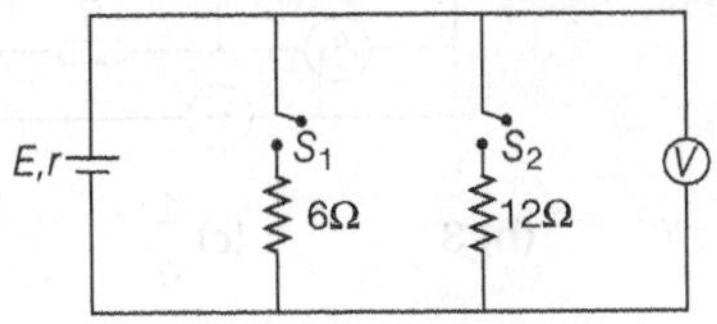

(a) 14.4 V (b) 20.6 V
(c) 24.2 V (d) 10.8 V

7 In the circuit shown in the figure, no current flows through the ideal ammeter. If the internal resistance of the cell is negligible, then find value of unknown resistance R.

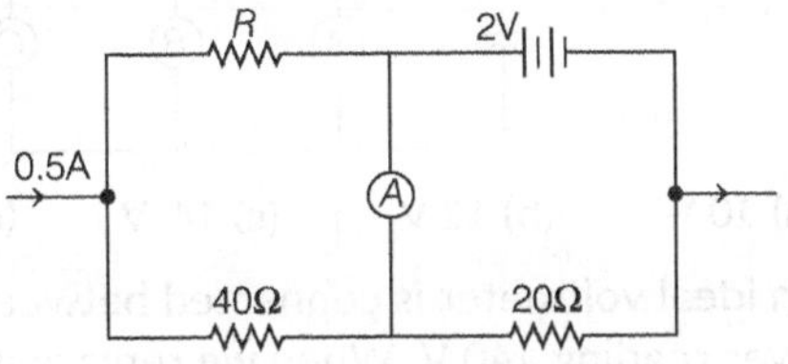

(a) 5 Ω (b) 10 Ω
(c) 15 Ω (d) 20 Ω

8 In the circuit shown, the reading of the ammeter (ideal) is the same with both switches open as with both closed. Find the value of resistance R in Ω.

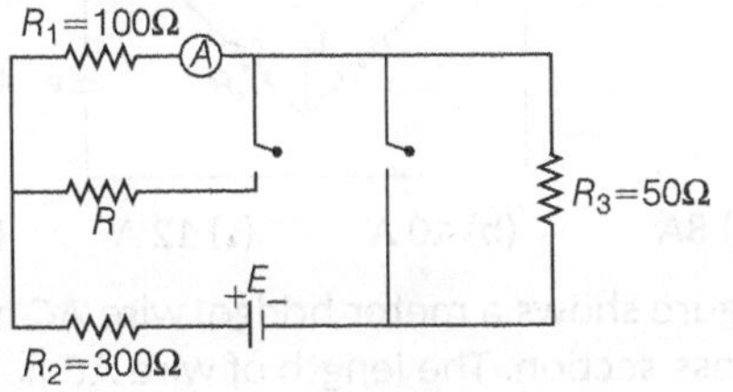

(a) 600 (b) 800
(c) 400 (d) 300

9 In the circuit shown, the variable resistance is adjusted to a particular value, so that the ammeter reading is same in both the positions 1 and 2 of the key. The reading of ammeter is 2A. If E = 10V, then value of x is

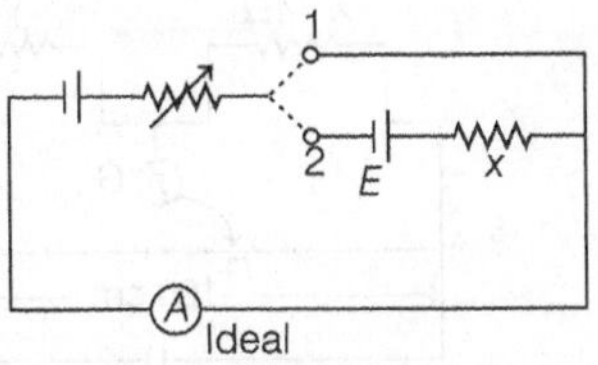

(a) 2 Ω (b) 5 Ω
(c) 10 Ω (d) 20 Ω

10 Four circuits are given in the options below. In all the circuits voltmeters, ammeter and cells are ideal. The readings of each ammeter and voltmeter are shown in the figure. In which pair of circuits shown below, readings of voltmeters V_1 and V_2 and ammeter A may be correct?

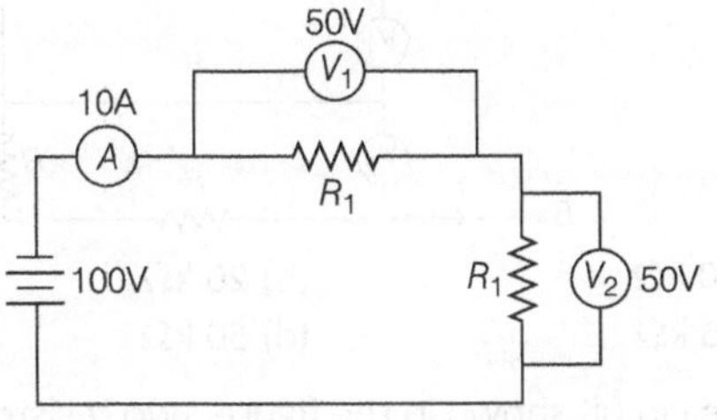

(1)

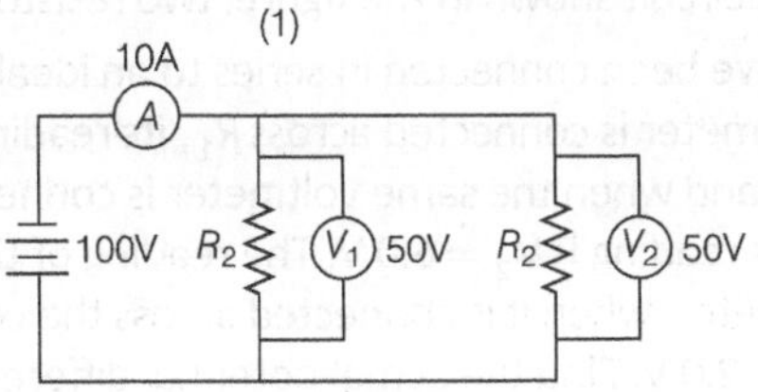

(2)

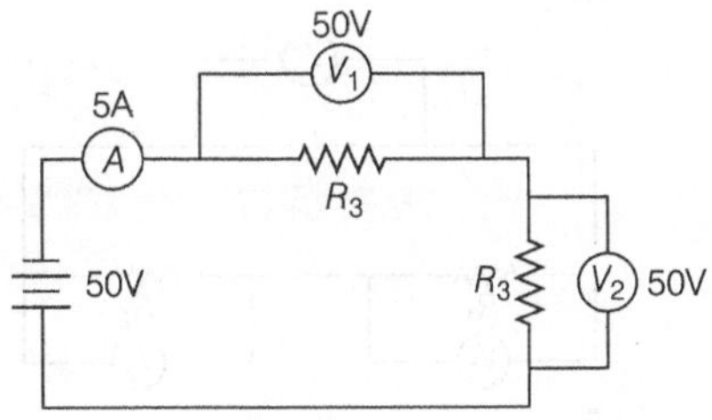

(3)

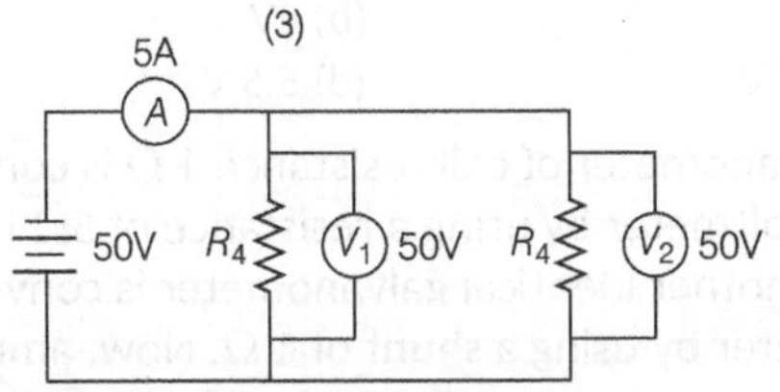

(4)

(a) 1 and 3 (b) 2 and 4 (c) 2 and 3 (d) 1 and 4

11 In the circuit shown, when keys K_1 and K_2 both are closed, the ammeter reads I_0. But when K_1 is open and K_2 is closed, the ammeter reads $I_0/2$. Assuming that, ammeter resistance is much less than R_2, the values of r and R_1 are

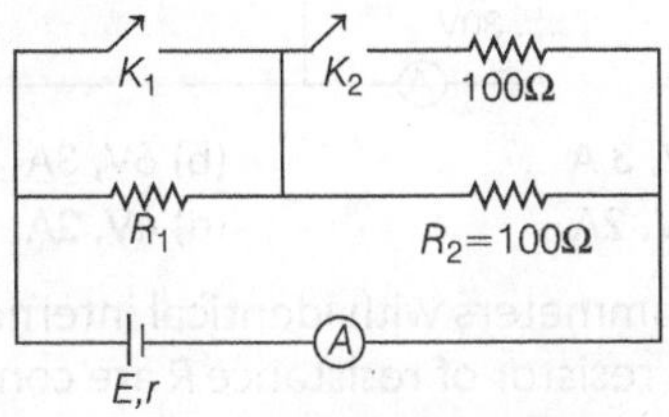

(a) 25 Ω, 50 Ω (b) 25 Ω, 100 Ω
(c) 0, 100 Ω (d) 0, 50 Ω

12 In the circuit shown in figure, a current $I = 600\,\mu A$ enters through A and leaves through B. Reading of the identical voltmeters V_1 and V_2 are 20V and 30V respectively. Find the value of R.

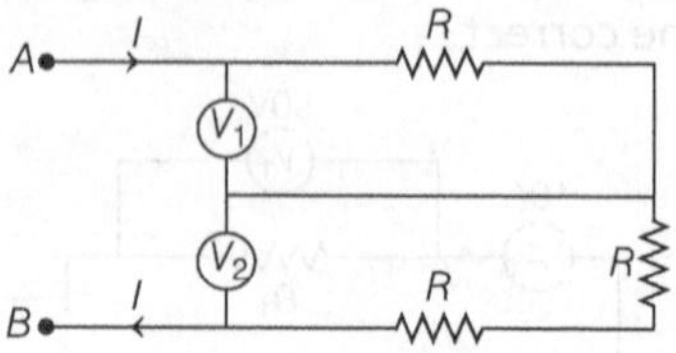

(a) $10\,k\Omega$ (b) $20\,k\Omega$
(c) $25\,k\Omega$ (d) $50\,k\Omega$

13 In the circuit shown in the figure, two resistors R_1 and R_2 have been connected in series to an ideal cell. When a voltmeter is connected across R_1, its reading is $V_1 =$ 4.0 V and when the same voltmeter is connected across R_2, its reading is $V_2 = 6.0$ V. The reading of the voltmeter, when it is connected across the cell is $V_3 = 12.0$ V. Find the actual potential difference across R_1 in the circuit.

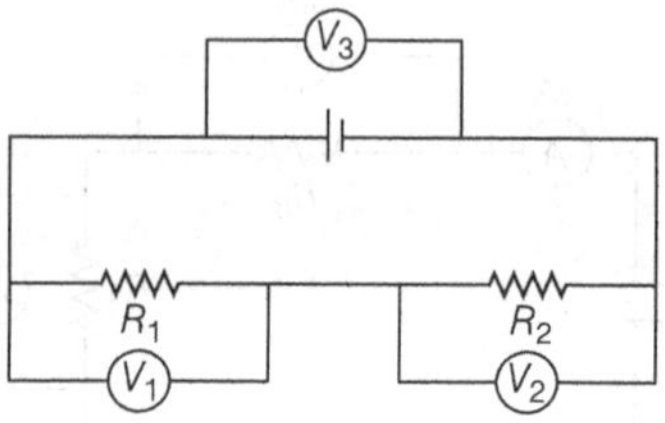

(a) 3V (b) 4V
(c) 4.8 V (d) 5.5 V

14 A galvanometer of coil resistance $1\,\Omega$ is converted into voltmeter by using a resistance of 5Ω in series and another identical galvanometer is converted into ammeter by using a shunt of $1\,\Omega$. Now, ammeter and voltmeter are connected in circuit as shown, the readings of voltmeter and ammeter respectively, are

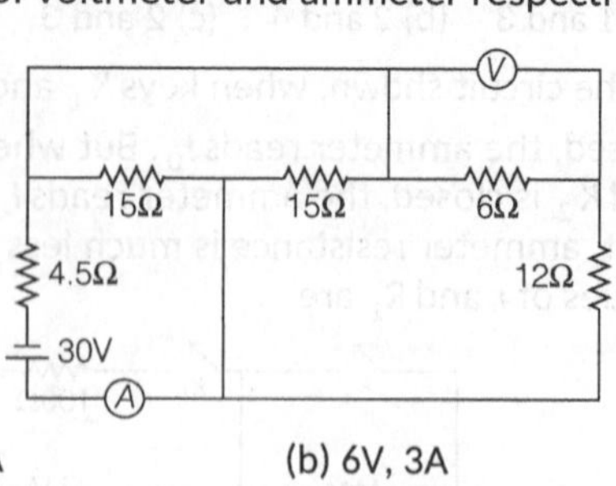

(a) 3V, 3 A (b) 6V, 3A
(c) 2 V, 2A (d) 4V, 2A

15 Four ammeters with identical internal resistance r and a resistor of resistance R are connected to a current source as shown in figure. It is known that, the reading of the ammeter A_1 is $I_1 = 3$A and the reading of the ammeter A_2 is $I_2 = 5$A. Determine the ratio of the resistances R/r.

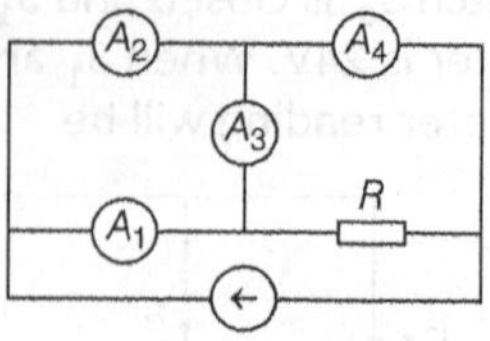

(a) 9 (b) 3 (c) $\frac{1}{9}$ (d) $\frac{1}{3}$

16 The circuit shown consists of three identical resistances and three identical voltmeters A, B and C. If the first voltmeter A reads $V_A = 22$ V and the third voltmeter C reads $V_C = 8$V, calculate reading of the second voltmeter B.

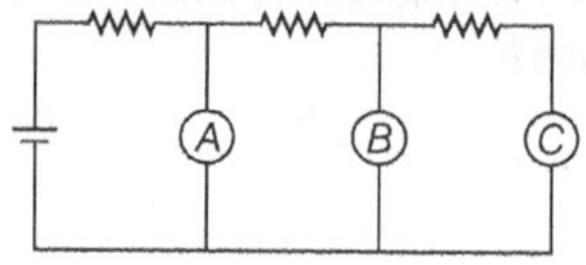

(a) 10 V (b) 12 V (c) 14 V (d) 15 V

17 An ideal voltmeter is connected between C and D gives reading 140 V. When we replace it with an ideal ammeter, its reading is 21 A. Now , we connect a resistor r between C and D. The current flowing through r is

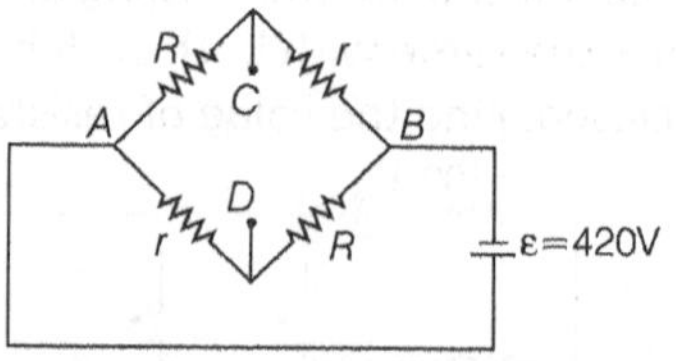

(a) 8A (b) 10 A (c) 12 A (d) 14 A

18 Figure shows a meter bridge, wire AC has uniform cross-section. The length of wire AC is 100 cm. X is a standard resistor of $4\,\Omega$ and Y is a coil. When Y is immersed in melting ice, the null point is at 40 cm from point A. When the coil Y is heated to 100°C, a $78\,\Omega$ resistor has to be connected in parallel with Y in order to keep the bridge balanced at the same point. Temperature coefficient of resistance of the coil is

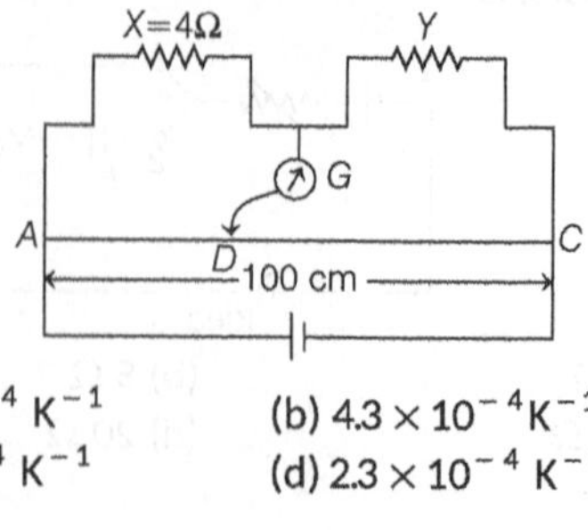

(a) $6.3 \times 10^{-4}\,K^{-1}$ (b) $4.3 \times 10^{-4}\,K^{-1}$
(c) $8.3 \times 10^{-4}\,K^{-1}$ (d) $2.3 \times 10^{-4}\,K^{-1}$

19 In a meter bridge, the wire of length 1 m has a non-uniform cross-section such that, the variation $\frac{dR}{dl}$ of its resistance R with length l is $\frac{dR}{dl} \propto \frac{1}{\sqrt{l}}$. Two equal resistances are connected as shown in the figure. The galvanometer has zero deflection when the jockey is at point P. What is the length AP?

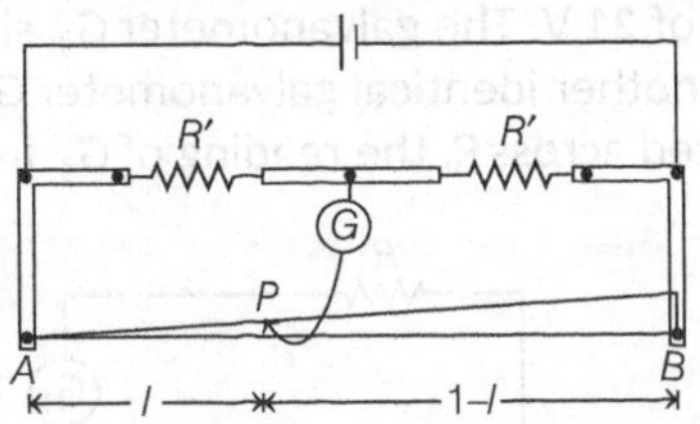

(a) 0.25 m (b) 0.3 m (c) 0.35 m (d) 0.2 m

20 Radius of wire AB of length 10 m changes from r to $2r$. At what distance from A, a jockey be contacted to give no deflection in the galvanometer?

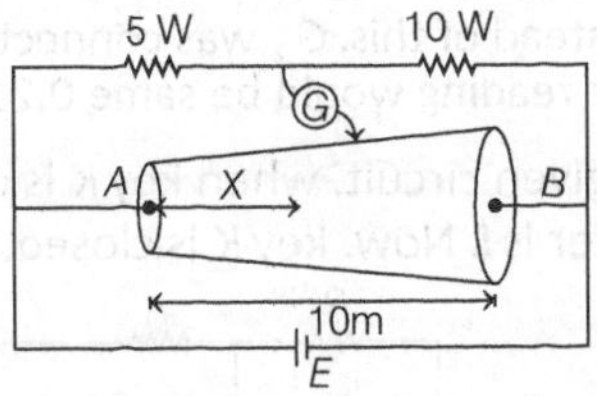

(a) 2 m (b) 4 m (c) 5 m (d) 6 m

21 In an experiment to measure the internal resistance of a cell by potentiometer, it is found that the balance point is at a length of 2m when the cell is shunted by a 5 Ω resistance, and is at a length of 3 m when the cell is shunted by a 10 Ω resistance. The internal resistance of the cell is

(a) 1 Ω (b) 1.5 Ω
(c) 10 Ω (d) 15 Ω

22 A battery of emf 10 V and internal resistance 2Ω is connected in primary circuit with a 100 cm long uniform potentiometer wire and a rheostat whose resistance is fixed at 998 Ω. A battery of unknown emf is being balanced on this potentiometer wire and balancing length is found to be 50 cm. When area of cross-section of potentiometer wire is doubled, then balancing length is found to be 75 cm. Calculate emf of the battery.

(a) 2.5 V (b) 4 V
(c) 5 V (d) 6 V

23 A uniform shape potentiometer wire AB (100 cm long) has specific resistance $\rho = kx$, where x is the position of point from starting end A. Then, at which position (in cm) null point of wire will come from the left end A for the given circuit ? Resistance of wire AB is 40 Ω.

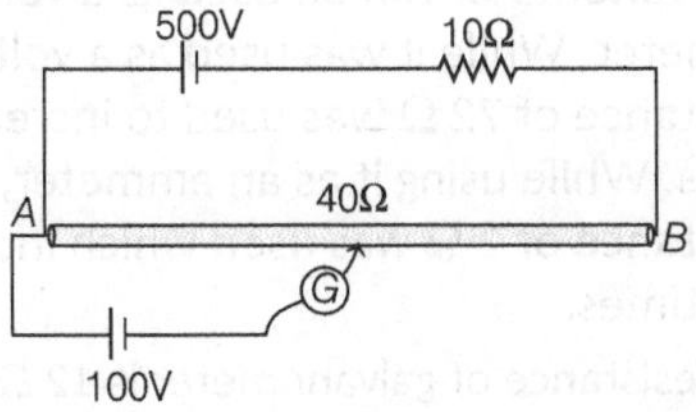

(a) 20 cm (b) 25 cm (c) 50 cm (d) 80 cm

24 A potentiometer wire AB as shown is 40 cm long of resistance 50 Ω/m; the free end of an ideal voltmeter is touching the potentiometer wire with the help of a jockey. What should be the velocity of the jockey as a function of time, so that reading of voltmeter varies with time as $(2 \sin \pi t)$ V.

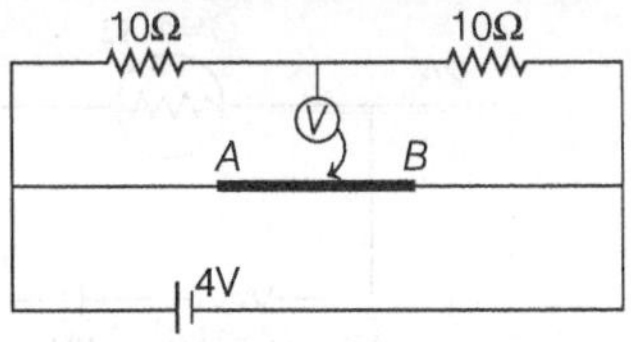

(a) $10\pi \sin \pi t \text{ cms}^{-1}$ (b) $10\pi \cos \pi t \text{ cms}^{-1}$
(c) $20\pi \sin \pi t \text{ cms}^{-1}$ (d) $20\pi \cos \pi t \text{ cms}^{-1}$

25 In the laboratory, the high emf of a battery is measured by using potentiometer and two resistances R_1 and R_2, where $R_1 << R_2$ as shown in the figure.

$R_1 = (100 \pm 0.10)\ \Omega$ and $R_2 = (9900 \pm 9.90)\ \Omega$, $AB = 1$ m.

The voltage across R_1, when switches S_1 and S_2 are connected to point 1 and point 2 is balanced against $l_1 = (60 \pm 0.06)$ cm. When the switches S_1 and S_2 are shifted to point 3 and point 4 as shown in the given figure, the potential difference of standard $E_0 = 2$ V is balanced against length $l_2 = (75 \pm 0.075)$ cm.

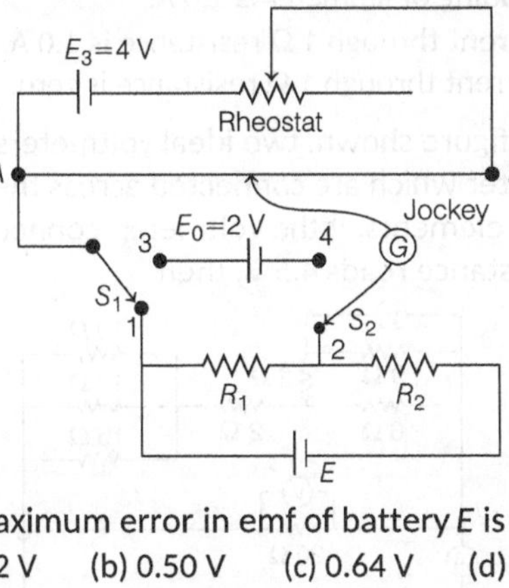

The maximum error in emf of battery E is

(a) 0.32 V (b) 0.50 V (c) 0.64 V (d) 0.80 V

Multiple Choice(s) Correct Questions

1 A galvanometer can be used as a voltmeter or an ammeter. While it was used as a voltmeter, a resistance of 72 Ω was used to increase its range to *n* times. While using it as an ammeter, a shunt resistance of 2 Ω was used which increased its range to *n* times.

(a) Resistance of galvanometer is 12 Ω
(b) Resistance of ammeter is 1.7 Ω
(c) Resistance of voltmeter is 84 Ω
(d) Resistance of ammeter is 3.4 Ω

2 The galvanometer shown in the figure has resistance 10 Ω. It is shunted by a series combination of a resistance $S = 1\,\Omega$ and an ideal cell of emf 2V. A current 2A passes as shown

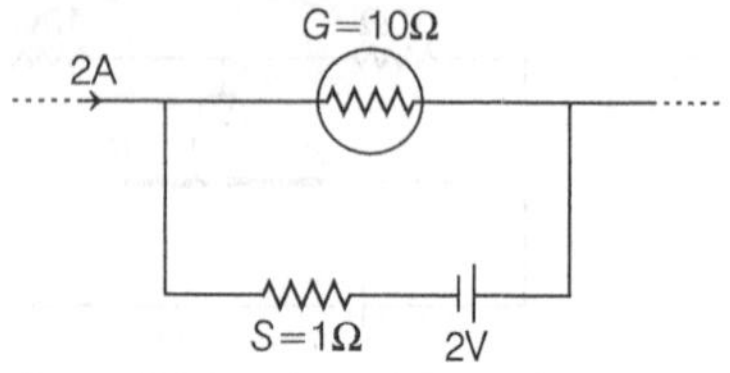

(a) The reading of the galvanometer is 1 A
(b) The reading of the galvanometer is zero
(c) The potential difference across the resistance *S* is 1.5 V
(d) The potential difference across the resistance *S* is 2 V

3 Voltmeter and ammeter shown in circuit diagram are ideal, then the correct statements.

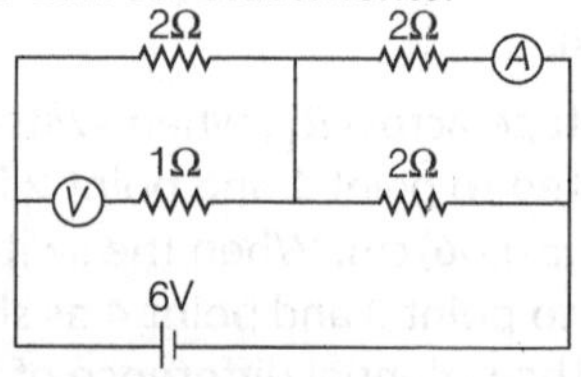

(a) Reading of voltmeter is 4 V.
(b) Reading of ammeter is 1.0 A.
(c) Current through 1 Ω resistance is 1.0 A.
(d) Current through 1 Ω resistance is zero.

4 In the figure shown, two ideal voltmeters and an ammeter which are connected across the various circuit elements. If the voltmeter connected across 9 Ω resistance reads 4.5 V, then

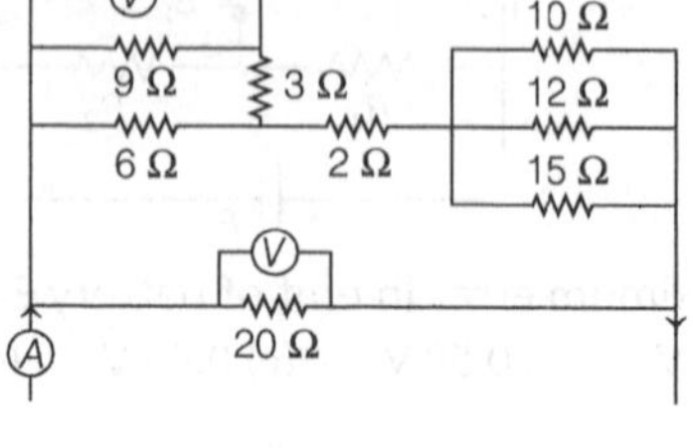

(a) the current through 12 Ω resistance is 0.5A
(b) the reading of the voltmeter connected across 20 Ω resistance, is 20 V
(c) the reading of the voltmeter connected across 20 Ω resistance, is 15 V
(d) the reading of the ammeter is 2.25 A

5 In the circuit shown, the battery is ideal. It has a voltage of 21 V. The galvanometer G_1 shows 0.42 A. When another identical galvanometer G_2 is connected across *R*, the reading of G_1 increases to 0.50 A.

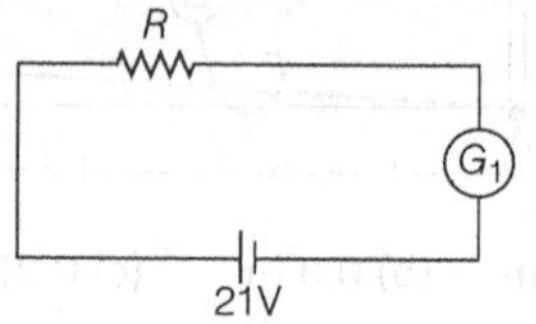

(a) The resistance of galvanometer is 30 Ω.
(b) The resistance *R* is 40 Ω.
(c) The reading of G_2 is 0.20A.
(d) If instead of this, G_2 was connected parallel to G_1, their reading would be same 0.21 A.

6 In the given circuit, when key *K* is open, reading of ammeter is *I*. Now, key *K* is closed.

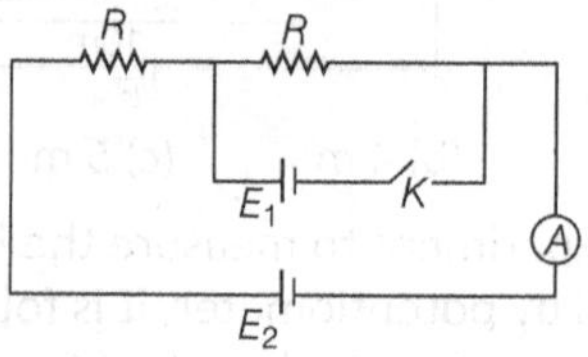

(a) If $E_1 = IR$, reading of the ammeter is *I*.
(b) If $IR < E_1 < 2IR$, reading of the ammeter is greater than *I*.
(c) If $E_1 = 2IR$, reading of the ammeter will be zero.
(d) Reading of the ammeter will not change.

7 By mistake, a voltmeter is placed in series and an ammeter is parallel with a resistance in an electric circuit, with a cell in series.

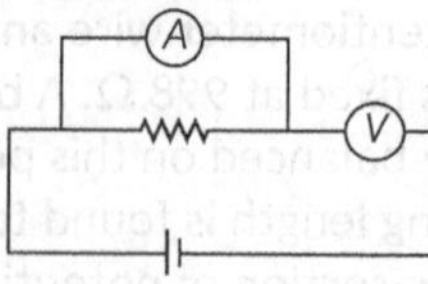

(a) If the devices are ideal, ammeter will read zero current and voltmeter will read the emf of cell.
(b) If the devices are ideal, a large current will flow through the ammeter and it will be damaged.
(c) The main current in the circuit will be very low and almost all current will flow through the ammeter, if resistance of ammeter is much smaller than the resistance in parallel.
(d) The devices may get damaged, if emf of the cell is very high and the meters are non-ideal.

8 In the given circuit, the potential difference between a and b is 300 V. The resistors are of 100 Ω each.

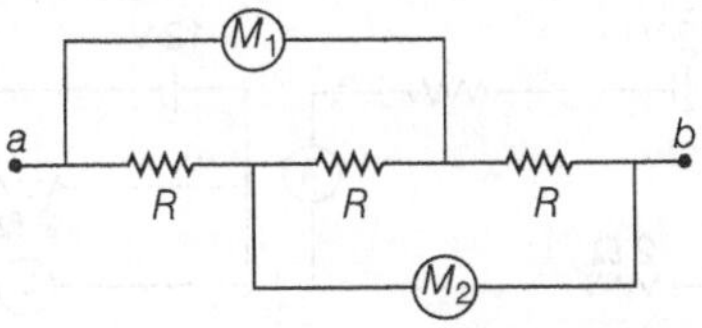

(a) If the upper meter M_1 is ideal voltmeter and lower is ideal ammeter M_2, reading of voltmeter is 300 V.
(b) If both meters are ideal voltmeters, they show 200 V each.
(c) If both meters are ideal ammeters, they read 6A each.
(d) If the upper meter M_1 is ideal voltmeter and lower M_2 is ideal ammeter, reading of ammeter is 3A.

9 In the circuit shown $R_1 = R_2 = 10\ \Omega$ and resistance per unit length of wire $PQ = 1\ \Omega$/cm and length $PQ = 10$ cm. S is mid-point of wire PQ. If R_2 is made 20 Ω, then to get zero deflection in galvanometer.

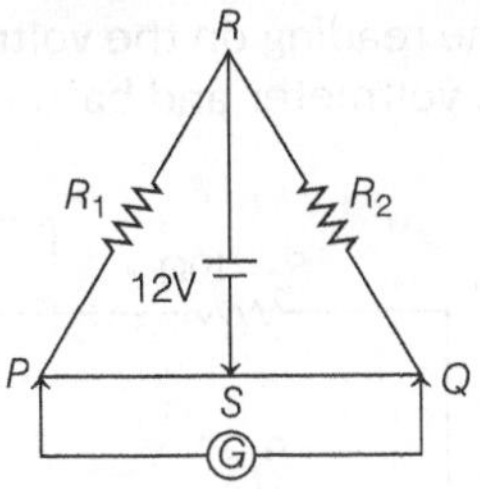

(a) The jockey at P can be moved towards S by 2 cm.
(b) The jockey at Q can be moved towards S by 2 cm.
(c) The jockey at S can be moved towards P by (5/3) cm.
(d) The jockey at all positions fixed and R_1 should be made 20 Ω.

10 In a potentiometer wire experiment, the emf of a battery in the primary circuit is 20 V and its internal resistance is 5 Ω. There is a resistance box (in series with the battery and the potentiometer wire) whose resistance can be varied from 120 Ω to 170 Ω. Resistance of the potentiometer wire is 75 Ω. The following potential differences can be measured using this potentiometer

(a) 5 V (b) 6 V
(c) 7 V (d) 8 V

11 The figure shows a potentiometer arrangement. D is the driving cell and C is the cell whose emf is to be determined. AB is the potentiometer wire and G is galvanometer. J is sliding contact which can touch any point on AB. Which of the following are essential conditions for obtaining balance?

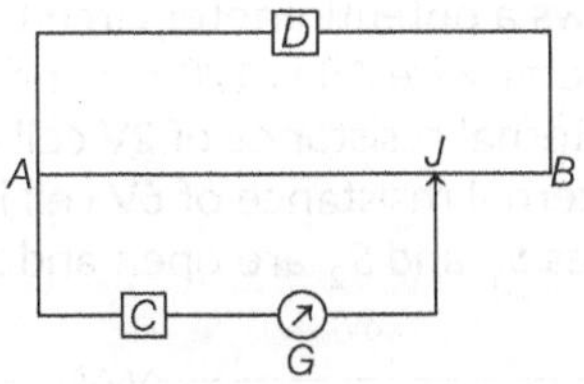

(a) The emf of D must be greater than the emf of C.
(b) Either the positive terminals of both D and C or the negative terminals of both D and C must be joined to A.
(c) The positive terminals of D and C must be joined.
(d) The resistance of G must be less than resistance of AB.

12 A student was given the experiment to measure the emf of a unknown cell using potentiometer. He cheated result and wrote the observation arbitrarily and was caught. Which reading helped the teacher to arrive at the conclusion that he cheated?

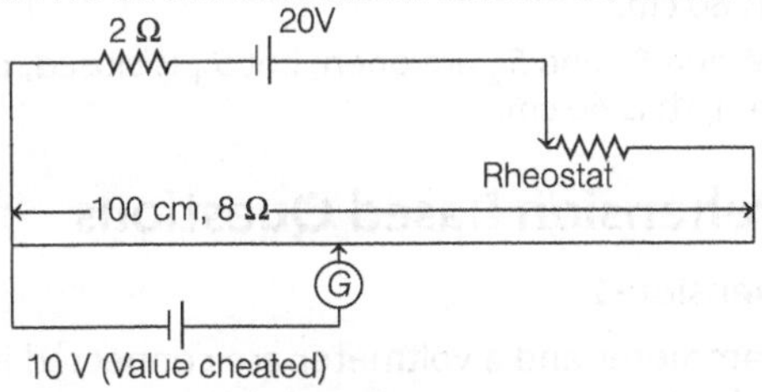

S.No.	Value of rheostat	Null point
1.	R_1	50 cm
2.	R_2	60 cm
3.	R_3	70 cm
4.	R_4	80 cm

(a) 1 (b) 2
(c) 3 (d) 4

13 In the potentiometer circuit of given figure, the galvanometer reveals a current in the direction shown wherever the sliding contact touches the wire. This could be caused by

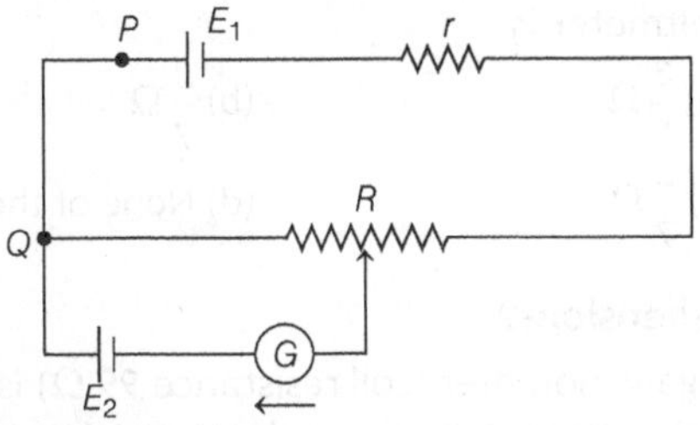

(a) E_1 being too low
(b) r being too high
(c) a break in PQ
(d) E_2 being too low

14 Figure shows a potentiometer circuit. The length of potentiometer wire AB is 120 cm and its resistance is 2Ω. The internal resistance of 2V cell is negligible and the internal resistance of 6V cell is $1\ \Omega$. Initially the switches S_1 and S_2 are open and S_3 is closed.

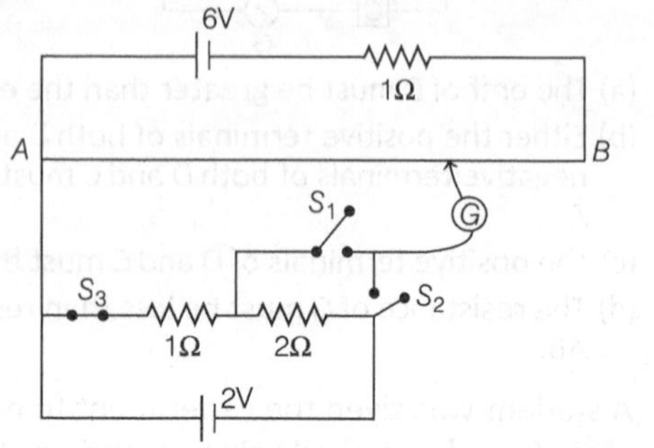

(a) When only S_2 is open, balanced length is 20 cm.
(b) When only S_1 is open, balanced length is 60 cm.
(c) When all three switches are closed, balanced length is 60 cm.
(d) When S_1 and S_2 are open, but S_3 is closed, balance length is 60 cm.

Comprehension Based Questions

Comprehension-1

An ammeter and a voltmeter are connected in series to a battery with an emf of 10V. When a certain resistance is connected in parallel with the voltmeter, the reading of the voltmeter decreases three times, whereas the reading of the ammeter increases the two times.

1 Find the voltmeter reading after the connection of the resistance.
(a) 1 V (b) 2 V (c) 3 V (d) 4 V

2 If resistance of the ammeter is $2\ \Omega$, then resistance of the voltmeter is
(a) $1\ \Omega$ (b) $2\ \Omega$ (c) $3\ \Omega$ (d) $4\ \Omega$

3 If resistance of the ammeter is $2\ \Omega$, then resistance of the resistor which is added in parallel to the voltmeter is
(a) $\frac{3}{5}\Omega$ (b) $\frac{2}{7}\Omega$
(c) $\frac{3}{7}\Omega$ (d) None of these

Comprehension-2

A galvanometer (coil resistance $99\ \Omega$) is converted into a ammeter using a shunt of $1\ \Omega$ and connected as shown in the Fig. (i). The ammeter reads 3A.

The same galvanometer is converted into a voltmeter by connecting a resistance of $101\ \Omega$ in series. This voltmeter is connected as shown in Fig. (ii). Its reading is found to be 4/5 times of the full scale reading.

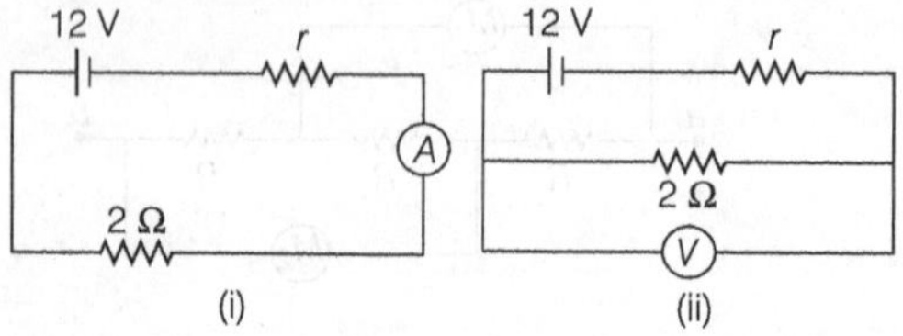

4 Internal resistance r of the cell is
(a) $1\ \Omega$ (b) $1.01\ \Omega$ (c) $1.05\ \Omega$ (d) $1.1\ \Omega$

5 Full scale deflection current of the galvanometer is
(a) 30 mA (b) 40 mA (c) 50 mA (d) 100 mA

6 Range of the ammeter and voltmeter respectively are
(a) 0-4 A, 0-5 V (b) 0-5 A, 0-10 V
(c) 0-8 A, 0-15 V (d) 0-10 A, 0-20 V

Comprehension-3

The power dissipated in resistor R_3 shown in the figure is 15 W. The reading on the ammeter is 500 mA and the reading on the voltmeter is 10V. Ammeter, voltmeter and battery are ideal.

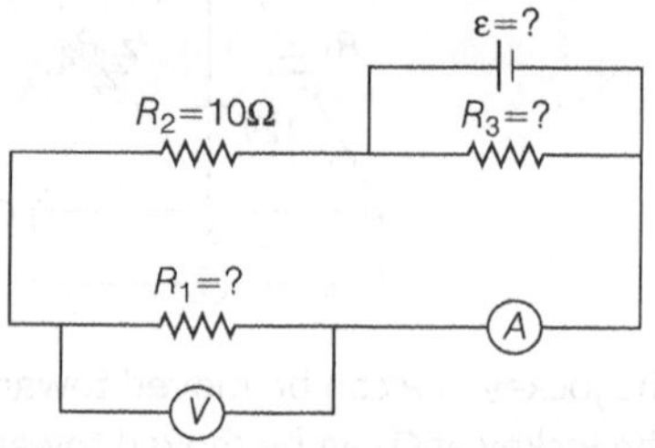

7 The resistance R_1 is
(a) $10\ \Omega$ (b) $15\ \Omega$ (c) $20\ \Omega$ (d) $25\ \Omega$

8 The emf ε of the supply battery is
(a) 10 V (b) 15 V (c) 20 V (d) 25 V

9 The resistance R_3 is
(a) $10\ \Omega$ (b) $15\ \Omega$ (c) $20\ \Omega$ (d) $25\ \Omega$

Comprehension-4

In a potentiometer circuit, two wires of same material of resistivity ρ, one of radius of cross-section a and other of radius of cross-section $2a$ are joined in series. They are of length L and $2L$, respectively. This combination acts as the potentiometer wire of length $3L$. The emf of the cell in the primary circuit is ε and internal resistance is $\rho L/2\pi a^2$. This cell is connected to the potentiometer wire by a conducting wire of negligible resistance with positive terminal of the cell connected to one end (call it A) of longer wire.

10 The maximum voltage which can be balanced on the potentiometer wire is

(a) ε (b) $\frac{\varepsilon}{2}$ (c) $\frac{3\varepsilon}{4}$ (d) $\frac{2\varepsilon}{5}$

11 The balancing length, measured from point *A*, obtained in measurement of emf of cell of emf $\frac{\varepsilon}{2}$ is

(a) L (b) $\frac{L}{2}$ (c) $\frac{2L}{5}$ (d) $\frac{5L}{2}$

12 If positive terminal of another cell of emf $\frac{\varepsilon}{2}$ and internal resistance $\rho L/2\pi a^2$ is connected to point *A* and other terminal of this cell is joined to other end of two wires, then the current through this cell is (Take, $R = \rho L/2\pi a^2$)

(a) $\frac{\varepsilon}{2R}$ (b) $\frac{\varepsilon}{3R}$ (c) $\frac{\varepsilon}{5R}$ (d) $\frac{\varepsilon}{7R}$

Comprehension-5

A wire *AB* (of length 1 m, area of cross-section πm^2) is used in potentiometer experiment to calculate emf and internal resistance (r) of battery.
The emf and internal resistance of driving battery are 15 V and 3Ω, respectively. The resistivity of wire *AB* varies as $\rho = \rho_0 x$ (where x is distance from *A* in metres and $\rho_0 = 24\pi\ \Omega$)
The distance of null point from *A* is obtained at $\sqrt{\frac{2}{3}}$ m when switch *S* is open and at $\frac{1}{\sqrt{2}}$ m when switch is closed.

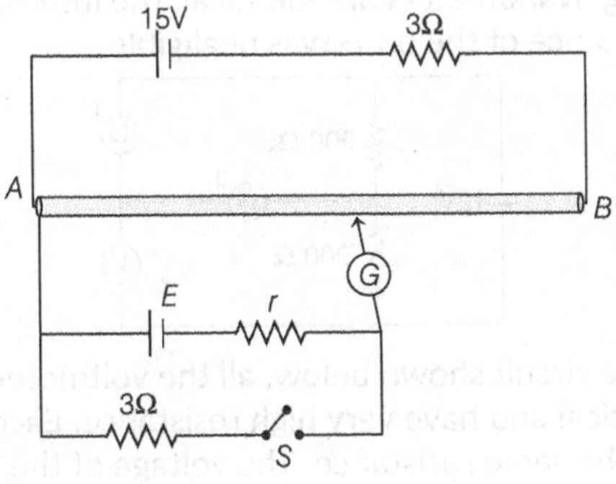

13 The resistance of whole wire *AB* is

(a) 6 Ω (b) 12 Ω (c) 18 Ω (d) 24 Ω

14 The emf *E* of battery is

(a) 4 V (b) 6 V (c) 8 V (d) 10 V

15 Internal resistance of battery *E* is

(a) 4 Ω (b) 3 Ω (c) 2 Ω (d) 1 Ω

Match the Columns Questions

1 Figure shows the internal wiring of a three range voltmeter whose binding posts are marked +, 2 V, 10 V and 100 V. When the meter is connected to the circuit being measured, one connection is made to the post marked + and the other to the post marked with the desired voltage range. The resistance of the moving coil galvanometer is 40 Ω and a current of 1 mA in the coil causes it to deflect full-scale, then match the following.

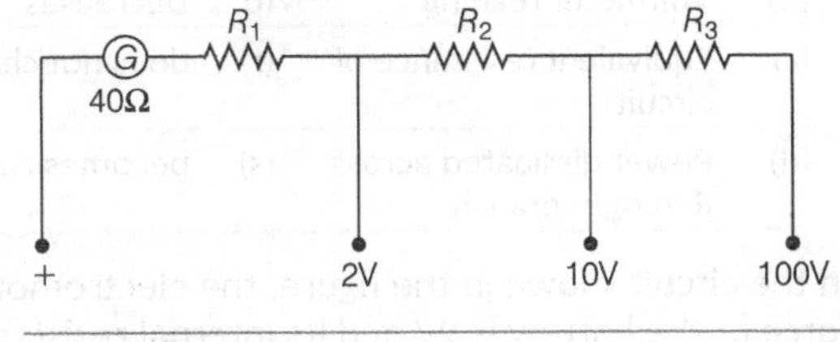

	Column I		Column II
(a)	Value of resistance R_1 in kΩ	(p)	100
(b)	Value of resistance R_3 in kΩ	(q)	2
(c)	Overall resistance of the meter in 100 V range in kΩ	(r)	1.96
(d)	Overall resistance of the meter in 2 V range in kΩ	(s)	90

2 Voltmeter of resistance 10 Ω and ammeter of resistance 10 Ω are attached in the following circuit with switches S_1 and S_2.

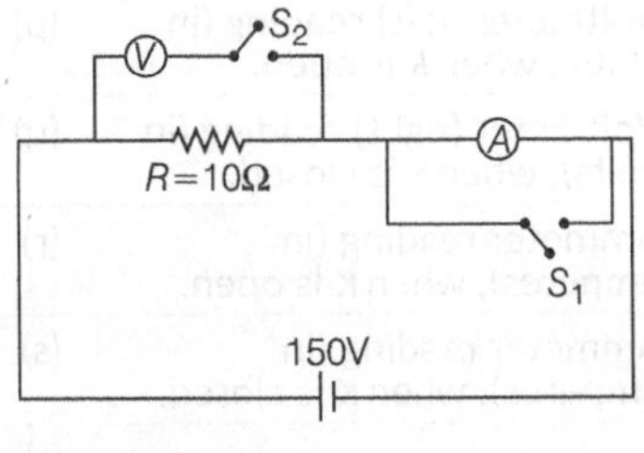

	Column I (switch position)		Column II (reading of voltmeter and ammeter)
(a)	S_1 open, S_2 closed	(p)	0, 7.5 A
(b)	S_1 closed, S_2 open	(q)	50 V, 10 A
(c)	S_1 open, S_2 open	(r)	0, 0
(d)	S_1 closed, S_2 closed	(s)	150 V, 0

3 The diagram shows a circuit with two identical resistors. The battery has a negligible internal resistance. What will the effect on the ammeter and voltmeter be if the switch *S* is closed?

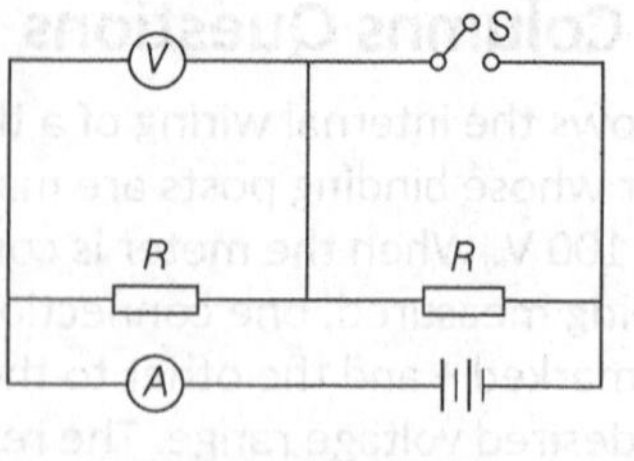

	Column I		Column II
(a)	Ammeter reading	(p)	Increases
(b)	Voltmeter reading	(q)	Decreases
(c)	Equivalent resistance of circuit	(r)	does not change
(d)	Power dissipated across R in right branch	(s)	becomes zero

4 In the circuit shown in the figure, the electromotive force of the battery is 9V and its internal resistance is 15 Ω. The two identical voltmeters and the ammeter can all be considered ideal (i.e. voltmeter is of very large resistance and ammeter is of negligible resistance).

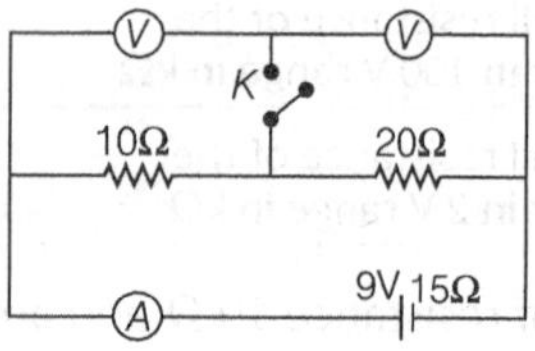

	Column-I		Column-II
(a)	Voltmeter (left) reading (in volts), when K is open.	(p)	4.5
(b)	Voltmeter (right) reading (in volts), when K is closed.	(q)	3
(c)	Ammeter reading (in amperes), when K is open.	(r)	4
(d)	Ammeter reading (in amperes), when K is closed.	(s)	0.2
		(t)	0

5 A potentiometer experiment set-up is shown in the given diagram. R is the point when there is no deflection in the galvanometer. E_1 is the source. Match the following.

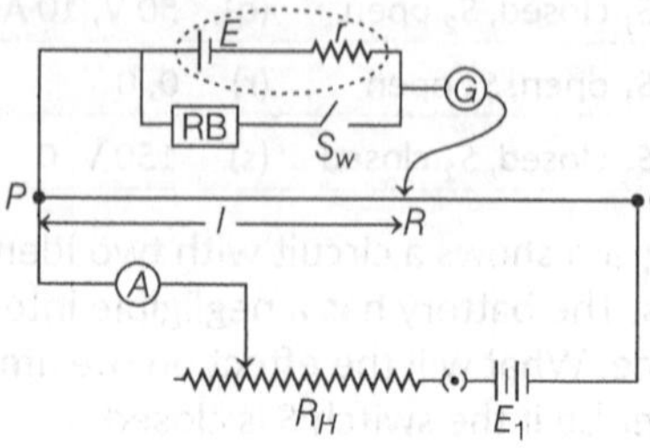

	Column I		Column II
(a)	If only emf of battery E_1 is increased	(p)	Point R will shift to left
(b)	If only resistance offered by rheostat is increased	(q)	Point R will shift to right
(c)	If resistance box (RB) is connected and resistance of RB is increased	(r)	Point R will remain unchanged
(d)	If an identical battery is connected in parallel to E	(s)	Point R may shift to left or right
		(t)	Reading of ammeter A changes

Numerical Value Questions

1 In the circuit shown, voltmeter is ideal but ammeter has a resistance 1 Ω. If the reading of ammeter and voltmeter are x A and yV respectively, then find value of $\frac{y}{x}$.

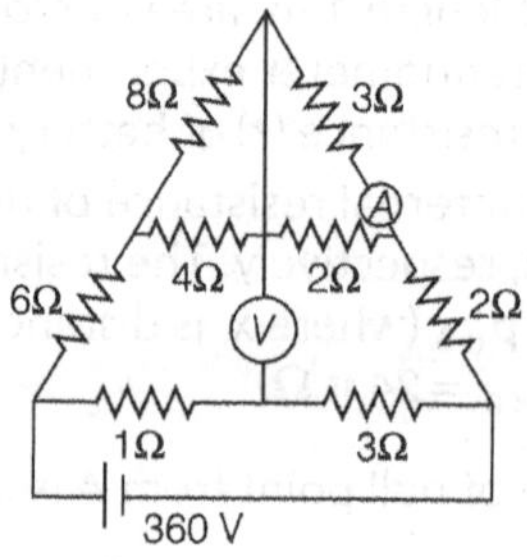

2 In the figure current in the galvanometer I is 10 mA, while the voltmeter reads a potential difference of 3 V. What is the current in galvanometer II (in mA)? The galvanometers are identical, the internal resistance of the battery is negligible.

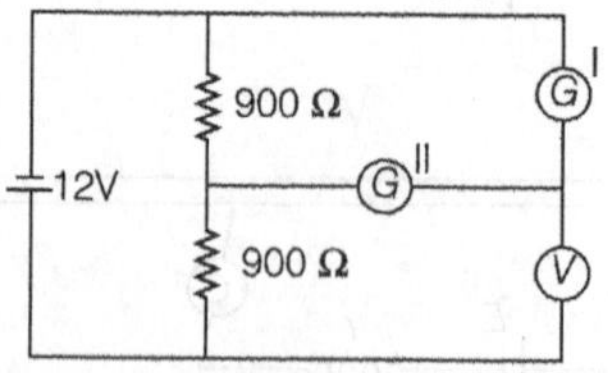

3 In the circuit shown below, all the voltmeters are identical and have very high resistance. Each resistor has the same resistance. The voltage of the ideal battery shown is 27 V. Find the reading of voltmeter V_3 (in volts).

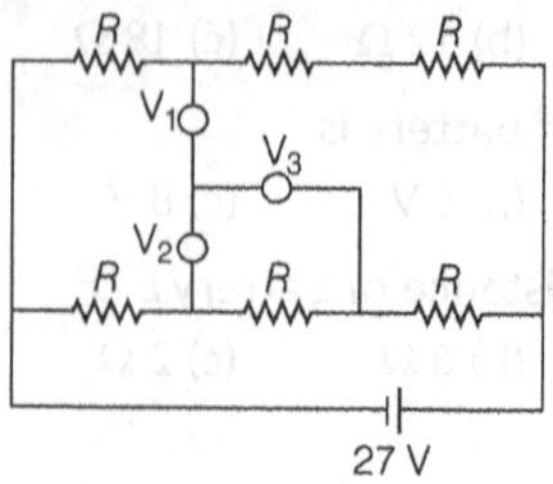

4 In the given circuit, the ammeters A_1 and A_2 are ideal and the ammeter A_3 has a resistance of 1.9×10^{-3} Ω. The reading in ampere of the ammeter A_2 is $\left(\frac{34}{K}\right)$. What is the value of K?

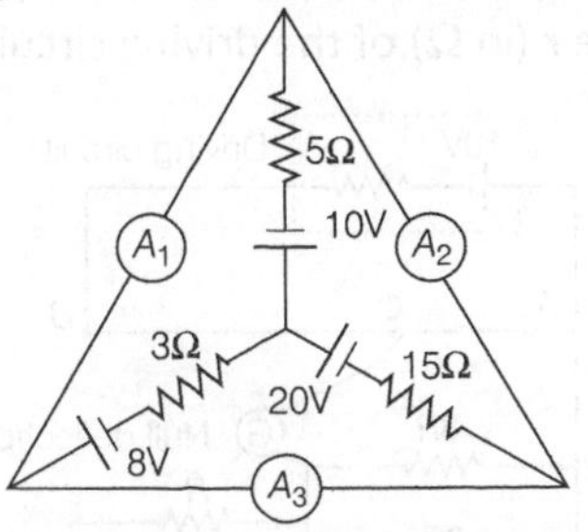

5 The figure shows a portion of an electric circuit. Resistors are known and are indicated on the diagram and the voltmeters are identical. If the voltmeters V_1 and V_2 read 7.5 V and 5.0 V, respectively. Find the reading of voltmeter V_3 (in V).

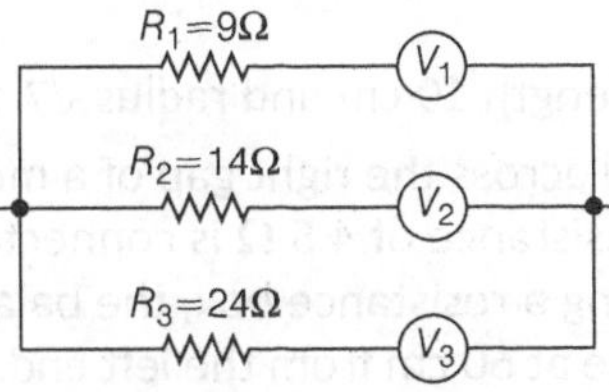

6 A constant voltage $V_0 (= 12 \text{ V})$ is applied to a potential divider of resistance $R (= 4\Omega)$, connected to an ideal ammeter. A constant resistor $r (= 2\ \Omega)$ is connected to the sliding contact of the potential divider (as shown). Find the minimum current (in A) measured by ammeter.

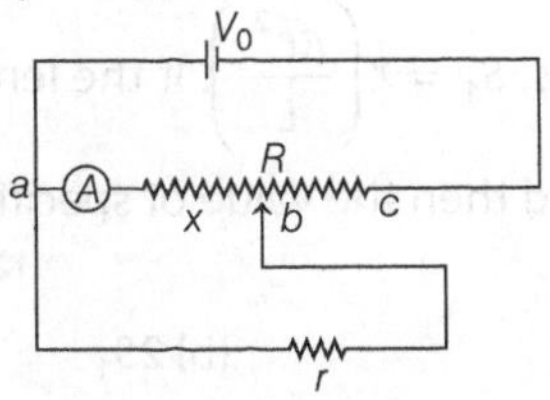

7 The circuit of a carbon arc lamp is shown in the figure (to ignite the lamp the carbon electrodes are touched together, then they are slowly drawn apart). The voltage across the gap between the carbon rods as a function of the current can be given by the following formula $V = A + B/I$, where A and B are constants.

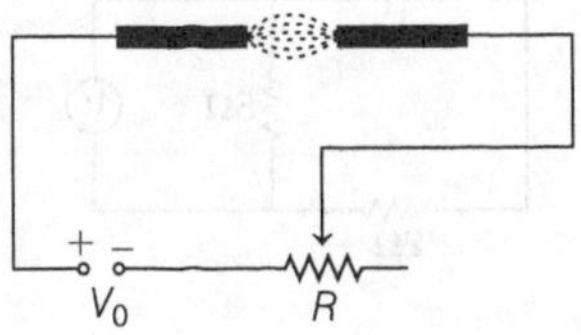

If the voltage of the battery V_0 can be considered constant, what is the maximum resistance(in Ω) of the rheostat R_{max}, that should be connected in series to ignite the lamp. Data $A = 40$ V, $B = 20$ W, $V_0 = 100$ V

8 Four wires of equal length 2 m are arranged as shown in diagram. Wires 2, 3 and 4 are of equal cross-sectional area and wire 1 is of half the cross-section of these wires. Jockey is moved through distance x cm on wire 1 to get null point, then find x.

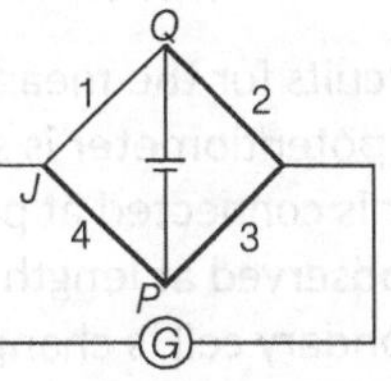

9 *ABCD* is a square frame made from different wires of same length and each having different uniform resistance per unit length. Resistances of wires forming sides *AB*, *BC*, *CD* and *DA* are 100 Ω, 400 Ω, 500 Ω and 200 Ω, respectively. An ideal cell is connected across *B* and *D*. A straight conducting wire containing a resistance and a galvanometer in series starts rotating about pivoted point *A* from initial position as shown with uniform angular velocity $\omega = \frac{\pi}{360}$ rad/s. One end of the straight wire (rotating) is pivoted at *A* and other end always in sliding contact with a side of the square. Find the time (in seconds) after start, when galvanometer shows zero deflection.

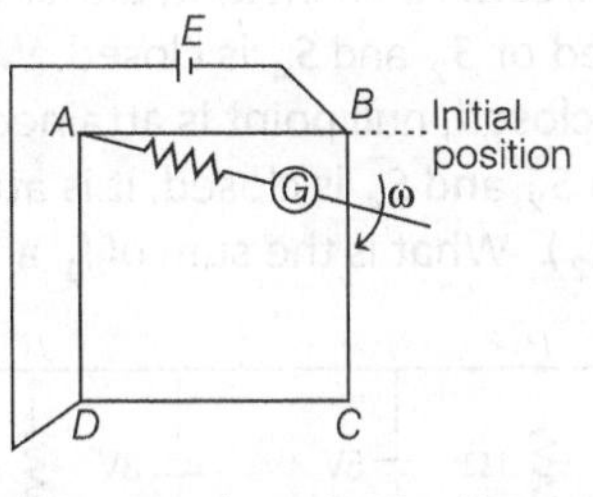

10 The circuit diagram given in the figure shows the experimental set-up for the measurement of unknown resistance by using a meter bridge. The wire connected between the points *P* and *Q* has non-uniform resistance such that resistance per unit length varies directly as the distance from the point *P*. Null point is obtained with the jockey *J* with R_1 and R_2 in the given position. On interchanging the positions R_1 and R_2 in the gaps, the jockey has to be displaced through a distance *D* from the previous position along the wire to establish the null point. If the ratio of $\frac{R_1}{R_2}=3$, find the value of D (in cm). Ignore any end corrections. (Take, $\sqrt{3}=1.7$)

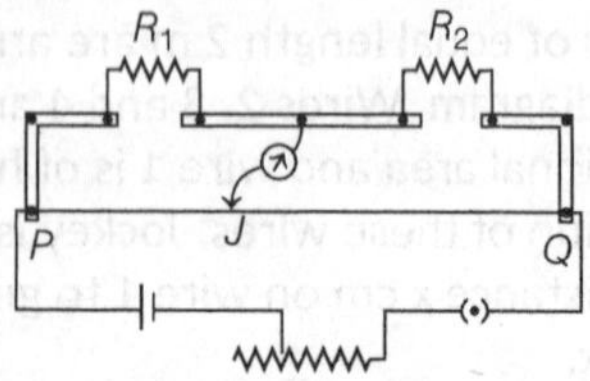

11 One of the circuits for the measurement of resistance by potentiometer is shown. The galvanometer is connected at point A and zero deflection is observed at length $PJ = 30$ cm. In second case, the secondary cell is changed.

Take, $E_s = 10$ V and $r = 1\,\Omega$ in 1st reading and $E_s = 5$ V and $r = 2\,\Omega$ in 2nd reading.

In second case, the zero deflection is observed at length $PJ = 10$ cm. What is the resistance R (in Ω)?

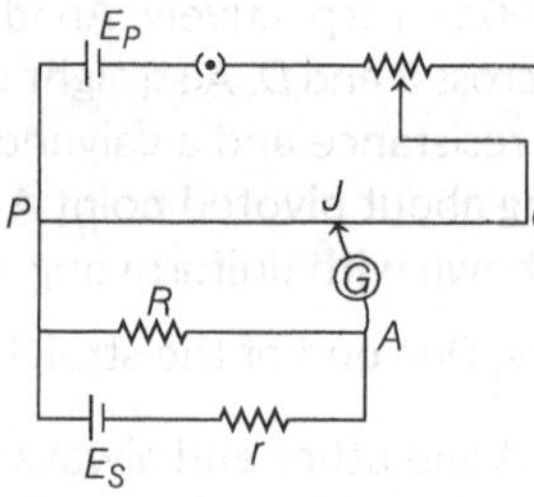

12 Figure shows a potentiometer connected to an external circuit. At an instant, either switch S_1 and S_3 is closed or S_2 and S_4 is closed. When switch S_1 and S_3 is closed, null point is attained at J_1 ($AJ_1 = l_1$) and when S_2 and S_4 is closed, it is attained at J_2 ($BJ_2 = l_2$). What is the sum of l_1 and l_2 in metre.

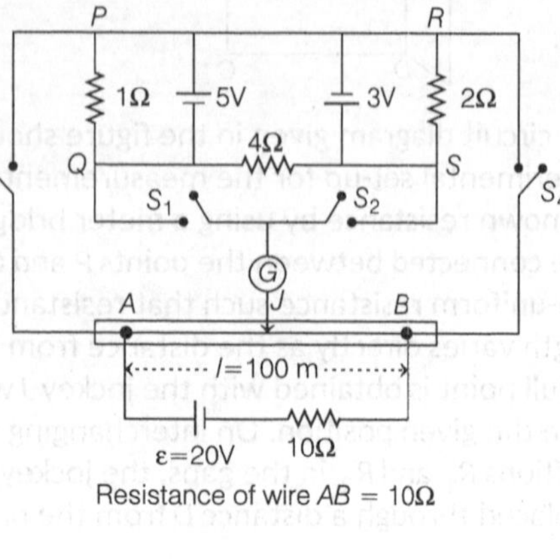

Resistance of wire AB = 10Ω

13 In the potentiometer circuit shown here, a potentiometer wire AB of length 100 cm and resistance 8 Ω is used. While measuring potential difference between points X and Y, balancing length AC is obtained to be equal to 25 cm. What is internal resistance r (in Ω) of the driving circuit?

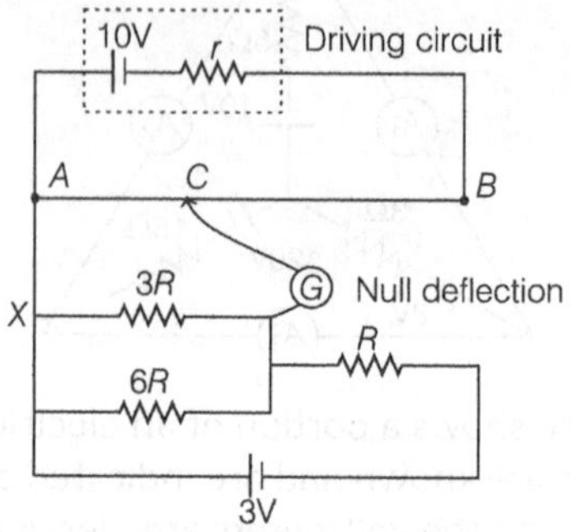

Previous Year's Questions

JEE Main

1 A wire of length 10 cm and radius $\sqrt{7}\times10^{-4}$ m is connected across the right gap of a meter bridge. When a resistance of 4.5 Ω is connected on the left gap by using a resistance box, the balance length is found to be at 60 cm from the left end. If the resistivity of the wire is $R\times10^{-7}\,\Omega$m, then value of R is **[2024, 27 Jan Shift-I]**

(a) 63 (b) 70 (c) 66 (d) 35

2 Wheatstone bridge principle is used to measure the specific resistance (S_1) of given wire, having length L, radius r. If X is the resistance of wire, then specific resistance is, $S_1 = X\left(\frac{\pi r^2}{L}\right)$. If the length of the wire gets doubled then the value of specific resistance will be **[2024, 29 Jan Shift-I]**

(a) $\frac{S_1}{4}$ (b) $2S_1$

(c) S_1 (d) $\frac{S_1}{2}$

3 As shown in the figure, the voltmeter reads 2 V across 5 Ω resistor. The resistance of the voltmeter is .... Ω. **[2023, 6 April Shift-I]**

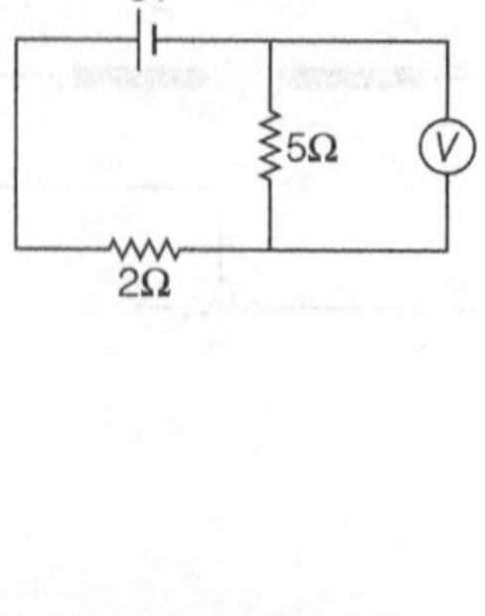

4 Two identical cells each of emf 1.5 V are connected in series across a 10 Ω resistance. An ideal voltmeter connected across 10 Ω resistance reads 1.5 V. The internal resistance of each cell is .... Ω. **[2023, 11 April Shift-II]**

5 With the help of potentiometer we can determine the value of emf of a given cell. The sensitivity of the potentiometer is

A. directly proportional to the length of the potentiometer wire
B. directly proportional to the potential gradient of the wire
C. inversely proportional to the potential gradient of the wire
D. inversely proportional to the length of the potentiometer wire

Choose the correct option for the above statements **[2023, 29 Jan Shift-II]**

(a) B and D only (b) A and C only
(c) C only (d) A only

6 In an experiment to find emf of a cell using potentiometer, the length of null point for a cell of emf 1.5 V is found to be 60 cm. If this cell is replaced by another cell of emf E, the length of null point increases by 40 cm. The value of E is $\frac{x}{10}$ V. The value of x is .... **[2023, 1 Feb Shift-I]**

7 In the given figure of meter bridge experiment, the balancing length AC corresponding to null deflection of the galvanometer is 40 cm. The balancing length, if the radius of the wire AB is doubled, will be .... cm. **[2022, 27 July Shift-II]**

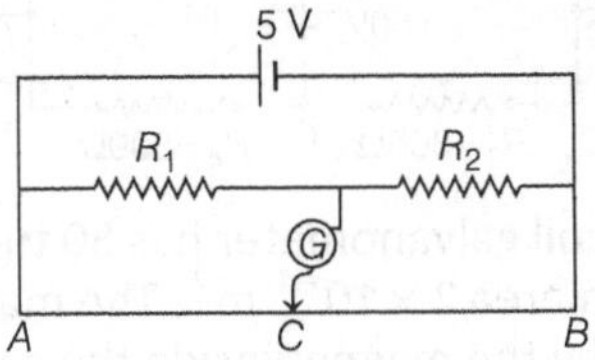

8 In a potentiometer arrangement, a cell of emf 1.20 V gives a balance point at 36 cm length of wire. This cell is now replaced by another cell of emf 1.80 V. The difference in balancing length of potentiometer wire in above conditions will be ...... cm. **[2022, 25 July Shift-II]**

9 A meter bridge setup is shown in the figure. It is used to determine an unknown resistance R using a given resistor of 15 Ω. The galvanometer G shows null deflection when tapping key is at 43 cm mark from end A. If the end correction for end A is 2 cm, then the determined value of R will be ...... Ω. **[2022, 28 June Shift-I]**

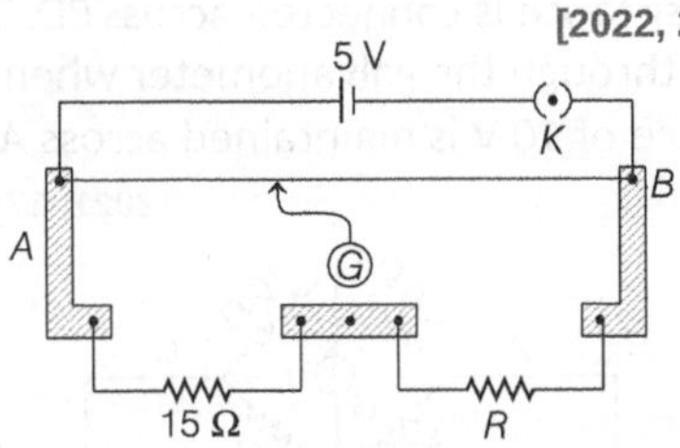

10 Current measured by the ammeter A in the reported circuit when no current flows through 10 Ω resistance, will be ...... A. **[2022, 28 June Shift-I]**

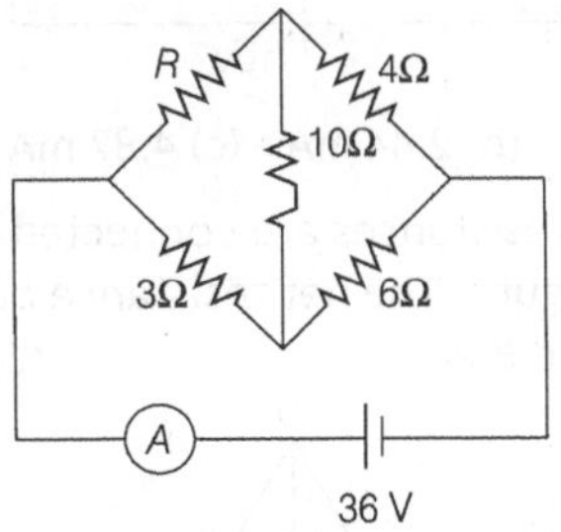

11 A cell, shunted by a 8 Ω resistance, is balanced across a potentiometer wire of length 3m. The balancing length is 2 m when the cell is shunted by 4 Ω resistance. The value of internal resistance of the cell will be ...... Ω. **[2022, 27 June Shift-I]**

12 In a potentiometer arrangement, a cell gives a balancing point at 75 cm length of wire. This cell is now replaced by another cell of unknown emf. If the ratio of the emf's of two cells, respectively is 3 : 2, the difference in the balancing length of the potentiometer wire in above two cases will be ...... cm. **[2022, 24 June Shift I]**

13 In the given potentiometer circuit arrangement, the balancing length AC is measured to be 250 cm. When the galvanometer connection is shifted from point (1) to point (2) in the given diagram, the balancing length becomes 400 cm. The ratio of the EMF of two cells, $\frac{\varepsilon_1}{\varepsilon_2}$ is **[2021, 25 July Shift-II]**

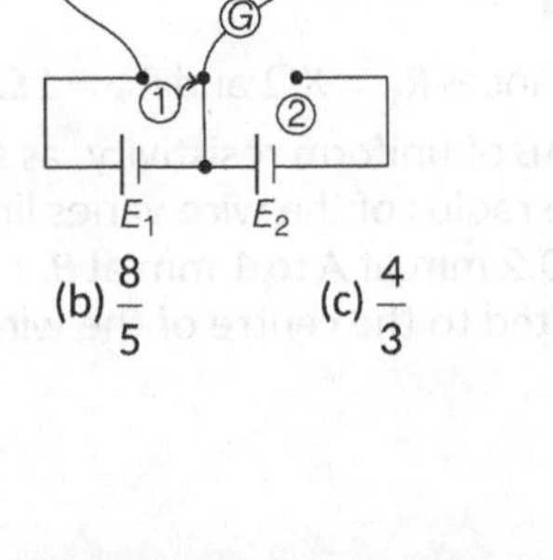

(a) $\frac{5}{3}$ (b) $\frac{8}{5}$ (c) $\frac{4}{3}$ (d) $\frac{3}{2}$

14 The four arms of a Wheatstone bridge have resistances as shown in the figure. A galvanometer of 15 Ω resistance is connected across BD. Calculate the current through the galvanometer when a potential difference of 10 V is maintained across AC.

[2021, 17 March Shift-II]

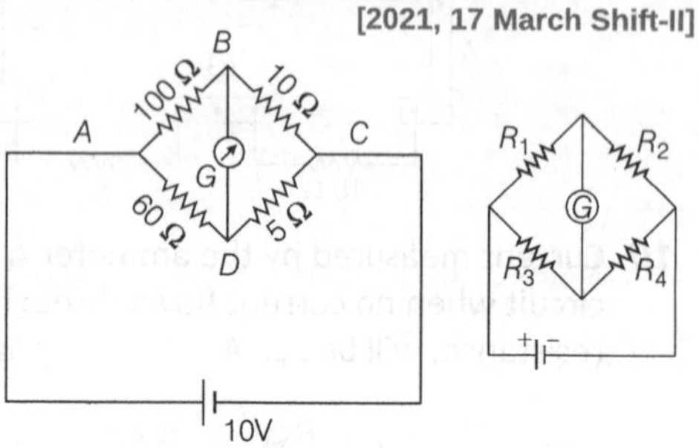

(a) 2.44 μA (b) 2.44 mA (c) 4.87 mA (d) 4.87 μA

15 Five equal resistances are connected in a network as shown in figure. The net resistance between the points A and B is

[2021, 26 Feb Shift-I]

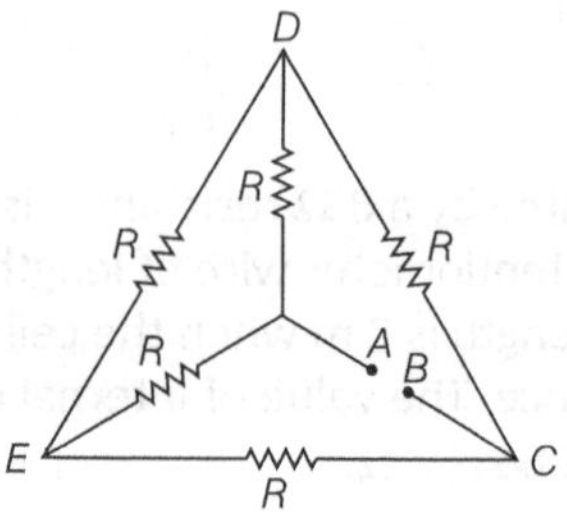

(a) $2R$ (b) $R/2$ (c) $3R/2$ (d) R

16 Consider a 72 cm long wire AB as shown in the figure. The galvanometer jockey is placed at P on AB at a distance x cm from A. The galvanometer shows zero deflection.

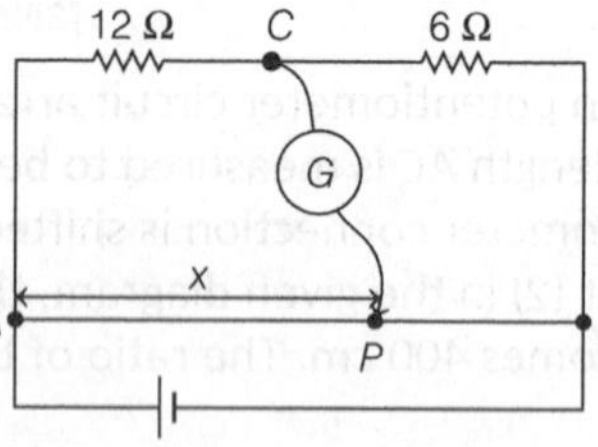

The value of x, to the nearest integer, is ....

[2021, 18 March Shift-II]

JEE Advanced

1. Two resistances $R_1 = X\Omega$ and $R_2 = 1\Omega$ are connected to a wire AB of uniform resistivity, as shown in the figure. The radius of the wire varies linearly along its axis from 0.2 mm at A to 1 mm at B. A galvanometer (G) connected to the centre of the wire, 50 cm from each end along its axis, shows zero deflection when A and B are connected to a battery. The value of X is ....

(2022 Adv.)

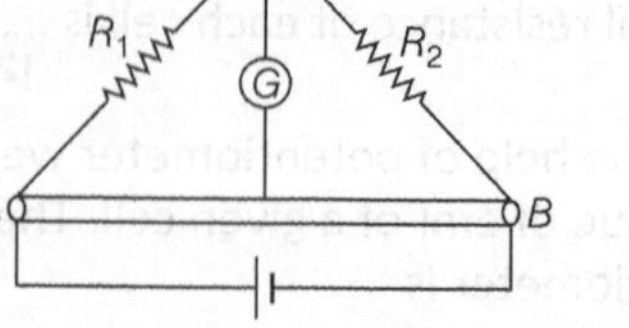

2. In order to measure the internal resistance r_1 of a cell of emf E, a meter bridge of wire resistance $R = 50\ \Omega$, a resistance $R_0/2$, another cell of emf $E/2$ (internal resistance r) and a galvanometer G are used in a circuit, as shown in the figure. If the null point is found at $l = 72$ cm, then the value of $r_1 =$ ________ Ω.

(2021 Adv.)

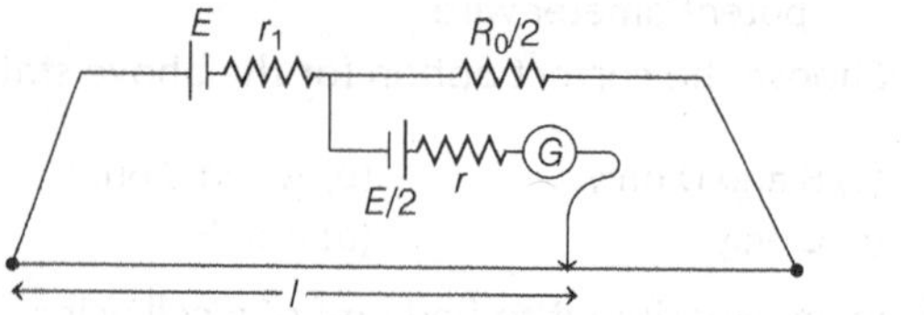

3. In the balanced condition, the values of the resistances of the four arms of a Wheatstone bridge are shown in the figure below. The resistance R_3 has temperature coefficient $0.0004°C^{-1}$. If the temperature of R_3 is increased by 100°C, the voltage developed between S and T will be ________ volt.

(2020 Adv.)

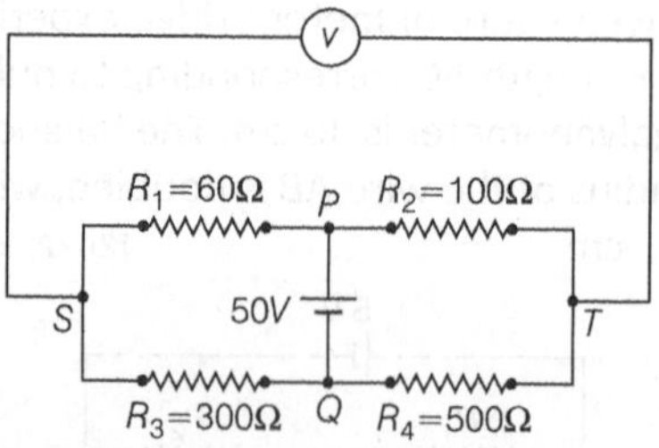

4 A moving coil galvanometer has 50 turns and each turn has an area $2 \times 10^{-4}\ m^2$. The magnetic field produced by the magnet inside the galvanometer is 0.02 T. The torsional constant of the suspension wire is 10^{-4} N-m rad^{-1}. When a current flows through the galvanometer, a full scale deflection occurs, if the coil rotates by 0.2 rad. The resistance of the coil of the galvanometer is 50 Ω. This galvanometer is to be converted into an ammeter capable of measuring current in the range 0-1.0 A. For this purpose, a shunt resistance is to be added in parallel to the galvanometer. The value of this shunt resistance in ohms, is ....

[JEE Advanced 2019]

5 Consider two identical galvanometers and two identical resistors with resistance R. If the internal resistance of the galvanometers $R_c < R/2$, which of the following statement(s) about any one of the galvanometers is (are) true? **[JEE Advanced 2016]**

(a) The maximum voltage range is obtained when all the components are connected in series

(b) The maximum voltage range is obtained when the two resistors and one galvanometer are connected in series, and the second galvanometer is connected in parallel to the first galvanometer

(c) The maximum current range is obtained when all the components are connected in parallel

(d) The maximum current range is obtained when the two galvanometers are connected in series, and the combination is connected in parallel with both the resistors

6 During an experiment with a meter bridge, the galvanometer shows a null point when the jockey is pressed at 40.0 cm using a standard resistance of 90 Ω, as shown in the scale used in the meter bridge is 1 mm. The unknown resistance is **[JEE Advanced 2014]**

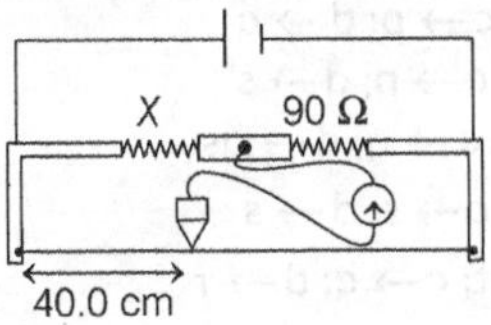

(a) $(60 \pm 0.15)\ \Omega$ (b) $(135 \pm 0.56)\ \Omega$

(c) $(60 \pm 0.25)\ \Omega$ (d) $(135 \pm 0.23)\ \Omega$

7 A galvanometer gives full scale deflection with 0.006 A current. By connecting it to a 4990 Ω resistance, it can be converted into a voltmeter of range 0-30 V. If connected to a $\frac{2n}{249}\ \Omega$ resistance, it becomes an ammeter of range 0-1.5 A. The value of n is .... **[JEE Advanced 2014]**

8 A meter bridge is set-up as shown in figure, to determine an unknown resistance X using a standard 10 Ω resistor. The galvanometer shows null point when tapping-key is at 52 cm mark. The end-corrections are 1 cm and 2 cm respectively for the ends A and B. The determined value of X is **[JEE Advanced 2011]**

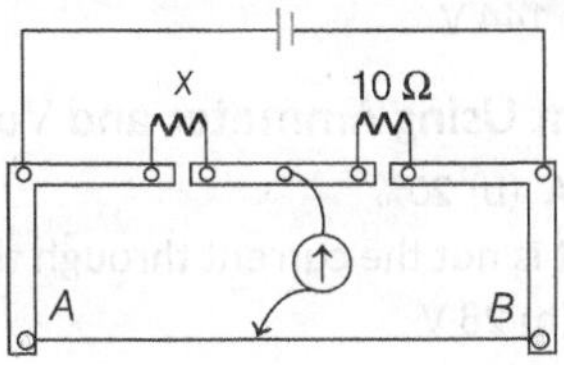

(a) 10.2 Ω (b) 10.6 Ω (c) 10.8 Ω (d) 11.1 Ω

9 To verify Ohm's law, a student is provided with a test resistor R_T, a high resistance R_1, a small resistance R_2, two identical galvanometers G_1 and G_2, and a variable voltage source V. The correct circuit to carry out the experiment is **[JEE Advanced 2010]**

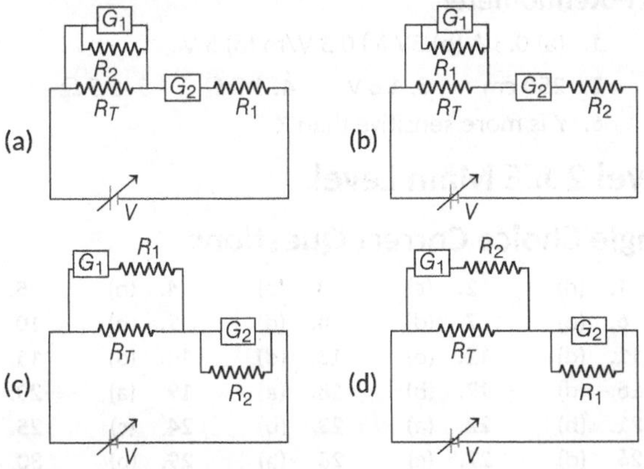

Answers

Level 1 Starter Level

7.1 Galvanometer, Ammeter and Voltmeter

1. 11 Ω 2. 48 Ω
3. (a) 0.06 Ω in parallel (b) 4970 Ω in series
4. 79.995 Ω
5. (a) 0.01 Ω in parallel (b) 9.995kΩ in series
6. 233.3 Ω; 144 V

7.2 Measurement Using Ammeter and Voltmeter

1. (a) 5A, 4A (b) 20%
2. 4A, No, it is not the current through the 6 Ω resistor.
3. (a) 24 V (b) 28 V
4. 400 Ω, 3.2 V, 3.238 V
5. 12 V 6. (a) 1 A, 40 V (b) 0.814 A, 44.8 V

7.3 Metre Bridge

1. 82.5 Ω 2. $R_1 = \frac{10}{3}\Omega$, $R_2 = 5\Omega$ 3. 10.6 Ω
4. The null point at *B* will give most accurate reading

7.4 Potentiometer

1. (a) 0.5 A (b) 5V (c) 0.5 V/m (d) 5 V
2. 250 cm 3. 1.6 V 4. 1.7 Ω 5. 1.5 Ω
6. *Y* is more sensitive than *X*

Level 2 JEE Main Level

Single Choice Correct Questions

1. (d)	2. (c)	3. (a)	4. (b)	5. (c)
6. (d)	7. (d)	8. (d)	9. (b)	10. (b)
11. (d)	12. (d)	13. (d)	14. (d)	15. (b)
16. (d)	17. (b)	18. (a)	19. (a)	20. (d)
21. (b)	22. (a)	23. (b)	24. (c)	25. (d)
26. (d)	27. (c)	28. (a)	29. (b)	30. (b)
31. (c)	32. (b)	33. (c)	34. (a)	35. (b)
36. (d)	37. (a)	38. (b)	39. (c)	40. (a)
41. (d)	42. (b)	43. (b)	44. (c)	45. (b)
46. (c)	47. (a)	48. (b)	49. (c)	50. (a)
51. (c)				

Numerical Value Questions

1. (3)	2. (6)	3. (2)	4. (290)	5. (30)
6. (7)	7. (6600)	8. (3)	9. (80)	10. (3)
11. (3)	12. (0.2)	13. (7.2)	14. (45)	15. (12)
16. (1)				

Level 3 JEE Advanced Level

Single Choice Correct Questions

1. (d)	2. (d)	3. (a)	4. (b)	5. (b)
6. (a)	7. (b)	8. (a)	9. (b)	10. (d)
11. (d)	12. (d)	13. (c)	14. (a)	15. (a)
16. (b)	17. (c)	18. (c)	19. (a)	20. (a)
21. (c)	22. (a)	23. (c)	24. (d)	25. (c)

Multiple Choice(s) Correct Questions

1. (abc)	2. (bd)	3. (abd)	4. (acd)	5. (ac)
6. (ac)	7. (acd)	8. (abcd)	9. (acd)	10. (abc)
11. (ab)	12. (ab)	13. (abc)	14. (abcd)	

Comprehension Based Questions

1. (b)	2. (c)	3. (a)	4. (b)	5. (c)
6. (b)	7. (c)	8. (b)	9. (b)	10. (c)
11. (d)	12. (d)	13. (b)	14. (c)	15. (d)

Match the Columns Questions

1. a → r; b → s; c → p; d → q
2. a → q; b → r; c → p; d → s
3. a → p; b → p; c → q; d → qs
4. a → q; b → r; c → s; d → s
5. a → pt; b → qt; c → q; d → r

Numerical Value Questions

1. 17	2. 2.22	3. 6	4. 27	5. 3
6. 2	7. 45	8. 50	9. 74	10. 35
11. 1	12. 80	13. 2		

Previous Year's Questions

JEE Main

1. (c)	2. (c)	3. (20)	4. (5)	5. (b)
6. (25)	7. (40)	8. (18)	9. (19)	10. (10)
11. (8)	12. (25)	13. (a)	14. (c)	15. (d)
16. (48)				

JEE Advanced

1. (5)	2. (3)	3. (0.27)	4. (5.55)	5. (a,c)
6. (c)	7. (5)	8. (b)	9. (c)	

SOLUTIONS

Level 1

7.1 Galvanometer, Ammeter and Voltmeter

1.

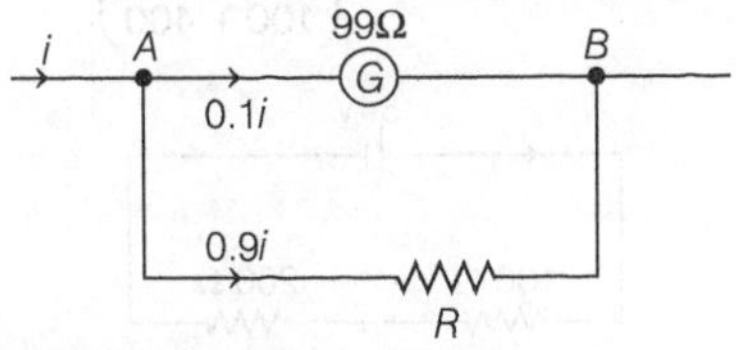

Let current in the main circuit be i.

Current passing through galvanometer $= i \times \dfrac{10}{100} = 0.1\,i$

Current passing through shunt $= i - 0.1\,i = 0.9\,i$

$$V_A - V_B = (0.1\,i)\,99 = (0.9\,i)R$$

$$\Rightarrow \quad R = 11\,\Omega$$

2. Let current be i through the galvanometer when deflection is 60 divisions.

So, when deflection falls to 12 divisions, current through galvanometer will be $\dfrac{i}{5}$.

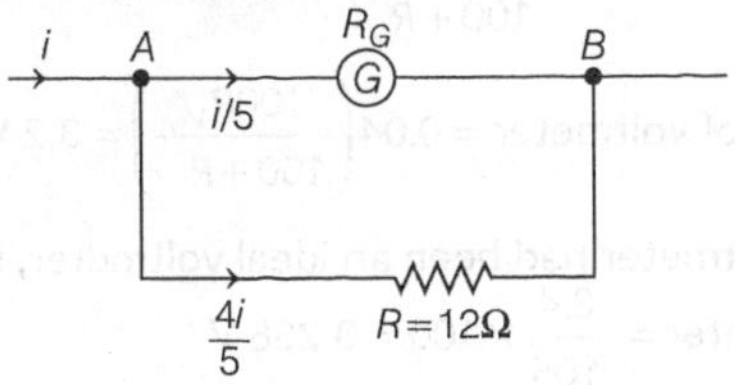

$$V_A - V_B = \left(\frac{i}{5}\right)R_G = \left(\frac{4i}{5}\right)12 \quad \Rightarrow \quad R_G = 48\,\Omega$$

3. (a)

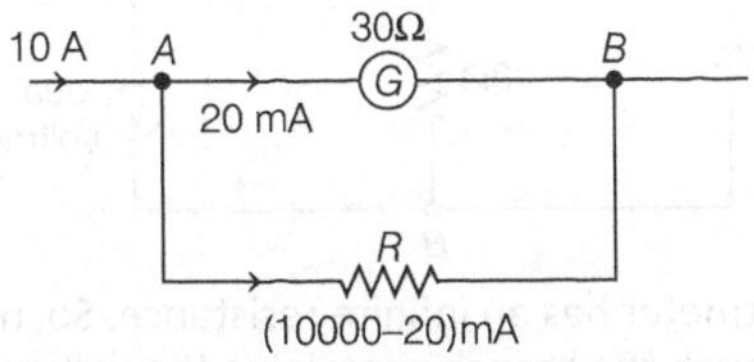

$$V_A - V_B = (20\text{ mA})30 = (10000 - 20)\text{ mA} \times R$$

$$\Rightarrow \quad R = \frac{600}{(10000 - 20)}\,\Omega$$

$$\Rightarrow \quad R \simeq 0.06\,\Omega$$

So, a resistance of 0.06 Ω should be connected in parallel to the galvanometer.

(b)

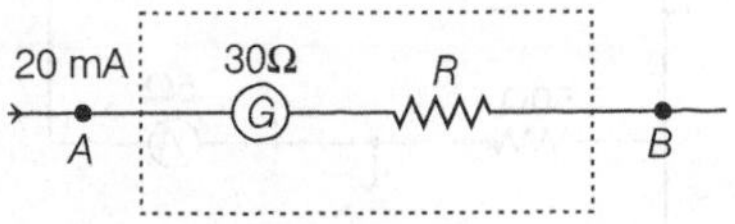

$$V_A - V_B = (20 \times 10^{-3})(30 + R) = 100$$

$$\Rightarrow \quad R = 4970\,\Omega$$

So, a resistance of 4970Ω should be connected in series to the galvanometer.

4.

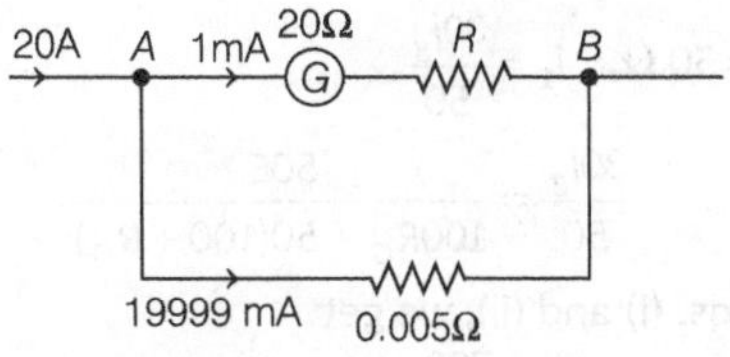

$$V_A - V_B = (1\text{ mA})\,(20 + R) = (20000 - 1)\text{ mA} \times (0.005)$$

$$\Rightarrow \quad R = 79.995\,\Omega$$

5.

$$i_g = \frac{100}{10} = 10\text{ mA}$$

$$V_g = \frac{100}{2} = 50\text{ mV}$$

$$R_g = \frac{V_g}{i_g} = \frac{50\text{ mV}}{10\text{ mA}} = 5\,\Omega$$

(a)

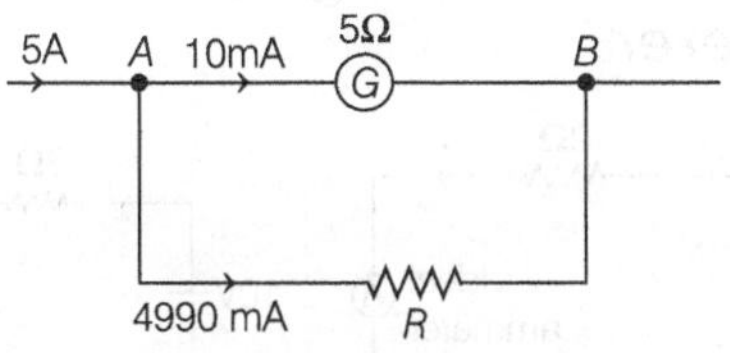

$$V_A - V_B = (10\text{ mA})5 = (4990\text{ mA})R \quad \Rightarrow \quad R = 0.01\,\Omega$$

So, a resistance of 0.01 Ω should be connected in parallel to the galvanometer.

(b) Full scale deflection $= 100 \times 1 = 100$ V

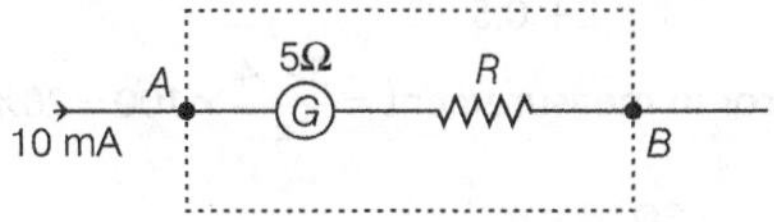

$$V_A - V_B = (10\text{ mA})\,(R + 5) = 100\text{ V}$$

$$\Rightarrow \quad R + 5 = 10000 \quad \Rightarrow \quad R = 9.995\text{ k}\Omega$$

So, a resistance of 9.995 kΩ should be connected in series to the galvanometer.

6.

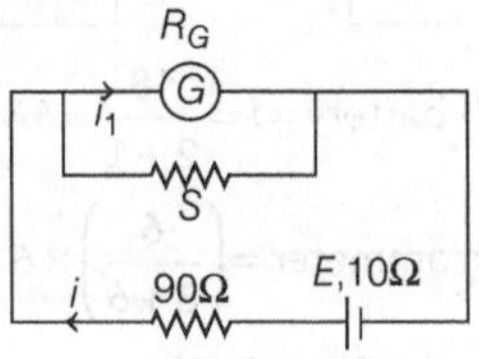

Let full scale deflection current of galvanometer be i_g.

i = current through battery

$$= \frac{E}{90 + 10 + \dfrac{R_G S}{R_G + S}} = \frac{E(R_G + S)}{100R_G + (100 + R_G S)}$$

i_1 = current through galvanometer

$$= i \times \frac{S}{R_G + R_S} = \frac{ES}{100R_G + (100 + R_G)S}$$

when, $S = 10\,\Omega, i_1 = \dfrac{9i_g}{50}$

$$\Rightarrow \quad \frac{9i_g}{50} = \frac{10E}{100R_G + 10(100 + R_G)} \quad \text{...(i)}$$

when $S = 50\,\Omega$, $i_1 = \dfrac{30i_g}{50}$

$$\Rightarrow \quad \frac{30i_g}{50} = \frac{50E}{100R_G + 50(100 + R_G)} \quad \text{...(ii)}$$

Solving Eqs. (i) and (ii), we get

$$R_G = \frac{700}{3}\,\Omega = 233.33\,\Omega$$

Now, $i_g = 300$ mA

$$\Rightarrow \quad \frac{9 \times 300 \times 10^{-3}}{50} = \frac{10E}{100 \times \frac{700}{3} + 10\left(100 + \frac{700}{3}\right)}$$

$$\Rightarrow \quad E = 144\text{ V}$$

7.2 Measurement using Ammeter and Voltmeter

1. (a)

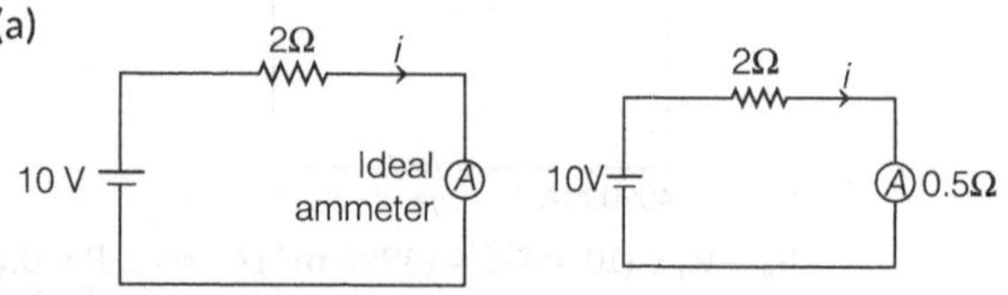

In circuit (a), $i = \dfrac{10}{2} = 5\text{A}$

In circuit (b), $i = \dfrac{10}{2 + 0.5} = 4\text{A}$

(b) % error in measurement $= \dfrac{5 - 4}{5} \times 100 = 20\%$

2.

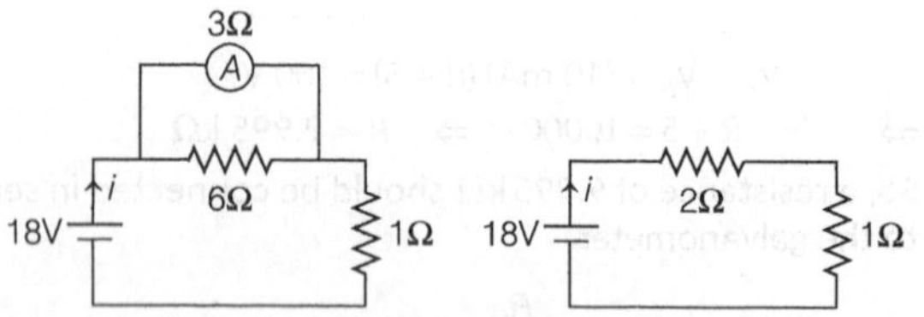

Current through battery $= i = \dfrac{18}{2 + 1} = 6\text{A}$

Current through ammeter $= \left(\dfrac{6}{3 + 6}\right) \times 6 = 4\text{A}$

No, it is not current through 6Ω.

3. (a)

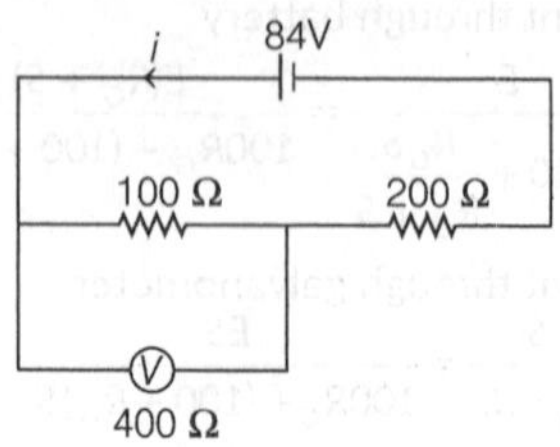

Equivalent resistance $= \dfrac{100 \times 400}{100 + 400} + 200 = 280\,\Omega$

Current through battery $= \dfrac{84}{280} = 0.3\text{A}$

Reading of voltmeter $= i\left(\dfrac{100 \times 400}{100 + 400}\right) = 0.3 \times 80 = 24\text{ V}$

(b)

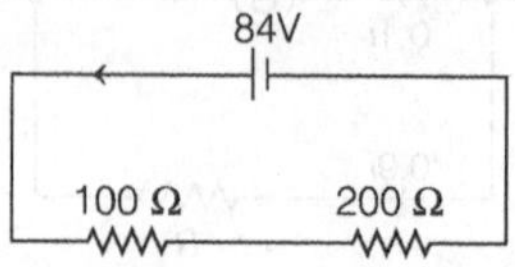

Potential difference across 100 Ω $= \dfrac{84}{300} \times 100 = 28\text{ V}$

4.

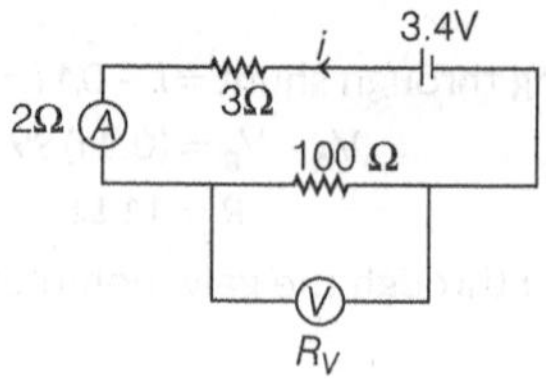

Current, $i = \dfrac{3.4}{3 + 2 + \dfrac{100R_V}{100 + R_V}} = 0.04 \quad \Rightarrow R_V = 400\,\Omega$

Reading of voltmeter $= 0.04\left(\dfrac{100R_V}{100 + R_V}\right) = 3.2\text{ V}$

If the voltmeter had been an ideal voltmeter, then reading of voltmeter $= \dfrac{3.4}{105} \times 100 = 3.238\text{ V}$

5.

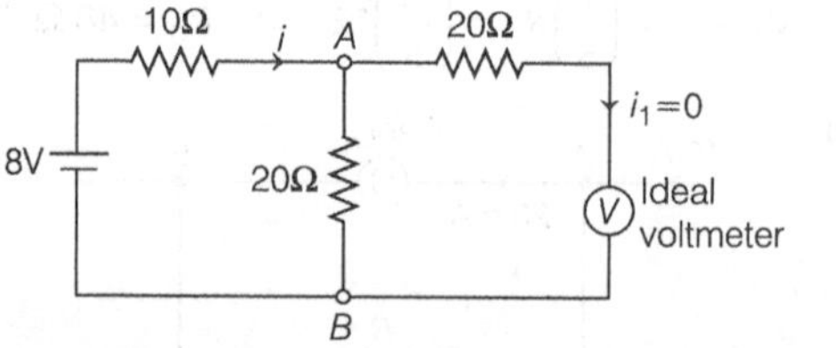

Ideal voltmeter has an infinite resistance. So, no current will pass through the branch containing the voltmeter.

$$i = \frac{18}{10 + 20} = 0.6\text{ A}$$

$$V_A - V_B = 20 \times 0.6 = 12\text{ V}$$

Reading of voltmeter $= V_A - V_B = 12\text{ V}$

6. (a)

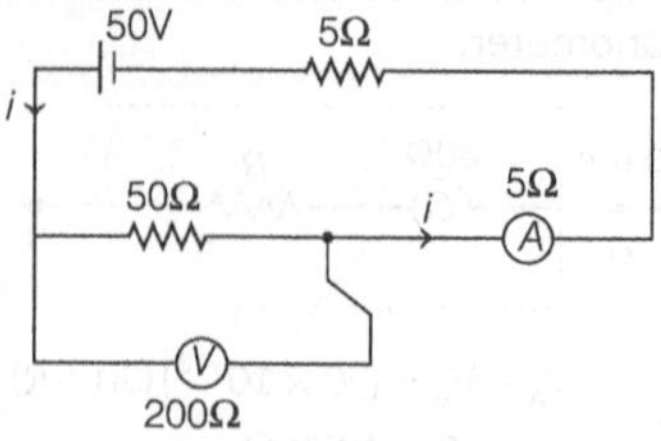

Equivalent resistance across battery $= 5 + 5 + \dfrac{50 \times 200}{50 + 200}$

$$= 50\,\Omega$$

Reading of ammeter $= i = \frac{50}{50} = 1\text{ A}$

Reading of voltmeter $= i\left(\frac{50 \times 200}{50 + 200}\right) = 40\text{ V}$

(b)

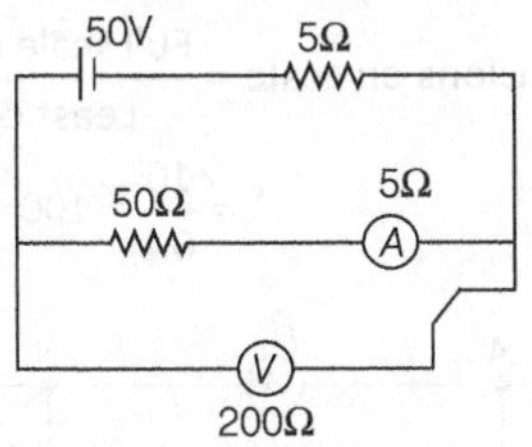

Equivalent resistance across battery $= 5 + \frac{200 \times 55}{200 + 55}$

$$= \frac{2455}{51}\,\Omega$$

Current through battery $= \frac{50}{\frac{2455}{51}} = \frac{510}{491}\text{ A}$

Reading of ammeter $= \frac{510}{491} \times \frac{200}{(200 + 55)} = 0.814\text{ A}$

Reading of voltmeter $= \frac{510}{491} \times \frac{200 \times 55}{(200 + 55)} = 44.8\text{ V}$

7.3 Meter Bridge

1. At null deflection,

$$55(100 - 40) = R \times 40$$

$$\Rightarrow \quad R = 82.5\ \Omega$$

2. $R_1 \times 60 = R_2 \times 40$ ...(i)

$$R_1 \times 50 = \left(\frac{10R_2}{10 + R_2}\right) \times 50 \quad \text{...(ii)}$$

Solving Eqs. (i) and (ii), we get

$$R_1 = \frac{10}{3}\,\Omega \text{ and } R_2 = 5\,\Omega$$

3. From given conditions, $l_1 = 52 + 1 = 53$ cm

$$l_2 = 48 + 2 = 50\text{ cm}$$

So, by balancing condition, $\frac{l_1}{l_2} = \frac{X}{R}$

$$\Rightarrow \quad \frac{53}{50} = \frac{X}{10} \quad \Rightarrow \quad X = 10.6\,\Omega$$

4. At null point,

$$Xl_2 = Rl_1 \quad \Rightarrow \quad X = \frac{Rl_1}{l_2}$$

$$\frac{\Delta X}{X} = \frac{\Delta l_1}{l_1} - \frac{\Delta l_2}{l_2}$$

$$= \frac{\Delta l_1}{l_1} - \frac{\Delta(100 - l_1)}{100 - l_1} \quad \{\because l_1 + l_2 = 100\}$$

$$= \frac{\Delta l_1}{l_1} + \frac{\Delta l_1}{100 - l_1} = \Delta l_1\left(\frac{1}{l_1} + \frac{1}{100 - l_1}\right)$$

For minimum error in the measurement of X,

$$\frac{d}{dl_1}(\Delta X) = 0$$

$$\Rightarrow \quad \Delta l_1\left(-\frac{1}{l_1^2} + \frac{1}{(100 - l_1)^2}\right) = 0 \Rightarrow l_1 = 50\text{ cm}$$

So, most accurate reading will be at B.

7.4 Potentiometer

1.

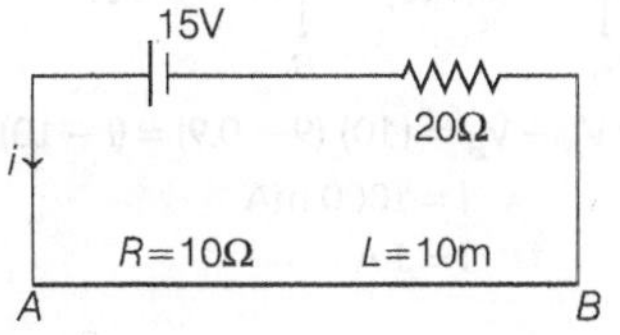

(a) $i = \frac{15}{20 + 10} = 0.5\text{ A}$

(b) Potential drop across potentiometer wire AB $= 0.5 \times 10 = 5\text{V}$

(c) Potential gradient $= \frac{5}{10} = 0.5$ V/m

(d) Maximum potential difference which can be measured with the potentiometer = Potential drop across wire AB $= 5\text{ V}$

2. Current in the primary circuit $= \frac{10}{9 + 1} = 1\text{ A}$

Potential drop across, $AB = 1 \times 9 = 9\text{V}$

Potential gradient $= x = \frac{9}{450} = \frac{1}{50}$ V/cm

For no deflection, $\varepsilon = xl$

$$\Rightarrow \quad 5 = \left(\frac{1}{50}\right)l \quad \Rightarrow \quad l = 250\text{ cm}$$

3. $$\frac{\varepsilon_1}{\varepsilon_2} = \frac{l_1}{l_2}$$

$$\Rightarrow \quad \varepsilon_1 = \varepsilon_2\left(\frac{l_1}{l_2}\right) = 1.12 \times \frac{80}{56} = 1.6\text{ V}$$

4. Let current in the secondary circuit be i.

$$i(10) = X(58.3) \quad \text{...(i)}$$

$$i(10 + X) = X(68.5) \quad \text{...(ii)}$$

Dividing Eq. (ii) by Eq. (i), we get

$$\frac{10 + X}{10} = \frac{68.5}{58.3} \Rightarrow X = 1.7\,\Omega$$

5. $r = \left(\frac{l_1}{l_2} - 1\right)R = \left(\frac{75}{60} - 1\right)6 = 1.5\,\Omega$

6. Sensitivity of a potentiometer is inversely proportional to its potential gradient.

Potential gradient $= \frac{dV}{dl}$ is lesser for Y.

So, Y is more sensitive than X and hence Y will give more accurate measurement.

Level 2

Single Choice Correct Questions

1. Resistance of an ideal voltmeter is infinite.

2.

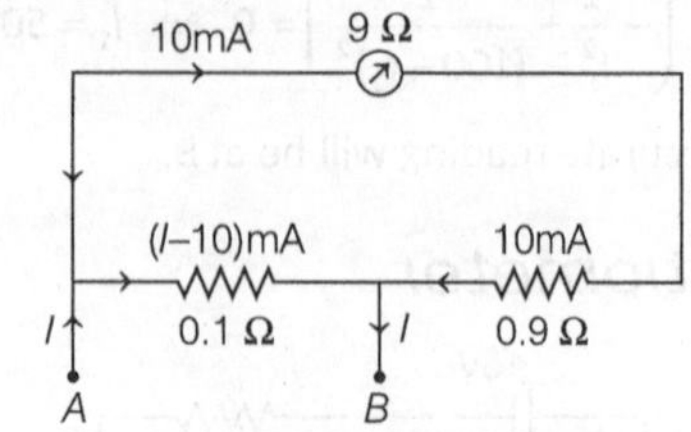

$$V_A - V_B = (10)\,(9+0.9) = (I-10)\,(0.1)$$

$\Rightarrow \quad I = 1000 \text{ mA}$

$\Rightarrow \quad I = 1 \text{ A}$

3.

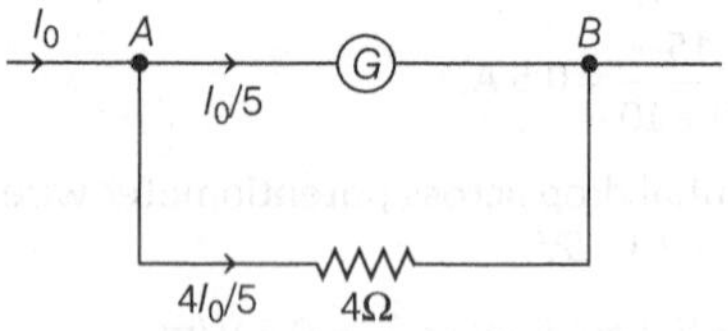

Let resistance of galvanometer be R_G.

$$V_A - V_B = \left(\frac{I_0}{5}\right) R_G = \left(\frac{4I_0}{5}\right) 4$$

$\Rightarrow \quad R_G = 16\,\Omega$

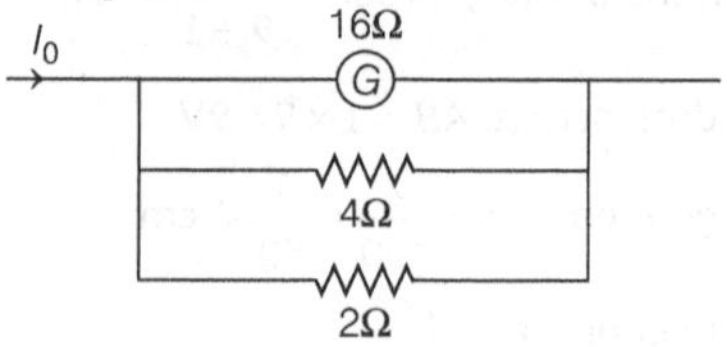

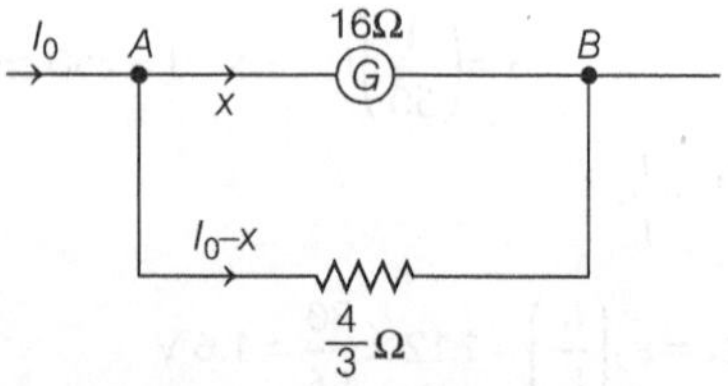

Let current through galvanometer be x.

$$V_A - V_B = x(16) = (I_0 - x)\frac{4}{3} \quad \Rightarrow \quad x = \frac{I_0}{13}$$

4. Full scale deflection current $= i_g = \dfrac{0.2}{20} = 0.01 \text{ A}$

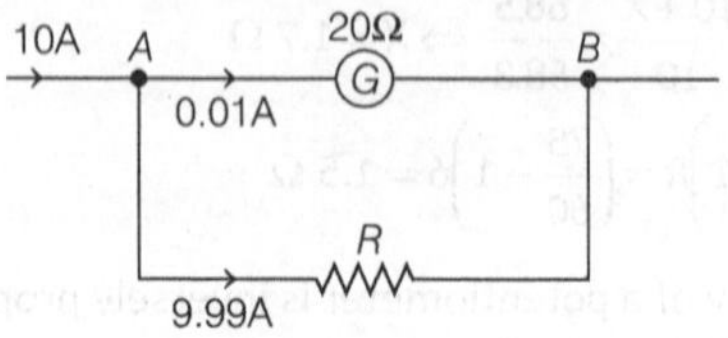

$$V_A - V_B = (0.01)(20) = 9.99\,R$$

$$R = 0.02\,\Omega$$

So, the galvanometer should have a $0.02\,\Omega$ resistance connected across it.

5.

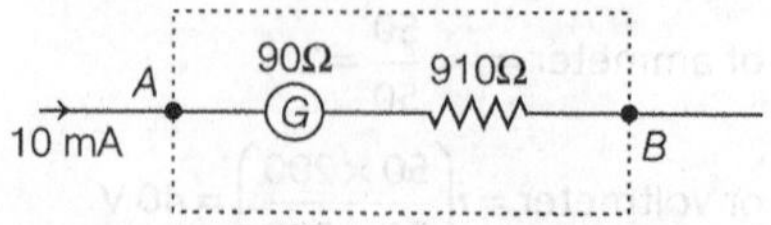

$$V = V_A - V_B = (10 \times 10^{-3})(90 + 910) = 10 \text{ V}$$

$$\text{Number of divisions on scale} = \frac{\text{Full scale reading}}{\text{Least count}} = \frac{10}{0.1} = 100$$

6.

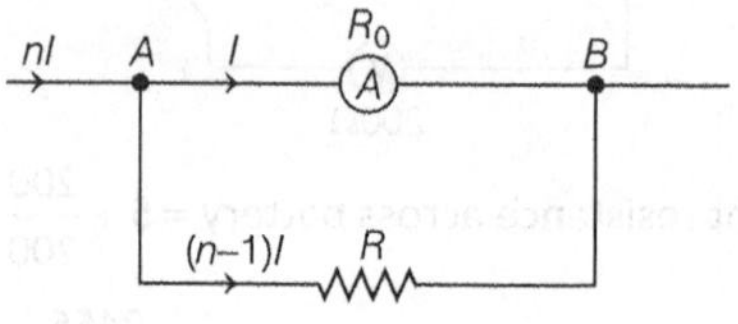

$$V_A - V_B = IR_0 = (n-1)\,IR \quad \Rightarrow \quad R = \frac{R_0}{n-1}$$

7. For galvanometer, $i \propto \theta$

If deflection becomes $\left(\frac{1}{5}\right)$th, then current through galvanometer will also become $\left(\frac{1}{5}\right)$th.

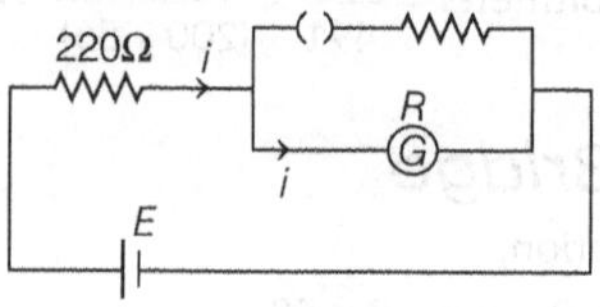

When K_1 is closed and K_2 is open, let current through the galvanometer be i.

Let R be resistance of the galvanometer.

$$\Rightarrow \quad i = \frac{E}{220 + R}$$

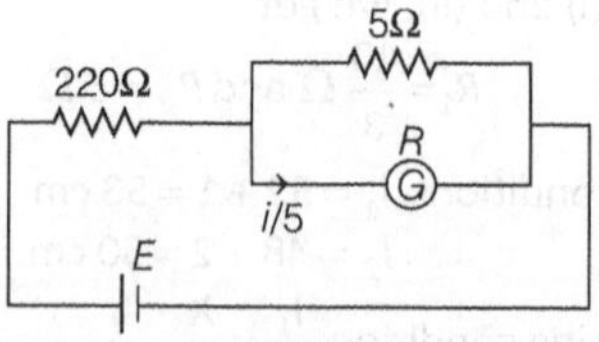

When K_2 is also closed, current through the galvanometer becomes $\dfrac{i}{5}$.

$$\frac{i}{5} = \left(\frac{E}{220 + \dfrac{5R}{5+R}}\right)\left(\frac{5}{5+R}\right)$$

$$\Rightarrow \quad \frac{1}{5}\left(\frac{E}{220+R}\right) = \left(\frac{E}{220 + \dfrac{5R}{5+R}}\right)\left(\frac{5}{5+R}\right)$$

$\Rightarrow \quad R = 22\,\Omega$

8. $V = i_g(R_G + R)$

$\Rightarrow \quad 20 = i_g(R_G + 1680)$ ...(i)

$\Rightarrow \quad 30 = i_g(R_G + 2930)$ ...(ii)

Solving Eqs. (i) and (ii), we get

$R_G = 820\,\Omega$ and $i_g = 8$ mA

9. $i_g = \dfrac{150}{10} = 15$ mA, $V_g = \dfrac{150}{2} = 75$ mV, $R_g = \dfrac{V_g}{i_g} = \dfrac{75}{15} = 5\,\Omega$

Full scale voltage $= 150 \times 1 = 150$ V

$V = i_g(R_g + R)$

$\Rightarrow \quad 150 = 15 \times 10^{-3}(5 + R)$

$\Rightarrow \quad R = 9995\,\Omega$

10.

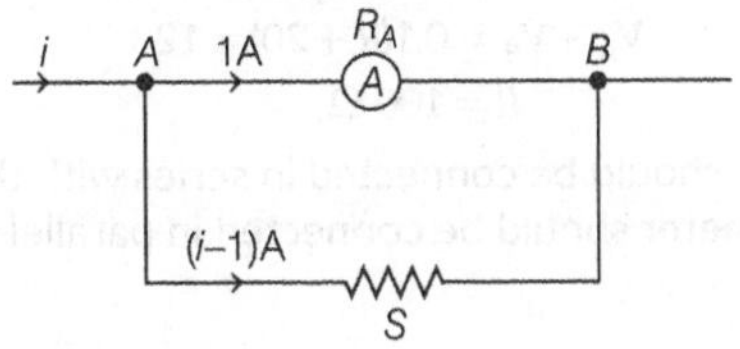

$V_A - V_B = (i-1)S = 1 \times R_A$

$\Rightarrow \quad S = \dfrac{R_A}{i-1} \Rightarrow S \propto \dfrac{1}{(i-1)}$

So, graph of S *versus* i will be hyperbola.

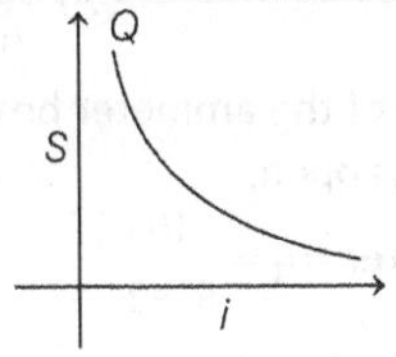

11.

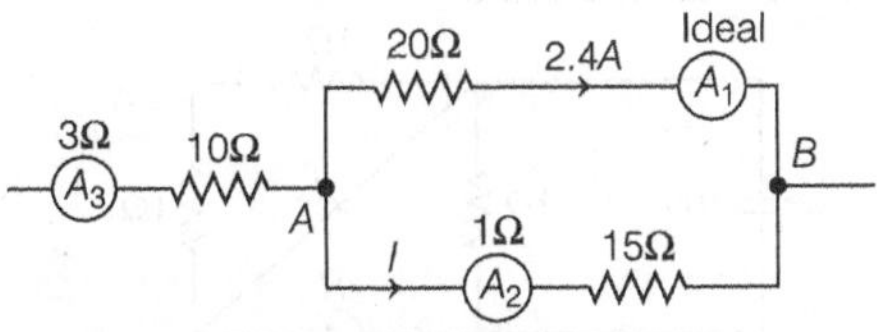

Let current through ammeter, A_2 be I.

$V_A - V_B = 20 \times 2.4 = I(1 + 15) \Rightarrow I = 3$A

Reading of ammeter, $A_3 = 2.4 + I$

$= 2.4 + 3 = 5.4$ A

12.

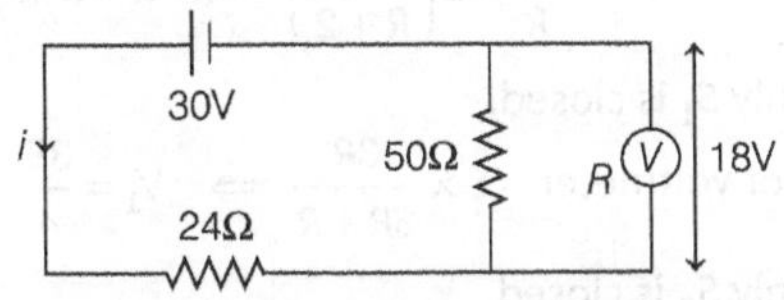

Let resistance of voltmeter be R.

i = current through battery $= \dfrac{30}{24 + \dfrac{50R}{50+R}}$

Reading of voltmeter $= i \times \dfrac{50R}{50+R}$

$$\Rightarrow \quad 18 = \left(\frac{30}{24 + \dfrac{50R}{50+R}}\right)\left(\frac{50R}{50+R}\right)$$

$$\Rightarrow \quad R = \frac{900}{7}\,\Omega$$

13. Ideal voltmeter has infinite resistance. So, current in the circuit will be nearly zero. Hence, voltmeter reading will be equal to emf of the battery.

14.

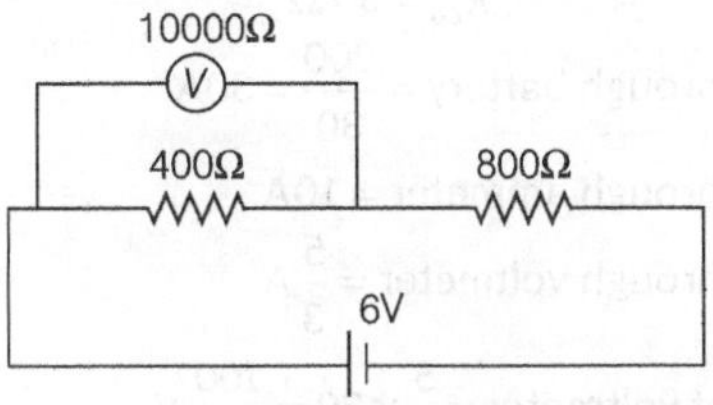

Actual potential difference across 400Ω resistance

$$= 6 \times \frac{400}{400 + 800} = 2\text{ V}$$

$$\text{Reading of voltmeter} = 6 \times \left(\frac{\dfrac{400 \times 10000}{400 + 10000}}{800 + \dfrac{400 \times 10000}{400 + 10000}}\right) = 1.95\text{ V}$$

Error in the measurement $= 2 - 1.95 = 0.05$ V

15. Let resistance of voltmeter be R.

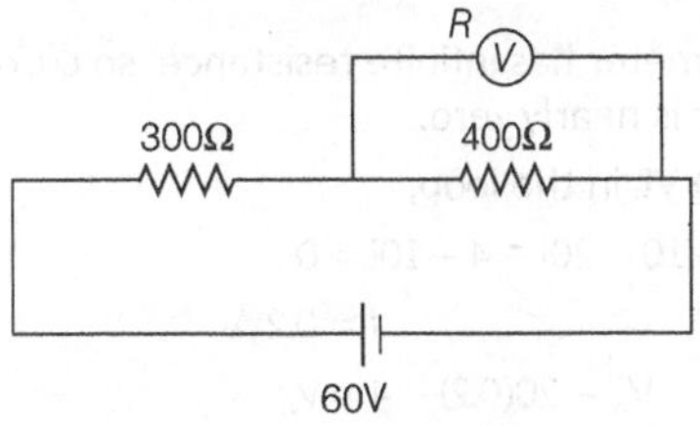

$$\text{Reading of voltmeter} = \frac{60 \times \dfrac{400R}{400+R}}{300 + \dfrac{400R}{400+R}} = 30$$

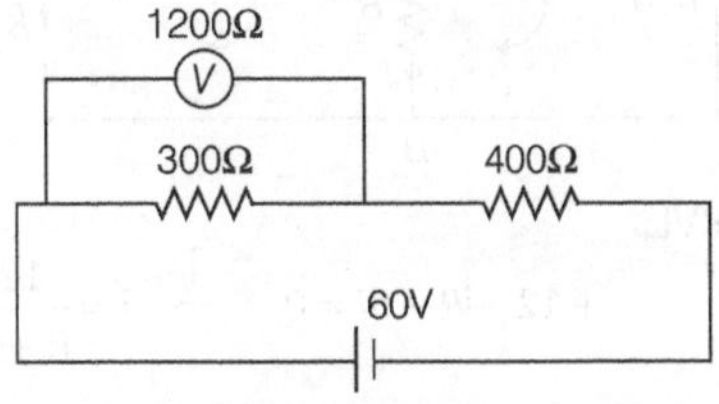

When voltmeter is connected across 300 Ω, reading of voltmeter

$$= 60 \times \frac{\dfrac{1200 \times 300}{1200 + 300}}{400 + \dfrac{1200 \times 300}{1200 + 300}} = 22.5\text{ V}$$

16.

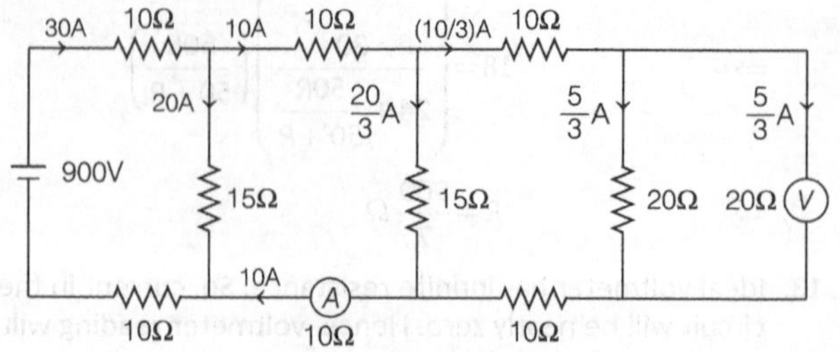

$$R_{eq} = 30\ \Omega$$

Current through battery $= \frac{900}{30} = 30\text{A}$

Current through ammeter $= 10\text{A}$

Current through voltmeter $= \frac{5}{3}\text{A}$

Reading of voltmeter $= \frac{5}{3} \times 20 = \frac{100}{3}\text{V}$

17.

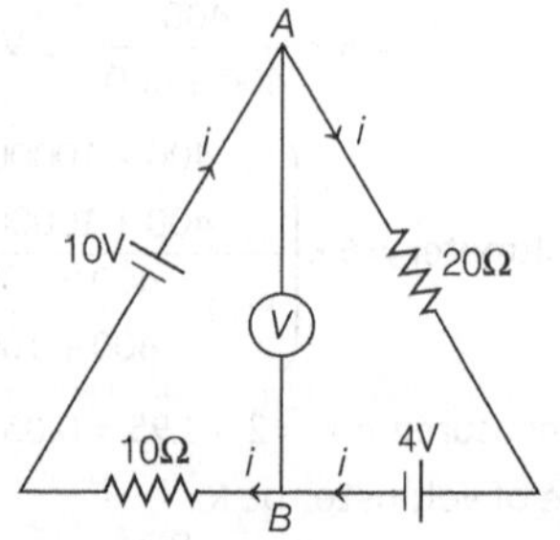

Ideal voltmeter has infinite resistance, so current through voltmeter is nearly zero.

Applying KVL in the loop,

$$+10 - 20i = 4 - 10i = 0$$

$$\Rightarrow \quad i = 0.2\text{ A}$$

$$V_A - 20(0.2) - 4 = V_B$$

$$V_A - V_B = 8\text{ V}$$

18.

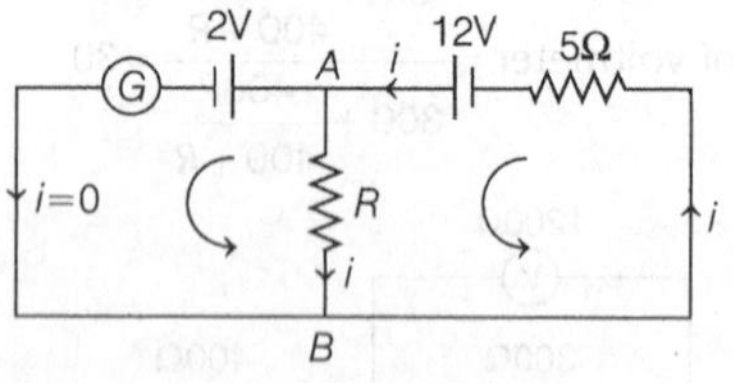

Applying KVL,

$$+12 - iR - 5i = 0 \quad \Rightarrow \quad i = \frac{12}{R+5}$$

$$V_A - 2 = V_B \Rightarrow V_A - V_B = 2$$

$$\Rightarrow \quad \left(\frac{12}{R+5}\right)R = 2 \quad \Rightarrow \quad R = 1\,\Omega$$

19. Reading of ideal voltmeter across cell 1 $= E - ir_1 = 0$

$$\Rightarrow \quad E - i(6) = 0$$

$$\Rightarrow \quad i = \frac{E}{6} \qquad \text{...(i)}$$

Applying KVL in the loop,

$$+E - ir_1 + E - ir_2 - iR = 0$$

$$\Rightarrow \quad i = \frac{E}{R+4} \qquad \text{...(ii)}$$

Solving Eqs. (i) and (ii), we get

$$R = 2\,\Omega$$

20.

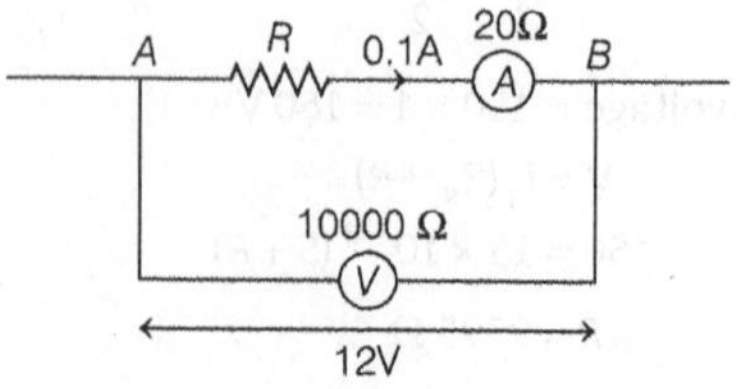

$$V_A - V_B = 0.1(R + 20) = 12$$

$$\Rightarrow \quad R = 100\,\Omega$$

21. Ammeter should be connected in series with the resistor and voltmeter should be connected in parallel across the resistor.

22.

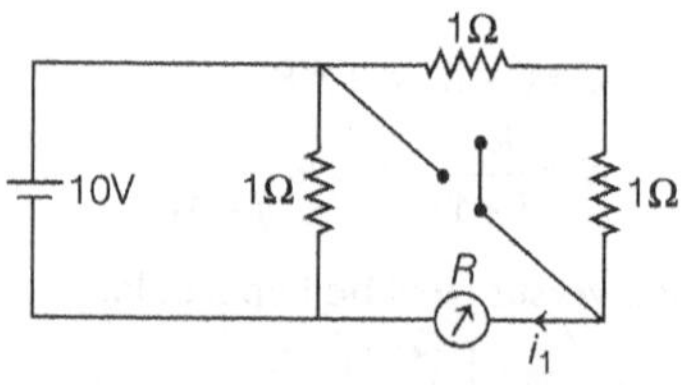

Let the resistance of the ammeter be R.

When the switch is open,

Reading of ammeter $= i_1 = \frac{10}{R+2}$

When the switch is closed.

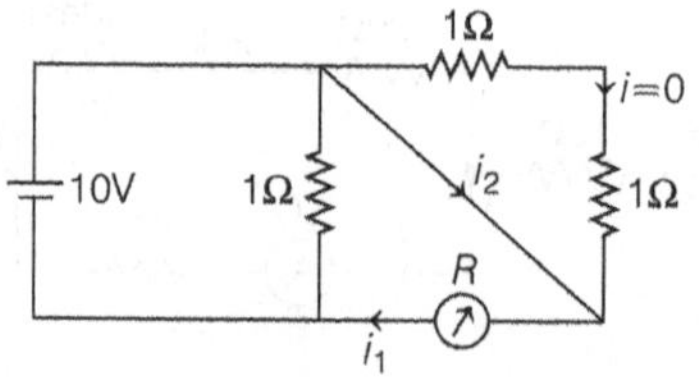

$$i_2 = \frac{10}{R}$$

$$i_2 = 2i_1$$

$$\Rightarrow \quad \frac{10}{R} = 2\left(\frac{10}{R+2}\right) \quad \Rightarrow \quad R = 2\,\Omega$$

23. When only S_1 is closed,

reading of voltmeter $= E \times \frac{3R}{3R+R} \quad \Rightarrow \quad V_1 = \frac{3E}{4}$

When only S_2 is closed,

reading of voltmeter $= E \times \frac{6R}{6R+R} \quad \Rightarrow \quad V_2 = \frac{6E}{7}$

When both S_1 and S_2 are closed,

reading of voltmeter $= E \times \frac{2R}{2R+R} \Rightarrow V_3 = \frac{2E}{3}$

So, $V_2 > V_1 > V_3$

24. Ammeter reading = 1 A

$$\Rightarrow \quad \frac{12}{X+Y+r} = 1 \qquad \text{...(i)}$$

Voltmeter reading across X = 1V

$$\Rightarrow \quad \left(\frac{12}{X+Y+r}\right)X = 1 \qquad \text{...(ii)}$$

When, Y is short-circuited,

Voltmeter reading across battery = 10 V

$$\Rightarrow \quad 12 - ir = 10$$

$$\Rightarrow \quad 12 - \left(\frac{12}{X+r}\right)r = 10$$

$$r = \frac{X}{5} \qquad \text{...(iii)}$$

Solving Eqs. (i), (ii) and (iii), we get

$$r = 0.2\ \Omega$$

25.

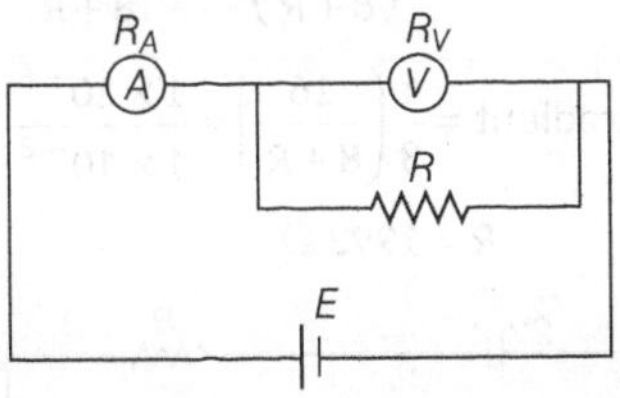

When a resistance is connected in parallel with the voltmeter, resistance of circuit will decrease. So, current through the ammeter will increase. Due to increased current, potential difference across ammeter will increase. Since, sum of potential difference across ammeter and voltmeter is emf of the battery potential difference across the voltmeter will decrease.

26. Potential difference between the terminals of the cell

$$= \varepsilon - ir$$

$\Rightarrow \quad V = \varepsilon - ir$

When $i = 0$, $\quad V = \varepsilon = y$

When $i = x$, $\quad 0 = \varepsilon - xr$

$\Rightarrow \quad 0 = y - xr \quad \Rightarrow \quad r = \dfrac{y}{x}$

27.

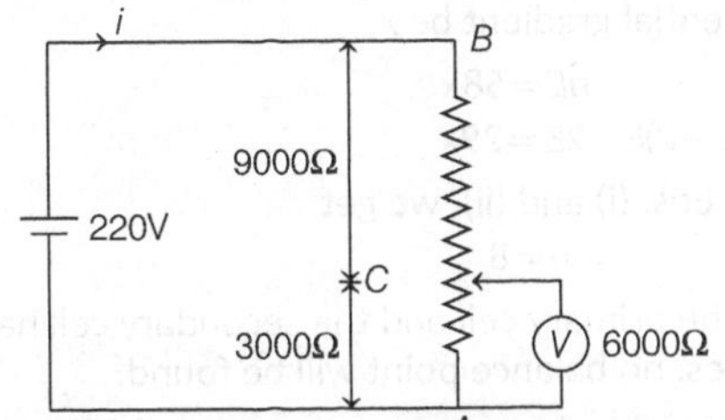

$$R_{CA} = \frac{1}{4}(12000) = 3000\ \Omega$$

$$R_{BC} = \frac{3}{4}(12000) = 9000\ \Omega$$

$$i = \frac{220}{9000 + \dfrac{6000 \times 3000}{6000 + 3000}} = 0.02\text{A}$$

$$\text{Reading of voltmeter} = (0.02)\left(\frac{6000 \times 3000}{6000 + 3000}\right) = 40\text{ V}$$

28. From the graph,

When $G \to \infty$, $V = 20$ V

Potential difference across resistor when $G \to \infty$

$$= \left(\frac{24}{R+1}\right)R = 20$$

$$\Rightarrow \quad 6R = 5R + 5 \quad \Rightarrow \quad R = 5\ \Omega$$

29. Let potential difference across ammeter and voltmeter be V_A and V_V respectively.

When both S_1 and S_2 are open,

$$V_A + V_V = 6 \qquad \text{...(i)}$$

When S_1 is closed,

$$2V_A + \frac{V_V}{2} = 6 \qquad \text{...(ii)}$$

Solving Eqs. (i) and (ii), we get

$$V_A = 2\text{ V and } V_V = 4\text{ V}$$

Now, when S_2 is also closed, voltmeter gets short-circuited.

So, $\quad V_A = 6$ V and $V_V = 0$

Potential difference across Y ammeter after closing $S_1 = 2V_A = 4$V

Potential difference across Y ammeter after closing

$$S_2 = 6\text{ V}$$

So, ammeter reading after closing, $S_2 = \dfrac{3}{2}$ times the value after closing S_1.

30. For balanced Wheatstone bridge,

$$P(625) = QS$$

$$\Rightarrow \quad \frac{P}{Q} = \frac{S}{625} \qquad \text{...(i)}$$

After interchanging P and Q, condition for the balanced Wheatstone bridge,

$$Q(625 + 51) = PS$$

$$\Rightarrow \quad \frac{P}{Q} = \frac{676}{S} \qquad \text{...(ii)}$$

From Eqs. (i) and (ii), we get

$$\frac{S}{625} = \frac{676}{S}$$

$$\Rightarrow \quad S = \sqrt{625 + 676} = 25 \times 26 = 650\ \Omega$$

31. For balanced Wheatstone bridge,

$$\frac{P}{Q} = \frac{R}{S}$$

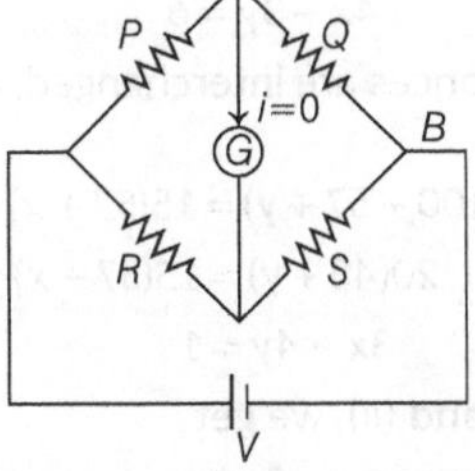

Current in the galvanometer will remain zero.

When, (1) battery emf is increased.

(3) all resistances are made five times.

(4) the battery and the galvanometer are interchanged.

32. Sensitivity of a potentiometer is inversely proportional to its potential gradient.

33.

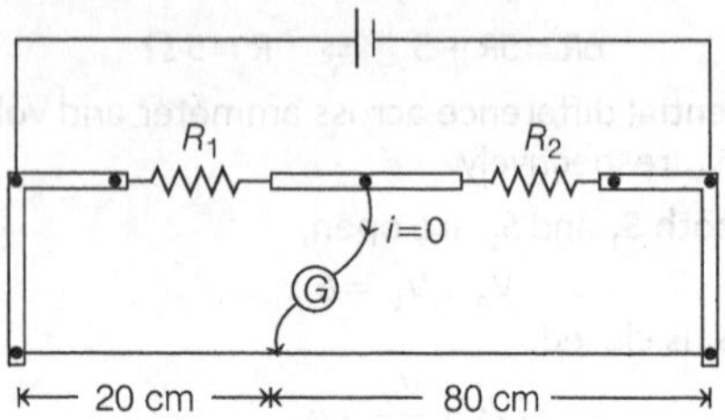

For null point, $R_1(80) = R_2(20)$

$\Rightarrow \quad R_2 = 4R_1$

When 15 Ω is connected in series with R_1, for null point,

$$(R_1 + 15)(60) = R_2(40)$$

$\Rightarrow \quad (R_1 + 15)(60) = 4R_1(40)$

$\Rightarrow \quad R_1 = 9\,\Omega$

34. For null point, $\dfrac{R_1}{R_2} = \dfrac{x}{100 - x}$

So, null point is independent of the radius of the wire *AB*.

35. For balance point, when R_1 is in the left gap $R_1(100 - 40) = X(40)$

$\Rightarrow \quad R_1 = \dfrac{2X}{3}$

When R_2 is in the left gap and $R_2(100 - 50) = X(50)$

$\Rightarrow \quad R_2 = X$

Now, when both R_1 and R_2 are in series in the left gap.

$$(R_1 + R_2)(100 - l) = X(l)$$

$\Rightarrow \quad \left(\dfrac{2X}{3} + X\right)(100 - l) = X(l)$

$\Rightarrow \quad l = 62.5$ cm

36. Let end corrections be *x* and *y* at end *A* and end *B*, respectively.

For null point,

$$15(100 - 42 + y) = 20(42 + x)$$

$\Rightarrow \quad 15(58 + y) = 20(42 + x)$

$\Rightarrow \quad 4x - 3y = 6 \qquad \text{...(i)}$

After the resistances are interchanged, condition for null point,

$$20(100 - 57 + y) = 15(57 + x)$$

$\Rightarrow \quad 20(43 + y) = 15(57 + x)$

$\Rightarrow \quad 3x - 4y = 1 \qquad \text{...(ii)}$

Solving Eqs. (i) and (ii), we get

$x = 3$ cm and $y = 2$ cm

37. When the first galvanometer is used,

$$R\left(L - \frac{L}{4}\right) = (R_1 + R_2)\frac{L}{4}$$

$\Rightarrow \quad R_1 + R_2 = 3R \qquad \text{...(i)}$

When the second galvanometer is used,

$$(R + R_1)\left(L - \frac{2L}{3}\right) = R_2\left(\frac{2L}{3}\right)$$

$\Rightarrow \quad 2R_2 - R_1 = R \qquad \text{...(ii)}$

Solving Eqs. (i) and (ii), we get

$$R_1 = \frac{5R}{3} \text{ and } R_2 = \frac{4R}{3}$$

38. Let value of resistance in the box be *R*.

Current in the primary circuit $= \dfrac{2}{8 + R}$

Potential drop across potentiometer wire

$$= \left(\frac{2}{8 + R}\right) \times 8 = \frac{16}{8 + R}$$

Potential gradient $= \dfrac{1}{8}\left(\dfrac{16}{8 + R}\right) = \dfrac{1 \times 10^{-6}}{1 \times 10^{-3}}$

$\Rightarrow \quad R = 1992\,\Omega$

39.

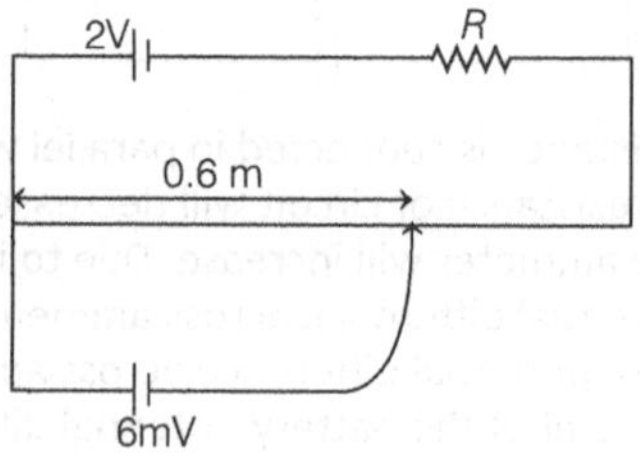

Potential gradient $= \dfrac{1}{1}\left(\dfrac{2}{5 + R}\right)$

For balance point,

$$\varepsilon = xl$$

$\Rightarrow \quad 6 \times 10^{-3} = \left(\dfrac{2}{5 + R}\right)(0.6)$

$$R = 195\,\Omega$$

40. Let potential gradient be *x*.

$$nE = 58x \qquad \text{...(i)}$$

$$(n - 2)E - 2E = 29x \qquad \text{...(ii)}$$

Solving Eqs. (i) and (ii), we get

$$n = 8$$

41. Since, the primary cell and the secondary cell have opposite polarities, no balance point will be found.

42. Potentiometer doesn't draw any current from the battery. So, emf of battery will be 1.44 V.

Voltmeter reading = 1.32 V

$\Rightarrow \quad \varepsilon - ir = 1.32$

$\Rightarrow \quad 1.44 - \left(\dfrac{1.44}{660 + r}\right)r = 1.32$

$\Rightarrow \quad r = 60\,\Omega$

43. Let emf of the primary cell be V.

Potential gradient $= \dfrac{V}{l}$

For balance point, $E = \left(\dfrac{V}{l}\right)\dfrac{l}{3}$

$\Rightarrow \quad V = 3E$

When the length of wire increased by l, new potential gradient $= \dfrac{V}{\frac{3l}{2}} = \dfrac{3E}{\left(\frac{3l}{2}\right)} = \dfrac{2E}{l}$

For balance point, $E = \left(\dfrac{2E}{l}\right)l' \Rightarrow l' = \dfrac{l}{2}$

44. $R \propto l$

$\Rightarrow \quad \dfrac{R_{AN}}{R_{AB}} = \dfrac{l}{L} \Rightarrow \dfrac{16}{20} = \dfrac{l}{L}$

$\Rightarrow \quad l = \dfrac{4L}{5}$

For null deflection,

$E = xl$

$\Rightarrow \quad E = \left(\dfrac{6}{L}\right)\left(\dfrac{4L}{5}\right) \Rightarrow E = 4.8 \text{ V}$

45. Sensitivity of a potentiometer is inversely proportional to its potential gradient. So, sensitivity will increase when potential gradient will decrease.

Potential gradient decreases when length of potentiometer wire is increased.

46. From the primary circuit.

Potential gradiant $= \dfrac{10}{1} = 10 \text{ V/m}$

At zero deflection,

current in the secondary loop $= \dfrac{5}{R+1}$

$V_A - V_C = 10(0.4) = \left(\dfrac{5}{R+1}\right)R$

$\Rightarrow \quad 4R + 4 = 5R \Rightarrow R = 4\Omega$

47. Let current in the secondary loop at null point be

$iR = x(10)$ ....(i)

$i(R + x) = x(30)$ ...(ii)

Solving Eqs. (i) and (ii), we get $x = 2R$

48. When switch S_2 is open

$6 = x\left(\dfrac{L}{2}\right) \Rightarrow 6 = \left(\dfrac{E}{L}\right)\left(\dfrac{L}{2}\right)$

$\Rightarrow \quad E = 12 \text{ V}$

When switch S_2 is closed,

$10\left(\dfrac{6}{10+r}\right) = x\left(\dfrac{5L}{12}\right)$

$\Rightarrow \quad \dfrac{60}{10+r} = \left(\dfrac{12}{L}\right)\left(\dfrac{5L}{12}\right) \Rightarrow r = 2\Omega$

49. Resistance of $AN = \dfrac{15r}{600} \times 560 = 14r$

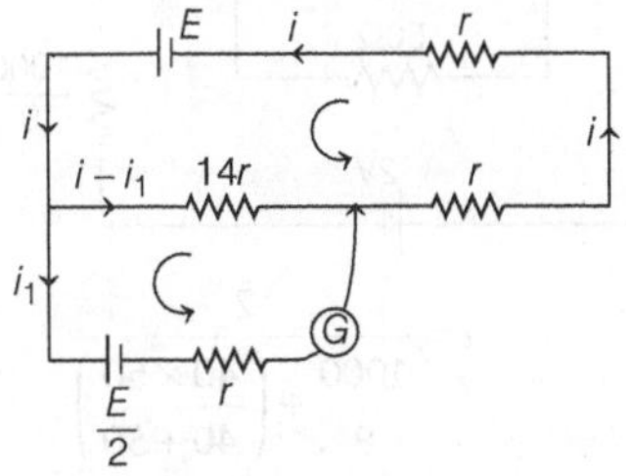

Using KVL,

$+E - (i - i_1)(14r) - ir - ir = 0$

$\Rightarrow \quad 16i - 14i_1 = \dfrac{E}{r}$ ...(i)

$-\dfrac{E}{2} - i_1 r + 14(i - i_1)r = 0$

$\Rightarrow \quad 28i - 30i_1 = \dfrac{E}{r}$ ...(ii)

Solving Eqs. (i) and (ii), we get

$i_1 = \dfrac{3E}{22r}$

50. If contact at Z has to be moved towards Y implies potential gradient decreases. So, the primary cell V_1 is running down.

51. In the primary circuit,

Potential gradient $= \dfrac{1}{4}\left(\dfrac{12}{16+8} \times 16\right) = 2 \text{ V/m}$

In the secondary circuit, $\varepsilon_{eq} = \dfrac{\frac{\varepsilon_1}{r_1} + \frac{\varepsilon_2}{r_2}}{\frac{1}{r_1} + \frac{1}{r_2}} = \dfrac{\frac{2}{2} - \frac{4}{6}}{\frac{1}{2} + \frac{1}{6}} = 0.5 \text{ V}$

For balance point, $\varepsilon_{eq} = xl$

$\Rightarrow \quad 0.5 = 2l$

$\Rightarrow \quad l = 0.25 \text{ m} = 25 \text{ cm}$

Numerical Value Questions

1.

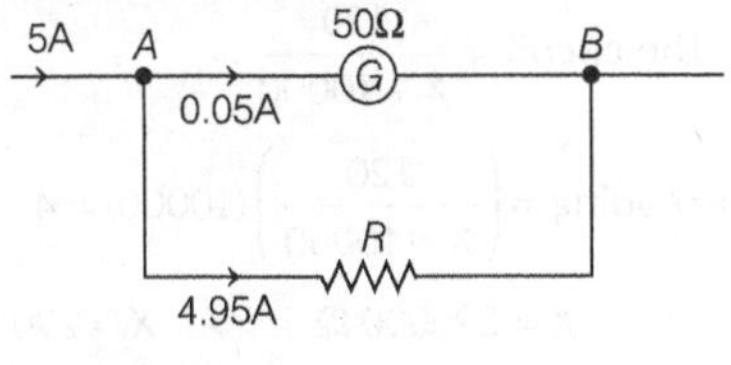

Let shunt resistance be R.

$V_A - V_B = 0.05 \times 50 = 4.95 \times R$

$\Rightarrow \quad R = \dfrac{50}{99}\,\Omega$

$R = \dfrac{\rho l}{A}$

$\Rightarrow \quad \dfrac{50}{99} = \dfrac{5 \times 10^{-7} \times l}{2.97 \times 10^{-2} \times 10^{-4}}$

$\Rightarrow \quad l = 3 \text{ m}$

2.

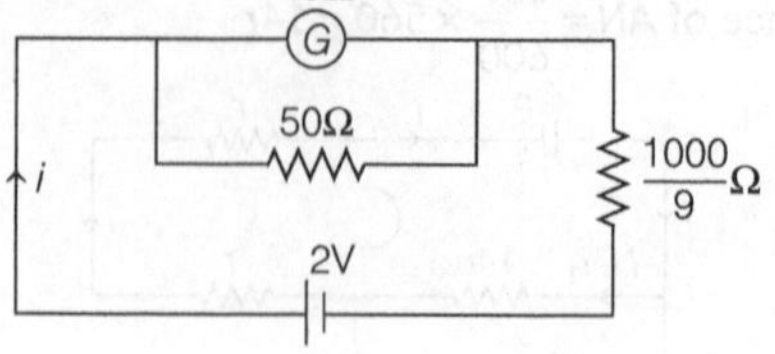

$$i = \frac{2}{\frac{1000}{9} + \left(\frac{40 \times 50}{40 + 50}\right)}$$

$$= 15 \times 10^{-3}\ \text{A} = 15\ \text{mA}$$

Current through galvanometer $= \left(\frac{50}{50+40}\right) \times (15\ \text{mA})$

$$= \frac{25}{3}\ \text{mA}$$

Current sensitivity $= \frac{50}{\frac{25}{3}} = 6$ div/mA

3.

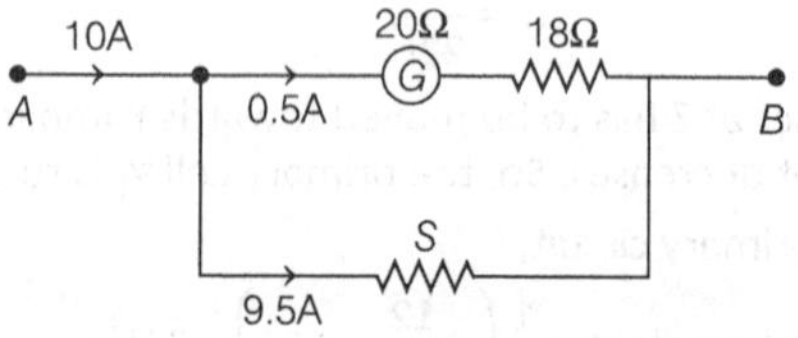

For half scale deflection, current through the galvanometer = 0.5 A

$$V_A - V_B = 0.5(20 + 18) = 9.5(S)$$

$$\Rightarrow \quad S = 2\Omega$$

4.

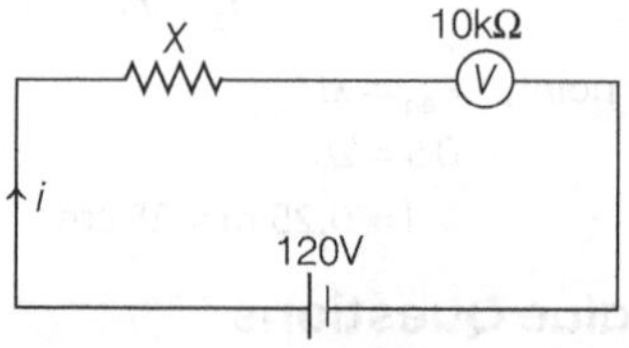

Current in the circuit $= \frac{120}{X + 10000}$

Voltmeter reading $= \left(\frac{120}{X + 10000}\right)(10000) = 4$

$$\Rightarrow \quad X = 290000\ \Omega \quad \Rightarrow \quad X = 290\ \text{k}\Omega$$

5.

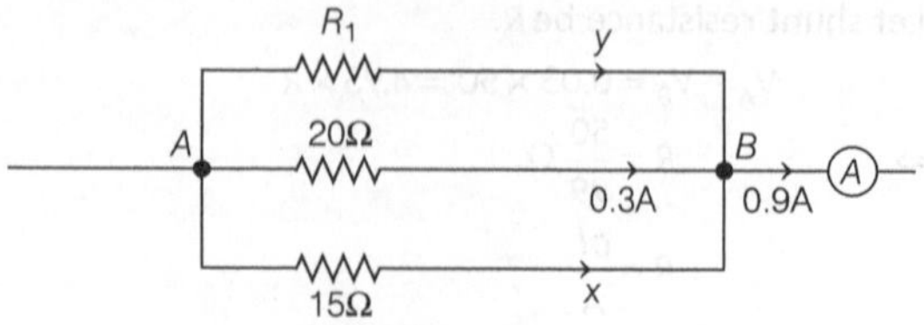

$$V_A - V_B = 20(0.3) = x(15) \quad \Rightarrow \quad x = 0.4\ \text{A}$$

$$x + y + 0.3 = 0.9 \quad \Rightarrow \quad y = 0.2\ \text{A}$$

$$V_A - V_B = 20(0.3) = (0.2)R_1$$

$$\Rightarrow \quad R_1 = 30\ \Omega$$

6.

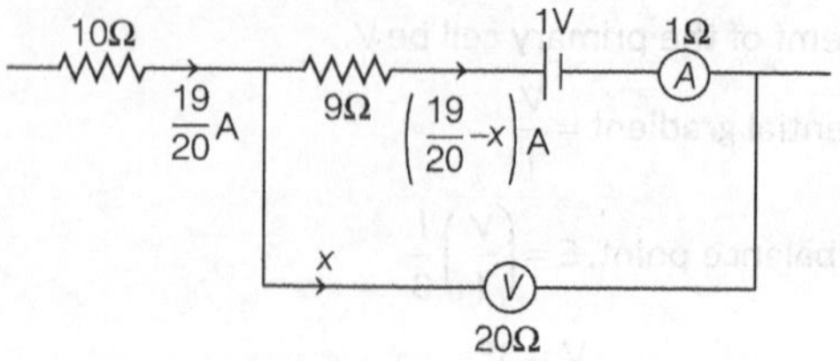

Using KVL in the loop,

$$-9\left(\frac{19}{20} - x\right) - 1 - 1\left(\frac{19}{20} - x\right) + 20x = 0$$

$$\Rightarrow \quad x = 0.35\ \text{A}$$

Reading of voltmeter $= x(20) = 0.35 \times 20 = 7$ V

7.

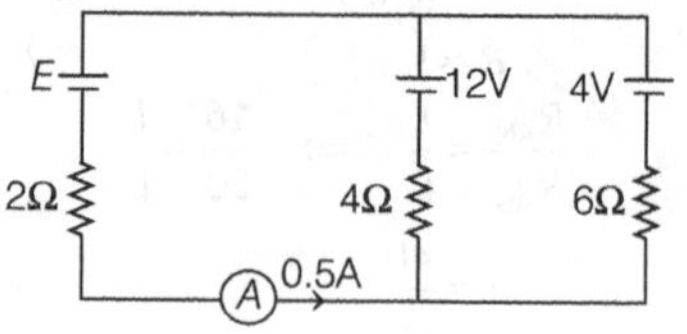

$$\varepsilon_{eq} = \frac{\frac{12}{4} + \frac{4}{6}}{\frac{1}{4} + \frac{1}{6}} = \frac{44}{5}\ \text{V}$$

$$\frac{1}{r_{eq}} = \frac{1}{4} + \frac{1}{6} \quad \Rightarrow \quad r_{eq} = \frac{12}{5}\ \Omega$$

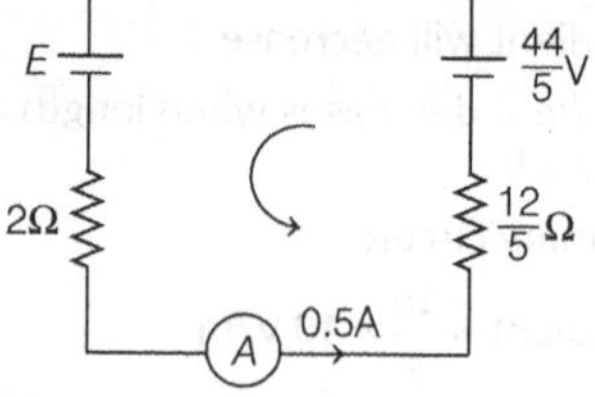

Applying KVL in the loop,

$$+\frac{44}{5} - E - 2(0.5) - \frac{12}{5}(0.5) = 0$$

$$\Rightarrow \quad E = 6.6\ \text{V} = 6600\ \text{mV}$$

8.

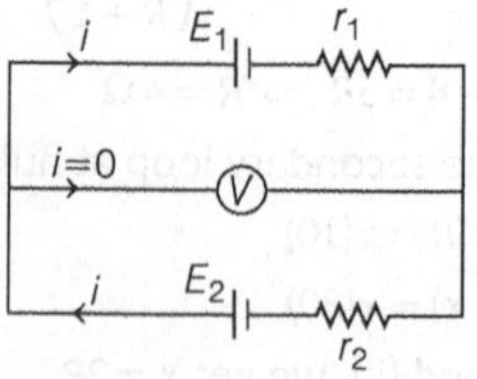

Applying KVL in the loop,

$$+E_2 - ir_2 - E_1 - ir_1 = 0 \quad \Rightarrow \quad i = \frac{E_2 - E_1}{r_1 + r_2}$$

Voltmeter reading $= E_1 + ir_1$

$$= E_1 + \left(\frac{E_2 - E_1}{r_1 + r_2}\right) r_1 = \frac{E_1 r_2 + E_2 r_1}{r_1 + r_2}$$

Voltmeter reading = 1.45 V

$$\Rightarrow \quad \frac{E_1 r_2 + E_2 r_1}{r_1 + r_2} = 1.45 \Rightarrow \frac{1.3 r_2 + 1.5 r_1}{r_1 + r_2} = 1.45$$

$$\Rightarrow \quad 1.3r_2 + 1.5r_1 = 1.45r_1 + 1.45r_2$$

$$\Rightarrow \quad 0.05r_1 = 0.15r_2 \Rightarrow \frac{r_1}{r_2} = 3$$

9.

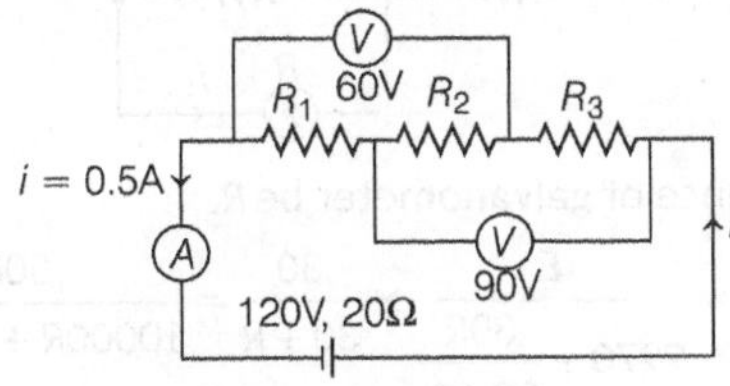

$$i(R_1 + R_2) = 60$$

$$\Rightarrow \quad 0.5(R_1 + R_2) = 60$$

$$\Rightarrow \quad R_1 + R_2 = 120\,\Omega \quad \text{...(i)}$$

$$i(R_2 + R_3) = 90$$

$$\Rightarrow \quad 0.5(R_2 + R_3) = 90$$

$$\Rightarrow \quad R_2 + R_3 = 180\,\Omega \quad \text{...(ii)}$$

$$i = \frac{120}{R_1 + R_2 + R_3 + 20} = 0.5$$

$$\Rightarrow \quad R_1 + R_2 + R_3 = 220 \quad \text{..(iii)}$$

Solving Eqs. (i), (ii) and (ii), we get

$$R_2 = 80\,\Omega$$

10. Let balance length be l and unknown resistance be R.

For null point,

$$2(100 - l) = R(l) \quad \text{...(i)}$$

When 2Ω and R are interchanged, balance point shifts by 20 cm. So,

for null point,

$$R(100 - (l + 20)) = 2(l + 20)$$

$$\Rightarrow \quad R(80 - l) = 2(l + 20) \quad \text{...(ii)}$$

Solving Eqs. (i) and (ii), we get

$$l = 40 \text{ cm and } R = 3\,\Omega$$

11.

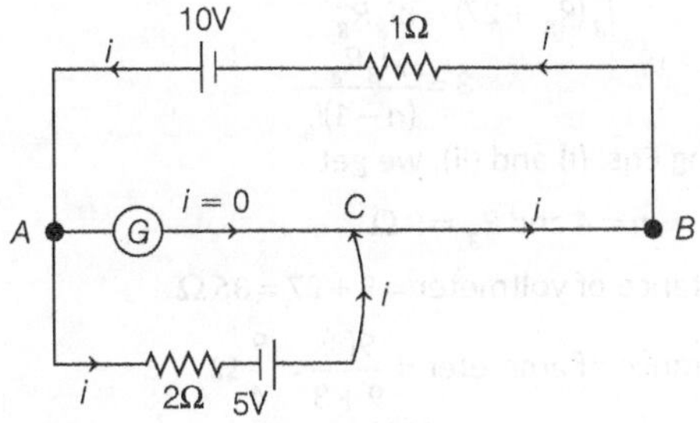

Applying KVL,

$$-i + 10 - 2i + 5 - iR_{BC} = 0$$

$$\Rightarrow \quad i = \frac{15}{3 + R_{BC}}$$

$$V_A - V_C = 5 - 2i = 0$$

$$\Rightarrow \quad i = 2.5 \text{ A}$$

$$2.5 = \frac{15}{3 + R_{BC}}$$

$$\Rightarrow \quad R_{BC} = 3\,\Omega$$

12. Current in the primary circuit $= \frac{3}{10 + 20} = 0.1$ A

Potential drop across the potentiometer wire

$$= 0.1 \times 20 = 2 \text{ V}$$

$$x = \text{potential gradient} = \frac{2}{10} = 0.2 \text{ V/m} = 0.2 \text{ mV/mm}$$

For balance point,

$$V = xl$$

$$\Delta V = x\Delta l = \left(0.2 \frac{\text{mV}}{\text{mm}}\right)(1 \text{ mm}) = 0.2 \text{ mV}$$

13. $x = \text{potential gradient} = \frac{2}{10} = 0.2$ V/m

For null point, $\varepsilon = xl$

$$\Rightarrow \quad \varepsilon = 0.2 \times 6.9 = 1.38 \text{ V}$$

Now a resistance 5Ω is put in series with the potentiometer wire,

$$x' = \text{new potential gradient} = \frac{1}{10}\left[\left(\frac{2}{115 + 5}\right) \times 115\right]$$

$$= \frac{23}{120} \text{ V/m}$$

For new null point,

$$\varepsilon = x'l'$$

$$\Rightarrow \quad 1.38 = \left(\frac{23}{120}\right)l' \Rightarrow l' = 7.2 \text{ m}$$

14. Let the potential gradient be x.

When only S_1 is closed, $\varepsilon_1 = x(40)$

When only S_2 is closed, $\varepsilon_2 = x(55)$

When both the keys are closed,

$$\varepsilon_{eq} = \frac{\frac{\varepsilon_1}{r} + \frac{\varepsilon_2}{2r}}{\frac{1}{r} + \frac{1}{2r}} = \frac{2\varepsilon_1 + \varepsilon_2}{3}$$

$$\varepsilon_{eq} = xl$$

$$\Rightarrow \quad \frac{2\varepsilon_1 + \varepsilon_2}{3} = xl$$

$$\Rightarrow \quad \frac{2(40x) + 55x}{3} = xl \Rightarrow l = 45 \text{ cm}$$

15. For wire AB,

$$\text{potential gradient} = x = \frac{5}{100} = 0.05 \text{ V/cm}$$

V_1 = potential drop across 40 cm of wire $AB = 40 \times 0.05 = 2$ V

For wire CD,

$$\text{Potential gradient} = \frac{1}{80}(2 \times R_{CD}) = \frac{R_{CD}}{40}$$

$$V_2 = \text{potential drop across 20 cm of wire } CD = \frac{R_{CD}}{40} \times 20$$

$$= \frac{R_{CD}}{2}$$

For null point,

$$V_1 = V_2$$

$$\Rightarrow \quad 2 = \frac{R_{CD}}{2} \Rightarrow R_{CD} = 4\,\Omega$$

Now, $\quad i = \frac{E}{2+4} = 2 \Rightarrow E = 12\text{ V}$

16. For wire w_1,

$$x = \text{potential gradient} = \frac{1}{l}\left(\frac{\varepsilon_P}{1+2} \times 2\right) = \frac{2\varepsilon_P}{3l}$$

For null point,

$$\varepsilon = x\left(\frac{l}{2}\right)$$

$$\Rightarrow \quad \varepsilon = \left(\frac{2\varepsilon_P}{3l}\right)\left(\frac{l}{2}\right) \Rightarrow \varepsilon_P = 3\varepsilon$$

For wire w_2, let its resistance be R.

$$x' = \text{potential gradient} = \frac{1}{l}\left(\frac{\varepsilon_P}{R+1}\right)R$$

For null point, $\varepsilon = x'\left(\frac{2l}{3}\right)$

$$\varepsilon = \frac{1}{l}\left(\frac{\varepsilon_P R}{R+1}\right)\left(\frac{2l}{3}\right)$$

$$\varepsilon = \frac{1}{l}\left(\frac{3\varepsilon_P R}{R+1}\right)\left(\frac{2l}{3}\right)$$

$$\Rightarrow \quad R = 1\,\Omega$$

Level 3

Single Choice Correct Questions

1. Let shunt resistance be S.

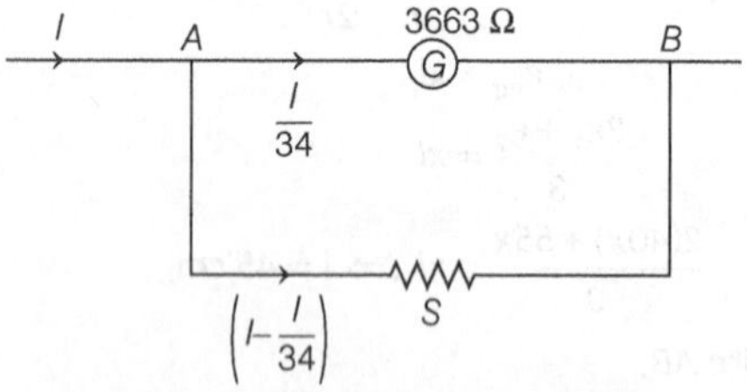

$$V_A - V_B = \left(\frac{I}{34}\right)(3663) = \left(I - \frac{I}{34}\right)S$$

$$\Rightarrow \quad S = 111\,\Omega$$

Let external resistance to be connected in series with the main circuit be R.

For total current in the main circuit to remain unaltered, total resistance should remain same.

$$3663 = \left(\frac{3663 \times 111}{3663 + 111}\right) + R$$

$$R = 3555.3\,\Omega$$

2.

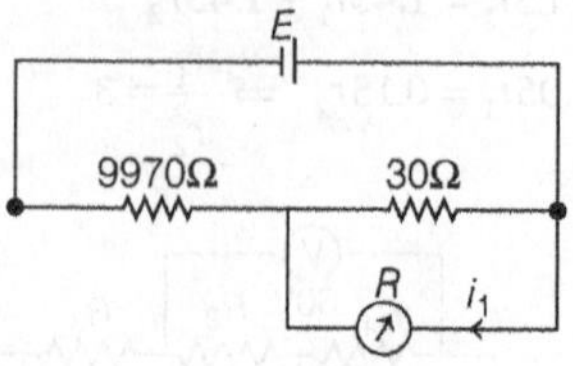

Let resistance of galvanometer be R.

$$i_1 = \frac{E}{9970 + \frac{30R}{30+R}} \times \frac{30}{30+R} = \frac{30E}{10000R + 299100}$$

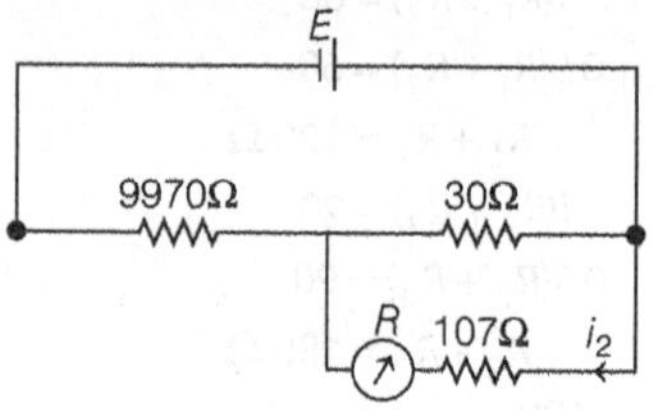

$$i_2 = \frac{E}{9970 + \frac{30(107+R)}{30+(107+R)}} \times \frac{30}{30+(107+R)}$$

For a galvanometer, deflection $\propto i$.

Since, deflection gets halved, current will also get halved. So

$$i_2 = \frac{i_1}{2}$$

$$\Rightarrow \quad \frac{30E}{10000R + 1369100} = \frac{1}{2}\left(\frac{30E}{10000R + 299100}\right)$$

$$\Rightarrow \quad R = 77.09\,\Omega$$

$$\Rightarrow \quad R \simeq 77\,\Omega$$

3. Let full scale deflection current and resistance of galvanometer be i_g and R_g, respectively.

$$i_g(R_g + 27) = n i_g R_g \qquad \text{...(i)}$$

$$3 = \frac{i_g R_g}{(n-1)i_g} \qquad \text{...(ii)}$$

Solving Eqs. (i) and (ii), we get

$$n = 4 \text{ and } R_g = 9\,\Omega$$

Resistance of voltmeter $= 9 + 27 = 36\,\Omega$

Resistance of ammeter $= \frac{9(3)}{9+3} = \frac{9}{4}\,\Omega$

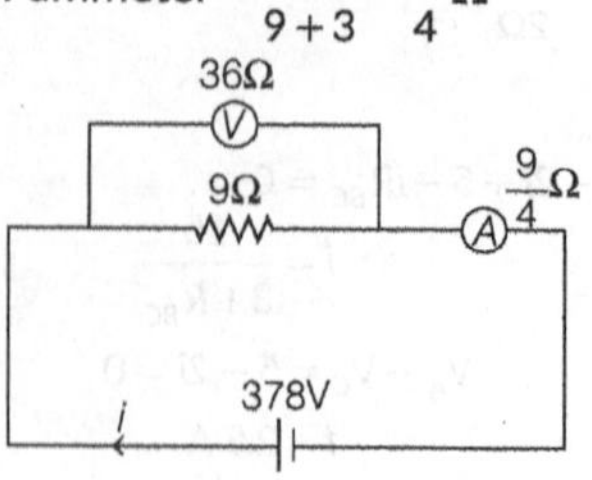

$$i = \frac{378}{\left(\frac{36 \times 9}{36+9}\right) + \frac{9}{4}} = 40\text{ A}$$

Current through galvanometer making up ammeter

$$= 40 \times \left(\frac{3}{3+9}\right) = 10\text{ A}$$

Current through galvanometer making up voltmeter

$$= 40 \times \left(\frac{90}{36+9}\right) = 8\text{ A}$$

4. Let emf of source be E.

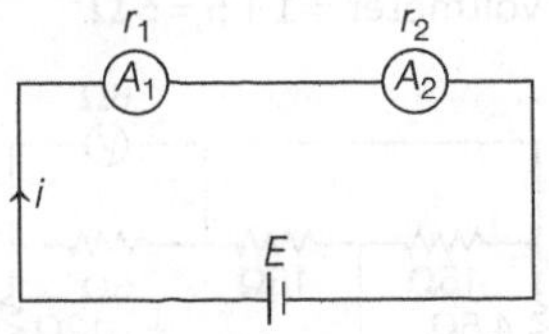

$$i = \frac{E}{r_1 + r_2}$$

$$\theta_1 \propto i \;\Rightarrow\; \theta_1 = K_1\left(\frac{E}{r_1 + r_2}\right)$$

$$\theta_2 \propto i \;\Rightarrow\; \theta_2 = K_2\left(\frac{E}{r_1 + r_2}\right)$$

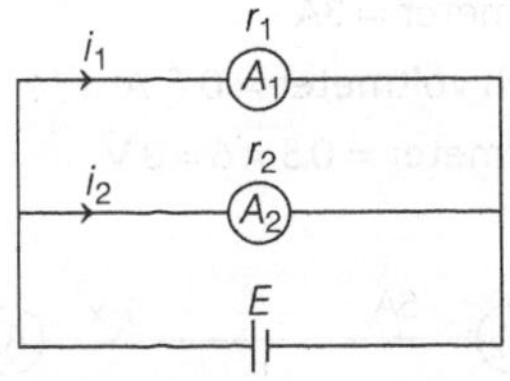

$$i_1 = \frac{E}{r_1} \text{ and } i_2 = \frac{E}{r_2}$$

$$\theta_1' = K_1\left(\frac{E}{r_1}\right) \text{ and } \theta_2' = K_2\left(\frac{E}{r_2}\right)$$

$$\frac{\theta_1}{\theta_2} = \frac{K_1}{K_2} \text{ and } \frac{\theta_1'}{\theta_2'} = \frac{K_1 r_2}{K_2 r_1}$$

$$\Rightarrow \quad \frac{\theta_1'}{\theta_2'} = \left(\frac{\theta_1}{\theta_2}\right)\frac{r_2}{r_1} \Rightarrow r_2 = \left(\frac{\theta_2\theta_1'}{\theta_1\theta_2'}\right) r_1$$

5.

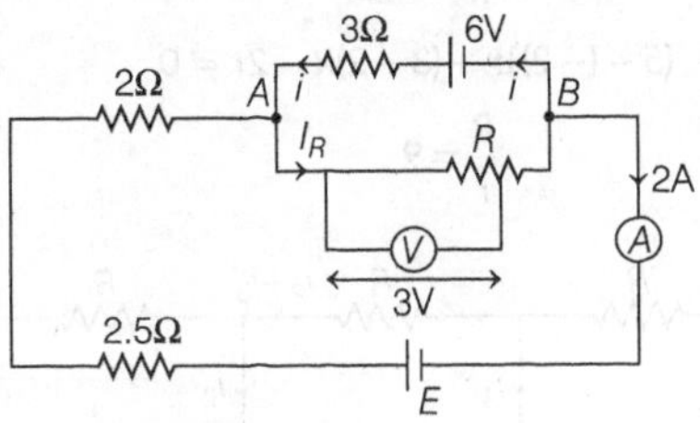

$$V_A - V_B = 3 = 6 - 3i$$

$$\Rightarrow \quad i = 1\text{ A}$$

At junction B,

$$I_R = i + 2 = 1 + 2 = 3\text{ A}$$

For resistor R, $V = iR$

$$\Rightarrow \quad 3 = 3(R)$$

$$\Rightarrow \quad R = 1\,\Omega$$

Applying KVL,

$$+E - 2.5 \times 2 - 2 \times 2 - 3 = 0$$

$$E = 12\text{ V}$$

6. When S_1 is closed and S_2 is open,

Voltmeter reading = 18

$$\Rightarrow \quad \left(\frac{E}{6+r}\right)6 = 18 \quad \text{...(i)}$$

When S_2 is closed and S_1 is open,

$$\text{Voltmeter reading} = \left(\frac{E}{12+r}\right)12 = 24 \quad \text{...(ii)}$$

Solving Eqs. (i) and (ii), we get

$$E = 36\text{ V and } r = 6\,\Omega$$

When both S_1 and S_2 are closed,

$$\text{Voltmeter reading} = \left(\frac{36}{4+6}\right) \times 4 = 14.4\text{ V}$$

7.

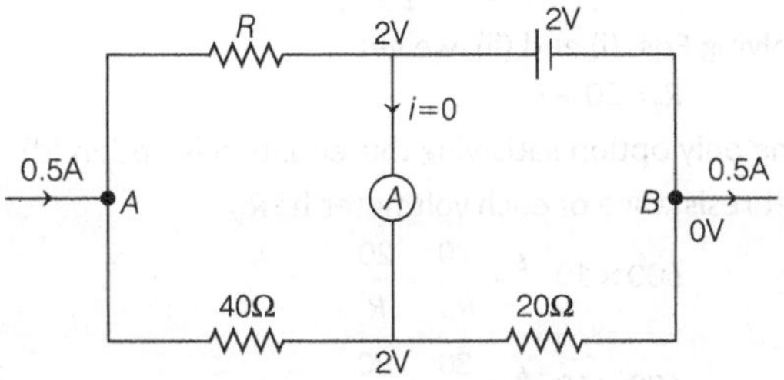

Let $V_B = 0$

$$\text{Current through } 20\,\Omega = \frac{2-0}{20} = 0.1\text{ A}$$

For 40 Ω resistance, $V = iR$

$$\Rightarrow \quad V_A - 2 = (0.1)(40)$$

$$\Rightarrow \quad V_A = 6\text{ V}$$

For resistance R,

$$R = \frac{V}{i} = \frac{V_A - 2}{0.5 - 0.1} = \frac{6-2}{0.4} = 10\,\Omega$$

8. When both the switches are open,

$$i_1 = \text{ reading of ammeter} = \frac{E}{300 + 100 + 50} = \frac{E}{450}$$

When both the switches are closed.

$$i_2 = \text{reading of ammeter} = \frac{E}{300 + \dfrac{100R}{(100+R)}} \times \left(\frac{R}{100+R}\right)$$

$$= \frac{ER}{30000 + 400R}$$

$$i_1 = i_2$$

$$\Rightarrow \quad \frac{E}{450} = \frac{ER}{30000 + 400R}$$

$$\Rightarrow \quad R = 600\,\Omega$$

9. In position 1,

Reading of ammeter $= \dfrac{V}{R} = 2$

$\Rightarrow \quad V = 2R$

In position 2,

Reading of ammeter $= \dfrac{V+E}{R+x} = 2$

$\Rightarrow \quad \dfrac{2R+10}{R+x} = 2$

$\Rightarrow \quad 2R + 10 = 2R + 2x \Rightarrow x = 5\,\Omega$

10. 1 and 4 may be correct.

11. When both keys K_1 and K_2 are closed.

Ammeter reading $= I_0 = \dfrac{E}{50+r}$ ..(i)

When K_1 is open and K_2 is closed.

Ammeter reading $= \dfrac{I_0}{2} = \dfrac{E}{R_1 + 50 + r}$ ...(ii)

Solving Eqs. (i) and (ii), we get

$R_1 = 50 + r$

The only option satisfying this equation is option (d).

12. Let resistance of each voltmeter be R_V.

$$600 \times 10^{-6} = \frac{20}{R_V} + \frac{20}{R} \quad \text{...(i)}$$

$$600 \times 10^{-6} = \frac{30}{R_V} + \frac{30}{2R} \quad \text{...(ii)}$$

Solving Eqs. (i) and (ii), we get

$R_V = 100\text{ k}\Omega$ and $R = 50\text{ k}\Omega$

13. Let resistance of voltmeter be R.

As the cell is ideal, reading of voltmeter $V_3 = 12\text{ V} =$ Emf of cell

Reading of voltmeter $(V_1) =$ Potential difference across R_1 (or R)

$$\Rightarrow \quad 4 = \frac{12}{\left(\frac{R_1R}{R+R_1} + R_2\right)} \times \left(\frac{R_1R}{R+R_1}\right)$$

$$\Rightarrow \quad \frac{R_1R_2 + RR_2}{RR_1} = 2 \quad \text{...(i)}$$

Reading of voltmeter $(V_2) =$ Potential difference across R_2 (or R)

$$6 = \frac{12}{\left(\frac{R_2R}{R+R_2} + R_1\right)} \times \frac{R_2R}{R+R_2}$$

$$\Rightarrow \quad \frac{R_1R_2 + RR_1}{R+R_2} = 1 \quad \text{...(ii)}$$

Eliminating R from Eqs. (i) and (ii), we get

$$\frac{R_1}{R_2} = \frac{2}{3}$$

Actual Potential difference across

$$R_1 = \frac{12}{R_1+R_2} \times R_1 = \frac{12}{1+\frac{R_2}{R_1}} = 4.8\text{ V}$$

14. Resistance of ammeter $= \dfrac{1(1)}{1+1} = 0.5\,\Omega$

Resistance of voltmeter $= 1 + 5 = 6\,\Omega$

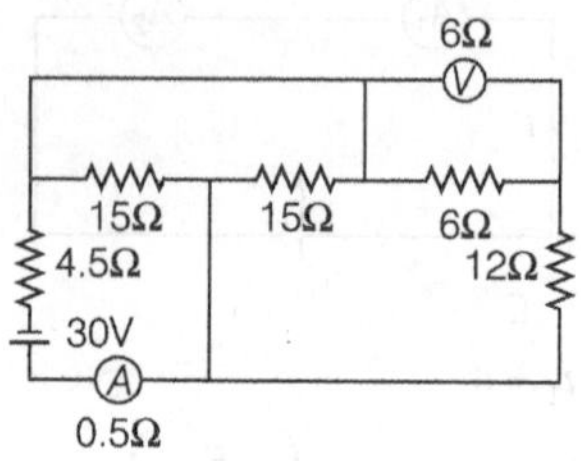

Equivalent resistance across battery $= 10\,\Omega$

Current though battery $= \dfrac{30}{10} = 3\text{ A}$

Reading of ammeter = 3A

Current through voltmeter = 0.5 A

Reading of voltmeter $= 0.5 \times 6 = 3\text{ V}$

15.

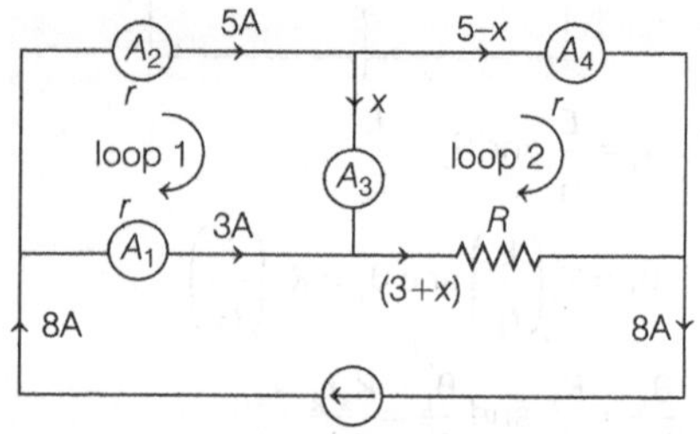

Using KVL,

Loop 1 $-5r - xr + 3r = 0$

$x = -2A$

Loop 2 $-(5-(-2))r + (3-2)R - 2r = 0$

$\Rightarrow \quad \dfrac{R}{r} = 9$

16.

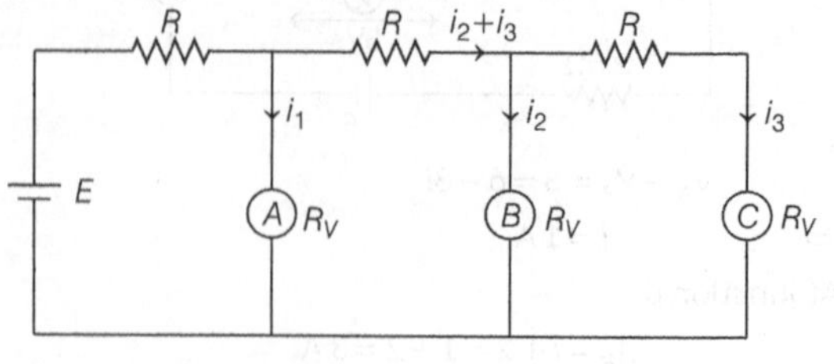

Let resistance of each resistor and each voltmeter be R and R_V, respectively.

Reading of voltmeter A = 22 V

$\Rightarrow \quad i_1 R_V = 22 \quad \Rightarrow \quad i_1 = \dfrac{22}{R_V}$

Reading of voltmeter $B = V_B$

$i_2 R_V = V_B \quad \Rightarrow \quad i_2 = \dfrac{V_B}{R_V}$

Reading of voltmeter $C = 8$ V

$i_3 R_V = 8 \quad \Rightarrow \quad i_3 = \dfrac{8}{R_V}$

$V_B = i_3(R + R_V) = V_B = \dfrac{8}{R_V}(R + R_V)$

$\Rightarrow \quad \dfrac{R}{R_V} = \dfrac{V_B}{8} - 1$

$V_A = (i_2 + i_3)R + i_2 R_V$

$\Rightarrow \quad 22 = (V_B + 8)\dfrac{R}{R_V} + V_B$

$\Rightarrow \quad 22 = (V_B + 8)\left(\dfrac{V_B}{8} - 1\right) + V_B$

$\Rightarrow \quad 176 = V_B^2 - 64 + 8V_B$

$\Rightarrow \quad V_B^2 + 8V_B - 240 = 0$

$\Rightarrow (V_B + 20)(V_B - 12) = 0$

$\Rightarrow \quad V_B = 12$ V

17. With an ideal voltmeter, C and D is open circuit.

I_1 = current from cell $= \dfrac{\varepsilon}{\left(\dfrac{R+r}{2}\right)} = \dfrac{2\varepsilon}{R+r}$

$V_C - V_D = \dfrac{I_1}{2}(R - r)$

$= \dfrac{420}{12 + r}(R + r) = 140$

$\Rightarrow \quad \dfrac{R - r}{R + r} = \dfrac{1}{3}$

$\Rightarrow \quad \dfrac{R}{r} = 2$

With an ideal ammeter, resistance between C and D is zero.

I_2 = current from cell $= \dfrac{\varepsilon}{\dfrac{3Rr}{R+r}} = \dfrac{\varepsilon}{2\left(\dfrac{2r}{3}\right)} = \dfrac{3\varepsilon}{4r}$

$= \dfrac{3 \times 420}{4r} = \dfrac{315}{r}$

Reading of ammeter $= I_2\left(\dfrac{R}{R+r}\right) - I_2\dfrac{r}{R+r}$

$\Rightarrow \quad 21 = \dfrac{315}{r}\left(\dfrac{R - r}{R + r}\right)$

$\Rightarrow \quad 21 = \dfrac{315}{r}\left(\dfrac{1}{3}\right)$

$\Rightarrow \quad r = 5\,\Omega$ and $R = 10\,\Omega$

Now,

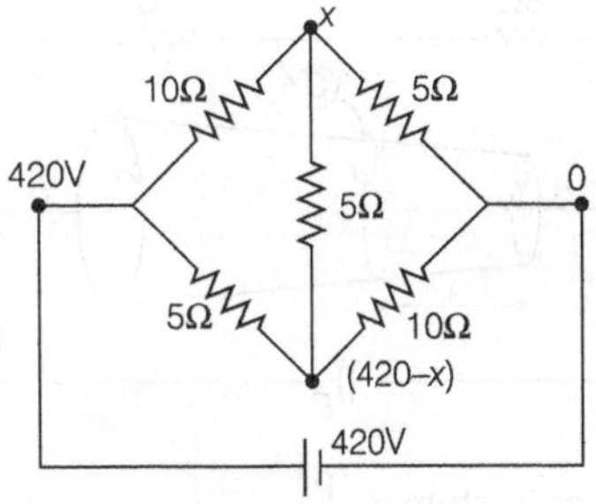

$\dfrac{420 - x}{10} + \dfrac{[(420 - x) - x]}{5} + \dfrac{0 - x}{5} = 0$

$\Rightarrow \quad 420 - x + 840 - 6x = 0$

$\Rightarrow \quad x = 180$ V

Current through r between C and $D = \dfrac{(420 - x) - x}{5}$

$= 12$ A

18. At melting point of ice (0°C).

For null point,

$4(100 - 40) = Y(40)$

$Y = 6\,\Omega$

Resistance of coil at 100°C $= Y(1 + \alpha\Delta T)$

$Y' = 6(1 + 100\alpha)$

Now, $\quad \dfrac{Y'(78)}{Y' + 78} = Y = 6$

$\Rightarrow \quad Y' = 6.5\,\Omega$

$\Rightarrow \quad 6(1 + 100\alpha) = 6.5$

$\Rightarrow \quad \alpha = 8.3 \times 10^{-4}\,K^{-1}$

19. $\dfrac{dR}{dl} \propto \dfrac{1}{\sqrt{l}}$

$\Rightarrow \quad \dfrac{dR}{dl} = \dfrac{K}{\sqrt{l}} \quad \Rightarrow \int dR = K\int \dfrac{dl}{\sqrt{l}}$

$\Rightarrow \quad R = K\int \dfrac{dl}{\sqrt{l}}$

$R_{AP} = K\int_0^{AP} \dfrac{dl}{\sqrt{l}} = 2K\sqrt{AP}$

$R_{PB} = K\int_{AP}^{l} \dfrac{dl}{\sqrt{l}} = 2K[\sqrt{l} - \sqrt{AP}]$

For null point,

$\dfrac{R'}{R'} = \dfrac{R_{AP}}{R_{PB}}$

$\Rightarrow \quad 1 = \dfrac{2K\sqrt{AP}}{2K[\sqrt{l} - \sqrt{AP}]}$

$\Rightarrow \quad \sqrt{AP} = \dfrac{1}{2}\sqrt{l}$

$\Rightarrow \quad \sqrt{AP} = \dfrac{l}{4} = \dfrac{1}{4} = 0.25$ m

20.

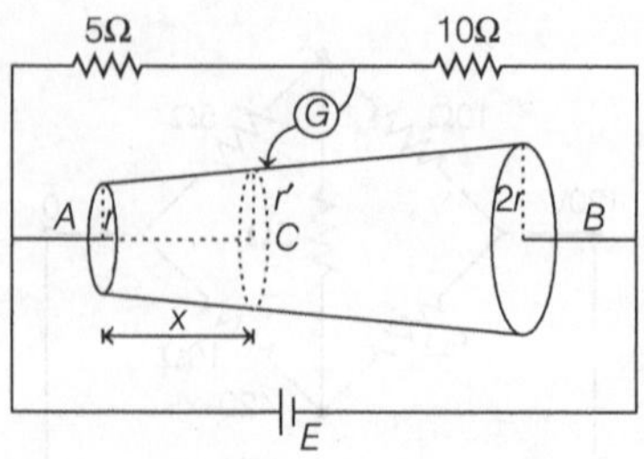

Resistance of frustum $= \dfrac{\rho l}{\pi r_1 r_2}$

$$R_{AC} = \frac{\rho x}{\pi r' r} \quad \text{and} \quad R_{CB} = \frac{\rho(10-x)}{\pi r'(2r)}$$

For null point,

$$\frac{5}{10} = \frac{R_{AC}}{R_{CB}}$$

$$\Rightarrow \quad \frac{1}{2} = \frac{2x}{10-x} \Rightarrow x = 2\text{ m}$$

21. Let potential gradient be x and emf and internal resistance of the secondary cell be ε and r, respectively.

$$\left(\frac{\varepsilon}{5+r}\right)5 = x(2) \qquad \text{...(i)}$$

$$\left(\frac{\varepsilon}{10+r}\right)10 = x(3) \qquad \text{...(ii)}$$

Dividing Eq. (i) by Eq. (ii), we get

$$\frac{1}{2}\left(\frac{10+r}{5+r}\right) = \frac{2}{3}$$

$$\Rightarrow \quad 30 + 3r = 20 + 4r$$

$$\Rightarrow \quad r = 10\,\Omega$$

22. Let resistance of potentiometer wire be R initially.

$$x = \text{potential gradient} = \left(\frac{10}{R+998+2}\right)\frac{R}{100}$$

$$\Rightarrow \quad x = \frac{R}{10(R+1000)}$$

For null point,

$$\varepsilon = xl$$

$$\varepsilon = \frac{R}{10(R+1000)} \times 50$$

$$\Rightarrow \quad \varepsilon = \frac{5R}{R+1000} \qquad \text{...(i)}$$

Now, area of cross-section is doubled.

New resistance of potentiometer wire $= \dfrac{R}{2}$

$$x' = \text{new potential gradient} = \frac{\frac{R}{2}}{10\left(\frac{R}{2}+1000\right)} = \frac{R}{10(R+2000)}$$

For null point,

$$\varepsilon = x'l'$$

$$\varepsilon = \frac{R}{10(R+2000)} \times 75$$

$$\varepsilon = \frac{7.5R}{R+2000} \qquad \text{...(ii)}$$

From Eqs. (i) and (ii), we get

$$\frac{5R}{R+1000} = \frac{7.5R}{R+2000}$$

$$\Rightarrow \quad 1.5R + 1500 = R + 2000$$

$$\Rightarrow \quad R = 1000\,\Omega$$

So, $\quad \varepsilon = \dfrac{5 \times 1000}{1000+1000} = 2.5\text{ V}$

23. Current in the primary circuit $= \dfrac{500}{10+40} = 10\text{ A}$

$$R_{AB} = \int_0^1 \frac{Kx\,dx}{A} = \frac{K}{2A} = 40 \Rightarrow \frac{K}{A} = 80$$

Let null point be at point C.

$$R_{AC} = \int_0^l \frac{Kx\,dx}{A} = \left(\frac{K}{A}\right)\frac{l^2}{2} = (80)\left(\frac{l^2}{2}\right) = 40l^2$$

For null point,

$$iR_{AC} = 100$$

$$\Rightarrow \quad 10(40l^2) = 100 \Rightarrow l = \frac{1}{2}$$

$$\Rightarrow \quad l = 0.5\text{ m} \Rightarrow l = 50\text{ cm}$$

24.

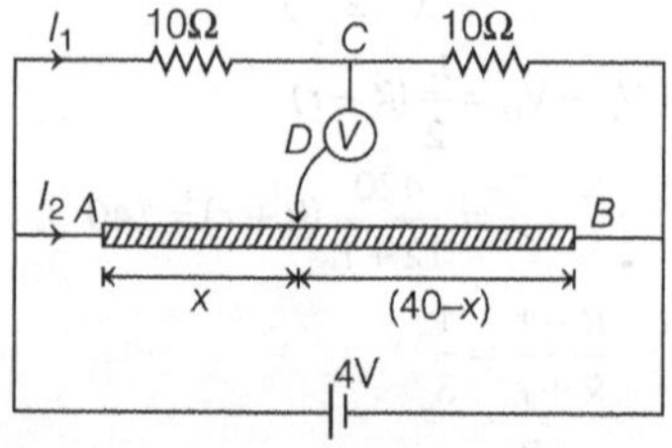

$$I_1 = \frac{4}{20} = 0.2\text{ A}$$

$$\Rightarrow \quad I_2 = \frac{4}{50 \times 0.4} = 0.2\text{ A}$$

$$V_A - V_C = 10I_1$$

and $\quad V_A - V_D = (50x)I_2$

$$V_C - V_D = (50x)I_2 - 10I_1$$

$$= (50x - 10)(0.2) = 10x - 2$$

$$V_C - V_D = 10x - 2 = 2\sin \pi t$$

$$x = \left(\frac{2(1+\sin \pi t)}{10}\right)\text{m}$$

$$x = (20(1+\sin \pi t))\text{ cm}$$

$$v = \frac{dx}{dt} = (20\pi \cos \pi t)\text{ cm/s}$$

25. $V_1 - V_2 = \dfrac{ER_1}{R_1 + R_2} = xl_1$ ...(i)

$E_0 = xl_2$ ...(ii)

From Eqs. (i) and (ii), we get

$$E = E_0 \frac{l_1}{l_2}\left(\frac{R_1 + R_2}{R_1}\right)$$

$$\Rightarrow \quad E = 2\left(\frac{60}{75}\right)\left(\frac{100 + 9900}{100}\right) = 160 \text{ V}$$

$$\Rightarrow \quad \frac{\Delta E}{E} = \frac{\Delta l_1}{l_1} + \frac{\Delta l_2}{l_2} + \frac{\Delta (R_1 + R_2)}{R_1 + R_2} + \frac{\Delta R_1}{R_1}$$

$$\Rightarrow \quad \frac{\Delta E}{160} = \frac{0.06}{60} + \frac{0.075}{75} + \frac{0.10 + 9.90}{100 + 9900} + \frac{0.10}{100}$$

$$\Rightarrow \quad \frac{\Delta E}{160} = \frac{4}{1000} \quad \Rightarrow \Delta E = 0.64 \text{ V}$$

Multiple Choice(s) Correct Questions

1. Let full scale deflection current and resistance of galvanometer be i_g and R_g, respectively.

When galvanometer is converted into voltmeter,

$$V = i_g (R_g + R)$$

$$\Rightarrow \quad n i_g R_g = i_g (R_g + 72)$$

$$\Rightarrow \quad (n-1)R_g = 72 \quad \text{...(i)}$$

When galvanometer is converted into ammeter

$$S = \frac{i_g R_g}{i - i_g} \Rightarrow 2 = \frac{i_g R_g}{n i_g - i_g} \Rightarrow (n-1)2 = R_g \quad \text{...(i)}$$

Solving Eqs. (i) and (ii), we get

$$n = 7 \text{ and } R_g = 12\,\Omega$$

Resistance of ammeter $= \dfrac{R_g S}{R_g + S} = \dfrac{12(2)}{12 + 2} = 1.7\,\Omega$

Resistance of voltmeter $= R_g + R = 12 + 72 = 84\,\Omega$

2.

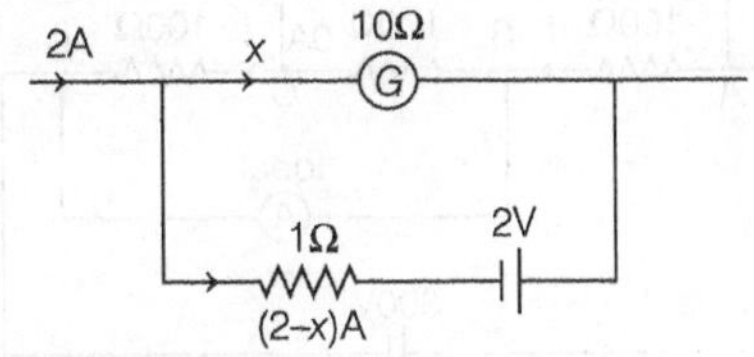

Using KVL in the loop,

$-10x - 2 + 1(2 - x) = 0 \quad \Rightarrow x = 0$

So, reading of galvanometer will be zero.

Potential difference across the resistance $S = (2 - x)1$

$= 2\text{ V}$

3.

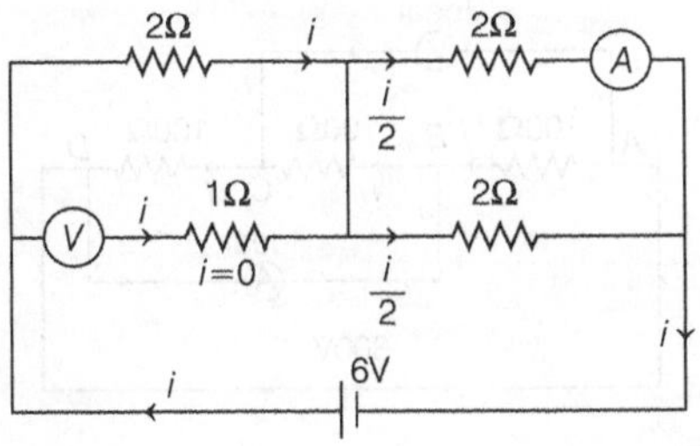

Since, voltmeter is ideal, it has infinite resistance and no current will pass through it. Resistance of ideal ammeter is zero.

Equivalent resistance across battery $= 2 + \dfrac{2 \times 2}{2 + 2} = 3\,\Omega$

$i =$ current through battery $= \dfrac{6}{3} = 2\text{A}$

Reading of voltmeter$= i(2) = 2(2) = 4\text{ V}$

Reading of ammeter $= \dfrac{i}{2} = \dfrac{2}{2} = 1\text{ A}$

Current through 1Ω resistor = 0

4.

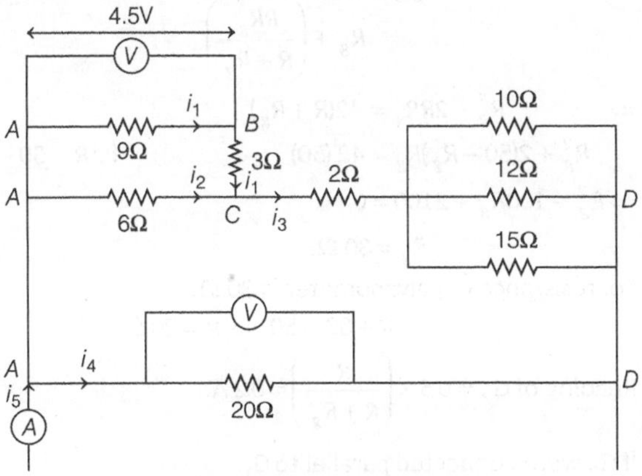

$$V_A - V_B = 4.5 = 9i_1$$

$$\Rightarrow \quad i_1 = 0.5\text{ A}$$

$$V_A - V_C = (9 + 3)i_1 = 6i_2$$

$$\Rightarrow \quad 12 \times 0.5 = 6i_2 \quad \Rightarrow \quad i_2 = 1\text{ A}$$

$$i_3 = i_1 + i_2 = 0.5 + 1 = 1.5\text{ A}$$

$$\frac{1}{R_{eq}} = \frac{1}{10} + \frac{1}{12} + \frac{1}{15} \quad \Rightarrow \quad R_{eq} = 4\,\Omega$$

$$V_A - V_D = 6i_2 + 2i_3 + 4i_3 = 15\text{ V}$$

$$V_A - V_D = 20i_4 = 15$$

$$\Rightarrow \quad i_4 = 0.75\text{ A}$$

Current through 12Ω resistance $= 1.5 \times \dfrac{\frac{1}{12}}{\frac{1}{12} + \frac{1}{10} + \frac{1}{15}}$

$= 0.5\text{ A}$

Reading of voltmeter connected across 20Ω resistance

$= 20i_4 = 20 \times 0.75 = 15\text{ V}$

Reading of ammeter $= i_5 = i_3 + i_4$

$= 1.5 + 0.75 = 2.25\text{ A}$

5.

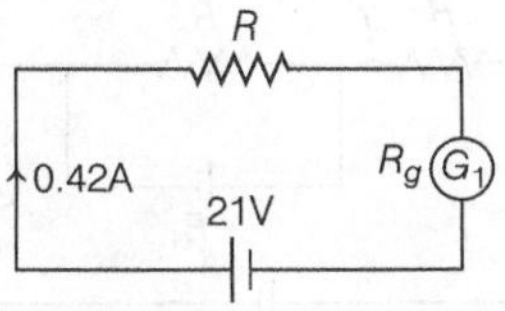

Let resistance of galvanometer G_1 and G_2 be R_g each

$$0.42 = \frac{21}{R + R_g} \Rightarrow R + R_g = 50$$

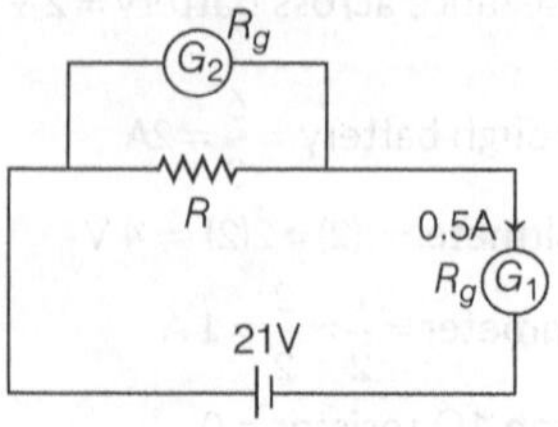

$$0.5 = \frac{21}{R_g + \left(\frac{RR_g}{R + R_g}\right)}$$

$$\Rightarrow \quad R_g^2 + 2RR_g = 42(R + R_g)$$

$$R_g^2 + 2(50 - R_g)R_g = 42(50) \qquad \{\because R = 50 - R_g\}$$

$$\Rightarrow R_g^2 - 100R_g + 2100 = 0$$

$$R_g = 30\ \Omega$$

So, resistance of galvanometer is 30 Ω.

$$R + 30 = 50 \Rightarrow R = 20\ \Omega$$

$$\text{Reading of } G_2 = 0.5 \times \left(\frac{R}{R + R_g}\right) = 0.2\ \text{A}$$

If G_2 were connected parallel to G_1,

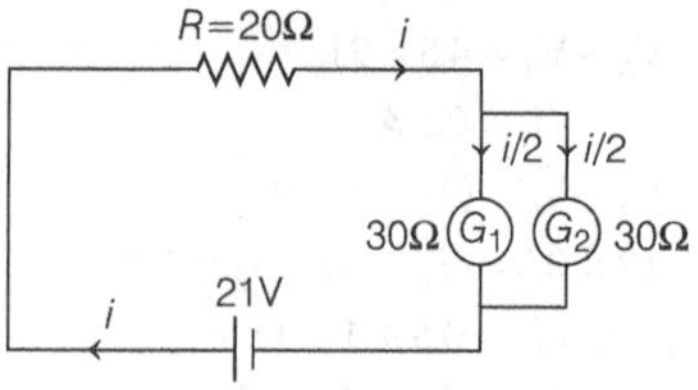

$$i = \frac{21}{20 + \frac{30 \times 30}{30 + 30}} = \frac{21}{35} = 0.6\ \text{A}$$

$$\text{Reading of } G_1 \text{ and } G_2 = \frac{i}{2} = 0.3\ \text{A}$$

6.

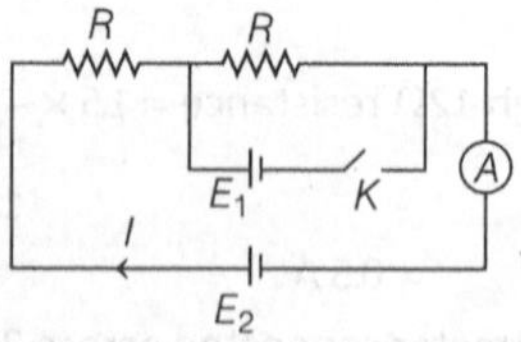

When key K is open.

$$\text{Reading of ammeter} = I = \frac{E_2}{2R} \Rightarrow E_2 = 2IR$$

When key K is closed, let reading of ammeter be I'.

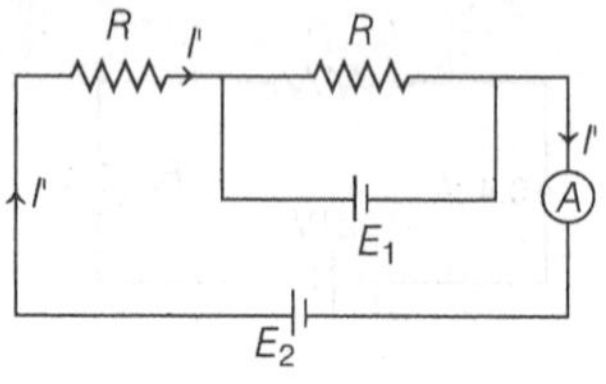

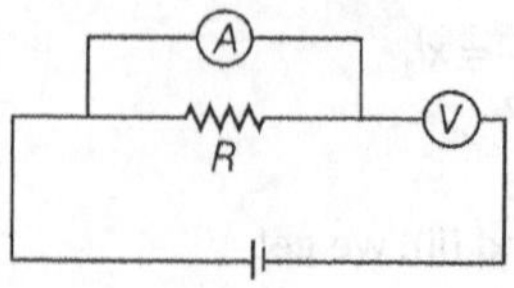

Using KVL,

$$+E_2 - I'R - E_1 = 0$$

$$\Rightarrow \quad I' = \frac{E_2 - E_1}{R} \Rightarrow I' = \frac{2IR - E_1}{R}$$

If $E_1 = IR$, then $I' = I$

If $IR < E_1 < 2IR$, then $I' < I$

If $E_1 = 2IR$, then $I' = 0$

7.

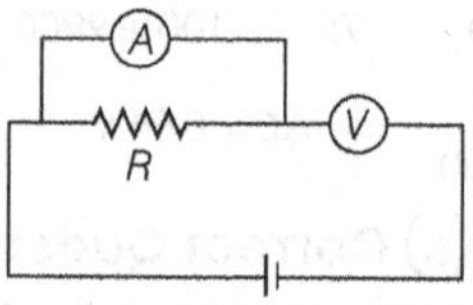

(a) If the devices are ideal, R will get short- circuit and current through battery will be nearly zero as voltmeter has infinite resistance. So, ammeter will read zero current and voltmeter will read to emf of the cell.

(b) Current through ammeter is nearly zero.

(c) The main current in the circuit will be very low as total resistance of circuit is very large due to voltmeter. Since, ammeter has very low resistance compared to R, most of the main current will pass through the ammeter.

(d) If emf of the cell is very high and the devices are non-ideal, then the devices may get damaged due to large current passing through them.

8. (a)

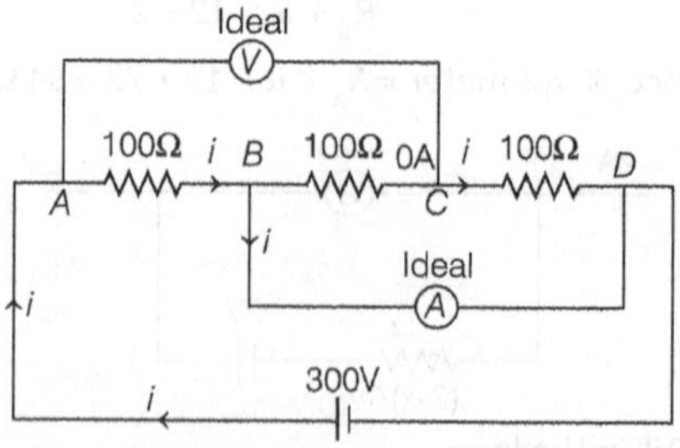

Since, M_2 is ideal ammeter, its resistance is zero and the two 100 Ω resistances on the right will get short-circuited.

So, voltmeter M, will read 300 V.

(b)

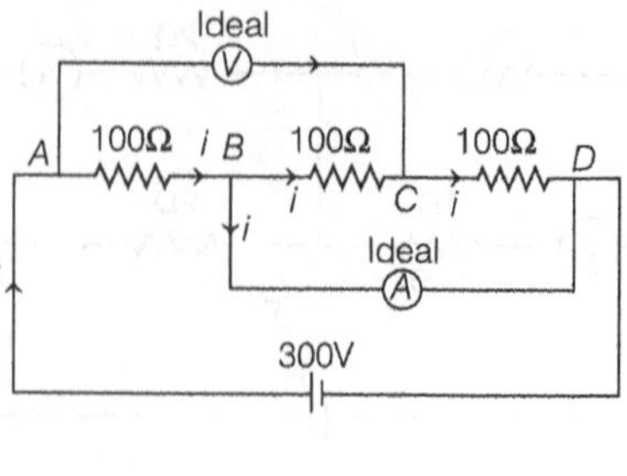

$$i=\frac{300}{300}=1\text{ A}$$

$V_A - V_C = 100\times1+100\times1=200$ V

$V_B - V_D = 100\times1+100\times1=200$ V

So, each voltmeter will read 200 V.

(c)

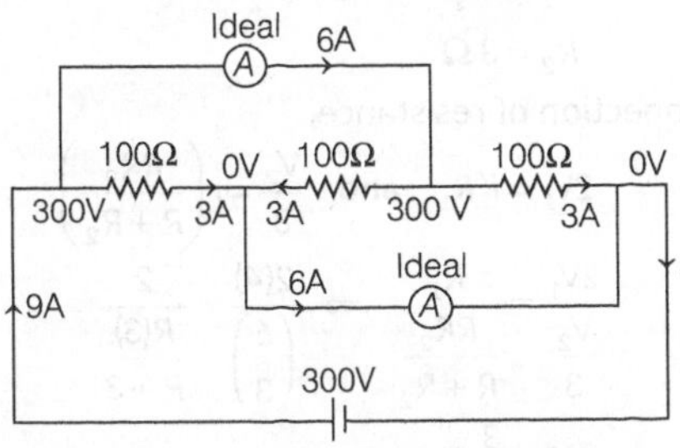

Current through each resistor $=\frac{300-0}{100}=3$ A

Current through each ammeter $=3+3=6$ A

(d)

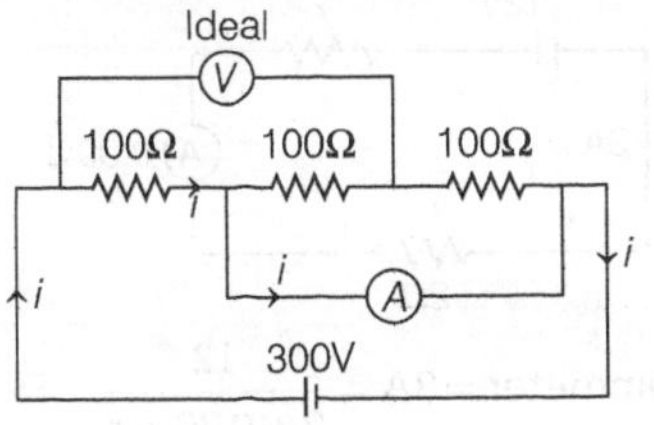

$$i=\frac{300}{100}=3\text{ A}$$

Reading of ammeter = 3A

9. Equivalent diagram of the given circuit is as shown

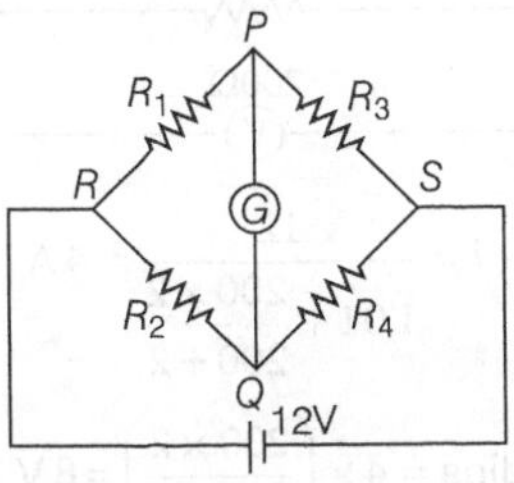

If jockey at P is moved towards S by 2 cm, then

$R_1 = 12\ \Omega$ and $R_2 = 3\ \Omega$

$\frac{R_1}{R_3}=\frac{12}{3}=4$ and $\frac{R_2}{R_4}=\frac{20}{5}=4$

Since, $\frac{R_1}{R_3}=\frac{R_2}{R_4}$, Wheatstone bridge will be balanced.

If jockey at Q is moved towards S by 2 cm,
then $R_1 = 10\ \Omega, R_2 = 22\ \Omega, R_3 = 5\ \Omega, R_4 = 3\ \Omega$

Since, $\frac{R_1}{R_3}\neq\frac{R_2}{R_4}$, Wheatstone bridge is not balanced.

If the jockey at S is moved towards P by $\frac{5}{3}$ cm, then $R_1 = 10$ $\Omega, R_2 = 20\ \Omega, R_3 = 5-\frac{5}{3}=\frac{10}{3}\ \Omega$ and $R_4 = 5+\frac{5}{3}=\frac{20}{3}\ \Omega$

Since, $\frac{R_1}{R_3}=\frac{R_2}{R_4}$, Wheatstone bridge is balanced.

If the jockey at all positions are fixed and R_1 is made 20 Ω, then

$R_1 = 20\ \Omega, R_2 = 20\ \Omega, R_3 = 5\ \Omega, R_4 = 5\ \Omega$

Since, $\frac{R_1}{R_3}=\frac{R_2}{R_4}$, Wheatstone bridge is balanced.

10. Let resistance of resistance box be R.

$$i=\frac{20}{5+75+R}=\frac{20}{80+R}$$

Potential drop across potentiometer wire,

$$V=\left(\frac{20}{80+R}\right)75=\frac{1500}{80+R}$$

Since, $120<R<170$

$\Rightarrow\quad 6<V<7.5$

11. For getting null point, emf of D must be greater than the emf of C and either the positive terminals of both D and C or the negative terminals of both D and C must be joined to A.

12. Let the rheostat resistance be R.

$$i=\frac{20}{2+8+R}=\frac{20}{10+R}$$

Potential drop across potentiometer wire

$$=\left(\frac{20}{10+R}\right)8=\frac{160}{10+R}$$

$x =$ potential gradient $=\frac{1}{100}\left(\frac{160}{10+R}\right)$ V/cm

For null point,

$\varepsilon = xl$

$$\varepsilon=\frac{1}{100}\left(\frac{160}{10+R}\right)l$$

If $l = 50$ cm, $\varepsilon=\frac{80}{10+R}\Rightarrow\ \varepsilon<8$ V

If $l = 60$ cm, $\varepsilon=\frac{96}{10+R}\Rightarrow\ \varepsilon<9.6$ V

If $l = 70$ cm, $\varepsilon=\frac{112}{10+R}$

$\Rightarrow\quad\varepsilon<11.2$ V

$128\ \Rightarrow\ \varepsilon<12.8$ V

Since, cheated value is 10 V, reading 1 and reading 2 helped the teacher to arrive at the conclusion that he cheated.

13. $V =$ potential drop across potentiometer wire $=\left(\frac{E_1}{R+r}\right)R$

For the direction of current shown, $E_2 > V$

$$\Rightarrow\quad E_2>\frac{E_1R}{R+r}$$

So, correct options are a, b and c.

14. Current in the primary loop $= \dfrac{6}{1+2} = 2\text{ A}$

Potential drop across wire $AB = 2 \times 2 = 4\text{V}$

Potential gradient $= x = \dfrac{4}{120} = \dfrac{1}{30}\text{ V/cm}$

(a) When only S_2 is open,

current in the secondary loop $= \dfrac{2}{3}\text{ A}$

potential difference across 1 Ω resistance $= \dfrac{2}{3} \times 1 = \dfrac{2}{3}\text{ V}$

For null point, $V = xl$

$$\Rightarrow \quad \frac{2}{3} = \frac{1}{30} l \quad \Rightarrow \quad l = 20 \text{ cm}$$

(b) When only S_1 is open,

For null point, $V = xl$

$$2 = \left(\frac{1}{30}\right) l \quad \Rightarrow \quad l = 60 \text{ cm}$$

(c) When all three switches are closed, for null point,

$$V = xl$$

$$\Rightarrow \quad 2 = \left(\frac{1}{30}\right) l \quad \Rightarrow \quad l = 60 \text{ cm}$$

(d) When S_3 and S_2 are open and S_1 is closed, for null point, $V = xl$

$$\Rightarrow \quad 2 = \left(\frac{1}{30}\right) l \quad \Rightarrow \quad l = 60 \text{ cm}$$

Comprehension Based Questions

1.

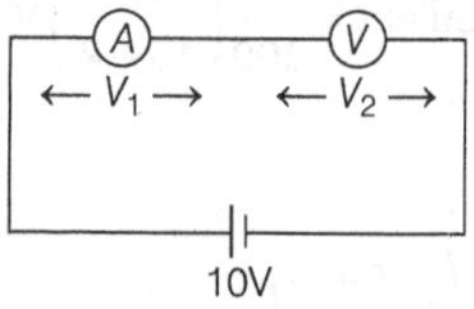

Let potential difference across ammeter and voltmeter be V_1 and V_2, respectively.

$$V_1 + V_2 = 10 \qquad \text{...(i)}$$

Now, resistance R is connected in parallel with the voltmeter.

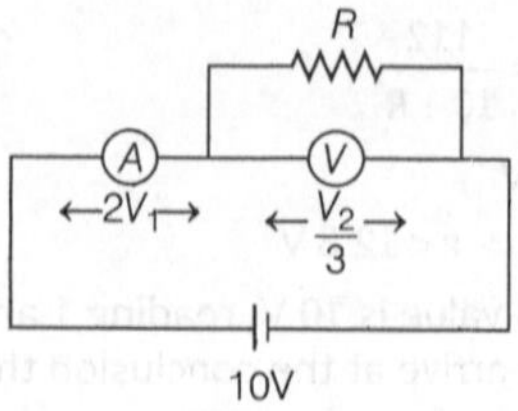

$$2V_1 + \frac{V_2}{3} = 10 \qquad \text{...(ii)}$$

Solving Eqs. (i) and (ii), we get

$$V_1 = 4\text{V and } V_2 = 6\text{V}$$

So, voltmeter reading after the connection of the resistance $= \dfrac{V_2}{3} = \dfrac{6}{3} = 2\text{ V}$

2. Let resistance of ammeter and voltmeter be R_1 and R_2 respectively,

$$V_1 = iR_1 \quad \text{and} \quad V_2 = iR_2$$

$$\frac{V_1}{V_2} = \frac{R_1}{R_2} \Rightarrow \frac{4}{6} = \frac{2}{R_2}$$

$$\Rightarrow \quad R_2 = 3\,\Omega$$

3. After connection of resistance,

$$2V_1 = i'R_1 \quad \text{and} \quad \frac{V_2}{3} = i\left(\frac{RR_2}{R+R_2}\right)$$

$$\Rightarrow \quad \frac{2V_1}{\frac{V_2}{3}} = \frac{R_1}{\frac{RR_2}{R+R_2}} \Rightarrow \frac{2(4)}{\left(\frac{6}{3}\right)} = \frac{2}{\frac{R(3)}{R+3}}$$

$$\Rightarrow \quad R = \frac{3}{5}\,\Omega$$

4. Resistance of ammeter $= \dfrac{99 \times 1}{99+1} = 0.99\,\Omega$

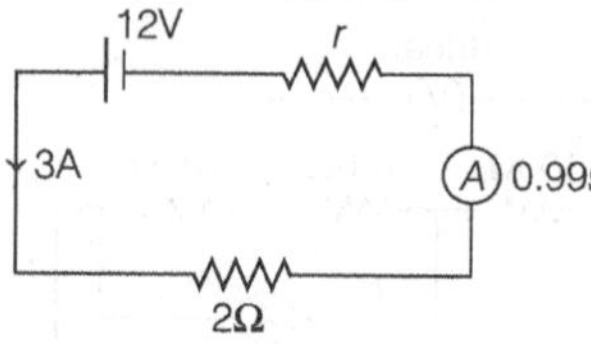

Reading of ammeter $= 3\text{A} = \dfrac{12}{2 + 0.99 + r} \Rightarrow r = 1.01\,\Omega$

5. Resistance of voltmeter $= 99 + 101 = 200\Omega$

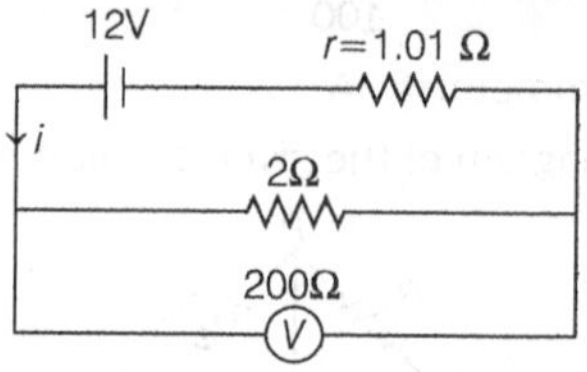

$$i = \frac{12}{1.01 + \frac{200 \times 2}{200+2}} = 4\text{ A}$$

Voltmeter reading $= 4 \times \left(\dfrac{200 \times 2}{200+2}\right) = 8\text{ V}$

Let full scale reading of voltmeter be V_{max}.

$$8 = \frac{4}{5}(V_{max}) \Rightarrow V_{max} = 10\text{ V}$$

Let full scale deflection current of galvanometer be i_g.

$$V = i_g(R_g + R)$$

$$\Rightarrow \quad 10 = i_g(99 + 101)$$

$$\Rightarrow \quad i_g = 0.05\text{ A} = 50\text{ mA}$$

6. For ammeter,

$$S = \frac{i_g R_g}{i - i_g} \Rightarrow 1 = \frac{50 \times 10^{-3} \times 99}{i - 50 \times 10^{-3}}$$

$$\Rightarrow \quad i = 5\text{ A}$$

So, range of ammeter = 0 -5 A

and range of voltmeter = 0 -10 V

7. Reading of voltmeter $= 10\text{ V}$

$$\Rightarrow \quad iR_1 = 10 \Rightarrow (500\times10^{-3})R_1 = 10$$

$$\Rightarrow \quad R_1 = 20\,\Omega$$

8. $\varepsilon = i(R_1 + R_2)$

$$\varepsilon = 500\times10^{-3}(20+10) = 15\text{ V}$$

9. Power dissipated in $R_3 = 15\text{ W}$

$$\Rightarrow \quad \frac{\varepsilon^2}{R_3} = 15 \Rightarrow \frac{(15)^2}{R_3} = 15 \Rightarrow R_3 = 15\,\Omega$$

10.

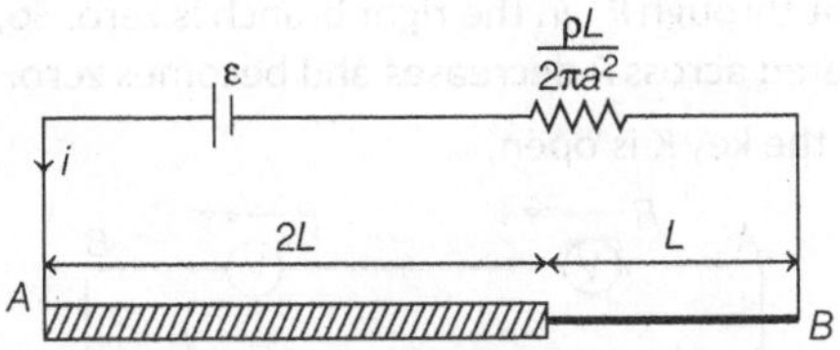

Resistance of longer wire $= \dfrac{\rho(2L)}{\pi(2a)^2} = \dfrac{\rho L}{2\pi a^2}$

Resistance of smaller wire $= \dfrac{\rho L}{\pi a^2}$

Current in the primary circuit $= \dfrac{\varepsilon}{\dfrac{\rho L}{2\pi a^2} + \dfrac{\rho L}{2\pi a^2} + \dfrac{\rho L}{\pi a^2}}$

$$\Rightarrow \quad i = \frac{\pi a^2 \varepsilon}{2\rho L}$$

Maximum voltage which can be measured on the potentiometer wire $AB = i\left(\dfrac{\rho L}{2\pi a^2} + \dfrac{\rho L}{\pi a^2}\right)$

$$= \frac{\pi a^2 \varepsilon}{2\rho L}\,\frac{3}{2}\,\frac{\rho L}{\pi a^2} = \frac{3\varepsilon}{4}$$

11. Let balance length be l.

$x_1 =$ potential gradient for longer wire $= \dfrac{1}{2L}\left[i\left(\dfrac{\rho l}{2\pi a^2}\right)\right] = \dfrac{\varepsilon}{8L}$

$x_2 =$ potential gradient for smaller wire $= \dfrac{1}{L}\left(i\dfrac{\rho L}{\pi a^2}\right) = \dfrac{\varepsilon}{2L}$

For balance point,

$$\frac{\varepsilon}{2} = x_1(2L) + x_2(l - 2L)$$

$$\Rightarrow \quad \frac{\varepsilon}{2} = \frac{\varepsilon}{8L}(2L) + \frac{\varepsilon}{2L}(l - 2L) \Rightarrow l = \frac{5L}{2}$$

12. $\dfrac{\rho L}{2\pi a^2} = R$

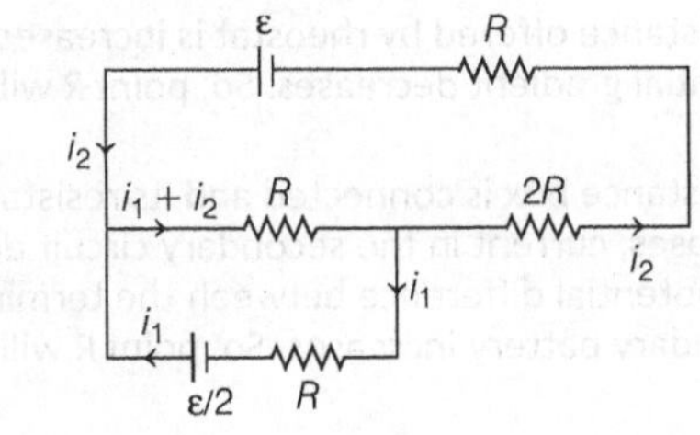

Applying KVL,

$$+\varepsilon - (I_1 + I_2)R - i_2(2R) - i_2 R = 0$$

$$\Rightarrow \quad i_1 + 4i_2 = \frac{\varepsilon}{R} \quad \text{...(i)}$$

$$+\frac{\varepsilon}{2} - (i_1 + i_2)R - i_1 R = 0$$

$$\Rightarrow \quad 2i_1 + i_2 = \frac{\varepsilon}{2R} \quad \text{...(ii)}$$

Solving Eqs. (i) and (ii), we get

$$i_1 = \frac{\varepsilon}{7R} \text{ and } i_2 = \frac{3\varepsilon}{14R}$$

So, current through the secondary cell $= \dfrac{\varepsilon}{7R}$

13. $dR = \dfrac{\rho dx}{A}$

$$\Rightarrow \quad dR = \frac{\rho_0 x dx}{A}$$

$$\Rightarrow \quad \int dR = \int_0^1 \frac{(24\pi)\,x dx}{\pi} \Rightarrow R = 12\,\Omega$$

14. Current in the primary circuit $= \dfrac{15}{12+3} = 1\text{ A}$

Potential drop across dx length $= dV$

$$\Rightarrow \quad dV = i\frac{\rho dx}{A} \Rightarrow dV = 1\frac{\rho_0 x dx}{A}$$

$$\Rightarrow \quad dV = \frac{(24\pi)\,x dx}{\pi} = 24x dx$$

When switch S is open, for null point,

$$E = \int dV = \int_0^{\sqrt{\frac{2}{3}}} 24x dx = 12[x^2]_0^{\sqrt{\frac{2}{3}}} = 8\text{ V}$$

15. When switch is closed, for null point

$$E - ir = \int_0^{\frac{1}{\sqrt{2}}} dV$$

$$\Rightarrow 8 - \left(\frac{8}{3+r}\right)r = \int_0^{\frac{1}{\sqrt{2}}} 24x dx$$

$$\Rightarrow \quad 8 - \frac{8r}{3+r} = 6 \Rightarrow r = 1\,\Omega$$

Match the Columns Questions

1. (a) For 2V range, $V = i_g(R_G + R)$

$$\Rightarrow \quad 2 = 1\times10^{-3}(40 + R_1)$$

$$\Rightarrow \quad R_1 = 1960\,\Omega = 1.96\text{ k}\Omega$$

(b) For 10 V range, $V = i_g(R_G + R)$

$$10 = 1\times10^{-3}(40 + 1960 + R_2)$$

$$\Rightarrow \quad R_2 = 8000\,\Omega = 8\text{ k}\Omega$$

For 100 V range, $V = i_g(R_G + R)$

$$100 = 1 \times 10^{-3}(40 + 1960 + 8000 + R_3)$$

$$\Rightarrow \quad R_3 = 90000\ \Omega = 90\ k\Omega$$

(c) Overall resistance for 100 V range

$$= (40 + 1960 + 8000 + 90000)\ \Omega = 100\ k\Omega$$

(d) Overall resistance for 2 V range

$$= (40 + 1960)\ \Omega = 2000\ \Omega = 2\ k\Omega$$

2. (a) S_1 is open and S_2 is closed

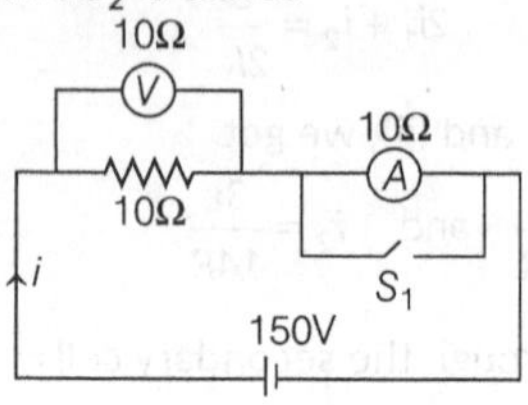

$$i = \frac{150}{10 + \left(\frac{10 \times 10}{10 + 10}\right)} = 10\text{A}$$

Reading of ammeter = 10A

Reading of voltmeter $= 10\left(\frac{10 \times 10}{10 + 10}\right) = 50$ V

(b) S_1 is closed, S_2 is open

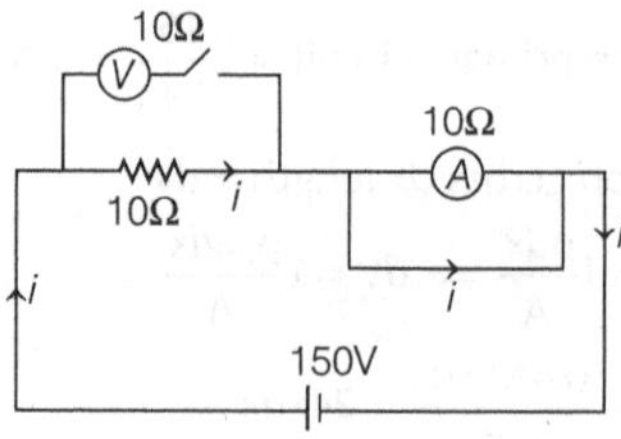

Ammeter gets short-circuited,

$$i = \frac{150}{10} = 15\ \text{A}$$

Reading of ammeter = 0

Reading of voltmeter = 0

(c) S_1 is open and S_2 is also open

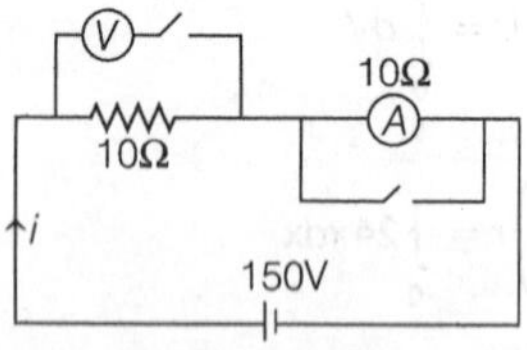

$$i = \frac{150}{(10 + 10)} = 7.5\ \text{A}$$

Reading of ammeter = 7.5 A

Reading of voltmeter = 0

(d) S_1 and S_2 both closed

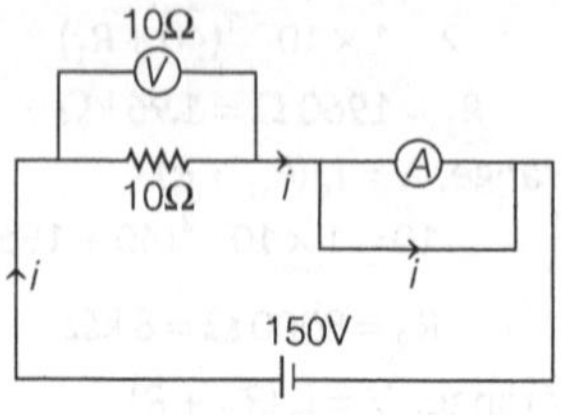

$$i = \frac{150}{\left(\frac{10 \times 10}{10 + 10}\right)} = 30\ \text{A}$$

Reading of ammeter = 0

Reading of voltmeter $= 30 \times 5 = 150$ V

3. When switch is closed, the resistor of resistance R on the right side gets short-circuited. So, equivalent resistance of circuit decreases and current through battery increases. Hence, reading of ammeter and voltmeter increases.

Current through R in the right branch is zero. So, power dissipated across R decreases and becomes zero.

4. When the key K is open,

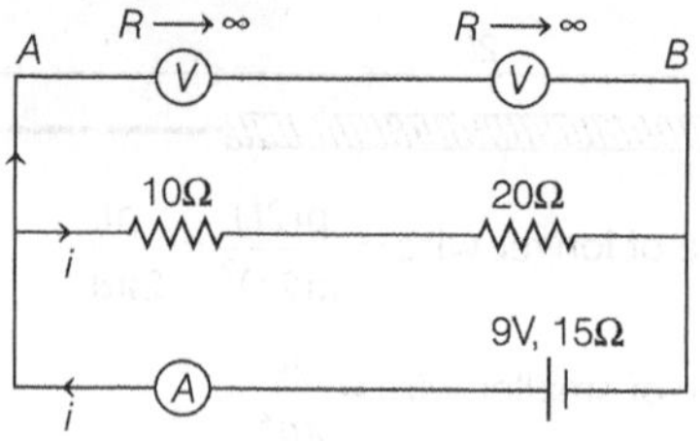

$$i = \frac{9}{15 + 10 + 20} = 0.2\ \text{A}$$

$$V_A - V_B = 0.2(10 + 20) = 6\ \text{V}$$

Since, both the voltmeters are identical and in series, their readings would be same.

Reading of each voltmeter $= \frac{6}{2} = 3$ V

When the key K is closed,

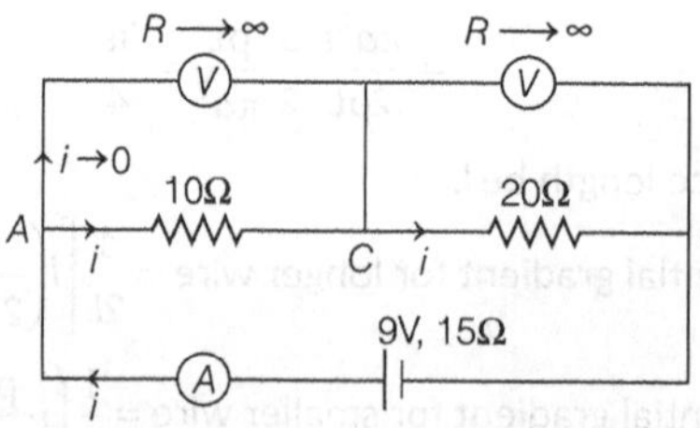

$$i = 0.2\ \text{A}$$

$$V_C - V_B = 20 \times 0.2 = 4\ \text{V}$$

Reading of right voltmeter = 4 V

Ammeter reading = 0.2 A

5. (a) If E_1 is increased, reading of ammeter increases and potential gradient increases. So, balance length will decrease and point R will shift to left.

(b) If resistance offered by rheostat is increased and potential gradient decreases. So, point R will shift to right.

(c) If resistance box is connected and its resistance increases, current in the secondary circuit decreases and potential difference between the terminals of the secondary battery increases. So, point R will shift to right.

(d) If an identical battery is connected in parallel to E, equivalent emf of the secondary battery will be E and equivalent interval resistance $\frac{r}{2}$. So, point R will remain unchanged.

Numerical Value Questions

1.

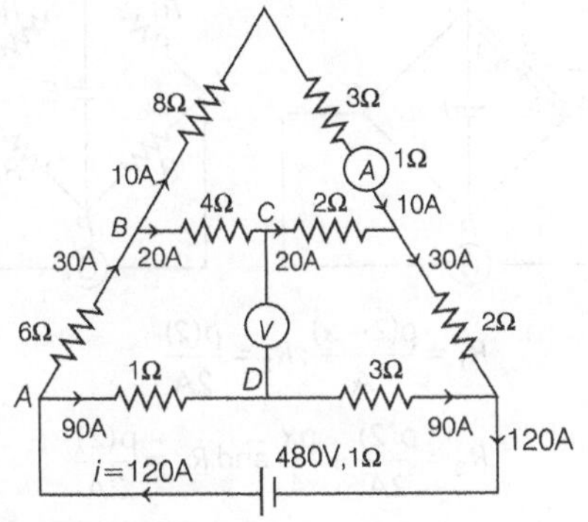

Equivalent resistance across battery = 3 Ω

$$i = \frac{480}{1+3} = 120 \text{ A}$$

Reading of ammeter = x = 10 A

$V_D + 90(1) - 6(30) - 4(20) = V_C$

$$V_D - V_C = 170 \text{ V}$$

Reading of voltmeter = $y = V_D - V_C = 170$ V

$$\frac{y}{x} = \frac{170}{10} = 17$$

2.

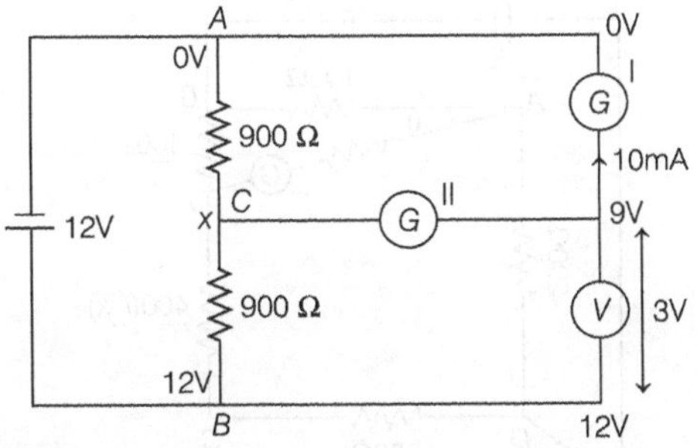

Let $\left.\begin{matrix} V_A = 0 \\ V_C = x \end{matrix}\right\}$ and resistance of each galvanometer be R.

For galvanometer I,

$$V = iR$$

$\Rightarrow$ $9 - 0 = 10 \times 10^{-3} \times R$

$\Rightarrow$ $R = 900\ \Omega$

Applying KCL at junction C,

$$\frac{0-x}{900} + \frac{12-x}{900} + \frac{9-x}{900} = 0$$

$\Rightarrow$ $x = 7$ V

Current through galvanometer II $= \frac{9-7}{900} = \frac{2}{900}$ A

$$= \frac{20}{9} \text{ mA} = 2.22 \text{ mA}$$

3.

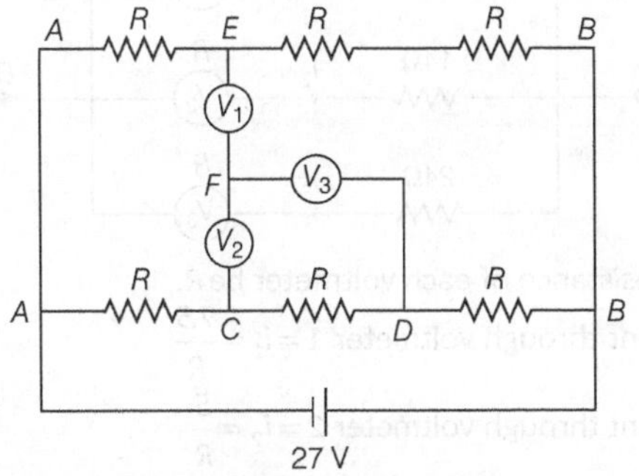

Let, $V_A = 0$

So, $V_B = 27$ V, $V_C = 9$ V, $V_D = 18$ V

and $V_E = 9$ V

Let resistance of each voltmeter be R.

Applying KCL at junction F,

$$\frac{V_E - V_F}{R} + \frac{V_C - V_F}{R} + \frac{V_D - V_F}{R} = 0$$

$$\Rightarrow \frac{9-V_F}{R} + \frac{9-V_F}{R} + \frac{18-V_F}{R} = 0$$

$\Rightarrow$ $V_F = 12$ V

Reading of voltmeter, $V_3 = V_D - V_F$

$= 18 - 12 = 6$ V

4.

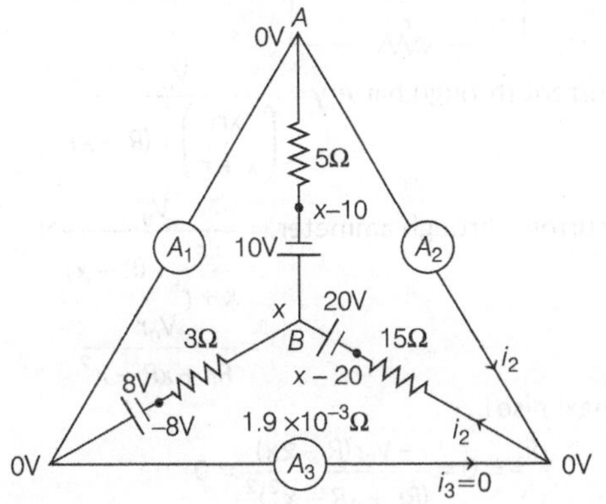

Let $V_A = 0$ V and $V_B = x$

Current through ammeter, $A_3 = \frac{0-0}{1.9 \times 10^{-3}} = 0$

Applying KCL at junction B,

$$\frac{-8-x}{3} + \frac{0-(x-20)}{15} + \frac{0-(x-10)}{5} = 0$$

$$x = \frac{10}{9} \text{ V} \Rightarrow i_2 = \frac{20 - \frac{10}{9}}{15} = \frac{170}{135} = \frac{34}{27} \text{ A}$$

Reading of ammeter, $A_2 = \frac{34}{27}$ A

5.

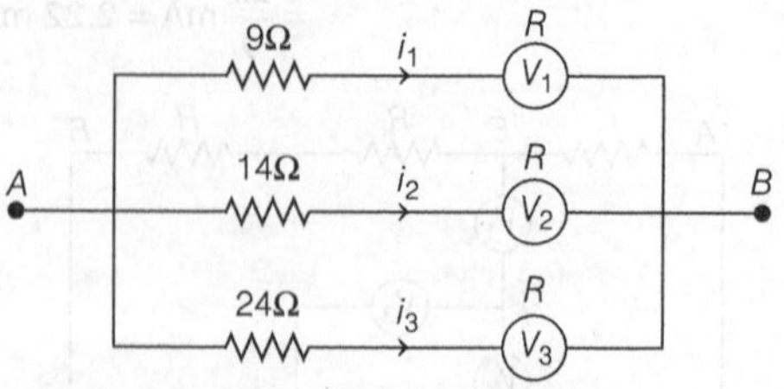

Let resistance of each voltmeter be R.

Current through voltmeter $1 = i_1 = \dfrac{7.5}{R}$

Current through voltmeter $2 = i_2 = \dfrac{5}{R}$

$$V_A - V_B = (R+9)i_1 = (14+R)i_2$$

$$\Rightarrow \quad (R+9)\left(\frac{7.5}{R}\right) = (R+14)\left(\frac{5}{R}\right)$$

$$\Rightarrow \quad R = 1\,\Omega$$

$$V_A - V_B = (1+9)\left(\frac{7.5}{1}\right) = (24+1)\,i_3$$

$$i_3 = 3\text{ A}$$

Reading of voltmeter $3 = 3 \times 1 = 3$ V

6.

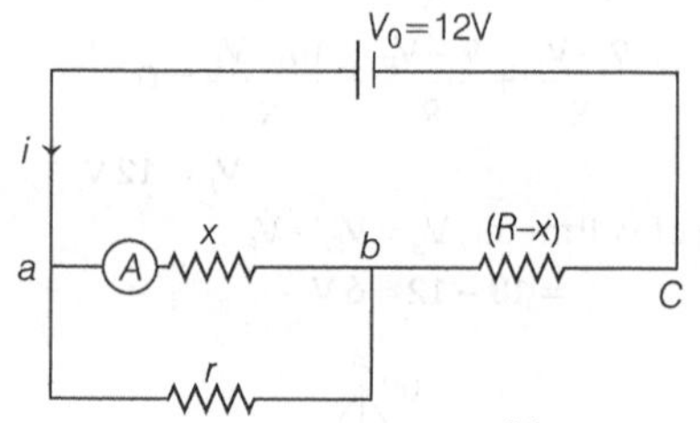

$$i = \text{current through battery} = \frac{V_0}{\left(\dfrac{xr}{x+r}\right) + (R-x)}$$

$$i_1 = \text{current through ammeter} = \frac{V_0}{\dfrac{xr}{x+r} + (R-x)} \times \frac{r}{x+r}$$

$$= \frac{V_0 r}{Rr + xR - x^2}$$

To maximise i_1,

$$\frac{di_1}{dx} = 0 = \frac{-V_0 r(R-2x)}{(Rr + xR - x^2)^2} = 0$$

$$\Rightarrow \quad x = \frac{R}{2} \quad \Rightarrow \quad (i_1)_{max} = \frac{12 \times 2}{4(2) + 2(4) - 2^2} = 2\text{ A}$$

7. Let current in the circuit be I.

V_0 = potential difference across R + potential difference across the gap

$$V_0 = IR + A + \frac{B}{I}$$

$$\Rightarrow \quad 100 = IR + 40 + \frac{20}{I}$$

$$\Rightarrow \quad R = \frac{1}{I}\left(60 - \frac{20}{I}\right) \quad \Rightarrow \quad R = \frac{60}{I} - \frac{20}{I^2}$$

To maximise R,

$$\frac{dR}{dI} = -\frac{60}{I^2} + \frac{40}{I^3} = 0 \quad \Rightarrow \quad I = \frac{2}{3}\text{ A}$$

$$R_{max} = \frac{1}{\left(\dfrac{2}{3}\right)}\left(60 - \frac{20}{\left(\dfrac{2}{3}\right)}\right) = 45\,\Omega$$

8.

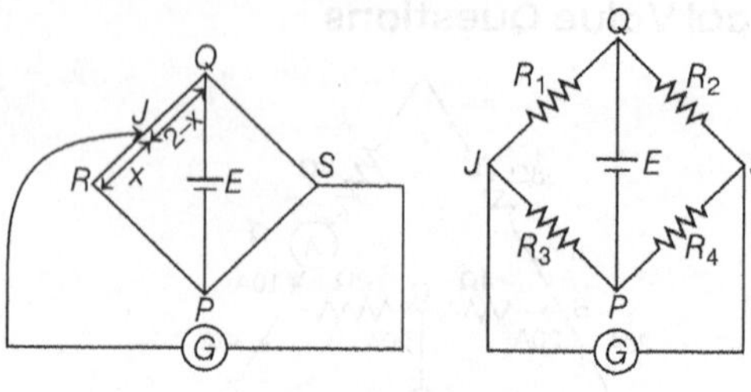

$$R_1 = \frac{\rho(2-x)}{A};\; R_2 = \frac{\rho(2)}{2A}$$

$$R_3 = \frac{\rho(2)}{2A} + \frac{\rho x}{A} \text{ and } R_4 = \frac{\rho(2)}{2A}$$

For null point,

$$\frac{R_1}{R_2} = \frac{R_3}{R_4}$$

$$\Rightarrow \quad \frac{\dfrac{\rho(2-x)}{A}}{\dfrac{\rho(2)}{2A}} = \frac{\dfrac{\rho(2)}{2A} + \dfrac{\rho x}{A}}{\dfrac{\rho(2)}{2A}}$$

$$\Rightarrow \quad x = 0.5\text{ m} = 50\text{ cm}$$

9. Equivalent circuit is as shown,

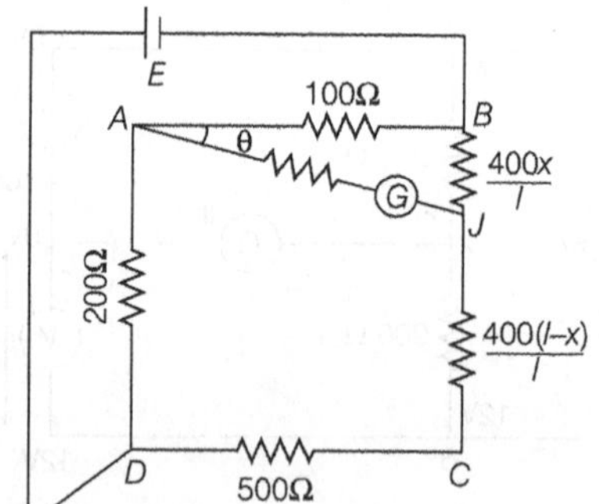

Let distance $BJ = x$ and side of square $= l$

$$\Rightarrow \quad CJ = l - x$$

$$R_{BJ} = \frac{400}{l}x \text{ and } R_{CJ} = \frac{400(l-x)}{l}$$

For null point,

$$\frac{R_{AB}}{R_{DA}} = \frac{R_{BJ}}{R_{DJ}}$$

$$\Rightarrow \quad \frac{100}{200} = \frac{\dfrac{400}{l}x}{500 + \dfrac{400(l+x)}{l}} \quad \Rightarrow \quad x = \frac{3l}{4}$$

$$\tan\theta = \frac{BJ}{AB} \Rightarrow \tan(\omega t) = \frac{\frac{3l}{4}}{l} = \frac{3}{4}$$

$$\Rightarrow \quad \omega t = \frac{37\pi}{180°} \Rightarrow \left(\frac{\pi}{360°}\right)t = 37\left(\frac{\pi}{180°}\right)$$

$$\Rightarrow \quad t = 74 \text{ s}$$

10.

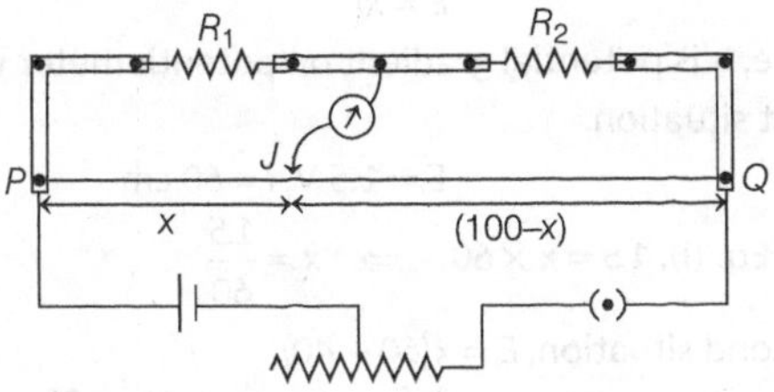

For wire PQ,

$$\frac{dR}{dx} \propto x \Rightarrow \frac{dR}{dx} = kx, \text{ where } k \text{ is a constant.}$$

$$\Rightarrow \quad \int dR = \int kxdx$$

$$R_{PJ} = \int_0^x kxdx = \frac{kx^2}{2}$$

$$R_{JQ} = \int_x^1 kxdx = \frac{k(1^2 - x^2)}{3} = \frac{k(1-x^2)}{2}$$

For null point,

$$\frac{R_1}{R_2} = \frac{R_{PJ}}{R_{JQ}} \Rightarrow 3 = \frac{\frac{kx^{-2}}{2}}{\frac{k(1-x^2)}{2}} \Rightarrow x = \frac{\sqrt{3}}{2} \text{ m}$$

On interchanging R_1 and R_2, let new null point happen when jockey is at J' and $PJ' = y$

$$R_{PJ'} = \int_0^y kxdx = \frac{ky^2}{2}, \quad R_{J'Q} = \int_y^1 kxdx = \frac{k(1-y^2)}{2}$$

For null point,

$$\frac{R_2}{R_1} = \frac{R_{PJ'}}{R_{J'Q}} \Rightarrow \frac{1}{3} = \frac{\frac{ky^2}{2}}{\frac{k(1-y^2)}{2}} \Rightarrow y = \frac{1}{2} \text{ m}$$

Displacement of jockey $\Rightarrow D = x - y$

$$= \frac{\sqrt{3}}{2} - \frac{1}{2} = \frac{\sqrt{3}-1}{2} = \frac{1.7-1}{2} = 0.35 \text{ m} = 35 \text{ cm}$$

11. Current in the secondary circuit $= \dfrac{E_S}{R+r}$

Potential difference across $R = iR = \dfrac{E_S R}{R+r}$

For null point,

$$\frac{E_S R}{R+R} = xl$$

$$\Rightarrow \quad \frac{10R}{R+1} = x \text{ (30 cm)} \quad \text{...(i)}$$

$$\Rightarrow \quad \frac{5R}{R+2} = x \text{ (10 cm)} \quad \text{...(ii)}$$

Solving Eqs. (i) and (ii), we get

$$R = 1\,\Omega$$

12. In the primary circuit, current $= \dfrac{20}{10+10} = 1$ A

Potential gradient $= x = \dfrac{10 \times 1}{100} = 0.1$ V/m.

When S_1 and S_3 is closed,

$$V = xl \Rightarrow 5 = (0.1)l_1 \Rightarrow l_1 = 50 \text{ m}$$

When S_2 and S_4 is closed,

$$V = xl \Rightarrow 3 = (0.1)l_2 \Rightarrow l_2 = 30 \text{ m}$$

$$\therefore \quad l_1 + l_2 = 50 + 30 = 80 \text{ m}$$

13. Current in the primary circuit $= \dfrac{10}{8+r}$

$$x = \text{potential gradient} = \left(\frac{10}{8+r}\right)\frac{8}{100} = \frac{4}{5(8+r)}$$

$$\text{Current in the secondary circuit} = \frac{3}{\frac{(3R)(6R)}{3R+6R} + R} = \frac{1}{R}$$

$$V_X - V_Y = \frac{1}{R}\left(\frac{3R(6R)}{3R+6R}\right) = 2 \text{ V}$$

For null point,

$$V_X - V_Y = xl$$

$$\Rightarrow \quad 2 = \frac{4}{5(8+r)} \times 25 \Rightarrow r = 2\,\Omega$$

Previous Year's Questions

JEE Main

1.

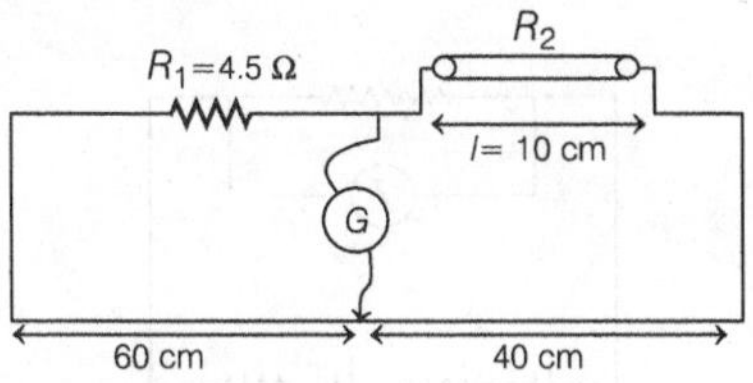

$$r = \sqrt{7} \times 10^{-4} \text{ m}$$

$$l = 10 \text{ cm} = 10 \times 10^{-2} \text{m} = \frac{1}{10} \text{m}$$

Under balance condition $\dfrac{R_1}{l_1} = \dfrac{R}{l_2}$

Here, $R_1 = 4.5\,\Omega, l_1 = 60$ cm

$$l_2 = 100 - l_1 = 40 \text{ cm}$$

$$R_2 = R$$

$$\frac{l_1}{l_2} = \frac{R_1}{R_2} \Rightarrow \frac{60}{40} = \frac{4.5\,\Omega}{R}$$

$R = 3\,\Omega$

$R = \rho\dfrac{l}{A} \Rightarrow 3 = \rho \times \dfrac{1}{\pi r^2}$

$3 = \rho \times \dfrac{1}{10 \times \pi \times 7 \times 10^{-8}}$

$\Rightarrow \quad \rho = 21\pi \times 10^{-7}$

$\rho = 21\pi \times 10^{-7}$

$\rho = 21 \times \dfrac{22}{7} \times 10^{-7} = 66 \times 10^{-7}$

$\rho = 66 \times 10^{-7} \Rightarrow R = 66$

2. Specific resistance does not depend on length of wire. It is depond on the material of wire.

Therefore, specific resistance remain same.

3.

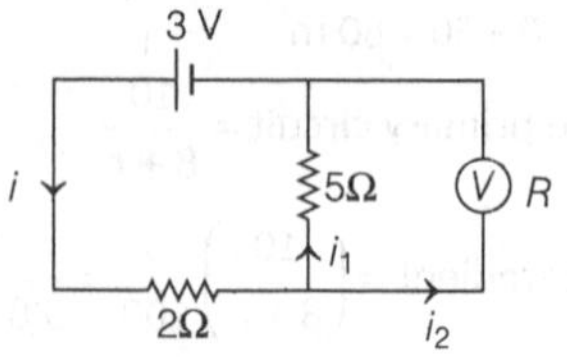

Given potential across 5Ω and voltmeter 2V to find resistance R of voltmeter.

Let current in 5Ω be i_1 and R is $\dfrac{V}{i_2}$, across 2Ω will be 1V and

$i = \dfrac{1}{2}$ A

Using junction law,

$$i = i_1 + i_2$$

$$\frac{1}{2} = \frac{2}{5} + \frac{2}{R}$$

$$\frac{2}{R} = \frac{1}{2} - \frac{2}{5} = \frac{1}{10}$$

$$R = 20\,\Omega$$

4.

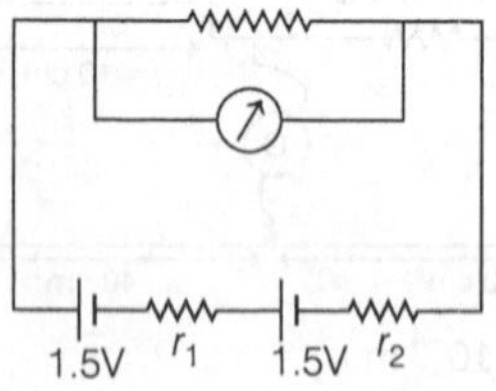

$$r = \left(\frac{E}{V} - 1\right)R$$

$$r = \left(\frac{3.0}{1.5} - 1\right) \times 10 = \left(\frac{30}{15} - 1\right) \times 10 = (2-1) \times 10$$

$V_{eq} = 10$

$r_1 = 5\Omega$ or $r_2 = 5\Omega$

5. A more sensitive potentiometer can measure a small potential drop or emf. So, its potential gradient, potential drop per unit length must be as small as possible. So, sensitivity of a potentiometer

$$\propto \frac{1}{\text{Potential gradient}} \propto \frac{l}{\Delta V}$$

6. If a cell of emf E is balanced on length l of potentiometer wire then emf E is given as

$$E = xl \qquad \text{...(i)}$$

Where, x is potential gradient on potentiometer wire

In first situation,

$$E = 1.5\text{ V}, l = 60\text{ cm}$$

From Eq. (i), $1.5 = x \times 60 \quad \Rightarrow \quad x = \dfrac{1.5}{60}$

In second situation, $E = x(60 + 40)$

$$E = \frac{1.5}{60} \times 100 \quad \Rightarrow \quad E = \frac{25}{10}\text{ V}$$

On comparing with, $\dfrac{x}{10}$ volt, we get $x = 25$

7. We know, in a balanced meter bridge,

$$\frac{R_1}{R_2} = \frac{AC}{CB} \qquad \text{...(i)}$$

$$\Rightarrow \quad \frac{R_1}{R_2} = \frac{40}{CB}$$

As we can clearly see from Eq. (i) that the condition for a balanced Wheatstone bridge (balanced meter bridge) is independent of the radius of wire AB, therefore the balancing length will not change and will remain 40 cm only.

8. In potentiometer arrangement we know that,

$$\frac{E_1}{E_2} = \frac{l_1}{l_2} \qquad \text{...(i)}$$

Given, $E_1 = 1.2\text{ V}, l_1 = 36\text{ cm}$

$E_2 = 1.8\text{ V}, l_2 = ?$

On putting these values in Eq. (i), we get

$$\frac{1.2}{1.8} = \frac{36}{l_2} \quad \Rightarrow \quad \frac{2}{3} = \frac{36}{l_2}$$

$$\Rightarrow \quad l_2 = \frac{36 \times 3}{2} = 54\text{ cm}$$

∴ Difference in balancing length,

$$\Delta l = l_2 - l_1 = 54 - 36 = 18\text{ cm}$$

9. Balance length is given 43 cm. So, other point's length will be

$$l_2 = (100 - l_1) = 100 - 43 = 57\text{cm}$$

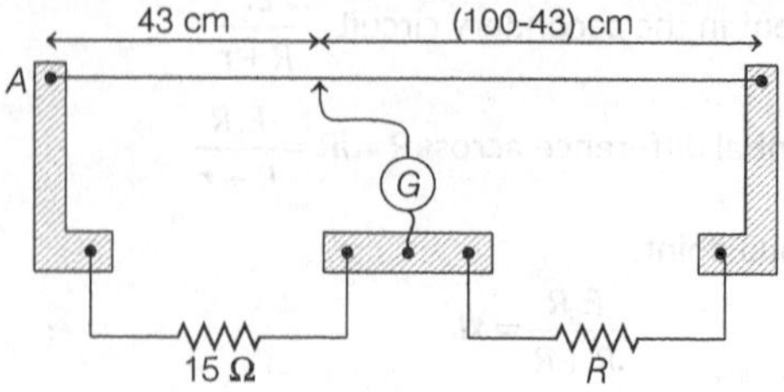

Now under balanced condition,

$$\frac{15}{l_1}=\frac{R}{l_2} \quad \text{(when there is no end error)}$$

$$\frac{15}{l_1+e_1}=\frac{R}{l_2+e_2}$$

(when there are errors e_1 at end A and e_2 at end B)

Here, $l_1 = 43$ cm, $l_2 = 100 - 43 = 57$ cm $e_1 = 2$ cm, $e_2 = 0$ (not given)

So, we have

$$\frac{15}{43+2}=\frac{R}{57}$$

$$\Rightarrow \quad R=\frac{15\times 57}{(43+2)}=19\ \Omega$$

10.

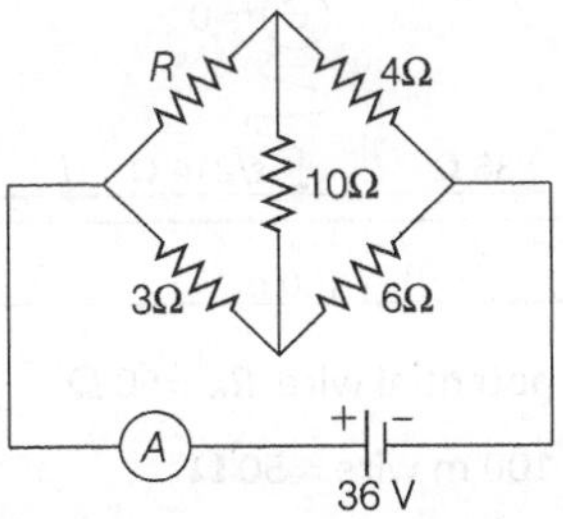

When no current flows through $10\,\Omega$ resistor, then given Wheatstone bridge will be balanced and so ratio of resistances are equal.

$$\Rightarrow \quad \frac{R}{3}=\frac{4}{6} \quad \Rightarrow \quad R=2\ \Omega$$

So, total resistance of circuit will be $(2+4)\,||\,(3+6)$

$$\Rightarrow \quad R_{\text{total}}=\frac{6\times 9}{6+9}=\frac{18}{5}\Omega$$

Current through ammeter,

$$I=\frac{V}{R_{\text{total}}}=\frac{36}{\frac{18}{5}}=10\text{ A}$$

11. According to question,

$$r=R\left[\frac{l_1}{l_2}-1\right]$$

Case 1 When balancing length is 3m.

$$l_1=L$$
$$l_2=3\text{ m}$$
$$R_1=8\Omega$$
$$r=8\left[\frac{L}{3}-1\right]$$
$$\left(\frac{r}{8}+1\right)\times 3=L \qquad \text{...(i)}$$

Case 2 When balancing length is 2m

$$l_1=L, l_2=2\text{m}, R_2=4\Omega$$
$$r=4\left[\frac{L}{2}-1\right]$$
$$\left(\frac{r}{4}+1\right)\times 2=L \qquad \text{...(ii)}$$

From Eqs. (i) and (ii), we get

$$3\times\left(\frac{r}{8}+1\right)=2\times\left(\frac{r}{4}+1\right)$$

$$\Rightarrow \quad \frac{r}{8}=1$$

$$r=8\Omega$$

12. Comparision of emfs of two cells using the experiment of potentiometer is given as

$$\frac{e_1}{e_2}=\frac{l_1}{l_2}$$

Where, l_1, and l_2 are their corresponding balancing length.

$$\therefore \quad \frac{3}{2}=\frac{75}{l_2} \qquad [\because l_1=75\text{ cm given}]$$

$$\Rightarrow \quad l_2=50\text{ cm}$$

$\therefore$ Difference in balancing length,

$$=l_1-l_2=75-50=25\text{ cm}$$

13. Given, balancing length for emf (ε_1),

$$l_1=250\text{ cm}=250\times 10^{-2}\text{ m}$$

and for balancing emf $(\varepsilon_1+\varepsilon_2)$, length,

$$l_2=400\text{ cm}=400\times 10^{-2}\text{ m}$$

As we know that,

$$\frac{\varepsilon_1}{\varepsilon_1+\varepsilon_2}=\frac{l_1}{l_2}$$

$$\Rightarrow \quad \frac{\varepsilon_1}{\varepsilon_1+\varepsilon_2}=\frac{250\times 10^{-2}}{400\times 10^{-2}} \quad \Rightarrow \quad \frac{\varepsilon_1}{\varepsilon_2}=\frac{5}{3}$$

14. As, A is directly connected to the positive terminal of the battery, $V_A = 10$V and $V_C = 0$

By nodal analysis at B,

$$\frac{V_B-10}{100}+\frac{V_B-V_D}{15}+\frac{V_B-0}{10}=0$$

$$53V_B-20V_D=30 \qquad \text{... (i)}$$

By nodal analysis at D,

$$\frac{V_D-10}{60}+\frac{V_D-V_B}{15}+\frac{V_D-0}{5}=0$$

$$-4V_B+17V_D=10 \qquad \text{...(ii)}$$

On solving Eqs. (i) and (ii) by substitution method, we get

$$V_D=0.792\text{ V}$$

$$\Rightarrow \quad V_B=0.865\text{ V}$$

The current through the galvanometer,

$$I=\frac{V_B-V_D}{R}$$

On substituting the values in the above equation, we get

$$I=\frac{0.865-0.792}{15}$$

$$\Rightarrow \quad I=4.87\text{ mA}$$

15. Given all resistances have same resistance R.
Now, we can redraw the circuit as below

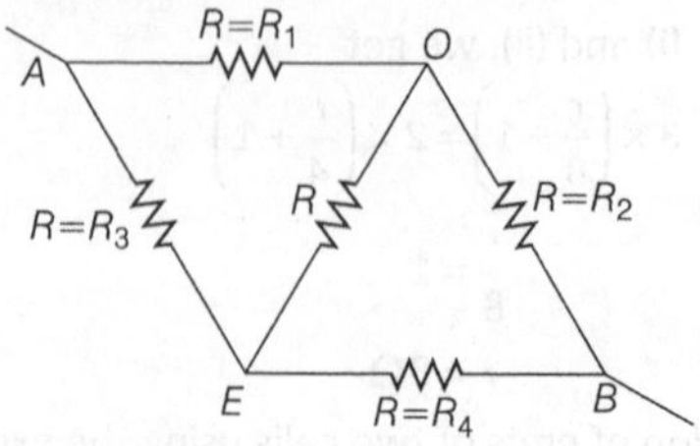

Let resistances be R_1, R_2, R_3 and R_4.

$$\because \quad \frac{R_1}{R_3} = \frac{R_2}{R_4}$$

So, circuit will behave as a Wheatstone bridge and no current will flow through middle resistor.

$$\therefore \quad R_{eq} = \frac{(R_1 + R_2)(R_3 + R_4)}{(R_1 + R_2) + (R_3 + R_4)}$$

$$= \frac{(R + R)(R + R)}{(R + R) + (R + R)} = R$$

16. At the balanced condition of the Wheatstone bridge,

$$\frac{R}{S} = \frac{L_1}{L - L_1} \Rightarrow \frac{12}{6} = \frac{x}{72 - x}$$

$$\Rightarrow \quad x = 48 \text{ cm}$$

$\therefore$ The galvanometer jockey is placed at P on AB at a distance of 48 cm from the A.

JEE Advanced

1. Resistance of frustum shaped conductor shown is

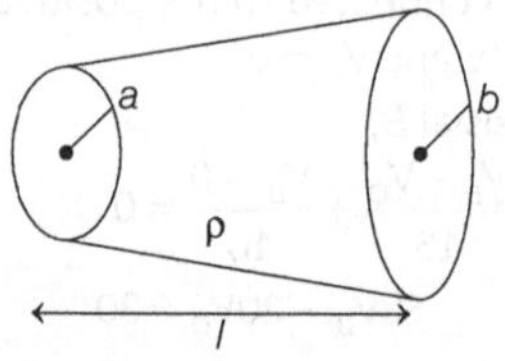

$$R = \rho \frac{l}{\pi ab}$$

For the shown conductor in the diagram,

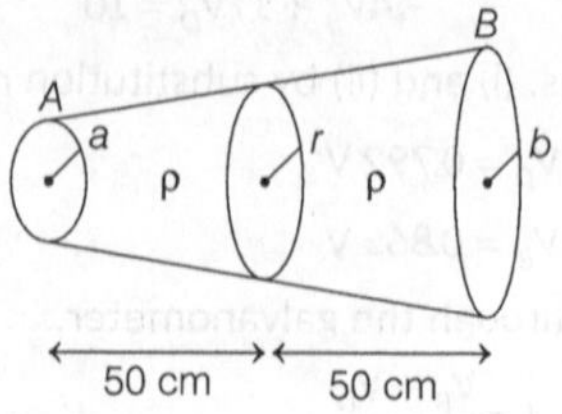

$$r = \frac{a + b}{2} = \frac{0.2 + 1}{2} = 0.6$$

Thus, the resistance of left half is $P = \dfrac{\rho \times 0.5 \times 10^6}{\pi \times 0.2 \times 0.6}$

and the resistance of right half is $Q = \dfrac{\rho \times 0.5 \times 10^6}{\pi \times 0.6 \times 1}$

For Wheatstone to be balanced,

$$\frac{R_1}{P} = \frac{R_2}{Q}$$

$$\Rightarrow \quad \frac{X\pi \times 0.2 \times 0.6}{\rho \times 0.5 \times 10^6} = \frac{1\pi \times 0.6 \times 1}{\rho \times 0.5 \times 10^6}$$

$$\Rightarrow \quad X = 5$$

2.

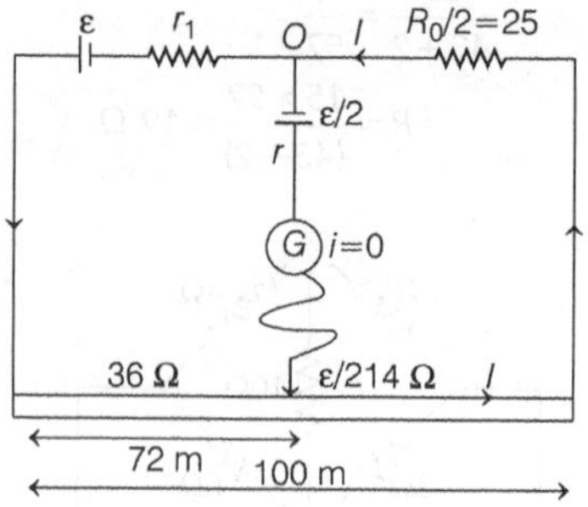

Resistance of potential wire, $R_0 = 50\ \Omega$

Resistance of 100 m wire $= 50\ \Omega$

So, resistance of 72 cm wire $= \dfrac{50}{100} \times 72 = 36\ \Omega$

$$\text{Current,} \quad I = \frac{\frac{\varepsilon}{2}}{14\Omega + 25\Omega} = \frac{\frac{\varepsilon}{2}}{r_1 + 36\ \Omega}$$

$$\Rightarrow \quad r_1 = 39 - 36 = 3\ \Omega$$

3. $R_3' = 300(1 + \alpha \Delta T) = 312\ \Omega$

Now,

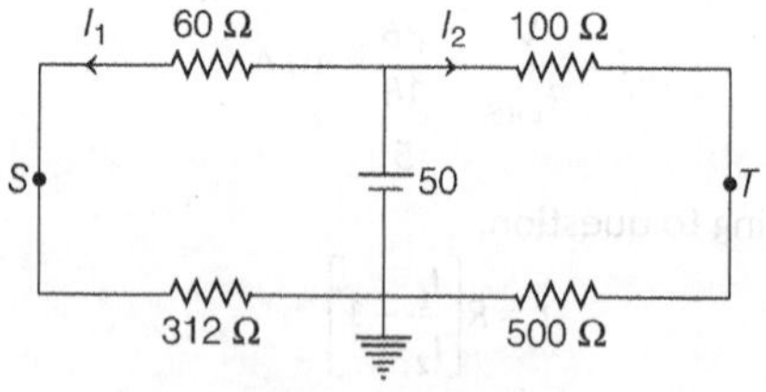

$$I_1 = \frac{50}{372} \text{ and } I_2 = \frac{50}{600}$$

$$V_S - V_T = 312 I_1 - 500 I_2$$

$$= 41.94 - 41.67 = 0.27 \text{ V}$$

4. Given, $N = 50$, $A = 2 \times 10^{-4} \text{m}^2$, $C = 10^{-4}$, $R = 50\Omega$,

$B = 0.02$ T, $\theta = 0.2$ rad

$$N i_g AB = C\theta$$

$$\Rightarrow \quad i_g = \frac{C\theta}{NAB} = \frac{10^{-4} \times 0.2}{50 \times 2 \times 10^{-4} \times 0.02} = 0.1 \text{ A}$$

$$\therefore \quad V_{ab} = i_g \times G = (i - i_g) S$$

$$\Rightarrow \quad 0.1\times 50 = (1-0.1)\times S$$

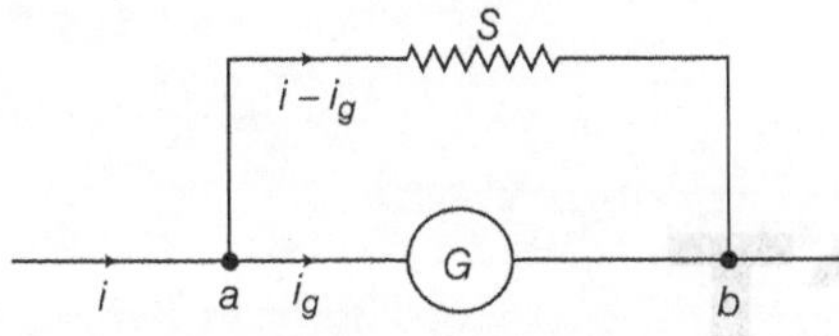

$$5 = 0.9\times S$$

$$\therefore \quad S = \frac{50}{9}\,\Omega = 5.55\,\Omega$$

5. For maximum range of voltage resistance should be maximum. So, all four should be connected in series. For maximum range of current, net resistance should be least. Therefore, all four should be connected in parallel.

6. For balanced meter bridge

$$\frac{X}{R} = \frac{l}{(100-l)} \qquad \text{(where, } R = 90\,\Omega)$$

$$\therefore \quad \frac{X}{90} = \frac{40}{100-40}$$

$$X = R\frac{l}{(100-l)}$$

$$\therefore \quad X = 60\,\Omega$$

$$\frac{\Delta X}{X} = \frac{\Delta l}{l} + \frac{\Delta l}{100-l} = \frac{0.1}{40} + \frac{0.1}{60}$$

$$\Delta X = 0.25$$

So, $X = (60 \pm 0.25)\,\Omega$

7.

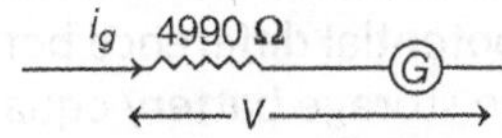

$$i_g(G+4990) = V$$

$$\Rightarrow \quad \frac{6}{1000}(G+4990) = 30$$

$$\Rightarrow \quad G + 4990 = \frac{30000}{6} = 5000$$

$$\Rightarrow \quad G = 10\,\Omega$$

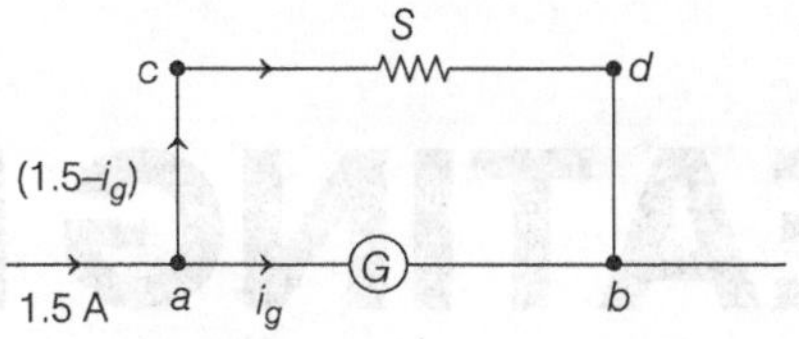

$$\therefore \quad V_{ab} = V_{cd}$$

$$\Rightarrow \quad i_g G = (1.5 - i_g)S$$

$$\Rightarrow \quad \frac{6}{1000}\times 10 = \left(1.5 - \frac{6}{1000}\right)S$$

$$\Rightarrow \quad S = \frac{60}{1494} = \frac{2n}{249}$$

$$\Rightarrow \quad n = \frac{249\times 30}{1494} = \frac{2490}{498} = 5$$

8. Using the concept of balanced Wheatstone bridge, we have

$$\frac{P}{Q} = \frac{R}{S}$$

$$\therefore \quad \frac{X}{(52+1)} = \frac{10}{(48+2)}$$

$$\therefore \quad X = \frac{10\times 53}{50} = 10.6\,\Omega$$

$\therefore$ Correct option is (b).

9. We will require a voltmeter, an ammeter, a test resistor and a variable battery to verify Ohm's law.
Voltmeter which is made by connecting a high resistance with a galvanometer is connected in parallel with the test resistor. Further, an ammeter which is formed by connecting a low resistance in parallel with galvanometer is required to measure the current through test resistor.
The correct option is (c).

CHAPTER~08

HEATING EFFECT OF CURRENT

LEVEL 01 Starter Level

8.1 Heating Effect of Current

1 Two wires of same mass, having ratio of the lengths 1 : 2, densities 1 : 3 and resistivities 2: 1. They are connected one by one to the same voltage supply. The rate of heat dissipation in the first wire is found to be 10 W. Find the rate of heat dissipation in the second wire.

2 In the following circuit, 5Ω resistor develops 45 J/s due to current flowing through it. Find the power developed across 12Ω resistor.

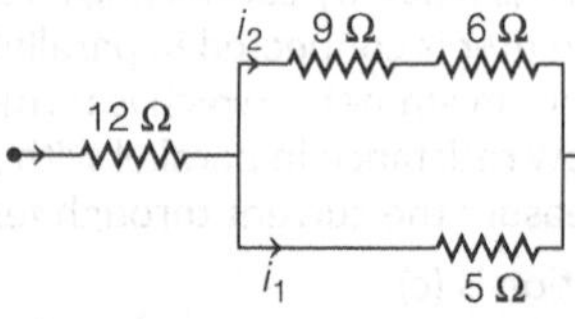

3 If bulb rating is 100 W and 220 V, then determine

(i) resistance of filament,

(ii) current through filament, if it is operated at a potential difference for which it is designed.

(iii) If bulb operates at 110 V power supply, then find power consumed by bulb.

4 A 500 W heater is designed to operate from a 200 V line. By what percentage will its heat output drop, if the line voltage drops to 160 V? Also, find the heat produced by it in 10 min.

5 How much time heater will take to increase the temperature of 100 g water by 50°C, if resistance of heating coil is 400Ω and supply voltage is 200 V?

6 An electric kettle taking 3 A at 210 V brings 1 L of water from 20°C to 80°C in 10 min. Find its efficiency.

7 A fuse of lead wire has an area of cross-section 0.2 mm^2. On short-circuiting, the current in the fuse wire reaches 30 A. How long after the short-circuiting, will the fuse begin to melt? For lead, take its specific heat 0.032 cal/g-°C, melting point 327°C, density 11.34g/cm^3 and the resistivity $= 22 \times 10^{-6}\ \Omega$-cm. The initial temperature of wire is 20°C. Neglect heat losses.

8 A storage battery with emf $E = 3.6$ V loaded with an external resistance produces a current $I = 2.0$ A. In this case, the potential difference between the terminals of the storage battery equals $V = 2.0$ V. Find the thermal power generated in the battery and the power supplied by the battery.

9 A series battery by 6 lead accumulators each of emf 2.0 V and internal resistance 0.5Ω is charged by a 100 V DC supply. What series resistance should be used in the charging circuit in order to limit the current to 8 A? Using the required resistor, calculate

(i) the power supplied by the DC source

(ii) the power dissipated as heat and

(iii) chemical energy stored in the battery in 15 min.

8.2 Series and Parallel Combinations of the Heating Elements

1 An electric heater and an electric bulb are rated 500 W, 220 V and 100 W, 220 V, respectively. Both are connected in series to a 220 V supply. Calculate power consumed by (i) heater (ii) bulb.

2 In the figure shown B_1, B_2 and B_3 are three bulbs rated as (200 V, 100 W), (200 V, 50W) and (200 V, 25 W), respectively.

(i) Which bulb is the brightest and also find power delivered by it?

(ii) What is the total power delivered by all the three bulbs?

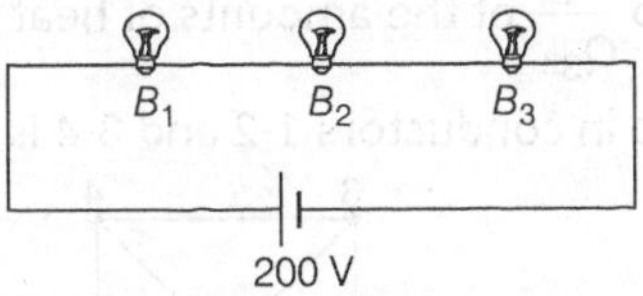

3 Two bulbs are rated 30 W-200 V and 60 W-200V. They are connected with a 400 V power supply. Find which bulb is likely to get fused, if they are connected in (i) series and (ii) parallel.

4 A 100 W bulb B_1 and two 60 W bulbs B_2 and B_3 are connected to a 250 V source as shown in the figure. Now, W_1, W_2 and W_3 are the output powers of the bulbs B_1, B_2 and B_3, respectively. Arrange W_1, W_2 and W_3 in the increasing or decreasing order.

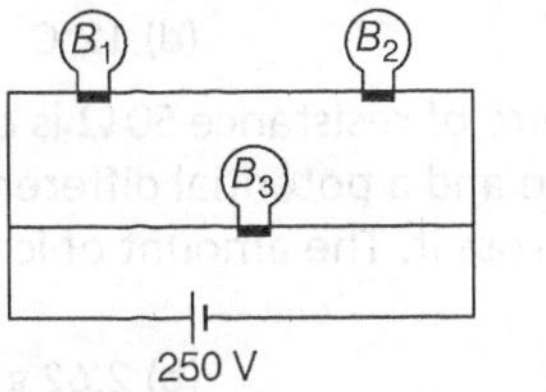

5 Four identical bulbs each rated 100 W, 220 V are connected across a battery as shown. What is total electric power consumed by the bulbs?

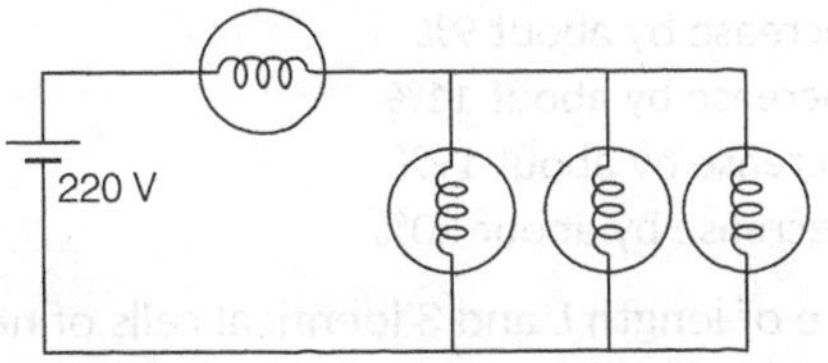

6 An electric tea kettle has two heating coils. When one of the coils is switched on, boiling begins in 12 min. When the other coil is switched on, the boiling begins in 6 min. In what time, will the boiling begin, if both coils are switched on simultaneously

(i) in series (ii) in parallel

7 A 100 W bulb designed to operate on 200 V is to be connected across a 500 V source. What resistance should be put in series, so that the bulb consumes 100 W?

8.3 Maximum Power Transfer Theorem

1 In the circuit as shown in figure, find value of external resistor R, so that the power dissipated in it is maximum. Also, find the maximum power dissipated in it.

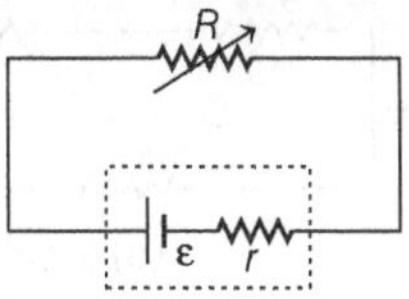

2 A battery has an open circuit potential difference of 36 V between its terminals. When a load resistance of 10Ω is connected across the battery, the power dissipated within the battery is 18 W. What should be the load resistance R, so that maximum power will be dissipated in R.

3 In the figure shown find R, so that the power generated in R is maximum.

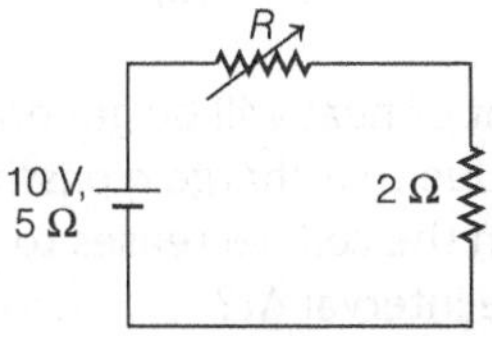

LEVEL 02 JEE Main Level

Single Choice Correct Questions

1 In the figure shown each resistor is of 20 Ω and the cell has emf 10 V with negligible internal resistance. Then, rate of joule heating in the circuit is

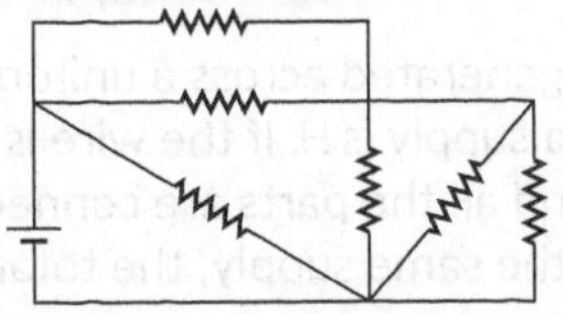

(a) $\frac{100}{11}$ W (b) $\frac{10000}{11}$ W (c) 11 W (d) None of these

2 Find the resistor in which the dissipated power is the greatest.

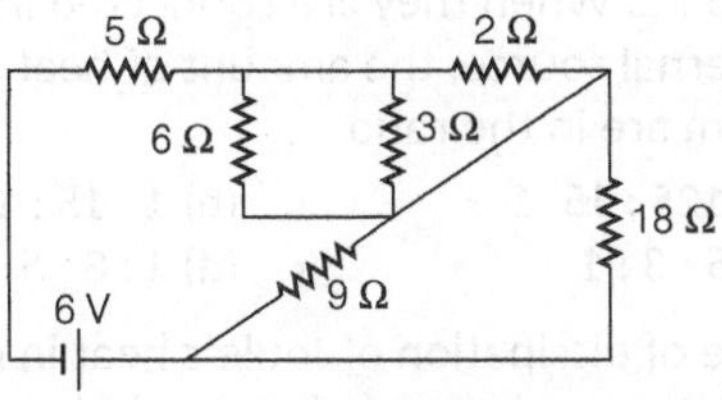

(a) 6Ω (b) 9Ω

(c) 18Ω (d) 5Ω

3 The ratio of powers dissipated respectively in R and $3R$, as shown is

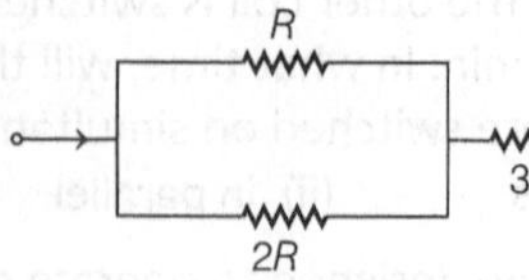

(a) 9 (b) $\frac{27}{4}$

(c) $\frac{4}{9}$ (d) $\frac{4}{27}$

4 In the circuit shown in figure, the heat produced in the 5Ω resistor due to the current flowing through it is 10 calories per second. The heat generated in the 4Ω resistor is

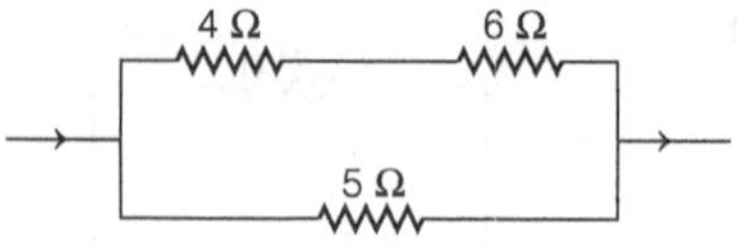

(a) 1 cal/s (b) 2 cal/s

(c) 3 cal/s (d) 4 cal/s

5 The charge flowing through a resistance R varies with time as $Q = 2t - 8t^2$. The total heat produced in the resistance is $\left(\text{for } 0 \le t \le \frac{1}{8}\right)$

(a) $\frac{R}{6}$ J (b) $\frac{R}{3}$ J

(c) $\frac{R}{2}$ J (d) R J

6 What amount of heat will be generated in a coil of resistance R due to a charge q passing through it, if the current in the coil decreases to zero uniformly during a time interval Δt?

(a) $\frac{4}{3}\frac{q^2R}{\Delta t}$ (b) $\ln\frac{q^2R}{2\Delta t}$

(c) $\frac{2q^2R}{3\Delta t}$ (d) $\ln\frac{(2\Delta t)}{q^2R}$

7 Masses of three wires of same material are in the ratio 1 : 3 : 5. Their lengths are in the ratio 5 : 3 : 1. When they are connected in series to an external source, the amount of heat produced in them are in the ratio

(a) 125 : 15 :1 (b) 1 : 15 : 125

(c) 5 : 3 : 1 (d) 1 : 3 : 5

8 Rate of dissipation of Joule's heat in resistance per unit volume is (symbols have their usual meanings)

(a) σE (b) σJ

(c) JE (d) None of these

9 The resistance of each arm in the circuit shown in figure has same value (i.e. $R_{12} = R_{10} = R_{13} = R_{20} = R_{24} = ...$ etc.). The ratio $\frac{Q_{12}}{Q_{34}}$ of the amounts of heat liberated per unit time in conductors 1-2 and 3-4 is

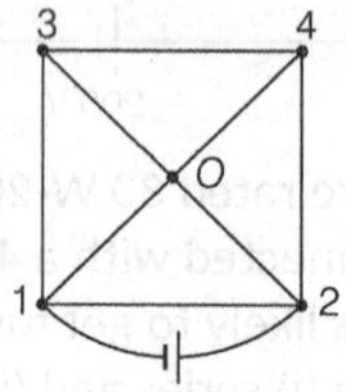

(a) 4 : 1 (b) 8 : 1

(c) 16 : 1 (d) None of these

10 A resistance coil of $60\,\Omega$ is immersed in 42 kg of water. A current of 7A is passed through it. The rise in temperature of water per minute is

(a) 4°C (b) 8°C

(c) 1.0°C (d) 12°C

11 A coil of wire of resistance $50\,\Omega$ is embedded in a block of ice and a potential difference of 210 V is applied across it. The amount of ice which melts in 1 s is

(a) 0.262 g (b) 2.62 g

(c) 26.2 g (d) 0.0262 g

12 If the length of the filament of a heater is reduced by 10%, the power of the heater will

(a) increase by about 9%

(b) increase by about 11%

(c) increase by about 19%

(d) decrease by about 10%

13 A wire of length L and 3 identical cells of negligible internal resistances are connected in series. Due to the current, the temperature of the wire is raised by ΔT in time t. N number of similar cells is now connected in series with a wire of the same material and cross-section but of length $2L$. The temperature of the wire is raised by the same amount ΔT in the same time t. The value of N is

(a) 4 (b) 6

(c) 8 (d) 9

14 Power generated across a uniform wire connected across a supply is H. If the wire is cut into n equal parts and all the parts are connected in parallel across the same supply, the total power generated in the wire is

(a) $\frac{H}{n^2}$ (b) n^2H (c) nH (d) $\frac{H}{n}$

15 Two resistances connected in parallel across a cell of negligible internal resistance, use 4.5 times the power that they would use when in series across the same cell. If one of the resistances is 8 Ω, the other is

(a) 8Ω (b) 12Ω
(c) 16Ω (d) 36Ω

16 A battery is supplying power to a tape-recorder by cable of resistance of 0.02 Ω. If the battery is generating 50 W power at 5 V, then power received by tape-recorder is (neglect internal resistance of battery)

(a) 50 W (b) 45 W
(c) 30 W (d) 48 W

17 When electric bulb of same power, but different marked voltage are connected in series across the power line, their brightness will be

(a) proportional to their marked voltage
(b) inversely proportional to their marked voltage
(c) proportional to the square of their marked voltage
(d) inversely proportional to the square of their marked voltage

18 Two bulbs rated (25 W - 220 V) and (100 W - 220 V) are connected in series to a 440 V line. Which one is likely to fuse?

(a) 25 W bulb (b) 100 W bulb
(c) Both bulbs (d) None of these

19 The wattage rating of a light bulb indicates the power dissipated by the bulb, if it is connected across 110 V DC potential difference. If 50 W and 100 W bulbs are connected in series to a 110 V DC source, how much power will be dissipated in the 50 W bulb?

(a) 50 W (b) 100 W (c) 22 W (d) 11 W

20 In the circuit shown, the battery is ideal. What is the total power consumed by the circuit approximately?

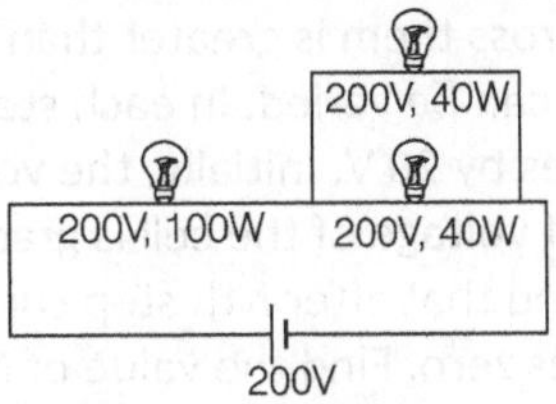

(a) 140 W (b) 44 W (c) 28 W (d) 56 W

21 Two bulbs of 500 W and 200 W are manufactured to operate on 220 V line. The ratio of heats produced in 500 W and 200 W in two cases when first they are joined in series and secondly in parallel, will be

(a) $\frac{5}{2}, \frac{2}{5}$ (b) $\frac{5}{2}, \frac{5}{2}$ (c) $\frac{2}{5}, \frac{5}{2}$ (d) $\frac{2}{5}, \frac{2}{5}$

22 The circuit given is made up using identical light bulbs. The light bulbs of maximum brightness of the following will be

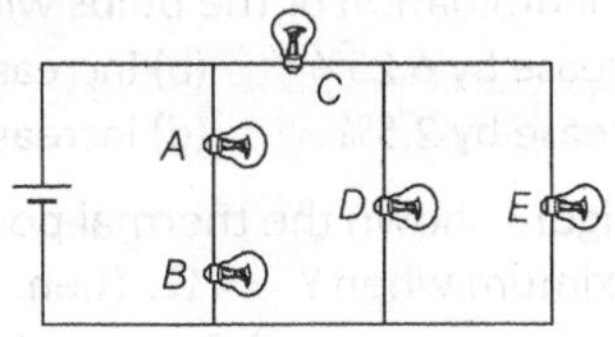

(a) bulb *A* (b) bulb *C* (c) bulb *D* (d) bulb *E*

23 In the circuit given, ammeter *A* reads 0.5 A. Bulbs L_1 and L_2 are brightly lit, but L_3 is not lit. What is the reason for L_3 not being lit?

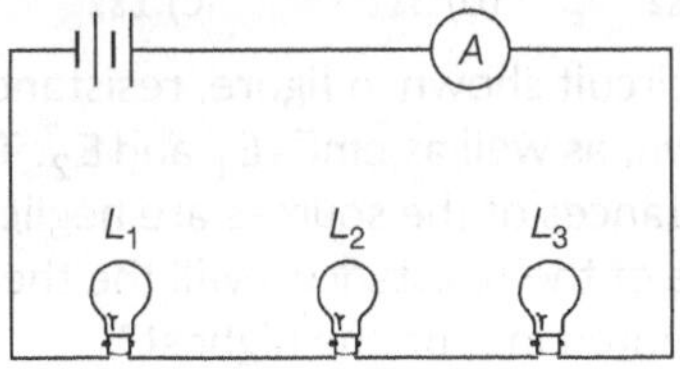

(a) The ammeter is faulty
(b) The filament of L_3 is broken
(c) The resistance of L_3 is much lower than that of L_1 and L_2
(d) There is a break in the connecting wire between L_2 and L_3

24 If *X*, *Y* and *Z* in the figure are identical lamps, which of the following changes to the brightness of the lamps occur when switch *S* is closed?

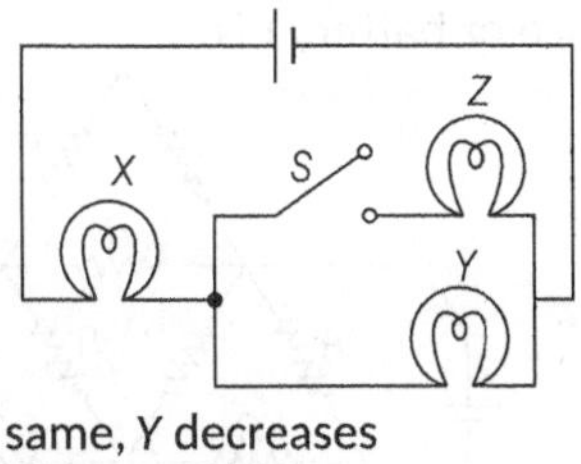

(a) *X* stays the same, *Y* decreases
(b) *X* increases, *Y* decreases
(c) *X* increases, *Y* stays the same
(d) *X* decreases, *Y* increases

25 The electrical installation in a building is protected by a 15 A fuse. If the supply voltage is 220 V, the maximum number of 60W bulbs that can be used in the building is

(a) 44 (b) 55 (c) 88 (d) 66

26 An electric kettle has two coils. When one of these is switched on, the water in the kettle boils in 6 min. When the other coil is switched on, the water boils in 3 min. If the two coils are connected in parallel, the time taken to boil the water in the kettle is

(a) 2 min (b) 3 min (c) 6 min (d) 9 min

27 40 electric bulbs are connected in series across a 220 V supply. After one bulb is fused, the remaining 39 are connected again in series across the same supply. Illumination of the bulbs will

(a) decrease by 6.25% (b) increase by 6.25%
(c) decrease by 2.5% (d) increase by 2.5%

28 In the figure shown the thermal power generated in Y is maximum when $Y = 4\,\Omega$. Then, X is

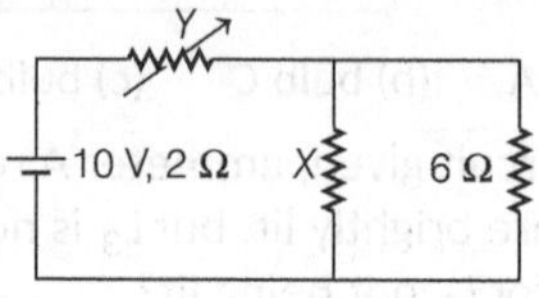

(a) 2Ω (b) 3Ω (c) 1Ω (d) 6Ω

29 In a circuit shown in figure, resistances R_1 and R_2 are known, as well as emf's E_1 and E_2. The internal resistances of the sources are negligible. At what value of the resistance R will the thermal power generated in it be the highest?

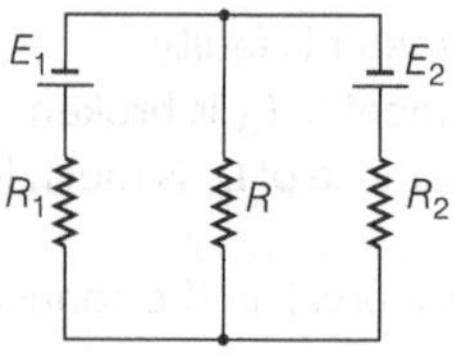

(a) $R_1 + R_2$ (b) $R_1 - R_2$ (c) $\sqrt{R_1 R_2}$ (d) $\dfrac{R_1 R_2}{R_1 + R_2}$

30 For maximum power from battery, the internal resistance of battery r is

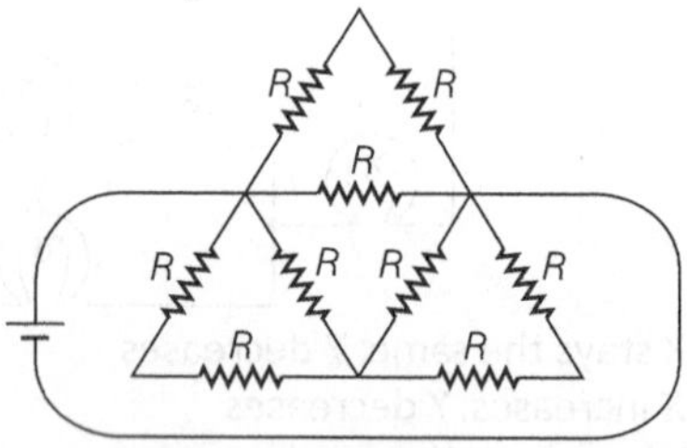

(a) $10R$ (b) $\dfrac{4R}{9}$ (c) $\dfrac{R}{8}$ (d) $\dfrac{10R}{9}$

Numerical Value Questions

1 A resistance $R = 12\,\Omega$ is connected across a source of varying emf as shown in figure. Its emf changes with time shown in the graph. What is the heat dissipated (in J) in the resistance in the first four second?

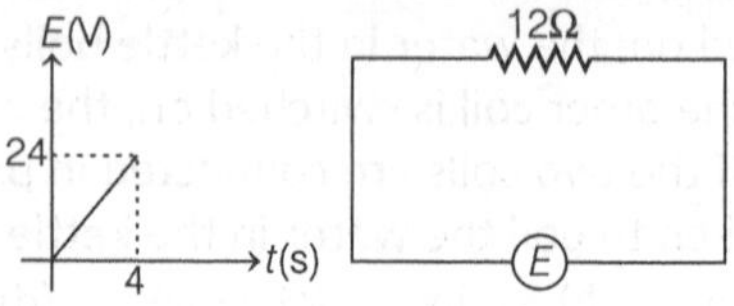

2 What should be the value of resistance R (in Ω) in the circuit shown in figure, so that the electric bulb consumes the rated power?

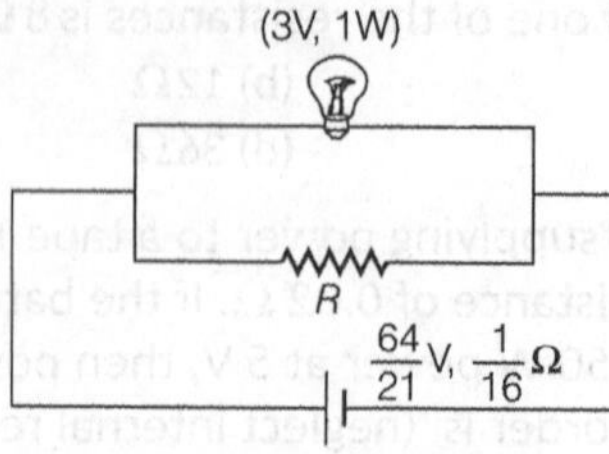

3 Two electric bulbs 40 W, 200 V and 100 W, 200 V are connected in series. Find the maximum voltage (in volts) that can be applied across the combination, without fusing either bulb.

4 Electric bulb 50W-100 V glowing at full power are to be used in parallel with battery 120 V, $10\,\Omega$. What is the maximum number of bulbs that can be connected, so that they glow in full power?

5 A fuse with a circular cross-sectional radius of 0.15 mm blows at 15 A. If the radius of a fuse, made of the same material is 0.60 mm, then find the current (in A) at which it blows.

6 A battery of internal resistance $6\,\Omega$ is connected to the network of resistance as shown in figure. In order to that the maximum power can be delivered to the network, what should be the value of R (in Ω)?

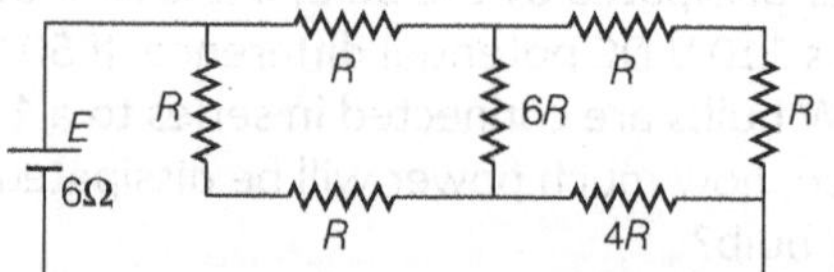

7 Figure shows three bulbs connected in series. Their voltage rating shows that they will fuse, if potential drop across them is greater than 100 V. Voltage of the cell can be varied. In each step voltage of the cell increases by 20 V. Initially, the voltage of the cell is 100 V. If voltage of the cell is gradually increased and it is found that after Nth step current in the circuit becomes zero. Find the value of N.

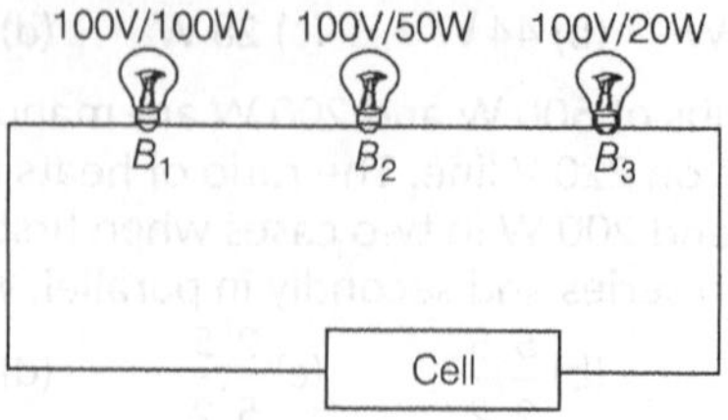

8 Circuit shows seven identical bulbs (A to G) connected through a battery of emf 200 V. The bulbs are rated at 200 V, 100 W. Find the power (in W) dissipated in the bulb which glow brightest.

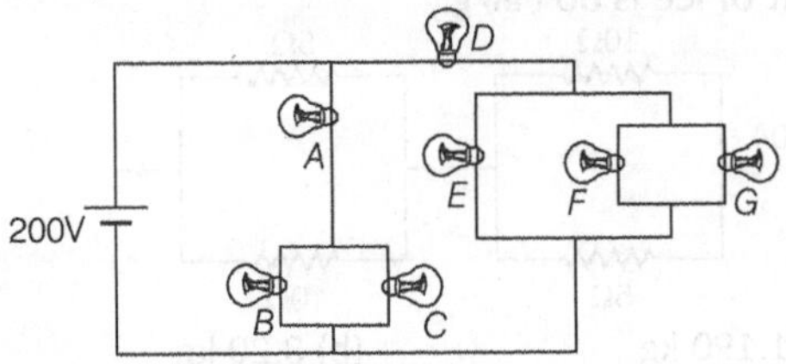

9 In a house, there are 3 lamps of 40 W each, 8 lamps of 60 W each, a radio of 40 W and a TV of 160 W. The lamps are in operation on an average for 2 h a day, the radio for 4 h a day and the TV for 1 h a day. On Sundays, an electric iron of 750 W is used for 1 h and the TV for an extra 3 h. Calculate the electricity bill (in ₹) for the month of february of a leap year at the rate of ₹ 5 per unit. The first Sunday falls on 3rd February.

10 The coil of a calorimeter C has a resistance of $R_1 = 60\,\Omega$. The coil R_1 is connected to the circuit as shown in figure. How many degrees (°C) will 240 g of water poured into the calorimeter be heated in 7 min during which a current flows through the coil, if the ammeter shows 3 A? The resistance of R_2 is $30\,\Omega$. Disregard the resistances of the battery and the ammeter; and the heat losses and heat capacity of the calorimeter and the resistor.

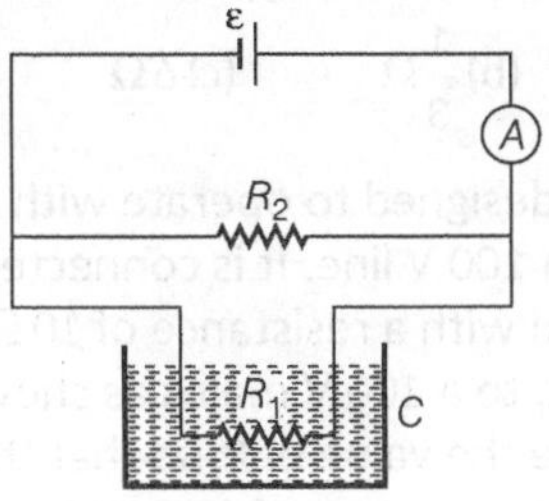

LEVEL 03 JEE Advanced Level

Single Choice Correct Questions

1 The charge supplied by source varies with time t as $Q = at - bt^2$. The total heat produced in the resistor $2R$ is (Assume that direction of current is not changing)

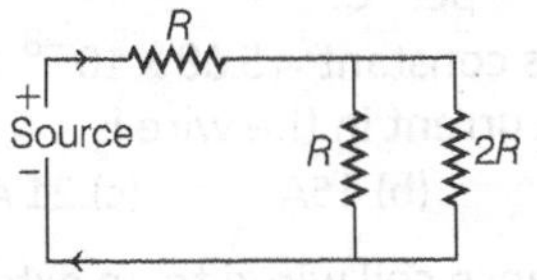

(a) $\frac{a^3R}{6b}$ (b) $\frac{a^3R}{27b}$ (c) $\frac{a^3R}{3b}$ (d) None of these

2 A total charge Q flows across a resistor R during a time interval, T in such a way that the current *versus* time graph for 0 to T is like the loop of a sine curve in the range 0 to π. The total heat generated in the resistor is

(a) $\frac{Q^2\pi^2R}{8T}$ (b) $\frac{2Q^2\pi^2R}{T}$ (c) $\frac{2Q^2\pi R}{T}$ (d) $\frac{Q^2v^2R}{2T}$

3 A time varying current i is passed through a resistance R as shown in figure. Total heat produced in the resistor is

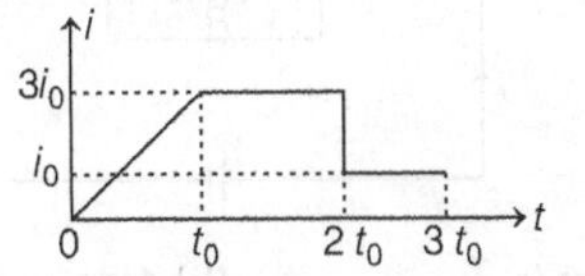

(a) $11i_0^2Rt_0$ (b) $13i_0^2Rt_0$ (c) $15i_0^2Rt_0$ (d) $17i_0^2Rt_0$

4 Two circular rings of identical radii and resistance of $36\,\Omega$ each are placed in such a way that cross each others centre C_1 and C_2 as shown in figure. Conducting joints are made at intersection points A and B of the rings. An ideal cell of emf 20 volts is connected across AB. The power delivered by cell is

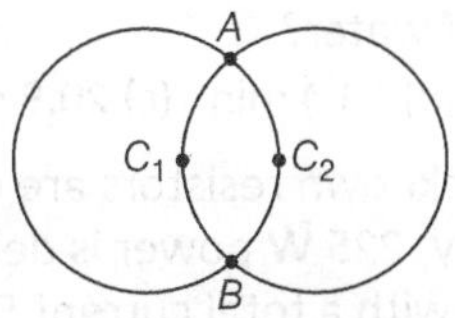

(a) 80 W (b) 100 W
(c) 120 W (d) 200 W

5 In the circuit shown in figure, the power which is dissipated as heat in the $6\,\Omega$ resistor is 6 W. What is the value of resistance R in the circuit?

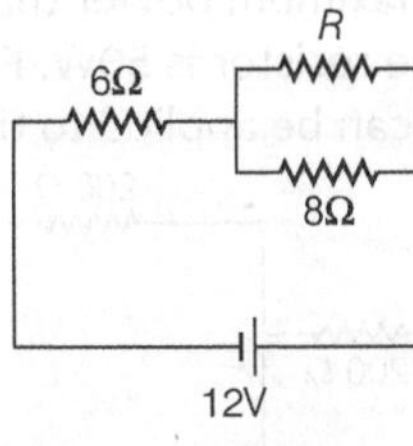

(a) $6\,\Omega$ (b) $8\,\Omega$
(c) $10\,\Omega$ (d) $24\,\Omega$

6 A metal oxide follows the relation $V = a\sqrt{I}$, where $a = 1 \frac{\text{volt}}{(\text{ampere})^{1/2}}$, V is potential drop across the oxide and I is current through it. If heat produced in resistor and metal oxide is same, then value of R is

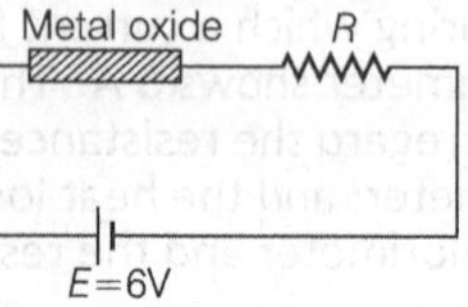

(a) 3Ω (b) $\frac{1}{3}\Omega$ (c) 6Ω (d) 9Ω

7 A heater is designed to operate with a power of 1000 W in a 100 V line. It is connected in combination with a resistance of $10\,\Omega$ and a resistance R, to a 100 V mains as shown in figure. What will be the value of R, so that the heater operates with a power of 62.5 W?

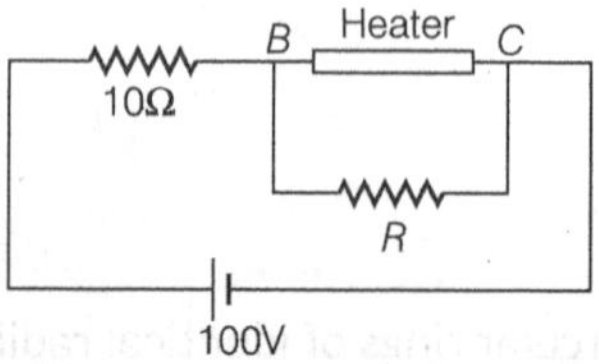

(a) 1Ω (b) 3Ω (c) 5Ω (d) 15Ω

8 It takes 16 min to boil some water in an electric kettle. Due to some defect, it becomes necessary to remove 10% turns of the heating coil of the kettle. After repairs, how much time will it take to boil the same mass of water?

(a) 17.7 min (b) 14.4 min (c) 20.9 min (d) 13.7 min

9 When two unknown resistors are connected in series with a battery, 225 W power is delivered to the combination with a total current 5A. For the same total current 50W is delivered when the resistors are connected in parallel. Find the ratio of two resistances.

(a) 9 (b) 12 (c) 2 (d) 4

10 Three $200\,\Omega$ resistors are connected as shown in figure. The maximum power that can be dissipated in anyone of the resistor is 50W. Find the maximum voltage that can be applied to the terminals A and B.

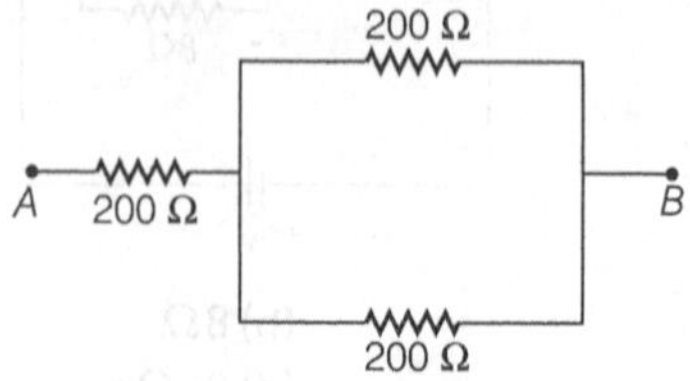

(a) 100 V (b) 150 V (c) 200 V (d) 250 V

11 Four resistors carrying a current shown in figure are immersed in a box containing ice at 0°C. How much ice must be put in the box every 10 min to keep the average quantity of ice in the box constant? Latent heat of ice is 80 cal/g.

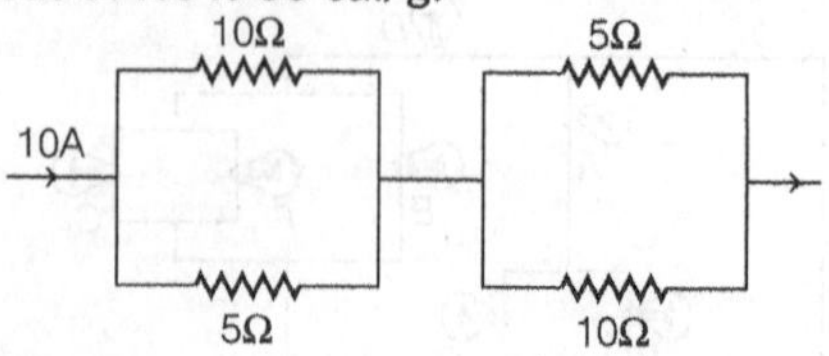

(a) 1.190 kg (b) 3.20 kg
(c) 4.2 kg (d) 0.25 kg

12 Six resistors, each of resistance R, are connected at their ends so as to form tetrahedral frame. Now, two cells of negligible internal resistance, and emf E is connected to the combination. One cell between any two corners and other cell between the remaining two corners. Thermal power developed will be

(a) $\frac{E^2}{R}$ (b) $\frac{2E^2}{R}$ (c) $\frac{4E^2}{R}$ (d) $\frac{8E^2}{R}$

13 A wire of length 1 m and radius 10^{-3} m is carrying a heavy current and is assumed to radiate as a black body. At equilibrium, its temperature is 900 K while that of the surroundings is 300 K. The resistivity of the material of the wire at 300 K is $\pi^2 \times 10^{-8}\,\Omega$-m and its temperature coefficient of resistance is 7.8×10^{-3} per °C.
(Stefan's constant $= 5.68 \times 10^{-8}$ W-m^{2}-K^{4}).
So, the current in the wire is

(a) 25A (b) 15A (c) 21 A (d) 36 A

14 A resistance coil wired to an external battery is placed inside a thermally insulated cylinder fitted with a frictionless piston and containing an ideal gas. A current $i = 240$ mA flows through the coil which has resistance $R = 490\,\Omega$. At what constant speed v must the piston of mass $m = 12$ kg move upward in order that the temperature of the gas remains unchanged? [Assume that 60% energy is utilised to do work by the gas, and neglect the work done by atmospheric pressure]

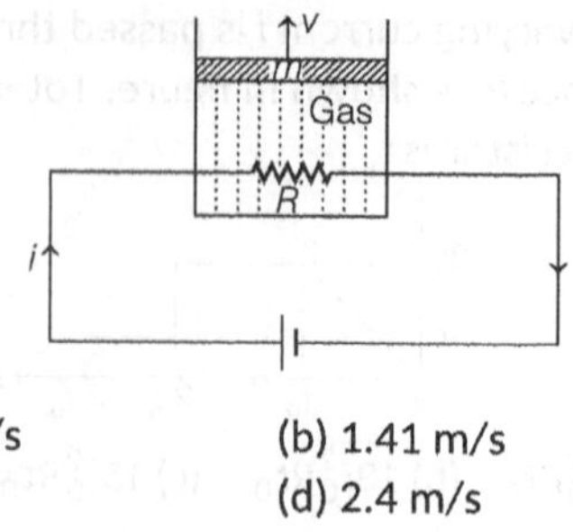

(a) 0.144 m/s (b) 1.41 m/s
(c) 0.24 m/s (d) 2.4 m/s

15 n identical light bulbs, each designed to draw P power from a certain voltage supply are joined in series and that combination is connected across that supply. The power consumed by one bulb will be

(a) nP (b) P (c) $\frac{P}{n}$ (d) $\frac{P}{n^2}$

16 The operating temperature of the filament of lamp is 2000°C. The temperature coefficient of the material of the filament is $0.005°C^{-1}$. If the atmospheric temperature is 0°C, then the current in the 100W-200V lamp when it is switched on is nearest to

(a) 2.5A (b) 3.5A
(c) 4.5A (d) 5.5A

17 Three light bulbs of 40W, 60W and 100 W are connected in series with a 240 V source. Then,

(a) the potential difference will be maximum across the 40 W bulb
(b) the current will be maximum in 100 W bulb
(c) the resistance of the 40 W bulb is minimum
(d) the current through the 60 W bulb will be 0.1 A

18 A house is fitted with certain number of 100 W, 230 V incandescent lamps. The power to the house is fed by a generator producing the power at 240 V. The resistance of the wires from the generator to the house is 2 Ω. The maximum number of lamps that can be illuminated, so that the voltage across none of the lamps drops below 230 V is

(a) 10 (b) 11 (c) 12 (d) 15

19 A torch bulb rated as 4.5 W, 1.5 V is connected as shown in the figure. The emf of the cell needed to make the bulb glow at full intensity is

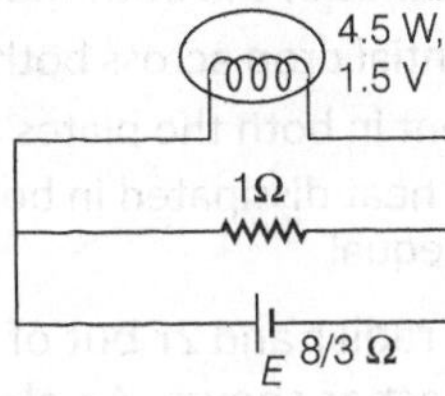

(a) 9 V (b) 12 V (c) 13.5 V (d) 15 V

20 The circuit shown in figure, contains a battery, a rheostat and two identical lamps. What will happen to the brightness of the lamps, if the resistance of the rheostat is increased?

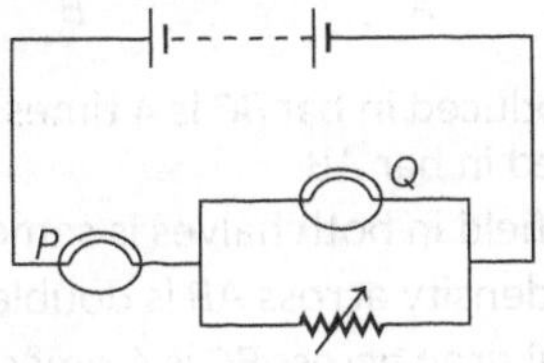

	Lamp P	Lamp Q
(a)	Less brighter	Brighter
(b)	Less brighter	Less brighter
(c)	Brighter	Less brighter
(d)	No change	Brighter

21 A circuit is connected as shown. All light bulbs are identical. When the switch in the circuit is closed illuminating bulb 4, which other bulb(s) also become brighter?

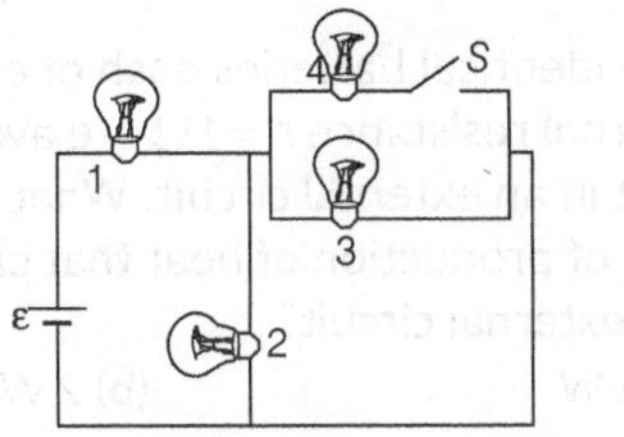

(a) Bulb 1 only (b) Bulb 2 only
(c) Bulbs 2 and 3 only (d) Bulbs 1, 2 and 3

22 The main supply voltage to a room is 120 V. The resistance of the lead wires is 6 Ω. A 60W bulb is already giving light. What is the decrease in the voltage across the bulb when a 240 W heater is switched on?

(a) No change (b) 10 V
(c) 20 V (d) More than 10 V

23 In the circuit shown, the bulb B glows equally bright whether the switch is closed or open. The resistance of bulb is

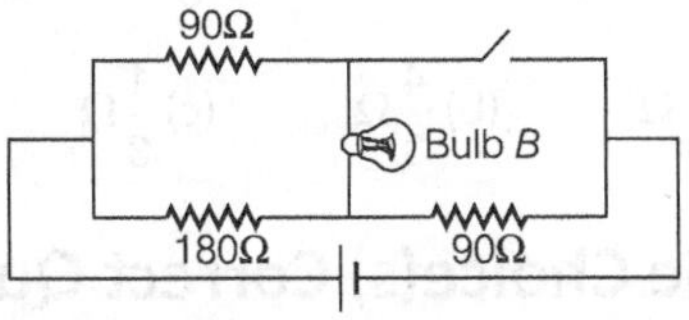

(a) 30Ω (b) 20Ω
(c) 60Ω (d) 120Ω

24 Assuming all bulbs are identical, rank the brightnesses of the bulbs from brightest to dimmest.

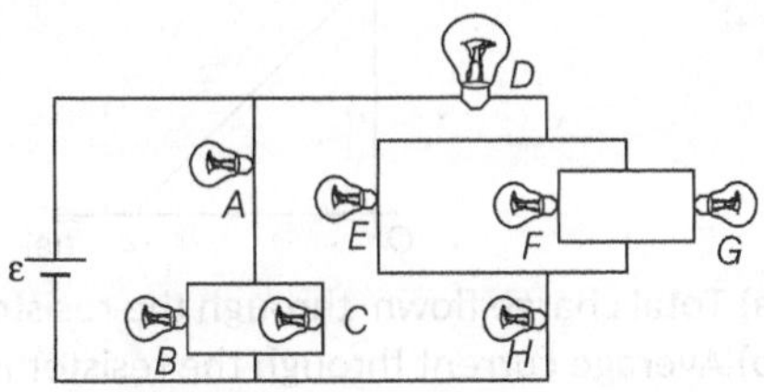

(a) $A > D = H > B = C > E = F = G$
(b) $A > B = C > D = H > E = F = G$
(c) $A > D = H > E = F = G > B = C$
(d) All have equal brightness

25 When a battery sends current through a resistance R_1 for time t, the heat produced in the resistor is Q. When the same battery sends current through another resistance R_2 for time t, the heat produced in R_2 is again Q. The internal resistance of battery is

(a) $\sqrt{R_1 R_2}$ (b) $R_1 + R_2$

(c) $R_1 - R_2$ (d) $\frac{R_1 + R_2}{2}$

26 Two identical batteries each of emf $E = 2$ V and internal resistance $r = 1\Omega$ are available to produce heat in an external circuit. What is the maximum rate of production of heat that can be obtained in the external circuit?

(a) 1 W (b) 2 W

(c) 4 W (d) 8 W

27 In the circuit shown the cell will deliver maximum power to the network, if the value of R is

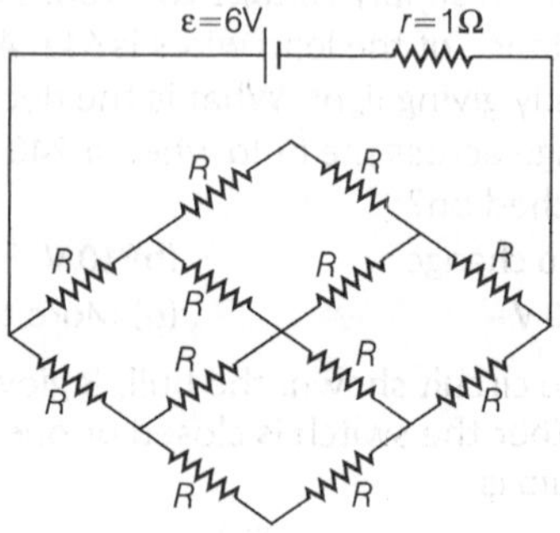

(a) $\frac{2}{3}\Omega$ (b) $\frac{4}{3}\Omega$ (c) $\frac{1}{3}\Omega$ (d) $\frac{5}{3}\Omega$

Multiple Choice(s) Correct Questions

1 A variable current flows through a 1Ω resistor for 2 s. Time dependence of the current is shown in the graph.

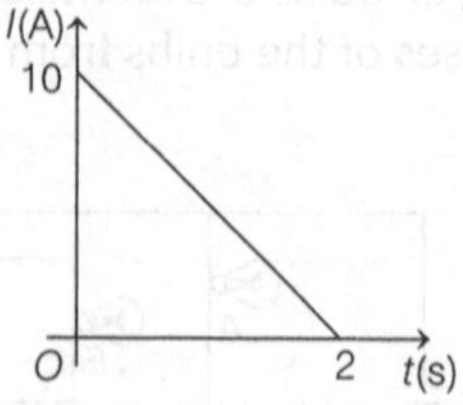

(a) Total charge flown through the resistor is 10 C

(b) Average current through the resistor is 5A

(c) Total heat produced in the resistor is 50 J

(d) Maximum power during the flow of current is 100 W

2 A conductor is made of an isotropic material and has shape of a truncated cone. A battery of constant emf is connected across it and its left end is earthed as shown in figure. If at a section distant x from left end, electric field intensity, potential and the rate of generation of heat per unit length are E, V and H respectively, which of the following graph(s) is/are correct?

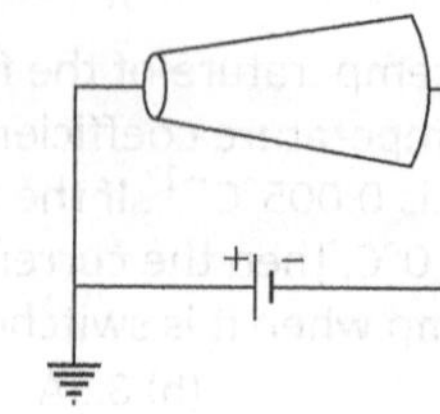

(a)

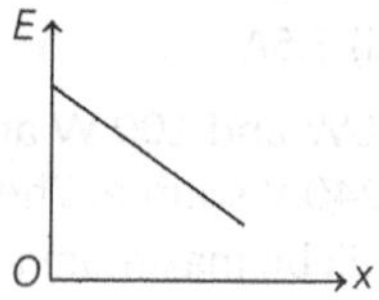

(b)

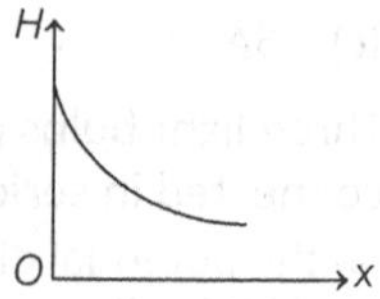

(c)

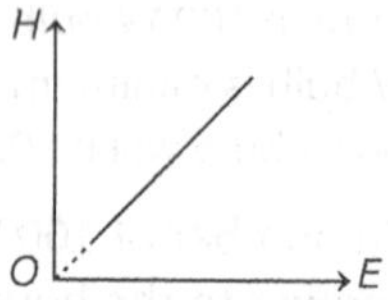

(d)

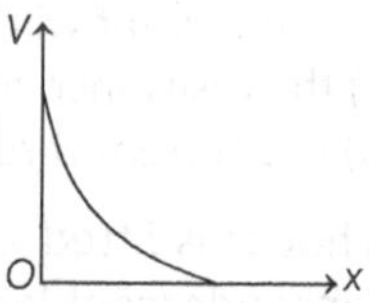

3 Square copper plates of equal thickness and having, area 1 cm^2 and 1 m^2, are connected in series as shown in the figure.

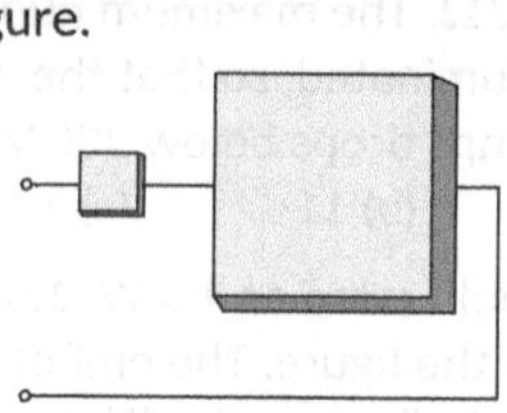

(a) The resistance of the both the plates are equal

(b) The potential drop across both the plates are equal

(c) The current in both the plates are equal

(d) The total heat dissipated in both the plates per unit time are equal

4 Two bars of radii r and $2r$ but of same material are kept in contact as shown. An electric current I is the passed through the bars. Then,

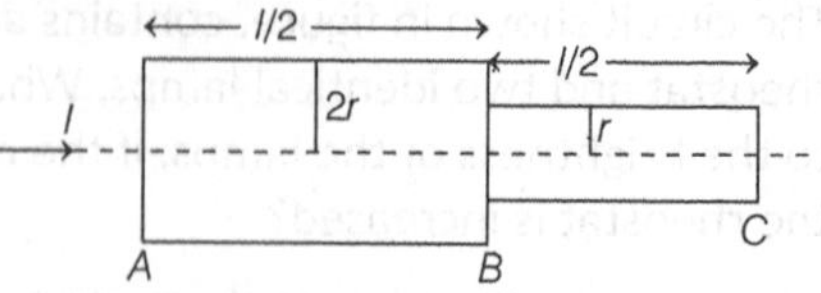

(a) heat produced in bar BC is 4 times the heat produced in bar AB

(b) electric field in both halves is same

(c) current density across AB is double that of across BC

(d) potential drop across BC is 4 times that of across AB

5 In the circuit as shown in figure,

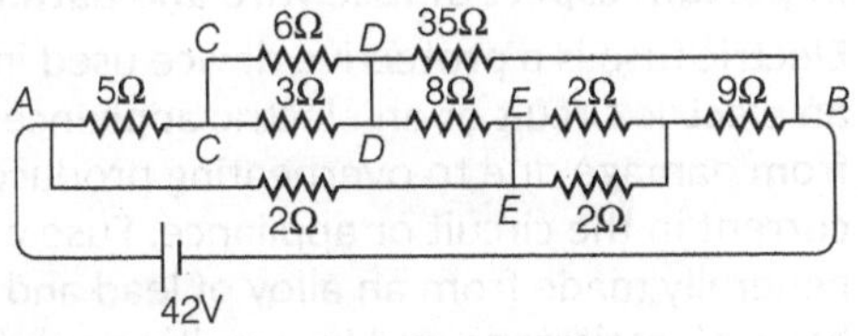

(a) power disputed in 5Ω resistor is 10 W
(b) power disputed in 5Ω resistor is 5 W
(c) power disputed in 8Ω resistor is zero
(d) power disputed in 8Ω resistor is 2 W

6 *AB* is part of a circuit as shown, that absorbs energy at a rate of 50W. *E* is an emf device that has no internal resistance.

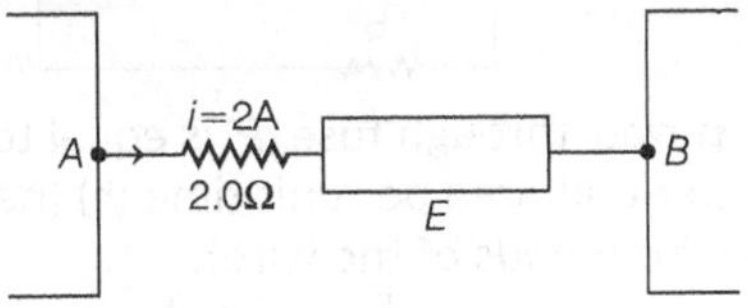

(a) Potential difference across *AB* is 17V
(b) Emf of the device is 21 V
(c) Point *B* is connected to the positive terminal of *E*
(d) Rate of conversion from electrical to chemical energy is 42 W in device *E*

7 Two bulbs consume same power when operated at 200 V and 300 V, respectively. When the bulbs are connected in series across a DC source of 500 V, then

(a) ratio of potential difference across them is $\frac{3}{2}$
(b) ratio of potential difference across them is $\frac{4}{9}$
(c) ratio of power consumed across them is $\frac{4}{9}$
(d) ratio of power consumed across them is $\frac{2}{3}$

8 Four identical bulbs *A*, *B*, *C* and *D* are connected in a circuit as shown in figure. Now, whenever any bulb fails, then it cannot conduct current through it. Then,

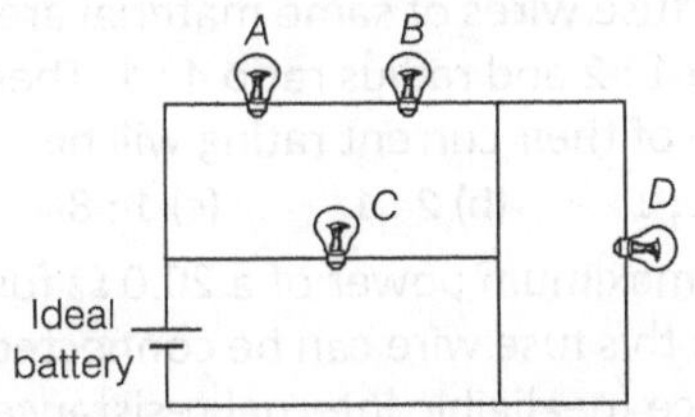

(a) brightness of bulb *C* is highest
(b) if bulb *C* fails, brightness of bulb *D* increases
(c) if bulb *C* fails, brightness of all bulbs remain same
(d) if bulb *A* fails, *B* will not glow

9 Two bulbs 25 W, 100 V (upper bulb in the figure) and 100 W, 200 V (lower bulb in the figure) are connected in the circuit as shown in figure.

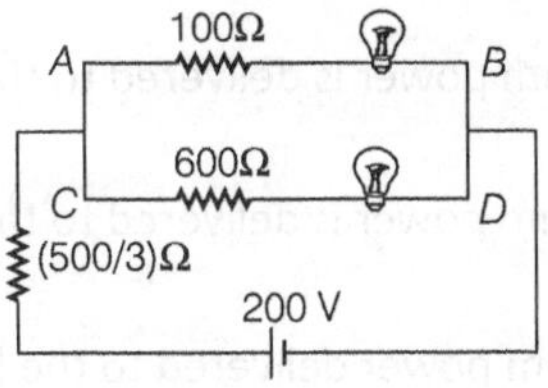

Choose the correct answer(s).
(a) Heat lost per second in the circuit will be 80 J
(b) Ratio of heat produced per second in the bulbs will be 1 : 1
(c) Ratio of heat produced in branch *AB* to that produced in branch *CD* will be 1 : 2
(d) Current drawn from the cell is 0.4A

10 An electric kettle heater has two coils. When one coil is switches on, the water in the kettle begins to boil after 15 min. When the other coil is switched on, the water boils in 30 min.

(a) The water will boil in 45 min, if the coils are connected in series.
(b) The water will boil in 10 min, if the coils are connected in parallel.
(c) Water boils in 22.5 min, if coils are connected in series.
(d) Water boils in 20 min, if coils are connected in parallel.

11 A battery of emf 2 V and internal resistance 1Ω is connected across terminals *A* and *B* of the circuit as shown in the given figure.

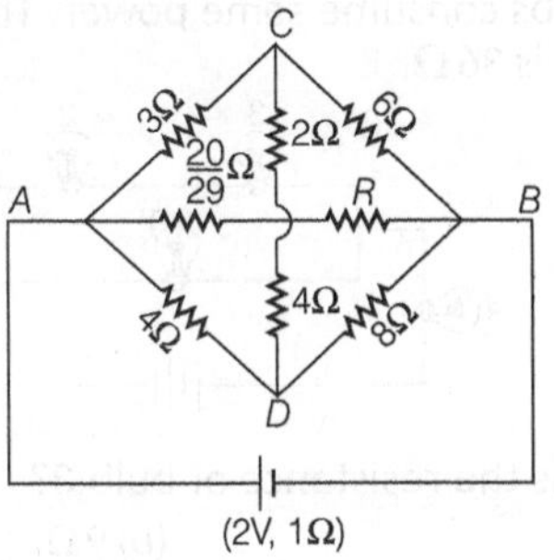

(a) Thermal power generated in external circuit will be maximum possible when $R = \frac{16}{29}\,\Omega$
(b) Maximum possible thermal power generated in external circuit is equal to 4 W
(c) The ratio of current through 6Ω to that through 4Ω is independent of *R*
(d) None of the above

12 N cells each of emf E and identical resistance r are grouped into sets of K cells connected in series. The (N/K) sets are connected in parallel to a load of resistance R, then

(a) maximum power is delivered to the load, if $K=\sqrt{\dfrac{NR}{r}}$

(b) maximum power is delivered to the load, if $K=\sqrt{\dfrac{r}{NR}}$

(c) maximum power delivered to the load is $\dfrac{NE^2}{4r}$

(d) maximum power delivered to the load is $\dfrac{E^2}{4Nr}$

Comprehension Based Questions

Comprehension-1

A car battery with a 12 V emf and an internal resistance of $0.04\,\Omega$ is being charged with a current of 50 A.

1 The potential difference V across the terminals of the battery are

(a) 10 V (b) 12 V (c) 14 V (d) 16 V

2 The rate at which energy is being dissipated as heat inside the battery is

(a) 100 W (b) 500 W
(c) 600 W (d) 700 W

3 The rate of energy conversion from electrical to chemical is

(a) 100 W (b) 500 W
(c) 600 W (d) 700 W

Comprehension-2

All bulbs consume same power. The resistance of bulb 1 is $36\,\Omega$.

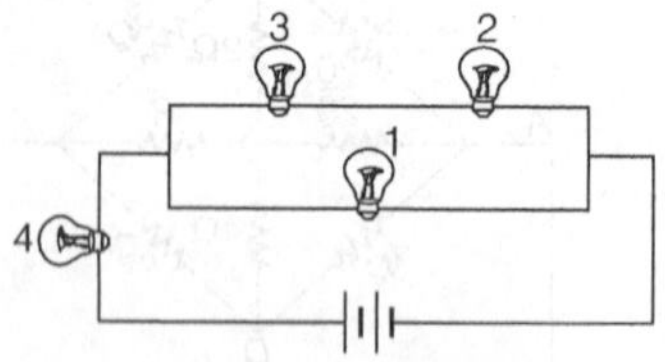

4 What is the resistance of bulb 3?

(a) 4Ω (b) 9Ω
(c) 12Ω (d) 18Ω

5 What is the resistance of bulb 4?

(a) 4Ω (b) 9Ω
(c) 12Ω (d) 18Ω

6 What is the voltage output of the battery, if the power of each bulb is 4W?

(a) 12 V (b) 16 V
(c) 24 V (d) None of these

Comprehension-3

Important aspect of fuse wire and battery

Electric fuse is a protective device used in series with an electric circuit or an electric appliance to save it from damage due to overheating produced by strong current in the circuit or appliance. Fuse wire is generally made from an alloy of lead and tin which has high resistance and low melting point. It is connected in series in an electric installation. If a circuit gets accidentally short-circuited, a large current flows, then fuse wire melts away which causes a break in the circuit.

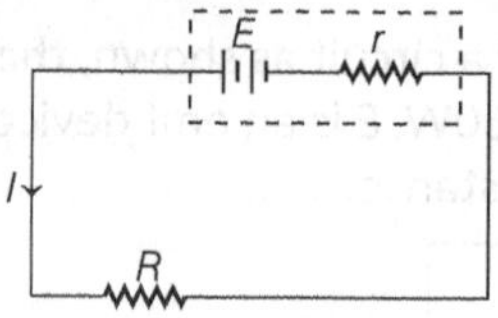

The power through fuse (P) is equal to heat energy lost per unit area per unit time (h) (neglecting heat loses from ends of the wire).

$P=I^2R=h\times 2\pi rl\ldots\left[R=\dfrac{\rho l}{\pi r^2}\right]$, where r and l are the length and radius of fuse wire, respectively. A battery is described by its emf (E) and internal resistance (r), efficiency of battery (η) is defined as the ratio of the output power and the input power.

$$\eta=\frac{\text{Output power}}{\text{Input power}}\times 100\%$$

But $I=\dfrac{E}{R+r}$, input power $=EI$,

output power $=EI-I^2r$, then

$$\eta=\left(\frac{EI-I^2r}{EI}\right)\times 100=\left(1-\frac{Ir}{E}\right)\times 100$$

$$=1-\left(\frac{E}{R+r}\right)\left(\frac{r}{E}\right)\times 100=\left(\frac{R}{R+r}\right)\times 100$$

We know that, output power of a source is maximum when the external resistance is equal to internal resistance, i.e. $R=r$.

7 Two fuse wires of same material are having length ratio 1 : 2 and radius ratio 4 : 1. Then, respective ratio of their current rating will be

(a) 8 : 1 (b) 2 : 1 (c) 1 : 8 (d) 4 : 1

8 The maximum power of a $20.0\,\Omega$ fuse wire is 2.0 kW, then this fuse wire can be connected safely to DC source (negligible internal resistance) of

(a) 300 V (b) 190 V (c) 250 V (d) 220 V

9 Efficiency of a battery (non-ideal) when delivering maximum power is

(a) 100% (b) 50% (c) 90% (d) 40%

Comprehension-4

A high tension wire is at a high potential with respect to a wire which is well grounded called earth wire. You must have seen such wires stretched parallel to roads. There is a high tension wire between two points A and B, 1 km apart. The distance between high tension wire and earth wire is 1 m. The resistance of the high tension (and also the earth wire) is 1Ω/m. This wire is at a potential of 11 kV at point A w.r.t. earth wire and is carrying 1A current which returns back to the generator through the earth wire. This wire is quite a thick wire. There is a sign board at a pole over which this wire is stretched reading 'DANGER, 11 kV'. You might think what would happen, if one touched this wire. Will one feel a shock or not. Well! it depends on whether the current through our body exceeds a particular value, which we may call critical current.

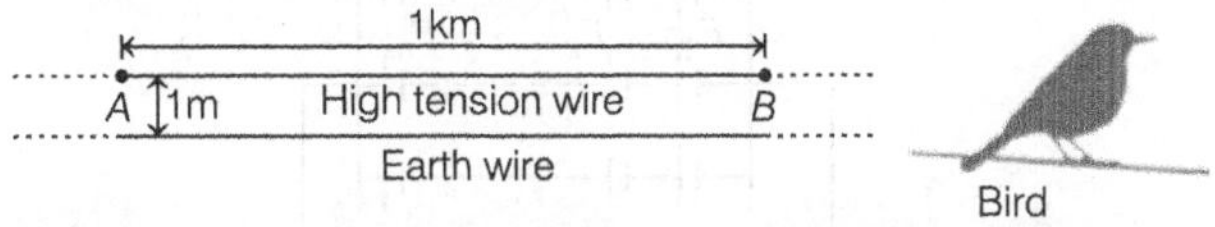

10 Consider a bird having effective resistance $10\,\Omega$ between its feet sitting on this high tension wire. The distance between its feet is 10 cm. The current through the bird is approximately
(a) 10A (b) 1A (c) 0.01A (d) 0.005A

11 If the critical current for the bird is 0.1 A, find the maximum power at 11 kV can be transmitted at point A, so that the bird may not get shock. Assume that the distance between the feet is 10 cm.
(a) 111 kW
(b) 11 kW
(c) 101 kW
(d) 110011 kW

Match the Columns Questions

1 For the circuit shown in figure, 4 cells are arranged. In Column I, the cell number is given while in Column II, some statements related to cells are given. Match the entries of Column I with the entries of Column II.

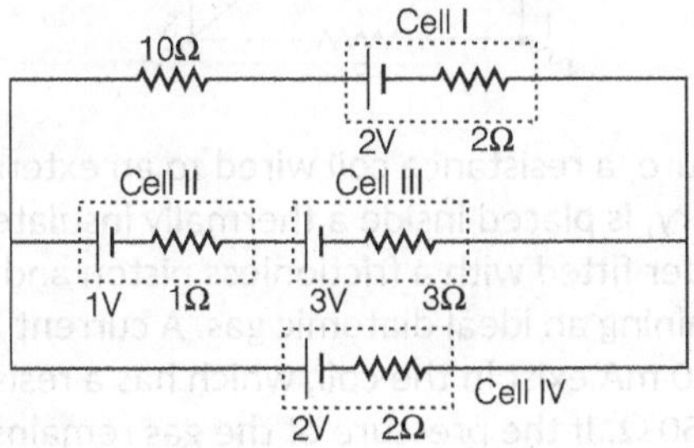

	Column I		Column II
(a)	Cell I	(p)	Chemical energy of cell is decreasing
(b)	Cell II	(q)	Chemical energy of cell is increasing
(c)	Cell III	(r)	Work done by cell is positive
(d)	Cell IV	(s)	Thermal energy developed in cell is positive

2 Referring to the circuit shown in figure match Column I with Column II

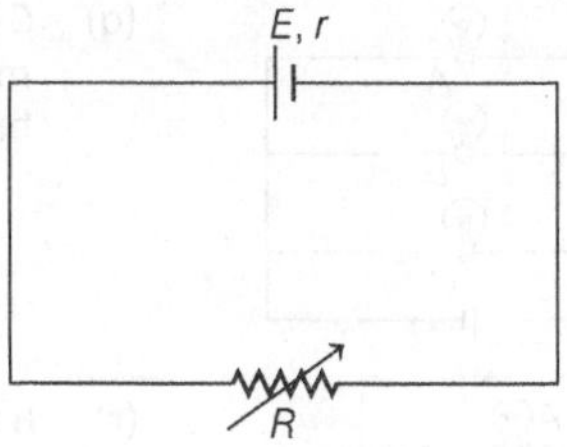

	Column I		Column II
(a)	Terminal potential difference across the cell will be maximum	(p)	$r > R$
(b)	Power transferred to resistance R is less than the maximum possible	(q)	$r < R$
(c)	Power dissipated in the cell is maximum	(r)	$R = \infty$
(d)	Faster drift of ions in the electrolyte in the cell will be for	(s)	$R = 0$

3 Consider two identical cells each of emf E and internal resistance r connected to a load resistance R.

	Column I		Column II
(a)	Maximum power transferred to load, if cells are connected in series	(p)	$\frac{4E^2}{9r}$
(b)	Maximum power transferred to load, if cells are connected in parallel	(q)	$\frac{E^2}{2r}$
(c)	Power transferred to load, if cells are connected in series and $R = r$	(r)	$E_{eq} = E$, $r_{eq} = \frac{r}{2}$
(d)	Power transferred to load, if cells are connected in parallel and $R = r$	(s)	$E_{eq} = 2E$, $r_{eq} = 2r$

4 Three bulbs A, B and C are having rated power P_A, P_B and P_C respectively, each bulb is designed to operate at rated voltage V. It is given that $P_A > P_B > P_C$. In Column I, the three bulbs are arranged in different configuration, while in Column II, the information about intensities of bulbs are mentioned. Match the entries of Column I with the entries of Column II. Neglect the variation, if resistance due to change in temperature.

	Column I		Column II
(a)	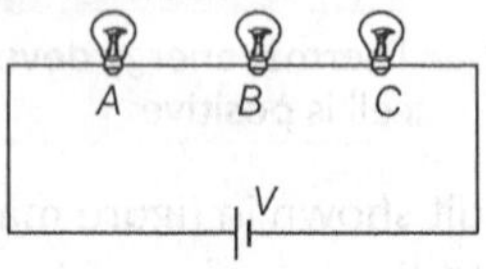	(p)	A is having minimum intensity
(b)	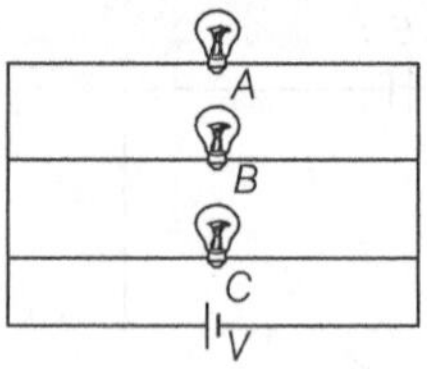	(q)	C is glowing with maximum brightness
(c)	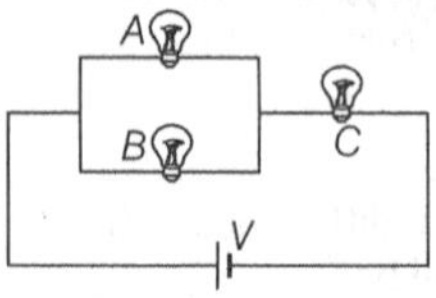	(r)	B is glowing with minimum brightness
(d)	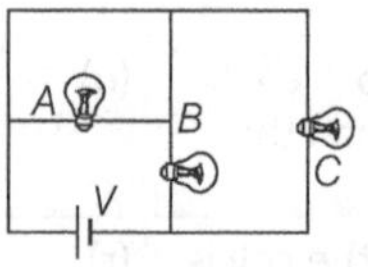	(s)	A is glowing with maximum brightness

Numerical Value Questions

1 In the given figure i-t graph, it is revealed that the current decreases by 50% in each time interval t. The heat dissipated in the resistor R is $\frac{Q^2R}{nT}$. The value of n is (Assuming total charge flows is Q)

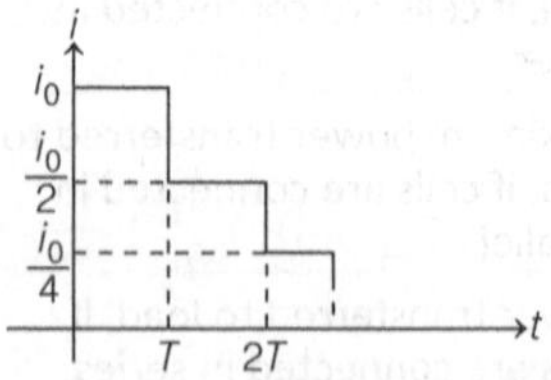

2 Figure shows a battery circuit with an unknown resistance x. If the value of maximum power dissipation in unknown resistance x is $\frac{5}{n}$ W, then find n.

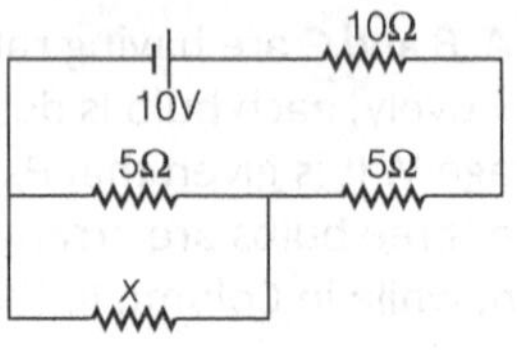

3 Each of 3 resistors in figure has a resistance of 2 Ω and can dissipate a maximum of 18 W without becoming excessively heated. Find the maximum power (in watts) that the circuit can dissipate.

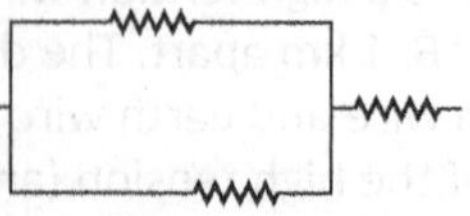

4 324 numbers of identical galvanic cells, each of internal resistance 9 Ω are arranged as several in series group of cells connected in parallel. The arrangement has been laid out, so that power output in an externally connected resistance of value 4 Ω is maximum. If n number of cells are connected in every series group that form parallel combination, then find value of n.

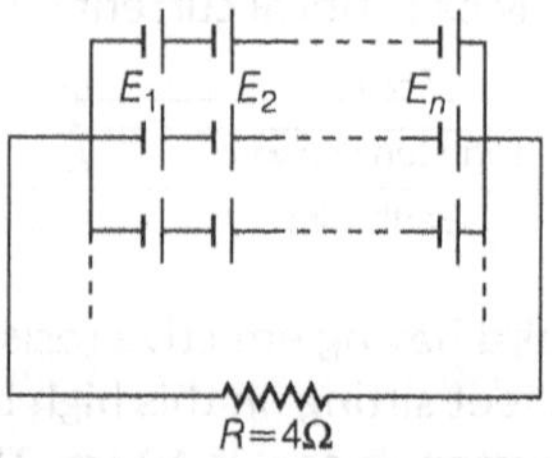

5 The resistances in a burner of an electric stove are connected together in an arrangement shown in figure. This arrangement is connected to the supply mains at points 1 and 2, and after a certain time, 500 grams of water are heated to the boiling point. How much water (in gram) can be heated to the boiling point in the same time interval when the arrangement of resistances is connected to the supply mains at points 1 and 3? The initial temperature of the water is the same in both cases. Neglect all heat loses.

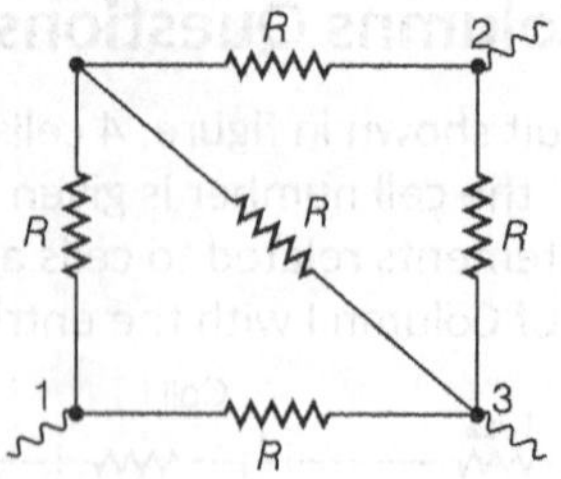

6 In figure, a resistance coil wired to an external battery, is placed inside a thermally insulated cylinder fitted with a frictionless piston and containing an ideal diatomic gas. A current $i = 200$ mA exist in the coil, which has a resistance $R = 350\,\Omega$. If the pressure of the gas remains constant, what should be the speed v (in cm/s) of the piston, of mass $m = 10$ kg? (Take $p_{atm} = 10^5$ Pa, $A = 10$ cm^2)

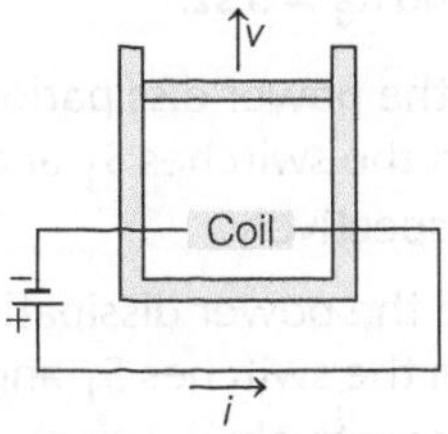

7 Figure shows an automobile circuit. How much power (in watt) is dissipated by the automobile circuit when switches A, B, C and D are closed.

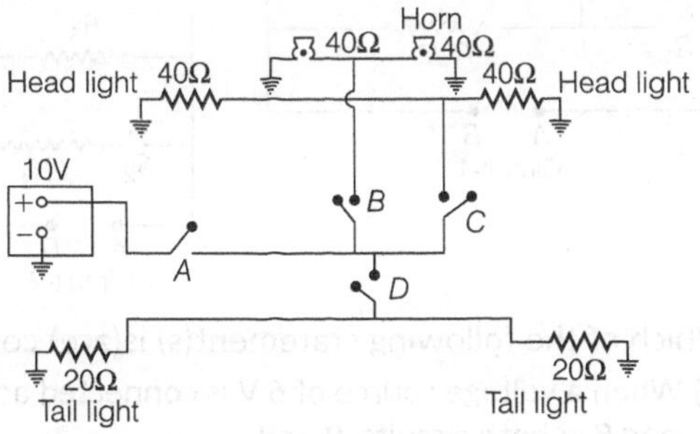

8 A battery of emf ε fitted with a resistor R in series supplies current to the resistors between A and B in the upper part of the circuit. If the power dissipated in the network between A and B as shown by rounded dotted line, does not get affected by closing the key K, find the value of R (in Ω), if $R' = 20\sqrt{2}\ \Omega$.

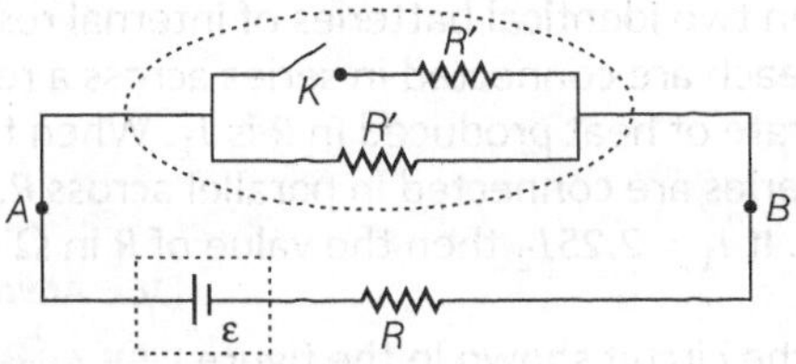

Previous Year's Questions

JEE Main

1 An electric toaster has resistance of 60 Ω at room temperature 27°C. The toaster is connected to a 220 V supply. If the current flowing through it reaches 2.75 A, the temperature attained by toaster is around (if, $\alpha = 2 \times 10^{-4}$/°C) **[2024, 30 Jan Shift-I]**

(a) 1667°C
(b) 1694°C
(c) 694°C
(d) 1235°C

2 When a potential difference V is applied across a wire of resistance R, it dissipates energy at a rate W. If the wire is cut into two halves and these halves are connected mutually parallel across the same supply, the energy dissipation rate will become **[2024, 31 Jan Shift-I]**

(a) $\frac{1}{2}W$ (b) $\frac{1}{4}W$ (c) $4W$ (d) $2W$

3 Different combination of 3 resistors of equal resistance R are shown in the figures. The increasing order for power dissipation is **[2023, 13 April Shift-I]**

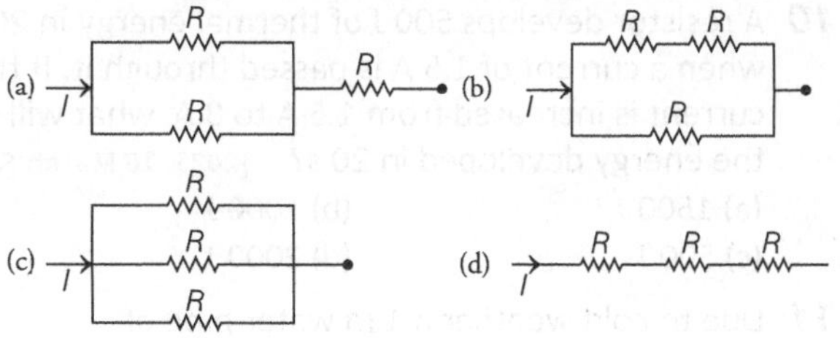

(a) $P_A < P_B < P_C < P_D$
(b) $P_C < P_D < P_A < P_B$
(c) $P_C < P_B < P_A < P_D$
(d) $P_B < P_C < P_D < P_A$

4 Two identical heater filaments are connected first in parallel and then in series. At the same applied voltage, the ratio of heat produced in same time for parallel to series will be **[2023, 11 April Shift-I]**

(a) 1 : 1 (b) 1 : 4
(c) 2 : 1 (d) 4 : 1

5 A potential V_0 is applied across a uniform wire of resistance R. The power dissipation is P_1. The wire is then cut into two equal halves and a potential of V_0 is applied across the length of each half. The total power dissipation ratio across two wires is P_2. The ratio $P_2 : P_1$ is $\sqrt{x} : 1$. The value of x is .... **[2023, 13 April Shift-I]**

6 An electrical bulb rated (220 V, 100 W) is connected in series with another bulb rated (220 V, 60 W). If the voltage across combination is 220 V, the power consumed by the 100 W bulb will be about .... W. **[2022, 28 July Shift-II]**

7 A resistor develops 300 J of thermal energy in 15 s when a current of 2 A is passed through it. If the current increases to 3 A, the energy developed in 10 s is .... J. **[2022, 25 June Shift-I]**

8 Two coils require 20 min and 60 min respectively to produce same amount of heat energy when connected separately to the same source. If they are connected in parallel arrangement to the same source; the time required to produce same amount of heat by the combination of coils will be .... min. **[2022, 29 June Shift-I]**

9 An electric bulb of 500 W at 100 V is used in a circuit having a 200 V supply. Calculate the resistance R to be connected in series with the bulb, so that the power delivered by the bulb is 500 W. **[2021, 26 Aug Shift-II]**

(a) 20 Ω (b) 30 Ω
(c) 5 Ω (d) 10 Ω

10 A resistor develops 500 J of thermal energy in 20 s, when a current of 1.5 A is passed through it. If the current is increased from 1.5 A to 3 A, what will be the energy developed in 20 s? **[2021, 16 March Shift-II]**

(a) 1500 J (b) 1000 J
(c) 500 J (d) 2000 J

11 Due to cold weather a 1 m water pipe of cross-sectional area 1 cm^2 is filled with ice at –10°C. Resistive heating is used to melt the ice. Current of 0.5 A is passed through a 4kΩ resistance. Assuming that all the heat produced is used for melting, what is the minimum time required?

(Given latent heat of fusion for water/ice $= 3.33 \times 10^5$ J kg^{-1}, specific heat of ice $= 2 \times 10^3$ J kg^{-1} and density of ice $= 10^3$ kg / m^3)

[2021, 1 Sep Shift-II]

(a) 3.53 s (b) 0.353 s (c) 35.3 s (d) 70.6 s

12 An electric bulb rated as 200 W at 100 V is used in a circuit having 200 V supply. The resistance R that must be put in series with the bulb so that the bulb delivers the same power is ....Ω **[2021, 25 July Shift-I]**

13 A uniform heating wire of resistance 36 Ω is connected across a potential difference of 240 V. The wire is then cut into half and potential difference of 240 V is applied across each half separately. The ratio of power dissipation in first case to the total power dissipation in the second case would be $1 : x$, where x is .... **[2021, 1 Sep Shift-II]**

14 A resistor dissipates 192 J of energy in 1 s when a current of 4 A is passed through it. Now, when the current is doubled, the amount of thermal energy dissipated in 5 s is .... J. **[2021, 31 Aug Shift-II]**

15 The energy dissipated by a resistor is 10 mJ in 1s when an electric current of 2 mA flows through it. The resistance is .... Ω.
(Round off to the nearest integer)
[2021, 16 March Shift-II]

JEE Advanced

1 In Circuit-1 and Circuit-2 shown in the figures, $R_1 = 1$ Ω, $R_2 = 2$ Ω and $R_3 = 3$ Ω.

P_1 and P_2 are the power dissipations in Circuit-1 and Circuit-2 when the switches S_1 and S_2 are in open conditions, respectively.

Q_1 and Q_2 are the power dissipations in Circuit-1 and Circuit-2 when the switches S_1 and S_2 are in closed conditions, respectively. **(2022 Adv.)**

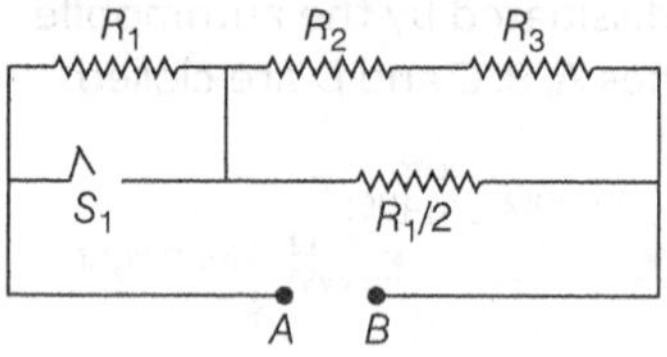

Circuit-1

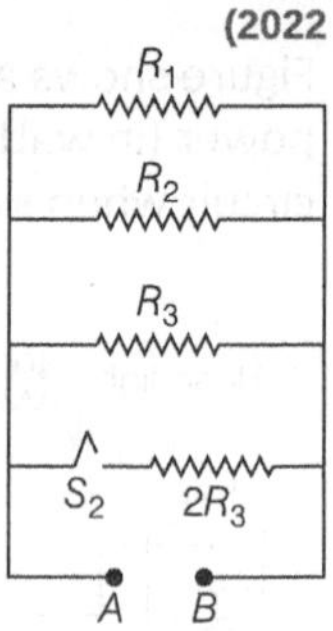

Circuit-2

Which of the following statement(s) is(are) correct?

(a) When a voltage source of 6 V is connected across A and B in both circuits, $P_1 < P_2$.
(b) When a constant current source of 2 A is connected across A and B in both circuits, $P_1 > P_2$.
(c) When a voltage source of 6 V is connected across A and B in Circuit-1, $Q_1 > P_1$.
(d) When a constant current source of 2 A is connected across A and B in both circuits, $Q_2 < Q_1$.

2 When two identical batteries of internal resistance 1 Ω each are connected in series across a resistor R, the rate of heat produced in R is J_1. When the same batteries are connected in parallel across R, the rate is J_2. If $J_1 = 2.25 J_2$ then the value of R in Ω is **[JEE Advanced 2010]**

3 For the circuit shown in the figure **[JEE Advanced 2009]**

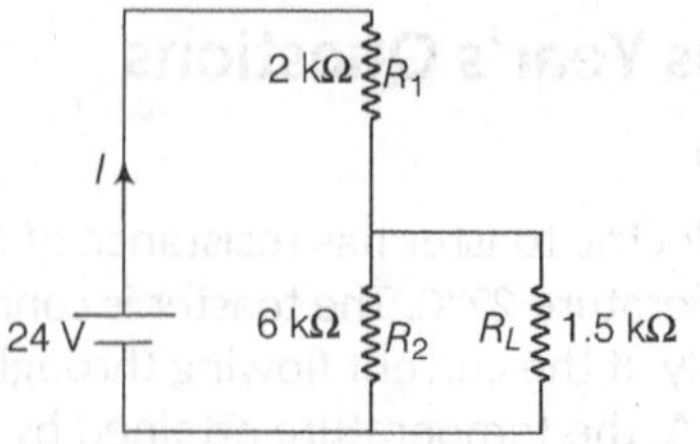

(a) the current I through the battery is 7.5 mA
(b) the potential difference across R_L is 18 V
(c) ratio of powers dissipated in R_1 and R_2 is 3
(d) if R_1 and R_2 are interchanged, magnitude of the power dissipated in R_L will decrease by a factor of 9

Answer Key

Level 1 Starter Level

8.1 Heating Effect of Current

1. $\frac{5}{3}$ W
2. 192 W
3. (i) $R = 484\,\Omega$ (ii) $\frac{5}{11}$ A (iii) 25 W
4. 36%, 192 kJ
5. 210 s
6. 66.67%
7. 0.095 s
8. 3.2 W, 4W
9. $8\,\Omega$ (i) 800W (ii) 704W (iii) 86400 J

8.2 Series and Parallel Combinations of the Heating Elements

1. (i) 13.88 W (ii) 69.44 W
2. (i) 8.16 W (ii) 14.28 W
3. (i) 30 W bulb (ii) both the bulbs
4. $W_3 > W_2 > W_1$
5. 75 W
6. (i) 18 min (ii) 4 min
7. $600\,\Omega$

8.3 Maximum Power Transfer Theorem

1. $r, \frac{\varepsilon^2}{4r}$
2. $2\,\Omega$
3. $7\,\Omega$

Level 2 JEE Main Level

Single Choice Correct Questions

1. (c)	2. (d)	3. (d)	4. (b)	5. (a)
6. (a)	7. (c)	8. (c)	9. (c)	10. (c)
11. (b)	12. (b)	13. (b)	14. (b)	15. (c)
16. (d)	17. (c)	18. (a)	19. (c)	20. (b)
21. (c)	22. (b)	23. (c)	24. (b)	25. (b)
26. (a)	27. (d)	28. (b)	29. (d)	30. (b)

Numerical Value Questions

1. (64)	2. (7)	3. (280)	4. (4)	5. (120)
6. (3)	7. (3)	8. (56.25)	9. (245)	10. (25)

Level 3 JEE Advanced Level

Single Choice correct Questions

1. (b)	2. (a)	3. (b)	4. (b)	5. (d)
6. (b)	7. (c)	8. (b)	9. (c)	10. (b)
11. (a)	12. (c)	13. (d)	14. (a)	15. (d)
16. (d)	17. (a)	18. (b)	19. (c)	20. (a)
21. (a)	22. (d)	23. (a)	24. (a)	25. (a)
26. (b)	27. (a)			

Multiple Choice(s) Correct Questions

1. (abd)	2. (bc)	3. (abcd)	4. (ad)	5. (bc)
6. (bd)	7. (bc)	8. (acd)	9. (ad)	10. (ab)
11. (ac)	12. (ac)			

Comprehension Based Questions

1. (c)	2. (a)	3. (c)	4. (b)	5. (a)
6. (b)	7. (a)	8. (b)	9. (b)	10. (c)
11. (a)				

Match the Columns Questions

1. (a) → qs; (b) → prs; (c) → prs; (d) → qs
2. (a) → r; (b) → pqrs; (c) → s; (d) → s
3. (a) → qs; (b) → qr; (c) → ps; (d) → pr
4. (a) → pq; (b) → s; (c) → qr; (d) → p

Numerical Value Questions

1. (3)	2. (12)	3. (27)	4. (12)	5. (800)
6. (2)	7. (20)	8. (20)		

Previous Year's Questions

JEE Main

1. (b)	2. (c)	3. (*)	4. (d)	5. (16)
6. (14)	7. (450)	8. (15)	9. (a)	10. (d)
11. (c)	12. (50)	13. (4)	14. (3840)	15. (2500)

JEE Advanced

1. (a,b,c)	2. (4)	3. (a,d)

SOLUTIONS

Level 1 Starter Level

8.1 Heating Effect of Current

1. $\dfrac{R_1}{R_2}=\dfrac{\dfrac{\rho_1 l_1}{A_1}}{\dfrac{\rho_2 l_2}{A_2}}=\dfrac{\dfrac{\rho_1 l_1^2}{A_1 l_1}}{\dfrac{\rho_2 l_2^2}{A_2 l_2}}=\left(\dfrac{\rho_1}{\rho_2}\right)\left(\dfrac{l_1}{l_2}\right)^2\left(\dfrac{V_2}{V_1}\right)$

$=\left(\dfrac{\rho_1}{\rho_2}\right)\left(\dfrac{l_1}{l_2}\right)^2\left(\dfrac{d_1}{d_2}\right) \qquad \left(\because d \propto \dfrac{1}{V}\right)$

$=\left(\dfrac{2}{1}\right)\left(\dfrac{1}{2}\right)^2\left(\dfrac{1}{3}\right)=\dfrac{1}{6}$

$P=\dfrac{V^2}{R} \Rightarrow \dfrac{P_1}{P_2}=\dfrac{R_2}{R_1}$

$\Rightarrow \dfrac{10}{P_2}=6 \Rightarrow P_2=\dfrac{5}{3}\text{ W}$

2.

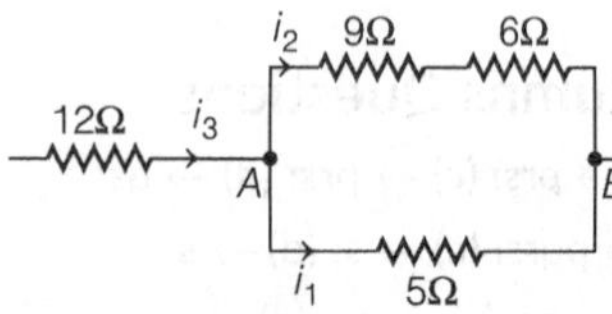

Power dissipated in 5 Ω = 45 W

$\Rightarrow \quad i_1^2(5)=45 \quad \Rightarrow \quad i_1=3\text{ A}$

$V_A-V_B=5(3)=(9+6)i_2$

$\Rightarrow \quad i_2=1\text{ A} \quad \Rightarrow \quad i_3=i_1+i_2$

$\Rightarrow \quad i_3=3+1=4\text{ A}$

Power developed across 12 Ω $=i_3^2R=(4)^2(12)=192\text{ W}$

3. (i) $R=\dfrac{V^2}{P}=\dfrac{(220)^2}{100}=484\,\Omega$

(ii) $P=Vi \Rightarrow i=\dfrac{P}{V}=\dfrac{100}{220}=\dfrac{5}{11}\text{ A}$

(iii) $P=\dfrac{V^2}{R}$

$100=\dfrac{(220)^2}{R}$ ...(i)

$P=\dfrac{(110)^2}{R}$ ...(ii)

Solving Eqs. (i) and (ii), we get

$P=25\text{ W}$

4. $R=\dfrac{V^2}{P}=\dfrac{(200)^2}{500}=80\,\Omega$

$P'=\dfrac{V'^2}{R}=\dfrac{(160)^2}{80}=320\text{ W}$

Percentage drop in heat output $=\left(\dfrac{500-320}{500}\right)\times 100=36\%$

Heat produced $=P't=(320)(10\times 60)=192\text{ kJ}$

5. $P=\dfrac{V^2}{R}=\dfrac{(200)^2}{400}=100\text{ W}$

Let time taken be t

Heat supplied to water $=ms\Delta T$

$\Rightarrow \quad P\times t=ms\Delta T$

$\Rightarrow \quad 100t=0.1\times 4200\times 50$

$\Rightarrow \quad t=210\text{ s}$

6. Power delivered by kettle $=Vi=210\times 3=630\text{ W}$

Power consumed by water $=\dfrac{ms\Delta T}{t}=\dfrac{1\times 4200\times 60}{600}$

$=420\text{ W}$

Efficiency of kettle $=\dfrac{P_{\text{consumed}}}{P_{\text{delivered}}}\times 100=\dfrac{420}{630}\times 100=66.67\%$

7. Let time taken be t.

$P=\dfrac{ms\Delta T}{t}$

$\Rightarrow \quad i^2R=\dfrac{ms\Delta T}{t}$

$\Rightarrow \quad t=\dfrac{ms\Delta T}{i^2R}=\dfrac{(dAl)s\Delta T}{i^2\left(\dfrac{\rho l}{A}\right)}=\dfrac{dA^2 s\Delta T}{\rho l^2}$

$=\dfrac{(11.34\times 10^3)(0.2\times 10^{-6})^2(0.032\times 4200)(327-20)}{(22\times 10^{-6}\times 10^{-2})(30)^2}$

$=0.095\text{ s}$

8. Potential difference between terminals of battery $=E-ir$

$\Rightarrow \quad 2=3.6-2r \Rightarrow r=0.8\,\Omega$

Thermal power generated in battery

$=i^2r=(2)^2(0.8)=3.2\text{ W}$

Power supplied by battery $=Ei-i^2r$

$=(3.6)(2)-(2)^2(0.8)=4\text{ W}$

9. Equivalent emf of battery $=2\times 6=12\text{ V}$

Equivalent internal resistance of battery $=0.5\times 6=3\Omega$

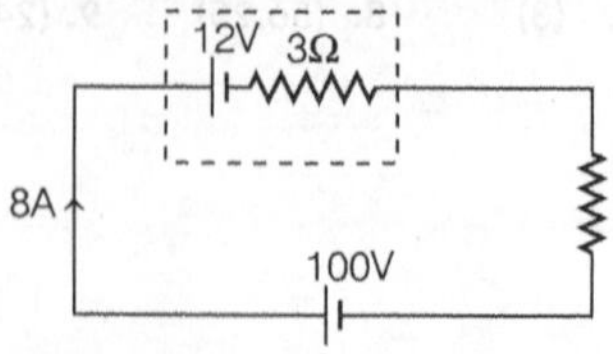

Using KVL, $+100-12-3(8)-8(R)=0$

$\Rightarrow \quad R=8\,\Omega$

(i) Power supplied by the DC source $=100\times 8=800\text{ W}$

(ii) Power dissipated as heat $=i^2R_{eq}=(8)^2(3+8)=704\text{ W}$

(iii) Chemical energy stored in battery in 15 min

$=E_{eq}\,it=12\times 8\times(15\times 60)=86400\text{ J}$

8.2 Series and Parallel Combinations of the Heating Elements

1.

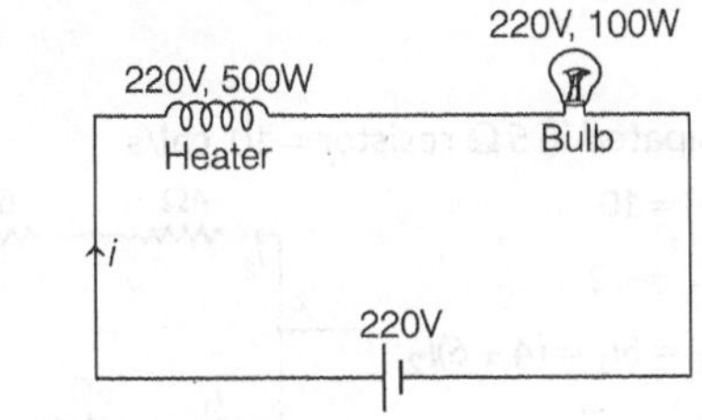

$$R_{heater} = \frac{(220)^2}{500}\,\Omega \text{ and } R_{bulb} = \frac{(220)^2}{100}$$

$$i = \frac{220}{\frac{(220)^2}{500} + \frac{(220)^2}{100}}$$

(i) Power consumed by heater $= i^2 R_{heater}$

$$= \left(\frac{220}{\frac{(220)^2}{500} + \frac{(220)^2}{100}}\right)^2 \times \frac{(220)^2}{500} = 13.88 \text{ W}$$

(ii) Power consumed by bulb $= i^2 R_{bulb}$

$$= \left(\frac{220}{\frac{(220)^2}{500} + \frac{(220)^2}{100}}\right)^2 \times \frac{(220)^2}{100} = 69.44 \text{ W}$$

2. (i) Bulb B_3 will be brightest as it has maximum resistance.
Power delivered by $B_3 = i^2 R_3$

$$= \left(\frac{200}{\frac{(200)^2}{100} + \frac{(200)^2}{50} + \frac{(200)^2}{25}}\right)^2 \times \frac{(200)^2}{25} = 8.16 \text{ W}$$

(ii) $\frac{1}{P_{eq}} = \frac{1}{P_1} + \frac{1}{P_2} + \frac{1}{P_3}$

$$\Rightarrow \quad \frac{1}{P_{eq}} = \frac{1}{100} + \frac{1}{50} + \frac{1}{25}$$

$$\Rightarrow \quad P = \frac{100}{7} = 14.28 \text{ W}$$

3. A bulb is likely to get fused when potential difference across it exceeds its rated voltage.
   (i) In series combination, potential difference across 30 W bulb will be more than 200 V as 30 W bulb has more resistance than 60 W bulb. So, 30 W bulb is likely to get fused.
   (ii) In parallel combination, potential difference across each bulb will be 400 V. So, both the bulbs are likely to get fused.

4. Bulbs B_1 and B_2 are in series. So, current through them is same and bulb with more resistance will give more power. B_2 has more resistance as it has lesser rated power. So, $W_2 > W_1$.
Potential difference across B_3 is greater than potential difference across B_2. So, B_3 will give more power than B_2. So, $W_3 > W_2 > W_1$

5. $$\frac{1}{P_{eq}} = \frac{1}{P} + \frac{1}{3P}$$

$$\Rightarrow \quad P_{eq} = \frac{3P}{4} = \frac{3}{4} \times 100 = 75 \text{ W}$$

6. Let power of first coil be P_1 and power of second coil be P_2.
Let heat required for boiling be Q.

$$P_1 = \frac{Q}{12} \text{ and } P_2 = \frac{Q}{6}$$

(i) In series combination,

$$P_{eq} = \frac{P_1 P_2}{P_1 + P_2} = \frac{\left(\frac{Q}{12}\right)\left(\frac{Q}{6}\right)}{\frac{Q}{12} + \frac{Q}{6}} = \frac{Q}{18}$$

So, time taken will be 18 min.

(ii) In parallel combination,

$$P_{eq} = P_1 + P_2 = \frac{Q}{12} + \frac{Q}{6} = \frac{Q}{4}$$

So, time taken will be 4 min.

7.

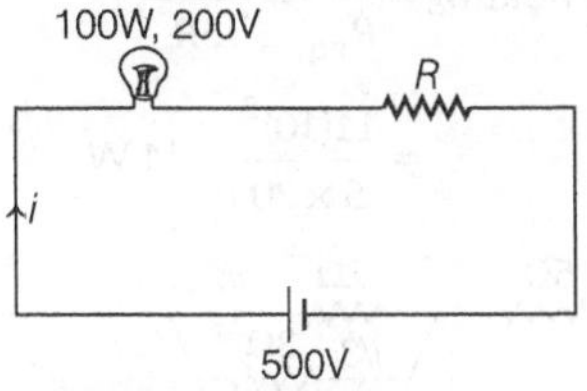

$$R_{bulb} = \frac{(200)^2}{100} = 400\,\Omega$$

$$i = \frac{P}{V} = \frac{100}{200} = 0.5 \text{ A}$$

$$i = \frac{500}{400 + R} = 0.5 \Rightarrow R = 600\,\Omega$$

8.3 Maximum Power Transfer Theorem

1. $$i = \frac{\varepsilon}{R + r}$$

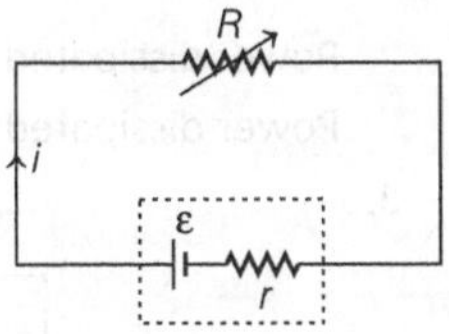

Power dissipated in $R = i^2 R$

$$\Rightarrow \quad P = \left(\frac{\varepsilon}{R + r}\right)^2 R = \frac{\varepsilon^2}{R + \frac{r^2}{R} + 2r}$$

To maximise power, we have to minimise denominator

$$R + \frac{r^2}{R} + 2r$$

Let $$y = R + \frac{r^2}{R} + 2r$$

$$\frac{dy}{dR} = 1 - \frac{r^2}{R^2} = 0 \Rightarrow R = r$$

$$P = \left(\frac{\varepsilon}{r + r}\right)^2 \cdot r \Rightarrow P = \frac{\varepsilon^2}{4r}$$

2. Let internal resistance of battery be r.

$$i = \frac{36}{10 + r}$$

Power dissipated by the battery $= i^2 r$

$$\Rightarrow \quad 18 = \left(\frac{36}{10 + r}\right)^2 r \Rightarrow r = 2\,\Omega$$

For maximum power, R should be $2\,\Omega$ from maximum power transfer theorem.

3. From maximum power transfer theorem,

$$R = 5 + 2 = 7\,\Omega$$

Level 2 JEE Main Level

Single Choice Correct Questions

1. $R_{eq} = \dfrac{R\left(\dfrac{R}{2} + \dfrac{R}{3}\right)}{R + \dfrac{R}{2} + \dfrac{R}{3}} = \dfrac{5R}{11}$

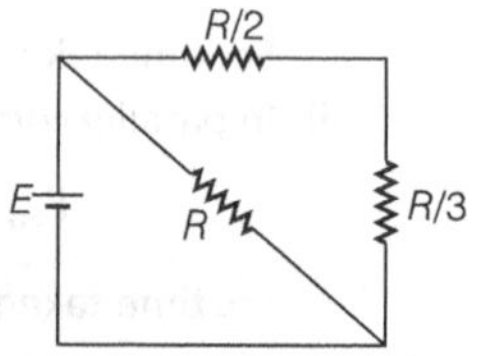

Rate of joule heating $= \dfrac{E^2}{R_{eq}} = \dfrac{11\,E^2}{5R}$

$$= \frac{11(10)^2}{5 \times 20} = 11\text{ W}$$

2.

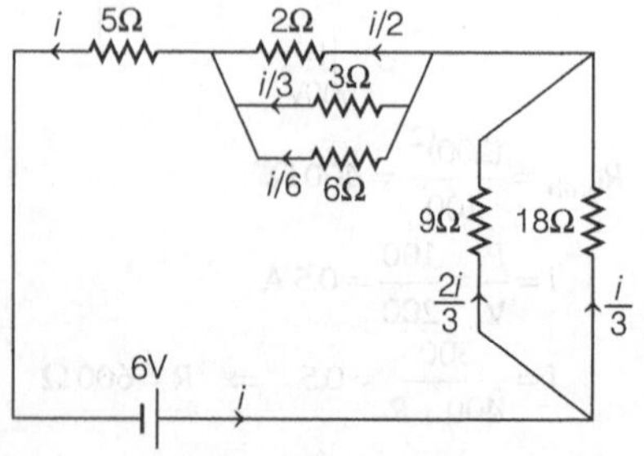

$$i = \frac{6}{R_{eq}} = \frac{6}{5 + 1 + 6} = 0.5\text{ A}$$

Power dissipated in $5\,\Omega = i^2 R = (0.5)^2 5 = 1.25$ W

Power dissipated in $5\,\Omega$ resistor will be maximum.

3.

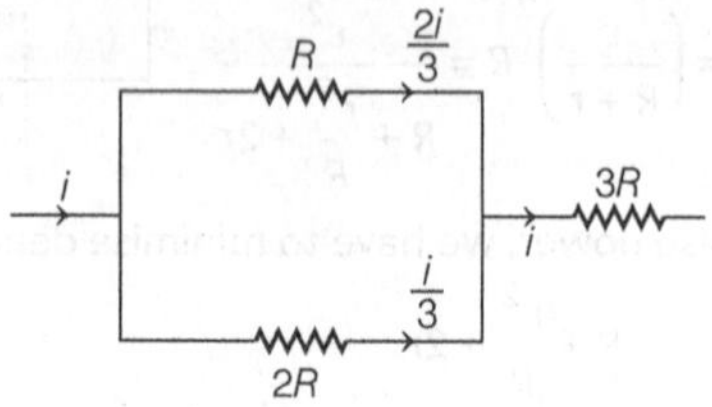

$$P_1 = \text{Power dissipated in } R = \left(\frac{2i}{3}\right)^2 R = \frac{4i^2 R}{9}$$

$$P_2 = \text{Power dissipated in } 3R = i^2(3R) = 3i^2 R$$

$$\frac{P_1}{P_2} = \frac{4}{27}$$

4.

Power dissipated in $5\,\Omega$ resistor $= 10$ cal/s

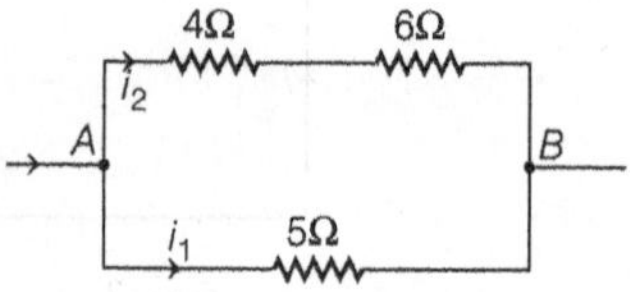

$$\Rightarrow \quad i_1^2(5) = 10$$

$$\Rightarrow \quad i_1 = \sqrt{2}$$

$$V_A - V_B = 5i_1 = (4 + 6)i_2$$

$$\Rightarrow \quad i_2 = \frac{i_1}{2} = \frac{\sqrt{2}}{2} = \frac{1}{\sqrt{2}}$$

Power dissipated in $4\,\Omega$ resistor $= i_2^2(4) = \left(\dfrac{1}{\sqrt{2}}\right)^2 4 = 2$ cal/s

5.

$$Q = 2t - 8t^2$$

$$i = \frac{dQ}{dt} = 2 - 16t$$

$$\text{Heat produced} = \int i^2 R\,dt = \int_0^{1/8} (2 - 16t)^2 R\,dt$$

$$= \left[\frac{(2 - 16t)^3 R}{-16 \times 3}\right]_0^{1/8} = \frac{R}{6}\text{ J}$$

6. Area under i - t curve = charge

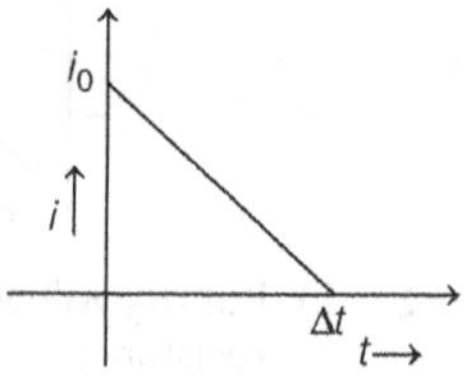

$$\Rightarrow \quad \frac{1}{2} i_0 \Delta t = q \Rightarrow i_0 = \frac{2q}{\Delta t}$$

Equation of straight line, $y = mx + C$

$$\Rightarrow \quad i = \left(-\frac{i_0}{\Delta t}\right)t + i_0 = \frac{2q}{\Delta t}\left(1 - \frac{t}{\Delta t}\right)$$

$$\text{Heat produced} = \int_0^{\Delta t} i^2 R\,dt = \int_0^{\Delta t} \left[\frac{2q}{\Delta t}\left(1 - \frac{t}{\Delta t}\right)\right]^2 R\,dt$$

$$= \frac{4q^2 R}{(\Delta t)^2} \left[\frac{\left(1 - \dfrac{t}{\Delta t}\right)^3}{3\left(\dfrac{-1}{\Delta t}\right)}\right]_0^{\Delta t} = \frac{4q^2 R}{3\Delta t}$$

7. $R = \dfrac{\rho l}{A} = \dfrac{\rho l^2}{Al} = \dfrac{\rho l^2}{V} = \dfrac{\rho l^2 d}{m}$

$$R \propto \frac{l^2}{m}$$

$$R_1 : R_2 : R_3 = \frac{5^2}{1} : \frac{3^2}{3} : \frac{1^2}{5}$$

$$= 25 : 3 : \frac{1}{5} = 125 : 15 : 1$$

Heat produced $= i^2 Rt$

Heat produced $\propto R$

So, heat produced in them will be in ratio

125 : 15 : 1

8. Rate of dissipation of Joule's heating per unit volume

$$= \frac{Vi}{(\text{Volume})} = \frac{(El)(JA)}{Al} = JE$$

9.

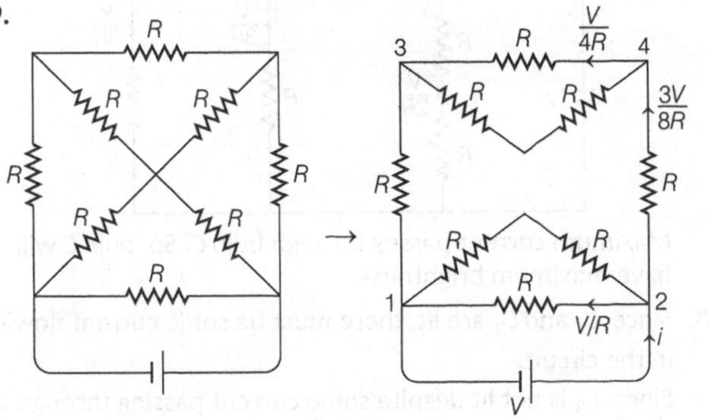

Current in conductor 1 - 2 $= \frac{V}{R}$

Current in conductor 3 - 4 $= \frac{V}{4R}$

Q = Heat liberated per unit time $= i^2R$

$$\frac{Q_{12}}{Q_{34}} = \frac{\left(\frac{V}{R}\right)^2 R}{\left(\frac{V}{4R}\right)^2 R} = 16:1$$

10. Heat produced $= i^2Rt = (7)^2(60)t$

Heat consumed by water $= ms\Delta T = 42 \times 4200 \times \Delta T$

$$i^2Rt = ms\Delta T$$

$$\Rightarrow \quad (7)^2(60)t = 42 \times 4200 \times \Delta T$$

$$\Rightarrow \quad \frac{\Delta T}{t} = \frac{49 \times 60}{42 \times 4200}$$

Rise in temperature per minute

$$= \frac{\Delta T}{t} \times 60 = \frac{49 \times 60}{42 \times 4200} \times 60 = 1°\text{C}$$

11. $P = \frac{V^2}{R}$

$$H = \left(\frac{V^2}{R}\right)t \text{ and } H = mL_f \quad \Rightarrow \quad \left(\frac{V^2}{R}\right)t = mL_f$$

$$\Rightarrow \quad \frac{(210)^2}{50} \times 1 = m\,(80 \times 4.2) \quad \Rightarrow \quad m = 2.62 \text{ g}$$

12. $P = \frac{V^2}{R}$

If length of filament of a heater is reduced by 10%, its resistance will reduce by 10%

$$P' = \frac{V^2}{R - \left(\frac{R \times 10}{100}\right)} = \frac{V^2}{0.9\,R}$$

$$\% \text{ change in power} = \frac{P' - P}{P} \times 100 = \frac{\frac{V^2}{0.9R} - \frac{V^2}{R}}{\frac{V^2}{R}} \times 100$$

$$= \frac{100}{9}\% = 11.11\%$$

13. Let emf of each cell be ε.

$$P = \frac{V^2}{R} = \frac{V^2}{\left(\frac{\rho L}{A}\right)} = \frac{V^2A}{\rho L}$$

Heat developed $= Pt = ms\Delta t$

$$\Rightarrow \quad Pt = dALs\Delta T$$

$$\frac{\Delta T}{t} = \frac{V^2}{d\rho L^2 s} \quad \Rightarrow \quad \frac{\Delta T}{t} \propto \frac{V^2}{L^2}$$

For 3 cells, equivalent emf $= 3\varepsilon$

$$\Rightarrow \quad \frac{\Delta T}{t} \propto \frac{(3\varepsilon)^2}{L^2} \qquad \text{...(i)}$$

For N cells, equivalent emf $= N\varepsilon$

$$\frac{\Delta T}{t} \propto \frac{(N\varepsilon)^2}{(2L)^2} \qquad \text{...(ii)}$$

Solving Eqs. (i) and (ii), we get

$$N = 6$$

14. When a wire of resistance R is cut into n equal parts, resistance of each part is $\frac{R}{n}$.

Now, all parts are connected in parallel.

So, $$R_{eq} = \frac{R/n}{n} = \frac{R}{n^2}$$

$$H = \frac{V^2}{R} \qquad \text{...(i)}$$

$$H' = \frac{V^2}{R_{eq}} = \frac{V^2}{\left(\frac{R}{n^2}\right)} = n^2\frac{V^2}{R} \qquad \text{...(ii)}$$

From Eqs. (i) and (ii), we get

$$H' = n^2H$$

15. Let the value of other resistance be R.

When connected in series,

$$P_1 = \frac{V^2}{(R+8)}$$

When connected in parallel,

$$P_2 = \frac{V^2}{\left(\frac{8R}{R+8}\right)} \quad \Rightarrow \quad P_2 = 4.5P_1$$

$$\frac{V^2}{\frac{8R}{8+R}} = 4.5\left(\frac{V^2}{R+8}\right)$$

$$\Rightarrow \quad (R+8)^2 = 36R$$

$$\Rightarrow \quad R^2 - 20R + 64 = 0$$

$$\Rightarrow \quad R = 4\Omega \text{ and } R = 16\Omega$$

16. Current in the circuit $= \frac{50}{5} = 10$ A

Power dissipated in circuit $= i^2R = (10)^2(0.02) = 2$ W

Power received by tape-recorder $= 50 - 2 = 48$ W

17. $R = \frac{V^2}{P}$

In series combination, $P = i^2R$

$$P = i^2\left(\frac{V^2}{P}\right)$$

$$P \propto V^2$$

So, brightness of bulbs will be proportional to square of their marked voltage.

18. Bulb with less rated power has more resistance. So, in series combination of bulbs across a 440 V supply, potential difference across 25 W bulb will be more than 220 V. So, 25 W bulb is likely to get fused.

19.

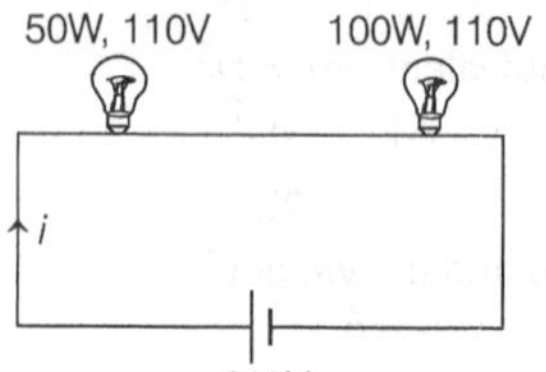

$$i = \frac{110}{\frac{(110)^2}{50} + \frac{(110)^2}{100}}$$

Power dissipated in 50 W bulb $= i^2R$

$$= \left(\frac{110}{\frac{(110)^2}{50} + \frac{(110)^2}{100}}\right)^2 \times \frac{(110)^2}{50} = \frac{200}{9} \text{ W} = 22.22 \text{ W}$$

20. $P_{eq} = \frac{P_1(P_2 + P_3)}{P_1 + P_2 + P_3}$

$$= \frac{100 \times 80}{100 + 80} = 44.44 \text{ W}$$

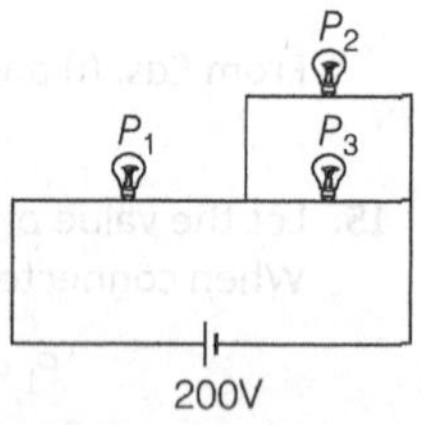

21. In series combination,

$$P = i^2R \Rightarrow P \propto R$$

$$\frac{P_1}{P_2} = \frac{R_1}{R_2} = \frac{\frac{(220)^2}{500}}{\frac{(220)^2}{200}} = \frac{2}{5}$$

In parallel combination,

$$P = \frac{V^2}{R} \Rightarrow P \propto \frac{1}{R}$$

$$\frac{P_1}{P_2} = \frac{R_2}{R_1} = \frac{\frac{(220)^2}{200}}{\frac{(220)^2}{500}} = \frac{5}{2}$$

22. Let resistance of each bulb be R.

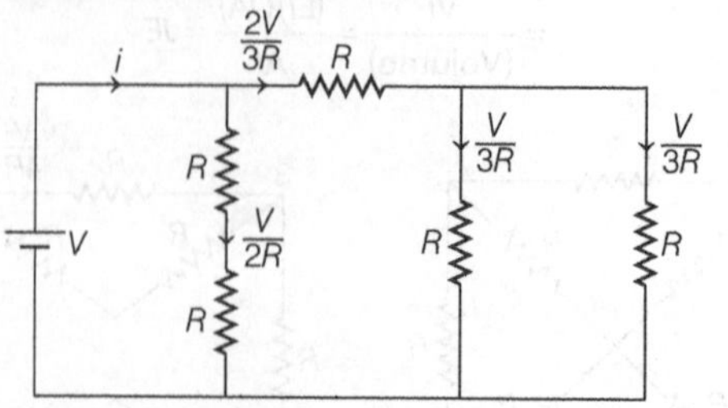

Maximum current passes through bulb C. So, bulb C will have maximum brightness.

23. Since, L_1 and L_2 are lit, there must be some current flowing in the circuit.

Since, L_3 is not lit despite some current passing through it, resistance of L_3 is much lower than that of L_1 and L_2.

24. When switch is closed, resistance of the circuit will decrease. So, current through X will decrease and brightness of X will increase.

Potential difference across Y decreases. So, brightness of Y decreases.

25. Current through each bulb $= \frac{60}{220} = \frac{3}{11}$ A

Let number of bulbs be n.

Current in the main supply $= n\left(\frac{3}{11}\right)$

$$n\left(\frac{3}{11}\right) = 15 \Rightarrow n = 55$$

26. Let heat required for boiling be Q.

$$P_1 = \text{power of first coil} = \frac{Q}{6}$$

$$P_2 = \text{power of second coil} = \frac{Q}{3}$$

In parallel combination of the coils,

$$P_{eq} = P_1 + P_2 = \frac{Q}{6} + \frac{Q}{3}$$

Time taken for boiling $= \frac{Q}{P_{eq}} = \frac{Q}{\frac{Q}{6} + \frac{Q}{3}} = 2$ min

27. Let resistance of each bulb be R.

When 40 bulbs are connected in series, $P_1 = \frac{(220)^2}{40R}$

When 39 bulbs are connected in series, $P_2 = \frac{(220)^2}{39R}$

% change in illumination $= \frac{P_2 - P_1}{P_1} \times 100$

$$= \frac{\frac{(220)^2}{39R} - \frac{(220)^2}{40R}}{\frac{(220)^2}{40R}} \times 100$$

$$= \frac{100}{39}\% \simeq 2.5\%$$

28. From maximum power transfer theorem,

$$Y = \frac{6X}{6+X} + 2$$

$$\Rightarrow \quad 4 = \frac{6X}{6+X} + 2$$

$$\Rightarrow \quad 12 + 2X = 6X \quad \Rightarrow \quad X = 3\,\Omega$$

29.

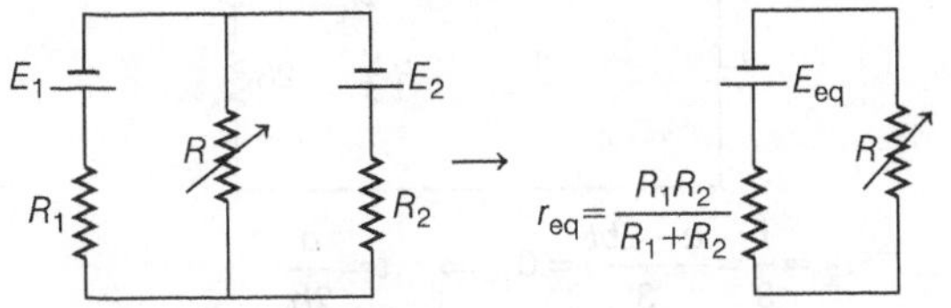

$$E_{eq} = \frac{\frac{E_1}{R_1} + \frac{E_2}{R_2}}{\frac{1}{R_1} + \frac{1}{R_2}} \quad \text{and} \quad r_{eq} = \frac{R_1R_2}{R_1 + R_2}$$

For maximum power in R, $R = r_{eq} = \frac{R_1R_2}{R_1 + R_2}$

30.

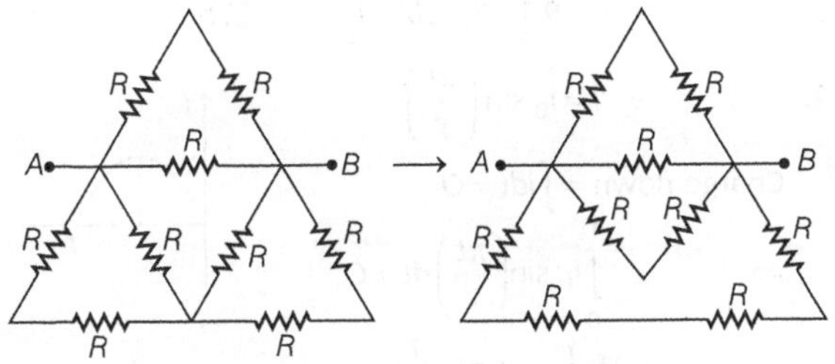

Equivalent resistance between A and B $= \frac{4R}{9}$

For maximum power from battery, $r = R_{eq} = \frac{4R}{9}$

Numerical Value Questions

1. From the graph, $E = 6t$

$$\text{Heat dissipated} = \int P dt = \int_0^4 \frac{E^2}{R} dt = 3\int_0^4 t^2 dt$$

$$= 3\left[\frac{t^3}{3}\right]_0^4 = 64 \text{ J}$$

2. Resistance of bulb $= \frac{V^2}{P} = \frac{(3)^2}{1} = 9\,\Omega$

Equivalent resistance across battery

$$= \frac{1}{16} + \frac{9R}{R+9} = \frac{145R+9}{16(R+9)}$$

$$\text{Current through battery} = \frac{\frac{64}{21}}{\frac{(145R+9)}{16(R+9)}} = \frac{1024(R+9)}{21(145R+9)}$$

$$\text{Current through bulb} = \frac{1024(R+9)}{21(145R+9)} \times \frac{R}{R+9} = \frac{1}{3}$$

$$\Rightarrow \quad \frac{1024R}{21(145R+9)} = \frac{1}{3}$$

$$\Rightarrow \quad 1024R = 7(145R+9)$$

$$\Rightarrow \quad R = 7\,\Omega$$

3. $R_{40\,W} = \frac{(200)^2}{40} = 1000\,\Omega$

and $R_{100\,W} = \frac{(200)^2}{100} = 400\,\Omega$

40 W bulb is likely to get fused before 100 W bulb.

If 40 W bulb operates at its rated specification, current through it is $\frac{40}{200} = \frac{1}{5}$ A

Now, potential difference across 100 W bulb $= 400\left(\frac{1}{5}\right)$

$$= 80 \text{ V}$$

So, maximum voltage across combination

$$= 200 + 80 = 280 \text{ V}$$

4. Resistance of each bulb $= \frac{(100)^2}{50} = 200\,\Omega$

Current through each bulb $= \frac{50}{100} = 0.5$ A

Let number of bulbs be n.

$$\text{Current through battery} = n(0.5) = \frac{120}{10 + \frac{200}{n}}$$

$$\Rightarrow \quad 240 = 10n + 200$$

$$\Rightarrow \quad n = 4$$

5. $i^2 \propto r^3$

$$\frac{i_1}{i_2} = \left(\frac{r_1}{r_2}\right)^{3/2}$$

$$\Rightarrow \quad \frac{15}{i_2} = \left(\frac{0.15}{0.60}\right)^{3/2}$$

$$\Rightarrow \quad i_2 = 120 \text{ A}$$

6. It is a balanced Wheatstone bridge.

$$R_{eq} = 2R$$

For maximum power to be delivered to network

$$R_{eq} = 2R = r$$

$$\Rightarrow \quad 2R = 6$$

$$\Rightarrow \quad R = 3\,\Omega$$

7. 20 W bulb has maximum resistance. So, it will get fused first.

$$R_{100\,W} = \frac{(100)^2}{100} = 100\,\Omega$$

$$R_{50\,W} = \frac{(100)^2}{50} = 200\,\Omega$$

$$R_{20\,W} = \frac{(100)^2}{20} = 500\,\Omega$$

When potential difference across 20 W bulb reaches 100 V, current through it is $\frac{20}{100} = \frac{1}{5}$ A.

Voltage of the cell $= i(R_{100\,W} + R_{50W} + R_{20W})$

$$= \frac{1}{5}(100 + 200 + 500)$$
$$= 160 \text{ V}$$

Voltage after Nth step $= 100 + 20N = 160$ V

$\Rightarrow \quad N = 3$

8. Resistance of each bulb $= \frac{(200)^2}{100} = 400\,\Omega$

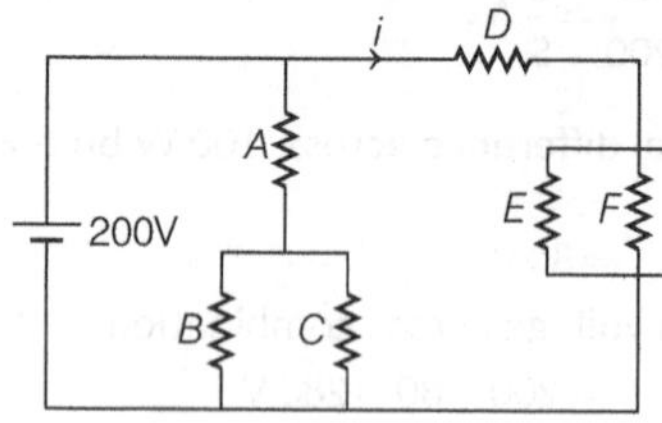

Bulb D will be brightest.

Current through bulb $D = \frac{200}{\frac{4}{3}(400)} = \frac{3}{8}$ A

Power dissipated in bulb $D = i^2R$

$$= \left(\frac{3}{8}\right)^2 400 = 56.25 \text{ W}$$

9. Energy consumed by 40 W lamps

$= 3 \times 40 \times 2 \times 29$ W-h $= 6960$ W-h

Energy consumed by 60 W lamps

$= 8 \times 60 \times 2 \times 29$ W-h $= 27840$ W-h

Energy consumed by radio

$= 40 \times 4 \times 29$ W-h $= 4640$ W-h

Energy consumed by TV $= 160 \times 1 \times 29 = 4640$ W-h

Additional energy consumed on 4 Sundays

$= 4 \times 750 \times 1 + 4 \times 160 \times 3 = 4920$ W-h

Total energy consumed

$= 6960 + 27840 + 4640 + 4640 + 4920$

$= 49000$ W-h

$= 49$ kWh $= 49$ units

Electricity bill $= 49 \times 5 =$ ₹245

10. Reading of ammeter $= 3$ A

Current through $R_1 = 3 \times \frac{R_2}{R_1 + R_2} = 3 \times \frac{30}{60 + 30} = 1$ A

Power dissipated $= i^2R$

Heat produced $= i^2Rt = ms\Delta T$

$$\Rightarrow \quad (1)^2(60)(7 \times 60) = \left(\frac{240}{1000}\right)(4200)\Delta T$$

$$\Rightarrow \quad \Delta T = 25°\text{ C}$$

Level 3 JEE Advanced Level

Single Choice Correct Questions

1. $Q = at - bt^2 \quad \Rightarrow \quad i = \frac{dQ}{dt} = a - 2bt$

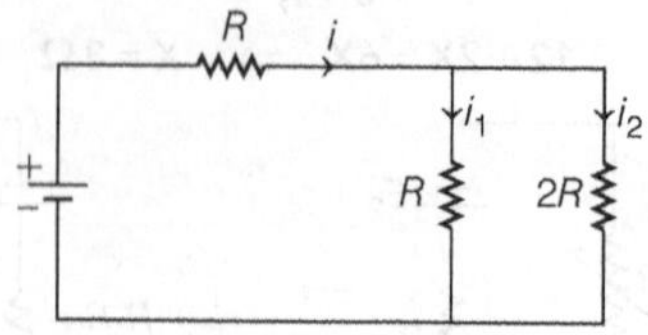

$$i_2 = \frac{i}{3} = \frac{a - 2bt}{3} = 0 \quad \Rightarrow \quad t = \frac{a}{2b}$$

Heat produced in resistor $2R = \int_0^{a/2b} i_2^2(2R)\,dt$

$$= \int_0^{a/2b} 2\left(\frac{a - 2bt}{3}\right)^2 R\,dt$$

$$= \frac{2R}{9}\left[\frac{(a - 2bt)^3}{3(-2b)}\right]_0^{a/2b} = \frac{a^3R}{27b}$$

2. $$i = i_0 \sin\left(\frac{\pi t}{T}\right)$$

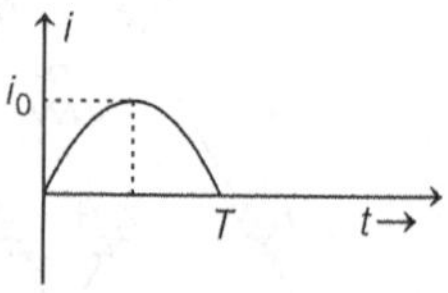

Charge flown $= \int i\,dt = Q$

$$\Rightarrow \quad \int_0^T i_0 \sin\left(\frac{\pi t}{T}\right) dt = Q$$

$$\Rightarrow \quad -\frac{Ti_0}{\pi}\left[\cos\left(\frac{\pi t}{T}\right)\right]_0^T = Q$$

$$\Rightarrow \quad -\frac{i_0 T}{\pi}[\cos \pi - \cos 0] = Q \Rightarrow i_0 = \frac{\pi Q}{2T}$$

Heat generated $= \int i^2R\,dt = \int_0^T i_0^2 R \sin^2\left(\frac{\pi t}{T}\right) dt$

$$= \frac{i_0^2 R}{2}\int_0^T \left[1 - \cos\left(\frac{2\pi t}{T}\right)\right] dt$$

$$= \frac{i_0^2 R}{2}\left[t - \frac{\sin\left(\frac{2\pi t}{T}\right)}{\frac{2\pi}{T}}\right]_0^T = \frac{i_0^2 RT}{2} = \frac{\pi^2 Q^2 R}{8T}$$

3. For $0 < t < t_0$; $i = \left(\frac{3i_0}{t_0}\right)t$

Heat produced $= \int_0^{t_0} i^2R\,dt = \int_0^{t_0}\left(\frac{3i_0 t}{t_0}\right)^2 R\,dt = 3i_0^2 R t_0$

For $t_0 < t < 2t_0$; $i = 3i_0$

Heat produced $= i^2R(2t_0 - t_0) = 9i_0^2 R t_0$

For $2t_0 < t < 3t_0$; $i = i_0$

Heat produced $= i_0^2 R(3t_0 - 2t_0) = i_0^2 R t_0$

Total heat produced $= 3i_0^2 R t_0 + 9i_0^2 R t_0 + i_0^2 R t_0 = 13 i_0^2 R t_0$

4.

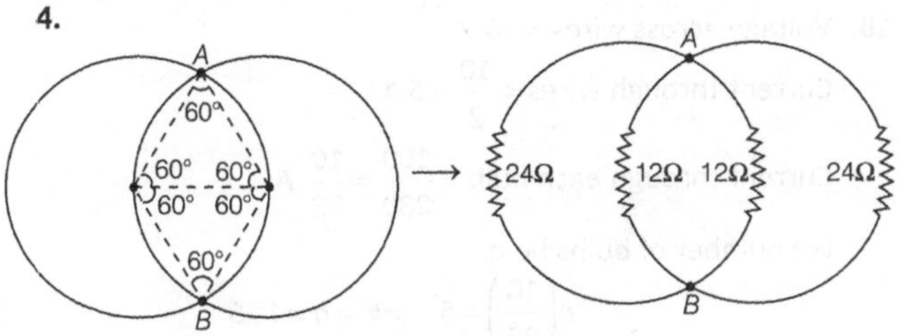

$R_{eq} = 4\,\Omega$

$P = \dfrac{V^2}{R_{eq}} = \dfrac{(20)^2}{4} = 100\text{ W}$

5. $P = i^2R$

$\Rightarrow \quad 6 = i^2(6) \Rightarrow i = 1\text{ A}$

$i = \dfrac{12}{6 + \dfrac{8R}{8+R}} = 1$

$\Rightarrow \quad 6 + \dfrac{8R}{8+R} = 12 \Rightarrow 4R = 24 + 3R$

$\Rightarrow \quad R = 24\,\Omega$

6. Let current in the circuit be I.

Potential difference across metal oxide + Potential difference across $R = 6$

$\Rightarrow \quad a\sqrt{I} + IR = 6$

$\Rightarrow \quad \sqrt{I} + IR = 6$

Power dissipated in metal oxide = Power dissipated in R

$\Rightarrow \quad VI = I^2R$

$\Rightarrow \quad (\sqrt{I})I = I^2R$

$\Rightarrow \quad I = \dfrac{1}{R^2}$

$\dfrac{1}{R} + \left(\dfrac{1}{R^2}\right)R = 6$

$\Rightarrow \quad \dfrac{2}{R} = 6 \Rightarrow R = \dfrac{1}{3}\,\Omega$

7. $R_{heater} = \dfrac{V^2}{P} = \dfrac{(100)^2}{1000} = 10\,\Omega$

$P = i^2R$

$\Rightarrow \quad 62.5 = i^2(10) \Rightarrow i = 2.5\text{ A}$

So, current through heater is 2.5A.

Current through battery $= \dfrac{100}{10 + \dfrac{10R}{10+R}}$

Current through heater $= \left(\dfrac{100}{10 + \dfrac{10R}{10+R}}\right)\left(\dfrac{R}{10+R}\right) = 2.5$

$\Rightarrow \quad \dfrac{100R}{100 + 20R} = 2.5$

$\Rightarrow \quad 100R = 250 + 50R \Rightarrow R = 5\,\Omega$

8. Let heat required to boil the given quantity of water be Q.

$Q = Pt$

$\Rightarrow \quad Q = \left(\dfrac{V^2}{R}\right)t$

$\Rightarrow \quad R = \left(\dfrac{V^2}{Q}\right)t \Rightarrow R \propto t$

$\Rightarrow \quad \dfrac{R_1}{R_2} = \dfrac{t_1}{t_2} \Rightarrow \dfrac{R}{0.9R} = \dfrac{16}{t} \Rightarrow t = 14.4\text{ min}$

9. $P = i^2R_{eq}$

$\Rightarrow \quad 225 = (5)^2(R_1 + R_2)$

$\Rightarrow \quad R_1 + R_2 = 9 \quad \text{...(i)}$

$P = i^2R_{eq}$

$\Rightarrow \quad 50 = (5)^2\left(\dfrac{R_1R_2}{R_1 + R_2}\right)$

$\Rightarrow \quad 50 = 25\left(\dfrac{R_1R_2}{9}\right)$

$\Rightarrow \quad R_1R_2 = 18 \quad \text{....(ii)}$

Solving Eqs. (i) and (ii), we get

$R_1 = 6\,\Omega$ and $R_2 = 3\,\Omega$

$\dfrac{R_1}{R_2} = \dfrac{6}{3} = 2$

10.

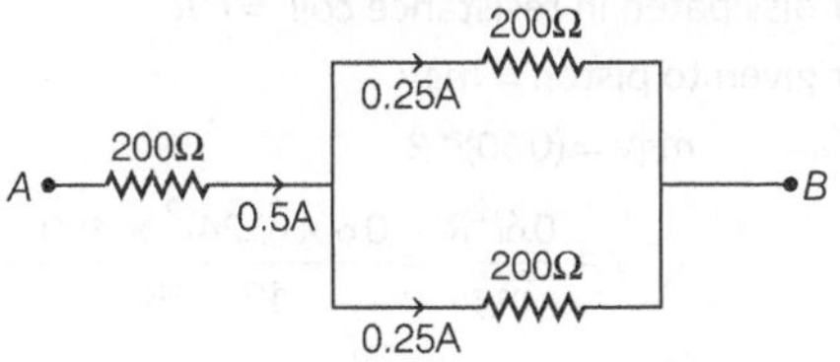

$P = i^2R \Rightarrow P_{max} = i_{max}^2R$

$\Rightarrow \quad 50 = i_{max}^2(200)$

$\Rightarrow \quad i_{max} = 0.5\text{ A}$

$V_{AB} = 200 \times 0.5 + 200 \times 0.25 = 150\text{ V}$

11. $R_{eq} = \dfrac{10 \times 5}{10 + 5} + \dfrac{5 \times 10}{5 + 10} = \dfrac{20}{3}\,\Omega$

Heat produced $= i^2R_{eq}t = mL_f$

$\Rightarrow \quad (10)^2\left(\dfrac{20}{3}\right)(10 \times 60) = m \times 80 \times 4200$

$\Rightarrow \quad m = 1.190\text{ kg}$

12.

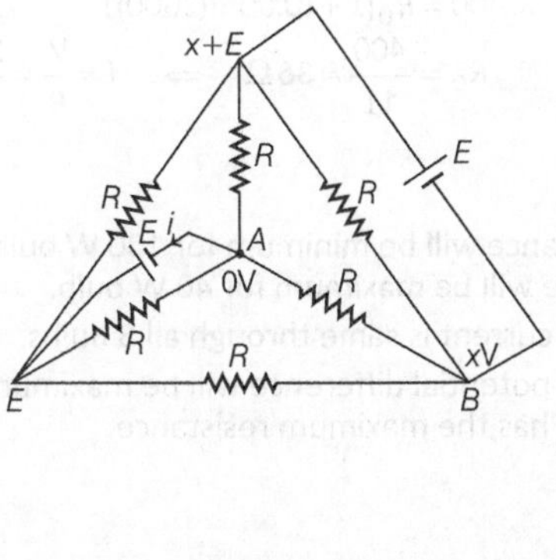

Let $V_A = 0$ and $V_B = x$

$$i = \frac{E-0}{R} + \frac{x-0}{R} + \frac{(x+E)-0}{R}$$
$$= \frac{E-x}{R} + \frac{E-0}{R} + \frac{E-(x+E)}{R}$$

$\Rightarrow$ $E + x + x + E = E - x + E + E - x - E$

$\Rightarrow$ $x = 0$

So, current through 2 resistors is zero and current through each of the remaining four resistors is $\frac{E}{R}$.

$$\text{Power} = \left(\frac{E}{R}\right)^2 R \times 4 = \frac{4E^2}{R}$$

13. $\rho = \rho_0(1+\alpha\Delta T) = \pi^2 \times 10^{-8}(1 + 7.8 \times 10^{-3} \times 600)$

$= \pi^2 \times 5.68 \times 10^{-8}\ \Omega\text{-m}$

In steady state,

$i^2R = Ae\sigma(T^4 - T_0^4)$

$\Rightarrow$ $i^2\left(\frac{\pi^2 \times 5.68 \times 10^{-8} \times \rho}{\pi r^2}\right)$

$= (2\pi rl)(1)(5.6 \times 10^{-8})[(900)^4 - (300)^4]$

$\Rightarrow$ $i^2 = 2r^3[(900)^4 - (300)^4]$

$\Rightarrow$ $i^2 = 2 \times (10^{-3})^3 \times 10^8 \times (6480)$

$\Rightarrow$ $i = \sqrt{1296} = 36\text{ A}$

14. Power dissipated in resistance coil $= i^2R$

Power given to piston $= mgv$

$mgv = (0.60)i^2R$

$\Rightarrow$ $v = \frac{0.6i^2R}{mg} = \frac{0.6 \times (0.24)^2 \times 490}{12 \times 9.8} = 0.144\text{ m/s}$

15. Resistance of each bulb, $R = \frac{V^2}{P}$

In series combination, potential difference across each bulb will be $\frac{V}{n}$.

$$\text{Power consumed by each bulb} = \frac{(V/n)^2}{R} = \frac{\left(\frac{V}{n}\right)^2}{\frac{V^2}{P}} = \frac{P}{n^2}$$

16. $R = \frac{V^2}{P} = \frac{(200)^2}{100} = 400\,\Omega$

$R = R_0(1+\alpha\Delta T)$

$\Rightarrow$ $400 = R_0[1 + (0.005)(2000)]$

$\Rightarrow$ $R_0 = \frac{400}{11} \approx 36\,\Omega$ $\Rightarrow$ $i = \frac{V}{R} = \frac{200}{36} = 5.5\text{ A}$

17. $R = \frac{V^2}{P}$

So, resistance will be minimum for 100 W bulb and resistance will be maximum for 40 W bulb.

In series, current is same through all 3 bulbs.

$V = iR$, so potential difference will be maximum across 40 W bulb as it has the maximum resistance.

18. Voltage across wires = 10 V

Current through wires $= \frac{10}{2} = 5\text{ A}$

Current through each bulb $= \frac{100}{230} = \frac{10}{23}\text{ A}$

Let number of bulbs be n.

$n\left(\frac{10}{23}\right) = 5$ $\Rightarrow$ $n = 11.5$

So, maximum number of bulbs will be 11.

19. Resistance of bulb $= \frac{V^2}{P} = \frac{(1.5)^2}{4.5} = 0.5\,\Omega$

Current through bulb $= \frac{4.5}{1.5} = 3\text{ A}$

Current through battery $= \frac{E}{\frac{8}{3} + \frac{(0.5)(1)}{1+0.5}} = \frac{E}{3}$

Current through bulb $= \frac{E}{3} \times \frac{1}{(1+0.5)} = 3$ $\Rightarrow$ $E = 13.5\text{ V}$

20. If resistance of rheostat is increased, resistance of circuit increases and current through battery decreases. So, brightness of lamp P decreases.

Potential difference across lamp P + Potential difference across lamp Q = Emf of battery

Due to decrement in current through lamp P, potential difference across lamp P decreases. Hence, potential difference across lamp Q increases and it gets brighter.

21. When the switch is closed, resistance of circuit decreases. So, current through battery increases. Hence, bulb 1 will get brighter.

Potential difference across bulb 1 increases and hence, potential difference across bulb 2 and bulb 3 decreases. So, bulb 2 and bulb 3 will get less brighter.

22. Resistance of 60 W bulb $= \frac{(120)^2}{60} = 240\,\Omega$

Current $= \frac{120}{(240+6)} = \frac{120}{246}\text{ A}$

Voltage across bulb $= \frac{120}{246} \times 240 = 117.1\text{ V}$

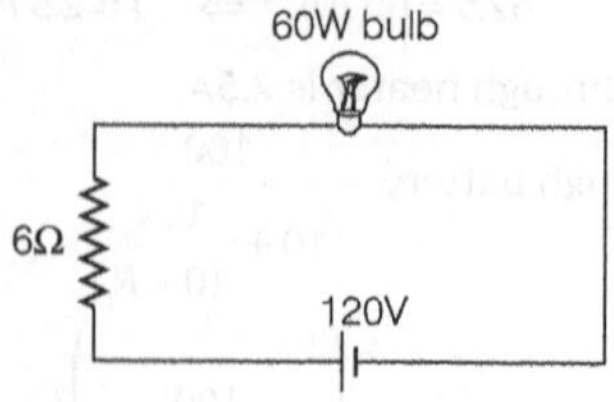

Resistance of heater $= \frac{(120)^2}{240} = 60\,\Omega$

Resistance of parallel combination $= \frac{60 \times 240}{60 + 240} = 48\,\Omega$

$R_{eq} = 48 + 6 = 54\,\Omega$

Voltage across bulb $= \frac{120}{54} \times 48 = 106.7$ V

Change in voltage $= 117.1 - 106.7 = 10.4$ V

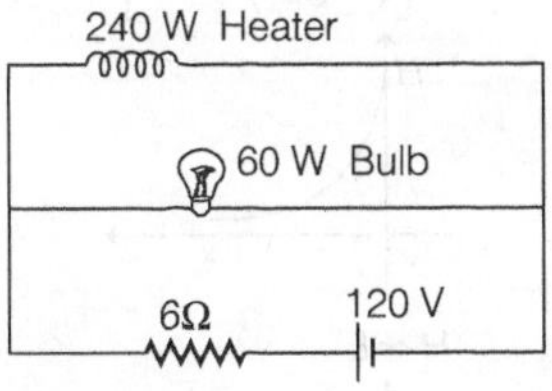

23. Let resistance of bulb be R.

When the switch is open,

$$R_{eq} = \frac{(90+R)(180)}{(90+R)+180} + 90$$

$$= 270\left(\frac{R+150}{R+270}\right)$$

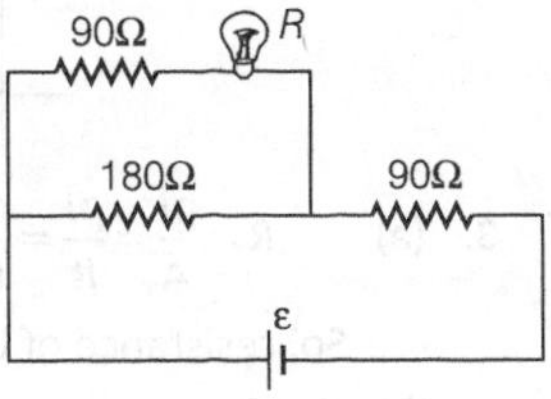

i_1 = Current through bulb

$$= \frac{\varepsilon}{R_{eq}} \times \frac{180}{180+(90+R)}$$

$$= \frac{\varepsilon}{270\left(\frac{R+150}{R+270}\right)} \times \frac{180}{(270+R)} = \frac{2\varepsilon}{3(R+150)}$$

When the switch is closed,

i_2 = Current through bulb

$$= \frac{\varepsilon}{\left(180 + \frac{90R}{90+R}\right)} \times \frac{90}{90+R}$$

$$= \frac{\varepsilon}{3(R+60)}$$

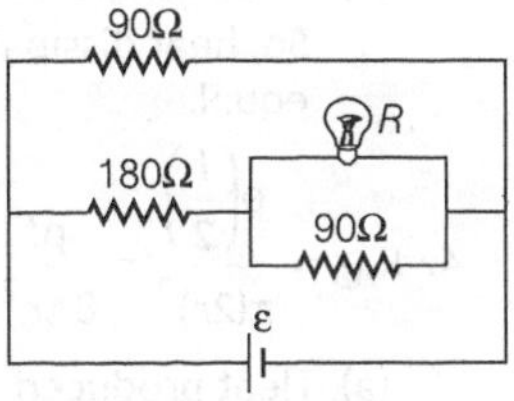

As, the bulb glows equally bright whether the switch is closed or open,

$$i_1 = i_2$$

$$\frac{2\varepsilon}{3(R+150)} = \frac{\varepsilon}{3(R+60)}$$

$$\Rightarrow \quad 2R + 120 = R + 150 \quad \Rightarrow \quad R = 30\,\Omega$$

24.

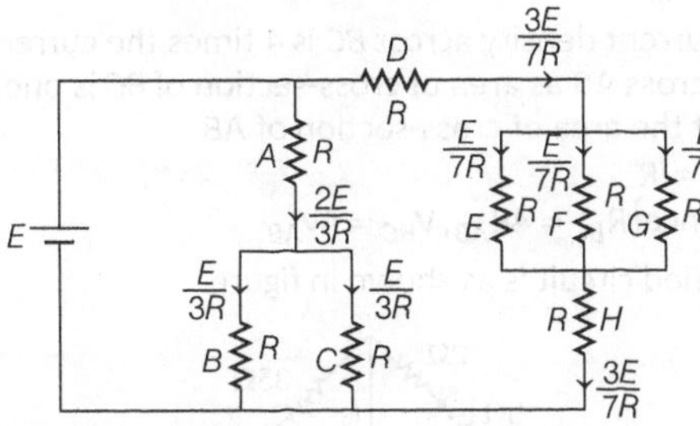

Let resistance of each bulb be R.

Currents through bulbs are in the following order

$$i_A > i_D = i_H > i_B = i_C > i_E = i_F = i_G$$

$$P = i^2 R$$

So, $P_A > P_D = P_H > P_B = P_C > P_E = P_F = P_G$

25. $\frac{Q}{t} = \left(\frac{E}{R_1+r}\right)^2 R_1$ ...(i)

$\frac{Q}{t} = \left(\frac{E}{R_2+r}\right)^2 R_2$ ...(ii)

From Eqs. (i) and (ii), we get

$$\left(\frac{E}{R_1+r}\right)^2 R_1 = \left(\frac{E}{R_2+R}\right)^2 R_2$$

$$\Rightarrow \quad (R_1+r)^2 R_2 = (R_2+r)^2 R_1$$

$$\Rightarrow R_1^2 R_2 + r^2 R_2 + 2R_1R_2 r = R_2^2 R_1 + r^2 R_1 + 2R_1R_2 r$$

$$\Rightarrow \quad R_1R_2(R_1 - R_2) = r^2(R_1 - R_2) \Rightarrow r = \sqrt{R_1R_2}$$

26. $i = \frac{E_{eq}}{R + r_{eq}}$

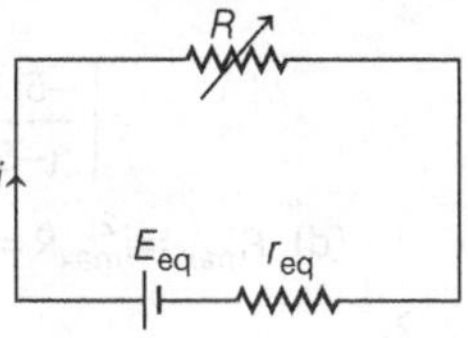

For maximum power, $R = r_{eq}$

$$\Rightarrow \quad i = \frac{E_{eq}}{r_{eq} + r_{eq}} = \frac{E_{eq}}{2r_{eq}}$$

$$P = i^2 R = \left(\frac{E_{eq}}{2r_{eq}}\right)^2 r_{eq} = \frac{E_{eq}^2}{4r_{eq}}$$

If the batteries are connected in series,

$$E_{eq} = 2E \text{ and } r_{eq} = 2r$$

$$\Rightarrow \quad P = \frac{(2E)^2}{4(2r)} = \frac{E^2}{2r}$$

If the batteries are connected in parallel,

$$E_{eq} = E \text{ and } r_{eq} = \frac{r}{2}$$

$$\Rightarrow \quad P = \frac{E^2}{4\left(\frac{r}{2}\right)} = \frac{E^2}{2r}$$

So, $\quad P = \frac{E^2}{2r} = \frac{(2)^2}{2(1)} = 2$ W

27.

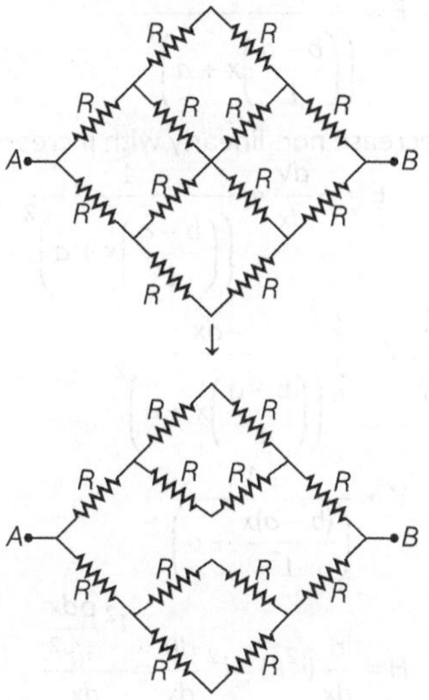

$$R_{eq} = \frac{3R}{2}$$

To deliver maximum power to network,

$$\frac{3R}{2} = r \Rightarrow \frac{3R}{2} = 1 \Rightarrow R = \frac{2}{3}\Omega$$

Multiple Choice(s) Correct Questions

1. (a) $q = \int i\,dt$ = Area under i-t curve $= \frac{1}{2} \times 2 \times 10 = 10$ C

(b) $i_{av} = \frac{\Delta q}{\Delta t} = \frac{10}{2} = 5$ A

(c) $i = -5t + 10$

$$H = \int i^2 R\,dt = \int_0^2 (-5t+10)^2 (1)\,dt$$

$$= \left[\frac{-5t+10}{(-5)(3)}\right]_0^2 = \frac{1}{15}[10]^3 = \frac{200}{3}\text{ J}$$

(d) $P_{max} = i_{max}^2 R = (10)^2(1) = 100$ W

2.

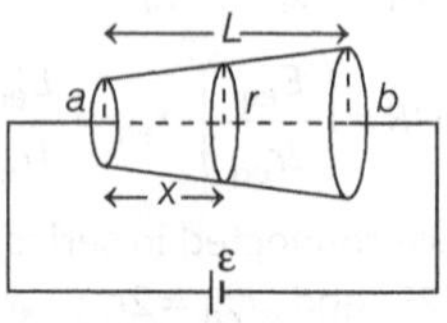

R = Resistance of cone $= \frac{\rho L}{\pi ab}$

Current through cone $= \frac{\varepsilon}{R} = \frac{\varepsilon \pi ab}{\rho L}$ = constant

$$r = \left(\frac{b-a}{L}\right)x + a$$

$$J = \frac{i}{\pi r^2} = \frac{i}{\pi\left(\left(\frac{b-a}{L}\right)x + a\right)^2}$$

$$J = \sigma E \Rightarrow E \propto J$$

$$\Rightarrow \quad E \propto \frac{1}{\left(\left(\frac{b-a}{L}\right)x + a\right)^2}$$

So, E will decrease non-linearly with increase in x.

$$E = -\frac{dV}{dx} \propto \frac{1}{\left(\left(\frac{b-a}{L}\right)x + a\right)^2}$$

$$\int_0^V dV \propto \int_0^x \frac{-dx}{\left(\left(\frac{b-a}{L}\right)x + a\right)^2}$$

$$\Rightarrow \quad V \propto \frac{-1}{\left(\frac{(b-a)x}{L} + a\right)}$$

$$H = \frac{d}{dx}(i^2 R) = i^2 \frac{dR}{dx} = \frac{i^2 \frac{\rho\,dx}{\pi r^2}}{dx}$$

$$H = \frac{\rho i^2}{\pi} \frac{1}{\left[\left(\frac{b-a}{L}\right)x + a\right]^2}$$

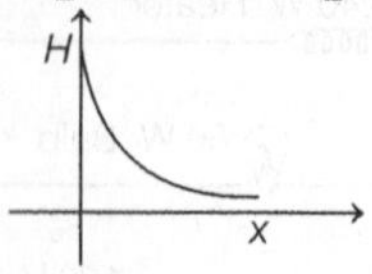

$H \propto E$

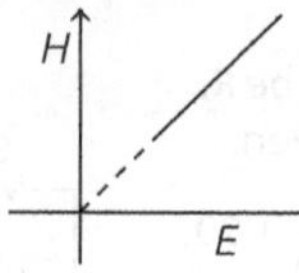

3. (a) $R = \frac{\rho l}{A} = \frac{\rho l}{lt} = \frac{\rho}{t}$

So, resistance of both the plates are equal.

(b) $V = iR$

Since, i and R are same, potential drop across both the plates are equal.

(c) Current in both the plates are equal as they are in series.

(d) Heat dissipated per unit time $= i^2 R$

So, heat dissipated in both the plates per unit time are equal.

4. $R_{AB} = \frac{\rho\left(\frac{l}{2}\right)}{\pi(2r)^2} = \frac{\rho l}{8\pi r^2}, \quad R_{BC} = \frac{\rho\left(\frac{l}{2}\right)}{\pi r^2} = \frac{\rho l}{2\pi r^2}$

(a) Heat produced $= i^2 Rt$

Heat produced in BC is 4 times the heat produced in AB as resistance of BC is 4 times the resistance of AB.

(b) $E \propto J \Rightarrow E \propto \frac{I}{A} \Rightarrow E \propto \frac{1}{A}$

Electric field will be different as cross-section area is different.

(c) $J = \frac{I}{A}$

Current density across BC is 4 times the current density across AB as area of cross-section of BC is one-fourth of the area of cross-section of AB.

(d) $V = iR$

Since, $R_{BC} = 4R_{AB}$, $V_{BC} = 4V_{AB}$

5. Simplified circuit is as shown in figure

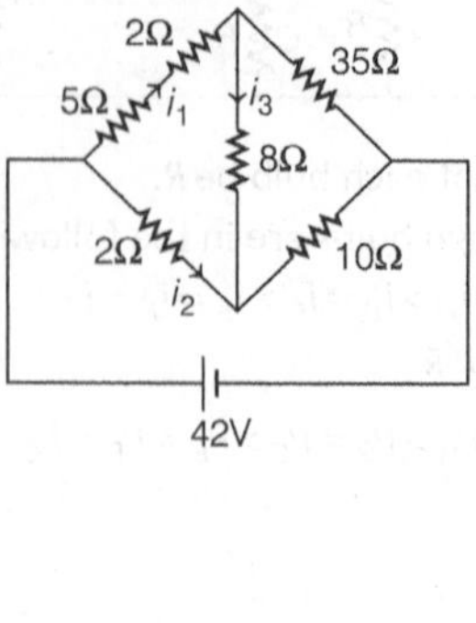

This is a balanced Wheatstone bridge.

$$i_1 = \frac{42}{(35+7)} = 1\text{ A}$$

Power dissipated in $5\,\Omega$ resistor $= (1)^2 5 = 5$ W

$$i_3 = 0$$

Power dissipated in $8\,\Omega$ resistor $= 0$

6. Power absorbed by $AB = i^2R + Ei$

$$\Rightarrow \quad 50 = (2)^2(2) + E(2) \Rightarrow E = 21\text{ V}$$

Potential difference across $AB = E + iR = 21 + (2)(2) = 25$ V

Point B is connected to negative terminal of E as it is getting charged.

Rate of conversion from electrical to chemical energy in device $E = Ei$

$$= (21)(2) = 42\text{ W}$$

7. $R_1 = \frac{(200)^2}{P}$ and $R_2 = \frac{(300)^2}{P}$

When they are connected in series across a DC supply of 500 V,

$$V = iR$$

$$\Rightarrow \quad \frac{V_1}{V_2} = \frac{R_1}{R_2} = \frac{\frac{(200)^2}{P}}{\frac{(300)^2}{P}} = \frac{4}{9}$$

$$P = i^2R \Rightarrow \frac{P_1}{P_2} = \frac{R_1}{R_2} = \frac{4}{9}$$

8. Potential difference across bulb C is maximum and is equal to emf of the battery. So, bulb C is brightest.

Bulb D is short-circuited. So, it does not glow.

If bulb C fails, potential differences across all other bulbs remain unchanged. So, brightness of all other bulbs will remain same.

It A fails, B will not glow.

9. Resistance of upper bulb, $R_1 = \frac{(100)^2}{25} = 400\,\Omega$

Resistance of lower bulb, $R_2 = \frac{(200)^2}{100} = 400\,\Omega$

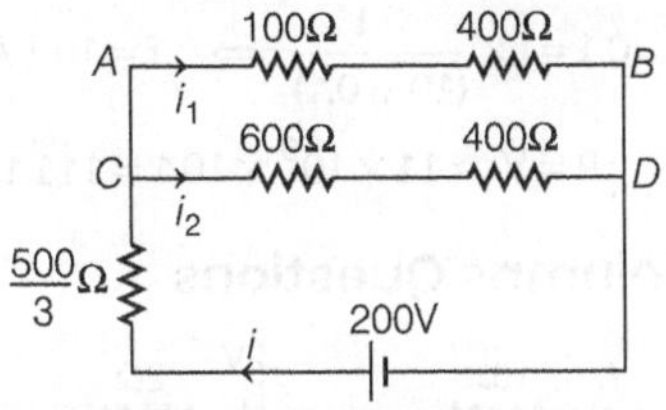

Equivalent resistance across battery $= 500\,\Omega$

$$i = \frac{200}{500} = 0.4\text{ A}$$

Power dissipated in circuit $= \frac{V^2}{R} = \frac{(200)^2}{500} = 80$ J/s

$$\frac{i_1}{i_2} = 2$$

Ratio of heat produced in the bulbs $= i_1^2R_1 : i_2^2R_2 = 4:1$

Ratio of heat produced in branch AB to branch CD

$$= \frac{V^2}{500} : \frac{V^2}{1000} = 2:1$$

10. Let heat required to boil water be Q.

$P_1 =$ Power of coil $1 = \frac{Q}{15}$

$P_2 =$ Power of coil $2 = \frac{Q}{30}$

When coils are connected in parallel,

$$P_{eq} = P_1 + P_2$$

$$\frac{Q}{t} = \frac{Q}{15} + \frac{Q}{30} \Rightarrow t = 10\text{ min}$$

When coils are connected in series,

$$\frac{1}{P_{eq}} = \frac{1}{P_1} + \frac{1}{P_2}$$

$$\Rightarrow \quad \frac{1}{\left(\frac{Q}{t}\right)} = \frac{1}{\left(\frac{Q}{15}\right)} + \frac{1}{\left(\frac{Q}{30}\right)} \Rightarrow t = 45\text{ min}$$

11. It is a balanced Wheatstone bridge. So, points C and D are equipotential and we can remove $2\,\Omega$ and $4\,\Omega$ between C and D.

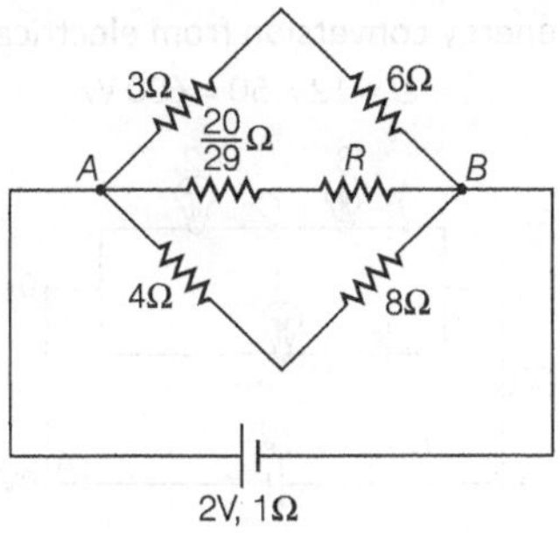

Between A and B,

$$\frac{1}{R_{eq}} = \frac{1}{9} + \frac{1}{12} + \frac{1}{\left(\frac{20}{29} + R\right)}$$

$$R_{eq} = \frac{\frac{36}{7}\left(\frac{20}{29} + R\right)}{\frac{36}{7} + \left(\frac{20}{29} + R\right)}$$

For maximum power in external circuit,

$$R_{eq} = r$$

$$\Rightarrow \quad \frac{\frac{36}{7}\left(\frac{20}{29} + R\right)}{\frac{36}{7} + \left(\frac{20}{29} + R\right)} = 1 \Rightarrow R = \frac{16}{29}\,\Omega$$

$$P_{max} = \left(\frac{E}{2r}\right)^2 r = \frac{E^2}{4r} = \frac{(2)^2}{4 \times 1} = 1\text{ W}$$

Ratio of current through $6\,\Omega$ to that through $4\,\Omega$ is independent of R.

12. For maximum power,

$$R = r_{eq}$$

$$\Rightarrow \quad R = \frac{Kr}{\left(\frac{N}{K}\right)} \quad \Rightarrow \quad K = \sqrt{\frac{NR}{r}}$$

$$P_{max} = i^2R = \left(\frac{E_{eq}}{R + r_{eq}}\right)^2 R = \left(\frac{KE}{R+R}\right)^2 R$$

$$= \frac{K^2E^2}{4R} = \frac{K^2E^2}{4\left(\frac{K^2r}{N}\right)} = \frac{NE^2}{4r}$$

Comprehension Based Questions

1.

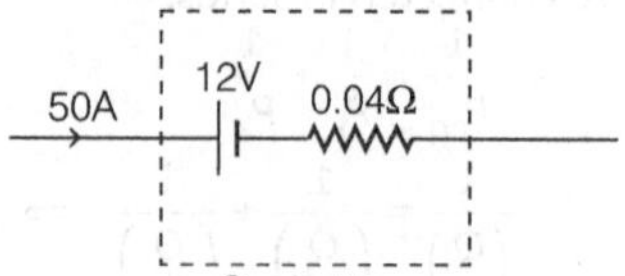

Car battery

Potential difference across the terminals of battery

$$= \varepsilon + ir = 12 + 50(0.04) = 14\text{ V}$$

2. Power dissipated inside battery $= i^2r = (50)^2(0.04) = 100$ W

3. The rate of energy conversion from electrical to chemical

$$= \varepsilon i = 12 \times 50 = 600\text{ W}$$

4.

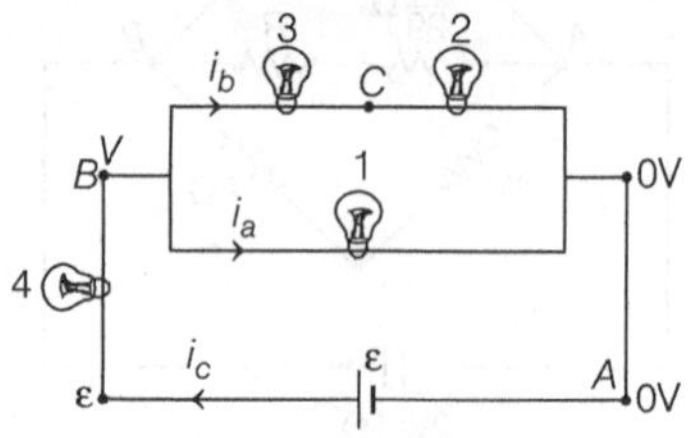

Let $\quad V_A = 0$ and $V_B = V$

$$P_2 = P_3$$

$$\Rightarrow \quad i_b^2R_2 = i_b^2R_3 \quad \Rightarrow \quad R_2 = R_3$$

$$\because \quad R_2 = R_3$$

$$\Rightarrow \quad V_B - V_C = V_C - V_A \quad \Rightarrow \quad V_C = \frac{V}{2}$$

$$\Rightarrow \quad P_1 = P_3$$

$$\Rightarrow \quad \frac{V^2}{36} = \frac{\left(\frac{V}{2}\right)^2}{R_3} \quad \Rightarrow \quad R_3 = 9\,\Omega$$

5. $R_2 = R_3 = 9\,\Omega$ and $R_1 = 36\,\Omega$

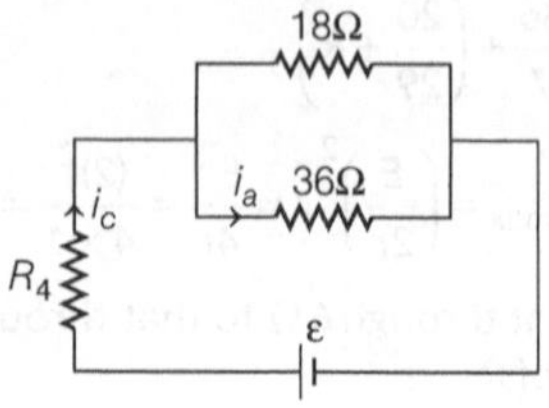

$$i_a = \frac{i_c}{3}$$

$$P_1 = P_4$$

$$\Rightarrow \quad i_a^2(36) = i_c^2R_4$$

$$\Rightarrow \quad \left(\frac{i_c}{3}\right)^2 36 = i_c^2R_4 \quad \Rightarrow \quad R_4 = 4\,\Omega$$

6. $P_4 = i_c^2R_4 \quad \Rightarrow \quad 4 = i_c^2(4)$

$$\Rightarrow \quad i_c = 1\text{ A}$$

$$R_{eq} = 4 + \frac{18 \times 36}{18 + 36} = 16\,\Omega$$

$$\varepsilon = iR_{eq} = 1(16) = 16\text{ V}$$

7. $I^2R = h(2\pi rl)$

$$\Rightarrow \quad I^2\left(\frac{\rho l}{\pi r^2}\right) = h(2\pi rl)$$

$$\Rightarrow \quad I^2 \propto r^3 \quad \Rightarrow \quad I \propto r^{3/2}$$

$$\frac{I_1}{I_2} = \left(\frac{r_1}{r_2}\right)^{3/2} \quad \Rightarrow \quad \frac{I_1}{I_2} = \left(\frac{4}{1}\right)^{3/2} = \frac{8}{1}$$

8. $P = \frac{V^2}{R} \quad \Rightarrow \quad 2 \times 10^3 = \frac{V^2}{20} \quad \Rightarrow \quad V = 200$ V

Voltage of DC source should be less than 200 V.

9. For maximum power, $R = r$

$$\text{Efficiency} = \left(\frac{R}{R+r}\right) \times 100 = \left(\frac{r}{r+r}\right) \times 100 = 50\%$$

10. Resistance of wire between the feet of the bird

$$= \left(\frac{1\,\Omega}{\text{m}}\right)(10\text{ cm}) = 0.1\,\Omega$$

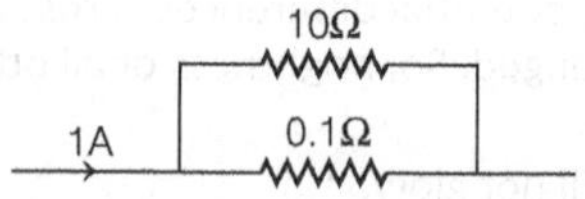

$$\text{Current through bird} = 1 \times \frac{0.1}{(10 + 0.1)} \simeq 0.01\text{ A}$$

11. Current through bird $= 0.1$ A

Let current in the high tension wire be i.

$$0.1 = i \times \frac{0.1}{(10 + 0.1)} \quad \Rightarrow \quad i = 10.1\text{ A}$$

$$P = Vi = 11 \times 10^3 \times 10.1 = 111.1\text{ kW} \simeq 111\text{ kW}$$

Match the Columns Questions

1.

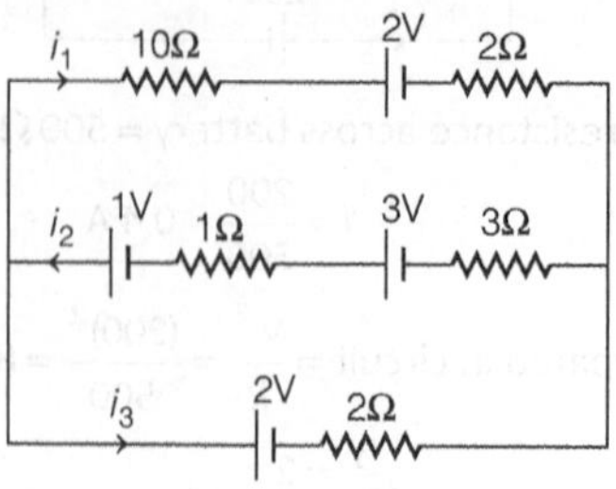

$$i_2 = i_1 + i_3 \quad ...(i)$$

Using KVL,

$$+3+1-3i_2-i_2-2-2i_3=0$$

$$\Rightarrow \quad 4i_2+2i_3=2 \quad ...(ii)$$

$$+3+1-3i_2-i_2-10i_1-2-2i_1=0$$

$$\Rightarrow \quad 12i_1+4i_2=2 \quad ...(iii)$$

Solving Eqs. (i), (ii) and (iii), we get

$$i_1=\frac{1}{20}\text{ A},\ i_2=\frac{7}{20}\text{ A} \quad \text{and} \quad i_3=\frac{6}{20}\text{ A}$$

In each cell, thermal energy will be dissipated due to internal resistance whether its discharging or getting charged. Cell I is getting charged. So, its chemical energy increases.

Cell II and Cell III are discharging. Hence, their chemical energies are decreasing and work done by both the cells is positive. Cell IV is getting charged, hence its chemical energy is increasing.

2. (a) Terminal potential difference across the cell is $V=E-ir$. It will be maximum when $i=0$. For $i=0$, $R=\infty$

(b) Power transferred to R is maximum, if $R=r$. In all other cases, it will be somewhat less.

(c) Power dissipated in the cell is i^2r which will be maximum when i is maximum.

For i to maximum, $R=0$

(d) For faster drift of ions in the electrolyte in the cell, current should be maximum. So, $R=0$.

3. (a) When cells are connected in series,

$$E_{eq}=2E, r_{eq}=2r$$

Power transferred to load will be maximum when

$$R=r_{eq}=2r$$

$$P_{max}=i^2R=\left(\frac{2E}{R+2r}\right)^2 R=\left(\frac{2E}{2r+2r}\right)^2 2r=\frac{E^2}{2r}$$

(b) When cells are connected in parallel,

$$E_{eq}=E,\ r_{eq}=\frac{r}{2}$$

Power transferred to load will be maximum when

$$R=r_{eq}=\frac{r}{2}$$

$$P_{max}=i^2R=\left(\frac{E}{R+\frac{r}{2}}\right)^2 R=\frac{E^2}{2r}$$

(c) Cells are connected in series and $R=r$.

$$E_{eq}=2E \text{ and } r_{eq}=2r$$

$$P=i^2R=\left(\frac{2E}{r+2r}\right)^2 r=\frac{4E^2}{9r}$$

(d) Cells are connected in parallel and $R=r$

$$E_{eq}=E \text{ and } r_{eq}=\frac{r}{2}$$

$$P=i^2R=\left(\frac{E}{r+\frac{r}{2}}\right)^2 r=\frac{4E^2}{9r}$$

4. Resistance of bulb $=\dfrac{V^2}{P}$

Since, rated voltage is same and

$$P_A>P_B>P_C$$

So, $$R_A<R_B<R_C$$

(a) All three bulbs are in series. So, current through them is same.

$$P=i^2R$$

C has maximum resistance. So, C is glowing with maximum brightness.

A has minimum resistance. So, A is having minimum intensity.

(b) Each bulb will deliver its rated power. So, A will be having maximum brightness and C will be glowing with minimum brightness.

(c) Let current through A and B be i_1 and i_2, respectively. Then, current through C is (i_1+i_2).

For C, i^2R is maximum. So, C is glowing with maximum brightness.

Further $\dfrac{V_1^2}{R_A}>\dfrac{V_2^2}{R_B}$. So, power delivered to B is minimum.

(d) Bulb A is short-circuited. So, A does not glow. Bulbs B and C are operating at them rated powers. So, B will be brightest.

Numerical Value Questions

1. Charge flown = Area under i-t graph

$$\Rightarrow \quad Q=i_0T+\frac{i_0}{2}T+\frac{i_0}{4}T+\ldots\infty$$

$$\Rightarrow \quad Q=i_0T\left(1+\frac{1}{2}+\frac{1}{4}+\ldots\infty\right)$$

$$\Rightarrow \quad Q=i_0T\left(\frac{1}{1-\frac{1}{2}}\right) \Rightarrow i_0=\frac{Q}{2T}$$

$$\text{Heat dissipated}=i_0^2RT+\left(\frac{i_0}{2}\right)^2RT+\left(\frac{i_0}{4}\right)^2RT+\ldots\infty$$

$$=i_0^2RT\left[1+\frac{1}{4}+\frac{1}{16}+\ldots\infty\right]$$

$$=i_0^2RT\frac{1}{\left(1-\frac{1}{4}\right)}=\frac{4i_0^2RT}{3}$$

$$=\frac{4}{3}\left(\frac{Q}{2T}\right)^2RT=\frac{Q^2R}{3T}$$

So, $n=3$

2. For maximum power,

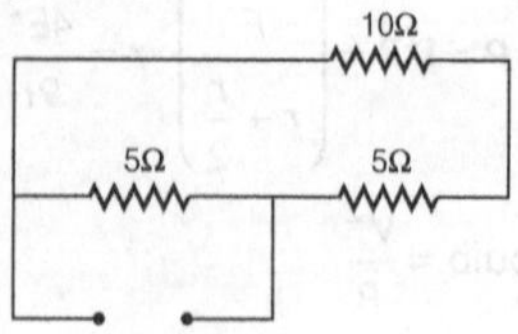

$$x = \frac{5(15)}{5+15} = \frac{15}{4}\Omega$$

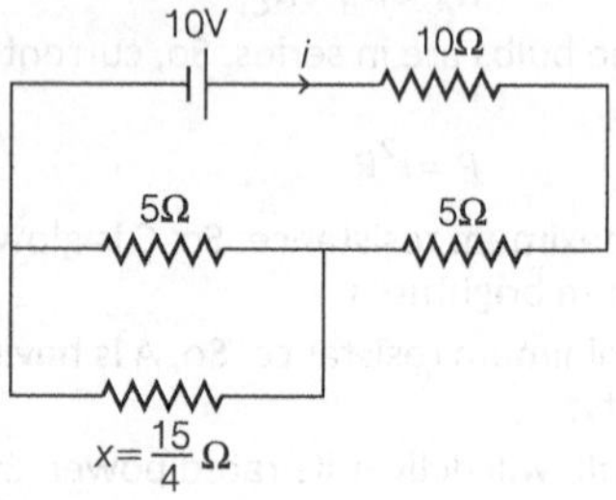

i = current through battery

$$= \frac{10}{\left(15 + \frac{5 \times \frac{15}{4}}{5 + \frac{15}{4}}\right)} = \frac{7}{12}\text{A}$$

Current through the unknown resistance x

$$= \frac{7}{12} \times \frac{5}{5 + \frac{15}{4}} = \frac{1}{3}\text{A}$$

Power dissipated in $x = \left(\frac{1}{3}\right)^2 \left(\frac{15}{4}\right) = \frac{5}{12}$ W

So, $n = 12$

3.

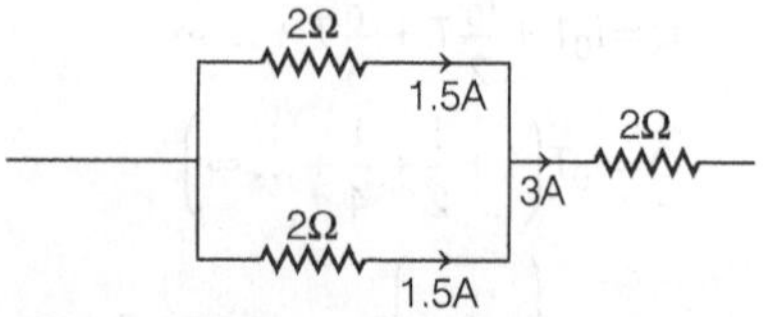

$$P = i^2R$$

$\Rightarrow \quad 18 = i^2(2) \Rightarrow i = 3\text{ A}$

$$P = (3)^2 2 + (1.5)^2 2 + (1.5)^2 2 = 27\text{ W}$$

4. Let there be m number of rows of cells in parallel.

Total number of cells = mn

$\Rightarrow \quad mn = 324$ ...(i)

$$E_{eq} = n\varepsilon \text{ and } r_{eq} = \frac{nr}{m}$$

For maximum power output,

$$R = r_{eq}$$

$\Rightarrow \quad 4 = \frac{nr}{m} \Rightarrow 4 = \frac{n(9)}{m}$

$\Rightarrow \quad m = \frac{9n}{4}$ ...(ii)

Solving Eqs. (i) and (ii), we get

$$\left(\frac{9n}{4}\right)n = 324$$

$\Rightarrow \quad n = 12$

5. $P \times t = ms\Delta T$

$\Rightarrow \quad \frac{V^2}{R_{eq}}t = ms\Delta T \Rightarrow \frac{m_1}{m_2} = \frac{R_{eq_2}}{R_{eq_1}}$

When supply is connected at points 1 and 2,

$$R_{eq_1} = R$$

When supply is connected at points 1 and 3,

$$R_{eq_2} = \frac{5R}{8}$$

$\Rightarrow \quad \frac{(500\text{ g})}{m_2} = \frac{\left(\frac{5R}{8}\right)}{R} \Rightarrow m_2 = 800\text{ g}$

6. Power dissipated in coil $= i^2R$

$$= (0.2)^2(350) = 14\text{ W}$$

Power consumed by gas = Power dissipated in coil

$\Rightarrow \quad nC_p\frac{dT}{dt} = 14$

$\Rightarrow \quad n\left(\frac{7R}{2}\right)\frac{dT}{dt} = 14$

$\Rightarrow \quad nR\frac{dT}{dt} = 4$

Applying work-energy theorem for the piston,

$$W_{gas} + W_{atm} + W_{mg} = \Delta K$$

$\Rightarrow \quad nRdT - p_{atm}Adx - mgdx = 0$

$\Rightarrow \quad nR\frac{dT}{dt} = (p_{atm}A + mg)\frac{dx}{dt}$

$\Rightarrow \quad nR\frac{dT}{dt} = (p_{atm}A + mg)v$

$\Rightarrow \quad v = \frac{nR\frac{dT}{dt}}{p_{atm}A + mg} = \frac{4}{10^5 \times 10 \times 10^{-4} + 10 \times 10}$

$$= 0.02\text{ m/s} = 2\text{ cm/s}$$

7. When switches A, B, C and D are closed, all resistances are in parallel.

$$\frac{1}{R_{eq}} = \frac{1}{40} + \frac{1}{40} + \frac{1}{40} + \frac{1}{40} + \frac{1}{20} + \frac{1}{20}$$

$\Rightarrow \quad R_{eq} = 5\,\Omega$

$$P = \frac{V^2}{R_{eq}} = \frac{(10)^2}{5} = 20\text{ W}$$

8. When the key K is open,

$$i = \frac{\varepsilon}{R + R'}$$

P_1 = Power dissipated in the network $= \left(\frac{\varepsilon}{R + R'}\right)^2 R'$

When the key K is closed, $i = \dfrac{\varepsilon}{R + \dfrac{R'}{2}}$

P_2 = Power dissipated in the network $= \left(\dfrac{\varepsilon}{R + \dfrac{R'}{2}}\right)\left(\dfrac{R'}{2}\right)$

Since, $\quad P_1 = P_2$

$$\Rightarrow \quad (R + R')^2 = 2\left(R + \frac{R'}{2}\right)^2$$

$$\Rightarrow \quad R + R' = \sqrt{2}\left(R + \frac{R'}{2}\right)$$

$$\Rightarrow \quad R = \frac{R'}{\sqrt{2}} = \frac{20\sqrt{2}}{\sqrt{2}} = 20\,\Omega$$

Previous Year's Questions

JEE Main

1. Given,

Resistance of toaster $= 60\ \Omega = R_0$

Supply voltage $= 220$ V

Current reaching at toaster $I_1 = 2.75$ A

Then, final resistance of toaster

$$R_F = \frac{V\ \text{(supply)}}{\text{Current}} = \frac{220}{2.75} = 80\ \Omega$$

Now, resistance dependency on temperature is given by

$$R_t = R_0(1 + \alpha t) \qquad [\because R_t = R_F]$$

$$80 = 60[1 + \alpha(T - 27)]$$

(Room temperature $= 27°$ given)

$$\alpha = 2 \times 10^{-4}/°\text{C (given)}$$

$$80 = 60[1 + 2 \times 10^{-4}(T - 27)]$$

$$\Rightarrow \quad \frac{4}{3} - 1 = 2 \times 10^{-4}(T - 27)$$

$$\Rightarrow \quad \frac{10000}{6} + 27 = T \quad \Rightarrow \quad T = 1694°\text{C}$$

2. Initially

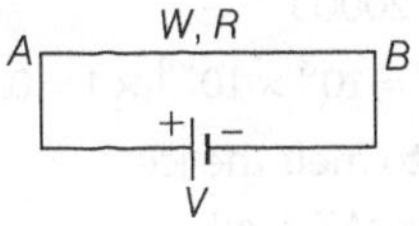

Finally

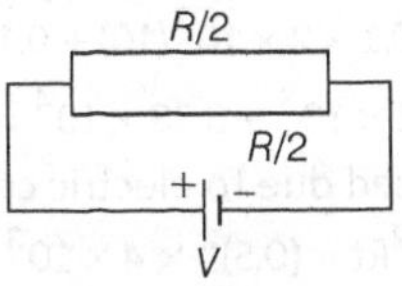

Initially energy dissipation rate = power

$$P_1 = W = \frac{V^2}{R}$$

When wire is cut into two parts, each part, has a resistance $\frac{R}{2}$. These are connected in parallel, so total resistance (R_{eq}) is given by

$$R_{eq} = \frac{R_1 R_2}{R_1 + R_2}$$

$$\Rightarrow \quad R_{eq} = \frac{\frac{R}{2} \times \frac{R}{2}}{\frac{R}{2} + \frac{R}{2}} = \frac{R}{4}$$

So, power dissipated will be

$$P_2 = \frac{V^2}{\frac{R}{4}} = 4\left(\frac{V^2}{R}\right) = 4\text{ W}$$

3. Suppose battery of emf ε is applied across each circuit.

$$R_{eq} = \frac{3R}{2}$$

(A) $P_{A_1} = \dfrac{\varepsilon^2}{R_{eq}} = \dfrac{\varepsilon^2}{\frac{3R}{2}} = \dfrac{2\varepsilon^2}{3R} = 0.67\dfrac{\varepsilon^2}{R}$

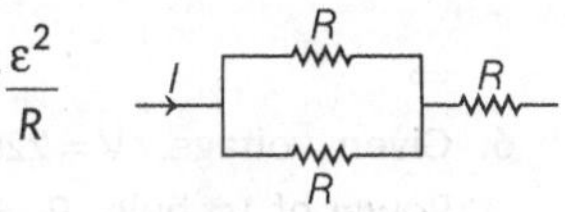

(B) $P_B = \dfrac{\varepsilon^2}{\frac{2R}{3}} = \dfrac{3}{2R}\varepsilon^2 = 1.5\dfrac{\varepsilon^2}{R}$

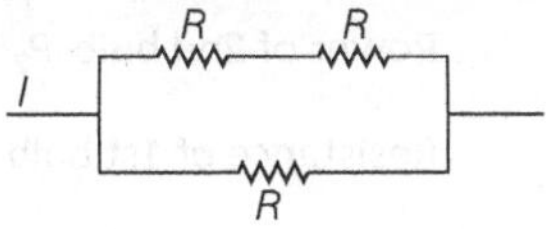

(C) $P_C = \dfrac{\varepsilon^2}{R/3} = \dfrac{3\varepsilon^2}{R}$

$R_{eq} = \dfrac{R}{3}; P_C = \dfrac{\varepsilon^2}{R}$

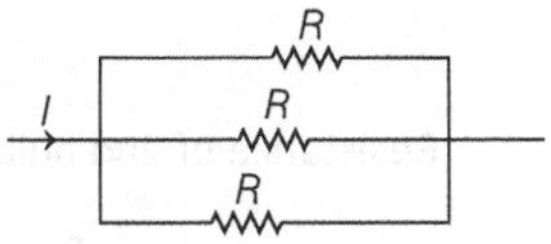

(D) $P_D = \dfrac{\varepsilon^2}{4R}$

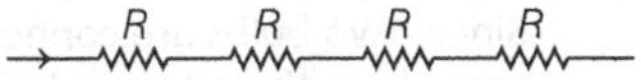

$P_D = 0.33\dfrac{\varepsilon^2}{R}$

From above we find, $\quad P_D < P_A < P_C > P_B$.

4. Given, $\quad H = \dfrac{V^2}{R_{eq}} \cdot t$

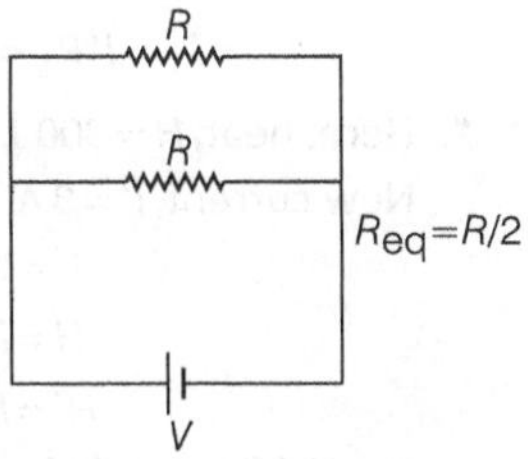

$$H_1 = \frac{V^2}{R/2} t$$

$$H_2 = \frac{V^2}{R_{eq}} \cdot t$$

$$\frac{1}{R_{eq}} = \frac{1}{R} + \frac{1}{R}$$

$$H_1 = \frac{2V^2}{R} \cdot t \qquad \text{...(i)}$$

$$H_2 = \frac{V^2}{2R} \cdot t \qquad \text{... (ii)}$$

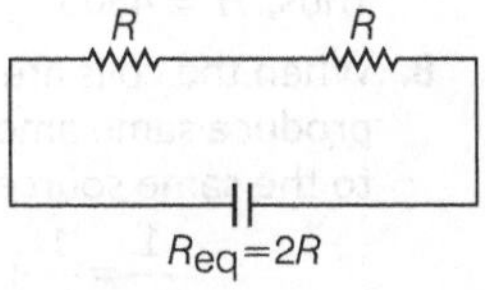

$$\frac{H_1}{H_2} = \frac{\frac{2V^2}{R} \cdot t}{\frac{V^2}{2R} \cdot t}$$

$$\frac{H_1}{H_2} = \frac{4}{1}$$

5. According to first condition, $P_1 = \frac{V_b^2}{R}$

According to second condition, when wire is cut into two halves, then

$$P_2 = \frac{V_0^2}{\frac{R}{2}} + \frac{V_0^2}{\frac{R}{2}}$$

$$\Rightarrow \quad P_2 = \frac{4V_0^2}{R} = 4P_1$$

$$\Rightarrow \quad \frac{P_2}{P_1} = \frac{4}{1} = \frac{\sqrt{x}}{1} \quad \text{(given)}$$

$$\therefore \quad \sqrt{x} = 4$$

$$\Rightarrow \quad x = 16$$

6. Given, voltage, $V = 220$ V

Power of 1st bulb, $P_1 = 100$ W

Power of 2nd bulb, $P_2 = 60$ W

Resistance of 1st bulb, $R_1 = \frac{V^2}{P_1} \quad \left[\because P = \frac{V^2}{R}\right]$

$$= \frac{(220)^2}{100} = 484\ \Omega$$

Resistance of 2nd bulb,

$$R_2 = \frac{V^2}{P_2} = \frac{(220)^2}{60} = 806.67\ \Omega$$

Since, two bulbs are connected in series, so current will be same in both and given by

$$I = \frac{V}{R_{\text{net}}} = \frac{V}{R_1 + R_2} = \frac{220}{(484 + 806.67)} = 0.17\text{ A}$$

So, power consumed by 100 W bulb is

$$P_1 = I^2 R_1 = (0.17)^2 \times 484 \simeq 14\text{ W}$$

7. Here, heat, $H = 300$ J, time, $t = 15$ s, current, $i = 2$ A

New current, $i' = 3$ A, New time,

$$t' = 10\text{ s}$$

$$H = i^2 Rt \quad \text{...(i)}$$

$$H' = i'^2 Rt' \quad \text{...(ii)}$$

On dividing Eq. (i) by (ii), we get

$$\frac{300}{H'} = \left(\frac{2}{3}\right)^2 \times \frac{15}{10};$$

$$\frac{300}{H'} = \frac{4}{9} \times \frac{15}{10}; H' = \frac{300 \times 9 \times 10}{4 \times 15}$$

Thus, $H' = 450$ J

8. When the coils are connected in parallel, the time taken to produce same amount of heat when connected Sparately to the same source, is

$$\frac{1}{t_p} = \frac{1}{t_1} + \frac{1}{t_2} \text{ or } t_p = \frac{t_1 t_2}{t_1 + t_2} = \frac{20 \times 60}{20 + 60}$$

$$\therefore \quad t_p = 15\text{ min}$$

9. Given, power rating of bulb, $P_B = 500$ W

Voltage across bulb, $V_B = 100$V

Supply voltage, $V_S = 200$ V

If a resistance R is attached in series with the bulb, then the voltage across resistance will be 100 V.

Now, current flowing in circuit when bulb delivers power of 500 W is given as

$$P_B = V_B I \Rightarrow 500 = 100 \times I \Rightarrow I = 5\text{A}$$

Same amount of current will flow from the resistance as it is connected in series.

Using Ohm's law,

$$V = IR \Rightarrow 100 = 5 \times R \Rightarrow R = 20\ \Omega$$

Thus, the resistance connected in series is 20 Ω.

10. Given, Heat energy, $H_1 = 500$ J

Initial current, $I_1 = 1.5$ A, final current,

$$I_2 = 3\text{ A}$$

and time, $t = 20$s

According to Joule's law of heating,

$$H = I^2 Rt$$

$$\Rightarrow \quad H_1 = I_1^2 Rt \quad \text{...(i)}$$

$$\text{and} \quad H_2 = I_2^2 Rt \quad \text{...(ii)}$$

[∵ Resistance and time being the same in both cases]

Dividing Eq. (i) by Eq. (ii), we get

$$\Rightarrow \quad \frac{H_1}{H_2} = \frac{I_1^2 Rt}{I_2^2 Rt} \Rightarrow \frac{H_1}{H_2} = \left(\frac{I_1}{I_2}\right)^2$$

$$\Rightarrow \quad \frac{H_1}{H_2} = \left(\frac{1.5}{3}\right)^2 = \left(\frac{15}{30}\right)^2$$

$$\Rightarrow \quad \frac{H_1}{H_2} = \left(\frac{1}{2}\right)^2$$

$$\Rightarrow \quad \frac{H_1}{H_2} = \frac{1}{4} \Rightarrow \frac{500}{H_2} = \frac{1}{4}$$

$$\Rightarrow \quad H_2 = 500 \times 4$$

$$\Rightarrow \quad H_2 = 2000\text{ J}$$

11. Mass of ice $= \rho Al = 10^3 \times 10^{-4} \times 1 = 0.1$ kg

Energy required to melt the ice

$$= ms\Delta T + mL$$

$$= 0.1 \times 2 \times 10^3 (10) + 0.1 \times 3.33 \times 10^5$$

$$= 2 \times 10^3 + 3.33 \times 10^4 = 3.53 \times 10^4\text{ J} \quad \text{...(i)}$$

Also, heat produced due to electric current

$$H = i^2 Rt = (0.5)^2 \times 4 \times 10^3 \times t$$

$$= 10^3 \times t \quad \text{...(ii)}$$

From Eqs. (i) and (ii),

$$3.53 \times 10^4 = 10^3 t$$

$$\therefore \quad t = 35.3\text{ s}$$

12. Rating of bulb = 200 W at 100 V

Supply voltage, $V = 200$ V

Resistance of bulb, $R' = \frac{100 \times 100}{200} = 50\Omega$

Let current be I, when resistance R is connected in series with the bulb.

Using, $p = VI$

$200 = 100 \times I \Rightarrow I = 2\,A$

Now, $V = I(R + R')$

$200 = 2(R + 50) \Rightarrow R = 50\,\Omega$

13. For **case I**,

The potential difference of the uniform wire, $V = 240\,V$

The resistance of the uniform wire, $R_1 = 36\,\Omega$

The power dissipation in the first case,

$$P_1 = \frac{V^2}{R_1} = \frac{(240)^2}{36}$$

For **case II**,

The resistance of each half,

$$R_2 = \frac{R_1}{2} = \frac{36}{2} = 18\,\Omega$$

$$P_2 = \frac{V^2}{R_2} + \frac{V^2}{R_2} = \frac{(240)^2}{18} + \frac{(240)^2}{18} = \frac{(240)^2}{9}$$

Thus, the ratio of the total power dissipation in the first case to the second case

$$\frac{P_1}{P_2} = \frac{(240)^2/36}{(240)^2/9} \Rightarrow \frac{P_1}{P_2} = \frac{1}{4}$$

On comparing with, $\frac{P_1}{P_2} = \frac{1}{x}$

The value of the $x = 4$.

14. Given that, initial current,

$I_1 = 4\,A$

Final current, $I_2 = 2I_1 = 8\,A$

Initial heat dissipated, $H_1 = 192\,J$

Initial time, $t_1 = 1\,s$

Final time, $t_2 = 5\,s$

Let final heat dissipated $= H_2$

By Joule's law of heating, $H \propto I^2RT$

Since, resistance remains same at initial and final condition,

$$\therefore \quad \frac{H_2}{H_1} = \frac{I_2^2Rt_2}{I_1^2Rt_1} = \frac{I_2^2t_2}{I_1^2t_1}$$

On substituting the given values, we get

$$\frac{H_2}{192} = \left(\frac{8}{4}\right)^2 \times \frac{5}{1}$$

$$\Rightarrow \quad H_2 = 3840\,J$$

15. Given, energy dissipated by a resistor,

$$H = 10\,mJ = 10 \times 10^{-3}\,J$$

Time, $t = 1\,s$

Electric current,

$$I = 2\,mA = 2 \times 10^{-3}\,A$$

Resistance, $R = ?$

According to Joule's law of heating,

$$H = I^2Rt$$

$$\Rightarrow \quad R = \frac{H}{I^2T} \quad \text{...(i)}$$

On substituting the given values in Eq. (i), we get

$$R = \frac{10 \times 10^{-3}}{(2 \times 10^{-3})^2 \times 1}$$

$$\Rightarrow \quad R = \frac{10^{-2}}{4 \times 10^{-6}}$$

$$\Rightarrow \quad R = 0.25 \times 10^4$$

$$\Rightarrow \quad R = 2500\,\Omega$$

JEE Advanced

1. When S_1 and S_2 are open

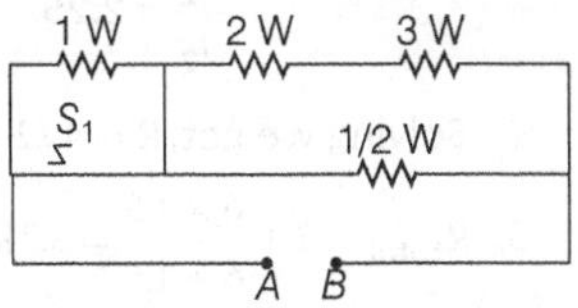

Circuit-1

$$(R_{eq})_1 = 1 + \frac{5 \times \frac{1}{2}}{5 + \frac{1}{2}}$$

$$= 1 + \frac{5}{11} = \frac{16}{11}$$

$$P_1 = \frac{V^2}{R_{eq}} = \frac{(6)^2}{16} \times 11$$

$$= \frac{36 \times 11}{16} = 24.75\,W$$

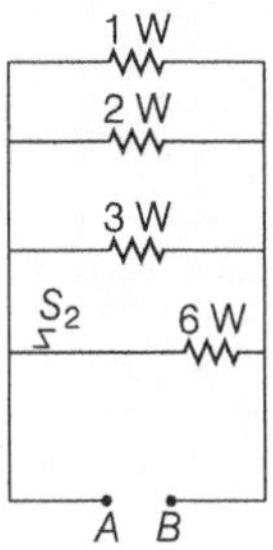

Circuit-2

$$(R_{eq})_2 = \frac{6}{11}\,\Omega$$

$$P_2 = \frac{V^2}{R_{eq}} = \frac{(6)^2}{6} \times 11$$

$$= \frac{36 \times 11}{6} = 66\,W$$

$P_2 > P_1$

Option (a) is correct.

$\Rightarrow$ If 2 A source is used in both the cases,

$$P_1 = i^2(R_{eq})_1 = (2)^2 \times \frac{16}{11} = \frac{64}{11} = 5.818\,W$$

$$P_2 = i^2(R_{eq})_2 = (2)^2 \times \frac{6}{11} = \frac{24}{11} = 2.1818\,W$$

$P_1 > P_2$

Option (b) is correct.

For Q_1,

$$R_{eq} = \frac{5}{11}\,\Omega$$

$$Q_1 = \frac{V^2}{R_{eq}} = \frac{(6)^2}{\frac{5}{11}} = \frac{36 \times 11}{5} = 79.2\,W$$

$P_1 = 24.75\,W$

$Q_1 > P_1$

Option (c) is correct.

For option (d),

$$Q_1 = i^2 R_{eq} = (2)^2 \times \frac{5}{11} = \frac{20}{11} = 1.81\ \text{W}$$

$$Q_2 = i^2 R_{eq} = (2)^2 \times \frac{1}{2} = \frac{4}{2} = 2\ \text{W}$$

$$Q_2 > Q_1$$

Option (d) is incorrect.

2. In series, $i = \dfrac{2E}{2+R} \Rightarrow J_1 = i^2 R = \left(\dfrac{2E}{2+R}\right)^2 \cdot R$

In parallel, $i = \dfrac{E}{0.5+R}$

$$\therefore \quad J_2 = i^2 R = \left(\frac{E}{0.5+R}\right)^2 \cdot R$$

$$\frac{J_1}{J_2} = 2.25$$

Solving we get, $R = 4\ \Omega$

3. $R_{total} = 2 + \dfrac{6 \times 1.5}{6 + 1.5} = 3.2\ \text{k}\Omega$

(a) $I = \dfrac{24\text{V}}{3.2\text{k}\Omega} = 7.5\ \text{mA} = I_{R_1}$

$$I_{R_2} = \left(\frac{R_L}{R_L + R_2}\right) I$$

$$I = \frac{1.5}{7.5} \times 7.5 = 1.5\text{mA}$$

$$I_{R_L} = 6\ \text{mA}$$

(b) $V_{R_L} = (I_{R_L})(R_L) = 9\ \text{V}$

(c) $\dfrac{P_{R_1}}{P_{R_2}} = \dfrac{(I_{R_1}^2)R_1}{(I_{R_2}^2)R_2} = \dfrac{(7.5)^2(2)}{(1.5)^2(6)} = \dfrac{25}{3}$

(d) When R_1 and R_2 are interchanged, then

$$\frac{R_2 R_L}{R_2 + R_L} = \frac{2 \times 1.5}{3.5} = \frac{6}{7}\text{k}\Omega$$

Now potential difference across R_L will be

$$V_L = 24\left[\frac{6/7}{6 + 6/7}\right] = 3\ \text{V}$$

Earlier it was 9 V

Since, $\quad P = \dfrac{V^2}{R} \quad$ or $\quad P \propto V^2$

In new situation potential difference has been decreased three times. Therefore, power dissipated will decrease by a factor of 9.

CHAPTER~09

CAPACITANCE

LEVEL 01 Starter Level

9.1 Capacitance of an Isolated Conductor

1 If $30\mu C$ charge is given to an isolated conductor of capacitance $5\mu F$, then find
(i) potential of the conductor and
(ii) energy stored in the electric field of conductor.

2 What is the capacitance of the earth? (Take, radius of the earth = 6400 km)

3 *n* identical spherical mercury drops each of capacitance *C* coalesce to form a bigger drop. Find the capacitance of the bigger drop.

4 Two conductors *A* and *B* of capacitances $3\mu F$ and $6\mu F$ have charges $6\mu C$ and $3\mu C$, respectively. They are placed at a large distance from each other. When they are joined by a conducting wire, find
(i) the final charges on *A* and *B*,
(ii) the common potential and
(iii) the heat produced during the process of flow of charges.

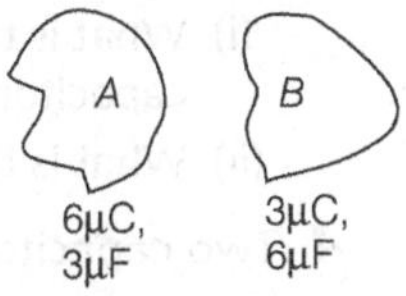

5 Two metallic spheres of radii 40cm and 10cm carry charges of 100 μC and $-20\mu C$, respectively. The two spheres are placed at a large distance from each other. If they are now connected by a metallic wire, then find
(i) the final charges on them
(ii) the charge flown through the metallic wire.

9.2 Capacitor

1 When 2.0×10^{12} electrons are transferred from one conductor to another, a potential difference of 10V appears between the conductors. Calculate the capacitance of the system of the conductors.

2 Charges $+q$ and $-q$ are given to plates of a parallel plate air capacitor having area of each plate *A* and separation between them is *d*, then find
(i) capacitance of the system,
(ii) electric field between the plates,
(iii) potential difference between the plates and
(iv) energy stored between the plates.

3 Two parallel conducting plates of a capacitor of capacitance *C* containing charges *Q* and $-2Q$ are at a distance *d* apart. Find
(i) potential difference between the plates and
(ii) energy stored in the capacitor

4 A parallel plate air capacitor is made using two square plates, each of edge 0.1m, spaced 1cm apart. It is connected to a 100 V battery.
(i) What is the capacitance?
(ii) What is the charge on each plate?
(iii) What is the energy stored in the capacitor?
(iv) What is the electric field between the plates?
(v) If the battery is disconnected and then the plates are pulled apart to a separation of 2 cm, what are the answers to the above parts?

5 The plates *S* and *T* of an uncharged parallel plate capacitor are connected across a battery. The battery is then disconnected and the charged plates are now connected in a system as shown in the figure. The system shown is in equilibrium. All the strings are insulating and massless. Find the magnitude of charge on one of the capacitor plates. (Area of plates = *A*)

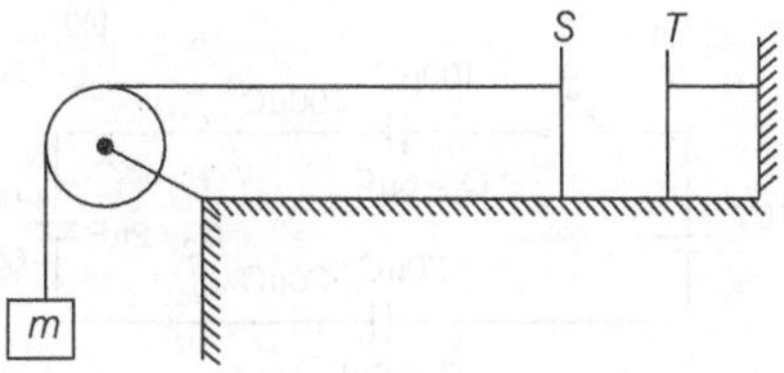

6 The stratosphere acts as a conducting layer for the earth. If the stratosphere extends beyond 50 km from the surface of earth, then calculate the capacitance of the spherical capacitor formed between stratosphere and earth's surface. (Take, radius of earth as 6400 km)

7 A cylindrical capacitor has two co-axial cylinders of length 15 cm and radii 1.5 cm and 1.4 cm. The outer cylinder is earthed and the inner cylinder is given a charge of 3.5 μC. Determine the capacitance of the system and the potential of the inner cylinder.

9.3 Applications of KCL and KVL

1 Initially, all capacitors are uncharged. Find the charges on all the capacitors in the following circuits using Kirchhoff's junction law.

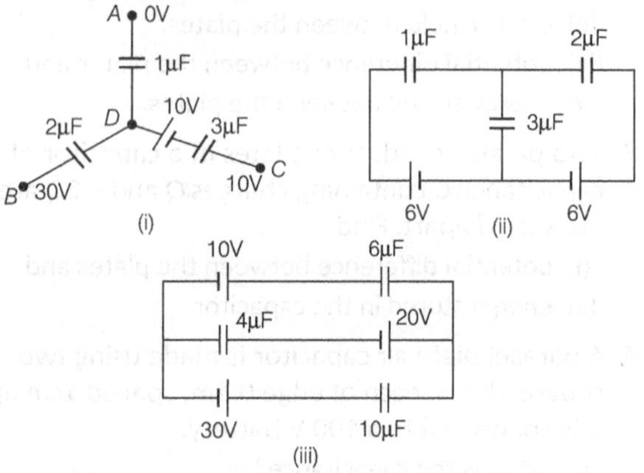

2 After closing the switch, find the charges on all the capacitors in the steady state in the following circuits using Kirchhoff s voltage law.

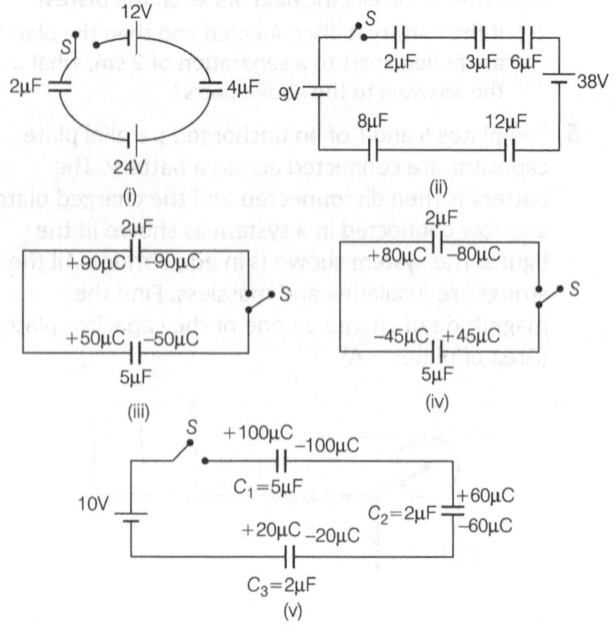

9.4 Redistribution of Charges

1 A capacitor of capacitance C which is initially uncharged is connected across a battery of emf E. Find work done by battery, energy stored in the capacitor and heat dissipated in the circuit during the process of charging.

2 In the following circuits, capacitor is initially charged as shown in figures. The switch is closed at $t = 0$, find heat produced in each circuit after a long time.

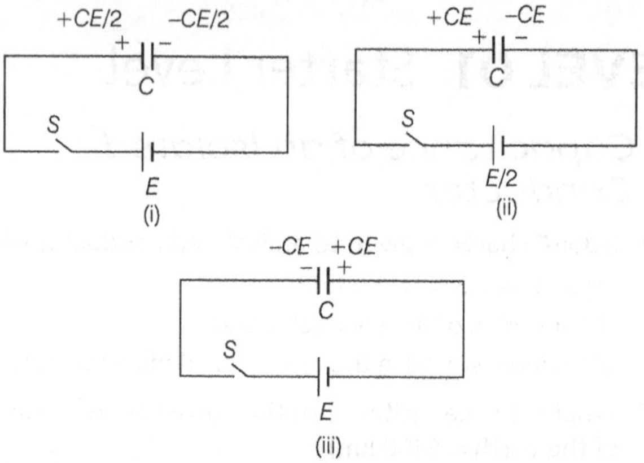

3 A 3 μF capacitor is charged to a potential of 100 V and is connected in parallel with an uncharged 2μF capacitor.

(i) What is the final potential difference across each capacitor?

(ii) What is the heat produced in the circuit?

4 Two capacitors of capacitances 2μF and 3μF are charged to potential difference 20 V and 10 V respectively as shown in figure.

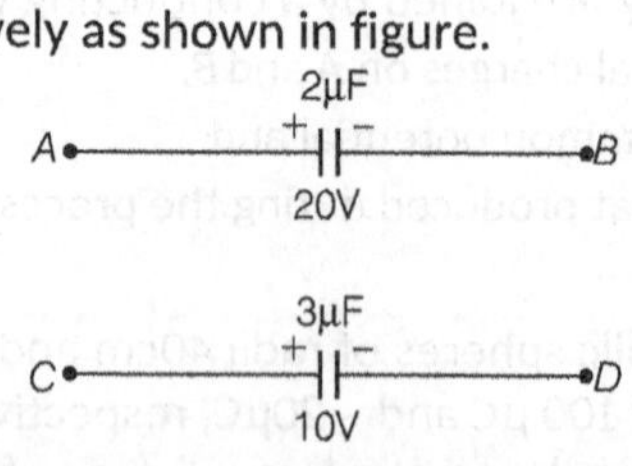

(i) If A is connected with C and B is connected with D, how much heat is produced in the circuit?

(ii) If A is connected with D and B is connected with C, how much heat is produced in the circuit?

5 Find the energy dissipated in the circuit after the switch is flipped from position 1 to 2.

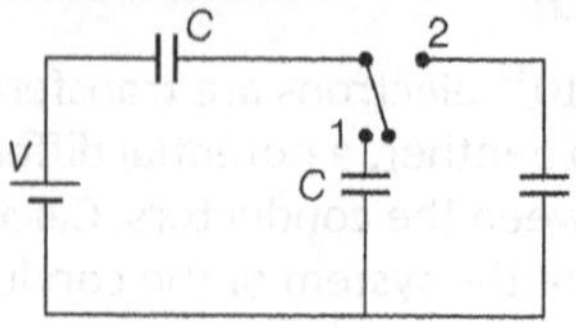

9.5 Series and Parallel Combinations

1 Three initially uncharged capacitors are connected in series as shown in circuit with a battery of emf 30V. Find out following

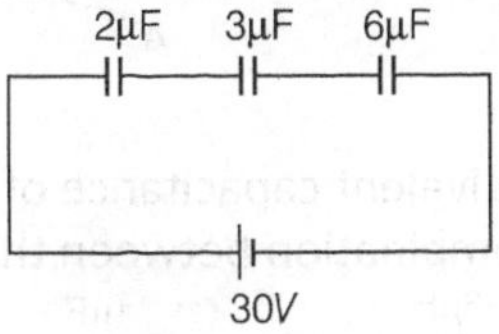

(i) equivalent capacitance across battery,
(ii) charge on each capacitor,
(iii) potential difference across 2μF capacitor and
(iv) energy stored in 3μF capacitor.

2 Three initially uncharged capacitors are connected to a battery of 10 V in parallel combination. Find out following

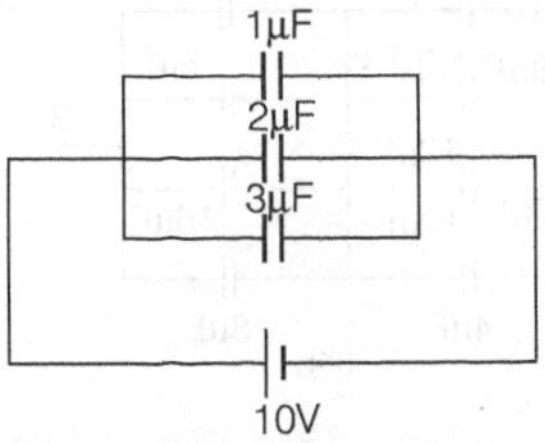

(i) equivalent capacitance across battery,
(ii) charge on 2μF capacitor,
(iii) total energy stored in all capacitors and
(iv) energy stored in the 3μF capacitor.

3 In the given circuit, find out

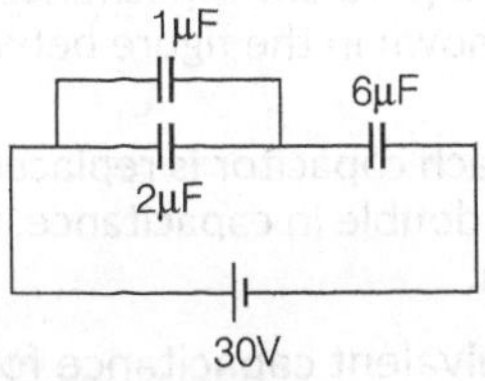

(i) charges on each capacitor,
(ii) potential difference across 1μF capacitor and
(iii) energy stored in 2μF capacitor.

4 In the circuit shown, find

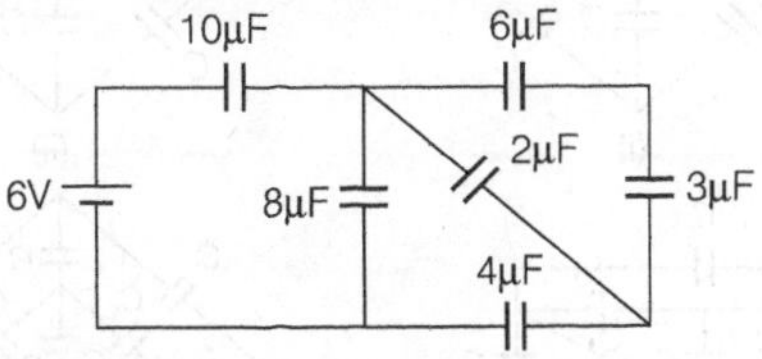

(i) the equivalent capacitance of the circuit across battery and
(ii) charge on each capacitor.

5 Find the potential difference between points *A* and *B* of the system shown in figure, if the emf is equal to $E = 110$ V and the capacitance ratio $C_2 / C_1 = 2.0$.

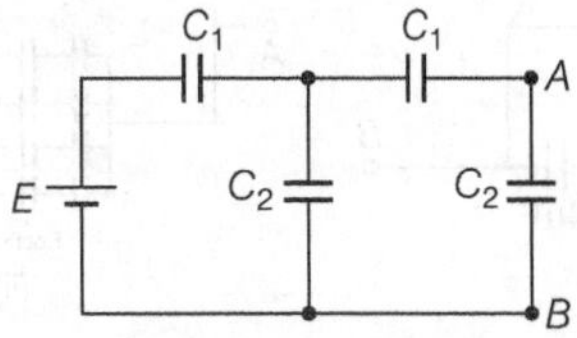

6

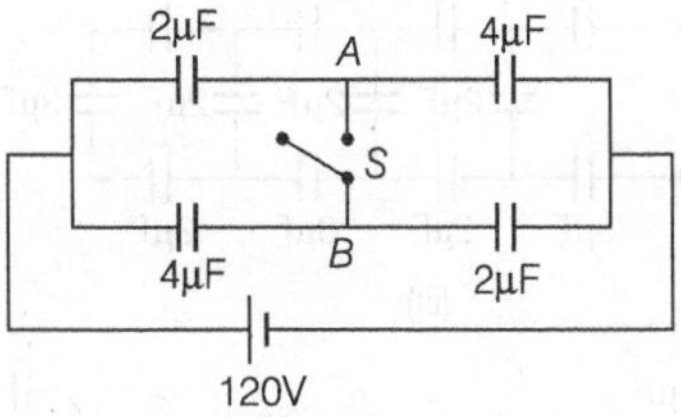

(i) Initially, switch *S* is open. What is the potential difference between *A* and *B*?
(ii) What charge will flow through the switch when it is closed?

7 Three capacitors each having capacitance $C = 2\mu F$ are connected with a batten of emf 30 V as shown in figure. When the switch *S* is closed, find

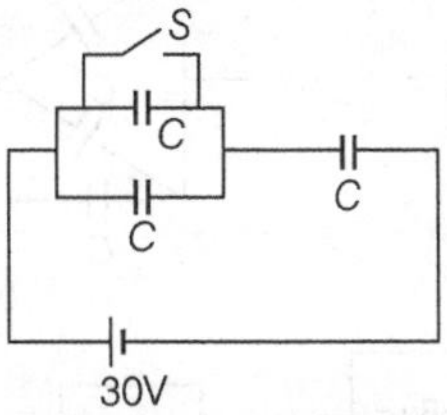

(i) the amount of charge flown through the battery,
(ii) the amount of charge flown through the switch *S*,
(iii) the energy supplied by the battery and
(iv) the heat generated in the circuit.

8 A capacitor of capacity $C_1 = 1\,\mu F$ withstands the maximum voltage $V_1 = 6$ kV while another capacitor of capacitance $C_2 = 2\,\mu F$ withstands the maximum voltage $V_2 = 4$ kV. What maximum voltage will the system of these two capacitors withstand, if they are connected in series?

9 From a supply of identical capacitors rated 8 μF, 200V, what is the minimum number of capacitors required to form a composite 16μF, 1000 V?

9.6 Equivalent Capacitance

1 Find the equivalent capacitance between the points *A* and *B* of the given assemblies.

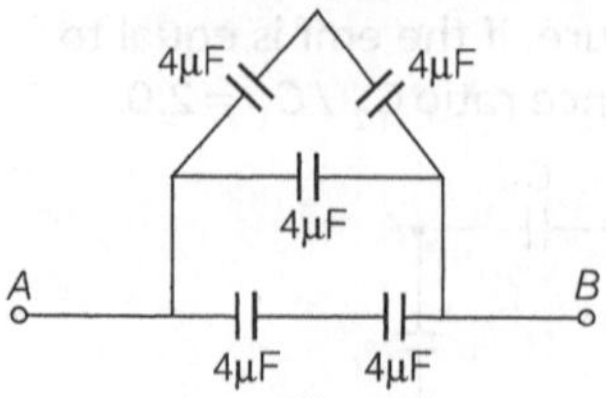

(i)

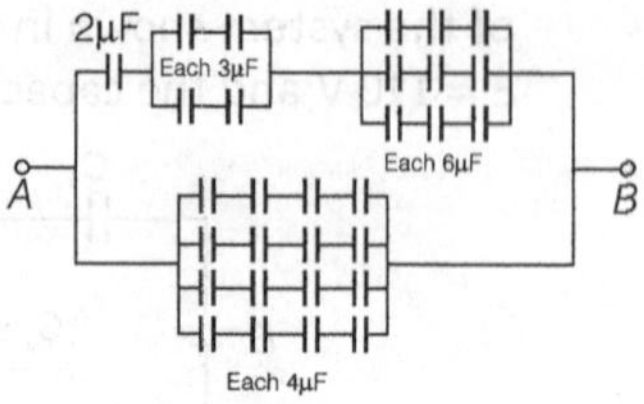

(ii)

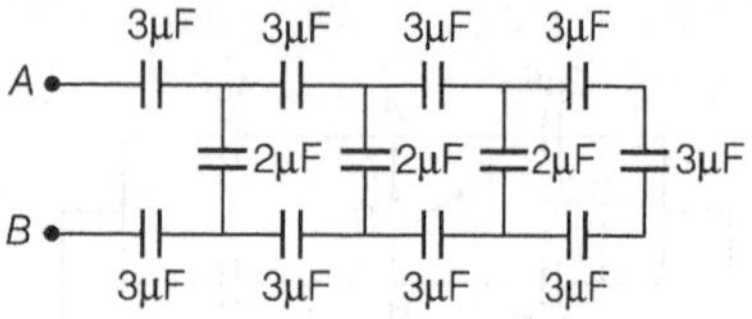

(iii)

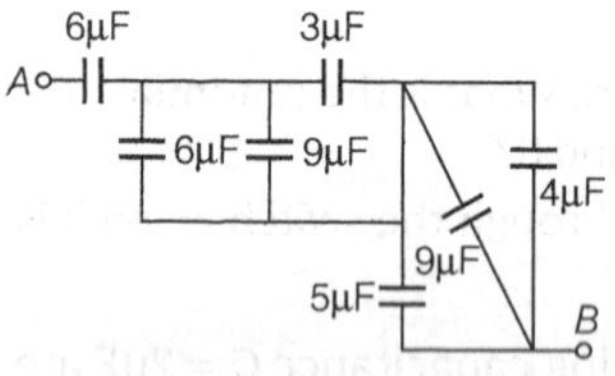

(iv)

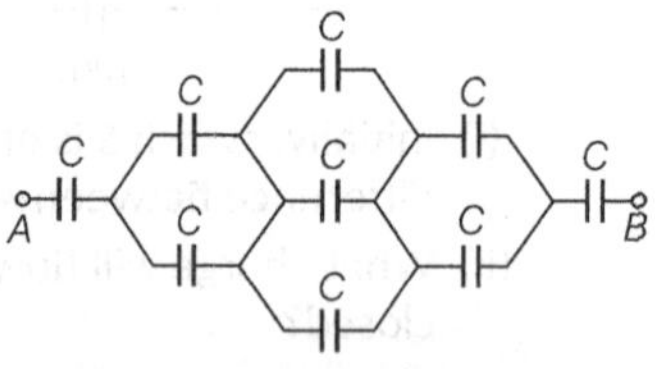

(v)

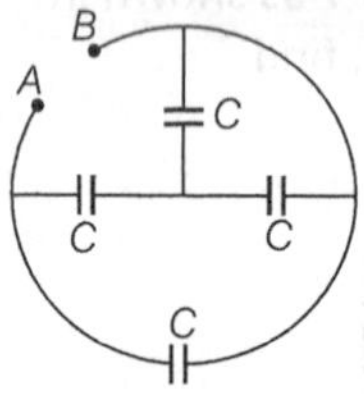

(vi)

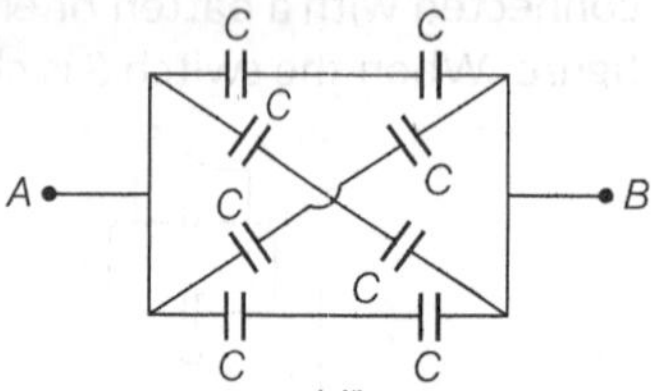

(vii)

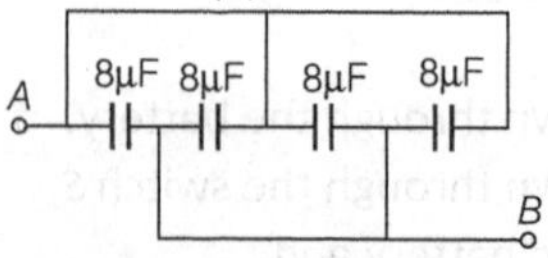

(viii)

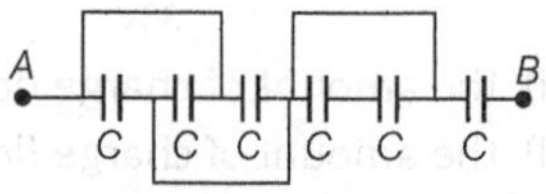

(ix)

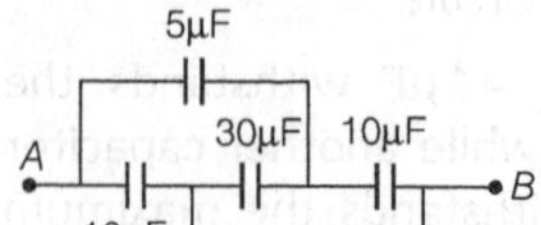

(x)

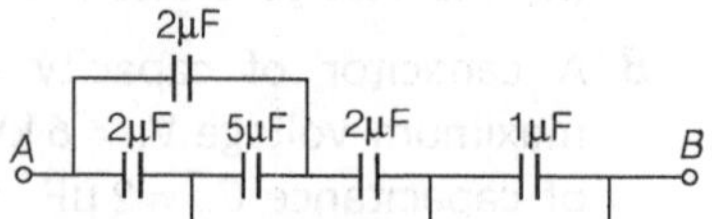

(xi)

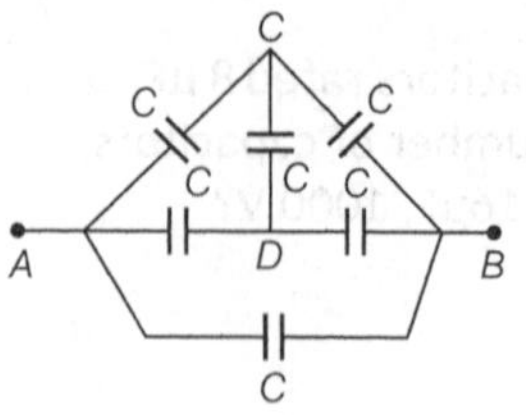

(xii)

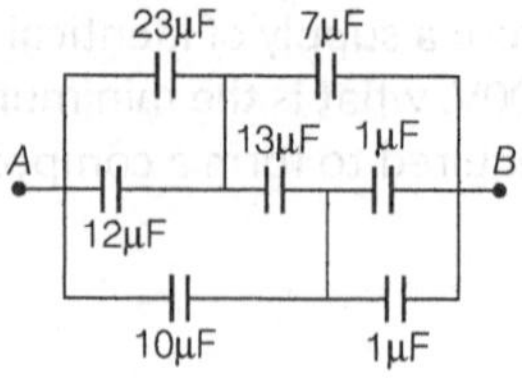

(xiii)

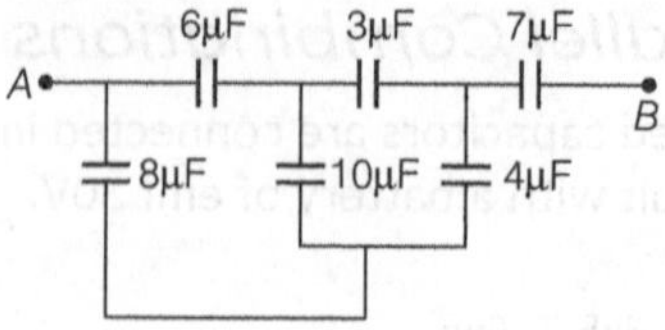

(xiv)

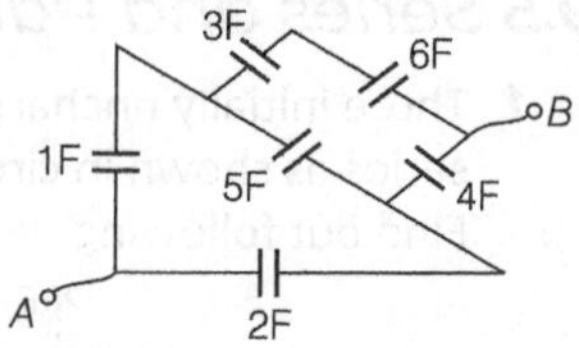

(xv)

2 Find the equivalent capacitance of each of the following combination between the points *A* and *B*.

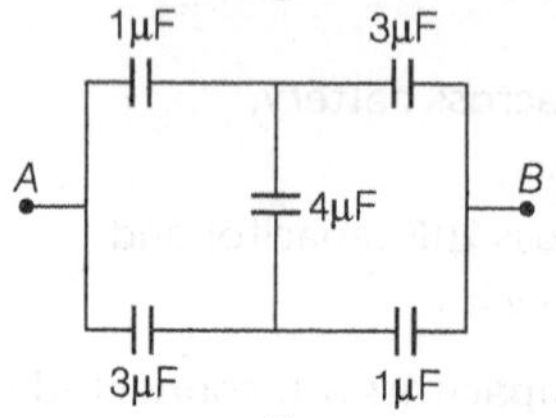

(i)

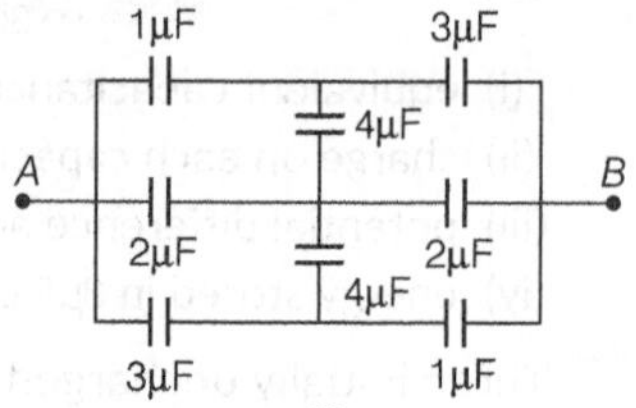

(ii)

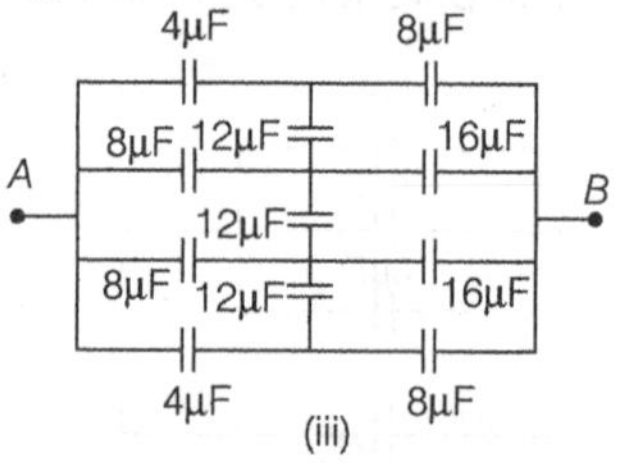

(iii)

3

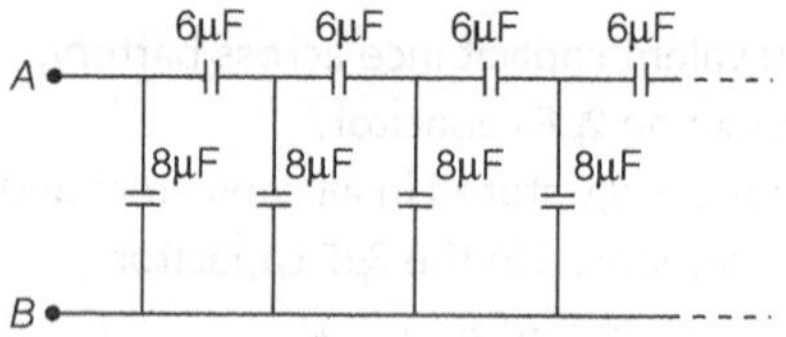

(i) Find the equivalent capacitance of the infinite ladder shown in the figure between the points *A* and *B*.

(ii) If now each capacitor is replaced by a capacitor which is double in capacitance, then repeat the question.

4 Find the equivalent capacitance for each of the following combinations between the points *A* and *B*.

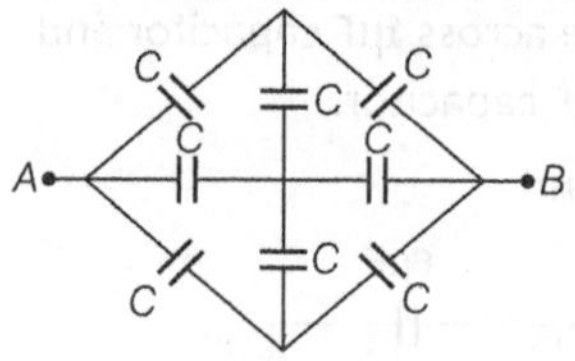

(i)

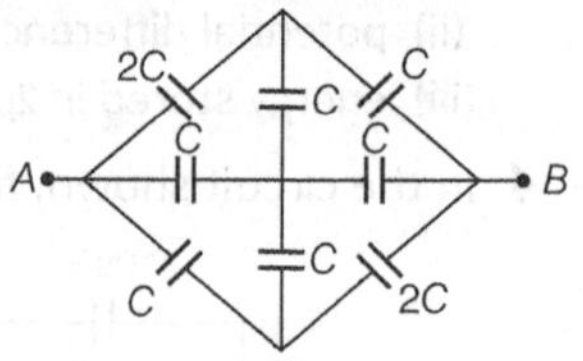

(ii)

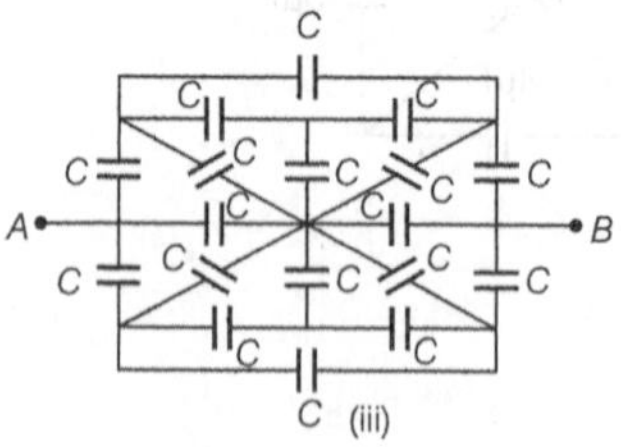

(iii)

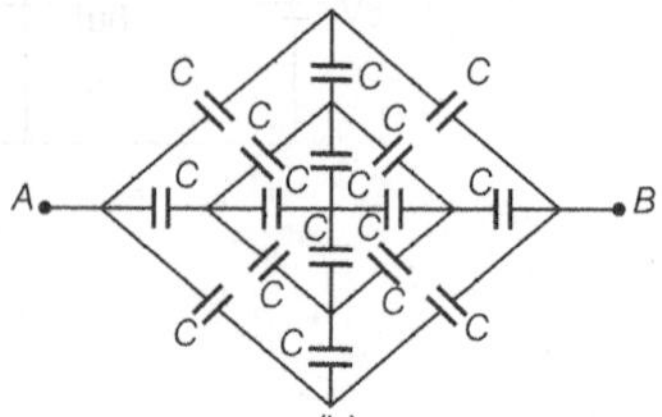

(iv)

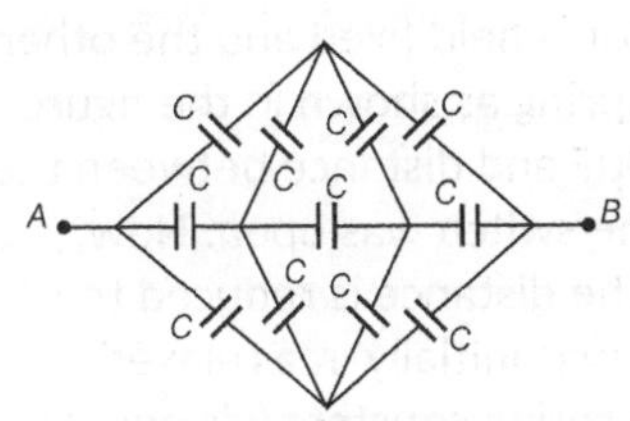
(v)

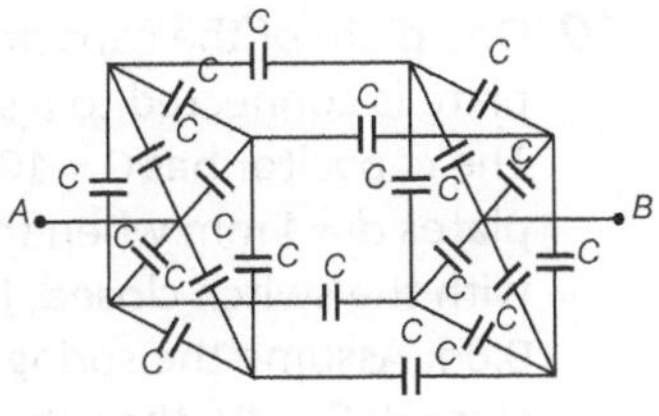
(vi)

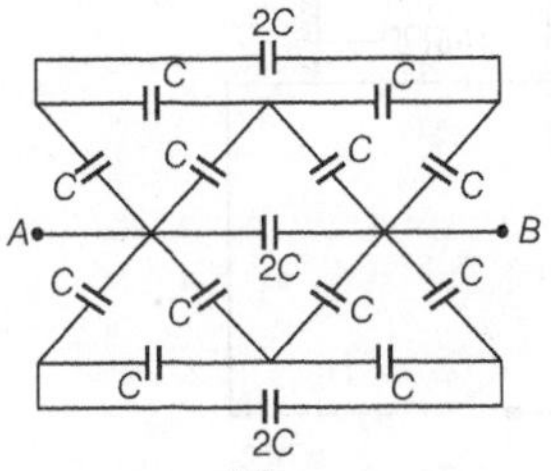
(vii)

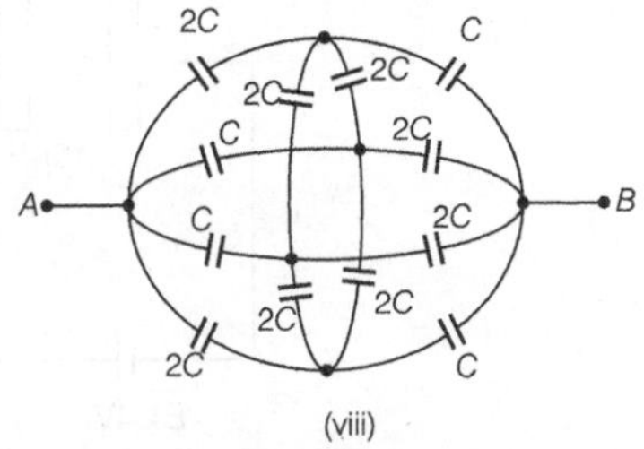
(viii)

9.7 Combination of Parallel Plates

1 Find out equivalent capacitance between A and B. (Take, each plate area = A and distance between two successive plates is d)

(i)
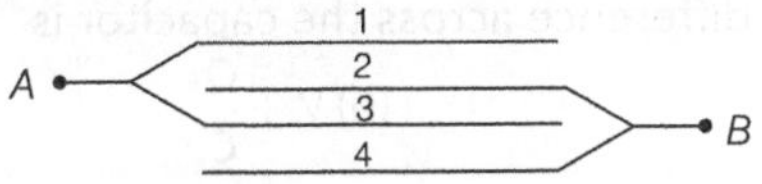

(ii)
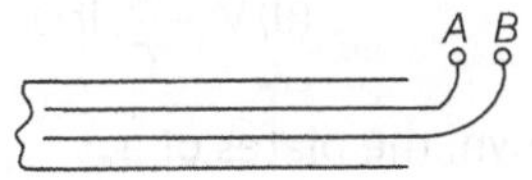

(iii)
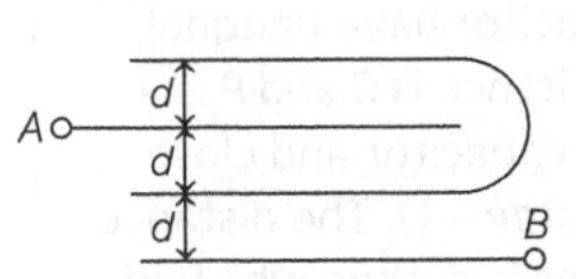

(iv)
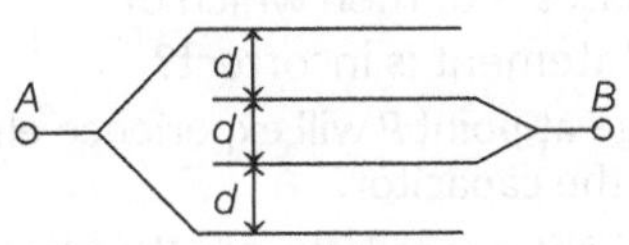

(v)
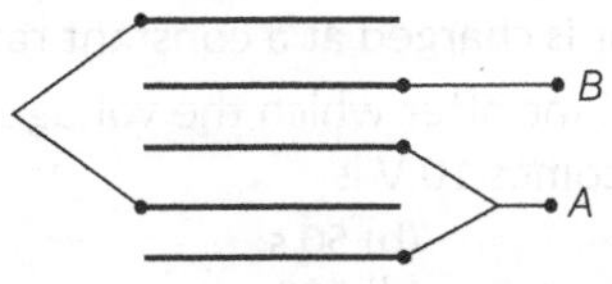

(vi)

2 Three identical very large conducting plates A, B and C are placed parallel to each other. Plates A and C are connected by thin conducting wire. A charge $+4Q$ is given to plate A and $-12Q$ is given to plate B. Find the final charges on each surfaces of plates. Here, separation between A and B is L and between B and C is $3L$.

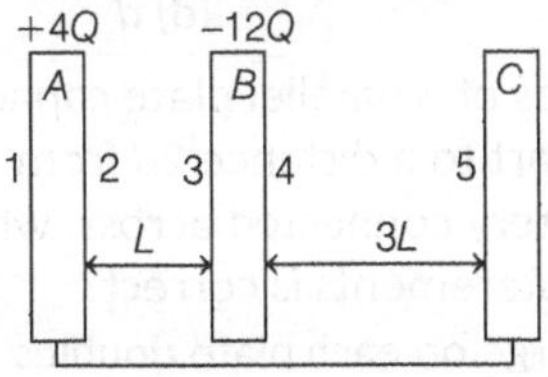

3 The metal plate on the left carries charge $+Q$ and on the right has charge $4Q$ respectively as shown in figure. The central plate has initially charge equal to $5Q$. When both S_1 and S_2 switches are closed simultaneously, then find the charge flown through S_1 upto steady state.

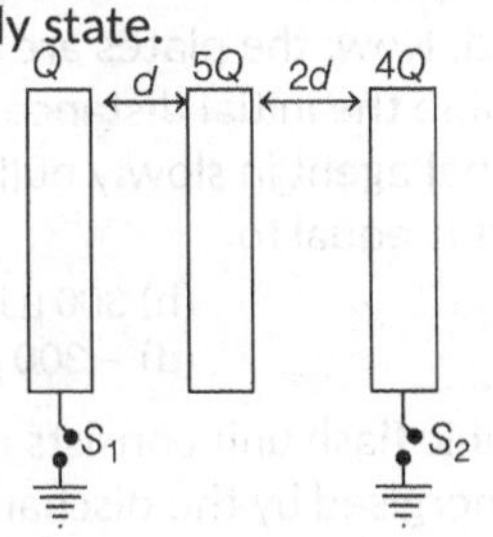

LEVEL 02 JEE Main Level

Single Choice Correct Questions

1 If two isolated charged metallic spheres of radii R_1 and R_2 having charges Q_1 and Q_2 respectively are connected to each other, then there is

(a) no change in the electrical energy of the system

(b) an increase in the electrical energy of the system

(c) a decrease in the electrical energy of the system in any case

(d) a decrease in electrical energy of the system, if $Q_1R_2 \neq Q_2R_1$

2 The distance between the plates of a circular parallel plate condenser of diameter 40 mm, in order to make its capacity equal to that of a metallic sphere of radius 1m, will be

(a) 0.1 mm

(b) 10 mm

(c) 0.01 mm

(d) 1 mm

3 A $800\mu F$ capacitor is charged at a constant rate of 50×10^{-6} A. The time after which the voltage across the capacitor becomes 10 V is

(a) 160 s (b) 50 s
(c) 10 s (d) 500 s

4 If the charge on a capacitor is increased by 2C, the energy stored in it increases by 21%. The original charge on the capacitor (in C) is

(a) 10 (b) 20
(c) 30 (d) 40

5 The plates of a parallel plate condenser are being moved away with a constant speed v. If the plate separation at any instant of time is d, then the rate of change of capacitance with time is proportional to

(a) $\frac{1}{d}$ (b) $\frac{1}{d^2}$
(c) d^2 (d) d

6 If the plates of a parallel plate capacitor are moved further apart to a distance $2d$ from initial distance d with a battery connected across, which of the following statements is correct?

(a) The charge on each plate doubles.
(b) The electric field in the region between the plates reduces to half of its initial value.
(c) The voltage across the plates doubles.
(d) The charge on each plate remains unaffected.

7 A parallel plate capacitor of $C = 12\mu F$ is charged to a potential difference of 10V and the battery disconnected. Now, the plates are pulled further apart to double the initial distance. The work done by the external agent in slowly pulling the plates further apart is equal to

(a) $-600\ \mu J$ (b) $300\ \mu J$
(c) $600\ \mu J$ (d) $-300\ \mu J$

8 A photographic flash unit consists of a Xenon-filled flash tube energised by the discharge of a capacitor, previously charged by a 1000 V source. The average power delivered to the tube is 2000 W in a time of 0.04 s. The capacitance of the capacitor can be estimated as

(a) $40\ \mu F$ (b) $80\ \mu F$
(c) $160\ \mu F$ (d) None of these

9 Capacity of an isolated sphere is increased n times when it is enclosed by an earthed concentric sphere. The ratio of their radii would be

(a) $\frac{n^2}{n-1}$ (b) $\frac{n}{n-1}$
(c) $\frac{2n}{n+1}$ (d) $\frac{2n+1}{n+1}$

10 One plate of the capacitor is held fixed and the other plate is connected to a spring as shown in the figure. The capacitor has $C = 10\mu F$ and distance between the plates $d = 1$ mm when the switch was open. Now, with the switch closed, the distance is reduced to $0.8d$. Assume the spring was initially in a relaxed state. If $E = 4V$, then the spring constant k is equal to

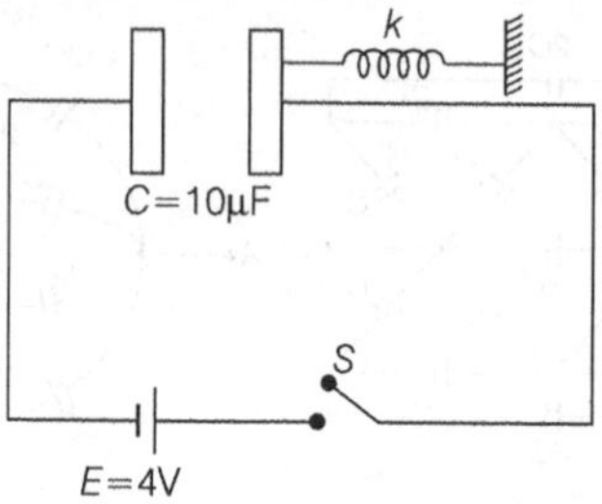

(a) 1500 N/m (b) 35 N/m
(c) 625 N/m (d) 125 N/m

11 A capacitor of capacitance C is charged to a potential difference V from a cell and then disconnected from it. A charge $+Q$ is now given to its positive plate. The potential difference across the capacitor is

(a) V (b) $V + \frac{Q}{C}$
(c) $V + \frac{Q}{2C}$ (d) $V - \frac{Q}{C}$, if $Q < CV$

12 In the figure shown, the plates of a parallel plate capacitor have unequal charges. Its capacitance is C and P is a point outside the capacitor and close to the plate of charge $-Q$. The distance between the plates is d, then which of the following statement is incorrect?

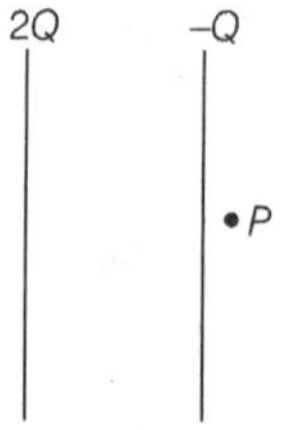

(a) A point charge at point P will experience electric force due to the capacitor.
(b) The potential difference between the plates will be $\frac{3Q}{2C}$.
(c) The energy stored in the electric field in the region between the plates is $\frac{9Q^2}{8C}$.
(d) The force on one plate due to the other plate is $\frac{9Q^2}{8\pi\varepsilon_0 A}$.

13 A capacitor having capacitance C is charged by a battery having emf 2V (battery is disconnected after charging). Now, this charged capacitor is connected to another battery having emf V. The positive plate of capacitor is connected with negative terminal of battery and *vice-versa*.

The amount of heat produced after connecting it with battery

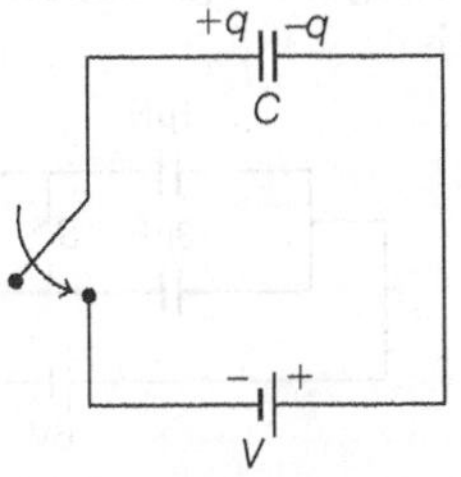

(a) $4.5\,CV^2$ (b) $1.5CV^2$
(c) $4\,CV^2$ (d) None of these

14 A 4μF capacitor is charged by a 200 V supply. It is then disconnected from the supply and is connected to another uncharged 2μF capacitor. What percentage of electrostatics energy of the first capacitor is dissipated in the form of heat and electromagnetic radiation?

(a) 20% (b) 25 %
(c) 33.33 % (d) 40 %

15 A parallel plate capacitor of capacitance *C* is connected to a battery and is charged to potential difference *V*. Another capacitor of capacitance 2*C* is similarly charged to a potential difference 2*V*. The charging battery is then disconnected and the capacitors are connected in parallel to each other in such a way that the positive terminal of one is connected to the negative terminal of the other. The final energy of the configuration is

(a) zero (b) $\frac{1}{2}CV^2$ (c) $\frac{25}{6}CV^2$ (d) $\frac{9}{2}CV^2$

16 Two identical capacitors, have the same capacitance *C*. One of them is charged to potential V_1 and the other to V_2. The negative ends of the capacitors are connected together. When the positive ends are also connected, the decrease in energy of the combined system is

(a) $\frac{1}{4}C(V_1^2 - V_2^2)$ (b) $\frac{1}{4}C(V_1^2 + V_2^2)$
(c) $\frac{1}{4}C(V_1 - V_2)^2$ (d) $\frac{1}{4}C(V_1 + V_2)^2$

17 The potential of the point *A* is greater than that of *B* by 19V. What is the potential difference across the 3μF capacitor?

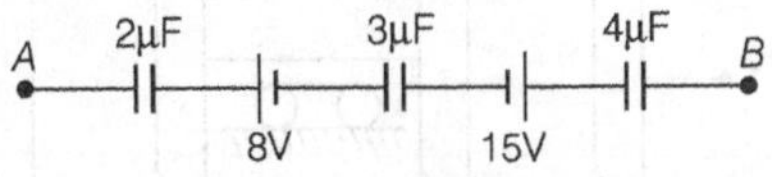

(a) 7 V (b) 8 V
(c) 23 V (d) 4 V

18 For the given circuit, the charge that appears across the 2μF capacitor is

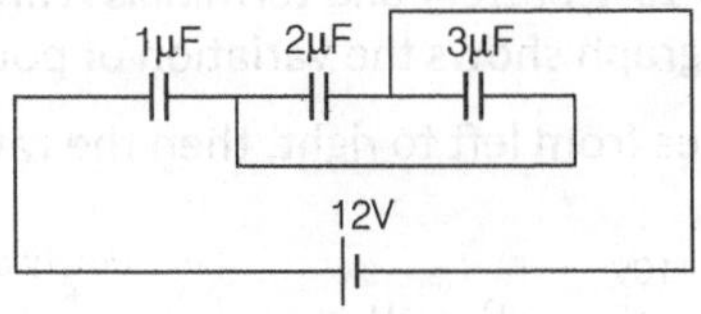

(a) 1μC (b) 4μC
(c) 3μC (d) 8μC

19 In the circuit shown, the energy stored in 1μF capacitor is

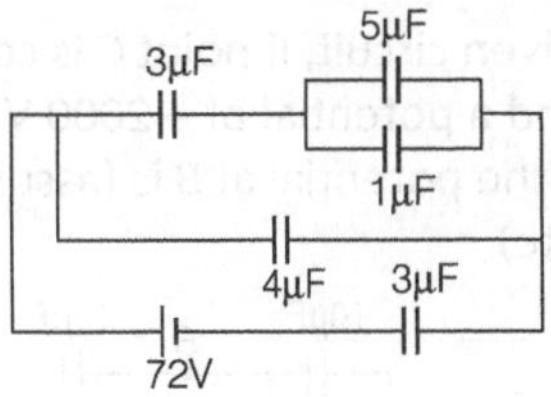

(a) 40μJ (b) 64μJ
(c) 32μJ (d) None of these

20 Three capacitors *A*, *B* and *C* are connected in a circuit as shown in figure. What is the charge (in μC) on the capacitor *B*?

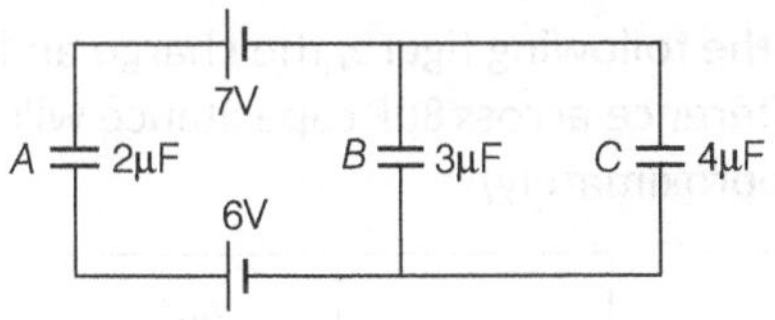

(a) 1/3 (b) 2/3 (c) 1 (d) 4/3

21 In the circuit shown in figure, the amount of charge that will flow through the key when it is closed is

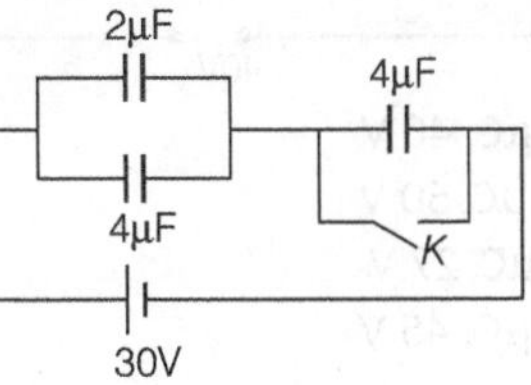

(a) 120μC (b) 150μC (c) 180μC (d) 0

22 The particle *P* shown in figure has a mass of 10 mg and a charge of − 0.01 μC. The plates are horizontal and each plate has a surface area 100 cm². What potential difference *V* should be applied to the combination to hold the particle *P* in equilibrium?

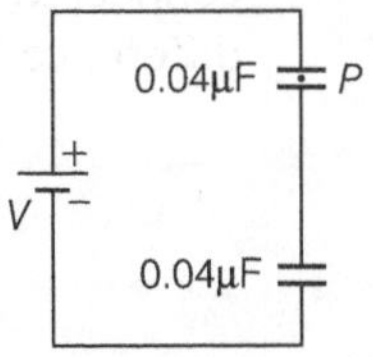

(a) 13 mV (b) 23 mV
(c) 43 mV (d) 93 mV

23 Figure shows two capacitors C_1 and C_2 connected with 10 V battery and terminals A and B are earthed. The graph shows the variation of potential as one moves from left to right, then the ratio of $\frac{C_1}{C_2}$ is

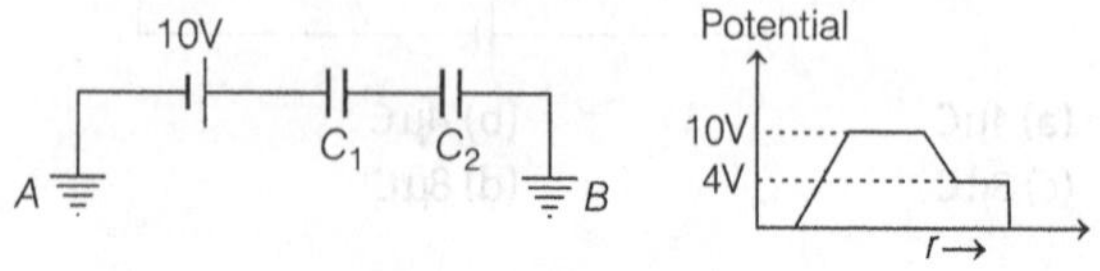

(a) $\frac{5}{2}$ (b) $\frac{2}{3}$ (c) $\frac{2}{5}$ (d) $\frac{3}{2}$

24 In the given circuit, if point C is connected to the earth and a potential of +2000 V is given to the point A, then the potential at B is (assume circuit is complete)

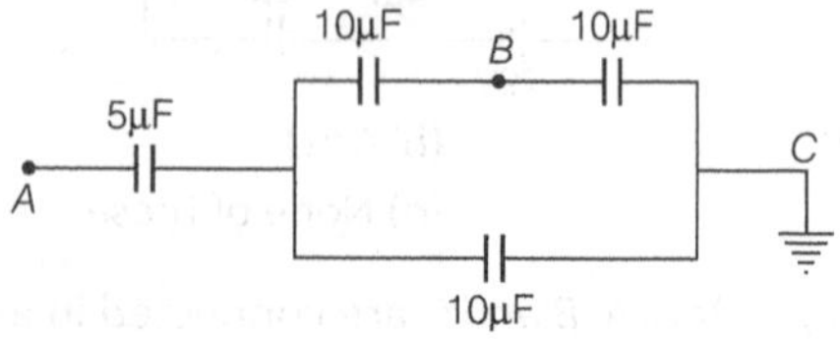

(a) 250 V (b) 500 V
(c) 750 V (d) 200 V

25 In the following figure, the charge and potential difference across 8μF capacitance will be respectively (approximately)

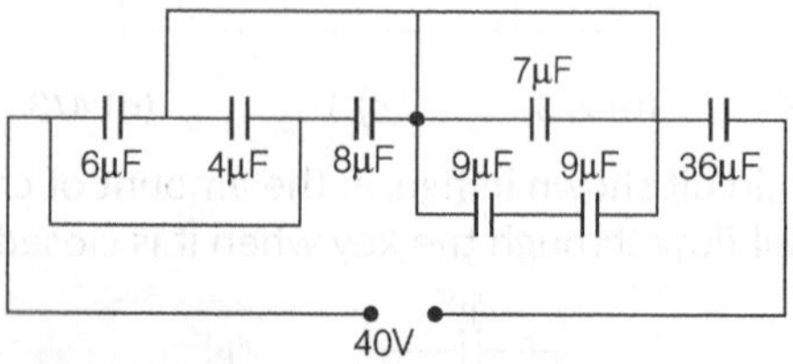

(a) 320 μC, 40 V
(b) 420 μC, 50 V
(c) 214 μC, 27 V
(d) 360 μC, 45 V

26 Four capacitors and two sources of emf are connected as shown in the figure. The potential difference between the points a and b is

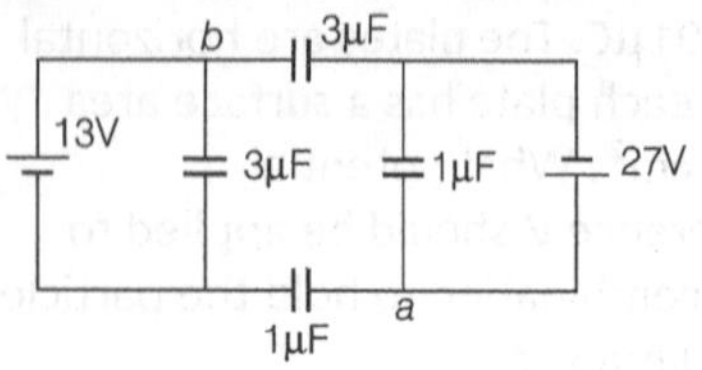

(a) zero (b) 13 V
(c) 17 V (d) 27 V

27 In the circuit when switch S is closed, the amount of charge passing through the switch is xμC, then the value of x is

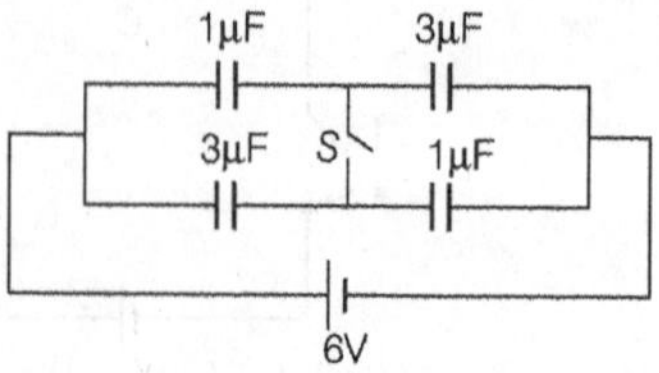

(a) 12 (b) 6
(c) 3 (d) 1

28 Find the charge flown through the switch when it is closed.

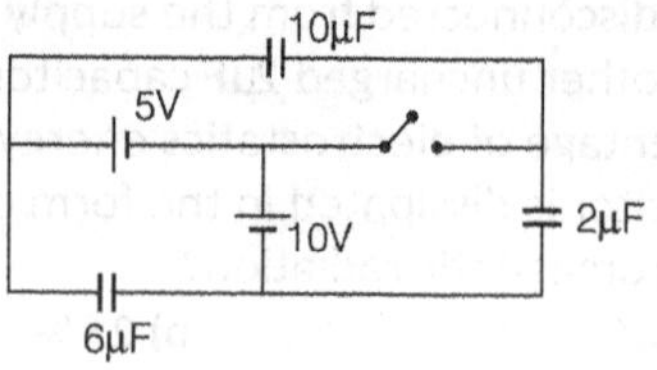

(a) 20 μC (b) 30 μC
(c) 42 μC (d) 60 μC

29 The circuit involves two ideal cells connected to a 1 μF capacitor *via* a key K. Initially, the key K is in position 1 and the capacitor is charged fully by 2V cell. The key is then pushed to position 2. The heat produced in circuit (in μJ) after pushing the key to position 2 is

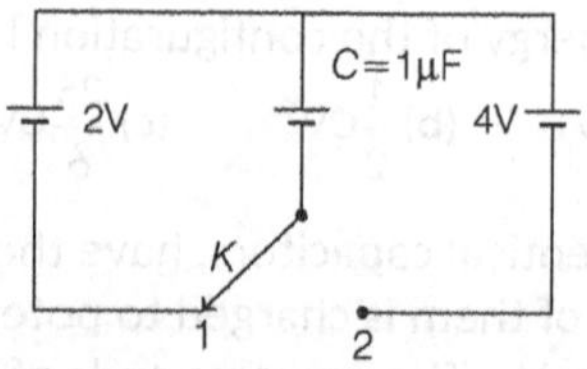

(a) 2 (b) 6 (c) 8 (d) 16

30 A, B, C and D are large conducting plates kept parallel to each other. A and D are fixed. Plates B are C connected to each other by a rigid conducting rod can slide over frictionless rails as shown in figure. Initially, the distance between plates A and B is same as that between plates C and D. If now the rod (along with plates B and C) is slightly moved towards right, the capacitance between the terminals 1 and 2

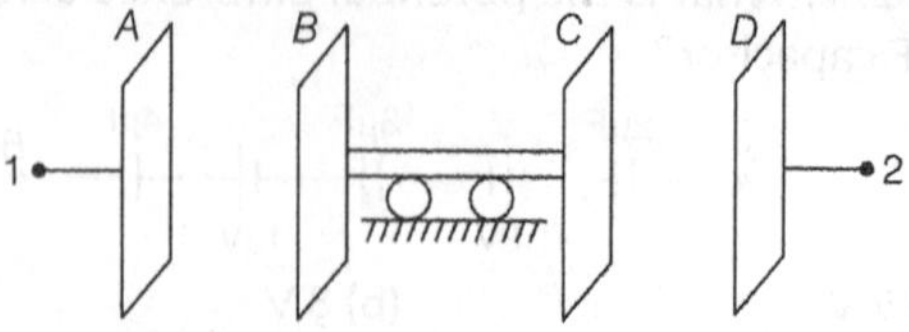

(a) remains unchanged (b) increases
(c) decreases (d) Nothing can be said

31 Twelve identical capacitors are connected in series between two points. Out of these for n capacitors, the spacing between the plates is reduced to half and for the remaining it is doubled. What is the value of n for which the effective capacitance remains unchanged?

(a) 4 (b) 6 (c) 8 (d) 2

32 The effective capacitance between points A and B will be

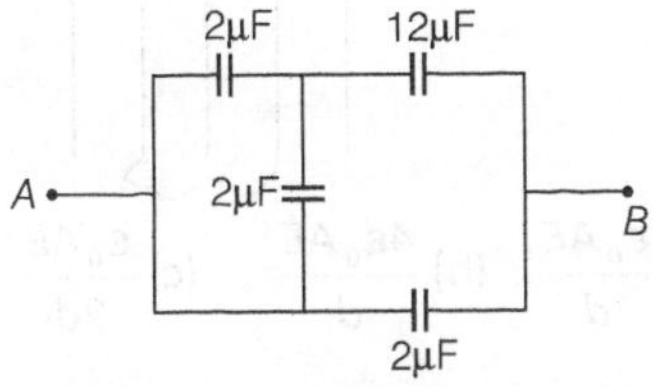

(a) $\frac{28}{9}$ μF (b) 5 μF

(c) 4 μF (d) None of these

33 The equivalent capacitance between points A and B is

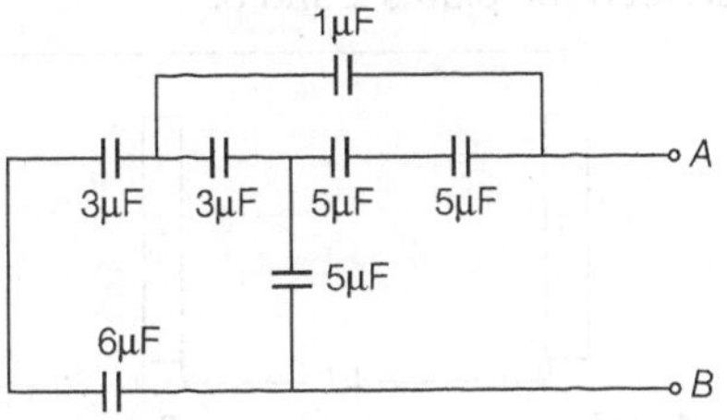

(a) $\frac{7}{3}$ μF (b) $\frac{7}{5}$ μF (c) $\frac{7}{6}$ μF (d) $\frac{11}{3}$ μF

34 Find equivalent capacitance between A and B.

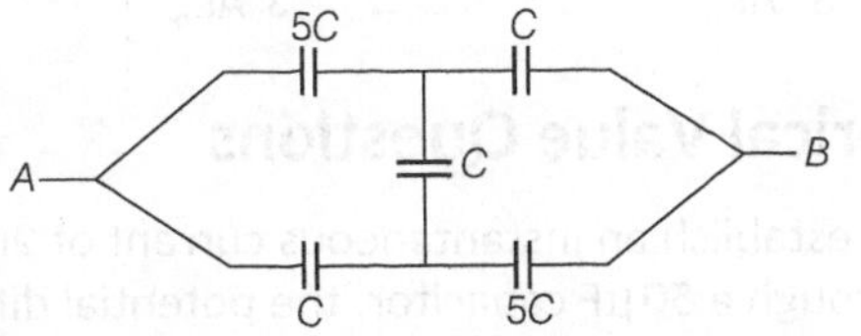

(a) 3C (b) 2C (c) $\frac{5C}{3}$ (d) $\frac{7C}{5}$

35 Find equivalent capacitance across AB (all capacitances in μF).

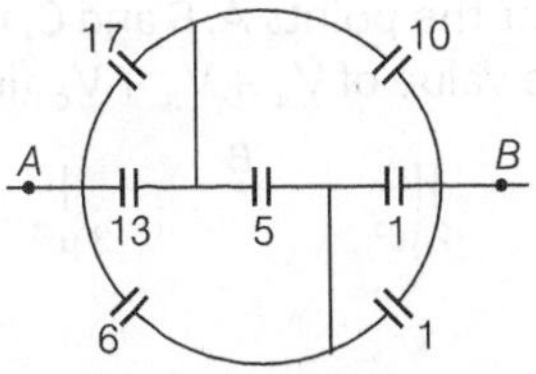

(a) $\frac{20}{3}$ μF (b) 9 μF

(c) 48 μF (d) None of the above

36 Find equivalent capacitance between points A and B.

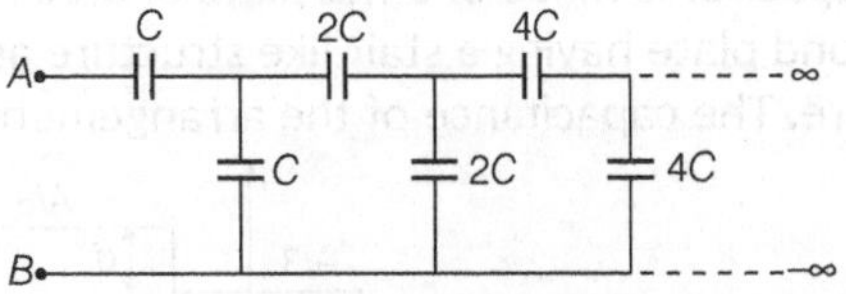

(a) $\frac{C}{\sqrt{2}}$ (b) $\frac{C}{\sqrt{2}+1}$ (c) $\frac{C}{\sqrt{2}-1}$ (d) $\frac{C}{2\sqrt{2}}$

37 Each edge of the cube contains a capacitance C. The equivalent capacitance between the points A and B will be

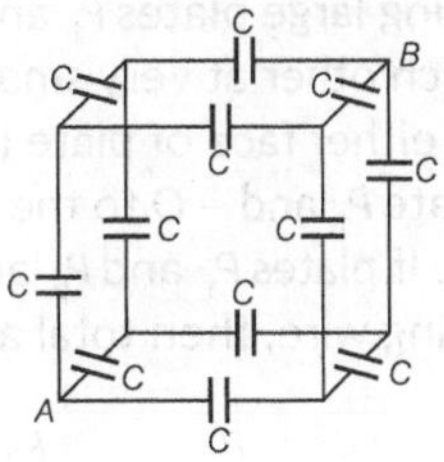

(a) $\frac{6C}{5}$ (b) $\frac{5C}{6}$ (c) $\frac{12C}{7}$ (d) $\frac{7C}{12}$

38 Three capacitors 2 μF, 3 μF and 5 μF can withstand voltages to 3V, 2V and 1V, respectively. Their series combination can withstand a maximum voltage equal to

(a) 5 V (b) 6 V (c) (26/5)V (d) (31/6) V

39 A circuit is made using five identical capacitors, each of which can withstand a maximum voltage of 2 V. The maximum voltage which can be safely applied across points A and B is

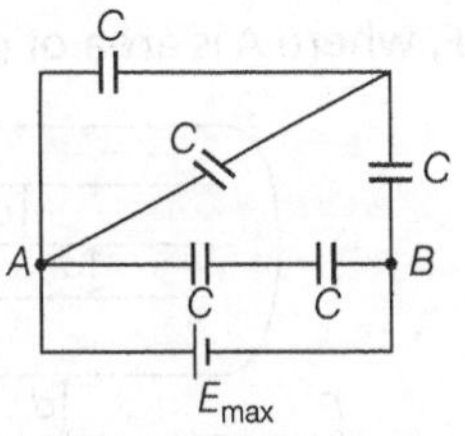

(a) 1 V (b) 2 V

(c) 3 V (d) 4V

40 Two spherical conductors A_1 and A_2 of radii r_1 and r_2 are placed concentrically in air. The two are connected by a copper wire as shown in figure, then the equivalent capacitance of the system is

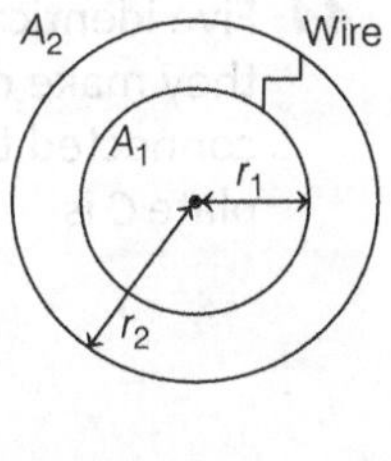

(a) $\frac{4\pi\varepsilon_0 r_1 r_2}{(r_2 - r_1)}$ (b) $4\pi\varepsilon_0 (r_1 + r_2)$

(c) $4\pi\varepsilon_0 r_2$ (d) $4\pi\varepsilon_0 r_1$

41 A capacitor is made of a flat plate of area A and a second plate having a stair like structure as shown in figure. The capacitance of the arrangement is

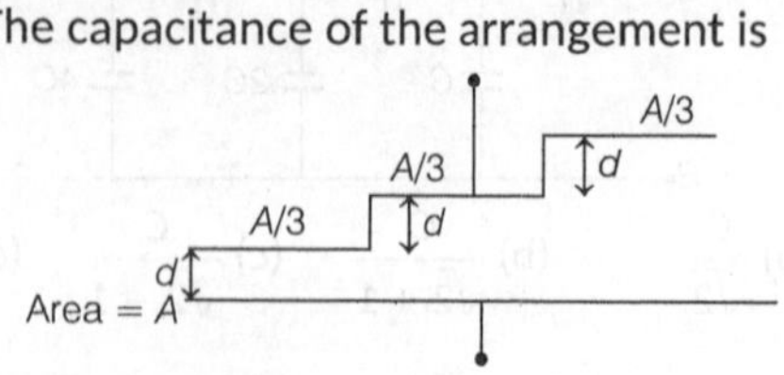

(a) $\frac{\varepsilon_0 A}{d}$ (b) $\frac{18}{11}\frac{\varepsilon_0 A}{d}$ (c) $\frac{11}{18}\frac{\varepsilon_0 A}{d}$ (d) $\frac{\varepsilon_0 A}{3d}$

42 Two conducting large plates P_1 and P_2 are placed parallel to each other at very small, separation d. The plate area of either face of plate is A. A charge $+2Q$ is given to plate P_1 and $-Q$ to the plate P_2 (neglect ends effects). If plates P_1 and P_2 are now connected by a conducting wire, then total amount of heat produced is

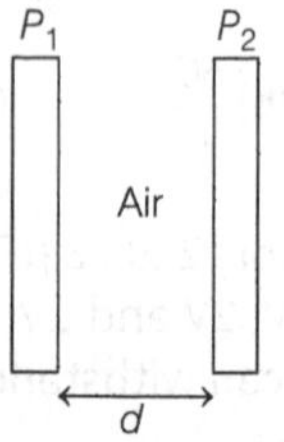

(a) $\frac{4Q^2 d}{3\varepsilon_0 A}$ (b) $\frac{9Q^2 d}{8\varepsilon_0 A}$ (c) $\frac{3Q^2 d}{4\varepsilon_0 A}$ (d) None of these

43 Find equivalent capacitance between A and B. [Assume, each conducting plate is having same dimensions and neglect the thickness of the plate, $\frac{\varepsilon_0 A}{d} = 7\mu\text{F}$, where A is area of plates and $A >> d$].

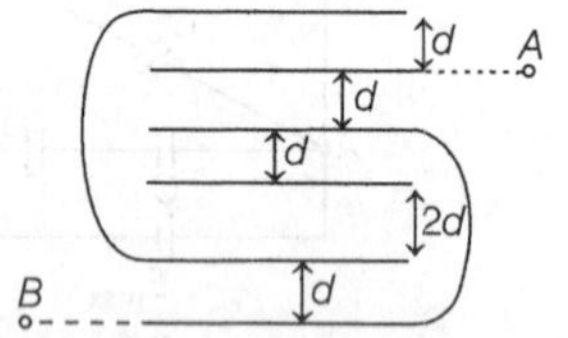

(a) 7 μF (b) 11 μF (c) 12 μF (d) 13 μF

44 Five identical capacitor plates are arranged such that they make capacitors each of 2 μF. The plates are connected to a source of emf 10 V. The charge on plate C is

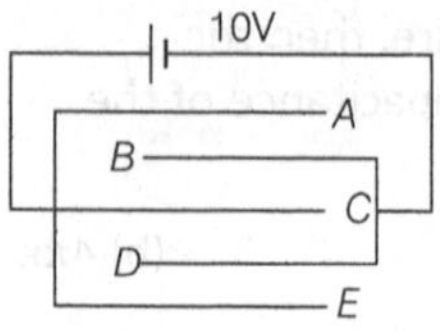

(a) + 20 μC (b) + 40 μC
(c) + 60 μC (d) + 80 μC

45 Five conducting parallel plates having area A and separation between them d, are placed as shown in the figure. Plate numbers 2 and 4 are connected wire and between point A and B, a cell of emf E is connected. The charge flown through the cell is

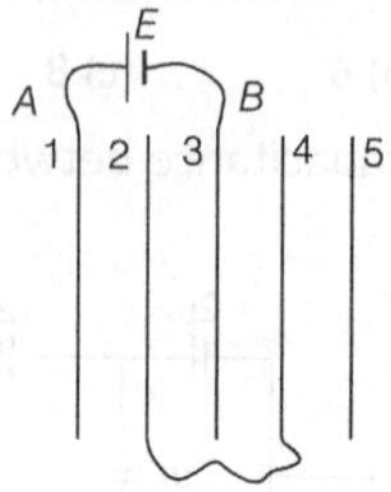

(a) $\frac{3}{4}\frac{\varepsilon_0 AE}{d}$ (b) $\frac{4\varepsilon_0 AE}{d}$ (c) $\frac{\varepsilon_0 AE}{2d}$ (d) $\frac{2}{3}\frac{\varepsilon_0 AE}{d}$

46 Three identical metal plates of large area A numbered 1,2 and 3 are arranged as shown in the figure. The plates 1 and 3 are connected by a conducting wire. The charge given to plate 2 is $2q$ and no other plate is given any charge. Find the potential difference between the plates 2 and 3.

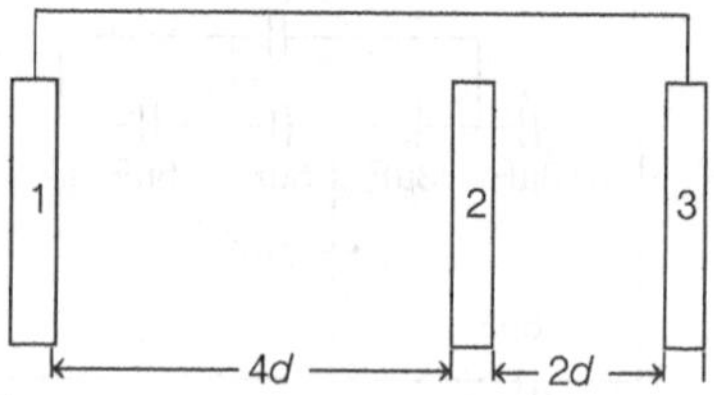

(a) $\frac{4}{3}\frac{qd}{A\varepsilon_0}$ (b) $\frac{8}{3}\frac{qd}{A\varepsilon_0}$

(c) $\frac{12}{3}\frac{qd}{A\varepsilon_0}$ (d) $\frac{2}{3}\frac{qd}{A\varepsilon_0}$

Numerical Value Questions

1 To establish an instantaneous current of 2mA through a 50 μF capacitor, the potential difference across the capacitor plates should be changed at the rate of β volt/second. Find the value of β.

2 Two uncharged capacitors are connected across a battery as shown in figure. V_A, V_B and V_C are potentials at the points A, B and C, respectively. What is the value of $V_A + V_B + V_C$ (in volts)?

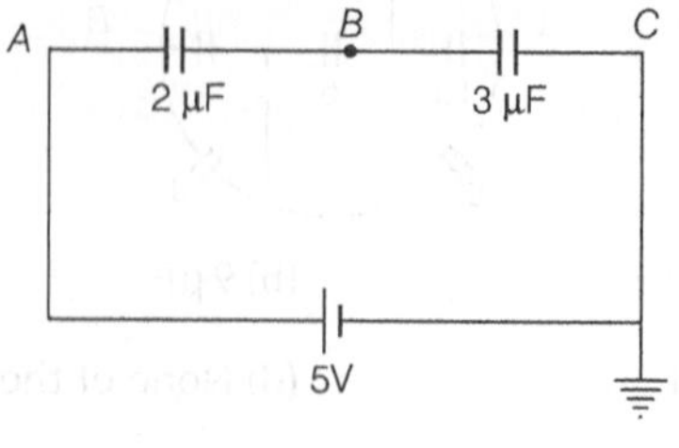

3 If potential of A is 5V, then find the potential of B (in volt).

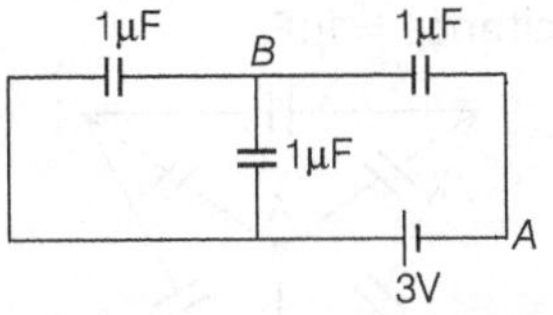

4 In the circuit as shown in figure, the potential difference between the points a and b is 4 V. Find the emf E (in V) of the battery.

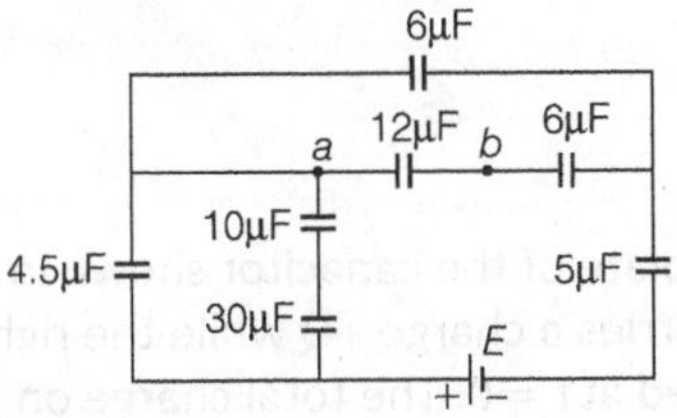

5 Figure shows a network of capacitors. Find the value of C (in μF), if the effective capacitance between the points A and B is 12μF.

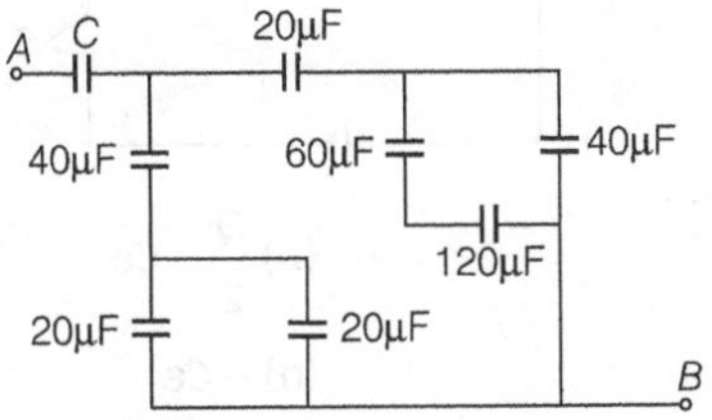

6 Find the equivalent capacitance (in μF) between points A and B of the arrangements shown in figure. Each capacitor has capacitance $C = 2$ μF.

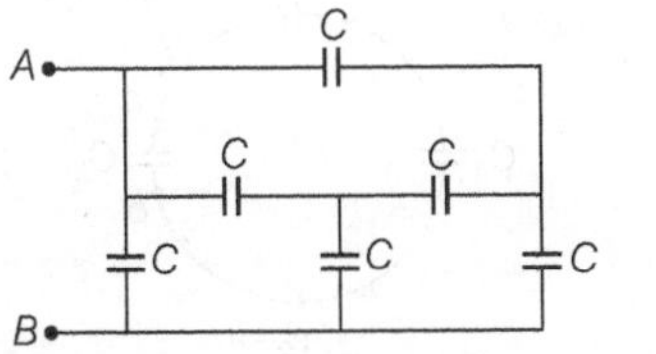

7 In figure $C_1 = 2$ μF, $C_2 = 6$ μF and $C_3 = 3$ μF. The breakdown voltages of the individual capacitors are $V_1 =$ 90 V, $V_2 = 60$V and $V_3 = 150$V, respectively. Find the maximum voltage(in V) that can be applied across points a and b, so that no capacitor breaks down.

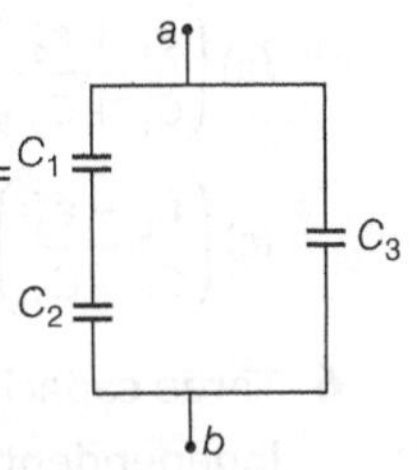

8 Plate 1 of a capacitor having capacitance 1.5 μF is given a charge of 30 μC while the other plate is uncharged. The capacitor is now connected with a battery of potential 40 V with plate 1 connected to the positive terminal. Work done by battery is __________ μJ.

9 A 8μF capacitor is charged by a 125V battery and then disconnected from the battery. When this capacitor is connected to a second (initially uncharged) capacitor C_0, the final voltage on each capacitor is 20V. What is the value of C_0 (in μF)?

10 Five plates of dimension 5 cm × 8 m are placed at separation of 8.85 mm from each other. If they are connected through a battery which provides constant potential difference of 20V as shown in figure, find the charge (in nC) flown through the battery.

11 Calculate the heat produced (in μJ) in the circuit when key is closed.

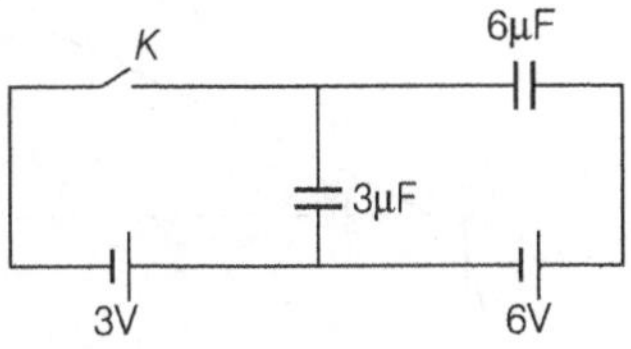

12 The amount of heat produced in the circuit after closing the switch S is $\frac{C\varepsilon^2}{n}$. Find the value of n.

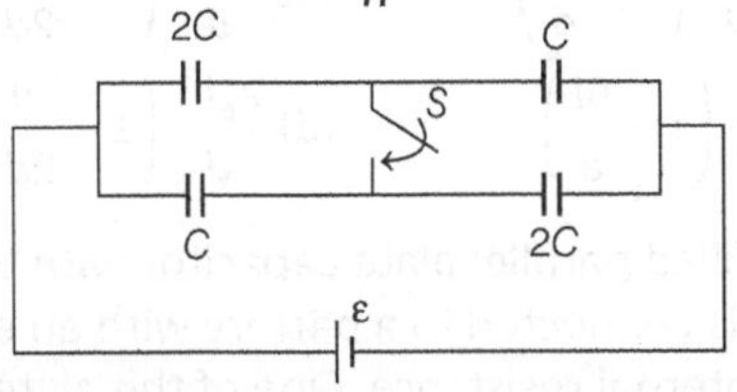

13 An electron with a kinetic energy of 100eV enters the space between the plates of plane capacitor made of two dense metal grids at an angle of 30° with the plates of capacitor and leaves this space at an angle of 45° with the plates. What is the potential difference (in V) of the capacitor?

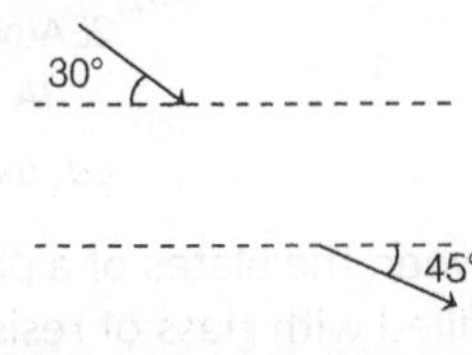

14 In the figure shown, the capacitor plates have a gap = 4 mm. The length of each plate is 10 cm. The capacitor plates are connected to a cell, so that the potential difference between them is 10 V. A particle of charge − 1 nC and mass 0.1 g enters the gap between the plates with a velocity is 50 cm/s as shown, exactly in the middle of the gap. What is the distance (in mm) of the point, where the particle hits the screen, from point O?

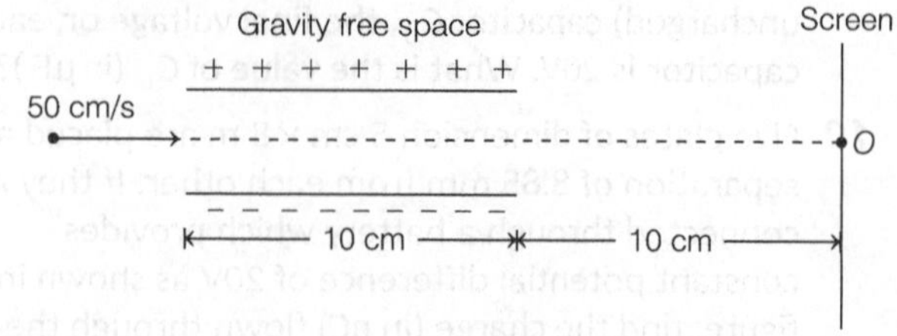

15 Find the effective capacitance(in μF) between points A and B in the networks shown below. All capacitors are of capacitance = 1μF.

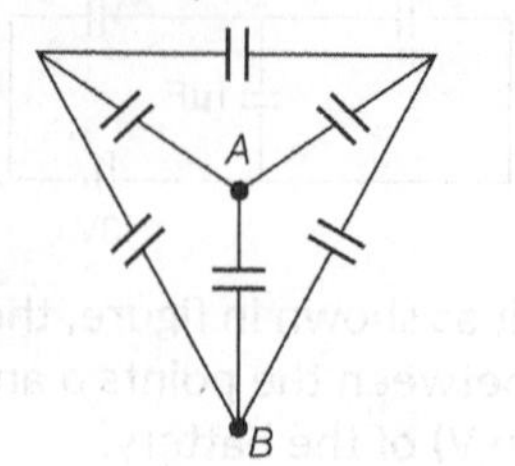

LEVEL 03 JEE Advanced Level

Single Choice Correct Questions

1 A capacitor has square plates, each of side l making an angle of θ with each other as shown in figure. The capacitance of the arrangement for small θ is

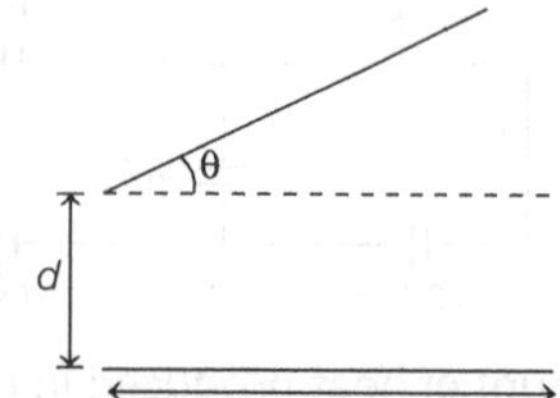

(a) $\frac{\varepsilon_0 l^2}{2d}\left(1+\frac{\theta l}{d}\right)$ (b) $\frac{\varepsilon_0 l^2}{d}\left(1+\frac{\theta l}{2d}\right)$

(c) $\frac{\varepsilon_0 l^2}{2d}\left(1-\frac{\theta l}{d}\right)$ (d) $\frac{\varepsilon_0 l^2}{d}\left(1-\frac{\theta l}{2d}\right)$

2 An air filled parallel plate capacitor with the plate area A is connected to a battery with an emf E and small internal resistance. One of the plates vibrates, so that the distance between plates varies as $d = d_0 + a\cos\omega t (a << d_0)$. The capacitor breaks down when the instantaneous current in the circuit reaches the value I. Maximum possible amplitude of vibration a is

(a) $\frac{Id_0^2}{EA\omega\varepsilon_0}$ (b) $\frac{Id_0^2}{2EA\omega\varepsilon_0}$

(c) $\frac{IA}{2Ed_0^2\omega\varepsilon_0}$ (d) $\frac{IA}{Ed_0^2\omega\varepsilon_0}$

3 The gap between the plates of a parallel plate capacitor is filled with glass of resistivity ρ. The capacitance of the capacitor without the glass equals C. The leakage current of the capacitor when a voltage V is applied to it is

(a) $\frac{V\rho}{C\varepsilon_0}$ (b) $\frac{CV}{\rho\varepsilon_0}$ (c) $\frac{V\varepsilon_0}{C\rho}$ (d) $\frac{CV\rho}{\varepsilon_0}$

4 The left plate of the capacitor shown in the figure above carries a charge +Q while the right plate is uncharged at $t = 0$. The total charge on the right plate after closing the switch will be

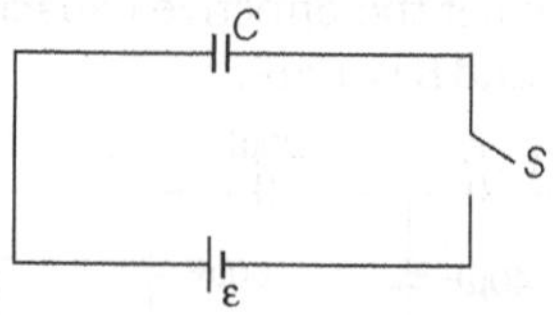

(a) $\frac{Q}{2} + C\varepsilon$ (b) $\frac{Q}{2} - C\varepsilon$

(c) $-\frac{Q}{2}$ (d) $-C\varepsilon$

5 Find the potential difference across point a and b as shown in figure.

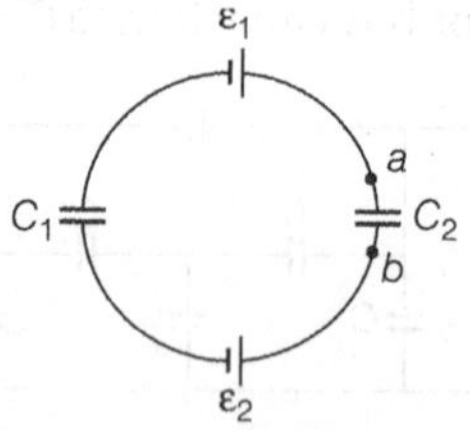

(a) $\left(\frac{\varepsilon_1+\varepsilon_2}{C_1+C_2}\right)C_1$ (b) $\left(\frac{\varepsilon_1+\varepsilon_2}{C_1+C_2}\right)C_2$

(c) $\left(\frac{\varepsilon_1-\varepsilon_2}{C_1+C_2}\right)C_1$ (d) $\left(\frac{\varepsilon_1-\varepsilon_2}{C_1+C_2}\right)C_2$

6 Three capacitors of 2μF, 3μF and 5μF are independently charged with batteries of emf's 5V, 20V and 10V, respectively. After disconnecting from the voltage sources, these capacitors are connected as shown in figure with their positive polarity plates connected to A and negative polarity is earthed. Now, a battery of 20V and an uncharged capacitor of 4μF capacitance are connected to the junction A as shown with a switch S. When switch is closed, the potential of the junction A is

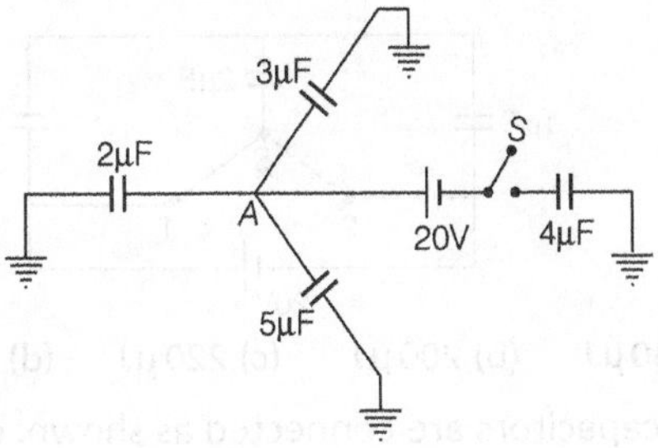

(a) $\frac{50}{7}$ V (b) $\frac{100}{7}$ V (c) $\frac{150}{7}$ V (d) $\frac{200}{7}$ V

7 In the given circuit, find the potential at point O.

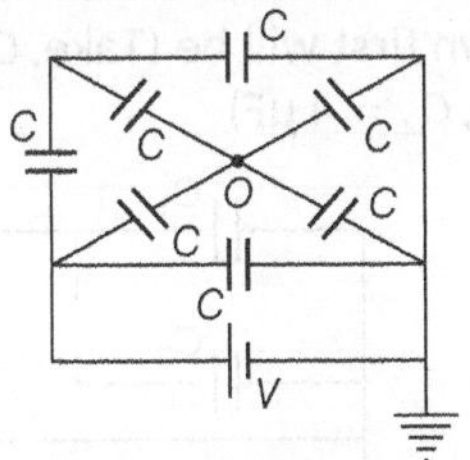

(a) $\frac{4V}{11}$ (b) $\frac{3V}{11}$

(c) $\frac{9V}{11}$ (d) None of these

8 Calculate the potential difference between the points a and b of the circuit shown.

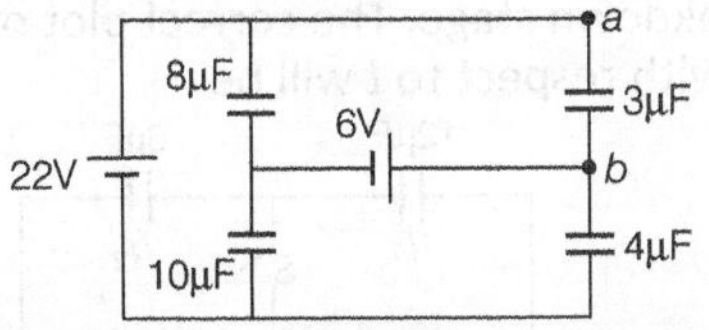

(a) 5 V (b) 7 V (c) 8 V (d) 14 V

9 Find the amount by which the total energy stored in the capacitors will increase in the circuit shown in the figure after switch K is closed. (Take, $C = 3\mu F$ and $V = 10$ V)

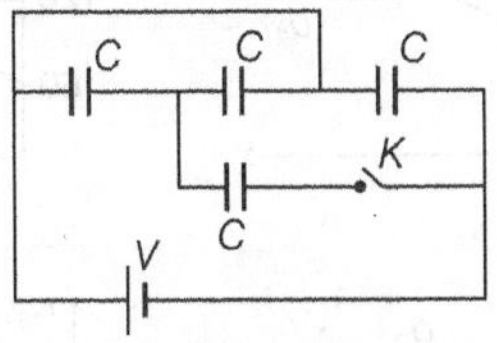

(a) 50 μJ (b) 100 μJ

(c) 150 μJ (d) 200 μJ

10 In the circuit shown, the potential of the topmost wire is maintained at 100 V and the lowermost wire is grounded. After closing the switch, the charge that flows through the switch is q_1 and the charge that flows into the earth is q_2. The ratio of $\left|\frac{q_1}{q_2}\right|$ is

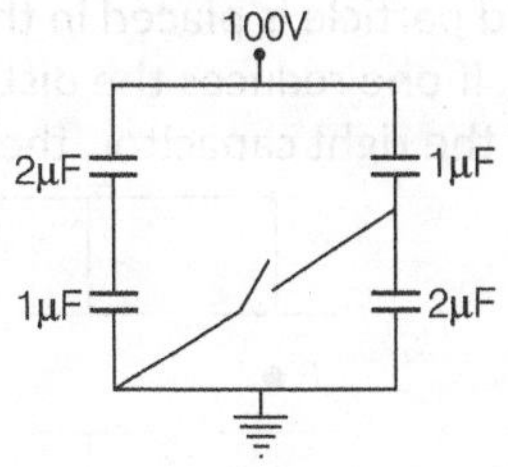

(a) 2 (b) 3 (c) 4 (d) 6

11 The charge which flows from point A to B, when switch is closed is

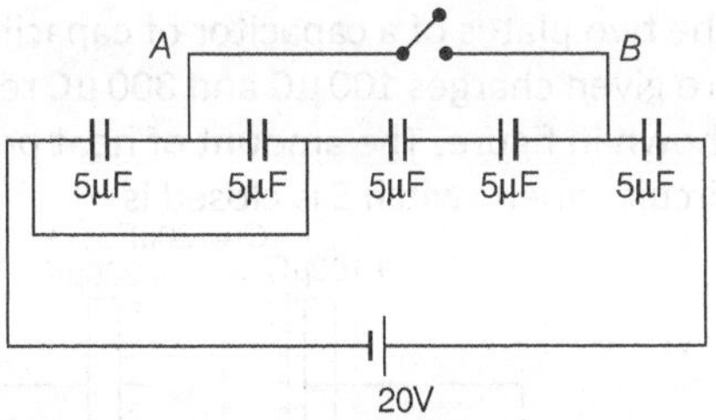

(a) $+\frac{300}{7}$ μC (b) $-\frac{300}{7}$ μC

(c) $+\frac{400}{7}$ μC (d) $-\frac{400}{7}$ μC

12 In the circuit shown, what charge will flow through the switch after it is closed. The switch was initially open since a long time. All capacitors have capacitances = 2μF and all cells have emf =10 V.

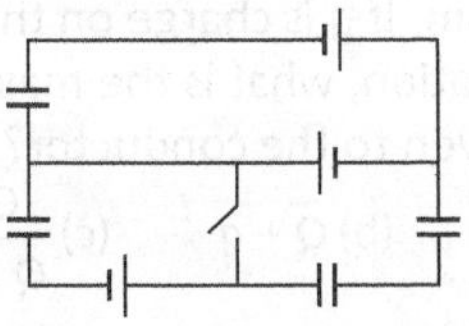

(a) 4 μC (b) 5 μC

(c) 8 μC (d) 10 μC

13 In the following circuit composed of identical capacitors, across which terminals would you connect a battery in order for all capacitors to charge up?

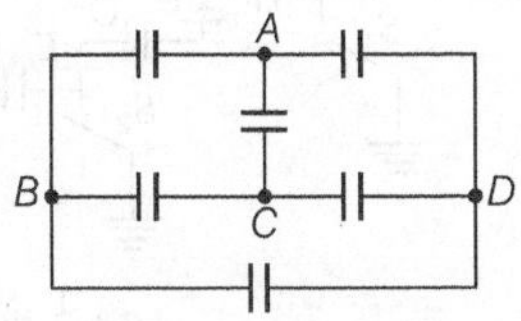

(a) AB (b) AC

(c) BD (d) None of these

14 Two parallel plate capacitors are placed horizontally and connected to a battery E as shown in figure. After charging the capacitors, the switch K is opened. A charged particle is placed in the left capacitor and is at rest. If one reduces the distance between the plates of the right capacitor, the particle will move

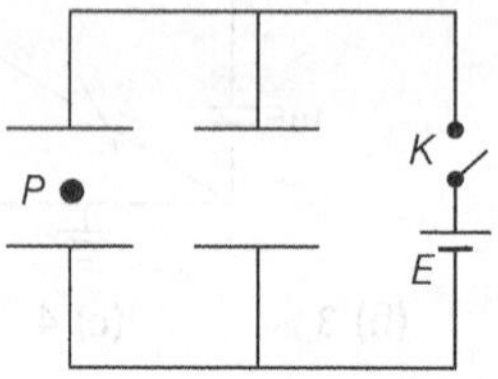

(a) horizontally (b) upwards
(c) downwards (d) in circle

15 The two plates of a capacitor of capacitance 20 μF are given charges 100 μC and 300 μC respectively as shown in figure. The amount of heat produced in the circuit, when switch S is closed is

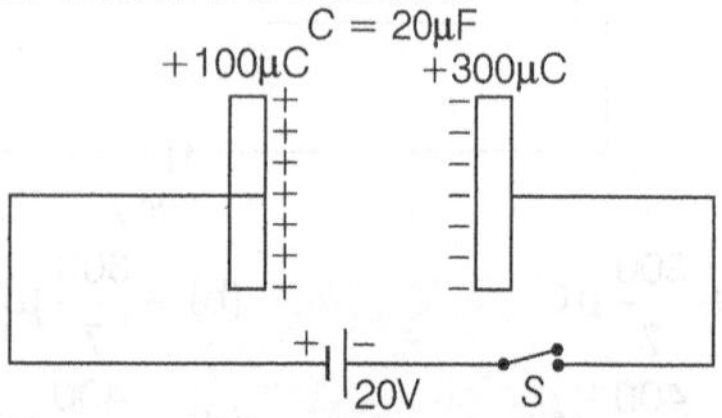

(a) 4.25 mJ (b) 6.75 mJ
(c) 6.25 mJ (d) 8.75 mJ

16 An insulated conductor initially free from charge is charged by repeated contacts with a plate which after each contact has a charge Q due to some mechanism. If q is charge on the conductor after the first operation, what is the maximum charge which can be given to the conductor?

(a) Q (b) $Q+q$ (c) $\frac{Qq}{Q+q}$ (d) $\frac{Qq}{Q-q}$

17 In the given circuit, all the capacitors are initially uncharged. After closing the switch S_1 for a long time, suddenly S_2 is also closed and kept closed for a long time. Total heat produced after closing S_2 will be

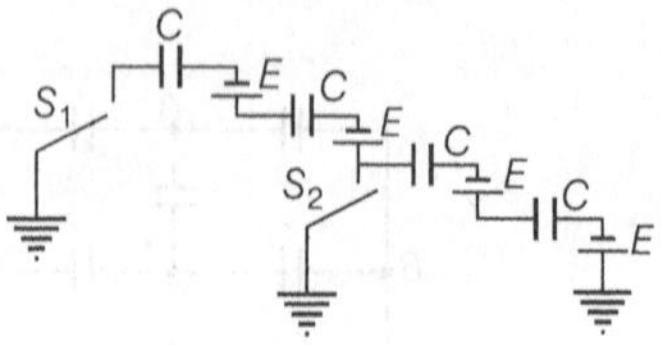

(a) $4\,CE^2$ (b) $\frac{1}{2}CE^2$
(c) $2\,CE^2$ (d) 0

18 The amount of heat liberated when the switch S is shifted from position 1 to 2 is

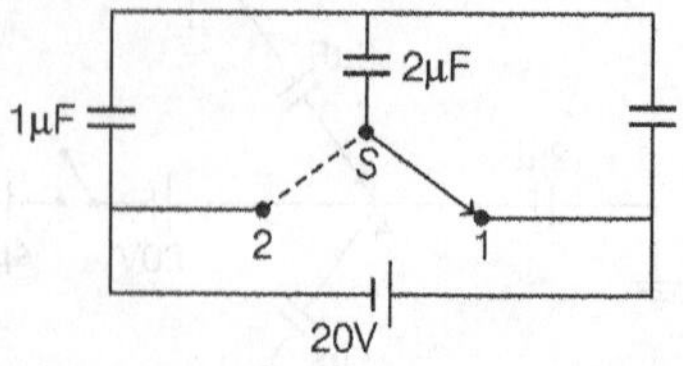

(a) 180 μJ (b) 200 μJ (c) 220 μJ (d) 210 μJ

19 Four capacitors are connected as shown, connected with a battery. Breakdown voltages of each capacitor C_1, C_2, C_3 and C_4 are 60V, 50V, 90V and 150V, respectively. If potential difference of battery is increased from zero, then the capacitor which will breakdown first will be (Take, $C_1 = 1\mu F$, $C_2 = 2\,\mu F$, $C_3 = 3\,\mu F$, $C_4 = 4\,\mu F$)

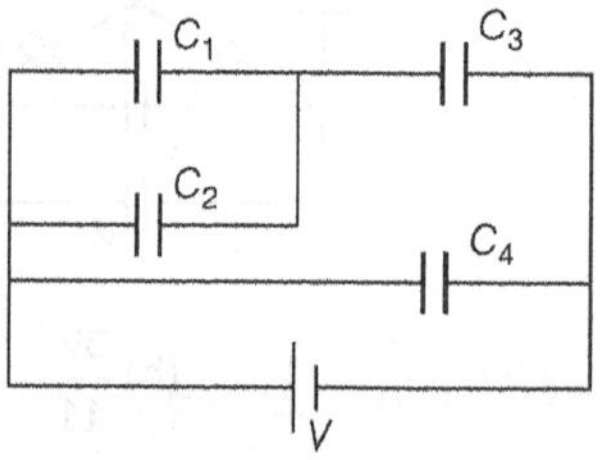

(a) C_1 (b) C_2 (c) C_3 (d) C_4

20 In the figure, switch S is closed and steady state is reached. Now at $t = 0$, voltage V_2 is increased according to equation $V = t + 10$; upto the breakdown stage. The correct plot of charges q_1 and q_2 with respect to t will be

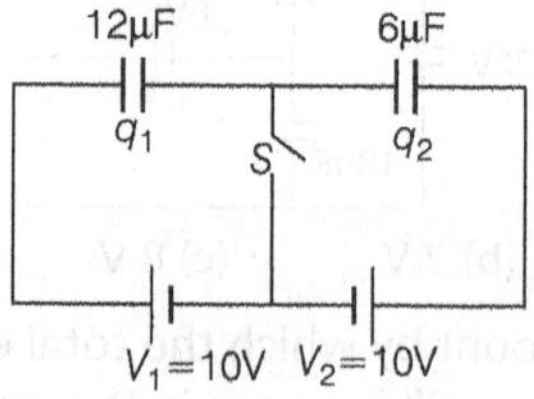

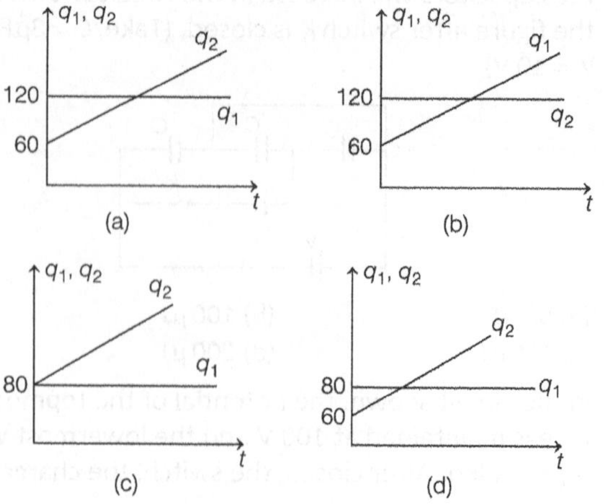

21 A capacitor of capacitance C_0 is charged to a voltage V_0 and then isolated. A capacitor C is then charged from C_0, discharged and charged again; the process is repeated n times. Due to this, potential of the C_0 is decreased to V, then value of C is

(a) $C_0(V_0/V)^{1/n}$ (b) $C_0[(V_0/V)^{1/n}-1]$
(c) $C_0[(V_0/V)-1]$ (d) $C_0[(V/V_0)^n+1]$

22 A parallel plate capacitor of capacitance 200 μF is charged by a battery of emf 100V. The battery is now disconnected and temperature of the plates is equal to atmospheric temperature. The plates are now connected by a thin wire of negligible heat capacity. Assume, 50% of their stored energy increases their temperature till the capacitor gets completely discharged and energy equally distributes over the plates. If thermal capacity of each plate is 0.5 JK^{-1} and coefficient of linear expansion is $2\times10^{-5}\,°C^{-1}$, percentage increase in the volume of the plates is

(a) 0.001% (b) 0.002% (c) 0.003% (d) 0.004%

23 Two parallel plate capacitors with area A are connected through a conducting spring of natural length l in series as shown in figure. Plates P and S have fixed positions at separation d. Now, the plates are connected by a battery of emf ε.

If the extension in the spring in equilibrium is equal to the separation between the plates, find the value of spring constant k.

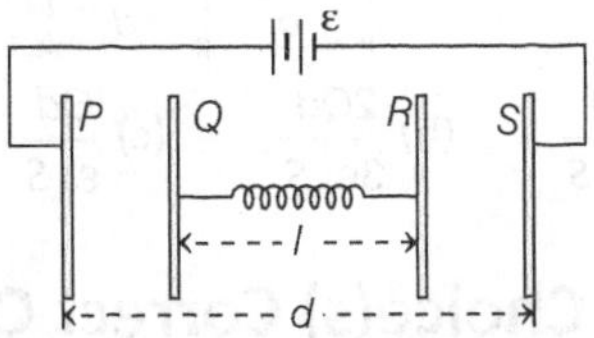

(a) $\dfrac{27}{8}\dfrac{A\varepsilon_0\varepsilon^2}{(d-l)^3}$ (b) $\dfrac{27}{16}\dfrac{A\varepsilon_0\varepsilon^2}{(d-l)^3}$
(c) $\dfrac{8}{27}\dfrac{A\varepsilon_0\varepsilon^2}{(d-l)^3}$ (d) $\dfrac{16}{27}\dfrac{A\varepsilon_0\varepsilon^2}{(d-l)^3}$

24 Conducting plates each are placed face-to-face and equi-spaced at distance d. Area of each plate is half of the previous plate. If area of first plate is A, then the equivalent capacitance of the system shown is

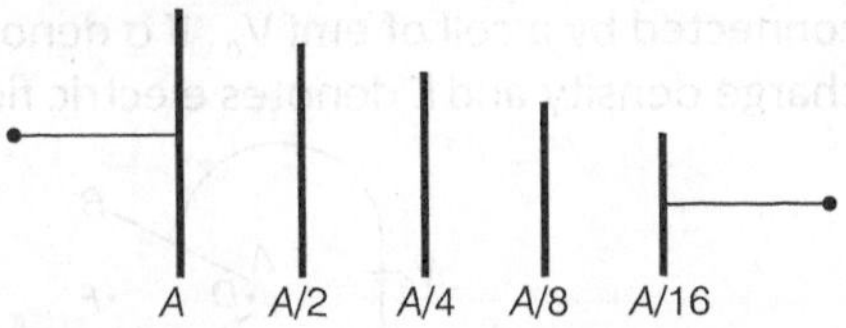

(a) $\dfrac{A\varepsilon_0}{d}$ (b) $\dfrac{A\varepsilon_0}{10d}$ (c) $\dfrac{A\varepsilon_0}{20d}$ (d) $\dfrac{A\varepsilon_0}{30d}$

25 What is the equivalent capacitance across the battery?

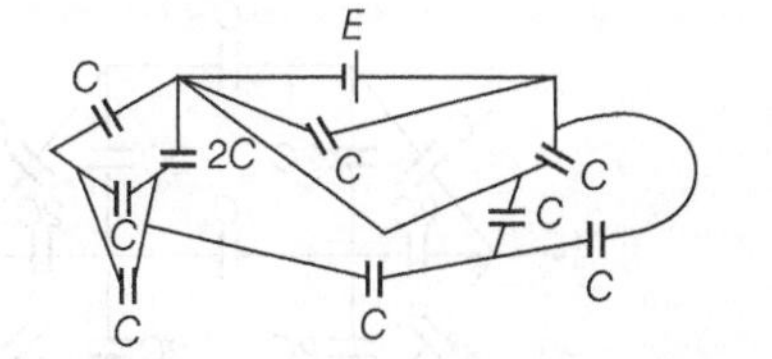

(a) $\dfrac{79}{30}C$ (b) $\dfrac{59}{30}C$ (c) $\dfrac{41}{30}C$ (d) $\dfrac{21}{30}C$

26 Find the equivalent capacitance of the circuit between point A and B.

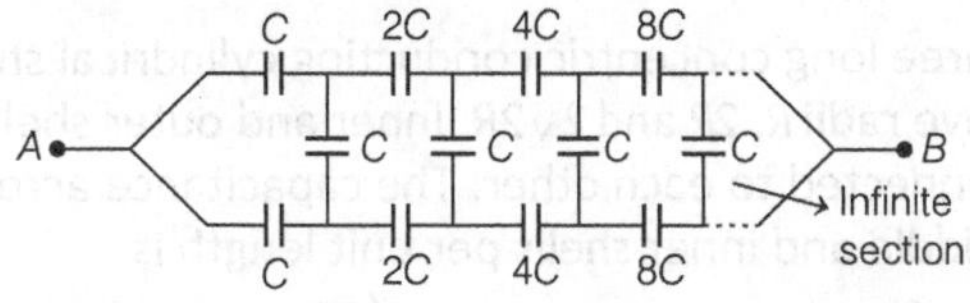

(a) C (b) $2C$ (c) $\dfrac{C}{2}$ (d) $\dfrac{C}{4}$

27 Find the equivalent capacitance of the combination shown in the figure. Each capacitor is of capacitance $C = 15\,\mu F$.

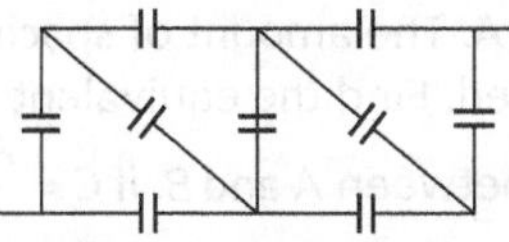

(a) 7 μF (b) 11 μF (c) 13 μF (d) 19 μF

28 A finite ladder is constructed by connecting several sections of 2 μF and 4 μF capacitor combinations as shown in the figure. It is terminated by a capacitor of capacitance C. What value should be chosen for C, such that equivalent capacitance of the ladder between the point A and B becomes independent of the number of sections in between?

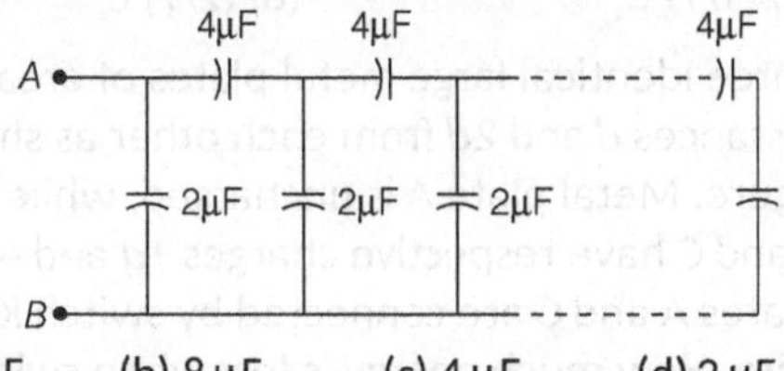

(a) 16 μF (b) 8 μF (c) 4 μF (d) 2 μF

29 The potential difference between the points A and B and that between E and F of the circuit shown in figure, respectively are

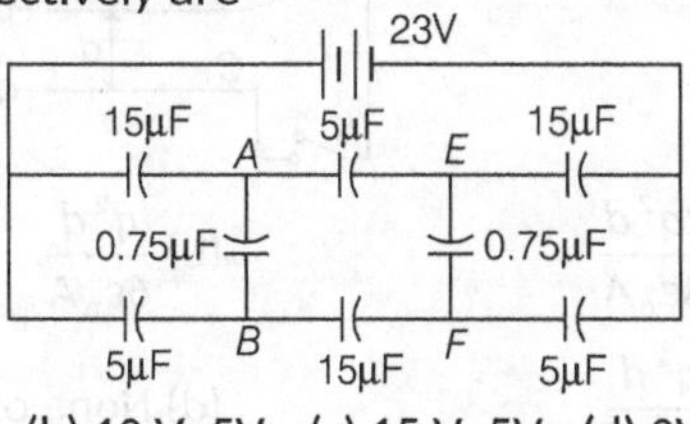

(a) 5V, 5V (b) 10 V, 5V (c) 15 V, 5V (d) 0V, 0V

30 Find equivalent capacitance between A and B.

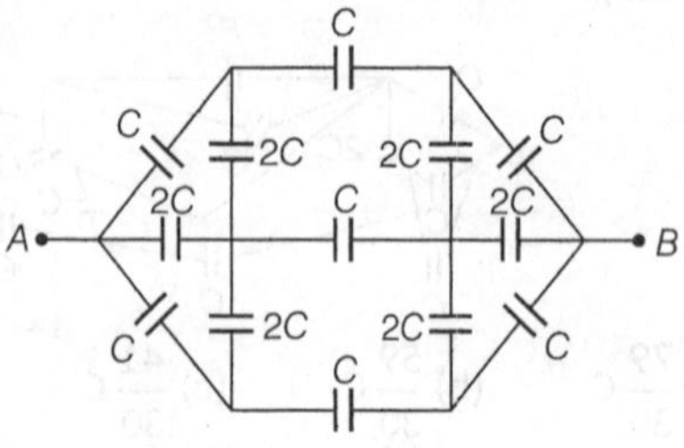

(a) $\frac{9C}{8}$ (b) $\frac{11C}{8}$ (c) $\frac{13C}{16}$ (d) $\frac{19C}{16}$

31 Three long concentric conducting cylindrical shells have radii R, $2R$ and $2\sqrt{2}R$. Inner and outer shells are connected to each other. The capacitance across middle and inner shells per unit length is

(a) $\frac{\varepsilon_0}{3\ln 2}$ (b) $\frac{6\pi\varepsilon_0}{\ln 2}$

(c) $\frac{\pi\varepsilon_0}{2\ln 2}$ (d) None of these

32 In the arrangement shown, all plates have equal area equal to A. The amount of spacing between plates is mentioned. Find the equivalent capacitance of the system between A and B, if $C = \frac{A\varepsilon_0}{L}$.

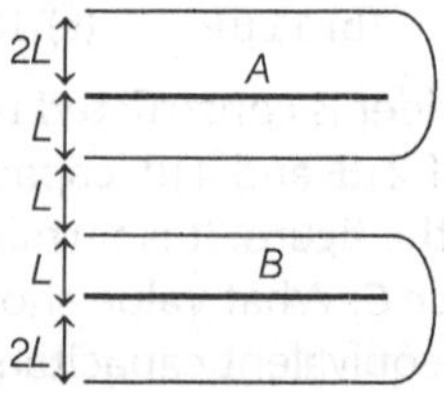

(a) (5/7) C (b) (3/7) C

(c) (1/7) C (d) (2/7) C

33 Three identical large metal plates of area A are at distances d and $2d$ from each other as shown in figure. Metal plate A is uncharged, while metal plates B and C have respective charges $+q$ and $-q$. Metal plates A and C are connected by switch K through a wire. How much energy is lost when switch is closed?

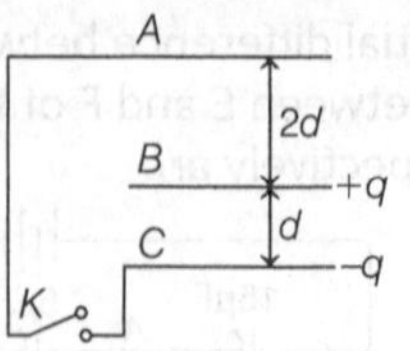

(a) $\frac{2q^2d}{3\varepsilon_0 A}$ (b) $\frac{q^2d}{6\varepsilon_0 A}$

(c) $\frac{q^2d}{3\varepsilon_0 A}$ (d) None of these

34 Consider a system of four identical uncharged infinite metal plates marked P, Q, R and S arranged as shown in figure. The key is now closed, what is potential difference between plates Q and S in steady state?

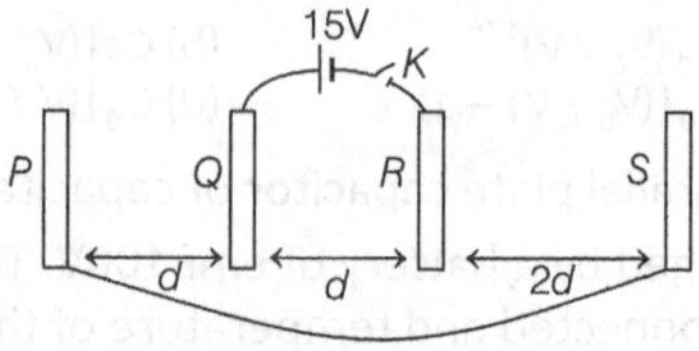

(a) 5 V (b) 8 V (c) 10 V (d) 12 V

35 Four identical large metal plates are arranged parallel to each other, with equal gaps in between. They are given charges q, $2q$, $3q$ and $4q$ (counting from any one side). The outermost plates are now shorted, the charge which flows through the shorting wire is

(a) $\frac{4q}{3}$ (b) $\frac{3q}{4}$ (c) $\frac{5q}{3}$ (d) None of these

36 Four parallel large plates separated by equal distance d are arranged as shown in figure. The area of the plate is S. Find the potential difference between the plates B and C, if the plate B is given charge Q.

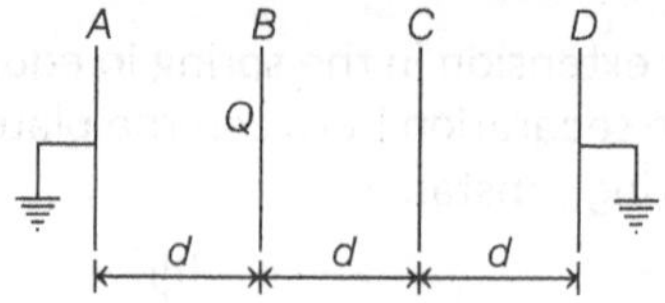

(a) $\frac{Qd}{3\varepsilon_0 S}$ (b) $\frac{2Qd}{3\varepsilon_0 S}$ (c) $\frac{Qd}{\varepsilon_0 S}$ (d) $\frac{2Qd}{\varepsilon_0 S}$

Multiple Choice(s) Correct Questions

1 A parallel plate capacitor is connected to a battery. If the distance between the plates is decreased,

(a) the charge on plates increases

(b) the electric field between the plates increases

(c) the potential difference between the plates increases

(d) force of attraction between the plates increases

2 In the given figure, a capacitor of non-parallel plates is as shown in figure. The plates of capacitor are connected by a cell of emf V_0. If σ denotes surface charge density and E denotes electric field, then

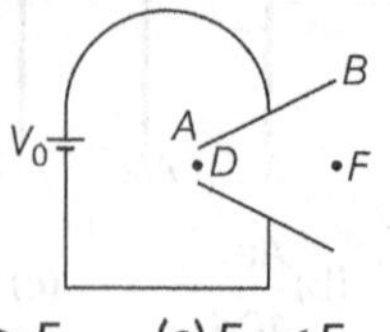

(a) $\sigma_A > \sigma_B$ (b) $E_F > E_D$ (c) $E_F < E_D$ (d) $\sigma_A < \sigma_B$

3 Rows of capacitors containing 1,2,4,8, ... ∞ capacitors, each of capacitance 2 μF, are connected in parallel as shown in figure. The potential difference across $AB = 10$ V, then

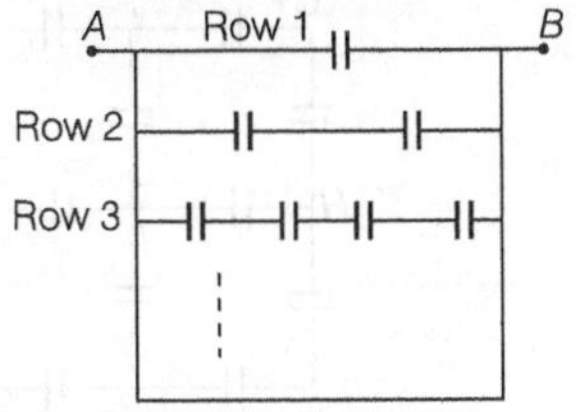

(a) total capacitance across AB is 4 μF
(b) charge on each capacitor will be same
(c) charge on the capacitor in the first row is more than on any other capacitor
(d) energy of all the capacitors is 100 μJ

4 In the circuit shown, in steady state

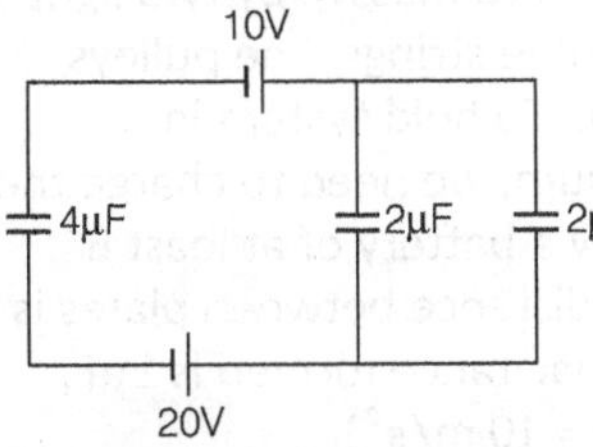

(a) charge on 4μF capacitor is 20μC
(b) charge on 2μF capacitor is 20μC
(c) the potential difference across 4μF capacitor is 5 V
(d) the potential difference across 4μF capacitor is 10 V

5 In the circuit diagram shown below,

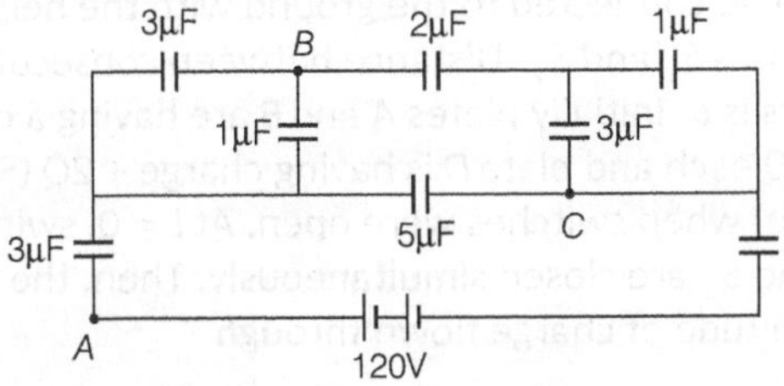

(a) the energy stored in all the capacitors is 7.2 mJ
(b) energy stored in 5μF capacitor is 1 mJ
(c) the potential difference between A and B is 45 V
(d) the potential difference between B and C is 15 V

6 Two identical plates P_1 and P_2 of cross-sectional area A are separated at a very small distance d, where $\frac{A\varepsilon_0}{d} = 2$ SI unit. Initially, charge on the plate P_1 is -10 C and charge on the plate P_2 is $+30$ C. Now, plates P_1 and P_2 are connected to positive and negative terminals of battery of potential difference 10 V with the help of switches S_1 and S_2, respectively. Choose the correct option(s).

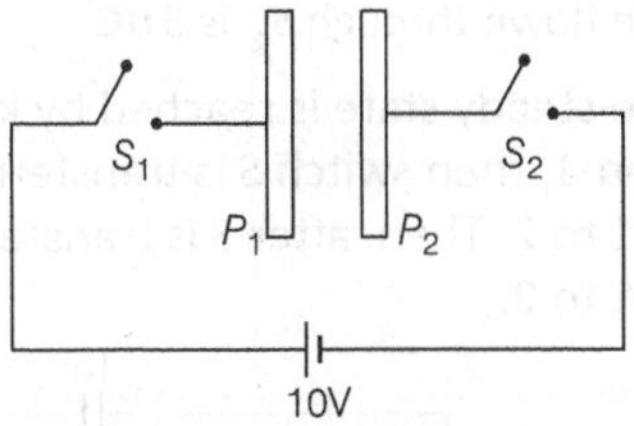

(a) The work done by the battery is 400 J.
(b) The net charge on the plate P_2 is -10C.
(c) The charge on the left side of the plate P_1 is 10C.
(d) Heat produced in the circuit is 200 J.

7 Two capacitors of capacitances 1μ F and 3μF are charged to the same voltages 5V. They are connected in parallel with oppositely charged plates connected together, then
(a) final common voltage will be 5V
(b) final common voltage will be 2.5 V
(c) heat produced in the circuit will be zero
(d) heat produced in the circuit will be 37.5 μJ

8 Negative plate of a 2 μF capacitor charged to 150 V is connected to the oppositely charged plate of 3 μF capacitor charged to 120 V. The other plates of each capacitor are connected to free wires. An uncharged capacitor of 1.5 μF is dropped on to free ends as shown in figure. After steady state, select the correct statements.

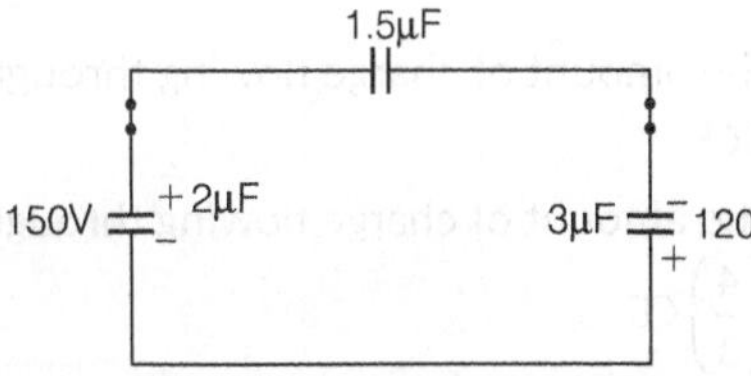

(a) Potential drop across 2 μF capacitor is 60V.
(b) Potential drop across 1.5 μF capacitor is 120 V.
(c) Potential drop across each capacitor is 90V.
(d) Charge on 3 μF capacitor is 180 μC .

9 Three capacitors $C_1 = 2\mu F$, $C_2 = 2\mu F$ and $C_3 = 3\mu F$ having initial charges 4 μC, zero and 1μC connected through a battery of emf 2V as shown in figure. On closing the switches S_1 and S_2,

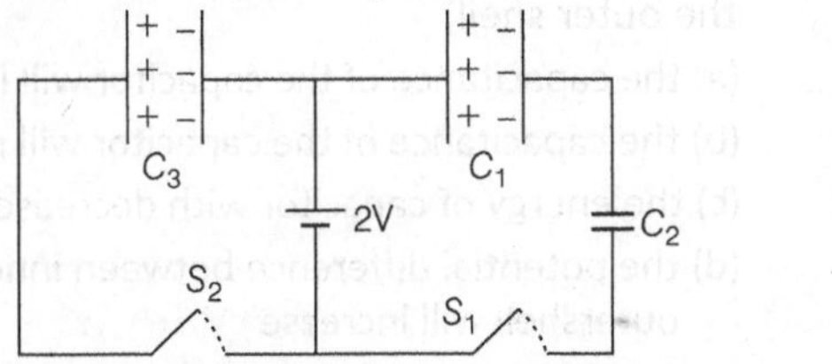

(a) charge on capacitor C_1 is $4\,\mu C$
(b) charge on capacitor C_2 is 0
(c) charge on capacitor C_3 is $6\,\mu C$
(d) charge flown through S_2 is $5\,\mu C$

10 When the steady state is reached by keeping switch in position-1, then switch S is transferred from position 1 to 2. Then, after S is transferred from position 1 to 2,

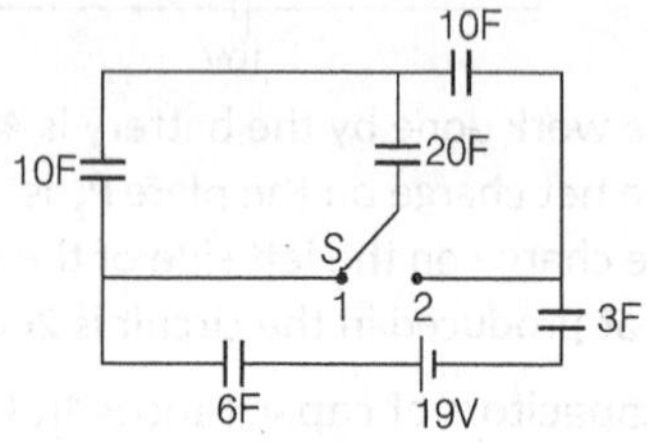

(a) charge on 3F capacitor is 30 C
(b) charge on 3F capacitor is (650/19) C
(c) work done by the battery is 380 J
(d) work done by the battery is 80 J

11 In the circuit shown in figure, each capacitor has a capacitance C. The emf of the cell is E and circuit already in steady state. If the switch S is closed,

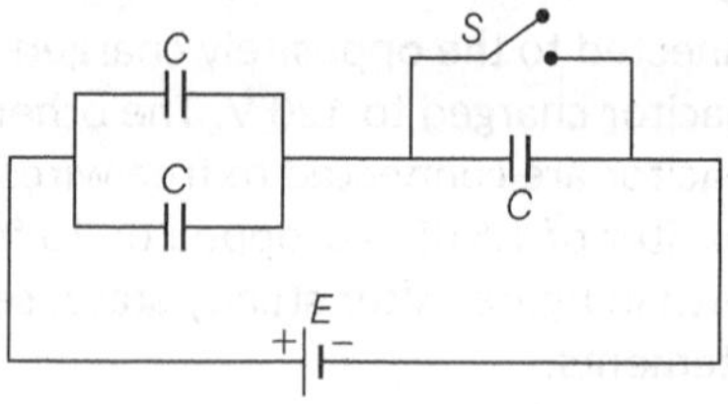

(a) the amount of charge flowing through the switch is $2CE$
(b) the amount of charge flowing through the cell is $\left(\frac{4}{3}\right)CE$
(c) heat produced in the circuit is $2CE^2$
(d) heat produced in the circuit is $\left(\frac{2}{3}\right)CE^2$

12 In a spherical capacitor, we have two concentric spherical shells, the inner one carrying a charge Q and outer one carrying a charge of $-Q$. If the inner shell is displaced from the centre without touching the outer shell,
(a) the capacitance of the capacitor will increase
(b) the capacitance of the capacitor will remain same
(c) the energy of capacitor with decrease
(d) the potential difference between inner and outershell will increase

13 Consider capacitance circuit consisting 12 identical capacitors each of capacitance 1μF as shown in the figure. The equivalent capacitance between the terminals

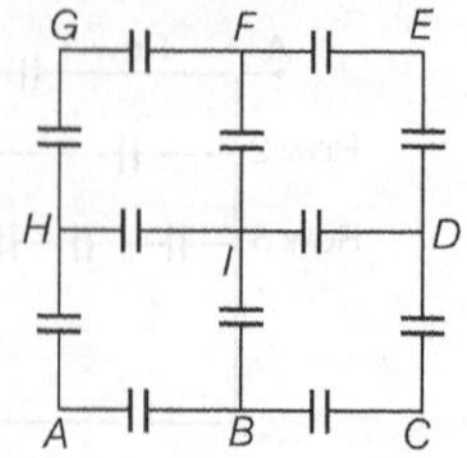

(a) A and E is $\frac{2}{3}\,\mu F$
(b) A and I is $\frac{8}{7}\,\mu F$
(c) H and I is $\frac{12}{7}\,\mu F$
(d) H and B is $\frac{5}{7}\,\mu F$

14 Two plates of mass m each are connected to mass M by two light inextensible strings. The pulleys are ideal. To hold system in equilibrium, we need to charge the plates by a battery of at least 8 volts. If distance between plates is 1μm, capacitance formed is 1 μF, then $(g = 10\text{ m/s}^2)$

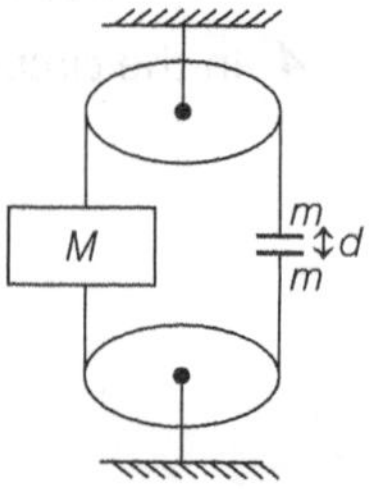

(a) $M = 12.8$ kg
(b) $m = 3.2$ kg
(c) $M = 6.4$ kg
(d) $m = 1.6$ kg

15 There is a system of four conducting parallel plates A, B, C and D. Plates A and C are connected to each other with the help of metallic wire and plates B and D can be connected to the ground with the help of switches S_1 and S_2. Distance between consecutive plates is d. Initially plates A and B are having a charge of $+Q$ each and plate D is having charge $+2Q$ (See figure) when switches were open. At $t = 0$, switches S_1 and S_2 are closed simultaneously. Then, the magnitude of charge flown through

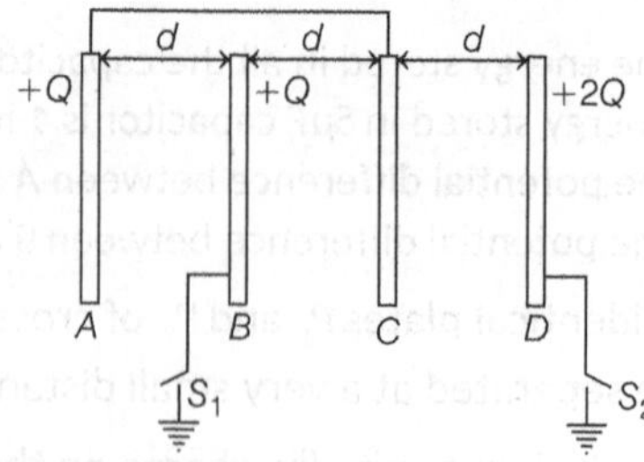

(a) S_1 is $5Q/3$
(b) S_1 is Q
(c) S_2 is $7Q/3$
(d) S_2 is $2Q$

16 Figure shows an arrangement of four identical rectangular plates A, B, C and D each of area S. Plates A and C are given charges Q_1 and Q_2, respectively. Ignore the separation between the plates in comparison to the plate dimensions.

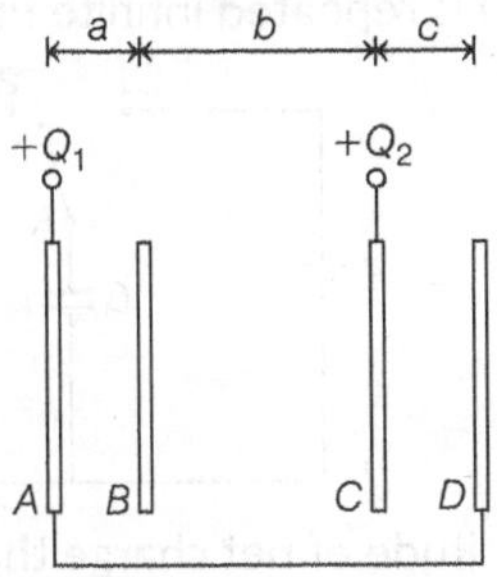

(a) Potential difference between plates A and B is independent of Q_1.

(b) Potential difference between plates C and D is independent of Q_1.

(c) Potential difference between plates A and B is independent of Q_2.

(d) Potential difference between plates C and D is independent of Q_2.

17 Two fixed very large conducting plates A and B of area S carry charges $-Q$ and q respectively, where $Q > q > 0$. A third identical plate C carrying a charge Q is released at distance d from B. Third plate collides with B. Assume collision is elastic and time of collision is sufficient to re-distribute charge among B and C (Neglect gravity).

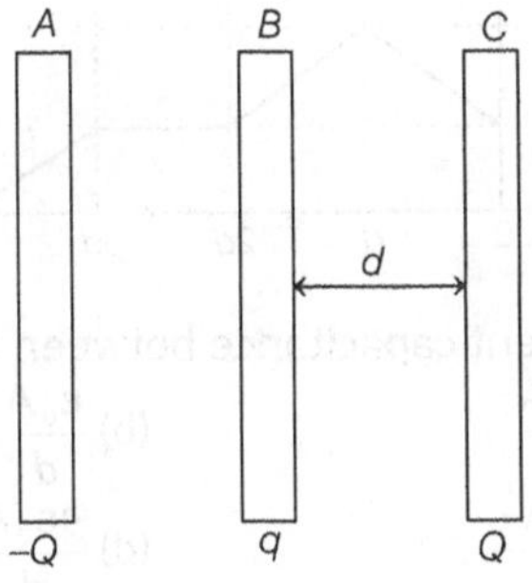

(a) Force acting on plate C before collision is $\dfrac{(Q-q)Q}{2\varepsilon_0 S}$

(b) Force acting on plate C after collision is $\dfrac{(q/2)^2}{2\varepsilon_0 S}$

(c) Subsequent to collision, kinetic energy of plate C increases

(d) Subsequent to collision, electric field between the plates B and C is zero

Comprehension Based Questions

Comprehension-1

Two conductors carry charges $+Q$ and $-Q$. They create a non-uniform electric field as shown in figure. A coordinate system is placed on the positive conductor, and the electric field strength along the X-axis is found to vary according to the function $E = \dfrac{\beta Q}{\varepsilon_0}\left(1 + \dfrac{x^2}{d^2}\right)$, where β is a constant and d is the least distance the conductors, answer the following equations.

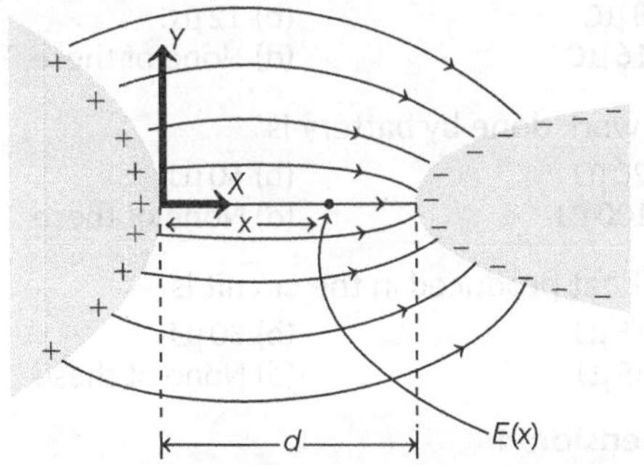

1 The potential difference between the conductors is

(a) $\dfrac{\beta Qd}{3\varepsilon_0}$ (b) $\dfrac{3\beta Qd}{2\varepsilon_0}$ (c) $\dfrac{4\beta Qd}{3\varepsilon_0}$ (d) None of these

2 The capacitance of the system is

(a) $\dfrac{3\varepsilon_0}{\beta d}$ (b) $\dfrac{2\varepsilon_0}{3\beta d}$

(c) $\dfrac{3\varepsilon_0}{4\beta d}$ (d) None of these

Comprehension-2

In the circuit shown in figure, five capacitors are connected to a battery.

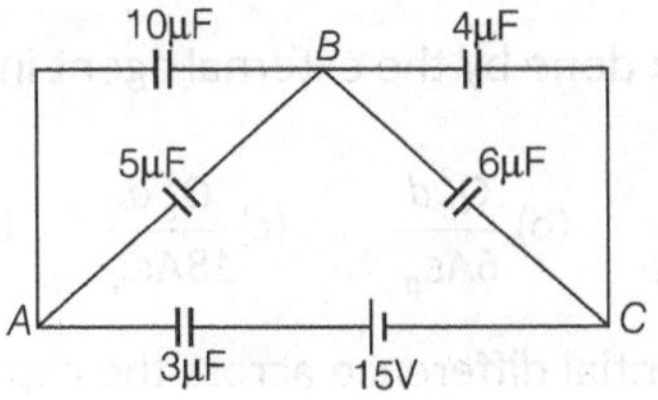

3 The charge on the 6 μF capacitor is

(a) 10μC (b) 12 μC (c) 18 μC (d) 24 μC

4 The potential difference across the 5 μF capacitor is

(a) 2 V (b) 3 V (c) 5 V (d) 10 V

5 The minimum energy is stored in the capacitor of

(a) 3 μF (b) 6 μF (c) 5 μF (d) 4 μF

Comprehension-3

Following figure shows the initial charges on the capacitor. After the switch S is closed,

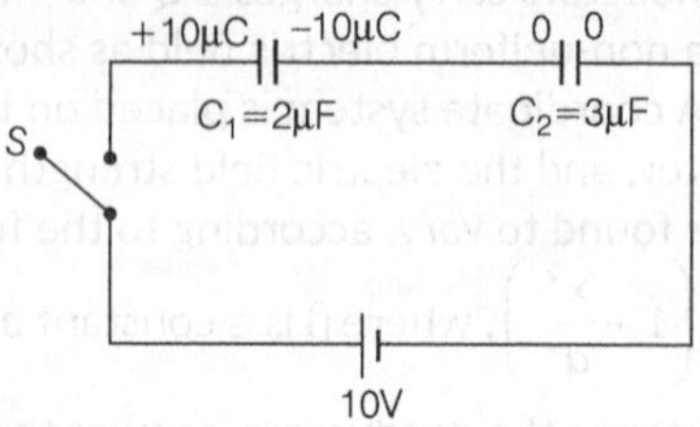

6 the charge on capacitor C_1 is

(a) 8 μC (b) 12 μC
(c) 16 μC (d) None of these

7 the work done by battery is

(a) 20 μJ (b) 60 μJ
(c) 100 μJ (d) None of these

8 the heat produced in the circuit is

(a) 15 μJ (b) 30 μJ
(c) 45 μJ (d) None of these

Comprehension-4

Two capacitors each having area A and plate separation d are connected as shown in the circuit. Each capacitor carries charge $Q_0/2$. The plates of one capacitor are slowly pulled apart by an external agent till the separation between them becomes $2d$. The other capacitor is not disturbed.

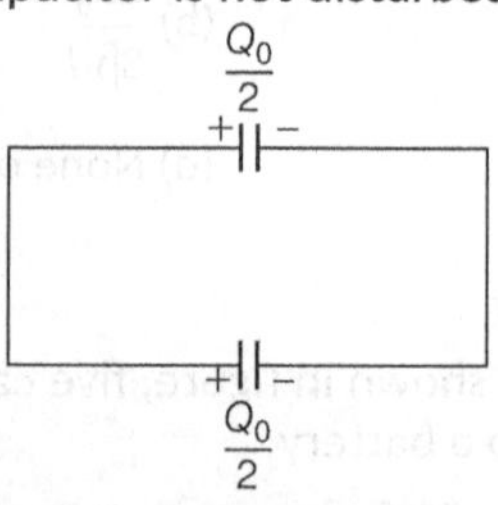

9 The work done by the external agent in this process will be

(a) $\frac{Q_0^2 d}{12A\varepsilon_0}$ (b) $\frac{Q_0^2 d}{6A\varepsilon_0}$ (c) $\frac{Q_0^2 d}{18A\varepsilon_0}$ (d) $\frac{Q_0^2 d}{9A\varepsilon_0}$

10 The potential difference across the capacitors when the separation between the plates is x, is

(a) $\frac{Q_0 xd}{2A\varepsilon_0 (x+d)}$ (b) $\frac{Q_0 xd}{A\varepsilon_0 (x+d)}$
(c) $\frac{Q_0 xd}{4A\varepsilon_0 (x+d)}$ (d) $\frac{Q_0 d}{2A\varepsilon_0 x}$

11 Heat produced in this process will be equal to

(a) $\frac{5Q_0^2 d}{72A\varepsilon_0}$ (b) $\frac{5Q_0^2 d}{36A\varepsilon_0}$ (c) $\frac{1Q_0^2 d}{2A\varepsilon_0}$ (d) 0

Comprehension-5

A circuit consists of two capacitors of capacitance C each and ideal cell of emf E volts as shown in figure. Initially, both the capacitors are uncharged. The key is pushed to position 1 and then to position 2. This operation is repeated infinite times.

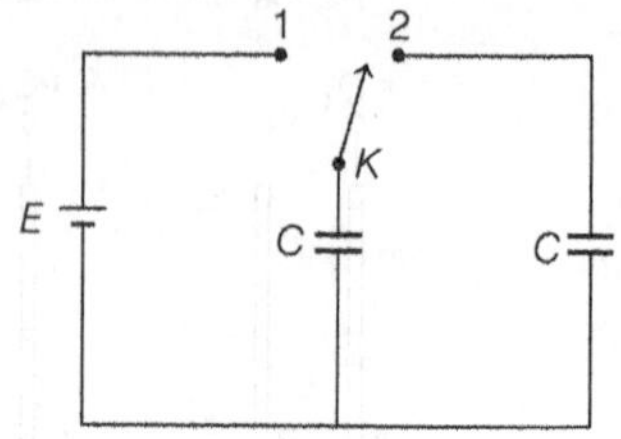

12 The magnitude of net charge that crosses the cell is

(a) CE (b) $1.5\,CE$
(c) $2\,CE$ (d) 0

13 The magnitude of net work done by the cell is

(a) CE^2 (b) $1.5\,CE^2$ (c) $2\,CE^2$ (d) 0

14 The net heat produced in the circuit is

(a) CE^2 (b) $1.5\,CE^2$ (c) $2\,CE^2$ (d) 0

Comprehension-6

The V *versus* x plot for six identical metal plates of cross-sectional area A is shown. The plates are placed with separation 'd'.

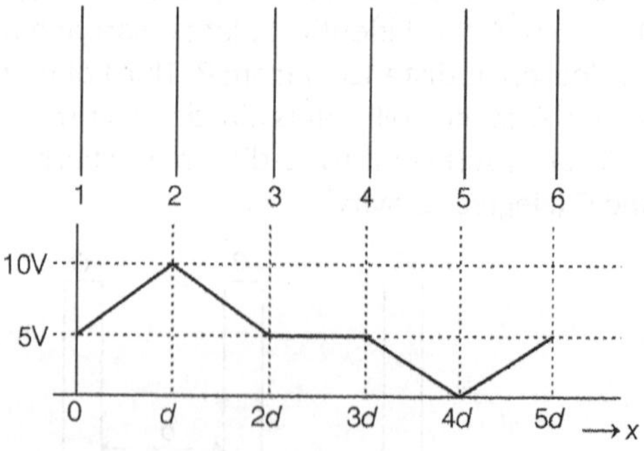

15 Equivalent capacitance between 2 and 5 is

(a) $\frac{2\varepsilon_0 A}{d}$ (b) $\frac{\varepsilon_0 A}{d}$
(c) $\frac{3\varepsilon_0 A}{d}$ (d) $\frac{4\varepsilon_0 A}{d}$

16 Total charge on plate 2 is

(a) $\frac{10\varepsilon_0 A}{d}$ (b) $\frac{5}{3}\frac{\varepsilon_0 A}{d}$
(c) $\frac{4}{3}\frac{\varepsilon_0 A}{d}$ (d) None of these

17 Ratio of charge on plate 2 to plate 5 i.e. $|Q_2 : Q_5|$, is

(a) 2 : 1 (b) 3 : 1
(c) 1 : 1 (d) None of these

Comprehension-7

A battery of voltage V and three large plates of area A are arranged as shown in diagram. Plates (1) and (3) are fixed and plate (2) is movable. Initial position of middle plates shown in Fig (1). Now, middle plate is shifted by a distance *d*/2 towards plate (3) and final position is shown in Fig.(2). Neglect external work done in process.

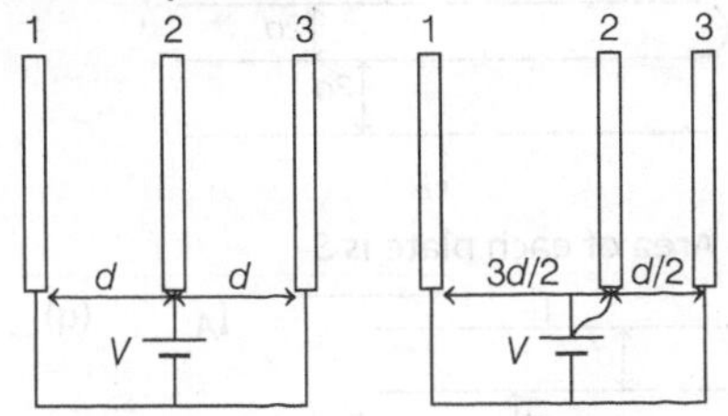

Fig. (1) Fig. (2)

18 If total charge on plate (2) initially is *x* and total charge on plate (2) finally is *y* then

(a) $x = \frac{\varepsilon_0 A}{2d} V$ (b) $x = \frac{2\varepsilon_0 A}{d} V$

(c) $y = \frac{8}{3}\frac{\varepsilon_0 A}{d} V$ (d) $y = \frac{3}{8}\frac{\varepsilon_0 A}{d} V$

19 If work done by the battery in shifting the plate (2) from initial position to final position is *x* and the amount of heat produced in doing so is *y*, then

(a) $x = \frac{2}{3}\frac{\varepsilon_0 A}{d} V^2$ (b) $x = \frac{3}{8}\frac{\varepsilon_0 A}{d} V^2$

(c) $y = \frac{\varepsilon_0 A V^2}{3d}$ (d) $y = \frac{\varepsilon_0 A V^2}{d}$

Comprehension-8

A parallel plate capacitor with air as a dielectric is arranged horizontally. The lower plate is fixed and the other connected with a vertical spring. The area of each plate is A. In the steady position, the distance between the plates is d_0. When the capacitor is connected with an electric source with the voltage *V*, a new equilibrium appears, with the distance between the plates as d_1. Mass of the upper plate is *m*.

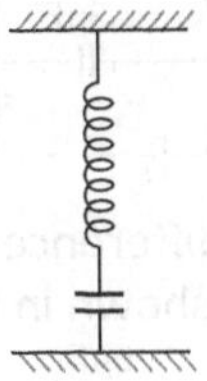

20 Spring constant *k* is

(a) $\frac{\varepsilon_0 A V^2}{(d_0 - d_1)^2 d_0}$ (b) $\frac{\varepsilon_0 A V^2}{2d_1^2 (d_0 - d_1)}$

(c) $\frac{\varepsilon_0 A V^2}{2(d_0 - d_1)^2 d_0}$ (d) $\frac{\varepsilon_0 A V^2}{3(d_0 - d_1)^2 d_0}$

21 Maximum voltage for a given *k* in which an equilibrium is possible, is

(a) $\sqrt{\frac{k}{A\varepsilon_0}\left(\frac{2}{3}d_0\right)^{3/2}}$ (b) $\sqrt{\frac{k}{2A\varepsilon_0}\left(\frac{2d_0}{3}\right)^{3/2}}$

(c) $\sqrt{\frac{2k}{A\varepsilon_0}\left(\frac{2}{3}d_0\right)^{3/2}}$ (d) $\sqrt{\frac{k}{A\varepsilon_0}\left(\frac{2d_0}{3}\right)^{1/2}}$

22 What is the angular frequency of the oscillating system around the equilibrium value d_1? (Amplitude of the oscillation << d_1)

(a) $\sqrt{\frac{k}{m}\left(\frac{2d_1 - 3d_0}{d_1}\right)}$ (b) $\sqrt{\frac{k}{m}\left(\frac{3d_1 - 2d_0}{d_1}\right)}$

(c) $\sqrt{\frac{k}{m}\left(\frac{d_1 - d_0}{d_1}\right)}$ (d) $\sqrt{\frac{k}{m}\left(\frac{2d_1 - d_0}{d_1}\right)}$

Match the Columns Questions

1 In the circuit, both capacitors are identical. Column I indicates action done on capacitor 1 and Column II indicates effect on capacitor 2.

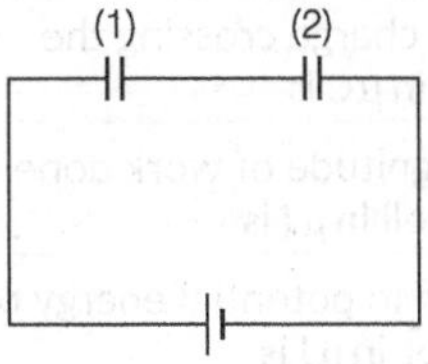

	Column I		Column II
(a)	Plates are moved further apart	(p)	Numerical value of charge on left plate increases
(b)	Area increased	(q)	Potential difference increases
(c)	Left plate is earthed	(r)	Numerical value of charge on right plate decreases
(d)	Its plates are short-circuited	(s)	None of the above effects

2 Match Column I against Column II referring to the adjacent figure.

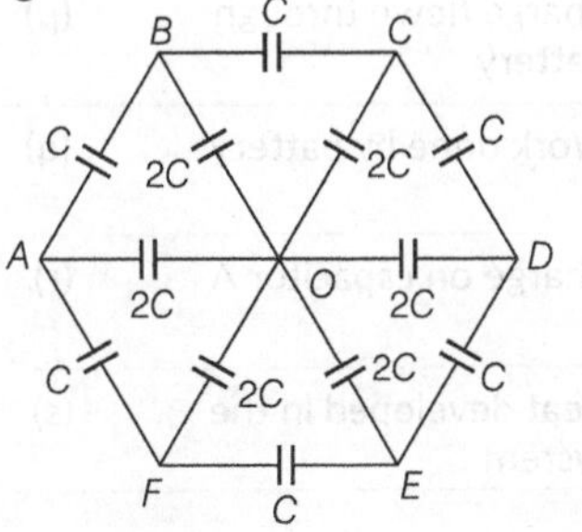

Column I		Column II
(a) Effective capacitance between A and D	(p)	$\frac{45}{13}C$
(b) Effective capacitance between F and E	(q)	$\frac{15}{8}C$
(c) Effective capacitance between A and E	(r)	$\frac{45}{19}C$
(d) Effective capacitance between A and O	(s)	$\frac{9}{5}C$

3 The circuit involves two ideal cells connected to a 1 μF capacitor *via* a key *K*. Initially the key *K* is in position 1 and the capacitor is charged fully by 2V cell.

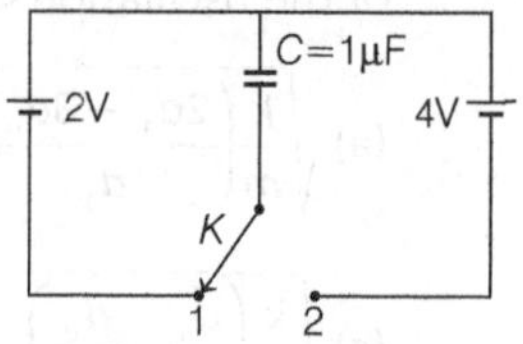

The key is then pushed to position 2. Column I gives physical quantities involving the circuit after the key is pushed from position 1 to position 2. Column II gives corresponding results. Match the statements in Column I with the corresponding values in Column II.

Column I		Column II
(a) The net charge crossing the 4 V cell in μC is	(p)	2
(b) The magnitude of work done by 4 V cell in μJ is	(q)	6
(c) The gain in potential energy of capacitor in μJ is	(r)	8
(d) The net heat produced in circuit in μJ is	(s)	16

4 Consider the situation shown. The switch *S* is open for a long time and then closed. Then, after closing *S*,

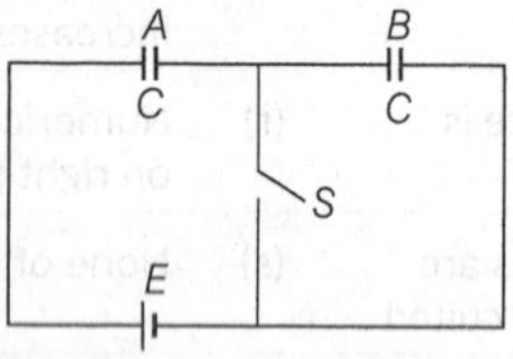

Column I		Column II
(a) Charge flown through battery	(p)	$\frac{CE^2}{2}$
(b) Work done by battery	(q)	$\frac{CE}{2}$
(c) Charge on capacitor *A*	(r)	$\frac{CE^2}{4}$
(d) Heat developed in the system	(s)	CE

5 The equivalent capacitance across *A* and *B* for the plates connected as shown in Column I, are given in Column II. Match the items in Column II with the items in Column I.

Column I		Column II
(a) 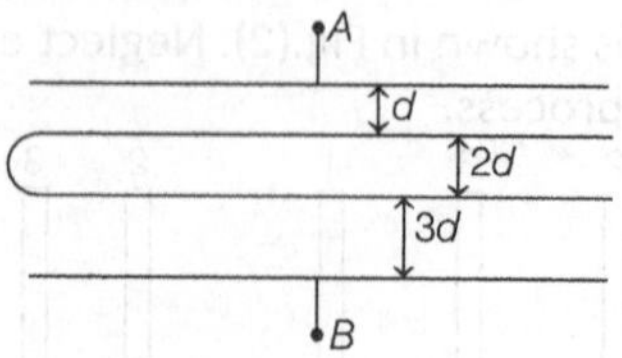 Area of each plate is *S*	(p)	$\frac{3\varepsilon_0 S}{4d}$
(b) 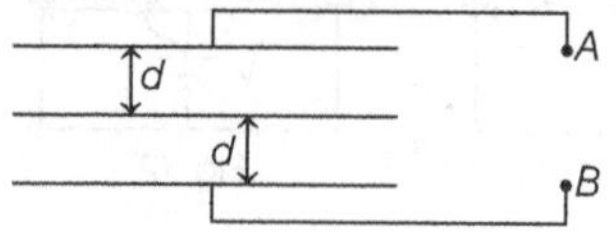 Area of each plate is *S*	(q)	$\frac{2\varepsilon_0 S}{3d}$
(c) 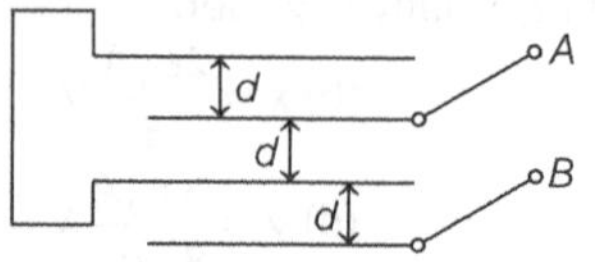 Area of each plate is *S*	(r)	$\frac{\varepsilon_0 S}{4d}$
(d) 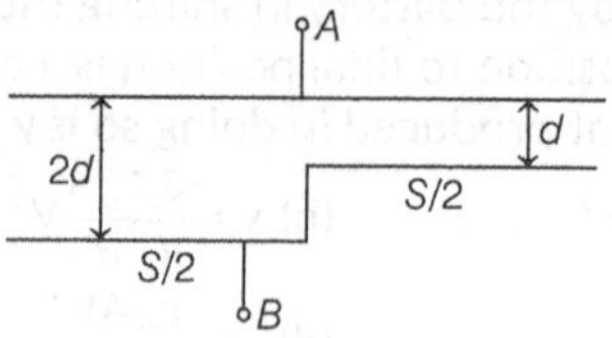 Area of upper plate is *S*	(s)	$\frac{\varepsilon_0 S}{2d}$
	(t)	$\frac{\varepsilon_0 S}{d}$

Numerical Value Questions

1 In the figure shown, the emf ε for which charge on 2 μF capacitor is 4 μC are ε_1 and ε_2. Find $\varepsilon_1 + \varepsilon_2$ (in volt).

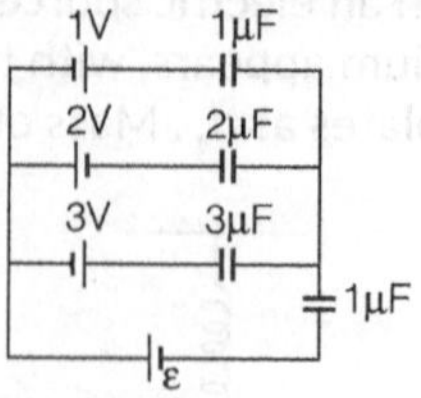

2 Find the potential difference (in V) across points *A* and *B* in the circuit shown in figure.

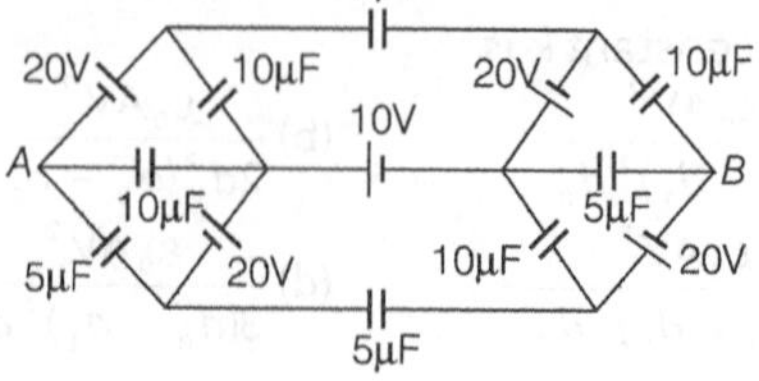

3 Find the charge (in μC) flown through the switch from A to B when it is closed.

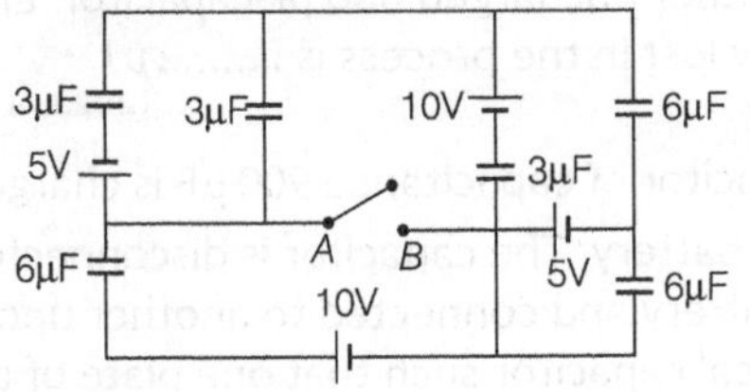

4 In given circuit, initially all capacitors were uncharged. First switch S_1 is closed and S_2 is kept open. After steady state, first S_1 is opened and then S_2 is closed. The capacitance of each capacitor is 6μF. Find the charge flown through switch S_2 after it is closed in μC.

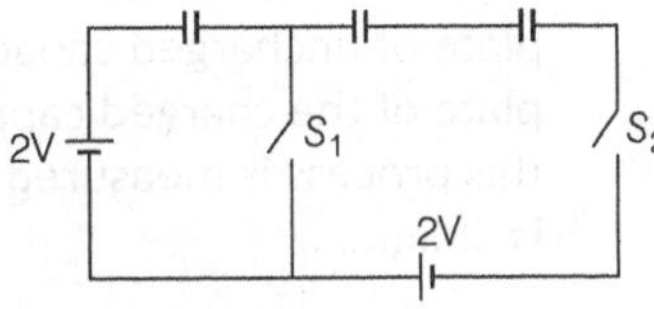

5 Two identical capacitors having plate separation d_0 are connected parallel to each other across points A and B as shown in figure. A charge Q is imparted to the system by connecting a battery across A and B and battery is removed. Now, first plate of first capacitor and second plate of second capacitor starts moving with constant velocity u_0 towards left. The magnitude of current flowing in the loop during this process at this instant is $\frac{Qu_0}{nd_0}$. Find the value of n, taking all quantities in SI units.

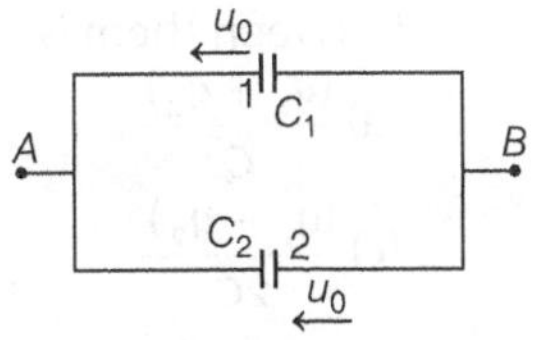

6 In a circuit, a branch carrying only capacitor has variable current $i = I_0 \sin 2\pi t$ and capacitor was uncharged at $t = 0$. The maximum magnitude of potential difference across capacitor is $\frac{2I_0}{k\pi C}$. Then, value of k will be

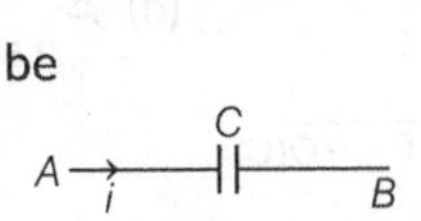

7 A charge of 8 μC is given to point A and point B is earthed. If each capacitance is 1 μF, what is the total energy (in μJ) of the system ?

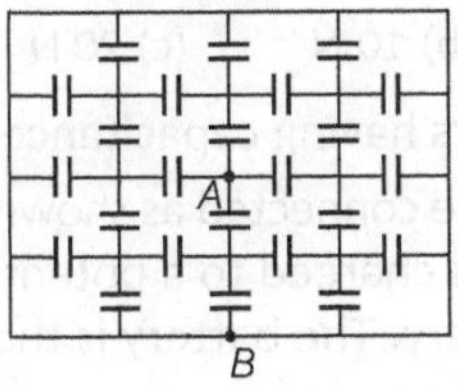

8 In the middle of two plates making a parallel plate capacitor, a plate was placed, having charge q. The plate is moved parallel to itself by a distance x. What is the charge (in μC) flowing through the external circuit of the capacitor, if the distance between its plates equal to d? (Take, $q = 8\mu C$, $x = 1$ mm, $d = 4$ mm)

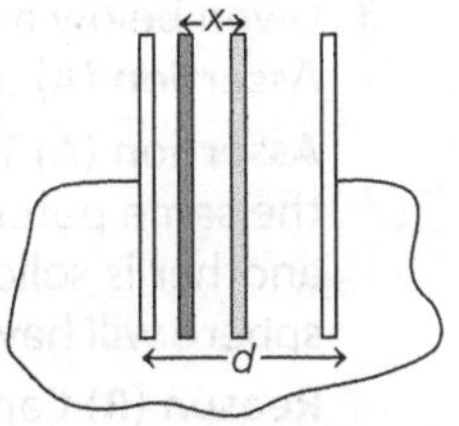

9 The figure shows four identical conducting plates each of area A. The separation between the consecutive plates is equal to L. When both the switches are closed, if charge present on the upper surface of the lowest plate from the top is written $\frac{xV_0\varepsilon_0 A}{L}$, then what is the value of x? Treat symbols as having usual meaning.

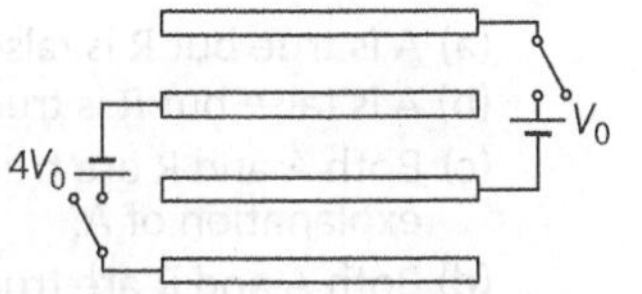

10 Four capacitors of capacitance 1μF each are connected with conducting wires between AB, BC, CD and DA, where $ABCD$ is a square. Considering the square to be horizontal, a point M is vertically above the centroid of the square. Four capacitors of capacitance 2 μF each are connected between AM, BM, CM and DM, thus forming a pyramid kind of a frame as shown. If the effective capacitance between points A - C is C_1 and between A - B is C_2, then find $\frac{C_2}{C_1}$.

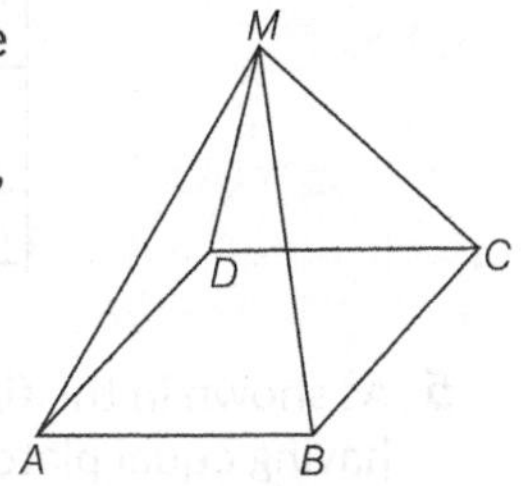

Previous Year's Questions

JEE Main

1 A capacitor of capacitance C and potential V has energy E. It is connected to another capacitor of capacitance $2C$ and potential $2V$. Then, the loss of energy is $\frac{x}{3}E$, where x is ....

[2024, 30 Jan Shift-I]

2 A capacitor of capacitance C is charged to a potential V. The flux of the electric field through a closed surface enclosing the positive plate of the capacitor is **[2023, 11 April Shift-II]**

(a) $\frac{CV}{2\varepsilon_0}$ (b) zero (c) $\frac{2CV}{\varepsilon_0}$ (d) $\frac{CV}{\varepsilon_0}$

3 Given below are two statements: One is labelled as **Assertion (A)** and the other is labelled as **Reason (R)**
Assertion (A) Two metallic spheres are charged to the same potential. One of them is hollow and another is solid and both have the same radii. Solid sphere will have lower charge than the hollow one.
Reason (R) Capacitance of metallic spheres depend on the radii of spheres.
In the light of the above statements, choose the correct answer from the options given below **[2023, 1 Feb Shift-II]**
(a) A is true but R is false.
(b) A is false but R is true.
(c) Both A and R are true and R is the correct explanation of A.
(d) Both A and R are true but R is not the correct explanation of A.

4 In the given figure the total charge stored in the combination of capacitors is 100 μC. The value of 'x' is .... **[2023, 15 April Shift-I]**

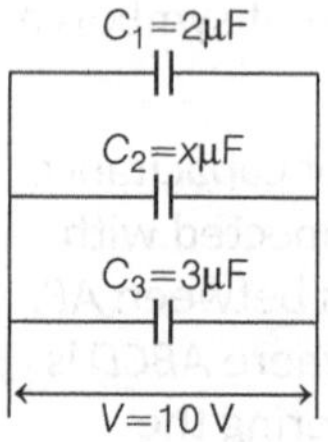

5 As shown in the figure, two parallel plate capacitors having equal plate area of 200 cm² are joined in such a way that $a \neq b$. The equivalent capacitance of the combination is $x\,\varepsilon_0 F$. The value of x is **[2023, 6 April Shift-II]**

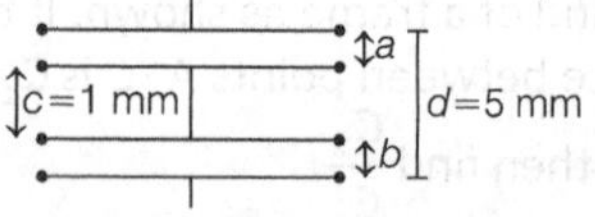

6 The equivalent capacitance of the combination shown is **[2023, 10 April Shift-I]**

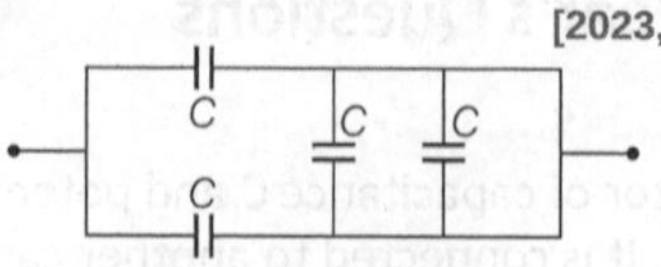

(a) $\frac{5}{3}C$ (b) 2C (c) $\frac{C}{2}$ (d) 4C

7 A parallel plate capacitor of capacitance 2F is charged to a potential V. The energy stored in the capacitor is E_1. The capacitor is now connected to another uncharged identical capacitor in parallel combination. The energy stored in the combination is E_2. The ratio E_2/E_1 is **[2023, 11 April Shift-I]**
(a) 1 : 2 (b) 1 : 4 (c) 2 : 3 (d) 2 : 1

8 A 600 pF capacitor is charged by 200 V supply. It is then disconnected from the supply and is connected to another uncharged 600 pF capacitor. Electrostatic energy lost in the process is .... μJ **[2023, 8 April Shift-II]**

9 A capacitor of capacitance 900 μF is charged by a 100 V battery. The capacitor is disconnected from the battery and connected to another uncharged identical capacitor such that one plate of uncharged capacitor connected to positive plate and another plate of uncharged capacitor connected to negative plate of the charged capacitor. The loss of energy in this process is measured as $x \times 10^{-2}$ J. The value of x is .... **[2023, 30 Jan Shift-I]**

10 Two identical thin metal plates has charge q_1 and q_2 respectively, such that $q_1 > q_2$. The plates were brought close to each other to form a parallel plate capacitor of capacitance C. The potential difference between them is **[2022, 29 July Shift-II]**
(a) $\frac{(q_1 + q_2)}{C}$ (b) $\frac{(q_1 - q_2)}{C}$
(c) $\frac{(q_1 - q_2)}{2C}$ (d) $\frac{2(q_1 - q_2)}{C}$

11 A condenser of 2 μF capacitance is charged steadily from 0 to 5 C. Which of the following graph represents correctly the variation of potential difference (V) across it's plates with respect to the charge (Q) on the condenser? **[2022, 25 July Shift-I]**

(a)
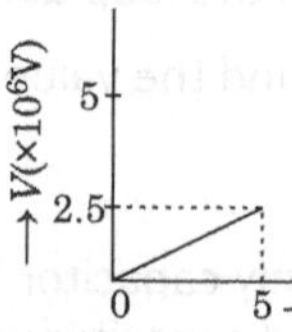

(b)
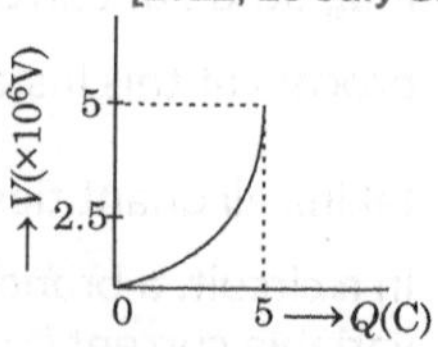

(c)
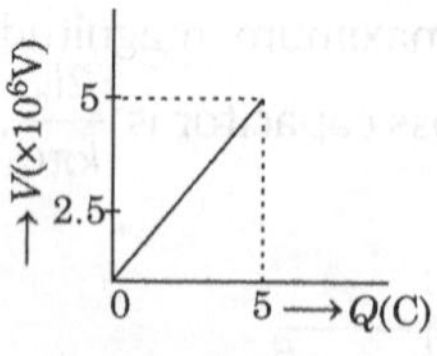

(d)
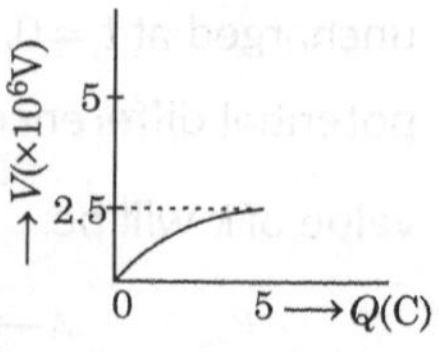

12 A force of 10 N acts on a charged particle placed between two plates of a charged capacitor. If one plate of capacitor is removed, then the force acting on that particle will be **[2022, 27 June Shift-I]**
(a) 5 N (b) 10 N (c) 20 N (d) Zero

13 Two capacitors having capacitance C_1 and C_2, respectively are connected as shown in figure. Initially, capacitor C_1 is charged to a potential difference V volt by a battery. The battery is then removed and the charged capacitor C_1 is now connected to uncharged capacitor C_2 by closing the switch S. The amount of charge on the capacitor C_2, after equilibrium is **[2022, 26 June Shift-I]**

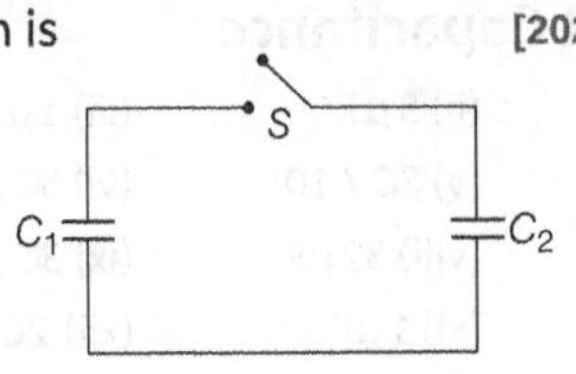

(a) $\frac{C_1 C_2}{(C_1 + C_2)}$V (b) $\frac{(C_1 + C_2)}{C_1 C_2}$V

(c) $(C_1 + C_2)$ V (d) $(C_1 - C_2)$ V

14 If the charge on a capacitor is increased by 2 C, the energy stored in it increases by 44%. The original charge on the capacitor is (in C) **[2022, 24 June Shift-II]**

(a) 10 (b) 20

(c) 30 (d) 40

15 Three capacitors $C_1 = 2\,\mu$F, $C_2 = 6\,\mu$F and $C_3 = 12\,\mu$F are connected as shown in figure. Find the ratio of the charges on capacitors C_1, C_2 and C_3, respectively. **[2021, 27 Aug Shift-II]**

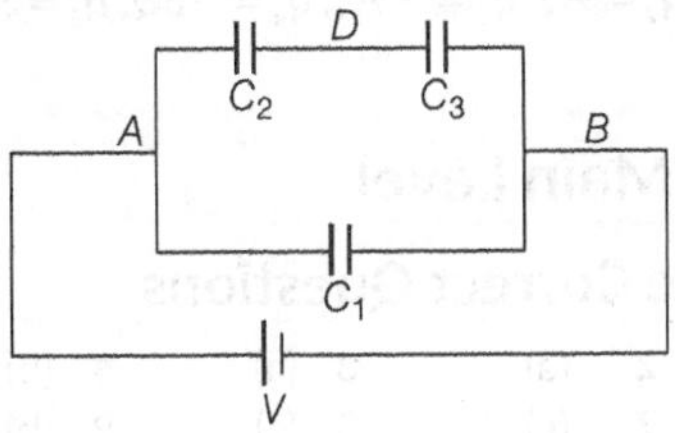

(a) 3 : 4 : 4 (b) 2 : 3 : 3

(c) 2 : 1 : 1 (d) 1 : 2 : 2

16 Consider the combination of two capacitors C_1 and C_2, with $C_2 > C_1$, when connected in parallel, the equivalent capacitance is 15/4 time the equivalent capacitance of the same connected in series. Calculate the ratio of capacitors $\frac{C_2}{C_1}$. **[2021, 26 Feb Shift-I]**

(a) $\frac{15}{11}$ (b) $\frac{111}{80}$

(b) $\frac{29}{15}$ (d) $\frac{15}{4}$

17 Two equal capacitors are first connected in series and then in parallel. The ratio of the equivalent capacities in the two cases will be **[2021, 24 Feb Shift-I]**

(a) 1 : 2 (b) 2 : 1 (c) 4 : 1 (d) 1 : 4

18 A 2 μF capacitor C_1 is first charged to a potential difference of 10 V using a battery. Then, the battery is removed and the capacitor is connected to an uncharged capacitor C_2 of 8 μF. The charge in C_2 on equilibrium condition is .... μC.
(Round off to the nearest integer) **[2021, 17 March Shift-II]**

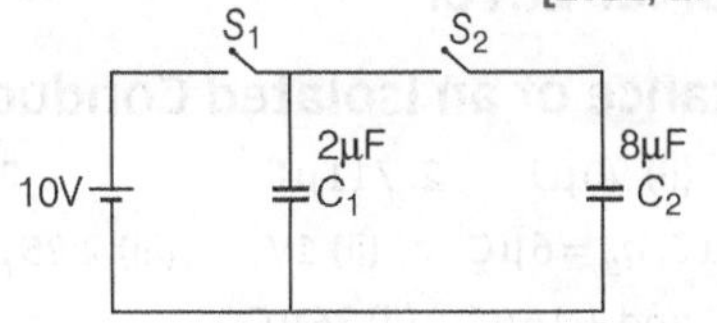

JEE Advanced

1 In the following circuit $C_1 = 12\,\mu$F, $C_2 = C_3 = 4\,\mu$F and $C_4 = C_5 = 2\,\mu$F. The charge stored in C_3 is .... μC. **(2022 Adv.)**

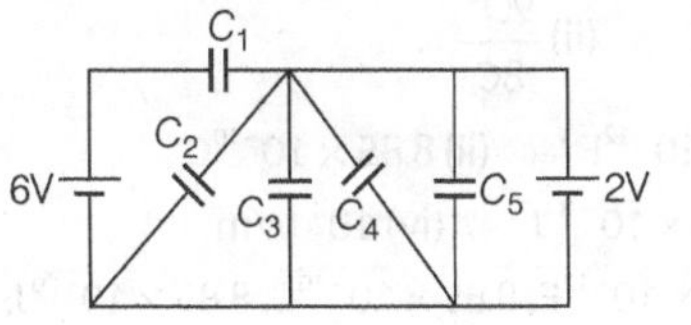

2 In the circuit shown in the figure, there are two parallel plate capacitors each of capacitance C. The switch S_1 is pressed first to fully charge the capacitor C_1 and then released. The switch S_2 is then pressed to charge the capacitor C_2. After some time, S_2 is released and then S_3 is pressed. After some time **(2013 Adv.)**

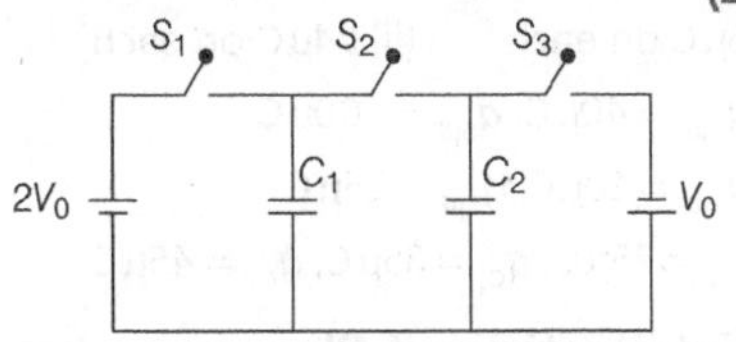

(a) the charge on the upper plate of C_1 is $2CV_0$
(b) the charge on the upper plate of C_1 is CV_0
(c) the charge on the upper plate of C_2 is 0
(d) the charge on the upper plate of C_2 is $-CV_0$

3 In the given circuit, a charge of $+80\,\mu$C is given to the upper plate of the 4 μF capacitor. Then in the steady state, the charge on the upper plate of the 3 μF capacitor is **(2012 Adv.)**

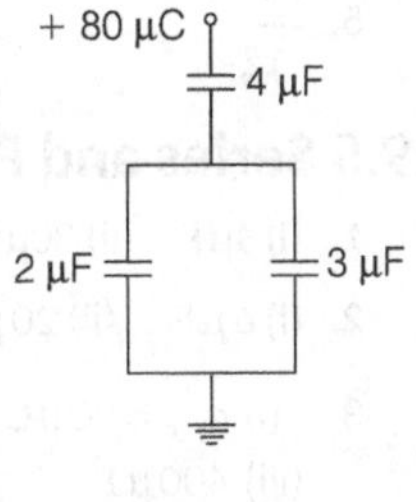

(a) + 32 μC (b) + 40 μC

(c) + 48 μC (d) + 80 μC

4 A 2 μF capacitor is charged as shown in the figure. The percentage of its stored energy dissipated after the switch S is turned to position 2 is **(2011 Adv.)**

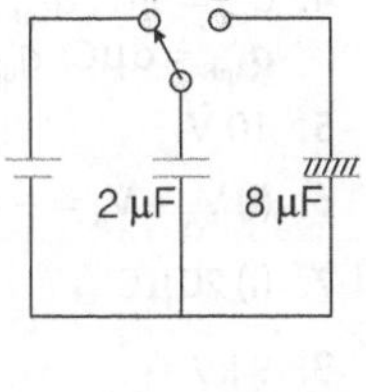

(a) 0% (b) 20%

(c) 75% (d) 80%

Answer Key

Level 1 Starter Level

9.1 Capacitance of an Isolated Conductor

1. (i) 6V (ii) 90 μJ 2. 711 μF 3. $n^{1/3}C$
4. (i) $q_A = 3\,\mu C$, $q_B = 6\,\mu C$ (ii) 1V (iii) 2.25 μJ
5. (i) + 64 μC and + 16 μC (ii) 36 μC

9.2 Capacitor

1. 32 nF 2. (i) $\frac{A\varepsilon_0}{d}$ (ii) $\frac{q}{A\varepsilon_0}$ (iii) $\frac{qd}{A\varepsilon_0}$ (iv) $\frac{q^2 d}{2A\varepsilon_0}$
3. (i) $V = \frac{3Q}{2C}$ (ii) $\frac{9Q^2}{8C}$
4. (i) 8.85×10^{-12}F (ii) 8.85×10^{-10}C
(iii) 4.425×10^{-8} J (iv) 10^4 V/m
(v) 4.425×10^{-12}F, 8.85×10^{-10}C, 8.85×10^{-10}J, 10^4 V/m
5. $\sqrt{2mgA\varepsilon_0}$ 6. 0.092 F 7. 1.21×10^{-10}F, 2.89×10^4V

9.3 Applications of KCL and KVL

1. (i) $q_{1\mu F} = 20\mu C$, $q_{2\mu F} = 20\mu C$, $q_{3\mu F} = 0$
(ii) $q_{1\mu F} = 3\mu C$, $q_{2\mu F} = 6\mu C$, $q_{3\mu F} = 9\mu C$
(iii) $q_{4\mu F} = 8\mu C$, $q_{6\mu F} = 72\mu C$, $q_{10\mu F} = 80\mu C$
2. (i) 16μC on each (ii) 24μC on each
(iii) $q_{2\mu F} = 40\mu C$, $q_{5\mu F} = 100\mu C$
(iv) $q_{2\mu F} = 10\mu C$, $q_{5\mu F} = 25\mu C$
(v) $q_{C_1} = 75\mu C$, $q_{C_2} = 35\mu C$, $q_{C_3} = 45\mu C$

9.4 Redistribution of Charges

1. $CE^2, \frac{CE^2}{2}, \frac{CE^2}{2}$ 2. (i) $\frac{CE^2}{8}$ (ii) $\frac{CE^2}{8}$ (iii) $2CE^2$
3. (i) 60 V (ii) 6 mJ 4. (i) 60 μJ (ii) 540 μJ
5. $\frac{CV^2}{12}$

9.5 Series and Parallel Combinations

1. (i) 1μF (ii) 30μC (iii) 15 V (iv) 150 μJ
2. (i) 6 μF (ii) 20 μC (iii) 300 μJ (iv) 150 μJ
3. (i) $q_{1\mu F} = 20\,\mu C$, $q_{2\mu F} = 40\,\mu C$, $q_{6\mu F} = 60\,\mu C$ (ii) 20 V
(iii) 400 μJ
4. $C_{eq} = 5\mu F$, $q_{2\mu F} = q_{3\mu F} = q_{6\mu F} = 3\,\mu C$,
$q_{4\mu F} = 6\,\mu C$, $q_{8\mu F} = 24\,\mu C$, $q_{10\mu F} = 30\,\mu C$
5. 10 V
6. (i) $V_A - V_B = -40$ V (ii) 120 μC
7. (i) 20 μC (ii) 60 μC (iii) 0.6 mJ (iv) 0.3 mJ
8. 9 kV 9. 50

9.6 Equivalent Capacitance

1. (i) 8 μF (ii) 5 μF (iii) 1 μF
(iv) 3.6 μF (v) 3C / 10 (vi) 5C / 3
(vii) 2C (viii) 32 μF (ix) 3C / 4
(x) 10 μF (xi) 1 μF (xii) 2C
(xiii) 7.5 μF (xiv) 2.8 μF (xv) 2F
2. (i) 11 / 6 μF (ii) 11 / 4 μF (iii) 16 μF
3. (i) 12 μF (ii) 24 μF
4. (i) 3C / 2 (ii) 15C / 8 (iii) 1.3 C
(iv) 11C / 8 (v) 7C / 5 (vi) 4C / 3
(vii) $\frac{23C}{6}$ (viii) 32C / 11

9.7 Combination of Parallel Plates

1. (i) $\frac{3A\varepsilon_0}{d}$ (ii) $\frac{3\varepsilon_0 A}{2d}$ (iii) $\frac{2A\varepsilon_0}{3d}$
(iv) $\frac{2A\varepsilon_0}{d}$ (v) $\frac{5}{3}\frac{\varepsilon_0 A}{d}$ (vi) $\frac{A\varepsilon_0}{d}$
2. $q_1 = -4Q$, $q_2 = 9Q$, $q_3 = -9Q$, $q_4 = -3Q$, $q_5 = 3Q$, $q_6 = -4Q$
3. 13Q / 3

Level 2 JEE Main Level

Single Choice Correct Questions

1	(d)	2	(a)	3	(a)	4	(b)	5	(b)
6	(b)	7	(c)	8	(c)	9	(b)	10	(c)
11	(c)	12	(d)	13	(a)	14	(c)	15	(b)
16	(c)	17	(b)	18	(b)	19	(c)	20	(b)
21	(c)	22	(c)	23	(b)	24	(a)	25	(c)
26	(c)	27	(b)	28	(b)	29	(a)	30	(a)
31	(c)	32	(b)	33	(a)	34	(b)	35	(b)
36	(a)	37	(a)	38	(d)	39	(c)	40	(c)
41	(c)	42	(b)	43	(b)	44	(b)	45	(d)
46	(b)								

Numerical Value Questions

1	(40)	2	(7)	3	(7)	4	(46)	5	(18)
6	(4)	7	(120)	8	(1800)	9	(42)	10	(8)
11	(220.50)	12	(12)	13	(50)	14	(1.50)	15	(2)

Level 3 JEE Advanced Level

Single Choice Correct Questions

1	(d)	2	(a)	3	(b)	4	(b)	5	(c)
6	(b)	7	(a)	8	(c)	9	(b)	10	(b)
11	(d)	12	(d)	13	(d)	14	(c)	15	(c)
16	(d)	17	(d)	18	(b)	19	(b)	20	(a)
21	(b)	22	(c)	23	(a)	24	(d)	25	(a)
26	(a)	27	(b)	28	(c)	29	(a)	30	(d)

31 (b)	32 (b)	33 (b)	34 (a)	35 (c)
36 (a)				

Multiple Choice(s) Correct Questions

1 (abd)	2 (ac)	3 (ac)	4 (ac)	5 (abcd)
6 (abc)	7 (bd)	8 (abd)	9 (abcd)	10 (bd)
11 (abd)	12 (ac)	13 (abc)	14 (bc)	15 (ac)
16 (ab)	17 (abcd)			

Comprehension Based Questions

1 (c)	2 (c)	3 (c)	4 (a)	5 (c)
6 (c)	7 (b)	8 (a)	9 (a)	10 (b)
11 (d)	12 (c)	13 (c)	14 (a)	15 (b)
16 (a)	17 (c)	18 (bc)	19 (ac)	20 (b)
21 (a)	22 (b)			

Match the Columns Questions

1. (a) → r, (b) → pq, (c) → s, (d) → pq
2. (a) → s; (b) → r; (c) → q; (d) → p
3. (a) → p; (b) → r; (c) → q; (d) → p
4. (a) → q; (b) → p; (c) → s; (d) → r
5. (a) → r; (b) → s; (c) → q; (d) → p

Numerical Value Type Questions

1. (40)	2. (10)	3. (69)	4. (4)	5. (2)
6. (2)	7. (12)	8. (2)	9. (3)	10. (1.20)

Previous Year's Questions

JEE Main

1 (2)	2 (d)	3 (b)	4 (5)	5 (5)
6 (b)	7 (b)	8 (6)	9 (2.25)	10 (c)
11 (a)	12 (a)	13 (a)	14 (a)	15 (d)
16 (*)	17 (d)	18 (16)		

JEE Advanced

1 (8)	2 (b,d)	3 (c)	4 (d)

SOLUTIONS

Level 1 Starter Level

9.1 Capacitance of an Isolated Conductor

1. (i) $V = \dfrac{q}{C} = \dfrac{30\ \mu C}{5\ \mu F} = 6\ V$

(ii) $U = \dfrac{q^2}{2C} = \dfrac{(30\times10^{-6})^2}{2\times5\times10^{-6}} = 90\ \mu J$

2. $C = 4\pi\varepsilon_0 R = \dfrac{6400\times10^3}{9\times10^9} \approx 711\ \mu F$

3. Let radius of each drop be r.

$$C = 4\pi\varepsilon_0 r$$

When n drops each of radius r coalesce,

$$n\frac{4}{3}\pi r^3 = \frac{4}{3}\pi R^3$$

Radius of bigger drop, $R = n^{1/3}r$

Capacitance of bigger drop $= 4\pi\varepsilon_0 R$

$$= 4\pi\varepsilon_0 n^{1/3} r = n^{1/3}C$$

4. (i)

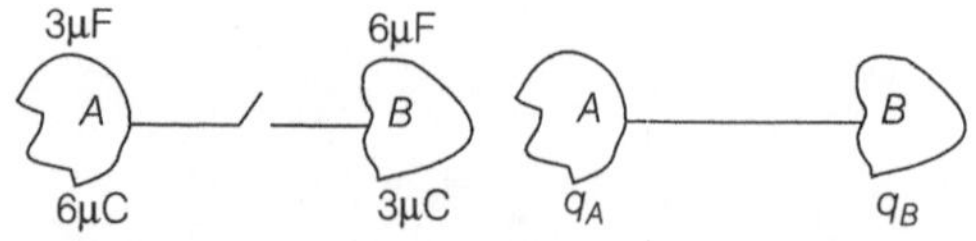

Finally, $V_A = V_B$

$\Rightarrow \dfrac{q_A}{3} = \dfrac{q_B}{6}$

$\Rightarrow \dfrac{q_A}{q_B} = \dfrac{1}{2}$ ... (i)

and $q_A + q_B = 9\ \mu C$ ... (ii)

Solving Eqs. (i) and (ii), we get

$$q_A = 3\ \mu C \text{ and } q_B = 6\ \mu C$$

(ii) Common potential $= \dfrac{q_A}{3} = \dfrac{3\ \mu C}{3\ \mu F} = 1\ V$

(iii) Heat produced $= \dfrac{1}{2}\dfrac{C_1C_2}{C_1+C_2}(V_1 - V_2)^2$

$$= \frac{1}{2}\times2\times10^{-6}\left(2-\frac{1}{2}\right)^2 = 2.25\ \mu J$$

5. (i) Let final charges on the two spheres be q_1 and q_2.

$q_1 + q_2 = +100 - 20 = 80\ \mu C$ ... (i)

and $\dfrac{q_1}{q_2} = \dfrac{R_1}{R_2}$

$\Rightarrow \dfrac{q_1}{q_2} = 4$ ... (ii)

Solving Eqs. (i) and (ii), we get

$$q_1 = 64\ \mu C \text{ and } q_2 = 16\ \mu C$$

(ii) Charge flown through the wire

$$= 100 - 64 = 36\ \mu C$$

9.2 Capacitor

1. $C = \dfrac{q}{V} = \dfrac{ne}{V} = \dfrac{2\times10^{12}\times1.6\times10^{-19}}{10} = 32\times10^{-9}F = 32\ nF$

2. (i) $C = \dfrac{A\varepsilon_0}{d}$

(ii) $E = \dfrac{\sigma}{\varepsilon_0} = \dfrac{q}{A\varepsilon_0}$

(iii) $V = Ed = \dfrac{qd}{A\varepsilon_0}$

(iv) $U = \dfrac{q^2}{2C} = \dfrac{q^2 d}{2A\varepsilon_0}$

3.

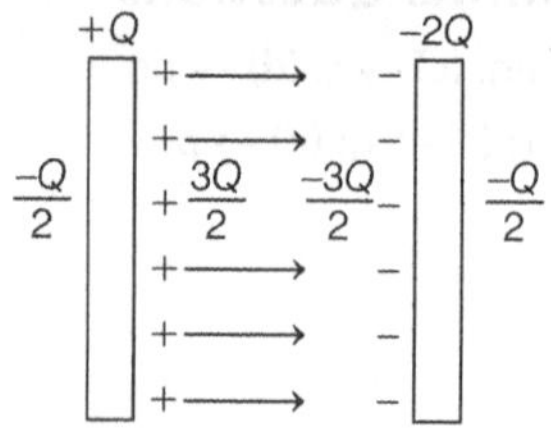

Charge on the facing surfaces $= \dfrac{3Q}{2}$

(i) $V = \dfrac{3Q/2}{C} = \dfrac{3Q}{2C}$

(ii) $U = \dfrac{(3Q/2)^2}{2C} = \dfrac{9Q^2}{8C}$

4. (i) $C = \dfrac{A\varepsilon_0}{d} = \dfrac{(0.1)^2(8.85\times10^{-12})}{10^{-2}} = 8.85\times10^{-12}F$

(ii) $q = CV$

$\Rightarrow q = (8.85\times10^{-12})(100) = 8.85\times10^{-10}C$

(iii) $U = \dfrac{1}{2}CV^2 = \dfrac{1}{2}\times8.85\times10^{-12}\times(100)^2 = 4.425\times10^{-8}\ J$

(iv) $E = \dfrac{V}{d} = \dfrac{100}{0.01} = 10^4\ V/m$

(v) $C' = \dfrac{A\varepsilon_0}{d'} = 4.425\times10^{-12}F$

$q' = q = 8.85\times10^{-10}C$

$U' = \dfrac{q^2}{2C'} = 8.85\times10^{-8}J$

$E' = \dfrac{q'}{A\varepsilon_0} = 10^4\ V/m$

5.

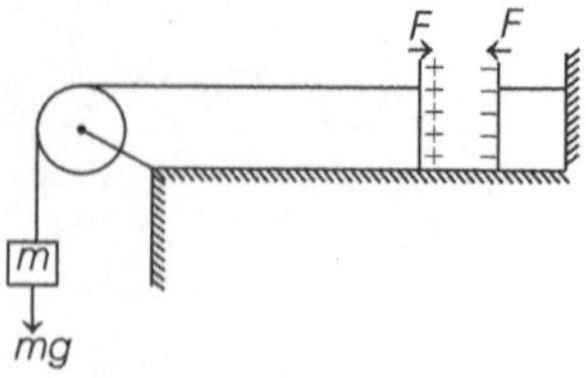

F = Attractive force between the plates $= \dfrac{q^2}{2A\varepsilon_0}$

For equilibrium of system,

$$\frac{q^2}{2A\varepsilon_0} = mg \Rightarrow q = \sqrt{2A\varepsilon_0 mg}$$

6. Capacitance of a spherical capacitor $= \dfrac{4\pi\varepsilon_0 R_1 R_2}{R_2 - R_1}$

$$C = \left(\frac{1}{9\times10^9}\right)\frac{6450\times10^3\times6400\times10^3}{50\times10^3} = 0.092\ \text{F}$$

7. $$C = \frac{2\pi\varepsilon_0 l}{\ln\left(\frac{b}{a}\right)} = \left(\frac{1}{18\times10^9}\right)\left(\frac{15\times10^{-2}}{\ln\left(\frac{15}{14}\right)}\right) = 1.21\times10^{-10}\text{F}$$

$$V = \frac{q}{C} = \frac{3.5\times10^{-6}}{1.21\times10^{-10}} = 2.89\times10^4\ \text{V}$$

9.3 Applications of KCL and KVL

1. (i) Let potential of junction D be x.

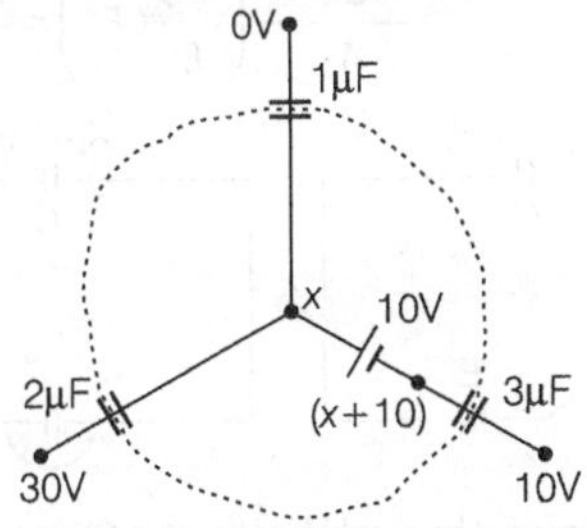

Sum of charges on the plates of isolated system = 0

$$1(x-0) + 2(x-30) + 3[(x-10)-10] = 0$$

$$\Rightarrow \quad x = 20\ \text{V}$$

$$q_{1\mu F} = 1(20-0) = 20\mu C$$

$$q_{2\mu F} = 2(30-20) = 20\mu C$$

$$q_{3\mu F} = 3(20-10-10) = 0$$

(ii)

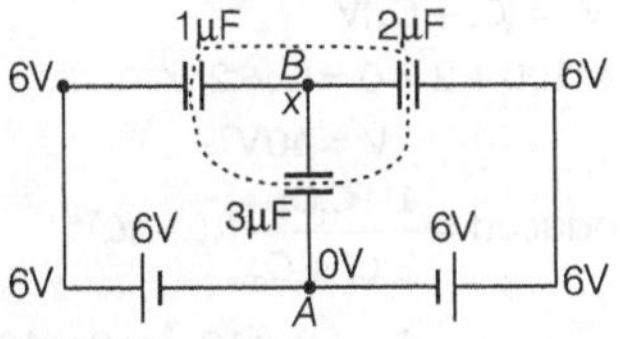

Let $V_A = 0$ and $V_B = x$

Sum of charges on the plates of isolated system $= 0$

$$\Rightarrow \quad 1(x-6) + 2(x-6) + 3(x-0) = 0$$

$$\Rightarrow \quad x = 3\text{V}$$

$$q_{1\mu F} = 1(6-3) = 3\,\mu C$$

$$q_{2\mu F} = 2(6-3) = 6\,\mu C$$

$$q_{3\mu F} = 3(3-0) = 9\,\mu C$$

(iii)

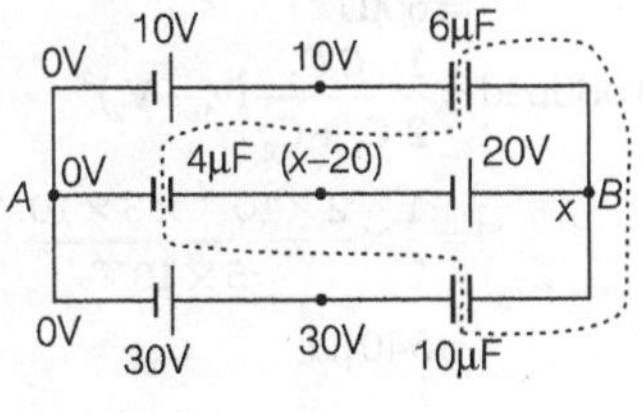

Let $V_A = 0$ and $V_B = x$

Sum of charges on the plates of the isolated system = 0

$$\Rightarrow +6(x-10) + 4[(x-20)-0] + 10(x-30) = 0$$

$$\Rightarrow \quad x = 22\text{V}$$

$$q_{6\mu F} = 6(22-10) = 72\,\mu C$$

$$q_{4\mu F} = 4[(22-20)-0] = 8\,\mu C$$

$$q_{10\mu F} = 10(30-22) = 80\,\mu C$$

2. (i)

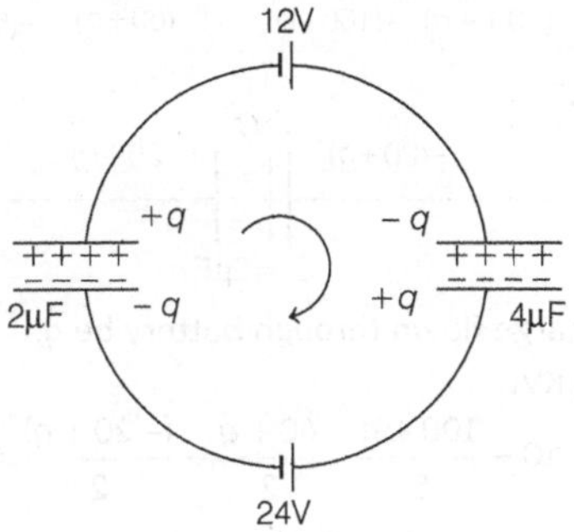

Applying KVL, $+\dfrac{q}{2} + 12 + \dfrac{q}{4} - 24 = 0$

$$q = 16\,\mu C$$

(ii)

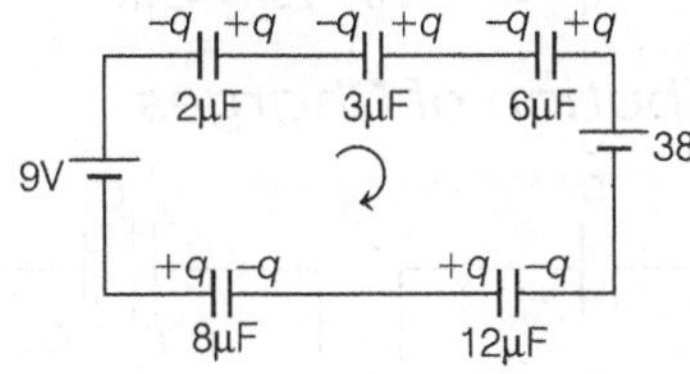

Applying KVL,

$$\Rightarrow \ +9 + \frac{q}{2} + \frac{q}{3} + \frac{q}{6} - 38 + \frac{q}{12} + \frac{q}{8} = 0 \ \Rightarrow \ q = 24\,\mu C$$

(iii)

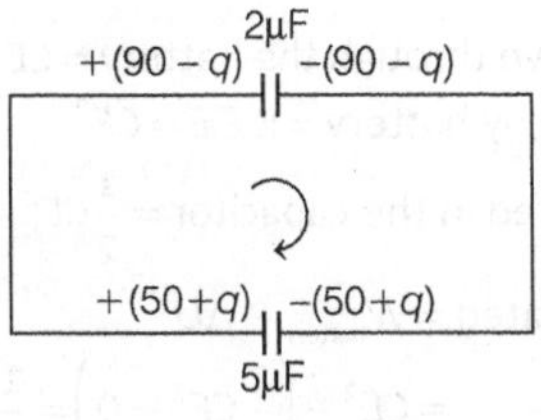

Applying KVL, $\dfrac{-(90-q)}{2} + \dfrac{50+q}{5} = 0$

$$\Rightarrow \quad -450 + 5q + 100 + 2q = 0$$

$$\Rightarrow \quad q = 50\,\mu C$$

$$q_{2\mu F} = 90 - 50 = 40\,\mu C$$

$$q_{5\mu F} = 50 + 50 = 100\,\mu C$$

(iv)

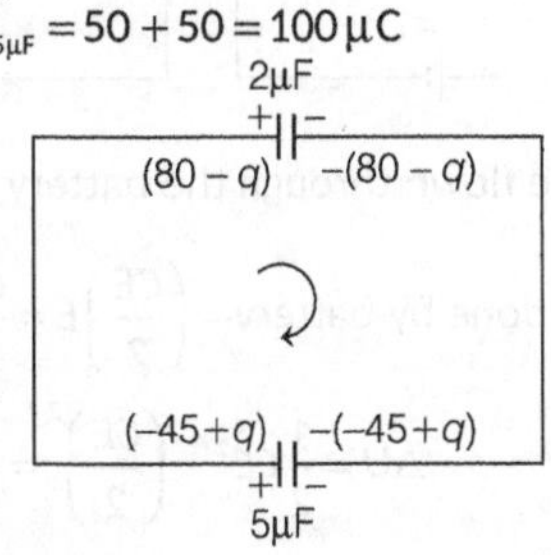

Using KVL, $\frac{-80-q}{2}+\frac{(-45+q)}{5}=0$

$\Rightarrow \quad q = 70\,\mu C$

$q_{2\mu F} = 80 - 70 = 10\,\mu C$

$q_{5\mu F} = -45 + 70 = 25\,\mu C$

(v)

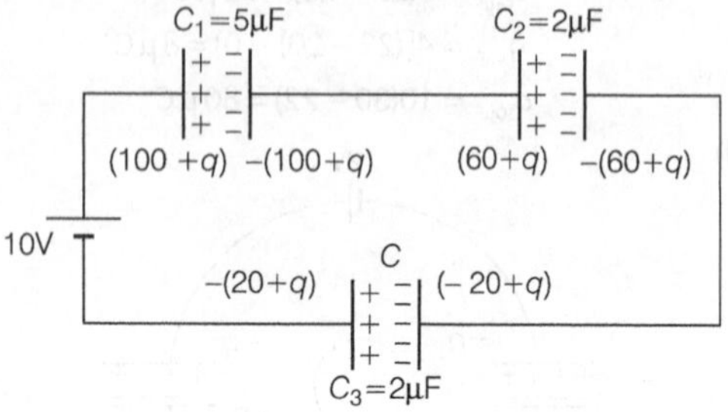

Let charge flown through battery be q.

Using KVL,

$$+10-\frac{100+q}{5}-\frac{60+q}{2}-\frac{(-20+q)}{2}=0$$

$\Rightarrow \quad q = -25\,\mu C$

$q_{C_1} = 100 - 25 = 75\,\mu C$

$q_{C_2} = 60 - 25 = 35\,\mu C$

$q_{C_3} = -(-20 - 25) = 45\,\mu C$

9.4 *Redistribution of Charges*

1.

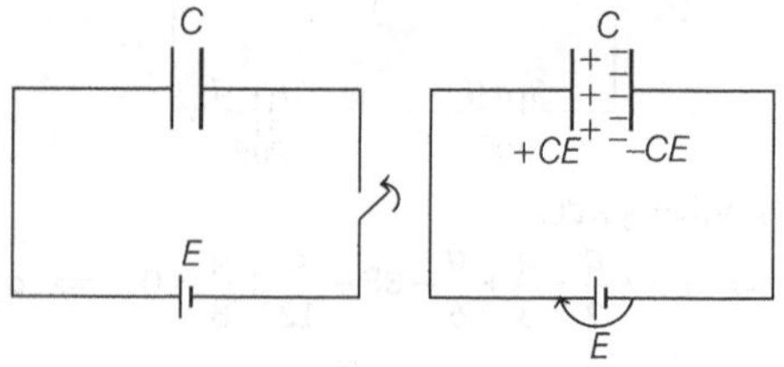

Charge flown through the battery $= CE$

Work done by battery $= (CE)E = CE^2$

Energy stored in the capacitor $= \frac{1}{2}CE^2$

Heat dissipated $= W_{battery} - \Delta U$

$$= CE^2 - \left(\frac{1}{2}CE^2 - 0\right) = \frac{1}{2}CE^2$$

2. (i)

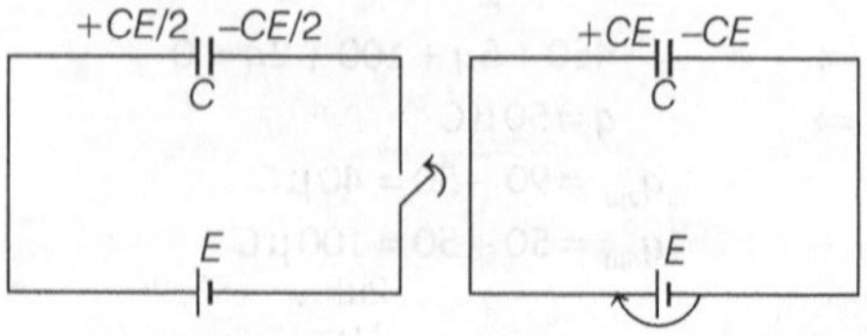

Charge flown through the battery $= CE - \frac{CE}{2} = \frac{CE}{2}$

Work done by battery $= \left(\frac{CE}{2}\right)E = \frac{CE^2}{2}$

$$\Delta U = \frac{1}{2}CE^2 - \left(\frac{CE}{2}\right)^2 = \frac{3}{8}CE^2$$

Heat produced $= W_{battery} - \Delta U$

$$= \frac{1}{2}CE^2 - \frac{3}{8}CE^2 = \frac{CE^2}{8}$$

(ii)

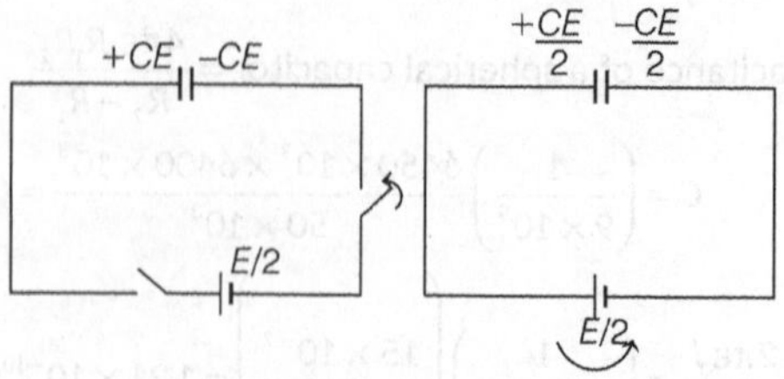

Charge flown through battery $= \frac{CE}{2} - CE = \frac{-CE}{2}$

Work done by battery $= \left(\frac{-CE}{2}\right)\frac{E}{2} = \frac{-CE^2}{4}$

$$\Delta U = \frac{(CE/2)^2}{2C} - \frac{(CE)^2}{2C} = \frac{-3}{8}CE^2$$

Heat produced $= W_{battery} - \Delta U$

$$= \frac{-CE^2}{4} - \left(\frac{-3}{8}CE^2\right) = \frac{CE^2}{8}$$

(iii)

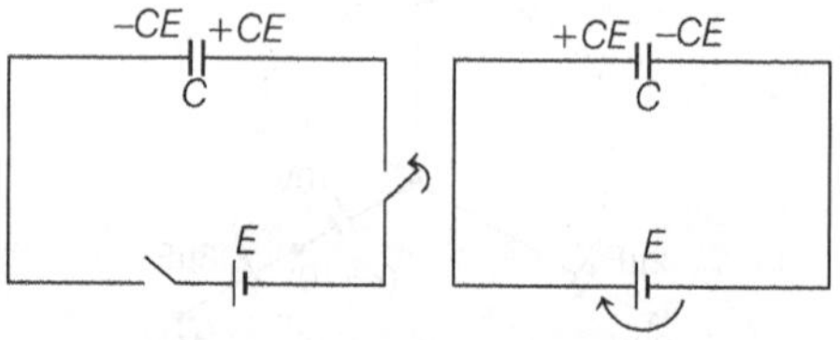

Charge flown through battery $= CE - (-CE) = 2CE$

$W_{battery} = (2CE)E = 2CE^2$

$$\Delta U = \frac{(CE)^2}{2C} - \frac{(CE)^2}{2C} = 0$$

Heat produced $= W_{battery} - \Delta U$

$= 2CE^2 - 0 = 2CE^2$

3. (i) $C_1V_1 + C_2V_2 = (C_1 + C_2)V$

$\Rightarrow \quad 3 \times 100 + 2 \times 0 = (3+2)V$

$\Rightarrow \quad V = 60\,V$

(ii) Heat produced $= \frac{1}{2}\frac{C_1C_2}{C_1+C_2}(V_1-V_2)^2$

$$= \frac{1}{2} \times \left(\frac{3\times10^{-6}\times2\times10^{-6}}{3\times10^{-6}+2\times10^{-6}}\right)(100-0)^2$$

$= 6\,mJ$

4. (i) Heat produced $= \frac{1}{2}\frac{C_1C_2}{C_1+C_2}(V_1-V_2)^2$

$$= \frac{1}{2} \times \frac{2\times10^{-6}\times3\times10^{-6}}{5\times10^{-6}}(20-10)^2$$

$= 60\,\mu J$

(ii) Heat produced $= \frac{1}{2}\frac{C_1C_2}{C_1+C_2}(V_1-V_2)^2$

$$= \frac{1}{2} \times \frac{2\times10^{-6}\times3\times10^{-6}}{5\times10^{-6}}[20-(-10)]^2$$

$= 540\,\mu J$

5.

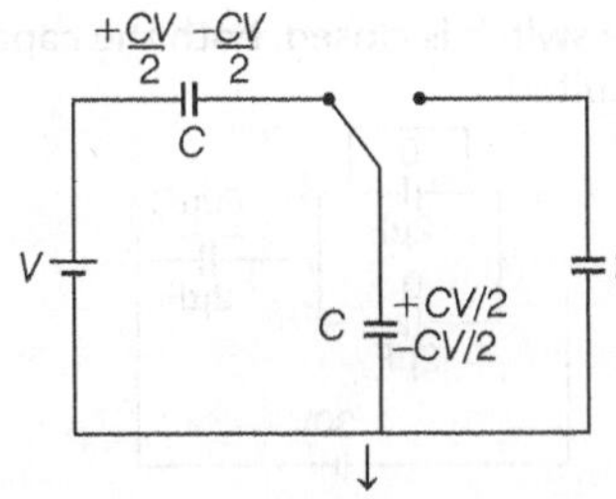

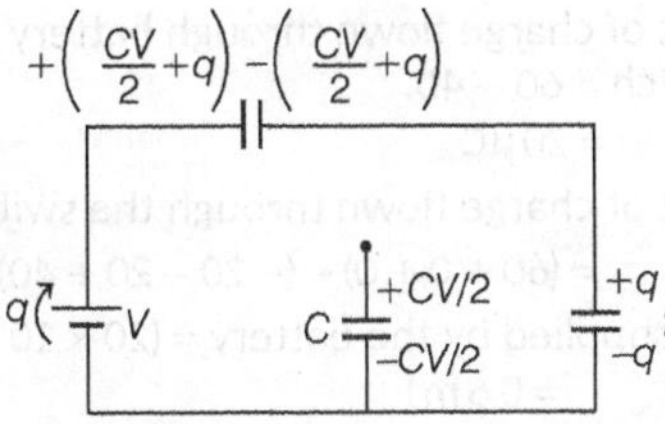

Let charge flown the battery after flipping the switch from 1 to 2 be q.

Using KVL,

$$+V-\frac{\frac{CV}{2}+q}{C}-\frac{q}{2C}=0$$

$$\Rightarrow \quad q=CV/3$$

$$\text{Work done by battery}=\left(\frac{CV}{3}\right)V=\frac{CV^2}{3}$$

$$U_1=\frac{(CV/2)^2}{2C}+\frac{(CV/2)^2}{2C}+0$$

$$U_2=\frac{(5CV/6)^2}{2C}+\frac{(CV/2)^2}{2C}+\frac{(CV/3)^2}{2(2C)}$$

$$\Delta U=U_2-U_1=\frac{1}{4}CV^2$$

$$\text{Heat produced}=W_{battery}-\Delta U=\frac{CV^2}{3}-\frac{CV^2}{4}=\frac{CV^2}{12}$$

9.5 *Series and Parallel Combinations*

1. (i) From given figure in question,

$$\frac{1}{C_{eq}}=\frac{1}{2}+\frac{1}{3}+\frac{1}{6} \quad \Rightarrow \quad C_{eq}=1\mu F$$

(ii) Charge flown through battery $=C_{eq}V=(1\mu F)(30V)$

$$=30\mu C$$

Charge on each capacitor $=30\mu C$

(iii) Potential difference across $2\mu F$ capacitor

$$=\frac{q}{C}=\frac{30\mu C}{2\mu F}=15V$$

(iv) Energy stored in $3\mu F$ capacitor $=\frac{q^2}{2C}$

$$=\frac{(30\times10^{-6})^2}{2\times3\times10^{-6}}=150\mu J$$

2. (i) $C_{eq}=1+2+3=6\mu F$

(ii) Charge on $2\mu F$ capacitor $=CV=(2\mu F)(10V)=20\mu C$

(iii) $U=\frac{1}{2}C_{eq}V^2=\frac{1}{2}(6\times10^{-6})(10)^2=300\mu J$

(iv) Energy stored in $3\mu F$ capacitor $=\frac{1}{2}CV^2$

$$=\frac{1}{2}\times3\times10^{-6}\times(10)^2=150\mu J$$

3. (i) $\frac{1}{C_{eq}}=\frac{1}{(1+2)}+\frac{1}{6} \Rightarrow C_{eq}=2\mu F$

Charge flown through battery $=C_{eq}V=(2)(30)=60\mu C$

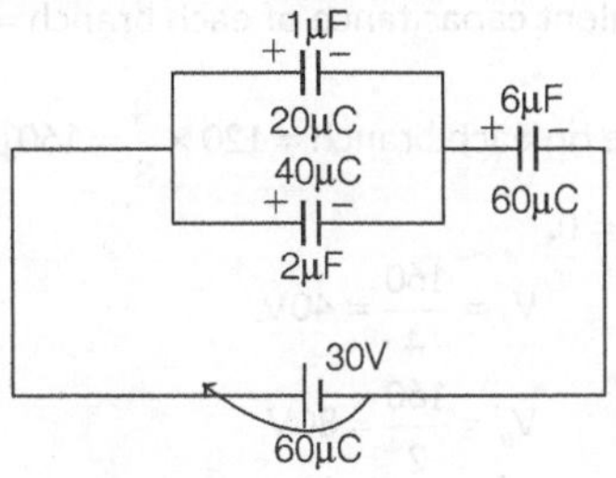

$$q_{1\mu F}=20\mu C,\ q_{2\mu F}=40\mu C \text{ and } q_{6\mu F}=60\mu C$$

(ii) $V=\frac{q}{C}=\frac{20\mu C}{1\mu F}=20V$

(iii) $U=\frac{q^2}{2C}=\frac{(40\times10^{-6})^2}{2\times2\times10^{-6}}=400\mu J$

4. (i) From given figure in question, Using series and parallel combination,

$$C_{eq}=5\mu F$$

(ii) Charge flown through battery $=C_{eq}V$

$$=(5\mu F)(6V)=30\mu C$$

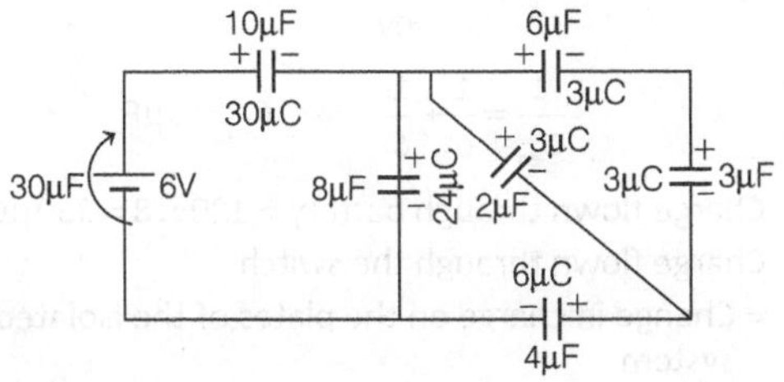

5. Let C_1 be C.

$$\Rightarrow \quad C_2=2C$$

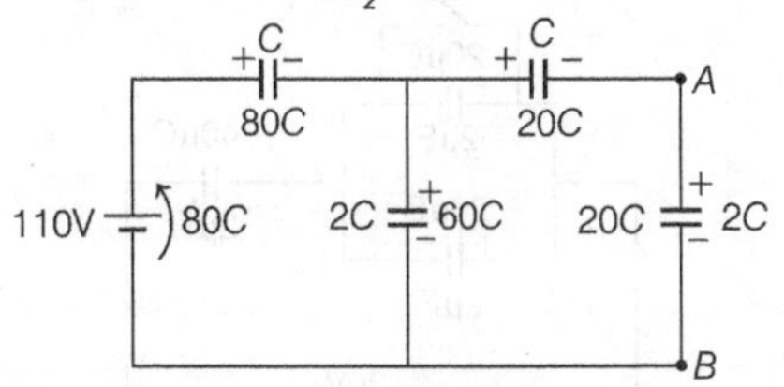

$$C_{eq}=\frac{8C}{11}$$

$$\text{Charge flown through battery}=\left(\frac{8C}{11}\right)(110)=80\,C$$

$$V_A-V_B=\frac{q}{C}=\frac{20C}{2C}=10\,V$$

6. (i)

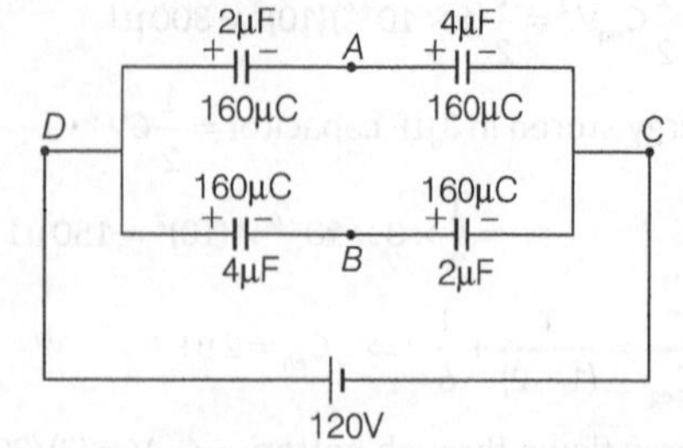

Equivalent capacitance of each branch $= \frac{2 \times 4}{2+4} = \frac{4}{3}\mu F$

Charge on each branch $= 120 \times \frac{4}{3} = 160\,\mu C$

Let $V_c = 0$.

$\Rightarrow \quad V_A = \frac{160}{4} = 40V$

$\Rightarrow \quad V_B = \frac{160}{2} = 80V$

$V_A - V_B = 40 - 80 = -40V$

(ii)

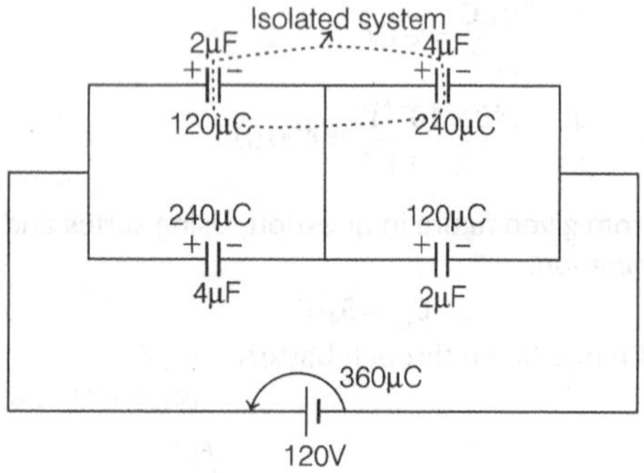

$$\frac{1}{C_{eq}} = \frac{1}{6} + \frac{1}{6} \Rightarrow C_{eq} = 3\mu F$$

Charge flown through battery $= 120 \times 3 = 360\,\mu C$

Charge flown through the switch

= Change in charge on the plates of the isolated system

$= (240 - 120) - (-160 + 160) = 120\,\mu C$

7. (i)

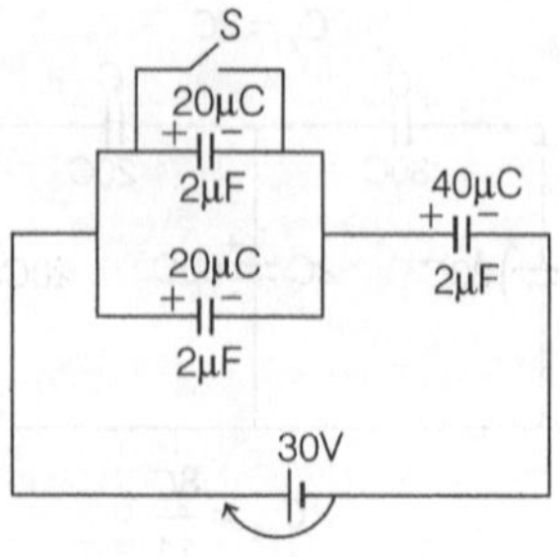

When the switch is open,

$$\frac{1}{C_{eq}} = \frac{1}{4} + \frac{1}{2} \Rightarrow C_{eq} = \frac{4}{3}\mu F$$

Charge flown through battery $= \frac{4}{3} \times 30 = 40\,\mu C$

When the switch is closed, both the capacitors will get short-circuited.

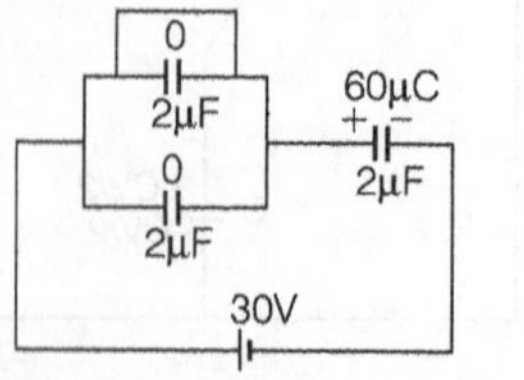

Amount of charge flown through battery after closing the switch $= 60 - 40$

$= 20\,\mu C$

(ii) Amount of charge flown through the switch

$= (60 + 0 + 0) - (-20 - 20 + 40) = 60\,\mu C$

(iii) Energy supplied by the battery $= (20 \times 10^{-6})\,30$

$= 0.6\,mJ$

(iv) $\Delta U = U_2 - U_1 = \frac{1}{2} \times 2 \times 10^{-6} \times (30)^2$

$- \frac{1}{2} \times \frac{4}{3} \times 10^{-6} \times (30)^2 = 0.3\,mJ$

Heat generated $= W_{battery} - \Delta U = 0.6 - 0.3 = 0.3\,mJ$

8. Maximum charge permissible on capacitor 1

$= 1 \times 10^{-6} \times 6 \times 10^3 = 6\,mC$

Maximum charge permissible on capacitor 2

$= 2 \times 10^{-6} \times 4 \times 10^3 = 8\,mC$

In series combination of the two capacitors, maximum charge permissible will be 6 mC.

Maximum voltage across combination

$$= \frac{6 \times 10^{-3}}{1 \times 10^{-6}} + \frac{6 \times 10^{-3}}{2 \times 10^{-6}} = 6 \times 10^3 + 3 \times 10^3 = 9\,kV$$

9.

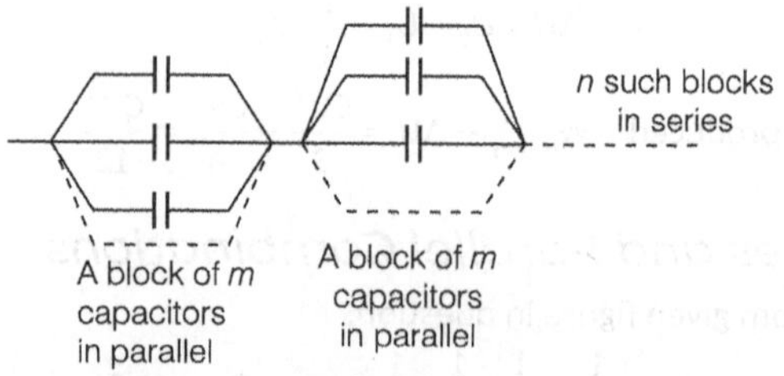

$n(200) = 1000 \Rightarrow n = 5$

$\frac{m(8)}{n} = 16 \Rightarrow m = 10$

9.6 Equivalent Capacitance

1. (i)

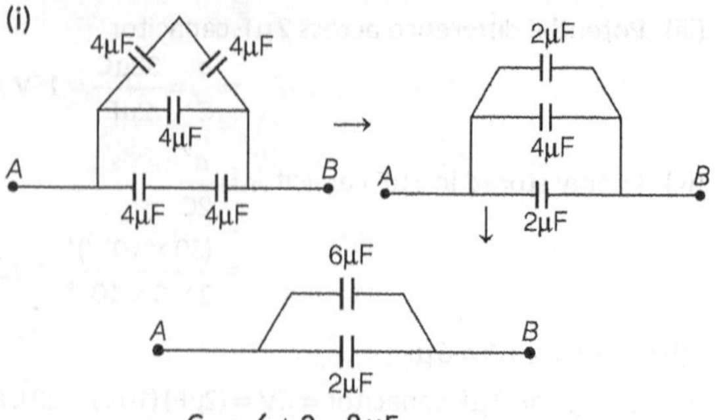

$C_{eq} = 6 + 2 = 8\,\mu F$

(ii)

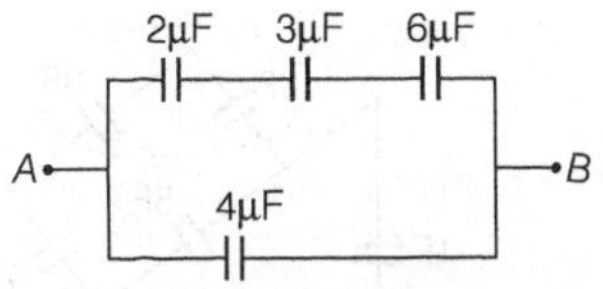

$$C_{eq} = 4 + 1 = 5\,\mu F$$

(iii)

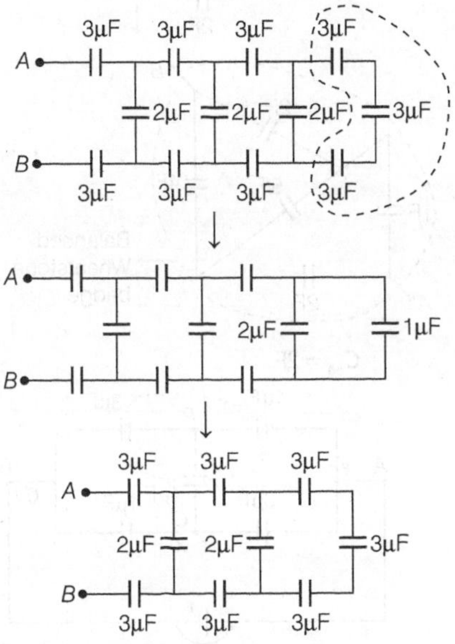

Finally, $\frac{1}{C_{eq}} = \frac{1}{3} + \frac{1}{3} + \frac{1}{3} \Rightarrow C_{eq} = 1\,\mu F$

(iv)

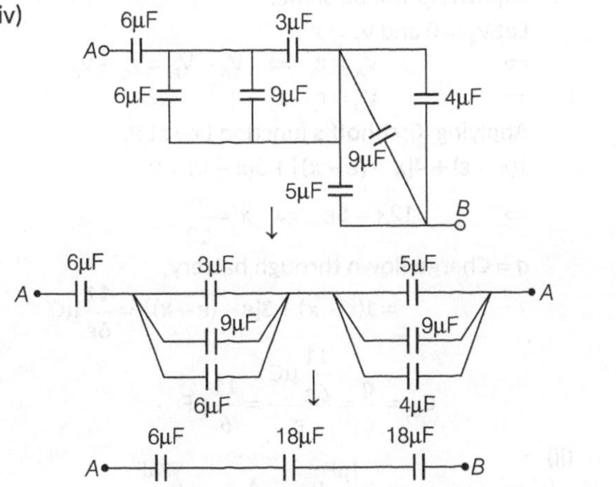

$$\frac{1}{C_{eq}} = \frac{1}{6} + \frac{1}{18} + \frac{1}{18} \Rightarrow C_{eq} = \frac{18}{5}\,\mu F = 3.6\,\mu F$$

(v)

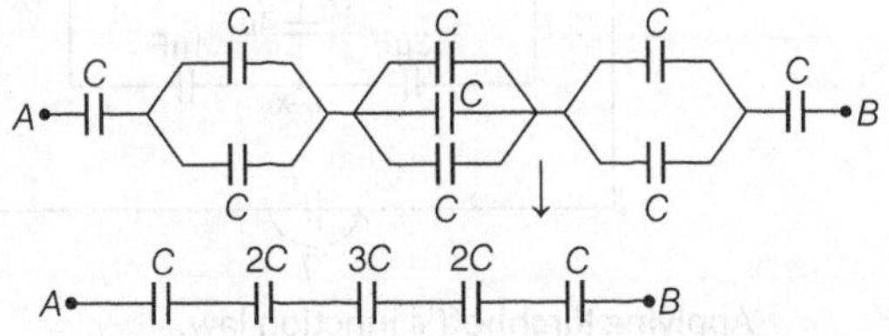

$$\frac{1}{C_{eq}} = \frac{1}{C} + \frac{1}{2C} + \frac{1}{3C} + \frac{1}{2C} + \frac{1}{C} \Rightarrow C_{eq} = \frac{3C}{10}$$

(vi)

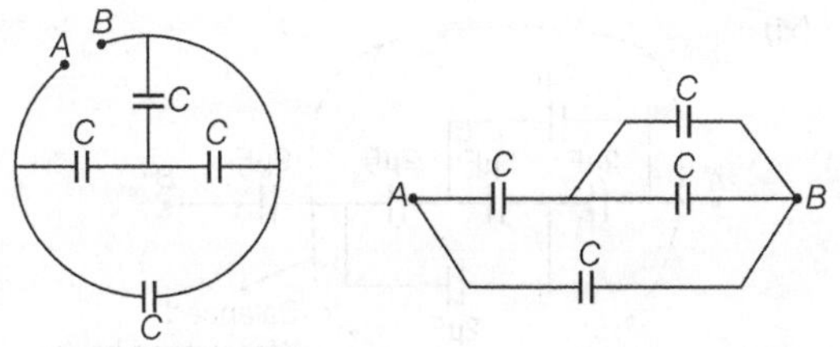

$$C_{eq} = \frac{5C}{3}$$

(vii)

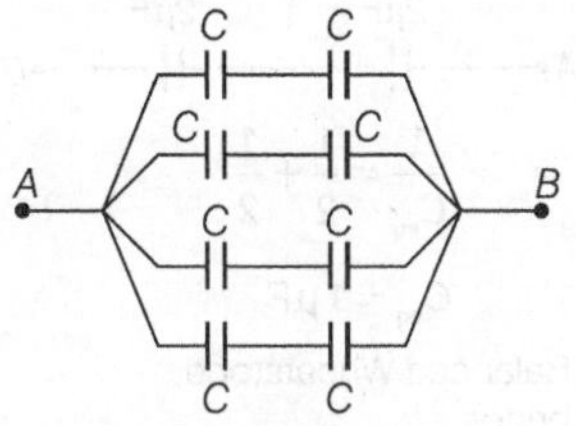

$$C_{eq} = \frac{C}{2} + \frac{C}{2} + \frac{C}{2} + \frac{C}{2} = 2C$$

(viii)

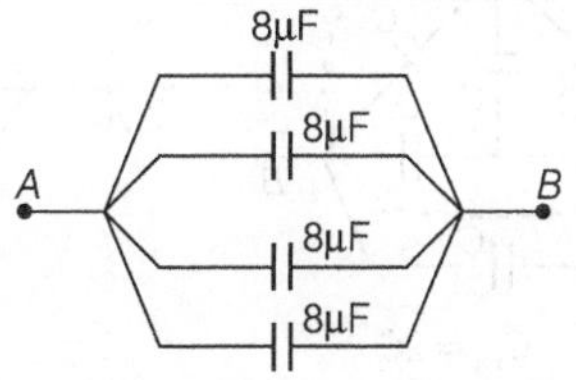

$$C_{eq} = 8 + 8 + 8 + 8 = 32\,\mu F$$

(ix)

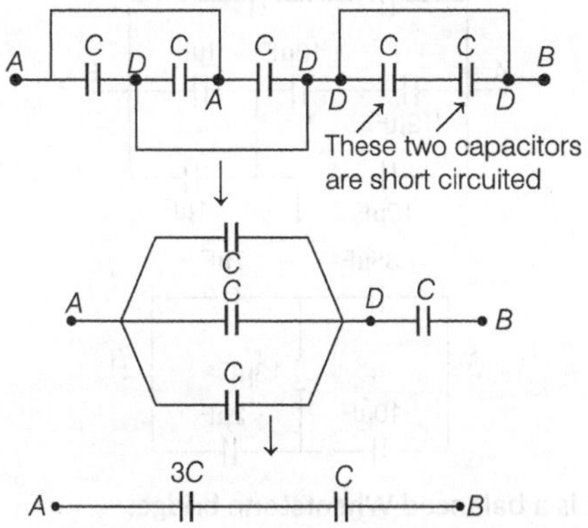

$$\frac{1}{C_{eq}} = \frac{1}{3C} + \frac{1}{C} \Rightarrow C_{eq} = \frac{3C}{4}$$

(x)

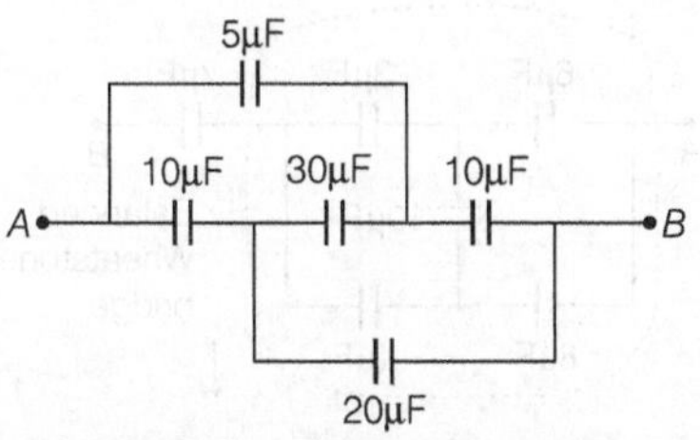

It is a balanced Wheatstone bridge. So, we can remove 30 μF capacitor.

Using series and parallel combination, now

$$C_{eq} = 10\,\mu F$$

(xi)

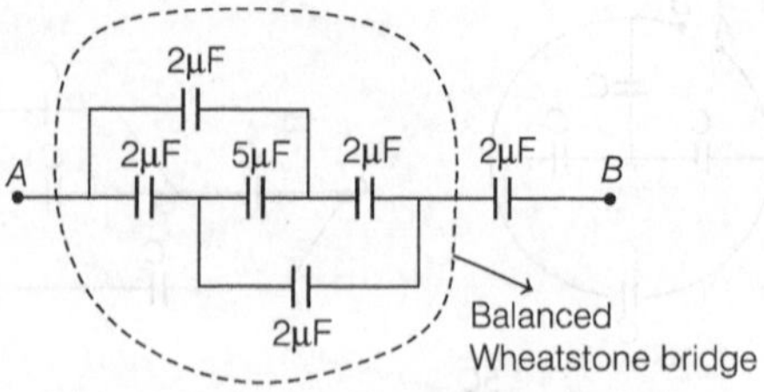

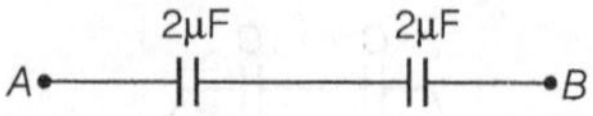

$$\frac{1}{C_{eq}} = \frac{1}{2} + \frac{1}{2}$$

$\Rightarrow \quad C_{eq} = 1\,\mu F$

(xii)

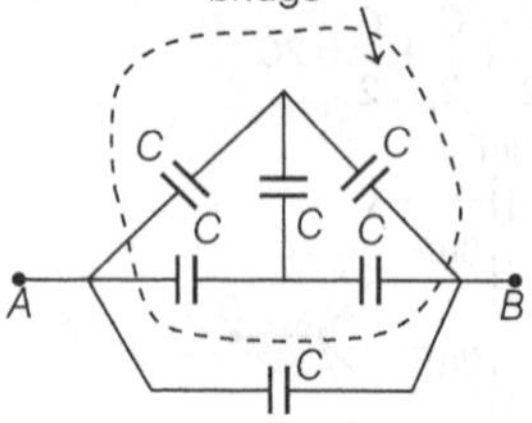

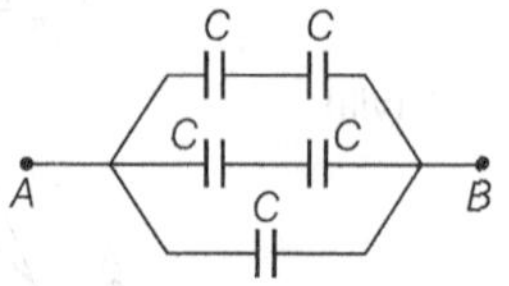

$C_{eq} = 2C$

(xiii)

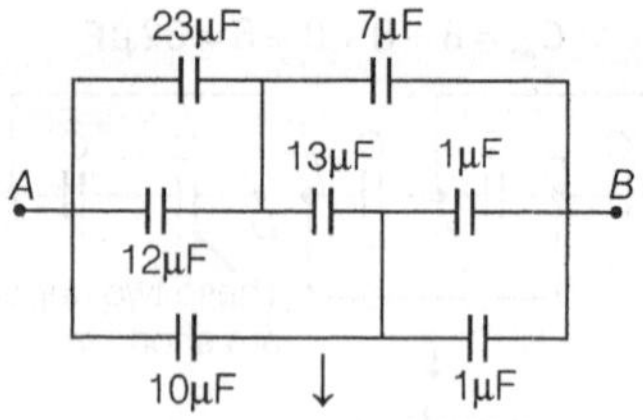

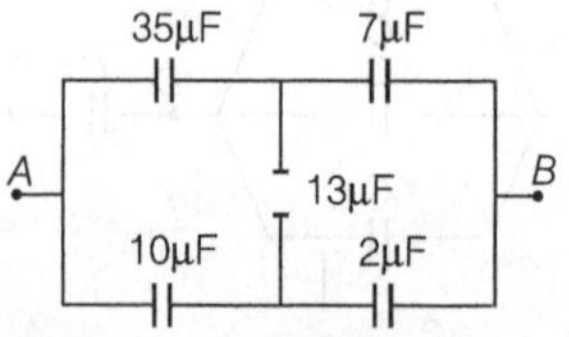

It is a balanced Wheatstone bridge.

$$C_{eq} = \frac{45 \times 9}{45 + 9} = \frac{15}{2}\,\mu F = 7.5\,\mu F$$

(xiv)

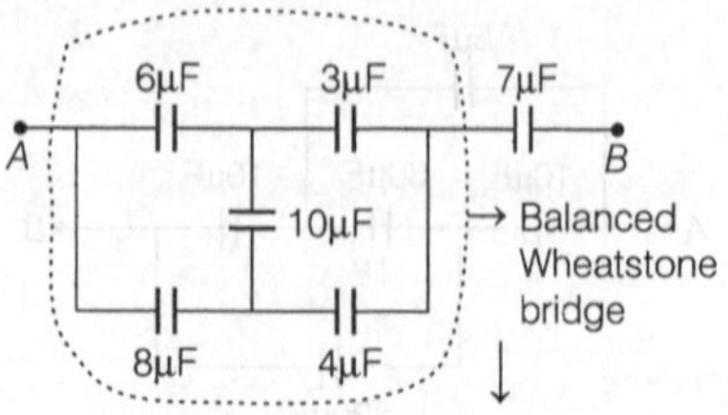

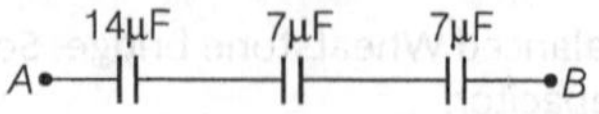

$$\frac{1}{C_{eq}} = \frac{1}{14} + \frac{1}{7} + \frac{1}{7} \quad \Rightarrow C_{eq} = \frac{14}{5}\,\mu F = 2.8\,\mu F$$

(xv)

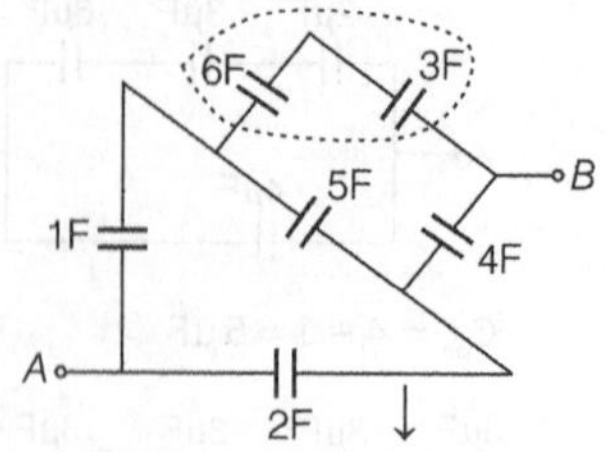

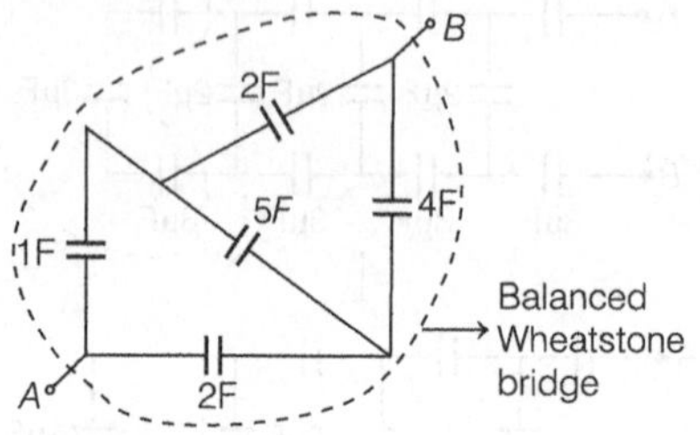

$C_{eq} = 2F$

2. (i)

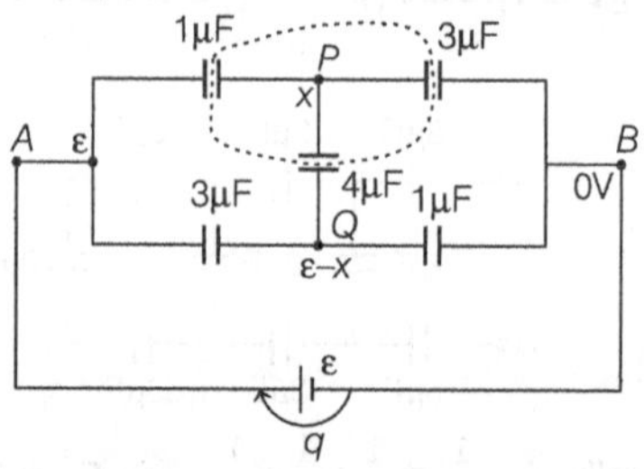

Due to symmetry, potential difference across both 1 μF capacitors will be same.

Let $V_B = 0$ and $V_P = x$

$\Rightarrow \quad V_A = \varepsilon \quad \Rightarrow \quad V_A - V_P = V_Q - V_B$

$\Rightarrow \quad V_Q = \varepsilon - x$

Applying Kirchhoff's junction law at P,

$$1(x - \varepsilon) + 4[x - (\varepsilon - x)] + 3(x - 0) = 0$$

$$\Rightarrow \quad 12x = 5\varepsilon \quad \Rightarrow \quad x = \frac{5\varepsilon}{12}$$

q = Charge flown through battery

$$= 1(\varepsilon - x) + 3[\varepsilon - (\varepsilon - x)] = \frac{11}{6\varepsilon}\,\mu C$$

$$C_{eq} = \frac{q}{\varepsilon} = \frac{\frac{11}{6\varepsilon}\,\mu C}{\varepsilon} = \frac{11}{6}\,\mu F$$

(ii)

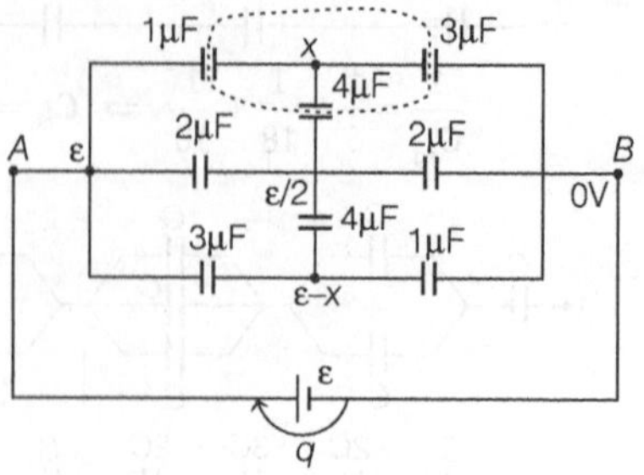

Applying Kirchhoff's junction law,

$$1(x - \varepsilon) + 4\left(x - \frac{\varepsilon}{2}\right) + 3(x - 0) = 0$$

$$\Rightarrow \quad 8x = 3\varepsilon \quad \Rightarrow \quad x = \frac{3\varepsilon}{8}$$

q = Charge flown through battery

$$= 1(\varepsilon - x) + 2\left(\varepsilon - \frac{\varepsilon}{2}\right) + 3[\varepsilon - (\varepsilon - x)]$$

$$= \frac{5\varepsilon}{8} + \varepsilon + \frac{9\varepsilon}{8} = \left(\frac{11\varepsilon}{4}\right)\mu C$$

$$C_{eq} = \frac{q}{\varepsilon} = \frac{\left(\frac{11\varepsilon}{4}\right)}{\varepsilon} = \frac{11}{4}\mu F$$

(iii)

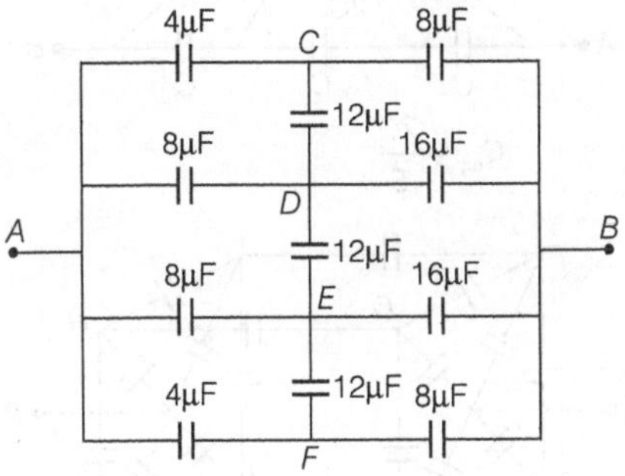

In each horizontal branch, capacitance ratio of the two capacitors is same. So, points C, D, E and F are equipotential. So, we can remove all 12μF capacitors.

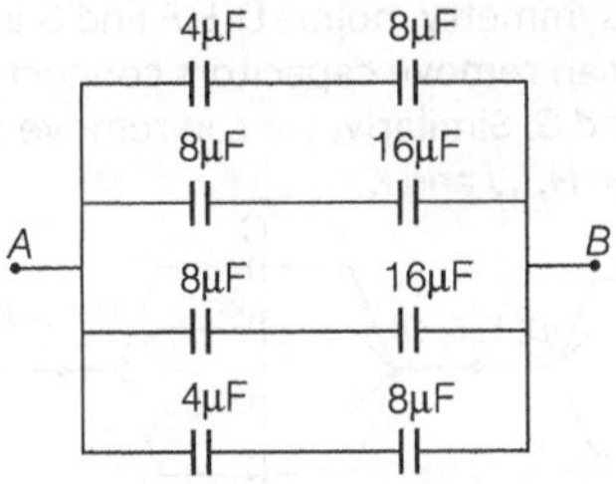

$$\frac{1}{C_{eq}} = \frac{1}{24} + \frac{1}{48} \Rightarrow C_{eq} = 16\,\mu F$$

3. (i)

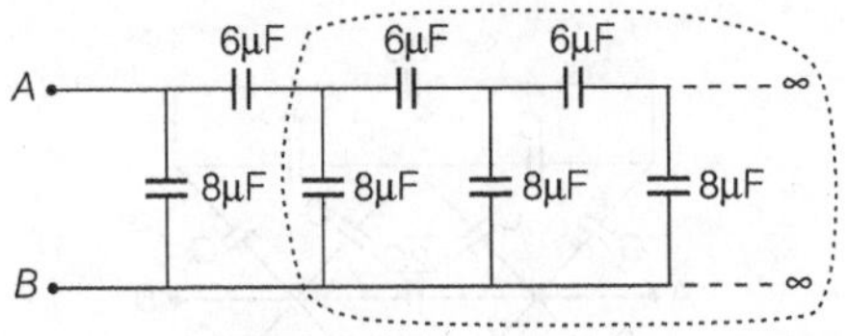

Let equivalent capacitance between A and B be x μF.

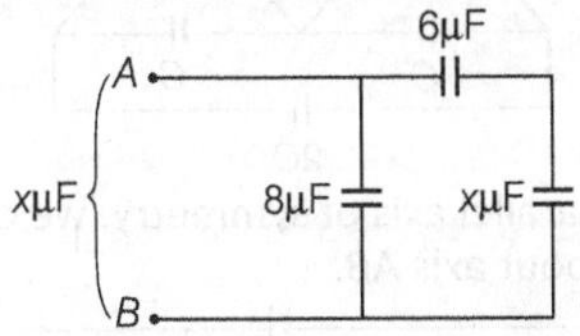

$$x = \frac{6x}{6+x} + 8 \Rightarrow 6x + x^2 = 48 + 14x$$

$$\Rightarrow \quad x^2 - 8x - 48 = 0 \Rightarrow x = 12\,\mu F$$

(ii) If each capacitor's capacitance is doubled, then equivalent capacitance will also get doubled.
Equivalent capacitance = 24μF

4. (i)

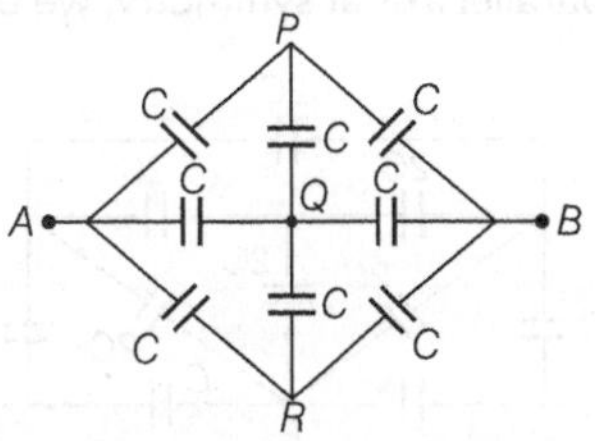

From symmetry, points P, Q and R are equipotential. So, we can remove capacitors between P & Q and Q & R.

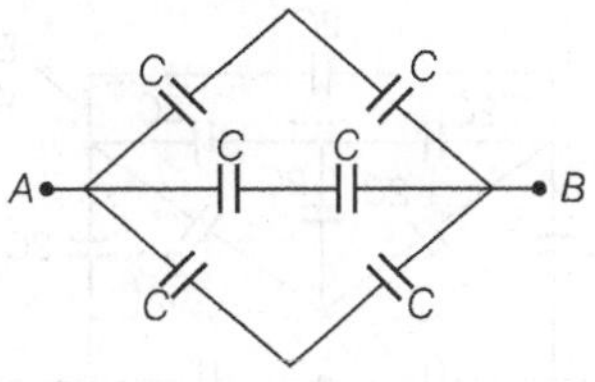

$C_{eq} = 3C/2$

(ii)

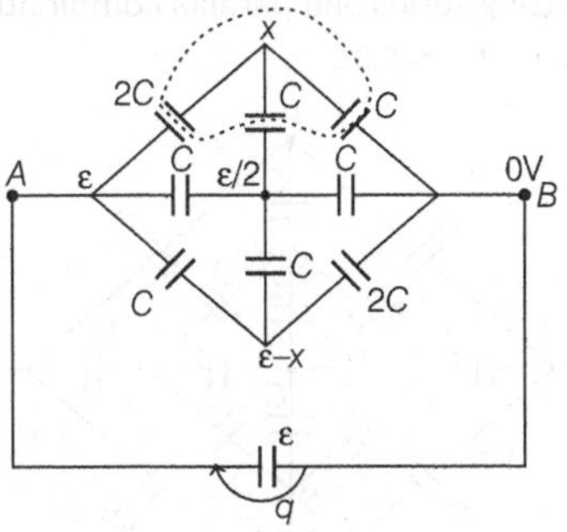

Applying Kirchhoff's junction law,

$$2C(x - \varepsilon) + C\left(x - \frac{\varepsilon}{2}\right) + C(x - 0) = 0$$

$$\Rightarrow \quad x = \frac{5\varepsilon}{8}$$

q = Charge flown through battery

$$= 2C(\varepsilon - x) + C\left(\varepsilon - \frac{\varepsilon}{2}\right) + C\,[\varepsilon - (\varepsilon - x)]$$

$$= \frac{6C\varepsilon}{8} + \frac{C\varepsilon}{2} + \frac{5C\varepsilon}{8} = \frac{15C\varepsilon}{8}$$

$$C_{eq} = \frac{q}{\varepsilon} = \frac{15C\varepsilon/8}{\varepsilon} = \frac{15C}{8}$$

(iii)

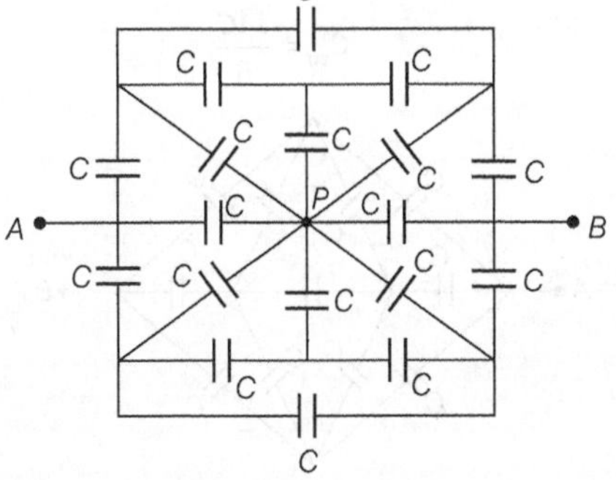

Due to parallel axis at symmetry, we can fold the circuit.

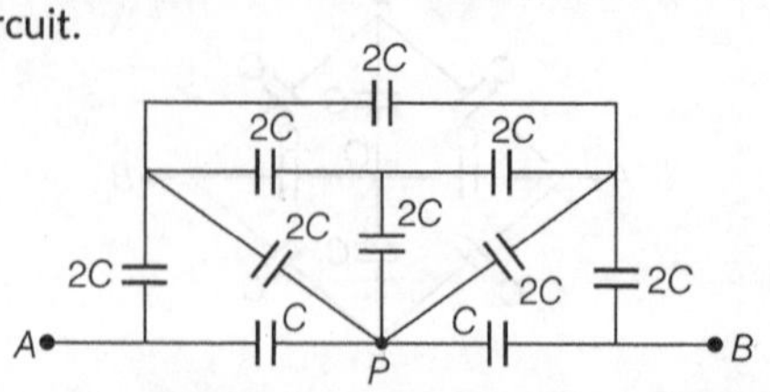

Due to perpendicular axis of symmetry, we can break junction at P as shown.

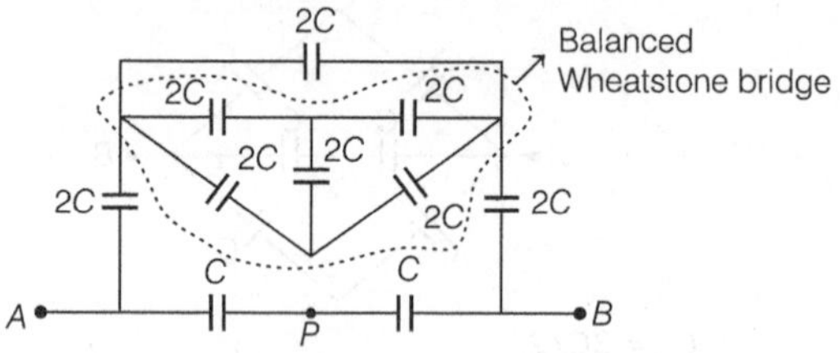

Now, using series and parallel combination,

$$C_{eq} = 1.3\,C$$

(iv)

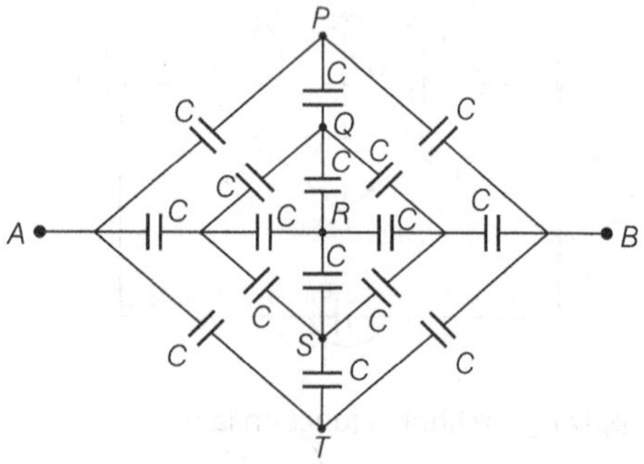

Due to perpendicular axis of symmetry, points P, Q, R, S and T are equipotential. So, we can remove capacitors connected between these points.

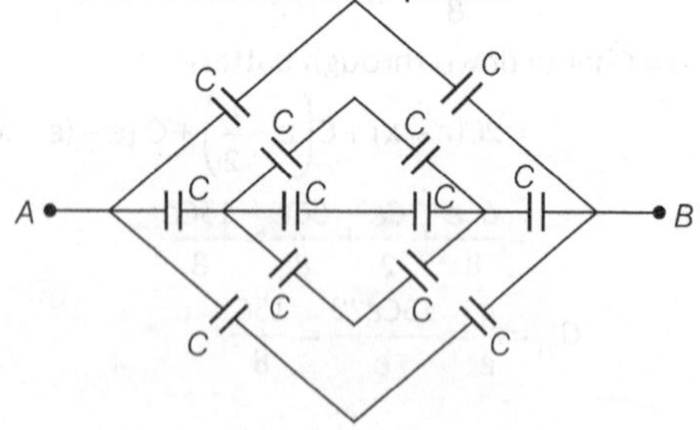

$$C_{eq} = \frac{11C}{8}$$

(v)

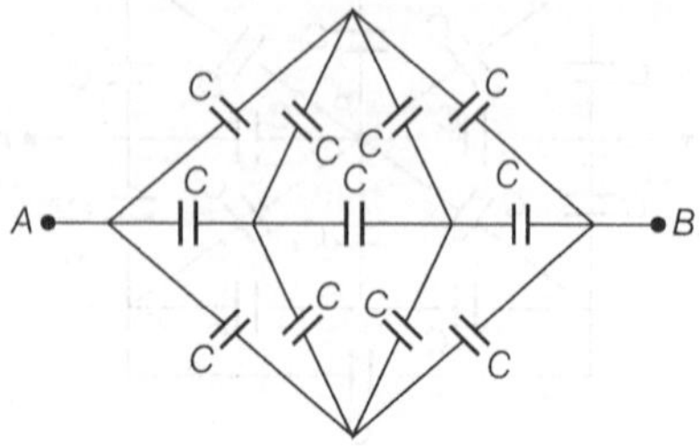

Due to parallel axis of symmetry, we can fold the circuit about line AB.

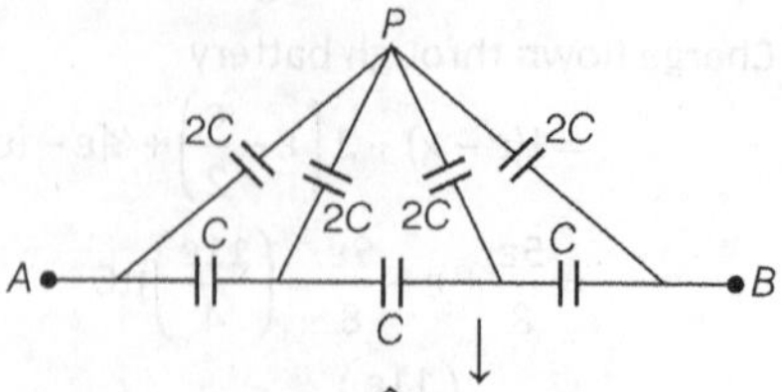

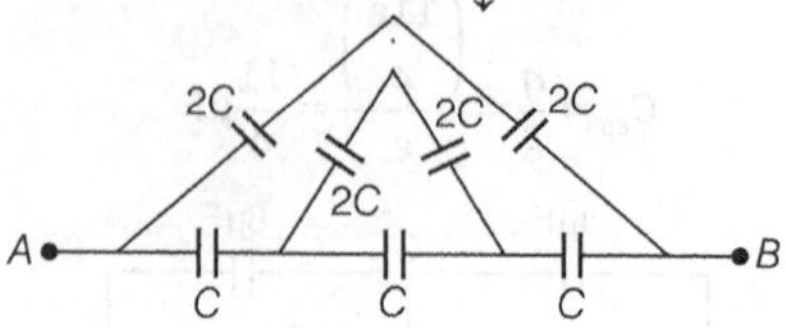

$$C_{eq} = \frac{7C}{5}$$

(vi)

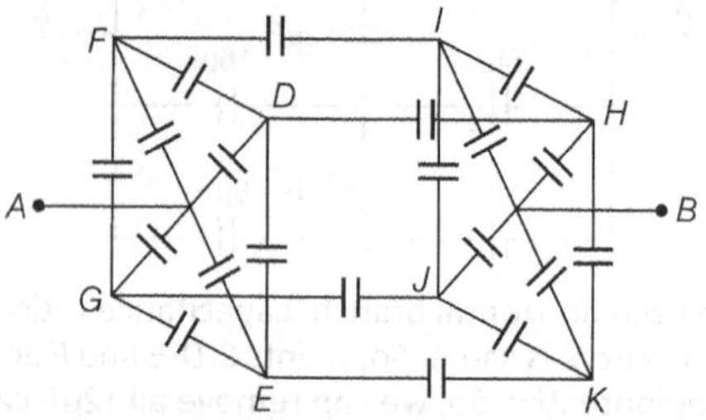

Due to symmetry, points D, E, F and G are equipotential. So, we can remove capacitors connected between D, E, F and G. Similarly, we can remove capacitors between H, I, J and K.

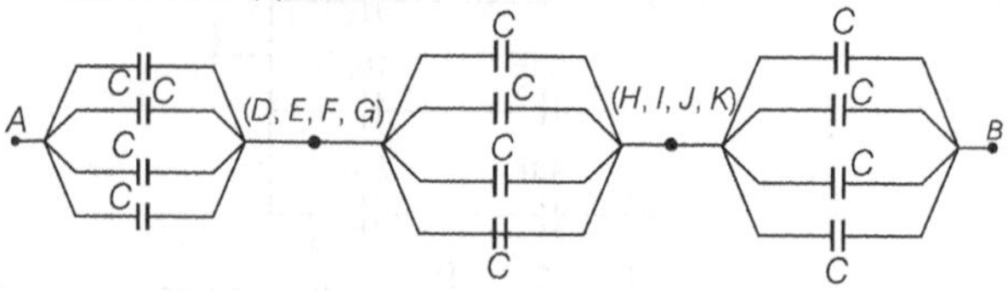

$$C_{eq} = \frac{4C}{3}$$

(vii)

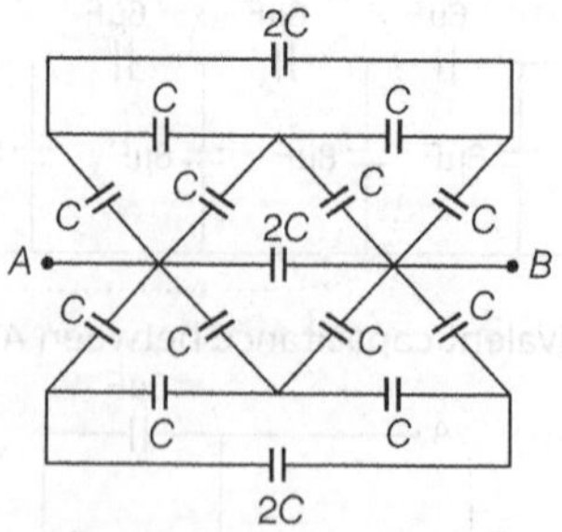

Due to parallel axis of symmetry, we can fold the circuit about axis AB.

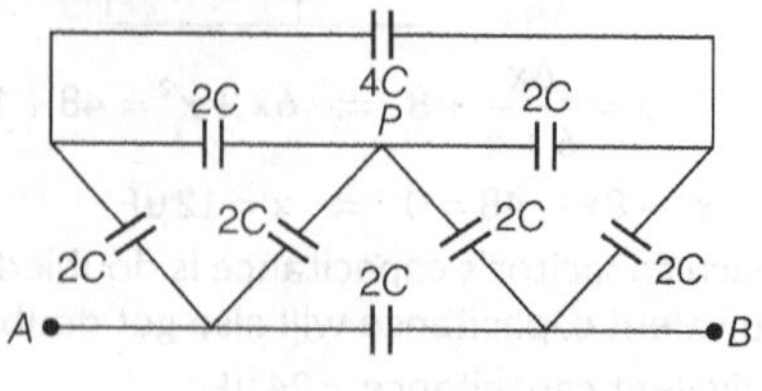

Due to perpendicular axis of symmetry, we can break junction at P as shown in figure.

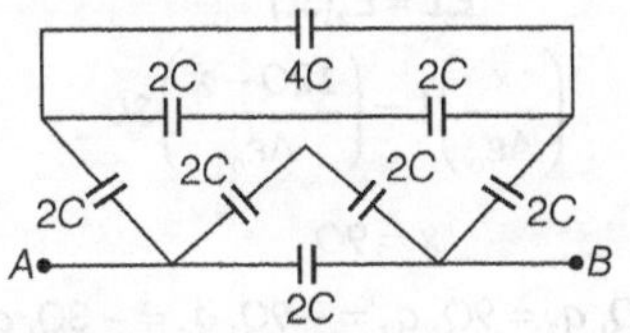

Now, using series and parallel combinations,

$$C_{eq} = \frac{23C}{6}$$

(viii)

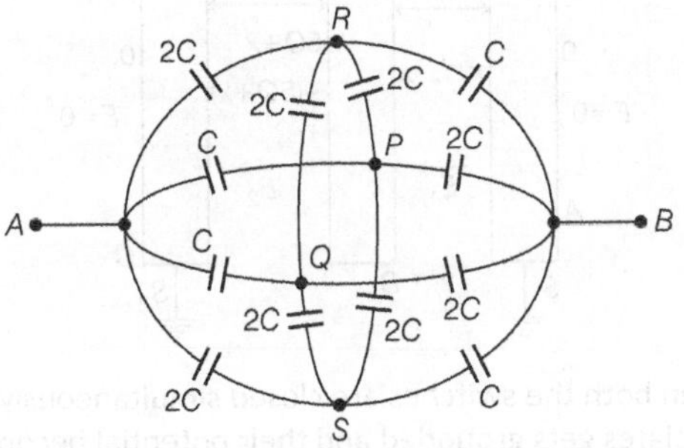

Due to symmetry, points P & Q and R & S are equipotential. So, we can join P & Q and R & S.

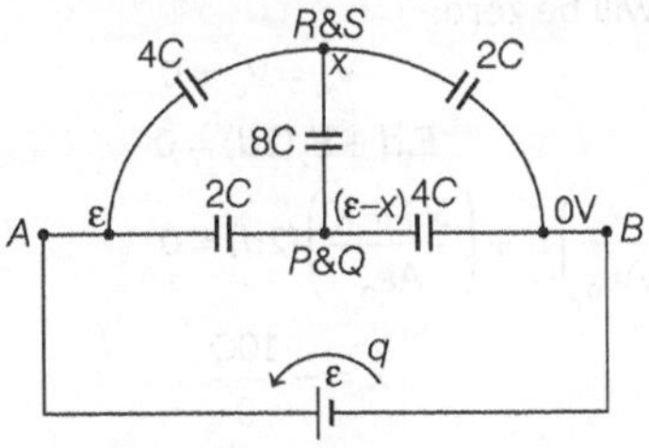

Using Kirchhoff's junction law,

$$4C(x-\varepsilon)+8C[x-(\varepsilon-x)]+2C(x-0)=0$$

$$\Rightarrow \quad 22x = 12\varepsilon$$

$$\Rightarrow \quad x = \frac{6\varepsilon}{11}$$

q = Charge flown through the battery

$$= 4C(\varepsilon - x) + 2C[\varepsilon - (\varepsilon - x)]$$

$$= \frac{20C\varepsilon}{11} + \frac{12C\varepsilon}{11} = \frac{32C\varepsilon}{11}$$

$$C_{eq} = \frac{q}{\varepsilon} = \frac{\frac{32C\varepsilon}{11}}{\varepsilon} = \frac{32C}{11}$$

9.7 Combination of Parallel Plates

1. (i)

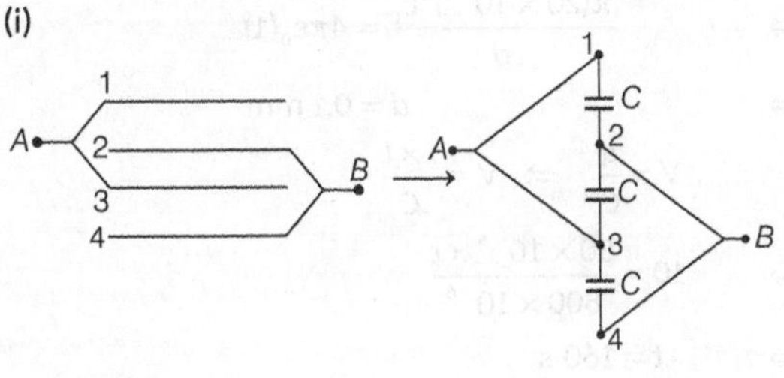

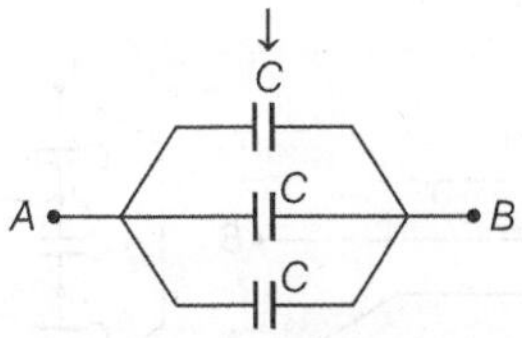

$$C_{eq} = 3C = \frac{3A\varepsilon_0}{d}$$

(ii)

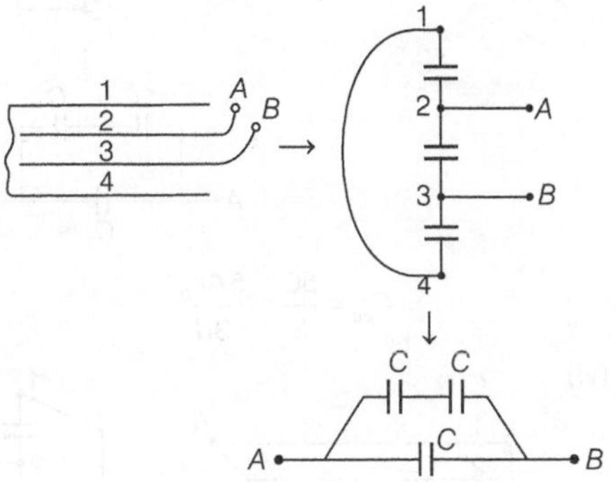

$$C_{eq} = \frac{3C}{2} = \frac{3}{2}\frac{A\varepsilon_0}{d}$$

(iii)

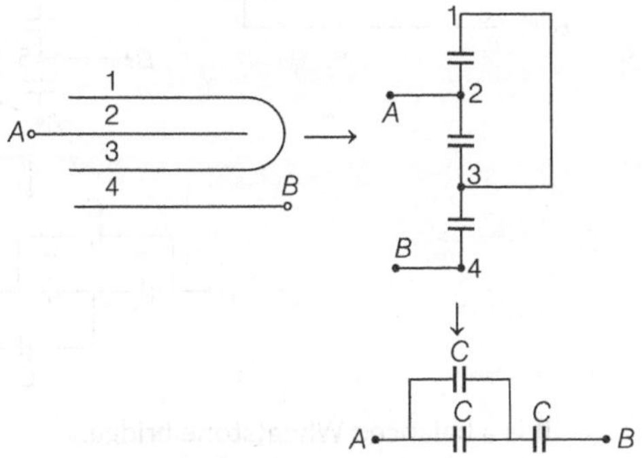

$$C_{eq} = \frac{2C}{3} = \frac{2}{3}\frac{A\varepsilon_0}{d}$$

(iv)

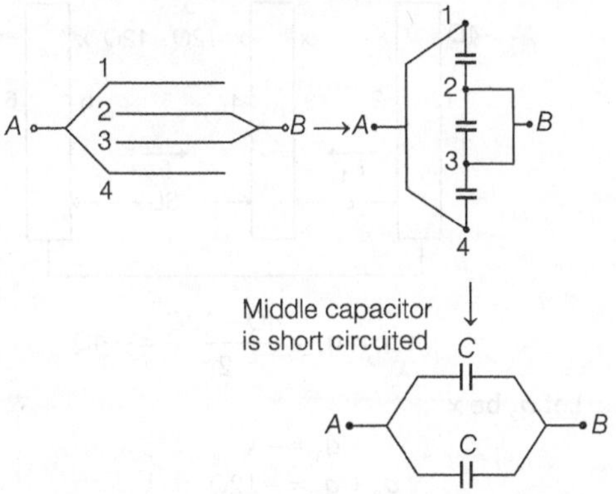

$$C_{eq} = 2C = \frac{2A\varepsilon_0}{d}$$

(v)

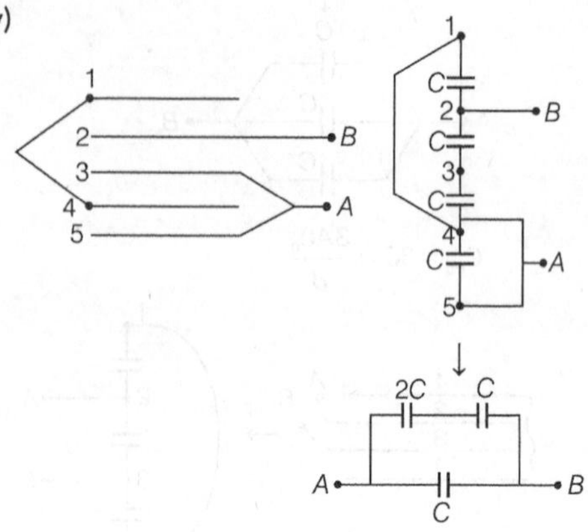

$$C_{eq} = \frac{5C}{3} = \frac{5A\varepsilon_0}{3d}$$

(vi)

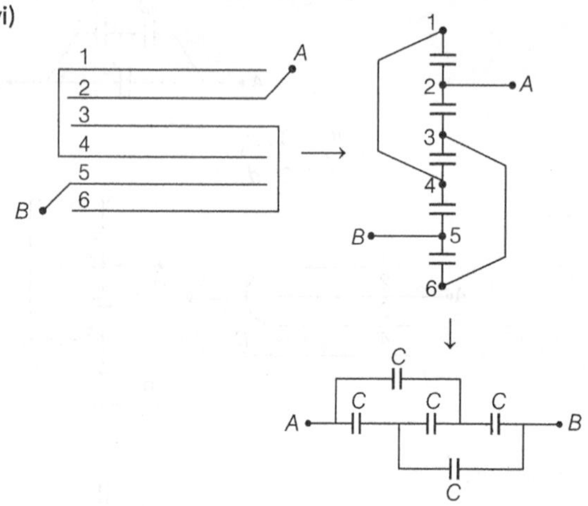

It is a balanced Wheatstone bridge.

$$C_{eq} = C = \frac{A\varepsilon_0}{d}$$

2.

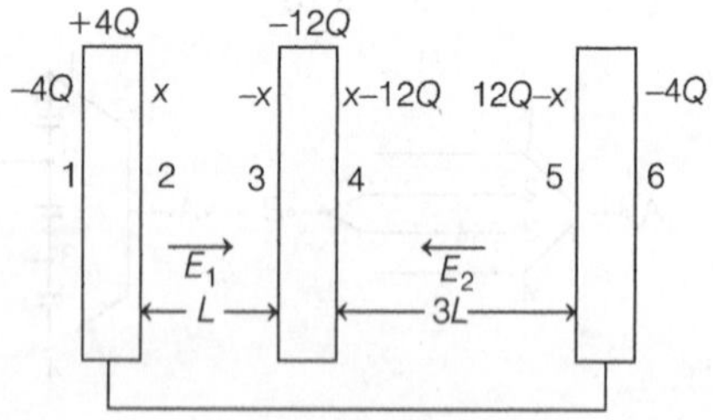

$$q_1 = q_6 = \frac{4Q - 12Q}{2} = -4Q$$

Let q_2 be x.

$$q_3 = -x$$

$$q_3 + q_4 = -12Q$$

$$\Rightarrow \quad q_4 = x - 12Q$$

$$q_5 = -q_4$$

$$\Rightarrow \quad q_5 = 12Q - x$$

Plates A and C are connected through a conducting wire,

$$V_A = V_C$$

$$\Rightarrow \quad V_A - V_B = V_C - V_B$$

$$\Rightarrow \quad E_1L = E_2(3L)$$

$$\Rightarrow \quad \left(\frac{x}{A\varepsilon_0}\right)L = \left(\frac{12Q - x}{A\varepsilon_0}\right)3L$$

$$\Rightarrow \quad x = 9Q$$

So, $q_1 = -4Q$, $q_2 = 9Q$, $q_3 = -9Q$, $q_4 = -3Q$, $q_5 = 3Q$ and $q_6 = -4Q$

3.

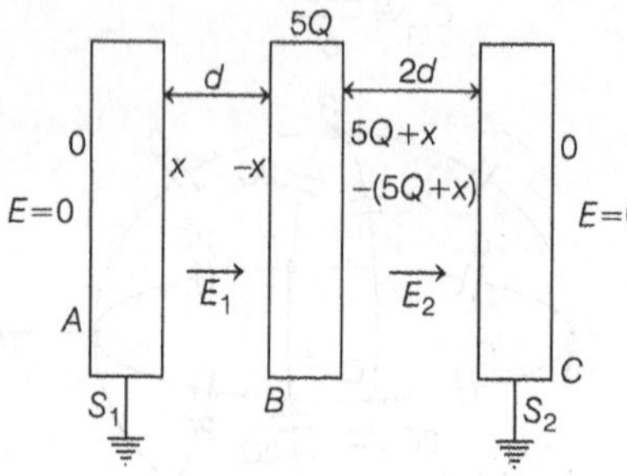

When both the switches are closed simultaneously, both the plates gets grounded and their potential become zero. So, there won't be any electric field in the region between the plates and infinity. Hence, charges on the outermost surfaces will be zero.

$$V_A = V_C = 0$$

$$\Rightarrow \quad E_1d + E_2(2d) = 0$$

$$\Rightarrow \quad \left(\frac{x}{A\varepsilon_0}\right)d + \left(\frac{5Q + x}{A\varepsilon_0}\right)(2d) = 0$$

$$\Rightarrow \quad x = -\frac{10Q}{3}$$

Charge flown through $S_1 = Q - \left(\frac{-10Q}{3}\right) = \frac{13Q}{3}$

Level 2 JEE Main Level

Single Choice Correct Questions

1. Charge will flow between them, if their potentials are not equal.

i.e. $\frac{KQ_1}{R_1} \neq \frac{KQ_2}{R_2}$

$$\Rightarrow \quad Q_1R_2 \neq Q_2R_1$$

2. $\frac{A\varepsilon_0}{d} = 4\pi\varepsilon_0 R$

$$\Rightarrow \quad \frac{\pi(20 \times 10^{-3})^2 \varepsilon_0}{d} = 4\pi\varepsilon_0(1)$$

$$\Rightarrow \quad d = 0.1 \text{ mm}$$

3. $V = \frac{q}{C} \Rightarrow V = \frac{i \times t}{C}$

$$\Rightarrow \quad 10 = \frac{50 \times 10^{-6} \times t}{800 \times 10^{-6}}$$

$$\Rightarrow \quad t = 160 \text{ s}$$

4. $$U = \frac{q^2}{2C} \quad \ldots \text{(i)}$$

$$1.21U = \frac{(q+2)^2}{2C} \quad \ldots \text{(ii)}$$

Dividing Eq. (ii) by Eq. (i), we get

$$\frac{(q+2)^2}{q^2} = 1.21$$

$$\Rightarrow \quad q + 2 = 1.1q$$

$$\Rightarrow \quad q = 20\text{C}$$

5. $C = \frac{A\varepsilon_0}{d}$

$$\frac{dC}{dt} = \frac{-A\varepsilon_0}{d^2}\frac{d(d)}{dt}$$

$$\Rightarrow \quad \frac{dC}{dt} = \frac{-A\varepsilon_0}{d^2}v$$

$$\Rightarrow \quad \frac{dC}{dt} \propto \frac{1}{d^2}$$

6. Capacitance will get halved. So, charge on capacitor will also get halved as voltage across the capacitor is constant.

$$E = \frac{V}{d}$$

Since, V is constant and d is doubled, electric field will become half of its initial value.

7. $U_1 = \frac{1}{2}C_1V^2 = \frac{1}{2} \times 12 \times 10^{-6} \times (10)^2 = 600\,\mu\text{J}$

$$U_2 = \frac{q^2}{2C_2} = \frac{(C_1V)^2}{2C_2} = \frac{(12 \times 10^{-6} \times 10)^2}{2 \times 6 \times 10^{-6}} = 1200\,\mu\text{J}$$

$$W_{\text{ext}} = \Delta U + \Delta K$$

$$= (1200 - 600) + 0 = 600\,\mu\text{J}$$

8. $U = \frac{1}{2}CV^2 \Rightarrow \quad Pt = \frac{1}{2}CV^2$

$\Rightarrow 2000 \times 0.04 = \frac{1}{2}C(1000)^2 \Rightarrow C = 160\,\mu\text{F}$

9. Capacitance of an isolated sphere $= 4\pi\varepsilon_0 a$

Capacitance of spherical capacitor $= \frac{4\pi\varepsilon_0 ab}{b-a}$

$$\frac{4\pi\varepsilon_0 ab}{b-a} = n(4\pi\varepsilon_0 a)$$

$$\Rightarrow \quad b = nb - na$$

$$\Rightarrow \quad \frac{b}{a} = \frac{n}{n-1}$$

10.

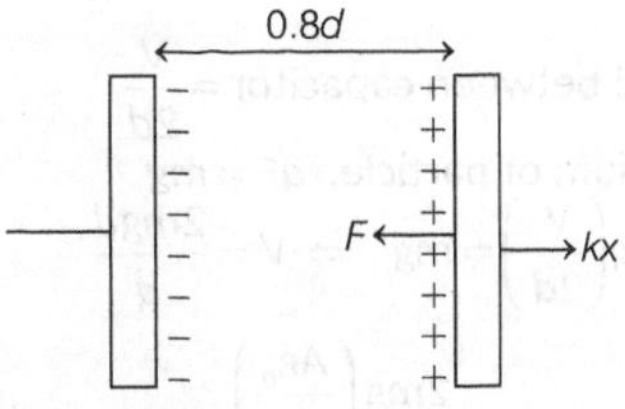

For equilibrium of right plate,

$$kx = F$$

$$\Rightarrow \quad k(d - 0.8d) = \frac{Q^2}{2A\varepsilon_0}$$

$$\Rightarrow \quad k(0.2)d = \frac{(CV)^2}{2A\varepsilon_0}$$

$$\Rightarrow \quad k(0.2)d = \frac{\left(\frac{A\varepsilon_0}{0.8d} \times 4\right)^2}{2A\varepsilon_0}$$

$$\Rightarrow \quad k = 625\text{ N/m}$$

11. When capacitor is disconnected from the battery, it carries charge CV.

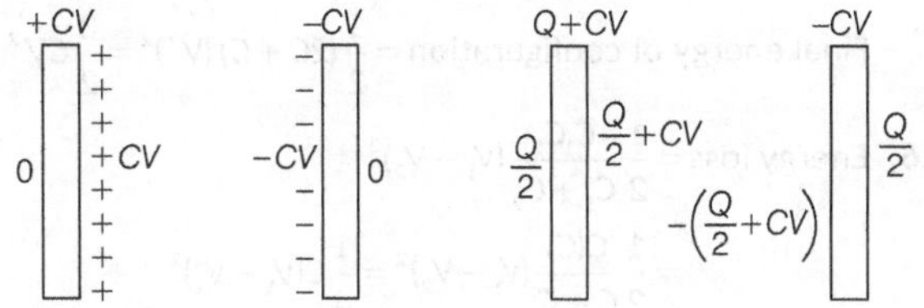

$$\text{Potential difference} = \frac{\frac{Q}{2} + CV}{C} = V + \frac{Q}{2C}$$

12.

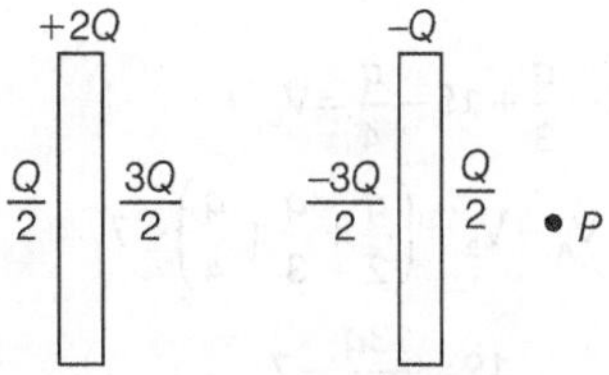

(a) A point charge at point P will experience force due to charge on the outer surfaces of the two plates.

(b) Potential difference $= \frac{3Q/2}{C} = \frac{3Q}{2C}$

(c) Energy stored $= \frac{(3Q/2)^2}{2C} = \frac{9Q^2}{8C}$

(d) $F = Q\left(\frac{(2Q)}{2A\varepsilon_0}\right) = \frac{Q^2}{A\varepsilon_0}$

13.

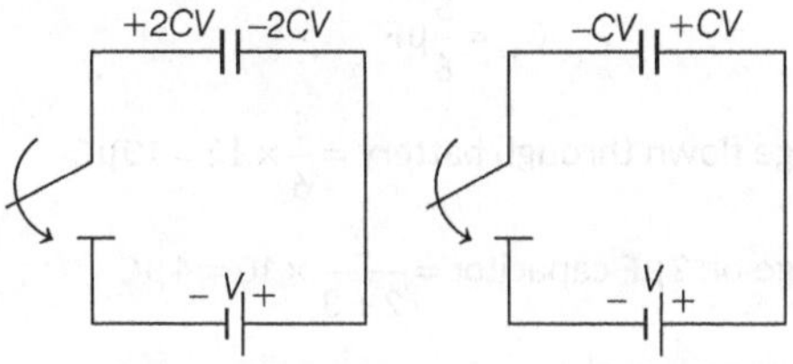

Charge flown through battery $= CV - (-2CV) = 3CV$

Work done by battery $= (3CV)V = 3CV^2$

$$\Delta U = U_2 - U_1 = \frac{1}{2}CV^2 - \frac{(2CV)^2}{2C} = \frac{-3}{2}CV^2$$

$$\text{Heat produced} = W_{\text{battery}} - \Delta U$$

$$= 3CV^2 - (-1.5\,CV^2)$$

$$= 4.5\,CV^2$$

14. Energy loss $= \dfrac{1}{2}\dfrac{C_1C_2}{C_1+C_2}(V_1 - V_2)^2$

$$= \frac{1}{2} \times \frac{4\times10^{-6}\times2\times10^{-6}}{6\times10^{-6}}(200-0)^2 = \frac{8}{3}\times10^{-2}$$

$$\% \text{ loss} = \frac{8/3\times10^{-2}}{\frac{1}{2}\times4\times10^{-6}\times(200)^2}\times100 = 33.33\%$$

15. $q_1 + q_2 = q_1' + q_2'$

$\Rightarrow \quad 2C(2V) - CV = (2C + C)V'$

$\Rightarrow \quad V' = V$

Final energy of configuration $= \dfrac{1}{2}(2C + C)(V')^2 = \dfrac{3}{2}CV^2$

16. Energy loss $= \dfrac{1}{2}\dfrac{C_1C_2}{C_1+C_2}(V_1 - V_2)^2$

$$= \frac{1}{2}\frac{C(C)}{C+C}(V_1 - V_2)^2 = \frac{1}{4}C(V_1 - V_2)^2$$

17.

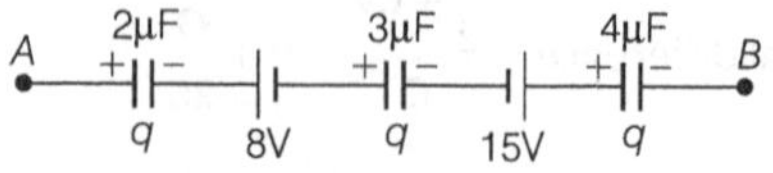

$$V_A - \frac{q}{2} - 8 - \frac{q}{3} + 15 - \frac{q}{4} = V_B$$

$\Rightarrow \quad V_A - V_B = \left(\dfrac{q}{2} + \dfrac{q}{3} + \dfrac{q}{4}\right) - 7$

$\Rightarrow \quad 19 = \dfrac{13q}{12} - 7$

$\Rightarrow \quad q = 24\,\mu C$

Potential difference across $3\,\mu F$ capacitor $= \dfrac{q}{C} = \dfrac{24\,\mu C}{3\,\mu F} = 8V$

18.

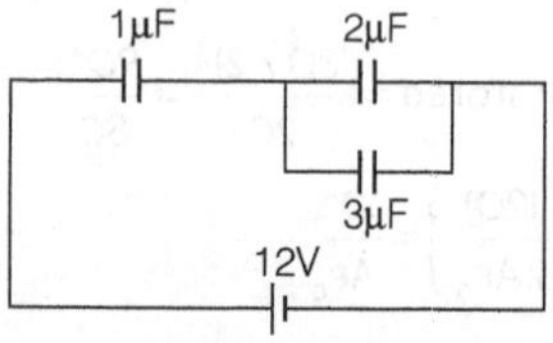

$$C_{eq} = \frac{5}{6}\mu F$$

Charge flown through battery $= \dfrac{5}{6}\times12 = 10\,\mu C$

Charge on $2\,\mu F$ capacitor $= \dfrac{2}{2+3}\times10 = 4\,\mu C$

19. Equivalent capacitance across battery $= 2\,\mu F$

Charge flown through battery $= 72\times2 = 144\,\mu C$

Charge on $1\,\mu F$ capacitor $= \left(\dfrac{1}{1+5}\right)\left(\dfrac{2}{2+4}\right)144 = 8\,\mu C$

Energy stored in $1\,\mu F$ capacitor $= \dfrac{q^2}{2C}$

$$= \frac{(8\times10^{-6})^2}{2\times1\times10^{-6}} = 32\,\mu J$$

20.

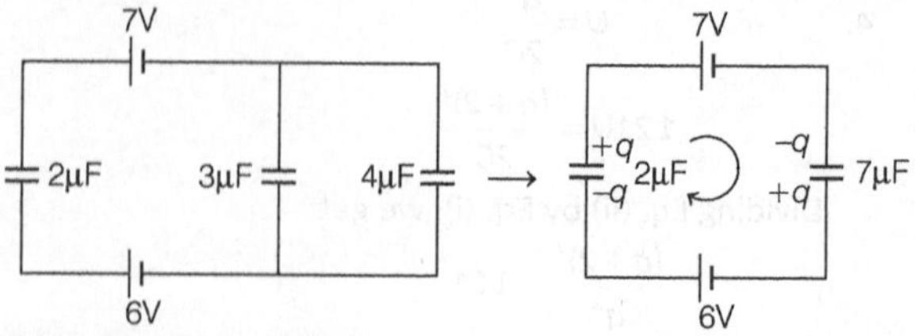

Applying KVL in the loop,

$$+\frac{q}{2} - 7 + \frac{q}{7} + 6 = 0 \Rightarrow q = \frac{14}{9}\mu C$$

Charge on $3\,\mu F$ capacitor $= \dfrac{3}{3+4}\times\dfrac{14}{9} = \dfrac{2}{3}\mu C$

21.

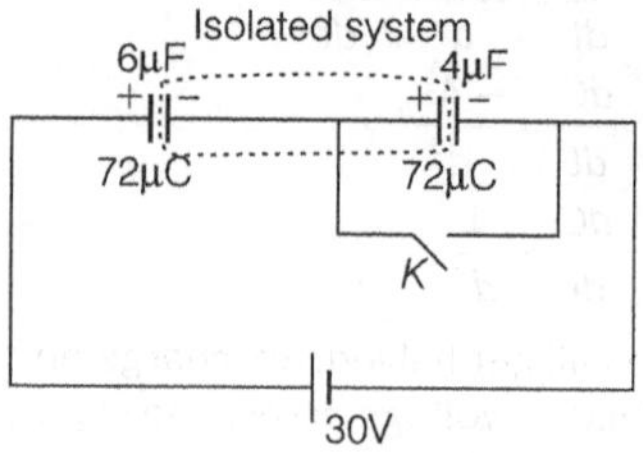

$$C_{eq} = \left(\frac{1}{6} + \frac{1}{4}\right)^{-1} = 2.4\,\mu F$$

Charge flown through battery $= 30\times2.4 = 72\,\mu C$

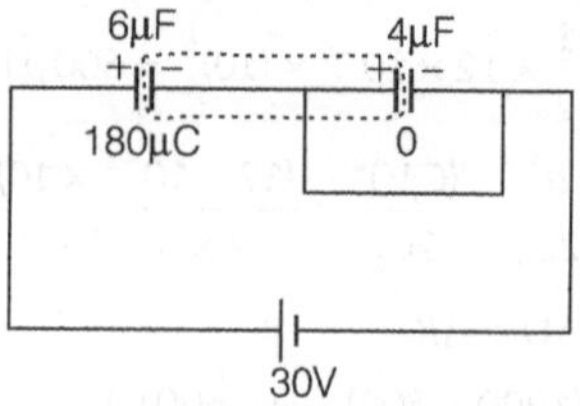

When key is closed, $4\,\mu F$ capacitor gets short-circuited.

Charge on $6\,\mu F$ capacitor will be $180\,\mu C$.

Charge flown through the key = Change in charge of isolated system

$$= (180 + 0) - (-72 + 72) = 180\,\mu C$$

22.

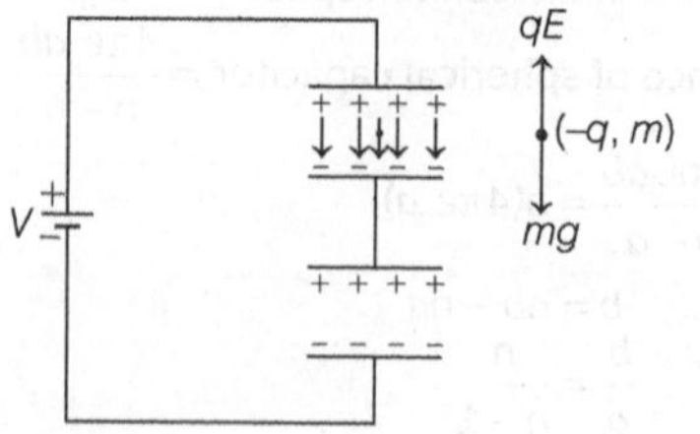

Potential difference across each capacitor $= \dfrac{V}{2}$

Electric field between capacitor $= \dfrac{V}{2d}$

For equilibrium of particle, $qE = mg$

$\Rightarrow \quad q\left(\dfrac{V}{2d}\right) = mg \Rightarrow V = \dfrac{2mgd}{q}$

$\Rightarrow \quad V = \dfrac{2mg\left(\dfrac{A\varepsilon_0}{C}\right)}{q} \qquad \left(\because C = \dfrac{A\varepsilon_0}{d}\right)$

$$\Rightarrow \quad V = \frac{2mgA\varepsilon_0}{qC}$$

$$= \frac{2\times 10\times 10^{-6}\times 9.8\times 100\times 10^{-4}\times 8.85\times 10^{-12}}{0.01\times 10^{-6}\times 0.04\times 10^{-6}}$$

$$= 43.37 \text{ mV}$$

Hence, the value of potential difference is close to option (c).

23. V_1 = Potential drop across $C_1 = 6V$

V_2 = Potential drop across $C_2 = 4V$

In series combination,

$$\frac{C_1}{C_2} = \frac{V_2}{V_1} \Rightarrow \frac{C_1}{C_2} = \frac{4}{6} = \frac{2}{3}$$

24.

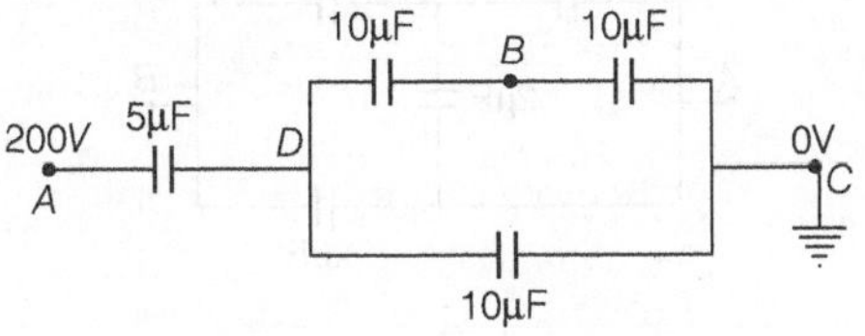

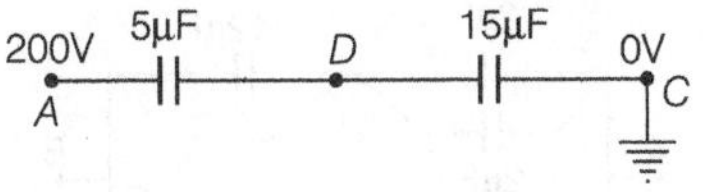

$$\frac{V_A - V_D}{V_D - V_C} = \frac{15}{5}$$

$$\Rightarrow \quad \frac{2000 - V_D}{V_D - 0} = 3 \Rightarrow V_D = 500V$$

$$\frac{V_D - V_B}{V_B - V_C} = \frac{10}{10} \Rightarrow \frac{500 - V_B}{V_B - 0} = 1$$

$$\Rightarrow \quad V_B = 250 \text{ V}$$

25.

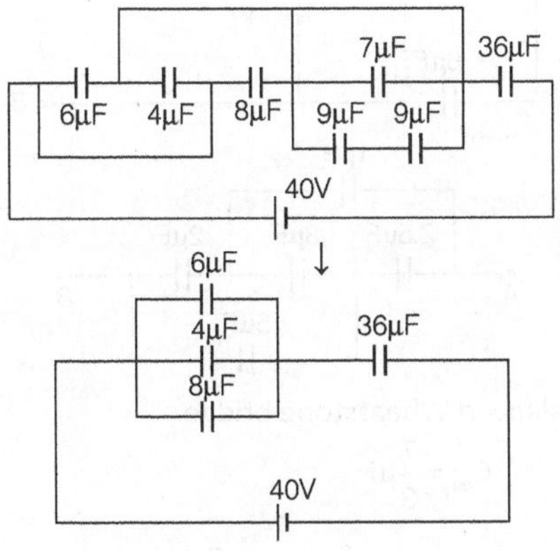

$$\frac{1}{C_{eq}} = \frac{1}{36} + \frac{1}{(6+4+8)}$$

$$C_{eq} = 12\,\mu F$$

Charge flown through battery $= 12 \times 40 = 480\,\mu C$

Charge on $8\,\mu F$ capacitor $= \frac{8}{18} \times 480 = 213.33\,\mu C \simeq 214\,\mu C$

Potential difference across $8\mu F$ capacitor

$$= \frac{q}{C} = \frac{214}{8} \simeq 27V$$

26.

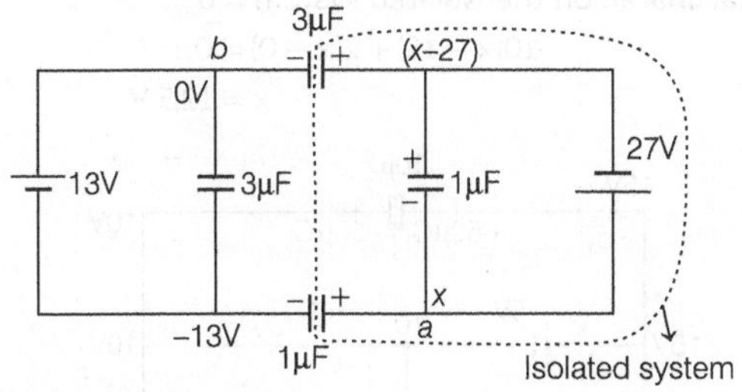

Let $V_b = 0$ and $V_a = x$

Applying charge conservation for the isolated system,

$$\Rightarrow \quad 3[(x-27)-0] + 1[x-(-13)] = 0$$

$$\Rightarrow \quad x = 17V$$

$$V_a - V_b = 17 - 0 = 17\text{ V}$$

27.

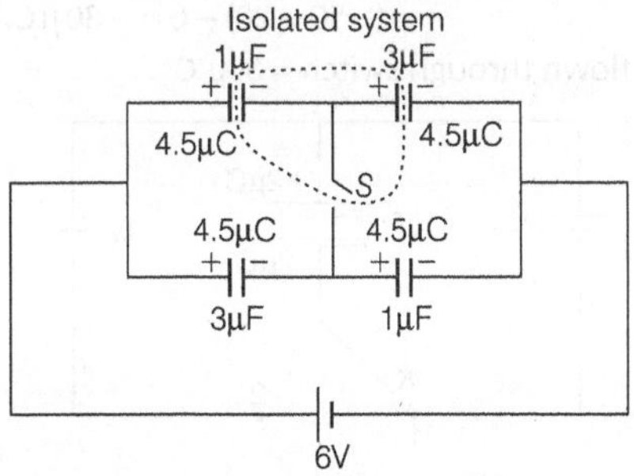

When switch is open, $C_{eq} = 1.5\,\mu F$

Charge flown through battery $= 6 \times 1.5 = 9\,\mu C$

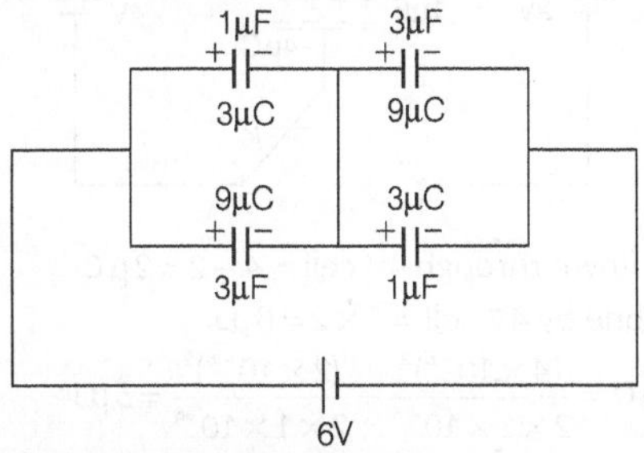

When the switch is closed, $C_{eq} = 2\,\mu F$

Charge flown through battery $= 6 \times 2 = 12\,\mu C$

Charge flown through switch = Change in charge of the isolated system

$$= (+9-3) - (-4.5+4.5) = 6\mu C$$

28.

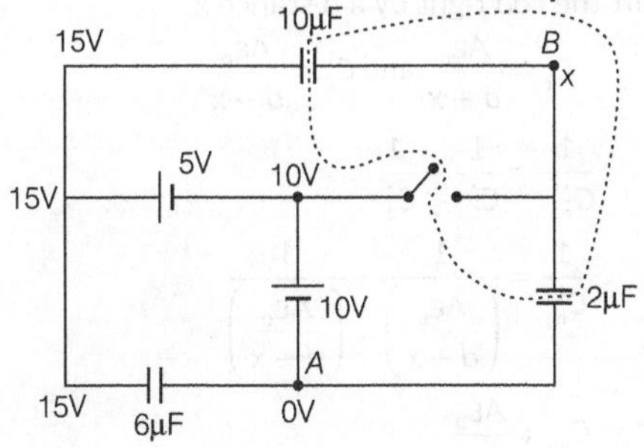

Let $V_A = 0$ and $V_B = x$

Total charge on the isolated system = 0

$\Rightarrow \quad 10(x-15)+2(x-0)=0$

$\Rightarrow \quad x = 12.5\text{ V}$

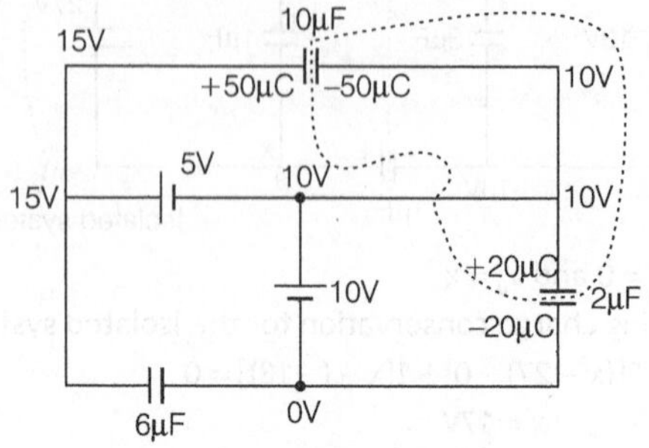

Change in charge of the isolated system

$=(-50+20)-0=-30\,\mu\text{C}$

Charge flown through switch = 30μ C

29.

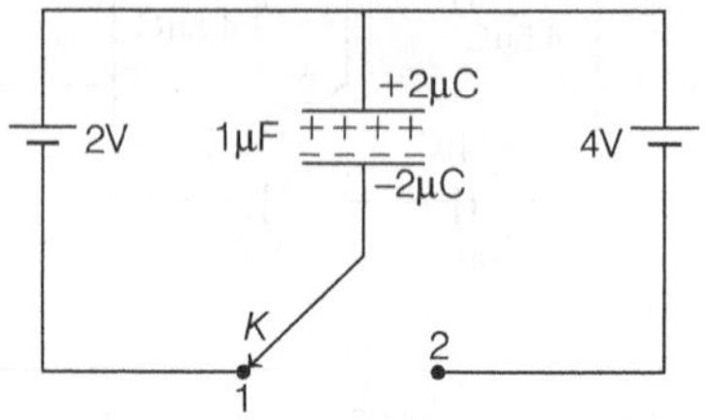

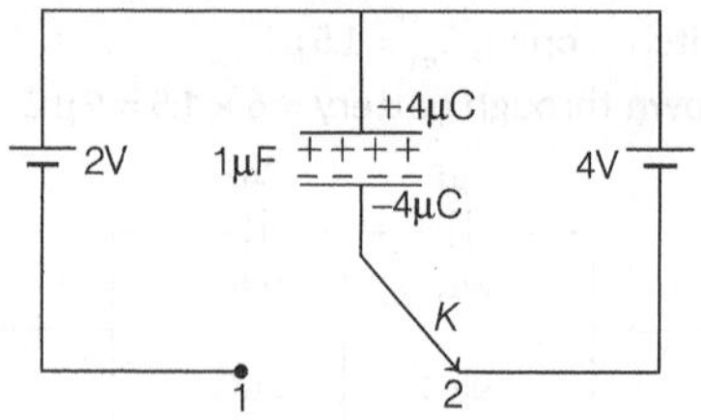

Charge flown through 4V cell $=4-2=2\,\mu\text{C}$

Work done by 4V cell $=4\times 2=8\,\mu\text{J}$

$$\Delta U=\frac{(4\times 10^{-6})^2}{2\times 1\times 10^{-6}}-\frac{(2\times 10^{-6})^2}{2\times 1\times 10^{-6}}=6\,\mu\text{J}$$

Heat produced $=W_{\text{cell}}-\Delta U=8-6=2\,\mu\text{J}$

30. Initially, $C_1=\dfrac{A\varepsilon_0}{d}$ and $C_2=\dfrac{A\varepsilon_0}{d}$

$$\frac{1}{C_{eq}}=\frac{1}{C_1}+\frac{1}{C_2}\Rightarrow C_{eq}=\frac{A\varepsilon_0}{2d}$$

Let shift the rod right by a distance x.

Now, $C_1'=\dfrac{A\varepsilon_0}{d+x}$ and $C_2'=\dfrac{A\varepsilon_0}{d-x}$

$$\frac{1}{C_{eq}'}=\frac{1}{C_1'}+\frac{1}{C_2'}$$

$$\frac{1}{C_{eq}'}=\frac{1}{\left(\dfrac{A\varepsilon_0}{d+x}\right)}+\frac{1}{\left(\dfrac{A\varepsilon_0}{d-x}\right)}$$

$$\Rightarrow \quad C_{eq}'=\frac{A\varepsilon_0}{2d}$$

So, capacitance between terminals 1 and 2 remains unchanged.

31. 12 identical capacitors in series, $C_{eq}=\dfrac{A\varepsilon_0}{12d}$

Now, $$\frac{1}{C_{eq}'}=\left(\frac{1}{\dfrac{A\varepsilon_0}{d/2}}\right)n+(12-n)\left(\frac{1}{\dfrac{A\varepsilon_0}{2d}}\right)$$

$$C_{eq}'=C_{eq}$$

$$\Rightarrow \quad \frac{n}{2}+2(12-n)=12\Rightarrow n=8$$

32.

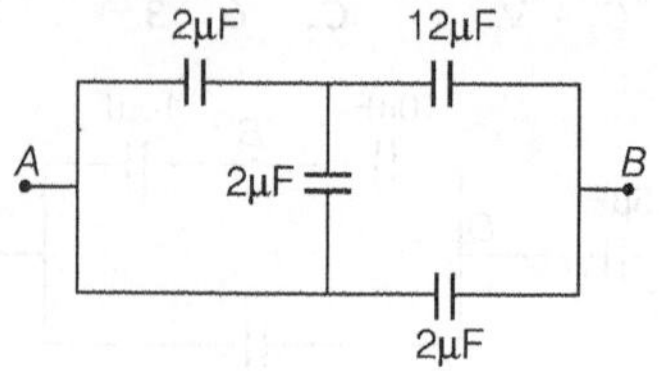

↓

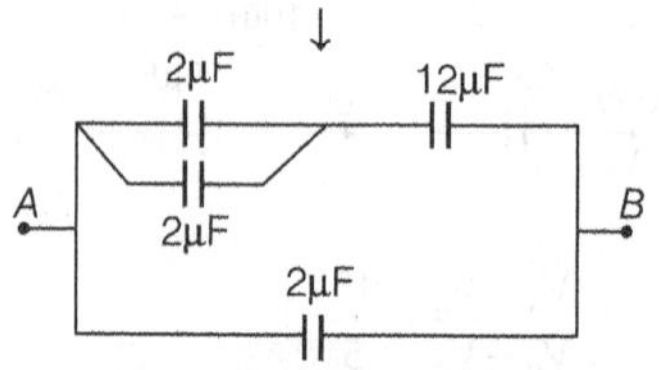

$C_{eq}=5\,\mu\text{F}$

33.

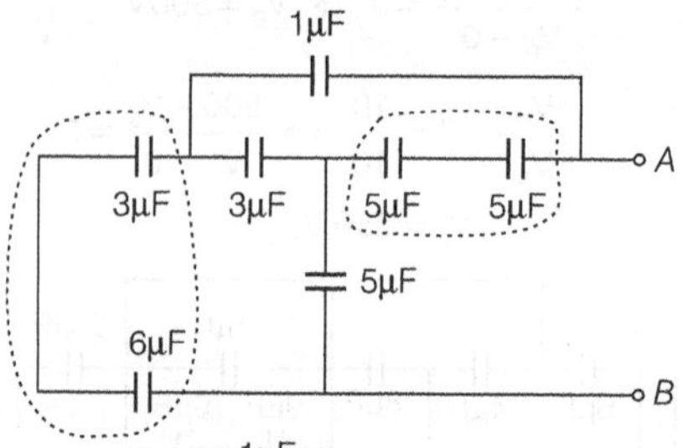

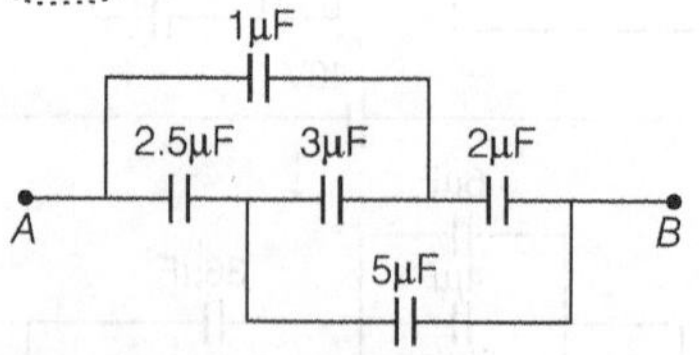

It is a balanced Wheatstone bridge.

$$C_{eq}=\frac{7}{3}\,\mu\text{F}$$

34.

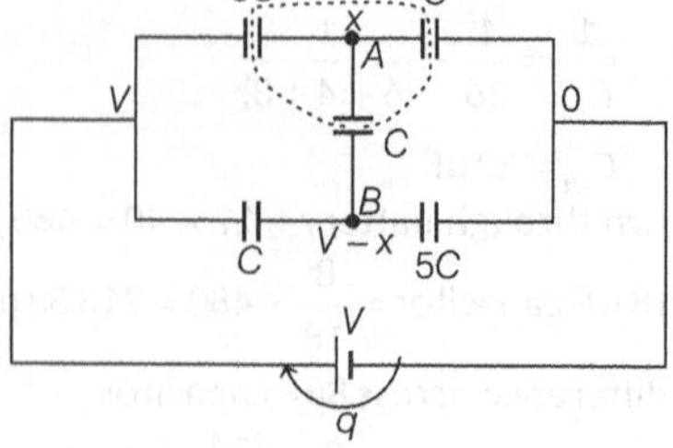

Applying KCL at junction A,

$$5C(x-V)+C[x-(V-x)]+C(x-0)=0$$

$$x=\frac{3V}{4}$$

$$q=\text{Charge flown the battery}=5C\left(V-\frac{3V}{4}\right)+C\left(\frac{3V}{4}\right)=2CV$$

$$C_{eq}=\frac{q}{V}=\frac{2CV}{V}=2C$$

35.

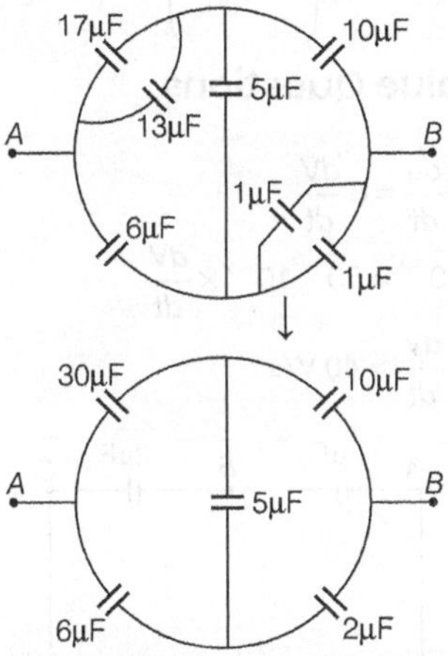

This is a balanced Wheatstone bridge.

$$C_{eq}=9\mu F$$

36. Let equivalent capacitance between A and B be x.

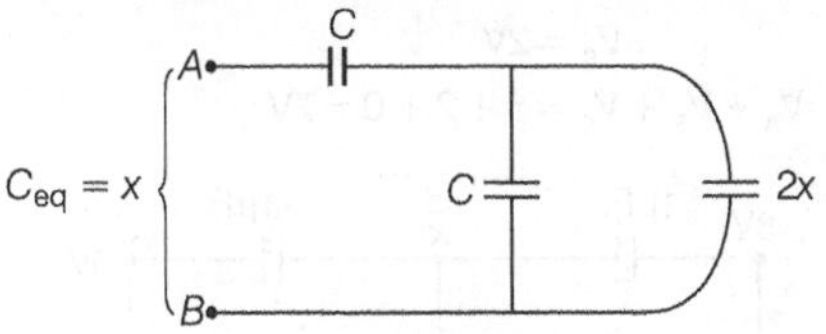

$$\frac{1}{x}=\frac{1}{C}+\frac{1}{(2x+C)}\Rightarrow\frac{1}{x}=\frac{2x+2C}{C(2x+C)}$$

$$\Rightarrow\quad 2x^2+2Cx=2Cx+C^2\Rightarrow x=\frac{C}{\sqrt{2}}$$

37.

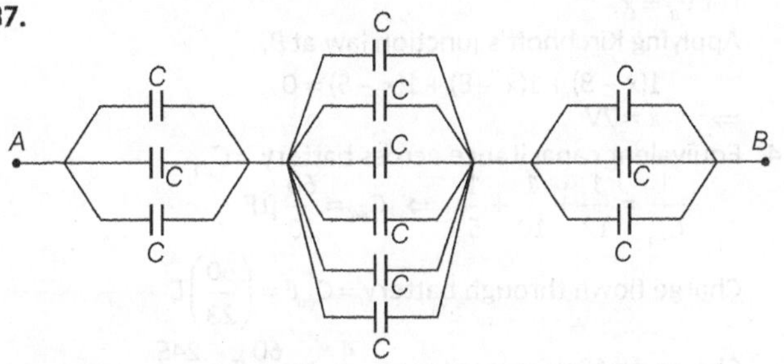

$$\frac{1}{C_{eq}}=\frac{1}{3C}+\frac{1}{6C}+\frac{1}{3C}\Rightarrow C_{eq}=\frac{6C}{5}$$

38. Maximum charge on $2\mu F$ capacitor $=2\times3=6\mu C$

Maximum charge on $3\mu F$ capacitor $=3\times2=6\mu C$

Maximum charge on $5\mu F$ capacitor $=5\times1=5\mu C$

If they are connected in series, maximum charge permissible will be $5\mu C$.

$$V=V_1+V_2+V_3=\frac{5}{2}+\frac{5}{3}+\frac{5}{5}=\frac{31}{6}V$$

39.

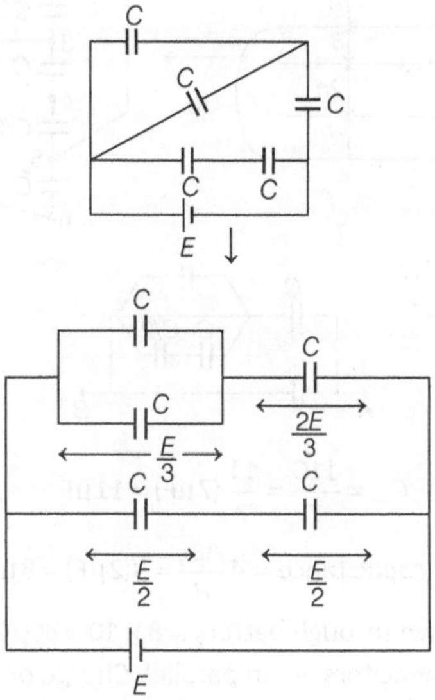

$$\text{Maximum voltage}=\frac{2E}{3}=2$$

$$\Rightarrow\quad E=3V$$

40. When they are connected by a copper wire, entire charge of inner conductor will go to the outer conductor.

So, capacitance $=4\pi\varepsilon_0 r_2$

41.

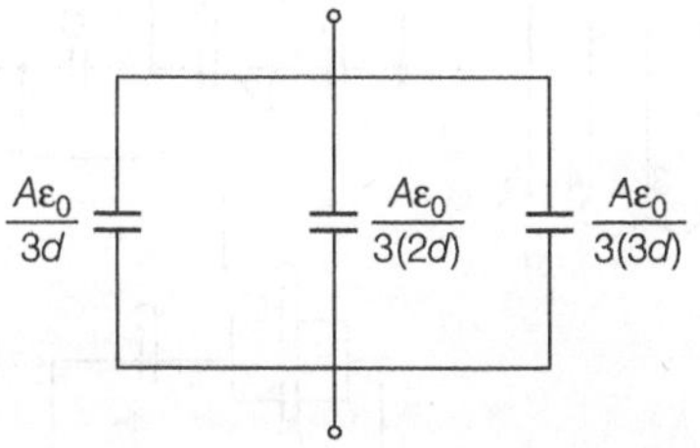

$$C_{eq}=C_1+C_2+C_3$$

$$=\frac{A\varepsilon_0}{3d}+\frac{A\varepsilon_0}{6d}+\frac{A\varepsilon_0}{9d}=\frac{11A\varepsilon_0}{18d}$$

42.

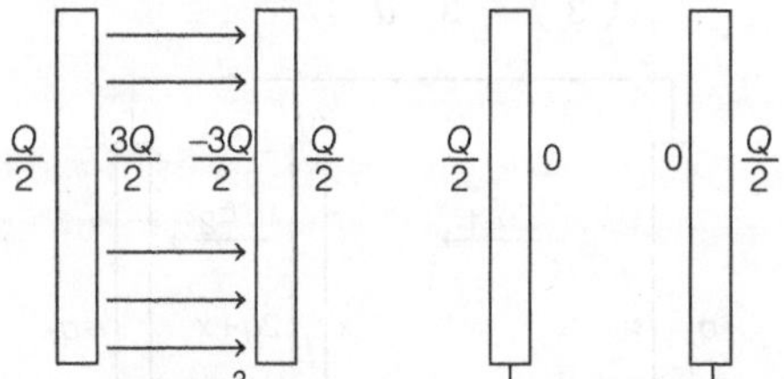

$$U_1=\frac{(3Q/2)^2}{2C}\qquad U_2=0$$

$$\text{Heat produced}=-\Delta U=U_1-U_2=\frac{9Q^2}{8C}=\frac{9Q^2d}{8A\varepsilon_0}$$

43. Let $\frac{A\varepsilon_0}{d} = C = 7\,\mu F$

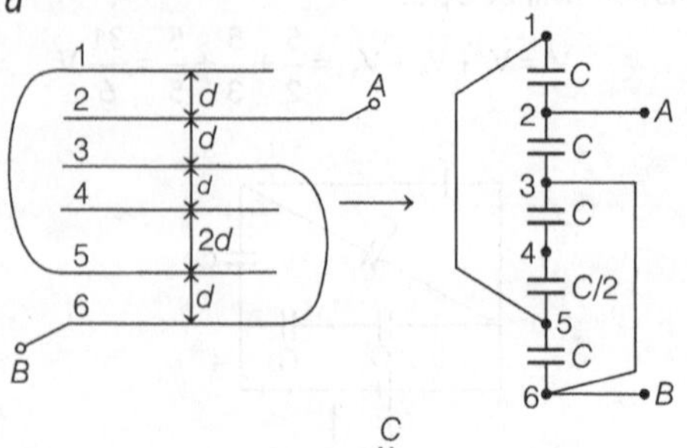

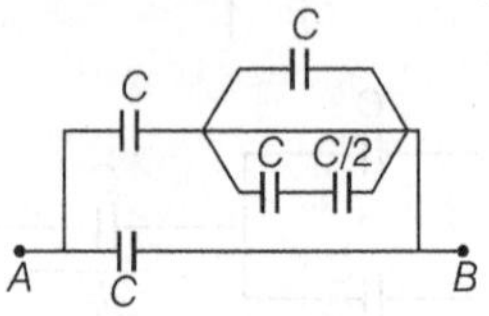

$$C_{eq} = \frac{11C}{7} = \frac{11}{7}(7\,\mu F) = 11\,\mu F$$

44. Equivalent capacitance $= 4\frac{A\varepsilon_0}{d} = 4(2\,\mu F) = 8\,\mu F$

Charge flown through battery $= 8 \times 10 = 80\mu C$

The four capacitors are in parallel. Charge on each capacitor $= 20\,\mu C$

Upper surface of plate C forms a capacitor with plate B and lower surface of plate C forms capacitor with plate D.

Total charge on plate $C = +20\,\mu C + 20\,\mu C = +40\,\mu C$

45.

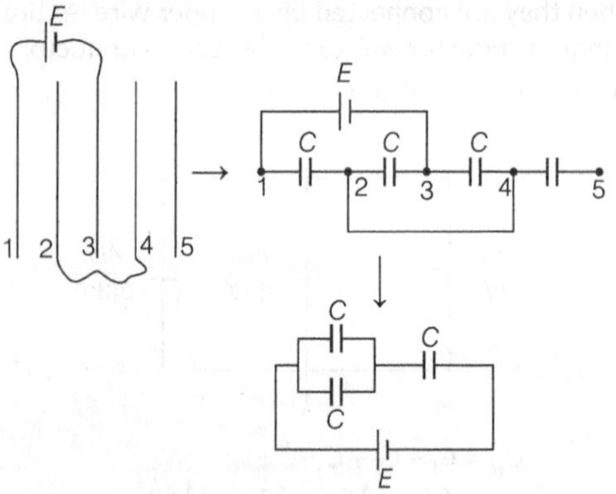

Charge flown through battery $= C_{eq}E$

$$= \left(\frac{2C}{3}\right)E = \frac{2}{3}\frac{\varepsilon_0 AE}{d}$$

46.

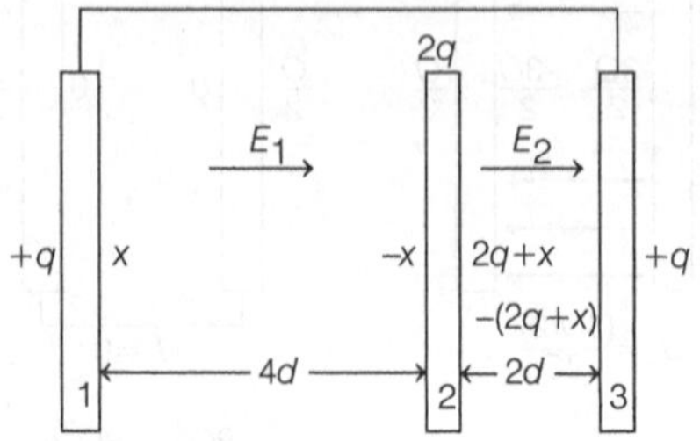

$$V_1 = V_3$$

$$\Rightarrow \quad V_1 - V_2 = V_3 - V_2$$

$$\Rightarrow \quad E_1(4d) = -E_2(2d)$$

$$\Rightarrow \quad \left(\frac{x}{A\varepsilon_0}\right)4d = -\left(\frac{2q+x}{A\varepsilon_0}\right)2d$$

$$\Rightarrow \quad 2x = -(2q+x) \quad \Rightarrow \quad x = -\frac{2q}{3}$$

$$V_2 - V_3 = E_2(2d) = \left(\frac{2q - \frac{2q}{3}}{A\varepsilon_0}\right)2d = \frac{8qd}{3A\varepsilon_0}$$

Numerical Value Questions

1. $q = CV$

$$\frac{dq}{dt} = C\frac{dV}{dt}$$

$$\Rightarrow \quad 2 \times 10^{-3} = 50 \times 10^{-6} \times \frac{dV}{dt}$$

$$\Rightarrow \quad \frac{dV}{dt} = 40 \text{ V/s}$$

2.

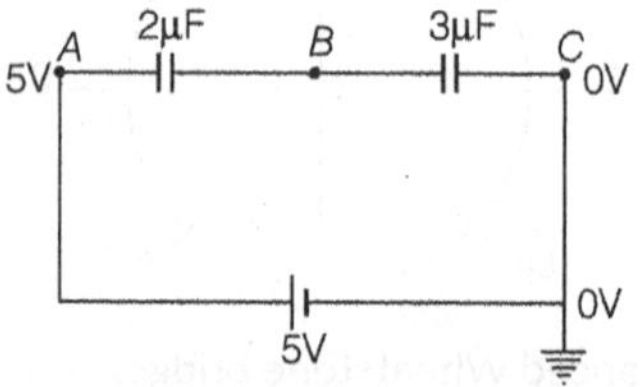

$$\frac{V_A - V_B}{V_B - V_C} = \frac{3}{2} \quad \Rightarrow \quad \frac{5 - V_B}{V_B - 0} = \frac{3}{2}$$

$$\Rightarrow \quad V_B = 2V$$

$$V_A + V_B + V_C = 5 + 2 + 0 = 7V$$

3.

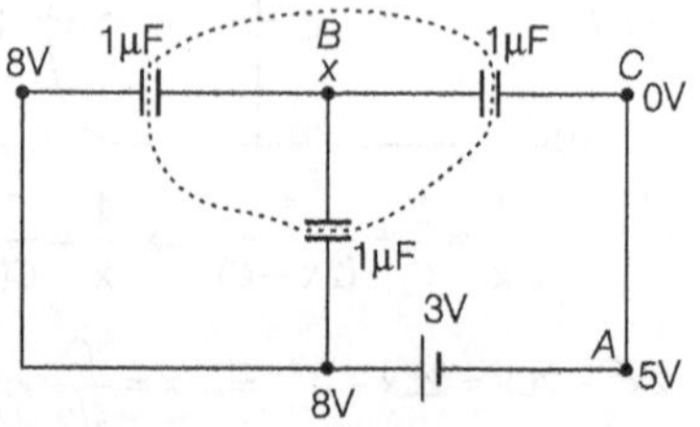

Let $V_B = x$.

Applying Kirchhoff's junction law at B,

$$1(x-8) + 1(x-8) + 1(x-5) = 0$$

$$\Rightarrow \quad x = 7V$$

4. Equivalent capacitance across battery $= C_{eq}$

$$\frac{1}{C_{eq}} = \frac{1}{12} + \frac{1}{10} + \frac{1}{5} \quad \Rightarrow \quad C_{eq} = \frac{60}{23}\,\mu F$$

Charge flown through battery $= C_{eq}E = \left(\frac{60}{23}\right)E$

Charge on $12\,\mu F$ capacitor $= \frac{4}{4+6} \times \frac{60}{23}E = \frac{24E}{23}$

Potential difference across $12\,\mu F$ capacitor

$$= \frac{q}{C} = \frac{24E/23}{12} = \frac{2E}{23}$$

$$\frac{2E}{23} = 4 \quad \Rightarrow \quad E = 46V$$

5.

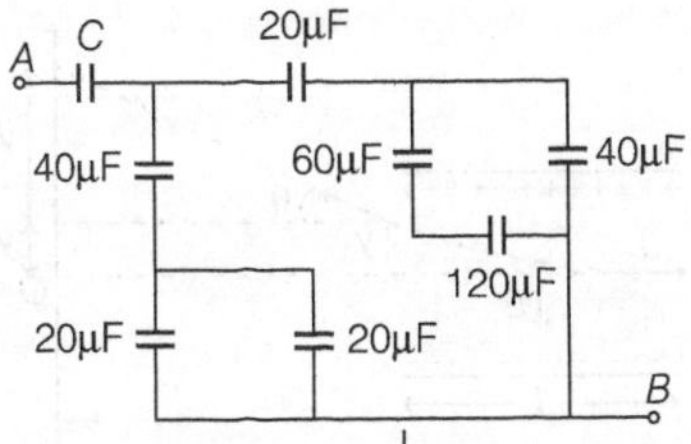

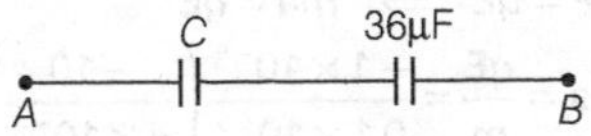

$$\frac{1}{C_{eq}} = \frac{1}{C} + \frac{1}{36} \Rightarrow \frac{1}{12} = \frac{1}{C} + \frac{1}{36}$$

$$\Rightarrow \quad C = 18\mu F$$

6.

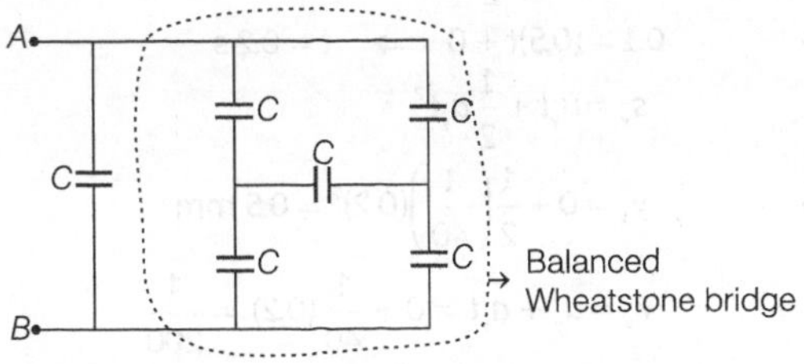

$$C_{eq} = 2C = 2(2\,\mu F) = 4\,\mu F$$

7.

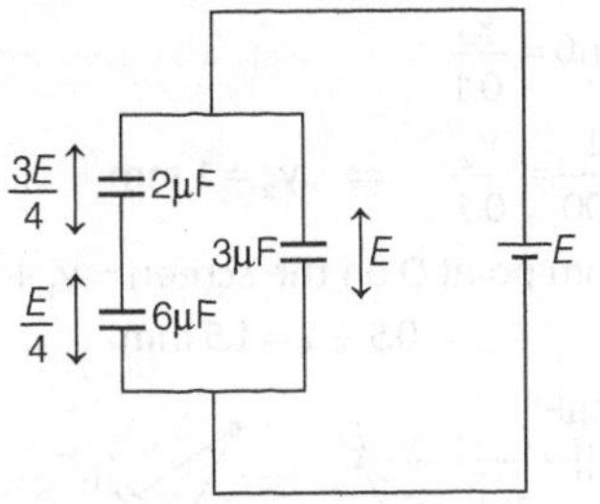

$$E < 150$$

$$\frac{3E}{4} < 90 \Rightarrow E < 120$$

$$\frac{E}{4} < 150 \Rightarrow E < 600$$

$$E_{max} = 120V$$

8.

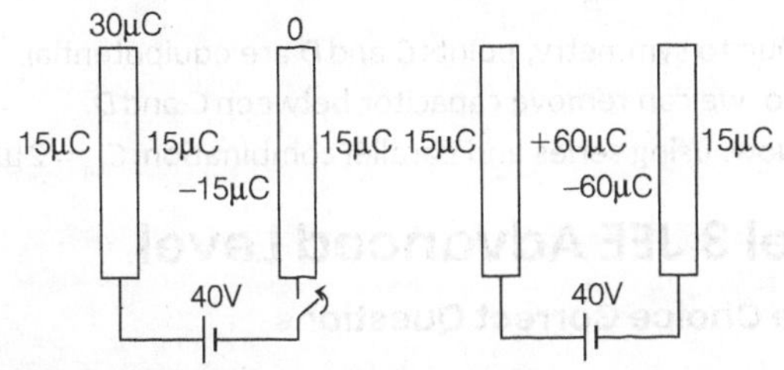

Charge flown through battery $= 60 - 15 = 45\,\mu C$

Work done by battery $= (45\,\mu C)(40\,V) = 1800\,\mu J$

9. $q_1 + q_2 = q_1' + q_2'$

$\Rightarrow \quad 8 \times 125 + 0 = (8 + C_0)20$

$\Rightarrow \quad C_0 = 42\,\mu F$

10.

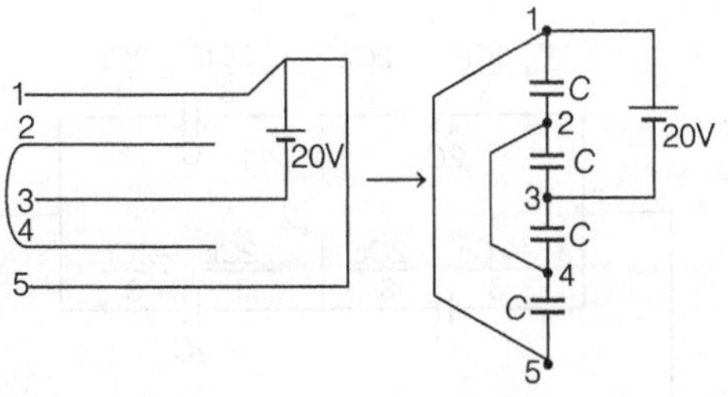

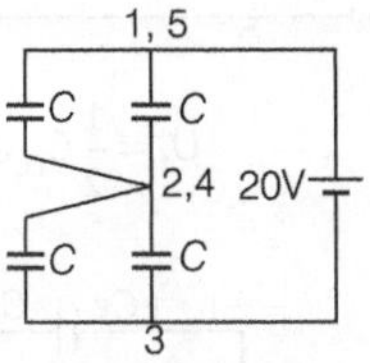

$$C_{eq} = C = \frac{A\varepsilon_0}{d} = \frac{(5 \times 10^{-2} \times 8)(8.85 \times 10^{-12})}{8.85 \times 10^{-3}}$$

$$= 4 \times 10^{-10} F$$

Charge flown through battery $= C_{eq}E = 4 \times 10^{-10} \times 20$

$= 8 \times 10^{-9} C = 8nC$

11.

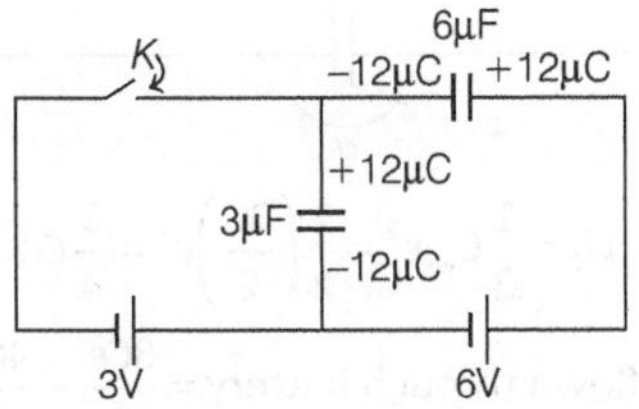

$$\frac{1}{C_{eq}} = \frac{1}{3} + \frac{1}{6}$$

$$\Rightarrow \quad C_{eq} = 2\,\mu F$$

$$q = C_{eq}V = (2\,\mu F)(6V) = 12\,\mu C$$

$$U_1 = \frac{1}{2}C_{eq}V^2 = \frac{1}{2} \times (2 \times 10^{-6})(6)^2 = 36\,\mu J$$

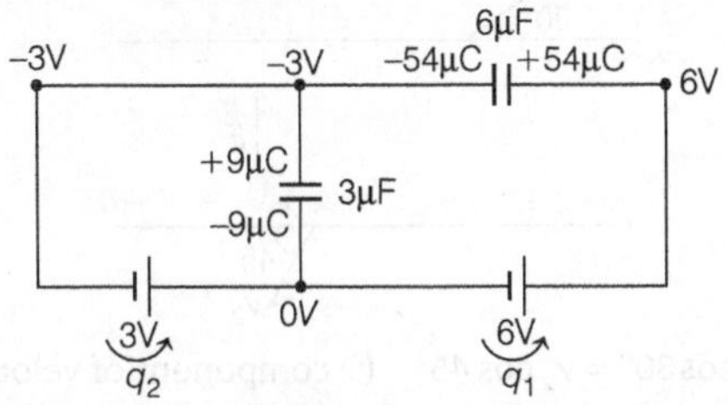

q_1 = Charge flown through 6V cell $= 54 - 12 = 42\,\mu C$

q_2 = Charge flown through 3V cell $= 63 - 0 = 63\,\mu C$

$$U_2 = \frac{(54 \times 10^{-6})^2}{2 \times 6 \times 10^{-6}} + \frac{(9 \times 10^{-6})^2}{2 \times 3 \times 10^{-6}}$$

$$= 243 + \frac{27}{2} = 256.5\,\mu J$$

Work done by both the cells $= 42 \times 6 + 63 \times 3 = 441\,\mu J$

Heat produced $= W_{cell} - \Delta U = 441 - (256.5 - 36)$

$= 220.5\,\mu J$

12.

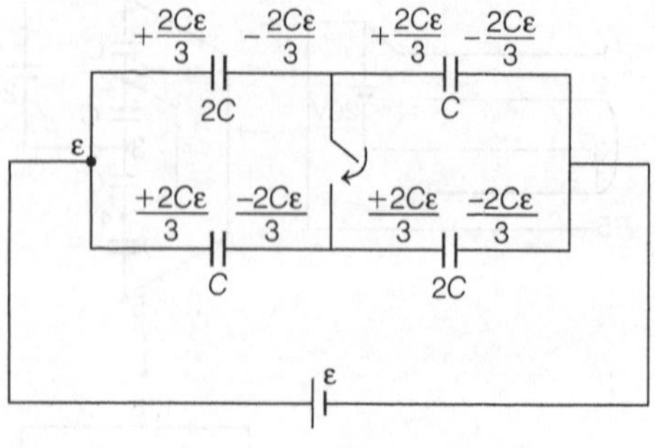

$$U_1 = \frac{1}{2}C_{eq}\varepsilon^2 = \frac{1}{2}\left(\frac{4C}{3}\right)\varepsilon^2 = \frac{2}{3}C\varepsilon^2$$

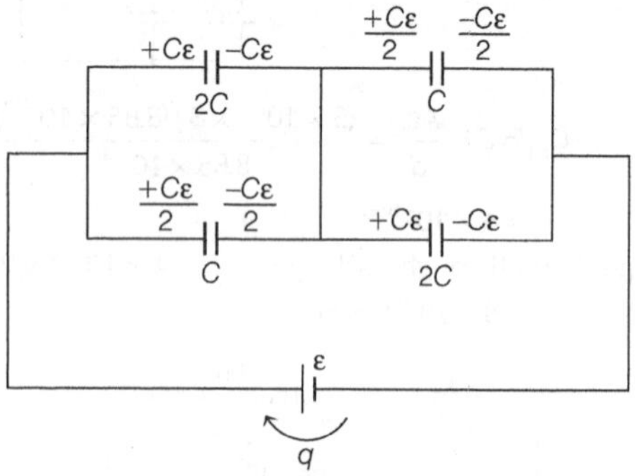

$$U_2 = \frac{1}{2}C_{eq}\varepsilon^2 = \frac{1}{2}\left(\frac{3C}{2}\right)\varepsilon^2 = \frac{3}{4}C\varepsilon^2$$

$q =$ Charge flown through battery $= \frac{3C\varepsilon}{2} - \frac{4C\varepsilon}{3} = \frac{C\varepsilon}{6}$

Heat produced $= W_{battery} - \Delta U$

$$= \left(\frac{C\varepsilon}{6}\right)\varepsilon - \left[\frac{3}{4}C\varepsilon^2 - \frac{2}{3}C\varepsilon^2\right]$$

$$= \left(\frac{1}{6} - \frac{1}{12}\right)C\varepsilon^2 = \frac{C\varepsilon^2}{12}$$

13.

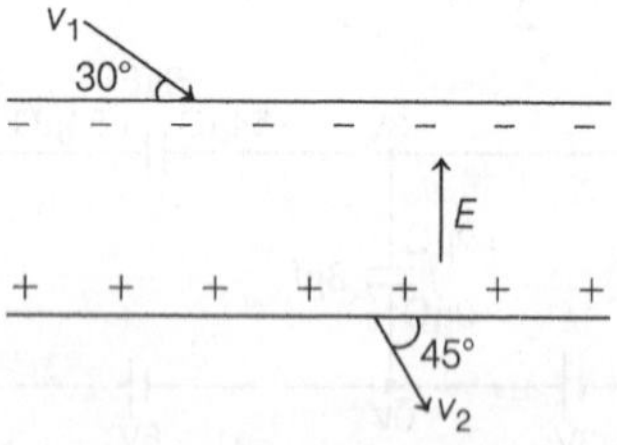

$v_1 \cos 30° = v_2 \cos 45°$ ($\because$ component of velocity parallel to plates remains constant)

$$\Rightarrow \quad v_2 = \frac{\sqrt{3}\,v_1}{\sqrt{2}}$$

$$K_2 = \frac{1}{2}mv_2^2 = \frac{1}{2}m\left(\frac{\sqrt{3}v_1}{\sqrt{2}}\right)^2$$

$$= \frac{3}{2}\left(\frac{1}{2}mv_1^2\right) = \frac{3}{2}(100\text{eV}) = 150\,\text{eV}$$

$$\Rightarrow \quad 150\text{ eV} - 100\text{eV} = e\Delta V$$

$$\Rightarrow \quad \Delta V = 50\text{V}$$

14.

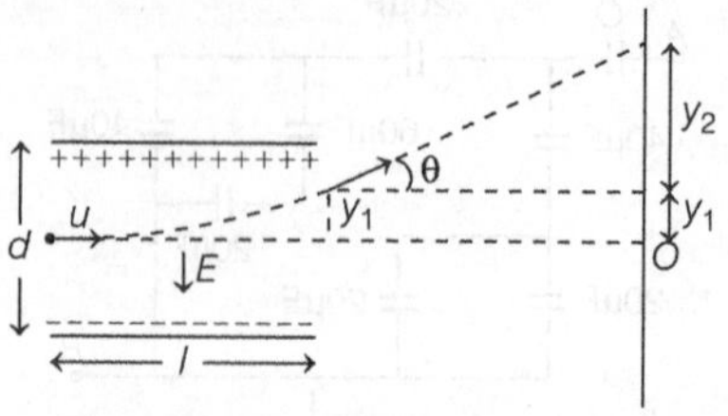

$$\mathbf{F} = q\mathbf{E} \quad \Rightarrow \quad m\mathbf{a} = q\mathbf{E}$$

$$\Rightarrow \quad \mathbf{a} = \frac{q\mathbf{E}}{m} = \frac{-1\times10^{-9}}{0.1\times10^{-3}}\left(\frac{-10}{4\times10^{-3}}\right)\hat{\mathbf{j}}$$

$$\Rightarrow \quad \mathbf{a} = +\frac{1}{40}\hat{\mathbf{j}}$$

$$s_x = u_x t + \frac{1}{2}a_x t^2$$

$$\Rightarrow \quad 0.1 = (0.5)t + 0 \quad \Rightarrow \quad t = 0.2\text{ s}$$

$$s_y = u_y t + \frac{1}{2}a_y t^2$$

$$\Rightarrow \quad y_1 = 0 + \frac{1}{2}\left(\frac{1}{40}\right)(0.2)^2 = 0.5\text{ mm}$$

$$v_y = u_y + a_y t = 0 + \frac{1}{40}(0.2) = \frac{1}{200}$$

$$\tan\theta = \frac{v_y}{v_x} = \frac{1/200}{0.5} = \frac{1}{100}$$

$$\tan\theta = \frac{y_2}{0.1}$$

$$\Rightarrow \quad \frac{1}{100} = \frac{y_2}{0.1} \quad \Rightarrow \quad y_2 = 1\text{ mm}$$

Distance from point O on the screen $= y_1 + y_2$

$= 0.5 + 1 = 1.5$ mm

15.

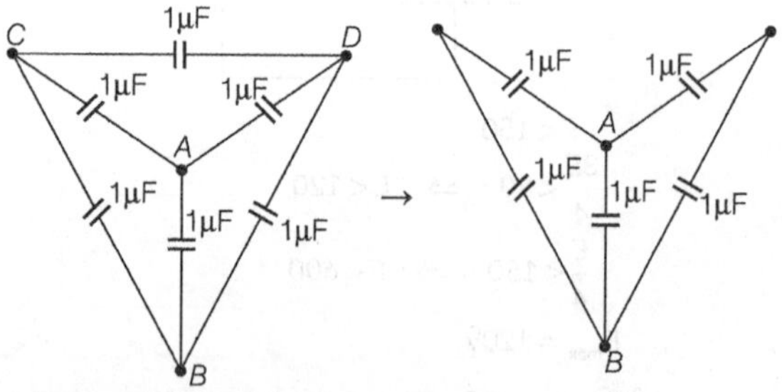

Due to symmetry, points C and D are equipotential.

So, we can remove capacitor between C and D.

Now, using series and parallel combination, $C_{eq} = 2\,\mu\text{F}$

Level 3 JEE Advanced Level

Single Choice Correct Questions

1.

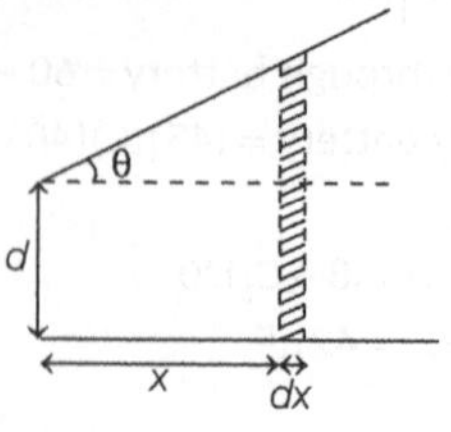

$$dC = \frac{(ldx)\varepsilon_0}{(d + x\tan\theta)}$$

$$dC = \frac{(ldx)\varepsilon_0}{d + x\theta} \qquad [\because \tan\theta \simeq \theta, \text{ for small } \theta]$$

$$dC = \frac{(ldx)\varepsilon_0}{d\left(1 + \frac{x\theta}{d}\right)}$$

$$dC = \frac{ldx\varepsilon_0}{d}\left(1 + \frac{x\theta}{d}\right)^{-1}$$

Using Binomial theorem,

$$dC = \frac{ldx\varepsilon_0}{d}\left(1 - \frac{x\theta}{d}\right)$$

$$\int dC = \frac{l\varepsilon_0}{d}\int_0^l \left(1 - \frac{x\theta}{d}\right)dx \Rightarrow C = \frac{\varepsilon_0 l^2}{d}\left(1 - \frac{\theta l}{2d}\right)$$

2. $q = CV$

$$q = \left(\frac{A\varepsilon_0}{d_0 + a\cos\omega t}\right)E$$

$$i = \frac{dq}{dt} = \frac{-A\varepsilon_0 E}{(d_0 + a\cos\omega t)^2} \times (-a\omega\sin\omega t)$$

$$\Rightarrow \quad i = \frac{EA\omega\varepsilon_0\, a\sin\omega t}{(d_0 + a\cos\omega t)^2}$$

$$\Rightarrow \quad i = \frac{EA\omega\varepsilon_0 a\sin\omega t}{d_0^2} \qquad [\because d_0 >> a]$$

$$\Rightarrow \quad i_{max} = \frac{EA\omega\varepsilon_0 a}{d_0^2} = I \quad \Rightarrow \quad a = \frac{Id_0^2}{EA\omega\varepsilon_0}$$

3.

$$J = \sigma E$$

$$\Rightarrow \quad \frac{i}{A} = \frac{1}{\rho}\frac{V}{d} \quad \Rightarrow \quad i = \frac{AV}{\rho d}$$

$$\Rightarrow \quad i = \left(\frac{A\varepsilon_0}{d}\right)\frac{V}{\rho\varepsilon_0} = \frac{CV}{\rho\varepsilon_0}$$

4.

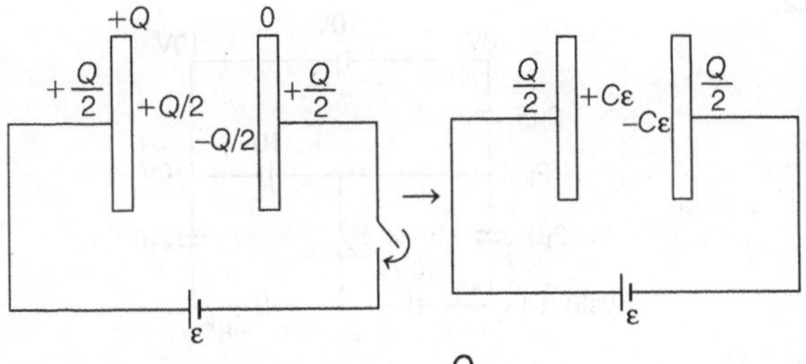

Total charge on the right plate $= \frac{Q}{2} - C\varepsilon$

5.

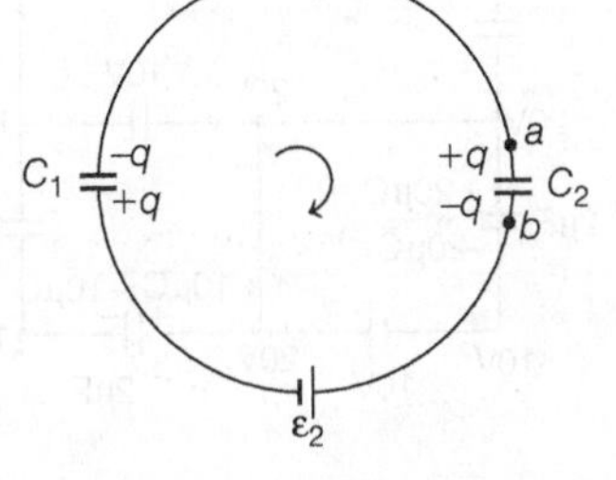

Applying KVL in the loop,

$$+\varepsilon_1 - \frac{q}{C_2} - \varepsilon_2 - \frac{q}{C_1} = 0$$

$$\Rightarrow \quad q = \frac{(\varepsilon_1 - \varepsilon_2)C_1C_2}{C_1 + C_2}$$

$$V_a - V_b = \frac{q}{C_2} = \left(\frac{\varepsilon_1 - \varepsilon_2}{C_1 + C_2}\right)C_1$$

6.

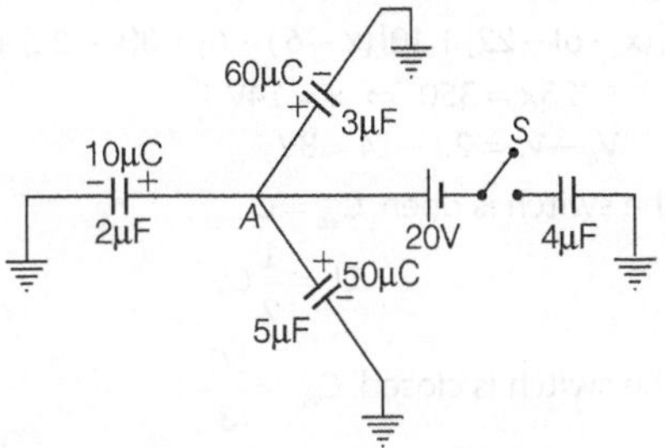

After closing the switch, let potential of junction A be x.

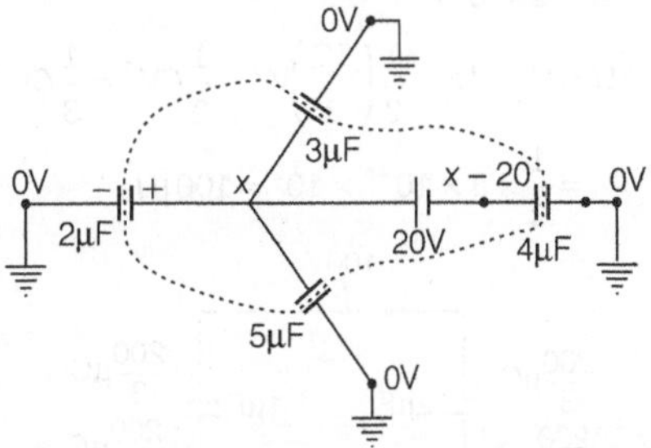

Applying Kirchhoff's junction law for the isolated system of plates,

$$2(x-0) + 3(x-0) + 5(x-0) + 4[(x-20) - 0]$$
$$= +10 + 60 + 50$$

$$\Rightarrow \quad 14x = 200 \quad \Rightarrow \quad x = \frac{100}{7}\text{ V}$$

7.

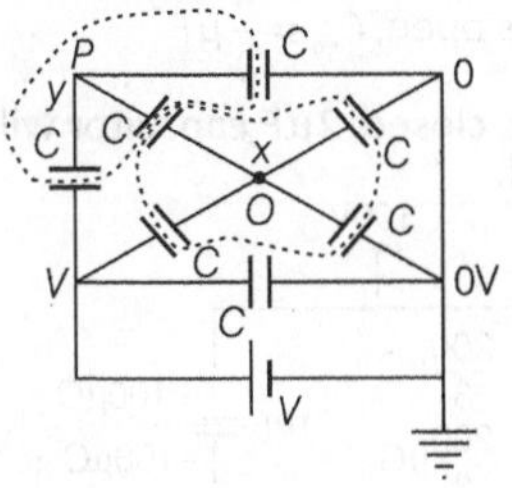

Let $V_O = x$ and $V_P = y$

Applying Kirchhoff's junction law at O,

$$C(x-y) + C(x-V) + C(x-0) + C(x-0) = 0$$

$$4x - y = V \qquad \text{... (i)}$$

Applying Kirchhoff's junction law at P,

$$C(y-0) + C(y-V) + C(y-x) = 0$$

$$\Rightarrow \quad 3y - x = V \qquad \text{... (ii)}$$

Solving Eqs. (i) and (ii), we get

$$x = \frac{4V}{11}$$

8.

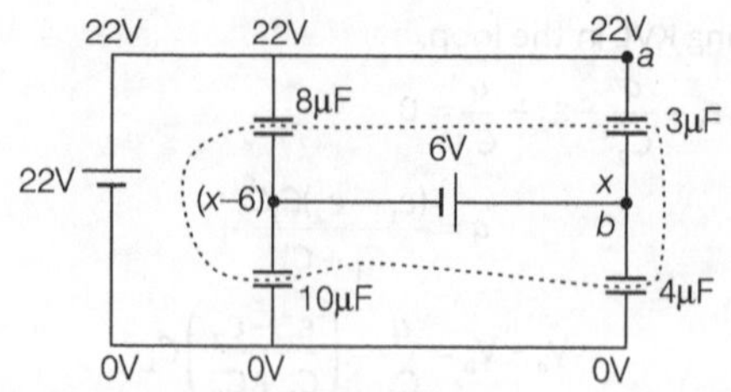

Applying Kirchhoff's junction law,

$$8[(x-6)-22]+10[(x-6)-0]+3(x-22)+4(x-0)=0$$

$$\Rightarrow \quad 25x=350 \Rightarrow x=14\text{V}$$

$$V_a-V_b=22-14=8\text{V}$$

9. When the switch is open, $C_{eq}=C$

$$U_1=\frac{1}{2}CV^2$$

When the switch is closed, $C_{eq}=\frac{5C}{3}$

$$U_2=\frac{1}{2}\left(\frac{5C}{3}\right)V^2$$

$$\Delta U=U_2-U_1=\frac{1}{2}\left(\frac{5C}{3}\right)V^2-\frac{1}{2}CV^2=\frac{1}{3}CV^2$$

$$=\frac{1}{3}\times 3\times 10^{-6}\times 10^2=100\,\mu\text{J}$$

10.

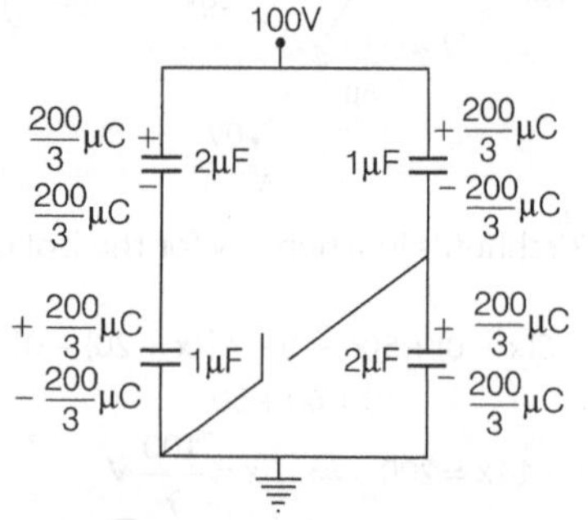

When switch is open, $C_{eq}=\frac{4}{3}\mu\text{F}$

When switch is closed, $2\mu\text{F}$ capacitor will get short-circuited.

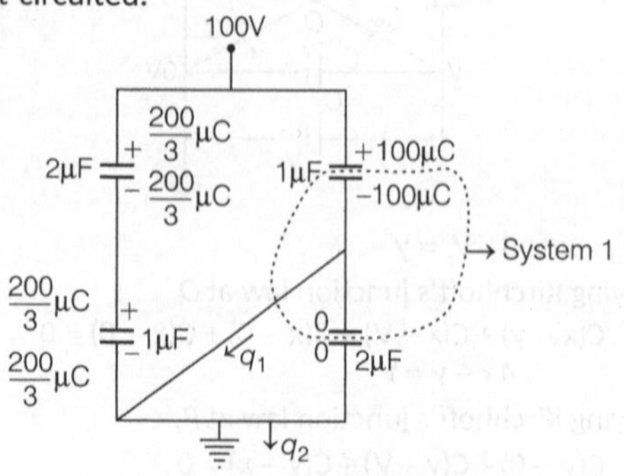

q_1 = Charge flown through switch

= Change in charge of system 1

$$=\left(\frac{-200}{3}+\frac{200}{3}\right)-(-100+0)=100\,\mu\text{C}$$

Change in charge of lower plate of right $2\,\mu\text{F}$

$$\text{capacitor}=0-\left(\frac{-200}{3}\right)$$

$$\Rightarrow \quad q_1-q_2=\frac{200}{3} \Rightarrow q_2=\frac{100}{3}\mu\text{C}$$

$$\frac{q_1}{q_2}=\frac{100}{\left(\frac{100}{3}\right)}=3$$

11.

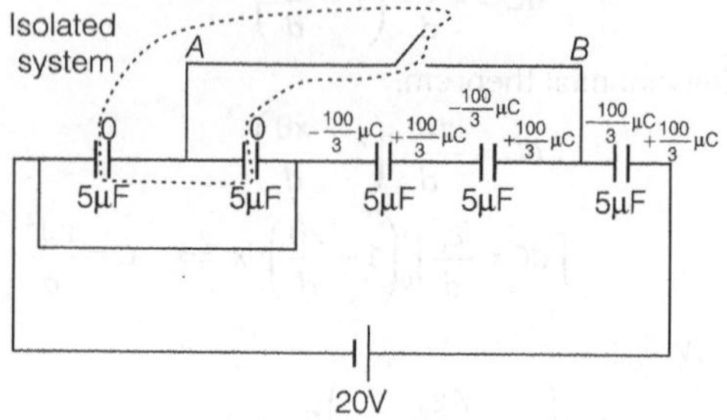

When the switch is open, $C_{eq}=\frac{5}{3}\mu\text{F}$ and first are short circuited.

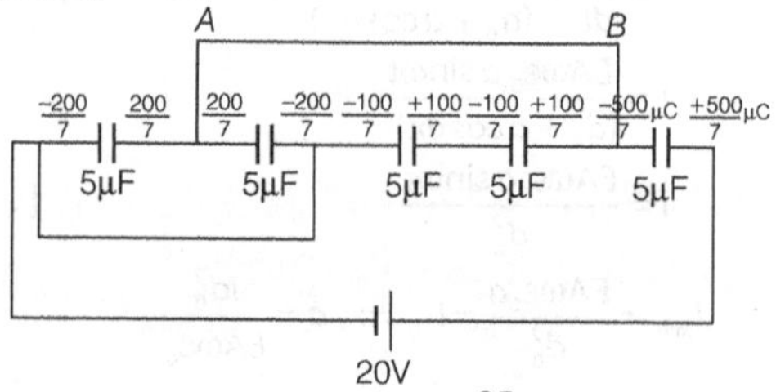

When the switch is closed, $C_{eq}=\frac{25}{7}\mu\text{F}$

Loss in charge of the isolated system $=0-\frac{400}{7}=-\frac{400}{7}\mu\text{C}$

So, charge flown from A to $B=-\frac{400}{7}\mu\text{C}$

12.

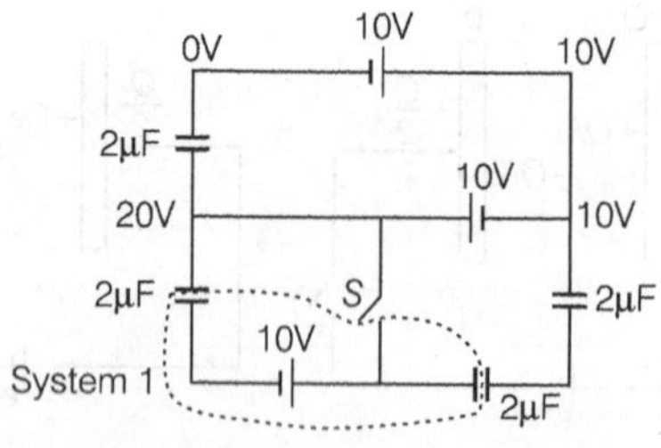

When the switch is open, total charge on system 1 = 0

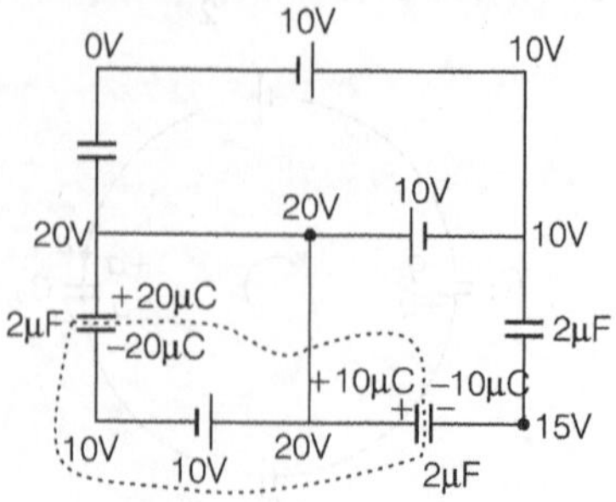

Charge flown through the switch = Change in charge of system 1 = 0 – (– 10) = 10μC

13. Given circuit can be reduced to regular tetrahedron. We can conclude from symmetry that irrespective of the pair of points between which we connect a battery, there is always an uncharged capacitor in the circuit.

14.

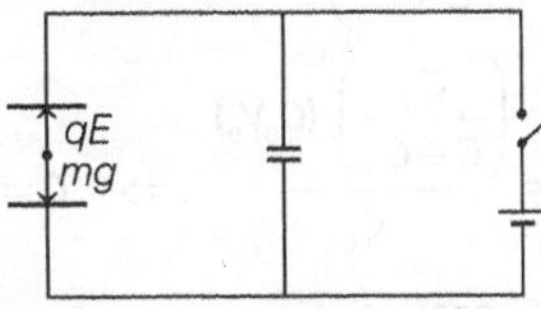

When distance between the plates of the right capacitor is reduced, its capacitance will increases. So, now there will be redistribution of charges on the two capacitors charge on the left capacitor will decreases as the right capacitor. has more capacitance now. So, electric field between the plates of the left capacitor will decrease and the particle will move downwards.

15.

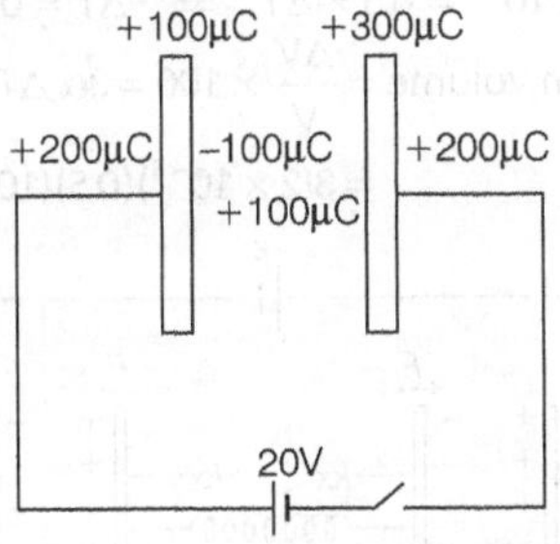

When the switch is open, $U_1 = \dfrac{q^2}{2C} = \dfrac{(100\times10^{-6})^2}{2\times20\times10^{-6}}$

$$= 250\times10^{-6}\text{J}$$

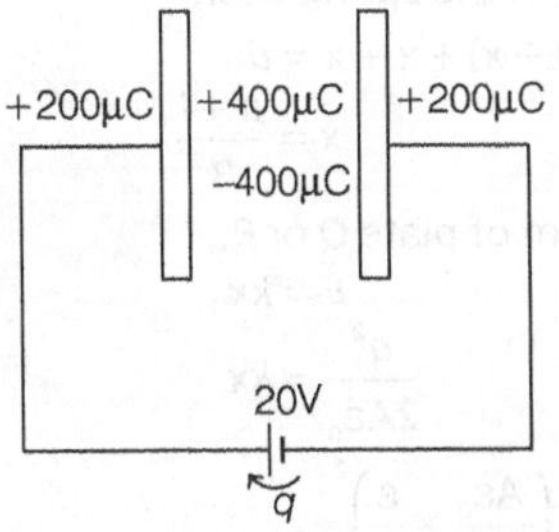

When the switch is closed, $U_2 = \dfrac{q^2}{2C} = \dfrac{(400\times10^{-6})^2}{2\times20\times10^{-6}}$

$$= 4000\times10^{-6}\text{J}$$

q = Charge flown through battery = 500 μC

Work done by battery = 20 × 500 × 10^{-6} = 10mJ

Heat produced = $W_{battery} - \Delta U = 10 - 3.75 = 6.25$ mJ

16. In every operation, total charge will be divided in the ratio of their capacitances.

After first operation,

$$\frac{Q-q}{q} = \frac{C_1}{C_2}$$

Charge will flow between the plate and the conductor till their potential are equal.

$$V_1 = V_2 \Rightarrow \frac{Q}{C_1} = \frac{q_{max}}{C_2}$$

$$q_{max} = Q\left(\frac{C_2}{C_1}\right) = Q\left(\frac{q}{Q-q}\right) = \frac{Qq}{Q-q}$$

17. When S_2 is open and S_1 is closed,

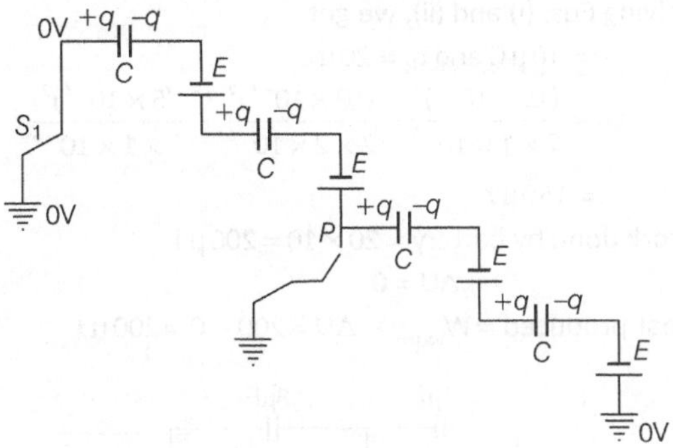

$$\frac{-q}{C} + E - \frac{q}{C} + E - \frac{q}{C} + E - \frac{q}{C} = -E \Rightarrow q = CE$$

When S_2 is also closed, there is no redistribution of charges as potential of point P is already 0.

So, heat produced = 0

18. When the switch is in position 1.

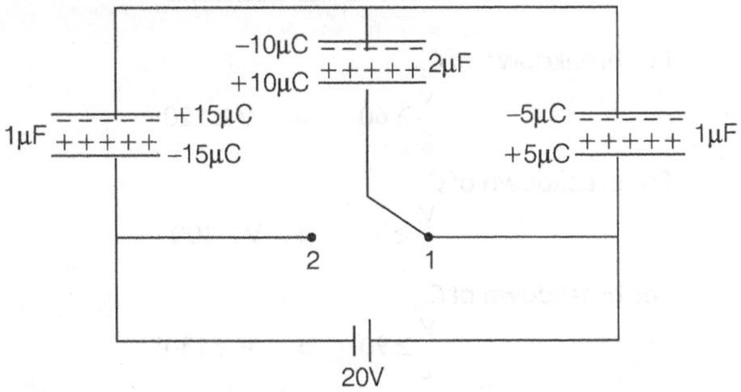

$$C_{eq} = \frac{3}{4}\mu\text{F}$$

Charge flown through battery = $20\times\dfrac{3}{4} = 15\,\mu$C

$$U_1 = \frac{1}{2}C_{eq}V^2 = \frac{1}{2}\times\frac{3}{4}\times(20)^2 = 150\,\mu\text{J}$$

When the switch is shifted to position 2, let charge flown through the battery be q.

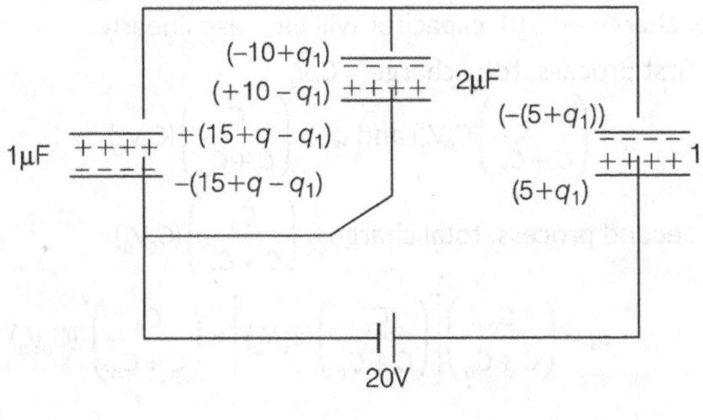

Applying KVL,

$$+20-\frac{5+q}{1}+\frac{10-q_1}{2}=0$$

$$\Rightarrow \qquad 2q+q_1=40 \qquad \text{...(i)}$$

$$+\frac{10-q_1}{2}+\frac{15+q-q_1}{1}=0$$

$$\Rightarrow \qquad 3q_1-2q=40 \qquad \text{...(ii)}$$

Solving Eqs. (i) and (ii), we get

$$q=10\,\mu\text{C and } q_1=20\,\mu\text{C}$$

$$U_2=\frac{(15\times10^{-6})^2}{2\times1\times10^{-6}}+\frac{(10\times10^{-6})^2}{2\times2\times10^{-6}}+\frac{(5\times10^{-6})^2}{2\times1\times10^{-6}}$$

$$=150\,\mu\text{J}$$

Work done by battery $=20\times10=200\,\mu\text{J}$

$$\Delta U=0$$

Heat produced $=W_{\text{battery}}-\Delta U=200-0=200\,\mu\text{J}$

19.

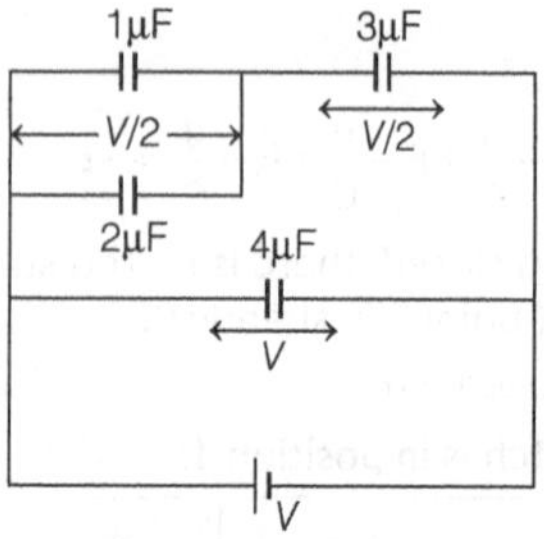

For breakdown of C_1,

$$\frac{V}{2}\geq 60 \Rightarrow V\geq 120$$

For breakdown of C_2,

$$\frac{V}{2}\geq 50 \Rightarrow V\geq 100$$

For breakdown of C_3,

$$\frac{V}{2}\geq 90 \Rightarrow V\geq 180$$

For breakdown of C_4,

$$V\geq 150$$

It V is gradually increased from zero, then the first capacitor to breakdown will be C_2 when $V=100$ V.

20. Potential difference across $12\,\mu$F capacitor is constant.

So, $q_1=10\times12=120\,\mu\text{C}$

$$q_2=C_2V_2=6(t+10)$$

$$\Rightarrow \qquad q_2=6t+60$$

So, charge on $6\,\mu$F capacitor will increase linearly.

21. In first process, total charge $=C_0V_0$

$$q_1=\left(\frac{C_0}{C+C_0}\right)(C_0V_0)\text{ and } q_2=\left(\frac{C}{C+C_0}\right)(C_0V_0)$$

In second process, total charge $=\left(\frac{C_0}{C+C_0}\right)(C_0V_0)$

$$q_1'=\left(\frac{C_0}{C+C_0}\right)\left[\left(\frac{C_0}{C+C_0}\right)(C_0V_0)\right]=\left(\frac{C_0}{C+C_0}\right)^2(C_0V_0)$$

and

$$q_2'=\frac{C}{C+C_0}\left[\left(\frac{C_0}{C+C_0}\right)(C_0V_0)\right]$$

After nth process;

Charge on capacitor of capacitance

$$C_0=\left(\frac{C_0}{C+C_0}\right)^n(C_0V_0)$$

$$V=\frac{\left(\frac{C_0}{C+C_0}\right)^n(C_0V_0)}{C_0} \Rightarrow C=C_0\left[\left(\frac{V_0}{V}\right)^{1/n}-1\right]$$

22. Heat produced $=50\%$ of energy stored

$$=\frac{50}{100}\times\frac{1}{2}CV^2=\frac{1}{2}\times\frac{1}{2}\times200\times10^{-6}\times(100)^2$$

$$=50\times10^{-2}\text{J}$$

Heat taken by each plate $=\frac{50\times10^{-2}}{2}=25\times10^{-2}$

Heat, $Q=C\Delta T$

$$\Rightarrow \qquad 25\times10^{-2}=0.5\times\Delta T \Rightarrow \Delta T=0.5\text{ K}$$

$$\%\text{ increase in volume}=\frac{\Delta V}{V}\times100=3\alpha\,\Delta T\times100$$

$$=3(2\times10^{-5})(0.5)(100)=0.003\%$$

23.

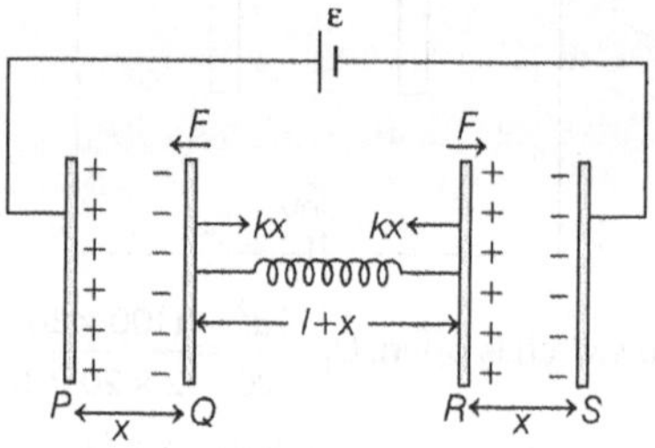

Let extension in the spring be x.

$$(l+x)+x+x=d$$

$$x=\frac{d-l}{3}$$

For equilibrium of plate Q or R,

$$F=kx$$

$$\frac{q^2}{2A\varepsilon_0}=kx$$

$$\frac{\left(\frac{A\varepsilon_0}{x}\times\frac{\varepsilon}{2}\right)^2}{2A\varepsilon_0}=kx$$

$$\Rightarrow \qquad k=\frac{A\varepsilon_0\varepsilon^2}{8x^3}=\frac{27A\varepsilon_0\varepsilon^2}{8(d-l)^3}$$

24.

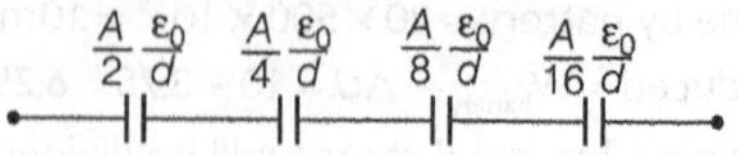

$$\frac{1}{C_{eq}}=\frac{1}{C_1}+\frac{1}{C_2}+\frac{1}{C_3}+\frac{1}{C_4}$$

$$\frac{1}{C_{eq}}=\frac{2d}{A\varepsilon_0}+\frac{4d}{A\varepsilon_0}+\frac{8d}{A\varepsilon_0}+\frac{16d}{A\varepsilon_0} \Rightarrow C_{eq}=\frac{A\varepsilon_0}{30d}$$

25.

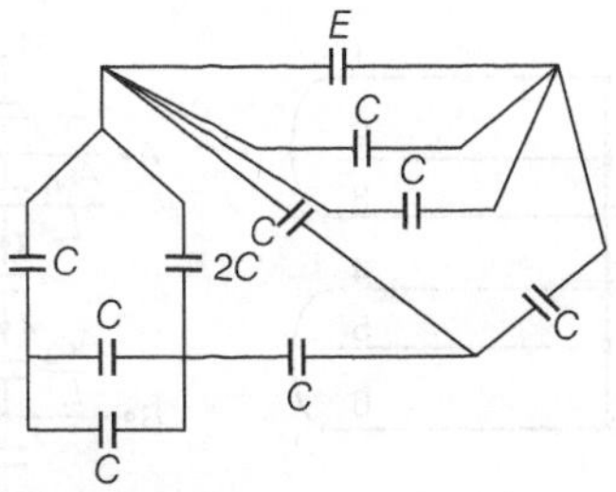

Using series and parallel combinations,

$$C_{eq} = \frac{79}{30}C$$

26.

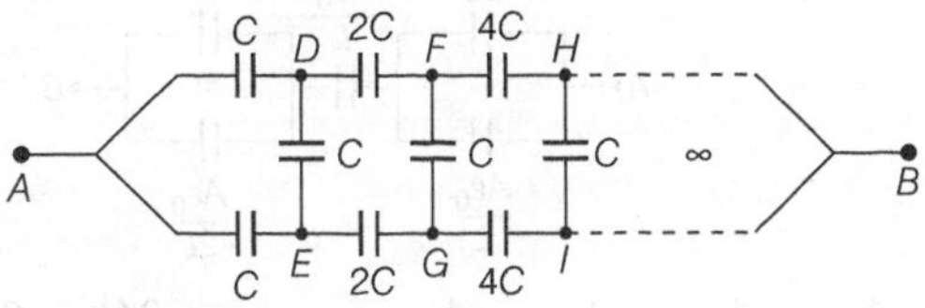

Due to symmetry, $V_D = V_E$

$V_F = V_G$

$V_H = V_I$ and so on.

So, we can remove capacitors between *D* and *E*, *F* and *G*, *H* and *I* and so on.

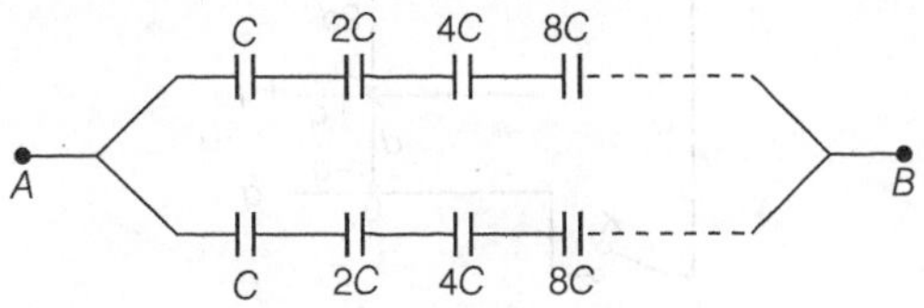

Let capacitance of each branch be *x*.

$$\frac{1}{x} = \frac{1}{C} + \frac{1}{2C} + \frac{1}{4C} + \frac{1}{8C} + \ldots\infty$$

$$\frac{1}{x} = \frac{1}{C}\left(\frac{1}{1-\frac{1}{2}}\right) \Rightarrow x = \frac{C}{2}$$

Equivalent capacitance between *A* and *B* = *x* + *x* = *C*

27.

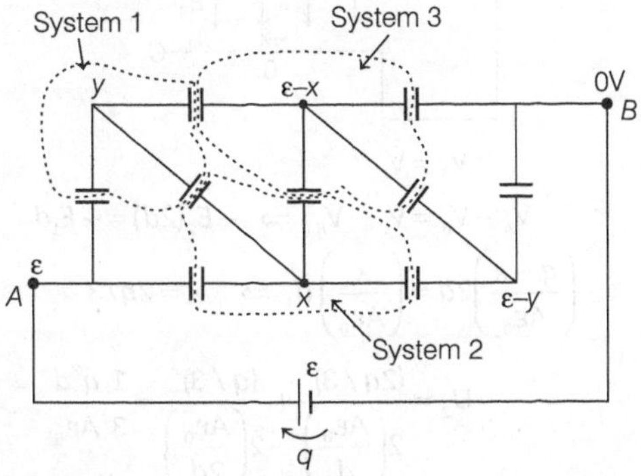

For system 1,

$$C(y-\varepsilon) + C(y-x) + C[y-(\varepsilon-x)] = 0$$

$$3y = 2\varepsilon \Rightarrow y = \frac{2\varepsilon}{3}$$

For system 2,

$$C(x-\varepsilon) + C(x-y) + c[x-(\varepsilon-x)] + C[x-(\varepsilon-y)] = 0$$

$$5x = 3\varepsilon$$

$$x = \frac{3\varepsilon}{5}$$

Let charge flown through battery be *q*.

$$q = C(\varepsilon - x) + C(\varepsilon - y)$$

$$= C\left(\varepsilon - \frac{3\varepsilon}{5}\right) + C\left(\varepsilon - \frac{2\varepsilon}{3}\right) = \frac{11C\varepsilon}{15}$$

$$C_{eq} = \frac{q}{\varepsilon} = \frac{11C\varepsilon/15}{\varepsilon}$$

$$= \frac{11C}{15} = \frac{11}{15} \times 15\,\mu F = 11\,\mu F$$

28. Circuit with one section

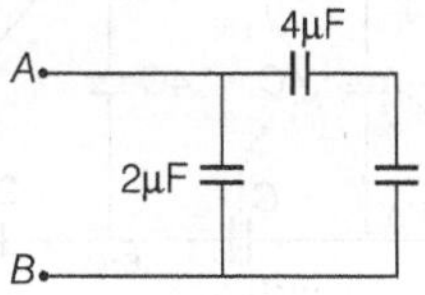

$$C_{eq} = 2 + \frac{4C}{C+4}$$

Circuit with no section

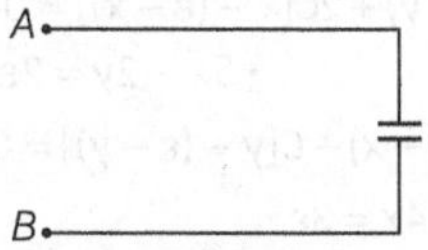

Since, equivalent capacitance between *A* and *B* is independent of number of sections.

$$2 + \frac{4C}{C+4} = C$$

$$\Rightarrow \quad 6C + 8 = C^2 + 4C$$

$$\Rightarrow \quad C^2 - 2C - 8 = 0 \Rightarrow C = 4\,\mu F$$

29.

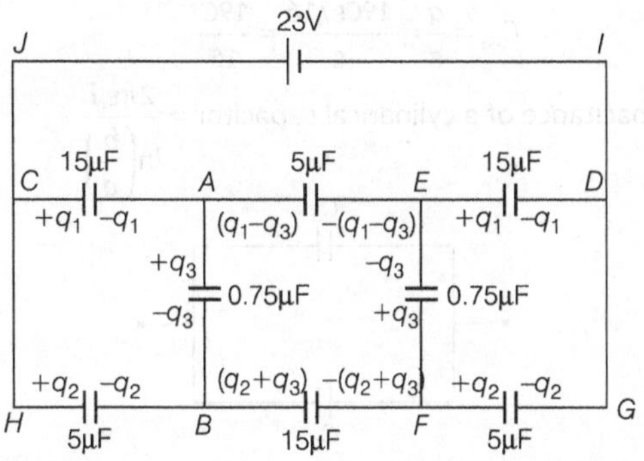

In loop *CABH*,

$$\frac{-q_1}{15} - \frac{q_3}{0.75} + \frac{q_2}{5} = 0 \qquad \ldots \text{(i)}$$

In loop *AEFB*,

$$\frac{+q_3}{0.75} - \frac{q_1 - q_3}{5} + \frac{q_3}{0.75} + \frac{q_2 + q_3}{15} = 0 \qquad \ldots \text{(ii)}$$

In loop *CAEDIJ*,

$$\frac{-q_1}{15}-\frac{q_1-q_3}{5}-\frac{q_1}{15}+23=0 \qquad \text{... (iii)}$$

Solving Eqs. (i), (ii) and (iii), we get

$$q_3=\frac{345}{92}$$

Potential difference between A and $B=\frac{q_3}{0.75}=5\text{V}$

Potential difference between E and F will also be 5V but with opposite polarity.

30. Due to parallel axis of symmetry, we can fold the circuit about axis AB.

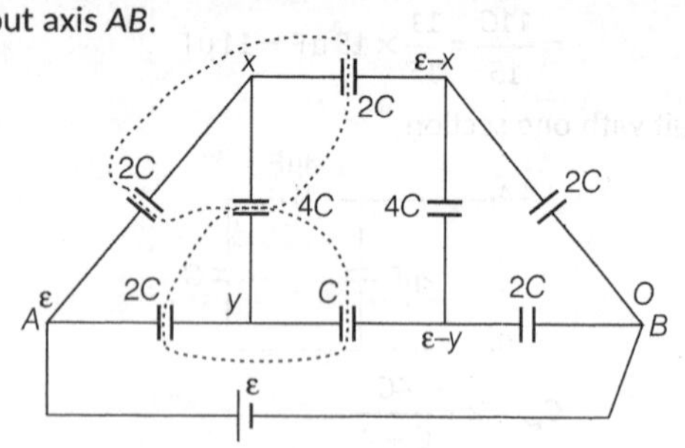

Now, lets connect a battery across A and B,

$$2C(x-\varepsilon)+4C(x-y)+2C[x-(\varepsilon-x)]=0$$

$$\Rightarrow \qquad 5x-2y=2\varepsilon \qquad \text{... (i)}$$

$$+2C(y-\varepsilon)+4C(y-x)+C[y-(\varepsilon-y)]=0$$

$$\Rightarrow \qquad 8y-4x=3\varepsilon \qquad \text{... (ii)}$$

Solving Eqs. (i) and (ii), we get

$$x=\frac{11\varepsilon}{16} \text{ and } y=\frac{23\varepsilon}{32}$$

Let charge flown through battery be q.

$$q=2C(\varepsilon-x)+2C(\varepsilon-y)=\frac{19C\varepsilon}{16}$$

$$C_{eq}=\frac{q}{\varepsilon}=\frac{19C\varepsilon/16}{\varepsilon}=\frac{19C}{16}$$

31. Capacitance of a cylindrical capacitor $=\frac{2\pi\varepsilon_0 l}{\ln\left(\frac{b}{a}\right)}$

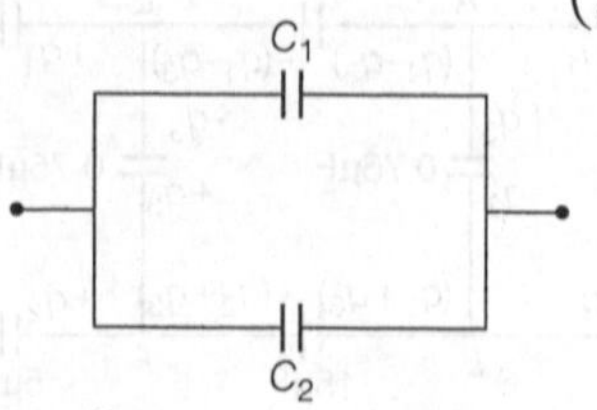

$$C_1=\frac{2\pi\varepsilon_0 l}{\ln\left(\frac{2R}{R}\right)} \text{ and } C_2=\frac{2\pi\varepsilon_0 l}{\ln\left(\frac{2\sqrt{2}R}{2R}\right)}$$

$$C_{eq}=C_1+C_2=\frac{2\pi\varepsilon_0 l}{\ln 2}+\frac{2\pi\varepsilon_0 l}{\ln\sqrt{2}}=\frac{6\pi\varepsilon_0 l}{\ln 2}$$

Capacitance per unit length $=\frac{6\pi\varepsilon_0}{\ln 2}$

32.

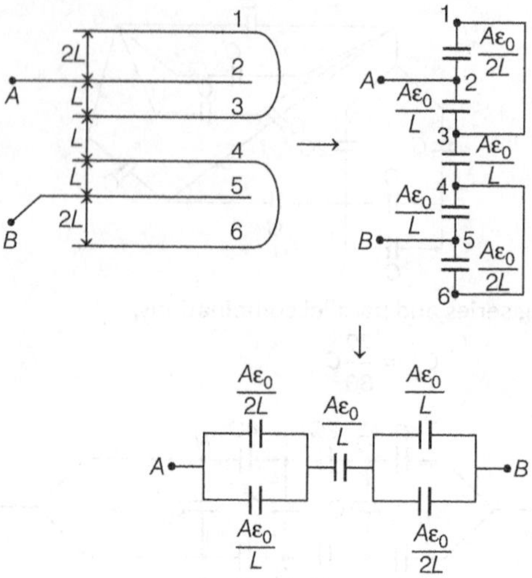

$$\frac{1}{C_{eq}}=\frac{1}{\frac{3}{2}\frac{A\varepsilon_0}{L}}+\frac{1}{\frac{A\varepsilon_0}{L}}+\frac{1}{\frac{3}{2}\frac{A\varepsilon_0}{L}} \Rightarrow C_{eq}=\frac{3A\varepsilon_0}{7L}=\frac{3C}{7}$$

33. When the switch is open,

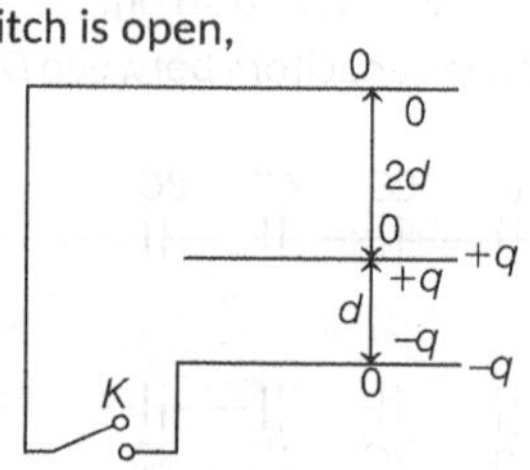

Energy stored, $U_1=\frac{q^2}{2\left(\frac{A\varepsilon_0}{d}\right)}=\frac{q^2 d}{2A\varepsilon_0}$

Now, when the switch is closed,

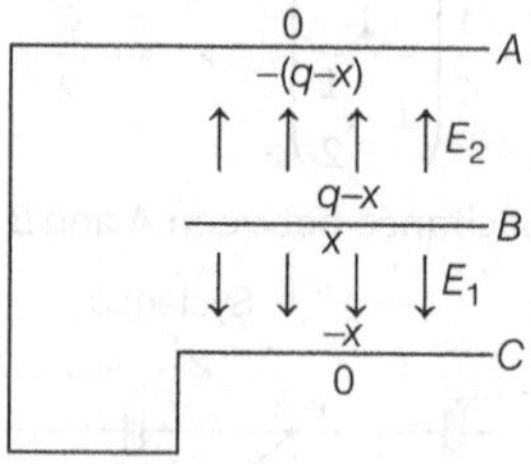

$$V_A=V_C$$

$$\Rightarrow \qquad V_A-V_B=V_C-V_B \Rightarrow -E_2(2d)=-E_1 d$$

$$\Rightarrow \qquad \left(\frac{q-x}{A\varepsilon_0}\right)2d=\left(\frac{x}{A\varepsilon_0}\right)d \Rightarrow x=2q/3$$

$$U_2=\frac{(2q/3)^2}{2\left(\frac{A\varepsilon_0}{d}\right)}+\frac{(q/3)^2}{2\left(\frac{A\varepsilon_0}{2d}\right)}=\frac{1}{3}\frac{q^2 d}{A\varepsilon_0}$$

Energy lost $=U_1-U_2$

$$=\frac{q^2 d}{2A\varepsilon_0}-\frac{q^2 d}{3A\varepsilon_0}=\frac{q^2 d}{6A\varepsilon_0}$$

34.

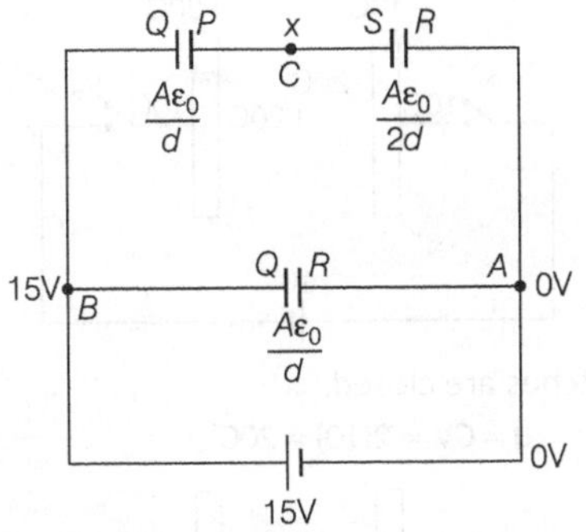

Let $V_A = 0$

$$V_B = 15\text{V} \quad \text{and} \quad V_C = x$$

In series combination, potential differences are in the inverse ratio of capacitances,

$$\frac{15 - x}{x} = \frac{A\varepsilon_0 / 2d}{A\varepsilon_0 / d}$$

$$\Rightarrow \quad 30 - 2x = x \quad \Rightarrow \quad x = 10\text{V}$$

Potential difference between plates Q and S

$$= V_B - V_C = 15 - 10 = 5\text{ V}$$

35. When the switch is open.

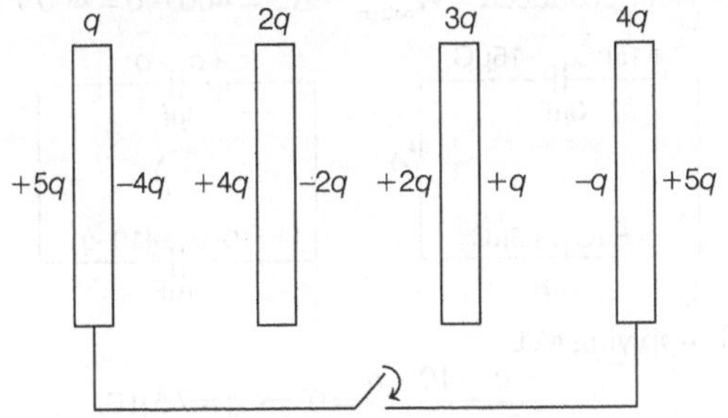

When the switch is closed.

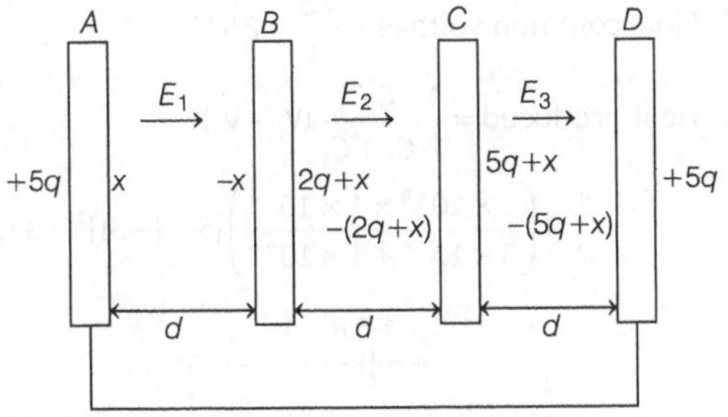

$$V_A = V_D$$

$$\Rightarrow \quad V_A - V_D = 0$$

$$\Rightarrow \quad E_1 d + E_2 d + E_3 d = 0$$

$$\Rightarrow \quad \left(\frac{x}{A\varepsilon_0} + \frac{2q + x}{A\varepsilon_0} + \frac{5q + x}{A\varepsilon_0}\right) d = 0$$

$$\Rightarrow \quad x = -\frac{7q}{3}$$

Charge flown the shorting wire = Gain in charge of plate A

$$= (5q + x) - q$$

$$= \left(5q - \frac{7q}{3}\right) - q = \frac{5q}{3}$$

36.

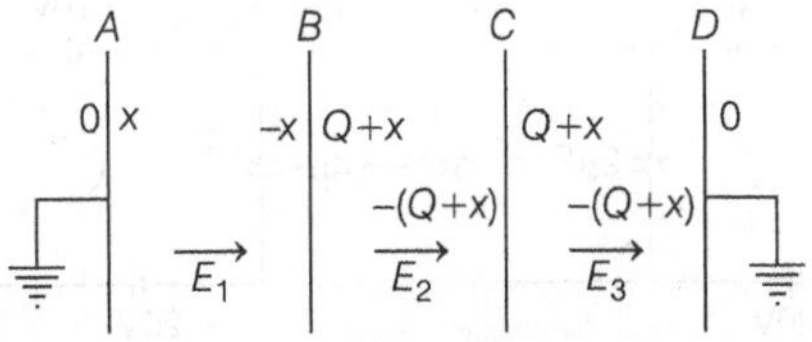

$$V_A = V_D = 0$$

$$\Rightarrow \quad V_A - V_D = 0$$

$$\Rightarrow \quad E_1 d + E_2 d + E_3 d = 0$$

$$\Rightarrow \quad \frac{x}{S\varepsilon_0} d + \left(\frac{Q + x}{S\varepsilon_0}\right) d + \left(\frac{Q + x}{S\varepsilon_0}\right) d = 0 \quad \Rightarrow \quad x = \frac{-2Q}{3}$$

Potential difference between plates B and $C = E_2 d$

$$= \left(\frac{Q + x}{S\varepsilon_0}\right) d = \frac{Qd}{3S\varepsilon_0}$$

Multiple Choice(s) Correct Questions

1. (a) $C = \frac{A\varepsilon_0}{d}$

If d decreases, capacitance increases, $q = CV$

Since, potential difference is constant and capacitance increases, so charge will increase.

(b) $E = \frac{V}{d}$

If d decreases, E increases.

(c) Potential difference between the plates is equal to emf of the battery. So, it will remain constant.

(d) $F = \frac{q^2}{2A\varepsilon_0}$

Since, q increases, F will increase.

2. Potential difference between the plates is constant.

$$E = \frac{V}{d}$$

$$E_D > E_F \quad \because \; d_D < d_F$$

$$E = \frac{\sigma}{\varepsilon_0}$$

$$\sigma_A > \sigma_B \quad \because \; E_D > E_F$$

3. (a) Capacitance of Ist row $= 2\,\mu\text{F}$

Capacitance of 2nd row $= \frac{2}{2} = 1\,\mu\text{F}$

Capacitance of 3rd row $= \frac{2}{4} = \frac{1}{2}\mu\text{F}$ and so on.

All rows are in parallel.

$$C_{eq} = C_1 + C_2 + C_3 + \ldots$$

$$= 2 + 1 + \frac{1}{2} + \frac{1}{4} + \ldots\infty = \frac{2}{1 - \frac{1}{2}} = 4\,\mu\text{F}$$

(b) Capacitance of each row is different. So, capacitors in different rows have different charges.

(c) Capacitance is maximum for the first row. So, charge will be maximum for capacitors in the first row.

(d) Energy $= \frac{1}{2}C_{eq}V^2 = \frac{1}{2}(4\,\mu\text{F})(10\text{V})^2 = 200\,\mu\text{J}$

4.

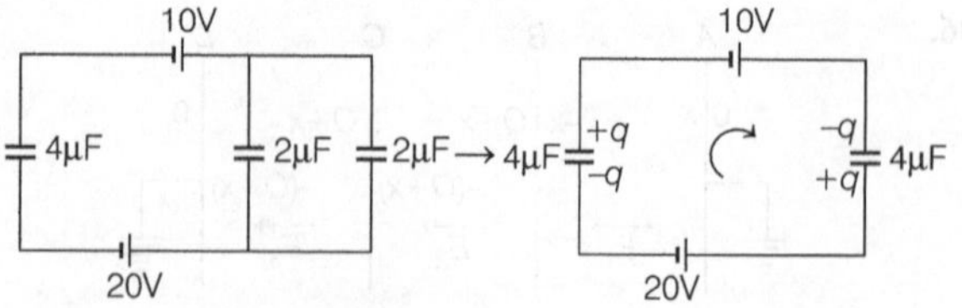

Applying KVL in the loop,

$$+10+\frac{q}{4}-20+\frac{q}{4}=0 \Rightarrow q=20\,\mu C$$

Potential difference across 4 μF capacitor

$$V=\frac{q}{C}=\frac{20\,\mu C}{4\,\mu F}=5V$$

5.

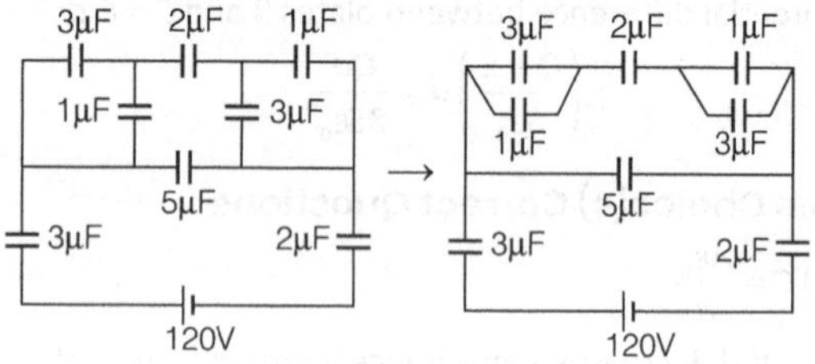

$$C_{eq}=1\,\mu F$$

(a) Energy stored in all the capacitors $=\frac{1}{2}C_{eq}V^2$

$$=\frac{1}{2}(1\times 10^{-6})(120)^2=7.2\text{ mJ}$$

(b)

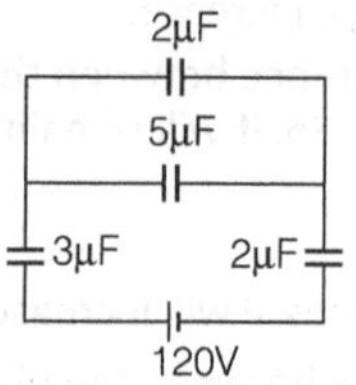

Charge flown through battery $=C_{eq}V$

$$=(1\,\mu F)(120\text{ V})=120\,\mu C$$

Charge on 5 μF capacitor $=\frac{5}{6}\times 120=100\,\mu C$

Energy stored in 5 μF capacitor $=\frac{q^2}{2C}$

$$=\frac{(100\times 10^{-6})^2}{2\times 5\times 10^{-6}}=1\text{ mJ}$$

(c)

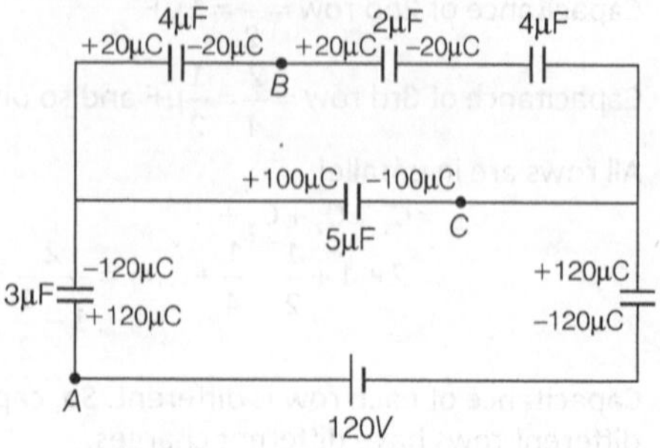

$$V_A-\frac{120}{3}-\frac{20}{4}=V_B \Rightarrow V_A-V_B=45V$$

(d) $V_B-\frac{20}{2}-\frac{20}{4}=V_C \Rightarrow V_B-V_C=15V$

6.

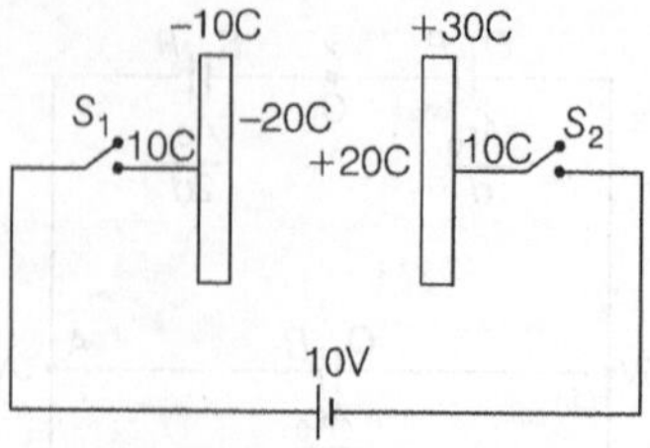

After switches are closed,

$$q=CV=2(10)=20C$$

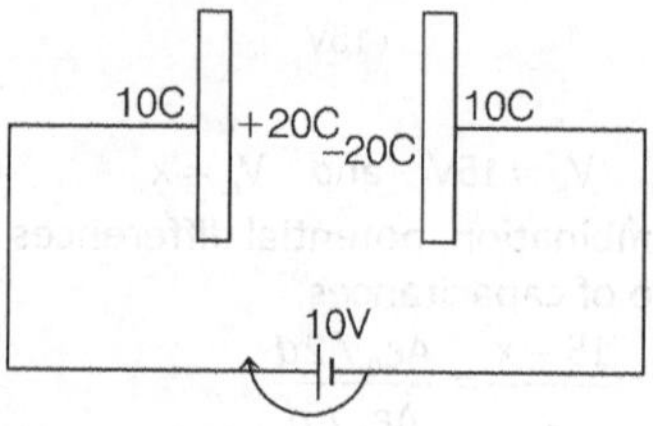

Charge flown through the battery = 20 − (− 20) = 40C

(a) Work done by battery = 10 × 40 = 400J

(b) Net charge on plate P_2 = − 20 + 10 = − 10 C

(c) Charge on the left side of plate P_1 is 10C.

(d) Heat produced $=W_{battery}-\Delta U=400-0=400$ J

7.

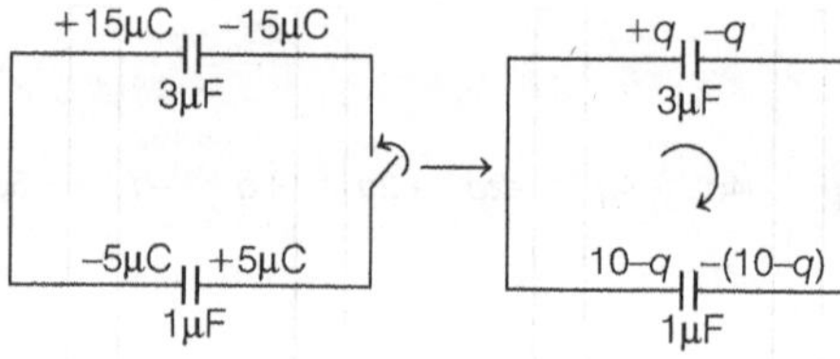

(a) Applying KVL,

$$\frac{-q}{3}+\frac{10-q}{1}=0 \Rightarrow q=7.5\,\mu C$$

(b) Final common voltage $=\frac{7.5}{3}=2.5$ V

(d) Heat produced $=\frac{1}{2}\frac{C_1C_2}{C_1+C_2}(V_1-V_2)^2$

$$=\frac{1}{2}\times\left(\frac{3\times 10^{-6}\times 1\times 10^{-6}}{3\times 10^{-6}+1\times 10^{-6}}\right)[5-(-5)]^2=37.5\,\mu J$$

8.

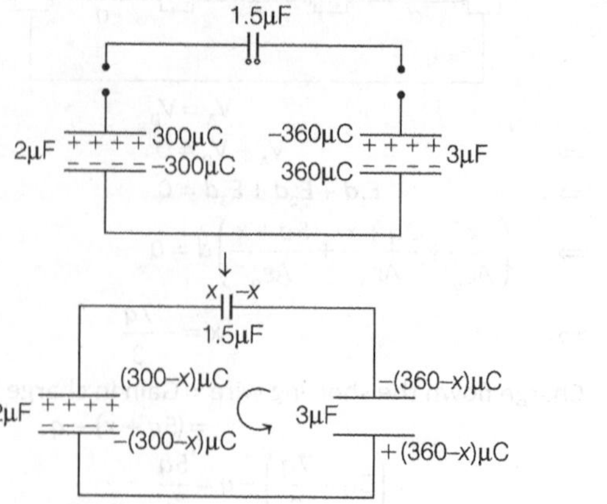

Applying KVL,

$$-\frac{x}{1.5}+\frac{360-x}{3}+\frac{300-x}{2}=0$$

$$\Rightarrow \quad 720-6x+900-3x=0$$

$$\Rightarrow \quad x=180\,\mu C$$

Potential drop across $2\,\mu F$ capacitor $=\dfrac{300-180}{2}=60$ V

Potential drop across $1.5\,\mu F$ capacitor $=\dfrac{180}{1.5}=120$ V

Charge on $3\,\mu F$ capacitor $=360-180=180\,\mu C$

9.

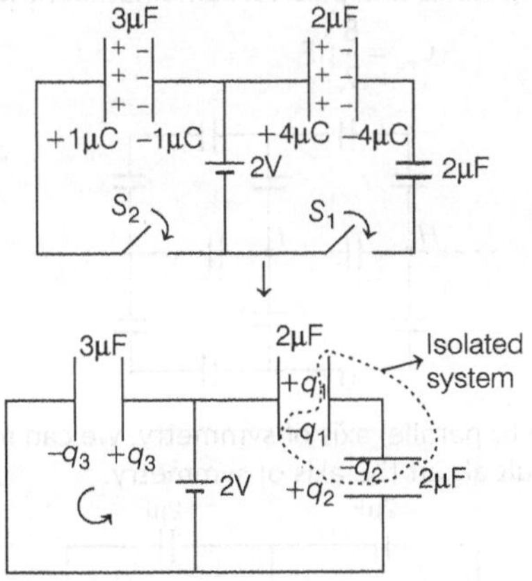

Applying KVL,

$$+2-\frac{q_3}{3}=0$$

$$\Rightarrow \quad q_3=6\,\mu C$$

$$+2-\frac{q_1}{2}+\frac{q_2}{2}=0$$

$$\Rightarrow \quad q_1-q_2=4 \quad \text{... (i)}$$

Charge conservation for isolated system,

$$-q_1-q_2=-4$$

$$\Rightarrow \quad q_1+q_2=4 \quad \text{... (ii)}$$

Solving Eqs. (i) and (ii), we get

$$q_1=4\,\mu C \text{ and } q_2=0$$

Charge flown through S_2 = Change in charge of left plate of C_3

$$=6-1=5\,\mu C$$

10.

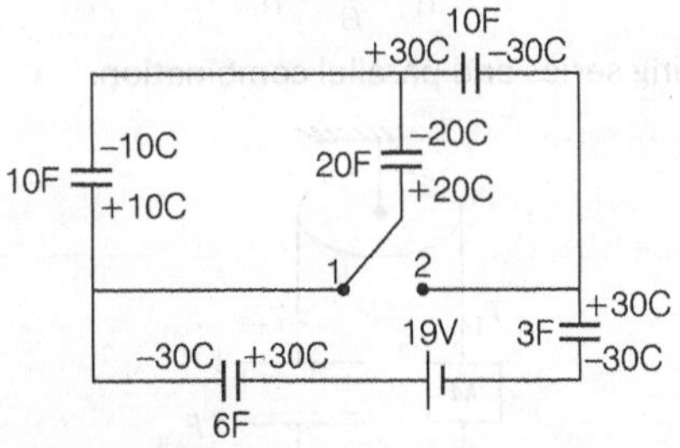

When the switch is in position 1,

$$\frac{1}{C_{eq}}=\frac{1}{6}+\frac{1}{(10+20)}+\frac{1}{10}+\frac{1}{3} \Rightarrow C_{eq}=\frac{30}{19}\text{F}$$

Charge flown through battery $=\dfrac{30}{19}\times 19=30$ C

Now, the switch is transferred to position 2,

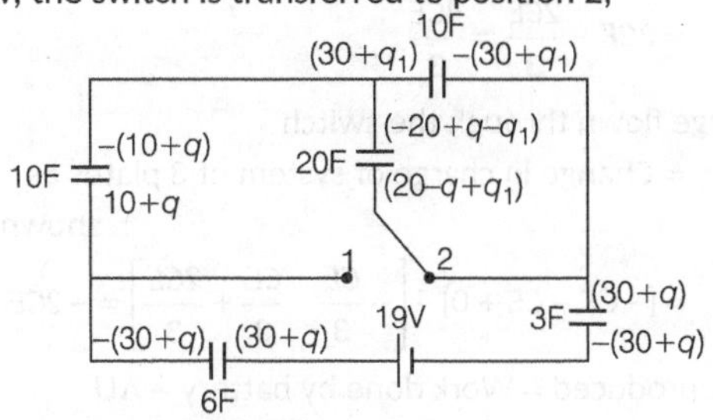

Let charge flown the battery be q.

For 10 F and 20 F capacitors, q is split as q_1 and $q-q_1$, respectively.

Applying KVL, $+19-\dfrac{(30+q)}{6}-\dfrac{(10+q)}{10}-\dfrac{(30+q_1)}{10}-\dfrac{(30+q)}{3}=0$

$$\Rightarrow \quad q_1+6q=0 \quad \text{... (i)}$$

$$-\frac{(30+q_1)}{10}-\frac{(20-q+q_1)}{20}=0$$

$$\Rightarrow \quad q-3q_1=80 \quad \text{... (ii)}$$

Solving Eqs. (i) and (ii), we get

$$q=\frac{80}{19}\text{C and } q_1=\frac{-480}{19}\text{C}$$

Charge on 3F capacitor $=30+q=30+\dfrac{80}{19}=\dfrac{650}{19}$ C

Work done by battery $=q\varepsilon=\left(\dfrac{80}{19}\right)(19)=80$ J

11.

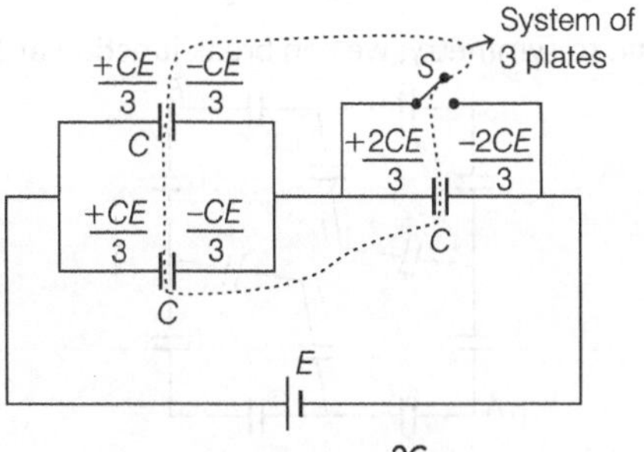

When the switch is open, $C_{eq}=\dfrac{2C}{3}$

When the switch is closed, the right most capacitor gets short-circuit and potential difference across each of the other two capacitors is E.

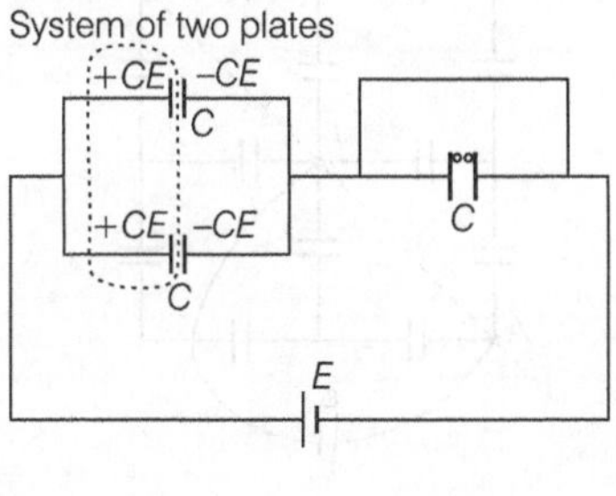

Charge flown through the cell = Change in charge of system of two plates as shown in figure

$$= 2CE - \frac{2CE}{3} = \frac{4CE}{3}$$

Charge flown through the switch

= Change in charge of system of 3 plates as shown in figure

$$= [-CE - CE + 0] - \left[-\frac{CE}{3} - \frac{CE}{3} + \frac{2CE}{3}\right] = -2CE$$

Heat produced = Work done by battery − ΔU

$$= \left(\frac{4}{3}CE\right)E - \left[\left(\frac{1}{2}CE^2 + \frac{1}{2}CE^2\right) - \frac{1}{2}\left(\frac{2C}{3}\right)E^2\right] = \frac{2}{3}CE^2$$

12. When the inner shell is displaced from the centre without touching the outer shell, there will be redistribution of charges on the two shells. Some energy will be dissipated as heat during redistribution. So, system will lose energy.

$$\text{Energy} = \frac{q^2}{2C} = \frac{1}{2}qV$$

Since, energy decreases, capacitance will increase and potential difference will decrease.

13. (a)

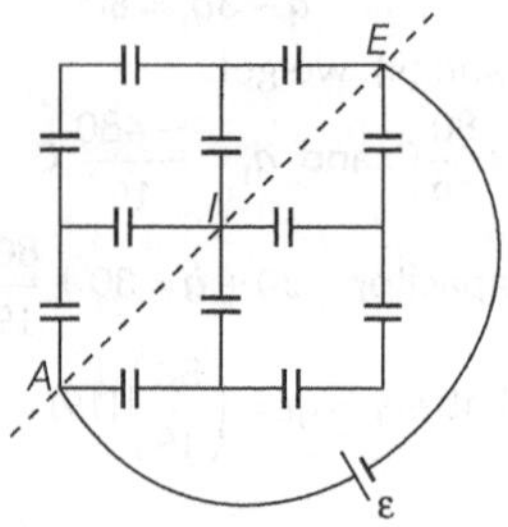

Due to symmetry, we can break junction at 1.

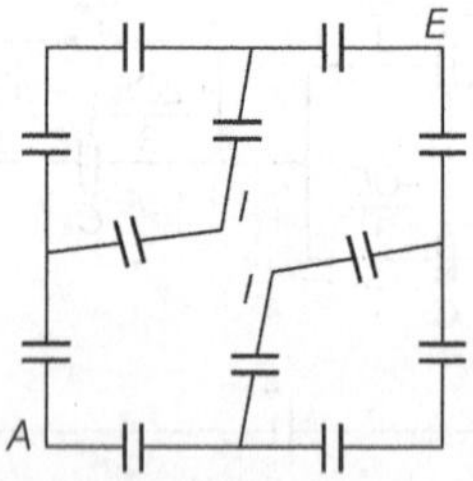

Using series and parallel combination,

$$C_{eq} = \frac{2}{3}\mu F$$

(b)

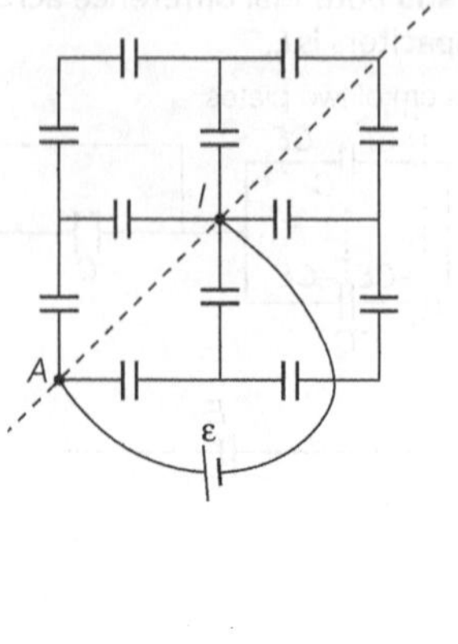

Due to parallel axis of symmetry, we can fold the circuit about the axis of symmetry.

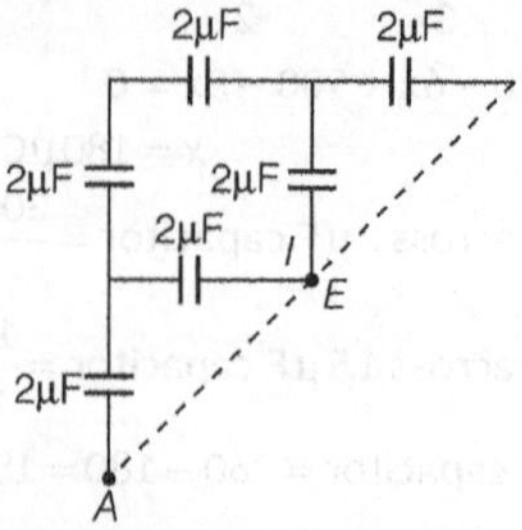

Using series and parallel combination now,

$$C_{eq} = \frac{8}{7}\mu F$$

(c)

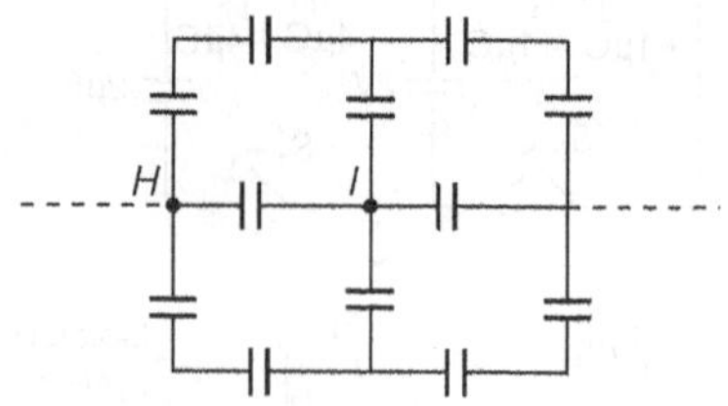

Due to parallel axis of symmetry, we can fold the circuit about the axis of symmetry.

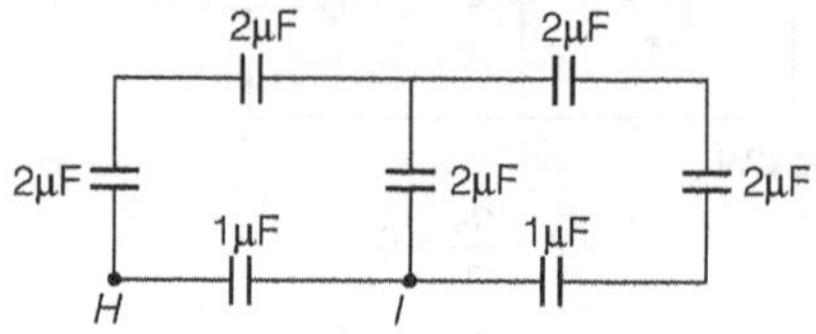

Using series and parallel combinations,

$$C_{eq} = \frac{12}{7}\mu F$$

(d) Due to symmetry, we can break the junction at I as shown.

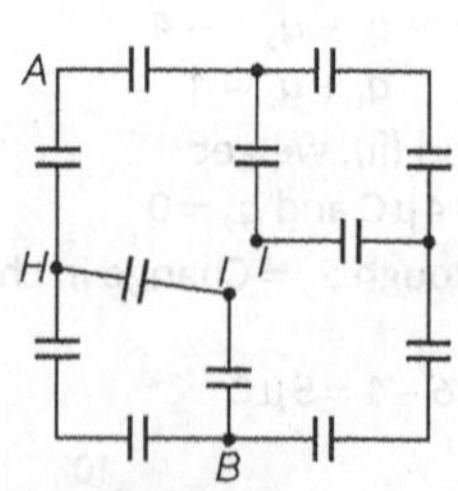

Using series and parallel combination.

14.

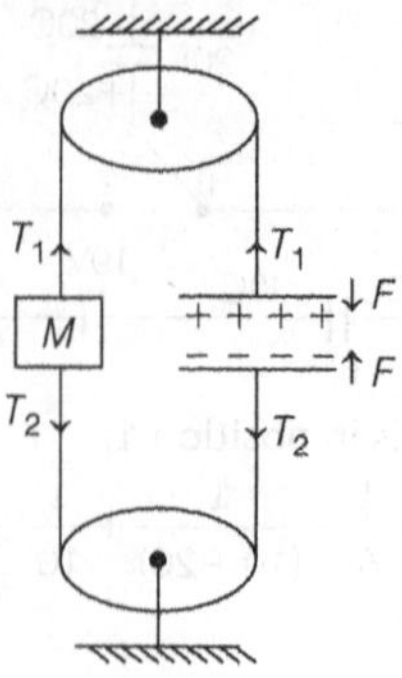

$$F_{min} = \text{Force between the plates}$$
$$= \frac{q^2}{2A\varepsilon_0} = \frac{CV^2}{2d} = \frac{10^{-6} \times 8^2}{2 \times 10^{-6}} = 32 \text{ N}$$

For the block, $T_1 = Mg + T_2$ ... (i)

For the upper plate, $T_1 = mg + F$ ... (ii)

For the lower plate, $F = mg + T_2$ ... (iii)

$$F = mg + T_2$$
$$\Rightarrow \quad F_{min} = mg \text{ when } T_2 = 0$$
$$\Rightarrow \quad 32 = mg \Rightarrow m = 3.2 \text{ kg}$$

Solving Eqs. (i), (ii) and (iii), we get

$$M = 2m \Rightarrow M = 6.4 \text{ kg}$$

15.

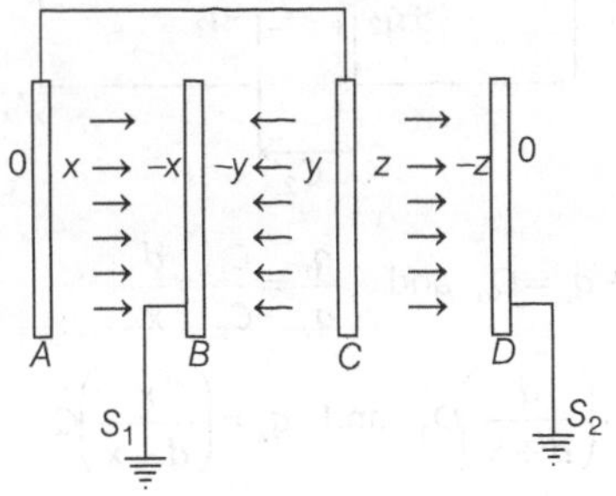

$$V_A = V_C$$
$$\Rightarrow \quad \left(\frac{x}{A\varepsilon_0}\right)d = \left(\frac{y}{A\varepsilon_0}\right)d$$
$$\Rightarrow \quad y = x \quad \text{... (i)}$$
$$V_B = V_D$$
$$\Rightarrow \quad \left(\frac{y}{A\varepsilon_0}\right)d = \left(\frac{z}{A\varepsilon_0}\right)d$$
$$\Rightarrow \quad y = z \quad \text{...(ii)}$$
$$q_A + q_C = Q$$
$$\Rightarrow \quad 0 + x + y + z = Q$$
$$\Rightarrow \quad x + y + z = Q \quad \text{... (iii)}$$

Solving Eqs. (i), (ii) and (iii), we get

$$x = y = z = \frac{Q}{3}$$

Charge flown through S_1 = Change in charge of plate B

$$= Q - \left(\frac{-2Q}{3}\right) = \frac{5Q}{3}$$

Charge flown through S_2 = Change in charge of plate D

$$= 2Q - \left(\frac{-Q}{3}\right) = \frac{7Q}{3}$$

16.

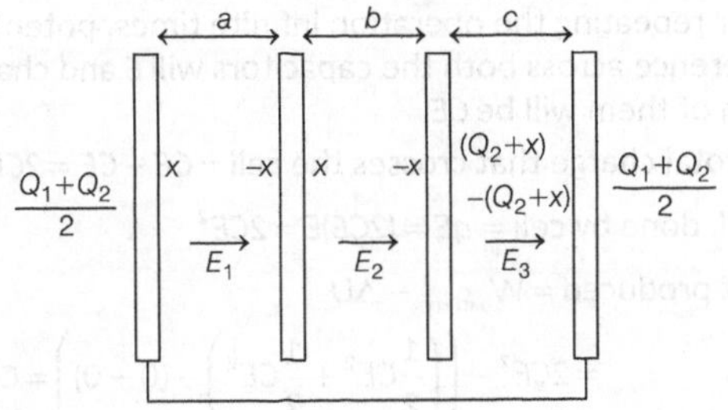

$$V_A = V_D$$
$$\Rightarrow \quad E_1 a + E_2 b + E_3 c = 0$$
$$\Rightarrow \quad \left(\frac{x}{A\varepsilon_0}\right)a + \left(\frac{x}{A\varepsilon_0}\right)b + \left(\frac{Q_2 + x}{A\varepsilon_0}\right)c = 0$$
$$\Rightarrow \quad xa + xb + cQ_2 + xc = 0$$
$$\Rightarrow \quad x = \frac{-cQ_2}{a+b+c}$$
$$V_A - V_B = \left(\frac{x}{A\varepsilon_0}\right)a = -\frac{caQ_2}{a+b+c}$$
$$V_C - V_D = \left(\frac{Q_2 + x}{A\varepsilon_0}\right)c = \frac{(a+b)Q_2}{a+b+c}$$

Potential difference between A and B and C and D depends on Q_2. It is independent of Q_1.

17. Before collision, electric field,

$$E_{A+B} = \frac{Q-q}{2\varepsilon_0 S} \text{ (towards left)}$$

$$\text{Force on plate } C = Q\left[\frac{Q-q}{2\varepsilon_0 S}\right] \text{ (towards left)}$$

During collision, redistribution of charges takes place between B and C, let charges on them are q_1 and q_2, respectively.

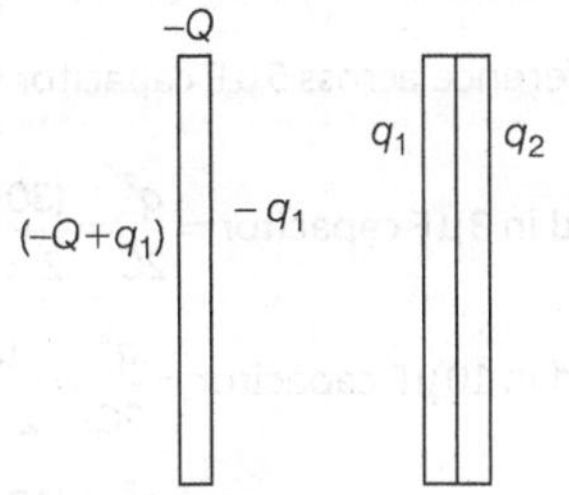

$$q_1 + q_2 = Q + q \quad \text{... (i)}$$
$$q_2 = -Q + q_1 \quad \text{... (ii)}$$

Solving Eqs. (i) and (ii), we get

$$q_1 = Q + \frac{q}{2} \quad \text{and} \quad q_2 = \frac{q}{2}$$

Force on plate C after collision,

$$F = q_C E_{(A+B)}$$
$$= \frac{q}{2}\left(\frac{-Q + Q + \frac{q}{2}}{2\varepsilon_0 S}\right) = \frac{(q/2)^2}{2\varepsilon_0 S} \quad \text{(towards right)}$$

After collision, electric field between plates B and C is zero. So, kinetic energy of plate C increases.

Comprehension Based Questions

1. $dV = -\mathbf{E} \cdot d\mathbf{r}$

$$dV = -E_x dx$$
$$\Rightarrow \quad \int dV = -\frac{\beta Q}{\varepsilon_0}\int\left(1 + \frac{x^2}{d^2}\right)dx$$

$$\Rightarrow \quad \Delta V = \frac{\beta Q}{\varepsilon_0}\int_0^d \left(1+\frac{x^2}{d^2}\right)dx$$

$$= \frac{\beta Q}{\varepsilon_0}\left[x+\frac{x^3}{3d^2}\right]_0^d = \frac{\beta Q}{\varepsilon_0}\left[d+\frac{d}{3}\right] = \frac{4\beta Qd}{3\varepsilon_0}$$

2. $C = \frac{Q}{\Delta V} = \frac{Q}{\frac{4\beta Qd}{3\varepsilon_0}} = \frac{3\varepsilon_0}{4\beta d}$

3.

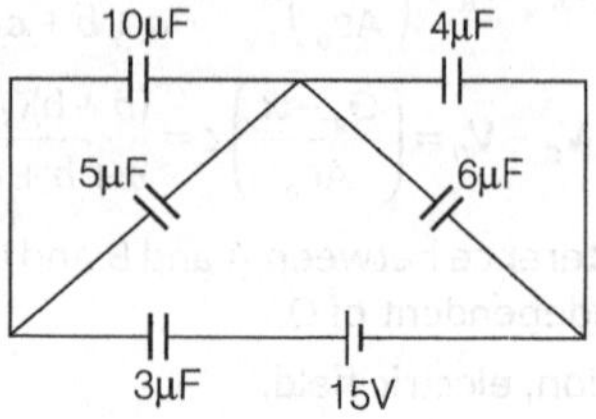

$$\frac{1}{C_{eq}} = \frac{1}{3} + \frac{1}{(10+5)} + \frac{1}{(4+6)} \Rightarrow C_{eq} = 2\,\mu F$$

Charge flown through battery $= C_{eq}\varepsilon = (2\,\mu F)(15V) = 30\,\mu C$

Charge on $4\,\mu F$ capacitor $= \left(\frac{6}{4+6}\right)(30)\,\mu C = 18\,\mu C$

4. Charge on $5\,\mu F$ capacitor $= \frac{5}{(10+5)} \times (30\,\mu C) = 10\,\mu C$

Potential difference across $5\,\mu F$ capacitor $= \frac{q}{C} = \frac{10\,\mu C}{5\,\mu F} = 2V$

5. Energy stored in $3\,\mu F$ capacitor $= \frac{q^2}{2C} = \frac{(30\,\mu C)^2}{2\times 3\,\mu F} = 150\,\mu J$

Energy stored in $10\,\mu F$ capacitor $= \frac{q^2}{2C} = \frac{(20\,\mu C)^2}{2\times(10\,\mu F)} = 20\,\mu J$

Energy stored in $5\,\mu F$ capacitor $= \frac{q^2}{2C} = \frac{(10\,\mu C)^2}{2\times 5\,\mu F} = 10\,\mu J$

Energy stored in $4\,\mu F$ capacitor $= \frac{q^2}{2C} = \frac{(12\,\mu C)^2}{2\times 4\,\mu F} = 18\,\mu J$

Energy stored in $6\,\mu F$ capacitor $= \frac{q^2}{2C} = \frac{(18\,\mu C)^2}{2\times 6\,\mu F} = 27\,\mu J$

So, energy stored is minimum in $5\,\mu F$ capacitor.

6.

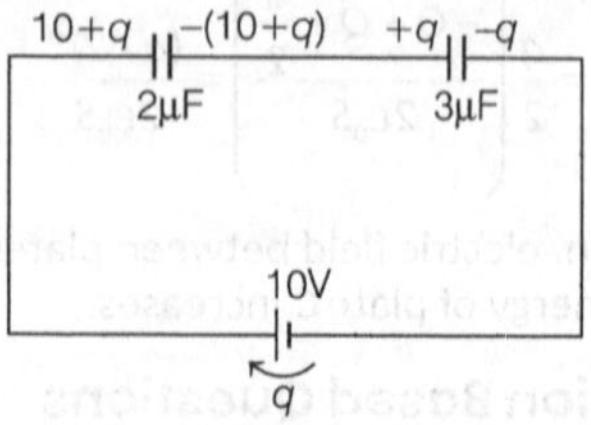

Let charge flown through battery after closing the switch be q.

Applying KVL, $\quad +10 - \frac{(10+q)}{2} - \frac{q}{3} = 0$

$$\Rightarrow \quad q = 6\,\mu C$$

Charge on capacitor $C_1 = (10+6)\,\mu C = 16\,\mu C$

7. Work done by battery $= q\varepsilon = (6\,\mu C)(10V) = 60\,\mu J$

8. Heat produced $= W_{battery} - \Delta U$

$$= 60 - \left(\left(\frac{(16)^2}{2\times 2} + \frac{6^2}{2\times 3}\right) - \left(\frac{10^2}{2\times 2}\right)\right) = 15\,\mu J$$

9.

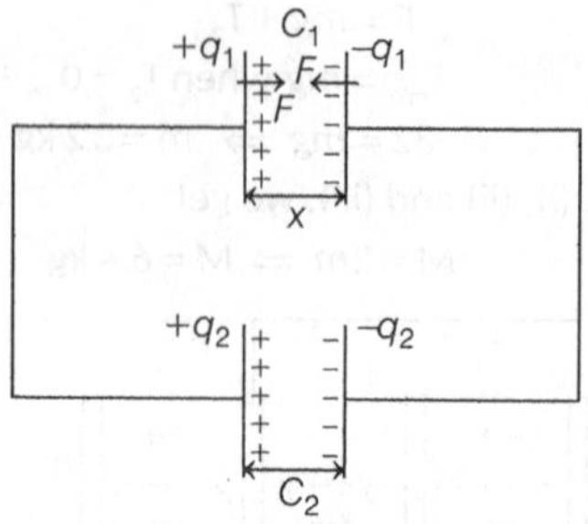

$$q_1 + q_2 = Q_0 \quad \text{and} \quad \frac{q_1}{q_2} = \frac{C_1}{C_2} = \frac{d}{x}$$

$$\Rightarrow \quad q_1 = \left(\frac{d}{d+x}\right)Q_0 \quad \text{and} \quad q_2 = \left(\frac{x}{d+x}\right)Q_0$$

$$F = \frac{q_1^2}{2A\varepsilon_0} = \left(\frac{d}{d+x}\right)^2 \frac{Q_0^2}{2A\varepsilon_0}$$

$$W_{ext} = \int F dx = \frac{Q_0^2 d^2}{2A\varepsilon_0}\int_d^{2d} \frac{1}{(d+x)^2}dx = \frac{Q_0^2 d}{12A\varepsilon_0}$$

10. $V = \frac{q_1}{C_1} = \left(\frac{d}{d+x}\right)\frac{Q_0}{\left(\frac{A\varepsilon_0}{x}\right)} = \frac{Q_0 xd}{A\varepsilon_0(x+d)}$

11. Heat produced $= W_{ext} - \Delta U$

$$W_{ext} = \frac{Q_0^2 d}{12A\varepsilon_0}$$

$$\Delta U = U_2 - U_1 = \left(\frac{q_1^2}{2C_1} + \frac{q_2^2}{2C_2}\right) - \left(\frac{Q_0^2}{8C} + \frac{Q_0^2}{8C}\right)$$

$$= \left(\frac{(Q_0/3)^2}{2\left(\frac{A\varepsilon_0}{2d}\right)} + \frac{(2Q_0/3)^2}{2\left(\frac{A\varepsilon_0}{d}\right)} - \frac{Q_0^2}{4\left(\frac{A\varepsilon_0}{d}\right)}\right) = \frac{Q_0^2 d}{12A\varepsilon_0}$$

Heat produced $= \frac{Q_0^2 d}{12A\varepsilon_0} - \frac{Q_0^2 d}{12A\varepsilon_0} = 0$

12. After repeating the operation infinite times, potential difference across both the capacitors will E and charge on each of them will be CE.

So, total charge that crosses the cell $= CE + CE = 2CE$

13. Work done by cell $= qE = (2CE)E = 2CE^2$

14. Heat produced $= W_{battery} - \Delta U$

$$= 2CE^2 - \left(\left(\frac{1}{2}CE^2 + \frac{1}{2}CE^2\right) - (0+0)\right) = CE^2$$

15.

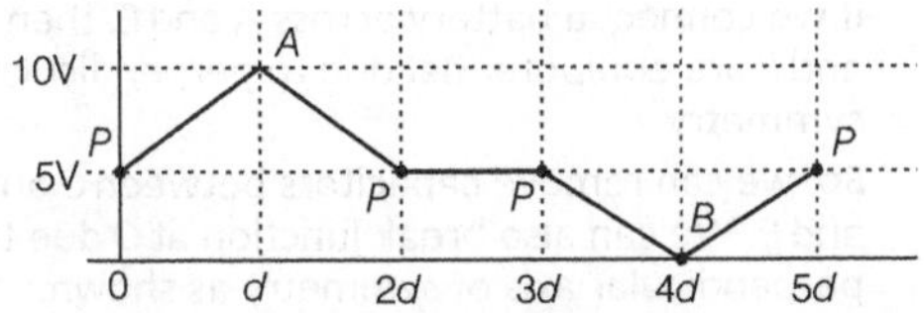

Capacitance of each capacitor $= \dfrac{A\varepsilon_0}{d}$

We have to find equivalent capacitance between A and B.

First two capacitors are between A and P.

Third capacitor is short-circuited.

Last two capacitors are between B and P.

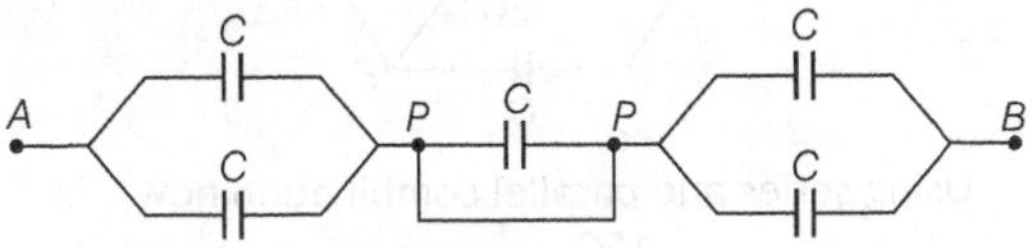

$$C_{eq} = \frac{(2C)(2C)}{2C+2C} = C = \frac{A\varepsilon_0}{d}$$

16. Total charge on plate $2 = C(5) + C(5) = 10C = \dfrac{10A\varepsilon_0}{d}$

17. $Q_2 = 10$ C and $Q_5 = -10$ C

$$\left|\frac{Q_2}{Q_5}\right| = 1:1$$

18. Figure 1,

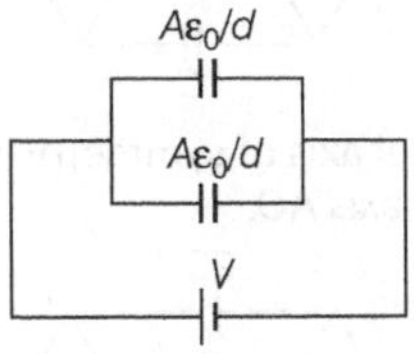

Total charge on plate $2 = x = \left(\dfrac{A\varepsilon_0}{d}\right)V + \left(\dfrac{A\varepsilon_0}{d}\right)V = \left(\dfrac{2A\varepsilon_0}{d}\right)V$

Figure 2,

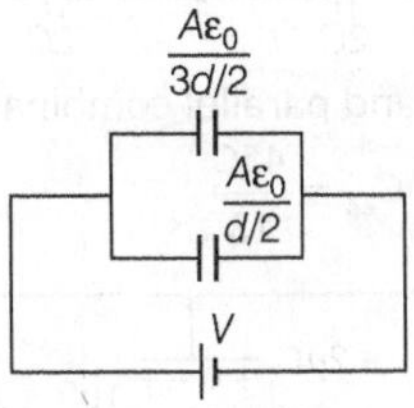

Total charge on plate $2 = y = \dfrac{A\varepsilon_0}{\left(\dfrac{3d}{2}\right)}V + \dfrac{A\varepsilon_0}{(d/2)}V = \left(\dfrac{8A\varepsilon_0}{3d}\right)V$

19. $W_{battery} = \left(\dfrac{8}{3}\dfrac{A\varepsilon_0}{d}V - \dfrac{2A\varepsilon_0}{d}V\right)V$

$$x = \frac{2}{3}\frac{A\varepsilon_0}{d}V^2$$

$y =$ Heat produced $= W_{battery} - \Delta U$

$$= \frac{2}{3}\frac{A\varepsilon_0}{d}V^2 - \left[\frac{1}{2}\left(\frac{A\varepsilon_0}{3d/2} + \frac{A\varepsilon_0}{d/2}\right)V^2 - \frac{1}{2}\times\frac{2A\varepsilon_0 V^2}{d}\right]$$

$$= \frac{A\varepsilon_0}{3d}V^2$$

20.

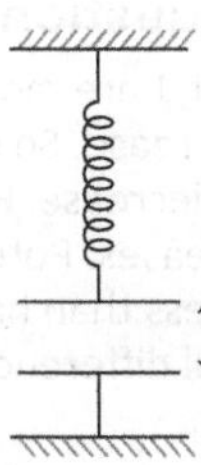

Attractive force between the plates $= \dfrac{q^2}{2A\varepsilon_0}$

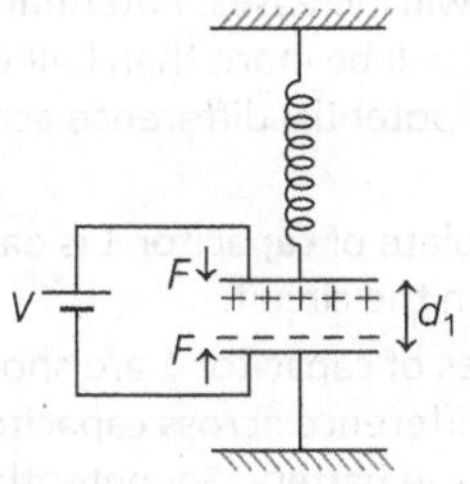

Additional elongation $= d_0 - d_1$

$$k(d_0 - d_1) = \frac{q^2}{2A\varepsilon_0}$$

$$\Rightarrow \quad k(d_0 - d_1) = \frac{(CV)^2}{2A\varepsilon_0} \Rightarrow k = \frac{A\varepsilon_0 V^2}{2d_1^2(d_0 - d_1)}$$

21. $V = \sqrt{\dfrac{2kd_1^2(d_0 - d_1)}{A\varepsilon_0}}$

For V to be maximum $\dfrac{dV}{d(d_1)} = 0$

$$\frac{dV}{d(d_1)} = \frac{1}{2\sqrt{\dfrac{2Kd_1^2(d_0 - d_1)}{A\varepsilon_0}}}2K(2d_1d_0 - 3d_1^2) = 0$$

$$\Rightarrow \quad d_1 = \frac{2d_0}{3}$$

$$V_{max} = \sqrt{\frac{2k\left(\dfrac{2d_0}{3}\right)^2\left(d_0 - \dfrac{2d_0}{3}\right)}{A\varepsilon_0}} = \sqrt{\frac{k}{A\varepsilon_0}}\left(\frac{2d_0}{3}\right)^{3/2}$$

22. Lets displace the upper plate by a distance x in down ward direction.

Restoring force $= -\left[kx - \left(\dfrac{A\varepsilon_0 V^2}{2(d_1 - x)^2} - \dfrac{A\varepsilon_0 V^2}{2d_1^2}\right)\right]$

$$F = -\left[kx - \frac{A\varepsilon_0 V^2}{2d_1^2}\left[\left[1 - \frac{x}{d_1}\right]^{-2} - 1\right]\right]$$

$$= -\left[kx - \frac{A\varepsilon_0 V^2}{2d_1^2}\left(\frac{2x}{d_1}\right)\right] = -\left[k - \frac{A\varepsilon_0 V^2}{d_1^3}\right]x$$

$$= -\left[k - \frac{2kd_1^2(d_0 - d_1)}{d_1^3}\right]x = -k\left[\frac{3d_1 - 2d_0}{d_1}\right]x$$

Angular frequency $= \sqrt{\dfrac{k(3d_1 - 2d_0)}{md_1}}$

Match the Columns Questions

1. (a) If plates of capacitor 1 are moved apart, its capacitance will decrease. So equivalent capacitance across battery will decrease. Hence charge on both the capacitors will decreases. Potential difference across capacitor 2 will be less than half of the emf of the battery. So potential difference across capacitor 2 decreases.

   (b) When area of plates of capacitor 1 is increased, its capacitance will increases. Charge on both the capacitors will increases. Potential difference across capacitor 2 will be more than half of the emf of the battery. So potential difference across capacitor 2 increases.

   (c) When left plate of capacitor 1 is earthed, there will be no effects in the circuit.

   (d) When plates of capacitor 1 are short-circuited, potential difference across capacitor 2 will be equal to the emf of the battery. So, potential difference and charge on capacitor 2 increases.

2. (a)

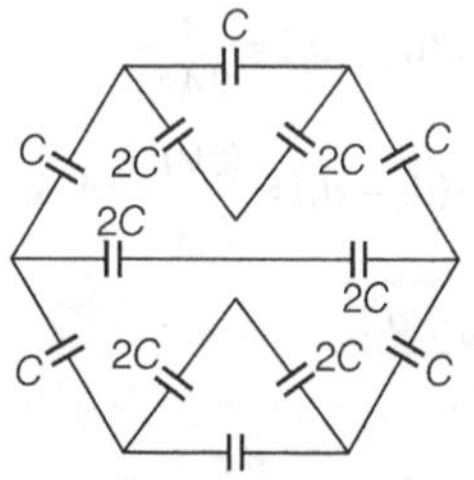

Due to input-output symmetry, we can break junction at O as shown in figure.

Now using series and parallel combinations, $C_{eq} = \frac{9C}{5}$

(b)

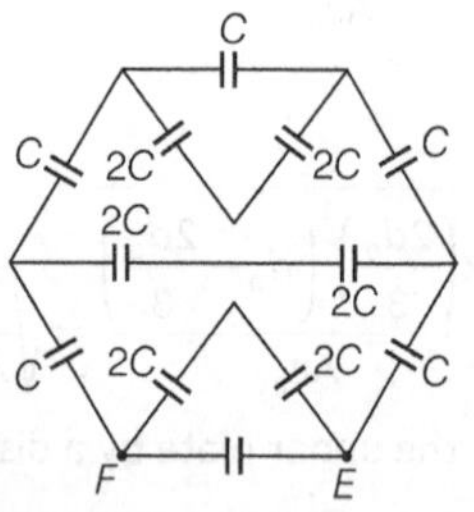

Due to input-output symmetry, we can break junction at O as shown in figure.

Now using series and parallel combinations $C_{eq} = \frac{45C}{19}$

(c)

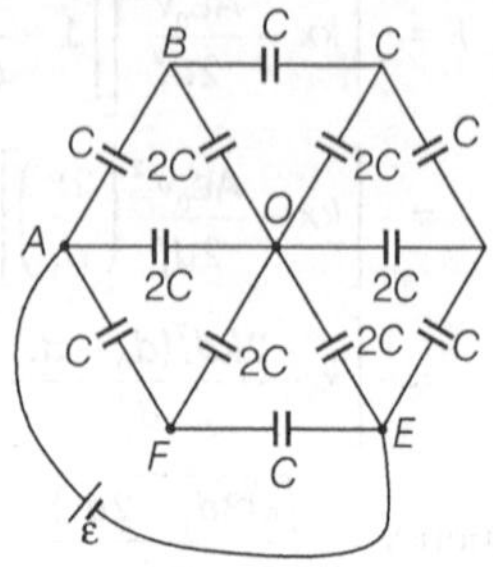

If we connect a battery across A and E, then points C, O and F are equipotential due to perpendicular axis of symmetry

So, we can remove capacitors between C and O and O and F. We can also break junction at O due to perpendicular axis of symmetry as shown.

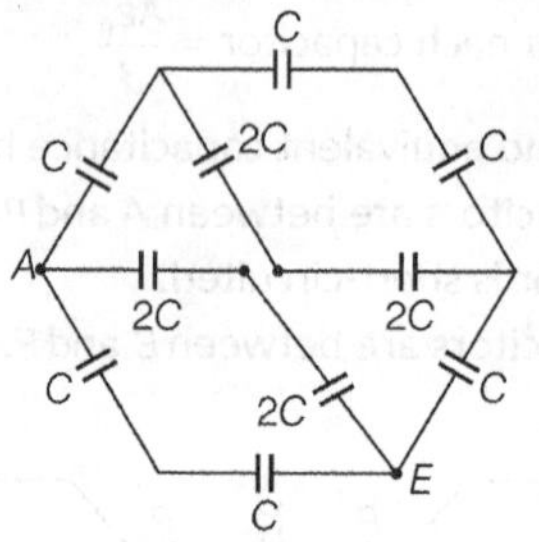

Using series and parallel combination now,

$$C_{eq} = \frac{15C}{8}$$

(d)

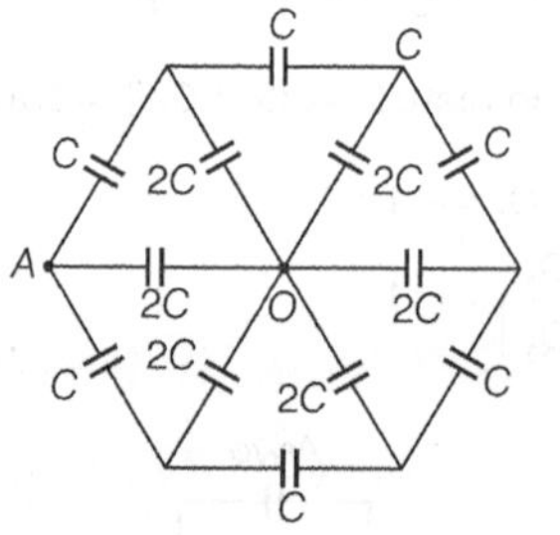

Due to parallel axis of symmetry, we can fold the circuit about axis AO.

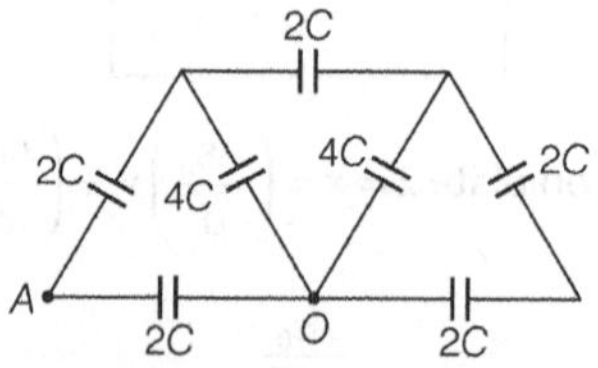

Using series and parallel combination now.

$$C_{eq} = \frac{45C}{13}$$

3.

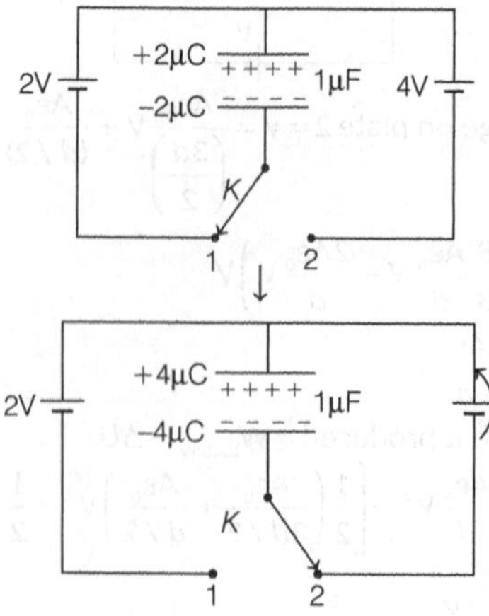

When the key is in position 1, charge on the capacitor is $2\,\mu C$. When the key is in position 2, charge on the capacitor is $4\,\mu C$.

q = Charge flown through 4V cell $= 4 - 2 = 2\,\mu C$

Work done by 4V cell $= (2\,\mu C)(4V) = 8\,\mu J$

$$\Delta U = U_2 - U_1 = \frac{1}{2}\times 1\times 10^{-6}\times 4^2 - \frac{1}{2}\times 1\times 10^{-6}\times 2^2 = 6\,\mu J$$

Heat produced $= W_{cell} - \Delta U = 8 - 6 = 2\,\mu J$

4.

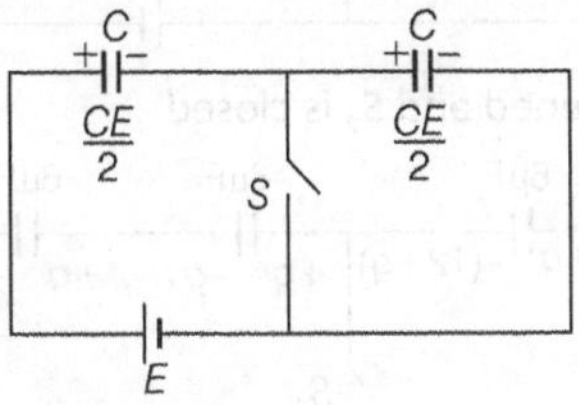

After the switch is closed

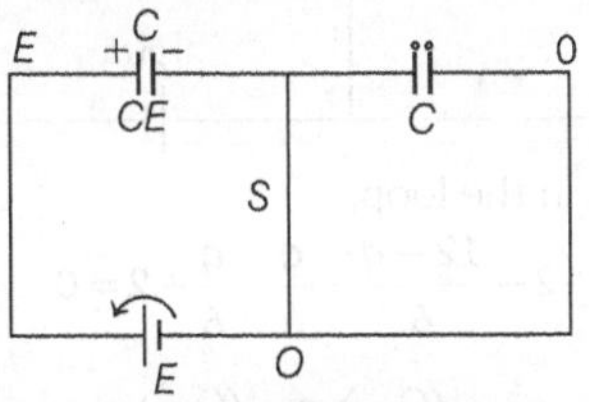

q = charge flown through battery when S is closed

$$= CE - \frac{CE}{2} = \frac{CE}{2}$$

$$\text{Work done by battery} = \left(\frac{CE}{2}\right)E = \frac{CE^2}{2}$$

Charge on capacitor $A = CE$

Heat developed $= W_{battery} - \Delta U$

$$= \frac{CE^2}{2} - \left(\left(\frac{1}{2}CE^2 + 0\right) - \left(\frac{1}{2}\left(\frac{C}{2}\right)E^2\right)\right) = \frac{CE^2}{4}$$

5. (a)

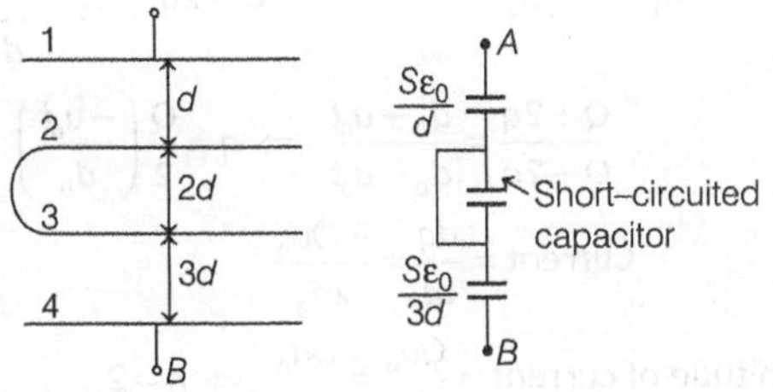

$$\frac{1}{C_{eq}} = \frac{1}{\frac{S\varepsilon_0}{d}} + \frac{1}{\frac{S\varepsilon_0}{3d}} \Rightarrow C_{eq} = \frac{S\varepsilon_0}{4d}$$

(b)

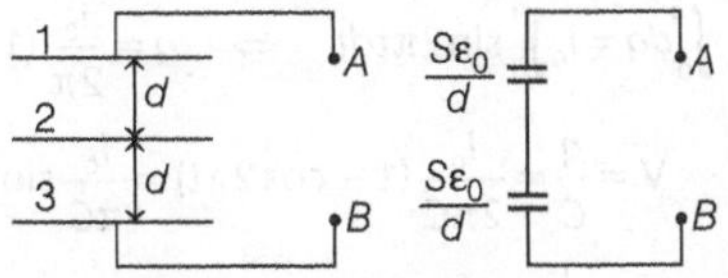

$$\frac{1}{C_{eq}} = \frac{1}{\left(\frac{S\varepsilon_0}{d}\right)} + \frac{1}{\left(\frac{S\varepsilon_0}{d}\right)} \Rightarrow C_{eq} = \frac{S\varepsilon_0}{2d}$$

(c)

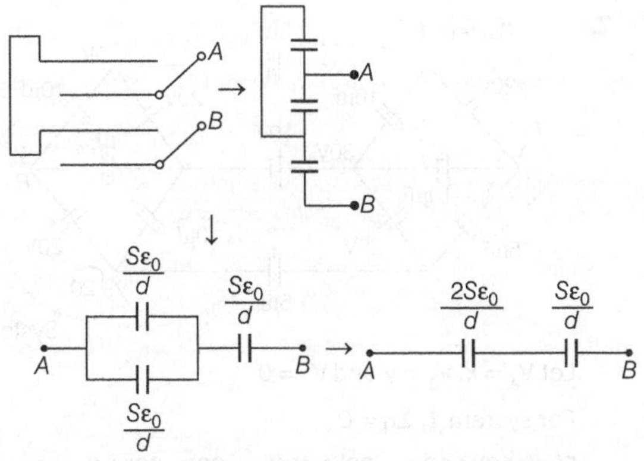

$$\frac{1}{C_{eq}} = \frac{1}{\left(\frac{2S\varepsilon_0}{d}\right)} + \frac{1}{\left(\frac{S\varepsilon_0}{d}\right)} \Rightarrow C_{eq} = \frac{2}{3}\frac{S\varepsilon_0}{d}$$

(d)

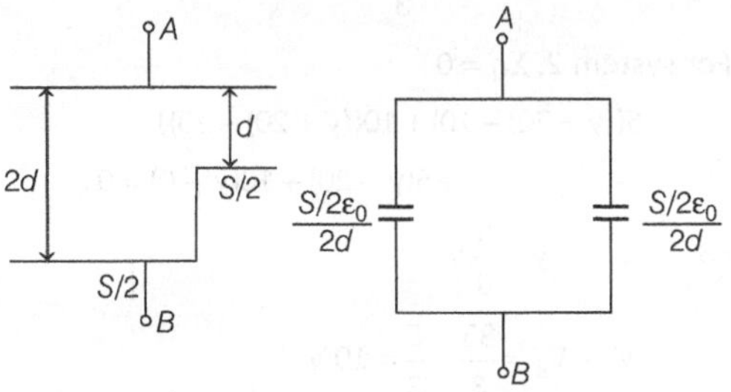

$$C_{eq} = \frac{S\varepsilon_0}{4d} + \frac{S\varepsilon_0}{2d} \Rightarrow C_{eq} = \frac{3}{4}\frac{S\varepsilon_0}{d}$$

Numerical Value Questions

1.

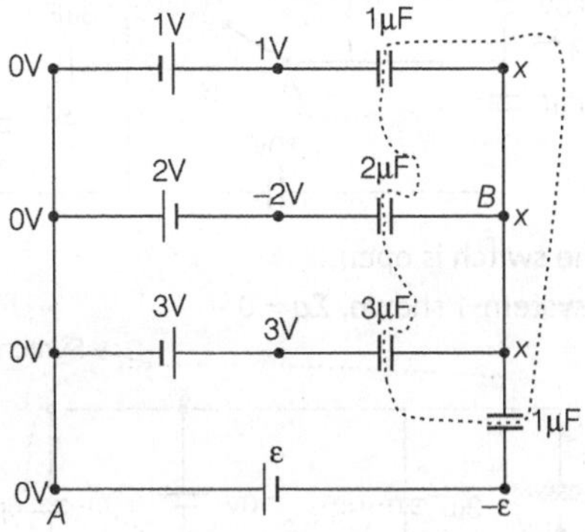

Let $V_A = 0V$ and $V_B = xV$

for the isolated system of plates

$$\varepsilon q = 0$$

$\Rightarrow$ $1(x-1) + 2(x-(-2)) + 3(x+3) + 1(x-(-\varepsilon)) = 0$

$\Rightarrow$ $7x - 6 + \varepsilon = 0$

$\Rightarrow$ $x = \dfrac{6-\varepsilon}{7}$

Charge on $2\,\mu F$ capacitor $= CV$

$\Rightarrow$ $\pm 4\,\mu C = (2\,\mu F)(x-(-2))$

$\Rightarrow$ $\pm 2 = \left(\dfrac{6-\varepsilon}{2} + 2\right)$

$\Rightarrow$ $\varepsilon = 6V$ and $\varepsilon = 34\,V$

2.

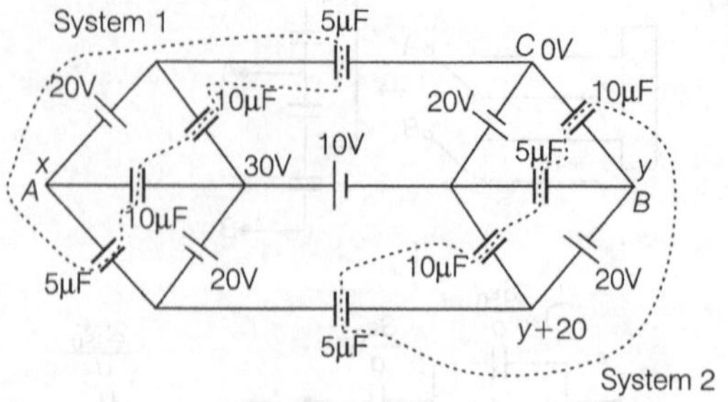

Let $V_A = x, V_B = y$ and $V_C = 0$

For system 1, $\Sigma q = 0$

$$5(x-10)+10(x-30)+10((x+20)-30)+5((x+20)-0)=0$$

$$\Rightarrow \quad x = \frac{35}{3}\text{ V}$$

For system 2, $\Sigma q = 0$

$$5((y+20)-10)+10((y+20)-20)) + 5(y-20)+10(y-0)=0$$

$$\Rightarrow \quad y = \frac{5}{3}\text{ V}$$

$$\Rightarrow \quad V_A - V_B = \frac{35}{3} - \frac{5}{3} = 10\text{ V}$$

3.

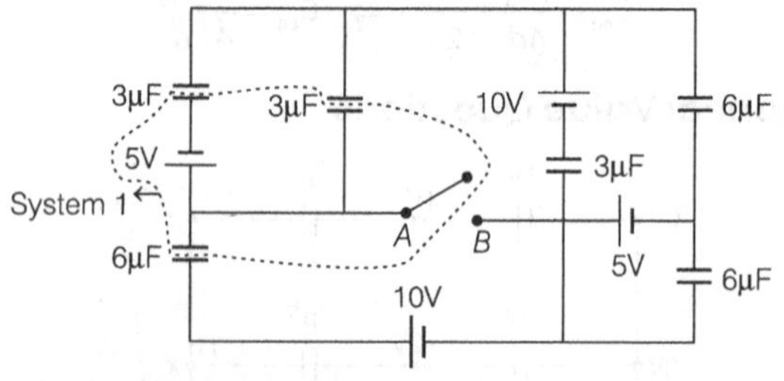

When the switch is open,

For the system-1 shown, $\Sigma q = 0$

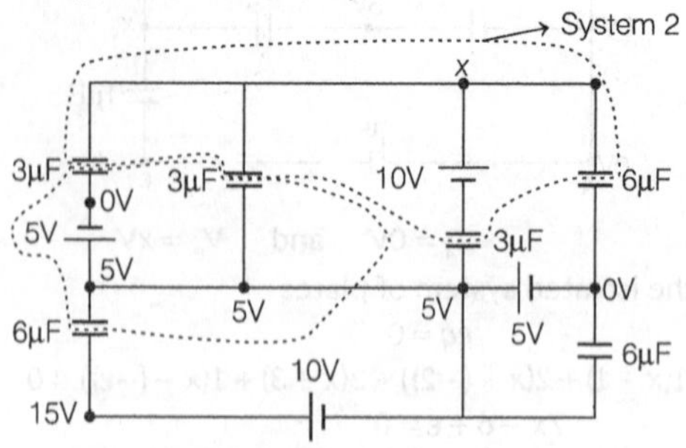

For system-2, $\Sigma q = 0$

$$3(x-0)+3(x-5)+3((x-10)-5)+6(x-0)=0$$

$$\Rightarrow \quad x = 4\text{V}$$

On system-1, $\Sigma q = 6(15-5)+3(4-0)+3(4-5) = 69\mu\text{C}$

Charge flown through switch $= 69 - 0 = 69\mu\text{C}$

4. When S_1 is closed and S_2 is open

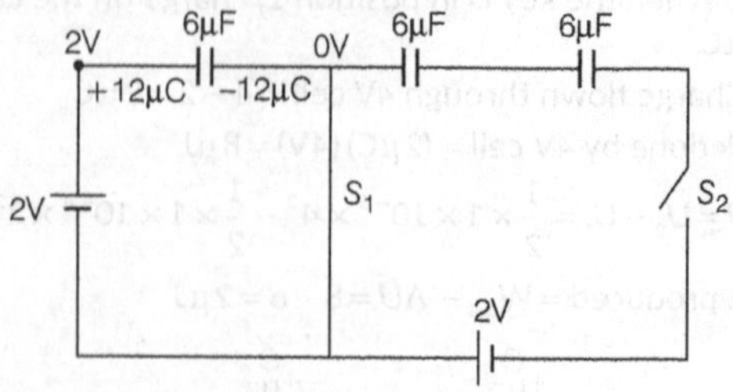

Now, S_1 is opened and S_2 is closed

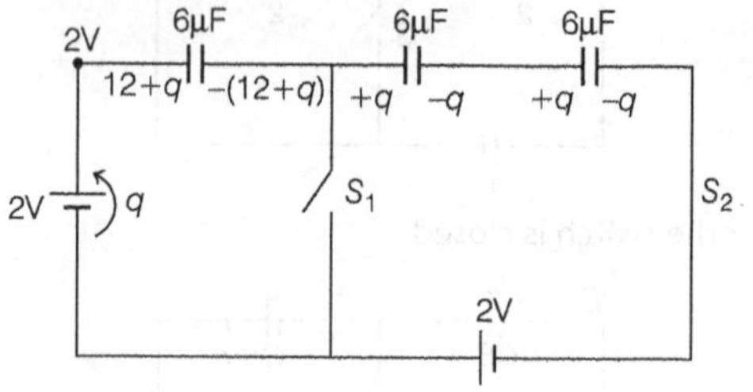

Applying KVL in the loop,

$$+2 - \frac{12+q}{6} - \frac{q}{6} - \frac{q}{6} + 2 = 0 \quad \Rightarrow q = 12C$$

5.

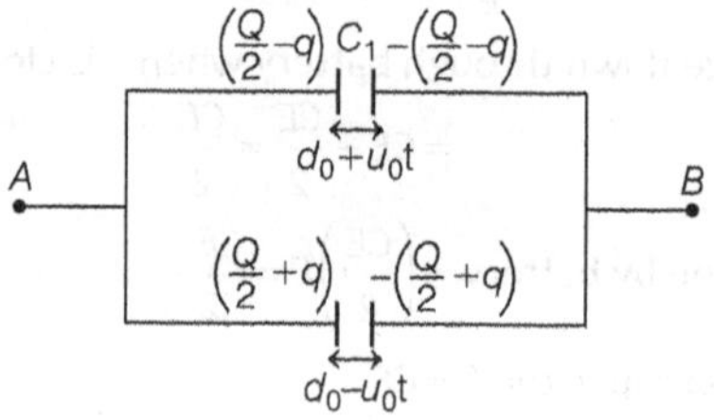

Applying KVL in the loop,

$$-\frac{\frac{Q}{2}-q}{C_1} + \frac{\frac{Q}{2}+q}{C_2} = 0 \quad \Rightarrow \quad \frac{Q+2q}{Q-2q} = \frac{C_2}{C_1} = \frac{\frac{A\varepsilon_0}{d_0-u_0t}}{\frac{A\varepsilon_0}{d_0+u_0t}}$$

$$\Rightarrow \quad \frac{Q+2q}{Q-2q} = \frac{d_0+u_0t}{d_0-u_0t} \quad \Rightarrow q = \frac{Q}{2}\left(\frac{-u_0t}{d_0}\right)$$

$$\text{Current} = \frac{dq}{dt} = \frac{-Qu_0}{2d_0}$$

$$\text{Magnitude of current} = \frac{Qu_0}{2d_0} = \frac{Qu_0}{nd_0} \quad \Rightarrow n = 2$$

6. $\frac{dq}{dt} = i = I_0 \sin 2\pi t$

$$\int_0^q dq = I_0 \int_0^t \sin 2\pi t dt \quad \Rightarrow \quad q = \frac{I_0}{2\pi}(1-\cos 2\pi t)$$

$$V = \frac{q}{C} = \frac{I_0}{2\pi C}(1-\cos 2\pi t) = \frac{I_0}{\pi C}\sin^2 \pi t$$

$$\Rightarrow \quad V_{max} = \frac{I_0}{\pi C} \text{ when } \sin \pi t = 1$$

$$\frac{I_0}{\pi C} = \frac{2I_0}{k\pi C} \quad \Rightarrow k = 2$$

7.

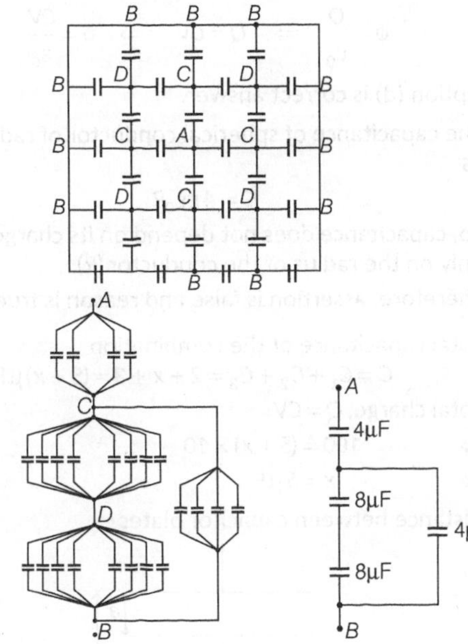

$$C_{eq} = \frac{8}{3}\mu F$$

$$\text{Energy stored} = \frac{q^2}{2C_{eq}} = \frac{(8\times10^{-6})^2}{2\left(\frac{8}{3}\times10^{-6}\right)} = 12\,\mu J$$

8. When the plate is kept in the middle of the capacitor.

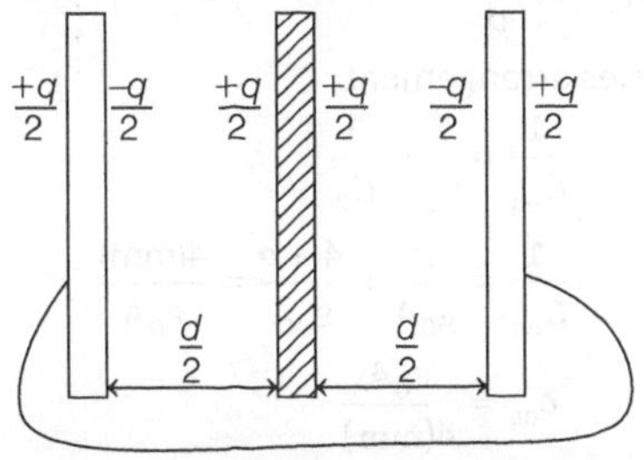

When the plate is shifted by $x = 1$ mm

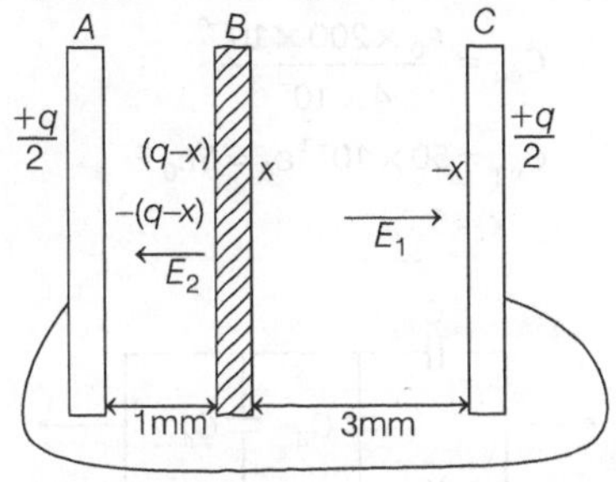

$$V_A = V_C \Rightarrow V_A - V_B = V_C - V_B$$

$$\Rightarrow \quad -E_2(1mm) = -E_1(3mm)$$

$$\Rightarrow \quad -\frac{q-x}{A\varepsilon_0}\times 1 = -\frac{x}{A\varepsilon_0}\times 3 \Rightarrow x = \frac{q}{4}$$

Final charge on plate $C = \frac{q}{2} - \frac{q}{4} = \frac{q}{4}$

Initial charge on plate $C = \frac{-q}{2} + \frac{q}{2} = 0$

Charge flown through external circuit $= \frac{q}{4} - 0 = \frac{8\mu C}{4} = 2\mu C$

9.

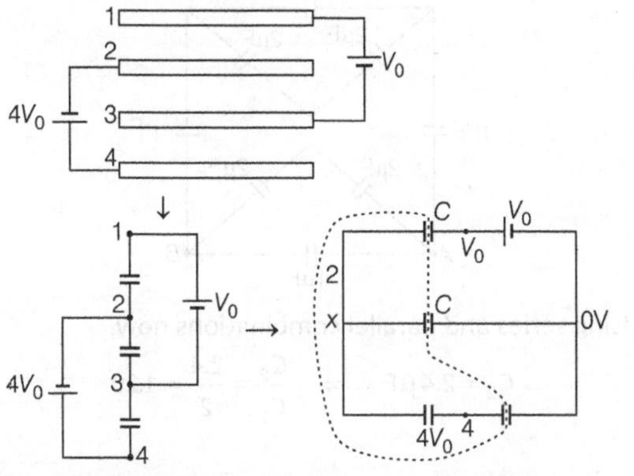

For the system shown $\Sigma q = 0$

$$C(x - V_0) + C(x - 0) + C((x + 4V_0) - 0) = 0 \Rightarrow x = -V_0$$

Charge on the upper surface of the lowest plate

$$= C((x + 4V_0) - 0) = C((-V_0 + 4V_0) - 0) = 3CV_0 = \frac{3V_0 A\varepsilon_0}{L}$$

10.

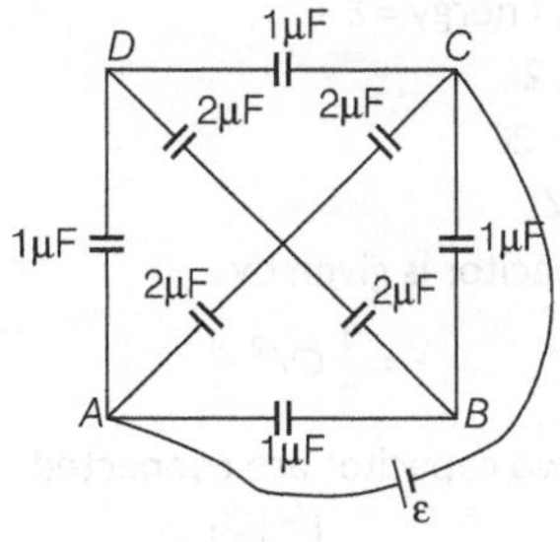

If a battery is connected across *A* and *C* then points *B* and *D* are equipotential. So we can join points *B* and *D*

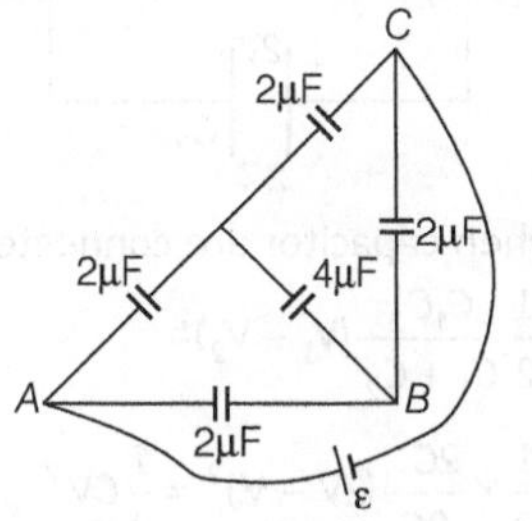

It is a balance wheat stone bridge now.
So, we can remove 4μF capacitor, $C_1 = 2\mu F$

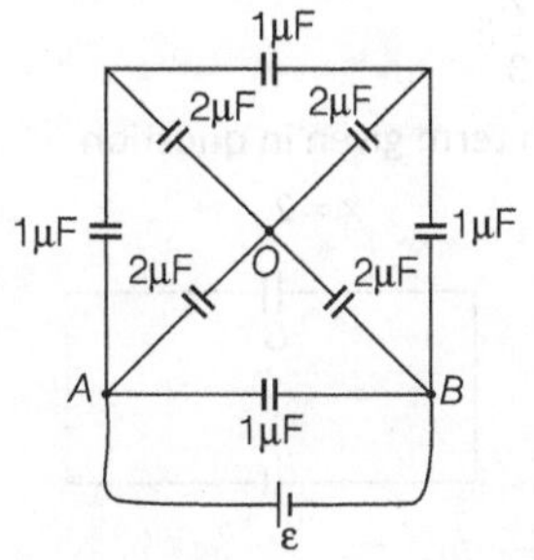

If a battery is connected between points A and B, then due to input-output symmetry we can break junction at O as shown in figure.

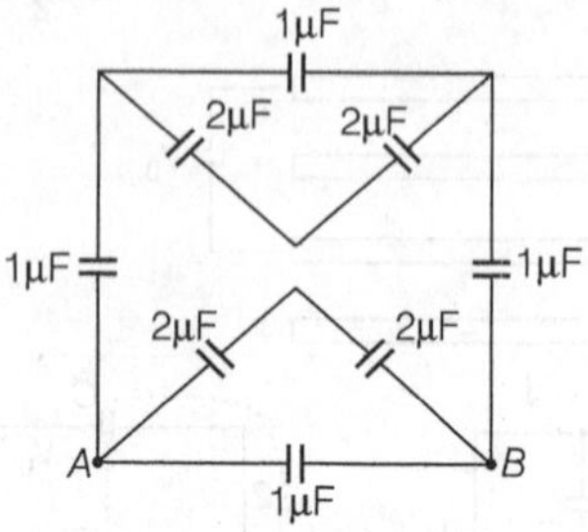

Using series and parallel combinations now,

$$C_2 = 2.4\,\mu\text{F} \quad \Rightarrow \quad \frac{C_2}{C_1} = \frac{2.4}{2} = 1.20$$

Previous Year's Questions

JEE Main

1. Given,

For capacitor 1 capacitance $= C$

Potential $= V$, Energy $= E$

For capacitor 2

Capacitance $= 2C$

Potential $= 2V$

Energy of capacitor is given by

$$E = \frac{1}{2}CV^2 \qquad \text{...(i)}$$

Now, these two capacitor are connected

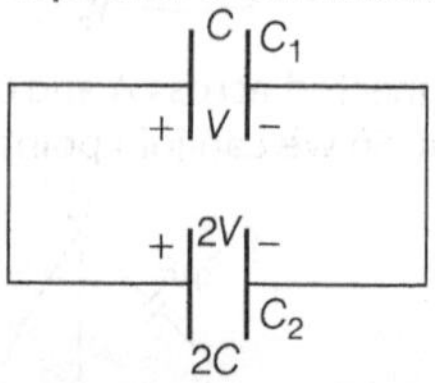

Energy loss when capacitor are connected is given by

$$U_{\text{Loss}} = \frac{1}{2}\frac{C_1C_2}{C_1 + C_2}(V_1 - V_2)^2$$

$$= \frac{1}{2} \times \frac{2C^2}{3C}(2V - V)^2 = \frac{1}{3}CV^2 \qquad \text{...(ii)}$$

From Eq. (i),

$$U_{\text{Loss}} = \frac{2}{3}E$$

Compare with term given in question

$$x = 2$$

2.

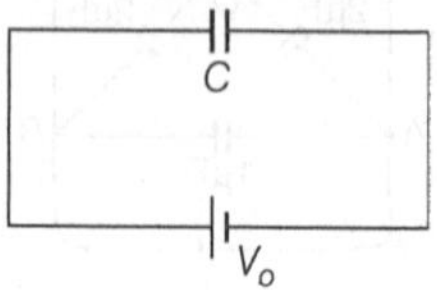

$$\phi = \frac{Q}{\varepsilon_0} \quad \Rightarrow \quad Q = CV \quad \Rightarrow \quad \phi = \frac{CV}{\varepsilon_0}$$

Option (d) is correct answer.

3. The capacitance of spherical conductor of radius R is given as

$$C = 4\pi\varepsilon_0 R$$

So, capacitance does not depend on its charge, it depends only on the radius of the conductor (R).

Therefore, assertion is false and reason is true.

4. Total capacitance of the combination

$$C = C_1 + C_2 + C_3 = 2 + x + 3 = (5 + x)\,\mu\text{F}$$

Total charge, $Q = CV$

$$\Rightarrow \qquad 100 = (5 + x) \times 10$$

$$\Rightarrow \qquad x = 5\,\mu\text{F}$$

5. Distance between capacitor plates

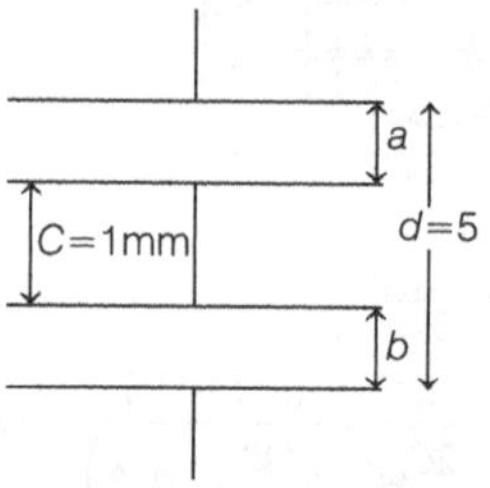

$$b = 5 - a - 1 = (4 - a)\text{ mm}$$

We know, $C = \dfrac{\varepsilon_0 A}{d}$

and in series arrangement,

$$\frac{1}{C_{eq}} = \frac{1}{C_1} + \frac{1}{C_2}$$

$$\frac{1}{C_{eq}} = \frac{a}{\varepsilon_0 A} + \frac{4 - a}{\varepsilon_0 A} = \frac{4(\text{mm})}{\varepsilon_0 A}$$

$$C_{eq} = \frac{\varepsilon_0 A}{4(\text{mm})}$$

given $\qquad A = 200\text{ cm}^2$

$$C_{eq} = \frac{\varepsilon_0 \times 200 \times 10^{-4}}{4 \times 10^{-3}}$$

$$C_{eq} = 50 \times 10^{-1}\varepsilon_0 = 5\varepsilon_0\text{ F}$$

$$x = 5$$

6.

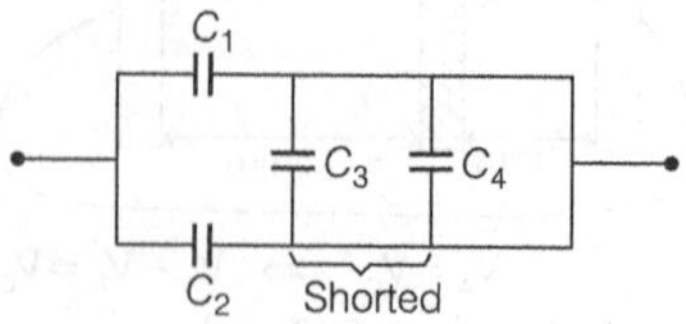

In given circuit, C_4 and C_3 are shorted so, capacitance of circuit is,

$$C_{CQ} = C_1 + C_2 = C + C = 2C$$

7. Given, $C = 2\text{F}$

Energy stored, $E_1 = \frac{1}{2}CV^2$ ...(i)

Now, common potential

$$V_C = \frac{C_1V_1 + C_2V_2}{C_1 + C_2} = \frac{CV + 0}{2C} = \frac{V}{2}$$

$$E_2 = \frac{1}{2}CV_C^2 = \frac{CV^2}{8} \quad ...(ii)$$

$$\frac{\text{Eq. (ii)}}{\text{Eq. (i)}} = \frac{E_2}{E_1} = \frac{CV^2/8}{CV^2/2} = \frac{1}{4}$$

8.

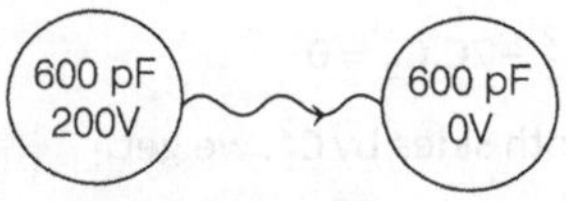

As both capacitors are identical, common potential after equilibrium is obtained is;

$$V' = \frac{Q_1 + Q_2}{C_1 + C_2} = \frac{C_1V_1 + C_2V_2}{C_1 + C_2}$$

$$= \frac{600 \times 200 + 600 \times 0}{600 + 600} = 100\text{ V}$$

Now, initial energy

$$= \frac{1}{2}C_1V^2 = \frac{1}{2} \times 600 \times 10^{-12} \times 200 \times 200$$

$$= 12 \times 10^{-6} \text{ joule}$$

Final energy $= \frac{1}{2}(C_1 + C_2)V'^2$

$$= \frac{1}{2} \times 1200 \times 10^{-12} \times (100)^2 = 6 \times 10^{-6}\text{ J}$$

∴ Energy cost = Initial energy − Final energy

$$= 6 \times 10^{-6}\text{ J} = 6\,\mu\text{J}$$

9.

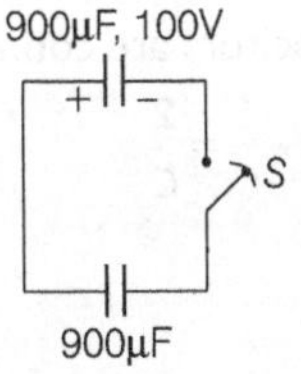

Common potential after redistribution of charges is

$$V' = \frac{C_1V_1 + C_2V_2}{C_1 + C_2} = \frac{900 \times 10^{-6} \times 100 + 0}{1800 \times 10^{-6}} = 50\text{ V}$$

Initial energy stored $= \frac{1}{2}CV^2 = \frac{1}{2} \times 900 \times 10^{-6} \times (100)^2$

$$= 4.5\text{ J} = 450 \times 10^{-2}\text{ J}$$

Final energy stored $= \frac{1}{2}(C_1 + C_2)V'^2$

$$= \frac{1}{2} \times 1800 \times 10^{-6} \times (50)^2$$

$$= 225 \times 10^{-2}\text{ J}$$

So, Loss of energy $= (450 - 225) \times 10^{-2}$

$$= 225 \times 10^{-2}\text{ J}$$

10. The given situation is shown below.

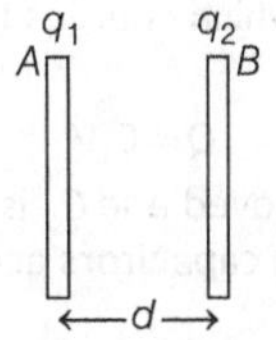

Net electric field inside the parallel plate capacitor.

$$E = \frac{\sigma_1}{2\varepsilon_0} - \frac{\sigma_2}{2\varepsilon_0} = \frac{1}{2\varepsilon_0}(\sigma_1 - \sigma_2) = \frac{1}{2\varepsilon_0}\left[\frac{q_1}{A_1} - \frac{q_2}{A_2}\right]$$

$\therefore\ A_1 = A_2 = A$

$$\Rightarrow E = \frac{1}{2\varepsilon_0}\left[\frac{q_1}{A} - \frac{q_2}{A}\right] = \frac{q_1 - q_2}{2\varepsilon_0 A}$$

∴ Potential difference between the plates.

$$V = E \cdot d = \frac{(q_1 - q_2)d}{2\varepsilon_0 A}$$

$$= \frac{q_1 - q_2}{2\left(\frac{\varepsilon_0 A}{d}\right)} = \frac{q_1 - q_2}{2C} \qquad \left(\text{where, } \frac{\varepsilon_0 A}{d} = C\right)$$

11. As, $C = \frac{Q}{V}$; $V = \frac{Q}{C}$

So, when capacitor is fully charged; given

$Q = 5\text{ C}$

and $C = 2 \times 10^{-6}\text{ F}$

$$V = \frac{5}{2 \times 10^{-6}} = 2.5 \times 10^6\text{ V}$$

Also, $V = \left(\frac{1}{C}\right) \times Q$

This is equation of a straight line with slope $\frac{1}{C}$.

Hence, correct graph is

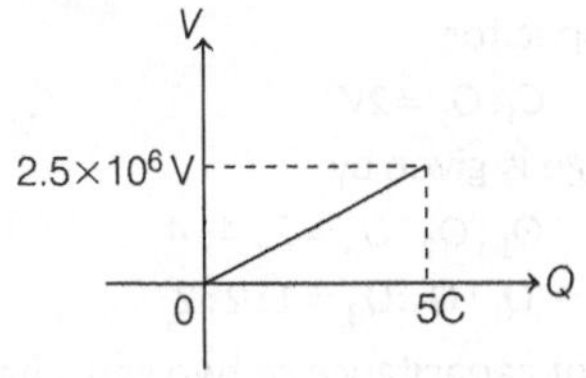

12.

Case 1 Force due to two charged plates in a capacitor

Case 2 Force due to single positively charged plate.

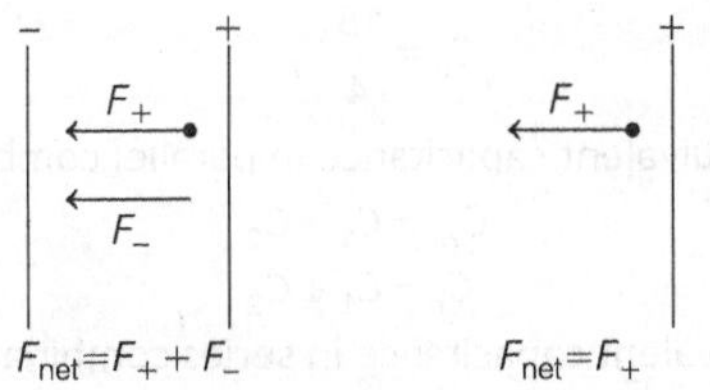

$$F_{\text{new}} = \frac{1}{2}F_{\text{net}} = \frac{1}{2} \times 10 = 5\text{ N}$$

13. Initially when capacitor C_1 is charged, total charge Q flows through the circuit which charges the capacitor C_1 by V volt. Thus

$$Q = C_1 V$$

When battery is removed and C_2 is connected to C_1, the C_1 discharges until both capacitors acquire a common potential.

$$V_{\text{com}} = \left(\frac{C_1}{C_1 + C_2}\right) V$$

Therefore, the amount of charge on capacitor C_2 is given as

$$Q_2 = C_2 V_{\text{com}} = \frac{C_2 C_1}{C_1 + C_2} V$$

14. Let the original charge is Q.

So, initial energy stored,

$$U_i = \frac{Q^2}{2C}$$

Final energy stored, $\dfrac{(Q+2)^2}{2C} = U_f$

% change in energy $= \dfrac{U_f - U_i}{U_i} \times 100 = 44$

$$\Rightarrow \quad \frac{(Q+2)^2 - Q^2}{Q^2} = 0.44$$

$$\Rightarrow \quad Q = 10\ \text{C}$$

15. Equivalent capacitance of the series combination of C_2 and C_3

$$C' = \frac{C_2 C_3}{C_2 + C_3}$$

$$\Rightarrow \quad C' = \frac{6 \times 12}{6 + 12} = 4\ \mu\text{F}$$

Charge on capacitors C_2 and C_3 is same.

$$\therefore \quad Q_2 = Q_3 = C'V = 4V$$

Charge on capacitor

$$C_1, Q_1 = 2V$$

Ratio of charge is given by

$$\therefore \quad Q_1 : Q_2 : Q_3 = 2 : 4 : 4$$

or

$$Q_1 : Q_2 : Q_3 = 1 : 2 : 2$$

16. Let, equivalent capacitance of two capacitors C_1 and C_2 connected in parallel be C_a and equivalent capacitance of same, when connected in series be C_b.

According to given data,

$$C_a = \frac{15}{4} C_b \qquad \text{...(i)}$$

Since, equivalent capacitance in parallel combination,

$$C_{\text{eq}} = C_1 + C_2$$

$$\therefore \quad C_a = C_1 + C_2 \qquad \text{...(ii)}$$

And equivalent capacitance in series combination,

$$\frac{1}{C'_{\text{eq}}} = \frac{1}{C_1} + \frac{1}{C_2}$$

$$\therefore \quad \frac{1}{C_b} = \frac{1}{C_1} + \frac{1}{C_2} = \frac{C_2 + C_1}{C_1 C_2}$$

$$C_b = \frac{C_1 C_2}{C_1 + C_2} \qquad \text{...(iii)}$$

On substituting Eqs. (ii) and (iii) in Eq. (i), we get

$$C_1 + C_2 = \frac{15}{4}\left(\frac{C_1 C_2}{C_1 + C_2}\right)$$

$$\Rightarrow \quad 4(C_1 + C_2)^2 = 15 C_1 C_2$$

$$\Rightarrow 4C_1^2 + 4C_2^2 + 8C_1C_2 = 15 C_1 C_2$$

$$\Rightarrow 4C_1^2 + 4C_2^2 - 7C_1C_2 = 0$$

On dividing both sides by C_1^2, we get

$$4 + 4\left(\frac{C_2}{C_1}\right)^2 - 7\frac{C_2}{C_1} = 0$$

or

$$4\left(\frac{C_2}{C_1}\right)^2 - 7\left(\frac{C_2}{C_1}\right) + 4 = 0$$

If $\dfrac{C_2}{C_1} = x$, then $4x^2 - 7x + 4 = 0$

By using the concept of quadratic equation,

$$x = \frac{-b \pm \sqrt{b^2 - 4ac}}{2a}$$

$$\Rightarrow \quad x = \frac{7 \pm \sqrt{49 - 64}}{8}$$

$$\Rightarrow \quad x = \frac{C_2}{C_1} = \frac{7 \pm \sqrt{-15}}{8} = \frac{7 \pm \sqrt{15}\,i}{8}$$

17. Given, $C_1 = C_2 = C$

When, both capacitors are connected in series,

$$\frac{1}{C_s} = \frac{1}{C} + \frac{1}{C} = \frac{2}{C}$$

$$\Rightarrow \quad C_s = \frac{C}{2}$$

When, both capacitors are connected in parallel,

$$C_p = C + C = 2C$$

∴ The ratio of equivalent capacitance in series and parallel combination is

$$\frac{C_s}{C_p} = \frac{C/2}{2C} = \frac{1}{4}$$

$$\Rightarrow \quad C_s : C_p = 1 : 4$$

18. Let V is the voltage across each capacitor,

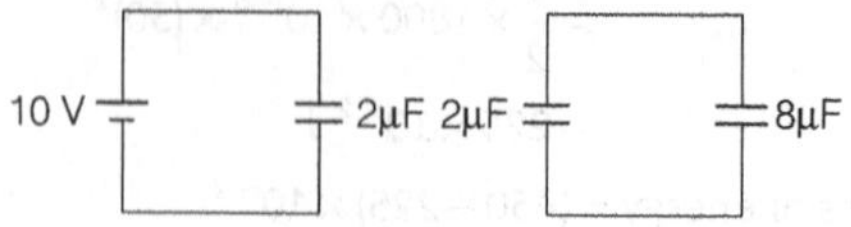

Now, after removing the battery the capacitor is connected.

So, using the law of conservation of charge,

$$2V + 8V = 2 \times 10 = 20$$

$$\Rightarrow \quad 10V = 20$$

$$\Rightarrow \quad V = 2\,V$$

As we know, $Q = CV = 8 \times 2 = 16\,\mu C$

JEE Advanced

1. 2 V battery is directly connected with C_3. Therefore, potential difference across $C_3 = 2\,V$
   Now, $q_3 = C_3V = (4\mu F)(2\,V) = 8\,\mu C$
2. After pressing S_1 charge on upper plate of C_1 is $+2CV_0$.
   After pressing S_2 this charge equally distributes in two capacitors. Therefore, charge on upper plates of both capacitors will be $+CV_0$.
   When S_2 is released and S_3 is pressed, charge on upper plate of C_1 remains unchanged $(= +CV_0)$ but charge on upper plate of C_2 is according to new battery $(= -CV_0)$.
3. Between $3\,\mu F$ and $2\,\mu F$ (in parallel), total charge of $80\,\mu C$ will distribute in direct ratio of capacity.

$$\frac{q_3}{q_2} = \frac{3}{2}$$

$$q_3 = \left(\frac{3}{3+2}\right)(80) = 48\,\mu C$$

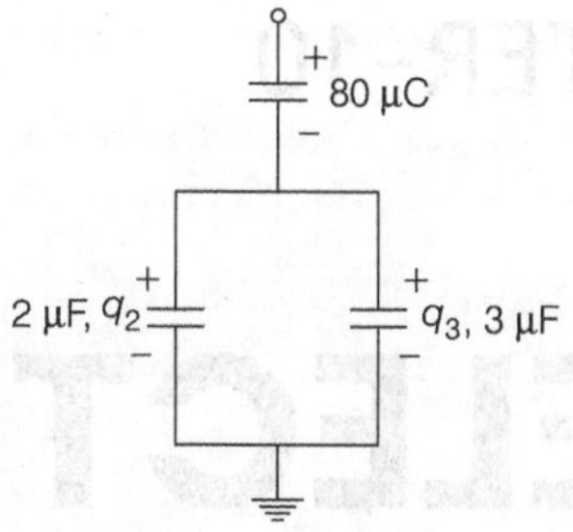

4. $q_i = C_iV = 2V = q$ (say)
   This charge will remain constant after switch is shifted from position 1 to position 2.

$$U_i = \frac{1}{2}\frac{q^2}{C_i} = \frac{q^2}{2 \times 2} = \frac{q^2}{4}$$

$$U_f = \frac{1}{2}\frac{q^2}{C_f} = \frac{q^2}{2 \times 10} = \frac{q^2}{20}$$

$$\therefore \text{Energy dissipated} = U_i - U_f = \frac{q^2}{5}$$

This energy dissipated $\left(= \frac{q^2}{5}\right)$ is 80% of the initial stored energy $\left(= \frac{q^2}{4}\right)$.

$\therefore$ Correct option is (d).

CHAPTER~10

DIELECTRICS

LEVEL 01 Starter Level

10.1 Capacitor Fully Filled with Dielectric

1 A parallel plate capacitor has plates of area A separated by distance d. The capacitor is connected across a cell of emf V.

(a) Find the capacitance (C_0), charge (q_0), electric field (E_0) and energy (U_0) of the capacitor.

(b) Find new capacitance (C), charge (q), electric field (E) and energy (U) of the capacitor in the following two cases.

Case-1 If battery is first disconnected and then a dielectric slab of dielectric constant K is inserted fully between the capacitor plates.

Case-2 If a dielectric slab of dielectric constant K is inserted fully between the capacitor plates while it is connected to battery.

2 A capacitor has two circular plates whose radii are 8 cm and distance between them is 1 mm. When mica (dielectric constant = 6) is placed between the plates, calculate the capacitance of this capacitor.

3 A parallel plate capacitor having plate area 100 cm^2 and separation 1.0 mm holds a charge of 0.12 μC when connected to a 120 V battery. Find the dielectric constant of the material filling the gap.

4 A parallel plate air capacitor has square plates of edge 10.0 cm separated by 1.0 mm. It is fully filled by a dielectric slab of dielectric constant 5.0 and connected across a 60.0 V battery. Then, find

(a) the charge supplied by the battery

(b) the induced charge on the dielectric

5 A parallel plate capacitor is formed by two plates, each of area 100 cm^2, separated by a distance of 1 mm. A dielectric of dielectric constant 5.0 and dielectric strength 1.9×10^7 V/m is filled between the plates. Find the maximum charge that can be stored on the capacitor without causing any dielectric breakdown.

10.2 Capacitor Partially Filled by a Dielectric

1 The distance between the plates of a parallel plate condenser is 5 cm. A field of 3×10^4 V/m is applied between the plates. It is then disconnected from the battery and an uncharged metal plate of thickness 1 cm is inserted into the condenser parallel to its plates. Find the potential difference between the plates;

(i) before the introduction of the metal plate,

(ii) after its introduction.

(iii) What would be the potential difference, if the metal plate is replaced by a plate of dielectric constant 2?

2 A potential difference of 130 V is applied across a plane air capacitor spaced 1 cm apart. A plane parallel glass layer with a thickness of 0.5 cm and a plane parallel paraffin layer with a thickness of 0.3 cm are placed in the space between the capacitor plates. Find

(i) intensity of electric field in each layer,

(ii) the drop of potential in each layer,

(iii) the surface charge density of the induced charges on each layer.

Given that: $K_{glass} = 6, K_{paraffin} = 2$.

3 A parallel plate air capacitor of capacitance 5 μF is connected to a battery of emf 30 V. The separation between the plates is 2 mm. Now, a dielectric slab of thickness 1 mm and dielectric constant 5 is inserted into the gap to occupy the lower half of it.

(i) Find the capacitance of the new combination.

(ii) How much charge has flown through the battery after the slab is inserted?

4 A parallel plate air capacitor of capacitance 15 μF is connected to a battery of 100 V. Separation between the plates 1 mm. A dielectric slab of thickness 0.5 mm and dielectric constant 5 is inserted into the gap.

(i) Find the increase in electrostatic energy.

(ii) If the battery is now disconnected and the dielectric slab is taken out, find the further increase in energy.

(iii) Why does the energy increase in inserting the slab as well as in taking it out?

10.3 Equivalent Capacitance with Dielectric

1 Some dielectric slabs are inserted between the plates of a parallel plate air capacitor of plates area A and separation d as shown in the following figures. Calculate capacitance for each case.

(i)
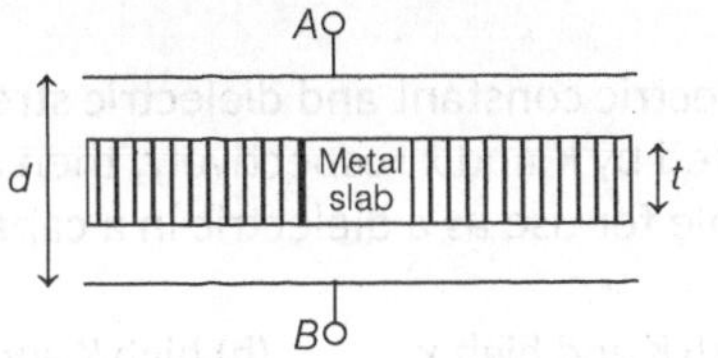

(ii)
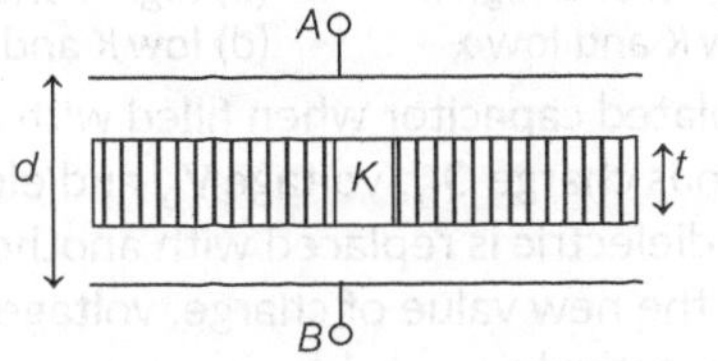

(iii)
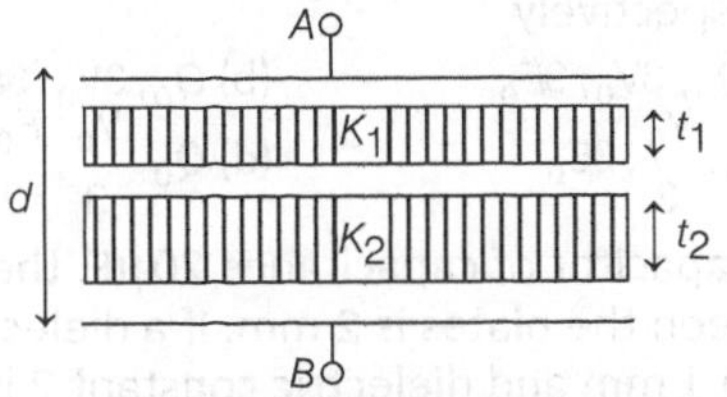

(iv)
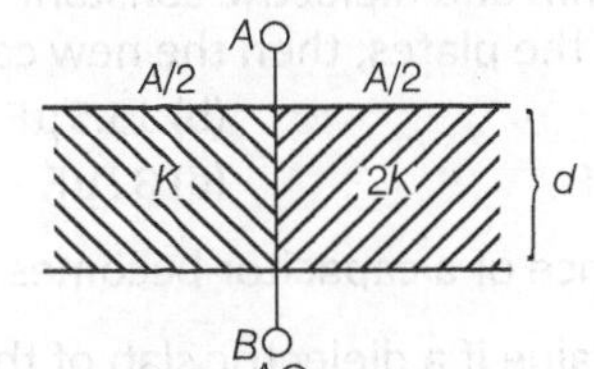

(v)
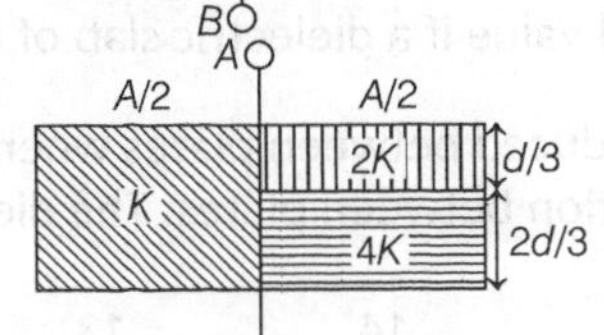

(vi)
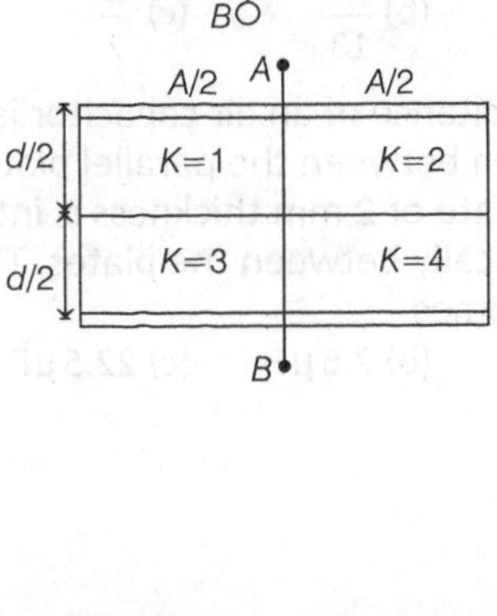

2 A parallel plate capacitor is having square plates of edge a and plate-separation d. The gap between the plates is filled with a dielectric. Calculate the capacitance for each case.

(i)
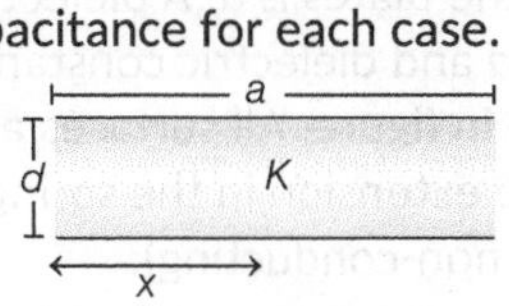

Dielectric constant K varies parallel to an edge as $K = K_0 + \lambda x$, where K_0 and λ are constants and x is the distance from the left end.

(ii)
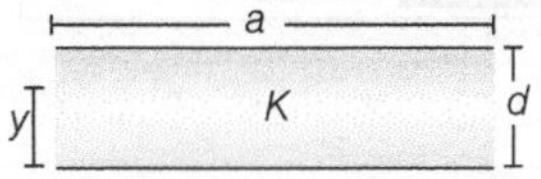

Dielectric constant K varies perpendicular to an edge as $K = K_0 + \lambda y$, where K_0 and λ are constants and y is the distance from an edge.

10.4 Capacitors with Dielectrics in Circuit

1 Two parallel plate air capacitors each of capacitance C were connected in series to a battery with emf. ε. Then, one of the capacitors was filled up with uniform dielectric with relative permittivity k.

(i) How many times did the electric field strength in that capacitor decrease?

(ii) What amount of charge flows through the battery?

2 Two parallel plate capacitors of capacitance 10 μF and 30 μF are connected in parallel and charged to a potential difference 300 V with the help of a battery. The battery is disconnected and the space between these two capacitors are filled with dielectric of constant 6 and 3 respectively. Find the voltage across the combination.

10.5 Force on Dielectric Slab

1 Figure shows a parallel plate capacitor with plates width b and length l. The separation between the plates is d. The plates are rigidly clamped and connected to a battery of e.m.f. V. Dielectric slab is of length l, width b, thickness d and dielectric constant K.

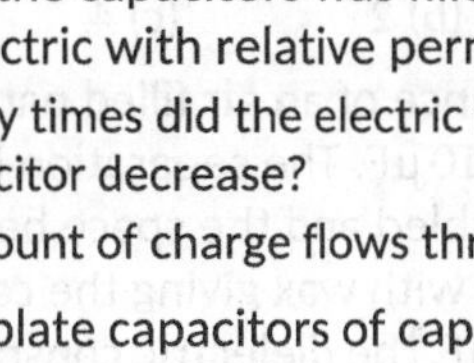

(i) Find the energy of the system when a length x of the slab is introduced into the capacitor.

(ii) What force is exerted on the slab by the capacitor?

2 The capacitor plates are fixed and connected to a battery of emf V. The width of each plate is b and separation between the plates is d. A dielectric slab of width b, thickness d and dielectric constant K is in equilibrium as shown in figure. All surfaces are smooth. Calculate the extension in the spring in equilibrium (spring is non-conducting).

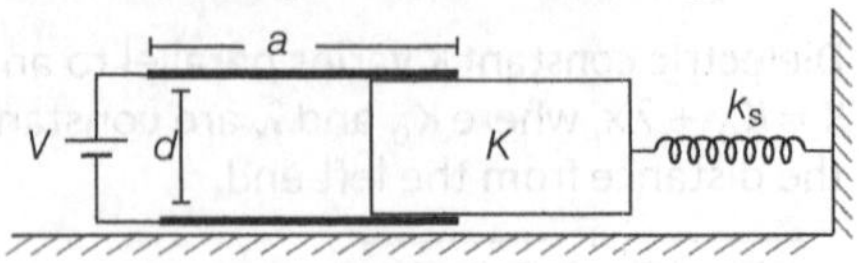

3 The rectangular plates ($l \times b$) of a capacitor are rigidly clamped as shown in figure. The dielectric slab is released from rest with a length a inside the capacitor. Neglecting friction and gravity, show that the slab will execute periodic motion and find its time period.

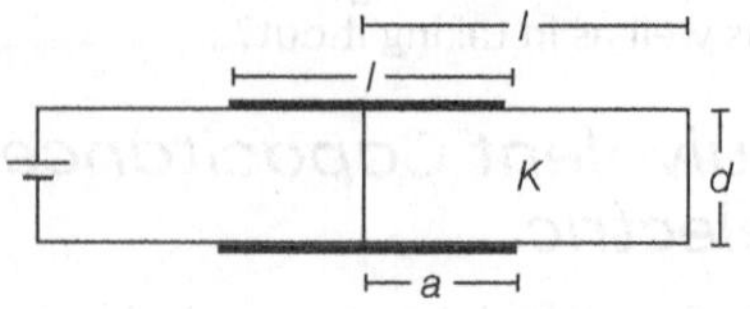

LEVEL 02 JEE Main Level

Single Choice Correct Questions

1 A capacitor stores 50 μC charge when connected across a battery. When the gap between the plates is filled with a dielectric, a charge of 100 μC flows through the battery. The dielectric constant of the material is

(a) 2.5 (b) 2 (c) 4 (d) 3

2 The capacitance of an air filled parallel plate capacitor is 10 μF. The separation between the plates is doubled and the space between the plates is then filled with wax giving the capacitance a new value of 40 μF.The dielectric constant of wax is

(a) 4 (b) 8 (c) 10 (d) 12

3 A capacitor is charged by using a battery which is then disconnected. A dielectric slab is then slipped between the plates which results in

(a) reduction of charges on the plates and increase of potential difference across the plates
(b) increase in the potential difference across the plates, reduction in stored energy, but no change in the charge on the plates
(c) decrease in the potential difference across the plates, reduction in stored energy, but no change in the charge on the plates.
(d) None of the above

4 Two square plates of capacitor are of length 32 cm each. Between the plates, material having thickness 640 μm is sandwiched whose dielectric strength is 20 MV/m. The maximum charge that can be put on the capacitor is (Permittivity of free space $=9\times10^{-12}$ SI unit and dielectric constant of material is 4)

(a) 4.6 μC (b) 5 μC (c) 73.7 μC (d) 18.4 μC

5 If dielectric constant and dielectric strength be denoted by K and x respectively, then a material suitable for use as a dielectric in a capacitor must have

(a) high K and high x (b) high K and low x
(c) low K and low x (d) low K and high x

6 An isolated capacitor when filled with a dielectric $K = 3$ has charge Q_0, voltage V_0 and electric field E_0. If the dielectric is replaced with another one having $K = 9$, the new value of charge, voltage and field will be respectively

(a) $3Q_0, 3V_0, 3E_0$ (b) $Q_0, 3V_0, 3E_0$
(c) $Q_0, \frac{V_0}{3}, 3E_0$ (d) $Q_0, \frac{V_0}{3}, \frac{E_0}{3}$

7 In a capacitor of capacitance 20 μF, the distance between the plates is 2 mm. If a dielectric slab of width 1 mm and dielectric constant 2 is inserted between the plates, then the new capacitance will be

(a) 2 μF (b) 15.5 μF
(c) 26.6 μF (d) 32 μF

8 Capacitance of a capacitor becomes 7/6 times its original value if a dielectric slab of thickness $t = \left(\frac{2}{3}\right)d$ is introduced between plates where d is the separation between plates. The dielectric constant of slab is

(a) $\frac{14}{11}$ (b) $\frac{14}{13}$ (c) $\frac{13}{7}$ (d) $\frac{11}{7}$

9 The capacitance of an air capacitor is 15 μF and the separation between the parallel plates is 6 mm. A copper plate of 2 mm thickness is introduced symmetrically between the plates. The capacitance now becomes

(a) 5 μF (b) 7.5 μF (c) 22.5 μF (d) 30 μF

10 Separation between the plates of a parallel-plate capacitor is 5 mm. This capacitor, having air as the dielectric medium between the plates, is charged to a potential difference 25 V using a battery. The battery is then disconnected and a dielectric slab of thickness 3 mm and dielectric constant $K = 10$ is placed between the plates, as shown. Potential difference between the plates after the dielectric slab has been introduced is

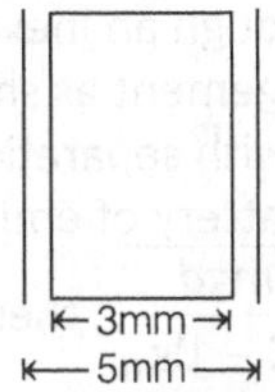

(a) 18.5 V (b) 13.5 V
(c) 11.5 V (d) 6.5 V

11 The plates of a parallel plate capacitor are charged upto 100 V. A 2 mm thick plate is inserted between the plates. To maintain the same potential difference, the distance between the capacitor plates is increased by 1.6 mm. The dielectric constant of the plate is

(a) 5 (b) 1.25 (c) 4 (d) 2.5

12 A parallel plate capacitor has two layers of dielectric as shown in figure. This capacitor is connected across a battery. The graph which shows the variation of electric field (E) and distance (x) from left plate.

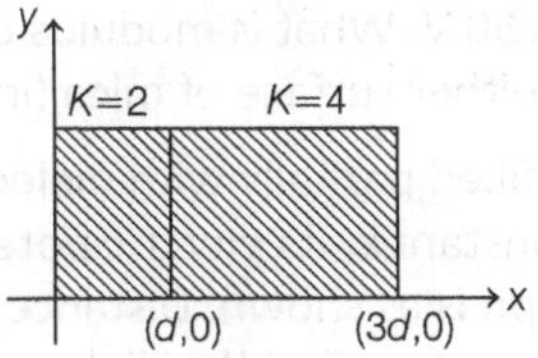

(a)

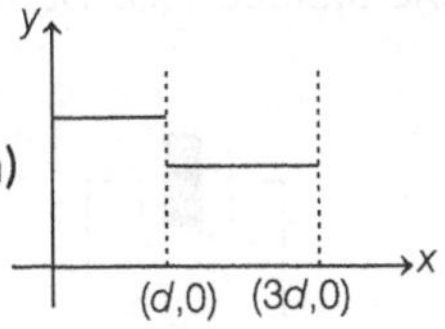

(b)

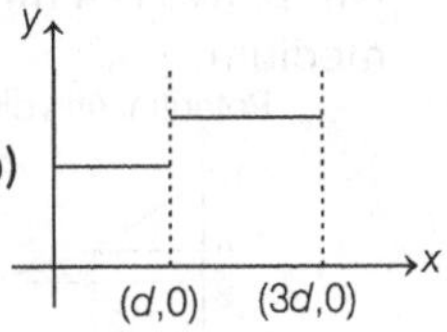

(c)

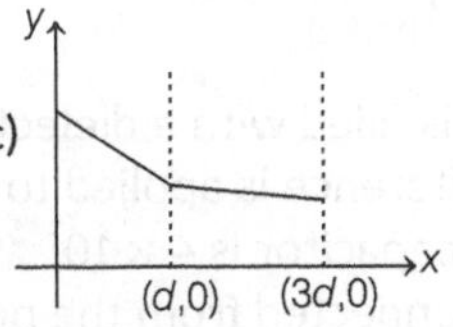

(d)

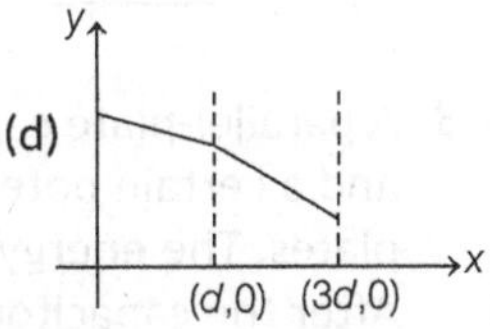

13 In the figure shown a parallel plate capacitor has a dielectric of width $d/2$ and dielectric constant $K = 2$. The other dimensions of the dielectric are same as that of the plates. The plates P_1 and P_2 of the capacitor have area A each. The energy of the capacitor is

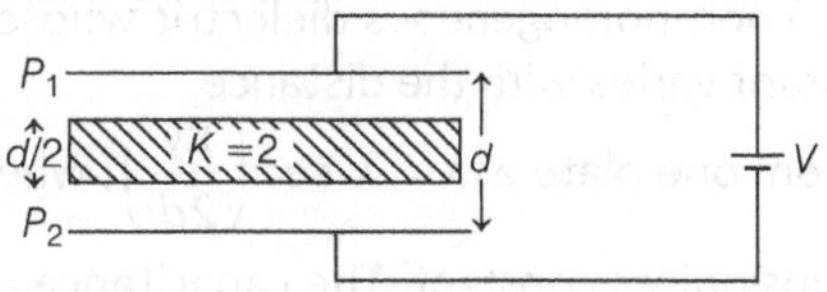

(a) $\frac{\varepsilon_0 AV^2}{3d}$ (b) $\frac{2\varepsilon_0 AV^2}{d}$ (c) $\frac{3}{2}\frac{\varepsilon_0 AV^2}{d}$ (d) $\frac{2\varepsilon_0 AV^2}{3d}$

14 A parallel plate capacitor is completely filled by an insulating material 3 mm thick and of relative permittivity 4. The distance between the plates is increased to allow the insertion of a second sheet 5 mm thick and of relative permittivity ε_r. If the capacitance of the capacitor so formed is one-half of the original capacitance, then the value of ε_r.

(a) $\frac{20}{3}$ (b) $\frac{16}{3}$
(c) $\frac{10}{3}$ (d) None of these

15 A parallel plate capacitor have distance between its plate is d and area of each plate is A. Now, half of capacitor is filled with a substance of dielectric constant K according to given figure. The capacity of the condenser, is

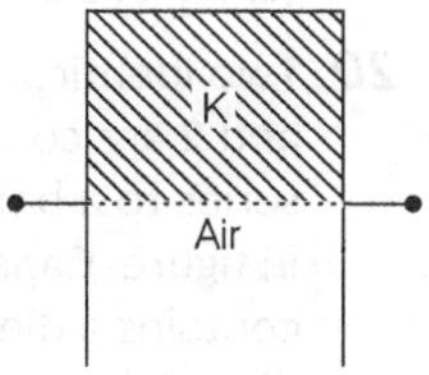

(a) $\frac{\varepsilon_0 A}{2d}(K+2)$ (b) $\frac{\varepsilon_0 A}{3d}(K+1)$
(c) $\frac{\varepsilon_0 A}{2d}(K+1)$ (d) $\frac{\varepsilon_0 A}{4d}(K+3)$

16 The two metallic plates of radius r are placed at a distance d apart and its capacity is C. If a plate of radius $\frac{r}{2}$ and thickness d of dielectric constant 6 is placed between the plates of the condenser, then its capacity will be

(a) $\frac{7C}{2}$ (b) $\frac{3C}{7}$ (c) $\frac{7C}{3}$ (d) $\frac{9C}{4}$

17 A parallel plate capacitor of capacitance C (without dielectrics) is filled by dielectric slabs as shown in figure. Then, the new capacitance of the capacitor is

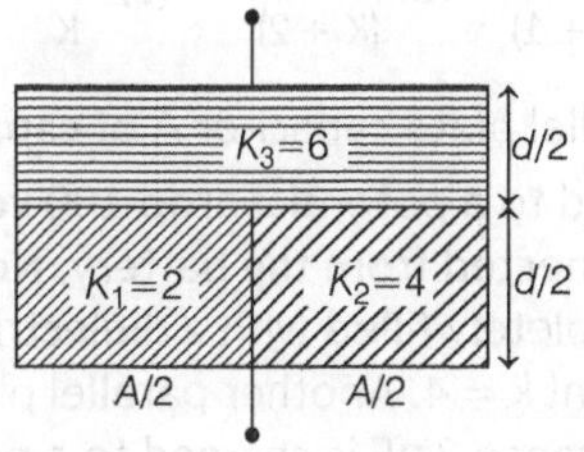

(a) 3.9 C (b) 4 C (c) 2.4 C (d) 3 C

18 The area of the plates of a parallel plate capacitor is A and the gap between them is d. The gap is filled with a non-homogeneous dielectric whose dielectric constant varies with the distance 'y' from one plate as $K = \lambda \sec\left(\frac{\pi y}{2d}\right)$, where λ is a dimensionless constant. The capacitance of this capacitor is

(a) $\pi\varepsilon_0\lambda \frac{A}{2d}$ (b) $\pi\varepsilon_0\lambda \frac{A}{d}$

(c) $2\pi\varepsilon_0\lambda \frac{A}{d}$ (d) None of these

19 In the circuit shown below, capacitors A and B have identical geometry, but a material of dielectric constant 3 is present between the plates of B. The potential differences across A and B are respectively

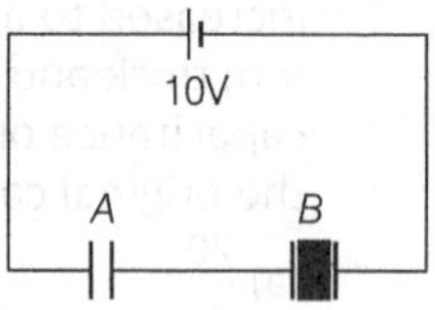

(a) 2.5 V, 7.5 V (b) 2 V, 8 V

(c) 7.5 V, 2.5 V (d) 8 V, 2 V

20 Two identical capacitors 1 and 2 are connected in series to a battery as shown in figure. Capacitor 2 contains a dielectric slab of dielectric constant K as shown. Q_1 and Q_2 are the charges stored in the capacitors. Now, the dielectric slab is removed and the corresponding charges are Q_1' and Q_2'. Then,

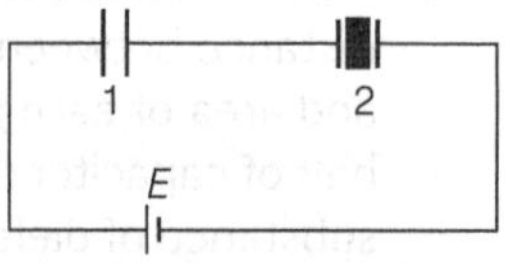

(a) $\frac{Q_1'}{Q_1} = \frac{K+1}{K}$ (b) $\frac{Q_2'}{Q_2} = \frac{K+1}{2}$

(c) $\frac{Q_2'}{Q_2} = \frac{K+1}{2K}$ (d) $\frac{Q_1'}{Q_1} = \frac{K}{2}$

21 Two parallel plate capacitors of capacitance C_0 and $2C_0$ are connected in parallel and charged to a potential difference V_0. The battery is disconnected and the region between the capacitor plates of capacitance C_0 is completely filled with a dielectric of dielectric constant K. The potential difference across the capacitors, now becomes

(a) $\frac{V_0}{(3K+1)}$ (b) $\frac{3V_0}{(K+2)}$ (c) $\frac{2V_0}{K}$ (d) $\frac{V_0}{(2K+1)}$

22 A parallel plate capacitor A of capacitance $1\,\mu F$ is charged to a potential drop 100 volt and then disconnected from the battery. Now, the capacitor A is completely filled with a dielectric slab of dielectric constant $k = 4$. Another parallel plate capacitor B of capacitance $2\,\mu F$ is charged to a potential drop 20 V and then disconnected from the battery. Now, the two capacitors A and B are connected with each other with opposite polarities. Then, the heat dissipated after connecting the capacitors is

(a) 1.15×10^{-3} J (b) 1.25×10^{-3} J

(c) 1.35×10^{-3} J (d) 1.45×10^{-3} J

23 A smooth dielectric slab A of mass m and dielectric constant k is placed between the plates of a parallel plate capacitor and connected to another block B of equal mass m through an inextensible string and a light pulley arrangement as shown in the figure. The capacitor plates with separation d and width b are connected to a battery of emf E as shown in the figure. If $E = \sqrt{\frac{mgd}{b(K-1)\varepsilon_0}}$, then acceleration of the dielectric slab will be

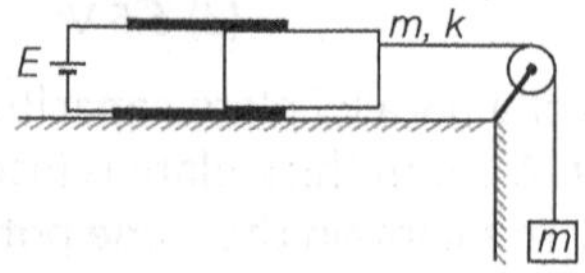

(a) g (b) $\frac{g}{2}$ (c) $\frac{g}{4}$ (d) $\frac{g}{8}$

Numerical Value Questions

1 A parallel plate capacitor has a capacitance of 120 pF (without dielectric) and plate area of 100 cm^2. The space between the plates is now filled with Mica ($k = 5.0$). The potential difference between the plates is 50 V. What is modulus of charge induced on either surface of mica (in nC)?

2 A capacitor filled partially with dielectric material of dielectric constant k. Its electric potential v/s position graph is as shown. Distance between the two plates is 4 mm. Find the dielectric constant of medium.

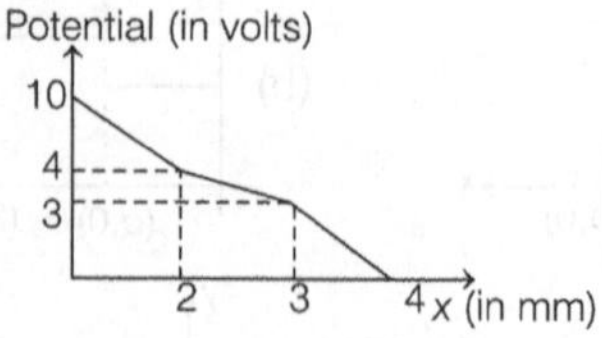

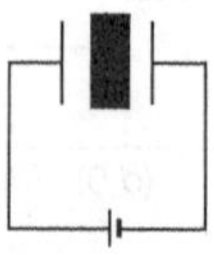

3 A parallel-plate capacitor is filled with a dielectric and a certain potential difference is applied to its plates. The energy of the capacitor is 4×10^{-5} J. After the capacitor is disconnected from the power source, the dielectric is extracted from the capacitor. The work performed against the forces of the electric field in extracting the dielectric is 12×10^{-5} J. Find the dielectric constant of the dielectric.

4 A parallel plate capacitor is to be designed which is to be connected across 1 kV potential difference. The dielectric material which is to be filled between the plates has dielectric constant $K = 6\pi$ and dielectric strength 10^7 V/m. For safety the electric field is never to exceed 10% of the dielectric strength. With such specifications, if we want a capacitor of capacitance 50pF, what minimum area (in mm^2) of plates is required for safe working? (use $\varepsilon_0 = \frac{1}{36\pi} \times 10^{-9}$ in SI unit)

5 If the equivalent capacitance between a and b is $\frac{nA\varepsilon_0}{15d}$, then find n.

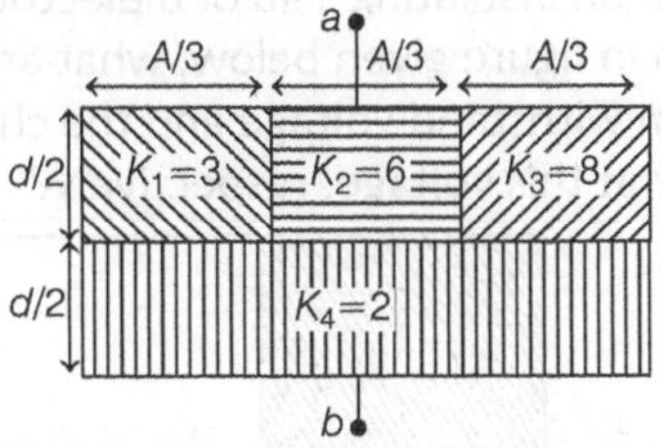

5 Condenser A has a capacity of 15 μF when it is filled with a medium of dielectric constant 15. Another condenser B has a capacity 1 μF with air between the plates. Both are charged separately by a battery of 100 V. After charging, both are connected in parallel without the battery and the dielectric material being removed. Find the common potential drop (in V) across each of them now.

7 Two conducting square plates with length l are arranged parallel to each other at a distance $d(<<l)$. The space between the plates is filled with a dielectric of relative permittivity $\varepsilon_r = 4$ up to a length $x = \frac{l}{3}$. The upper plate is given a charge Q and the lower plate is given a charge $-Q$ as shown in the figure. If $Q = 6$ μC then find how much charge (in μC) is present on the portion of upper plate which is in contact with the dielectric?

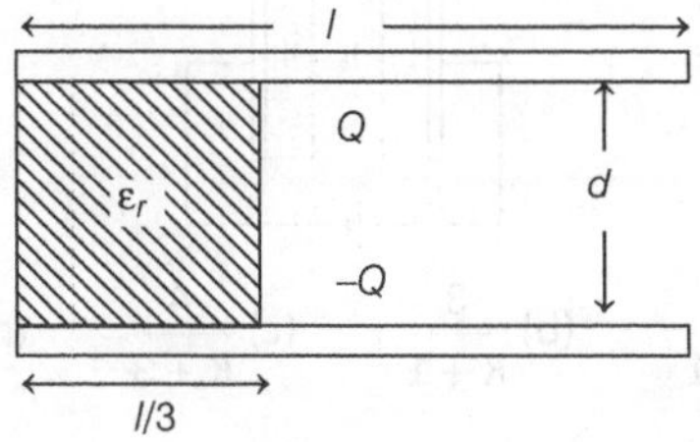

8 A parallel plate capacitor is made by fixing two large plates 2 mm apart inside of a container as shown in figure. The plates are connected to a battery of voltage 90 V. If at $t = 0$, the tap is opened from which a liquid of dielectric constant 5 starts filling in the container at a constant rate of 4π m^3/s, find the current (in mA) in connecting wires as a function of time. Neglect any resistance in connecting wires.

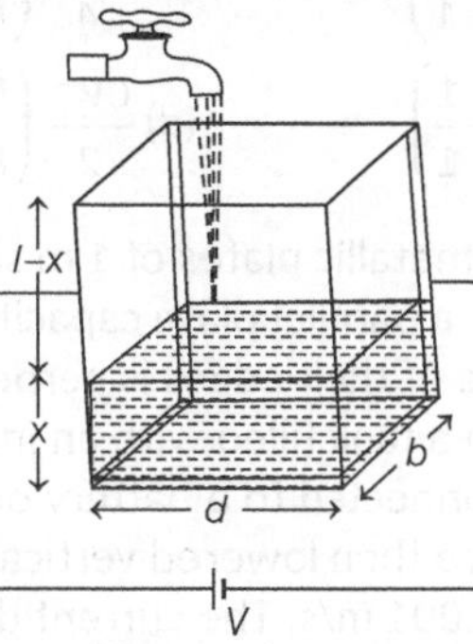

LEVEL 03 JEE Advanced Level

Single Choice Correct Questions

1 When a dielectric slab is introduced inside a parallel plate capacitor then

(a) charge appearing on the surface of slab is due to free electrons inside the dielectric

(b) dielectric gets uniformly charged throughout the volume

(c) charge appearing at the surface is due to bound charge

(d) if σ is surface charge density at the surface of dielectric then electric field due to surface charge on dielectric will be $\frac{\sigma}{k\varepsilon_0}$

2 In a parallel plate capacitor, the distance between the plates is 10 cm. Two dielectric slabs of thickness 5 cm each and dielectric constants $K_1 = 2$ and $K_2 = 4$ respectively, are inserted between the plates. A potential of 100 V is applied across the capacitor as shown in the figure. The value of the net bound surface charge density at the interface of the two dielectrics is

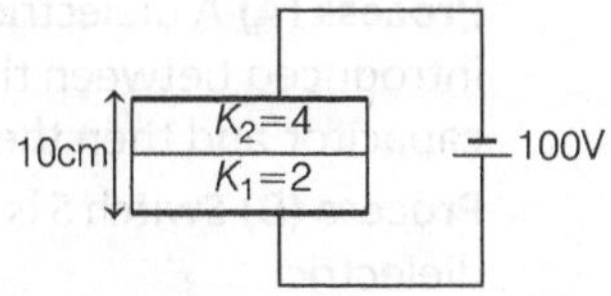

(a) $-\frac{2000}{3}\varepsilon_0$ (b) $-\frac{1000}{3}\varepsilon_0$

(c) $-250\varepsilon_0$ (d) $\frac{2000}{3}\varepsilon_0$

3 The figure shows a capacitor having three layers of equal thickness and same area as that of plate. Layer I is vacuum, layer II is conductor and layer III is dielectric of dielectric constant K. The ratio of energy stored in region III to total energy stored in capacitor is

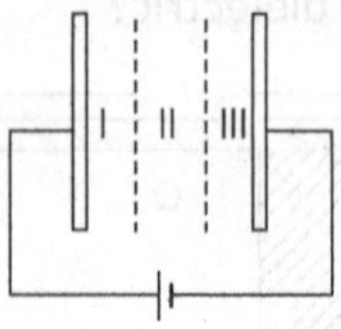

(a) $\frac{1}{K+1}$ (b) $\frac{3}{K+1}$ (c) $\frac{4}{K+3}$ (d) $\frac{4}{3K+1}$

4 The work done in placing the dielectric slab inside one of the capacitors as shown in diagram is

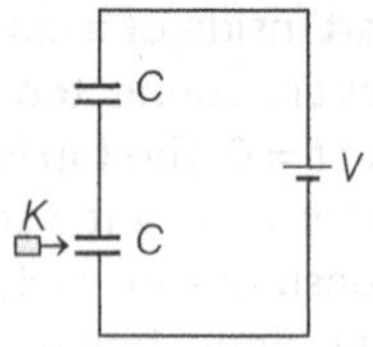

(a) $\frac{CV^2}{2}\left(\frac{K-1}{K+1}\right)$ (b) $\frac{CV^2}{4}\left(\frac{K-1}{K+1}\right)$

(c) $\frac{CV^2}{4}\left(\frac{K+1}{K-1}\right)$ (d) $\frac{CV^2}{2}\left(\frac{K+1}{K-1}\right)$

5 Two square metallic plates of 1 m side are kept 0.01 m apart, like a parallel plate capacitor, in air in such a way that one of their edges is perpendicular, to an oil surface in a tank filled with an insulating oil. The plates are connected to a battery of emf 500 volt. The plates are then lowered vertically into the oil at a speed of 0.001 m/s. The current drawn from the battery during the process is

[Dielectric constant of oil = 11, $\varepsilon_0 = 8.85 \times 10^{-12}$ $C^2/N^2\ m^2$]

(a) 8.85×10^{-9} A (b) 9.735×10^{-9} A

(c) 4.425×10^{-9} A (d) 1.77×10^{-9} A

6 In the given figure, two identical capacitors are shown, with one of them having charge Q and the other being uncharged.

Process (A) A dielectric of dielectric constant k is introduced between the plates of the charged capacitor and then the switch S is closed.

Process (B) Switch S is closed without inserting the dielectric.

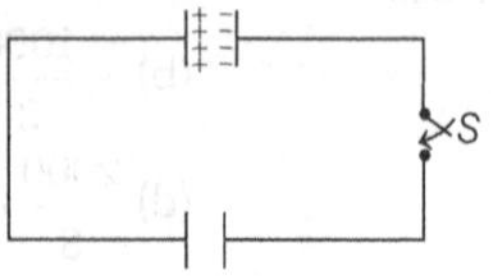

Find the Incorrect statement.

(a) Energy lost during process (A) is less as compared to process (B)

(b) Charge transferred to the uncharged capacitor in process (A) is more as compared to process (B)

(c) Common potential difference after redistribution of charge is more in process (B) as compared to process (A)

(d) In process (B), electric field between the plates, in both the capacitors, becomes same, after redistribution of charge.

7 A parallel plate air capacitor carries a charge Q at its maximum withstand voltage V. If the capacitor is half filled with an insulating slab of dielectric constant 4 as shown in figure given below, what are the maximum withstand voltage and the charge on the capacitor at this voltage, respectively?

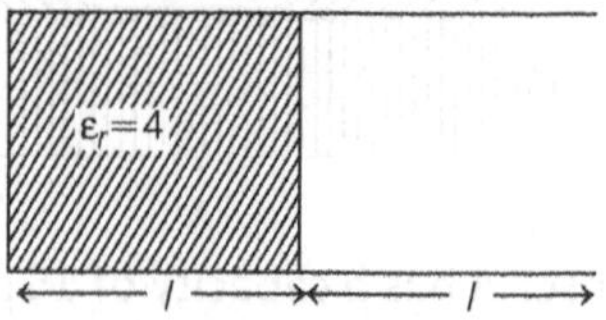

(a) 2.5 V, Q (b) 4 V, 2.5 Q

(c) V, 2.5 Q (d) $\frac{V}{4}$, Q

8 A thin metallic partition of negligible thickness is inserted between two shaded metallic plates as shown. The remaining ends are then packed with insulating plates to form a container like structure. 2 taps shown are opened at $t = 0$ and finally closed at $t = 5$ s. Find capacitance of system between A and B after closing taps. (Assume liquid to be non-conducting) Volumetric flow rates and dielectric constants of liquid are given.

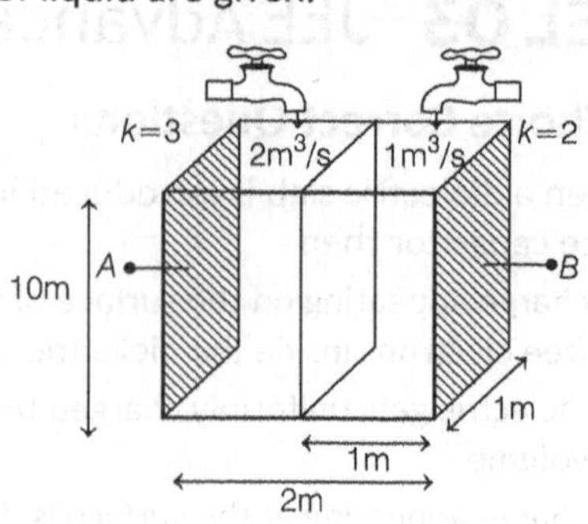

(a) 8.85×10^{-11} F

(b) 8.85×10^{-10} F

(c) 8.63×10^{-10} F

(d) 8.63×10^{-11} F

9 Find the capacitance between the inner and outer curved cylindrical conductor surface as shown in figure. Space between conductor surface is filled with dielectric of dielectric constant K. Consider $b << R$.

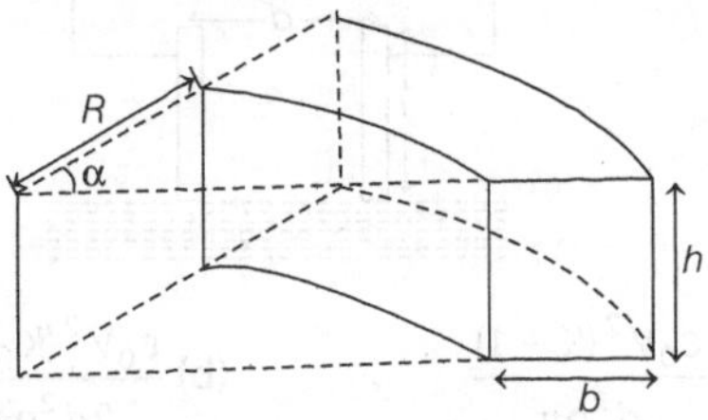

(a) $\frac{\varepsilon_0 KhR\alpha}{b}$ (b) $\frac{\varepsilon_0 KbR\alpha}{h}$

(c) $\frac{\varepsilon_0 KhR\alpha}{2b}$ (d) $\frac{\varepsilon_0 KbR\alpha}{2h}$

10 The gap between the plates of a parallel-plate capacitor is filled with a dielectric material whose relative permittivity ε varies linearly from ε_1 to ε_2 $(\varepsilon_2 > \varepsilon_1)$ in the direction perpendicular to the plates. The area of each plate equals to S and the separation between the plates is equal to d. The capacitance of the capacitor is

(a) $\frac{\varepsilon_0(\varepsilon_2 - \varepsilon_1)S}{d \ln\left(\frac{\varepsilon_2}{\varepsilon_1}\right)}$ (b) $\frac{\varepsilon_0(\varepsilon_2 + \varepsilon_1)S}{d \ln\left(\frac{\varepsilon_2}{\varepsilon_1}\right)}$

(c) $\frac{\varepsilon_0 S}{d \ln\left(\frac{\varepsilon_2}{\varepsilon_1}\right)}$ (d) None of these

11 A parallel plate capacitor is made of two square plates of side a, separated by a distance d $(d << a)$. The lower triangular portion is filled with a dielectric of dielectric constant K, as shown in the figure. Capacitance of this capacitor is

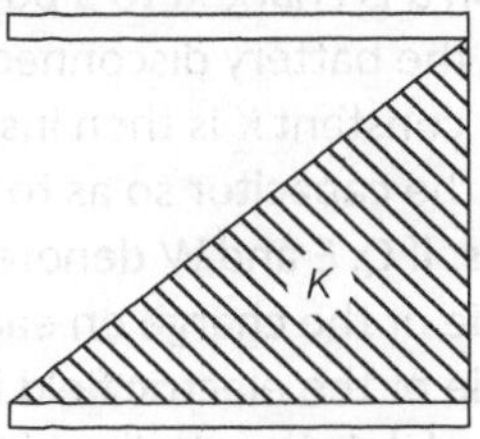

(a) $\frac{K\varepsilon_0 a^2}{2d}$ (b) $\frac{K\varepsilon_0 a^2}{d} \ln K$

(c) $\frac{K\varepsilon_0 a^2}{d(K-1)} \ln K$ (d) $\frac{K\varepsilon_0 a^2}{2d(K+1)}$

12 A spherical capacitor is made of two conducting spherical shells of radii a and $b = 3a$. The space between the shells is filled with a dielectric of dielectric constant $K = 3$ upto a radius $c = 2a$ as shown. If the capacitance of given arrangement is n times the capacitance of an isolated spherical conducting shell of radius a, then value of n is

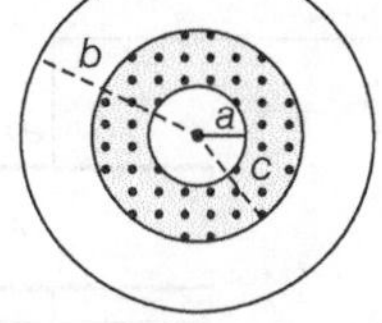

(a) 2 (b) 3 (c) 4 (d) 6

13 Four identical plates 1, 2, 3 and 4 are placed parallel to each other at equal distance as shown in the figure. Plates 1 and 4 are joined together and the space between 2 and 3 is filled with a dielectric of dielectric constant $k = 2$. The capacitance of the system between 1 and 3, 2 and 3 are C_1 and C_2 respectively. The ratio of $\frac{C_1}{C_2}$ is

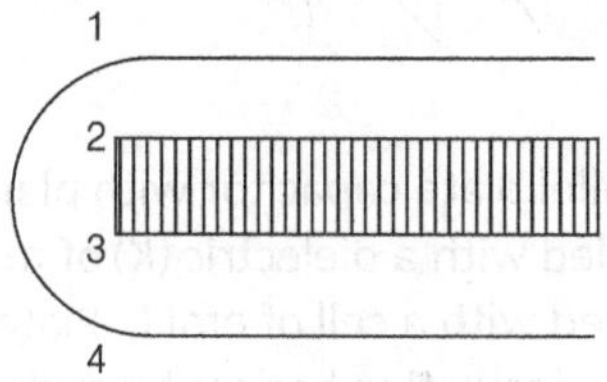

(a) 1 (b) $\frac{3}{2}$ (c) $\frac{2}{3}$ (d) $\frac{2}{5}$

14 Three identical metallic plates A, B and C of size $(l \times l)$ are placed parallel to each other at distances d. The region between A and B has a dielectric medium of constant k. If A is given charge $+Q$ while B and C are neutral, calculate the potential difference $(V_A - V_C)$.

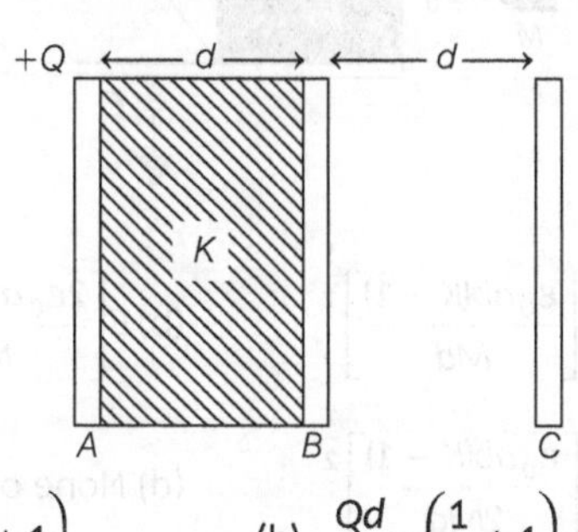

(a) $\frac{Qd}{\varepsilon_0 l^2}\left(\frac{1}{K}+1\right)$ (b) $\frac{Qd}{2\varepsilon_0 l^2}\left(\frac{1}{K}+1\right)$

(c) $\frac{Qd}{\varepsilon_0 l^2}(K+1)$ (d) $\frac{Qd}{2\varepsilon_0 l^2}(K+1)$

15 In the below figure a dielectric is released inside the capacitor at $t = 0$ from the end of the capacitor. Then which of the following current (i) *versus* time (t) graph is correct in one complete oscillation if clockwise current is taken as positive and anticlockwise as negative? ($a > c$). Neglect electrical and mechanical resistance.

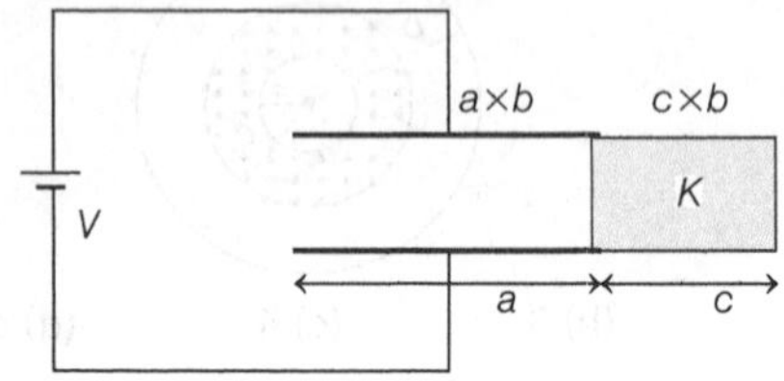

(a) 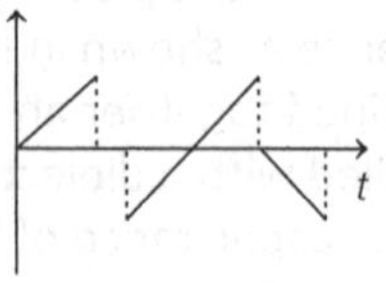

(b) 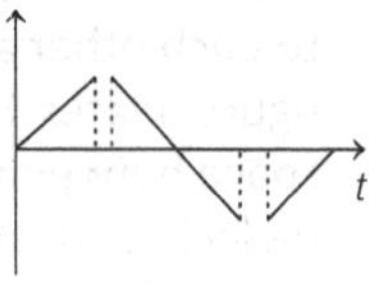

(c) 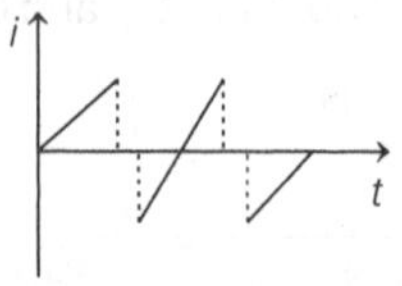

(d) 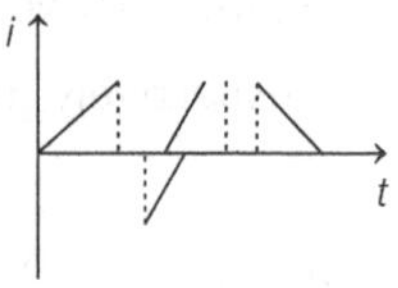

16 A parallel plate capacitor with plate separation d, is half filled with a dielectric (K) of mass M. Capacitor is attached with a cell of emf E. Plates are held fixed on smooth insulating horizontal surface. A bullet of mass M hits the dielectric elastically and it is found that dielectric just leaves out the capacitor. The speed of bullet is

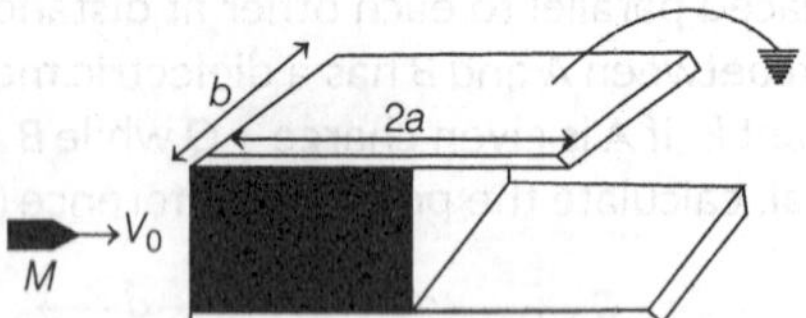

(a) $E\left[\dfrac{\varepsilon_0 ab(K-1)}{Md}\right]^{\frac{1}{2}}$ (b) $E\left[\dfrac{2\varepsilon_0 ab(K-1)}{Md}\right]^{\frac{1}{2}}$

(c) $E\left[\dfrac{\varepsilon_0 ab(K-1)}{2Md}\right]^{\frac{1}{2}}$ (d) None of these

17 A parallel plate capacitor of plate area $A = lb$ with separation d is connected to a battery via a switch S as shown in figure. Capacitor plates are kept vertical and touched on the surface of a liquid of density ρ as shown. If S is closed, find the height between plates to which the liquid level will rise.

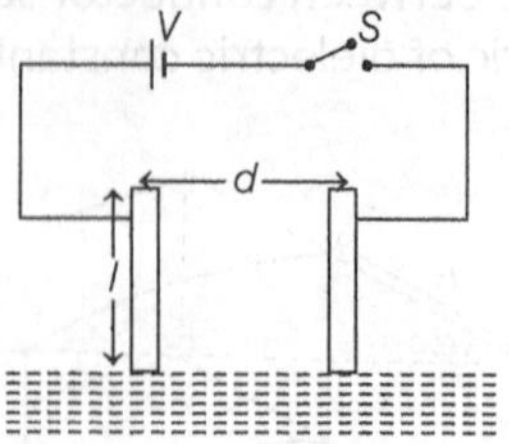

(a) $\dfrac{\varepsilon_0 V^2(K-1)}{d^2\rho g}$ (b) $\dfrac{\varepsilon_0 V^2(K-1)}{2d^2\rho g}$

(c) $\dfrac{2\varepsilon_0 V^2(K-1)}{d^2\rho g}$ (d) $\dfrac{\varepsilon_0 V^2 K}{d^2\rho g}$

18 A horizontal parallel-plate capacitor is lowered on a liquid surface in such a way that its lower plate is just submerged in the liquid of dielectric constant K as shown in figure. Find the height to which the liquid level will be raised between the plates, if the capacitor plates are given a surface charge density $+\sigma$ and $-\sigma$ on its plates.

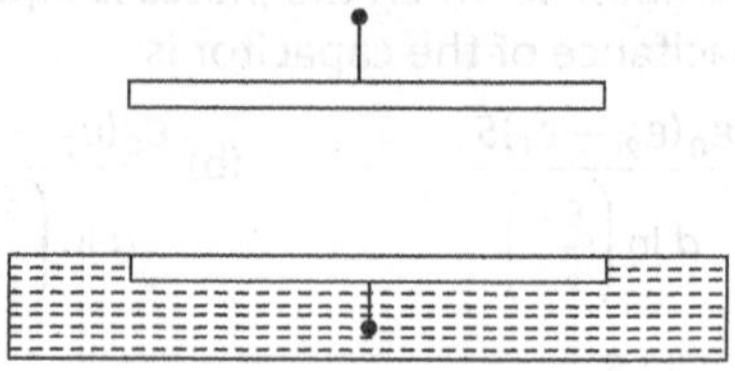

(a) $\dfrac{\sigma^2(K-1)}{\varepsilon_0 K\rho g}$ (b) $\dfrac{\sigma^2(K-1)}{2\varepsilon_0 K\rho g}$

(c) $\dfrac{\sigma^2(K^2-1)}{\varepsilon_0 K^2\rho g}$ (d) $\dfrac{\sigma^2(K^2-1)}{2\varepsilon_0 K^2\rho g}$

Multiple Choice(s) Correct Questions

1 A parallel plate capacitor of plate area A and plate separation d is charged to a potential difference V and then the battery disconnected. A slab of dielectric constant K is then inserted between the plates of the capacitor so as to fill the space between the plates. If Q, E and W denote respectively, the magnitude of the charge on each plate, the magnitude of the electric field between the plates (after the slab is inserted) and the magnitude of the work done on the system, in the process of inserting the slab, then

(a) $Q = \dfrac{\varepsilon_0 AV}{d}$ (b) $Q = \dfrac{\varepsilon_0 KAV}{d}$

(c) $E = \dfrac{V}{Kd}$ (d) $W = \dfrac{\varepsilon_0 AV^2}{2d}\left(1 - \dfrac{1}{K}\right)$

2 A capacitor of capacity C_0 is connected to a battery of emf V_0. When steady state is attained, a dielectric slab of dielectric constant K is slowly introduced in the capacitor to fill the capacitor completely. Mark the correct statement(s), in final steady state.

(a) Magnitude of induced charge on the each surface of slab is $C_0V_0(K-1)$

(b) Electric force due to induced charges on any plate is zero.

(c) Force of attraction between plates of capacitor is $\dfrac{K(C_0V_0)^2}{2\varepsilon_0 A}$

(d) Field due to induced charges in dielectric slab is $\dfrac{(K-1)C_0V_0}{\varepsilon_0 A}$

3 On a parallel plate capacitor following operations can be performed.

P – connect the capacitor to a battery of emf V.
Q – disconnect the battery,
R – reconnect the battery with polarity reversed,
S – insert a dielectric slab in the capacitor.

(a) In PQR (perform P, then Q, then R), the stored electric energy remains unchanged and no thermal energy is developed.

(b) The charge appearing on the capacitor is greater after the action PSQ than after the action PQS.

(c) The electric energy stored in the capacitor is greater after the action SPQ than after the action PQS.

(d) The electric field in the capacitor after the action PS is the same as that after SP.

4 A parallel plate capacitor of area A and separation d is charged to potential difference V and removed from the charging source. A dielectric slab of constant $K = 2$, thickness d and area $\dfrac{A}{2}$ is inserted, as shown in the figure. Let σ_1 be free charge density at the conductor-dielectric surface and σ_2 be the charge density at the conductor-vacuum surface.

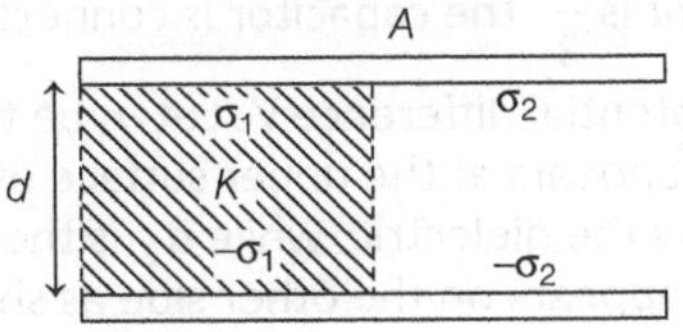

(a) The electric field has the same value inside the dielectric as that in the free space between the plates.

(b) The ratio $\dfrac{\sigma_1}{\sigma_2}$ is equal to $\dfrac{2}{1}$.

(c) The new capacitance is $\dfrac{3\varepsilon_0 A}{2d}$.

(d) The new potential difference between the plates is $\dfrac{2}{3}V$.

5 A dielectric slab fills the space between the plates of a parallel-plate capacitor. The magnitude of the bound charge on the slab is 75% of the magnitude of the free charge on the plates. The capacitance is 480 μF and the maximum charge that can be stored on the capacitor is $240\,\varepsilon_0 L^2 E_{max}$, where E_{max} is the breakdown field.

(a) The dielectric constant for the dielectric slab is 4.

(b) Without the dielectric, the capacitance of the capacitor would be 360 μF.

(c) The plate area is $60\,L^2$.

(d) If the dielectric slab is having the same area as the capacitor plate but the width half that of the capacitor, the capacitance would be 192 μF.

6 In the figure shown

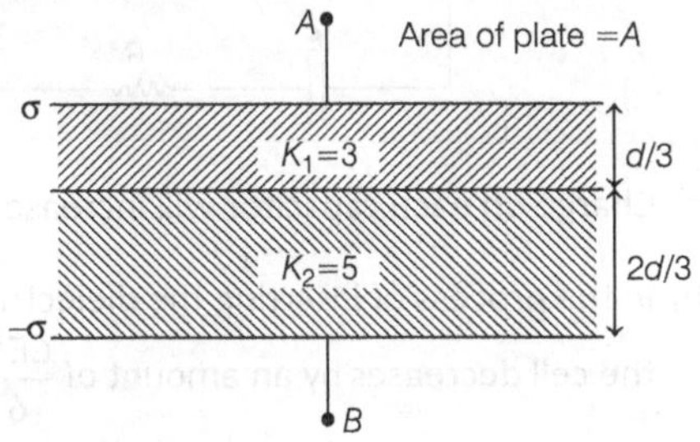

(a) The ratio of energy density in first dielectric to second dielectric is $\dfrac{5}{3}$.

(b) The ratio of energy density in first dielectric to second dielectric is $\dfrac{3}{5}$.

(c) Net induced surface charge density on the interface of the two dielectrics is $\dfrac{2\sigma}{15}$.

(d) Net induced surface charge density on the interface of the two dielectrics is $-\dfrac{2\sigma}{15}$.

7 Identical dielectric slabs are inserted into two identical capacitors A and B. These capacitors and a battery are connected as shown in figure. Now, the slab of capacitor B is pulled out with battery remaining connected.

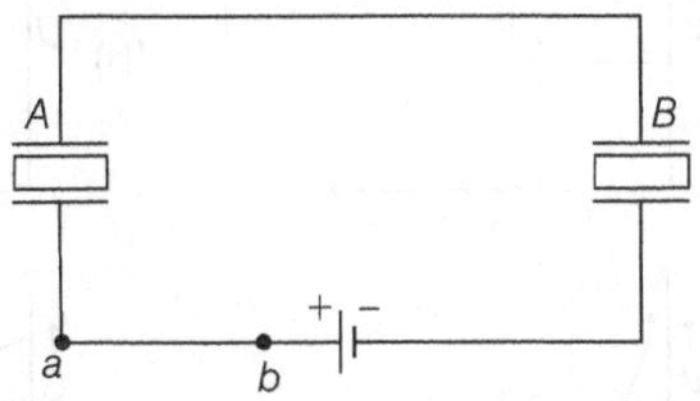

(a) During the process, positive charge flows from a to b.

(b) Finally charge on capacitor B will be less than that on capacitor A.

(c) During the process, a work is done by the external force F, which completely appears as heat in the circuit.

(d) During the process, internal energy of the battery increases.

8 In the figure shown capacitors A and B of capacitance C each are in steady state. A dielectric slab of dielectric constant $K = 2$ and dimensions equal to the inner dimensions of the capacitor is inserted in the space between the plates of the capacitor B. Choose the correct option(s)

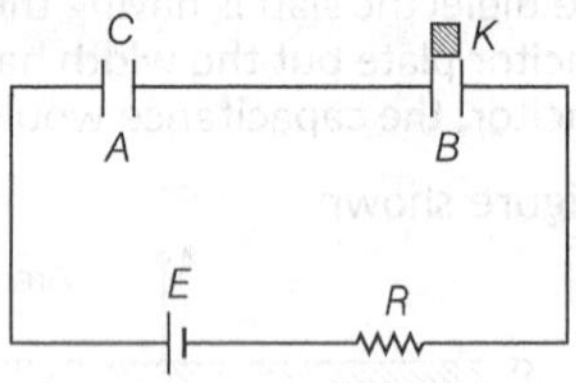

(a) Charge on each capacitor will increase by $\frac{CE}{6}$.

(b) In the process of inserting the dielectric, energy of the cell decreases by an amount of $\frac{CE^2}{6}$.

(c) In the process of inserting the dielectric, energy of the cell increases by an amount of $\frac{CE^2}{6}$.

(d) In the process of inserting the dielectric, energy in the capacitor A increases by an amount of $\frac{7CE^2}{72}$.

9 A parallel plate capacitor has a dielectric slab in it. The slab just fills the space inside the capacitor. The capacitor is charged by a battery and the battery is disconnected. Now, an external agent starts pulling the slab out uniformly at $t = 0$. If at time t, capacitance of the capacitor is C, potential difference across plate is V, and energy stored in it is U, then which of the following graph is/are correct?

(a)
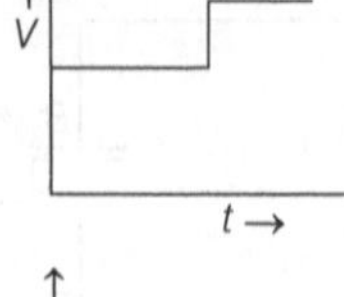

(b)
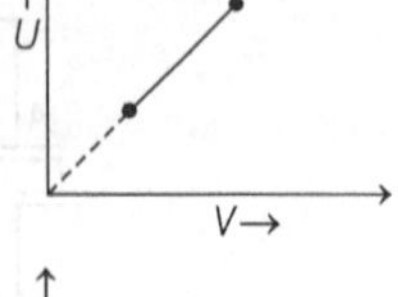

(c)
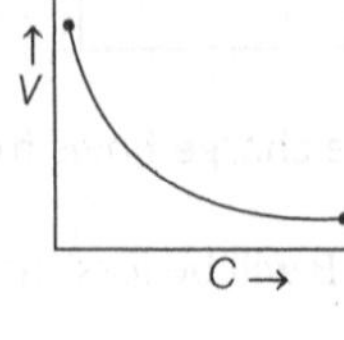

(d)
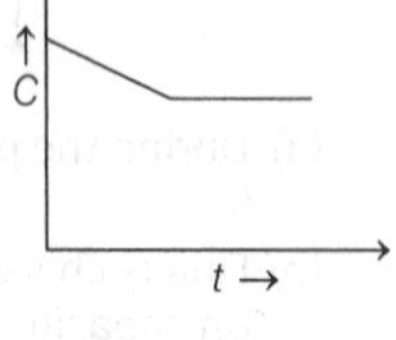

Comprehension Based Questions

Comprehension-1

Consider a series combination of capacitor C_1, C_2 and C_3. Capacitor C_1 and C_3 have air as the dielectric medium between the plates while C_2 has a medium of dielectric constant $K = 3$ filled uniformly between the plates. A potential difference V is applied across the combination. It is observed that potential difference across C_3 is 12 V.

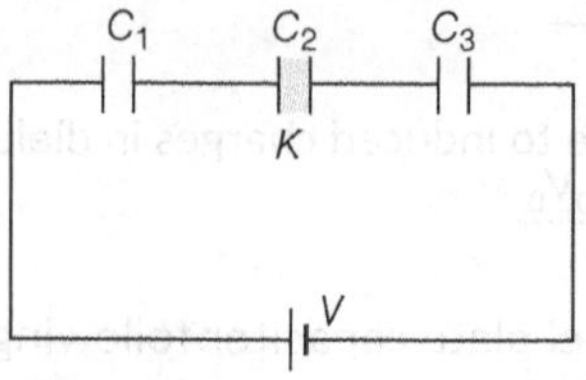

The dielectric material ($K = 3$) between the plates of C_2 is now removed. In this situation, potential difference across C_3 is found to change by 3 V. It is also found that potential differences across C_1 and C_2 are equal. (Capacitance of C_2 without dielectric is 2 μF).

1 Applied potential difference V is

(a) 10 V (b) 20 V (c) 30 V (d) 36 V

2 Capacitance C_3 is

(a) 8 μF (b) 6 μF (c) 3 μF (d) 2 μF

3 Capacitance C_1 is

(a) 8 μF (b) 6 μF (c) 3 μF (d) 2 μF

Comprehension-2

Figure shows a parallel plate capacitor having an insulator of dielectric constant $K = 2$. The plate area of the capacitor is A and separation between them is d, while the surface area of the dielectric is $\frac{A}{3}$ and its height is $\frac{d}{3}$. The capacitor is connected to a battery of potential difference V. Let q_1 be the free charge that appears at the upper surface of lower plate, just below the dielectric, while q_2 is the surface charge that appears on the other side as shown.

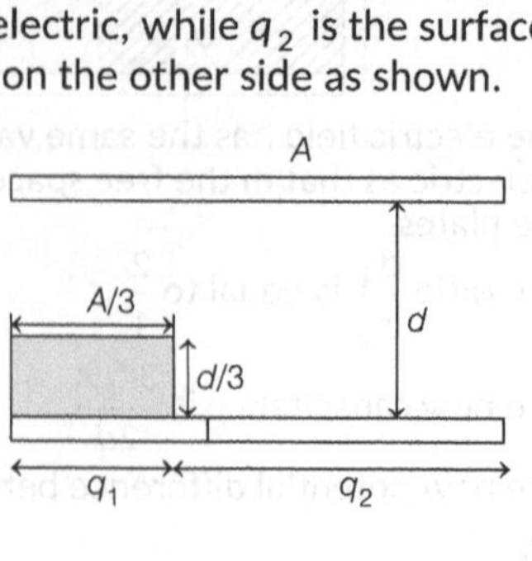

4 The equivalent capacitance of the system is

(a) $\frac{12}{11}\frac{\varepsilon_0 A}{d}$ (b) $\frac{11}{12}\frac{\varepsilon_0 A}{d}$ (c) $\frac{16}{15}\frac{\varepsilon_0 A}{d}$ (d) $\frac{15}{16}\frac{\varepsilon_0 A}{d}$

5 The ratio of charge $\frac{q_1}{q_2}$ on the lower plate of capacitor is

(a) 1 (b) $\frac{3}{5}$ (c) $\frac{3}{8}$ (d) $\frac{5}{3}$

Comprehension-3

Two metal plates form a parallel-plate capacitor. The separation between the plates is $2d$. Now, half of the separation between the plates is filled with a material of dielectric constant 2 as shown in figure. The new arrangement gets punctured when a potential difference just exceeding 1200 V is applied.

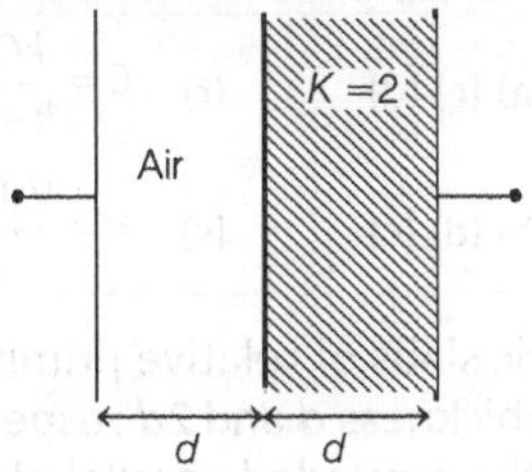

6 The ratio of capacitance before and after insertion of dielectric is

(a) 1 : 2 (b) 2 : 1 (c) 3 : 4 (d) 4 : 3

7 The maximum potential difference that can exist across the dielectric is

(a) 300 V (b) 400 V (c) 600 V (d) 800 V

8 The ratio of electrostatic energy stored by air and dielectric parts of capacitor is

(a) 1 : 2 (b) 2 : 1 (c) 3 : 4 (d) 4 : 3

Comprehension-4

In the circuit shown, capacitor A has capacitance $C_1 = 2\,\mu F$ when filled with dielectric slab ($k = 2$). Capacitor B and C are air capacitors and have capacitances $C_2 = 3\,\mu F$ and $C_3 = 6\,\mu F$ respectively.

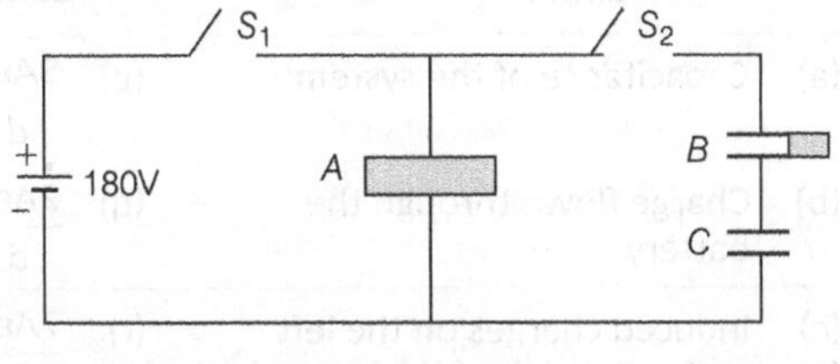

9 Calculate the energy supplied by battery during process of charging when switch S_1 is closed alone.

(a) 32.4 mJ (b) 64.8 mJ (c) 15 mJ (d) 30 mJ

10 Switch S_1 is opened and S_2 is closed. The charge on capacitor B is

(a) 240 μC (b) 280 μC (c) 180 μC (d) 200 μC

11 Now switch S_2 is opened, slab of A is removed. Another dielectric slab $k = 2$ which can just fill the space in B, is inserted into it and then switch S_2 is closed. The charge on capacitor B is

(a) 90 μC (b) 240 μC (c) 180 μC (d) 270 μC

Comprehension-5

An isolated spherical capacitor has charge $+Q$ on its inner conductor of radius a and $-Q$ on its outer conductor of radius b. Half of volume between the two conductors is then filled with a liquid dielectric of constant K as shown in figure

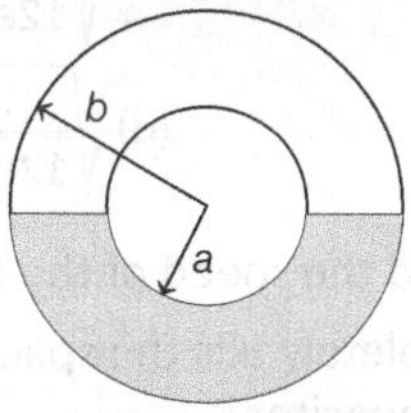

12 The capacity of half filled spherical capacitor is

(a) $\frac{4\pi\varepsilon_0 Kab}{b-a}$ (b) $\frac{2\pi\varepsilon_0 (K+1)ab}{b-a}$

(c) $\frac{2\pi\varepsilon_0 Kab}{b-a}$ (d) $\frac{4\pi\varepsilon_0 (K+1)ab}{b-a}$

13 The electric field between the two plates of capacitor as a function of distance r from centre is

(a) $\frac{Q}{2\pi\varepsilon_0 Kr^2}$ (b) $\frac{Q}{4\pi\varepsilon_0 Kr^2}$

(c) $\frac{Q}{2\pi\varepsilon_0 (K+1)r^2}$ (d) $\frac{Q}{4\pi\varepsilon_0 (K+1)r^2}$

14 Surface density of charge on lower half of inner conductor is

(a) $\frac{Q}{4\pi a^2(1+K)}$ (b) $\frac{Q}{4\pi b^2(1+K)}$

(c) $\frac{KQ}{2\pi a^2(1+K)}$ (d) $\frac{KQ}{4\pi b^2(1+K)}$

Comprehension-6

A block A of mass m kept on a rough horizontal surface is connected to a dielectric slab of mass $\frac{m}{6}$ and dielectric constant K by means of a light and inextensible string passing over a fixed pulley as shown in figure. The dielectric can completely fill the space between the parallel plate capacitor of plate area $l \times l$ and separation between the plates d kept in vertical position. Initially switch S is open and length of the dielectric inside the capacitor is b. The coefficient of friction between the block A and the surface is $\mu = \frac{1}{4}$. Ignore any other friction.

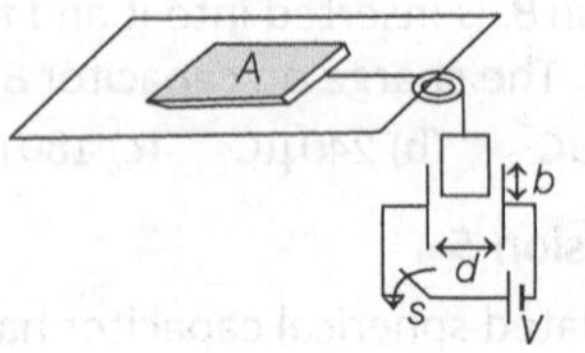

15 The minimum value of the emf V_{min} of the battery so that after closing the switch the block A will move

(a) $\sqrt{\frac{mgd}{6\varepsilon_0 lK}}$ (b) $\sqrt{\frac{mgd}{12\varepsilon_0 lK}}$

(c) $\sqrt{\frac{mgd}{6\varepsilon_0 l(K-1)}}$ (d) $\sqrt{\frac{mgd}{12\varepsilon_0 l(K-1)}}$

16 If $V = 2V_{min}$ find the speed of the block A when the dielectric completely fills the space between the plates of the capacitor.

(a) $\sqrt{\frac{3}{7}g(l-b)}$ (b) $\sqrt{\frac{6}{7}g(l-b)}$

(c) $\sqrt{\frac{3}{11}g(l-b)}$ (d) $\sqrt{\frac{6}{11}g(l-b)}$

Match the Columns Questions

1 Some events related to a capacitor are listed in column-I. Match these events with their effect(s) in column-II.

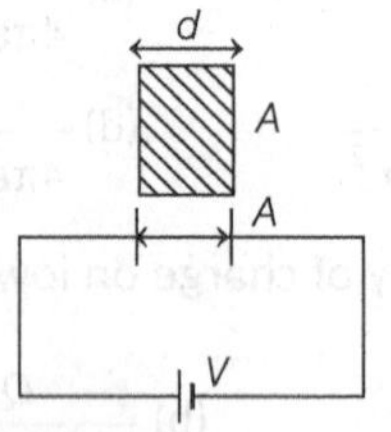

	Column I (Events)		Column II (Effects)
(a)	Insertion of dielectric while battery remains attached	(p)	Electric field changes between plates
(b)	Removal of dielectric while battery is not present	(q)	Charge present on plates changes
(c)	Slow decrease in separation between plates while battery is attached	(r)	Energy stored in capacitor increases
(d)	Slow increase of separation between plates while battery is not present	(s)	Work done by external agent is positive

2 On a capacitor of capacitance C_0 following steps are performed in the order as given in column-I.

(a) Capacitor is charged by connecting it across a battery of Emf V_0.

(b) Dielectric of dielectric constant k and thickness d is inserted.

(c) Capacitor is disconnected from battery.

(d) Separation between plates is doubled.

	Column-I (Steps performed)		Column-II Final value of Quantity (Symbols have usual meaning)
(a)	(a) (d) (c) (b)	(p)	$Q = \frac{C_0V_0}{2}$
(b)	(d) (a) (c) (b)	(q)	$Q = \frac{kC_0V_0}{k+1}$
(c)	(b) (a) (c) (d)	(r)	$C = \frac{kC_0}{k+1}$
(d)	(a) (b) (d) (c)	(s)	$V = \frac{V_0(k+1)}{2k}$

3 Two dielectric slabs of relative primitivities $\varepsilon_{r_1} = 2$, $\varepsilon_{r_2} = 3$ and thickness d and $2d$ respectively are filled in between the grounded parallel plates each of area A. If a battery of emf $\varepsilon = 2$ volt is connected to the middle conducting plate find all the quantity in SI unit. (Assume initially uncharged).

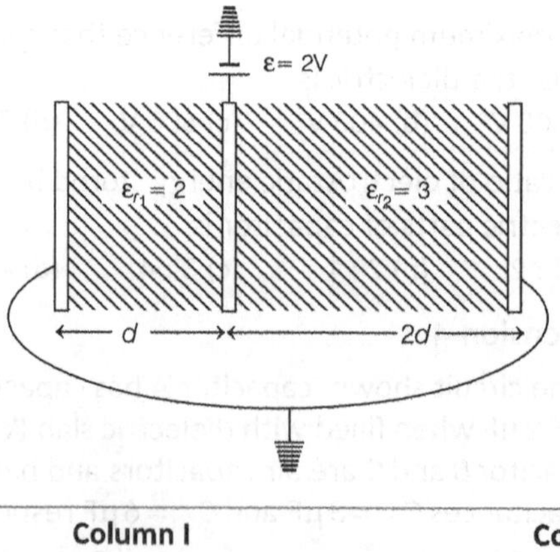

	Column I		Column II
(a)	Capacitance of the system	(p)	$\frac{5A\varepsilon_0}{d}$
(b)	Charge flown through the battery	(q)	$\frac{2A\varepsilon_0}{d}$
(c)	Induced charges on the left surface of slab of thickness d	(r)	$\frac{7A\varepsilon_0}{d}$
(d)	Energy stored in the system	(s)	$\frac{7A\varepsilon_0}{2d}$

Numerical Value Questions

1 A parallel plate capacitor is filled by a dielectric whose dielectric constant varies with the applied voltage according to the law $K = \alpha V$, where $\alpha = 1$ per volt. The same (but containing no dielectric) capacitor charged to a voltage $V = 156$ volt is connected in parallel to the first non-linear, uncharged capacitor. Find the final voltage V_f (in volt) across the capacitors.

2 Between the plates of a parallel-plate capacitor there is a metallic plate whose thickness takes up $\eta = 0.60$ of the capacitor gap. When that plate is absent the capacitor has a capacity $C = 20$ nF. The capacitor is connected to a dc voltage source $V = 100$ V. The metallic plate is slowly extracted from the gap. Find the mechanical work performed in the process of plate extraction. (in μJ)

3 A capacitor consists of two fixed semicircular plates of radius R and a movable slab of thickness d and dielectric constant K placed between them. The slab can freely rotate about the axis O and practically fills the entire gap between the fixed plate. A constant voltage V is maintained between the plates. If the torque acting on the dielectric slab when the slab is displaced to an angle θ as shown in the figure, due to electrostatic force is $\tau = \frac{(K-1)\varepsilon_0 R^2 V^2}{nd}$, find the value of n.

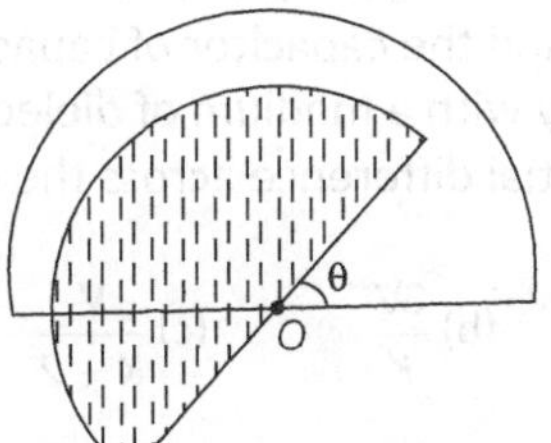

4 One end of an open coaxial cable is immersed vertically in a liquid dielectric of unknown permittivity. The cable is connected to a source of potential difference V. The electrostatic forces draw the liquid dielectric into the annular space of the cable for a height h above the level of the dielectric outside the cable. The radius of the inner conductor is a, that of the outer conductor is b ($b > a$), and the mass density of the liquid is ρ_m. Determine the relative permittivity of the liquid dielectric, if $V = 1000$ V, $h = 3.29$ cm, $a = 0.5$ mm, $b = 1.5$ mm, $\rho_m = 1$ gm/cm^3 ($g = 10$ ms^{-2}) (Assume that electrostatic force balances the weight of the liquid) (Take, ln 3 = 1.1)

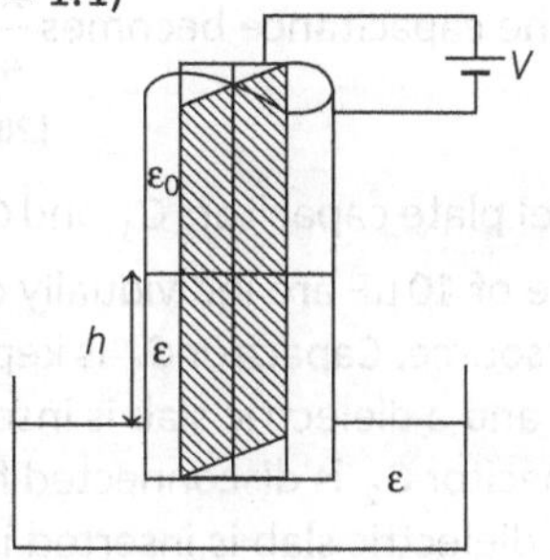

5 A parallel plate capacitor consists of two square plates of side length $a = 6$ cm. There is dielectric slab in the shape of a cylinder of parabolic cross-section between the plates, as shown in figure. The dielectric constant of the material is $K = 2$. The length of latus rectum of the parabola is equal to the side length of the plate. Then, the capacitance is given by $4\pi\varepsilon_0 N \times 10^{-2}$ farad, then find the value of N.

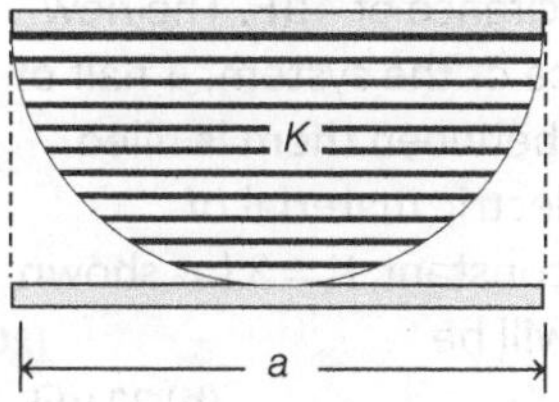

Previous Year's Questions

JEE Main

1 A parallel plate capacitor with plate separation 5 mm is charged up by a battery. It is found that on introducing a dielectric sheet of thickness 2mm, while keeping the battery connections intact, the capacitor draws 25% more charge from the battery than before. The dielectric constant of the sheet is ....

[2024, 27 Jan Shift-II]

2 The distance between two plates of a capacitor is d and its capacitance is C_1, when air is the medium between the plates. If a metal sheet of thickness $\frac{2d}{3}$ and of the same area as plate is introduced between the plates, the capacitance of the capacitor becomes C_2. The ratio $\frac{C_2}{C_1}$ is

[2023, 10 April Shift-II]

(a) 3 : 1 (b) 1 : 1 (c) 4 : 1 (d) 2 : 1

3 A parallel plate capacitor with air between the plates has a capacitance of 15 pF. The separation between the plate becomes twice and the space between them is filled with a medium of dielectric constant 3.5. Then the capacitance becomes $\frac{x}{4}$ pF. the value of x is **[2023, 24 Jan Shift-II]**

4 Two parallel plate capacitors C_1 and C_2 each having capacitance of 10 μF are individually charged by a 100 V D.C. source. Capacitor C_1 is kept connected to the source and a dielectric slab is inserted between it plates. Capacitor C_2 is disconnected from the source and then a dielectric slab is inserted in it. Afterwards the capacitor C_1 is also disconnected from the source and the two capacitors are finally connected in parallel combination. The common potential of the combination will be .... V.
(Assuming Dielectric constant = 10) **[2023, 31 Jan Shift-II]**

5 A parallel plate capacitor with plate area A and plate separation $d = 2$ m has a capacitance of 4μF. The new capacitance of the system, if half of the space between them is filled with a dielectric material of dielectric constant, $K = 3$ (as shown in figure) will be **[2022, 26 June shift-II]**

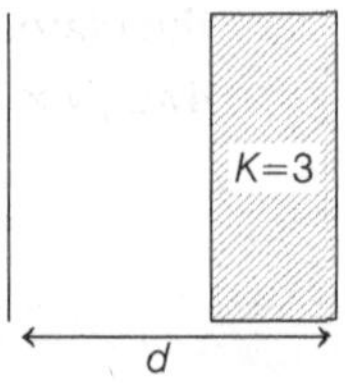

(a) 2 μF (b) 32 μFF
(c) 6 μF (d) 8 μF

6 Two metallic plates form a parallel plate capacitor. The distance between the plates is d. A metal sheet of thickness $d/2$ and of area equal to area of each plate is introduced between the plates. What will be the ratio of the new capacitance to the original capacitance of the capacitor? **[2022, 25 June Shift-II]**

(a) 2 : 1 (b) 1 : 2 (c) 1 : 4 (d) 4 : 1

7 Two capacitors, each having capacitance 40 μF are connected in series. The space between one of the capacitors is filled with dielectric material of dielectric constant K such that the equivalence capacitance of the system became 24 μF. The value of K will be **[2022, 28 July Shift-I]**

(a) 1.5 (b) 2.5 (c) 1.2 (d) 3

8 A parallel plate capacitor filled with a medium of dielectric constant 10, is connected across a battery and is charged. The dielectric slab is replaced by another slab of dielectric constant 15, then the energy of capacitor will **[2022, 29 June Shift-I]**

(a) increased by 50% (b) decreased by 15%
(c) increased by 25% (d) increased by 33%

9 A parallel plate capacitor with width 4 cm, length 8 cm and separation between the plates of 4 mm is connected to a battery of 20 V. A dielectric slab of dielectric constant 5 having length 1 cm, width 4 cm and thickness 4 mm is inserted between the plates of parallel plate capacitor. The electrostatic energy of this system will be .... ε_0 J.
(where, ε_0 is the permittivity of free space) **[2022, 27 July Shift-II]**

10 Two capacitors of capacities $2C$ and C are joined in parallel and charged upto potential V. The battery is removed and the capacitor of capacity C is filled completely with a medium of dielectric constant K. The potential difference across the capacitors will now be **[2021, 27 July Shift-I]**

(a $\frac{V}{K+2}$ (b) $\frac{V}{K}$ (c) $\frac{3V}{K+2}$ (d) $\frac{3V}{K}$

11 A parallel plate capacitor has plate area 100 m^2 and plate separation of 10 m. The space between the plates is filled upto a thickness 5 m with a material of dielectric constant of 10. The resultant capacitance of the system is x pF.
The value of $\varepsilon_0 = 8.85 \times 10^{-12}$ fm^{-1}.
The value of x to the nearest integer is .... **[2021, 18 March Shift-I]**

12 Two capacitors of capacities $2C$ and C are joined in parallel and charged up to potential V. The battery is removed and the capacitor of capacity C is filled completely with a medium of dielectric constant K. The potential difference across the capacitors will now be **[2021, 27 July Shift-I]**

(a) $\frac{3V}{K+2}$ (b) $\frac{3V}{K}$ (c) $\frac{V}{K+2}$ (d) $\frac{V}{K}$

13 In the reported figure, a capacitor is formed by placing a compound dielectric between the plates of parallel plate capacitor. The expression for the capacity of the said capacitor will be (Take, area of plate = A) **[2021, 27 July Shift-II]**

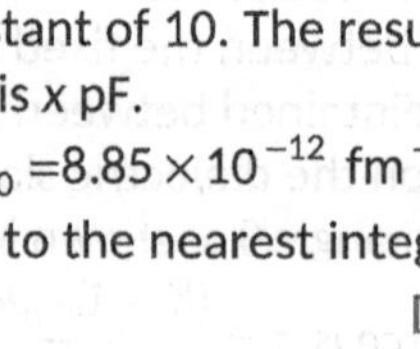

(a) $\frac{15}{34}\frac{K\varepsilon_0 A}{d}$ (b) $\frac{15}{6}\frac{K\varepsilon_0 A}{d}$
(c) $\frac{25}{6}\frac{K\varepsilon_0 A}{d}$ (d) $\frac{9}{6}\frac{K\varepsilon_0 A}{d}$

14 A parallel plate capacitor whose capacitance C is 14 pF is charged by a battery to a potential difference $V = 12\,V$ between its plates. The charging battery is now disconnected and a porcelain plate with $K = 7$ is inserted between the plates, then the plate would oscillate back and forth between the plates with a constant mechanical energy of .... pJ. (Assume no friction) **[2021, 17 March Shift-I]**

JEE Advanced

1 A container has a base of 50 cm × 5 cm and height 50 cm, as shown in the figure. It has two parallel electrically conducting walls each of area 50 cm × 50 cm. The remaining walls of the container are thin and non-condcting. The container is being filled with a liquid of dielectric constant 3 at a uniform rate of 250 $cm^3\ s^{-1}$. What is the value of the capacitance of the container after10 seconds? (Given : Permittivity of free space $\varepsilon_0 = 9 \times 10^{-12}\ C^2N^{-2}$, the effects of the non-conducting walls on the capacitance are negligible) **[JEE Advanced 2023]**

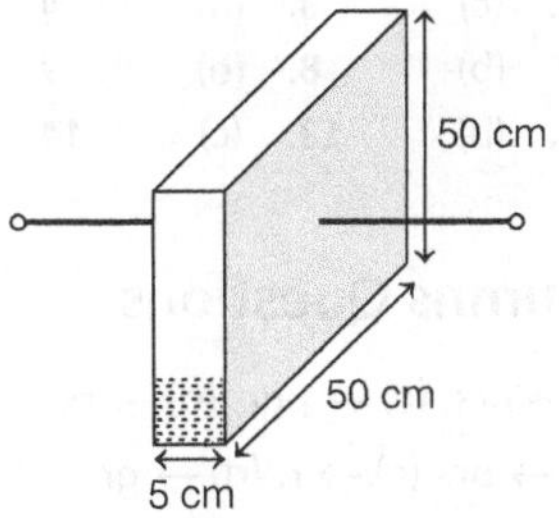

(a) 27 pF
(b) 63 pF
(c) 81 pF
(d) 135 pF

2 Three identical capacitors C_1, C_2 and C_3 have a capacitance of 1.0 μF each and they are uncharged initially. They are connected in a circuit as shown in the figure and C_1 is then filled completely with a dielectric material of relative permittivity ε_r. The cell electromotive force (emf) $V_0 = 8V$. First the switch S_1 is closed while the switch S_2 is kept open. When the capacitor C_3 is fully charged, S_1 is opened and S_2 is closed simultaneously. When all the capacitors reach equilibrium, the charge on C_3 is found to be 5μC. The value of $\varepsilon_r = ...$ **[JEE Advanced 2018]**

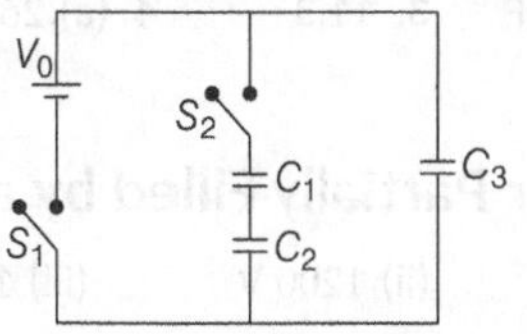

3 A parallel plate capacitor having plates of area S and plate separation d, has capacitance C_1 in air. When two dielectrics of different relative permittivities ($\varepsilon_1 = 2$ and $\varepsilon_2 = 4$) are introduced between the two plates as shown in the figure, the capacitance becomes C_2. The ratio $\frac{C_2}{C_1}$ is **[JEE Advanced 2015]**

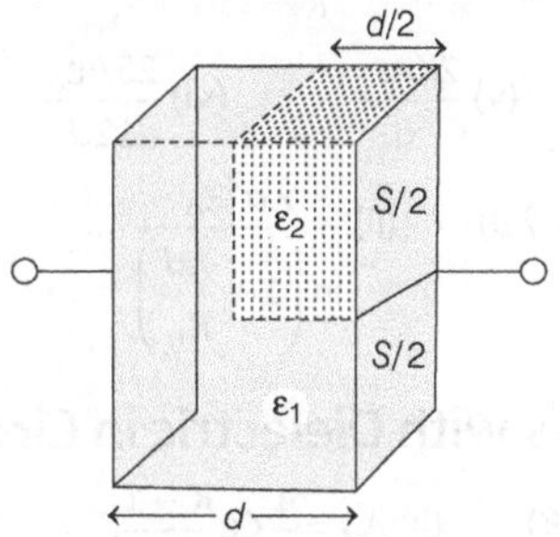

(a) $\frac{6}{5}$ (b) $\frac{5}{3}$ (c) $\frac{7}{5}$ (d) $\frac{7}{3}$

Answer Key

Level 1 Starter Level

10.1 Capacitor Fully Filled with Dielectric

1. (i) $C_0 = \frac{A\varepsilon_0}{d}, q_0 = \frac{A\varepsilon_0 V}{d}, E_0 = \frac{V}{d}, U_0 = \frac{1}{2}\frac{A\varepsilon_0}{d}V^2$

   (ii) $C = KC_0, q = q_0, E = \frac{E_0}{K}, U = \frac{U_0}{K}$

   (iii) $C = KC_0, q = Kq_0, E = E_0, U = KU_0$

2. 1.067×10^{-9} F   3. 11.3   4. (a) 26.6 nC, (b) 21.3 nC

5. 8.4 μC

10.2 Capacitor Partially Filled by a Dielectric

1. (i) 1500 V   (ii) 1200 V   (iii) 1350 V
2. (i) 5×10^3 V/m, 1.5×10^4 V/m   (ii) 25 V, 45 V

   (iii) 22.2×10^{-8} C/m^2, 13.3×10^{-8} C/m^2
3. (i) 8.3 μF, (ii) 99 μC   4. (i) 0.05 J (ii) 0.083 J

10.3 Equivalent Capacitance with Dielectric

1. (i) $\frac{A\varepsilon_0}{d-t}$ (ii) $\frac{A\varepsilon_0}{d-t+\frac{t}{K}}$ (iii) $\frac{A\varepsilon_0}{(d-t_1-t_2)+\frac{t_1}{K_1}+\frac{t_2}{K_2}}$

   (iv) $\frac{3KA\varepsilon_0}{2d}$ (v) $\frac{2KA\varepsilon_0}{d}$ (vi) $\frac{25A\varepsilon_0}{12d}$

2. (i) $\frac{a^2\varepsilon_0}{2d}(2K_0 + \lambda a)$ (ii) $\frac{\lambda a^2 \varepsilon_0}{\ln\left(1+\frac{\lambda d}{K_0}\right)}$

10.4 Capacitors with Dielectric in Circuit

1. (i) $\frac{E_i}{E_f} = \frac{1}{2}(1+K)$ (ii) $\Delta q = \frac{1}{2}C\varepsilon\frac{K-1}{K+1}$ 2. 80 V

10.5 Force on Dielectric Slab

1. (i) $U = \frac{\varepsilon_0 bV^2}{2d}[(K-1)x + l]$ (ii) $F = \frac{\varepsilon_0 bV^2(K-1)}{2d}$

2. $\frac{\varepsilon_0 bV^2(K-1)}{2dK_s}$ 3. $8\sqrt{\frac{md(l-a)}{b\varepsilon_0\varepsilon^2(K-1)}}$

Level 2 JEE Main Level

Single Choice Correct Questions

1. (d)	2. (b)	3. (c)	4. (c)	5. (a)
6. (d)	7. (c)	8. (a)	9. (c)	10. (c)
11. (a)	12. (a)	13. (d)	14. (a)	15. (c)
16. (d)	17. (a)	18. (a)	19. (c)	20. (c)
21. (b)	22. (c)	23. (c)		

Numerical Value Questions

1. (24)	2. (3)	3. (4)	4. (300)	5. (43)
6. (800)	7. (4)	8. (10)		

Level 3 JEE Advanced Level

1. (c)	2. (a)	3. (a)	4. (b)	5. (c)
6. (b)	7. (c)	8. (d)	9. (a)	10. (a)
11. (c)	12. (b)	13. (c)	14. (b)	15. (c)
16. (a)	17. (b)	18. (b)		

Multiple Choice(s) Correct Questions

1. (acd)	2. (abd)	3. (bcd)	4. (abcd)	5. (acd)
6. (ad)	7. (ad)	8. (abd)	9. (bcd)	

Comprehension Based Questions

1. (d)	2. (c)	3. (d)	4. (c)	5. (b)
6. (c)	7. (b)	8. (b)	9. (b)	10. (c)
11. (d)	12. (b)	13. (c)	14. (c)	15. (c)
16. (a)				

Match the Columns Questions

1. (a) $\rightarrow$ qr, (b) $\rightarrow$ prs, (c) $\rightarrow$ pqr, (d) $\rightarrow$ rs
2. (a) $\rightarrow$ prs, (b) $\rightarrow$ prs (c) $\rightarrow$ r, (d) $\rightarrow$ qr
3. (a) $\rightarrow$ s, (b) $\rightarrow$ r, (c) $\rightarrow$ q, (d) $\rightarrow$ r

Numerical Value Questions

1. (12)	2. (150)	3. (4)	4. (82.78)	5. (3)

Previous Year's Questions

JEE Main

1. (2)	2. (a)	3. (105)	4. (55)	5. (c)
6. (a)	7. (a)	8. (a)	9. (240)	10. (c)
11. (161)	12. (a)	13. (a)	14. (864)	

JEE Advanced

1. (b)	2. (1.50)	3. (d)

SOLUTIONS

Level 1 Starter Level

10.1 Capacitor Fully Filled with Dielectric

1. (a) $C_0 = \frac{A\varepsilon_0}{d}$

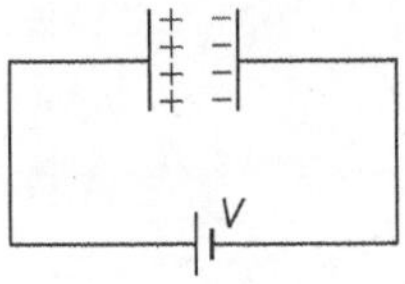

$q_0 = \left(\frac{A\varepsilon_0}{d}\right)V$

$E_0 = \frac{V}{d}$

$U_0 = \frac{1}{2}\left(\frac{A\varepsilon_0}{d}\right)V^2$

(b) **Case 1**

If battery is disconnected, charge on the capacitor will be same.

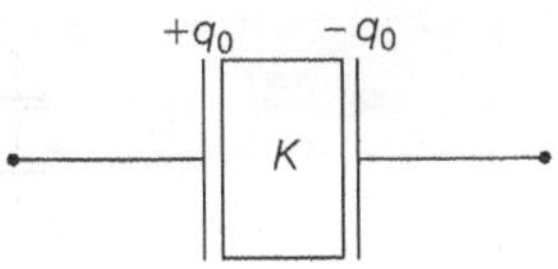

Charge, $q = q_0$

Electric field, $E = \frac{E_0}{K}$

$V' =$ Potential difference $= \left(\frac{E_0}{K}\right)d = \frac{V}{K}$

Capacitance, $C = \frac{q}{V'} = \frac{q_0}{(V_0/K)} = KC_0$

Energy stored, $U = \frac{q^2}{2C} = \frac{q_0^2}{2(KC_0)} = \frac{U_0}{K}$

Case 2

Capacitance, $C = KC_0$

Charge, $q = (KC_0)V = Kq_0$

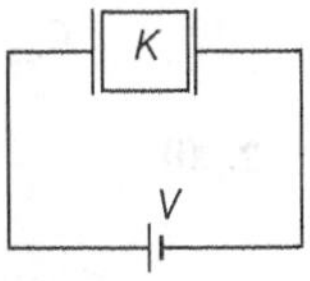

Electric field, $E = \frac{V}{d} = E_0$

Energy stored, $U = \frac{1}{2}(KC_0)V^2 = KU_0$

2. $C = \frac{KA\varepsilon_0}{d} = \frac{6 \times 3.14 \times (8 \times 10^{-2})^2 \times 8.85 \times 10^{-12}}{1 \times 10^{-3}}$

$= 1.067 \times 10^{-9}$ F

3. $q = CV$

$\Rightarrow q = (KC_0)V$

$\Rightarrow 0.12 \times 10^{-6} = K\left(\frac{100 \times 10^{-4} \times 8.85 \times 10^{-12}}{10^{-3}}\right)(120)$

$\Rightarrow K = 11.3$

4. (a) $q = CV = \left[\frac{5 \times (10 \times 10^{-2})^2 \times 8.85 \times 10^{-12}}{1 \times 10^{-3}}\right](60)$

$= 26.6 \times 10^{-9}$ C $= 26.6$ nC

(b) Induced charge on dielectric $= q\left(1 - \frac{1}{K}\right) = 26.6\left(1 - \frac{1}{5}\right)$

$= 21.3$ nC

5. Dielectric strength $= \frac{q_{max}}{KA\varepsilon_0}$

$\Rightarrow 1.9 \times 10^7 = \frac{q_{max}}{5 \times 100 \times 10^{-4} \times 8.85 \times 10^{-12}}$

$\Rightarrow q_{max} = 8.4 \times 10^{-6}$ C $= 8.4\,\mu$C

10.2 Capacitor Partially Filled by a Dielectric

1. (i) Potential difference between the plates before the introduction of the metal plate

$\Rightarrow Ed = (3 \times 10^4)(5 \times 10^{-2}) = 1500$ V

(ii) Potential difference after the introduction of the metal plate $= (3 \times 10^4)(4 \times 10^{-2}) + (0 \times 1 \times 10^{-2}) = 1200$ V

(iii) If metal plate is replaced by a plate of dielectric constant 2, then

Potential difference

$= (3 \times 10^4)(4 \times 10^{-2}) + \left(\frac{3 \times 10^4}{2}\right)(1 \times 10^{-2}) = 1350$ V

2. (i)

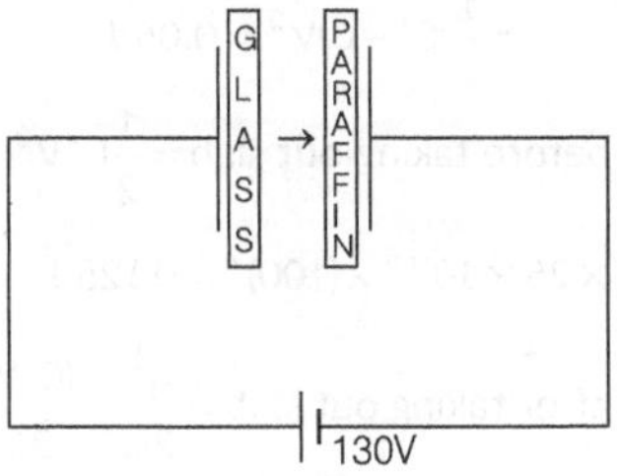

Let electric field in air be E.

Electric field in glass layer $= \frac{E}{6}$

Electric field in paraffin layer $= \frac{E}{2}$

$E(0.2 \text{ cm}) + \frac{E}{6}(0.5 \text{ cm}) + \frac{E}{2}(0.3 \text{ cm}) = 130$

$E = 3 \times 10^4$ V/m

Electric field in glass layer $= \frac{3 \times 10^4}{6} = 5 \times 10^3$ V/m

Electric field in paraffin layer $= \frac{3 \times 10^4}{2} = 1.5 \times 10^4$ V/m

(ii) Potential drop across glass layer

$= 5 \times 10^3 \times 0.5 \times 10^{-2} = 25$ V

Potential drop across paraffin layer

$= 1.5 \times 10^4 \times 0.3 \times 10^{-2} = 45$ V

(iii) $E = \frac{\sigma}{\varepsilon_0} = 3 \times 10^4$

$\Rightarrow \sigma = 3 \times 10^4 \times 8.854 \times 10^{-12} = 26.6 \times 10^{-8}$ C/m^2

Surface charge density on glass layer

$$=\sigma\left(1-\frac{1}{K}\right)=26.6\times10^{-8}\left(1-\frac{1}{6}\right)$$

$$=22.2\times10^{-8}\ \text{C/m}^2$$

Surface charge density on paraffin layer

$$=26.6\times10^{-8}\left(1-\frac{1}{2}\right)=13.3\times10^{-8}\ \text{C/m}^2$$

3. (i) $C=\dfrac{A\varepsilon_0}{d}=\dfrac{A\varepsilon_0}{2\text{mm}}=5\,\mu\text{F}$

$$C'=\frac{A\varepsilon_0}{(d-t)+\dfrac{t}{K}}=\frac{(5\mu\text{F})\times(2\text{mm})}{1\text{mm}+\left(\dfrac{1\text{mm}}{5}\right)}=8.3\,\mu\text{F}$$

(ii) Charge flown through battery $=C'V-CV$

$$=(8.3-5)\times10^{-6}\times30=99\,\mu\text{C}$$

4. (i) $C=15\,\mu\text{F}=\dfrac{A\varepsilon_0}{1\text{mm}}$

$$C'=\frac{A\varepsilon_0}{(d-t)+\dfrac{t}{K}}=\frac{(15\mu\text{F})\,(1\text{mm})}{0.5\text{mm}+\left(\dfrac{0.5\text{mm}}{5}\right)}=25\,\mu\text{F}$$

$$\Delta U=\frac{1}{2}C'V^2-\frac{1}{2}CV^2$$

$$=\frac{1}{2}(C'-C)V^2=0.05\ \text{J}$$

(ii) Energy before taking out slab $=\dfrac{1}{2}C'V^2$

$$=\frac{1}{2}\times25\times10^{-6}\times(100)^2=0.125\ \text{J}$$

Energy after taking out slab $=\dfrac{q^2}{2C}=\dfrac{(C'V)^2}{2C}$

$$=\frac{(25\times10^{-6}\times100)^2}{2\times15\times10^{-6}}=0.208\ \text{J}$$

$$\Delta E=0.208-0.125=0.083\ \text{J}$$

10.3 Equivalent Capacitance with Dielectric

1. (i) $C=\dfrac{A\varepsilon_0}{(d-t)+\dfrac{t}{K}}=\dfrac{A\varepsilon_0}{(d-t)+\dfrac{t}{\infty}}=\dfrac{A\varepsilon_0}{d-t}$

(ii) $C=\dfrac{A\varepsilon_0}{(d-t)+\dfrac{t}{K}}$ (iii) $C=\dfrac{A\varepsilon_0}{(d-t_1-t_2)+\dfrac{t_1}{K_1}+\dfrac{t_2}{K_2}}$

(iv)

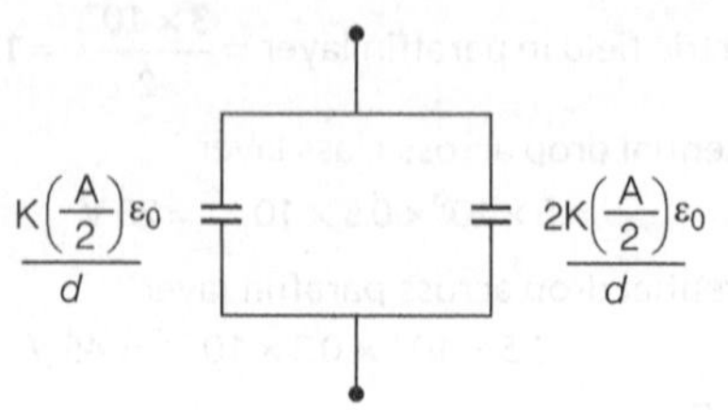

$$C_{eq}=C_1+C_2=\frac{K\left(\dfrac{A}{2}\right)\varepsilon_0}{d}+\frac{2K\left(\dfrac{A}{2}\right)\varepsilon_0}{d}=\frac{3KA\varepsilon_0}{2d}$$

(v)

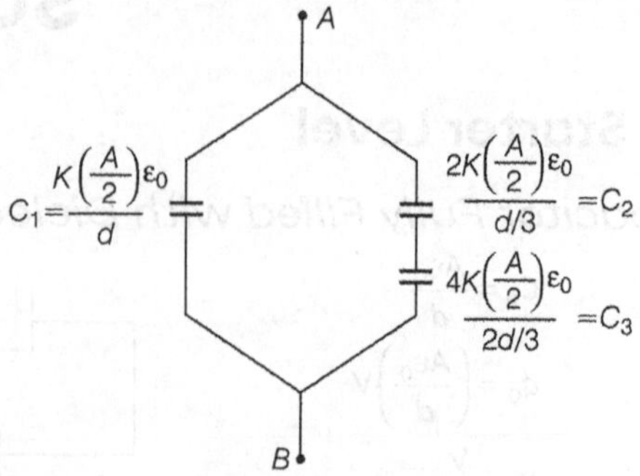

$$C_{eq}=C_1+\frac{C_2C_3}{C_2+C_3}=\frac{2KA\varepsilon_0}{d}$$

(vi)

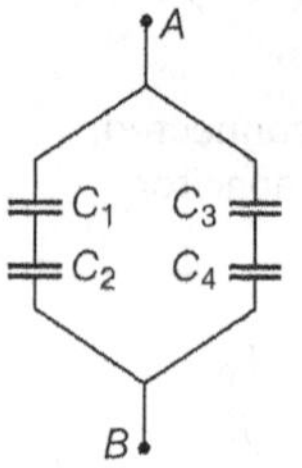

$$C_1=\frac{1\left(\dfrac{A}{2}\right)\varepsilon_0}{d/2},\qquad C_2=\frac{3\left(\dfrac{A}{2}\right)\varepsilon_0}{d/2},$$

$$C_3=\frac{2\left(\dfrac{A}{2}\right)\varepsilon_0}{d/2},\qquad C_4=\frac{4\left(\dfrac{A}{2}\right)\varepsilon_0}{d/2}$$

$$C_{eq}=\frac{C_1C_2}{C_1+C_2}+\frac{C_3C_4}{C_3+C_4}=\frac{25A\varepsilon_0}{12d}$$

2. (i)

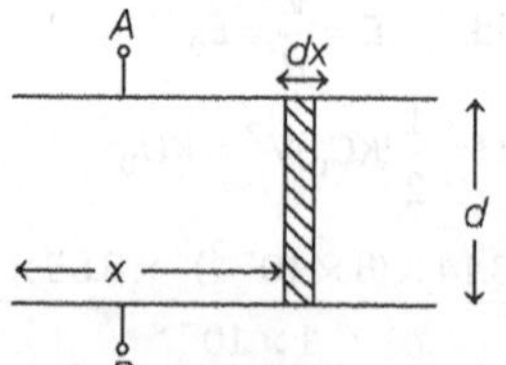

$$dC=\frac{K(adx)\varepsilon_0}{d}$$

$$\Rightarrow\quad \int dC=\int_0^a\frac{(K_0+\lambda x)\,adx\,\varepsilon_0}{d}$$

$$\Rightarrow\quad C=\frac{a\varepsilon_0}{d}\left[K_0x+\frac{\lambda x^2}{2}\right]_0^a=\frac{a^2\varepsilon_0}{2d}(2K_0+\lambda a)$$

(ii)

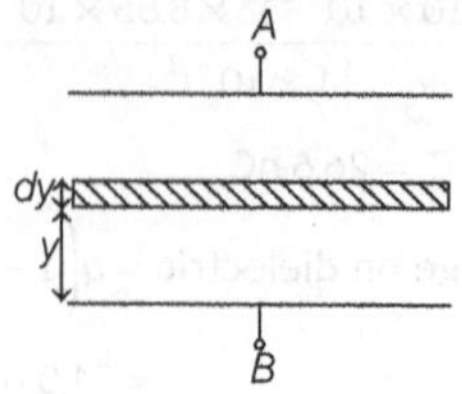

$$dC = \frac{(K_0+\lambda y)a^2\varepsilon_0}{dy}$$

$$\frac{1}{C} = \int \frac{1}{dC}$$

$$\Rightarrow \quad \frac{1}{C} = \int_0^d \frac{dy}{(k_0+\lambda y)a^2\varepsilon_0}$$

$$\Rightarrow \quad \frac{1}{C} = \frac{1}{a^2\varepsilon_0\lambda}\ln\left(\frac{K_0+\lambda d}{K_0}\right)$$

$$\Rightarrow \quad C = \frac{\lambda a^2\varepsilon_0}{\ln\left(1+\frac{\lambda d}{K_0}\right)}$$

10.4 Capacitors with Dielectrics in Circuit

1. (i)

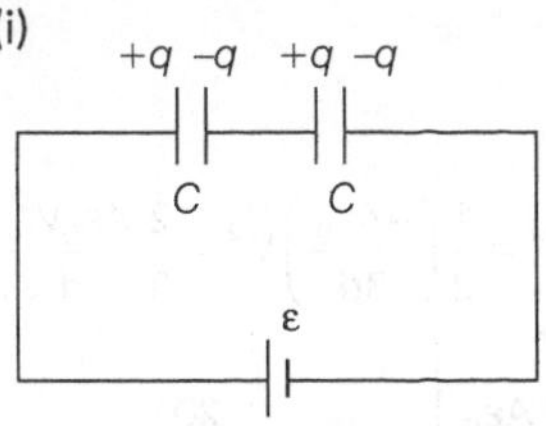

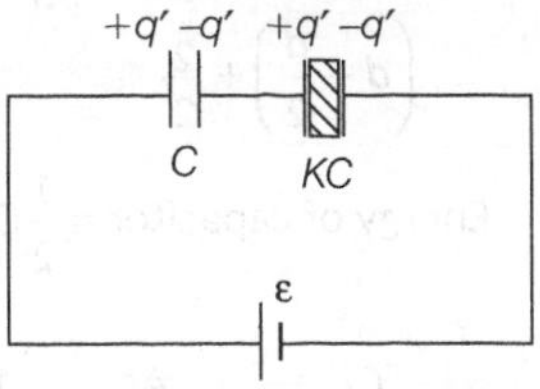

$$q = C_{eq}\varepsilon = \left(\frac{C}{2}\right)\varepsilon$$

$$q' = C'_{eq}\varepsilon = \left[\frac{(C)(KC)}{C+KC}\right]\varepsilon = \frac{KC\varepsilon}{K+1}$$

$$E = \frac{q}{A\varepsilon_0} \text{ and } E' = \frac{q'}{KA\varepsilon_0}$$

$$\frac{E}{E'} = \frac{\frac{q}{A\varepsilon_0}}{\frac{q'}{KA\varepsilon_0}} = \frac{Kq}{q'} = \frac{K\left(\frac{C\varepsilon}{2}\right)}{\left(\frac{KC\varepsilon}{K+1}\right)} = \frac{K+1}{2}$$

(ii) Charge flown through battery $= q' - q$

$$\Delta q = \frac{KC\varepsilon}{K+1} - \frac{C\varepsilon}{2} = \left(\frac{K-1}{K+1}\right)\left(\frac{C\varepsilon}{2}\right)$$

2. $q_1 + q_2 = q'_1 + q'_2$

$$\Rightarrow \quad C_1V_1 + C_2V_2 = C'_1V + C'_2V$$

$$\Rightarrow \quad 10(300) + 30(300) = (6\times 10)\,V + (3\times 30)\,V$$

$$\Rightarrow \quad V = 80\text{ V}$$

10.5 Force on Dielectric Slab

1. (i)

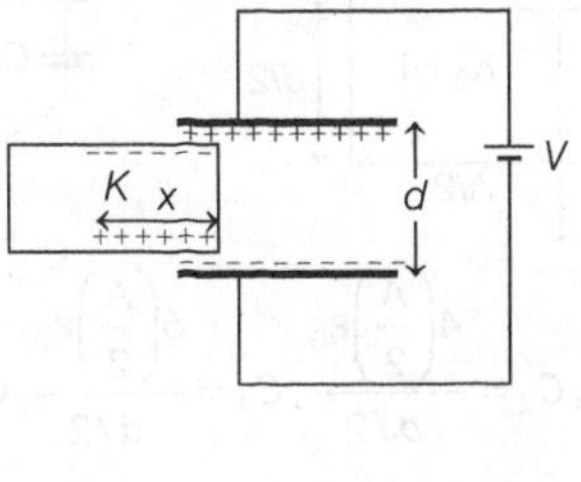

$$C = \frac{K(bx)\varepsilon_0}{d} + \frac{1(l-x)b\varepsilon_0}{d} = \frac{b\varepsilon_0}{d}(l+(K-1)x)$$

$$U = \frac{1}{2}CV^2 = \frac{1}{2}\frac{b\varepsilon_0}{d}[l+(K-1)x]V^2$$

(ii) $$F = -\frac{dU}{dx} = -\frac{1}{2}\frac{b\varepsilon_0V^2}{d}(K-1)$$

$$|F| = \frac{1}{2}\frac{b\varepsilon_0V^2}{d}(K-1)$$

2. In equilibrium, $F = Kx$

$$\Rightarrow \quad \frac{1}{2}\frac{b\varepsilon_0V^2}{d}(K-1) = K_sx$$

$$\Rightarrow \quad x = \frac{b\varepsilon_0V^2(K-1)}{2K_sd}$$

3. F = Force on dielectric $= \dfrac{b\varepsilon_0\varepsilon^2(K-1)}{2d}$

So, dielectric experiences a force of constant magnitude.

$$F = ma = \frac{b\varepsilon_0\varepsilon^2(K-1)}{2d}$$

$$a = \frac{b\varepsilon_0\varepsilon^2(K-1)}{2md}$$

$$s = ut + \frac{1}{2}at^2$$

$$\Rightarrow \quad l - a = 0 + \frac{1}{2}\left(\frac{b\varepsilon_0\varepsilon^2(K-1)}{2md}\right)t^2$$

$$t = 2\sqrt{\frac{md(l-a)}{b\varepsilon_0\varepsilon^2(K-1)}}$$

$$T = 4t = 8\sqrt{\frac{md(l-a)}{b\varepsilon_0\varepsilon^2(K-1)}}$$

Level 2 JEE Main Level

Single Choice Correct Questions

1. $q = 50\,\mu C$

$$q' = 50 + 100 = 150\,\mu C$$

$$q' = Kq$$

$$\Rightarrow \quad 150\,\mu C = K(50\,\mu C) \quad \Rightarrow \quad K = 3$$

2. $C = \dfrac{A\varepsilon_0}{d} = 10\,\mu F$

$$C' = K\frac{A\varepsilon_0}{2d} = 40\,\mu F$$

$$\Rightarrow \quad \frac{K}{2}\left(\frac{A\varepsilon_0}{d}\right) = 40\,\mu F$$

$$\Rightarrow \quad \frac{K}{2}(10\,\mu F) = 40\,\mu F \quad \Rightarrow \quad K = 8$$

3. Charge will be same.

$$q' = q$$

Capacitance will become K times, i.e. $C' = KC$

Potential difference $= \frac{q}{C}$ and energy stored $= \frac{q^2}{2C}$

As charge is same and capacitance increases, potential difference and energy stored will decrease.

4. Dielectric strength $= \frac{q_{max}}{KA\varepsilon_0}$

$$\Rightarrow \quad 20 \times 10^6 = \frac{q_{max}}{4 \times (32 \times 10^{-2})^2 \times 9 \times 10^{-12}}$$

$$\Rightarrow \quad q_{max} = 73.7\,\mu C$$

5. High dielectric constant for high capacitance and high dielectric strength, so that it doesn't breakdown.

6. Charge will remain same as the capacitor is isolated.

$$E = \frac{E_0}{K} \text{ and } V = \left(\frac{E_0}{K}\right)d = \frac{V_0}{K}$$

As dielectric constant becomes three times,

$$E = \frac{E_0}{3} \text{ and } V = \frac{V_0}{3}$$

7. $$C = \frac{A\varepsilon_0}{d} = 20\,\mu F$$

$$\Rightarrow \quad \frac{A\varepsilon_0}{2\text{ mm}} = 20\,\mu F$$

$$C' = \frac{A\varepsilon_0}{(d-t) + \frac{t}{K}} = \frac{(20\,\mu F) \times (2\text{ mm})}{1\text{mm} + \left(\frac{1\text{ mm}}{2}\right)}$$

$$= \frac{80}{3}\,\mu F = 26.6\,\mu F$$

8. $$C' = \frac{A\varepsilon_0}{(d-t) + \frac{t}{K}} \Rightarrow \frac{7}{6}\frac{A\varepsilon_0}{d} = \frac{A\varepsilon_0}{\frac{d}{3} + \frac{2d}{3K}}$$

$$\Rightarrow \quad \frac{7}{6} = \frac{3K}{K+2} \Rightarrow K = \frac{14}{11}$$

9. $$C = \frac{A\varepsilon_0}{d} = 15\,\mu F$$

$$\frac{A\varepsilon_0}{6\text{mm}} = 15\mu F$$

$$C' = \frac{A\varepsilon_0}{(d-t) + \frac{t}{K}} = \frac{A\varepsilon_0}{(6-2) + \frac{2}{\infty}} = 22.5\,\mu F$$

10. $V = Ed \Rightarrow 25 = E(5\text{ mm})$

$$\Rightarrow \quad E = 5\text{ V/mm}$$

$$V' = E(2\text{ mm}) + \left(\frac{E}{K}\right)(3\text{ mm})$$

$$= 5 \times 2 + \frac{5}{10} \times 3 = 11.5\text{ V}$$

11. For an isolated capacitor, charge will be same.

$$V = \frac{q}{C}$$

So to maintain the same potential difference, capacitance must be same.

$$C_1 = C_2$$

$$\Rightarrow \quad \frac{A\varepsilon_0}{d} = \frac{A\varepsilon_0}{(d + 1.6 - 2) + \frac{2}{K}} \Rightarrow K = 5$$

12. For $0 < x < d$; $E = \frac{E_0}{2}$ and for $d < x < 3d$; $E = \frac{E_0}{4}$

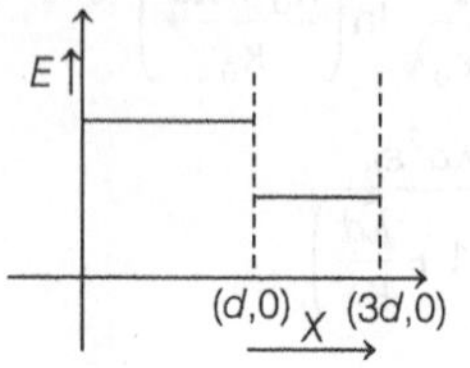

13. $$C = \frac{A\varepsilon_0}{\left(d - \frac{d}{2}\right) + \frac{d}{2}\cdot\frac{2}{2}}$$

$$C = \frac{A\varepsilon_0}{\left(d - \frac{d}{2}\right) + \frac{\frac{d}{2}}{2}} = \frac{4A\varepsilon_0}{3d}$$

Energy of capacitor $= \frac{1}{2}CV^2 = \frac{1}{2}\left(\frac{4A\varepsilon_0}{3d}\right)V^2 = \frac{2}{3}\frac{A\varepsilon_0 V^2}{d}$

14. $$C_2 = \frac{C_1}{2} \Rightarrow \frac{A\varepsilon_0}{\frac{3}{4} + \frac{5}{\varepsilon_r}} = \frac{1}{2}\left(\frac{A\varepsilon_0}{\frac{3}{4}}\right) \Rightarrow \varepsilon_r = \frac{20}{3}$$

15.

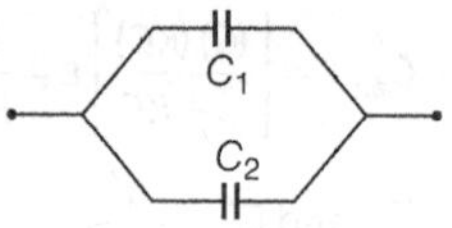

$$C_1 = K\frac{A}{2}\frac{\varepsilon_0}{d}, \quad C_2 = \left(\frac{A}{2}\right)\frac{\varepsilon_0}{d}$$

$$C = C_1 + C_2$$

$$= K\frac{A}{2}\frac{\varepsilon_0}{d} + \frac{A}{2}\frac{\varepsilon_0}{d} = (K+1)\frac{A\varepsilon_0}{2d}$$

16. $$C = C_1 + C_2$$

$$= \frac{6\left[\pi\left(\frac{r}{2}\right)^2\right]\varepsilon_0}{d} + \frac{1\left[\pi r^2 - \pi\left(\frac{r}{2}\right)^2\right]\varepsilon_0}{d}$$

$$= \frac{9}{4}\frac{(\pi r^2)\varepsilon_0}{d} = \frac{9C}{4}$$

17.

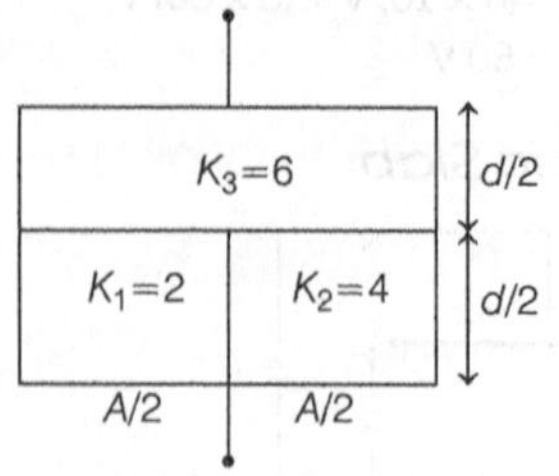

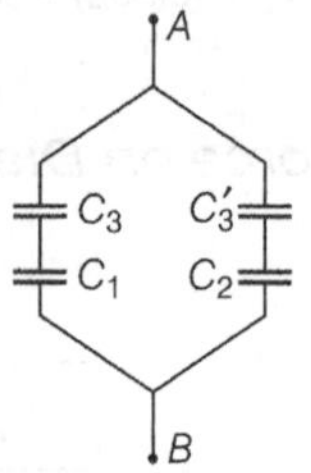

$$C_1 = \frac{2\left(\frac{A}{2}\right)\varepsilon_0}{d/2}, C_2 = \frac{4\left(\frac{A}{2}\right)\varepsilon_0}{d/2}, C_3 = \frac{6\left(\frac{A}{2}\right)\varepsilon_0}{d/2}, C_3' = \frac{6\left(\frac{A}{2}\right)\varepsilon_0}{d/2}$$

$$C_{eq} = \frac{C_1C_3}{C_1+C_3} + \frac{C_2C_3'}{C_2+C_3'}$$

$$= \frac{3}{2}\frac{A\varepsilon_0}{d} + \frac{12}{5}\frac{A\varepsilon_0}{d} = \frac{39}{10}\frac{A\varepsilon_0}{d} = 3.9\ C$$

18.

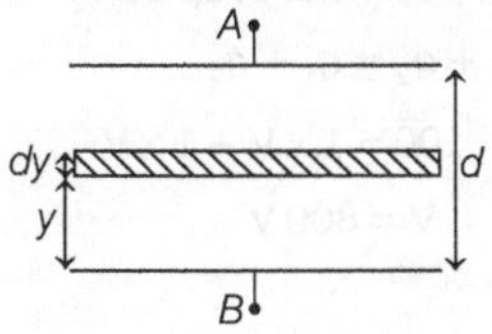

$$dC = \frac{KA\varepsilon_0}{dy} = \frac{\lambda \sec\left(\frac{\pi y}{2d}\right)A\varepsilon_0}{dy}$$

$$\frac{1}{dC} = \frac{dy}{\lambda A\varepsilon_0 \sec\left(\frac{\pi y}{2d}\right)}$$

$$\Rightarrow \quad \int \frac{1}{dC} = \frac{1}{\lambda A\varepsilon_0}\int_0^d \cos\left(\frac{\pi y}{2d}\right)dy$$

$$\Rightarrow \quad \frac{1}{C} = \frac{1}{\lambda A\varepsilon_0}\left[\frac{\sin\left(\frac{\pi y}{2d}\right)}{\frac{\pi}{2d}}\right]_0^d$$

$$C = \frac{\lambda A\varepsilon_0 \pi}{2d}$$

19.

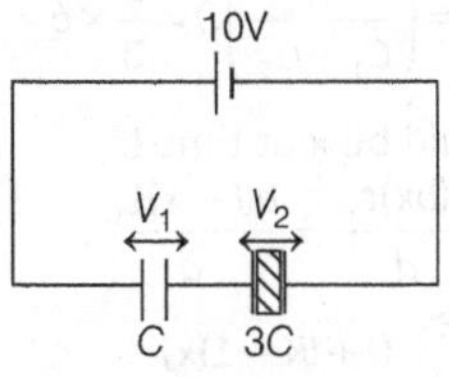

$$V_1 + V_2 = 10 \qquad \text{...(i)}$$

and $$\frac{V_1}{V_2} = \frac{3}{1} \qquad \text{...(ii)}$$

Solving equations (i) and (ii), we get

$$V_1 = 7.5\text{ V} \quad \text{and} \quad V_2 = 2.5\text{ V}$$

20.

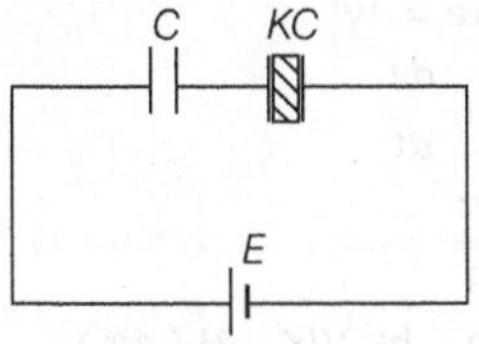

$$Q_1 = Q_2 = C_{eq}E = \left[\frac{(KC)C}{KC+C}\right]E = \left(\frac{K}{K+1}\right)CE$$

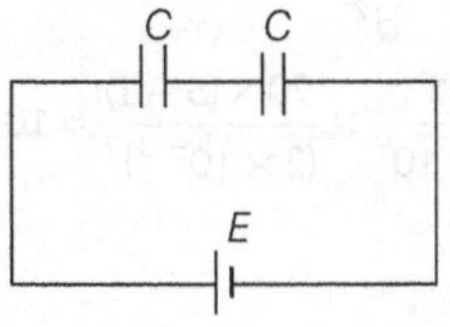

$$Q_1' = Q_2' = C_{eq}E = \frac{C}{2}E$$

$$\frac{Q_2'}{Q_2} = \frac{\frac{CE}{2}}{\left(\frac{K}{K+1}\right)CE} = \frac{K+1}{2K}$$

21. $q_1 + q_2 = q_1' + q_2'$

$$\Rightarrow \quad C_0V_0 + 2C_0V_0 = (KC_0)V + (2C_0)V$$

$$\Rightarrow \quad V = \frac{3V_0}{K+2}$$

22. Let the final common potential drop be V.

$$q_1 + q_2 = q_1' + q_2'$$

$$\Rightarrow \quad 1\times 100 - 2\times 20 = (1\times 4)\,V + 2V$$

$$\Rightarrow \quad V = 10\text{ V}$$

$$U_1 = \frac{(1\times 100\times 10^{-6})^2}{2\times 4\times 10^{-6}} + \frac{1}{2}\times 2\times 10^{-6}\times (20)^2$$

$$= 1.65\times 10^{-3}\text{ J}$$

$$U_2 = \frac{1}{2}\times (4\times 10^{-6})(10)^2 + \frac{1}{2}\times (2\times 10^{-6})(10)^2$$

$$= 0.3\times 10^{-3}\text{ J}$$

Heat dissipated $= U_1 - U_2 = 1.65\times 10^{-3} - 0.3\times 10^{-3}$

$$= 1.35\times 10^{-3}\text{ J}$$

23. Force on dielectric slab due to capacitor $= \frac{1}{2}\frac{b\varepsilon_0 V^2}{d}(K-1)$

$$\Rightarrow \quad F = \frac{1}{2}\frac{b\varepsilon_0}{d}\left(\sqrt{\frac{mgd}{b(K-1)\varepsilon_0}}\right)^2 (K-1)$$

$$\Rightarrow \quad F = \frac{mg}{2}$$

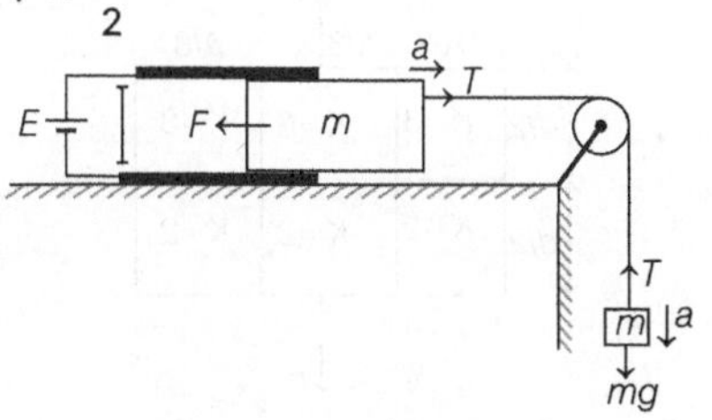

$$mg - T = ma \qquad \text{...(i)}$$

$$T - F = ma \qquad \text{...(ii)}$$

Solving equations (i) and (ii), we get

$$a = \frac{mg - F}{2m} = \frac{mg - \frac{mg}{2}}{2m} = \frac{g}{4}$$

Numerical Value Questions

1. Charge on capacitor $q = CV$

$$= 5\times 120\times 10^{-12}\times 50 = 30\times 10^{-9}\text{ C} = 30\text{ nC}$$

Induced charges on mica $= q\left(1 - \frac{1}{K}\right) = (30\text{ nC})\left(1 - \frac{1}{5}\right)$

$$= 24\text{ nC}$$

2. For $x<2$; $E_0=-\dfrac{dV}{dx}=\dfrac{10-4}{2-0}=3\text{ V/mm}$

For $2<x<3$; $E=-\dfrac{dV}{dx}=\dfrac{4-3}{3-2}=1\text{ V/mm}$

$$E=\frac{E_0}{K} \Rightarrow 1\text{ V/mm}=\frac{3\text{ V/mm}}{K} \Rightarrow K=3$$

3. $$U_1=\frac{q^2}{2(KC)}=4\times10^{-5}\text{ J},\ U_2=\frac{q^2}{2C}$$

$$W_{ext}=U_2-U_1$$

$$\Rightarrow 12\times10^{-5}=U_2-4\times10^{-5}$$

$$\Rightarrow U_2=16\times10^{-5}$$

$$\therefore \frac{U_2}{U_1}=\frac{\dfrac{q^2}{2C}}{\dfrac{q^2}{2KC}}=\frac{16\times10^{-5}}{4\times10^{-5}} \Rightarrow K=4$$

4. $E=\text{Electric field}=\dfrac{1000}{d}$

$$E=10^7\times\frac{10}{100}$$

$$\Rightarrow \frac{1000}{d}=10^7\times\frac{10}{100} \Rightarrow d=1\text{ mm}$$

$$C=\frac{KA\varepsilon_0}{d}$$

$$\Rightarrow 50\times10^{-12}=\frac{6\pi A\left(\dfrac{1}{36\pi}\times10^{-9}\right)}{10^{-3}}$$

$$\Rightarrow A=300\times10^{-6}\text{ m}^2=300\text{ mm}^2$$

5.

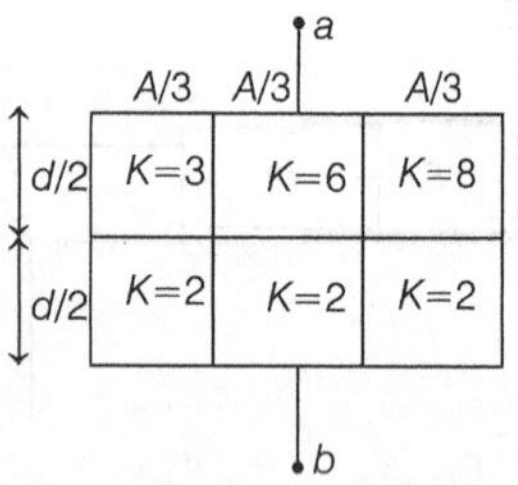

Let $\dfrac{\dfrac{A}{3}\varepsilon_0}{\dfrac{d}{2}}=C \Rightarrow C=\dfrac{2A\varepsilon_0}{3d}$

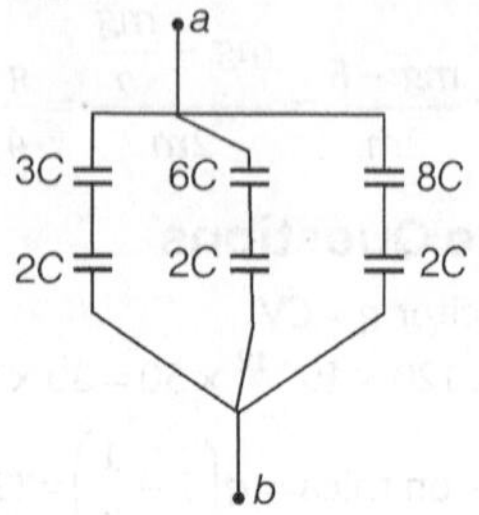

$$C_{eq}=\frac{(3C)(2C)}{3C+2C}+\frac{(6C)(2C)}{6C+2C}+\frac{(8C)(2C)}{8C+2C}$$

$$=\frac{43C}{10}=\frac{43}{10}\times\frac{2A\varepsilon_0}{3d}=\frac{43}{15}\frac{A\varepsilon_0}{d}$$

6. Let the common potential drop be V.

$$q_1+q_2=q_1'+q_2'$$

$$\Rightarrow 15\times100+1\times100=1\times V+1\times V$$

$$\Rightarrow V=800\text{ V}$$

7.

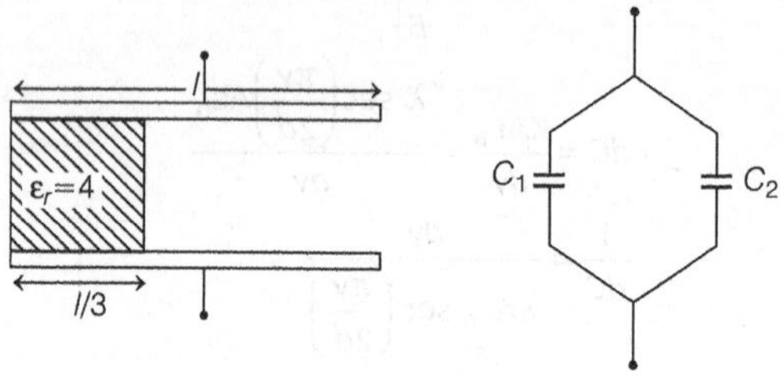

$$C_1=\frac{4\left(l\times\dfrac{l}{3}\right)\varepsilon_0}{d}=\frac{4l^2\varepsilon_0}{3d}$$

$$C_2=\frac{\left(l\times\dfrac{2l}{3}\right)\varepsilon_0}{d}=\frac{2l^2\varepsilon_0}{3d}$$

$$\Rightarrow \frac{C_1}{C_2}=2$$

$$q=\left(\frac{C_1}{C_1+C_2}\right)Q=\frac{2}{3}\times6=4\,\mu\text{C}$$

8. Let height of liquid be x at time t.

$$C=\frac{K(bx)\varepsilon_0}{d}+\frac{b(l-x)\varepsilon_0}{d}$$

$$=\frac{b\varepsilon_0}{d}\,(l+(K-1)x)$$

$q=$ charge on capacitor $=CV$

$$\Rightarrow q=\frac{b\varepsilon_0V}{d}[l+(K-1)\,x]$$

$$i=\frac{dq}{dt}=\frac{b\varepsilon_0V}{d}(K-1)\frac{dx}{dt}$$

Volume flow rate $=Av$

$$\Rightarrow 4\pi=(bd)\frac{dx}{dt}$$

$$\Rightarrow \frac{dx}{dt}=\frac{4\pi}{bd}$$

$$i=\frac{dq}{dt}=\frac{b\varepsilon_0V(K-1)}{d}\left(\frac{4\pi}{bd}\right)$$

$$=\frac{4\pi\varepsilon_0V(K-1)}{d^2}$$

$$=\frac{1}{9\times10^9}\times\frac{90\times(5-1)}{(2\times10^{-3})^2}=10\text{ mA}$$

Level 3 JEE Advanced Level

Single Choice Correct Questions

1. Charge appearing at the surface is due to bound charge.

2. $q = C_{eq}V$

$$\Rightarrow \quad q = \left(\frac{A\varepsilon_0}{\frac{5}{2}+\frac{5}{4}}\right)100$$

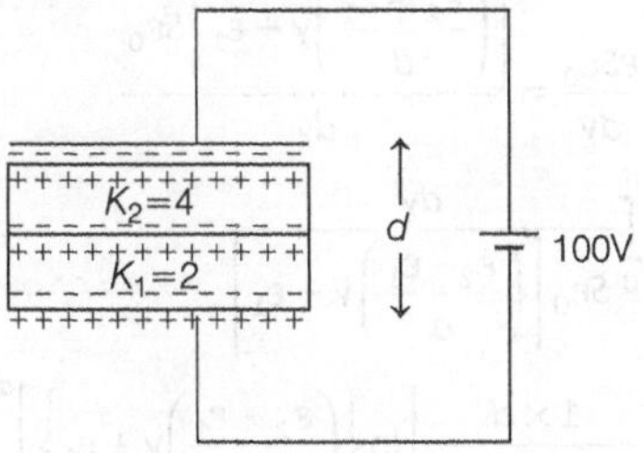

$$\Rightarrow \quad \frac{q}{A} = \frac{8000}{3}\varepsilon_0 \quad \Rightarrow \sigma = \frac{8000}{3}\varepsilon_0$$

Net bound surface charge density at the interface

$$= \sigma\left(1-\frac{1}{K_1}\right) - \sigma\left(1-\frac{1}{K_2}\right)$$

$$= \frac{8000\varepsilon_0}{3}\times\left(1-\frac{1}{2}\right) - \frac{8000\varepsilon_0}{3}\left(1-\frac{1}{4}\right)$$

$$= \frac{8000\varepsilon_0}{3}\times\left(-\frac{1}{4}\right) = -\frac{2000}{3}\varepsilon_0$$

3.

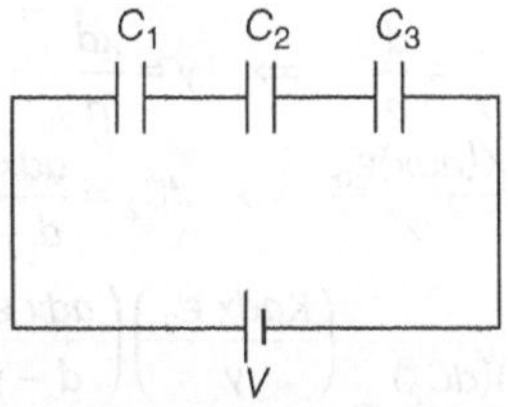

$$\frac{1}{C_{eq}} = \frac{1}{C_1} + \frac{1}{C_2} + \frac{1}{C_3}$$

$$\frac{1}{C_{eq}} = \frac{1}{\left(\frac{A\varepsilon_0}{\frac{d}{3}}\right)} + \frac{1}{\infty} + \frac{1}{\left(\frac{KA\varepsilon_0}{\frac{d}{3}}\right)}$$

$$\Rightarrow \quad C_{eq} = \left(\frac{K}{K+1}\right)\frac{3A\varepsilon_0}{d}$$

$$\frac{U_3}{U} = \frac{\frac{q^2}{2C_3}}{\frac{q^2}{2C_{eq}}} = \frac{C_{eq}}{C_3} = \frac{\left(\frac{K}{K+1}\right)\frac{3A\varepsilon_0}{d}}{\left[K\frac{A\varepsilon_0}{\left(\frac{d}{3}\right)}\right]} = \frac{1}{K+1}$$

4. $U_1 = \frac{1}{2}C_{eq}V^2 = \frac{1}{2}\left(\frac{C}{2}\right)V^2$

$$U_2 = \frac{1}{2}C'_{eq}V^2 = \frac{1}{2}\left[\frac{C(KC)}{C+KC}\right]V^2$$

$$W_{ext} = \Delta U = U_2 - U_1$$

$$= \frac{1}{2}\left(\frac{KC}{K+1}\right)V^2 - \frac{1}{2}\left(\frac{C}{2}\right)V^2$$

$$= \frac{1}{2}CV^2\left[\frac{K}{K+1} - \frac{1}{2}\right] = \frac{CV^2}{4}\left[\frac{K-1}{K+1}\right]$$

5.

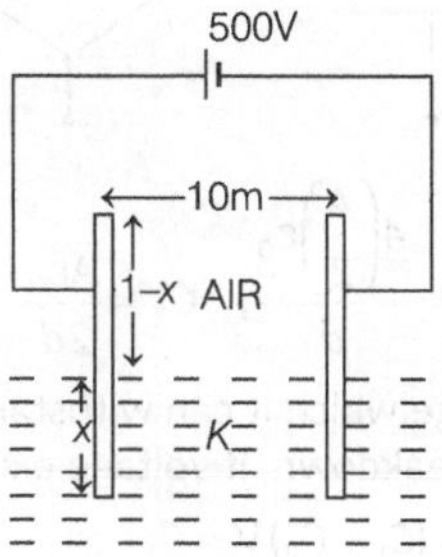

$$C = K\frac{1(x)\varepsilon_0}{0.01} + \frac{(1-x)(1)\varepsilon_0}{0.01}$$

$$= 100\varepsilon_0[1+(K-1)x] = 100\varepsilon_0(1+10x)$$

$$q = CV = 100\varepsilon_0(1+10x)(500)$$

$$i = \frac{dq}{dt} = (100\varepsilon_0)(10)\frac{dx}{dt}(500)$$

$$= 1000\varepsilon_0 \times 0.001 \times 500 = 4.425\times10^{-9}\ \text{A}$$

6.

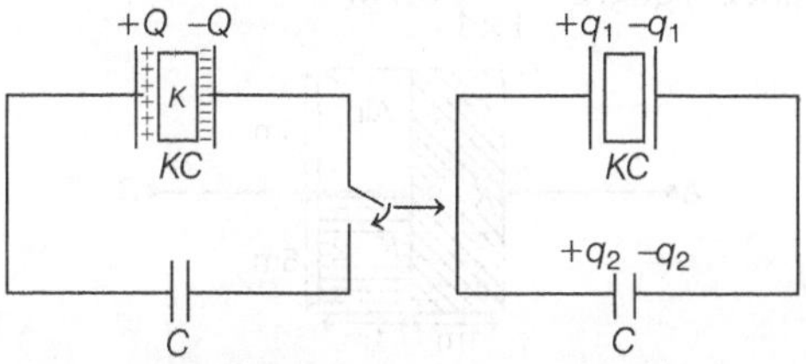

$$q_1 = \left(\frac{K}{K+1}\right)Q \text{ and } q_2 = \left(\frac{1}{K+1}\right)Q$$

Common potential difference after redistribution

$$= \frac{q_1}{KC} = \frac{Q}{(K+1)C}$$

$$\text{Energy lost} = \frac{1}{2}\frac{(KC)C}{KC+C}\left(\frac{Q}{KC}-0\right)^2 = \frac{Q^2}{2C}\left[\frac{1}{K(K+1)}\right]$$

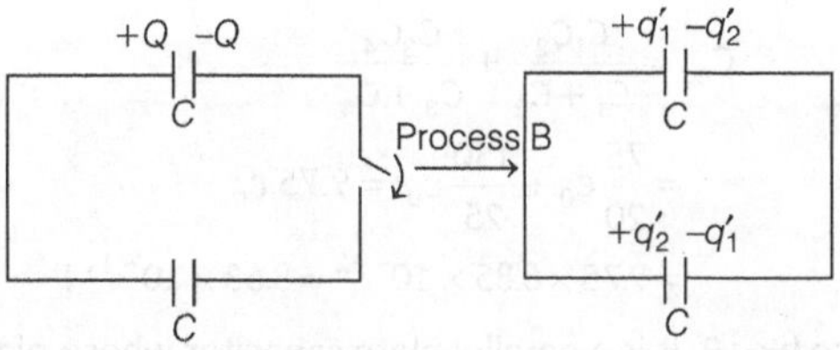

$$q'_1 = q'_2 = \frac{Q}{2}$$

Common potential difference after redistribution $= \dfrac{Q}{2C}$

Energy lost $= \dfrac{1}{2}\dfrac{C(C)}{C+C}\left(\dfrac{Q}{C}-0\right)^2 = \dfrac{Q^2}{4C}$

7. $Q = CV = \left(\dfrac{A\varepsilon_0}{d}\right)V$

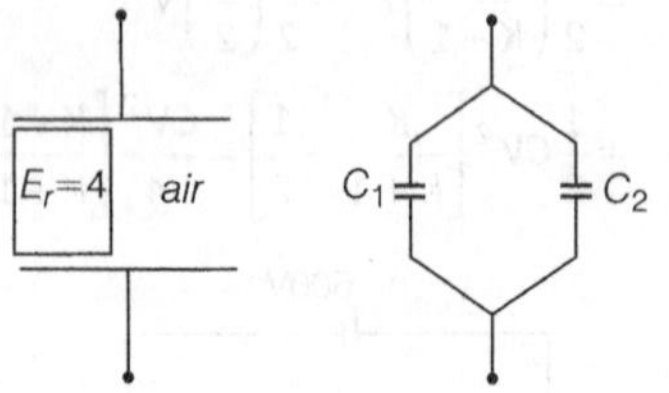

$$C_1 = \frac{4\left(\frac{A}{2}\right)\varepsilon_0}{d}, \quad C_2 = \frac{A\varepsilon_0}{2d}$$

Maximum voltage which it can withstand will be V as air capacitor will breakdown, if voltage exceeds V.

$$Q' = (C_1 + C_2)V$$
$$= \left(\frac{2A\varepsilon_0}{d} + \frac{A\varepsilon_0}{2d}\right)V = 2.5\left(\frac{A\varepsilon_0}{d}\right)V = 2.5\,Q$$

8. Volume of liquid 1 collected in 5 sec $= 2\times 5 = 10\ \text{m}^3$

Weight of liquid 1 $= \dfrac{10}{(1\times 1)} = 10$ m

Volume of liquid 2 collected in 5 sec $= 1\times 5 = 5\ \text{m}^3$

Weight of liquid 2 $= \dfrac{5}{1\times 1} = 5$ m

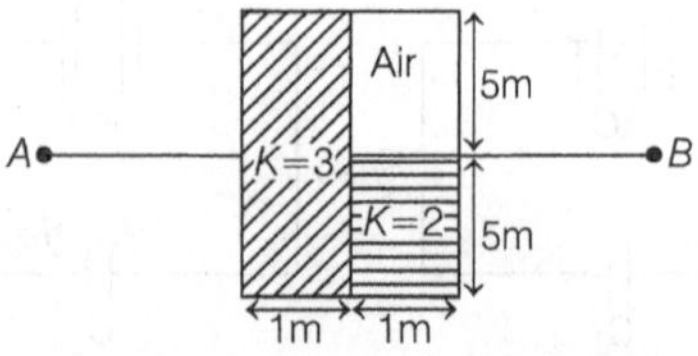

$$C_1 = \frac{3(5\times 1)\varepsilon_0}{1}, \quad C_2 = \frac{1(5\times 1)\varepsilon_0}{1}$$

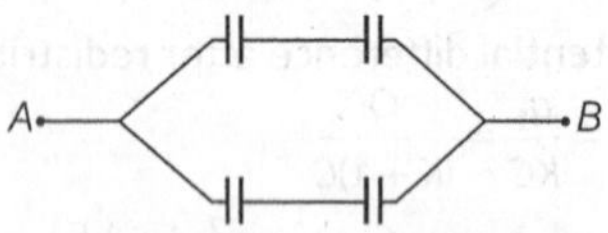

$$C_3 = \frac{3(5\times 1)\varepsilon_0}{1}, \quad C_4 = \frac{2(5\times 1)\varepsilon_0}{1}$$

$$C_{eq} = \frac{C_1C_2}{C_1+C_2} + \frac{C_3C_4}{C_3+C_4}$$
$$= \frac{75}{20}\varepsilon_0 + \frac{150}{25}\varepsilon_0 = 9.75\,\varepsilon_0$$
$$= 9.75\times 8.85\times 10^{-12} = 8.63\times 10^{-11}\ \text{F}$$

9. Since $b << R$, it is a parallel plate capacitor whose plate area is $(R\alpha)h$ and separation between the plates is b.

$$C = \frac{KA\varepsilon_0}{d} = \frac{K(R\alpha)h\varepsilon_0}{b}$$

10.

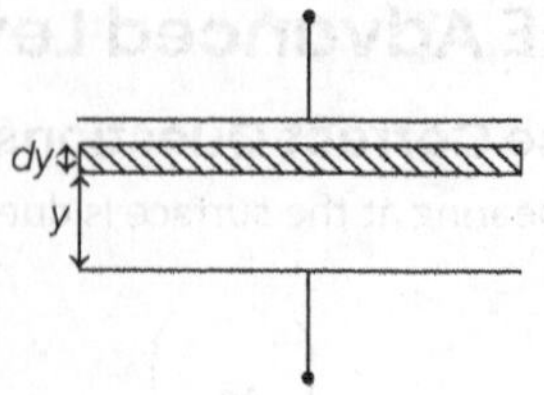

$$\varepsilon = \left(\frac{\varepsilon_2 - \varepsilon_1}{d}\right)y + \varepsilon_1$$

$$dC = \frac{\varepsilon S\varepsilon_0}{dy} = \frac{\left[\left(\frac{\varepsilon_2-\varepsilon_1}{d}\right)y + \varepsilon_1\right]S\varepsilon_0}{dy}$$

$$\int \frac{1}{dC} = \int_0^d \frac{dy}{S\varepsilon_0\left[\left(\frac{\varepsilon_2-\varepsilon_1}{d}\right)y+\varepsilon_1\right]}$$

$$\frac{1}{C} = \frac{1\times d}{S\varepsilon_0(\varepsilon_2-\varepsilon_1)}\left[\ln\left\{\left(\frac{\varepsilon_2-\varepsilon_1}{d}\right)y+\varepsilon_1\right\}\right]_0^d$$

$$\Rightarrow \quad C = \frac{\varepsilon_0 S(\varepsilon_2-\varepsilon_1)}{d\ln\left(\frac{\varepsilon_2}{\varepsilon_1}\right)}$$

11.

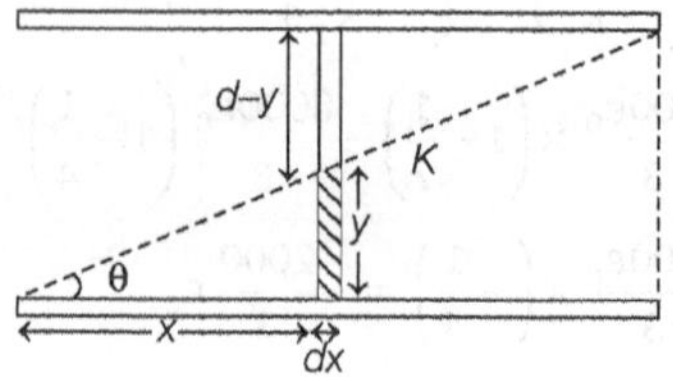

$$\tan\theta = \frac{y}{x} = \frac{d}{a} \quad\Rightarrow\quad y = \frac{xd}{a}$$

$$dC_1 = \frac{K(adx)\varepsilon_0}{y} \quad\Rightarrow\quad dC_2 = \frac{adx\varepsilon_0}{d-y}$$

$$dC = \frac{(dC_1)(dC_2)}{dC_1+dC_2} = \frac{\left(\frac{Kadx\,\varepsilon_0}{y}\right)\left(\frac{adx\,\varepsilon_0}{d-y}\right)}{\frac{Kadx\,\varepsilon_0}{y} + \frac{adx\,\varepsilon_0}{d-y}}$$

$$\Rightarrow \quad dC = \frac{Kadx\,\varepsilon_0}{Kd+(1-K)y}$$

$$\int dC = Ka\varepsilon_0\int\frac{dx}{Kd+(1-K)y}$$

$$\Rightarrow \quad C = Ka\varepsilon_0\int_0^a \frac{dx}{Kd+(1-K)\left(\frac{xd}{a}\right)}$$

$$= \frac{Ka^2\varepsilon_0}{d}\int_0^a\frac{dx}{Ka+(1-K)x}$$

$$= \frac{Ka^2\varepsilon_0}{d}\left(\frac{1}{1-K}\right)[\ln(Ka+(1-K)x]_0^a$$

$$= \frac{Ka^2\varepsilon_0}{d(1-K)}\ln\left(\frac{a}{Ka}\right) = \frac{Ka^2\varepsilon_0}{d(K-1)}\ln K$$

12.

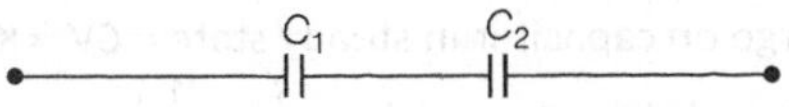

$$C_1 = K4\pi\varepsilon_0\left(\frac{ca}{c-a}\right) = 3(4\pi\varepsilon_0)\left[\frac{(2a)(a)}{2a-a}\right] = 24\pi\varepsilon_0 a$$

$$C_2 = 4\pi\varepsilon_0\left(\frac{bc}{b-c}\right) = 4\pi\varepsilon_0\left[\frac{(3a)(2a)}{3a-2a}\right] = 24\pi\varepsilon_0 a$$

$$C = \frac{C_1C_2}{C_1+C_2} = 12\pi\varepsilon_0 a$$

C' = Capacitance of an isolated spherical conducting shell of radius $a = 4\pi\varepsilon_0 a$

$$C = nC'$$

$$\Rightarrow \quad 12\pi\varepsilon_0 a = n(4\pi\varepsilon_0 a) \quad \Rightarrow \quad n = 3$$

13. Let $\frac{A\varepsilon_0}{d} = C$

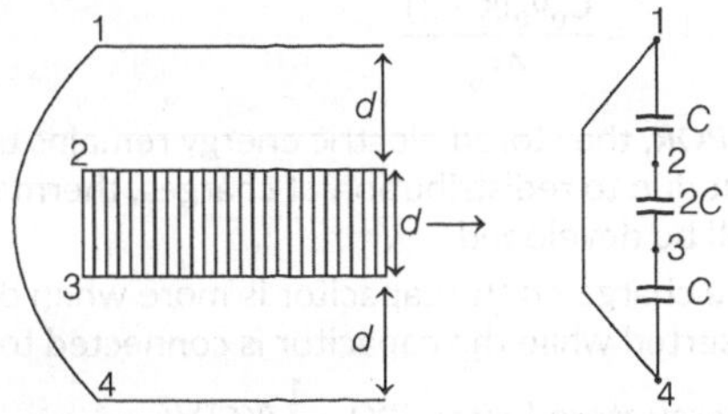

Between 1 and 3

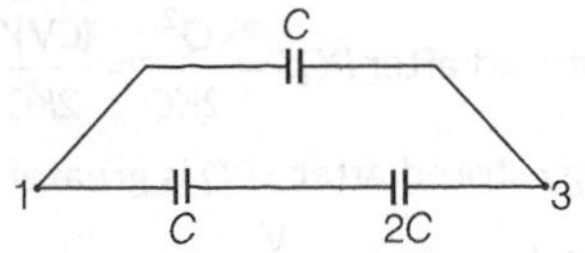

$$C_1 = \frac{2C}{3} + C = \frac{5C}{3}$$

Between 2 and 3

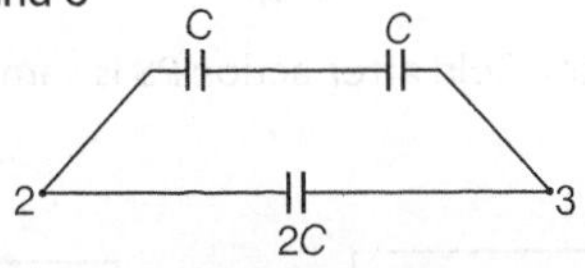

$$C_2 = 2C + \frac{C}{2} = \frac{5C}{2}$$

$$\therefore \quad \frac{C_1}{C_2} = \frac{\frac{5C}{3}}{\frac{5C}{2}} = \frac{2}{3}$$

14.

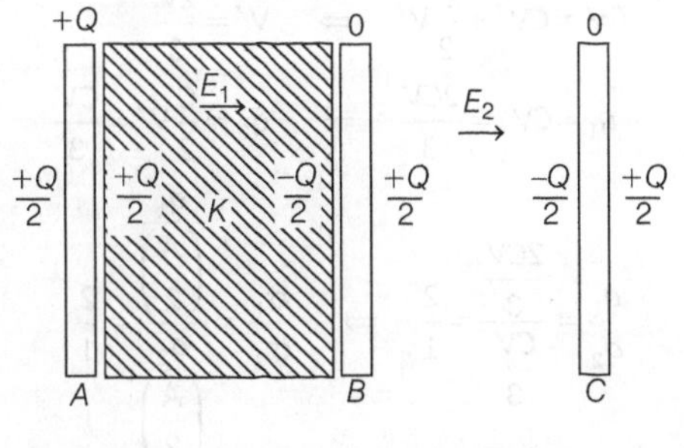

$$V_A - V_C = E_1 d + E_2 d$$

$$= \left(\frac{\frac{Q}{2}}{KA\varepsilon_0}\right)d + \left(\frac{\frac{Q}{2}}{A\varepsilon_0}\right)d = \frac{Qd}{2\varepsilon_0 l^2}\left(\frac{1}{K}+1\right)$$

15.

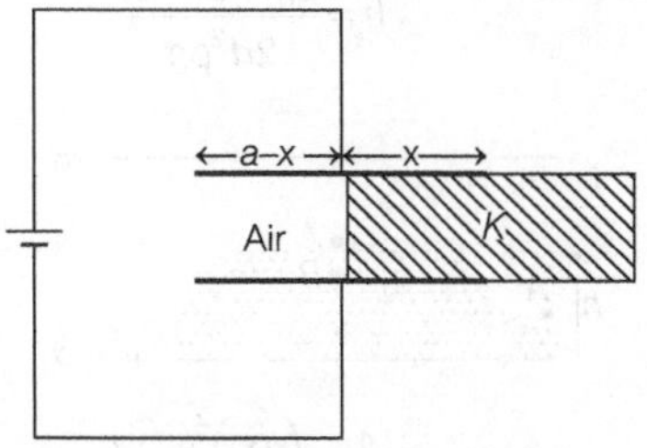

When x length of dielectric is inside capacitor,

$$C = \frac{K(bx)\varepsilon_0}{d} + \frac{1[b(a-x)]\varepsilon_0}{d}$$

$$C = \frac{b\varepsilon_0}{d}(a+(K-1)x)$$

$$U = \frac{1}{2}CV^2 = \frac{1}{2}\frac{b\varepsilon_0}{d}[a+(K-1)x]V^2$$

$$F = -\frac{dU}{dx} = -\frac{1}{2}\frac{b\varepsilon_0}{d}(K-1)V^2$$

So, the dielectric slab experiences a constant force. Thus it will have constant acceleration.

$$v = u + at \quad \Rightarrow \quad v \propto t$$

$$q = CV \quad \Rightarrow \quad q = \frac{b\varepsilon_0}{d}(a+(k-1)x)V$$

$$i = \frac{dq}{dt} = \frac{b\varepsilon_0 V}{d}(K-1)\frac{dx}{dt} = \frac{b\varepsilon_0 V}{d}(K-1)v$$

$$\Rightarrow \quad i \propto t$$

When dielectric slab is completely inside the capacitor, it experiences zero force and capacitance is constant. So current will be zero.

16. Just after collision, bullet will come to rest and dielectric will start moving with velocity v_0.

As long as dielectric slab is completely inside the capacitor, force on dielectric is zero. Dielectric will start experiencing a constant force F when it begins to come out of the capacitor.

$$F = \frac{1}{2}\frac{b\varepsilon_0 E^2}{d}(K-1)$$

$$W_F = \Delta K$$

$$\Rightarrow \quad -Fa = 0 - \frac{1}{2}mv_0^2$$

$$\Rightarrow \quad -\frac{1}{2}\frac{b\varepsilon_0 E^2}{d}(K-1)a = -\frac{1}{2}Mv_0^2$$

$$\Rightarrow \quad v_0 = E\left[\frac{\varepsilon_0 ab(K-1)}{Md}\right]^{\frac{1}{2}}$$

17. In equilibrium, let height of liquid be h.

$$F = mg$$

$$\Rightarrow \quad \frac{1}{2}\frac{b\varepsilon_0 V^2}{d}(K-1) = \rho(bhd)g$$

$$\Rightarrow \quad h = \frac{\varepsilon_0 V^2 (K-1)}{2d^2 \rho g}$$

18.

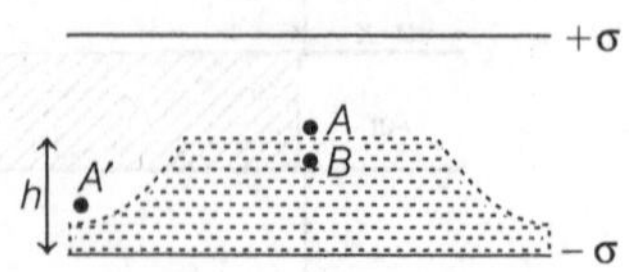

$$P_{A'} = P_A = P_0 + \frac{1}{2}\varepsilon_0\left(\frac{\sigma}{\varepsilon_0}\right)^2$$

$$P_B = P_0 + \frac{1}{2}K\varepsilon_0\left(\frac{\sigma}{K\varepsilon_0}\right)^2$$

$$P_A - P_B = \frac{1}{2}\varepsilon_0\left(\frac{\sigma}{\varepsilon_0}\right)^2 - \frac{1}{2}K\varepsilon_0\left(\frac{\sigma}{K\varepsilon_0}\right)^2$$

$$\Rightarrow \quad h\rho g = \frac{(K-1)\sigma^2}{2\varepsilon_0 K}$$

$$\Rightarrow \quad h = \frac{\sigma^2(K-1)}{2\varepsilon_0 K\rho g}$$

Multiple Choice(s) Correct Questions

1.

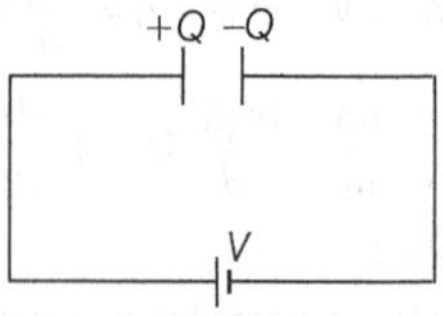

$$Q = CV = \left(\frac{A\varepsilon_0}{d}\right)V$$

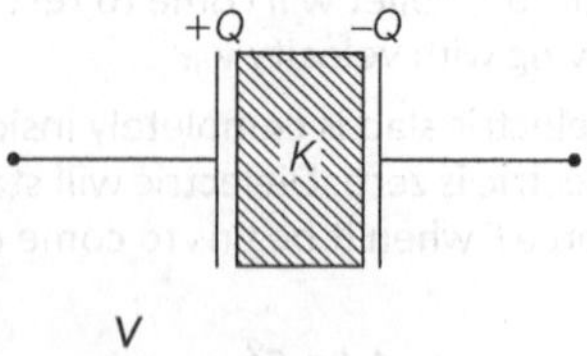

$$E = \frac{E_0}{K} = \frac{\frac{V}{d}}{K} = \frac{V}{Kd}$$

$$W = \Delta U = U_2 - U_1$$

$$= \frac{Q^2}{2KC} - \frac{Q^2}{2C} = \frac{Q^2}{2C}\left(\frac{1}{K} - 1\right)$$

$$W = \frac{Q^2}{2C}\left(1 - \frac{1}{K}\right)$$

$$= \frac{A\varepsilon_0}{2d}V^2\left(1 - \frac{1}{K}\right)$$

2. (A) Charge on capacitor in steady state $= CV = KC_0V_0$

Induced charges on slab $= Q\left(1 - \frac{1}{K}\right)$

$$= KC_0V_0\left(1 - \frac{1}{K}\right) = C_0V_0(K-1)$$

(B) Electric field due to induced charges at any point outside the slab is zero. So, force on any plate of the capacitor due to induced charges is zero.

(C) Force of attraction between the plates is $\frac{Q^2}{2A\varepsilon_0}$, where $Q = KC_0V_0$

(D) Electric field due to induced charges in the slab

$$= \frac{\sigma_i}{\varepsilon_0} = \frac{\sigma\left(1 - \frac{1}{K}\right)}{\varepsilon_0} = \left(\frac{KC_0V_0}{A}\right)\frac{\left(1 - \frac{1}{K}\right)}{\varepsilon_0}$$

$$= \frac{C_0V_0(K-1)}{A\varepsilon_0}$$

3. (A) In PQR, the stored electric energy remains unchanged but due to redistribution of charges, thermal energy will be developed.

(B) The charge on the capacitor is more when dielectric is inserted while the capacitor is connected to battery.

(C) Energy stored after $SPQ = \frac{1}{2}(KC)V^2$

Energy stored after $PQS = \frac{Q^2}{2KC} = \frac{(CV)^2}{2KC} = \frac{1}{2}\frac{CV^2}{K}$

So, energy stored after SPQ is greater than after PQS.

(D) Electric field after $PS = \frac{V}{d}$

Electric field after $SP = \frac{V}{d}$

So, electric field after action PS is same as that after SP.

4. Let $\frac{A\varepsilon_0}{d} = C$

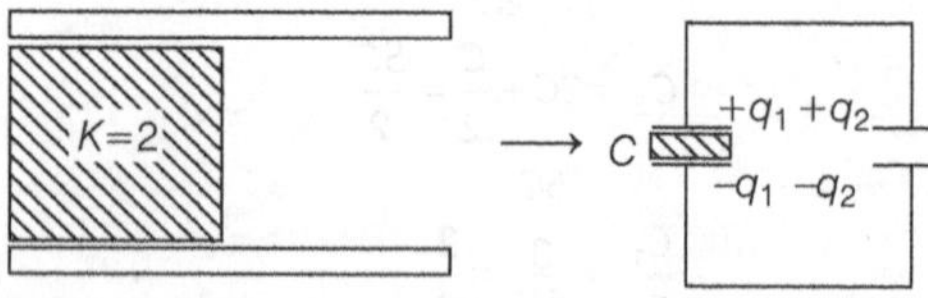

From charge conservation, $CV = q_1 + q_2$

$$\Rightarrow \quad CV = CV' + \frac{C}{2}V' \quad \Rightarrow \quad V' = \frac{2V}{3}$$

$$q_1 = CV' = \frac{2CV}{3} \quad \Rightarrow \quad q_2 = \frac{C}{2}V' = \frac{CV}{3}$$

$$\frac{q_1}{q_2} = \frac{\frac{2CV}{3}}{\frac{CV}{3}} = \frac{2}{1} \quad \Rightarrow \quad \frac{\sigma_1}{\sigma_2} = \frac{\frac{q_1}{\left(\frac{A}{2}\right)}}{\frac{q_2}{\left(\frac{A}{2}\right)}} = \frac{2}{1}$$

New capacitance $= C + \frac{C}{2} = \frac{3C}{2} = \frac{3}{2}\frac{A\varepsilon_0}{d}$

Electric field $= \frac{V'}{d}$

5. (A) $q_i = q\left(1 - \frac{1}{K}\right)$

$$\Rightarrow \quad \frac{75}{100} \times q = q\left(1 - \frac{1}{K}\right)$$

$$\Rightarrow \quad 1 - \frac{1}{K} = \frac{3}{4}$$

$$\Rightarrow \quad K = 4$$

(B) Capacitance without dielectric $= \frac{480}{4} = 120\,\mu\text{F}$

(C) $$E_{max} = \frac{q_{max}}{KA\varepsilon_0}$$

$$\Rightarrow \quad q_{max} = KA\varepsilon_0 E_{max}$$

$$\Rightarrow \quad 240\varepsilon_0 L^2 E_{max} = 4A\varepsilon_0 E_{max}$$

$$\Rightarrow \quad A = 60L^2$$

(D) $C = \frac{A\varepsilon_0}{\frac{d}{2} + \frac{d}{4(2)}} = \frac{8}{5}\frac{A\varepsilon_0}{d} = \frac{8}{5} \times 120 = 192\,\mu\text{F}$

6. Energy density $= \frac{1}{2}\varepsilon E^2 = \frac{1}{2}(K\varepsilon_0)\left(\frac{E_0}{K}\right)^2 = \left(\frac{1}{2}\varepsilon_0 E_0^2\right)\frac{1}{K}$

$\Rightarrow$ Energy density $\propto \frac{1}{K}$

$$\frac{\text{Energy density in first dielectric}}{\text{Energy density in second dielectric}} = \frac{K_2}{K_1} = \frac{5}{3}$$

Total induced surface charge density on the interface

$$= \sigma\left(1 - \frac{1}{K_1}\right) - \sigma\left(1 - \frac{1}{K_2}\right)$$

$$= \sigma\left(1 - \frac{1}{3}\right) - \sigma\left(1 - \frac{1}{5}\right) = -\frac{2\sigma}{15}$$

7.

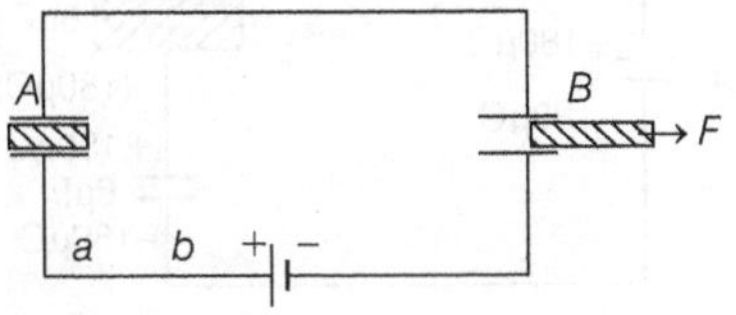

As dielectric slab of capacitor *B* is pulled out, equivalent capacitance of the circuit will decrease. So charge on the two capacitors will decrease but they will have same charge as they are in series.

Charge will flow from *a* to *b* and battery will get charged. So, its internal energy will increase.

Using energy conservation,

$$W_{ext} + W_{battery} = \Delta U + \text{Heat produced.}$$

8. (a)

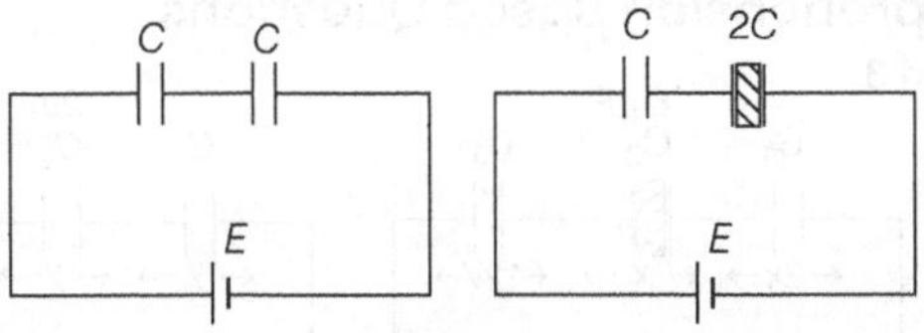

Without dielectric, $C_{eq} = \frac{C}{2}$

Charge on each capacitor $= \frac{CE}{2}$

With the dielectric, $C_{eq} = \frac{2C}{3}$

Charge on each capacitor $= \frac{2CE}{3}$

Increment in charge $= \frac{2CE}{3} - \frac{CE}{2} = \frac{CE}{6}$

(B) $W_{battery} = qE = \left(\frac{CE}{6}\right)E = \frac{CE^2}{6}$

So, energy of cell decreases by $\frac{CE^2}{6}$.

(D) $\Delta U_A = \frac{\left(\frac{2CE}{3}\right)^2}{2C} - \frac{\left(\frac{CE}{2}\right)^2}{2C} = \frac{7CE^2}{72}$

9. Let length of plate $= l$

Width of plate $= b$

$$C = \frac{Kbx\varepsilon_0}{d} + \frac{(l-x)b\varepsilon_0}{d}$$

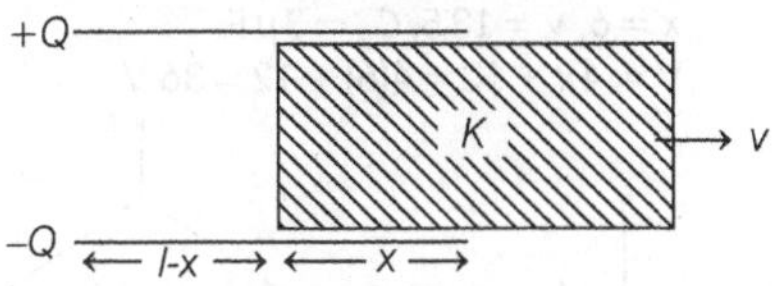

$$C = \frac{b\varepsilon_0}{d}[(l + (k-1)x)]$$

$$\frac{dC}{dt} = \frac{b\varepsilon_0}{d}(K-1)\frac{dx}{dt} = -\frac{b\varepsilon_0(K-1)v}{d}$$

So, capacitance decreases at constant rate and becomes constant after the slab comes out of the capacitor plates completely.

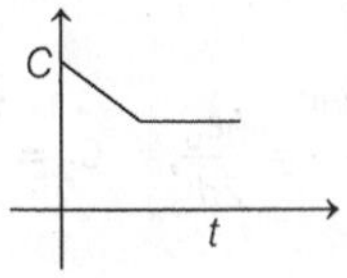

$V = \frac{Q}{C}$

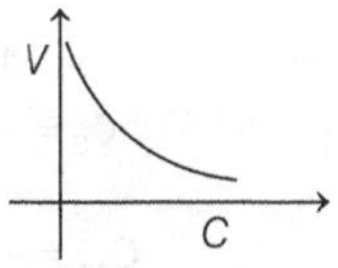

$U = \frac{1}{2}QV$

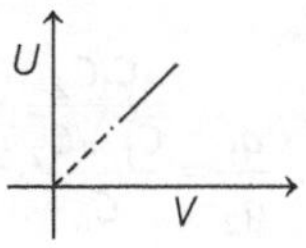

Comprehension Based Questions

1, 2 and 3

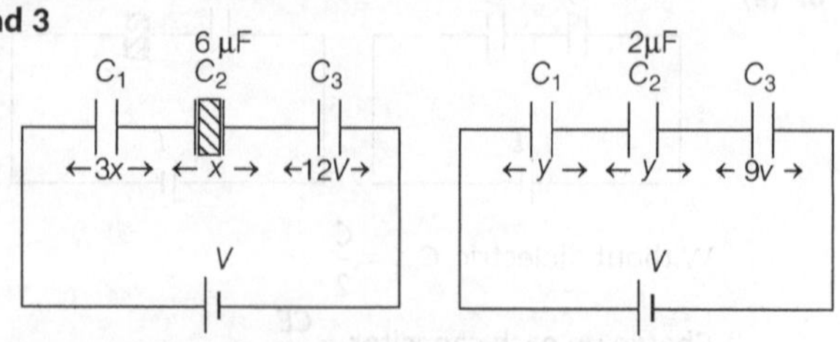

After removing dielectric, capacitance of C_2 decreases. So, potential difference across C_2 increases and potential difference across C_3 decreases.

So, potential difference across C_3 will decrease by 3V.

Since potential difference across C_1 and C_2 are equal, $C_1 = C_2 = 2\mu F$.

Let potential difference across C_1 and C_2 after removing dielectric is y.

With the dielectric, let potential difference across C_2 be x.

Since, $V \propto \frac{1}{C}$ in series combination, potential difference across C_1 will be $3x$.

$$V = 3x + x + 12 = y + y + 9$$

$$\Rightarrow \quad 2y - 4x = 3 \quad \text{...(i)}$$

Since, $$V \propto \frac{1}{C} \Rightarrow \frac{x}{12} = \frac{C_3}{6} \quad \text{...(ii)}$$

and $$\frac{y}{9} = \frac{C_3}{2} \quad \text{...(iii)}$$

Solving equations (i) and (ii), we get

$$x = 6,\ y = 13.5,\ C_3 = 3\mu F$$

$$V = 4x + 12 = 4(6) + 12 = 36 \text{ V}$$

4.

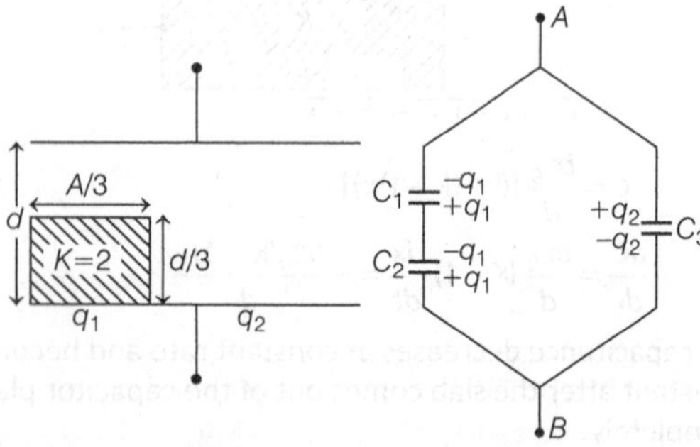

$$C_1 = \frac{1\left(\frac{A}{3}\right)\varepsilon_0}{\frac{2d}{3}} = \frac{A\varepsilon_0}{2d}, \quad C_2 = \frac{2\left(\frac{A}{3}\right)\varepsilon_0}{\frac{d}{3}} = \frac{2A\varepsilon_0}{d}$$

$$C_3 = \frac{1\left(\frac{2A}{3}\right)\varepsilon_0}{d} = \frac{2A\varepsilon_0}{3d}$$

$$C_{eq} = \frac{C_1C_2}{C_1 + C_2} + C_3 = \frac{16}{15}\frac{A\varepsilon_0}{d}$$

5. $$\frac{q_1}{q_2} = \frac{\frac{C_1C_2}{C_1 + C_2}}{C_3} = \frac{\frac{2}{5}\frac{A\varepsilon_0}{d}}{\frac{2}{3}\frac{A\varepsilon_0}{d}} = \frac{3}{5}$$

6. $$C_1 = \frac{A\varepsilon_0}{2d}, \quad C_2 = \frac{A\varepsilon_0}{d + \frac{d}{2}} = \frac{2A\varepsilon_0}{3d}$$

$$C_1 : C_2 = \frac{A\varepsilon_0}{2d} : \frac{2A\varepsilon_0}{3d} = 3 : 4$$

7. Let electric field in air be E.

$$Ed + \left(\frac{E}{2}\right)d = 1200 \Rightarrow Ed = 800 \text{ V}$$

Maximum potential difference

across dielectric $= \frac{E}{2}d = 400$ V

8. $$U = \frac{q^2}{2C}$$

$$\frac{U_{air}}{U_{dielectric}} = \frac{C_{dielectric}}{C_{air}} = \frac{\frac{2A\varepsilon_0}{d}}{\frac{A\varepsilon_0}{d}} = 2:1$$

9. When only S_1 is closed,

$$q = CV = 2 \times 10^{-6} \times 180 = 360\mu C$$

Work done by battery $= qV$

$$= 360 \times 10^{-6} \times 180$$

$$= 64.8 \times 10^{-3} \text{ J} = 64.8 \text{ mJ}$$

10. When S_1 is opened and S_2 is closed.

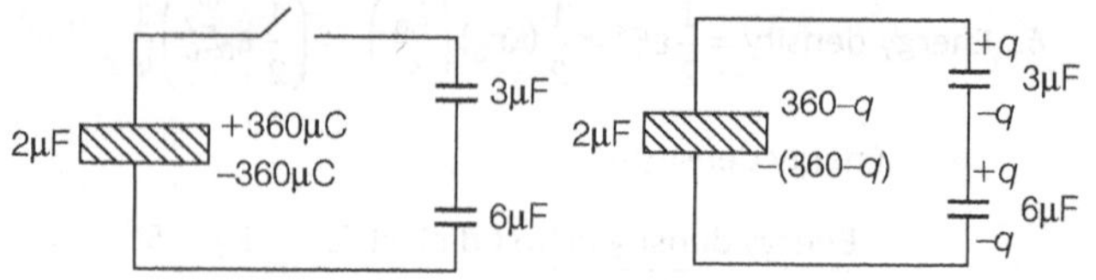

Applying KVL,

$$\frac{+360 - q}{2} - \frac{q}{3} - \frac{q}{6} = 0 \Rightarrow q = 180\mu C$$

11.

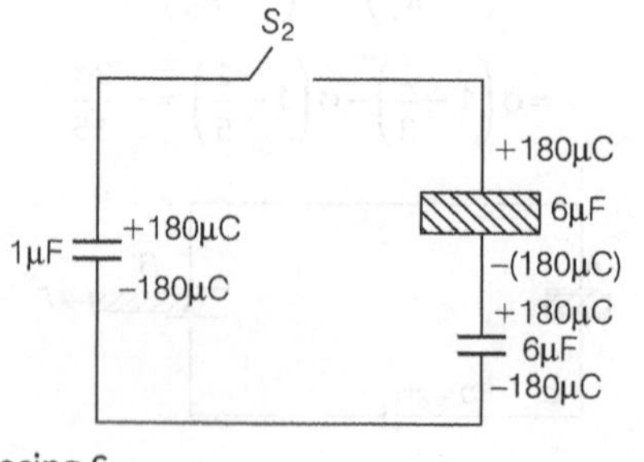

After closing S_2

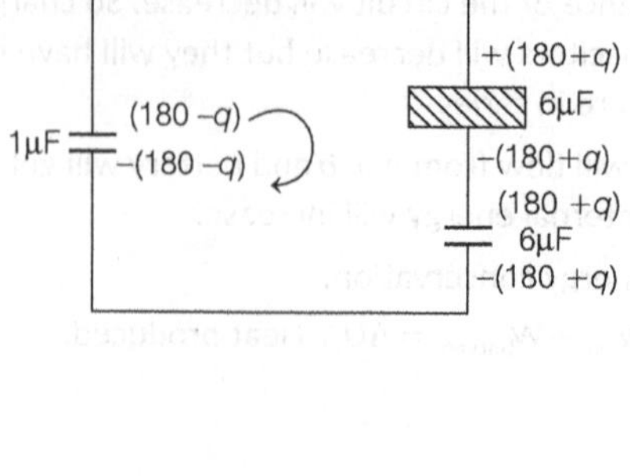

Applying KVL,

$$+\frac{180-q}{1}-\frac{180+q}{6}-\frac{180+q}{6}=0$$

$$\Rightarrow \quad 540-3q=180+q \quad \Rightarrow \quad q=90\,\mu C$$

Charge on capacitor, $B=180+90=270\,\mu C$

12.

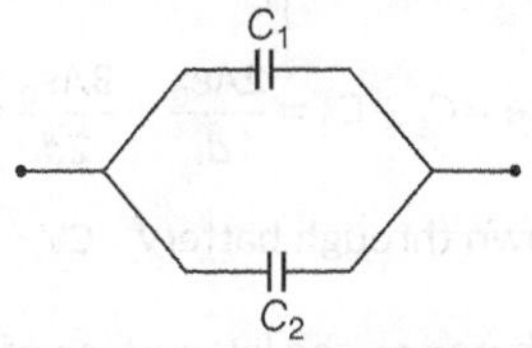

$$C_1=\frac{2\pi\varepsilon_0 ab}{b-a},\quad C_2=\frac{K(2\pi\varepsilon_0)ab}{b-a}$$

$$C_{eq}=C_1+C_2=\frac{2\pi\varepsilon_0(K+1)\,ab}{b-a}$$

13. Let charges on upper half and lower half be q_1 and q_2 respectively.

$$q_1+q_2=Q \quad \text{and} \quad \frac{q_1}{q_2}=\frac{C_1}{C_2}=\frac{1}{K}$$

$$\Rightarrow \quad q_1=\frac{Q}{K+1} \quad \text{and} \quad q_2=\frac{KQ}{K+1}$$

Electric field in the upper half

$$=\frac{1}{2\pi\varepsilon_0}\frac{q_1}{r^2}=\frac{1}{2\pi\varepsilon_0}\frac{Q}{(K+1)r^2}$$

Electric field in the lower half

$$=\frac{1}{2\pi\varepsilon_0 K}\frac{q_2}{r^2}=\frac{1}{2\pi\varepsilon_0}\frac{Q}{(K+1)r^2}$$

14. Surface charge density on the lower half

$$=\frac{q_2}{2\pi r^2}=\frac{KQ/K+1}{2\pi r^2}=\frac{KQ}{2\pi a^2(K+1)}$$

15.

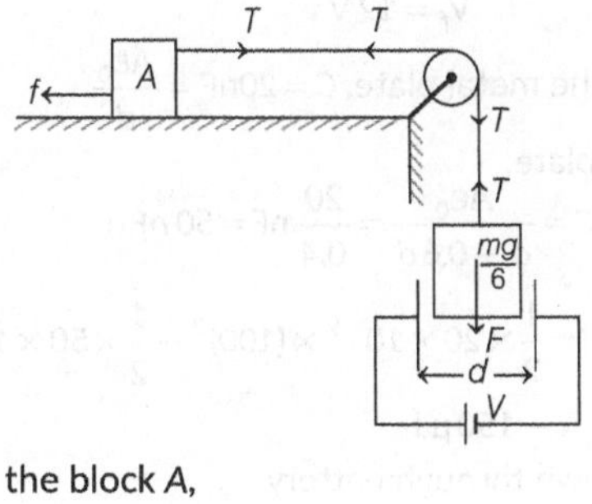

To move the block A,

$$F+\frac{mg}{6}\geq f_L$$

$$\Rightarrow \quad \frac{1}{2}\frac{l\varepsilon_0 V^2(K-1)}{d}+\frac{mg}{6}\geq\frac{1}{4}mg$$

$$\Rightarrow \quad \frac{1}{2}\frac{l\varepsilon_0 V^2(K-1)}{d}\geq\frac{mg}{4}-\frac{mg}{6}$$

$$\Rightarrow \quad V\geq\sqrt{\frac{mgd}{6\varepsilon_0 l(K-1)}}$$

$$\Rightarrow \quad V_{min}=\sqrt{\frac{mgd}{6\varepsilon_0 l(K-1)}}$$

16. If $V=2V_{min}$, then $F=\frac{1}{2}\frac{l\varepsilon_0(K-1)}{d}\left[2\sqrt{\frac{mgd}{6\varepsilon_0 l(K-1)}}\right]^2$

$$\Rightarrow \quad F=\frac{mg}{3}$$

$$a=\frac{\frac{mg}{6}+F-\frac{1}{4}mg}{m+\frac{m}{6}}=\frac{3g}{14}$$

For block A,

$$v^2=u^2+2as$$

$$\Rightarrow \quad v^2=0^2+2\left(\frac{3g}{14}\right)(l-b)$$

$$\Rightarrow \quad v=\sqrt{\frac{3g}{7}(l-b)}$$

Match the Columns Questions

1. (a) When dielectric is inserted while battery remains connected, capacitance increases. Since $q=CV$, charge will increase.

$U=\frac{1}{2}CV^2$, energy stored increases.

Capacitor will pull the slab into it. So, work done by external agent will be negative for slowly inserting the slab.

Electric field will be constant.

$$E=\frac{V}{d}$$

(b) When dielectric is removed while battery is not present, capacitance decreases and charge on the capacitor doesn't change.

Electric field will increase.

Energy stored $=\frac{q^2}{2C}$

Since, $q=$ constant and capacitance decreases, energy stored increases.

For the external agent, force applied and displacement of slab are in the same direction. So, work done by external agent is positive.

(c) Due to decrease in separation between plates, capacitance increases.

$E=\frac{V}{d}$, since battery is connected, V is constant and due to decrease in d, electric field will increase.

$q=CV$, charge will increase.

$U=\frac{1}{2}CV^2$; Energy stored will increase.

Plates attract each other. So, work done by external agent will be negative.

(d) $C = \frac{A\varepsilon_0}{d}$

Since, separation is increased, capacitance decreases. Charge will not change as battery is not present.

$E = \frac{Q}{A\varepsilon_0} \Rightarrow$ Electric field doesn't change.

$U = \frac{Q^2}{2C} \Rightarrow$ Energy stored increases as capacitance decreases.

Work done by external agent will be positive as force applied and displacement are in the same direction.

2. (a) Step (a) $\Rightarrow$ Capacitor connected across battery

Step (d) $\Rightarrow$ Separation is doubled, so capacitance becomes $\frac{C_0}{2}$ and charge on capacitor $Q = \left(\frac{C_0}{2}\right)V_0$.

Step (c) $\Rightarrow$ Capacitor is disconnected from battery.

Step (b) $\Rightarrow C = \frac{A\varepsilon_0}{d + \frac{d}{K}} = \frac{K}{K+1}\frac{A\varepsilon_0}{d} = \frac{KC_0}{K+1}$

$$Q = \frac{C_0V_0}{2}$$

and $$V = \frac{Q}{C} = \frac{\frac{C_0V_0}{2}}{\frac{KC_0}{K+1}} = \frac{(K+1)V_0}{2K}$$

(b) Step (d) $\Rightarrow$ Separation is doubled.

Step (a) $\Rightarrow Q = \left(\frac{C_0}{2}\right)V_0$

Step (c) $\Rightarrow$ Battery disconnected.

Step (b) $\Rightarrow$ Dielectric inserted

$$C = \frac{KC_0}{K+1}, Q = \frac{C_0V_0}{2}$$

and $$V = \frac{Q}{C} = \frac{(K+1)V_0}{2K}$$

(c) Step (b) $\Rightarrow$ Dielectric inserted

Step (a) $\Rightarrow$ Battery is connected

$\Rightarrow Q = KC_0V_0$

Step (c) $\Rightarrow$ Battery disconnected.

Step (d) $\Rightarrow$ Separation between plates is doubled.

$$C = \frac{KC_0}{K+1}, Q = KC_0V_0 \text{ and } V = \frac{Q}{C} = (K+1)V_0$$

(d) Step (a) $\Rightarrow$ Battery is connected.

Step (b) $\Rightarrow Q = KC_0V_0$

Step (d) $\Rightarrow$ Separation is doubled.

$$C = \frac{KC_0}{K+1} \text{ and } Q = \frac{KC_0V_0}{K+1}$$

$$V = V_0$$

Step (c) $\Rightarrow$ Battery is disconnected.

3.

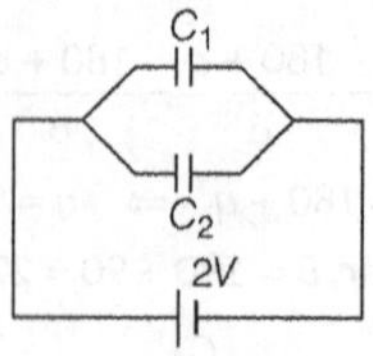

(a) Capacitance $= C_1 + C_2 = \frac{2A\varepsilon_0}{d} + \frac{3A\varepsilon_0}{2d} = \frac{7A\varepsilon_0}{2d}$

(b) Charge flown through battery $= CV = \left(\frac{7A\varepsilon_0}{2d}\right)(2) = \frac{7A\varepsilon_0}{d}$

(c) Induced charge on the left surface of slab of thickness d

$$= q_1\left(1 - \frac{1}{\varepsilon_{r_1}}\right) = C_1V\left(1 - \frac{1}{\varepsilon_{r_1}}\right)$$

$$= \left(\frac{2A\varepsilon_0}{d}\right)(2)\left(1 - \frac{1}{2}\right) = \frac{2A\varepsilon_0}{d}$$

(d) Energy stored $= \frac{1}{2}CV^2 = \frac{1}{2}\left(\frac{7A\varepsilon_0}{2d}\right)(2)^2 = \frac{7A\varepsilon_0}{d}$

Numerical Value Questions

1.

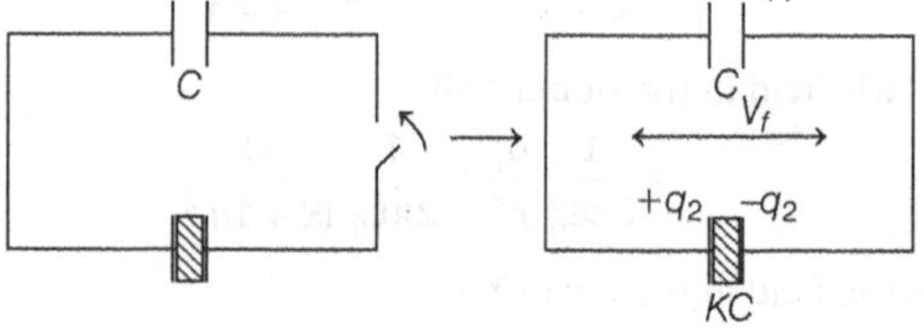

From charge conservation,

$$q = q_1 + q_2$$

$\Rightarrow \quad C(156) = CV_f + KCV_f$

$\Rightarrow \quad C(156) = CV_f + (\alpha V_f)CV_f$

$\Rightarrow \quad V_f^2 + V_f - 156 = 0$

$\Rightarrow \quad V_f = 12\text{ V}$

2. Without the metal plate, $C = 20\text{nF} = \frac{A\varepsilon_0}{d}$

With the plate;

$$C = \frac{A\varepsilon_0}{d - 0.6d} = \frac{20}{0.4}\text{nF} = 50\text{ nF}$$

$$\Delta U = \frac{1}{2} \times 20 \times 10^{-9} \times (100)^2 - \frac{1}{2} \times 50 \times 10^{-9} \times (100)^2$$

$$= -150\,\mu\text{J}$$

Charge flown through battery

$$= 20 \times 10^{-9} \times 100 - 50 \times 10^{-9} \times 100$$

$$= -30 \times 10^{-7}\text{ C}$$

Work done by battery $= q\varepsilon = -30 \times 10^{-7} \times 100 = -300\,\mu\text{J}$

From energy conservation,

$$W_{battery} + W_{ext} = \Delta U$$

$\Rightarrow \quad -300 + W_{ext} = -150$

$\Rightarrow \quad W_{ext} = 150\,\mu\text{J}$

3. $C = C_1 + C_2 = \dfrac{1\left(\dfrac{R^2\theta}{2}\right)\varepsilon_0}{d} + \dfrac{K\left(\dfrac{R^2(\pi-\theta)}{2}\right)\varepsilon_0}{d}$

$$= \frac{\varepsilon_0 R^2}{2d}(\pi K + (1-K)\theta)$$

Energy stored $= \dfrac{1}{2}CV^2 = \dfrac{\varepsilon_0 R^2 V^2}{4d}[\pi K + (1-K)\theta]$

$$\tau = -\frac{dU}{d\theta} = -\frac{\varepsilon_0 R^2 V^2}{4d}(1-K) = \frac{(K-1)\varepsilon_0 R^2 V^2}{4d}$$

So, $n = 4$

4. $C = C_1 + C_2 = \dfrac{2\pi\varepsilon_0\varepsilon_r h}{\ln\left(\dfrac{b}{a}\right)} + \dfrac{2\pi\varepsilon_0(L-h)}{\ln\left(\dfrac{b}{a}\right)} = \dfrac{2\pi\varepsilon_0}{\ln\left(\dfrac{b}{a}\right)}[L + (\varepsilon_r - 1)h]$

$$U = \frac{1}{2}CV^2 = \frac{\pi\varepsilon_0 V^2}{\ln\left(\dfrac{b}{a}\right)}[L + (\varepsilon_r - 1)h]$$

$$F = -\frac{dU}{dh} = -\frac{\pi\varepsilon_0 V^2}{\ln\left(\dfrac{b}{a}\right)}(\varepsilon_r - 1)$$

In equilibrium, $F = mg$

$$\Rightarrow \frac{\pi\varepsilon_0 V^2}{\ln\left(\dfrac{b}{a}\right)}(\varepsilon_r - 1) = [\rho_m \pi(b^2 - a^2)h]g$$

$$\Rightarrow \quad \varepsilon_r = 1 + \frac{\rho_m(b^2 - a^2)hg\ln\left(\dfrac{b}{a}\right)}{\varepsilon_0 V^2}$$

$$\Rightarrow \varepsilon_r = 1 + \frac{1000[(1.5)^2 - (0.5)^2]\times 10^{-6}\times 3.29\times 10^{-2}\times 10\times 1.1}{8.85\times 10^{-12}\times(1000)^2}$$

$$= 82.78$$

5. Consider the coordinate axes as shown in the figure. Equation of parabola, $x^2 = ay$

Now, consider an elementary capacitor at a distance x from the axis of parabola as shown.

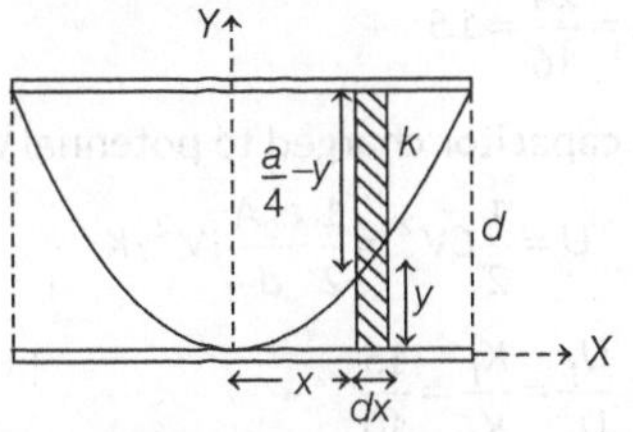

Then, the capacitance of this elementary capacitor will be

$$dC = \frac{\varepsilon_0 a dx}{\dfrac{a}{4} + \dfrac{1}{K}\left(\dfrac{a}{4} - y\right)} = \frac{\varepsilon_0 a dx}{\dfrac{a}{4K} + \left(1 - \dfrac{1}{K}\right)y}$$

$$\int dC = \int_{-\frac{a}{2}}^{\frac{a}{2}} \frac{\varepsilon_0 a dx}{\dfrac{a}{4K} + \left(1 - \dfrac{1}{K}\right)\dfrac{x^2}{a}}$$

$$\Rightarrow \quad C = \frac{2\varepsilon_0 a^2 K}{K-1}\int_0^{\frac{a}{2}} \frac{dx}{x^2 + \left(\dfrac{a}{2\sqrt{K-1}}\right)^2}$$

$$\Rightarrow \quad C = \frac{4\varepsilon_0 aK}{\sqrt{K-1}}\tan^{-1}(\sqrt{K-1})$$

$$= \frac{4\varepsilon_0(6\times 10^{-2})(2)}{\sqrt{2-1}}\tan^{-1}(\sqrt{2}-1) = 4\pi\varepsilon_0(3)\times 10^{-2}\text{ F}$$

So, $N = 3$

Previous Year's Questions

JEE Main

1. As battery remains connected potential difference between plates remains same before and after insertion of dielectric. Capacitance before insertion is,

$$C_1 = \frac{\varepsilon_0 A}{d}$$

Capacity after insertion of dielectric is,

$$C_2 = \frac{\varepsilon_0 A}{\left(d - t + \dfrac{t}{K}\right)}$$

As charge stored is $Q = CV$

$\therefore$ Charge before insertion of dielectric

$$Q_1 = C_1 V = \frac{\varepsilon_0 A}{d}\cdot V$$

and charge after introduction of dielectric

$$Q_2 = C_2 V = \frac{\varepsilon_0 AV}{\left(d - t + \dfrac{t}{K}\right)}$$

Now given, $Q_2 = \dfrac{125}{100}Q_1$

$$\Rightarrow \quad \frac{\varepsilon_0 AV}{\left(d - t + \dfrac{t}{K}\right)} = \frac{125}{100}\frac{\varepsilon_0 AV}{d}$$

$$\Rightarrow \quad 125\left(d - t + \frac{t}{K}\right) = 100d$$

$$\Rightarrow \quad 125\left(3 + \frac{2}{K}\right) = 100\times 5$$

$$\Rightarrow \quad K = 2$$

2. Given, dielectric constant for metallic sheet, $k = \infty$

Thickness of (metallic plate), $t = \dfrac{2d}{3}$

Distance between two plates of capacitor $= d$

According to question, $C_1 = \dfrac{\varepsilon_0 A}{d}$

$$C_2 = \frac{\varepsilon_0 A}{d - t + \dfrac{t}{k}} = \frac{\varepsilon_0 A}{d - \dfrac{2d}{3} + 0} = 3C_1$$

$\Rightarrow \quad \dfrac{C_2}{C_1} = 3$

3. Initially, capacity of capacitor,

$$C = \frac{\varepsilon_0 A}{d} = 15 \text{ pF} \quad \text{[Given]}$$

When separation is doubled and space is filled with dielectric $K = 3.5$, capacity of capacitor becomes

$$C' = \frac{\varepsilon_0 KA}{2d} = \frac{K}{2}\left(\frac{\varepsilon_0 A}{d}\right)$$

$$= \frac{3.5}{2} \times 15 \text{ pF} = \frac{105}{4} \text{ pF}$$

4. Given, situations in question are as follows

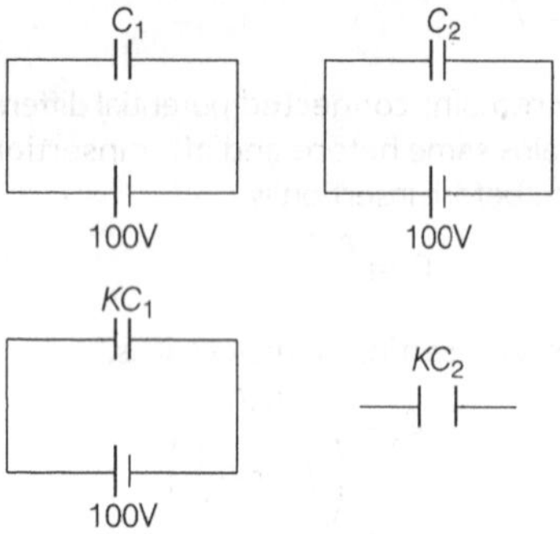

$$Q_1 = KC_1 \times 100 = 10 \times 10 \times 10^{-6} \times 100$$

$$Q_1 = 1000 \,\mu\text{C}$$

$$Q_2 = 100 \times 10^{-6} = 100 \,\mu\text{C} \quad \text{(As isolated capacitor)}$$

Now, both capacitors are joined together as

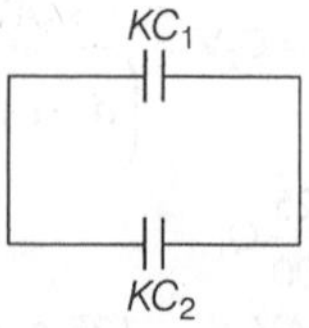

$$V_{\text{common}} = \frac{Q_1 + Q_2}{C_1' + C_2'} = \frac{(1000 + 100)\,\mu\text{C}}{(10 + 10)\,\mu\text{F}} = \frac{1100}{20} \text{ V}$$

$$V_{\text{common}} = 55 \text{ V}$$

5. Initial capacitance

$$C_1 = \frac{\varepsilon_0 A}{d} \quad \text{...(i)}$$

When dielectric material of dielectric constant ($K = 3$) is filled in half the space i.e. $t = d/2$, then new capacitance

$$C_2 = \frac{\varepsilon_0 A}{(d - t) + \left(\frac{t}{K}\right)} = \frac{\varepsilon_0 A}{\left(d - \frac{d}{2}\right) + \left(\frac{d/2}{K}\right)}$$

$$= \frac{\varepsilon_0 A}{\frac{d}{2} + \frac{d}{2K}} = \frac{\varepsilon_0 A}{d\left(\frac{1}{2} + \frac{1}{2K}\right)} = \frac{C_1}{\frac{1}{2} + \frac{1}{2K}} \quad \text{[Using Eq. (i)]}$$

$$= \frac{4}{\frac{1}{2} + \frac{1}{2 \times 3}} = \frac{4}{4/6} = 6 \,\mu\text{F}$$

6. Initial capacitance of parallel plate capacitor

$$C = \frac{\varepsilon_0 A}{d} \quad \text{...(i)}$$

Dielectric constant of metal sheet, $K = \infty$, when a metal sheet of thickness $t = \dfrac{d}{2}$ is introduced between the plates of capacitor, then new capacitance,

$$C' = \frac{\varepsilon_0 A}{(d - t) + \frac{t}{K}} = \frac{\varepsilon_0 A}{\left(d - \frac{d}{2}\right) + \frac{d/2}{\infty}} = \frac{\varepsilon_0 A}{d/2 + 0}$$

$$\Rightarrow \quad C' = \frac{2\varepsilon_0 A}{d}$$

$$\Rightarrow \quad C' = 2C \quad \text{[from Eq. (i)]}$$

$$\Rightarrow \quad \frac{C'}{C} = \frac{2}{1} \quad \Rightarrow \quad C' : C = 2 : 1$$

7. According to first condition,

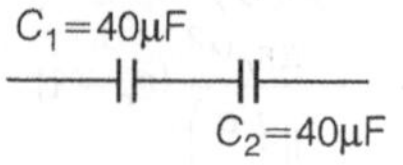

Equivalent capacitance,

$$C = \frac{C_1 \times C_2}{C_1 + C_2} = \frac{40 \times 40}{40 + 40} = 20 \,\mu\text{F}$$

When the space between the one of the capacitor is filled dielectric material of dielectric constant K then.

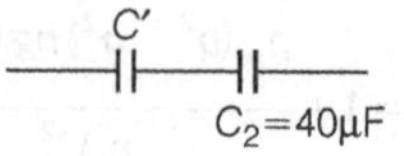

$$C' = C_1 K = K \times 40 \mu\text{F} = 40 K\mu\text{F}$$

$\therefore$ Equivalent capacitance,

$$C'' = \frac{C' \times C_2}{C' + C_2}$$

$$\Rightarrow \quad 24 = \frac{40K \times 40}{40K + 40} \Rightarrow 24 = \frac{40K}{K + 1}$$

$$\Rightarrow 24K + 24 = 40K \quad \Rightarrow \quad 24 = 16K$$

$$\Rightarrow \quad K = \frac{24}{16} = 1.5$$

8. Energy of a capacitor charged to potential V,

$$U = \frac{1}{2} CV^2 = \frac{1}{2} \frac{\varepsilon_0 A}{d} \cdot V^2 \cdot K \quad \left[\because C = \frac{\varepsilon_0 KA}{d}\right]$$

$$\Rightarrow \quad \frac{U_f}{U_i} = \frac{K_f}{K_i} = \frac{15}{10}$$

(as all other parameters remain constant)

Percentage change in energy,

$$\frac{U_f - U_i}{U_i} \times 100 = \frac{K_f - K_i}{K_i} \times 100 = \left[\frac{K_f}{K_i} - 1\right] \times 100$$

$$= \left[\frac{15}{10} - 1\right] \times 100$$

$$= \frac{15 - 10}{10} \times 100 = 50\%$$

9. According to the question,

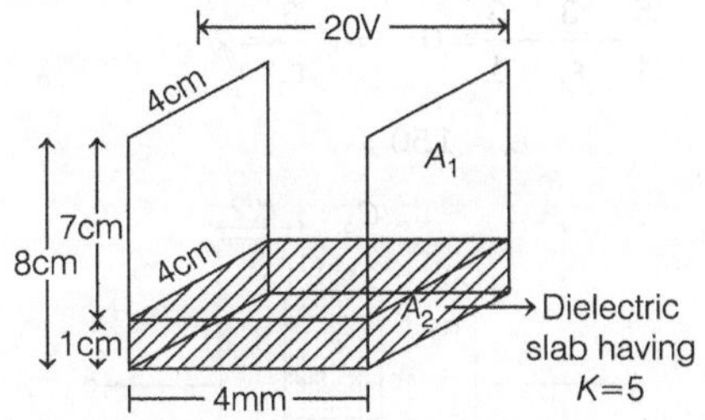

The above situation is a parallel combination of two capacitors,

$\therefore \quad C_{\text{equivalent}} = C_1 + C_2$

$$C_{\text{equivalent}} = \frac{\varepsilon_0 A_1}{d} + \frac{K\varepsilon_0 A_2}{d} \quad \text{...(i)}$$

(Since, on inserting dielectric the capacitance increases K times)

But, $A_1 = (7 \times 4)\text{ cm}^2 = 28 \times 10^{-4}\text{ m}^2$

and $A_2 = (1 \times 4)\text{ cm}^2 = 4 \times 10^{-4}\text{ m}^2$

$\therefore$ On putting these values in Eq. (i), we get

$$C_{\text{equivalent}} = \frac{\varepsilon_0}{d}[A_1 + A_2 K]$$

$$= \frac{\varepsilon_0}{4 \times 10^{-3}}[(28 \times 10^{-4}) + (4 \times 10^{-4} \times 5)]$$

$$C_{\text{equivalent}} = \frac{\varepsilon_0}{4 \times 10^{-3}}[48 \times 10^{-4}] = 12 \times 10^{-1}\,\varepsilon_0$$

$\therefore$ The electrostatic energy of this system,

$$= \frac{1}{2}C_{\text{equivalent}}V^2 = \frac{1}{2} \times 12 \times 10^{-1} \times 20^2\,\varepsilon_0$$

$$= \frac{1}{2} \times 12 \times 10^{-1} \times 400\,\varepsilon_0$$

$$= 24 \times 10\varepsilon_0 = 240\varepsilon_0$$

10. Total charge on both capacitors,

$$Q = Q_1 + Q_2 = C_1V + C_2V$$

$$= 2CV + CV = 3CV$$

$\Rightarrow \quad Q = 3CV$

When dielectric material is filled within the capacitor of capacitance C after removing the battery, then its charge will remain same but its capacitance becomes KC.

Now, potential difference across the capacitors will be common potential given as

$$V_C = \frac{Q}{KC + 2C} = \frac{3CV}{C(K+2)} = \frac{3V}{K+2}$$

11. As we know, the expression of the capacitor with dielectric constant

$$C = \frac{A\varepsilon_0}{\left(d - t + \frac{t}{K}\right)}$$

$$\Rightarrow \quad C = \frac{100 \times 8.85 \times 10^{-12}}{\left(10 - 5 + \frac{5}{10}\right)}$$

$$\Rightarrow \quad C = 161 \times 10^{-12}\text{ F} = 161\text{ pF}$$

12. Let the potential be V.

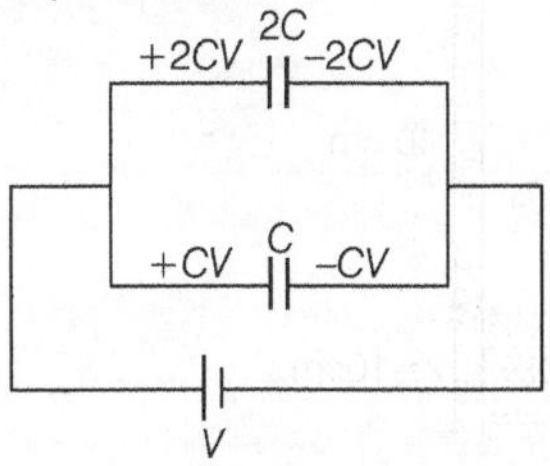

and

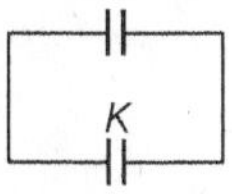

$$V_C = \frac{Q_1 + Q_2}{C_1 + C_2} = \frac{2CV + CV}{KC + 2C}$$

$$\therefore \quad V_C = \frac{3CV}{(K+2)C} = \frac{3V}{K+2}$$

13. The value of C_1, C_2 and C_3 can be given as

$$C_1 = \frac{K\varepsilon_0 A}{d}, C_2 = \frac{3K\varepsilon_0 A}{2d}, C_3 = \frac{5K\varepsilon_0 A}{3d}$$

$\because$ In the above figure, we can see that C_1, C_2 and C_3 are in series combination.

$$\Rightarrow \quad \frac{1}{C_{eq}} = \frac{1}{C_1} + \frac{1}{C_2} + \frac{1}{C_3}$$

$$\Rightarrow \quad \frac{1}{C_{eq}} = \frac{1}{\frac{K\varepsilon_0 A}{d}} + \frac{1}{\frac{3K\varepsilon_0 A}{2d}} + \frac{1}{\frac{5K\varepsilon_0 A}{3d}}$$

$$\Rightarrow \quad \frac{1}{C_{eq}} = \frac{d}{K\varepsilon_0 A} + \frac{2d}{3K\varepsilon_0 A} + \frac{3d}{5K\varepsilon_0 A}$$

$$\Rightarrow \quad \frac{1}{C_{eq}} = \frac{d}{K\varepsilon_0 A}\left(1 + \frac{2}{3} + \frac{3}{5}\right)$$

$$\Rightarrow \quad \frac{1}{C_{eq}} = \frac{d}{K\varepsilon_0 A}\left(\frac{15 + 10 + 9}{15}\right)$$

$$\Rightarrow \quad \frac{1}{C_{eq}} = \frac{34d}{15K\varepsilon_0 A}$$

$$\Rightarrow \quad C_{eq} = \frac{15}{34}\left(\frac{K\varepsilon_0 A}{d}\right)$$

14. Given, capacitance of capacitor, $C = 14$ pF

Potential difference, $V = 12$V

Energy of capacitor, $E_i = \frac{1}{2}CV^2$

$$= \frac{1}{2} \times 14 \times 12 \times 12 = 1008\text{ pJ}$$

Now, the charging battery is disconnected and a porcelain plate with $K = 7$ is inserted between the plates

$$\therefore \quad E_f = \frac{E_i}{7} \Rightarrow E_f = \frac{1008}{7}\text{ pJ}$$

$$\Rightarrow \quad E_f = 144\text{ pJ}$$

Mechanical energy with which the plate would oscillate back and forth between the plates will be

$$= (1008 - 144)\text{ pJ} = 864\text{ pJ}$$

JEE Advanced

1. Let container is filled upto height x in 10 s

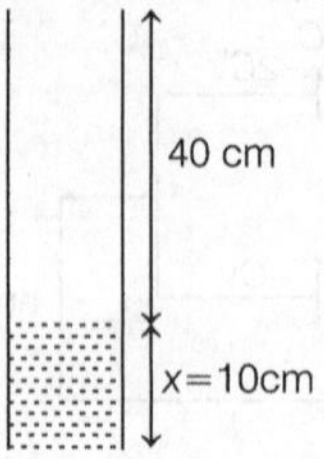

$$250\times10=50\times5\times x$$
$$x=10\text{ cm}$$
$$C=C_1+C_2$$
$$C=\frac{A_1\varepsilon_0}{d}+\frac{KA_2\varepsilon_0}{d}$$
$$C=\frac{9\times10^{-12}}{5\times10^{-2}}[40\times50\times10^{-4}+3\times50\times10\times10^{-4}]$$
$$=63\times10^{-12}\text{F}$$
$$C=63\text{ pF}$$

2.

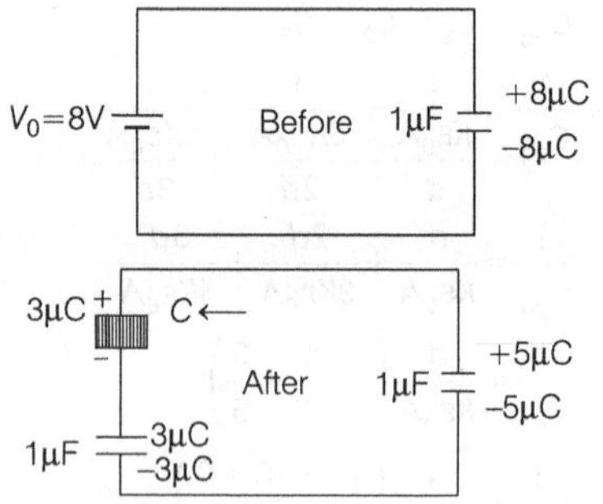

$$C=\varepsilon_r C_1=(\varepsilon_r)\,\mu\text{F}$$

Applying loop rule,

$$\frac{5}{1}-\frac{3}{\varepsilon_r}-\frac{3}{1}=0\Rightarrow\frac{3}{\varepsilon_r}=2$$
$$\varepsilon_r=1.50$$

3.

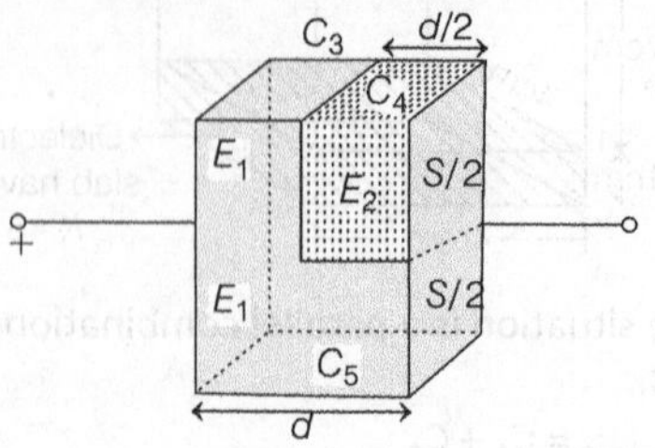

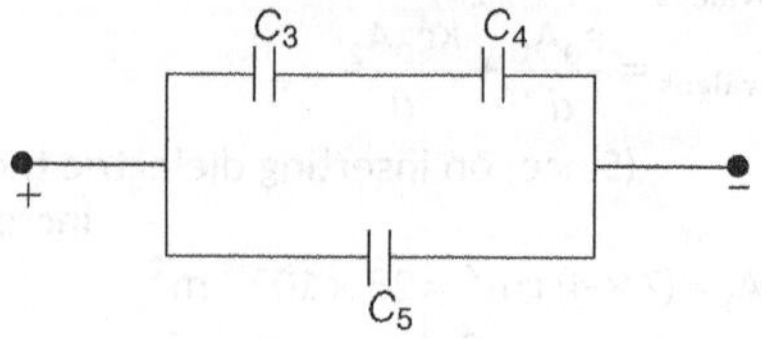

$$C_1=\frac{\varepsilon_0 s}{d},\ C_3=\frac{2\varepsilon_0\frac{s}{2}}{\frac{d}{2}}=\frac{2\varepsilon_0 s}{d}$$

$$\Rightarrow\quad C_4=\frac{4\varepsilon_0\frac{s}{2}}{\frac{d}{2}}=\frac{4\varepsilon_0 s}{d}$$

and $$C_5=\frac{2\varepsilon_0\frac{s}{2}}{d}=\frac{\varepsilon_0 s}{d}$$

$$C_2=\frac{C_3C_4}{C_3+C_4}+C_5=\frac{4}{3}\frac{\varepsilon_0 s}{d}+\frac{\varepsilon_0 s}{d}=\frac{7}{3}\frac{\varepsilon_0 s}{d}=\frac{7}{3}C_1$$

$$\Rightarrow\quad\frac{C_2}{C_1}=\frac{7}{3}$$

CHAPTER-11

R-C CIRCUIT

LEVEL 01 Starter Level

11.1 R-C Circuit at $t = 0$ (Initial State) and $t = \infty$ (Final State)

1 Find out current in the circuit and charge on capacitor which is initially uncharged in the following situations.

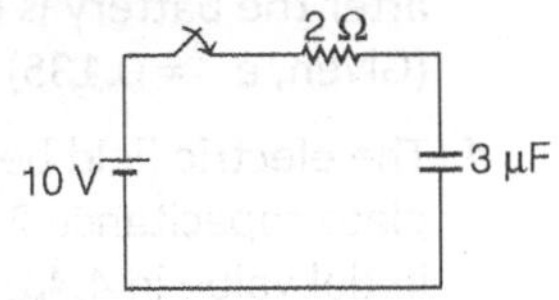

(i) Just after the switch is closed

(ii) After a long time when switch was closed.

2 Find out current i_1, i_2, i_3 and charge on the capacitor in the circuit when it is initially uncharged in the following situations.

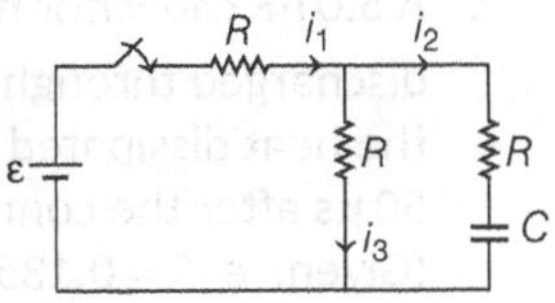

(i) Just after the switch is closed

(ii) After a long time when switch is closed.

3 Find the charge on each capacitor in steady state

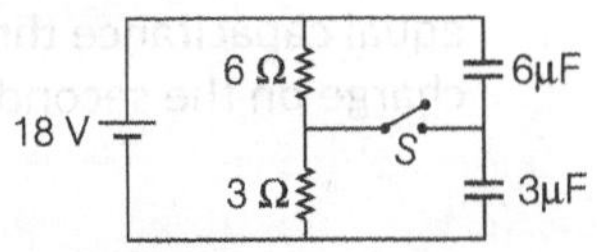

(i) when switch S is open

(ii) when switch S is closed.

4 Find the charge on each capacitor of the given circuit in steady state.

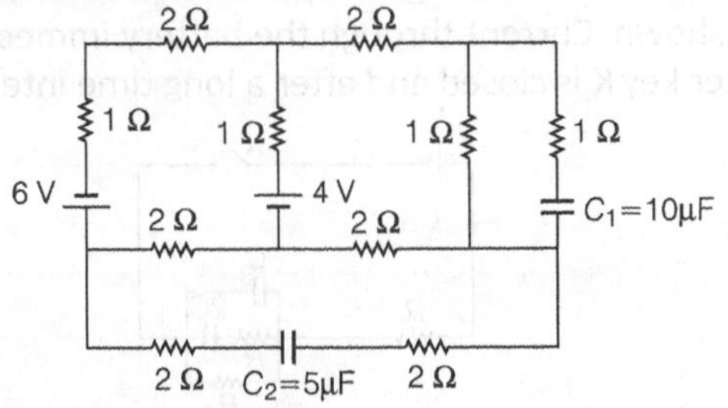

11.2 R-C Series Circuit (Charging)

1 A capacitor of capacitance 10 μF is connected to a battery of emf 2 V. It is found that it takes 50 ms for the charge on the capacitor to become 12.6 μC. Find the resistance of the circuit.

2 A 2 μF capacitor is joined to a battery of emf 50 V through a resistance of 1 kΩ. Find the charge on the capacitor 4 ms after the connections are made.

3 A capacitor is connected to a 12 V battery through a resistance of 10 Ω. It is found that the potential difference across the resistor is 8 V after 1 μs. Find the capacitance of the capacitor.
(Given, $\ln 3 = 1.0986, \ln 2 = 0.693$)

4 A parallel plate capacitor of plate area 40 cm^2 and separation between the plates 0.10 mm is connected to a battery of emf 2.0 V through a 16 Ω resistor. Find the electric field in the capacitor 10 ns after the connections are made.

5 A capacitor of capacitance 12.0 μF is connected to a battery of emf 6.00 V and internal resistance 1.00 Ω through resistanceless leads. 12.0 μs after the connections are made, what will be (i) the current in the circuit, (ii) the power delivered by the battery, (iii) the power dissipated in heat and (iv) the rate at which the energy stored in the capacitor is increasing.

6 How many time constants will elapse before the charge on the capacitor in a charging R-C circuit reaches half of its steady state value?

7 How many time constants will elapse before the energy stored in the capacitor reaches half of its equilibrium value in a charging R-C circuit?

8 How many time constants will elapse before the power delivered by the battery drops to half of its maximum value in an R-C circuit?

9 A capacitor of capacitance C is connected to a battery of emf ε at $t = 0$ through a resistance R. Find the maximum rate at which energy is stored in the capacitor. When does the rate has this maximum value?

10 By evaluating $\int i^2 R dt$, show that when a capacitor is charged by connecting it to a battery through a resistor, the energy dissipated as heat equals the energy stored in the capacitor.

11 A capacitor of capacitance C is given a charge q. At $t = 0$, it is connected to an ideal battery of emf E through a resistance R. Find the charge on the capacitor at time t.

12 Find the charge on each of the capacitors 0.20 ms after the switch S is closed in figure.

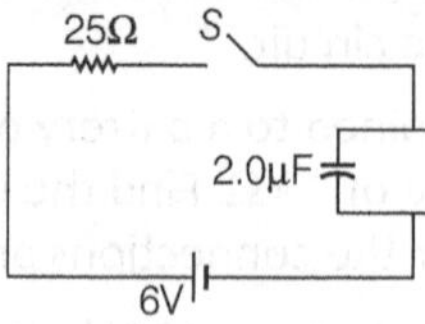

13 Initially, the capacitor is uncharged. Find the charge on capacitor as a function of time, if switch is closed at $t = 0$.

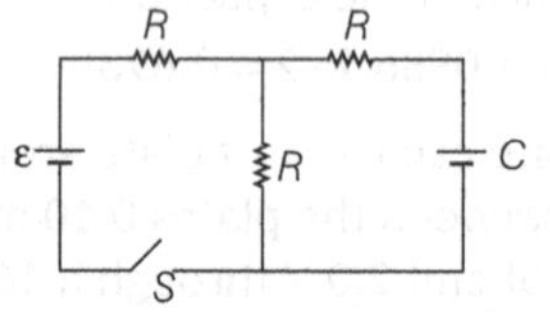

11.3 R-C Circuit (Discharging)

1 The plates of a capacitor of capacitance 10 μF, charged to 60 μC, are joined together by a wire of resistance 10 Ω at $t = 0$. Find the charge on the capacitor in the circuit at
(i) $t = 0$ (ii) $t = 100$ μs
(iii) $t = 200$ μs and (iv) $t = 1.0$ ms.

LEVEL 02 JEE Main Level

Single Choice Correct Questions

1 The magnitude of charge in steady state on either of the plates of condenser C in the adjoining circuit is

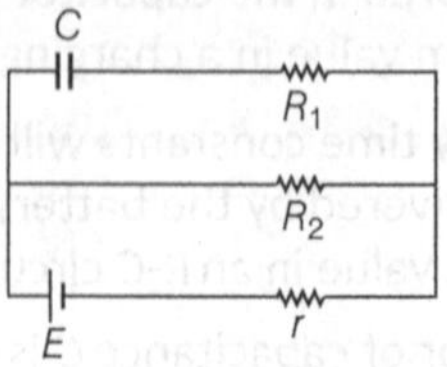

(a) CE (b) $\frac{CER_2}{(R_1 + r)}$

(c) $\frac{CER_2}{(R_2 + r)}$ (d) $\frac{CER_1}{(R_2 + r)}$

2 The switch S shown in figure is kept closed for a long time and is then opened at $t = 0$. Find the current in the middle 10 Ω resistor at $t = 1.0$ ms.

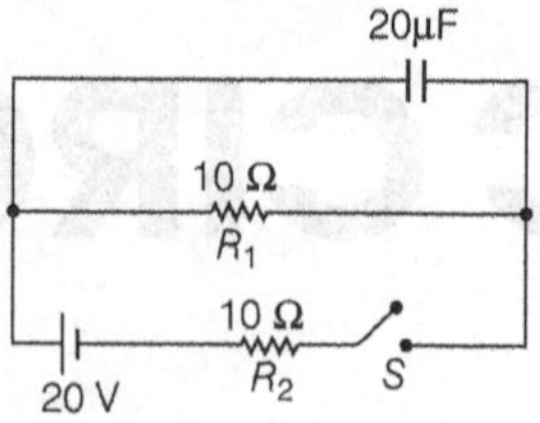

3 A capacitor of capacitance 200μF is connected across a battery of emf 10.0 V through a resistance of 40 kΩ for 16.0 s. The battery is then replaced by a thick wire. What will be the charge on the capacitor 16.0s after the battery is disconnected?
(Given, $e^{-2} = 0.135$)

4 The electric field between the plates of a parallel plate capacitance 2.0μF drops to one-third of its initial value in 4.4μs when the plates are connected by a thin wire. Find the resistance of the wire.
(Given, $\ln 3 = 1.0986$)

5 A 5.0 μF capacitor having a charge of 20 μC is discharged through a wire of resistance 5.0 Ω. Find the heat dissipated in the wire between 25 μs to 50 μs after the connections are made.
(Given, $e^{-2} = 0.135$)

6 A capacitor of capacitance C is given a charge Q. At $t = 0$, it is connected to an uncharged capacitor of equal capacitance through a resistance R. Find the charge on the second capacitor as a function of time.

2 A network of uncharged capacitors and resistances is as shown. Current through the battery immediately after key K is closed and after a long time interval is

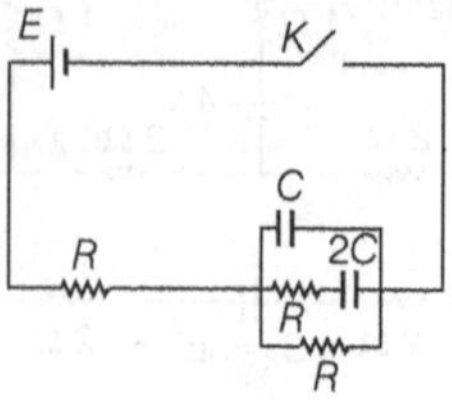

(a) $\frac{E}{R}, \frac{E}{2R}$ (b) $\frac{E}{2R}, \frac{2E}{3R}$

(c) zero, $\frac{E}{R}$ (d) $\frac{2E}{3R}, \frac{E}{R}$

3 The capacitor shown in the figure is in steady state. The energy stored in the capacitor is

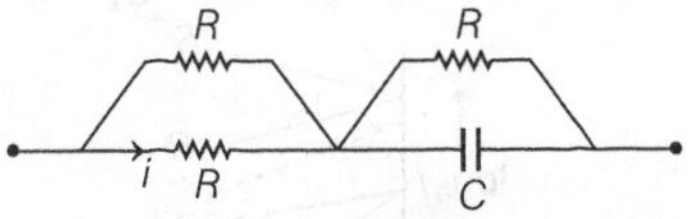

(a) Ci^2R^2 (b) $2Ci^2R^2$
(c) $4Ci^2R^2$ (d) None of these

4 In the given circuit with steady current, the potential drop across the capacitor must be

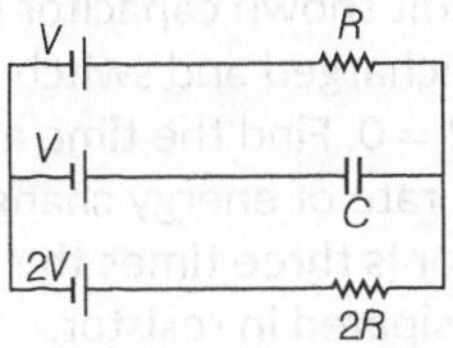

(a) V (b) $\frac{V}{2}$ (c) $\frac{V}{3}$ (d) $\frac{2V}{3}$

5 Ratio of charges on capacitor C_1 after long time when switch S is open and closed respectively, in the given circuit, is

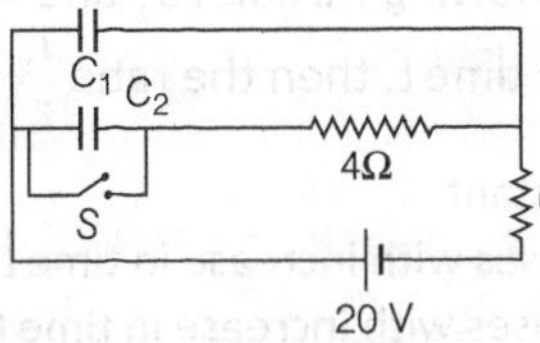

(a) 1 : 1 (b) 1 : 8
(c) 5 : 2 (d) Data insufficient

6 The charge on the capacitor in the steady state in the circuit shown is

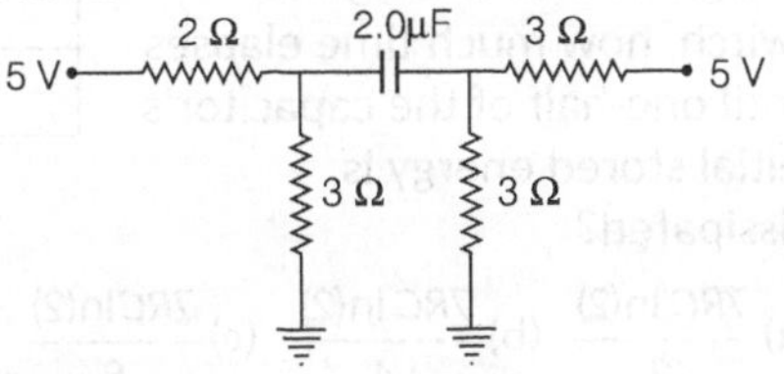

(a) 0.5 μC (b) 1 μC (c) 2 μC (d) 4 μC

7 In the circuit shown, switch S_2 is closed first and is kept closed for a long time. Now, S_1 is closed. Just after that instant, the current through S_1 is

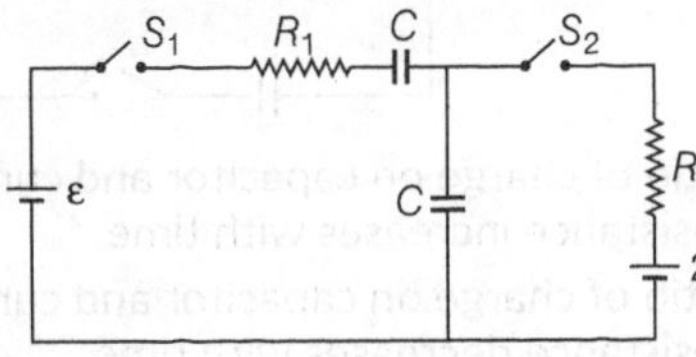

(a) $\frac{\varepsilon}{R_1}$ toward right (b) $\frac{\varepsilon}{R_1}$ toward left
(c) $\frac{2\varepsilon}{R_1}$ (d) zero

8 In the given circuit, the potential difference across the capacitor is 12 V in steady state. Each resistor have 3 Ω resistance. The emf of the ideal battery is

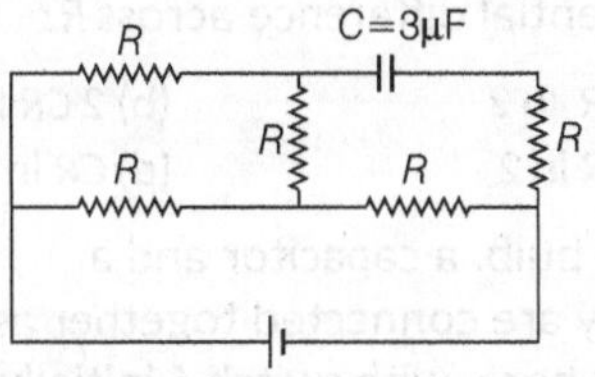

(a) 15 V (b) 9 V (c) 12 V (d) 24 V

9 Initially switch S is connected to position 1 for a long time. The net amount of heat generated in the circuit after it shifted to position 2 is

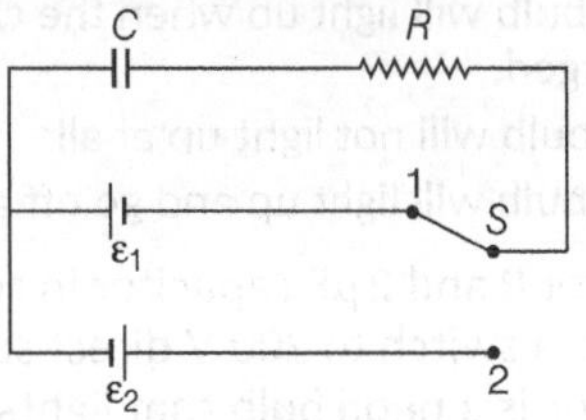

(a) $\frac{C}{2}(\varepsilon_1+\varepsilon_2)\varepsilon_2$ (b) $C(\varepsilon_1+\varepsilon_2)\varepsilon_2$
(c) $\frac{C}{2}(\varepsilon_1+\varepsilon_2)^2$ (d) $C(\varepsilon_1+\varepsilon_2)^2$

10 Heat produced in the circuit shown in the figure when switch is closed, is

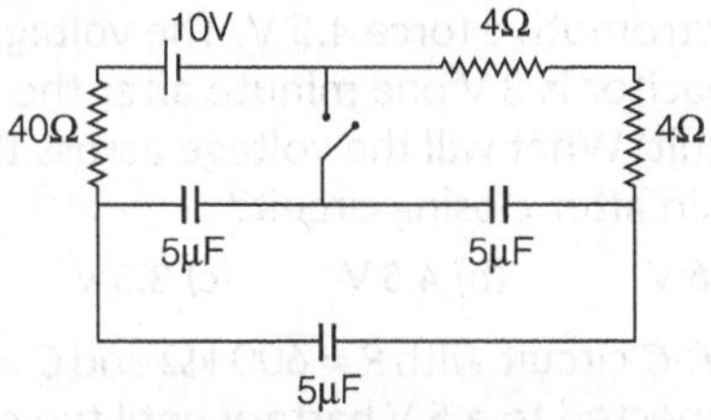

(a) 125 μJ (b) 250 μJ (c) 375 μJ (d) 500 μJ

11 In the circuit, if no current flows through the galvanometer when the key K is closed, the bridge is balanced. The balancing condition for bridge is

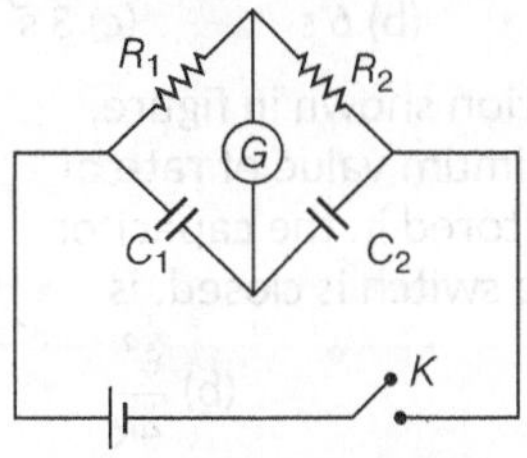

(a) $\frac{C_1}{C_2}=\frac{R_1}{R_2}$ (b) $\frac{C_1}{C_2}=\frac{R_2}{R_1}$
(c) $\frac{C_1^2}{C_2^2}=\frac{R_1^2}{R_2^2}$ (d) $\frac{C_1^2}{C_2^2}=\frac{R_2}{R_1}$

12 In given circuit, switch S is closed at $t = 0$. After what time, voltage across capacitor becomes 7 times of potential difference across R?

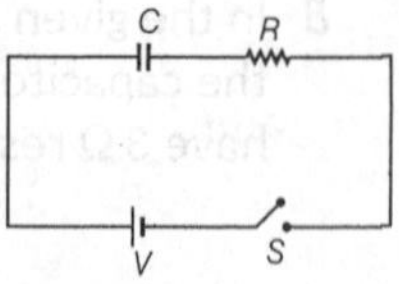

(a) $3\,CR \ln 2$ (b) $2\,CR \ln 2$
(c) $8\,CR \ln 2$ (d) $CR \ln 2$

13 A light bulb, a capacitor and a battery are connected together as shown here, with switch S initially open. When the switch S is closed, which one of the following is true?

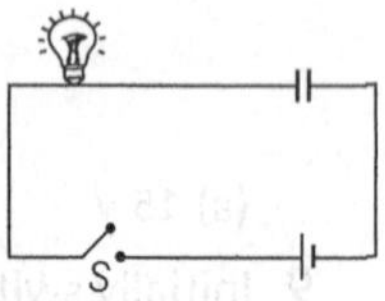

(a) The bulb will light up for some time interval after the capacitor starts charging.
(b) The bulb will light up when the capacitor is fully charged.
(c) The bulb will not light up at all.
(d) The bulb will light up and go off at regular intervals.

14 A resistor R and 2 μF capacitor in series is connected through a switch to 200 V direct supply. Across the capacitor is a neon bulb that lights up at 100 V. Calculate the value of R to make the bulb light up 6.93 s after the switch has been closed.

(a) $5 \times 10^6\ \Omega$ (b) $2 \times 10^7\ \Omega$
(c) $10 \times 10^4\ \Omega$ (d) $2 \times 10^5\ \Omega$

15 An uncharged capacitor and a resistor of big resistance are connected in series to a battery of electromotive force 4.5 V. The voltage across the capacitor is 3 V one minute after the closing the circuit. What will the voltage across the capacitor be 2 min after closing circuit?

(a) 6 V (b) 4.5 V (c) 3.5 V (d) 4 V

16 An R-C circuit with $R = 600\ \text{k}\Omega$ and $C = 10\ \mu\text{F}$, is connected to a 5 V battery until the capacitor is fully charged. Then, the battery is suddenly replaced with a new 3 V battery of opposite polarity. At what time after this replacement will the energy stored in the capacitor be zero? (Given, $e \simeq \frac{8}{3}$)

(a) 12 s (b) 6 s (c) 3 s (d) 1.5 s

17 As situation shown in figure, the maximum value of rate of energy stored in the capacitor after the switch is closed, is

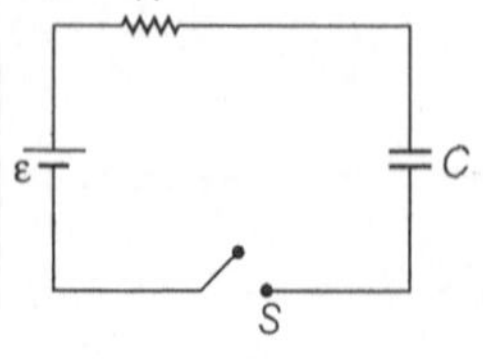

(a) $\frac{\varepsilon^2}{2R}$ (b) $\frac{\varepsilon^2}{4R}$
(c) $\frac{\varepsilon^2}{8R}$ (d) None of these

18 In an R-C circuit while charging, the graph of $\log_e i$ *versus* time is shown by dotted line in the diagram, where i is the current. When the value of the resistance is doubled, which of the solid curves best represents the variation of $\log_e i$ *versus* time?

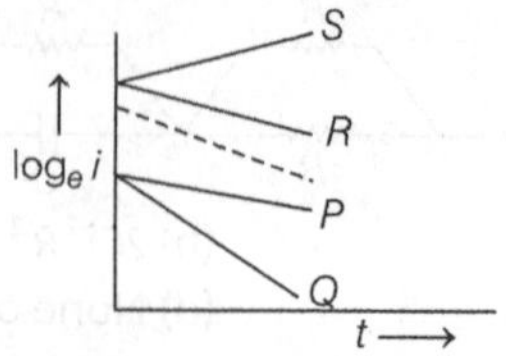

(a) P (b) Q (c) R (d) S

19 In the circuit shown capacitor is initially uncharged and switch is closed at $t = 0$. Find the time at which the rate of energy change in capacitor is three times the power dissipated in resistor.

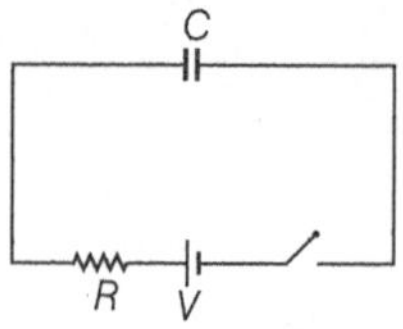

(a) $RC \ln 3$ (b) $2RC \ln 3$ (c) $RC \ln 2$ (d) $2RC \ln 2$

20 In the circuit shown in figure $C_1 = 2C_2$. Switch S is closed at time $t = 0$. Let i_1 and i_2 be the currents flowing through C_1 and C_2 at any time t, then the ratio $\frac{i_1}{i_2}$

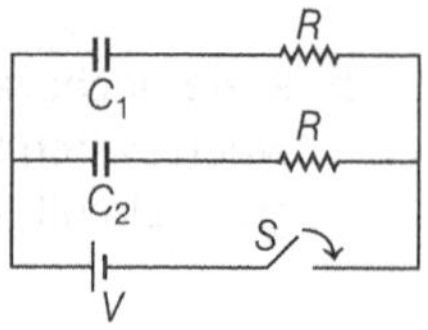

(a) is constant
(b) increases with increase in time t
(c) decreases with increase in time t
(d) first increases then decreases

21 The capacitor in the circuit shown in figure is initially charged. After closing the switch, how much time elapses until one-half of the capacitor's initial stored energy is dissipated?

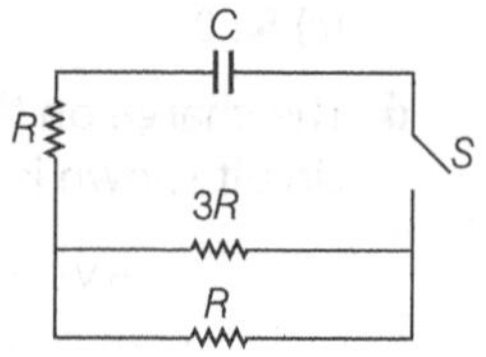

(a) $\frac{7RC \ln(2)}{2}$ (b) $\frac{7RC \ln(2)}{4}$ (c) $\frac{7RC \ln(2)}{8}$ (d) $7RC \ln(2)$

22 In a discharging R-C circuit,

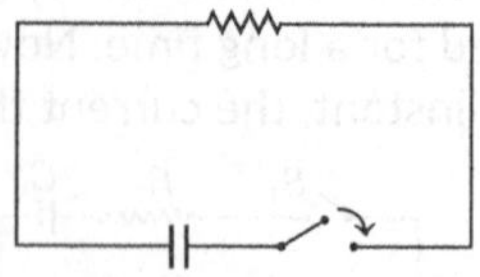

(a) ratio of charge on capacitor and current in resistance increases with time.
(b) ratio of charge on capacitor and current in resistance decreases with time.
(c) ratio of charge on capacitor and current in resistance remains constant.
(d) ratio of charge on capacitor and current in resistance first decreases, then increases with time.

23 A charged capacitor is allowed to discharge through a resistor by closing the key at the instant $t = 0$. At the instant $t = (\ln 4)\,\mu s$, the reading of the ammeter falls half the initial value. The resistance of the ammeter is equal to

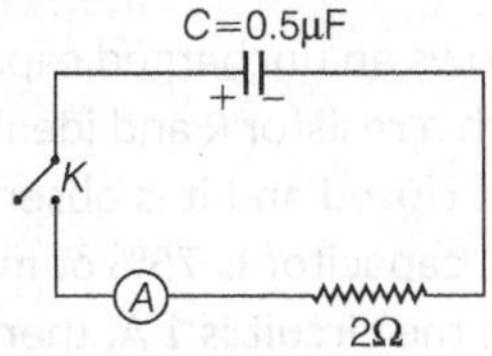

(a) 1Ω (b) 2Ω
(c) 3Ω (d) 4Ω

24 In the R-C circuit shown in the figure, the total energy of 3.6×10^{-3} J is dissipated in the 10Ω resistor when the switch S is closed. The initial charge on the capacitor is

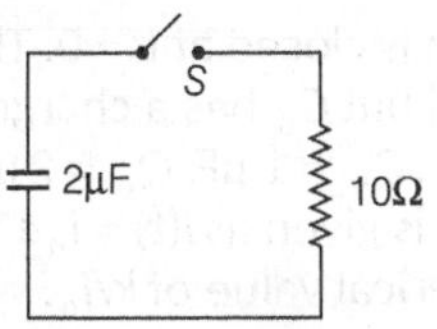

(a) $60\,\mu C$ (b) $60\sqrt{2}\,\mu C$
(c) $\frac{60}{\sqrt{2}}\,\mu C$ (d) $120\,\mu C$

25 Consider the R-C circuit shown below. What combination of values R and C will result in the slowest rate of capacitor discharge when switch S is closed?

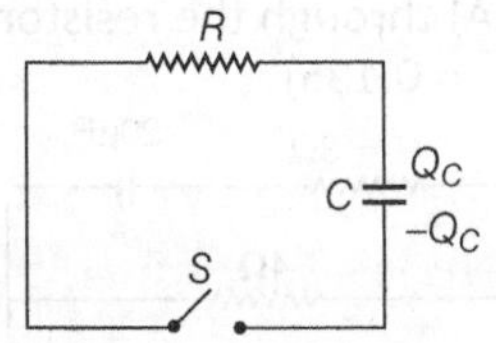

(a) $10\,\Omega$ and $50\,\mu F$ (b) $100\,\Omega$ and $5\,\mu F$
(c) $10\,\Omega$ and $5\,\mu F$ (d) $100\,\Omega$ and $50\,\mu F$

26 The switch S shown in figure is kept closed for a long time and then opened at $t = 0$, then the current in the middle $20\,\Omega$ resistor at $t = 0.25$ ms is

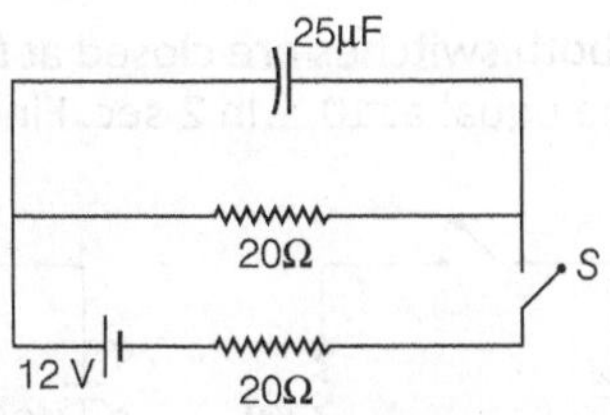

(a) 329 mA (b) 285 mA
(c) 182 mA (d) 28 mA

27 The figure shows an experimental plot for discharging of a capacitor in an R-C circuit. The time constant τ of this circuit lies between

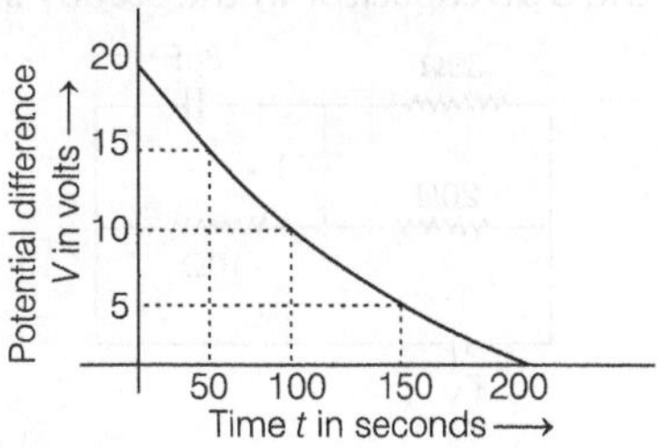

(a) 100 s and 150 s (b) 150 s and 200 s
(c) 0 and 50 s (d) 50 s and 100 s

28 In the transient circuit shown, the time constant of the circuit is

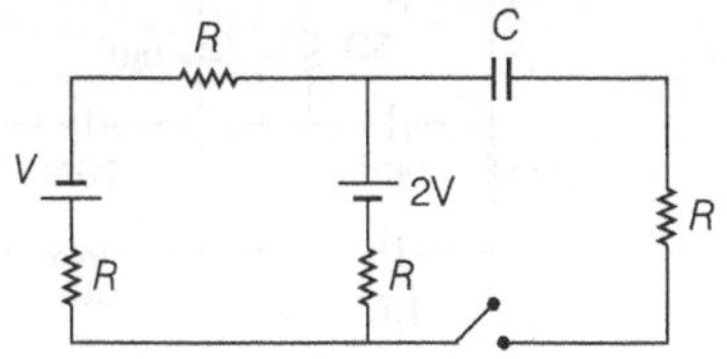

(a) $\frac{5}{3}RC$ (b) $\frac{5}{2}RC$ (c) $\frac{4}{5}RC$ (d) $\frac{7}{5}RC$

29 A capacitor $C = 100\,\mu F$ is connected to three resistors each of resistance $1\,k\Omega$ and a battery of emf 9V. The switch S has been closed for long time so as to charge the capacitor. When switch S is opened, the capacitor discharges with time constant.

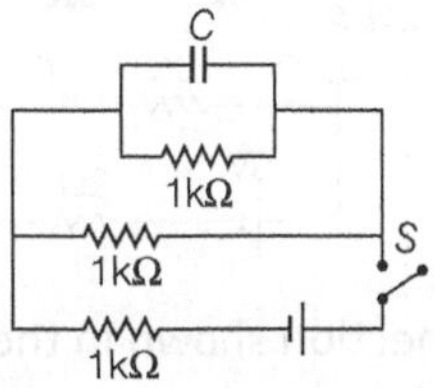

(a) 33 ms (b) 5 ms (c) 3.3 ms (d) 50 ms

30 The switch S in the circuit diagram is closed at $t = 0$. The charge on each capacitor at any time t is

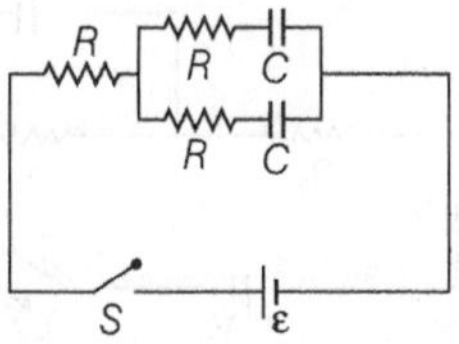

(a) $q = C\varepsilon\left(1 - e^{-\frac{2t}{3RC}}\right)$ (b) $q = C\varepsilon\left(1 - e^{-\frac{t}{2RC}}\right)$
(c) $q = C\varepsilon\left(1 - e^{-\frac{t}{3RC}}\right)$ (d) $q = C\varepsilon\left(1 - e^{-\frac{3t}{2RC}}\right)$

Numerical Value Questions

1 For the circuit shown in the figure, find the charge (in μC) on the 8 μF capacitor in the steady state.

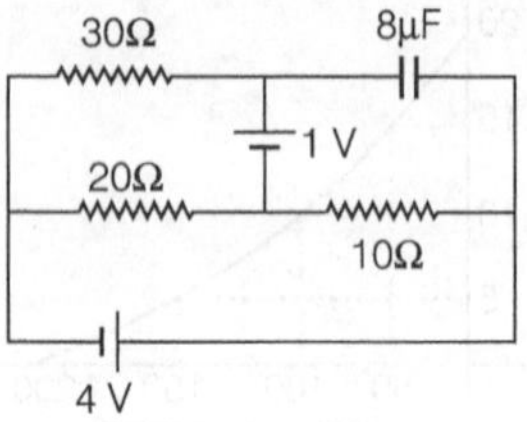

2 The ratio of charges on 5 μF and 10 μF capacitor when circuit is in steady state is $\frac{\alpha}{38}$. Find α.

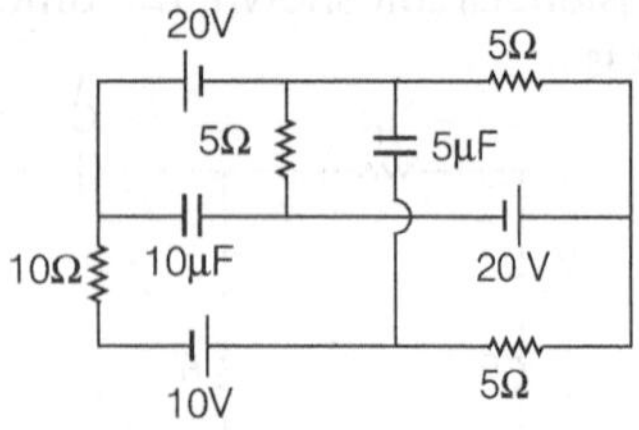

3 The capacitors C_1 and C_2 have capacitances 1 μF and 3 μF respectively in the given circuit. The circuit is in steady state. Find the total energy (in μJ) stored in the capacitors.

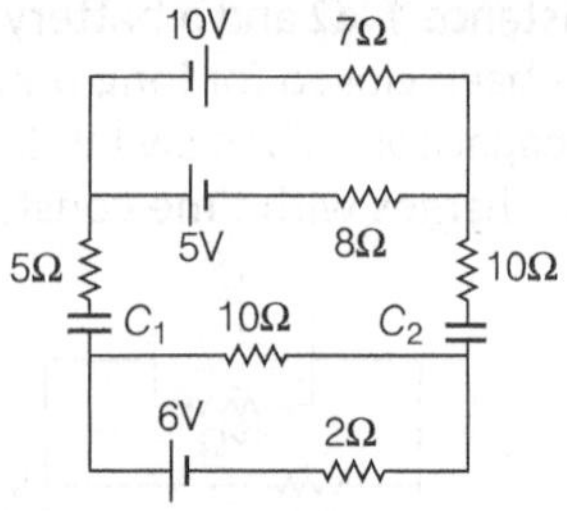

4 In the connection shown in the figure, the switch *K* is open and the capacitor is uncharged. Then, we close the switch and let the capacitor charge up to the maximum and open the switch again. Then,

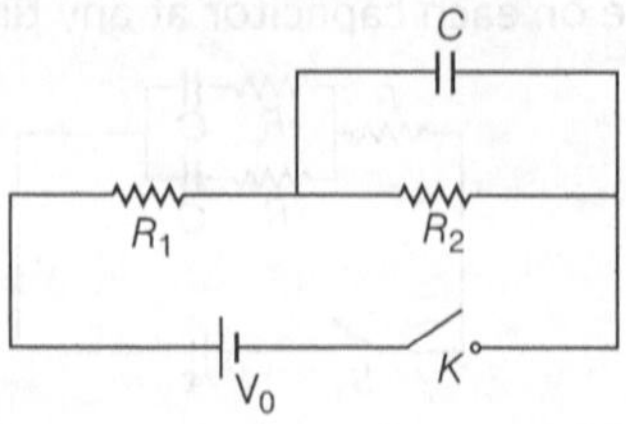

(a) the current through R_1 be i_1 immediately after closing the switch

(b) the current through R_2 be i_2 a long time after the switch was closed

(c) the current through R_2 be i_3 immediately after reopening the switch.

Find $\frac{i_1}{i_2 i_3}$ (in ampere^{-1}) (Use the following data: $V_0 = 30$ V, $R_1 = 10$ kΩ, $R_2 = 5$ kΩ)

5 Figure shows an uncharged capacitor connected in series with a resistor *R* and ideal battery. At $t = 0$, switch *S* is closed and it is observed that when charge on capacitor is 75% of maximum value, then current in the circuit is 1 A, then find the value of *R* (in Ω).

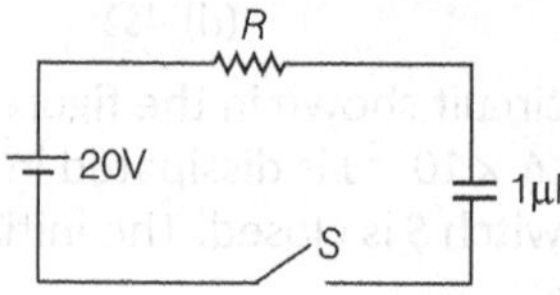

6 The switch is closed at $t = 0$. The capacitor *C* is uncharged but C_0 has a charge Q_0 at $t = 0$. If $R = 100$ Ω, $C = 2$ μF, $C_0 = 1$ μF, $Q_0 = 2$ μC, $E = 4$V. Current in the circuit is given as $i(t) = i_0 e^{-kt}$. Find numerical value of k/I_0.

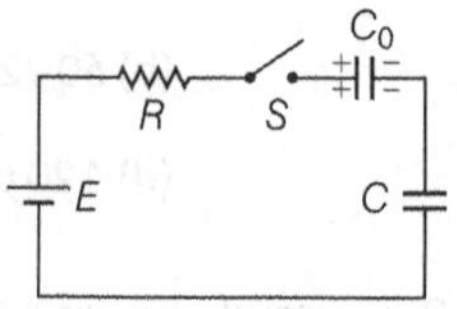

7 In the circuit shown, the switch *S* is closed at $t = 0$. The capacitor is initially uncharged. Then, find the current (in mA) through the resistor $R = 8$ Ω at $t = 0.4$ ms. (Take, $e^{-2} = 0.135$)

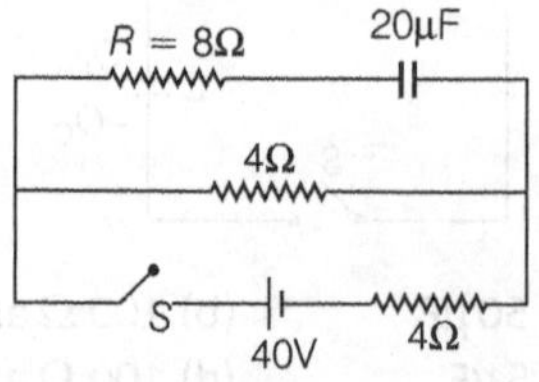

8 The figure shows two circuits with a charged capacitor that is to be discharged through a resistor as shown. The ratio of initial charge on capacitors $\frac{q_2}{q_1} = 2$. If both switches are closed at $t = 0$, the charges become equal at 10^{-4} In 2 sec. Find the resistance *R* (in Ω).

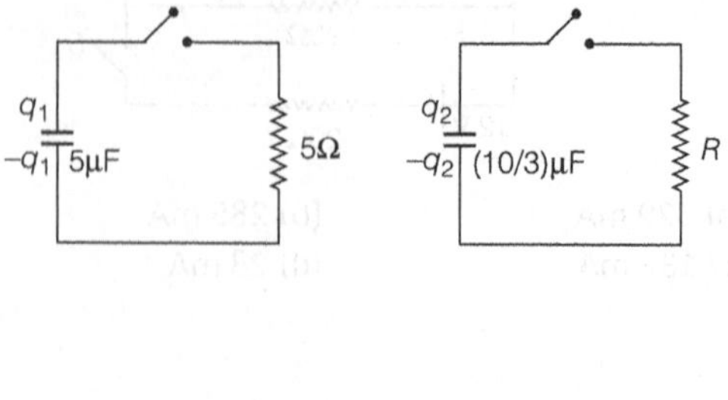

LEVEL 03 JEE Advanced Level

Single Choice Correct Questions

1 The capacitor C shown in figure is charged by closing switch S for a long time. Find the charge on it in steady state.

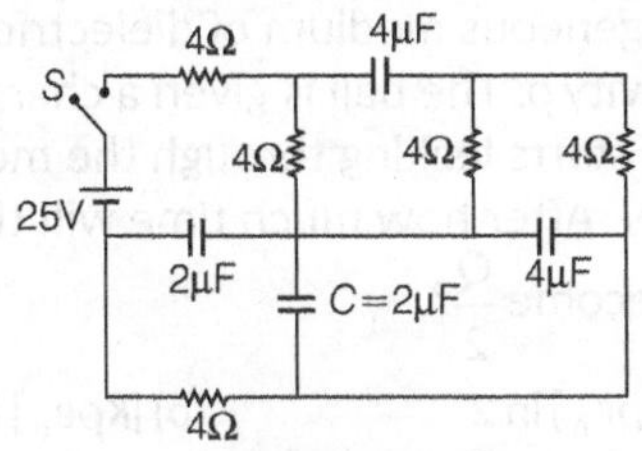

(a) 8 μC (b) 10 μC
(c) 16 μC (d) 20 μC

2 In the shown circuit, all three capacitors are identical and have capacitance C each. Each resistor has resistance of R. An ideal cell of emf V volts is connected as shown. Then, the magnitude of potential difference across capacitor C_3 in steady state is

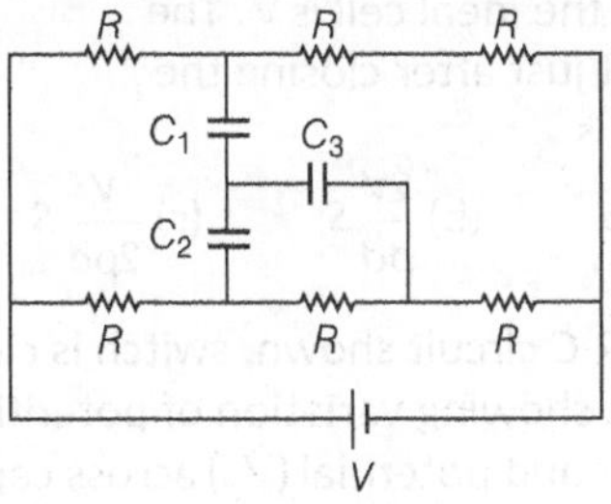

(a) $\frac{V}{3}$ (b) $\frac{V}{2}$
(c) $\frac{2V}{9}$ (d) $\frac{3V}{4}$

3 The circuit shown below shows a steady state with S open. When S is closed,

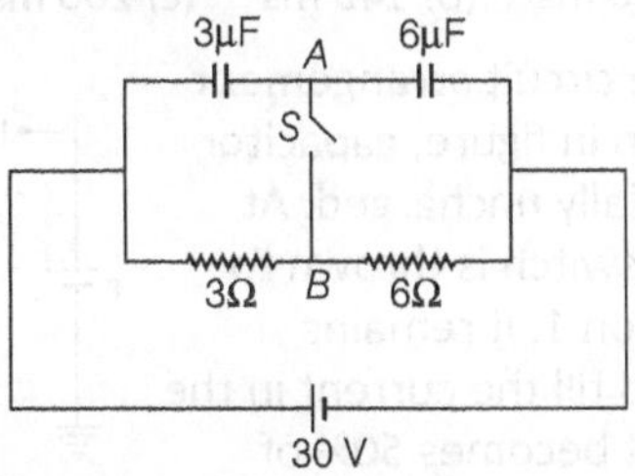

(a) no charge/current passes through S
(b) a steady current of 30 A flows through S
(c) 90 μC of charge flows from B to A
(d) 120 μC of charge flows from A to B

4 Switch S is closed at $t = 0$. Find the total heat (all types of losses included) generated in the resistors after closing the switch. (All capacitors are initially uncharged)

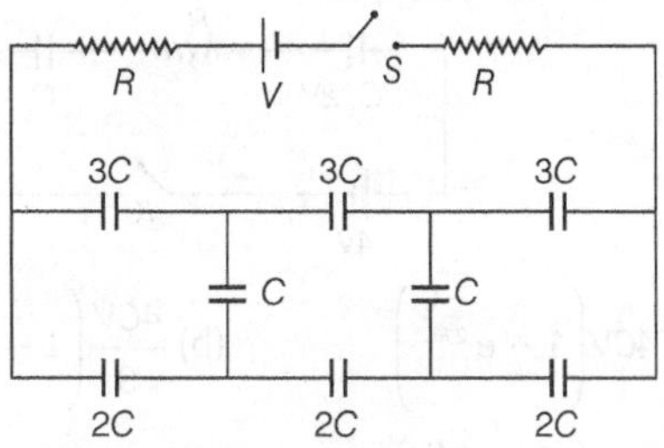

(a) $\frac{5CV^2}{3}$ (b) $\frac{6CV^2}{3}$
(c) $\frac{5CV^2}{6}$ (d) $3CV^2$

5 In below figure, a part of circuit in steady state is shown. If energy stored in the capacitor is $x \times 10^{-4}$ J, then find value of x.

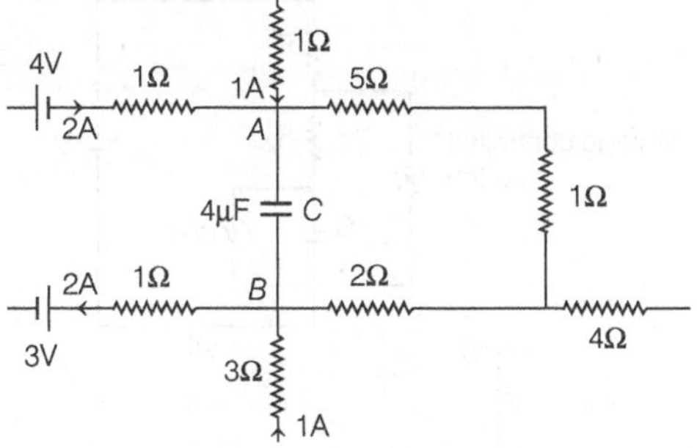

(a) 5 (b) 6 (c) 7 (d) 8

6 In the given circuit, the capacitor of capacitance C is charged by closing key K at $t = 0$. Find the time required to charge the capacitor upto maximum charge for the given circuit, if it were to be charged with the constant initial charging rate at $t = 0$ in the given circuit.

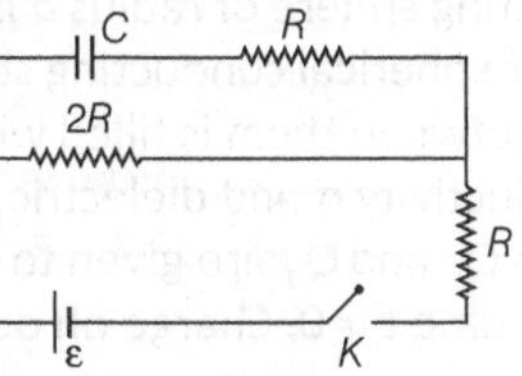

(a) $\frac{RC}{3}$ (b) $\frac{2RC}{5}$
(c) $\frac{2RC}{3}$ (d) $\frac{5RC}{3}$

7 A capacitor of capacitance 2C is charged to a potential 2V and then connected to an uncharged capacitor of capacitance C with a resistance R to a battery of emf 4V as shown. The key is closed at t = 0. The charge on uncharged capacitor as a function of time will be

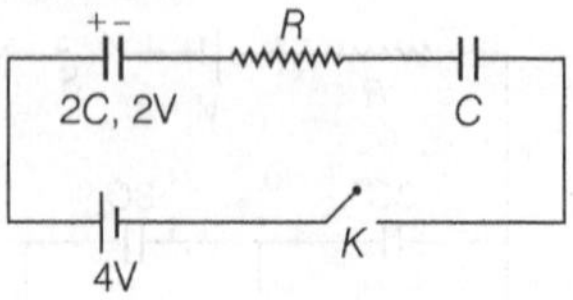

(a) $4CV\left(1-e^{\frac{-t}{2RC}}\right)$ (b) $\frac{4CV}{3}\left(1-e^{\frac{-t}{2RC}}\right)$

(c) $4CV\left(1-e^{\frac{-3t}{2RC}}\right)$ (d) $\frac{4CV}{3}\left(1-e^{\frac{-3t}{2RC}}\right)$

8 The switch in figure (a) closes when $V_C = \frac{2V}{3}$ and opens when $V_C = \frac{V}{3}$. The voltmeter reads a voltage as plotted in figure (b). What is the period T of the waveform? (Take, $R_1 = 6R$ and $R_2 = 3R$)

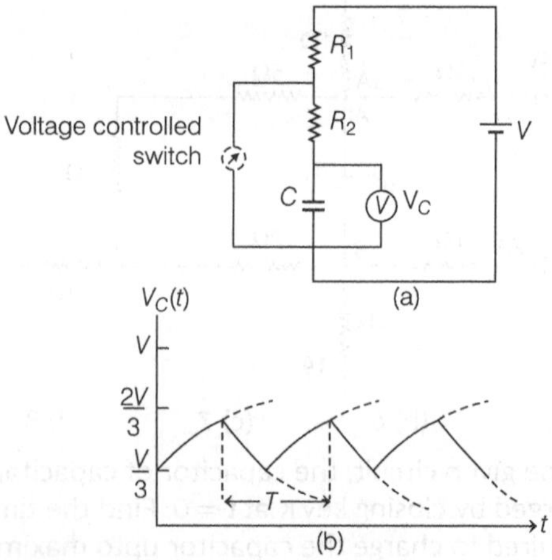

(a) 12 RC ln 2 (b) 18 RC ln 2

(c) 21 RC ln 2 (d) None of these

9 Conducting sphere of radius a is surrounded by another spherical conducting shell of radius b. The space between them is filled with dielectric material of conductivity σ and dielectric constant K. The charges Q_1 and Q_2 are given to the inner and outer shell at time t = 0. Charge on outer shell at time t is

(a) $Q_1 + Q_2\left(1-\exp\left(-\frac{\sigma t}{\varepsilon_0 K}\right)\right)$

(b) $Q_2 - Q_1\left(1-\exp\left(-\frac{\sigma t}{\varepsilon_0 K}\right)\right)$

(c) $Q_1 - Q_2\left(1-\exp\left(-\frac{\sigma t}{\varepsilon_0 K}\right)\right)$

(d) $Q_2 + Q_1\left(1-\exp\left(-\frac{\sigma t}{\varepsilon_0 K}\right)\right)$

10 A metal ball of radius R is surrounded by a homogeneous medium of dielectric constant K and resistivity ρ. The ball is given a charge Q at t = 0, which starts leaking through the medium towards infinity. After how much time will the charge on the ball become $\frac{Q}{2}$?

(a) $[2K\rho\varepsilon_0]\ln 2$ (b) $[K\rho\varepsilon_0]\ln 2$

(c) $[K\rho\varepsilon_0/2]\ln 2$ (d) None of these

11 The area of the plates of the capacitor shown in figure is S. The dielectric constant and resistivity of the material of the slab inserted in the capacitor are K = 1 and ρ, respectively. The emf of the ideal cell is V. The current just after closing the switch is

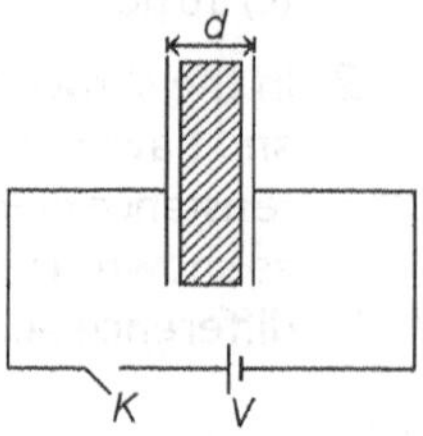

(a) $\frac{V}{\rho d}S$ (b) $\frac{2V}{\rho d}S$ (c) $\frac{V}{2\rho d}S$ (d) zero

12 In the R-C circuit shown, switch is closed at t = 0. Graphs showing variation of potential (V_R) across resistor and potential (V_C) across capacitor are given. Time constant of circuit is approximately equal to

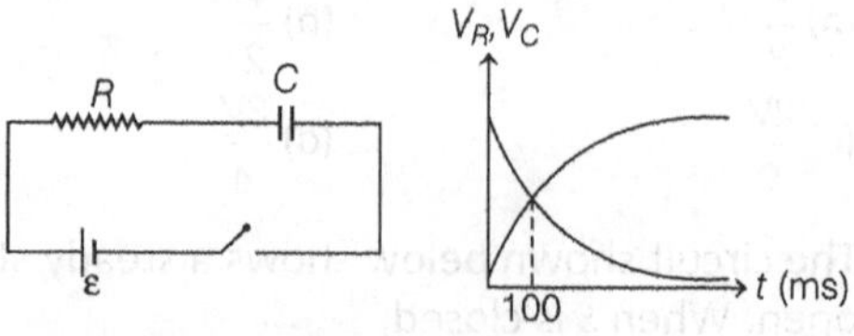

(a) 100 ms (b) 145 ms (c) 200 ms (d) 300 ms

13 In the circuit arrangement shown in figure, capacitor is initially uncharged. At t = 0, switch is thrown to position 1. It remains closed till the current in the circuit becomes 50% of maximum current, then suddenly switch is shifted to position 2. Amount of work done by battery of emf 2ε long after switch is shifted to position 2 is (Assume all batteries are ideal)

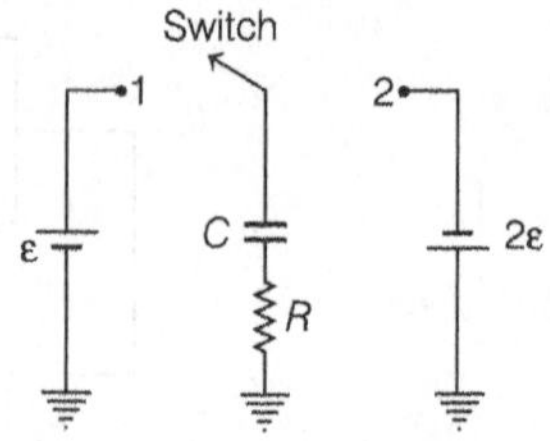

(a) $\frac{5C\varepsilon^2}{2}$ (b) $3C\varepsilon^2$ (c) $\frac{3C\varepsilon^2}{2}$ (d) $5C\varepsilon^2$

14 A graph between current and time during charging of a capacitor by a battery in series with a resistor is shown. The graphs are drawn for two circuits. R_1, C_1 and V_1 are the values of resistance, capacitance and emf of the cell in one circuit and R_2, C_2 and V_2 for another circuit, respectively. If only two parameters (out of resistance, capacitance, emf) are different in the two circuits, what is the correct option?

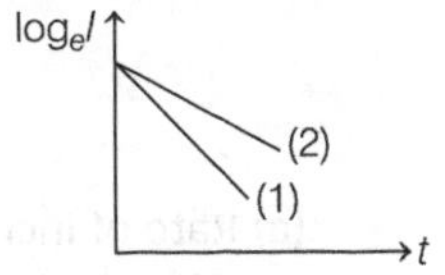

(a) $V_1 = V_2, R_1 > R_2, C_1 > C_2$

(b) $V_1 > V_2, R_1 > R_2, C_1 = C_2$

(c) $V_1 < V_2, R_1 < R_2, C_1 = C_2$

(c) $V_1 < V_2, C_1 < C_2, R_1 = R_2$

15 A charged capacitor C_1 is discharged through a resistor R. When the discharge current attains the value I_0, the key is shifted from 1 to 2. Then, the amount of heat Q liberated in the resistor starting from this moment, is

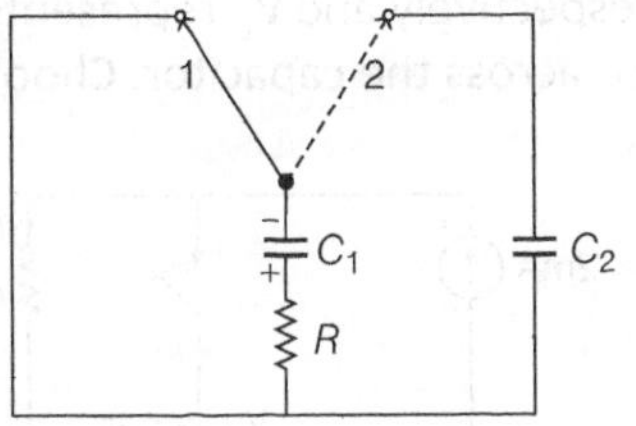

(a) $\dfrac{i_0^2 R^2 C_1 C_2}{2(C_1 + C_2)}$ (b) $\dfrac{i_0^2 R^2 C_1 C_2}{4(C_1 + C_2)}$

(c) $\dfrac{i_0^2 R^2}{2}\left(\dfrac{C_1 + C_2}{C_1 C_2}\right)$ (d) None of these

16 The capacitor C is initially uncharged. Switch S_1 is closed for a long time while S_2 remains open. Now, at $t = 0$, S_2 is closed while S_1 is opened. All the batteries are ideal and connecting wires are resistanceless. Find incorrect statement.

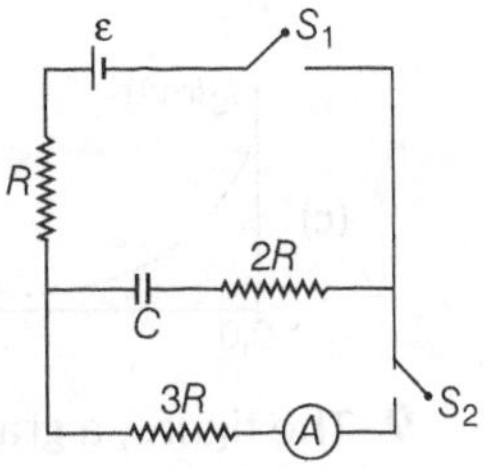

(a) At time $t = 0$ (just after S_2 is closed), reading of ammeter is $\dfrac{\varepsilon}{5R}$.

(b) At time $t = 5RC \ln 2$, reading of ammeter is $\dfrac{\varepsilon}{5eR}$.

(c) Heat developed till time $t = 5\,RC \ln 2$ in resistance $3R$ is $\dfrac{9}{40} C\varepsilon^2$.

(d) After time $t > 0$, charge on the capacitor follows the equation $C\varepsilon\, e^{-\frac{t}{5RC}}$

17 Initially S_1 is open and S_2 is kept closed for a long time. Now at $t = 0$, switch S_2 is opened and S_1 is closed. At $t = R_1 C$, switch S_1 is opened and S_2 is closed. The charge on the capacitor at $t = 2R_1 C + R_2 C$ is

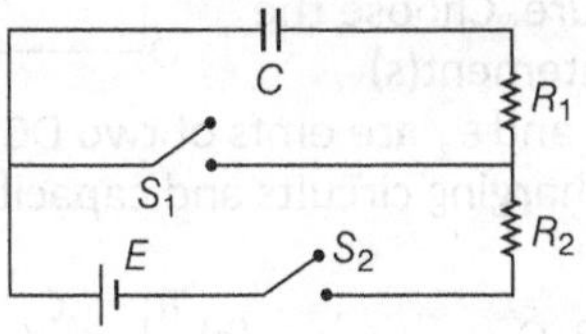

(a) $CE\left(1 - \dfrac{1}{e} + \dfrac{1}{e^2}\right)$ (b) $CE\left(\dfrac{1}{e} - \dfrac{1}{e^2}\right)$

(c) $CE\left(1 + \dfrac{1}{e} - \dfrac{1}{e^2}\right)$ (d) $CE\left(\dfrac{1}{e} + \dfrac{1}{e^2}\right)$

Multiple Choice(s) Correct Questions

1 In the circuit shown, there is steady state with the switch closed. The switch is opened at $t = 0$. Choose the correct option(s).
(Given, $\varepsilon = 24$ V, $C_1 = 3$ F and $C_2 = 2$F)

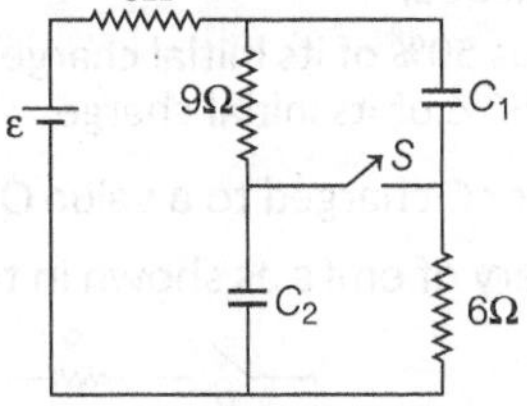

(a) The voltage across C_1 before the switch is open is 12 V.

(b) The voltage across C_2 before the switch is open is 8 V.

(c) The voltage across C_1 after a long time after the switch is open is 12 V.

(d) The voltage across C_2 after a long time after the switch is open is 24 V.

2 In the circuit shown in figure, if the galvanometer resistance is 6Ω, then in the steady state,

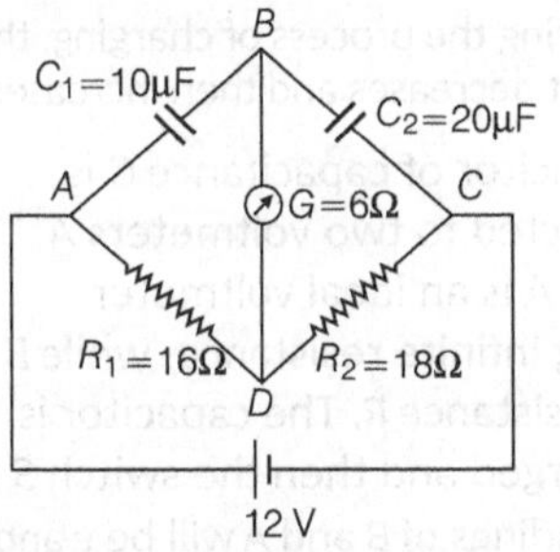

(a) no current flows through the galvanometer

(b) the current through R_2 is 4 A

(c) the charge on C_1 is 80 μC

(d) the charge on C_2 is 80 μC

3 The instantaneous charge on capacitor in two discharging *R-C* circuits is plotted with respect to time in figure. Choose the correct statement(s) (where, ε_1 and ε_2 are emfs of two DC sources in two different charging circuits and capacitors are fully charged).

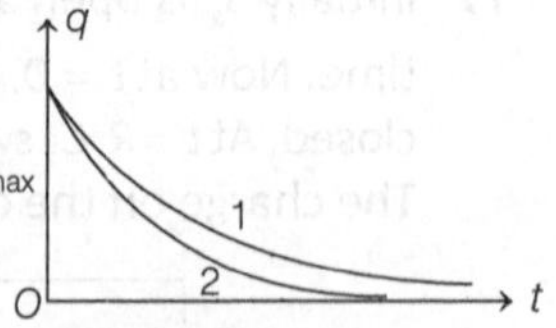

(a) $R_1C_1 > R_2C_2$ (b) $\frac{R_1}{R_2} < \frac{C_2}{C_1}$

(c) $R_1 > R_2$, if $\varepsilon_1 = \varepsilon_2$ (d) $C_2 > C_1$, if $\varepsilon_1 = \varepsilon_2$

4 Capacitors $C_1 = 1\mu F$ and $C_2 = 2\mu F$ are separately charged from the same battery. They are then allowed to discharge separately through equal resistors.

(a) The current in the two discharging circuits at $t = 0$ is zero

(b) The currents in the two discharging circuits at $t = 0$ are equal but not zero

(c) The currents in the two discharging circuits at $t = 0$ are unequal

(d) C_1 loses 50% of its initial charge sooner than C_2 loses 50% of its initial charge

5 A capacitor *C* charged to a value $Q = \varepsilon C$ is connected to a battery of emf ε as shown in the figure.

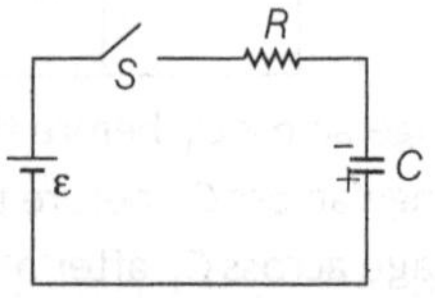

(a) Charge on the capacitor is zero at time *RC* ln 2 after the switch *S* is closed

(b) Charged on the capacitor is zero very long time after the switch *S* is closed

(c) Maximum charge on the capacitor during the process of charging is εC

(d) During the process of charging, the charging current first decreases and then increases exponentially

6 A capacitor of capacitance *C* is connected to two voltmeters *A* and *B*. *A* is an ideal voltmeter having infinite resistance, while *B* has resistance *R*. The capacitor is uncharged and then the switch *S* is closed at $t = 0$,

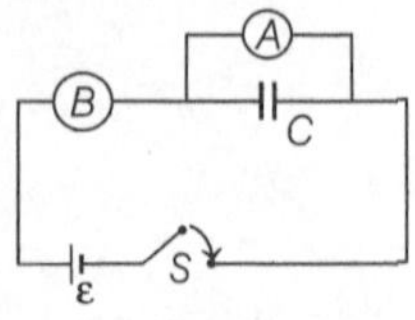

(a) Readings of *B* and *A* will be ε and zero respectively at $t = 0$

(b) During time interval $(0 \le t \le \infty)$, readings of *B* and *A* are changing

(c) Reading of *A* and *B* will be equal at $t = RC \ln 2$

(d) None of the above

7 In the circuit shown in the figure, switch *S* is closed at time $t = 0$. Select the correct statements.

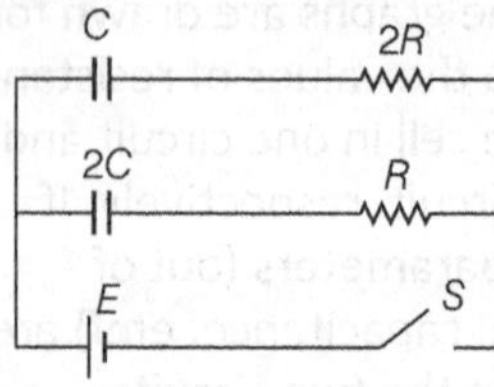

(a) Rate of increase of charge is same in both the capacitor.

(b) Ratio of charge stored in capacitors *C* and 2*C* at any time *t* would be 1 : 2.

(c) Time constant of both the capacitors are equal.

(d) Steady state charge in capacitors *C* and 2*C* are in the ratio 1 : 2.

8 Consider a circuit with a constant current source of $i_s = 2$ mA with a capacitor of 2 μF and resistor of 5 kΩ as shown in figure. At $t = 0$, the switch is closed. i_C and i_R denotes current in the capacitor and resistor branch respectively and V_C represents potential difference across the capacitor. Choose the correct graph(s).

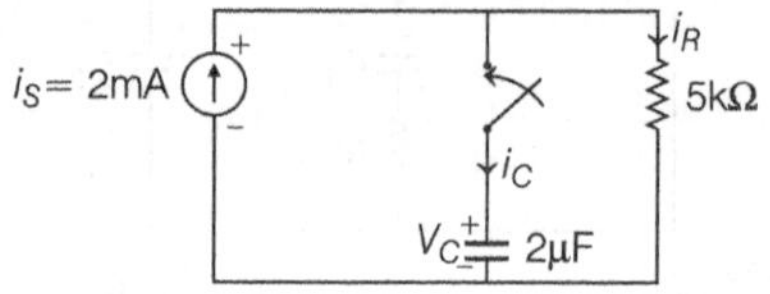

(a)

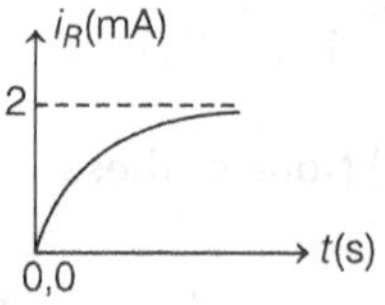

(b)

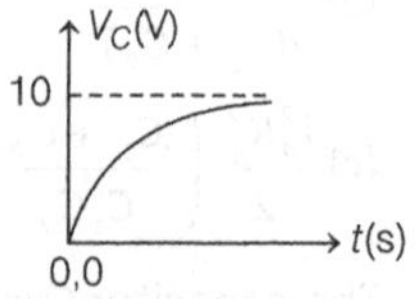

(c)

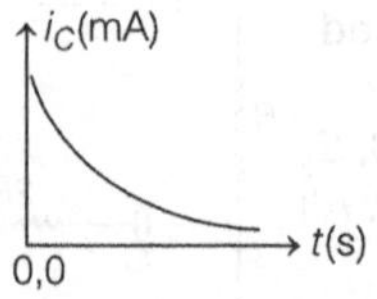

(d)

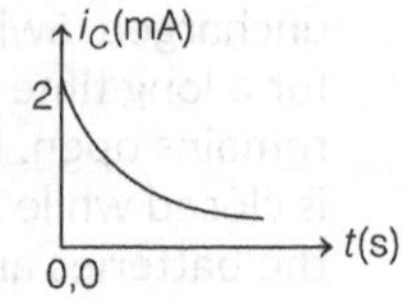

9 The figure, a graph of the current in a discharging circuit of a capacitor through a resistor of resistance 10Ω.

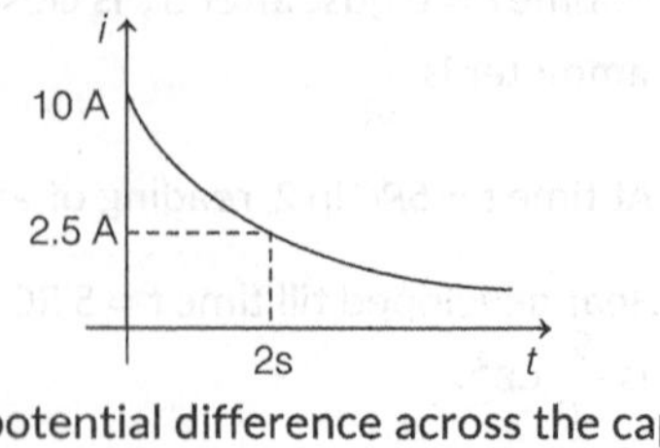

(a) The initial potential difference across the capacitor is 100 V.

(b) The capacitance of the capacitor is $\frac{1}{10 \ln 2}$ F.

(c) The total heat produced in the circuit will be $\frac{500}{\ln 2}$ J.

(d) The thermal power in the resistor will decrease with a time constant $\frac{1}{2\ln 2}$ s.

Comprehension Based Questions

Comprehension-1

In the circuit shown in figure, the battery is an ideal one with emf *V*. The capacitor is initially uncharged. The switch *S* is closed at time $t = 0$.

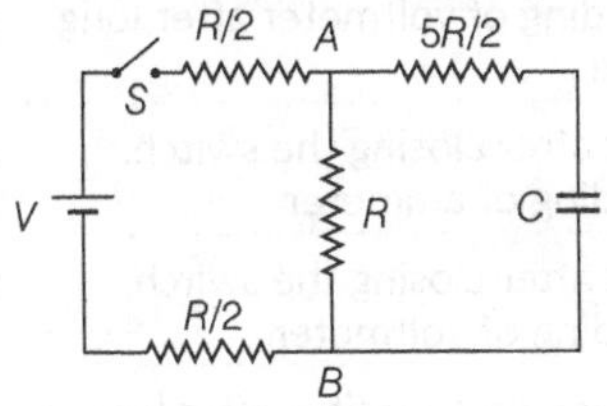

1 The charge *Q* on the capacitor at time *t* is

(a) $\frac{CV}{2}\left(1-e^{-\frac{2t}{5RC}}\right)$ (b) $\frac{CV}{2}\left(1-e^{-\frac{t}{3RC}}\right)$

(c) $\frac{CV}{6}\left(1-e^{-\frac{2t}{5RC}}\right)$ (d) $\frac{CV}{6}\left(1-e^{-\frac{t}{3RC}}\right)$

2 The current in *AB* at time *t* is

(a) $\frac{V}{2R}\left(1-e^{-\frac{2t}{5RC}}\right)$ (b) $\frac{2V}{R}\left(1-e^{-\frac{t}{3RC}}\right)$

(c) $\frac{2V}{R}\left(1-\frac{e^{-\frac{2t}{5RC}}}{6}\right)$ (d) $\frac{V}{2R}\left(1-\frac{e^{-\frac{t}{3RC}}}{6}\right)$

3 What is its limiting value i_{AB} at $t \to \infty$?

(a) $\frac{V}{2R}$ (b) $\frac{V}{6R}$

(c) $\frac{2V}{R}$ (d) $\frac{V}{3R}$

Comprehension-2

In the circuit shown in figure, switch *S* is closed at time $t = 0$. Thereafter the constant current source by varying its emf, maintains a constant current *i* out of its upper terminal.

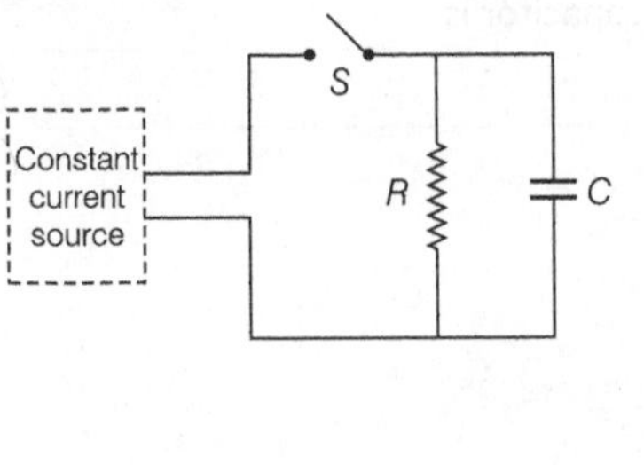

4 The expression for the charge on the capacitor as a function of time is

(a) $q = iRC\left(e^{-\frac{t}{RC}}\right)$ (b) $q = iRC\left(1-e^{-\frac{t}{RC}}\right)$

(c) $q = it\left(1-e^{-\frac{t}{RC}}\right)$ (d) $q = \frac{i}{RC}\left(1-e^{-\frac{t}{RC}}\right)$

5 Find the time at which the rate of energy storage on capacitor is equal to the rate of heat dissipation through resistor.

(a) $t = \frac{RC\ln}{2}$ (b) $t = 2RC\ln 2$

(c) $t = RC\ln 2$ (d) Not possible

Comprehension-3

A highway emergency flasher uses a 120 V battery, a 1 MΩ resistor, a 1 μF capacitor, a neon flash lamp in the circuit shown in the figure. The flash lamp has a resistance more than 10^{10} Ω when the voltage across it is less than 110 V. Above 110 V, the neon gas ionises, the lamp's resistance drops to 10 Ω, and the capacitor discharges completely. Until the capacitor voltage reaches the breakdown voltage $V_b = 110$ V, the large resistance of the flash lamp ensures that it draws a negligible current.

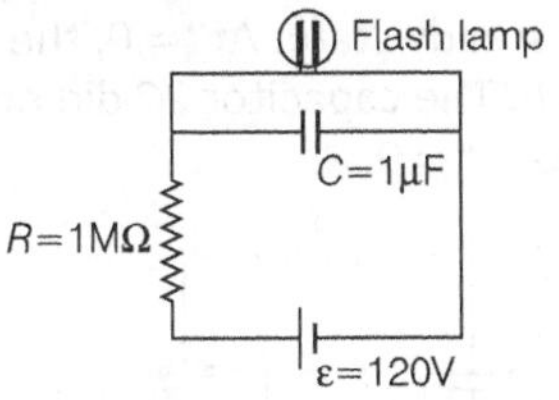

The capacitor charges as if the lamp were absent. At V_b, however the lamp resistance quickly becomes negligible, and the capacitor discharges through the lamp as if the battery and the series resistor were absent. The time between the flashes is the time for the capacitor to charge to V_b. The flash duration is roughly the time for the capacitor to discharge through the lamp, or about 3 time constant of the capacitor-lamp circuit. The flash energy is the stored energy in the capacitor at 110 V.

6 Time constant (τ_c) of the capacitor-lamp circuit is

(a) 20 μs (b) 15 μs (c) 30 μs (d) 10 μs

7 Flash duration is

(a) 10 μs (b) 20 μs

(c) 30 μs (d) 5 μs

8 The energy in the flash is

(a) 6.1 mJ (b) 3.2 mJ

(c) 6.4 mJ (d) 12.2 mJ

Comprehension-4

The charge across the capacitor in two different R-C circuits 1 and 2 are plotted as shown in figure.

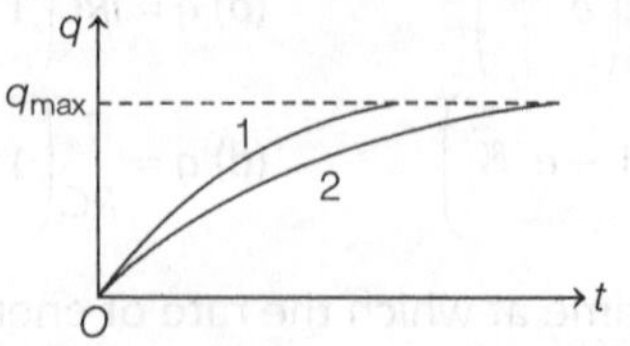

9 Choose the correct statement(s) related to the two circuits.

(a) Both the capacitors are charged to the same charge.
(b) The emf's of cells in both the circuit are equal.
(c) The emf's of the cells may be different.
(d) The emf ε_1 is more than ε_2.

10 Identify the correct statement(s) related to the R_1, R_2, C_1 and C_2 of the two R-C circuits.

(a) $R_1 > R_2$, if $\varepsilon_1 = \varepsilon_2$ (b) $C_1 < C_2$, if $\varepsilon_1 = \varepsilon_2$
(c) $R_1C_1 > R_2C_2$ (d) $\frac{R_1}{R_2} < \frac{C_2}{C_1}$

Comprehension-5

Consider the circuit in the figure. The switch is initially in position A for a sufficiently long time to establish a steady state. At $t = 0$, the switch is turned to position B. The capacitor 2C did not hold any charge before $t = 0$.

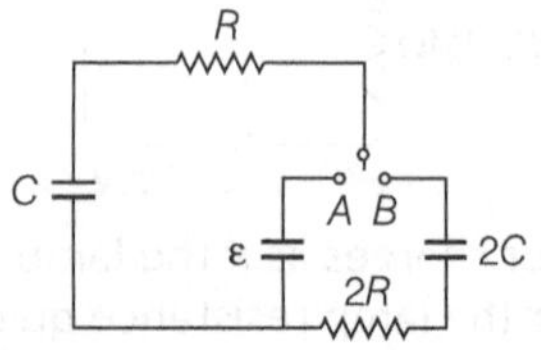

11 At $t \to \infty$, when a new steady state has been established, the charges held by capacitors C and 2C will respectively be

(a) $C\varepsilon$ and $2C\varepsilon$ (b) $\frac{C\varepsilon}{2}$ and $C\varepsilon$
(c) $\frac{C\varepsilon}{3}$ and $\frac{2C\varepsilon}{3}$ (d) $\frac{2C\varepsilon}{3}$ and $C\varepsilon$

12 The current decreases exponentially between $t = 0$ to $t = \infty$. The time constant is

(a) $9RC$ (b) $2RC$ (c) $3RC$ (d) $\frac{3RC}{2}$

13 The time, at which charge in the capacitor C is reduced to half of the value it had at $t = 0$, is

(a) $6RC \ln 2$ (b) $3RC \ln 2$ (c) $2RC \ln 2$ (d) $4RC \ln 2$

Match the Columns Questions

1 Initially capacitor was uncharged and switch was open. Switch is closed at $t = 0$. Ammeter and voltmeter are ideal. [All units are in SI]

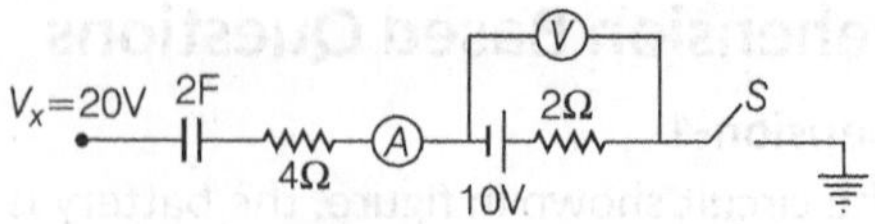

	Column I		Column II
(a)	Reading of voltmeter after long time	(p)	0
(b)	Just after closing the switch, reading of ammeter	(q)	5
(c)	Just after closing the switch, reading of voltmeter	(r)	10
(d)	Charge on capacitor after long time	(s)	20
		(t)	60

2 Consider the circuit shown in figure. There are three switches S_1, S_2, S_3. Match the following columns.

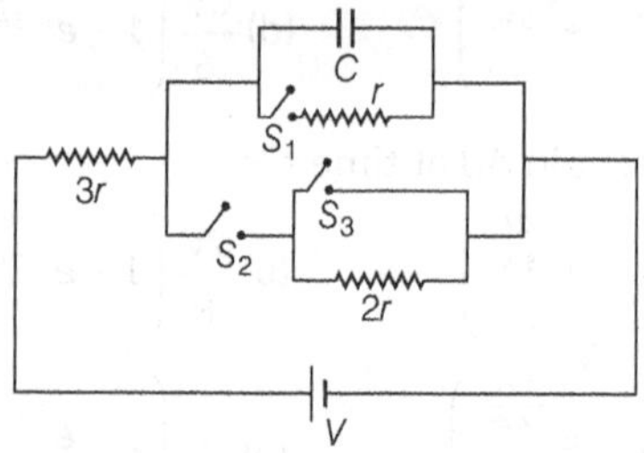

	Column I		Column II
(a)	If S_1 and S_3 are opened and S_2 is closed, then in steady state, charge on capacitor equals	(p)	$\frac{CV}{4}$
(b)	If S_2 and S_3 are opened and S_1 is closed, then in steady state, charge on capacitor equals	(q)	$\frac{2CV}{5}$
(c)	If S_1 and S_2 are closed and S_3 is opened, then in steady state, charge on capacitor equals	(r)	$\frac{CV}{3}$
(d)	If all the switches are closed, then in steady state, charge on capacitor is	(s)	$\frac{2CV}{11}$
		(t)	zero

3 In the shown circuit initially capacitor has some charge, the switch is closed at $t = 0$.

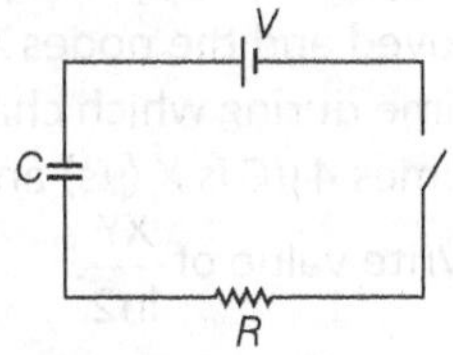

Variables		Possible graphs	
(a)	Charge on upper plate of capacitor *versus* time	(p)	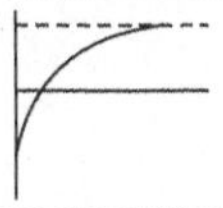
(b)	Current *versus* time	(q)	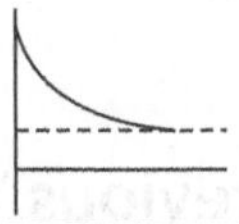
(c)	Charge *versus* current	(r)	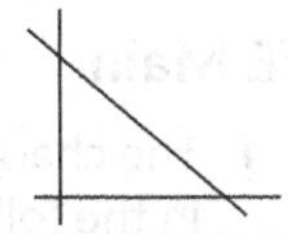
(d)	Energy stored in capacitor *versus* time	(s)	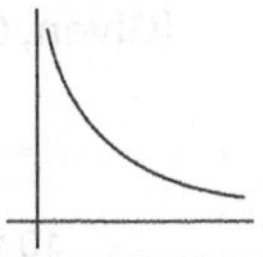

4 In the circuit shown the figure, the capacitor is initially uncharged. At $t = 0$, the switch is closed at position (1) and remains closed for a long time. Then at $t = t'$, the switch is shifted to position (2). Match the following.

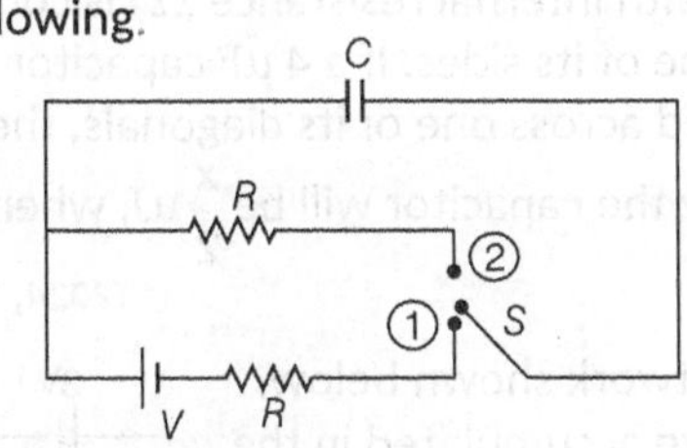

	Column I		Column II
(a)	As the capacitor charges from $t = 0$ to $t = t'$	(p)	Current in the circuit falls exponentially
(b)	As the capacitor discharges, i.e. for $t > t'$	(q)	Current in the circuit grows exponentially
(c)	Maximum current in the circuit depends on	(r)	R, C
(d)	Time to achieve 50% charging of the capacitor depends on	(s)	R
		(t)	None of these

Numerical Value Questions

1 In the circuit shown in figure, find the charge (in μC) on capacitor C_2 in steady state.

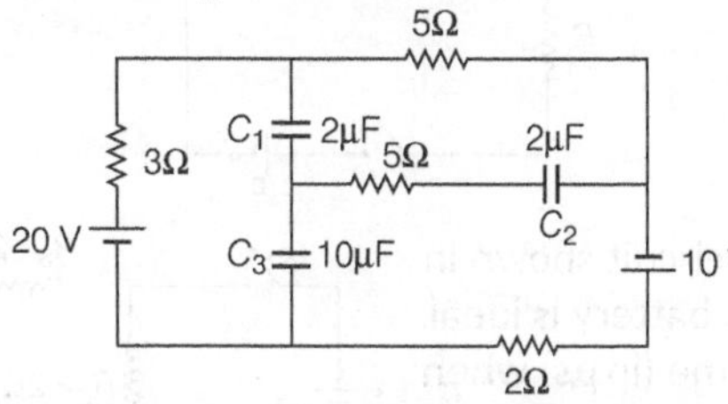

2 A system of capacitor and resistors are connected to an ideal battery of emf V as shown in figure. Initially all the capacitors are uncharged and switch is open. Now, switch S is closed at $t = 0$. Capacitance of each capacitor is C and resistance of each resistor is R and all of the symbols have their usual meanings. Current through battery just after switch is closed is $\left(\frac{nV}{3R}\right)$.

What is the value of n ?

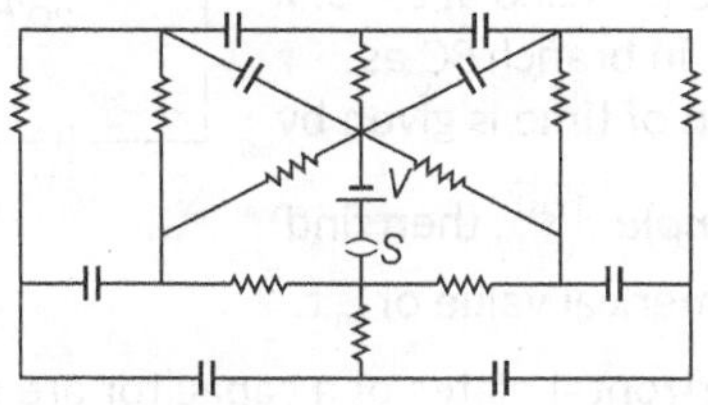

3 A parallel plate capacitor with plates of length l is included in a circuit as shown in figure. Given are the emf of the current source ε, its internal resistance r and the distance d between the plates. An electron with a velocity v_0 flies into the capacitor, parallel to the plates. Find the resistance R (in Ω) that should be connected in parallel with the capacitor, so that the electron flies out of the capacitor at an angle of 37° to the plates. Assume that circuit is in steady state and neglect gravity. (Take, $l = 91$cm, $\varepsilon = 3$V, $r = 2\Omega$, $d = \frac{1}{3}$ mm, $v_0 = 4 \times 10^7$ m/s, $e = 1.6 \times 10^{-19}$ C, mass of electron $= 9.1 \times 10^{-31}$ kg)

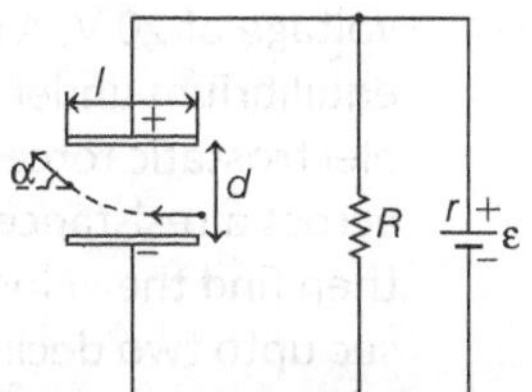

4 The figure shows a R-C circuit with a parallel plate capacitor. Before switching on the circuit, plate A of the capacitor was given a charge $-Q$. While plate B has no net charge. Now at $t = 0$, the circuit is switched on how much time (in second) will elapse before the net charge on plate A becomes zero.

(Take, $C = 1\mu F$, $Q = 1$ mC, $\varepsilon = 1000$ V and $R = \frac{2}{\ln 3}$ MΩ)

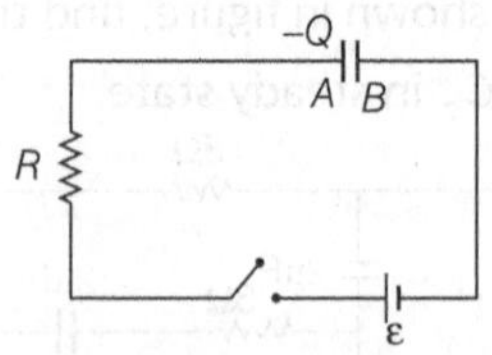

5 In the circuit shown in figure, battery is ideal. Find time (in μs) when the current in R_3 becomes $\frac{1}{e}$ time of maximum current through it. (At time $t = 0$, the key S is closed, Initially capacitor is uncharged)

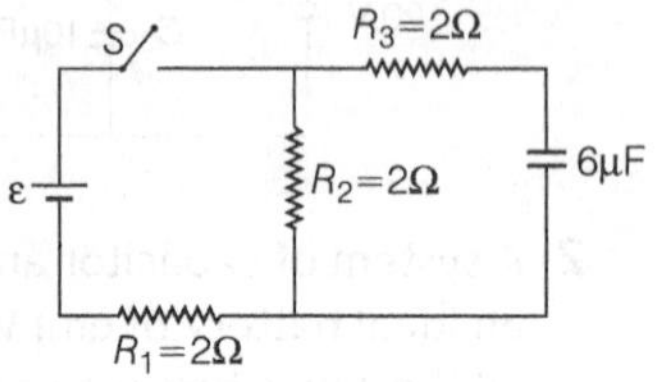

6 An uncharged capacitor of capacitance C is connected in given circuit diagram, switch S is closed at $t = 0$. If current in branch BC as function of time is given by $I = I_0 (Amp) e^{\frac{t}{\tau(\text{in}\,\mu s)}}$, then find the numerical value of $I_0 \tau$.

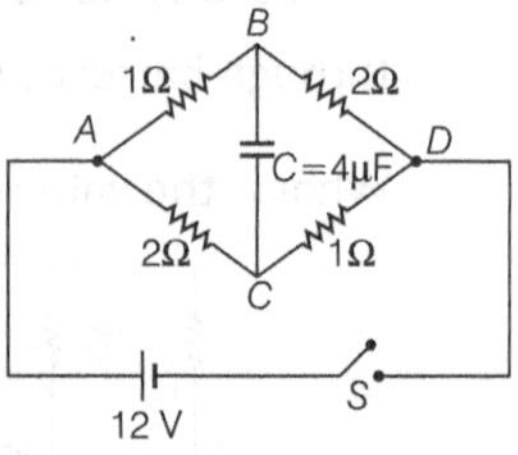

7 The horizontal plates of a capacitor are charged to a voltage of 20 V. A particle carrying a charge is in equilibrium under the influence of gravitational and electrostatic forces. Capacitor is now connected across a resistance 4 kΩ. If capacitance is 500 μF, then find the velocity (in m/s) of the particle at $t = 2$ sec upto two decimal places.
(Take, $g = 10$ m/s^2)

8 A parallel plate capacitor has plate area A and separation d between the plates. The space between plates is filled with a dielectric of dielectric constant K and resistivity ρ. The capacitor is initially charged to Q_0 using a battery. After removing battery at $t = 0$, current density in the dielectric at any time t is $\frac{nQ_0}{\rho K \varepsilon_0 A} e^{-\left(\frac{mt}{\rho K \varepsilon_0}\right)}$. Find $n + m$.

9 Consider the shown network, the capacitor C_1 ($= 6$ μF) has an initial charge $q_0 = \frac{30e}{e-1}$ μC, $C_2 = 4$ μF and $R = 80\Omega$. Initially C_2 is uncharged. At $t = 0$, the switch S is closed. Obtain the charge on C_2 (in μC) at $t = 192$ μs.

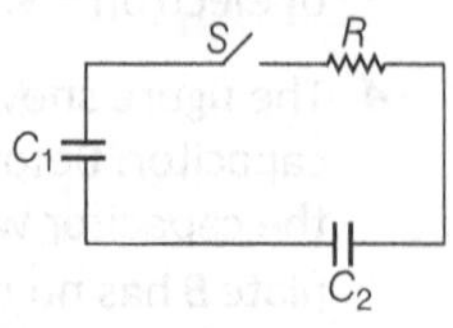

10 For the given circuit in the steady state condition, charge on the capacitor is $q_0 = 16$ μC. If now the battery is removed and the nodes A and C are shorted. The time during which charge on the capacitor becomes 4 μC is X (μs) and emf of battery was Y (volt). Write value of $\frac{XY}{\ln 2}$.

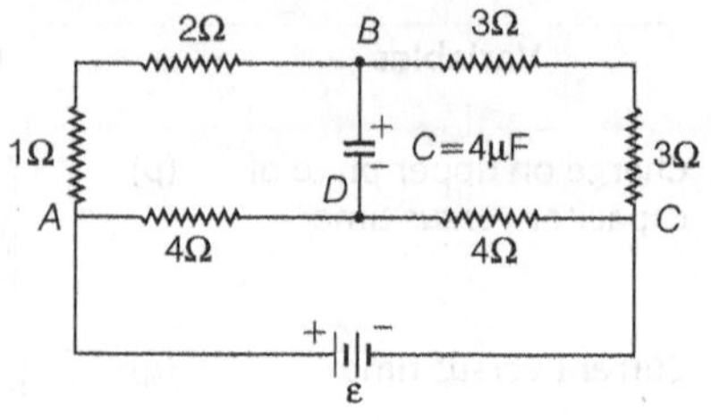

Previous Year's Questions

JEE Main

1 The charge accumulated on the capacitor connected in the following circuit is .... μC.
(Given, $C = 150$ μF) **[2024, 27 Jan Shift-I]**

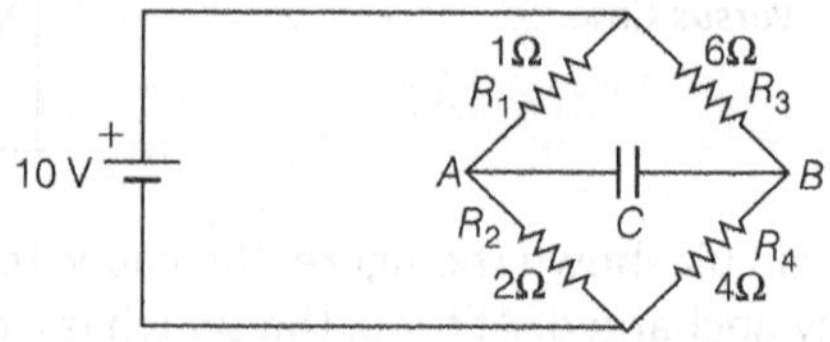

2 A 16 Ω wire is bend to form a square loop. A 9 V battery with internal resistance 1 Ω is connected across one of its sides. If a 4 μF capacitor is connected across one of its diagonals, the energy stored by the capacitor will be $\frac{x}{2}$ μJ, where $x =$ .... **[2024, 29 Jan Shift-I]**

3 In the network shown below, the charge accumulated in the capacitor in steady state will be **[2023, 13 April Shift-II]**

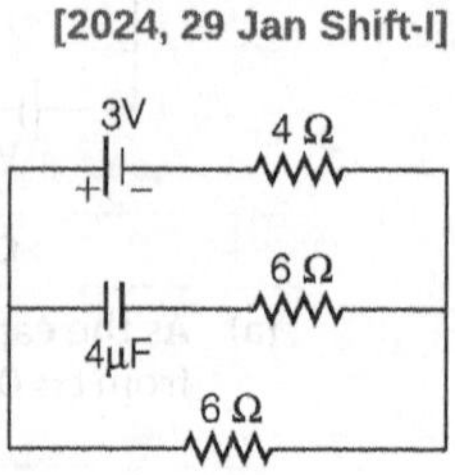

(a) 12 μC (b) 4.8 μC
(c) 7.2 μC (d) 10.3 μC

4 In the circuit shown, the energy stored in the capacitor is n μJ. The value of n is **[2023, 13 April Shift-II]**

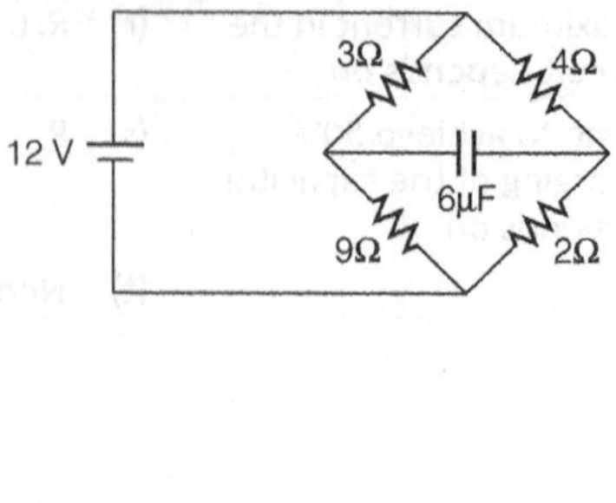

5 A capacitor of 50 μF is connected in a circuit as shown in figure. The charge on the upper plate of the capacitor is .... μC. **[2021, 31 Aug Shift-I]**

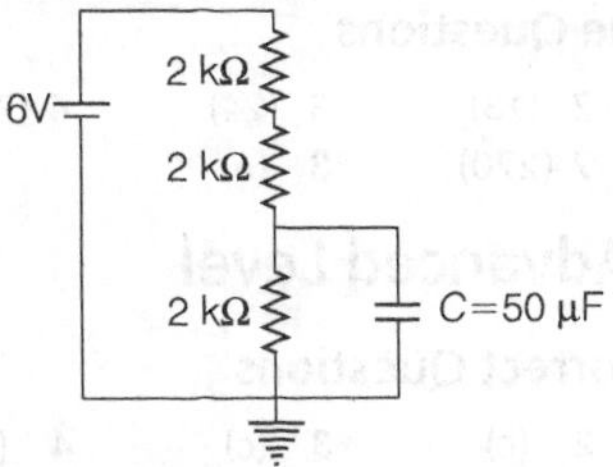

6 The circuit shown in the figure consists of a charged capacitor of capacity 3 μF and a charge of 30 μC. At time $t = 0$, when the key is closed, the value of current flowing through the 5 MΩ resistor is x μA. The value of x to the nearest integer is .... **[2021, 18 March Shift-I]**

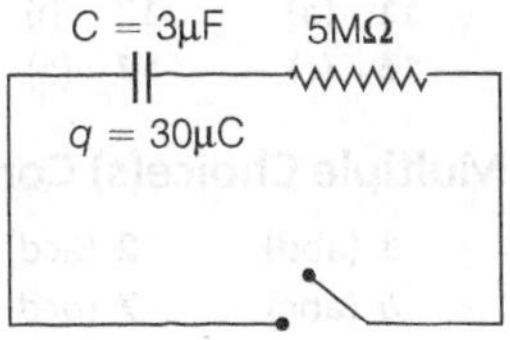

JEE Advanced

1 In a circuit shown in the figure, the capacitor C is initially uncharged and the key K is open. In this condition, a current of 1 A flows through the 1Ω resistor. The key is closed at time $t = t_0$. Which of the following statement(s) is(are) correct?

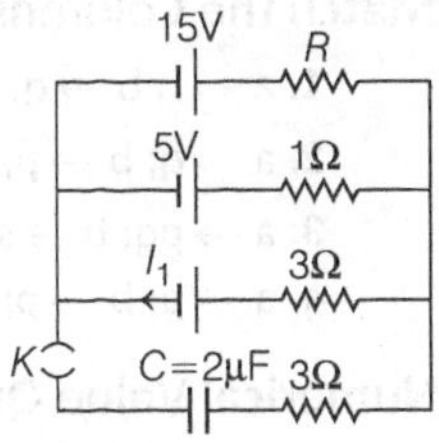

(Given, $e^{-1} = 0.36$) **(2023)**

(a) The value of the resistance R is 3Ω

(b) For $t < t_0$, the value of current I_1 is $2a$.

(c) At $t = t_0 + 7.2$ μs, the current in the capacitor is 0.6 A.

(d) For $t \to \infty$, the charge on the capacitor is 12 μC.

Passage Based Questions

Passage Consider a simple R-C circuit as shown in Figure 1.

Process 1 In the circuit, the switch S is closed at $t = 0$ and the capacitor is fully charged to voltage V_0 (i.e. charging continues for time $T >> RC$). In the process, some dissipation (E_D) occurs across the resistance R. The amount of energy finally stored in the fully charged capacitor is E_C.

Process 2 In a different process the voltage is first set to $\frac{V_0}{3}$ and maintained for a charging time $T >> RC$. Then, the voltage is raised to $\frac{2V_0}{3}$ without discharging the capacitor and again maintained for a time $T >> RC$. The process is repeated one more time by raising the voltage to V_0 and the capacitor is charged to the same final voltage V_0 as in process 1.

These two processes are depicted in Figure 2. **[JEE Advanced 2017]**

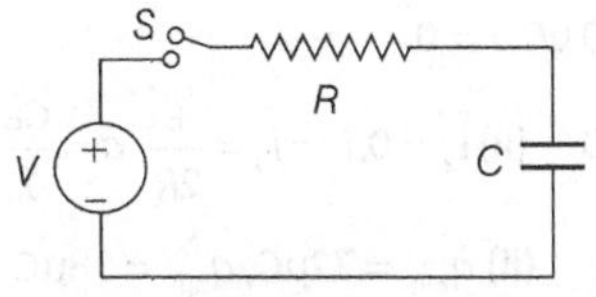

Figure 1

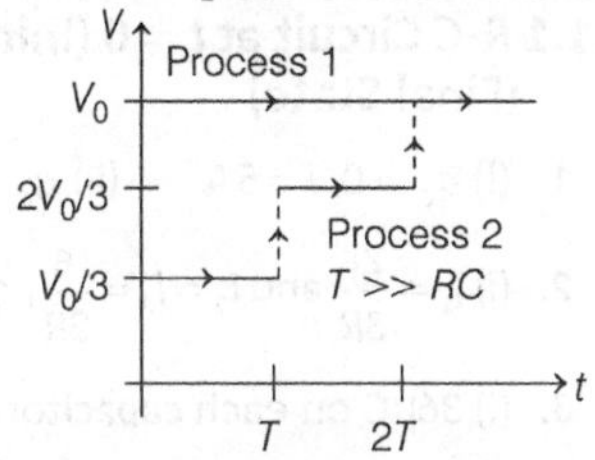

Figure 2

2 In process 1, the energy stored in the capacitor E_C and heat dissipated across resistance E_D are related by

(a) $E_C = E_D \ln 2$ (b) $E_C = E_D$ (c) $E_C = 2E_D$ (d) $E_C = \frac{1}{2}E_D$

3 In process 2, total energy dissipated across the resistance E_D is

(a) $E_D = \frac{1}{3}\left(\frac{1}{2}CV_0^2\right)$ (b) $E_D = 3\left(\frac{1}{2}CV_0^2\right)$

(c) $E_D = 3CV_0^2$ (d) $E_D = \frac{1}{2}CV_0^2$

4 At time $t = 0$, a battery of 10 V is connected across points A and B in the given circuit. If the capacitors have no charge initially, at what time (in second) does the voltage across them become 4 V? [Take : $\ln 5 = 1.6$, $\ln 3 = 1.1$] **[JEE Advanced 2010]**

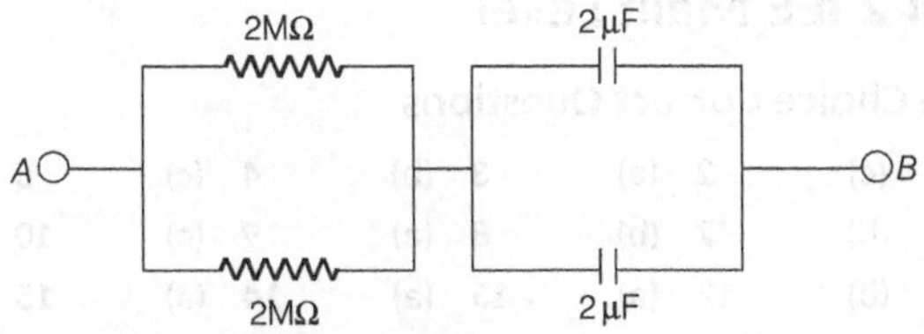

5 A parallel plate capacitor C with plates of unit area and separation d is filled with a liquid of dielectric constant $K = 2$. The level of liquid is $d/3$ initially. Suppose the liquid level decreases at a constant speed v, the time constant as a function of time t is **[JEE Advanced 2008]**

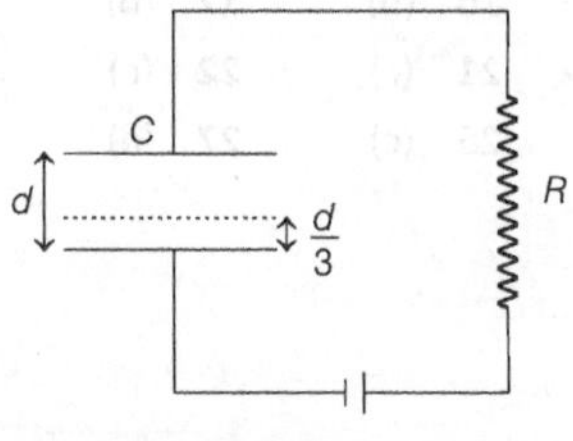

(a) $\frac{6\varepsilon_0 R}{5d + 3vt}$ (b) $\frac{(15d + 9vt)\varepsilon_0 R}{2d^2 - 3dvt - 9v^2t^2}$

(c) $\frac{6\varepsilon_0 R}{5d - 3vt}$ (d) $\frac{(15d - 9vt)\varepsilon_0 R}{2d^2 + 3dvt - 9v^2t^2}$

Answer Key

Level 1 Starter Level

11.1 *R-C* Circuit at $t = 0$ (Initial State) and $t = \infty$ (Final State)

1. (i) $q_C = 0, i = 5A$ (ii) $q_C = 30\,\mu C, i = 0$
2. (i) $i_1 = \frac{2\varepsilon}{3R}$ and $i_2 = i_3 = \frac{\varepsilon}{3R}, q = 0$ (ii) $i_2 = 0, i_1 = i_3 = \frac{\varepsilon}{2R}, q = \frac{C\varepsilon}{2}$
3. (i) 36μC on each capacitor (ii) $q_{6\mu F} = 72\mu C, q_{3\mu F} = 18\mu C$
4. $q_1 = 4\mu C, \quad q_2 = 12\mu C$

11.2 *R-C* Series Circuit (Charging)

1. 5 kΩ 2. 86.5 μC 3. 0.25 μF 4. 1.7×10^4 V/m
5. (i) 2.21 A (ii) 13.2 W (iii) 4.87 W (iv) 8.37 W
6. 0.693 7. 1.23 8. 0.693 9. $RC \ln 2$
10. $\frac{1}{2}CV^2$ 11. $CE\left(1 - e^{-\frac{t}{RC}}\right) + qe^{-\frac{t}{RC}}$
12. 10.37 μC 13. $q = \frac{C\varepsilon}{2}\left(1 - e^{-\frac{2t}{3RC}}\right)$

11.3 *R-C* Circuit (Discharging)

1. (i) 60 μC, (ii) 22 μC (iii) 8.12 μC (iv) 0.003 μC
2. 6.7 mA 3. 233.55 μC
4. 2.0 Ω 5. 4.7 μJ 6. $q = \frac{Q}{2}\left(1 - e^{-\frac{2t}{RC}}\right)$

Level 2 JEE Main Level

Single Choice Correct Questions

1 (c)	2 (a)	3 (b)	4 (c)	5 (c)
6 (b)	7 (b)	8 (a)	9 (c)	10 (a)
11 (b)	12 (a)	13 (a)	14 (a)	15 (d)
16 (b)	17 (b)	18 (a)	19 (d)	20 (b)
21 (c)	22 (c)	23 (b)	24 (d)	25 (d)
26 (c)	27 (a)	28 (a)	29 (d)	30 (c)

Numerical Value Questions

1 (8)	2 (13)	3 (24)	4 (750)	5 (5)
6 (300)	7 (270)	8 (6)		

Level 3 JEE Advanced Level

Single Choice Correct Questions

1 (d)	2 (c)	3 (c)	4 (c)	5 (d)
6 (d)	7 (d)	8 (a)	9 (d)	10 (b)
11 (a)	12 (b)	13 (d)	14 (c)	15 (a)
16 (c)	17 (a)			

Multiple Choice(s) Correct Questions

1 (abd)	2 (acd)	3 (ac)	4 (bd)	5 (ac)
6 (abc)	7 (bcd)	8 (abd)	9 (abcd)	

Comprehension Based Questions

1 (b)	2 (d)	3 (a)	4 (b)	5 (c)
6 (d)	7 (c)	8 (a)	9 (c)	10 (d)
11 (c)	12 (b)	13 (d)		

Match the Columns Questions

1. a → r; b → q; c → p; d → t
2. a → q; b → p; c → s; d → t
3. a → pq; b → s; c → r; d → q
4. a → p; b → p; c → s; d → r

Numerical Value Questions

1 (10)	2 (6)	3 (10)	4 (2)	5 (18)
6 (16)	7 (7.36)	8 (2)	9 (12)	10 (768)

Previous Year's Questions

JEE Main

1 (400)	2 (81)	3 (c)	4 (75)	5. (100)
6. (2)				

JEE Advanced

1 (a,b,c,d)	2 (b)	3 (a)	4 (2)	5 (a)

SOLUTIONS

Level 1 Starter Level

11.1 R-C Circuit at t = 0 (Initial State) and t = ∞ (Final State)

1. (i) Just after the switch is closed.

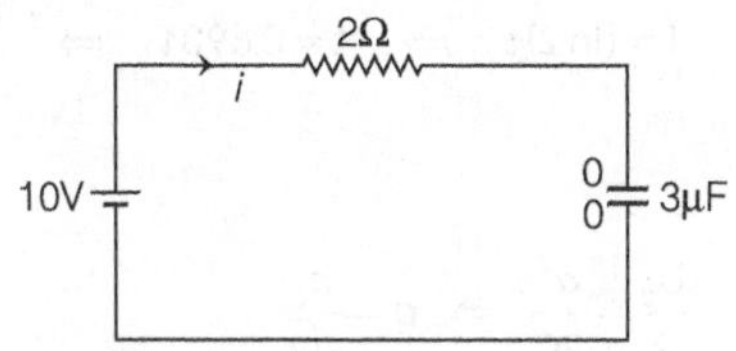

Charge on capacitor = 0

Current in the circuit $= \frac{10}{2} = 5\text{A}$

(ii) After a long time, when switch is closed.

Current in the circuit = 0

Potential difference across capacitor = 10 V

So, charge on capacitor $= (3 \times 10^{-6}) \times 10 = 30\,\mu\text{C}$

2. (i) Just after the switch is closed.

Charge on capacitor = 0

and capacitor acts as a conducting wire.

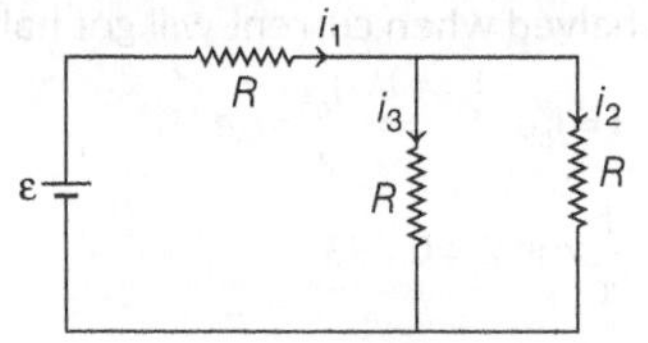

$$i_1 = \frac{\varepsilon}{R_{eq}} = \frac{\varepsilon}{\left(\frac{3R}{2}\right)} = \frac{2\varepsilon}{3R}$$

$$i_2 = \frac{\varepsilon}{3R} \text{ and } i_3 = \frac{\varepsilon}{3R}$$

(ii) After a long time, when switch is closed.

Current through branch containing capacitor = 0

$\Rightarrow i_2 = 0$ and the capacitor acts as open circuit.

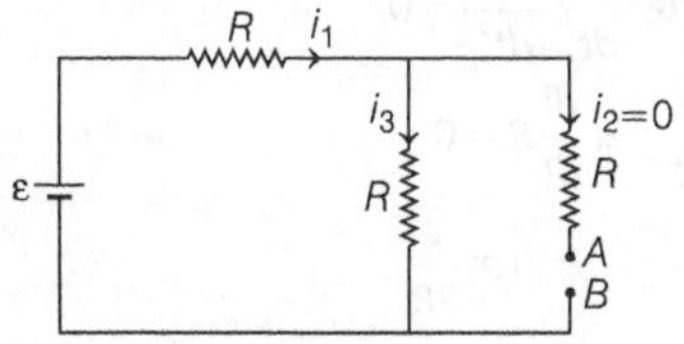

$$i_1 = i_3 = \frac{\varepsilon}{2R}$$

$$V_A - V_B = i_3 R = \left(\frac{\varepsilon}{2R}\right) R = \frac{\varepsilon}{2}$$

Charge on capacitor $= C(V_A - V_B) = \frac{C\varepsilon}{2}$

3. (i) When switch S is open,

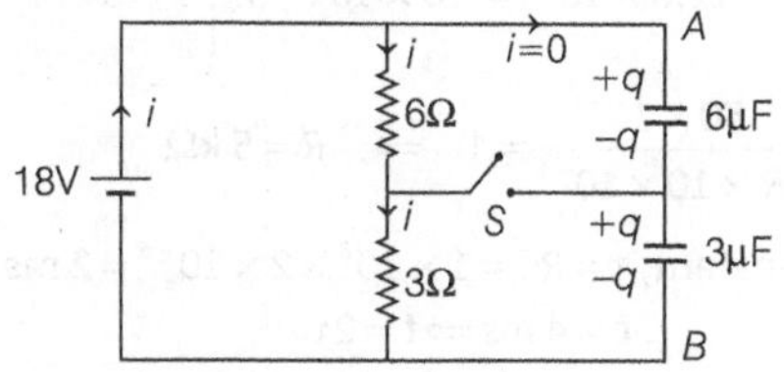

$$\frac{q}{6} + \frac{q}{3} = 18 \Rightarrow q = 36\,\mu\text{C}$$

(ii) When switch S is closed,

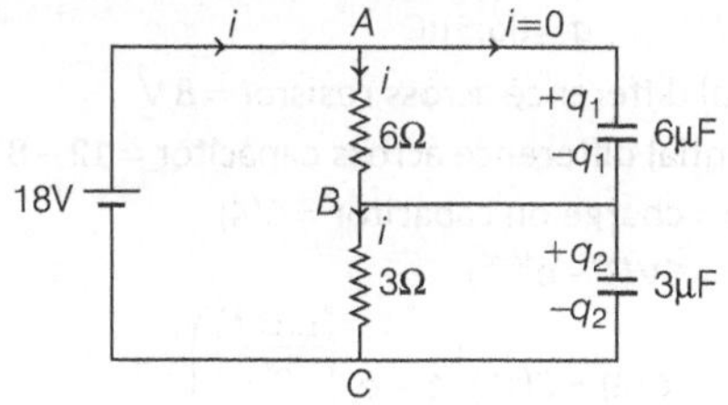

$$i = \frac{18}{(6+3)} = 2\text{A}$$

$$V_A - V_B = 2 \times 6 = 12\text{ V}$$

$$V_B - V_C = 2 \times 3 = 6\text{ V}$$

Charge on 6 μF capacitor $= CV = C(V_A - V_B)$

$= (6\,\mu\text{F})\,(12\text{ V}) = 72\,\mu\text{C}$

Charge on 3 μF capacitor $= CV = C(V_B - V_C)$

$= (3\,\mu\text{F})\,(6\text{V}) = 18\,\mu\text{C}$

4. In steady state, both capacitors act as open circuit.

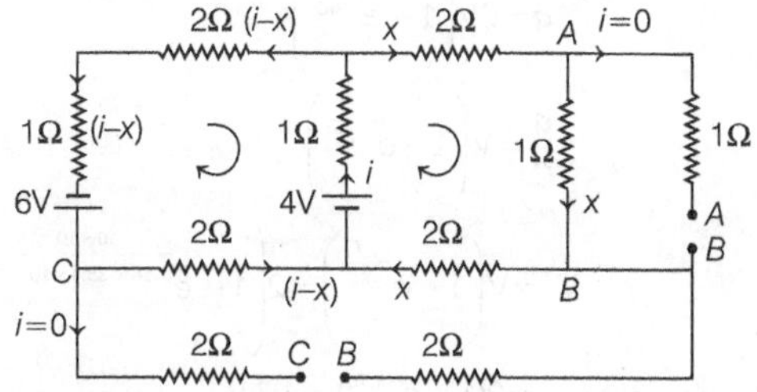

Using KVL,

$$-6 + (i - x) + 2(i - x) + i - 4 + 2(i - x) = 0$$

$$\Rightarrow \quad 6i - 5x = 10 \qquad \text{...(i)}$$

$$+4 - i(1) - 2x - x - 2x = 0$$

$$\Rightarrow \quad i + 5x = 4 \qquad \text{...(ii)}$$

Solving Eqs. (i) and (ii), we get

$$i = 2\text{A and } x = 0.4\text{ A}$$

$$V_A - V_B = x(1) = 0.4\text{ V}$$

$$V_C - V_B = 2(i - x) - 2x$$

$$= 2(2 - 0.4) - 2(0.4) = 2.4\text{ V}$$

$$q_1 = CV = C_1(V_A - V_B) = (10\mu\text{F})\,(0.4\text{V}) = 4\mu\text{C}$$

$$q_2 = CV = C_2(V_C - V_B) = (5\mu\text{F})\,(2.4\text{V}) = 12\,\mu\text{C}$$

11.2 R-C Series Circuit (Charging)

1. $q = CV(1 - e^{-\frac{t}{RC}})$

$$\Rightarrow \quad 12.6 \times 10^{-6} = (10 \times 10^{-6})(2)\left(1 - e^{-\left(\frac{50 \times 10^{-3}}{R \times 10 \times 10^{-6}}\right)}\right)$$

$$\Rightarrow \quad \frac{50 \times 10^{-3}}{R \times 10 \times 10^{-6}} = 1 \Rightarrow R = 5\,\text{k}\Omega$$

2. Time constant, $\tau = RC = 1 \times 10^3 \times 2 \times 10^{-6} = 2$ ms

$$t = 4\text{ ms} \Rightarrow t = 2\tau$$

$$q = CV\left(1 - e^{-\frac{t}{\tau}}\right)$$

$$\Rightarrow \quad q = (2\mu\text{F})(50\text{ V})(1 - e^{-2})$$

$$\Rightarrow \quad q = 86.5\,\mu\text{C}$$

3. Potential difference across resistor = 8 V

$\Rightarrow$ Potential difference across capacitor = 12 − 8 = 4 V

$\Rightarrow$ q = charge on capacitor = $C(4)$

$$q = CV(1 - e^{t/RC})$$

$$\Rightarrow \quad C(4) = C(12)\left(1 - e^{-\left(\frac{1 \times 10^{-6}}{10C}\right)}\right)$$

$$\Rightarrow \quad \frac{10^{-7}}{C} = \ln\left(\frac{3}{2}\right)$$

$$\Rightarrow \quad C = \frac{10^{-7}}{\ln\left(\frac{3}{2}\right)} = 0.25\,\mu\text{F}$$

4. $C = \frac{A\varepsilon_0}{d} = \frac{(40 \times 10^{-4})(8.85 \times 10^{-12})}{(0.10 \times 10^{-3})} = 35.4 \times 10^{-11}$ F

$$q = CV\left(1 - e^{-\frac{t}{RC}}\right)$$

$$\Rightarrow \quad \frac{q}{C} = V\left(1 - e^{-\frac{t}{RC}}\right)$$

$$\Rightarrow \quad V' = V\left(1 - e^{-\frac{t}{RC}}\right) = 2\left(1 - e^{-\frac{10 \times 10^{-9}}{16 \times 35.4 \times 10^{-11}}}\right)$$

$$= 2(1 - e^{-1.76}) = 1.7\text{ V}$$

Electric field $= \frac{V'}{d} = \frac{1.7}{0.1 \times 10^{-3}} = 1.7 \times 10^4$ V/m

5. (i) $$i = \frac{V}{R} e^{-\frac{t}{RC}}$$

$$\Rightarrow \quad i = \left(\frac{6.00}{1.00}\right) e^{-\left(\frac{12 \times 10^{-6}}{1.00 \times 12 \times 10^{-6}}\right)} \Rightarrow i = 2.21\text{ A}$$

(ii) Power delivered by battery $= Vi = 6.00 \times 2.21 = 13.2$ W

(iii) Power dissipated in heat $= i^2R = \left(\frac{6}{e}\right)^2 (1.00) = 4.87$ W

(iv) Rate at which energy stored in the capacitor is increasing $= Vi - i^2R$

$$= 13.2 - 4.87 = 8.37\text{ W}$$

6. Charge on capacitor in steady state = CV

$$q = CV\left(1 - e^{-\frac{t}{\tau}}\right)$$

$$\Rightarrow \quad \frac{CV}{2} = CV\left(1 - e^{-\frac{t}{\tau}}\right)$$

$$\Rightarrow \quad e^{-\frac{t}{\tau}} = \frac{1}{2} \Rightarrow \frac{t}{\tau} = \ln 2$$

$$\Rightarrow \quad t = (\ln 2)\tau \Rightarrow t = 0.693\tau \Rightarrow \frac{t}{\tau} = 0.693$$

7. $U_0 = \frac{q_0^2}{2C}$

$$\Rightarrow \quad \frac{U_0}{2} = \frac{q^2}{2C} \Rightarrow q = \frac{q_0}{\sqrt{2}}$$

$$q = CV\left(1 - e^{-\frac{t}{\tau}}\right)$$

$$\Rightarrow \quad \frac{q_0}{\sqrt{2}} = q_0\left(1 - e^{-\frac{t}{\tau}}\right)$$

$$\Rightarrow \quad t = -\tau \ln\left(1 - \frac{1}{\sqrt{2}}\right)$$

$$\Rightarrow \quad t = 1.23\tau \Rightarrow \frac{t}{\tau} = 1.23$$

8. Power delivered by battery = Vi

Power gets halved when current will get halved.

$$i = i_0 e^{-\frac{t}{\tau}} \Rightarrow \frac{i_0}{2} = i_0 e^{-\frac{t}{\tau}}$$

$$\Rightarrow \quad \frac{t}{\tau} = \ln 2 = 0.693$$

9.

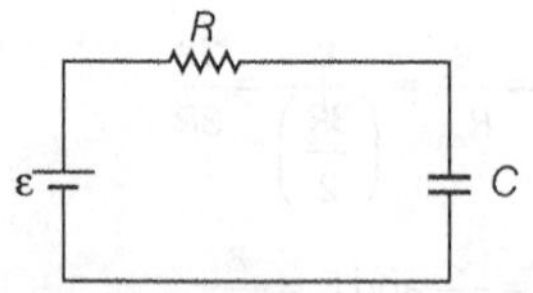

Rate at which energy is stored in the capacitor

$$= \frac{dU}{dt} = \varepsilon i - i^2R$$

To maximize $\frac{dU}{dt}$; $\frac{d^2U}{dt^2} = 0$

$$\Rightarrow \quad \varepsilon\frac{di}{dt} - 2i\frac{di}{dt}R = 0$$

$$\Rightarrow \quad i = \frac{\varepsilon}{2R}$$

$$\left(\frac{dU}{dt}\right)_{\max} = \varepsilon\left(\frac{\varepsilon}{2R}\right) - \left(\frac{\varepsilon}{2R}\right)^2 R = \frac{\varepsilon^2}{4R}$$

$$i = \frac{\varepsilon}{R} e^{-\frac{t}{\tau}}$$

$$\Rightarrow \quad \frac{\varepsilon}{2R} = \frac{\varepsilon}{R} e^{-\frac{t}{RC}} \Rightarrow t = RC \ln 2$$

10. Energy stored in the capacitor in steady state $= \frac{1}{2}CV^2$

Heat dissipated $= \int i^2 R\, dt$

$$= \int_0^\infty \left(\frac{V}{R} e^{-\frac{t}{RC}}\right)^2 R\, dt$$

$$= \frac{V^2}{R} \frac{1}{\left(-\frac{2}{RC}\right)} \left[e^{-\frac{2t}{RC}}\right]_0^\infty = \frac{1}{2}CV^2$$

11.

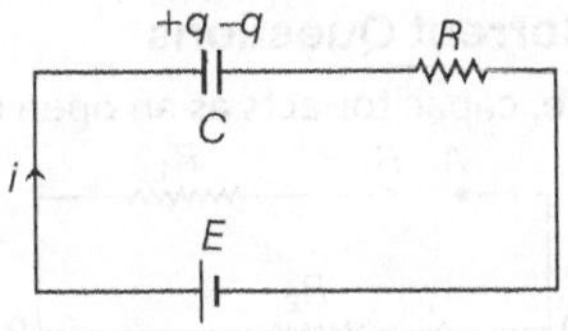

Let charge on capacitor at $t = t$ be q.

Applying KVL in the loop,

$$+E - \frac{q}{C} - iR = 0$$

$$\Rightarrow \quad i = \frac{CE - q}{RC}$$

$$\Rightarrow \quad \frac{dq}{dt} = \frac{CE - q}{RC}$$

$$\Rightarrow \quad \int_Q^q \frac{dq}{CE - q} = \frac{1}{RC}\int_0^t dt$$

$$\Rightarrow \quad \frac{1}{(-1)}[\ln(CE - q)]_Q^q = \frac{1}{RC}[t]_0^t$$

$$\Rightarrow \quad \ln\left(\frac{CE - q}{CE - Q}\right) = -\frac{t}{RC}$$

$$\Rightarrow \quad CE - q = (CE - Q)e^{-\frac{t}{RC}}$$

$$\Rightarrow \quad q = CE - (CE - Q)e^{-\frac{t}{RC}}$$

$$= CE\left(1 - e^{-\frac{t}{RC}}\right) + Qe^{-\frac{t}{RC}}$$

12.

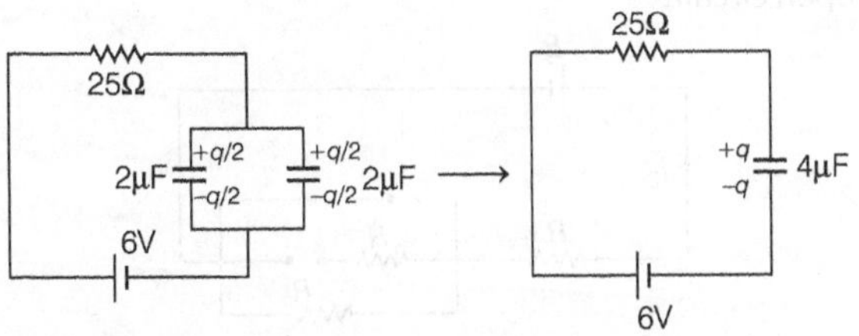

$$q = CV\left(1 - e^{-\frac{t}{RC}}\right)$$

$$= (4 \times 10^{-6} \times 6.0)\left(1 - e^{-\frac{0.2\times 10^{-3}}{25\times 4\times 10^{-6}}}\right)$$

$$= (24 \times 10^{-6})(1 - e^{-2}) = 20.75\,\mu C$$

Charge on each capacitor $= \frac{q}{2} = \frac{20.75}{2} = 10.37\,\mu C$

13.

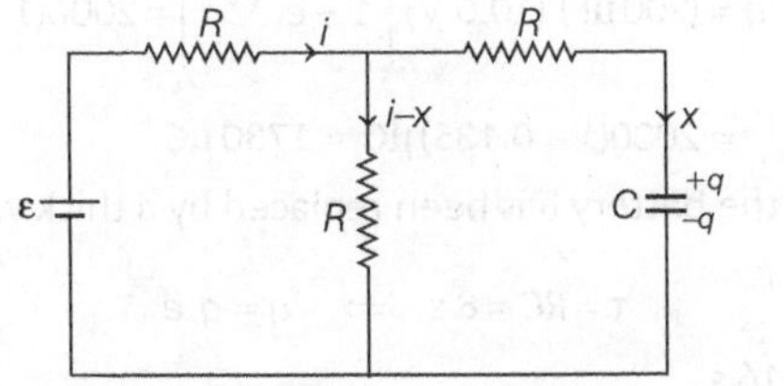

Let charge on capacitor be q and current through it be x at $t = t$.

Applying KVL,

$$+\varepsilon - iR - (i - x)R = 0 \qquad \text{...(i)}$$

$$+\varepsilon - iR - xR - \frac{q}{C} = 0 \qquad \text{...(ii)}$$

From Eqs. (i) and (ii), we get

$$x = \frac{C\varepsilon - 2q}{3RC}$$

$$\Rightarrow \quad \frac{dq}{dt} = \frac{C\varepsilon - 2q}{3RC}$$

$$\Rightarrow \quad \int_0^q \frac{dq}{C\varepsilon - 2q} = \int_0^t \frac{1}{3RC} dt$$

$$\Rightarrow \quad q = \frac{C\varepsilon}{2}\left(1 - e^{-\frac{2t}{3RC}}\right)$$

11.3 R-C Circuit (Discharging)

1. $q = q_0 e^{-\frac{t}{RC}}$

(i) At $t = 0$; $q = q_0 = 60\,\mu C$

(ii) At $t = 100\,\mu s$; $q = (60\,\mu C)\left(e^{-\frac{100\times 10^{-6}}{10\times 10\times 10^{-6}}}\right) = 22\,\mu C$

(iii) At $t = 200\,\mu s$; $q = (60\,\mu C)\left(e^{-\frac{200\times 10^{-6}}{10\times 10\times 10^{-6}}}\right) = 8.12\,\mu C$

(iv) At $t = 1$ ms; $q = (60\,\mu C)\left(e^{-\frac{10^{-3}}{10\times 10\times 10^{-6}}}\right) = 0.003\,\mu C$

2. At $t = 0$, charge on capacitor $= CV$

$$= (20 \times 10^{-6})\left(\frac{20}{(10 + 10)} \times 10\right) = 200\,\mu C$$

After opening the switch,

$$i = \frac{Q}{RC} e^{-\frac{t}{RC}}$$

$$\Rightarrow \quad i = \left(\frac{200 \times 10^{-6}}{10 \times 20 \times 10^{-6}}\right) e^{-\left(\frac{1\times 10^{-3}}{10\times 20\times 10^{-6}}\right)} = 1 \times e^{(-5)} = 6.7\text{ mA}$$

3. While battery is connected,

$$\tau = RC = 40 \times 10^3 \times 200 \times 10^{-6} = 8\text{ s}$$

$$q = CV\left(1 - e^{-\frac{t}{\tau}}\right)$$

At $t = 16$ s,

$$q = (200\,\mu\text{F})\,(10.0\text{ V})\left(1 - e^{-\left(\frac{16}{8}\right)}\right) = 2000(1 - e^{-2})\,\mu\text{C}$$

$$= 2000(1 - 0.135)\,\mu\text{C} = 1730\,\mu\text{C}$$

After the battery has been replaced by a thick wire,

$$\tau = RC = 8\text{ s} \Rightarrow q = q_0 e^{-\frac{t}{\tau}}$$

At $t = 16$ s,

$$q = (1730 \times 10^{-6})\left(e^{-\frac{16}{8}}\right) = (1730\,\mu\text{C})\,(e^{-2})$$

$$= (1730\,\mu\text{C})\,(0.135) = 233.55\,\mu\text{C}$$

4. When electric field drops to one-third of its initial value, charge on capacitor will also drop to one-third of the initial charge.

$$q = q_0 e^{-\frac{t}{RC}}$$

$$\Rightarrow \quad \frac{q_0}{3} = q_0 e^{-\frac{4.4 \times 10^{-6}}{R \times 2 \times 10^{-6}}}$$

$$\Rightarrow \quad R = \frac{11}{5\ln 3} = 2.0\,\Omega$$

5. $\tau = RC = 5.0 \times (5.0 \times 10^{-6}) = 25\,\mu\text{s}$

$$q_0 = 20\,\mu\text{C} \Rightarrow q = q_0 e^{-\frac{t}{\tau}}$$

At $t = 25\,\mu$s; $q_1 = (20\,\mu\text{C})\left(e^{-\left(\frac{25}{25}\right)}\right) = \left(\frac{20}{e}\right)\mu\text{C}$

At $t = 50\,\mu$s; $q_2 = (20\,\mu\text{C})\left(e^{-\left(\frac{50}{25}\right)}\right) = \left(\frac{20}{e^2}\right)\mu\text{C}$

Heat dissipated $= \frac{q_1^2}{2C} - \frac{q_2^2}{2C}$

$$= \left(\frac{1}{2 \times 5 \times 10^{-6}}\right)\left(\left(\frac{20}{e}\right)^2 - \left(\frac{20}{e^2}\right)^2\right) \times 10^{-12}$$

$$= (40 \times 10^{-6})(1 - e^{-2})e^{-2} = 4.7\,\mu\text{J}$$

6.

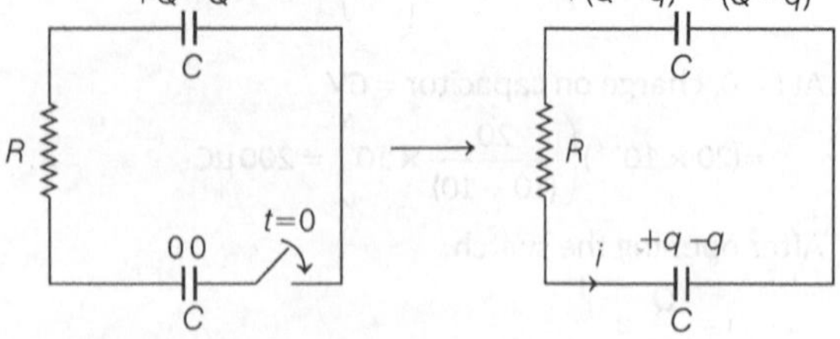

Let charge on the second capacitor be q at time t.

Applying KVL in the loop,

$$-iR - \frac{q}{C} + \frac{Q - q}{C} = 0$$

$$\Rightarrow \quad i = \frac{Q - 2q}{RC}$$

$$\Rightarrow \quad \frac{dq}{dt} = \frac{Q - 2q}{RC}$$

$$\Rightarrow \quad \int_0^q \frac{dq}{Q - 2q} = \frac{1}{RC}\int_0^t dt$$

$$\Rightarrow \quad \frac{1}{(-2)}[\ln(Q - 2q)]_0^q = \frac{1}{RC}[t]_0^t$$

$$\Rightarrow \quad q = \frac{Q}{2}\left(1 - e^{-\frac{2t}{RC}}\right)$$

Level 2 JEE Main Level

Single Choice Correct Questions

1. In steady state, capacitor acts as an open circuit.

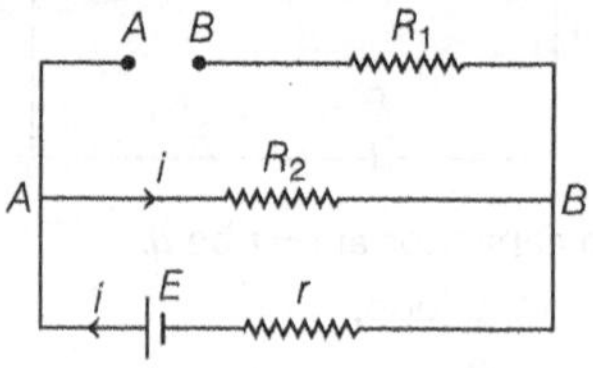

$$i = \frac{E}{R_2 + r}$$

$$V_A - V_B = iR_2 = \frac{ER_2}{R_2 + r}$$

Charge on capacitor $= CV = C(V_A - V_B) = \frac{CER_2}{R_2 + r}$

2. Immediately after closing the key, a capacitor acts as a conducting wire.

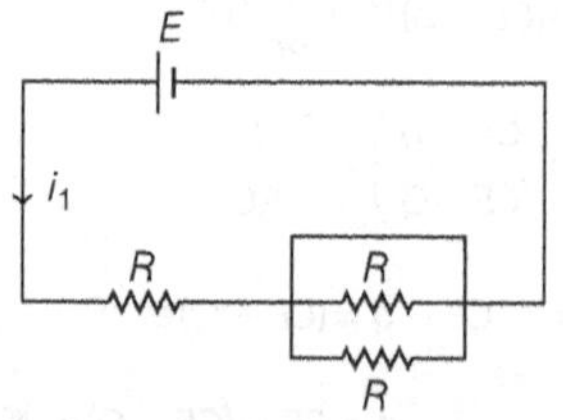

$$i_1 = \frac{E}{R}$$

After a long time interval, a capacitor acts as an open circuit.

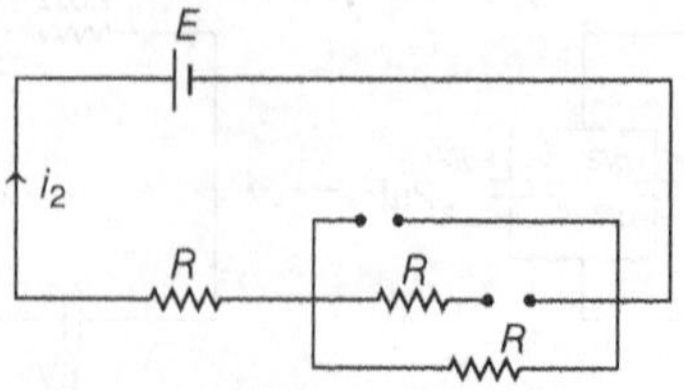

$$i_2 = \frac{E}{2R}$$

3. In steady state, a capacitor acts as an open circuit.

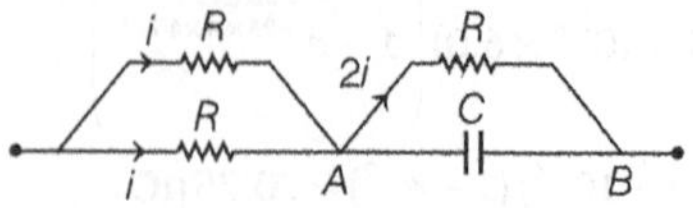

$$V_A - V_B = (2i)R$$

Energy stored in the capacitor $= \frac{1}{2}C(V_A - V_B)^2 = \frac{1}{2}C(2iR)^2$

$$= 2Ci^2R^2$$

4. In steady state, a capacitor acts as an open circuit.

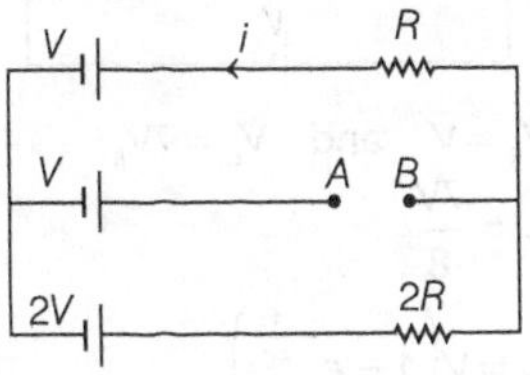

Applying KVL,

$$+2V - i(2R) - iR - V = 0 \Rightarrow i = \frac{V}{3R}$$

$$V_A - V + V + iR = V_B$$

$$V_B - V_A = iR = \left(\frac{V}{3R}\right)R = \frac{V}{3}$$

5. When switch S is open,

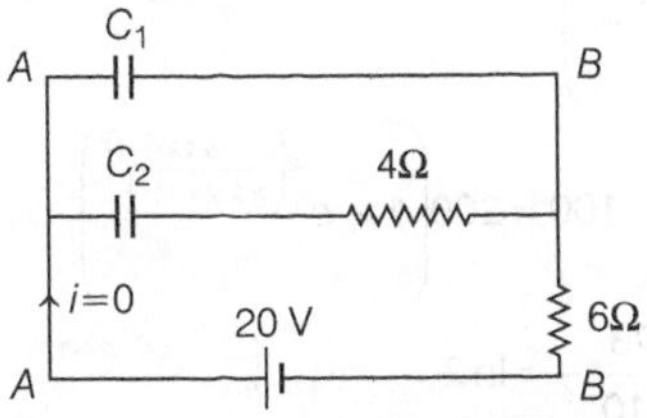

$$V_A - V_B = 20\text{ V}$$

q_1 = charge on capacitor $C_1 = C_1(V_A - V_B) = C_1(20)$

When switch S is closed, C_2 will get short-circuited.

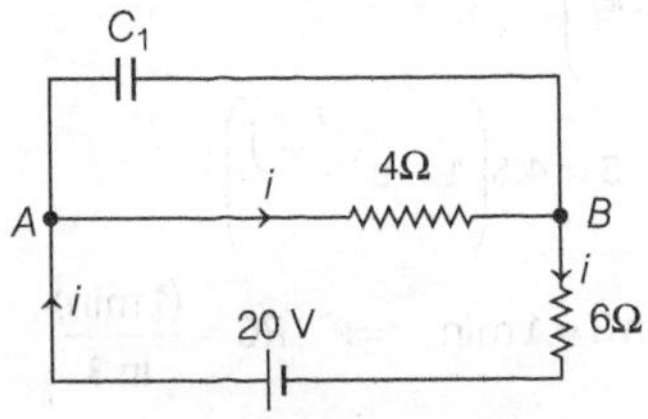

$$i = \frac{20}{(4+6)} = 2\text{A}$$

$$V_A - V_B = i(4) = 8\text{V}$$

q_2 = charge on capacitor $C_1 = C_1(V_A - V_B) = C_1(8)$

$$\frac{q_1}{q_2} = \frac{20C_1}{8C_1} = \frac{5}{2}$$

$\Rightarrow \quad q_1 : q_2 = 5:2$

6.

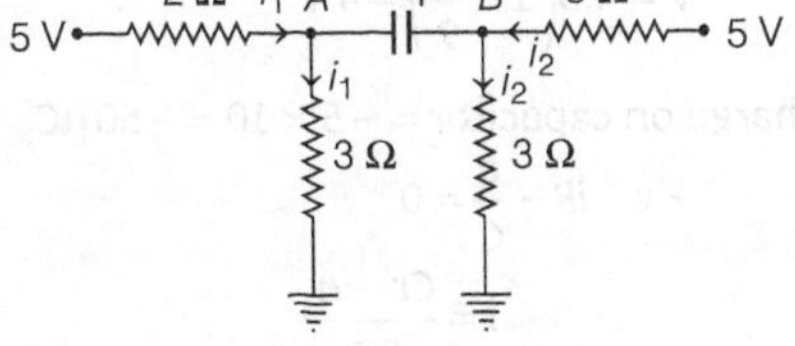

$$i_1 = \frac{5}{(2+3)} = 1\text{A}$$

$$i_2 = \frac{5}{(3+3)} = \frac{5}{6}\text{A}$$

$$V_A = 3i_1 = 3(1) = 3\text{V}$$

$$V_B = 3i_2 = 3\left(\frac{5}{6}\right) = 2.5\text{V}$$

$$V_A - V_B = 3 - 2.5 = 0.5\text{ V}$$

Charge on capacitor $= C(V_A - V_B) = (2\mu\text{F})(0.5\text{V}) = 1\,\mu\text{C}$

7. When switch S_2 is kept closed for a long time, charge on capacitor $= C(2\varepsilon) = 2C\varepsilon$

Now, just after closing switch S_1,

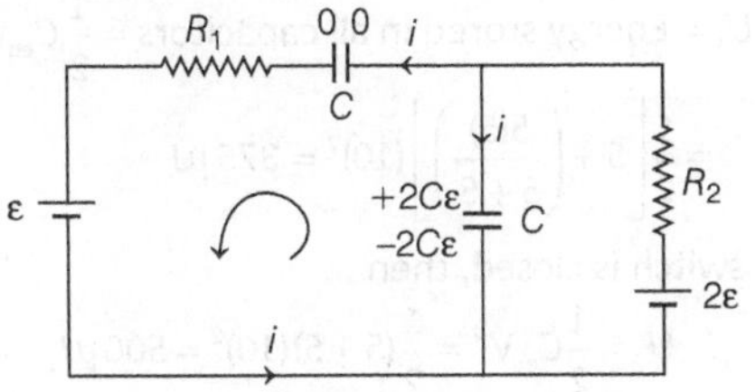

Applying KVL in the left loop,

$$+\varepsilon + iR_1 - \frac{2C\varepsilon}{C} = 0 \quad \Rightarrow \quad i = \frac{\varepsilon}{R_1}$$

So, current through S_1 is $\frac{\varepsilon}{R_1}$ toward left.

8.

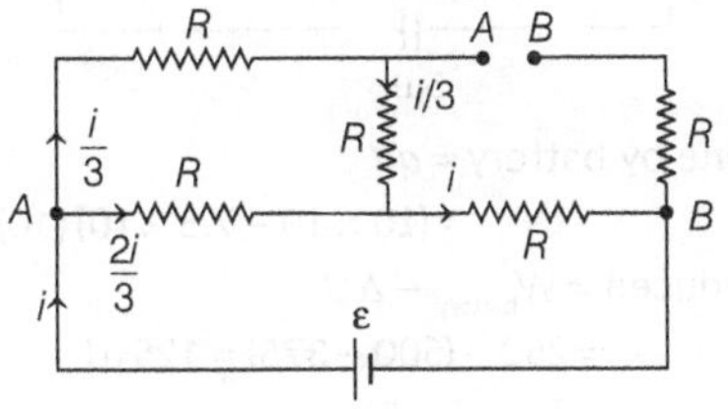

In steady state, capacitor acts as an open circuit.

$$i = \frac{\varepsilon}{R_{eq}} = \frac{\varepsilon}{\left(\frac{5R}{3}\right)} = \frac{3\varepsilon}{5R}$$

$$V_A - V_B = \left(\frac{i}{3}\right)R + iR = \frac{4}{3}iR$$

$$\Rightarrow \quad V_A - V_B = \frac{4}{3}\left(\frac{3\varepsilon}{5R}\right)R = 12 \quad \Rightarrow \quad \varepsilon = 15\text{ V}$$

9. When switch is in position 1, charge on capacitor $= C\varepsilon_1$

U_1 = Energy stored in capacitor $= \frac{1}{2}C\varepsilon_1^2$

When switch is shifted to position 2, charge on capacitor $= C\varepsilon_2$ (reverse polarity)

Charge flown through cell $\varepsilon_2 = C(\varepsilon_1 + \varepsilon_2)$

Work done by cell $\varepsilon_2 = C\varepsilon_2(\varepsilon_1 + \varepsilon_2)$

$$U_2 = \frac{1}{2}C\varepsilon_2^2$$

Heat generated $= W_{cell} - \Delta U$

$$= C\varepsilon_2(\varepsilon_1 + \varepsilon_2) - \left(\frac{1}{2}C\varepsilon_2^2 - \frac{1}{2}C\varepsilon_1^2\right) = \frac{1}{2}C(\varepsilon_1 + \varepsilon_2)^2$$

10. When switch is open, then

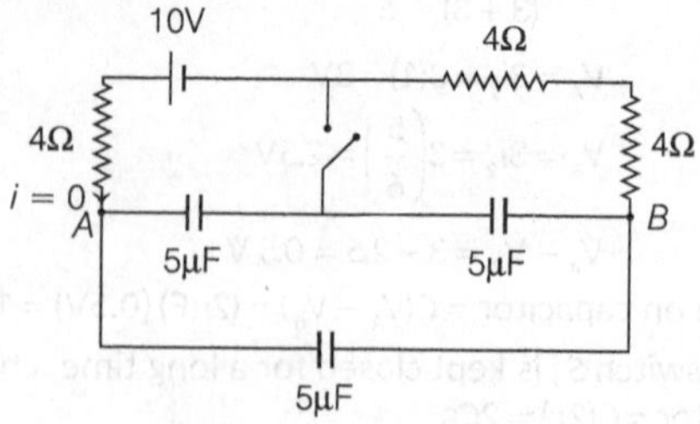

$$V_A - V_B = 10\text{ V}$$

$$U_1 = \text{Energy stored in all capacitors} = \frac{1}{2}C_{eq}V^2$$

$$= \frac{1}{2}\left[5 + \left(\frac{5(5)}{5+5}\right)\right](10)^2 = 375\ \mu\text{J}$$

When switch is closed, then

$$U_2 = \frac{1}{2}C_{eq}V^2 = \frac{1}{2}(5+5)(10)^2 = 500\ \mu\text{J}$$

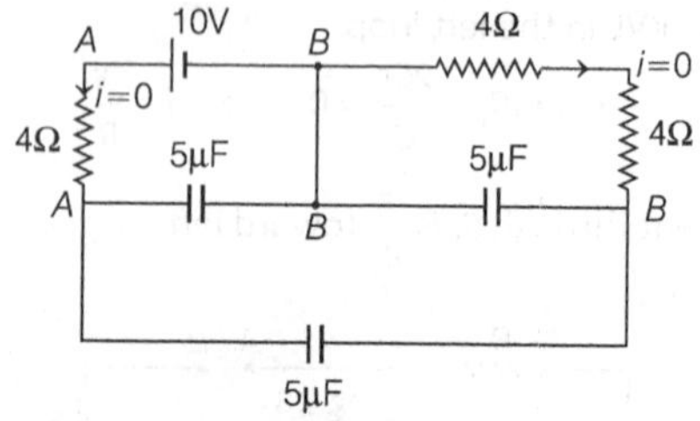

Work done by battery $= qV$

$$= (10\times 10 - 7.5\times 10)(10) = 250\ \mu\text{J}$$

Heat produced $= W_{\text{battery}} - \Delta U$

$$= 250 - (500 - 375) = 125\ \mu\text{J}$$

11.

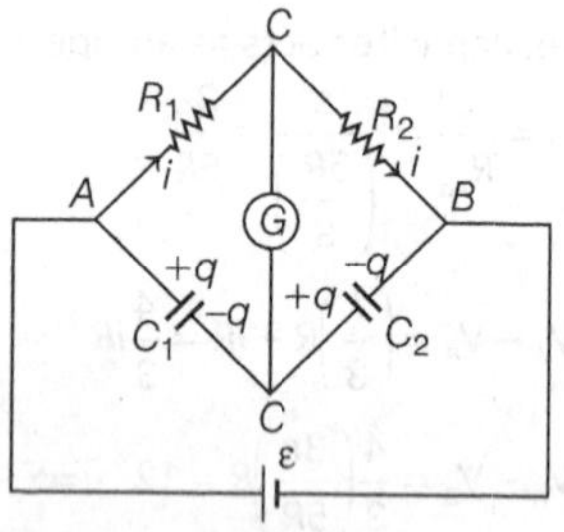

$$V_A - V_C = iR_1 \text{ and } V_C - V_B = iR_2$$

$$\frac{V_A - V_C}{V_C - V_B} = \frac{iR_1}{iR_2} = \frac{R_1}{R_2} \quad \text{...(i)}$$

$$V_A - V_C = \frac{q}{C_1} \text{ and } V_C - V_B = \frac{q}{C_2}$$

$$\Rightarrow \quad \frac{V_A - V_C}{V_C - V_B} = \frac{\frac{q}{C_1}}{\frac{q}{C_2}} = \frac{C_2}{C_1} \quad \text{...(ii)}$$

From Eqs. (i) and (ii), we get

$$\frac{R_1}{R_2} = \frac{C_2}{C_1}$$

12.

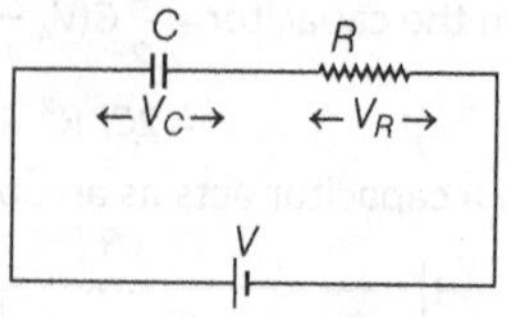

$$V_C + V_R = V \quad \text{and} \quad V_C = 7V_R$$

$$\Rightarrow \quad V_C = \frac{7V}{8}$$

$$V_C = V\left(1 - e^{-\frac{t}{RC}}\right)$$

$$\Rightarrow \quad \frac{7V}{8} = V\left(1 - e^{-\frac{t}{RC}}\right) \Rightarrow t = 3RC\ln 2$$

13. Current in the circuit gradually decreases to zero. So, the bulb will light up for some time interval after the capacitor starts charging.

14. $V = E\left(1 - e^{-\frac{t}{RC}}\right)$

$$\Rightarrow \quad 100 = 200\left(1 - e^{-\left(\frac{6.93}{R\times 2\times 10^{-6}}\right)}\right)$$

$$\Rightarrow \quad \frac{6.93}{2R\times 10^{-6}} = \ln 2$$

$$\Rightarrow \quad R = \frac{6.93\times 10^6}{2\ln 2} = \frac{6.93\times 10^6}{2\times 0.693} = 5\times 10^6\ \Omega$$

15. $V = E\left(1 - e^{-\frac{t}{RC}}\right)$

$$\Rightarrow \quad 3 = 4.5\left(1 - e^{-\left(\frac{1\text{ min}}{RC}\right)}\right)$$

$$\Rightarrow \quad RC\ln 3 = 1\text{ min} \Rightarrow RC = \frac{(1\text{ min})}{\ln 3}$$

$$V = E\left(1 - e^{-\frac{t}{RC}}\right)$$

At $t = 2$ min,

$$V = 4.5\left(1 - e^{-\left(\frac{2\text{ min}}{\left(\frac{1\text{ min}}{\ln 3}\right)}\right)}\right)$$

$$\Rightarrow \quad V = 4.5\left(1 - \frac{1}{9}\right) = 4\text{ V}$$

16. Initial charge on capacitor $= -5\times 10 = -50\,\mu\text{C}$

$$+\varepsilon - iR - \frac{q}{C} = 0$$

$$\Rightarrow \quad i = \frac{C\varepsilon - q}{RC}$$

$$\Rightarrow \quad \frac{dq}{dt} = \frac{C\varepsilon - q}{RC} = \frac{30 - q}{6}$$

$$\Rightarrow \quad \int_{-50}^{0} \frac{dq}{30-q} = \frac{1}{6}\int_{0}^{t} dt$$

$$\Rightarrow \quad \frac{1}{(-1)}[\ln(30-q)]_{-50}^{0} = \frac{1}{6}[t]_0^t$$

$$\Rightarrow \quad \ln\left(\frac{30-0}{30-(-50)}\right) = -\frac{t}{6}$$

$$\Rightarrow \quad t = 6\ln\left(\frac{8}{3}\right) \Rightarrow t = 6\text{ s}$$

17.

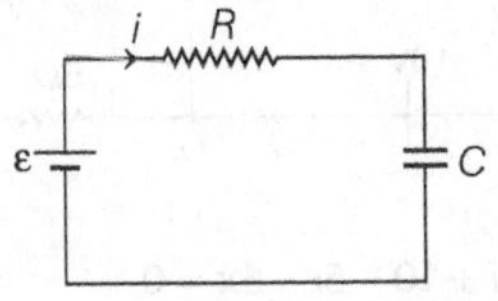

Rate of energy stored in the capacitor $= \varepsilon i - i^2R$

$$\frac{dU}{dt} = \varepsilon i - i^2 R$$

To maximize $\frac{dU}{dt}, \frac{d^2U}{dt^2} = 0$

$$\Rightarrow \quad \varepsilon\frac{di}{dt} - 2i\frac{di}{dt}R = 0 \Rightarrow i = \frac{\varepsilon}{2R}$$

$$\left(\frac{dU}{dt}\right)_{max} = \varepsilon\left(\frac{\varepsilon}{2R}\right) - \left(\frac{\varepsilon}{2R}\right)^2 R = \frac{\varepsilon^2}{4R}$$

18. $i = \frac{\varepsilon}{R}e^{-\frac{t}{RC}}$

$$\Rightarrow \quad \log_e i = \log_e\left(\frac{\varepsilon}{R}\right) + \log_e e^{-\frac{t}{RC}}$$

$$\Rightarrow \quad \log_e i = \log_e\left(\frac{\varepsilon}{R}\right) - \left(\frac{1}{RC}\right)t$$

When the value of resistance is doubled, y-intercept decreases and magnitude of slope also decreases.

So, correct graph will be P.

19. Power dissipated in resistor $= i^2R$

Rate of energy change in capacitor $= Vi - i^2R$

$$Vi - i^2R = 3(i^2R)$$

$$\Rightarrow \quad i = \frac{V}{4R}$$

$$i = \frac{V}{R}e^{-\frac{t}{RC}}$$

$$\Rightarrow \quad \frac{V}{4R} = \frac{V}{R}e^{-\frac{t}{RC}}$$

$$\Rightarrow \quad t = 2RC\ln 2$$

20. $i_1 = \frac{V}{R}e^{-\frac{t}{RC_1}}$ and $i_2 = \frac{V}{R}e^{-\frac{t}{RC_2}}$

$$\frac{i_1}{i_2} = e^{-\frac{t}{R}\left(\frac{1}{C_1}-\frac{1}{C_2}\right)} = e^{-\frac{t}{R}\left(\frac{1}{2C_2}-\frac{1}{C_2}\right)} \Rightarrow \frac{i_1}{i_2} = e^{\frac{t}{2RC_2}}$$

So, $\frac{i_1}{i_2}$ increases with increase in time t.

21. $U_1 = \frac{q_0^2}{2C}$

$$U_2 = \frac{q^2}{2C}$$

$$\because \quad U_2 = \frac{U_1}{2} \Rightarrow q = \frac{q_0}{\sqrt{2}}$$

$$q = q_0 e^{-\frac{t}{R_{eq}C}}$$

$$\Rightarrow \quad \frac{q_0}{\sqrt{2}} = q_0 e^{-\frac{t}{R_{eq}C}}$$

$$\Rightarrow \quad t = \frac{R_{eq}C\ln 2}{2} = \frac{7RC\ln 2}{8}$$

22. $q = q_0 e^{-\frac{t}{RC}}$

$$i = i_0 e^{-\frac{t}{RC}}$$

$$\frac{q}{i} = \frac{q_0}{i_0} = \text{constant}$$

23. $i = i_0 e^{-\frac{t}{R_{eq}C}}$

$$\Rightarrow \quad \frac{i_0}{2} = i_0 e^{-\frac{t}{R_{eq}C}} \Rightarrow t = R_{eq}C\ln 2$$

$$\Rightarrow \quad (\ln 4)\times 10^{-6} = R_{eq}(0.5\times 10^{-6})\ln 2$$

$$\Rightarrow \quad R_{eq} = 4\,\Omega$$

$$R_{eq} = 2 + R_A$$

$$\Rightarrow \quad 4 = 2 + R_A \Rightarrow R_A = 2\,\Omega$$

24.

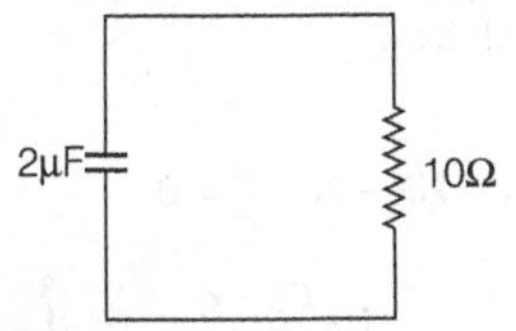

Let initial charge be q_0.

Initial energy stored in the capacitor

= Energy dissipated in resistor

$$\Rightarrow \quad \frac{q_0^2}{2C} = 3.6\times 10^{-3}$$

$$\Rightarrow \quad q_0^2 = 2\times 2\times 10^{-6}\times 3.6\times 10^{-3}$$

$$\Rightarrow \quad q_0 = 12\times 10^{-5}\text{C} = 120\,\mu\text{C}$$

25. Slowest rate of discharge will happen when time constant of the circuit is largest.

Time constant $= RC$ is largest

when, $R = 100\,\Omega$ and $C = 50\,\mu\text{F}$

26. At $t = 0$, current through middle $20\,\Omega$ resistor

$$= \frac{12}{20+20} = \frac{3}{10}\text{A}$$

$$i = i_0 e^{-\frac{t}{RC}}$$

$$\Rightarrow \quad i = (0.3)\,e^{-\left(\frac{0.25\times 10^{-3}}{20\times 25\times 10^{-6}}\right)}$$

$$\Rightarrow \quad i = 0.3\,e^{-0.5} = 0.3\times 0.606 = 0.182\text{ A} = 182\text{ mA}$$

27. $V = V_0 e^{-\frac{t}{\tau}}$

In one time constant,

$$V = V_0 e^{-1} = \frac{V_0}{e} = 20 \times 0.37 = 7.4\text{ V}$$

So, time constant of the circuit lies between 100 s and 150 s.

28.

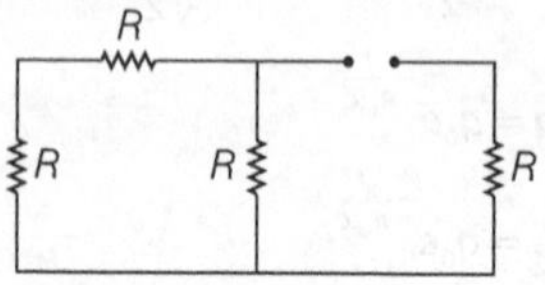

$$\tau = R_{eq} C = \left(\frac{5R}{3}\right) C$$

29. When switch is opened, time constant for discharging circuit $= R_{eq} C$

$$= \left(\frac{(1\text{ k}\Omega)(1\text{ k}\Omega)}{1\text{ k}\Omega + 1\text{ k}\Omega}\right) \times 100 \times 10^{-6}$$

$$= 0.5 \times 10^3 \times 100 \times 10^{-6} = 50 \times 10^{-3} = 50\text{ ms}$$

30.

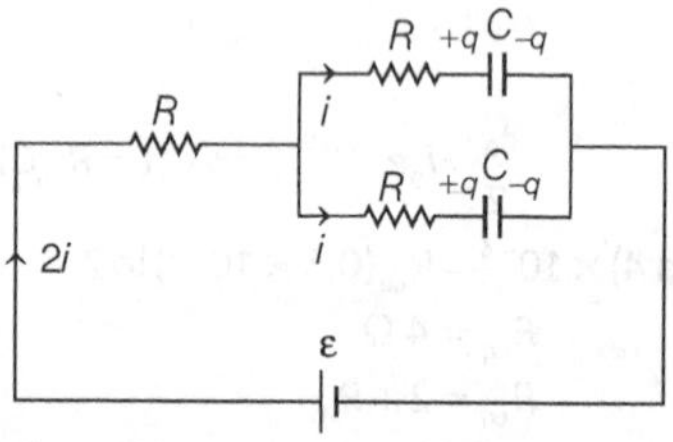

Let charge on capacitor at $t = t$ be q and current through capacitor branch be i.

Applying KVL,

$$+\varepsilon - 2iR - iR - \frac{q}{C} = 0$$

$$\Rightarrow \quad i = \frac{C\varepsilon - q}{3RC} \Rightarrow \int_0^q \frac{dq}{C\varepsilon - q} = \frac{1}{3RC} \int_0^t dt$$

$$\Rightarrow \quad \frac{1}{(-1)} [\ln(C\varepsilon - q)]_0^q = \frac{1}{3RC} [t]_0^t \Rightarrow q = C\varepsilon\left(1 - e^{-\frac{t}{3RC}}\right)$$

Numerical Value Questions

1. In steady state, a capacitor acts as an open circuit.

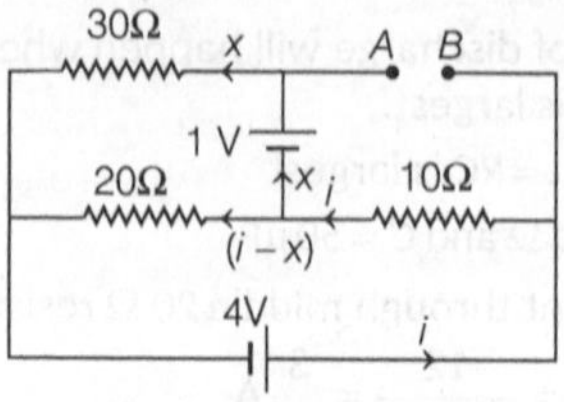

Applying KVL,

$$+4 - 10i - 20(i - x) = 0$$

$$15i - 10x = 2 \quad \text{...(i)}$$

$$+1 - 30x + 20(i - x) = 0$$

$$\Rightarrow \quad 50x - 20i = 1 \quad \text{...(ii)}$$

Solving Eqs. (i) and (ii), we get

$$i = 0.2\text{ A} \quad \text{and} \quad x = 0.1\text{ A}$$

$$V_A - 1 + 10i = V_B$$

$$\Rightarrow \quad V_B - V_A = 10(0.2) - 1 = 1\text{ V}$$

Charge on capacitor $= (8\,\mu\text{F})\,(1\text{V}) = 8\,\mu\text{C}$

2.

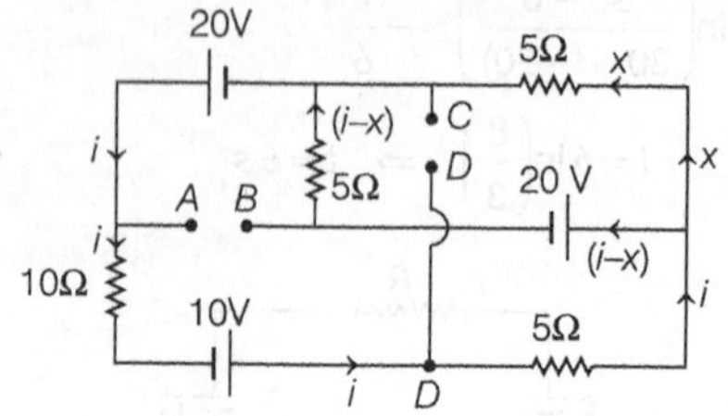

Applying KVL,

$$+20 - 10i + 10 - 5i - 5x = 0$$

$$\Rightarrow \quad 3i + x = 6 \quad \text{...(i)}$$

$$+20 - 5x + 5(i - x) = 0$$

$$2x - i = 4 \quad \text{...(ii)}$$

Solving Eqs. (i) and (ii), we get

$$x = \frac{18}{7}\text{ A and } i = \frac{8}{7}\text{ A}$$

$$V_A - 20 + 5(i - x) = V_B$$

$$\Rightarrow \quad V_A - V_B = \frac{190}{7}\text{ V}$$

$$V_D - 5i - 5x = V_C \Rightarrow V_D - V_C = \frac{130}{7}\text{ V}$$

Charge on 5 μF capacitor, $q_1 = (5\,\mu\text{F})\,(V_D - V_C)$

$$= 5 \times \frac{130}{7}\,\mu\text{C} = \frac{650}{7}\,\mu\text{C}$$

Charge on 10 μF capacitor, $q_2 = (10\,\mu\text{F})\,(V_A - V_B)$

$$= 10 \times \frac{190}{7}\,\mu\text{C} = \frac{1900}{7}\,\mu\text{C}$$

$$\frac{q_1}{q_2} = \frac{\frac{650}{7}}{\frac{1900}{7}} = \frac{13}{38}$$

3. Using KVL,

$$+10 - 7i_2 - 8i_2 + 5 = 0 \Rightarrow i_2 = 1\text{A}$$

$$+6 - 10i_1 - 2i_1 = 0$$

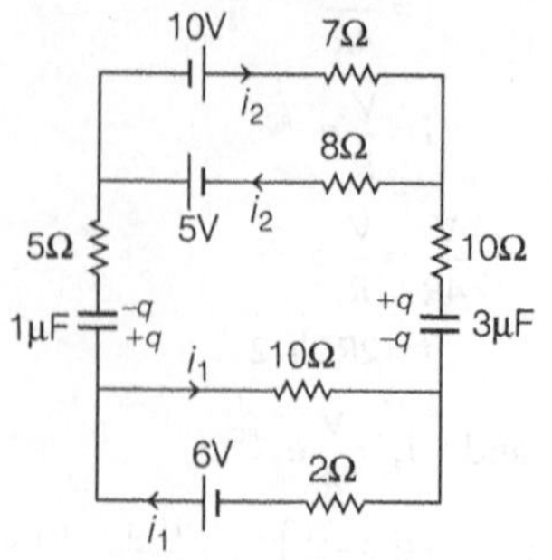

$$\Rightarrow \quad i_1 = 0.5\text{A}$$

$$-\frac{q}{1} - 5 + 8(i_2) - \frac{q}{3} + 10i_1 = 0$$

$$\Rightarrow \quad q = 6\,\mu\text{C}$$

Energy stored in the capacitors $= \dfrac{q_1^2}{2C_1} + \dfrac{q_2^2}{2C_2} = 24\,\mu J$

4. $i_1 = \dfrac{V_0}{R_1} = \dfrac{30}{10\times 10^3} = 3\times 10^{-3}$ A

$i_2 = \dfrac{V_0}{R_1 + R_2} = \dfrac{30}{10\times 10^3 + 5\times 10^3} = 2\times 10^{-3}$ A

$i_3 = \dfrac{V_0}{R_1 + R_2} = 2\times 10^{-3}$ A

$\dfrac{i_1}{i_2 i_3} = \dfrac{3\times 10^{-3}}{(2\times 10^{-3})\times(2\times 10^{-3})} = 750$

5. Maximum charge on capacitor $= 1\times 20 = 20\,\mu C$

Potential difference across capacitor when charge is 75% of maximum value $= \dfrac{20\times 0.75}{1} = 15$ V

Potential difference across resistor $= 20 - 15 = 5$ V

$i = \dfrac{V}{R} \Rightarrow 1 = \dfrac{5}{R} \Rightarrow R = 5\,\Omega$

6.

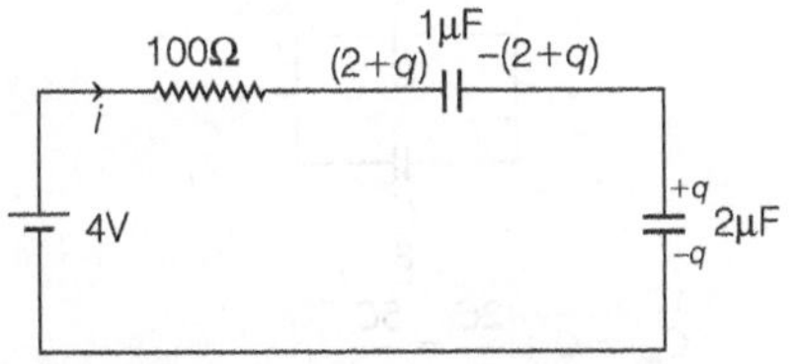

Let $q\,\mu C$ charge flows through battery in time t.

Using KVL in the loop,

$+4 - 100i - \dfrac{(2+q)\times 10^{-6}}{1\times 10^{-6}} - \dfrac{q\times 10^{-6}}{2\times 10^{-6}} = 0$

$\Rightarrow \quad 4 - 100i - (2+q) - \dfrac{q}{2} = 0$

$\Rightarrow \quad i = \dfrac{4-3q}{200}$

$\Rightarrow \quad \dfrac{dq}{dt} = \left(\dfrac{4-3q}{200}\right)\times 10^6$

$\Rightarrow \quad \displaystyle\int_0^q \frac{dq}{4-3q} = \frac{10^6}{200}\int_0^t dt$

$\Rightarrow \quad \ln\left(\dfrac{4-3q}{4}\right) = -\dfrac{3\times 10^6 t}{200}$

$q = \dfrac{4}{3}(1 - e^{-15000t})$

$i = \dfrac{dq}{dt}\times 10^{-6} = \dfrac{4}{3}\times 10^{-6}\times(-15000)\times(-e^{-15000t})$

$i = \dfrac{1}{50}e^{-15000\,t}$

$\dfrac{k}{i_0} = \dfrac{15000}{50} = 300$

7. Charge on capacitor in steady state $= CV$

$= (20\,\mu F)\left(\dfrac{40}{(4+4)}\times 4\right) = 400\,\mu C$

Time constant, $\tau = R_{eq}C$

For finding R_{eq},

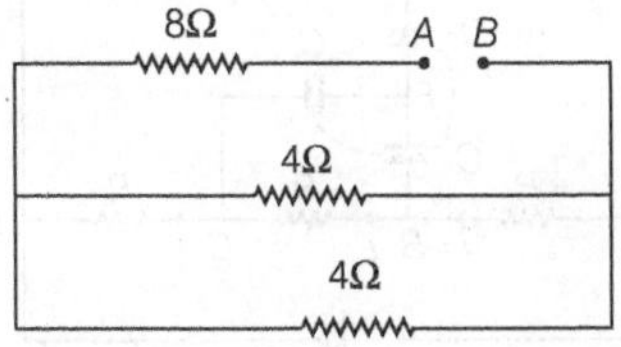

$R_{eq} = 10\Omega$

$\tau = 10\times 20\times 10^{-6} = 200\times 10^{-6}$ sec

$q = 400\times 10^{-6}\left(1 - e^{-\left(\frac{t}{200\times 10^{-6}}\right)}\right)$

$i = \dfrac{dq}{dt} = \left(400\times 10^{-6}\times\dfrac{1}{200\times 10^{-6}}\right)e^{-\left(\frac{t}{200\times 10^{-6}}\right)}$

$i = 2e^{-5000t}$

At $t = 0.4\times 10^{-3}$ s, $i = 2e^{-5000\times 0.4\times 10^{-3}}$

$= 2e^{-2} = 0.27$ A $= 270$ mA

8. $q'_1 = q_1 e^{-\frac{t}{R_1C_1}}$ and $q'_2 = q_2 e^{-\frac{t}{R_2C_2}}$

$q'_1 = q'_2$

$\Rightarrow \quad q_1 e^{-\frac{t}{R_1C_1}} = q_2 e^{-\frac{t}{R_2C_2}} \Rightarrow e^{\left(\frac{1}{R_2C_2} - \frac{1}{R_1C_1}\right)t} = \dfrac{q_2}{q_1}$

$\Rightarrow \quad \left(\dfrac{1}{R_2C_2} - \dfrac{1}{R_1C_1}\right)t = \ln\left(\dfrac{q_2}{q_1}\right)$

$\Rightarrow \quad \left(\dfrac{1}{R\left(\dfrac{10}{3}\times 10^{-6}\right)} - \dfrac{1}{5\times 5\times 10^{-6}}\right)(10^{-4}\ln 2) = \ln 2$

$\Rightarrow \quad 100\times\dfrac{3}{10R} - \dfrac{100}{25} = 1 \Rightarrow R = 6\,\Omega$

Level 3 JEE Advanced Level

Single Choice Correct Questions

1.

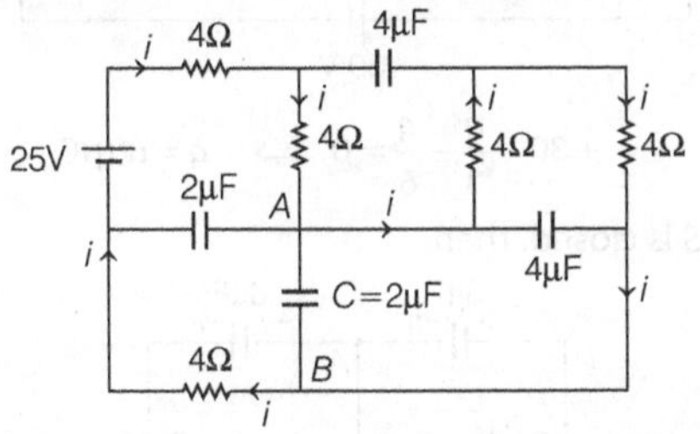

$i = \dfrac{25}{(4+4+4+4+4)} = \dfrac{25}{20} = \dfrac{5}{4}$ A

$V_A - V_B = 8i = 8\left(\dfrac{5}{4}\right) = 10$V

Charge on $C = 2\,\mu F$ capacitor $= (2\,\mu F)(10V) = 20\,\mu C$

2.

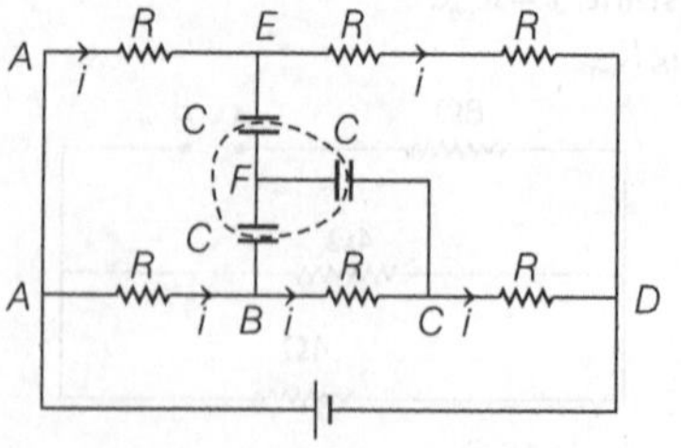

$$i=\frac{V}{3R}$$

Let $V_D=0 \Rightarrow V_A=V$

$$V_A-V_B=iR=\left(\frac{V}{3R}\right)R=\frac{V}{3} \quad \Rightarrow \quad V_B=\frac{2V}{3}$$

$$V_B-V_C=\left(\frac{V}{3R}\right)R=\frac{V}{3} \quad \Rightarrow \quad V_C=\frac{V}{3}$$

$$V_A-V_E=\left(\frac{V}{3R}\right)R=\frac{V}{3} \quad \Rightarrow \quad V_E=\frac{2V}{3}$$

Let potential of junction F be x.

At junction F, $\Sigma q=0$

$$\Rightarrow \quad C(V_F-V_E)+C(V_F-V_B)+C(V_F-V_C)=0$$

$$\Rightarrow \quad C\left(x-\frac{2V}{3}\right)+C\left(x-\frac{2V}{3}\right)+C\left(x-\frac{V}{3}\right)=0$$

$$\Rightarrow \quad x=\frac{5V}{9}$$

Potential difference across, $C_3=V_F-V_C$

$$=\frac{5V}{9}-\frac{V}{3}=\frac{2V}{9}$$

3. When S is opened, then

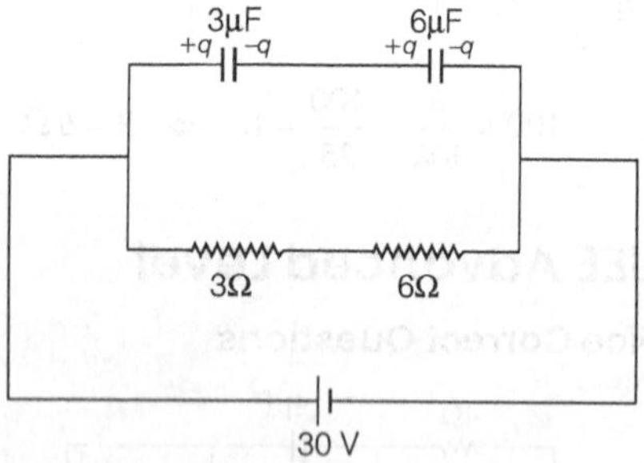

$$+30-\frac{q}{3}-\frac{q}{6}=0 \Rightarrow q=60\,\mu\text{C}$$

When S is closed, then

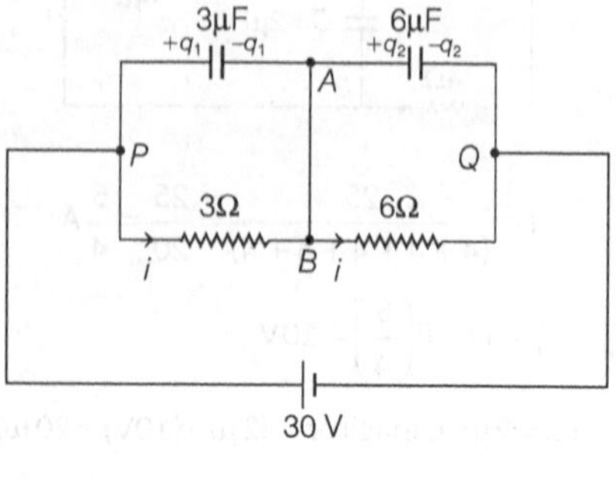

$$i=\frac{30}{6+3}=\frac{10}{3}\text{ A}$$

$$q_1=3(V_P-V_A)=3[i(3)]=3\left(\frac{10}{3}\times 3\right)=30\,\mu\text{C}$$

$$q_2=6(V_A-V_Q)=6[i(6)]=6\left(\frac{10}{3}\times 6\right)=120\,\mu\text{C}$$

Charge flown through $S=(-30+120)-(-60+60)$

$=90\,\mu$C from B to A

4.

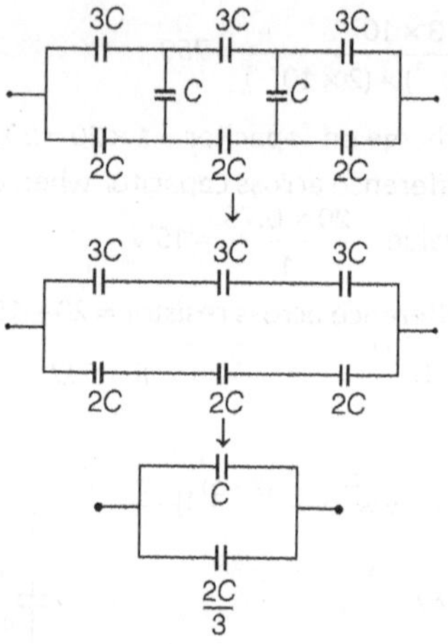

$$C_{eq}=C+\frac{2C}{3}=\frac{5C}{3}$$

Charge flown through battery $=\left(\frac{5C}{3}\right)V=\frac{5CV}{3}$

Work done by battery $=\left(\frac{5CV}{3}\right)V=\frac{5CV^2}{3}$

$$\Delta U=U_2-U_1=\frac{1}{2}\left(\frac{5C}{3}\right)V^2-0=\frac{5CV^2}{6}$$

Heat generated $=W_{\text{battery}}-\Delta U=\frac{5CV^2}{3}-\frac{5CV^2}{6}=\frac{5CV^2}{6}$

5.

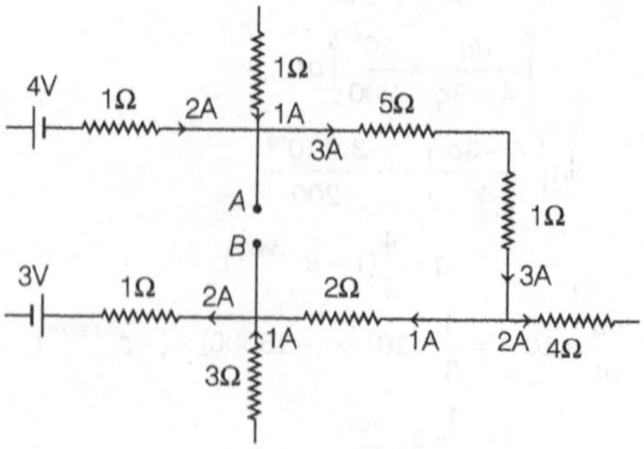

$$V_A-3(5)-3(1)-1(2)=V_B$$

$$\Rightarrow \quad V_A-V_B=20\text{V}$$

Energy stored in capacitor $=\frac{1}{2}CV^2$

$$=\frac{1}{2}\times 4\times 10^{-6}\times(20)^2=8\times 10^{-4}\text{J}$$

6. At $t = 0$, capacitor acts as a conducting wire.

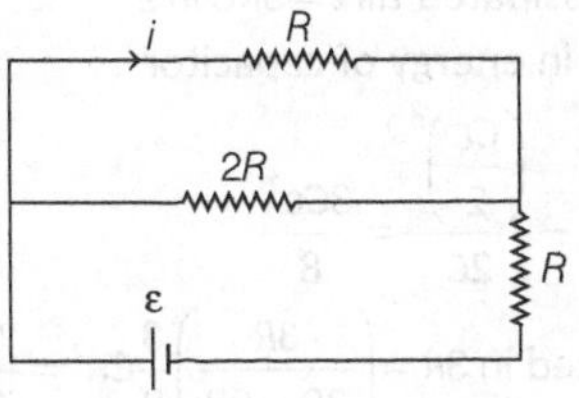

$$i = \text{Initial charging rate} = \frac{\varepsilon}{\left(R + \frac{(2R)R}{2R+R}\right)}\left(\frac{2R}{2R+R}\right) = \frac{2\varepsilon}{5R}$$

At $t = \infty$, capacitor acts as an open circuit

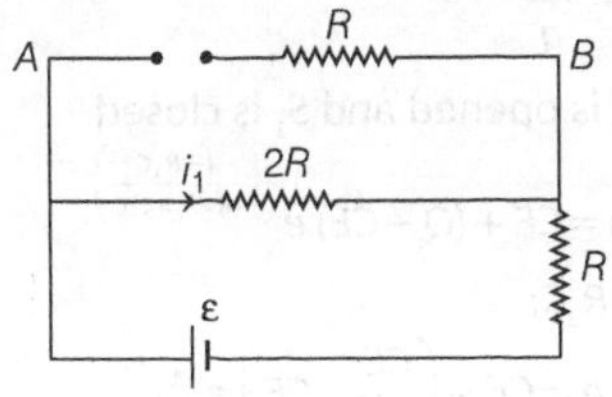

$$i_1 = \frac{\varepsilon}{3R}$$

$$V_A - V_B = i_1(2R) = \frac{2\varepsilon}{3}$$

$$q = \text{charge on capacitor} = C(V_A - V_B) = \frac{2C\varepsilon}{3}$$

If capacitor is charged with constant initial charging rate, then

$$q = it$$

$$\Rightarrow \quad \frac{2C\varepsilon}{3} = \left(\frac{2\varepsilon}{5R}\right)t \quad \Rightarrow \quad t = \frac{5RC}{3}$$

7. Let charge flown through battery be q.

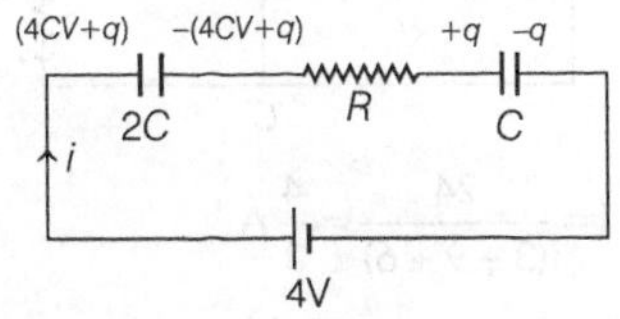

Applying KVL,

$$+4V - \frac{4CV+q}{2C} - iR - \frac{q}{C} = 0$$

$$\Rightarrow \quad i = \frac{4CV - 3q}{2RC}$$

$$\Rightarrow \quad \int_0^q \frac{dq}{4CV - 3q} = \frac{1}{2RC}\int_0^t dt$$

$$\Rightarrow \quad \ln\left(\frac{4CV - 3q}{4CV}\right) = -\frac{3t}{2RC}$$

$$\Rightarrow \quad q = \frac{4CV}{3}\left(1 - e^{-\frac{3t}{2RC}}\right)$$

8. In charging circuit, let time taken to from $\frac{V}{3}$ to $\frac{2V}{3}$ be T_1.

$$T_1 = R_{eq}C\ln 2 = 9RC\ln 2$$

In discharging circuit, let time taken to go from $\frac{2V}{3}$ to $\frac{V}{3}$ be T_2.

$$T_2 = R'_{eq}\, C\ln 2 = 3RC\ln 2$$

$$T = T_1 + T_2 = 9RC\ln 2 + 3RC\ln 2 = 12\,RC\ln 2$$

9. $E = \frac{1}{4\pi\varepsilon_0 K}\left(\frac{Q_1 - q}{r^2}\right)$

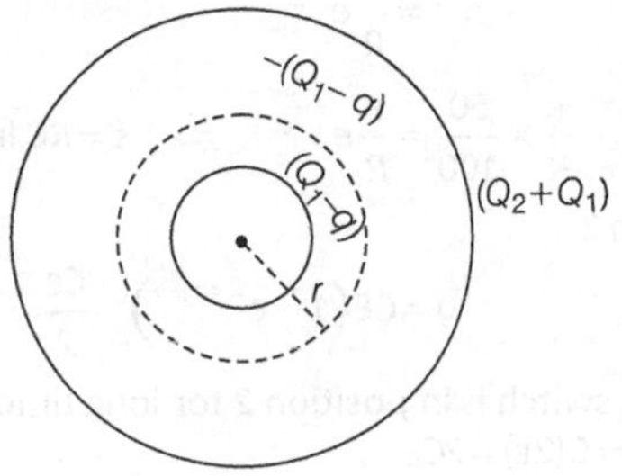

$$J = \sigma E$$

$$\Rightarrow \quad \frac{i}{4\pi r^2} = \sigma\left(\frac{1}{4\pi\varepsilon_0 K}\right)\left(\frac{Q_1 - q}{r^2}\right)$$

$$\Rightarrow \quad i = \frac{\sigma(Q_1 - q)}{\varepsilon_0 K}$$

$$\Rightarrow \quad \int_0^q \frac{dq}{Q_1 - q} = \frac{\sigma}{\varepsilon_0 K}\int_0^t dt$$

$$\Rightarrow \quad q = Q_1\left(1 - e^{-\frac{\sigma t}{K\varepsilon_0}}\right)$$

$$\text{Charge on outer shell} = Q_2 + q = Q_2 + Q_1\left(1 - e^{-\frac{\sigma t}{\varepsilon_0 K}}\right)$$

10. $q = Qe^{-\frac{t}{RC}} = Qe^{-\frac{t}{\tau}}$, $\quad R = \int_R^\infty \frac{\rho dr}{4\pi r^2} = \frac{\rho}{4\pi R}$

$$C = 4\pi\varepsilon_0 KR, \quad \tau = RC = \left(\frac{\rho}{4\pi R}\right)(4\pi\varepsilon_0 KR) = K\rho\varepsilon_0$$

$$q = Qe^{-\frac{t}{K\rho\varepsilon_0}} \quad \Rightarrow \quad \frac{Q}{2} = Qe^{-\frac{t}{K\rho\varepsilon_0}} \quad \Rightarrow \quad t = K\rho\varepsilon_0\ln 2$$

11. Equivalent diagram is shown in figure.

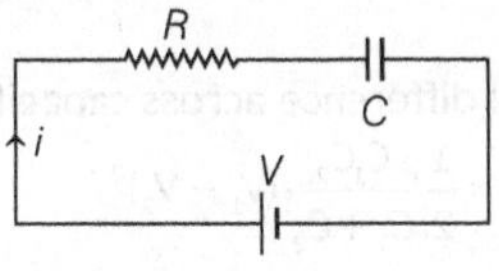

$$i = \frac{V}{R} = \frac{V}{\left(\frac{\rho d}{S}\right)} = \frac{VS}{\rho d}$$

12. $V_C = \varepsilon\left(1 - e^{-\frac{t}{RC}}\right)$, $\quad V_R = \varepsilon e^{-\frac{t}{RC}}$

$$V_C = V_R$$

$$\Rightarrow \quad \varepsilon\left(1 - e^{-\frac{t}{RC}}\right) = \varepsilon e^{-\frac{t}{RC}}$$

$\Rightarrow \quad 2e^{\frac{t}{RC}} = 1 \quad \Rightarrow \quad t = RC\ln 2$

$\Rightarrow \quad 100 = \tau \ln 2 \quad \Rightarrow \quad \tau = \dfrac{100}{\ln 2} \simeq 145$ ms

13. When the switch is in position 1,

$$i = \frac{\varepsilon}{R} e^{-\frac{t}{RC}}$$

$$\Rightarrow \quad \frac{\varepsilon}{R} \times \frac{50}{100} = \frac{\varepsilon}{R} e^{-\frac{t}{RC}} \quad \Rightarrow \quad t = RC\ln 2$$

At $t = RC\ln 2$,

$$q = CE\left(1 - e^{-RC\ln 2}\right) = \frac{C\varepsilon}{2}$$

When the switch is in position 2 for long time, charge on capacitor $= C(2\varepsilon) = 2C\varepsilon$

Charge flown through battery of emf 2ε

$$= 2C\varepsilon - \left(-\frac{C\varepsilon}{2}\right) = \frac{5C\varepsilon}{2}$$

Work done by battery of emf $2\varepsilon = \left(\dfrac{5C\varepsilon}{2}\right) 2\varepsilon = 5C\varepsilon^2$

14. $i = \dfrac{\varepsilon}{R} e^{-\frac{t}{RC}}$

$$\Rightarrow \quad \log i = -\frac{t}{RC} + \log\left(\frac{\varepsilon}{R}\right)$$

y-intercept is same for both the graphs.

$$\Rightarrow \quad \log\left(\frac{\varepsilon_1}{R_1}\right) = \log\left(\frac{\varepsilon_2}{R_2}\right) \quad \Rightarrow \quad \frac{\varepsilon_1}{R_1} = \frac{\varepsilon_2}{R_2}$$

Since, only two parameters out of C, R and ε are different

$\Rightarrow \quad C_1 = C_2$

Magnitude of slope of graph 1 > Magnitude of slope of graph 2

$$\Rightarrow \quad \frac{1}{R_1C_1} > \frac{1}{R_2C_2}$$

$$\Rightarrow \quad R_2C_2 > R_1C_1 \quad \Rightarrow \quad R_2 > R_1 \qquad (\because C_1 = C_2)$$

We know that $V \propto R$

Hence, $V_1 < V_2$

15. Initial potential difference across capacitor $= i_0R$

Heat liberated $= \dfrac{1}{2}\dfrac{C_1C_2}{C_1 + C_2}(V_1 - V_2)^2$

$$= \frac{1}{2}\frac{C_1C_2}{C_1 + C_2}(i_0R - 0)^2 = \frac{C_1C_2 i_0^2 R^2}{2(C_1 + C_2)}$$

16. At $t = 0$; charge on capacitor $= C\varepsilon$

At $t = t$; $q = C\varepsilon\, e^{-\frac{t}{R_{eq}C}} = C\varepsilon\, e^{-\frac{t}{5RC}}$

$$i = \frac{dq}{dt} = \frac{\varepsilon}{5R} e^{-\frac{t}{5RC}}$$

At $t = 0$; $i = \dfrac{\varepsilon}{5R}$

At $t = 5RC\ln 2$; $i = \dfrac{\varepsilon}{10R}$

Total heat dissipated till $t = 5RC\ln 2$

= Loss in energy of capacitor

$$= \frac{(C\varepsilon)^2}{2C} - \frac{\left(\frac{C\varepsilon}{2}\right)^2}{2C} = \frac{3C\varepsilon^2}{8}$$

Heat dissipated in $3R = \left(\dfrac{3R}{3R + 2R}\right)\dfrac{3}{8}C\varepsilon^2 = \dfrac{9}{40}C\varepsilon^2$

17. At $t = 0$; charge on capacitor $= CE$

$0 < t \le R_1C$; $q = CE\, e^{-\frac{t}{R_1C}}$

At $t = R_1C$; $q = \dfrac{CE}{q}$

At $t = R_1C$; S_2 is opened and S_1 is closed

For $t > R_1C$; $q = CE + (Q - CE)\, e^{\left(\frac{t - R_1C}{(R_1 + R_2)C}\right)}$

At $t = 2R_1C + R_2C$;

$$q = CE + \left(\frac{CE}{e} - CE\right)e^{-1}$$

$$q = CE\left(1 - \frac{1}{e} + \frac{1}{e^2}\right)$$

Multiple Choice(s) Correct Questions

1. When the switch is closed,

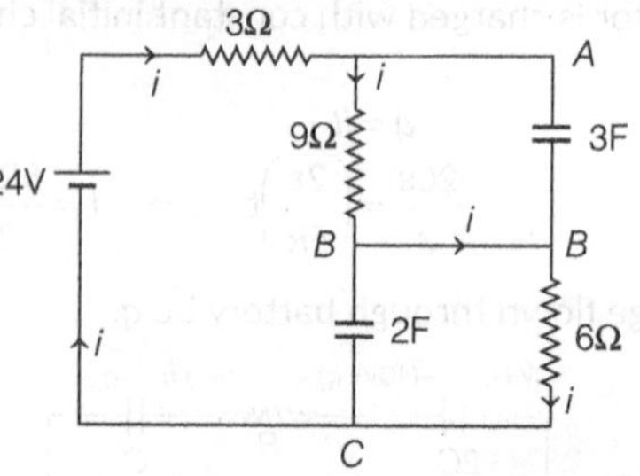

$$i = \frac{24}{(3 + 9 + 6)} = \frac{4}{3}\text{ A}$$

$$V_A - V_B = 9i = 9\left(\frac{4}{3}\right) = 12\text{V}$$

$$V_B - V_C = 6i = 6\left(\frac{4}{3}\right) = 8\text{V}$$

After a long time after the switch is open, potential difference across each capacitor will be equal to emf of the battery as there is no current in the circuit.

2.

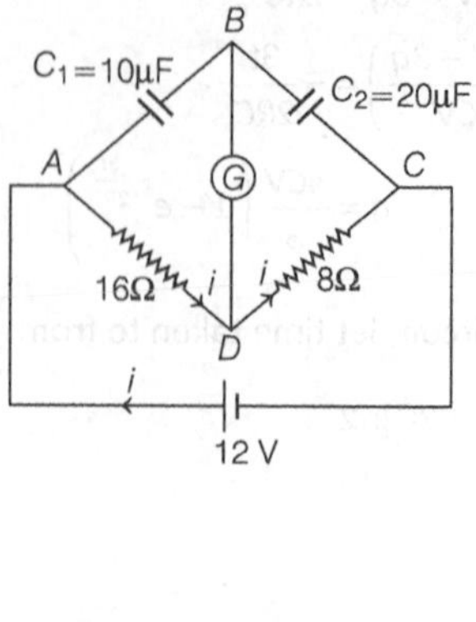